OXFORD ECONOMIC ATLAS OF THE WORLD

FOURTH EDITION

PREPARED BY
THE CARTOGRAPHIC DEPARTMENT OF THE CLARENDON PRESS

ADVISORY EDITOR
D. B. JONES, INSTITUTE OF ECONOMICS AND STATISTICS,
UNIVERSITY OF OXFORD

OXFORD UNIVERSITY PRESS

Oxford University Press, Ely House, London W.1

GLASGOW NEW YORK TORONTO MELBOURNE WELLINGTON
CAPE TOWN IBADAN NAIROBI DAR ES SALAAM LUSAKA ADDIS ABABA
DELHI BOMBAY CALCUTTA MADRAS KARACHI LAHORE DACCA
KUALA LUMPUR SINGAPORE HONG KONG TOKYO

CASED ISBN 0 19 894106 4
PAPERBACK ISBN 0 19 894107 2

FIRST EDITION 1954
SECOND EDITION 1959
THIRD EDITION 1965
FOURTH EDITION 1972
REPRINTED 1973

Compiled, drawn and photomechanically processed by
The Cartographic Department of the Clarendon Press

Printed in Great Britain,
maps by Cook, Hammond and Kell, Ltd, London
gazetteer and statistical supplement at the University Press, Oxford

ACKNOWLEDGEMENTS

We acknowledge with gratitude the co-operation and assistance given by numerous government bodies and statistical agencies, national trade associations, and private companies throughout the world. Some individuals and organizations deserving special mention are listed here.

Aluminium Federation, Birmingham, U.K.
Prof. J. S. Anderson, Dept. of Inorganic Chemistry, University of Oxford
Anglo American Corporation of South Africa Ltd., Johannesburg
Anglo American International (U.K.) Ltd., London
Dr. J. H. Appleton, Dept. of Geography, University of Hull, U.K.
K. W. Ashberry, British Rail
G. R. Bamber, Editor of *Water Power*, London
Dr. L. M. Bechelli, Division of Communicable Diseases, W.H.O., Geneva
Dr. P. Beckett, Dept. of Soil Science, University of Oxford
D. P. Bickmore, Royal College of Art, London
N. Bittner, Special Committee for Machinery, O.E.C.D., Paris
Prof. G. E. Blackman, Dept. of Agricultural Science, University of Oxford
Board of Trade Library, London
Bodleian Library, University of Oxford
T. A. Boley, Electricity Council, London
K. E. Boome, International Road Federation, Geneva
British Man-Made Fibres Federation
British Paper and Board Makers' Association, London
Dr. D. G. Browning, School of Geography, University of Oxford
Dr. L. J. Bruce-Chwatt, Division of Malaria Eradication, W.H.O., Geneva
Prof. J. H. Burnett, Dept. of Agricultural Science, University of Oxford
Cadbury Schweppes Ltd., Birmingham, U.K.
A. A. L. Caesar, Dept. of Geography, University of Cambridge
J. Cashman, Lloyd's, London
Prof. S. B. Cohen, Dept. of Geography, Clark University, Worcester, Massachusetts
Commodities Division, Commonwealth Secretariat, London
Miss P. Cook, Medical Research Council, London
S. G. Cooper, International Civil Aviation Organization, Montreal
Cyanamid International, Wayne, New Jersey
P. A. Delafield, British Association of Synthetic Rubber Manufacturers Ltd., London
Dr. A. J. Duggan, Wellcome Institute, London
Economist Intelligence Unit, London
D. B. Evans, British Bureau of Non-ferrous Metal Statistics, Birmingham, U.K.
Dr. B. E. F. Fender, Dept. of Inorganic Chemistry, University of Oxford
R. Fountain, British Aircraft Corporation, Weybridge, U.K.
Prof. J. Gottmann, School of Geography, University of Oxford
Guildhall Library, London
J. Guthrie-Brown, Sir Alexander Gibb and Partners, London
R. Hankinson, International Planned Parenthood Federation, London
G. W. Hemy, Crosfield Chemicals, Warrington, U.K.
T. V. Hill, Intelligence Dept., Lloyd's, London
K. E. Hunt, Institute of Agricultural Economics, University of Oxford
M. C. Hyde, Editor of *Chemical Age*, London
Imperial Tobacco Group Limited, London
Institute of Commonwealth Studies Library, University of Oxford
Institute of Economics and Statistics, University of Oxford
A. Jeffery, International Synthetic Rubber Co. Ltd., Southampton
D. G. Jones, British Sulphur Corporation Ltd., London
W. G. G. Kellett, Rubber Growers' Association, London
A. La Spada, International Tin Council, London
Lead Development Association, London
Dr. M. J. M. Leask, Dept. of Physics, University of Oxford
J. J. MacGregor, Dept. of Forestry, University of Oxford
G. B. Masefield, Dept. of Agricultural Science, University of Oxford
Miss M. McAfee, United Nations Library, London
Mineral Resources Division, Institute of Geological Sciences, London
W. A. Campbell, Dr. R. S. Collins, R. A. Healing, D. E. Highley, D. S. Paterson, Dr. D. Slater, I. A. Thomas, A. H. J. Todd, Dr. D. C. Turner
Ministry of Agriculture, Fisheries and Food, London
Ministry of Overseas Development, London
National Coal Board, London
Natural Rubber Producers' Research Association, Welwyn Garden City, U.K.
P. W. Allen, Dr. L. Mullins
Miss B. Needham, Textile Council, Manchester, U.K.
N. G. Osman, International Sugar Organization, London
Overseas Activities Section, Electricity Council, London
Overseas Development Institute Ltd., London
Dr. E. R. Oxburgh, Dept. of Geology, University of Oxford
Pan American Coffee Bureau, New York
J. H. C. Patten, School of Geography, University of Oxford
M. L. Pearl, Iron and Steel Institute, London
L. Perk Vlaanderen, Secretariat of the International Rubber Study Group, London
B. A. Proctor, Economic Intelligence Dept., Barclays Bank Ltd., London
Railway Technical Centre Library, Wilmorton, U.K.
Reed Paper and Board (U.K.) Ltd., London
C. I. M. Reekie, Unilever Ltd., London
Rhodes House Library, University of Oxford
G. B. Richardson, Faculty of Social Studies, University of Oxford
G. R. Robinson, British Computer Society Library, London
Dr. J. S. Rollett, University Computing Laboratory, Oxford
Royal Automobile Club, Croydon, U.K.
Royal School of Mines Library, Imperial College, London
Royal Society for the Prevention of Accidents, London
A. E. Schreck, U.S. Bureau of Mines, Washington, D.C.
J. Slater, Mathematical Institute, University of Oxford
Dr. E. B. Smith, Dept. of Physical Chemistry, University of Oxford
C. G. Smith, School of Geography, University of Oxford
Dr. A. M. Stewart, Faculty of Medicine, University of Oxford
Dr. M. M. Sweeting, School of Geography, University of Oxford
E. J. Taaffe, Dept. of Geography, Ohio State University, Columbus
Unigate Limited, London
United Kingdom Atomic Energy Authority, London
United Nations Statistical Office, New York
Dr. B. B. Waddy, Ross Institute of Tropical Medicine, London
Dr. K. Warren, School of Geography, University of Oxford
G. Weber, Editor of *Oil and Gas Journal*, Tulsa, Oklahoma
J. Weinthal, Society of Motor Manufacturers and Traders Ltd., London
Wellcome Institute, London
Westminster Commercial Reference Library, London
Wool Industry Bureau of Statistics, Bradford, U.K.
Zinc Development Association, London

For technical assistance:
Church Army Press & Supplies Ltd., Oxford
William Clowes & Sons Ltd., Beccles
Cook, Hammond & Kell Ltd., London
Fairey Surveys Ltd., Maidenhead
David L. Fryer & Co., Henley-on-Thames
S. Glossop & Sons Ltd., Cardiff
Oxford Litho Plates Ltd., Oxford

CONTENTS

SUBJECT INDEX

INTRODUCTION

The **arrangement** of the atlas has two main parts: maps grouped into thirteen sections, and the Statistical Supplement arranged in alphabetical order by country.

The maps include eight sections based on commodity groups, one introductory section of physical geography and summary maps, and four sections providing background information on demography, disease, social and political factors, and communications.

The maps and Supplement are complementary and should be used together. The maps provide a world view of any topic while the Supplement gives precise statistics for each country, showing the relative importance of any commodity in the country's economy.

The atlas is in series with the Oxford Regional Economic Atlases, which deal separately and in much greater detail with *Western Europe*, *North America*, *Africa*, the *U.S.S.R. and Eastern Europe*, and the *Middle East and North Africa*. The regional atlases contain larger scale topographic and economic maps, and they have maps of commodities which are important regionally but not on a world scale. The world atlas shows the world distribution pattern of all the more important commodities, industries and resources; in this edition these are supplemented by larger scale treatment of congested areas on each map.

For the economic maps, **commodities** were chosen mainly on the basis of their importance in world trade, with the minimum value being U.S.$100,000. Exceptionally, commodities that would not on their own have qualified for inclusion have been added expressly to increase the usefulness of maps of other associated commodities. Demographic and other non-economic topics were chosen on the basis of their relevance to economics taking into account the availability of information, the feasibility of mapping it, and the validity of the maps which would result.

Most maps are based on the **period** 1963-5. Comparative statistics for 1953-5 are given in tabular form, both accompanying the maps and in the Statistical Supplement. However, where industries were changing rapidly, and if there were more recent data available for the whole world, more up-to-date information was used, and comparative statistics for 1963-5 and 1953-5 added where possible. In some instances it was difficult to obtain data as recent even as 1963-5, particularly for China P.R. Where earlier information was considered likely to affect significantly the validity of the map its date is given.

Major **sources** of information are listed. Whenever possible statistics were obtained from international bodies for maximum comparability. Often, however, such data do not exist, and many of the statistics were obtained from national associations and statistical offices and from private companies and individuals. Others who have been advisers on collection and presentation of data are listed in the acknowledgements.

Detailed **data** for most maps have been adjusted to standard estimates of statistics on a national basis. These estimates were supplied for all countries by organizations collecting statistics on an international level, such as the United Nations, the Food and Agriculture Organization, the United States Bureau of Mines, and the Institute of Geological Sciences.

Data for each topic are presented whenever possible in statistically significant numerical categories. Exceptionally they were available only in predetermined categories, or in insufficient detail for this to be done. Most maps give an indication of the range of the statistics by stating the minimum values involved; many give maximum values as well.

Symbols are centred on the point to which they refer. The point indicated by a sector or a semi-circle is the centre of the circle of which it is a part. Symbols representing the total production of a region or province are located on the main area of production when this is known, and the location may therefore differ from the geographic centre of the region as given in the gazetteer. Symbols representing the total production of scattered centres may be placed in a box to avoid confusion with symbols for specific centres. The location of the boxed symbol does not necessarily indicate the centre of the producing area which it represents.

Insets have been used to show at a larger scale the more congested areas of the world maps; they are normally positioned just below the main map, but are occasionally on adjoining pages.

The **projection** is a modified Gall which is not an equal area projection. However, distortion of area is excessive only in polar and near-polar latitudes where economic activity is minimal. To reduce still further the effect of distortion, the method of representing data by areal shading has been little used except where the balance can be restored by including a dot distribution as the base to which the data apply. Approximate equatorial scale, on both maps and the insets, is given only as a basis for comparison between them and, in broad terms, with other maps of which the reader has knowledge. It is not appropriate to use the scale to measure distances.

The international **boundaries** used are those which existed in 1965. They have been compiled from U.N. Boundary Commission and other geographic reports and from large scale topographic maps. The internal divisions of Australia, Brazil, Canada, China P.R., the U.S.A. and the U.S.S.R. are also shown because these countries cover such large areas.

The atlas is presented in metric **units.** However, although data in the metric system formed the basis for the environment maps, data in the English system of inches, degrees Farenheit, etc., were used in the agriculture notes. In these two cases therefore, data are given in both systems. Since original data of this nature are to some extent approximate, conversion from one system to the other has also been approximate.

Certain **standard symbols** have been used in statistical tables throughout the atlas:

*	estimate	—	nil, negligible
. . .	not applicable	NA, na	data not available

Standard symbols have also been used on the maps themselves. On dot distribution maps countries which are known to produce the commodity in significant quantities, but for which detailed data are not available, have been shaded. On maps of industry, known centres of production for which detailed statistics are not available are indicated by a cross.

For most commodities mapped there are also tables listing the leading producing countries and the percentage of total world production for which they were responsible. In some instances this information is given for two or more associated commodities in one table. Although not all countries included in such composite tables were leading producers of all the commodities, their ratings for all commodities are given. For this reason, the ratings of the leading producers are emphasized by backing them with grey rectangles. A rating which is not grey-backed is not therefore among the leaders; its presence is incidental for that commodity and there is at least one other country whose production of that commodity is higher, although its production of none of the commodities is high enough to warrant its inclusion in the table.

English versions of **country names** are used throughout. Some countries have more than one of these, and the few names used in the atlas which might not be immediately identifiable with other versions are listed below, along with some of the alternatives. Here and elsewhere, the word Republic as part of a country name has been abbreviated to R.

China P.R.	People's Republic of China/Mainland China/China
Congo D.R.	Democratic Republic of the Congo/Congo (Kinshasa)/Zaïre
Congo R.	Republic of the Congo/Congo (Brazzaville)
Germany D.R.	German Democratic Republic/East Germany
Germany F.R.	Federal Republic of Germany/West Germany
Irish R.	Republic of Ireland/Eire
North Korea	Democratic People's Republic of Korea
South Korea	Republic of Korea
Taiwan	Nationalist China/Formosa
U.A.R.	Egypt
North Vietnam	Democratic Republic of Vietnam
South Vietnam	Republic of Vietnam

All **other names** are in the forms used in the countries concerned (transliterated into the Roman alphabet where applicable). In countries with two or more official languages, the nationally recommended version is used. If a place name has a well-known English version which is not clearly recognizable from the vernacular form, the English is normally added in parenthesis. The spelling and locations of most place names have been taken from the United States Board on Geographic Names publications; a fuller list of sources accompanies the gazetteer.

Names in upright type indicate specific places. Names in italic type indicate administrative and other statistical regions, areas around towns, and geographical features. The letter (a) in parenthesis after a name in italic type indicates that a town name has been used as a means of identifying either a producing centre which can be located only in relation to the nearest populated place, or the amalgamation of small centres represented by one symbol. Geographical features are further differentiated by letters in parenthesis following their names as follows:

b	bay	h	hill(s), ridge	pen	peninsula
bn	basin	i	island	pl	plain, plateau uplands
cl	canal	l	loch(s), lake(s), lagoon(s)		
ct	coast			pt	point
d	deposit	m	mountain range, mountain(s)	r	river
dt	desert			s	sea
e	estuary	o	oasis	st	straits
f	fjord	p	pass		

When centres of activity are so close together that there is insufficient space to name all of them individually without ambiguity, one of three courses has been adopted. Where two names refer to a single symbol, the names are placed one after the other, that of the larger centre first, and joined by a stroke (/). Where two symbols are named together the individual names are placed one after the other, that of the larger symbol first, and joined by an ampersand (&). Where more than two symbols are involved, their names have been placed in a box and grouped according to size, with a horizontal line separating names of different sized symbols. The names of the largest symbol size are first, followed by other size groups in descending order. Within each size group the names are arranged according to the position of the symbols, not by size within that category. Boxes containing names of more than one type of symbol may include spots of colour or other indicators to assist the assigning of names to symbols.

Trade flow mapped in this atlas is defined as the value of trade in one direction between a pair of countries. The flows shown for different commodities (or groups of associated commodities) are the few largest which, taken together, account for much of world trade in each commodity or group and, individually are appreciably larger than the hundreds of much smaller flows making up the balance. They vary considerably in number for different commodities. They are essentially bilateral links and, although they are the most important ones, they do not necessarily involve all major exporters or importers.

Trade tables accompanying the maps list the major exporters and importers with their percentage of world trade, and the Statistical Supplement gives absolute figures for total exports and imports for every country (where data are available).

The source of the data is the United Nations Statistical Office Data Bank (International Trade Statistics Centre). Data were obtained for 60 reporting countries which together accounted for over 90% of total world trade in each commodity in 1966, excluding trade within the bloc of countries with centrally-planned economies. Wherever possible, data were based on both imports and exports as reported by two trading partners but, where only one partner was a reporting country, only its imports or exports have been used. Data have been adjusted for maximum comparability, for example by excluding transport costs.

Commodities and commodity groups used are found in the 'Standard International Trade Classification, Revised' U.N. Statistical Papers, Series M, No. 34. They were selected according to the availability of data and of space on the map and the relevance to the rest of the map.

The flows have been drawn schematically, no attempt being made to follow actual routes. Those to and from Europe have been grouped according to whether the link is with a country in Southern, NE. or NW. Europe, or in Scandinavia. Those to and from countries of North Africa, the Middle East, and the Caribbean have been similarly grouped. Otherwise, two or more flows have been amalgamated only where they originate from, or are destined for, the same country. In all cases the identity of individual flows is preserved.

The width of each flow represents the value of that link. The scale used for value varies from map to map according to the range to be shown and the space available. The precise value of each flow, in U.S. $ millions, is given. If provenance and/or destination are not clear, this information is also given. Where necessary, flows are represented in boxes in which provenance is stated, and destination and value are treated in the same manner as on the map.

Details of precise value, and provenance and destination where necessary, are given by labelling individual or grouped flow lines, for example:

E TO D(6) F(4) GB(3)

indicating exports from Spain to Germany F.R., France and the U.K. valued at $6 million, $4 million and $3 million, respectively.

The international automobile registration letters, as established by the International Conventions of 1926 and 1949, have been used. Those countries not included among them have been assigned appropriate letters. A complete list of the letters used appears below; those countries not given official registration letters by the Conventions are asterisked.

A	Austria	LI	Libya*
AUS	Australia	MA	Morocco
B	Belgium	MEX	Mexico
BR	Brazil	MS	Mauritius
BS	Bahamas	N	Norway
CDN	Canada	NA	Netherlands Antilles
CGO	Congo D.R.	NIC	Nicaragua
CH	Switzerland	NIG	Niger
CPR	China P.R.*	NL	Netherlands
CS	Czechoslovakia	P	Portugal
CY	Cyprus	PA	Panama
D	Germany F.R.*	PAK	Pakistan
DE	Germany D.R.*	PL	Poland
DK	Denmark	PTM	Malaysia
DZ	Algeria	R	Romania
E	Spain	RA	Argentina
EAU	Uganda	RCH	Chile
EC	Ecuador	RF	Réunion*
ES	El Salvador*	RI	Indonesia
ET	U.A.R.	RL	Lebanon
F	France	RNR	Zambia
FJ	Fiji*	S	Sweden
GB	U.K.	SA	Saudi Arabia*
GH	Ghana	SF	Finland
GR	Greece	SGP	Singapore
HK	Hong Kong	SU	U.S.S.R.
I	Italy	SUD	Sudan
IL	Israel	T	Thailand
IND	India	TN	Tunisia
IR	Iran	TR	Turkey
IRL	Irish R.	TT	Trinidad/Tobago
IRQ	Iraq	USA	U.S.A.
J	Japan	VNS	South Vietnam*
JA	Jamaica	WAN	Nigeria
KS	South Korea*	YU	Yugoslavia
KWT	Kuwait	ZA	South Africa
L	Luxembourg		

Political Units

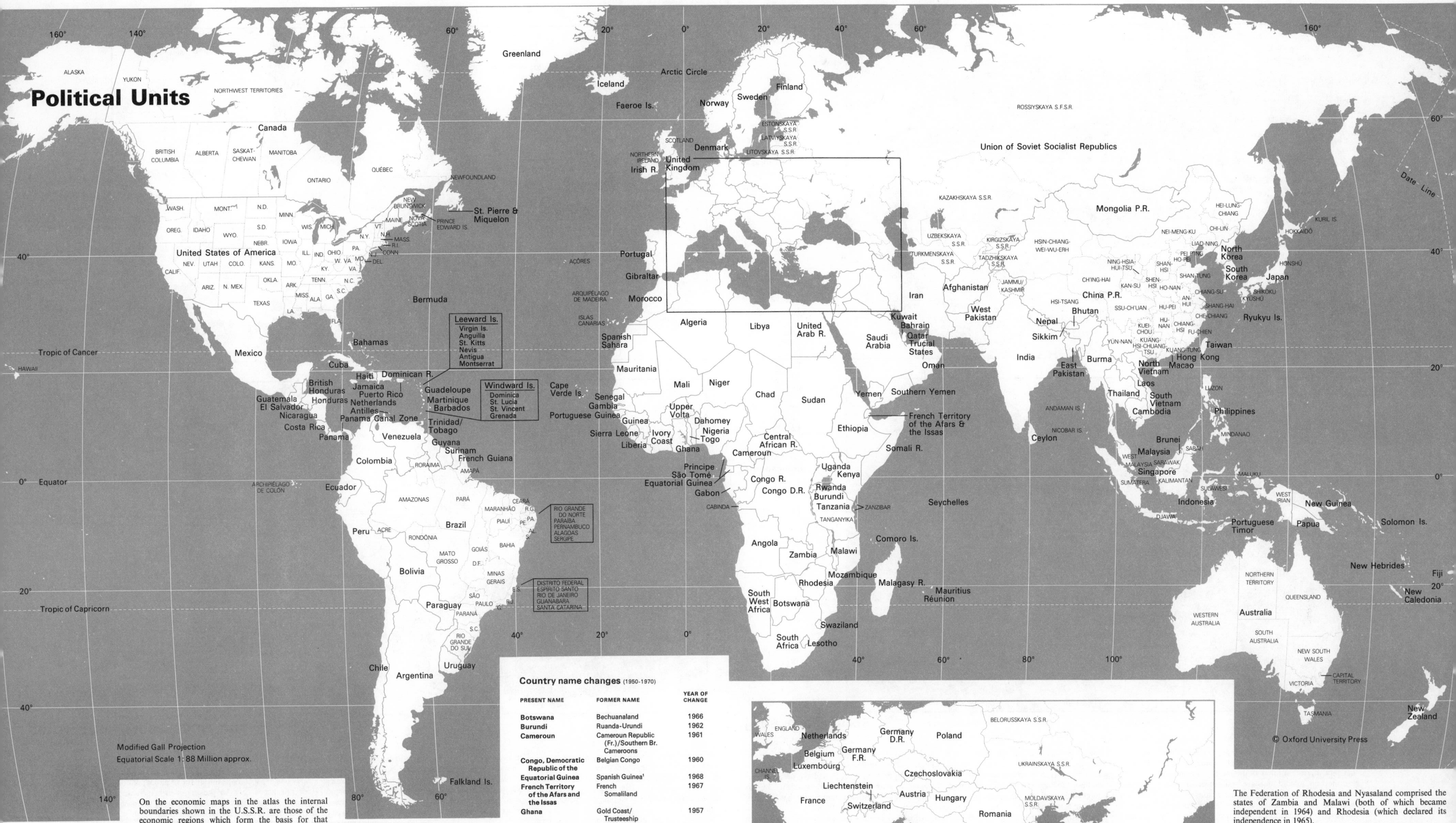

On the economic maps in the atlas the internal boundaries shown in the U.S.S.R. are those of the economic regions which form the basis for that country's statistical reports. Some of these economic regions are subdivisions of the S.S.R.s; others comprise several small S.S.R.s. The divisions are:
S.S.R.: *Economic Region*
Rossiyskaya (R.S.F.S.R.): *Severo-Zapad, Tsentr, Volgo-Vyatsk, Tsentralno-Chernozem, Povolzhsk, Severo-Kavkaz, Ural, Zapadno-Sibir', Vostochno-Sibir', Dal'nevostock*
Ukrainskaya: *Donetsko-Pridneprovsk, Yugo-Zapad, Yuzhniy*
Uzbekskaya, Kirgizskaya, Tadzhikskaya, Turkmenskaya: *Srednezazia*
Litovskaya, Latviyskaya, Estonskaya, Kaliningradskaya (Oblast'): *Pribaltika*[1]
Armyanskaya, Gruzinskaya, Azerbaydzhanskaya: *Zakavkaz*[2]
The S.S.R.s of Kazakh, Belorossiya and Moldavia are coincident with the economic regions of the same name.

[1]On all economic maps the S.S.R. boundaries are shown.
[2]On all economic maps the boundary for the economic region only is shown.

On some economic maps in the atlas data have been reported for first order administrative divisions and for their sub-divisions, most of which are too small to be shown on a world map of this scale. Examples of these are: the provinces, states, departments, etc. of most countries; the counties of the U.S.A., which are subdivisions of the states; and the prefectures (-ken) of Japan, which are subdivisions of the islands. Occasionally regional names have been used in reference to clearly defined physical units such as the Red Basin of Szechwan (Ssu-ch'uan P'en-ti), the North European Plain and the Ganges Plain, or to areas unified by their economic activity, such as the Corn Belt (of the U.S.A. and Canada), the Maize Triangle (of South Africa) and the Ruhr (the major industrial conurbation of Germany F.R.).

Political units

Boundaries (1965)

- International
- Internal

Names (1970)

- Mexico — Country names (in the anglicized form)
- OHIO — Major administrative divisions (in the vernacular form, transliterated where necessary)

For complete forms of U.S.A. state abbreviations see the introduction to the gazetteer

Country name changes (1950-1970)

PRESENT NAME	FORMER NAME	YEAR OF CHANGE
Botswana	Bechuanaland	1966
Burundi	Ruanda-Urundi	1962
Cameroun	Cameroun Republic (Fr.)/Southern Br. Cameroons	1961
Congo, Democratic Republic of the	Belgian Congo	1960
Equatorial Guinea	Spanish Guinea[1]	1968
French Territory of the Afars and the Issas	French Somaliland	1967
Ghana	Gold Coast/ Trusteeship Territory of Togoland	1957
Guyana	British Guiana	1966
Lesotho	Basutoland	1966
Malagasy Republic	Madagascar	1960
Malawi	Nyasaland	1964
Malaysia	Malaya/Sabah/ Sarawak	1963
Oman	Muscat & Oman	1970
Rhodesia	Southern Rhodesia	1965
Rwanda	Ruanda-Urundi	1962
Somali Republic	Br. Somaliland/ Somalia	1960
Southern Yemen	Federation of South Arabia	1967
Tanzania	Tanganyika/ Zanzibar	1964
United Arab Republic	Egypt	1958
Zambia	Northern Rhodesia	1964

[1]Incl. Fernando Póo and Rio Muni

The Federation of Rhodesia and Nyasaland comprised the states of Zambia and Malawi (both of which became independent in 1964) and Rhodesia (which declared its independence in 1965).
Indo-China comprised the states of Laos (1949), Cambodia (1953), North Vietnam (1954) and South Vietnam (1954), which became independent in the years shown.
Spanish West Africa retains only the province of Spanish Sahara. Ifni was returned to Morocco in 1968.
French West Africa comprised the sovereign states of Guinea (which became independent in 1958), Ivory Coast, Togo, Niger, Dahomey, Senegal, Mali (formerly the territory of French Sudan) Mauritania and Upper Volta, all of which became independent in 1960.
French Equatorial Africa comprised the states of Central African Republic (formerly the territory of Ubangi Shari), the Republic of the Congo (formerly the territory of Middle Congo), Chad and Gabon, all of which became independent in 1960.
The Federation of Malaysia, which came into being in 1963, comprised the Federation of Malaya, the State of Singapore and the colonies of North Borneo (renamed Sabah) and Sarawak. In 1965 Singapore seceded from the Federation and became an independent sovereign state.

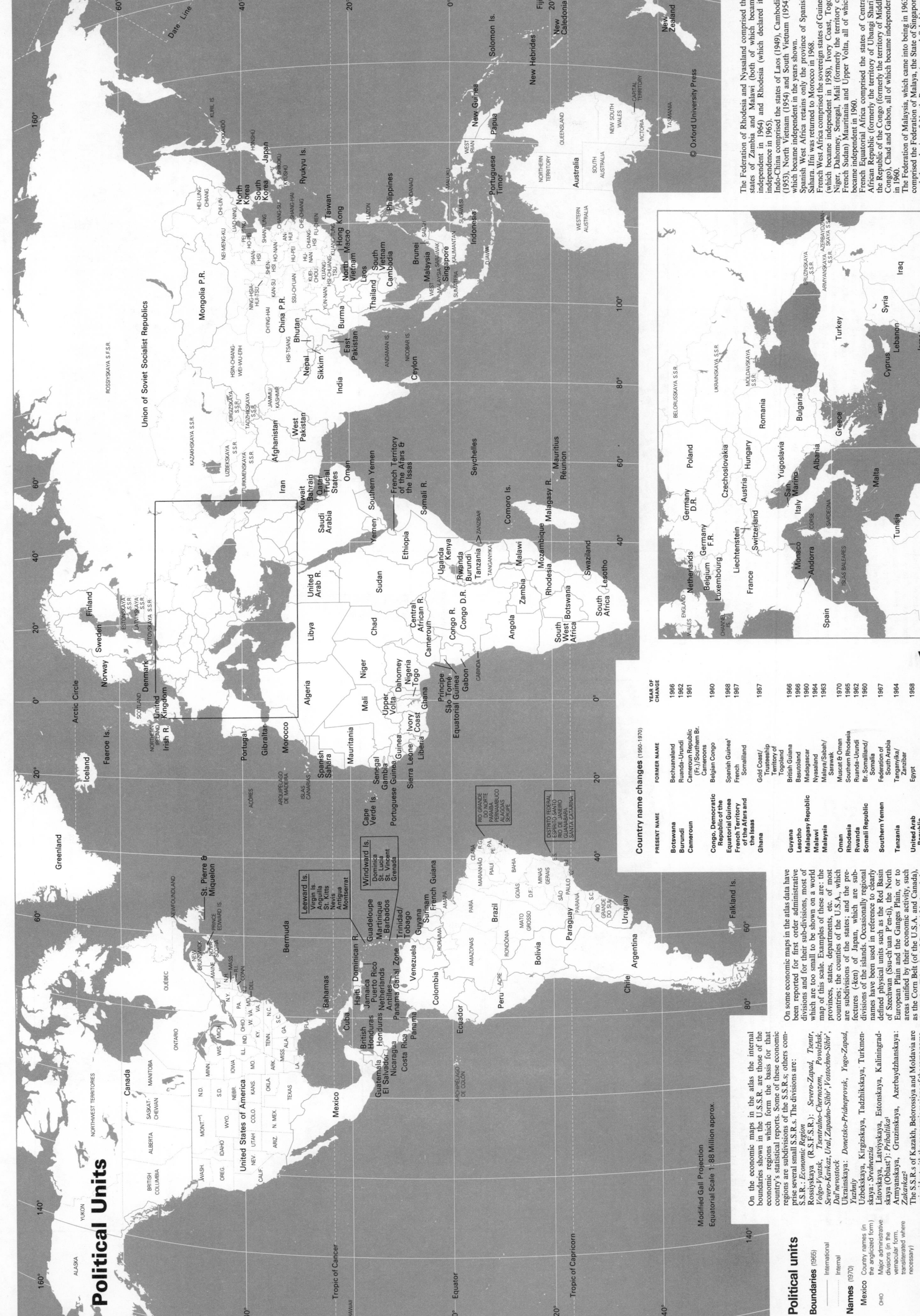

Environment

For individual country data see Statistical Supplement

The economic activity of any area and the degree to which it has been developed are influenced to some extent by the prevalent physical conditions and the resources available. However, the nature of man's activity is also influenced by such social and economic factors as his technical knowledge and skills, cultural preferences, the efficiency of his systems of communication, world demand for commodities and local and national policies. These may override physical conditions.

The majority of the maps in this section present those components of the physical environment which most influence human activities. The last three maps of the section give a general summary of the ways in which man has responded to his environment, information which is presented in detail in the sections following.

Climate, rock type, relief, soil, vegetation and geomorphic processes acting on the land are all important components of man's environment. In any one area the landscape represents the complex interaction of all these factors through time, together with the effect of human activity which is itself an integral part of the environment and of its development. Man's activity has led to an alteration of many characteristics of the landscape as it was before his appearance, and to a disturbance of the interrelations between the elements of the environment. The extent to which this has occurred has varied through time, depending to a large extent on his need for materials and his technical understanding and abilities.

Since early in his history man has played a major role in altering the vegetation cover of a large proportion of the earth's surface. Vast areas of forest have been cleared to provide land for crop cultivation and wood for building, fuel, and other uses. Changes in the vegetation have caused a disruption of the balance which existed between the different elements of the environment. Soils, for example, are more subject to erosion without the protection afforded by the vegetation, and changes in the hydrological cycle have also been initiated. The alteration of the vegetation pattern is but one example of the part man has played in fashioning his environment. Urbanization, industrialization and mining are all responsible for changes of various kinds. More efficient use of resources, becoming ever more necessary as population growth increases the pressure on existing resources, is an important factor in economic development. Man's ability to modify his environment and to use it so as to increase its economic potential has improved as his knowledge and technical skills have advanced. This modification of the environment is exemplified by the development of irrigation schemes and the use of wind breaks, glass-houses and smudge pots in order to make climatic conditions more favourable for crops; the use of organic and inorganic fertilizers to increase the productivity of the soil; selective breeding of crops and of animals; and development of new methods of overcoming the problems posed by permafrost. Furthermore the increase in the extent and efficiency of the communications system makes possible the economic development of areas where such development has been for a long time impossible or uneconomic because of their inaccessibility.

It is important to note that for all these activities a knowledge of the physical characteristics of the environment is vital. Further development of resources will depend on an increased understanding both of the nature of the individual elements which make up the environment and of their interrelationships.

Lack of knowledge of the working of the environment, together with pressure on resources, has often led to indiscriminate and careless exploitation, resulting in the destruction or depletion of resources, pollution and the dereliction of land.

There is an increasing realization of the importance of conserving the earth's natural resources and minimizing the disruption of the environment. This involves not only the rehabilitation of those areas which have suffered through exploitation (for example by reafforestation and improvement of farming techniques) but also the employment of conservation measures concurrently with economic development, to ensure that areas at present unspoilt will remain so. Conservation requires careful and efficient planning, based on thorough knowledge of every aspect of the environment.

Temperature/Ocean currents

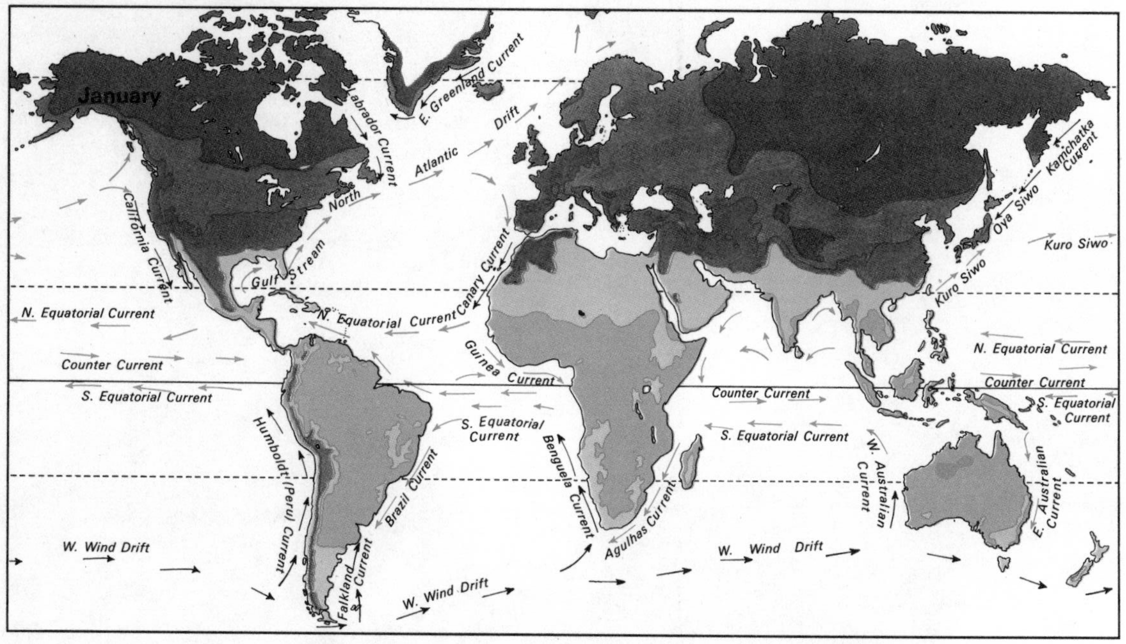

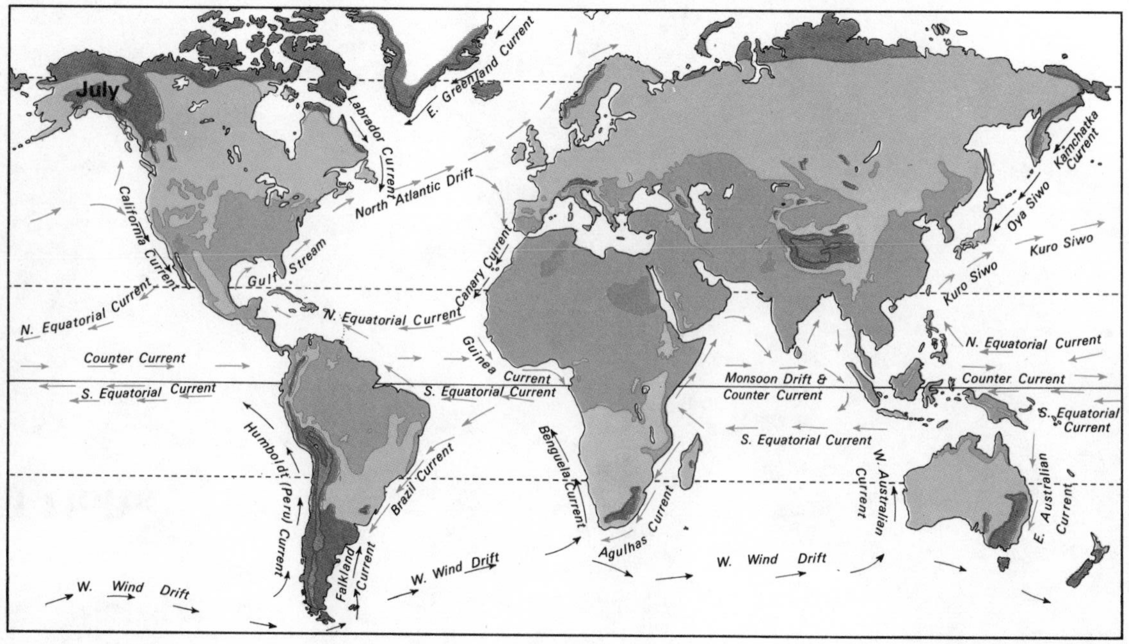

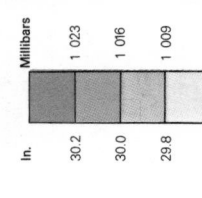

Actual temperature

°F	°C
90	32
70	21
50	10
30	-1
0	-18

Ocean currents

cold

warm

Pressure/Winds

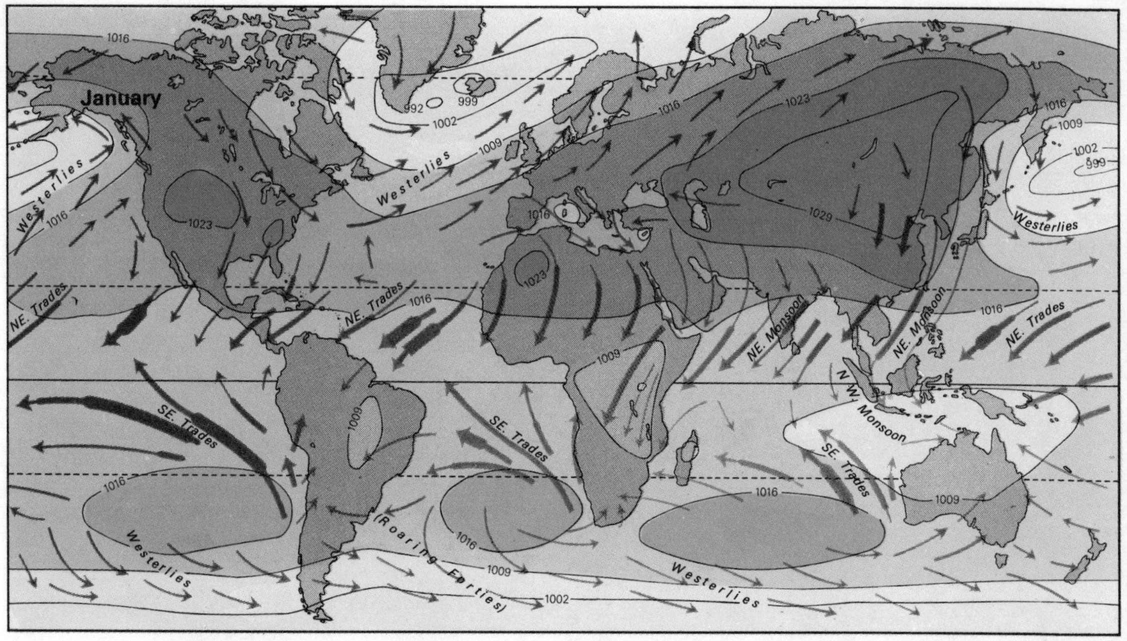

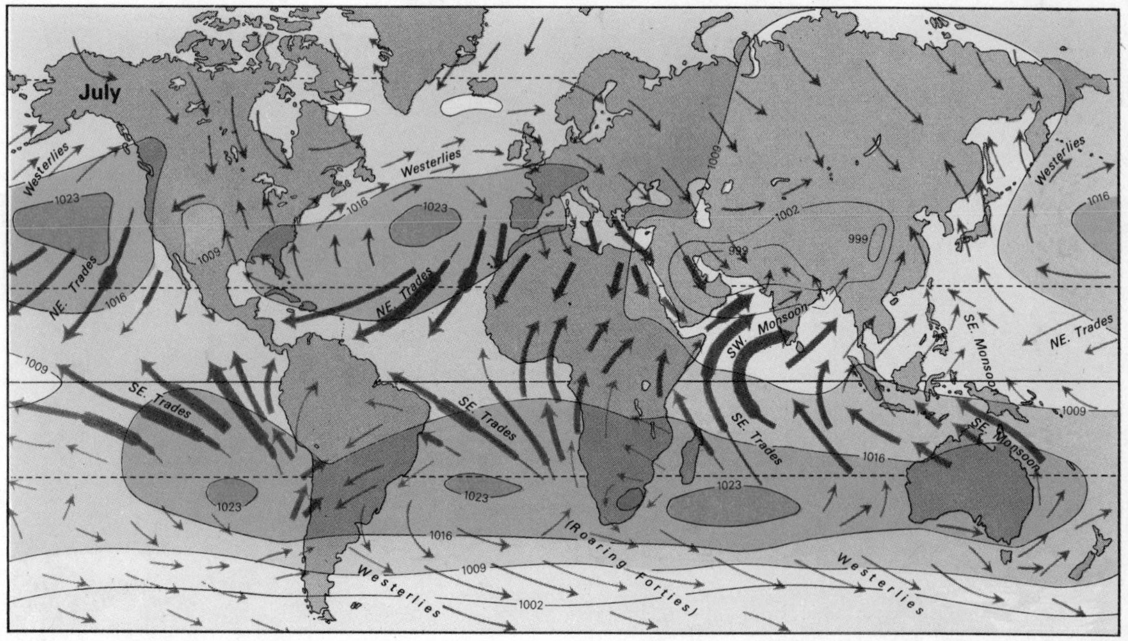

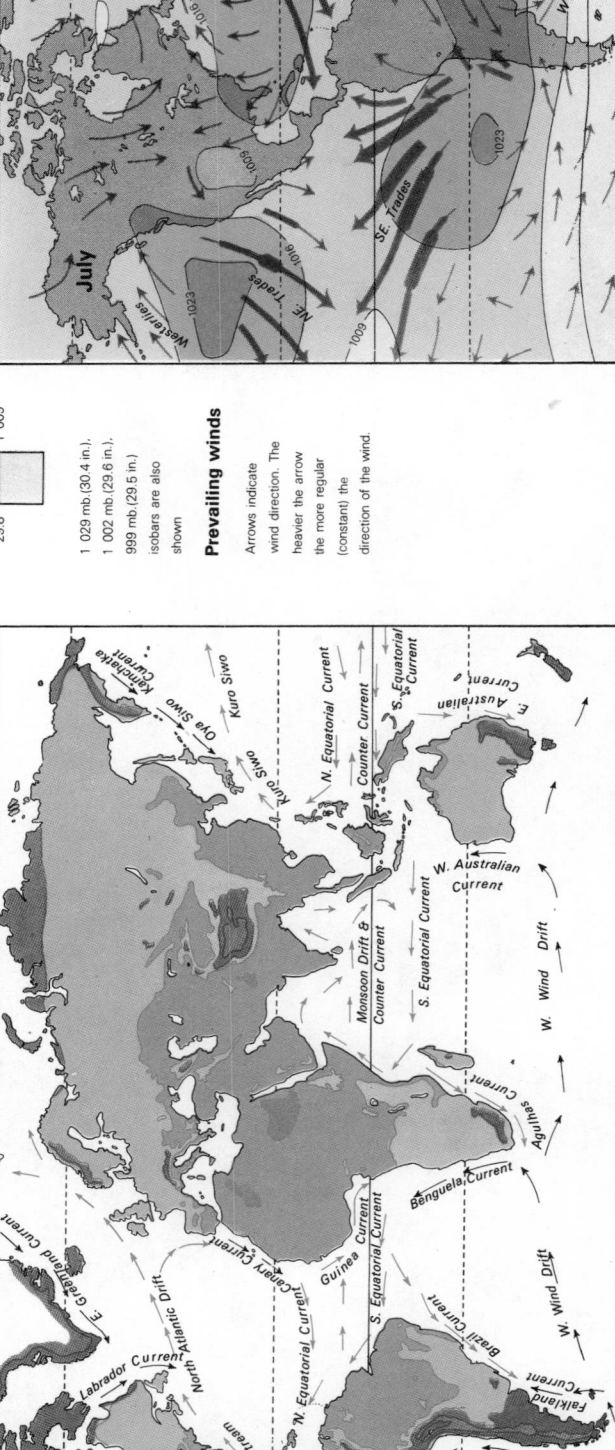

Atmospheric pressure

In.	Millibars
30.2	1 023
30.0	1 016
29.8	1 009

1 029 mb.(30.4 in.).
1 002 mb.(29.6 in.).
999 mb.(29.5 in.)
isobars are also shown

Prevailing winds

Arrows indicate wind direction. The heavier the arrow the more regular (constant) the direction of the wind.

Frost Incidence

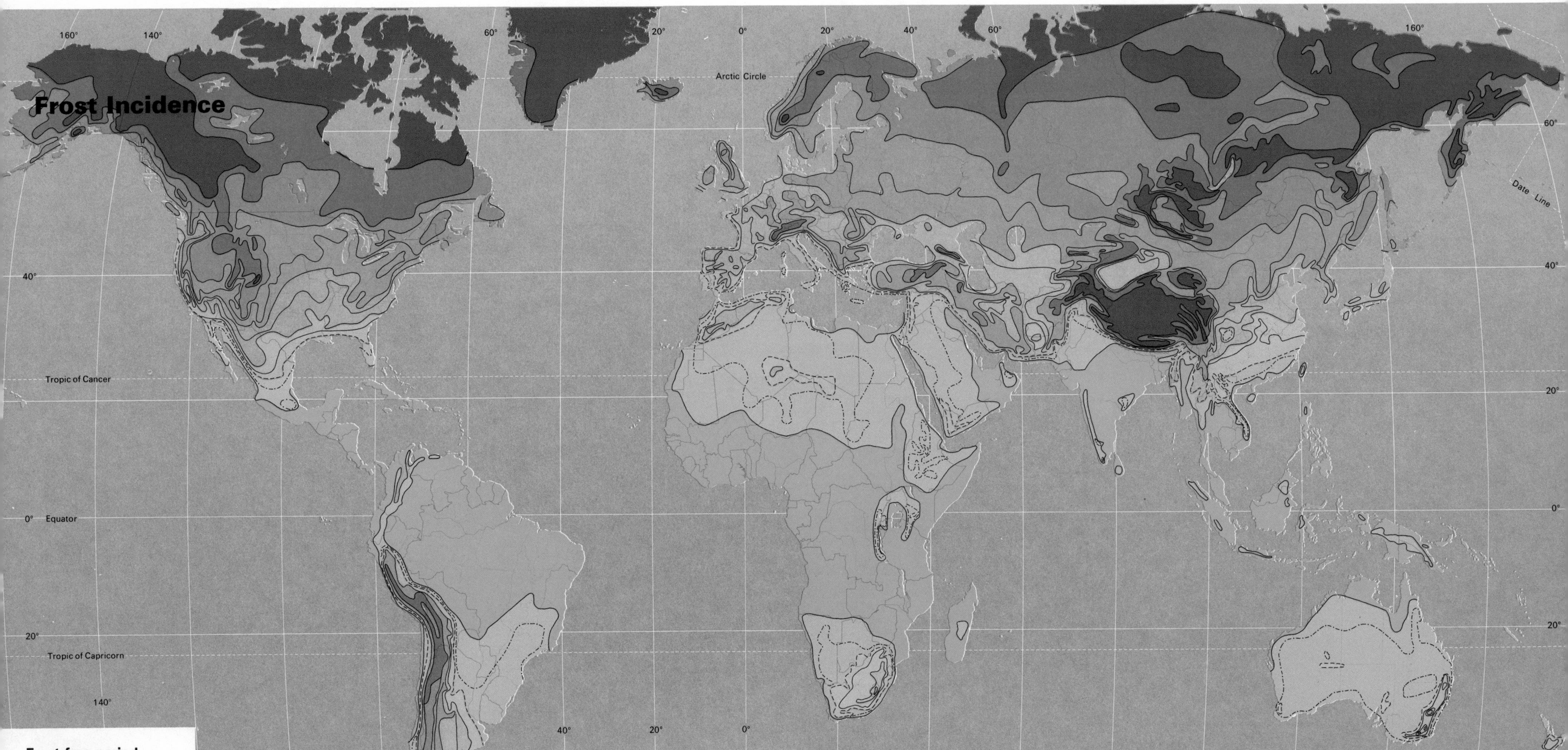

Arctic Circle
Tropic of Cancer
Equator
Tropic of Capricorn
Date Line
160°
140°
60°
20°
0°
40°
80°
100°
120°
© Oxford University Press

Frost-free period

Number of days with minimum temperature above 0°C (32°F)

60, 90 — Summer frosts may occur where frost-free period is less than 90 days

120, 150, 180, 210, 240, 270 — No summer frosts where frost-free period is more than 90 days

Frosts occur in some years only

Absence of frosts

Boundaries of frost probability

- - - - - 100%

-·-·-·-·- 50%

Modified Gall Projection

Equatorial Scale 1: 88 Million approx.

Permafrost (perennially frozen ground) occurs extensively in Canada, Alaska and the U.S.S.R. It can be differentiated into 3 main zones: (a) continuous permafrost, where very little land is unfrozen and where permafrost may reach depths over 600 m. (approx 2 000 ft.); (b) discontinuous permafrost, where scattered patches of unfrozen land occur; and (c) sporadic permafrost, where patches of permafrost occur in a generally unfrozen area. Overlying permafrost is an 'active' layer of rock or soil which thaws in summer and freezes in winter. Permafrost creates both technical and financial problems for economic development. Melting of permafrost due to heat from buildings may lead to flooding and land subsidence, thus necessitating the careful siting of buildings and the use of effective insulation. Similarly, roads, railways, bridges, dams, sewerage and water-supply systems are affected by flooding, slumping and freezing, and maintenance is costly. Mining operations are hindered by the hardness of the ground, the thawing of permafrost in mine shafts and the formation of ice on machines. Agriculture is virtually negligible where permafrost near the ground surface limits the amount of soil available for plant growth. Also, apart from restrictions imposed by flooding and slumping, it is especially affected by the poorly developed soils and short growing season which are found in permafrost zones.

Permafrost zones

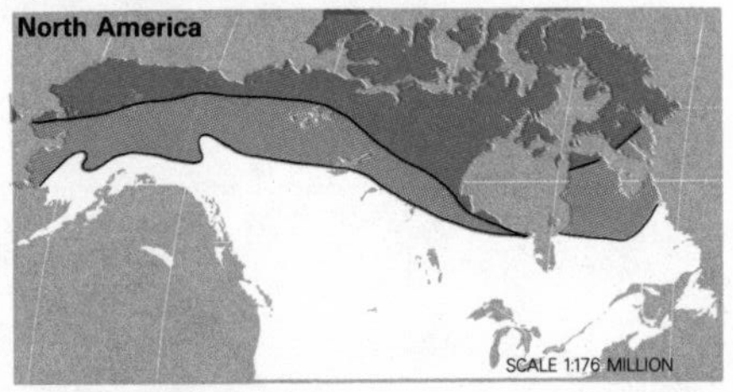

North America
SCALE 1:176 MILLION

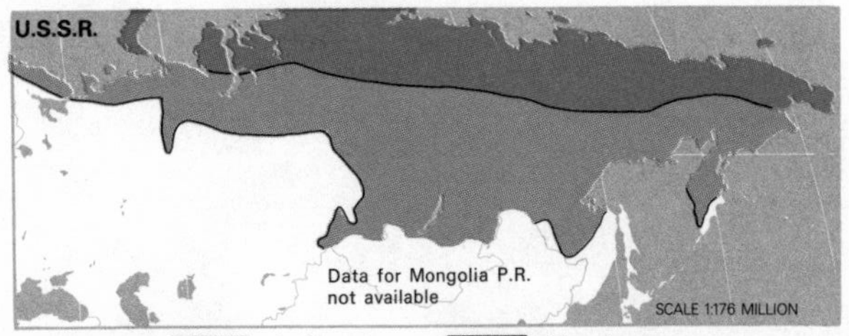

U.S.S.R.
Data for Mongolia P.R. not available
SCALE 1:176 MILLION

Continuous permafrost

Discontinuous permafrost

Sporadic permafrost and permafrost in mountain areas outside discontinuous zone excluded

Plants vary quite considerably in their tolerance to low temperature conditions; some are killed when temperatures approach or reach freezing point whereas others can withstand such conditions although growth is negligible. In general, all plant activity is extremely low when temperatures are at or near freezing point and plant growth is not of economic significance when temperatures are below 4°C (approx. 40°F). The accompanying small world map indicates those areas where the mean monthly temperature is below 4°C for part or all of the year.

The length of the frost-free period gives a general indication of the length of the growing season and hence the suitability of different areas for the production of various crops. It may also serve to indicate whether double cropping is possible during the year. The length of the frost-free period is not, however, the only criterion for determining whether an area is suitable for the production of a particular crop. Other conditions may be equally important, including the following: light intensity; photoperiod (number of daylight hours), for example in temperate rice growing areas; day and night temperature intensities, for example in the production of tomatoes; and water regime.

In some areas, where the occurrence of frosts threatens crops which are otherwise suited to the area, protective measures may be employed to avoid losses. Fruit crops are particularly susceptible to frosts, especially at blossom time. Consequently in some fruit growing areas, particularly the citrus groves of Florida and California, the use of smudge pots to create smoke palls, or of oil heaters, combats damaging frosts. The spreading of straw and mulch over early vegetable crops is another method of frost protection. Also, advances are being made in the development of crops which mature in a shorter, but favourable growing season, so permitting the extension of crop production in such areas as Alaska, Northern Canada and Siberia.

Mean January and July temperatures

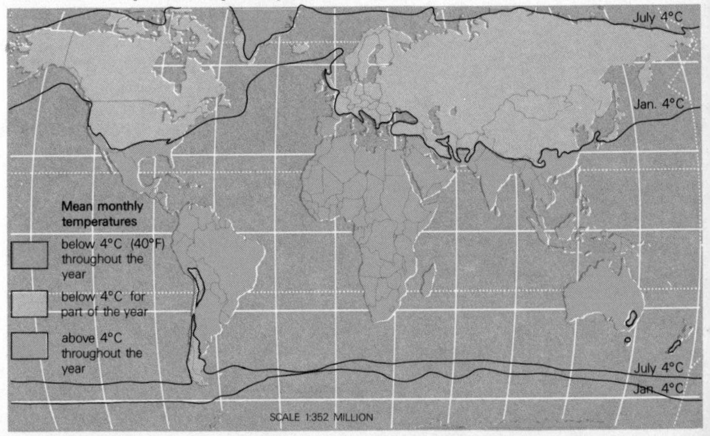

July 4°C
Jan. 4°C
Mean monthly temperatures
below 4°C (40°F) throughout the year
below 4°C for part of the year
above 4°C throughout the year
SCALE 1:352 MILLION

Mean Annual Precipitation

Arctic Circle
Tropic of Cancer
Date Line
Bergen
Moskva
Valentia Island
Kew
Berlin
Perpignan
Athínai
Hulwân
Irkutsk
Tōkyō
Bombay
Kumasi
Bulawayo
Perth
Brisbane
Prince George
Regina
Montréal
Little Rock
Phoenix
Rochambeau
Lima
Rosario
Isohyet intervals
mm.
ins. (approx.)
3 000
120
2 500
100
2 000
80
1 500
60
1 000
40
750
30
500
20
250
10
100
4
Modified Gall Projection
Equatorial Scale 1 : 88 Million approx.
© Oxford University Press

Precipitation data for selected stations (1931–60 av.)[1]

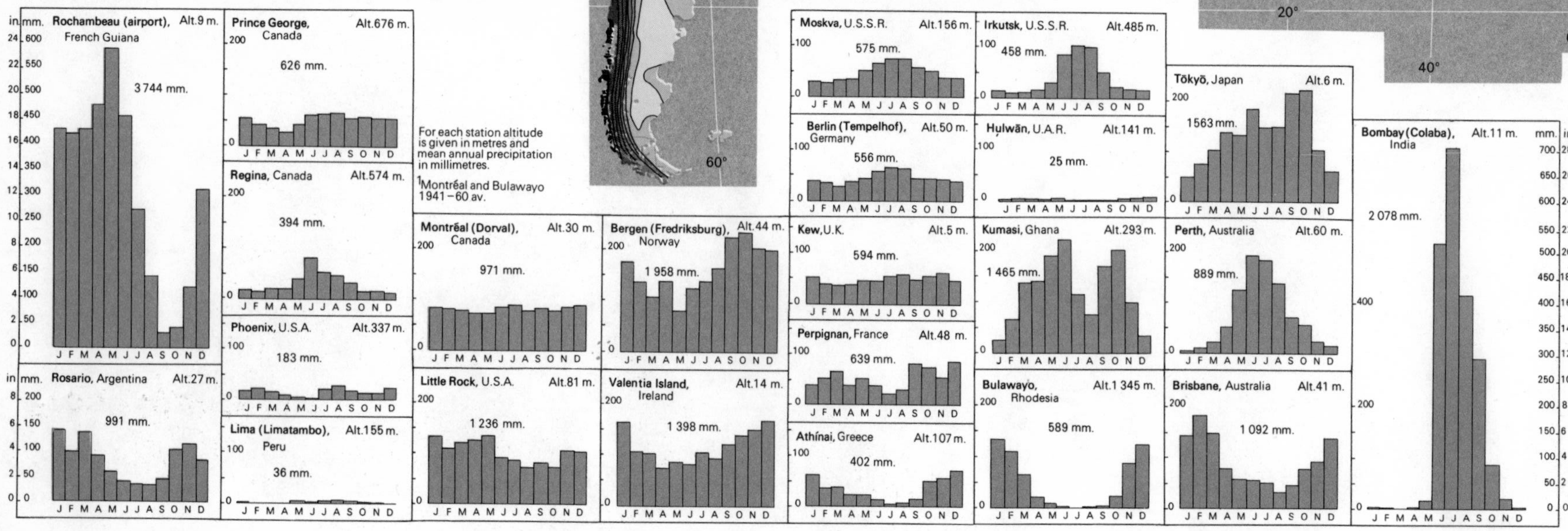
Rochambeau (airport), French Guiana Alt.9 m. 3 744 mm.
Rosario, Argentina Alt.27 m. 991 mm.
Prince George, Canada Alt.676 m. 626 mm.
Regina, Canada Alt.574 m. 394 mm.
Phoenix, U.S.A. Alt.337 m. 183 mm.
Lima (Limatambo), Peru Alt.155 m. 36 mm.
Montréal (Dorval), Canada Alt.30 m. 971 mm.
Little Rock, U.S.A. Alt.81 m. 1 236 mm.
Bergen (Fredriksburg), Norway Alt.44 m. 1 958 mm.
Valentia Island, Ireland Alt.14 m. 1 398 mm.
Moskva, U.S.S.R. Alt.156 m. 575 mm.
Berlin (Tempelhof), Germany Alt.50 m. 556 mm.
Kew, U.K. Alt.5 m. 594 mm.
Perpignan, France Alt.48 m. 639 mm.
Athínai, Greece Alt.107 m. 402 mm.
Irkutsk, U.S.S.R. Alt.485 m. 458 mm.
Hulwân, U.A.R. Alt.141 m. 25 mm.
Kumasi, Ghana Alt.293 m. 1 465 mm.
Bulawayo, Rhodesia Alt.1 345 m. 589 mm.
Tōkyō, Japan Alt.6 m. 1563 mm.
Perth, Australia Alt.60 m. 889 mm.
Brisbane, Australia Alt.41 m. 1 092 mm.
Bombay (Colaba), India Alt.11 m. 2 078 mm.
J F M A M J J A S O N D
in mm.

For each station altitude is given in metres and mean annual precipitation in millimetres.

[1] Montréal and Bulawayo 1941–60 av.

Potential evaporation (evapotranspiration)

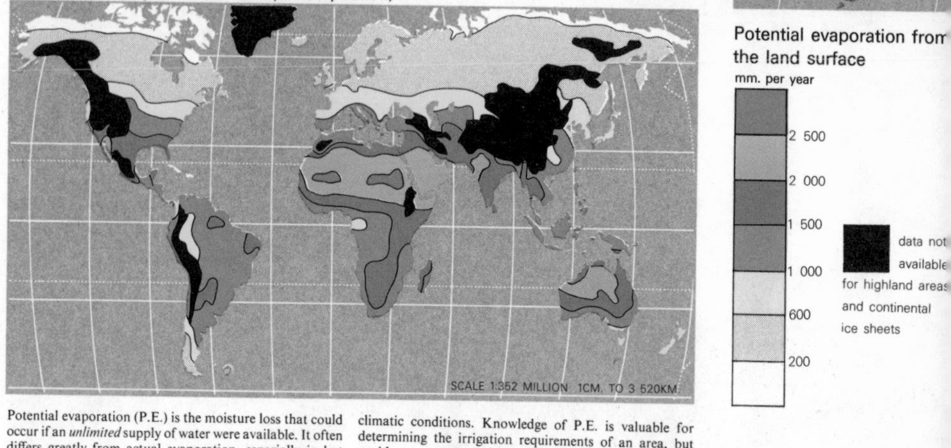
SCALE 1:352 MILLION 1CM. TO 3 520KM
Potential evaporation from the land surface
mm. per year
2 500
2 000
1 500
1 000
600
200
data not available for highland areas and continental ice sheets

Potential evaporation (P.E.) is the moisture loss that could occur if an *unlimited* supply of water were available. It often differs greatly from actual evaporation, especially in hot deserts where water transfer rate is far less than the rate at which evaporation could occur under the prevailing climatic conditions. Knowledge of P.E. is valuable for determining the irrigation requirements of an area, but problems may arise in areas of high P.E. since water added to the land is rapidly evaporated, leading to increased soil salinity which may be harmful to crops.

Seasonal Climates

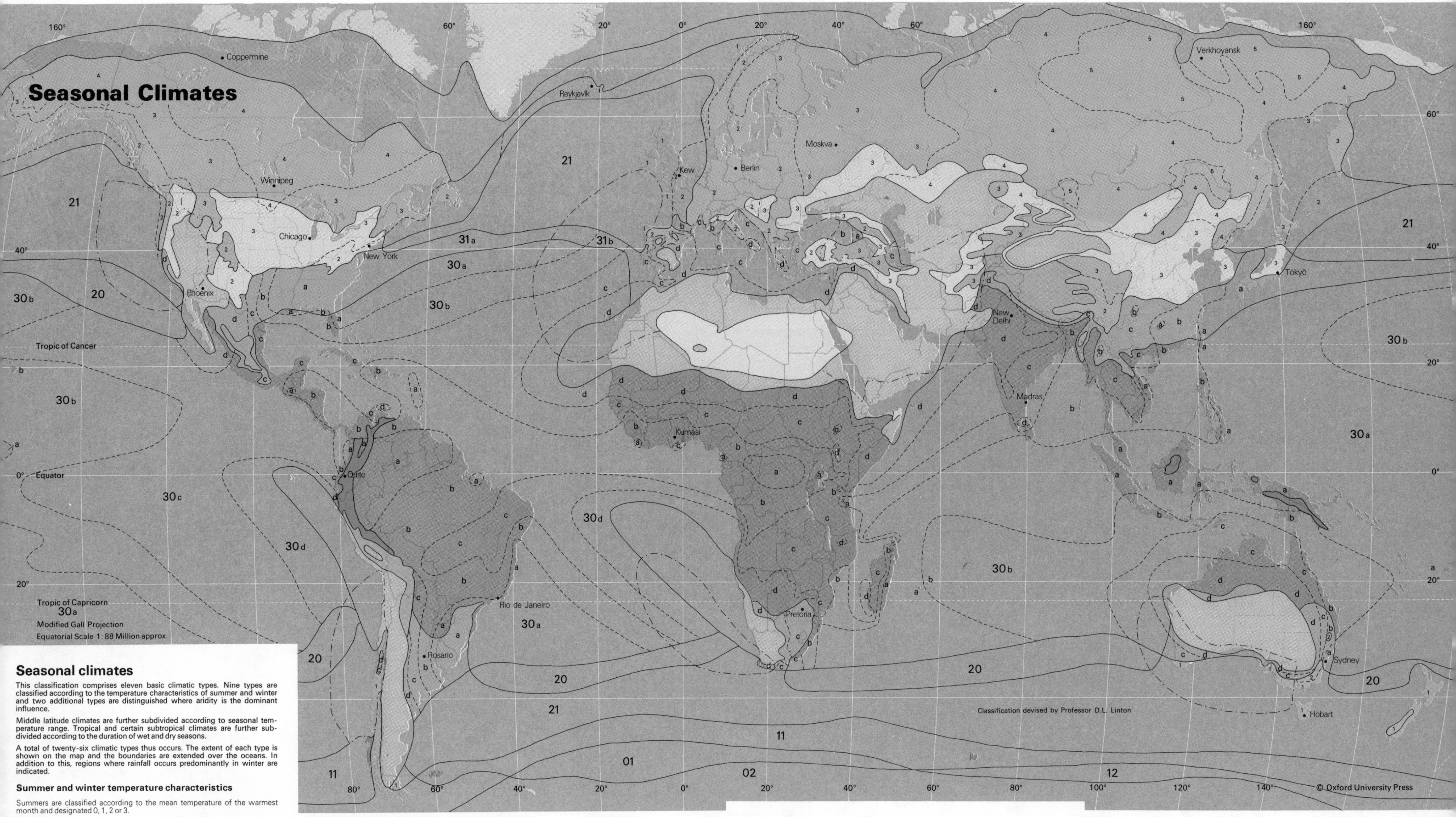

Seasonal climates

This classification comprises eleven basic climatic types. Nine types are classified according to the temperature characteristics of summer and winter and two additional types are distinguished where aridity is the dominant influence.

Middle latitude climates are further subdivided according to seasonal temperature range. Tropical and certain subtropical climates are further subdivided according to the duration of wet and dry seasons.

A total of twenty-six climatic types thus occurs. The extent of each type is shown on the map and the boundaries are extended over the oceans. In addition to this, regions where rainfall occurs predominantly in winter are indicated.

Summer and winter temperature characteristics

Summers are classified according to the mean temperature of the warmest month and designated 0, 1, 2 or 3.

		MEAN TEMPERATURE OF THE WARMEST MONTH
0	No summer	6 °C (43 °F) and under.
1	Very cool summer	6°-10°C (43°-50°F)
2	Cool summer	10°-20°C (50°-68°F)
3	Full summer	over 20 °C (68 °F)

Winters are classified according to the mean temperature of the coldest month and designated 0, 1 or 2.

		MEAN TEMPERATURE OF THE COLDEST MONTH
0	No winter	over 13 °C (55 °F)
1	Mild winter	2°-13°C (36°-55°F)
2	Cold winter	below 2 °C (36 °F)

Combinations of summer and winter conditions are used to indicate climatic types. These are shown on land areas by colour and on sea areas by figures, in which case the digit for summer is always given first. Thus 02 indicates no summer, cold winter.

Combinations of summer and winter conditions

- No summer, Cold winter
- Very cool summer, Cold winter
- Very cool summer, Mild winter
- Cool summer, Cold winter
- Cool summer, Mild winter
- Cool summer, No winter
- Full summer, Cold winter
- Full summer, Mild winter
- Full summer, No winter

Arid climates

- Arid

Arid climates are those climates in middle and low latitudes in which no month receives as much as 50 mm. (2 in.) rainfall.

- Extremely arid

Extremely arid climates are perennially rainless with no more than 2.5 mm. (0.1 in.) rainfall per month for at least 10 months of the year.

Seasonal temperature range

For areas 21, 22 and 32 outside the tropics

1 Oceanic
Seasonal range under 12°C (22° F)

2 Sub Continental
Seasonal range 12°-24°C (22°-43°F)

3 Continental
Seasonal range 24°-36°C (43°-65°F)

4 Very Continental
Seasonal range 36°-48°C (65°-86°F)

5 Extremely Continental
Seasonal range over 48°C (86°F)

Duration of wet and dry seasons

For areas 30 and 31 only

a All months rainy
i.e. with over 50 mm. (2 in.) rainfall

b Rainy season predominant
8-11 months with over 50 mm.

c Rainy and dry seasons approx. equal
5, 6 or 7 months with over 50 mm.

d Dry season predominant
1-4 months with over 50 mm.

Winter rain regions

(–·–·–) Boundary of region where rainfall occurs predominantly in winter

Mean monthly temperatures for January and July (1931–60)

Selected stations *(with altitude in metres)*

	Jan. °C	Jan. °F	July °C	July °F
Coppermine *(0)*	**–28.6**	–19	**9.3**	49
Verkhoyansk *(137)*	**–46.8**	–52	**15.7**	60
Winnipeg *(240)*	**–17.7**	0	**20.2**	68
Moskva *(156)*	**–9.9**	14	**19.0**	66
Berlin *(50)*	**–0.5**	31	**19.4**	67
Reykjavík *(16)*	**–0.4**	31	**11.2**	52
Kew *(5)*	**4.2**	40	**17.6**	64
Hobart *(54)*	**16.3**	61	**7.8**	46
Quito *(2812)*	**13.0**	55	**12.9**	55
Tōkyō *(6)*	**3.7**	39	**25.1**	77
Chicago *(190)*	**–3.3**	26	**24.3**	76
New York *(16)*	**0.9**	34	**24.9**	77
Sydney *(42)*	**21.9**	71	**12.3**	54
Rosario *(27)*[1]	**23.8**	75	**9.9**	50
Pretoria *(1400)*[2]	**21.0**	70	**10.3**	51
Rio de Janeiro *(27)*	**26.0**	79	**20.8**	69
Kumasi *(293)*[1]	**25.2**	77	**24.2**	76
Madras *(16)*	**24.5**	76	**30.7**	87
New Delhi *(216)*[1]	**14.3**	58	**31.2**	88
Phoenix *(337)*	**10.4**	51	**32.9**	91

Temperatures decrease with increasing altitude at a rate of about 2°C (3.6°F) for every 300m. (1 000 ft). Location, season and time of day all influence the actual rate.

[1]1941–60 [2]1951–60

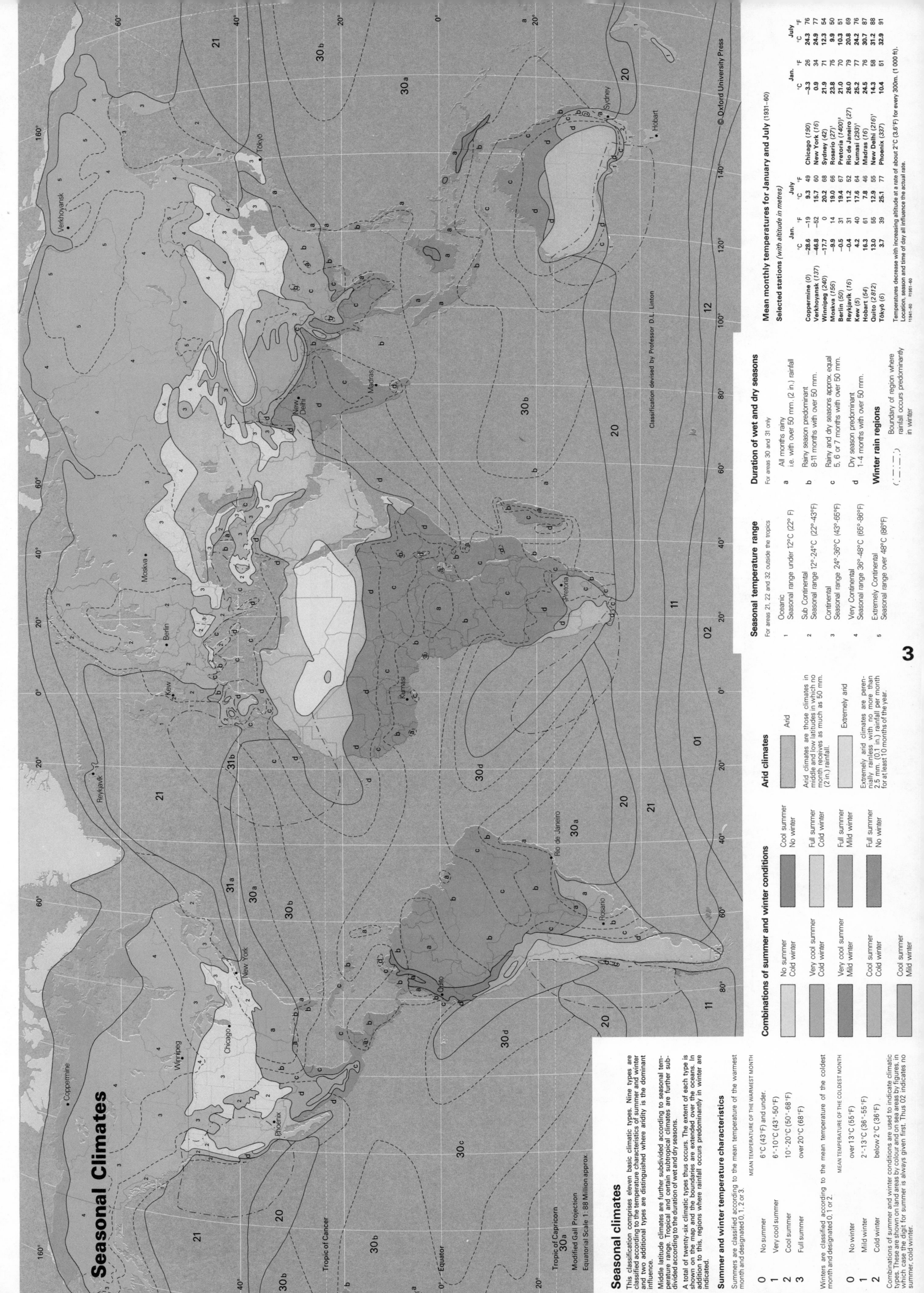

Relief

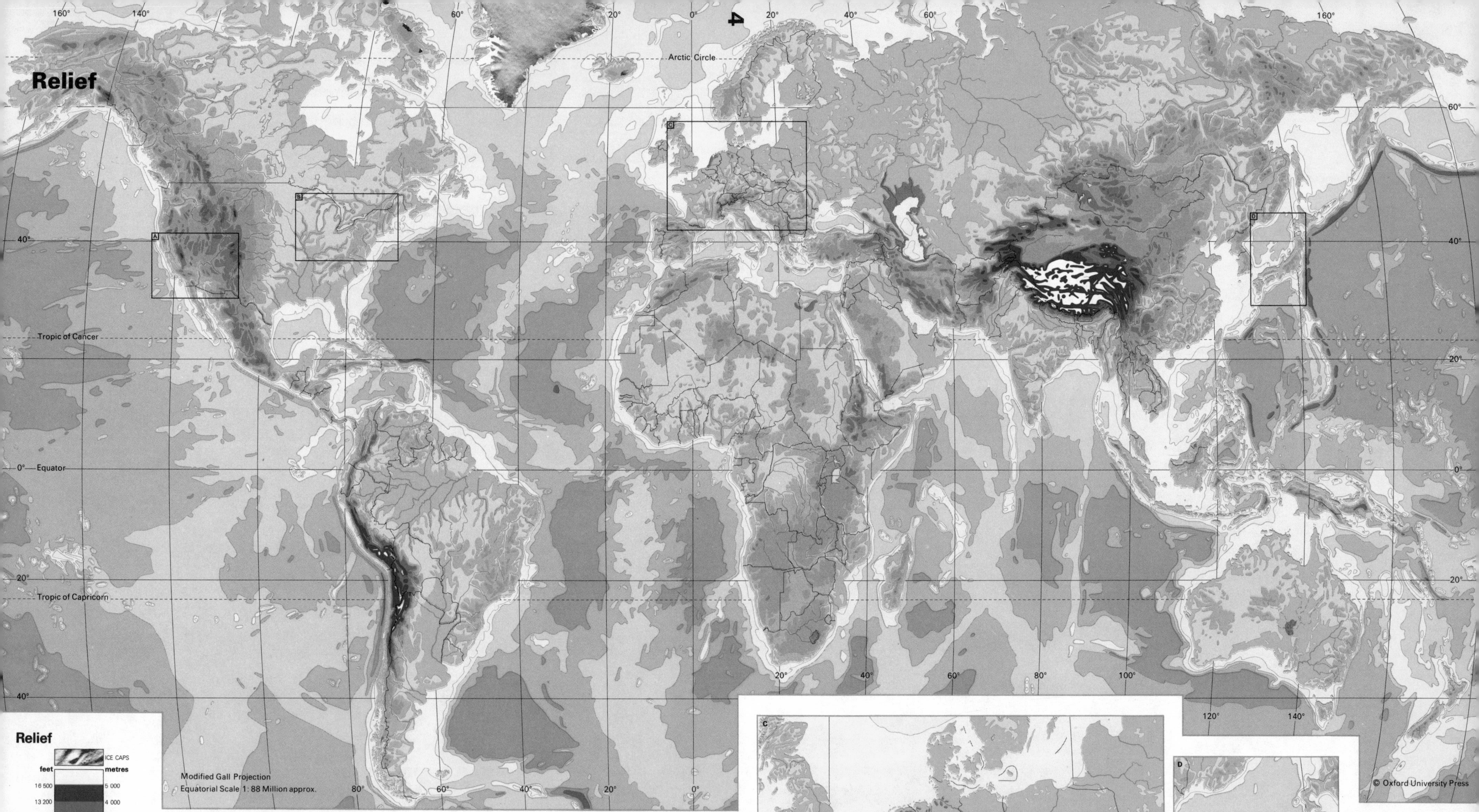
160°
140°
60°
20°
0°
20°
40°
60°
160°
Arctic Circle
60°
40°
Tropic of Cancer
20°
0° Equator
20°
Tropic of Capricorn
40°
80°
100°
120°
140°
A
B
C
D
© Oxford University Press

Modified Gall Projection
Equatorial Scale 1: 88 Million approx.

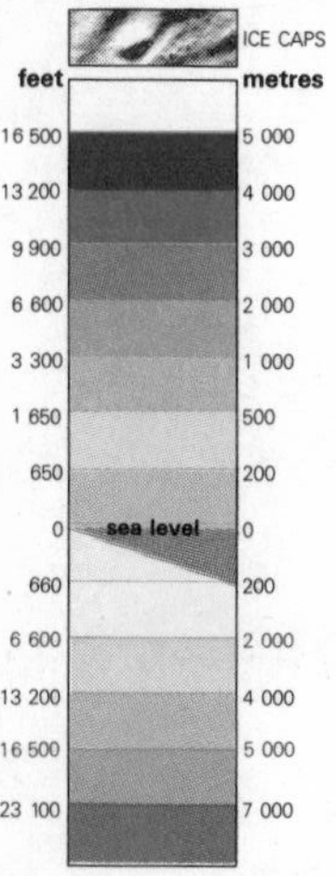
Relief
ICE CAPS
feet
metres
16 500
13 200
9 900
6 600
3 300
1 650
650
0
660
6 600
13 200
16 500
23 100
5 000
4 000
3 000
2 000
1 000
500
200
0
200
2 000
4 000
5 000
7 000
sea level

A
SCALE 1:29 MILLION

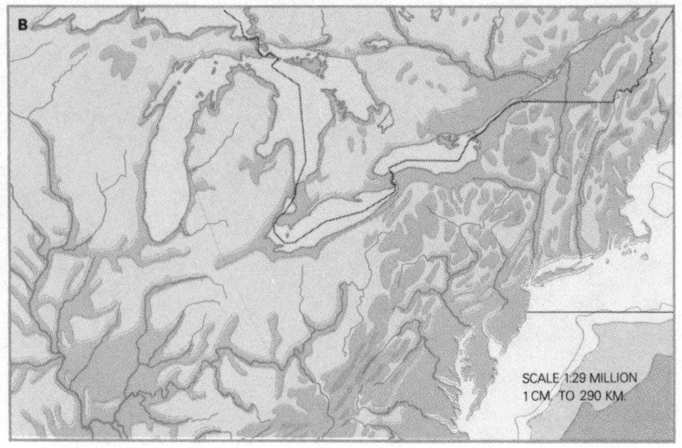
B
SCALE 1:29 MILLION
1 CM. TO 290 KM.

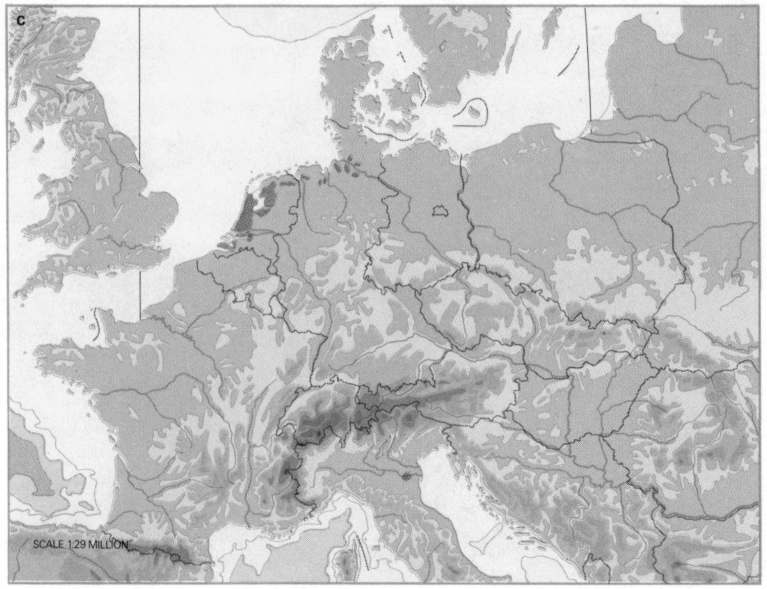
C
SCALE 1:29 MILLION

D
SCALE 1:29 MILLION

Relief

	METRES
Land	
Highest point:	
Mt. Everest	8 848
Lowest point:	
Shores of the Dead Sea	-392
Average height	840
Oceans and seas	
Greatest known depth:	
Marianas Trench	11 022
Average depth	3 808

Area

	MILLION SQ. KM.
Land	149
Water surface	361
Total	510
of which:	
Ice sheets and glaciers	16

Soil

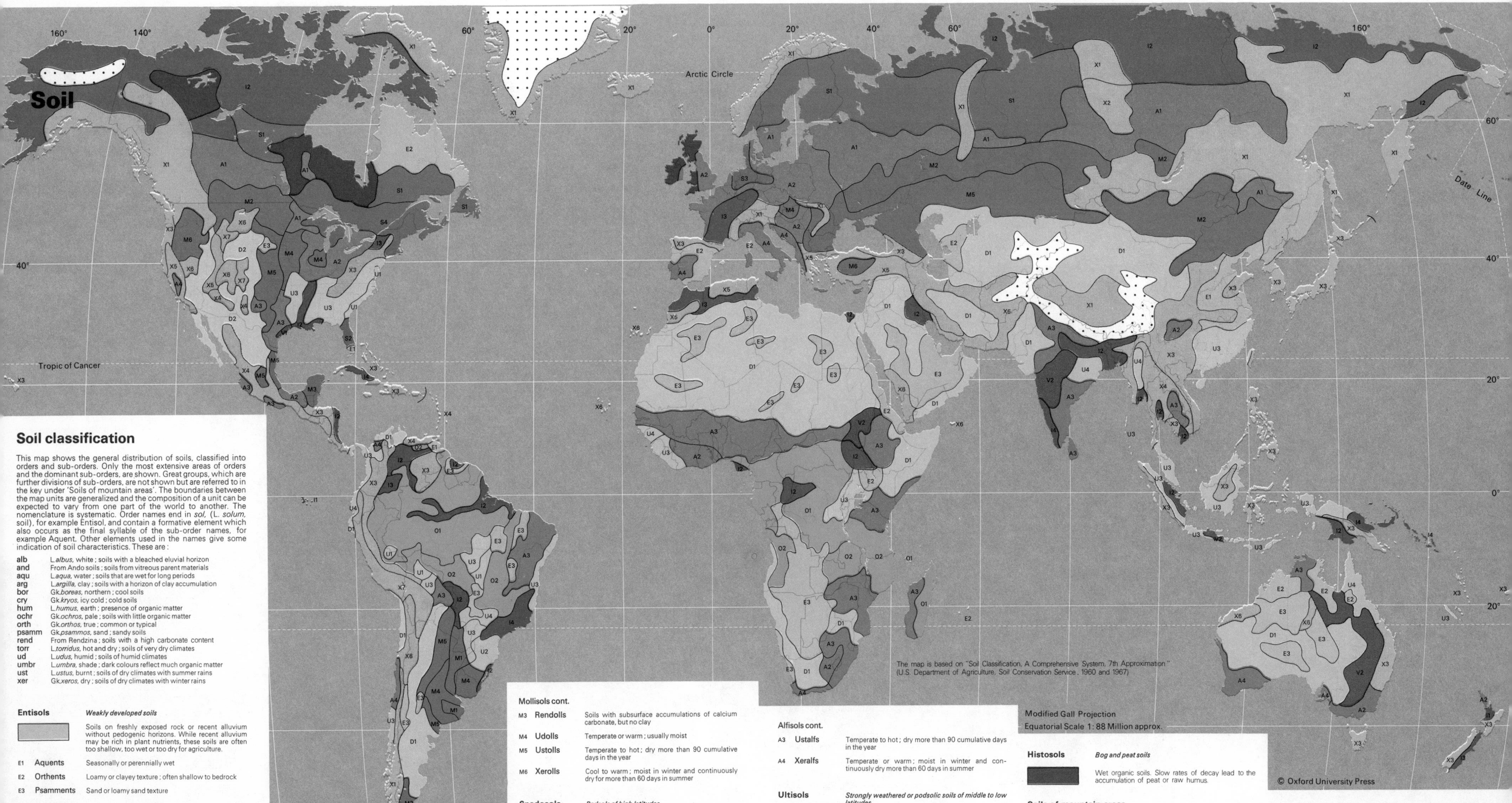

The map is based on "Soil Classification, A Comprehensive System, 7th Approximation" (U.S. Department of Agriculture, Soil Conservation Service, 1960 and 1967)

Modified Gall Projection
Equatorial Scale 1: 88 Million approx.

Soil classification

This map shows the general distribution of soils, classified into orders and sub-orders. Only the most extensive areas of orders and the dominant sub-orders, are shown. Great groups, which are further divisions of sub-orders, are not shown but are referred to in the key under 'Soils of mountain areas'. The boundaries between the map units are generalized and the composition of a unit can be expected to vary from one part of the world to another. The nomenclature is systematic. Order names end in *sol*, (L. *solum*, soil), for example Entisol, and contain a formative element which also occurs as the final syllable of the sub-order names, for example Aquent. Other elements used in the names give some indication of soil characteristics. These are:

alb	L.*albus*, white; soils with a bleached eluvial horizon
and	From Ando soils; soils from vitreous parent materials
aqu	L.*aqua*, water; soils that are wet for long periods
arg	L.*argilla*, clay; soils with a horizon of clay accumulation
bor	Gk.*boreas*, northern; cool soils
cry	Gk.*kryos*, icy cold; cold soils
hum	L.*humus*, earth; presence of organic matter
ochr	Gk.*ochros*, pale; soils with little organic matter
orth	Gk.*orthos*, true; common or typical
psamm	Gk.*psammos*, sand; sandy soils
rend	From Rendzina; soils with a high carbonate content
torr	L.*torridus*, hot and dry; soils of very dry climates
ud	L.*udus*, humid; soils of humid climates
umbr	L.*umbra*, shade; dark colours reflect much organic matter
ust	L.*ustus*, burnt; soils of dry climates with summer rains
xer	Gk.*xeros*, dry; soils of dry climates with winter rains

Entisols — *Weakly developed soils*

Soils on freshly exposed rock or recent alluvium without pedogenic horizons. While recent alluvium may be rich in plant nutrients, these soils are often too shallow, too wet or too dry for agriculture.

- E1 Aquents — Seasonally or perennially wet
- E2 Orthents — Loamy or clayey texture; often shallow to bedrock
- E3 Psamments — Sand or loamy sand texture

Vertisols — *Grumusols*

Soils with a high content of active clays which swell when wet and develop deep, wide cracks when dry. Usually have a moderate to high nutrient status, but may be difficult to manage.

- V1 Uderts — Usually moist, with cracks open less than 90 cumulative days in the year
- V2 Usterts — Dry and cracked more than 90 cumulative days in the year

Inceptisols — *Moderately developed soils*

Soils with some horizons of pedogenic alteration, or concentration of weathering products, but no horizons of redistributed materials except possibly silica or carbonates. Usually moist; base supply usually medium to high. May support a variety of crops.

- I1 Andepts — Soils containing amorphous or allophanic clay, often associated with volcanic ash and/or pumice
- I2 Aquepts — Seasonally or perennially wet
- I3 Ochrepts — Soils with thin, light-coloured surface horizons
- I4 Tropepts — Continuously warm or hot
- I5 Umbrepts — Dark surface horizons; medium to low base supply

Aridisols — *Desert or saline soils*

Soils with pedogenic horizons, which contain little organic matter or nitrogen, and are usually dry for more than 6 months in the year. In many areas salts accumulate on or near the soil surface to form crusts or hardpans. Since their nutrient content, excepting nitrogen, is often high, these soils can be productive with irrigation, but are vulnerable to salt accumulation.

- D1 Aridisols — Undifferentiated
- D2 Argids — Soils with horizons of clay accumulation (U.S.A.)

Mollisols — *Brown forest, chernozem or chestnut soils*

Soils with dark, organic-rich surface horizons, high base supply and which are either usually moist or usually dry. They are highly fertile and can support a variety of crops.

- M1 Albolls — Soils with a seasonally perched water table
- M2 Borolls — Cool or cold

Mollisols cont.

- M3 Rendolls — Soils with subsurface accumulations of calcium carbonate, but no clay
- M4 Udolls — Temperate or warm; usually moist
- M5 Ustolls — Temperate to hot; dry more than 90 cumulative days in the year
- M6 Xerolls — Cool to warm; moist in winter and continuously dry for more than 60 days in summer

Spodosols — *Podsols of high latitudes*

Soils with subsurface accumulations of amorphous materials (mainly iron and aluminium oxides); usually moist or wet, and generally strongly leached (therefore poor in mineral elements), acid and almost structureless, in upper layers. Can be agriculturally productive with the addition of lime and fertilizer.

- S1 Spodosols — Undifferentiated
- S2 Aquods — Seasonally wet
- S3 Humods — Soils with subsurface accumulations of organic matter
- S4 Orthods — Soils with subsurface accumulations of organic matter, iron and aluminium

Alfisols — *Podsolic soils of middle latitudes and degraded grassland soils*

Soils with grey to brown surface horizons, subsurface clay accumulation and a medium to high base supply. They have a better organic status and structure than spodosols and are less acidic. With adequate lime and fertilizer, they will support the continued production of a variety of crops.

- A1 Boralfs — Cool
- A2 Udalfs — Temperate to hot, and usually moist

Alfisols cont.

- A3 Ustalfs — Temperate to hot; dry more than 90 cumulative days in the year
- A4 Xeralfs — Temperate or warm; moist in winter and continuously dry more than 60 days in summer

Ultisols — *Strongly weathered or podsolic soils of middle to low latitudes*

Soils with subsurface horizons of clay accumulation and low base supply; usually moist and usually low in organic matter. Lower horizons may contain iron concretions. Natural agricultural capacity not high, but can be productive with fertilization and good management.

- U1 Aquults — Seasonally wet
- U2 Humults — Temperate or warm; moist all of the year; high content of organic matter
- U3 Udults — Temperate to hot; usually moist
- U4 Ustults — Warm or hot; dry more than 90 cumulative days in the year

Oxisols — *Strongly weathered soils of middle to low latitudes (laterites, latosols)*

Soils with pedogenic horizons that are mixtures principally of kaolin, hydrated oxides and quartz and are low in weatherable minerals. Humus breakdown is rapid and the soils are usually deep and porous. They require fertilization to support continued crop production.

- O1 Orthox — Hot and nearly always moist
- O2 Ustox — Warm or hot; dry for long periods, but moist for a period of more than 90 days in the year

Histosols — *Bog and peat soils*

Wet organic soils. Slow rates of decay lead to the accumulation of peat or raw humus.

Soils of mountain areas

Soils with various temperature and moisture regimes. Altitude, aspect, steepness of slope and relief cause soils to vary greatly within short distances, and vertical zonation is common. In many places soils are absent.

- X1 Cryic great groups of Entisols, Inceptisols and Spodosols
- X2 Boralfs and cryic great groups of Entisols and Inceptisols
- X3 Udic great groups of Alfisols, Entisols and Ultisols; Inceptisols
- X4 Ustic great groups of Alfisols, Inceptisols, Mollisols and Ultisols
- X5 Xeric great groups of Alfisols, Entisols, Inceptisols, Mollisols and Ultisols
- X6 Torric great groups of Entisols; Aridisols
- X7 Ustic and cryic great groups of Alfisols, Entisols, Inceptisols and Mollisols; ustic great groups of Ultisols; cryic great groups of Spodosols
- X8 Aridisols; torric and cryic great groups of Entisols; cryic great groups of Spodosols and Inceptisols

Areas where soils are largely absent

Icefields and rugged mountains

Soil erosion is a natural and continual process which is normally balanced by soil-forming processes so that the basic character of a soil is maintained. In some areas however, the rate of erosion has been greatly accelerated resulting in the removal of part or all of the soil within a relatively short time. Thus, many areas have become either useless for cultivation or else very costly to cultivate due to the large amounts of fertilizer required. Only in those areas where the most fertile horizons are low down in the soil profile can the removal of the upper layers be beneficial, and it may therefore be induced. Accelerated erosion is usually initiated when the equilibrium of an environment is disturbed through human interference, for example by the clearing of land for cultivation, overcultivation or overstocking of sloping land, and the cultivation of steep slopes without terracing. Once the soil has lost its protective covering of vegetation and its surface has been broken up by ploughing, it is less able to withstand erosion, and rapid removal of material by wind and by water (for example sheetwash and gullying) may result. The actual rate of erosion depends on the type of soil, the climatic conditions, and the relief. Attempts are now being made to prevent further destruction and to reclaim land which has suffered extensive erosion. Conservation measures include the use of more suitable crop rotations, strip cropping, contour ploughing, terracing and destocking and a return to either forest or pasture, of land which has proved unsuitable for cultivation.

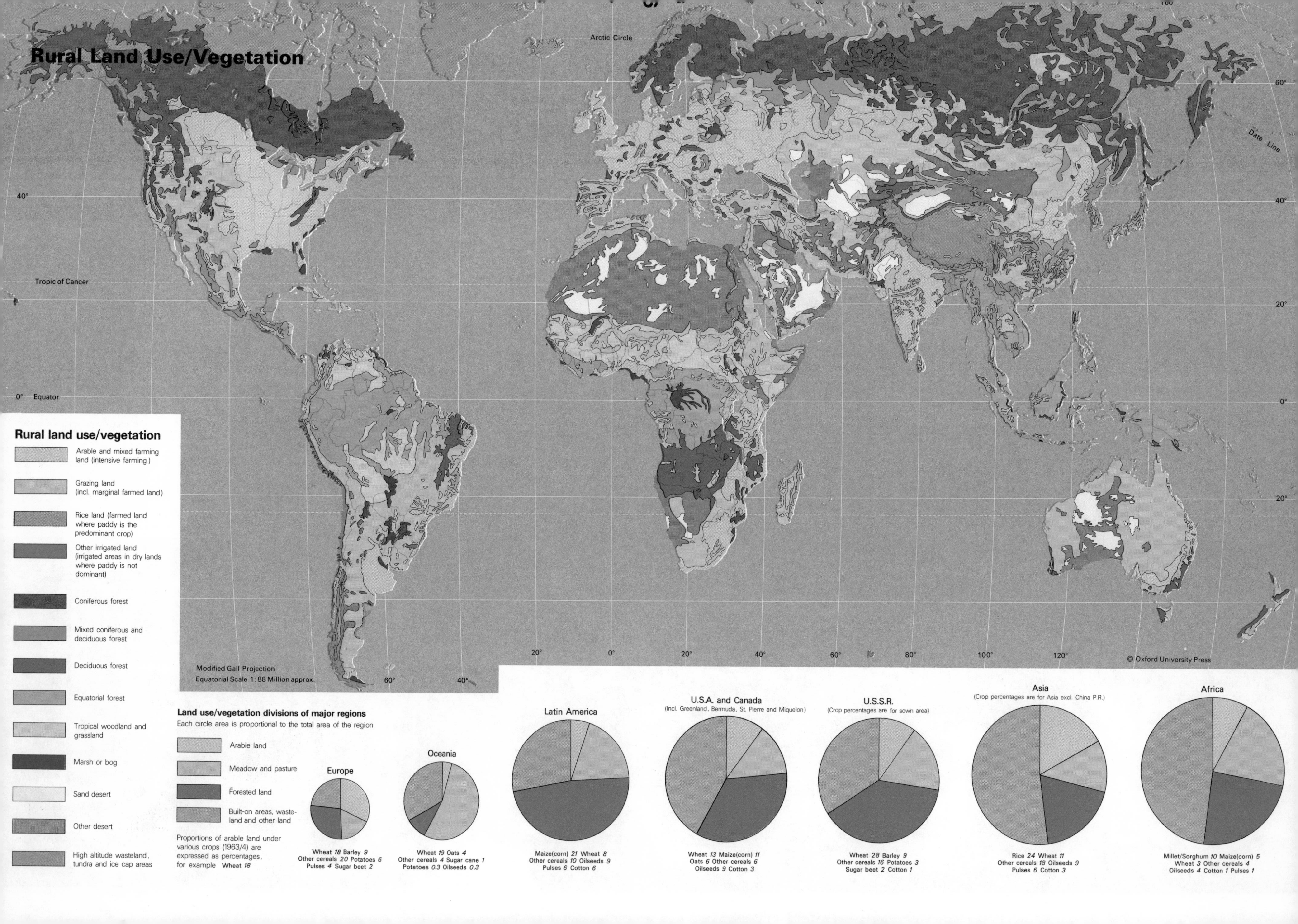
Rural Land Use/Vegetation
Arctic Circle
Tropic of Cancer
Equator
Date Line
Rural land use/vegetation
Arable and mixed farming land (intensive farming)
Grazing land (incl. marginal farmed land)
Rice land (farmed land where paddy is the predominant crop)
Other irrigated land (irrigated areas in dry lands where paddy is not dominant)
Coniferous forest
Mixed coniferous and deciduous forest
Deciduous forest
Equatorial forest
Tropical woodland and grassland
Marsh or bog
Sand desert
Other desert
High altitude wasteland, tundra and ice cap areas
Modified Gall Projection
Equatorial Scale 1: 88 Million approx.
© Oxford University Press
Land use/vegetation divisions of major regions
Each circle area is proportional to the total area of the region
Arable land
Meadow and pasture
Forested land
Built-on areas, waste-land and other land
Proportions of arable land under various crops (1963/4) are expressed as percentages, for example Wheat 18
Europe
Wheat 18 Barley 9
Other cereals 20 Potatoes 6
Pulses 4 Sugar beet 2
Oceania
Wheat 19 Oats 4
Other cereals 4 Sugar cane 1
Potatoes 0.3 Oilseeds 0.3
Latin America
Maize(corn) 21 Wheat 8
Other cereals 10 Oilseeds 9
Pulses 6 Cotton 6
U.S.A. and Canada
(Incl. Greenland, Bermuda, St. Pierre and Miquelon)
Wheat 13 Maize(corn) 11
Oats 6 Other cereals 6
Oilseeds 9 Cotton 3
U.S.S.R.
(Crop percentages are for sown area)
Wheat 28 Barley 9
Other cereals 16 Potatoes 3
Sugar beet 2 Cotton 1
Asia
(Crop percentages are for Asia excl. China P.R.)
Rice 24 Wheat 11
Other cereals 18 Oilseeds 9
Pulses 6 Cotton 3
Africa
Millet/Sorghum 10 Maize(corn) 5
Wheat 3 Other cereals 4
Oilseeds 4 Cotton 1 Pulses 1

Predominant Economies

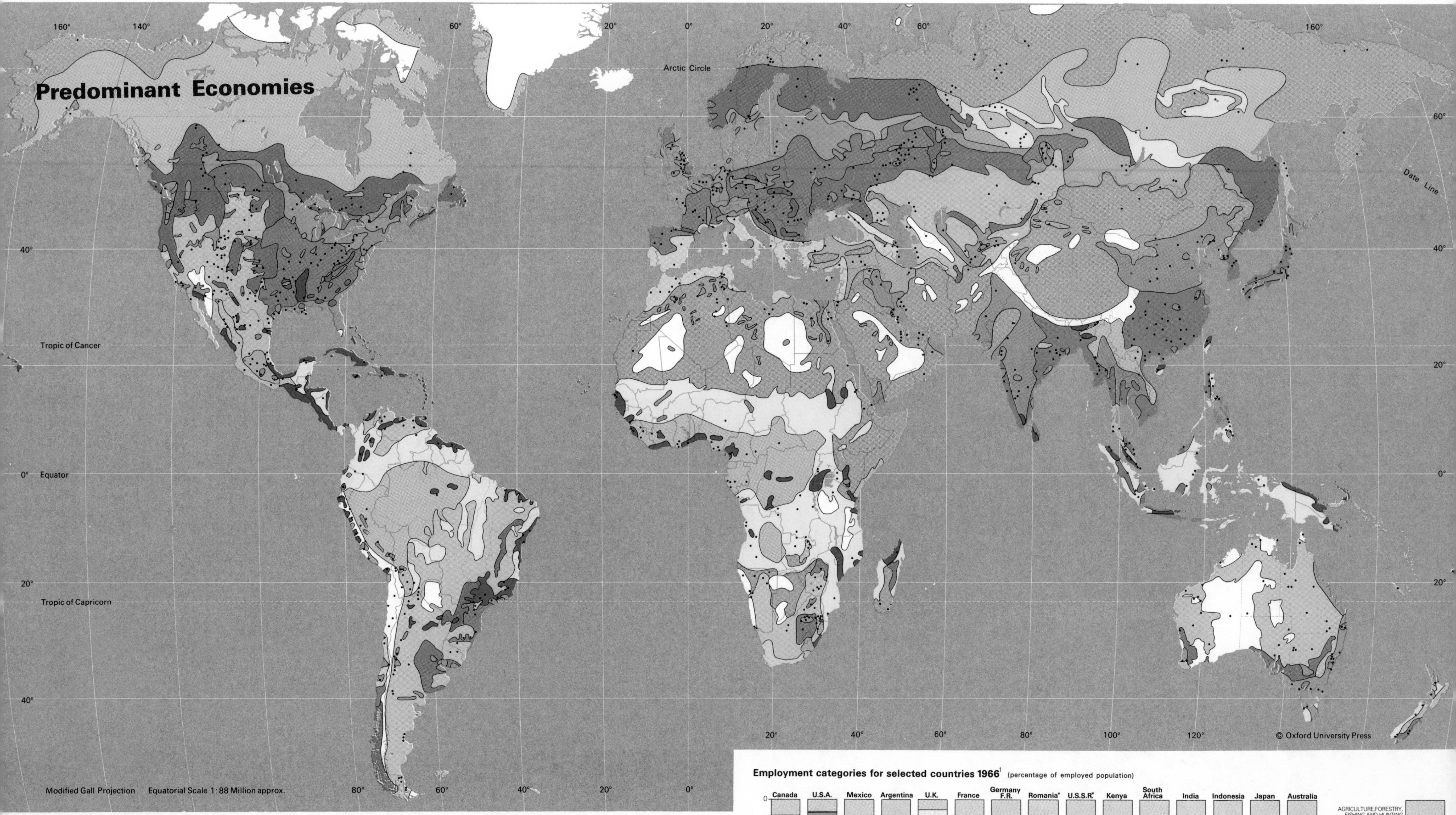

Arctic Circle
Tropic of Cancer
Equator
Tropic of Capricorn
Date Line
160°
140°
60°
20°
0°
20°
40°
60°
160°
40°
20°
0°
20°
40°
80°
100°
120°
© Oxford University Press
Modified Gall Projection
Equatorial Scale 1 : 88 Million approx.

Predominant economies

- Little or no economic activity
- Nomadic herding
- Hunting, gathering, fishing and primitive cultivation
- Shifting and marginal cultivation
- Commercial forestry
- Extensive grazing or stock raising
- Subsistence agriculture: rice dominant
- Subsistence agriculture: rice unimportant
- Subsistence agriculture: mixed crop and livestock
- Mediterranean agriculture
- Plantation crops
- Specialized horticulture
- Other commercial crops: grain dominant
- Commercial agriculture: mixed crop and livestock
- Dairy farming
- Manufacturing and service industries
- Isolated industrial centres
- Mining and extractive industries (1965)

Employment categories for selected countries 1966[1] (percentage of employed population)

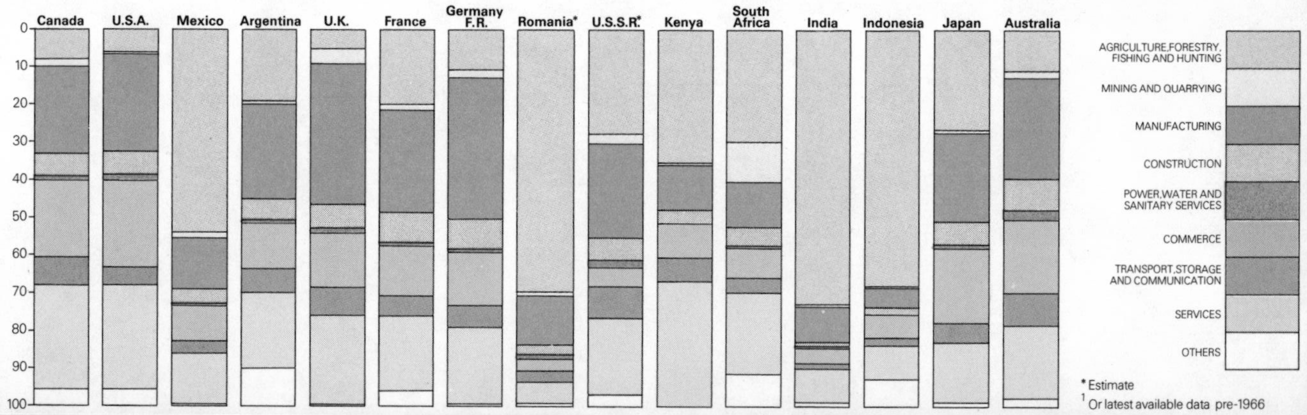

Canada
U.S.A.
Mexico
Argentina
U.K.
France
Germany F.R.
Romania*
U.S.S.R.*
Kenya
South Africa
India
Indonesia
Japan
Australia
0
10
20
30
40
50
60
70
80
90
100
AGRICULTURE, FORESTRY, FISHING AND HUNTING
MINING AND QUARRYING
MANUFACTURING
CONSTRUCTION
POWER, WATER AND SANITARY SERVICES
COMMERCE
TRANSPORT, STORAGE AND COMMUNICATION
SERVICES
OTHERS

* Estimate
[1] Or latest available data pre-1966

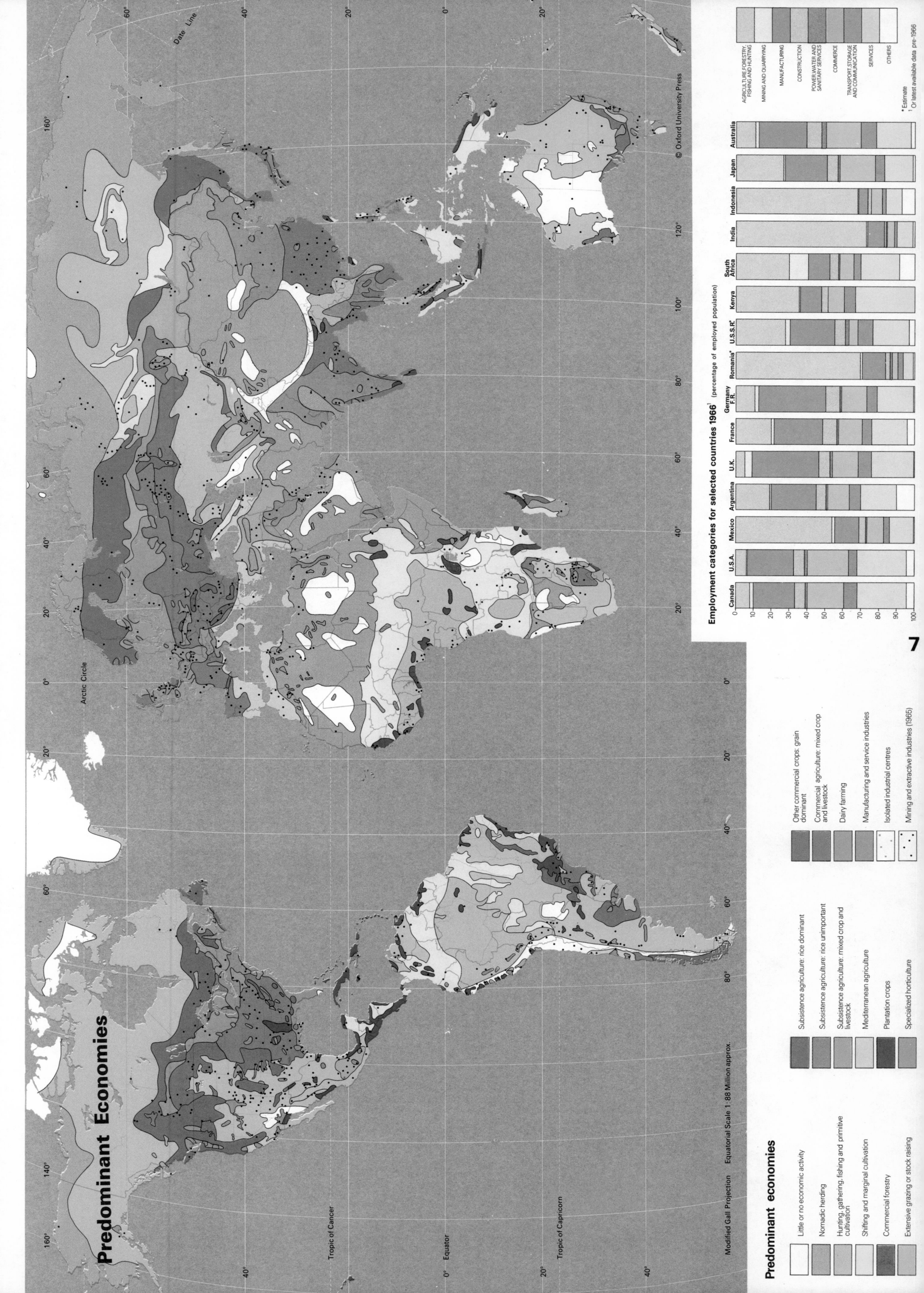

Economic Geology

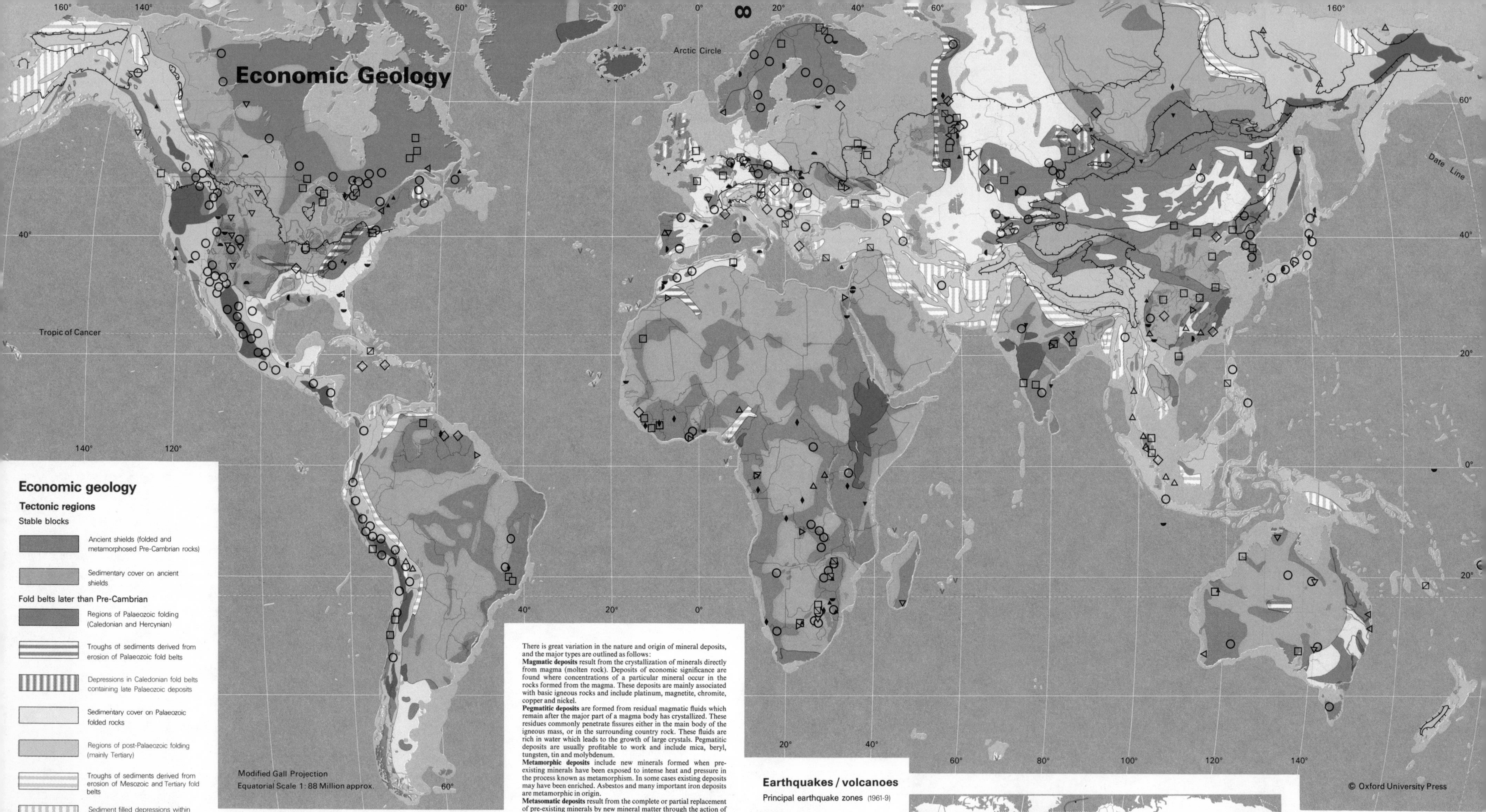

Arctic Circle
Tropic of Cancer
Date Line
160°
140°
120°
60°
40°
20°
0°
Modified Gall Projection
Equatorial Scale 1: 88 Million approx.

Economic geology

Tectonic regions

Stable blocks

- Ancient shields (folded and metamorphosed Pre-Cambrian rocks)
- Sedimentary cover on ancient shields

Fold belts later than Pre-Cambrian

- Regions of Palaeozoic folding (Caledonian and Hercynian)
- Troughs of sediments derived from erosion of Palaeozoic fold belts
- Depressions in Caledonian fold belts containing late Palaeozoic deposits
- Sedimentary cover on Palaeozoic folded rocks
- Regions of post-Palaeozoic folding (mainly Tertiary)
- Troughs of sediments derived from erosion of Mesozoic and Tertiary fold belts
- Sediment filled depressions within Mesozoic and Tertiary fold belts

Extrusive and intrusive igneous rocks

- Post-Palaeozoic lava fields
- Post-Palaeozoic granitoid intrusions
- VVVVVVVVV Principal volcanic islands

Continental shelf/ocean shallows

- Represented approximately by those areas lying between 0 and 200 m. below sea level

Pleistocene glaciation

- Approximate limit of maximum extent of Pleistocene glaciation

Minerals (major areas)

Worked mineral deposits

- ○ gold, silver, lead, zinc, copper[1]
- □ iron
- ◇ bauxite
- △ tin
- ▽ uranium
- ◁ titanium
- ▷ manganese
- nickel
- chrome
- diamond
- asbestos
- mica
- potash
- phosphates
- sulphur
- pyrites

Fossil fuels

- FIELD / BASIN Coal and lignite
- Crude oil fields (incl.oil shales)
- Natural gas fields

[1]These ores are grouped together as two or more occur frequently in association

There is great variation in the nature and origin of mineral deposits, and the major types are outlined as follows:

Magmatic deposits result from the crystallization of minerals directly from magma (molten rock). Deposits of economic significance are found where concentrations of a particular mineral occur in the rocks formed from the magma. These deposits are mainly associated with basic igneous rocks and include platinum, magnetite, chromite, copper and nickel.

Pegmatitic deposits are formed from residual magmatic fluids which remain after the major part of a magma body has crystallized. These residues commonly penetrate fissures either in the main body of the igneous mass, or in the surrounding country rock. These fluids are rich in water which leads to the growth of large crystals. Pegmatitic deposits are usually profitable to work and include mica, beryl, tungsten, tin and molybdenum.

Metamorphic deposits include new minerals formed when pre-existing minerals have been exposed to intense heat and pressure in the process known as metamorphism. In some cases existing deposits may have been enriched. Asbestos and many important iron deposits are metamorphic in origin.

Metasomatic deposits result from the complete or partial replacement of pre-existing minerals by new mineral matter through the action of circulating waters, which either originate in cooling igneous bodies or come from higher levels in the earth's crust. Certain deposits of iron, lead and zinc are examples.

Sedimentary deposits result from the accumulation of material by processes of sedimentation. They include coal (which is derived from an accumulation of plant material), salt deposits and some iron deposits.

Placer deposits are concentrations of mineral particles which have been removed by weathering from the parent rock, transported and eventually deposited by streams. The point of deposition of the mineral particles is determined largely by their specific gravity and therefore particles of one type of mineral are deposited in the same area. Placer deposits are important sources of tin, gold and diamonds. Ancient placer deposits form the source of much of South Africa's gold.

Weathering deposits are derived from the alteration of minerals by weathering processes. Bauxite, for example, is formed when weathering causes the removal of silica from feldspars (important constituent minerals of igneous rocks).

Crude oil and natural gas deposits occur either in 'traps' produced by the juxtaposition of porous and non-porous sedimentary rocks as a result of earth movements, or in association with salt domes (as in the U.S. Gulf coast). The exact origin of oil is not known, but it has been ascertained that it contains compounds that must have come from living matter once inhabiting a shallow, calm, tropical sea.

Earthquakes / volcanoes

Principal earthquake zones (1961-9)

- Areas with a high frequency of earthquakes
- Areas with a lower frequency of earthquakes

Volcanoes

- · Active volcanoes

Volcanoes which have shown no major activity during this century have been omitted.

Most earthquake zones coincide with active volcanic districts, but this is not always so. All volcanoes occur in tectonic fault zones in which tensional forces have caused fissuring of the crust.

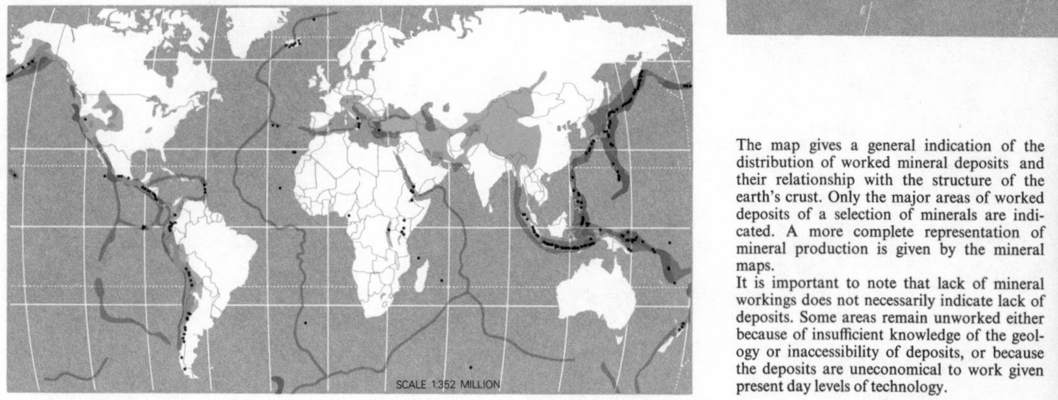

SCALE 1:352 MILLION

The map gives a general indication of the distribution of worked mineral deposits and their relationship with the structure of the earth's crust. Only the major areas of worked deposits of a selection of minerals are indicated. A more complete representation of mineral production is given by the mineral maps.

It is important to note that lack of mineral workings does not necessarily indicate lack of deposits. Some areas remain unworked either because of insufficient knowledge of the geology or inaccessibility of deposits, or because the deposits are uneconomical to work given present day levels of technology.

Cereals/Potatoes

Barley p.10 · Maize-Corn p.10 · Nutrition p. 20 · Potatoes p. 11 · Rice p.11 · Wheat p.12

For individual country data see Statistical Supplement

Cereals include those members of the grain family which have starchy edible seeds; the most common being rice, wheat, barley, oats, maize, sorghums and some millets. Potatoes, though not a cereal, are mapped in this section because they are a starch-producing crop and possess similar dietary properties.
Cereals have been grown throughout historical times, and every major civilization has been founded on them as the principal source of food. It was largely owing to their cultivation that settled communities were formed. Cereals and potatoes are still the world's basic foods.
The pre-eminence of cereals as a foodstuff is partly explained by the ease with which they can be produced, stored and transported. They yield more food, both in bulk and in nutritive value, per unit of land and labour than most other crops. This is why they are so vital to large communities crowded on small areas. Also, cereals provide the basis for man's diet, either in direct human consumption, or as a food for animals producing meat, milk, eggs and fats. As living standards rise, consumption of cereals per head at first rises with them; but, after a point, more expensive and attractive food is sought, and direct consumption begins to decline.
Wheat ranks as the leading bread grain. Rye predominates for bread-making only in East Europe and the U.S.S.R. Elsewhere rye is mainly an animal feed, and as such the least important of feed grains. Whereas wheat is the bread grain of the temperate zones, rice is the principal cereal, and, indeed, the principal food, of the warmer humid areas, especially in Asia. That continent grows and consumes about nine-tenths of the world's rice.
As a source of human food potatoes rival wheat and rice. In terms of potential dry matter potatoes yield more per hectare than wheat. Potatoes are grown in vast quantities in Europe, the U.S.A. and the U.S.S.R., and they are a main item of the diet of hundreds of millions. Oats and barley are grown usually to provide food for livestock; but, by volume of output, the most important animal feed grain is maize, of which the United States produces almost half the total.
Other cereals are grown primarily as subsistence crops. These include millets and sorghums which are major food crops in India and Africa, and are grown for animal consumption in the U.S.A. or as forage crops in Europe and elsewhere. Cassava (manioc) is a starch-producing crop occurring in most tropical countries especially in South America; allied crops are sweet potatoes and yams.
Data for oats, rye, millets and sorghums, sweet potatoes and yams are given in the statistical index but are not mapped.
Although cereals are chiefly consumed in the form of grain or processed products there are other important applications, particularly the brewing of beer from barley or in Africa from sorghum. All cereals (and potatoes) are used in varying degrees for the distillation of potable spirits and industrial alcohols.
World production of grains has greatly expanded in the past 100 years to keep pace with the growth of population and with rising living standards. Although the extension of grain areas, notably in North America, partly accounts for the expansion of output, increases in yield have had a far greater effect. These have resulted from the breeding of more productive strains, the use of nitrogenous and other fertilizers, the control of diseases and pests, the spraying of crops with weed killers and continual improvement in cultivation and harvesting. Naturally, it is in highly-developed countries and where scarcity of farm land in relation to population encourages intensive farming methods that the biggest returns are obtained. Yield, therefore, varies considerably; during 1963-5 wheat yields ranged from 0.56 metric tons per hectare in Africa to 4.42 metric tons per hectare in the Netherlands.
The tables below indicate the relative importance of cereals and other starchy foods in the national average diet of selected countries.

Percent of total calorie intake derived from cereals/starches

Selected countries

	1961-4 av.	1951-4 av.
Malagasy R.	86[1]	*NA*
Afghanistan	82	*NA*
Bolivia	72[1]	*NA*
Ethiopia	71	*NA*
Turkey	71	*72*
Uganda	70[1]	*NA*
Guatemala	68[1]	*NA*
Japan	68	*78*
India	68	*69*
Romania	68	*NA*
Yugoslavia	64	*73*
South Africa	58	*59*
Poland	55	*NA*
Brazil	51	*51*
Colombia	50[1]	*NA*
Israel	42	*55*
Finland	40	*44*
Argentina	39	*40*
France	37	*48*
Switzerland	33	*38*
U.K.	30	*36*
Denmark	29	*35*
U.S.A.	24	*26*

[1]Incl. plantains

Both cereals and starchy roots contain large amounts of carbohydrates but are relatively poor in proteins and other essential nutrients. Thus the proportion of calories derived from them gives an approximate idea of the nutritional value of the diet as a whole. The lower the proportion of these foods in the diet, the higher generally would be the proportion of the more nutritious foods. However, the nutritive value of the diet is influenced not only by this proportion but also by the precise nature of the foods comprising the group of cereals and starchy roots as well as the nutrients provided by the rest of the foods in the diet. Nevertheless, this indicator has the merit of simplicity, and since in almost all countries cereals and starchy roots are staples of diet, it is fairly widely applicable.

Consumption of principal food commodities[1] (1960 - 3 av.)

Selected countries *(kg. per capita)*

	CEREALS	STARCHY ROOTS	SUGAR	NUTS/ PULSES	VEGE-TABLES	FRUIT	MEAT	EGGS	FISH	MILK FAT	MILK PROTEIN	FAT
Turkey	223	39	17	13	105	89	14	2	3	4	4	8
Romania	196	66	13	9	62	44	35	5	2	5	5	5
Afghanistan	174	—	3	—	23	27	13	1	*NA*	4	4	1
Japan	149	69	16	16[3]	90	26	8	6	27	1	1	5
Ethiopia	149	19	2	19	13	2	27	2	—	3	3	5
Poland	146	221	31	2	92	16	54	8	4	7	7	10
Guatemala	141	8[2]	26	9	39	28	12	2	—	1	1	3
India	140	11	18	23	3	18	2	—	1	3	2[4]	4[5]
Israel	116	38	32	10	112	142	40	20	7	4	5	18
Brazil	109	149	40	30	8	112	28	3	3	2	2	8
Finland	107	111	40	2	15	44	34	8	11	12	12	20
France	98	99	29	6	142	64	78	11	7	6	7	22
Switzerland	96	69	43	8	75	162	60	10	4	10	9	20
Argentina	91	88	35	3	48	80	100	8	2	4	3	16
Australia	84	47	50	4	64	104	109	12	5	7	7	15
U.K.	81	98	49	6	58	55	74	15	10	8	8	23
U.S.A.	66	48	40	8	99	101	96	19	5	8	9	21
Colombia	65	206	50	5	12	45	36	3	1	2	2	4
Uganda	61	476[2]	13	27	23	7	10	1	4	2	1	2
Dominican R.[6]	57	124[2]	21	17	23	220	19	4	4	3	3	4

[1]At the retail level [2]Incl. plantains [3]Incl. soya bean preparations in terms of soya bean [4]Incl. milk for making butter [5]Excl. butter [6]Data for 1959

Cereals contribute more than any other food group to the energy value and protein content of diets. Starchy roots generally provide the cheapest source of energy. Sugar consists entirely of carbohydrates and is thus a source only of energy. Pulses and nuts are nutritionally important, being a source of energy, protein, some minerals and B-complex vitamins. Fruit and vegetables provide many essential minerals and vitamins. Products of animal origin provide high-quality protein and are a rich source of essential nutrients. Cereals and starchy roots are commonly known as 'staple foods'; pulses, fruit, vegetables and foods of animal origin are known as 'protective foods' because of their high nutritional quality.

International trade in cereals (1963-5 av.)

Wheat (S.I.T.C. no. 041)[2]

Production
260 093 700 met. tons 1963-5 av.
157 900 000 1953-5 av.[1]

Percentage exported
19% 1963-5 av.
16% 1953-5 av.[1]

Exports
48 156 200 met. tons 1963-5 av.
25 143 700 1953-5 av.

	PERCENTAGE 1963-5 av.	1953-5 av.
U.S.A.	39	*28*
Canada	25	*30*
Australia	12	*10*
Argentina	8	*12*
France	7	*7*
U.S.S.R.	5	*3*
Mexico	1	—
Sweden	1	*1*
Others	2	*9*
	100	*100*

Imports
47 145 100 met. tons 1963-5 av.
24 848 000 1953-5 av.

	PERCENTAGE 1963-5 av.	1953-5 av.
U.S.S.R.	12	—
India	11	*3*
China P.R.	11	—
U.K.	9	*19*
Japan	7	*8*
Brazil	5	*7*
Poland	4	*2*
Germany F.R.	4	*10*
Others	37	*51*
	100	*100*

Maize-Corn (S.I.T.C. no. 044)

Production
221 111 000 met. tons 1963-5 av.
152 700 000 1953-5 av.[1]

Percentage exported
10% 1963-5 av.
3% 1953-5 av.[1]

Exports
22 805 200 met. tons 1963-5 av.
5 309 300 1953-5 av.

	PERCENTAGE 1963-5 av.	1953-5 av.
U.S.A.	56	*50*
Argentina	13	*23*
South Africa	6	*8*
Thailand	4	*1*
Romania	4	*2*
U.S.S.R.	3	*1*
France	3	—
Brazil	2	*1*
Others	9	*14*
	100	*100*

Imports
21 908 100 met. tons 1963-5 av.
5 285 000 1953-5 av.

	PERCENTAGE 1963-5 av.	1953-5 av.
Italy	19	*3*
U.K.	16	*27*
Japan	14	*5*
Germany F.R.	9	*10*
Netherlands	9	*10*
Belg./Lux.	3	*8*
France	3	*6*
Canada	2	*2*
Others	25	*29*
	100	*100*

Barley (S.I.T.C. no. 043)

Production
104 450 700 met. tons 1963-5 av.
63 933 000 1953-5 av.[1]

Percentage exported
7% 1963-5 av.
9% 1953-5 av.[1]

Exports
7 154 900 met. tons 1963-5 av.
5 542 300 1953-5 av.

	PERCENTAGE 1963-5 av.	1953-5 av.
France	28	*1*
U.S.A.	19	*15*
U.S.S.R.	16	*2**
Canada	10	*33*
Australia	5	*9*
Argentina	4	*10*
Syria	4	*4*
Others	14	*26*
	100	*100*

Imports
7 039 700 met. tons 1963-5 av.
5 445 000 1953-5 av.

	PERCENTAGE 1963-5 av.	1953-5 av.
Germany F.R.	16	*16*
Italy	10	*1*
Spain	8	*1[3]*
Japan	6	*13*
Poland	6	—
Czechoslovakia	6	—
Denmark	5	*4[4]*
Others	43	*65*
	100	*100*

Millets/Sorghums

Production
77 237 000 met. tons 1963-5 av.
62 533 000 1953-5 av.

Percentage exported
5% 1963-5 av.
2% 1953-5 av.

Exports
3 998 600 met. tons 1963-5 av.
1 126 700 1953-5 av.

	PERCENTAGE 1963-5 av.	1953-5 av.
U.S.A.	72	*68*
Argentina	15	*3*
South Africa	3	*4[5]*
Sudan	2	*4*
Morocco	1	*3*
Netherlands	1	—
Australia	1	*5*
Others	5	*13*
	100	*100*

Imports
4 066 900 met. tons 1963-5 av.
1 000 300 1953-5 av.

	PERCENTAGE 1963-5 av.	1953-5 av.
Japan	27	*4*
Netherlands	17	*12*
Belg./Lux.	13	*11*
U.K.	10	*21*
Germany F.R.	7	*14*
Israel	4	*5*
Poland	4	—
Others	18	*33*
	100	*100*

Rice (S.I.T.C. no. 042)

Production
256 652 000 met. tons 1963-5 av.
185 900 000 1953-5 av.[1]

Percentage exported
3% 1963-5 av.
3% 1953-5 av.[1]

Exports
7 412 000 met. tons 1963-5 av.
4 717 000 1953-5 av.

	PERCENTAGE 1963-5 av.	1953-5 av.
Thailand	24	*25*
Burma	20	*29*
U.S.A.	18	*13*
China P.R.	10	*6*
Cambodia	6	*4[6]*
U.A.R.	6	*2*
Taiwan	2	*2*
Pakistan	2	*3*
S. Vietnam	2	*NA[6]*
Italy	1	*4*
Others	9	*12*
	100	*100*

Imports
7 270 300 met. tons 1963-5 av.
4 555 000 1953-5 av.

	PERCENTAGE 1963-5 av.	1953-5 av.
Indonesia	10	*5*
Malaysia	10	*11*
India	9	*8*
Japan	7	*27*
Ceylon	7	*9*
Hong Kong	5	*5*
Philippines	5	*1*
U.S.S.R.	4	*2*
Cuba	3	*4*
Germany F.R.	2	*2*
Others	38	*26*
	100	*100*

Potatoes (S.I.T.C. no. 054.1)

Production
288 080 000 met. tons 1963-5 av.
163 233 300 1953-5 av.[1]

Percentage exported
1% 1963-5 av.
1% 1953-5 av.[1]

Exports
3 359 300 met. tons 1963-5 av.
2 084 300 1953-5 av.

	PERCENTAGE 1963-5 av.	1953-5 av.
Poland	19	—
Netherlands	19	*24*
France	12	*11*
Italy	6	*8*
Belg./Lux.	6	*6*
Canada	6	*6*
Spain	4	*3[3]*
U.S.A.	3	*7*
Morocco	3	*1*
U.K.	3	*4*
Others	19	*30*
	100	*100*

Imports
3 318 100 met. tons 1963-5 av.
1 975 000 1953-5 av.

	PERCENTAGE 1963-5 av.	1953-5 av.
Germany F.R.	16	*8*
Czechoslovakia	11	—
U.K.	10	*12*
Italy	8	*6*
Spain	6	*3[3]*
France	6	*13*
Germany D.R.	6	—
Belg./Lux.	4	*6*
Hungary	3	—
U.S.A.	3	*3*
Others	27	*49*
	100	*100*

Oats (S.I.T.C. no. 045.2)

Production
46 296 000 met. tons 1963-5 av.
50 800 000 1953-5 av.[1]

Percentage exported
3% 1963-5 av.
2% 1953-5 av.[1]

Exports
1 433 800 met. tons 1963-5 av.
1 436 700 1953-5 av.

	PERCENTAGE 1963-5 av.	1953-5 av.
Australia	23	*8*
Canada	22	*48*
Argentina	21	*23*
U.S.A.	13	*9*
Sweden	6	*1*
Netherlands	6	*2*
France	3	*1*
Germany F.R.	3	—
U.S.S.R.	1	*2*
Denmark	1	*2*
Others	1	*4*
	100	*100*

Imports
1 370 800 met. tons 1963-5 av.
1 459 000 1953-5 av.

	PERCENTAGE 1963-5 av.	1953-5 av.
Germany F.R.	30	*6*
Italy	12	*3*
Netherlands	11	*14*
Switzerland	10	*8*
Denmark	6	*4*
China P.R.	5*	—
Belg./Lux.	5	*7*
U.S.A.	4	*44*
U.K.	2	*4*
Finland	2	*1*
Others	13	*9*
	100	*100*

Rye (S.I.T.C. no. 045.1)

Production
32 832 000 met. tons 1963-5 av.
19 800 000 1953-5 av.[1]

Percentage exported
3% 1963-5 av.
6% 1953-5 av.[1]

Exports
888 300 met. tons 1963-5 av.
1 546 000 1953-5 av.

	PERCENTAGE 1963-5 av.	1953-5 av.
U.S.S.R.	38	*28*
U.S.A.	22	*4*
Canada	14	*19*
Argentina	8	*32*
Turkey	4	*3*
Denmark	3	—
France	2	—
Netherlands	2	*2*
Romania	2	—
Czechoslovakia	2	—
Others	3	*12*
	100	*100*

Imports
904 100 met. tons 1963-5 av.
1 546 700 1953-5 av.

	PERCENTAGE 1963-5 av.	1953-5 av.
Netherlands	20	*9*
Poland	15	*26*
Germany D.R.	14	—
Germany F.R.	9	*10*
Sweden	9	*2*
Czechoslovakia	5	—
Norway	5	*4*
Finland	5	*6*
Belg./Lux.	5	*9*
U.S.A.	4	*13*
Others	9	*21*
	100	*100*

*Estimate [1]Excl. U.S.S.R. [2]Incl. Meslin [3]Incl. Canary Is. [4]Excl. Faeroes [5]Incl. South West Africa [6]Data for Cambodia includes Laos and Vietnam

Barley/Maize-Corn

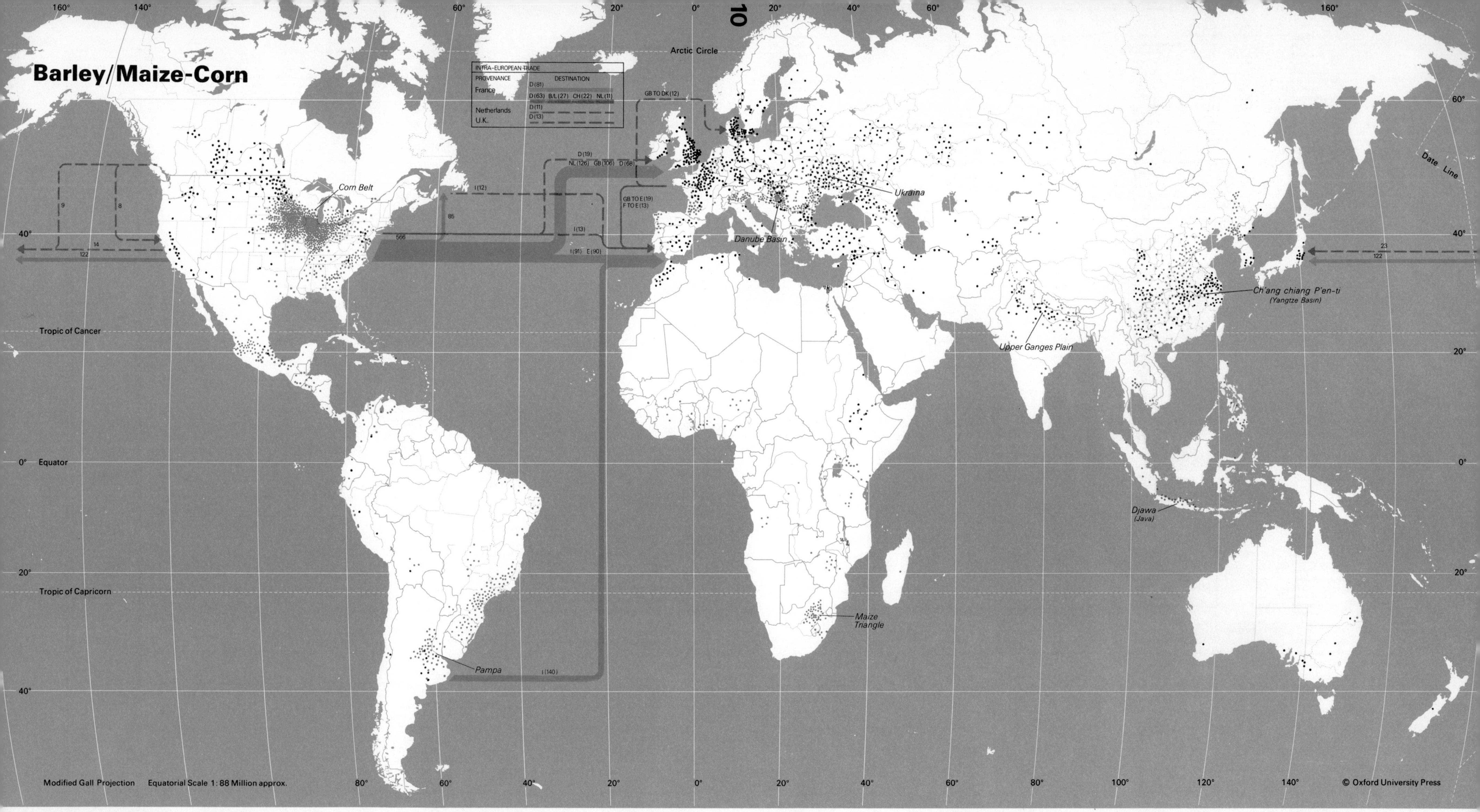

Barley/Maize-Corn

(1963 - 5 av.)[1]

One dot represents 100 000 met. tons

• barley • maize

Major trade flows (1966)

Commodity: S.I.T.C. no.

BARLEY (UNMILLED) 043

MAIZE-CORN (UNMILLED) : 044

Value ($ U.S.)

0.5 mm represents increments of $50 million

($ MILLIONS) 450 250 50

UNDER $25 MILLION

122 VALUE IN $ MILLIONS

[1] Data for China P. R. 1952-6 av.

Barley production

104 450 700 met. tons 1963-5 av.[1]

63 933 000 1953-5 av.[2]

	PERCENTAGE 1963-5 av.	1953-5 av.
U.S.S.R.	22	...[2]
U.S.A.	8	*12*
U.K.	7	*4*
France	7	*4*
Canada	4	*8*
Denmark	4	*3*
Germany F.R.	3	*3*
Turkey	3	*5*
India	2	*5*
Others	40	*56*
	100	*100*

[1] Excl. China P.R.
[2] Excl. U.S.S.R.

Barley yield

Selected countries

(metric tons per hectare)

	1963-5 av.
Netherlands	3.98
Denmark	3.90
U.K.	3.65
Germany F.R.	3.11
France	2.94
Czechoslovakia	2.20
U.S.A.	2.07
Canada	1.83
Turkey	1.28
U.S.S.R.	1.11
India	0.82
World average	1.49

Maize-corn production

221 111 000 met. tons 1963-5 av.[1]

152 700 000 1953-5 av.[2]

	PERCENTAGE 1963-5 av.	1953-5 av.
U.S.A.	44	*53*
U.S.S.R.	5	...[2]
Brazil	5	*4*
Mexico	4	*3*
Romania	3	*4*
Yugoslavia	3	*2*
South Africa	2	*2*
Argentina	2	*2*
India	2	*2*
Others	30	*28*
	100	*100*

[1] Excl. China P.R.
[2] Excl. U.S.S.R.

Maize-corn yield

Selected countries

(metric tons per hectare)

	1963-5 av.
Canada	4.71
U.S.A.	4.28
Yugoslavia	2.47
U.S.S.R.	2.25
Romania	1.86
Argentina	1.71
Brazil	1.28
South Africa	1.15
Mexico	1.09
India	1.00
Philippines	0.69
World average	2.20

Barley has the shortest growing season of all cereals and when spring-sown can be grown further north, at higher altitudes, and in more arid regions than any other cereal. The requirements for malting barley differ from those for barley for direct consumption.
Where autumn-sown crops are exposed to mild winters, or where the soil in the spring still retains much of the moisture due to winter precipitation, barley for food purposes can withstand hot arid—but not humid—conditions in the heading and post-heading stage; malting barley demands cooler conditions in the ripening phase. Barley is a crop of both the woodland and grassland climax, and is specific in its soil requirements; it demands good drainage and relatively fertile soils without acid conditions.
In most countries barley is used more for animal feeding than for direct human consumption. But some higher-grade barley is used in the malting industry for beer and to a small extent for the production of whisky and of industrial alcohol.

Maize is susceptible to frost, thus the length of frost-free periods limits distribution. Optimum grain yields result when the growing period is at least 140 days and the mean summer temperatures are approximately 75°F (24°C) by day, 57°F (14°C) by night.
Varieties differ in their temperature requirement; early-maturing types will succeed when the summer temperature is approximately 66°F (19°C), or less if the growing season is cool but long.

Most crops are grown with 25–40 in. (650–1 000 mm.) annual rainfall but there must be adequate water available during mid-seasonal growth. Maize grows on a wide range of soils provided there is a high availability of mineral nutrients, especially nitrogen, in the later phases of vegetative growth.
Selective cross-breeding has resulted in hybrids that are more uniform and productive. Yields have been raised 20-50%, and in 1960, 96% of the maize-sown area in the U.S.A. was planted with hybrid strains. The diversity of types of maize makes it suitable for cultivation in most tropical to warm temperate areas of the world. Maize is an important subsistence crop in Asia and Africa, but most of the maize entering international trade is as a livestock feed. Large quantities are converted into compound feeding stuffs or used as a source of glucose, starch, oil, dextrins, alcohol and breakfast foods.

Rice/Potatoes

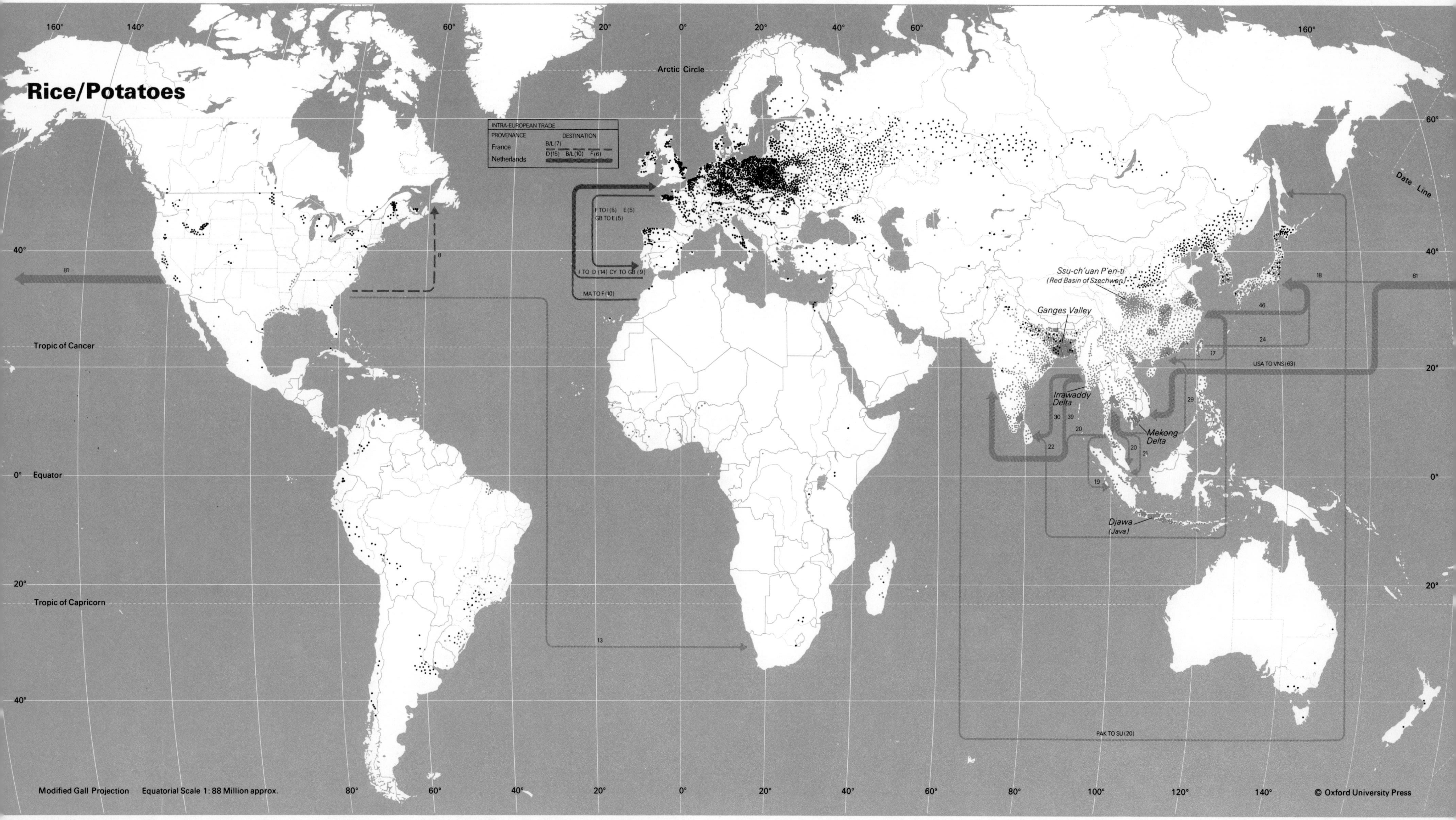

Rice/Potatoes (1963-5 av.)

One dot represents 100 000 met. tons

◦ rice • potatoes

Major trade flows (1966)

Commodity : S.I.T.C. no.

RICE : 042

POTATOES (FRESH, EXCL. SWEET POTATOES) : 054.1

Value ($ U.S.)

0.5 mm represents increments of $ 20 million

($ MILLIONS) 180 100 20

UNDER $10 MILLION

39 VALUE IN $ MILLIONS

Rice production

256 652 000 met. tons 1963-5 av.

185 900 000 1953-5 av.[1]

	PERCENTAGE 1963-5 av.	1953-5 av.
China P.R.	33	*35*
India	21	*22*
Pakistan	7	*7*
Japan	6	*7*
Indonesia	5	*6*
Thailand	4	*4*
Burma	3	*3*
Brazil	3	*2*
S. Vietnam	2	*NA*[2]
Others	16	*NA*
	100	*100*

[1]Excl. U.S.S.R.
[2]Vietnam data not divided

Rice yield

Selected countries

(metric tons per hectare)

	1963-5 av.
Spain	6.17
Japan	5.02
Taiwan	3.64
S. Vietnam	2.04
Indonesia	1.79
Pakistan	1.69
Burma	1.66
Brazil	1.57
India	1.49
China P.R.	1.15[1]
World average	2.06

[1]Data for 1956-8

Potato production

288 080 000 met. tons 1963-5 av.

163 233 000 1953-5 av.[1]

	PERCENTAGE 1963-5 av.	1953-5 av.
U.S.S.R.	29	*...*[1]
Poland	16	*19*
Germany F.R.	7	*15*
France	4	*10*
Germany D.R.	4	*9*
U.S.A.	4	*6*
U.K.	2	*5*
Czechoslovakia	2	*5*
Spain	2	*2*
Others	30	*29*
	100	*100*

[1]Excl. U.S.S.R.

Potato yield

Selected countries

(metric tons per hectare)

	1963-5 av.
Netherlands	29.33
Germany F.R.	25.07
U.K.	23.07
U.S.A.	22.17
France	18.37
Germany D.R.	17.43
Poland	16.03
Australia	14.33
Czechoslovakia	12.37
Spain	11.73
U.S.S.R.	9.90
World average	12.20

Potatoes require a long cool growing season with adequate moisture throughout. Growth starts at about 45°F (7°C); if mean maximum temperature exceeds 64°F (18°C) yields are lower. High temperatures combined with high humidity lead to attacks of 'blight'. Where the springs are mild but the summers hot, the less productive early-maturing types are cultivated. These can also be grown in the extreme north of Europe, where the season is short but the days long. Potatoes, like rye, can be grown in exposed acid sands; the best soils are loams or silts, with a good content of organic matter. A high level of mineral nutrients is needed and heavy applications of fertilizers normally give economic returns.

Under good conditions the potato can produce more food per hectare than any of the cereals. This was an important factor in the rapid increase in population in NW. Europe in the nineteenth century. Today in East and Central Europe the potato is the staple food for millions of people. In some parts of Europe as much as 40% of the crop may be fed to livestock. Potatoes are also a source of industrial alcohol and potable spirits, especially in East Europe and the U.S.S.R.

Rice is normally grown in standing water for most of the growth cycle, while other requirements are high temperature and, for maximum yields, high light intensities. Varieties of 'upland' rice can be cultivated without irrigation or flooding as long as the rainfall is heavy and very frequent, such as 60 in. (1 500 mm.) minimum during the season in the Philippines. In the warm temperate zones the limits of production are associated with the length of the frost-free period combined with minimal temperatures during germination, vegetative growth and ripening; varieties differ in these requirements but the minimal limits for the phases are 64°–68°F (18°–20°C), 72°–75°F (22°–24°C) and 66°F (19°C). Unlike other cereals, rice can tolerate very high temperatures combined with high humidities. Rich alluvial soils with an impervious subsoil are best, but other soils are suitable as long as they can hold the irrigation or flood water.

Until recently the highest yields of rice have been obtained in the warm temperate zones with a Mediterranean type of climate. However, yields in the tropics should be substantially increased following the introduction of new varieties bred at the International Rice Research Institute in the Philippines.

The high productivity of rice coupled with its ability to maintain good yields under a system of continuous cultivation have contributed to its historical position as the staple food of millions of people in Asia. Unfortunately milled rice (the form in which it is usually eaten) is a deficient diet.

Only about 5% of the world's rice enters into trade. The bulk of this trade is carried on within the Asiatic continent.

Rice growing does extend beyond areas shown on the map, but reliable statistics for such areas are not available.

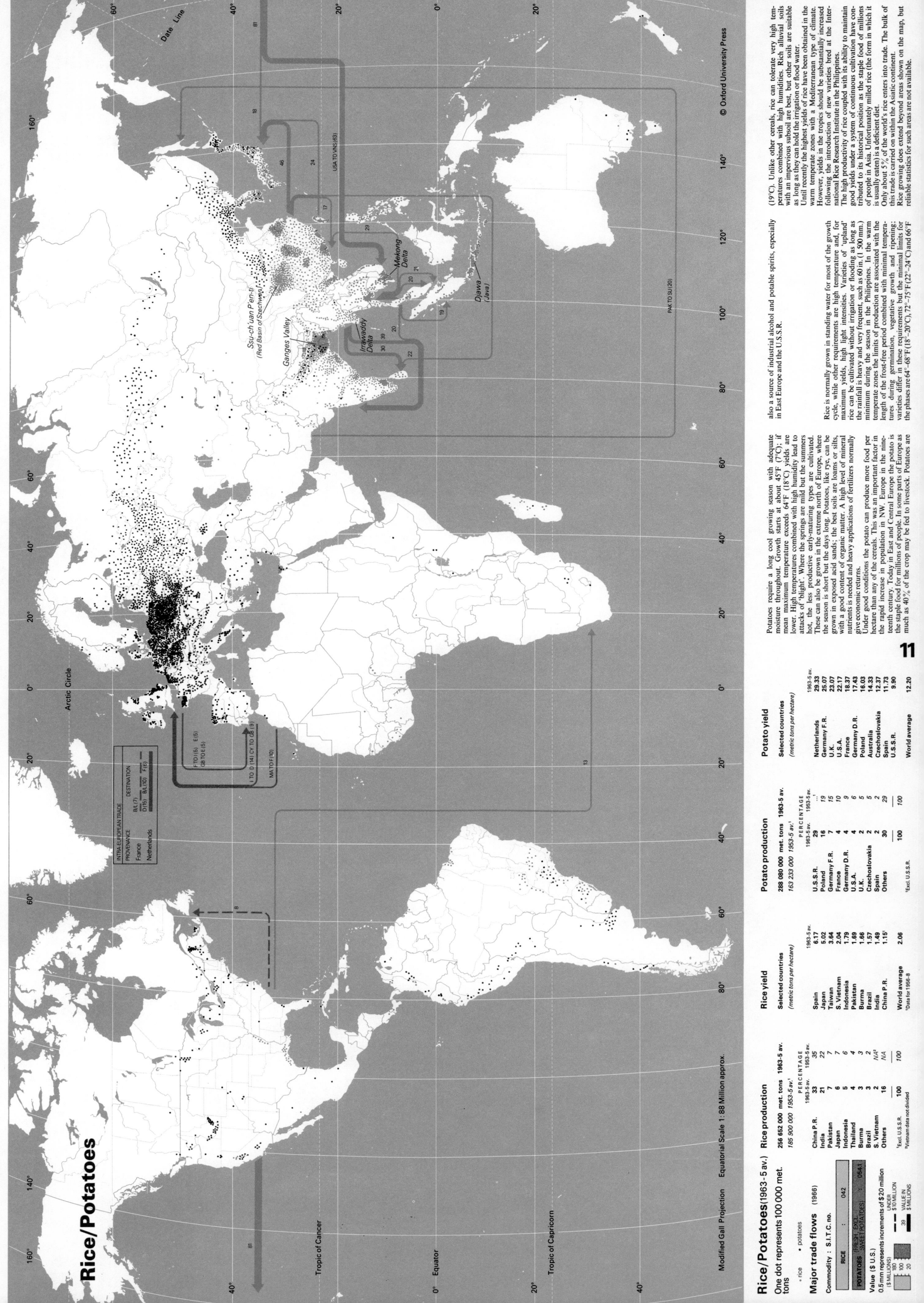

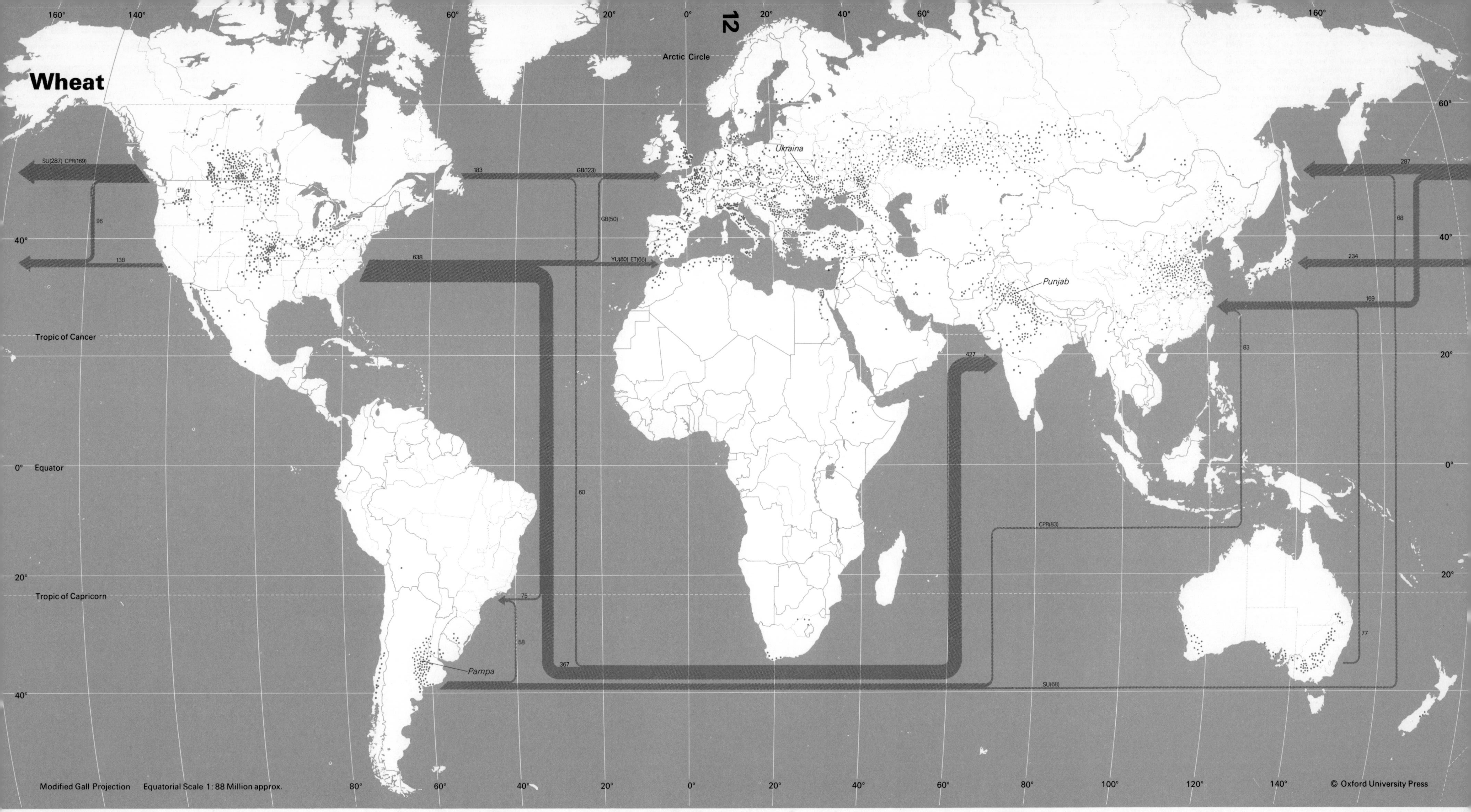

Wheat (1963-5 av.)

One dot represents 100 000 met. tons

Major trade flows (1966)

Commodity: S.I.T.C.no.

WHEAT (INCL. SPELT/MESLIN) : 041

Value ($ U.S.)
0.5mm represents increments of $60 million

780 ($ MILLIONS)
540
300
60

96 VALUE IN $ MILLIONS

Wheat production

260 093 670 met. tons 1963-5 av.
157 900 000 1953-5 av.[1]

	PERCENTAGE 1963-5 av.	1953-5 av.
U.S.S.R.	24	...[1]
U.S.A.	13	18
China P.R.	9	14
Canada	7	8
France	5	6
India	4	5
Turkey	3	4
Italy	3	5
Australia	3	3
Argentina	3	4
Others	26	33
	100	100

[1]Excl. U.S.S.R.

Wheat production by region

(million metric tons)

	1934-8 av.	1948-52 av.	1955	1965
World[2]	129	140	158	205
Europe[2]	43	41	49	67
France	8	8	10	15
N. America	27	44	39	53
Latin America	9	8	10	10
Middle East	10	11	14	14
Asia	34	27	37	47
China P.R.	23	18[1]	23	26
Africa	2	3	4	7
Oceania	4	5	5	7
U.S.S.R.	38	NA	NA	61

[1]Data for 1952
[2]Excl. U.S.S.R.

Wheat yield

Selected countries
(metric tons per hectare)

	1963-5 av.
Netherlands	4.42
U.K.	4.04
France	3.03
U.A.R.	2.72
Czechoslovakia	2.37
U.S.A.	1.74
Argentina	1.57
Australia	1.24
Turkey	1.13
U.S.S.R.	0.91
China P.R.	0.87
World average	1.21

Wheat is a basic food for human consumption within the temperate zones. It ranks with rice as the most important of all crops. Three-quarters of the crop is autumn-sown. Spring sowing is practised where winters are too cold for autumn-sown crops. Rainfall requirements are normally from 10-35 in. (250-900 mm.), but at the lower end of this scale fallowing in alternate years may be necessary. Wheat requires warm moist conditions for its early growth and a minimum temperature of 60°F (15.5°C) for ripening the grain. The normal growth period for spring wheats is about 90 days but with new varieties, or in high latitudes, may be shorter. Wheat is hardy but will not tolerate extreme cold. The northern limit corresponds with the May isotherm of 50°F (10°C). High temperature and humidity in the growing period also inhibit wheat growing—the limit in the U.S.A. is a mean temperature of 68°F (20°C) and annual rainfall above 50 in. (1 250 mm.). A recent development has been the breeding in Mexico and elsewhere of short high-yielding varieties suitable for the tropics. Wheat is associated with a grassland, and more rarely a woodland,climax, and is most productive on fertile, medium-textured soils with reasonable drainage.

Hard wheats are the best bread-making varieties, and are grown where the climate ensures rapid maturity, i.e. in countries such as the U.S.A., Canada, Argentina and Australia. Britain and some other countries in general produce soft wheat used for biscuits and cakes, and import hard wheat, which may be mixed with home-grown soft wheat, for bread-making. Wheat is also used for alcohol production.

Wheat is one of the most widely grown cereals and has become a major world export commodity. About 21% of production enters world trade. Some European and Asiatic countries are partly dependent on imports, while one of the bigger wheat consumers, the U.K., relies on supplies from overseas for almost two-thirds of its requirements. In contrast the U.S.A., Canada, Argentina and Australia rely on exporting about half of their production and wheat exports are an important source of foreign currency.

The U.S.S.R. is a traditional exporter of wheat, in 1961 accounting for 12% of total world exports. By 1965, this had fallen to 3% and the U.S.S.R. had become the world's largest single importer accounting for 13% of total world imports of wheat. In the mid-fifties this position was held by the U.K., but now both India and China P.R. besides the U.S.S.R., import more than the U.K. which is 4th on the world scale, Japan following closely in 5th place.

As much as one fifth of world output may enter into international trade, but wheat has become one of the world's chief export commodities only in the last 90 years. This rise followed the development, after 1870, of the new wheat-growing areas of the great plains of North America, especially Canada, and later the opening up of the Argentinian Pampa and southern parts of Australia. Improved transport played an important part in this development: the introduction of grain elevators and devices for mechanical handling, extension of the railway network, and the building of ocean-going ships able to make rapid crossings of the Atlantic.

This revolution in transport brought the new wheat lands in distant continents within reach of importing countries and so stimulated further production and trade. But the great increase in output since then has been due to modern science and farming technology. New and more resistant strains, which are earlier maturing or resistant to insect and disease attacks, are continually being developed; selective weed killers, fertilizers to improve yields and prevent soil exhaustion, soil conservation to avoid recurrences of the 'dust-bowl' of the American Midwest, and ever-growing efficiency in sowing and harvesting have all combined to achieve steep rises in yield per unit area sown. Further increases in world production are likely to result more from improvement in yield than in extension of sown area.

In 1963-5 64% of world wheat exports came from North America, the bulk of this exported through Montréal, New York and Vancouver. Ice blocks the St.Lawrence River and prevents shipments from Montréal during the first three months of the year, but due to the St. Lawrence Seaway more wheat can be shipped while the river is ice-free. Exports from the southern hemisphere, mainly Argentina and Australia, while smaller, are still important, particularly as the crop is harvested at a different time; importers thus receive a more regular supply than would otherwise be possible, and need store less wheat for a shorter time.

Because of the great importance of wheat in world trade there have been, since 1949, a series of International Wheat Agreements to counteract the vagaries of a wholly free market. The fifth International Wheat Agreement came into force in July 1962. The international price limits of marketing covered by the agreement are fixed in advance by buyers and sellers and impose on both the obligation to maintain a minimum volume of trade at these prices; if exporters' prices rise above the 'ceiling', importers are released from their percentage of imports quota. Price agreements also exist in the domestic markets.

Beverages, Tobacco and Sugar

Cocoa p.15 Sugar p.14 Tobacco p.15
Coffee p.15 Tea p.15 Consumption maps p.15

For individual country data see Statistical Supplement

All these crops, except tobacco and sugar beet, are grown mainly for export to economically advanced countries, and even tobacco is important in world trade. In varying degrees the beverages act as stimulants, and all are wanted for taste and flavour rather than nutritive value. Equally they all come more or less within the category of semi-luxuries, the amounts consumed being dependent on the prosperity of the consumer.

Tea has the distinction of being the world's principal and cheapest beverage. Although more expensive by unit weight than coffee, it is more economical in use. Yet, outside China and Japan, where green tea is grown, the tea-drinking habit was comparatively unknown until about 150 years ago. Cultivation of black tea in India and Ceylon, nowadays the chief exporters, is of still more recent origin. India did not begin commercial production before about 1830. Ceylon, where tea dramatically superseded coffee after its destruction by disease, followed forty years later. In both countries the tea industries were initially financed and developed by British enterprise. Britain still is dominant in world tea trade, as well as being the largest consumer of imported tea.

The demand for tea is inelastic—fairly small change in supply causes a big change in price. An international agreement aimed at restricting output in order to stabilize prices lapsed in 1955 because of heavy demand in the immediate post-war years. But with increased world production due to developments in Africa and South America and higher yields in the Asian countries, the price of tea at the London auctions has declined from the record 1954 level.

Coffee has been known to the West longer than tea. Enjoyed for its flavour and stimulating effect, coffee began to gain wider popularity from the seventeenth century onwards, first in the famous coffee houses of Britain and Continental Europe, later in the houses of the well-to-do. Though no longer a luxury, coffee is still more expensive than tea when made up into a beverage. The U.S.A. is the largest single coffee consuming country but per capita consumption is highest in Sweden.

Production is concentrated in Latin America which grows almost 70% of the world crop. African and Far Eastern production is increasing and in 1965 made up 25% and 5% of the world production respectively. Brazil accounted for about 58% of Latin American production in 1965; compared with 68% pre-war; Colombian and Mexican production is substantially higher than pre-war.

Coffee exports are important in that they provide many of the developing countries with an invaluable source of foreign exchange from more prosperous countries. In Colombia, for example, coffee accounts for almost 68% of all exports. Coffee ranks amongst the most important traded commodities in the world. In terms of volume it is relatively small but in value it accounts for over 13% of all commodity exports and represents 1.2% of total international trade. In recent years the volume of coffee exported has risen considerably.

The demand for coffee is also inelastic, and the history of production is characterized by a series of surpluses and shortages. For example, as a result of over-production in the 1930's about four million tons of coffee had to be destroyed in Brazil. An International Coffee Agreement has played an important role in stabilizing world trade by the restriction of exports to avoid cyclical shortages and surpluses.

It seems probable that in the next few years there will be a relative coffee shortage. Stocks have been declining as consumption has exceeded production in the past few years, and in addition to this, disastrous frosts destroyed many trees in Brazil in July, 1969. Until the new trees planted begin to bear fruit an increase in production will depend on improved farming methods and greater use of fertilizer.

Cocoa (cacao) which is produced mainly in West Africa and South America is usually included with the beverages. As a beverage, however, it has far less stimulating effect than either tea or coffee. Its main use is in the manufacture of chocolate.

The main constituent of chocolate is cocoa-butter, which is extracted from the bean, while the rest of the bean forms the powder with which drinking cocoa is made. Chocolate is one of the most appetizing and most nutritious of foods. Its manufacture is a complex process and one of the world's major industrial enterprises.

There has been considerable expansion in production since the beginning of the century and this has had an important effect on the economies of several countries, especially Ghana. In 1900, 78% of world cocoa production was from the Americas (mainly Brazil and Ecuador) and the West Indies, but by 1959 Ghana alone was producing more than the whole of the Americas.

World consumption of cocoa has exceeded production in the last few years, and demand has doubled in the last 15 years and is continuing to increase. Higher standards of living are partly responsible for the rise in demand, and the need to meet it has necessitated research and the use of new methods. More intensive production is required rather than simply an increase in acreage, and the use of insecticides, fungicides and higher yielding strains of tree are important in this respect.

Much trade in cocoa is handled by cocoa marketing boards which protect farmers from fluctuations in world market prices and also provide financial support for research and development. An International Cocoa Agreement acceptable to both producers and consumers has not yet been formulated. The aim of such an Agreement would be to stabilize world prices and encourage production and consumption.

Without **sugar,** the palatability and, therefore, the use of tea, coffee and cocoa would be greatly diminished. But not only does sugar add taste to drink and food; it is itself a major foodstuff. All countries with high living standards consume sugar in large quantities, though elsewhere it is frequently beyond the means of millions. The great expansion in sugar consumption was made possible by the development of low-cost production in sugar cane countries, which provide almost all of the sugar entering international trade.

Many of these countries are excessively dependent on sugar growing. Most of the Caribbean Islands and Mauritius can be said to have "one crop economies" although attempts are now being made at a measure of diversification. The low prices of the 1930's affected them very severely; demand was high immediately post-war, but after 1951 supply began to exceed demand and an International Sugar Agreement was set up in 1953 to stabilize the world free market price of raw sugar through the operation of a system of export quotas. New agreements have since emerged and the latest came into operation from the beginning of 1969.

The Commonwealth Sugar Agreement imposes quotas on Commonwealth countries. By far the larger part of world sugar consumption is traded subject to protective measures, subsidies or preferential arrangements extended by governments.

Sugar was first extracted from beet by a German chemist in 1747 but commercial development dates from the Napoleonic wars, when sugar supplies to continental Europe were cut off by the British naval blockade. European governments have since protected beet sugar partly to secure supplies in times of war and partly because it takes a valuable place in the rotation of crops; since 1880 beet has been the principal source of sugar consumed in Europe.

As a stimulant **tobacco** exceeds even coffee and tea in importance. At least as early as the first century B.C. the smoking of tobacco was practised by the Mayan Indians of Central America. It was introduced to other parts of the world by early explorers (especially the Spanish), and commercial trading in tobacco on an international basis dates from the mid-sixteenth century when a demand for it was being created in several countries. The spread of smoking (which was at first a luxury enjoyed only by the rich) and the consequent increase in demand for tobacco necessitated an increase in production. Existing plantations were therefore extended and new ones established. Tobacco farming began in Europe in the late sixteenth century.

Tobacco is usually heavily taxed and the vast sums spent on it constitute considerable revenue. Tobacco has been taxed in Britain since 1590 when Queen Elizabeth I introduced a duty on tobacco imported into England. In 1969 tobacco provided 8% (£1 105 millions) of the U.K. government's revenue.

In recent years the relationship between smoking and respiratory disease, notably lung cancer, has been the subject of much research. In some countries cigarette packets are now required to carry a note warning people that cigarette smoking may be hazardous to health.

Tobacco products

Cigarette production[1,2]

2 198 000 million 1963-5 av.[3]
1 401 000 million 1953-5 av.[3,4]

	PERCENTAGE 1963-5 av.	1953-5 av.
U.S.A.	25	29
U.S.S.R.	13	14
Japan	7	7
U.K.[5]	5	8[6]
Germany F.R.[7]	4	3[5]
Brazil	3	...[4]
Italy[7]	3	3
Poland[7]	3	2
France[7]	2	3
India	2	1
Others	33	30
	100	100

Cigar production

World total not available

	MILLIONS 1963-5 av.	1953-5 av.
U.S.A.	8 062	5 837
Germany F.R.[7]	3 970	4 692
Netherlands[7]	1 883	1 113
Germany D.R.[7]	1 844	NA
Switzerland	652	499
Colombia	476	531
U.K.[5]	461	119
Canada	455	245
Belgium	366	105
Spain	350	592

Tobacco production[8]

374 000 met. tons 1963-5 av.[9]
277 000 1953-5.[9]

	'000 MET. TONS 1963-5 av.	1953-5 av.
Bulgaria	115	NA
U.S.A.	78	93
France	18	19
U.K.[5]	16	16
Netherlands	14	10
South Africa	11	10
Canada	10	12
S. Korea	9	4
Germany F.R.	9	17
Norway	5	3

[1]Where reported by weight a conversion factor of 1 million cigarettes per metric ton was used [2]Incl. cigarillos for most countries [3]Excl. China P.R. and N. Korea [4]Excl. Brazil [5]Sales [6]1954 only [7]Cigarillos included with cigars [8]For smoking, chewing and snuff [9]Incomplete world total

International trade in beverages, tobacco, sugar and chocolate (1963-5 av.)

Tobacco (S.I.T.C. no. 121)

Production
4 383 000 met. tons 1963-5 av.
3 297 000 1953-5 av.[1]

Percentage exported
22% 1963-5 av.
19% 1953-5 av.

Exports[2]
944 700 met. tons 1963-5 av.
641 000 1953-5 av.

	PERCENTAGE 1963-5 av.	1953-5 av.
U.S.A.	24	36
Rhodesia[3]	12	NA
Bulgaria	9	3*
India	7	5
Greece	7	8
Turkey	6	10
Brazil	6	4
Philippines	3	1
Others	26	NA
	100	100

Imports[2]
934 000 met. tons 1963-5 av.
608 000 1953-5 av.

	PERCENTAGE 1963-5 av.	1953-5 av.
U.K.	15	24
Germany F.R.	14	10
U.S.S.R.	12	4
U.S.A.	8	8
France	5	6
Netherlands	5	6
Spain	4	3
Belg./Lux.	3	4
Germany D.R.	3	1
Others	31	34
	100	100

Coffee (S.I.T.C. no. 071.1)

Production
4 090 300 met. tons 1963-5 av.
2 607 000 1953-5 av.

Percentage exported
71% 1963-5 av.
76% 1953-5 av.

Exports[4]
2 892 100 met. tons 1963-5 av.
1 973 000 1953-5 av.

	PERCENTAGE 1963-5 av.	1953-5 av.
Brazil	33	41
Colombia	13	19
Ivory Coast	7	NA
Uganda	5	3
Angola	5	3
El Salvador	4	3
Guatemala	3	3
Mexico	3	4
Indonesia	3	2
Others	24	NA
	100	100

Imports[4]
2 933 000 met. tons 1963-5 av.
1 978 000 1953-5 av.

	PERCENTAGE 1963-5 av.	1953-5 av.
U.S.A.	46	58
Germany F.R.	9	5
France	8	9
Italy	4	4
Sweden	3	3
Netherlands	3	1
Canada	3	2
U.K.	2	2
Belg./Lux.	2	2
Others	20	14
	100	100

Cocoa (cacao) (S.I.T.C. no. 072.1)

Production
1 303 800 met. tons 1963-5 av.
795 000 1953-5 av.

Percentage exported
87% 1963-5 av.
92% 1953-5 av.

Exports[5]
1 134 900 met. tons 1963-5 av.
731 700 1953-5 av.

	PERCENTAGE 1963-5 av.	1953-5 av.
Ghana	38	30
Nigeria	20	13
Ivory Coast	10	NA
Brazil	7	16
Cameroun	6	8
Ecuador	3	3
Equatorial Guinea	3	2
Dominican R.	2	3
New Guinea	1	—
Others	10	NA
	100	100

Imports[5]
1 104 700 met. tons 1963-5 av.
730 000 1953-5 av.

	PERCENTAGE 1963-5 av.	1953-5 av.
U.S.A.	28	34
Germany F.R.	13	10
Netherlands	10	8
U.K.	8	19
U.S.S.R.	6	2
France	6	7
Italy	4	3
Japan	3	1
Spain	2	2
Others	20	14
	100	100

Chocolate and chocolate products

(S.I.T.C. no. 073.0)

Exports
161 300 met. tons 1963-5 av.
90 900 1952-6 av.

	PERCENTAGE 1963-5 av.	1952-6 av.
Irish R.[6]	27	50
Netherlands	19	10
U.K.	16	20
Belgium	10	2
Switzerland[7]	7	4
France	5	4
Germany F.R.	4	1
U.S.A.	3	3
Italy	2	—
Canada	2	—
Sweden	1	1
Denmark	1	2
Others	3	3
	100	100

Imports
148 100 met. tons 1963-5 av.
80 000 1952-6 av.

	PERCENTAGE 1963-5 av.	1952-6 av.
U.K.[6]	28	68
Germany F.R.	23	4
U.S.A.	10	3
Belgium	7	4
France	6	1
Netherlands	6	1
Canada	4	5
Denmark	2	—
Austria	2	—
Sweden	2	1
Japan	1	1
Hong Kong	1	1
Others	8	11
	100	100

Tea (S.I.T.C. no. 074.1)

Production
1 112 200 met. tons 1963-5 av.
645 000 1953-5 av.

Percentage exported
55% 1963-5 av.
76% 1953-5 av.

Exports
613 900 met. tons 1963-5 av.
490 000 1953 av.

	PERCENTAGE 1963-5 av.	1953-5 av.
Ceylon	35	33
India	34	41
China P.R.*	5	3
Indonesia	4	5
Kenya	4	1
U.K.[8]	3	3
Taiwan	3	2
Malawi	2[3]	1[9]
Argentina	2	—
Others	8	11
	100	100

Imports
613 600 met. tons 1963-5 av.
485 000 1953-5 av.

	PERCENTAGE 1963-5 av.	1953-5 av.
U.K.	41	48
U.S.A.	10	10
U.S.S.R.	5	—
Australia	5	5
U.A.R.	4	4
Canada	3	4
Iraq	3	3
South Africa	3	2
Irish R.	2	2
Others	24	22
	100	100

Sugar (S.I.T.C. no. 061.1, 2)

Production[10]
59 133 900 met. tons 1963-5 av.
38 289 000 1953-5 av.

Percentage exported
31% 1963-5 av.
35% 1953-5 av.

Exports[11]
18 134 600 met. tons 1963-5 av.
13 496 300 1953-5 av.[12]

	PERCENTAGE 1963-5 av.	1953-5 av.
Cuba	24*	35
Australia	7	5
Philippines	6	7
France	5	4
Taiwan	4*	5
U.S.S.R.	4	1*
Dominican R.	3	4
Mauritius	3	4
South Africa	3	1
Others	41	34
	100	100

Imports
17 637 700 met. tons 1963-5 av.
13 370 700 1953-5 av.

	PERCENTAGE 1963-5 av.	1953-5 av.
U.S.A.	20	26
U.K.	13	19
U.S.S.R.	10	3*
Japan	9	8
Canada	4	4
China P.R.	2*	—
France	2	3
Italy	2	—
Iran	2	2
Others	36	35
	100	100

*Estimate [1]Excluding U.S.S.R. [2]Unmanufactured tobacco [3]1964-5 av. [4]Coffee, green or roasted, and coffee substitutes containing coffee [5]Beans, raw or roasted [6]Including milk crumb [7]Including filled chocolate since 1954 [8]Re-exports [9]1953 only [10]Centrifugal sugar [11]Raw and refined (raw basis) [12]Excluding trade between continental U.S.A. and Hawaii and Puerto Rico

Consumption of beverages and tobacco (1963-5 av.)

Tobacco

Selected countries
(kg. per adult 15 yrs. and over)

	1963-5 av.
Canada	4.5
U.S.A.	4.5
Netherlands	4.0
Switzerland	3.8
Australia	3.4
Iceland	3.0
U.K.	2.9
Germany F.R.	2.8
France	2.3
Japan	2.3
South Africa	2.0
Brazil	1.7
Portugal	1.2
India	0.8
Av. of available countries	2.6

Coffee

Selected countries
(kg. per capita)

	1962-4 av.
Sweden	11.5
Switzerland	9.9
U.S.A.	7.0
Brazil	5.5
France	4.6
Colombia	3.7
Algeria	2.6
U.K.	1.4
Australia	1.1
Yugoslavia[1]	0.8
South Africa	0.7
Japan	0.2
Congo D.R.	0.2
Thailand	0.1
Av. of available countries	2.3

Cocoa (cacao)[2]

Selected countries
(kg. per capita)

	1963-5 av.
Switzerland	3.4
Netherlands	2.5
U.K.	2.2
New Zealand	1.8
U.S.A.	1.8
France	1.4
Czechoslovakia	1.0
Argentina	0.4
U.S.S.R.	0.3
Brazil	0.2
Tunisia	0.1
Ghana	0.05
Iran	0.01
India	0.001
Av. of available countries	0.4

Tea

Selected countries
(kg. per capita)

	1963-5 av.
U.K.	4.2
Irish R.	4.0
Libya	2.9
Australia	2.6
Ceylon	1.4
Japan	0.8
Chile	0.7
Israel	0.5
India	0.3
U.S.A.	0.3
U.S.S.R.	0.3
Norway	0.1
Italy	0.05
Ghana	0.01
Av. of available countries	0.6

[1]1963-4 av. [2]Consumption of cocoa beans and cocoa products in terms of beans

Sugar

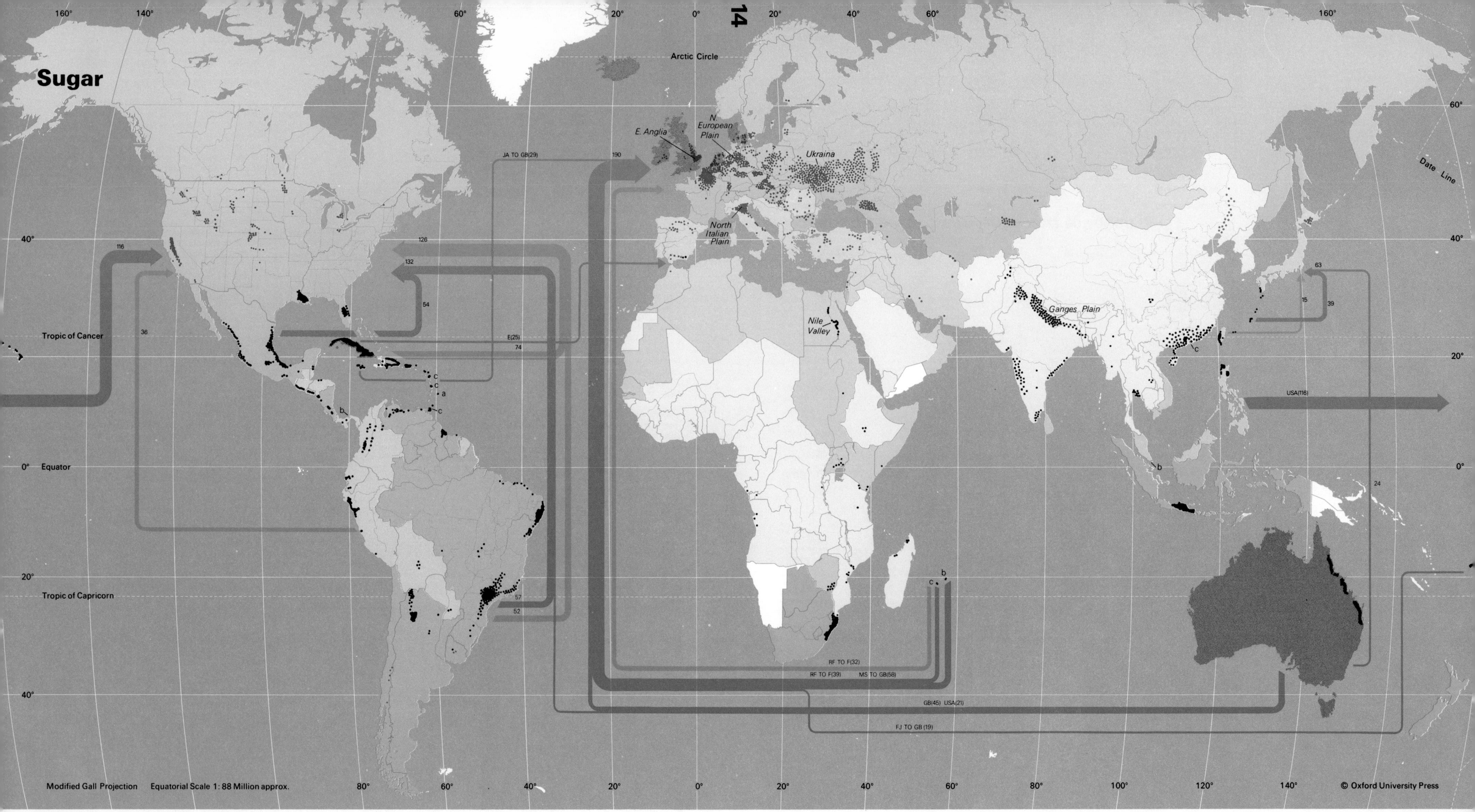

Sugar cane/beet

Production (1963-5 av.)

One dot represents 20 000 met. tons of centrifugal sugar.[1]

• SUGAR CANE • SUGAR BEET

Consumption (1963-5 av.)

(kg. per capita per year)

a[2]	51 & OVER		0–10
b	31–50		DATA N.A.
c	11–30		

[1]Raw value: i.e. 92% net sucrose content. [2]Letters are used where shading cannot be shown.

Major trade flows (1966)

Commodity : S.I.T.C.[1] no.

RAW SUGAR (CANE & BEET) : 061.1

REFINED SUGAR : 061.2

Value ($ U.S.)

0.5mm represents increments of $20 million

($ MILLIONS) 260 180 100 20

36 VALUE IN $ MILLIONS

[1]S.I.T.C.= STANDARD INTERNATIONAL TRADE CLASSIFICATION

Centrifugal sugar

59 133 934 met. tons 1963-5 av.

38 289 000 1953-5 av.

	PERCENTAGE 1963-5 av.	1953-5 av.
U.S.S.R.	13	*9*
Cuba	8	*13*
U.S.A.	8	*8*
Brazil	6	*5*
India	5	*4*
France	4	*4*
China P.R.	3	*2*
Australia	3	*3*
Mexico	3	*2*
Others	47	*50*
	100	*100*

Centrifugal sugar : beet

25 639 872 met. tons 1963-5 av.

15 532 000 1953-5 av.

	PERCENTAGE 1963-5 av.	1953-5 av.
U.S.S.R.	30	*22*
U.S.A.	11	*11*
France	9	*10*
Germany F.R.	7	*8*
Poland	6	*7*
Italy	4	*5*
Czechoslovakia	3	*6*
U.K.	3	*5*
Germany D.R.	3	*5*
Others	24	*21*
	100	*100*

Centrifugal sugar : cane

33 494 062 met. tons 1963-5 av.

22 757 000 1953-5 av.

	PERCENTAGE 1963-5 av.	1953-5 av.
Cuba	14	*21*
Brazil	11	*9*
India	9	*6*
U.S.A.	6	*7*
Australia	6	*5*
Mexico	6	*4*
Philippines	5	*5*
China P.R.	5	*3*
South Africa	4	*3*
Others	34	*37*
	100	*100*

Sugar consumption

Selected countries

(kg. centrifugal sugar per capita)

	1963-5 av.
Cuba	61
Australia	60
U.K.	54
U.S.A.	47
Argentina	39
U.S.S.R.	38
France	34
Colombia	21
Algeria	20
Greece	16
India	6
China P.R.	3
Nigeria	1
World average	16

Raw sugar is derived from sugar cane and sugar beet (which has been grown commercially in Europe since about 1870). The raw sugar is first extracted from the cane and beet and then refined to produce white sugar. Beet pulp and cane molasses are valuable by-products; both are used for cattle-feed, and molasses is also used in the production of rum and alcohol. Much of the cane sugar is exported raw, whereas beet sugar is generally refined and consumed in the countries which produce it. In the twentieth century production has sometimes tended to exceed demand.

Sugar beet demands a temperate climate, a long growing season, (preferably 5 – 6 months), a regular supply of water, long days, and high light intensities. In the autumn it requires either a dry period or cool nights to check growth and thereby accelerate sugar accumulation in the roots. The highest yield is obtained when the crop is irrigated, or the annual rainfall is more than 25 in. (650mm.), and the summer temperature ranges around 60°–70°F (15.5°–21°C). Sugar beet is usually grown on medium to light soils; the drainage must be good and the nutrient status high.

Sugar cane is essentially a perennial plant of the tropics and highest yields are obtained when frequent heavy rainfall is interspersed with bright sunshine. Under these conditions the rate of sugar accumulation in the stem of the mature plant is highest. The crop is generally ready for harvesting after 12 – 24 months. If frost shortens the season, as in Louisiana, the crop is cut when immature and the sugar yield is lower. The minimum annual rainfall requirement is about 50 – 65 in. (1 250 – 1 650 mm.) and in many areas the crop is irrigated.

Temperature requirement varies according to species. In general growth is slow below 59°F (15°C) and active only above 70°F (21°C). Plants regenerate after the first harvest but such 'ratoon' crops have a lower sugar yield. Sugar cane will grow in a variety of soils but the best are deep soils which are well drained but retain moisture. A high level of fertility, or heavy application of fertilizer, particularly nitrogen, is necessary for maximum production. Given suitable conditions of soil and climate, sugar cane can be grown on the same land for several years.

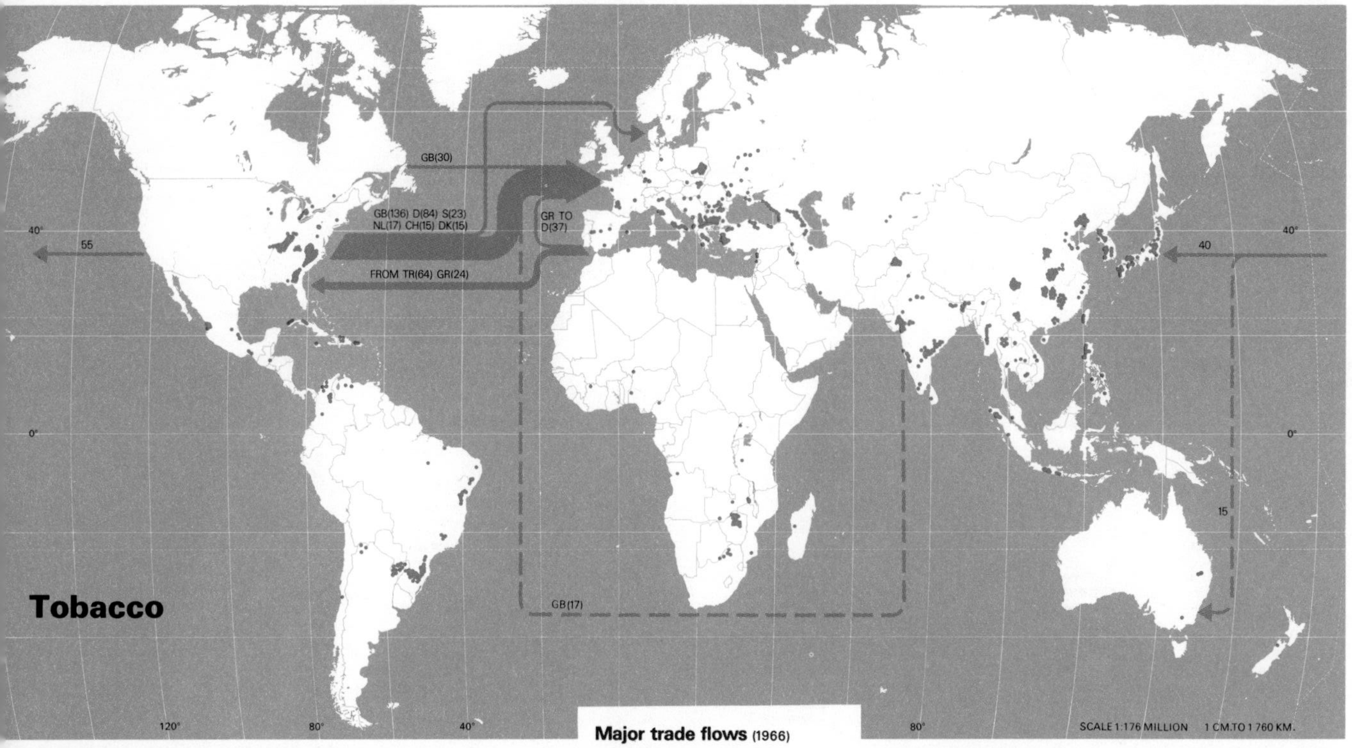
Tobacco
GB(30)
GB(136) D(84) S(23)
NL(17) CH(15) DK(15)
GR TO D(37)
FROM TR(64) GR(24)
55
40
15
GB(17)
120°
80°
40°
0°
SCALE 1:176 MILLION 1 CM.TO 1 760 KM.

Tobacco

Major trade flows (1966)

Commodity: S.I.T.C. no.

TOBACCO (UNMANUFACTURED) : 121

Value ($ U.S.)
0.5mm. represents increments of $40 million
520 / 360 / 200 / 40 ($ MILLIONS)
UNDER $20 MILLION
88 VALUE IN $ MILLIONS

Production (1963-5 av.)
One dot represents 5 000 metric tons

Major producers	U.S.A.	CHINA P.R.	INDIA	BRAZIL	U.S.S.R.	OTHERS	MET. TONS WORLD
	PERCENTAGE						
1963-5 av.	**22**	**10**	**8**	**5**	**4**	**51**	**4 383 000**
1953-5 av.	*30*	*11*	*8*	*4*	*...*[1]	*47*	*3 297 000*[1]

[1]Excluding U.S.S.R.

The tobacco plant originated in tropical America, but can tolerate climates ranging from the humid tropical to the dry temperate: it grows best where temperature and water supply are fairly constant, the atmosphere is humid and the soil well-drained and rich in nitrogen and potassium. The type of tobacco, the climate and soil conditions and the way in which the leaves are processed and dried (curing) all affect the flavour of the tobacco. After curing the tobacco is sold to the manufacturer and may be stored up to two years before being used in the production of cigarettes, cigars, pipe and chewing tobacco and snuff. Tobacco is grown in many countries, though mostly only on a small scale and for local consumption.

Tobacco consumption (1963-5 av.)

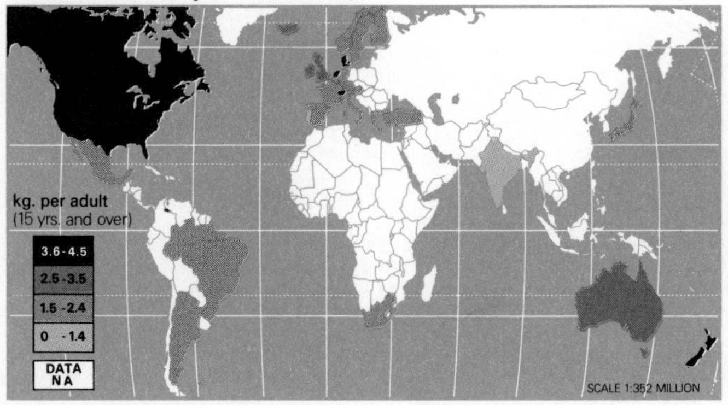
kg. per adult (15 yrs. and over)
3.6 - 4.5
2.5 - 3.5
1.5 - 2.4
0 - 1.4
DATA N A
SCALE 1:352 MILLION

Coffee consumption (1962-4 av.)

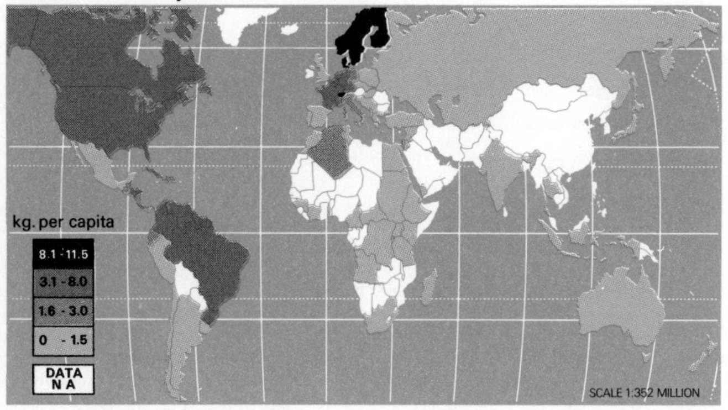
kg. per capita
8.1 - 11.5
3.1 - 8.0
1.6 - 3.0
0 - 1.5
DATA N A
SCALE 1:352 MILLION

Cocoa consumption (1963-5 av.)

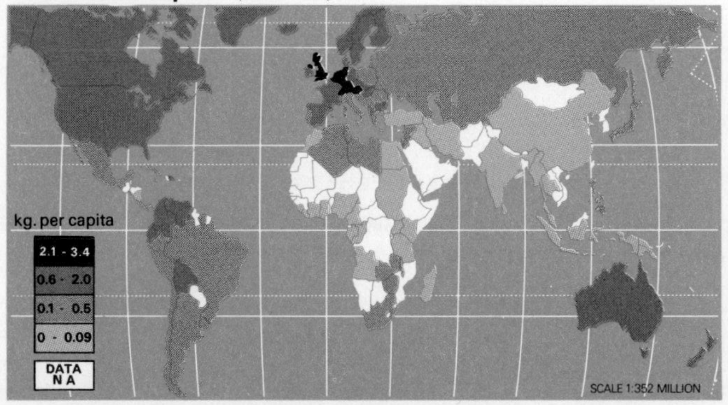
kg. per capita
2.1 - 3.4
0.6 - 2.0
0.1 - 0.5
0 - 0.09
DATA N A
SCALE 1:352 MILLION

Consumption of cocoa beans and cocoa products in terms of beans

Tea consumption (1963-5 av.)

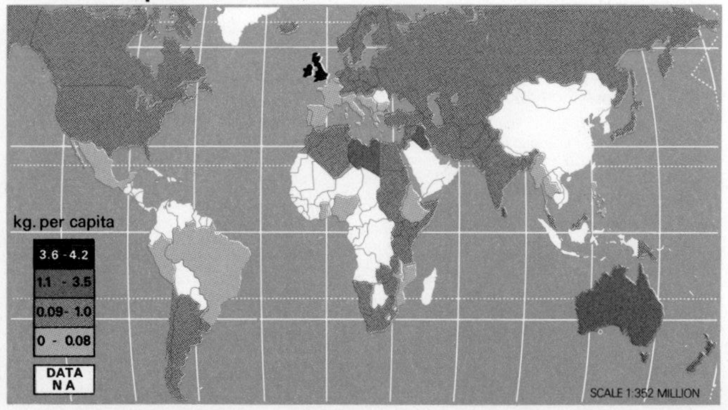
kg. per capita
3.6 - 4.2
1.1 - 3.5
0.09 - 1.0
0 - 0.08
DATA N A
SCALE 1:352 MILLION

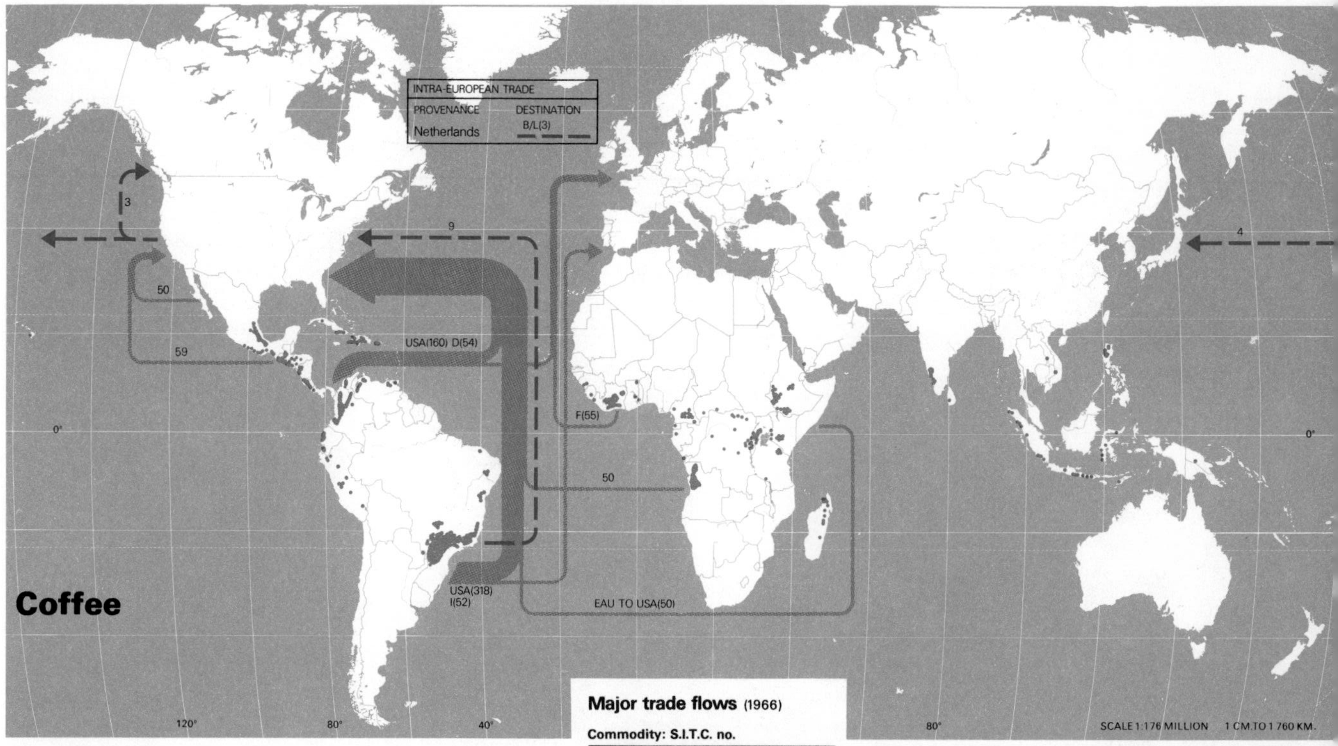
Coffee
INTRA-EUROPEAN TRADE
PROVENANCE DESTINATION
Netherlands B/L(3)
3
9
4
50
59
USA(160) D(54)
F(55)
50
USA(318) I(52)
EAU TO USA(50)
120°
80°
40°
0°
SCALE 1:176 MILLION 1 CM TO 1 760 KM.

Coffee

Major trade flows (1966)

Commodity: S.I.T.C. no.

COFFEE (GREEN/ROASTED) : 071.1

COFFEE EXTRACTS/ESSENCES : 071.3

Value ($ U.S.)
0.5mm. represents increments of $60 million
540 / 300 / 60 ($ MILLIONS)
UNDER $30 MILLION
50 VALUE IN $ MILLIONS

Production (1963-5 av.)
One dot represents 5 000 metric tons

Major producers	BRAZIL	COLOMBIA	IVORY COAST	UGANDA	OTHERS	MET. TONS WORLD
	PERCENTAGE					
1963-5 av.	**37**	**12**	**6**	**5**	**40**	**4 090 300**
1953-5 av.	*45*	*14*	*4*[1]	*2*	*35*	*2 607 000*

[1]This figure is for former French West Africa of which Ivory Coast was a part

Coffee is mainly obtained from two species of tree, *Coffea arabica*, which grows from 3 300-6 600 ft. (1 000-2 000m.) and is most widely cultivated, and *C. robusta*, which grows from sea level to 1 000m. The trees require a deep, rich, well-drained soil and an annual rainfall of 60-120in. (1 500-3 000mm.) is most favourable for cultivation. They will not tolerate frost or long periods of direct heat. Harvesting is carried out by hand and a large labour force is needed. Coffee beans are the seeds inside the fruits (or 'cherries') and extraction involves either drying alone, or more commonly washing and drying. After grading the beans are then stored or exported.

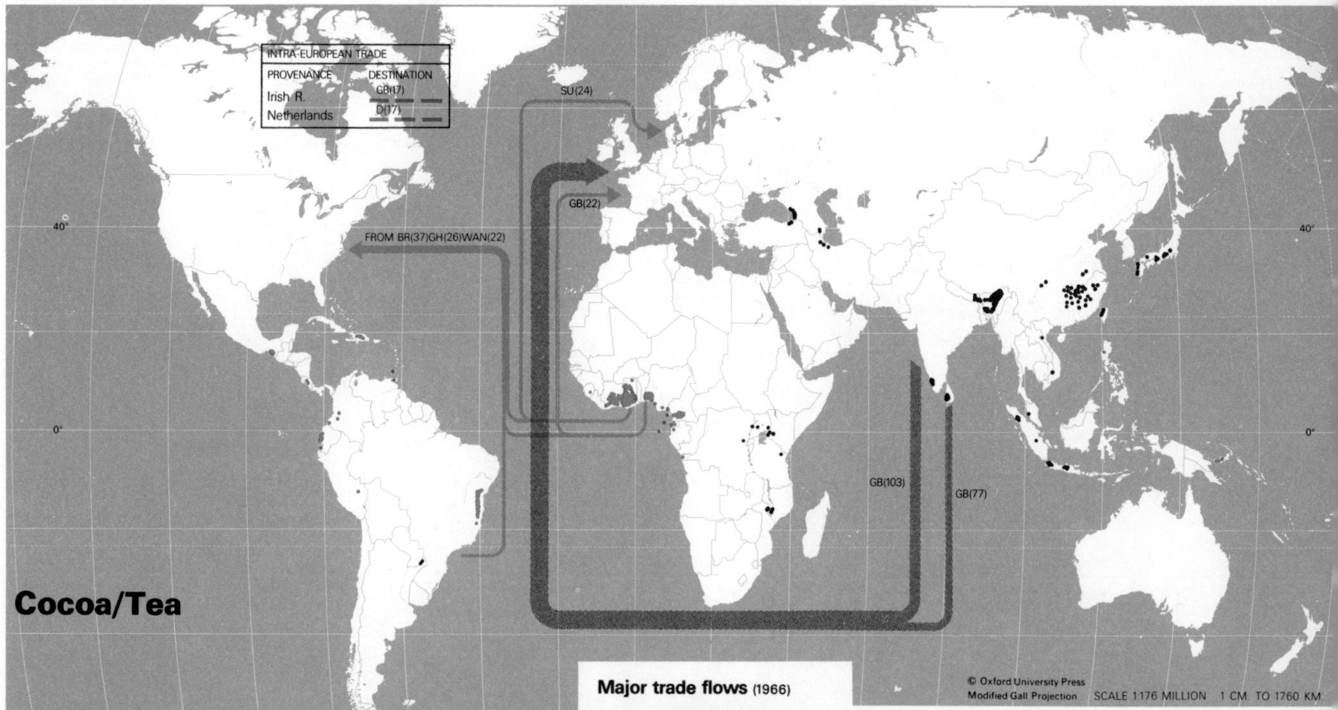
Cocoa/Tea
INTRA-EUROPEAN TRADE
PROVENANCE DESTINATION
Irish R. GB(17)
Netherlands D(17)
SU(24)
GB(22)
FROM BR(37)GH(26)WAN(22)
GB(103)
GB(77)
120°
80°
40°
0°
© Oxford University Press
Modified Gall Projection
SCALE 1:176 MILLION 1 CM TO 1760 KM

Cocoa/Tea

Major trade flows (1966)

Commodity: S.I.T.C. no.

TEA : 074.1 COCOA : 072

CHOCOLATE/PRODUCTS : 073

Value ($ U.S.)
0.5mm. represents increments of $40 million
360 / 200 / 40 ($ MILLIONS)
UNDER $20 MILLION
77 VALUE IN $ MILLIONS

Production (1963-5 av.)
One dot represents 5 000 metric tons ▪ cocoa • tea

Major producers		GHANA	NIGERIA	BRAZIL	IVORY COAST	OTHERS	'000 MET. TONS WORLD
		PERCENTAGE					
Cocoa	**1963-5 av.**	**36**	**18**	**9**	**9**	**28**	**1 303.8**
	1953-5 av.	*28*	*13*	*19*	*8*[1]	*32*	*795*
		INDIA	CEYLON	CHINA P.R.	INDONESIA	OTHERS	WORLD
Tea	**1963-5 av.**	**33**	**20**	**14***	**8**	**25**	**1 112.3**
	1953-5 av.	*44*	*25*	*2**	*6*	*23*	*656*

*Estimate [1]Former French West Africa

Cocoa (cacao) is a tropical forest crop which flourishes in a hot, rainy uniform climate with a mean annual temperature of at least 70°F (21°C) and a well distributed rainfall of at least 50in. (1 250mm.). It is normally grown under shade trees, but this is not essential for established plantations. Cultivation is mainly in the hands of peasant farmers.

Tea is a perennial crop which grows best where monthly maximum temperatures range from 70°-84°F (21°-29°C), annual rainfall is at least 50in. (1 250mm.) and the soils acid, well-drained and porous. It will grow at heights of up to 8 000ft. (2 440m.). In the tropics harvesting is mainly by hand, and only the tops of young shoots are plucked.

Fruit

Apples p. 16 Citrus Fruit p. 16 Wine p. 17
Bananas p. 16 Grapes p. 17
For individual country data see Statistical Supplement

The cultivation of fruit has been carried on in one form or another for many thousands of years. Certainly figs, dates, olives, and bananas have been cultivated for at least 4 000 years, and citrus fruit, apples, pears, plums and apricots for half that time. Cultivation of soft fruit, such as raspberries, gooseberries, currants, etc., is of comparatively recent origin.
More recently, demand for fruit has been further stimulated by the appreciation of the medical value of vitamin C and of the importance of many fruits as a source of this vitamin.
Commercial fruit growing has led to the development of special methods of preserving and marketing its products. Canning and drying have been long established, but a recent development is the production of 'fresh frozen' fruits. Soft fruit is particularly suited to being frozen, and an increasing amount is being processed in this way. The expansion of trade has been assisted by developments in transport and refrigeration, which now make it possible for costly fruit to be shipped cheaply across the world and to arrive at its destination in good condition.
Pears are widely cultivated in the temperate zones of both the northern and southern hemispheres. Of a total world production of 5 587 000 met. tons, 1963-5 av., Italy produced 18%, China P.R. 15%, the U.S.A. 9%, France 7%, Germany F.R. 7% and Japan 6%. Turkey, Australia and Argentina are also significant producers, and Germany F.R., the U.K. and France are the major importers. The distribution of pear production is similar to that of apples.
Pineapples grow throughout the tropics. Total recorded world production, 1963-5 av., was 3 264 000 met. tons of which Hawaii produced 29%, Venezuela 12%, West Malaysia 10%, Thailand 9%, Brazil 9% and Ghana 7%. A large proportion of production is canned.
The date palm thrives best in a sunny and arid environment where a low relative humidity is maintained. Total world date production, 1963-5 av., was 1 825 000 met. tons of which the U.A.R. produced 21%, Iraq 18%, Iran 16%, Saudi Arabia 15% and Algeria 6%. India, China P.R., Germany D.R. and the U.S.S.R. are the main importers. World fig production, 1963-5 av., was 1 489 000 met. tons of which Portugal produced 24%, Italy 18%, Turkey 14%, Spain 10% and Greece 8%.
The tomato is a native fruit of South and Central America but is cultivated in the open in the warm temperate zones during the frost-free periods; it has also become a major greenhouse product. Total world production, 1963-5 av., was 18 697 000 met. tons of which the U.S.A. produced 26%, Italy 16%, Spain 7% and the U.A.R. 6%.

Citrus fruit consumption (1963/4)

	ISRAEL	LEBANON	GREECE	ARGENTINA	U.S.A.	BRAZIL	CANADA	SWITZERLAND	AUSTRALIA	SPAIN	GERMANY F.R.	U.K.	JAPAN	SOUTH AFRICA	WORLD
Total ('000 metric tons)	212	89	346	837	5 191	2 115	515	138*	256	668	1 206	789	1 077	178	22 818*
Kg. per capita	89*	46	41	39	28	28	27	24*	24	21	21	15	11	11	10*[1,2]

* Estimate [1]Excl. China P.R. [2]Average

International trade in fruit (1963-5 av.)

Apples (S.I.T.C. no. 051.4)

Production
19 071 700 met. tons 1963-5 av.
13 667 000 1953-5 av.

Percentage exported
9% 1963-5 av.
6% 1953-5 av.

Exports
1 740 810 met. tons 1963-5 av.
831 670 1953-5 av.

	PERCENTAGE 1963-5 av.	1953-5 av.
Italy	26	28
Argentina	12	7
Australia	8	10
Hungary	7	2
France	6	9
U.S.A.	5	4
China P.R.	5	—
South Africa	5	2
Netherlands	4	11
Canada	4	5
Others	18	22
	100	100

Imports
1 709 900 met. tons 1963-5 av.
754 330 1953-5 av.

	PERCENTAGE 1963-5 av.	1953-5 av.
Germany F.R.	31	35
U.K.	14	20
U.S.S.R.	8	—
France	6	4
Germany D.R.	4	4
Austria	3	3
Czechoslovakia	3	2
Belg./Lux.	3	1
Sweden	3	4
Brazil	3	5
Finland	2	2
Others	20	20
	100	100

Bananas (S.I.T.C. no. 051.3)

Production
21 840 000 met. tons 1963-5 av.
11 200 000 1953-5 av.

Percentage exported
20% 1963-5 av.
25% 1953-5 av.

Exports
4 408 970 met. tons 1963-5 av.
2 958 000 1953-5 av.

	PERCENTAGE 1963-5 av.	1953-5 av.
Ecuador	29	17
Costa Rica	7	12
Honduras	10	10
Panama	7	7
Brazil	5	7
Colombia	5	7
Jamaica	4	6
Taiwan	4	1
Cameroun	3	3
Ivory Coast	3	NA
Others	23	NA
	100	100

Imports
4 211 430 met. tons 1963-5 av.
2 944 330 1953-5 av.

	PERCENTAGE 1963-5 av.	1953-5 av.
U.S.A.	35	51
Germany F.R.	12	6
France	9	9
U.K.	9	10
Japan	8	1
Italy	5	1
Argentina	4	5
Canada	4	5
Netherlands	2	1
Others	12	11
	100	100

Citrus fruit (S.I.T.C. no. 051.1,2)

Production
24 971 000 met. tons 1963-5 av.
17 467 000 1953-5 av.

Percentage exported
17% 1963-5 av.
16% 1953-5 av.

Exports
4 150 570 met. tons 1963-5 av.
2 800 000 1953-5 av.

	PERCENTAGE 1963-5 av.	1953-5 av.
Spain	26	35
Italy	12	13
Israel	12	9
Morocco	10	5
U.S.A.	9	15
South Africa	7	7
Algeria	5	8
Brazil	3	1
Lebanon	3	1
Greece	2	—
Others	11	6
	100	100

Imports
4 186 040 met. tons 1963-5 av.
2 770 000 1953-5 av.

	PERCENTAGE 1963-5 av.	1953-5 av.
Germany F.R.	23	19
France	20	24
U.K.	12	17
Canada	6	9
Netherlands	6	4
U.S.S.R.	4	2
Sweden	3	4
Others	26	21
	100	100

Grapes (S.I.T.C. no. 051.5)

Production
50 859 700 met. tons 1963-5 av.
39 433 000 1953-5 av.

Percentage exported
2% 1963-5 av.
1% 1953-5 av.

Exports
824 320 met. tons 1963-5 av.
310 000 1953-5 av.

	PERCENTAGE 1963-5 av.	1953-5 av.
Italy	24	20
Bulgaria	23	9
U.S.A.	12	17
Spain	11	14
Romania	6	—
France	4	12
South Africa	4	6
Hungary	3	3
Afghanistan	3	NA
Yugoslavia	2	2
Others	8	NA
	100	100

Imports
798 760 met. tons 1963-5 av.
287 000 1953-5 av.

	PERCENTAGE 1963-5 av.	1953-5 av.
Germany F.R.	29	35
Canada	13	16
U.S.S.R.	13	2
U.K.	7	13
Czechoslovakia	5	2
Germany D.R.	5	2
Switzerland	4	6
Poland	4	—
Sweden	3	4
Austria	3	3
Others	14	17
	100	100

Apples/Bananas

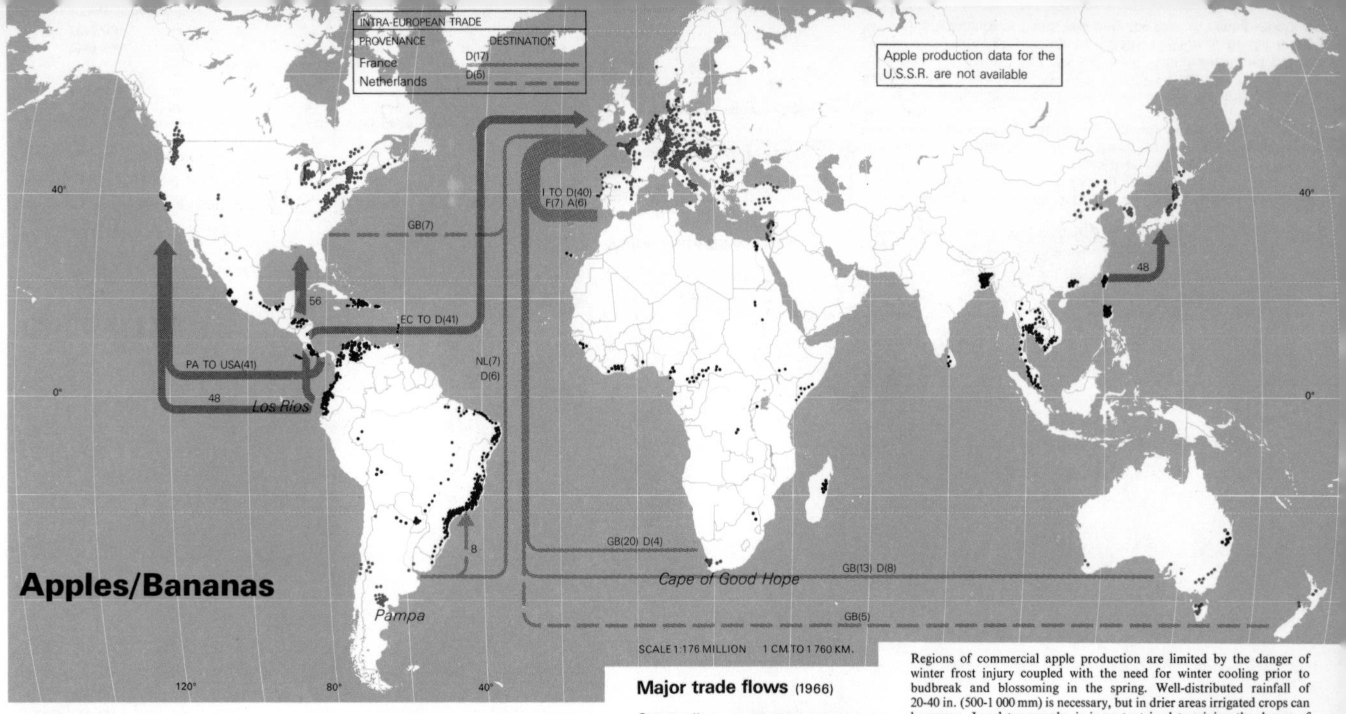

Production (1963-5 av.)
One dot represents 20 000 metric tons • apples • bananas

Major producers	FRANCE	U.S.A.	ITALY	GERMANY F.R.	JAPAN	U.K.	OTHERS	MET. TONS WORLD[2]
Apples 1963-5 av.	18	15	12	8	6	3	38	19 071 700
1953-5 av.	*30*	*17*	*7*	*9*	*3*	*4*	*30*	*13 667 000*

	BRAZIL	ECUADOR[1]	INDIA	VENEZUELA	PAKISTAN	OTHERS	WORLD
Bananas 1963-5 av.	20	13	12	6	5	44	21 840 000
1953-5 av.	*34*	*5*	*17*	–	*NA*	*NA*	*11 200 000*

[1]Exports only [2]Excl. U.S.S.R.

Major trade flows (1966)
Commodity : S.I.T.C. no.
APPLES : 051.4
BANANAS : 051.3
Value ($ U.S.)
0.5mm represents increments of $20 million
($ MILLIONS) 180 100 20
UNDER $10 MILLION
41 VALUE IN $ MILLIONS

Regions of commercial apple production are limited by the danger of winter frost injury coupled with the need for winter cooling prior to budbreak and blossoming in the spring. Well-distributed rainfall of 20-40 in. (500-1 000 mm) is necessary, but in drier areas irrigated crops can be grown. Local topography is important in determining the degree of risk to blossom and young fruit from late spring frost. Other limiting factors are those affecting the 'finish' and quality of dessert apples; the link between climate and disease, for example high summer humidity and scab in England; and adequate storage and transport facilities. Dessert and cooking apples are most important but some are produced for cider. Bananas (incl. plantains) are grown in most humid tropical areas; often plantains are an important subsistence crop. Extensive plantations in Central America are sited on well-drained and aerated sandy to medium clay loams, usually in rain-forest alluvial regions with a well-distributed rainfall of at least 80 in. (2 000 mm.) In drier areas supplementary irrigation may be practised. Diverse soils and localities may be used, provided high fertility can be maintained.

Citrus Fruit

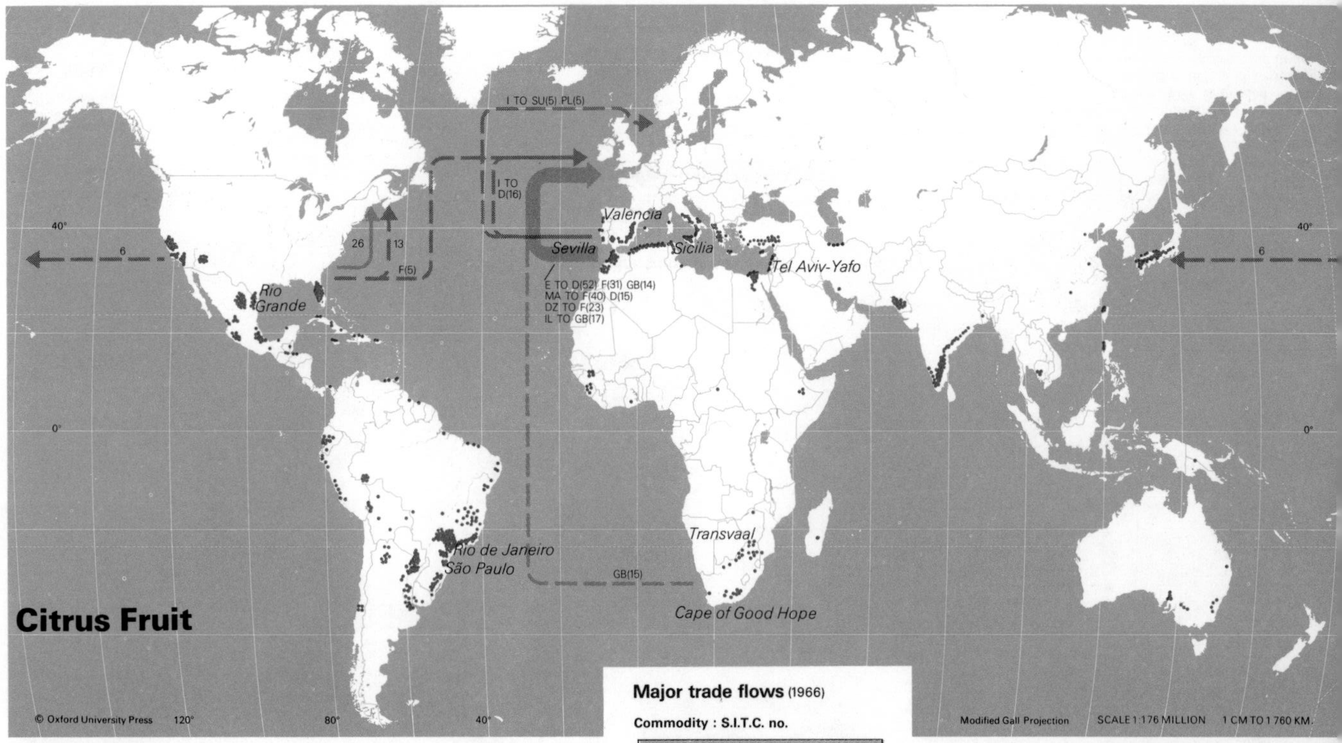

Production (1963-5 av.)
One dot represents 20 000 metric tons

Major producers	U.S.A.	BRAZIL	SPAIN	ITALY	JAPAN	INDIA	OTHERS	MET. TONS WORLD
Citrus 1963-5 av.	28	9	8	7	6	5	37	24 971 000
1953-5 av.	*42*	*8*	*7*	*6*	*3*	*4*	*30*	*17 467 000*

Major trade flows (1966)
Commodity : S.I.T.C. no.
ORANGES/TANGERINES : 051.1
OTHER CITRUS FRUIT : 051.2
Value ($ U.S.)
0.5mm represents increments of $40 million
($ MILLIONS) 360 200 40
UNDER $20 MILLION
26 VALUE IN $ MILLIONS

Citrus includes eight species of the *Rutacea* family varying in characteristics and commercial importance. The lime and citron are tropical and frost-susceptible, while the hardiest, the Seville orange, can tolerate several degrees of frost. Average temperature limits are 40°F (4.5°C) in the coldest month with 70°-75°F (21°-24°C) for most of the summer. Where citrus is grown in the tropics the temperatures may reach 120°F (49°C). Citrus tolerates a wide range of rainfall and extensive irrigation may be practised. Most non-alkaline, well-drained soils are suitable. In 1965 the main producers were: of oranges, the U.S.A. (24%) and Brazil (12%); of lemons/limes, the U.S.A. (21%) and Italy (20%); and of grapefruit, the U.S.A. (75%) and Israel (7%).

Grapes / Wine

Grapes

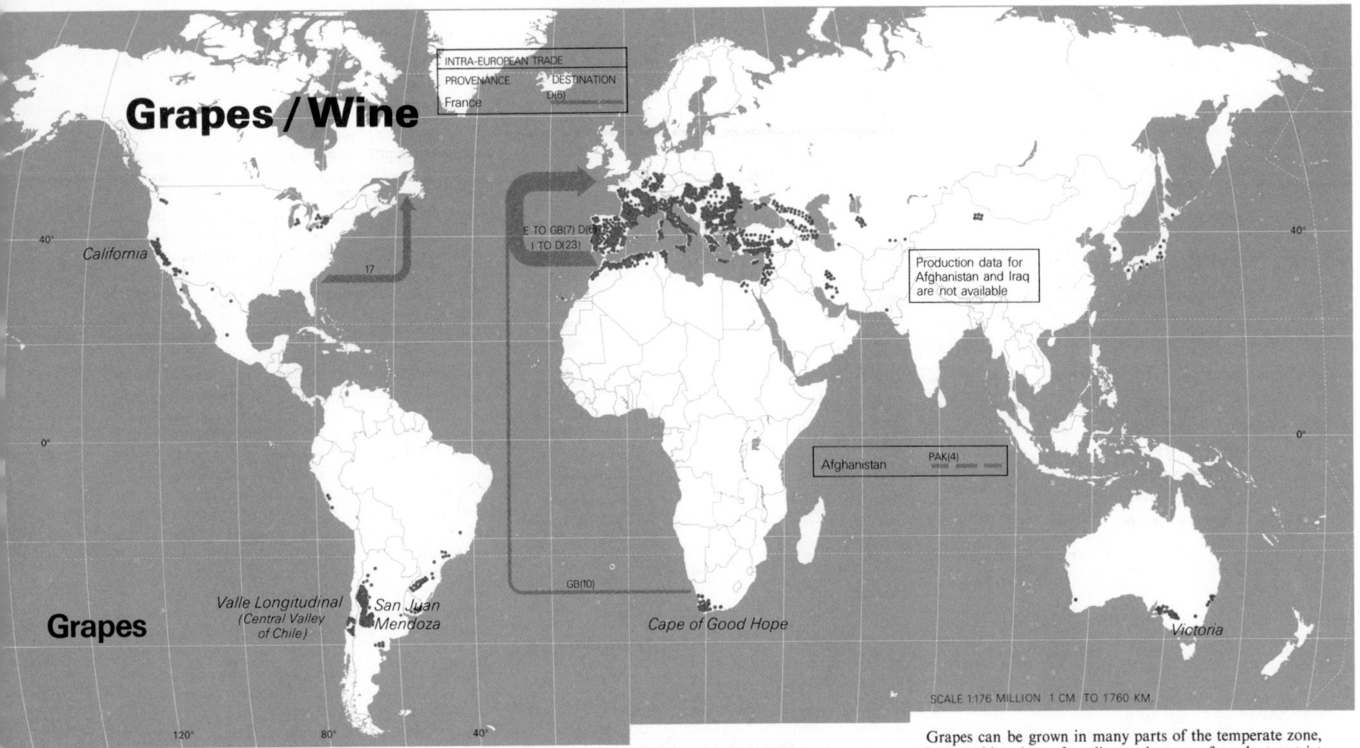

Production (1963-5 av.)

One dot represents 20 000 metric tons

Major producers	ITALY	FRANCE	SPAIN	U.S.A.	U.S.S.R.	TURKEY	OTHERS	WORLD (MET. TONS)
1963-5 av.	19	19	9	6	6	6	35	50 859 700
1953-5 av.	*22*	*23*	*8*	*7*	*...*[1]	*5*	*35*	*39 433 000*[1]

PERCENTAGE

[1] Excl. U.S.S.R.

Major trade flows (1966)

Commodity: S.I.T.C. no.

FRESH GRAPES : 051.5

Value ($ U.S.)
0.5mm. represents increments of $10 million

($ MILLIONS) 50, 10 — UNDER $5 MILLION — 17 VALUE IN $ MILLIONS

Grapes can be grown in many parts of the temperate zone, but considerations of quality or the type of product restrict the localities of commercial cultivation. Conditions for growth vary with the species of vine and the nature of the rootstock. All European vines are descended from one species, *Vitis vinifera.* Vines require a good supply of water in the vegetative phase and dry sunny weather during ripening and harvesting: high summer temperatures of about 65°-72°F (18.5°-22°C) for a prolonged period are inimical. At least 80% of the world's grapes are grown for wine. The North African muscat is grown primarily for dessert, while the U.S.A., Turkey, Greece, Australia and Iran produce large quantities of raisins or sultanas.

Wine

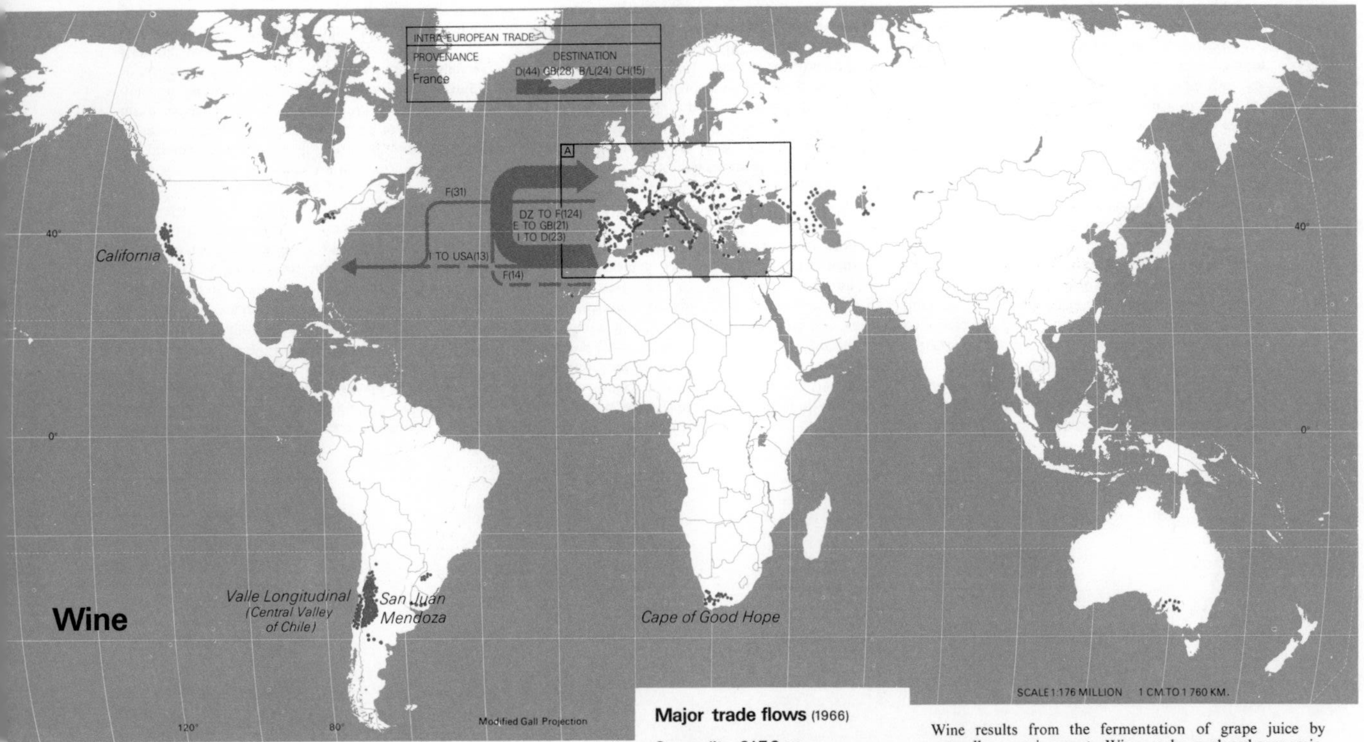

Production (1963-5 av.)

One dot represents 200 000 hectolitres

Major producers	ITALY	FRANCE	SPAIN	ARGENTINA	ALGERIA	PORTUGAL	OTHERS	WORLD ('000 HECTO-LITRES)
1963-5 av.	23	23	11	7	5	5	26	274 666
1953-5 av.	*24*	*27*	*9*	*6*	*8*	*5*	*21*	*225 473*

PERCENTAGE

Major trade flows (1966)

Commodity: S.I.T.C. no.

WINE OF FRESH GRAPES : 112.1

Value ($ U.S.)
0.5mm. represents increments of $30 million

($ MILLIONS) 150, 30 — UNDER $15 MILLION — 31 VALUE IN $ MILLIONS

Wine results from the fermentation of grape juice by naturally occurring yeasts. Wine can be produced economically in the northern hemisphere between lats. 30°-50° and in the southern hemisphere between lats. 30°-45°. Wines are classified according to strength and appearance. Table wines contain between 8-14% ethyl-alcohol, those with a higher alcohol content being grown in regions with much sun during the ripening period. Fortified wines, such as Sherry, are those in which spirits, usually brandy, have been added to increase the alcoholic content to 18-21%. Aromatic wines, such as Vermouths and Dubonnet, are fortified wines to which herbs and spices have been added.

A European wine areas

Each dot represents the production of 200 000 hectolitres of wine, located in the major wine-grape areas of each province. The names form a selection of wine-producing centres which are usually settlements but occasionally provinces. They are not primarily wine names although some places, such as Barsac and Chablis, have obviously given their names to many well-known wines.

[1] Area around the volcano

Consumption of alcoholic beverages (1966)

Wine

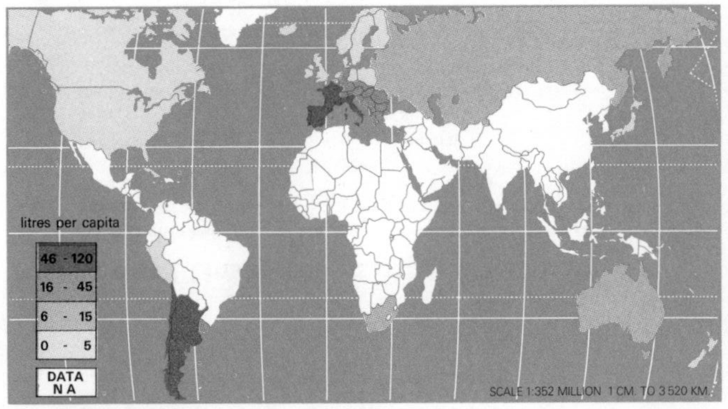

Beer

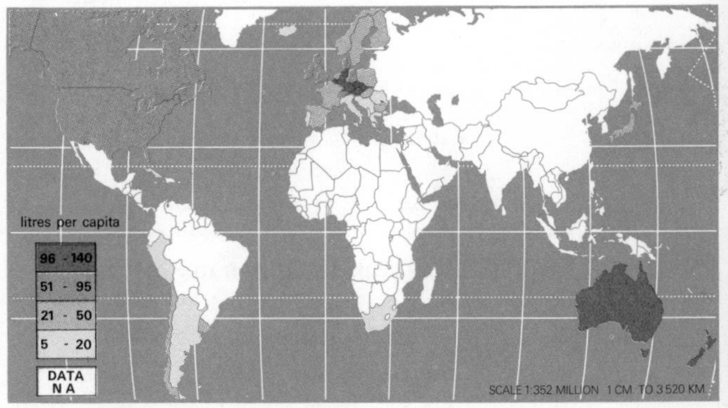

Spirit (100% proof)

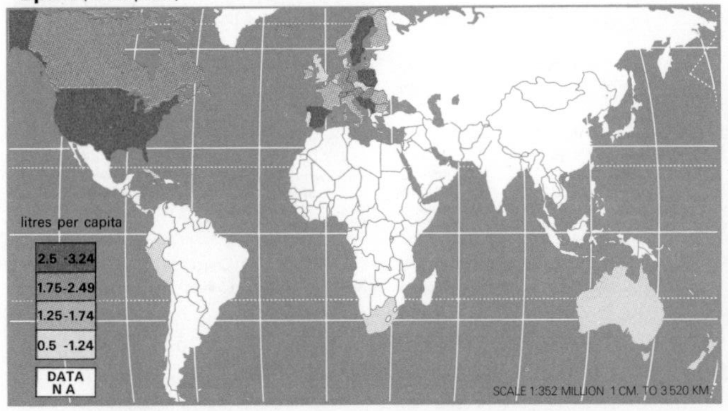

Total alcohol (100% proof)

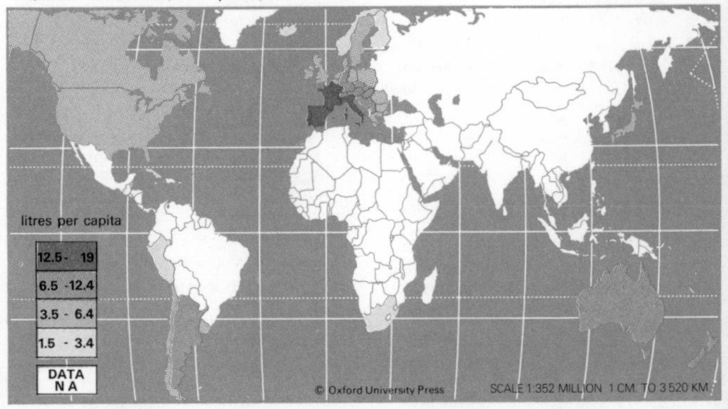

The consumption maps for wine and beer are based upon the total volume of the drink consumed. Total alcohol and spirit consumption maps are based upon the volume adjusted to show the consumption of 100% proof potable total alcohol and spirit.

The wine and beer data may be recalculated on the same basis by assuming an average alcohol content of 12% for wine and 5% for beer. It should be noted that the true range of individual figures is quite high: a Rhine wine may have an average alcohol content of 10% while that of a Sherry may be 18%.

Data for South Africa exclude Bantu-produced alcohol. No data are available for much of Latin America and most of Africa and Asia although much non-commercial brewing and distilling, both legal and illegal, are known to exist. Data for the U.S.S.R. are estimated.

Vegetable Oilseeds and Oils

Groundnuts p.19 Soya Beans p.19
Rapeseed p.19 Sunflower Seed p.19

For individual country data see Statistical Supplement

It is estimated that in recent years vegetable oils have accounted for just under three-fifths of the total world supply of fats and oils. World production of the main vegetable oil crops, in oil equivalent, mounted from 14 million tons in 1939 to 21.5 million tons in 1960 and to 39.6 million tons in 1968.

With animal fats lagging behind the growth of world population, more and more vegetable oils have been consumed as food; their use in paints, varnishes, lubricants, synthetic fabrics and other manufactures has also been expanded. Valuable by-products remain after extracting the oil from the seed, which can be used as livestock feed, as fertilizer, or, with soya beans, as protein-meal for human consumption.

As prosperity increases, the consumption of vegetable oils rises; more fats are added to the diet and more technical uses are discovered for oilseed products as industry advances. In 1960-2 consumption of fat varied from 1.1 kg. per capita in the Malagasy Republic to 35.9 kg. per capita in Denmark.

Consumption of fats and oils also expands with population growth. From 1850 to 1950 the population of Western Europe about doubled. In the same period the consumption of vegetable oils quadrupled, owing partly to population growth, partly to the swift rise of living standards.

The increasing demand could not be met by the traditional forms and sources of fats. The Dutch butter producers, the Jurgens, were therefore forced to supply an edible fat made from flour, milk and suet, which was called margarine by its inventor Hippolyte Mège Mouriès. But this margarine had relied on a solid animal fat, and until Crosfield invented in 1909 a method of making liquid vegetable oils solid by hydrogenation, and until refining processes were introduced, the enormous potentialities of tropical oils for producing a cheap edible fat lay unrealized.

In 1965 world output of margarine was over two-and-a-half times as great as in 1938, although the rate of increase in world production recently has been considerably slower than in the 1951-4 period. The United States is the largest producer, and with the progressive removal of restrictions and a price ratio in favour of margarine, consumption has risen steadily at the expense of butter. In 1965, in the U.S.A. consumption of margarine was 4.4 kg. per capita while that of butter was 2.8 kg. per capita. Corresponding figures for the U.K. are 5.4 kg. and 8.7 kg. per capita.

Since the development of hydrogenation and refining processes the demand for oilseed products greatly expanded, both for making margarine and for industrial products including soap and cattle cake. Palm oil production in West Africa and copra production in the Pacific Islands became increasingly profitable and new methods were evolved to increase production and improve quality. At the same time more efficient methods of crushing enable more and better quality oil to be extracted from the seed. For example, by traditional methods the Nigerian can extract only about 45% of the oil from the pericarp of the oil palm fruit, with a hand press about 65%, while in a mechanized mill some 85-90% of the available oil is extracted.

Since 1945 the patterns of world trade in oils and oilseeds have been radically altered. Wartime shortages, higher consumption in the producing countries, and a tendency to crush the seed within the producing country have all left a lasting mark. The last world war, for instance, cut off imports into America of the Chinese soya bean and of copra from Indonesia and the Philippines. This resulted in the expansion of oilseed crops in the U.S.A. Acreages of groundnuts, cottonseed, linseed, and particularly soya beans, rose. Tung trees were planted to supply the valuable drying oil which was formerly obtained only from China P.R. Mechanical harvesting was used for all these crops.

Also the substitution of one vegetable oil for another, as a result of improvements in processing, enabled margarine producers to use the oils of soya beans, groundnuts or cottonseed according to their availability, just as it allowed different oils to be used in industry. This freed paint-makers, for example, from their former exclusive reliance on linseed oil and tung oil.

In this way the U.S.A., which before the war was a heavy importer of most of the major oilseeds, is now increasingly a net exporter; in the period 1958-60 nearly 25% of the total domestic production was exported, though some of this was for charitable purposes. Although world production has risen, world trade has remained at the same level. Increased world demand has been met by growing the oilseeds best suited to local conditions and consuming them locally.

Since the 1940's vegetable oils have encountered strong competition from growing world output of synthetic chemical products and animal and marine fats. With the expanding production of synthetic detergents in the U.K., other West European countries, the U.S.A. and Canada, the use of vegetable oils in soap has tended to decline. In the U.S.A. where this trend has been particularly marked, oil consumption in soap averaged only 66 000 metric tons between 1963-65 compared with 242 000 metric tons in 1938. The rise of detergents has done much to allay fears of a long term shortage of oils and fats. In addition synthetic resins are now used in paint, and new surface coatings have begun to replace industrial oils.

The increased use of lard and marine oils in the manufacture of margarine, particularly in the U.K., is seen in the following figures. In 1954 they accounted for 16.6% of the total oils and fats used for margarine in the U.K., by 1965 the proportion had risen to 62.5%. Corresponding figures for the U.S.A., where 75% of margarine production is from soya bean oil, are 1.4% and 5.4%.

Despite these facts the demand for oilseeds is certain to increase. In the foreseeable future the need for edible fats and oils can only be met by oil-bearing plants. While synthetics make further inroads on the use of vegetable oils in soap and in industry, food is the major use; with rising living standards and a growing world population consumption will continue to rise. In many of the developing countries consumption of fat is below the level required for a balanced diet.

Vegetable oils

('000 met. tons)

	Extraction rate[1]	Production[2] 1963-5 av.	Production[2] *1953-5 av.*	Exports[3] 1963-5 av.	Exports[3] *1953-5 av.*	Imports[3] 1963-5 av.	Imports[3] *1953-5 av.*	Major exporters 1963-5 av.
Edible								
Soya bean oil	18%	6 038	*3 504*	685	*79*	621	*80*	U.S.A., Denmark
Groundnut oil	46%[4]	4 996	*3 682*	401	*271*	425	*249*	Senegal, Nigeria
Cottonseed oil	18%	3 831	*2 472*	272	*239*	286	*180*	U.S.A., Sudan
Sunflower oil	35%	2 646	*589*	294	*32*	298	*29*	U.S.S.R., Bulgaria
Rapeseed oil	38%	1 669	*1 900*	59	*32*	50	*30*	Germany F.R., France
Olive oil	—	1 411	*1 080*	168	*114*	183	*124*	Spain, Tunisia
Sesame oil	48%	784	*861*	NA	*NA*	NA	*NA*	NA
Edible/ Industrial								
Coconut oil	64%	2 117	*1 856*	462	*328*	448	*333*	Philippines, Ceylon
Palm oil	—	1 326	*1 110*	564	*578*	553	*574*	Nigeria, Malaysia
Palm kernel oil	48%	504	*462*	81	*61*	83	*51*	Congo D.R., Netherlands
Industrial								
Linseed oil	34%	1 187	*894*	276	*372*	292	*358*	Argentina, Uruguay
Castor oil	45%	323	*194*	149	*69*	141	*67*	Brazil, India
Tung oil	—	1 050	*107*	43	*59*	43	*56*	China P.R., Argentina

[1]Average yield from commercial sources [2]Oil equivalent of oilseed where extraction rate is given [3]Traded as oil [4]Ex-shell groundnut extraction rate

International trade in vegetable oilseeds and oils (1963-5 av.)

Soya beans/Soya bean oil (S.I.T.C. no. 221.4/421.2)

Production *(beans)*
33 543 000 met. tons 1963-5 av.
19 467 000 1953-5 av.[1]

Percentage exported *(beans)*
18% 1963-5 av.
9% 1953-5 av.[1]

Exports
Beans
6 155 300 met. tons 1963-5 av.*
*1 734 000 1953-5 av.**

	Percentage 1963-5 av.	*1953-5 av.*
U.S.A.	90	*80*
China P.R.*	8	*14*
Canada	1	*1*
Others	1	*5*
	100	*100*

Imports
Beans
5 999 500 met. tons 1963-5 av.
1 616 000 1953-5 av.

	Percentage 1963-5 av.	*1953-5 av.*
Japan	28	*36*
Germany F.R.	21	*19*
Canada	7	*11*
Others	44	*34*
	100	*100*

Oil (exports)
685 100 met. tons 1963-5 av.
78 800 1953-5 av.

	Percentage 1963-5 av.	*1953-5 av.*
U.S.A.	79	*49*
Denmark	6	*2*
Israel	3	*—*
Others	12	*49*
	100	*100*

Oil (imports)
620 900 met. tons 1963-5 av.
80 200 1953-5 av.

	Percentage 1963-5 av.	*1953-5 av.*
Spain	14	*—*
Pakistan	12	*—*
Turkey	6	*—*
Others	68	*100*[2]
	100	*100*

Groundnuts[3]/Groundnut oil (S.I.T.C. no. 221.1/421.4)

Production *(nuts)*
10 860 500 met. tons 1963-5 av.
8 003 300 1953-5 av.[1]

Percentage exported *(nuts)*
13% 1963-5 av.
12% 1953-5 av.[1]

Exports
Nuts
1 443 700 met. tons 1963-5 av.
937 000 1953-5 av.

	Percentage 1963-5 av.	*1953-5 av.*
Nigeria	42	*41*
Senegal	15	*23*[4]
Sudan	10	*3*
Others	32	*33*
	100	*100*

Imports
Nuts
1 392 300 met. tons 1963-5 av.
929 000 1953-5 av.

	Percentage 1963-5 av.	*1953-5 av.*
France	35	*33*
U.K.	10	*39*
Italy	9	*2*
Others	46	*26*
	100	*100*

Oil (exports)
401 000 met. tons 1963-5 av.
270 700 1953-5 av.

	Percentage 1963-5 av.	*1953-5 av.*
Senegal	31	*34*[4]
Nigeria	20	*10*
India	11	*27*
Others	38	*29*
	100	*100*

Oil (imports)
425 200 met. tons 1963-5 av.*
248 600 1953-5 av.

	Percentage 1963-5 av.	*1953-5 av.*
France	34*	*34*
U.K.	13	*15*
Spain	11	*—*
Others	42	*51*
	100	*100*

Linseed/Linseed oil (S.I.T.C. no. 221.5/422.1)

Production *(seed)*
3 490 000 met. tons 1963-5 av.
2 630 000 1953-5 av.[1]

Percentage exported *(seed)*
17% 1963-5 av.
15% 1953-5 av.[1]

Exports
Seed
599 000 met. tons 1963-5 av.
391 000 1953-5 av.

	Percentage 1963-5 av.	*1953-5 av.*
Canada	60	*39*
U.S.A.	20	*32*
Belg./Lux.	5	*2*
Others	15	*27*
	100	*100*

Imports
Seed
572 800 met. tons 1963-5 av.
390 000 1953-5 av.

	Percentage 1963-5 av.	*1953-5 av.*
U.K.	21	*7*
Japan	17	*13*
France	13	*30*
Others	49	*50*
	100	*100*

Oil (exports)
276 200 met. tons 1963-5 av.
372 500 1953-5 av.

	Percentage 1963-5 av.	*1953-5 av.*
Argentina	79	*46*
Uruguay	7	*8*
U.S.A.	4	*27*
Others	10	*19*
	100	*100*

Oil (imports)
292 100 met. tons 1963-5 av.
357 900 1953-5 av.

	Percentage 1963-5 av.	*1953-5 av.*
Germany F.R.	25	*23*
U.K.	15	*27*
U.S.S.R.	10	*11*
Others	50	*39*
	100	*100*

Sunflower seed/Sunflower seed oil (S.I.T.C. no. 221.8/421.6)

Production *(seed)*
7 558 700 met. tons 1963-5 av.
1 683 000 1953-5 av.[1]

Percentage exported *(seed)*
3% 1963-5 av.
3% 1953-5 av.[1]

Exports
Seed
230 100 met. tons 1963-5 av.
102 900 1953-5 av.

	Percentage 1963-5 av.	*1953-5 av.*
U.S.S.R.	42	*52*
Bulgaria	34	*8*
Hungary	6	*35*
Others	18	*5*
	100	*100*

Imports
Seed
217 500 met. tons 1963-5 av.
*90 400 1953-5 av.**

	Percentage 1963-5 av.	*1953-5 av.*
Germany D.R.	32	*4**
Italy	29	*3*
Germany F.R.	14	*31*
Others	25	*62*
	100	*100*

Oil (exports)
293 900 met. tons 1963-5 av.
*31 800 1953-5 av.**

	Percentage 1963-5 av.	*1953-5 av.*
U.S.S.R.	71	*—*
Romania	12	*—*
Hungary	7	*55**
Others	10	*45*
	100	*100*

Oil (imports)
297 900 met. tons 1963-5 av.*
28 900 1953-5 av.

	Percentage 1963-5 av.	*1953-5 av.*
Germany D.R.	22	*—*
Germany F.R.	20	*21*
Cuba	12*	*—*
Others	46	*79*
	100	*100*

Copra/Coconut oil (S.I.T.C. no. 221.2/422.3)

Production *(kernels)*
3 307 200 met. tons 1963-5 av.
2 900 000 1953-5 av.

Percentage exported *(kernels)*
46% 1963-5 av.
50% 1953-5 av.

Exports
Kernels
1 513 000 met. tons 1963-5 av.
1 448 300 1953-5 av.

	Percentage 1963-5 av.	*1953-5 av.*
Philippines	61	*53*
Indonesia	9	*20*
New Guinea	4	*5*
Others	26	*22*
	100	*100*

Imports
Kernels
1 401 500 met. tons 1963-5 av.
1 446 000 1953-5 av.

	Percentage 1963-5 av.	*1953-5 av.*
U.S.A.	18	*21*
Germany F.R.	18	*14*
Netherlands	9	*10*
Others	55	*55*
	100	*100*

Oil (exports)
462 400 met. tons 1963-5 av.
328 100 1953-5 av.

	Percentage 1963-5 av.	*1953-5 av.*
Philippines	48	*20*
Ceylon	21	*26*
Netherlands	8	*11*
Others	23	*43*
	100	*100*

Oil (imports)
447 700 met. tons 1963-5 av.
333 100 1953-5 av.

	Percentage 1963-5 av.	*1953-5 av.*
U.S.A.	40	*19*
Germany F.R.	11	*17*
U.K.	10	*10*
Others	39	*54*
	100	*100*

Palm kernels/Palm kernel oil (S.I.T.C. no. 221.3/422.4)

Production *(kernels)*
1 049 700 met. tons 1963-5 av.
963 000 1953-5 av.

Percentage exported *(kernels)*
64% 1963-5 av.
83% 1953-5 av.

Exports
Kernels
667 500 met. tons 1963-5 av.
800 000 1953-5 av.

	Percentage 1963-5 av.	*1953-5 av.*
Nigeria	61	*55*
Sierra Leone	8	*8*
Dahomey	6	*10*[4]
Others	25	*27*
	100	*100*

Imports
Kernels
666 900 met. tons 1963-5 av.
802 000 1953-5 av.

	Percentage 1963-5 av.	*1953-5 av.*
U.K.	31	*47*
Germany F.R.	19	*16*
Netherlands	19	*11*
Others	31	*26*
	100	*100*

Oil (exports)
81 400 met. tons 1963-5 av.
61 300 1953-5 av.

	Percentage 1963-5 av.	*1953-5 av.*
Congo D.R.	44	*40*[5]
Netherlands	24	*19*
U.K.	9	*31*
Others	23	*10*
	100	*100*

Oil (imports)
83 400 met. tons 1963-5 av.
50 700 1953-5 av.

	Percentage 1963-5 av.	*1953-5 av.*
U.S.A.	46	*44*
Germany F.R.	18	*27*
Italy	10	*—*
Others	26	*29*
	100	*100*

*Estimate [1]Excl. U.S.S.R. [2]Germany F.R. was the major importer [3]Ex-shell basis [4]French West Africa (incl. Dahomey, Ivory Coast, Niger, Senegal, Upper Volta and Mali) [5]Belgian Congo

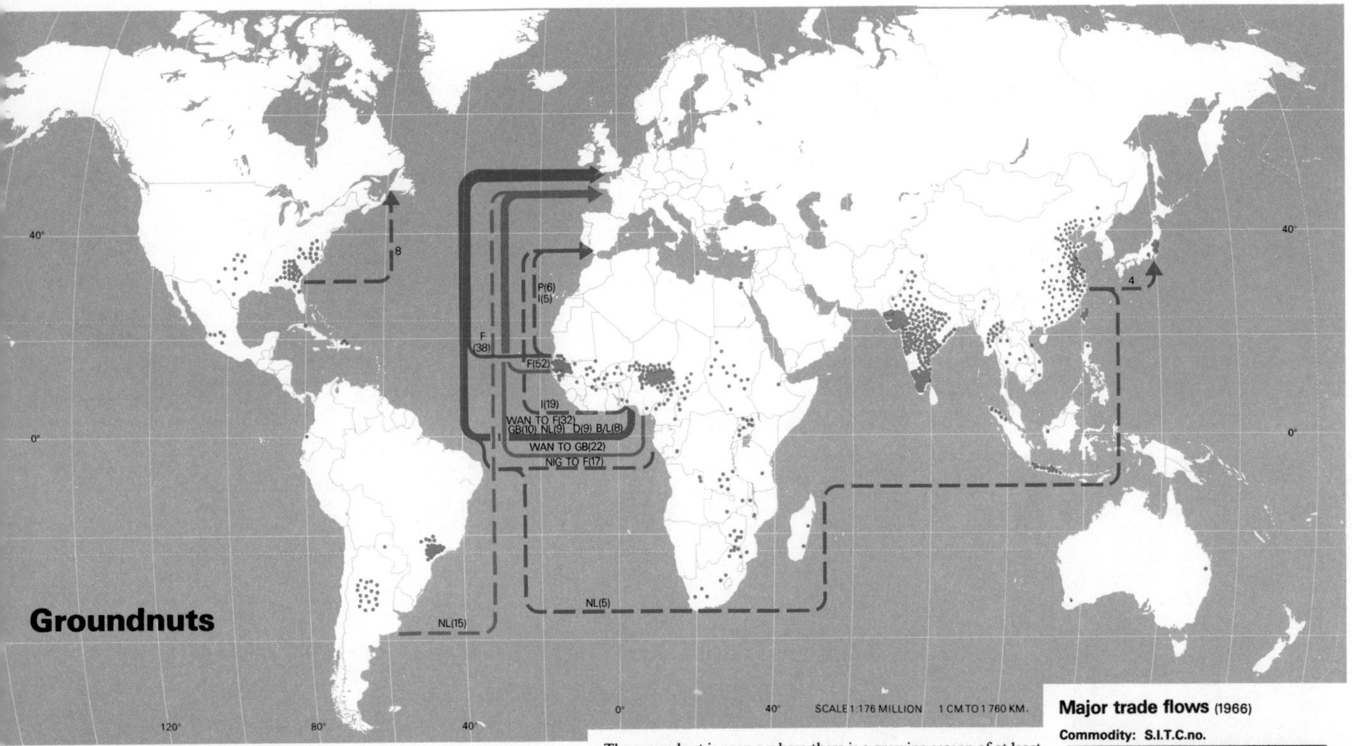
Groundnuts
NL(15)
NL(5)
F
(38)
P(6)
I(5)
F(52)
I(19)
WAN TO F(32)
GB(10) NL(9) D(9) B/L(8)
WAN TO GB(22)
NIG TO F(17)
8
4
SCALE 1:176 MILLION 1 CM.TO 1 760 KM.

Groundnuts

Production (1963-5 av.)

One dot represents 20 000 metric tons (in shell)

Major producers	INDIA	CHINA P.R.	NIGERIA	SENEGAL	U.S.A.	OTHERS	MET. TONS WORLD[1]
	PERCENTAGE						
1963-5 av.	**32**	**14**	**9**	**7**	**6**	**32**	**15 515 000**
1953-5 av.	*34*	*23*	*8*	*8*	*6*	*21*	*11 433 000*

[1]Excl. U.S.S.R.

The groundnut is grown where there is a growing season of at least four months with mean temperatures of about 80°F (26.5°C) for most of the period. Much of the crop is cultivated in regions with 40 in. (1 000 mm.) or more annual rainfall although seasonal rainfall may be as low as 20–30 in. (500–750 mm.), and a dry period during harvesting is necessary. In Africa and Asia groundnuts are an important subsistence crop; since the buried pods are collected by hand they can be grown on soils unsuitable for mechanical harvesting due to their heavy texture or liability to compaction. The highest quality kernels are produced on fertile light soils. Groundnuts are a valuable source of edible oil, and the meal is used as animal feed.

Major trade flows (1966)

Commodity: S.I.T.C.no.

GROUNDNUTS/PEANUTS (GREEN) : 221.1

GROUNDNUT/PEANUT OIL : 421.4

Value ($U.S.)

0.5mm represents increments of $40 million ($ MILLIONS) 360 200 40

UNDER $20 MILLION

52 VALUE IN $ MILLIONS

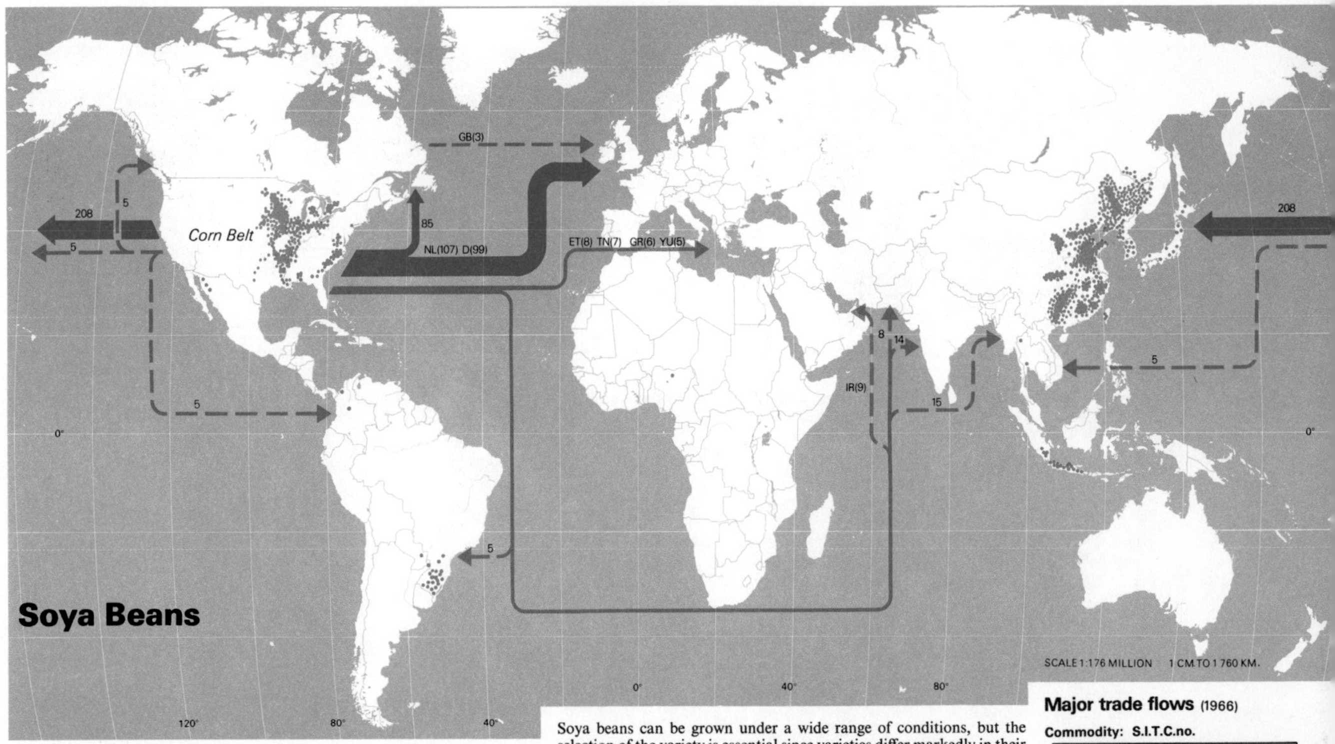
Soya Beans
Corn Belt
208
5
5
GB(3)
85
NL(107) D(99)
ET(8) TN(7) GR(6) YU(5)
5
8
14
IR(9)
15
5
208
SCALE 1:176 MILLION 1 CM.TO 1 760 KM.

Soya Beans

Production (1963-5 av.)

One dot represents 20 000 metric tons

Major producers	U.S.A.	CHINA P.R.	BRAZIL	U.S.S.R.	OTHERS	MET. TONS WORLD
	PERCENTAGE					
1963-5 av.	**61**	**33**	**1**	**1**	**4**	**33 543 000**
1953-5 av.	*46*	*47*	*1*	*...[1]*	*6*	*19 467 000[1]*

[1]Excl. U.S.S.R.

Soya beans can be grown under a wide range of conditions, but the selection of the variety is essential since varieties differ markedly in their environmental requirements such as the length of day which initiates flowering. In general the climatic conditions demanded are similar to those of maize (corn). Fertile well-drained soils are the most productive but a wide range are tolerated depending on the variety. The seedlings of some varieties are susceptible to frost, and low night temperatures of about 55°F (13°C) greatly retard development. The plants can tolerate short droughts when past the seedling stage, but a relatively even distribution of rainfall during the growth cycle is needed. The oil is used as an edible oil for margarine or as a drying oil for paint-making. The residual meal is a valuable source of protein for animal or human consumption.

Major trade flows (1966)

Commodity: S.I.T.C.no.

SOYA BEANS(EXCL.FLOUR/MEAL): 221.4

SOYA BEAN OIL : 421.2

Value ($U.S.)

0.5mm represents increments of $40 million ($ MILLIONS) 360 200 40

UNDER $20 MILLION

85 VALUE IN $ MILLIONS

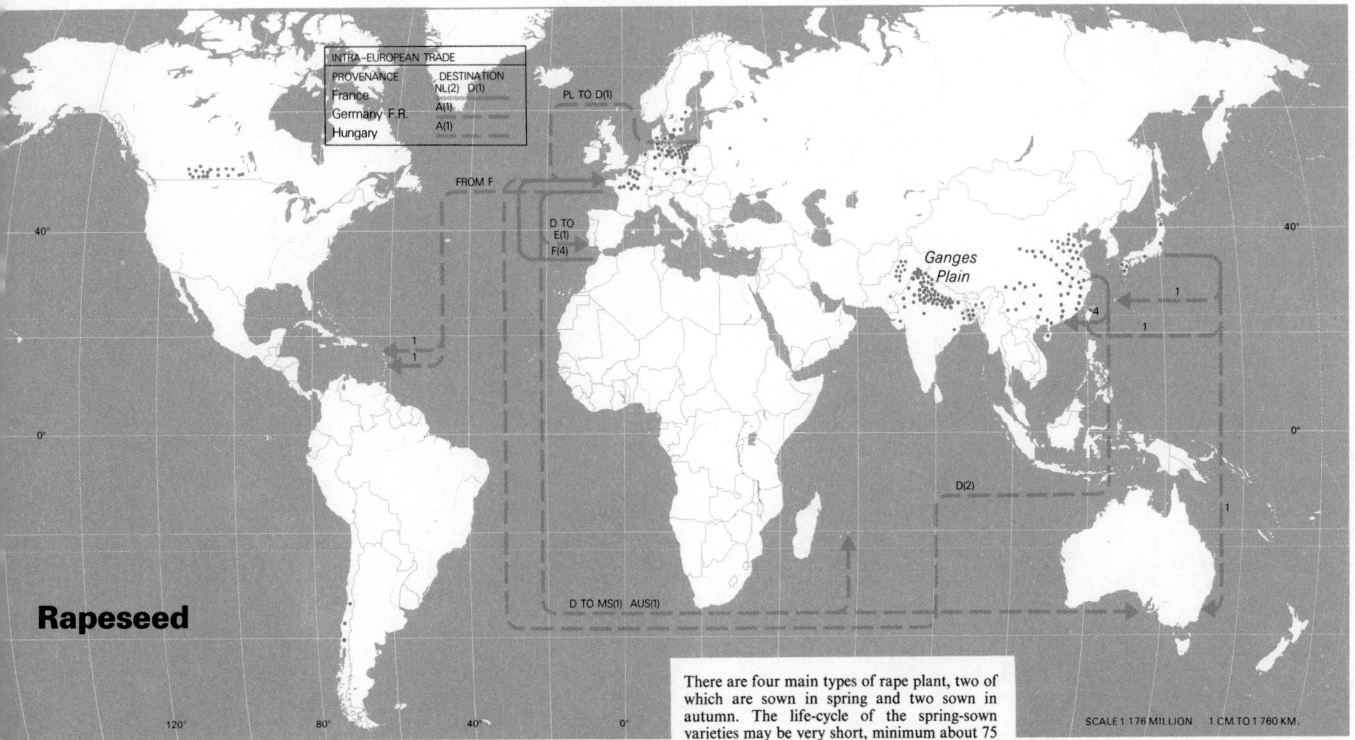
Rapeseed
INTRA-EUROPEAN TRADE
PROVENANCE DESTINATION
France NL(2) D(1)
Germany F.R. A(1)
Hungary A(1)
PL TO D(1)
FROM F
D TO
E(1)
F(4)
Ganges Plain
1
1
4
1
D(2)
1
D TO MS(1) AUS(1)
SCALE 1:176 MILLION 1 CM.TO 1 760 KM.

Rapeseed

Production (1963-5 av.)

One dot represents 20 000 metric tons

Major producers	INDIA	CHINA P.R.	CANADA	POLAND	PAKISTAN	FRANCE	OTHERS	MET. TONS WORLD
	PERCENTAGE							
1963-5 av.	**28**	**25**	**8**	**8**	**7**	**5**	**19**	**4 392 300**
1953-5 av.	*18*	*56*	*—*	*NA*	*6*	*2*	*NA*	*5 000 000[1]*

[1]Excl. U.S.S.R.

There are four main types of rape plant, two of which are sown in spring and two sown in autumn. The life-cycle of the spring-sown varieties may be very short, minimum about 75 days, while the more productive autumn sown types are grown where winters are not severe. They are adapted to temperate conditions and in the sub-tropics are grown in the cool season. The water requirements vary with type of plant, although the rape is often grown where annual rainfall is less than 20 in. (500 mm.). Soils may vary considerably; neutral fertile soils with high nitrogen content are best. Rapeseed oil is mainly used for edible purposes, although it also has specialized industrial uses.

Major trade flows (1966)

Commodity: S.I.T.C.no.

RAPE,COLZA & MUSTARD OILS : 421.7

Value ($U.S.)

0.5mm represents increments of $5 million

UNDER $2.5 MILLION

4 VALUE IN $ MILLIONS

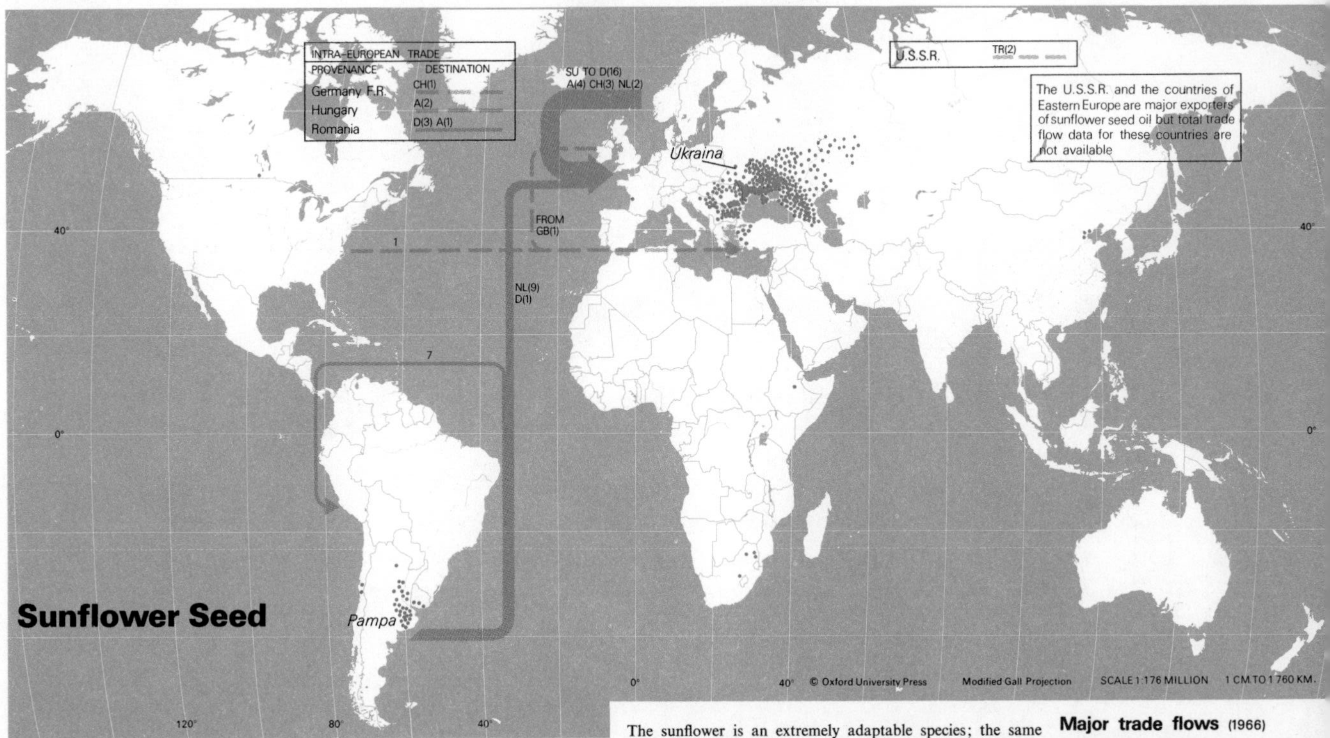
Sunflower Seed
INTRA-EUROPEAN TRADE
PROVENANCE DESTINATION
Germany F.R. CH(1)
Hungary A(2)
Romania D(3) A(1)
SU TO D(16)
A(4) CH(3) NL(2)
U.S.S.R. TR(2)
The U.S.S.R. and the countries of Eastern Europe are major exporters of sunflower seed oil but total trade flow data for these countries are not available
Ukraina
FROM GB(1)
1
NL(9)
D(1)
7
Pampa
© Oxford University Press
Modified Gall Projection
SCALE 1:176 MILLION 1 CM.TO 1 760 KM.

Sunflower Seed

Production (1963-5 av.)

One dot represents 20 000 metric tons

Major producers	U.S.S.R.	ARGENTINA	ROMANIA	BULGARIA	YUGOSLAVIA	OTHERS	MET. TONS WORLD
	PERCENTAGE						
1963-5 av.	**69**	**7**	**7**	**5**	**3**	**9**	**7 558 700**
1953-5 av.	*...[1]*	*27*	*NA*	*NA*	*7*	*NA*	*1 683 000[1]*

[1]Excl. U.S.S.R.

The sunflower is an extremely adaptable species; the same variety has been grown successfully in the tropics and at latitude 50°N with a July temperature of about 68°F (20°C). Much of the crop is grown where the annual rainfall is less than 20 in. (500 mm.), but greater rainfall gives yields as long as there is a dry period during the later stages of ripening. A wide range of soils of moderate fertility is used. In some areas large-scale production is limited by the supply of pollinating insects. In the major centres of production the heads are mechanically harvested and threshed but elsewhere hand collection is common. Sunflower seed oil can be used for margarine or salad oil and the residue can be made into cattle cake.

Major trade flows (1966)

Commodity: S.I.T.C. no.

SUNFLOWER SEED OIL : 421.6

Value ($U.S.)

0.5mm represents increments of $5 million ($ MILLIONS) 45 25 5

UNDER $2.5 MILLION

7 VALUE IN $ MILLIONS

Nutrition

Arctic Circle
Tropic of Cancer
Equator
Tropic of Capricorn
Date Line
Wheat
Corn
Sugar
Millet
Cassava
Bananas
Potatoes
Rice
Barley
Rye
Fruit
Teff
Yams
Modified Gall Projection Equatorial Scale 1: 88 Million approx.
© Oxford University Press

Basic food crops

Production areas of production of selected crops

(One dot: 100 000 metric tons) Rice, Wheat, Corn, Barley, Rye, Millet, Teff

Cassava, Yams, Potatoes

(One dot: 20 000 metric tons) Sugar (beet & cane) Bananas (incl. plantains) Other Fruit

Consumption estimated domestic consumption from national production of those crops shown

(calories per capita per day)

1 660-1 220	1 220-750	750-450	450-160	DATA NA

For each country are shown per capita domestic consumption and areas of production for one or more basic food crop. The crops selected are those carbohydrates which contribute the highest number of calories per capita of any home-grown crop. Selection has been based on national averages, and does not take account of regional or other variations; for example, rice is the basic crop shown for Pakistan, but if shown regionally rice would remain the basic crop for East Pakistan although wheat would probably be more important for West Pakistan.

A further crop is shown for a country if its contribution to the national average calorific intake is at least 75% of that of the first crop selected. When this occurs, the consumption category is based on the aggregate for both crops; for example, in Brazil rice provides 394 calories per capita per day and corn 302 (76.7% of the rice). Both crops are mapped and calorific intake is given as 696 calories per capita per day.

Fat levels per capita

Selected countries

(grammes per day)

	1961-3 av.
New Zealand	157.2
U.K.	143.4
U.S.A.	142.7
Argentina	109.1
Greece	88.1
Uganda	39.0
Japan	36.3
Iraq	35.5
Bolivia	28.2
India	26.6
Malagasy R.	16.8

[1]Data for 1962

In general there are two methods employed in increasing food production. The first is to improve the existing methods of husbandry at a minimal cost. The second, which is used to raise the levels of yield further, entails the breeding and selection of seeds or crops best fitted to the environment coupled with the efficient use of fertilizers, pesticides and farm mechanization. Increased productivity of the agrarian labour force is also a requirement. In some areas a high level of mechanization is essential to ensure that the crops are sown and harvested at the right times, as in the Canadian wheat belt. In other regions where, as a consequence of industrialization, farm workers must be paid high wages, mechanization is essential to keep down costs of production. Tractors are only a part of mechanization but the following table gives an idea of one aspect of the labour-mechanization balance.

	Agrarian labour as % of total	Tractors per arable 10 000 ha.
Cambodia	80.9	—[1]
India	72.9	2
Bulgaria	64.1	133
Ghana	58.0	25
Brazil	51.6	21
Peru	49.7	25
Jordan	35.3	13
U.S.S.R.	35.2	67
Kenya	35.2	36
Japan	26.9	29
New Zealand	14.4	1 096
Netherlands	10.7	1 115
U.S.A.	6.2	250
U.K.	5.1	508

[1]Three tractors per 1 000 000 ha.

Estimated calories per capita per day

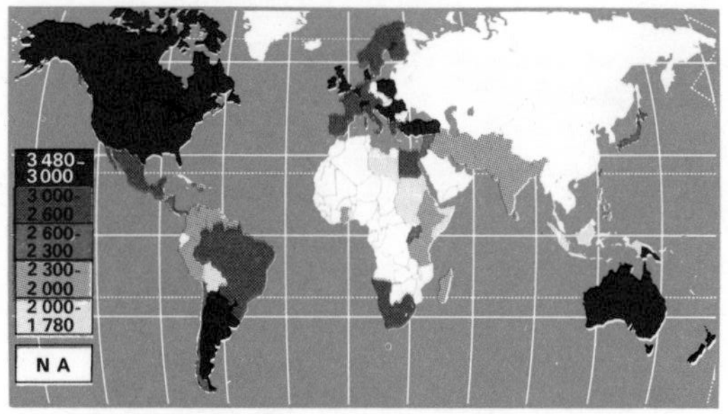

3 480-3 000
3 000-2 600
2 600-2 300
2 300-2 000
2 000-1 780
N A

Estimated minimum calorie requirement to avoid malnutrition, by region

Europe[1]	2 590
North America	2 590
Latin America	2 410
Middle East	2 400
Africa	2 340
Asia[2]	2 300

Estimated gm. per day of protein available, by region

North America	93
Europe[1]	88
Middle East	76
Latin America	67
Africa	61
Asia[2]	56

[1]Incl. U.S.S.R. [2]Incl. China P.R.

Estimated protein per capita (gm. per day)

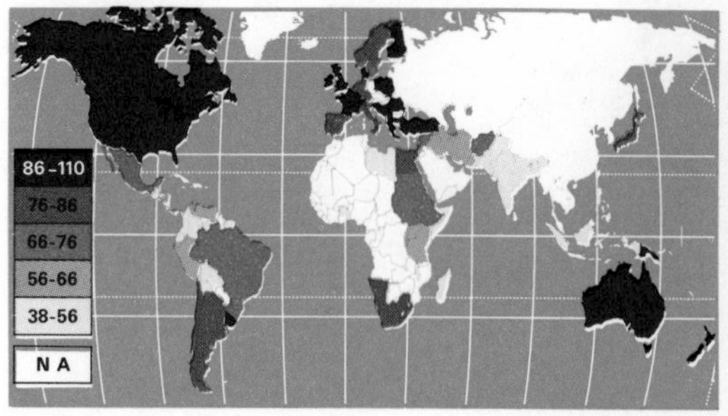

86-110
76-86
66-76
56-66
38-56
N A

Livestock/Livestock Products

Cattle p. 22 Pigs p. 23 Sheep p. 23

For individual country data see Statistical Supplement

Man uses livestock for food, power and sport. Food from livestock – meat, eggs and dairy products – is eaten mainly by those with a high standard of living. Livestock is used for power largely in developing areas, where the ox ploughing or drawing a cart is a familiar sight. The most important use of animals for sport is horse racing.

Food from livestock is generally expensive when compared, for example, with cereals. Man can obtain up to ten times as many calories by eating a crop instead of the livestock products which would result from feeding beasts off land on which crops can be grown for human consumption. But the raising of livestock is not always at the expense of grains for human consumption, since much grazing land is unsuitable for cultivation, and good husbandry often requires a rotation which includes grass or fodder crops.

The output of meat and dairy products could be greatly increased in many countries by proper management. It can also be raised by careful breeding and by controlling disease, which in a normal year causes the loss of about 15% of the total output of livestock products in the U.K. The world total of livestock has increased substantially since 1945 but at a rate sufficient only to keep pace with growing population. Numbers of livestock per head of population are shown in the table below.

Cattle. In Europe most of the cattle are of breeds good for producing both milk and beef, for which the relatively high local standard of living provides a ready demand. Grazing land is usually limited, and cattle are therefore often kept in courts or yards and fed largely on farm by-products and root crops grown for them on mixed farms. In winter they are generally kept warm in sheds so as to economize on feed. In the Western U.S.A., Australia and Argentina cattle can usually be grazed on open range, and it is mainly beef types that are raised. A large part of the beef production of Australia, Argentina and New Zealand is refrigerated and exported. In India the climate is more suitable for Zebu or humped cattle, which are used primarily as a source of milk and as draught animals, although the hides are also valuable and important in international trade.

In the more industrialized countries great progress has been made not only in the care and feeding of animals but also in improving the quality of the herds. This is done by breeding from registered stock and by the use of artificial insemination, which greatly extends the influence of the best bulls. Beef steers, which used to be slaughtered when four to six years old, can now often be fattened for market in eighteen months. In Europe since 1945 milk and beef yields per animal have been rising by about two per cent per annum. Milk marketing has been improved by the development of the canning and dehydrating industries, which enable large quantities of milk to be stored and transported over long distances.

Sheep and Goats. Most sheep are raised for wool and meat; the merino yields a particularly fine wool, and crossbreds are superior for meat. Although both meat and wool must be produced together, it is possible to vary the proportion in which they are supplied by varying the breeds or the age at which the animals are killed.

Although wool and meat are by far the most important products, sheep are raised chiefly for their skins in some countries and in parts of Southern Europe cheese is made from their milk. Milk is also the chief product of goats raised in European countries, although elsewhere meat and hides are usually most important. The Angora goat, a native of the Turkish steppes but now also reared in the U.S.A., South Africa, Lesotho and elsewhere, is the source of mohair, used in plushes, linings and carpets. Sheep can normally be left to graze in open pasture; goats, unless they are tethered, eat the bark and branches of trees and shrubs.

Poultry. More people keep poultry than any other type of livestock; production is highest in North America, but there are large numbers in other countries, notably India and China P.R. Most chickens are kept for egg production, usually on general farms and often with free range, but there are also intensive producers using battery or deep-litter systems. The specialist systems sell the birds after one year's laying. Since 1945 a broiler industry has grown up in North America and Europe producing birds for meat only.

The use of incubators enables numbers to be increased cheaply and rapidly and production levels to be maintained throughout the year. Marketing difficulties have been reduced in some countries by co-operatives and by egg preservation and deep freezing of dressed birds. Chickens are the most common poultry, but ducks are raised for eggs and meat in many countries; geese and turkeys, which are widely distributed, are mainly kept for meat.

Equines. Horses, ponies, donkeys and mules are used mainly as draught or pack animals, but their hides are valuable, and in some countries their meat and milk are also valued. In more industrialized countries animals are being replaced by motor vehicles; in the U.S.A. the number of horses has fallen by over 80% since 1939. Camels, while not equines, serve much the same purpose.

Pigs. Pigs are normally kept on mixed farms where they can be fed cheaply on farm by-products or coarse grains. In Denmark, for example, the Landrace pig, which has been carefully bred to produce bacon economically, is fed on barley and the skim milk left over from butter-making. Pigs eat less and fatten more quickly if warm and dry, and this helps to cover the high capital cost of the buildings which are essential for housing them during the winter in northern countries.

It takes about four months to fatten a pig for pork, and rather longer for bacon. The breeding cycle can be completed in six months, and pigs normally litter 8-10, so it is possible to increase the supply of pigmeat rapidly. This causes large cyclical fluctuations, when scarcity of pigs, resulting in high prices, alternates with abundance, which lowers prices.

Livestock population

	HEAD		MILLION HEAD									
	LIVESTOCK PER CAPITA		TOTAL LIVESTOCK		CAMELS/HORSES		CATTLE[1]		SHEEP		PIGS	
	1963-5 av.	1953-5 av.	1963-5 av.	1953-5 av.	1963-5 av.	1953-5 av.	1963-5 av.	1953-5 av.	1963-5 av.	1953-5 av.	1963-5 av.	1953-5 av.
Oceania	14.5	*12.7*	246	*190*	1	*1*	26	*22*	217	*165*	2	*2*
South America	2.6	*2.9*	415	*361*	27	*26*	170	*145*	148	*145*	70	*45*
Africa	1.4	*1.6*	416	*348*	24	*20*	128	*102*	258	*222*	6	*4*
Central America	1.3	*1.2*	102	*68*	12	*9*	47	*28*	22	*18*	21	*13*
U.S.A./Canada	1.0	*1.1*	215	*200*	3	*6*	117	*105*	33	*35*	62	*54*
Europe[2]	0.9	*0.9*	395	*368*	14	*21*	118	*106*	147	*151*	116	*90*
U.S.S.R.	1.3	*1.2*	290	*247*	10	*16**	87	*61*	139	*128*	54	*42*
Asia[3]	0.7	*0.7*	730	*598*	19	*18*	365	*301*	305	*255*	41	*24*
China P.R.*	0.6	*0.4*	429	*259*	21	*21*	90	*63*	120	*79*	198	*96*
World	1.0	*1.0*	3 238	*2 639*	131	*138*	1 148	*933*	1 389	*1 198*	570	*370*

*Estimate [1]Including buffaloes [2]Excluding the U.S.S.R. [3]Excluding China P.R.

International trade in livestock/livestock products (1963-5 av.)

Bovine cattle (S.I.T.C. no. 001.1)

Production
1 030 730 300 head 1963-5 av.
842 333 000 1953-5 av.

Percentage exported
0.4% 1963-5 av.
0.2% 1953-5 av.

Exports
4 016 800 head 1963-5 av.
1 845 700 1953-5 av.

	PERCENTAGE 1963-5 av.	1953-5 av.
Irish R.	17	*25*
Mexico	12	*4*
Canada	9	*3*
Denmark	7	*19*
Others	55	*49*
	100	*100*

Imports
3 948 700 head 1963-5 av.
1 801 000 1953-5 av.

	PERCENTAGE 1963-5 av.	1953-5 av.
U.S.A.	21	*11*
Italy	17	*5*
U.K.	16	*31*
Germany F.R.	10	*14*
Others	36	*39*
	100	*100*

Milk and cream[1] (S.I.T.C. no. 022)

Production[2]
331 603 000 met. tons 1963-5 av.
226 033 000 1953-5 av.

Percentage exported
3% 1963-5 av.
2% 1953-5 av.

Exports[3]
11 320 000 met. tons 1963-5 av.
4 288 000 1953-5 av.

	PERCENTAGE 1963-5 av.	1953-5 av.
U.S.A.	46	*41*
Netherlands	14	*23*
France	8	*1*
New Zealand	7	*11*
Others	25	*24*
	100	*100*

Imports[3]
9 969 000 met. tons 1963-5 av.
3 471 000 1953-5 av.

	PERCENTAGE 1963-5 av.	1953-5 av.
Netherlands	10	*1*
U.K.	9	*17*
Japan	7	*3*
Venezuela	4	*5**
Others	70	*74*
	100	*100*

Butter (S.I.T.C. no. 023)

Production
4 813 300 met. tons 1963-5 av.
3 418 000 1953-5 av.

Percentage exported
14% 1963-5 av.
14% 1953-5 av.

Exports
660 100 met. tons 1963-5 av.
484 000 1953-5 av.

	PERCENTAGE 1963-5 av.	1953-5 av.
New Zealand	27	*31*
Denmark	16	*28*
Australia	14	*12*
U.S.S.R.	7	*—*
Others	36	*29*
	100	*100*

Imports
687 400 met. tons 1963-5 av.
442 700 1953-5 av.

	PERCENTAGE 1963-5 av.	1953-5 av.
U.K.	65	*67*
Germany D.R.	5	*3**
Italy	5	*2*
Germany F.R.	3	*4*
Others	22	*24*
	100	*100*

Cheese and curd (S.I.T.C. no. 024)

Production
5 217 700 met. tons 1963-5 av.
2 812 000 1953-5 av.

Percentage exported
11% 1963-5 av.
14% 1953-5 av.

Exports
576 100 met. tons 1963-5 av.
392 000 1953-5 av.

	PERCENTAGE 1963-5 av.	1953-5 av.
Netherlands	20	*23*
New Zealand	16	*24*
Denmark	14	*15*
France	10	*5*
Others	40	*33*
	100	*100*

Imports
572 800 met. tons 1963-5 av.
374 300 1953-5 av.

	PERCENTAGE 1963-5 av.	1953-5 av.
U.K.	26	*37*
Germany F.R.	22	*16*
Italy	11	*6*
Belg./Lux.	6	*9*
Others	35	*32*
	100	*100*

Eggs[4] (S.I.T.C. no. 025.01)

Production[5]
14 629 900 met. tons 1963-5 av.
10 120 000 1953-5 av.[6]

Percentage exported
3% 1963-5 av.
4% 1953-5 av.

Exports
370 000 met. tons 1963-5 av.
393 700 1953-5 av.

	PERCENTAGE 1963-5 av.	1953-5 av.
Netherlands	29	*29*
Poland	11	*5*
China P.R.	10	*7**
Belg./Lux.	9	*1*
Denmark	8	*26*
Others	33	*32*
	100	*100*

Imports
345 700 met. tons 1963-5 av.
367 300 1953-5 av.

	PERCENTAGE 1963-5 av.	1953-5 av.
Germany F.R.	40	*39*
Italy	11	*6*
Hong Kong	11	*6*
U.S.S.R.	7	*1*
Switzerland	7	*4*
Others	24	*44*
	100	*100*

Meat of swine (S.I.T.C. no. 011.3/012.1)

Production
30 669 000 met. tons 1963-5 av.
17 723 000 1953-5 av.

Percentage exported *(pork)*
1% 1963-5 av.
1% 1953-5 av.

Exports

Pork[7]
354 200 met. tons 1963-5 av.
141 000 1953-5 av.

	PERCENTAGE 1963-5 av.	1953-5 av.
Denmark	21	*24*
Netherlands	21	*9*
Yugoslavia	11	*4*
U.S.A.	10	*2*
Canada	5	*13*
Others	32	*48*
	100	*100*

Bacon[8]
435 300 met. tons 1963-5 av.
369 700 1953-5 av.

	PERCENTAGE 1963-5 av.	1953-5 av.
Denmark	69	*61*
Poland	12	*15**
Irish R.	6	*2*
U.S.A.	3	*7*
Netherlands	2	*10*
Others	8	*5*
	100	*100*

Imports

Pork[7]
377 000 met. tons 1963-5 av.
130 300 1953-5 av.

	PERCENTAGE 1963-5 av.	1953-5 av.
France	22	*12*
Germany F.R.	8	*13*
Italy	8	*2*
Poland	7	*—*
Canada	6	*—*
Others	49	*73*
	100	*100*

Bacon[8]
434 600 met. tons 1963-5 av.
348 300 1953-5 av.

	PERCENTAGE 1963-5 av.	1953-5 av.
U.K.	91	*89*
U.S.A.	1	*2*
Canada	1	*—*
Hong Kong	1	*—*
Others	6	*9*
	100	*100*

Meat of bovine animals[7] (S.I.T.C. no. 011.1)

Production
32 641 000 met. tons 1963-5 av.
22 160 000 1953-5 av.

Percentage exported
5% 1963-5 av.
3% 1953-5 av.

Exports
1 506 300 met. tons 1963-5 av.
564 300 1953-5 av.

	PERCENTAGE 1963-5 av.	1953-5 av.
Argentina	29	*24*
Australia	19	*25*
New Zealand	8	*12*
Uruguay	6	*5*
Others	38	*34*
	100	*100*

Imports
1 452 100 met. tons 1963-5 av.
516 700 1953-5 av.

	PERCENTAGE 1963-5 av.	1953-5 av.
U.S.A.	24	*2*
U.K.	23	*61*
Italy	18	*7*
Germany F.R.	8	*2*
Others	27	*28*
	100	*100*

Meat of sheep and goats[7] (S.I.T.C. no. 011.2)

Production
5 942 000 met. tons 1963-5 av.
4 140 000 1953-5 av.

Percentage exported
9% 1963-5 av.
10% 1953-5 av.

Exports
525 400 met. tons 1963-5 av.
406 700 1953-5 av.

	PERCENTAGE 1963-5 av.	1953-5 av.
New Zealand	69	*66*
Australia	17	*15*
Argentina	5	*15*
Irish R.	3	*1*
Others	6	*3*
	100	*100*

Imports
519 000 met. tons 1963-5 av.
386 700 1953-5 av.

	PERCENTAGE 1963-5 av.	1953-5 av.
U.K.	67	*90*
Japan	11	*—*
U.S.A.	5	*—*
Greece	4	*—*
Others	13	*10*
	100	*100*

Meat (S.I.T.C. no. 011, 012, 013)

Net exports

	'000 METRIC TONS 1963-5 av.	1953-4 av.
South America	659	*417*
Africa	9	*...*
Oceania	919	*706*
Total	1 587	*1 123*

Net imports

	'000 METRIC TONS 1963-5 av.	1953-4 av.
Europe	1 223	*767*
U.S.S.R.	298	*71*
North America[9]	142	*76*
Asia	81	*41*
Africa	...	*15*
Total	1 744	*970*

Types traded

Fresh, chilled and frozen
3 367 000 met. tons 1963-5 av.
1 260 000 1953-4 av.

	PERCENTAGE 1963-5 av.	1953-4 av.
Beef	45	*41*
Mutton/lamb	16	*33*
Pork	10	*10*
Poultry and others	29	*16*
	100	*100*

Prepared and canned
1 063 000 met. tons 1963-5 av.
1 092 000 1953-4 av.

	PERCENTAGE 1963-5 av.	1953-4 av.
Bacon[8]	41	*43*
Canned meat and preparations	56	*52*
Others	3	*5*
	100	*100*

*Estimate [1]Incl. condensed evaporated and dried milk [2]From cows [3]Milk equivalent [4]In the shell [5]From hens [6]Excl. U.S.S.R. [7]Fresh, chilled and frozen [8]Incl. ham and other dried, salted and smoked pigmeat [9]Incl. Central America

Cattle

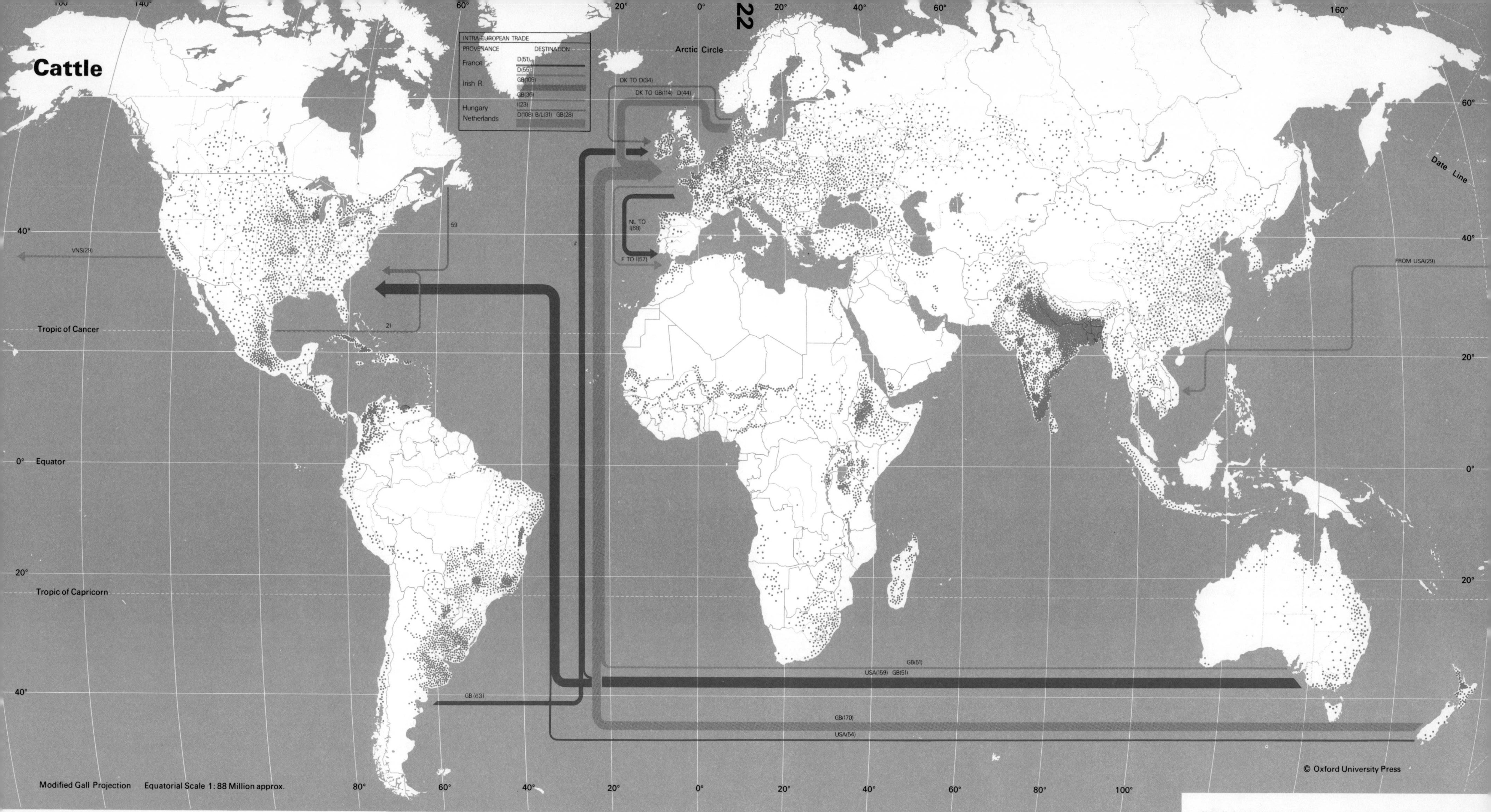
Cattle
INTRA-EUROPEAN TRADE
PROVENANCE
DESTINATION
France
D(51)
D(55)
Irish R.
GB(108)
GB(36)
Hungary
I(23)
Netherlands
D(108) B/L(31) GB(28)
Arctic Circle
DK TO D(34)
DK TO GB(114) D(44)
NL TO I(68)
F TO I(57)
VNS(29)
59
21
FROM USA(29)
Date Line
Tropic of Cancer
Equator
Tropic of Capricorn
GB(51)
USA(159) GB(51)
GB (63)
GB(170)
USA(54)
Modified Gall Projection
Equatorial Scale 1: 88 Million approx.

Cattle (1963-5av.)

Distribution One dot represents 100 000 head

Major trade flows (1966)

Commodity: S.I.T.C no.

- BOVINE CATTLE (INCL. BUFFALOES) : 001.1
- MEAT OF BOVINE CATTLE (FRESH/FROZEN) : 011.1
- DAIRY PRODUCTS/EGGS : 02

Value ($ U.S.)
0.5mm represents increments of $40 million
($ MILLIONS) 360 200 40
63 VALUE IN $ MILLIONS

Cattle population

1 030 730 300 head 1963-5 av.
842 333 000 1953-5 av.

	PERCENTAGE 1963-5 av.	1953-5 av.
India	18	*NA*
U.S.A.	10	*11*
U.S.S.R.	8	*7*
Brazil	8	*7*
China P.R.	6	*5*
Argentina	4	*5*
Pakistan	3	*4*
Mexico	3	*2*
Ethiopia	2	*NA*
Others	38	*NA*
	100	*100*

Milk production (from cows)

331 603 000 met. tons 1963-5 av.
226 033 000 1953-5 av.

	PERCENTAGE 1963-5 av.	1953-5 av.
U.S.S.R.	19	*NA*
U.S.A.	17	*24*
Germany F.R.	6	*7*
Poland	4	*4*
U.K.	4	*5*
India	3	*NA*
Italy	3	*3*
Canada	3	*3*
Netherlands	2	*3*
Others	39	*NA*
	100	*100*

Milk yield per milk cow

Selected countries
(kg. per annum)

	1963-5 av.
Netherlands	4 156
Japan	3 971
Denmark	3 783
U.K.	3 711
Germany F.R.	3 571
U.S.A.	3 558
S. Korea	3 033
France	2 795
Chile	1 667
U.S.S.R.	1 606
Peru	680
Pakistan	421
Uganda	284

Cheese production

5 217 700 met. tons 1963-5 av.
2 812 000 1953-5 av.

	PERCENTAGE 1963-5 av.	1953-5 av.
U.S.A.	20	*29*
France	10	*11*
U.S.S.R.	9	*NA*
Italy	7	*11*
Germany F.R.	7	*9*
U.A.R.	5	*NA*
Netherlands	4	*6*
Poland	3	*–*
Argentina	3	*4*
Others	32	*NA*
	100	*100*

Butter production

4 813 300 met. tons 1963-5 av.
3 418 000 1953-5 av.

	PERCENTAGE 1963-5 av.	1953-5 av.
U.S.S.R.	21	*12*
U.S.A.	13	*21*
Germany F.R.	10	*10*
France	9	*9*
New Zealand	5	*6*
Australia	4	*5*
Germany D.R.	4	*4*
Poland	3	*2*
Canada	3	*4*
Others	28	*27*
	100	*100*

Beef & veal production[1]

32 532 000 met. tons 1963-5 av.
22 847 000 1953-5 av.[2]

	PERCENTAGE 1963-5 av.	1953-5 av.
U.S.A.	26	*29*
U.S.S.R.	10	*...[2]*
Argentina	7	*8*
China P.R.	6	*NA*
France	5	*NA*
Brazil	4	*5*
Germany F.R.	3	*3*
Australia	3	*3*
Others	36	*NA*
	100	*100*

[1]From indigenous animals only
[2]Excl. U.S.S.R.

Hides & skins (cattle & buffalo)

Major producers
('000 metric tons)

	1963-5 av.	1953-5 av.
Brazil	183	*47*
Germany F.R.	106	*84*
U.K.	89	*70*
Mexico	59	*NA*
Poland	40	*NA*
Uruguay	36	*NA*
Yugoslavia	26	*NA*
Netherlands	26	*16*
New Zealand	22	*NA*
Belgium	21	*19*
Japan	19	*10*

Two distinct types of cattle exist—European cattle, found mainly in temperate zones; and Zebu, or humped cattle, in the tropics. The former thrive best in areas where mean monthly temperatures are below 64°F (18°C), while the latter thrive best at temperatures above 70°F (21°C). Cattle are kept primarily for milk, meat or work, or for any combination of these purposes. Work cattle are found mainly in the tropics, Southern Europe and Asia, while in the U.S.A., Argentina, Uruguay and Australia there are large numbers of pure beef cattle. Specialized dairy farming tends to occur near densely populated areas with a high standard of living, and is most important in NE. U.S.A. and NW. Europe. In the U.S.A., and to some extent the U.K., specialized dairy breeds are important. In most of Europe dual-purpose milk-beef types predominate. In general the size of the cattle in any area depends on environmental and nutritional conditions. In areas of high rainfall where soils are leached of calcium and phosphorus, the native breeds of cattle are usually small, whereas in arid areas they are large. From prehistoric times man in his migrations has tended to bring his own native breeds with him, and the present distribution of the different breeds throughout the world reflects this general pattern, although there are exceptions.

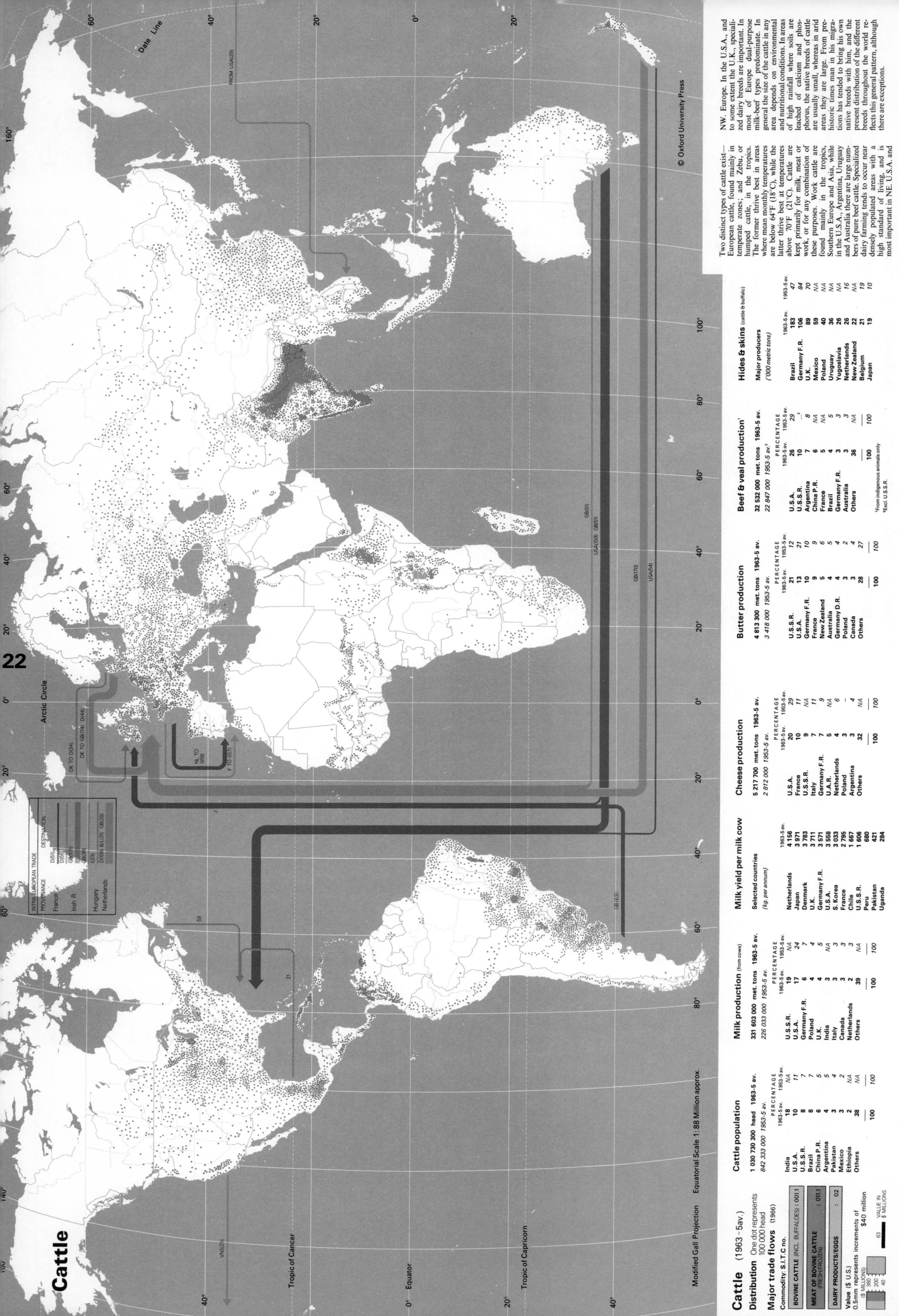

Sheep/Pigs

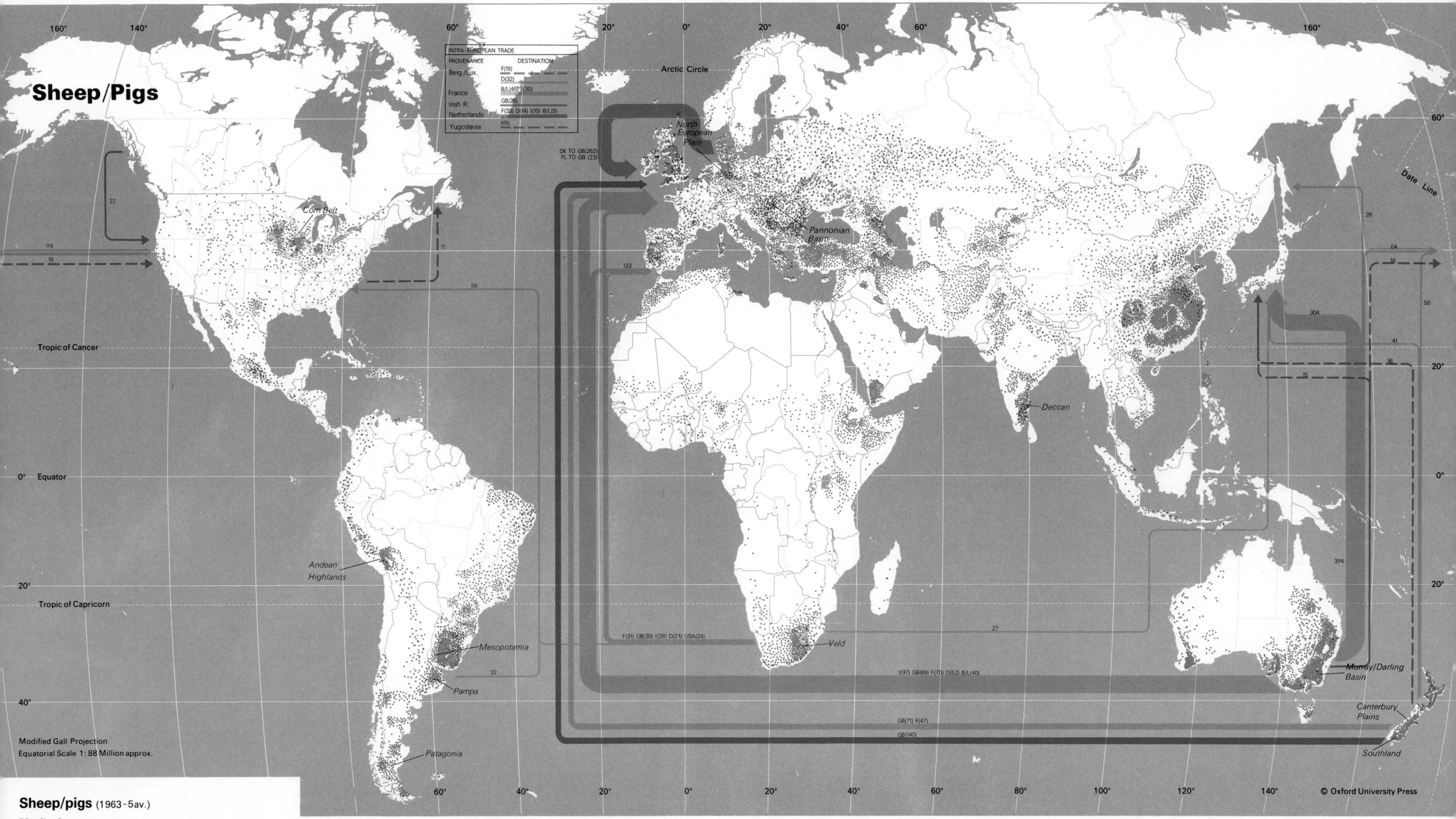

Sheep/pigs (1963-5av.)

Distribution One dot represents 100 000 head
· sheep · pigs

Major trade flows (1966)

Commodity: S.I.T.C. no.

- WOOL/ANIMAL HAIR :262
- MEAT-SHEEP/GOATS (FRESH/FROZEN) :011.2
- MEAT-SWINE { FRESH/FROZEN :001.3; DRIED/SALTED :012.1

Value ($ U.S.)
0.5mm represents increments of $40 million
520, 360, 200, 40 ($ MILLIONS)
UNDER $20 MILLION
64 VALUE IN $ MILLIONS

Trade in meat of sheep/goats is, by value, three times that of live sheep/goats. There are no particularly predominant flows of the latter and trade is mainly among the countries of the Middle East and Eastern Europe. The main flows (which account for 11% of total trade) in live sheep/goats are from Iran to Kuwait and from Bulgaria to Greece .
Trade in meat of pigs is, by value, four times that of live pigs. The main flows (which account for 40% of total trade) in live pigs are from China P.R. to Hong Kong and from Denmark to Germany F.R.

Sheep population

1 030 418 700 head 1963-5 av.
871 000 000 1953-5 av.

	PERCENTAGE 1963-5 av.	1953-5 av.
Australia	**16**	*15*
U.S.S.R.	**13**	*13*
China P.R.	**6**	*5*
New Zealand	**5**	*4*
Argentina	**4**	*6*
India	**4**	*NA*
South Africa	**4**	*4*
Turkey	**3**	*3*
Iran	**3**	*2*
Others	**42**	*NA*
	100	*100*

Pig population

569 366 000 head 1963-5 av.
370 133 000 1953-5 av.

	PERCENTAGE 1963-5 av.	1953-5 av.
China P.R.	**35**	*26*
U.S.A.	**10**	*13*
Brazil	**10**	*9*
U.S.S.R.	**10**	*11*
Germany F.R.	**3**	*4*
Mexico	**2**	*2*
Poland	**2**	*3*
France	**2**	*2*
Germany D.R.	**2**	*4*
Others	**24**	*26*
	100	*100*

Goat population

368 613 000 head 1963-5 av.
327 000 000 1953-5 av.

	PERCENTAGE 1963-5 av.	1953-5 av.
India	**18**	*NA*
China P.R.	**15**	*12*
Turkey	**6**	*6*
Nigeria	**6**	*NA*
Ethiopia	**5**	*NA*
Brazil	**4**	*3*
Iran	**4**	*NA*
Mexico	**3**	*2*
Pakistan	**3**	*1*
Others	**36**	*NA*
	100	*100*

Sheep are raised primarily either for meat or for wool, though in many countries dual-purpose animals are common. In Southern Europe another minor product is cheese made from ewe-milk.
There are three main types of wool. Fine Merino comes from areas of low rainfall. Medium crossbred is produced where the rainfall is higher and the pasturage better and here the dual-purpose animal is often kept. Coarse carpet wool is associated with 'hill' sheep.
Australia is the chief producer of Merino wool, though important quantities come also from South Africa and to some extent from Argentina. Considerable amounts of lamb are produced in New Zealand and the U.S.A.
Of minor economic importance in some parts of Africa and the Middle East are the fat-tailed and fat-rumped sheep.

The distribution of pigs is based mainly on food supply and not climate; they are often kept in buildings, and so protected from the rigours of northern winters. The pig converts perishable by-products into human food—in Denmark and New Zealand from the butter and cheese-making industries, in Germany and Poland from small potatoes, in Canada and Australia from shrivelled grain unsuitable for milling. The maize growing areas of the 'corn belt' of America and SE. Europe also support large numbers and tend to produce a lard type. The pig (especially the Chinese and Bantu type) is also a scavenger, and converts into food substances otherwise unfit for human consumption. The main products are pork, bacon and lard.

Wool production (clean basis)

1 507 000 met. tons 1963-5 av.
1 060 000 1953-5 av.[1]

	PERCENTAGE 1963-5 av.	1953-5 av.
Australia	**30**	*31*
U.S.S.R.	**14**	*...*[1]
New Zealand	**14**	*13*
Argentina	**7**	*10*
South Africa	**4**	*6*
U.S.A.	**4**	*6*
Uruguay	**3**	*5*
China P.R.	**3**	*3*
U.K.	**3**	*3*
Others	**18**	*23*
	100	*100*

[1]Excl. U.S.S.R.

Meat production[1] (1965)

Mutton/lamb
5 923 000 met. tons

	PERCENTAGE
U.S.S.R.	**14**
Australia	**10**
China P.R.	**9**
New Zealand	**8**
India	**6**
U.S.A.	**5**
U.K.	**4**
Iran	**3**
Ethiopia	**3**
Argentina	**2**
Others	**36**
	100

Pork
31 453 000 met. tons

	PERCENTAGE
China P.R.	**30**
U.S.A.	**16**
U.S.S.R.	**10**
Germany F.R.	**6**
Poland	**4**
France	**4**
U.K.	**3**
Denmark	**2**
Germany D.R.	**2**
Brazil	**2**
Others	**21**
	100

[1]From indigenous animals only

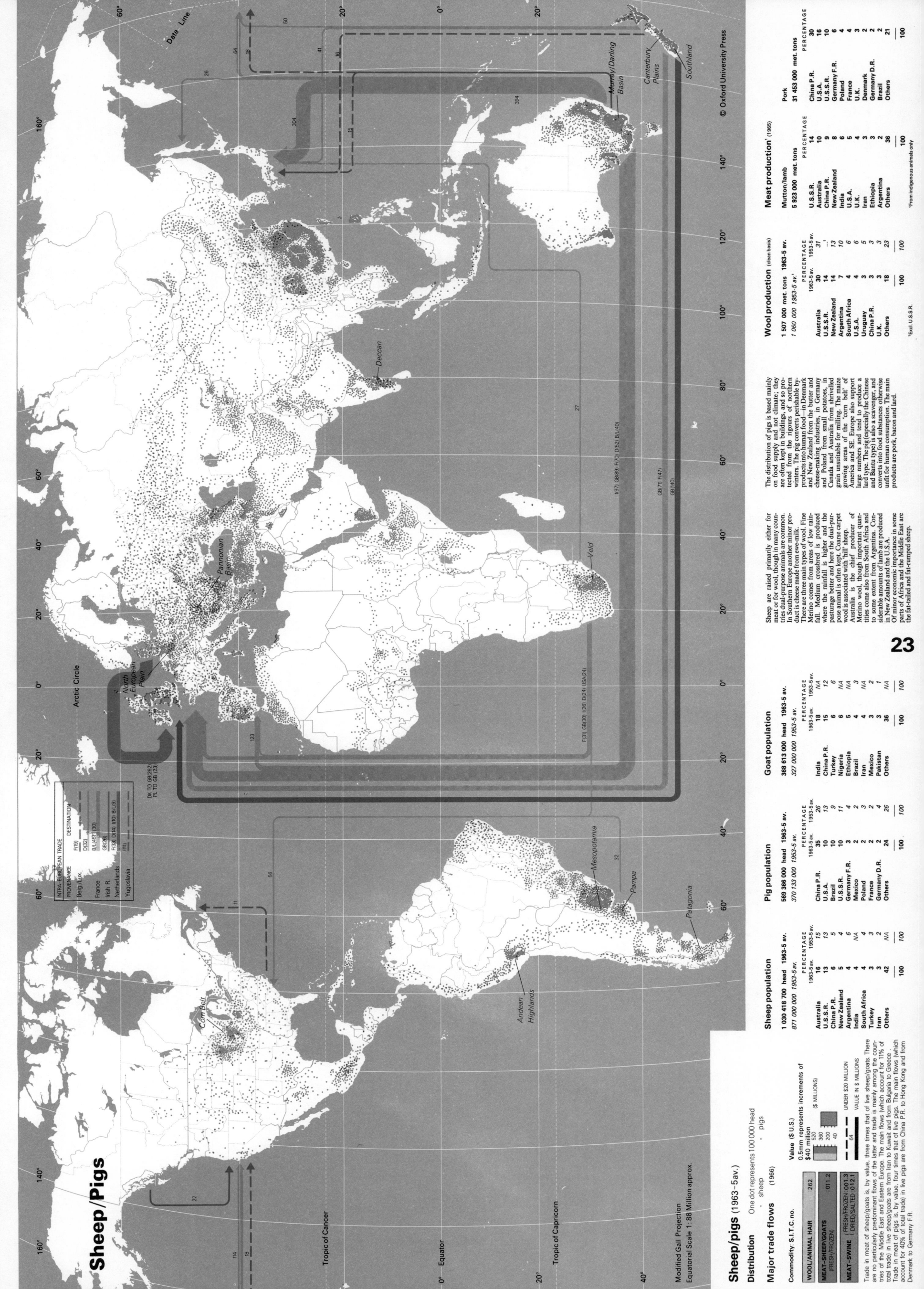

Forest Products

Forests p. 25 Paper p. 25

For individual country data see Statistical Supplement

Forests cover about 4 100 million hectares, 30% of the world's land surface. Their extent is just greater than the total agricultural area. Broadleaved forests are the more widespread, yet coniferous forests are of far greater industrial use and much more heavily cut. In 1963-5, 55% of total fellings were absorbed by industry; the rest was used as firewood. Sawlogs and veneer logs are the chief industrial uses taking 40% of total fellings in 1963-5. The largest single user is the pulp and paper industry, based on the coniferous forest belt of the northern hemisphere.

Conifers predominate in cool temperate climates; the northern limits are independent of the severity of the winter but require mean July temperatures of over 50°F (10°C). Where similar conditions prevail in mountainous regions conifers are dominant even in the tropics, but although in a more favourable environment conifers give way to hardwoods, they are not completely eliminated except in the wet tropics. The coniferous forest is tolerant of low rainfall but typically experiences a heavy snowfall.

Temperate hardwoods are the principal trees where the mean annual temperature lies between 40°-65°F (4.5°-18.5°C), frosts together with varying amounts of snow occur during the winter, and the annual rainfall exceeds 20 in. (500 mm.). A few hardwoods, such as birch, extend northwards or upwards almost as far as the conifers.

Tropical hardwoods are limited to regions which are frost-free and receive annually more than 20 in. (500 mm.) of rain. A reasonably distributed annual rainfall of at least 80 in. (2 000 mm.) is necessary for full development, but good timber may be produced with only 30 in. (750 mm.) falling during four months. If the precipitation is between 20-30 in. (500-750 mm.), the resulting small trees are only useful for special purposes. The mean annual temperature is normally over 75°F (24°C) and the coldest month not below 60°F (15.5°C).

Paper (and paperboard) is made from cellulose fibre usually obtained from wood. The main types of wood used are pine, spruce, poplar and aspen, but the use of harder woods such as beech and chestnut is extending. It is sometimes made from other fibres such as those derived from waste paper, cotton, linen, jute, hemp, straw, bagasse, esparto grass and papyrus (from which paper gets its name).

There are two main methods of treating woodpulp. It can either be ground into pulp by mechanical milling under a flow of water, or reduced to small pieces and treated with chemicals which remove most of the lignin and other non-cellulose material. Pulp made in this way is stronger and superior in quality to that made by the mechanical method. Pulp derived from other fibrous materials is always made by the second (chemical) method. The pulp is drawn on to a continuous belt. As the fibres dry they adhere together to form the paper, which is finally wound on to reels.

Cheap types of printing paper, like newsprint, are made from a mechanical or part mechanical pulp. Other printing and writing papers are usually made from chemical woodpulp, though a pulp with a high cotton rag or esparto grass content is used for fine grade book papers where special characteristics are required. For strong wrapping papers and packaging boards pure woodpulp (mechanical or chemical) is used, but for the cheaper types waste paper pulp is most frequently used.

Woodpulp can be treated to make the resultant paper and board waterproof, fire proof and resistant to acids. It can be beaten out to make the paper totally transparent. Once it is made, the paper can be coated with various substances. The coating most frequently used is china clay which gives the paper an extra smooth surface suitable for printing.

In this way paper and board can be made to suit many different applications from household and facial tissues to filter paper and insulating board; from book papers to building boards. This means that paper and board can successfully replace other materials such as wood, cloth, glass and metals. The rate of paper consumption per capita is regarded as a reliable indicator of national standards of living, with more affluent nations using more paper.

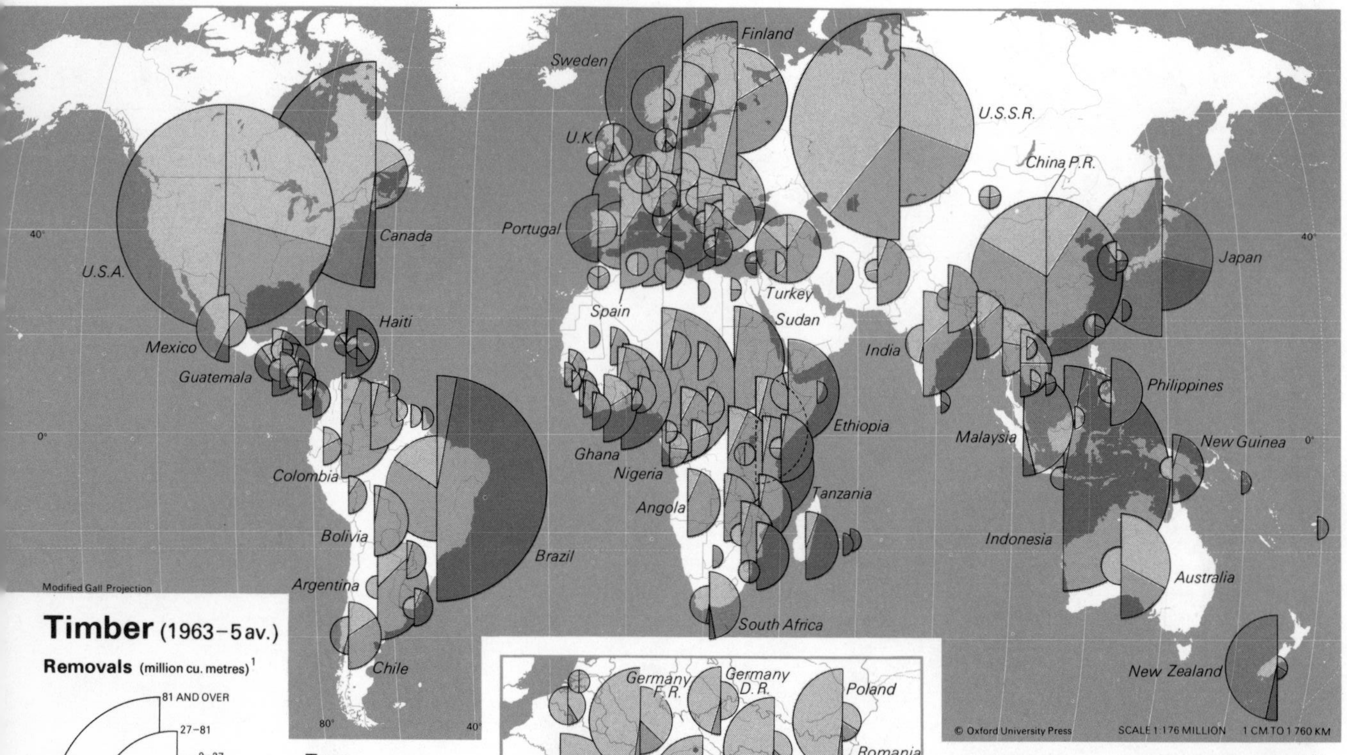

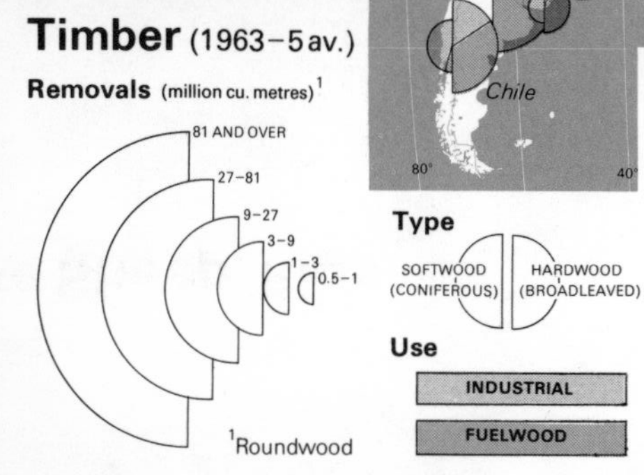

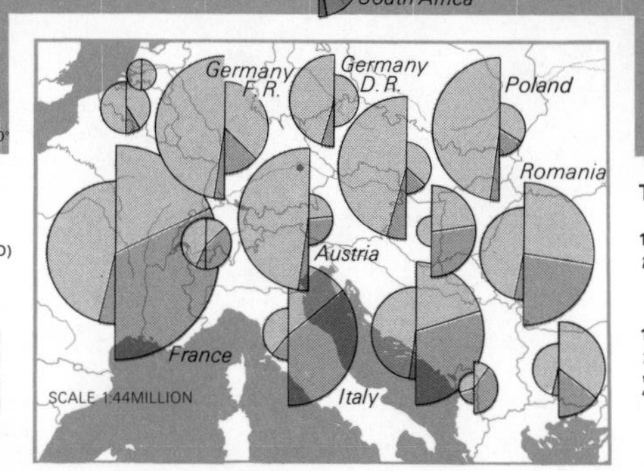

Total removals

	PERCENTAGE					MILLION CU. METRES
	U.S.S.R.	U.S.A.	BRAZIL	CHINA P.R.	OTHERS	WORLD[2]
1963-5 av.	19	16	7	7	51	1 934
1953-5 av.	*23*	*23*	*8*	*...[1]*	*46*	*1 312[1]*

	NORTH AMERICA[3]	ASIA	EUROPE[4]	AFRICA	SOUTH AMERICA	PACIFIC
1963-5 av.	23	18	17	11	11	1
1953-5 av.	*31*	*8*	*18*	*7*	*11*	*2*

[1] Excl. China P.R. [2] Roundwood volume [3] Incl. Central America
[4] Excl. U.S.S.R. which is given in table above

International trade in forest products (1963-5 av.)

Softwood[1] (S.I.T.C. no. 242.2/243.2)

Production[2]
955 087 700 cu. metres 1963-5 av.
734 953 000 1953-5 av.[3]

Percentage exported
9% 1963-5 av.
6% 1953-5 av.

Exports[4]
82 401 000 cu. metres 1963-5 av.
47 281 000 1953-5 av.[3]

	PERCENTAGE 1963-5 av.	1953-5 av.
Canada	31	*34*
U.S.S.R.	19	*5*
Sweden	11	*16*
U.S.A.	9	*6*
Finland	9	*12*
Austria	6	*11*
Romania	3	*2*
Brazil	2	*3*
Czechoslovakia	2	*1*
Poland	2	*1*
Others	6	*9*
	100	*100*

Imports[4]
80 781 000 cu. metres 1963-5 av.
47 256 000 1953-5 av.[3]

	PERCENTAGE 1963-5 av.	1953-5 av.
U.S.A.	24	*25*
U.K.	18	*25*
Germany F.R.	9	*9*
Japan	8	*1*
Italy	7	*6*
Netherlands	5	*6*
France	3	*2*
Germany D.R.	3	*—*
Canada	2	*2*
Denmark	2	*2*
Others	19	*22*
	100	*100*

Hardwood[1] (S.I.T.C. no. 242.3/243.3)

Production[2]
978 419 300 cu. metres 1963-5 av.
576 570 000 1953-5 av.[3]

Percentage exported
3% 1963-5 av.
2% 1953-5 av.

Exports[4]
27 733 000 cu. metres 1963-5 av.
10 990 000 1953-5 av.[3]

	PERCENTAGE 1963-5 av.	1953-5 av.
Philippines	24	*22*
Sabah	12	*4*
Ivory Coast	7	*NA*
Malaya	5	*3*
Sarawak	5	*4*
Gabon	4	*NA*
France	4	*9*
Romania	4	*1*
Ghana	4	*6*
Nigeria	3	*4*
Others	28	*NA*
	100	*100*

Imports[4]
27 065 000 cu. metres 1963-5 av.
9 998 000 1953-5 av.[3]

	PERCENTAGE 1963-5 av.	1953-5 av.
Japan	32	*16*
Germany F.R.	8	*8*
U.K.	7	*17*
Italy	7	*4*
France	5	*3*
U.S.A.	5	*14*
Singapore	3	*NA*
Netherlands	2	*4*
Canada	2	*3*
Belg./Lux.	2	*3*
Others	27	*NA*
	100	*100*

Wood pulp[5,6] (S.I.T.C. no. 251.2, 6, 7, 8, 9)

Production
74 381 700 met. tons 1963-5 av.
42 473 300 1953-5 av.

Percentage exported
16% 1963-5 av.
16% 1953-5 av.

Exports
12 132 000 met. tons 1963-5 av.
6 767 000 1953-5 av.

	PERCENTAGE 1963-5 av.	1953-5 av.
Sweden	28	*33*
Canada	27	*29*
Finland	17	*17*
U.S.A.	11	*6*
Norway	7	*10*
U.S.S.R.	2	*1*
Austria	1	*2*
South Africa	1	*NA*
Others	6	*NA*
	100	*100*

Imports
12 023 300 met. tons 1963-5 av.
6 649 000 1953-5 av.

	PERCENTAGE 1963-5 av.	1953-5 av.
U.K.	24	*29*
U.S.A.	22	*29*
Germany F.R.	9	*7*
France	8	*7*
Italy	7	*4*
Japan	4	*2*
Netherlands	4	*3*
Austria	2	*—*
Others	20	*19*
	100	*100*

Paper[7] (S.I.T.C. no. 641 [excl. 641.1/641.6])

Production
75 362 000 met. tons 1963-5 av.
40 700 000 1953-5 av.

Percentage exported
9% 1963-5 av.
7% 1953-5 av.

Exports
6 716 000 met. tons 1963-5 av.[3]
2 667 000 1953-5 av.[3]

	PERCENTAGE 1963-5 av.	1953-5 av.
Finland	22	*17*
Sweden	21	*22*
U.S.A.	18	*14*
Netherlands	6	*11*
Norway	6	*8*
Canada	5	*4*
Austria	4	*6*
Japan	3	*2*
Others	15	*16*
	100	*100*

Imports
6 446 700 met. tons 1963-5 av.[3]
2 546 700 1953-5 av.[3]

	PERCENTAGE 1963-5 av.	1953-5 av.
Germany F.R.	19	*9*
U.K.	16	*22*
France	6	*2*
Belg./Lux.	6	*4*
Netherlands	6	*5*
Italy	4	*2*
Denmark	3	*3*
U.S.A.	3	*7*
Others	37	*46*
	100	*100*

Newsprint (S.I.T.C. no. 641.1)

Production
16 086 000 met. tons 1963-5 av.
10 600 000 1953-5 av.

Percentage exported
52% 1963-5 av.
59% 1953-5 av.

Exports
8 442 700 met. tons 1963-5 av.
6 227 000 1953-5 av.

	PERCENTAGE 1963-5 av.	1953-5 av.
Canada	72	*81*
Finland	12	*7*
Sweden	5	*3*
Norway	3	*2*
U.S.S.R.	1	*—*
New Zealand	1	*—*
U.S.A.	1	*2*
Austria	1	*1*
Chile	1	*—*
Others	3	*4*
	100	*100*

Imports
8 412 300 met. tons 1963-5 av.
6 163 000 1953-5 av.

	PERCENTAGE 1963-5 av.	1953-5 av.
U.S.A.	64	*74*
U.K.	8	*5*
Germany F.R.	6	*2*
Australia	3	*3*
Argentina	2	*1*
Denmark	1	*1*
India	1	*1*
France	1	*1*
Brazil	1	*2*
Others	13	*10*
	100	*100*

Use of softwood and hardwood (1963-5 av.)

	SOFTWOOD	HARDWOOD
Production	955 087 700 cu. metres	978 419 300 cu. metres
	PERCENTAGE	
Sawlogs, veneer logs, logs for sleepers	53	18
Pulpwood and pitprops	22	6
Other industrial wood	8	4
Fuelwood (incl. wood for charcoal)	17	72
	100	100

Proportion of land area forested

Figures in brackets indicate percentages of regional land areas[8]

	MILLION HECTARES FOREST	ARABLE	MEADOW[9]	OTHER	TOTAL[8]
South America	911 *(51)*	75 *(4)*	309 *(17)*	485 *(28)*	1 780
U.S.S.R.	880 *(39)*	230 *(10)*	370 *(17)*	760 *(34)*	2 240
North America[10]	810 *(33)*	256 *(11)*	364 *(15)*	997 *(41)*	2 427
Africa	727 *(24)*	254 *(8)*	598 *(20)*	1 444 *(48)*	3 023
Asia[3]	449 *(26)*	350 *(20)*	152 *(9)*	790 *(45)*	1 741
Europe[11]	137 *(28)*	152 *(31)*	90 *(18)*	114 *(23)*	493
Oceania	79 *(9)*	35 *(4)*	460 *(54)*	279 *(33)*	853
China P.R.	77 *(8)*	109 *(11)*	178 *(18)*	612 *(63)*	976
World	4 070 *(30)*	1 461 *(11)*	2 521 *(19)*	5 481 *(40)*	13 533

Production of forest products (1963-5 av.)

Softwood removals[1,2]

955 087 700 cu. metres 1963-5 av.
734 953 000 1953-5 av.[3]

	PERCENTAGE 1963-5 av.	1953-5 av.
U.S.S.R.*	32	*32*
U.S.A.	23	*27*
Canada	9	*11*
China P.R.	6*	*...[3]*
Sweden	4	*5*
Japan	4	*4*
Finland	3	*4*
Brazil	2*	*2*
Germany F.R.	2	*2*
Others	15	*13*
	100	*100*

Hardwood removals[1,2]

978 419 300 cu. metres 1963-5 av.
576 570 000 1953-5 av.[3]

	PERCENTAGE 1963-5 av.	1953-5 av.
Brazil	12*	*14*
U.S.A.	9	*16*
Indonesia	9	*1*
China P.R.	7*	*...[3]*
U.S.S.R.*	7	*11*
Nigeria	3	*—*
France	3*	*4*
Japan	3	*4*
Colombia	3	*1*
Others	44	*49*
	100	*100*

Wood pulp production[5,6]

74 381 700 met. tons 1963-5 av.
42 473 300 1953-5 av.[3]

	PERCENTAGE 1953-5 av.	1953-5 av.
U.S.A.	39	*40*
Canada	16	*20*
Sweden	8	*9*
Finland	7	*6*
Japan	7	*4*
U.S.S.R.	5	*4**
Norway	2	*3*
Germany F.R.	2	*3*
France	2	*3*
Others	12	*8*
	100	*100*

Paper production[7]

75 362 000 met. tons 1963-5 av.
40 700 000 1953-5 av.[3]

	PERCENTAGE 1963-5 av.	1953-5 av.
U.S.A.	45	*55*
Japan	8	*4*
Germany F.R.	5	*5*
U.K.	5	*6*
U.S.S.R.*	4	*5*
France	4	*3*
China P.R.	3*	*...[3]*
Canada	3*	*4*
Sweden*	3	*3*
Others	20	*15*
	100	*100*

Newsprint production

16 086 000 met. tons 1963-5 av.
10 600 000 1953-5 av.[3]

	PERCENTAGE 1963-5 av.	1953-5 av.
Canada	41	*51*
U.S.A.	12	*11*
Japan	7	*4*
Finland	7	*5*
U.K.	5	*6*
Sweden	4	*3*
U.S.S.R.	4	*4**
France	3	*4*
China P.R.	2*	*...[3]*
Others	15	*12*
	100	*100*

*Estimate [1]Roundwood volume [2]Industrial and fuel [3]Excl. China P.R. [4]Sawlogs, veneer logs, logs for sleepers and sawnwood only [5]Chemical and mechanical [6]Air dry weight [7]Excl. newsprint [8]Incl. inland water bodies
[9]Permanent meadow [10]Incl. Central America [11]Excl. U.S.S.R.

Paper

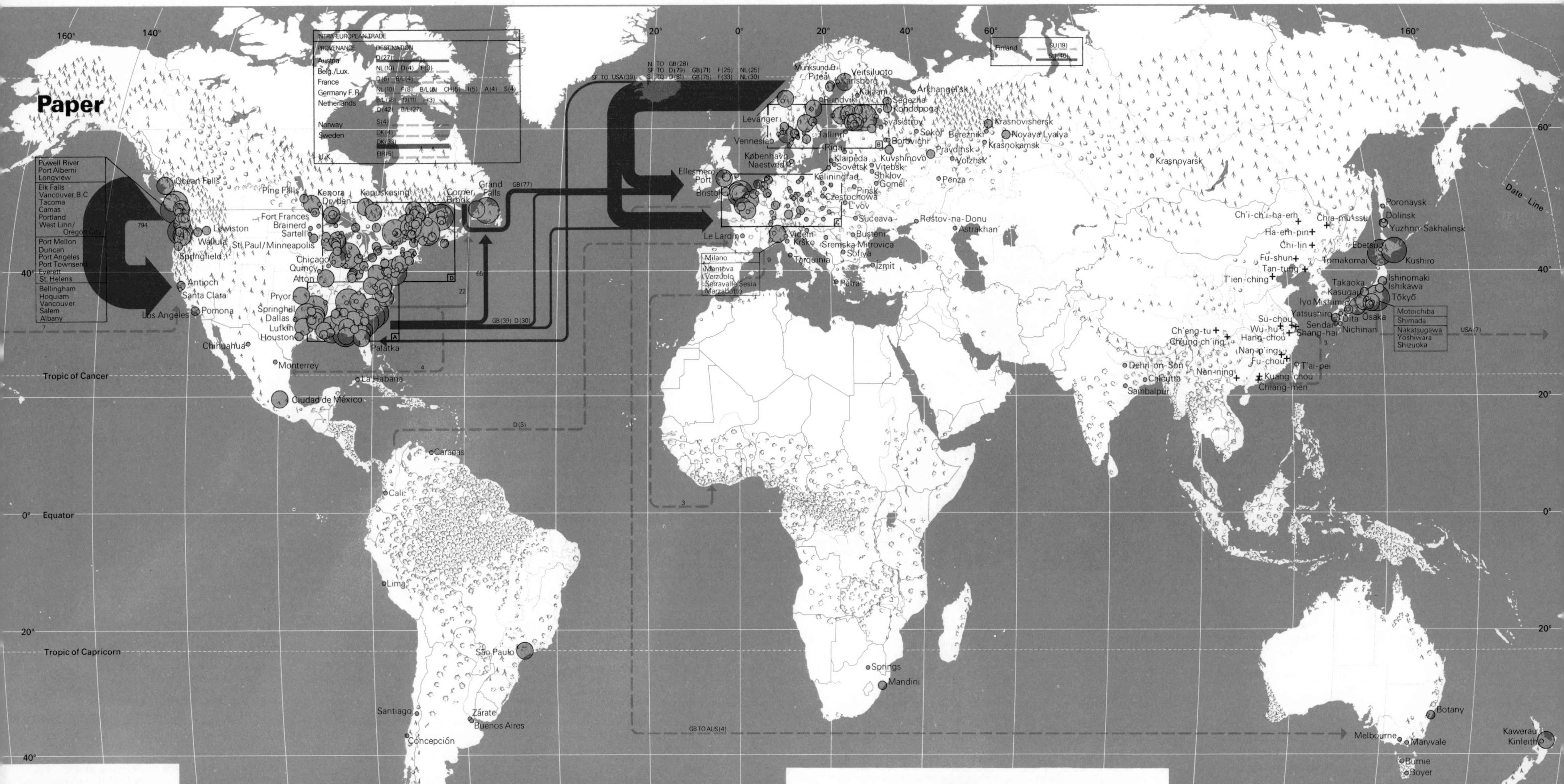

© Oxford University Press

Modified Gall Projection
Equatorial Scale 1 : 88 Million approx.

Paper

Production centres (1965)

Annual output ('000 met. tons)

- 400 & OVER
- 200 – 400
- 100 – 200
- 50 – 100

+ Data not available but reported to be in at least the smallest category

Forests

Predominant types

- BROADLEAVED
- CONIFEROUS
- MIXED

Major trade flows (1966)

Commodity : S.I.T.C.no.

- PAPER/PAPERBOARD 641
- PAPER PRODUCTS 642

Value ($ U.S.)
0.5 mm represents increments of $40 million

680 / 520 / 360 / 200 / 40 ($ MILLIONS)

- UNDER $20 MILLION
- 77 VALUE IN $ MILLIONS

Paper production

91 422 000 met. tons 1963-5 av.
51 247 000 1953-5 av.[1]

	PERCENTAGE	
	1963-5 av.	1953-5 av.
U.S.A.	39	46
Canada	10	13
Japan	8	4
U.K.	5	6
Germany F.R.	4	4
U.S.S.R.	4	4
France	3	3
Finland	3	2
China P.R.	3	..[1]
Others	21	18
	100	100

[1]Excl. China P. R.

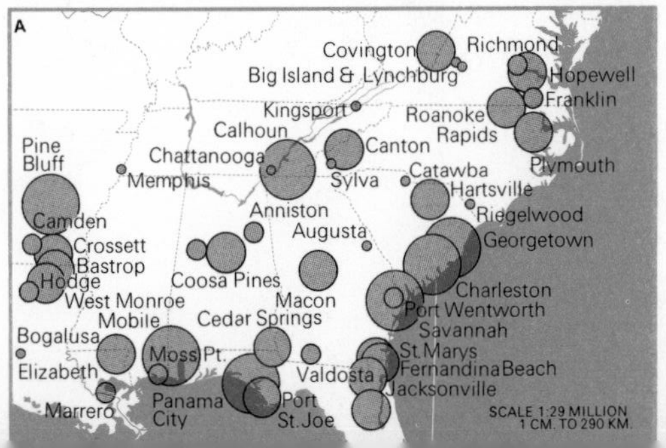

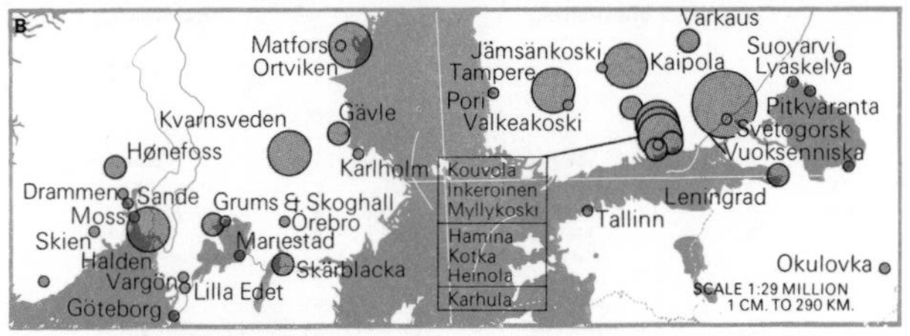

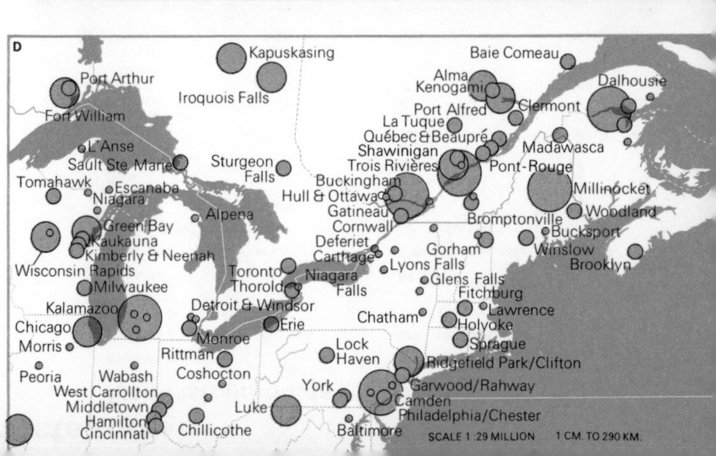

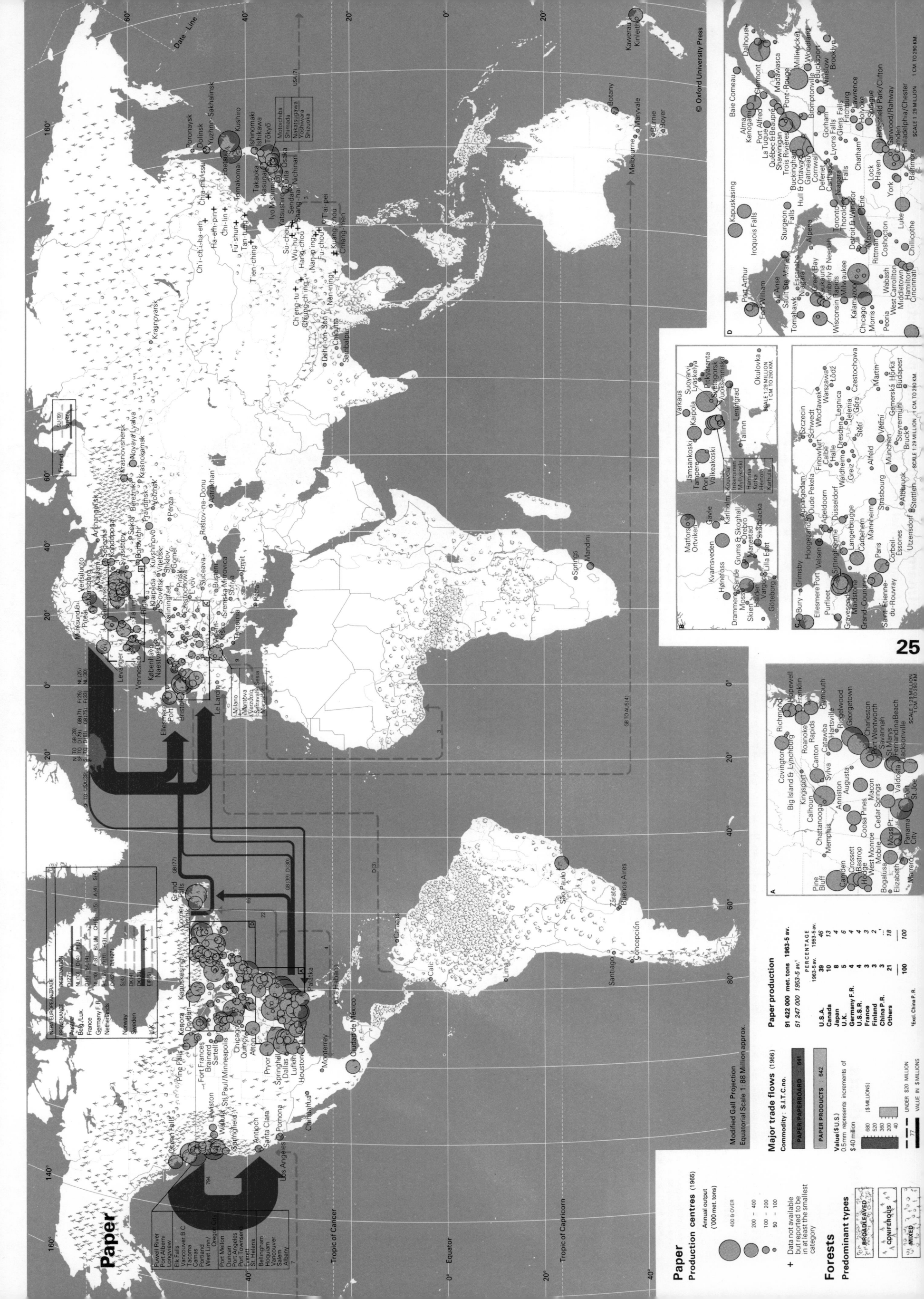

Fish/Fish Products

Fish p.27

For individual country data see Statistical Supplement

In general fish feed on minute organisms in sea water, called plankton, or the small invertebrates (and/or other fish) which themselves feed on plankton. The productivity of the oceans in these organisms varies with climatological, physiological and oceanographical conditions, and the number of fish and other large sea animals is directly dependent on the fertility of the water. On the whole the open ocean of the tropics is less productive than the open ocean of higher latitudes. However there are some regions in the tropics which show a marked fertility, where the upwelling currents, such as the Humboldt current off the coast of Peru, bring the deeper, richer water to the surface and encourage a high rate of production, sometimes even exceeding that of the Antarctic.

The marine fisheries are of two kinds, pelagic and demersal. Pelagic fisheries exploit fish living near the surface (herring) while demersal fisheries exploit fish feeding on the bottom-living invertebrate animals found in the shallow regions of seas (cod) and in coastal waters (shrimps).

Successful commercial fishing requires large shoals of fish of one species, numerous enough to withstand regular exploitation, within economic distances of markets. The areas most heavily fished at present are the commercial fishing grounds shown on the map, although almost all other coastal areas are fished to some extent. The fertile tropical waters are, as yet, only exploited for tuna, which is also caught in coastal waters.

Fish is a rich source of protein, and could become a valuable addition to the diet of many undernourished peoples. With modern technology more distant grounds, such as those of the North Atlantic and Arctic, have been fished, and markets further inland have been penetrated. But demand is still limited by a lack of taste for fish in many countries and by inadequate technical resources in others. Developing countries find it hard to provide trained crews and the large and costly trawlers needed for modern ocean fishing, and the marketing of fresh fish presents special difficulties.

Not only is demand very variable, but there are daily and seasonal variations in supply and fresh fish is extremely perishable. It is therefore necessary to have expensive facilities for the rapid distribution of fresh fish and for preserving what cannot be sold immediately by freezing, salting, smoking, drying or canning. Some fish are also used to make oils, meals, glues and fertilizers. Preserving and processing give the trade some protection from violent fluctuations in the price of fresh fish, and sometimes provide the main market, as with the canning of salmon and sardines and the manufacture of oil and meal from South African pilchards, the American menhaden and the Peruvian anchovy.

The following table shows the relative importance of various species in total world catch.

Catch by species[1]

51 340 000 met.tons 1963-5 av.

27 470 000 1953-5 av.

	PERCENTAGE 1963-5 av.	1953-5 av.
Herring, sardine, anchovy	33	*23*
Freshwater fish[2]/diadromous fish	13	*14*
Cod, hake, haddock	12	*16*
Mullet, jack, sea bass etc.	10	*11*
Molluscs	5	*7*
Tuna, bonito, mackerel etc.	5	*6*
Crustacea/other invertebrates	2	*3*
Flounder, halibut, sole	2	*2*
Salmon, trout, smelt	1	*2*
Shark, ray etc.	1	*1*
Aquatic animals and plants	1	*1*
Unsorted/unidentified	15	*14*
	100	*100*

[1]Excl. whales [2]Excl. salmon, trout, smelt

Freshwater fishing is an important sector of the fishing industry. The most important fish caught in freshwater is the salmon. The Atlantic salmon is found on both sides of the North Atlantic, while the Pacific salmon species, chum, pink and red salmon, are found from northern Japan to Alaska and southwards as far as San Francisco Bay, California. Red and pink salmon are mainly used in the canning industry. The salmon is caught in the rivers to which it returns to spawn after it has spent two or more years in the sea. The Pacific salmon usually dies after spawning. Pollution of rivers has severely affected catches in many countries and rivers have to be restocked periodically. In Canada artificial salmon pools have been constructed.

The main centres of the sturgeon fishing industry are the U.S.S.R. and the U.S.A. where the meat is either canned or fresh-frozen. The sturgeon, fished for both its meat and roe (from which caviar is made) is found from Scandinavia to the Mediterranean and from the St. Lawrence to the Gulf of Mexico. It has been greatly depleted by over-fishing.

Fishing in the North American Great Lakes and in British Columbia exploits the salmon trout. Another economically important fish is the Lake Whitefish of Canada and the U.S.A.

Commercial breeding of carp, a fish originally indigenous to Asia, is widespread in Europe and Asia. It has also been introduced into North America, where an annual catch of some 15 000 tons comes largely from the Mississippi River basin.

Pond and lake breeding of fish is practised in many countries to increase supplies of protein foods. In the U.S.S.R., Israel, China P.R. (where fish culture goes back to 2000 B.C.), Hungary, Italy, the Netherlands, Denmark, Czechoslovakia (where fish culture began in the sixteenth century), India, Malaya and the U.S.A. mainly carp and eel are bred. Fish meal is used as a cheap means of feeding and fattening the fish.

Whales are widely distributed in both hemispheres and generally migrate to tropical waters during the winter and into higher latitudes during the summer. It is during the summer feeding period that they are taken, mainly in the Antarctic. Overfishing is a danger as whales breed slowly compared with fish. To combat this the International Whaling Commission decides the number to be killed in the Antarctic from year to year. Processing of whales today is almost entirely carried out on factory ships, which form part of the whaling fleets.

Catch by species (1965)

Selected countries

('000 met. tons)

	FRESHWATER[1]	SALMON SMELT TROUT	STURGEON	FLOUNDER HALIBUT	COD HAKE HADDOCK	HERRING SARDINE ANCHOVY	TUNA BONITO MACKEREL	MULLET JACK SEA BASS	SHARK RAY	CRUSTACEA	MOLLUSCS	OTHERS	TOTAL
Peru	80.0	—	—	0.2	—	7 256.8	78.5	28.4	7.6	0.6	4.6	5.2	7 461.9
Japan	59.9	184.5	—	216.3	781.0	494.4	1 396.7	1 455.0	66.9	134.2	1 138.1	980.7	6 907.7
U.S.S.R.	807.0	153.2	16.8	158.8	1 380.8	1 347.3	36.5	881.6	3.7	49.3	NA	NA	5 099.9
U.S.A.	90.2	158.4	0.5	106.9	168.6	841.1	159.9	257.8	7.2	283.1	646.9	3.7	2 724.3
Norway	0.5	219.2	—	23.7	648.0	1 089.2	161.0	23.5	32.2	14.4	10.8	84.8	2 307.3
Spain	10.7[2]	1.8	—	14.1	475.0	250.2	88.0	205.1	11.4	17.9	109.3	NA	1 341.5
India	517.6	—	—	9.8	5.5	359.8	97.9	207.3	31.4	79.7	0.3	22.0	1 331.3
Canada	37.6	75.0	0.2	126.7	414.4	385.3	17.5	63.8	0.4	20.8	89.4	31.2	1 262.3
Iceland	—	49.7	—	9.8	330.0	762.9	—	38.0	0.4	4.6	0.2	3.4	1 199.0
U.K.	0.8	2.6	—	63.9	701.8	161.3	3.3[3]	32.8	24.7	13.3	14.5	28.3	1 047.3
Denmark	3.5	14.3	—	61.1	210.3	350.2	6.9	139.7	1.5	6.9	18.3	28.1	840.8
Chile	—	—	—	0.3	106.0	481.6	25.4	26.4	0.4	24.5	36.7	7.2	708.5
Philippines	80.7	—	—	4.7	—	95.9	36.5	425.6	NA	22.9	10.0	NA	685.7
South Africa	0.1	—	—	1.8	87.0	412.7	54.0	67.0	0.5	8.4	1.8	30.6	663.9
Mexico	3.9	—	—	0.3	—	30.8	17.9	32.9	5.1	62.2	40.9	62.4	256.4
Greece	12.0	—	—	1.8	4.1	30.7	5.7	21.3	4.4	2.8	4.9	36.3	124.0
Australia	0.6	—	—	0.1	—	0.7	11.2	24.1	4.8	17.9	18.5	1.7	79.6
Ghana	2.0	—	—	1.7	—	7.8	11.0	29.3	4.8	—	4.0	11.9	72.5

[1]Excl. salmon, smelt, trout, sturgeon [2]Incomplete data [3]Mackerel only

International trade in fish/fish products (1963-5 av.)

Aquatic animal oils and fats

Production

721 000 met. tons 1963-5 av.[1]

Data for 1953-5 av. not available

Percentage exported

97% 1963-5 av.

NA 1953-5 av.

Exports

697 000 met. tons 1963-5 av.

371 200 1953

	PERCENTAGE 1963-5 av.	1953
Peru	19	*NA*
Japan	18	*5*
U.S.A.	12	*13*
Iceland	11	*6*
Norway	9	*34*
South Africa[2]	7	*9*
U.S.S.R.	6	*NA*
Denmark	5	*NA*
Germany F.R.	2	*NA*
Others	11	*NA*
	100	*100*

Imports

759 000 met. tons 1963-5 av.

586 400 1953

	PERCENTAGE 1963-5 av.	1953
U.K.	23	*28*
Germany F.R.	16	*35*
Netherlands	12	*7*
Norway	9	*4*
Sweden	6	*4*
U.S.A.	5	*6*
France	5	*3*
U.S.S.R.	4	*NA*
Denmark	4	*NA*
Others	16	*NA*
	100	*100*

Whale oil

Production[3]

379 200 met. tons 1963-5 av.

464 300 1953-5 av.

Percentage exported

NA 1963-5 av.

NA 1953-5 av.

Exports

Specific export data are not available but the major exporters in both 1963–5 and 1953–5 were Norway and Japan. In 1953–5 Norway exported mostly to the U.K. and Japan to Germany F.R. By 1963–5 both had extended their markets to include other countries of Western Europe, and Japan also exported to China P.R. The other major producer of whale oil in 1963–5, the U.S.S.R., retained the whole of its production for domestic consumption.

Imports

182 900 met. tons 1963-5 av.

312 300 1953-5 av.

	PERCENTAGE 1963-5 av.	1953-5 av.
Germany F. R.	31[3]	*35*
U.K.	18	*36*
U.S.A.	16	*6[3]*
Netherlands	13	*16*
France	10	—
Belgium	6	—
Norway	2	*3*
Italy	2	—
Others	2	*4*
	100	*100*

[1]Fish oil [2]Incl. South West Africa [3]Incl. sperm oil

Fish/Fish products (S.I.T.C. no. 03)

Production

51 330 000 met. tons 1963-5 av.

27 470 000 1953-5 av.

Percentage exported

12% 1963-5 av.

NA 1953-5 av.

Exports

5 912 000 met. tons 1963-5 av.

Data for 1953-5 av. not available

	PERCENTAGE 1963-5 av.
Peru	25
Japan	9
Norway	8
Iceland	7
South Africa	6
Denmark	6
Canada	6
Sweden	4
U.S.S.R.	3
Others	26
	100

Imports

5 898 000 met. tons 1963-5 av.

NA 1953-5 av.

	PERCENTAGE 1963-5 av.
U.S.A.	15
Germany F.R.	13
U.K.	12
France	5
Netherlands	5
Italy	5
Denmark	4
Belg./Lux.	3
Japan	3
Others	35
	100

Types of fish and products traded

	1963-5 av. 5 806 000 met. tons	1950-3 av. 2 457 000 met. tons
	PERCENTAGE	
Aquatic animal meals and solubles	38	*13*
Fresh and frozen fish	26	*22*
Aquatic animal oils and fats	12	*23*
Canned fish and preparations	9	*11*
Dried, salted and smoked fish	9	*21*
Crustacea and molluscs	5	*7*
Canned crustacea and molluscs	1	*3*
	100	*100*

Whale oil production[3]

Major producers	JAPAN	U.S.S.R.	NORWAY	SOUTH AFRICA	OTHERS	WORLD (MET. TONS)
	PERCENTAGE					
1963-5 av.	40	31	11	4	14	379 200
1953-5 av.	*14*	*9*	*34*	*7*	*34*	*464 300*

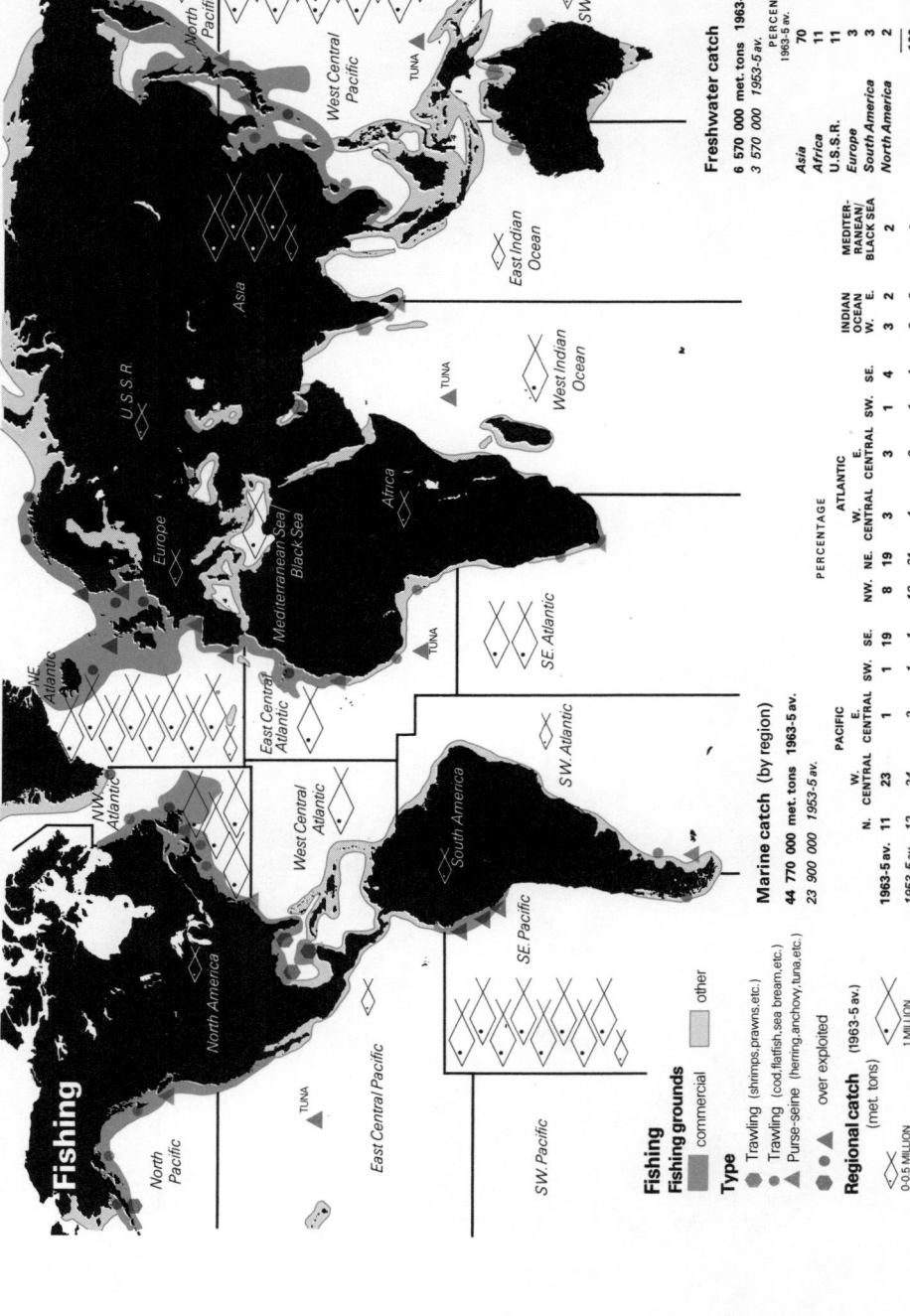

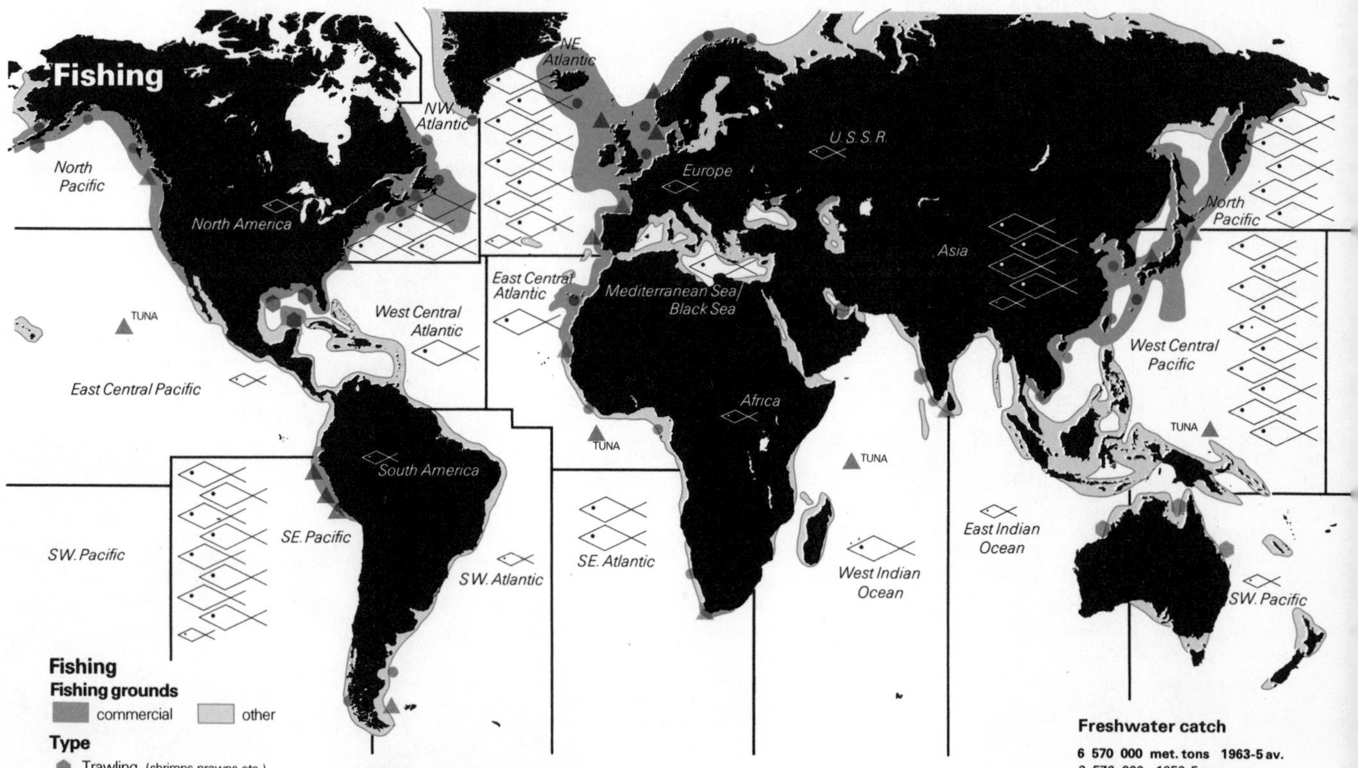

Marine catch (by region)

44 770 000 met. tons 1963-5 av.

23 900 000 1953-5 av.

PERCENTAGE

	PACIFIC N.	PACIFIC W. CENTRAL	PACIFIC E. CENTRAL	PACIFIC SW.	PACIFIC SE.	ATLANTIC NW.	ATLANTIC NE.	ATLANTIC W. CENTRAL	ATLANTIC E. CENTRAL	ATLANTIC SW.	ATLANTIC SE.	INDIAN OCEAN W.	INDIAN OCEAN E.	MEDITERRANEAN/ BLACK SEA
1963-5 av.	11	23	1	1	19	8	19	3	3	1	4	3	2	2
1953-5 av.	*12*	*24*	*2*	*1*	*1*	*10*	*31*	*4*	*2*	*1*	*4*	*3*	*2*	*3*

Freshwater catch

6 570 000 met. tons 1963-5 av.

3 570 000 1953-5 av.

	PERCENTAGE 1963-5 av.	1953-5 av.
Asia	70	*56*
Africa	11	*14*
U.S.S.R.	11	*21*
Europe	3	*3*
South America	3	*3*
North America	2	*3*
	100	*100*

Fish

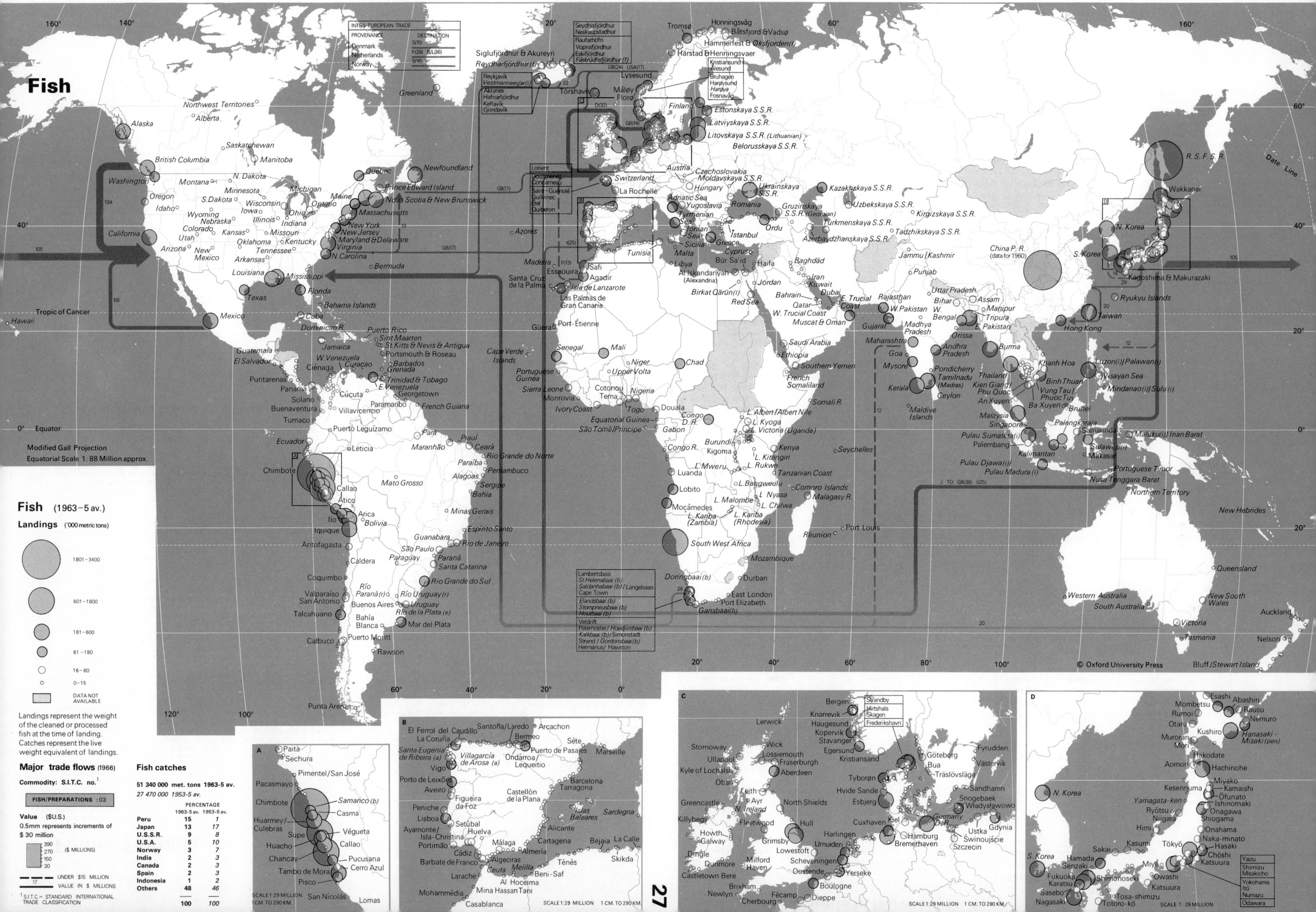

Fish (1963–5 av.)

Landings ('000 metric tons)

- 1801–3400
- 601–1800
- 181–600
- 61–180
- 16–60
- 0–15
- DATA NOT AVAILABLE

Landings represent the weight of the cleaned or processed fish at the time of landing. Catches represent the live weight equivalent of landings.

Major trade flows (1966)

Commodity: S.I.T.C. no.[1]

FISH/PREPARATIONS : 03

Value ($U.S.)

0.5mm represents increments of $ 30 million

390 / 270 / 150 / 30 ($ MILLIONS)

UNDER $15 MILLION

VALUE IN $ MILLIONS

[1] S.I.T.C. = STANDARD INTERNATIONAL TRADE CLASSIFICATION

Fish catches

51 340 000 met. tons 1963-5 av.

27 470 000 1953-5 av.

	PERCENTAGE 1963-5 av.	1953-5 av.
Peru	15	*1*
Japan	13	*17*
U.S.S.R.	9	*8*
U.S.A.	5	*10*
Norway	3	*7*
India	2	*3*
Canada	2	*3*
Spain	2	*3*
Indonesia	1	*2*
Others	48	*46*
	100	*100*

Fibres/Textiles

Cotton Lint p.32 | Flax p.30 | Man-made Fibres p.32 | Wool Yarn p.29
Cotton Yarn p.31 | Jute p.30 | Rubber p.30

For individual country data see Statistical Supplement

The manufacture of textiles in their various forms is one of the world's leading industries, and in many of the less-industrialized countries it is the biggest single source of industrial employment. Textiles are manufactured from natural fibres, man-made fibres or mixtures of both. Natural fibres are still by far the most important, but man-made fibres now make up about 30% of world consumption, as shown below.

Consumption of fibres (kg. per capita)

	1938	1954-6	1959-61	1964-6
Cotton	2.9	3.3	3.4	3.2
Wool	0.4	0.5	0.5	0.5
Cellulosic fibre	0.4	0.8	0.9	1.0
Non-cellulosic fibre	—	0.1	0.2	0.6

Coir is a soft, water-resistant fibre found between the outer husk of the coconut and the shell of the inner kernel. It is of three main types: bristle fibre; curl, tow or mattress fibre; and mat fibre, used in ropes, twinings and matting. The only important producers are India, which exports mainly manufactured articles, and Ceylon, which exports mainly fibre.

Kapok is the floss obtained from the pods of the kapok tree, cultivated in Java and to a lesser degree in other parts of Indonesia, India, Pakistan, Ceylon, Ecuador, Indo-China and other tropical areas. It is very light, resilient, moisture-proof and is used in bedding, upholstery, in thermal and sound insulation and as a substitute for cork.

Hemp is found between the bark and the pith in the stem of the *Cannabis sativa* plant found in humid regions within the temperate zone, where the mid-season temperatures average between 60°F (15.5°C) and 80°F (26.5°C), and the frost-free period exceeds four months. Moist soils, rich in organic matter, are the most suitable especially if they are calcareous. Hemp fibre is used mainly for small cordage.

Agave fibres are used primarily in cordage industries. Abaca (Manila hemp) is a strong, hard fibre with a natural resistance to wind, rain, sun and rubbing, making abaca rope particularly useful as marine hawser. It is obtained from *Musa textilis*, a species of banana, grown in the Philippines and Central America under warm humid conditions. Sisal is the most widely used substitute for abaca, although used more for twine than for rope. It is particularly drought resistant and is grown in the dry tropical climates of East Africa, Brazil, Haiti and Java. Henequen, a soft fibre, is similar to sisal, although it is not so strong and is used mostly for inferior twines. It is grown in Cuba and Mexico.

Some **flax** plants are grown for fibre, others primarily for linseed, though they yield fibre as a by-product. From this fibre a variety of linen goods are produced for domestic and industrial use, but demand is declining, partly as a result of substitution. **Jute** is vital to the world food economy because it is a cheap material readily converted into sacking for agricultural produce. Yet only two countries, India and Pakistan, grow it to any extent. Jute, sisal, abaca and hemp, with their specialized industrial uses, do not seriously compete with cotton, wool and man-made fibres.

Cotton is unsurpassed for sheer volume of output and versatility in use among fibres. The U.A.R. produces the finest long staple cotton but the greatest production is of cheap, medium staple in the U.S.A. India produces mainly the coarse and short varieties. Cotton demands a long hot growing season but is grown under a wide range of annual rainfall. Best results are obtained when the period of maturation coincides with a dry period. The summer isotherm of 77°F (25°C) and a 200-day frost-free period are the economic limits of cultivation in the U.S.A., although the rainfall variation is 23–60 in. (600–1 500 mm). After cotton has been picked, the seed is separated from the fibre (ginning), crushed to extract oil, and the residue used as cattle feed. The fibres are pressed into bales and subsequently made into a wide range of products from light cloth to heavy tarpaulins.

Wool gives warmth without weight and will absorb water without feeling wet and is thus an important fibre in the clothing industry. There are two types of wool yarn: worsted, where the fibres are combed parallel and tightly spun to form a firm smooth yarn used to make worsted cloth; and woollen, where the fibres lie in all directions and result in a soft, fuzzy yarn used to make blankets and woollen cloth.

Man-made fibres, in contrast to the older fibres, are produced mainly from materials readily available in Western Europe and North America. They are of two main origins. Regenerated fibres, of which the principal example is viscose rayon, derive from vegetable or animal materials in which the physical or chemical form has been changed. Synthetic fibres, such as nylon, polyester or glass fibres, are built up from chemical or mineral constituents. Thus there is a very close relationship between the synthetic fibre industry and the chemical industry.

Fibres are, for the most part, grown for the **textile industries,** of which the cotton industry is by far the largest and most widely spread; cotton manufacturing often appears in the earliest stages of industrialization, particularly in cotton growing areas. The British, West European and Japanese industries can obtain cotton only from imports, and a highly organized market for raw cotton has grown up, with New Orleans, Memphis, New York, Alexandria and Liverpool as the main centres. In Japan and the U.S.A. the bulk of cotton cloth comes from integrated concerns which both spin and weave. Elsewhere this vertical integration is much less marked, despite the existence of large combines.

The wool industry produces both woollens made from a variety of raw materials from new wool to shoddy (i.e. re-manufactured fibres), and worsteds which use only new wool. In many countries, the wool industry was originally based on domestic raw materials, but this is no longer true of the world's major producers. Much of the raw wool entering world trade is sold by auction in London and Sydney. The silk industry, heavily concentrated in Japan, has suffered severely from first rayon and then nylon, which has come to displace silk in the manufacture of high-grade hosiery for women. The rapid development of man-made fibres is breaking down some of the traditional distinction between the cotton and wool textile industries; mixtures of such fibres with either wool or cotton are becoming increasingly common.

International trade in yarns/textiles (1963-5 av.)

Cotton yarn

Production[1]
8 131 000 met. tons 1963-5 av.
6 958 000 1953-5 av.

Percentage exported
3% 1963-5 av.[1]
2% 1953-5 av.[2]

Exports
231 900 met. tons 1963-5 av.[1]
123 700 1953-5 av.[2]

	PERCENTAGE 1963-5 av.	1953-5 av.
U.A.R.	14	7
Pakistan	10	—
Italy	9	10
Belgium	7	18
Others	60	65
	100	100

Imports[1]
205 000 met. tons 1963-5 av.[1]
*101 300 1953-5 av.**[2]

	PERCENTAGE 1963-5 av.	1953-5 av.
Germany F.R.	14	5
Netherlands	8	13
U.K.	8	4
Belgium	7	2
Others	63	76
	100	100

Wool yarn[3]

Production[1]
1 860 700 met. tons 1963-5 av.
1 366 400 1953-5 av.

Percentage exported[1]
6% 1963-5 av.
4% 1953-5 av.

Exports[1]
104 800 met. tons 1963-5 av.*
56 000 1953-5 av.

	PERCENTAGE 1963-5 av.	1953-5 av.
France	24	32
Belgium	24	21
U.K.	14	22
Italy	11	4
Others	27	21
	100	100

Imports[1]
96 500 met. tons 1963-5 av.
51 100 1953-5 av.

	PERCENTAGE 1963-5 av.	1953-5 av.
Germany F.R.	35	26
Netherlands	13	17
Belgium	7	5
Denmark	5	4
Others	40	48
	100	100

Cotton cloth

Production
5 500 800 met. tons 1963-5 av.[1,4]
3 440 900 1953-5 av.[2]

Percentage exported
13% 1963-5 av.[1]
15% 1963-5 av.[2]

Exports
786 200 met. tons 1963-5 av.*
525 000 1953-5 av.[2]

	PERCENTAGE 1963-5 av.	1953-5 av.
Japan	18	21
India	9	16
China P.R.*	8	...[2]
Hong Kong	6	3
Others	59	60
	100	100

Imports
735 100 met. tons 1963-5 av.[1]
488 100 1953-5 av.[2]

	PERCENTAGE 1963-5 av.	1953-5 av.
U.K.	13	5
U.S.A.	9	2
Indonesia	5	12
Hong Kong	5	3
Others	68	78
	100	100

Woven wool fabrics[2,5]

Production
685 100 met. tons 1963-5 av.
256 800 1953-5 av.

Percentage exported
18% 1963-5 av.
32% 1953-5 av.

Exports
125 500 met. tons 1963-5 av.*
83 000 1953-5 av.

	PERCENTAGE 1963-5 av.	1953-5 av.
Italy	45	33
U.K.	18	35
Belgium	9	9
Japan	8	4
Others	20	19
	100	100

Imports
99 600 met. tons 1963-5 av.*
57 400 1953-5 av.

	PERCENTAGE 1963-5 av.	1953-5 av.
Germany F.R.	27	19
U.S.A.	11	10
Netherlands	9	7
U.K.	9	7
Others	44	57
	100	100

*Estimate [1]Excl. China P.R. [2]Excl. China P.R., U.S.S.R. and Eastern Europe [3]Worsted and woollen [4]Total of available countries [5]Incl. blankets, excl. carpets

International trade in fibres (1963-5 av.)

Cotton lint[1] (S.I.T.C. no. 263)

Production
11 493 000 met. tons 1963-5 av.
7 367 000 1953-5 av.[2]

Percentage exported
33% 1963-5 av.
33% 1953-5 av.[2]

Exports
3 766 400 met. tons 1963-5 av.
2 549 000 1953-5 av.

	PERCENTAGE 1963-5 av.	1953-5 av.
U.S.A.	27	28
U.S.S.R.	10	4
Mexico	10	11
U.A.R.	8	12
Others	45	45
	100	100

Imports
3 738 800 met. tons 1963-5 av.
2 553 300 1953-5 av.

	PERCENTAGE 1963-5 av.	1953-5 av.
Japan	19	18
Germany F.R.	8	10
France	7	11
U.K.	6	13
Others	60	48
	100	100

Wool[3] (S.I.T.C. no. 262.1/262.2)

Production
1 507 000 met. tons 1963-5 av.
1 060 000 1953-5 av.[2]

Percentage exported
59% 1963-5 av.
69% 1953-5 av.[2]

Exports
895 500 met. tons 1963-5 av.
732 000 1953-5 av.

	PERCENTAGE 1963-5 av.	1953-5 av.
Australia	43	41
New Zealand	21	19
Argentina	8	10
South Africa	7	8
Others	21	22
	100	100

Imports
934 900 met. tons 1963-5 av.
722 000 1953-5 av.

	PERCENTAGE 1963-5 av.	1953-5 av.
U.K.	19	31
Japan	15	7
U.S.A.	10	16
France	10	14
Others	46	32
	100	100

Flax[4] (S.I.T.C. no. 265.1)

Production
666 100 met. tons 1963-5 av.
247 000 1953-5 av.[2]

Percentage exported
64% 1963-5 av.
49% 1953-5 av.[2]

Exports
426 400 met. tons 1963-5 av.
121 300 1953-5 av.

	PERCENTAGE 1963-5 av.	1953-5 av.
Netherlands	34	18
France	29	5
Belg./Lux.	22	70
Others	15	7
	100	100

Imports
408 100 met. tons 1963-5 av.
121 700 1953-5 av.

	PERCENTAGE 1963-5 av.	1953-5 av.
Belg./Lux.	62	12
U.K.	11	35
France	5	9
Others	22	44
	100	100

Jute[5] (S.I.T.C. no. 264)

Production
3 283 000 met. tons 1963-5 av.
1 833 000 1953-5 av.[6]

Percentage exported
26% 1963-5 av.
53% 1953-5 av.[6]

Exports
856 300 met. tons 1963-5 av.
974 300 1953-5 av.

	PERCENTAGE 1963-5 av.	1953-5 av.
Pakistan	89	98
India	3	—
Belg./Lux.	3	—
Others	5	2
	100	100

Imports
983 300 met. tons 1963-5 av.
951 700 1953-5 av.

	PERCENTAGE 1963-5 av.	1953-5 av.
U.K.	13	15
France	10	10
Belg./Lux.	10	8
Others	67	67
	100	100

Abaca–Manila hemp (S.I.T.C. no. 265.5)

Production
116 700 met. tons 1963-5
130 000 1953-5 av.

Percentage exported
97% 1963-5 av.
94% 1953-5 av.

Exports
113 600 met. tons 1963-5 av.
122 000 1953-5 av.

	PERCENTAGE 1963-5 av.	1953-5 av.
Philippines	93	87
Malaysia	4	2
Others	3	11
	100	100

Imports
107 400 met. tons 1963-5 av.
118 000 1953-5 av.

	PERCENTAGE 1963-5 av.	1953-5 av.
U.S.A.	28	35
Japan	28	26
U.K.	16	14
Others	28	25
	100	100

Sisal/Henequen[7] (S.I.T.C. no. 265.4)

Production
871 500 met. tons 1963-5 av.
536 700 1953-5 av.

Percentage exported
71% 1963-5 av.
86% 1953-5 av.

Exports
622 300 met. tons 1963-5 av.
460 700 1953-5 av.

	PERCENTAGE 1963-5 av.	1953-5 av.
Tanzania	34	39
Brazil	22	11
Kenya	10	8
Others	34	42
	100	100

Imports
600 000 met. tons 1963-5 av.
443 300 1953-5 av.

	PERCENTAGE 1963-5 av.	1953-5 av.
U.S.A.	15	34
U.K.	12	15
France	10	8
Others	63	43
	100	100

Hemp (S.I.T.C. no. 265.2)

Production
336 500 met. tons 1963-5 av.
346 700 1953-5 av.[2]

Percentage exported
12% 1963-5 av.
16% 1953-5 av.[2]

Exports
41 200 met. tons 1963-5 av.
55 500 1953-5 av.

	PERCENTAGE 1963-5 av.	1953-5 av.
India	27	30
Yugoslavia	26	17
Hungary	11	—
Others	36	53
	100	100

Imports
35 600 met. tons 1963-5 av.
55 700 1953-5 av.

	PERCENTAGE 1963-5 av.	1953-5 av.
Italy	22	2
Germany F.R.	20	27
U.K.	12	21
Others	46	50
	100	100

Silk[8] (S.I.T.C. no. 261)

Production
32 400 met. tons 1963-5 av.
24 000 1953-5 av.[2]

Percentage exported
36% 1963-5 av.
29% 1953-5 av.[2]

Exports
11 700 met. tons 1963-5 av.
7 000 1953-5 av.

	PERCENTAGE 1963-5 av.	1953-5 av.
Japan	26	65
China P.R.*	18	16
U.S.S.R.	13	—
Others	43	19
	100	100

Imports
11 900 met. tons 1963-5 av.
6 000 1953-5 av.

	PERCENTAGE 1963-5 av.	1953-5 av.
Italy	30	5
U.S.A.	25	51
Japan	13	2
Others	32	42
	100	100

Cellulosic fibres

Production
3 227 900 met. tons 1963-5 av.
2 065 900 1953-5 av.[6]

Percentage exported
18% 1963-5 av.
13% 1953-5 av.[6]

Exports
574 400 met. tons 1963-5 av.
269 000 1953-5 av.[9]

	PERCENTAGE 1963-5 av.	1953-5 av.
Germany F.R.	18	16
Japan	17	3
Italy	13	20
U.K.	9	9
France	8	9
Others	35	43
	100	100

Imports
447 500 met. tons 1963-5 av.
145 700 1953-5 av.[9]

	PERCENTAGE 1963-5 av.	1953-5 av.
U.S.S.R.	13[10]	...[9]
U.S.A.	11	32
China P.R.	10[10]	...[9]
Germany F.R.	7	12
South Africa	7	4
Others	52	52
	100	100

Non-cellulosic fibres

Production
1 692 000 met. tons 1963-5 av.
205 900 1953-5 av.

Percentage exported
17% 1963-5 av.
NA 1953-5 av.

Exports
282 700 met. tons 1963-5 av.
Data for 1953-5 av. not available

	PERCENTAGE 1963-5 av.
Germany F.R.	16
U.S.A.	16
Italy	15
Japan	14
U.K.	12
Others	27
	100

Imports
258 500 met. tons 1963-5 av.
Data for 1953-5 av. not available

	PERCENTAGE 1963-5 av.
U.K.	9
Germany F.R.	8
Belgium	7
France	6
U.S.A.	6
Others	64
	100

*Estimate [1]1963-5 data for raw cotton other than linters [2]Excl. U.S.S.R. [3]Clean basis [4]Fibre, tow and waste [5]Incl. kenaf [6]Excl. China P.R.
[7]Incl. other agave fibres [8]Raw [9]Excl. China P.R., U.S.S.R. and Eastern Europe [10]Data for 1965

Wool Yarn

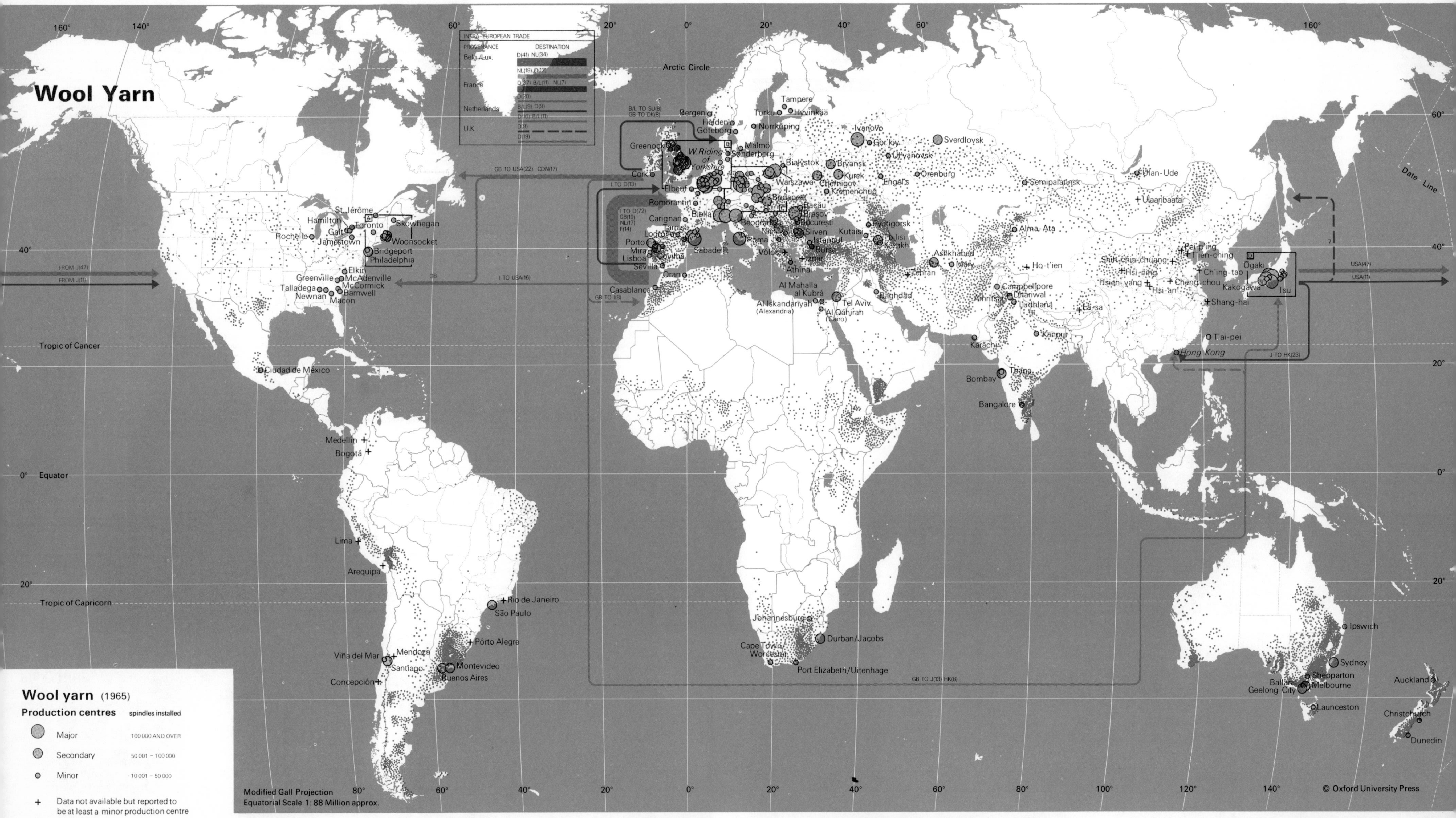

Wool yarn (1965)

Production centres spindles installed

- Major — 100 000 AND OVER
- Secondary — 50 001 – 100 000
- Minor — 10 001 – 50 000
- + Data not available but reported to be at least a minor production centre

Sheep

One dot represents 100 000 head of sheep

Major trade flows (1966)

Commodity: S.I.T.C.no.

WOOL YARN & THREAD (INCLUDING WOOL FROM ANIMALS OTHER THAN SHEEP) 651.2

WOOL FABRICS (NOT INCLUDING TRADE IN MADE-UP CLOTHES OR 'RAW' WOOL) 653.2

Value (\$U.S.)

0.5mm represents increments of \$20 million

(\$ MILLIONS) 260 180 100 20

UNDER \$10 MILLION

47 VALUE IN \$ MILLIONS

Wool spindles

Number installed, end of year

(in thousands)

	1965	1955
U.K.	3 697	*4 971*
Italy	1 700	*1 608*
Japan	1 510[2]	*1 779*
U.S.A.	1 223[2]	*1 768*
France	1 191	*2 124*
Germany F.R.	1 042	*1 201*
Spain	560	*589*
Poland	554[1]	*NA*
Belgium	485	*717*
Argentina	375[2]	*NA*

[1]Data for 1962

[2]Data for 1964

Wool yarn production

1 860 700 met. tons 1963-5 av.[1]

1 366 400 1953-5 av.[1]

	PERCENTAGE 1963-5 av.	1953-5 av.
U.K.	14	*18*
U.S.S.R.	13	*11*
U.S.A.	13	*23*
Italy	9	*NA*
Japan	8	*6*
France	8	*9*
Germany F.R.	6	*8*
Belgium	3	*3*
Poland	3	*4*
Others	23	*NA*
	100	*100*

[1]Excl. China P.R.

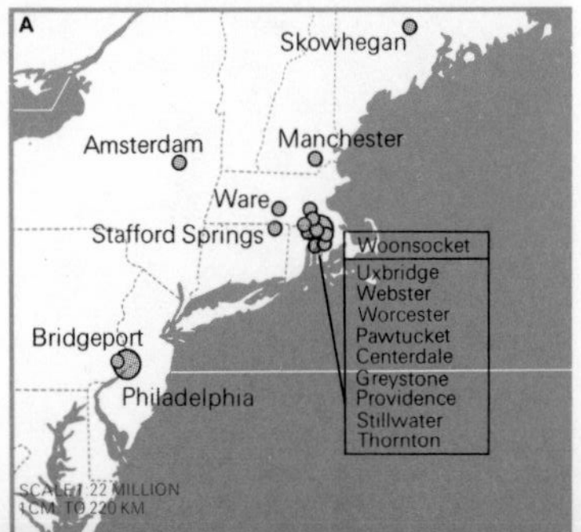

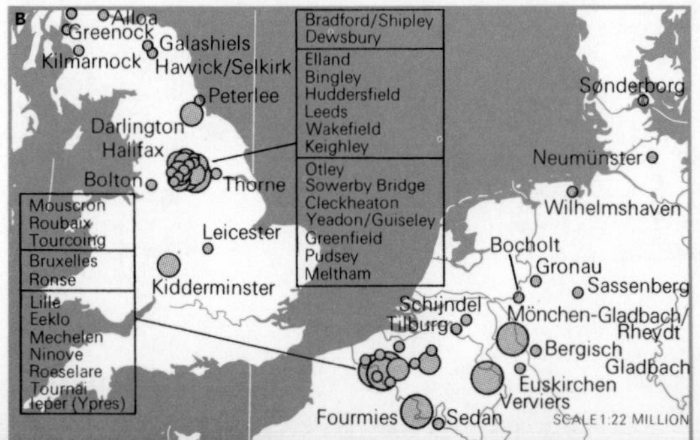

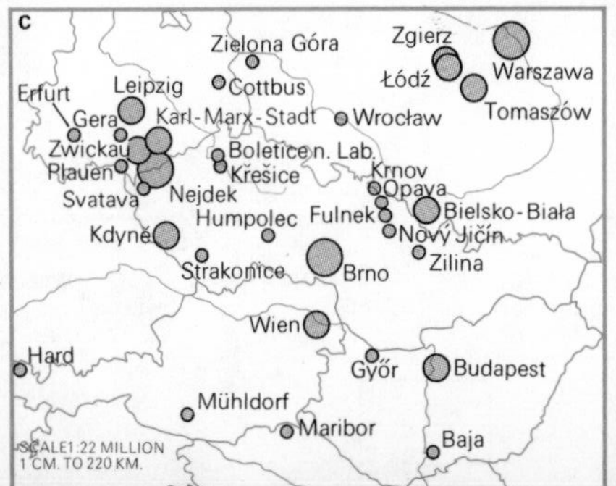

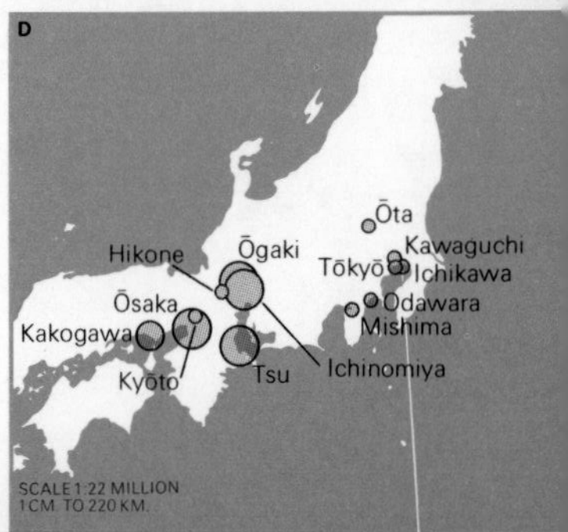

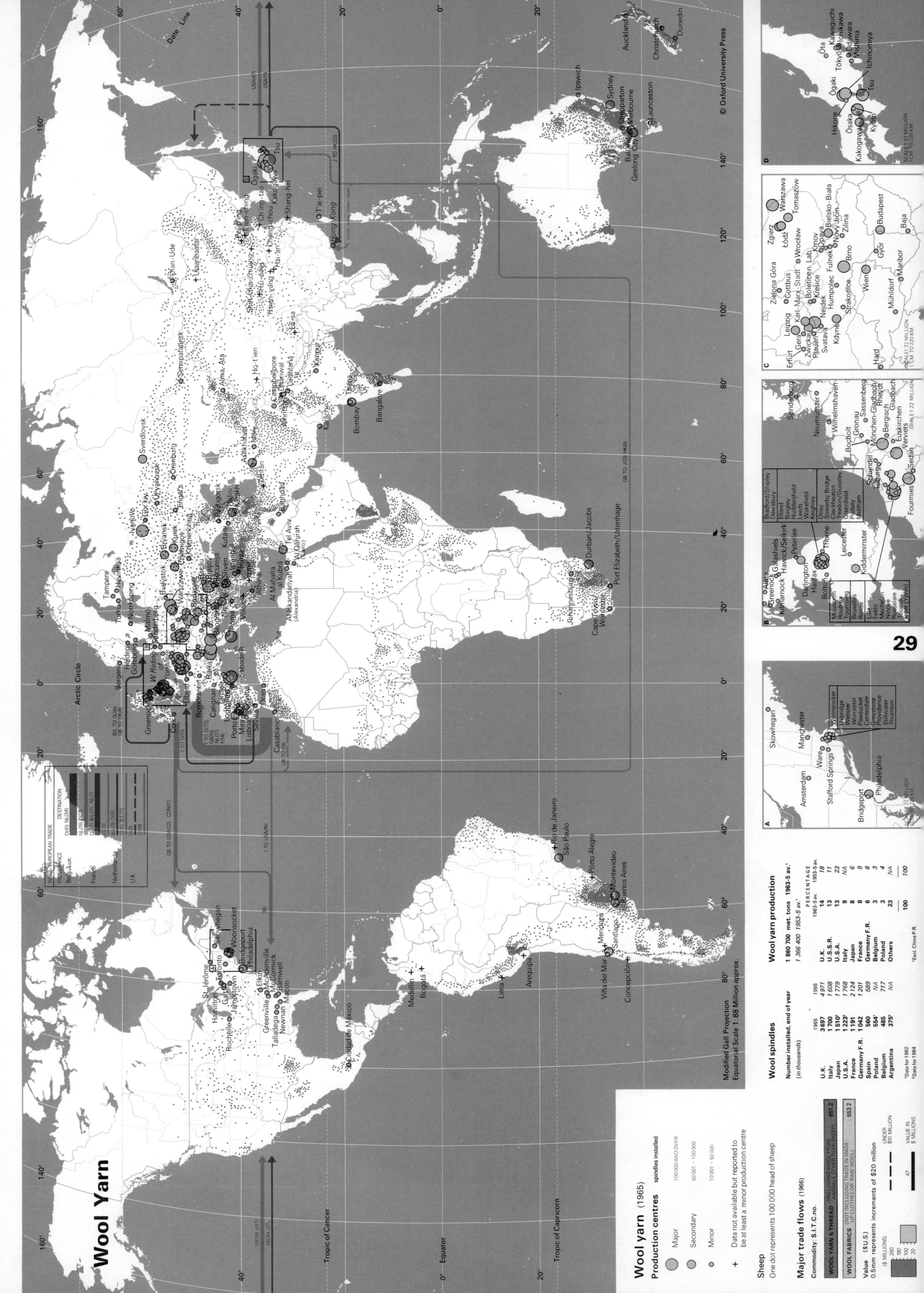

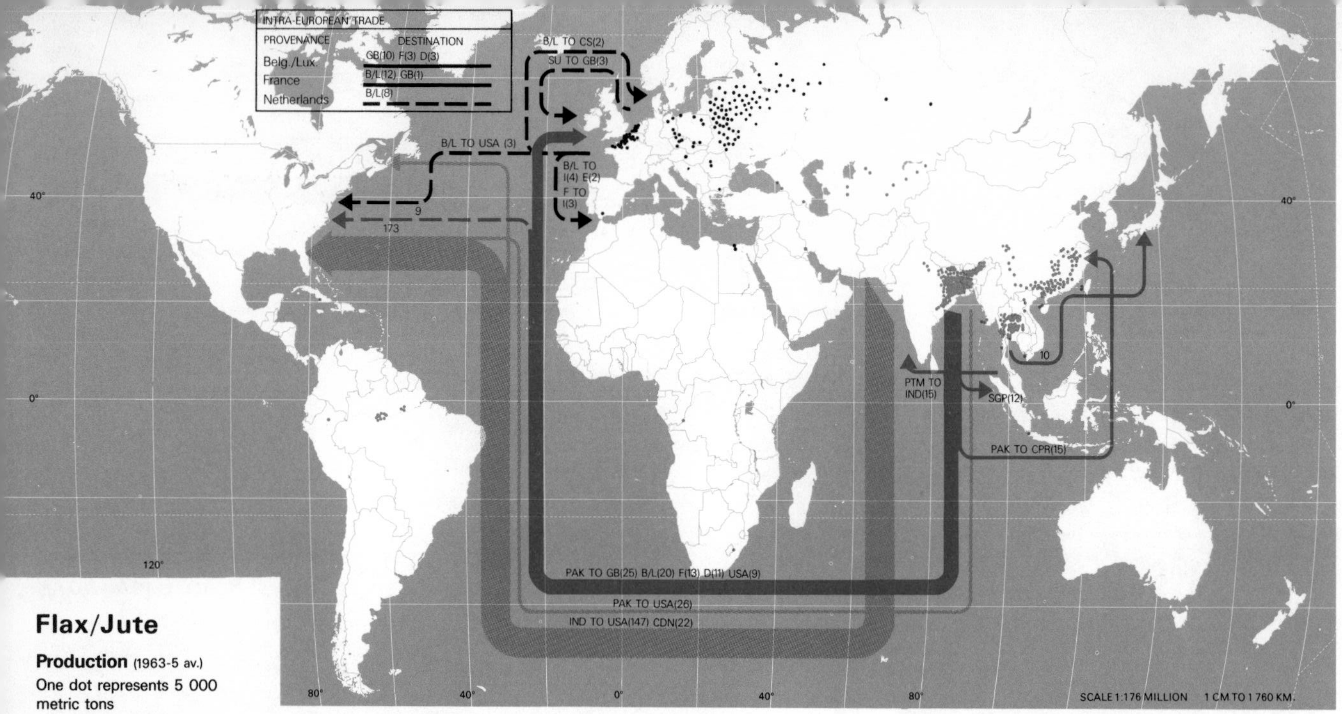

Flax/Jute

Production (1963-5 av.)

One dot represents 5 000 metric tons

- flax
- jute (including kenaf)

Major trade flows (1966)

Commodity : S.I.T.C.no.

FLAX,FLAX TOW,WASTE : 265.1

JUTE (NOT SPUN) : 264

JUTE WOVEN FABRICS : 653.4

Value ($ U.S.)

0.5mm represents increments of $20 million

($ MILLIONS) 180 100 20 — UNDER $10 MILLION — 15 VALUE IN $ MILLIONS

Flax fibre production

666 100 met. tons 1963-5 av.

247 000 1953–5 av.[1]

	PERCENTAGE 1963-5 av.	1953-5 av.
U.S.S.R.	59	...[1]
France	11	15
Poland	8	21
Belgium	6	16
Netherlands	5	15
Czechoslovakia	3	NA
U.A.R.	1	NA
Others	7	NA
	100	100

[1] Excl. U.S.S.R.

Jute production[1]

3 283 000 met. tons 1963-5 av.

1 833 000 1953–5 av.[2]

	PERCENTAGE 1963-5 av.	1953-5 av.
India	39	44
Pakistan	33	46
China P.R.	12	...[2]
Thailand	9	—
Brazil	2	1
U.S.S.R.	2[3]	NA
Nepal	1	—
Others	2	NA
	100	100

[1] Incl. kenaf
[2] Excl. China P.R. [3] Only kenaf

Flax fibre and linseed seed are obtained from selected types of a common parent. Their environment and soil criteria are somewhat similar, but for the production of fibre the requirements are more exacting. The quality of the fibre in the stems is highest under moist, cool conditions, [59°-64°F (15°-18°C) in July] and well drained, fertile soils. In warmer and drier areas dual purpose varieties are grown and the shorter fibres (tow) can be obtained from linseed straw. Thus although U.S.S.R. grows 59% of the world's output, more favourable conditions in Western Europe give higher yields and superior quality flax so that the Netherlands, France and Belgium are the main exporters. Although nylon is now largely replacing it in rope production, flax is still used to make fine linen and thread.

Jute fibres are derived from the stems of two closely related tropical species of the genus *Corchorus*. Both are tall annuals (3-4 metres) the stems of which are harvested within 3 or 4 months of planting, while the plants are flowering. *Corchorus* requires flooding, hot moist conditions and soils of high fertility. It also demands much hand labour. Jute is used mainly for making cheap, strong sacks and burlap, but also for twine, tarpaulin, carpets and linoleum backing. Although there has been a considerable increase in the world production of packable commodities over the last 20 years, the relative increase in the production of jute goods has been very small. This is mainly due to modern methods of bulk carrying and only partly to the use of synthetics.

Natural and synthetic rubber

Natural rubber is primarily derived from the bast tissues just underneath the bark of the tree, *Hevea brasiliensis*. When a shallow incision is made in the bark (tapping) a white viscous juice, latex (which is 60% water) flows out. This is collected and processed in one of two ways: either the juice is taken direct to the factory where the water is largely removed by a centrifuge to produce concentrated latex—see later—or acid is added to encourage coagulation of the rubber particles and partial separation of the water. This coagulum is further processed to remove dirt followed by the removal of water by mechanical pressure and drying.

Hevea, a native of the Amazon was first introduced into Ceylon, Indonesia and Malaya in the 1870's. The subsequent rapid expansion of the planted areas arose from the tremendous demand for rubber for the new motor industry. Few commodities have ever achieved so fast a pre-eminent place amongst the world's key raw materials. The great growth of natural rubber output in this century can be ascribed to a variety of factors. The introduction of *Hevea* required the clearance of indigenous forests and therefore the input of much capital which lead to the development of large estates with well-organized systems of production. Secondly, by breeding and selection, the application of chemicals to prolong the latex flow and advances in the techniques of tapping and other plantation practices, yields of rubber have been greatly increased. More recently improved methods of processing have led to the production of more closely standardized grades of rubber. In Malaysia and Indonesia the production of rubber by smallholders has been encouraged and today world output is roughly equally divided between estates and smallholdings.

Industrial application of rubber began only in the early nineteenth century with the work of Hancock on rubber processing and the introduction by Mackintosh of a patented process for waterproofing cloth. Later the discovery of vulcanization by Goodyear opened up a whole new range of end products, above all the invention by Dunlop of the pneumatic tube and the production of rubber tyres.

In 1948 more than 90% of the world supply was natural rubber; today over 60% is synthetic, made mainly from hydrocarbon monomers produced by the petro-chemical industry. Such chemicals can also be obtained from other sources such as coal.

The synthetic rubber industry, which began in Germany in the 1930's was developed in the U.S.A. in the early 1940's and also in the U.S.S.R. In the 1950's the U.K. and France built plants, and Germany F.R. began to produce again. The 1960's heralded a wider spread still to the newer manufacturing countries, particularly Japan. Synthetic production during World War II enabled the rapidly growing world demand for general rubber products and for tyres in particular to be met, when supplies of natural rubber were disrupted. Since then further increases in production have helped both to meet rising demand and to steady the prices of an essential raw material which in the past had fluctuated wildly.

Today natural rubber's share of world consumption is declining although its actual rate of consumption is still increasing. In many applications, and these include tyre production, the best characteristics in a product are obtained by blending synthetic and natural rubbers or by using different rubbers in different parts such as the treads and sidewalls of tyres. Because of the specific properties of polymers the emergence of SMR (Standard Malaysian Rubber)—a technically specified natural rubber—reflects the industry's awareness that its customers require consistent quality.

Styrene/Butadiene Synthetic rubber (SBR) is the chief general purpose synthetic rubber and slightly more SBR is currently produced than natural rubber on a world wide basis.

The other types of synthetic rubber are more specialized in their use. For example Butyl rubber holds air and gases well, resists heat and the harmful effects of acids, and is thus used in the manufacture of inner tubes, and linings for tubeless tyres. Cis-Polyisoprene rubber is very much like natural rubber and is used mainly for tyres. Polychloroprene rubber resists the normally harmful effects of oxygen, sunlight, oil and petrol (gasoline) and is therefore ideal for the manufacture of gasoline hose, insulation for wires and cables used in conjunction with oil, and gaskets for sealing against gas and oil. Nitrile rubbers have a high resistance to gasoline, grease, oil, wax and solvents and are also heat-resistant to 349°F (176°C). These are used for paper and leather products. Polysulphide rubber resists chemical ageing, air, sunlight and the normally harmful effects of grease so is used for lining gasoline hoses, printing plates and rollers. Polyurethane also resists age and heat and withstands stresses and pressures so that it outlasts natural rubber. This is used mainly for upholstery, mattresses and insulating materials. Silicone rubber can be used at temperatures ranging from −130°F to 707°F (−90°C to 375°C) and is therefore used for seals, gaskets and components for jet planes and machinery exposed to high temperatures. Other uses for synthetic rubbers are footwear, floor coverings, belting and waterproof clothing.

Polybutadiene's resistance to abrasion and low temperatures has enabled it to establish for itself a very important role in tyre technology, and it is currently branching out successfully into many other applications, not least of which is in the reinforcement of plastics materials.

Lastly, Ethylene/Propylene rubbers may prove to be the fastest growing rubber polymer during the next decade.

Of all consumers of both natural and synthetic rubber the motor industry is the largest. Over 50% of all rubber used goes into tyres. But tyres are not the only outlet for rubber in the automotive industry; it has been estimated that there are approximately 300 components made of rubber in a car.

Latex

In addition to the concentration of the latex by a centrifuge, ammonia or other preservatives are added to suppress the activities of micro-organisms during shipment abroad and storage in bulk. Latex is employed in the manufacture of foam rubber used extensively for cushions, upholstery and mattresses. It is also used in paper/fabric coating and for dipped goods, such as surgeons' gloves.

Very large quantities of natural and synthetic latices are currently being used by the carpet industry; firstly as primary backing to tufted carpets and secondly in the form of spread foam, as either attached or separate foam underlays, adding that touch of luxury to the product.

Rubber consumption

Figures in brackets indicate percentages used in tyres and tyre products, where known.

Natural 1960	Natural 1970*	('000 met. tons)	Synthetic 1970*	Synthetic 1960
2 098	2 947	World	4 643	1 832
486 (68)	589	U.S.A.	2 179	1 096 (62)
169 (46)	269	Japan	460	62 (35)
148 (51)	194	Germany F.R.	298	106 (59)
183 (46)	193	U.K.	259	118 (63)
129 (59)	140	France	230	92 (54)
75 (60)	110	Italy	190	58 (45)
193	254	U.S.S.R.[1]	5	13
36 (69)	53	Canada	128	57 (68)
50	100	India	37	7
49	40	Brazil	82	18
41	42	Australia	52	28
NA	46	Czechoslovakia	36	NA
NA	26	Sweden	53	18[1]
NA	891	Others	634	NA

* Estimates [1] Data refers to imports

Rubber

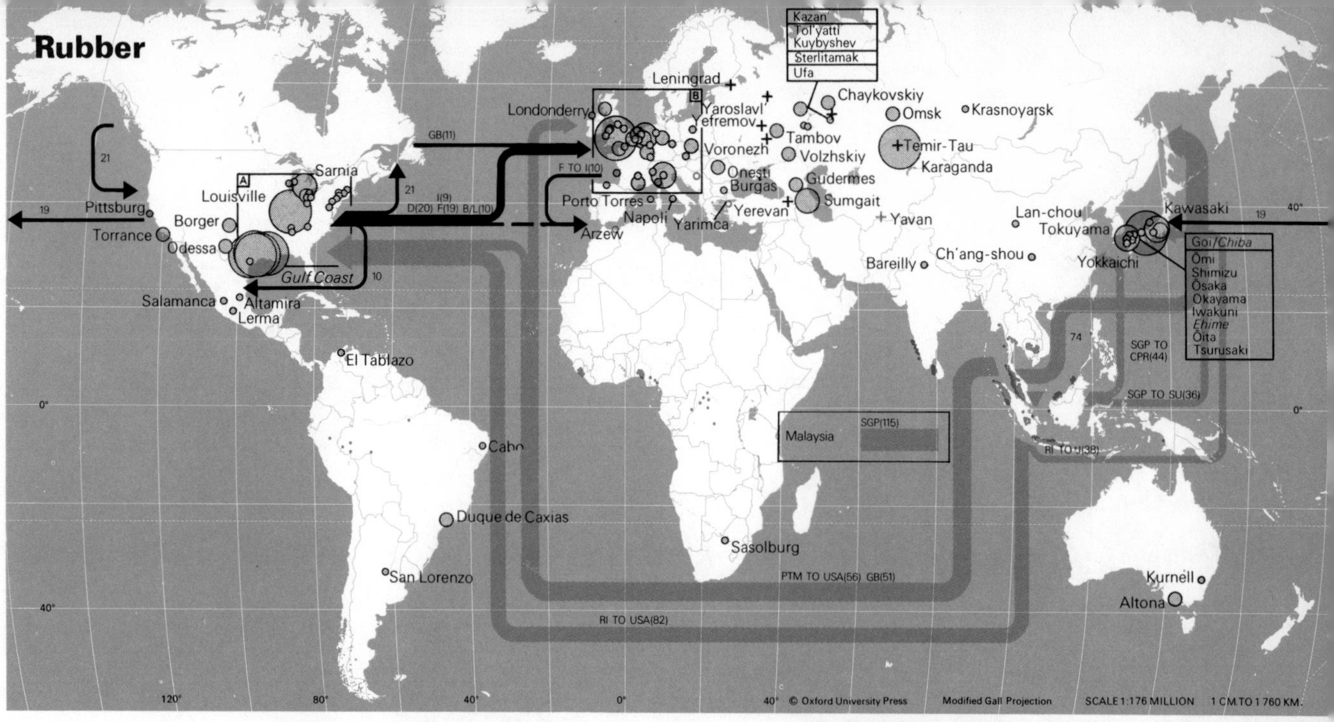

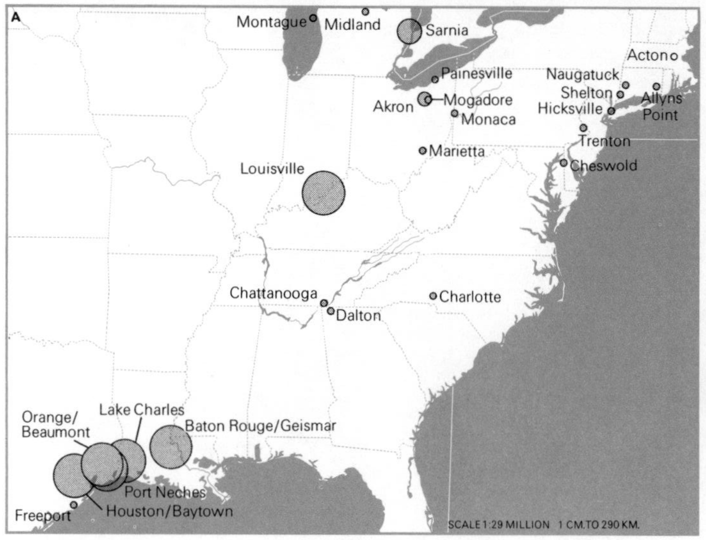

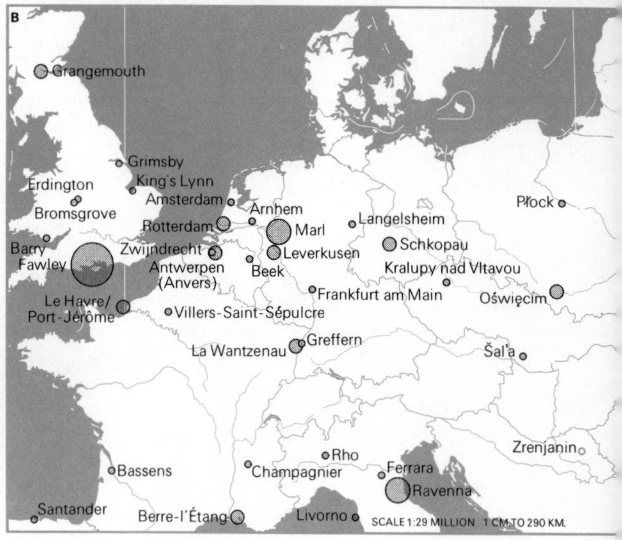

Natural rubber

Production (1963–5 av.)

One dot represents 5 000 metric tons

Synthetic rubber (1969)

Producing capacity (met.tons)

- OVER 260 000
- 160 000–260 000
- 60 000 – 160 000
- 60 000 & UNDER
- + capacity unknown
- ○ plant under construction
- + plant under construction ultimate capacity unknown

Major trade flows (1966)

Commodity: S.I.T.C.no. (Brussels no.)

NATURAL RUBBER : 231.1 (40.01)

SYNTHETIC RUBBER : 231.2 (40.02)

Value ($ U.S.)

0.5mm represents increments of $20 million

($ MILLIONS) 180 100 20 — UNDER $10 MILLION — 38 VALUE IN $ MILLIONS

Natural rubber production

2 957 000 met. tons 1970*
2 252 200 1963-5 av.
1 843 000 1953-5 av.

	PERCENTAGE 1970*	1963-5 av.	1953-5 av.
Malaysia[1]	44	40	36
Indonesia	26	29	40
Thailand	9	9	6
Ceylon	5	5	5
Others	16	17	13
	100	100	100

*Estimates [1] Incl. Singapore

Reclaimed rubber production

374 396 met. tons 1968
403 700 1963-5 av.
378 100 1953-5 av.

	PERCENTAGE 1968	1963-5 av.	1953-5 av.
U.S.A.	70	70	79
Germany F.R.	9	11	9
U.K.	9	11	9
Brazil	5	3	—
Australia	3	3	2
Canada	4	2	1
	100	100	100

Synthetic rubber production[1]

4 770 000 met. tons 1970[2]
2 925 000 1963-5 av.
927 000 1953-5 av.

	PERCENTAGE 1970[2]	1963-5 av.	1953-5 av.
U.S.A.	50	60	89
Japan	11	4	—
U.K.	6	5	—
France	6	4	—
Germany F.R.	6	5	1
Canada	5	7	10
Netherlands	4	3	—
Italy	3	4	—
Brazil	1	1	—
Others	8	7	—
	100	100	100

[1] Excl. U.S.S.R. and some minor producers
[2] Data for 1970 is based on estimates and excludes Eastern Europe

The data for reclaimed rubber includes both natural and synthetic reclaimed rubber and shows only the six countries for which regular production data is available.

Natural rubber imports

2 743 335 met. tons 1968
2 443 970 1963-5 av.
2 118 000 1953-5 av.

	PERCENTAGE 1968	1963-5 av.	1953-5 av.
U.S.A.	19	18	30
U.S.S.R.	12	10	1
Japan	9	8	4
China P.R.	8	6	3
U.K.	7	8	13
Germany F.R.	6	7	7
Malaysia	NA	7	16
France	5	5	6
Italy	4	4	3
Others	NA	27	17
	100	100	100

Natural rubber is now obtained mainly from plantations of *Hevea brasiliensis*, particularly in Southeast Asia, although *Hevea* plantations have also been established in West Africa. *Hevea* was introduced from the tropical rain forests of the Amazon. It requires an equable temperature within limits of *c.* 75°-95°F (24°-35°C). Optimum annual rainfall is 100-120 in. (2 550-3 050 mm.) although on suitable soils the trees will tolerate a minimum of 60 in. (1 500 mm.) rainfall provided that it is evenly distributed throughout the year. For optimal growth the soil should be deep, fertile, well drained and not alkaline, although the application of fertilizers allows the use of otherwise unsuitable soils. Above 300 metres *Hevea* is liable to attack by the fungus *Oidium*, and in Central and South America the establishment of plantations has been greatly hampered by the leaf blight disease *Dothidella ulei*.

Natural rubber exports

2 494 403 met. tons 1968
2 478 730 1963-5 av.
2 116 000 1953-5 av.

	PERCENTAGE 1968	1963-5 av.	1953-5 av.
Malaysia	45	43	44
Indonesia	29	27	33
Thailand	10	8	6
Ceylon	6	4	5
Others	10	18	12
	100	100	100

Synthetic rubber trade

('000 met. tons)	Imports	Exports
1968	880	1 034
1963-5 av.	635	751[1]

[1] U.S.A., Canada and Netherlands .. 68%

Cotton Yarn

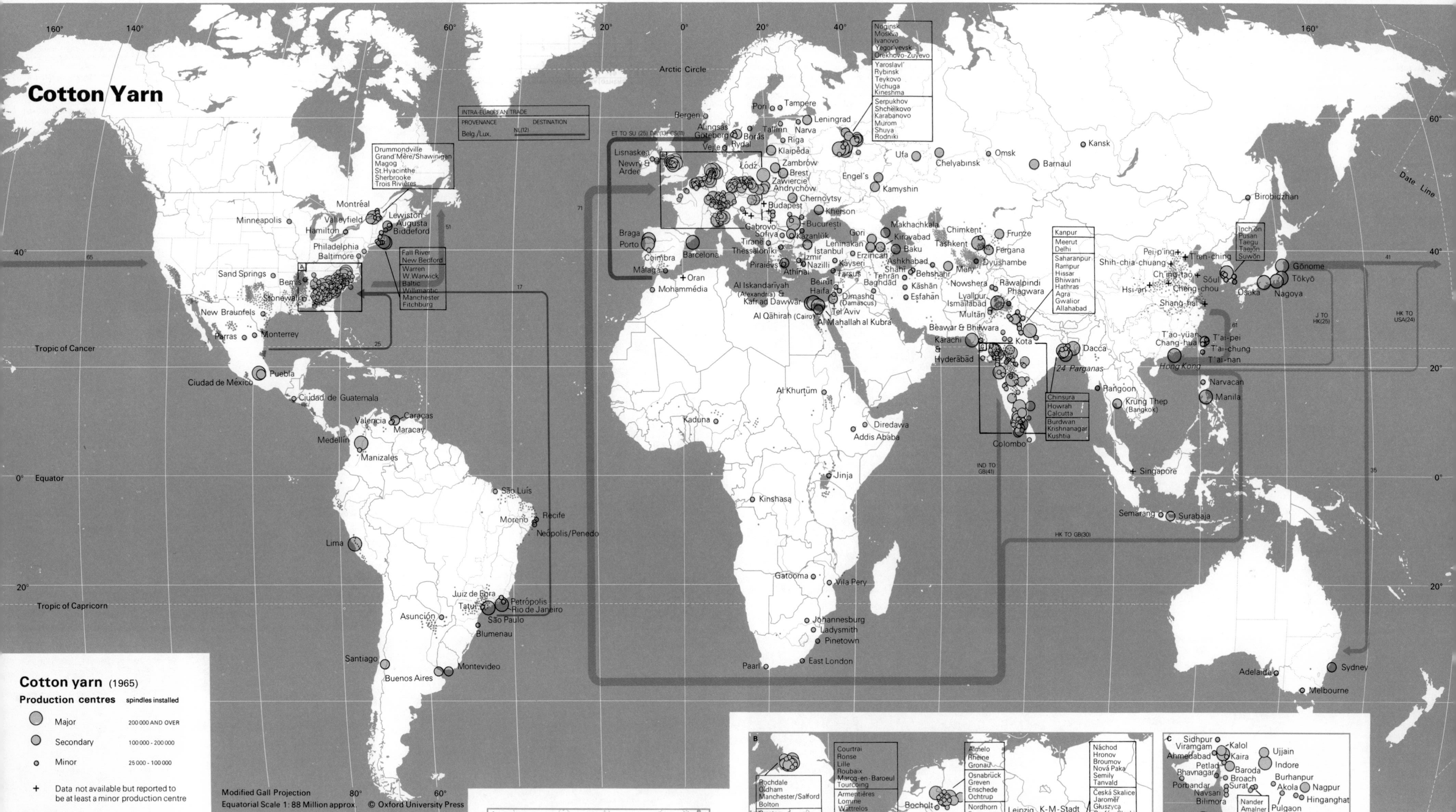

Cotton yarn (1965)

Production centres spindles installed

◯	Major	200 000 AND OVER
◯	Secondary	100 000 - 200 000
○	Minor	25 000 - 100 000
+	Data not available but reported to be at least a minor production centre	

Cotton lint

One dot represents 100 000 met. tons of cotton lint production

Major trade flows (1966)

Commodity: S.I.T.C.no.

COTTON YARN	(AND THREAD)	651.3/4
COTTON CLOTH	(NOT MADE UP)	652.1/2

Value ($U.S.)
0.5mm represents increments of $20 million

($ MILLIONS) 180 100 20

51 VALUE IN $ MILLIONS

Cotton yarn production

8 131 000 met. tons 1963-5 av.[1]
6 958 000 1953-5 av.[1]

	PERCENTAGE 1963-5 av.	1953-5 av.
U.S.A.	23	24
U.S.S.R.	16	14
India	11	10
Japan	6	6
Germany F.R.	5	5
France	4	4
Pakistan	3	1
U.K.	3	5
Italy	2	2
Others	27	29
	100	100

[1]Excl. China P.R.

Cotton spindles

Number installed, end of year
130 495 000 1965
103 400 000 1955[1]

	PERCENTAGE 1965	1955
U.S.A.	15	22
India	12	11
Japan	10	8
U.S.S.R.	10	...[1]
China P.R.	9	NA
Germany F.R.	4	6
U.K.	3	11
Italy	3	5
France	3	7
Others	31	NA
	100	100

[1]Excl. U.S.S.R.

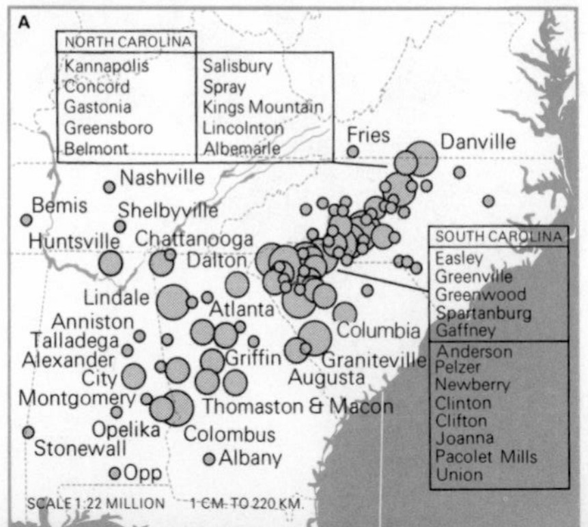

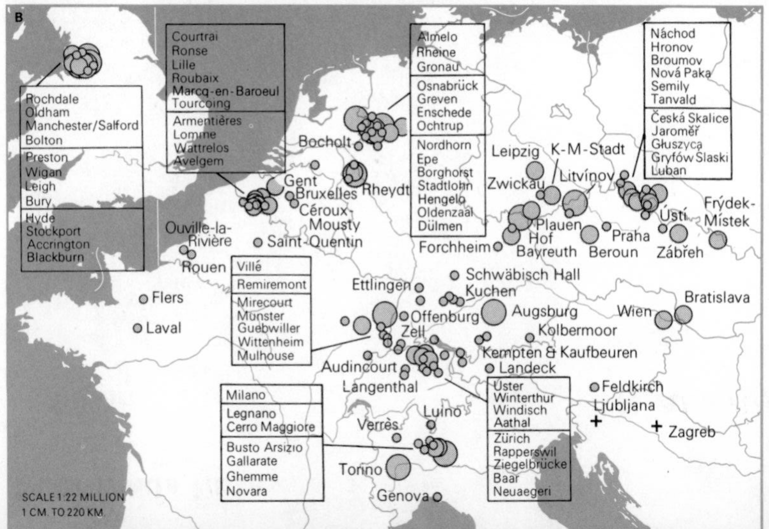

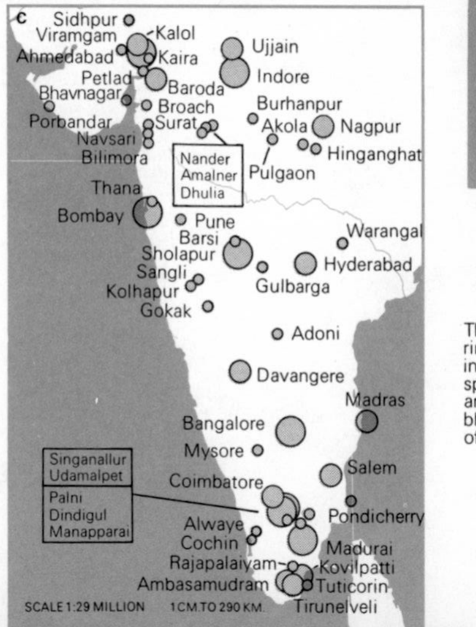

This map shows ring spindles installed for spinning cotton and cotton blend yarn as of 1965.

Cotton lint

Production (1963–5 av.)

One dot represents 5 000 met. tons

Major trade flows (1966)

Commodity: S.I.T.C. No. COTTON: 263

Value ($U.S.)

0.5mm. represents increments of $20 million

260 ($ MILLIONS) 180 100 20

32 VALUE IN $ MILLIONS

Cotton statistics

PERCENTAGES UNLESS OTHERWISE STATED — MET. TONS

		U.S.A.	U.S.S.R.	CHINA P.R.	INDIA	BRAZIL	MEXICO	U.A.R.	PAKISTAN	TURKEY	JAPAN	GERMANY F.R.	OTHERS	WORLD
Lint consumption	**1963-5 av.**	**18**	**14**	**12**	**11**	**3**	**1**	**1**	**3**	**1**	**7**	**3**	**26**	**10 737 000**
production	**1963-5 av.**	**29**	**16**	**10**	**9**	**6**	**5**	**4**	**4**	**3**	—	—	**14**	**11 493 000**
	1953-5 av.	*44*	...[1]	*10*	*10*	*5*	*5*	*5*	*4*	*2*	—	—	*15*	*7 367 000*[1]
Yield kg. per hectare	**1963-5 av.**	**583**	**740**	**261**	**131**	**217**	**649**	**687**	**263**	**452**	...	...	...	NA
Seed production	**1963-5 av.**	**26**	**17**	**11**	**10**	**6**	**5**	**4**	—	**2**	—	—	**19**	**21 285 000**
	1953-5 av.	*41*	...[1]	*11*	*11*	*6*	*5*	*5*	—	*2*	—	—	*19*	*13 733 000*[1]

[1] Excl. U.S.S.R.

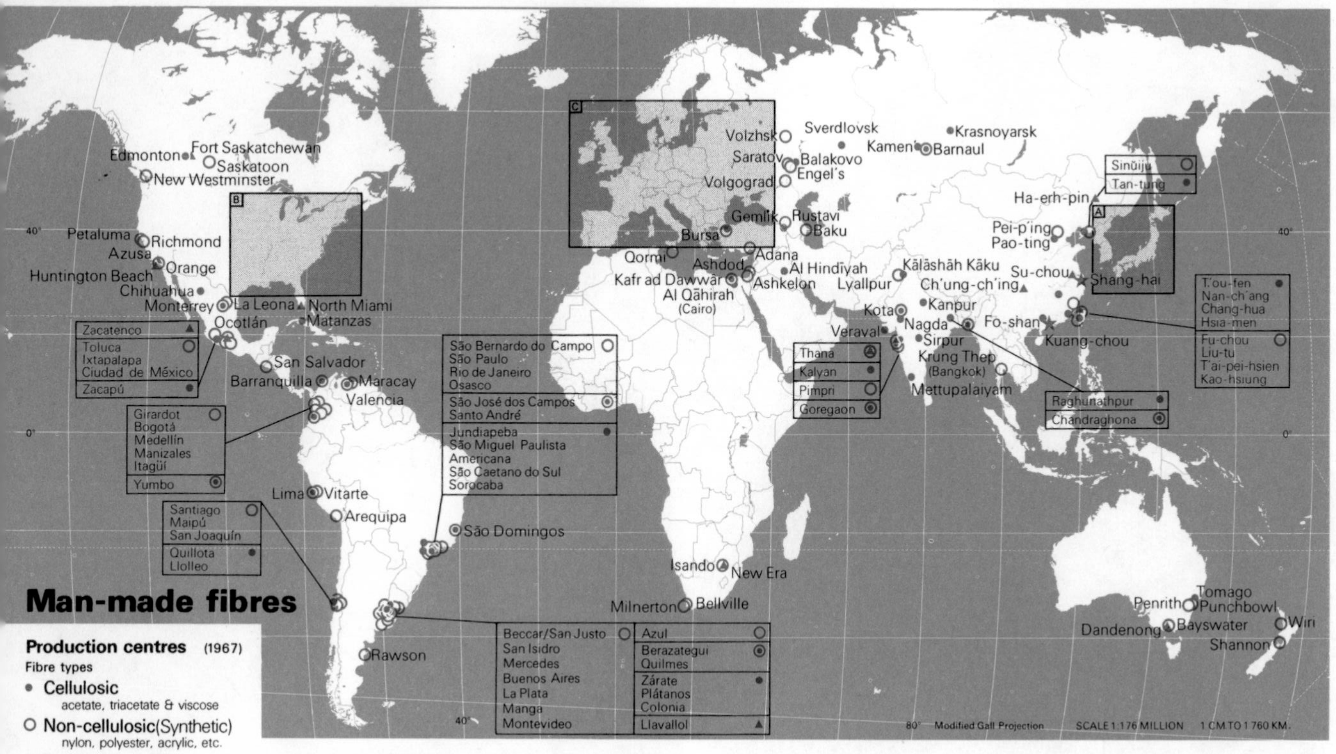

Man-made fibres

Production centres (1967)

Fibre types

- ● Cellulosic — acetate, triacetate & viscose
- ○ Non-cellulosic (Synthetic) — nylon, polyester, acrylic, etc.
- ▲ Textile glass fibre
- ★ All of the above

Major trade flows (1966)

Trade flows in synthetic and regenerated yarn are predominantly intra-European although flows within Asia and North America are also important. The main flows are from the Netherlands to Germany F.R. and from Japan to S. Korea.

Man-made yarn/staple

PERCENTAGE — MET. TONS

Major producers		U.S.A.	JAPAN	U.S.S.R.	GERMANY F.R.	U.K.	ITALY	GERMANY D.R.	FRANCE	POLAND	NETHERLANDS	CANADA	OTHERS	WORLD
Cellulosic	**1963-5 av.**	**20**	**15**	**9**	**9**	**7**	**6**	**5**	**4**	**2**	**2**	**2**	**19**	**3 227 903**
	1953-5 av.	*26*	*14*	*4*	*10*	*9*	*6*	*6*	*5*	*2*	*2*	*2*	*14*	*2 065 904*
Non-cellulosic	**1963-5 av.**	**39**	**19**	**3**	**8**	**7**	**6**	**1**	**5**	**1**	**2**	**2**	**7**	**1 692 053**
	1953-5 av.	*67*	*5*	*2*	*4*	*6*	*3*	*1*	*4*	*1*	*1*	*3*	*3*	*205 856*

Man-made fibres

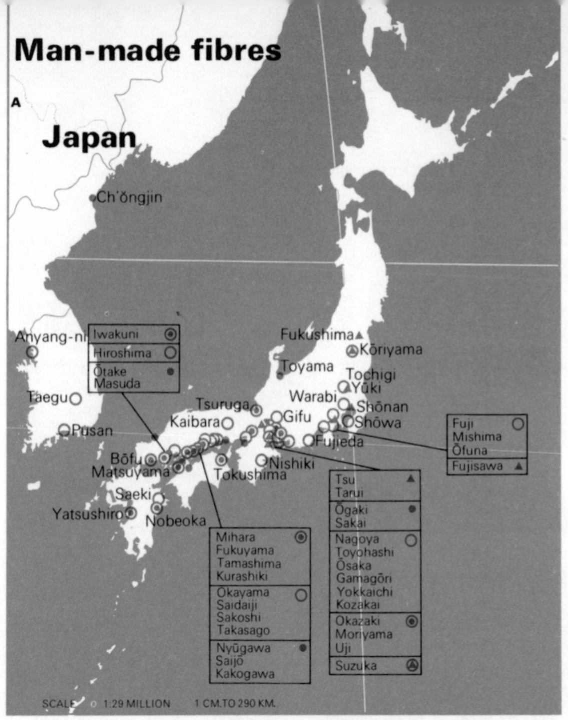

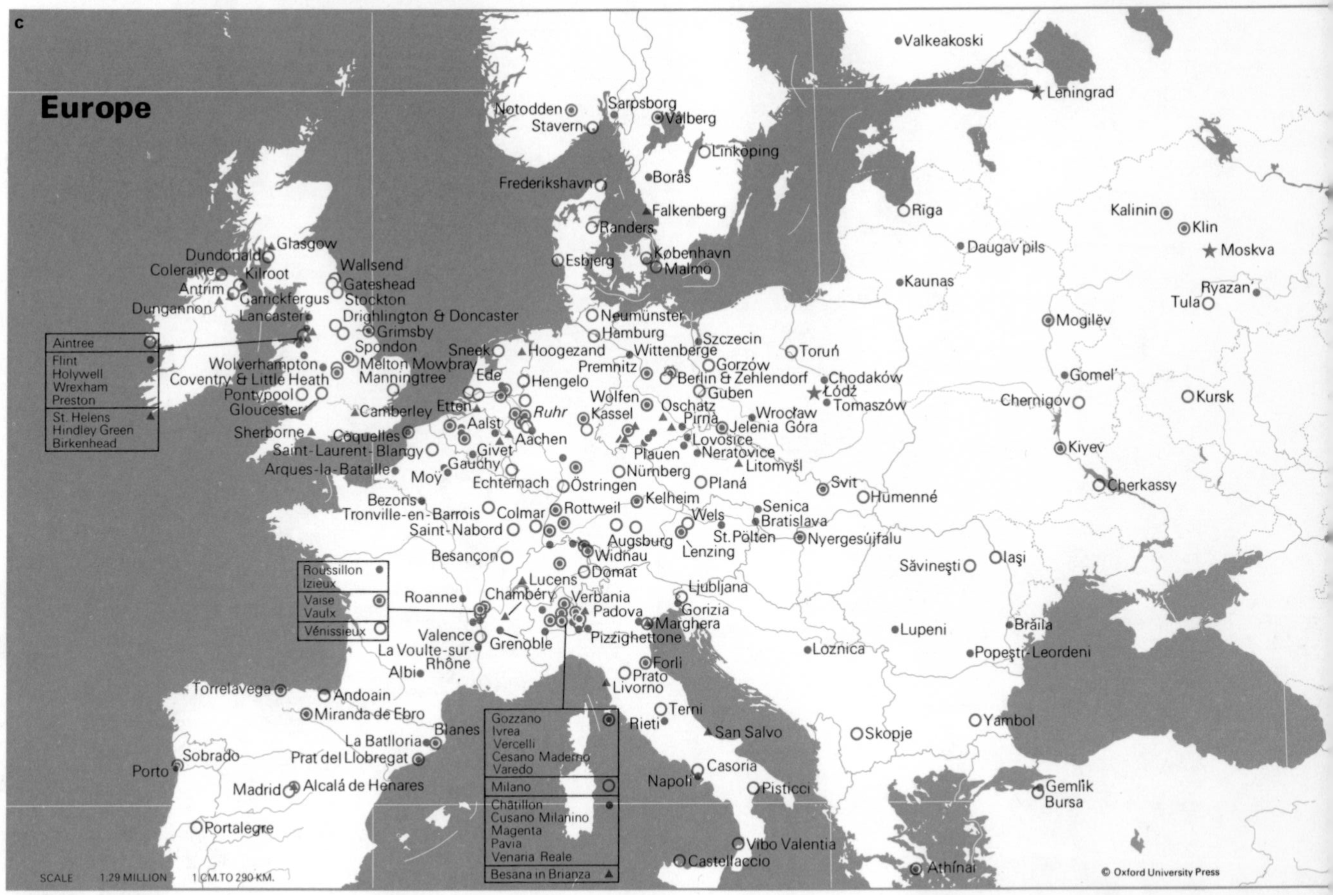

Total production of man-made fibre in 1965 was 5 389 000 metric tons, 62% of which was cellulosic fibre. Non-cellulosic production was over two-thirds as large as rayon production and increasing rapidly. 1968 producing capacity was more than double the actual 1965 production and sixteen times that of 1955.

The main types of non-cellulosic fibre are:

1. Nylon (Polyamide), based on coal, petroleum and castor oil;
2. Acrylic (Acrilan, Courtelle, Orlon, etc.);
3. Polyester (Terylene, Dacron, etc.);
4. Other fibres such as Vinyl, Azlon, Olefin, Saran, Spandex, Vinyon, Alginate and TFE-fluorocarbon.

In 1965 of a total of 2 050 700 metric tons produced, 50% was nylon, 22% was polyester and 20% was acrylic and modacrylic. Rayon is regenerated cellulose, (viscose or cuprammonium depending on the process of manufacture). Acetate and triacetate are cellulose acetate. In 1965 76% of the world output of rayon and acetate filament yarn was of the viscose type. Rayon can be produced as continuous filament ready for weaving or as staple cut into short lengths which subsequently can be spun into yarn.

Textile glass fibre is glass in the form of fine threads twisted into yarns and cords and subsequently woven into cloth and tape. These threads can be finer than human hair and may look and feel like silk. The fibres are stronger than steel and will not burn, stretch, rot or fade.

Energy

For individual country data see Statistical Supplement

Large supplies of energy are a vital adjunct to our present way of life. The process of industrialization which has improved living standards for the people of many countries, requires a plentiful energy source. Between 1958 and 1968 world consumption of energy rose almost continuously both absolutely and on a per capita basis.

Energy sources are normally classified into two categories: primary and secondary fuels. Primary fuels are those which occur naturally such as coal, crude oil, natural gas, peat, wood and dung. Whilst the last three of these are important sources of energy in certain countries, such as India, available data on consumption are poor and, with the occasional exception of peat, they are rarely included in official statistics. Three other primary fuels are hydro, nuclear and geothermal energy which are used to produce the secondary fuel, electricity. Other secondary fuels are manufactured gas, various manufactured solid fuels and refined oil products.

The distribution of energy sources throughout the world is governed by geological and geographical factors. However the pattern of production differs from that of consumption because the consumption of energy is linked with stages of economic development. North America is able to produce approximately enough energy from its own resources, but Western Europe has to import over half of its consumption, whereas in 1968 Western Asia exported twelve times its own total energy consumption, principally in the form of oil. The world balance of energy production and consumption is shown on the table below.

Energy production and consumption

In kg. per capita of coal equivalent (1963-5 av.)

	PRODUCTION	CONSUMPTION
North America[1]	8 032	8 732
Western Asia[2]	5 765	469
Caribbean America[3]	2 962	939
Oceania	2 297	3 416
Western Europe	1 702	2 980
U.S.S.R./China P.R./ Eastern Europe	1 467	1 392
Africa	527	270
Other America[4]	362	569
Far East	198	306
World average	1 572	1 543

[1]Mainly Canada and U.S.A.
[2]Mainly Middle East
[3]Incl. Caribbean islands, Central America, Colombia and Venezuela
[4]South America excl. Colombia and Venezuela

Until the end of the 1960's solid fuel had been the major energy source for the world. However by 1968 this position had been taken over by liquid fuels. Third was natural gas which has grown rapidly in importance. Hydro, nuclear and geothermal energy accounted for only 2% of world consumption.

In absolute terms, world-wide consumption of solid fuel has increased, but it has declined in certain areas and countries. In most areas, the decrease in the share of energy consumption held by solid fuel has occurred since the beginning of the 1950's, although in North America, which has large indigenous oil and gas resources, it started much earlier. The increasing importance of liquid fuels has been due partly to the rapid growth in transport, where liquid fuels have a captive market, and partly to substitution for solid fuel. This substitution has been caused both by technical factors which enable liquid fuel to be used more easily than solid fuel and also by a favourable price ratio. Because of the ease of transport by pipeline or tanker, the growth of liquid fuel consumption has occurred in practically all countries, whereas natural gas use has been concentrated in countries with indigenous sources. Although the share of hydro and nuclear electricity has remained fairly static over many years, increasing numbers of nuclear power stations are now being planned throughout the world.

There are three main types of **coal** which, in descending order of thermal value, are anthracite, bituminous coal and lignite (or brown coal). The coal reserves of the world are extremely large and those that have been measured could supply several hundred times the present annual consumption. About 60% of the world reserves are believed to lie in the U.S.S.R. with about another 15% in both the U.S.A. and China P.R.

Most coal is obtained from deep mines as opposed to open-cast mines where only a thin layer of top soil needs to be removed to expose the coal seams. In industrialized countries, the most easily worked seams have already been mined and consequently strenuous efforts are being made to mechanize production in deep mines in order to make it economic to extract coal from thin seams in geologically difficult conditions. The great bulk of all the coal mined is either burnt directly as a fuel or is converted into other solid fuels such as coke. Only certain types of bituminous coal have the correct coking qualities, and the major buyer of such coals is the steel industry. When coking coals are heated in a sealed oven with little air, the volatile matter is driven off and the coke, mainly fixed carbon, remains. Coke is an essential material in steel-making as it is used in the blast furnaces which smelt the iron ore.

About $1\frac{1}{2}$ tons of coal are needed to produce 1 ton of coke, and the volatile matter driven off in the carbonization process can itself be used for heating purposes. This gas may be used in the steel works or added to town (coal) gas supplies. It can also be used for manufacturing certain chemicals such as dyes, detergents and plastics. In industrial countries the principal uses of coal burnt directly are electricity production, steam raising in industry and domestic heating. Coal may also be used to produce synthetic gasoline (petrol) and this, together with the underground gasification of coal, may provide new markets for coal in the future.

Crude oil varies considerably in composition and appearance both between countries and between fields in a country. The major impurity is sulphur, in various compound forms, which is released as sulphur dioxide when the oil is burnt. With increasing concern about air pollution, those oils with a low sulphur content, notably from North Africa, are becoming more valuable. The most important refined oil products are gasoline and fuel oils, the former being used for transport and the latter mainly for providing heat in, for example, industrial furnaces. Only about 10% of oil consumption is used for non-energy purposes.

Over the last 30 years, there has been a steady movement of oil refining away from the producing areas to the consuming areas. This movement has been due to both economic and strategic factors. As oil consumption has increased, the cost of shipping crude oil and building medium size refineries close to the demand centres has become less than that of putting large refineries on the oilfields and shipping refined products. From the strategic viewpoint, the increasing importance of oil in the consuming countries meant that supply disruptions were increasingly serious, but home-based refineries can be adjusted to take crude oil from alternative supply sources. In addition, the producing countries have realized the value of what is, in many cases, their only natural asset and their ability to dictate, with limits, their own supply terms. The Organization of Petroleum Exporting Countries (OPEC) has been formed to increase their bargaining power through the presentation of a united front.

Natural gas occurs both alone and in conjunction with oil, and its principal component is methane. Much of the natural gas occurring with oil is burnt at the point of production because of the difficulty of transporting it to the consuming areas. However pipeline development in the United States in the 1920's and 1930's led to natural gas taking an increasing share of the energy market there. The rising world-wide demand for energy has increased exploration, and new reserves of natural gas have been found so that proved reserves now total about half those of oil. Technical developments are making it economic to liquefy natural gas and transport it in refrigerated tankers to other countries, and several inter-country pipelines are under construction.

Natural gas must, like oil, be produced from wells at a steady rate in order to obtain the maximum percentage of the reserves but, unlike oil, it cannot easily be stored. In order to meet fluctuations in demand either liquefied gas storage tanks are used or the gas is pumped into naturally occurring underground reservoirs. Natural gas is an attractive fuel as it is non-toxic, virtually free of sulphur and has a calorific value twice that of coal gas. Being sulphur-free, it can be used for direct process heating in industry without affecting the product, so it has a premium value over oil. However for general use in steam raising it must compete directly on price. Whilst the bulk of the natural gas is used by industry, a large proportion also goes into the domestic market for heating and cooking. The availability of natural gas has supplanted coal or oil in the town gas industry, as the higher calorific value doubles the capacity of the existing assets and the price is usually very much lower than that of manufactured gas. Natural gas can also be used as a chemical feedstock.

Particularly in the U.S.A., natural gas has been identified with 'total energy' schemes whereby all the energy requirements in an establishment are supplied by the one fuel. A gas-driven engine connected to a generator provides the electrical requirements and the exhaust heat from the engine is used, together with more gas if necessary, to supply the heating requirements. Whilst the thermal efficiency of such schemes is high, the increased capital cost remains a barrier to their widespread adoption.

Electricity is a versatile and refined fuel capable of providing services such as lighting, heating and motive power with great flexibility. Throughout the world, its importance in the energy market has increased very rapidly. Although the overland transmission of electricity is relatively simple, so that inter-country exchanges are quite important, very few undersea connections have been built owing to technical difficulties. Two factors which put constraints on the type of plant used and hence on the final selling price of the fuel are that it is not economically feasible to store electricity in large quantities and that the majority of electricity is produced from other primary fuels through a conversion process which is only about 30% efficient. In order to eliminate the remaining heat large quantities of cooling water are used so plants are sited on rivers, lakes or the coast.

For many decades, the demand for electricity has increased by over 7% per annum and growth rates much higher than this are occurring in those countries beginning a period of industrialization. Out of a total world production of over 4 200 000 million kilowatt hours in 1968, 26% was supplied by the primary sources of hydro, geothermal and nuclear energy and the remainder by the conversion of the other primary fuels. In any particular area, the choice of fuel to generate electricity is mainly a function of the relative capital costs of the various types of plant, the expected future cost and availability of the various fuels, the existing generating system and the expected growth in electrical load. Although the capital costs of hydro and nuclear generating plants are high, in relation to fossil-fuel fired ones, their running costs are very low. As the capital costs of fossil-fuel fired plant burning either coal, oil, gas or peat are very similar, the choice between them depends mainly on the local cost and availability of each fuel.

Hydro-electric schemes use a flow of water from a river, which may be retained by a dam, to drive turbines which in turn drive electricity generators. Although in some countries nearly all the electricity is generated this way, the hydro-electric share of world production has been decreasing. The cheapest sites have already been developed, and the relative economics have changed in favour of fossil-fuel fired power stations. However the world potential for hydro-electricity is basically untapped. In many cases, the hydro-electric plant is only part of a general irrigation scheme so that the resource, water, can have more than one use. Given favourable conditions it is also possible to make use of the energy in the tides, and one such scheme is in operation on the Rance estuary in Northern France. Another variant which is being developed is pumped storage, where water is pumped to a high-level reservoir when the electrical load on the system is low and is then released at peak times to generate electricity in the normal way.

Geothermal energy is unimportant on a world scale, being only about half of one percent of hydro generation, but power stations based on steam wells are operating in such countries as the United States, New Zealand, Iceland, Mexico and Italy.

Nuclear energy arises from the heat generated by the fission of uranium atoms. In natural uranium the component isotope U_{235}, which represents only 0.7% of the metal, is fissile and emits neutrons. When the nucleus of a U_{235} atom is struck by a neutron the atom splits into two, releasing more neutrons which in turn strike other nuclei and hence sustain a chain reaction. Large quantities of heat are emitted by such a reaction. This heat can be transferred to a coolant and, through heat exchangers, used to raise steam for turbines. In order to slow down the speed of the neutrons to make the chain reaction sustainable and controllable a moderator is needed. Three types have been developed and are in commercial use. The United States has concentrated on light water moderated and cooled systems, Canada and Sweden on heavy water moderator and coolant and France and the U.K. on the gas-cooled, graphite-moderated system.

An important aspect of nuclear reactors is that some of the non-fissile uranium isotope U_{238} is converted into plutonium, which is fissile. A prototype reactor, using plutonium, is being built in the U.K. with liquid sodium as the coolant. Another fissile isotope is U_{233}, and it is possible that this could be bred from thorium. A more remote possibility is that the fusion of two separate nuclei, which also produces large quantities of heat, could be used to produce electricity. However this process has yet to be handled successfully even in the laboratory.

Nuclear power plants are still relatively new, and the oldest commercial plant is far from retirement so the technical problems of dealing with the safety of obsolete radio-active plant have still to be tackled in practice. Small experimental reactors have, of course, been dismantled satisfactorily.

Most electricity is not used directly, but it is an integral part of industrialized society because of the widespread use of lighting, electric motors, communications and countless other devices. One direct use of electricity is in electro-chemistry including the manufacture of chlorine and ozone, the manufacture of aluminium from its oxide and in copper refining. Electricity can also be used directly in the fabrication of components by electro-discharge techniques either induced magnetically or through a fluid. Such techniques are being used in the U.S.A. in the aerospace industry. Machining can also be done electrically either by electrochemical corrosion, spark erosion or glow discharge techniques. Material cutting, which is difficult by mechanical methods at high speeds, can also be done electrically by electron beams, lasers or plasmas. Paint deposition on variable contour surfaces can be aided electrically by the use of electrostatic fields.

The use of electricity in the transport industry is also expanding. The advantages of electric traction on the railways, given heavily used lines, are being increasingly realized and even higher speed travel is promised by the hovertrain which can be driven by a newly developed linear type of electric motor. Electric vehicles are at present confined to short distance service operations because of the energy storage limitations of the lead-acid battery. However the potential advantages of electric vehicles have led to battery research throughout the world and several experimental batteries are under consideration.

The future development of the various energy industries is part of a complex economic process. Many of the decisions taken by a particular industry react on the others both nationally and internationally and on society as a whole by, for example, the resulting impact on the landscape, water resources and the atmosphere. Although techniques are being developed to attempt to quantify these 'external' effects a substantial amount of subjective judgement must still be used in order to balance the conflicting requirements that exist.

Production and consumption of fuel and energy (1963-5 av.)

Million metric tons coal equivalent

Regional totals	Solid fuel[1,2]	Liquid fuel[3]	Natural gas[1]	H.E.P./ Nuclear energy
Production				
Consumption				
World totals				
Production	2 225	1 865	871	107
Consumption	2 218	1 783	865	107

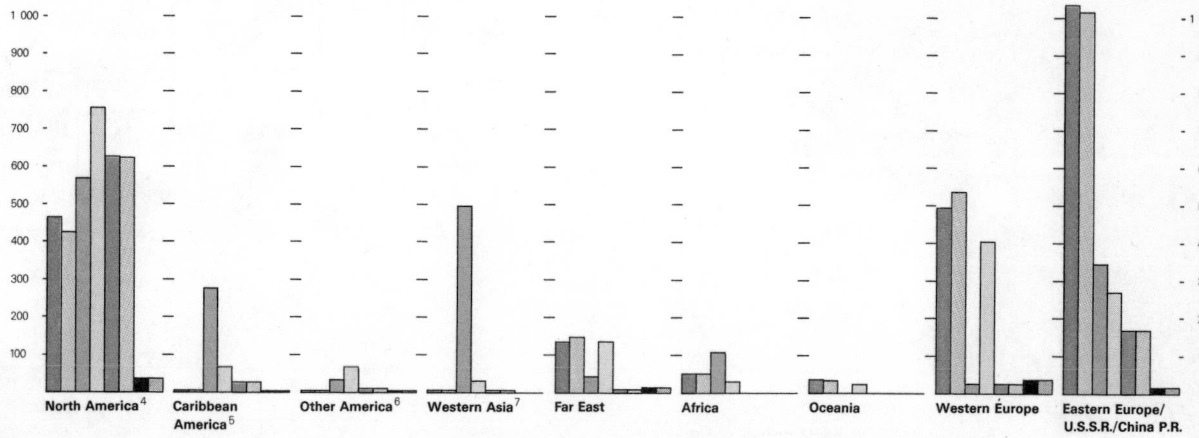

[1]External trade in coke and manufactured gas is subtracted from the consumption of the exporting country and added to that of the importing country [2]Mainly coal and lignite but incl. peat where important; excl. wood and dung [3]Consumption for energy purposes only [4]Canada, U.S.A., Greenland and St. Pierre/Miquelon [5]Incl. Colombia and Venezuela [6]South America excl. Colombia and Venezuela [7]Bahrain, Cyprus, Iran, Iraq, Israel, Jordan, Kuwait, Lebanon, Neutral Zone, Qatar, Saudi Arabia, Southern Yemen, Syria, Trucial Oman, Turkey and Yemen

Natural Gas

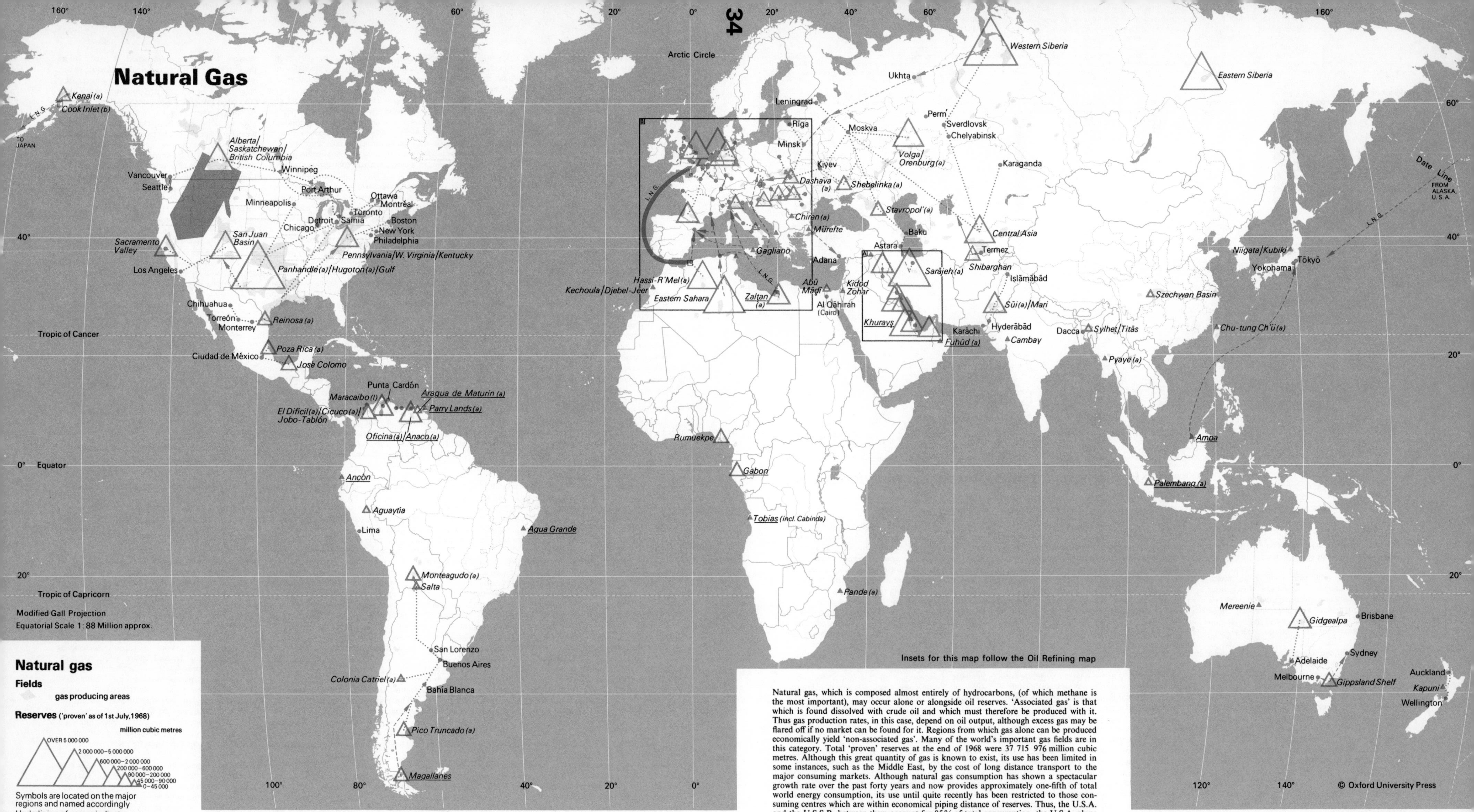

Natural gas

Fields

gas producing areas

Reserves ('proven' as of 1st July, 1968)

million cubic metres

OVER 5 000 000
2 000 000–5 000 000
600 000–2 000 000
200 000–600 000
90 000–200 000
45 000–90 000
0–45 000

Symbols are located on the major regions and named accordingly
Underlining of names indicates that reserves are found predominantly in association with crude oil;
e.g. *Mereenie* ; *Ampa*

Annual movements (1967)

- where international trade is below 500 million cu. metres
- Thereafter every additional 500 million cu. metres is shown by 0.5 mm. width, thus represents 1 000 million cu. m.
- major internal movements (not quantified)
- planned internal and international movements
- L.N.G. Liquified Natural Gas movements
- □ liquefaction plants
- • centres of distribution and/or consumption

Natural gas, which is composed almost entirely of hydrocarbons, (of which methane is the most important), may occur alone or alongside oil reserves. 'Associated gas' is that which is found dissolved with crude oil and which must therefore be produced with it. Thus gas production rates, in this case, depend on oil output, although excess gas may be flared off if no market can be found for it. Regions from which gas alone can be produced economically yield 'non-associated gas'. Many of the world's important gas fields are in this category. Total 'proven' reserves at the end of 1968 were 37 715 976 million cubic metres. Although this great quantity of gas is known to exist, its use has been limited in some instances, such as the Middle East, by the cost of long distance transport to the major consuming markets. Although natural gas consumption has shown a spectacular growth rate over the past forty years and now provides approximately one-fifth of total world energy consumption, its use until quite recently has been restricted to those consuming centres which are within economical piping distance of reserves. Thus, the U.S.A. and the U.S.S.R. between them account for 85% of total consumption, the U.S.A. alone accounting for 65%. This pattern is now showing signs of change. The more recent discovery of reserves of non-associated gas in the North Sea, the Netherlands, Algeria, Australia and many other countries and the development of new transport techniques, has meant the emergence of the great energy market of Europe as a market for gas. Other regions and countries have also become gas markets in recent years. Natural gas can be liquified by cooling it to –258°F (–161°C) when it is known as L.N.G. (Liquified Natural Gas). L.N.G. occupies only 1/600th of its previous volume, thus transport in specially insulated tankers is possible. L.N.G. links have been established between Arzew (Algeria) and Canvey Island (U.K.) and Le Havre (France), between Alaska and Japan and between Libya and Italy and Spain. Other L.N.G. movements are in the active planning or construction phase. The propane and butane elements of natural gas can also be stripped out and are then known as L.P.G. (Liquified Petroleum Gas). When liquified they occupy only 1/250th of their original volume, and can be stored and shipped in relatively small quantities economically. L.P.G. supply links between Kuwait, Saudi Arabia, Iran and Japan already exist; there are also links between Venezuela and Brazil and Argentina, and other trans-ocean movements are projected. At present the percentage of total energy requirements met by natural gas varies greatly from 34% in the U.S.A. and 17% in the U.S.S.R. to 5% in France. It is estimated that Europe as a whole will meet some 11% of her energy demand with natural gas by 1975, although of course the percentage will be higher in certain individual countries, for example the Netherlands.

Natural gas 'proven' reserves

(as of 1st July, 1968)

37 626 000 million cu. metres

	PERCENTAGE	
Eastern Europe/China	*25*	
U.S.S.R.		24
North America	*25*	
U.S.A.		22
Middle East	*17*	
Iran		8
Kuwait		3
Saudi Arabia		3
Africa	*13*	
Algeria		11
Western Europe	*11*	
Netherlands		6
U.K.		2
Latin America	*5*	
Asia Pacific	*4*	

Natural gas production

821 650 million cubic metres 1967
704 130 million 1965
300 450 million 1955

	PERCENTAGE 1967	1965	1955
U.S.A.	63	65	*89*
U.S.S.R.	19	18	*3*
Canada	6	6	*1*
Romania	2	2	*2*
Mexico	2	2	—
Italy	1	1	*1*
Venezuela	1	1	*1*
Netherlands	1	—	—
France	1	1	—
Others	4	4	*3*
	100	100	*100*

Natural gas consumption

816 720 million cubic metres 1967
700 730 million 1965
(equivalent data for 1955 not available)

	KG. PER CAPITA 1967	PERCENTAGE 1967	1965
U.S.A.	697	64	66
U.S.S.R.	208	19	18
Canada	47	4	4
Romania	25	2	2
Mexico	19	2	2
Italy	12	1	1
Venezuela	10	1	1
France	8	1	1
Netherlands	8	1	—
Others	...	5	5
		100	100

Natural gas exports

21 640 million cubic metres 1967
15 180 million 1965
1 279 million 1955

	PERCENTAGE 1967	1965	1955
Canada	66	75	*25*
U.S.A.	8	5	*69*
Mexico	7	10	—
U.S.S.R.	6	3	—
Algeria	5	5	—
Netherlands	5	—	—
Afghanistan	1	—	—
Romania	1	1	—
Others	1	1	*6*
	100	100	*100*

Natural gas imports

21 940 million cubic metres 1967
15 120 million 1965
1 257 million 1955

	PERCENTAGE 1967	1965	1955
U.S.A.	73	85	*25*
Canada	7	3	*25*
Poland	5	3	*44*
U.K.	3	4	—
France	3	1	—
Belg./Lux.	2	—	—
Germany F.R.	2	—	—
Mexico	2	2	—
Czechoslovakia	1	—	—
Others	2	2	*6*
	100	100	*100*

Crude Oil

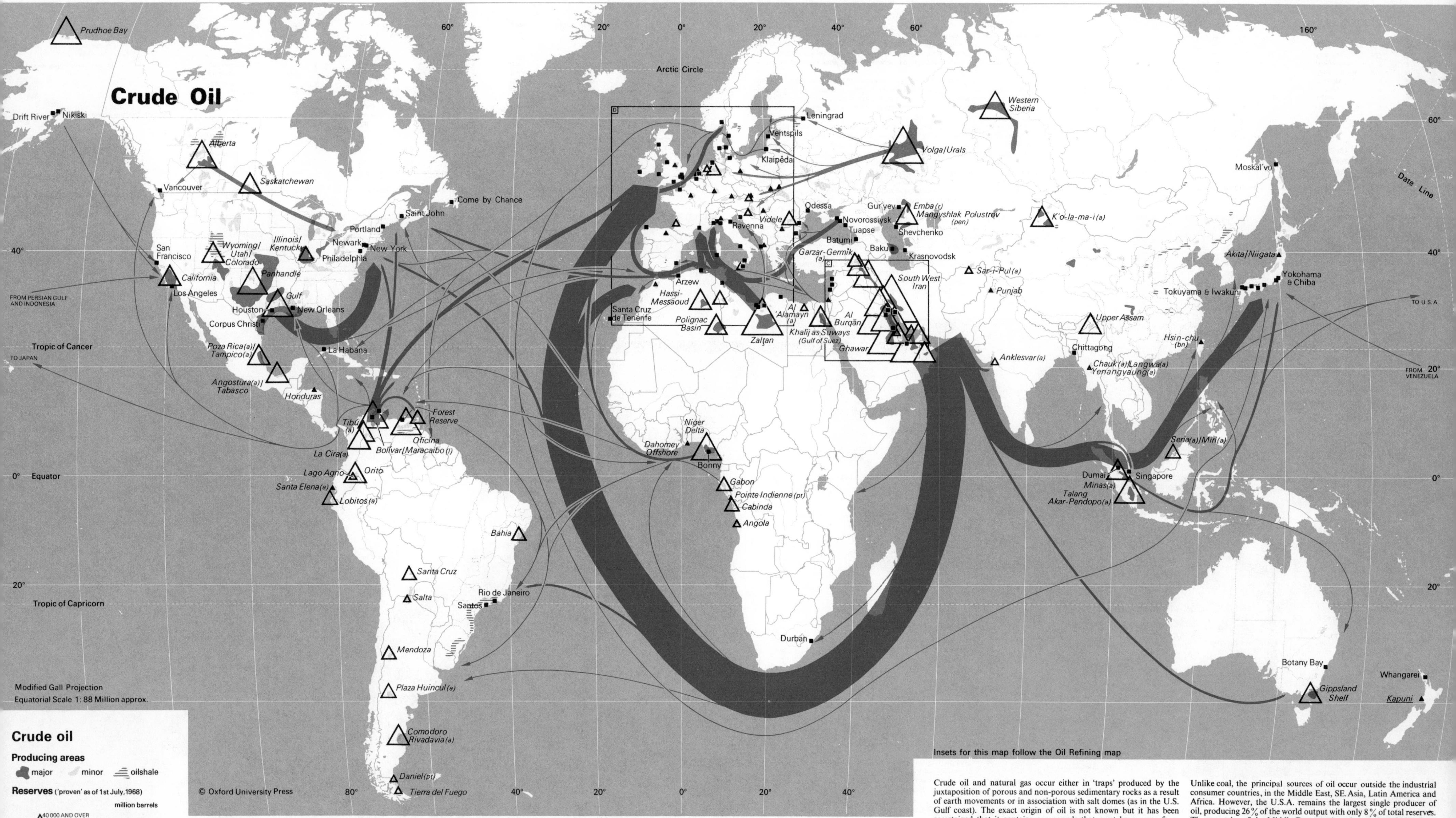

Crude oil

Producing areas

major · minor · oilshale

Reserves ('proven' as of 1st July, 1968)

million barrels

40 000 AND OVER
17 500–40 000
4 500–17 500
900–4 500
350–900
100–350
UNDER 100

Symbols are located on the major regions

Kapuni — underlining indicates condensate reserves only

Annual movements (1967)

→ where movement is below 45 million barrels

Thereafter every additional 90 million barrels is shown by 0.5 mm. width, thus: represents 180 million barrels

■ major tanker terminals

One barrel of crude oil (world average gravity) is equal to 0.137 metric tons

Crude oil 'proven' reserves

453 526 million barrels (1st July 1968)

	PERCENTAGE	
Middle East	*59*	
South Arabia		17
Kuwait		15
Iran		12
East Europe/China	*12*	
U.S.S.R.		8
Africa	*10*	
Libya		7
North America	*9*	
U.S.A.		7
Latin America	*7*	
Venezuela		3
Asia Pacific	*3*	
Indonesia		2
Europe	—	

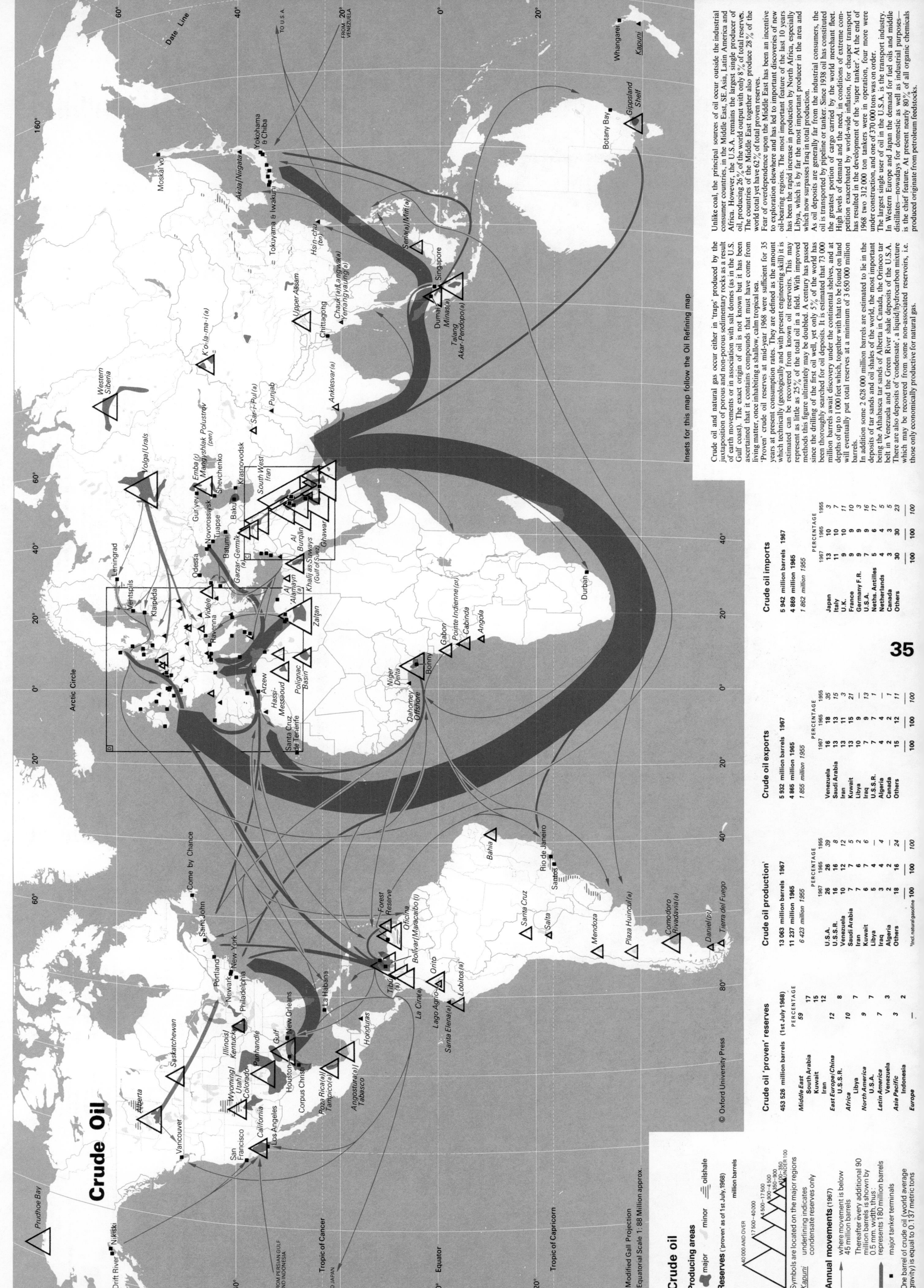

Crude oil production[1]

13 063 million barrels 1967
11 237 million 1965
6 423 million 1955

	1967	1965	1955
U.S.A.	26	26	*39*
U.S.S.R.	16	16	*8*
Venezuela	10	12	*12*
Saudi Arabia	7	7	*5*
Iran	7	6	*2*
Kuwait	6	7	*6*
Libya	5	4	—
Iraq	3	4	*4*
Algeria	2	2	—
Others	18	16	*24*
	100	100	*100*

[1]Incl. natural gasoline

Crude oil exports

5 932 million barrels 1967
4 865 million 1965
1 855 million 1955

	1967	1965	1955
Venezuela	16	18	*35*
Saudi Arabia	13	13	*15*
Iran	13	11	*3*
Kuwait	13	15	*21*
Libya	10	9	—
Iraq	7	9	*13*
U.S.S.R.	7	7	*1*
Algeria	4	4	—
Canada	2	2	*1*
Others	15	12	*11*
	100	100	*100*

Crude oil imports

5 942 million barrels 1967
4 869 million 1965
1 862 million 1955

	1967	1965	1955
Japan	13	10	*3*
Italy	11	10	*7*
U.K.	9	10	*11*
France	9	9	*10*
Germany F.R.	9	9	*3*
U.S.A.	7	9	*16*
Neths. Antilles	5	6	*17*
Netherlands	4	4	*5*
Canada	3	3	*5*
Others	30	30	*23*
	100	100	*100*

Insets for this map follow the Oil Refining map

Crude oil and natural gas occur either in 'traps' produced by the juxtaposition of porous and non-porous sedimentary rocks as a result of earth movements or in association with salt domes (as in the U.S. Gulf coast). The exact origin of oil is not known but it has been ascertained that it contains compounds that must have come from living matter, once inhabiting a shallow, calm tropical sea.

'Proven' crude oil reserves at mid-year 1968 were sufficient for 35 years at present consumption rates. They are defined as the amount which technically (geologically and with present engineering skill) it is estimated can be recovered from known oil reservoirs. This may represent as little as 25% of the total oil in a field. With improved methods this figure ultimately may be doubled. A century has passed since the drilling of the first oil well, yet only 5% of the world has been thoroughly searched for oil deposits. It is estimated that 73 000 million barrels await discovery under the continental shelves, and at depths of up to 1 000 feet which, together with that to be found on land will eventually put total reserves at a minimum of 3 650 000 million barrels.

In addition some 2 628 000 million barrels are estimated to lie in the deposits of tar sands and oil shales of the world, the most important being the Athabasca tar sands of Alberta in Canada, the Orinoco tar belt in Venezuela and the Green River shale deposits of the U.S.A. There are also deposits of 'condensate', a liquid/hydrocarbon mixture which may be recovered from some non-associated reservoirs, i.e. those only economically productive for natural gas.

Unlike coal, the principal sources of oil occur outside the industrial consumer countries, in the Middle East, SE. Asia, Latin America and Africa. However, the U.S.A. remains the largest single producer of oil, producing 26% of the world output with only 8% of total reserves. The countries of the Middle East together also produce 28% of the world total yet have 62% of total proven reserves.

Fear of overdependence upon the Middle East has been an incentive to exploration elsewhere and has led to important discoveries of new oil-bearing regions. The most important feature of the last 10 years has been the rapid increase in production by North Africa, especially Libya, which is by far the most important producer in the area and which now surpasses Iraq in total production.

As oil deposits are generally far from the industrial consumers, the oil is transported by pipeline or tanker. Since 1938 oil has constituted the greatest portion of cargo carried by the world merchant fleet. High levels of demand and the need, in conditions of extreme competition exacerbated by world-wide inflation, for cheaper transport has resulted in the development of the 'super tanker'. At the end of 1968 two 312 000 ton tankers were in operation, four more were under construction, and one of 370 000 tons was on order.

The largest single user of oil in the U.S.A. is the transport industry. In Western Europe and Japan the demand for fuel oils and middle distillates—nowadays for domestic as well as industrial purposes—is the chief feature. At present nearly 80% of all organic chemicals produced originate from petroleum feedstocks.

Oil Refining

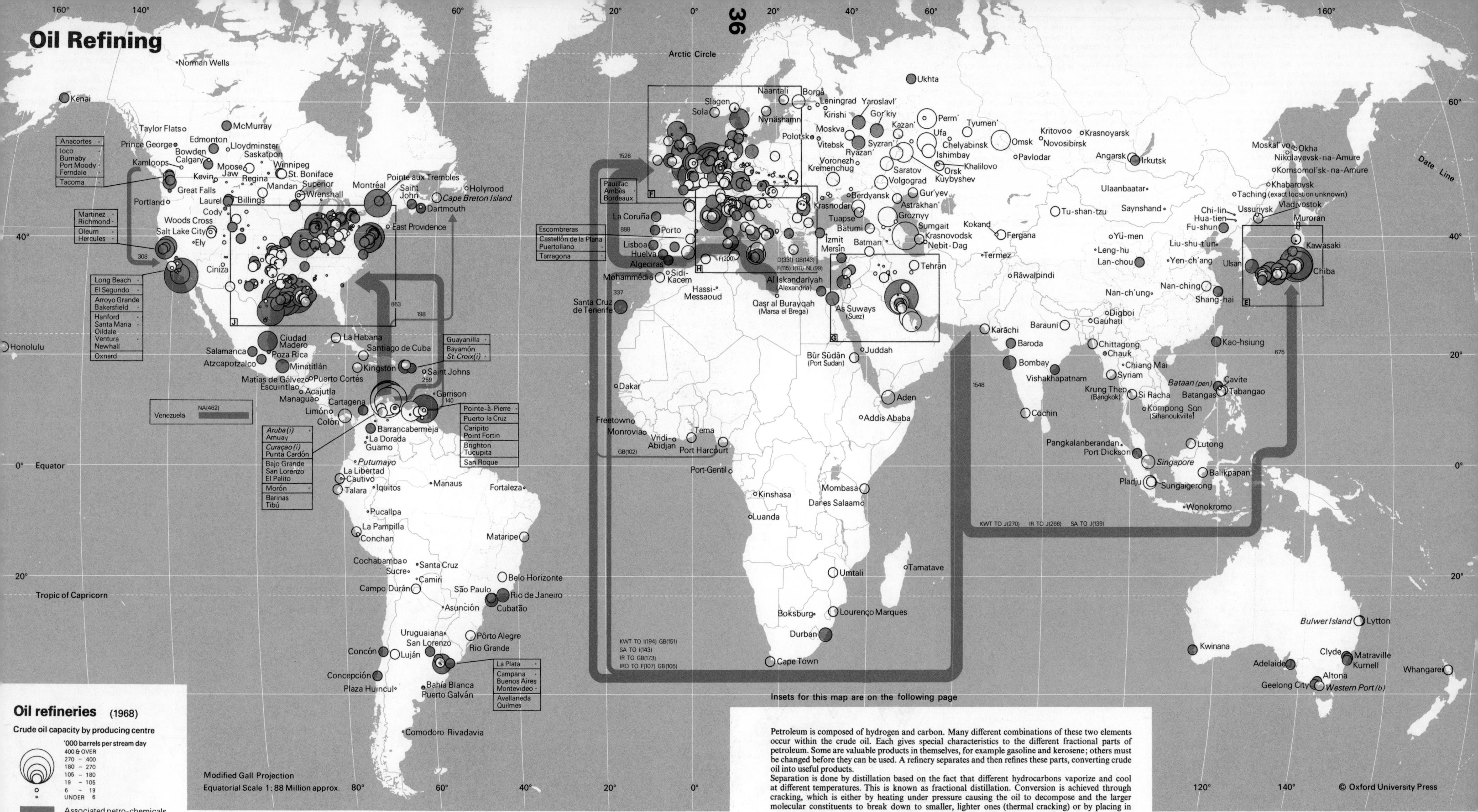

Oil refineries (1968)

Crude oil capacity by producing centre

'000 barrels per stream day

- 400 & OVER
- 270 – 400
- 180 – 270
- 105 – 180
- 19 – 105
- 6 – 19
- UNDER 6

Associated petro-chemicals

Major trade flows (1966)

Commodity : S.I.T.C. no.[1]

PETROLEUM: CRUDE / REFINED / BY-PRODUCTS } 33

Value ($ U.S.)
0.5mm represents increments of $150 million

1350 / 750 / 150 ($ MILLIONS)

308 VALUE IN $ MILLIONS

Trade flow shows only major trading partners, not total trade

[1]S. I. T. C. - STANDARD INTERNATIONAL TRADE CLASSIFICATION

Refining capacity (end 1968)

44 911 000 barrels per stream day

	PERCENTAGE	
North America	*30*	
U.S.A.		27
Western Europe	*28*	
Italy		6
U.K.		5
Germany F.R.		5
France		5
Eastern Europe/China	*14*	
U.S.S.R.		12
Latin America	*11*	
Venezuela		3
Asia Pacific	*10*	
Japan		6
Middle East	*5*	
Africa	*2*	

Refined oil fuel production[1]

34 454 000 barrels per calendar day 1967
29 874 000 1965
14 914 000 1955

	PERCENTAGE 1967	1965	1955
U.S.A.	30	31	*49*
U.S.S.R.	13	13	*9*
Japan	6	4	*1*
Italy	5	4	*2*
Germany F.R.	4	4	*1*
U.K.	4	4	*4*
France	4	4	*3*
Venezuela	4	4	*4*
Others	30	32	*27*
	100	100	*100*

[1]Gasoline, kerosene and fuel oil only

Refined oil fuel consumption[1]

31 310 430 barrels per calendar day 1967
27 074 740 1965
16 046 860 1955

	KG. PER CAPITA	PERCENTAGE 1967	1965	1955
U.S.A.	2 649	36	38	*45*
U.S.S.R.	790	13	13	*8*
Japan	930	6	5	*1*
Germany F.R.	1 274	5	5	*1*
U.K.	1 298	5	5	*3*
Canada	2 570	4	4	*3*
France	1 036	4	3	*2*
Italy	1 003	4	3	*1*
Others	…	23	24	*36*
		100	100	*100*

[1]Gasoline, kerosene and fuel oil only

Petroleum is composed of hydrogen and carbon. Many different combinations of these two elements occur within the crude oil. Each gives special characteristics to the different fractional parts of petroleum. Some are valuable products in themselves, for example gasoline and kerosene; others must be changed before they can be used. A refinery separates and then refines these parts, converting crude oil into useful products.

Separation is done by distillation based on the fact that different hydrocarbons vaporize and cool at different temperatures. This is known as fractional distillation. Conversion is achieved through cracking, which is either by heating under pressure causing the oil to decompose and the larger molecular constituents to break down to smaller, lighter ones (thermal cracking) or by placing in contact with a catalyst (catalytic cracking). Polymerization is the reverse of this process, combining the smaller molecular parts to form heavy oils. Alkylation is the combining of gaseous hydrocarbons into a liquid state suitable for gasoline. Hydrogenation is a process whereby the addition of extra hydrogen to heavy oils (which are hydrogen deficient) produces light oils. Reforming (thermal and catalytic) produces aromatics (benzene, toluene and xylene) the basis for the petro-chemical industry.

The location of refineries is greatly dependent upon logistic considerations both economic and strategic. The reduction in unit costs of transportation which has resulted from the development of ever-larger crude oil carriers has permitted a shift of location away from the centres of oil production to those of oil consumption—a trend which both large and small current governments have encouraged. Because of the need of deep water facilities and abundant supplies of cooling water, the rule has been for refineries to be located on the coast. Recently, however, Europe has seen refineries located inland in the industrial areas such as the Saar, Ruhr and Bavaria, where the volumetric increase in demand has been greatest. This has only been possible since the development of air-cooling and long-distance, large diameter pipeline systems, which run overland to the refineries from the ports of discharge: Rotterdam, Wilhelmshaven, Marseilles, Genoa and Trieste.

Refining capacity may be expressed in barrels per stream day which represents the out-turn when periods of shutdown for maintenance and so forth have been allowed for.

Barrels per calendar day is another measure used and may be calculated either on the capacity at the end of the year or by averaging capacity over the year. To convert from barrels per stream day multiply by 0.9.

Refined oil fuel exports[1]

6 203 233 barrels per calendar day 1967
5 585 916 1965
2 850 303 1955

	PERCENTAGE 1967	1965	1955
Venezuela	17	23	*16*
Neths. Antilles	12	13	*27*
U.S.S.R.	8	8	*4*
Italy	7	6	*4*
Trinidad/Tobago	5	6	*3*
France	4	4	*4*
Netherlands	4	4	*5*
U.K.	4	4	*5*
Others	39	32	*32*
	100	100	*100*

[1]Gasoline, kerosene and fuel oil only

Refined oil fuel imports[1]

5 671 020 barrels per calendar day 1967
5 010 092 1965
2 783 628 1955

	PERCENTAGE 1967	1965	1955
U.S.A.	26	25	*19*
U.K.	9	8	*6*
Germany F.R.	7	7	*2*
Japan	6	6	*3*
Sweden	6	6	*5*
Canada	3	3	*4*
Netherlands	3	3	*2*
Singapore	3	3	*—*
Others	37	39	*59*
	100	100	*100*

[1]Gasoline, kerosene and fuel oil only

Natural Gas

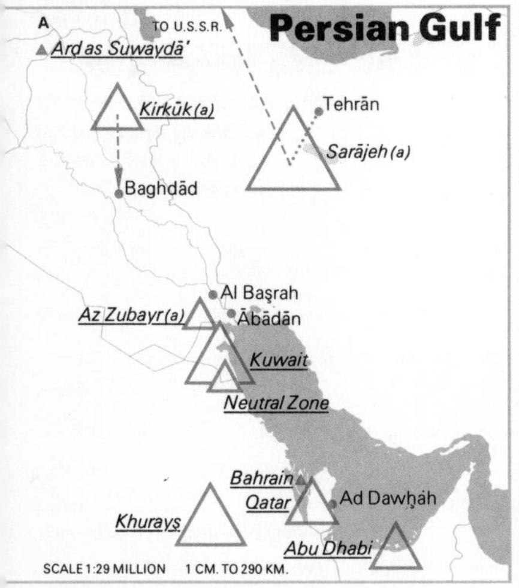

Natural gas

Fields gas producing areas

Reserves ('proven' as of 1st July 1968) million cubic metres

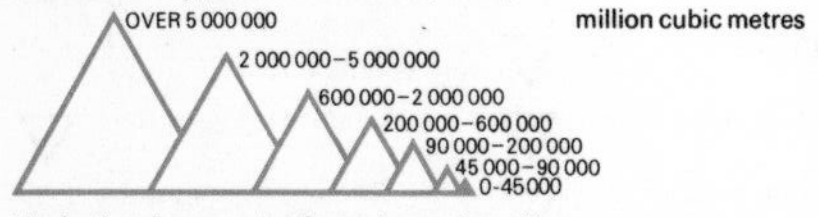

Underlined names indicate 'associated' gas

Annual movements (1967)

- where international trade is below 500 million cu.m.
- represents 1 000 million cu.m. international trade
- major internal movements (not quantified)
- planned internal and international movements
- L.N.G. Liquified Natural Gas movements
- liquefaction plants
- centres of distribution and/or consumption

Crude Oil

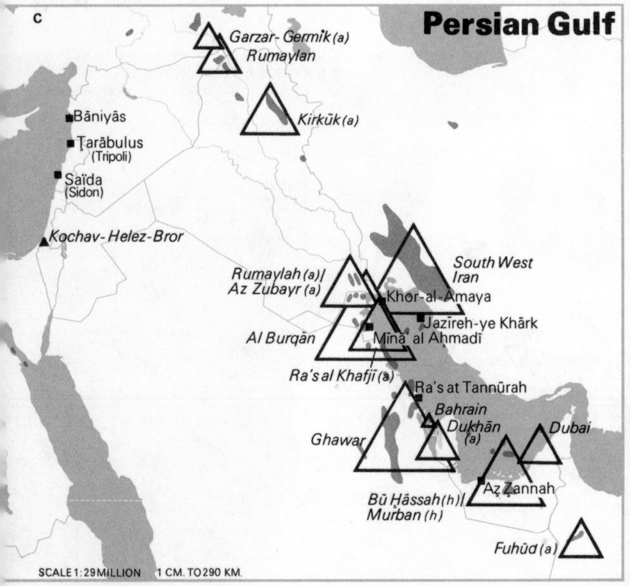

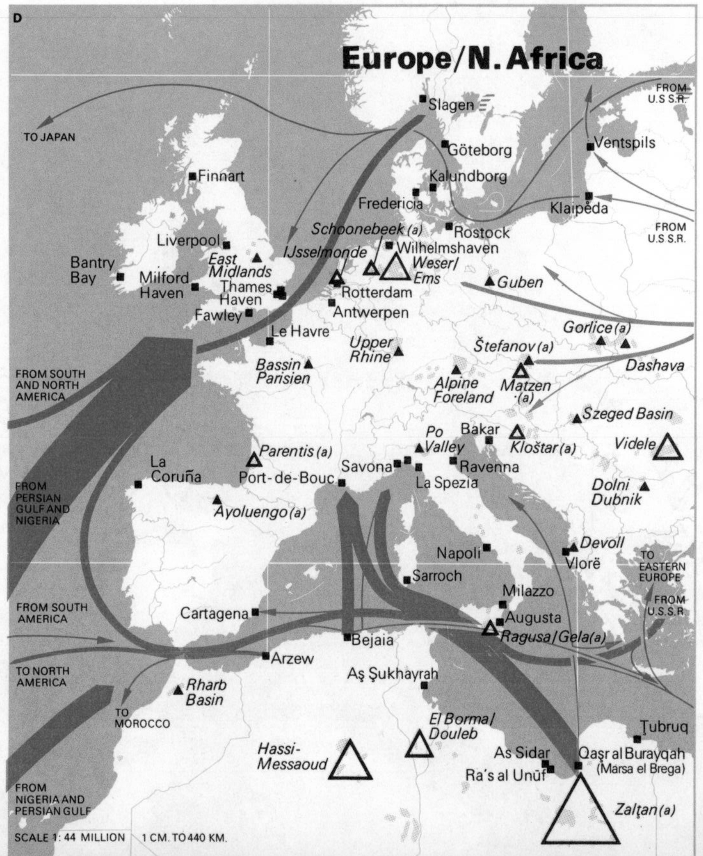

Crude oil

Producing areas major minor oilshale

Reserves ('proven' as of 1st July 1968) million barrels

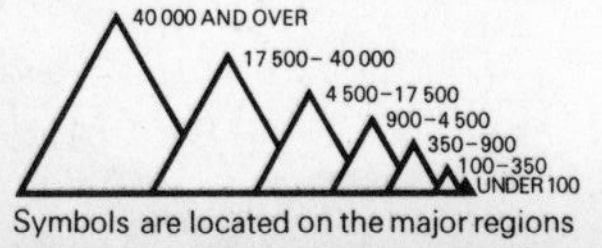

Symbols are located on the major regions

Annual movements (1967)

- where movement is below 45 million barrels
- represents 180 million barrels
- major tanker terminals

One barrel of crude oil (world average gravity) is equal to 0.137 metric tons

Oil Refining

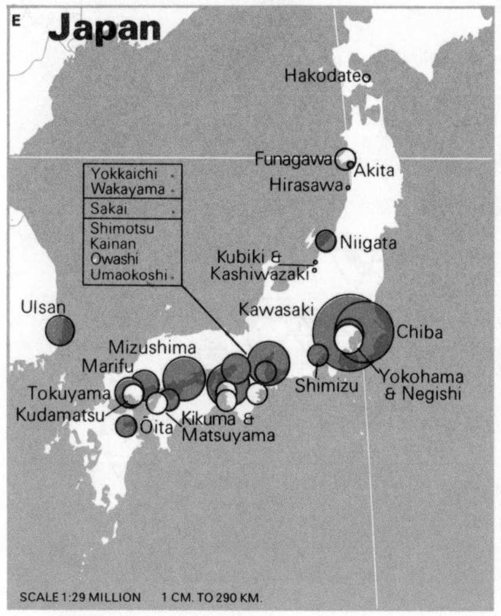

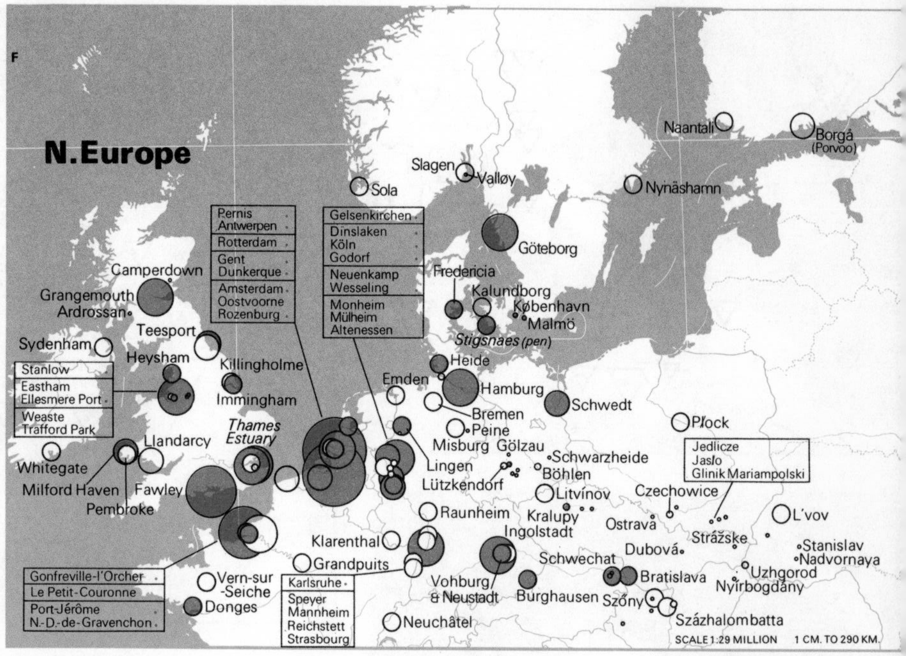

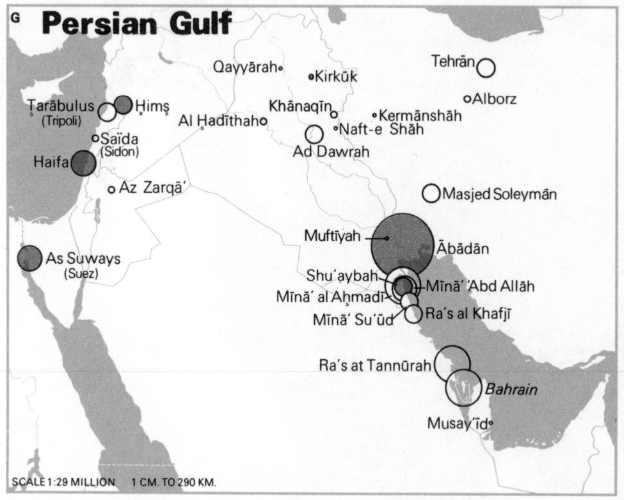

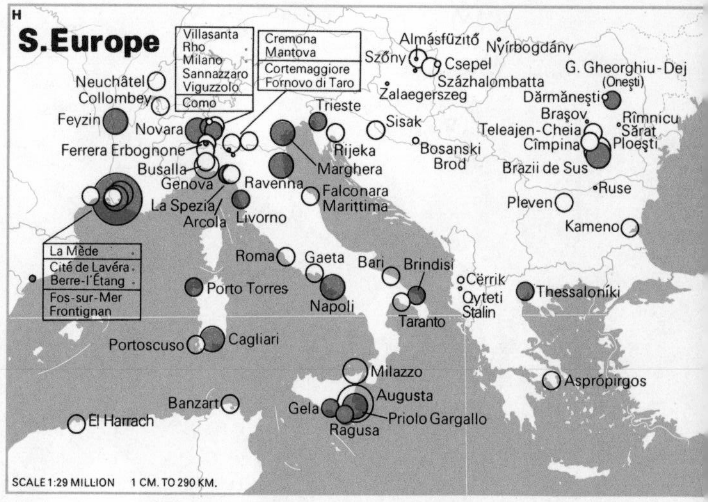

Oil refineries (1968)

Crude oil capacity by producing centre

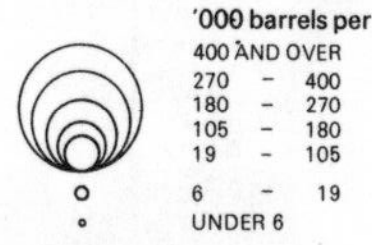

Associated petro-chemicals

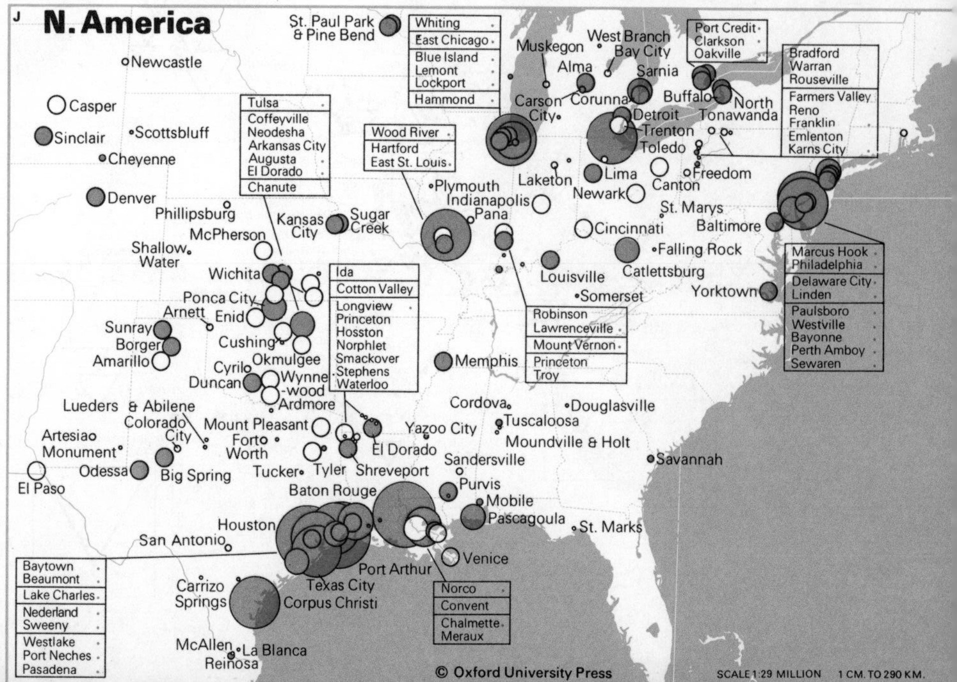

Petro-chemicals are derived from petroleum 'feed-stock'—crude oil and natural gas. The primary products, ethylene, ammonia and aromatic hydro-carbons, are the 'building blocks' for many other petro-chemicals, including organic monomers and polymers, synthetic resins, plastics, synthetic rubber and fibres.

In 1945 of a total world production of 1 million tons of organic chemicals very little originated from petroleum. In 1965 79% of the 34 million tons produced were petro-chemicals.

Petro-chemicals were first produced in the U.S.A. which had both the raw materials and the markets. The U.S.A. has long been the largest producer of petro-chemicals but the shift of oil refining into the consumer markets of Western Europe post-1945 paved the way for the development of a major petro-chemical industry. Now Japan and Australia are developing their own refining com-plexes and the oil producing areas of the Middle East and Caribbean have similar aims.

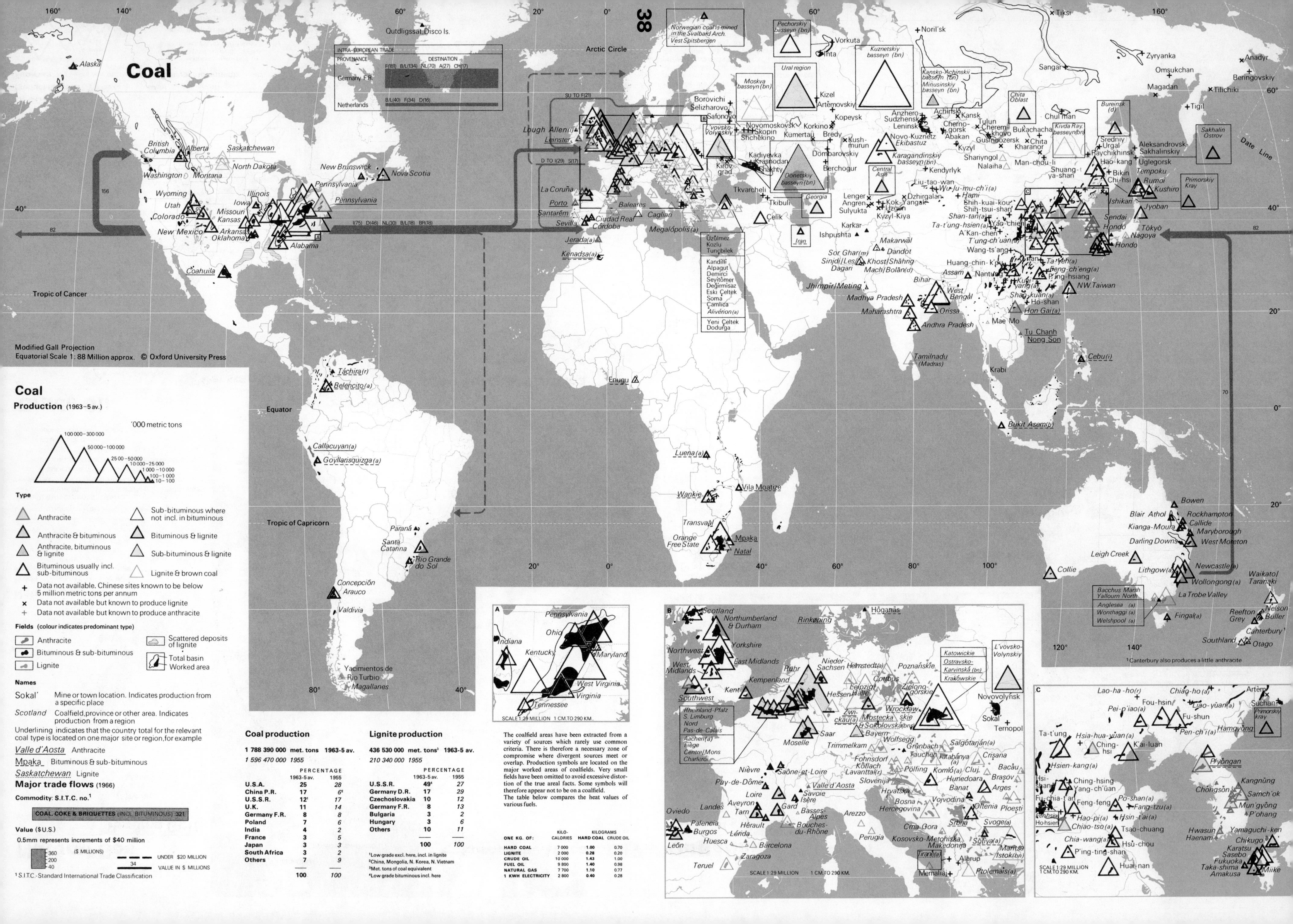

38
Coal
Modified Gall Projection
Equatorial Scale 1: 88 Million approx. © Oxford University Press
Coal
Production (1963-5 av.)
'000 metric tons
100 000-300 000
50 000-100 000
25 00-50 000
10 000-25 000
1 000-10 000
100-1 000
10-100
Type
Anthracite
Anthracite & bituminous
Anthracite, bituminous & lignite
Bituminous usually incl. sub-bituminous
Sub-bituminous where not incl. in bituminous
Bituminous & lignite
Sub-bituminous & lignite
Lignite & brown coal
Data not available. Chinese sites known to be below 5 million metric tons per annum
Data not available but known to produce lignite
Data not available but known to produce anthracite
Fields (colour indicates predominant type)
Anthracite
Bituminous & sub-bituminous
Lignite
Scattered deposits of lignite
Total basin
Worked area
Names
Sokal' Mine or town location. Indicates production from a specific place
Scotland Coalfield, province or other area. Indicates production from a region
Underlining indicates that the country total for the relevant coal type is located on one major site or region, for example
Valle d'Aosta Anthracite
Mpaka Bituminous & sub-bituminous
Saskatchewan Lignite
Major trade flows (1966)
Commodity: S.I.T.C. no.[1]
COAL, COKE & BRIQUETTES (INCL. BITUMINOUS) 321
Value ($U.S.)
0.5mm represents increments of $40 million
($ MILLIONS) 360 200 40
UNDER $20 MILLION
VALUE IN $ MILLIONS
[1] S.I.T.C.-Standard International Trade Classification
INTRA-EUROPEAN TRADE
PROVENANCE
DESTINATION
Germany F.R. F(181) B/L(134) NL(70) A(27) CH(17)
Netherlands B/L(40) F(34) D(16)
Arctic Circle
Tropic of Cancer
Equator
Tropic of Capricorn
Date Line
Norwegian coal is mined in the Svalbard Arch. Vest Spitsbergen
[1] Canterbury also produces a little anthracite
SCALE 1:29 MILLION 1 CM.TO 290 KM.

Coal production

1 788 390 000 met. tons 1963-5 av.
1 596 470 000 1955

	PERCENTAGE 1963-5 av.	1955
U.S.A.	25	28
China P.R.	17	6[2]
U.S.S.R.	12[1]	17
U.K.	11	14
Germany F.R.	8	8
Poland	7	6
India	4	2
France	3	5
Japan	3	3
South Africa	3	2
Others	7	9
	100	100

Lignite production

436 530 000 met. tons[3] 1963-5 av.
210 340 000 1955

	PERCENTAGE 1963-5 av.	1955
U.S.S.R.	49[4]	27
Germany D.R.	17	29
Czechoslovakia	10	12
Germany F.R.	8	13
Bulgaria	3	2
Hungary	3	6
Others	10	11
	100	100

[1] Low grade excl. here, incl. in lignite
[2] China, Mongolia, N. Korea, N. Vietnam
[3] Met. tons of coal equivalent
[4] Low grade bituminous incl. here

The coalfield areas have been extracted from a variety of sources which rarely use common criteria. There is therefore a necessary zone of compromise where divergent sources meet or overlap. Production symbols are located on the major worked areas of coalfields. Very small fields have been omitted to avoid excessive distortion of the true areal facts. Some symbols will therefore appear not to be on a coalfield.
The table below compares the heat values of various fuels.

ONE KG. OF:	KILO-CALORIES	KILOGRAMS HARD COAL	CRUDE OIL
HARD COAL	7 000	1.00	0.70
LIGNITE	2 000	0.28	0.20
CRUDE OIL	10 000	1.43	1.00
FUEL OIL	9 800	1.40	0.98
NATURAL GAS	7 700	1.10	0.77
1 KWH ELECTRICITY	2 800	0.40	0.28

Hydro-electric Power

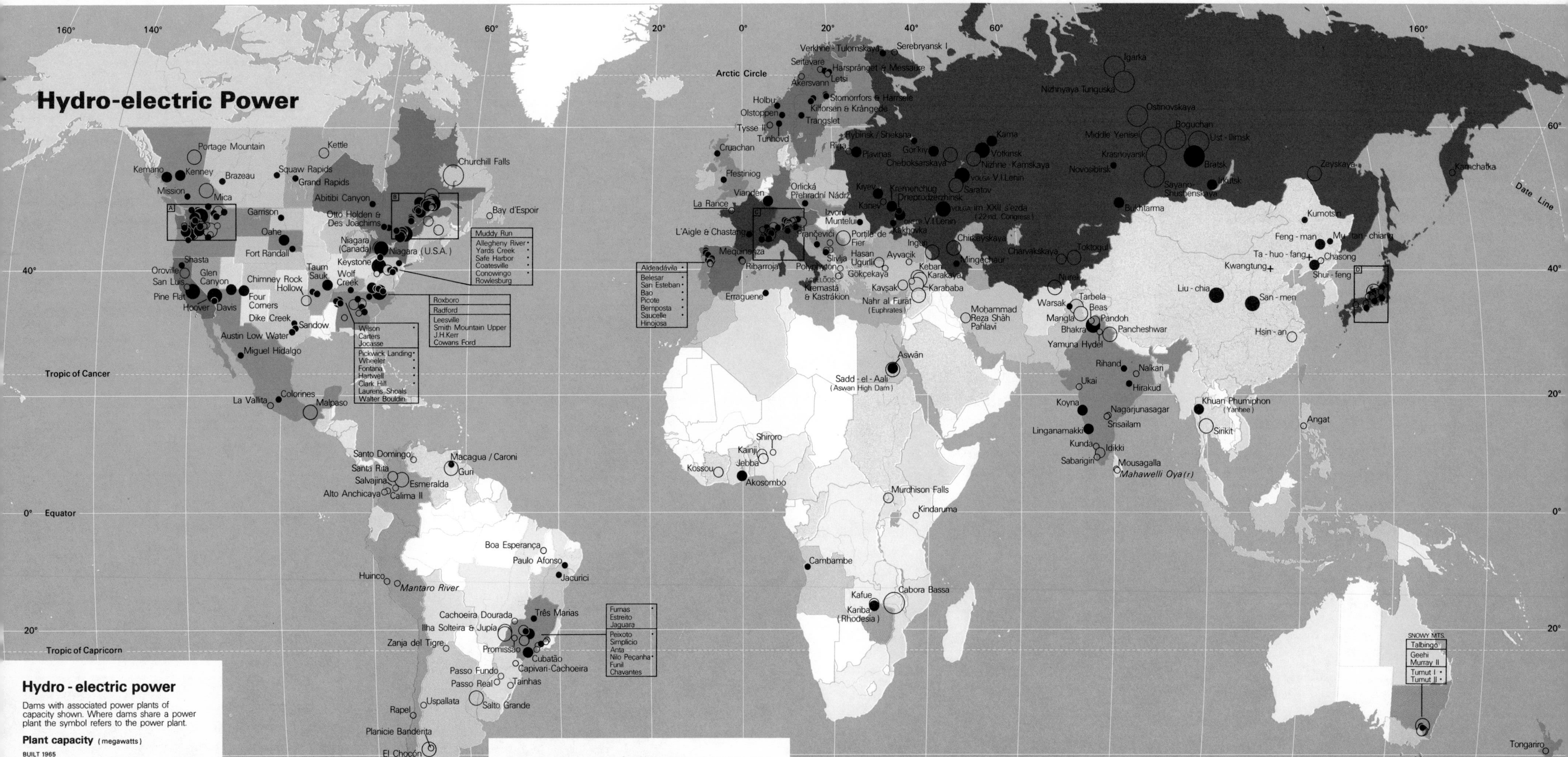

Hydro - electric power

Dams with associated power plants of capacity shown. Where dams share a power plant the symbol refers to the power plant.

Plant capacity (megawatts)

BUILT 1965

200 - 500	500 - 1 000	1 000 - 3 500	3 500 AND OVER

UNDER CONSTRUCTION / PROPOSED BEFORE 1970

200 - 500	500 - 1 000	1 000 - 3 500	3 500 AND OVER

La Rance : Tidal power plant

+ Capacity data not available but believed to be at least 200 MW

Where several dams together form one river system this is named in CAPITALS with the individual dam names following, for example ACHELÔOS : Kremastá and Kastrákion

Total installed capacity by region
(1963-5 av. in megawatts)

10 000 AND OVER	200 — 500
3 500 — 10 000	50 — 200
1 000 — 3 500	0 — 50
500 — 1 000	NIL
DATA NA	

H.E.P. installed capacity

202 200 MW 1963-5 av.[1]
95 698 1953-5 av.[1]

	PERCENTAGE 1963-5 av.	1953-5 av.
U.S.A.	21	*25*
U.S.S.R.	11	*5*
Canada	10	*11*
Japan	8	*9*
Italy	7	*10*
France	6	*8*
Sweden	4	*5*
Norway	4	*4*
Switzerland	4	*4*
Others	25	*19*
	100	*100*

[1]Excl. China P.R.

H.E.P. production

839 679 million kWh 1963-5 av.[1]
440 330 million 1953-5 av.[1]

	PERCENTAGE 1963-5 av.	1953-5 av.
U.S.A.	22	*26*
Canada	13	*16*
U.S.S.R.	9	*5*
Japan	9	*10*
Norway	5	*5*
France	5	*5*
Sweden	5	*5*
Italy	5	*7*
Brazil	3	*2*
Others	24	*19*
	100	*100*

[1]Excl. China P.R.

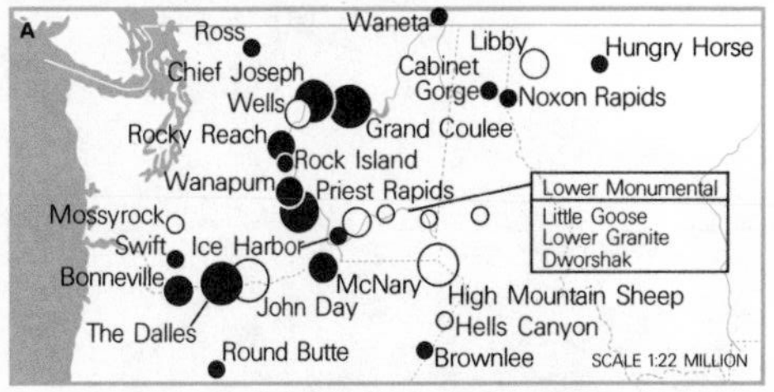

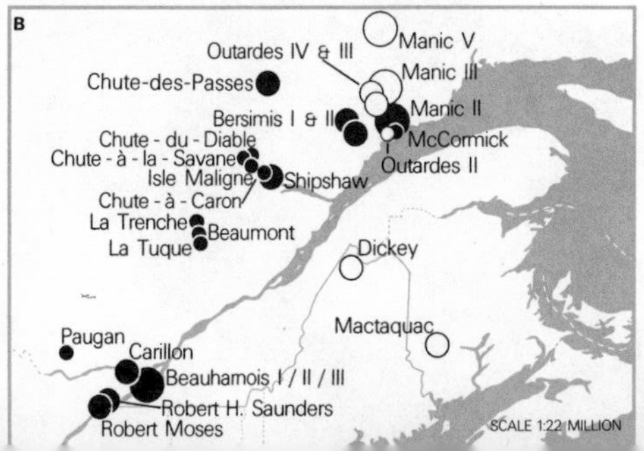

Hydro-electric power production (1963-5 av.)

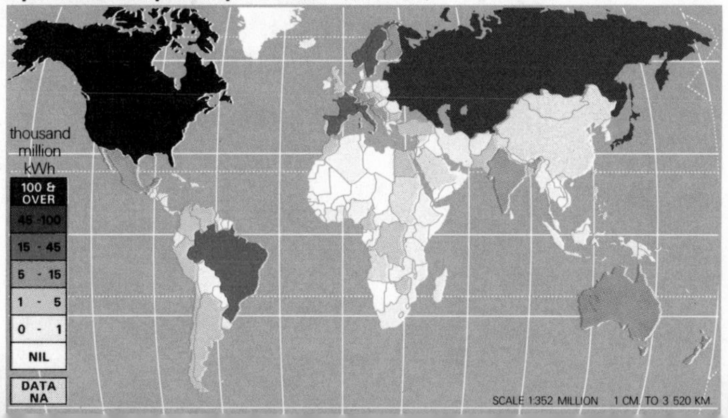

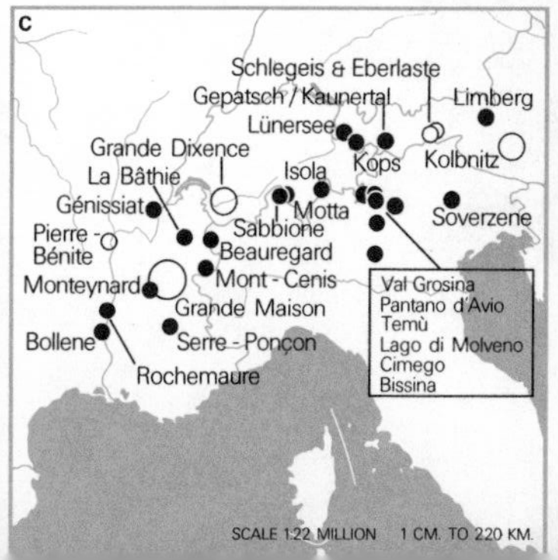

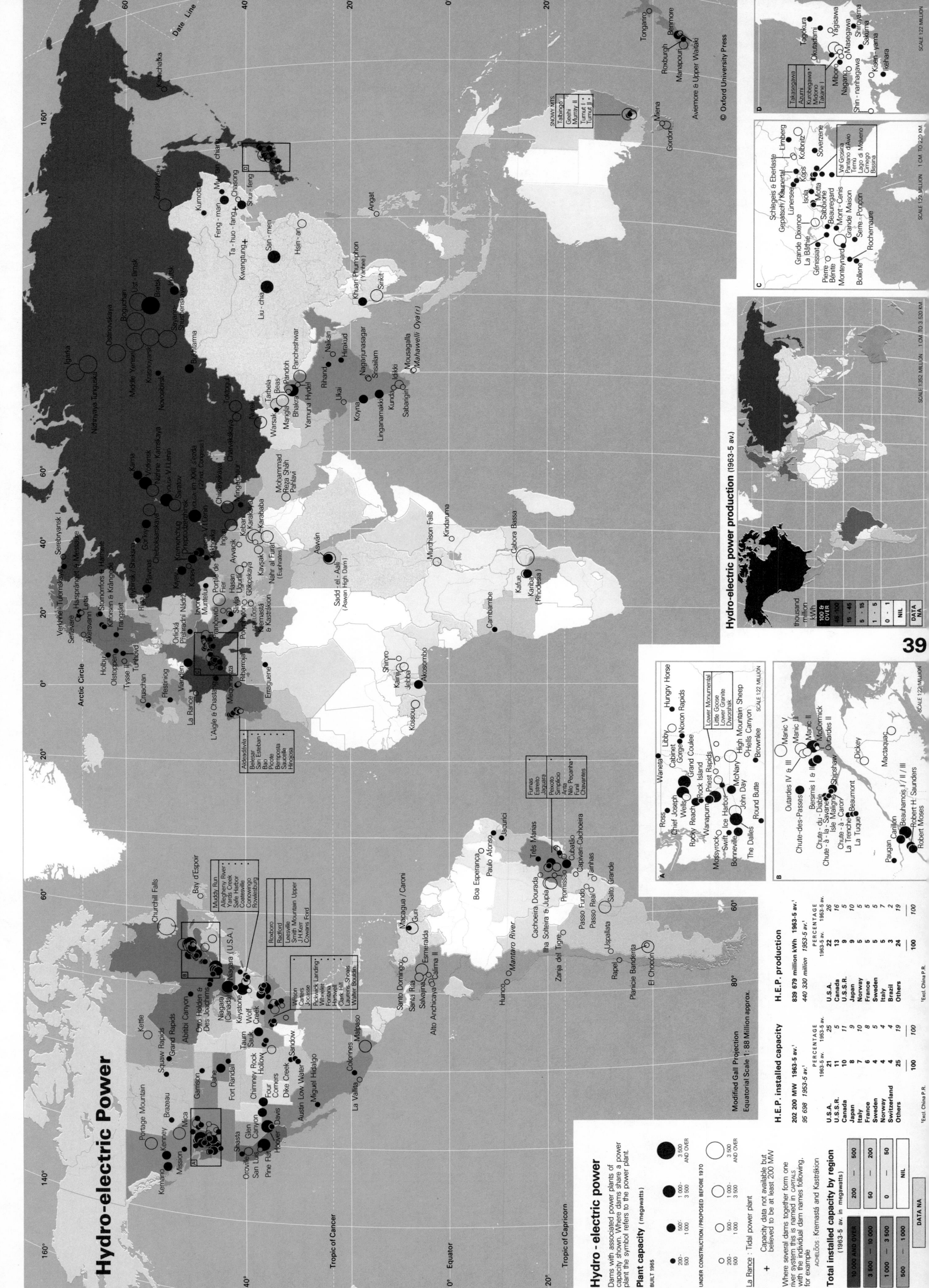

Uranium/Rare Earths/Nuclear Energy

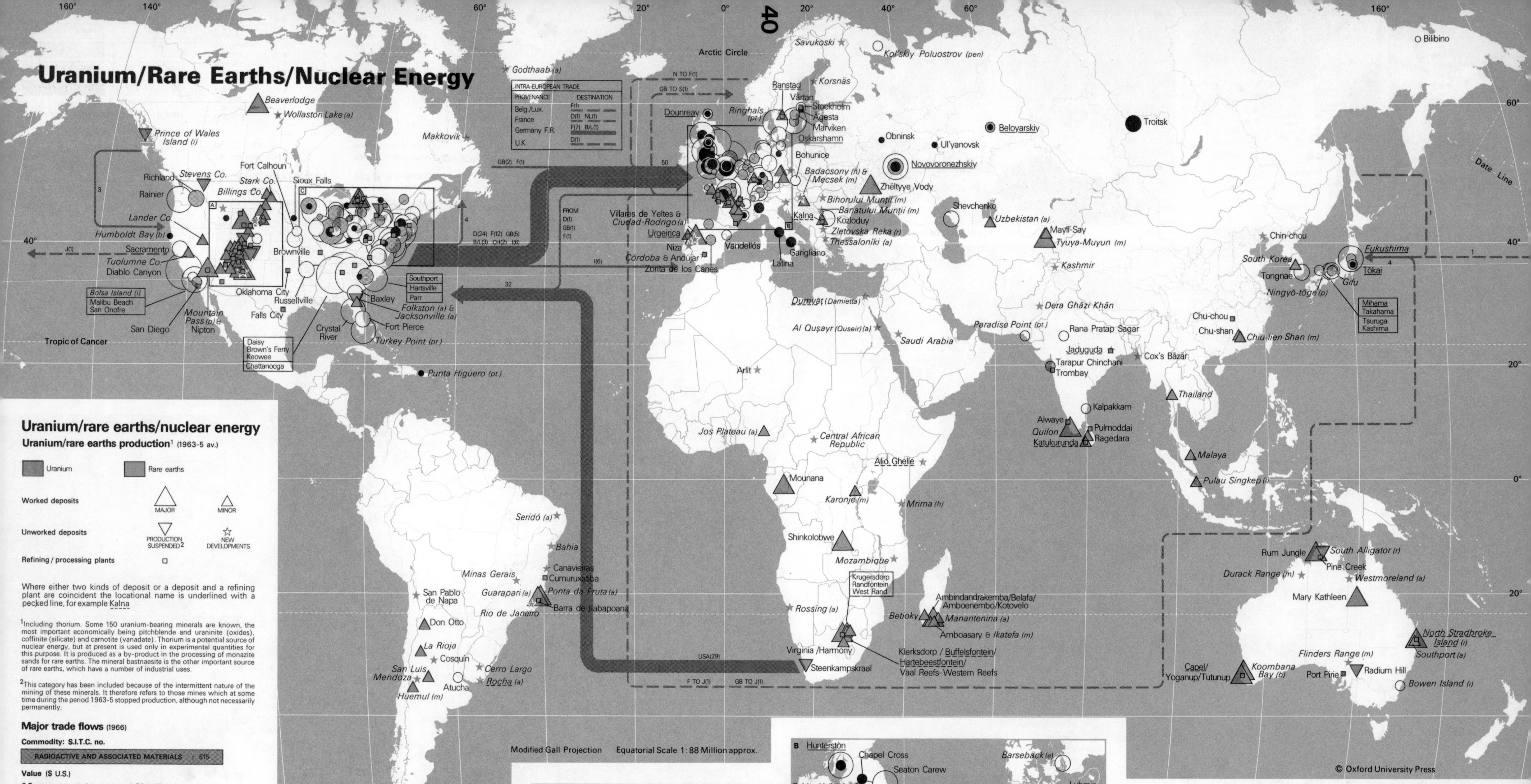

Uranium/rare earths/nuclear energy

Uranium/rare earths production[1] (1963-5 av.)

Uranium — Rare earths

Worked deposits — MAJOR — MINOR

Unworked deposits — PRODUCTION SUSPENDED[2] — NEW DEVELOPMENTS

Refining / processing plants

Where either two kinds of deposit or a deposit and a refining plant are coincident the locational name is underlined with a pecked line, for example Kalna

[1]Including thorium. Some 150 uranium-bearing minerals are known, the most important economically being pitchblende and uraninite (oxides), coffinite (silicate) and carnotite (vanadate). Thorium is a potential source of nuclear energy, but at present is used only in experimental quantities for this purpose. It is produced as a by-product in the processing of monazite sands for rare earths. The mineral bastnaesite is the other important source of rare earths, which have a number of industrial uses.

[2]This category has been included because of the intermittent nature of the mining of these minerals. It therefore refers to those mines which at some time during the period 1963-5 stopped production, although not necessarily permanently.

Major trade flows (1966)

Commodity: S.I.T.C. no.

RADIOACTIVE AND ASSOCIATED MATERIALS : 515

Value ($ U.S.)

0.5mm represents increments of $5 million

($ MILLIONS) 65 45 25 5 — UNDER $2.5 MILLION — VALUE IN $ MILLIONS

Nuclear power stations

Operational by 1965

Operational 1966-70

Under construction 1970

Station capacity (MW)

2 001 & OVER; 1001 - 2000; 501 - 1000; 101 - 500; 1 - 100

Where two or more circles are concentric, parts of the total capacity of a power station have become operational at different times, and the locational name is underlined, for example Dounreay

Uranium production[1]

27 433 met. tons 1963-5 av.[2]

16 257 1956

	PERCENTAGE 1963-5 av.	1956
U.S.A.	34	28
Canada	19	11
South Africa	11	27
France	4	NA
Australia	2	—
Gabon	2	—
Others	28[2]	NA[3]
	100	100

[1]Metal content of ore
[2]Incl. estimates for U.S.S.R., China P.R, India, Germany F.R., as well as small production in Argentina, Malagsay R., Spain and Portugal
[3]Incl. U.S.S.R., Congo D.R., Rhodesia, Portugal and Argentina

Rare earths production[1]

7 800 met. tons 1963-5 av.[1]

2 454 1956[2]

	PERCENTAGE 1963-5 av.	1956
India	30	...[2]
Australia	25	10
Malagasy R.	18	6
South Africa	9	...[2]
W. Malaysia	8	26
Brazil	7	...[2]
Indonesia	1	—
Nigeria	1	33
Ceylon	1	2
Others	—	23[3]
	100	100

[1]Excl. U.S.A. and Canada
[2]Excl. U.S.A., Brazil, India and South Africa
[3]Incl. Congo D.R. and S. Korea

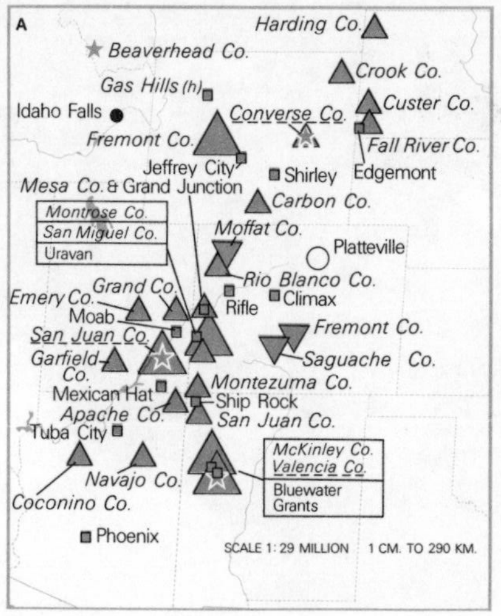

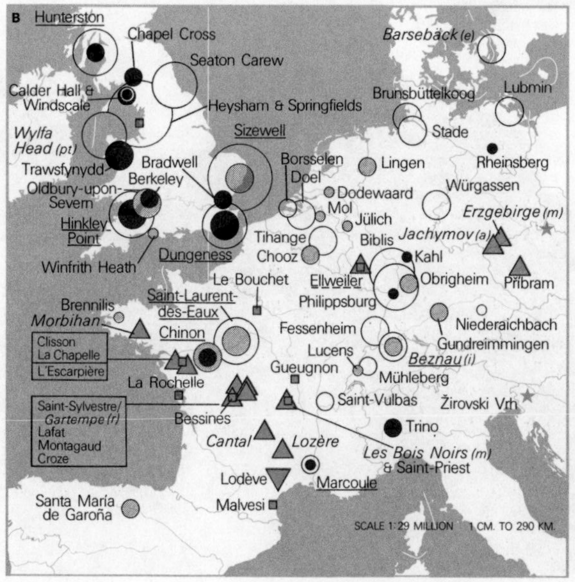

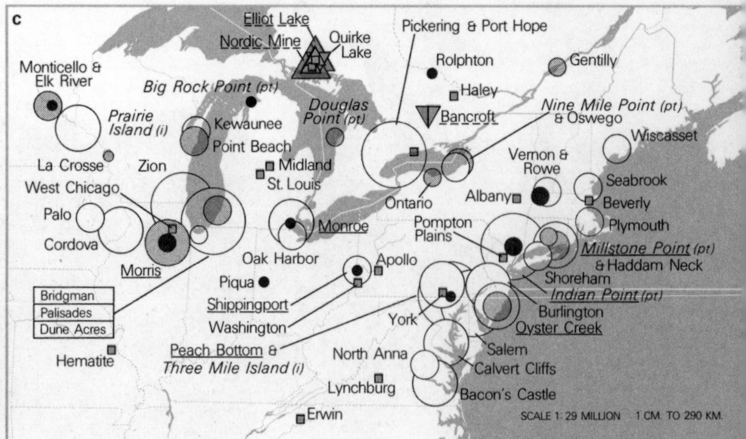

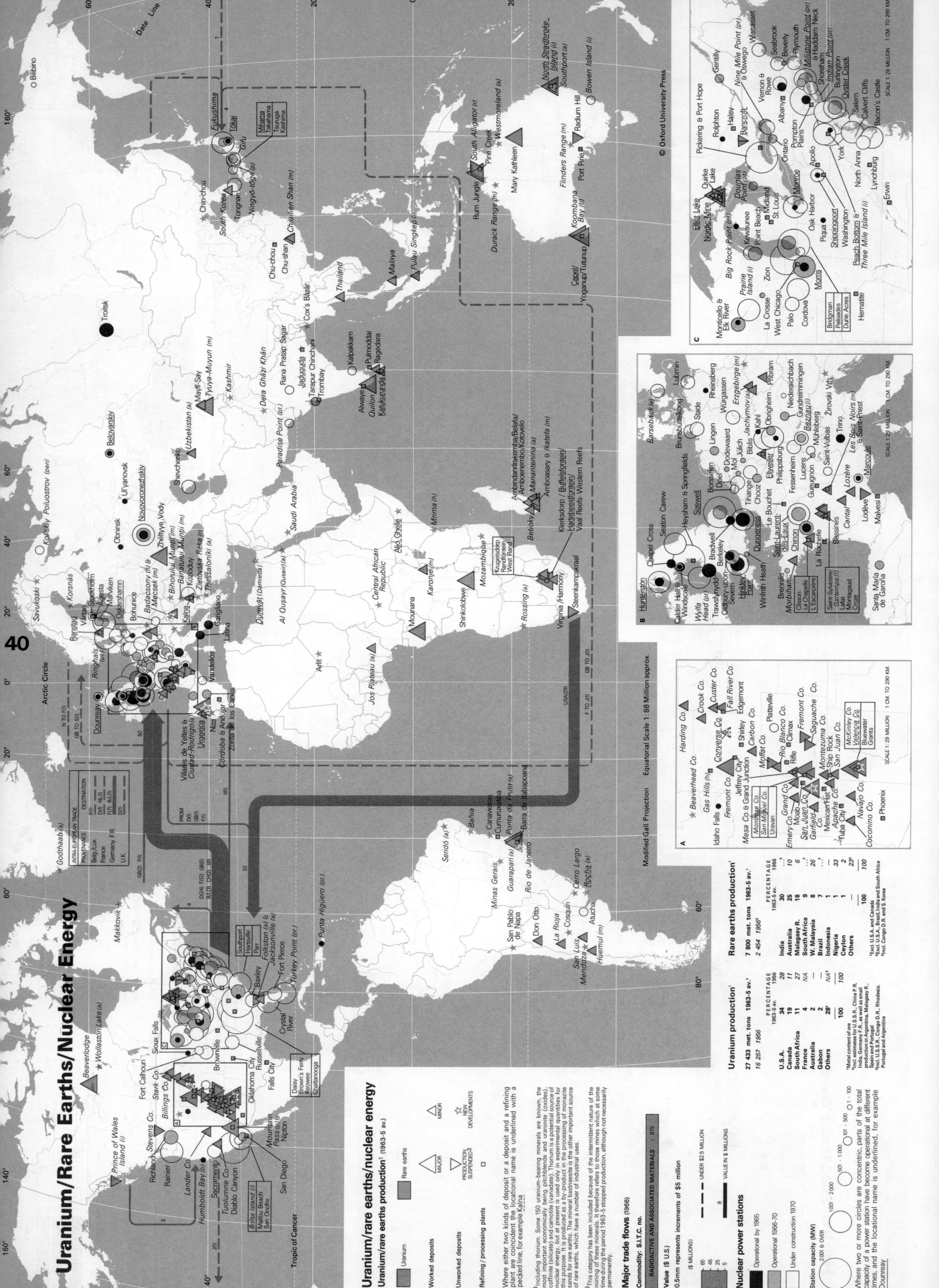

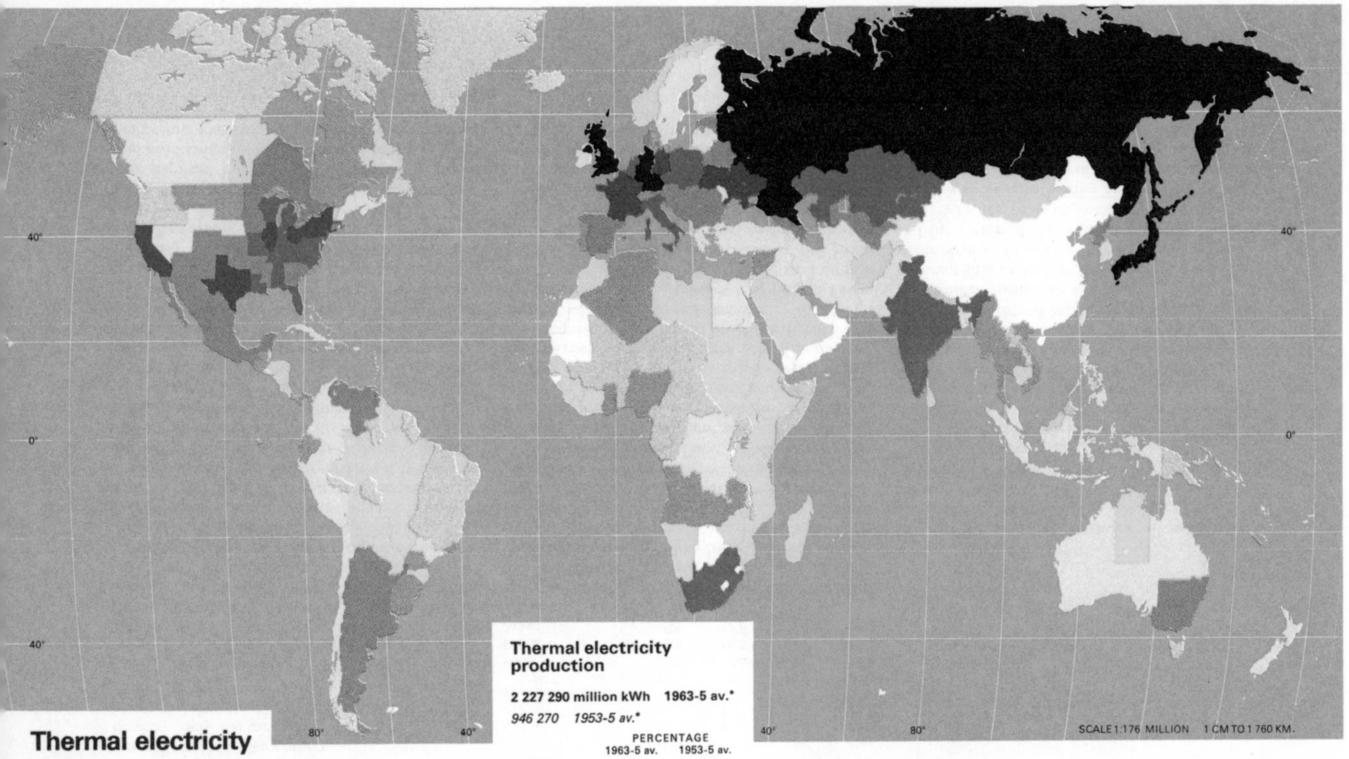
SCALE 1:176 MILLION 1 CM TO 1 760 KM.

Thermal electricity

Annual production in million kWh (1963-5 av.)[1]

OVER 100 000	5 000 - 15 000	50 - 250
45 000 - 100 000	1 000 - 5 000	0 - 50
15 000 - 45 000	250 - 1 000	DATA NA

[1]Data for Australia, Brazil, Canada, the U.S.A. and the U.S.S.R. are by administrative division. For the U.S.S.R. they refer to total electricity; however non-thermal production is estimated to be not so high as to alter the categories.

Thermal electricity production

2 227 290 million kWh 1963-5 av.*

*946 270 1953-5 av.**

	PERCENTAGE 1963-5 av.	1953-5 av.
U.S.A.	40	*48*
U.S.S.R.	17	*14*
U.K.	8	*9*
Germany F.R.	7	*6*
Japan	5	*2*
France	2	*2*
Germany D.R.	2	*3*[1]
Others	19	*16*
	100	*100*

*Estimate
[1]Data refer to total electricity

Thermal electricity

Production in kWh per capita for selected countries

	1963-5 av.	1953-5 av.		1963-5 av.	1953-5 av.
U.S.A.	4 680	*2 761*	Japan	1 093	*170*
U.K.	3 142	*1 656*	France	896	*509*
Germany F.R.	2 598	*1 167*	Venezuela	739	*159*
Australia	2 223	*1 308*	Yugoslavia	323	*93*
Belgium	2 164	*1 141*	Uruguay	245	*120*
South Africa	1 674	*1 077*	Mexico	201	*116*
U.S.S.R.	1 674	*682*	India	40	*18*
Israel	1 474	*639*	Nigeria	16	*NA*

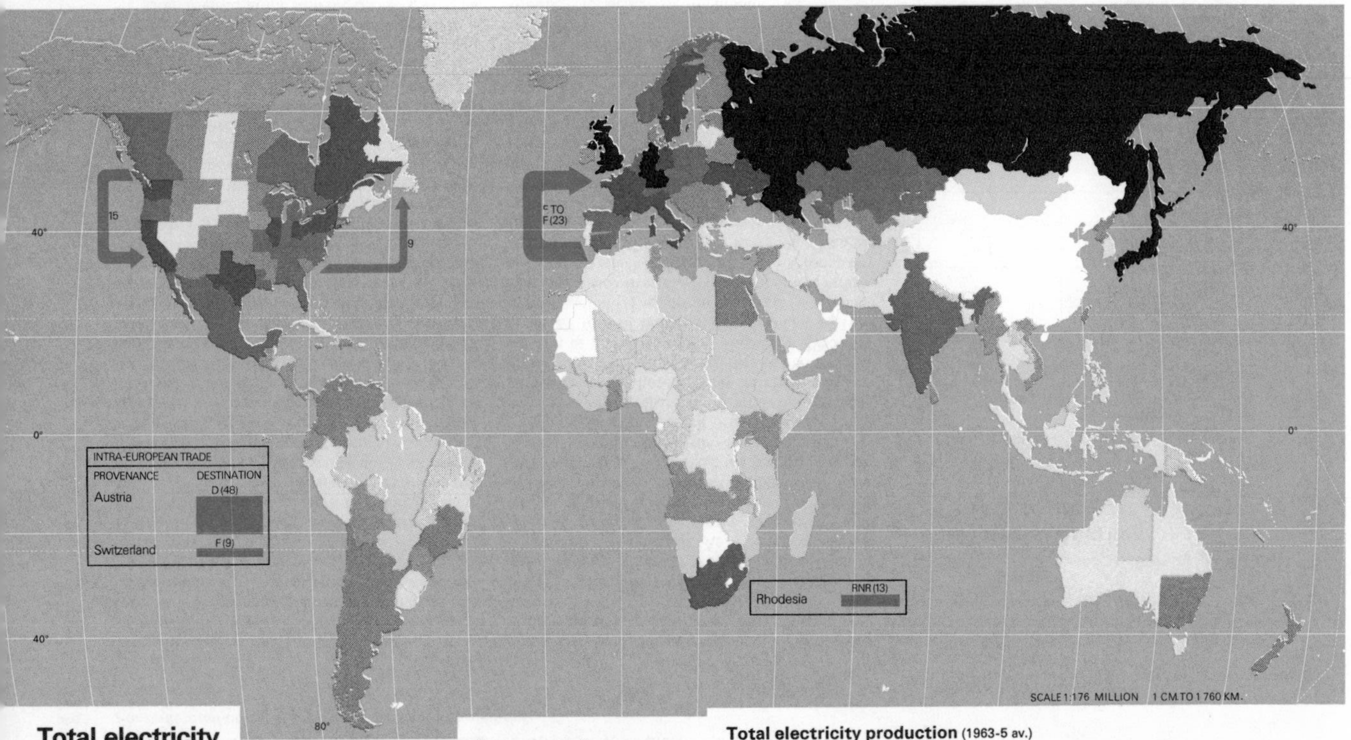
INTRA-EUROPEAN TRADE
PROVENANCE
DESTINATION
Austria
D (48)
Switzerland
F (9)
Rhodesia
RNR (13)
SCALE 1:176 MILLION 1 CM TO 1 760 KM.

Total electricity

Annual production in million kWh (1963-5 av.)[1]

OVER 100 000	5 000 - 15 000	50 - 250
45 000 - 100 000	1 000 - 5 000	0 - 50
15 000 - 45 000	250 - 1 000	DATA NA

[1]Data for Australia, Brazil, Canada, the U.S.S.R. and the U.S.A. are by administrative division; other data are national totals.

Major trade flows (1966)

Commodity : S.I.T.C. no.

ELECTRIC ENERGY : 351

Value ($U.S.)
0.5 mm represents increments of $5 million

45 ($ MILLIONS) 25 5 — 9 VALUE IN $ MILLIONS

Total electricity production (1963-5 av.)

Percentage production by type of plant for selected countries

	Thermal	H.E.P.	Nuclear		Thermal	H.E.P.	Nuclear
Australia	76	24	...	Sweden	6	94	...
Brazil	21	79	...	U.S.S.R.	83[1]	17	*NA*
Canada	17	83	—	U.A.R.	68	32	...
France	55	44	1	U.K.	92	2	6
Germany F.R.	92	8	—	U.S.A.	83	17	—
India	56	44	...	Venezuela	84	16	...
Italy	41	56	3	Zambia	58	42	—
Japan	60	40	—	World	73	27	—

[1]Incl. nuclear

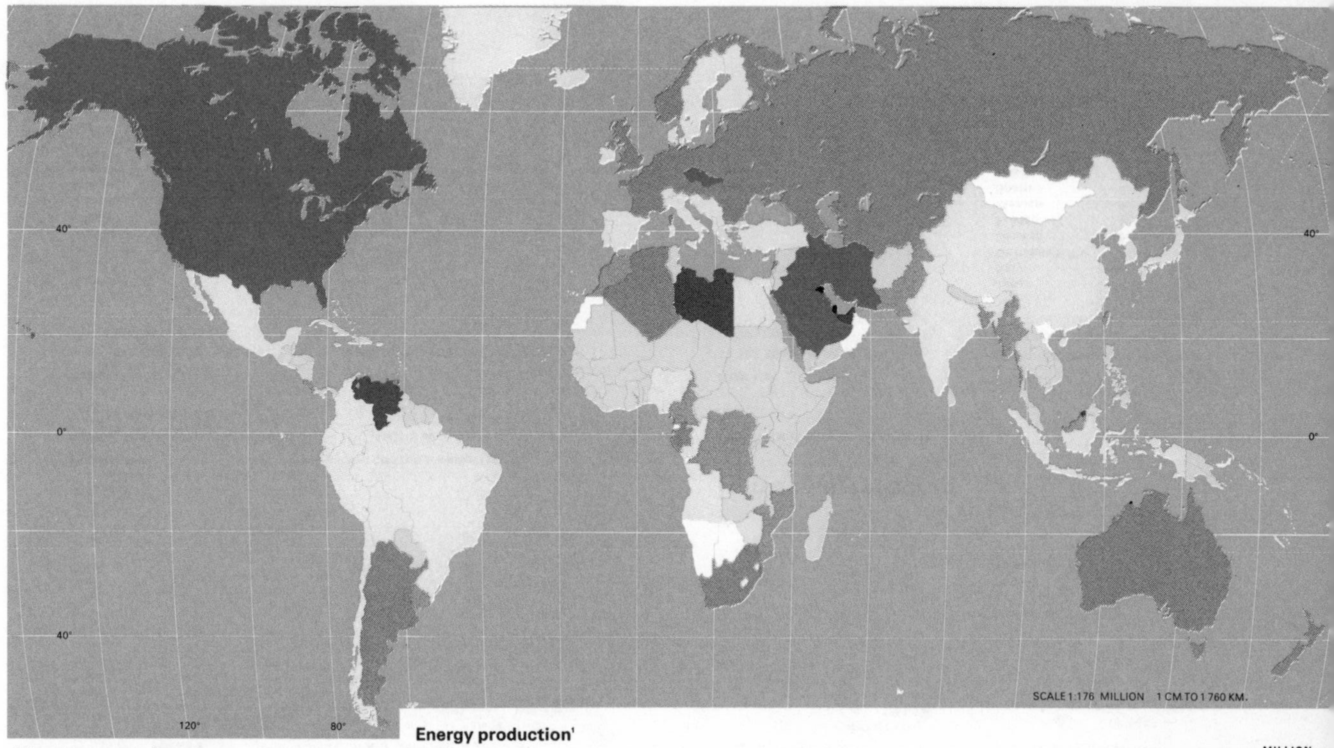
SCALE 1:176 MILLION 1 CM TO 1 760 KM.

Energy production (1963-5 av.)

Kg. per capita in coal equivalent

OVER 100 000[1]	1 000 - 5 000	0 - 20
20 000 - 100 000	100 - 1 000	DATA NA
5 000 - 20 000	20 - 100	

[1]Kuwait 320 774

Energy production[1]

Major producers — PERCENTAGE

	U.S.A.	U.S.S.R.	CHINA P.R.[2]	VENEZUELA	U.K.	GERMANY F.R.	KUWAIT	CANADA	SAUDI ARABIA	POLAND	OTHERS	WORLD (MILLION MET. TONS)
1965	31	17	6	5	4	3	3	3	3	2	23	5 327
1955	*39*	*13*	*3*	*5*	*7*	*5*	*2*	*2*	*2*	*3*	*19*	*3 295*

Selected countries — KG. PER CAPITA

	VENEZUELA	CANADA	U.S.S.R.	U.K.	AUSTRALIA	ALGERIA	ROMANIA	ARGENTINA	INDIA	CHINA P.R.	WORLD AVERAGE
1965	28 273	6 867	4 029	3 553	3 551	3 112	2 308	1 096	850	480	1 617
1955	*25 028*	*3 185*	*2 247*	*4 406*	*2 530*	*42*	*1 490*	*371*	*103*	*166*	*1 187*

[1]Coal equivalent [2]Incl. N. Vietnam, N. Korea and Mongolia

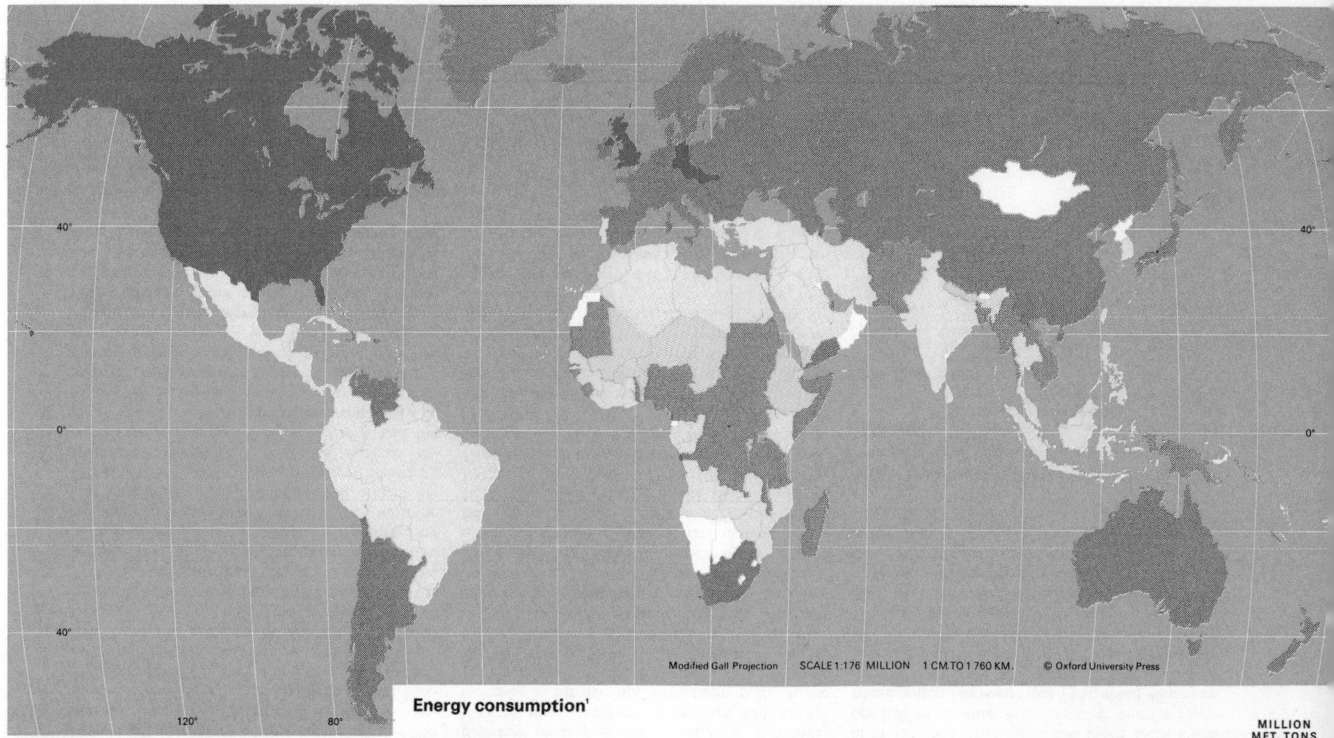
Modified Gall Projection SCALE 1:176 MILLION 1 CM TO 1 760 KM.

Energy consumption (1963-5 av.)

Kg. per capita in coal equivalent

5 000 - 20 000	20 - 100
1 000 - 5 000	0 - 20
100 - 1 000	DATA NA

Energy consumption[1]

Major consumers — PERCENTAGE

	U.S.A.	U.S.S.R.	CHINA P.R.[2]	U.K.	GERMANY F.R.	JAPAN	CANADA	FRANCE	POLAND	GERMANY D.R.	OTHERS	WORLD (MILLION MET. TONS)
1965	34	16	6	5	5	3	3	3	2	2	21	5 223
1955	*40*	*13*[3]	*NA*	*7*	*5*	*3*	*3*	*3*	*2*[4]	*2*[4]	*NA*	*3 426*

Selected countries — KG. PER CAPITA

	U.S.A.	CZECHO-SLOVAKIA	AUSTRALIA	U.S.S.R.	JAPAN	ARGENTINA	YUGOSLAVIA	CHINA P.R.[2]	U.A.R.	INDIA	NIGERIA	WORLD AVERAGE
1965	9 201	5 676	4 795	3 611	1 783	1 341	1 192	461	301	172	44	1 594
1955	*8 250*	*3 760*[4]	*3 660*	*2 020*[3]	*990*	*890*	*470*	*160*[4]	*230*	*120*	*40*	*1 290*

[1]Coal equivalent. [2]Incl. N. Vietnam, N. Korea and Mongolia [3]Production, partially corrected for trade; believed to correspond closely to consumption [4]Production data

Iron/Steel

Ferro-alloy Minerals p. 50 Iron Ore p. 43 Steel p. 43
For individual country data see Statistical Supplement

Iron and steel are the commonest, as well as the cheapest, of the metals. They provide a basic material for a host of secondary industries, including mechanical engineering, constructional engineering, motors, hardware and hollow-ware, shipbuilding, and also railways and collieries.

Historically, the industry has usually arisen where iron ore and coking coal were found in proximity and where there was a demand for iron and steel products. Typical examples are the northeast coast of England, South Wales and the Ruhr. The American steel industry, however, with the growth in importance of the Lake Superior iron ore fields, has become less concentrated on the coalfields and more dependent on sites close to its markets and where the costs of assembling both the coke and the ores are lowest, leading to development of lakeside steel centres. In Japan and increasingly in other countries the industry depends on seaborne ore. Once the industry is established in a particular location, there is a strong tendency for it to remain and develop there.

Iron was not used by man until long after such metals as copper and its alloy, bronze, which gave the name to the Bronze Age which preceded the Iron Age. Pure iron is too soft for use in implements, and until engines and railways were built there was no great need for iron.

The principal ores are hematite (Fe_2O_3), magnetite (Fe_3O_4), limonite ($2Fe_2O_3.3H_2O$), siderite or chalybite ($FeCO_3$). Magnetite is the richest, with about 72% iron; hematite about 70%, limonite about 60% and siderite about 48%. These theoretical percentages are never attained in the iron ore deposits, even the best and most productive magnetite ores of Kiruna and Gällivare, in Northern Sweden, contain not more than 68% iron. The most productive carbonate iron ores of Cleveland in Yorkshire and the iron mines of Northamptonshire average less than 30% iron (lean ores). Magnetite and hematite deposits in general are of primary geological origin, being formed in igneous and in sedimentary rocks by mineralizing solutions. Limonite deposits are of secondary origin, and siderite deposits may be of primary or of secondary origin.

Broadly, only the rich ores (over 50% Fe) enter international trade, though an understandable exception is the export of lean Lorraine ore from France to Germany and Belgium/Luxembourg. Newly-developed fields are changing the established pattern of iron ore production. The U.S.A. is taking increasing amounts from Canada, with the development of the Labrador deposits, as well as from the newer Venezuelan, Brazilian and Liberian fields. The U.S.S.R. has become a major exporter since the war; other relatively new exporters are China P.R., Chile, Peru and Australia. Most iron ore business is done on the basis of long-term contracts as the investment involved is so large. Thus it is common for major iron and steel firms to have a financial interest in iron mines and to build special ore-carrying vessels and dock facilities.

Ore is smelted in the blast furnace to produce pig iron, which generally contains about 4% of carbon and smaller amounts of phosphorus, sulphur, silicon and manganese. There were considerable advances in iron-making and in the efficiency of the blast furnace in the period 1950-1965. Coal cleaning, coal pulverization, and scientific blending permitted the use of previously unsuitable coals for the manufacture of coke. Exploration and exploitation of substantial deposits of high-iron content ore, particularly in South America, Canada, Africa and Australia, and their shipment by very large carriers to the major steel producers provided a valuable source of good quality raw material, while the improved sintering of ore fines and the pelletization of inferior ores made it possible to utilize low-iron content home ores.

Blast furnace efficiency was also improved by larger furnaces, better refractory linings, and reduced coke consumption. As a result, *in the best practices throughout the world*, the average iron content of metallic bearing materials charged into the blast furnace increased from about 52% Fe in 1950 to over 60% Fe in 1965; the raw iron ore part of the burden decreased from about eight-tenths of the charge in 1950 to about one-third in 1965. The downward trend of tons of total blast furnace burden per ton of hot metal pig iron produced continued, about 3.3 tons being required to produce one ton of pig iron in 1950 whereas in 1965 only about 2.4 tons of burden materials including coke were required. The production rate was much increased, rising from the typical large blast furnace of 1950-1955 which produced about 1 500 tons a day to a production of about 2 750 tons a day from the largest units in 1965.

In foundries the molten iron is poured into moulds to make cast iron products, such as pipes, railway chairs, parts of machinery and of internal combustion engines, etc. Though hard and strong, cast iron is generally brittle and incapable of being rolled, forged or drawn, as steel can be. Indeed, steel is remarkably versatile, being worked into such diverse products as girders, rails, bars, plates, sheets, strip, tinplate, tubes and wires, besides various castings and forgings. It has virtually eliminated wrought iron and is replacing cast iron in some uses.

About 75% of the world's steel production comes from the highly industrialized areas of the U.S.A., Western Europe and Japan – where most of it is also converted into various manufactures, such as motor vehicles etc. The table below shows further steel production data for selected countries.

Crude steel production
Selected countries

	MILLION MET. TONS			
	1955	1960	1965	1969
U.S.A.	106.2	90.1	119.3	128.0
U.K.	20.1	24.7	27.4	26.8
European Coal & Steel Community	52.5	72.8	86.0	107.3
India	1.7	3.3	6.4	6.5
U.S.S.R.	45.3	65.3	91.0	110.2
Japan	9.5	22.5	41.1	82.2

In the U.S.A. the industry is largely concentrated on the Northern Appalachian coalfield around Pittsburgh (its original location), but more recent expansion has tended to take place on the lake shores (Chicago, Detroit, Cleveland) at the trans-shipment point of waterborne ores from Lake Superior. New plants have also been built on the eastern seaboard, at such sites as Sparrows Point. The British industry is widely dispersed on inland and coastal sites, all with access to good coal. With the gradual exhaustion of most of its rich ore deposits, the U.K. imports nearly half of its ore requirements, mainly from Sweden, Canada and Venezuela. The industry in Western Europe is based on Ruhr, Belgian and French coal and on the local lean ores.

By 1965 the U.S.S.R., Eastern Europe and China P.R. accounted for one-third of crude steel output. The U.S.S.R. was the major producer of this group with a fivefold increase over the immediate pre-war level, and China P.R. ranked seventh in world production with the greatest rate of increase in the period since 1958.

In 1959 Japan overtook France to become the fifth world producer, due to very large additions to capacity in 1957, and by 1965 she was third in world production. For an historical representation of world steel production see the diagram below.

Crude steel and pig iron
World production 1880–1967[1]

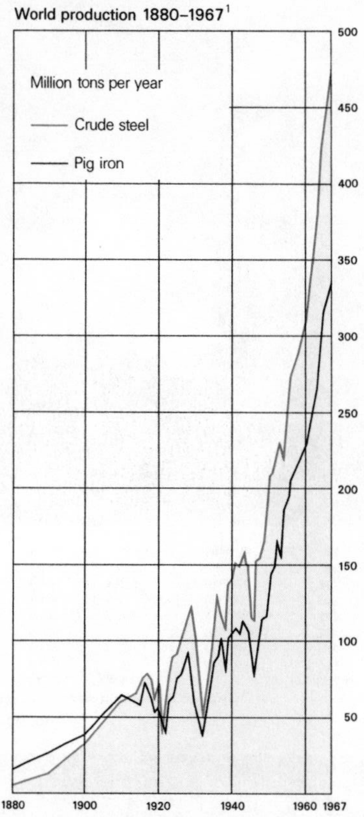

[1] Excl. China P. R. whose estimated production for 1955 and 1965, in million met. tons, was as follows: pig iron, 3.7 and 19; steel, 2.9 and 15.

In the U.K. the chief consumers of steel are the construction and engineering industries (19%) and the motor vehicles industry (16%). In the U.S.A. the automobile industry consumes 28%, construction 17% and containers 12%.

Steel is made from pig iron by removing much of the carbon, as well as the phosphorus and sulphur. The addition of various ferro-alloys is required for the production of alloy steels, which are in growing demand as a result of the invention of the gas turbine (which requires for its blades a steel which can withstand extremely high temperatures) and of other engineering advances.

Different steel-making processes are used according to the quality of the pig iron and the melting charge and the nature of the required product. Until the late 1960's, the most important in Britain and the U.S.A. was the open hearth ('Siemens-Martin') process. Here a proportion of scrap is used with the pig iron. The furnaces vary greatly in size with capacities up to 350 tons or more, and the steel-making process may take from 8 to 20 hours. By contrast, the Bessemer converter (*acid* Bessemer process invented by Henry Bessemer in 1856 and *basic* process about twenty years later by Thomas and Gilchrist) generally has a capacity of 25 to 50 tons and uses molten iron almost exclusively, air being blown through the molten metal (no fuel being used) and refining being completed in 12-15 minutes. The basic Bessemer ('Thomas') process was most important in France, Belgium and Luxembourg, being the only suitable process to deal with the high phosphoric irons produced by the local ores. The Bessemer process producing great quantities of cheap mild steel provided material for much of the industrial advance throughout the world in the nineteenth century and displaced wrought iron as the chief constructional material. Its dominance was in turn gradually challenged by the rise of the open-hearth process which took the lead in production in Britain in 1891 and in the U.S.A. in 1908. The crucible process (invented by Huntsman in 1740) has universally declined, especially since the end of World War I and the emergence of the electric processes mainly used to make alloy and other special steels and used with particular advantage in areas of cheap electric power (see table below showing major innovations).

With the availability of low-cost high purity tonnage oxygen after World War II, the lead of basic open hearth process began to be threatened. Various oxygen steel-making processes have been developed and have achieved rapid application. Chief among these is the Linz-Donawitz process (named from two neighbouring Austrian towns where the process was originally developed) abbreviated to the 'L-D' process and also known as 'BOP' and 'BOF' after basic oxygen process or furnace. In its operation, a stream of oxygen of more than 99.5% purity is directed by a lance onto a bath consisting of blast furnace hot metal and scrap iron coolant. As in the Bessemer process no fuel is required. A normal blowing time is about 25 minutes and several increases in furnace size have taken place in the years between 1954 and 1965, rising in many places from 35 tons per heat to 150-ton heats. With fast blowing and charging, production rates of the order of 300 to 400 tons an hour have been achieved; advances have also been promoted by the introduction of large rotating furnace vessels such as in the 'Kaldo' and 'Rotor' processes. By 1965, some of the major steel producers were making a substantial proportion of their steel in the BOF: Japan 55%, Australia 34%, the ECSC countries 19%, and the U.S.A. and the U.K. around 17%. There is no doubt that these proportions will grow and that in time the process will displace the open hearth.

The replacement boom after World War II and the demand resulting from the Korean War led to increased production up to 1952. Since then there have been three periods of lower world production, in 1952, 1954, and 1957-58, caused mainly by reductions in North American output. By 1959 output had recovered and 1960 showed a 13% increase over the previous year. Since then production has constantly increased. World crude steel production exceeded 400 million tons for the first time in 1964 and during the decade ending in 1965 almost doubled with an average annual increase of over 20 million tons. From the end of World War II to 1965 there were appreciable changes in the world distribution of iron- and steel-making plants, as is indicated in the figures for the U.S.A., whose share of world steel production has fallen from about one-half to one-quarter in this time, and for Japan where output has risen from 7½ to about 40 million tons in the decade 1955-1965. By 1965, however, over three-quarters of the world steel capacity was still concentrated in seven countries: the U.S.A., the U.S.S.R., Japan, Germany F.R., the U.K., France and Italy. The major technical changes that have most profoundly affected the iron and steel industry in just over one hundred years are summarized in the following table.

Major iron/steel industry innovations
Periods of development and application

1856-1880	Bessemer pneumatic steel-making Thomas Gilchrist basic process Siemens-Martin open hearth steel-making
1910-1930	Stainless steel Universal rolling mill By-product coke ovens Electric arc steel-making Continuous hot strip mill Agglomeration of flue dust and fine ores
1946-1965	Oxygen steel-making Continuous casting Vacuum degassing Pelletization

Estimated crude steel consumption and production
Selected countries

KG. PER CAPITA

		AUSTRALIA	BELG./LUX.	BRAZIL	CANADA	GERMANY F.R.	INDIA	JAPAN	SOUTH AFRICA	SPAIN	SWEDEN	U.K.	U.S.A.	U.S.S.R.	VENEZUELA
Consumption	1965	514	330	39	531	540	16	294	210	194	682	424	656	376	138
	1955	*333*	*292*	*26*	*322*	*410*	*7*	*82*	*138*	*50*	*402*	*367*	*620*	*225*	*116*
Production	1965	480	1 404	37	466	648	13	420	184	111	611	505	613	395	78
	1955	*243*	*995*	*21*	*261*	*425*	*5*	*106*	*112*	*45*	*293*	*393*	*643*	*208*	—

International trade in iron ore, iron and steel (1963-5 av.)

Iron ore[1]

Production
586 600 000 met. tons 1963-5 av.
340 716 000 1953-5 av.

Percentage exported
33% 1963-5 av.
23% 1953-5 av.

Exports
194 888 800 met. tons 1963-5 av.
77 548 000 1953-5 av.

	PERCENTAGE 1963-5 av.	1953-5 av.
Canada	15	*10*
U.S.S.R.	12	*11*
Sweden	12	*19*
France	11	*15*
Venezuela	8	*7*
Liberia	6	*2*
India	6	*2*
Brazil	5	*2*
Others	25	*32*
	100	*100*

Imports
194 374 000 met. tons 1963-5 av.
76 818 000 1953-5 av.

	PERCENTAGE 1963-5 av.	1953-5 av.
U.S.A.	21	*22*
Germany F.R.	18	*17*
Japan	17	*6*
Belg./Lux.	11	*17*
U.K.	9	*16*
Poland	5	*5*
Czechoslovakia	5	*5*
Italy	3	*1*
Others	11	*11*
	100	*100*

Pig iron/Ferro-alloys

Production
311 366 000 met. tons 1963-5 av.
*173 362 000 1953-5 av.**

Percentage exported
3% 1963-5 av.
*2% 1953-5 av.**

Exports
8 254 000 met. tons 1963-5 av.
3 592 000 1953-5 av.

	PERCENTAGE 1963-5 av.	1953-5 av.
U.S.S.R.	40	*33*
Germany F.R.	9	*9*
Norway	7	*6*
South Africa	7	—
Canada	7	*9*
Finland	6	—
France	4	*10*
Rhodesia	3	—
Others	17	*33*
	100	*100*

Imports
9 407 000 met. tons 1963-5 av.
3 616 000 1953-5 av.

	PERCENTAGE 1963-5 av.	1953-5 av.
Japan	27	—
U.S.A.	10	*13*
Italy	9	*6*
Germany D.R.	8	*7*
U.K.	6	*19*
Germany F.R.	6	*5*
Belg./Lux.	5	*9*
Poland	4	—
Sweden	3	*2*
Others	22	*39*
	100	*100*

Steel

Production
428 044 000 met. tons 1963-5 av.*
*242 792 000 1953-5 av.**

Percentage exported
1% 1963-5 av.
*1% 1953-5 av.**

Exports
4 751 000 met. tons 1963-5 av.
1 977 000 1953-5 av.

	PERCENTAGE 1963-5 av.	1953-5 av.
Germany F.R.	22	*14*
U.S.S.R.	17	*9*
Belg./Lux.	13	*19*
U.S.A.	13	*11*
France	10	*22*
Canada	7	*6*
Japan	4	*10*
Sweden	2	—
Others	12	*9*
	100	*100*

Imports
5 732 000 met. tons 1963-5 av.
1 711 000 1953-5 av.

	PERCENTAGE 1963-5 av.	1953-5 av.
Italy	17	*8*
France	10	*9*
Argentina	10	*22*
Spain	8	—
Hungary	7	—
Germany F.R.	6	*7*
Pakistan	5	*3*
Belg./Lux.	4	*4*
Others	33	*47*
	100	*100*

Iron and steel scrap

Production data not available

Exports
13 185 000 met. tons 1963-5 av.
4 988 000 1953-5 av.

	PERCENTAGE 1963-5 av.	1953-5 av.
U.S.A.	49	*43*
Germany F.R.	12	*12*
France	11	*11*
U.K.	6	—
U.S.S.R.	3	*1*
Canada	3	*10*
Netherlands	3	*3*
India	3	*5*
Others	10	*15*
	100	*100*

Imports
13 069 000 met. tons 1963-5 av.
5 891 000 1953-5 av.

	PERCENTAGE 1963-5 av.	1953-5 av.
Japan	33	*19*
Italy	30	*27*
Germany F.R.	9	*11*
Canada	6	*3*
France	4	*3*
Mexico	4	*3*
Spain	2	*1*
U.S.A.	2	*3*
Others	10	*30*
	100	*100*

*Estimate [1] Including pyrites

Iron Ore/Steel

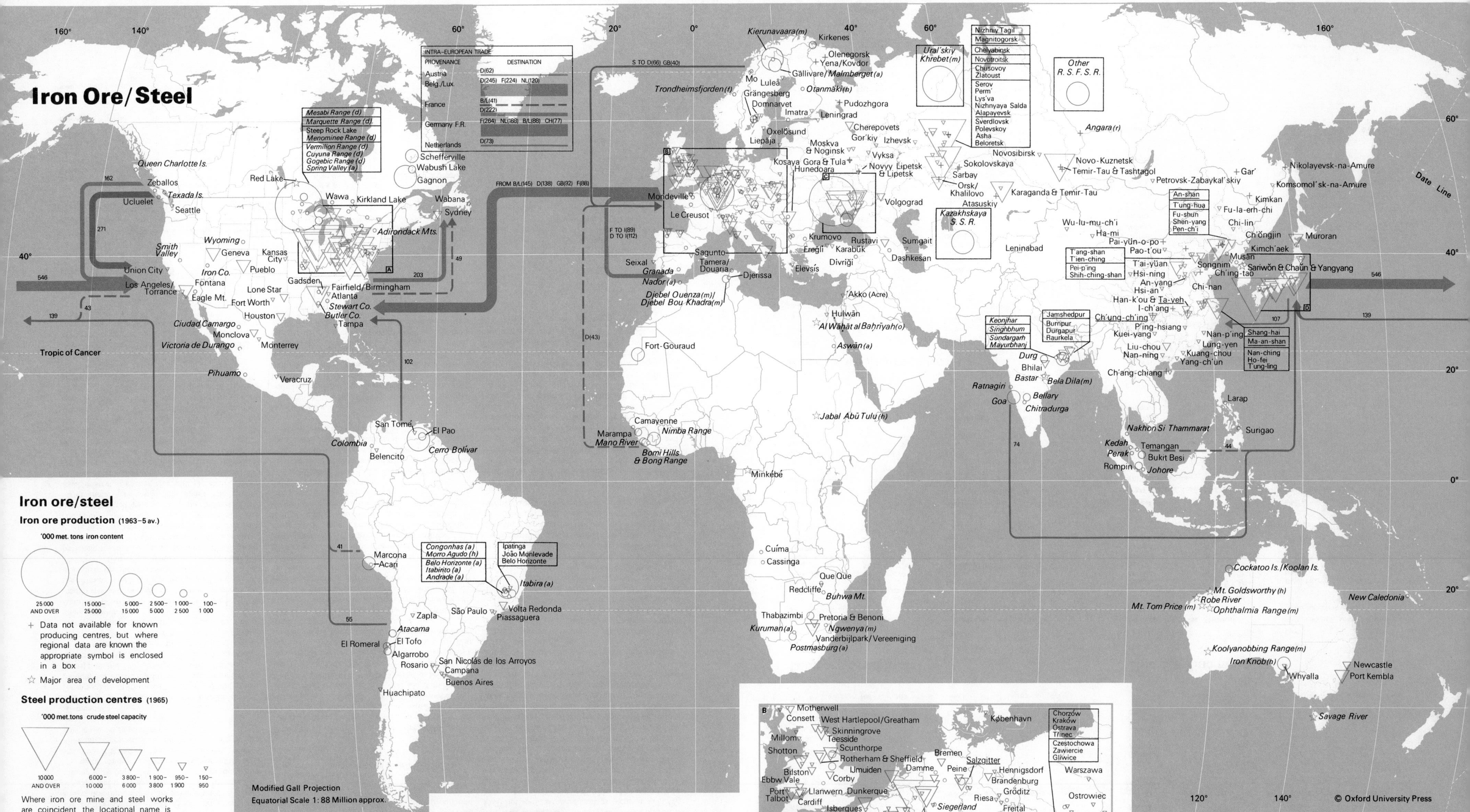

Iron ore/steel

Iron ore production (1963–5 av.)

'000 met. tons iron content

25 000 AND OVER · 15 000–25 000 · 5 000–15 000 · 2 500–5 000 · 1 000–2 500 · 100–1 000

+ Data not available for known producing centres, but where regional data are known the appropriate symbol is enclosed in a box

☆ Major area of development

Steel production centres (1965)

'000 met.tons crude steel capacity

10 000 AND OVER · 6 000–10 000 · 3 800–6 000 · 1 900–3 800 · 950–1 900 · 150–950

Where iron ore mine and steel works are coincident the locational name is underlined, for example Kamaishi

Major trade flows (1966)

Commodity: S.I.T.C.[1] no.

IRON ORE AND CONCENTRATES: 281.3

IRON AND STEEL: 67

Value ($U.S.)

0.5mm represents increments of $100 million

($ MILLIONS) 900 · 500 · 100 — UNDER $50 MILLION — 203 VALUE IN $ MILLIONS

Trade flow is defined as trade in one direction between two countries. This indicates major trading partners but not necessarily major traders.

[1] S.I.T.C. STANDARD INTERNATIONAL TRADE CLASSIFICATION

Iron ore production[1]			Steel production	
309 707 000*		met. tons 1963-5 av.	428 044 000*	
164 977 000*		1953-5 av.	242 792 000*	
PERCENTAGE			PERCENTAGE	
1953-5 av.	1963-5 av.		1963-5 av.	1953-5 av.
23	28	U.S.S.R.	20	17
31	15	U.S.A.	26	39
3	8	China P.R.	3*	1*
3	6	Canada	2	1
8	6	France	4	5
6	5	Sweden	1	1
1	—	Japan	9	3
2	1	Germany F.R.	8	9
3	1	U.K.	6	8
20	30	Others	21	16
100	100		100	100

*Estimate [1] Iron content

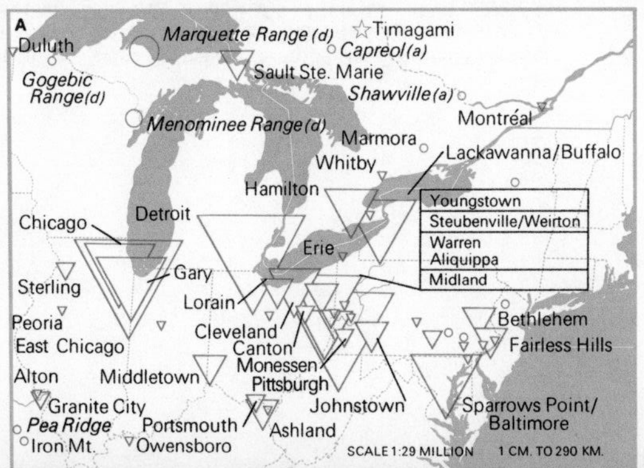

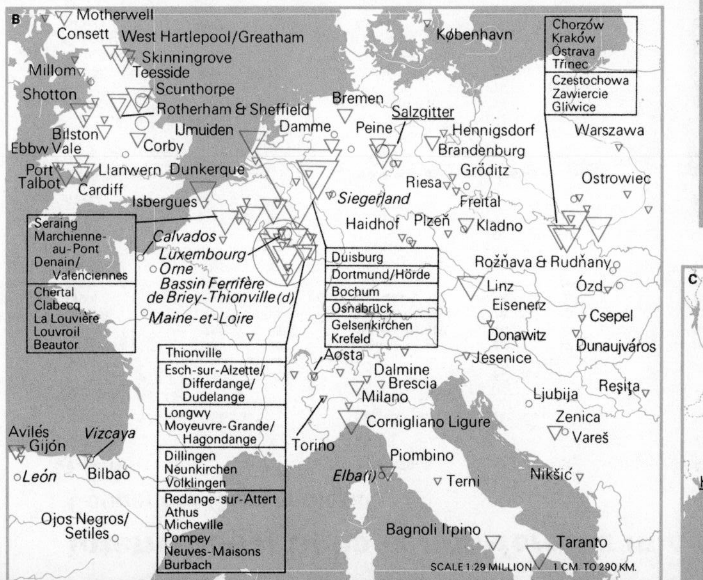

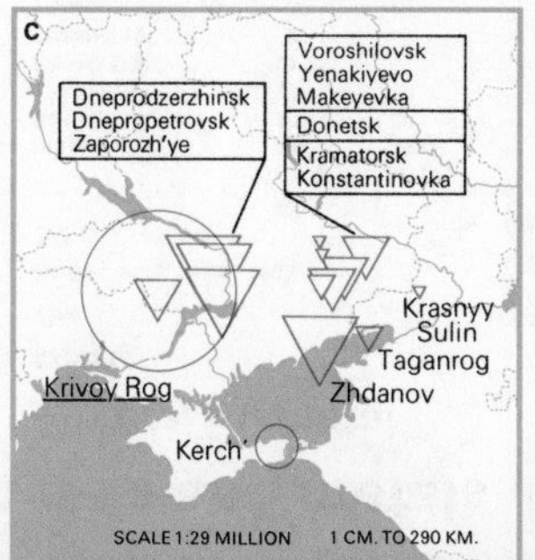

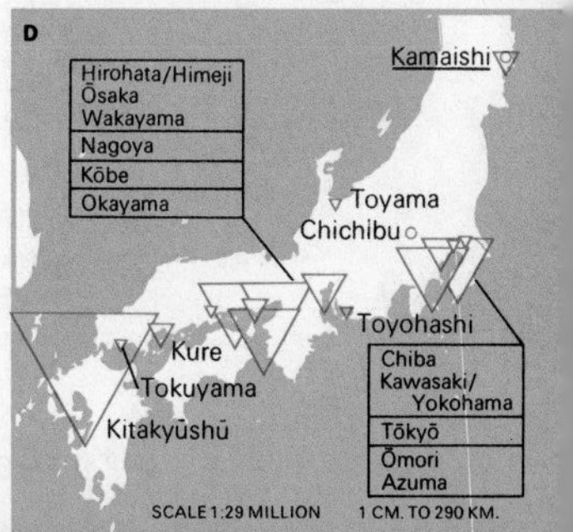

Non-ferrous Minerals and Metals

Aluminium p. 47 · Bauxite p. 47 · Copper p. 45 · Lead p. 46 · Tin p. 45 · Zinc p. 46

For individual country data see Statistical Supplement

The ability to extract metals from the ores in which the earth's crust abounds marked one of man's most important steps towards civilization. Some of the earth's mineral resources remain unexploited today, notably those in the sea and under the polar ice-caps and other deposits which are too small for mining to be profitable. Nevertheless, production of the major non-ferrous metals is widespread throughout the world and the five most important metals—aluminium, copper, lead, zinc and tin—play a vital part in the world economy.

Aluminium

Aluminium is the most abundant metallic element, forming 8% of the earth's crust. Although aluminium can be obtained from many common rocks, bauxite is the only important ore, consisting of hydrated aluminium oxides together with impurities of iron, silicon, and titanium oxides. Bauxite deposits are formed on or near the earth's surface through humid tropical weathering of rocks containing aluminium silicates.

Alumina (aluminium oxide) is produced by the reaction of caustic soda on bauxite dissolving out the alumina which is then precipitated and roasted in a kiln to produce a white powder.

The production of aluminium metal from alumina by smelting requires great amounts of electricity, which accounts for the industry being established where there is cheap hydro-electric power available. Aluminium has many valuable properties which have encouraged its use. It is the lightest of the major metals, weighing only about one-third as much as steel, copper or zinc, and a quarter as much as lead. It is second only to copper as a heat and electricity conductor, and it reflects light and radiant heat well. It also has a strong resistance to corrosion. World consumption has grown during the past 25 years at a faster rate than any of the other major metals, initially as a result of the growth of the aircraft industry. The applications for aluminium have steadily widened, however, and more recently its use in the building and electrical industries has grown considerably.

Copper

Copper, the oldest of the major metals, is produced in over 50 countries and this number will rise during coming years as new mines come into operation in Mauritania, Indonesia, Malaysia and Bougainville Island. At present the four major production areas account for 80% of total world mine production. They are listed below with their 1969 production statistics.

	'000 MET. TONS
North America (U.S.A. and Canada)	1 901
African Copper Belt (Zambia and Congo)	1 084
Western Andes (Chile and Peru)	887
Urals and Kazakhstan, U.S.S.R.	875

Products made of copper or containing copper components are used in every country in the world. As copper is malleable and ductile and has a high electrical conductivity, over 50% of world consumption is in the electrical and allied industries. Copper's ability to withstand corrosion leads to its use in shipbuilding and construction, as does its capacity for forming strong and easily worked alloys, such as bronze and brass, many of which are also used in general engineering and the motor industry.

Most copper ore is concentrated, smelted and refined in the countries in which it is produced, although there are some important exceptions to this. At present, for example, the whole of the rapidly expanding production by the Philippines is shipped in the form of concentrates to the U.S.A. and Japan while part of the smelter production of the Congo D.R., South Africa, Zambia, Chile and Peru is exported for refining in other countries.

Since one of copper's greatest virtues is its durability, it is possible to recover considerable quantities of copper from scrap materials. "Secondary" copper recovered in this way accounts for 40% of total world copper consumption.

In 1967 Chile, Congo D.R., Peru and Zambia, who between them produce a third of world mine output held a conference at Lusaka, Zambia, and formed the Conseil Intergouvernemental des Pays Exportateurs de Cuivre, known as CIPEC.

Lead and Zinc

Lead and zinc ores are very often found together and contain important quantities of silver and gold. For producing the metals by the electrolytic and well established thermal processes, the ores must be treated to yield separate lead and zinc concentrates. The Imperial Smelting process, which uses a blast furnace can, however, produce both metals from mixed concentrates. Zinc and lead are widely distributed throughout the world, and Canada, Australia, the U.S.A. and U.S.S.R. are the biggest producers.

The chief source of lead is galena (lead sulphide, PbS) but some is also found as cerussite ($PbCO_3$) formed by the oxidation of galena. The main use of lead is in storage batteries (used in motor vehicles), which takes about 30% of world production. Other important uses are for sheathing electric power cables; for anti-knock compounds to adjust the octane rating of petrol; as building materials in the form of sheet and pipe; for solders and other alloys such as printing metal and for paint pigments and other compounds such as ceramic glazes. Lead also has a wide range of miscellaneous uses, including shielding for radio-active materials, shot and bullet rod for ammunition, foil and seals for packaging, balance and fishing weights.

The chief source of zinc is the mineral sphalerite or zinc blende (ZnS), but smithsonite ("calamine", $ZnCO_3$) and various silicates which are formed by the action of air and water on zinc blende are important in some parts of the world. Nearly a half of the world's annual zinc production is used to protect steel products in the form of galvanized and other zinc coatings. Brass, an alloy with copper, is another very important use, and special high purity zinc alloyed with 4% aluminium and a little magnesium is pressure diecast on a very large scale to produce components of cars, household equipments, hardware etc. Zinc sheet and strip are important building materials and zinc compounds are used in the manufacture of rubber, paints and ceramic goods.

Tin

Most of the world's tin deposits occur as cassiterite (SnO_2), either in alluvial deposits, for example in Malaysia and Nigeria, where it is recovered mainly by dredging and gravel pumps, or as veins and lodes, for example in Bolivia, where it is mined by conventional methods. Because it is unusually malleable and resists corrosion, it is largely used in the making of tin plate for the canning industry. With the development of electrolytic methods of tin plating, in which the coating of tin is very thin, the quantity of tin used per ton of tinplate has decreased but a greater amount of tin plate is being produced. Other uses include alloys (such as whitemetal, bronze and gunmetal), solder and tin oxide and tin powders.

Metal production

Copper

5 230 000 met. tons 1963-5 av.*

*3 081 000 1953-5 av.**

	PERCENTAGE 1963-5 av.	1953-5 av.
U.S.A.	24	30
U.S.S.R.*	12	11
Zambia	12	12[1]
Chile	11	12
Canada	7	6
Japan	6	2
Germany F.R.	6	8
Congo D.R.	5	7
Peru	3	1
Others	14	11
	100	100

Tin

197 000 met. tons 1963-5 av.*

*197 000 1953-5 av.**

	PERCENTAGE 1963-5 av.	1953-5 av.
Malaysia	39	35
China P.R.*	13	5
U.S.S.R.*	11	5
U.K.	9	14
Netherlands	7	14
Nigeria	5	—
Belgium	3	5
Thailand	3	—
U.S.A.	2	13
Others	8	9
	100	100

Lead

2 520 000 met. tons 1963-5 av.*

*1 959 000 1953-5 av.**

	PERCENTAGE 1963-5 av.	1953-5 av.
U.S.A.	15	22
U.S.S.R.*	13	11
Australia	11	12
Mexico	7	11
Canada	6	7
Germany F.R.	4	6
Yugoslavia	4	4
Japan	4	1
Belgium	4	4
Others	32	22
	100	100

Zinc

3 727 000 met. tons 1963-5 av.*

*2 501 000 1953-5 av.**

	PERCENTAGE 1963-5 av.	1953-5 av.
U.S.A.	23	32
U.S.S.R.*	13	10
Japan	9	4
Canada	8	9
Belgium	6	8
Australia	5	4
Poland	5	6
France	5	4
Germany F.R.	3	7
Others	23	16
	100	100

Aluminium

5 843 000 met. tons 1963-5 av.*

*2 805 000 1953-5 av.**

	PERCENTAGE 1963-5 av.	1953-5 av.
U.S.A.	39	46
U.S.S.R.*	14	13
Canada	12	19
France	5	4
Japan	4	2
Norway	4	2
Germany F.R.	4	4
Italy	2	2
China P.R.*	2	—
Others	14	8
	100	100

*Estimate [1]Incl. Rhodesia

International trade in non-ferrous minerals and metals[1] (1963-5 av.)

Copper ore/Copper metal

Exports

Ore

731 000 met. tons 1963-5 av.

381 000 1953-5 av.

	PERCENTAGE 1963-5 av.	1953-5 av.
Philippines	37	20[3]
Cyprus	28	6[4]
Canada	12[2]	11
Chile	5	8
Peru	3	3
Others	15	52
	100	100

Metal

3 720 000 met. tons 1963-5 av.

2 046 000 1953-5 av.

	PERCENTAGE 1963-5 av.	1953-5 av.
Zambia	18	18[7]
Chile	15	18
U.S.A.	10	12
Belg./Lux.	9	8
Congo D.R.	8*	11
Others	40	33
	100	100

Imports

Ore

967 000 met. tons 1963-5 av.

549 000 1953-5 av.

	PERCENTAGE 1963-5 av.	1953-5 av.
Japan	63	7
Germany F.R.[5]	15	28
Sweden	9	8
Norway	6	6[6]
U.S.A.[2]	2	19
Others	5	32
	100	100

Metal

3 576 000 met. tons 1963-5 av.

1 783 000 1953-5 av.

	PERCENTAGE 1963-5 av.	1953-5 av.
Germany F.R.	16	14
U.K.	15	21
U.S.A.	13	26
Belg./Lux.	10	1
France	8	8
Others	38	30
	100	100

Tin ore/Tin metal

Exports

Ore

73 000 met. tons 1963-5 av.

121 000 1953-5 av.

	PERCENTAGE 1963-5 av.	1953-5 av.
Indonesia	29	38
Bolivia[2]	29	25
Thailand[2]	19	9
Congo D.R.	11*[8]	15
Argentina	3[9]	—
Others	9	13
	100	100

Metal

144 000 met. tons 1963-5 av.

147 000 1953-5 av.

	PERCENTAGE 1963-5 av.	1953-5 av.
Malaysia	52	47
Netherlands	9	19
U.K.	7	8
Nigeria	7	—
China P.R.*	6	3
Others	19	23
	100	100

Imports

Ore

103 000 met. tons 1963-5 av.

153 000 1953-5 av.

	PERCENTAGE 1963-5 av.	1953-5 av.
U.K.	44	40
Netherlands	20	24
Malaysia	11	8
Germany F.R.	8	1
Belg./Lux.	7	9
Others	10	18
	100	100

Metal

149 000 met. tons 1963-5 av.

140 000 1953-5 av.

	PERCENTAGE 1963-5 av.	1953-5 av.
U.S.A.	28	48
Japan	10	4
Germany F.R.	9	5
France	7	6
U.K.	6	1
Others	40	36
	100	100

Lead ore/Lead metal[10]

Exports

Ore

619 000 met. tons 1963-5 av.

392 000 1953-5 av.

	PERCENTAGE 1963-5 av.	1953-5 av.
Morocco	20	21
Australia	15[2]	10
Peru	11	12[2]
South West Africa[2]	9	16
Sweden	7	3
Others	38	38
	100	100

Metal

1 132 000 met. tons 1963-5 av.

936 000 1953-5 av.

	PERCENTAGE 1963-5 av.	1953-5 av.
Australia	22	22
Mexico	13	22
Canada	9	10
U.S.S.R.	9	3
Peru	7	6
Others	40	37
	100	100

Imports

Ore

637 000 met. tons 1963-5 av.

430 000 1953-5 av.

	PERCENTAGE 1963-5 av.	1953-5 av.
Belg./Lux.	22	27
France	21	20
Germany F.R.	19	16
U.S.A.[2]	19	30
Japan	10	4
Others	9	3
	100	100

Metal

1 073 000 met. tons 1963-5 av.

884 000 1953-5 av.

	PERCENTAGE 1963-5 av.	1953-5 av.
U.S.A.	19	33
U.K.	17	23
Germany F.R.	11	6
Italy	6	2
Netherlands	6	5
Others	41	31
	100	100

Zinc ore/Zinc metal

Exports

Ore

1 908 000 met. tons 1963-5 av.

1 520 000 1953-5 av.

	PERCENTAGE 1963-5 av.	1953-5 av.
Canada[2]	17	11
Mexico	16	22
Peru[2]	10	7
Sweden	8	6
Finland	8	1
Others	41	53
	100	100

Metal

1 277 000 met. tons 1963-5 av.

875 000 1953-5 av.

	PERCENTAGE 1963-5 av.	1953-5 av.
Canada	17	21
Belg./Lux.	14	18
U.S.S.R.	10	4
Poland	9	11
Australia	7	5
Others	43	41
	100	100

Imports

Ore

2 132 000 met. tons 1963-5 av.

1 580 000 1953-5 av.

	PERCENTAGE 1963-5 av.	1953-5 av.
Belg./Lux.	22	29
U.S.A.	15	25
France	15[2]	15
Japan	13	—
U.K.	12	12
Others	23	19
	100	100

Metal

1 219 000 met. tons 1963-5 av.

765 000 1953-5 av.

	PERCENTAGE 1963-5 av.	1953-5 av.
U.K.	16	20
Germany F.R.	15	8
U.S.A.	12	24
India	7	4
U.S.S.R.	6	6
Others	44	38
	100	100

Bauxite ore[11]/Aluminium

Exports

Ore

18 378 000 met. tons 1963-5 av.

10 416 000 1953-5 av.

	PERCENTAGE 1963-5 av.	1953-5 av.
Jamaica	33*	19
Surinam	21	31
Guyana	8*	21
Greece	6	4
Yugoslavia	5	5
Others	27	20
	100	100

Metal

2 291 000 met. tons 1963-5 av.

944 000 1953-5 av.

	PERCENTAGE 1963-5 av.	1953-5 av.
Canada	28	49
U.S.A.	14	5
Norway	11	6
France	9	3
U.S.S.R.	9	4*
Others	29	33
	100	100

Imports

Ore

17 610 000 met. tons 1963-5 av.

9 387 000 1953-5 av.

	PERCENTAGE 1963-5 av.	1953-5 av.
U.S.A.	60	52
Canada	10	28[13]
Germany F.R.	9	11
Japan	9	3
U.S.S.R.	3[12]	—
Others	9	6
	100	100

Metal

2 090 000 met. tons 1963-5 av.

868 000 1953-5 av.

	PERCENTAGE 1963-5 av.	1953-5 av.
U.S.A.	23	30
U.K.	17	25
Germany F.R.	11	6
Belg./Lux.	6	4
Italy	5	2
Others	38	33
	100	100

Annual consumption of major non-ferrous metals

Selected countries (1963-5 av.)

'000 MET. TONS

	COPPER	TIN	LEAD	ZINC	ALUMINIUM
U.S.A.	1 679	61[14]	966	1 099	2 576
U.S.S.R.	749	30	319	323	858*
U.K.	612	22	301	276	341
Germany F.R.	539	13	258	312	363
Japan	412	18	150	321	256
France	276	11[15]	162	190	247
Italy	208	6	93	102	125
China P.R.	120	15	71	80	88
Australia	92	5	56	102	67[16]
India	69	5	42	60	63
Mexico	34	1	53	20	18
Poland	—	3	55	112	56
World	5 800	229	2 800	3 900	6 000

*Estimate [1]Incl. alloys, scrap and salts [2]Metal content of ore [3]Incl. copper-gold-silver concentrate [4]Incl. Cu content of cement copper and cupreous pyrites [5]Excl. burnt cupreous pyrites [6]Incl. copper-nickel matte [7]Incl. blister and electrolytic copper [8]Incl. Rwanda and Burundi [9]Incl. tin-silver ore [10]Incl. Pb content of base bullion [11]Incl. cryolite [12]Imports from Greece only [13]Incl. alumina [14]Primary and secondary tin [15]Incl. Saar [16]Oceania

Copper/Tin

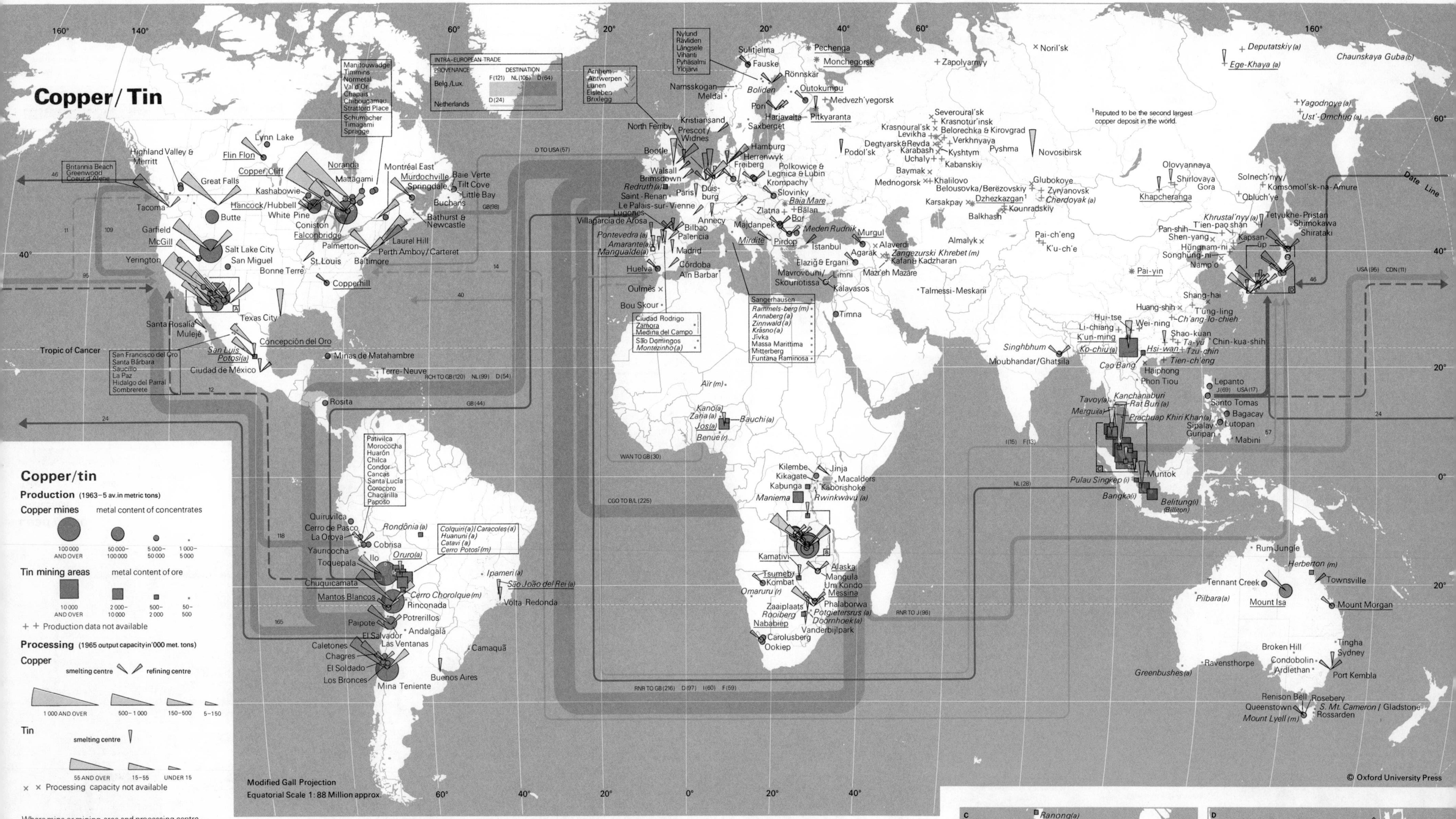

Copper/tin

Production (1963–5 av. in metric tons)

Copper mines metal content of concentrates

100 000 AND OVER · 50 000–100 000 · 5 000–50 000 · 1 000–5 000

Tin mining areas metal content of ore

10 000 AND OVER · 2 000–10 000 · 500–2 000 · 50–500

+ + Production data not available

Processing (1965 output capacity in '000 met. tons)

Copper smelting centre · refining centre

1 000 AND OVER · 500–1 000 · 150–500 · 5–150

Tin smelting centre

55 AND OVER · 15–55 · UNDER 15

× × Processing capacity not available

Where mine or mining area and processing centre are coincident the locational name is underlined for example, McGill or *Baia Mare*

Major trade flows (1966)

Commodity: S.I.T.C. no.

COPPER ORE/MATTE/CONCENTRATES : 283.1

TIN ORE/CONCENTRATES : 283.6

COPPER METAL : 682 (WORKED/UNWORKED)

TIN METAL : 687 (WORKED/UNWORKED)

Value ($ U.S.)

0.5 mm. represents increments of $40 million

1000 ($ MILLIONS) · 840 · 680 · 520 · 360 · 200 · 40

UNDER $20 MILLION

95 VALUE IN $ MILLIONS

Copper ore production[1]

4 883 000 met. tons 1963-5 av.*

*2 891 000 1953-5 av.**

	PERCENTAGE 1963-5 av.	1953-5 av.
U.S.A.	24	*29*
U.S.S.R.*	15	*11*
Zambia	13	*13*
Chile	12	*13*
Canada	9	*9*
Congo D.R.	6	*8*
Peru	4	*1*
Japan	2	*2*
Australia	2	*1*
Others	13	*13*
	100	*100*

*Estimate [1]Metal content

Tin ore production[1]

198 000 met. tons 1963-5 av.*

*193 000 1953-5 av.**

	PERCENTAGE 1963-5 av.	1953-5 av.
Malaysia	31	*31*
China P.R.*	13	*6*
Bolivia	12	*16*
U.S.S.R.*	10	*5*
Thailand	9	*5*
Indonesia	7	*18*
Nigeria	5	*4*
Congo D.R.	4	*8*
Australia	2	*1*
Others	6	*6*
	100	*100*

*Estimate [1]Metal content

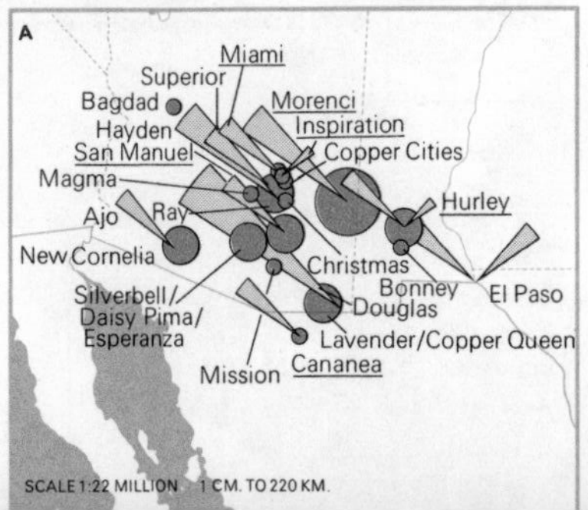

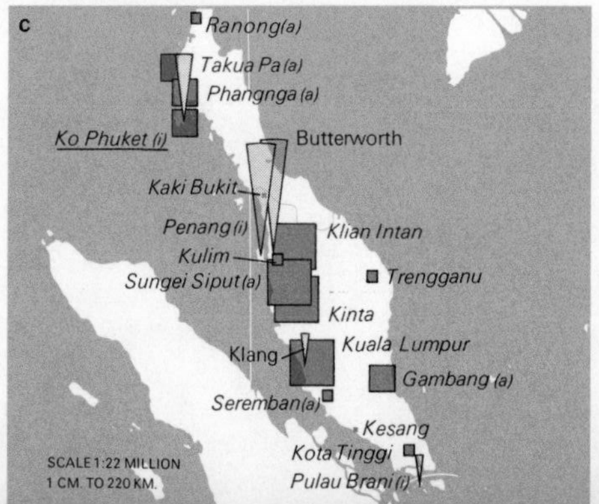

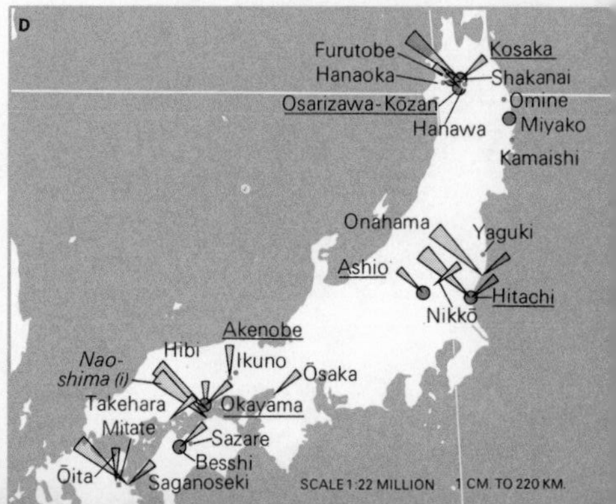

Lead / Zinc

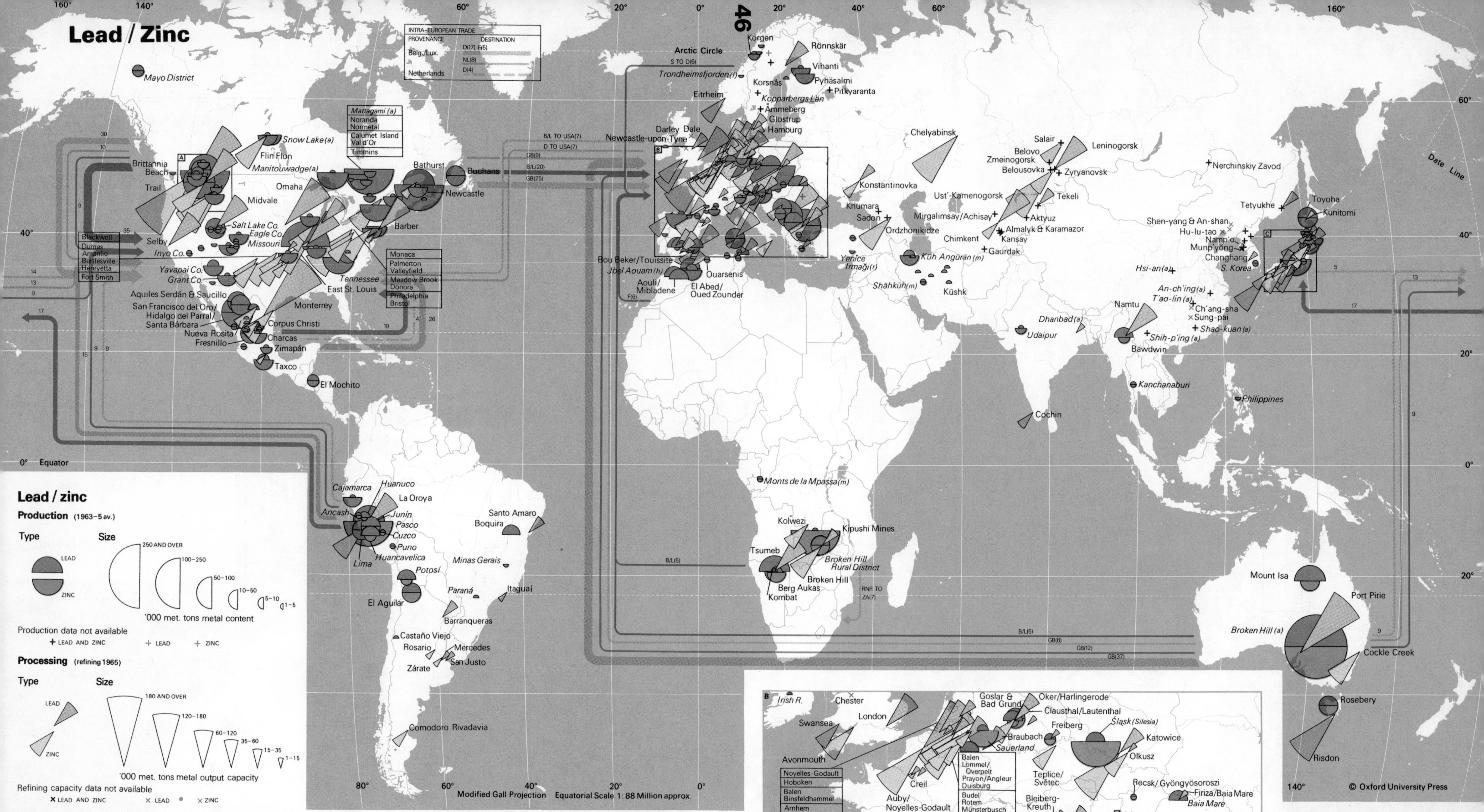

Lead / zinc

Production (1963–5 av.)

Type — LEAD / ZINC

Size — 250 AND OVER; 100–250; 50–100; 10–50; 5–10; 1–5

'000 met. tons metal content

Production data not available
+ LEAD AND ZINC + LEAD + ZINC

Processing (refining 1965)

Type — LEAD / ZINC

Size — 180 AND OVER; 120–180; 60–120; 35–60; 15–35; 1–15

'000 met. tons metal output capacity

Refining capacity data not available
× LEAD AND ZINC × LEAD × ZINC

Cadmium is recovered as a by-product of zinc and, to a much lesser extent, lead and copper processing. The largest producers, in order, are the U.S.A., the U.S.S.R., Japan and Canada. They produced 71% of the estimated total of 12 150 met. tons of cadmium metal recovered 1963-5 av. This metal was recovered from domestic or imported ores.

Major trade flows (1966)

Commodity: S.I.T.C. no.

LEAD ORES/CONCENTRATES : 283.4
ZINC ORES/CONCENTRATES : 283.5
LEAD METAL(WORKED/UNWORKED): 685
ZINC METAL(WORKED/UNWORKED): 686

Value ($U.S.)

0.5 mm represents increments of $10 million

90 / 50 / 10 ($ MILLIONS)
UNDER $5 MILLION
20 — VALUE IN $ MILLIONS

Lead production[1]

2 583 000 met. tons 1963-5 av.*
2 029 000 1953-5 av.*

	PERCENTAGE 1963-5 av.	1953-5 av.
Australia	15	14
U.S.S.R.	13	10
U.S.A.	10	15
Canada	8	9
Mexico	7	11
Peru	6	6
Yugoslavia	4	4
China P.R.	4	—
Bulgaria	4	NA
Others	29	NA
	100	100

*Estimate [1]Content of ore

Zinc production[1]

3 997 500 met. tons 1963-5 av.*[2]
2 736 700 1953-5 av.*

	PERCENTAGE 1963-5 av.	1953-5 av.
Canada	16	13
U.S.A.	13	17
U.S.S.R.	11	9
Australia	9	9
Mexico	6	9
Peru	6	6
Japan	5	4
Poland	4	4
Italy	3	4
Others	27	25
	100	100

*Estimate
[1]Content of ore
[2]Excl. Czechoslovakia, Romania & N. Vietnam

Modified Gall Projection Equatorial Scale 1: 88 Million approx.

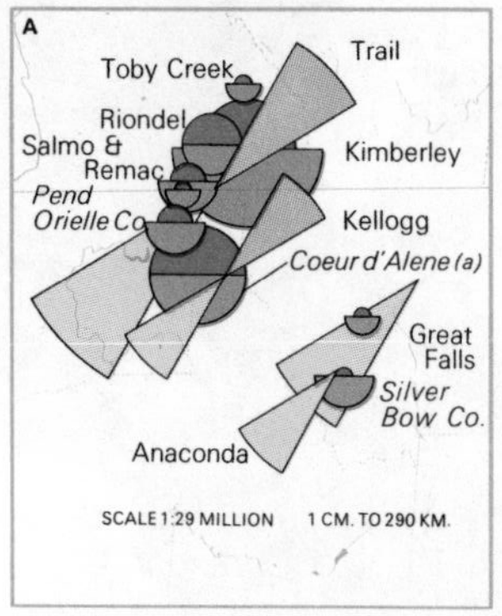

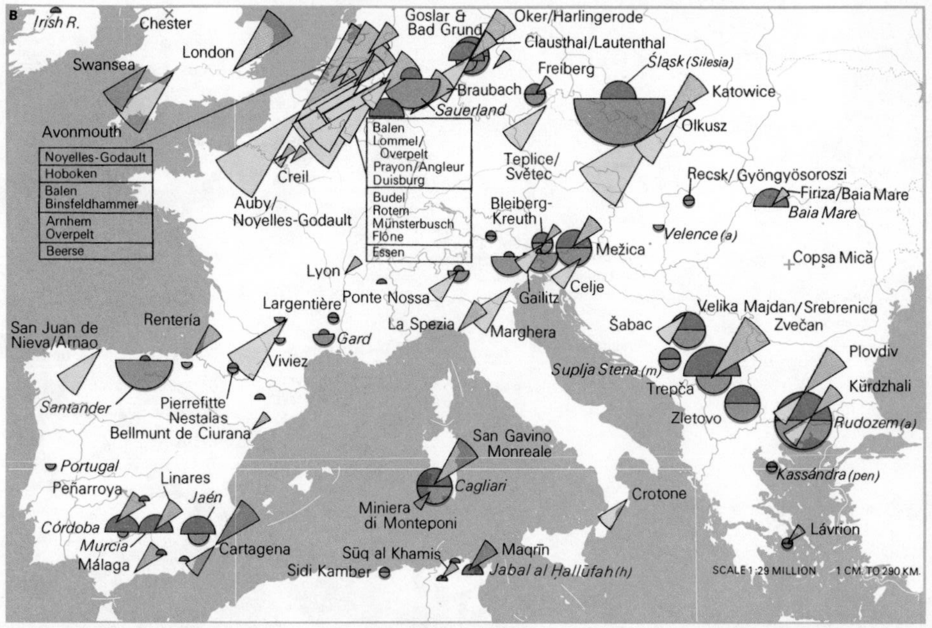

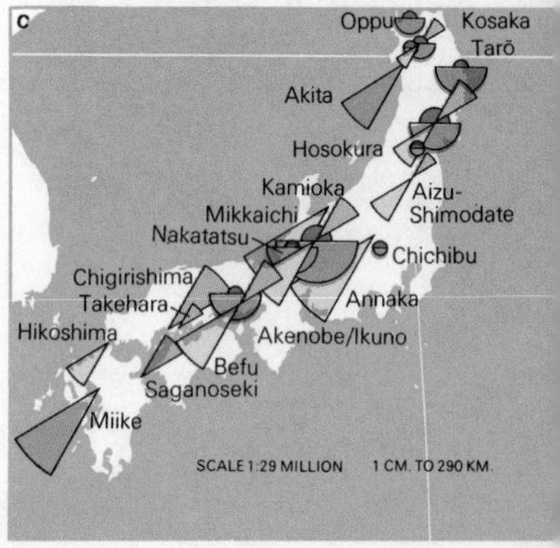

Bauxite (and Aluminium)/Titanium

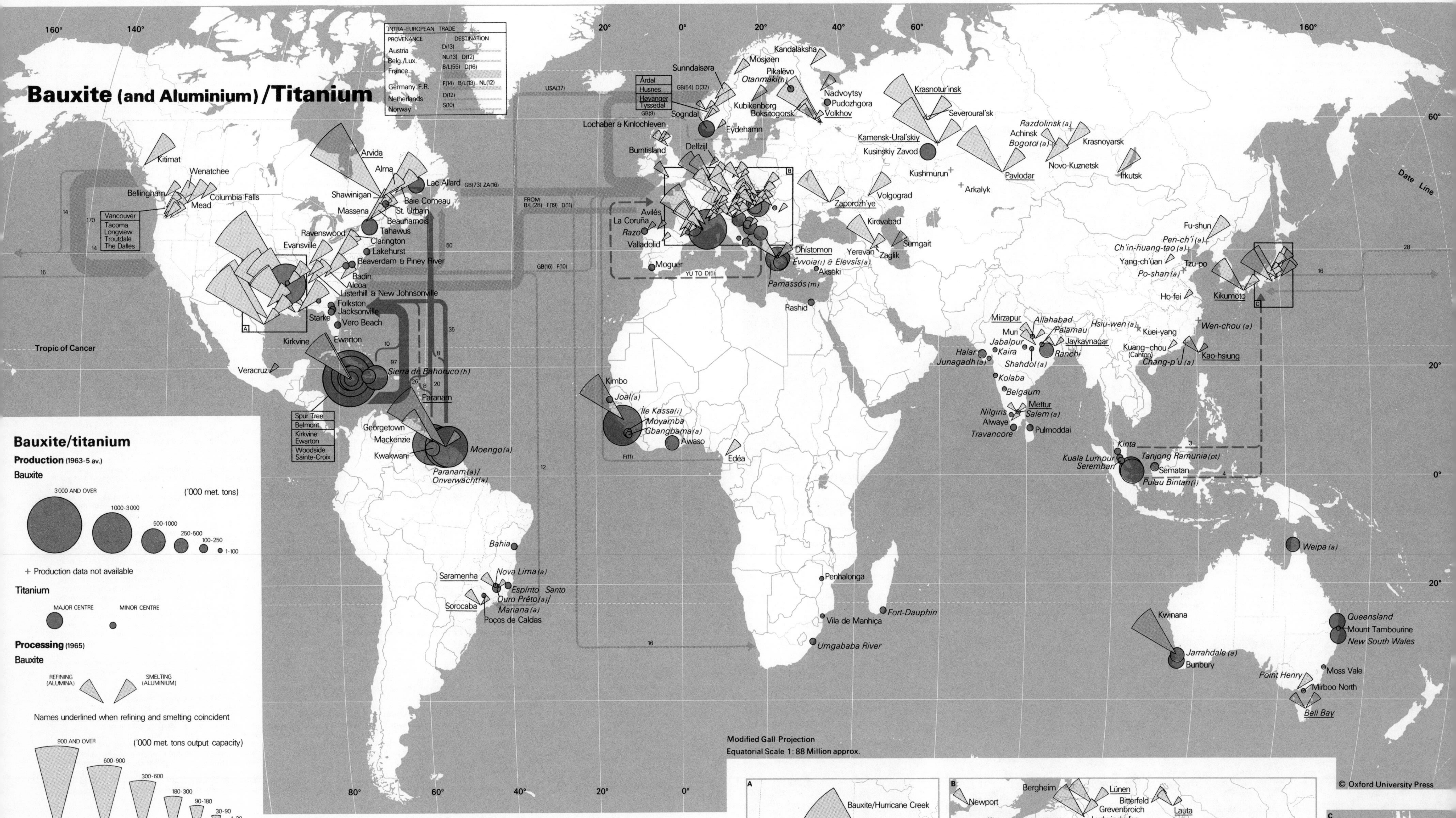

Bauxite/titanium

Production (1963-5 av.)

Bauxite

('000 met. tons)

3 000 AND OVER · 1000-3 000 · 500-1000 · 250-500 · 100-250 · 1-100

+ Production data not available

Titanium

MAJOR CENTRE · MINOR CENTRE

Processing (1965)

Bauxite

REFINING (ALUMINA) · SMELTING (ALUMINIUM)

Names underlined when refining and smelting coincident

('000 met. tons output capacity)

900 AND OVER · 600-900 · 300-600 · 180-300 · 90-180 · 30-90 · 1-30

× Refining capacity data not available

Major trade flows (1966)

Commodity: S.I.T.C.[1] no.

BAUXITE/ALUMINIUM CONCENTRATES : 283.3

ALUMINIUM METAL (WORKED/UNWORKED) **: 684**

Value($U.S.)

0.5mm represents increments of $20 million

180 · 100 · 20 ($ MILLIONS) — UNDER $10 MILLION — 37 VALUE IN $ MILLIONS

[1] S.I.T.C. = STANDARD INTERNATIONAL TRADE CLASSIFICATION

Bauxite production

33 830 000 met. tons 1963-5 av.*

*15 783 000 1953-5 av.**

	PERCENTAGE 1963-5 av.	1953-5 av.
Jamaica	**23**	*13*
U.S.S.R.*	**13**	*6*
Surinam	**12**	*21*
Guyana	**8**	*15*
France	**7**	*8*
Guinea	**5**	*—*
U.S.A.	**5**	*11*
Hungary	**4**	*8*
Yugoslavia	**4**	*4*
Others	**19**	*14*
	100	*100*

*Estimate

Aluminium production

5 843 000 met. tons 1963-5 av.*

*2 805 000 1953-5 av.**

	PERCENTAGE 1963-5 av.	1953-5 av.
U.S.A.	**39**	*46*
U.S.S.R.*	**14**	*13*
Canada	**12**	*19*
France	**5**	*4*
Japan	**4**	*2*
Norway	**4**	*2*
Germany F.R.	**4**	*4*
Italy	**2**	*2*
China P.R.*	**2**	*—*
Others	**14**	*8*
	100	*100*

*Estimate

Titanium production[1]

2 482 000 met. tons 1963-5 av.*

*1 185 000 1953-5 av.**

	PERCENTAGE 1963-5 av.	1953-5 av.
U.S.A.	**35**	*43*
Australia	**21**	*4*
Canada	**18**	*11*
Norway	**11**	*12*
Malaysia[2]	**5**	*4*
Finland	**5**	*4*
Spain	**2**	*—*
Others	**3**	*22*
	100	*100*

*Estimate
[1] Ilmenite and rutile
[2] Exports

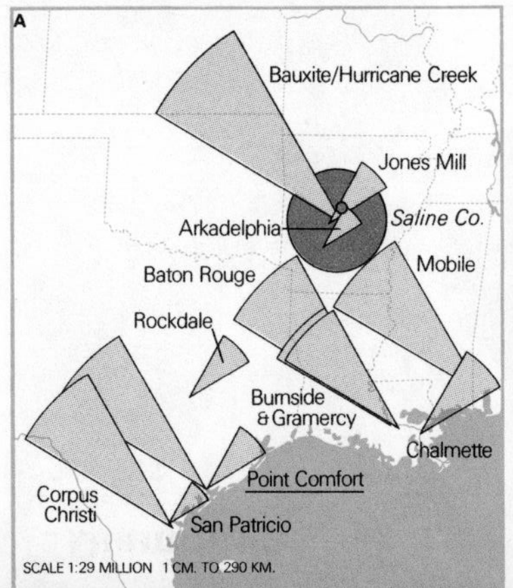

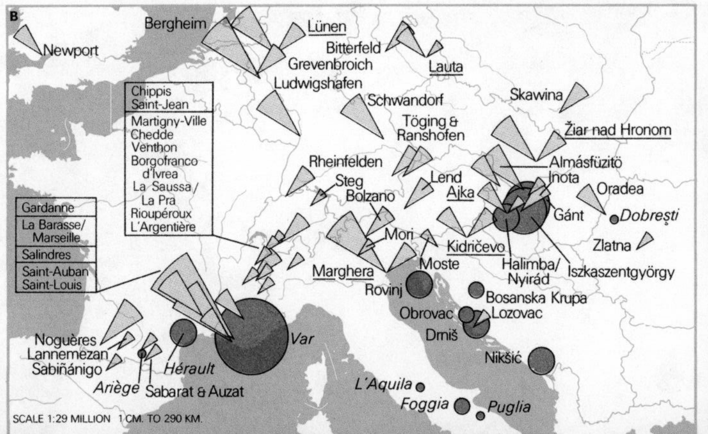

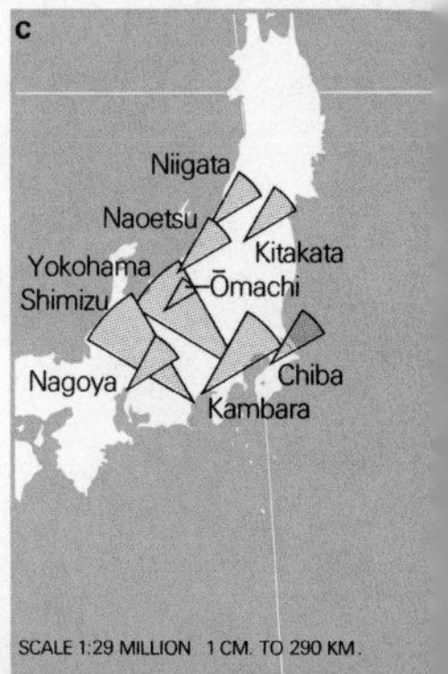

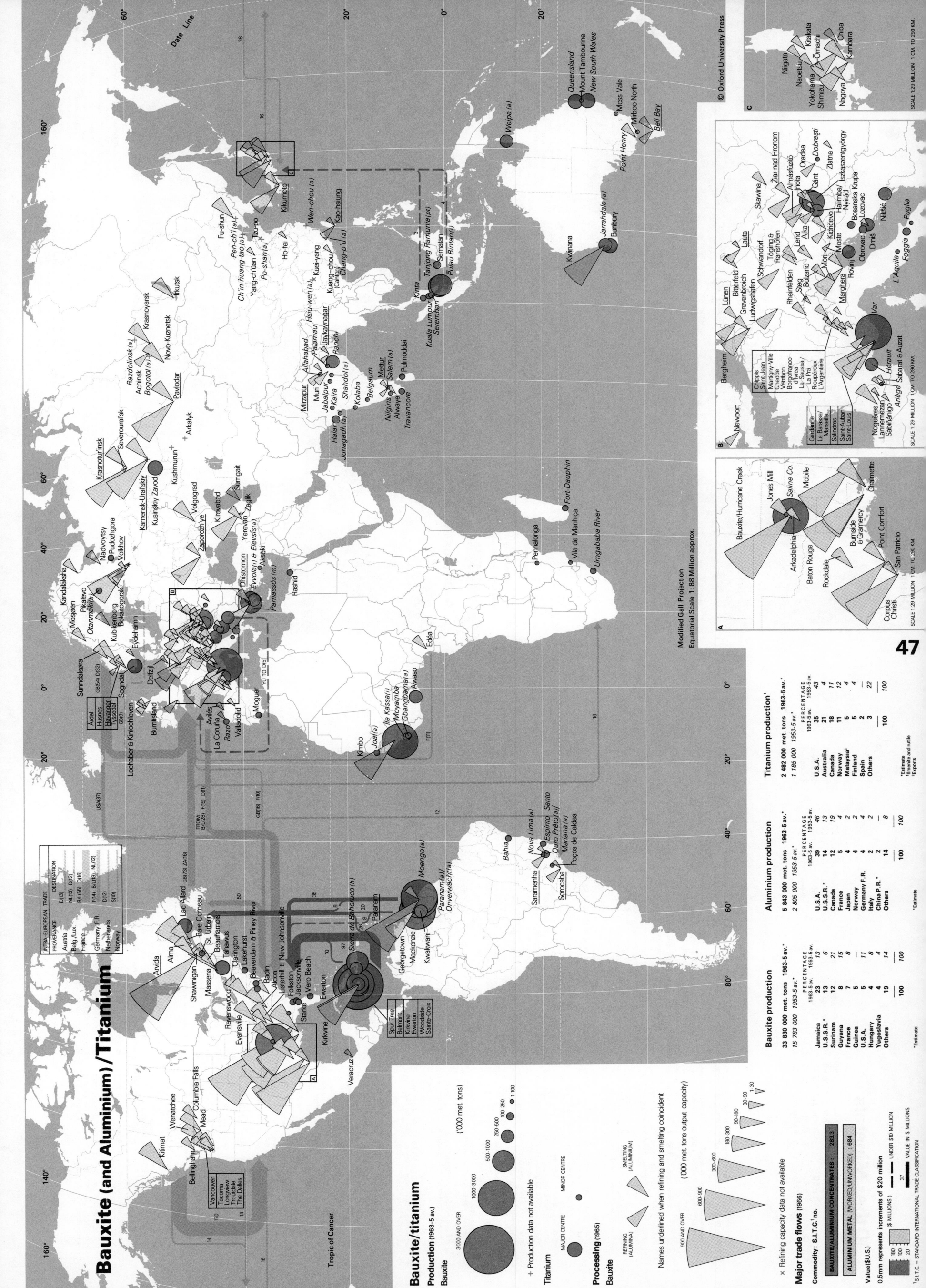

Other Minerals

For individual country data see Statistical Supplement

Ferro-alloys are used to make various types of steels with physical and mechanical properties which would not otherwise be obtainable.

Manganese is used principally as a cleanser in the manufacture of steel, where it acts as a deoxidizer and desulphurizer. Steels containing about 1% manganese are employed for structural work and for rails; steels of 12% manganese have high tensile strength and resistance to abrasives for use in rock-crushers, sprockets, railway points and crossings, etc. Compounds of manganese are important in the production of disinfectants and batteries.

About 45% of the world's production of **nickel** is used in steels, either alone or in combination with chromium, manganese, or other metals. Stainless steel is the most important single resultant product, followed by high nickel alloys and plating and constructional steels. Nickel steels with less than 6% nickel have high strength, ductility and toughness suitable for automobile and aircraft construction and heavy machinery. Steels with 7% - 35% nickel and some chromium are heat— and corrosion—resistant and are used for chemical apparatus, marine fittings and turbine blades. Nickel cast irons are employed in motor car and diesel engines. Highly magnetic alloys with 45% - 85% nickel are used in sub-marine cable sheathing, radio transformers, and telephone and telegraph relay parts. About half the world's production of nickel comes from Canada's Sudbury district, although production in the U.S.S.R. is rising.

Chromium is obtained from chromite found in chrome ore. Stainless chromium - nickel steel has many uses in electrical and marine engineering, and in the dyeing and dairying industries where its resistance to corrosion makes it a valuable material for containers and machinery parts in contact with liquids. Aircraft parts, warship superstructures, armour-plating and rifle barrels are also frequently made from it. Chrome ore is used as a refractory (in the form of bricks, cements, and plasters) in constructing furnaces, and the metal and its salts are employed in the chemical industry.

Tungsten steels are used principally for high-speed machine tools and cutting instruments. Tungsten carbide, one of the hardest materials available, is widely used in cutting tools, drill bits and machine parts. Tungsten alloys are used in jet engines, rockets, and missiles. Tungsten also forms the filament in electric light bulbs. The chief sources of tungsten are the minerals wolframite, (Fe, Mn)WO_4, and scheelite, $CaWO_4$.

Cobalt, when alloyed, is very hard and resistant to high temperatures and is used in cutting tools. Cobalt alloys are used in jet engines and in the production of atomic energy. Cobalt is magnetic, it is a colouring pigment, it has medicinal uses and the radio-active isotope can be used in radio-therapy. Almost all the world's cobalt is obtained as a by-product from complex ores worked chiefly for the other metals they contain.

By far the most important use of **molybdenum** is as an alloy in steel, particularly for stainless and high-speed steels. Molybdenum can be used as a substitute for tungsten in the manufacture of high-speed steels, only half as much molybdenum as tungsten being required; this is strategically important as about half the world's production of tungsten comes from China P.R. Molybdenum is used for increasing strength and creep resistance of steel at high temperatures. A small amount of molybdenum is used as a metal, especially for high-temperature purposes, and some is used in chemicals, pigments and catalysts and for improving lubricants. The Climax mine in the U.S.A. produces molybdenite, MoS_2, but the balance of world production is a by-product, mainly of copper and tungsten mining.

Vanadium reduces and controls the grain of steel and imparts strength, toughness, resistance to impact and abrasion, and makes it easier to machine and weld. Steel with up to 1% vanadium is used in construction and engineering, in springs, forging, and uses involving high stresses. It is used instead of platinum as a catalyst in sulphuric acid manufacturing, and the salts are used in paints, dyes and insecticides. Much ferrovanadium is produced and used as well as vanadium oxide, these being the two vendable products of vanadium ore besides the metal.

There are many other minerals of great economic and industrial importance of which only a few are shown on the maps in this section.

Mercury has many unique properties, being liquid at room temperature, with high electrical conductivity, high density, chemical stability and uniform volume expansion. The principal uses are in electrical apparatus, agriculture, pharmaceuticals, and the electrolytic preparation of chlorine and caustic soda. Almost all the world's mercury is obtained from the red sulphide mineral cinnabar, HgS, but a little native metal occurs. With surface mining, ore with about 1.5 kg. of mercury per ton is an economic proposition, but with underground methods the proportion must be about 4.5 kg. per ton.

Zirconium is mainly used in nuclear reactors, being corrosion-resistant, especially in water at high temperatures, and absorbing very few neutrons. It is also used in the chemical industry, due to its resistance to corrosion by acids and alkalis. Zirconium is also used in the electrical industry, being readily machined, in porcelain manufacture and as a de-oxidizing agent in steel-making. Almost all zirconium is derived from the two minerals zircon, $ZrSiO_4$ (itself a valuable refractory much used in foundries and aluminium furnaces), and baddeleyite, ZrO_2. Zircon is found with ilmenite, rutile and monazite in beach sands; baddeleyite is found in stream gravels in Brazil.

Magnesium is recovered from seawater, natural brine and the rocks dolomite and magnesite. It is alloyed with aluminium and lithium to produce a light, strong, workable metal suitable for aircraft, vehicles, spacecraft and marine applications. It is also used in nuclear reactor fuel cans and in the reduction of uranium, titanium and other rare metals. Magnesium minerals are used extensively in the metallurgical and chemical industries. Magnesite, although very important in the production of basic refractories, is being replaced as a source of magnesium compounds and metal by the seawater-magnesia processes. Magnesium salt deposits are exploited by the chemical industry.

The most important source of **beryllium** is the mineral beryl, $Be_3Al_2Si_6O_{18}$, which contains only about 5% beryllium. Except for a few sporadic occurrences, deposits containing beryl are rarely workable for that mineral unless it is associated with other useful minerals. Large low-grade deposits of bertrandite, $Be_4Si_2O_7(OH)_2$, have recently been discovered and may eventually become the main source of beryllium. A major use is in alloys with copper; about 2% of beryllium in copper greatly increases the tensile strength and durability of the material. The alloy is especially suitable for springs in electrical devices, motion-picture cameras, aircraft under-carriage springs, etc. Pure beryllium is mainly used in X-ray tube windows and with radium as a source of neutrons. The future of the metal now depends largely on its use in nuclear energy projects and in the aerospace industry.

Antimony is not normally used by itself, but is commonly alloyed with lead in battery plates, cable sheathings, and sulphuric acid-resistant sheet and pipe. It is also used in making bearing-metal solder and low-melting-point alloys. Type-metal is basically a lead-antimony-tin alloy, and antimony enters into the composition of Brittania metal and some pewters. Some of the antimony salts are important in the chemical industry, in making paints and enamels, and in treating textiles to make them flameproof. Potential uses in electronics are numerous. The metal is derived chiefly from stibnite, Sb_2S_3, which is usually found in association with the ores of other metals, especially mercury.

The principal use of **titanium** in recent years is in the form of titanium oxide, TiO_2, as a white paint pigment of truly remarkable opacity, which is rapidly replacing lithopone, white lead and zinc oxide in paints. Titanium oxide is used also in toilet preparations, linoleum and rubber. The metal has high resistance to corrosion, is very light and strong and can be substituted for aluminium, making it very important in the aircraft and chemical industries and in space and marine technology. The metal is used in making the alloys of ferrotitanium and ferrocarbon-titanium; and titanium carbide has beneficial effects in the manufacture of chromium steels. An alloy of titanium carbide and molybdenum carbide is used for extra-hard cutting tools. The minerals ilmenite, $FeTiO_3$, and rutile, TiO_2 are the chief sources of titanium. The "black sands" of certain sea and lake beaches yield part of the world's supply of titanium, the most productive beach deposits being on the eastern coast of Australia. This region is especially important for rutile production.

Cadmium is a relatively rare element recovered as a by-product of zinc and, to a much lesser extent, lead and copper production from ores associated with zinc. Since the only significant cadmium mineral, greenockite, CdS, never occurs as a separate mineral in sufficient quantities to be workable, greater production of cadmium can be achieved only by increased output of zinc or improved methods of recovery. More than half the supply is consumed in protective coatings for iron and steel. A considerable amount of cadmium is used in alloys for electricity transmission cables, storage batteries, type founding metal and solders. It can also be used for fission control in nuclear reactors. Cadmium is also used for low friction bearings and in cadmium salts and compounds, used principally in pigments for stable oil, water and ceramic colours.

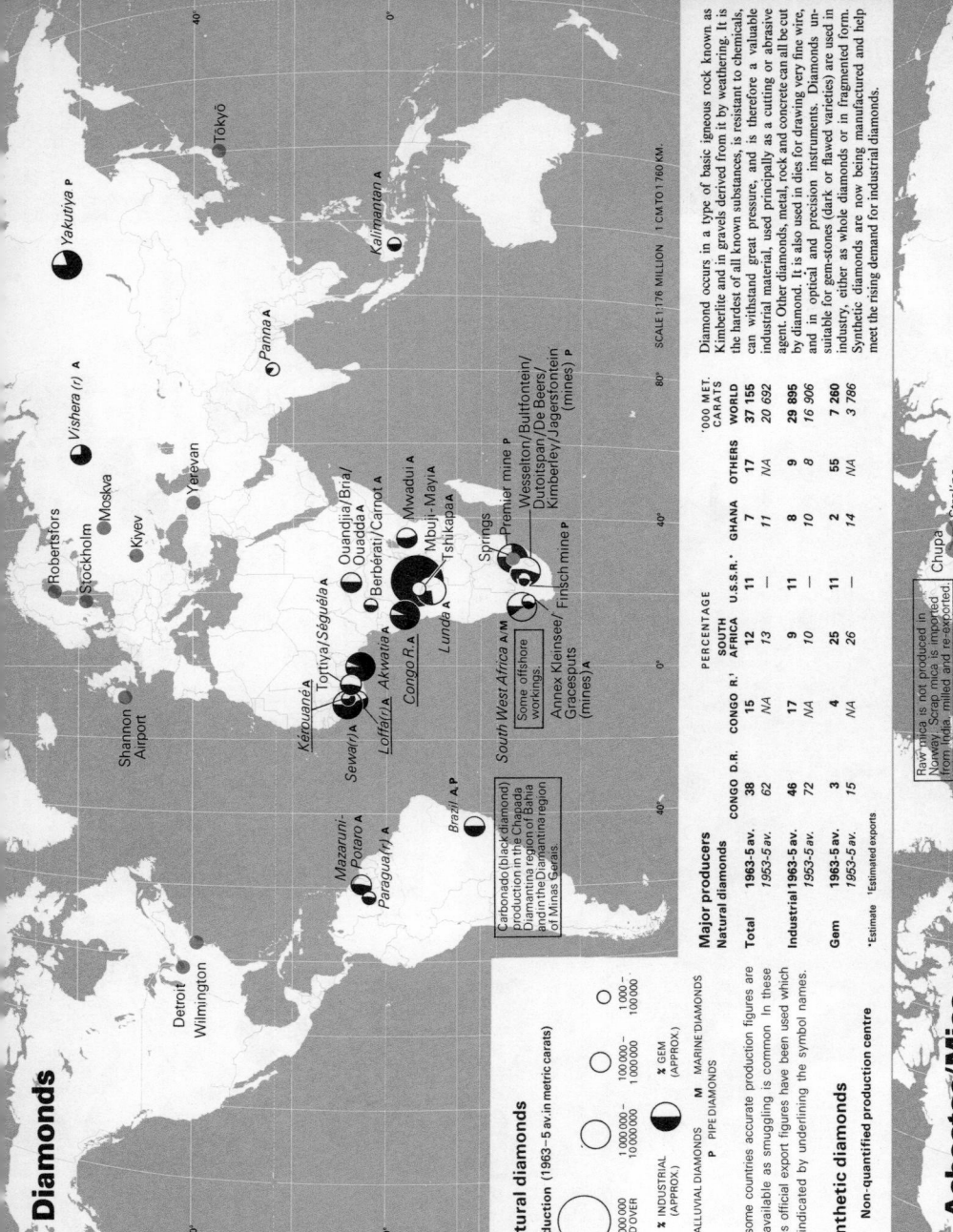

Notes relating to **diamonds, asbestos,** and **mica** can be found with the maps.

Precious metals, including gold, silver and the platinum group, have important industrial, as well as decorative and monetary, uses.

The principal use of **gold** is as the standard for monetary systems in the form of coinage or as ingots of the metal (bullion). Gold is also used as a conductor in the electronics industry, and in dental and other alloys. An important use of gold is in jewellery, for which it is alloyed with other metals because it is too soft when pure. Most of the world's gold is obtained from "native gold", or the yellow metallic mineral which is rarely pure, almost invariably containing some silver. In the past production was from surface gold-bearing gravels, but for several decades the main source has been deep mines, such as those in the Witwatersrand goldfield in South Africa.

About 80% of the **silver** consumption of the world (excl. the U.S.S.R., Eastern Europe and China P.R., for whom no data are available) is by art and industry. Monetary use has a decreasing proportion, as newer coins use less silver or none at all. Silver has increasing industrial uses, particularly in the fields of photography, electrical engineering, and electronics. The principal mineral source of the metal is argentite, Ag_2S; it also occurs naturally in metallic form. Most of the world's production is as a by-product of argentiferous lead, zinc and copper ores or of gold ores.

The **platinum** group metals, including osmium, rhodium, iridium, ruthenium, palladium and platinum, are particularly important in the chemical, petroleum, glass and electronics industries. Considerably more palladium than platinum is used in industry; however, the total value of the platinum used is the greater. Platinum is a catalyst in the petrochemical industry, and platinum rhodium alloys are used in the conversion of ammonia to nitric acid. Platinum group metals are used in glass manufacture and glass seals and in thermocouples. A thin coating of platinum gives protection against oxidation and corrosion at high temperatures to tungsten, molybdenum and tantalum steels, which is particularly useful in jet and missile technology. Production of platinum in South Africa is from ore mined primarily for its platinum content. In Canada platinum metal is produced as a by-product of nickel production. In Colombia and the U.S.A. platinum production is from placer deposits.

Diamonds

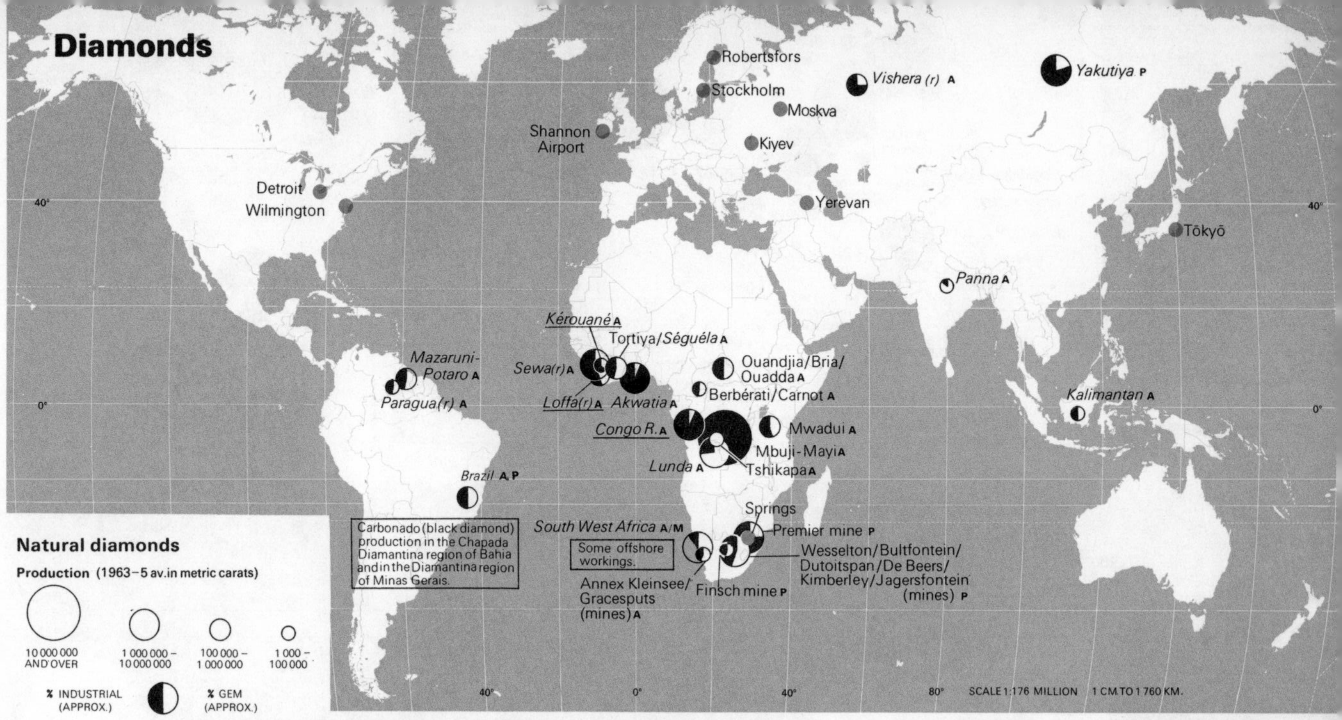

Major producers

Natural diamonds

		PERCENTAGE						'000 MET. CARATS
		CONGO D.R.	CONGO R.[1]	SOUTH AFRICA	U.S.S.R.*	GHANA	OTHERS	WORLD
Total	**1963-5 av.**	**38**	**15**	**12**	**11**	**7**	**17**	**37 155**
	1953-5 av.	*62*	*NA*	*13*	—	*11*	*NA*	*20 692*
Industrial	**1963-5 av.**	**46**	**17**	**9**	**11**	**8**	**9**	**29 895**
	1953-5 av.	*72*	*NA*	*10*	—	*10*	*8*	*16 906*
Gem	**1963-5 av.**	**3**	**4**	**25**	**11**	**2**	**55**	**7 260**
	1953-5 av.	*15*	*NA*	*26*	—	*14*	*NA*	*3 786*

*Estimate [1]Estimated exports

Diamond occurs in a type of basic igneous rock known as Kimberlite and in gravels derived from it by weathering. It is the hardest of all known substances, is resistant to chemicals, can withstand great pressure, and is therefore a valuable industrial material, used principally as a cutting or abrasive agent. Other diamonds, metal, rock and concrete can all be cut by diamond. It is also used in dies for drawing very fine wire, and in optical and precision instruments. Diamonds unsuitable for gem-stones (dark or flawed varieties) are used in industry, either as whole diamonds or in fragmented form. Synthetic diamonds are now being manufactured and help meet the rising demand for industrial diamonds.

Asbestos/Mica

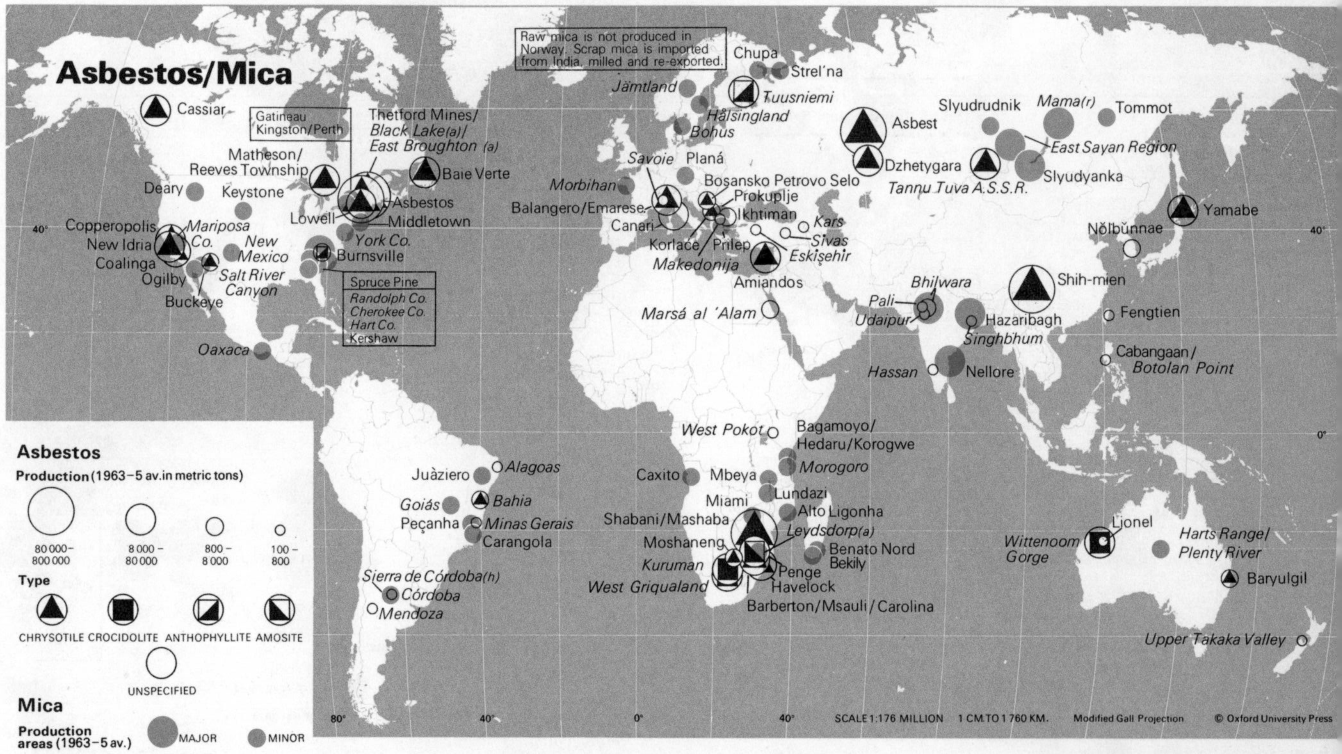

Major producers

Asbestos

	PERCENTAGE					MET. TONS
	CANADA[1]	U.S.S.R.*	SOUTH AFRICA	RHODESIA	OTHERS	WORLD
1963-5 av.	**46**	**27**	**7**	**5**	**15**	**2 709 000***
1953-5 av.	*56*	*22*	*6*	*5*	*11*	*1 563 700**

Mica (incl. scrap)

	U.S.A.	INDIA[2]	NORWAY[3]	SOUTH AFRICA	OTHERS	WORLD[4]
1963-5 av.	**70**	**23**	**2**	**2**	**3**	**149 200***
1953-5 av.	*75*	*17*	*1*	*2*	*5*	*101 500**

*Estimate [1]Sales [2]Exports [3]Re-exports [4]Excl. China P.R., N. Korea, Romania, U.S.S.R.

Asbestos is a fibrous mineral which, due to its properties, is an invaluable material for many types of industry. It is resistant to heat, fire, rot, friction and corrosion, is a poor conductor of electricity and sound, and most varieties possess a high tensile strength, similar to that of steel. The uses of asbestos are many and varied, including a wide range of fireproof and building materials. Of the different types of asbestos, chrysotile, which accounts for over 90% of world production, is commercially the most valuable and is used for such commodities as fireproof clothing, brake linings and asbestos cement. Amphibole fibres (crocidolite, amosite and anthophyllite) are harsher and are used for building and thermal insulating materials.

Mica is also a valuable industrial mineral on account of its properties which include perfect cleavage, flexibility, elasticity, infusibility, low thermal conductivity, transparency and in particular, high dielectric strength. Muscovite, the most important kind is found in workable quantities in coarse-grained granite pegmatites, and much of the world supply of high grade sheet muscovite is from India. It is used for electric condensers and in telephones, dynamos and domestic heating equipment. Another variety, phlogopite, is used in commutators; ground mica, largely from waste, is used as a powder in paint and for coating and filler in roofing and rubber material. Synthetic mica is now being produced.

Gold/Silver/Platinum

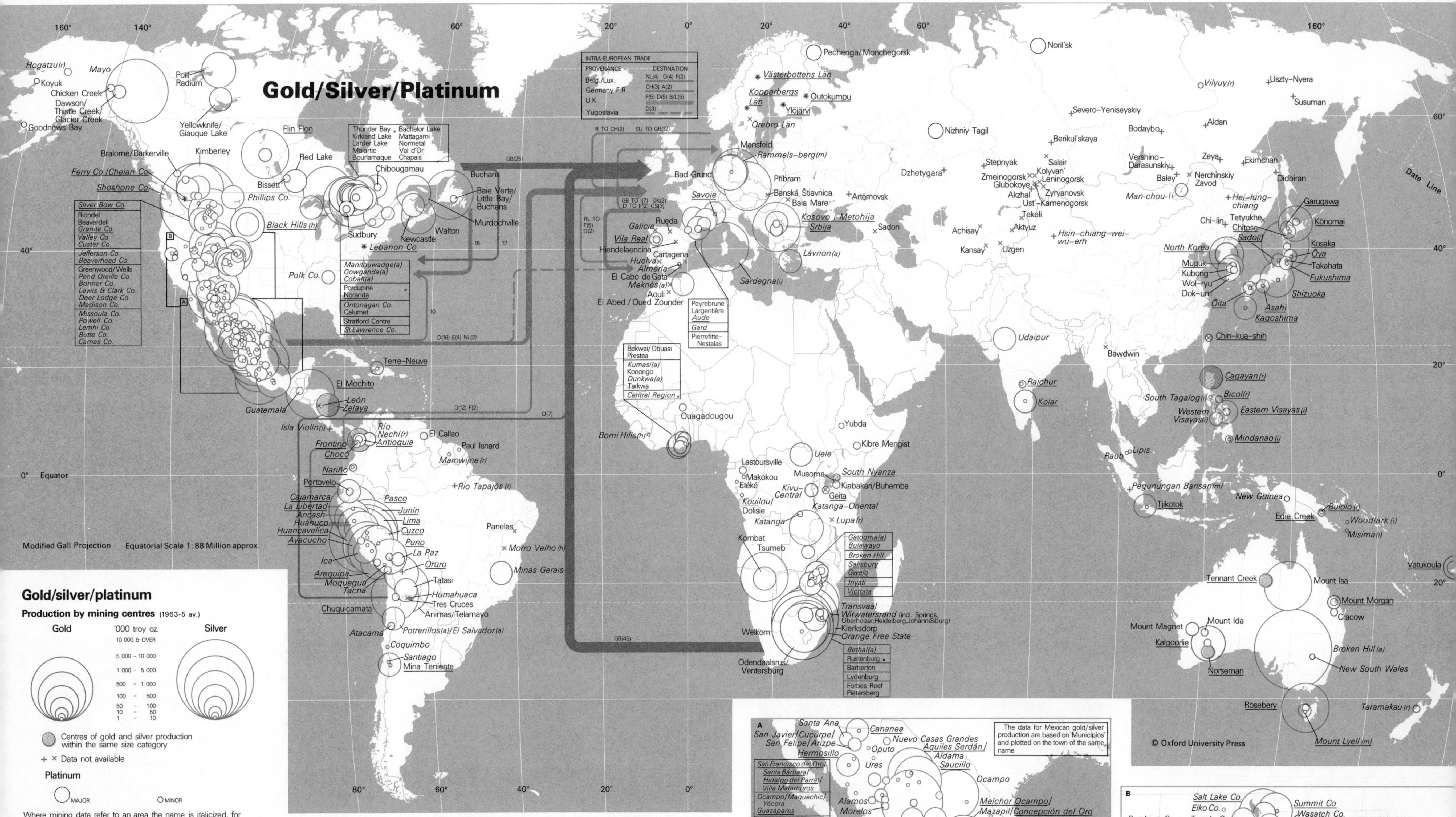

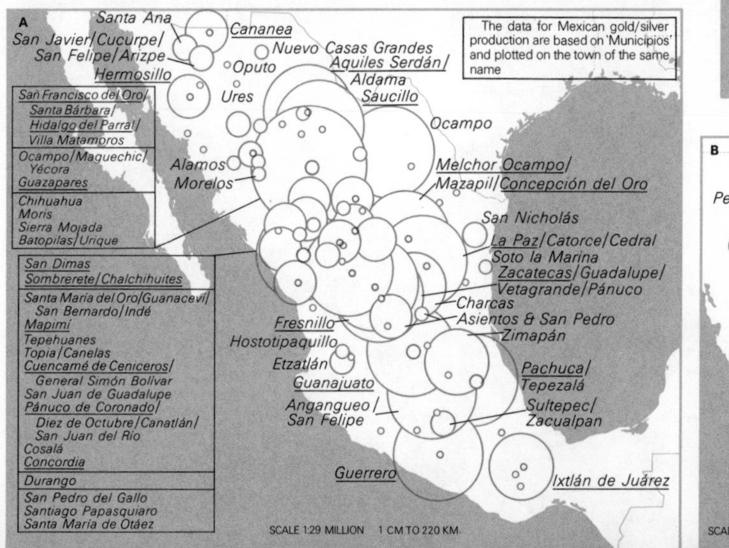

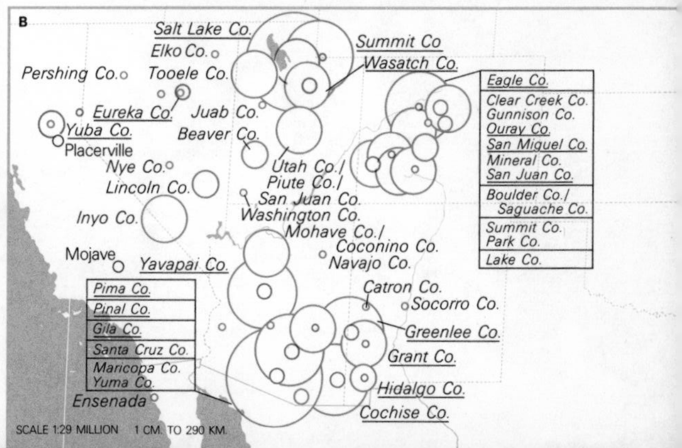

Gold/silver/platinum

Production by mining centres (1963-5 av.)

Gold — '000 troy oz. — Silver

10 000 & OVER
5 000 - 10 000
1 000 - 5 000
500 - 1 000
100 - 500
50 - 100
10 - 50
1 - 10

Centres of gold and silver production within the same size category

+ × Data not available

Platinum

MAJOR — MINOR

Where mining data refer to an area the name is italicized, for example *Atacama*

Where gold and silver mining centres are coincident the name is underlined, for example Terre-Neuve

Major trade flows (1966)

Commodity: S.I.T.C.[1] no.

SILVER/PLATINUM ORES AND CONCENTRATES : 285 — SILVER (UNWORKED/ PARTLY WORKED) : 681.1

Trade flows for gold are excluded because it is impossible to isolate monetary movements

Value (\$U.S.)

0.5mm. represents increments of \$10 million

90 / 50 / 10 (\$ MILLIONS)

UNDER \$5 MILLION

VALUE IN \$ MILLIONS

[1] STANDARD INTERNATIONAL TRADE CLASSIFICATION

Gold production

44 736 000 troy oz. 1963-5 av.*

*35 067 000 1953-5 av.**

	PERCENTAGE 1963-5 av.	1953-5 av.
South Africa	65	*38*
U.S.S.R.*	10	*26*
Canada	9	*12*
U.S.A.	3	*5*
Australia	2	*3*
Ghana	2	*2*
Rhodesia	1	*1*
Others	8	*13*
	100	*100*

*Estimate

Silver production

251 632 000 troy oz. 1963-5 av.*

*216 967 000 1953-5 av.**

	PERCENTAGE 1963-5 av.	1953-5 av.
Mexico	16	*21*
U.S.A.	15	*17*
Peru	14	*10*
Canada	12	*13*
U.S.S.R.*	12	*12*
Australia	7	*6*
Japan	4	*3*
Germany D.R.	2	*2*
Others	18	*16*
	100	*100*

*Estimate

Platinum[1] production

2 352 000 troy oz. 1963-5 av.*

*858 000 1953-5 av.**

	PERCENTAGE 1963-5 av.	1953-5 av.
U.S.S.R.*	57	*13*
South Africa	24*	*40*
Canada	17	*40*
U.S.A.	1	*3*
Others	1	*4*
	100	*100*

*Estimate
[1]Platinum group metals

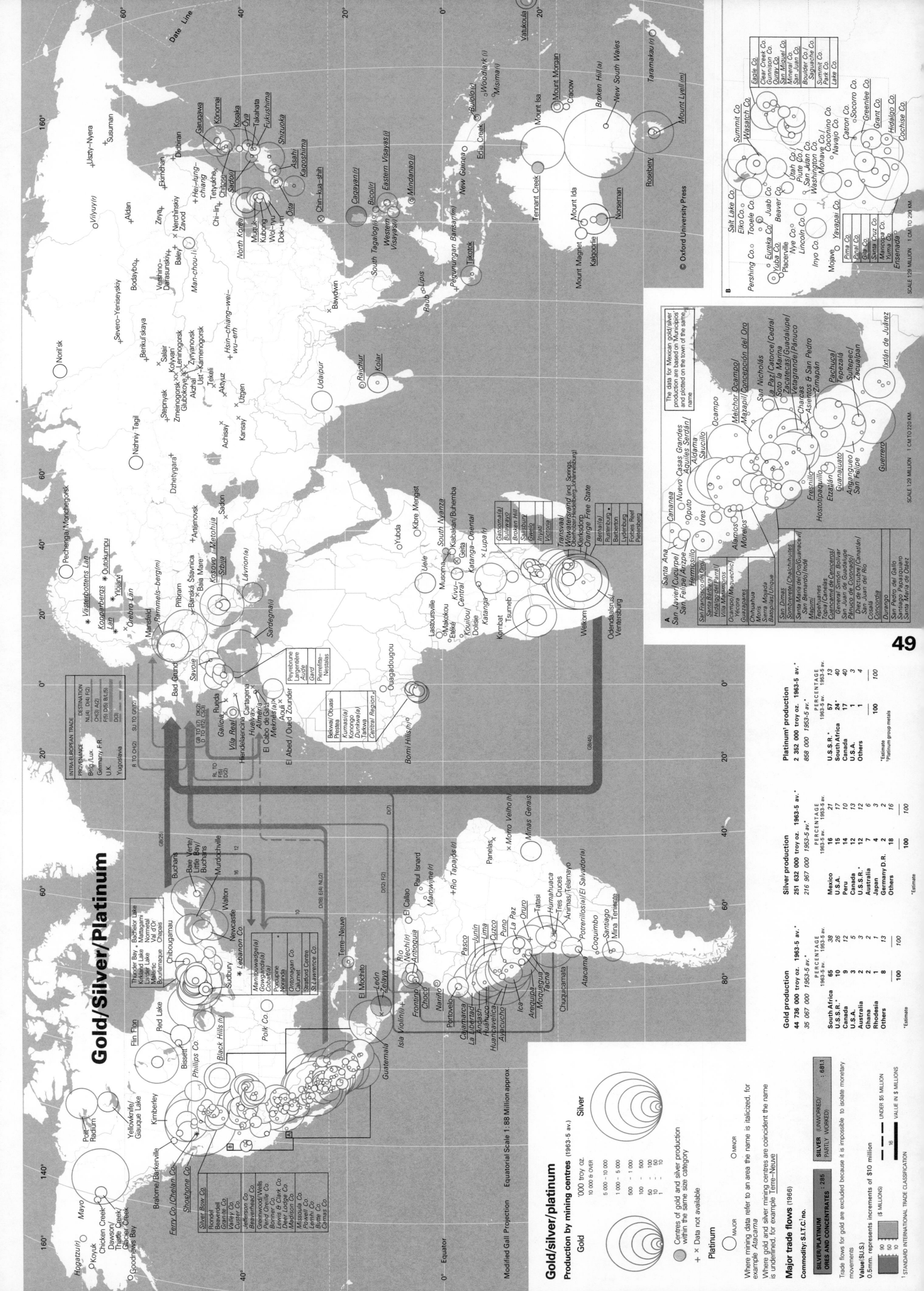

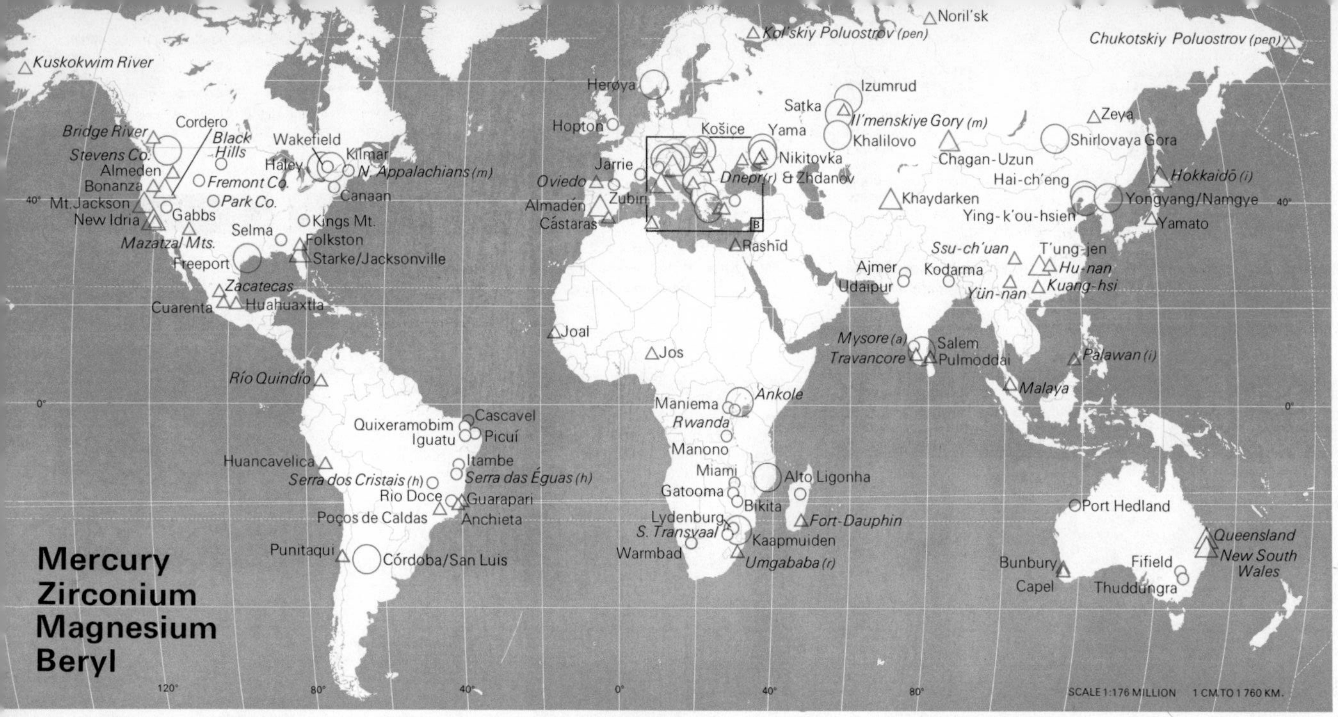

Mercury Zirconium Magnesium Beryl

SCALE 1:176 MILLION 1 CM. TO 1 760 KM.

Major producers

	(PERCENTAGE)	AUSTRALIA	ARGENTINA	BRAZIL	CANADA	CHINA P.R.	INDIA	ITALY	NORWAY	SENEGAL	SPAIN	U.S.S.R.	U.S.A.	OTHERS	WORLD (MET. TONS)
Mercury	**1963-5 av.**	–	–	–	–	10*	–	22	–	–	28	14*	7	19	8 850*
	1953-5 av.	–	–	–	–	NA	–	30	–	–	23	7*	10	NA	6 030*
Zirconium	**1963-5 av.**[1]	98	–	–	–	–	...[1]	–	–	1	–	...[1]	...[1]	1	204 730*
	1953-5 av.[1,2]	91	–	8	–	–	–	–	–	1[3]	–	–	...[1]	–	43 350*
Magnesium (primary)	**1963-5 av.**	–	–	–	6	1*	–	4	15	–	–	21*	47	6	152 530*
	1953-5 av.	–	–	–	5	NA	–	1	4	–	–	35*	50	NA	135 170*
Beryl	**1963-5 av.**	2	8	28	–	–	8	–	–	–	–	19*	4	31	5 380*
	1953-5 av.	2	12	23	–	–	6	–	–	–	–	NA	8	NA	7 500*

*Estimate [1]Excl. U.S.A., U.S.S.R., & India [2]Production by U.S.A. was 53% of that by Australia; comparable 1963-5 data NA [3]Former French West Africa

Manganese Nickel Antimony Chrome ore

SCALE 1:176 MILLION 1 CM. TO 1 760 KM.

Major producers

	(PERCENTAGE)	BOLIVIA	BRAZIL	CANADA	CHINA P.R.	CUBA	INDIA[1]	NEW CALEDONIA	PHILIPPINES	RHODESIA	SOUTH AFRICA	U.S.S.R.	OTHERS	WORLD (MET. TONS)
Manganese ore (high grade: 30 % Mn & over)[2]	**1963-5 av.**	–	8	–	6*	–	9	–	–	–	9	44*	24	16 043 250*
	1953-5 av.	–	2	–	NA	3	17	–	–	–	7	44*	NA	10 474 960*
Nickel	**1963-5 av.**	–	–	55	–	6	–	11	–	–	1	21*	6	391 900*
	1953-5 av.[3]	–	–	83	–	7	–	8	–	NA	1	...[3]	NA	175 690*
Antimony (content of ore)	**1963-5 av.**	15	–	1	25*	–	–	–	–	–	21	10*	28	59 450*
	1953-5 av.[3]	14	–	2	27*	–	–	–	–	–	21	...[3]	36	39 920*
Chromite	**1963-5 av.**	–	–	–	–	1	1	–	11	11	20	30*	26	4 384 730*
	1953-5 av.	–	–	–	–	2	2	2	15	12	18	15*	34	3 538 020*

*Estimate [1]Incl. Goa [2]Percent Mn varies by country; all above 30% except U.S.S.R. (grade NA) [3]Excl. U.S.S.R.

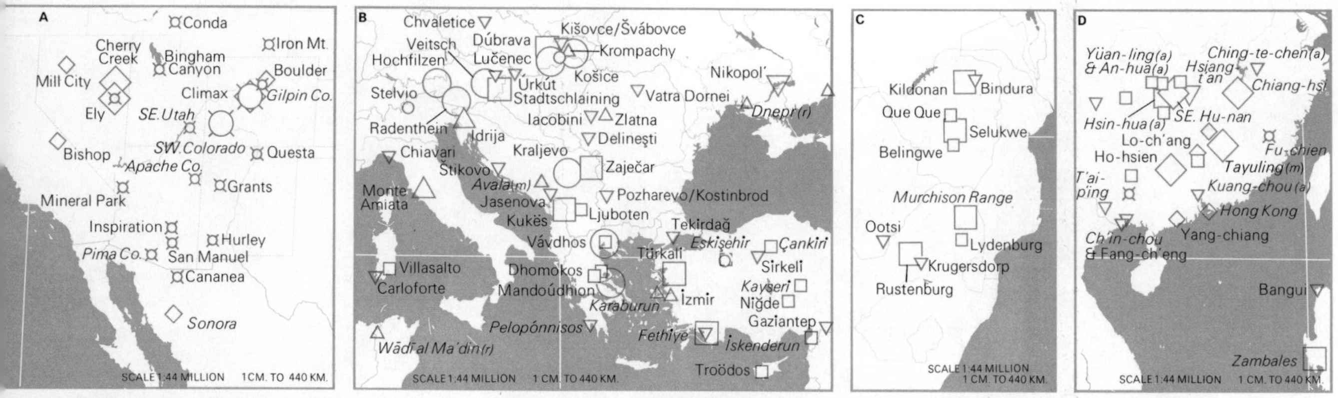

SCALE 1:44 MILLION 1 CM. TO 440 KM.

Ferro-alloy and other minerals

Producing districts[1] (1963-5 av.)

	MAJOR	MINOR
Cinnabar (Mercury)	△	△
Zirconium minerals	△	△
Magnesium minerals	○	○
Beryl	○	○
Manganese minerals	▽	▽
Nickel minerals	▽	▽
Antimony minerals	□	□
Chrome ore	□	□
Tungsten minerals	◇	◇
Cobalt minerals	◇	◇
Molybdenum minerals	¤	¤
Vanadium minerals	¤	¤

[1]Mines, *mining areas* or processing centres

Trade in ferro-alloy minerals

Nickel The major sources of the ore in world trade are Canada and New Caledonia; metal is exported by Canada, Norway and the U.K. Chief importers of ores, matte and other nickel-bearing raw materials are Japan, the U.K., Norway and France.

Tungsten Most is traded in the form of ores and concentrates. The chief exporters of these are Australia, Bolivia, S. Korea and China P.R.; they are imported mainly by the U.S.S.R., Germany F.R. and the U.K. The U.K. exports two-thirds of the ferro-tungsten reported in international trade data; Sweden is the major importer. Tungsten metal is exported by Germany F.R., the U.S.A. and France.

Molybdenum The U.S.A. and Chile are the major exporters, mainly in the form of ores and concentrates. Chief exporters of ferro-molybdenum are the U.S.S.R., the U.S.A. and France. Molybdenum is imported by Germany F.R., the U.K., Japan and France.

Cobalt The Congo D.R. is the largest exporter; Zambia and Morocco are also major exporters. Main importers are France, the U.S.A., the U.K. and Japan.

Vanadium The U.S.A., South West Africa and Finland are principal exporters; France, Belgium/Luxembourg and Italy are the major importers.

Chrome ore exports

3 166 850 met. tons 1963-5 av.*
*2 297 160 1953-5 av.**[1]

	PERCENTAGE 1963-5 av.	1953-5 av.
U.S.S.R.	21	7
South Africa	20	21
Philippines	17	21
Rhodesia	14	16
Turkey	10	23
Others	18	12
	100	100

Manganese ore exports

7 106 670 met. tons 1963-5 av.*[2]
*5 237 630 1953-5 av.**[2]

	PERCENTAGE 1963-5 av.	1953-5 av.
India	18	30
U.S.S.R.	14	17
South Africa	13	10
Brazil	13	3
Gabon	12	–
Others	30	40
	100	100

Chrome ore imports

3 015 520 met. tons 1963-5 av.*[1]
*2 389 590 1953-5 av.**[1,2]

	PERCENTAGE 1963-5 av.	1953-5 av.
U.S.A.	43	70
Japan	11	2
Germany F.R.	8	8
U.K.	7	6
France	6	3
Others	25	11
	100	100

Manganese ore imports

7 623 700 met. tons 1963-5 av.*
*4 417 460 1953-5 av.**[1]

	PERCENTAGE 1963-5 av.	1953-5 av.
U.S.A.	37	55
Japan	10	3
France	10	12
Germany F.R.	10	7
U.K.	6	11
Others	27	12
	100	100

*Estimate [1]Excl. Eastern Europe [2]Excl. China P.R.

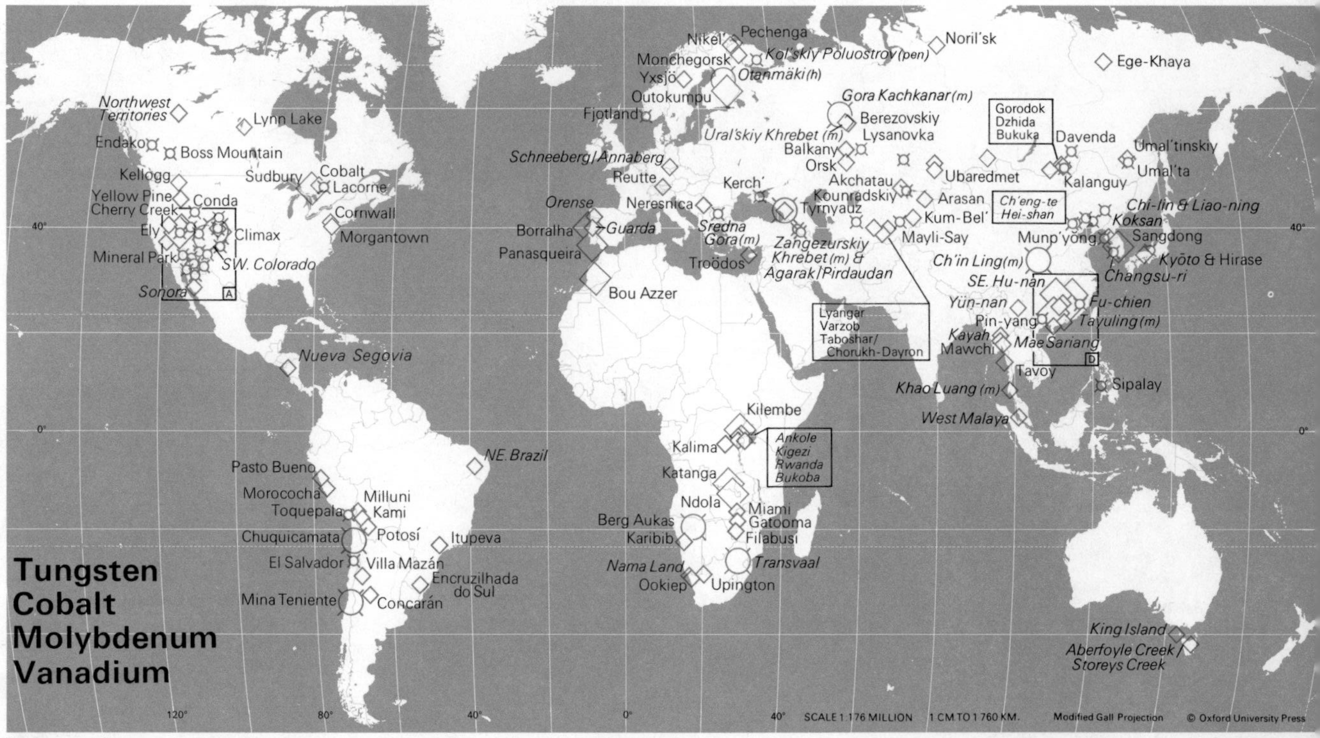

Tungsten Cobalt Molybdenum Vanadium

SCALE 1:176 MILLION 1 CM. TO 1 760 KM. Modified Gall Projection

Major producers

	(PERCENTAGE)	CANADA	CHILE	CHINA P.R.	CONGO D.R.	FINLAND	S. KOREA	MOROCCO	SOUTH AFRICA	SOUTH WEST AFRICA	U.S.S.R.	U.S.A.	OTHERS	WORLD (MET. TONS)
Tungsten (concentrates & ores: 60 % WO_3 basis)	**1963-5 av.**	2	–	35*	–	–	9	–	–	–	19*	12	23	57 910*
	1953-5 av.	2	–	24*	2[1]	–	7	–	–	–	10*	17	38	72 270*
Cobalt	**1963-5 av.**	9	–	–	49	11	–	10	–	–	8	2*	11	16 030*
	1953-5 av.[2]	9	–	–	67	NA	NA	6	–	–	...[2]	5	NA	12 640*
Molybdenum (in ores & concentrates)	**1963-5 av.**[3]	4	8	4*	–	–	–	–	–	–	13*	69	2	45 430*
	1953-5 av.[4]	1	4	...[4]	–	–	–	–	–	–	...[4]	91	4	29 570*
Vanadium (in ores & concentrates)	**1963-5 av.**	–	–	–	–	12	–	–	17	15	–	56	–	7 280*
	1953-5 av.	–	–	–	–	–	–	–	–	16	–	79	5	3 590*

*Estimate [1]Incl. Rwanda and Burundi [2]Excl. U.S.S.R. [3]Excl. Eastern Europe [4]Excl. U.S.S.R., China P.R. and Eastern Europe

Transport Industries

Aircraft p. 53 Railway Vehicles p. 54
Motor Vehicles p. 55 Shipbuilding p. 52
For individual country data see Statistical Supplement

Shipbuilding
The distribution of the shipbuilding industry shows the predominance of Europe, where there is a long history of shipbuilding, and of Japan, which has always had a traditional industry but which in this century has made such progress that in 1970 she launched almost half of the world's tonnage.
The most dramatic event in modern shipbuilding has been the increase in size of the largest ships constructed. In 1963 the largest ship launched in the world was 58 000 gross registered tonnage (G.R.T.). In 1968 the largest ship launched was 150 000 G.R.T. and in 1970 54 ships (of which 30 were built in Japan) each exceeded 100 000 G.R.T. All but one of these were oil tankers. These giant ships, too large to transit the Suez Canal fully laden, have considerable economic advantages over smaller ones on long sea voyages. Closure of Suez in 1967, therefore, by denying to smaller tankers the shorter route for oil from the Persian Gulf to Europe, effectively accelerated the demand for the supertanker.

Sizes of ships launched (1966)

Total number of ships launched[1] 2 561
of which tankers 210

'000 G.R.T.	PERCENTAGE Total	Tankers
0.1 — 1	61	*30*
1 — 4	14	*12*
4 — 8	5	*1*
8 — 15	9	*4*
15 — 25	4	*4*
25 — 50	5	*33*
50 & above	2	*16*
	100	*100*

[1]Excl. ships of less than 100 G.R.T.

Bulk carriers, which transport chiefly ore or grain, are an important part of world shipping fleets. In 1970 they formed 28% of all merchant tonnage launched, compared with 46% for oil tankers. This type of ship has now emulated the oil tanker in size. There are orders in hand for single purpose bulk carriers of 80 000 G.R.T. while the combination type ore/bulk/oil carrier ship is now of the 140 000 G.R.T. size.
General cargo ships are being replaced by the new fast container ships which average about 27 000 G.R.T. as compared to a maximum size of about 14 000 G.R.T. for a conventional cargo liner. Container ships are also growing in size and there are now orders in hand for fully refrigerated container ships of 40 000 G.R.T. If container ships are generally adopted on established routes, the number of ships needed to deal with the general cargo trade could be greatly reduced. For example, before the introduction of container ships nearly 100 conventional cargo ships carried the regular trade between Australia and the U.K. It has been said that, in theory, 9 container ships would be capable of carrying 80% of this trade.
Large passenger ships are rarely built nowadays; the *Queen Elizabeth 2* could well be the last of the great passenger liners, but there is a continuing demand for smaller passenger ships which are used as ferries or for holiday cruises. The demand for small ships of quality, such as coasters and fishing vessels, will always remain. Many of these are built in shipyards with a production too small to appear on the shipbuilding map. These small shipbuilding places are particularly numerous along the coast of Norway and on the waterways of the Netherlands, but they exist in smaller shipbuilding countries such as Peru, Pakistan, Angola and Greece.
Ships have traditionally been custom built but this is now changing and series, or standard, shipbuilding is the foremost factor influencing shipbuilding today. This method can be used for ships of any size, including the giant tankers. During the building of a series, the benefits of mass prefabrication become evident and costs per ton gradually decrease.
Most shipbuilding industries are to some extent assisted by their own governments, because of their value to the country's economy and because of the social problems which the closure of a shipyard can cause. Government protection is even greater in the young industries of developing countries. Here, costs of production are high because complex parts and equipment must be imported from a distance. The prices of new ships built in Brazil, for example, are between 25% and 40% above world average.
The main importing countries are those with large merchant fleets; such countries may also have important shipbuilding industries of their own. Liberia provides a 'flag of convenience' offering special privileges for shipowners.
The pattern of naval shipbuilding differs considerably from that of merchant shipbuilding. The leading producers are the two great military powers, the U.S.A. and the U.S.S.R., and the industry seems to be of importance also in China. New naval ships are normally supplied by a country's own industry, and imported only by those countries which have insufficient shipbuilding industries.

Motor vehicles
Motor vehicles, in particular motor cars, are now recognized as an essential part of modern industrial life, and the motor vehicle industry has become one of the major indicators of industrial and economic advance. Its effect on the economy is difficult to determine, but it is estimated that 10% of the U.K.'s industrial production depends either directly or indirectly on vehicle manufacture and the effect on other European countries is probably much greater.
The importance of the motor industry to industrial growth lies in the vast number of associated industries which supply and service it, some of these being metal manufacturing, glass, rubber and plastics.
Motor vehicle production necessitates the development of roads, servicing, parts and fuel supply stations. Some countries, such as the U.S.S.R., have in the past been unwilling or unable to invest in this kind of development and the motor industry, particularly private vehicle production, has been held back.
In both Europe and North America it is the production of private cars which forms the most important part of total vehicle production. In 1969 the U.S.A. produced 8 224 327 private vehicles and 1 980 719 commercial vehicles whereas the U.S.S.R. produced 293 600 private vehicles and 974 100 commercial vehicles. In developing countries the mechanization of agriculture plus the overriding initial importance of road transport for carrying goods, creates a demand for commercial vehicles which is sustained until further developments in other forms of transport produce a levelling off of demand.
In most developing countries the motor car is still very much a luxury, but as industrialization takes place demand increases and new markets emerge. Recognizing these new markets, motor manufacturers are now breaking away from their national origins and building new factories or setting up new companies wherever it is most profitable or convenient to do so. The experience of Belgium shows in a dramatic form the way in which this process is occurring all over the world. Belgium's output of motor vehicles increased from 216 000 in 1960 to 475 000 in 1965 and to 766 896 in 1969 yet there is no domestic manufacturer; every plant is owned, or licensed, by one of the big American or European companies. Even small, newly independent countries are establishing their own motor vehicle industry; for example, Trinidad, where the market is so small that the Rootes, Ford and British Leyland Motor Corporation dealers have joined to run a co-operative plant. The waiving of the 25% import duty on completed cars is just sufficient to offset the extra cost of assembling in Trinidad instead of in the U.K. This arrangement of assembly plant is an advantage not only to the companies involved but also to the host country, particularly to developing nations where lack of sufficient technical knowledge and foreign currency and, frequently, high tariff barriers on imports of foreign goods are partially circumvented by part assembly of European and American manufactured components. The next step, already taken in Brazil, is to move to full-scale production.
Assembly plant has now been established in countries such as Chile, Argentina, Venezuela, Ghana, South Africa, South Korea, India and Australia. In order to make full use of cheaper labour in developing countries, some big manufacturers are beginning to sub-contract to plants in countries such as Mexico where, for example, a Volkswagen factory is producing spare parts which are exported to Germany and to the U.S.A. Some countries are assembling vehicles not only for home consumption but also for re-export to a third market.
The increasingly wider distribution of the industry has meant that the U.S.A. no longer produces more than half of the total world output of cars. This is due in part to an increase in assembly plant throughout the world but more particularly to increased production from countries such as Italy, Germany F.R., and Japan, whose industry had its beginning some years after that of the U.S.A. The Japanese industry more than doubled its production between 1960 and 1965 and increased it almost tenfold from 481 551 in 1960 to 4 674 340 in 1969. Japan is now proving to be a serious competitor on the American market.
Although the percentage of two car families in Europe has risen from 1.9% in 1963 to 6.3% in 1969, demand in the established markets of Northwestern Europe and North America is beginning to level off and the industry is seeking new markets for the future. Plans for these new export markets, apart from the building of assembly plant, have centred on the two rapidly advancing areas of Southern Europe and Asia.
Just as social and economic changes affect the *demand* for motor vehicles, so too they affect the *type* of vehicle produced. In the Western world increased congestion in cities has produced a demand for a smaller more manoeuvrable car. Competition from foreign imports of smaller cars has forced the U.S.A. to design and produce smaller cars for their home market, which forms 95% of American vehicle sales.
A question now beginning seriously to affect the motor vehicle industry is that of pollution from poisonous exhaust fumes. If traffic congestion and air pollution in cities continue to increase, drastic solutions will have to be sought and those alternatives already submitted could seriously affect the motor industry. Alternatives, such as increased public transport services using monorail systems and overhead railways, could completely change the present demand for private motor vehicles.

Aircraft
The aircraft industry is divided into two distinct sections, the military and the civil. Both types of aircraft production are important and both types of aircraft are exported, but statistics relating to the production and trade of military aircraft are classified. Some countries, of which Sweden is an example, produce only military aircraft but many produce both, and many advances in civil aviation have been a direct result of research conducted for military purposes.
The cost of developing a new aircraft from drawing-board to operational readiness is very high and for this reason is often subsidized to a considerable extent by governments. The aircraft industry is, therefore, particularly vulnerable to changes in government or in government policy. The U.S.A. has far more resources available for research into new aircraft than any individual country of Europe and some attempts have been made within Europe to answer American competition by co-operative ventures. A famous example of this is the Anglo-French supersonic airliner Concorde. A similar aeroplane is being developed in the U.S.S.R. and is expected to be in service before Concorde. Another recent development, pioneered in the U.S.A., is the very large airliner, the so-called jumbo-jet, carrying more than 300 passengers, which is already in commercial service.
During the 1960's production of civil airliners increased partly because of an increase in the number of passengers and the amount of freight to be transported and partly because of a widespread change from piston-engined aircraft to faster and more powerful jet aeroplanes. The replacement of piston-engined aircraft by jets is still far from complete but the proportion of piston-engined planes in the fleets of I.C.A.O.[1] countries has declined both absolutely and proportionally from 4 178 (91%) in 1958 to 3 069 (52%) in 1966 and to 1 995 (27%) in 1970. The changeover is not likely ever to reach 100% unless economic considerations are sacrificed to prestige because some routes are too short to justify the use of jets.
The production of light aircraft for business or pleasure is increasing and, being relatively simple, is carried out in some countries such as Argentina and Brazil which do not produce larger aircraft though the largest growth has been in the U.S.A. where the number of light aircraft produced rose from less than 7 000 to almost 16 000 between 1962 and 1966.
The distribution of the aircraft industry is complex. Many companies own a number of plants in different locations and also sub-contract the assembly of important parts of aircraft, such as the wings, to other companies, not necessarily in the same country. Like the motor industry the aircraft industry draws on other industries for the supply of such things as tyres, special glass, and electrical equipment. It is also important to realize that many aircraft manufacturers, whether of air-frames or of aero-engines, are also engaged in space technology.

Railway vehicles
In the OECD countries output of railway vehicles reached peaks in the years 1955-63 which have never since been surpassed. In many of the developed countries the industry has actually been declining in more recent years. Output, however, is not the sole measure of the importance of the industry. According to an estimate made for the OECD countries the industry accounts for only 5% of the total output of the transport industries (other figures are: road vehicles 61%; aircraft 25%; ships and boats 9%) but these railway vehicles carry an estimated 40% of internal freight traffic and 25% of passenger traffic. Another important consideration is that the diesel locomotives which are now being produced are more powerful than those they replace. In the U.S.A. diesels of 1 200 – 1 400 h.p. are now being replaced by diesels of 2 000 – 3 000 h.p. Electric locomotives are favoured in Europe and Japan where conditions are more favourable for their use than in the U.S.A. These are even more powerful than the new diesels, averaging between 3 000 and 5 000 h.p. Since the end of the first world war alternative means of transport have cut the amount of passenger traffic handled by the railways in the U.S.A. and Western Europe.
There is considerable surplus capacity for the production of railway vehicles, both locomotives and trailers (including self-powered cars). This is caused not only by the growth of other forms of transport but also by the growth of production centres in the developing countries, who consequently import less; by the growth of railway workshops which do work formerly done by private producers; and by gross fluctuations in demand. As a result of this some firms producing railway vehicles have diversified whilst others have merged or closed down completely.
One of the few growth points in the industry is in self-propelled cars. These cars are increasingly used for medium distance journeys but they are particularly suitable for sub-ways and commuter services which are the very sections of passenger service which have not declined in importance. In rolling stock production passenger cars are far outnumbered by freight cars which account for up to two-thirds of the annual value of all railway vehicles delivered. Fewer of the basic box or flat type of freight cars are now produced but there has been a growth in the demand for special purpose cars, e.g. those for quick turn around for bulk transport and for motor vehicle transport.
It is highly unusual for the countries producing railway vehicles to compete in each other's home markets. Where there is an export trade in railway vehicles it is generally to the developing countries and is therefore financed to a very considerable extent by some form of foreign aid. One exception to this is that the COMECON countries manufacture railway vehicles which are sold to the U.S.S.R.

[1]International Civil Aviation Organization which has 120 member states, excluding China P.R.

International trade in transport equipment[1]

Merchant ships[4] (1966)

Exports[2,3]
G.R.T. 7 132 031
Data for 1953-5 av. not available

	PERCENTAGE 1966
Japan	56
Sweden	11
Germany F.R.	8
U.K.	4
Poland	4
Germany D.R.	3
Yugoslavia	2
Denmark	2
Others	10
	100

Imports
G.R.T. 7 132 031
Data for 1953-5 av. not available

	PERCENTAGE 1966
Norway	32
Liberia	25
U.S.S.R.	11
U.K.	7
Greece	3
Netherlands	2
Romania	1
Poland	1
Others	18
	100

Aircraft

Exports
$1 827 million 1963-5 av.
$908 million 1953-5 av.

	PERCENTAGE 1963-5 av.	1953-5 av.
U.S.A.	55	*82[8]*
U.K.	9	*12[8]*
Netherlands	8[5]	*1*
Canada	8[6]	*3[8]*
France	7[7]	*1*
Belg./Lux.	5	—
Italy	4	*1*
Germany F.R.	3	—
Others	1	—
	100	*100*

Imports
$1 085 million 1963-5 av.
$727 million 1953-5 av.

	PERCENTAGE 1963-5 av.	1953-5 av.
Germany F.R.	11	—
Canada	10	*16*
U.S.A.	10	*4*
Netherlands	7	*2*
Australia	6	*2*
Japan	6	*1*
Belg./Lux.	6	*2*
France	5	*5*
Others	39	*68*
	100	*100*

Motor vehicles

Exports
$7 985 million 1963-5 av.
$3 350 million 1953-5 av.

	PERCENTAGE 1963-5 av.	1953-5 av.
Germany F.R.	27	*14*
U.S.A.	22	*39*
U.K.	19	*21*
France	9	*7*
Italy	6	*3*
Belg./Lux.	4	*1*
Japan	4	—
Sweden	3	*1*
Others	6	*14*
	100	*100*

Imports
$7 600 million 1963-5 av.
$2 369 million 1953-5 av.

	PERCENTAGE 1963-5 av.	1953-5 av.
U.S.A.	11	*3*
Canada	10	*14*
Belg./Lux.	6	*5*
Netherlands	5	*5*
Sweden	4	*6*
Germany F.R.	4	*1*
France	4	*1*
Australia	4	*7*
Others	52	*58*
	100	*100*

Railway vehicles

Exports
$724 million 1963-5 av.
$400 million 1953-5 av.

	PERCENTAGE 1963-5 av.	1953-5 av.
Germany D.R.	19	*...[1]*
U.S.A.	18	*28*
Germany F.R.	13	*15*
Poland	10[9]	*...[1]*
Czechoslovakia	9[10]	*...[1]*
U.K.	7	*30*
Japan	5	*3*
Italy	5	*2*
Others	14	*22*
	100	*100*

Imports
$518 million 1963-5 av.
$332 million 1953-5 av.

	PERCENTAGE 1963-5 av.	1953-5 av.
U.S.S.R.	30[11]	*...[1]*
India	10	*5[12]*
Argentina	9	*6[13]*
Pakistan	6	—
Mexico	6	*3*
South Africa	3	*...[1]*
Brazil	3	*6*
Indonesia	3	*2*
Others	30	*78*
	100	*100*

[1]Total of available countries [2]Export data from the U.S.S.R. and China P.R. are not available [3]Figures for individual countries within the British Commonwealth are not available [4]Excl. ships of less than 100 G.R.T. [5]Incl. second-hand aircraft when they first cross the frontier after purchase or sale [6]Incl. second-hand aircraft [7]Incl. second-hand aircraft purchased or sold abroad [8]Excl. parts [9]Freight and passenger cars only [10]Locomotives only [11]Locomotives and passenger coaches only [12]Railway carriages, wagons and parts [13]Locomotives and railway materials

Shipbuilding

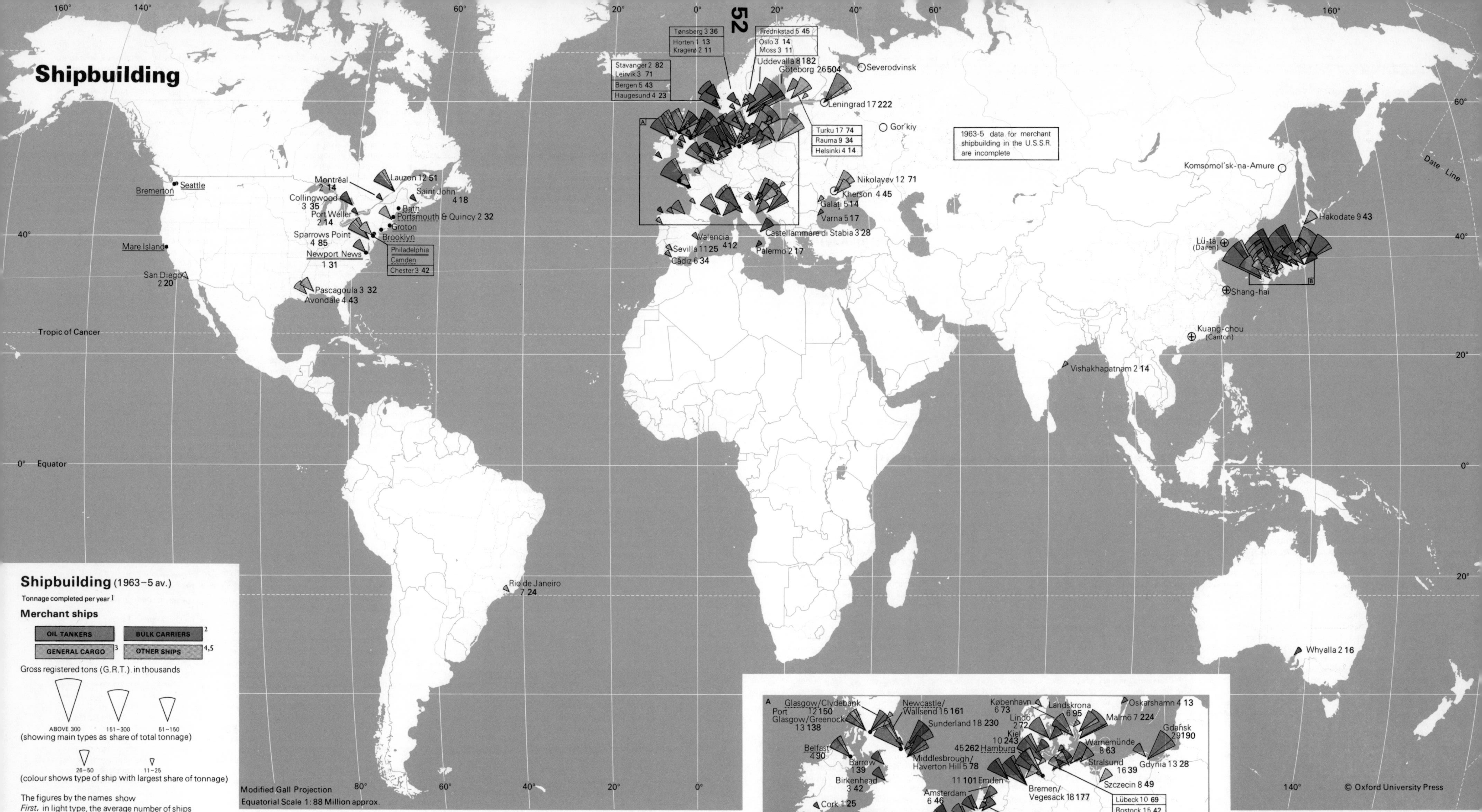

Shipbuilding (1963–5 av.)

Tonnage completed per year 1

Merchant ships

OIL TANKERS | BULK CARRIERS 2
GENERAL CARGO 3 | OTHER SHIPS 4,5

Gross registered tons (G.R.T.) in thousands

ABOVE 300 · 151–300 · 51–150
(showing main types as share of total tonnage)

26–50 · 11–25
(colour shows type of ship with largest share of tonnage)

The figures by the names show
First, in light type, the average number of ships completed, 1963–5
Second, in heavier type, the average gross registered tonnage completed, 1963–5, in thousands

+ Data not available

Ships of under 100 G.R.T. are excluded

Naval ships

Displacement tons, in thousands

e.g. Philadelphia — ABOVE 20
Bremerton — 11 – 20
Hamburg — 6 – 10

• Indicates location

○ Data not available

Non-combat naval ships are included

1. Although ships are allocated to the year of completion they are not necessarily allocated to the place of completion. They are always shown as having been built at the place where the hull was constructed before launching.

2. Bulk carriers are especially designed for handling bulk cargoes such as ore or grain.

3. 'General cargo' includes cargo ships of at least 2000 G.R.T. and with a capacity of less than 100 passengers.

4. 'Other ships' are mainly fishing or passenger ships or small cargo ships.

5. 'Other ships' may include one or more type of ship with too small a share of total tonnage to be shown separately as a distinct sector.

Merchant ships completed[1]

10 771 997 G.R.T. 1963-5 av.[2,3]
5 208 487 G.R.T. 1954-5 av.[4]

	PERCENTAGE 1963-5 av.	1954-5 av.
Japan	34	*10*
Sweden	10	*10*
U.K.	10	*27*
Germany F.R.	9	*18*
France	5	*6*
Italy	4	*4*
U.S.S.R.	4[3]	*...*[4]
Others	24	*25*
	100	*100*

[1] Excl. ships below 100 G.R.T.
[2] Excl. China P.R. [3] U.S.S.R. figure incomplete
[4] Excl. China P.R., Germany D.R. & U.S.S.R.

Ships and boats (S.I.T.C. no. 735)

Total value of exports
$1 964 million 1963-5 av.

	PERCENTAGE 1963-5 av.
Japan	27
Sweden	13
Germany F.R.	11
Netherlands	6
France	6
Norway	5
Poland	5
U.K.	5
Denmark	4
U.S.A.	3
Others	15
	100

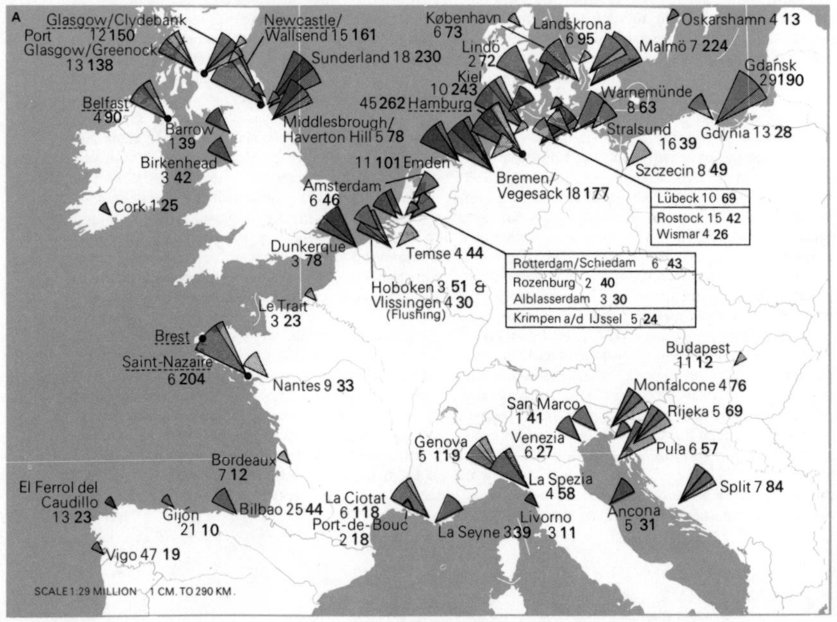

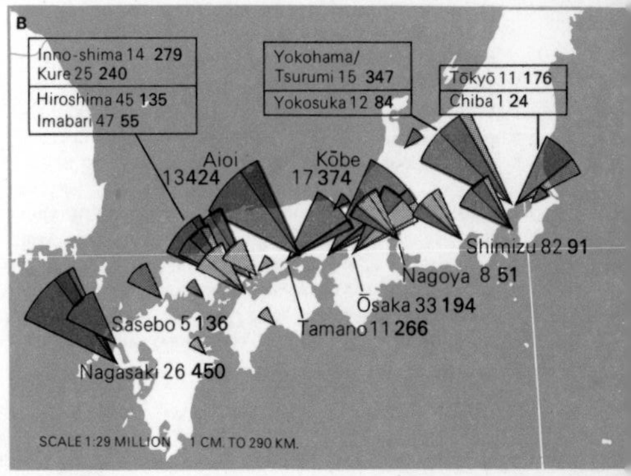

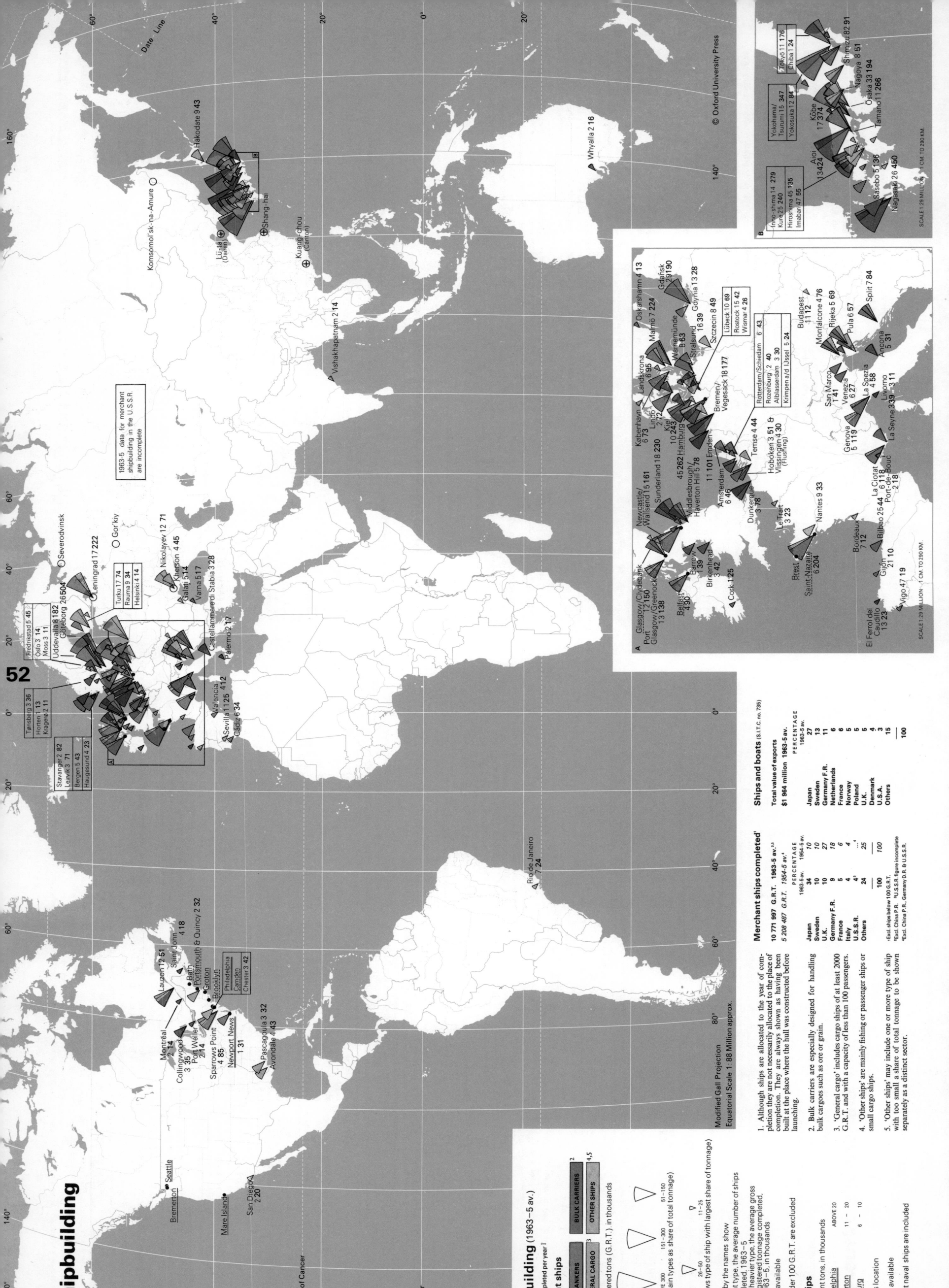

Aircraft

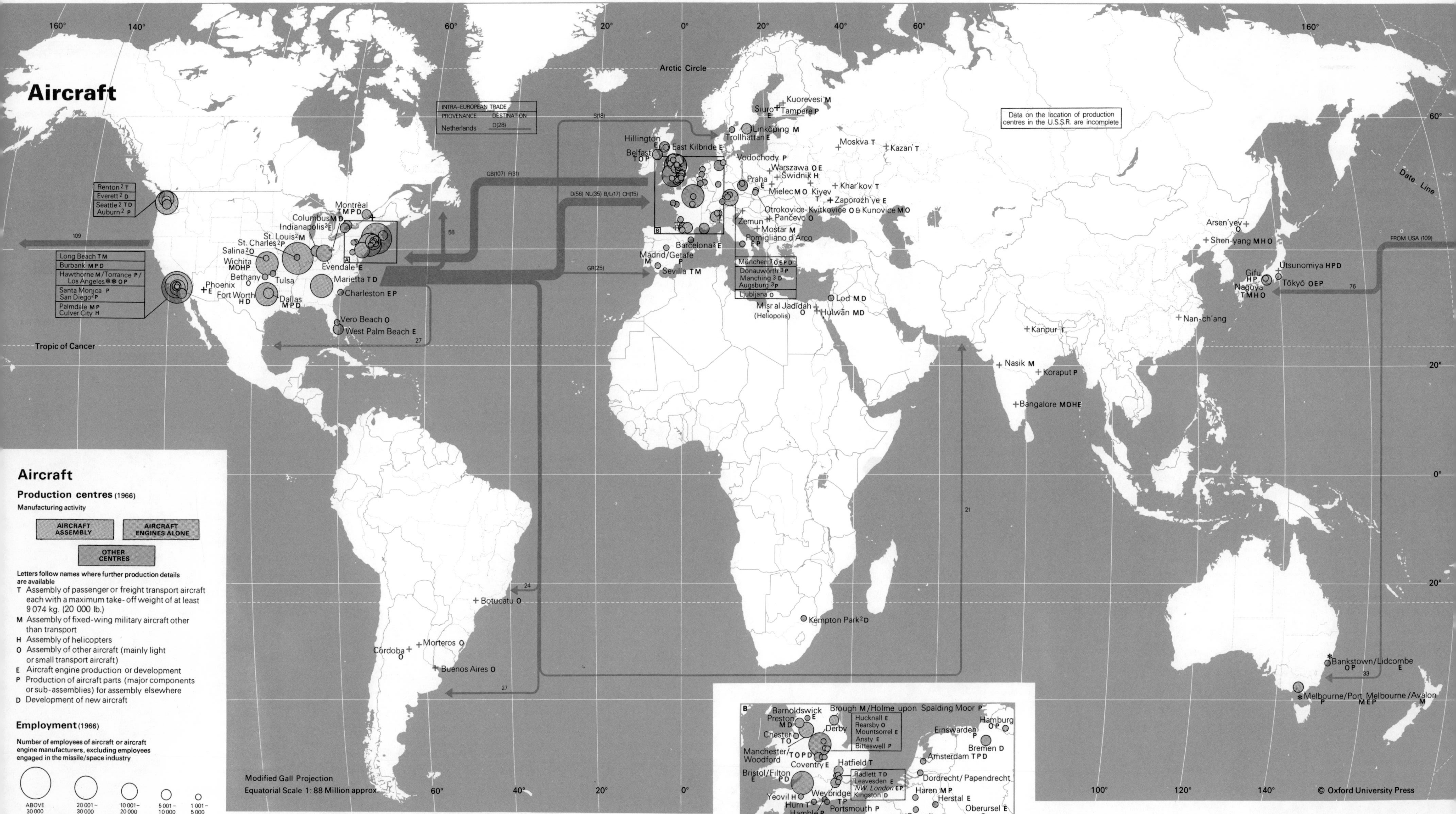

Aircraft

Production centres (1966)

Manufacturing activity

AIRCRAFT ASSEMBLY | AIRCRAFT ENGINES ALONE | OTHER CENTRES

Letters follow names where further production details are available

- T Assembly of passenger or freight transport aircraft each with a maximum take-off weight of at least 9 074 kg. (20 000 lb.)
- M Assembly of fixed-wing military aircraft other than transport
- H Assembly of helicopters
- O Assembly of other aircraft (mainly light or small transport aircraft)
- E Aircraft engine production or development
- P Production of aircraft parts (major components or sub-assemblies) for assembly elsewhere
- D Development of new aircraft

Employment (1966)

Number of employees of aircraft or aircraft engine manufacturers, excluding employees engaged in the missile/space industry

ABOVE 30 000 | 20 001–30 000 | 10 001–20 000 | 5 001–10 000 | 1 001–5 000

+ + + Employment data not available
* Employment figures estimated
** Employment figures incomplete
1,2,3 Where 1966 employment figures were not available, later figures were used
[1] 1967 [2] 1968 [3] 1969

Major trade flows (1966)

Commodity: S.I.T.C.no.[1]

AIRCRAFT (HEAVIER THAN AIR) :734.1

Value ($U.S.)
0.5mm. represents increments of $30 million

($ MILLIONS) 270 150 30 — 58 VALUE IN $ MILLIONS

[1] S.I.T.C. Standard International Trade Classification

Aircraft exports (S.I.T.C. no. 734)

$2 212 million 1965-7 av.
$1 827 million 1963-5 av.[1]
$908 million 1953-5 av.[1]

	PERCENTAGE 1965-7 av.	1963-5 av.	1953-5 av.
U.S.A.	56	55	*82*
U.K.	13	9	*12*
France	8	7	*1*
Canada	8	8	*3*
Netherlands	4	8	*1*
Germany F.R.	3	3	—
Italy	3	4	*1*
U.S.S.R.	2[2]	...[1]	...[1]
Belg./Lux.	2	5	—
Others	1	1	—
	100	100	*100*

[1] Excl. U.S.S.R.
[2] 1966/7 only

Aircraft deliveries

Total value in $U.S.[1]
$13 835 million 1965-7 av.[2]

	PERCENTAGE 1965-7 av.
U.S.A.	76
U.K.	8
France	8
Canada	3
Japan	1
Italy	1
Germany F.R.	1
Netherlands	1
Others	1
	100

[1] Incl. parts and excl. engines
[2] Estimated from data for Japan, Western Europe & North America only

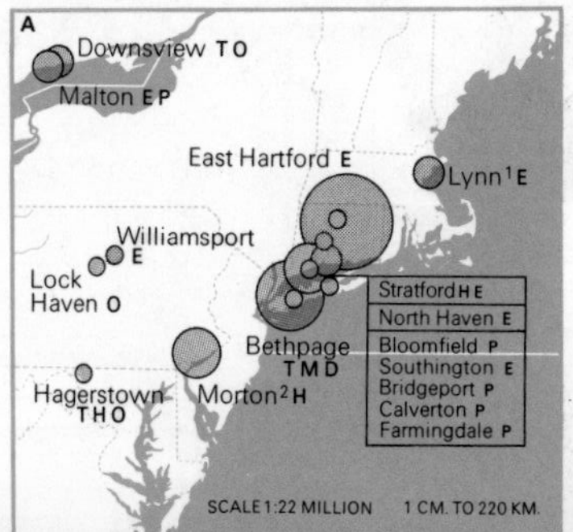

53

Civil airliner production (1965-7 av.)

Turbo-jet and turbo-prop aircraft with a maximum take-off weight of at least 9 074 kg. delivered to civil airlines of the member states of I.C.A.O.[1]

Symbols, located at the place of airliner assembly, are graded into 5 sizes according to weight of production.

Figures after names show *first*, in light type, the average number of airliners delivered; *second*, in heavier type, the total weight (empty) of the airliners delivered, measured in thousand kilograms.

[1] International Civil Aviation Organization

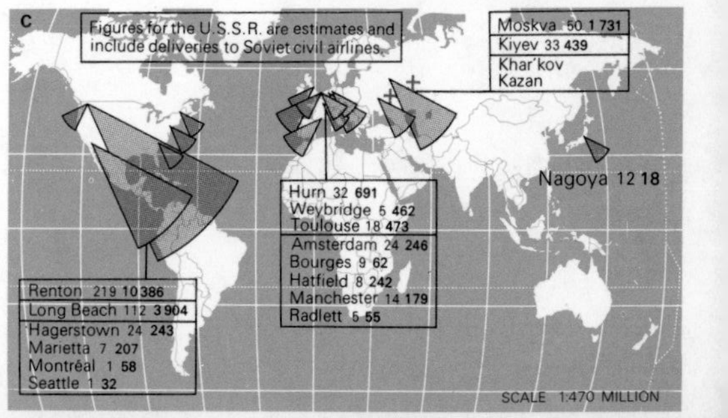

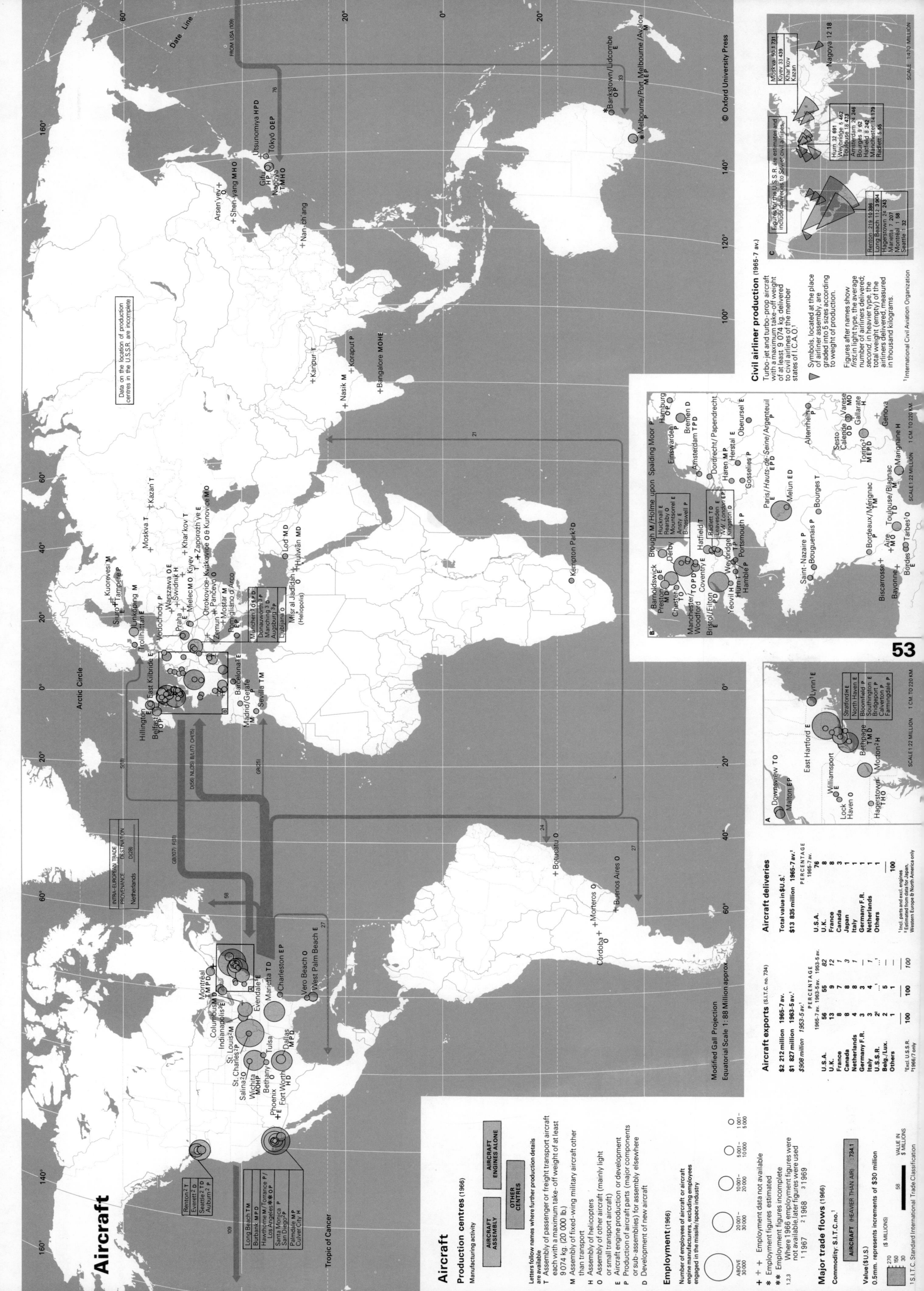

Railway Vehicles

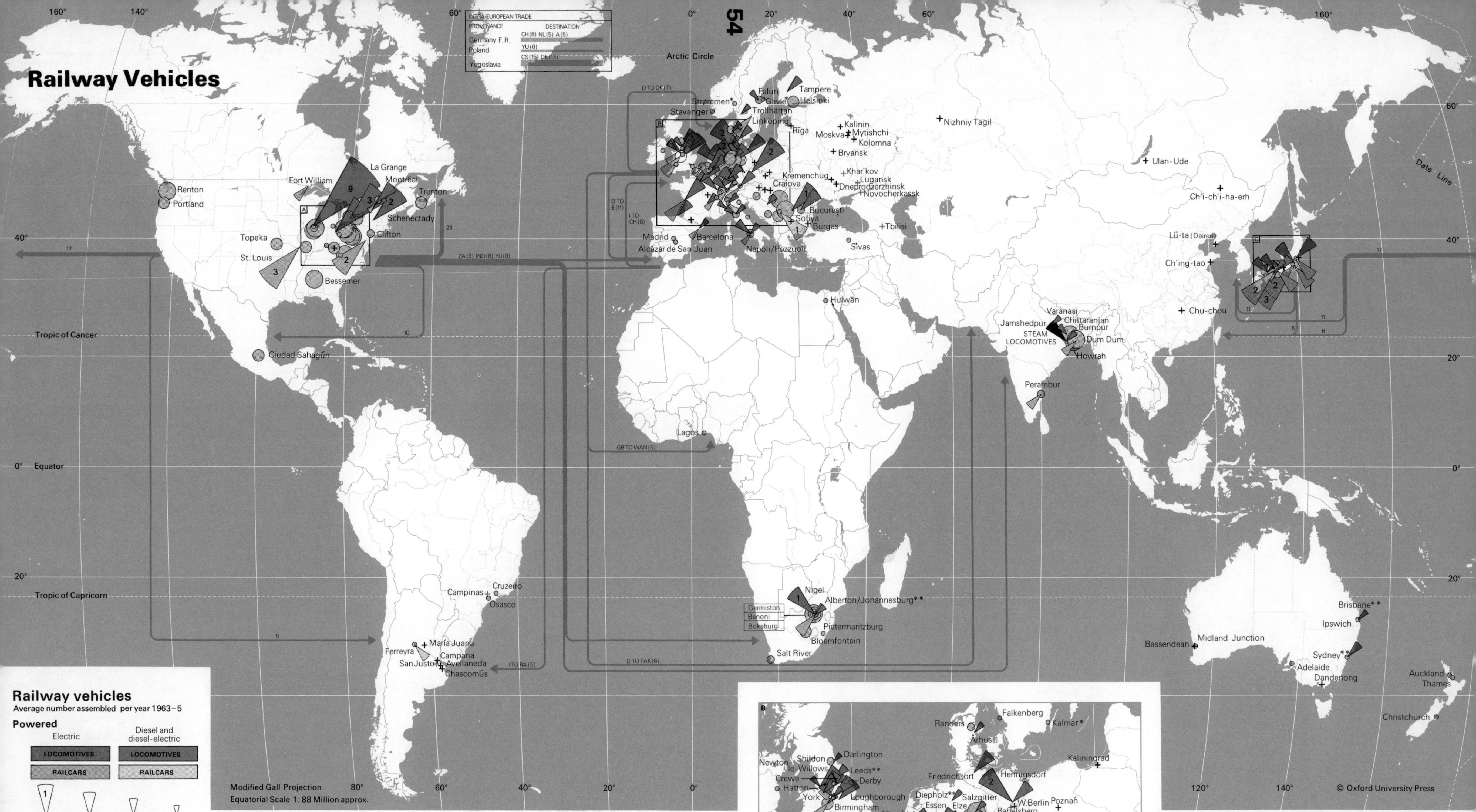

Railway vehicles

Average number assembled per year 1963–5

Powered

Electric	Diesel and diesel-electric
LOCOMOTIVES	LOCOMOTIVES
RAILCARS	RAILCARS

1: 101–200; 51–100; 26–50; 11–25

Higher categories increase by units of 100

e.g. 3 shows production of 301–400

Locomotives of under 100 h. p. are excluded

Non-powered rolling stock

ABOVE 2 000; 1 001–2 000; 501–1 000; 101–500

\+ Data not available (specialized locomotive production shown in the appropriate colour)

* Estimate

** Data incomplete

Locomotives (number produced)

9 250 1963-5 av.[1]

5 551 1953-4 av.[2]

	PERCENTAGE 1963-5 av.	1953-4 av.
U.S.S.R.	23	*18*
U.S.A.	16	*30**
Germany F.R.	11	*13*
U.K.	8	*21*
Germany D.R.	6	...[3]
Czechoslovakia	6	*1*
Others	30	*17*
	100	*100*

*Estimate

[1]Estimated from 24 major producers excluding China P.R.

[2]11 countries only

[3]Not included in 1953-4 total

Railway vehicles (S.I.T.C. no. 731)

Total value of exports[1]

$724 million 1963-5 av.

	PERCENTAGE 1963-5 av.
Germany D.R.	19
U.S.A.	18
Germany F.R.	13
Poland[2]	10
Czechoslovakia[3]	9
U.K.	7
Japan	5
Italy	5
Others	14
	100

[1]20 countries only

[2]Freight & passenger cars only

[3]Locomotives only

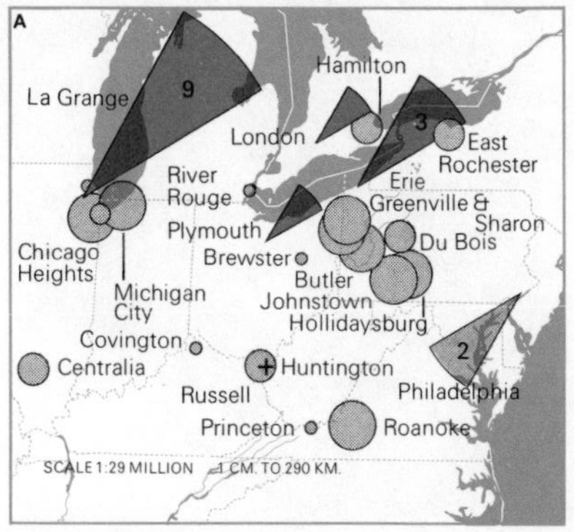

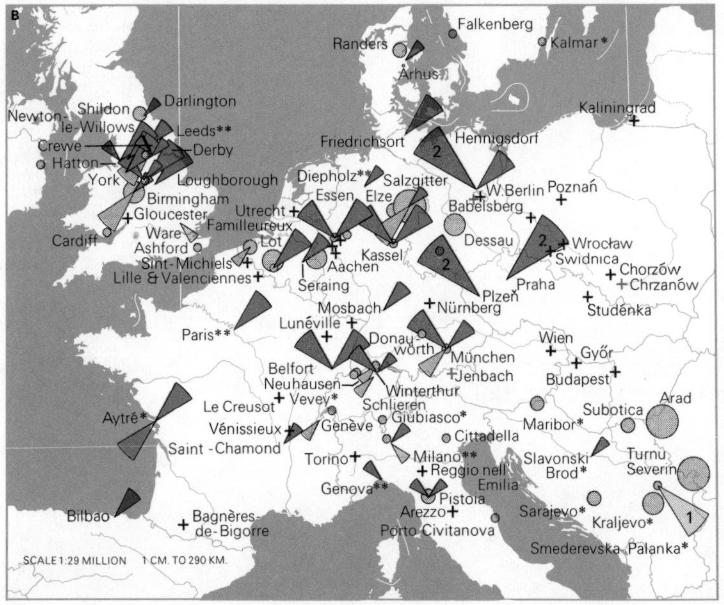

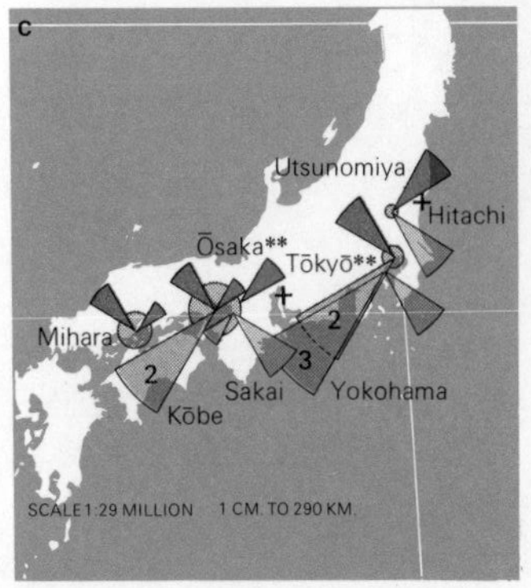

Major trade flows (1966)

Commodity: S.I.T.C.no.

RAILWAY VEHICLES : 731

Value ($ U.S.)

0.5 mm represents increments of $10 million

90 / 50 / 10 ($ MILLIONS)

17 VALUE IN $ MILLIONS

A trade flow is defined as trade in one direction only between any two countries. This indicates major trading partners but not necessarily major traders.

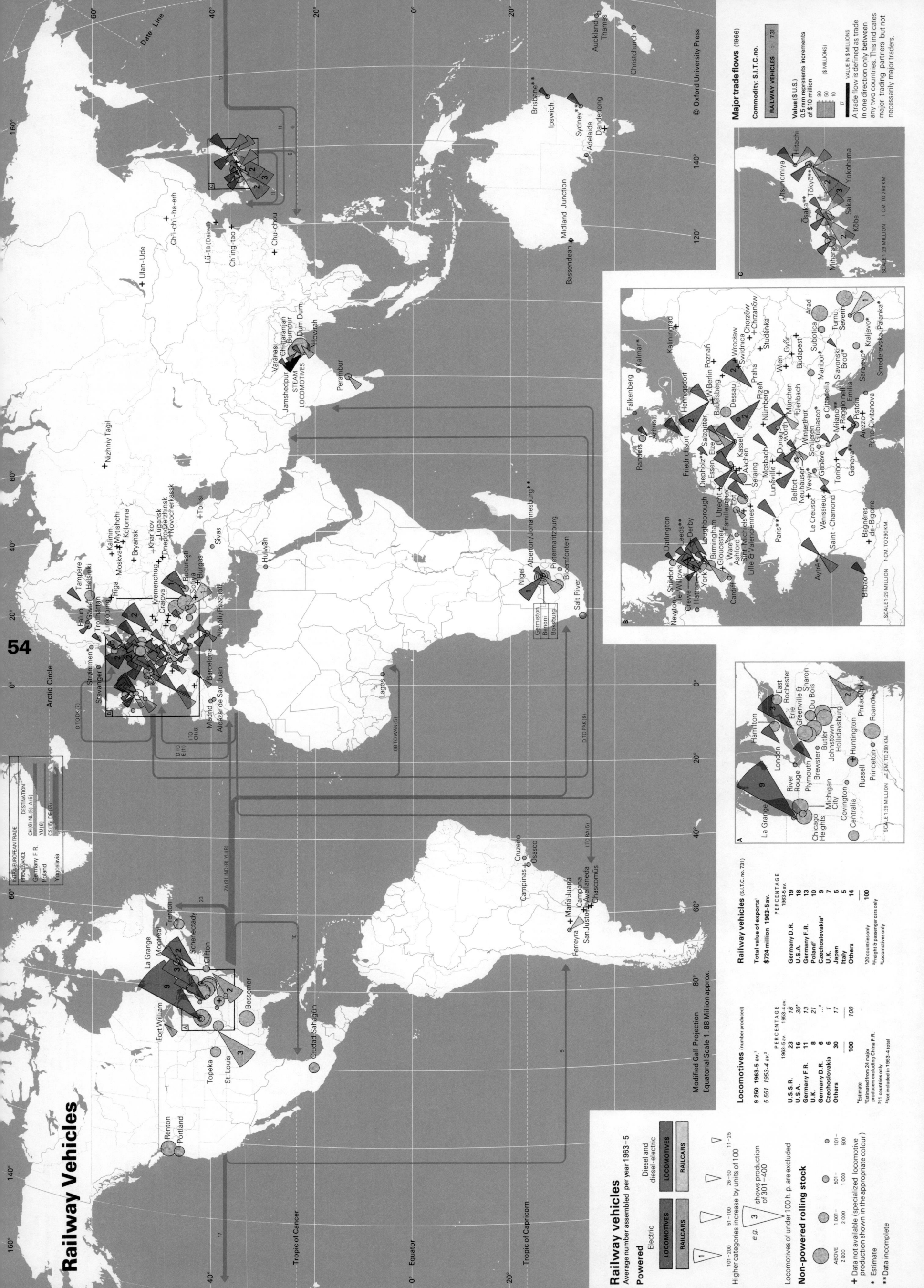

Motor Vehicles

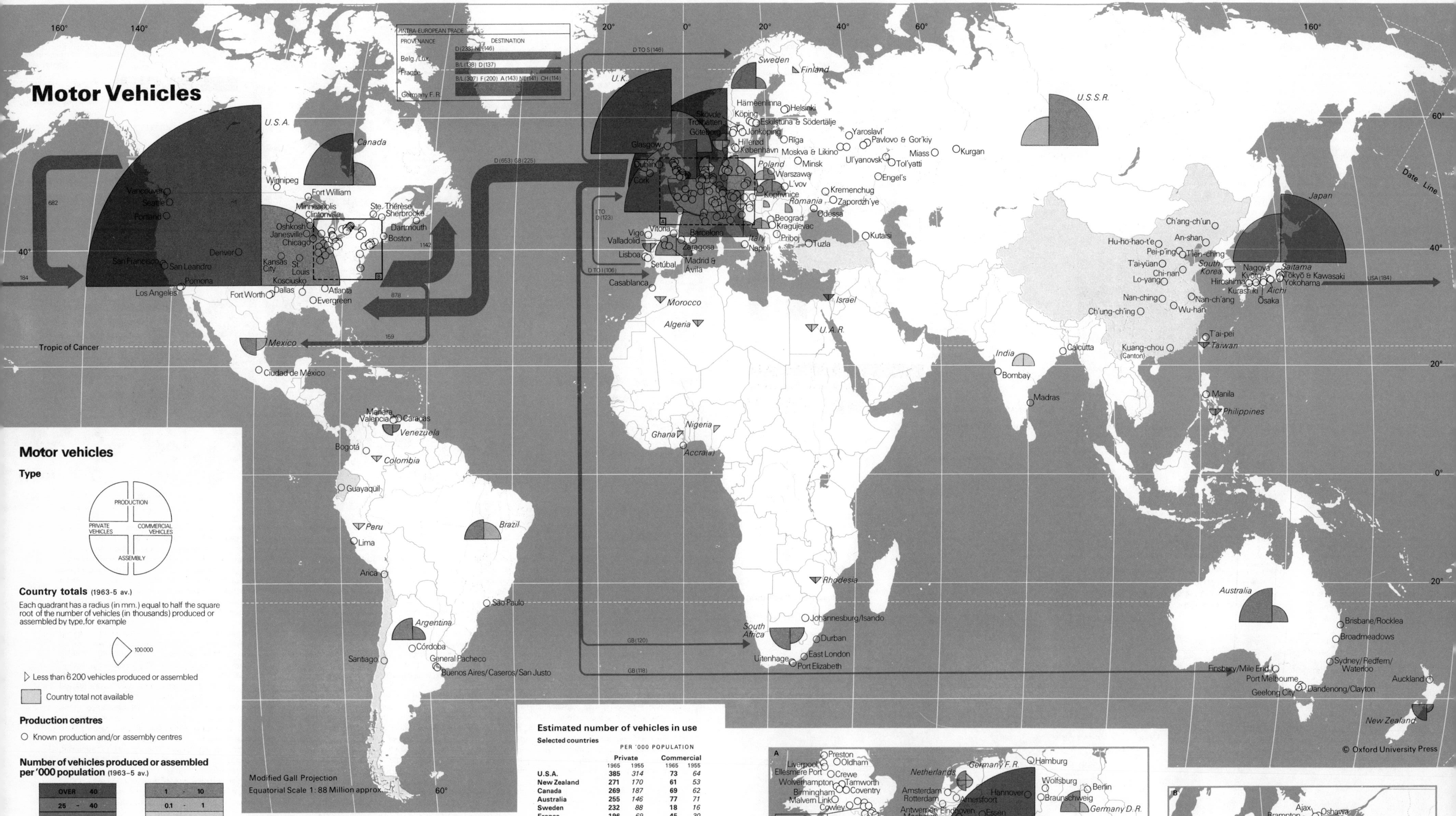

Motor vehicles

Type

Country totals (1963-5 av.)

Each quadrant has a radius (in mm.) equal to half the square root of the number of vehicles (in thousands) produced or assembled by type, for example

100 000

▷ Less than 6 200 vehicles produced or assembled

Country total not available

Production centres

○ Known production and/or assembly centres

Number of vehicles produced or assembled per '000 population (1963–5 av.)

OVER 40	1 - 10
25 - 40	0.1 - 1
10 - 25	UNDER 0.1

Major trade flows (1966)

Commodity: S.I.T.C. no.

ROAD MOTOR VEHICLES : 732

Value ($ U.S.)

0.5 mm represents increments of $ 100 million

1700 ($ MILLIONS) 1300 900 500 100

184 VALUE IN $ MILLIONS

Trade flow is defined as trade in one direction between two countries. This indicates major trading partners but not necessarily major traders.

Motor vehicle production

Private vehicles

17 460 000 units 1963-5 av.

9 013 000 1953-5 av.

	PERCENTAGE 1963-5 av.	PERCENTAGE 1953-5 av.
U.S.A.	47	*72*
Germany F.R.	15	*6*
U.K.	10	*8*
France	8	*5*
Italy	6	*2*
Canada	3	*4*
Japan	3	—
Australia	2	*1*
U.S.S.R.	1	*1*
Others	5	*1*
	100	*100*

Commercial vehicles

4 893 000 units 1963-5 av.

2 293 000 1953-5 av.

	PERCENTAGE 1963-5 av.	PERCENTAGE 1953-5 av.
U.S.A.	32	*51*
Japan	23	*2*
U.S.S.R.	12	*13*
U.K.	9	*12*
France	5	*7*
Germany F.R.	5	*7*
Canada	2	*4*
Brazil	1	—
Italy	1	*2*
Others	10	*2*
	100	*100*

Estimated number of vehicles in use

Selected countries

	Private 1965 (per '000 population)	Private 1955	Commercial 1965	Commercial 1955
U.S.A.	385	*314*	73	*64*
New Zealand	271	*170*	61	*53*
Canada	269	*187*	69	*62*
Australia	255	*146*	77	*71*
Sweden	232	*88*	18	*16*
France	196	*69*	45	*30*
U.K.	170	*69*	33	*23*
Germany F.R.	158	*36*	15	*22*
Kuwait	123	*NA*	46	*NA*
Austria	109	*21*	41	*9*
Italy	106	*18*	13	*8*
Netherlands	104	*25*	19	*11*
South Africa	63	*42*	16	*12*
Venezuela	44	*24*	19	*16*
Argentina	41	*18*	26	*14*
Israel	30	*10*	16	*10*
Spain	25	*5*	12	*3*
Japan	22	*2*	44	*3*
Mexico	18	*10*	9	*8*
Brazil	14	*6*	12	*6*
Morocco	12	*11*	5	*5*
Kenya	8	*4*	1	*4*
Poland	8	*1*	6	*3*
Colombia	7	*6*	6	*5*
Philippines	5	*2*	3	*3*
India	1	*1*	1	—

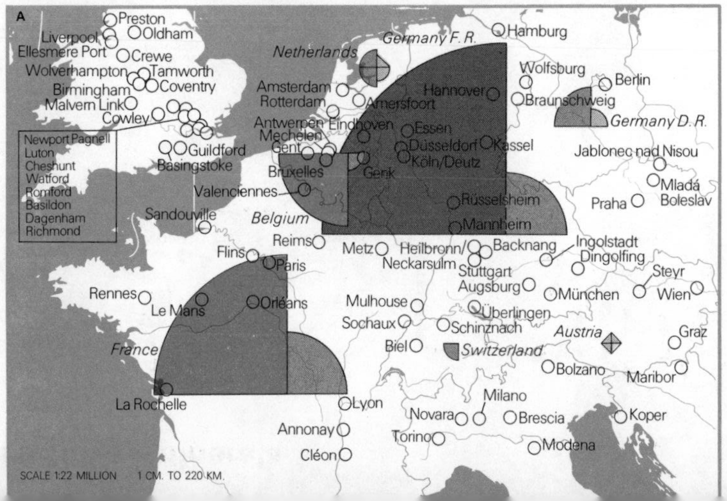

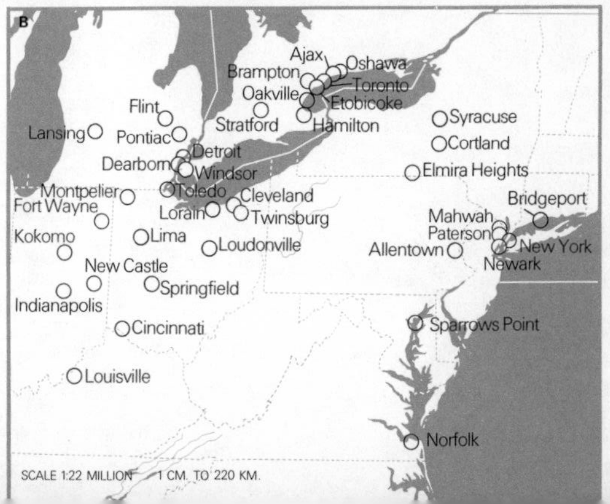

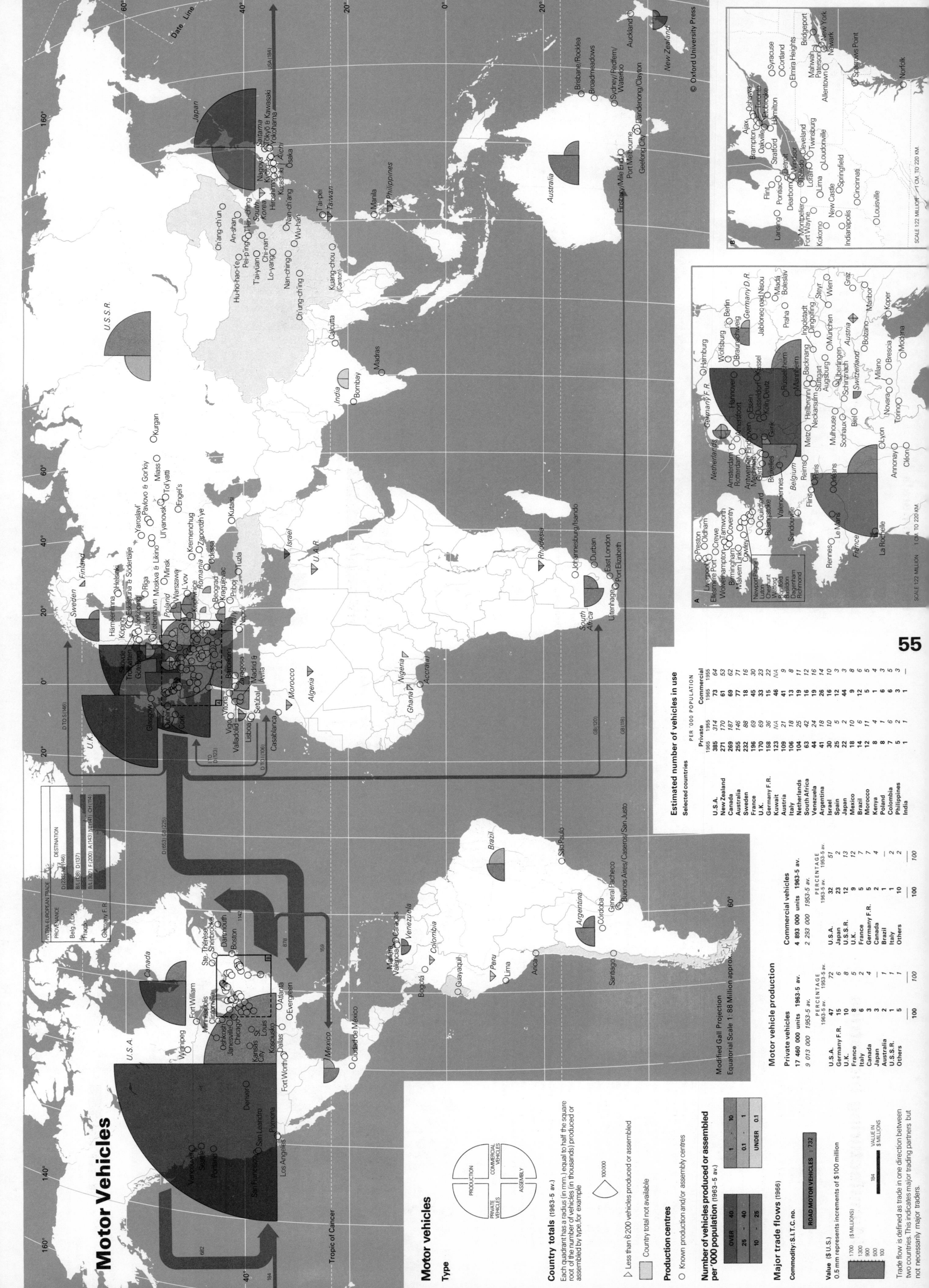

Manufacturing Industries

For individual country data see Statistical Supplement

The manufacturing industries as they are known in the industrialized nations today may be said to have begun with the invention of the water frame for cotton spinning in 1769. This machine was too big to be used in the home so its adoption marked the beginning of the factory system. Of the manufacturing industries which are of importance today only textiles and pottery have continued right through from the early days of the industrial revolution. Many new light industries have started and become important since then. Some of these important newer industries, including computers and electrical engineering, have been the direct result of scientific research. One particular scientific breakthrough, the synthesis of urea from inorganic substances, has been important in the development of the chemical industry, but even more important has been the development of the petroleum industry. Petro-chemicals are made from the by-products of petroleum refining, and these constitute a very important part of the chemicals industry. Industry repays its debt to science by the manufacture of ever more sophisticated scientific instruments.

The manufacturing industries offer a growth potential to the developing countries because one or more of them can often be developed in areas where the raw materials, the technical skill, or the financial resources for the development of heavy industry are lacking but where centuries of skill in domestic crafts can be used as the basis of a manufacturing industry. Too rapid industrialization can bring many problems to a developing country. Urban areas become overcrowded and unemployment is caused by the change from cottage industry to factory industry as well as by the shift from agriculture to industry. Even the most labour intensive industry is less labour intensive than simple agriculture and concealed under-employment on the land becomes overt unemployment in the factories.

The cement industry is a particularly interesting example of the role of industry in development. The basis of cement is lime which is widely available, and the manufacture of cement is relatively cheap and straightforward. When it is made into concrete, cement gives a building material which is strong and durable as well as being fireproof and watertight. Cement is also extremely costly to transport and for this reason, as well as for those stated above, the cement industry is very widely spread and may even be one of the first signs that a country is beginning to industrialize. The beer industry is also very widespread, much more so than the statistics for the commercial industry would suggest. Beer does not travel well and therefore there is little trade in it but more important is the fact that most beer is produced only for local consumption and much of it is never even bottled and labelled.

The chemical industry is both one of the most important and also one of those which has a large potential for growth because there is no immediate danger of a decline in the petroleum industry which serves it and because it serves other industries which are themselves growing and spends a considerable sum on research and development. Chemicals are important in every aspect of life; providing fertilizers, drugs, paint, and plastics among many other things.

In the industrialized nations the major factor influencing the further development of the manufacturing industries is the relatively high cost of labour. The cost of labour is one of the factors which favours the employment of women in these industries. The garments industry and the electronics industry both employ more women than men, thus making use of their temperament and dexterity and bringing into the labour force many women who would not otherwise be wage earners. An increasingly greater emphasis is also being given to automation which uses computer-controlled machines. In industrialized countries the future development of new manufacturing industries is likely to be the result of advances in scientific research.

Beer

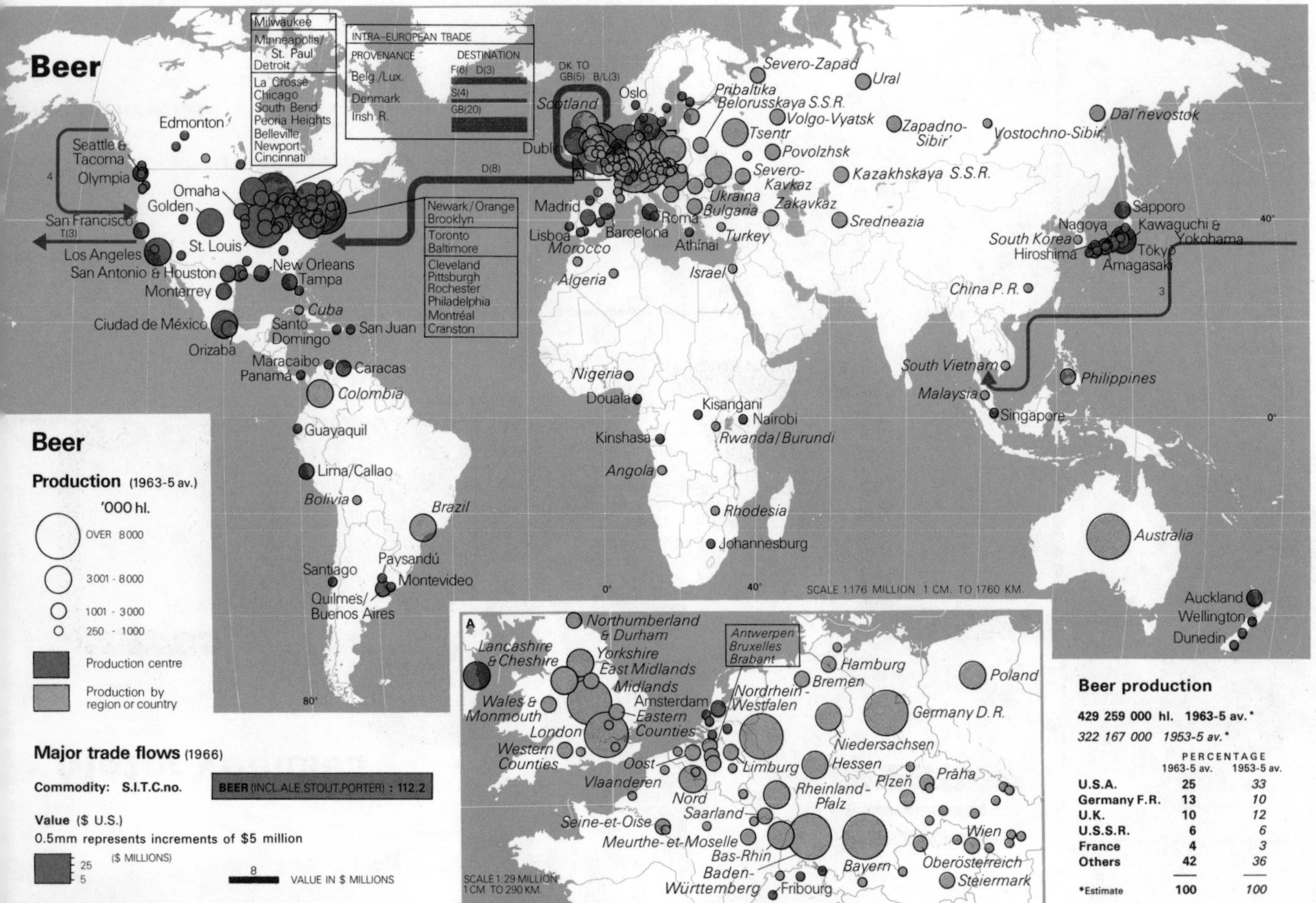

Beer

Production (1963-5 av.)

'000 hl.

- OVER 8000
- 3001 - 8000
- 1001 - 3000
- 250 - 1000
- Production centre
- Production by region or country

Major trade flows (1966)

Commodity: S.I.T.C.no. BEER (INCL.ALE,STOUT,PORTER) : 112.2

Value ($ U.S.)

0.5mm represents increments of $5 million

($ MILLIONS) 25, 5

8 VALUE IN $ MILLIONS

Beer production

429 259 000 hl. 1963-5 av.*

*322 167 000 1953-5 av.**

	PERCENTAGE 1963-5 av.	1953-5 av.
U.S.A.	25	33
Germany F.R.	13	10
U.K.	10	12
U.S.S.R.	6	6
France	4	3
Others	42	36
	100	100

*Estimate

Fertilizer Minerals

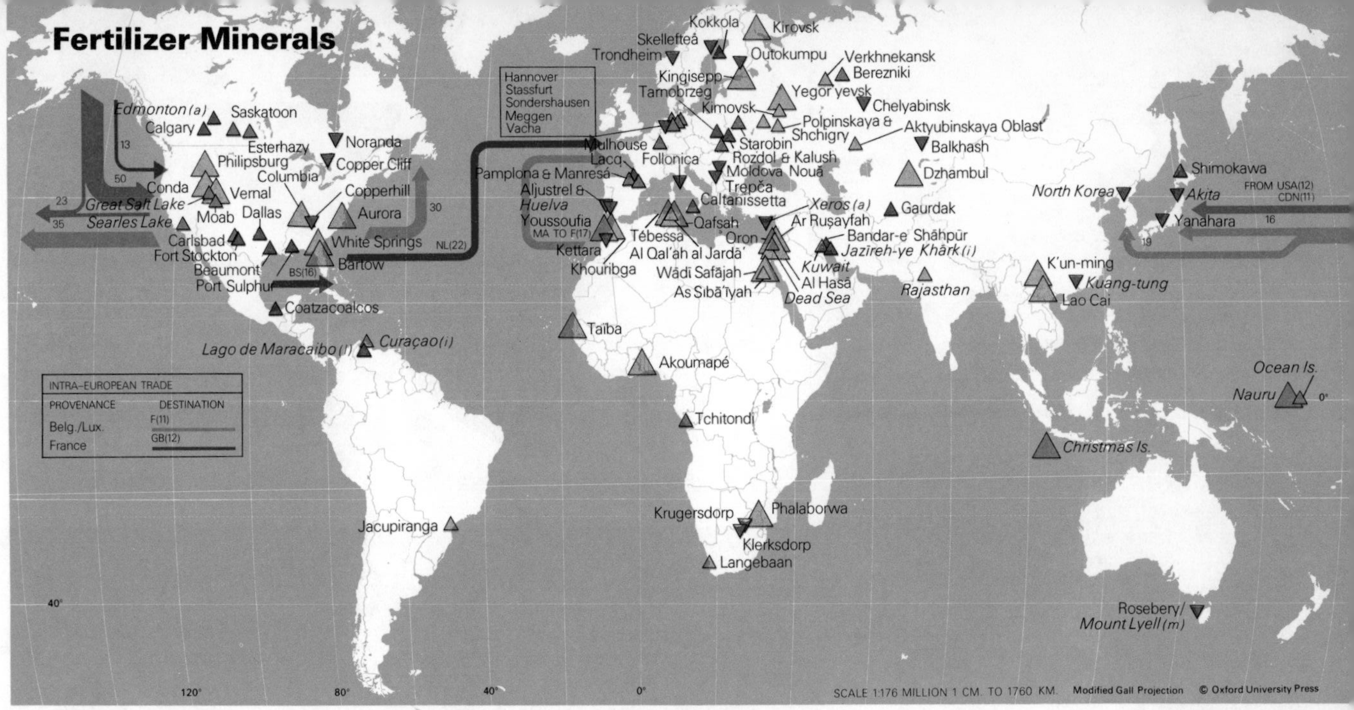

Fertilizer minerals

Producing districts (1969)

Annual production capacity in '000 met. tons

Phosphates (phosphate rock)
- OVER 500
- 100 - 500

Potash (K_2O)
- OVER 100

Sulphur
- OVER 100

Pyrites (sulphur equivalent)
- OVER 100

Major trade flows (1966)

Commodity: S.I.T.C.no.

PHOSPHATES[1]/FERTS./MATERIALS	271.3 / 561.2
POTASSIC SALTS/FERTS./MATERIALS	271.4 / 561.3
SULPHUR/IRON PYRITES (UNROASTED)	274

Value ($ U.S.)

0.5mm represents increments of $10 million

($ MILLIONS) 90, 50, 10

22 VALUE IN $ MILLIONS

Trade flow is defined as trade in one direction between two countries. This indicates major trading partners but not necessarily major traders.

[1]Natural minerals

Potash[1] production

12 450 000 met. tons 1963-5 av.*

*6 560 000 1953-5 av.**

	PERCENTAGE 1963-5 av.	1953-5 av.
U.S.A.	22	27
U.S.S.R.*	18	9
Germany F.R.	17	24
Germany D.R.	15	21*
France	14	16
Canada	7	—
Spain	3	3
Israel	2*	—
Others	2	—
	100	100

*Estimate [1]K_2O equivalent

Phosphate[1] production

56 571 000 met. tons 1963-5 av.*

*29 380 000 1953-5 av.**

	PERCENTAGE 1963-5 av.	1953-5 av.
U.S.A.	41	44
U.S.S.R.*	20	15
Morocco	17	16
Tunisia	5	6
Nauru Is.[2]	3	4
N. Vietnam	2*	—
China P.R.*	1	1
Senegal	1	—
Togo	1	—
Others	9	14
	100	100

*Estimate [1]Rock [2]Exports

Sulphur production

Native sulphur

8 960 000 met. tons 1963-5 av.*

*6 500 000 1953-5 av.**

	PERCENTAGE 1963-5 av.	1953-5 av.
U.S.A.	61	86
Mexico	18	3
U.S.S.R.*	11	NA
Poland	4	—
Japan	3	3
China P.R.	1*	—
Italy	1	3[1]
Others	1	NA
	100	100

*Estimate [1]Crude sulphur

Recovered sulphur

5 297 000 met. tons 1963-5 av.*

Data for 1953-5 not available

	PERCENTAGE 1963-5 av.
Canada	29
France	28
U.S.A.	20
U.S.S.R.	8
China P.R.	2
Germany D.R.	2
Germany F.R.	2
Spain	1
Iran	1
Others	7
	100

*Estimate

Pyrites[1]

9 400 000 met. tons 1963-5 av.*

*6 300 000 1953-5 av.**

	PERCENTAGE 1963-5 av.	1953-5 av.
Japan	19	17
U.S.S.R.*	18	NA
Spain	11	15
Italy	7	9
China P.R.*	6	NA
Cyprus	4	9*
U.S.A.	4	6
Norway	4	6
Portugal	3	5
Others	24	NA
	100	100

*Estimate [1]Sulphur equivalent

Consumption of fertilizer nutrients N, K_2O and P_2O_5 (1964/5)

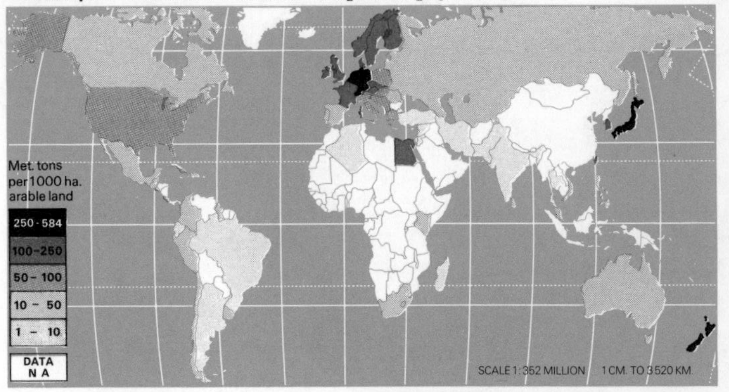

The use of artificial fertilizers, in areas which also have a high standard of cultivation and adequate water supply, increases crop yield. The contents of plant nutrients in fertilizers are measured by N (nitrogen), P_2O_5 (phosphorus pentoxide) and K_2O (potassium oxide), although the fertilizers do not contain those ingredients or do not contain them in those particular chemical combinations.

The main use of *phosphate* deposits is as a source of fertilizers. The two principal varieties and sources of natural phosphates are: (1) rock phosphates such as phosphorite, phosphatic limestone, guano and bone-beds and (2) the mineral apatite, $3Ca_3P_2O_8CaF_2$. The U.S.A. and the U.S.S.R. are more or less self-sufficient in phosphates, but most European countries have to import large amounts from the rich deposits of North Africa and the islands of the Pacific and Indian Oceans. China P.R. and North Vietnam also have large reserves. Morocco, the U.S.A., the U.S.S.R., Tunisia and Nauru Island are the main exporters of phosphate rock. Japan, France, Germany F.R., Italy, the U.K., Canada and Australia are the main importers.

About 90% of world *potash* production is employed as a fertilizer in agriculture and horticulture, but until early this century the principal uses of potash were in dyeing and tanning and for making glass, porcelain, soap, matches and explosives. Most of the world's mineral potash fertilizer comes from salt beds, formed in past geological times when the evaporation of sea water in enclosed but extensive basins resulted in the accumulation of saline residues containing the chlorides and sulphates of potassium. Some of these now form deposits of great economic importance, such as those of Stassfurt in Germany D.R. which once virtually monopolized the potassium salt production in Europe. Similar deposits occur near Mulhouse in France and in the Berezniki region of the U.S.S.R. The Canadian province of Saskatchewan is another important source. The U.S.A., Japan, the U.K. and Poland are the major importers.

In the manufacture of fertilizers, phosphate rock can be treated with sulphuric acid to form either superphosphate or phosphoric acid—the latter being an important intermediate in the production of high analysis compound fertilizers. *Sulphur*, in the uncombined form, is used as an insecticide and fungicide, and large amounts are used in making vulcanized rubber goods. Large deposits of sulphur occur at and near volcanic craters, active and extinct; but the most productive deposits are those formed in the cap-rocks overlying great plug-like intrusions of rock salt, or salt domes, such as those along the U.S. Gulf Coast in the vicinity of Beaumont, Texas and Port Sulphur, Louisiana. Apart from the 'native' sulphur already mentioned, 'recovered' sulphur accounts for nearly 50% of world sulphur production. It is derived primarily from natural gas and oil refinery gases. Sulphur is also obtained in considerable quantities by roasting pyrite (iron pyrites), FeS_2. This mineral is frequently found in copper mines. The U.S.A., Mexico, France, Canada and Poland are the principal exporters of sulphur; this group of five countries is significant as being major exporters of elemental sulphur. The U.S.A., the U.K., Australia and India are the chief importers.

Cement

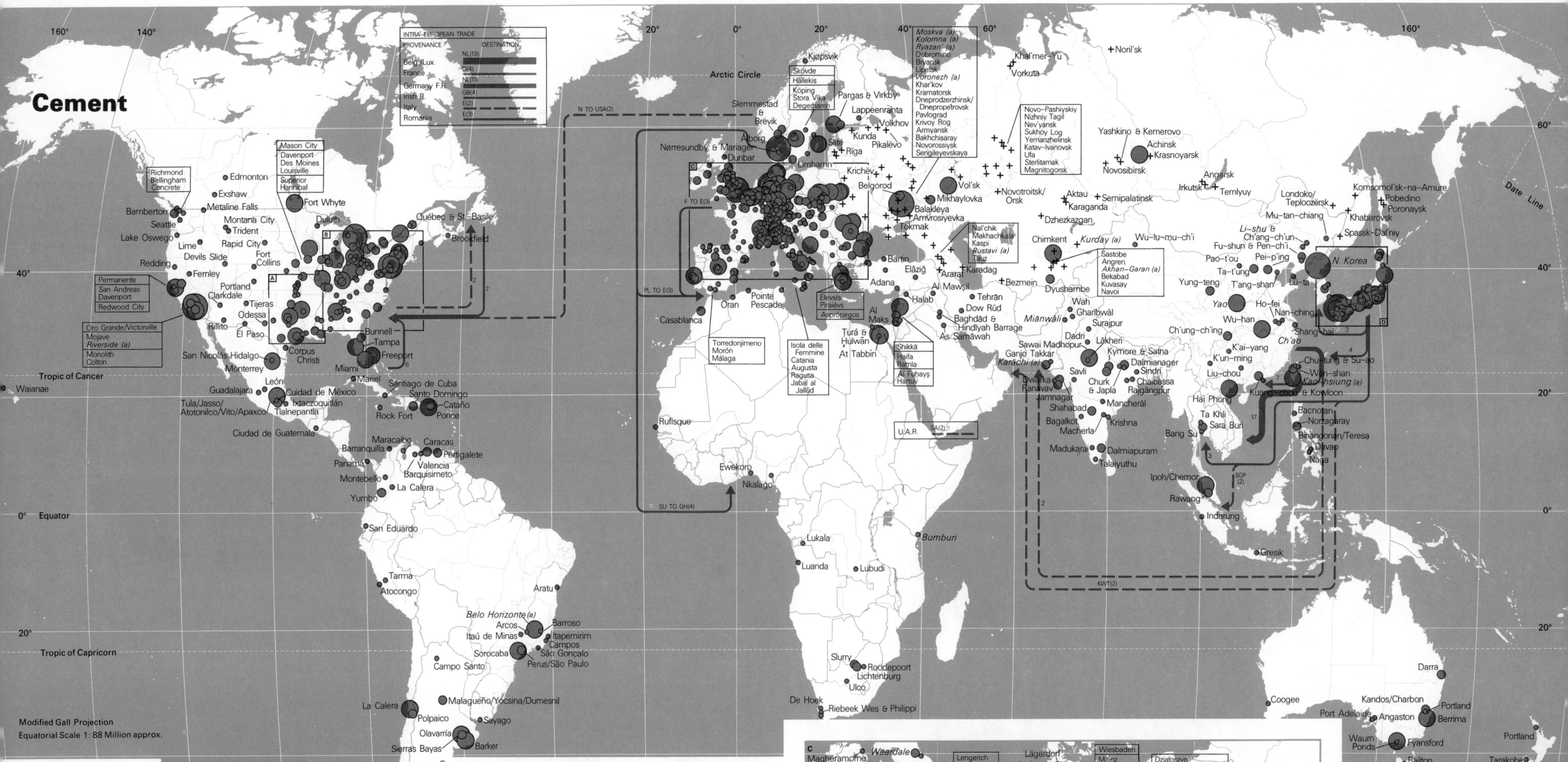

Modified Gall Projection
Equatorial Scale 1: 88 Million approx.

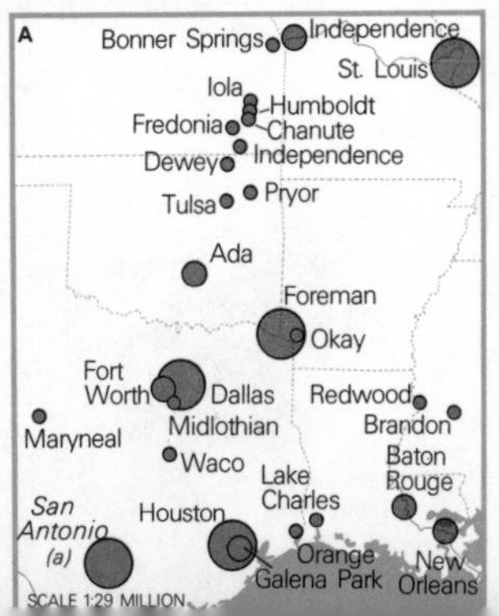

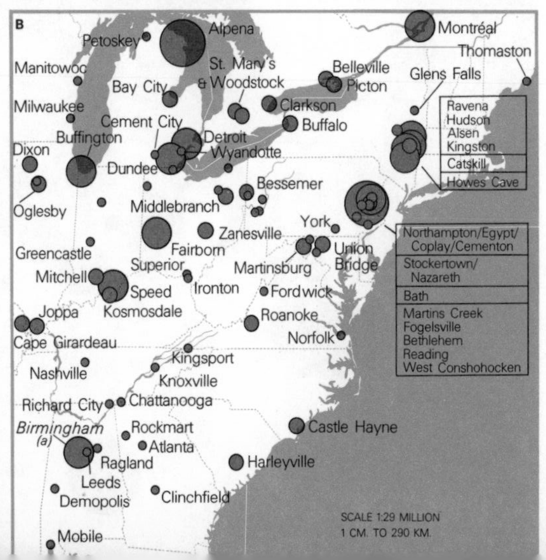

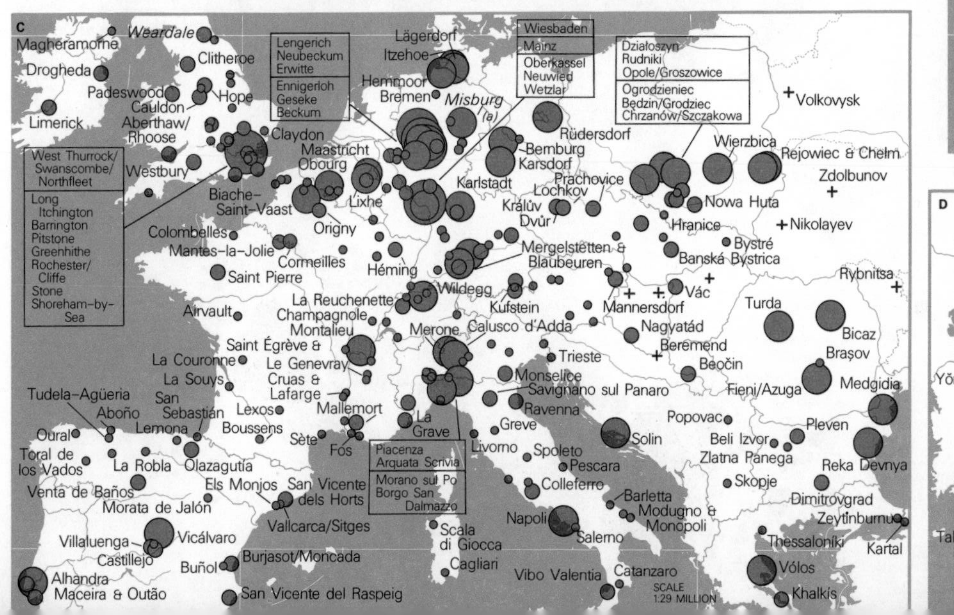

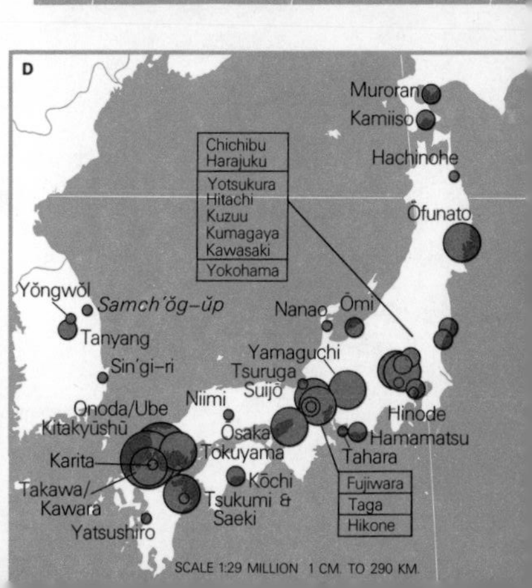

Cement

Producing centres (1965)

'000 met. tons capacity

- 2 000 AND OVER
- 800 - 2 000
- 500 - 800
- 200 - 500
- \+ Data not available

Major trade flows (1966)

Commodity: S.I.T.C. no.

CEMENT : 661.2

Value ($ U.S.)

0.5mm. represents increments of $5 million

45 / 25 / 5 ($ MILLIONS)

UNDER $2.5 MILLION

9 VALUE IN $ MILLIONS

Cement production

405 200 000 met. tons 1963-5 av.*

*195 400 000 1953-5 av.**

	PERCENTAGE 1963-5 av.	1953-5 av.
U.S.S.R.*	16	10
U.S.A.	15	24
Japan	8	5
Germany F.R.	8	9
Italy	5	5
France	5	5
U.K.	4	6
China P.R.*	3	2[1]
India	2	2
Others	34	32
	100	100

*Estimate [1]Incl. N. Korea

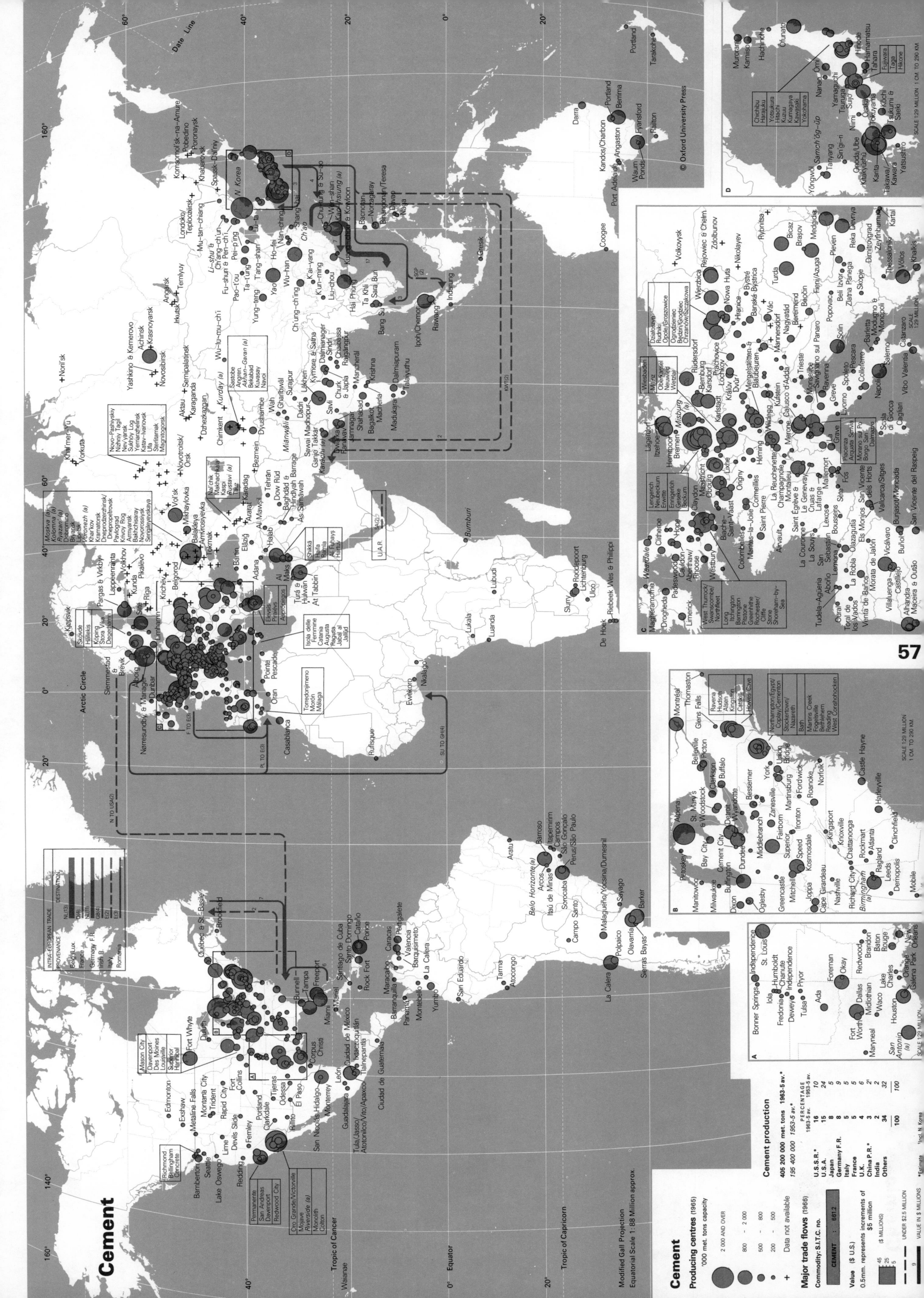

Chemicals I

Benzene/Phthalic Anhydride

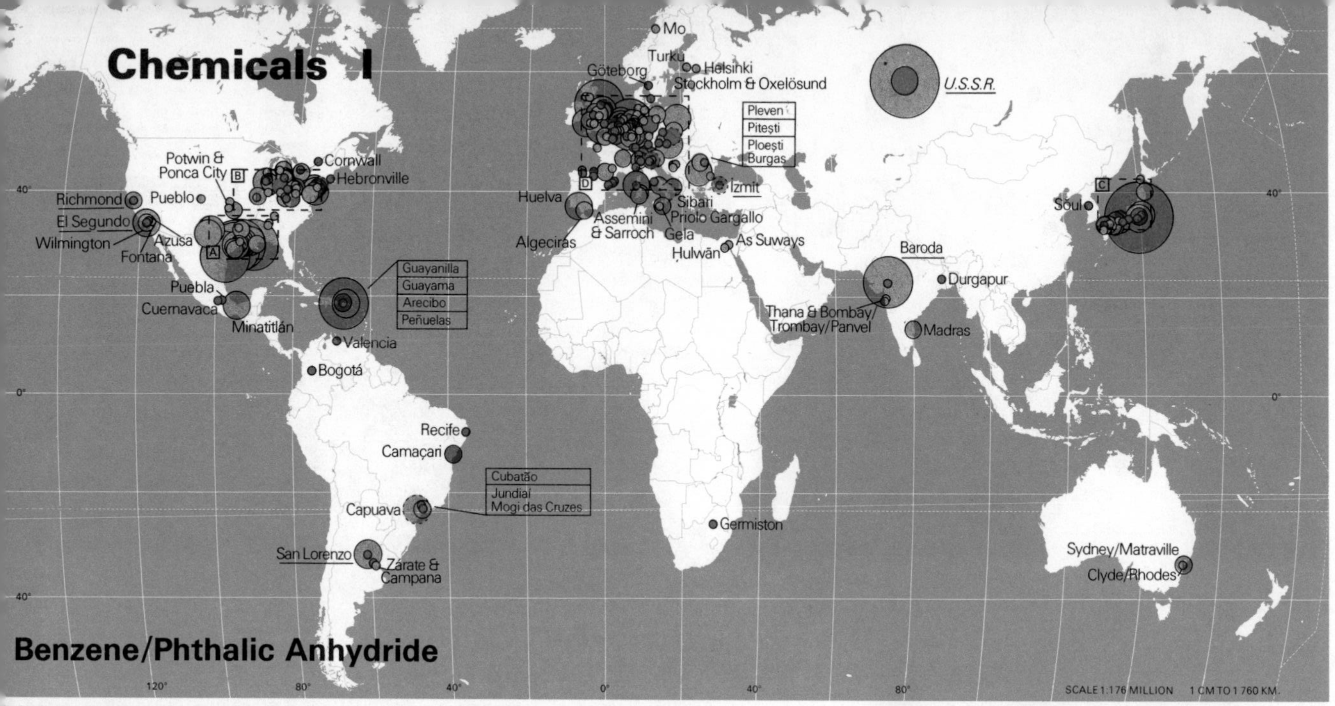

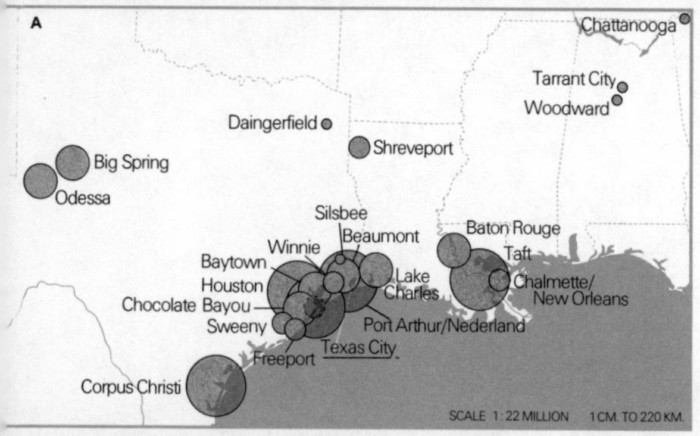

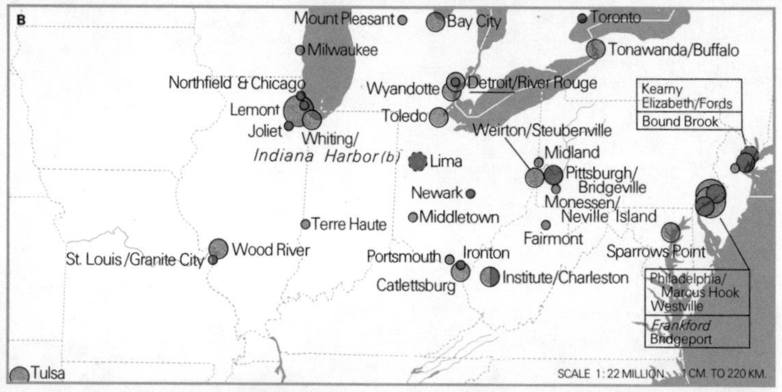

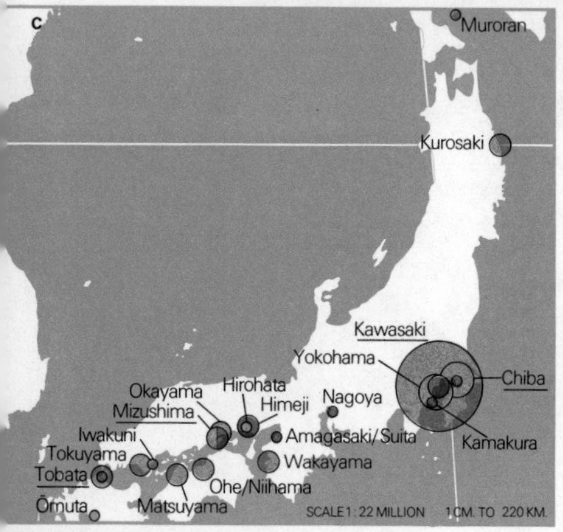

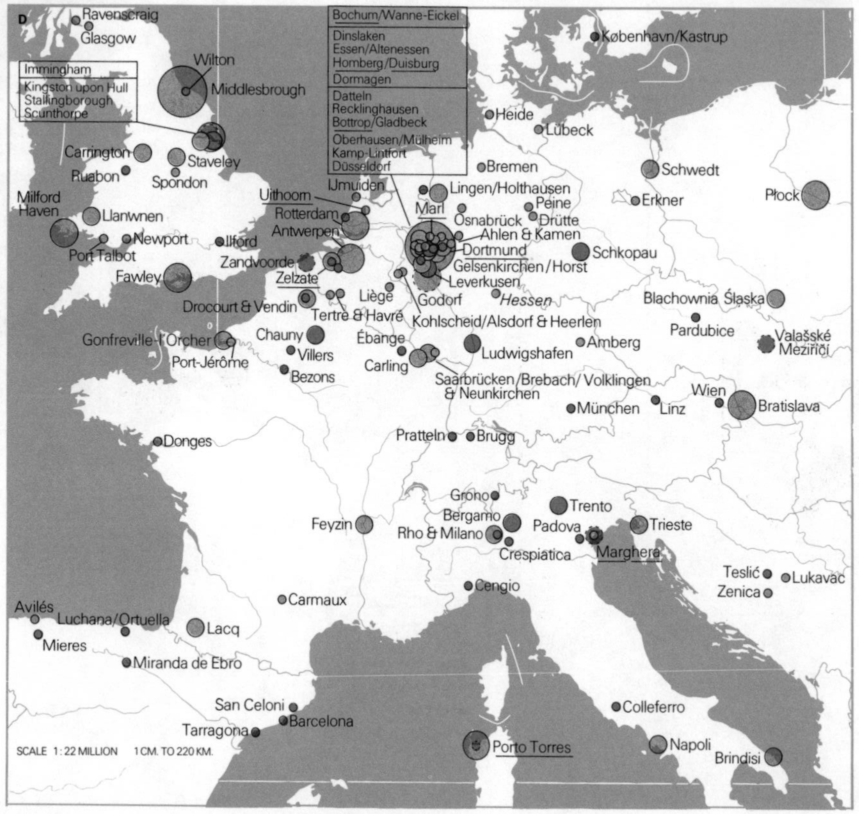

Benzene/phthalic anhydride

Production centres (1970)

'000 metric tons capacity

601 - 1 000; 301 - 600; 101 - 300; 31 - 100; 0 - 30

Under construction/planned

\+ Data not available

Benzene

Phthalic anhydride

Where two symbols of the same size are coincident the colour fill is divided

Names of centres producing more than one of these chemicals are underlined

Methanol/Phenol/Ethylene

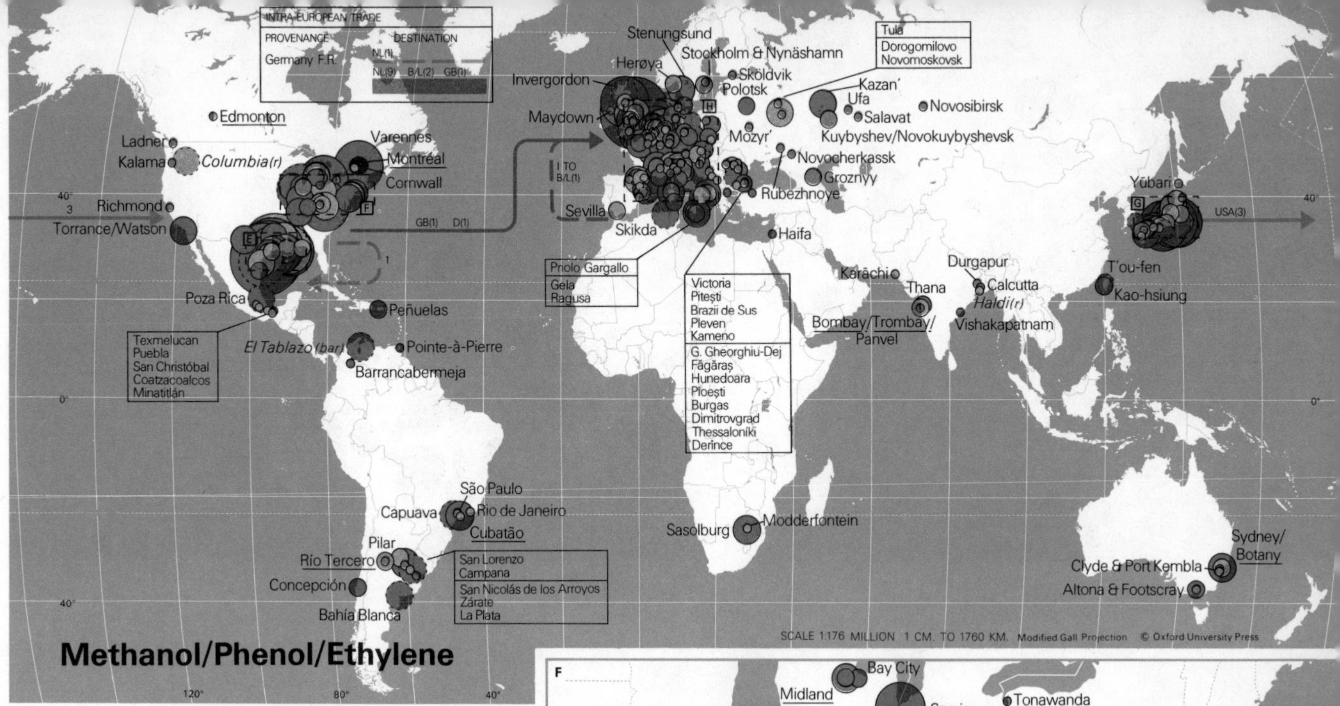

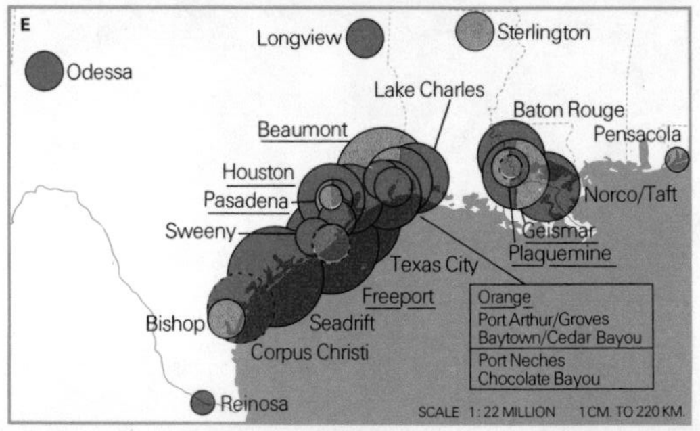

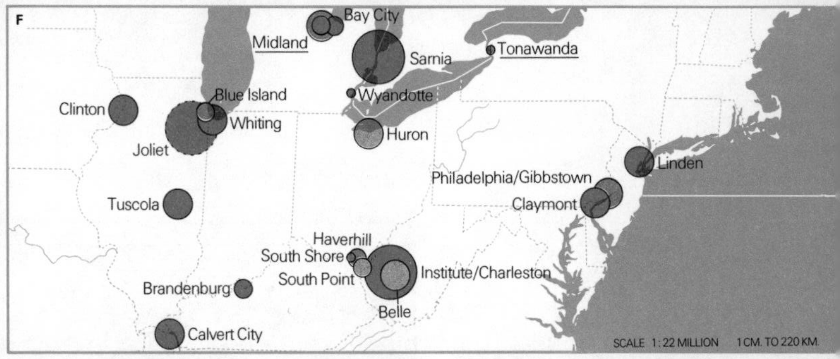

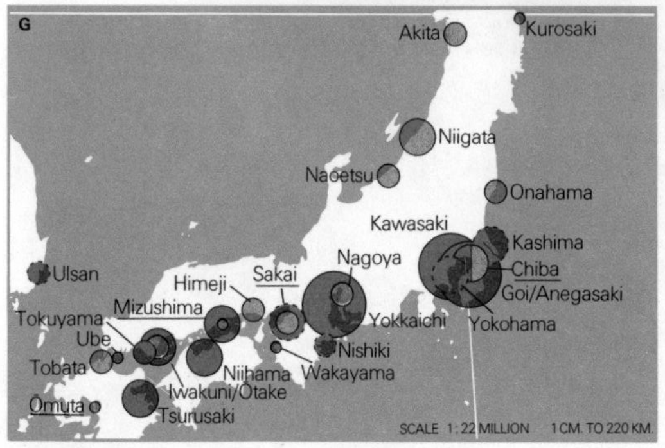

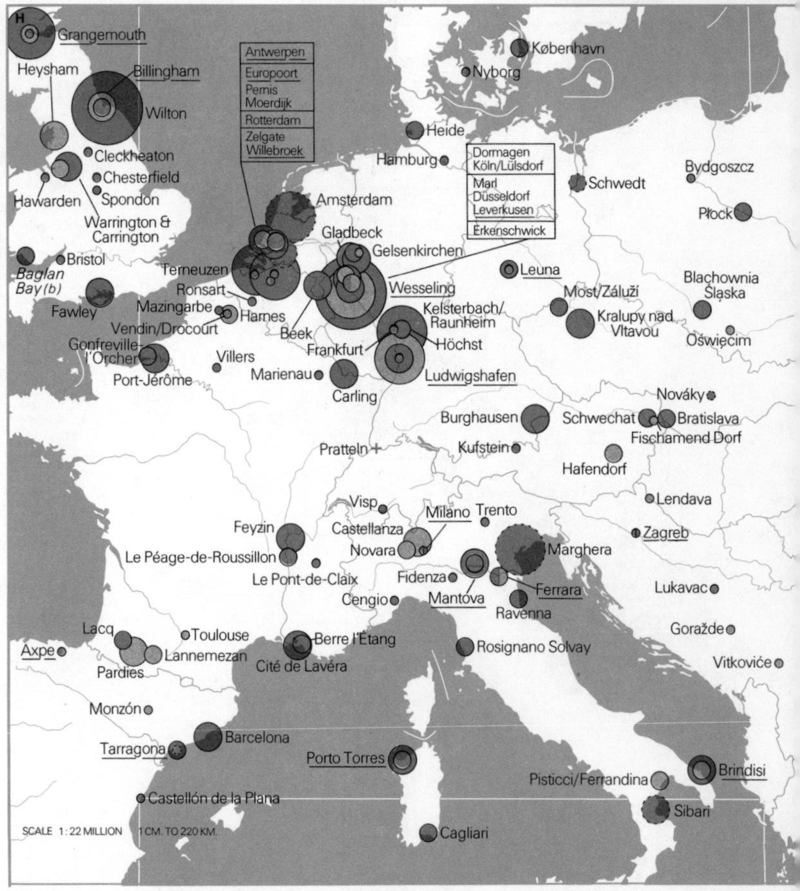

Methanol/phenol/ethylene

Production centres (1970)

'000 metric tons capacity

601 - 1 000; 301 - 600; 101 - 300; 31 - 100; 0 - 30

Under construction/planned

\+ Data not available

Methanol

Phenol

Ethylene

Where two symbols of the same size are coincident the colour fill is divided

Where three symbols of the same size are coincident

Names of centres producing more than one of these chemicals are underlined

Major trade flows (1966)

Commodity : S.I.T.C. no.	Value ($ U.S.)
METHYL ALCOHOL (METHANOL) : 512.21	0.5 mm. represents increments of $3 million
PHENOLS/PHENOL-ALCOHOL : 512.27	($ MILLIONS) 15, 3

UNDER $1.5 MILLION

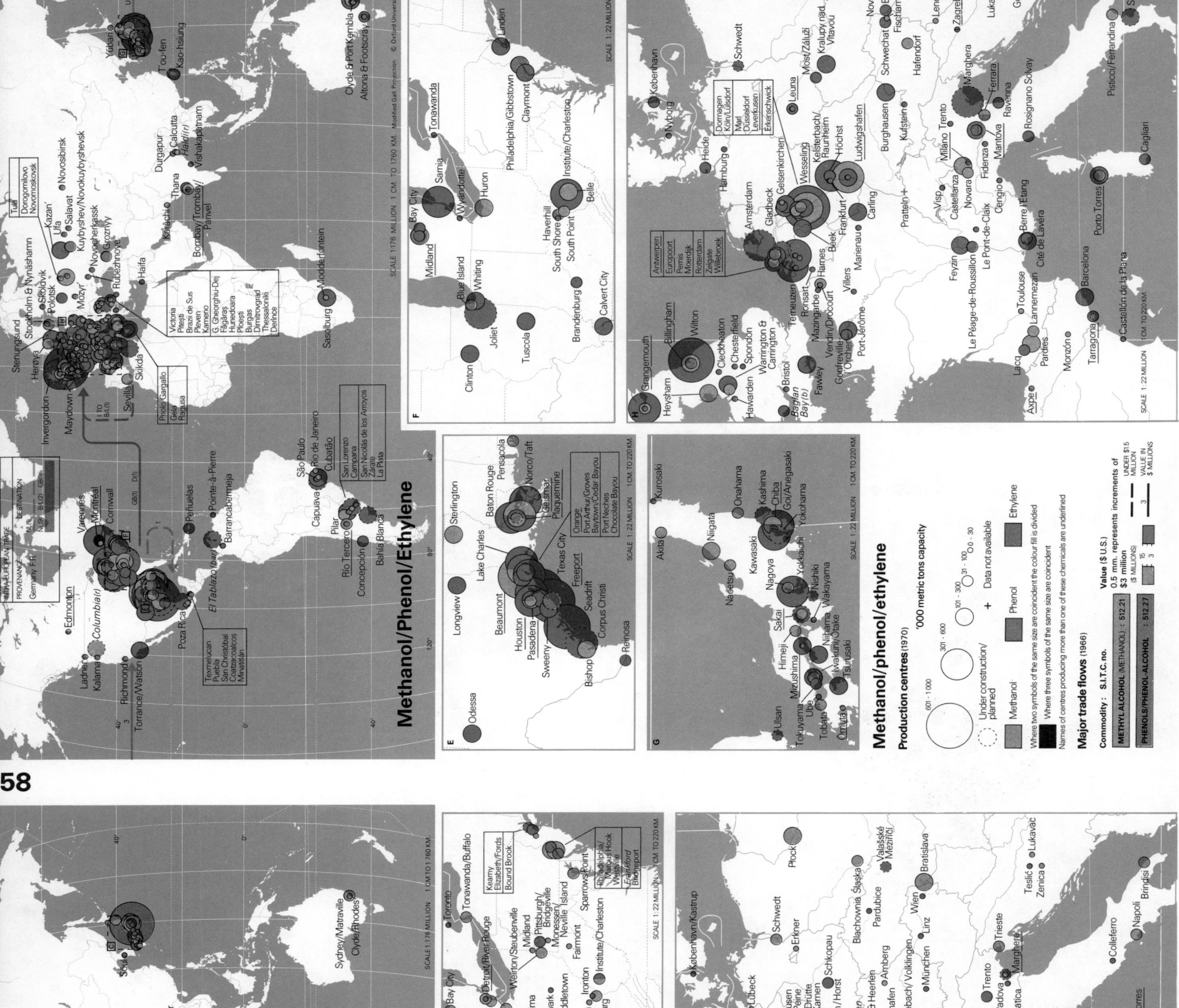

VALUE IN $ MILLIONS

Chemicals II

Heavy Inorganics

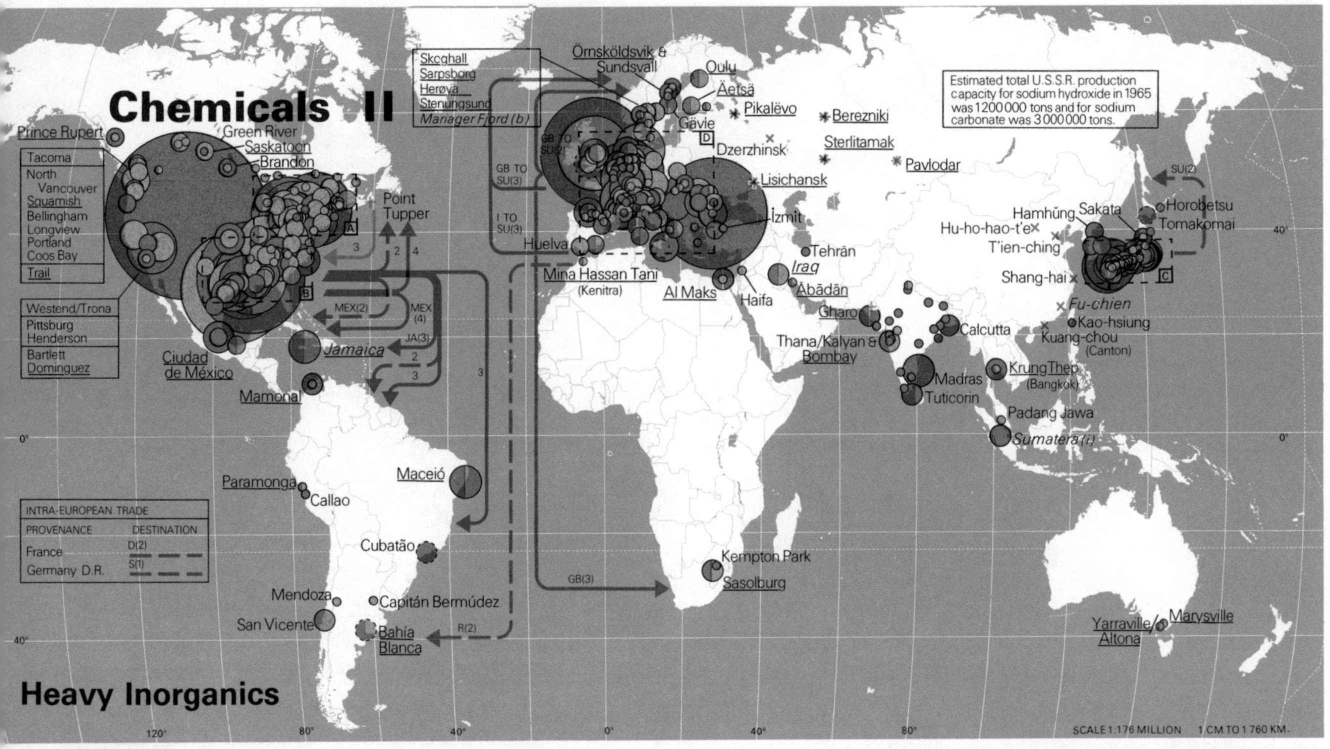

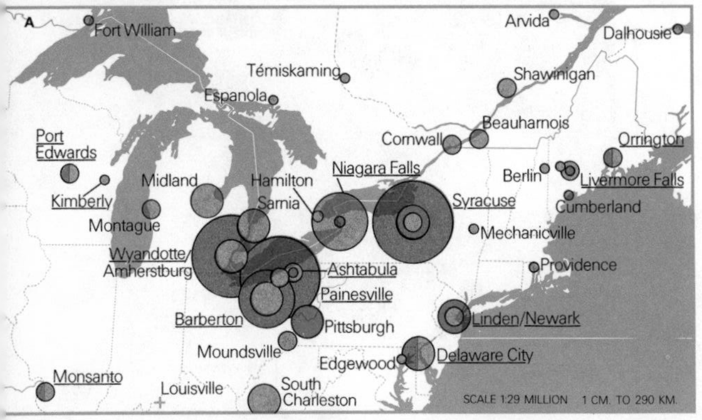

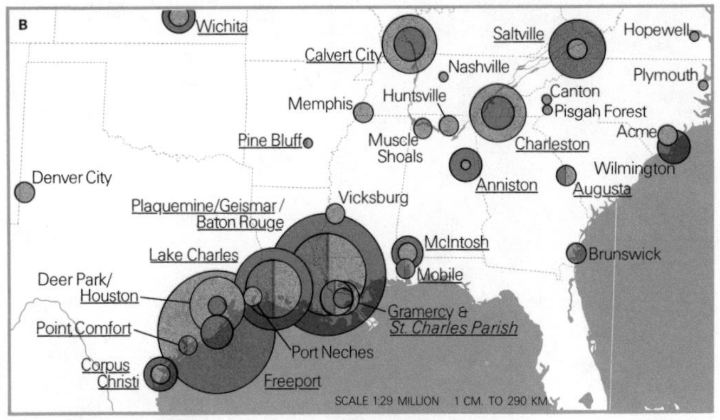

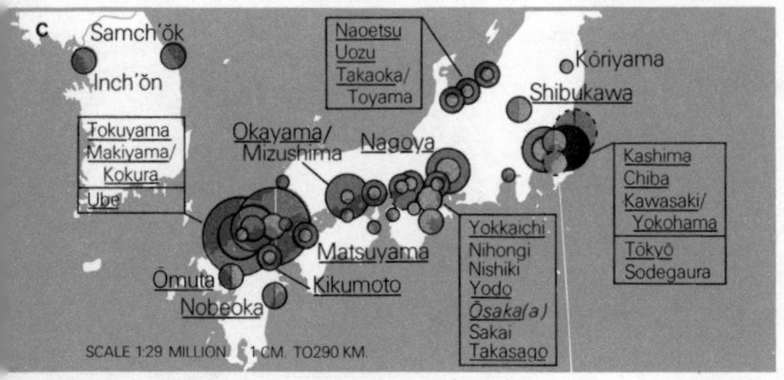

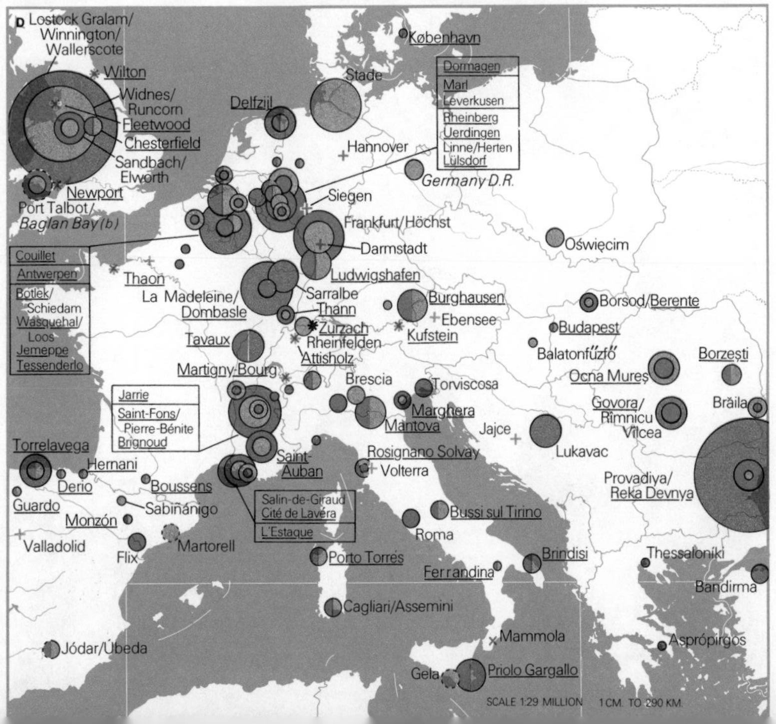

Estimated total U.S.S.R. production capacity for sodium hydroxide in 1965 was 1 200 000 tons and for sodium carbonate was 3 000 000 tons.

France D(2)

Heavy inorganics
Production centres (1970)

'000 met. tons capacity

2 001 & OVER
1 001 - 2 000
601 - 1 000
301 - 600
101 - 300
31 - 100
0 - 30

CHLORINE
SODIUM HYDROXIDE
SODIUM CARBONATE

Where two symbols of the same size coincide the colour fill is divided

Where three symbols of the same size coincide

Names of centres producing more than one of these chemicals are underlined

UNDER CONSTRUCTION/ PLANNED

+ × DATA NA

Major trade flows (1966)

Commodity : S.I.T.C. no.	
CHLORINE	513.21
CAUSTIC SODA	513.62
SODIUM CARBONATE	514.28

Value ($ U.S.)

0.5mm. represents increments of $5 million

($ MILLIONS) 45 25 5

UNDER $2.5 MILLION

VALUE IN $ MILLIONS

Sulphuric Acid

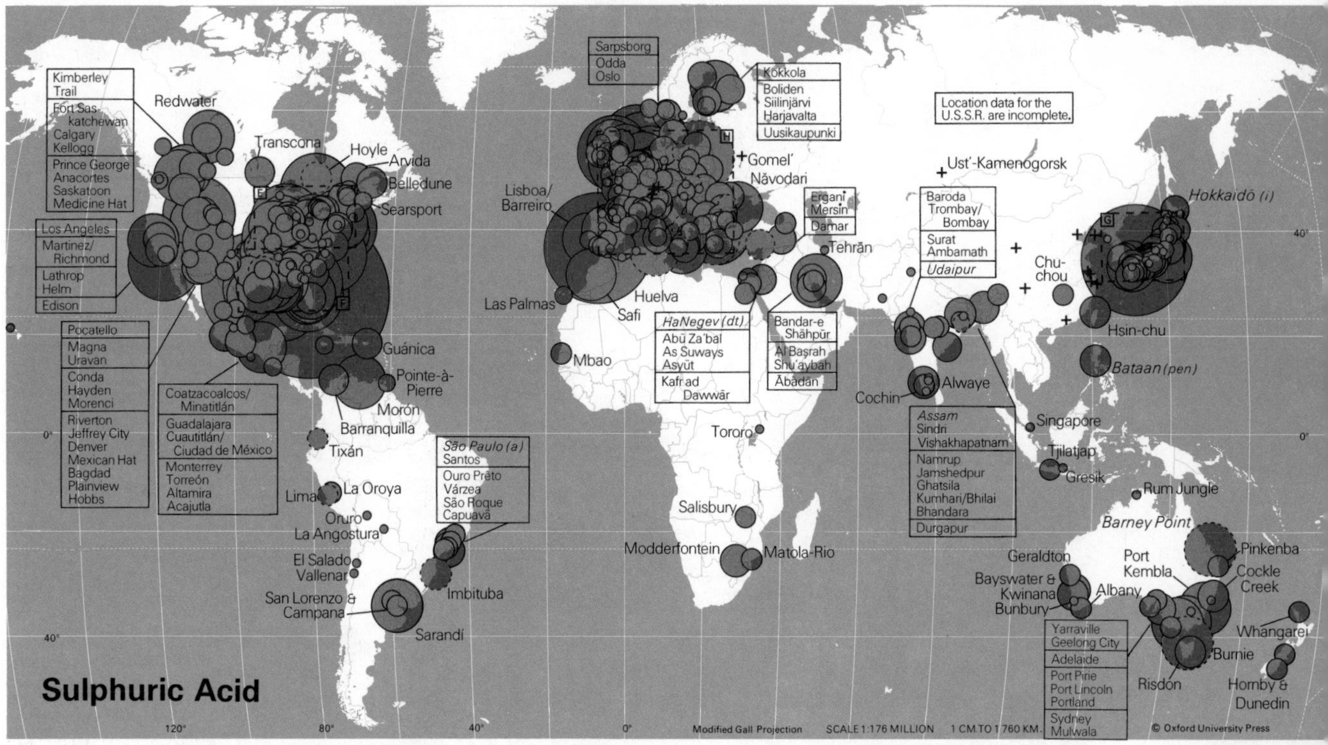

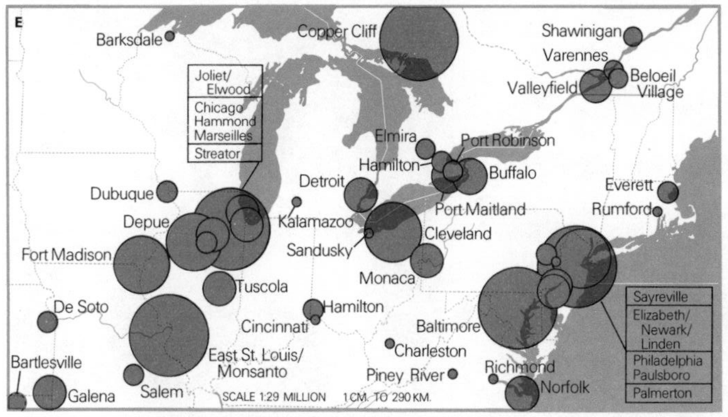

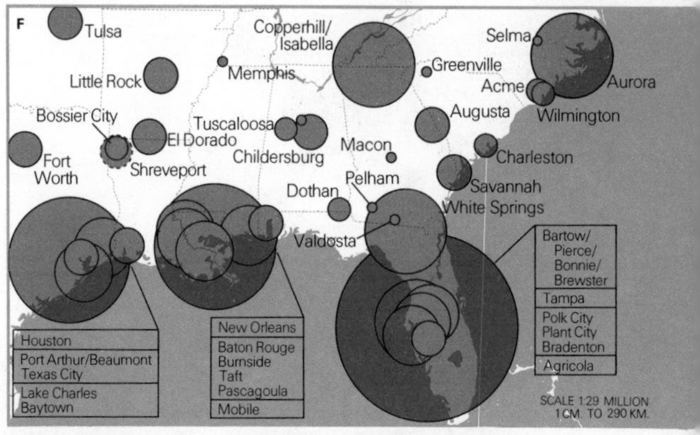

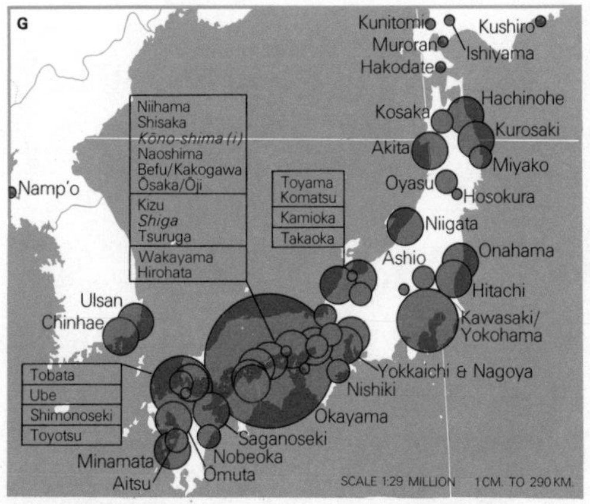

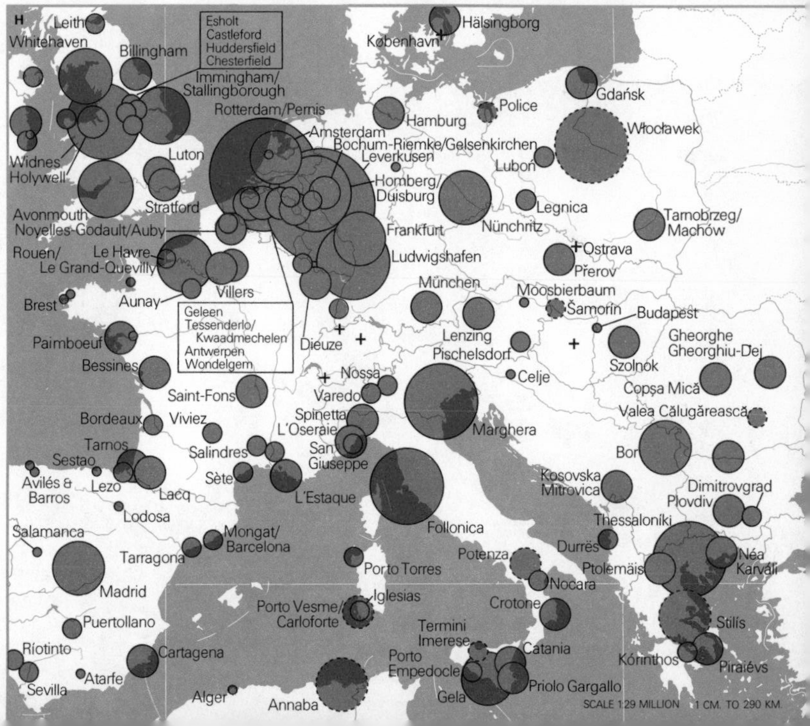

Location data for the U.S.S.R. are incomplete.

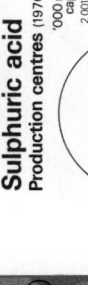

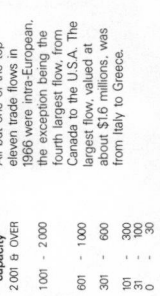

Sulphuric acid
Production centres (1970)

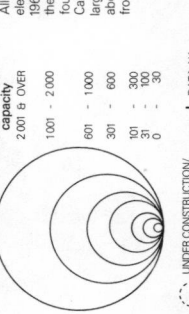

'000 met. tons capacity

2 001 & OVER
1 001 - 2 000
601 - 1 000
301 - 600
101 - 300
31 - 100
0 - 30

UNDER CONSTRUCTION/ PLANNED

+ DATA NA

Major trade flows

All but one of the top eleven trade flows in 1966 were intra-European, the exception being the fourth largest flow, from Canada to the U.S.A. The largest flow, valued at about $1.6 millions, was from Italy to Greece.

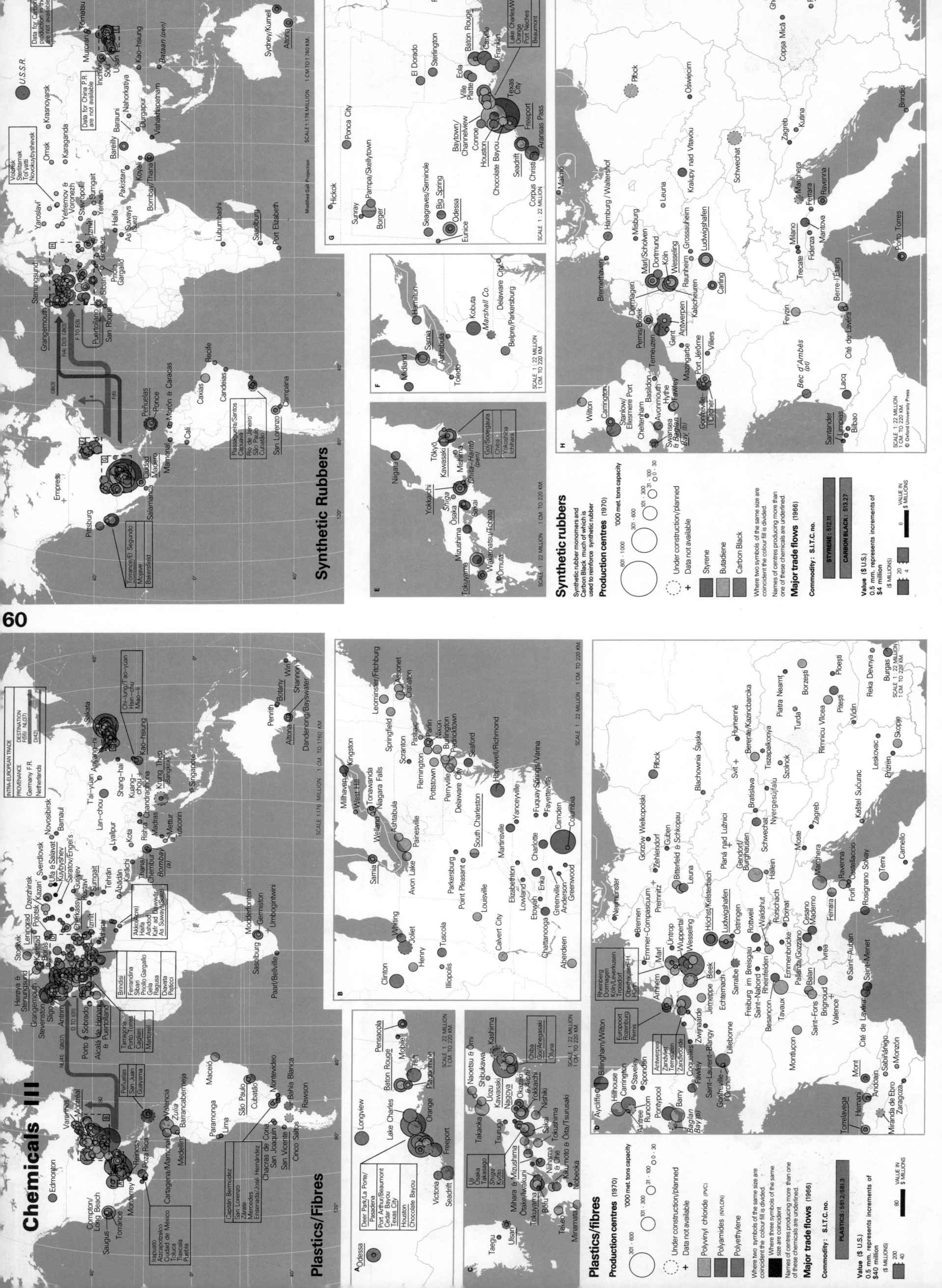

Chemicals III

Plastics/Fibres

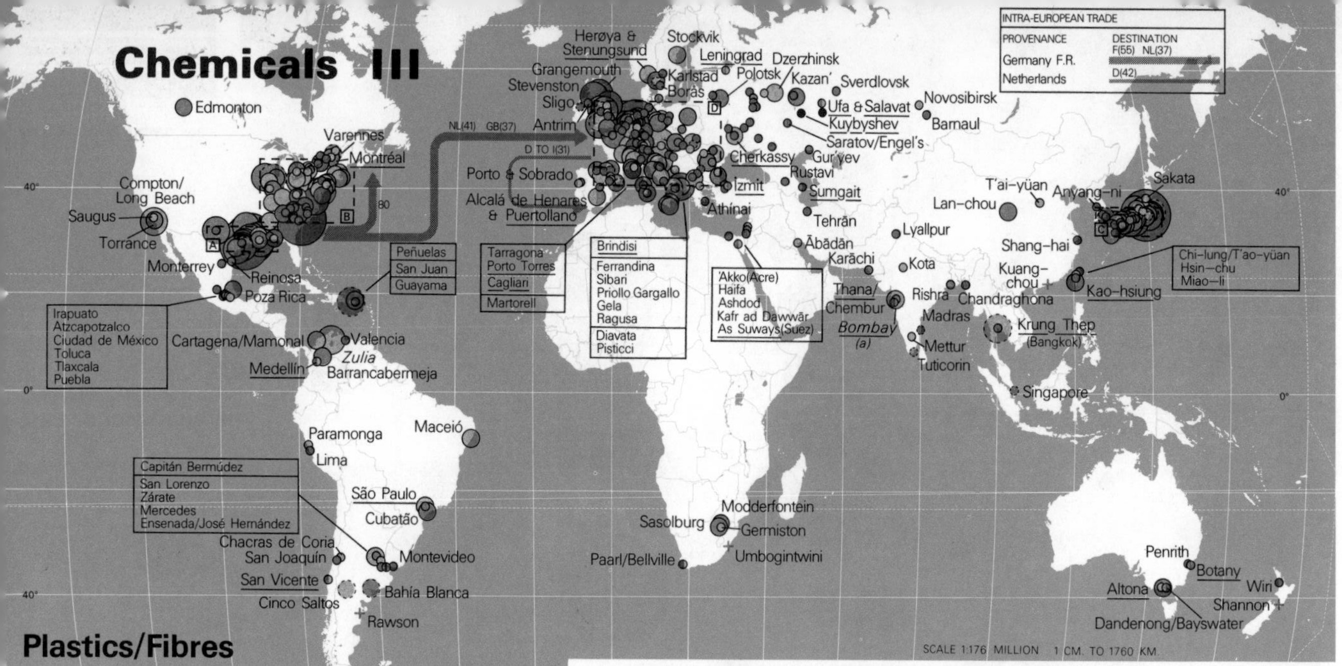

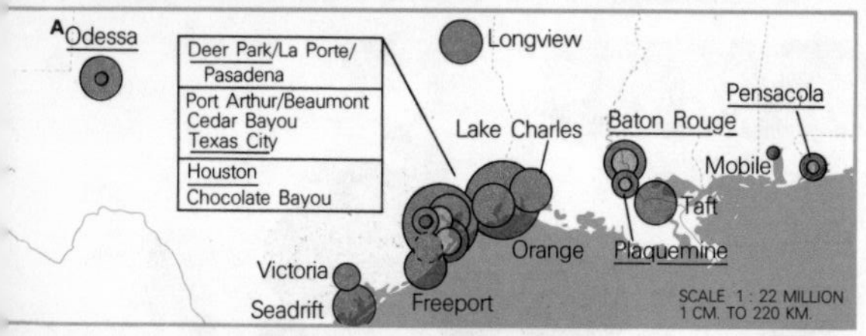

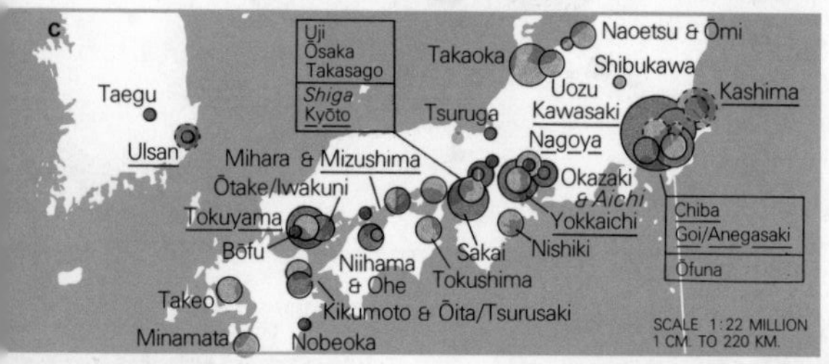

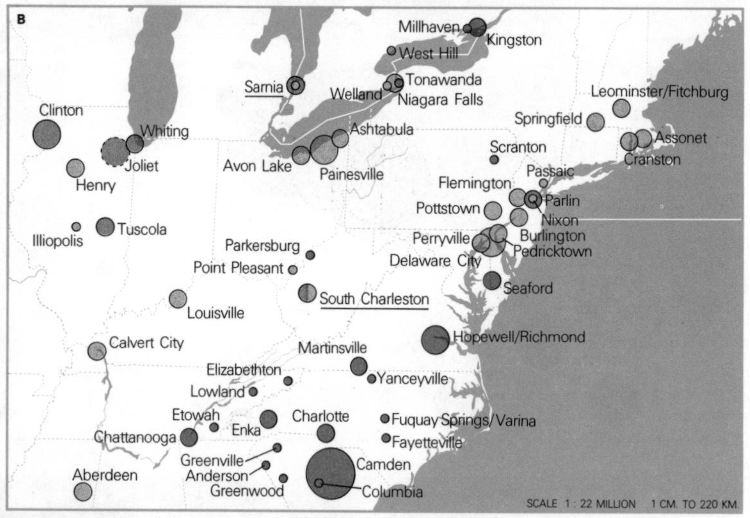

Plastics/fibres

Production centres (1970)

'000 met. tons capacity: 301 - 600; 101 - 300; 31 - 100; 0 - 30

Under construction/planned

+ Data not available

Polyvinyl chloride (PVC)

Polyamides (NYLON)

Polyethylene

Where two symbols of the same size are coincident the colour fill is divided.

Where three symbols of the same size are coincident

Names of centres producing more than one of these chemicals are underlined.

Major trade flows (1966)

Commodity: S.I.T.C. no.

PLASTICS : 581.2/581.3

Value ($ U.S.)

0.5 mm. represents increments of $40 million

($ MILLIONS) 200 40

80 VALUE IN $ MILLIONS

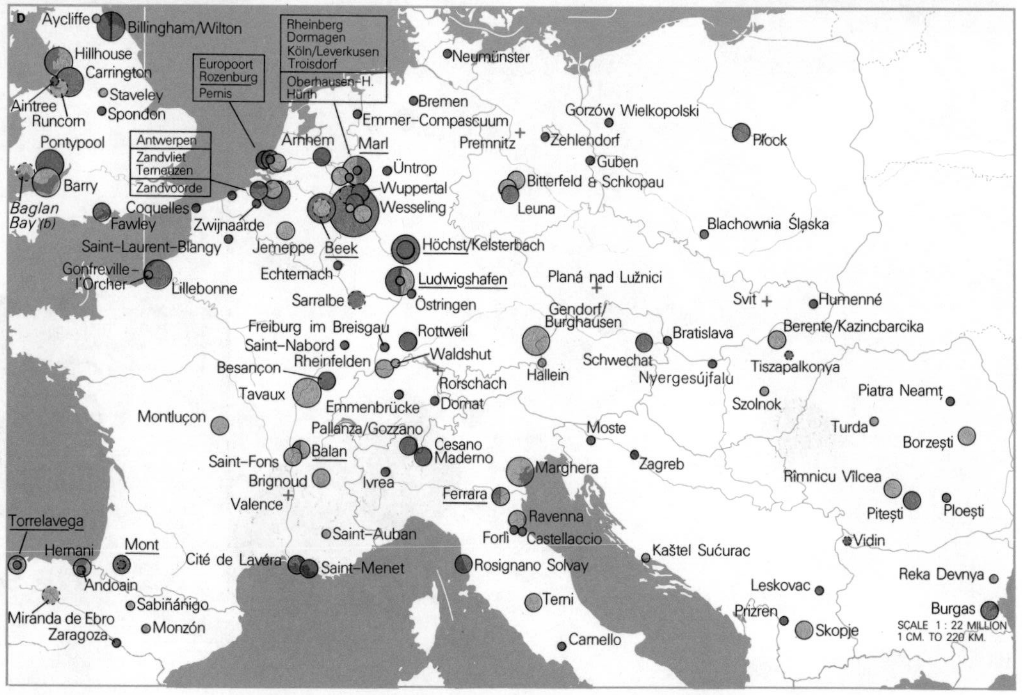

Synthetic Rubbers

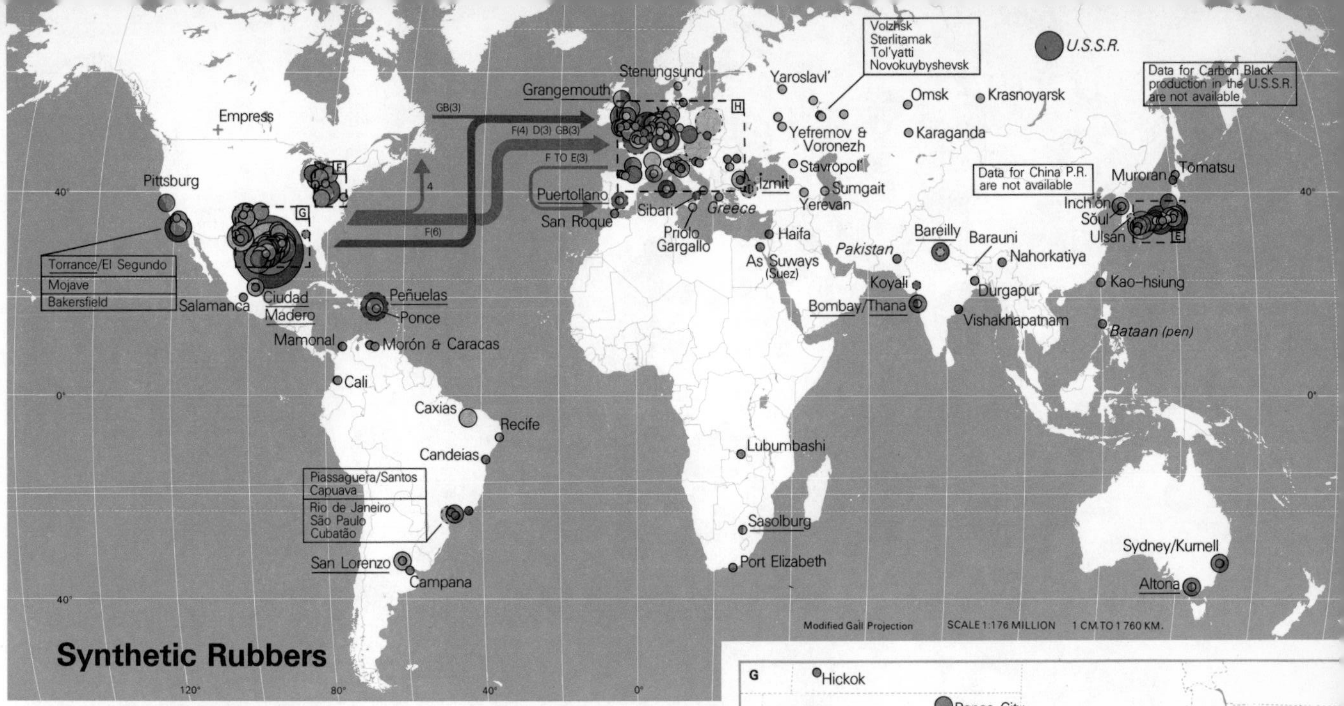

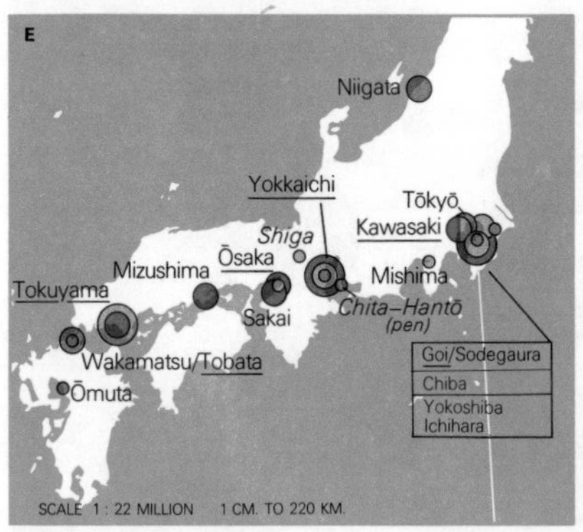

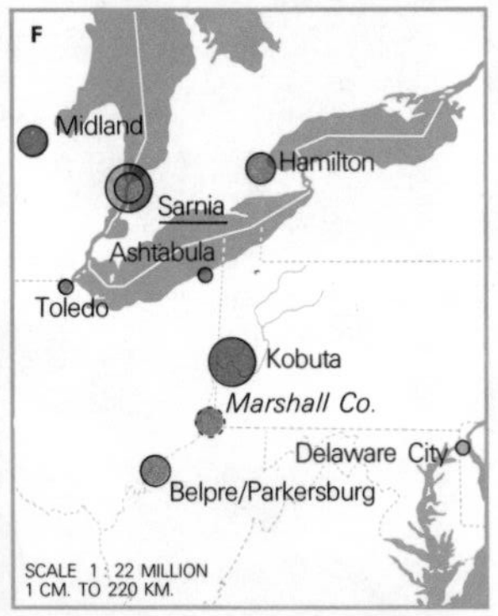

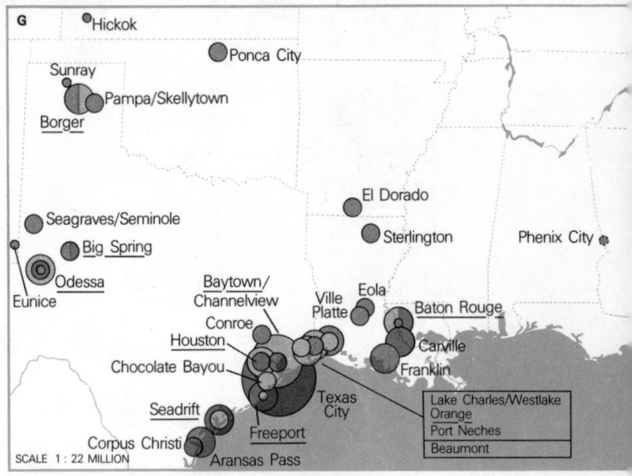

Synthetic rubbers

Synthetic rubber monomers and Carbon Black much of which is used to reinforce synthetic rubber

Production centres (1970)

'000 met. tons capacity: 601 - 1000; 301 - 600; 101 - 300; 31 - 100; 0 - 30

Under construction/planned

+ Data not available

Styrene

Butadiene

Carbon Black

Where two symbols of the same size are coincident the colour fill is divided.

Names of centres producing more than one of these chemicals are underlined.

Major trade flows (1966)

Commodity: S.I.T.C. no.

STYRENE : 512.11

CARBON BLACK : 513.27

Value ($ U.S.)

0.5 mm. represents increments of $4 million

($ MILLIONS) 20 4

6 VALUE IN $ MILLIONS

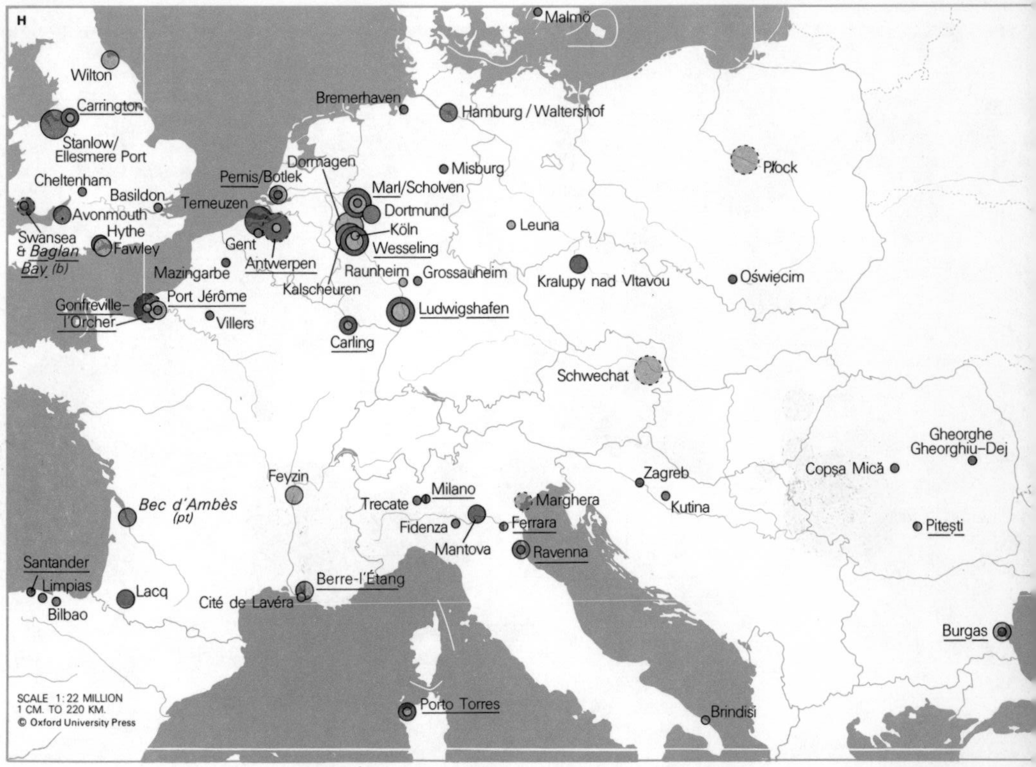

Chemicals IV

Ammonia

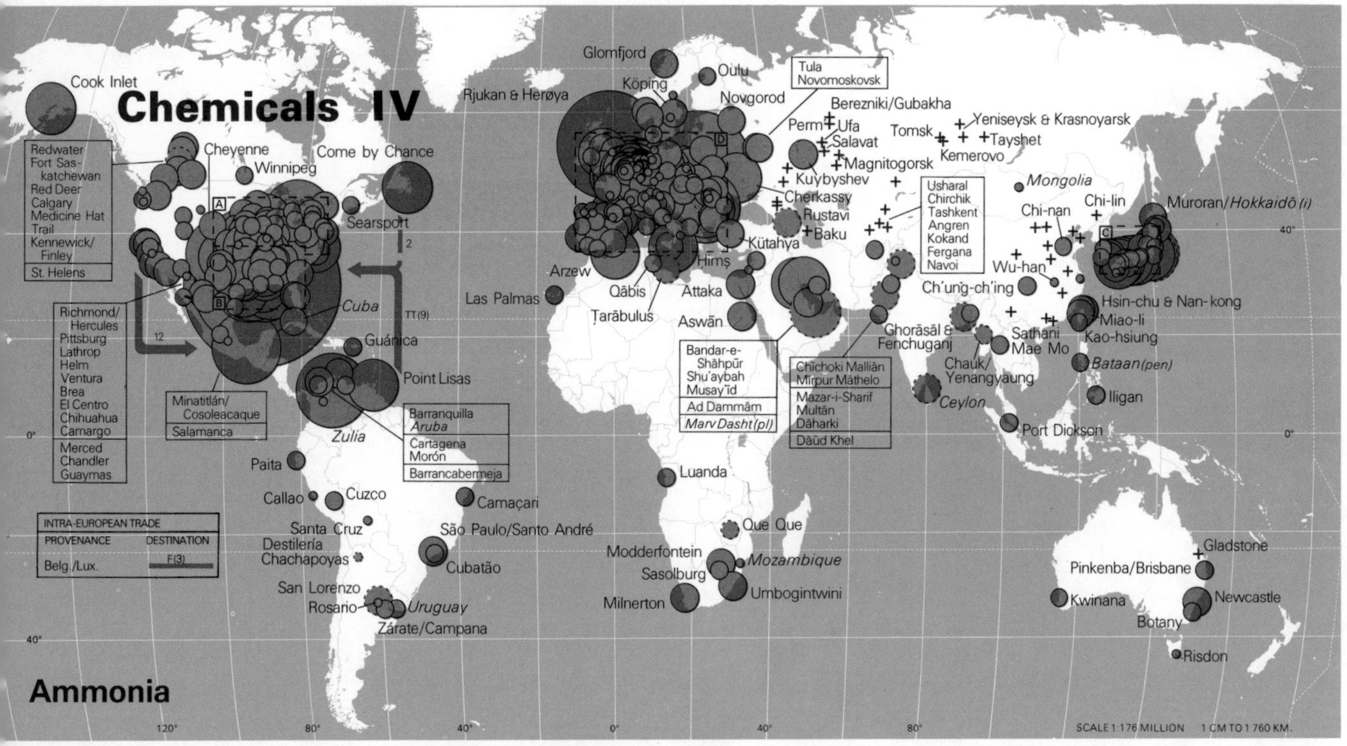

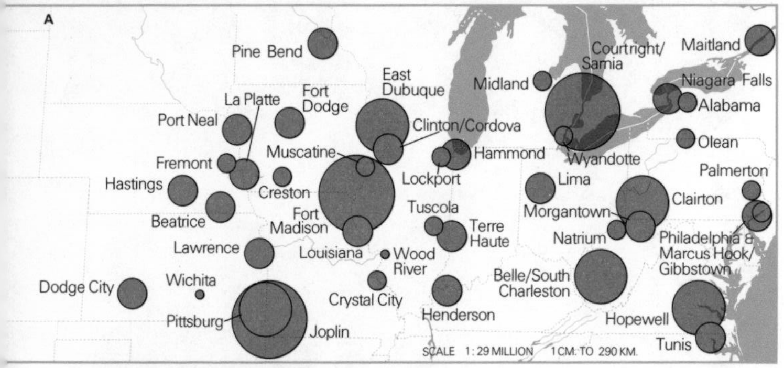

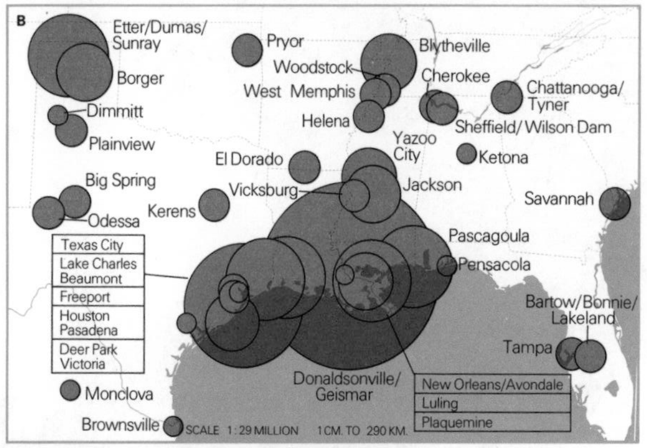

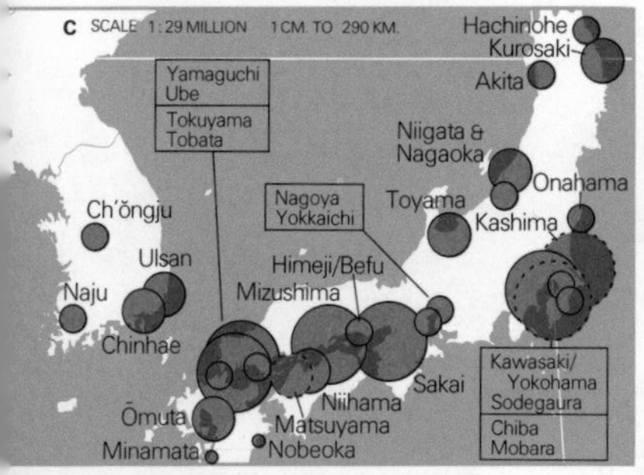

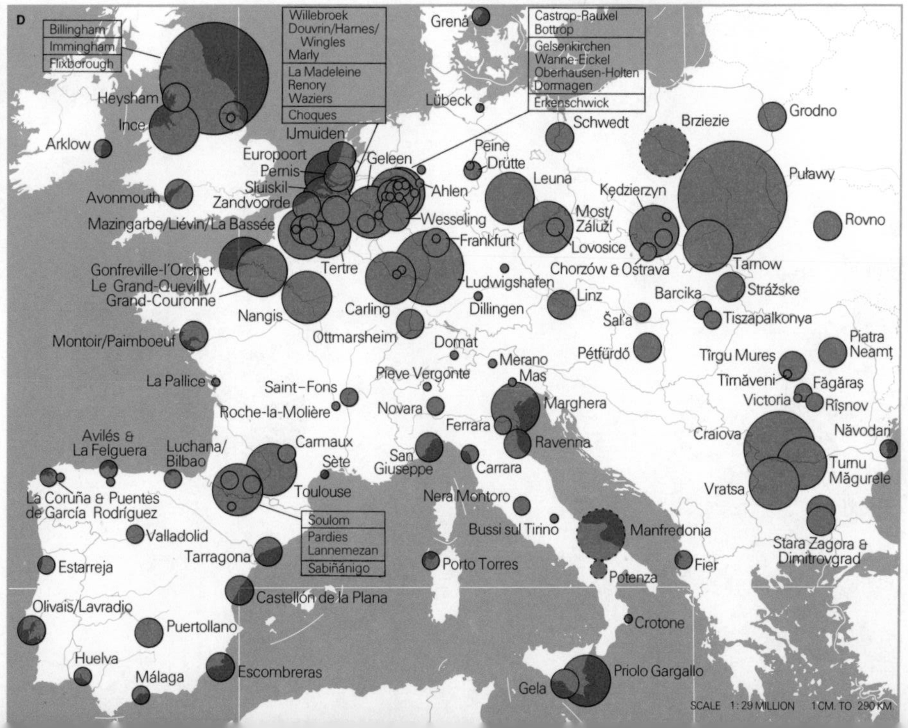

Ammonia

Production centres (1970)

'000 met. tons capacity

- 2 001 & OVER
- 1001 - 2000
- 601 - 1000
- 301 - 600
- 101 - 300
- 31 - 100
- 0 - 30

UNDER CONSTRUCTION/PLANNED

+ DATA NOT AVAILABLE

Major trade flows (1966)

Commodity : S.I.T.C. no. AMMONIA : 513.61

Value ($ U.S.)

0.5 mm represents increments of $5 million

($ MILLIONS) 25 5

UNDER $2.5 MILLION

9 VALUE IN $ MILLIONS

Urea/Nitric Acid

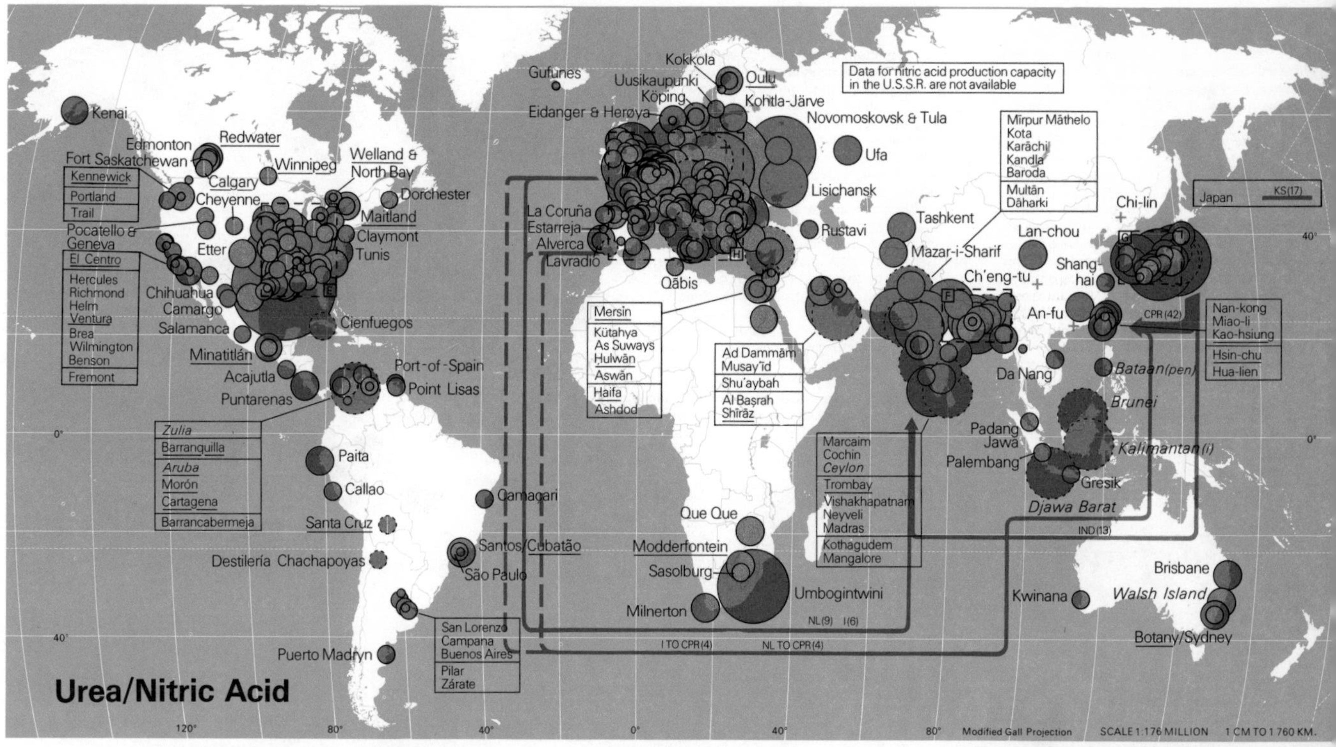

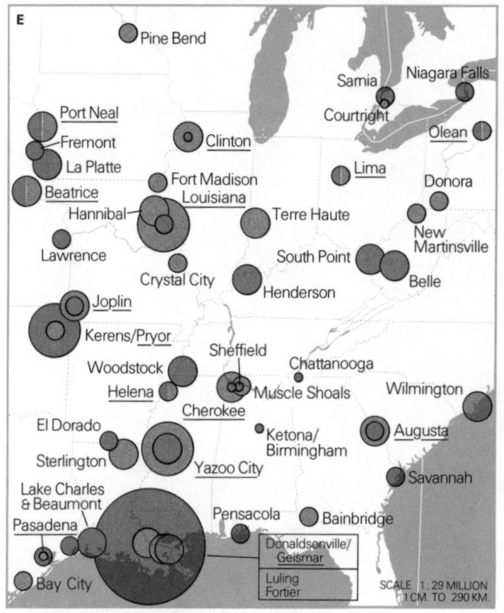

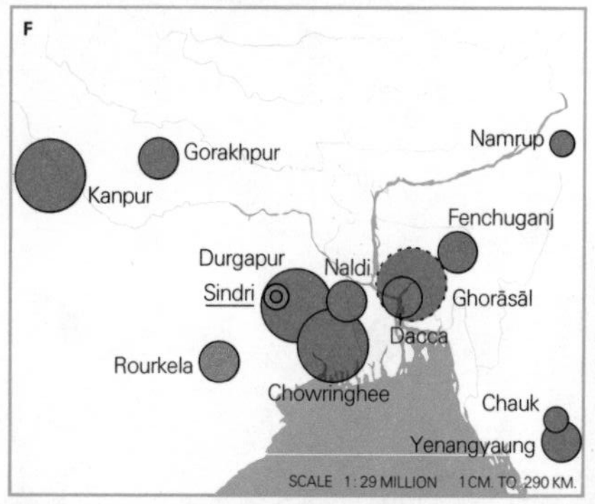

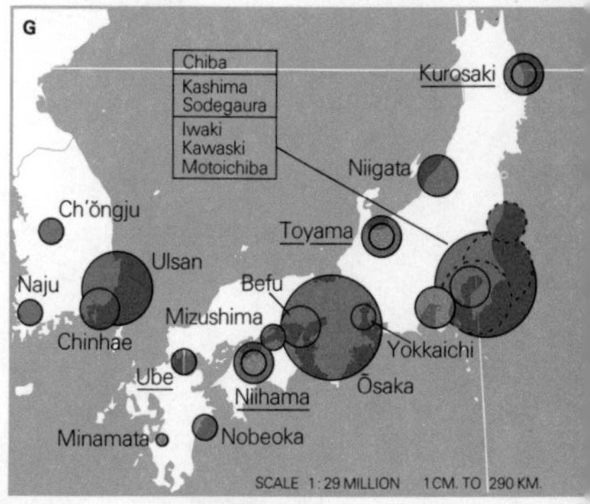

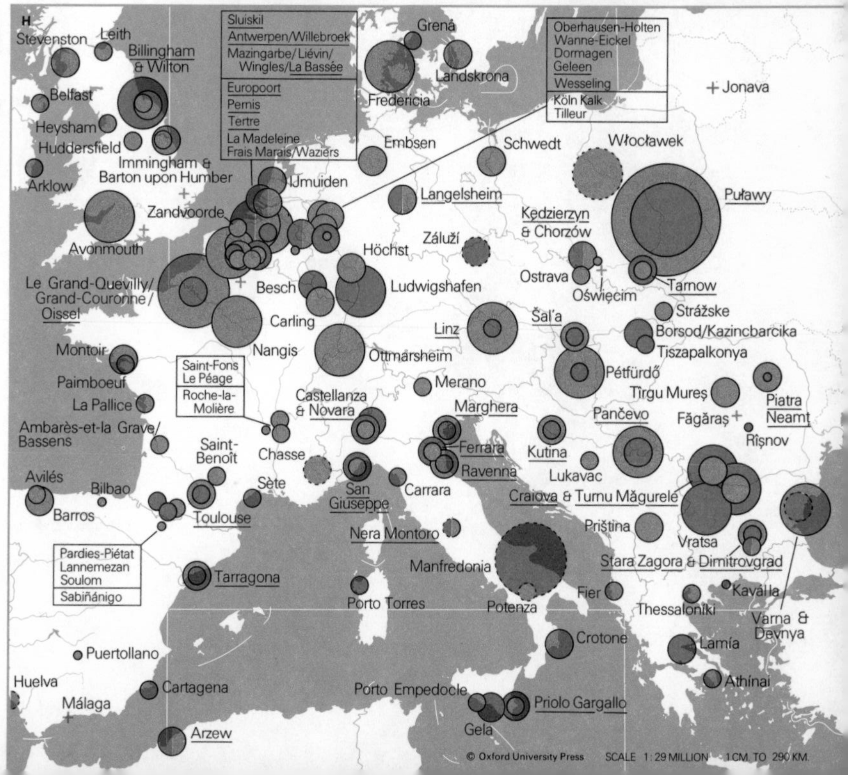

Urea/nitric acid

Production centres (1970)

'000 met. tons capacity

- 1001 & OVER
- 601 - 1000
- 301 - 600
- 101 - 300
- 31 - 100
- 0 - 30

UREA

NITRIC ACID

Where two symbols of the same size are coincident the colour fill is divided

Names of centres producing both of these chemicals are underlined

UNDER CONSTRUCTION/PLANNED

+ DATA NOT AVAILABLE

Major trade flows (1966)

Commodity: S.I.T.C.no. AMIDE - FUNCTION COMPOUNDS : 512.74

Value ($ U.S.)

0.5 mm represents increments of $ 15 million

($ MILLIONS) 75 15

UNDER $7.5 MILLION

28 VALUE IN $ MILLIONS

Trade flows in Nitric Acid are predominantly intra-European. The largest flow, which is less than $0.5 million in value, is between Belgium/Luxembourg and Germany F.R.

Computers

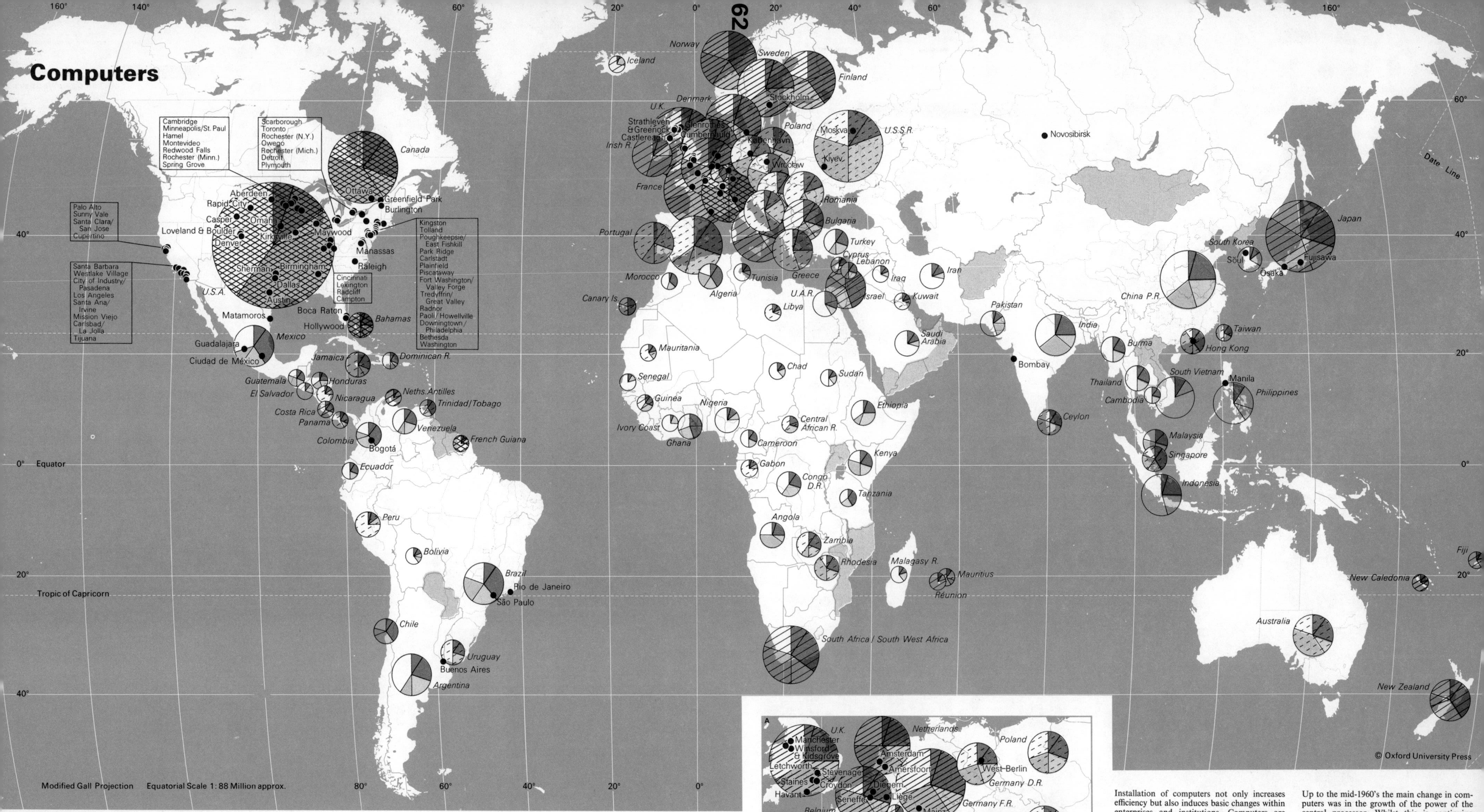

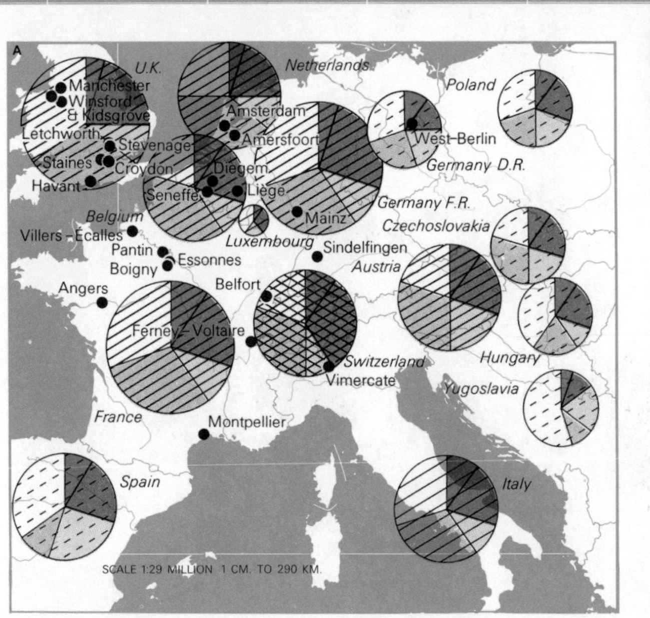

Computers (as at 1st March, 1970*)

Number installed

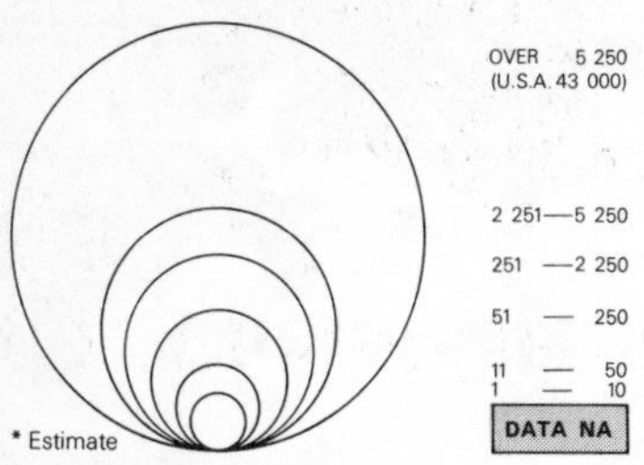

* Estimate

Type of user

- EDUCATION
- FINANCE
- GOVERNMENT
- MANUFACTURING
- OTHER

Investment in computers

($ U.S. per capita)

- 30 AND OVER
- 15 — 30
- 5 — 15
- 1 — 5
- UNDER 1

Production centres

● Location (not quantified)

Production centres include both assembly and component manufacturing facilities. Those shown represent locations of producers responsible for 95% of computer output. Data for smaller producers were not available at time of publication.

Computers installed

U.S.$18 698 million 1970* Total value

	PERCENTAGE 1970
U.S.A.	**45**
U.K.	**9**
Japan	**7**
Germany F.R.	**6**
France	**5**
U.S.S.R.	**5**
Canada	**4**
China P.R.	**3**
Italy	**2**
Switzerland	**2**
Others	**12**
	100

*Estimate as of 1st March

Installation of computers not only increases efficiency but also induces basic changes within enterprises and institutions. Computers are faster and thus have a greater productive capacity than humans; they are universal in their ability to process information.

Computer operations can be simply described: a computer accepts information from outside as input, combines this, according to the rules of a program which is stored in its memory, with information already received and stored, and returns information to its environment as output.

The input and output devices (peripherals), arithmetic and control circuits and the memory (central processor) form the 'hardware' of the computer. The instructions or programs which set the system to work are known as the 'software'. Computers lack the ability to think or reason for themselves. Their efficiency, ability and accuracy depend on the state of the art and science of programming as well as on the speed and memory capacity of the computer.

Up to the mid-1960's the main change in computers was in the growth of the power of the central processor. Whilst this is continuing more effort has since been made to improve the methods of passing information to and from the computer. The use of remote terminals utilizing the power of one central processor, visual display units enabling a user to 'converse' with the computer, and the technique of time sharing where the computer can be working on more than one problem at once, will all extend the role of the computer in the 1970's. The future development of computer-based information services using these tools will mean that the computer will become a significant factor not only in commerce and industry, but also in society as a whole.

The ability of the computer to make calculations which were previously laboriously made manually has not always been well received. Some developing countries have restricted their use because of the unemployment problems that they might cause.

Top Firms

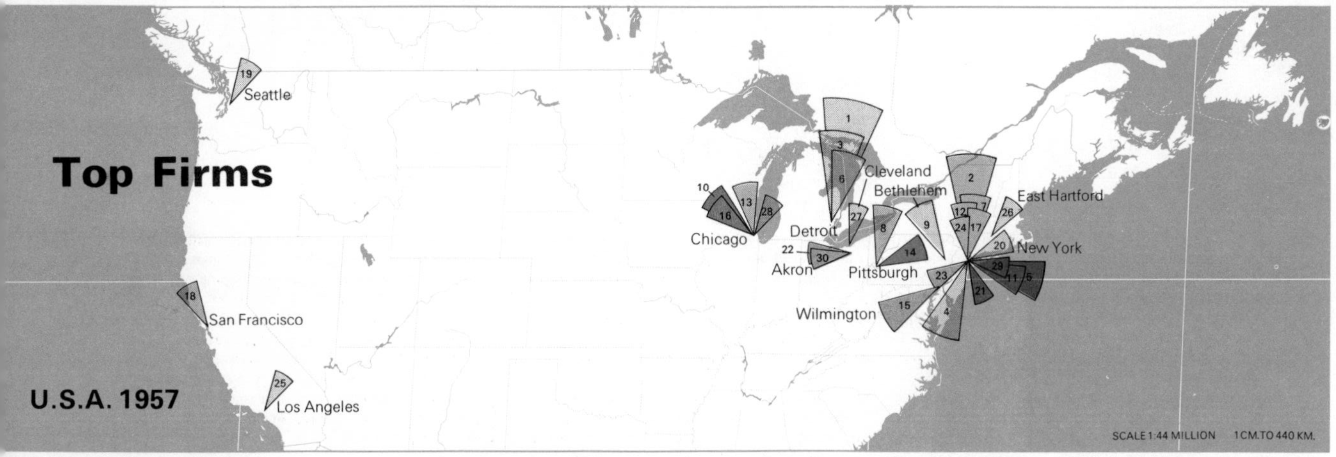
U.S.A. 1957
Seattle
San Francisco
Los Angeles
Chicago
Detroit
Akron
Cleveland
Bethlehem
East Hartford
New York
Pittsburgh
Wilmington
SCALE 1:44 MILLION 1 CM.TO 440 KM.

The largest industrial corporations in the U.S.A. 1957 (top 30 ranked by sales)

RANK 1957	COMPANY	HEADQUARTERS	SALES (Million $ U.S.)	ASSETS (Million $ U.S.)
1	**General Motors**	Detroit	10 990	7 498
2	**Standard Oil (N.J.)**	New York	7 830	8 712
3	**Ford Motor**	Detroit	5 771	3 348
4	**U.S. Steel**	New York	4 414	4 373
5	**General Electric**	New York	4 336	2 361
6	**Chrysler**	Detroit	3 565	1 497
7	**Socony Mobil Oil**	New York	2 976	3 105
8	**Gulf Oil**	Pittsburgh	2 730	3 241
9	**Bethlehem Steel**	Bethlehem, Pa.	2 604	2 260
10	**Swift**	Chicago	2 542	545
11	**Western Electric**	New York	2 480	1 329
12	**Texas Co.**	New York	2 344	2 729
13	**Standard Oil (Ind.)**	Chicago	2 010	2 535
14	**Westinghouse Electric**	Pittsburgh	2 009	1 401
15	**Du Pont (E.I.) de Nemours**	Wilmington, Del.	1 964	2 756
16	**Armour**	Chicago	1 936	443
17	**Shell Oil**	New York	1 765	1 407
18	**Standard Oil (Calif.)**	San Francisco	1 651	2 246
19	**Boeing Airplane**	Seattle	1 597	491
20	**General Dynamics**	New York	1 563	571
21	**National Dairy Products**	New York	1 432	554
22	**Goodyear Tire & Rubber**	Akron, Ohio	1 422	929
23	**Union Carbide**	New York	1 395	1 456
24	**Sinclair Oil**	New York	1 251	1 481
25	**North American Aviation**	Los Angeles	1 244	350
26	**United Aircraft**	E. Hartford, Conn.	1 233	451
27	**Republic Steel**	Cleveland	1 227	980
28	**International Harvester**	Chicago	1 171	1 021
29	**Radio Corp. of America**	New York	1 171	752
30	**Firestone Tire & Rubber**	Akron, Ohio	1 159	780

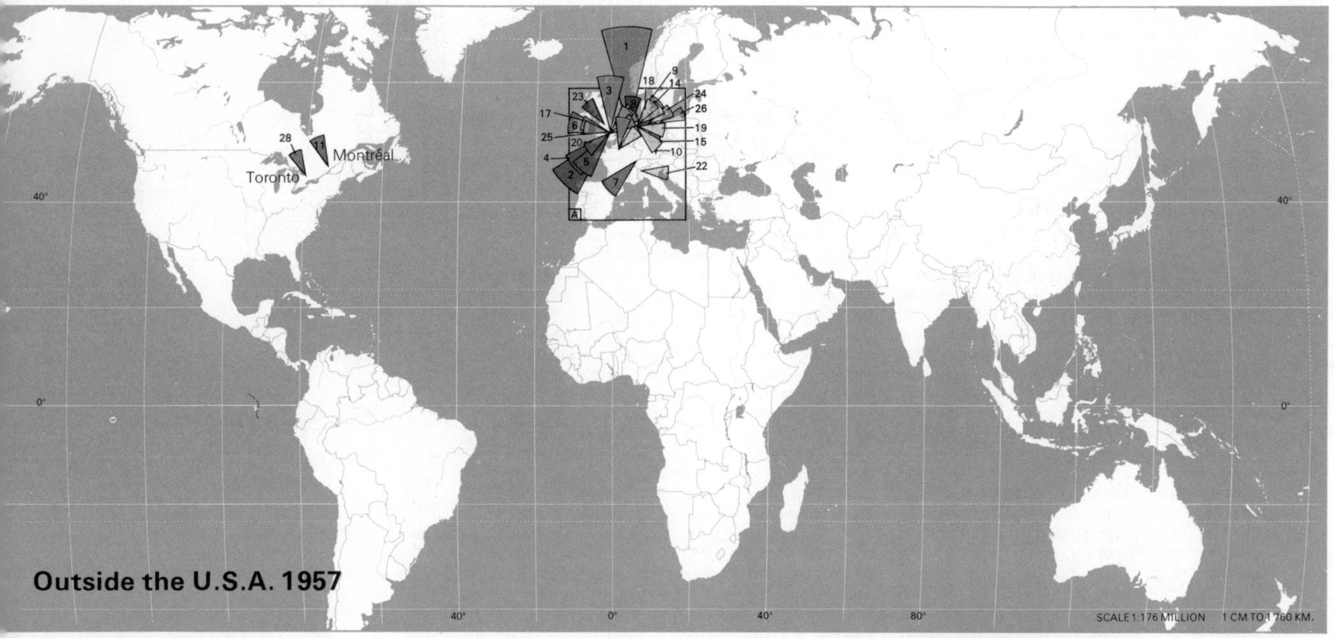
Outside the U.S.A. 1957
Toronto
Montréal
SCALE 1:176 MILLION 1 CM.TO 1 760 KM.

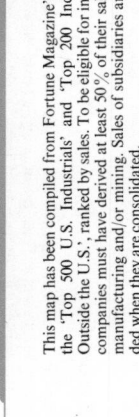

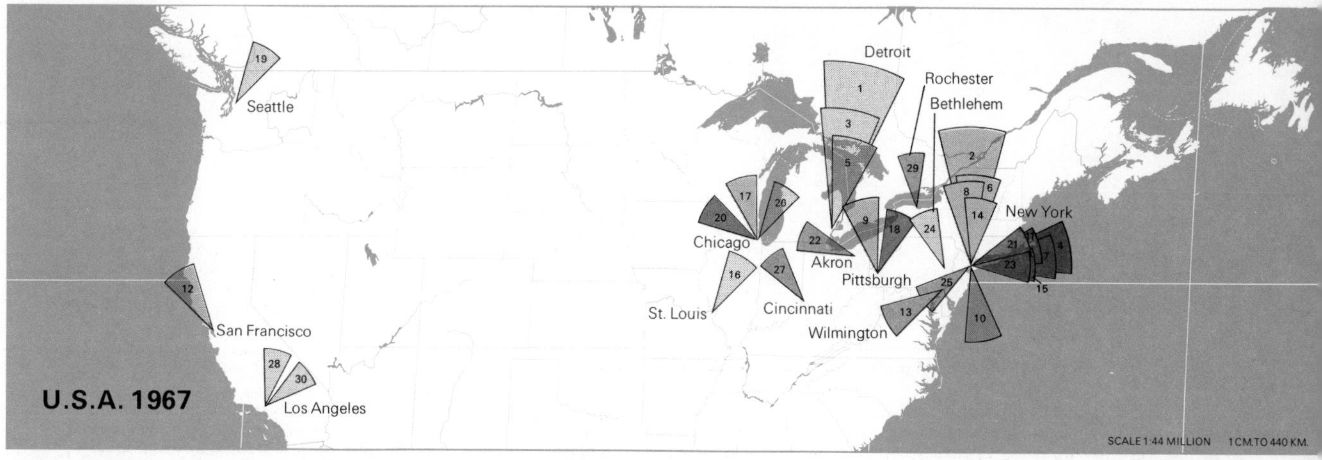
U.S.A. 1967
Seattle
San Francisco
Los Angeles
St. Louis
Chicago
Cincinnati
Akron
Detroit
Rochester
Bethlehem
New York
Pittsburgh
Wilmington
SCALE 1:44 MILLION 1 CM.TO 440 KM.

The largest industrial corporations in the U.S.A. 1967 (top 30 ranked by sales)

RANK 1967	COMPANY	HEADQUARTERS	SALES (Million $ U.S.)	ASSETS (Million $ U.S.)
1	**General Motors**	Detroit	20 026	13 273
2	**Standard Oil (N.J.)**	New York	13 266	15 197
3	**Ford Motor**	Detroit	10 516	7 967
4	**General Electric**	New York	7 741	5 347
5	**Chrysler**	Detroit	6 213	3 855
6	**Mobil Oil**	New York	5 772	6 224
7	**I.B.M.**	Armonk, N.Y.	5 345	5 599
8	**Texaco**	New York	5 121	7 163
9	**Gulf Oil**	Pittsburgh	4 202	6 458
10	**U.S. Steel**	New York	4 006	5 606
11	**Western Electric**	New York	3 718	2 553
12	**Standard Oil (Calif.)**	San Francisco	3 298	5 310
13	**Du Pont (E.I.) de Nemours**	Wilmington, Del.	3 102	3 071
14	**Shell Oil**	New York	3 073	3 421
15	**Radio Corp. of America**	New York	3 014	2 084
16	**McDonnell Douglas**	St. Louis	2 934	1 366
17	**Standard Oil (Ind.)**	Chicago	2 918	4 058
18	**Westinghouse Electric**	Pittsburgh	2 901	2 075
19	**Boeing**	Seattle	2 880	2 030
20	**Swift**	Chicago	2 835	758
21	**International Tel. & Tel.**	New York	2 761	2 961
22	**Goodyear Tire & Rubber**	Akron, Ohio	2 638	2 083
23	**General Tel. & Electronics**	New York	2 622	5 431
24	**Bethlehem Steel**	Bethlehem, Pa.	2 594	3 084
25	**Union Carbide**	New York	2 546	3 088
26	**International Harvester**	Chicago	2 542	1 812
27	**Proctor & Gamble**	Cincinnati	2 439	1 483
28	**North American Rockwell**	Los Angeles	2 438	1 144
29	**Eastman Kodak**	Rochester, N.Y.	2 392	2 233
30	**Lockheed Aircraft**	Los Angeles	2 335	881

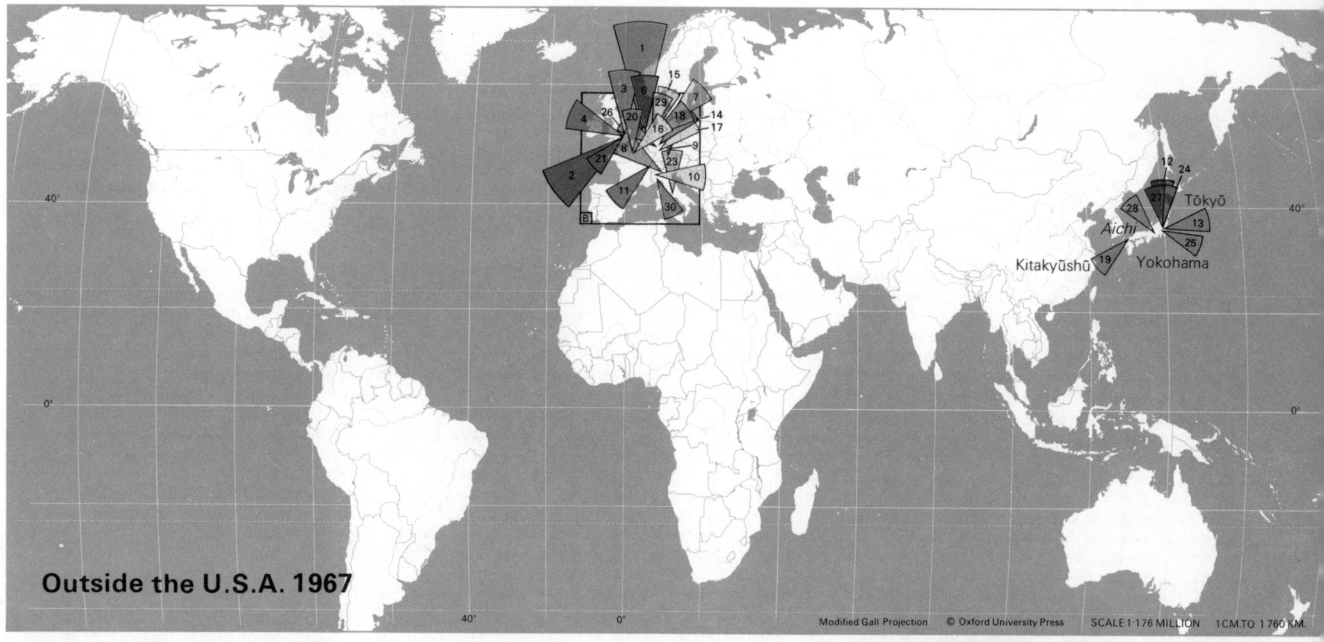
Outside the U.S.A. 1967
Tōkyō
Aichi
Yokohama
Kitakyūshū
Modified Gall Projection
© Oxford University Press
SCALE 1:176 MILLION 1 CM.TO 1 760 KM.

Top firms

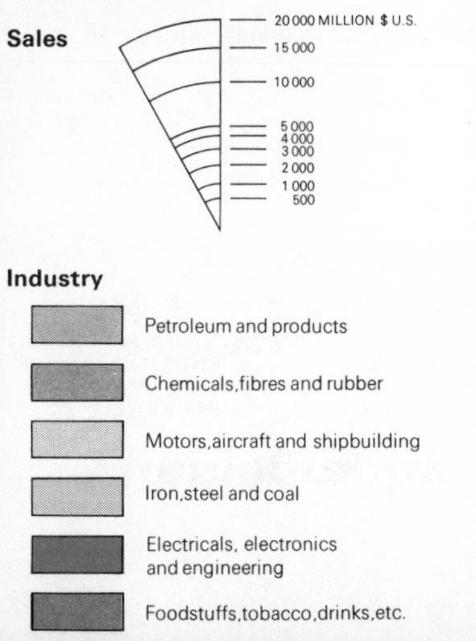
Sales
20 000 MILLION $ U.S.
15 000
10 000
5 000
4 000
3 000
2 000
1 000
500
Industry
Petroleum and products
Chemicals, fibres and rubber
Motors, aircraft and shipbuilding
Iron, steel and coal
Electricals, electronics and engineering
Foodstuffs, tobacco, drinks, etc.

This map has been compiled from Fortune Magazine's lists of the 'Top 500 U.S. Industrials' and 'Top 200 Industrials Outside the U.S.', ranked by sales. To be eligible for inclusion, companies must have derived at least 50% of their sales from manufacturing and/or mining. Sales of subsidiaries are included when they are consolidated.

Figures have been converted into U.S. dollars at official exchange rates. For British companies, whose financial year ended after the devaluation of the pound in November 1967, sales have been converted to $ U.S. using an exchange rate that represents the whole financial year. Total assets, shown in the tables, have been converted at the exchange rate prevailing at the end of each company's financial year.

As sales and assets may be assessed by various methods, close comparisons between figures are inadvisable, particularly between U.S. firms and those in the rest of the world. The classification of firms into six groups is somewhat arbitrary. Many firms are diversified into a wide range of industries other than their original ones, and in these cases they have been classified according to their main products. There is also a trend towards multi-national companies such as Royal Dutch/Shell and Unilever who are both owned jointly by Britain and the Netherlands.

Sales are not the only yardstick for assessing a company's size or economic success. High sales, even when coupled with high assets, do not necessarily produce high profits. For instance, in 1967 the National Coal Board (N.C.B.) registered sales of U.S. $2 439 million, placing them fifth in Fortune's ranking; yet their net profit was only U.S. $958 000, lower than any firm in the top 120.

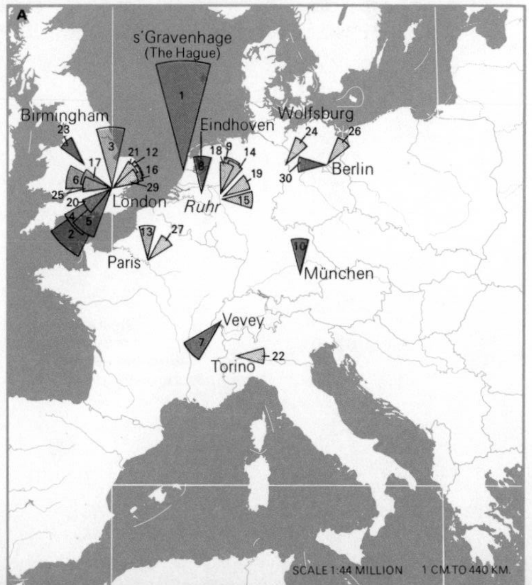
A
s'Gravenhage (The Hague)
Birmingham
Eindhoven
Wolfsburg
Berlin
London
Ruhr
Paris
München
Vevey
Torino
SCALE 1:44 MILLION 1 CM.TO 440 KM.

The largest industrial companies outside the U.S.A. (top 30 ranked by sales)

1957

RANK	COMPANY	HEADQUARTERS	SALES (Million $ U.S.)	ASSETS (Million $ U.S.)
1	**Royal Dutch/Shell**	s'Gravenhage	7 377	6 512
2	**Unilever**	London	3 415	1 909
3	**British Petroleum**	London	2 220	1 356
4	**Imperial Tobacco**	London	1 850	764
5	**British-American Tobacco**	London	1 650	962
6	**I.C.I.**	London	1 296	1 836
7	**Nestlé**	Vevey	1 150	157
8	**Philips' Gloeilampenfabrieken**	Eindhoven	836	988
9	**Fried. Krupp**	Essen	817	N A
10	**Siemens**	München	800	647
11	**Distillers Corp.-Seagrams**	Montréal	746	499
12	**Hawker Siddeley**	London	730	403
13	**Cie Française des Pétroles**	Paris	714	253
14	**Rheinische Stahlwerke**	Essen	667	476
15	**Mannesmann**	Düsseldorf	659	672
16	**British Motor**	London	650	295
17	**Dunlop**	London	647	520
18	**Gelsenkirchener Bergwerks-A.G.**	Essen	643	524
19	**Gutehoffnungshütte**	Oberhausen	599	N A
20	**Gallaher**	London	571	289
21	**Vickers**	London	568	469
22	**Fiat**	Torino	560	1 019
23	**Tube Investments**	Birmingham	560	279
24	**Volkswagenwerk**	Wolfsburg	538	175
25	**Courtaulds**	London	537	523
26	**Phoenix-Rheinrohr**	Berlin	531	402
27	**Renault**	Paris	515	211
28	**Canada Packers**	Toronto	482	88
29	**Ford Motor**	Dagenham	465	368
30	**A.E.G.**	Berlin	462	279

1967

RANK	COMPANY	HEADQUARTERS	SALES (Million $ U.S.)	ASSETS (Million $ U.S.)
1	**Royal Dutch/Shell**	s'Gravenhage	8 376	12 870
2	**Unilever**	London	5 560	3 271
3	**British Petroleum**	London	2 974	4 686
4	**I.C.I.**	London	2 692	4 014
5	**National Coal Board**	London	2 439	2 736
6	**Philips' Gloeilampenfabrieken**	Eindhoven	2 402	3 064
7	**Volkswagonwerk**	Wolfsburg	2 334	1 405
8	**Montecatini Edison**	Milano	2·092	4 463
9	**Siemens**	München	1 984	1 406
10	**Fiat**	Torino	1 911	1 511
11	**Nestlé**	Vevey	1 796	415
12	**Hitachi**	Tōkyō	1 749	2 097
13	**Mitsubishi Heavy Industries**	Tōkyō	1 651	2 463
14	**Farbwerke Hoechst**	Frankfurt	1 650	1 495
15	**August Thyssen-Hütte**	Duisburg	1 638	1 363
16	**Renault**	Paris	1 519	632
17	**Daimler-Benz**	Stuttgart	1 491	735
18	**Farbenfabriken Bayer**	Leverkusen	1 459	1 424
19	**Yawata Iron & Steel**	Kitakyūshū	1 376	2 032
20	**Cie Française des Pétroles**	Paris	1 343	788
21	**British-American Tobacco**	London	1 320	1 815
22	**British Motor**	London	1 308	884
23	**E.N.I.**	Roma	1 295	3 037
24	**Matsushita Electric Industrial**	Tōkyō	1 280	1 071
25	**Nissan Motor**	Yokohama	1 273	1 598
26	**B.A.S.F.**	Ludwigshafen	1 259	1 318
27	**Tokyo Shibaura Electric**	Tōkyō	1 258	1 621
28	**Toyota Motor**	Aichi-ken	1 258	1 106
29	**Krupp-Konzern**	Essen	1 233	1 300
30	**Finsider**	Genova	1 203	3 680

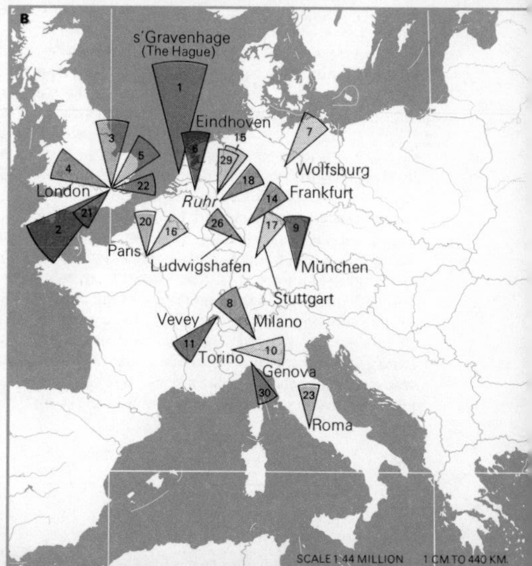
B
s'Gravenhage (The Hague)
Eindhoven
Wolfsburg
Frankfurt
London
Ruhr
Paris
Ludwigshafen
München
Stuttgart
Vevey
Milano
Torino
Genova
Roma
SCALE 1:44 MILLION 1 CM.TO 440 KM.

Demography

For individual country data see Statistical Supplement

The development of world population

That the future stability and welfare of the world as a whole is closely linked to the changes in the numbers of its people has long been widely recognized. Recent increases in population are striking for the short period over which they have taken place; the predicted future growth for its enormous size and speed of development.
The following diagram illustrates population increase from 1800.

Estimated world population

In millions 1800–1970

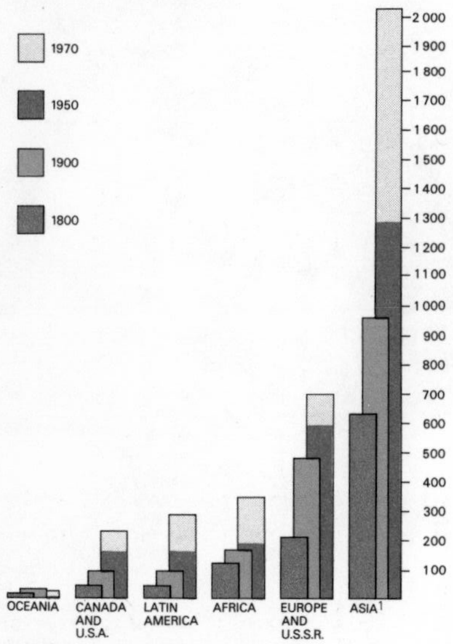

[1]Incl. Turkey

Many of the figures on which it is based are estimates; the world-wide taking of accurate and regular censuses has still to be completely achieved, and totals for the nineteenth century, as for some developing countries today, must be regarded with reserve. It is from about 1650, in Western Europe at least, that the beginnings of the sudden spurt of population growth can be traced. Undoubtedly this growth was closely connected with the industrial and scientific revolutions of the eighteenth and nineteenth centuries; it was also involved with important associated economic, social and political changes. Three centuries ago most of the world had, by the standards of today, a near stationary population, the result of a high and erratic death rate cancelling a high but fluctuating birth rate. In this situation probably half the children died before reaching the age of ten or twelve; 50% of the population was under 20 and expectation of life was short for most. There were perhaps 500-600 million people in the world in 1650, at least a half of these being in East and SE. Asia, a proportion close to that found today; the concentration of population here over a long period is one of the primary features of the distribution of the earth's people. Over the 300 years since, the situation has been dramatically altered, although with many regional differences in the rate and timing of advance. A five-fold multiplication between 1650 and 1950 has been the result.
Until about 1900 this growth was moderate and restricted to parts of Europe and Asia; population was advancing at a rate by which the world total doubled about every century. From 1900 onwards all over the world the rate of increase has dramatically altered; the population will soon be doubling in 30 or 40 years. In the early modern period scattered and inaccurate sources make it difficult to decide whether it was rising fertility, declining mortality or a combination of both that aided the sudden acceleration in Europe: today mortality rates continue to fall there, albeit very slowly, but they have declined much more dramatically in the developing countries in recent years. The differences in mortality are thus beginning to vanish under the impetus of world-wide changes in standards of public health and hygiene.
Expectation of life for the developing countries still, of course, falls below the 67-72 years at birth to be found for most men and women in Europe and North America. It ranges between 30 and 60 years on average. This in itself represents a great and ever-growing improvement on the situation before the days of the world-wide spread of scientific medicine and higher standards of sanitation, when the expectation of life reached only about 30 years.
It is thus the astonishing fertility of the peoples of most of Africa, Asia and Latin America which, tied to their falling death rates, allows a clear distinction to be drawn between "developing" and "developed" countries in a demographic sense; they represent, at the moment, two separate population types.
It is to be expected that mortality will continue to fall: any decrease in the rate of population growth of the last few decades and its projected future developments must come through an induced decline in the birth rate.
The rates of recent growth in different areas vary widely. In the period 1920-1960 the population of Latin America grew by 135%, of South Asia by 85% and of East Asia by about 45%. This last figure is the most uncertain of all owing to the lack of reliable demographic information emanating from the giant country of China P.R. Europe as a whole, on the other hand, reached only a 40% increase.
The divergence between the growth rates of the two major population types naturally affects their relative size within the world total. There has been and will continue to be an increase in the share of the developing countries at the expense of the more developed, such as Europe, the U.S.S.R., North America, Japan, Australia, New Zealand, and parts of temperate South America and South Africa, whose portion has dropped from 35% to 30% in recent years, and which may fall below 20% by the year 2000. At present the population of the developing countries is increasing at an annual rate of 1.5 – 3.5%, save in those with a still high mortality rate; the equivalent rate for most developed countries is between 0.5 – 1.0%. The expected increase over the next decade is shown in the table below.

Forecast of population increase 1970-1980

	PERCENTAGE		
Latin America	34	North America	15
Africa	30	East Asia	14
South Asia	28	U.S.S.R.	13
Oceania	21	Europe	6

If fertility remains high and constant in the developing nations, however, or declines no faster than it did in the West from the nineteenth century, unmanageable increases could result. Africa's great advances in population could be still to come, although that of Latin America which began in the 1920's shows signs of levelling off, as it does in some parts of Asia. The pressing problem is the length of time that will be taken for the fall in birth rates now apparently beginning in island and peninsular countries around the edge of the Asian mainland to spread effectively through the one and a half billion (1 500 000 000) people on the continent.
Some regions, especially in Asia itself, start out with population numbers and densities greatly in excess of those in the West at the beginning of its rapid growth, so the increase of people and the resulting pressure on resources and agricultural land will be far, far greater. Furthermore, the West's period of advance was paralleled by a rapidly expanding industrial economy that was able to support more and more people at ever higher standards of living. This is certainly not the case in most developing countries, where there is no guarantee that even with Western style industrialization and economic advance a similar fall in net population growth will occur in the same way.
The probability is of a world population of 7 000 million by the end of the millenium with the peak still to come; and of the total doubling and quadrupling thereafter with frightening speed according to some projections. Past experience has often shown these to be underestimates, although on the other hand, projections for France and the U.S.A. in recent years have proved to be overestimates. This presents two great problems: the limitation of fertility to reduce births and the feeding of the natural increase that does occur.
Much more is known today about birth control than during the great period of European population growth, and so perhaps fertility decline can be initiated at an earlier stage of demographic development. The post-war period in particular has seen great advances in the techniques and effectiveness of birth control devices; the lowering of their cost and the efforts of many national and international agencies have spread their use throughout the developing world in various forms.
The degree of their acceptance by the indigenous populations of different countries has varied, and ratios of effectiveness have often been rather low: indeed a high proportion of unplanned conceptions even in Europe in recent years has occurred despite the use of contraceptive devices. In some developing countries the proportion of women of childbearing age practising birth control is still only about 10%.
The problems therefore concern less-educated and economically advanced peoples with different social standards; but it is through family planning programmes that the modifying effect on population must come, unless catastrophic losses through famine and epidemic disease take their toll. These last dangers are under twin-pronged attack by improvements in medical and agricultural practice.
A true 'agricultural revolution' in a modern sense is still awaited in many parts of the developing world, as new techniques and crops are uncertainly and sometimes unsuccessfully tried in an attempt to meet increasing population pressure on the availability of foodstuffs. Food supply is unlikely to present any great problem in future years in the developed and industrialized countries. A number of these, the U.S.A., Canada, Australia and New Zealand, have great agricultural resources, and surpluses of staples like grain are often produced. Some is exported to such countries as the U.K. or Germany F.R., whose dense industrial populations are partially dependent on imported foodstuffs. Such produce is often more difficult to redistribute in times of need to the developing countries themselves. The social habits of the people often resist the introduction of new foodstuffs, political problems are sometimes difficult to overcome, even though Canada, for example, has sent vast shipments of grain to China P.R. in some recent years.
But such movements of foodstuffs are only a temporary palliative for developing countries like India and Pakistan. These are unquestionably overpopulated in terms both of agricultural land and employment opportunities. In such areas the impetus must come from within. This is necessary in order to establish productive capacity and to meet the demands not only of more mouths to feed but of eventually rising living standards. Agricultural advances when achieved will also undoubtedly eventually lead, with growing efficiency, to the economic redundancy of much of the already underemployed agricultural sector. These people will increasingly look to industry and to the city for employment and place of residence.
Certainly it is unlikely that there will be any solution found to problems of overpopulation in large scale migration. There will probably never again be movements on the scale of the great transatlantic exodus of European peoples to the new world of the Americas, and to a lesser extent Australia and New Zealand; such a mass transfer of people was probably the biggest in human history. Recent movement into the new lands of Siberia and of China P.R. is probably considerable, but lack of reliable information makes this difficult to quantify. Since the sixteenth century it is estimated that over 75 million people have emigrated to the new lands, at least 45 million of these going to Anglo-America. Besides re-distributing population, such movements led to the opening up of new regions and the adoption of more productive agricultural techniques, bringing about an enormous increase in the world's production of foodstuffs.
There have been few recent examples of large population increases due to long range international migration, except perhaps the doubling of Israel's size between 1948 and 1951 when the natural rate of increase was only moderate. Political and national considerations have led to the closing of many former channels of migration; the level of intake into the U.S.A. has dropped to between 250 000 and 350 000 per year, and that country and others like Canada and Australia are now very selective in the choice of their new nationals.
On the other hand, shorter distance and less permanent movements may be expected to increase as barriers to the free movement of labour drop in response to the organization of units like the European Economic Community; for example, some of the industries of Germany F.R., France and Belgium depend on a regular supply of workers from Italy. As a whole the Southern European countries of Italy, Spain, Portugal, Yugoslavia and Greece have suffered a net loss of about 300 000 a year since 1945, with fewer crossing the Atlantic as European opportunities began to open. The effects of such relatively small movements on the density and distribution of world population is, however, likely to remain slight.

Increasing urbanization of the world's population

By far the most marked characteristic of today's accelerating world population growth is its very great rate of urbanization. The increase in the total is associated with an ever continuing shift towards employment in non-agricultural activities. Similarly, parallel with the spread of popular education, material and cultural aspirations are undergoing continuing transformation while social relationships are altering within an urban framework. These are some of the changes, amongst many others, marking the last century or so, which part in response and part in stimulation to urbanization act as a total mechanism which pushes the process into an ever increasing upward spiral. Indeed the very character of urbanity itself has undergone much change in recent decades because of the shifts from manufacturing to service and higher level activities. Entire regions are now affected by this process, for example much of the NE. seaboard of the U.S.A. has been identified as one continuous urban agglomeration, megalopolis. Others can be seen perceptibly growing around the Great Lakes, in Western Europe (the Rhine-Ruhr axis, for example) and in Japan. The conurbation stretching between Kobe and Tokyo is now merging imperceptibly into 'Tokaido'. With the great increase in the number of urban activities and attributes and their ever widening diffusion it is doubtful whether the traditional division of the world's population into rural and urban components is any longer valid, at least for many developed countries. This trend is likely to continue in the future throughout the developing countries, and to be undoubtedly the most important change in the future life style of the world's burgeoning population.
Urbanization, with even the possible development of a true world city, may in the long term retard the growth of population which is actually being tackled in the short term by the spread of birth control. Much evidence, admittedly largely drawn from already industrialized Western society which may not necessarily provide generally applicable principles, exists to suggest that levels of fertility are invariably lower in more urbanized societies. This has been attributed to higher levels of income and education, as well as to a greater variety of types of employment opportunity for women found in cities. Rising aspirations have historically led to smaller families. Indeed the very way of life in a city environment may have a profound psychological effect on attitudes to fertility as it does on other matters of individual as well as mass behaviour. Even if these limiting effects on the growth of the human population are found in the future to apply on a world-wide scale, the time that this will take will inevitably be long.
In recent years the most conspicuous rates of urbanization have been experienced in Asia and Latin America; but, growing from 200 million to 450 million in the 40 years up to 1960, the urban population of the developed Western world has more than doubled and may do so again by the end of the century. In the same period, but from a much lower starting point, the urban population of the developing world has quadrupled to over 300 million; it is likely to quadruple again to about 1 500 million by the year 2000. The ever changing relationships of "urban" and "rural" populations in the developing and developed countries is illustrated in the table below.
Despite the increasing momentum of urbanization in both parts of the populated world nearly half of the increase up to the year 2000 is estimated to be going to take place in what are still conventionally described as rural and small town sectors of the population, and about half of this will occur in an already overcrowded South Asia struggling with the twin problems of sometimes near starvation and the difficulties of initiating true industrial advance.

Comparison of the world's urban and rural population 1920-2000

YEAR	MILLIONS WORLD POPULATION	PERCENTAGE OF WORLD TOTAL: DEVELOPED REGIONS URBAN	RURAL	TOTAL	DEVELOPING REGIONS URBAN	RURAL	TOTAL
1920	1 860	11	25	36	4	60	64
1940	2 295	13	23	36	5	59	64
1960	2 991	15	18	33	10	57	67
1980	4 318	15	12	27	16	57	73
2000	6 112	15	9	24	23	53	76

Population I

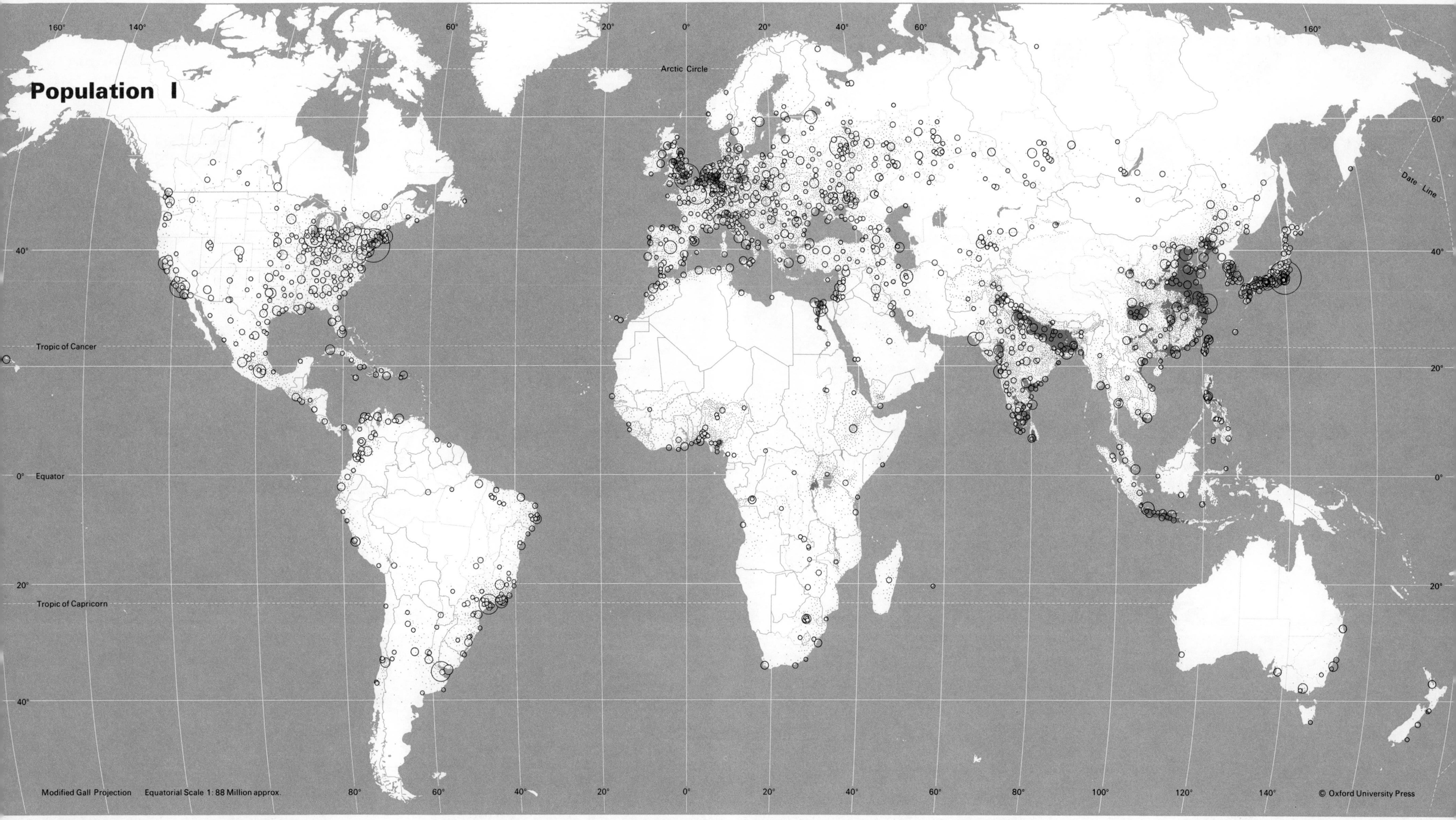

Arctic Circle
Tropic of Cancer
Equator
Tropic of Capricorn
Date Line
160°
140°
60°
40°
20°
0°
80°
100°
120°
Modified Gall Projection
Equatorial Scale 1: 88 Million approx.

Population distribution

Towns of at least 100 000 population

OVER 10 000 000
7 500 001 – 10 000 000
5 000 001 – 7 500 000
2 500 001 – 5 000 000
1 000 001 – 2 500 000
500 001 – 1 000 000
200 001 – 500 000
100 001 – 200 000

One dot per 100 000 population outside the towns shown

Population statistics for selected countries

Latest census available in 1968

	BURMA	NIGERIA	SAUDI ARABIA	YUGO-SLAVIA	CHINA P.R.	INDIA	INDO-NESIA	ALGERIA	PHILIP-PINES	PARAGUAY	TURKEY
Total population (thousands)	16 823	55 670	6 990	18 549	582 603	435 512	96 319	12 102	27 088	1 817	31 391
Population density (persons/sq. km.)[1]	38	67	3	78	75	156	74	5	116	5	42
Percentage urbanized	7	9	9	9	10	10	10	14	15	17	19
Size of largest urban agglomeration (thousands)	821	665	225	585	6 900	4 903	2 907	903	1 402	305	2 052

	POLAND	U.S.S.R.	SOUTH AFRICA	MEXICO	TAIWAN	SWEDEN	GERMANY F.R.	FRANCE	IRAQ	U.A.R.	BRAZIL	ISRAEL	U.S.A.	NETHER-LANDS	U.K.	JAPAN	CANADA	ARGENTINA	AUSTRALIA
Total population (thousands)	29 776	208 827	15 994	34 923	13 383	7 766	53 977	46 520	8 262	25 984	70 119	2 183	179 323	11 462	52 709	98 275	18 238	23 031	11 541
Population density (persons/sq. km.)[1]	102	11	15	23	365	17	233	91	19	31	10	129	21	375	226	270	2	8	2
Percentage urbanized	23	24	27	28	29	31	32	34	34	35	36	41	45	47	49	50	52	57	63
Size of largest urban agglomeration (thousands)	1 261	6 507	1 153	3 353	1 155	1 262	2 191	7 369	1 745	4 220	5 383	390	11 410	1 048	7 914	11 005	2 437	7 000	2 445

[1]1967

Population II

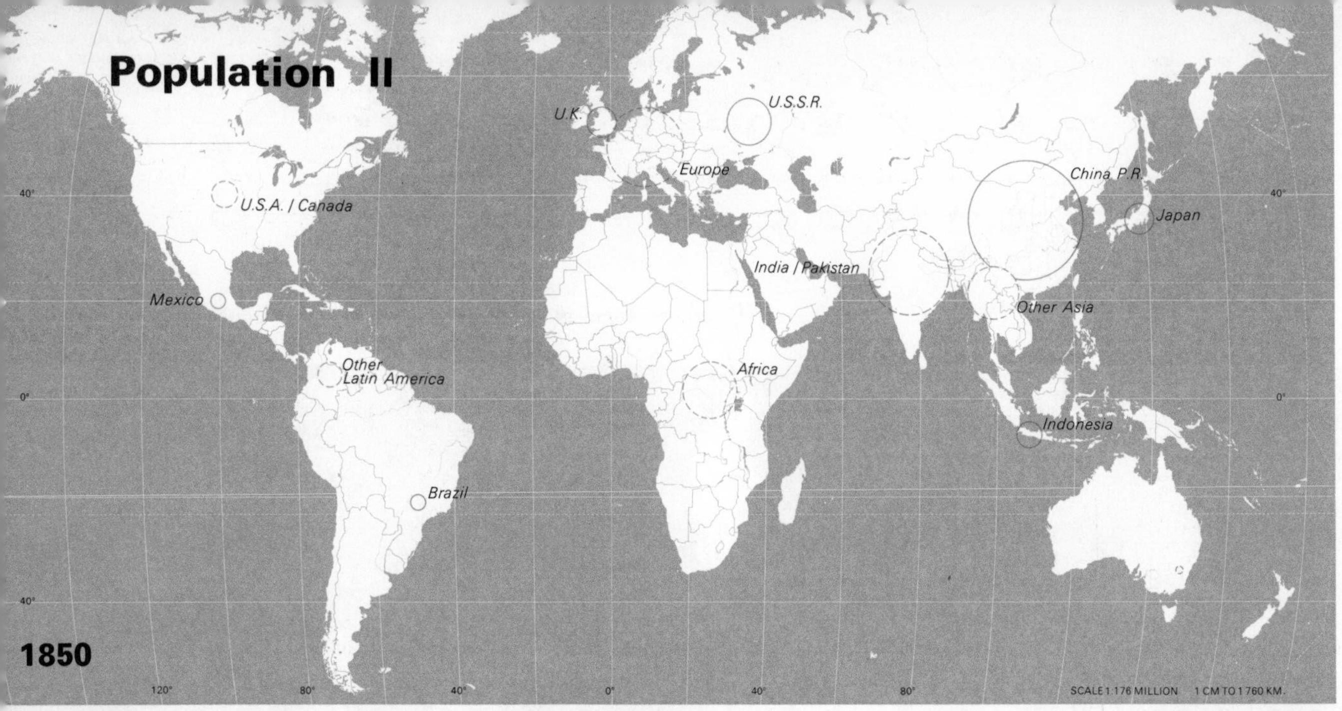

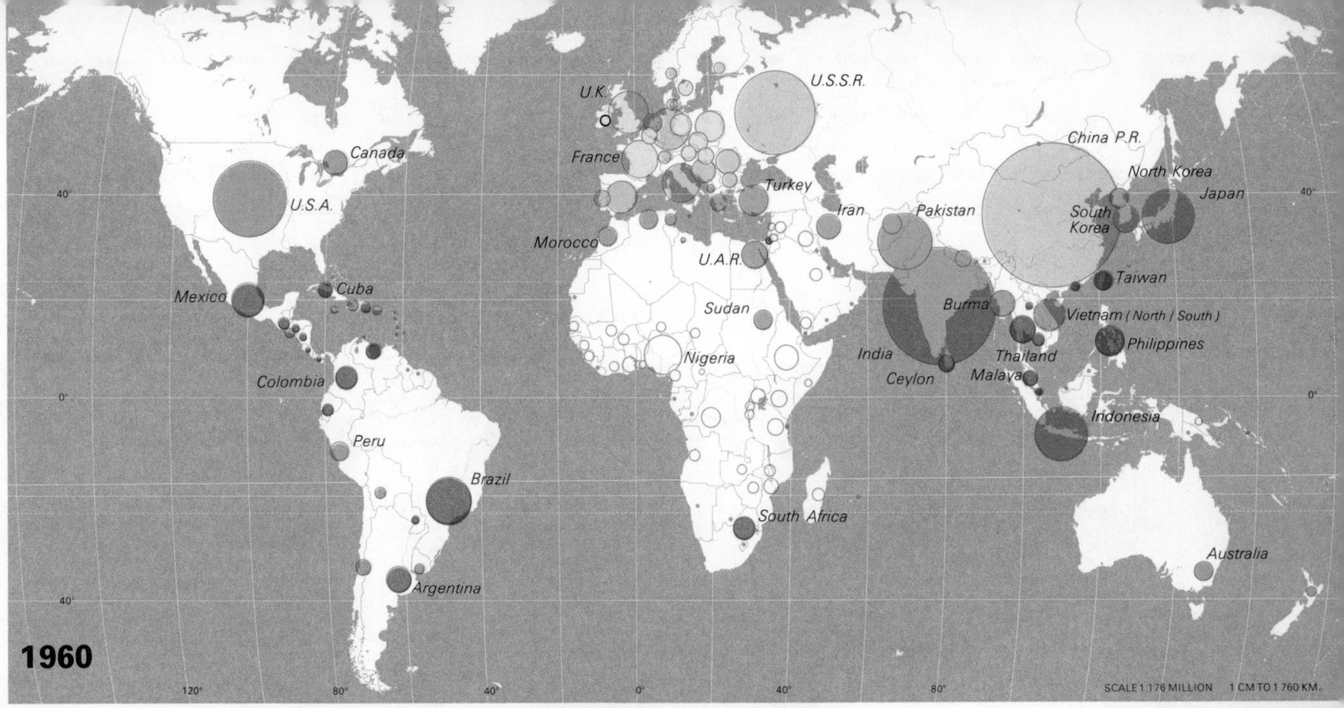

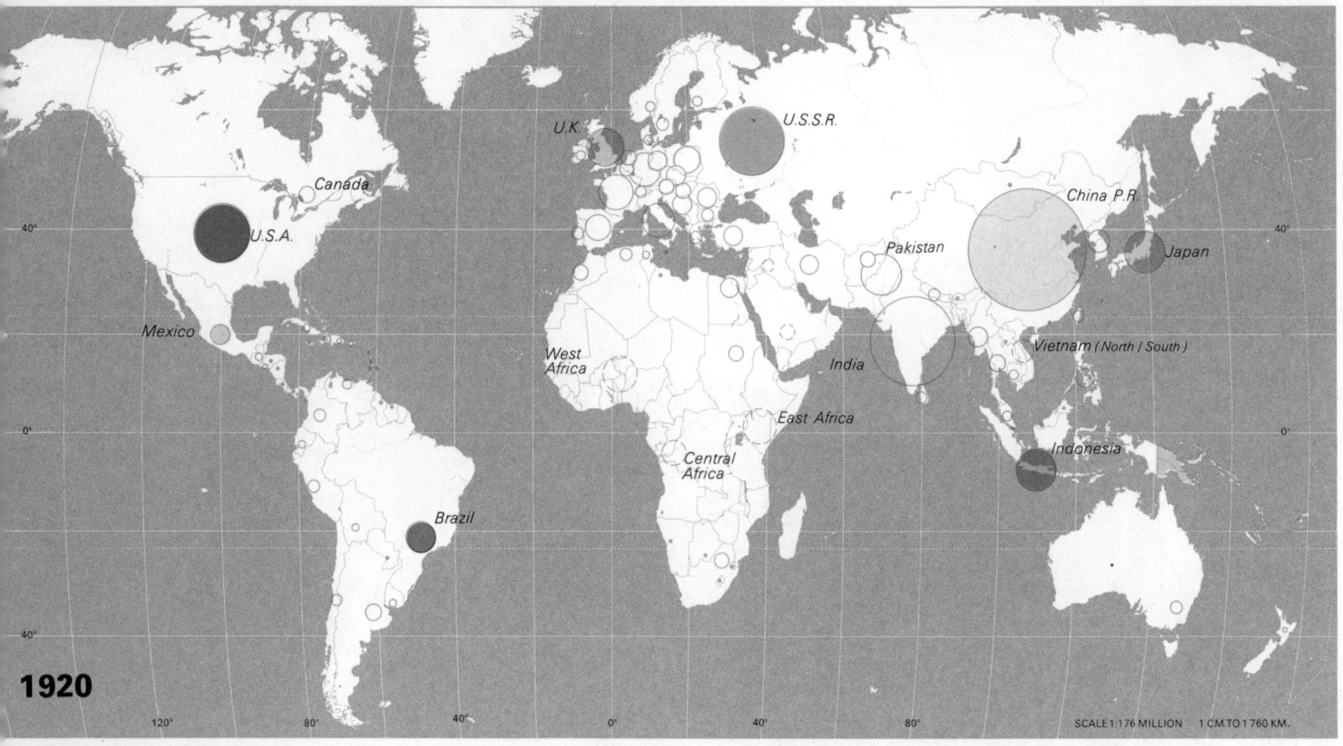

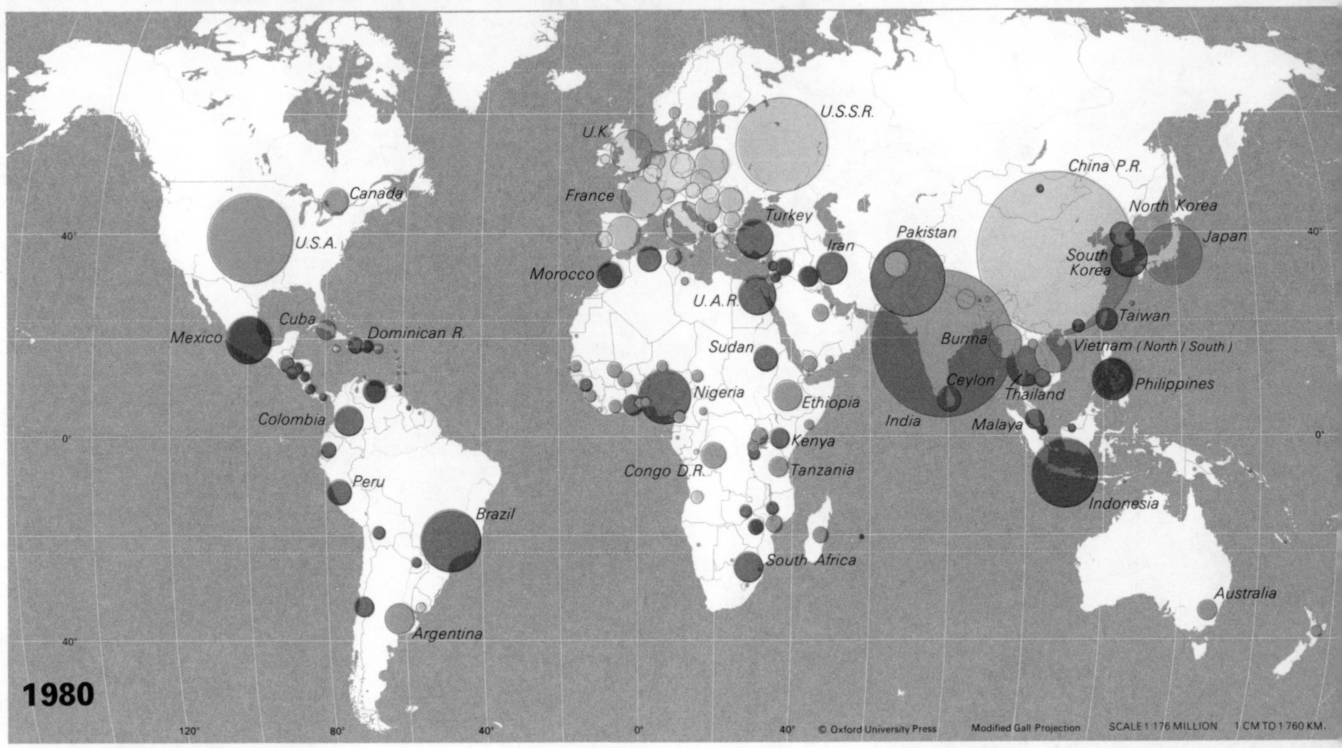

Population (historical distribution)

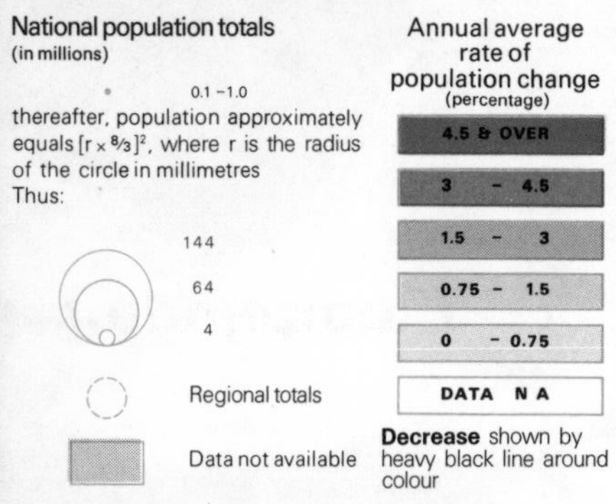

This series of maps is intended to show the accelerating growth of the world's population since 1850 and its expected increase in the immediate future.

In 1850 the total population was about 1 000 million compared with the present figure of 3 500 million, and precise information about the population was scarce. At that time only a few nations had carried out national censuses. Most of the figures are based upon rough estimates made by various organizations and individuals. A large majority of the population lived in South and East Asia, where the agriculture-based economy was very similar to that found in many areas of the region today. It was only in Western Europe and North America that industrialization was leading to diversification in the employment of the labour force, making censuses more important for social planning.

By 1920 statistical information had improved considerably and only in tropical Africa and parts of the Middle East was there still an almost complete lack of demographic data. Thus, a general pattern of population distribution could be seen, major concentrations being in South and East Asia and Europe, with the U.S.A. having the fastest rate of increase (1850-1920) mainly because of large-scale immigration. This came first from North and West Europe, and then, at the end of the nineteenth century and the beginning of the twentieth century, from South and East Europe, until the introduction of immigration restrictions, particularly after 1924.

The population distribution in 1960 was similar to that in 1920. It is estimated that the world population increased by 473 millions during the 1950's. If current growth rates are maintained, the world population would be 7 000 million by the end of the century, and 12 000 million by 2030. Latin America showed the fastest rate of increase (1920-60). Other areas of rapid increase were a result of exceptional political situations, such as the creation of Israel as a Jewish state in 1948, and emigration from the Chinese mainland to Taiwan and Hong Kong after the revolution in 1949.

The forecast rates of increase (1960-80), based when possible on the 'medium' population projections of the 'UN Report on World Population Prospects as Assessed in 1963', are similar to those of 1920-60. Central America has particularly high growth rates while Europe has a low rate of increase, having reached a stable demographic equilibrium of low birth and death rates.

Population pyramids (% of population in each ten-year age group)

These pyramids show the structure of the population of selected countries in terms of age and sex. They are based on ten-year age groups up to the age of 80.[1] The difference in age structures between nations is largely a result of their level of development. Thus Ghana, India and Venezuela have very large 0-9 age groups and a low number of older people. On the other hand, the U.K. and France in particular have a nearly constant number of people in each age group up to 60, signifying a lower birth-rate and better medical standards. The pyramids also show that although more males than females are born, the females tend to live longer, as seen clearly in the U.K.

Population by region

	PERCENTAGE OF WORLD TOTAL		
	1920	1960	1980
Europe	17.6	14.2	11.2
U.S.S.R.	8.3	7.2	6.5
North America	6.2	6.7	6.1
Latin America	4.8	7.1	8.8
East Asia[2]	29.7	26.5	24.4
South Asia	25.2	28.7	32.0
Africa	7.7	9.1	10.5
Oceania	0.5	0.5	0.5

[2] East Asia: China P.R., Japan, Taiwan, Korea, Mongolia, Hong Kong, Macao, Ryukyu Is.

[1] Data for Germany D.R. and Venezuela, undifferentiated above the age of 70.

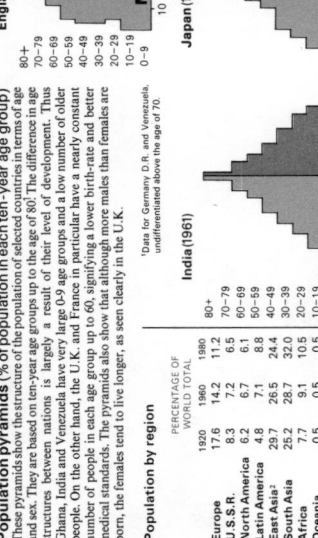

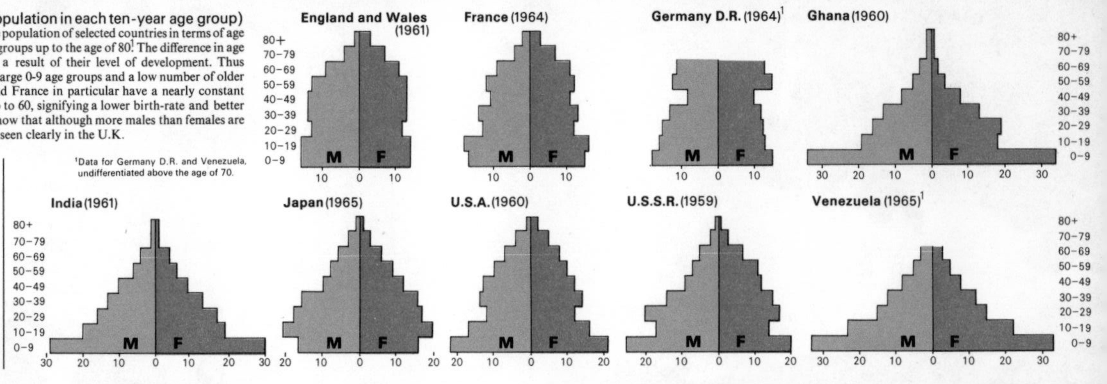

Population III

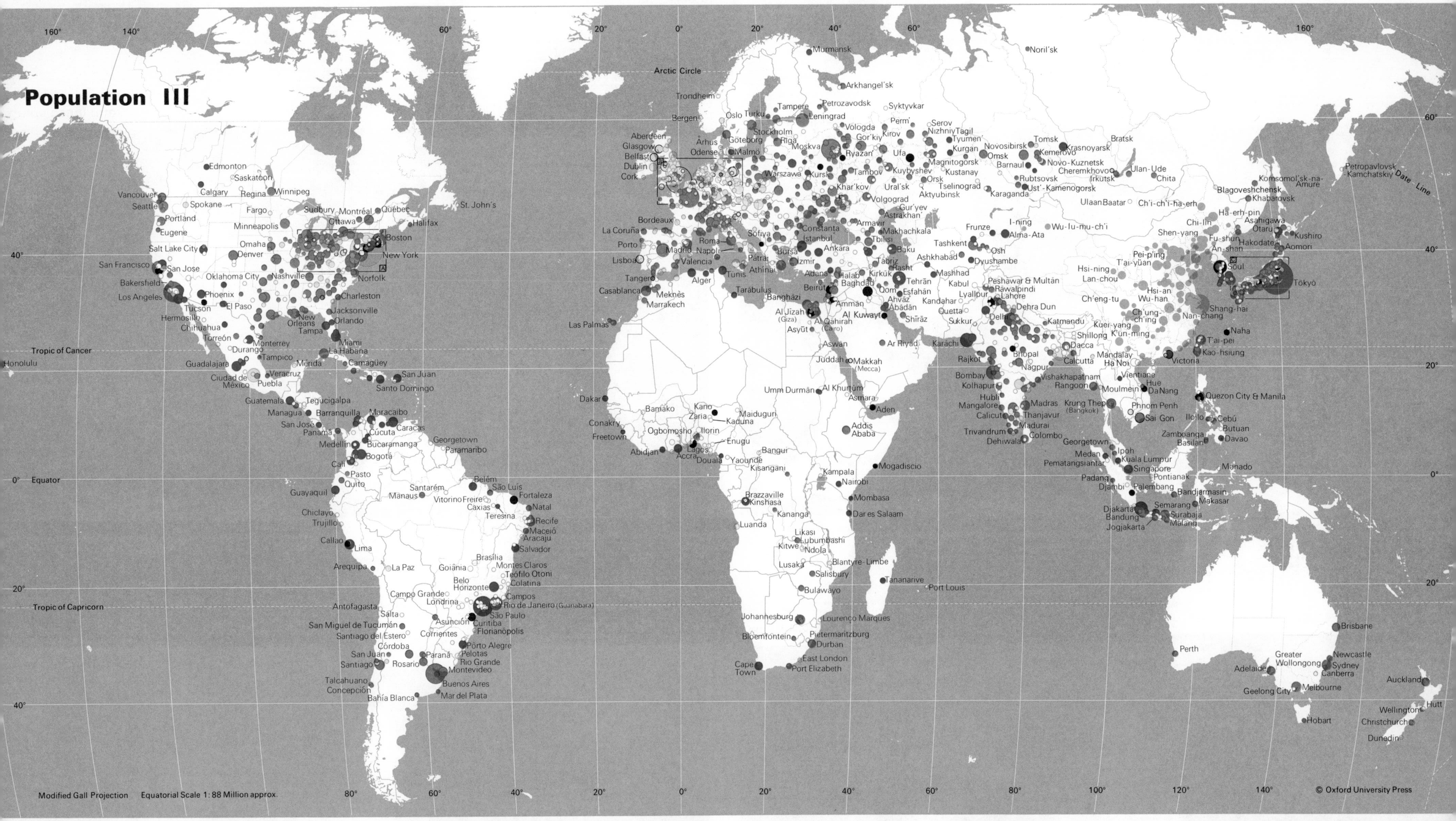

Urban change

In those cities of at least 100 000 population at the last census

Size at last census shown by graded circles

OVER 10 000 000
7 500 001 - 10 000 000
5 000 001 - 7 500 000
2 500 001 - 5 000 000
1 000 001 - 2 500 000
500 001 - 1 000 000
200 001 - 500 000
100 001 - 200 000

Percentage change in previous decade shown by colour

0–5%	30–60%
5–15%	60–120%
15–30%	OVER 120%
DATA N A	

decreases shown by black line around colour

cities below 100 000 population at the beginning of the decade shown by open circles because data on change are not available

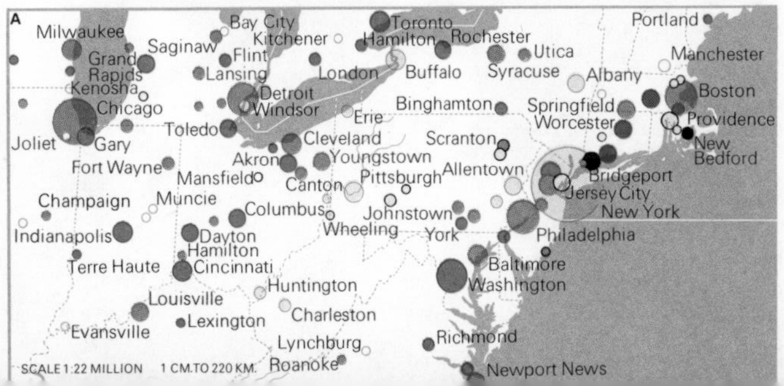

It must be noted that data on change are applied only to those cities which had 100 000 population at the beginning of the decade, and are shown as percentages over the 10 years, p%.

To convert to an average annual rate, r% p.a., use the compound interest formula:

$$r = \left(100 \times \sqrt[10]{\frac{p+100}{100}}\right) - 100$$

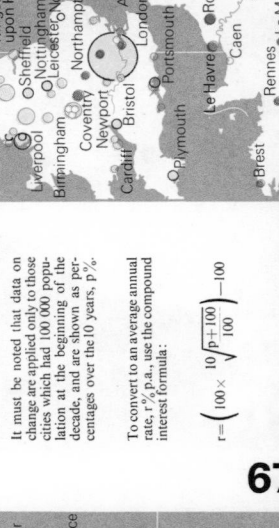

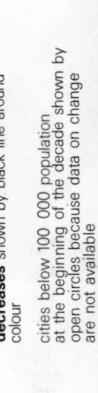

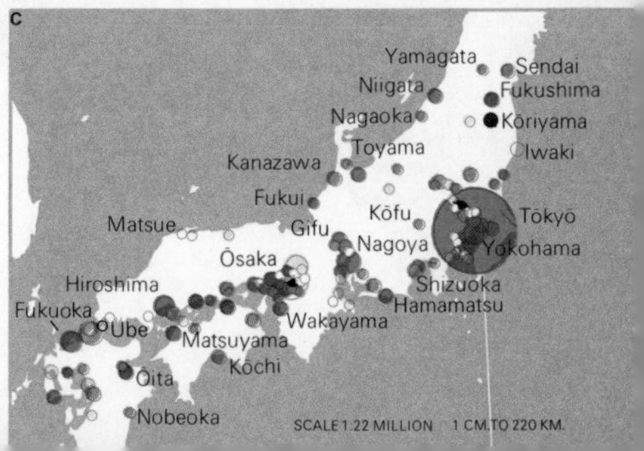

Population IV

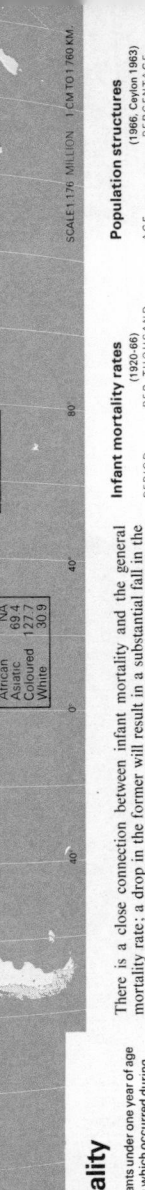

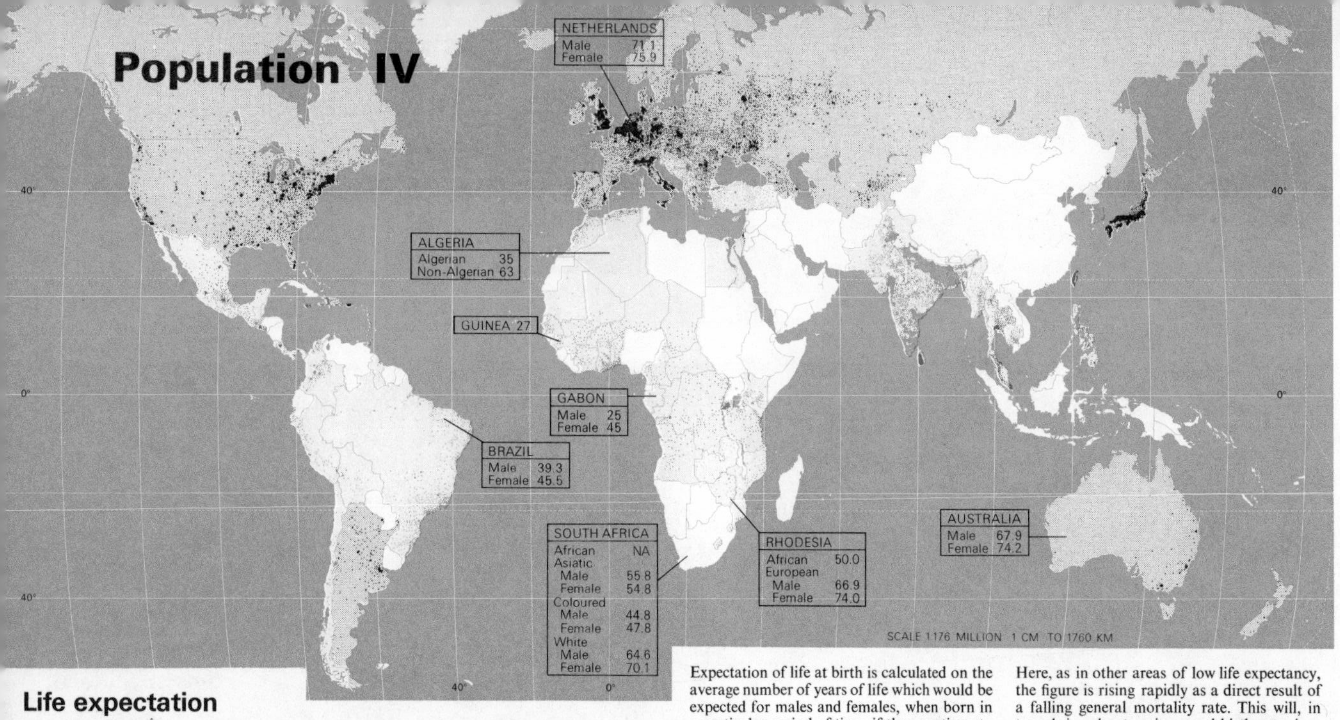
NETHERLANDS
Male 71.1
Female 75.9
ALGERIA
Algerian 35
Non-Algerian 63
GUINEA 27
GABON
Male 25
Female 45
BRAZIL
Male 39.3
Female 45.5
SOUTH AFRICA
African NA
Asiatic
Male 55.8
Female 54.8
Coloured
Male 44.8
Female 47.8
White
Male 64.6
Female 70.1
RHODESIA
African 50.0
European
Male 66.9
Female 74.0
AUSTRALIA
Male 67.9
Female 74.2
SCALE 1:176 MILLION 1 CM TO 1760 KM

Life expectation at birth[1]

- 65 & OVER
- 55 – 65
- 40 – 55
- UNDER 40
- DATA NA

One dot to 100 000 population

[1] Data based on latest available national censuses and may be as early as 1940

Increases in life expectation at birth

		AGE			
		1900-10	1920-30	1947-49	1966
Netherlands	*Male*	51	62	69	71
	Female	53	64	72	76
Japan	*Male*	44	45[1]	50[2]	68
	Female	45	47[1]	54[2]	74
India	*Male*	23	27	32[3]	42[4]
	Female	23	27	32[3]	41[4]

[1] 1926-30 [2] 1947 [3] 1941-50 [4] 1951-60 latest available

Expectation of life at birth is calculated on the average number of years of life which would be expected for males and females, when born in a particular period of time, if they continue to be subject to the same mortality conditions as existed in that period of time. It is important to reach separate figures for males and females, since generally throughout the world women have a longer life expectation than men and it is only in a very few countries, of those for which data are available, that the reverse is true; these include India, Pakistan, Ceylon, Cambodia and Upper Volta. Central Africa is the area of lowest life expectancy in the world.

Here, as in other areas of low life expectancy, the figure is rising rapidly as a direct result of a falling general mortality rate. This will, in turn, bring about an increased birth rate since more women will live throughout all their possible childbearing years. Consequently, in the developing nations the number of elderly, unproductive persons will rise as well as the number of young persons. A severe strain will be placed upon the developing economies as more persons need to be employed and supported, necessitating an ever-increasing capital investment, which the nations concerned are finding difficult to maintain.

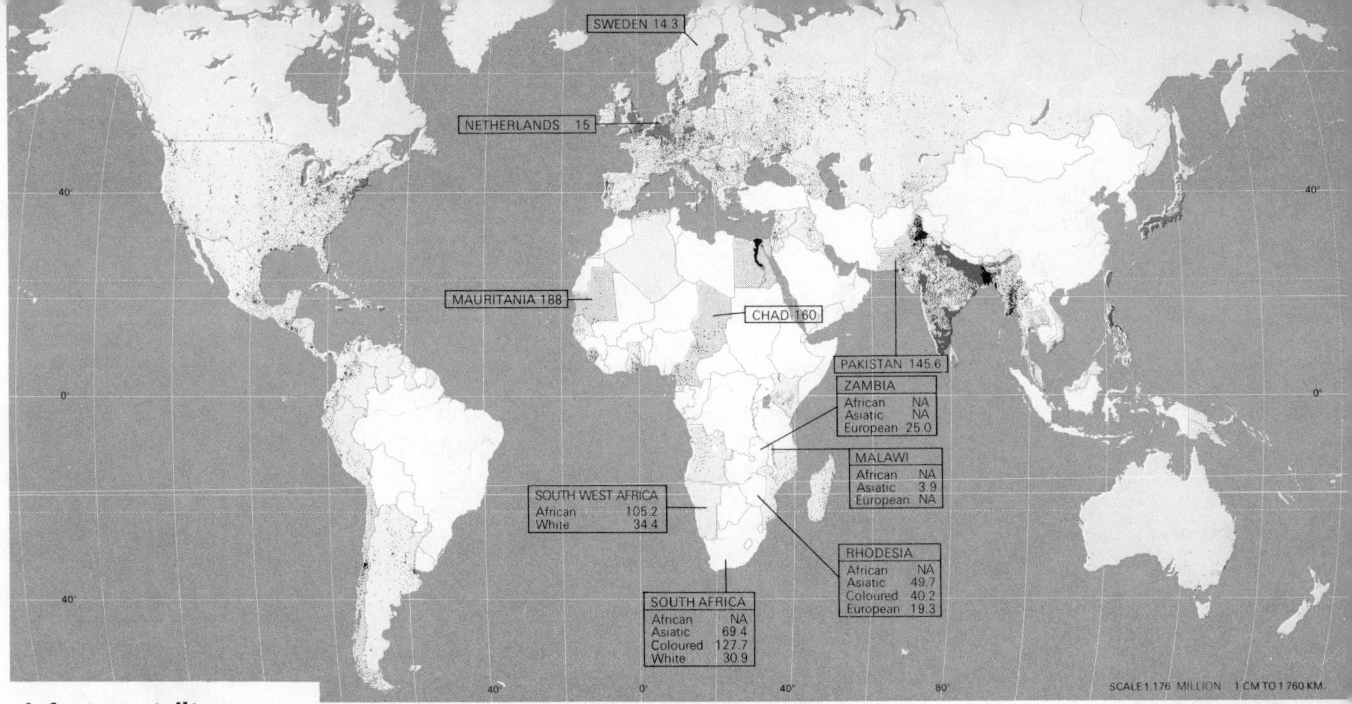
SWEDEN 14.3
NETHERLANDS 15
MAURITANIA 188
CHAD 160
PAKISTAN 145.6
ZAMBIA
African NA
Asiatic NA
European 25.0
MALAWI
African NA
Asiatic 3.9
European NA
SOUTH WEST AFRICA
African 105.2
White 34.4
RHODESIA
African NA
Asiatic 49.7
Coloured 40.2
European 19.3
SOUTH AFRICA
African NA
Asiatic 69.4
Coloured 127.7
White 30.9
SCALE 1:176 MILLION 1 CM TO 1 760 KM.

Infant mortality

Number of deaths of infants under one year of age per thousand live births which occurred during the same period (1963-5 av.)

- 100 & OVER
- 60 – 100
- 30 – 60
- UNDER 30
- DATA NA

One dot to 100 000 population

There is a close connection between infant mortality and the general mortality rate; a drop in the former will result in a substantial fall in the latter, since infant mortality is an important quantitative part of mortality rates in general. Deaths during the first year of life can be divided into two major causes differing in importance with time from birth. Those occurring during the first month after birth are primarily due to genetic causes, while the majority in the remaining eleven months are the result of the environment. The latter are far easier to control, and most work in reducing the rates of infant mortality is being done in this sphere.

Infant mortality rates

(1920-66)

PERIOD	U.K.	JAPAN	CEYLON
	PER THOUSAND		
1920-29	76.2	152.7	183.1
1930-39	61.6	117.3	173.9
1940-49	48.2	79.8	122.6
1950-59	26.4	45.2	71.2
1960-64	21.9	27.3	54.9
1965	19.5	18.5	NA
1966	19.6	19.3	NA

Population structures

(1966, Ceylon 1963)

AGE	U.K.	JAPAN	CEYLON
	PERCENTAGE		
0- 9	16.5	15.9	28.9
10-19	14.7	20.4	22.3
20-29	13.1	17.3	15.5
30-39	12.2	16.2	12.6
40-49	12.9	11.4	8.7
50-59	12.8	9.0	5.9
60+	17.8	9.8	6.1

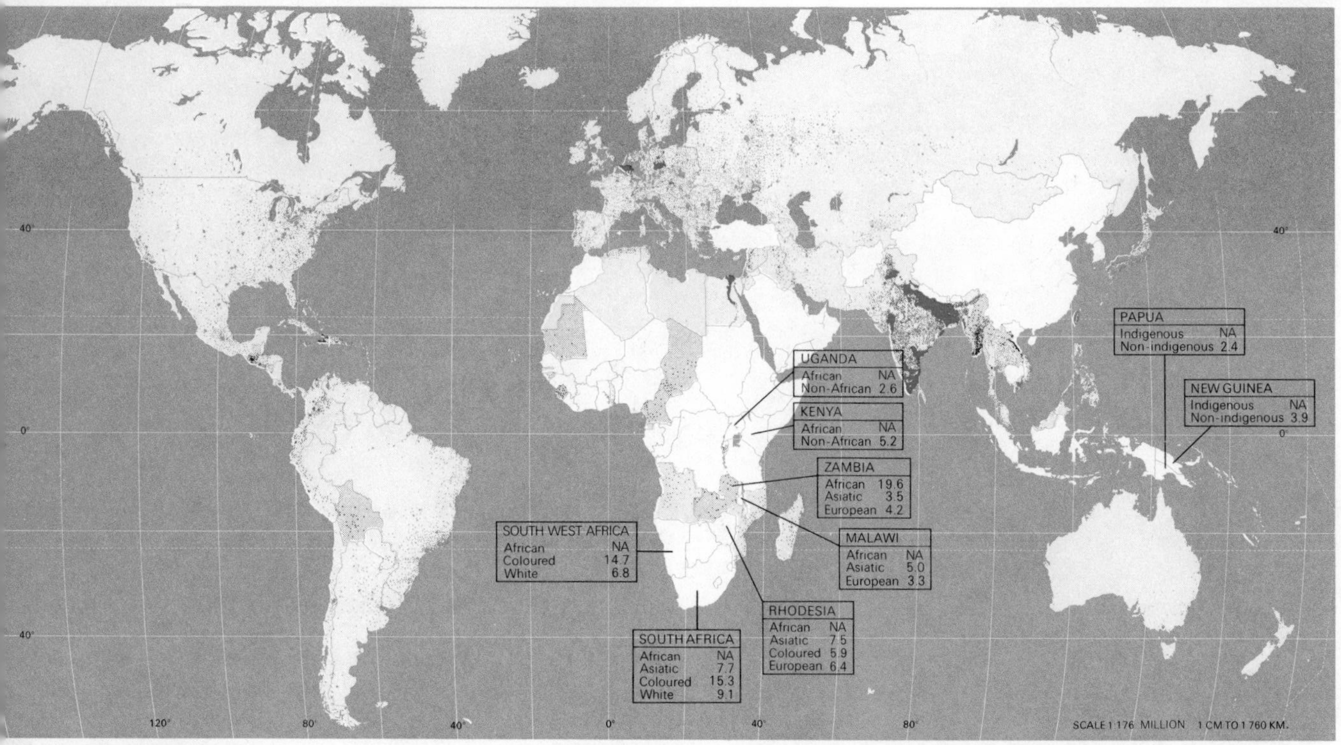
PAPUA
Indigenous NA
Non-indigenous 2.4
NEW GUINEA
Indigenous NA
Non-indigenous 3.9
UGANDA
African NA
Non-African 2.6
KENYA
African NA
Non-African 5.2
ZAMBIA
African 19.6
Asiatic 3.5
European 4.2
MALAWI
African NA
Asiatic 5.0
European 3.3
SOUTH WEST AFRICA
African NA
Coloured 14.7
White 6.8
RHODESIA
African NA
Asiatic 7.5
Coloured 5.9
European 6.4
SOUTH AFRICA
African NA
Asiatic 7.7
Coloured 15.3
White 9.1
SCALE 1:176 MILLION 1 CM TO 1 760 KM.

Crude death rate

Rate per thousand population (1963-5 av.)

- 18 & OVER
- 12 – 18
- 6 – 12
- UNDER 6
- DATA NA

One dot to 100 000 population

There are many difficulties in obtaining accurate mortality statistics. A major problem is the variation among countries in the basis of tabulation, that is, by date of occurrence or by date of registration. If registration is prompt the difference is slight, but if registration is delayed internationally comparable data will not be produced, especially since the number of events registered may vary due to temporary incentives to encourage registration. There is also a real danger of excluding the deaths of infants who died before registration of their births. Large areas of Latin America, North Africa, the Middle East and Asia are particularly suspect.

Although death rates are still high in many developing nations, great advances are being made with the introduction of advanced medical methods such as in the campaign to fight malaria in Ceylon which started in 1946. The rapidly falling death rates, which are linked with medical technology and socio-political organization, are not matched by equally declining birth rates, which are more responsive to cultural conditions.

Ceylon Death rates

1921-25	27.8
1940-44	19.7
1946	19.8
1948	12.9
1955	10.8
1965	8.1

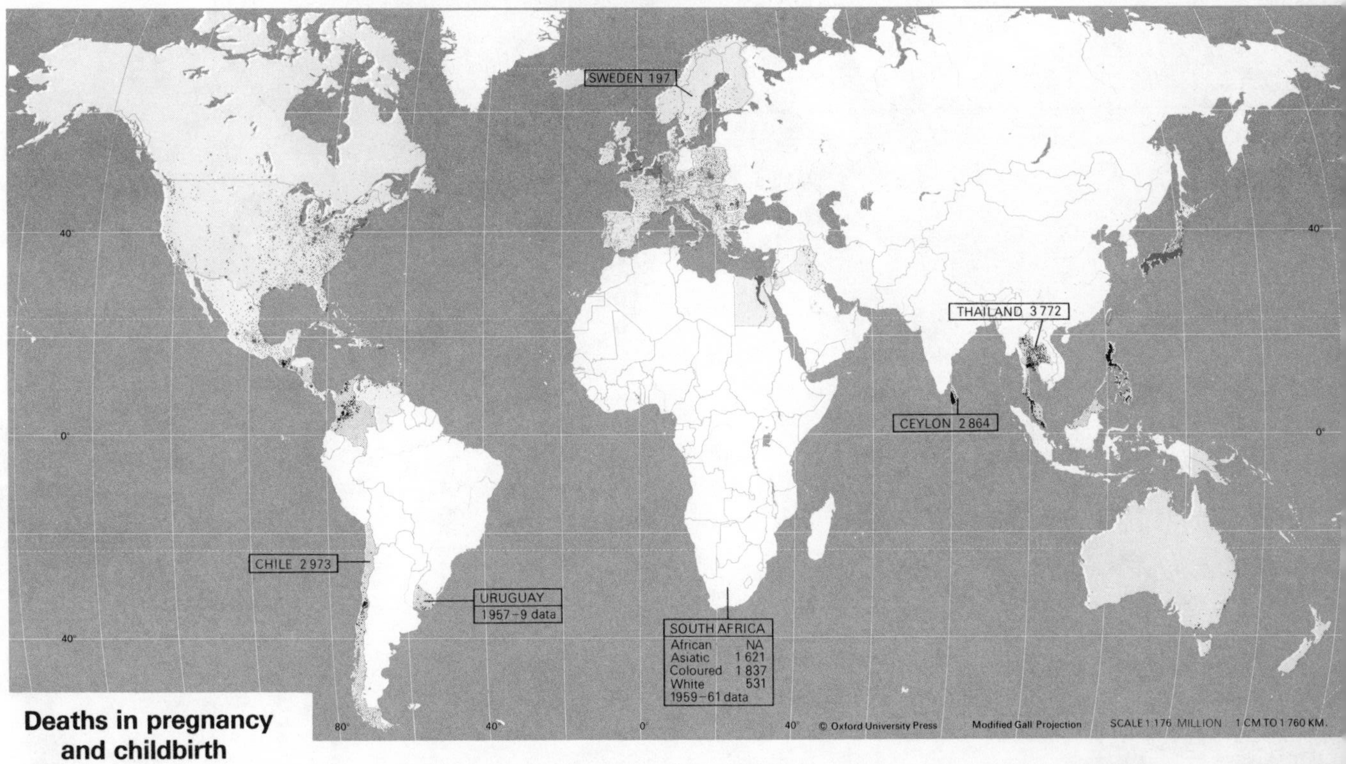
SWEDEN 197
THAILAND 3 772
CEYLON 2 864
CHILE 2 973
URUGUAY
1957-9 data
SOUTH AFRICA
African NA
Asiatic 1 621
Coloured 1 837
White 531
1959-61 data
Modified Gall Projection
SCALE 1:176 MILLION 1 CM TO 1 760 KM.

Deaths in pregnancy and childbirth

Number of deaths of women in pregnancy and childbirth per million babies born alive (1962–4)

- 2 000 & OVER
- 1000 – 2 000
- 500 – 1000
- UNDER 500
- DATA NA

One dot to 100 000 population

Like all mortality rates, the number of deaths caused by complications of pregnancy and childbirth are falling. Several factors responsible for this reduction are commonly affecting all forms of mortality. There is the general spread of health facilities which now reach an ever-growing proportion of the population. Public measures are being taken to produce general improvements in the environment, such as water purification schemes, better sewage disposal, vaccinations, and the use of chemicals in large-scale drives against certain diseases. Also, public awareness of health hazards has increased, and individuals are making correspondingly greater efforts to protect themselves. All this has been made possible by an increase in the real income per capita, enabling people to live at higher socio-economic levels: better food and housing making for stronger resistance to disease. However, deaths in maternity are still high in certain developing areas since the introduction of more advanced medical science is hampered by traditional customs and taboos often harmful to the mother and child, which are linked with fertility, marriage and childbirth.

Population V

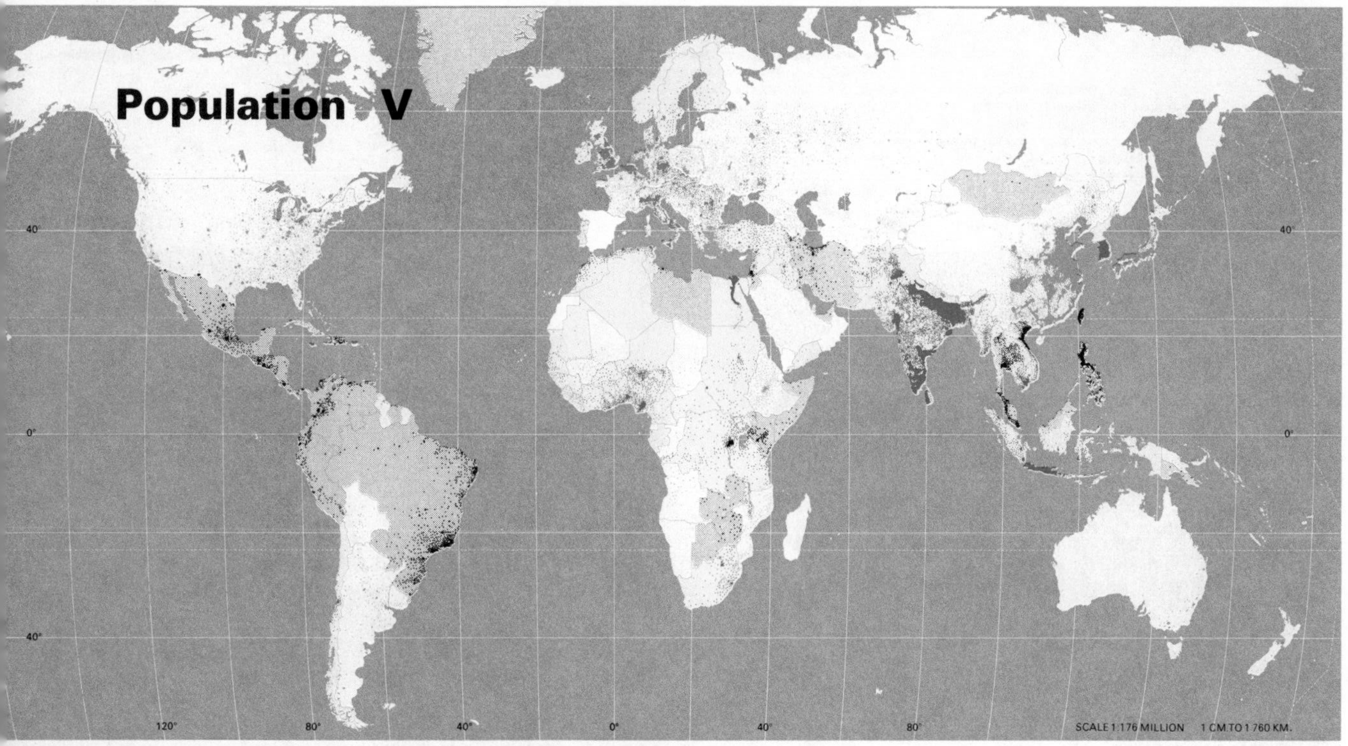

SCALE 1:176 MILLION 1 CM.TO 1 760 KM.

Population growth rates

Percentage annual growth (1963-7 av.)

3 & OVER | 1 – 2
2 – 3 | UNDER 1
DATA N.A.

One dot to 100 000 population

Growth per year	*Population doubles in*
3%	23½ yrs
2%	35 yrs
1%	70 yrs

Data for much of Asia, Africa, Latin America and Oceania are of dubious reliability.

For some years now economists and others have been disturbed by the rate of population growth. Prior to the nineteenth century this growth was almost undetectable, and surpluses from Western Europe could be absorbed by 'New Lands', a movement which started as early as the sixteenth century. Now the pressures are much greater. In many countries a high rate of growth is combined with a low income especially in parts of Africa, Asia and Latin America. New methods of agriculture can help where finance, land and initiative are available; however in many countries changes in the social framework must take place if such methods are to flourish. Much has been achieved by these new methods already in the attempt to increase world food supplies. The spread of modern birth control entails many social adjustments but is certainly one of the most important means now widely available of arriving at a balance between population and food supply. These maps serve to indicate in a small way the need for, and progress of, family planning throughout the world in 1968.

SCALE 1:176 MILLION 1 CM.TO 1 760 KM.

Development of family planning

As indicated by the level of national and international co-operation in 1968

Countries which have:

- Government: effective programme
- Government: commitment only
- Some degree of anti-contraceptive legislation
- Membership of I. P. P. F.[1]
- Family planning association[2]
- Data not available

[1]International Planned Parenthood Federation [2]Not shown if already a member of I. P. P. F.

An effective government family planning programme may be assumed to reach 10% or more of eligible women: this category excludes countries with high contraceptive practice but without a government policy.
Government commitment to provide family planning services may be *either* as a health measure or as a means of slowing population growth. In Europe it means that legislation has been passed to encourage the use of contraception; for example, Danish doctors must give advice after child birth or abortion.
It should be noted that the anti-contraceptive legislation may be by-passed in some countries, such as Canada and the Netherlands. However it is still significant as it affects *government* involvement in family planning.

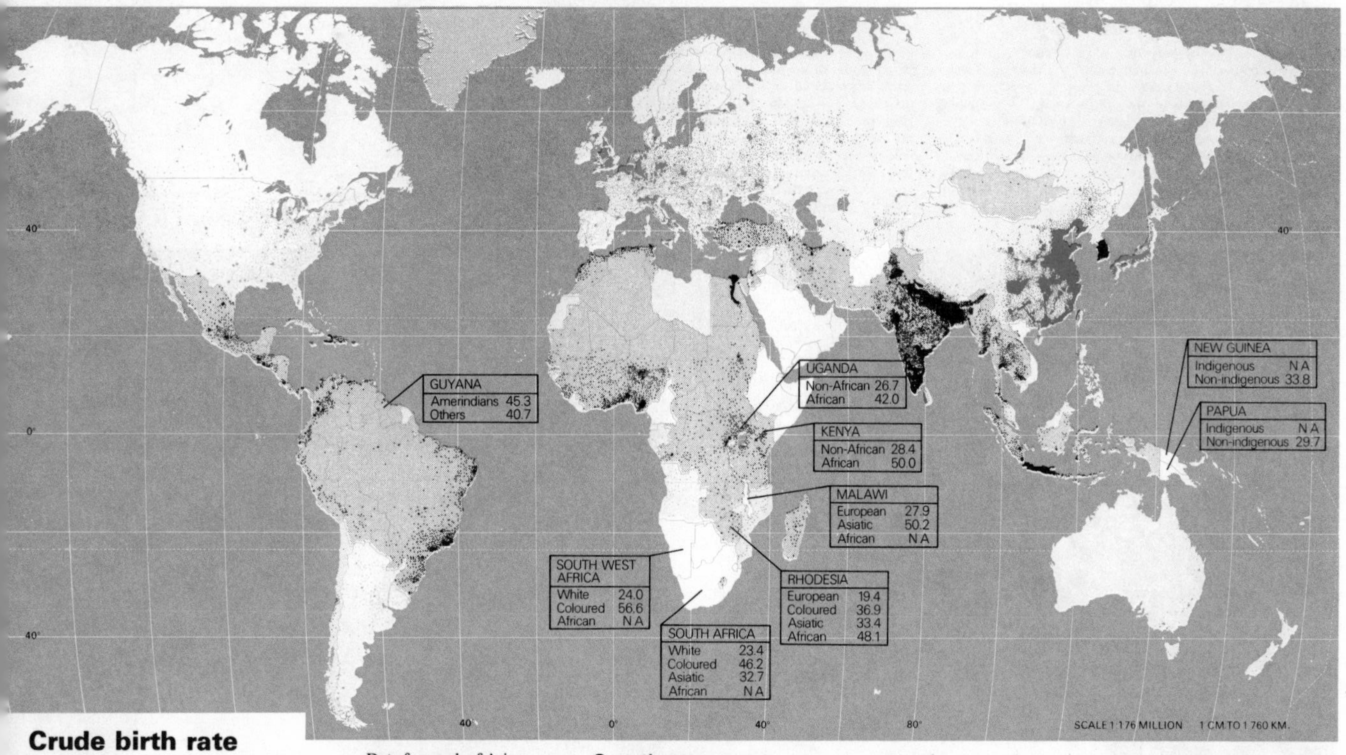

GUYANA
Amerindians 45.3
Others 40.7
UGANDA
Non-African 26.7
African 42.0
KENYA
Non-African 28.4
African 50.0
MALAWI
European 27.9
Asiatic 50.2
African N.A.
SOUTH WEST AFRICA
White 24.0
Coloured 56.6
African N.A.
RHODESIA
European 19.4
Coloured 36.9
Asiatic 33.4
African 48.1
SOUTH AFRICA
White 23.4
Coloured 46.2
Asiatic 32.7
African N.A.
NEW GUINEA
Indigenous N.A.
Non-indigenous 33.8
PAPUA
Indigenous N.A.
Non-indigenous 29.7
SCALE 1:176 MILLION 1 CM.TO 1 760 KM.

Crude birth rate

Annual rate per '000 (1963-5 av. or latest available data pre-1963)

40 & OVER | 20 – 30
30 – 40 | 5 – 20
DATA N.A.

One dot to 100 000 population

Data for much of Asia, Africa, Latin America and Oceania are of dubious reliability. Comparison between *any* countries should be treated with care. The extent and type of survey, variation in basis and year of data will all affect the rate.

Growth rates		AFRICA	ASIA	EUROPE	N. AMERICA	LAT. AMERICA	OCEANIA	U.S.S.R.	WORLD
Population (millions)	1950	*222*	*1 381*	*392*	*166*	*163*	*13*	*180*	*2 517*
Population (millions)	1960	318	1 868	449	217	253	18	233	3 356
Av. annual birth rate (‰)	1960-66	46	38	18	22	41	26	22	34
Av. annual death rate (‰)	1960-66	23	18	10	9	13	11	7	16
Av. rate of population increase (%)	1960-66	2.3	2.3	0.9	1.5	2.8	2.1	1.4	1.9

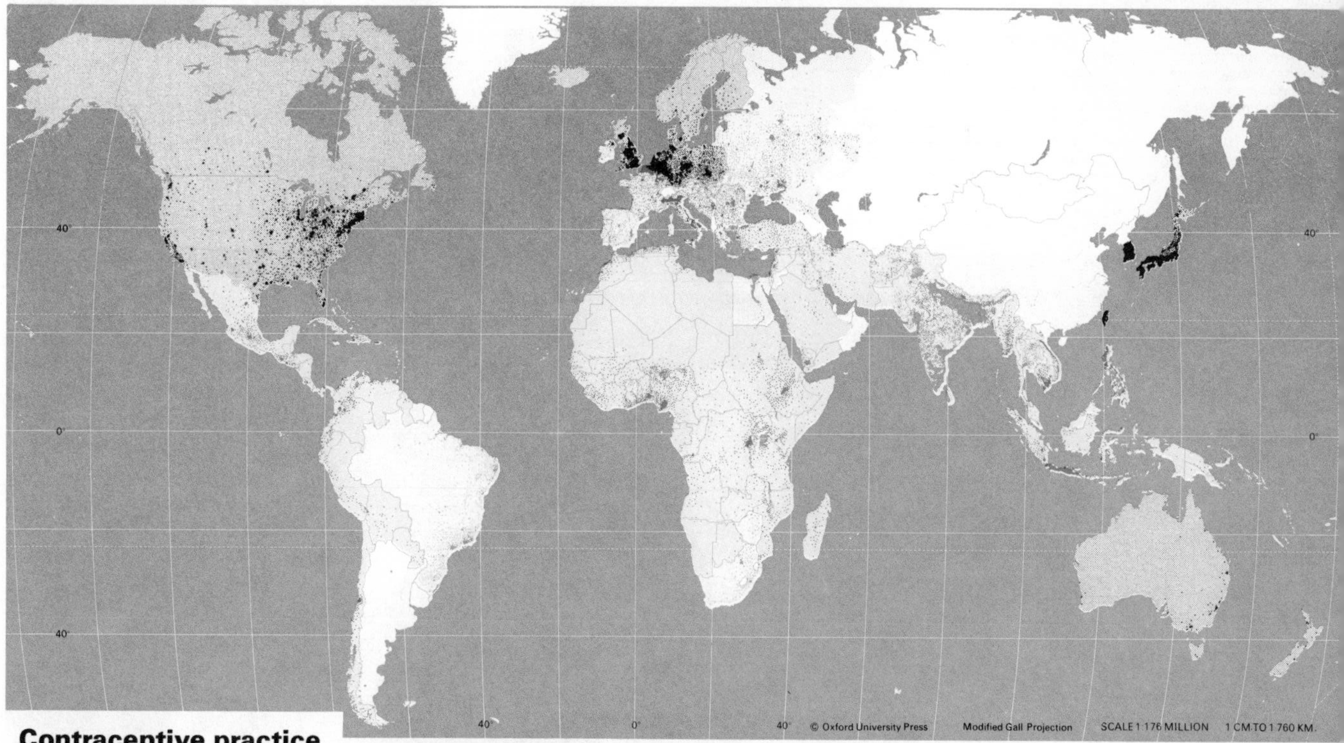

© Oxford University Press Modified Gall Projection SCALE 1:176 MILLION 1 CM.TO 1 760 KM.

Contraceptive practice

Percentage of eligible females using effective contraceptive measures in 1968

30 & OVER | 5 – 10
10 – 30 | 0 – 5
DATA N.A.

One dot to 100 000 population

Effective contraceptive measures are *here*[1] defined as:—

a Barrier methods
b Intra-uterine devices
c Oral method—'the pill'
d Rhythm method—if teaching supplied
e Sterilization

Eligible females are defined as those aged 15-45 years.

[1]Coitus interruptus and abortion may be as effective a control in many cases.

African statistics are fairly reliable; it is known that contraceptive practice is very low. Latin America is mainly Roman Catholic, hence figures are virtually non-existent. The estimates shown are based on manufacturers' figures, social surveys, etc. Data for the Caribbean and North America are most reliable. Estimates for Asia are quite well supported, notable exceptions being former Indo-China and the Middle East. China P.R., Mongolia, N. Vietnam and N. Korea are omitted as, although there is no evidence, contraceptive practice may be quite high, especially in China P.R. and N. Vietnam. Oceania and Europe are considered to be reasonable estimates. The map does not show the wide variations in urban and rural areas.

Migrations

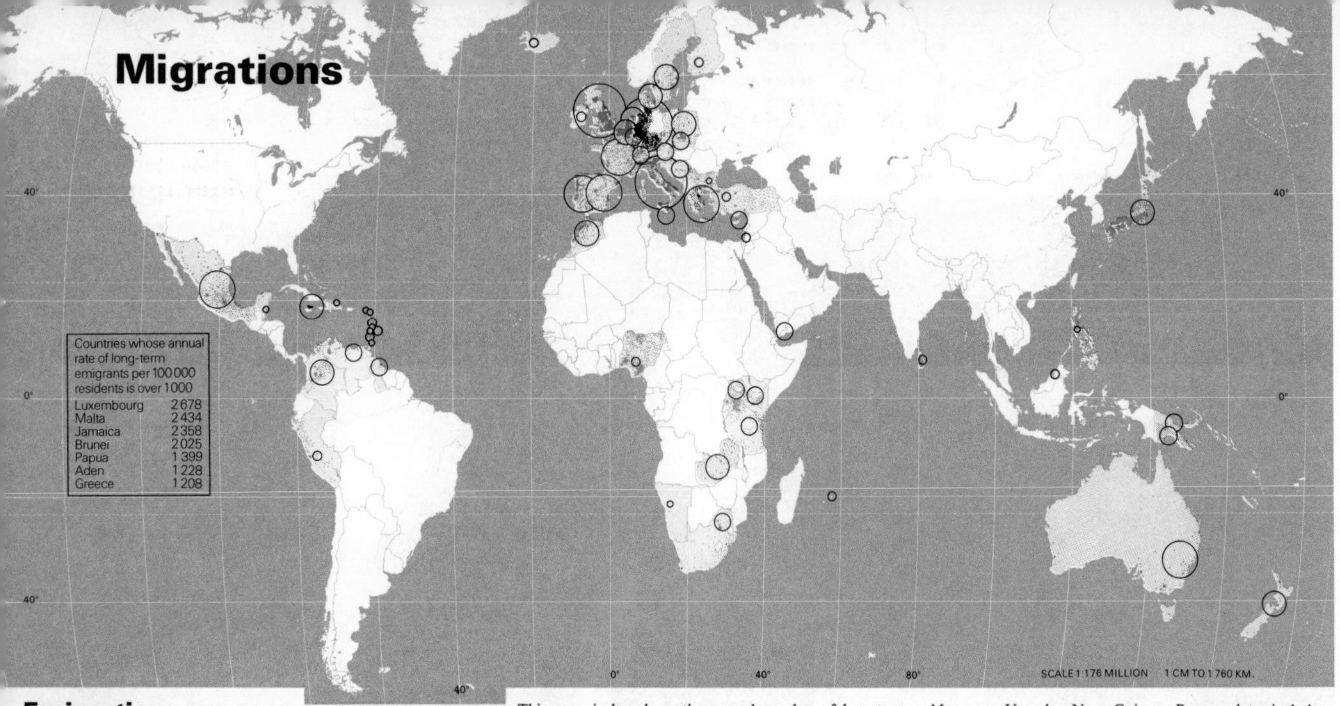
Countries whose annual rate of long-term emigrants per 100 000 residents is over 1 000
Luxembourg 2 678
Malta 2 434
Jamaica 2 358
Brunei 2 025
Papua 1 399
Aden 1 228
Greece 1 208
SCALE 1:176 MILLION 1 CM TO 1 760 KM.

Emigration (1963-5 av.)

Annual rate of long-term emigrants per 100 000 residents

OVER 750 | 101 – 750 | 26 – 100 | 0 – 25 | DATA N A

One dot to 100 000 population

Annual number of long-term emigrants

OVER 250 000 | 50 001 – 250 000 | 10 001 – 50 000 | 2 501 – 10 000 | 501 – 2 500 | 1 – 500

This map is based on the annual number of long-term emigrants from each country, that is, the number of residents leaving a country for a period longer than one year. The value of the data for both emigration and immigration is restricted by a number of factors. International comparability is limited since even when frontier checks are numerically accurate, the definitions and categories used in such checks vary widely. These records are based on the stated intentions of travellers, who may change their plans. Also clandestine movements, known to occur across certain frontiers, escape statistical recording.

Morocco, Uganda, New Guinea, Papua—data include short-term immigrants leaving.
Jamaica—data exclude movements to other parts of the West Indies.
Germany F.R.—data exclude movements to Germany D.R.
U.K.—data for intercontinental migrants using ships sailing between the U.K. and places outside Europe.
Scandinavia—data exclude all movements between the five countries of the Nordic passport zone.
Israel—data for declaring long-term emigrants only; other long-term emigrants were estimated to be about 6 000 in 1965.

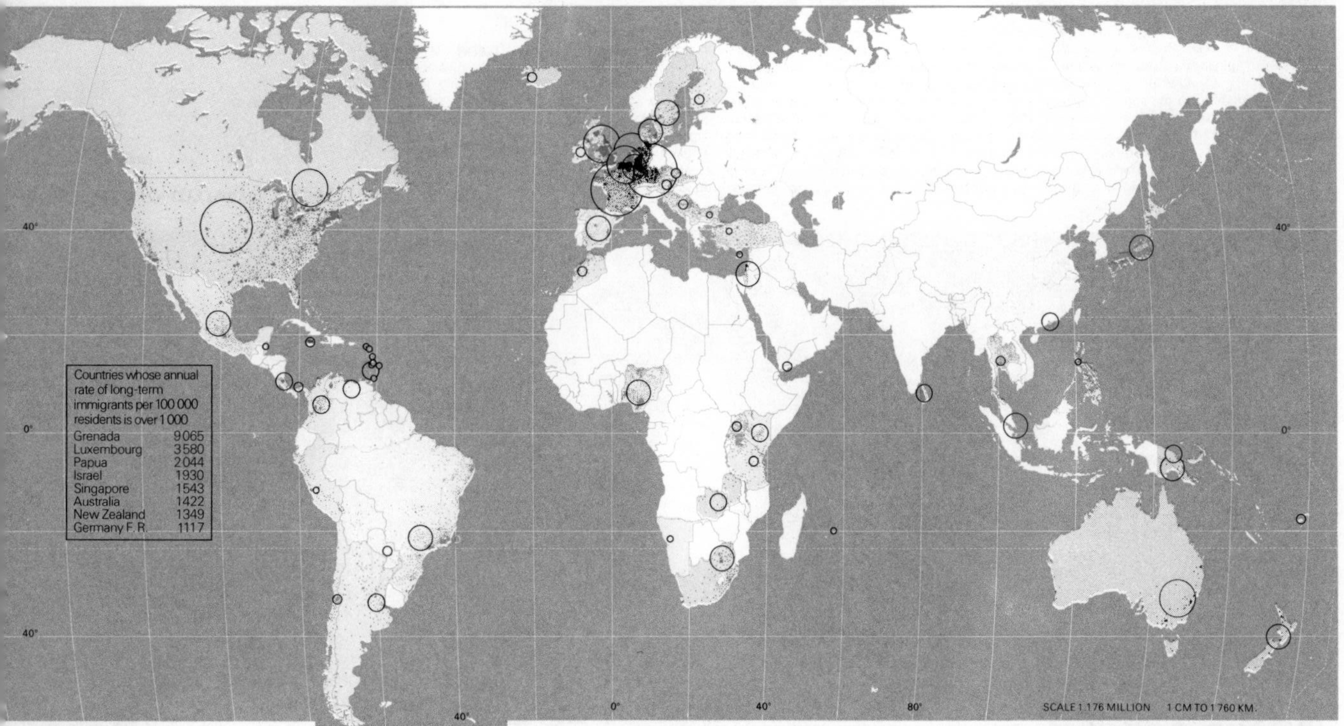
Countries whose annual rate of long-term immigrants per 100 000 residents is over 1 000
Grenada 9065
Luxembourg 3580
Papua 2044
Israel 1930
Singapore 1543
Australia 1422
New Zealand 1349
Germany F.R. 1117
SCALE 1:176 MILLION 1 CM TO 1 760 KM.

Immigration (1963-5 av.)

Annual rate of long-term immigrants per 100 000 residents

OVER 750 | 101 – 750 | 26 – 100 | 0 – 25 | DATA N A

One dot to 100 000 population

Annual number of long-term immigrants

OVER 250 000 | 50 001 – 250 000 | 10 001 – 50 000 | 2 501 – 10 000 | 501 – 2 500 | 1 – 500

This map is based on the annual number of long-term immigrants to each country, that is, the number of non-residents (nationals and aliens) intending to remain for longer than one year.
Barbados, Ceylon, Fiji Is., Grenada, Jamaica, Kenya, Luxembourg, Morocco, Singapore, South Africa, South West Africa, Tanzania, Uganda, Zambia—data include short-term immigrants, that is, non-residents intending to exercise, for a period of one year or less, an occupation remunerated from within the country.
France—over 50% of immigrants are Algerian workers.

Germany F.R.—movements from Germany D.R. excluded.
Scandinavia—data exclude all movements between the five countries of the Nordic passport zone.
Spain—data for intercontinental movements only.
U.K.—data for intercontinental movements using ships sailing between the U.K. and places outside Europe.
U.S.A.—data represent aliens admitted for the first time for permanent residence and alien residents returning after one year or more abroad.

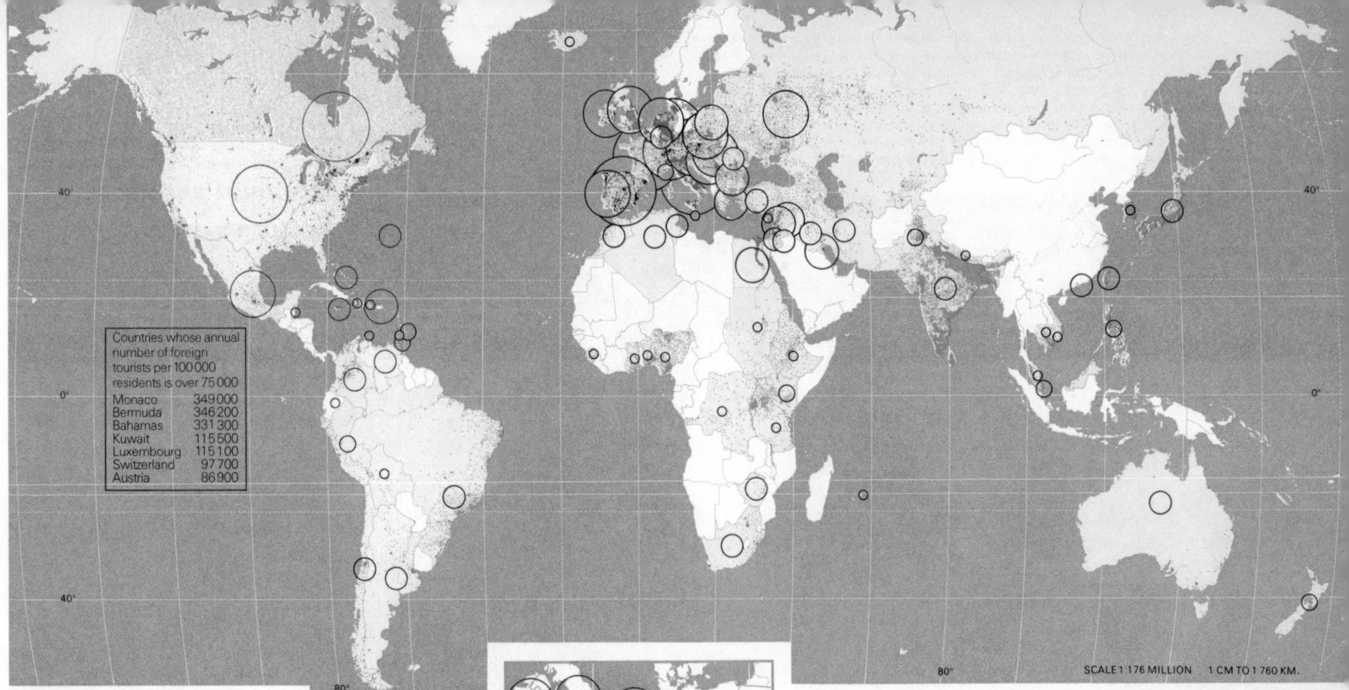
Countries whose annual number of foreign tourists per 100 000 residents is over 75 000
Monaco 349 000
Bermuda 346 200
Bahamas 331 300
Kuwait 115 500
Luxembourg 115 100
Switzerland 97 700
Austria 86 900
SCALE 1:176 MILLION 1 CM TO 1 760 KM.

Tourists (1964-5 av.)

Annual number of foreign tourists per 100 000 residents

OVER 30 000 | 10 001 – 30 000 | 1 001 – 10 000 | 0 – 1 000 | DATA N A

One dot to 100 000 population

Annual number of tourist arrivals (in millions)

OVER 10 | 5 – 10 | 1 – 5 | 0.5 – 1 | 0.1 – 0.5 | 0.05 – 0.1 | 0.05 & UNDER

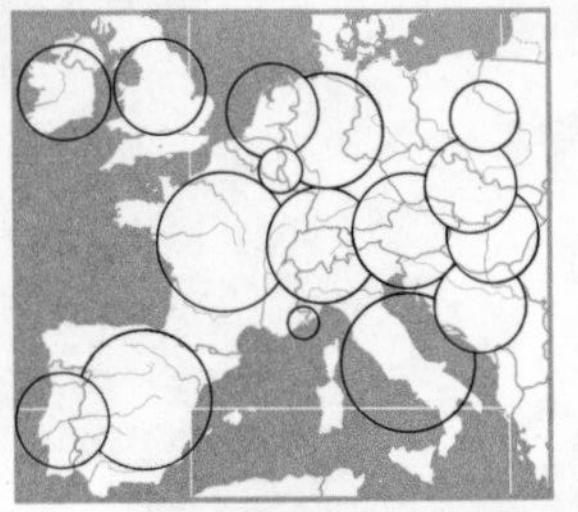

These maps are based on data from the International Travel Statistics published by the International Union of Official Travel Organisations (I.U.O.T.O.). Most of the countries which provided data used the I.U.O.T.O. definition of a tourist—'a temporary visitor staying at least 24 hours in the country visited and the purpose of whose journey can be classified under one of the following headings:

a) leisure (recreation, holiday, health, study, religion, sport)
b) business, family, mission, meeting.'

The rapid growth in the number of tourists in recent years is a result of higher socio-economic levels; in particular an annual leave of absence and a wage level high enough to permit a holiday. Thus most tourists come from Western Europe and North America, and since intercontinental holidays are, as yet, rare, these are also the main centres of the tourist industry.

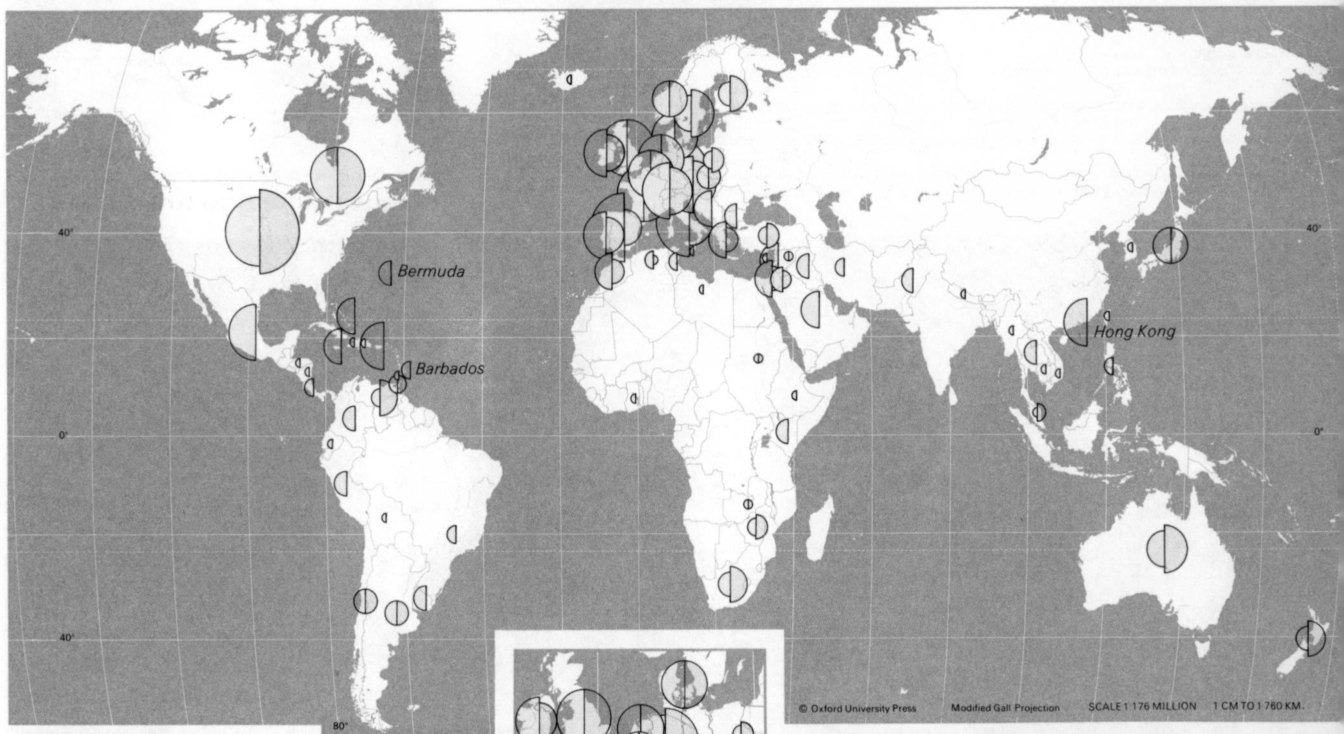
Bermuda
Barbados
Hong Kong
© Oxford University Press Modified Gall Projection SCALE 1:176 MILLION 1 CM TO 1 760 KM.

Tourism (1964-5 av.)

Receipts from foreign tourists and expenditures by residents abroad in million $ U.S.

RECEIPTS | EXPENDITURES

OVER 2 000 | 1 001 – 2 000 | 501 – 1 000 | 101 – 500 | 51 – 100 | 21 – 50 | 11 – 20 | 0 – 10

Where one or both semicircles are missing, the relevant data are not available

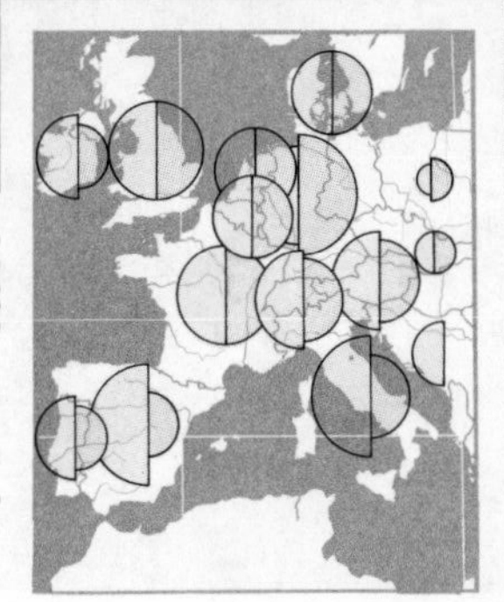

Tourism, besides being of sociological interest, is also of growing economic importance. Nationally, the major factor is the difference between expenditure and receipts. In some countries there is a substantial gain of foreign capital (Spain and Italy annually gain almost $1 000 million each) while in others, the loss of capital through tourism is a major concern as in the U.S.A. and Germany F.R. which each year lose $1 200 and $700 million respectively.
Tourism may affect the development of particular regions, for it provides the capital and also the incentive for development, in order to attract more tourists. Not only is better accommodation provided, but also new communication systems and other physical and social amenities, such as more advanced water supplies, helping to alter the nature of the region's economy.

Fatal Accidents

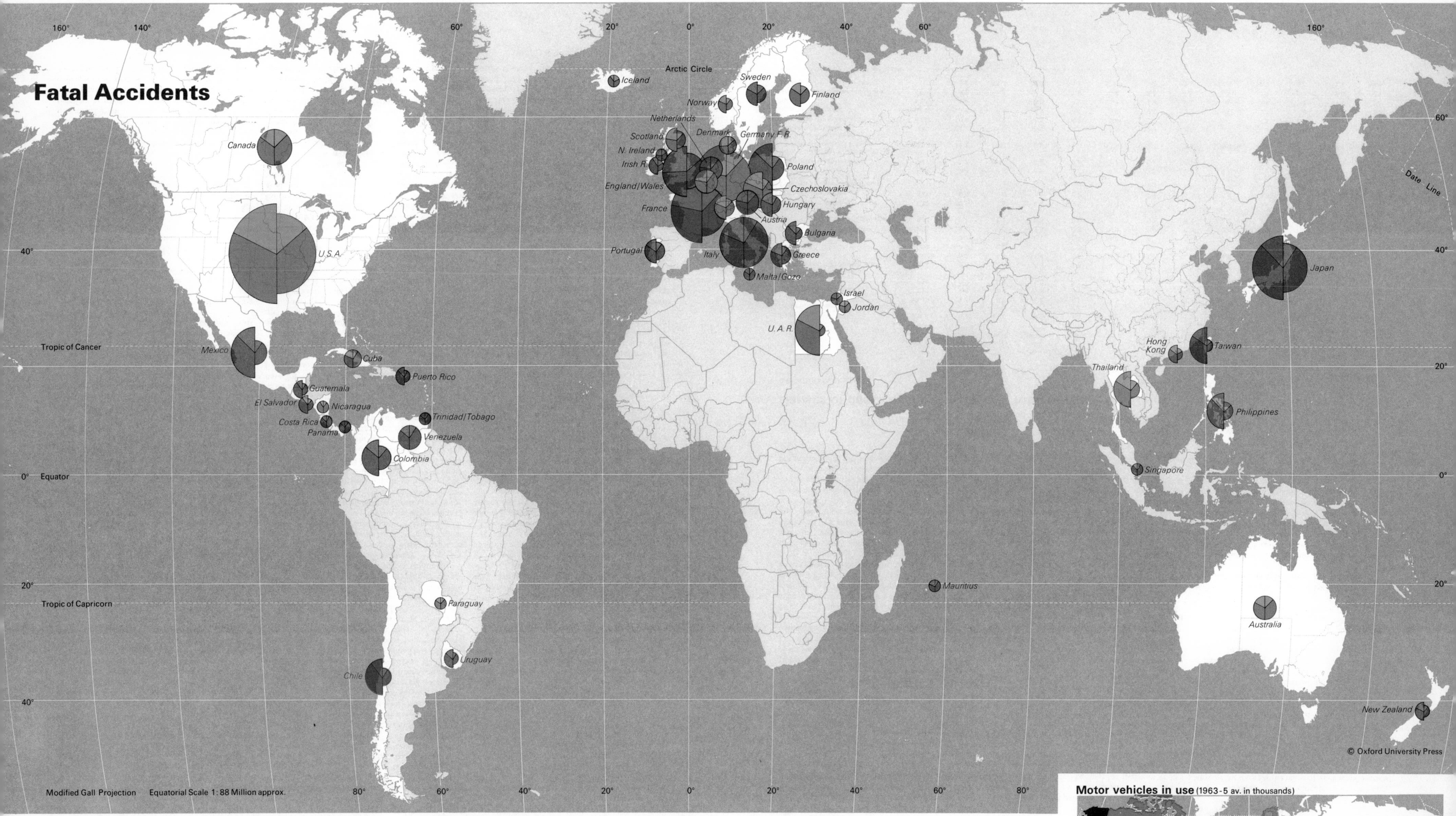

Arctic Circle
Tropic of Cancer
Equator
Tropic of Capricorn
Date Line
Iceland
Sweden
Finland
Norway
Netherlands
Denmark
Germany F.R.
Scotland
N. Ireland
Irish R.
Poland
England/Wales
Czechoslovakia
Hungary
France
Austria
Bulgaria
Portugal
Italy
Greece
Malta/Gozo
Israel
Jordan
U.A.R.
Canada
U.S.A.
Mexico
Cuba
Puerto Rico
Guatemala
El Salvador
Nicaragua
Costa Rica
Panama
Trinidad/Tobago
Venezuela
Colombia
Paraguay
Uruguay
Chile
Japan
Hong Kong
Taiwan
Thailand
Philippines
Singapore
Mauritius
Australia
New Zealand
© Oxford University Press
Modified Gall Projection Equatorial Scale 1: 88 Million approx.

Fatal accidents (1963-4 av. for age group 15-64)

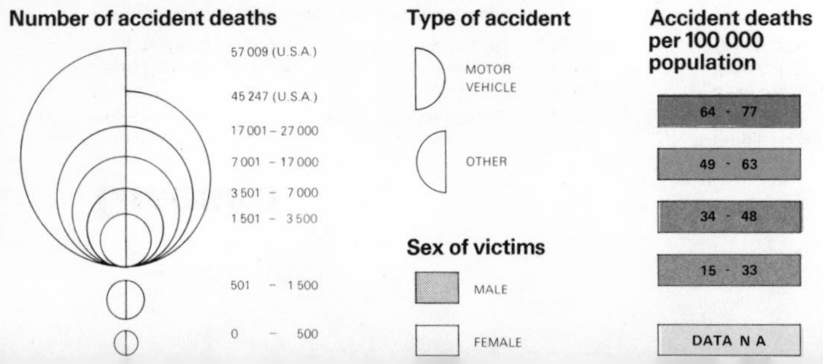

Number of accident deaths
57 009 (U.S.A.)
45 247 (U.S.A.)
17 001 – 27 000
7 001 – 17 000
3 501 – 7 000
1 501 – 3 500
501 – 1 500
0 – 500
Type of accident
MOTOR VEHICLE
OTHER
Sex of victims
MALE
FEMALE
Accident deaths per 100 000 population
64 - 77
49 - 63
34 - 48
15 - 33
DATA N A

The annual toll of accidents throughout the world, whether in industry, the home, on the roads, or any other area of human activity, is constantly rising. The cost in human life, misery and money is enormous, and in spite of the most prolonged efforts to counteract the trend, there seems to be no really effective way of preventing this lamentable waste. Education, training and legislation help, but the effects are difficult to measure and many think that a high proportion of accidents arise from human inadequacies which cannot entirely be covered by these approaches. Obviously, where hazards exist there will always be a proportion of casualties; it is also generally accepted that the majority of accidents are preventable, so the waste in human life and the suffering caused by unnecessary risk-taking are made all the more pronounced.

In the United States the cost of all accidents in 1969 was estimated at $25 000 million. In that year the number of working days lost through injuries at work in the United States was 245 million. In Great Britain in an average year 22 million working days are lost through industrial injuries compared with 5 million for industrial disputes. The most effective controls can perhaps be operated in industry where statutory legislation in the factory ensures a certain basic protection. But carelessness, neglect and lack of proper instruction and supervision still lead to a high proportion of industrial accidents.

Accidents in the home in Great Britain account for 7 500 deaths a year, with a further 120 000 casualties being admitted to hospital. Another 1.5 million attend casualty outpatient departments. In an average year in Great Britain fatal home accidents exceed those on the road, but in the United States the fatal home accident figure is about half the road fatality total. It is estimated in Britain that the cost of each personal-injury accident on the road is about £400. In spite of vehicle tests, tyre regulations, research into driver behaviour and constant propaganda, the casualty rate is rising.

Accidents of all kinds are the fourth leading cause of death (following heart disease, cancer and strokes) in the United States, Canada, Australia and the majority of European countries. Further, in the United States accidents of all kinds are the leading cause of death for the 1-37 age-group.

The international comparability of statistics on accidents is limited by the lack of published data and the variation in definition of the terms employed. For example, in some countries an accident is considered fatal if the victim dies many months after its occurrence; in other countries death must occur at the time of the accident or within a few hours. Also, many countries include in occupational accident statistics those injuries or deaths which occur in commuting to and from work. These differences in data collection do not alter the fact that accidents have important consequences in economic, as well as human, terms.

Motor vehicles in use (1963-5 av. in thousands)

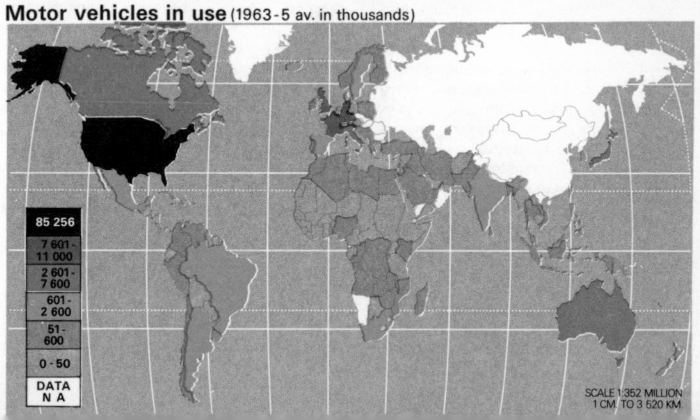

85 256
7 601 - 11 000
2 601 - 7 600
601 - 2 600
51 - 600
0 - 50
DATA N A
SCALE 1:352 MILLION 1 CM TO 3 520 KM

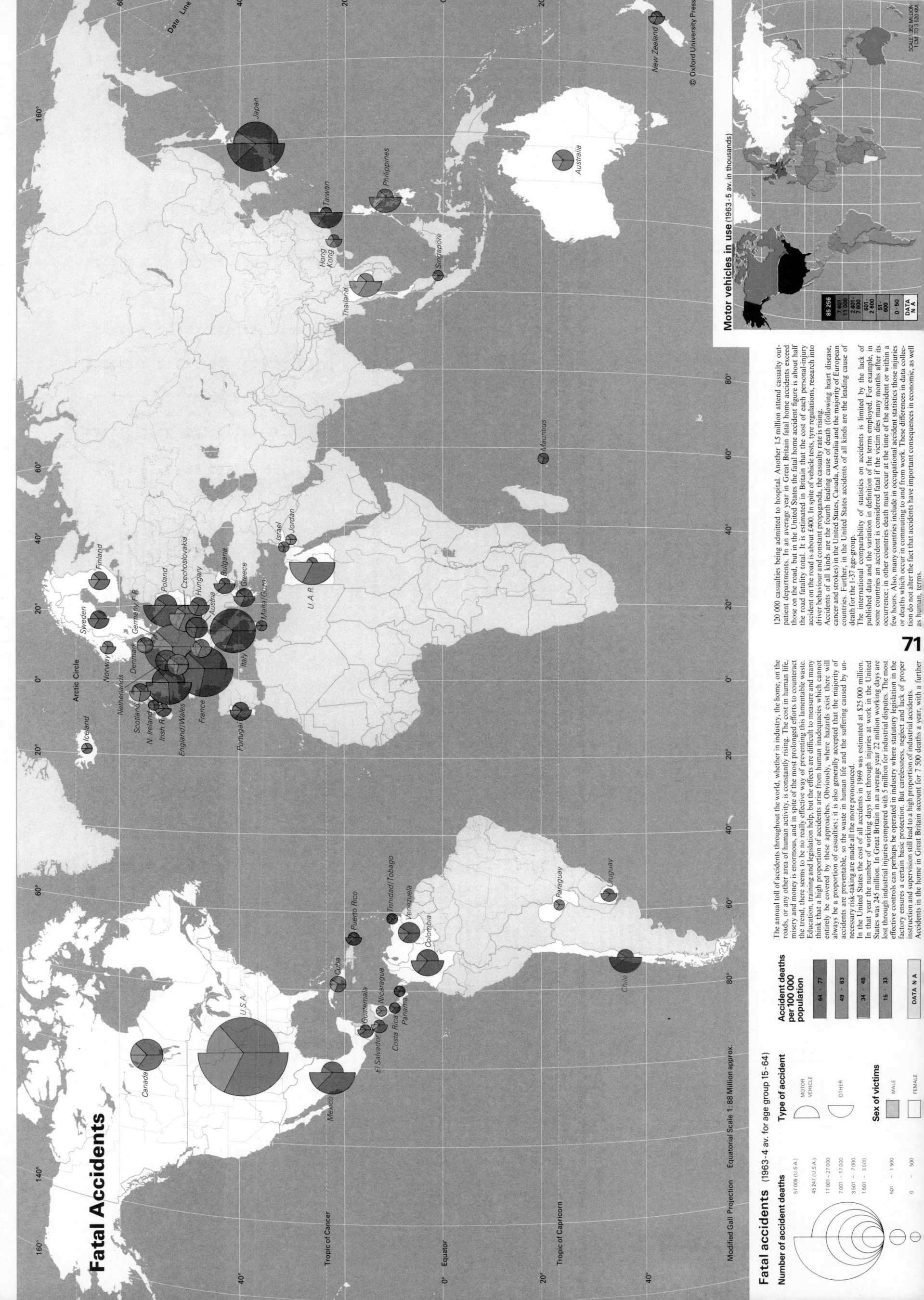

Disease

For individual country data see Statistical Supplement

The present world pattern of disease distribution broadly reflects economic conditions rather than aspects of the physical or biological environments. In developing countries infectious diseases are still rife, and malnutrition and intestinal parasites affect large sections of the population, sapping energy and stunting ability. These are mostly conditions of known origin (typhoid, cholera, smallpox, rabies, plague, malaria, tuberculosis and kwashiakor) which could be greatly reduced in frequency and almost eliminated as they have been elsewhere in the world, if only sufficient money could be devoted to raising the level of nutrition and sanitation and to implementing the necessary programmes of vaccination and control of insect vectors.

In the economically more prosperous countries, where the control of infections and malnutrition has largely been achieved, the major hazards are now the degenerative conditions such as cancer and heart disease which for the most part affect the older age groups but which even so reduce by twenty or thirty years the potential lives of the majority of those affected. Mental sickness has also become a major health problem and many deaths and disabilities are caused by accidents, especially accidents involving motor vehicles.

Within the broad economic framework the detailed distribution of individual diseases is determined by a complex of environmental and social factors. Climate and topography affect the distribution of the vectors which carry sleeping sickness, onchocerciasis and schistosomiasis and, as these require warm temperatures for their survival, the infectious diseases which they transmit add to the already heavy burden of disease in the developing world.

Iron and zinc deficiencies occur in areas of drier climate, for example parts of the U.A.R. or Iran, where lack of rainfall prevents the cultivation of an adequate range of foodstuffs and where there is an excessive loss of essential elements through heavy sweating. Geology is an important factor in the distribution of diseases such as goitre and cretinism which are due to iodine deficiency and which are common in limestone areas of recent mountain ranges such as the Swiss Alps. Geology may also play a part in the occurrence of coronary heart disease, which in several areas of the world shows a clear association with the hardness of the drinking water.

With other diseases the causative factors seem to lie more in the social and cultural environments. Both cigarette smoking which is a major cause of lung cancer, and air pollution which has a contributory effect, are features of a man-made environment. Deaths from liver cirrhosis are common in France as a result of high alcohol intake. Cancer of the mouth is far more common in India than in other parts of the world, apparently from the habit of chewing a quid of tobacco and lime wrapped in betel leaves.

The origin of most degenerative diseases is still unknown, but the marked geographical variation in frequency which many display suggests that, as with the examples given above, some environmental factor is involved in their development and that they could therefore be prevented. At present all that is possible against most degenerative disorders is curative or palliative treatment after the symptoms of disease have appeared. Enormous sums of money have been spent on such medical treatment in the developed world since the scientific advances of the past century and a half (vaccination and chemotherapy in medicine and anaesthetics and antiseptics in surgery) showed an ideal of physical well-being in which the discomfort of disease need not be accepted as a normal part of life. This is reflected in the fact that nations such as the U.K. or the U.S.A. spend almost 100 times as much per capita per annum maintaining their health as some developing countries. Paradoxically, epidemiological research is beginning to suggest that much of this expenditure perhaps need not have been incurred because it seems that many of the diseases of economic prosperity are themselves caused by the way of life that such prosperity permits or demands. Heart disease, appendicitis, varicose veins, diabetis, lung cancer and bowel cancer are all very common in Western society but are practically unknown in rural communities of Asia and Africa.

As the environmental or social conditions change so, too, does the characteristic pattern of disease. Very valuable epidemiological information can be gained by studying morbidity and mortality among the migrant communities of the world. Black Americans have a disease pattern which is far more similar to that of white Americans than to present day inhabitants of Africa, thus stressing the importance of environment rather than genetic constitution in the development of most diseases. However, recent migrants retain the disease pattern of their original community for a period of time after immigration, sometimes for as long as several generations if major cultural customs such as diet continue to be followed in the new environment. A good example of this are the Asian inhabitants of Africa who are of Indian origin and who show differences both from local Africans because they have continued their own cultural traditions in relatively closed communities, and from Indians in India because they have for the most part improved their standard of living after migration to Africa.

Obviously all disease places an economic burden on a community but in choosing the diseases to map for an economic atlas it was decided to concentrate mainly on those which attack the adult population and thus impose the particular economic burden of loss of efficiency and loss of working hours among a country's labour force. Some were chosen as typical of the developing world, — tuberculosis, sleeping sickness, malaria, cholera and leprosy. Others such as heart disease, bronchitis and cancer play a similar role in economically developed communities.

The choice of diseases mapped has also been determined partly by the availability of data. Conditions such as bilharzia and syphilis could not be considered for inclusion because no adequate statistics are available. The principal source of data has been the various reports of the World Health Organization supplemented by cancer registry material for the cancer maps. A more detailed source list can be found in the section of sources at the end of the atlas. The large areas on the maps indicating lack of data reflect the very uneven distribution of medical care in the world. In much of Asia and Africa there is less than one doctor to every 100 000 inhabitants, compared with over one per 1 000 in most of Western Europe and America, and under these circumstances the fact of death, let alone the cause, often goes unrecorded. The maps which show the distribution of doctors and the availability of hospital beds in the section on medical care can therefore also be used as an index of the reliability of data shown in the disease maps. A further indication is given by the proportion of all deaths ascribed to 'senility or unknown causes', which varies in the selected countries shown in the table below from 0.6% in Canada to 22.3% in the U.A.R.

Various indices have been used to measure disease frequency. The most informative is the *incidence* rate which is based on the number of new cases developing each year, but it is also possible to measure the total number of people affected at a given point in time (to give a *prevalence* rate) or the number of deaths caused by a disease (to give a *mortality* rate). The prevalence and mortality rates reflect not only the frequency of a disease but also its duration and the extent to which it can be treated and cured and so are artificially lowered in countries which have highly developed medical services. However they are generally easier to study than incidence since mortality statistics are routinely collected by many governments and since prevalence can be measured in a specially organized study on a single day instead of over a period of months or years.

Certain infectious diseases are notifiable by international agreement so that their spread can be controlled and it has therefore been possible to map incidence for cholera, sleeping sickness and malaria. It must be remembered though that in countries where these diseases are most frequent the medical services are very poorly staffed and that a case can be only notified if the disease has first come to the notice of a doctor. The incidence in the high frequency areas is therefore only a minimal estimate of the true frequency.

Research interest in the unsolved problems of cancer aetiology has led many countries to establish cancer registries which record each new case as it is diagnosed. It has therefore also been possible to base the cancer maps largely on incidence data. Where only mortality figures are available an adjustment has been made for each specific type of cancer to allow for the probable difference between the incidence and mortality rates from the average difference observed in countries for which both are available.

The bronchitis, tuberculosis and heart disease maps are based on mortality figures. For bronchitis the death rates indicate the pattern of regional variation but greatly underestimate the extent of the disease. In parts of NE. England, for example, a survey of the population indicated that one in six women is affected by chronic bronchitis. The number who actually die from the disease is very much lower. The condition generally lasts many years and it is estimated that about one-third of sufferers are incapacitated from their normal occupation for over one month every year.

For tuberculosis the mortality figures are affected by the availability of treatment in different countries. They fail to distinguish therefore between the situation in Denmark where very few cases occur and the situation in Britain where the frequency of air-borne infection is such that new cases still develop but where the disease is controlled by treatment and mortality is again very low.

The leprosy map is based on prevalence rates estimated from various W.H.O. investigations. The estimates are for the most part based on the number of registered patients with the addition of from 25% to 300% extra cases according to the degree of underreporting anticipated in each country.

In calculating disease rates it is necessary to take account not only of the number of persons affected but also of the size and structure of the population at risk. For a disease with such marked geographical variation as cholera a simple dot map of cases would give a fairly clear picture of the world distribution, but in order to distinguish more subtle variation it is necessary to relate the number of cases to the total population so that the disease map is not merely a pale reflection of population density.

The simplest allowance is to divide the total number of cases by the total population in which they occur. This gives a measure known as a *crude* disease rate. However many diseases show a sharp rise in frequency with age and where this occurs it is essential to make allowance also for the age structure of the population at risk. For example, many old people retire to the south coast of England and for this reason a town in that area, such as Bournemouth, appears to have a higher crude death rate than a town elsewhere in the country, such as Bradford. If the death rates at each age of life (age specific death rates) were compared, Bournemouth would appear the healthier town at all ages but the crude death rate is inflated by the elderly structure of the population at risk.

If the number of people in each age group is known in each area (and preferably also the local age specific disease rates) the statistical procedure of 'age standardization' can be applied to the frequency rates for specific diseases, and it then becomes possible to compare the disease experience of the 'young' countries of the developing world with that of Western Europe where the expectation of life is so much greater. Heart disease, bronchitis and many types of cancer all become increasingly frequent at older ages, and age standardized incidence and mortality rates have been mapped for these diseases. Only with 'age standardization' did it become apparent that cancer was not specifically a disease of economically developed countries but that it occured almost as frequently among the middle aged and elderly of Africa and Asia.

Data which are adequate for age standardization are not available for the other diseases mapped here, but this is of less importance because comparisons are largely being made within the areas where life expectation is still low.

Standards of diagnosis, especially on death certificates, tend to vary not only between countries but also between different sectors of the population in the same country. They are generally least good among the elderly where symptoms are ascribed simply to 'senility' without a more detailed investigation. The level of mis-diagnosis varies from country to country, and for this reason it is advisable to restrict comparisons of frequency to persons under the age of sixty-five.

The maps for heart disease, bronchitis and cancers of the lung, stomach and breast have been drawn for the age group 35-64 partly for this reason and partly because relatively few cases in adults occur under this lower age limit. The map for liver cancer has been drawn for the age group 15-44 because, although primary liver cancer continues to occur with increasing frequency in older people, tumours of other sites commonly metastasize to the liver and, at older ages, it is difficult to distinguish primary from secondary growths in the cancer statistics. However, liver cancer is also distinctive in occurring at younger ages than is common for the other tumours mapped here.

For malaria, cholera, tuberculosis and sleeping sickness, in keeping with the policy of mapping diseases which cause death and disability in people who are normally economically active, an attempt was made to calculate the frequency rates for the age span of the working population. However, the data were nowhere good enough to permit such refinement and crude rates had to be used instead.

Most of the data published by the World Health Organization are given at a national level, but incidence and mortality rates calculated on this basis can disguise wide regional differences within a country. Disease boundaries rarely coincide with national boundaries, and for a proper understanding of the different causative factors which may play a part in the development of any disease it is usually necessary to study the frequency in more limited sectors of the population and therefore in smaller areas, or in different occupational, social class or ethnic groups. The relative importance of the various suspected factors involved in the development of bronchitis (domestic and industrial air pollution, cigarette smoking, cold and humidity and industrial hazards such as dust from mining activities) have only been disentangled by detailed studies within national territories and not by broad comparisons between countries. However detailed information of this kind is routinely available only for a very few countries and most of the maps published here have had to be based on national figures.

Where figures for different ethnic groups are available they have been included. The importance of this kind of breakdown is clear from the example of tuberculosis in South Africa, where the death rate per million varies from 1436 for Coloureds (non-African) to 295 for Asians and 61 for Whites.

The World Health Organization, from whose reports most of the data for the maps of disease and medical care have been drawn, is one of the specialized agencies of the United Nations. It came into being in 1948 and through its organization the public health authorities and medical professions of more than 100 countries exchange knowledge and experience and collaborate in an effort to improve the level of health throughout the world.

The speed of modern travel has so shrunk distances that diseases can be carried thousands of miles within a few hours. Without an effective world system of epidemic control no community would be really safe and dramatic changes could occur in the world pattern of disease distribution. One of the major roles of W.H.O. is to broadcast daily epidemic bulletins from Geneva of the appearance in any new area of the world of the pestilential diseases, or of outbreaks of conditions such as influenza or polio, and to lay down and revise international regulations for quarantine, inoculations and vaccinations.

The purpose of drawing maps of disease, and the ultimate aim of research by organizations such as W.H.O. and the various national medical institutions, is to understand better the causes of each disease so that the distribution patterns which the maps show can be destroyed. The present series of maps indicate the situation at one point in time; the more quickly they become out of date because of diminishing frequencies the better for the health of mankind.

Causes of death as a percentage of total deaths (1966)

Selected countries

(figures in brackets indicate G.N.P. per capita in $ U.S.)

	W.H.O. I.C.D. NUMBER[1]	U.A.R. (160)	PHILIPPINES (160)	PORTUGAL (380)	MEXICO (470)	CHILE (510)	SINGAPORE (570)	JAPAN (860)	ISRAEL (1 160)	ENGLAND/WALES (1 620)[2]	FRANCE (1 730)	CANADA (2 240)	SWEDEN (2 270)
Tuberculosis	B1, B2	0.7	11.9	2.7	2.3	3.9	5.4	3.0	0.5	0.4	1.2	0.5	0.4
Other infective or parasitic diseases	B3-B17	1.2	6.2	1.2	6.1	3.3	1.1	0.9	0.8	0.4	0.6	0.4	0.3
Malignant neoplasms	B18	1.4	3.0	10.6	3.7	9.9	12.8	16.4	18.1	19.2	19.4	17.9	18.9
Diabetis mellitus	B20	0.3	0.3	0.8	1.0	0.6	0.9	0.9	0.7	0.8	1.6	1.7	1.7
Vascular lesions affecting the central nervous system	B22	0.6	2.0	15.8	2.3	5.6	7.2	25.7	12.6	14.0	12.1	10.4	11.7
Heart disease	B24-28	6.9	4.4	14.4	3.6	8.7	11.0	12.3	32.6	31.3	18.8	36.1	35.8
Influenza	B30	0.0	0.8	0.5	1.2	1.5	0.2	0.1	0.1	0.7	0.6	0.4	0.2
Pneumonia	B31	2.2	15.1	8.1	13.1	14.6	7.7	3.2	1.9	6.3	1.8	3.6	5.0
Bronchitis	B32	8.5	5.7	2.8	2.8	0.9	1.4	0.8	0.6	5.7	0.4	0.9	0.6
Ulcer of stomach and duodenum	B33	0.1	1.1	0.8	0.5	0.4	0.5	1.3	0.8	0.7	0.3	0.6	0.9
Gastritis, duodenitis, enteritis and colitis	B36	32.5	7.6	4.6	9.6	5.9	2.0	1.2	0.7	0.5	0.1	0.4	0.4
Cirrhosis of the liver	B37	0.0	0.5	3.1	2.0	3.2	1.0	1.5	0.8	0.3	3.3	0.9	0.7
Deliveries and complications of pregnancy, childbirth and the puerperium	B40	0.3	0.8	0.2	0.3	0.9	0.3	0.2	0.2	0.0	0.1	0.1	0.0
Congenital malformations	B41	0.1	0.7	0.6	0.8	1.2	1.5	0.7	1.9	0.8	0.7	1.5	0.7
Birth injuries and diseases of the newborn and early infancy	B42-44	11.1	8.6	4.6	12.3	13.9	7.7	2.1	4.3	1.5	1.6	3.4	1.2
Senility and ill-defined or unknown causes	B45	22.3	11.0	15.6	18.2	5.9	17.9	8.5	3.3	0.8	13.0	0.6	1.0
Motor vehicle accidents	BE47	0.0	0.2	1.5	0.7	1.5	2.5	2.7	1.7	1.3	2.3	3.6	1.8
All other accidents	BE48	2.8	2.9	2.7	4.1	5.8	2.8	3.7	3.1	2.1	4.3	4.0	2.8
Suicide	BE49	0.0	0.1	0.8	0.2	0.7	1.8	2.2	1.0	0.9	1.5	1.1	2.0
Homicide and operations of war	BE50	0.0	1.4	0.1	1.9	0.6	0.3	0.2	0.1	0.1	0.1	0.2	0.1
Others		9.0	15.7	8.5	13.3	11.0	14.0	12.4	14.2	12.2	16.2	11.7	13.8

[1]World Health Organization International Classification of Disease 7th edition Geneva 1955

[2]Average for U.K., including Northern Ireland and Scotland

Disease I

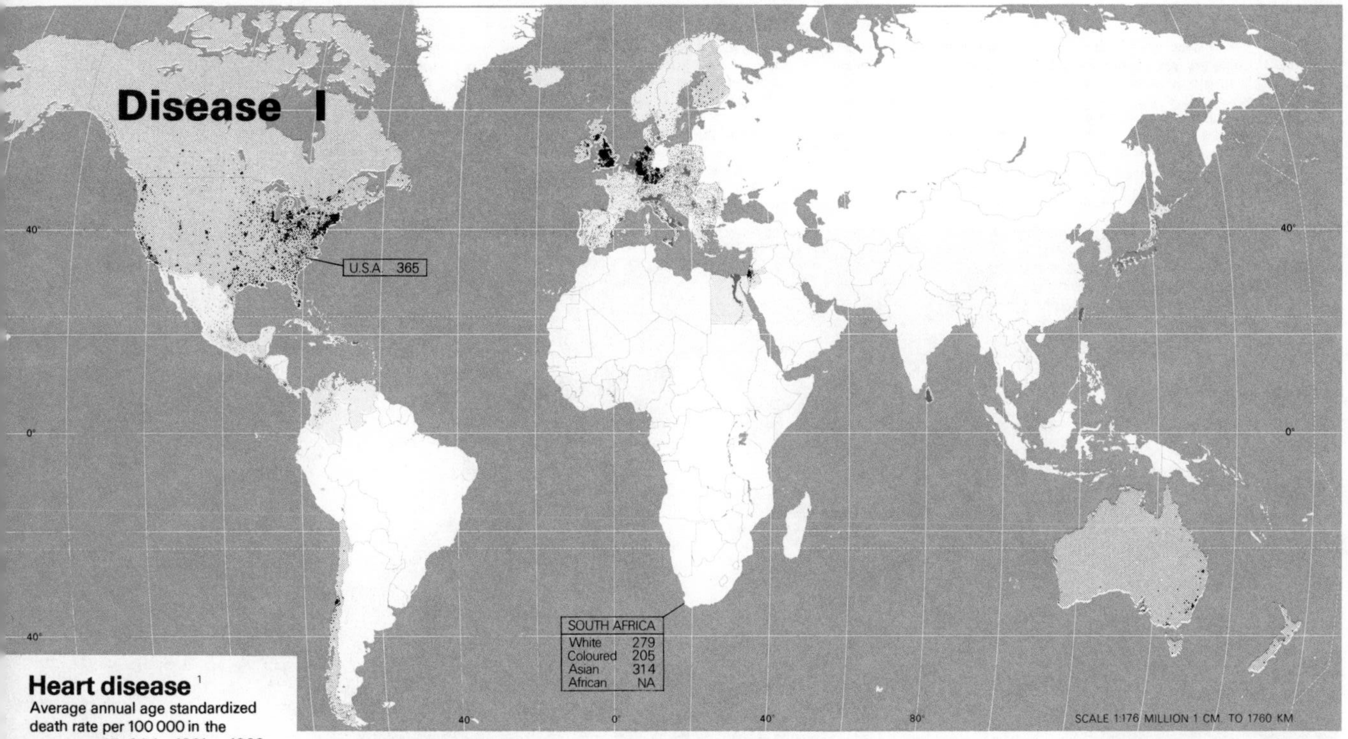
U.S.A. 365
SOUTH AFRICA
White 279
Coloured 205
Asian 314
African NA
SCALE 1:176 MILLION 1 CM. TO 1760 KM.

Heart disease[1]

Average annual age standardized death rate per 100 000 in the age group 35-64 for 1961 or 1962

140 & OVER
70 – 140
35 – 70
2 – 35
DATA NA

One dot to 100 000 population

[1] WORLD HEALTH ORGANIZATION (WHO) INTERNATIONAL CLASSIFICATION OF DISEASE NUMBER 420-422

Mortality from arteriosclerotic heart disease is highest in the economically more developed English-speaking communities with the white population of the U.S.A. at the forefront followed by the Asian, white and coloured populations of South Africa, and by Australia, Canada, New Zealand, the U.K. and Ireland. The only non-English-speaking country with an exceptionally high incidence is Finland. The rest of North and West Europe has rates a little lower than those in England and Wales, but the total variations between the U.S.A. and the lowest of these countries (Spain and Iceland) is only about threefold. (The mortality in France is apparently exceptionally low for Western Europe but it may be that this represents a national difference in diagnostic practice.)

In developing countries, though little statistical evidence is available, the total mortality from cardiovascular disease is known to be very small (even allowing for the much younger age structure of the population). This has led to the suggestion that the white race has a genetic pre-disposition to heart disease, but such a hypothesis is belied by the evidence from America and South Africa where negroes and Asians have a rate very much higher than is common in most of Africa or in India.

A diet rich in sugar, fats or refined carbohydrates, the psychological stresses of modern urban society and lack of exercise have all been suggested as possible causes of heart disease. Any or all of these may be in some way involved, but at present the specific cause is unknown.

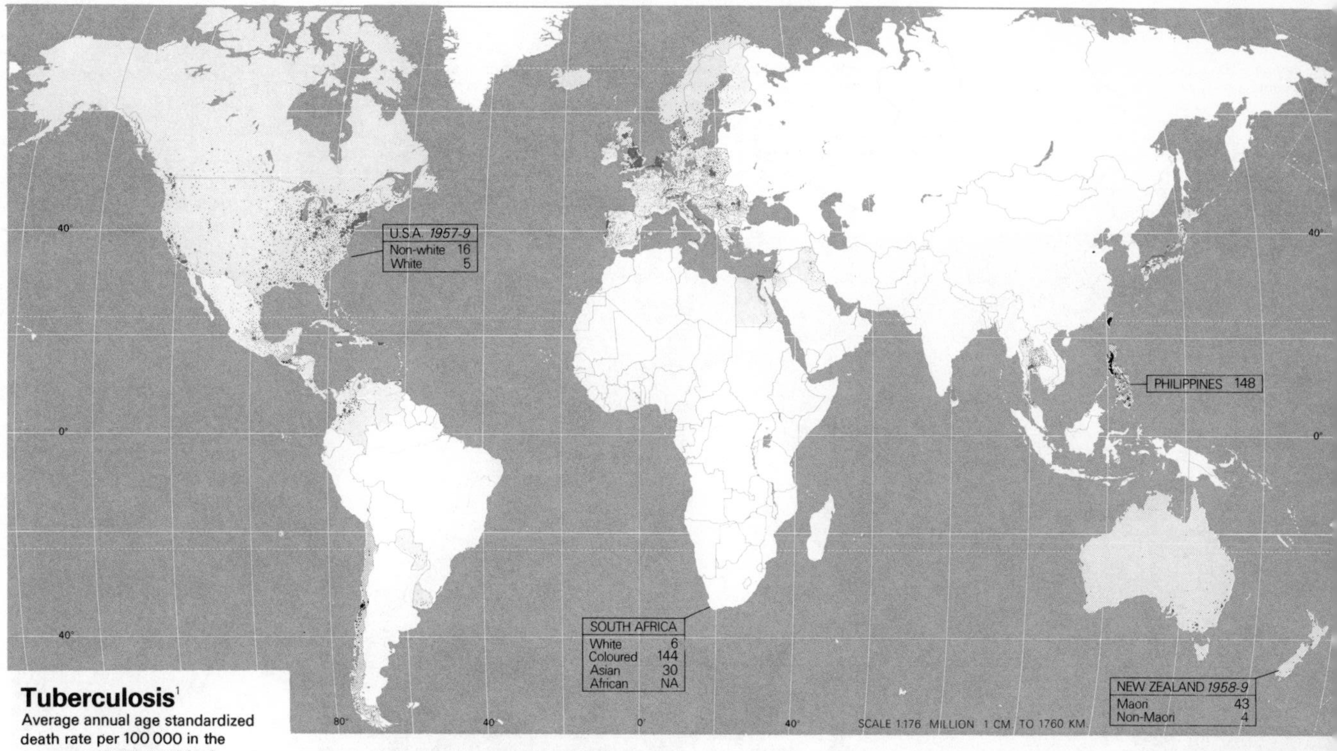
U.S.A. 1957-9
Non-white 16
White 5
PHILIPPINES 148
SOUTH AFRICA
White 6
Coloured 144
Asian 30
African NA
NEW ZEALAND 1958-9
Maori 43
Non-Maori 4
SCALE 1:176 MILLION 1 CM. TO 1760 KM.

Tuberculosis[1]

Average annual age standardized death rate per 100 000 in the age group 15-64 for 1961-3

60 & OVER
30 – 60
10 – 30
1 – 10
DATA NA

One dot to 100 000 population

[1] WHO INTERNATIONAL CLASSIFICATION OF DISEASE NUMBER 001-008

Tuberculosis in man is caused either by the human or the bovine type of tubercle bacillus (*mycobacterium tuberculosis*). The human type is spread by the cough spray and expectoration of sufferers, the bovine type by infected milk from cows with udder tuberculosis. Pulmonary tuberculosis which is principally a disease of adults, is the most prevalent form of tuberculosis and is almost all of the human type. Bovine tuberculosis mainly affects children. Wherever possible the figures mapped are for pulmonary tuberculosis because of the incapacity which it causes among the adult working population. The mode of transmission is such that pulmonary tuberculosis is most common in conditions of poverty and overcrowding, and it is thus more common in towns than in rural areas.

In industrialized societies it has tended to reach a peak in the early stages of industrialization. In England and Wales from 1780 to 1800 the mortality rate is estimated to have reached 1 000 per 100 000 and to have declined steadily since, apart from a sharp increase during the two world wars. Although tuberculosis has been known in the world since earliest history, lack of communications formerly limited its spread. Large areas were free until it was introduced by the infected, economically more developed nations. It then spread with devastating severity in Africa, Asia and South America where there was no protection from acquired immunity. BCG vaccination can now give a considerable measure of protection and tuberculosis can also be cured by treatment with drugs.

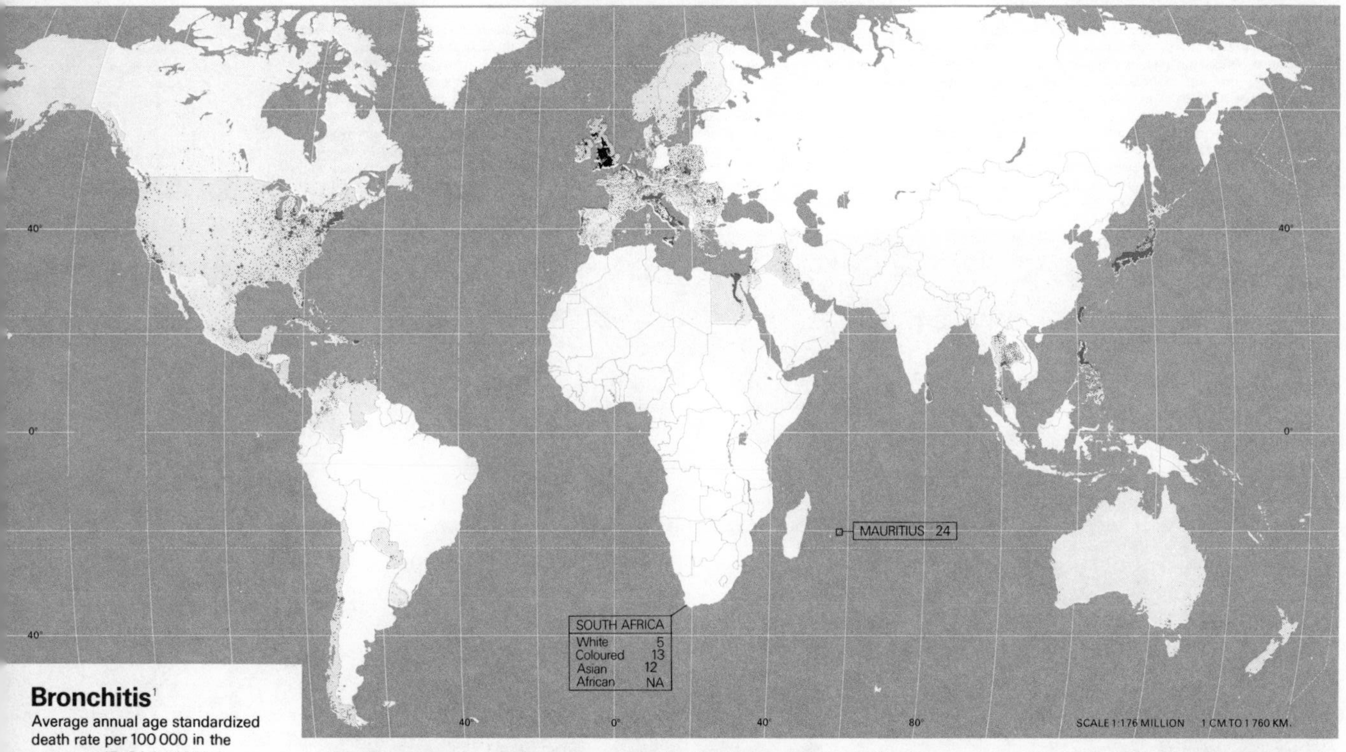
MAURITIUS 24
SOUTH AFRICA
White 5
Coloured 13
Asian 12
African NA
SCALE 1:176 MILLION 1 CM TO 1 760 KM.

Bronchitis[1]

Average annual age standardized death rate per 100 000 in the age group 15-64 for 1961-3

17.5 & OVER
7.5 – 17.5
2.5 – 7.5
0.6 – 2.5
DATA NA

One dot to 100 000 population

[1] WHO INTERNATIONAL CLASSIFICATION OF DISEASE NUMBER 500-502

Bronchitis occurs either as an isolated acute attack in which the symptoms of cough and expectoration of mucus are exaggerations of the normal mechanisms for clearing the throat or as a chronic disease in which long-standing inflammation of the bronchi causes permanent injury and serious disablement. Onset of chronic bronchitis is commonest after the age of thirty and the average duration is over twenty-five years. The most striking feature of the regional distribution is that the mortality in the British Isles is about thirty times greater than in the U.S.A. and five or six times greater than in most of Western Europe. Within England and Wales it is largely a disease of poor, overcrowded urban areas. The most important causative factor seems to be air pollution and in particular pollution from domestic chimneys rather than industrial sources. However, the problem is most probably aggravated in Britain by the natural climatic conditions. Certainly attacks in individuals suffering from chronic bronchitis are precipitated by damp, cold weather and by fog. The disease also occurs quite commonly among South American Indians who sleep with very little shelter at high altitudes where the cold and damp towards dawn are considerable. As might be expected in a disease so clearly associated with air pollution, smokers are far more prone to bronchitis than non-smokers.

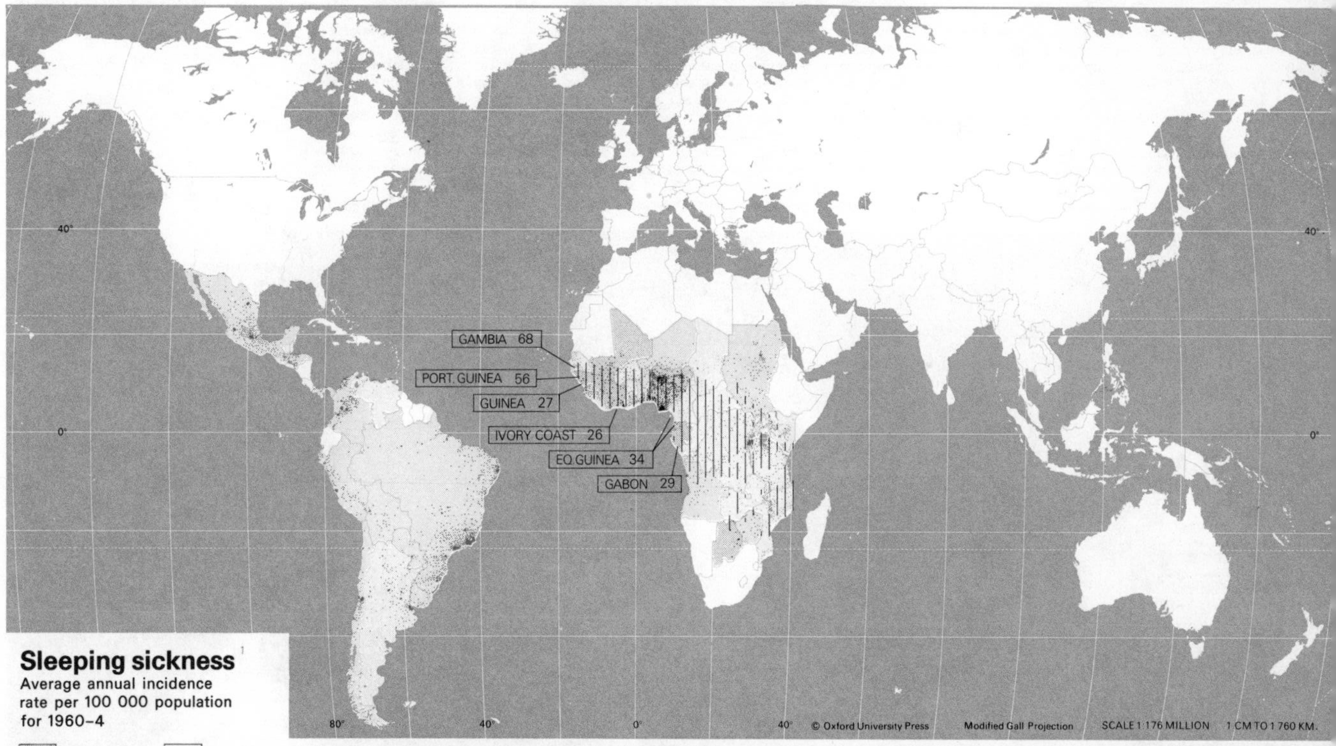
GAMBIA 68
PORT. GUINEA 56
GUINEA 27
IVORY COAST 26
EQ. GUINEA 34
GABON 29
© Oxford University Press
Modified Gall Projection
SCALE 1:176 MILLION 1 CM TO 1 760 KM.

Sleeping sickness[1]

Average annual incidence rate per 100 000 population for 1960-4

10.5 & OVER
5.5 – 10.5
0.5 – 5.5
0 – 0.5
DATA NA

One dot to 100 000 population

MAIN DISTRIBUTION OF TSETSE FLY

[1] WHO INTERNATIONAL CLASSIFICATION OF DISEASE NUMBER 121

African trypanosomiasis (sleeping sickness) occurs in humans and animals infected by the protozoa trypanosome which is transmitted by the blood-sucking tsetse fly (glossina spp.), an insect found only in the African continent. In man the disease is characterized initially by fever and intense headache and secondarily by wasting and somnolence as the central nervous system is affected. Untreated, it is fatal in about 90% of cases, but the widespread epidemics in man which used to occur and which led to the abandonment of large areas of fertile land following tsetse infestation have largely been controlled. However, trypanosomiasis also has a high fatality among domestic animals, and this has had a crippling effect on the agricultural development of much of Africa. In affected areas stockraising is impracticable, diet is badly lacking in animal protein and cultivation is severely restricted because of the lack of draught animals. The disease is most typical of sparsely settled savanna woodland with 30-60 in. (750-1 500 mm.) of rain a year and poor soils. In drier areas it is found mainly near rivers and lakes. It can be controlled by clearing bush, by killing game animals which are also affected, and by spraying the favoured resting sites of the fly. In South America another variety of trypanosomes causes an infection known as Chagas disease. Unlike African trypanosomiasis it is rarely fatal.

Disease II

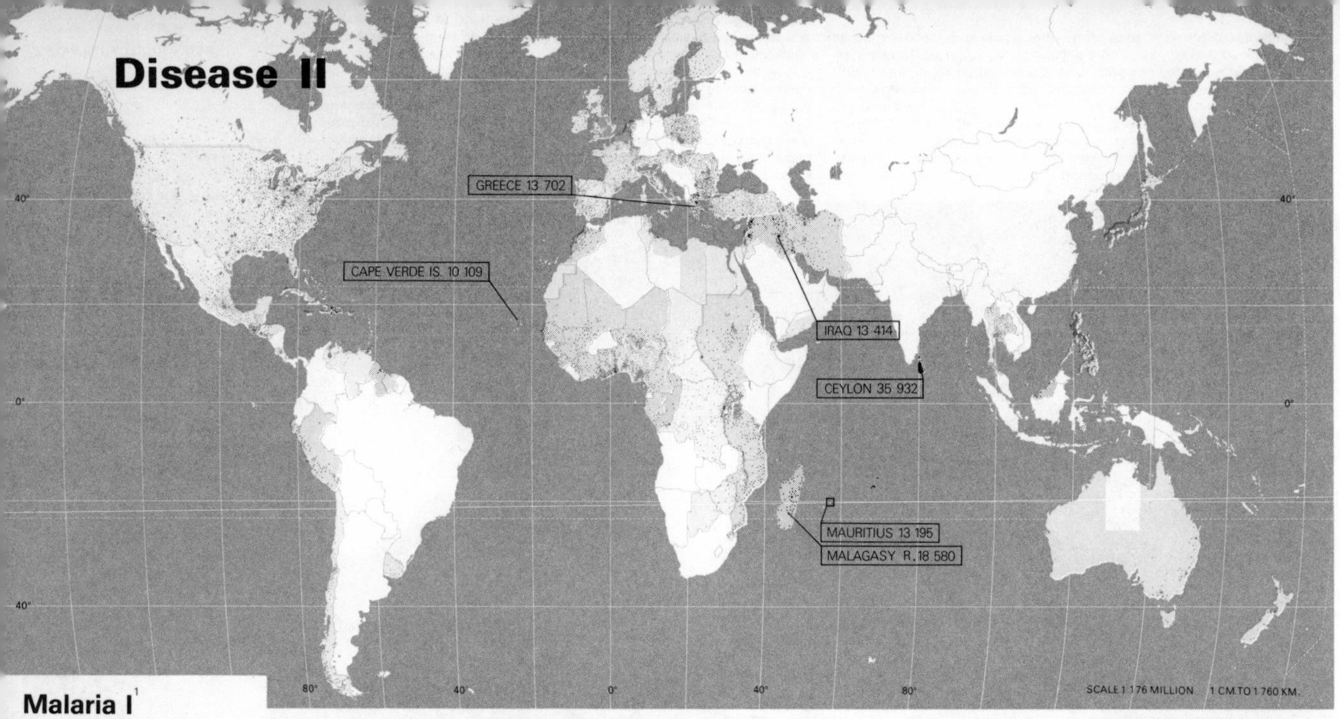

GREECE 13 702
CAPE VERDE IS. 10 109
IRAQ 13 414
CEYLON 35 932
MAURITIUS 13 195
MALAGASY R. 18 580
SCALE 1:176 MILLION 1 CM TO 1 760 KM.

Malaria I[1]

Average annual incidence rate per 100 000 for 1944 - 6

4 000 & OVER	5 - 85
900 - 4 000	0 - 5
85 - 900	DATA NA

One dot to 100 000 population

[1] WORLD HEALTH ORGANIZATION (WHO) INTERNATIONAL CLASSIFICATION OF DISEASE NUMBER 110 - 117

Malaria is caused by parasites, protozoa of the genus *plasmodium*, which multiply in the blood stream where they attack and destroy red blood cells. The resulting anaemia and accompanying bouts of fever are extremely debilitating and account for an enormous loss of work potential in the tropical and sub-tropical areas where malaria is still endemic. However, adults in endemic areas have acquired a degree of immunity from repeated attack and few die of the disease; children, after weaning, have no such immunity and the death rate up to the age of two may be as high as 50%. The malaria parasites are transmitted from one human being to another by the bite of female anopheline mosquitoes, of which over sixty species are recognized as vectors of human malaria. The majority of these thrive where temperatures and humidity are high, but the climatic limits are broad [a summer temperature not falling below 60°F (15.5°C) with rainfall and drainage such as to give stretches of stagnant or slow moving water in which the mosquitoes can breed], and malaria has been recorded as far north as 60°N. Seasonal variation in the intensity of malarial infection follows closely the distribution of rainfall. Malaria transmission is perennial only in an equatorial belt (from about 10°N to 10°S) where it is possible for the mosquito vector to breed throughout the year. Outside this belt the occurrence varies from regular seasonal outbreaks to occasional disastrous epidemics. This map shows the extent of the disease before the introduction of any major control or eradication programme.

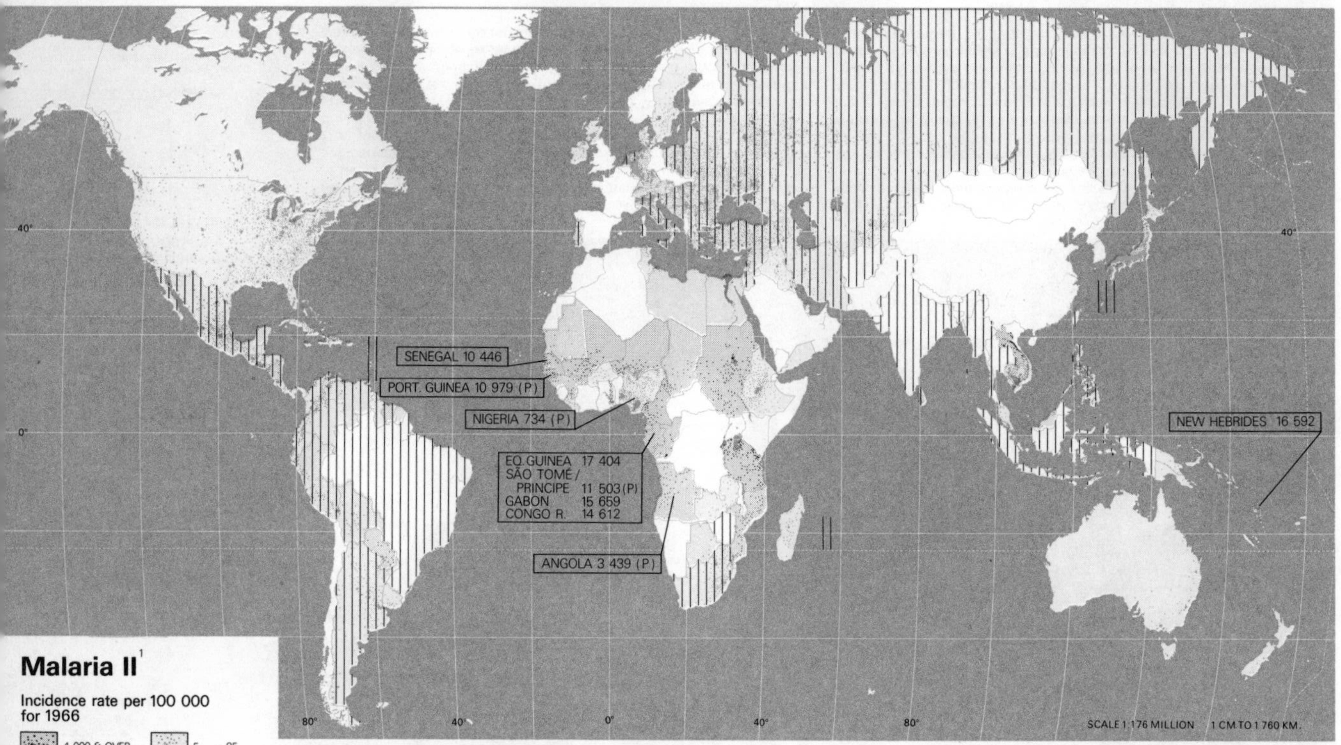

SENEGAL 10 446
PORT. GUINEA 10 979 (P)
NIGERIA 734 (P)
EQ.GUINEA 17 404
SÃO TOMÉ / PRINCIPE 11 503 (P)
GABON 15 659
CONGO R. 14 612
ANGOLA 3 439 (P)
NEW HEBRIDES 16 592
SCALE 1:176 MILLION 1 CM TO 1 760 KM.

Malaria II[1]

Incidence rate per 100 000 for 1966

4 000 & OVER	5 - 85
900 - 4 000	0 - 5
85 - 900	DATA NA

(P) 'Prevalence rate'

One dot to 100 000 population

COUNTRIES WITH ERADICATION PROGRAMMES IN 1965

[1] WHO INTERNATIONAL CLASSIFICATION OF DISEASE NUMBER 110 - 117

Programmes to control malaria have concentrated mainly on attacking the mosquito vectors. If the number can be reduced and held at a low level for several years, malaria will die out from the control area. The mosquito population may subsequently increase but there will be no infection to be spread. Early measures were directed at the mosquito breeding grounds either by draining swamps, by spraying stretches of water with oil or by destroying larvae with chemicals. Later much cheaper insecticides such as DDT were developed which would kill adult mosquitoes, and which would remain effective for several months after being sprayed on the house walls where the mosquitoes normally rest after biting. As the mosquitoes developed resistance to various insecticides, it became necessary to shift the emphasis from "malaria control" to "malaria eradication". So far, however, only the richer countries have successfully carried out eradication programmes. Malaria has now disappeared from Europe, North America and the U.S.S.R. It is still an enormous problem throughout Africa from Rhodesia to the Sahara and in much of SE. Asia. A major obstacle to control in poorer areas is the large number of immigrants, either traditional pastoralists or families seeking a higher standard of living in the towns, who are liable to reintroduce the disease into areas from which it has been cleared.

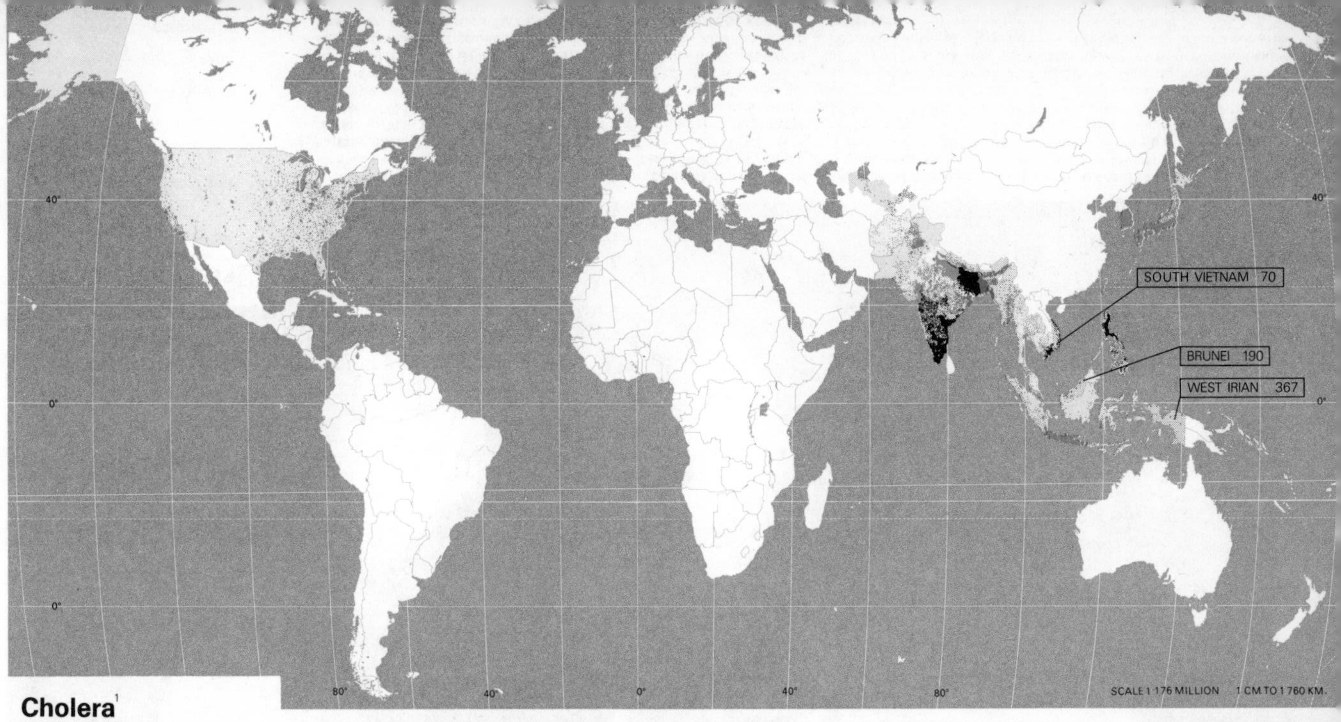

SOUTH VIETNAM 70
BRUNEI 190
WEST IRIAN 367
SCALE 1:176 MILLION 1 CM TO 1 760 KM.

Cholera[1]

Average annual incidence rate per 100 000 for 1963 - 5

10 & OVER	1 - 5
5 - 10	0 - 1
DATA NA	

One dot to 100 000 population

[1] WHO INTERNATIONAL CLASSIFICATION OF DISEASE NUMBER 043

Cholera is an acute intestinal disease which is spread directly from person to person by water contaminated by infected sewage. The disease has been endemic in India since the beginning of recorded society, and during the nineteenth century it several times exploded in epidemic waves which spread almost throughout the world following the routes of traders, pilgrims, and soldiers. The fatality among untreated cases is 50 or 60% but only about 10% in treated cases. The disease predominates in children in endemic areas, but in newly invaded areas where there is no acquired immunity it attacks all ages. With improved sanitation and with the establishment of quarantine stations there has been no epidemic of cholera in the Americas during the present century and none in Europe since 1923. There was an isolated outbreak in Egypt in 1947 and since then the disease has also disappeared from Africa. Two strains of cholera exist, the Classical and El Tor. Up to 1960 classical cholera had retreated to its original endemic foci in India and a few neighbouring territories, and El Tor was endemic only in Sulawezi Island in Indonesia. During the last decade Classical Cholera has increased in India and El Tor has spread to entirely new areas as far west as the Persian Gulf and as far north as Soviet Uzbekistan. In most countries so far there have only been sporadic outbreaks but with rapidly expanding populations and the attendant threat of overcrowding, cholera could again spread disastrously, especially in developing areas.

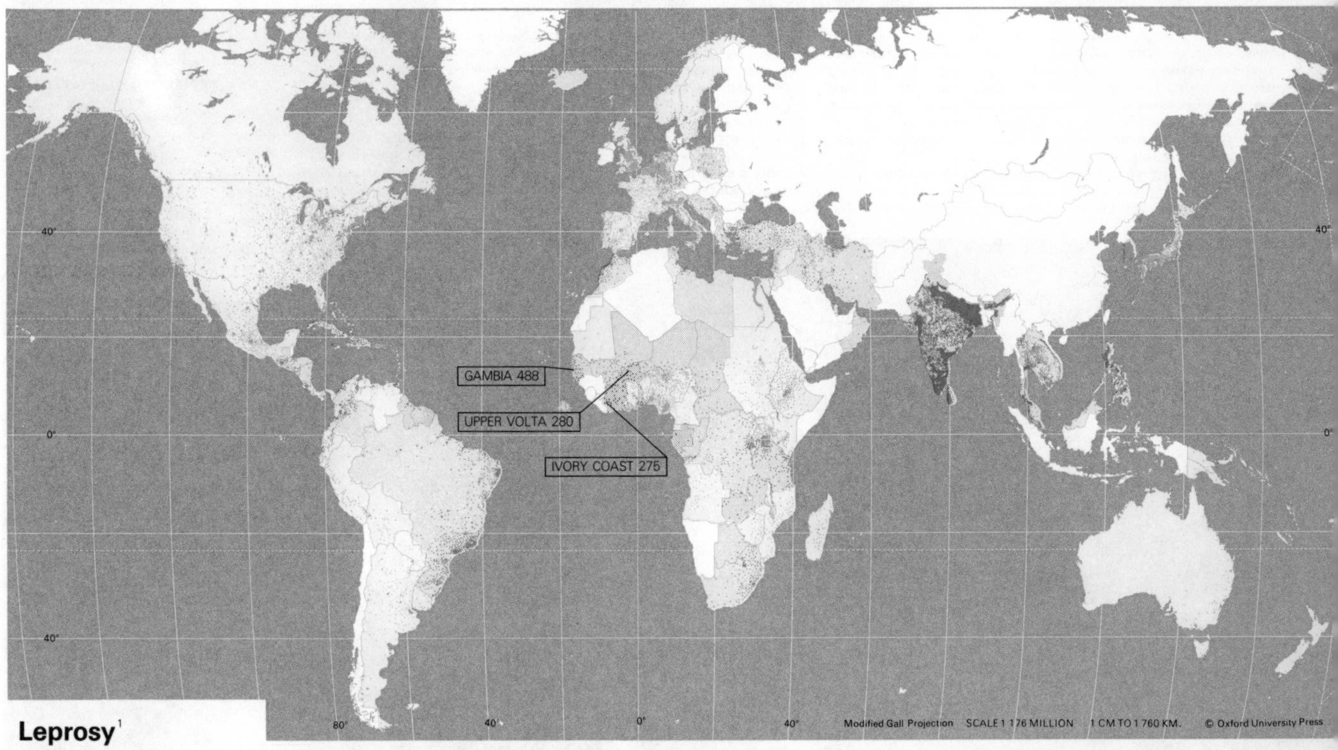

GAMBIA 488
UPPER VOLTA 280
IVORY COAST 275
Modified Gall Projection SCALE 1:176 MILLION 1 CM TO 1 760 KM.

Leprosy[1]

Average annual incidence rate per 100 000 for 1963 - 5

150 & OVER	1 - 5
50 - 150	0 - 1
5 - 50	DATA NA

One dot to 100 000 population

[1] WHO INTERNATIONAL CLASSIFICATION OF DISEASE NUMBER 060

Two-thirds of the world's population live in areas where leprosy has a prevalence of over 0.5 per 1 000. In parts of the West and Central Africa over 4% of the population are affected. The disease is of long duration, degenerative and disfiguring. Not only is it an enormous economic handicap in the countries affected, but prejudice against those afflicted is greater than with almost any other disease, causing great individual suffering. Among those exposed to leprosy about 20% are particularly susceptible. Children have a higher attack rate than adults. The disease is transmitted by direct person to person contact in which the *mycobacterium leprae* penetrates either through abrasions of the skin or through the mucosa of the nose. During the Middle Ages leprosy was widespread in Europe. The reasons for its disappearance in the sixteenth century are not properly understood and neither are there satisfactory physical or cultural explanations for the present geographical distribution. It is not always possible to ascertain whether published data cover only new cases notified during the year or the total number of cases treated, and similarly an apparent increase within a country may simply indicate a drive to register and treat more cases. International comparisons of frequency are therefore only very approximate.

Disease III

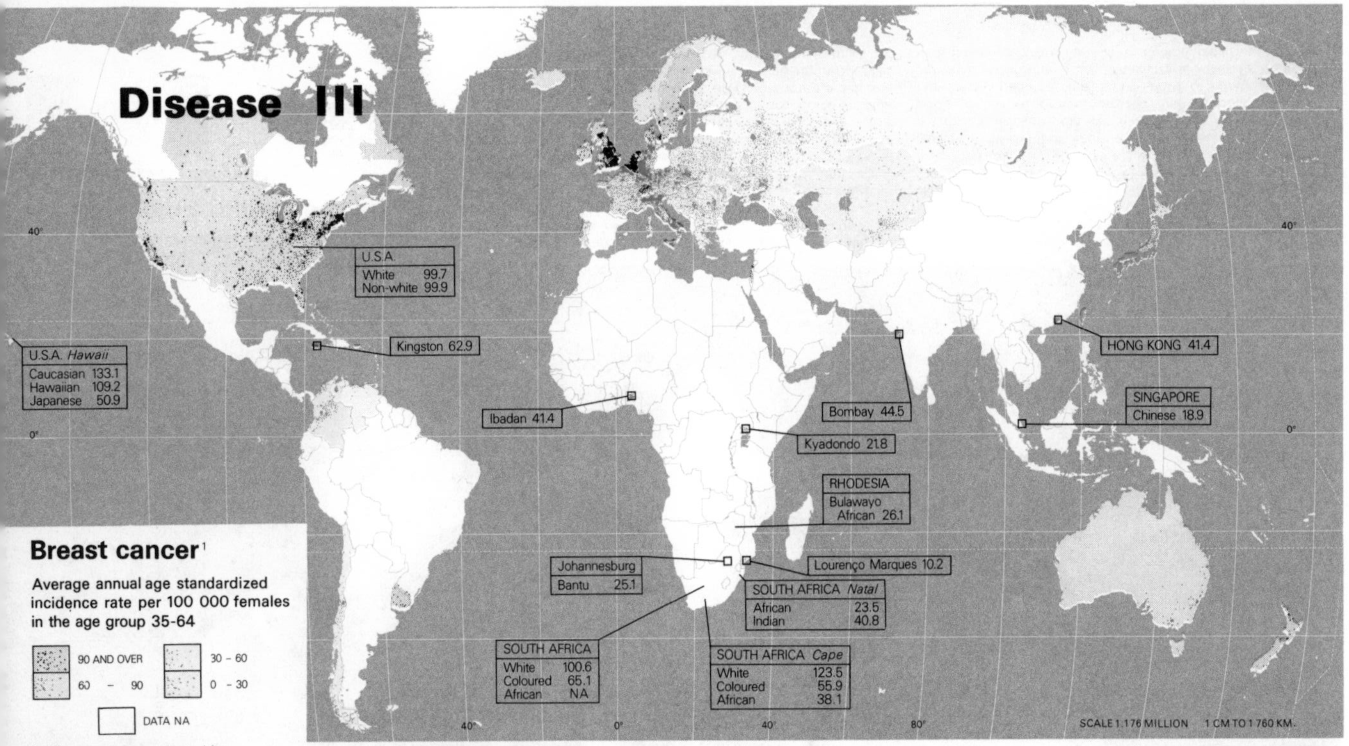

U.S.A. White 99.7 Non-white 99.9
U.S.A. Hawaii Caucasian 133.1 Hawaiian 109.2 Japanese 50.9
Kingston 62.9
Ibadan 41.4
Bombay 44.5
HONG KONG 41.4
SINGAPORE Chinese 18.9
Kyadondo 21.8
RHODESIA Bulawayo African 26.1
Johannesburg Bantu 25.1
Lourenço Marques 10.2
SOUTH AFRICA Natal African 23.5 Indian 40.8
SOUTH AFRICA White 100.6 Coloured 65.1 African NA
SOUTH AFRICA Cape White 123.5 Coloured 55.9 African 38.1
SCALE 1:176 MILLION 1 CM TO 1 760 KM.

Breast cancer[1]

Average annual age standardized incidence rate per 100 000 females in the age group 35-64

90 AND OVER; 60 - 90; 30 - 60; 0 - 30; DATA NA

Incidence rates are estimated from mortality rates for all except these countries: Canada, Chile, Denmark, England/Wales, Finland, Iceland, India, Israel, Jamaica, Mozambique, New Zealand, Nigeria, Norway, Puerto Rico, Rhodesia, Singapore, Sweden, Uganda, U.S.A.(Hawaii)

U.S.S.R. data are based on towns within the republics

One dot to 100 000 population

[1] WORLD HEALTH ORGANIZATION (WHO) INTERNATIONAL CLASSIFICATION OF DISEASE NUMBER 170

Cancer of the breast in women occurs most commonly in Canada and the United States. From this area of high incidence it shows a steady reduction in frequency eastward across the northern hemisphere through Western and Central Europe and into Central Asia. The incidence in India and the Far East is also much lower than in Western Europe or America. To a certain extent the world pattern reflects the situation in Britain where breast cancer occurs more commonly among women in the higher socio-economic groups but there are some notable exceptions, in particular the similar incidence in whites and non-whites in the U.S.A. and the high frequency in Colombia in South America. There is some tendency for cancer of the breast to run in families, but genetic factors cannot explain the geographical variation; the difference in frequency between Africans in Africa and non-whites in America, or between the Japanese in Hawaii and in Japan, points strongly to some social or environmental influence. Fertility and prolonged lactation are associated with lower incidence but recent work suggests that age at first pregnancy may be a more decisive factor. Between the ages of twenty-five and fifty there is a sharp increase in the incidence of cancer of the breast after which the rate of increase with age slows down. Many other tumours show a continued progressive rise in frequency with age, and the shape of the age curve for cancer of the breast may indicate that the carcinogenic agent ceases to be active after a number of years, possibly at the time of the menopause.

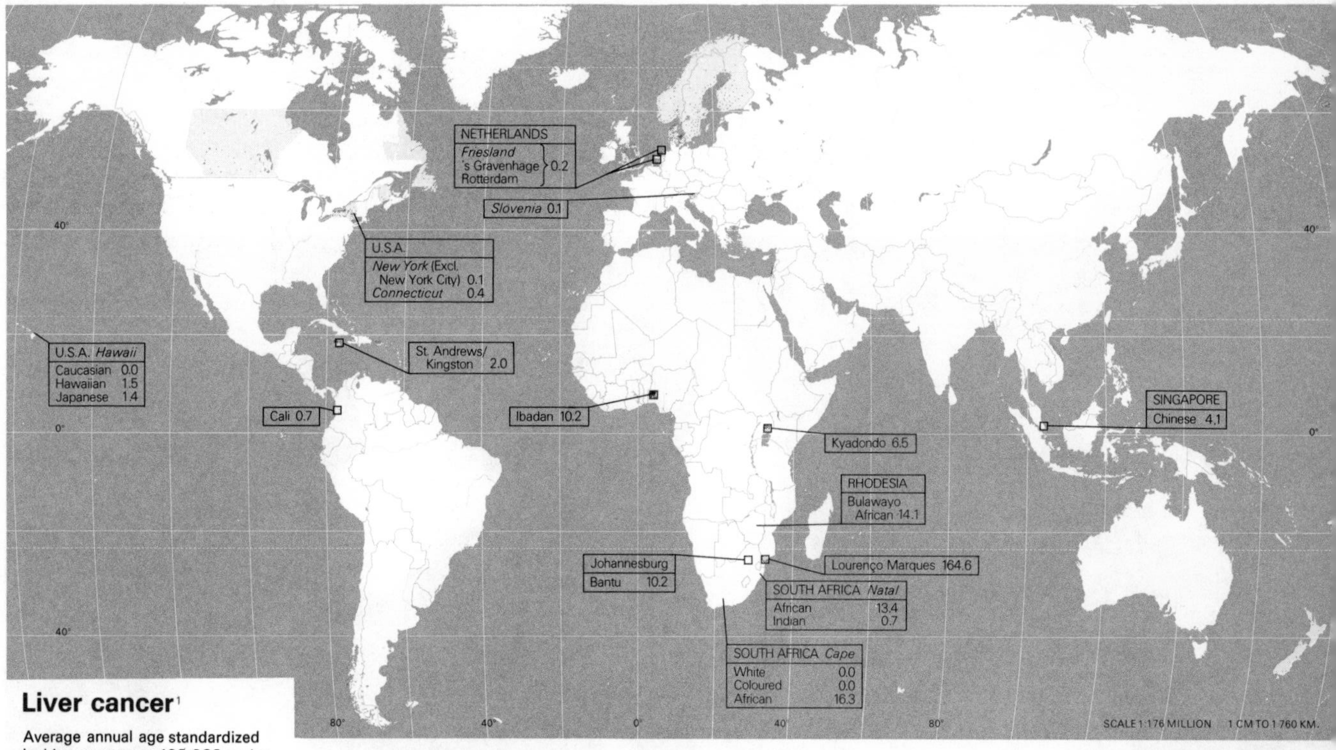

NETHERLANDS Friesland 's Gravenhage Rotterdam 0.2
Slovenia 0.1
U.S.A. New York (Excl. New York City) 0.1 Connecticut 0.4
U.S.A. Hawaii Caucasian 0.0 Hawaiian 1.5 Japanese 1.4
St. Andrews/ Kingston 2.0
Cali 0.7
Ibadan 10.2
SINGAPORE Chinese 4.1
Kyadondo 6.5
RHODESIA Bulawayo African 14.1
Johannesburg Bantu 10.2
Lourenço Marques 164.6
SOUTH AFRICA Natal African 13.4 Indian 0.7
SOUTH AFRICA Cape White 0.0 Coloured 0.0 African 16.3
SCALE 1:176 MILLION 1 CM TO 1 760 KM.

Liver cancer[1]

Average annual age standardized incidence rate per 100 000 males in the age group 15-44

6 AND OVER; 1 - 6; 0.5 - 1; 0 - 0.5; DATA NA

One dot to 100 000 population

[1] WHO INTERNATIONAL CLASSIFICATION OF DISEASE NUMBER 155

Primary liver cancer is the most consistently common tumour in Africa south of the Sahara, representing almost everywhere over 10% of all malignant tumours diagnosed in men and a substantial, though lower, proportion of tumours in women. By contrast it is almost unknown in Western Europe and North America. The highest recorded incidence is in Lourenço Marques, Mozambique, where it represents over half of cancer of all sites and where the incidence in men aged 20–44 is as high as lung cancer in England among men twenty years older. The range of frequency between Lourenço Marques and Canada, Scandinavia or England is about a thousand-fold whereas the world-wide variation in cancer of the lung is only forty-fold and in stomach cancer thirty-fold. Within Africa south of the Sahara there seems to be only about a five-fold variation. A possible clue to the aetiology of primary liver cancer was the discovery that aflotoxin, a product of the mould *aspergilus flavus* commonly found in the tropics on stored crops such as groundnuts and cereals, was highly toxic to the livers of turkeys and was capable of producing a high incidence of liver cancer in experimental animals. Much work is being done to see whether a relationship between aflotoxin and liver cancer exists in man. The research would be greatly facilitated if it were possible to establish an area of genuinely lower frequency in Africa.

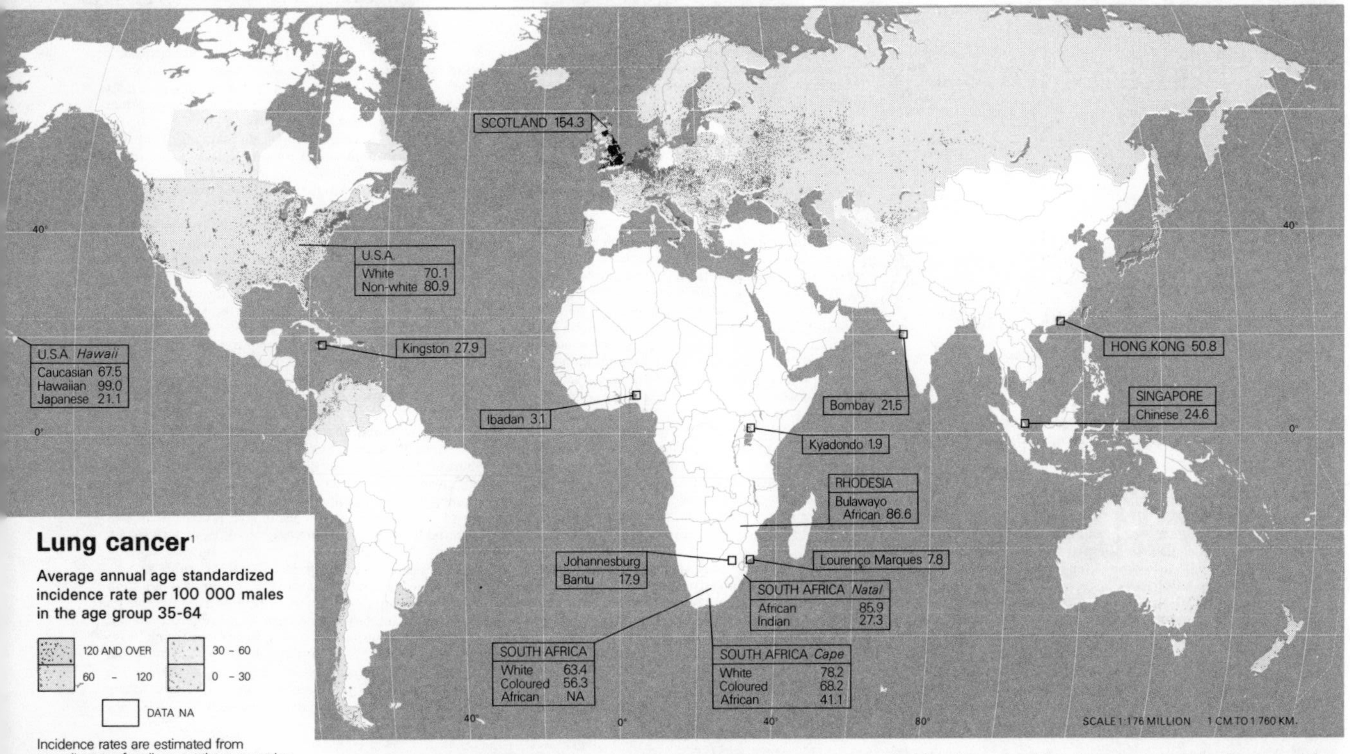

SCOTLAND 154.3
U.S.A. White 70.1 Non-white 80.9
U.S.A. Hawaii Caucasian 67.5 Hawaiian 99.0 Japanese 21.1
Kingston 27.9
Ibadan 3.1
Bombay 21.5
HONG KONG 50.8
SINGAPORE Chinese 24.6
Kyadondo 1.9
RHODESIA Bulawayo African 86.6
Johannesburg Bantu 17.9
Lourenço Marques 7.8
SOUTH AFRICA Natal African 85.9 Indian 27.3
SOUTH AFRICA White 63.4 Coloured 56.3 African NA
SOUTH AFRICA Cape White 78.2 Coloured 68.2 African 41.1
SCALE 1:176 MILLION 1 CM TO 1 760 KM.

Lung cancer[1]

Average annual age standardized incidence rate per 100 000 males in the age group 35-64

120 AND OVER; 60 - 120; 30 - 60; 0 - 30; DATA NA

Incidence rates are estimated from mortality rates for all except these countries: Canada, Chile, Denmark, England/Wales, Finland, Iceland, India, Israel, Jamaica, Mozambique, New Zealand, Nigeria, Norway, Puerto Rico, Rhodesia, Singapore, Sweden, Uganda, U.S.A.(Hawaii)

U.S.S.R. data are based on towns within the republics

One dot to 100 000 population

[1] WHO INTERNATIONAL CLASSIFICATION OF DISEASE NUMBER 162-163

Like bronchitis, cancer of the lung is more common in Britain than anywhere else in the world. However, the difference between Britain and other countries is less pronounced than with bronchitis since lung cancer is also common in Central and Eastern Europe, the U.S.S.R. and the U.S.A. Incidence is slightly less in Canada, Australia and among the white population of South Africa, and considerably less in Scandinavia, South America and Asia. In East and West Africa it is virtually unknown, but among Africans in urban Zambia and South Africa it has become one of the more commonly diagnosed tumours. Wherever the disease is now common it has become so only in the last thirty or forty years and there is considerable evidence that this is due to an increase in cigarette smoking. Everywhere the increase in incidence has been greater among men than women, but in Britain in recent years the female incidence has started to increase faster than the male, probably reflecting the time-lag before smoking became widely acceptable for women. The geographical distribution is not wholly explained by the number of cigarettes smoked, and it may be that cigarette smoking is more harmful to tissue already affected by some agent such as air pollution. However, studies of the length of butt discarded or the number of puffs taken from each cigarette indicate national differences in the exposure levels from cigarette smoking.

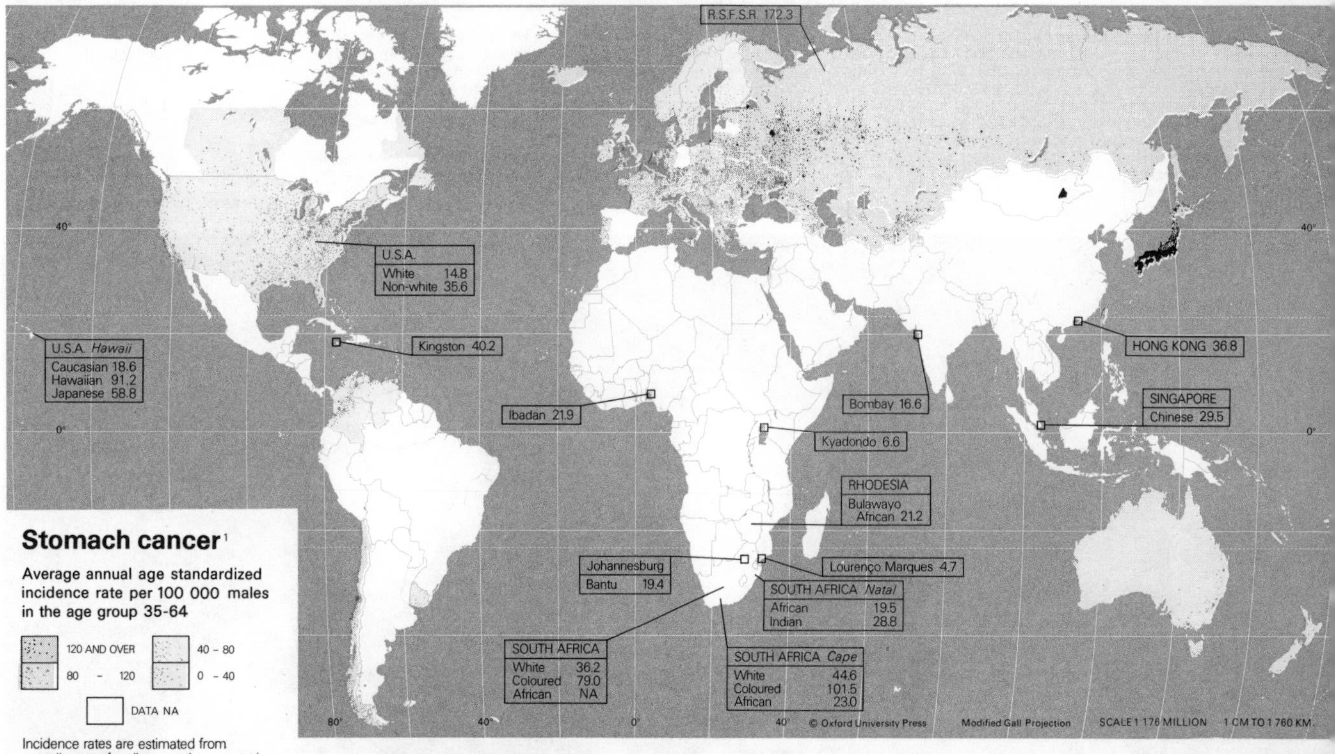

R.S.F.S.R. 172.3
U.S.A. White 14.8 Non-white 35.6
U.S.A. Hawaii Caucasian 18.6 Hawaiian 91.2 Japanese 58.8
Kingston 40.2
Ibadan 21.9
Bombay 16.6
HONG KONG 36.8
SINGAPORE Chinese 29.5
Kyadondo 6.6
RHODESIA Bulawayo African 21.2
Johannesburg Bantu 19.4
Lourenço Marques 4.7
SOUTH AFRICA Natal African 19.5 Indian 28.8
SOUTH AFRICA White 36.2 Coloured 79.0 African NA
SOUTH AFRICA Cape White 44.6 Coloured 101.5 African 23.0
© Oxford University Press Modified Gall Projection SCALE 1:176 MILLION 1 CM TO 1 760 KM.

Stomach cancer[1]

Average annual age standardized incidence rate per 100 000 males in the age group 35-64

120 AND OVER; 80 - 120; 40 - 80; 0 - 40; DATA NA

Incidence rates are estimated from mortality rates for all except these countries: Canada, Chile, Denmark, England/Wales, Finland, Iceland, India, Israel, Jamaica, Mozambique, New Zealand, Nigeria, Norway, Puerto Rico, Rhodesia, Singapore, Sweden, Uganda, U.S.A.(Hawaii)

U.S.S.R. data are based on towns within the republics

One dot to 100 000 population

[1] WHO INTERNATIONAL CLASSIFICATION OF DISEASE NUMBER 157

The highest recorded incidence of stomach cancer is in Japan, but it is very common also throughout Central Soviet Asia. From there the incidence declines steadily westward to a much lower level in North America. The only exception to this trend is Iceland where the incidence is unexpectedly high. In the southern hemisphere the distribution is less regular. Incidence in Africa is generally low, but frequency studies from some parts of the continent such as the eastern Congo Republic indicate areas in the continent where it is most commonly diagnosed tumour in men. In South America the incidence is very high on the east coast, in Colombia and throughout Chile. People belonging to blood group A have an increased risk of developing stomach cancer but this is true in areas of both high and low frequency, and this genetic factor is insufficient to explain the world-wide geographical variation. The Japanese population of Hawaii have far less stomach cancer than the Japanese in Japan, which strongly suggests an environmental influence. Stomach cancer is unusual among tumours in that there has been a general reduction in mortality in recent years, especially in Europe and North America. This has led to the suggestion that carcinogenic agents could be produced by the deterioration of stored foodstuffs, which has largely been checked in the West with the widespread introduction of refrigeration and better methods of food preservation.

Medical Care

The type of health service available to any individual is determined by the social history and present wealth of his country. Almost all governments have now taken responsibility for organizing some aspects of medical care, but there may also be a confused mixture of private medicine, compulsory and voluntary insurance schemes, industrial health clinics, philanthropic institutions and traditional remedies provided by local healers. For example, in Iran compulsory insurance schemes provide benefits to 6% of the population and in Yugoslavia to 98%. In Peru and Costa Rica employers play an important part in the provision of medical care. In Jamaica beds in private hospitals and clinics accounted for 5% of the total in the country; in Cyprus 38%. In East Africa herbalists supplement western medicine to some extent, while in Pakistan there are an estimated 50 000 ayurvedic practitioners compared with only 3 300 western trained doctors.

The great variety of authorities responsible for organizing and financing medical care in different countries make valid international comparisons of the actual level of care very difficult. The three indices mapped here (the proportion of doctors and hospital beds relative to the total population and the expenditure per capita on health services by public institutions) give some idea of the world situation, but they give no indication, for example, of whether the majority of doctors are in public service or private practice, or of whether the hospital bed is in a fully equipped western teaching hospital or in a corrugated iron mission hut where the doctor is desperately short even of such simple necessities as cotton wool and aspirins. There is also great variation between countries in the proportion of beds devoted to different specialist services. In the U.K. and Finland 31% of time in hospital is spent in general hospitals; in Ceylon and Chile the proportion is over 70%. In the U.K. and the U.S.A. 45% of all bed-days are spent in psychiatric hospital while in Yugoslavia and Czechoslovakia the proportion is only 10%.

The figures mapped for public health expenditure are for 'indirect' payments (that is, payments by governments, employers, insurers and charities) because details of 'direct' payments (private expenditure by the patient) are very difficult to obtain. Estimates of total expenditure have been made for a few countries and are presented in the table below. Among high-income countries it is not those which rely most heavily on government financing that allocate the highest proportion of their resources to health services.

There is obviously no relationship between the level of medical care available and the health needs of a country, but given the very uneven distribution of resources there is also very little systematic knowledge about the optimum use of available funds so as best to solve local health problems. In part this results from lack of detailed knowledge about patterns of morbidity and mortality in developing countries, and faced with this lack of data W.H.O. is at present organizing research programmes to investigate in depth the real medical needs of communities in developing areas. In part it results from a natural desire on the part of governments in poorer countries to copy the best facilities of western medicine and to build, for example, a lavishly equipped medical school in the capital city when the needs of the majority of people might be better served by improving the network of rural clinics. Some adjustments to local conditions are being made. For example, the loss of medical manpower through doctors seeking employment abroad has reached such serious proportions in some developing countries that governments are beginning to concentrate resources more on the training of semi-skilled medical assistants who will be able to contribute more to solving the health problems of their own people.

In part the lack of knowledge about the best use of resources results from ignorance as to what is genuinely best for the patient. There can for example be no sound medical reason why the average length of stay in maternity hospitals is $5\frac{1}{2}$ days in the U.S.A. and Israel, 8 days in Finland and over 9 days in Yugoslavia. Most wealthy countries have increased their health expenditure in recent years and if the present trends continue there will be countries which before the end of the century spend over 10% of their gross national product on medical services. This results partly from the scientific advances of medicine with the introduction of more expensive drugs and equipment and partly from the expectation by patients of better personal care in hospital and in the home. These services can be provided only by more nurses, more medical social workers and more domiciliary helps, and all such ancillary help is very expensive to provide in countries with a high material standard of living.

Total annual expenditure on health services
Including direct payments by recipients
(early 1960s)

	Current/capital expenditure as a percentage of G.N.P.	Current expenditure in $U.S. per capita	Direct payments by recipients as a percentage of current payments
Israel	6.3	90	27
Canada	6.0	108	36
U.S.A.	5.8	163	48
Chile	5.6	37	57
Sweden	5.4	4	22
Australia	5.2	74	39
Yugoslavia	5.0	12	6
Netherlands	4.8	56	33
Finland	4.8	48	40
France	4.4	72	10
Federation of Rhodesia and Nyasaland	4.2	6	39
U.K.	4.2	58	14
Ceylon	4.0	94	38
Czechoslovakia	3.6	37	7
Kenya	3.5	3	51
Tanganyika	2.5	2	32

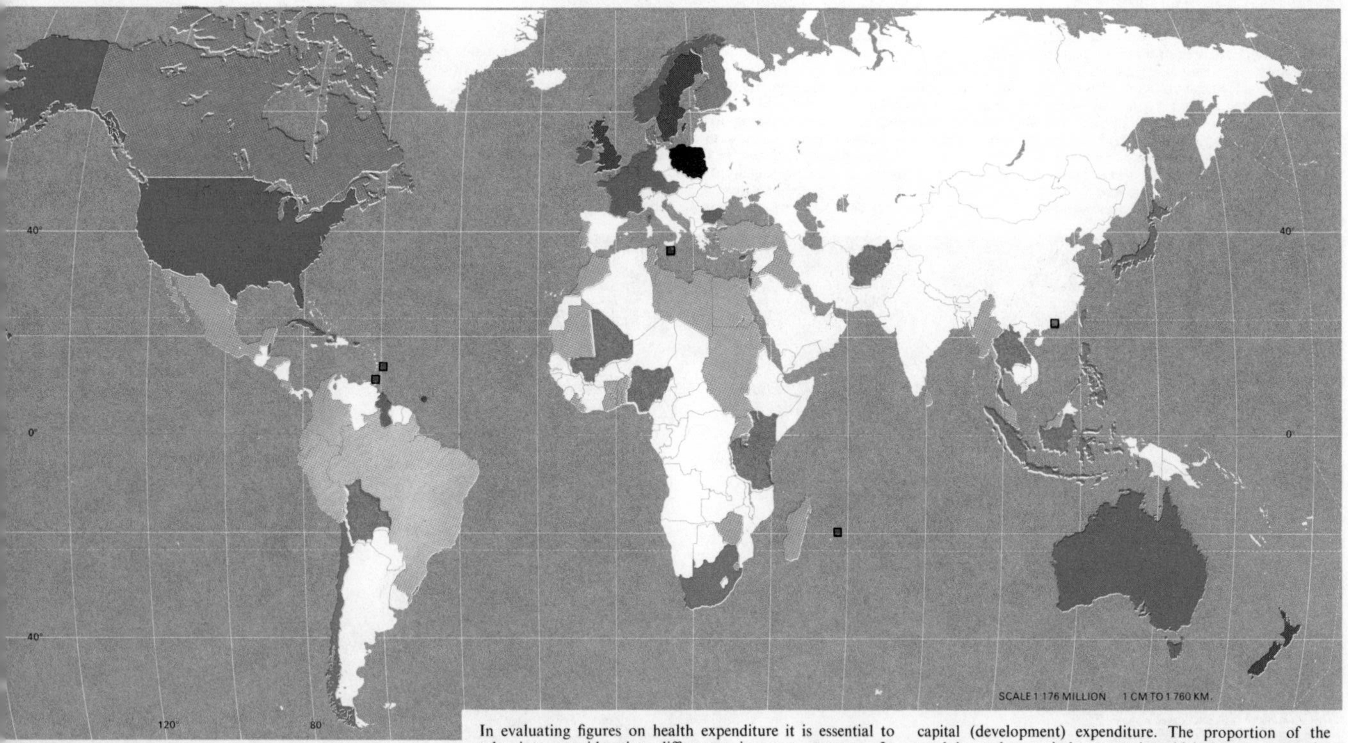

120°
80°
40°
0°
40°
40°
0°
40°
SCALE 1:176 MILLION 1 CM TO 1 760 KM.

Public health expenditure (1966)[1]

Annual expenditure per capita in $ U.S.

70 & OVER	20 - 30	1 - 5
50 - 70	10 - 20	0 - 1
30 - 50	5 - 10	DATA N A

[1] Or latest available previous data

In evaluating figures on health expenditure it is essential to take into consideration differences in wage structure. In countries where doctors have incomes well above average a higher proportional expenditure is inevitable. This applies both to high income countries such as the U.S.A. and to low income countries with particularly wide discrepancies in personal earnings. It also means that in terms of the actual services provided the differences between countries may not be so great as they appear from the figures of per capita expenditure since health services are major users of labour (in addition to doctors) which is very expensive in wealthy countries. The figures mapped mostly include both current (operating) and capital (development) expenditure. The proportion of the total devoted to capital costs varies widely between countries and from year to year since capital expenditure can be more easily reduced or postponed in times of economic stress. In the years shown here the proportion varies from over 20% in Swaziland and Hong Kong to 4% in the U.K. Over 90% of both current and capital expenditure in most countries is spent on personal health care; the remainder is spent on items such as public health education, research and training of doctors. Hospital treatment accounts for two-thirds of the money spent on personal health in the U.S.A., Sweden and Australia, compared with about one-half in Yugoslavia, Poland, Israel and France.

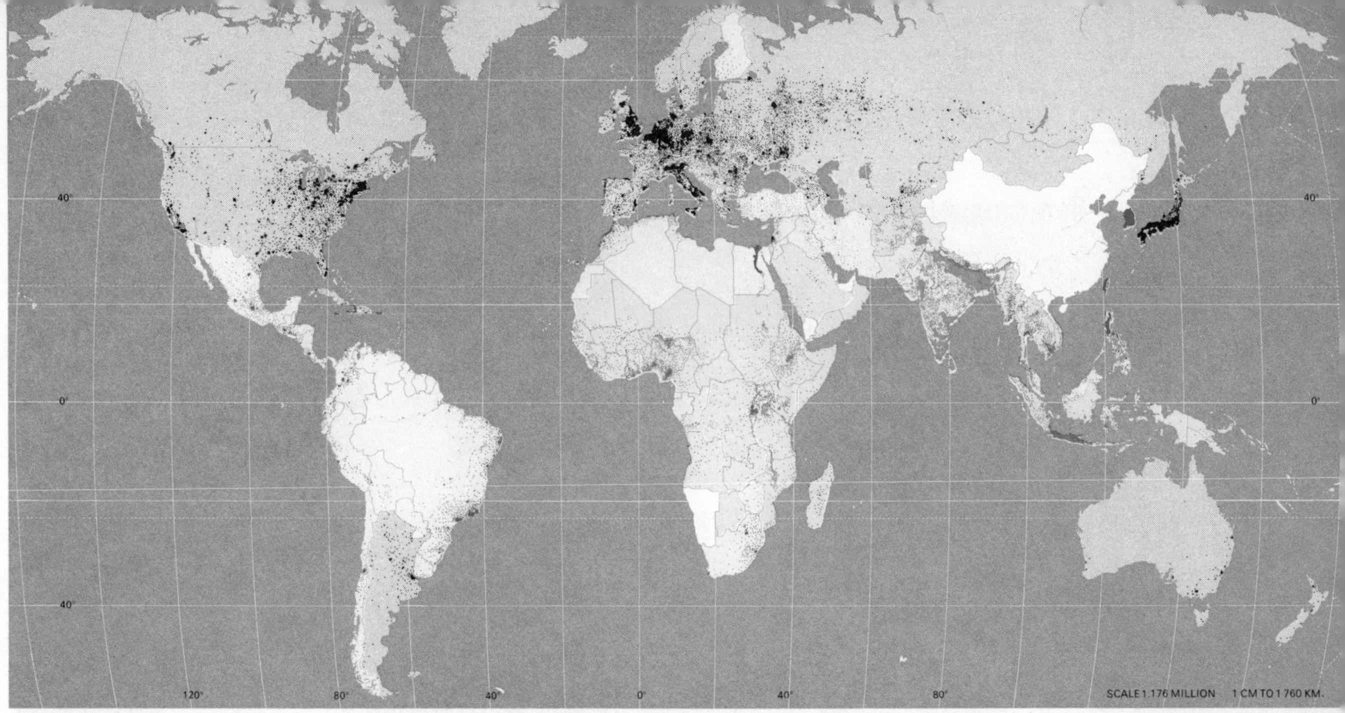

40°
0°
40°
120°
80°
40°
0°
40°
80°
SCALE 1:176 MILLION 1 CM TO 1 760 KM.

Physicians (1960-5 av.)

Number of people per physician

UNDER 1 000	8 000 - 18 000
1000 - 4 000	18 000 & OVER
4 000 - 8 000	DATA NA

One dot to 100 000 population

The number of people served by one doctor varies from 410 in Israel or 480 in the U.S.S.R. to 97 000 in Rwanda. In most European countries the number is less than 1 000 and in most African countries south of the Sahara it is over 10 000. The actual discrepancies are even more marked than is indicated by the national figures since in all countries there is a tendency for doctors to work in cities rather than rural areas, partly because specialist facilities are concentrated there and partly because they themselves prefer the amenities of living in an urban area. In a poorer country this can result in over half the total doctors working in a single town. In Senegal, for example, in 1966, 69% of all doctors in the country were working in Dakar. Inevitably this means that over vast tracts of rural territory each doctor may serve well over 100 000 persons. Many countries which are large in area have a Flying Doctor service, but this can help only very few people unless sophisticated communications systems are widely developed. In more prosperous countries there are still serious regional differences in the distribution of doctors. Most of the counties of SE. England have fewer than 500 people per doctor while in many northern counties the number is over 1 000. Some countries try to overcome this problem by requiring young doctors to work in remote areas for a period immediately following their training; others attempt, by providing incentive payments within a state system of medicine, to encourage doctors to work in rural or poor urban areas.

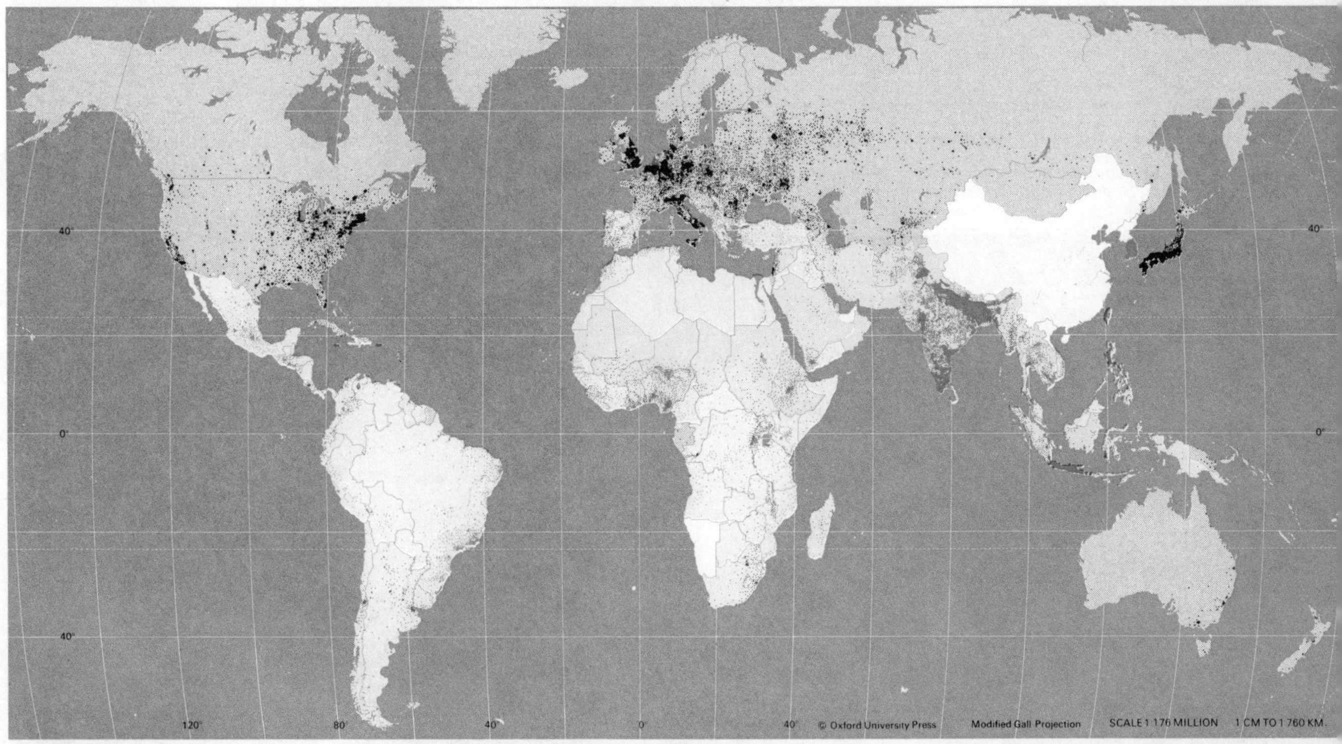

40°
0°
40°
120°
80°
40°
0°
40°
© Oxford University Press
Modified Gall Projection
SCALE 1:176 MILLION 1 CM TO 1 760 KM.

Hospital beds (1962-6 av.)

Number of people per hospital bed

UNDER 150	800 - 1600
150 - 250	1600 & OVER
250 - 800	DATA NA

One dot to 100 000 population

The number of hospital beds available divides the world in the same way as the ratio of doctors to population—a crude division into rich and poor nations. In most developed countries there is one hospital bed to every hundred or so people; in Afghanistan the number of people to a hospital bed is over 8 000 and in East Pakistan over 10 000. The cost of hospital care is paid for "indirectly" (see Medical Care introduction above) in most countries but in terms of yearly per capita national income the average cost of a stay in a general hospital varies from 13% in the U.S.A. or Sweden to 87% in Taiwan and 95% in Senegal. Even so, many African countries are relatively better provided with hospital places than with doctors. In Europe and North America there are generally 5 to 10 hospital beds to each doctor; in most African countries the number is between 20 and 70. This reflects the fact that, whereas in a country such as England approximately half the doctors are in general practice without direct responsibility for hospital beds, in Africa south of the Sahara almost all trained doctors are working in hospitals. In the poorer countries of Asia doctors and hospital places tend to be equally scarce. The actual number of beds is only a very approximate guide to the standard of hospital service available because so much depends on the staffing and resources of the various units.

Income

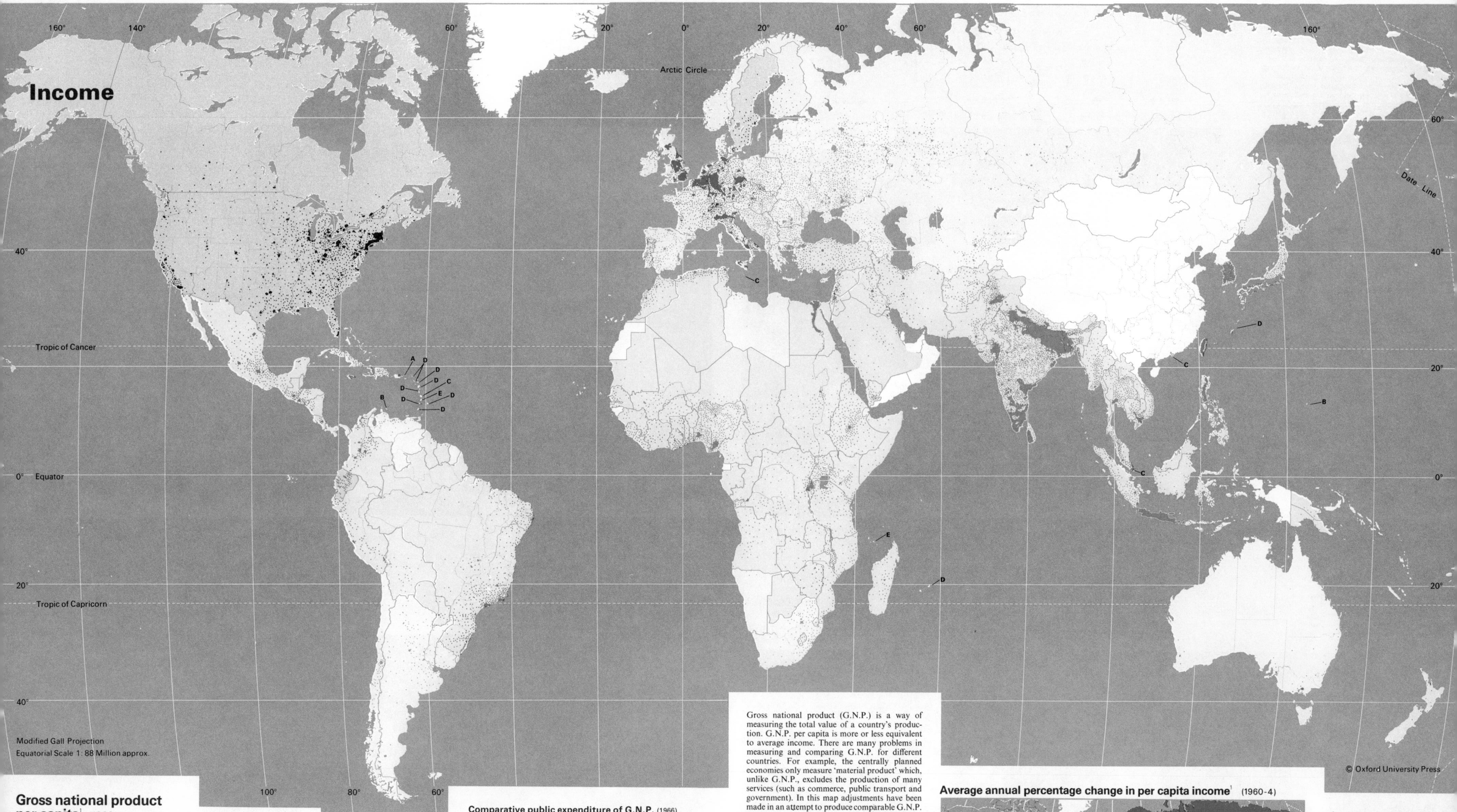

Arctic Circle
Tropic of Cancer
Equator
Tropic of Capricorn
Date Line
160°
140°
100°
80°
60°
40°
20°
0°
A
B
C
D
E
Modified Gall Projection
Equatorial Scale 1 : 88 Million approx.

Gross national product per capita[1] (1966)

	$ U.S.
A	2 000 & OVER
B	1000 — 2 000
C	500 — 1000
D	200 — 500
E	0 — 200
	DATA N A

One dot represents 100 000 population

[1] G.N.P. shown by letters for very small areas

G.N.P. per capita (1966)

Selected countries	$ U.S.
U.S.A.	3 520
Sweden	2 270
Australia	1 840
France	1 730
U.K.	1 620
Germany D.R.	1 220
Israel	1 160
U.S.S.R.	890
Japan	860
Romania	650
South Africa[1]	550
Mexico	470
Peru	320
Brazil	240
India	90
Nigeria	80

[1] Incl. South West Africa

The table to the right is based on data from a survey of 120 countries by the U.S. Arms Control and Disarmament Agency. The amount spent on public health and education may be augmented by varying amounts of private spending, depending on the extent to which these services are provided by governments or supported by the private sector. The expenditure of even a small percentage of G.N.P. for military purposes is a burden to developing countries, whose limited capital resources could be otherwise invested in projects which would aid long-term growth and raise the standard of living.

Comparative public expenditure of G.N.P. (1966)

REGION AND COUNTRY	G.N.P. '000 MILLION $U.S.	PUBLIC EXPENDITURE PERCENTAGE OF G.N.P. Military	Education	Health
North America	*800.9*	*8.1*	*4.7*	*1.7*
U.S.A.	747.6	8.5	4.6	1.6
Europe	*1 037.3*	*7.4*	*5.6*	*3.2*
European NATO	466.6	4.6	4.0	1.3
Warsaw Pact	478.5	NA	7.6	5.3
U.S.S.R.	(357.0)	NA	8.6	5.9
Other Europe	92.2	3.1	3.7	2.2
Latin America	*102.4*	*2.1*	*2.4*	*1.6*
Far East	*218.7*	*4.3*	*3.7*	*0.7*
China P.R.	80.0	8.1	3.5	1.4
Japan	97.5	1.0	4.2	0.1
South Asia	*54.2*	*3.5*	*2.4*	*0.4*
India	36.9	4.0	2.7	0.5
Middle East	*24.8*	*7.5*	*4.0*	*2.4*
Africa	*42.5*	*2.5*	*2.8*	*1.2*
Oceania	*30.6*	*3.9*	*3.3*	*1.6*
World	*2 311.1*	*6.9*	*4.8*	*2.3*

Gross national product (G.N.P.) is a way of measuring the total value of a country's production. G.N.P. per capita is more or less equivalent to average income. There are many problems in measuring and comparing G.N.P. for different countries. For example, the centrally planned economies only measure 'material product' which, unlike G.N.P., excludes the production of many services (such as commerce, public transport and government). In this map adjustments have been made in an attempt to produce comparable G.N.P. figures for as many countries as possible, but there is no perfect way of comparing the value of production in countries where tastes and consumption patterns are completely different.

Per capita G.N.P. figures also fail to show the distribution of income. Both rich and poor countries have some areas which are vastly richer than others, although these contrasts are often most pronounced in poor countries. Poor countries also generally have greater proportional differences in incomes between the rich and the poor, irrespective of regional differences.

No conceptual or statistical problems can, however, hide the enormous variation in per capita G.N.P. between countries. This income gap between the very rich and very poor countries is tending to increase, not decrease. The East European countries generally have lower per capita incomes than the developed Western group, but are catching them up because of their higher growth rates.

Average annual percentage change in per capita income[1] (1960-4)

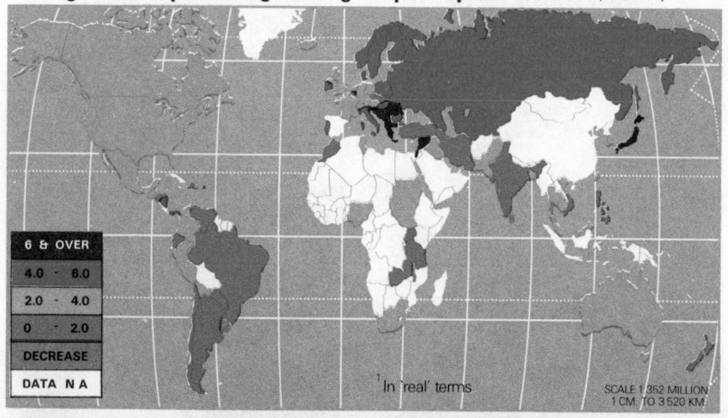

6 & OVER
4.0 - 6.0
2.0 - 4.0
0 - 2.0
DECREASE
DATA N A
SCALE 1:352 MILLION
1 CM TO 3 520 KM

[1] In 'real' terms

Average annual rate of increase in 'real'[1] per capita income (1960-4)

Selected countries	PERCENTAGE
Japan	9.7
Romania	8.2
Israel	6.5
U.S.S.R.	4.8
Sweden	4.7
France	3.8
South Africa	3.5
Peru	3.4
Mexico	3.0
U.S.A.	2.7
Australia	2.6
U.K.	2.6
Nigeria	2.5
Germany D.R.	2.4
Brazil	1.5
India	0.7

[1] At constant market prices

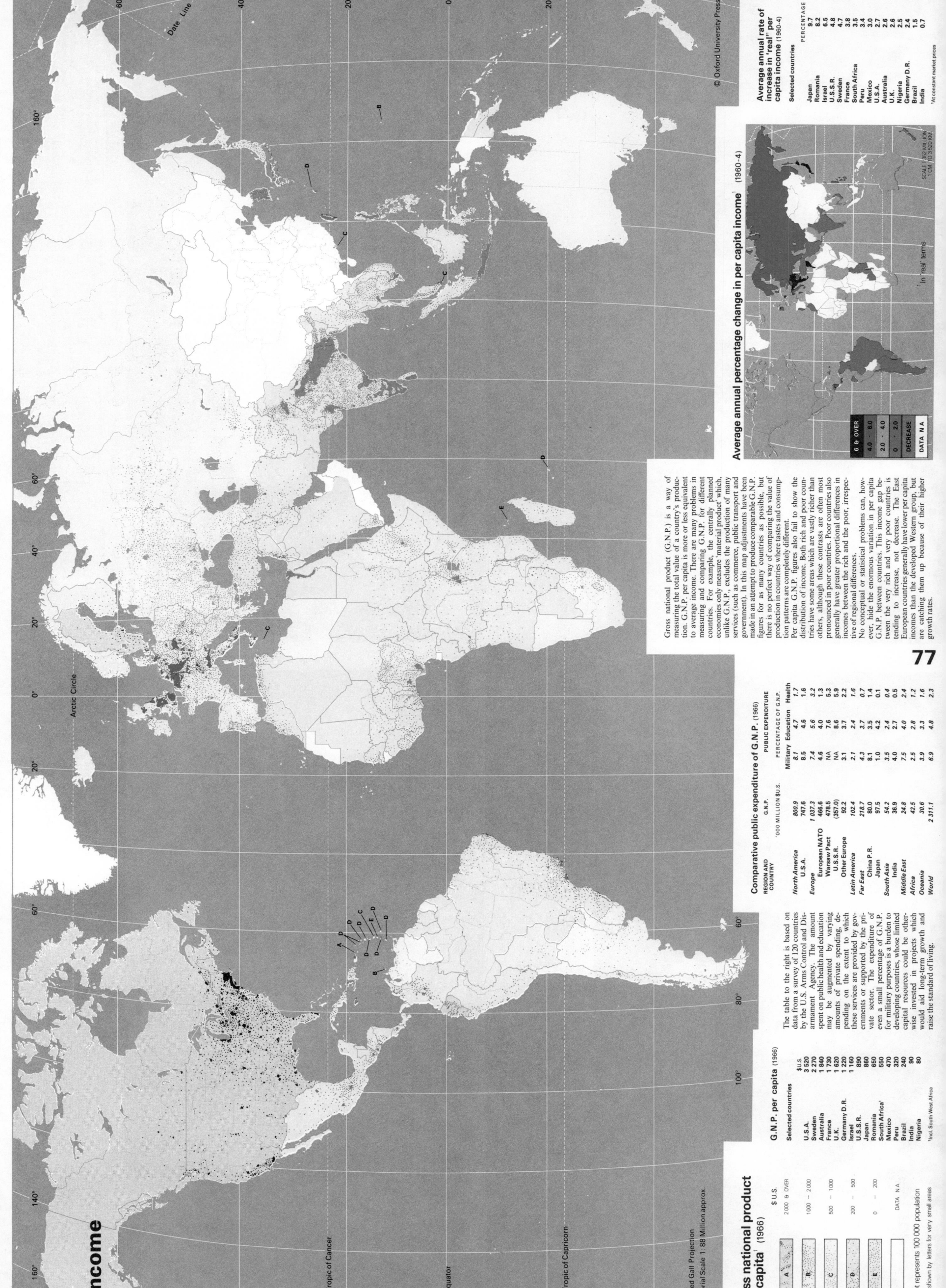

Education

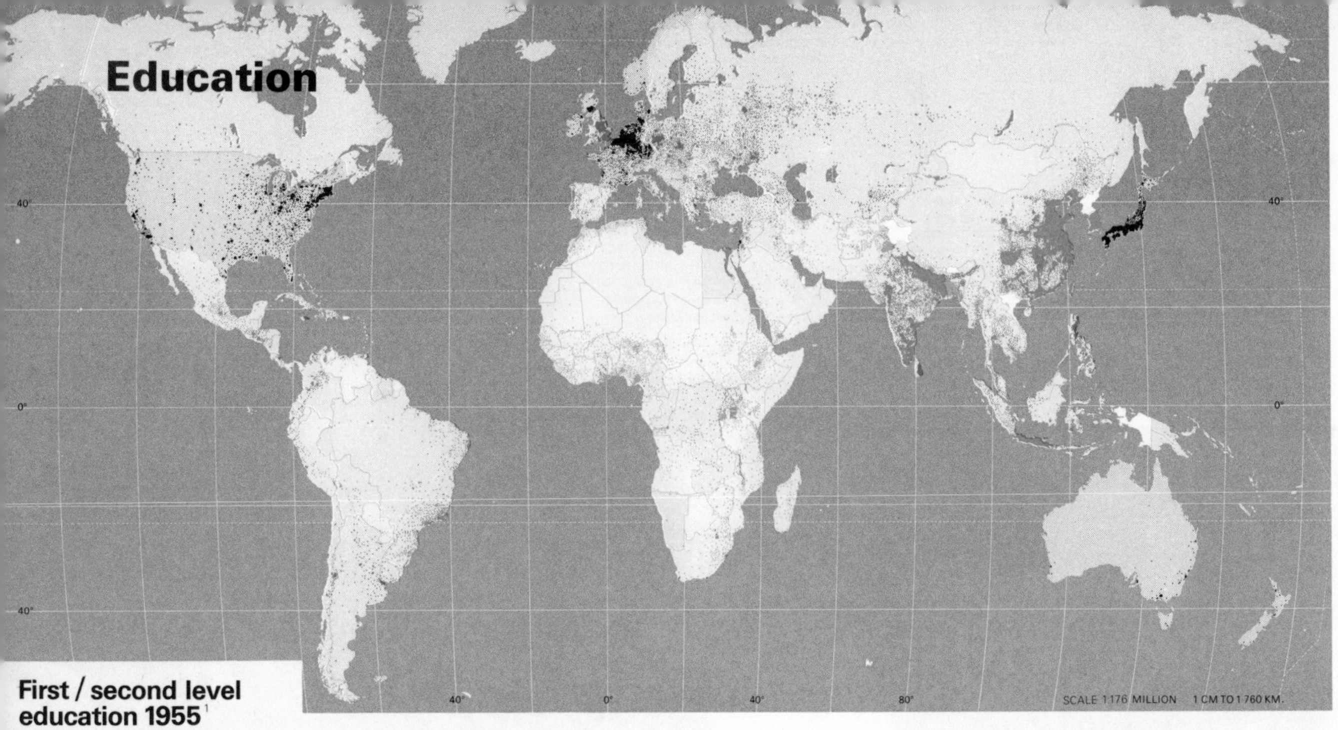
SCALE 1:176 MILLION 1 CM TO 1 760 KM.

First / second level education 1955[1]

Percentage of 5-19 year-olds enrolled in schools

- 85 AND OVER
- 65 – 85
- 45 – 65
- 25 – 45
- UNDER 25
- DATA NA

One dot to 100 000 population

[1]Adjusted

The school enrolment figures on which these maps are based have been compiled on the principle of enrolment figures in all types of school related to the estimated population figures of 5–19 year olds and adjusted to minimize the effect of differences in the national school systems. It should be emphasized that these ratios can be regarded only as indicators of the development of education at the first and second levels for a given country, and they should be treated with great caution in international comparisons.

Education at the first level is taken as 'basic instruction in the tools of learning' which continues for about 6 years in most countries, where it may be compulsory unless there is no suitable school within reach and may also be free. In some countries secondary education is an alternative to primary, or they may overlap, but normally the second level of education provides general or specialized instruction for a pupil who has had at least four years schooling at the first level. From 1950–1966 total enrolment at first and second levels of education increased by 70% and 154% respectively.

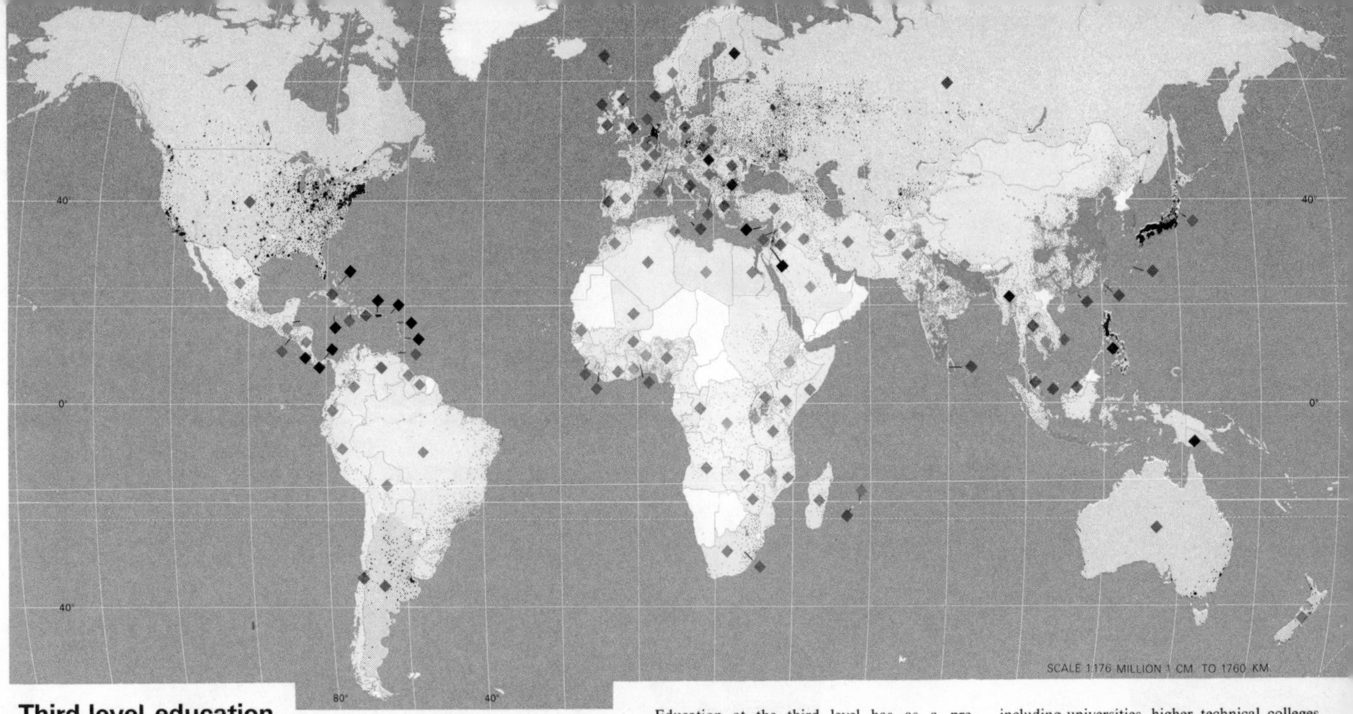
SCALE 1:176 MILLION 1 CM. TO 1 760 KM.

Third level education

Number of students per 100 000 population (1963-5 av.)

- 1000 – 3 000
- 760 – 1000
- 360 – 760
- 60 – 360
- UNDER 60
- DATA NA

One dot to 100 000 population

Percentage of students who are female (1965)

- 40 – 55
- 30 – 39
- 20 – 29
- 10 – 19
- UNDER 10

Education at the third level has as a prerequisite successful completion of education at the second level or evidence of attainment of the equivalent. From 1950–1965 the enrolment at the third level of education increased by 216%, the estimated world enrolment in 1950 being 6.5 millions, in 1960 11.5 millions and in 1965 18 millions. During this time the total population increase was 31%. Education at this level comprises all types of institution, public or private, which are concerned with higher education—whether they grant degrees or not—including universities, higher technical colleges, teacher training colleges (except those included at the second level of education) and theological colleges. As far as possible the figures include part-time students but exclude those taking correspondence courses (except in the U.S.S.R. and Hungary). Where there are no figures available for a locality it may mean that third level education is undertaken in another country; some or all of the third level students in many countries may be attending educational institutions abroad.

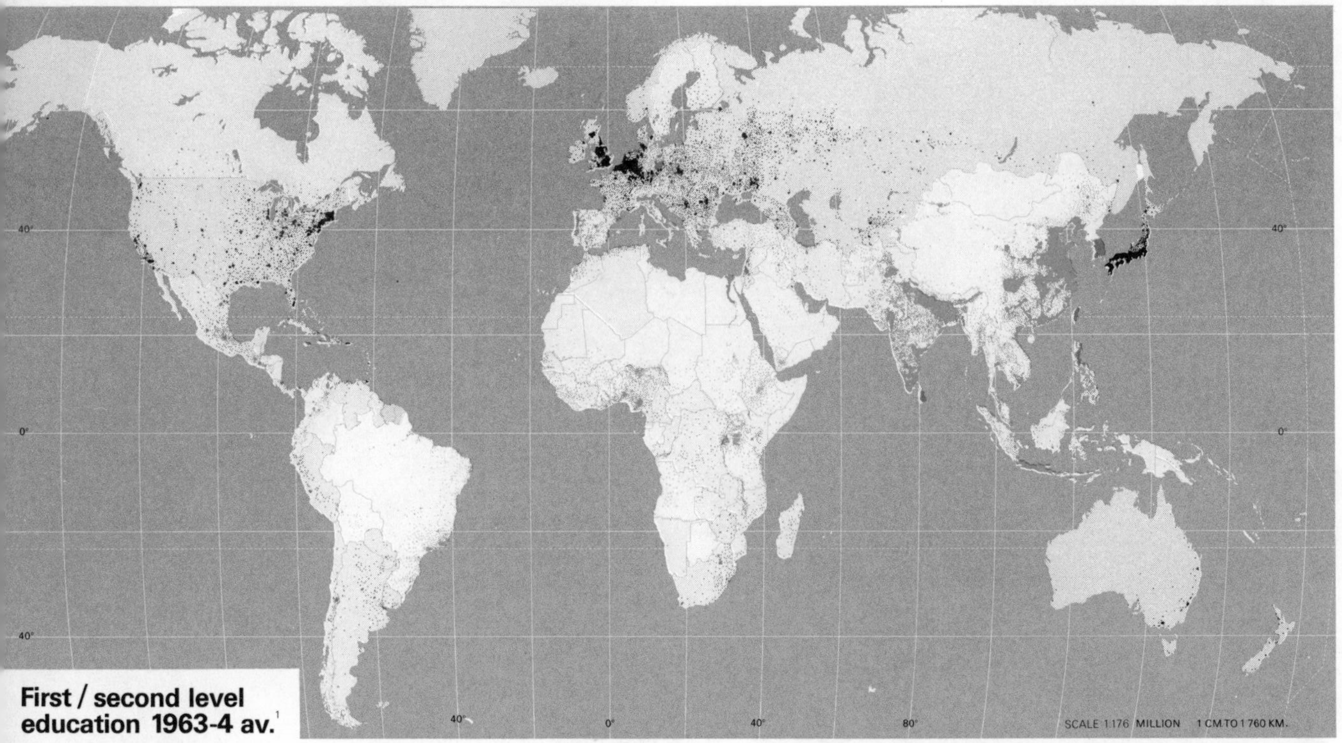
SCALE 1:176 MILLION 1 CM TO 1 760 KM.

First / second level education 1963-4 av.[1]

Percentage of 5-19 year-olds enrolled in schools

- 85 AND OVER
- 65 – 85
- 45 – 65
- 25 – 45
- UNDER 25
- DATA NA

One dot to 100 000 population

[1]Adjusted

Education programmes at both first and second levels in developing countries are frequently hampered by shortages of money, equipment and teachers, and in some cases there is great dependence on outside help to supply teaching assistance. Poor communications are another hindrance to the spread of education, but in many areas increased educational development has been encouraged by increased mechanization of industry and farming bringing greater demands by employers for educational attainment.

The second level of education may include teacher training, but teachers trained at this level may often be restricted to pre-school, first level or vocational teaching; some countries (such as Israel and Colombia) include all teacher training with their second level of education figures. In Argentina, where there is high enrolment for third level education, 87% of the teachers training at the second level are women, but in Ethiopia and Liberia, where third level enrolment is low, only 10% and 6% of those training at the second level are women, suggesting that there may be a correlation between the education level of women and the overall enrolment for third level education.

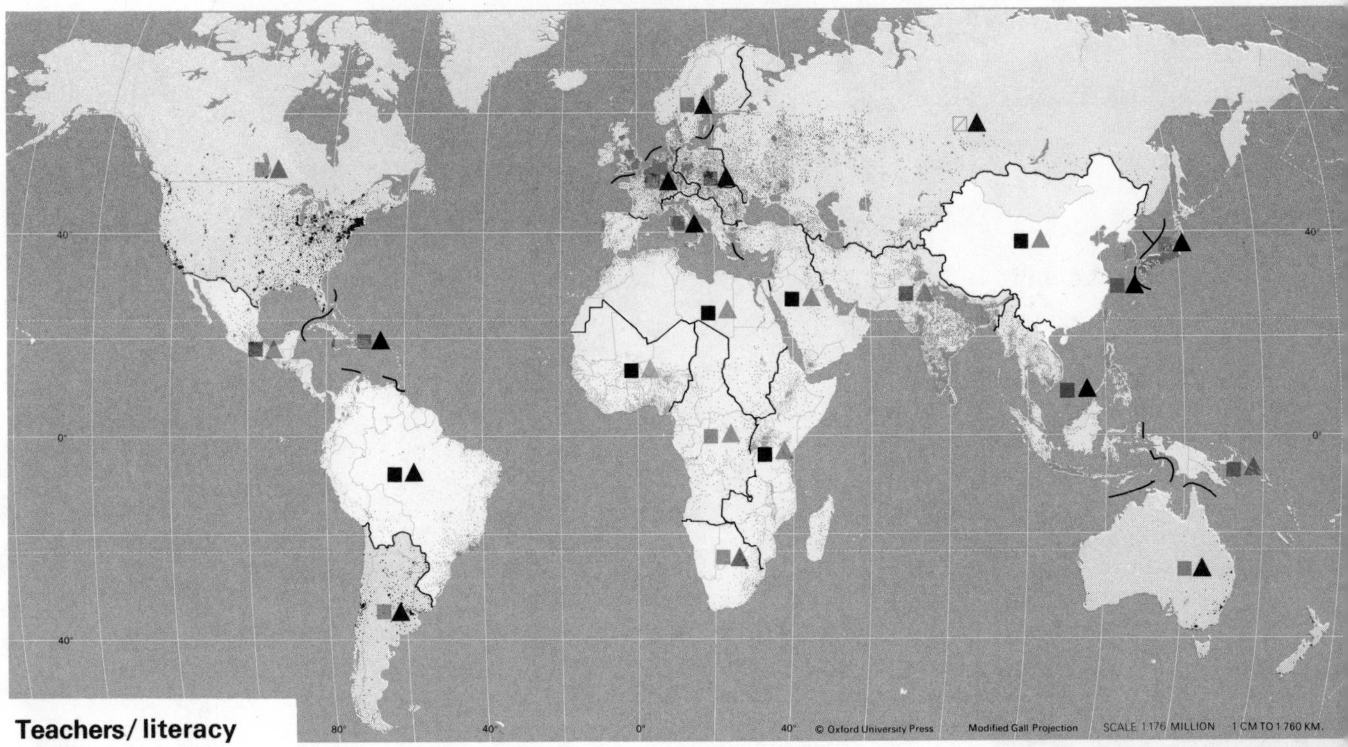
© Oxford University Press
Modified Gall Projection
SCALE 1:176 MILLION 1 CM TO 1 760 KM.

Teachers / literacy

Number at all levels per '000 population by area (1965)[1]

- 10 – 12
- 8 – 10
- 5 – 8
- 2.5 – 5
- UNDER 2.5
- DATA NA

One dot to 100 000 population

Increase in number of teachers

Percentage increase for all levels by area (1950-65)[1]

- 200 – 260
- 150 – 199
- 100 – 149
- 50 – 99
- UNDER 50
- DATA NA

Annual increase in adult literacy[2]

Percentage of annual adult population increase by area (1950-60)[1]

- 100 AND OVER
- 86 – 99
- 40 – 85
- 20 – 39
- UNDER 20

[1]As used by UNESCO [2] World average 86.6%

Adult literacy is here defined as the ability both to read and to write at the age of 15 years. Where the increased number of adult literates is equal to the increase in adult population the percentage increase in adult literacy is 100; where the increase exceeds 100%, illiteracy is being overcome; where it is below 100%, education is falling behind population increase.

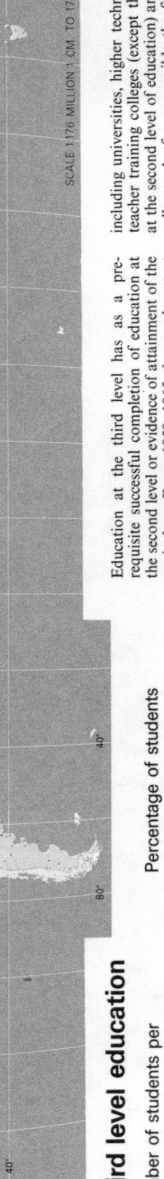

Employment

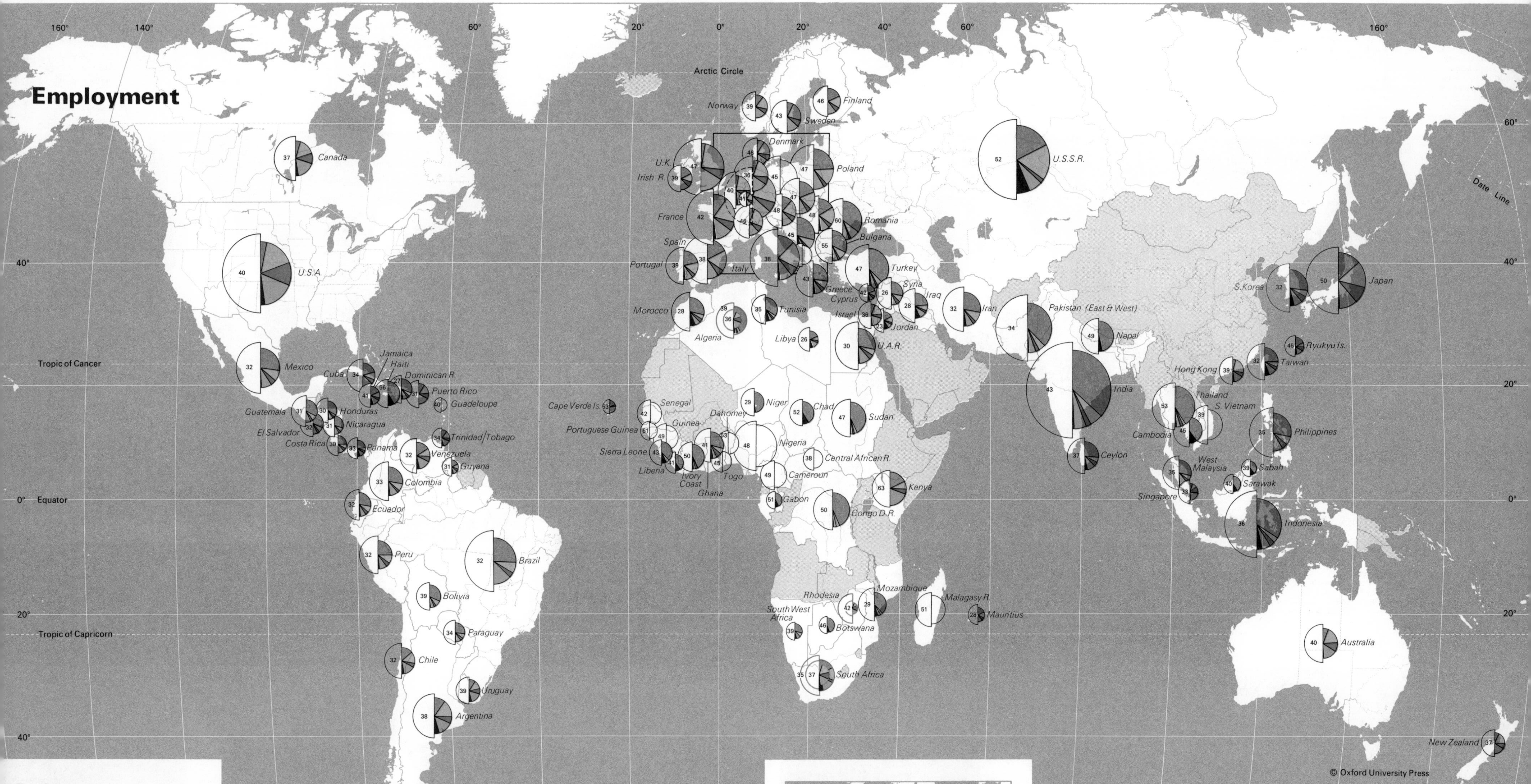

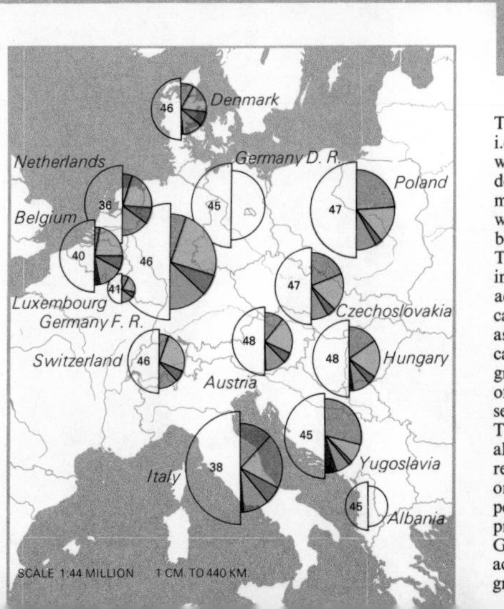

Employment

Population (latest census)

TOTAL — ECONOMICALLY ACTIVE

42 PERCENTAGE ECONOMICALLY ACTIVE

Red and green outlines are used to differentiate between ethnic groups where data are available (see note).

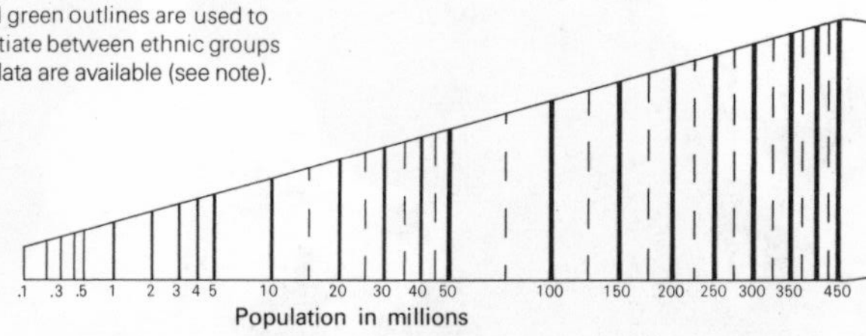

Economic activity [1]

GROUP A (U.N. GROUP 0)	Agriculture, forestry, fishing and hunting
GROUP B (U.N. GROUPS 1-4)	Manufacturing, construction, mining and quarrying
GROUP C (U.N. GROUP 6)	Commerce
GROUP D (U.N. GROUPS 5,7,8)	Services, including electricity, gas, water, sanitary services, transport, etc.
GROUP E (U.N. GROUP 9)	Others (see note), including the above categories when too small to show separately

[1] Based on data from the United Nations International Labour Office 'Yearbook of Labour Statistics 1966'

The data presented refer to the economically active population, i.e., to the total of employed persons. This excludes students, women occupied solely in domestic duties, retired persons and dependents. The treatment of such groups as armed forces, inmates of institutions, occupants of reservations, persons seeking work for the first time, seasonal and part-time workers varies between countries.

The comparability of the data is further hampered by differences in methods of collection and tabulation. Definitions of economic activity also vary, as does the minimum age at which the term can apply. For example, the extent to which family workers, who assist in family enterprises, are included amongst the 'economically active' varies from country to country. The employment groupings are also subject to some inconsistency. However, none of these dissimilarities is so great that the value of the map is seriously impaired.

The nine United Nations employment groups have been reallocated into five main employment categories to simplify representation. Where the right-hand semi-circle is empty, data on the division of labour are not available. Where data on the percentage economically active are unavailable, a black tone is printed over that country.

Group E (United Nations Group 9) consists of the economically active population which cannot be categorized according to groups A-D. Where the unemployed are not classified according to their last job, they are frequently included under group E, as are those seeking work for the first time. Group E also includes any groups of A-D, which would be too small to be shown as distinct sectors.

In Algeria, Rhodesia and South Africa, superimposed symbols facilitate a comparison between the economic activities of different ethnic groups. In Algeria the green circle represents Europeans and the red circle non-Europeans. In Rhodesia the green circle represents non-Africans and the red circle Africans, and in South Africa, the green circle represents 'whites' and the red circle 'non-whites'.

It is significant to note the dependence upon primary industries (agriculture, fishing etc.) in developing countries. These countries are characterized by small service industries and little commerce.

Secondary industries (such as manufacturing) and tertiary industries (services) develop as a country becomes more industrialized —Canada, the U.S.A. and the U.K. have noticeably large service industries.

When developed countries have large agricultural industries these are often so highly mechanized that they employ comparatively few people, as in the U.S.A., Canada and Australia. Therefore, it should be emphasized that the sectors refer to the numbers employed in each category and not the financial importance of the industries in that category.

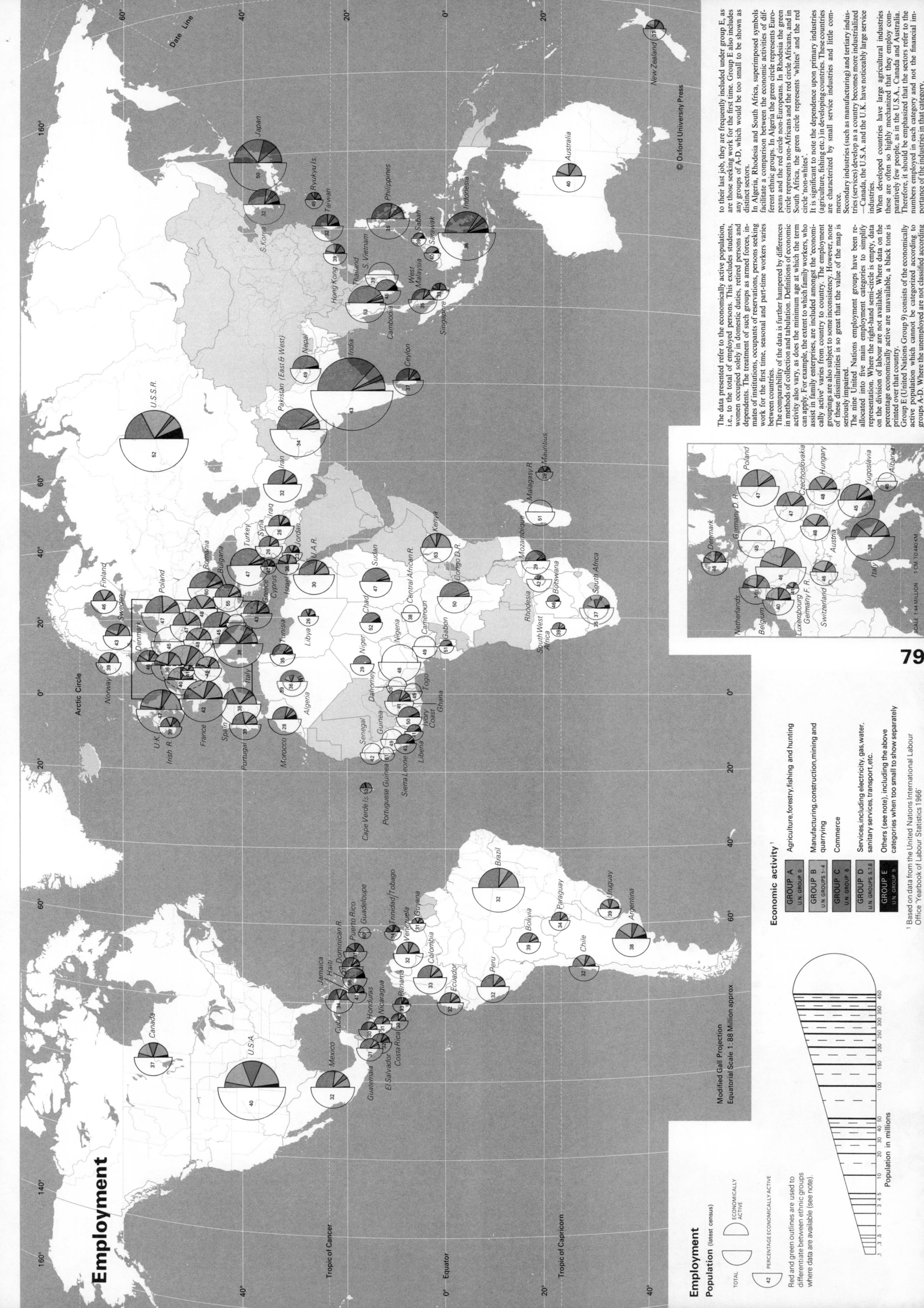

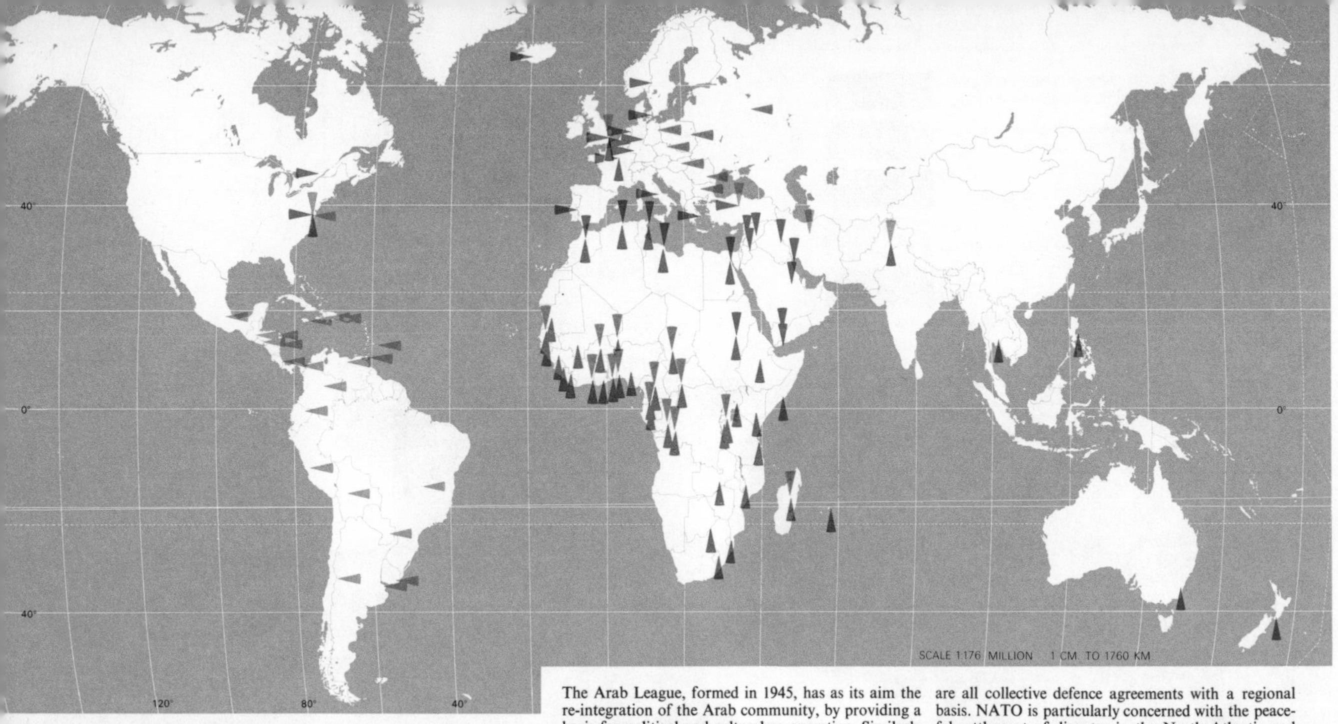

Political / defence blocs

Membership of multilateral organizations (1969)

- Arab League
- OAS (Organization of American States)
- OAU (Organization of African Unity)
- OCAM (Afro–Malagasy Common Organization)
- CENTO (Central Treaty Organization)
- Warsaw Pact
- NATO (North Atlantic Treaty Organization)
- SEATO (South East Asia Treaty Organization)

The Arab League, formed in 1945, has as its aim the re-integration of the Arab community, by providing a basis for political and cultural co-operation. Similarly the more recently formed Organization of African Unity (1963) has as its chief objective the furtherance of African solidarity and unity. The Organization of American States(1948) differs in that it aims at mutual co-operation starting from a geographic basis as a hemisphere rather than from a common cultural framework. It includes the U.S.A. as a member along with the majority of Latin American nations. The North Atlantic Treaty Organization (1949), the South-East Asia Treaty Organization (1954) and the Central Treaty Organization (previously the Baghdad Pact 1955) are all collective defence agreements with a regional basis. NATO is particularly concerned with the peaceful settlement of disputes in the North Atlantic and Mediterranean areas. SEATO provides for collective security action in SE. Asia and the SW. Pacific. CENTO deals with disputes and political or economic problems in the general area of its member states. The Warsaw Pact (1955) is a mutual defence agreement signed by the U.S.S.R. and most East European countries.

Apart from regional political groupings, the United Nations organization, an international peace-keeping body with membership covering most of the world, has been in existence since 1945.

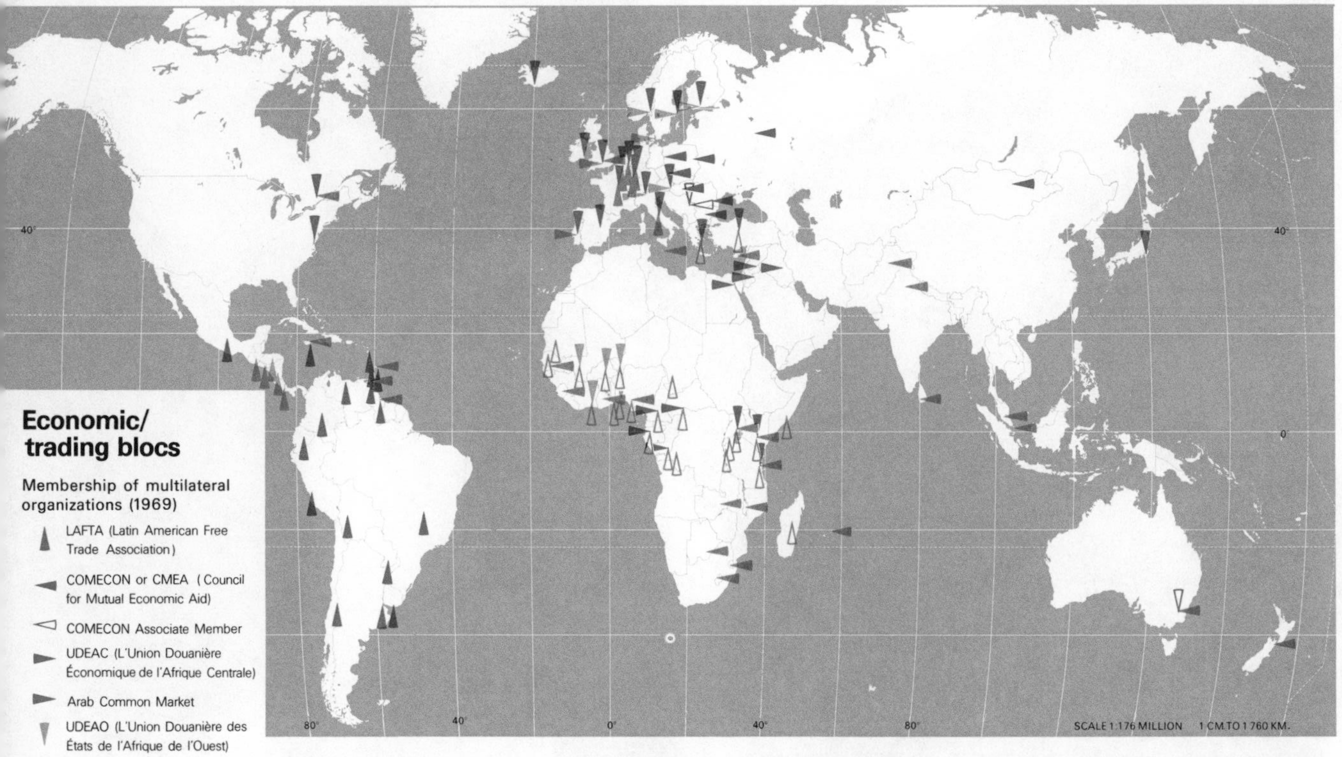

Economic/ trading blocs

Membership of multilateral organizations (1969)

- LAFTA (Latin American Free Trade Association)
- COMECON or CMEA (Council for Mutual Economic Aid)
- COMECON Associate Member
- UDEAC (L'Union Douanière Économique de l'Afrique Centrale)
- Arab Common Market
- UDEAO (L'Union Douanière des États de l'Afrique de l'Ouest)
- EEC (European Economic Community)
- EEC Associate Member
- CACM (Central American Common Market)
- CARIFTA (Caribbean Free Trade Area)
- East African Community
- EFTA (European Free Trade Association)
- EFTA Associate Member
- Commonwealth
- OECD (Organization for Economic Co-operation and Development)
- OECD Associate Member

The main regional economic groupings in the world are indicated above, but several more broadly based economic agreements also exist, in close relationship to the main United Nations organization. The General Agreement on Tariffs and Trade, (GATT 1948), with 76 full members by 1969, lays down regulations and controls on world trade. Notably absent are many developing countries especially in Latin America and the Middle East. Also in existence are the International Monetary Fund, (IMF), aiming at promoting international monetary co-operation; the International Bank for Reconstruction and Development, (World Bank), which provides capital to facilitate investment and economic development; and the closely affiliated International Finance Corporation, (IFC), which supplements World Bank activities.

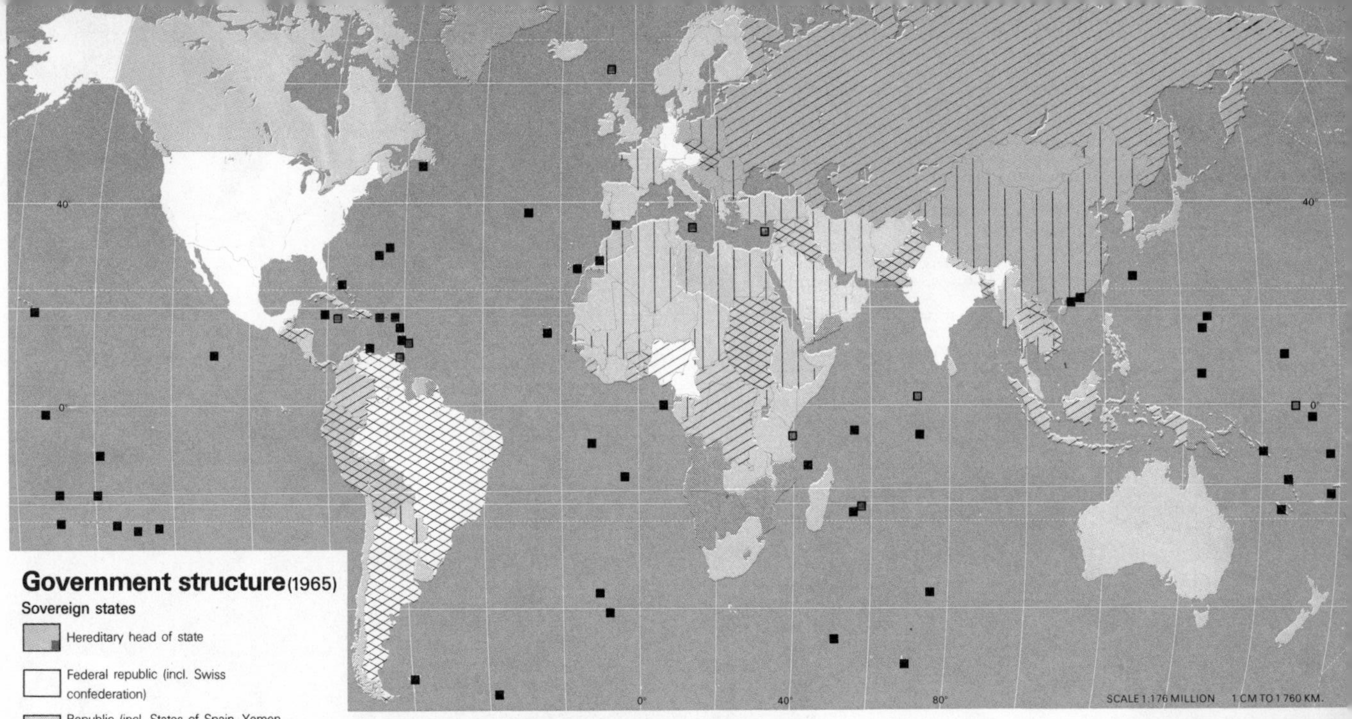

Government structure (1965)

Sovereign states

- Hereditary head of state
- Federal republic (incl. Swiss confederation)
- Republic (incl. States of Spain, Yemen and Kuwait)
- Socialist republic (incl. People's Republic, Socialist Federal Republic, Federation of Soviet Republics)

Non–sovereign states

- Overseas province or department and other non–sovereign areas (incl. associate states, territories and British colonies)

Political instability[1] (1945–70)

Number of unconstitutional changes in governmental leadership since 1945 (or year of independence if later)[2]

1   2   3 OR MORE

[1] Criteria were military and political coups, abdication under pressure, elimination of opposition parties and suspension of constitution.

[2] Only states independent before 1965 are included.

Between 1965 and 1970 several countries saw a change in their type of government structure. British Guiana (now Guyana), Bechuanaland (now Botswana), Basutoland (now Lesotho) and Barbados all became independent members of the Commonwealth in 1966. Mauritius and Swaziland attained this status in 1968. Rhodesia unilaterally declared independence in November 1965. South Arabia was declared the Southern Yemen People's Republic in 1967. Constantine II fled Greece after failing to restore civilian and democratic government in 1967. Spain plans to have the monarchy reinstated.

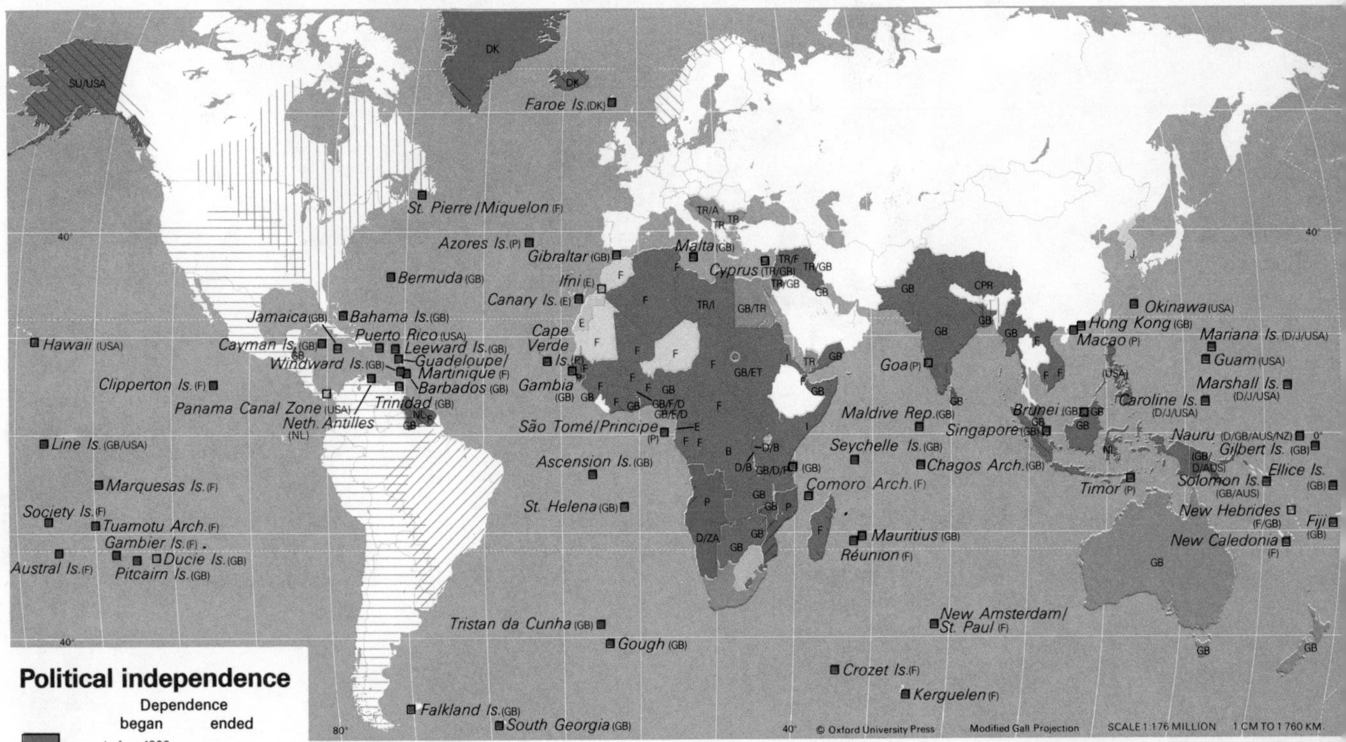

Political independence

Dependence began	ended
before 1900 / after 1900	not before 31st Dec. 1970
before 1900 / after 1900	1930–70
before 1900 / after 1900	1900–30

Suzerain nation

A	Austria	I	Italy
AUS	Australia	J	Japan
B	Belgium	NL	Netherlands
CPR	China P.R.	NZ	New Zealand
D	Germany	P	Portugal
DK	Denmark	SU	U.S.S.R.
E	Spain	TR	Turkey
ET	Egypt	USA	United States
GB	Britain	ZA	South Africa

Areas colonized by 1763

Colonizing nation: Spain, Portugal, Britain, Others

Incl. only colonization of overseas territories. Excl. Ottoman, Chinese and Russian land empires.

Colonial status and political dependence vary in form and degree, so that precise comparison of status is difficult. Furthermore, the nature of transition to independence also varies from a sudden violent overthrow of colonial rule to the final deliberate acknowledgement of an independence which has been complete in all but name for decades. The map shows the spread of political independence, defined here as the attainment of self-government by an area, or its merging with a larger independent state of which it becomes an integral part. Military occupation and changes of boundary resulting from major wars have been excluded from consideration. In addition, areas which achieved their independence before 1900 have been excluded.

Direction of Trade

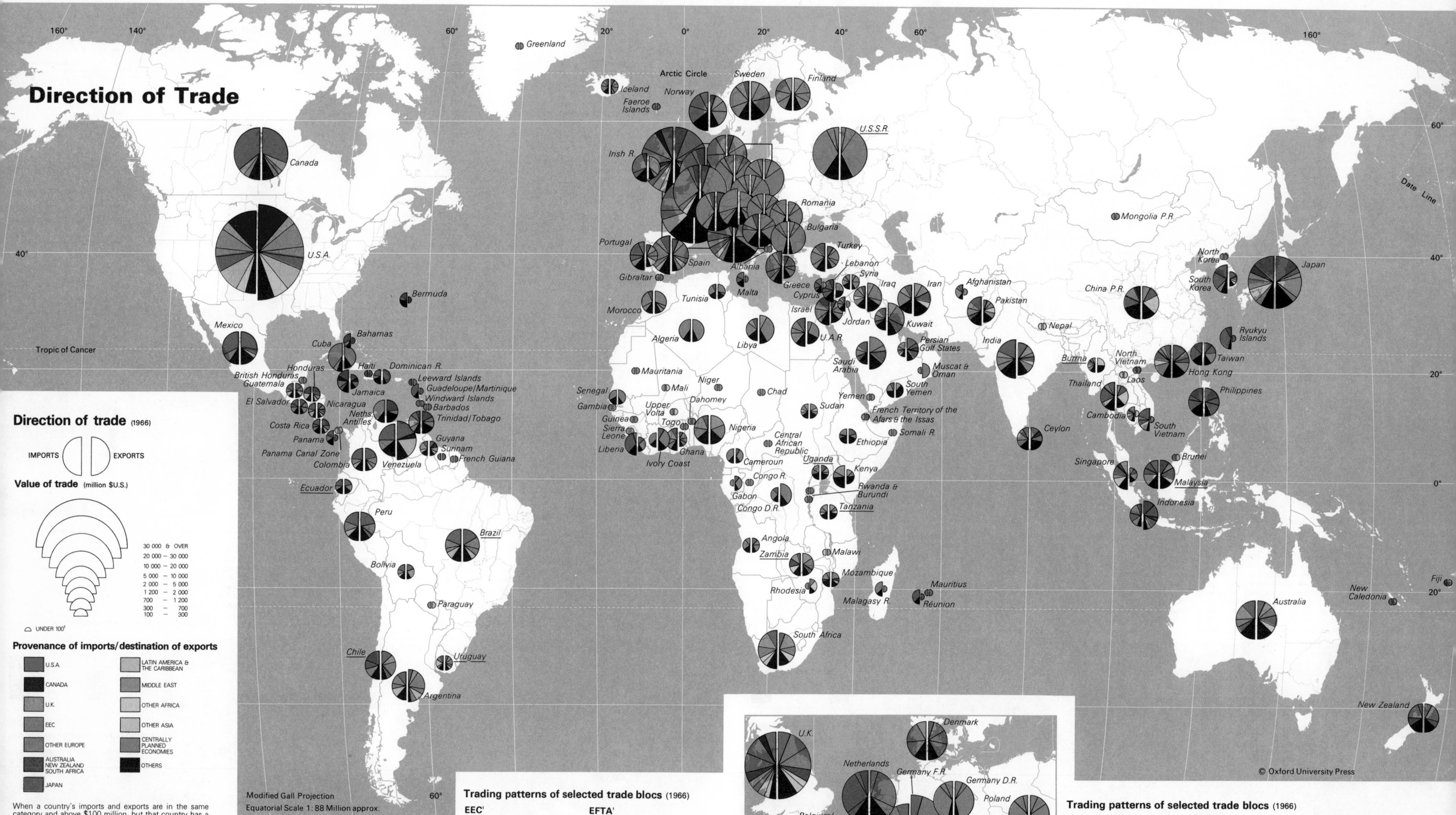

Direction of trade (1966)

IMPORTS EXPORTS

Value of trade (million $U.S.)

30 000 & OVER
20 000 – 30 000
10 000 – 20 000
5 000 – 10 000
2 000 – 5 000
1 200 – 2 000
700 – 1 200
300 – 700
100 – 300

UNDER 100[1]

Provenance of imports/destination of exports

U.S.A.
CANADA
U.K.
EEC
OTHER EUROPE
AUSTRALIA NEW ZEALAND SOUTH AFRICA
JAPAN
LATIN AMERICA & THE CARIBBEAN
MIDDLE EAST
OTHER AFRICA
OTHER ASIA
CENTRALLY PLANNED ECONOMIES
OTHERS

When a country's imports and exports are in the same category and above $100 million, but that country has a trade surplus of at least 10%, its name is underlined.

Other Europe excludes the East European states of COMECON and includes Turkey and Yugoslavia. The Middle East includes Cyprus, Iran, Iraq, Israel, Jordan, Lebanon, Syria, the U.A.R. and the Arabian Peninsula States. Other Africa refers to the African continent excluding South Africa and the U.A.R. The Centrally Planned Economies refers to the Sino-Soviet bloc, including Albania, Bulgaria, China P.R., Cuba, Czechoslovakia, Germany D.R., Hungary, Mongolia P.R., North Korea, North Vietnam, Poland, Romania and the U.S.S.R. For every country 'Others' refers to countries not elsewhere specified, such as Greenland. However for each country 'Others' also includes those categories too small to be shown separately.

[1]For this category only the largest provenance and/or destination of trade is shown.

This map includes trade in 'visible' commodities only; it excludes trade in 'invisibles', such as banking, insurance, shipping and tourism, which play a significant role in the trading pattern and balance of payments of countries such as the U.K., Switzerland, Liberia and Greece.

Modified Gall Projection
Equatorial Scale 1: 88 Million approx.

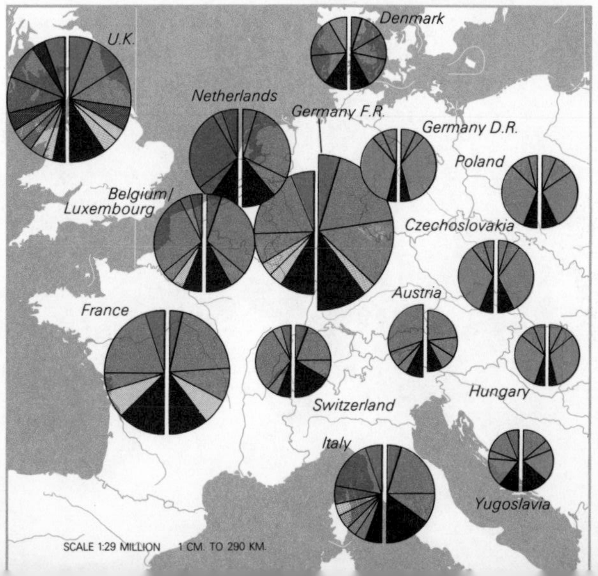

Total value of world trade (1966) $419 200 million

Proportion accounted for by selected countries and groups of countries (see legend for colour code)

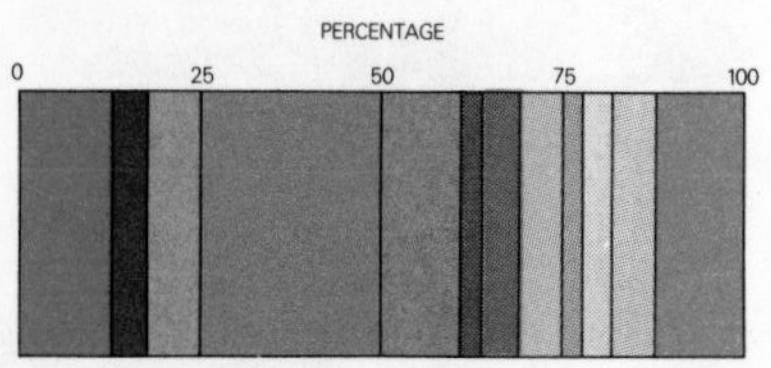

Trading patterns of selected trade blocs (1966)

EEC[1]

Total value of trade $106 492 million
Internal trade 43%
External trade 57%
Imports $30 881 million
Exports $29 426 million

	PERCENTAGE IMPORTS	PERCENTAGE EXPORTS
EFTA	25	36
U.S.A.	20	14
Other Africa[2]	14	9
Middle East	9	5
LAFTA	8	5
COMECON	6	6
Other Europe	4	9
Others	14	16
	100	100

[1]Includes Belgium, France, Germany F.R., Italy, Luxembourg and Netherlands
[2]Excludes U.A.R. and South Africa

EFTA[1]

Total value of trade $65 738 million
Internal trade 24%
External trade 76%
Imports $27 640 million
Exports $22 573 million

	PERCENTAGE IMPORTS	PERCENTAGE EXPORTS
EEC	40	34
U.S.A.	13	14
COMECON	6	6
Other Africa[2]	6	6
LAFTA	5	4
Other Europe	4	8
Middle East	4	5
Others	22	23
	100	100

[1]Includes Austria, Denmark, Norway, Portugal, Sweden, Switzerland, U.K. and Finland (associate member)
[2]Excludes U.A.R. and South Africa

Trading patterns of selected trade blocs (1966)

COMECON*,[1]

Total value of trade $41 826 million
Internal trade 61%
External trade 39%
Imports $8 048 million
Exports $8 320 million

	PERCENTAGE IMPORTS	PERCENTAGE EXPORTS
EEC	27	25
EFTA	21	21
Other Sino-Soviet bloc	11	14
Other Europe	8	10
Other Asia[2]	7	6
Others	26	24
	100	100

*Estimated
[1]Includes Bulgaria, Czechoslovakia, Germany D.R., Hungary, Mongolia P.R. Poland, Romania and U.S.S.R.
[2]Excludes Japan

LAFTA[1]

Total value of trade $18 252 million
Internal trade 10%
External trade 90%
Imports $7 232 million
Exports $9 163 million

	PERCENTAGE IMPORTS	PERCENTAGE EXPORTS
U.S.A.	50	36
EEC	22	23
EFTA	12	12
Other Latin America	1	10[2]
Others	15	19
	100	100

[1]Includes Argentina, Bolivia, Brazil, Chile, Colombia, Ecuador, Mexico, Paraguay Peru, Uruguay and Venezuela
[2]Three-fifths of which was Venezuela exports to Netherlands Antilles

CACM[1]

Total value of trade $1 778 million
Internal trade 20%
External trade 80%
Imports $756 million
Exports $674 million

	PERCENTAGE IMPORTS	PERCENTAGE EXPORTS
U.S.A.	51	44
EEC	19	29
Japan	8	13
LAFTA	6	—
Other Latin America	3	1
Others	13	13
	100	100

[1]Includes Costa Rica, El Salvador, Guatemala, Honduras and Nicaragua

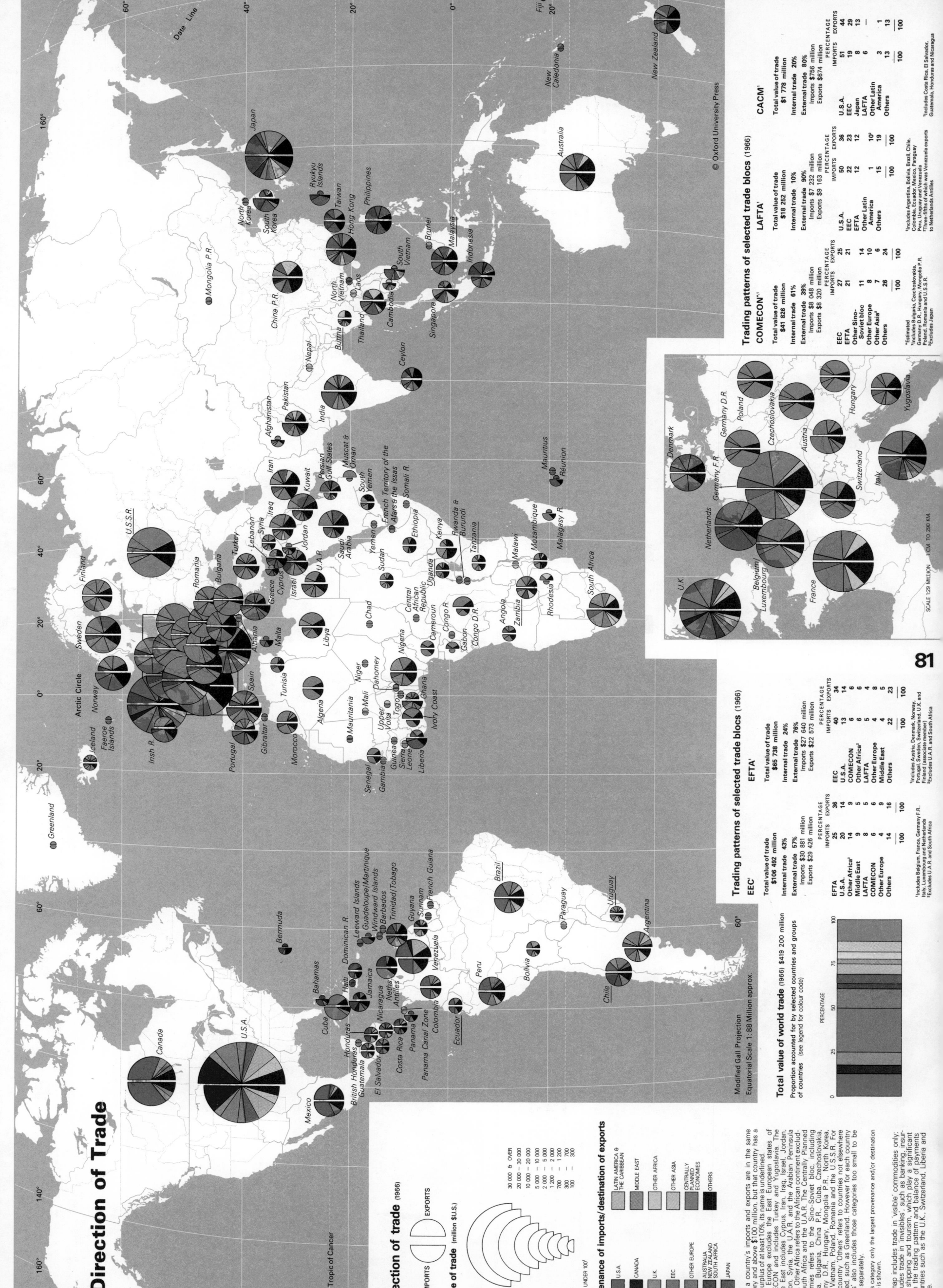

Foreign Aid/Trade

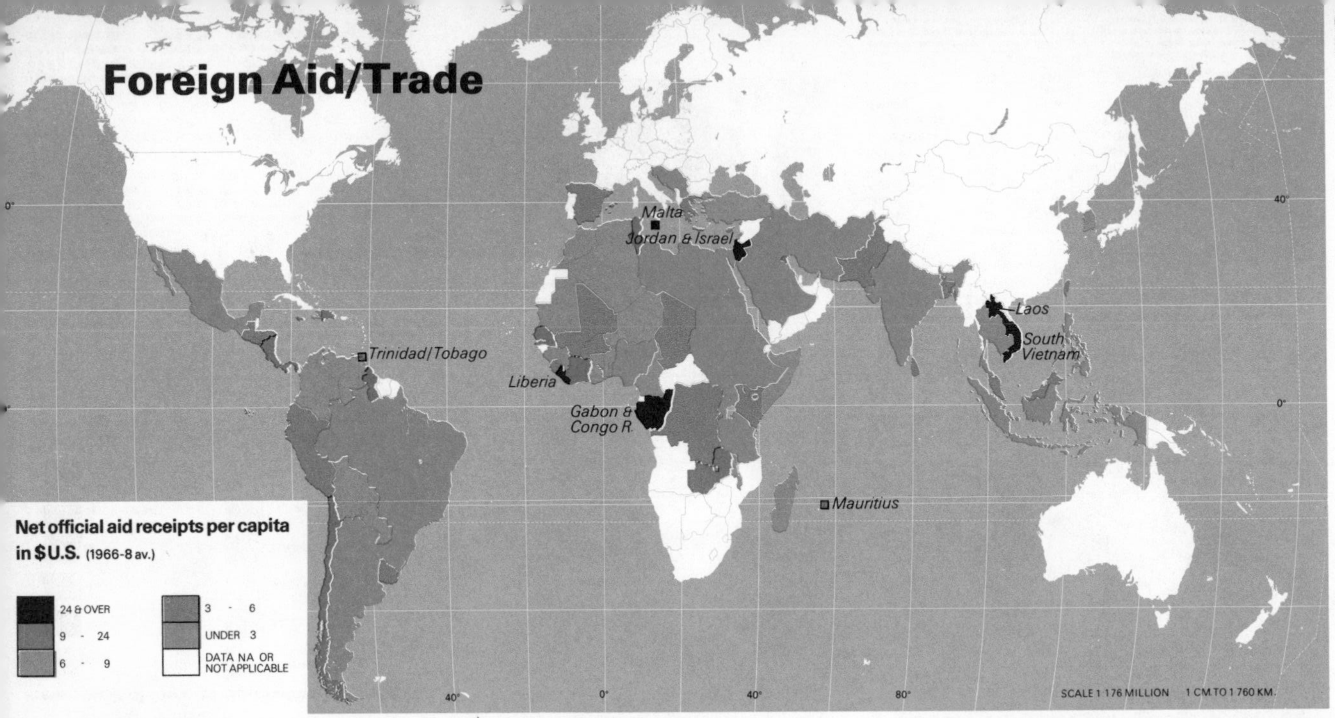

Net official aid receipts per capita in $U.S. (1966-8 av.)

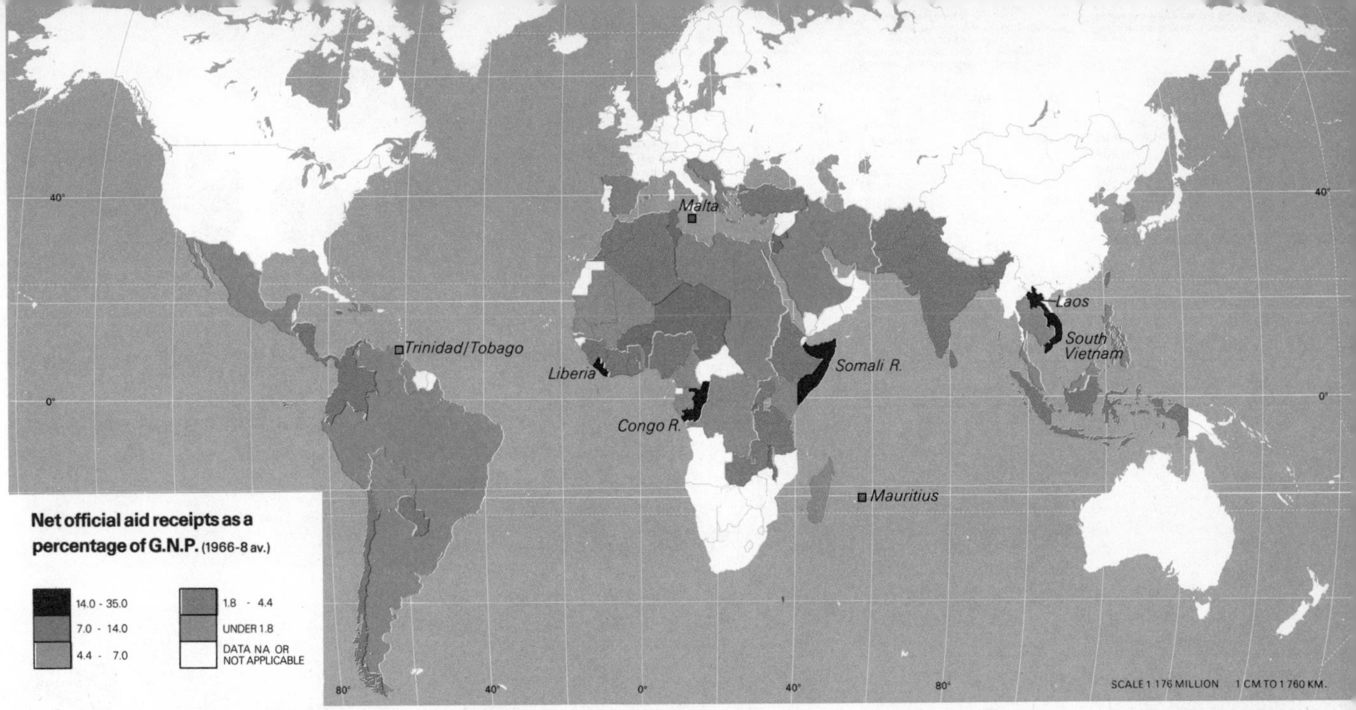

Net official aid receipts as a percentage of G.N.P. (1966-8 av.)

Most developing countries are trying to raise incomes by investing more in agriculture, industry and economic infrastructure such as roads and ports. They must maintain or increase social expenditure on education and health, and in many cases political independence has led to a greatly increased military expenditure. This leads to two 'gaps'—firstly between the revenue governments can raise from domestic taxation and savings, and the expenditures to which they are committed; and secondly, a gap between export earnings and import requirements. Foreign aid helps to fill these two gaps.

In general aid is a far more important factor to the recipient countries than to the donor countries. Few donor countries contribute as much as one per cent of their G.N.P. yet this can play a vital part in the development programmes of the recipient countries.

Unfortunately aid is not always given in ways that produce the greatest benefit to recipient countries. Donor countries prefer to give aid directly rather than through international organizations and, not unnaturally, tend to give it in ways that lead to the greatest political advantages, and the least economic sacrifices.

Thus aid is often 'tied' to imports from the donor country, which may be more expensive or technically less suitable than similar goods from other sources; or it may be 'tied' to projects which are attractive to the donor country, sometimes resulting in unnecessary prestige projects.

'Food aid' may stave off famine, but is often a convenient way for the donor to dispose of surplus stocks and can, in the process, damage the development of food and agricultural industries of the recipent country. Construction projects may be tied to contractors from the donor country, with the result that much of the 'aid' immediately flows back to the donor country, even when local firms could have done the work. Technical assistance (skilled personnel) is invariably tied to personnel from the donor countries. Various estimates suggest that if all forms of 'tying' were abandoned, the real value of aid to recipients would rise by at least fifty per cent.

Another factor reducing the value of 'aid' is that, *despite the name*, much consists of loans at various rates of interest. Some are merely commercial loans from suppliers of equipment, guaranteed by the government of the donor country. In other cases 'soft' loans are given with low interest rates and long repayment periods. However, combined debt repayment and interest payments from recipients to donors now make up about 19% of the gross outflow of aid.

Donors also concentrate their aid on countries within their 'sphere of influence' or where they have important commercial investments. This can be a powerful weapon to influence economic and political policies of recipient countries.

The result is that the distribution of aid between countries bears little relationship to population, or to development needs, while global figures of the amounts given or received give a faulty picture of the real cost to the donor, or the real benefit to the recipient. Many of these drawbacks would be remedied if more aid was given through international agencies like the United Nations, but donors are unwilling to relinquish the political influence their aid carries with it.

Some of the deficiencies in the official aid programmes are compensated for by investment from private companies. In 1968 of the total net disbursements to developing countries, investment by private companies accounted for over 40%. Developing nations offer tax benefits and other inducements in an effort to offset the fears of foreign investors that their industries might be nationalized and confiscated.

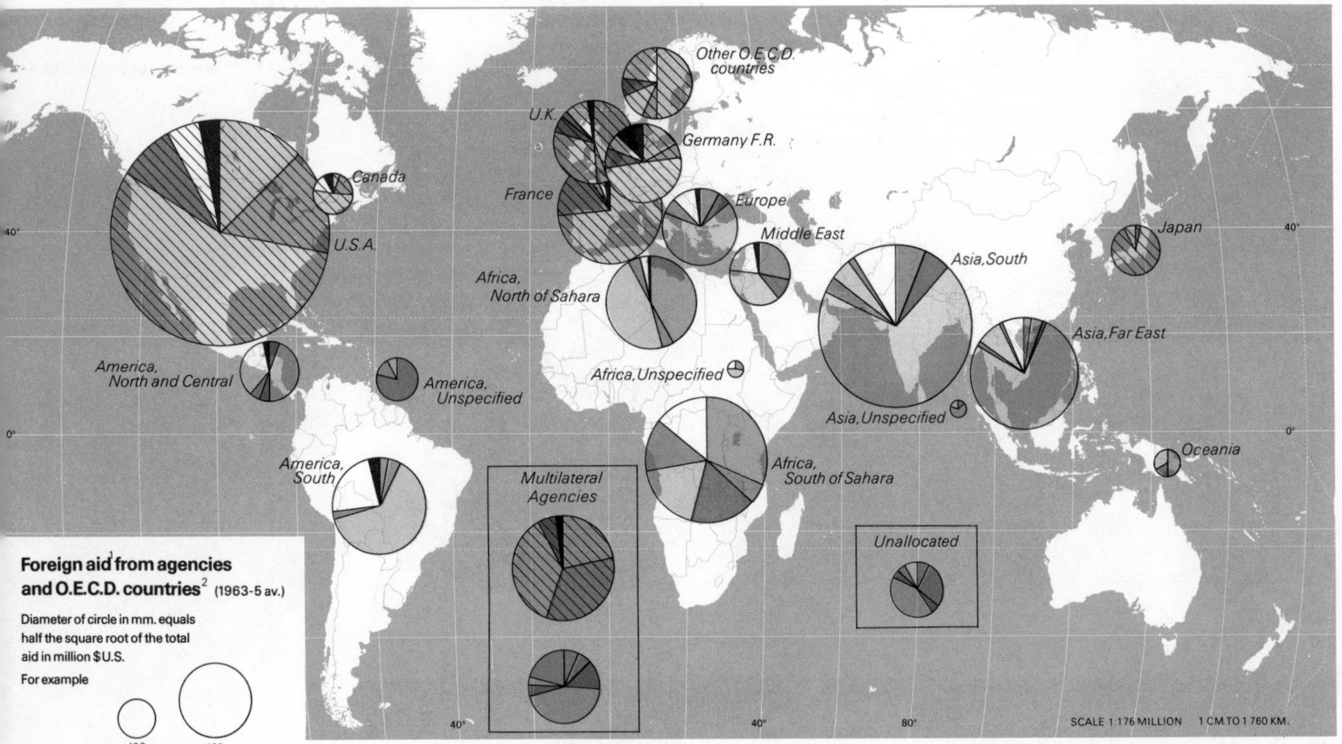

Foreign aid[1] from agencies and O.E.C.D. countries[2] (1963-5 av.)

Total aid to each recipient region divided in proportion to the amount given by the following donor countries :

FRANCE, GERMANY F.R., U.K., U.S.A., CANADA, JAPAN, OTHER O.E.C.D., MULTILATERAL AGENCIES, UNDIFFERENTIATED

Total aid from each donor country divided in proportion to the amount given to the following recipient regions :

AFRICA, AMERICA, ASIA, EUROPE, OCEANIA, MULTILATERAL AGENCIES, OTHER/UNALLOCATED

[1]Net flow of total official financial resources. Incl. money donations by governments as bilateral aid or through multilateral agencies. Incl. repayment of loans but not interest paid on official debt. Excl. aid from the U.S.S.R. and China P.R. (roughly estimated to be $350 million in 1966). Excl. unofficial, or private, aid or investment and aid in non-monetary form.

[2]Incl. Austria, Belgium, Canada, Denmark, France, Germany F.R., Greece, Iceland, Irish R., Italy, Japan, Luxembourg, Netherlands, Norway, Portugal, Spain, Sweden, Switzerland, Turkey, U.K., and U.S.A.

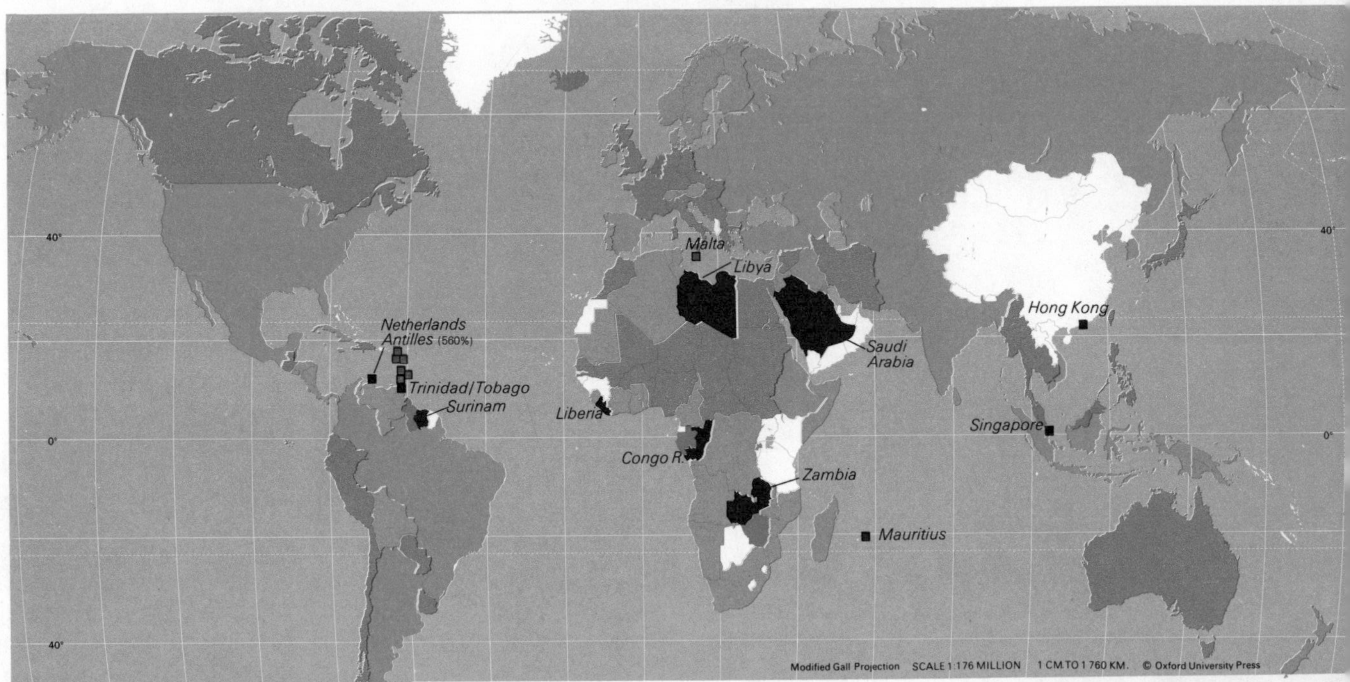

International trade[1] as a percentage of G.N.P. (1965)

100 & OVER; 70 - 100; 40 - 70; 20 - 40; 5 - 20; DATA NA

[1]Exports plus imports

The larger and more developed a country, the greater is the range of goods it can produce efficiently within its national boundaries with less reliance on trade. This depends more on its having a wide range of industries than on its having extensive natural resources. Thus, the U.S. and the U.S.S.R. both have very low dependence on trade, but even Japan with meagre natural resources but high G.N.P. has fairly low trade dependence. The picture is less clear for developing countries. A few (India and Pakistan) have large enough populations to support a wide range of industries, despite very low per capita incomes, and have low dependence on trade. The majority, however, have smaller and less sophisticated economies, and have to import most manufactured goods, which they pay for by exporting primary products. For countries rich in primary products this can lead to very high dependence on trade, which ties their economic growth to the primary products needs of the developed countries. Many developing countries have therefore tried to increase their economic growth by reducing dependence on trade through industrialization. Paradoxically this may initially lead to greater dependence on trade, since more primary products have to be exported to pay for imports of plant and equipment. A few resource-poor areas (Singapore) have achieved high dependence on trade based on exports of manufactured goods, whilst some countries have low dependence on trade simply because they lack potential exports. Policies to reduce trade dependence for political or strategic reasons, or in response to balance of payments problems and demands for protection by domestic producers, also have an impact. However this can be offset by attempts to increase trade within trade blocs. Although not included in this map, it is important to remember that 'invisible' trade in services like tourism, shipping, insurance, or the profits on investment has the same economic role as 'visible' trade in goods. Some countries specialize in exports of such services (Liberia and Greece in shipping; Switzerland and Lebanon in financial services), and to this extent their dependence on trade is underestimated.

Mass Communications

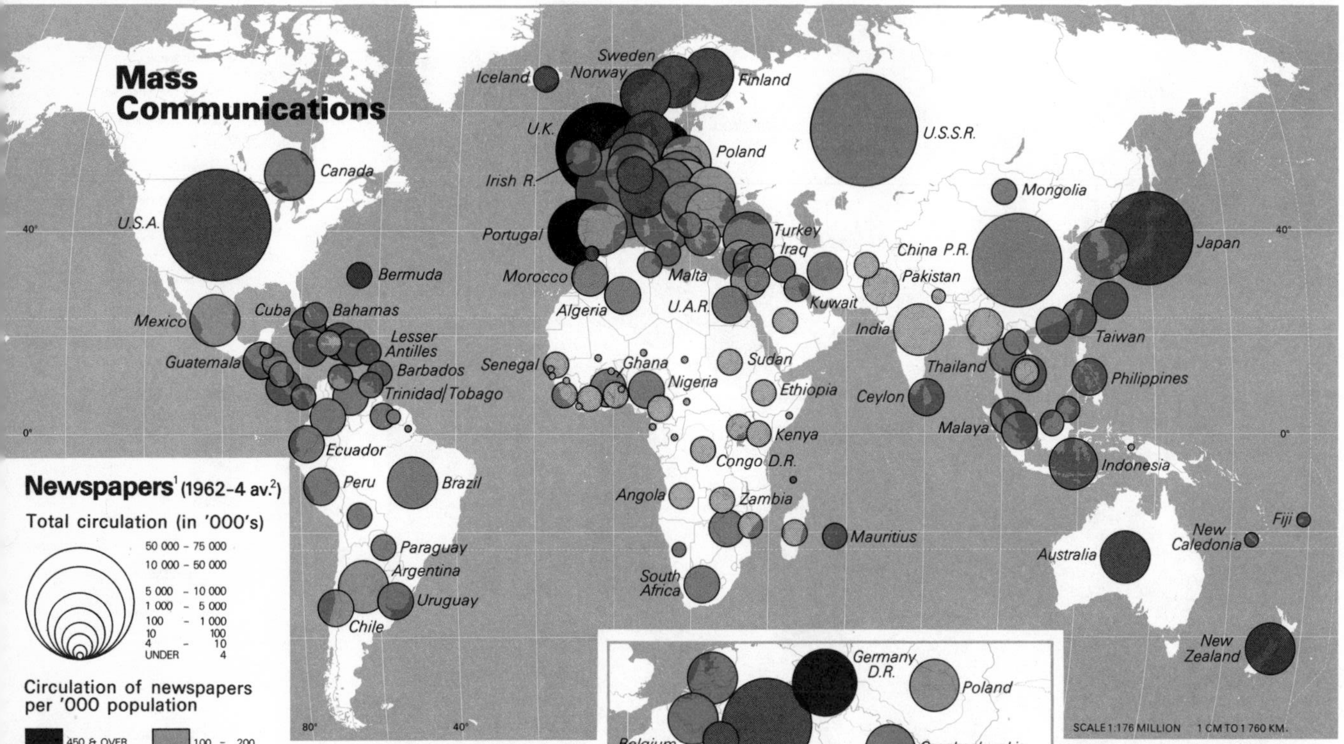
SCALE 1:176 MILLION 1 CM TO 1 760 KM.

Newspapers[1] (1962–4 av.[2])

Total circulation (in '000's)

50 000 – 75 000
10 000 – 50 000
5 000 – 10 000
1 000 – 5 000
100 – 1 000
10 – 100
4 – 10
UNDER 4

Circulation of newspapers per '000 population

450 & OVER | 300 – 450 | 200 – 300 | 100 – 200 | 10 – 100 | UNDER 10

[1]Daily [2]Or latest available previous data. Data are available only for selected newspapers for the following countries: Australia, Chile, Costa Rica, Ethiopia, Honduras, India, Israel, Libya, Morocco, Nigeria, Panama, Syria, Venezuela. Data for the U.S.A. include only English language and for Canada only English and French language newspapers.

Daily newspapers are here defined as publications containing general news and appearing at least four times a week. The size of these publications may vary from a single sheet to fifty or more pages. The data for total circulation represent the total **daily** circulation and refer to the number of copies sold, both inside and outside the country of publication. These figures are generally only estimates, usually official but of varying accuracy.

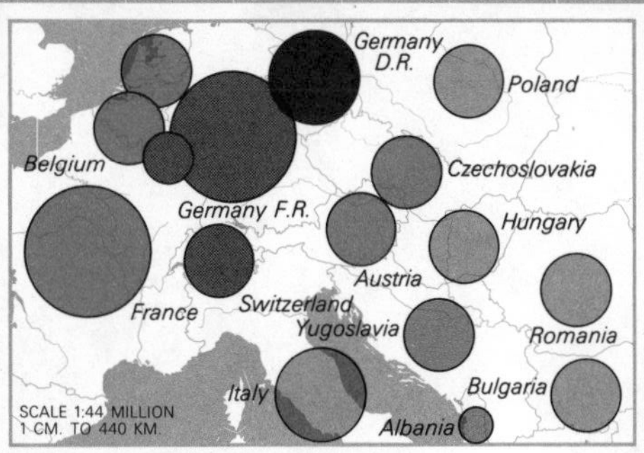
SCALE 1:44 MILLION 1 CM. TO 440 KM.

In recent years increased competition from radio and television has forced the press, particularly of industrialized countries, to consolidate and/or diversify in order to compete more strongly for the advertising revenue which forms its major source of income. However, the transitory nature of radio and television signals, and the need for detailed and local information in more permanent form, have enabled the press to continue expanding despite increased competition.

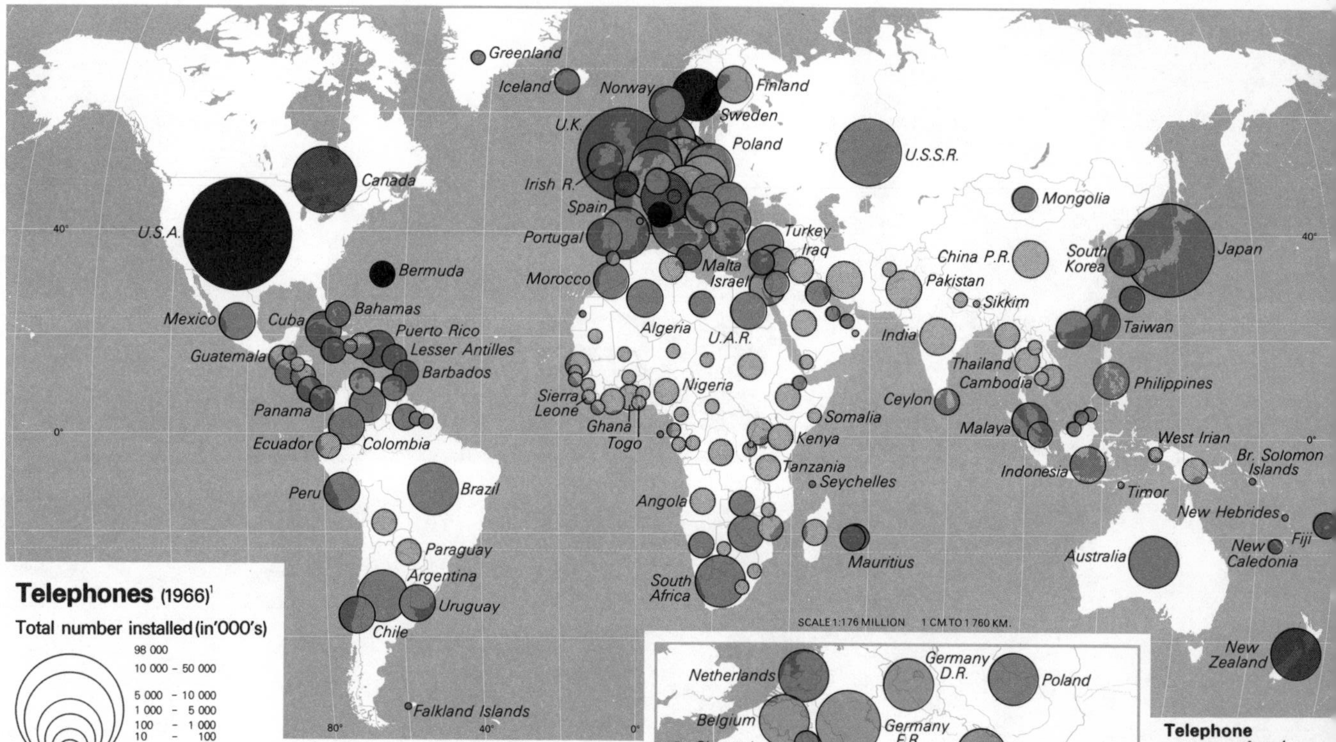
SCALE 1:176 MILLION 1 CM TO 1 760 KM.

Telephones (1966)[1]

Total number installed (in '000's)

98 000
10 000 – 50 000
5 000 – 10 000
1 000 – 5 000
100 – 1 000
10 – 100
1 – 10
UNDER 1

Number of telephones per '000 population

450 & OVER | 300 – 450 | 200 – 300 | 100 – 200 | 10 – 100 | UNDER 10

[1]Or latest available for Albania (1959), China P.R. (1948)

Telephones installed (1966)

	ARGENTINA	JAPAN	SOUTH AFRICA	SPAIN	U.K.	U.S.A.
	PERCENTAGE					
Business[1]	42	68	54	66	54	28
Residence[1]	58	32	46	34	46	72
Ext. & P.B.X.[1] [2]	22	27	34	37	44	39
Increase 1957–1966	32	330	65	156	58	64

[1]Percentage of country total [2]Extension and Private Branch Extension

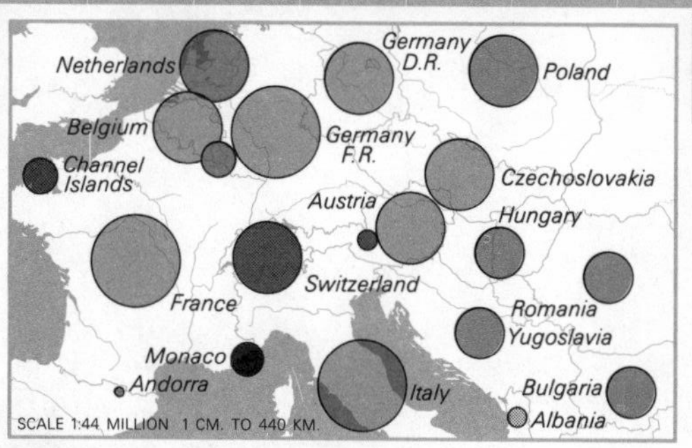
SCALE 1:44 MILLION 1 CM. TO 440 KM.

Telephone conversations[1] (1966)

	AV. NUMBER PER CAPITA
U.S.A.	648
Sweden	585
Australia	194
Italy	157
U.K.	136
Brazil	103
South Africa	100
Mexico	47
Ghana	4

[1]For selected countries

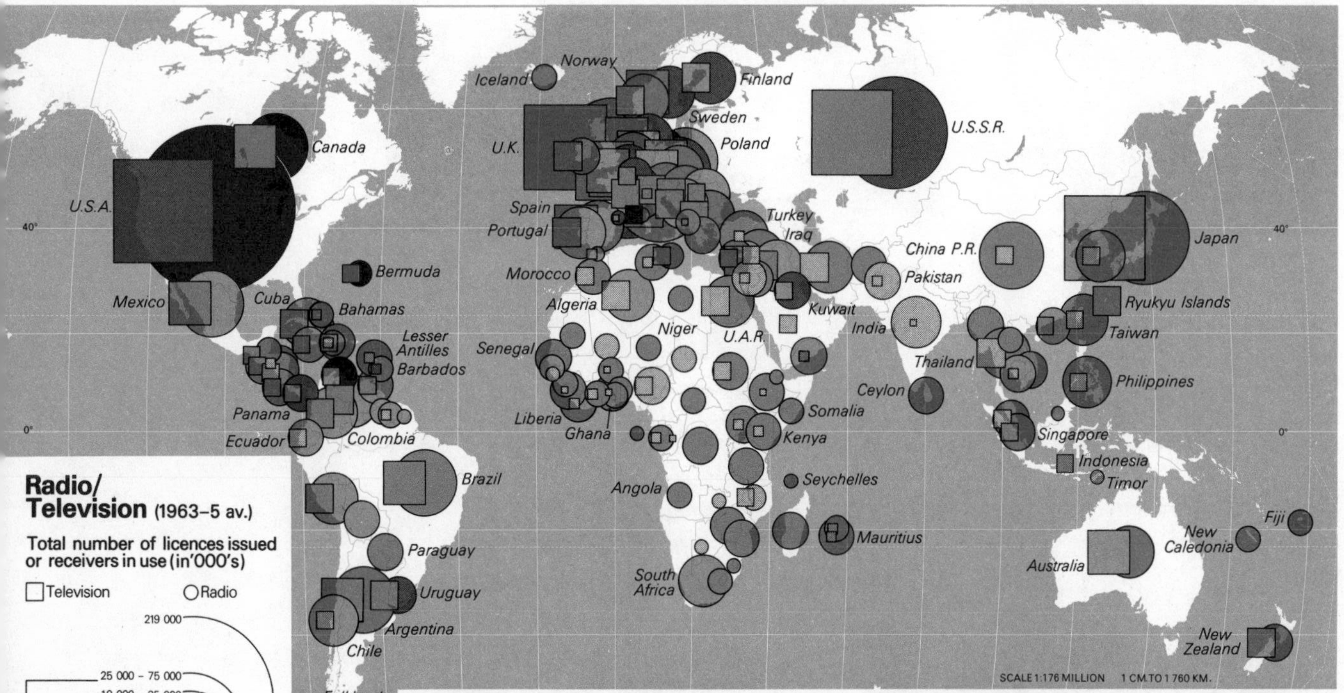
SCALE 1:176 MILLION 1 CM TO 1 760 KM.

Radio/ Television (1963–5 av.)

Total number of licences issued or receivers in use (in '000's)

Television | Radio

219 000
25 000 – 75 000
10 000 – 25 000
5 000 – 10 000
1 000 – 5 000
100 – 1 000
10 – 100
1 – 10
UNDER 1

Number of licences issued or receivers in use per '000 population

450 & OVER[1] | 300 – 450 | 200 – 300 | 100 – 200 | 10 – 100 | UNDER 10

[1]U.S.A.:1 140 radio receivers per '000 population

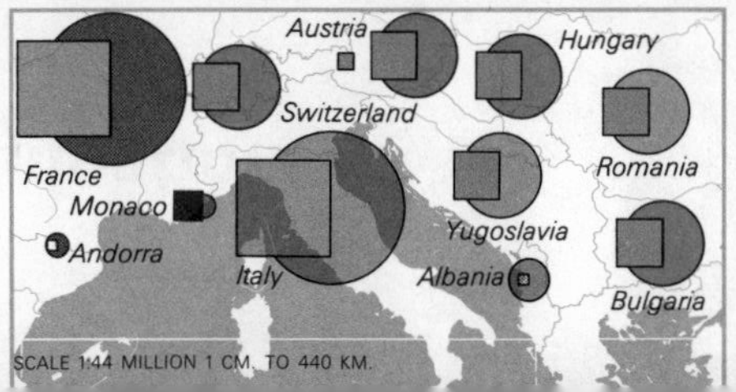
SCALE 1:44 MILLION 1 CM. TO 440 KM.

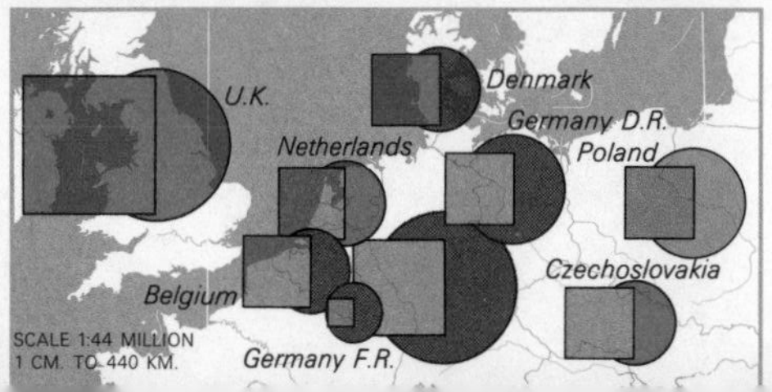
SCALE 1:44 MILLION 1 CM. TO 440 KM.

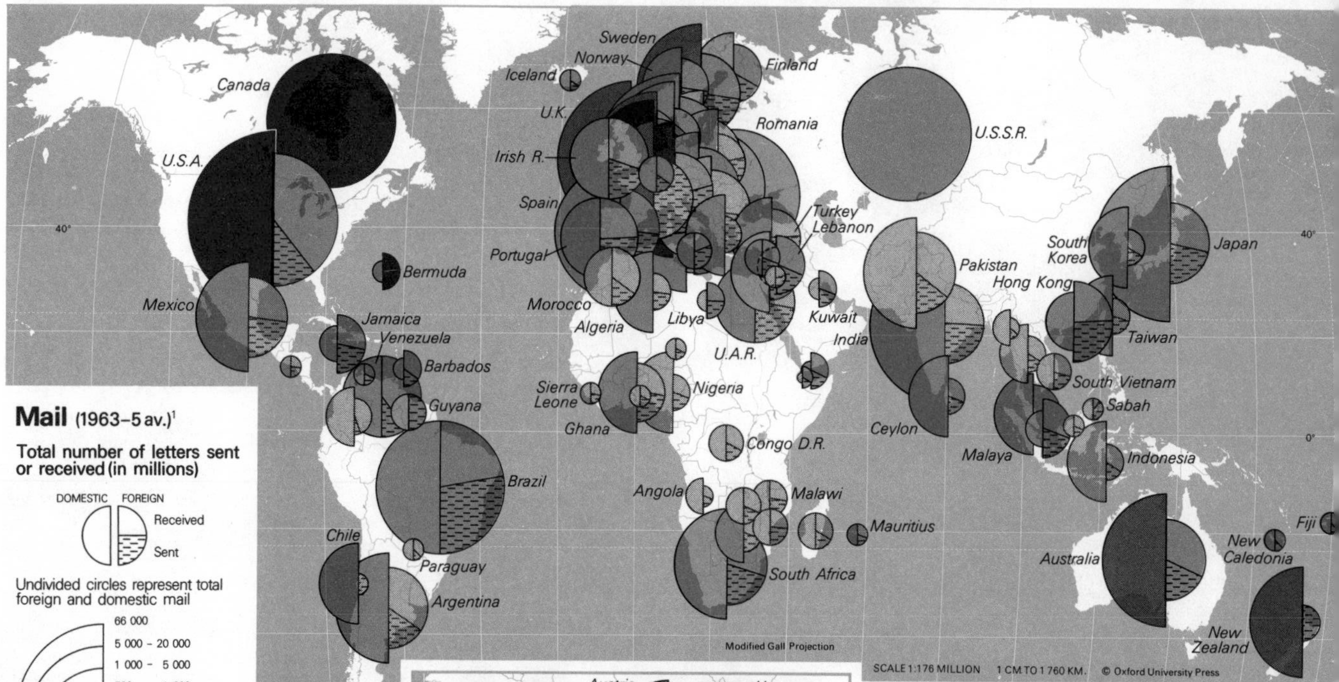
Modified Gall Projection
SCALE 1:176 MILLION 1 CM TO 1 760 KM.

Mail (1963–5 av.)[1]

Total number of letters sent or received (in millions)

DOMESTIC FOREIGN Received Sent

Undivided circles represent total foreign and domestic mail

66 000
5 000 – 20 000
1 000 – 5 000
500 – 1 000
100 – 500
50 – 100
10 – 50
1 – 10
UNDER 1

Domestic and foreign[2] mail per capita

200 & OVER | 150 – 200 | 100 – 150 | 50 – 100 | 10 – 50 | UNDER 10

[1]Or latest available previous data [2]Total foreign mail

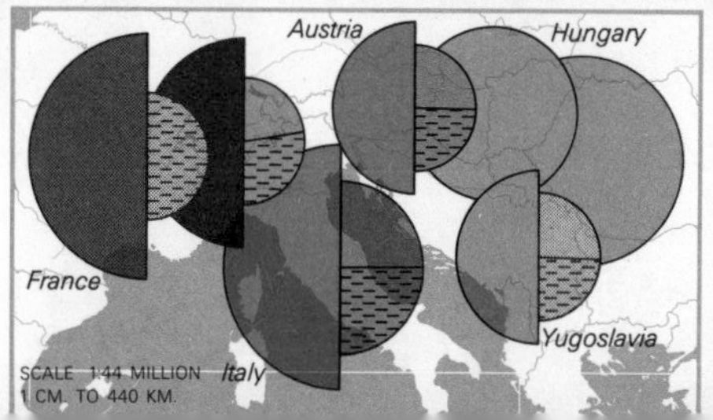
SCALE 1:44 MILLION 1 CM. TO 440 KM.

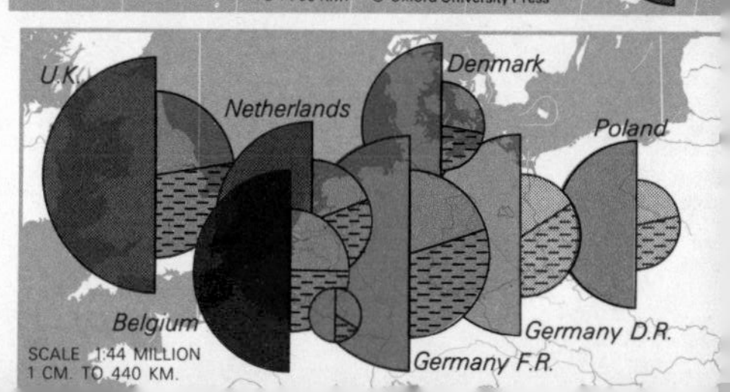
SCALE 1:44 MILLION 1 CM. TO 440 KM.

Surface Communications I

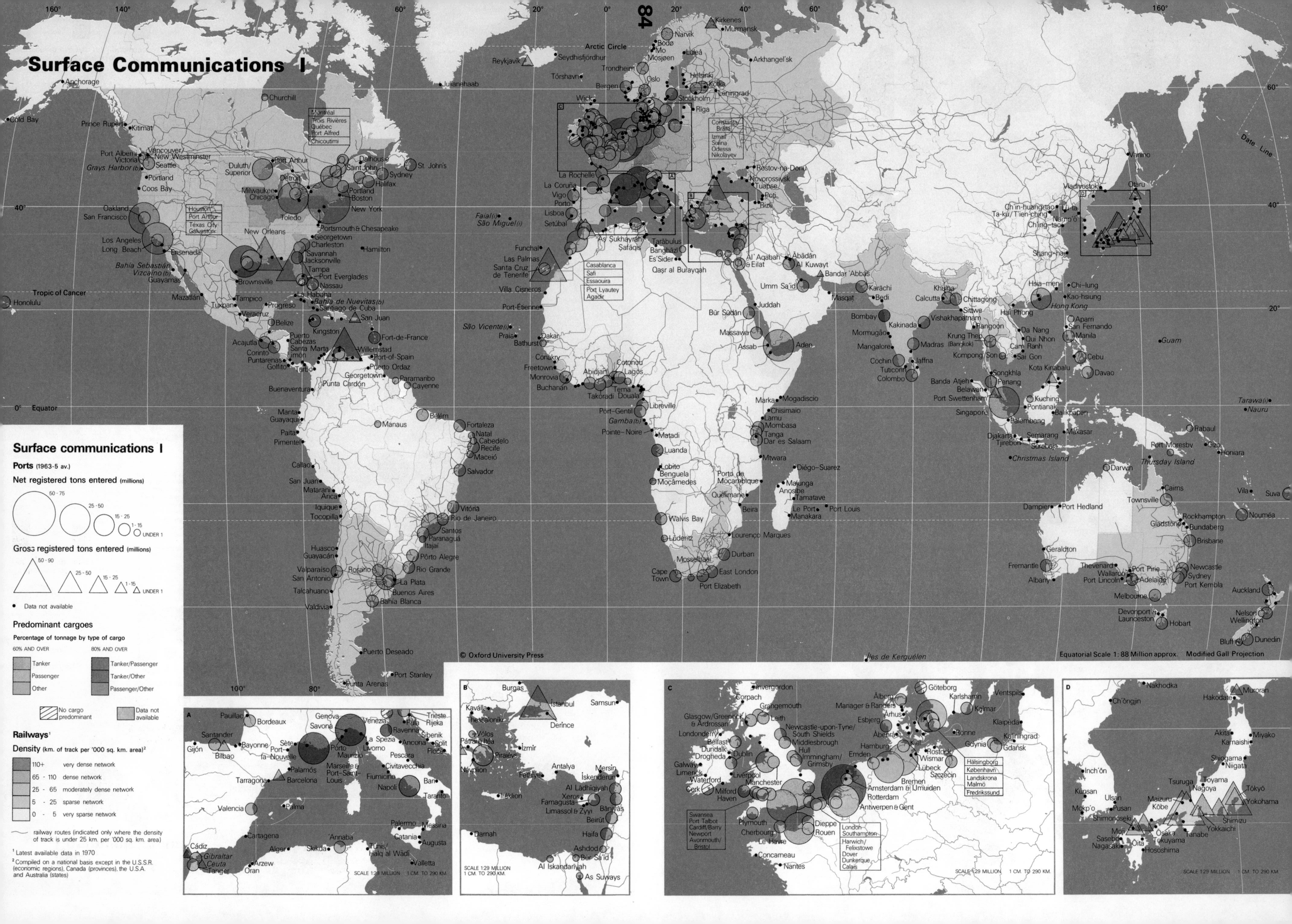
Surface communications I
Ports (1963-5 av.)
Net registered tons entered (millions)
50 - 75
25 - 50
15 - 25
1 - 15
UNDER 1
Gross registered tons entered (millions)
50 - 90
25 - 50
15 - 25
1 - 15
UNDER 1
Data not available
Predominant cargoes
Percentage of tonnage by type of cargo
60% AND OVER
Tanker
Passenger
Other
80% AND OVER
Tanker/Passenger
Tanker/Other
Passenger/Other
No cargo predominant
Data not available
Railways[1]
Density (km. of track per '000 sq. km. area)[2]
110+ very dense network
65 - 110 dense network
25 - 65 moderately dense network
5 - 25 sparse network
0 - 5 very sparse network
railway routes (indicated only where the density of track is under 25 km. per '000 sq. km. area)
[1] Latest available data in 1970
[2] Compiled on a national basis except in the U.S.S.R. (economic regions), Canada (provinces), the U.S.A. and Australia (states)
Equatorial Scale 1: 88 Million approx. Modified Gall Projection
A
SCALE 1:29 MILLION 1 CM. TO 290 KM.
B
SCALE 1:29 MILLION 1 CM. TO 290 KM.
C
SCALE 1:29 MILLION 1 CM. TO 290 KM.
D
SCALE 1:29 MILLION 1 CM. TO 290 KM.

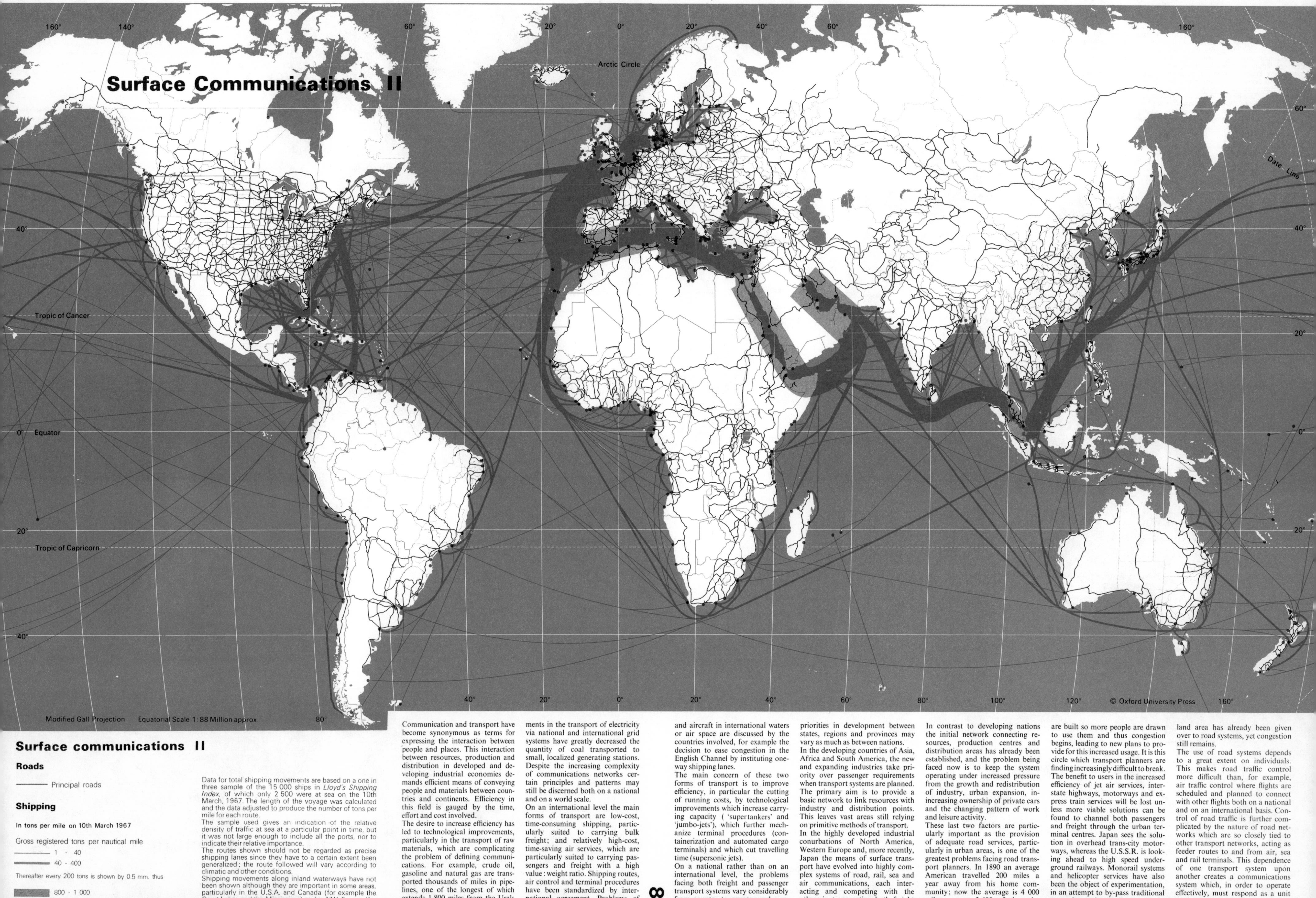

Surface communications II

Roads

——— Principal roads

Shipping

In tons per mile on 10th March 1967

Gross registered tons per nautical mile

——— 1 - 40

——— 40 - 400

Thereafter every 200 tons is shown by 0.5 mm. thus

800 - 1 000

Ports

Data for total shipping movements are based on a one in three sample of the 15 000 ships in *Lloyd's Shipping Index*, of which only 2 500 were at sea on the 10th March, 1967. The length of the voyage was calculated and the data adjusted to produce the number of tons per mile for each route.

The sample used gives an indication of the relative density of traffic at sea at a particular point in time, but it was not large enough to include all the ports, nor to indicate their relative importance.

The routes shown should not be regarded as precise shipping lanes since they have to a certain extent been generalized; the route followed will vary according to climatic and other conditions.

Shipping movements along inland waterways have not been shown although they are important in some areas, particularly in the U.S.A. and Canada (for example the Great Lakes and the Mississippi) and in NW. Europe (for example the Rhine/Rhône Waterway).

Communication and transport have become synonymous as terms for expressing the interaction between people and places. This interaction between resources, production and distribution in developed and developing industrial economies demands efficient means of conveying people and materials between countries and continents. Efficiency in this field is gauged by the time, effort and cost involved.

The desire to increase efficiency has led to technological improvements, particularly in the transport of raw materials, which are complicating the problem of defining communications. For example, crude oil, gasoline and natural gas are transported thousands of miles in pipelines, one of the longest of which extends 1 800 miles from the Urals to Eastern Europe. Also, improvements in the transport of electricity via national and international grid systems have greatly decreased the quantity of coal transported to small, localized generating stations.

Despite the increasing complexity of communications networks certain principles and patterns may still be discerned both on a national and on a world scale.

On an international level the main forms of transport are low-cost, time-consuming shipping, particularly suited to carrying bulk freight; and relatively high-cost, time-saving air services, which are particularly suited to carrying passengers and freight with a high value: weight ratio. Shipping routes, air control and terminal procedures have been standardized by international agreement. Problems of traffic control and safety of vessels and aircraft in international waters or air space are discussed by the countries involved, for example the decision to ease congestion in the English Channel by instituting one-way shipping lanes.

The main concern of these two forms of transport is to improve efficiency, in particular the cutting of running costs, by technological improvements which increase carrying capacity ('supertankers' and 'jumbo-jets'), which further mechanize terminal procedures (containerization and automated cargo terminals) and which cut travelling time (supersonic jets).

On a national rather than on an international level, the problems facing both freight and passenger transport systems vary considerably from country to country and even within a national framework. The priorities in development between states, regions and provinces may vary as much as between nations.

In the developing countries of Asia, Africa and South America, the new and expanding industries take priority over passenger requirements when transport systems are planned. The primary aim is to provide a basic network to link resources with industry and distribution points. This leaves vast areas still relying on primitive methods of transport.

In the highly developed industrial conurbations of North America, Western Europe and, more recently, Japan the means of surface transport have evolved into highly complex systems of road, rail, sea and air communications, each interacting and competing with the others in transporting both freight and passengers.

In contrast to developing nations the initial network connecting resources, production centres and distribution areas has already been established, and the problem being faced now is to keep the system operating under increased pressure from the growth and redistribution of industry, urban expansion, increasing ownership of private cars and the changing pattern of work and leisure activity.

These last two factors are particularly important as the provision of adequate road services, particularly in urban areas, is one of the greatest problems facing road transport planners. In 1890 an average American travelled 200 miles a year away from his home community; now the average is 4 000 miles a year, 3 600 of these by motor car. As more road systems are built so more people are drawn to use them and thus congestion begins, leading to new plans to provide for this increased usage. It is this circle which transport planners are finding increasingly difficult to break.

The benefit to users in the increased efficiency of jet air services, interstate highways, motorways and express train services will be lost unless more viable solutions can be found to channel both passengers and freight through the urban terminal centres. Japan sees the solution in overhead trans-city motorways, whereas the U.S.S.R. is looking ahead to high speed underground railways. Monorail systems and helicopter services have also been the object of experimentation, in an attempt to by-pass traditional trans-city road and rail networks. In some American cities 30-40% of the land area has already been given over to road systems, yet congestion still remains.

The use of road systems depends to a great extent on individuals. This makes road traffic control more difficult than, for example, air traffic control where flights are scheduled and planned to connect with other flights both on a national and on an international basis. Control of road traffic is further complicated by the nature of road networks which are so closely tied to other transport networks, acting as feeder routes to and from air, sea and rail terminals. This dependence of one transport system upon another creates a communications system which, in order to operate effectively, must respond as a unit to the changing demands and pressures placed upon it.

Surface Communications III

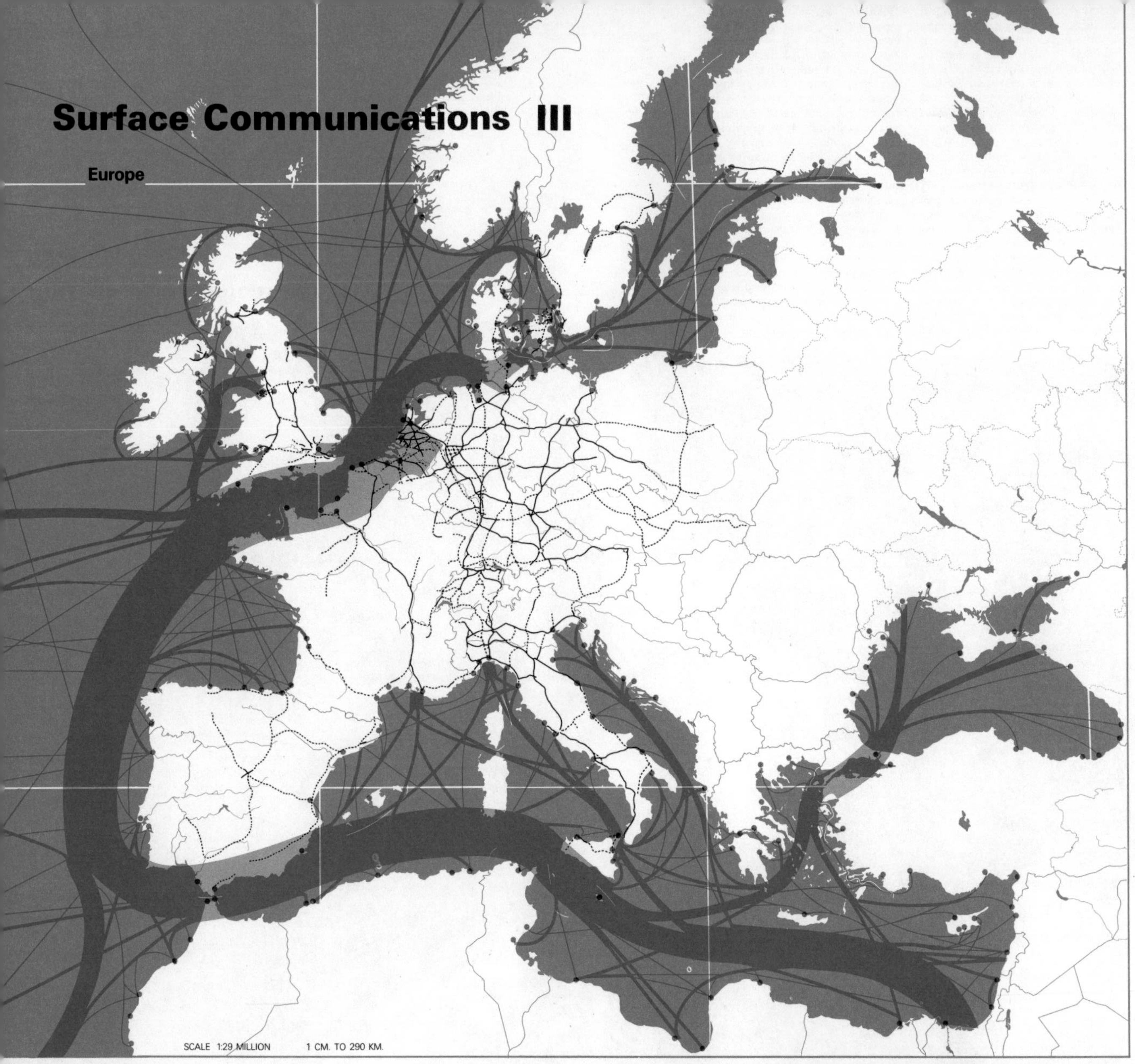
Europe
SCALE 1:29 MILLION
1 CM. TO 290 KM.

Surface communications III

Shipping

In tons per mile of route on 10th March 1967

Gross registered tons per nautical mile

- 1 - 40
- 40 - 400

Thereafter every 200 tons is shown by 0.5mm. width , thus

- 800 - 1 000
- • Ports

Motorways

Dual carriage, two or more lane roads with limited access and curves and gradients designed for fast motor traffic[1]

- ——— COMPLETED BY THE END OF 1970
- .... UNDER CONSTRUCTION / PLANNED

Data for the U.S.A. represent the situation at the end of 1966. Over 90% of the network shown is the Interstate Highway System which is scheduled for completion by the end of 1972.

[1]Excl. urban motorway systems

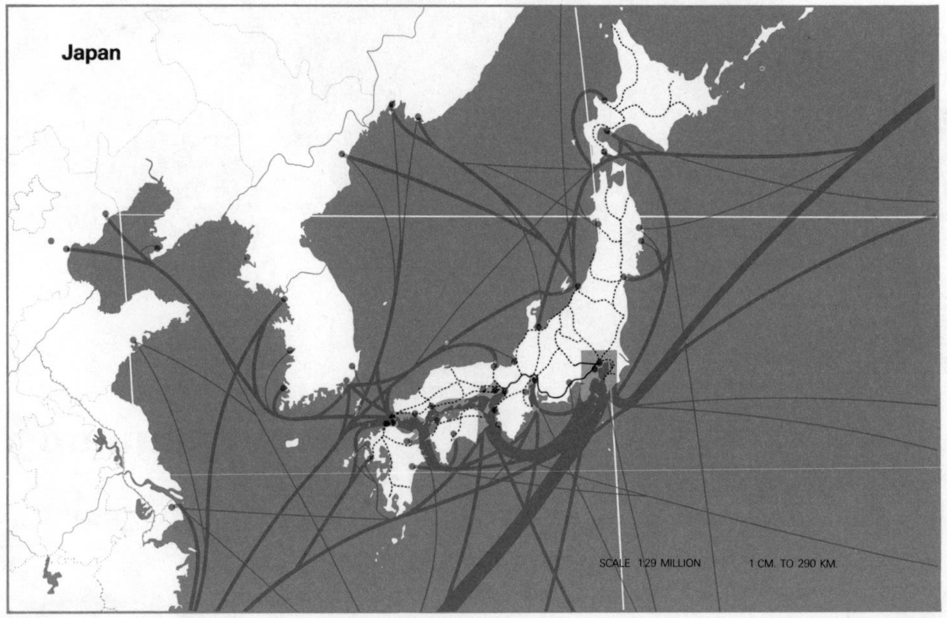
Japan
SCALE 1:29 MILLION
1 CM. TO 290 KM.

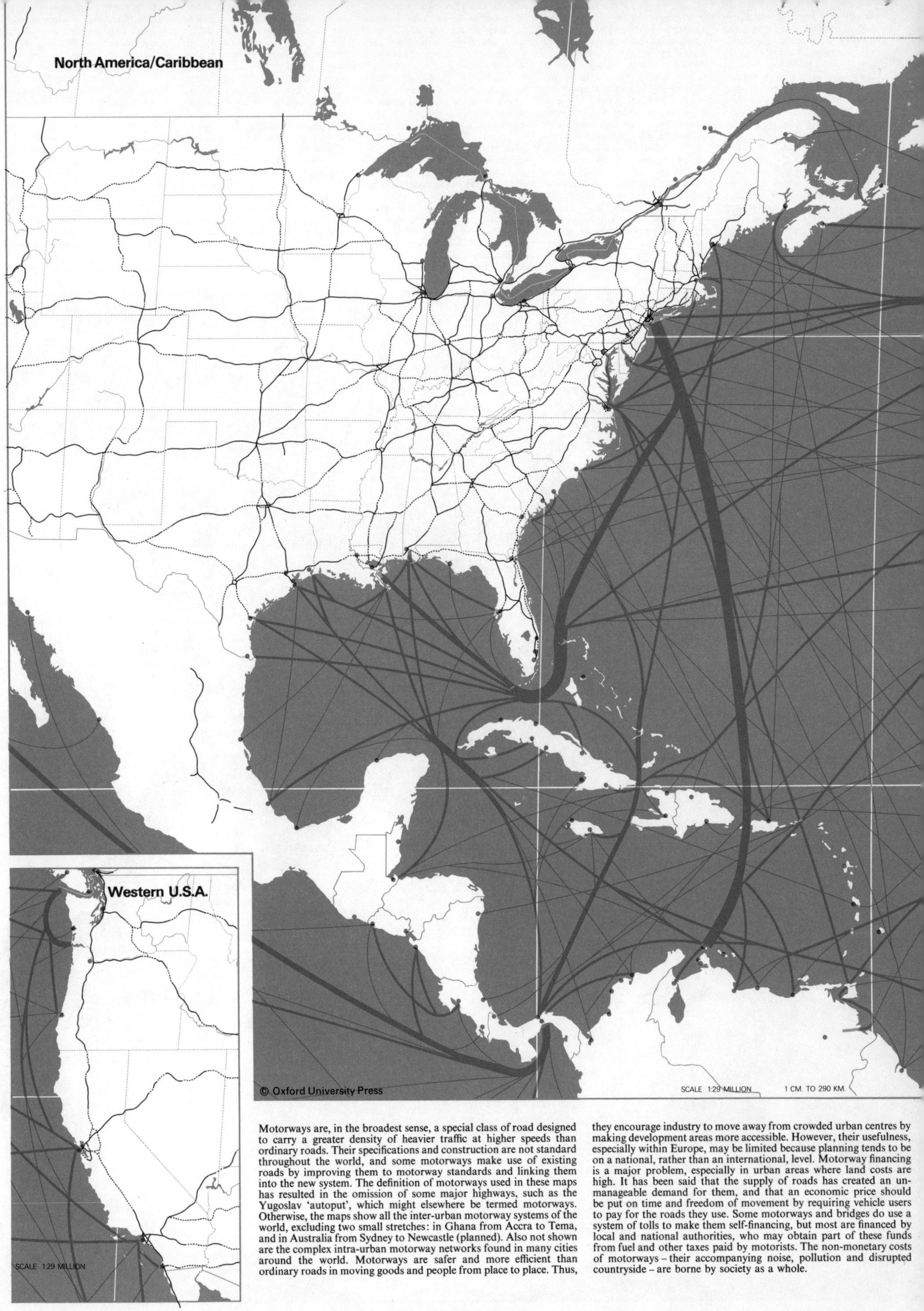
North America/Caribbean
SCALE 1:29 MILLION
1 CM. TO 290 KM.
Western U.S.A.
SCALE 1:29 MILLION

Motorways are, in the broadest sense, a special class of road designed to carry a greater density of heavier traffic at higher speeds than ordinary roads. Their specifications and construction are not standard throughout the world, and some motorways make use of existing roads by improving them to motorway standards and linking them into the new system. The definition of motorways used in these maps has resulted in the omission of some major highways, such as the Yugoslav 'autoput', which might elsewhere be termed motorways. Otherwise, the maps show all the inter-urban motorway systems of the world, excluding two small stretches: in Ghana from Accra to Tema, and in Australia from Sydney to Newcastle (planned). Also not shown are the complex intra-urban motorway networks found in many cities around the world. Motorways are safer and more efficient than ordinary roads in moving goods and people from place to place. Thus, they encourage industry to move away from crowded urban centres by making development areas more accessible. However, their usefulness, especially within Europe, may be limited because planning tends to be on a national, rather than an international, level. Motorway financing is a major problem, especially in urban areas where land costs are high. It has been said that the supply of roads has created an unmanageable demand for them, and that an economic price should be put on time and freedom of movement by requiring vehicle users to pay for the roads they use. Some motorways and bridges do use a system of tolls to make them self-financing, but most are financed by local and national authorities, who may obtain part of these funds from fuel and other taxes paid by motorists. The non-monetary costs of motorways – their accompanying noise, pollution and disrupted countryside – are borne by society as a whole.

Air Communications I

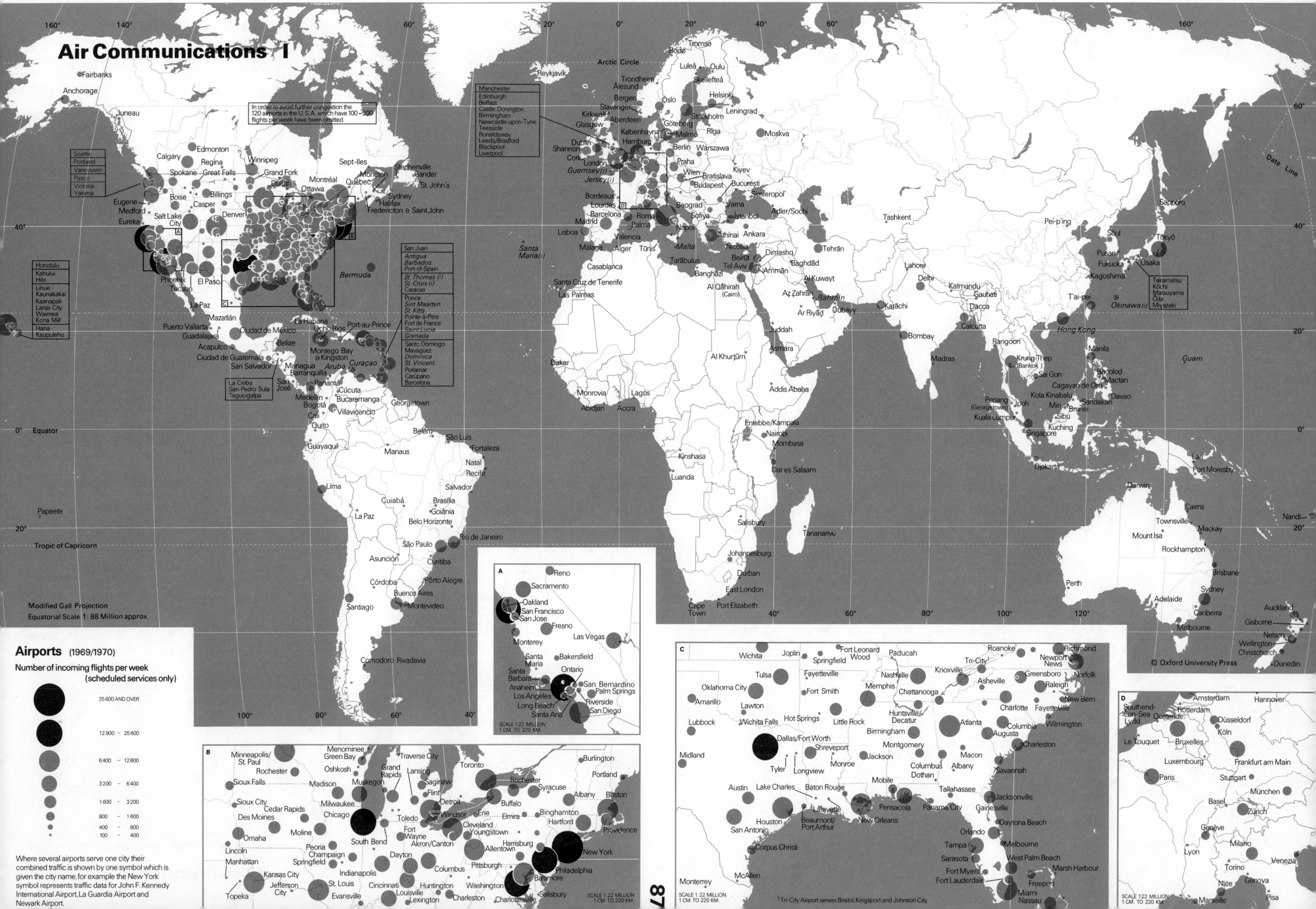

Airports (1969/1970)

Number of incoming flights per week
(scheduled services only)

- 25 600 AND OVER
- 12 800 - 25 600
- 6400 - 12 800
- 3200 - 6400
- 1600 - 3200
- 800 - 1600
- 400 - 800
- 100 - 400

Where several airports serve one city their combined traffic is shown by one symbol which is given the city name, for example the New York symbol represents traffic data for John F. Kennedy International Airport, La Guardia Airport and Newark Airport.

Air Communications II

Jet flights to New York, London, Moskva and Tōkyō during April 1970 (from cities of one million population in 1966)

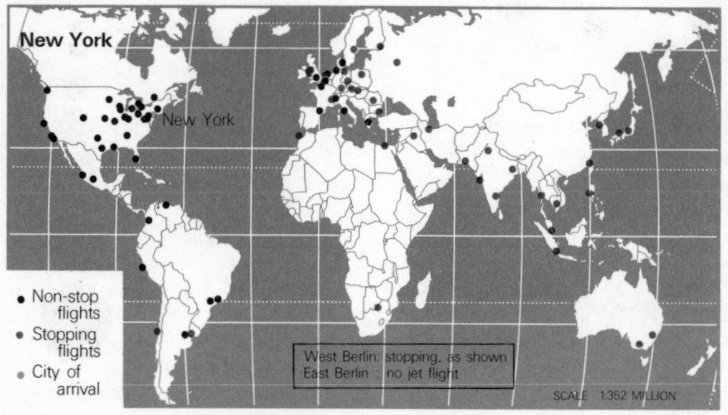
New York
New York
• Non-stop flights
• Stopping flights
• City of arrival
West Berlin: stopping, as shown
East Berlin: no jet flight
SCALE 1:352 MILLION

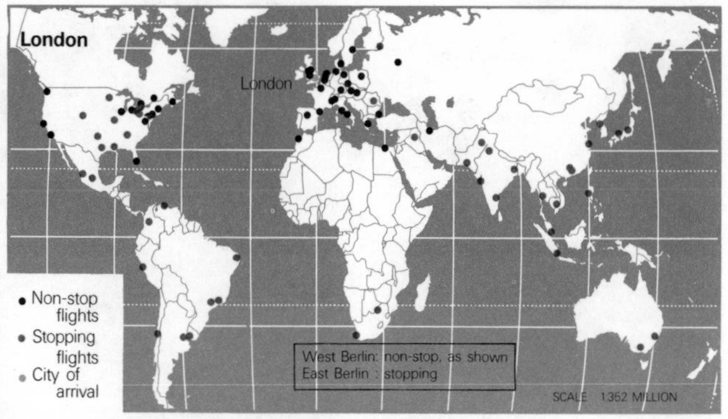
London
London
• Non-stop flights
• Stopping flights
• City of arrival
West Berlin: non-stop, as shown
East Berlin: stopping
SCALE 1:352 MILLION

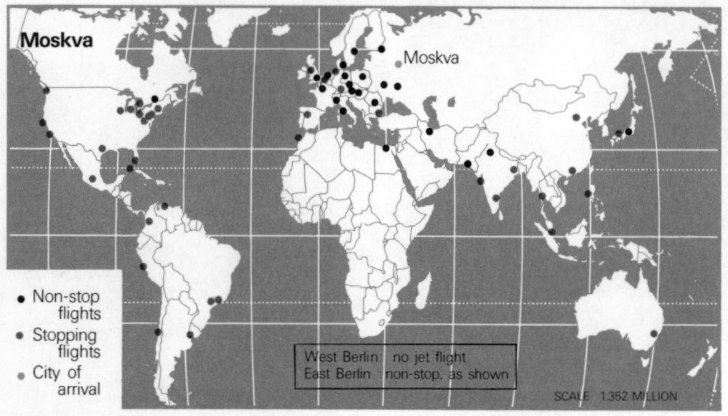
Moskva
Moskva
• Non-stop flights
• Stopping flights
• City of arrival
West Berlin: no jet flight
East Berlin: non-stop, as shown
SCALE 1:352 MILLION

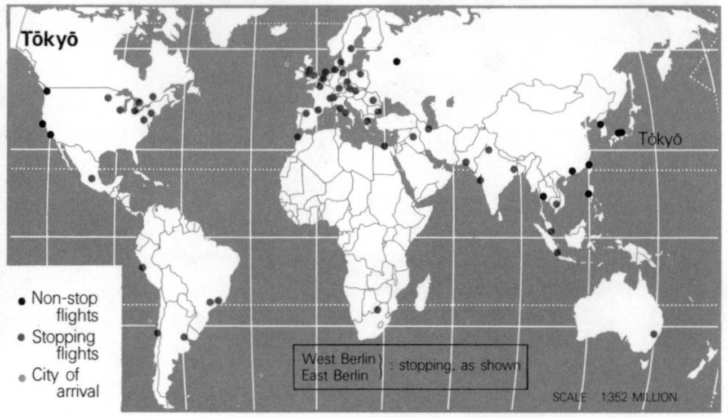
Tōkyō
Tōkyō
• Non-stop flights
• Stopping flights
• City of arrival
West Berlin / East Berlin : stopping, as shown
SCALE 1:352 MILLION

Cities of one million population in 1966

Ahmadābād
Al Iskandarīyah
Al Qāhirah (Cairo)
Amsterdam
Anaheim
Athínai
Atlanta
Baghdād
Baku
Baltimore
Bangalore
Barcelona
Belo Horizonte
Berlin (East & West)
Birmingham (U.K.)
Bogotá
Bombay
Boston
Bruxelles
Bucureşti
Budapest
Buenos Aires
Buffalo
Calcutta
Caracas
Casablanca
Ch'eng-tu
Chicago
Ch'ing-tao
Ch'ung-ch'ing
Cincinnati
Ciudad de México
Cleveland
Dallas
Delhi
Denver
Detroit
Djakarta
Gor'kiy
Guadalajara
Ha-erh-pin
Hamburg
Hong Kong
Houston
Hsi-an
Hyderābād
Indianapolis
İstanbul
Johannesburg
Kanpur
Kansas City
Karāchi
Khar'kov
Kitakyūshū
Kiyev
Kōbe
København
Krung Thep (Bangkok)
Kyōto
Kuang-chou (Canton)
La Habana
Lahore
Leeds
Leningrad
Lima
Liverpool
London
Los Angeles
Lü-ta
Madras
Madrid
Manchester
Manila
Melbourne
Miami
Milano
Milwaukee
Minneapolis/St. Paul
Montevideo
Montréal
Moskva
München
Nagoya
Nan-ching
Napoli
Newark
New Orleans
New York
Novosibirsk
Ōsaka
Paris
Paterson
Pei-p'ing
Philadelphia
Pittsburgh
Praha
Pusan
Recife
Rio de Janeiro
Roma
Rotterdam
Sai Gon
St. Louis
San Bernardino
San Diego
San Fransisco
Santiago
São Paulo
Seattle
Shang-hai
Shen-yang
Singapore
Sŏul
Stockholm
Surabaja
Sydney
T'ai-pei
T'ai-yüan
Tashkent
Tehrān
T'ien-ching
Tōkyō
Torino
Toronto
Warszawa
Washington
Wien
Wu-han
Yokohama

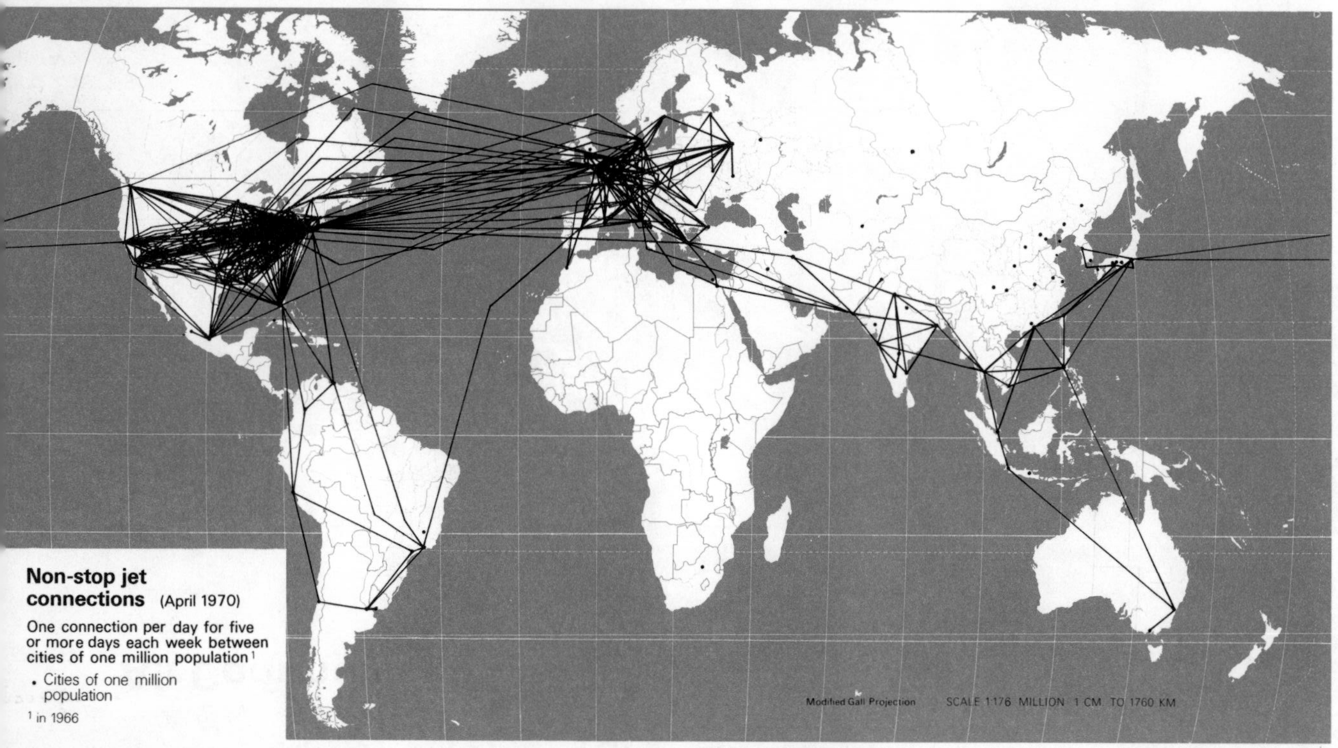
Modified Gall Projection
SCALE 1:176 MILLION 1 CM. TO 1760 KM

Non-stop jet connections (April 1970)

One connection per day for five or more days each week between cities of one million population[1]

• Cities of one million population

[1] in 1966

Intra-North American non-stop jet connections

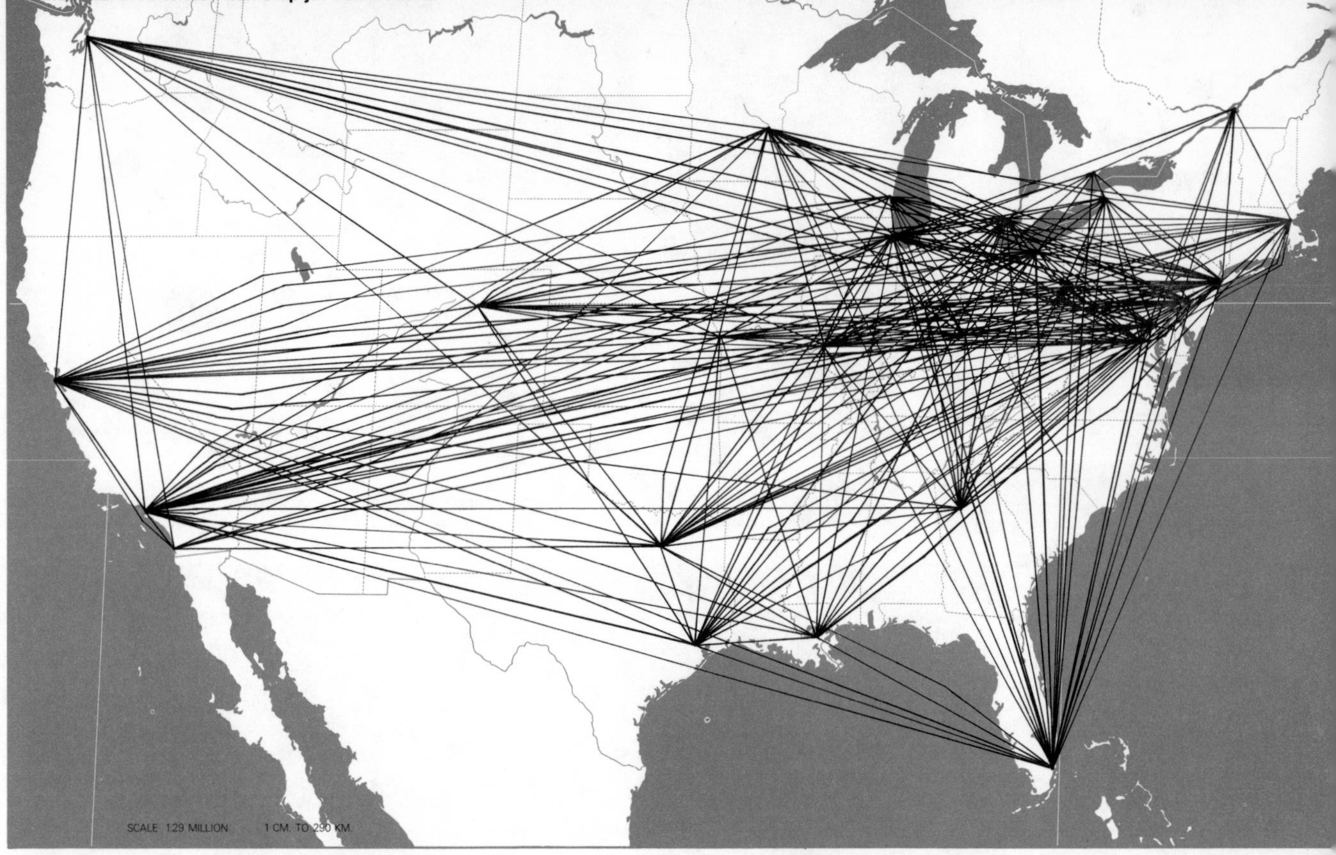
SCALE 1:29 MILLION 1 CM. TO 290 KM

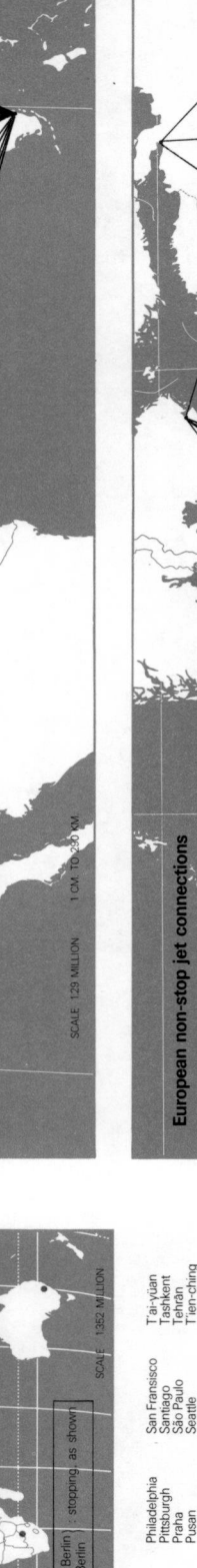

European non-stop jet connections

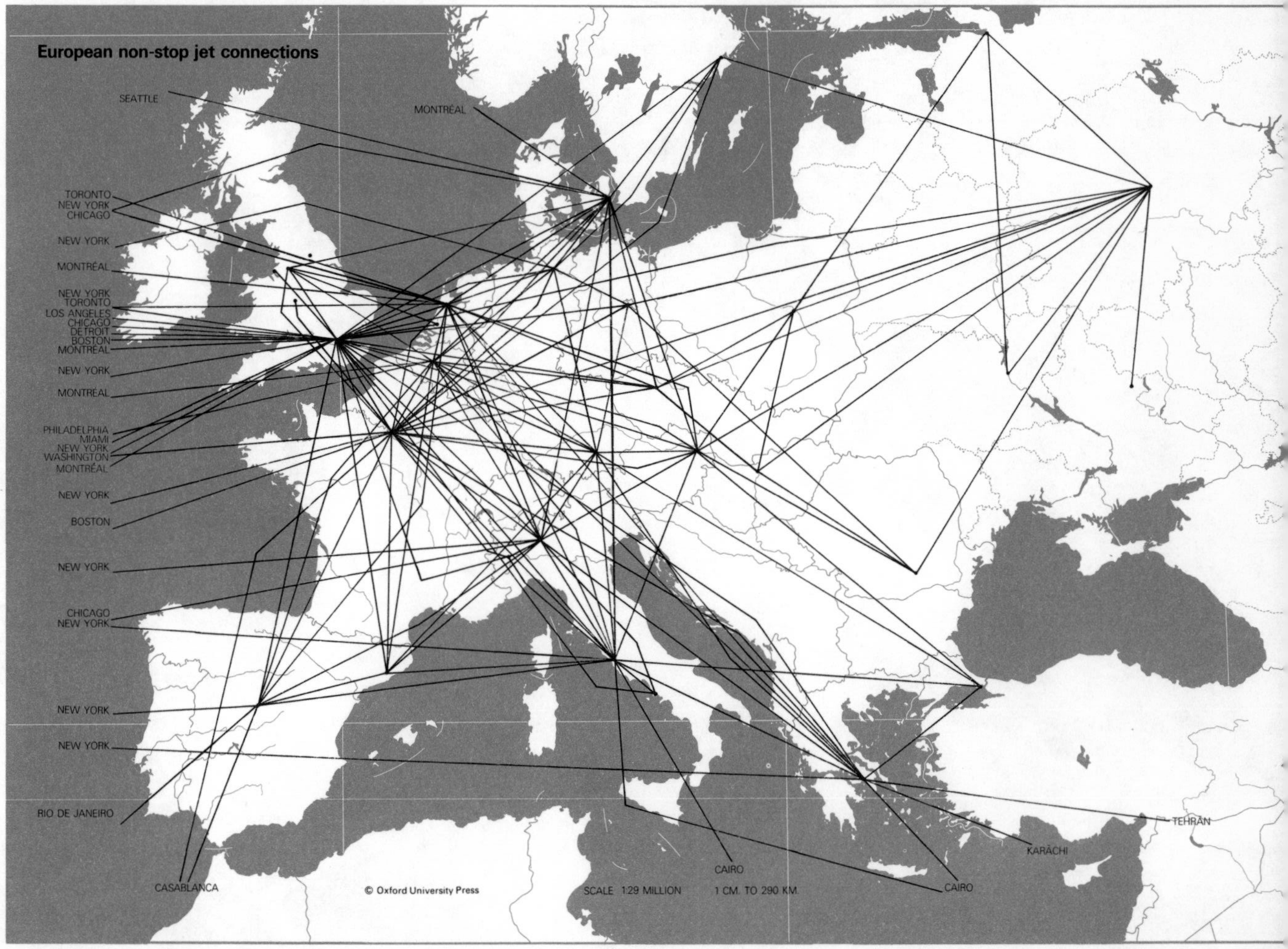
SEATTLE
MONTRÉAL
TORONTO
NEW YORK
CHICAGO
NEW YORK
MONTRÉAL
NEW YORK
TORONTO
LOS ANGELES
CHICAGO
DETROIT
BOSTON
MONTRÉAL
NEW YORK
MONTRÉAL
PHILADELPHIA
MIAMI
NEW YORK
WASHINGTON
MONTRÉAL
NEW YORK
BOSTON
NEW YORK
CHICAGO
NEW YORK
NEW YORK
NEW YORK
RIO DE JANEIRO
CASABLANCA
TEHRĀN
KARĀCHI
CAIRO
CAIRO
SCALE 1:29 MILLION 1 CM. TO 290 KM

Air Communications III

Travel times by jet from New York, London, Moskva, Tōkyō during April 1970

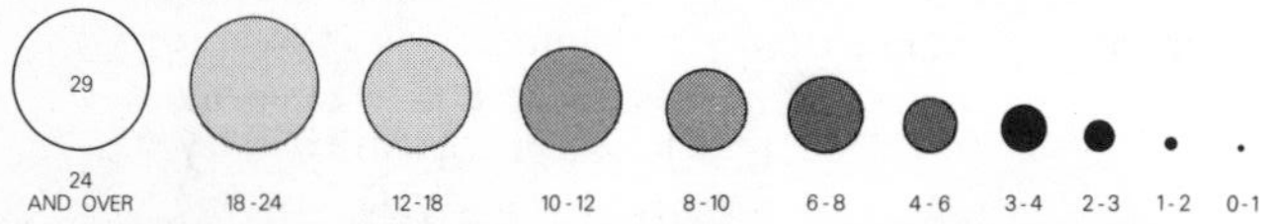

29
24 AND OVER
18-24
12-18
10-12
8-10
6-8
4-6
3-4
2-3
1-2
0-1

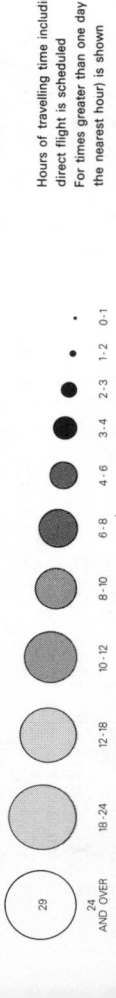

Hours of travelling time including transfer time where no direct flight is scheduled
For times greater than one day the number of hours (to the nearest hour) is shown

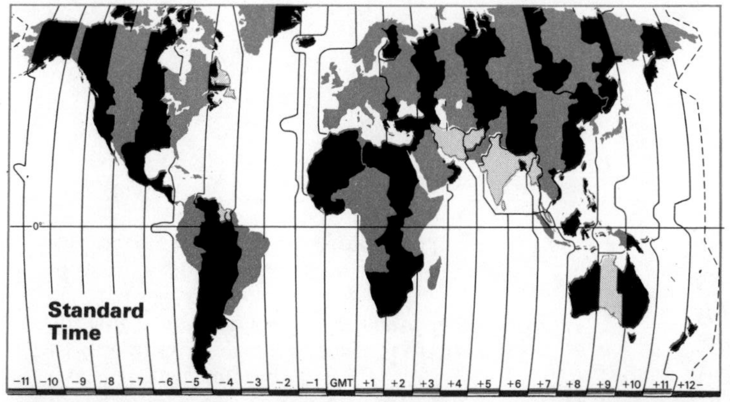

Standard Time
−11 −10 −9 −8 −7 −6 −5 −4 −3 −2 −1 GMT +1 +2 +3 +4 +5 +6 +7 +8 +9 +10 +11 +12

Standard time 1970

Numbers indicate hours ahead or behind GMT (Greenwich Mean Time)

- - - - - - International Date Line

Areas where legal time is less or more than one hour different from the adjacent zone

	HOURS FROM GMT
Afghanistan	+4.5
Australia (South Australia/ Northern Territory)	+9.5
Burma	+6.5
Canada (Newfoundland)	−3.5
Guyana	−3.75
India/Nepal/Ceylon	+5.5
Iran	+3.5
Liberia	−0.75
Surinam	−3.5
Singapore/Malaya	+7.5

The standard time system is based on the division of the world's surface into 24 zones of 15° (1 hour) of longitude, each using the mean (solar) time of the central meridian of the zone. This system is applied with modifications, principally to allow political or economic regions to maintain the same time. The time used in each country, whether it is the time of the theoretical zone or a modification of it, is fixed by law and is known as 'standard time'. For economic reasons certain countries adjust their standard time for part of the year, usually the summer (Daylight Saving Time), advancing it by an hour or some other amount of time. Where such deviations operate throughout the year that time is considered to be 'standard time'. In the U.S.S.R. standard times are one hour in advance of the theoretical zone times.

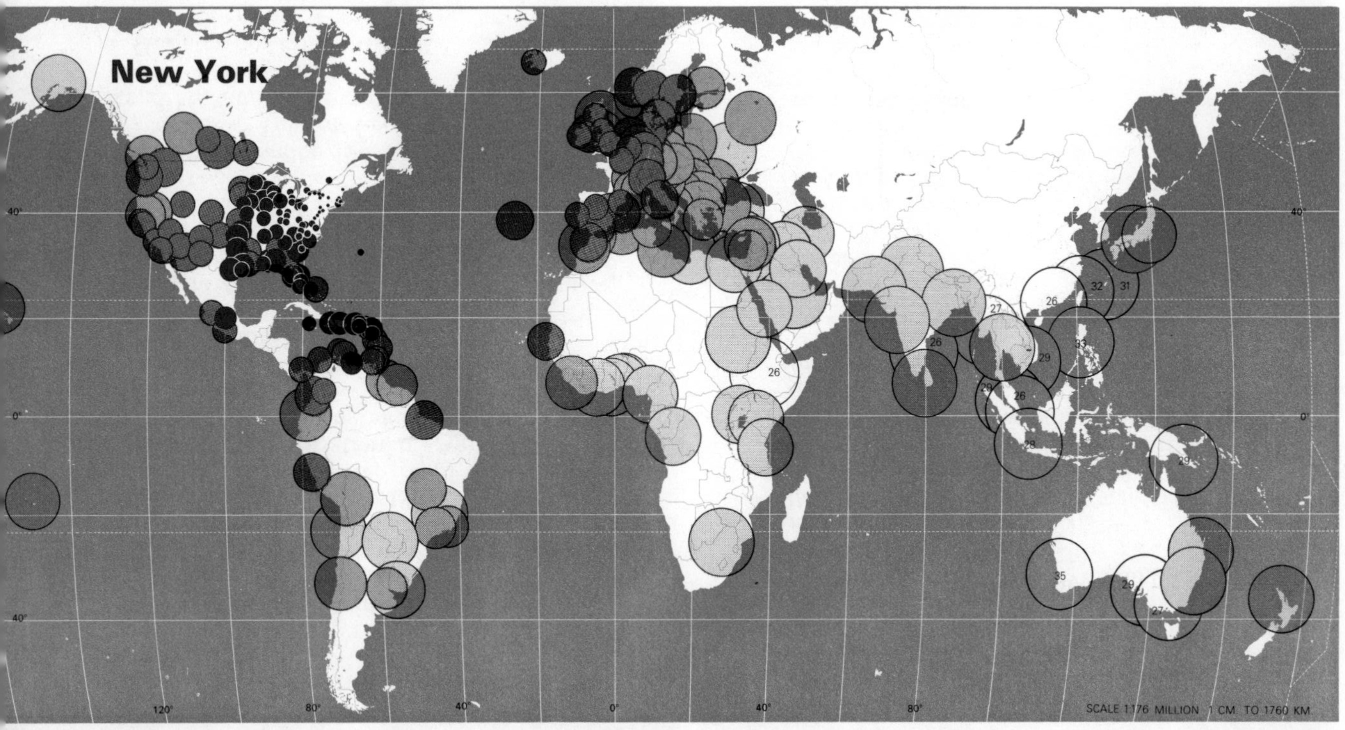

New York
SCALE 1:176 MILLION 1 CM. TO 1760 KM

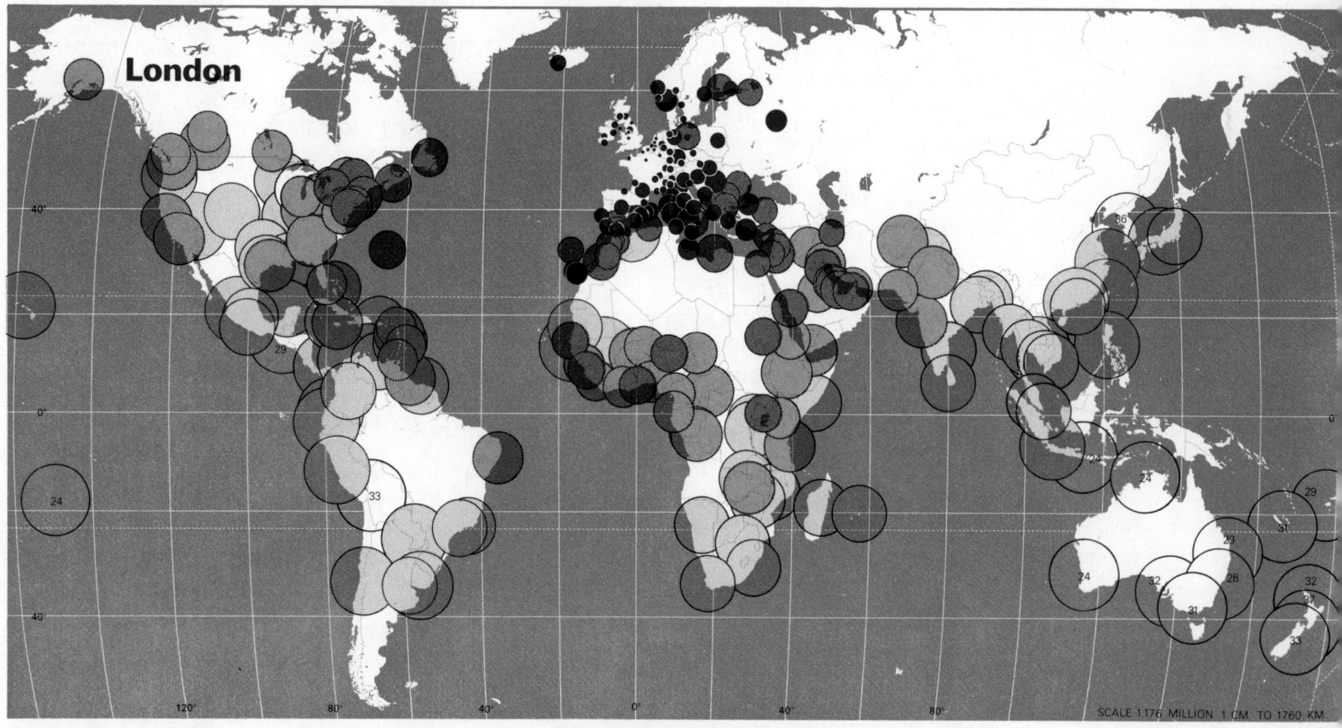

London
SCALE 1:176 MILLION 1 CM. TO 1760 KM

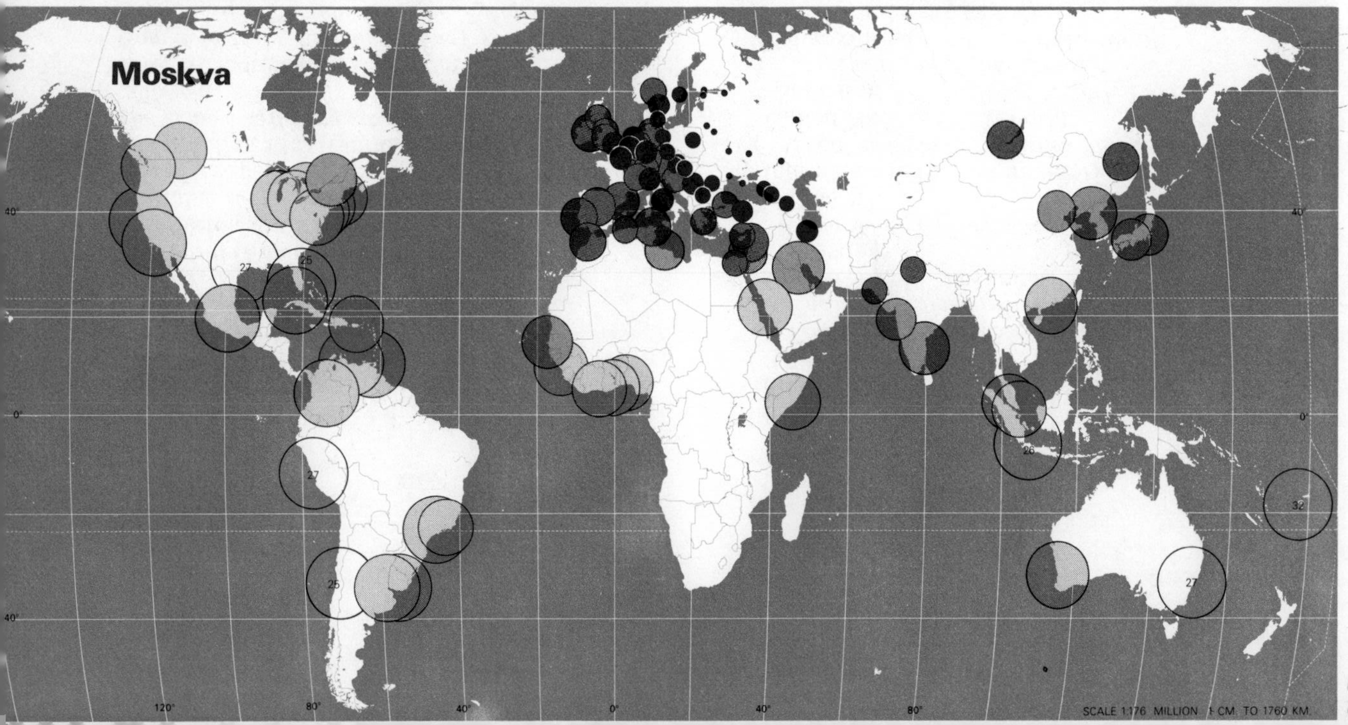

Moskva
SCALE 1:176 MILLION 1 CM. TO 1760 KM

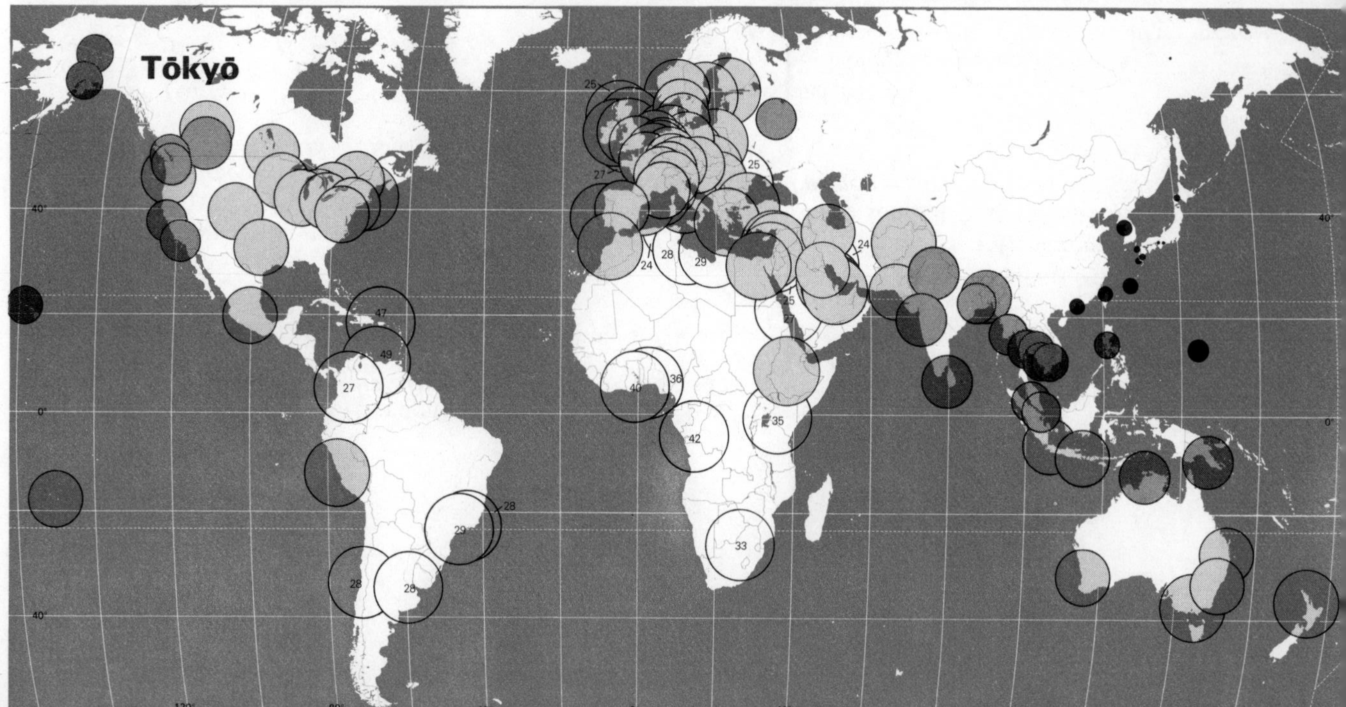

Tōkyō
SCALE 1:176 MILLION 1 CM. TO 1760 KM

Modified Gall Projection

SOURCES

Environment

Academy of Sciences U.S.S.R./Main Administration of Geodesy Cartography, S.G.C. U.S.S.R. (Moskva 1964):
Fiziko-Geograficheskiy Atlas Mira
K. H. W. Klages (New York 1942):
Ecological Crop Geography
C. Embleton & C. A. M. King (London 1968):
Glacial & Periglacial Geomorphology
Times Newspapers Ltd. (London)/John Bartholomew & Son Ltd. (Edinburgh):
The Times Atlas of the World, Comprehensive Edition 1967
World Meteorological Organization (Geneva):
Climatological Normals (Clino) for Climat and Climat Ship Stations for the Period 1931–1960 (WMO/OMM—No. 117. TP.52)
WMO/OMM No. 9. TP.4 Volume A Stations
Prof. D. L. Linton, Dept. of Geography, University of Birmingham, U.K.
U.S. Dept. of Agriculture, Soil Conservation Service (Hyattsville, Maryland):
Soil Map of the World based on *Soil Classification, A Comprehensive System, 7th Approximation*
G. T. Trewartha, A. H. Robinson, and E. H. Hammond (New York 1967):
Physical Elements of Geography
International Association of Agricultural Economists, Istituto Geografico de Agostini, S.p.A. (Novara 1970):
World Atlas of Agriculture
Haack (Leipzig 1969):
Weltatlas
Food and Agriculture Organization (Roma):
Production Yearbook 1964
Clarendon Press (Oxford):
Oxford Regional Economic Atlas of the United States and Canada
A. Holmes (London 1965):
Principles of Physical Geology
Rand McNally & Company (Chicago 1964):
Goode's World Atlas
J. H. Paterson (London 1970):
North America
International Labour Organization (Geneva):
Yearbook of Labour Statistics
H. F. Gregor (Princeton 1963):
Environment and Economic Life
U.S. Dept. of Commerce, Environmental Science Services Administration (Washington, D.C.):
World Seismicity 1961–9

Crops

Food and Agriculture Organization (Roma):
Production Yearbook 1956, 1966
Trade Yearbook 1955, 1957, 1966
Cocoa Statistics Vol. 12 1969
Unilever Ltd., Economics and Statistics Dept. (London):
World Oils and Fats Statistics 1963/1966 and 1964/1967
International Tea Committee (London):
Annual Bulletin of Statistics 1969
United Nations (New York):
Statistical Yearbook 1957, 1967, 1968
Compendium of Social Statistics 1967
Tobacco Research Council (London):
Research Paper 6 (Ed. 2)
International Sugar Organization (London):
Sugar Yearbook 1966, 1968
Alexis Lichine (London 1967):
Encyclopaedia of Wines and Spirits
Hugh Johnson (London 1966):
Wine
U.S. Dept. of Agriculture (Washington, D.C.):
The World Food Budget 1970
James Lambe (London 1967):
Rich World, Poor World
International Coffee Organization (London):
World Coffee Requirements, 1953–75
Produktschap voor Gedistilleerde Dranken (Schiedam):
Hoevel Alcoholhoudende Dranken Worden er in de Wereld Gedronken

Livestock

F.A.O. (Roma):
Production Yearbook 1955, 1956, 1966
Trade Yearbook 1955, 1957, 1966

Forestry and Fishing

F.A.O. (Roma):
Yearbook of Fishery Statistics 1966
Yearbook of Forest Products Statistics 1965, 1966
Production Yearbook 1964
U.N. (New York):
Statistical Yearbook 1956, 1966
Commonwealth Economic Committee (London):
Vegetable Oils and Oilseeds 1968
J. A. Gulland, Fishery Resources and Exploitation Division of the F.A.O. (Roma)

Admark Publishing Co. Ltd. (London):
Paper Makers' and Merchants' Directory of all Nations 1966
S. C. Phillips and Co. Ltd. (London):
Phillips' Paper Trade Directory of the World 1965

Fibres and Textiles

F.A.O. (Roma):
Production Yearbook 1955, 1957, 1966
Trade Yearbook 1955, 1957, 1966
U.N. (New York):
Statistical Yearbook 1956, 1966
Thomas Skinner & Co. Ltd. (London):
Skinner's Wool Trade Directory of the World 1965–1966
Skinner's Cotton and Man-Made Fibres Directory of the World 1967
Textile Economics Bureau, Inc. (New York):
Textile Organon 1956, 1965, 1966
Rubber and Plastics Age (London):
Technical and Marketing Data
International Rubber Study Group (London):
Rubber Statistical Bulletin 1966
International Synthetic Rubber Co. Ltd. (Southampton)
International Cotton Advisory Committee (Washington, D.C.):
Cotton—World Statistics Oct. 1967
Comité International de la Rayonne et des Fibres Synthétiques (Paris):
CIRFS 1967

Energy

U.N. (New York):
World Energy Supplies 'Statistical Papers' Series J, Nos. 3, 11, 12
Statistical Yearbook 1956, 1966, 1967
The Petroleum Publishing Co. (Tulsa, Oklahoma):
International Petroleum Encyclopedia 1969
Oil and Gas Journal
Petroleum Information Bureau (London):
Publications of production by region
International Commission on Large Dams (Paris):
World Register of Dams
Institute of Geological Sciences (London):
Statistical Summary of the Mineral Industry 1952–1957, 1962–1967
Mineral Resources Division
Radiogeology and Rare Minerals Unit

U.S. Department of the Interior (Washington, D.C.):
Bureau of Mines, Minerals Yearbook 1956, 1965, 1966
Vol. II Mineral Fuels
Vol. III Area Reports: Domestic
Vol. IV Area Reports: International
N.T.P. Business Journals Ltd. (London):
Nuclear Engineering International Jan/Feb 1971

Minerals and Metals

Institute of Geological Sciences (London):
Statistical Summary of the Mineral Industry 1952–1957, 1962–1967
Mineral Resources Division
U.S. Dept. of the Interior (Washington, D.C.):
Bureau of Mines, Minerals Yearbook 1956, 1965, 1966
Vol. I Metals and Minerals
Vol. III Area Reports: Domestic
Vol. IV Area Reports: International
American Bureau of Metal Statistics (New York):
Year Book 1963–1965
Metal Bulletin Ltd. (London):
Iron and Steel Works of the World 1965
British Iron and Steel Federation, Intelligence Dept. (London)
Alluminio, Direzione, Redazione e Publicita (Milano):
Alluminio
A.M.M.I. S.p.A. (Roma):
Non Ferrous Metals and Ferroalloys
Metallgesellschaft Aktiengesellschaft (Frankfurt am Main):
Metal Statistics 1958–1967
The British Bureau of Non-ferrous Metal Statistics (Birmingham, U.K.):
World Non-ferrous Metal Statistics 1968
Thomas Skinner & Co. Ltd. (London):
Skinner's Mining Yearbook 1963–1969
International Tin Council (London):
Statistical Year Book 1964
Minerais et Métaux 1965
Asbestos Information Committee (London)
Industrial Diamond Information Bureau (London)

Transport Industries

Sampson Low, Marston & Co. (Great Missenden, U.K.):
Jane's World Railways
Jane's All the World's Aircraft

Transport and Technical Publications Ltd. (London):
Railway Directory and Yearbook 1967/1968

Organization for Economic Co-operation and Development (Paris):
The Engineering Industries in North America, Europe and Japan 1966/67

Railway Age (New York):
Railway Age Statistical Review 1962–1965

International Civil Aviation Organization (Montréal)

American Aviation Publications (Washington, D.C.):
American Aviation

Lloyd's (London):
Register of Ships 1967/8
Annual Summary of Merchant Ships Launched in the World 1953–1955 and 1964–1966

U.N. (New York):
Statistical Yearbook 1957, 1967
Yearbook of International Trade Statistics 1965
Repertoire International de l'Industrie Automobile 1965

Society of Motor Manufacturers and Traders Ltd. (London):
Motor Industry of Great Britain

Automobile Club of Italy:
World Car Club

Manufacturing Industries

CEMBUREAU, The European Cement Association (Malmö, Sweden):
World Cement Directory

U.N. (New York):
Statistical Yearbook 1957, 1966, 1968

Computer Consultants Limited (Llandudno, U.K.):
European Computer Survey 1968/9
European Computer Users' Handbook 1964
British Commercial Computer Digest 1963

The British Sulphur Corporation Limited (London)

U.S. Dept. of the Interior (Washington, D.C.):
Bureau of Mines, Minerals Yearbook
Vol. I Metals and Minerals

F.A.O. (Roma):
Fertilizers—An Annual Review of World Production, Consumption and Trade 1966

European Chemical News (London):
'Chemical Product Data' 1969
'Chemical Plant Data' 1969

Verlag für Internationale Wirtschaftsliteratur GmbH. (Zürich):
International Brewers' Directory and Soft Drink Guide 1965

William Reed Ltd. (London):
The Brewers Journal

Modern Brewery Age (Stamford, Connecticut):
Blue Book 1968

Time, Inc. (Chicago):
The Fortune Directory of the 500 Largest U.S. Industrial Corporations 1957 and 1967
The Fortune Directory of the 200 Largest Industrial Companies Outside the U.S. 1957 and 1967

Demography

U.N. (New York):
Demographic Yearbook
Report on World Population Prospects, as Assessed in 1963
Statistical Yearbook 1967

International Planned Parenthood Federation (London)

International Union of Official Travel Organizations (London):
International Travel Statistics

World Health Organization (Geneva):
Statistics Annual Vol. I, 1962, 1963, 1964
Third Report on the World Health Situation 1961–1964
Epidemiological and Vital Statistics Report 1959–61, 1966

Disease

World Health Organization (Geneva):
Epidemiological and Vital Statistics Reports
Statistics Annual 1957–1966
Epidemiological Assessment on the Status of Malaria—Official Records of the World Health Organization No. 118
Official Records of the W.H.O. No. 127
W.H.O. Chronicle
Bulletin
Vol. 28: J. Ford, 'Distribution of Vectors of African Pathogenic Trypanosomes' and
Vol. 34: L. M. Bechelli & V. M. Domingues, 'The Leprosy Problem in the World'
Second and Third Reports on the World Health Situation
Public Health Papers
No. 32: B. Abel-Smith, 'An International Study of Health Expenditure'
World Health Magazine

U.N. (New York):
Demographic Yearbook 1966

International Leprosy Association (Washington, D.C.):
International Journal of Leprosy

J. May (New York 1958):
Ecology of Human Disease

American Society of Tropical Medicine and Hygiene (Baltimore, Maryland):
American Journal of Tropical Medicine and Hygiene

A. H. Gale (London 1959):
Epidemic Diseases

American Public Health Association (New York 1960):
Control of Communicable Diseases in Man

Ross Institute Records (London)

T. H. Davey and W. P. H. Lightbody (London 1961):
The Control of Diseases in the Tropics

E. Rodenwalt (Hamburg 1952–7):
World Atlas of Epidemic Diseases

U.I.C.C., International Union Against Cancer (Berlin 1966):
R. Doll, P. Payne, J. Waterhouse (eds.), *Cancer Incidence in Five Continents*

Dept. of Public Health, University School of Medicine (Sendai, Japan 1966):
Segi, Mitsuo, et al., *Cancer Mortality for Selected Sites in 24 Countries*

British Journal of Cancer (Vol. 23, 1969):
R. Doll, *The Geographical Distribution of Cancer*

Nuffield Provincial Hospitals Trust, 1967:
R. Doll, *Epidemiology of Cancer*

R. M. Prothero (London 1965):
Migrants and Malaria

Society and Politics

International Labour Organization (Geneva):
Yearbook of Labour Statistics 1966

U.N. (New York):
Yearbook of National Accounts Statistics 1965
UNESCO Statistical Yearbook 1965–1968
Yearbook of International Trade Statistics
Statistical Yearbook 1964–1967

International Monetary Fund (Washington, D.C.):
Direction of Trade Annual 1963–7

International Bank for Reconstruction and Development (Washington, D.C.):
World Bank Atlas

American Telephone and Telegraph Company New York):
The World's Telephones 1967

O.E.C.D. (Paris):
Development Assistance Efforts and Policies 1968 and 1969

Macmillan & Co. Ltd. (London):
The Statesman's Year Book

Europa Publications Limited (London):
Europa Year Book

P. Robson (London 1968):
Economic Integration in Africa

Cambridge University Press (London 1970):
The New Cambridge Modern History Atlas

J. Wreford Watson (London 1968):
North America, Its Countries and Regions

G. Pendle (London 1968):
A History of Latin America

Surface and Air Communications

Macmillan & Co. Ltd. (London):
The Statesman's Year Book

Kultura (Budapest):
Cartactual

Lloyd's (London):
Shipping Index
Register of Shipping
Voyage Supplement
Maritime Atlas

Dr. B. J. Turton, Dept. of Geography, University of Keele, U.K.

Thomas Skinner & Co. Ltd. (London):
ABC World Airways Guide April 1970

Reuben H. Donnelly Corp. (Oak Brook, Illinois):
Official Airline Guide
International Edition, Sept. 1969
North American Edition, March 1970

GAZETTEER

The gazetteer lists more than eight thousand names of populated places, specific sites (such as mines or dams), physical features and administrative divisions which are named on the maps. It does not list country names.

The gazetteer uses the vernacular form of all place names, transliterated into the Roman alphabet where appropriate, according to the system used by the United States Board on Geographic Names. Where the vernacular form of a name may be unfamiliar to English-speaking readers and there is a common English form, this English form is given as a cross-reference. Entries for places recently renamed also may include a cross-reference to the previous name. For each place the name used is a de facto representation of the situation at the time of the compilation of the gazetteer and does not imply any political comment or bias.

The names in the gazetteer are arranged in alphabetical order taking no account of diacritical marks or letters not found in the Roman alphabet. Names which begin St. or Ste. are alphabetized as though written out in full. Names beginning Le, La, Les, Los, etc. are alphabetized under the pronoun. Names which have had to be abbreviated on the maps are written out in full in the gazetteer and alphabetized accordingly.

Any name which is not that of a populated place is followed by a description in italic type except that where the descriptive term forms part of the name it is italicized but not repeated. No distinction of size is made in respect of administrative divisions; but the counties of the U.S.A., the names of which are not familiar, are described simply as *Co.* Every entry is identified by the name of the country in which it is to be found, and entries for places in the U.S.A. are further specified by their state location.

Wherever possible co-ordinates have been given to the nearest minute, enabling entries to be located on maps at any scale. The majority of such co-ordinates have been taken from a printed source as specified below but in some cases, particularly for dams and mines, they have been plotted for this atlas (as accurately as possible) from less authoritative maps. Regions or physical features which are not well defined have not been located with such precision. References to large geographical or administrative areas are generalized, and each refers to the approximate centre of the area. The co-ordinates given for large areas will not, therefore, necessarily coincide with the position of a symbol on a map. The same is true of the co-ordinates given for rivers which refer always to the location of the mouth of the river.

Each entry is followed by a list of all the pages on which the name occurs. Where a name occurs on an inset map, rather than on the main world map, this is indicated by the use of a capital letter which corresponds to the letter of the inset on which the name occurs.

Sources. The gazetteers of official standard names which are published by the United States Board on Geographic Names have been taken as authoritative for both the location of places and the spelling of place names for all countries with the following major exceptions:

Algeria	New Zealand
Canada	Nigeria
Cyprus	Peru
Czechoslovakia	Philippines
Greece	Poland
India	South Africa
Irish Republic	Switzerland
Israel	U.K.
Netherlands	U.S.A.

For all of these the *Index-Gazetteer of the World* published by The Times Publishing Company Ltd., has been taken as authoritative for the location of places and, supplemented where appropriate by national atlases, has been used as the major source for spellings. The U.S.B.G.N. gazetteer for Morocco appeared too late to be used as an authority on spellings but has been used for locations. Moroccan names are spelt as in the Atlas du Maroc published by the Comité de Géographie du Maroc.

The Comprehensive edition of the *Atlas of the World*, published by The Times Newspapers Ltd., and the *International Atlas* published by Rand McNally and Co. (George Philip & Son Ltd. in the U.K.), have also been used extensively.

Of the many atlases and maps which have been consulted during the preparation of this gazetteer, the following are the most important and most frequently used:

The National Atlases of Canada and Czechoslovakia
Pergamon Press: *Pergamon World Atlas*
Touring Club Italiano: *Atlante Internazionale del T.C.I.*
Rand McNally & Co.: *International World Atlas*
Clarendon Press: *The Atlas of Britain*
Kartogràfiai Vàllalat Budapest: *Kèpes Politikai ès Gazdasàgi Vilàgatlasz*
Columbia University Press: *The Columbia Lippincott Gazetteer of the World*
Kultura: *Cartactual*
National and State road maps
The Petroleum Publishing Co.: *International Petroleum Encyclopedia*
George Philip & Son Ltd.: *Geographical Digest* (used particularly to verify name changes)

Generic terms. The following generic terms in foreign languages appear in the gazetteer. English equivalents are taken from the U.S.B.G.N. gazetteers.

Basseyn (*Russian*)	basin	Lough (*Gaelic*)	lake
Berg (*German*)	hill, mountain	Marsá (*Arabic*)	anchorage, bay
Birkat (*Arabic*)	lake, marsh	Misaki (*Japanese*)	peninsula
Bukit (*Indonesian*)	hill, mountain, peninsula	Morro (*Portuguese*)	hill(s), mountain(s)
Būr (*Arabic*)	port	Ostov, Ostova (*Russian*)	island(s)
Cerro(s) (*Spanish*)	hill(s), mountain(s)	Oya (*Ceylonese*)	stream
Deresi (*Turkish*)	stream	Pegunungan (*Indonesian*)	mountains, mountain range
Ghar (*Pakistani*)	mountain(s), mountain range	P'en-ti (*Chinese*)	basin
Gora, Gory (*Russian*)	mountain, mountains	Pereval (*Russian*)	mountain pass
Guba (*Russian*)	bay	Poluostrov (*Russian*)	peninsula
Ho (*Spanish*)	lake, stream	Pulau (*Indonesian*)	island, reef
Jabal, Jbel, Djebel (*Arabic*)	hill(s), mountain(s)	Río (*Spanish*)	river, stream
Jazireh (*Persian*)	island	Serra (*Portuguese*)	mountain range
Khalij (*Arabic*)	gulf	Shima (*Japanese*)	island(s)
Khao (*Thai*)	hill, mountain	Sierra (*Spanish*)	hill(s), mountain(s)
Khrebet (*Russian*)	mountains, mountain range	Stena (*Yugoslav*)	mountain
Khuan (*Thai*)	dam	Tanjong (*Malay*)	point
Ko (*Thai*)	island, peninsula, point	Wādī (*Arabic*)	stream, irrigation canal
Kuh (*Persian*)	hill(s), mountain(s)	Wāḩāt (*Arabic*)	oasis
Ling (*Chinese*)	hill(s), mountain(s), pass	Yama (*Japanese*)	hill, mountain(s)

Abbreviations. The abbreviations listed below have been used in the gazetteer.

admin.	administrative division	G.F.R. / Germany F.R.	Federal Republic of Germany	Okla.	Oklahoma
Ala.	Alabama	Ice.	Iceland	Oreg.	Oregon
arch.	archipelago	Ill.	Illinois	Pa.	Pennsylvania
Arg.	Argentina	Ind.	Indiana	*pen.*	peninsula
Ariz.	Arizona	Indon.	Indonesia	*pt.*	point
Ark.	Arkansas	Irish R.	Irish Republic	*reg.*	region
Austl.	Australia	*is.*	island or islands	R.I.	Rhode Island
Calif.	California	Kans.	Kansas	*riv.*	river
Cent. Af. R.	Central African Republic	Ky.	Kentucky	S. Africa	South Africa
China P.R.	The People's Republic of China	La.	Louisiana	S. Vietnam	South Vietnam
Co.	County	Malagasy R.	Malagasy Republic	S.C.	South Carolina
Colo.	Colorado	Mass.	Massachusetts	S.D.	South Dakota
Congo D.R.	Democratic Republic of the Congo	Md.	Maryland	S.S.R.	Sovietskaya Sotsialisticheskaya Respublika
Congo R.	Republic of the Congo	Mich.	Michigan	St. Maarten	Sint Maarten
Conn.	Connecticut	Minn.	Minnesota	Tenn.	Tennessee
Czech.	Czechoslovakia	Miss.	Mississippi	Thai.	Thailand
Del.	Delaware	Mo.	Missouri	U.A.R.	United Arab Republic
Den.	Denmark	Mont.	Montana	U.S.A.	United States of America
Dom. R.	Dominican Republic	Mor.	Morocco	U.S.S.R.	Union of Soviet Socialist Republics
Eng.	England	*mtn.(s)*	mountain(s)	Va.	Virginia
Fla.	Florida	N.C.	North Carolina	Vt.	Vermont
Fr. Guiana	French Guiana	N.D.	North Dakota	Wash.	Washington
Ga.	Georgia (U.S.A.)	Nebr.	Nebraska	Wis.	Wisconsin
G.D.R. / Germany D.R.	German Democratic Republic	Neths.	Netherlands	W. Va.	West Virginia
		Nev.	Nevada	Wyo.	Wyoming
		N.H.	New Hampshire	Yugo.	Yugoslavia
		N.J.	New Jersey		
		N. Korea	North Korea		
		N. Mex.	New Mexico		
		N.Y.	New York		

A

	° ′	° ′	Page(s)
Aachen: Germany F.R.	50 46 N	6 06 E	32C, 38B, 54B
Aalst: Belgium	50 56 N	4 02 E	32C
Aathal: Switzerland	47 20 N	8 30 E	31B
Ābādān: Iran	30 20 N	48 16 E	37A, 37G, 59, 60, 67, 84
Abakan: U.S.S.R.	53 43 N	91 26 E	38
Abashiri: Japan	44 01 N	144 17 E	27D
Åbenrå: Denmark	55 02 N	9 26 E	84C
Aberdeen: Miss., U.S.A.	33 49 N	88 34 W	60B
Aberdeen: Scotland	57 10 N	2 04 W	27C, 67, 87
Aberdeen: S.D., U.S.A.	45 28 N	98 30 W	62
Aberfoyle Creek: *stream*, Austl.	41 44 S	147 48 E	50
Aberthaw: Wales	51 24 N	3 23 W	57C
Abidjan: Ivory Coast	5 19 N	4 02 W	67, 84, 87
Abilene: Texas, U.S.A.	32 27 N	99 45 W	37J
Abitibi Canyon: *dam*, Canada	49 53 N	81 34 W	39
Åbo *see* Turku: Finland	60 27 N	22 17 E	29, 52, 58, 67
Aboño: Spain	43 34 N	5 43 W	57C
Abruzzi e Molise: *admin.*, Italy	42 20 N	13 45 E	17
Abshirsay: *river*, U.S.S.R.	40 29 N	72 12 E	50
Abū Māḍī: *region*, U.A.R.	31 30 N	31 20 E	34
Abū Tulu, Jabal: *hill*, Sudan	11 41 N	28 40 E	43
Abū Za'bal: U.A.R.	30 15 N	31 21 E	59
Acajutla: El Salvador	13 36 N	89 50 W	36, 59, 61, 84
Acapulco de Juaréz: Mexico	16 51 N	99 55 W	87
Acari: Peru	15 25 S	74 37 W	43
Accra: Ghana	5 33 N	0 13 W	55, 67, 87
Accrington: England	53 46 N	2 21 W	31B
Achinsk: U.S.S.R.	56 17 N	90 30 E	38, 47, 57
Achisay: U.S.S.R.	43 35 N	68 53 E	46, 49
Acme: N.C., U.S.A.	34 20 N	78 11 W	59B, 59F
Acre *see* 'Akko: Israel	32 55 N	35 04 E	43, 59, 60
Acton: Mass., U.S.A.	42 28 N	71 26 W	30A
Ada: Okla., U.S.A.	34 47 N	96 41 W	57A
Adana: Turkey	37 01 N	35 18 E	32, 34, 57, 67
Ad Dammām: Saudi Arabia	26 26 N	50 07 E	61
Ad Dawḥah: Qatar	25 17 N	51 32 E	37A
Ad Dawrah: Iraq	33 16 N	44 21 E	37G
Addis: La., U.S.A.	30 20 N	91 18 W	30A
Addis Ababa: Ethiopia	9 03 N	38 42 E	31, 36, 67, 87
Adelaide: Australia	34 56 S	138 56 E	31, 34, 36, 54, 59, 67, 84, 87
Aden: Southern Yemen	12 50 N	45 03 E	36, 67, 84
Adirondack *Mountains*: N.Y., U.S.A.	44 00 N	74 30 W	43
Adler: U.S.S.R.	43 25 N	39 56 E	87
Adoni: India	15 38 N	77 16 E	31C
Adriatic *Sea*: Europe	42 30 N	16 00 E	27
Äetsä: Finland	61 18 N	22 42 E	59
Agadir: Morocco	30 24 N	9 36 W	27, 84
Agarak: U.S.S.R.	39 13 N	46 33 E	45, 50
Ågesta: Sweden	59 14 N	18 05 E	40
Agra: India	27 09 N	78 00 E	31
Agricola: Fla., U.S.A.	27 30 N	81 50 W	59F
Agua Grande: *region*, Brazil	11 30 S	38 00 W	34
Aguaytía: *region*, Peru	8 30 S	74 40 W	34
Agudo, Morro: *hill*, Brazil	20 42 S	42 09 W	43
Ahlen: Germany F.R.	51 45 N	7 55 E	58D, 61D
Ahmadabad: India	23 03 N	72 40 E	31C
Ahvāz: Iran	31 19 N	48 42 E	67
Aichi-ken: *admin.*, Japan	35 00 N	137 15 E	55, 60C, 63
Aiken: S.C., U.S.A.	33 34 N	81 44 W	32B
Aïn Barbar: Algeria	36 54 N	7 47 E	45
Aintree: England	53 29 N	2 57 W	32C, 60D
Aioi: Japan	34 48 N	134 28 E	52B
Aïr: *plateau*, Niger	18 00 N	8 30 E	45
Aire-sur-l'Adour: France	43 42 N	0 16 W	53B
Airvault: France	46 50 N	0 09 W	57C
Aitsu: Japan	32 30 N	130 26 E	59G
Aiud: Romania	46 18 N	23 43 E	17
Aizu-Shimodate: Japan	37 34 N	140 08 E	46C
Ajax: Canada	43 51 N	79 02 W	55A
Ajka: Hungary	47 06 N	17 34 E	47B
Ajmer: India	26 29 N	74 40 E	50
Ajo: Ariz., U.S.A.	32 24 N	112 51 W	45A
A'kan-chen: China P.R.	35 57 N	103 49 E	38
Akchatau: U.S.S.R.	47 59 N	74 02 E	50
Akenobe: Japan	35 05 N	134 35 E	45D, 46C
Akersvann: *dam*, Norway	66 15 N	14 00 E	39
Akhan-Gharan: U.S.S.R.	40 54 N	69 37 E	57
Akita: Japan	39 43 N	140 07 E	37E, 46C, 58G, 59G, 61C, 84D
Akita-ken: *admin.*, Japan	40 00 N	140 30 E	35, 56
'Akko (Acre): Israel	32 55 N	35 04 E	43, 59, 60
Akola: India	20 40 N	77 05 E	31C
Akosombo: *dam*, Ghana	6 16 N	0 03 W	39
Akoumapé: Togo	6 23 N	1 27 E	56
Akranes: Iceland	64 19 N	22 06 W	27
Akron: Ohio, U.S.A.	41 04 N	81 31 W	30A, 63, 67A, 87B
Akseki: Turkey	37 02 N	31 48 E	47
Aktau: U.S.S.R.	50 13 N	73 03 E	57
Aktyubinsk: U.S.S.R.	50 17 N	57 10 E	67
Aktyubinskaya Oblast': *admin.*, U.S.S.R.	48 00 N	58 00 E	56
Aktyuz: U.S.S.R.	42 54 N	76 07 E	46, 49
Akureyri: Iceland	65 40 N	18 06 W	27
Akwatia: Ghana	6 03 N	0 48 W	48C
Akzhal: U.S.S.R.	49 13 N	81 25 E	49
Alabama: *admin.*, U.S.A.	33 00 N	38 00 W	38
Alabama: N.Y., U.S.A.	43 05 N	78 27 W	61A
Alagoas: *admin.*, Brazil	9 00 S	36 00 W	27, 48D
Al 'Alamayn: U.A.R.	30 49 N	28 57 E	35
'Alam, Marsá al: *anchorage*, U.A.R.	25 05 N	34 54 E	48
Alamos: Mexico	27 01 N	108 56 W	49A
Alapayevsk: U.S.S.R.	57 52 N	61 42 E	43
Al 'Aqabah (Aqaba): Jordan	29 31 N	35 00 E	84
Alarup: Albania	40 52 N	20 48 E	38B
Alaska: *admin.*, U.S.A.	65 00 N	153 00 W	27, 35, 38
Alaska: Rhodesia	17 22 S	30 05 E	45
Alaverdi: U.S.S.R.	41 08 N	44 39 E	45
Albany: Australia	35 02 S	117 53 E	59, 84
Albany: Ga., U.S.A.	31 37 N	84 10 W	31A, 87C
Albany: N.Y., U.S.A.	42 40 N	73 49 W	40C, 67A, 87B
Albany: Oreg., U.S.A.	44 38 N	123 07 W	25
Al Başrah (Basra): Iraq	30 30 N	47 47 E	37A, 59, 61
Albbruck: Germany F.R.	47 36 N	8 08 E	25C
Albemarle: N.C., U.S.A.	35 21 N	80 12 W	31A
Alberta: *admin.*, Canada	54 00 N	113 00 W	27, 34, 35, 38
Albert, *Lake*: Africa	1 40 N	31 00 E	27
Albert Nile: *river*, Uganda	3 36 N	32 02 E	27
Alberton: South Africa	26 16 S	28 08 E	54
Albi: France	43 56 N	2 09 E	32C
Alblasserdam: Netherlands	51 52 N	4 40 E	52A
Ålborg: Denmark	57 03 N	9 56 E	57, 84C
Alborz: Iran	34 43 N	50 59 E	37G
Al Burqān: *region*, Kuwait	28 58 N	47 58 E	35, 37C
Alburquerque: Spain	39 13 N	7 00 W	50
Alcalá de Henares: Spain	40 29 N	3 22 W	32C, 60
Alcázar de San Juan: Spain	39 24 N	3 12 W	54
Alcoa: Tenn., U.S.A.	35 47 N	84 00 W	47
Aldama: Mexico	28 51 N	105 54 W	49A
Aldan: U.S.S.R.	58 37 N	125 24 E	49
Aldeadávila: *dam*, Spain	41 14 N	6 44 W	39
Aleksandrovac: Yugoslavia	44 27 N	21 13 E	17
Aleksandrovsk-Sakhalinskiy: U.S.S.R.	50 54 N	142 10 E	38
Alella: Spain	41 29 N	2 18 E	17
Aleppo *see* Ḥalab: Syria	36 12 N	37 10 E	57
Ålesund: Norway	62 28 N	6 09 E	27, 87
Alexander City: Ala., U.S.A.	32 57 N	86 00 W	31A
Alexandria *see* Al Iskandarīyah: U.A.R.	31 12 N	29 54 E	27, 29, 36, 84B
Alfeld: Germany F.R.	49 26 N	11 33 E	25C
Al Fuḥayş: Jordan	32 01 N	35 46 E	57
Algarrobo: Chile	30 30 S	71 07 W	43
Algeciras: Spain	36 08 N	5 30 W	27B, 36, 58
Alger: Algeria	36 50 N	3 00 E	17, 59H, 67, 84A, 87
Al Ḥadīthah: Iraq	34 07 N	42 23 E	37G
Al Ḥallūfah, Jabal: *hill*, Tunisia	36 40 N	10 25 E	46B
Alhandra: Portugal	38 55 N	9 00 W	57C
Al Ḥasā: Jordan	30 51 N	35 56 E	56
Al Hindīyah: Iraq	32 32 N	44 13 E	32
Al Hoceima: Morocco	35 14 N	3 56 W	27B
Alicante: *admin.*, Spain	38 30 N	0 30 W	17
Alicante: Spain	38 21 N	0 29 W	27B
Alingsås: Sweden	57 56 N	12 31 E	31
Alio Ghelle: Somali Republic	3 00 N	44 00 E	40
Aliquippa: Pa., U.S.A.	40 38 N	80 16 W	43A
Al Iskandarīyah (Alexandria): U.A.R.	31 12 N	29 54 E	27, 29, 36, 84B
Alivérion: Greece	38 24 N	24 02 E	38
Al Jīzah (Giza): U.A.R.	30 01 N	31 13 E	67
Aljustrel: Portugal	32 52 N	8 10 W	56
Al Khurṭūm (Khartoum): Sudan	15 36 N	32 32 E	31, 67, 87
Al Kuwayt (Kuwait): Kuwait	29 20 N	47 59 E	56, 67, 84, 87
Al Lādhiqiyah: Syria	35 31 N	35 47 E	84B
Allahabad: *admin.*, India	25 30 N	81 45 E	47
Allahabad: India	25 27 N	81 50 E	31
Allegheny River: *dam*, Pa., U.S.A.	41 50 N	79 01 W	39
Allen, Lough: *lake*, Irish R.	54 08 N	8 08 W	38
Allentown: Pa., U.S.A.	40 37 N	75 30 W	55B, 67A, 87B
Alloa: Scotland	56 07 N	3 49 W	29B
Allyns Point: Conn., U.S.A.	41 26 N	72 05 W	30A
Alma: Canada	48 32 N	71 41 W	25, 47
Alma: Mich., U.S.A.	43 23 N	84 40 W	37J
Alma-Ata: U.S.S.R.	43 15 N	76 57 E	29, 67
Almadén: Spain	38 46 N	4 50 W	50
Al Maḥallah al Kubrá: U.A.R.	30 58 N	31 10 E	29, 31
Al Maks: U.A.R.	31 09 N	29 51 E	57, 59
Almalyk: U.S.S.R.	40 50 N	69 35 E	45, 46
Almásfüzitő: Hungary	47 43 N	18 16 E	37H, 47B
Al Mawşil: Iraq	36 20 N	43 08 E	57
Almeden: Idaho, U.S.A.	44 30 N	116 45 W	50
Almelo: Netherlands	52 21 N	6 40 E	31B
Almería: *admin.*, Spain	37 10 N	2 20 W	49
Almería: Spain	36 50 N	2 27 W	27B
Alpagut: Turkey	40 20 N	34 51 E	38
Alpena: Mich., U.S.A.	45 04 N	83 27 W	25D, 57B
Alpine Foreland: *region*, G.F.R.	48 30 N	12 30 E	37D
Al Qāhirah (Cairo): U.A.R.	30 03 N	31 15 E	29, 31, 32, 34, 67, 87
Al Qal'ah al Jardā': Tunisia	35 40 N	8 35 E	56
Al Quşayr (Quseir): U.A.R.	26 06 N	34 17 E	40
Alsdorf: Germany F.R.	50 53 N	6 10 E	58D
Alsen: N.Y., U.S.A.	42 11 N	73 55 W	57B
Altamira: Mexico	22 24 N	97 55 W	30, 59
Altenessen: Germany F.R.	51 29 N	7 00 E	37F, 58D
Altenrhein: Switzerland	47 28 N	9 30 E	53B
Alto Anchicaya: *dam*, Colombia	3 46 N	77 10 W	39
Alto Ligonha: Mozambique	15 31 S	38 16 E	48, 50
Alton: Ill., U.S.A.	38 55 N	90 10 W	25, 43A
Altona: Australia	37 52 S	144 50 E	30, 36, 58, 59, 60
Alverca: Portugal	38 54 N	9 02 W	61
Al Wāḥāt al Baḥrīyah: *region*, U.A.R.	28 15 N	28 57 E	43
Alwaye: India	10 06 N	76 23 E	31C, 40, 47, 59
Amagasaki: Japan	34 43 N	135 25 E	56, 58C
Amakusa-shimo-jima: *is.*, Japan	32 20 N	130 05 E	38C
Amalfi: Italy	40 38 N	14 36 E	17
Amalner: India	21 01 N	75 09 E	31C
Amapá: Brazil	2 03 N	50 48 W	50
Amarante: Portugal	41 16 N	8 05 W	45
Amarillo: Texas, U.S.A.	35 14 N	101 50 W	37J, 46, 87C
Ambarès-et-la Grave: France	44 55 N	0 29 W	61H
Ambarnath: India	19 11 N	73 11 E	59
Ambasamudram: India	8 45 N	77 27 E	31C
Amberg: Germany F.R.	49 27 N	11 52 E	58D
Ambès: France	45 01 N	0 32 W	36
Ambès, Bec d': *point*, France	45 03 N	0 37 W	60H
Ambindandrakemba: Malagasy Republic	25 02 S	46 23 E	40
Amboasary: Malagasy R.	25 02 S	46 23 E	40
Amboenembo: Malagasy R.	25 02 S	46 23 E	40
Americana: Brazil	22 45 S	47 20 W	32
Amersfoort: Netherlands	52 09 N	5 23 E	55A, 62A
Amherstburg: Canada	42 06 N	83 06 W	59A
Amiandos: Cyprus	34 55 N	32 55 E	48D
Amiens: France	49 54 N	2 18 E	67B
'Ammān (Rabbah): Jordan	31 57 N	35 56 E	67, 87
Åmmeberg: Sweden	58 52 N	15 00 E	46
Amoy *see* Hsia-men: China P.R.	24 27 N	118 05 E	32, 84
Ampa: *region*, Brunei	5 00 N	114 30 E	34
Amritsar: India	31 35 N	74 56 E	29
Amsterdam: Netherlands	52 21 N	4 54 E	30B, 37B, 37F, 52A, 53B, 53C, 55A, 56A, 58H, 59H, 62A, 67B, 84C, 87D
Amsterdam: N.Y., U.S.A.	42 56 N	74 12 W	29A, 32B
Amuay: Venezuela	11 47 N	70 15 W	36
Amvrosiyevka: U.S.S.R.	47 47 N	38 30 E	57
Anaco: Venezuela	9 27 N	64 28 W	34
Anaconda: Mont., U.S.A.	46 09 N	112 56 W	46A
Anacortes: Wash., U.S.A.	48 30 N	122 42 W	36, 59
Anadyr': U.S.S.R.	64 45 N	177 29 E	38
Anaheim: Calif., U.S.A.	33 50 N	117 56 W	87A
Anauchi: Japan	33 20 N	133 00 E	50
Ancash: *admin.*, Peru	9 30 S	77 45 W	46, 49
Anchieta: Brazil	20 48 S	40 39 W	50
An-ch'ing: China P.R.	30 31 N	117 02 E	46
Anchorage: Alaska, U.S.A.	61 10 N	150 00 W	84, 87
Ancón: Ecuador	2 20 S	80 52 W	34
Ancona: Italy	43 38 N	13 30 E	52A, 84A
Andalgalá: Argentina	27 36 S	66 19 W	45
Andean Highland: *region*, Peru	16 00 S	71 00 W	23
Anderson: S.C., U.S.A.	34 30 N	82 39 W	31A, 32B, 60B
Andhra Pradesh: *admin.*, India	16 00 N	79 00 E	27, 38
Andoain: Spain	43 13 N	2 01 W	32C, 60D
Andrade: Brazil	21 01 S	42 58 W	43
Andrychów: Poland	49 51 N	19 18 E	31
Andújar: Spain	38 03 N	4 04 W	40
Anegasaki: Japan	35 28 N	140 02 E	58G, 60C
An-fu: China P.R.	27 23 N	114 37 E	61
Angara: *river*, U.S.S.R.	58 06 N	93 00 E	43
Angarsk: U.S.S.R.	52 34 N	103 54 E	36, 57
Angaston: Australia	34 30 S	139 02 E	57
Angat: *dam*, Philippines	14 55 N	121 01 E	39
Angers: France	47 28 N	0 33 W	17, 62A
Anglesea: Australia	38 25 S	144 10 E	38
Angleur: Belgium	50 37 N	5 36 E	46B
Angostura: Mexico	18 15 N	102 31 W	35
Angren: U.S.S.R.	41 01 N	70 12 E	38, 57, 61
Angūrān, Kūh: *mtn.*, Iran	36 44 N	48 38 E	46
An-hua: China P.R.	28 24 N	111 13 E	50D
Ánimas: Bolivia	18 22 S	67 35 W	49
Ankara: Turkey	39 56 N	32 52 E	67, 87
Anklesvar: India	21 38 N	73 02 E	35
Ankole: *admin.*, Uganda	0 30 S	30 30 E	50
'Annaba: Algeria	36 55 N	7 47 E	59H, 84A
Annaberg: *admin.*, G.D.R.	50 35 N	13 00 E	45, 50
Annaka: Japan	36 19 N	138 54 E	46C
Annecy: France	45 54 N	6 07 W	45
Annex Kleinsee: *mine*, S. Africa	29 43 S	17 03 E	48
Anniston: Ala., U.S.A.	33 38 N	85 50 W	25A, 31A, 59B
Annonay: France	45 14 N	4 40 E	55A
Anosibe: Malagasy Republic	16 17 S	44 54 E	84
An-shan: China P.R.	41 07 N	122 57 E	43, 46, 55, 67
Ansty: England	52 26 N	1 24 W	53B
Anta: *dam*, Brazil	22 03 S	42 59 W	39
Antalya: Turkey	36 53 N	30 42 E	84B
Antananarivo (Tananarive): Malagasy Republic	18 55 S	47 31 E	67, 87
Antioch: Calif., U.S.A.	38 01 N	121 49 W	25
Antioquia: *admin.*, Colombia	7 00 N	75 30 W	49
Antofagasta: Chile	23 39 S	70 24 W	27, 67
Antrim: Northern Ireland	54 43 N	6 13 W	32C, 60
Antung *see* Tan-tung: China P.R.	40 08 N	124 24 E	25, 32
Antwerpen: *admin.*, Belgium	51 13 N	4 25 E	56A
Antwerpen (Anvers): Belgium	51 13 N	4 25 E	30B, 37D, 37F, 45, 55A, 58D, 58H, 59D, 59H, 60D, 60H, 61H, 67B, 84C
Anvers *see* Antwerpen: Belgium			
An Xuyen: *admin.*, S. Vietnam	9 00 N	105 05 E	27
An-yang: China P.R.	36 05 N	114 21 E	43
Anyang-ni: South Korea	37 23 N	126 55 E	32A, 60
Anzhero-Sudzhensk: U.S.S.R.	56 07 N	86 00 E	38
Aomori: Japan	40 49 N	140 45 E	27D, 67
Aomori-ken: *admin.*, Japan	40 45 N	141 00 E	50
Aosta: Italy	45 44 N	7 20 E	43B
Aouam, Jbel: *hill*, Morocco	33 10 N	5 40 W	43
Aouli: Morocco	32 50 N	4 34 W	46, 49
Apache *Co.*: Ariz., U.S.A.	35 30 N	109 30 W	40A, 50A
Aparri: Philippines	18 22 N	121 40 E	84
Apaxco de Ocampo: Mexico	19 59 N	99 10 W	57
Apeldoorn: Netherlands	52 13 N	5 57 E	25C
Apollo: Pa., U.S.A.	40 34 N	79 34 W	40C
Appalachian Mountains, North: *mtns.*, Maine, U.S.A.	45 00 N	70 00 W	50
Appingedam: Netherlands	53 18 N	6 52 E	25C
Aqaba *see* Al 'Aqabah: Jordan	29 31 N	35 00 E	84
Aquiles Serdán: Mexico	28 36 N	105 53 W	46, 49A
Aracaju: Brazil	10 55 S	37 04 W	67
Arad: Romania	46 11 N	21 19 E	37B, 54
Aragua de Maturín: Venezuela	9 58 N	63 29 W	34
Arakaka: Guyana	7 35 N	60 07 W	50
Aransas Pass: Texas, U.S.A.	27 55 N	97 10 W	60G
Ararat: U.S.S.R.	39 50 N	44 42 E	57
Arasan: U.S.S.R.	45 17 N	79 22 E	50
Aratu: Brazil	12 49 S	38 27 W	57
Arauco: *admin.*, Chile	37 50 S	73 15 W	38
Arcachon: France	44 39 N	1 10 W	27B
Archangel *see* Arkhangel'sk: U.S.S.R.	64 34 N	40 32 E	25, 67, 84
Arcola: Italy	44 07 N	9 54 E	37H
Arcos: Brazil	20 17 S	45 32 W	57
Årdal: Norway	61 14 N	7 43 E	47
Arḍ as Suwaydā': *region*, Syria	35 41 N	36 45 E	37A
Ardee: Irish Republic	53 52 N	6 33 W	31
Ardlethan: Australia	34 21 S	146 54 E	45
Ardmore: Okla., U.S.A.	34 11 N	97 08 W	37J
Ardrossan: Scotland	55 39 N	4 49 W	37F, 84C
Arecibo: Puerto Rico	18 28 N	66 43 W	58
Arequipa: *admin.*, Peru	16 00 S	72 50 W	49
Arequipa: Peru	16 25 S	71 32 W	29, 32, 67
Arezzo: *admin.*, Italy	43 32 N	11 50 E	38
Arezzo: Italy	43 25 N	11 53 E	54B
Argenteuil: France	48 57 N	2 15 E	53B
Argeş: *region*, Romania	44 04 N	26 37 E	38B
Arhbar: Morocco	30 32 N	6 49 W	50
Århus: Denmark	56 09 N	10 13 E	54B, 67, 84C
Arica: Chile	18 29 S	70 20 W	27, 55, 84
Ariège: *admin.*, France	43 00 N	1 30 E	47B
Arizona: *admin.*, U.S.A.	34 00 N	112 00 W	27
Arizpe: Mexico	30 20 N	110 10 W	49A
Arkadelphia: Ark., U.S.A.	34 07 N	93 06 W	47A
Arkalyk: U.S.S.R.	50 13 N	66 50 E	47
Arkansas: *admin.*, U.S.A.	35 00 N	94 00 W	27, 38
Arkansas City: Kans., U.S.A.	37 03 N	97 02 W	37J
Arkhangel'sk (Archangel): U.S.S.R.	64 34 N	40 32 E	25, 67, 84
Arklow: Irish Republic	52 48 N	6 09 W	61D, 61H
Arlit: Niger	18 50 N	7 50 E	40
Armavir: U.S.S.R.	45 00 N	41 08 E	67
Armentières: France	50 41 N	2 53 E	31B
Armyansk: U.S.S.R.	46 06 N	33 42 E	57
Arnao: Spain	43 35 N	5 58 W	46B
Arnett: Okla., U.S.A.	36 08 N	99 46 W	37J
Arnhem: Netherlands	52 00 N	5 53 E	30B, 45, 46B, 60D
Arnprior: Canada	45 26 N	76 24 W	32B
Arquata Scrivia: Italy	44 41 N	8 53 E	57C
Arques-la-Bataille: France	49 53 N	1 08 E	32C
Ar Riyāḍ (Riyadh): Saudi Arabia	24 38 N	46 43 E	67, 87
Arroyo Grande: Calif., U.S.A.	35 08 N	120 34 W	36
Ar Ruşayfah: Jordan	32 01 N	36 02 E	56
Arsen'yev: U.S.S.R.	44 10 N	133 15 E	53
Artëm: U.S.S.R.	43 22 N	132 13 E	38C
Artëmovsk: U.S.S.R.	48 35 N	38 00 E	49
Artëmovskiy: U.S.S.R.	57 21 N	61 54 E	38
Artesia: N. Mex., U.S.A.	32 51 N	104 24 W	37J
Arvida: Canada	48 26 N	71 11 W	47, 59, 59A
Arzew: Algeria	35 50 N	0 19 W	30, 35, 37B, 37D, 61, 84A
Asahigawa: Japan	43 46 N	142 22 E	67
Asahi-mura: *admin.*, Japan	35 39 N	140 12 E	49
Asbest: U.S.S.R.	57 00 N	61 30 E	48
Asbestos: Canada	45 46 N	71 56 W	48
Asem, Bukit: *hill*, Indonesia	3 46 S	103 46 E	38
Asha: U.S.S.R.	55 00 N	57 16 E	43
Ashdod: Israel	31 45 N	34 40 E	32, 60, 61, 84B
Asheville: N.C., U.S.A.	35 35 N	82 35 W	87C
Ashford: England	51 09 N	0 53 E	54B
Ashio: Japan	36 38 N	139 27 E	45D, 59G
Ashkelon: Israel	31 40 N	34 33 E	32

	° ′	° ′	Page(s)
Ashkhabad: U.S.S.R.	37 57 N	58 23 E	29, 31, 67
Ashland: Ky., U.S.A.	38 28 N	82 40 W	43A
Ashtabula: Ohio, U.S.A.	41 53 N	80 47 W	59A, 60B, 60F
Ashton: R.I., U.S.A.	41 56 N	71 26 W	32B
Asia, Central: *reg.*, U.S.S.R.	41 00 N	73 00 E	34, 38
Asientos: Mexico	22 14 N	102 06 W	49A
Asmara: Ethiopia	15 20 N	38 58 E	67, 87
Asprópirgos: Greece	38 03 N	23 35 E	37H, 57, 59D
Assab: Ethiopia	13 01 N	42 47 E	84
Assam: *admin.*, India	26 00 N	92 00 E	27, 35, 38, 59
As Samāwah: Iraq	31 18 N	45 17 E	57
Assemini: Italy	39 17 N	9 00 E	58, 59D
As Sibāʻīyah: U.A.R.	25 11 N	32 41 E	56
As Sidar: Libya	30 37 N	19 44 E	37B
Assonet: Mass., U.S.A.	41 48 N	71 04 W	60B
Aş Şukhayrah: Tunisia	34 17 N	10 06 E	37D, 84
As Suways (Suez): U.A.R.	29 58 N	32 33 E	36, 37G, 58, 59, 60, 61, 84B
Astara: U.S.S.R.	38 26 N	48 53 E	34
Astrakhan': U.S.S.R.	46 21 N	48 03 E	25, 36, 67
Asunción: Paraguay	25 16 S	57 40 W	31, 36, 67, 87
Aswān: *dam*, U.A.R.	23 57 N	32 53 E	39
Aswān: United Arab Republic	24 05 N	32 53 E	43, 61, 67
Aswan High Dam *see* Sadd-el-Aali: *dam*, U.A.R.	23 56 N	32 53 E	39
Asyūt: United Arab Republic	27 11 N	31 11 E	59, 67
Atacama: *admin.*, Chile	27 30 S	70 00 W	43, 49
Atarfe: Spain	37 13 N	3 41 W	59H
Atasuskiy: U.S.S.R.	48 42 N	71 38 E	43
Athens *see* Athínai: Greece			
Athínai (Athens): Greece	38 00 N	23 44 E	2, 29, 31, 32C, 56, 60, 61H, 67, 87
Athus: Belgium	49 34 N	5 50 E	43B
Atico: Peru	16 14 S	73 40 W	27
Atlanta: Ga., U.S.A.	33 45 N	84 23 W	31A, 43, 55, 57B, 87
Atocongo: Peru	12 07 S	77 02 W	57
Atotonilco Tula: Mexico	20 00 N	99 13 W	57
At Tabbīn: U.A.R.	29 47 N	31 18 E	57
Attaka: U.A.R.	29 58 N	32 33 E	61
Attisholz: Switzerland	47 13 N	7 34 E	59D
Atucha: Argentina	33 58 S	59 18 W	40
Atzcapotzalco: Mexico	19 28 N	99 12 W	36, 60
Auburn: N.Y., U.S.A.	42 57 N	76 34 W	32B
Auburn: Wash., U.S.A.	47 19 N	122 14 W	53
Auby: France	50 25 N	3 03 E	46B, 59H
Auckland: New Zealand	36 55 S	174 45 E	27, 29, 34, 54, 55, 56, 67, 84, 87
Aude: *admin.*, France	43 05 N	2 30 E	49
Audincourt: France	47 29 N	6 50 E	31B
Augsburg: Germany F.R.	48 22 N	10 53 E	31B, 32C, 53, 55A
Augusta: Ga., U.S.A.	33 29 N	82 00 W	25, 31A, 59B, 59F, 61E, 87C
Augusta: Italy	37 13 N	15 13 E	37D, 37H, 57, 84A
Augusta: Kans., U.S.A.	37 41 N	96 58 W	37J
Augusta: Maine, U.S.A.	44 17 N	69 50 W	31
Aunay-sous-Crécy: France	48 40 N	1 18 E	59H
Aurora: N.C., U.S.A.	35 18 N	76 48 W	56, 59F
Austin: Texas, U.S.A.	30 18 N	97 47 W	62, 87C
Austin Low Water: *dam*, Texas, U.S.A.	30 18 N	97 47 W	39
Autlán de Navarro: Mexico	19 46 N	104 22 W	50
Auzat: France	42 46 N	1 29 E	47B
Avala: *mtn.*, Yugoslavia	44 25 N	19 55 E	50B
Avalon: Australia	38 01 S	144 25 E	53
Aveiro: Portugal	40 38 N	8 39 W	27B
Avelgem: Belgium	50 46 N	3 26 E	31B
Avellaneda: Argentina	34 39 S	58 23 W	36, 54
Aveyron: *admin.*, France	44 15 N	2 30 E	38B
Aviemore: *dam*, New Zealand	44 46 S	170 30 E	39
Ávila de los Caballeros: Spain	40 39 N	4 42 W	55
Avilés: Spain	43 33 N	5 55 W	43B, 47, 58D, 59H, 61D, 61H
Avondale: La., U.S.A.	29 55 N	90 11 W	52, 61B
Avon Lake: Ohio, U.S.A.	41 31 N	82 01 W	60B
Avonmouth: England	51 31 N	2 42 W	46B, 59H, 60H, 61D, 61H, 84C
Awaso: Ghana	6 14 N	2 16 W	47
Axpe: Spain	43 07 N	2 36 W	58H
Ayacucho: *admin.*, Peru	14 00 S	74 00 W	49
Ayamonte: Spain	37 13 N	7 24 W	27B
Aycliffe: England	54 36 N	1 34 W	60D
Ayoluengo: Spain	42 45 N	3 52 W	37D
Ayr: Scotland	55 28 N	4 38 W	27C
Aytré: France	46 08 N	1 06 E	54B
Ayvacik: *dam*, Turkey	41 00 N	36 39 E	39
Azerbaydzhanskaya S.S.R.: *admin.*, U.S.S.R.	40 30 N	47 30 E	27
Azuga: Romania	45 27 N	25 33 E	57C
Azul: Argentina	36 47 S	59 51 W	32
Azuma: Japan	35 56 N	140 30 E	43D
Azumi: *dam*, Japan	36 11 N	137 47 E	39D
Azusa: Calif., U.S.A.	34 12 N	117 48 W	32, 58
Az Zahrān: Saudi Arabia	26 18 N	50 08 E	87
Az Zannah: Abu Dhabi	24 11 N	52 35 E	37C
Az Zarqā' (Zarqā'): Jordan	32 04 N	36 05 E	37G
Az Zubayr: Iraq	30 23 N	47 43 E	37A, 37C

B

	° ′	° ′	Page(s)
Baar: Switzerland	47 12 N	8 32 E	31B
Babelsberg: Germany D.R.	52 24 N	13 06 E	54B
Bacău: *admin.*, Romania	46 40 N	26 40 E	38B
Bacău: Romania	46 34 N	26 54 E	29, 37B
Bacchus Marsh: Australia	37 41 S	144 27 E	38
Bachelor *Lake*: Canada	49 30 N	76 30 W	49
Backnang: Germany F.R.	48 57 N	9 26 E	55A
Bacnotan: Philippines	16 45 N	120 21 E	57
Bacolod: Philippines	10 38 N	122 58 E	87
Bacon's Castle: Va., U.S.A.	37 10 N	76 40 W	40C
Bacton: England	52 52 N	1 28 E	37B
Badacsony: *hill*, Hungary	46 48 N	17 30 E	17, 40
Baden-Württemberg: *admin.*, Germany F.R.	48 30 N	9 00 E	56A
Bad Grund: Germany F.R.	51 49 N	10 14 E	46B, 49
Badin: N.C., U.S.A.	35 28 N	80 06 W	47
Bad Kreuznach: Germany F.R.	49 50 N	7 52 E	17
Bagacay: Philippines	11 50 N	125 00 E	45
Bagalkot: India	16 14 N	74 47 E	57
Bagamoyo: Tanzania	4 33 S	37 52 E	48
Bagdad: Ariz., U.S.A.	34 35 N	113 11 W	45A, 59
Baghdād: *admin.*, Iraq	34 00 N	43 46 E	27
Baghdād: Iraq	33 21 N	44 25 E	29, 31, 37A, 57, 67, 87
Baglan *Bay*: Wales	51 36 N	3 47 W	58H, 59D, 60D, 60H
Bagnères-de-Bigorre: France	43 04 N	0 09 E	54B
Bagnoli Irpino: Italy	40 50 N	15 04 E	43B
Bahia: *admin.*, Brazil	12 00 S	42 00 W	27, 35, 40, 47, 48,
Bahía Blanca: Argentina	38 43 S	62 17 W	27, 34, 36, 58, 59 60, 67, 84
Bahía de Nuevitas: *bay*, Cuba	21 30 N	77 12 W	84
Bahía Sebastián Vizcaíno: *bay*, Mexico	28 00 N	114 30 W	84
Bahoruco, Sierra de: *ridge*, Dominican Republic	18 10 N	71 25 W	47
Baḩrīyah, Al Wāḩāt al: *region*, U.A.R.	28 15 N	28 57 E	43
Baia Mare: *admin.*, Romania	47 40 N	23 35 E	45, 46B
Baia Mare: Romania	47 40 N	23 35 E	46B, 49
Baie Comeau: Canada	49 12 N	68 10 W	25D, 47
Baie Verte: Canada	49 55 N	56 12 W	45, 48, 49
Bainbridge: Ga., U.S.A.	30 54 N	84 33 W	61E
Baixo Alentejo: *admin.*, Portugal	37 55 N	8 10 W	50
Baja: Hungary	46 11 N	18 58 E	29C
Baja California: *admin.*, Mexico	30 00 N	115 00 W	50
Bajo Grande: Venezuela	10 30 N	71 38 W	36
Bakar: Yugoslavia	45 18 N	14 32 E	37D
Bakersfield: Calif., U.S.A.	35 25 N	119 00 W	36, 60, 67, 87
Bakhchisaray: U.S.S.R.	44 45 N	33 52 E	57
Baku: U.S.S.R.	40 23 N	49 51 E	29, 31, 32, 34, 35, 61, 67
Bakwanga *see* Mbuji-Mayi: Congo D.R.	6 09 S	23 36 E	48
Balaghat: India	21 48 N	80 16 E	50
Balakleya: U.S.S.R.	49 27 N	36 52 E	57
Balakovo: U.S.S.R.	52 02 N	47 47 E	32
Balan: France	45 50 N	5 06 E	60D
Bălan: Romania	46 39 N	25 49 E	45
Balangero: Italy	45 16 N	7 31 E	48
Balatonfűzfő: Hungary	47 04 N	18 03 E	59D
Baleares: *admin.*, Spain	39 30 N	3 00 E	27B, 38
Balen: Belgium	51 10 N	5 09 E	46B
Baley: U.S.S.R.	51 36 N	116 38 E	49
Balikpapan: Indonesia	1 17 S	116 50 E	36, 84
Balkany: U.S.S.R.	53 26 N	59 37 E	50
Balkhash: U.S.S.R.	46 49 N	75 00 E	45, 56
Ballarat: Australia	37 33 S	143 51 E	29
Baltic: Conn., U.S.A.	41 36 N	72 08 W	31
Baltimore: Md., U.S.A.	39 18 N	76 38 W	25D, 31, 37J, 43A, 45, 56, 59E, 67, 87B
Bamako: Mali	12 39 N	8 00 W	67
Bamberton: Canada	48 35 N	123 31 W	57
Banat: *region*, Romania	45 30 N	21 00 E	38B
Banatului Munţii: *mtns.*, Romania	45 00 N	22 10 E	40
Bancroft: Canada	45 03 N	77 52 W	40C
Bancroft: Zambia	12 18 S	27 43 E	45B
Banda Atjeh: Indonesia	5 34 N	95 20 E	84
Bandar ʻAbbās: Iran	27 11 N	56 17 E	84
Bandar-e Shāhpūr: Iran	30 25 N	49 05 E	56, 59, 61
Bandirma: Turkey	40 20 N	27 58 E	59, 59D
Bandjarmasin: Indonesia	3 20 S	114 35 E	67
Bandol: France	43 08 N	5 45 E	17
Bandung: Indonesia	0 32 N	103 18 E	67
Bangalore: India	12 58 N	77 35 E	29, 31C, 53
Banghāzī (Bengasi): Libya	32 07 N	20 04 E	67, 84, 87
Bangka: *island*, Indonesia	2 15 S	106 00 E	45
Bangkok *see* Krung Thep: Thailand	13 45 N	100 31 E	31, 32, 36, 59, 60, 67, 84, 87
Bang Su: Thailand	13 48 N	100 33 E	57
Bangui: Cent. Af. R.	4 22 N	18 35 E	67
Bangui: Philippines	18 33 N	120 45 E	50, 50D
Bangweule, *Lake*: Zambia	11 05 S	29 45 E	27
Bāniyās: Syria	35 11 N	35 57 E	37C, 84B
Bankstown: Australia	33 55 S	151 02 E	53
Ban Sang: *admin.*, Thailand	13 55 N	101 15 E	50
Banská Bystrica: Czech.	48 44 N	19 10 E	57C
Banská Štiavnica: Czech.	48 29 N	18 50 E	49
Bantry *Bay*: Irish Republic	51 41 N	9 27 W	37D
Banzart (Bizerte): Tunisia	37 17 N	9 52 E	37H
Bao: *dam*, Spain	42 15 N	7 10 W	39
Barauni: India	25 28 N	85 59 E	36, 60
Barbate de Franco: Spain	36 12 N	5 55 W	27B
Barber: N.J., U.S.A.	40 32 N	74 16 W	46
Barberton: Ohio, U.S.A.	41 02 N	81 37 W	59A
Barberton: South Africa	25 48 S	31 03 E	48, 49
Barcelona: *admin.*, Spain	41 40 N	2 00 E	38B
Barcelona: Spain	41 23 N	2 11 E	27B, 31, 37B, 53, 54, 55, 56, 58D, 58H, 59H, 84A, 87
Barcelona: Venezuela	10 08 N	64 42 W	87
Barcika: Hungary	48 16 N	20 38 E	61D
Bareilly: India	28 20 N	79 24 E	30, 60
Bari: Italy	41 08 N	16 51 E	37H, 84A
Barima: Guyana	7 30 N	60 08 W	50
Barinas: Venezuela	8 38 N	70 12 W	36
Barisan, Pegunungan: *mtns.*, Indonesia	3 00 S	102 15 E	49
Barker: Argentina	37 38 S	59 24 W	57
Barkerville: Canada	53 06 N	121 35 W	49
Barksdale: Wis., U.S.A.	46 37 N	90 56 W	59E
Barletta: Italy	41 19 N	16 17 E	57C
Barnaul: U.S.S.R.	53 22 N	83 45 E	31, 32C, 60, 67
Barney *Point*: Australia	23 50 S	151 16 E	59
Barnoldswick: England	53 55 N	2 11 W	53B
Barnwell: S.C., U.S.A.	33 14 N	81 21 W	29
Baroda: India	22 19 N	73 14 E	31C, 36, 58, 59, 61
Barquisimeto: Venezuela	10 04 N	69 19 W	57
Barra de Itabapoana: Brazil	21 18 S	40 58 W	40
Barrancabermeja: Colombia	7 03 N	73 52 W	36, 58, 60, 61
Barranqueras: Argentina	27 29 S	58 56 W	46
Barranquilla: Colombia	10 59 N	74 48 W	32, 57, 59, 61, 67, 87
Barreiro: Portugal	38 40 N	9 04 W	59
Barrington: England	52 08 N	0 02 E	57C
Barros: Spain	43 18 N	5 42 W	59H, 61H
Barroso: Brazil	20 12 S	42 31 W	57
Barrow (Barrow-in-Furness): England	54 07 N	3 14 W	52A
Barry: Wales	51 24 N	3 18 W	30B, 60D, 84C
Barsac: France	44 37 N	0 19 W	17
Barsebäck: *estuary*, Sweden	55 48 N	12 57 E	40B
Barsi: India	18 14 N	75 48 E	31C
Bartin: Turkey	41 38 N	32 21 E	57
Bartlesville: Okla., U.S.A.	36 44 N	95 59 W	46, 59E
Bartlett: Calif., U.S.A.	36 30 N	118 03 W	59
Barton upon Humber: England	53 41 N	0 26 W	61H
Bartow: Fla., U.S.A.	27 54 N	81 51 W	56, 59F, 61B
Baryulgil: Australia	29 13 S	152 36 E	48
Basarabi: Romania	44 11 N	28 25 E	17
Basel: Switzerland	47 33 N	7 36 E	37B, 87D
Basilan: Philippines	6 40 N	121 59 E	67
Basildon: England	51 34 N	0 25 E	55A, 60H
Basingstoke: England	51 16 N	1 05 W	55A
Basra *see* Al Başrah: Iraq	30 30 N	47 47 E	37A, 59, 61
Bas-Rhin: *admin.*, France	48 35 N	7 40 E	56A
Bassendean: Australia	31 54 S	115 57 E	54
Bassens: France	44 54 N	0 31 W	30B, 61H
Basses-Alpes: *admin.*, France	44 10 N	6 00 E	38B
Bassin Ferrifère de Briey-Thionville: *deposit*, France	49 15 N	6 00 E	43B
Bassin Parisien: *basin*, France	49 00 N	2 00 E	37D
Bastar: *admin.*, India	19 00 N	81 00 E	43
Bastrop: La., U.S.A.	32 49 N	91 54 W	25A
Bataan: *pen.*, Philippines	14 30 N	120 15 E	36, 59, 60, 61
Batangas: Philippines	13 46 N	121 01 E	36
Bath: Maine, U.S.A.	43 56 N	69 50 W	52
Bath: Pa., U.S.A.	40 43 N	75 24 W	57B
Bâthie, La: *dam*, France	45 38 N	6 27 E	39C
Bathurst: Canada	47 37 N	65 40 W	45, 46
Bathurst: Gambia	13 27 N	16 35 W	84
Batman: Turkey	37 52 N	41 07 E	36
Baton Rouge: La., U.S.A.	30 30 N	91 10 W	30A, 37J, 47A, 57A, 58A, 58E, 59B, 59F, 60A, 60G, 87C
Batopilas: Mexico	27 01 N	107 44 W	49A
Båtsfjord: Norway	70 38 N	29 44 E	27
Batumi: U.S.S.R.	41 38 N	41 38 E	35, 36
Bau: Malaysia	1 25 N	110 09 E	50
Bauchi: Nigeria	10 16 N	9 50 E	45
Bauxite: Ark., U.S.A.	34 33 N	92 31 W	47A
Bawdwin: Burma	23 06 N	97 18 E	46, 49, 50
Baxley: Ga., U.S.A.	31 47 N	82 21 W	40
Ba Xuyen: *admin.*, S. Vietnam	9 20 N	105 45 E	27
Bayamo: Cuba	20 23 N	76 39 W	50
Bayamón: Puerto Rico	18 24 N	66 09 W	36
Bay City: Mich., U.S.A.	43 35 N	83 52 W	37J, 57B, 58B, 58F, 67A
Bay City: Texas, U.S.A.	28 59 N	96 00 W	61E
Bay d'Espoir: *dam*, Canada	47 56 N	55 47 W	39
Bayern: *admin.*, Germany F.R.	49 00 N	11 30 E	38B, 56A
Baymak: U.S.S.R.	52 28 N	58 15 E	45
Bayonne: France	43 29 N	1 29 W	53B, 84A
Bayonne: N.J., U.S.A.	40 39 N	74 08 W	37J
Bayreuth: Germany F.R.	49 57 N	11 35 E	31B
Bayswater: Australia	37 51 S	145 16 E	32, 59, 60
Baytown: Texas, U.S.A.	29 43 N	94 59 W	30A, 37J, 58A, 58E, 59F, 60G
Beas: *dam*, India	31 57 N	75 50 E	39
Beatrice: Nebr., U.S.A.	40 17 N	96 45 W	61A, 61E
Beauharnois: Canada	45 18 N	73 52 W	47, 59A
Beauharnois: *dam*, Canada	45 18 N	73 52 W	39B
Beaumont: *dam*, Canada	47 33 N	72 44 W	39B
Beaumont: Texas, U.S.A.	30 04 N	94 06 W	30A, 37J, 56, 58A, 58E, 59F, 60A, 60G, 61B, 61E, 87C
Beauregard: *dam*, Italy	45 35 N	7 04 E	39C
Beautor: France	49 39 N	3 20 E	43B
Beaver *Co.*: Utah, U.S.A.	38 25 N	113 10 W	49B
Beaverdam: Va., U.S.A.	37 55 N	77 40 W	47
Beaverdell: Canada	49 26 N	119 05 W	49
Beaverhead *Co.*: Mont., U.S.A.	45 00 N	113 00 W	40A, 49
Beaverlodge: Canada	59 35 N	108 30 W	40
Beawar: India	26 02 N	74 20 E	31
Beccar: Argentina	34 28 S	58 32 W	32
Bec d'Ambès: *point*, France	45 03 N	0 37 W	60H
Beckum: Germany F.R.	51 21 N	7 54 E	57C
Bedi: India	22 32 N	70 02 E	84
Będzin: Poland	50 20 N	19 10 E	57C
Beek: Netherlands	50 56 N	5 47 E	30B, 58H, 60D
Beerse: Belgium	51 19 N	4 52 E	46B
Befu: Japan	34 43 N	134 51 E	46C, 59G, 61C, 61G
Behshahr: Iran	36 43 N	53 34 E	31
Beira: Mozambique	19 50 S	34 52 E	84
Beirūt: Lebanon	33 52 N	35 30 E	31, 67, 84B, 87
Bejaia: Algeria	36 49 N	5 03 E	27B, 37D
Bekabad: U.S.S.R.	40 13 N	69 14 E	57
Bekily: Malagasy Republic	24 13 S	45 19 E	48
Bekwai: Ghana	5 39 N	2 10 W	49
Bela Dila: *mtn.*, India	18 46 N	81 21 E	43
Belafa: Malagasy Republic	25 02 S	46 23 E	40
Belawan: Indonesia	3 47 N	98 41 E	84
Belém: Brazil	1 27 S	48 29 W	67, 84, 87
Belencito: Colombia	5 47 N	72 54 W	38, 43
Belesar: *dam*, Spain	42 39 N	7 42 W	39
Belfast: Northern Ireland	54 35 N	5 55 W	52A, 53, 61H, 67, 84C, 87
Belfort: France	47 38 N	6 52 E	54B, 62A
Belgaum: *admin.*, India	16 00 N	75 00 E	47
Belgorod: U.S.S.R.	50 36 N	36 34 E	57
Belgrade *see* Beograd: Yugo.	44 50 N	20 30 E	29, 55, 67, 87
Beli Izvor: Bulgaria	43 16 N	23 28 E	57C
Belingwe: Rhodesia	20 29 S	29 55 E	50C
Belitung (Billiton): *island*, Indonesia	2 50 S	107 56 E	45
Belize: British Honduras	17 29 N	88 10 W	84, 87
Bellary: *admin.*, India	15 00 N	76 15 E	43
Bell *Bay*: Australia	41 08 S	146 53 E	47
Belle: W. Va., U.S.A.	38 15 N	81 34 W	58F, 61A, 61E
Belledune: Canada	47 53 N	65 49 W	59
Belleterre: Canada	47 25 N	78 41 W	50
Belleville: Canada	44 10 N	77 22 W	57B
Belleville: Ill., U.S.A.	38 31 N	89 59 W	56
Bellingham: Wash., U.S.A.	48 45 N	122 29 W	25, 47, 57, 59
Bellmunt de Ciurana: Spain	41 09 N	0 46 E	46B
Bellville: South Africa	33 55 S	18 38 E	32, 60
Belmont: Jamaica	18 19 N	77 08 W	47
Belmont: N.C., U.S.A.	35 13 N	81 03 W	31A
Beloeil Village: Canada	45 34 N	73 12 W	59E
Belo Horizonte: Brazil	19 55 S	43 56 W	36, 43, 57, 67, 87
Belorechka: U.S.S.R.	57 20 N	60 02 E	45
Beloretsk: U.S.S.R.	53 58 N	58 24 E	43
Belorusskaya S.S.R.: *admin.*, U.S.S.R.	53 00 N	28 00 E	27, 56
Belousovka: U.S.S.R.	50 08 N	82 33 E	45, 46
Belovo: U.S.S.R.	54 25 N	86 18 E	46
Beloyarskiy: U.S.S.R.	56 45 N	61 24 E	40
Belpre: Ohio, U.S.A.	39 17 N	81 36 W	60F
Bemis: Tenn., U.S.A.	35 34 N	88 50 W	31, 31A
Bemposta: *dam*, Portugal	41 16 N	6 30 W	39
Benares *see* Varanasi: India	25 20 N	83 00 E	54
Benato Nord: Malagasy R.	23 05 S	45 52 E	48
Bengasi *see* Banghāzī: Libya	32 07 N	20 04 E	67, 84, 87
Benguela: Angola	12 35 S	13 25 E	84
Beni-Saf: Algeria	35 28 N	1 22 W	27B
Benmore: *dam*, New Zealand	44 34 S	170 11 E	39
Benoni: South Africa	26 12 S	28 18 E	43, 54
Benson: Ariz., U.S.A.	31 58 N	110 19 W	61
Benue: *river*, Nigeria	7 50 N	6 45 E	45
Beočin: Yugoslavia	45 12 N	19 44 E	57C
Beograd (Belgrade): Yugoslavia	44 50 N	20 30 E	29, 55, 67, 87
Berazategui: Argentina	34 46 S	58 13 W	32
Berbérati: Cent. Af. R.	4 16 N	15 47 E	48
Berchogur: U.S.S.R.	48 25 N	58 44 E	38
Berdyansk: U.S.S.R.	46 45 N	36 47 E	36
Beremend: Hungary	45 47 N	18 26 E	57C
Berente: Hungary	48 14 N	20 40 E	59D, 60D
Berezniki: U.S.S.R.	59 24 N	56 46 E	25, 56, 59, 61
Berezovskiy: U.S.S.R.	56 55 N	60 49 E	50
Berëzovskiy: U.S.S.R.	50 35 N	82 38 E	45
Bergamo: Italy	45 41 N	9 43 E	58D
Berg Aukas: South West Africa	19 20 S	18 10 E	46, 50

	° ′	° ′	*Page(s)*
Bergen: Norway	60 23 N	5 20 E	2, 27C, 29, 31, 52, 67, 84, 87
Bergheim: Germany F.R.	50 58 N	6 39 E	47B
Bergisch Gladbach: G.F.R.	50 59 N	7 08 E	29B
Berikul'skaya: U.S.S.R.	56 12 N	87 12 E	49
Beringovskiy: U.S.S.R.	63 03 N	179 19 E	38
Berkeley: England	51 42 N	2 27 W	40B
Berlin: G.D.R./G.F.R.	52 31 N	13 24 E	2, 3, 32C, 55A, 63A, 67B, 87
Berlin: N.H., U.S.A.	44 27 N	71 13 W	59A
Bermeo: Spain	43 26 N	2 43 W	27B
Bernburg: Germany D.R.	51 48 N	11 44 E	57B
Bernkastel-Kues: G.F.R.	49 55 N	7 04 E	17
Beroun: Czechoslovakia	49 58 N	14 05 E	31B
Berre-l'Étang: France	43 28 N	5 11 E	30B, 37H, 58H, 60H
Berrima: Australia	34 29 S	150 20 E	57
Bersimis I: *dam*, Canada	49 18 N	69 32 W	39B
Bersimis II: *dam*, Canada	49 10 N	69 17 W	39B
Besana in Brianza: Italy	45 42 N	9 17 E	32C
Besançon: France	47 15 N	6 02 E	32C, 60D
Besch: Germany F.R.	49 30 N	6 22 E	61H
Bessemer: Ala., U.S.A.	33 22 N	87 00 W	54
Bessemer: Pa., U.S.A.	40 59 N	80 31 W	57B
Besshi: Japan	33 55 N	133 10 E	45D
Bessines: France	46 18 N	0 30 W	59H
Bessines-sur-Gartempe: France	46 06 N	1 22 E	40B
Bethal: South Africa	26 27 S	29 28 E	49
Bethany: Okla., U.S.A.	35 33 N	97 37 W	53
Bethesda: Md., U.S.A.	39 00 N	77 05 W	62
Bethlehem: Pa., U.S.A.	40 36 N	75 22 W	43A, 57B, 63
Bethpage: N.Y., U.S.A.	40 46 N	73 27 W	53A
Betioky: *admin.*, Malagasy R.	23 45 S	44 45 E	40
Beverly: Mass., U.S.A.	42 35 N	70 52 W	40C
Beverly: N.J., U.S.A.	40 04 N	74 55 W	32B
Bezmein: U.S.S.R.	38 05 N	58 12 E	57
Beznau: *island*, Switzerland	47 34 N	8 16 E	40B
Bezons: France	48 56 N	2 13 E	32C, 58D
Bhakra: *dam*, India	31 24 N	76 30 E	39
Bhandara: India	21 10 N	79 41 E	59
Bhavnagar: India	21 46 N	72 14 E	31C
Bhilai: India	21 12 N	81 26 E	43, 59
Bhilwara: *admin.*, India	25 23 N	74 39 E	48
Bhilwara: India	25 23 N	74 39 E	31
Bhiwani: India	28 50 N	76 10 E	31
Bhopal: India	23 17 N	77 28 E	67
Biache-Saint-Vaast: France	50 18 N	2 57 E	57C
Białystok: Poland	53 09 N	23 10 E	29
Biblis: Germany F.R.	49 41 N	8 27 E	40B
Bicaz: Romania	46 55 N	26 04 W	57C
Bicol: *river*, Philippines	13 44 N	123 08 E	49
Biddeford: Maine, U.S.A.	43 29 N	70 27 W	31
Biel: Switzerland	47 09 N	7 16 E	55A
Biella: Italy	45 34 N	8 03 E	29
Bielsko-Biała: Poland	49 50 N	19 00 E	29C
Big Island: Va., U.S.A.	37 33 N	79 24 W	25A
Big Rock Point: Mich., U.S.A.	45 22 N	85 11 W	40C
Big Spring: Texas, U.S.A.	32 15 N	101 30 W	37J, 58A, 60G, 61B
Bihar: *admin.*, India	25 00 N	86 00 E	27, 38
Bihorului Munţii: *mtns.*, Romania	46 40 N	22 45 E	40
Bikin: U.S.S.R.	46 48 N	134 16 E	38
Bikita: Rhodesia	20 06 S	31 38 E	50
Bilbao: Spain	43 15 N	2 58 W	43B, 45, 52A, 54B, 60H, 61D, 61H, 84A
Bilibino: U.S.S.R.	68 03 N	166 20 E	40
Bilimora: India	20 45 N	73 00 E	31C
Billingham: England	54 36 N	1 17 W	58H, 59H, 60D, 61D, 61H
Billings: Mont., U.S.A.	45 47 N	108 30 W	36, 87
Billings *Co.*: N.D., U.S.A.	47 00 N	103 30 W	40A
Billiton *see* Belitung: *island*, Indonesia	2 50 S	107 56 E	45
Bilston: England	52 34 N	2 04 W	43B
Binangonan: Philippines	14 28 N	121 11 E	57
Bindura: Rhodesia	17 19 S	31 20 E	50C
Bingham *Canyon*: Utah, U.S.A.	40 33 N	112 09 W	50A
Binghamton, N.Y., U.S.A.	42 06 N	75 55 W	67A, 87B
Bingley: England	53 51 N	1 50 W	29B
Binh Thuan: *admin.*, South Vietnam	11 10 N	108 20 E	27
Binsfeldhammer: G.F.R.	50 45 N	6 15 E	46B
Bintan, Pulau: *island*, Indonesia	1 05 N	104 30 E	47
Birkat Qārūn: *lake*, U.A.R.	29 28 N	30 40 E	27
Birkenhead: England	53 24 N	3 02 W	32C, 52A
Birmingham: Ala., U.S.A.	33 30 N	86 55 W	43, 57B, 61E, 62, 87C
Birmingham: England	52 30 N	1 50 W	37B, 54B, 55A, 63A, 63B, 67B, 87
Birobidzhan: U.S.S.R.	48 48 N	132 57 E	31
Biscarrosse: France	44 24 N	1 10 W	53B
Bishop: Calif., U.S.A.	37 20 N	118 24 W	50A
Bishop: Texas, U.S.A.	27 36 N	97 49 W	58E
Bissett: Canada	51 01 N	95 40 W	49
Bissina: *dam*, Italy	45 38 N	10 30 E	39C
Bistriţa: Romania	44 35 N	22 47 E	17
Bitterfeld: Germany D.R.	51 37 N	12 19 E	47B, 60D
Bitteswell: England	52 28 N	1 13 W	53B
Bizerte *see* Banzart: Tunisia	37 17 N	9 52 E	37H

	° ′	° ′	*Page(s)*
Blachownia Śląska: Poland	50 24 N	18 18 E	58D, 58H, 60D
Blackburn: England	53 45 N	2 29 W	31B
Black *Hills*: S.D., U.S.A.	44 00 N	104 00 W	49, 50
Black Lake: Canada	46 03 N	71 21 W	48
Blackpool: England	53 50 N	3 03 W	87
Blackwell: Okla., U.S.A.	36 47 N	97 18 W	46
Blagnac: France	43 38 N	1 24 E	53B
Blagoveshchensk: U.S.S.R.	50 16 N	127 32 E	67
Blair Athol: Australia	22 42 S	147 33 E	38
Blanes: Spain	41 41 N	2 48 E	32C
Blantyre: Malawi	15 47 S	35 00 E	67
Blaubeuren: Germany F.R.	48 24 N	9 47 E	57B
Bleiberg-Kreuth: Austria	46 38 N	13 38 E	46B
Blida: Algeria	36 30 N	2 50 E	17
Bloemfontein: South Africa	29 07 S	26 14 E	54, 67
Bloomfield: Conn., U.S.A.	41 50 N	72 45 W	53A
Blue Island: Ill., U.S.A.	41 40 N	87 42 W	37J, 58F
Bluewater: N. Mex., U.S.A.	35 16 N	107 58 W	40A
Bluff: New Zealand	46 38 S	168 21 E	27, 84
Blumenau: Brazil	26 56 S	49 03 W	31
Blytheville: Ark., U.S.A.	35 56 N	89 56 W	61B
Boa Esperança: *dam*, Brazil	6 47 S	43 01 W	39
Boca Raton: Fla., U.S.A.	26 22 N	80 05 W	62
Bocholt: Germany F.R.	51 50 N	6 36 E	29B, 31B
Bochum: Germany F.R.	51 29 N	7 13 E	43B, 58D
Bochum-Riemke: G.F.R.	51 30 N	7 12 E	59H
Bodaybo: U.S.S.R.	57 51 N	114 10 E	49
Bodø: Norway	67 17 N	14 23 E	84, 87
Bōfu: Japan	34 03 N	131 34 E	32A, 60C
Bogalusa: La., U.S.A.	30 56 N	89 53 W	25A
Bogotá: Colombia	4 36 N	74 05 W	29, 32, 55, 58, 62, 67, 87
Bogotol: U.S.S.R.	56 10 N	89 35 E	47
Boguchan: *dam*, U.S.S.R.	58 23 N	97 29 E	39
Böhlen: Germany D.R.	51 16 N	13 18 E	37F
Bohunice: Czechoslovakia	49 11 N	16 39 E	40
Bohus: Sweden	57 51 N	12 01 E	48
Boigny: France	48 30 N	2 22 E	62A
Boise: Idaho, U.S.A.	43 38 N	116 12 W	87
Bois Noirs, Les: *mtns.*, France	45 55 N	3 45 E	40B
Boksburg: South Africa	26 13 S	28 15 E	36, 54
Boksitogorsk: U.S.S.R.	59 28 N	33 51 E	47
Bolān: *deposit*, Pakistan	29 45 N	67 35 E	38
Boletice nad Labem: Czech.	50 44 N	14 12 E	29C
Boliden: Sweden	64 52 N	20 23 E	45, 59
Bolívar: *admin.*, Venezuela	10 15 N	71 05 W	35
Bolívar, Cerro: *mtn.*, Venezuela	7 27 N	63 25 W	43
Bollene: *dam*, France	44 27 N	4 43 E	39C
Bologna: Italy	44 29 N	11 20 E	17
Bolsa *Island*: Calif., U.S.A.	33 40 N	118 00 W	40
Bolton: England	53 35 N	2 26 W	29B, 31B
Bolzano: Italy	46 31 N	11 22 E	17, 47B, 55A
Bombay: India	18 56 N	72 51 E	2, 29, 31C, 36, 55, 58, 59, 60, 62, 67, 84, 87
Bomi *Hills*: Liberia	6 54 N	10 50 W	43, 49
Bonanza: Oreg., U.S.A.	42 11 N	121 26 W	50
Bong Range: *mtns.*, Liberia	6 52 N	10 10 W	43
Bonner *Co.*: Idaho, U.S.A.	48 25 N	116 30 W	49
Bonner Springs: Kans., U.S.A.	39 04 N	94 54 W	57A
Bonne Terre: Mo., U.S.A.	37 56 N	90 33 W	45
Bonneville: *dam*, Wash./Oreg., U.S.A.	45 38 N	121 59 W	39A
Bonney: N. Mex., U.S.A.	32 22 N	108 44 W	45A
Bonnie: Fla., U.S.A.	27 53 N	81 52 W	59F, 61B
Bonny: Nigeria	4 25 N	7 10 E	35
Bootle: England	53 28 N	3 00 W	45
Boquira: Brazil	12 49 S	42 46 W	46
Bor: Yugoslavia	44 06 N	22 06 E	45, 59H
Borås: Sweden	57 43 N	12 55 E	31, 32C, 60
Bordeaux: France	44 50 N	0 34 W	17, 36, 52A, 53B, 59H, 67, 84A, 87
Bordes: France	43 14 N	0 17 W	53B
Borgå (Porvoo): Finland	60 24 N	25 40 E	36, 37F
Borger: Texas, U.S.A.	35 39 N	101 24 W	30A, 37J, 60G, 61B
Borghorst: Germany F.R.	52 08 N	7 25 E	31B
Borgofranco d'Ivrea: Italy	45 30 N	7 51 E	47B
Borgo San Dalmazzo: Italy	44 20 N	7 30 E	57C
Borma, El: *region*, Tunisia	32 00 N	9 00 E	37D
Borneo *see* Kalimantan: *island*, Indonesia	1 00 S	114 00 E	27, 48, 61
Borovichi: U.S.S.R.	58 24 N	33 55 E	25, 38
Borralha: Portugal	40 34 N	8 26 W	50
Borsod: Hungary	48 19 N	20 45 E	59D, 61H
Borsselen: Netherlands	51 25 N	3 45 E	40B
Borzeşti: Romania	46 14 N	26 49 E	59D, 60D
Bosanska Krupa: Yugoslavia	44 53 N	16 10 E	47B
Bosanski Brod: Yugoslavia	45 08 N	18 01 E	37H
Bosansko Petrovo Selo: Yugo.	44 38 N	18 22 E	48
Bosna i Hercegovina: *admin.*, Yugoslavia	44 15 N	17 50 E	38B
Boss Mountain: Canada	53 00 N	120 00 W	50
Bossier City: La., U.S.A.	32 31 N	93 44 W	59F
Boston: Mass., U.S.A.	42 20 N	71 05 W	34, 55, 67, 84, 87B
Botany: Australia	33 58 S	151 12 E	25, 35, 58, 60, 61
Botlek: Netherlands	51 53 N	4 18 E	59D, 60H
Botolan *Point*: Philippines	15 15 N	120 00 E	48
Bottrop: Germany F.R.	51 31 N	6 55 E	58D, 61D
Botucatu: Brazil	22 52 S	48 26 W	53
Bou Azzer: Morocco	30 32 N	6 55 W	50

	° ′	° ′	*Page(s)*
Bou Beker: Morocco	34 30 N	1 48 W	46
Bouches-du-Rhône: *admin.*, France	43 30 N	5 00 E	38B
Bougie: Algeria	36 49 N	5 03 E	17
Bouguenais: France	47 11 N	1 37 W	53B
Bou Khadra, Djebel: *mtn.*, Algeria	35 45 N	8 00 E	43
Boulder: Colo., U.S.A.	40 02 N	105 16 W	50A, 62
Boulder *Co.*: Colo., U.S.A.	40 00 N	105 10 W	49B
Boulogne-sur-Mer: France	50 43 N	1 37 E	27C
Bound Brook: N.J., U.S.A.	40 33 N	74 32 W	32B, 58B
Bourges: France	47 05 N	2 24 E	53B, 53C
Bourlamaque: Canada	48 05 N	77 56 W	49
Bou Skour: Morocco	30 56 N	6 18 W	45
Boussens: France	43 11 N	0 58 E	57C, 59D
Bowden: Canada	51 58 N	114 01 W	36
Bowen: Australia	20 01 S	148 14 E	38
Bowen *Island*: Australia	35 08 S	150 46 E	40
Boyer: Australia	42 47 S	147 06 E	25
Brabant: *admin.*, Belgium	50 45 N	4 30 E	56A
Bradenton: Fla., U.S.A.	27 29 N	82 33 W	59F
Bradford: England	53 48 N	1 45 W	29, 87
Bradford: Pa., U.S.A.	41 57 N	78 39 W	37J
Bradwell: England	51 44 N	0 54 W	40B
Braga: Portugal	41 33 N	8 26 W	31
Brăila: Romania	45 16 N	27 59 E	32C, 59D, 84
Brainerd: Minn., U.S.A.	46 20 N	94 10 W	25
Bralorne: Canada	50 46 N	122 51 W	49
Brampton: Canada	43 41 N	79 46 W	55A
Brandenburg: Germany D.R.	52 25 N	12 33 E	43B
Brandenburg: Ky., U.S.A.	38 00 N	86 11 W	58F
Brandon: Canada	49 50 N	99 57 W	36, 59
Brandon: Miss., U.S.A.	32 16 N	89 59 W	57A
Brani, Pulau: *island*, Singapore	1 15 N	103 50 E	45C
Brantford: Canada	43 09 N	80 17 W	32B
Brasília: Brazil	15 47 S	47 55 W	67, 87
Braşov: Romania	45 38 N	25 35 E	29, 38C, 37H, 57C
Bratislava (Pressburg): Czechoslovakia	48 10 N	17 08 E	31B, 32C, 37B, 37F, 58D, 58H, 60D, 87
Bratsk: *dam*, U.S.S.R.	56 05 N	101 48 E	39
Bratsk: U.S.S.R.	56 21 N	101 55 E	67
Braubach: Germany F.R.	50 17 N	7 40 E	46B
Braunschweig: Germany F.R.	52 16 N	10 32 E	55A
Brazeau: *dam*, Canada	52 56 N	115 25 W	39
Brazii de Sus: Romania	44 52 N	26 01 E	37H, 58
Brazzaville: Congo Republic	4 16 S	15 17 E	67
Brea: Calif., U.S.A.	33 55 N	117 54 W	61
Brebach: Germany F.R.	49 13 N	7 02 E	58D
Breda: Netherlands	51 35 N	4 46 E	67B
Bredy: U.S.S.R.	52 26 N	60 21 E	38
Bremen: *admin.*, Germany F.R.	53 05 N	8 50 E	56A
Bremen: Germany F.R.	53 05 N	8 48 E	37F, 43B, 52A, 53B, 57C, 58D, 60D, 67B, 84C
Bremen: Ohio, U.S.A.	39 43 N	82 26 W	32B
Bremerhaven: Germany F.R.	53 33 N	8 35 E	27C, 60H
Bremerton: Wash., U.S.A.	47 34 N	122 40 W	52
Brennilis: France	48 21 N	3 51 W	40B
Brescia: Italy	45 33 N	10 15 E	43B, 55A, 59D
Brest: France	48 24 N	4 29 W	52A, 59H, 67B
Brest: U.S.S.R.	52 06 N	23 42 E	31
Brevik: Norway	59 04 N	9 42 E	57
Brewster: Fla., U.S.A.	27 45 N	81 59 W	59F
Brewster: Ohio, U.S.A.	40 43 N	81 37 W	54A
Bria: Central African Republic	6 32 N	21 59 E	48
Bridgeport: Conn., U.S.A.	41 12 N	73 12 W	53A, 55B, 67A
Bridgeport: N.J., U.S.A.	39 48 N	75 21 W	58B
Bridgeport: Pa., U.S.A.	40 06 N	75 20 W	29A
Bridge *River*: Canada	50 43 N	122 12 W	50
Bridgeville: Pa., U.S.A.	40 20 N	80 08 W	58B
Bridgman: Mich., U.S.A.	41 57 N	86 32 W	40C
Briey-Thionville, Bassin Ferrifère de: *deposit*, France	49 15 N	6 00 E	43B
Brighton: Trinidad	10 15 N	61 38 W	36
Brignoud: France	45 15 N	5 54 E	59D, 60D
Brimsdown: England	51 40 N	0 15 W	45
Brindisi: Italy	40 38 N	17 56 E	37H, 58D, 58H, 59D, 60, 60H
Brisbane: Australia	27 30 S	153 01 E	2, 34, 54, 55, 61, 67, 84, 87
Bristol: England	51 27 N	2 35 W	25, 53B, 58H, 67B, 84C
Bristol: Pa., U.S.A.	40 06 N	74 52 W	46
Bristol: R.I., U.S.A.	41 41 N	71 12 W	32B
Britannia Beach: Canada	49 38 N	123 11 W	45, 46
British Columbia: *admin.*, Canada	54 00 N	125 00 W	16, 27, 34, 38
Brixham: England	50 24 N	3 30 W	27C
Brixlegg: Austria	47 25 N	11 53 E	45
Brno: Czechoslovakia	49 11 N	16 39 E	29C
Broach: India	21 40 N	73 02 E	31C
Broadmeadows: Australia	29 51 S	152 18 E	55
Broken Hill: *admin.*, Zambia	14 30 S	27 45 E	46, 49
Broken Hill: Australia	31 57 S	141 26 E	45, 46, 49, 50
Broken Hill: Zambia	14 27 S	28 27 E	46
Bromptonville: Canada	45 28 N	71 56 W	25D
Bromsgrove: England	52 20 N	2 03 W	30B
Brookfield: Canada	45 15 N	63 18 W	57
Brooklyn: Canada	44 04 N	64 42 W	25D

	° ′	° ′	*Page(s)*
Brooklyn: N.Y., U.S.A.	40 30 N	73 55 W	32B, 52, 56
Brough: England	53 44 N	0 36 W	53B
Broumov: Czechoslovakia	50 36 N	16 20 E	31B
Brownlee: *dam*, Idaho, U.S.A.	44 47 N	116 59 W	39A
Brown's Ferry: Ala., U.S.A.	34 36 N	87 00 W	40
Brownsville: Texas, U.S.A.	25 54 N	97 30 W	61B, 84
Brownville: Nebr., U.S.A.	40 23 N	96 40 W	40
Bruck an der Mur: Austria	47 25 N	15 17 E	25C
Brugg: Switzerland	47 29 N	8 13 E	58D
Bruhagen: Norway	63 02 N	7 45 E	27
Brunei: Brunei	4 53 N	114 56 E	87
Brunsbüttelkoog: Germany F.R.	53 54 N	9 08 E	40B
Brunswick: Ga., U.S.A.	31 09 N	81 30 W	59B
Bruxelles: *admin.*, Belgium	50 50 N	4 20 E	56A
Bruxelles: Belgium	50 50 N	4 20 E	29B, 31B, 37B, 55A, 67B, 87D
Bryansk: U.S.S.R.	53 15 N	34 22 E	29, 54, 57
Brziezie: Poland	52 39 N	19 01 E	61D
Bua: Sweden	57 14 N	12 07 E	27C
Bucaramanga: Colombia	7 08 N	73 09 W	67, 87
Bucelas: Portugal	38 54 N	9 07 W	17
Buchanan: Liberia	5 53 N	10 03 W	84
Buchans: Canada	48 49 N	56 53 W	45, 46, 49
Bucharest *see* Bucureşti: Romania	44 26 N	26 06 E	29, 31, 54, 87
Buckeye: Ariz., U.S.A.	33 25 N	112 34 W	48
Buckingham: Canada	45 35 N	75 25 W	25D
Bucksport: Maine, U.S.A.	44 35 N	68 47 W	25D
Bucureşti (Bucharest): Romania	44 26 N	26 06 E	29, 31, 54, 87
Budapest: Hungary	47 30 N	19 05 E	25, 29C, 31, 37B, 52A, 54B, 59D, 59H, 87
Budel: Netherlands	51 17 N	5 35 E	46B
Buenaventura: Colombia	3 53 N	77 04 W	27, 84
Buenos Aires: Argentina	34 36 S	58 27 W	25, 27, 29, 31, 32, 34, 36, 43, 45, 53, 55, 56, 61, 62, 67, 84, 87
Buffalo: N.Y., U.S.A.	42 52 N	78 55 W	37J, 43A, 57B, 58D, 59E, 67A, 87B
Buffelsfontein: South Africa	26 52 S	26 39 E	40
Buffington: Ind., U.S.A.	41 38 N	87 25 W	57B
Bū Ḥassah: *hill*, Abu Dhabi	23 54 N	53 17 E	37C
Buhemba: Tanzania	1 46 S	34 05 E	49
Buhwa *Mountain*: Rhodesia	20 38 S	30 20 E	43
Bukachacha: U.S.S.R.	52 59 N	116 55 E	38
Bukhtarma: *dam*, U.S.S.R.	49 36 N	83 25 E	39
Bukit Asem: *hill*, Indonesia	3 46 S	103 46 E	38
Bukit Besi: Malaysia	4 46 N	103 11 E	43
Bukoba: *admin.*, Tanzania	1 35 S	31 30 E	50
Bukuka: U.S.S.R.	51 11 N	116 39 E	50
Bulawayo: Rhodesia	20 09 S	28 36 E	2, 49, 67
Buller: New Zealand	41 44 N	171 36 E	38
Bulolo *River*: New Guinea	7 08 S	146 37 E	49
Bultfontein: *mine*, South Africa	28 48 S	24 48 E	48
Bulwer *Island*: Australia	27 25 S	153 08 E	36
Bumburi: *region*, Kenya	4 00 S	39 43 E	57
Bunbury: Australia	33 20 S	115 38 E	47, 50, 59
Bundaberg: Australia	24 51 S	152 21 E	84
Bunnell: Fla., U.S.A.	29 28 N	81 16 W	57
Buñol: Spain	39 25 N	0 47 W	57C
Burbach: Germany F.R.	49 41 N	7 13 E	43B
Burbank: Calif., U.S.A.	34 10 N	118 25 W	53
Burdwan: India	23 15 N	87 52 E	31
Bureinsk: *deposit*, U.S.S.R.	51 15 N	133 00 E	38
Burgas: Bulgaria	42 30 N	27 28 E	17, 30, 54, 58, 58D, 60D, 60H, 84B
Burghausen: Germany F.R.	48 10 N	12 50 E	37F, 58H, 59D, 60D
Burgos: *admin.*, Spain	42 20 N	3 40 W	38B
Burhanpur: India	21 18 N	76 08 E	31C
Burjasot: Spain	39 31 N	0 25 W	57C
Burlington: N.J., U.S.A.	40 05 N	74 51 W	40C, 60B
Burlington: Vt., U.S.A.	44 28 N	73 14 W	62, 87B
Burnaby: Canada	49 16 N	122 58 W	36
Burnie: Australia	41 04 S	145 55 E	25, 59
Burnpur: India	23 40 N	86 55 E	43, 54
Burnside: La., U.S.A.	30 05 N	90 55 W	47A, 59F
Burnsville: N.C., U.S.A.	35 56 N	82 18 W	48
Burntisland: Scotland	56 03 N	3 15 W	47
Burqān, Al: *region*, Kuwait	28 58 N	47 58 E	35, 37C
Bursa: Turkey	40 11 N	29 04 E	29, 32, 32C, 67
Būr Sa'īd (Port Said): U.A.R.	31 16 N	32 18 E	27, 84B
Būr Sūdān (Port Sudan): Sudan	19 37 N	37 14 E	36, 84
Bury: England	53 36 N	2 17 W	25C, 31B
Busalla: Italy	44 34 N	8 57 E	37H
Busan *see* Pusan: South Korea	35 06 N	129 03 E	31, 32, 84D, 87
Bussi sul Tirino: Italy	42 12 N	13 49 E	59D, 61D
Buşteni: Romania	45 24 N	25 32 E	25
Busto Arsizio: Italy	45 37 N	8 51 E	31B
Butler *Co.*: Ala., U.S.A.	31 45 N	86 50 W	43
Butler: Pa., U.S.A.	40 51 N	79 55 W	54A
Butte *Co.*: Idaho, U.S.A.	43 50 N	113 10 W	49
Butte: Mont., U.S.A.	46 00 N	112 31 W	45
Butterworth: Malaysia	5 25 N	100 24 E	45C
Butuan: Philippines	8 56 N	125 31 E	67
Buziaş: Romania	45 39 N	21 36 E	17
Bydgoszcz: Poland	53 10 N	18 00 E	58H
Bystré: Czechoslovakia	49 01 N	21 32 E	57C

C

	° ′	° ′	*Page(s)*
Cabangaan: Philippines	14 53 N	120 13 E	48
Cabedelo: Brazil	6 58 S	34 50 W	84
Cabinet Gorge: *dam*, Idaho, U.S.A.	48 06 N	116 02 W	39A
Cabo: Brazil	8 17 S	35 02 W	30
Cabora Bassa: *dam*, Mozambique	15 30 S	33 00 E	39
Cachoeira Dourada: *dam*, Brazil	18 30 S	49 30 W	39
Cádiz: Spain	36 32 N	6 18 W	27B, 52, 84A
Caen: France	49 11 N	0 21 W	67B
Cagayan de Oro: Philippines	8 29 N	124 40 E	87
Cagayan: *river*, Philippines	18 17 N	121 38 E	49
Cagliari: *admin.*, Italy	39 30 N	8 45 E	38, 46B
Cagliari: Italy	39 13 N	9 07 E	37H, 57C, 58H, 59D, 60
Cairns: Australia	16 55 S	145 46 E	84, 87
Cairo *see* Al Qāhirah: U.A.R.	30 03 N	31 15 E	29, 31, 32, 34, 67, 87
Cajamarca: *admin.*, Peru	6 15 S	78 50 W	46, 49
Calais: France	50 57 N	1 50 E	84C
Calbe: Germany D.R.	51 54 N	11 46 E	25C
Calbuco: Chile	41 46 S	73 08 W	27
Calcutta: India	22 35 N	88 21 E	25, 31, 55, 58, 59, 67, 84, 87
Caldera: Chile	27 04 S	70 50 W	27
Calder Hall *Atomic Energy Station*: England	54 23 N	3 32 W	40B
Caletones: Chile	34 06 S	70 27 W	45
Calgary: Canada	51 05 N	114 05 W	36, 56, 59, 61, 67, 87
Calhoun: Tenn., U.S.A.	35 13 N	84 45 W	25A
Cali: Colombia	3 27 N	76 31 W	25, 60, 67, 87
Calicut (Kozhikode): India	11 15 N	75 45 E	67
California: *admin.*, U.S.A.	37 00 N	120 00 W	16, 17, 27, 35
Calima II: *dam*, Colombia	3 56 N	76 31 W	39
Callacuyan: Peru	7 40 S	78 30 W	38
Callao: Peru	12 05 S	77 08 W	27, 27A, 56, 59, 61, 67, 84
Callide: Australia	24 19 S	150 28 E	38
Caltanissetta: Italy	37 29 N	14 04 E	56
Calumet: Canada	45 39 N	74 38 W	49
Calumet Island: Canada	45 40 N	76 42 W	46
Calusco d'Adda: Italy	45 41 N	9 28 E	57C
Calvados: *admin.*, France	49 10 N	0 30 W	43B
Calvert City: Ky., U.S.A.	37 02 N	88 22 W	58F, 59B, 60B
Calvert Cliffs: Md., U.S.A.	38 25 N	76 25 W	40C
Calverton: N.Y., U.S.A.	40 55 N	72 46 W	53A
Camaçari: Brazil	12 41 S	38 18 W	58, 61
Camagüey: Cuba	21 23 N	77 55 W	67
Camaquã: Brazil	30 51 S	51 49 W	45
Camas: Wash., U.S.A.	45 35 N	122 26 W	25
Camas *Co.*: Idaho, U.S.A.	43 30 N	114 50 W	49
Camayenne: Guinea	9 32 N	13 41 W	43
Cambambe: *dam*, Angola	9 38 S	14 23 E	39
Cambay: *region*, India	22 30 N	72 30 E	34
Camberley: England	51 21 N	0 45 W	32C
Cambridge: Minn., U.S.A.	45 34 N	93 11 W	62
Camden: Ark., U.S.A.	33 32 N	92 49 W	25A
Camden: N.J., U.S.A.	39 57 N	75 06 W	25D, 52
Camden: S.C., U.S.A.	34 16 N	80 36 W	32B, 60B
Camiri: Bolivia	20 06 S	63 32 W	36
Çamlica: Turkey	38 45 N	27 18 E	38
Campana: Argentina	34 10 S	58 57 W	36, 43, 54, 58, 59, 60, 61
Campbellpore: Pakistan	33 46 N	72 22 E	29
Camperdown: Scotland	56 29 N	3 03 W	37F
Campinas: Brazil	22 54 S	47 05 W	54
Campine *see* Kempenland: *region*, Belgium	51 10 N	5 20 E	38B
Campo Durán: Argentina	22 14 S	63 42 W	36
Campo Grande: Brazil	20 27 S	54 37 W	67
Campos: Brazil	21 45 S	41 18 W	57, 67
Campo Santo: Argentina	24 40 S	65 06 W	57
Campton: Ky., U.S.A.	37 44 N	83 35 W	62
Cam Ranh: South Vietnam	11 54 N	109 12 E	84
Canaan: N.Y., U.S.A.	42 25 N	73 27 W	50
Canal du Centre: *canal*, Belgium	50 27 N	3 56 E	38B
Cananea: Mexico	30 57 N	110 18 W	45A, 49A, 50A
Canari: France	42 51 N	9 21 E	48
Canatlán: Mexico	24 31 N	104 47 W	49A
Canavieiras: Brazil	15 43 S	38 58 W	40
Canberra: Australia	35 20 S	149 10 E	67, 87
Cancas: Peru	13 49 S	75 42 W	45
Candeias: Brazil	12 40 S	38 33 S	60
Candela: Italy	41 08 N	15 31 E	37B
Canelas: Mexico	25 06 N	106 34 W	49A
Çankiri: *admin.*, Turkey	40 30 N	33 35 E	50B
Cantal: *admin.*, France	45 05 N	2 40 E	40B, 50
Canterbury: *admin.*, New Zealand	44 20 S	171 20 E	38
Canterbury *Plains*: New Zealand	43 45 S	171 45 E	23
Canton: N.C., U.S.A.	35 33 N	82 51 W	25A, 59B
Canton: Ohio, U.S.A.	40 48 N	81 23 W	37J, 43A, 67A, 87B
Canton *see* Kuang-chou: China P.R.	23 07 N	113 15 E	25, 32, 43, 50D, 52, 55, 57, 59, 60
Canvey Island: England	51 32 N	0 35 E	37B
Cao Bang: *admin.*, North Vietnam	22 40 N	106 15 E	45
Cape Breton *Island*: Canada	46 00 N	60 30 W	36
Cape Girardeau: Mo., U.S.A.	37 19 N	89 31 W	57B
Capel: Australia	33 34 S	115 33 E	40, 50
Cape of Good Hope: *admin.*, South Africa	31 00 S	23 00 E	16, 17
Cape Town: South Africa	33 56 S	18 28 E	27, 29, 36, 67, 84, 87
Capitán Bermúdez: Argentina	32 49 S	60 43 W	59, 60
Capivari-Cachoeira: *dam*, Brazil	25 25 S	49 15 W	39
Capreol: Canada	46 43 N	80 56 W	43A
Capri: *island*, Italy	40 33 N	14 13 E	17
Capuava: Brazil	23 56 S	47 58 W	58, 59, 60
Caracas: Venezuela	10 30 N	66 55 W	25, 31, 55, 56, 57, 60, 67, 87
Caracoles: Bolivia	16 59 S	67 24 W	45
Carangola: Brazil	20 44 S	42 02 W	48D
Carbon *Co.*: Wyo., U.S.A.	41 30 N	107 00 W	40A
Cardiff: Wales	51 30 N	3 13 W	43B, 54B, 67B, 84C
Carignan: France	44 48 N	0 29 W	29
Carillon: *dam*, Canada	45 34 N	74 21 W	39B
Caripito: Venezuela	10 08 N	63 06 W	36
Carling: France	49 10 N	6 43 E	58D, 58H, 60H, 61D, 61H
Carloforte: Italy	39 08 N	8 18 E	50B, 59H
Carlsbad: Calif., U.S.A.	33 09 N	117 20 W	62
Carlsbad: N. Mex., U.S.A.	32 25 N	104 14 W	56
Carlstadt: N.J., U.S.A.	40 50 N	74 05 W	62
Carmaux: France	44 03 N	2 09 E	58D, 61D
Carnello: Italy	41 41 N	13 37 E	60D
Carnot: Cent. Af. R.	4 56 N	15 52 E	48
Carolina: South Africa	26 05 S	30 07 E	48
Carolusberg: South Africa	28 38 S	17 54 E	45
Carrara: Italy	44 05 N	10 06 E	61D, 61H
Carrickfergus: Northern Ireland	54 43 N	5 49 W	32C
Carrington: England	53 26 N	2 24 W	58D, 58H, 60D, 60H
Carrizo Springs: Texas, U.S.A.	28 33 N	99 54 W	37J
Carson City: Mich., U.S.A.	43 11 N	84 50 W	37J
Cartagena: Colombia	10 25 N	75 32 W	36, 60, 61
Cartagena: Spain	37 36 N	0 59 W	27B, 37D, 46B, 49, 59H, 61H, 84A
Carteret: N.J., U.S.A.	40 35 N	74 14 W	45
Carters: *dam*, Ga., U.S.A.	34 37 N	84 21 W	39
Carthage: N.Y., U.S.A.	43 59 N	75 37 W	25D
Carúpano: Venezuela	10 40 N	63 14 W	87
Carville: La., U.S.A.	30 10 N	91 06 W	60G
Casablanca: Morocco	33 39 N	7 35 W	17, 27B, 29, 55, 57, 67, 84, 87
Cascavel: Brazil	4 07 S	38 14 W	50
Caseros: Argentina	34 36 S	58 33 W	55
Casma: Peru	9 30 S	78 18 W	27A
Casoria: Italy	40 54 N	14 17 E	32C
Casper: Wyo., U.S.A.	42 50 N	106 20 W	36, 37J, 62, 87
Cassiar: Canada	59 15 N	129 49 W	48
Cassinga: Angola	15 08 S	16 05 E	43
Cassis: France	43 13 N	5 32 E	17
Castaño Viejo: Argentina	30 59 S	69 34 W	46
Cástaras: Spain	36 56 N	3 16 W	50
Castellaccio: Italy	44 09 N	12 23 E	32C, 60D
Castellammare di Stabia: Italy	40 42 N	14 29 E	52
Castellanza: Italy	45 37 N	8 54 E	58H, 61H
Castellón de la Plana: Spain	39 59 N	0 02 W	27B, 36, 58H, 61D
Castillejo: Spain	39 57 N	3 44 W	57C
Castle Donington: England	52 51 N	1 19 W	87
Castleford: England	53 44 N	1 21 W	59H
Castle Hayne: N.C., U.S.A.	34 21 N	77 54 W	57B
Castlereagh: Northern Ireland	54 34 N	5 54 W	62
Castletown Bere: Irish Republic	51 39 N	9 55 W	27C
Castrop-Rauxel: Germany F.R.	51 33 N	7 19 E	61D
Catania: Italy	37 30 N	15 06 E	57, 59H, 84A
Cataño: Puerto Rico	18 27 N	66 07 W	57
Catanzaro: Italy	38 54 N	16 35 E	57C
Catavi: Bolivia	18 24 S	66 36 W	45
Catawba: S.C., U.S.A.	34 51 N	80 57 W	25A
Catlettsburg: Ky., U.S.A.	38 24 N	82 37 W	37J, 58B
Catorce: Mexico	23 42 N	100 54 W	49A
Catron *Co.*: N. Mex., U.S.A.	34 00 N	108 30 W	49B
Catskill: N.Y., U.S.A.	42 14 N	73 52 N	57B
Cauldon: England	53 02 N	1 54 W	57C
Cautivo: Ecuador	2 12 S	80 54 W	36
Cavite: Philippines	14 30 N	120 54 E	36
Cawnpore *see* Kanpur: India	26 27 N	80 14 E	29, 31, 32, 53, 61F
Caxias: Brazil	4 50 S	43 21 W	60, 67
Caxito: Angola	8 33 S	13 36 E	48
Cayenne: French Guiana	4 55 N	52 18 W	84
Cayo Guam, Río: *river*, Cuba	20 37 N	74 51 W	50
Ceará: *admin.*, Brazil	5 00 S	40 00 W	27
Cebu: *island*, Philippines	10 15 N	123 40 E	38
Cebu: Philippines	10 17 N	123 56 E	67, 84
Cedar Bayou: Texas, U.S.A.	29 41 N	94 56 W	58E, 60A
Cedar Rapids: Iowa, U.S.A.	41 59 N	91 39 W	87B
Cedar Springs: Ga., U.S.A.	31 10 N	85 03 W	25A
Cedral: Mexico	23 48 N	100 44 W	49A
Celebes *see* Sulawesi: *island*, Indonesia	2 00 S	121 00 E	27, 50
Çelik: Turkey	38 23 N	40 33 E	38
Celje: Yugoslavia	46 14 N	15 16 E	46B, 59H
Cellino: *region*, Italy	42 35 N	13 50 E	37B
Cement City: Mich., U.S.A.	42 03 N	84 18 W	57B
Cementon: Pa., U.S.A.	40 42 N	75 31 W	57B
Cengio: Italy	44 23 N	8 12 E	58D, 58H
Centerdale: R.I., U.S.A.	41 53 N	71 30 W	29A
Central Asia: *reg.*, U.S.S.R.	41 00 N	73 00 E	34, 38
Centralia: Ill., U.S.A.	38 32 N	89 08 W	54A
Central Region: *admin.*, Ghana	5 30 N	1 00 W	49
Central Valley of Chile *see* Valle Longitudinal: *valley*, Chile	36 00 S	72 00 W	17
Centre Atomique de Marcoule: France	44 08 N	4 42 E	40B
Centre/Mons: *region*, Belgium	50 25 N	3 55 E	38B
Ceres: South Africa	33 23 S	19 19 E	50
Céroux-Mousty: Belgium	50 40 N	4 31 E	31B
Cërrik: Albania	41 02 N	19 57 E	37H
Cerro Azul: Peru	13 05 S	76 29 W	27A
Cerro Bolívar: *mtn.*, Venezuela	7 27 N	63 25 W	43
Cerro Chorolque: *mtn.*, Bolivia	20 56 S	66 01 W	45
Cerro de Pasco: Peru	10 43 S	76 15 W	45
Cerro de San Pedro: Mexico	22 13 N	100 49 W	49A
Cerro Huemul: *mtn.*, Argentina	35 45 S	69 39 W	40
Cerro Largo: *admin.*, Uruguay	32 20 S	54 20 W	40
Cerro Maggiore: Italy	45 36 N	8 57 E	31B
Cerro Potosí: *mtn.*, Bolivia	19 37 S	65 45 W	45
Çesano Maderno: Italy	45 38 N	9 08 E	32C, 60D
Česká Skalice: Czechoslovakia	50 24 N	16 03 E	31B
Chablis: France	47 49 N	3 48 E	17
Chacarilla: Bolivia	17 40 S	68 19 W	45
Chacras de Coria: Argentina	33 00 S	68 52 W	60
Chagan-Uzun: U.S.S.R.	50 06 N	88 21 E	50
Chagres: Chile	32 48 S	70 58 W	45
Chaibassa: India	22 31 N	85 50 E	57
Chalchihuites: Mexico	23 29 N	103 53 W	49A
Challapata: Bolivia	18 54 S	66 47 W	50
Chalmette: La., U.S.A.	29 54 N	89 58 W	37J, 47A, 58A
Chalon-sur-Sâone: France	46 47 N	4 51 E	17
Chambéry: France	45 34 N	5 56 E	17, 32C
Chambishi: Zambia	12 40 S	28 03 E	45B
Champagnier: France	45 06 N	5 43 E	30B
Champagnole: France	46 45 N	5 55 E	57C
Champaign: Ill., U.S.A.	40 07 N	88 14 W	67A, 87B
Chancay: Peru	11 36 S	77 14 W	27A
Chandler: Ariz., U.S.A.	33 19 N	111 49 W	61
Chandraghona: Pakistan	22 28 N	92 09 E	32, 60
Ch'ang-chiang: China P.R.	19 12 N	109 01 E	43
Ch'ang-chiang P'en-ti (Yangtze Basin): *basin*, China P.R.	31 48 N	121 10 E	10
Ch'ang-ch'un: China P.R.	43 52 N	125 21 E	55, 57
Changhang: South Korea	36 01 N	126 42 E	46
Chang-hua: Taiwan	24 06 N	120 31 E	31, 32
Ch'ang-lo-chieh: China P.R.	28 50 N	113 14 E	45
Chang-p'u: China P.R.	24 06 N	117 37 E	47
Ch'ang-sha: China P.R.	28 12 N	112 58 E	46
Ch'ang-shou: China P.R.	29 50 N	107 04 E	30
Changsu-ri: South Korea	35 39 N	127 31 E	50
Channelview: Texas, U.S.A.	29 46 N	95 07 W	60G
Chanute: Kans., U.S.A.	37 41 N	95 26 W	37J, 57A
Ch'ao Hsien: *admin.*, China P.R.	31 36 N	117 52 E	57
Chapais: Canada	49 47 N	74 54 W	45, 49
Chapel Cross: England	55 05 N	3 15 W	40B
Charbon: Australia	32 53 S	149 58 E	57
Charcas: Mexico	23 08 N	101 07 W	46, 49A
Charleroi: Belgium	50 25 N	4 26 E	38B, 67B
Charleston: S.C., U.S.A.	32 48 N	79 58 W	59F, 67, 84, 87C
Charleston: Tenn., U.S.A.	35 17 N	84 45 W	59B
Charleston: W. Va., U.S.A.	32 48 N	79 58 W	25A, 53, 58B, 58F, 59E, 67A, 87C
Charlotte: N.C., U.S.A.	35 03 N	80 50 W	30A, 60B, 87C
Charlottesville: Va., U.S.A.	38 02 N	78 29 W	87C
Charvakskaya: *dam*, U.S.S.R.	41 35 N	69 54 E	39
Chascomús: Argentina	35 34 S	58 01 W	54
Chasong: *dam*, North Korea	41 25 N	126 32 E	39
Chasse: France	44 11 N	6 35 E	61H
Chastang: *dam*, France	45 09 N	2 02 E	39
Châteauneuf-du-Pape: France	44 03 N	4 50 E	17
Chatham: N.Y., U.S.A.	42 22 N	73 36 W	25D
Châtillon: Italy	45 45 N	7 37 E	32C
Chattanooga: Tenn., U.S.A.	35 02 N	85 18 W	25A, 30A, 31A, 32B, 40, 57B, 58A, 60B, 61B, 61E, 87C
Chauk: Burma	20 53 N	94 49 E	35, 36, 61, 61F
Chaŭn: South Korea	37 52 N	128 00 E	43
Chaunskaya Guba: *bay*, U.S.S.R.	69 20 N	170 00 E	45
Chauny: France	49 37 N	3 13 E	58D
Chavantes: *dam*, Brazil	23 02 S	44 43 W	39
Chaykovskiy: U.S.S.R.	56 47 N	54 09 E	30
Cheboksarskaya: *dam*, U.S.S.R.	56 08 N	46 52 E	39
Chedde: France	45 56 N	6 43 E	47B
Chelan *Co.*: Wash., U.S.A.	47 50 N	120 30 W	49
Chełm: Poland	51 08 N	23 29 E	57C
Cheltenham: England	51 54 N	2 04 W	60H
Chelyabinsk: U.S.S.R.	55 10 N	61 24 E	31, 34, 36, 43, 46, 56
Chembur: India	19 03 N	72 54 E	60
Chemnitz *see* Karl-Marx-Stadt: Germany D.R.	50 50 N	12 55 E	29C, 31B
Chemor: Malaysia	4 43 N	101 07 E	57
Cheng-chou: China P.R.	34 45 N	113 40 E	29, 31
Ch'eng-te: China P.R.	40 58 N	117 53 E	50
Ch'eng-tu: China P.R.	30 40 N	104 04 E	25, 61, 67
Cherbourg: France	49 39 N	1 39 W	27C, 84C
Cherdoyak: U.S.S.R.	48 48 N	84 00 E	45
Cheremkhovo: U.S.S.R.	53 09 N	103 05 E	38, 67
Cherepovets: U.S.S.R.	59 08 N	37 54 E	43
Cherkassy: U.S.S.R.	49 26 N	32 04 E	32C, 60, 61
Chernigov: U.S.S.R.	51 30 N	31 18 E	29, 32C
Chernogorsk: U.S.S.R.	53 49 N	91 18 E	38
Chernovtsy: U.S.S.R.	48 18 N	25 56 E	31
Cherokee: Ala., U.S.A.	34 44 N	87 59 W	61B, 61E
Cherokee *Co.*: Ga., U.S.A.	34 13 N	84 29 W	48
Cherry Creek: Nev., U.S.A.	39 54 N	114 53 W	50, 50A
Chertal: Belgium	50 41 N	5 40 E	43B
Chesapeake: Va., U.S.A.	36 43 N	76 15 W	84
Cheshire, Lancashire and: *region*, England	53 30 N	2 30 W	56A
Cheshunt: England	51 43 N	0 02 W	55A
Chester: England	53 12 N	2 54 W	46B, 53B
Chester: Pa., U.S.A.	39 50 N	75 23 W	25D, 52
Chester: S.C., U.S.A.	34 43 N	81 14 W	32B
Chesterfield: England	53 15 N	1 25 W	58H, 59D, 59H
Cheswold: Del., U.S.A.	39 13 N	75 36 W	30A
Cheyenne: Wyo., U.S.A.	41 08 N	104 50 W	36, 37J, 61
Chia-mu-ssu: China P.R.	46 50 N	130 21 E	25
Chiang-hsi (Kiangsi): *admin.*, China P.R.	28 00 N	116 00 E	50D
Chiang Mai: Thailand	18 47 N	98 59 E	36
Chiang-men: China P.R.	22 35 N	113 05 E	25
Chiao-ho: China P.R.	43 42 N	127 19 E	38C
Chiao-tso: China P.R.	35 15 N	113 13 E	38C
Chiatura: U.S.S.R.	42 19 N	43 18 E	50
Chiavari: Italy	44 19 N	9 19 E	50B
Chia-wang: China P.R.	34 27 N	117 27 E	38C
Chiba: Japan	35 36 N	140 07 E	35, 36, 37E, 43D, 47C, 52B, 58C, 58G, 59C, 60C, 60E, 61C, 61G
Chibougamau: Canada	49 56 N	74 24 W	45, 49
Chibuluma: Zambia	12 43 S	28 07 E	45B
Chicago: Ill., U.S.A.	41 50 N	87 45 W	3, 25, 25D, 34, 43A, 55, 56, 58D, 59E, 63, 67A, 84, 87B
Chicago Heights: Ill., U.S.A.	41 31 N	87 39 W	54A
Chichibu: Japan	35 59 N	139 05 E	43D, 46C, 57D
Ch'i-ch'i-ha-erh (Tsitsihar): China P.R.	47 22 N	123 57 E	25, 54, 67
Chīchoki Malliān: Pakistan	31 42 N	74 05 E	61
Chicken Creek: Alaska, U.S.A.	64 04 N	142 00 W	49
Chiclayo: Peru	6 47 S	79 47 W	67
Chicoutimi: Canada	48 26 N	71 04 W	84
Chief Joseph: *dam*, Wash., U.S.A.	48 04 N	119 43 W	39A
Chigirishima: Japan	34 15 N	132 40 E	46C
Chi-hsi: China P.R.	45 18 N	130 58 E	38
Chihuahua: *admin.*, Mexico	28 30 N	106 00 W	50
Chihuahua: Mexico	28 38 N	106 05 W	25, 32, 34, 49A, 61, 67
Chikugo: Japan	33 15 N	130 27 E	38C
Chilca: Peru	12 35 S	76 41 W	45
Childersburg: Ala., U.S.A.	33 16 N	86 21 W	32B, 59F
Chi-lin (Kirin): *admin.*, China P.R.	43 00 N	126 00 E	50
Chi-lin (Kirin): China P.R.	43 51 N	126 33 E	25, 36, 43, 49, 61, 67
Chillicothe: Ohio, U.S.A.	38 20 N	83 00 W	25D
Chi-lung: Taiwan	25 08 N	121 44 E	60, 84
Chilwa, *Lake*: Malawi	15 12 S	35 50 E	27
Chimbote: Peru	9 04 S	78 34 W	27, 27A
Chimkent: U.S.S.R.	42 18 N	69 36 E	31, 46, 57
Chimney Rock Hollow: *dam*, Okla., U.S.A.	36 15 N	95 10 W	39
Chi-nan (Tsinan): China P.R.	36 40 N	117 00 E	43, 55, 61
Ch'in-chou: China P.R.	21 57 N	108 37 E	50D
Chin-chou: China P.R.	41 07 N	121 06 E	40
Chinghai *see* Hsi-ning: China P.R.	36 37 N	101 46 E	29, 43, 67
Ching-hsi: China P.R.	39 56 N	116 24 E	38C
Ching-hsing: China P.R.	38 00 N	114 01 E	38C
Ch'ing-tao (Tsingtao): China P.R.	36 04 N	120 19 E	29, 31, 43, 54, 84
Ching-te-chen: China P.R.	29 16 N	117 11 E	50D
Chinhae: South Korea	35 08 N	128 40 E	59G, 61C, 61G
Ch'in-huang-tao: China P.R.	39 56 N	119 37 E	47, 84
Chin-kua-shih: Taiwan	25 07 N	121 51 E	45, 49
Ch'in Ling (Tsinling Shan): *mtns.*, China P.R.	34 00 N	108 00 E	50
Chinon: France	47 10 N	0 15 E	17, 40B
Chinsura: India	22 53 N	88 25 E	31
Chippis: Switzerland	46 17 N	7 33 E	47B
Chirchik: U.S.S.R.	41 29 N	69 35 E	61
Chiren: Bulgaria	43 20 N	23 35 E	34, 37B
Chirkeyskaya: *dam*, U.S.S.R.	43 06 N	46 50 E	39
Chisimaio: Somali Republic	00 23 S	42 30 E	84
Chita: U.S.S.R.	52 03 N	113 30 E	38, 67
Chita-Hantō: *pen.*, Japan	34 50 N	136 53 E	60E

	° ′	° ′	*Page(s)*
Chitanga: Zambia	15 35 S	28 19 E	57
Chitinskaya Oblast' (Chita Oblast): *admin.*, U.S.S.R.	52 00 N	117 00 E	38
Chitose: Japan	42 49 N	141 39 E	49
Chitradurga: *admin.*, India	14 14 N	76 24 E	43
Chittagong: Pakistan	22 20 N	91 50 E	35, 36, 84
Chittaranjan: India	23 50 N	87 00 E	54
Chiu-lien Shan: *mtn.*, China P.R.	24 30 N	114 42 E	40
Chiwefwe: Zambia	13 38 S	29 27 E	50
Chocó: *admin.*, Colombia	6 00 N	77 00 W	49
Chocolate Bayou: Texas, U.S.A.	29 20 N	95 16 W	58A, 58E, 60A, 60G
Chocques: France	50 32 N	2 34 E	61D
Chodaków: Poland	52 15 N	20 15 E	32C
Ch'ŏngjin: North Korea	41 46 N	129 49 E	32, 43, 84D
Ch'ŏngju: South Korea	36 38 N	127 30 E	61C, 61G
Chŏngsŏn: South Korea	37 22 N	128 39 E	38C
Chooz: France	50 06 N	4 48 E	40B
Chorolque, Cerro: *mtn.*, Bolivia	20 56 S	66 01 W	45
Chorukh-Dayron: U.S.S.R.	40 24 N	69 40 E	50
Chorzów: Poland	50 19 N	18 56 E	43B, 54B, 61D, 61H
Chōshi: Japan	35 44 N	140 50 E	27D
Chowringhee: India	22 35 N	88 21 E	61F
Christchurch: New Zealand	43 33 S	172 40 E	29, 54, 67, 87
Christmas: Ariz., U.S.A.	33 02 N	110 44 W	45A
Chrzanów: Poland	50 10 N	19 21 E	54B, 57C
Chu-chou: China P.R.	27 50 N	113 09 E	40, 54, 59
Chukotskiy Poluostrov: *pen.*, U.S.S.R.	66 00 N	174 00 W	50
Chul'man: U.S.S.R.	56 52 N	124 52 E	38
Ch'ung-ch'ing: China P.R.	29 34 N	106 35 E	25, 32, 43, 55, 57, 61, 67
Chupa: U.S.S.R.	66 16 N	33 04 E	48
Chuquicamata: Chile	22 19 S	68 56 W	45, 49, 50
Churchill: Canada	58 46 N	94 10 W	84
Churchill Falls: *dam*, Canada	53 35 N	64 27 W	39
Church Point: La., U.S.A.	30 22 N	92 15 W	37J
Churk: India	24 40 N	83 06 E	57
Chu-shan: China P.R.	24 57 N	114 30 E	40
Chusovoy: U.S.S.R.	58 17 N	57 49 E	43
Chute-à-Caron: *dam*, Canada	48 31 N	71 15 W	39B
Chute-à-la-Savane: *dam*, Canada	48 43 N	71 53 W	39B
Chute-des-Passes: *dam*, Canada	49 55 N	71 20 W	39B
Chute-du-Diable: *dam*, Canada	48 46 N	71 40 W	39B
Chu-tung: Taiwan	24 44 N	121 05 E	57
Chu-tung ch'ü: *admin.*, Taiwan	24 40 N	121 10 E	34
Chvaletice: Czechoslovakia	50 02 N	15 26 E	50B
Cicuco: Colombia	9 03 N	74 31 W	34
Ciénaga: Colombia	11 01 N	74 15 W	27
Cienfuegos: Cuba	22 09 N	80 27 W	61
Cimego: *dam*, Italy	45 50 N	10 32 E	39C
Cîmpina: Romania	45 08 N	25 44 E	37H
Cincinnati: Ohio, U.S.A.	39 10 N	84 30 W	25D, 37J, 55B, 56, 59F, 62, 63, 67A, 87B
Cinco Saltos: Argentina	38 49 S	68 04 W	60
Ciniza: N. Mex., U.S.A.	32 32 N	108 46 W	36
Cité de Lavéra: France	43 23 N	5 02 E	37H, 58H, 59D, 60D, 60H
Cittadella: Italy	45 39 N	11 47 E	54B
City of Industry: Calif., U.S.A.	34 01 N	117 51 W	62
Ciudad Camargo: Mexico	27 40 N	105 10 W	43, 61
Ciudad de Guatemala: Guatemala	14 38 N	90 31 W	31, 57, 67, 87
Ciudad de México (Mexico City): Mexico	19 24 N	99 09 W	25, 29, 31, 32, 34, 45, 55, 56, 57, 59, 60, 62, 67, 87
Ciudad Madero: Mexico	22 16 N	97 50 W	36, 60
Ciudad Real: *admin.*, Spain	39 00 N	4 00 W	38
Ciudad-Rodrigo: Spain	40 36 N	6 32 W	40, 45
Ciudad Sahagún: Mexico	19 47 N	98 33 W	54
Civitavecchia: Italy	42 06 N	11 48 E	84A
Clabecq: Belgium	50 41 N	4 13 E	43B
Clairton: Pa., U.S.A.	40 17 N	79 56 W	61A
Clarington: Ohio, U.S.A.	39 47 N	80 53 W	47
Clarkdale: Ariz., U.S.A.	34 49 N	112 03 W	57
Clark Hill: *dam*, Ga., U.S.A.	33 39 N	82 12 W	39
Clarkson: Canada	43 30 N	79 38 W	37J, 57B
Clausthal: Germany F.R.	51 48 N	10 20 E	46B
Claydon: England	52 06 N	1 07 E	57C
Claymont: Del., U.S.A.	39 48 N	75 28 W	58B, 61
Clayton: Australia	37 55 S	145 07 E	55
Clear Creek *Co.*: Colo., U.S.A.	39 30 N	105 45 W	49B
Cleckheaton: England	53 44 N	1 43 W	29B, 58H
Cléon: France	44 37 N	4 56 E	55A
Clermont: Canada	47 42 N	70 14 W	25D
Cleveland: Ohio, U.S.A.	41 30 N	81 41 W	43A, 55B, 56, 59E, 63, 67A, 87B
Cliffe: England	51 28 N	0 30 E	57C
Clifton: N.J., U.S.A.	40 52 N	74 09 W	25D, 54
Clifton: S.C., U.S.A.	34 58 N	81 50 W	31A
Climax: Colo., U.S.A.	39 22 N	106 11 W	40A, 50, 50A
Clinchfield: Ga., U.S.A.	32 25 N	83 40 W	57B
Clinton: Iowa, U.S.A.	41 51 N	90 12 W	58B, 60B, 61A, 61E
Clinton: S.C., U.S.A.	34 27 N	81 52 W	31A
Clintonville: Wis., U.S.A.	44 37 N	88 46 W	55
Clisson: France	47 05 N	1 17 W	40B
Clitheroe: England	53 53 N	2 23 W	57C
Cluj: *admin.*, Romania	46 50 N	24 00 E	38B
Clyde: Australia	33 50 S	151 01 E	36, 58
Clydebank: *region*, Scotland	55 54 N	4 24 W	52A
Coahuila: *admin.*, Mexico	27 20 N	102 00 W	38
Coalinga: Calif., U.S.A.	36 08 N	120 22 W	48
Coatesville: *dam*, Pa., U.S.A.	39 56 N	75 40 W	39
Coatzacoalcos: Mexico	18 09 N	94 25 W	56, 58, 59
Cobalt: Canada	47 24 N	79 41 W	49, 50
Cobourg: Canada	43 58 N	78 11 W	32B
Cobrisa: Peru	12 00 S	74 12 W	45
Cochabamba: Bolivia	17 24 S	66 09 W	36
Cochin: India	9 56 N	76 15 E	31C, 36, 46, 59, 61, 84
Cochise *Co.*: Ariz., U.S.A.	32 00 N	109 30 W	49B
Cockatoo *Island*: Australia	16 06 S	123 37 E	43
Cockle Creek: Australia	32 57 S	151 38 E	46, 59
Coconino *Co.*: Ariz., U.S.A.	35 30 N	112 30 W	40A, 49B
Cody: Wyo., U.S.A.	44 31 N	109 04 W	36
Coeur d'Alene: Idaho, U.S.A.	47 40 N	116 46 W	45, 46A, 50
Coffeyville: Kans., U.S.A.	37 02 N	95 37 W	37J
Cognac: France	45 42 N	0 20 W	17
Coimbatore: India	11 00 N	76 57 E	31C
Coimbra: Portugal	40 12 N	8 25 W	17, 31
Colares: Portugal	38 48 N	9 27 W	17
Colatina: Brazil	19 32 S	40 37 W	67
Cold Bay: Alaska, U.S.A.	55 11 N	162 30 W	84
Coleraine: Northern Ireland	55 08 N	6 40 W	32C
Colleferro: Italy	41 44 N	12 59 E	57C, 58D
Collie: Australia	33 22 S	116 09 E	38
Collingwood: Canada	44 30 N	80 14 W	52
Collombey: Switzerland	46 17 N	6 56 E	37F, 37H
Colmar: France	48 05 N	7 22 E	32C
Cologne *see* Köln: G.F.R.	50 56 N	6 57 E	37F, 55A, 58H, 60H, 67B, 87D
Colombelles: France	49 12 N	0 18 W	57C
Colombo: Ceylon	6 56 N	79 51 E	31, 67, 84
Colón: Panama	9 22 N	79 54 W	36
Colonia Catriel: Argentina	37 51 S	67 50 W	34
Colonia del Sacramento: Uruguay	34 28 S	57 51 W	32
Colorado: *admin.*, U.S.A.	40 00 N	106 00 W	27, 35, 38
Colorado City: Texas, U.S.A.	32 24 N	100 51 W	37J
Colorado, South West: *reg.*, Colo., U.S.A.	38 00 N	108 00 W	50, 50A
Colorines: *dam*, Mexico	19 11 N	100 08 W	39
Colquiri: Bolivia	17 25 S	67 08 W	45
Colton: Calif., U.S.A.	34 05 N	117 20 W	57
Columbia: *river*, Oreg./Wash., U.S.A.	46 15 N	123 30 W	58
Columbia: S.C., U.S.A.	34 00 N	81 00 W	31A, 32B, 60B, 87C
Columbia: Tenn., U.S.A.	35 37 N	87 02 W	56
Columbia Falls: Mont., U.S.A.	48 24 N	114 11 W	47
Columbus: Ga., U.S.A.	32 28 N	84 59 W	31A, 87C
Columbus: Ohio, U.S.A.	39 59 N	83 03 W	53, 67A, 87B
Come by Chance: Canada	47 51 N	53 59 W	35, 61
Como: Italy	45 47 N	9 05 E	37H
Comodoro Rivadavia: Argentina	45 52 S	67 30 W	35, 36, 46, 87
Compton: Calif., U.S.A.	33 55 N	118 14 W	60
Conakry: Guinea	9 31 N	13 43 W	67, 84
Concarán: Argentina	32 34 S	65 15 W	50
Concarneau: France	47 52 N	3 55 W	27, 84C
Concepción: *admin.*, Chile	37 00 S	72 30 W	38
Concepción: Chile	36 50 S	73 03 W	25, 29, 36, 58, 67
Concepción del Oro: Mexico	24 38 N	101 25 W	45, 49A
Conchan: Peru	12 30 S	76 30 W	36
Concón: Chile	32 55 S	71 31 W	36
Concord: N.C., U.S.A.	35 25 N	80 34 W	31A
Concordia: Mexico	23 17 N	106 04 W	49A
Concrete: Wash., U.S.A.	48 32 N	121 46 W	57
Conda: Idaho, U.S.A.	42 44 N	111 33 W	50, 50A, 56, 59
Condobolin: Australia	33 05 S	147 09 E	45
Condor: Peru	13 37 S	75 39 W	45
Condrieu: France	45 27 N	4 46 E	17
Conegliano: Italy	45 53 N	12 18 E	17
Congonhas: Brazil	20 30 S	43 52 W	43
Congo *River*: Central Africa	6 04 S	12 24 E	48
Coniston: Canada	46 29 N	80 51 W	45
Conowingo: *dam*, Md., U.S.A.	39 41 N	76 17 W	39
Conroe: Texas, U.S.A.	30 19 N	95 28 W	60G
Conselheiro Lafaiete: Brazil	20 40 S	43 48 W	50
Consett: England	54 51 N	1 49 W	43B
Conshohocken: Pa., U.S.A.	40 05 N	75 18 W	32B
Constanța: Romania	44 11 N	28 39 E	67, 84
Convent: La., U.S.A.	29 57 N	90 49 W	37J
Converse *Co.*: Wyo., U.S.A.	43 00 N	105 30 W	40A
Coogee: Australia	32 07 S	115 46 E	57
Cook Inlet: *bay*, Alaska, U.S.A.	60 30 N	152 00 W	34, 61
Coosa Pines: Ala., U.S.A.	33 17 N	86 22 W	25A
Coos Bay: Oreg., U.S.A.	43 23 N	124 12 W	59, 84
Copenhagen *see* København: Denmark	55 40 N	12 35 E	25, 32C, 37F, 43B, 52A, 55, 58D, 58H, 59D, 59H, 62, 84C, 87
Coplay: Pa., U.S.A.	40 40 N	75 30 W	57B
Copper Cities: Ariz., U.S.A.	33 22 N	110 48 W	45A
Copper Cliff: Canada	46 28 N	81 05 W	45, 56, 59E
Copperhill: Tenn., U.S.A.	35 00 N	84 21 W	45, 56, 59F
Coppermine: Canada	67 49 N	115 12 W	3
Copperopolis: Calif., U.S.A.	37 58 N	120 38 W	48
Copper Queen: Ariz., U.S.A.	31 27 N	110 00 W	45A
Copşa Mică: Romania	46 07 N	24 15 E	46B, 59H, 60H
Coquelles: France	50 56 N	1 48 E	32C, 60D
Coquimbana: Chile	28 21 S	70 56 W	50
Coquimbo: *admin.*, Chile	31 00 S	71 00 W	49
Coquimbo: Chile	29 58 S	71 21 W	27
Corbehem: France	50 20 N	3 03 E	25C
Corbeil-Essonnes: France	48 36 N	2 29 E	25C
Corby: England	52 29 N	0 40 W	43B
Cordero: Nev., U.S.A.	41 50 N	117 40 W	50
Córdoba: *admin.*, Argentina	32 00 S	64 00 W	48
Córdoba: *admin.*, Spain	38 00 N	4 50 W	38, 40, 46B
Córdoba: Argentina	31 24 S	64 11 W	50, 53, 55, 67, 87
Córdoba: Spain	37 53 N	4 46 W	45
Córdoba, Sierra de: *hill*, Arg.	31 24 S	64 11 W	48
Cordova: Ala., U.S.A.	33 45 N	87 10 W	37J
Cordova: Ill., U.S.A.	41 42 N	90 19 W	40C, 61A
Corinth *see* Kórinthos: Greece	37 56 N	22 55 E	17, 59H
Corinto: Nicaragua	12 29 N	87 12 W	84
Cork: Irish Republic	51 54 N	8 28 W	29, 52A, 55, 67, 84C, 87
Cormeilles-en-Parisis: France	48 59 N	2 12 E	57C
Cornas: France	44 58 N	4 51 E	17
Corn Belt: *region* Iowa/Kans., U.S.A.	40 00 N	95 00 W	10, 14, 19, 23
Corner Brook: Canada	48 58 N	57 58 W	25
Cornigliano Ligure: Italy	44 25 N	8 53 E	43B
Cornwall: Canada	45 02 N	74 45 W	25D, 32B, 58, 59A
Cornwall: Pa., U.S.A.	40 17 N	76 24 W	50
Corocoro: Bolivia	17 12 S	68 29 W	45
Coron: *island*, Philippines	12 00 N	120 30 E	50
Corpach: Scotland	56 51 N	5 08 W	84C
Corpus Christi: Texas, U.S.A.	27 47 N	97 26 W	35, 37J, 46, 47A, 57, 58A, 58E, 59B, 60G, 87C
Corral Quemado: Chile	30 20 S	70 58 W	50
Corrientes: Argentina	27 28 S	58 50 W	67
Cortemaggiore: Italy	44 59 N	9 56 E	37H
Cortland: N.Y., U.S.A.	42 36 N	76 10 W	55B
Corunna: Canada	42 53 N	82 26 W	37J
Coryton: England	51 32 N	0 31 E	37F
Cosalá: Mexico	24 23 N	106 41 W	49A
Coshocton: Ohio, U.S.A.	40 16 N	81 53 W	25D
Cosoleacaque: Mexico	18 00 N	94 37 W	61
Cosquín: Argentina	31 15 S	64 29 W	40
Cotonou: Dahomey	6 21 N	2 26 E	27, 84
Cottbus: *admin.*, Germany D.R.	51 45 N	14 18 E	38B
Cottbus: Germany D.R.	51 46 N	14 20 E	29C
Cotton Valley: La., U.S.A.	32 49 N	93 25 W	37J
Couillet: Belgium	50 23 N	4 27 E	59D
Courtrai *see* Kortrijk: Belgium	50 50 N	3 16 E	31B
Courtright: Canada	42 47 N	82 27 W	61A, 61E
Coventry: England	52 25 N	1 30 W	32C, 53B, 55A, 67B
Covilhã: Portugal	40 17 N	7 30 W	29
Covington: Ky., U.S.A.	39 04 N	84 30 W	54A
Covington: Va., U.S.A.	37 48 N	80 01 W	25A, 32B
Cowans Ford: *dam*, N.C., U.S.A.	35 44 N	81 06 W	39
Cowley: England	51 44 N	1 14 W	55A
Cox's Bāzār: Pakistan	21 26 N	91 59 E	40
Cracow: Australia	25 18 S	150 18 E	49
Craiova: Romania	44 19 N	23 48 E	54, 61D, 61H
Cranston: R.I., U.S.A.	41 47 N	71 27 W	56, 60B
Creil: France	49 16 N	2 29 E	46B
Cremona: Italy	45 07 N	10 02 E	37H
Crespiatica: Italy	45 21 N	9 34 E	58D
Creston: Iowa, U.S.A.	41 04 N	94 20 W	61A
Crewe: England	53 05 N	2 27 W	54B, 55A
Crişana: Romania	46 37 N	21 31 E	38B
Cristais, Serra dos: *hill*, Brazil	16 37 S	47 37 W	50
Crna Gora (Montenegro): *admin.*, Yugoslavia	42 30 N	19 18 E	38B
Croatia *see* Hrvatska: *admin.*, Yugoslavia	45 10 N	15 30 E	38B
Crook *Co.*: Wyo., U.S.A.	44 30 N	104 30 W	40A
Crossett: Ark., U.S.A.	33 09 N	91 59 W	25A
Crotone: Italy	39 05 N	17 08 E	46B, 59H, 61D 61H
Croydon: England	51 23 N	0 06 W	62A
Croze: France	46 12 N	1 55 E	40B
Cruachan: *dam*, Scotland	56 26 N	5 09 W	39
Cruas: France	44 39 N	4 46 E	57C
Cruzeiro: Brazil	22 34 S	44 58 W	54
Crystal City: Mo., U.S.A.	38 11 N	90 22 W	61A, 61E
Crystal River: Fla., U.S.A.	28 54 N	82 36 W	40
Csepel: Hungary	47 25 N	19 05 E	37H, 43B
Cuarenta: Mexico	21 30 N	101 46 W	50
Cuautitlán de Romero Rubio: Mexico	19 40 N	99 11 W	59
Cubatão: Brazil	23 53 S	46 25 W	36, 58, 59, 60, 61
Cubatão: *dam*, Brazil	23 40 S	46 43 W	39
Cucurpe: Mexico	30 20 N	110 43 W	49A
Cúcuta: Colombia	7 54 N	72 31 W	27, 67, 87
Cuencamé de Ceniceros: Mexico	24 53 N	103 42 W	49A
Cuernavaca: Mexico	18 55 N	99 15 W	58
Cuiabá: Brazil	15 32 S	56 05 W	87
Cuíma: Angola	13 16 S	15 42 E	43
Culebras: Peru	9 53 S	78 13 W	27A
Culver City: Calif., U.S.A.	34 01 N	118 24 W	53
Cumberland: Maine, U.S.A.	43 45 N	70 13 W	59A
Cumberland: Md., U.S.A.	39 40 N	78 47 W	32B
Cumbernauld: Scotland	55 58 N	3 59 W	62
Cumuruxatiba: Brazil	17 06 S	39 11 W	40
Cupertino: Calif., U.S.A.	37 19 N	122 02 W	62
Curitiba: Brazil	25 25 S	49 15 W	67, 87
Cusano Milanino: Italy	45 33 N	9 11 E	32C
Cushing: Okla., U.S.A.	35 59 N	96 47 W	37J
Custer *Co.*: Idaho, U.S.A.	44 20 N	114 30 W	49
Custer *Co.*: S.D., U.S.A.	43 40 N	103 30 W	40A
Cuxhaven: Germany F.R.	53 53 N	8 42 E	27C
Cuyuna Range: *deposit*, Minn., U.S.A.	46 30 N	93 55 W	43, 50
Cuzco: *admin.*, Peru	12 30 S	72 30 W	46, 49
Cuzco: Peru	13 32 S	71 57 W	61
Cyril: Okla., U.S.A.	34 55 N	98 11 W	37J
Czechowice: Poland	49 50 N	19 02 E	37F
Czestochowa: Poland	50 49 N	19 07 E	25C, 43B

D

	° ′	° ′	*Page(s)*
Dacca: Pakistan	23 43 N	90 25 E	31, 34, 61F, 67, 87
Daegu *see* Taegu: South Korea	35 52 N	128 36 E	31, 32, 60C
Daejeon *see* Taejŏn: S. Korea	36 20 N	127 26 E	31
Daerat Tingkat i Djawa Barat: *admin.*, Indonesia	7 00 S	107 00 E	61
Dagari: Pakistan	30 04 N	67 13 E	38
Dagenham: England	51 33 N	0 08 E	55A
Dāharki: Pakistan	24 55 N	68 30 E	61
Daingerfield: Texas, U.S.A.	33 02 N	94 44 W	58A
Dairen *see* Lü-ta: China P.R.	38 55 N	121 39 E	52, 54, 57, 84
Daisy: Tenn., U.S.A.	35 10 N	85 12 W	40
Daisy Pima: Ariz., U.S.A.	32 21 N	111 30 W	45A
Dakar: Senegal	14 40 N	17 26 W	36, 67, 84, 87
Dalhousie: Canada	48 03 N	66 22 W	25D, 59A, 84
Dallas: Texas, U.S.A.	32 47 N	96 48 W	25, 53, 55, 56, 57A, 62, 87C
Dalmia Dadri: India	28 37 N	76 19 E	57
Dalmianager: India	24 55 N	84 11 E	57
Dalmiapuram: India	10 53 N	78 53 E	57
Dalmine: Italy	45 39 N	9 36 E	43B
Dal'nevostok: *region*, U.S.S.R.	52 30 N	130 30 E	56
Dalton: Ga., U.S.A.	34 46 N	84 59 W	30A, 31A
Damar: Turkey	41 15 N	41 34 E	59
Damascus *see* Dimashq: Syria	33 30 N	36 15 E	31, 87
Damietta *see* Dumyāţ: *admin.*, U.A.R.	31 20 N	31 45 E	40
Damme: Germany F.R.	52 31 N	8 12 E	43B
Dampier: Australia	20 39 S	116 45 E	84
Da Nang: South Vietnam	16 04 N	108 13 E	61, 67, 84
Danao: Philippines	10 33 N	124 01 E	57
Dandenong: Australia	37 59 S	145 12 E	32, 54, 55, 60
Dandot: Pakistan	32 39 N	72 58 E	38
Daniel: *point*, Chile	52 19 S	68 48 W	35
Danube *Basin*: Austria	45 20 N	29 40 E	10
Danville: Va., U.S.A.	36 34 N	79 25 W	31A
Danzig *see* Gdańsk: Poland	54 22 N	18 38 E	52A, 59H, 84C
Dar es Salaam: Tanzania	6 48 S	39 17 S	36, 67, 84, 87
Darley Dale: England	53 09 N	1 36 W	46
Darling Downs: *region*, Austl.	27 30 S	150 30 E	38
Darlington: England	54 31 N	1 34 W	29B, 54B
Dărmăneşti: Romania	46 22 N	26 29 E	37H
Darmstadt: Germany F.R.	49 52 N	8 39 E	59D
Darnah: Libya	32 45 N	22 39 E	84B
Darra: Australia	27 34 S	152 58 E	57
Dartmouth: Canada	44 40 N	63 35 W	36, 55
Darwin: Australia	12 28 S	130 50 E	84, 87
Dashava: U.S.S.R.	49 16 N	24 00 E	34, 37B, 37D
Dashkesan: U.S.S.R.	40 30 N	46 04 E	43
Datteln: Germany F.R.	51 40 N	7 23 E	58D
Dāūd Khel: Pakistan	32 53 N	71 34 E	61
Daugav'pils: U.S.S.R.	55 53 N	26 32 E	32C
Davangere: India	14 30 N	75 52 E	31C
Davao: Philippines	7 05 N	125 38 E	57, 67, 84, 87
Davenda: U.S.S.R.	53 33 N	119 18 E	50
Davenport: Calif., U.S.A.	37 01 N	122 14 W	57
Davenport: Iowa, U.S.A.	41 32 N	90 36 W	57
Davis: *dam*, Ariz., U.S.A.	35 10 N	114 34 W	39
Dawson: Canada	64 04 N	139 24 W	49
Dayton: Ohio, U.S.A.	39 45 N	84 10 W	67A, 87B
Daytona Beach: Fla., U.S.A.	29 11 N	81 01 W	87C
Dead Sea: *lake*, Middle East	31 30 N	35 30 E	56
Déan Funes: Argentina	30 25 S	64 22 W	50
Dearborn: Mich., U.S.A.	42 18 N	83 14 W	55B
Deary: Idaho, U.S.A.	46 48 N	116 32 W	48
De Beers: *mine*, South Africa	28 45 S	24 46 E	48
Decatur: Ala., U.S.A.	34 36 N	87 00 W	32B, 87C
Decatur: Tenn., U.S.A.	35 21 N	84 28 W	32B
Deccan: *plateau*, India	17 30 N	78 00 E	23
Deer Lodge *Co.*: Mont., U.S.A.	46 00 N	113 00 W	49
Deer Park: Texas, U.S.A.	29 43 N	95 08 W	59B, 60A, 61B
Deferiet: N.Y., U.S.A.	44 03 N	75 41 W	25D
Degerhamn: Sweden	56 21 N	16 24 E	57
Değirmisaz: Turkey	39 29 N	29 14 E	38
Degtyarsk: U.S.S.R.	56 42 N	60 06 E	45
Dehiwala: Ceylon	6 51 N	79 52 E	67
De Hoek: South Africa	32 57 S	18 46 E	57

	° ′	° ′	Page(s)
Ettlingen: Germany F.R.	48 57 N	8 24 E	31B
Etzatlán: Mexico	20 46 N	104 05 W	49A
Euboea *see* Évvoia: *island*, Greece	38 24 N	23 50 E	17, 47
Eugene: Oreg., U.S.A.	44 03 N	123 04 W	67, 87
Eunice: N. Mex., U.S.A.	32 26 N	103 09 W	60G
Euphrates *see* Nahr al Furāt: *dam*, Syria	35 52 N	38 34 E	39
Eureka: Calif., U.S.A.	40 49 N	124 10 W	87
Eureka *Co.*: Nev., U.S.A.	40 00 N	116 20 W	49B
Europoort: Netherlands	51 58 N	4 00 E	58H, 60D, 61D, 61H
Euskirchen: Germany F.R.	50 40 N	6 47 E	29B
Evansville: Ind., U.S.A.	38 00 N	87 33 W	32B, 47, 67A, 87B
Evendale: Ohio, U.S.A.	39 15 N	84 25 W	53
Everett: Mass., U.S.A.	42 23 N	71 03 W	59F
Everett: Wash., U.S.A.	47 59 N	122 14 W	25, 53
Evergreen: Ala., U.S.A.	31 25 N	86 59 W	55
Évvoia (Euboea): *island*, Greece	38 24 N	23 50 E	17, 47
Ewarton: Jamaica	18 11 N	77 05 W	47
Ewekoro: Nigeria	6 54 N	3 20 E	57
Exshaw: Canada	51 07 N	115 08 W	57
Eydehamn: Norway	58 31 N	8 53 E	47

F

	° ′	° ′	Page(s)
Făgăraş: Romania	45 51 N	24 58 E	58, 61D, 61H
Faial: *island*, Azores	38 35 N	28 42 W	84
Fairbanks: Alaska, U.S.A.	64 50 N	147 50 W	87
Fairborn: Ohio, U.S.A.	39 48 N	84 03 W	57B
Fairfield: Ala., U.S.A.	33 29 N	86 59 W	43
Fair Haven: Vt., U.S.A.	43 35 N	73 16 W	32B
Fairless Hills: Pa., U.S.A.	40 10 N	74 53 W	43A
Fairmont: W. Va., U.S.A.	39 28 N	80 08 W	58B
Falconara Marittima: Italy	43 37 N	13 24 E	37H
Falconbridge: Canada	46 35 N	80 48 W	45
Falkenberg: Sweden	56 54 N	12 28 E	32C, 54B
Falling Rock: W. Va., U.S.A.	38 28 N	81 23 W	37J
Fall River: Mass., U.S.A.	41 42 N	71 08 W	31, 32B
Fall River *Co.*: S.D., U.S.A.	43 15 N	103 30 W	40A
Falls City: Texas, U.S.A.	29 00 N	98 02 W	40A
Falun: Sweden	60 36 N	15 38 E	54
Famagusta: Cyprus	35 07 N	33 56 E	84B
Familleureux: Belgium	50 31 N	4 12 E	54B
Fang-ch'eng: China P.R.	21 46 N	108 21 E	50D
Fang-tzu: China P.R.	36 37 N	119 09 E	38C
Fargo: N.D., U.S.A.	46 52 N	96 49 W	67
Farmers Valley: Pa., U.S.A.	41 50 N	78 27 W	37J
Farmingdale: N.Y., U.S.A.	40 44 N	73 26 W	53A
Fáskrúdhsfjördhur: *fjord*, Ice.	64 54 N	13 52 W	27
Fauske: Norway	67 15 N	15 24 E	45
Fawley: England	50 49 N	1 20 W	30B, 37D, 37F, 58D, 58H, 60D, 60H
Fayetteville: Ark., U.S.A.	36 03 N	94 10 W	87C
Fayetteville: N.C., U.S.A.	35 03 N	78 53 W	32B, 60B, 87C
Fécamp: France	49 45 N	0 22 E	27C
Feldkirch: Austria	47 14 N	9 36 E	31B
Felixstowe: England	51 58 N	1 20 E	84C
Fenchuganj: Pakistan	24 42 N	91 57 E	61, 61F
Feng-ch'eng: China P.R.	28 12 N	115 46 E	38
Feng-feng: China P.R.	36 28 N	114 12 E	38C
Feng-man: *dam*, China P.R.	43 43 N	126 41 E	39
Fengtein: Taiwan	23 58 N	121 35 E	48
Fen-hsi: China P.R.	36 38 N	111 31 E	38C
Fergana: U.S.S.R.	40 23 N	71 46 E	31, 36, 61
Fernandina Beach: Fla., U.S.A.	30 30 N	81 26 W	25A
Ferndale: Wash., U.S.A.	48 51 N	122 36 W	36
Ferney-Voltaire: France	46 15 N	6 07 E	62A
Fernley: Nev., U.S.A.	39 36 N	119 14 W	57
Ferrandina: Italy	40 29 N	16 27 E	58H, 59D, 60
Ferrara: Italy	44 50 N	11 35 E	30B, 58H, 60D, 60H, 61D, 61H
Ferrera Erbognone: Italy	45 07 N	8 52 E	37H
Ferreyra: Argentina	31 28 S	64 08 W	54
Ferry *Co.*: Wash., U.S.A.	48 30 N	118 40 W	49
Fessenheim: France	47 55 N	7 32 E	40B
Fethiye: *admin.*, Turkey	36 39 N	29 20 E	50B
Fethiye: Turkey	36 37 N	29 07 E	84B
Feyzin: France	45 40 N	4 51 E	37H, 58D, 58H, 60H
Ffestiniog: *dam*, Wales	52 59 N	3 57 W	39
Fidenza: Italy	44 52 N	10 03 E	58H, 60H
Fieni: Romania	45 08 N	25 25 E	57C
Fier: Albania	40 43 N	19 34 E	61D, 61H
Fifield: Australia	32 48 S	147 28 E	50
Figueira da Foz: Portugal	40 09 N	8 52 W	27B
Filabusi: Rhodesia	20 33 S	29 18 E	50
Filton: England	51 31 N	2 35 W	53B
Fingal: Australia	41 38 S	147 58 E	38
Finley: Wash., U.S.A.	46 04 N	119 04 W	61
Finnart: Scotland	56 07 N	4 50 W	37D
Finowfurt: Germany D.R.	52 51 N	13 41 E	25C
Finsbury: Australia	34 52 S	138 32 E	55
Finsch: *mine*, South Africa	28 00 S	23 00 E	48
Firiza: Romania	47 45 N	23 36 E	46B
Fischamend Dorf: Austria	48 07 N	16 36 E	58H
Fitchburg: Mass., U.S.A.	42 35 N	71 50 W	25D, 31, 60B
Fiumicino: Italy	41 46 N	12 14 E	84A
Fjotland: Norway	58 32 N	7 00 E	50
Fleetwood: England	53 56 N	3 01 W	27C, 59D
Flemington: N.J., U.S.A.	40 31 N	74 52 W	60B
Flers: France	48 45 N	0 34 W	31B
Flinders Range: *mtns.*, Austl.	31 25 S	138 45 E	40
Flin Flon: Canada	54 47 N	101 51 W	45, 46, 49
Flins-sur-Seine: France	48 58 N	1 52 E	55A
Flint: Mich., U.S.A.	43 03 N	83 40 W	55B, 67A, 87B
Flint: Wales	53 15 N	3 07 W	32C
Flix: Spain	41 14 N	0 33 E	59D
Flixborough: England	53 37 N	0 41 W	61D
Flône: Belgium	50 34 N	5 20 E	46B
Florianópolis: Brazil	27 35 S	48 34 W	67
Florida: *admin.*, U.S.A.	28 00 N	82 00 W	16, 27
Florø: Norway	61 36 N	5 00 E	27
Flushing *see* Vlissingen: Neths.	51 27 N	3 35 E	52A
Focşani: Romania	45 42 N	27 11 E	17
Fogelsville: Pa., U.S.A.	40 35 N	75 40 W	57B
Foggia: *admin.*, Italy	41 27 N	15 32 E	47B
Fohnsdorf: Austria	47 12 N	14 41 E	38B
Folkston: Ga., U.S.A.	30 49 N	82 02 W	40, 47, 50
Follonica: Italy	42 55 N	10 45 E	56, 59H
Fontana: Calif., U.S.A.	34 06 N	117 26 W	43, 58
Fontana: *dam*, N.C., U.S.A.	35 30 N	83 56 W	3
Footscray: Australia	37 48 S	144 54 E	58
Forbes Reef: Swaziland	26 10 S	31 05 E	49
Forchheim: Germany F.R.	49 43 N	11 04 E	31B
Fords: N.J., U.S.A.	40 32 N	74 19 W	58B
Fordwick: Va., U.S.A.	38 05 N	79 22 W	57B
Foreman: Ark., U.S.A.	33 43 N	94 24 W	57A
Forest Reserve: *reg.*, Trinidad	10 10 N	61 40 W	35
Forlì: Italy	44 13 N	12 03 E	32C, 60D
Fornovo di Taro: Italy	44 42 N	10 06 E	37H
Fortaleza: Brazil	3 43 S	38 30 W	36, 67, 84, 87
Fort Calhoun: Nebr., U.S.A.	41 26 N	96 01 W	40
Fort Collins: Colo., U.S.A.	40 35 N	105 05 W	57
Fort-Dauphin: *admin.*, Malagasy Republic	24 35 S	47 00 E	47, 50
Fort-de-France: Martinique	14 36 N	61 05 W	84, 87
Fort Dodge: Iowa, U.S.A.	42 31 N	94 10 W	61A
Fort Frances: Canada	48 37 N	93 23 W	25
Fort-Gouraud: Mauritania	22 41 N	12 43 W	43
Fortier: La., U.S.A.	29 55 N	90 11 W	61E
Fort Lauderdale: Fla., U.S.A.	26 08 N	80 08 W	87C
Fort Leonard Wood: Mo., U.S.A.	37 45 N	92 07 W	87C
Fort Madison: Iowa, U.S.A.	40 38 N	91 21 W	59E, 61A, 61E
Fort Myers: Fla., U.S.A.	26 39 N	81 51 W	87C
Fort Pierce: Fla., U.S.A.	27 28 N	80 20 W	40
Fort Randall: *dam*, S.D., U.S.A.	43 03 N	98 34 W	39
Fort Saskatchewan: Canada	53 42 N	113 12 W	32, 59, 61
Fort Smith: Ark., U.S.A.	35 22 N	94 27 W	46, 87C
Fort Stockton: Texas, U.S.A.	30 54 N	102 54 W	56
Fort Washington: Pa., U.S.A.	40 08 N	75 14 W	62
Fort Wayne: Ind., U.S.A.	41 05 N	85 08 W	55B, 67A, 87B
Fort Whyte: Canada	49 49 N	97 30 W	57
Fort William: Canada	48 23 N	89 16 W	25D, 54, 55, 59A
Fort Worth: Texas, U.S.A.	32 45 N	97 20 W	37J, 43, 53, 55, 57A, 59F, 87C
Forūmad: Iran	36 28 N	56 40 E	50
Fo-shan: China P.R.	23 02 N	113 07 E	32
Fosnavåg: Norway	62 21 N	5 39 E	27
Fos-sur-Mer: France	43 26 N	4 57 E	37H, 57C
Fou-hsin: China P.R.	42 04 N	121 44 E	38C
Four Corners: *dam*, N. Mex., U.S.A.	36 43 N	108 12 W	39
Fourmies: France	50 00 N	4 03 E	29B
Frais Marais: France	50 24 N	3 08 E	61H
Frankford: *admin.*, Pa., U.S.A.	40 01 N	75 05 W	58B
Frankfurt am Main: G.F.R.	50 07 N	8 41 E	30B, 58H, 59D, 59H, 61D, 63B, 67B, 87D
Franklin: La., U.S.A.	29 48 N	91 31 W	60G
Franklin: Pa., U.S.A.	41 24 N	79 49 W	37J
Franklin: Va., U.S.A.	36 41 N	76 58 W	25A
Frascati: Italy	41 48 N	12 41 E	17
Fraserburgh: Scotland	57 42 N	2 00 W	27C
Fredericia: Denmark	55 35 N	9 46 E	37B, 37F, 61
Fredericton: Canada	45 57 N	66 40 W	87
Frederikshavn: Denmark	57 26 N	10 32 E	27C, 32C
Fredonia: Kans., U.S.A.	37 32 N	95 50 W	57A
Fredrikssund: Denmark	55 51 N	12 05 E	84
Fredrikstad: Norway	59 13 N	10 57 E	52
Freedom: Pa., U.S.A.	40 40 N	80 18 W	37J
Freehold: N.J., U.S.A.	40 16 N	74 16 W	32B
Freeport: Bahamas	26 30 N	78 47 W	57, 87C
Freeport: Texas, U.S.A.	28 56 N	95 20 W	30A, 50, 58A, 58E, 59B, 60A, 60F, 61C
Freetown: Sierra Leone	8 30 N	13 15 W	36, 67, 84
Freiberg: Germany D.R.	50 55 N	13 22 E	45, 46B
Freiburg im Breisgau: G.F.R.	48 00 N	7 51 E	60D
Freital: Germany D.R.	51 01 N	13 39 E	43B
Fremantle: Australia	32 03 S	115 46 E	84
Fremont: Calif., U.S.A.	37 32 N	121 57 W	61
Fremont: Nebr., U.S.A.	41 26 N	96 30 W	61A, 61E
Fremont *Co.*: Colo., U.S.A.	38 30 N	105 30 W	40A
Fremont *Co.*: Wyo., U.S.A.	43 00 N	109 00 W	40A, 50
Fresnillo de González Echeverría: Mexico	23 10 N	102 53 W	46, 49A
Fresno: Calif., U.S.A.	36 41 N	119 47 W	87A
Fribourg: Switzerland	46 50 N	7 10 E	56A
Friedrichsort: Germany F.R.	54 24 N	10 11 E	54B
Fries: Va., U.S.A.	36 43 N	81 00 W	31A
Friuli: *region*, Italy	46 00 N	13 00 E	17
Frontignan: France	43 27 N	3 45 E	17, 37H
Frontino: *admin.*, Colombia	6 40 N	76 20 W	49
Front Royal: Va., U.S.A.	38 56 N	78 13 W	32B
Frunze: U.S.S.R.	40 07 N	71 44 E	50
Frunze: U.S.S.R.	42 54 N	74 36 E	31, 67
Frýdek-Místek: Czechoslovakia	49 42 N	18 20 E	31B
Fu-chia-t'an: China P.R.	36 45 N	111 40 E	38C
Fu-chien: *admin.*, China P.R.	26 00 N	118 00 E	50, 50D, 59
Fu-chou: China P.R.	26 05 N	119 18 E	25, 32
Fuhūd: Muscat and Oman	22 18 N	56 28 E	34, 37C
Fuji: Japan	35 09 N	138 39 E	32A
Fujieda: Japan	34 52 N	138 16 E	32A
Fujisawa: Japan	35 21 N	139 29 E	32A, 62
Fujiwara: Japan	35 09 N	136 30 E	57D
Fukui: Japan	36 04 N	136 13 E	67C
Fukuoka: Japan	33 35 N	130 24 E	27D, 38C, 67C, 87
Fukushima: Japan	37 45 N	140 28 E	32A, 67C
Fukushima-ken: *admin.*, Japan	37 30 N	140 15 E	40, 49
Fukuyama: Japan	34 29 N	133 22 E	32A
Fu-la-erh-chi: China P.R.	47 15 N	123 40 E	43
Fulnek: Czechoslovakia	49 43 N	17 55 E	29C
Funagawa: Japan	39 53 N	139 51 E	37E
Funchal: Madeira	32 38 N	16 54 W	84
Funil: *dam*, Brazil	22 28 S	44 26 W	39
Funtana Raminosa: Italy	39 55 N	9 11 E	45
Fuquay Springs: N.C., U.S.A.	35 35 N	78 50 W	32B, 60B
Furnas: *dam*, Brazil	20 40 S	46 20 W	39
Furutobe: Japan	40 18 N	140 40 E	45D
Fu-shun: China P.R.	41 52 N	123 53 E	25, 32C, 36, 43, 47, 57, 67
Fusina: Italy	45 25 N	7 51 E	47B
Fyansford: Australia	38 08 S	144 19 E	57
Fyrudden: Sweden	58 10 N	16 50 E	27C

G

	° ′	° ′	Page(s)
Gabbs: Nev., U.S.A.	38 53 N	117 57 W	50
Gabrovo: Bulgaria	42 52 N	25 19 E	31
Gadsden: Ala., U.S.A.	34 00 N	86 00 W	43
Gaeta: Italy	41 12 N	13 35 E	37H
Gaffney: S.C., U.S.A.	35 03 N	81 40 W	31A
Gagliano: *region*, Italy	37 40 N	14 30 E	34, 37B
Gagnon: Canada	51 56 N	68 16 W	43
Gailitz: Austria	46 33 N	13 42 E	46B
Gaillac: France	43 54 N	1 55 E	17
Gainesville: Fla., U.S.A.	29 37 N	82 21 W	87C
Galashiels: Scotland	55 37 N	2 49 W	29B
Galaţi: Romania	45 27 N	28 03 E	52
Galena: Kans., U.S.A.	37 05 N	94 39 W	59E
Galena Park: Texas, U.S.A.	29 44 N	95 16 W	57A
Galicia: *region*, Spain	43 00 N	8 00 W	49
Gallarate: Italy	45 40 N	8 47 E	31B, 53B
Gällivare: Sweden	67 08 N	20 42 E	43
Galt: Canada	43 21 N	80 19 W	29, 32B
Galveston: Texas, U.S.A.	29 17 N	94 48 W	84
Galway: Irish Republic	53 16 N	9 03 W	27C, 84C
Gamagōri: Japan	34 50 N	137 14 E	32A
Gamba: *bay*, Gabon	2 39 S	9 59 E	84
Gambang: Malaysia	3 43 N	103 06 E	45C
Gamlakarleby *see* Kokkola: Finland	63 50 N	23 07 E	56, 59, 61
Gand *see* Gent: Belgium	51 03 N	3 43 E	31B, 37F, 55A, 60H, 67B, 84C
Gander: Canada	48 58 N	54 34 W	87
Ganges *Plain*: India	23 22 N	90 32 E	10, 11, 14, 19
Ganjo Takkar: Pakistan	25 17 N	68 22 E	57
Gansbaai: *bay*, South Africa	34 35 S	19 20 E	27
Gánt: Hungary	47 23 N	18 24 E	47B
Gar': U.S.S.R.	52 35 N	129 08 E	43
Gard: *admin.*, France	44 00 N	4 00 E	38B, 46B, 49
Gardanne: France	43 27 N	5 28 E	47B
Garfield: Utah, U.S.A.	40 44 N	112 11 W	45
Garfield *Co.*: Utah, U.S.A.	37 45 N	111 30 W	40A
Garigliano: Italy	40 03 N	15 29 E	40
Garrison: Barbados	13 05 N	59 36 W	36
Garrison: *dam*, N.D., U.S.A.	47 30 N	101 26 W	39
Gartempe: *river*, France	46 47 N	0 50 E	40B
Garugawa: Japan	43 07 N	141 15 E	49
Garwood: N.J., U.S.A.	40 39 N	74 20 W	25D
Gary: Ind., U.S.A.	41 34 N	87 20 W	43A, 67A
Garzan: *admin.*, Turkey	38 02 N	41 33 E	37A
Garzar-Germik: Turkey	37 18 N	40 18 E	35, 37C
Gas *Hills*: Wyo., U.S.A.	44 00 N	109 00 W	40A
Gastonia: N.C., U.S.A.	35 14 N	81 12 W	31A, 32B
Gateshead: England	54 58 N	1 35 W	32C
Gatineau: Canada	45 29 N	75 40 W	25D, 48
Gatooma: Rhodesia	18 21 S	29 55 E	31, 49, 50
Gauchy: France	49 49 N	3 16 E	32C
Gauhati: India	26 10 N	91 45 E	36, 87
Gaurdak: U.S.S.R.	37 50 N	66 04 E	46, 56
Gavi: Italy	44 41 N	8 49 E	17
Gävle: Sweden	60 40 N	17 10 E	25B, 54, 59
Gaziantep: *admin.*, Turkey	37 00 N	37 20 E	50B
Gbangbama: Sierra Leone	7 42 N	12 19 W	47
Gdańsk (Danzig): Poland	54 22 N	18 38 E	52A, 59H, 84C
Gdynia: Poland	54 31 N	18 30 E	27C, 52A, 84C
Geehi: *dam*, Australia	36 14 S	148 11 E	39
Geelong City: Australia	38 09 S	144 21 E	29, 36, 55, 59, 67
Geismar: La., U.S.A.	30 13 N	91 03 W	30A, 58A, 59B, 61B, 61E
Geita: Tanzania	2 52 S	32 10 E	49
Gela: Italy	37 04 N	14 15 E	37D, 37H, 58, 59D, 59H, 60, 61D, 61H
Geleen: Netherlands	50 58 N	5 45 E	59H, 61D, 61H
Gelsenkirchen: Germany F.R.	51 31 N	7 06 E	37F, 43B, 58D, 58H, 59H, 61D
Gemerská Hôrka: Czech.	48 32 N	20 23 E	25C
Gemlik: Turkey	40 26 N	29 09 E	32, 32C
Gendorf: Germany F.R.	48 11 N	12 44 E	60D
General Pacheco: Argentina	34 28 S	58 38 W	55
General Simón Bolívar: Mexico	24 41 N	103 13 W	49A
Geneva: Utah, U.S.A.	40 19 N	111 45 W	43, 61
Genève: Switzerland	46 13 N	6 09 E	54B, 87D
Génissiat: *dam*, France	46 03 N	5 48 E	39C
Genk: Belgium	50 58 N	5 30 E	55A
Genoa *see* Genova: Italy			
Genova (Genoa): Italy	44 25 N	8 57 E	31B, 37H, 52A, 53B, 54B, 63B, 84A, 87D
Gent (Gand, Ghent): Belgium	51 03 N	3 43 E	31B, 37F, 55A, 60H, 67B, 84C
Gentilly: Canada	46 24 N	72 34 W	40C
Georgetown (Demerara): Guyana	6 46 N	58 10 W	27, 47, 67, 84, 87
Georgetown *see* Penang: Malaysia	5 26 N	100 16 E	67, 84, 87
Georgetown: S.C., U.S.A.	33 23 N	79 18 W	25A, 84
Georgia *see* Gruziya: *reg.*, U.S.S.R.	42 00 N	43 30 E	38
Gepatsch: *dam*, Austria	46 57 N	10 45 E	39C
Gera: Germany D.R.	50 52 N	12 05 E	29C, 67B
Geraldton: Australia	28 46 S	114 36 E	59, 84
Germik: Turkey	37 18 N	40 18 E	37A
Germiston: South Africa	26 15 S	28 10 E	54, 58, 60
Geseke: Germany F.R.	51 39 N	8 31 E	57C
Getafe: Spain	40 18 N	3 43 W	53
Gharībwāl: Pakistan	32 41 N	73 10 E	57
Gharo: Pakistan	24 44 N	67 35 E	59
Ghar Sor: *mtn.*, Pakistan	30 09 N	67 13 E	38
Ghatsila: India	22 36 N	86 34 E	45, 59
Ghawar: *region*, Saudi Arabia	25 30 N	49 30 E	35, 37C
Ghemme: Italy	45 36 N	8 25 E	31B
Ghent *see* Gent: Belgium	51 03 N	3 43 E	31B, 37F, 55A, 60H, 67B, 84C
Gheorghe Gheorghiu-Dej (Oneşti): Romania	46 15 N	26 45 E	37H, 58, 59H, 60H
Ghorāsāl: Pakistan	23 56 N	90 38 E	61, 61F
Giauque Lake: Canada	63 00 N	114 00 W	49
Gibbstown: N.J., U.S.A.	39 50 N	75 18 W	58F, 61B
Gidgealpa: *region*, Australia	28 30 S	140 00 E	34
Gifu: Japan	35 25 N	136 45 E	32A, 53, 67C
Gifu-ken: *admin.*, Japan	35 45 N	137 00 E	40, 50
Gigondas: France	44 10 N	5 00 E	17
Gijón: Spain	43 32 N	5 40 W	43B, 52A, 84A
Gila *Co.*: Ariz., U.S.A.	33 30 N	110 30 W	49B
Gilpin *Co.*: Colo., U.S.A.	39 50 N	105 30 W	50A
Gippsland Shelf: *region*, Austl.	38 30 S	147 30 E	34, 35
Girardot: Colombia	4 18 N	74 48 W	32
Gisborne: New Zealand	38 41 S	178 02 E	87
Giubiasco: Switzerland	46 11 N	9 01 E	54B
Givet: France	50 08 N	4 50 E	32C
Giza *see* Al Jīzah: U.A.R.	30 01 N	31 13 E	67
Gizo: Solomon Is.	8 07 S	156 52 E	84
Glacier Creek: Canada	64 01 N	140 42 W	49
Gladbeck: Germany F.R.	51 34 N	6 59 E	58D, 58H
Gladstone: Australia	23 51 S	151 15 E	45, 61, 84
Glasgow: Scotland	55 53 N	4 15 W	32C, 37B, 52A, 55, 58D, 67, 84C, 87
Glen Canyon: *dam*, Ariz., U.S.A.	36 58 N	111 30 W	39
Glenrothes: Scotland	56 12 N	3 10 W	62
Glens Falls: N.Y., U.S.A.	43 17 N	73 41 W	25D, 57B
Glinik Mariampolski: Poland	49 43 N	20 59 E	37F
Gliwice: Poland	50 20 N	18 40 E	43B
Głogów: Poland	51 40 N	16 06 E	50
Glomfjord: Norway	66 49 N	13 58 E	61
Glostrup: Denmark	55 40 N	12 24 E	46
Gloucester: England	51 53 N	2 14 W	32C, 54B
Glubokoye: U.S.S.R.	50 06 N	82 19 E	45, 49
Głuszyca: Poland	50 41 N	16 22 E	31B
Goa: *admin.*, India	15 30 N	74 00 E	27, 43, 50
Godorf: Germany F.R.	50 51 N	6 59 E	37F, 58D
Godthaab: Greenland	64 10 N	51 40 W	40
Gogebic Range: *deposit*, Mich./Wis., U.S.A.	46 45 N	89 25 W	43, 43A
Goi: Japan	35 31 N	140 05 E	30, 58G, 59G, 60C, 60E
Goiânia: Brazil	16 40 S	49 16 W	67, 87
Goiás: *admin.*, Brazil	12 00 S	48 00 W	48
Gokak: India	16 13 N	74 54 E	31C
Gökçekaya: *dam*, Turkey	40 02 N	31 18 E	39
Golden: Colo., U.S.A.	39 45 N	105 15 W	56

	° ′	° ′	*Page(s)*
Goldsworthy, *Mount*: Austl.	20 21 S	119 32 E	43
Golfito: Costa Rica	8 38 N	83 11 W	84
Gölzau: Germany D.R.	51 39 N	12 05 E	37F
Gomel': U.S.S.R.	52 25 N	31 00 E	25, 32C, 59
Gonfreville-l'Orcher: France	49 30 N	0 14 E	37F, 58D, 58H, 60D, 60H, 61D
Gōnome: Japan	37 44 N	140 28 E	31
Goodnews Bay: Alaska, U.S.A.	59 06 N	161 38 W	49
Gora Kachkanar: *mtn.*, U.S.S.R.	58 47 N	59 23 E	50
Gorakhpur: India	26 45 N	83 23 E	61F
Gora Tyuya-Muyun: *mtn.*, U.S.S.R.	40 25 N	72 12 E	40
Goražde: Yugoslavia	43 40 N	18 59 E	58H
Gordon: *dam*, Australia	42 35 S	146 24 E	39
Gordonsbaai: *bay*, South Africa	34 10 S	18 52 E	27
Goregaon: India	19 08 N	72 50 E	32
Gorham: N.H., U.S.A.	44 23 N	71 11 W	25D
Gori: U.S.S.R.	41 58 N	44 07 E	31
Gorizia: Italy	45 57 N	13 38 E	32C
Gor'kiy: *dam*, U.S.S.R.	56 40 N	43 30 E	39
Gor'kiy: U.S.S.R.	56 20 N	44 00 E	29, 36, 43, 52, 55, 67
Gorlice: Poland	49 40 N	21 09 E	37D
Gorodok: U.S.S.R.	50 23 N	103 17 E	50
Gorzów Wielkopolski: Poland	52 42 N	15 12 E	32C, 60D
Goslar: Germany F.R.	51 54 N	10 26 E	46B
Gosselies: Belgium	50 28 N	4 25 E	53B
Göteborg: Sweden	57 43 N	11 58 E	25B, 27C, 29, 31, 37B, 37H, 52, 55, 58, 67, 84C, 87
Govora: Romania	45 04 N	24 14 E	59D
Gowganda: Canada	47 39 N	80 46 W	49
Goyllarisquizga: Peru	10 31 S	76 24 W	38
Gozzano: Italy	45 45 N	8 26 E	32C, 60D
Gracesputs: *mine*, South Africa	29 43 S	17 03 E	48
Grafton: Mass., U.S.A.	42 13 N	71 40 W	32B
Gramercy: La., U.S.A.	30 00 N	90 42 W	47A, 59B
Granada: *admin.*, Spain	37 15 N	3 15 W	43
Grand Coulee: *dam*, Wash., U.S.A.	47 59 N	118 58 W	39A
Grand *Co.*: Utah, U.S.A.	39 00 N	109 30 W	40A
Grand-Couronne: France	49 21 N	1 00 E	25C, 61D, 61H
Grande Dixence: *dam*, Switzerland	46 05 N	7 25 E	39C
Grande Maison: *dam*, France	45 03 N	6 08 E	39C
Grand Falls: Canada	48 57 N	55 40 W	25
Grand Fork: N.D., U.S.A.	47 57 N	97 05 W	87
Grand Junction: Colo., U.S.A.	39 04 N	108 33 W	36, 40A
Grand-Lahou: Ivory Coast	5 08 N	5 01 W	50
Grand'Mère: Canada	46 36 N	72 41 W	31
Grandpuits: France	48 35 N	2 58 E	37F
Grand Rapids: *dam*, Canada	53 10 N	99 15 W	39
Grand Rapids: Mich., U.S.A.	42 57 N	86 40 W	67A, 87B
Grangemouth: Scotland	56 01 N	3 44 W	30B, 37F, 58H, 60, 84C
Grängesberg: Sweden	60 05 N	14 59 E	43
Granite City: Ill., U.S.A.	38 43 N	90 04 W	43A, 58B
Granite *Co.*: Mont., U.S.A.	46 20 N	113 30 W	49
Graniteville: S.C., U.S.A.	33 34 N	81 48 W	31A
Grant *Co.*: N. Mex., U.S.A.	33 00 N	108 30 W	46, 49B, 50
Grants: N. Mex., U.S.A.	35 10 N	107 51 W	40A, 50A
Gravesend: England	51 27 N	0 24 E	25C
Grays Harbor: *bay*, Wash., U.S.A.	46 56 N	124 05 W	84
Graz: Austria	47 04 N	15 27 E	55A
Great Falls: Mont., U.S.A.	47 30 N	111 16 W	36, 45, 46A, 87
Greatham: England	54 39 N	1 14 W	43B
Great Salt *Lake*: Utah, U.S.A.	41 00 N	112 30 W	56
Great Valley: Pa., U.S.A.	40 03 N	75 12 W	62
Green Bay: Wis., U.S.A.	44 32 N	88 00 W	25D, 87B
Greenbushes: Australia	33 51 S	116 03 E	45
Greencastle: Ind., U.S.A.	39 39 N	86 51 W	57B
Greencastle: Irish Republic	55 12 N	6 59 W	27C
Greenfield: England	53 33 N	2 00 W	29B
Greenfield Park: Canada	45 28 N	73 29 W	62
Greenhithe: England	51 28 N	0 17 E	57C
Greenlee *Co.*: Ariz., U.S.A.	33 25 N	109 00 W	49B
Greenock: Scotland	55 57 N	4 45 W	29B, 52A, 62, 84C
Green River: Wyo., U.S.A.	41 33 N	109 27 W	59
Greensboro: N.C., U.S.A.	36 03 N	79 50 W	31A, 87C
Greenville: Pa., U.S.A.	41 24 N	80 24 W	54A
Greenville: S.C., U.S.A.	34 52 N	82 25 W	29, 31A, 32B, 59F, 60B
Greenwood: Canada	49 08 N	118 41 W	45, 49
Greenwood: S.C., U.S.A.	34 11 N	82 10 W	31A, 32B, 60B
Greffern: Germany F.R.	48 45 N	8 00 E	30B
Greiz: Germany D.R.	50 39 N	12 12 E	25C
Grenå: Denmark	56 25 N	10 53 E	61D, 61H
Grenoble: France	45 10 N	5 43 E	32C
Gresik: Indonesia	7 09 S	112 28 E	57, 59, 61
Greve: Italy	43 35 N	11 19 E	57C
Greven: Germany F.R.	52 06 N	7 37 E	31B
Grevenbroich: Germany F.R.	51 05 N	6 35 E	47B
Grey: New Zealand	42 27 S	171 12 E	38
Greystone: R.I., U.S.A.	41 52 N	71 30 W	29
Griffin: Ga., U.S.A.	33 15 N	84 17 W	31A
Grimsby: England	53 35 N	0 05 W	25C, 27C, 30B, 32C, 84C
Grindavík: Iceland	63 50 N	22 26 W	27

	° ′	° ′	*Page(s)*
Griqualand, West: *region*, South Africa	28 40 S	23 30 W	48
Gröditz: Germany D.R.	51 25 N	13 27 E	43B
Grodno: U.S.S.R.	53 41 N	23 50 E	61D
Grodziec: Poland	50 21 N	19 04 E	57C
Gronau: Germany F.R.	52 12 N	7 02 E	29B, 31B
Groningen: *admin.*, Neths.	53 15 N	6 45 E	37B
Groningen: Netherlands	53 13 N	6 35 E	67B
Grono: Switzerland	46 15 N	9 09 E	58D
Groote Eylandt: *island*, Austl.	14 00 S	136 40 E	50
Grossauheim: Germany F.R.	50 06 N	8 57 E	60H
Groszowice: Poland	50 38 N	17 57 E	57C
Groton: Conn., U.S.A.	41 22 N	72 05 W	52
Groves: Texas, U.S.A.	29 57 N	93 55 W	58E
Groznyy: U.S.S.R.	43 20 N	45 42 E	36, 58
Grums: Sweden	59 21 N	13 06 E	25B
Grünbach: Austria	47 47 N	15 59 E	38B
Gruzinskaya S.S.R.: *admin.*, U.S.S.R.	42 00 N	43 30 E	27
Gruziya (Georgia): *reg.*, U.S.S.R.	42 00 N	43 30 E	38
Gryfów Śląski: Poland	51 02 N	15 25 E	31B
Guadalajara: Mexico	20 40 N	103 20 W	57, 59, 62, 67, 87
Guadalupe: Mexico	22 45 N	102 31 W	49A
Guamo: Colombia	4 02 N	74 58 W	36
Guanabara: *admin.*, Brazil	22 55 S	43 30 W	27, 67
Guanaceví: Mexico	25 56 N	105 57 W	49A
Guanajuato: Mexico	21 01 N	101 15 W	49A
Guánica: Puerto Rico	17 58 N	66 55 W	59, 61
Guarapari: Brazil	20 40 S	40 30 W	40, 50
Guarda: *admin.*, Portugal	40 40 N	7 10 W	50
Guardo: Spain	42 47 N	4 50 W	59D
Guayacán: Chile	29 58 S	71 22 W	84
Guayama: Puerto Rico	17 59 N	66 07 W	58, 60
Guayamas: Mexico	27 56 N	110 54 W	84
Guayanilla: Puerto Rico	18 01 N	66 47 W	36, 58
Guayaquil: Ecuador	2 10 S	79 50 W	55, 56, 67, 84, 87
Guaymas: Mexico	27 56 N	110 54 W	61
Guazapares: Mexico	27 22 N	108 15 W	49A
Gubakha: U.S.S.R.	58 52 N	57 36 E	61
Guben: *admin.*, Germany D.R.	51 55 N	14 35 E	37D
Guben: Germany D.R.	51 57 N	14 43 E	32C, 60D
Gudermes: U.S.S.R.	43 21 N	46 06 E	30
Guebwiller: France	47 55 N	7 12 E	31B
Guelph: Canada	43 34 N	80 16 W	32B
Güera: Spanish Sahara	20 50 N	17 06 W	27
Guernsey: *island*, Channel Is.	49 27 N	2 35 W	87
Guerrero: *admin.*, Mexico	17 40 N	100 00 W	49A, 50
Gueugnon: France	46 36 N	4 04 E	40B
Gufunes: Iceland	64 09 N	21 49 W	61
Guildford: England	51 14 N	0 35 W	55A
Guilvinec: France	47 47 N	4 17 W	27
Guiseley: England	53 53 N	1 42 W	29B
Gujarat: *admin.*, India	23 00 N	72 00 E	27
Gulbarga: India	17 22 N	76 47 E	31C
Guleman: Turkey	38 25 N	39 54 E	50
Gulf of Suez *see* Khalīj as Suways: *region*, U.A.R.	28 10 N	33 27 E	35
Gumpoldskirchen: Austria	48 03 N	16 17 E	17
Gundreimmingen: G.F.R.	48 30 N	10 24 E	40B
Gunnison *Co.*: Colo., U.S.A.	38 40 N	107 00 W	49B
Guri: *dam*, Venezuela	7 39 N	62 50 W	39
Guripan: Philippines	7 50 N	123 20 E	45
Gur'yev: U.S.S.R.	47 07 N	51 53 E	35, 36, 60, 67
Gusinoozërsk: U.S.S.R.	51 17 N	106 30 E	38
Guyra: Australia	30 14 S	151 40 E	50
Gwalior: India	26 12 N	78 09 E	31
Gwelo: *admin.*, Rhodesia	19 10 S	29 30 E	49
Gyöngyös: Hungary	47 47 N	19 56 E	17
Gyöngyösoroszi: Hungary	47 50 N	19 54 E	46B
Győr: Hungary	47 41 N	17 38 E	29C, 54B

H

	° ′	° ′	*Page(s)*
Haarlem: Netherlands	52 23 N	4 38 E	67B
Hachinohe: Japan	40 30 N	141 29 E	27D, 57D, 59G, 61C
Haddam Neck: Conn., U.S.A.	41 31 N	72 31 W	40C
Haenam: South Korea	34 34 N	126 36 E	38C
Ha-erh-pin (Harbin): China P.R.	45 45 N	126 39 E	25, 32, 67
Hafendorf: Austria	47 27 N	15 19 E	58H
Hafnarfjördhur: Iceland	64 04 N	21 57 W	27
Hagerstown: Md., U.S.A.	39 39 N	77 44 W	53A, 57B
Hagondange: France	49 15 N	6 10 E	43B
Hai-ch'eng: China P.R.	40 52 N	122 45 E	50
Haidhof: Germany F.R.	49 41 N	11 13 E	43B
Haifa: Israel	32 49 N	34 59 E	27, 31, 37G, 57, 58, 59, 60, 61, 84B
Hai Phong: North Vietnam	20 52 N	106 41 E	45, 57, 84
Hakodate: Japan	41 45 N	140 43 E	27D, 37E, 52B, 59G, 67, 84D
Ḥalab (Aleppo): Syria	36 12 N	37 10 E	57, 67
Ḥalā'ib: Sudan	22 13 N	36 38 E	50
Halar: *admin.*, India	22 15 N	70 00 E	47
Halden: Norway	59 09 N	11 23 E	25B, 29
Haldi: *river*, India	22 00 N	88 00 E	58
Haley: Canada	45 34 N	76 47 W	40C, 50
Halifax: Canada	44 38 N	63 35 W	67, 84, 87

	° ′	° ′	*Page(s)*
Halifax: England	53 44 N	1 52 W	29B
Halimba: Hungary	47 02 N	17 32 E	47B
Halle: *admin.*, Germany D.R.	51 30 N	12 00 E	38B
Halle: Germany D.R.	51 30 N	12 00 E	25C, 67B
Hallein: Austria	47 41 N	13 06 E	60D
Hällekis: Sweden	58 38 N	13 25 E	57
Ḥalq al Wādī: Tunisia	36 49 N	10 18 E	84A
Hälsingborg: Sweden	56 03 N	12 42 E	59H, 84C
Hälsingland: *reg.*, Sweden	61 30 N	17 00 E	48
Hamada: Japan	34 53 N	132 05 E	27D
Hamamatsu: Japan	34 42 N	137 44 E	57D, 67C
Ḥamāṭah, Jabal: *mtn.*, U.A.R.	24 12 N	35 00 E	50
Hamble: England	50 52 N	1 19 W	53B
Hamburg: *admin.*, G.F.R.	53 35 N	10 00 E	56A
Hamburg: Germany F.R.	53 33 N	10 00 E	27C, 32C, 37B, 37F, 45, 46, 52A, 53B, 55A, 58H, 59H, 60H, 67B, 84C, 87
Hämeenlinna: Finland	61 00 N	24 27 E	55
Hamel: Minn., U.S.A.	45 03 N	93 30 W	62
Hamgyŏng-pukto: *admin.*, North Korea	41 45 N	129 50 E	38C
Hamhŭng: North Korea	39 54 N	127 32 E	59
Ha-mi: China P.R.	42 48 N	93 27 E	38, 43
Hamilton: Bermuda	32 18 N	64 48 W	84
Hamilton: Canada	43 15 N	79 50 W	29, 31, 43A, 54A, 55A, 59A, 59E, 60F, 67A
Hamilton: Ohio, U.S.A.	39 23 N	84 33 W	25D, 59E, 67A
Hamina: Finland	60 34 N	27 12 E	25B
Hammerfest: Norway	70 40 N	23 42 E	27
Hammond: Ind., U.S.A.	41 37 N	87 30 W	37J, 59E, 61A
Hana: Hawaii, U.S.A.	20 45 N	155 59 E	87
Hanaoka: Japan	40 15 N	140 20 E	45D
Hanasaki-Misaki: *pen.*, Japan	43 17 N	145 36 E	27D
Hanawa: Japan	40 11 N	140 47 E	45D
Hancock: Mich., U.S.A.	47 08 N	88 34 W	45
HaNegev (Negev): *desert*, Israel	30 45 N	34 50 E	59
Hanford: Calif., U.S.A.	36 19 N	119 39 W	36
Hang-chou: China P.R.	30 15 N	120 10 E	25
Hangha: Sierra Leone	7 56 N	11 09 W	50
Han-K'ou: China P.R.	30 35 N	114 16 E	43
Hannibal: Mo., U.S.A.	39 41 N	91 20 W	57, 61E
Hannover: Germany F.R.	52 22 N	9 43 E	55A, 56, 59D, 67B, 87D
Ha Noi: North Vietnam	21 02 N	105 51 E	67
Hao-kang: China P.R.	47 24 N	130 22 E	38
Hao-pi: China P.R.	35 57 N	114 13 E	38C
Harajuku: Japan	35 54 N	139 21 E	57D
Harbin *see* Ha-erh-pin: China P.R.	45 45 N	126 39 E	25, 32, 67
Hard: Austria	47 29 N	9 41 E	29C
Harding *Co.*: S.D., U.S.A.	45 30 N	103 30 W	40A
Haren: Belgium	50 53 N	4 25 E	53B
Harjavalta: Finland	61 19 N	22 08 E	45, 59
Harleyville: S.C., U.S.A.	33 14 N	80 26 W	57B
Harlingen: Netherlands	53 10 N	5 25 E	27C
Harlingerode: Germany F.R.	51 55 N	10 31 E	46B
Harmony: South Africa	28 06 S	26 52 E	40
Harnes: France	50 27 N	2 54 E	58H, 61D
Haro: Spain	42 35 N	2 51 W	17
Harøya: *island*, Norway	62 45 N	6 27 E	27
Harøysund: Norway	62 52 N	6 57 E	27
Harrisburg: Pa., U.S.A.	40 17 N	76 54 W	87B
Harrsele: *dam*, Sweden	63 57 N	19 25 E	39
Harsprånget: *dam*, Sweden	66 52 N	19 49 E	39
Harstad: Norway	68 47 N	16 33 E	27
Hart *Co.*: Ga., U.S.A.	34 18 N	83 00 W	48
Hartebeestfontein: South Africa	26 52 S	26 39 E	40
Hartford: Conn., U.S.A.	41 45 N	72 42 W	87B
Hartford: Ill., U.S.A.	38 48 N	90 06 W	37J
Harts Range: *mtns.*, Australia	23 10 S	134 50 E	48
Hartsville: S.C., U.S.A.	34 23 N	80 05 W	25A, 40
Hartuv: Israel	31 45 N	35 00 E	57
Hartwell: *dam*, Ga., U.S.A.	34 22 N	82 57 W	39
Harwich: England	51 57 N	1 17 E	84C
Hasaki: Japan	35 44 N	140 50 E	27D
Hasan Ugurlli: *dam*, Turkey	41 00 N	30 15 E	39
Hassan: *admin.*, India	13 01 N	76 03 E	48, 50
Hassi-Messaoud: Algeria	31 52 N	5 43 E	35, 36, 37D
Hassi-R'Mel: Algeria	32 52 N	3 12 E	34, 37B
Hastings: Nebr., U.S.A.	40 37 N	98 22 W	61A
Hatfield: England	51 46 N	0 13 W	53B, 53C
Hathras: India	27 36 N	78 02 E	31
Hatton: England	52 52 N	1 40 W	54B
Haugesund: Norway	59 25 N	5 18 E	27C, 52
Hauts-de-Seine: *admin.*, France	45 50 N	2 10 E	53B
Havana *see* La Habana: Cuba	23 08 N	82 22 W	25, 35, 36, 67, 84, 87
Havant: England	50 51 N	0 59 W	62A
Havelock: Swaziland	25 58 S	31 08 E	48
Haverhill: Ohio, U.S.A.	38 40 N	82 50 W	58F
Haverton Hill: England	54 36 N	1 14 W	52A
Havré: Belgium	50 28 N	4 02 E	58D
Hawaii: *admin.*, U.S.A.	19 30 N	155 30 W	27
Hawarden: Wales	53 11 N	3 02 W	58H
Hawick: Scotland	55 25 N	2 47 W	29B
Hawston: South Africa	34 24 S	19 08 E	27
Hawthorne: Calif., U.S.A.	33 56 N	122 38 W	53
Hayden: Ariz., U.S.A.	33 01 N	110 48 W	45A, 59

	° ′	° ′	*Page(s)*
Hazaribagh: India	24 00 N	85 23 E	48
Hazlehurst: Ga., U.S.A.	31 53 N	82 34 W	32B
Hebronville: Mass., U.S.A.	41 54 N	71 18 W	58
Hedaru: Tanzania	4 30 S	37 54 E	48
Heerlen: Netherlands	50 53 N	5 59 E	58D
Heide: Germany F.R.	54 12 N	9 06 E	37F, 58D, 58H
Heidebreck *see* Kędzierzyn: Poland	50 20 N	18 12 E	61D, 61H
Heidelberg: South Africa	26 31 S	28 21 E	49
Heilbronn: Germany F.R.	49 08 N	9 13 E	55A
Hei-lung-chiang: *admin.*, China P.R.	48 00 N	128 00 E	49
Heinola: Finland	61 13 N	26 02 E	25B
Hei-shan: China P.R.	41 40 N	122 03 E	50
Helena: Ark., U.S.A.	34 30 N	90 35 W	61B, 61E
Heliopolis *see* Miṣr al Jadīdah: U.A.R.	30 06 N	31 20 E	53
Hells Canyon: *dam*, Oreg., U.S.A.	45 18 N	116 37 W	39A
Helm: Calif., U.S.A.	36 31 N	120 09 W	59, 61
Helmstedt: Germany F.R.	52 14 N	11 00 E	38B
Helsinki: Finland	61 10 N	24 58 E	52, 54, 55, 58, 84, 87
Hematite: Mo., U.S.A.	38 10 N	90 29 W	40C
Héming: France	48 42 N	6 57 E	57C
Hemmoor: Germany F.R.	53 42 N	9 07 E	57C
Henderson: Nev., U.S.A.	36 01 N	115 00 W	59, 61A, 61E
Hengelo: Netherlands	52 16 N	6 46 E	31B, 32C
Hennigsdorf: Germany D.R.	52 38 N	13 12 E	43B, 54B
Henningsvaer: Norway	68 09 N	14 13 E	27
Henry: Ill., U.S.A.	41 07 N	89 23 W	60B
Henryetta: Okla., U.S.A.	35 27 N	96 00 W	46
Henry, *Point*: Australia	38 08 S	144 26 E	47
Hérault: *admin.*, France	43 40 N	3 30 E	38B, 47B
Herberton: Australia	17 24 S	145 23 E	45
Hercules: Calif., U.S.A.	38 01 N	122 17 W	36, 61
Hermanus: South Africa	34 25 S	19 14 E	27
Hermosillo: Mexico	29 04 N	110 58 W	49A, 67
Hernani: Spain	43 16 N	1 58 W	59D, 60D
Herøya: Norway	59 07 N	9 38 E	50, 58, 59, 60, 61
Herrenwyk: Germany F.R.	53 54 N	10 48 E	45
Herstal: Belgium	50 40 N	5 38 E	53B
Herten: Netherlands	51 11 N	5 59 E	59D
Hessen: *admin.*, Germany F.R.	50 30 N	9 15 E	38B, 56A, 58D
Heysham: England	54 02 N	2 54 W	37F, 40B, 58H, 61D, 61H
Hibi: Japan	34 27 N	133 55 E	45
Hickok: Kans., U.S.A.	37 34 N	101 14 W	60G
Hicksville: N.Y., U.S.A.	40 47 N	73 32 W	30A
Hidalgo *Co.*: N. Mex., U.S.A.	32 00 N	108 30 W	49B
Hidalgo del Parral: Mexico	26 56 N	105 40 W	45, 46, 49A
Hiendelaencina: Spain	41 05 N	3 00 W	49
Highland *Valley*: Canada	50 20 N	121 20 W	45
High Mountain Sheep: *dam*, Idaho, U.S.A.	45 51 N	116 50 W	39A
Higüero, Punta: *point*, Puerto Rico	18 22 N	67 16 W	40
Hikone: Japan	35 15 N	136 15 E	29D, 57D
Hikoshima: Japan	34 00 N	130 57 E	46C
Hillerød: Denmark	55 56 N	12 19 E	55
Hillhouse: England	53 56 N	2 50 W	60D
Hillington: Scotland	55 48 N	4 15 W	53
Hilo: Hawaii, U.S.A.	19 44 N	155 05 E	87
Himeji: Japan	34 49 N	134 42 E	43D, 58C, 58G, 61C
Himi: Japan	36 51 N	136 59 E	27D
Ḥimṣ: Syria	34 44 N	36 43 E	61
Hindīyah Barrage: Iraq	32 43 N	44 18 E	57
Hindley Green: England	53 31 N	2 33 W	32C
Hindubāgh: Pakistan	30 49 N	67 45 E	50
Hinganghat: India	20 32 N	78 52 E	31C
Hinkley Point *Atomic Energy Station*: England	51 12 N	3 09 W	40B
Hinode: Japan	35 45 N	139 14 E	57D
Hinojosa: *dam*, Spain	40 59 N	6 47 W	39
Hirakud: *dam*, India	21 32 N	83 55 E	39
Hirasawa: Japan	39 17 N	139 58 E	37E
Hirase: Japan	36 10 N	137 00 E	50
Hirohata: Japan	34 48 N	134 38 E	43D, 58C, 59G
Hirose: Japan	35 22 N	133 10 E	50
Hiroshima: Japan	34 24 N	132 27 E	32A, 52B, 55, 56, 67C
Hirtshals: Denmark	57 35 N	9 58 E	27C
Hissar: India	29 10 N	75 45 E	31
Hitachi: Japan	36 36 N	140 39 E	45D, 54C, 57D, 59G
Hiyama: Japan	40 10 N	140 07 E	50
Hobart: Australia	42 55 S	147 20 E	3, 67, 84
Hobbs: N. Mex., U.S.A.	32 42 N	103 08 W	59
Hoboken: Belgium	51 10 N	4 21 E	46B, 52A
Hochfilzen: Austria	47 28 N	12 37 E	50B
Höchst: Germany F.R.	50 06 N	8 33 E	58H, 59D, 60D, 61H
Hodge: La., U.S.A.	32 18 N	92 42 W	25A
Hoedjiesbaai: *bay*, S. Africa	32 50 S	17 55 E	27
Hof: Germany F.R.	50 19 N	11 55 E	31B
Ho-fei: China P.R.	31 51 N	117 17 E	43, 47, 57
Höganäs: Sweden	56 12 N	12 33 E	38B
Hogatzu: *river*, Alaska, U.S.A.	66 12 N	154 20 W	49
Ho-hsien: China P.R.	24 25 N	111 31 E	50D
Ho-hsien: China P.R.	36 35 N	111 44 E	38C

	° ′	° ′	*Page(s)*
Hokkaidō: *island*, Japan	44 00 N	143 00 E	**50, 59, 61**
Ho Lao-ha: *river*, China P.R.	43 24 N	120 39 E	**38**
Holbu: *dam*, Norway	62 32 N	8 28 E	**39**
Hollidaysburg: Pa., U.S.A.	40 26 N	78 24 W	**54A**
Hollywood: Fla., U.S.A.	26 01 N	80 09 W	**62**
Holme upon Spalding Moor: England	53 51 N	0 46 W	**53B**
Holt: Ala., U.S.A.	33 14 N	87 30 W	**37J**
Holthausen: Germany F.R.	52 33 N	7 17 E	**58D**
Holyoke: Mass., U.S.A.	42 12 N	72 37 W	**25D**
Holyrood: Canada	47 24 N	53 10 W	**36**
Holywell: Wales	53 17 N	3 13 W	**32C, 59H**
Homberg: Germany F.R.	51 28 N	6 43 E	**58D, 59H**
Homer: N.Y., U.S.A.	42 39 N	76 11 W	**32B**
Hondo: Japan	36 03 N	133 08 E	**38**
Hondō: Japan	33 13 N	133 11 E	**38**
Hønefoss: Norway	60 10 N	10 18 E	**25B**
Hon Gai: North Vietnam	20 57 N	107 05 E	**38**
Honiara: Solomon Is.	9 28 S	159 52 E	**84**
Honningsvåg: Norway	70 59 N	25 59 E	**27**
Honolulu: Hawaii, U.S.A.	21 19 N	157 50 W	**36, 67, 84, 87**
Hoogezand: Netherlands	53 10 N	6 45 E	**25C, 32C**
Hoover: *dam*, Ariz./Nev., U.S.A.	36 01 N	114 45 W	**39**
Hope: Canada	49 21 N	121 28 W	**50**
Hope: England	53 22 N	1 45 W	**57C**
Hopeh *see* T'ang-shan: China P.R.	39 38 N	118 11 E	**43, 57**
Hopewell: Va., U.S.A.	37 17 N	77 19 W	**25A, 32B, 59B, 60B, 61A**
Hopton: England	53 03 N	1 34 W	**50**
Hoquiam: Wash., U.S.A.	46 59 N	123 55 W	**25**
Hörde: Germany F.R.	51 29 N	7 30 E	**43B**
Hornby: New Zealand	43 33 S	172 32 E	**59**
Horobetsu: Japan	44 05 N	145 01 E	**59**
Horst: Germany F.R.	51 32 N	7 02 E	**58D**
Horten: Norway	59 25 N	10 30 E	**52**
Ho-shan: China P.R.	22 19 N	110 16 E	**38**
Hosokura: Japan	38 40 N	141 00 E	**46C, 59G**
Hososhima: Japan	32 26 N	131 40 E	**84D**
Hosston: La., U.S.A.	32 52 N	93 53 W	**37J**
Hostotipaquillo: Mexico	21 04 N	104 04 W	**49A**
Ho-t'ien (Khotan): China P.R.	37 07 N	79 55 E	**29**
Hot Springs: Ark., U.S.A.	34 30 N	93 02 W	**87C**
Houston: Texas, U.S.A.	29 45 N	95 25 W	**25, 30A, 35, 37J, 43, 56, 57A, 58A, 58E, 59B, 59F, 60A, 60G, 61B, 84, 87C**
Houtbaai: *bay*, South Africa	34 03 S	18 21 E	**27**
Howellville: Pa., U.S.A.	40 04 N	75 08 W	**62**
Howes Cave: N.Y., U.S.A.	42 41 N	74 23 W	**57B**
Howrah: India	22 35 N	88 20 E	**31, 54**
Howth: Irish Republic	53 23 N	6 04 W	**27C**
Høyanger: Norway	61 13 N	6 05 E	**47**
Hoyle: Canada	48 35 N	81 03 W	**59**
Hranice: Czechoslovakia	49 34 N	17 45 E	**57C**
Hronov: Czechoslovakia	50 29 N	16 11 E	**31B**
Hrvatska (Croatia): *admin.*, Yugoslavia	45 10 N	15 30 E	**38B**
Hsia-hua-yüan: China P.R.	40 30 N	115 15 E	**38C**
Hsia-men (Amoy): China P.R.	24 27 N	118 05 E	**32, 84**
Hsi-an: China P.R.	34 16 N	108 54 E	**29, 31, 43, 46, 67**
Hsiang-t'an: China P.R.	27 51 N	112 54 E	**50D**
Hsien-kang: China P.R.	38 54 N	112 25 E	**38C**
Hsien-yang: China P.R.	34 22 N	108 42 E	**29**
Hsin-an: *dam*, China P.R.	29 29 N	119 13 E	**39**
Hsin-chiang-wei-wu-erh (Sinkiang Uighur): *admin.*, China P.R.	42 00 N	86 00 E	**49**
Hsin-chu: *basin*, Taiwan	24 50 N	121 30 E	**35**
Hsin-chu: Taiwan	24 48 N	120 58 E	**59, 60, 61**
Hsin-hua: China P.R.	27 45 N	111 18 E	**50D**
Hsi-ning (Chinghai): China P.R.	36 37 N	101 46 E	**29, 43, 67**
Hsin-t'ai: China P.R.	35 54 N	117 44 E	**38C**
Hsi-shan: China P.R.	37 52 N	112 33 E	**38C**
Hsiu-wen: China P.R.	26 51 N	106 35 E	**47**
Hsi-wan: China P.R.	24 29 N	111 39 E	**45**
Hsü-chou (Süchow): China P.R.	34 16 N	117 11 E	**38C**
Huachipato: Chile	36 45 S	73 07 W	**43**
Huacho: Peru	11 14 S	77 35 W	**27A**
Huahuaxtla: Mexico	19 55 N	97 37 W	**50**
Huai-nan: China P.R.	32 40 N	117 00 E	**38C**
Hua-lien: Taiwan	23 58 N	121 36 E	**61**
Huancavelica: *admin.*, Peru	13 00 S	75 00 W	**46, 49**
Huancavelica: Peru	12 45 S	75 03 W	**50**
Huang-chin-k'ou: China P.R.	30 00 N	105 00 E	**38**
Huang-shih: China P.R.	30 13 N	115 06 E	**45**
Huánuco: *admin.*, Peru	9 55 S	76 14 W	**46, 49**
Huanuni: Bolivia	18 16 S	66 51 W	**45**
Huarmey: Peru	10 03 S	78 08 W	**27A**
Huaron: Peru	11 03 S	76 24 W	**45**
Huasco: Chile	28 28 S	71 14 W	**84**
Hua-tien: China P.R.	42 56 N	126 42 E	**36**
Hubbell: Mich., U.S.A.	47 10 N	88 27 W	**45**
Hubli: India	15 20 N	75 14 E	**67**
Hucknall Torkard: England	53 02 N	1 11 W	**53B**
Huddersfield: England	53 39 N	1 47 W	**29B, 59H, 61H**
Hudson: N.Y., U.S.A.	42 15 N	73 47 W	**57B**
Hue: South Vietnam	16 28 N	107 36 E	**67**
Huelva: *admin.*, Spain	37 40 N	7 00 W	**49, 56**

	° ′	° ′	*Page(s)*
Huelva: Spain	37 16 N	6 57 W	**27B, 36, 45, 58, 59, 61D, 61H**
Huemul, Cerro: *mtn.*, Arg.	35 45 S	69 39 W	**40**
Huesca: *admin.*, Spain	42 10 N	0 10 W	**38B**
Hugoton: Kans., U.S.A.	37 11 N	101 22 W	**34**
Hu-ho-hao-t'e: China P.R.	40 47 N	111 37 E	**55, 59**
Huinco: *dam*, Peru	11 52 S	76 45 W	**39**
Hui-tse: China P.R.	26 21 N	103 25 E	**45**
Hull: Canada	45 26 N	75 45 W	**25D**
Hull (Kingston upon Hull): Eng.	53 45 N	0 20 W	**27C, 58D, 67B, 84C**
Hu-lu-tao: China P.R.	40 43 N	121 00 E	**46**
Ḩulwān: United Arab Republic	29 51 N	31 20 E	**2, 43, 53, 54, 57, 58, 61**
Humahuaca: *admin.*, Argentina	23 05 S	65 20 W	**49**
Humboldt: Kans., U.S.A.	37 50 N	95 26 W	**57A**
Humboldt Bay: Calif., U.S.A.	40 47 N	124 11 W	**40**
Humenné: Czechoslovakia	48 57 N	21 54 E	**32C, 60D**
Humpolec: Czechoslovakia	49 33 N	15 20 E	**29C**
Hu-nan: *admin.*, China P.R.	28 00 N	112 00 E	**50**
Hunedoara: *admin.*, Romania	45 45 N	23 15 E	**38B, 58**
Hunedoara: Romania	45 45 N	22 54 E	**38B, 43**
Hŭngnam-ni: North Korea	39 30 N	127 14 E	**45**
Hungry Horse: *dam*, Mont., U.S.A.	48 20 N	114 00 W	**39A**
Hunterston: Scotland	55 40 N	4 55 W	**40B**
Huntingdon: Pa., U.S.A.	40 31 N	78 02 W	**32B**
Huntington: W. Va., U.S.A.	38 24 N	82 26 W	**54A, 67A, 87B**
Huntington Beach: Calif., U.S.A.	33 40 N	118 00 W	**32**
Huntsville: Ala., U.S.A.	34 44 N	86 35 W	**31A, 59B, 87C**
Hurley: N. Mex., U.S.A.	32 41 N	108 07 W	**45A, 50A**
Hurn: England	50 47 N	1 49 W	**53B, 53C**
Huron: Ohio, U.S.A.	41 23 N	82 33 W	**58F**
Hurricane Creek: Ark., U.S.A.	34 33 N	92 31 W	**47A**
Hürth: Germany F.R.	50 52 N	6 52 E	**60D**
Husnes: Norway	59 52 N	5 46 E	**47**
Hutt: New Zealand	41 10 S	174 56 E	**67**
Hvide Sande: Denmark	55 59 N	8 08 E	**27C**
Hwasun: South Korea	35 04 N	126 59 E	**38C**
Hyde: England	53 27 N	2 04 W	**31B**
Hyderabad: India	17 22 N	78 26 E	**31C**
Hyderābād: Pakistan	25 22 N	68 22 E	**31, 34**
Hythe: England	50 51 N	1 24 W	**60H**
Hyvinkää: Finland	60 38 N	24 52 E	**29**

I

	° ′	° ′	*Page(s)*
Iacobini: Romania	46 14 N	22 21 E	**50B**
Iaşi: Romania	47 10 N	27 36 E	**17, 32C**
Ica: *admin.*, Peru	14 20 S	75 30 W	**49**
Ice Harbor: *dam*, Wash., U.S.A.	46 16 N	118 51 W	**39A**
I-ch'ang: China P.R.	30 42 N	111 17 E	**43**
Ichihara: Japan	35 32 N	140 04 E	**60E**
Ichikawa: Japan	35 44 N	139 55 E	**29D**
Ichinomiya: Japan	35 18 N	136 48 E	**29D**
Ida: La., U.S.A.	33 00 N	93 55 W	**37J**
Idaho: *admin.*, U.S.A.	45 00 N	115 00 W	**27**
Idaho Falls: Idaho, U.S.A.	43 30 N	112 01 W	**40A**
Idikki: *dam*, India	10 05 N	77 00 E	**39**
Idrija: Yugoslavia	46 00 N	14 02 E	**50B**
Ieper (Ypres): Belgium	50 51 N	2 53 E	**29B**
Igarka: *dam*, U.S.S.R.	67 28 N	86 35 E	**39**
Iglesias: Italy	39 19 N	8 32 E	**59H**
Iguatu: Brazil	6 22 S	39 18 W	**50**
IJmuiden: Netherlands	52 28 N	4 38 E	**27C, 43B, 58D, 61D, 61H, 84C**
IJsselmonde: Netherlands	51 54 N	4 33 E	**37D**
Ikatefa: *mtn.*, Malagasy R.	25 02 S	46 32 E	**40**
Ikehara: *dam*, Japan	34 02 N	135 57 E	**39D**
Ikhtiman: Bulgaria	42 26 N	23 49 E	**48**
Ikuno: Japan	35 10 N	134 48 E	**45D, 46C**
Île Kassa: *island*, Guinea	9 29 N	13 45 W	**47**
Ilford: England	51 33 N	0 06 E	**58D**
Ilha Solteira: *dam*, Brazil	20 30 S	51 20 W	**39**
Iligan: Philippines	8 15 N	124 18 E	**61**
Illinois: *admin.*, U.S.A.	40 00 N	89 00 W	**27, 38, 35**
Illiopolis: Ill., U.S.A.	39 50 N	89 13 W	**60B**
Il'menskiye Gory: *mtns.*, U.S.S.R.	55 15 N	60 12 E	**50**
Ilo: Peru	17 42 S	71 20 W	**27, 45**
Iloilo: Philippines	10 41 N	122 33 E	**67**
Ilorin: Nigeria	8 32 N	4 34 E	**67**
Imabari: Japan	34 03 N	133 00 E	**52B**
Imatra: Finland	61 10 N	28 46 E	**43**
Imbituba: Brazil	28 14 S	48 40 W	**59**
Imini: Morocco	31 06 N	7 17 W	**50**
Immingham: England	53 37 N	0 14 W	**37F, 58D, 59H, 61D, 61H, 84C**
Im XXII s'ezda (22nd Congress): *dam*, U.S.S.R.	48 49 N	44 44 E	**39**
Ince: England	53 17 N	2 50 W	**61D**
Inch'ŏn: South Korea	37 28 N	126 38 E	**31, 59G, 60, 84D**
Indarung: Indonesia	0 56 S	100 28 E	**57**
Indé: Mexico	25 54 N	105 13 W	**49A**
Independence: Kans., U.S.A.	37 13 N	95 43 W	**57A**
Independence: Mo., U.S.A.	39 04 N	94 27 W	**57A**

	° ′	° ′	*Page(s)*
Indiana: *admin.*, U.S.A.	40 00 N	86 00 W	**27, 38A**
Indiana Harbor: *bay*, Ind., U.S.A.	41 40 N	87 27 W	**58B**
Indianapolis: Ind., U.S.A.	39 45 N	86 10 W	**37J, 53, 55B, 67A, 87B**
Indian Point: N.J., U.S.A.	41 16 N	73 56 W	**40C**
Indore: India	22 42 N	75 54 E	**31C**
Ingessana *Hills*: Sudan	11 27 N	33 59 E	**50**
Ingolstadt: Germany F.R.	48 46 N	11 26 E	**37F, 55A**
Inguri: *dam*, U.S.S.R.	42 35 N	42 00 E	**39**
I-ning (Kuldja): China P.R.	43 54 N	81 21 E	**67**
Inkeroinen: Finland	60 42 N	26 51 E	**25B**
Inno-shima: *island*, Japan	34 19 N	133 10 E	**52B**
Inota: Hungary	47 12 N	18 11 E	**47B**
Inspiration: Ariz., U.S.A.	33 23 N	110 52 W	**45A, 50A**
Institute: W. Va., U.S.A.	38 23 N	81 45 W	**32B, 58B, 58F**
Inta: U.S.S.R.	66 05 N	60 08 E	**38**
Invergordon: Scotland	57 42 N	4 10 W	**58, 84C**
Inyati: Rhodesia	19 41 S	28 52 E	**49**
Inyo *Co.*: Calif., U.S.A.	36 45 N	117 30 W	**46, 49B**
Ioco: Canada	49 19 N	122 54 W	**36**
Iola: Kans., U.S.A.	37 57 N	95 26 W	**57A**
Ionian *Sea*: Europe	39 00 N	19 00 E	**27**
Iowa: *admin.*, U.S.A.	42 00 N	93 00 W	**27, 38**
Ipameri: Brazil	17 43 S	48 09 W	**45**
Ipatinga: Brazil	19 30 S	42 32 W	**43**
Ipoh: Malaysia	4 35 N	101 05 E	**57, 67, 87**
Ipswich: Australia	27 37 S	152 46 E	**29, 54**
Iquique: Chile	20 13 S	70 10 W	**27, 84**
Iquitos: Peru	3 51 S	73 13 W	**36**
Iráklion: Greece	35 20 N	25 08 E	**84B**
Irancy: France	47 43 N	3 40 E	**17**
Irapuato: Mexico	20 41 N	101 28 W	**60**
Irian Barat (West New Guinea): *admin.*, Indonesia	5 00 S	138 00 E	**27**
Irkutsk: *dam*, U.S.S.R.	52 16 N	104 20 E	**39**
Irkutsk: U.S.S.R.	52 16 N	104 20 E	**2, 36, 47, 57, 67**
Irmaği Yenice: *river*, Turkey	37 36 N	35 35 E	**46**
Iron *Co.*: Utah, U.S.A.	38 00 N	113 00 W	**43**
Iron Gate *see* Porţile de Fier: Romania	44 41 N	22 31 E	**39**
Iron Knob: *hill*, Australia	32 45 S	137 08 E	**43**
Iron Mountain: Mo., U.S.A.	37 40 N	90 46 W	**43A**
Iron Mountain: Wyo., U.S.A.	41 32 N	105 13 W	**50A**
Ironton: Ohio, U.S.A.	38 32 N	82 40 W	**57B, 58B**
Iroquois Falls: Canada	48 47 N	80 41 W	**25D**
Irrawaddy *Delta*: Burma	16 30 N	95 00 E	**11**
Irvine: Calif., U.S.A.	33 35 N	117 48 W	**62**
Isabella: Tenn., U.S.A.	34 58 N	84 22 W	**59F**
Isando: South Africa	26 09 S	28 12 E	**32, 55**
Isbergues: France	50 37 N	2 27 E	**43B**
Ischia: *island*, Italy	40 43 N	13 54 E	**17**
Isère: *admin.*, France	45 10 N	5 50 E	**38B**
Ishikari: Japan	43 15 N	141 22 E	**38**
Ishikawa: Japan	37 09 N	140 27 E	**25**
Ishikawa-ken: *admin.*, Japan	36 45 N	136 45 E	**50**
Ishimbay: U.S.S.R.	53 28 N	56 02 E	**36**
Ishinomaki: Japan	38 25 N	141 18 E	**25, 27D**
Ishiyama: Japan	42 58 N	141 20 E	**59G**
Ishpushta: Afghanistan	35 20 N	66 05 E	**38**
İskenderun: *admin.*, Turkey	36 30 N	36 05 E	**50B**
İskenderun: Turkey	36 37 N	36 07 E	**84B**
Isla-Cristina: Spain	37 12 N	7 19 W	**27B**
Isla de Lanzarote: *island*, Spain	29 00 N	13 40 W	**27**
Islāmābād: Pakistan	33 42 N	73 10 E	**34**
Isla Violín: Costa Rica	8 50 N	83 38 W	**49**
Isle Maligne: *dam*, Canada	48 34 N	71 38 W	**39B**
Ismāīlābād: Pakistan	30 08 N	71 21 E	**31**
Isola: *dam*, Italy	46 26 N	9 19 E	**39C**
Isola delle Femmine: Italy	38 12 N	13 15 E	**57**
İstanbul: Turkey	41 01 N	28 58 E	**27, 29, 31, 45, 67, 84B, 87**
Iszkaszentgyörgy: Hungary	47 14 N	18 18 E	**47B**
Itabira: Brazil	19 37 S	43 13 W	**43**
Itabirito: Brazil	20 15 S	43 48 W	**43**
Itaguaí: Brazil	22 52 S	43 47 W	**46**
Itagüí: Colombia	6 10 N	75 36 W	**32**
Itajaí: Brazil	26 53 S	48 39 W	**84**
Itambe: Brazil	12 48 S	40 48 W	**50**
Itapemirim: Brazil	21 01 S	40 50 W	**57**
Itaú de Minas: Brazil	20 43 S	46 45 W	**57**
Itéa: Greece	38 26 N	22 25 E	**84B**
Itō: Japan	34 58 N	139 05 E	**27D**
Itupeva: Brazil	23 09 S	47 04 W	**50**
Itzehoe: Germany F.R.	53 55 N	9 31 E	**57C**
Ivanovo: U.S.S.R.	57 12 N	41 42 E	**29, 31**
Ivrea: Italy	45 28 N	7 52 E	**32C, 60D**
Iwaki: Japan	36 58 N	140 56 E	**61G, 67C**
Iwakuni: Japan	34 09 N	132 11 E	**32A, 35, 58C, 58G, 60C**
Ixtaczoquitlán: Mexico	18 51 N	97 04 W	**57**
Ixtapalapa: Mexico	19 21 N	99 06 W	**32**
Ixtlán de Juárez: Mexico	17 20 N	96 29 W	**49A**
Iyo Mishima: Japan	33 58 N	133 30 E	**25**
Izhevsk: U.S.S.R.	56 51 N	53 14 E	**43**
Izieux: France	45 28 N	4 30 E	**32C**
Izmail: U.S.S.R.	45 21 N	28 50 E	**84**
İzmir: Turkey	38 25 N	27 09 E	**17, 29, 31, 50B, 67, 84B**

	° ′	° ′	*Page(s)*
İzmit: Turkey	40 46 N	29 55 E	**25, 36, 58, 59, 60**
Izumrud: U.S.S.R.	57 05 N	61 23 E	**50**
Izvoru Muntelui: *dam*, Romania	46 57 N	26 06 E	**39**

J

	° ′	° ′	*Page(s)*
Jabal Abū Tulu: *hill*, Sudan	11 41 N	28 40 E	**43**
Jabal al Ḩallūfah: *hill*, Tunisia	36 40 N	10 25 E	**46B**
Jabal al Jallūd: Tunisia	36 46 N	10 13 E	**57**
Jabal Ḩamāţah: *mtn.*, U.A.R.	24 12 N	35 00 E	**50**
Jabalpur: *admin.*, India	23 30 N	80 00 E	**47**
Jabal Sīdī 'Abd ar Raḩmān: *ridge*, Tunisia	36 47 N	10 44 E	**37B**
Jablonec nad Nisou: Czech.	50 44 N	15 10 E	**55A**
Jachymov: Czechoslovakia	50 22 N	12 55 E	**40B**
Jackson: Miss., U.S.A.	32 20 N	90 11 W	**61B, 87C**
Jacksonville: Fla., U.S.A.	30 20 N	81 40 W	**25A, 32B, 40, 47, 50, 67, 84, 87C**
Jacobs: South Africa	29 53 S	31 00 E	**29**
Jacupiranga: Brazil	24 42 S	48 00 W	**56**
Jacurici: *dam*, Brazil	10 51 S	39 43 W	**39**
Jadotville *see* Likasi: Congo D.R.	10 59 S	26 44 E	**45, 67**
Jaduguda: India	22 42 N	85 56 E	**40**
Jaén: *admin.*, Spain	38 00 N	3 30 W	**46B**
Jaffa *see* Yafo: Israel	32 03 N	34 45 E	**16, 17**
Jaffna: Ceylon	9 38 N	80 02 E	**84**
Jagersfontein: *mine*, S. Africa	29 45 S	25 25 E	**48**
Jaguara: *dam*, Brazil	21 58 S	47 30 W	**39**
Jahrom: Iran	28 31 N	53 33 E	**50**
Jajce: Yugoslavia	44 21 N	17 17 E	**59D**
Jamestown: N.Y., U.S.A.	42 05 N	79 15 W	**29**
Jamnagar: India	22 28 N	70 06 E	**57**
Jämsänkoski: Finland	61 55 N	25 11 E	**25B**
Jamshedpur: India	22 47 N	86 12 E	**43, 54, 59**
Jämtland: Sweden	63 26 N	14 04 E	**48**
Janesville: Wis., U.S.A.	42 42 N	89 02 W	**55**
Janja Lipa: Yugoslavia	45 27 N	17 00 E	**37B**
Japla: India	24 33 N	84 01 E	**57**
Jaroměř: Czechoslovakia	50 22 N	15 55 E	**31B**
Jarrahdale: Australia	32 21 S	116 04 E	**47**
Jarrie: France	45 07 N	5 46 E	**50, 59D**
Jasenova: Yugoslavia	42 45 N	19 23 E	**50B**
Jasło: Poland	49 45 N	21 28 E	**37F**
Jasso: Mexico	20 01 N	99 19 W	**57**
Java *see* Djawa: *is.*, Indon.	7 30 S	110 00 E	**10, 11, 27**
Jaykaynagar: India	23 40 N	87 01 E	**47**
Jazīreh-ye Khārk: *island*, Iran	29 15 N	50 20 E	**37C, 56**
Jbel Aouam: *hill*, Morocco	33 09 N	5 39 W	**43, 46**
Jebba: *dam*, Nigeria	9 08 N	4 50 E	**39**
Jeddah *see* Juddah: Saudi Arabia	21 30 N	39 12 E	**36, 67, 84, 87**
Jedlicze: Poland	49 43 N	21 42 E	**37F**
Jefferson City: Mo., U.S.A.	38 33 N	92 10 W	**87B**
Jefferson *Co.*: Mont., U.S.A.	46 20 N	112 00 W	**49**
Jeffrey City: Wyo., U.S.A.	42 29 N	107 49 W	**40A, 59**
Jelenia Góra: Poland	50 55 N	15 45 E	**25C, 32C**
Jemeppe: Belgium	50 28 N	4 40 E	**59D, 60D**
Jenbach: Austria	47 24 N	11 47 E	**54B**
Jerada: Morocco	34 17 N	2 13 W	**38**
Jerez de la Frontera: Spain	36 41 N	6 08 W	**17**
Jersey: *island*, Channel Is.	49 13 N	2 07 W	**87**
Jersey City: N.J., U.S.A.	40 44 N	74 04 W	**67A**
Jesenice: Yugoslavia	46 27 N	14 04 E	**43B**
Jesselton *see* Kota Kinabalu: Malaysia	5 59 N	116 04 E	**84, 87**
Jhimpīr: Pakistan	25 01 N	68 01 E	**38**
J. H. Kerr: *dam*, Va., U.S.A.	36 35 N	78 16 W	**39**
Jinja: Uganda	0 26 N	33 12 E	**31, 45**
Jivka: Czechoslovakia	50 35 N	16 10 E	**45**
Joal: Senegal	14 10 N	16 51 W	**47, 50**
Joanna: S.C., U.S.A.	34 21 N	81 50 W	**31**
João Monlevade: Brazil	19 50 S	43 08 W	**43**
Jobo-Tablón: *region*, Colombia	9 00 N	75 15 W	**34**
Jocasse: *dam*, S.C., U.S.A.	34 58 N	82 56 W	**39**
Jódar: Spain	37 50 N	3 21 W	**59D**
Jogjakarta (Djokjakarta): Indonesia	7 48 S	110 22 E	**67**
Johannesburg: South Africa	26 10 S	28 02 E	**29, 31, 49, 54, 55, 56, 67, 87**
John Day: *dam*, Oreg., U.S.A.	45 43 N	120 41 W	**39A**
Johnsonville: S.C., U.S.A.	33 48 N	79 28 W	**32B**
Johnstown: Pa., U.S.A.	40 20 N	78 56 W	**43A, 54A, 67A**
Johore: *admin.*, Malaysia	2 00 N	103 30 E	**43**
Joliet: Ill., U.S.A.	41 32 N	88 05 W	**58B, 58F, 59E, 60B, 67A**
Jonava: U.S.S.R.	55 05 N	24 17 E	**61H**
Jones Mill: Ark., U.S.A.	34 27 N	92 50 W	**47A**
Jönköping: Sweden	57 47 N	14 11 E	**55**
Joplin: Mo., U.S.A.	37 04 N	94 31 W	**61A, 61E, 87C**
Joppa: Ill., U.S.A.	37 13 N	88 52 W	**57B**
Joppa *see* Yafo: Israel	32 03 N	34 45 E	**16, 17**
Jos: Nigeria	9 54 N	8 53 E	**45, 50**
José Colomo: *region*, Mexico	18 00 N	92 30 W	**34**
José Hernández: Argentina	34 54 S	58 00 W	**60**
Jos *Plateau*: Nigeria	9 30 N	9 00 E	**40**
Juab *Co.*: Utah, U.S.A.	39 40 N	113 00 W	**49B**
Juàziero: Brazil	9 25 S	40 30 W	**48**

	° ′	° ′	Page(s)
Juddah (Jeddah): Saudi Arabia	21 30 N	39 12 E	36, 67, 84, 87
Juiz de Fora: Brazil	21 45 S	43 20 W	31
Julianehaab: Greenland	60 45 N	46 00 W	84
Jülich: Germany F.R.	50 56 N	6 22 E	40B
Junagadh: *admin.*, India	21 32 N	70 32 E	47
Jundiaí: Brazil	23 11 S	46 52 W	58
Jundiapeba: Brazil	23 33 S	46 15 W	32
Juneau: Alaska, U.S.A.	58 20 N	134 20 W	87
Junín: *admin.*, Peru	11 30 S	75 00 W	46, 49
Jupiá: *dam*, Brazil	20 48 S	51 40 W	39
Jurançon: France	43 18 N	0 23 W	17
Jyoban: Japan	39 00 N	141 00 E	38

K

	° ′	° ′	Page(s)
Kaanapali: Hawaii, U.S.A.	20 56 N	156 42 W	87
Kaapmuiden: South Africa	25 33 S	31 20 E	50
Kabanskiy: U.S.S.R.	54 28 N	61 04 E	45
Kaborishoke: Tanzania	1 40 S	31 00 E	45
Kabul: Afghanistan	34 30 N	69 10 E	67
Kabunga: Congo D.R.	1 42 S	28 08 E	45
Kachkanar, Gora: *mtn.*, U.S.S.R.	58 47 N	59 23 E	50
Kadiyevka: U.S.S.R.	48 34 N	38 40 E	38
Kaduna: Nigeria	10 28 N	7 25 E	31, 67
Kadzharan: U.S.S.R.	39 10 N	46 08 E	45
Kafan: U.S.S.R.	39 12 N	46 24 E	45
Kafr ad Dawwār: U.A.R.	31 08 N	30 07 E	31, 32, 59, 60
Kafue: *dam*, Zambia	15 55 S	28 50 E	39
Kagoshima: Japan	31 36 N	130 33 E	27, 87
Kagoshima-ken: *admin.*, Japan	30 00 N	130 00 E	49, 50
Kahl am Main: Germany F.R.	50 05 N	9 00 E	40B
Kahului: Hawaii, U.S.A.	20 54 N	156 28 W	87
Kaibara: Japan	35 08 N	135 05 E	32A
K'ai-luan: China P.R.	39 56 N	119 37 E	38C
Kainan: Japan	34 09 N	135 12 E	37E
Kainji: *dam*, Nigeria	9 55 N	4 35 E	39
Kaipola: Finland	61 49 N	25 15 E	25B
Kaira: *admin.*, India	23 00 N	73 00 E	47
Kaira: India	22 44 N	72 44 E	31C
K'ai-yang: China P.R.	27 04 N	106 58 E	57
Kajaani: Finland	64 14 N	27 41 E	25
Kakanda: Congo D.R.	10 44 S	26 23 E	45
Kakhovka: *dam*, U.S.S.R.	46 46 N	33 22 E	39
Kaki Bukit: Malaysia	6 39 N	100 12 E	45C
Kakinada: India	16 59 N	82 20 E	84
Kakogawa: Japan	34 46 N	134 51 E	29D, 32A, 59G
Kalama: Wash., U.S.A.	46 01 N	122 50 W	58
Kalamazoo: Mich., U.S.A.	42 17 N	85 36 W	25D, 59E
Kalanguy: U.S.S.R.	50 01 N	116 13 E	50
Kālāshāh Kāku: Pakistan	31 43 N	74 16 E	32
Kalavasos: Cyprus	34 46 N	33 18 E	45
Kalgoorlie: Australia	30 45 S	121 28 E	49
Kalima: Congo D.R.	2 34 S	26 37 E	50
Kalimantan (Borneo): *island*, Indonesia	1 00 S	114 00 E	27, 48, 61
Kalinin: U.S.S.R.	56 52 N	35 55 E	32C, 54
Kaliningrad (Königsberg): U.S.S.R.	54 43 N	20 30 E	25, 54B, 84C
Kalkbaai: *bay*, South Africa	34 10 S	18 25 E	27
Kalmar: Sweden	56 40 N	16 22 E	54, 84C
Kalna: Yugoslavia	43 25 N	22 25 E	40
Kalol: India	23 15 N	72 32 E	31C
Kalpakkam: India	12 37 N	80 13 E	40
Kalscheuren: Germany F.R.	50 53 N	6 54 E	60H
Kalundborg: Denmark	55 41 N	11 06 E	37B, 37F
Kalush: U.S.S.R.	49 01 N	24 22 E	56
Kalyan: India	19 17 N	73 11 E	32, 59
Kama: *dam*, U.S.S.R.	58 00 N	56 15 E	39
Kamaishi: Japan	39 16 N	141 53 E	27D, 43D, 45D, 84D
Kamakura: Japan	35 19 N	139 33 E	58C
Kamativi: Rhodesia	18 10 S	26 15 E	45
Kambara: Japan	35 07 N	138 36 E	47C
Kambove: Congo D.R.	10 52 S	26 38 E	45
Kamchatka: *dam*, U.S.S.R.	54 00 N	158 00 E	39
Kamen: Germany F.R.	51 36 N	7 40 E	58D
Kamen': U.S.S.R.	53 47 N	81 20 E	32
Kameno: Bulgaria	42 43 N	27 18 E	37H, 58
Kamensk-Ural'skiy: U.S.S.R.	56 25 N	61 54 E	47
Kami: Bolivia	17 26 S	66 50 W	50
Kamiiso: Japan	41 49 N	140 39 E	57D
Kami-Nakaze: Japan	36 14 N	139 17 E	50
Kamioka: Japan	36 16 N	137 18 E	46C, 59G
Kamloops: Canada	50 39 N	120 24 W	36
Kamoto: Congo D.R.	10 45 S	25 23 E	45
Kampala: Uganda	0 19 N	32 35 E	67, 87
Kamp-Lintfort: Germany F.R.	51 30 N	6 32 E	58D
Kampumbu: *stream*, Zambia	12 55 S	30 01 E	50
Kamyshin: U.S.S.R.	50 06 N	45 24 E	31
Kananga (Luluabourg): Congo D.R.	5 54 S	22 25 E	67
Kanazawa: Japan	36 34 N	136 39 E	67C
Kanchanaburi: *admin.*, Thailand	14 38 N	99 06 E	46
Kanchanaburi: Thailand	14 01 N	99 32 E	45
Kandahar: Afghanistan	31 36 N	65 47 E	67
Kandalaksha: U.S.S.R.	67 09 N	32 25 E	47
Kandilli: Turkey	41 21 N	31 30 E	38
Kandla: India	23 00 N	70 10 E	61
Kandos: Australia	32 51 S	149 58 E	57
Kanev: *dam*, U.S.S.R.	49 44 N	31 28 E	39
Kangnŭng: South Korea	37 44 N	128 54 E	38C
Kannapolis: N.C., U.S.A.	35 30 N	80 36 W	31A
Kano: Nigeria	12 00 N	8 31 E	45, 67
Kanpur (Cawnpore): India	26 27 N	80 14 E	29, 31, 32, 53, 61F
Kansas: *admin.*, U.S.A.	39 00 N	98 00 W	27, 38
Kansas City: Kans., U.S.A.	39 05 N	94 37 W	37J
Kansas City: Mo., U.S.A.	39 02 N	94 33 W	32B, 43, 55, 87B
Kansay: U.S.S.R.	40 30 N	69 41 E	46, 49
Kansk: U.S.S.R.	56 13 N	95 41 E	31, 38
Kansko-Achinskii Basseyn: *basin*, U.S.S.R.	56 15 N	92 50 E	38
Kao-hsiung: Taiwan	22 38 N	120 17 E	32, 47, 57, 58, 59C, 60, 61, 67, 84
Kapsan-ŭp: North Korea	41 05 N	128 18 E	45
Kapuni: *region*, New Zealand	39 30 S	174 20 E	34, 35
Kapuskasing: Canada	49 25 N	82 26 W	25, 25D
Karababa: *dam*, Turkey	37 25 N	38 26 E	39
Karabanovo: U.S.S.R.	56 19 N	38 42 E	31
Karabash: U.S.S.R.	55 29 N	60 14 E	45
Karabük: Turkey	41 12 N	32 37 E	43
Karaburun: *admin.*, Turkey	38 35 N	26 28 E	50B
Karāchi: Pakistan	24 52 N	67 03 E	29, 31, 34, 36, 57, 58, 60, 61, 67, 84, 87
Karadag: U.S.S.R.	40 16 N	49 36 E	57
Karaganda: U.S.S.R.	49 50 N	73 10 E	30, 34, 43, 57, 60, 67
Karagandinskiy Ugol'nyy Basseyn: *basin*, U.S.S.R.	50 00 N	73 00 E	38
Karakaya: *dam*, Turkey	38 16 N	39 10 E	39
Karamai *see* K'o-la-ma-i: China P.R.	45 30 N	84 55 E	35
Karamazor: U.S.S.R.	40 42 N	69 58 E	46
Karatsu: Japan	33 26 N	129 58 E	27D, 38C
Karhula: Finland	60 31 N	26 57 E	25B
Kariba: *dam*, Rhodesia	16 30 S	28 50 E	39
Kariba, *Lake*: Africa	17 00 S	28 00 E	27
Karibib: South West Africa	21 59 S	15 51 E	50
Karita: Japan	33 47 N	130 59 E	57D
Karkar: Afghanistan	35 55 N	68 35 E	38
Karlholm: Sweden	60 31 N	17 37 E	25B
Karl-Marx-Stadt (Chemnitz): Germany D.R.	50 50 N	12 55 E	29C, 31B
Karlsborg: Sweden	65 48 N	23 17 E	25
Karlshamn: Sweden	56 10 N	14 51 E	84C
Karlsruhe: Germany F.R.	49 01 N	8 24 E	37F
Karlstad: Sweden	59 22 N	13 30 E	60
Karlstadt: Germany F.R.	49 57 N	9 46 E	57C
Karns City: Pa., U.S.A.	40 59 N	79 41 W	37J
Karonje: *mtn.*, Rwanda	2 10 S	29 20 E	40
Kars: Turkey	40 37 N	43 05 E	48
Karsakpay: U.S.S.R.	47 50 N	66 45 E	45
Karsdorf: Germany D.R.	51 17 N	11 39 E	57B
Kartal: Turkey	40 53 N	29 10 E	57C
Kartaly: U.S.S.R.	53 03 N	60 40 E	50
Kasekelesa: Congo D.R.	10 39 S	24 56 E	50
Kashabowie: Canada	48 40 N	90 26 W	45
Kāshān: Iran	33 59 N	51 29 E	31
Kashima: Japan	35 30 N	133 01 E	40, 58G, 59C, 60C, 61C, 61G
Kashiwazaki: Japan	37 22 N	138 33 E	37E
Kaspi: U.S.S.R.	41 56 N	44 25 E	57
Kassa, Île: *island*, Guinea	9 29 N	13 45 W	47
Kassan: U.S.S.R.	39 02 N	65 35 E	50
Kassándra: *peninsula*, Greece	40 06 N	23 22 E	46B
Kassel: Germany F.R.	51 19 N	9 30 E	32C, 54B, 55A
Kaštel Sućurac: Yugoslavia	43 32 N	16 25 E	60D
Kastrákion: *dam*, Greece	38 45 N	21 36 E	39
Kastrup: Denmark	55 38 N	12 39 E	58D
Kasugai: Japan	35 15 N	136 57 E	25
Kasumi: Japan	35 38 N	134 38 E	27D
Katanga: Congo D.R.	11 07 S	27 06 E	49, 50, 57
Katanga-Oriental: *admin.*, Congo D.R.	10 00 S	27 30 E	49
Katav-Ivanovsk: U.S.S.R.	54 45 N	58 12 E	57
Katmandu: Nepal	27 42 N	85 19 E	67, 87
Katowice: Poland	50 15 N	18 59 E	46B
Katowickie: *admin.*, Poland	50 15 N	18 59 E	38B
Katsuura: Japan	33 37 N	135 56 E	27D
Katsuura: Japan	35 08 N	140 18 E	27D
Katukurunda: Ceylon	6 34 N	79 58 E	40
Kaufbeuren: Germany F.R.	47 53 N	10 37 E	31B
Kaukauna: Wis., U.S.A.	44 20 N	88 16 W	25D
Kaunakakai: Hawaii, U.S.A.	21 05 N	157 02 W	87
Kaunas: U.S.S.R.	54 54 N	23 54 E	32C
Kaunertal: *dam*, Austria	46 57 N	10 45 E	39C
Kaupulehu: Hawaii, U.S.A.	19 50 N	155 59 W	87
Kaválla: Greece	40 56 N	24 25 E	61H, 84B
Kavşak: *dam*, Turkey	37 32 N	35 34 E	39
Kawaguchi: Japan	35 48 N	139 43 E	29D, 56
Kawara: Japan	33 40 N	130 51 E	57D
Kawasaki: Japan	35 32 N	139 43 E	36, 37E, 43D, 55, 57D, 58C, 58G, 59C, 59G, 60C, 60E, 61C, 61G
Kawerau: New Zealand	38 03 S	176 43 E	25
Kayah: *admin.*, Burma	19 15 N	97 30 E	50
Kayseri: *admin.*, Turkey	38 45 N	35 30 E	50B
Kazakh: U.S.S.R.	41 05 N	45 22 E	29
Kazakhskaya S.S.R.: *admin.*, U.S.S.R.	48 00 N	68 00 E	27, 43, 56
Kazan': U.S.S.R.	55 45 N	49 08 E	30, 36, 53, 58, 60
Kazanlŭk: Bulgaria	42 37 N	25 24 E	31
Kazincbarcika: Hungary	48 15 N	20 38 E	60D, 61H
Kdyně: Czechoslovakia	49 24 N	13 03 E	29C
Kearny: N.J., U.S.A.	40 46 N	74 09 W	58B
Keban: *dam*, Turkey	38 49 N	38 45 E	39
Kechoula: *region*, Morocco	31 30 N	9 00 W	34, 37B
Kedah: *admin.*, Malaysia	6 00 N	100 40 E	43
Kędzierzyn (Heidebreck): Poland	50 20 N	18 12 E	61D, 61H
Keflavík: Iceland	64 01 N	22 34 W	27
Keighley: England	53 52 N	1 54 W	29B
Kelheim: Germany F.R.	48 55 N	11 52 E	32C
Kellogg: Idaho, U.S.A.	47 33 N	116 06 W	46A, 50, 59
Kelsterbach: Germany F.R.	50 04 N	8 32 E	58H, 60D
Kemano: *dam*, Canada	53 31 N	127 56 W	39
Kemerovo: U.S.S.R.	55 20 N	86 05 E	57, 61, 67
Kempenland (Campine): *region*, Belgium	51 10 N	5 20 E	38B
Kempten: Germany F.R.	47 43 N	10 19 E	31B
Kempton Park: South Africa	26 07 S	28 14 E	53, 59
Kenadsa: Algeria	31 30 N	2 30 W	38
Kenai: Alaska, U.S.A.	60 35 N	151 19 W	34, 36, 61
Kendyrlyk: U.S.S.R.	47 30 N	85 12 E	38
Kenitra *see* Mina Hassan Tani: Morocco	34 20 N	6 34 W	27B, 59
Kennewick: Wash., U.S.A.	46 13 N	119 08 W	61
Kenney: *dam*, Canada	53 38 N	124 59 W	39
Kenogami: Canada	48 26 N	71 16 W	25D
Kenora: Canada	49 47 N	94 26 W	25
Kenosha: Wis., U.S.A.	42 34 N	87 50 W	67A
Kent: *admin.*, England	51 00 N	0 30 E	38B
Kentucky: *admin.*, U.S.A.	38 00 N	85 00 W	27, 34, 35, 38A
Keonjhar: *admin.*, India	22 00 N	85 30 E	43, 50
Keowee: S.C., U.S.A.	34 40 N	82 55 W	40
Kerala: *admin.*, India	10 00 N	76 30 E	27
Kerch': U.S.S.R.	45 21 N	36 28 E	43, 50
Kerens: Texas, U.S.A.	32 07 N	96 15 W	61A, 61B
Kermānshāh: Iran	34 19 N	47 04 E	37G
Kérouané: *admin.*, Guinea	9 10 N	9 05 W	48
Kerr, J. H.: *dam*, Va., U.S.A.	36 35 N	78 16 W	39
Kershaw: S.C., U.S.A.	34 33 N	80 36 W	48
Kesang: Malaysia	2 07 N	102 30 E	45C
Kesennuma: Japan	38 54 N	141 35 E	27D
Ketona: Ala., U.S.A.	33 34 N	86 42 W	61B, 61E
Kettara: Morocco	31 52 N	8 10 W	56
Kettle: *dam*, Canada	56 21 N	94 43 W	39
Kevin: Mont., U.S.A.	48 44 N	111 58 W	36
Kew: England	51 29 N	0 18 W	2, 3
Kewaunee: Wis., U.S.A.	44 27 N	87 31 W	40C
Keystone: *dam*, Pa., U.S.A.	40 41 N	79 11 W	39
Keystone: S.D., U.S.A.	43 55 N	103 28 W	48
Khabarovsk: U.S.S.R.	48 30 N	135 06 E	36, 57, 67
Khafji, Ra's al: *pt.*, Neutral Zone	28 24 N	48 33 E	37C, 37G
Khalīj as Suways (Gulf of Suez): *region*, U.A.R.	28 10 N	33 27 E	35
Khalilovo: U.S.S.R.	51 24 N	58 09 E	36, 43, 45, 50
Khalkís: Greece	38 28 N	23 36 E	57C
Khal'mer-Yu: U.S.S.R.	67 58 N	64 50 E	57
Khānaqīn: Iraq	34 21 N	45 22 E	37G
Khanh Hoa: *admin.*, South Vietnam	12 20 N	109 00 E	27
Khanqat al Ḥājjāj: Tunisia	36 37 N	10 25 E	17
Khao Luang: *mtn.*, Thailand	8 30 N	99 40 E	50
Khapcheranga: U.S.S.R.	49 42 N	112 24 E	45
Kharanor: U.S.S.R.	50 05 N	116 40 E	38
Khārk, Jazīreh-ye: *island*, Iran	29 15 N	50 20 E	37C, 56
Khar'kov: U.S.S.R.	50 00 N	36 15 E	53, 54, 57, 67
Khartoum *see* Al Khurṭūm: Sudan	15 36 N	32 32 E	31, 67, 87
Khaydarken: U.S.S.R.	39 57 N	71 20 E	50
Kherson: U.S.S.R.	46 38 N	32 36 E	31, 52
Khor-al-Amaya: Iraq	29 47 N	48 41 E	37C
Khost: Pakistan	30 13 N	67 35 E	38
Khotan *see* Ho-t'ien: China P.R.	37 07 N	79 55 E	29
Khouribga: Morocco	32 54 N	6 57 W	56
Khrustal'nyy: U.S.S.R.	44 21 N	135 06 E	45
Khuan Phumiphon (Yanhee): *dam*, Thailand	17 15 N	98 58 E	39
Khulna: Pakistan	22 48 N	89 33 E	84
Khumara: U.S.S.R.	43 50 N	41 56 E	46
Khurayş: *region*, Saudi Arabia	25 05 N	48 02 E	34, 37A
Kiabakari: Tanzania	1 46 S	33 50 E	49
Kianga-Moura: *region*, Austl.	24 40 S	150 05 E	38
Kiangsi *see* Chiang-hsi: *admin.*, China P.R.	28 00 N	116 00 E	50, 50D
Kibre Mengist: Ethiopia	5 52 N	39 00 E	49
Kidderminster: England	52 23 N	2 14 W	29B
Kidod Zohar: *region*, Israel	31 00 N	35 00 E	34
Kidričevo: Yugoslavia	46 24 N	15 47 E	47B
Kidsgrove: England	53 05 N	2 16 W	62A
Kiel: Germany F.R.	54 20 N	10 08 E	27C, 52A, 67B, 84C
Kien Giang: *admin.*, S. Vietnam	10 00 N	105 15 E	27
Kierunavaara: *mtn.*, Sweden	67 50 N	20 12 E	43
Kiev *see* Kiyev: U.S.S.R.	50 26 N	30 31 E	32C, 34, 48, 53, 62, 87
Kigezi: *admin.*, Uganda	1 00 S	29 45 E	50
Kigoma: Tanzania	4 52 S	29 38 E	27
Kikagati: Uganda	1 02 S	30 40 E	45
Kikuma: Japan	34 03 N	132 53 E	37E
Kikumoto: Japan	33 25 N	131 37 E	47, 59C, 60C
Kildonan: Rhodesia	17 21 S	30 37 E	50, 50C
Kilembe: Uganda	0 12 N	30 00 E	45, 50
Kilforsen: *dam*, Sweden	63 27 N	16 45 E	39
Killingholme: England	53 30 N	0 21 W	37F
Killybegs: Irish Republic	54 38 N	8 27 W	27C
Kilmar: Canada	45 46 N	74 37 W	50
Kilmarnock: Scotland	55 37 N	4 30 W	29B
Kilroot: Northern Ireland	54 43 N	5 46 W	32C
Kimberley: Canada	49 41 N	115 59 W	46, 49, 50A, 59
Kimberley: *mine*, S. Africa	28 45 S	24 46 E	48
Kimberly: Wis., U.S.A.	44 15 N	88 19 W	25D, 59A
Kimbo: Guinea	10 24 N	13 33 W	47
Kimch'aek: North Korea	40 41 N	129 12 E	43
Kimkan: U.S.S.R.	48 58 N	131 26 E	43
Kimovsk: U.S.S.R.	53 58 N	38 32 E	56
Kindaruma: *dam*, Kenya	0 49 S	37 46 E	39
Kineshma: U.S.S.R.	57 28 N	42 07 E	31
Kingisepp: U.S.S.R.	59 22 N	28 40 E	56
King *Island*: Australia	39 50 S	144 00 E	50
King's Lynn: England	52 45 N	0 24 W	30B,
Kings Mountain: N.C., U.S.A.	35 14 N	81 21 W	31A, 50
Kingsport: Tenn., U.S.A.	36 33 N	82 34 W	25A, 32B, 57B
Kingston: Canada	44 14 N	76 30 W	32B, 48, 60B
Kingston: Jamaica	18 00 N	76 48 W	36, 84, 87
Kingston: N.Y., U.S.A.	41 55 N	74 00 W	57B, 62
Kingston upon Hull *see* Hull: England	53 45 N	0 20 W	27C, 58D, 67B, 84C
Kingston-upon-Thames: Eng.	51 25 N	0 17 W	53B
Kinleith: New Zealand	38 15 S	175 56 E	25
Kinlochleven: Scotland	56 43 N	4 58 W	47
Kinshasa (Léopoldville): Congo D.R.	4 18 N	15 18 E	31, 36, 56, 67, 87
Kinston: N.C., U.S.A.	35 15 N	77 34 W	32B
Kinta: *admin.*, Malaysia	4 30 N	101 12 E	45C, 47
Kipushi *Mines*: Congo D.R.	11 43 S	27 14 E	45, 46
Kirgizskaya S.S.R.: *admin.*, U.S.S.R.	41 00 N	75 00 E	27
Kirin *see* Chi-lin: *admin.*, China P.R.	43 00 N	126 00 E	50
Kirin *see* Chi-lin: China P.R.	43 51 N	126 33 E	25, 36, 43, 49, 61, 67
Kirishi: U.S.S.R.	59 27 N	32 02 E	36
Kirkenes: Norway	69 43 N	30 03 E	43, 84
Kirkland Lake: Canada	48 10 N	80 02 W	43, 49
Kirksville: Mo., U.S.A.	40 12 N	92 35 W	62
Kirkūk: Iraq	35 28 N	44 28 E	34, 37A, 37C, 37G, 67
Kirkvine: Jamaica	18 04 N	77 28 W	47
Kirkwall: Scotland	58 59 N	2 58 W	87
Kirov: U.S.S.R.	58 33 N	49 42 E	67
Kirovabad: U.S.S.R.	40 41 N	46 22 E	31, 47
Kirovgrad: U.S.S.R.	57 26 N	60 04 E	45
Kirovograd: U.S.S.R.	48 30 N	32 18 E	38
Kirovsk: U.S.S.R.	67 37 N	33 40 E	56
Kisangani (Stanleyville): Congo D.R.	0 30 N	25 12 E	56, 67
Kisenga: Congo D.R.	10 41 S	23 10 E	50
Kisen-yama: *dam*, Japan	34 56 N	135 54 E	39D
Kišovce: Czechoslovakia	49 01 N	20 25 E	50B
Kitakata: Japan	37 39 N	139 52 E	47C
Kitakyūshū: Japan	33 52 N	130 49 E	43D, 57D
Kitangiri, *Lake*: Tanzania	4 04 S	34 19 E	27
Kitchener: Canada	43 27 N	80 30 W	32B, 67A
Kitimat: Canada	54 05 N	128 38 W	47, 84
Kitwe: Zambia	12 49 S	28 13 E	67
Kivda-Raychikhinsk Basseyn: *basin*, U.S.S.R.	49 45 N	129 25 E	38
Kivu-Central: *admin.*, Congo D.R.	3 00 S	28 30 E	49
Kiyev: *dam*, U.S.S.R.	50 47 N	30 31 E	39
Kiyev (Kiev): U.S.S.R.	50 26 N	30 31 E	32C, 34, 48, 53, 62, 87
Kizel: U.S.S.R.	59 03 N	57 40 E	38
Kizu: Japan	34 44 N	135 49 E	59G
Kjøpsvik: Norway	68 06 N	16 21 E	57
Kladno: Czechoslovakia	50 10 N	14 05 E	43B
Klaipėda: U.S.S.R.	55 43 N	21 07 E	25, 31, 35, 37D, 84C
Klang: Malaysia	3 02 N	101 27 E	45C
Klarenthal: Germany F.R.	49 13 N	6 53 E	37F
Klerksdorp: South Africa	26 52 S	26 39 E	40, 49, 56
Klian Intan: Malaysia	5 39 N	101 02 E	45C
Klin: U.S.S.R.	56 20 N	36 44 E	32C
Kloštar Podravski: Yugoslavia	45 59 N	17 10 E	37D
Knarrevik: Norway	60 22 N	5 10 E	27C
Knoxville: Tenn., U.S.A.	36 00 N	83 57 W	57B, 87C
Kōbe: Japan	34 41 N	135 10 E	43D, 52B, 54C, 84D
København (Copenhagen): Denmark	55 40 N	12 35 E	25, 32C, 37F, 43B, 52A, 55, 58D, 58H, 59D, 59H, 62, 84C, 87

	° ′	° ′	Page(s)
Koblenz: Germany F.R.	50 21 N	7 36 E	67B
Kobuta: Pa., U.S.A.	40 41 N	80 19 W	60F
Kochav-Helez-Bror: *region*, Israel	31 36 N	34 39 E	37C
Kōchi: Japan	33 33 N	133 33 E	57D, 67C, 87
Kōchi-ken: *admin.*, Japan	33 40 N	133 30 E	50
Ko-chiu: China P.R.	23 23 N	103 09 E	45
Kodarma: India	24 28 N	85 36 E	50
Köflach: Austria	47 04 N	15 05 E	38B
Kōfu: Japan	35 39 N	138 35 E	67C
Kohlscheid: Germany F.R.	50 50 N	6 06 E	58D
Kohtla-Järve: U.S.S.R.	59 24 N	27 15 E	61
Kokand: U.S.S.R.	40 30 N	70 57 E	36, 61
Kokkola (Gamlakarleby): Finland	63 50 N	23 07 E	56, 59, 61
Kokomo: Ind., U.S.A.	40 30 N	86 09 W	55B
Koksan-gun: *admin.*, N. Korea	38 45 N	126 40 E	50
Kokura: Japan	33 53 N	130 53 E	59C
Kok-Yangak: U.S.S.R.	41 02 N	73 12 E	38
Kolaba: *admin.*, India	18 30 N	73 00 E	47
K'o-la-ma-i (Karamai): China P.R.	45 30 N	84 55 E	35
Kolar: *admin.*, India	13 08 N	78 08 E	49
Kolbermoor: Germany F.R.	47 51 N	12 04 E	31B
Kolbnitz: *dam*, Austria	46 56 N	13 32 E	39C
Kolhapur: India	16 42 N	74 19 E	31C, 67
Köln (Cologne): G.F.R.	50 56 N	6 57 E	37F, 55A, 58H, 60H, 67B, 87D
Köln-Kalk: Germany F.R.	50 55 N	7 00 E	61H
Kolomna: U.S.S.R.	55 05 N	38 47 E	54, 57
Kol'skiy Poluostrov: *pen.*, U.S.S.R.	67 20 N	37 00 E	40, 50
Kolwezi: Congo D.R.	10 43 S	25 28 E	46
Kolyvan': U.S.S.R.	51 18 N	82 34 E	49
Komarovo: U.S.S.R.	53 48 N	57 23 E	50
Komatsu: Japan	36 24 N	136 27 E	59G
Kombat: South West Africa	19 12 S	17 41 E	45, 46, 49
Komló: *admin.*, Hungary	46 12 N	18 16 E	38B
Kompong Son (Sihanoukville): Cambodia	10 38 N	103 30 E	36, 84
Komsomol'sk-na-Amure: U.S.S.R.	50 35 N	137 02 E	36, 43, 45, 52, 57, 67
Kona Mill: Hawaii, U.S.A.	19 38 N	155 58 W	87
Kondopoga: U.S.S.R.	62 12 N	34 17 E	25
Königsberg *see* Kaliningrad: U.S.S.R.	54 43 N	20 30 E	25, 54B, 84C
Kōnomai: Japan	44 08 N	143 21 E	49
Konongo: Ghana	6 37 N	1 13 W	49
Kōno-shima: *island*, Japan	34 27 N	133 30 E	59G
Konstantinovka: U.S.S.R.	48 32 N	37 43 E	43C, 46
Koolan *Island*: Australia	16 08 S	123 45 E	43
Koolyanobbing Range: *mtns.*, Australia	30 49 S	119 36 E	43
Koombana *Bay*: Australia	33 18 S	115 39 E	40
Koper: Yugoslavia	45 33 N	13 44 E	37B, 55A
Kopervik: Norway	59 17 N	5 18 E	27C
Kopeysk: U.S.S.R.	55 07 N	61 37 E	38
Ko Phuket: *is.*, Thailand	8 00 N	98 20 E	45C
Köping: Sweden	59 31 N	16 00 E	55, 57, 61
Kopparbergs: *admin.*, Sweden	61 00 N	14 30 E	46, 49
Kopřivnice: Czechoslovakia	49 36 N	18 09 E	55
Kops: *dam*, Austria	46 58 N	10 07 E	39C
Koraput: India	18 48 N	82 41 E	53
Korgen: Norway	66 05 N	13 50 E	46
Kórinthos (Corinth): Greece	37 56 N	22 55 E	17, 59H
Kōriyama: Japan	37 24 N	140 23 E	32A, 59C, 67C
Korkino: U.S.S.R.	54 54 N	61 23 E	38
Korlaće: Yugoslavia	43 22 N	20 39 E	48
Korogwe: Tanzania	5 09 S	38 29 E	48
Korsnäs: *admin.*, Finland	62 45 N	21 15 E	40, 46
Kortrijk (Courtrai): Belgium	50 50 N	3 16 E	31B
Kosaka: Japan	40 19 N	140 44 E	45D, 46C, 49, 59G
Kosaya Gora: U.S.S.R.	54 07 N	37 33 E	43
Kosciusko: Miss., U.S.A.	33 02 N	89 36 W	55
Košice: Czechoslovakia	48 43 N	21 14 E	50, 50B
Kosmosdale: Ky., U.S.A.	38 06 N	85 55 W	57B
Kosovo i Metohija: *admin.*, Yugoslavia	43 35 N	21 00 E	49
Kosovska Mitrovica: Yugo.	42 53 N	20 52 E	38B, 59H
Kossou: *dam*, Ivory Coast	6 57 N	4 58 W	39
Kostinbrod: Bulgaria	42 49 N	23 13 E	50B
Kota: India	25 11 N	75 58 E	31, 32, 60, 61
Kota Kinabalu (Jesselton): Malaysia	5 59 N	116 04 E	84, 87
Kotalahti: Finland	62 33 N	27 33 E	50
Kota Tinggi: *region*, Malaysia	1 49 N	103 58 E	45C
Kothagudem: India	17 30 N	80 20 E	61
Kotka: Finland	60 28 N	26 55 E	25B, 84
Kotovelo: Malagasy Republic	25 02 S	46 23 E	40
Kouilou: *admin.*, Congo R.	4 00 S	12 00 E	49
Kounradskiy: U.S.S.R.	46 59 N	75 00 E	45, 50
Kouvola: Finland	60 52 N	26 42 E	25B
Kovdor: U.S.S.R.	67 34 N	30 28 E	43
Kovilpatti: India	9 12 N	77 55 E	31C
Kowloon: Hong Kong	22 18 N	114 10 E	57
Koyali: India	22 16 N	72 55 E	60
Koyna: *dam*, India	17 25 N	73 45 E	39
Koyuk: Alaska, U.S.A.	64 55 N	161 20 W	49
Kozakai: Japan	34 48 N	137 22 E	32A
Kozhikode *see* Calicut: India	11 15 N	75 45 E	67
Kozloduy: Bulgaria	43 47 N	23 44 E	40
Kozlu: Turkey	41 26 N	31 46 E	38
Krabi: Thailand	8 04 N	98 55 E	38
Kragerø: Norway	58 52 N	9 25 E	48, 52
Kragujevac: Yugoslavia	44 01 N	20 55 E	55
Kraków: Poland	50 04 N	19 57 E	43B
Krakówskie: *admin.*, Poland	50 03 N	19 55 E	38B
Kraljevo: Yugoslavia	43 44 N	20 43 E	50B, 54B
Kralupy: Czechoslovakia	50 26 N	13 20 E	37F
Kralupy nad Vltavou: Czech.	50 14 N	14 19 E	30, 58H, 59H, 60H
Králův Dvůr: Czechoslovakia	49 59 N	14 03 E	57C
Kramatorsk: U.S.S.R.	48 43 N	37 32 E	43C, 57
Krångede: *dam*, Sweden	63 09 N	16 01 E	39
Krásno: Czechoslovakia	50 06 N	12 48 E	45
Krasnodar: U.S.S.R.	45 02 N	39 00 E	36
Krasnodon: U.S.S.R.	48 17 N	39 48 E	38
Krasnogvardeyskiy: U.S.S.R.	57 22 N	62 20 E	45
Krasnokamsk: U.S.S.R.	58 04 N	55 48 E	25
Krasnotur'insk: U.S.S.R.	59 46 N	60 12 E	45, 47
Krasnoural'sk: U.S.S.R.	58 21 N	60 03 E	45
Krasnovishersk: U.S.S.R.	60 23 N	57 03 E	25
Krasnovodsk: U.S.S.R.	40 00 N	53 00 E	35, 36
Krasnoyarsk: *dam*, U.S.S.R.	56 01 N	92 50 E	39
Krasnoyarsk: U.S.S.R.	56 01 N	92 50 E	25, 30, 32C, 36, 47, 57, 60, 61, 67
Krasnyy Sulin: U.S.S.R.	47 54 N	40 03 E	43C
Krefeld: Germany F.R.	51 20 N	6 34 E	43B
Kremastá: *dam*, Greece	38 54 N	21 34 E	39
Kremenchug: *dam*, U.S.S.R.	49 04 N	33 25 E	39
Kremenchug: U.S.S.R.	49 04 N	33 25 E	29, 36, 54, 55
Krems an der Donau: Austria	48 25 N	15 36 E	17
Křešice: Czechoslovakia	50 33 N	14 15 E	29C
Krichëv: U.S.S.	53 42 N	31 43 E	57
Krimpen a/d. IJssel: Neths.	51 55 N	4 35 E	52A
Krishna: India	16 30 N	80 30 E	57
Krishnanagar: India	23 22 N	88 32 E	31
Kristiansand: Norway	58 10 N	8 00 E	27C, 45
Kristiansund: Norway	63 07 N	7 45 E	27
Kritovo: U.S.S.R.	56 15 N	90 00 E	36
Krivoy Rog: U.S.S.R.	47 55 N	33 21 E	43C, 57
Krnov: Czechoslovakia	50 05 N	17 40 E	29C
Krompachy: Czechoslovakia	48 55 N	20 52 E	45, 50B
Krugersdorp: South Africa	26 06 S	27 46 E	40, 50, 50C, 56
Krumovo: Bulgaria	42 16 N	26 24 E	43
Krung Thep (Bangkok): Thai.	13 45 N	100 31 E	31, 32, 36, 59, 60, 67, 84, 87
Krušné Hory *see* Erzgebirge: *mtns.*, Germany D.R.	50 30 N	13 10 E	40B
Kuala Lumpur: *admin.*, Malaysia	3 14 N	101 40 E	45C, 47
Kuala Lumpur: Malaysia	3 10 N	101 42 E	67, 87
Kuang-chou: *admin.*, China P.R.	23 07 N	113 15 E	25, 43, 47, 50D, 52
Kuang-chou (Canton): China P.R.	23 07 N	113 15 E	25, 32, 43, 50D, 52, 55, 57, 59, 60
Kuang-hsi: *admin.*, China P.R.	24 00 N	109 00 E	50
Kuang-tung: *admin.*, China P.R.	23 00 N	113 00 E	58
Kubikenborg: Sweden	62 23 N	17 21 E	47
Kubiki: *region*, Japan	37 00 N	139 00 E	34, 37E
Kubong: South Korea	36 25 N	126 55 E	49
K'u-ch'e: China P.R.	41 43 N	82 54 E	45
Kuchen: Germany F.R.	48 38 N	9 48 E	31B
Kuching: Malaysia	1 33 N	110 20 E	84, 87
Kudamatsu: Japan	34 00 N	131 52 E	37E
Kuei-yang: China P.R.	26 35 N	106 43 E	38, 43, 47, 67
Kufstein: Austria	47 35 N	12 10 E	57C, 58H, 59D
Kūh Angūrān: *mtn.*, Iran	36 44 N	48 38 E	46
Kukës: Albania	42 05 N	20 24 E	50B
Kuldja *see* I-ning: China P.R.	43 54 N	81 21 E	67
Kulim: *admin.*, Malaysia	5 22 N	100 39 E	45C
Kulon Progo: *admin.*, Indon.	7 50 S	110 15 E	50
Kumagaya: Japan	36 08 N	139 23 E	57D
Kumasi: Ghana	6 41 N	1 37 W	2, 3, 49
Kum-Bel': U.S.S.R.	41 44 N	75 40 E	50
Kumertau: U.S.S.R.	52 46 N	55 47 E	38
Kumhari: India	21 15 N	81 30 E	59
Kumotsin: *dam*, China P.R.	47 25 N	127 57 E	39
Kunda: *dam*, India	11 10 N	76 30 E	39
Kunda: U.S.S.R.	59 29 N	26 32 E	57
Kunitomi: Japan	42 45 N	140 30 E	46, 59G
K'un-ming: China P.R.	25 04 N	102 41 E	27, 45, 56, 57, 67
Kunovice: Czechoslovakia	49 03 N	17 28 E	53
Kunsan: South Korea	35 59 N	126 43 E	84D
Kuorevesi: Finland	61 56 N	24 43 E	53
Kurashiki: Japan	34 35 N	133 46 E	32A, 55
Kurday: U.S.S.R.	43 35 N	75 00 E	57
Kŭrdzhali: Bulgaria	41 39 N	25 22 E	46B
Kure: Japan	34 14 N	132 34 E	43D, 52B
Kurgan: U.S.S.R.	55 26 N	65 18 E	55, 67
Kurnell: Australia	34 01 S	151 12 E	30, 36, 60
Kurobegawa: *dam*, Japan	36 36 N	137 38 E	39D
Kurosaki: Japan	40 00 N	141 56 E	58C, 58G, 59G, 61C, 61G
Kursk: U.S.S.R.	51 42 N	36 12 E	29, 32C, 67
Kuruman: *admin.*, S. Africa	27 28 S	23 27 E	43, 48
Kushiro: Japan	42 58 N	144 23 E	25, 27D, 38, 59G, 67
Kūshk: Iran	31 50 N	55 45 E	46
Kushmurun: U.S.S.R.	52 27 N	64 36 E	38, 47
Kushtia: Pakistan	23 55 N	89 07 E	31
Kusinskiy Zavod: U.S.S.R.	55 21 N	59 24 E	47
Kuskokwim *River*: Alaska, U.S.A.	61 30 N	160 00 W	50
Kustanay: U.S.S.R.	53 10 N	63 35 E	67
Kütahya: Turkey	39 25 N	29 59 E	61
Kutaisi: U.S.S.R.	42 15 N	42 40 E	29, 55
Kutina: Yugoslavia	45 29 N	16 47 E	60H, 61H
Kutjevo: Yugoslavia	45 25 N	17 53 E	17
Kuvasay: U.S.S.R.	40 18 N	71 59 E	57
Kuvshinovo: U.S.S.R.	57 02 N	34 12 E	25
Kuwait *see* Al Kuwayt: Kuwait	29 20 N	47 59 E	56, 67, 84, 87
Kuybyshev: U.S.S.R.	53 12 N	50 09 E	30, 36, 58, 60, 61, 67
Kuznetskiy Basseyn: *basin*, U.S.S.R.	54 00 N	86 00 E	38
Kuzuu: Japan	36 24 N	139 37 E	57D
Kvarnsveden: Sweden	60 31 N	15 24 E	25B
Kwaadmechelen: Belgium	51 06 N	5 08 E	59H
Kwakwani: Guyana	5 16 N	58 04 W	47
Kwangtung: *dam*, China P.R.	40 15 N	115 38 E	39
Kwinana: Australia	32 15 S	115 46 E	36, 47, 59, 61
Kyle of Lochalsh: Scotland	57 17 N	5 43 W	27C
Kymore: India	23 47 N	80 29 E	57
Kyoga, *Lake*: Uganda	1 30 N	33 00 E	27
Kyōto: Japan	35 00 N	135 45 E	29D, 55, 60C
Kyoto-fu: *admin.*, Japan	35 10 N	135 30 E	50
Kyshtym: U.S.S.R.	55 42 N	60 34 E	45
Kyzyl: U.S.S.R.	51 42 N	94 27 E	38
Kyzyl-Kiya: U.S.S.R.	40 16 N	72 08 E	38

L

	° ′	° ′	Page(s)
La Angostura: Bolivia	19 57 S	62 58 W	59
La Barasse: France	43 17 N	5 28 E	47B
La Bassée: France	50 32 N	2 48 E	61D, 61H
La Bâthie: *dam*, France	45 38 N	6 27 E	39C
La Batlloria: Spain	41 43 N	2 33 E	32C
La Blanca: Texas, U.S.A.	26 20 N	98 02 W	37J
La Calera: Chile	32 47 S	71 12 W	57
La Calera: Colombia	4 37 N	74 04 W	57
Lac Allard: Canada	50 31 N	63 31 W	47
La Calle: Algeria	36 53 N	8 29 E	27B
La Ceiba: Honduras	15 47 N	86 50 W	87
La Chapelle-Largeau: France	46 57 N	0 50 W	40B
La Ciotat: France	43 10 N	5 36 E	52A
La Cira: Colombia	7 00 N	73 47 W	35
Lackawanna: N.Y., U.S.A.	42 49 N	78 49 W	43A
Lacorne: Canada	48 22 N	78 00 W	50
La Coruña: *admin.*, Spain	43 10 N	8 25 W	38
La Coruña: Spain	43 22 N	8 23 W	27B, 36, 37D, 38, 47, 61, 61D, 67, 84,
La Couronne: France	45 37 N	0 06 E	57C
Lacq: France	43 25 N	0 38 W	34, 37B, 56, 58D, 58H, 59H, 60H
La Crosse: Wis., U.S.A.	43 48 N	91 04 W	40C, 56
Ladner: Canada	49 06 N	123 05 W	58
La Dorada: Colombia	5 27 N	74 40 W	36
Ladysmith: South Africa	28 34 S	29 47 E	31
Lae: New Guinea	6 45 S	147 00 E	87
Lafarge: France	44 31 N	4 41 E	57C
Lafat: France	46 20 N	1 37 E	40B
Lafayette: La., U.S.A.	30 12 N	92 18 W	87C
La Felguera: Spain	43 19 N	5 41 W	61D
Lagenthal: Switzerland	47 13 N	7 48 E	31B
Lägerdorf: Germany F.R.	53 53 N	9 35 E	57C
Lago Agrio: *region*, Ecuador	0 00 N	76 30 W	35
Lago de Maracaibo: *lake*, Venezuela	9 40 N	71 30 W	34, 35, 56
Lago di Molveno: *dam*, Italy	46 08 N	10 57 E	39C
Lagos: Nigeria	6 27 N	3 28 E	54, 67, 84, 87
La Grange: Ga., U.S.A.	33 02 N	85 02 W	32B
La Grange: Ill., U.S.A.	41 47 N	87 53 W	54A
La Grave: France	43 48 N	7 22 E	57C
La Habana (Havana): Cuba	23 08 N	82 22 W	25, 35, 36, 67, 84 87
Lahore: Pakistan	31 35 N	74 18 E	67, 87
L'Aigle: *dam*, France	45 17 N	2 15 E	39
La Jolla: Calif., U.S.A.	32 50 N	117 16 W	62
Lake Albert: *lake*, Africa	1 40 N	31 00 E	27
Lake Bangweule: *lake*, Zambia	11 05 S	29 45 E	27
Lake Charles: La., U.S.A.	30 13 N	93 13 W	30A, 37J, 57A, 58A, 58E, 59B, 59F, 60A, 60G, 61B, 61E, 87C
Lake *Co.*: Colo., U.S.A.	39 15 N	106 30 W	49B
Lakehurst: N.J., U.S.A.	40 01 N	74 19 W	47
Lake Kariba: *lake*, Africa	17 00 S	28 00 E	27
Lake Kitangiri: *lake*, Tanzania	4 04 S	34 19 E	27
Lake Kyoga: *lake*, Uganda	1 30 N	33 00 E	27
Lakeland: Fla., U.S.A.	28 02 N	81 59 W	61B
Lake Malawi *see* Lake Nyasa: *lake*, Africa	12 00 S	34 30 E	27
Lake Malombe: *lake*, Malawi	14 38 S	35 12 E	27
Lake Mweru: *lake*, Africa	9 00 S	28 45 E	27
Lake Nyasa (Lake Malawi): *lake*, Africa	12 00 S	34 30 E	27
Lake Oswego: Oreg., U.S.A.	45 25 N	122 42 W	57
Lake Rukwa: *lake*, Tanzania	8 00 S	32 25 E	27
Laketon: Ind., U.S.A.	40 58 N	85 49 W	37J
Lake Victoria: *lake*, Africa	1 00 S	33 00 E	27
Lake Woollaston: *lake*, Canada	58 15 N	103 20 W	40
Lākheri: India	25 40 N	76 25 E	57
La Leona: Mexico	25 34 N	101 37 W	32
La Libertad: *admin.*, Peru	8 00 S	78 30 W	49
La Libertad: Ecuador	2 14 S	80 57 W	36
La Louvière: Belgium	50 28 N	4 11 E	43B
La Madeleine: France	48 39 N	6 15 E	59D, 61D, 61H
La Mancha: *plain*, Spain	39 05 N	3 00 W	17
Lambertsbaai: South Africa	32 04 S	18 20 E	27
La Mède: France	43 24 N	5 07 E	37H
Lamía: Greece	38 55 N	22 26 E	61H
La Motte: Canada	48 19 N	78 08 W	50
Lamu: Kenya	2 16 S	40 54 E	84
Lanai City: Hawaii, U.S.A.	20 50 N	156 55 W	87
Lancashire and Cheshire: *region*, England	53 30 N	2 30 W	56A
Lancaster: England	54 03 N	2 48 W	32C
Lan-chou: China P.R.	36 03 N	103 41 E	30, 36, 60, 61, 67
Landeck: Austria	47 08 N	10 34 E	31B
Lander *Co.*: Nev., U.S.A.	40 00 N	117 00 W	40A
Landes: *admin.*, France	44 00 N	0 50 W	38B
Landskrona: Sweden	55 52 N	12 50 E	52A, 61, 84C
Langebaan: South Africa	33 06 S	18 03 E	27, 56
Langelsheim: Germany F.R.	51 56 N	10 20 E	30B, 61H
Langensalza: *admin.*, G.D.R.	51 05 N	10 40 E	37B
Langenthal: Switzerland	47 13 N	7 48 E	31B
Langerbrugge: Belgium	51 07 N	3 44 E	25C
Långsele: Sweden	64 49 N	20 15 E	45
Langwa: Burma	21 23 N	96 11 E	35
Lannemezan: France	43 08 N	0 23 E	47B, 58H, 61D, 61H
L'Anse: Mich., U.S.A.	46 45 N	88 27 W	25D
Lansing: Mich., U.S.A.	42 44 N	85 34 W	55B, 67A, 87B
Lanzarote, Isla de: *island*, Spain	29 00 N	13 40 W	27
Lanžhot: Czechoslovakia	48 44 N	16 58 E	37B
Lao Cai: North Vietnam	22 30 N	103 57 E	56
Lao-ha Ho: *river*, China P.R.	43 24 N	120 39 E	38
La Oroya: Peru	11 36 S	75 54 W	45, 46, 50, 59
La Pallice: France	46 10 N	1 13 W	61D, 61H
La Pampilla: Peru	12 00 S	77 00 W	36
La Paz: *admin.*, Bolivia	15 30 S	68 00 W	49
La Paz: Bolivia	16 30 S	68 09 W	67, 87
La Paz: Mexico	23 41 N	100 43 W	49A
La Paz: Mexico	24 10 N	110 18 W	87
La Paz: Mexico	26 59 N	105 02 W	45
La Plata: Argentina	34 55 S	57 57 W	32, 36, 58, 84
La Platte: Nebr., U.S.A.	41 05 N	95 55 W	61A, 61E
La Porte: Texas, U.S.A.	29 38 N	95 03 W	60A
Lappeenranta: Finland	61 04 N	28 11 E	57
La Pra: France	45 12 N	6 35 E	47B
La Quiaca: Argentina	22 06 S	65 37 W	50
L'Aquila: *admin.*, Italy	42 05 N	13 40 E	47B
Larache: Morocco	35 12 N	6 10 W	27B
La Rance: *dam*, France	48 37 N	2 01 W	39
Larap: Philippines	14 07 N	122 35 E	43
Larder Lake: Canada	48 06 N	79 44 W	49
Laredo: Spain	43 24 N	3 25 W	27B
La Reuchenette: Switzerland	47 11 N	7 15 E	57C
Largentière: France	44 32 N	4 18 E	46B, 49
L'Argentière-la-Bessée: France	44 47 N	6 33 E	47B
La Rioja: *admin.*, Argentina	30 00 S	67 30 W	40
La Rioja: *region*, Spain	42 20 N	2 20 W	17
La Robla: Spain	42 48 N	5 37 W	57C
La Rochelle: France	46 10 N	1 09 W	27, 40B, 55A, 84
La-sa: China P.R.	24 25 N	97 48 E	29
La Saussa: France	45 13 N	6 29 E	47B
La Seyne-sur-Mer: France	43 06 N	5 53 E	52A
La Souys: France	44 50 N	0 32 W	57C
Las Palmas: *admin.*, Canary Is.	28 20 N	14 20 W	16
Las Palmas de Gran Canaria: Canary Is.	28 06 N	15 24 W	27, 59, 61, 67, 84, 87
La Spezia: Italy	44 07 N	9 50E	37B, 37D, 37H, 46B, 52A, 84A
Lastoursville: Gabon	0 49 S	12 42 E	49
Las Vegas: Nev., U.S.A.	36 10 N	105 15 W	87A
Las Ventanas: Chile	32 44 S	71 29 W	45
Lathrop: Calif., U.S.A.	37 50 N	121 17 W	59, 61
Latina: Italy	41 28 N	12 52 E	40
La Trenche: *dam*, Canada	47 45 N	72 53 W	39B
La Trobe *Valley*: Australia	38 07 S	147 13 E	38
La Tuque: Canada	47 26 N	72 47 W	25D
La Tuque: *dam*, Canada	47 29 N	72 48 W	39B
Latviyskaya S.S.R.: *admin.*, U.S.S.R.	57 00 N	25 00 E	27
Launceston: Australia	41 25 S	147 08 E	29, 84
Laurel: Mont., U.S.A.	45 40 N	108 46 W	36
Laurel Hill: N.Y., U.S.A.	40 46 N	70 55 W	45
Laurens Shoals: *dam*, Ga., U.S.A.	33 19 N	83 24 W	39
Lauta: Germany D.R.	51 28 N	14 04 E	47B
Lautenthal: Germany F.R.	51 52 N	10 18 E	46B
Lauzon: Canada	46 49 N	71 10 W	52
Laval: France	48 04 N	0 46 W	31B
La Vallita: *dam*, Mexico	18 15 N	101 55 W	39
Lavanttal: *valley*, Austria	46 40 N	14 50 E	38B
Lavender: Ariz., U.S.A.	31 27 N	109 56 W	45A
La Voulte-sur-Rhône: France	44 48 N	4 47 E	32C
Lavradio: Portugal	38 40 N	9 03 W	61, 61D

	° ′	° ′	Page(s)
Lávrion: Greece	37 43 N	24 03 E	46B, 49
La Wantzenau: France	48 40 N	7 50 E	30B
Lawrence: Kans., U.S.A.	38 58 N	95 15 W	61A, 61E
Lawrence: Mass., U.S.A.	42 41 N	71 12 W	25D
Lawrenceville: Ill., U.S.A.	38 44 N	87 42 W	37J
Lawton: Okla., U.S.A.	34 36 N	98 25 W	87C
Leavesden: England	51 44 N	0 26 W	53B
Lebanon *Co.*: Pa., U.S.A.	40 20 N	76 30 W	49
Le Bouchet: France	48 32 N	2 22 E	40B
Lechinţa: Romania	47 56 N	23 18 E	17
Le Creusot: France	46 48 N	4 26 E	43, 54B
Leeds: Ala., U.S.A.	33 33 N	86 33 W	57B
Leeds: England	51 15 N	0 36 E	29B, 37B, 54B, 67B, 87
Leesville: *dam*, Va., U.S.A.	37 03 N	79 29 W	39
Le Genevray: France	45 02 N	5 39 E	57C
Leghorn *see* Livorno: Italy	43 33 N	10 19 E	30B, 32C, 37H, 52A, 57C, 84A
Legnago: Italy	45 11 N	11 18 E	59H
Legnano: Italy	45 36 N	8 54 E	31B
Legnica: Poland	51 12 N	16 10 E	25C, 45, 59H
Le Grand-Quevilly: France	49 25 N	1 02 E	59D, 61D, 61H
Le Havre: France	49 30 N	0 08 E	30B, 37B, 37D, 59H, 67B, 84C
Leicester: England	52 38 N	1 05 W	29B, 67B
Leigh: England	53 30 N	2 33 W	31B
Leigh Creek: *river*, Australia	29 47 S	138 11 E	38
Leinster: *region*, Irish Republic	53 00 N	7 30 W	38
Leipzig: *admin.*, Germany D.R.	51 20 N	12 20 E	38B
Leipzig: Germany D.R.	51 18 N	12 20 E	29C, 31B, 67B
Leirvik: Norway	59 47 N	5 30 E	52
Leith: Scotland	55 59 N	3 10 W	27C, 59H, 61H, 84C
Le Lardin: France	45 08 N	1 13 E	25
Le Mans: France	48 00 N	0 12 W	55A, 67B
Lemhi *Co.*: Idaho, U.S.A.	45 00 N	114 25 W	49
Lemona: Spain	43 13 N	2 46 W	57C
Lemont: Ill., U.S.A.	41 39 N	87 59 W	37J, 58B
Le Moyne: Ala., U.S.A.	30 40 N	88 05 W	32B
Lend: Austria	47 18 N	13 04 E	47B
Lendava: Yugoslavia	46 34 N	16 27 E	58H
Lenger: U.S.S.R.	42 12 N	69 54 E	38
Lengerich: Germany F.R.	52 11 N	7 52 E	57C
Leng-hu: China P.R.	38 57 N	93 25 E	36
Leninabad: U.S.S.R.	40 56 N	72 01 E	43
Leninakan: U.S.S.R.	40 48 N	43 50 E	31
Leningrad: U.S.S.R.	59 55 N	30 15 E	25B, 30, 31, 32C, 34, 35, 36, 43, 52, 60, 67, 84, 87
Leninogorsk: U.S.S.R.	50 22 N	83 32 E	46, 49
Leninsk-Kuznetskiy: U.S.S.R.	54 38 N	86 10 E	38
Leninskoye: U.S.S.R.	47 56 N	132 38 E	50
Lenin, V.I.: *dam*, (Dnepr), U.S.S.R.	47 49 N	35 11 E	39
Lenin, V.I.: *dam*, (Volga), U.S.S.R.	53 25 N	49 30 E	39
Lenzing: Austria	47 58 N	13 37 E	32C, 59H
Leominster: Mass., U.S.A.	42 31 N	71 45 W	60B
León: *admin.*, Nicaragua	12 35 N	86 35 W	49
León: *admin.*, Spain	42 40 N	6 00 W	38B, 43B
León: Mexico	21 07 N	101 40 W	57
Léopoldville *see* Kinshasa: Congo D.R.	4 18 N	15 18 E	31, 36, 56, 67, 87
Le Palais-sur-Vienne: France	45 52 N	1 19 E	45
Lepanto: Philippines	16 55 N	120 50 E	45
Le Péage-de-Roussillon: France	45 22 N	4 48 E	58H, 61H
Le Petit-Couronne: France	49 23 N	1 01 E	37F
Le Pont-de-Claix: France	45 07 N	5 42 E	58H
Le Port: Réunion	20 55 S	55 18 E	84
Lequeitio: Spain	43 22 N	2 30 W	27B
Lérida: *admin.*, Spain	42 00 N	1 10 E	38B
Lerma: Mexico	19 48 N	90 36 W	30
Lerwick: Scotland	60 09 N	1 09 W	27C
Les: Pakistan	30 30 N	66 50 E	38
Les Bois Noirs: *mtns.*, France	45 55 N	3 45 E	40B
L'Escarpière: France	47 05 N	1 11 W	40B
Leskovac: Yugoslavia	42 59 N	21 57 E	60D
L'Estaque: France	43 22 N	5 20 E	59D, 59H
Letchworth: England	51 58 N	0 14 W	62A
Leticia: Colombia	4 09 S	69 57 W	27
Le Touquet-Paris-Plage: France	50 31 N	1 35 E	87D
Le Trait: France	49 28 N	0 49 E	52A
Letsi: *dam*, Sweden	66 31 N	20 04 E	39
Leuna: Germany D.R.	51 19 N	12 01 E	58H, 60D, 60H, 61D
Levanger: Norway	63 45 N	11 18 E	25
Leverkusen: Germany F.R.	51 01 N	6 59 E	30B, 58D, 58H, 59D, 59H, 60D
Levikha: U.S.S.R.	57 36 N	59 55 E	45
Levskigrad: Bulgaria	42 38 N	24 48 E	17
Lewis and Clark *Co.*: Mont., U.S.A.	47 00 N	112 30 W	49
Lewiston: Idaho, U.S.A.	46 25 N	117 00 W	25
Lewiston: Maine, U.S.A.	44 06 N	70 14 W	31
Lewistown: Pa., U.S.A.	40 37 N	77 36 W	32B
Lexington: Ky., U.S.A.	38 02 N	84 30 W	62, 67A, 87B
Lexington: N.C., U.S.A.	35 50 N	80 27 W	32B
Lexos: France	44 09 N	1 52 E	57C
Leydsdorp: South Africa	23 59 S	30 30 E	48
Lezo: Spain	43 19 N	1 54 W	59H
Liao-ning: *admin.*, China P.R.	41 00 N	123 00 E	50

	° ′	° ′	Page(s)
Liao-yüan: China P.R.	42 55 N	125 09 E	38C
Libby: *dam*, Mont., U.S.A.	48 25 N	115 33 W	39A
Liberdade: Brazil	22 01 S	44 19 W	50
Libreville: Gabon	0 23 N	9 27 E	84
Li-chiang: China P.R.	26 48 N	100 16 E	45
Lichtenburg: South Africa	26 09 S	26 11 E	57
Lidcombe: Australia	33 52 S	151 02 E	53
Liège (Luik): Belgium	50 38 N	5 34 E	38B, 58D, 62A, 67B
Liepāja: U.S.S.R.	56 31 N	21 01 E	43
Liévin: France	50 25 N	2 46 E	61D, 61H
Liguria: *admin.*, Italy	44 30 N	8 50 E	17
Lihue: Hawaii, U.S.A.	21 59 N	159 22 W	87
Likasi (Jadotville): Congo D.R.	10 59 S	26 44 E	45, 67
Likino: U.S.S.R.	55 44 N	38 57 E	55
Lilla Edet: Sweden	58 08 N	12 08 E	25B
Lille: France	50 38 N	3 04 E	29B, 31B, 37B, 54B, 67B
Lillebonne: France	49 31 N	0 33 E	60D
Lima: *admin.*, Peru	12 00 S	76 35 W	46, 49
Lima: Ohio, U.S.A.	40 43 N	84 06 W	37J, 55B, 58B, 61A, 61E
Lima: Peru	12 06 S	77 03 W	2, 25, 29, 31, 32, 34, 55, 56, 59, 60, 67, 87
Limassol: Cyprus	34 40 N	33 03 E	17, 84B
Limbe: Malawi	15 49 S	35 03 E	67
Limberg: *dam*, Austria	47 17 N	12 46 E	39C
Limburg: *admin.*, Belgium	51 00 N	5 30 E	56A
Limburg, Southern: *region*, Netherlands	50 53 N	5 59 E	38B
Lime: Oreg., U.S.A.	44 24 N	117 18 W	57
Limerick: Irish Republic	52 40 N	8 38 W	57C, 84C
Limhamn: Sweden	55 35 N	12 54 E	57
Limni: Cyprus	35 02 N	32 28 E	45
Limón: Costa Rica	10 00 N	83 02 W	36, 84
Limoux: France	43 04 N	2 14 E	17
Limpias: Spain	43 22 N	3 25 W	60H
Linares: Spain	38 05 N	3 38 W	46B
Lincoln: Nebr., U.S.A.	40 49 N	96 41 W	87B
Lincoln *Co.*: Nev., U.S.A.	37 30 N	115 00 W	49B
Lincolnton: N.C., U.S.A.	35 27 N	81 16 W	31A
Lindale: Ga., U.S.A.	34 09 N	85 10 W	31A
Linden: N.J., U.S.A.	40 38 N	74 15 W	37J, 58F, 59A, 59E
Lindö: Denmark	55 30 N	10 30 E	52A
Linganamakki: *dam*, India	14 05 N	74 55 E	39
Lingen: Germany F.R.	52 31 N	7 19 E	37F, 40B, 58D
Linköping: Sweden	58 25 N	15 37 E	32C, 53, 54
Linne: Netherlands	51 09 N	5 56 E	59D
Linz: Austria	48 18 N	14 18 E	43B, 58D, 61D, 61H
Lionel: Australia	21 39 S	120 07 E	48
Lipetsk: U.S.S.R.	52 37 N	39 35 E	43, 57
Lipis: *admin.*, Malaysia	4 20 N	102 10 E	49
Lisas, *Point*: Trinidad	10 22 N	61 29 W	61
Lisboa: Portugal	38 43 N	9 08 W	27B, 29, 36, 55, 56, 59, 67, 84, 87
Li-shu: *admin.*, China P.R.	43 20 N	124 37 E	57
Lisichansk: U.S.S.R.	48 55 N	36 26 E	59, 61
Lisnaskea: Northern Ireland	54 15 N	7 26 W	31
Listerhill: Ala., U.S.A.	34 45 N	87 40 W	47
Lithgow: Australia	33 29 S	150 09 E	38
Litoměřice: Czechoslovakia	50 33 N	14 10 E	17
Litomyšl: Czechoslovakia	49 52 N	16 20 E	32C
Litovskaya S.S.R.: *admin.*, U.S.S.R.	56 00 N	24 00 E	27
Little Bay: Canada	49 40 N	55 55 W	45, 49
Little Goose: *dam*, Wash., U.S.A.	46 36 N	118 01 W	39A
Little Heath: England	52 29 N	1 30 W	32C
Little Rock: Ark., U.S.A.	34 42 N	92 17 W	2, 59F, 87C
Litvínov: Czechoslovakia	50 38 N	13 30 E	31B, 37F
Liu-chia: *dam*, China P.R.	35 55 N	103 25 E	39
Liu-chou: China P.R.	24 19 N	109 24 E	43, 57
Liu-shu-t'un: China P.R.	39 01 N	121 43 E	36
Liu-tao-wan: China P.R.	43 49 N	87 34 E	38
Liu-tu: Taiwan	25 05 N	121 42 E	32
Livermore Falls: Maine, U.S.A.	44 28 N	70 11 W	59A
Liverpool: England	53 25 N	2 55 W	37D, 55A, 67B, 84C, 87
Livorno (Leghorn): Italy	43 33 N	10 19 E	30B, 32C, 37H, 52A, 57C, 84A
Lixhe: Belgium	50 45 N	5 40 E	57C
Ljubija: Yugoslavia	44 57 N	16 38 E	43B
Ljubljana: Yugoslavia	46 02 N	14 30 E	31B, 32C, 53
Ljuboten: Yugoslavia	42 06 N	21 29 E	50B
Llandarcy: Wales	51 38 N	3 48 W	37F
Llanwern: England/Wales	51 35 N	2 55 W	43B
Llanwnen: Wales	52 06 N	4 09 W	58D
Llavallol: Argentina	34 47 S	58 26 W	32
Llolleo: Chile	33 37 S	71 37 W	32
Lloydminster: Canada	53 18 N	110 00 W	36
Lobito: Angola	12 20 S	13 34 E	27, 84
Lobitos: Peru	4 30 S	81 15 W	35
Lochaber: Scotland	56 57 N	5 30 W	47
Lo-ch'ang: China P.R.	25 08 N	113 20 E	50D
Lochkov: Czechoslovakia	49 59 N	14 23 E	57C
Lock Haven: Pa., U.S.A.	41 09 N	77 28 W	25D, 53A
Lockport: Ill., U.S.A.	41 34 N	88 03 W	37J, 61A
Lod: Israel	31 57 N	34 54 E	53

	° ′	° ′	Page(s)
Lodève: France	43 43 N	3 19 E	40B
Lodosa: Spain	42 25 N	2 05 W	59H
Łódź: Poland	51 49 N	19 28 E	25C, 29C, 31, 32C
Loffa *River*: Liberia	6 36 N	11 08 W	48
Logroño: Spain	42 28 N	2 27 W	17, 29
Loire: *admin.*, France	45 30 N	4 00 E	38B
Lomas: Peru	15 33 S	74 50 W	27A
Lomme: France	50 39 N	2 59 E	31B
Lommel: Belgium	51 14 N	5 18 E	46B
Londoko: U.S.S.R.	49 02 N	131 59 E	57
London: Canada	42 58 N	81 15 W	54A, 67A
London: England	51 30 N	0 10 W	37B, 46B, 63A, 63B, 67, 84C, 87
London: *region*, England	51 30 N	0 15 W	56A
Londonderry: Northern Ireland	55 00 N	7 19 W	30, 84C
London, North West: *region*, England	51 34 N	0 15 W	53B
Londrina: Brazil	23 18 S	51 09 W	67
Lone Star: Texas, U.S.A.	32 56 N	94 43 W	43
Long Beach: Calif., U.S.A.	33 47 N	118 15 W	36, 53, 60, 84, 87A
Long Itchington: England	52 17 N	1 24 W	57C
Longview: Texas, U.S.A.	32 30 N	94 45 W	37J, 58E, 60A, 87C
Longview: Wash., U.S.A.	46 08 N	122 56 W	25, 47, 59
Longwy: France	49 31 N	5 46 E	43B
Loos: France	50 37 N	3 01 E	59D
Lorain: Ohio, U.S.A.	41 28 N	82 11 W	43A, 55B
Lorient: France	47 45 N	3 22 W	27, 37B
Los Angeles: Calif., U.S.A.	34 00 N	118 15 W	25, 34, 35, 43, 53, 55, 56, 59, 62, 63, 67, 84, 87A
Los Bronces: Chile	33 08 S	70 18 W	45
L'Oseraie: France	43 59 N	4 52 E	59H
Los Ríos: *admin.*, Ecuador	1 30 S	79 25 W	16
Lossiemouth: Scotland	57 43 N	3 18 W	27C
Lostock Gralam: England	53 16 N	2 28 W	59D
Lot: Belgium	50 46 N	4 16 E	54B
Loudonville: Ohio, U.S.A.	40 39 N	82 14 W	55B
Lough Allen: *lake*, Irish R.	54 08 N	8 08 W	38
Loughborough: England	52 47 N	1 11 W	54B
Louisiana: *admin.*, U.S.A.	31 00 N	92 00 W	27
Louisiana: Mo., U.S.A.	39 27 N	91 02 W	61A, 61E
Louisville: Ky., U.S.A.	38 13 N	85 48 W	30A, 32B, 37J, 55B, 59A, 60, 67A, 87B
Louisville: Nebr., U.S.A.	41 00 N	96 10 W	57
Lourdes: France	43 06 N	0 03 W	87
Lourenço Marques: Mozambique	25 58 S	32 34 E	36, 67, 84
Louvroil: France	50 16 N	3 58 E	43B
Loveland: Colo., U.S.A.	40 24 N	105 06 W	62
Lovosice: Czechoslovakia	50 31 N	14 04 E	32C, 61D
Lowell: Vt., U.S.A.	44 47 N	72 27 W	48
Lower Granite: *dam*, Wash., U.S.A.	46 40 N	117 25 W	39A
Lower Monumental: *dam*, Wash., U.S.A.	46 30 N	118 30 W	39A
Lowestoft: England	52 29 N	1 45 E	27C
Lowland: Tenn., U.S.A.	36 06 N	83 14 W	32B, 60B
Lo-yang: China P.R.	34 41 N	112 28 E	55
Lozère: *admin.*, France	44 30 N	3 30 E	40B
Loznica: Yugoslavia	44 32 N	19 13 E	32C
Lozovac: Yugoslavia	43 48 N	15 58 E	47B
Luanda: Angola	8 48 S	13 14 E	27, 36, 57, 61, 67, 84, 87
Luang, Khao: *mtn.*, Thailand	8 30 N	99 40 E	50
Luanshya: Zambia	13 08 S	28 24 E	45B
Lubaczów: Poland	50 11 N	23 08 E	37B
Luban: Poland	51 07 N	15 17 E	31B
Lubbock: Texas, U.S.A.	33 35 N	101 53 W	87C
Lübeck: Germany F.R.	53 52 N	10 42 E	37B, 45, 52A, 58D, 61D, 67B, 84C
Lubin: Poland	51 23 N	16 10 E	45
Lubmin: Germany D.R.	54 07 N	13 36 E	40B
Luboń: Poland	52 25 N	16 55 E	59H
Lubudi: Congo D.R.	9 57 S	25 58 E	57
Lubumbashi (Élisabethville): Congo D.R.	11 40 S	27 28 E	45, 60, 67
Lučenec: Czechoslovakia	48 20 N	19 40 E	50B
Lucens: Switzerland	46 43 N	6 51 E	32C, 40B
Luchana: Spain	43 17 N	2 59 W	58D, 61D
Lüderitz: South West Africa	26 38 S	15 10 E	84
Ludhiana: India	30 56 N	75 52 E	29
Ludwigshafen: Germany F.R.	49 29 N	8 27 E	47B, 58D, 58H, 59D, 59H, 60D, 60H, 61D, 61H, 63B
Lueders: Texas, U.S.A.	32 47 N	99 37 W	37J
Luena: Congo D.R.	9 27 S	25 47 E	38
Lufkin: Texas, U.S.A.	31 21 N	94 47 W	25
Lugansk: U.S.S.R.	48 34 N	39 20 E	54
Lugones: Spain	43 24 N	5 48 W	45
Luik *see* Liège: Belgium	50 38 N	5 34 E	38B, 58D, 62A, 67B
Luilo: Congo D.R.	10 40 S	25 45 E	45
Luino: Italy	46 00 N	8 44 E	31B
Luján de Cuyo: Argentina	33 03 S	68 52 W	36
Lukala: Congo D.R.	5 31 S	14 32 E	57
Lukavac: Yugoslavia	44 33 N	18 32 E	58D, 58H, 59D, 59H
Luke: Md., U.S.A.	39 30 N	79 04 W	25D

	° ′	° ′	Page(s)
Luleå: Sweden	65 34 N	22 10 E	43, 84, 87
Luling: La., U.S.A.	29 56 N	90 24 W	61B, 61E
Lülsdorf: Germany F.R.	50 50 N	7 00 E	58H, 59D
Luluabourg *see* Kananga: Congo D.R.	5 54 S	22 25 E	67
Lumberton: N.C., U.S.A.	34 37 N	79 03 W	32B
Lunda: *admin.*, Angola	9 30 S	20 00 E	48
Lundazi: Zambia	12 19 S	33 13 E	48
Lünen: Germany F.R.	51 37 N	7 31 E	45, 47B
Lünersee: *dam*, Austria	47 04 N	9 45 E	39C
Lunéville: France	48 36 N	6 30 E	54B
Lung-yen: China P.R.	25 11 N	117 00 E	43
Lupa: *river*, Tanzania	8 39 S	33 12 E	49
Lupeni: Rhodesia	45 21 N	23 14 E	32C
Lusaka: Zambia	15 25 S	28 17 E	67
Lü-ta (Dairen): China P.R.	38 55 N	121 39 E	52, 54, 57, 84
Luton: England	51 53 N	0 25 W	55A, 59H
Lutong: Malaysia	4 28 N	114 00 E	36
Lutopan: Philippines	10 30 N	123 38 E	45
Lutry: Switzerland	46 31 N	6 42 E	17
Lützkendorf: Germany D.R.	51 18 N	11 51 E	37F
Luxembourg: Luxembourg	49 37 N	6 08 E	87D
Luzon: *is.*, Philippines	16 00 N	121 00 E	27
L'vov: U.S.S.R.	49 50 N	24 00 E	25, 37F, 55
L'vovsko-Volynskiy Basseyn: *basin*, U.S.S.R.	51 00 N	24 15 E	38
Lyallpur: Pakistan	31 25 N	73 09 E	31, 32, 60, 67
Lyangar: U.S.S.R.	40 25 N	65 59 E	50
Lyaskelya: U.S.S.R.	61 46 N	31 01 E	25B
Lydd: England	50 57 N	0 55 E	87D
Lydenburg: South Africa	25 10 S	30 29 E	49, 50, 50C
Lyell, *Mount*: Australia	42 03 S	145 38 E	45, 49, 56
Lynchburg: Va., U.S.A.	37 24 N	79 09 W	25A, 40C, 67A
Lynn: Mass., U.S.A.	42 29 N	70 57 W	53A
Lynn Lake: Canada	56 51 N	101 01 W	45, 50
Lyon: France	45 45 N	4 51 E	37B, 46B, 55A, 87D
Lyons Falls: N.Y., U.S.A.	43 36 N	75 22 W	25D
Lysanovka: U.S.S.R.	53 31 N	63 06 E	50
Lysesund: Norway	63 53 N	9 52 E	27
Lys'va: U.S.S.R.	58 07 N	57 47 E	43
Lytton: Australia	27 25 S	153 10 E	36

M

	° ′	° ′	Page(s)
Ma-an-shan: China P.R.	31 44 N	118 28 E	43
Maastricht: Netherlands	50 51 N	5 42 E	57C
Mabini: Philippines	7 00 N	126 20 E	45
McAdenville: N.C., U.S.A.	35 16 N	81 05 W	29
Macagua-Caroni: *dam*, Venezuela	8 15 N	62 45 W	39
Macalders: Kenya	0 58 S	34 17 E	45
McAllen: Texas, U.S.A.	26 13 N	98 15 W	37J, 87C
McCormick: *dam*, Canada	49 10 N	68 18 W	39B
McCormick: S.C., U.S.A.	33 55 N	82 19 W	29
Macedonia *see* Makedonija: *admin.*, Yugoslavia	41 50 N	22 00 E	38B, 48
Maceió: Brazil	9 40 S	35 43 W	59, 60, 67, 84
Maceira: Portugal	38 52 N	9 19 W	57C
McGill: Nev., U.S.A.	39 24 N	114 47 W	45
Mach: *basin*, Pakistan	29 50 N	67 20 E	38
Macherla: India	16 29 N	79 25 E	57
Machias: Maine, U.S.A.	44 44 N	67 28 W	35
Machów: Poland	50 31 N	21 34 E	59H
McIntosh: Ala., U.S.A.	31 15 N	88 03 W	59B
Mackay: Australia	21 09 S	149 12 E	87
Mackenzie: Guyana	5 58 N	58 17 W	47
McKinley *Co.*: N. Mex., U.S.A.	35 30 N	108 00 W	40A
McMurray: Canada	56 45 N	111 27 W	36
McNary: *dam*, Wash./Oreg., U.S.A.	45 55 N	119 17 W	39A
Mâcon: France	46 18 N	4 50 E	17
Macon: Ga., U.S.A.	32 49 N	83 37 W	25A, 29, 31A, 59F, 87C
McPherson: Kans., U.S.A.	38 22 N	97 41 W	37J
Mactan: Philippines	10 16 N	123 58 E	87
Mactaquac: *dam*, Canada	45 55 N	66 55 W	39B
Madawaska: Maine, U.S.A.	47 21 N	68 21 W	25D
Madhya Pradesh: *admin.*, India	23 00 N	79 00 E	27, 38
Ma'din, Wādī al: *stream*, Tunisia	36 33 N	8 26 E	50B
Madison: Wis., U.S.A.	43 04 N	89 22 W	87B
Madison *Co.*: Mont., U.S.A.	45 20 N	112 00 W	49
Madras: India	13 05 N	80 18 E	3, 31C, 55, 58, 59, 60, 61, 67, 84, 87
Madras *see* Tamilnadu: *admin.*, India	11 00 N	78 15 E	27, 38
Madrid: Spain	40 24 N	3 41 W	32C, 45, 53, 54, 55, 56, 59H, 67, 87
Madukarai: India	10 56 N	77 00 E	57
Madura: *island*, Indonesia	7 00 S	113 20 E	27
Madurai: India	9 55 N	78 07 E	31C, 67
Mae Mo: Thailand	18 16 N	99 43 E	38, 61
Mae Sariang: *admin.*, Thailand	18 10 N	97 55 E	50
Magadan: U.S.S.R.	59 34 N	150 48 E	38
Magallanes: *admin.*, Chile	51 30 S	73 30 W	34, 38
Magenta: Italy	45 28 N	8 53 E	32C

	° ′	° ′	*Page(s)*
Magheramorne: Northern Ireland	54 50 N	5 49 W	**57C**
Magma: Ariz., U.S.A.	33 10 N	111 29 W	**45A**
Magna: Utah, U.S.A.	40 43 N	112 06 W	**59**
Magnitogorsk: U.S.S.R.	53 27 N	59 04 E	**43, 57, 61, 67**
Magog: Canada	45 16 N	72 09 W	**31**
Maguechic: Mexico	28 21 N	108 40 W	**49A**
Maharashtra: *admin.*, India	19 00 N	76 00 E	**27, 38**
Mahawelli Oya: *river*, Ceylon	7 20 N	80 57 E	**39**
Mahwah: N.J., U.S.A.	41 06 N	74 09 W	**55B**
Maidstone: England	51 17 N	0 32 E	**25, 25C**
Maiduguri: Nigeria	11 53 N	13 16 E	**67**
Maine: *admin.*, U.S.A.	45 00 N	69 00 W	**27**
Maine-et-Loire: *admin.*, France	47 30 N	0 20 W	**43B**
Mainz: Germany F.R.	50 00 N	8 15 E	**57C, 62A**
Maipú: Chile	33 31 S	70 46 W	**32**
Maitland: Canada	44 38 N	75 37 W	**32B, 61, 61A**
Maize Triangle: *reg*, S. Africa	30 30 S	25 00 E	**10**
Maizuru: Japan	35 27 N	135 20 E	**84D**
Majdanpek: Yugoslavia	44 25 N	21 56 E	**45**
Majunga: Malagasy Republic	15 43 S	46 19 E	**84**
Makarwāl Kheji: Pakistan	32 53 N	71 09 E	**38**
Makasar: Indonesia	5 07 S	119 24 E	**27, 67, 84**
Makedonija (Macedonia): *admin.*, Yugoslavia	41 50 N	22 00 E	**38B, 48**
Makeyevka: U.S.S.R.	48 02 N	37 58 E	**43C**
Makhachkala: U.S.S.R.	42 58 N	47 30 E	**31, 57, 67**
Makiyama: Japan	33 53 N	130 52 E	**59C**
Makkah (Mecca): Saudi Arabia	21 27 N	39 49 E	**67**
Makkovik: Canada	55 00 N	59 10 W	**40**
Makokou: Gabon	0 34 N	12 52 E	**49**
Makurazaki: Japan	31 16 N	130 19 E	**27D**
Málaga: Spain	36 43 N	4 25 W	**27B, 31, 46B, 57, 61D, 61H, 87**
Malagueño: Argentina	31 28 S	64 22 W	**57**
Malang: Indonesia	7 59 S	112 37 E	**67**
Malartic: Canada	48 09 N	78 09 W	**49**
Malawi, *Lake see* Nyasa, *Lake*: Africa	12 00 S	34 30 E	**27**
Malibu Beach: Calif., U.S.A.	34 04 N	118 35 W	**40**
Mallemort: France	43 44 N	5 11 E	**57C**
Malmberget: Sweden	67 10 N	20 40 E	**43**
Malmö: Sweden	55 36 N	13 00 E	**29, 32C, 37F, 52A, 60H, 67, 84C, 87**
Malombe, *Lake*: Malawi	14 38 S	35 12 E	**27**
Måløy: Norway	61 56 N	5 07 E	**27**
Malpaso: *dam*, Mexico	17 03 N	93 40 W	**39**
Malton: Canada	43 42 N	79 39 W	**53A**
Maluku (Moluccas): *island*, Indonesia	2 00 S	128 00 E	**27**
Malvern Link: England	52 08 N	2 18 W	**55A**
Malvesi: France	42 56 N	3 01 E	**40B**
Mama: *river*, U.S.S.R.	58 18 N	112 55 E	**48**
Mammola: Italy	38 22 N	16 14 E	**59D**
Mamonal: Colombia	10 19 N	75 31 W	**59, 60**
Manado: Indonesia	1 29 N	124 51 E	**67**
Managua: Nicaragua	12 09 N	86 17 W	**36, 67, 87**
Manakara: Malagasy Republic	22 08 S	48 01 E	**84**
Manantenina: Malagasy R.	24 17 S	47 19 E	**40**
Manapouri: *dam*, New Zealand	45 35 S	167 38 E	**39**
Manapparai: India	10 34 N	78 27 E	**31C**
Manassas: Va., U.S.A.	38 45 N	77 39 W	**62**
Manaus: Brazil	3 08 S	60 01 W	**36, 67, 84, 87**
Mancherāl: India	18 52 N	79 25 E	**57**
Manchester: England	53 30 N	2 15 W	**31B, 37B, 53B, 62A, 84C, 87**
Manchester: N.H., U.S.A.	42 59 N	71 28 W	**29A, 31, 67A**
Manching: Germany F.R.	48 43 N	11 30 E	**53**
Man-chou-li: *admin.*, China P.R.	49 36 N	117 26 E	**49**
Man-chou-li: China P.R.	49 36 N	117 26 E	**38**
Mandalay: Burma	22 00 N	96 05 E	**67**
Mandan: N.D., U.S.A.	46 50 N	100 54 W	**36**
Mandini: South Africa	29 09 S	31 25 E	**25**
Mandoúdhion: Greece	38 48 N	23 29 E	**50B**
Manfredonia: Italy	41 38 N	15 55 E	**61D, 61H**
Manga: Uruguay	34 48 S	56 09 W	**32**
Mangalore: India	12 54 N	74 51 E	**61, 67, 84**
Mangla: *dam*, Pakistan	33 09 N	73 44 E	**39**
Mangualde: Portugal	40 36 N	7 46 W	**45**
Mangula: Rhodesia	16 55 S	30 12 E	**45**
Mangyshlak Polustrov: *pen.*, U.S.S.R.	44 18 N	51 00 E	**35**
Manhattan: Kans., U.S.A.	39 11 N	96 35 W	**87B**
Manic II: *dam*, Canada	49 19 N	68 19 W	**39B**
Manic III: *dam*, Canada	49 50 N	68 34 W	**39B**
Manic V: *dam*, Canada	50 38 N	68 35 W	**39B**
Maniema: *admin.*, Congo D.R.	3 00 S	26 00 E	**45**
Maniema: Congo D.R.	1 11 S	28 37 E	**50**
Manila: Philippines	14 36 N	120 59 E	**31, 55, 62, 67, 84, 87**
Manipur: *admin.*, India	25 00 N	94 00 E	**27**
Manitoba: *admin.*, Canada	54 00 N	97 00 W	**27**
Manitouwadge: Canada	49 08 N	85 49 W	**45, 46, 49**
Manitowoc: Wis., U.S.A.	44 04 N	87 40 W	**57B**
Manizales: Colombia	5 05 N	75 32 W	**31, 32**
Mannersdorf: Austria	47 58 N	16 36 E	**57C**
Mannheim: Germany F.R	49 29 N	8 28 E	**25C, 37B, 37F, 55A, 67B**
Manningtree: England	51 57 N	1 04 E	**32C**
Manono: Congo D.R.	7 18 S	27 25 E	**45, 50**
Mano *River*: Liberia	6 56 N	11 31 W	**43**
Manresá: Spain	41 44 N	1 50 E	**56**
Mansfeld: Germany D.R.	51 35 N	11 28 E	**49**
Mansfield: Ohio, U.S.A.	40 46 N	82 31 W	**67A**
Manta: Ecuador	0 59 S	80 44 W	**84**
Mantaro River: *dam*, Peru	12 10 S	74 32 W	**39**
Mantes-la-Jolie: France	48 59 N	1 43 E	**57C**
Mantos Blancos: Chile	23 25 S	70 05 W	**45**
Mantova (Mantua): Italy	45 09 N	10 48 E	**25, 37H, 58H, 59D, 60H**
Mantua *see* Mantova: Italy			
Mapimí: Mexico	25 49 N	103 51 W	**49A**
Maqrīn: Tunisia	36 46 N	10 14 E	**46B**
Maracaibo, Lago de: *lake*, Venezuela	9 40 N	71 30 W	**34, 35, 56**
Maracaibo: Venezuela	10 44 N	71 37 W	**35, 56, 57, 67**
Maracay: Venezuela	10 15 N	67 36 W	**31, 32**
Marampa: Sierra Leone	8 41 N	12 28 W	**43**
Maranhão: *admin.*, Brazil	5 00 S	45 00 W	**27**
Marcaim: India	15 31 N	73 52 E	**61**
Marchienne-au-Pont: Belgium	50 24 N	4 23 E	**43B**
Marcona: Peru	15 10 S	75 02 W	**43**
Marcoule, *Centre Atomique* de: France	44 08 N	4 42 E	**40B**
Marcq-en-Baroeul: France	50 40 N	3 05 E	**31B**
Marcus Hook: Pa., U.S.A.	39 50 N	72 25 W	**37J, 58B, 61A**
Mar del Plata: Argentina	38 00 S	57 33 W	**27, 67**
Mare Island: Calif., U.S.A.	38 04 N	122 15 W	**52**
Marganets: U.S.S.R.	48 04 N	67 05 E	**50**
Marghera: Italy	45 48 N	12 14 E	**32C, 37H, 46B, 47B, 58D, 58H, 59D, 59H, 60D, 60H, 61D, 61H**
Mari: *region*, Pakistan	28 00 N	67 45 E	**34**
María Juana: Argentina	31 41 S	61 44 W	**54**
Mariager: Denmark	56 39 N	10 00 E	**57, 84C**
Mariager Fjord: *bay*, Denmark	56 41 N	10 20 E	**59**
Mariana: Brazil	20 23 S	43 25 W	**47**
Mariara: Venezuela	10 17 N	67 43 W	**55**
Maribor: Yugoslavia	46 33 N	15 39 E	**29C, 54B, 55A**
Maricopa *Co.*: Ariz., U.S.A.	33 35 N	112 15 W	**49B**
Mariel: Cuba	22 59 N	82 45 W	**57**
Marienau: France	49 11 N	6 52 E	**58H**
Mariestad: Sweden	58 43 N	13 51 E	**25B**
Marietta: Ga., U.S.A.	33 57 N	84 34 W	**53**
Marietta: Ohio, U.S.A.	39 26 N	81 27 W	**30A**
Marifu: Japan	34 23 N	132 20 E	**37E**
Marignane: France	43 25 N	5 13 E	**53B**
Mariposa *Co.*: Calif., U.S.A.	37 30 N	119 58 W	**48**
Maritsa-Istok: *basin*, Bulgaria	42 00 N	25 50 E	**38B**
Marka: Somali Republic	1 47 N	44 52 E	**84**
Marl: Germany F.R.	51 39 N	7 05 E	**30B, 58D, 58H, 59D, 60D, 60H**
Marly: France	50 21 N	3 33 E	**61D**
Marmora: Canada	44 29 N	77 40 W	**43A**
Marowijne: *river*, Surinam	4 00 N	56 00 W	**49**
Marquette Range: *deposit*, Mich., U.S.A.	46 35 N	87 25 W	**43A**
Marrakech: Morocco	31 49 N	8 00 W	**17, 67**
Marrero: La., U.S.A.	29 52 N	90 06 W	**25A**
Marsá al ‘Alam: *anchorage*, U.A.R.	25 05 N	34 54 E	**48**
Marsa el Brega *see* Qaşr al Burayqah: Libya	30 25 N	19 34 E	**36, 37B, 37D, 84**
Marseille: France	43 18 N	5 24 E	**27B, 37B, 47B, 84A, 87D**
Marseilles: Ill., U.S.A.	41 20 N	88 42 W	**59E**
Marshall *Co.*: W. Va., U.S.A.	39 50 N	80 30 W	**60F**
Marsh Harbour: Bahamas	26 33 N	77 03 W	**87C**
Marsyaty: U.S.S.R.	60 02 N	60 29 E	**50**
Martigny-Bourg: Switzerland	46 06 N	7 04 E	**59D**
Martigny-Ville: Switzerland	46 07 N	7 05 E	**47B**
Martin: Czechoslovakia	49 05 N	18 55 E	**25C**
Martinez: Calif., U.S.A.	38 00 N	122 10 W	**36, 59**
Martinsburg: W. Va., U.S.A.	39 28 N	77 49 W	**57B**
Martins Creek: Pa., U.S.A.	40 47 N	75 12 W	**57B**
Martinsville: Va., U.S.A.	36 43 N	79 53 W	**32B, 60B**
Martorell: Spain	41 28 N	1 56 E	**59D, 60D**
Marv Dasht: *plain*, Iran	29 50 N	52 40 E	**61**
Marviken: Sweden	58 34 N	16 51 E	**40**
Mary: U.S.S.R.	37 36 N	61 50 E	**29, 31**
Maryborough: Australia	25 32 S	152 42 E	**38**
Mary Kathleen: Australia	20 44 S	140 01 E	**40**
Maryland: *admin.*, U.S.A.	39 00 N	77 00 W	**27, 38A**
Maryneal: Texas, U.S.A.	32 14 N	100 26 W	**57A**
Marysville: Australia	37 31 S	145 45 E	**59**
Maryvale: Australia	38 10 S	146 25 E	**25**
Marzabotto: Italy	44 20 N	11 12 E	**25**
Mas: Italy	46 09 N	12 07 E	**61**
Masegawa: *dam*, Japan	35 40 N	137 10 E	**39D**
Mashaba: Rhodesia	20 03 S	30 29 E	**48**
Mashhad (Meshed): Iran	36 18 N	59 36 E	**67**
Masjed Soleymān: Iran	31 58 N	49 18 E	**37G**
Mason City: Iowa, U.S.A.	43 10 N	93 10 W	**57**
Masqaţ (Muscat): Muscat and Oman	23 37 N	58 38 E	**84**
Massachusetts: *admin.*, U.S.A.	42 00 N	72 00 W	**27**
Massa Marittima: Italy	43 03 N	10 53 E	**45**
Massawa: Ethiopia	15 37 N	39 28 E	**84**
Massena: N.Y., U.S.A.	44 56 N	74 57 W	**47**
Masuda: Japan	34 40 N	131 51 E	**32A**
Matadi: Congo D.R.	5 49 S	13 27 E	**84**
Matamoros: Mexico	25 53 N	97 30 W	**62**
Matanzas: Cuba	23 03 N	81 35 W	**32**
Matarani: Peru	17 00 S	72 07 W	**84**
Mataripe: Brazil	12 41 S	38 35 W	**36**
Mataró: Spain	41 32 N	2 27 E	**17**
Matfors: Sweden	62 21 N	17 02 E	**25B**
Matheson: Canada	48 33 N	80 28 W	**48**
Matías de Gálvez: Guatemala	15 42 N	88 37 W	**36**
Māţir: Tunisia	37 03 N	9 40 E	**17**
Mato Grosso: *admin.*, Brazil	16 00 S	56 00 W	**27, 48**
Matola-Rio: Mozambique	25 49 S	32 27 E	**59**
Matraville: Australia	33 57 S	151 14 E	**36, 58**
Matsue: Japan	35 28 N	133 04 E	**67C**
Matsuyama: Japan	33 50 N	132 45 E	**32A, 37E, 58C, 59C, 61C, 67C, 87**
Mattagami: Canada	49 47 N	77 38 W	**45, 46, 49**
Matzen: Austria	48 24 N	16 42 E	**37D**
Mavrovouni: Cyprus	35 06 N	32 51 E	**45**
Mawchi: Burma	18 49 N	97 09 E	**50**
Mayagüez: Puerto Rico	18 12 N	67 09 W	**87**
Maydown: Northern Ireland	54 59 N	7 19 W	**58**
Mayli-Say: U.S.S.R.	41 17 N	72 24 E	**40, 50**
Mayo *District*: Canada	63 30 N	136 00 W	**46, 49**
Mayurbhanj: *admin.*, India	21 50 N	86 30 E	**43**
Maywood: Ill., U.S.A.	41 51 N	87 48 W	**62**
Mazapil: Mexico	24 38 N	101 34 W	**49A**
Mazar-i-Sharif: Afghanistan	36 43 N	67 05 E	**61**
Mazaruni-Potaro: *admin.*, Guyana	6 00 N	59 30 W	**48**
Mazatlán: Mexico	23 13 N	106 25 W	**84, 87**
Mazatzal *Mountains*: Ariz., U.S.A.	34 00 N	111 30 W	**50**
Mazingarbe: France	50 28 N	2 42 E	**58H, 60H, 61D, 61H**
Mazra‘eh Mazāre‘: Iran	38 36 N	47 03 E	**45**
Mazul'skiy: U.S.S.R.	56 16 N	90 22 E	**50**
Mbao: Senegal	15 48 N	16 31 W	**59**
Mbeya: Tanzania	8 54 S	33 27 E	**48**
Mbuji-Mayi (Bakwanga): Congo D.R.	6 09 S	23 36 E	**48**
Mead: Wash., U.S.A.	47 45 N	117 20 W	**47**
Meadow Brook: W. Va., U.S.A.	39 21 N	80 20 W	**46**
Meadville: Pa., U.S.A.	41 38 N	80 10 W	**32B**
Mecca *see* Makkah: Saudi Arabia	21 27 N	39 49 E	**67**
Mechanicville: N.Y., U.S.A.	42 55 N	73 42 W	**59A**
Mechelen: Belgium	51 02 N	4 28 E	**29B, 55A**
Mecsek: *mtns.*, Hungary	46 10 N	18 18 E	**40**
Medan: Indonesia	3 35 N	98 40 E	**67**
Medellín: Colombia	6 15 N	75 35 W	**29, 31, 32, 60, 67, 87**
Meden Rudnik: Bulgaria	42 27 N	27 24 E	**45**
Medford: Oreg., U.S.A.	42 20 N	122 52 W	**87**
Medgidia: Romania	44 15 N	28 17 E	**57C**
Mediaş: Romania	46 10 N	24 21 E	**17**
Medicine Hat: Canada	50 03 N	110 41 W	**59, 61**
Medina del Campo: Spain	41 18 N	4 55 W	**45**
Mednogorsk: U.S.S.R.	51 24 N	57 37 E	**45**
Medvezh'yegorsk: U.S.S.R.	62 55 N	34 28 E	**45**
Meerut: India	29 00 N	77 42 E	**31**
Megalópolis: Greece	37 24 N	22 08 E	**38**
Meggen: Germany F.R.	51 08 N	8 04 E	**56**
Meknès: Morocco	33 53 N	5 37 W	**17, 49, 67**
Mekong *Delta*: South Vietnam	10 00 N	106 00 E	**11**
Melbourne: Australia	37 50 S	145 00 E	**25, 29, 31, 34, 53, 67, 84, 87**
Melbourne: Fla., U.S.A.	28 04 N	80 38 W	**87C**
Melchor Ocampo: Mexico	24 51 N	101 39 W	**49A**
Meldal: Norway	63 03 N	9 45 E	**45**
Melnik: Bulgaria	41 31 N	23 24 E	**17**
Meltham: England	53 36 N	1 52 W	**29B**
Melton Mowbray: England	52 46 N	0 53 W	**32C**
Melun: France	48 32 N	2 40 E	**53B**
Memaliaj: Albania	40 20 N	19 58 E	**38B**
Memphis: Tenn., U.S.A.	35 10 N	90 00 W	**25A, 37J, 59B, 59F, 87C**
Mendoza: *admin.*, Argentina	34 30 S	68 30 W	**17, 35, 40, 48**
Mendoza: Argentina	32 53 S	68 49 W	**29, 59**
Menominee: Mich., U.S.A.	45 07 N	87 37 W	**25D, 87B**
Menominee Range: *deposit*, Mich., U.S.A.	45 07 N	87 37 W	**43A**
Mequinenza: *dam*, Spain	41 22 N	0 17 E	**39**
Merano: Italy	46 40 N	11 09 E	**61D, 61H**
Meraux: La., U.S.A.	29 54 N	89 55 W	**37J**
Merced: Calif., U.S.A.	37 17 N	120 29 W	**61**
Mercedes: Argentina	34 39 S	59 27 W	**46, 60**
Mercedes: Argentina	33 40 S	65 28 W	**32**
Mereenie: *region*, Australia	25 30 S	130 30 E	**34**
Mergelstetten: Germany F.R.	48 39 N	10 09 E	**57C**
Mergui: Burma	12 26 N	98 36 E	**45**
Mérida: Mexico	20 58 N	89 37 W	**67**
Mérignac: France	44 50 N	0 38 W	**53B**
Merone: Italy	45 47 N	9 15 E	**57C**
Merritt: Canada	50 09 N	120 49 W	**45**
Mersin: Turkey	36 48 N	34 38 E	**36, 59, 61, 84B**
Mesabi Range: *deposit*, Minn., U.S.A.	47 30 N	92 50 W	**43**
Mesa *Co.*: Colo., U.S.A.	39 00 N	108 30 W	**40A**
Meshed *see* Mashhad: Iran	36 18 N	59 36 E	**67**
Mesopotamia Argentina: *reg.*, Argentina	30 00 S	58 00 W	**23**
Messaure: *dam*, Sweden	66 40 N	20 21 E	**39**
Messina: Italy	38 11 N	15 34 E	**17, 84A**
Messina: South Africa	22 23 S	30 00 E	**45**
Metaline Falls: Wash., U.S.A.	48 52 N	117 20 W	**57**
Meting: Pakistan	25 43 N	68 01 E	**38**
Mettupalaiyam: India	11 18 N	76 57 E	**32**
Mettur: India	11 53 N	77 51 E	**47, 60**
Metuchen: N.J., U.S.A.	40 33 N	74 23 W	**32B**
Metz: France	49 08 N	6 10 E	**55A, 67B**
Meurthe-et-Moselle: *admin.*, France	48 35 N	6 10 E	**56A**
Mexican Hat: Utah, U.S.A.	37 10 N	109 54 W	**40A, 59**
Mexico City *see* Ciudad de México: Mexico	19 24 N	99 09 W	**25, 29, 31, 32, 34, 45, 55, 56, 57, 59, 60, 62, 67, 87**
Mežica: Yugoslavia	46 31 N	14 52 E	**46B**
Miami: Ariz., U.S.A.	33 24 N	110 54 W	**45A**
Miami: Fla., U.S.A.	25 45 N	80 15 W	**57, 67, 87C**
Miami: Rhodesia	16 40 S	29 46 E	**48, 50**
Miānwāli: *admin.*, Pakistan	32 10 N	71 30 E	**57**
Miao-li: Taiwan	24 33 N	120 49 E	**60, 61**
Miass: U.S.S.R.	54 59 N	60 06 E	**55**
Mibladene: Morocco	32 46 N	4 38 W	**46**
Miboro: *dam*, Japan	36 08 N	136 55 E	**39D**
Mica: *dam*, Canada	51 30 N	118 30 W	**39**
Micheville: France	49 28 N	5 56 E	**43B**
Michigan: *admin.*, U.S.A.	44 00 N	85 00 W	**27**
Michigan City: Ind., U.S.A.	41 43 N	86 54 W	**54A**
Middlebranch: Ohio., U.S.A.	40 52 N	81 21 W	**57B**
Middlesbrough: England	54 35 N	1 14 W	**52A, 58D, 84C**
Middletown: Conn., U.S.A.	41 34 N	72 39 W	**48**
Middletown: Ohio, U.S.A.	39 31 N	84 13 W	**25D, 43A, 58B**
Middle Yenisei: *dam*, U.S.S.R.	65 20 N	88 05 E	**39**
Midland: Mich., U.S.A.	43 38 N	84 14 W	**30A, 40C, 58B, 58F, 59A, 60F, 61A**
Midland: Pa., U.S.A.	40 38 N	80 28 W	**43A**
Midland: Texas, U.S.A.	32 00 N	102 09 W	**87C**
Midland Junction: Australia	31 54 S	116 00 E	**54**
Midlands: *region*, England	52 30 N	2 00 W	**56A**
Midlands, East: *region*, England	53 30 N	1 00 W	**37D, 38B, 56A**
Midlands, West: *region*, England	52 30 N	2 30 W	**38B**
Midlothian: Texas., U.S.A.	32 30 N	97 01 W	**57A**
Midono: *dam*, Japan	36 13 N	137 35 E	**39D**
Midvale: Utah, U.S.A.	40 37 N	111 55 W	**46**
Mielec: Poland	50 18 N	21 25 E	**53**
Miena: *dam*, Australia	41 59 S	146 44 E	**39**
Mieres: Spain	43 15 N	5 46 W	**58D**
Miguel Burnier: Brazil	20 26 S	43 47 W	**50**
Miguel Hidalgo: *dam*, Mexico	26 28 N	108 35 W	**39**
Mihama: Japan	35 36 N	135 56 E	**40**
Mihara: Japan	34 24 N	133 05 E	**32A, 54C, 60C**
Miike: Japan	33 03 N	130 29 E	**38C, 46C**
Mikhaylovka: U.S.S.R.	50 04 N	43 15 E	**57**
Mikkaichi: Japan	36 52 N	137 27 E	**46C**
Milano: Italy	45 28 N	9 12 E	**25, 31B, 32C, 37B, 37H, 43B, 53B, 54B, 55B, 58D, 58H, 60H, 87D**
Milazzo: Italy	38 13 N	15 14 E	**37D, 37H**
Mile End: Australia	34 56 S	138 35 E	**55**
Milford Haven: Wales	51 44 N	5 02 W	**27C, 37D, 37F, 58D, 84C**
Mill City: Nev., U.S.A.	40 42 N	118 03 W	**50A**
Millhaven: Canada	44 15 N	76 55 W	**60B**
Millinocket: Maine, U.S.A.	45 42 N	68 43 W	**25D**
Millom: England	54 13 N	3 18 W	**43B**
Millstone *Point*: Conn., U.S.A.	41 19 N	72 10 W	**40C**
Milluni: Bolivia	16 20 S	68 09 W	**50**
Milnerton: South Africa	33 54 S	18 30 E	**32, 61**
Milwaukee: Wis., U.S.A.	43 03 N	87 56 W	**25D, 56, 57B, 58B, 67A, 84. 87B**
Mīnā' ‘Abd Allah: Kuwait	29 01 N	48 10 E	**37G**
Mīnā' al Aḩmadī: Kuwait	29 04 N	48 02 E	**37C, 37G**
Mina Hassan Tani (Kenitra): Morocco	34 20 N	6 34 W	**27B, 59**
Minamata: Japan	32 13 N	130 24 E	**59G, 60C, 61C, 61G**
Minas: Indonesia	0 50 N	101 29 E	**35**
Minas de Matahambre: Cuba	22 35 N	83 57 W	**45**
Minas Gerais: *admin.*, Brazil	18 00 S	44 00 W	**27, 40, 46, 48, 49**
Mīnā' Su‘ūd: Neutral Zone	28 43 N	48 25 E	**37G**
Mina Teniente: Chile	34 05 S	70 21 W	**45, 49, 50**
Minatitlán: Mexico	17 59 N	94 31 W	**36, 58, 59, 61**
Mindanao: *is.*, Philippines	7 30 N	125 00 E	**27, 49**
Mineral *Co.*: Colo., U.S.A.	37 40 N	107 00 W	**49B**
Mineral de Angangueo: Mexico	19 37 N	100 18 W	**49A**
Mineral Park: Ariz., U.S.A.	35 12 N	114 02 W	**50, 50A**
Mingechaur: *dam*, U.S.S.R.	40 45 N	47 03 E	**39**
Miniera di Monteponi: Italy	39 18 N	8 29 E	**46B**
Miniş: Romania	46 08 N	21 36 E	**17**
Minkébé: Gabon	1 46 N	12 48 E	**43**
Minneapolis: Minn., U.S.A.	45 00 N	93 15 W	**25, 31, 34, 55, 56, 62, 67, 87B**
Minnesota: *admin.*, U.S.A.	46 00 N	94 00 W	**27**
Minsk: U.S.S.R.	53 54 N	27 34 E	**34, 37B, 55**
Minusinskiy Ugol'nyy Basseyn: *basin*, U.S.S.R.	53 35 N	91 20 E	**38**
Mira: Portugal	39 32 N	8 43 W	**29**

	° ′	° ′	*Page(s)*
Miranda de Ebro: Spain	42 41 N	2 57 W	32C, 58D, 60D
Mirboo North: Australia	38 24 S	146 09 E	47
Mirditë: Albania	41 49 N	19 56E	45
Mirecourt: France	48 18 N	8 08 E	31B
Mirgalimsay: U.S.S.R.	43 32 N	68 36 E	46
Miri: Malaysia	4 23 N	113 59 E	35, 87
Mīrpur Māthelo: Pakistan	28 02 N	69 33 E	61
Mirzapur: India	25 09 N	82 34 E	47
Misakicho: Japan	35 14 N	139 38 E	27D
Misburg: Germany F.R.	52 23 N	9 51 E	37F, 57C, 60H
Mishima: Japan	35 07 N	138 55 E	29D, 32A, 60E
Misima *Island*: Papua	9 06 S	152 45 E	49
Miṣr al Jadīdah (Heliopolis): U.A.R.	30 06 N	31 20 E	53
Mission: Ariz., U.S.A.	32 00 N	110 59 W	45A
Mission: *dam*, Canada	50 41 N	122 15 W	39
Mission Viejo: Calif., U.S.A.	33 36 N	117 42 W	62
Mississippi: *admin.*, U.S.A.	33 00 N	90 00 W	27
Missoula *Co.*: Mont., U.S.A.	47 00 N	114 00 W	49
Missouri: *admin.*, U.S.A.	39 00 N	94 00 W	27, 38, 46
Mitate: Japan	33 15 N	131 40 E	45D
Mitchell: Ind., U.S.A.	38 43 N	86 29 W	57B
Mitterberg: Austria	47 25 N	13 08 E	45
Miya: Japan	34 48 N	137 15 E	27D
Miyako: Japan	39 38 N	141 57 E	27D, 45D, 59G, 84D
Miyazaki: Japan	31 54 N	131 26 E	87
Mizushima: Japan	34 35 N	133 50 E	37E, 58C, 58G, 59C, 60C, 60E, 61C, 61G
Mladá Boleslav: Czechoslovakia	50 26 N	14 55 E	55A
Mo: Norway	66 19 N	14 10 E	43, 58, 84
Moab: Utah, U.S.A.	38 35 N	109 34 W	40, 56
Mobara: Japan	35 25 N	140 18 E	61C
Mobile: Ala., U.S.A.	30 40 N	88 05 W	25A, 37J, 47A, 57B, 59B, 59F, 60A, 87C
Moçâmedes: Angola	15 10 S	12 09 E	27, 84
Modderfontein: South Africa	26 05 S	28 10 E	58, 59, 60, 61
Modena: Italy	44 40 N	10 55 E	55A
Modra: Czechoslovakia	48 20 N	17 19 E	17
Modugno: Italy	41 05 N	16 47 E	57C
Moengo: Surinam	5 36 N	54 25 W	47
Moerdijk: Netherlands	51 42 N	4 38 E	58H
Moffat *Co.*: Colo., U.S.A.	40 30 N	108 00 W	40A
Mogadiscio: Somali Republic	2 02 N	45 21 E	67, 84
Mogadore: Ohio, U.S.A.	41 03 N	81 24 W	30A
Mogi das Cruzes: Brazil	23 31 S	46 11 W	58
Mogilëv: U.S.S.R.	53 54 N	30 21 E	32C
Moguer: Spain	37 16 N	6 50 W	47
Moḥammad Reẕa Shāh Pahlavī: *dam*, Iran	32 43 N	48 30 E	39
Mohammédia: Morocco	33 44 N	7 24 W	27B, 31, 36
Mohave *Co.*: Ariz., U.S.A.	35 30 N	114 00 W	49B
Mojave: Calif., U.S.A.	35 02 N	118 11 W	49B, 57, 60
Moji: Japan	33 57 N	130 58 E	84D
Mokp'o: South Korea	34 47 N	126 23 E	84D
Mol: Belgium	51 11 N	5 06 E	40B
Molango: Mexico	20 47 N	98 43 W	50
Moldavskaya S.S.R.: *admin.*, U.S.S.R.	47 00 N	29 00 E	17, 27
Moldova Nouă: Romania	44 44 N	21 41 E	56
Moline: Ill., U.S.A.	41 31 N	90 26 W	87B
Moluccas *see* Maluku: *island*, Indonesia	2 00 S	128 00 E	27
Molveno, Lago di: *dam*, Italy	46 08 N	10 57 E	39C
Mombasa: Kenya	4 03 S	39 40 E	36, 67, 84, 87
Mombetsu: Japan	44 21 N	143 22 E	27D
Monaca: Pa., U.S.A.	40 42 N	80 19 W	30A, 46, 59E
Moncada: Spain	39 33 N	0 24 W	57C
Monchegorsk: U.S.S.R.	67 56 N	32 58 E	45, 49, 50
Mönchen-Gladbach: G.F.R.	51 12 N	6 26 E	29B
Monclova: Mexico	26 54 N	101 25 W	43, 61, 61B
Moncton: Canada	46 04 N	64 50 W	87
Mondeville: France	49 10 N	0 19 W	43
Monessen: Pa., U.S.A.	40 08 N	79 54 W	43A, 58B
Monfalcone: Italy	45 49 N	13 32 E	52A
Mongat: Spain	41 28 N	2 18 E	59H
Monheim: Germany F.R.	51 05 N	6 53 E	37F
Monmouth: *admin.*, Eng./Wales	52 30 N	33 0 W	56A
Monolith: Calif., U.S.A.	35 07 N	118 23 W	57
Monopoli: Italy	40 57 N	17 18 E	57C
Monroe: La., U.S.A.	32 31 N	92 06 W	87C
Monroe: Mich., U.S.A.	41 56 N	83 21 W	25D, 40C
Monrovia: Liberia	6 19 N	10 48 W	27, 36, 84, 87
Mons: *region*, Belgium	50 27 N	3 56 E	38B
Monsanto: Ill., U.S.A.	38 35 N	90 10 W	59A, 59E
Monselice: Italy	45 14 N	11 45 E	57C
Mont: France	43 26 N	0 39 W	60D
Montagaud: France	46 19 N	1 59 E	40B
Montague: Mich., U.S.A.	43 26 N	86 22 W	30A, 59B
Montalieu-Vercieu: France	45 49 N	5 24 E	57C
Montana: *admin.*, U.S.A.	47 00 N	110 00 W	27, 38
Montana City: Mont., U.S.A.	46 30 N	112 60 W	57
Mont-Cenis: *dam*, France	45 14 N	6 55 E	39C
Monteagudo: Bolivia	19 49 S	63 59 W	34
Monte Amiata: Italy	42 58 N	11 33 E	50B
Montebello: Colombia	6 14 N	75 35 W	57
Montego Bay: Jamaica	18 28 N	77 55 W	87
Montenegro *see* Crna Gora: *admin.*, Yugoslavia	42 30 N	19 18 E	38B

	° ′	° ′	*Page(s)*
Monterey: Calif., U.S.A.	36 35 N	121 55 W	87A
Monterrey: Mexico	25 40 N	100 19 W	25, 31, 32, 34, 43, 46, 56, 57, 59, 60, 61, 67, 87C
Montes Claros: Brazil	16 43 S	43 52 W	67
Montevideo: Minn., U.S.A.	44 58 N	95 21 W	62
Montevideo: Uruguay	34 53 S	56 11 W	29, 31, 32, 36, 56, 60, 67, 87
Monteynard: *dam*, France	44 58 N	5 42 E	39C
Montezinho: Portugal	41 56 N	6 46 W	45
Montezuma *Co.*: Colo., U.S.A.	37 15 N	108 30 W	40A
Montgolfier: Algeria	35 34 N	1 00 E	17
Montgomery: Ala., U.S.A.	32 22 N	86 20 W	31A, 87C
Monticello: Minn., U.S.A.	45 17 N	93 44 W	40C
Montilla: Spain	37 35 N	4 38 W	17
Montluçon: France	46 20 N	2 36 E	60D
Montoir-de-Bretagne: France	47 20 N	2 09 W	61D, 61H
Montpelier: Ohio, U.S.A.	41 35 N	84 35 W	55B
Montpellier: France	43 36 N	3 53 E	62A
Montréal: Canada	45 30 N	73 36 W	2, 31, 34, 36, 43A, 45, 52, 53, 54, 56, 57B, 58, 60, 63, 67, 84, 87
Montrose *Co.*: Colo., U.S.A.	38 15 N	108 15 W	40A
Monts de la Mpassa: *mtns.*, Congo R.	2 30 S	14 05 E	46
Mont-sur-Rolle: Switzerland	46 38 N	6 21 E	17
Monument: N. Mex., U.S.A.	32 38 N	103 16 W	37J
Monzón: Spain	41 55 N	0 12 E	58H, 59D, 60D
Moosbierbaum: Austria	48 18 N	15 54 E	59H
Moose Jaw: Canada	50 23 N	105 35 W	36
Moquegua: *admin.*, Peru	16 50 S	70 55 W	49
Mór: Hungary	47 23 N	18 12 E	17
Morano sul Po: Italy	45 10 N	8 22 E	57C
Morata de Jalón: Spain	41 28 N	1 28 W	57C
Morbihan: *admin.*, France	47 55 N	2 50 W	40B, 48
Morenci: Ariz., U.S.A.	33 05 N	109 22 W	45A, 59
Moreno: Brazil	8 07 S	35 06 W	31
Morgantown: Pa., U.S.A.	40 09 N	75 53 W	50
Morgantown: W. Va., U.S.A.	39 38 N	79 57 W	61A
Mori: Italy	45 51 N	10 59 E	47B
Mori: Japan	42 06 N	140 35 E	27D
Moris: Mexico	28 06 N	107 45 W	49A
Moriyama: Japan	35 04 N	135 59 E	32A
Mormugão: India	15 24 N	73 48 E	84
Morococha: Peru	11 39 S	76 07 W	45, 50
Morogoro: Tanzania	6 49 S	37 40 E	48
Morón: Venezuela	10 29 N	68 11 W	36, 58, 59, 60, 61
Morón de la Frontera: Spain	37 08 N	5 27 W	57
Morris: Ill., U.S.A.	41 22 N	88 25 W	25D, 40C
Morro Agudo: *hill*, Brazil	20 42 S	42 09 W	43
Morro Velho: *hill*, Brazil	13 40 S	43 19 W	49
Morteros: Argentina	30 42 S	62 00 W	53
Morton: Pa., U.S.A.	39 55 N	75 20 W	53A
Mosbach: Germany F.R.	49 21 N	9 09 E	54B
Moscow *see* Moskva: U.S.S.R.	55 45 N	37 35 E	2, 3, 31, 32C, 34, 36, 43, 48, 53, 54, 55, 57, 62, 67, 87
Moselle: *admin.*, France	49 00 N	6 30 E	38B
Moses, Robert: *dam*, N.Y., U.S.A.	45 00 N	74 50 W	39B
Moshaneng: Botswana	24 59 S	25 15 E	48
Mosjøen: Norway	65 50 N	13 12 E	47, 84
Moskal'vo: U.S.S.R.	53 35 N	142 30 E	35, 36
Moskva Basseyn: *basin*, U.S.S.R.	55 45 N	37 30 E	38
Moskva (Moscow): U.S.S.R.	55 45 N	37 35 E	2, 3, 31, 32C, 34, 36, 43, 48, 53, 54, 55, 57, 62, 67, 87
Moss: Norway	59 26 N	10 42 E	25B, 52
Mosselbaai: South Africa	34 12 S	22 08 E	84
Moss Point: Miss., U.S.A.	30 25 N	88 31 W	25A
Moss Vale: Australia	34 33 S	150 23 E	47
Mossyrock: *dam*, Wash., U.S.A.	46 32 N	122 25 W	39A
Most: Czechoslovakia	50 31 N	13 39 E	58H, 61D
Mostaganem: Algeria	35 54 N	0 05 E	17
Mostar: Yugoslavia	43 21 N	17 49 E	53
Moste: Yugoslavia	46 03 N	14 33 E	47B, 60D
Mostecká: *basin*, Czechoslovakia	50 30 N	13 40 E	38B
Motherwell: Scotland	55 48 N	4 00 W	43B
Motoichiba: Japan	35 09 N	138 39 E	25, 61G
Motta: *dam*, Italy	46 23 N	8 21 E	39C
Mouanda: Gabon	1 34 S	13 11 E	50
Moubhandar: India	22 36 N	86 34 E	45
Moulmein: Burma	16 30 N	97 38 E	67
Mounana: Gabon	1 18 S	13 13 E	40
Moundsville: W. Va., U.S.A.	39 54 N	80 44 W	59A
Moundville: Ala., U.S.A.	33 00 N	87 38 W	37J
Mountain *Pass*: Calif., U.S.A.	35 28 N	115 25 W	40
Mount Goldsworthy: *hill*, Austl.	20 21 S	119 32 E	43
Mount Ida: Australia	29 03 S	120 30 E	49
Mount Isa: Australia	20 44 S	139 30 E	45, 46, 49, 87
Mount Jackson: Calif., U.S.A.	38 30 N	123 00 W	50
Mount Lyell: *mtn.*, Australia	42 03 S	145 38 E	45, 49, 56
Mount Magnet: Australia	28 04 S	117 49 E	49
Mount Morgan: Australia	23 39 S	150 23 E	45, 49
Mount Pleasant: Mich., U.S.A.	43 36 N	84 46 W	58B
Mount Pleasant: Texas, U.S.A.	33 10 N	94 59 W	37J
Mountsorrel: England	52 44 N	1 07 W	53B
Mount Tambourine: Australia	27 58 S	153 12 E	47
Mount Tom Price: *mtn.*, Austl.	22 49 S	117 51 E	43
Mount Vernon: Ind., U.S.A.	37 55 N	87 55 W	37J

	° ′	° ′	*Page(s)*
Mousagalla: *dam*, Ceylon	7 29 N	80 42 E	39
Mouscron: Belgium	50 44 N	3 13 E	29B
Moyamba: *admin.*, Sierra Leone	8 00 N	12 30 W	47
Moÿ-de-l'Aisne: France	49 45 N	3 22 E	32C
Moyeuvre-Grande: France	49 15 N	6 02 E	43B
Mozyr': U.S.S.R.	52 03 N	29 16 E	58
Mpaka: Swaziland	26 26 S	31 47 E	38
Mpassa, Monts de la: *mtns.*, Congo R.	2 30 S	14 05 E	46
Mrima: *hill*, Kenya	4 29 S	39 16 E	40
Msauli: South Africa	26 00 S	31 05 E	48
Mtwara: Tanzania	10 17 S	40 11 E	84
Muddy Run: *dam*, Pa., U.S.A.	39 47 N	77 18 W	39
Muftīyah: Iraq	30 32 N	47 48 E	37G
Mufulira: Zambia	12 33 S	28 14 E	45B
Muguk: South Korea	36 55 N	127 35 E	49
Mühldorf: Austria	46 51 N	13 21 E	29C
Mühleberg: Switzerland	46 57 N	7 16 E	40B
Mukden *see* Shen-yang: China P.R.	41 48 N	123 27 E	43, 45, 46, 53, 67
Mulejé: Mexico	26 53 N	112 01 W	45
Mülheim an der Ruhr: G.F.R.	51 26 N	6 53 E	37F, 58D
Mulhouse: France	47 45 N	7 20 E	31B, 55A, 56
Multān: Pakistan	30 11 N	71 29 E	31, 61, 67
Mulwala: Australia	35 59 S	146 01 E	59
München (Munich): G.F.R.	48 09 N	11 35 E	25C, 53, 54B, 55A, 58D, 59D, 59H, 63A, 63B, 67B, 87D
Muncie: Ind., U.S.A.	40 11 N	85 22 W	67A
Mun'gyŏng: South Korea	36 44 N	128 07 E	38C
Munich *see* München: G.F.R.	48 09 N	11 35 E	25C, 53, 54B, 55A, 58D, 59D, 59H, 63A, 63B, 67B, 87D
Munksund: Sweden	65 17 N	21 29 E	25
Munp'yŏng: North Korea	38 07 N	125 23 E	46, 50
Munster: France	48 03 N	7 08 E	31B
Münsterbusch: Germany F.R.	50 46 N	6 13 E	46B
Munţii, Banatului: *mtns.*, Romania	45 00 N	22 10 E	40
Munţii, Bihorului: *mtns.*, Romania	46 40 N	22 45 E	40
Muntok: Indonesia	2 04 S	105 11 E	45
Murban: *hill*, Abu Dhabi	23 58 N	53 40 E	37C
Murchison Falls: *dam*, Uganda	2 17 N	31 41 E	39
Murchison Range: *hills*, South Africa	23 50 S	30 40 E	50, 50C
Murcia: *admin.*, Spain	38 00 N	1 30 W	46B
Murdochville: Canada	48 57 N	65 30 W	45, 49
Mürefte: *admin.*, Turkey	40 40 N	27 14 E	34, 37B
Murgul: Turkey	41 15 N	41 34 E	45
Muri: India	23 51 N	82 34 E	47
Murmansk: U.S.S.R.	68 58 N	33 05 E	67, 84
Murom: U.S.S.R.	55 34 N	42 02 E	31
Muroran: Japan	42 18 N	140 59 E	27D, 36, 43D, 57D, 58C, 59G, 60, 61, 84D
Murray/Darling *Basin*: Australia	33 00 S	141 00 E	23
Murray II: *dam*, Australia	36 14 S	148 08 E	39
Musan: North Korea	39 54 N	124 36 E	43
Musay'īd: Qatar	24 59 N	51 32 E	37G, 61
Muscat *see* Masqaţ: Muscat and Oman	23 37 N	58 38 E	84
Muscatine: Iowa, U.S.A.	41 25 N	91 05 W	61A
Muscle Shoals: Ala., U.S.A.	34 45 N	87 38 W	59B, 61E
Muskegon: Mich., U.S.A.	43 13 N	86 15 W	37J, 87B
Musoma: Tanzania	1 30 S	33 48 E	49
Musonoi: Congo D.R.	10 41 S	25 26 E	45
Mu-tan-chiang: China P.R.	44 35 N	129 36 E	57
Mu-tan-chiang: *dam*, China P.R.	44 05 N	129 00 E	39
Mwadui: Tanzania	3 33 S	33 36 E	48
Mweru, *Lake*: Africa	9 00 S	28 45 E	27
Myllykoski: Finland	60 47 N	26 48 E	25B
Mysore: *admin.*, India	14 00 N	76 00 E	27
Mysore: India	12 18 N	76 37 E	31C, 50
Mytishchi: U.S.S.R.	55 55 N	37 46 E	54

N

	° ′	° ′	*Page(s)*
Naantali: Finland	60 27 N	22 02 E	36, 37F
Nababiep: South Africa	29 36 S	17 46 E	45
Náchod: Czechoslovakia	50 26 N	16 10 E	31B
Nador: Morocco	35 12 N	2 55 W	43
Nadvornaya: U.S.S.R.	48 38 N	24 34 E	37F
Nadvoytsy: U.S.S.R.	63 52 N	34 19 E	47
Naestved: Denmark	55 14 N	11 46 E	25
Naft-e Shāh: Iran	33 59 N	45 30 E	37G
Naga: Philippines	10 15 N	123 46 E	57
Nagano: *dam*, Japan	35 50 N	136 33 E	39D
Nagaoka: Japan	37 27 N	138 51 E	61C, 67C
Nagarjunasagar: *dam*, India	16 35 N	79 17 E	39
Nagasaki: Japan	32 48 N	129 55 E	27D, 52B, 84D
Nagda: India	23 30 N	75 29 E	32
Nagoya: Japan	35 10 N	136 55 E	31, 32A, 38, 43D, 47C, 52B, 53, 55, 56, 58C, 58G 59C, 59G, 60,C, 61C, 67C, 84D

	° ′	° ′	*Page(s)*
Nagpur: India	21 10 N	79 12 E	31C, 67
Nagyatád: Hungary	46 13 N	17 22 E	57C
Naha: Ryukyu Is.	26 10 N	127 40 E	67
Nahorkatiya: India	27 02 N	95 05 E	60
Nahr al Furāt (Euphrates): *dam*, Syria	35 52 N	38 34 E	39
Nairobi: Kenya	1 17 S	36 49 E	56, 67, 87
Naju: South Korea	35 02 N	126 43 E	61C, 61G
Naka-minato: Japan	36 20 N	140 36 E	27D
Nakatatsu: Japan	36 00 N	136 30 E	46C
Nakatsugawa: Japan	35 29 N	137 30 E	25
Nakhodka: U.S.S.R.	42 48 N	132 52 E	84D
Nakhon Si Thammarat: Thai.	8 15 N	100 00 E	43
Nalaiha: Mongolia	47 45 N	107 20 E	38
Nal'chik: U.S.S.R.	43 29 N	43 37 E	57
Naldi: India	23 35 N	88 45 E	61F
Nalkari: *dam*, India	23 22 N	85 20 E	39
Nama Land: *region*, S. Africa	29 00 S	17 00 E	50
Namgye: North Korea	41 13 N	128 49 E	50
Namp'o: North Korea	38 44 N	125 24 E	45, 46, 59G, 84
Namrup: India	27 12 N	95 20 E	59, 61F
Namsskogan: Norway	64 55 N	13 10 E	45
Namtu: Burma	23 05 N	97 24 E	46
Nanao: Japan	37 03 N	136 58 E	57D
Nan-ch'ang: China P.R.	28 41 N	115 53 E	53
Nan-chang: China P.R.	31 47 N	111 42 E	32, 55, 67
Nan-ching (Nanking): China P.R.	32 03 N	118 47 E	36, 43, 55, 57
Nan-ch'ung: China P.R.	30 48 N	106 04 E	36
Nancy: France	48 41 N	6 12 E	37B, 67B
Nander: India	19 11 N	77 21 E	31C
Nandi: Fiji	17 47 S	177 29 E	87
Nangis: France	48 33 N	3 00 E	61D, 61H
Nanking *see* Nan-ching: China P.R.	32 03 N	118 47 E	36, 43, 55, 57
Nan-kong: Taiwan	25 05 N	121 35 E	61
Nan-ning: China P.R.	22 49 N	108 19 E	25, 43
Nan-p'ing: China P.R.	26 38 N	118 10 E	25, 43
Nantes: France	47 13 N	1 33 W	52A, 84C
Nan-tung: China P.R.	29 34 N	106 35 E	38
Naoetsu: Japan	37 11 N	138 15 E	47C, 58G, 59C, 60C
Nao-shima: *island*, Japan	34 26 N	133 59 E	45D
Naoshima: Japan	34 26 N	133 59 E	59G
Naples *see* Napoli: Italy			
Napoli (Naples): Italy	40 50 N	14 15 E	30B, 32C, 37B, 37D, 37H, 54, 55, 57C, 58D, 67, 84A, 87
Nariño: *admin.*, Colombia	1 30 N	78 00 W	49
Narrows: Va., U.S.A.	37 20 N	80 50 W	32B
Narva: U.S.S.R.	59 23 N	28 12 E	31
Narvacan: Philippines	17 29 N	120 28 E	31
Narvik: Norway	68 26 N	17 25 E	84
Nashville: Tenn., U.S.A.	36 10 N	86 50 W	31A, 32B, 57B, 59, 67, 87C
Nasik: India	20 00 N	73 52 E	53
Nassau: Bahamas	25 05 N	77 21 W	84, 87C
Natal: *admin.*, South Africa	28 45 S	30 45 E	38
Natal: Brazil	5 47 S	35 13 W	67, 84, 87
Natrium: W. Va., U.S.A.	39 46 N	80 50 W	61A
Naugatuck: Conn., U.S.A.	41 30 N	73 04 W	30A
Navajo *Co.*: Ariz., U.S.A.	35 30 N	110 20 W	40A, 49B
Năvodari: Romania	44 19 N	28 36 E	59, 61D
Navoi: U.S.S.R.	40 09 N	65 22 E	57, 61
Návplion: Greece	37 34 N	22 48 E	84B
Navsari: India	20 58 N	73 01 E	31C
Nazaré: Brazil	13 02 S	39 00 W	50
Nazareth: Pa., U.S.A.	40 44 N	75 18 W	57B
Nazilli: Turkey	37 55 N	28 21 E	31
Nchanga: Zambia	12 30 S	27 53 E	45B
Ndola: Zambia	12 58 S	28 38 E	45B, 50, 67
Néa Karváli: Greece	40 57 N	24 29 E	59H
Nebit-Dag: U.S.S.R.	39 30 N	54 22 E	36
Nebraska: *admin.*, U.S.A.	41 30 N	100 00 W	27
Nechí, Río: *river*, Colombia	8 08 N	74 46 W	49
Neckarsulm: Germany F.R.	49 11 N	9 14 E	55A
Nederland: Texas, U.S.A.	29 59 N	94 00 W	37J, 58A
Neenah: Wis., U.S.A.	44 10 N	88 29 W	25D
Negev *see* HaNegev: *desert*, Israel	30 45 N	34 50 E	59
Negishi: Japan	35 26 N	139 37 E	37E
Negotin: Yugoslavia	44 13 N	22 32 E	17
Nejdek: Czechoslovakia	50 20 N	12 44 E	29C
Nellore: India	14 29 N	80 00 E	48
Nelson: *admin.*, New Zealand	41 25 S	172 20 E	38C
Nelson: New Zealand	41 18 S	173 17 E	27, 84, 87
Nemuro: Japan	43 20 N	145 36 E	27D
Neodesha: Kans., U.S.A.	37 26 N	95 42 W	37J
Neópolis: Brazil	10 18 S	36 35 W	31
Nera Montoro: Italy	42 30 N	12 28 E	61D, 61H
Neratovice: Czechoslovakia	50 16 N	14 31 E	32C
Nerchinskiy Zavod: U.S.S.R.	51 19 N	119 36 E	46, 49
Neresnica: Yugoslavia	44 27 N	21 44 E	50
Neskaupstadhur: Iceland	65 09 N	13 42 W	27
Neuaegeri: Switzerland	47 10 N	8 33 E	31B
Neubeckum: Germany F.R.	51 48 N	8 03 E	57C
Neuchâtel: Switzerland	47 00 N	6 56 E	37F, 37H
Neuenkamp: Germany F.R.	51 26 N	6 44 E	37F
Neuhausen: Switzerland	47 42 N	8 37 E	54B
Neumünster: Germany F.R.	54 04 N	9 59 E	29B, 32C, 60D
Neunkirchen: Germany F.R.	49 21 N	7 11 E	43B, 58D

	° ′	° ′	*Page(s)*
Neustadt an der Donau: G.F.R.	48 48 N	11 46 E	37F
Neuves-Maisons: France	48 37 N	6 06 E	43B
Neuwied: Germany F.R.	50 26 N	7 28 E	57C
Neville Island: Pa., U.S.A.	40 31 N	80 08 W	58B
Nev'yansk: U.S.S.R.	57 30 N	60 13 E	57
Newark: N.J., U.S.A.	40 44 N	74 11 W	35, 55B, 56, 59A, 59E
Newark: Ohio, U.S.A.	40 03 N	82 25 W	37J, 58B
New Bedford: Mass., U.S.A.	41 38 N	70 55 W	31, 32B, 67A
New Bern: N.C., U.S.A.	35 05 N	77 04 W	87C
Newberry: S.C., U.S.A.	34 17 N	81 39 W	31A
New Braunfels: Texas, U.S.A.	29 43 N	98 09 W	31
New Brunswick: *admin.*, Canada	47 00 N	66 00 W	27, 38
Newcastle: Australia	32 55 S	151 45 E	38, 43, 61, 67, 84
Newcastle: Canada	47 01 N	65 36 W	45, 46, 49
New Castle: Ind., U.S.A.	39 56 N	85 21 W	55B
Newcastle: Wyo., U.S.A.	43 52 N	104 14 W	36, 37H
Newcastle-upon-Tyne: England	54 59 N	1 35 W	37B, 46, 52A, 62A, 84C, 87
New Cornelia: Ariz., U.S.A.	32 25 N	112 50 W	45A
New Delhi: India	28 37 N	77 13 E	3
New Era: South Africa	26 16 S	28 24 E	32
Newfoundland: *admin.*, Canada	52 00 N	56 00 W	27
Newhall: Calif., U.S.A.	34 23 N	118 33 W	36
New Idria: Calif., U.S.A.	36 30 N	121 20 W	48, 50
New Jersey: *admin.*, U.S.A.	40 00 N	75 00 W	27
New Johnsonville: Tenn., U.S.A.	35 59 N	87 59 W	47
Newlyn: England	50 06 N	5 34 W	27C
New Martinsville: W. Va., U.S.A.	39 39 N	80 52 W	61E
New Mexico: *admin.*, U.S.A.	35 00 N	106 00 W	27, 38, 48
Newnan: Ga., U.S.A.	33 23 N	84 48 W	29
New Orleans: La., U.S.A.	30 00 N	90 03 W	32B, 35, 56, 57A, 58A, 59F, 61B, 67, 84, 87C
Newport: England/Wales	51 35 N	3 00 W	47B, 58D, 59D, 67B, 84C
Newport: Ky., U.S.A.	39 05 N	84 27 W	56
Newport News: Va., U.S.A.	36 59 N	76 26 W	52, 67A, 87C
Newport Pagnell: England	52 05 N	0 44 W	55A
Newry: Northern Ireland	54 11 N	6 20 W	31
New South Wales: *admin.*, Australia	33 00 S	146 00 E	27, 47, 49, 50
Newton-le-Willows: England	54 17 N	1 40 W	54B
New Westminster: Canada	49 10 N	122 58 W	32, 84
New York: *admin.*, U.S.A.	43 00 N	75 00 W	16, 27
New York: N.Y., U.S.A.	40 40 N	73 50 W	3, 34, 35, 55B, 63, 67, 84, 87B
Neyveli: India	11 36 N	79 26 E	61
Ngwenya: *mtn.*, Swaziland	26 11 S	31 02 E	43
Niagara: *dam*, Canada	43 09 N	79 03 W	39
Niagara: *dam*, N.Y., U.S.A.	43 07 N	79 04 W	39
Niagara: Wis., U.S.A.	45 47 N	88 00 W	25D
Niagara Falls: Canada	43 05 N	79 06 W	61A, 61E
Niagara Falls: N.Y., U.S.A.	43 06 N	79 04 W	25D, 32B, 59A, 60B
Nicaro: Cuba	20 42 N	75 33 W	50
Nice: France	43 42 N	7 15 E	87D
Nichinan: Japan	31 36 N	131 23 E	25
Nicosia: Cyprus	35 11 N	33 23 E	87
Niederaichbach: Germany F.R.	48 36 N	12 19 E	40B
Niedersachsen: *admin.*, G.F.R.	52 00 N	10 00 E	38B, 56A
Nierstein: Germany F.R.	49 53 N	8 20 E	17
Nièvre: *admin.*, France	47 05 N	3 30 E	38B
Niğde: *admin.*, Turkey	38 05 N	34 40 E	50B
Nigel: South Africa	26 25 S	28 28 E	54
Niger *Delta*: Nigeria	5 00 N	6 30 E	35
Nihongi: Japan	34 39 N	136 23 E	59C
Niigata: Japan	37 55 N	139 03 E	27D, 34, 37E, 47C, 58G, 59G, 60E, 61C, 61G, 67C, 84D
Niigata-ken: *admin.*, Japan	37 30 N	139 00 E	34, 35
Niihama: Japan	33 58 N	133 16 E	58C, 58G, 59G, 60C, 61C, 61G
Niimi: Japan	34 59 N	133 28 E	57D
Nikel': U.S.S.R.	69 24 N	30 12 E	50
Nikiski: Alaska, U.S.A.	60 40 N	151 40 W	35
Nikitovka: U.S.S.R.	48 21 N	38 02 E	50
Nikkō: Japan	36 45 N	139 37 E	45D
Nikolayev: U.S.S.R.	46 58 N	32 00 E	17, 52, 57C, 84
Nikolayevsk-na-Amure: U.S.S.R.	53 08 N	140 44 E	36, 43
Nikopol': U.S.S.R.	47 34 N	34 24 E	50B
Nikšić: Yugoslavia	42 46 N	18 58 E	43B, 47B
Nile *Valley*: U.A.R.	30 10 N	31 06 E	14, 31
Nilgiris: *admin.*, India	11 20 N	76 30 E	47
Nilo Peçanha: *dam*, Brazil	22 28 S	43 50 W	39
Nimba Range: *mtns.*, Liberia	7 35 N	8 28 W	43
Nine Mile Point: N.Y., U.S.A.	43 35 N	76 25 W	40C
Ningyō-tōge: *pass*, Japan	35 19 N	133 56 E	40C
Ninove: Belgium	50 50 N	4 01 E	29B
Nipton: Calif., U.S.A.	35 27 N	115 16 W	40
Niš: Yugoslavia	43 19 N	21 54 E	29
Nishiki: Japan	34 13 N	136 24 E	32A, 58G, 59C, 59G, 60C
Nitro: W. Va., U.S.A.	38 26 N	81 51 W	32B
Nixon: N.J., U.S.A.	40 30 N	74 23 W	60B
Niza: Portugal	39 31 N	7 39 W	40
Nizhne-Kamskaya: *dam*, U.S.S.R.	55 45 N	52 00 E	39

	° ′	° ′	*Page(s)*
Nizhniy Tagil: U.S.S.R.	57 55 N	59 57 E	43, 49, 54, 57, 67
Nizhnyaya Salda: U.S.S.R.	58 05 N	60 43 E	43
Nizhnyaya Tunguska: *dam*, U.S.S.R.	65 48 N	88 04 E	39
Nkalago: Nigeria	6 22 N	7 48 E	57
Nkana-Kitwe: Zambia	12 49 S	28 15 E	45B
Nobeoka: Japan	32 35 N	131 40 E	32A, 59C, 59G, 60C, 61C, 61G, 67C
Nocara: Italy	40 06 N	16 29 E	59H
Noginsk: U.S.S.R.	55 51 N	38 27 E	31, 43
Noguères: France	43 22 N	0 36 W	47B
Nŏlbŭnnae: South Korea	36 53 N	128 09 E	48
Noranda: Canada	48 16 N	79 03 W	45, 46, 49, 56
Norco: La., U.S.A.	30 01 N	90 24 W	37J, 58E
Nord: *admin.*, France	50 20 N	3 40 E	38B, 56A
Nordhorn: Germany F.R.	52 26 N	7 05 E	31B
Nordic Mine: Canada	46 19 N	82 43 W	40C
Nordrhein-Westfalen: *admin.*, Germany F.R.	51 30 N	7 00 E	56A
Norfolk: Va., U.S.A.	36 54 N	76 18 W	55, 57B, 59E, 67, 87C
Noril'sk: U.S.S.R.	69 20 N	88 06 E	38, 45, 49, 50, 57, 67
Norman Wells: Canada	65 19 N	126 46 W	36
Normetal: Canada	49 00 N	79 22 W	45, 46, 49
Norphlet: Ark., U.S.A.	33 18 N	92 40 W	37J
Nørresundby: Denmark	57 04 N	9 55 E	57
Norrköping: Sweden	58 36 N	16 11 E	29
Norseman: Australia	32 12 S	121 46 E	49
Northampton: England	52 14 N	0 54 W	67B
Northampton: Pa., U.S.A.	40 40 N	75 29 W	57B
North Anna: Va., U.S.A.	37 48 N	77 25 W	40C
North Appalachian *Mountains*: Maine, U.S.A.	45 00 N	70 00 W	50
North Bay: Canada	46 20 N	79 28 W	61
North Carolina: *admin.*, U.S.A.	36 00 N	80 00 W	27
North China *Plain*: China P.R.	37 00 N	117 00 E	19, 31
North Dakota: *admin.*, U.S.A.	48 00 N	100 00 W	27, 38
Northern Territory: *admin.*, Australia	20 00 S	134 00 E	27
North European *Plain*: Europe	53 00 N	16 00 E	14, 23
North Ferriby: England	53 44 N	0 31 W	45
Northfield: Ill., U.S.A.	42 06 N	87 46 W	58B
Northfleet: England	51 27 N	0 20 E	57C
North Haven: Conn., U.S.A.	41 23 N	72 52 W	53A
North Italian *Plain*: Italy	45 00 N	11 00 E	14
North Miami: Fla., U.S.A.	25 53 N	80 10 W	32
North *Sea*: Europe	55 20 N	3 00 E	37B
North Shields: England	55 01 N	1 26 W	27C
North Stradbroke *Island*: Austl.	27 35 S	153 28 E	40
North Tonawanda: N.Y., U.S.A.	43 02 N	78 54 W	37J
Northumberland: *admin.*, Eng.	55 00 N	2 00 W	38B
Northumberland and Durham: *region*, England	55 00 N	2 00 W	56A
North Vancouver: Canada	49 59 N	123 05 W	59
North West London: *region*, England	51 35 N	0 15 W	53B
Northwest Territories: *admin.*, Canada	70 00 N	100 00 W	27, 50
Norwich: England	52 38 N	1 18 E	67B
Norzagaray: Philippines	14 53 N	121 02 E	57
Nossa: Italy	45 52 N	9 53 E	59H
Noto: Italy	36 53 N	15 04 E	17
Notodden: Norway	59 34 N	9 17 E	32C
Notre-Dame-de-Gravenchon: France	49 29 N	0 35 E	37F
Nottingham: England	52 58 N	1 10 W	67B
Nouméa: New Caledonia	22 16 S	166 27 E	84
Nováky: Czechoslovakia	48 43 N	18 33 E	58H
Nova Lima: Brazil	19 59 S	43 51 W	47
Nová Paka: Czechoslovakia	50 30 N	15 30 E	31B
Novara: Italy	45 28 N	8 38 E	31B, 37H, 55A, 58H, 61D, 61H
Nova Scotia: *admin.*, Canada	45 00 N	63 00 W	27, 38
Novaya Lyalya: U.S.S.R.	59 03 N	60 36 E	25
Novgorod: U.S.S.R.	58 31 N	31 17 E	61
Novocherkassk: U.S.S.R.	47 25 N	40 06 E	54, 58
Novokuybyshevsk: U.S.S.R.	53 07 N	49 58 E	58, 60
Novo-Kuznetsk (Stalinsk): U.S.S.R.	53 45 N	87 06 E	38, 43, 47, 67
Novomoskovsk (Stalinogorsk): U.S.S.R.	54 05 N	38 13 E	38, 58, 61
Novo-Pashiyskiy: U.S.S.R.	58 23 N	58 19 E	57
Novorossiysk: U.S.S.R.	44 43 N	37 47 E	35, 57, 84
Novosibirsk: *dam*, U.S.S.R.	54 47 N	83 02 E	39
Novosibirsk: U.S.S.R.	55 02 N	82 55 E	36, 43, 45, 57, 58, 60, 62, 67
Novotroitsk: U.S.S.R.	51 12 N	58 20 E	43, 57
Novovolynsk: U.S.S.R.	50 43 N	24 06 E	38B
Novovoronezhskiy: U.S.S.R.	51 19 N	39 13 E	40
Nový Jičín: Czechoslovakia	49 37 N	18 00 E	29C
Novyy Lipetsk: U.S.S.R.	52 35 N	39 37 E	43
Nowa Huta: Poland	50 04 N	20 02 E	57C
Nowshera: Pakistan	34 01 N	71 59 E	31
Noxon Rapids: *dam*, Mont., U.S.A.	47 58 N	115 47 W	39A
Noyelles-Godault: France	50 25 N	2 59 E	46B, 59H
Nsuta: Ghana	5 16 N	1 59 W	50
Nueva Rosita: Mexico	27 57 N	101 13 W	46

	° ′	° ′	*Page(s)*
Nueva Segovia: *admin.*, Nicaragua	13 40 N	86 10 W	50
Nuevitas, Bahía de: *bay*, Cuba	21 30 N	77 12 W	84
Nuevo Casas Grandes: Mexico	30 25 N	107 55 W	49A
Numazu: Japan	35 06 N	138 52 E	27D
Nünchritz: Germany D.R.	51 18 N	13 24 E	59H
Nurek: *dam*, U.S.S.R.	37 01 N	68 16 E	39
Nuremberg *see* Nürnberg: Germany F.R.			
Nürnberg (Nuremberg): G.F.R.	49 27 N	11 05 E	32C, 54B, 67B
Nusa Tenggara Barat: *admin.*, Indonesia	8 50 S	117 30 E	27
Nyasa, *Lake* (Lake Malawi): Africa	12 00 S	34 30 E	27
Nyborg: Denmark	55 19 N	10 48 E	58H
Nye *Co.*: Nev., U.S.A.	38 00 N	116 30 W	49B
Nyergesújfalu: Hungary	47 46 N	18 33 E	32C, 60D
Nyirád: Hungary	47 00 N	17 27 E	47B
Nyírbogdány: Hungary	48 03 N	21 53 E	37F, 37H
Nylund: Sweden	65 21 N	18 37 E	45
Nynäshamn: Sweden	58 54 N	17 57 E	36, 37F, 58
Nyūgawa: Japan	33 56 N	133 05 E	32A

O

	° ′	° ′	*Page(s)*
Oahe: *dam*, S.D., U.S.A.	44 25 N	100 23 W	39
Oak Harbor: Ohio, U.S.A.	41 31 N	83 10 W	40C
Oakland: Calif., U.S.A.	37 50 N	122 15 W	84, 87A
Oakville: Canada	43 27 N	79 41 W	37J, 55A
Oaxaca: *admin.*, Mexico	17 00 N	96 30 W	48, 50
Oban: Scotland	56 25 N	5 29 W	27C
Oberhausen: Germany F.R.	51 28 N	6 51 E	58D
Oberhausen-Holten: G.F.R.	51 33 N	6 48 E	60D, 61D, 61H
Oberholzer: South Africa	26 20 S	27 25 E	49
Oberkassel: Germany F.R.	50 43 N	7 10 E	57C
Oberösterreich: *admin.*, Austria	48 15 N	14 00 E	56A
Oberursel: Germany F.R.	50 12 N	8 35 E	53B
Obluch'ye: U.S.S.R.	49 00 N	131 05 E	45
Obninsk: U.S.S.R.	55 05 N	36 37 E	40
Obourg: Belgium	50 28 N	4 00 E	57C
Obrigheim: Germany F.R.	49 21 N	9 06 E	40B
Obrovac: Yugoslavia	44 12 N	15 41 E	47B
Obuasi: Ghana	6 12 N	1 40 W	49
Ocampo: Mexico	28 11 N	108 23 W	49A
Ocampo: Mexico	27 20 N	102 21 W	49A
Ocean Falls: Canada	52 24 N	127 42 W	25
Ocho Rios: Jamaica	18 25 N	77 07 W	87
Ochtrup: Germany F.R.	52 13 N	7 11 E	31B
Ocna Mureş: Romania	46 23 N	23 51 E	59D
Ocotlán: Mexico	20 21 N	102 46 W	32
Odawara: Japan	35 15 N	139 10 E	27D, 29D
Odda: Norway	60 04 N	6 33 E	59
Odendaalsrus: South Africa	27 52 S	26 42 E	49
Odense: Denmark	55 24 N	10 23 E	67
Odenton: Md., U.S.A.	39 05 N	76 41 W	32B
Odessa: Texas, U.S.A.	31 50 N	102 23 W	30A, 37J, 57, 58A, 58E, 60A, 60G, 61B
Odessa: U.S.S.R.	46 28 N	30 44 E	17, 35, 55, 84
Offenburg: Germany F.R.	48 29 N	7 56 E	31B
Oficina: Venezuela	8 53 N	64 18 W	34, 35
Ōfuna: Japan	35 21 N	139 32 E	32A, 60C
Ōfunato: Japan	39 04 N	141 43 E	27D, 57D
Ōgaki: Japan	35 21 N	136 37 E	29D, 32A
Ogbomosho: Nigeria	8 05 N	4 11 E	67
Ogilby: Calif., U.S.A.	32 49 N	114 50 W	48
Oglesby: Ill., U.S.A.	41 16 N	89 02 W	57B
Ogrodzieniec: Poland	50 27 N	19 31 E	57C
Ohe: Japan	33 55 N	133 25 E	58C, 60C
Ohio: *admin.*, U.S.A.	40 15 N	82 45 W	27, 38A
Oildale: Calif., U.S.A.	35 25 N	119 00 W	36
Oissel: France	49 20 N	1 06 E	61D
Ōita: Japan	33 14 N	131 36 E	25, 37E, 45, 60C, 67C, 84D, 87
Ōita-ken: *admin.*, Japan	33 15 N	131 30 E	49
Ōji: Japan	34 59 N	135 37 E	59G
Ojos Negros: Spain	40 44 N	1 30 W	43B
Okay: Ark., U.S.A.	33 45 N	93 56 W	57A
Okayama: Japan	34 39 N	133 55 E	32A, 43D, 45D, 58C, 59C, 59G
Okazaki: Japan	34 57 N	137 10 E	32A, 60C
Oker: Germany F.R.	51 54 N	10 29 E	46B
Okha: U.S.S.R.	53 34 N	142 56 E	36
Okinawa: *island*, Ryukyu Is.	26 30 N	128 10 E	87
Oklahoma: *admin.*, U.S.A.	36 00 N	98 00 W	27, 38
Oklahoma City: Okla., U.S.A.	35 28 N	97 33 W	40, 67, 87C
Okmulgee: Okla., U.S.A.	35 38 N	95 59 W	37J
Øksfjorden: *fjord*, Norway	70 16 N	22 20 E	27
Okulovka: U.S.S.R.	58 22 N	33 18 E	25B
Okutadami: *dam*, Japan	37 09 N	139 15 E	39D
Olavarría: Argentina	36 54 S	60 17 W	57
Olazagutía: Spain	42 53 N	2 12 W	57C
Oldbury-upon-Severn: England	51 29 N	2 31 W	40B
Oldenzaal: Netherlands	52 19 N	6 55 E	31B
Oldham: England	53 33 N	2 07 W	31B, 55A
Old Hickory: Tenn., U.S.A.	36 15 N	86 39 W	32B
Olean: N.Y., U.S.A.	42 05 N	78 26 W	61A, 61E
Olenegorsk: U.S.S.R.	68 09 N	33 18 E	43
Oleum: Calif., U.S.A.	37 58 N	122 21 W	36

	° ′	° ′	*Page(s)*
Olivais: Portugal	38 46 N	9 06 W	61D
Olkusz: Poland	50 18 N	19 33 E	46B
Olovyannaya: U.S.S.R.	50 56 N	115 35 E	45
Olstoppen: *dam*, Norway	61 29 N	9 23 E	39
Oltenia: *region*, Romania	44 30 N	23 30 E	38B
Olympia: Wash., U.S.A.	47 03 N	122 53 W	56
Ōmachi: Japan	36 30 N	137 52 E	47C
Omaha: Nebr., U.S.A.	41 15 N	96 00 W	46, 56, 62, 67, 87B
Omaruru: South West Africa	21 28 S	15 56 E	45
Omdurman *see* Umm Durmān: Sudan	15 38 N	32 30 E	67
Ōmi: Japan	37 01 N	137 48 E	30, 57D, 60C
Ōmine: Japan	39 58 N	141 54 E	45D
Ōmori: Japan	35 50 N	140 09 E	43D
Omsk: U.S.S.R.	55 00 N	73 24 E	30, 31, 36, 60, 67
Omsukchan: U.S.S.R.	62 32 N	155 48 E	38
Ōmuta: Japan	33 02 N	130 27 E	58C, 58G, 59C, 59G, 60E, 61C
Onagawa: Japan	38 26 N	141 27 E	27D
Onahama: Japan	36 57 N	140 54 E	27D, 45D, 58G, 59G, 61C
O'nan: China P.R.	30 32 N	114 18 E	38
Ondárroa: Spain	43 19 N	2 25 W	27B
Oneşti *see* Gheorghe Gheorgiu-Dej: Romania	46 15 N	26 45 E	30, 37H, 58, 59H, 60H
Onoda: Japan	33 59 N	131 11 E	57D
Ontario: *admin.*, Canada	51 00 N	85 00 W	27
Ontario: Calif., U.S.A.	34 04 N	117 38 W	87A
Ontario: N.Y., U.S.A.	43 10 N	77 24 W	40C
Ontonagan *Co.*: Mich., U.S.A.	46 30 N	89 30 W	49
Onverwacht: Surinam	5 36 N	55 14 W	47
Ookiep: South Africa	29 38 S	17 54 E	45, 50
Oostende (Ostend): Belgium	51 13 N	2 55 E	27C, 87D
Oost-Vlaanderen: *admin.*, Belgium	51 00 N	3 45 E	56A
Oostvoorne: Netherlands	51 55 N	4 06 E	37F
Ootsi: Botswana	25 00 S	25 30 E	50, 50C
Opava: Czechoslovakia	49 58 N	17 55 E	29C
Opelika: Ala., U.S.A.	32 39 N	85 26 W	31A
Ophthalmia Range: *mtns.*, Australia	23 17 S	119 30 E	43
Opole: Poland	50 40 N	17 56 E	57C
Opp: Ala., U.S.A.	31 16 N	86 18 W	31A
Oppu: Japan	40 45 N	140 30 E	46C
Oputo: Mexico	30 03 N	109 20 W	49A
Oradea: Romania	47 03 N	21 55 E	47B
Oran: Algeria	35 45 N	0 38 W	29, 31, 57, 84A
Orange: Calif., U.S.A.	33 48 N	117 51 W	30A, 32
Orange: N.J., U.S.A.	40 47 N	74 15 W	56
Orange: Texas, U.S.A.	30 05 N	93 43 W	57A, 58F, 60A, 60G
Orange Free State: *admin.*, South Africa	29 00 S	27 00 E	38, 49
Ordu: *admin.*, Turkey	40 50 N	37 30 E	27
Ordzhonikidze: U.S.S.R.	43 00 N	44 40 E	46
Örebro: *admin.*, Sweden	59 30 N	15 00 E	49
Örebro: Sweden	59 17 N	15 13 E	25B
Oregon: *admin.*, U.S.A.	44 00 N	121 00 W	27
Oregon City: Oreg., U.S.A.	45 21 N	122 36 W	25
Orekhovo-Zuyevo: U.S.S.R.	55 49 N	38 59 E	31
Orenburg: U.S.S.R.	51 45 N	55 06 E	29, 34
Orense: *admin.*, Spain	42 10 N	7 30 W	50
Origny-Sainte-Benoîte: France	49 50 N	3 30 E	57C
Orissa: *admin.*, India	20 00 N	84 00 E	27, 38
Orito: *region*, Colombia	0 45 N	77 00 W	35
Orizaba: Mexico	18 51 N	97 06 W	56
Orlando: Fla., U.S.A.	28 33 N	81 21 W	67, 87C
Orléans: France	47 55 N	1 54 E	55A
Orlická Přehradní Nádrž: *dam*, Czechoslovakia	49 31 N	14 09 E	39
Orne: *admin.*, France	48 40 N	0 05 E	43B
Örnsköldsvik: Sweden	63 18 N	18 43 E	59
Oro Grande: Calif., U.S.A.	34 36 N	117 20 W	57
Oron: Israel	30 55 N	35 01 E	56
Oroville: *dam*, Calif., U.S.A.	39 26 N	121 27 W	39
Orrington: Maine, U.S.A.	44 42 N	68 49 W	59A
Orsk: U.S.S.R.	51 12 N	58 34 E	36, 43, 50, 57, 67
Ortuella: Spain	43 19 N	3 04 W	58D
Ortviken: Sweden	62 24 N	17 21 E	25B
Oruro: *admin.*, Bolivia	18 40 S	67 30 W	49
Oruro: Bolivia	17 59 S	67 09 W	45, 50, 59
Orvieto: Italy	42 43 N	12 07 E	17
Ōsaka: Japan	34 40 N	135 30 E	25, 29D, 31, 32A, 43D, 45D, 52B, 54C, 55, 57D, 59C, 59G, 60C, 60E, 61G, 62, 67, 84D, 87
Osarizawa-kōzan: Japan	40 11 N	140 45 E	45
Osasco: Brazil	23 32 S	46 46 W	32, 54
Oschatz: Germany D.R.	51 18 N	13 07 E	32C
Osh: U.S.S.R.	40 32 N	72 48 E	67
Oshawa: Canada	43 53 N	78 51 W	55A
Oshkosh: Wis., U.S.A.	44 01 N	88 32 W	55, 87B
Oskarshamn: Sweden	57 16 N	16 26 E	40, 52A
Oslo: Norway	59 55 N	10 45 E	52, 56, 59, 67, 84, 87
Osnabrück: Germany F.R.	52 16 N	8 03 E	31B, 43B, 58D
Ostend *see* Oostende: Belgium	51 13 N	2 55 E	27C, 87D

P

Q

R

	° ′	° ′	Page(s)
Reinosa: Mexico	26 07 N	98 18 W	34, 37J, 58E, 60
Rejowiec: Poland	51 06 N	23 18 E	57C
Reka Devnya: Bulgaria	43 13 N	27 36 E	57C, 59D, 60D
Reka Zletovska: *river*, Yugo.	41 51 N	22 17 E	40
Remac: Canada	49 01 N	117 22 W	46A
Remiremont: France	48 01 N	6 35 E	31B
Renison Bell: Australia	41 48 S	145 25 E	45
Renkum: Netherlands	51 58 N	5 44 E	25C
Rennes: France	48 05 N	1 41 W	55A, 67B
Reno: Nev., U.S.A.	39 32 N	119 49 W	87A
Reno: Pa., U.S.A.	41 26 N	79 46 W	37J
Renory: Belgium	50 36 N	5 33 E	61D
Rentería: Spain	43 19 N	1 54 W	46B
Renton: Wash., U.S.A.	47 28 N	122 11 W	53, 54
Reşiţa: Romania	45 18 N	21 55 E	43B
Reutte: Austria	47 29 N	10 43 E	50
Revda: U.S.S.R.	56 48 N	59 57 E	45
Reydharfjördhur: *fjord*, Iceland	65 01 N	14 00 W	27
Reykjavík: Iceland	64 09 N	21 57 W	3, 27, 84, 87
Rharb *Basin*: Morocco	34 00 N	6 00 W	37C
Rheinberg: Germany F.R.	51 33 N	6 36 E	59D, 60D
Rheine: Germany F.R.	52 17 N	7 27 E	31B
Rheinfelden: Germany F.R.	47 34 N	7 48 E	47B, 59D, 60D
Rheinland-Pfalz: *admin.*, G.F.R.	49 40 N	7 30 E	38B, 56A
Rheinsberg: Germany D.R.	53 06 N	12 53 E	40B
Rheydt: Germany F.R.	51 10 N	6 27 E	29B, 31B
Rho: Italy	45 32 N	9 02 E	30B, 37H, 58D
Rhodes: Australia	33 50 S	151 05 E	58
Rhodes *see* Ródhos: *island*, Greece	36 26 N	28 13 E	17
Rhoose: Wales	51 24 N	3 18 W	57C
Ribarroja: *dam*, Spain	41 15 N	0 21 E	39
Richard City: Tenn., U.S.A.	35 00 N	85 41 W	57B
Richland: Wash., U.S.A.	46 17 N	119 17 W	40
Richmond: B.C., Canada	40 11 N	123 08 W	57
Richmond: Calif., U.S.A.	37 56 N	122 20 W	32, 36, 58, 59, 61
Richmond: England	51 28 N	0 18 W	55A
Richmond: Québec, Canada	45 40 N	72 08 W	32B
Richmond: Va., U.S.A.	37 34 N	77 27 W	25A, 32B, 59E, 60B, 67A, 87C
Riddle: Oreg., U.S.A.	42 56 N	123 24 W	50
Ridgefield Park: N.J., U.S.A.	40 52 N	74 02 W	25D
Riebeek Wes: South Africa	33 20 S	18 51 E	57
Riegelwood: N.C., U.S.A.	34 17 N	78 21 W	25A
Riesa: Germany D.R.	51 18 N	13 18 E	43B
Rieti: Italy	42 24 N	12 51 E	32C
Rifle: Colo., U.S.A.	39 32 N	107 47 W	40A
Rīga: *dam*, U.S.S.R.	56 51 N	24 15 E	39
Rīga: U.S.S.R.	56 57 N	24 06 E	25, 31, 32C, 34, 37B, 54, 55, 57, 67, 84, 87
Rihand: *dam*, India	24 09 N	83 02 E	39
Rijeka: Yugoslavia	45 21 N	14 24 E	37H, 52A, 84A
Rillito: Ariz., U.S.A.	32 23 N	111 08 W	57
Rimnicu Sărat: Romania	45 23 N	27 03 E	37H
Rimnicu Vîlcea: Romania	45 06 N	24 22 E	59D, 60D
Rinconada: Argentina	22 26 S	66 10 W	45
Ringhals: *point*, Sweden	57 15 N	12 05 E	40
Ringkøbing: *admin.*, Denmark	56 08 N	9 00 E	38B
Rio Blanco *Co.*: Colo., U.S.A.	40 00 N	108 15 W	40A
Rio Cayo Guam: *river*, Cuba	20 37 N	74 51 W	50
Rio de Janeiro: *admin.*, Brazil	22 00 S	42 30 W	16, 27, 40
Rio de Janeiro: Brazil	22 54 S	43 14 W	3, 29, 31, 32, 35, 36, 52, 58, 60, 62, 67, 84, 87
Río de la Plata: *estuary*, Arg.	35 00 S	57 00 W	27
Rio Doce: Brazil	20 15 S	42 54 W	50
Rio Grande: Brazil	32 02 S	52 05 W	36, 67, 84
Rio Grande: *region*, Mexico/U.S.A.	26 00 N	98 00 W	16
Rio Grande do Norte: *admin.*, Brazil	5 45 S	36 00 W	27
Rio Grande do Sul: *admin.*, Brazil	30 00 S	54 00 W	27, 38
Riondel: Canada	49 46 N	116 51 W	46A, 49
Rio Nechí: *river*, Colombia	8 08 N	74 46 W	49
Rio Paraná: *river*, Argentina	33 43 S	59 15 W	27
Rio Quindío: *river*, Colombia	4 24 N	75 46 W	50
Rio Tapajós: *river*, Brazil	2 24 S	54 41 W	49
Rio Tercero: Argentina	32 11 S	64 06 W	58
Ríotinto: Spain	37 40 N	6 39 W	59H
Rioupéroux: France	45 05 N	5 54 E	47B
Rio Uruguay: *river*, South America	34 12 S	58 18 W	27
Río Yamanigüey: *river*, Cuba	20 35 N	74 44 W	50
Riquewihr: France	48 10 N	7 18 E	17
Risdon: Australia	42 48 S	147 20 E	46, 59, 61
Rishra: India	22 43 N	88 21 E	60
Rîşnov: Romania	45 35 N	25 27 E	61D, 61H
Rittersgrün: Germany D.R.	50 28 N	12 47 E	25C
Rittman: Ohio, U.S.A.	40 58 N	81 47 W	25D
River Rouge: Mich., U.S.A.	42 15 N	83 09 W	54A, 58B
Riverside: Calif., U.S.A.	33 59 N	117 22 W	57, 87A
Riverton: Wyo., U.S.A.	43 02 N	108 22 W	59
Riyadh *see* Ar Riyāḑ: Saudi Arabia	24 38 N	46 43 E	67, 87
Rize: Turkey	41 02 N	40 31 E	84
Rjukan: Norway	59 52 N	8 34 E	61
Roanne: France	46 02 N	4 04 E	32C
Roanoke: Va., U.S.A.	37 15 N	79 58 W	54A, 57B, 67A, 87C

	° ′	° ′	Page(s)
Roanoke Rapids: N.C., U.S.A.	36 27 N	77 40 W	25A
Robe *River*: Australia	21 19 S	115 40 E	43
Robert H. Saunders: *dam*, Canada	45 02 N	74 45 W	39B
Robert Moses: *dam*, N.Y., U.S.A.	45 00 N	74 50 W	39B
Robertsfors: Sweden	64 11 N	20 51 E	48
Robinson: Ill., U.S.A.	39 00 N	87 43 W	37J
Rocha: Uruguay	34 29 S	54 20 W	40
Rochambeau: *airport*, Fr. Guiana	4 45 N	52 22 W	2
Rochdale: England	53 38 N	2 09 W	31B
Roche-la-Molière: France	45 26 N	4 19 E	61D, 61H
Rochelle: Ill., U.S.A.	41 55 N	89 05 W	29
Rochemaure: *dam*, France	44 35 N	4 44 E	39C
Rochester: England	51 24 N	0 30 E	57C
Rochester: Mich., U.S.A.	42 41 N	83 08 W	62
Rochester: Minn., U.S.A.	44 01 N	92 27 W	62, 87B
Rochester: N.Y., U.S.A.	43 12 N	77 37 W	32B, 56, 62, 63, 67A, 87B
Rockdale: Texas, U.S.A.	30 40 N	97 00 W	47A
Rock Fort: Jamaica	18 00 N	76 47 W	57
Rockhampton: Australia	23 23 S	150 30 E	38, 84, 87
Rock Hill: S.C., U.S.A.	34 55 N	81 01 W	32B
Rock Island: *dam*, Wash., U.S.A.	47 21 N	120 07 W	39A
Rocklea: Australia	27 33 S	153 01 E	55
Rockmart: Ga., U.S.A.	34 01 N	85 02 W	57B
Rocky Mount: N.C., U.S.A.	35 56 N	77 48 W	32B
Rocky Reach: *dam*, Wash., U.S.A.	47 36 N	120 14 W	39A
Ródhos (Rhodes): *is.*, Greece	36 26 N	28 13 E	17
Rodniki: U.S.S.R.	57 06 N	41 44 E	31
Roeselare: Belgium	50 57 N	3 08 E	29B
Rolle *see* Mont-sur-Rolle: Switzerland	46 38 N	6 21 E	17
Rolphton: Canada	46 11 N	77 41 W	40C
Roma: Italy	41 54 N	12 29 E	29, 37B, 37H, 56, 59D, 63B, 67, 87
Rome: Ga., U.S.A.	34 01 N	85 02 W	32B
Romford: England	51 35 N	0 11 E	55A
Romorantin: France	47 22 N	1 45 E	29
Rompin: Malaysia	2 42 N	102 31 E	43
Ronaldsway *Airport*: Isle of Man	54 04 N	4 33 W	87
Rondônia: Brazil	10 52 S	61 57 W	45
Rönnskär: Sweden	64 40 N	21 16 E	45, 46
Ronsart: Belgium	50 42 N	3 41 E	58H
Ronse: Belgium	50 45 N	3 36 E	29B, 31B
Roodepoort: South Africa	26 10 S	27 53 E	57
Rooiberg: South Africa	24 30 S	27 40 E	45
Rorschach: Switzerland	47 28 N	9 30 E	60D
Rosario: Argentina	32 57 S	60 40 W	2, 3, 43, 46, 61, 67, 84
Roseau: Dominica	15 18 N	61 24 W	27
Rosebery: Australia	41 47 S	145 31 E	45, 46, 49, 56
Rosignano Solvay: Italy	43 23 N	10 26 E	58H, 59D, 60D
Rosita: Nicaragua	13 53 N	84 24 W	45
Ross: *dam*, Wash., U.S.A.	48 50 N	121 02 W	39A
Rossarden: Australia	41 40 S	147 45 E	45
Rossing: South West Africa	22 31 S	14 52 E	40
Rossiyskaya Sovietskaya Federativnaya Sotsialistich-eskaya Respublika (R.S.F.S.R.): *admin.*, U.S.S.R.	60 00 N	100 00 E	27, 43
Rostock: Germany D.R.	54 05 N	12 08 E	37D, 52A, 67B, 84C
Rostov-na-Donu: U.S.S.R.	47 14 N	39 42 E	25, 84
Rotem: Belgium	51 03 N	5 44 E	46B
Rotherham: England	53 26 N	1 20 W	43B
Rotterdam: Netherlands	51 55 N	4 29 E	30B, 37B, 37D, 37F, 52A, 55A, 58D, 58H, 59H, 67B, 84C, 87D
Rottweil: Germany F.R.	48 10 N	8 37 E	32C, 60D
Roubaix: France	50 42 N	3 10 E	29B, 31B, 67B
Rouen: France	49 26 N	1 05 E	31B, 59H, 67B, 84C
Round Butte: *dam*, Oreg., U.S.A.	44 34 N	121 10 W	39A
Rourkela: India	22 16 N	85 01 E	61F
Rouseville: Pa., U.S.A.	41 28 N	79 42 W	37J
Roussillon: France	45 22 N	4 49 E	32C
Rovinj: Yugoslavia	45 05 N	13 38 E	47B
Rovno: U.S.S.R.	50 37 N	26 15 E	61D
Rowe: Mass., U.S.A.	42 50 N	72 50 W	40C
Rowlesburg: *dam*, W. Va., U.S.A.	39 21 N	79 40 W	39
Roxboro: *dam*, N.C., U.S.A.	36 24 N	79 00 W	39
Roxburgh: *dam*, New Zealand	45 34 S	169 21 E	39
Rozdol: U.S.S.R.	49 28 N	24 04 E	56
Rozenburg: Netherlands	51 55 N	4 15 E	37F, 52A, 60D
Rožňava: Czechoslovakia	48 40 N	20 32 E	43B
Ruabon: Wales	52 59 N	3 02 W	58D
Rubezhnoye: U.S.S.R.	48 30 N	37 11 E	58
Rubtsovsk: U.S.S.R.	51 30 N	81 15 E	45
Rüdersdorf: Germany D.R.	52 27 N	13 47 E	57C
Rüdesheim: Germany F.R.	49 59 N	7 55 E	17
Rudňany: Czechoslovakia	48 52 N	20 40 E	43B
Rudník: Czechoslovakia	50 35 N	15 43 E	32C
Rudniki: Poland	50 53 N	19 16 E	57C
Rudozem: Bulgaria	41 29 N	24 51 E	46B
Rueda: Spain	42 51 N	4 25 W	49

	° ′	° ′	Page(s)
Rufisque: Senegal	14 43 N	17 17 E	57
Ruhr: *region*, Germany F.R.	51 25 N	7 00 E	32C, 38B, 63A, 63B
Rukwa, *Lake*: Tanzania	8 00 S	32 25 E	27
Rumaylah: Iraq	30 47 N	47 37 E	37C
Rumaylan: *mtn.*, Syria	37 01 N	41 58 E	37C
Rumford: R.I., U.S.A.	41 51 N	71 21 W	59E
Rum Jungle: Australia	13 01 S	131 00 E	40, 45, 59
Rumoi: Japan	43 56 N	141 39 E	27D, 38
Rumuekpe: *region*, Nigeria	5 00 N	6 45 E	34
Runcorn: England	53 20 N	2 44 W	59D, 60D
Rundvik: Sweden	63 32 N	19 26 E	25
Ruse: Bulgaria	43 50 N	25 57 E	37H
Russell: Ky., U.S.A.	38 32 N	82 42 W	54A
Russellville: Ark., U.S.A.	35 17 N	93 06 W	40
Rüsselsheim: Germany F.R.	50 00 N	8 25 E	55A
Rustavi: U.S.S.R.	41 33 N	45 03 E	32, 43, 57, 60, 61
Rustenburg: South Africa	25 40 S	27 15 E	49, 50C
Ruwe: Congo D.R.	10 39 S	25 30 E	45
Rwinkwavu: Rwanda	1 58 S	30 34 E	45
Ryazan': U.S.S.R.	54 38 N	39 44 E	32C, 36, 57, 67
Rybinsk: U.S.S.R.	58 03 N	38 50 E	31
Rybinsk/Sheksna: *dam*, U.S.S.R.	58 03 N	38 50 E	39
Rybnitsa: U.S.S.R.	47 45 N	29 00 E	57C
Rydal: Sweden	57 33 N	12 41 E	31
Ryōtsu: Japan	38 05 N	138 26 E	27D

S

	° ′	° ′	Page(s)
Saarbrücken: Germany F.R.	49 14 N	7 00 E	58D
Saarland: *admin.*, G.F.R.	49 15 N	7 00 E	38B, 56A
Šabac: Yugoslavia	44 45 N	19 43 E	46B
Sabadell: Spain	41 33 N	2 06 E	29
Sabarat: France	43 06 N	1 24 E	47B
Sabarigiri: *dam*, India	9 35 N	76 32 E	39
Sabbione: *dam*, Italy	46 25 N	8 20 E	39C
Sabiñánigo: Spain	42 31 N	0 22 W	47B, 59D, 60D, 61D, 61H
Sacramento: Calif., U.S.A.	38 32 N	121 30 W	40, 87A
Sacramento *Valley*: Calif., U.S.A.	39 15 N	122 00 W	34
Sadd-el-Aali (Aswan High Dam): *dam*, U.A.R.	23 56 N	32 53 E	39
Sado: *is.*, Japan	38 00 N	138 25 E	49
Sadon: U.S.S.R.	42 51 N	44 00 E	46, 49
Saeki: Japan	32 57 N	131 54 E	32A, 57D
Safājah, Wādī: *stream*, U.A.R.	26 38 N	33 59 E	56
Şafāqis: Tunisia	34 44 N	10 46 E	84
Safe Harbor: *dam*, Pa., U.S.A.	39 56 N	76 24 W	39
Safi: Morocco	32 20 N	9 17 W	27, 59, 84
Safonovo: U.S.S.R.	55 06 N	33 15 E	38
Saganoseki: Japan	33 15 N	131 53 E	45D, 46C, 59G
Saginaw: Mich., U.S.A.	43 25 N	83 54 W	67A, 87B
Saguache *Co.*: Colo., U.S.A.	38 10 N	106 10 W	40A, 49B
Sagunto: Spain	39 41 N	0 16 W	43
Saharanpur: India	29 58 N	77 33 E	31
Saïda: Algeria	34 50 N	0 10 E	17
Saïda (Sidon): Lebanon	33 32 N	35 22 E	37C, 37G
Saidaiji: Japan	34 39 N	134 02 E	32A
Sai Gon: South Vietnam	10 45 N	106 40 E	67, 84, 87
Saijō: Japan	33 55 N	133 11 E	32A
Ste. Anne de Beaupré: Canada	47 02 N	70 58 W	25D
Saint-Auban: France	44 04 N	6 00 E	47B, 59D, 60D
Saint-Basile: Canada	46 45 N	71 49 W	57
Saint-Benoît-de-Carmaux: France	44 03 N	2 08 E	61H
St. Boniface: Canada	49 54 N	97 07 W	36
Saint-Chamond: France	45 28 N	4 30 E	54B
St. Charles: Mo., U.S.A.	38 48 N	91 29 W	53
St. Charles Parish: *admin.*, La., U.S.A.	29 55 N	90 25 W	59B
Sainte-Croix: Haiti	18 25 N	73 09 W	47
St. Croix: *island*, Virgin Is., (U.S.A.)	17 45 N	64 45 W	36, 87
Saint-Egrève: France	45 14 N	5 41 E	57C
Saint-Émilion: France	44 53 N	0 09 W	17
Saint-Étienne-du-Rouvray: France	49 23 N	1 06 E	25C
Saint-Fons: France	45 42 N	4 52 E	59D, 59H, 60D, 61D, 61H
Saint-Guénolé: France	47 49 N	4 22 W	27
St. Helenabaai: *bay*, S. Africa	32 43 S	18 05 E	27
St. Helens: England	53 28 N	2 44 W	32C
St. Helens: Oreg., U.S.A.	45 54 N	122 50 W	25, 61
St. Hyacinthe: Canada	45 38 N	72 57 W	31
Saint-Jean-de-Maurienne: France	45 17 N	6 21 E	47B
St. Jérôme: Canada	45 47 N	74 01 W	29
Saint John: Canada	45 16 N	66 03 W	35, 36, 52, 84, 87
Saint Johns: Antigua	17 06 N	61 51 W	36
St. John's: Canada	47 34 N	52 41 W	67, 84, 87
Saint-Laurent-Blangy: France	50 18 N	2 48 E	32C, 60D
Saint-Laurent-des-Eaux: France	47 43 N	1 36 E	40B
St. Lawrence *Co.*: N.Y., U.S.A.	44 25 N	75 00 W	49
Saint-Louis: France	43 21 N	5 22 E	47B
St. Louis: Mich., U.S.A.	43 24 N	84 35 W	40C

	° ′	° ′	Page(s)
St. Louis: Mo., U.S.A.	38 40 N	90 15 W	32B, 45, 53, 54, 55, 56, 57A, 58B, 63, 87B
Saint-Marcet: France	43 12 N	0 45 E	37B
St. Marks: Fla., U.S.A.	30 12 N	84 12 W	37J
St. Mary's: Canada	43 15 N	81 09 W	57B
St. Marys: Ga., U.S.A.	30 43 N	81 34 W	25A
St. Marys: W. Va., U.S.A.	39 24 N	81 13 W	37J
Saint-Menet: France	43 17 N	5 27 E	60D
Saint-Nabord: France	48 03 N	6 35 E	32C, 60D
Saint-Nazaire: France	47 17 N	2 12 W	52A, 53B
St. Paul: Minn., U.S.A.	45 00 N	93 10 W	25, 56, 62, 87B
St. Paul Park: Minn., U.S.A.	44 50 N	93 00 W	37J
Saint-Pierre-la-Cour: France	48 07 N	1 02 W	57C
St. Pölten: Austria	48 12 N	15 38 E	32C
Saint-Pourçain-sur-Besbre: France	46 28 N	3 39 E	17
Saint-Priest-la-Prugne: France	45 58 N	3 45 E	40B
Saint-Quentin: France	49 51 N	3 17 E	31B
Saint-Renan: France	48 26 N	4 37 W	45
Saint-Sylvestre: France	46 00 N	1 23 E	40B
Ste. Thérèse: Canada	45 38 N	73 50 W	32B, 55
St. Thomas: *island*, Virgin Is., (U.S.A.)	18 21 N	64 55 W	87
St. Urbain: Canada	47 35 N	70 33 W	47
Saint-Vulbas: France	45 50 N	5 17 E	40B
Saitama-ken: *admin.*, Japan	36 00 N	139 30 E	55
Sakai: Japan	34 35 N	135 28 E	32A, 37E, 54C, 58G, 59C, 60C, 60E, 61C
Sakai: Japan	35 33 N	133 14 E	27D
Sakata: Japan	38 55 N	139 50 E	59, 60C
Sakhalin Ostrov: *is.*, U.S.S.R.	51 00 N	143 00 E	38
Sakoshi: Japan	34 46 N	134 26 E	32A
Sakuma: *dam*, Japan	35 05 N	137 47 E	39D
Salair: U.S.S.R.	54 13 N	85 47 E	46, 49
Salamanca: Mexico	20 34 N	101 12 W	30, 36, 60, 61
Salamanca: Spain	40 58 N	5 39 W	59H
Šala-nod-Vahom: Czech.	48 09 N	17 51 E	30, 61D, 61H
Salavat: U.S.S.R.	53 21 N	55 55 E	58, 60, 61
Saldanhabaai: *bay*, S. Africa	33 00 S	17 56 E	27
Salem: India	11 38 N	78 08 E	31C, 47, 50
Salem: Mo., U.S.A.	37 38 N	91 34 W	59E
Salem: N.J., U.S.A.	39 35 N	75 28 W	40C
Salem: Oreg., U.S.A.	44 57 N	123 01 W	25
Salerno: Italy	40 41 N	14 47 E	57C
Salford: England	53 30 N	2 16 W	31B
Salgótarján: Hungary	48 07 N	19 49 E	38B
Salina: Kans., U.S.A.	38 53 N	97 36 W	53
Salin-de-Giraud: France	43 25 N	4 44 E	59D
Salindres: France	44 10 N	4 10 E	47B, 59H
Saline *Co.*: Ark., U.S.A.	34 40 N	92 45 W	47A
Salisbury: *admin.*, Rhodesia	18 00 S	30 55 E	49
Salisbury: Md., U.S.A.	38 22 N	75 37 W	87B
Salisbury: N.C., U.S.A.	35 20 N	80 30 W	31A, 32B
Salisbury: Rhodesia	17 50 S	31 03 E	59, 67, 87
Salmo: Canada	49 11 N	117 16 W	46A
Salta: *admin.*, Argentina	25 00 S	64 06 W	34, 35
Salta: Argentina	24 47 S	65 25 W	67
Salt Lake City: Utah, U.S.A.	40 45 N	111 55 W	36, 45, 67, 87
Salt Lake *Co.*: Utah, U.S.A.	40 45 N	112 00 W	46, 49B
Salto Grande: *dam*, Argentina	31 14 S	57 55 W	39
Salt River: South Africa	33 56 S	18 28 E	54
Salt River *Canyon*: Ariz., U.S.A.	33 45 N	110 45 W	48
Saltville: Va., U.S.A.	36 52 N	81 48 W	59B
Salvador: Brazil	12 59 S	38 31 W	67, 84, 87
Salvajina: *dam*, Colombia	4 03 N	74 50 W	39
Salzgitter: Germany F.R.	52 05 N	10 20 E	43B, 54B
Samanco: *bay*, Peru	9 13 S	78 33 W	27A
Samarinda: Indonesia	0 30 S	117 09 E	27
Sambalpur: India	21 28 N	84 04 E	25
Samch'ŏg-ŭp: *admin.*, South Korea	37 26 N	129 08 E	57D
Samch'ŏk: South Korea	37 27 N	129 10 E	38C, 59C
Šamorín: Czechoslovakia	48 02 N	17 19 E	59H
Samsun: Turkey	41 17 N	36 20 E	84B
San Andreas: Calif., U.S.A.	38 10 N	120 41 W	57
San Antonio: Chile	33 35 S	71 38 W	27, 84
San Antonio: Texas, U.S.A.	29 25 N	98 30 W	37J, 56, 57A, 87C
San Bernardino: Calif., U.S.A.	34 04 N	117 18 W	87A
San Bernardo: Mexico	25 59 N	105 33 W	49A
San Celoni: Spain	41 41 N	2 29 E	58D
San Cristóbal: Mexico	18 23 N	95 44 W	58
Sandakan: Malaysia	5 50 N	118 07 E	87
Sandbach: England	53 09 N	2 22 W	59D
Sande: Norway	59 36 N	10 12 E	25B
Sandersville: Miss., U.S.A.	31 47 N	89 02 W	37J
San Diego: Calif., U.S.A.	32 45 N	117 10 W	40, 52, 53, 87A
Sandhamn: Sweden	56 06 N	15 51 E	27C
San Dimas: Mexico	24 08 N	105 58 W	49A
Sandouville: France	49 30 N	0 19 E	55A
Sandow: *dam*, Texas, U.S.A.	30 40 N	97 00 W	39
Sand Springs: Okla., U.S.A.	36 08 N	96 07 W	31
Sandur: India	15 06 N	76 31 E	50
Sandusky: Ohio, U.S.A.	41 27 N	82 42 W	59E
San Eduardo: Ecuador	2 12 S	79 56 W	57
San Esteban: *dam*, Spain	42 25 N	7 40 W	39
San Felipe: Mexico	30 22 N	110 13 W	49A
San Felipe del Progresso: Mexico	19 43 N	99 57 W	49A
San Fernando: Philippines	16 39 N	120 19 E	84

	° ′	° ′	Page(s)
San Francisco: Calif., U.S.A.	37 45 N	122 27 W	35, 55, 56, 63, 67, 84, 87A
San Francisco del Oro: Mexico	26 52 N	105 51 W	45, 46, 49A
Sangar: U.S.S.R.	63 55 N	127 31 E	38
San Gavino Monreale: Italy	39 33 N	8 47 E	46B
Sangdong: South Korea	36 59 N	128 52 E	50
Sangerhausen: Germany D.R.	51 28 N	11 18 E	45
San Giuseppe: Italy	44 22 N	8 18 E	59H, 61D, 61H
Sangli: India	16 55 N	74 37 E	31C
San Isidro: Argentina	34 27 S	58 30 W	32
San Javier de Arriba: Mexico	30 13 N	110 44 W	49A
San Joaquín: Chile	33 36 S	70 41 W	32, 60
San Jose: Calif., U.S.A.	37 20 N	121 55 W	62, 67, 87A
San José: Costa Rica	9 56 N	84 05 W	67, 87
San José: Peru	6 40 S	79 55 W	27A
San Juan: *admin.*, Argentina	31 00 S	69 00 W	17
San Juan: Argentina	31 32 S	68 31 W	67
San Juan: *basin*, N. Mex., U.S.A.	36 15 N	108 20 W	34
San Juan: Chile	23 07 S	69 01 W	50
San Juan: Peru	15 22 S	75 07 W	84
San Juan: Puerto Rico	18 28 N	66 07 W	56, 60, 67, 84, 87
San Juan *Co.*: Colo., U.S.A.	37 40 N	107 40 W	49B
San Juan *Co.*: N. Mex., U.S.A.	36 30 N	108 30 W	40A
San Juan *Co.*: Utah, U.S.A.	37 45 N	109 50 W	40A, 49B
San Juan de Guadalupe: Mexico	24 38 N	102 44 W	49A
San Juan del Río: Mexico	24 47 N	104 27 W	49A
San Juan de Nieva: Spain	43 35 N	5 56 W	46B
San Justo: Argentina	34 40 S	58 33 W	32, 46, 54, 55
San Leandro: Calif., U.S.A.	37 43 N	122 10 W	55
San Lorenzo: Argentina	32 45 S	60 44 W	30, 34, 36, 58, 59, 60, 61
San Lorenzo: Venezuela	9 47 N	71 04 W	36
Sanlúcar de Barrameda: Spain	36 47 N	6 21 W	17
San Luis: *admin.*, Argentina	34 00 S	66 00 W	40
San Luis: Argentina	33 18 S	66 21 W	50
San Luis: *dam*, Calif., U.S.A.	37 04 N	121 07 W	39
San Luis Potosí: *admin.*, Mexico	22 30 N	100 30 W	50
San Luis Potosí: Mexico	22 09 N	100 59 W	45
San Manuel: Ariz., U.S.A.	32 35 N	110 40 W	45A, 50A
San Marco: Italy	45 42 N	13 05 E	52A
San Martín Texmelucan: Mexico	19 17 N	98 26 W	58
San-men: *dam*, China P.R.	34 40 N	111 00 E	39
San Miguel: Colo., U.S.A.	37 49 N	107 43 W	45
San Miguel *Co.*: Colo., U.S.A.	38 00 N	108 30 W	40A, 49B
San Miguel de Tucumán: Arg.	26 49 S	65 13 W	67
Sannazzaro de' Burgondi: Italy	45 06 N	8 54 E	37H
San Nicholás: Mexico	24 41 N	98 48 W	49A
San Nicolás: Peru	15 11 S	75 12 W	27A
San Nicolás de los Arroyos: Arg.	33 20 S	60 13 W	43, 58
San Nicolás Hidalgo: Mexico	25 59 N	100 27 W	57
San Onofre: Calif., U.S.A.	33 22 N	117 33 W	40
San Pablo de Napa: Bolivia	20 29 S	68 39 W	40
San Patricio: Texas, U.S.A.	27 52 N	97 27 W	47A
San Pedro del Gallo: Mexico	25 33 N	104 18 W	49A
San Pedro Sula: Honduras	15 27 N	88 02 W	87
San Roque: Spain	36 13 N	5 24 W	60
San Roque: Venezuela	9 17 N	64 43 W	36
San Salvador: El Salvador	13 42 N	89 12 W	32, 87
San Salvo: Italy	42 03 N	14 44 E	32C
San Sebastián: Spain	43 19 N	1 59 W	57C
Santa Ana: Calif., U.S.A.	33 44 N	117 54 W	62, 87A
Santa Ana: Mexico	30 33 N	111 07 W	49A
Santa Barbara: Calif., U.S.A.	34 25 N	119 41 W	62, 87A
Santa Bárbara: Mexico	26 48 N	105 49 W	45, 46, 49A
Santa Catarina: *admin.*, Brazil	27 00 S	50 00 W	27, 38
Santa Catarina de Tepehuanes: Mexico	25 21 N	105 44 W	49A
Santa Clara: Calif., U.S.A.	37 21 N	121 58 W	25, 62
Santa Cruz: *admin.*, Bolivia	17 30 S	61 30 W	35
Santa Cruz: Bolivia	17 48 S	63 10 W	36, 61
Santa Cruz *Co.*: Ariz., U.S.A.	31 30 N	110 50 W	49B
Santa Cruz de la Palma: Canary Is.	28 41 N	17 45 E	27
Santa Cruz de Tenerife: *admin.*, Canary Is.	28 10 N	17 20 W	16
Santa Cruz de Tenerife: Canary Is.	28 27 N	16 14 W	35, 36, 84, 87
Santa Elena: Ecuador	2 14 S	80 51 W	35
Santa Eugenia de Ribeira: Spain	42 33 N	9 00 W	27B
Santa Lucía: Peru	15 40 S	70 30 W	45
Santa Maria: Calif., U.S.A.	34 56 N	120 25 W	36, 87A
Santa María de Garoña: Spain	42 46 N	3 12 W	40B
Santa María del Oro: Mexico	25 56 N	105 22 W	49A
Santa María de Otáez: Mexico	24 42 N	106 00 W	49A
Santa Maria: *island*, Azores	36 58 N	25 07 W	87
Santa Marta: Colombia	11 15 N	74 13 W	84
Santa Monica: Calif., U.S.A.	34 00 N	118 25 W	53
Santander: *admin.*, Spain	43 10 N	4 00 W	46B
Santander: Spain	43 28 N	3 48 W	30B, 60H, 84A
Santarém: *admin.*, Portugal	39 15 N	8 35 W	38
Santarém: Brazil	2 26 S	54 42 W	67
Santa Rita: *dam*, Colombia	6 02 N	75 26 W	39
Santa Rosalía: Mexico	27 19 N	112 17 W	45
Santiago: *admin.*, Chile	33 30 S	70 50 W	49
Santiago: Chile	33 27 S	70 40 W	25, 29, 31, 32, 55, 56, 67, 87
Santiago de Cuba: Cuba	20 01 N	75 49 W	36, 57, 84
Santiago del Estero: Argentina	27 47 S	64 16 W	67
Santiago Papasquiaro: Mexico	25 03 N	105 25 W	49A

	° ′	° ′	Page(s)
Santo Amaro: Brazil	12 32 S	38 43 W	46
Santo André: Brazil	23 40 S	46 31 W	32, 61
Santo Domingo: *dam*, Venezuela	9 00 N	71 00 W	39
Santo Domingo: Dom. R.	18 28 N	69 54 W	56, 57, 67, 87
San Tomé: Venezuela	8 58 N	64 08 W	43
Santoña: Spain	43 27 N	3 27 W	27B
Santos: Brazil	23 57 S	46 20 W	35, 59, 60, 61, 84
Santo Tomas: Philippines	16 02 N	120 47 E	45
San Vicente: Chile	36 43 S	73 08 W	59, 60
San Vicente del Raspeig: Spain	38 24 N	0 31 W	57C
San Vicente dels Horts: Spain	41 24 N	2 01 E	57C
São Bernardo do Campo: Brazil	23 42 S	46 33 W	32
São Caetano do Sul: Brazil	23 36 S	46 34 W	32
São Domingos: Brazil	19 09 S	40 37 W	32
São Domingos: Portugal	37 40 N	7 30 W	45
São Gonçalo: Brazil	22 51 S	43 04 W	57
São João del Rei: Brazil	21 09 S	44 16 W	45
São José dos Campos: Brazil	23 11 S	45 53 W	32
São Luís: Brazil	2 31 S	44 16 W	31, 67, 87
São Miguel: *island*, Azores	37 47 N	25 30 W	84
São Miguel Paulista: Brazil	23 30 S	46 26 W	32
Saône-et-Loire: *admin.*, France	46 40 N	4 30 E	38B
São Paulo: *admin.*, Brazil	22 00 S	49 00 W	16, 27
São Paulo: Brazil	23 32 S	46 37 W	25, 29, 31, 32, 36, 43, 55, 57, 58, 59, 60, 61, 62, 67, 87
São Roque: Brazil	23 32 S	47 08 W	59
São Vicente: *is.*, Cape Verde Is.	16 50 N	25 00 W	84
Sapporo: Japan	43 03 N	141 21 E	56, 87
Sara Buri: Thailand	14 32 N	100 55 E	57
Saragossa *see* Zaragoza: Spain	41 38 N	0 53 W	55, 60D
Sarājeh: Iran	34 36 N	51 04 E	34, 37A
Sarajevo: Yugoslavia	43 50 N	18 25 E	54B
Saramenha: Brazil	20 24 S	43 31 W	47
Sarandí: Argentina	34 40 S	58 20 W	59
Sarany: U.S.S.R.	58 32 N	58 46 E	50
Sarasota: Fla., U.S.A.	27 20 N	82 32 W	87C
Saratov: *dam*, U.S.S.R.	52 02 N	47 47 E	39
Saratov: U.S.S.R.	51 34 N	46 02 E	32C, 36, 60
Sarbay: U.S.S.R.	52 58 N	63 07 E	43
Sardegna (Sardinia): *is.*, Italy	40 00 N	9 00 E	27, 49
Sardinia *see* Sardegna: *is.*, Italy			
Sargun: Japan	42 30 N	143 00 E	50
Sar-i-Pul: Afghanistan	35 30 N	66 40 E	35
Sariwŏn: North Korea	38 30 N	125 45 E	43
Sarnia: Canada	42 57 N	82 24 W	30A, 34, 37J, 58, 59A, 60B, 60F, 61A, 61E
Şaroş: *admin.*, Romania	46 15 N	24 20 E	37B
Sarpsborg: Norway	59 17 N	11 07 E	32C, 59
Sarralbe: France	49 00 N	7 01 E	59D, 60D
Sarroch: Italy	39 04 N	9 00 E	37D, 58D
Sartell: Minn., U.S.A.	45 36 N	94 13 W	25
Sasebo: Japan	33 10 N	129 43 E	27D, 38C, 52B, 84D
Saskatchewan: *admin.*, Canada	54 00 N	105 00 W	27, 34, 35, 38,
Saskatoon: Canada	52 10 N	106 40 W	32, 36, 56, 59, 67
Sasolburg: South Africa	26 50 S	27 51 E	30, 58, 59, 60, 61
Sassenberg: Germany F.R.	52 00 N	8 03 E	29B
Satobe: U.S.S.R.	42 32 N	70 00 E	57
Satka: U.S.S.R.	55 03 N	59 01 E	50
Satna: India	24 33 N	80 50 E	57
Saucelle: *dam*, Spain	41 03 N	6 48 W	39
Saucillo: Mexico	28 01 N	105 17 W	45, 46, 49A
Sauerland: *region*, G.F.R.	51 20 N	7 50 E	46B
Saugus: Calif., U.S.A.	34 25 N	118 31 W	60
Sault Ste. Marie: Canada	46 32 N	84 20 W	25D, 43A
Saunders, Robert H.: *dam*, Canada	45 02 N	74 45 W	39B
Sauternes: France	44 32 N	0 20 W	17
Savage *River*: Australia	41 38 S	145 04 E	43
Savannah: Ga., U.S.A.	32 04 N	81 07 W	25A, 37J, 59F, 61B, 61E, 84, 87C
Savennières: France	47 23 N	0 39 W	17
Savignano sul Panaro: Italy	44 29 N	11 02 E	57C
Săvinești: Romania	46 51 N	26 28 E	32C
Savli: India	22 33 N	73 16 E	57
Savoie: *admin.*, France	45 30 N	6 25 E	38B, 48, 49
Savona: Italy	44 17 N	8 30 E	37D, 84A
Savukoski: *admin.*, Finland	67 40 N	28 30 E	40
Sawai Madhopur: India	26 00 N	76 28 E	57
Saxberget: Sweden	60 07 N	14 58 E	45
Sayago: Uruguay	34 53 S	56 11 W	57
Sayano-Shushenskaya: *dam*, U.S.S.R.	53 17 N	91 59 E	39
Saynshand: Mongolia	44 58 N	110 10 E	36
Sayreville: N.J., U.S.A.	40 28 N	74 21 W	59E
Sazare: Japan	33 58 N	133 20 E	45D
Scala di Giocca: Italy	40 43 N	8 36 E	57C
Scarborough: Canada	43 44 N	79 16 W	62
Schefferville: Canada	54 50 N	67 00 W	43
Schenectady: N.Y., U.S.A.	42 48 N	73 57 W	54
Scheveningen: Netherlands	52 05 N	4 16 E	27C
Schiedam: Netherlands	51 55 N	4 25 E	52A, 59D
Schijndel: Netherlands	51 37 N	5 27 E	29B
Schinznach: Switzerland	47 28 N	8 08 E	55A
Schkopau: Germany D.R.	51 23 N	11 59 E	30B, 58D; 60D
Schlegeis: *dam*, Austria	47 08 N	11 48 E	39C
Schlieren: Switzerland	47 28 N	8 27 E	54B
Schneeberg: *admin.*, G.D.R.	50 35 N	12 38 E	50
Scholven: Germany F.R.	51 36 N	7 01 E	60H

	° ′	° ′	Page(s)
Schoonebeek: Netherlands	52 39 N	6 52 E	37D
Schumacher: Canada	48 30 N	81 16 W	45
Schwäbisch Hall: G.F.R.	49 06 N	9 44 E	31B
Schwandorf im Bayern: G.F.R.	49 20 N	12 07 E	47B
Schwarzheide: Germany D.R.	51 29 N	13 52 E	37F
Schwechat: Austria	48 08 N	16 28 E	37F, 58, 60D, 60H
Schwedt: Germany D.R.	53 04 N	14 18 E	25C, 37F, 58D, 58H, 61D, 61H
Scottsbluff: Nebr., U.S.A.	41 52 N	103 40 W	37J
Scranton: Pa., U.S.A.	41 25 N	75 40 W	32B, 60B, 67A
Scunthorpe: England	53 36 N	0 38 W	43B, 58D
Seabrook: N.H., U.S.A.	42 53 N	70 53 W	40C
Seadrift: Texas, U.S.A.	28 25 N	96 44 W	58E, 60A, 60G
Seaford: Del., U.S.A.	38 39 N	75 35 W	32B, 60B
Seagraves: Texas, U.S.A.	32 56 N	102 35 W	60G
Searles *Lake*: Calif., U.S.A.	35 45 N	117 20 W	56
Searsport: Maine, U.S.A.	44 27 N	68 56 W	59, 61
Seaton Carew: England	54 40 N	1 11 W	40B
Seattle: Wash., U.S.A.	47 35 N	122 20 W	34, 43, 52, 53, 55, 56, 57, 63, 67, 84, 87
Sebastián Vizcaíno, Bahía: *bay*, Mexico	28 00 N	114 30 W	84
Sechura: Peru	5 39 S	80 50 W	27A
Sedan: France	49 42 N	4 57 E	29B
Segezha: U.S.S.R.	63 44 N	34 19 E	25
Séguéla: *admin.*, Ivory Coast	8 05 N	6 32 W	48
Seine-et-Oise: *admin.*, France	48 45 N	2 00 E	56A
Seitevare: *dam*, Sweden	67 01 N	18 32 E	39
Seixal: Portugal	38 38 N	9 06 W	43
Selby: Calif., U.S.A.	38 06 N	122 14 W	46
Selizharovo: U.S.S.R.	56 51 N	33 27 E	38
Selkirk: Scotland	55 33 N	2 50 W	29B
Selma: Ala., U.S.A.	32 24 N	87 01 W	50
Selma: N.C., U.S.A.	35 32 N	78 18 W	59F
Selnech'nyy: U.S.S.R.	50 45 N	136 50 E	45
Selukwe: Rhodesia	19 40 S	30 00 E	50, 50C
Semarang: Indonesia	6 58 S	110 25 E	31, 67, 84
Sematan: Malaysia	1 48 N	109 46 E	47
Semily: Czechoslovakia	50 38 N	15 22 E	31B
Seminole: Texas, U.S.A.	32 43 N	102 39 W	60G
Semipalatinsk: U.S.S.R.	50 28 N	80 13 E	29, 57
Sendai: Japan	38 15 N	140 53 E	25, 38, 67C
Seneffe: Belgium	50 31 N	4 15 E	62A
Sengileyevskaya: U.S.S.R.	45 03 N	41 40 E	57
Senica nad Myjavou: Czech.	48 40 N	17 20 E	32C
Senzaki: Japan	34 23 N	131 12 E	27D
Seoul *see* Sŏul: South Korea	37 34 N	127 00 E	31, 58, 60, 62, 67, 87
Sept-Iles: Canada	50 13 N	66 22 W	87
Seraing: Belgium	50 36 N	5 29 E	43B, 54B
Serebryansk I: *dam*, U.S.S.R.	69 07 N	35 55 E	39
Seremban: *region*, Malaysia	2 45 N	101 55 E	45C, 47
Sergipe: *admin.*, Brazil	10 30 S	37 30 W	27
Seria: Brunei	4 37 N	114 19 E	35
Seridó: Brazil	6 51 S	36 25 W	40
Serov: U.S.S.R.	59 36 N	60 35 E	43, 67
Serpukhov: U.S.S.R.	54 55 N	37 25 E	31
Serra das Éguas: *ridge*, Brazil	14 08 S	41 44 W	50
Serra dos Cristais: *hill*, Brazil	16 37 S	47 37 W	50
Serravalle Sesia: Italy	45 41 N	8 18 E	25
Serre-Ponçon: *dam*, France	44 27 N	6 16 E	39C
Sestao: Spain	43 18 N	3 00 W	59H
Sesto Calende: Italy	45 44 N	8 38 E	53B
Sète: France	43 24 N	3 41 E	27B, 57C, 59H, 61D, 61H, 84A
Setiles: Spain	40 44 N	1 37 W	43B
Setúbal: Portugal	38 32 N	8 54 W	17, 27B, 55, 84
Severodvinsk: U.S.S.R.	64 34 N	39 50 E	52
Severo-Kavkaz: *region*, U.S.S.R.	45 30 N	39 00 E	56
Severoural'sk: U.S.S.R.	60 09 N	59 57 E	45, 47
Severo-Yeniseyskiy: U.S.S.R.	60 22 N	93 01 E	49
Severo-Zapad: *region*, U.S.S.R.	63 00 N	44 00 E	56
Sevilla: *admin.*, Spain	37 30 N	5 30 W	16, 38
Sevilla: Spain	37 23 N	5 59 W	29, 52, 53, 58H, 59H
Sewa: *river*, Sierra Leone	7 18 N	12 08 W	48
Sewaren: N.J., U.S.A.	40 33 N	74 16 W	37J
Seydhisfjördhur: Iceland	65 16 N	14 00 W	27, 84
Seyitömer: Turkey	39 34 N	29 52 E	38
's Gravenhage (Den Haag, The Hague): Netherlands	52 05 N	4 16 E	63A, 63B
Shabani: Rhodesia	20 20 S	30 02 E	48
Shahabad: India	17 07 N	76 54 E	57
Shahdol: India	23 13 N	81 32 E	47
Shāhī: Iran	36 28 N	52 53 E	31
Shāhkūh: *mtns.*, Iran	32 30 N	51 38 E	46
Shahrezā: Iran	32 01 N	51 52 E	50
Shāhrig: Pakistan	30 11 N	67 42 E	38
Shakanai: Japan	40 18 N	140 34 E	45D
Shakhty: U.S.S.R.	47 42 N	40 13 E	38
Shallow Water: Kans., U.S.A.	38 23 N	100 53 W	37J
Shang-hai: China P.R.	31 14 N	121 28 E	25, 29, 31, 32, 36, 43, 45, 52, 57, 59, 60, 61, 67, 84
Shannon: New Zealand	40 32 N	175 24 E	32, 60
Shannon *Airport*: Irish Republic	52 42 N	8 57 W	48, 87
Shan-tan: China P.R.	38 45 N	101 15 E	38
Shao-kuan: China P.R.	24 48 N	113 35 E	38, 45, 46
Shariyn gol: Mongolia	49 15 N	106 30 E	38

	° ′	° ′	Page(s)
Sharon: Pa., U.S.A.	41 16 N	80 30 W	54A
Shasta: *dam*, Calif., U.S.A.	40 37 N	122 28 W	39
Shawinigan: Canada	46 33 N	72 45 W	25D, 31, 47, 59A, 59E
Shawville: Canada	45 36 N	76 30 W	43A
Shchëkino: U.S.S.R.	53 59 N	37 38 E	38
Shchëlkovo: U.S.S.R.	55 55 N	38 00 E	31
Shchigry: U.S.S.R.	51 52 N	36 54 E	56
Shebelinka: U.S.S.R.	49 27 N	36 31 E	34
Sheffield: Ala., U.S.A.	34 45 N	87 40 W	61B, 61E
Sheffield: England	53 23 N	1 30 W	43B, 58D, 67B
Sheksna/Rybinsk: *dam*, U.S.S.R.	58 03 N	38 50 E	39
Shelby: N.C., U.S.A.	35 16 N	81 34 W	32B
Shelbyville: Ind., U.S.A.	39 31 N	85 46 W	32B
Shelbyville: Tenn., U.S.A.	35 29 N	86 30 W	31A
Shelton: Conn., U.S.A.	41 19 N	73 06 W	30A
Shen-yang (Mukden): China P.R.	41 48 N	123 27 E	43, 45, 46, 53, 67
Shepparton: Australia	36 23 S	145 24 E	29
Sherborne: England	50 57 N	2 31 W	32C
Sherbrooke: Canada	45 24 N	71 54 W	31, 55
Sherman: Texas, U.S.A.	33 39 N	96 35 W	62
Shevchenko: U.S.S.R.	43 37 N	51 11 E	35, 40
Shibarghan: Afghanistan	36 40 N	65 42 E	34
Shibukawa: Japan	36 29 N	139 00 E	59C, 60C
Shiga-ken: *admin.*, Japan	35 15 N	136 00 E	59G, 60C, 60E
Shih-chia-chuang: China P.R.	38 03 N	114 29 E	29, 31
Shih-ching-shan: China P.R.	39 55 N	116 08 E	43
Shih-kuai-kou: China P.R.	40 42 N	110 20 E	38
Shih-mien: China P.R.	29 20 N	102 28 E	48
Shih-p'ing: China P.R.	23 43 N	102 30 E	46
Shih-tsui-shan: China P.R.	39 10 N	106 45 E	38
Shikkā: Lebanon	34 20 N	35 44 E	57
Shildon: England	54 38 N	1 39 W	54B
Shillong: India	25 34 N	91 53 E	67
Shimada: Japan	34 49 N	138 11 E	25
Shimizu: Japan	35 01 N	138 29 E	27D, 37E, 47C, 52B, 84D
Shimokawa: Japan	44 18 N	142 39 E	45, 56
Shimonoseki: Japan	33 57 N	130 57 E	27D, 59G, 84D
Shimotsu: Japan	33 51 N	135 10 E	37E
Shindy, Pereval: *pass*, U.S.S.R.	37 36 N	74 54 E	50
Shinkolobwe: Congo D.R.	11 02 S	26 35 E	40
Shin-narihagawa: *dam*, Japan	34 47 N	133 33 E	39D
Shiogama: Japan	38 19 N	141 01 E	27D, 84D
Shipley: England	53 50 N	1 47 W	29B
Shippingport: Pa., U.S.A.	40 38 N	80 25 W	40C
Ship Rock: N. Mex., U.S.A.	36 46 N	108 42 W	40A
Shipshaw: *dam*, Canada	48 30 N	71 14 W	39B
Shirataki: Japan	43 53 N	143 11 E	45
Shīrāz: Iran	29 36 N	52 32 E	61, 67
Shiribeshi-yama: *mtn.*, Japan	42 49 N	140 49 E	50
Shirley: Wyo., U.S.A.	42 12 N	106 30 W	40A
Shirlovaya Gora: U.S.S.R.	50 34 N	116 15 E	45, 50
Shiroro: *dam*, Nigeria	10 03 N	6 50 E	39
Shiroyama: *dam*, Japan	35 35 N	139 17 E	39D
Shisaka: Japan	34 06 N	133 11 E	59G
Shizuoka: Japan	34 58 N	138 23 E	25, 67C
Shizuoka-ken: *admin.*, Japan	35 00 N	138 00 E	49
Shklov: U.S.S.R.	54 13 N	30 18 E	25
Sholapur: India	17 43 N	75 56 E	31C
Shōnan: Japan	35 50 N	140 03 E	32A
Shoreham: N.Y., U.S.A.	40 57 N	72 53 W	40C
Shoreham-by-Sea: England	50 49 N	0 16 W	57C
Shoshone *Co.*: Idaho, U.S.A.	47 30 N	116 00 W	49
Shotton: Wales	53 12 N	3 02 W	43B
Shōwa: Japan	35 27 N	139 59 E	32A
Shreveport: La., U.S.A.	32 30 N	93 46 W	37J, 58A, 59F, 87C
Shuang-ya-shan: China P.R.	46 40 N	131 21 E	38
Shu'aybah: Kuwait	29 02 N	48 10 E	37G, 59, 61
Shui-feng: *dam*, China P.R.	40 30 N	125 05 E	39
Shuya: U.S.S.R.	56 50 N	41 25 E	31
Sibari: Italy	39 45 N	16 27 E	58, 58H, 60
Šibenik: Yugoslavia	43 44 N	15 53 E	84A
Sibu: Malaysia	2 18 N	111 49 E	87
Sicilia: *island*, Italy	37 30 N	14 00 E	16, 27
Sidhpur: India	23 57 N	72 28 E	31C
Sīdī 'Abd ar Raḥmān, Jabal: *ridge*, Tunisia	36 47 N	10 44 E	37B
Sidi-Kacem: Morocco	34 15 N	5 49 W	36
Sidi Kamber: Algeria	36 45 N	6 30 E	46B
Sidon *see* Saïda: Lebanon	33 32 N	35 22 E	37C, 37G
Siegen: Germany F.R.	50 52 N	8 02 E	59D
Siegerland: *region*, G.F.R.	50 55 N	8 05 E	43B
Siena: Italy	43 19 N	11 21 E	17
Sierra de Bahoruco: *ridge*, Dom. R.	18 10 N	71 25 W	47
Sierra de Córdoba: *hill*, Arg.	31 24 S	64 11 W	48
Sierra Mojada: Mexico	27 17 N	103 42 W	49A
Sierras Bayas: Argentina	36 57 S	60 09 W	57
Siglufjördhur: Iceland	66 09 N	18 55 W	27
Sihanoukville *see* Kompong Son: Cambodia	10 38 N	103 30 E	36, 84
Siilinjärvi: Finland	63 05 N	27 40 E	59
Silesia *see* Śląsk: *region*, Poland	50 40 N	17 00 E	46B
Silsbee: Texas, U.S.A.	30 20 N	94 10 W	58A
Silverbell: Ariz., U.S.A.	32 22 N	111 31 W	45A
Silver Bow *Co.*: Mont., U.S.A.	46 00 N	112 45 W	46A, 49
Sîmburești: Romania	44 48 N	24 25 E	17

T

	° ′	° ′	Page(s)
Takeo: Japan	33 12 N	130 01 E	60C
Ta Khli: Thailand	15 15 N	100 21 E	57
Takoradi: Ghana	4 55 N	1 45 W	84
Ta-ku: China P.R.	38 59 N	117 41 E	84
Takua Pa: Thailand	8 52 N	98 21 E	45C
Talaiyuthu: India	9 00 N	77 30 E	57
Talang Akar: Indonesia	3 16 S	103 51 E	35
Talara: Peru	4 38 S	81 18 W	36
Talbingo: *dam*, Australia	35 36 S	148 18 E	39
Talcahuano: Chile	36 43 S	73 07 W	27, 67, 84
Talladega: Ala., U.S.A.	33 25 N	86 07 W	29, 31A
Tallahassee: Fla., U.S.A.	30 26 N	84 19 W	87C
Tallinn: U.S.S.R.	59 25 N	24 45 E	25, 25B, 31
Talmessi-Meskani: Iran	33 28 N	53 30 E	45
Tamano: Japan	34 29 N	133 56 E	52B
Tamashima: Japan	34 32 N	133 40 E	32A
Tamatave: Malagasy Republic	18 10 S	49 23 E	36, 84
Tambo de Mora: Peru	13 30 S	76 08 W	27A
Tambov: U.S.S.R.	52 43 N	41 27 E	30, 67
Tamera: Tunisia	37 01 N	9 09 E	43
Tamilnadu (Madras): *admin.*, India	11 00 N	78 15 E	27, 38
Tampa: Fla., U.S.A.	27 58 N	82 38 W	43, 56, 57, 59F, 61B, 67, 84, 87C
Tampere: Finland	61 30 N	23 45 E	25B, 29, 31, 53, 54, 67
Tampico: Mexico	22 13 N	97 51 W	35, 67, 84
Tamworth: England	52 39 N	1 40 W	55A
Tanabe: Japan	33 44 N	135 22 E	84D
Tananarive *see* Antananarivo: Malagasy Republic	18 55 S	47 31 E	67, 87
Tanga: Tanzania	5 07 S	39 05 E	84
Tanger: Morocco	35 48 N	5 45 W	67, 84
T'ang-shan (Hopeh): China P.R.	39 38 N	118 11 E	43, 57
Tanjong Ramunia: *point*, Malaysia	1 22 N	104 16 E	47
Tannu Tuva: *reg.*, U.S.S.R.	53 00 N	96 00 E	48
Tan-tung (Antung): China P.R.	40 08 N	124 24 E	25, 32
Tanvald: Czechoslovakia	50 46 N	15 19 E	31B
Tanyang: South Korea	36 56 N	128 19 E	57D
T'ao-lin: China P.R.	28 55 N	113 07 E	46
Taormina: Italy	37 51 N	15 17 E	17
T'ao-yüan: Taiwan	24 59 N	121 19 E	31, 60
Tapajós, Rio: *river*, Brazil	2 24 S	54 41 W	49
Ţarābulus (Tripoli): Lebanon	34 27 N	35 50 E	37C, 37G,
Ţarābulus (Tripoli): Libya	32 54 N	13 11 E	61, 67, 84, 87
Tarakohe: New Zealand	40 51 S	172 54 E	57
Taramakau *River*: New Zealand	42 34 S	171 08 E	49
Taranaki: *admin.*, New Zealand	39 20 S	174 30 E	38C
Taranto: Italy	40 28 N	17 14 E	37H, 43B, 84A
Tarapur Chinchani: India	19 52 N	72 42 E	40
Tarbela: *dam*, Pakistan	34 08 N	72 49 E	39
Tarbes: France	43 14 N	0 05 E	53B
Tarkwa: Ghana	5 18 N	1 59 W	49
Tarma: Peru	11 28 S	75 41 W	57
Tarn: *admin.*, France	43 50 N	2 00 E	38B
Tarnobrzeg: Poland	50 35 N	21 40 E	56, 59H
Tarnos: France	43 32 N	1 28 W	59H
Tarnow: Poland	50 01 N	20 59 E	61D, 61H
Tarō: Japan	39 44 N	141 58 E	46C
Tarquinia: Italy	42 15 N	11 45 E	25
Tarragona: *admin.*, Spain	41 10 N	1 00 E	17
Tarragona: Spain	41 07 N	1 15 E	27B, 36, 58D, 58H, 59H, 60, 61D, 61H, 84A
Tarrant City: Ala., U.S.A.	33 38 N	86 46 W	58A
Tarrasa: Spain	41 34 N	2 01 E	29
Tarsus: Turkey	36 55 N	34 53 E	31
Tarui: Japan	35 22 N	136 32 E	32A
Tashkent: U.S.S.R.	41 20 N	69 18 E	31, 61, 67, 87
Tashtagol: U.S.S.R.	52 47 N	87 53 E	43
Tasmania: *admin.*, Australia	42 00 S	147 00 E	27
Tatabánya: Hungary	47 34 N	18 25 E	38B
Tatasi: Bolivia	21 10 S	66 08 W	49
Tatuí: Brazil	23 21 S	47 51 W	31
Ta-t'ung: China P.R.	40 05 N	113 18 E	38C, 57
Ta-t'ung-hsien: *admin.*, China P.R.	36 56 N	101 40 E	38
Tauchen: Austria	47 24 N	16 13 E	38B
Taum Sauk: *dam*, Mo., U.S.A.	37 25 N	90 48 W	39
Tauz: U.S.S.R.	40 59 N	45 36 E	57
Tavaux: France	47 02 N	5 24 E	59D, 60D
Tavoy: Burma	14 05 N	98 12 E	45, 50
Taxco de Alarcón: Mexico	18 33 N	99 36 W	46
Ta-yeh: China P.R.	30 05 N	114 57 E	38, 43
Taylor Flats: Canada	56 09 N	120 40 W	36
Tayshet: U.S.S.R.	55 57 N	98 00 E	61
Ta-yü: China P.R.	25 24 N	114 22 E	45
Tayu Ling: *mtn.*, China P.R.	25 30 N	114 30 E	50, 50D
Tbilisi (Tiflis): U.S.S.R.	41 42 N	44 45 E	29, 54, 67
Tchitondi: Congo Republic	4 33 S	12 08 E	56
Tébessa: Algeria	35 21 N	8 06 E	56
Teesport: England	54 36 N	1 08 W	37F
Teesside: England	54 35 N	1 14 W	43B, 87
Tegucigalpa: Honduras	14 06 N	87 13 W	67, 87
Tehrān: Iran	35 40 N	51 26 E	29, 31, 36, 37A, 37G, 57, 59, 60, 67, 87
Tekeli: U.S.S.R.	44 48 N	78 57 E	46, 49
Tekirdağ: Turkey	40 59 N	27 31 E	50B
Telamayo: Bolivia	21 08 S	66 19 W	49
Tel Aviv: Israel	32 05 N	34 46 E	16, 17, 29, 31, 87
Teleajen-cheia: Romania	45 27 N	25 56 E	37H
Tema: Ghana	5 37 N	0 01 W	27, 36, 84
Temangan: Malaysia	5 42 N	102 09 E	43
Temir-Tau: U.S.S.R.	50 05 N	72 56 E	30, 43
Temir-Tau: U.S.S.R.	53 08 N	87 28 E	43
Témiskaming: Canada	46 44 N	79 05 W	59A
Temlyuy: U.S.S.R.	51 59 N	106 34 E	57
Tempoku: *basin*, Japan	45 00 N	142 00 E	38
Temse: Belgium	51 08 N	4 13 E	52A
Temù: *dam*, Italy	46 15 N	10 28 E	39C
Ténès: Algeria	36 34 N	1 18 E	27B
Tennant Creek: Australia	19 39 S	134 12 E	45, 49
Tennessee: *admin.*, U.S.A.	36 00 N	86 00 W	27, 38A, 46
Teófilo Otoni: Brazil	17 51 S	41 30 W	67
Tepezalá: Mexico	20 09 N	98 33 W	49A
Teplice: Czechoslovakia	50 40 N	13 50 E	46B
Teploozërsk: U.S.S.R.	49 00 N	131 54 E	57
Terek: U.S.S.R.	40 01 N	73 33 E	50
Teresa: Philippines	14 35 N	121 00 E	57
Teresina: Brazil	5 05 S	42 49 W	67
Termez: U.S.S.R.	37 14 N	67 16 E	34, 36
Termini Imerese: Italy	37 59 N	13 42 E	59H
Terneuzen: Netherlands	51 20 N	3 50 E	58H, 60D, 60H
Terni: Italy	42 34 N	12 37 E	32C, 43B, 60D
Ternopol': U.S.S.R.	49 33 N	25 35 E	38B
Terre Haute: Ind., U.S.A.	39 27 N	87 24 W	58B, 61A, 61E, 67A
Terre-Neuve: Haiti	19 36 N	72 47 W	45, 49
Tertre: Belgium	50 28 N	3 48 E	58D, 61D, 61H
Teruel: *admin.*, Spain	40 40 N	0 40 W	38B
Teslić: Yugoslavia	44 37 N	17 52 E	58D
Tessenderlo: Belgium	51 04 N	5 05 E	59D, 59H
Tetyukhe: U.S.S.R.	44 35 N	135 35 E	46, 49
Tetyukhe-Pristan: U.S.S.R.	44 21 N	135 49 E	45
Texada *Island*: Canada	49 38 N	124 30 W	43
Texas: *admin.*, U.S.A.	32 00 N	99 00 W	27
Texas City: Texas, U.S.A.	29 23 N	94 55 W	37J, 45, 58A, 58E, 59F, 60A, 60G, 61B, 84
Teykovo: U.S.S.R.	56 52 N	40 34 E	31
Thabazimbi: South Africa	24 41 S	27 21 E	43
Thames: New Zealand	37 08 S	175 35 E	54
Thames *Estuary*: England	51 30 N	0 40 E	37F
Thames Haven: England	51 31 N	0 31 E	37D
Thana: India	19 14 N	73 02 E	29, 31C, 32, 58, 59, 60
Thanjavur: India	10 46 N	79 09 E	67
Thann: France	47 49 N	7 05 E	59D
Thaon: France	49 16 N	0 27 W	59D
The Dalles: *dam*, Oreg., U.S.A.	45 37 N	121 08 W	39A
The Dalles: Oreg., U.S.A.	45 36 N	121 10 W	47
Thessaloníki: Greece	40 38 N	22 58 E	17, 31, 37H, 40, 57C, 58, 59D, 59H, 61H, 84B
Thetford Mines: Canada	46 06 N	71 18 W	48
Thevenard: Australia	32 10 S	133 38 E	84
Thionville: France	49 22 N	6 10 E	43B, 67B
Thistle Creek: Canada	62 57 N	139 29 W	49
Thomaston: Ga., U.S.A.	32 55 N	84 20 W	31A
Thomaston: Maine, U.S.A.	44 04 N	69 14 W	57B
Thompson: Canada	55 45 N	97 54 W	50
Thorne: England	53 37 N	0 58 W	29B
Thornton: R.I., U.S.A.	41 48 N	71 30 W	29A
Thorold: Canada	43 08 N	79 14 W	25D
Three Mile Island: Pa., U.S.A.	40 09 N	76 45 W	40C
Thuddungra: Australia	34 09 S	148 07 E	50
Thunder *Bay*: Canada	48 20 N	80 15 W	49
Thursday *Island*: Australia	10 35 S	142 13 E	84
Tibú: Colombia	8 39 N	72 42 W	35, 36
Tien-ch'eng: China P.R.	21 31 N	111 18 E	45
T'ien-ching (Tientsin): China P.R.	39 08 N	117 12 E	25, 29, 31, 43, 55, 59, 84
T'ien-pao-shan: China P.R.	42 57 N	128 57 E	45
Tientsin *see* T'ien-ching: China P.R.	39 08 N	117 12 E	25, 29, 31, 43, 55, 59, 84
Tierra del Fuego: *admin.*, Arg.	54 00 S	67 00 W	35
Tiflis *see* Tbilisi: U.S.S.R.	41 42 N	44 45 E	29, 54, 67
Tigil: U.S.S.R.	57 48 N	158 40 E	38
Tihange: Belgium	50 32 N	5 16 E	40B
Tijeras: N. Mex., U.S.A.	35 04 N	106 23 W	57
Tijuana: Mexico	32 32 N	117 01 W	62
Tiksi: U.S.S.R.	71 36 N	128 48 E	38
Tilburg: Netherlands	51 34 N	5 05 E	29B
Tilichiki: U.S.S.R.	60 28 N	166 06 E	38
Tilleur: Belgium	50 37 N	5 32 E	61H
Tilt Cove: Canada	50 00 N	55 55 W	45
Timagami: Canada	47 04 N	79 47 W	43A, 45
Timmins: Canada	48 30 N	81 20 W	45, 46
Timna': Israel	29 45 N	34 59 E	45
Tingha: Australia	29 57 S	151 13 E	45
Tiranë: Albania	41 20 N	19 50 E	31, 38B
Tîrgu Mureş: Romania	46 33 N	24 34 E	61D, 61H
Tîrnăveni: Romania	46 20 N	24 17 E	61D
Tirunelveli: India	8 45 N	77 43 E	31C
Tiszapalkonya: Hungary	47 53 N	21 04 E	60D, 61D, 61H
Titās: *region*, Pakistan	24 00 N	91 00 E	34
Tixán: Ecuador	2 08 S	78 48 W	59
Tjikotok: Indonesia	6 03 S	106 19 E	49
Tjilatjap: Indonesia	7 44 S	109 00 E	59
Tjirebon: Indonesia	6 44 S	108 34 E	84
Tkibuli: U.S.S.R.	42 22 N	42 59 E	38
Tkvarcheli: U.S.S.R.	42 51 N	41 41 E	38
Tlalnepantla: Mexico	19 00 N	98 59 W	57
Tlaxcala de Xicohténcatl: Mexico	19 19 N	98 14 W	60
Tobata: Japan	33 53 N	130 50 E	58C, 58G, 59G, 60E, 61C
Tobias: *region*, Angola	9 40 S	13 16 E	34
Tobruk *see* Ţubruq: Libya	32 05 N	23 59 E	37D
Toby Creek: Canada	50 30 N	116 15 W	46A
Tochigi: Japan	36 23 N	139 44 E	32A
Tocopilla: Chile	22 05 S	70 12 W	84
Töging: Germany F.R.	48 15 N	12 35 E	47B
Tōkai: Japan	36 27 N	140 54 E	40
Tokaj: Hungary	48 07 N	21 25 E	17
Tokmak: U.S.S.R.	47 14 N	35 44 E	57
Toktogul: *dam*, U.S.S.R.	41 35 N	72 42 E	39
Tokushima: Japan	34 04 N	134 34 E	32A, 60C
Tokuyama: Japan	34 03 N	131 49 E	35, 37E, 43D, 57D, 58C, 58G, 59C, 60C, 60E, 61C, 84D
Tōkyō: Japan	35 42 N	139 46 E	2, 3, 25, 27D, 29D, 31, 34, 38, 43D, 48, 52B, 53, 54C, 55, 56, 59C, 60E, 63, 67, 84D, 87
Toledo: Ohio, U.S.A.	41 40 N	83 35 W	37J, 55B, 58B, 60F, 67B, 84, 87B
Tolland: Conn., U.S.A.	41 52 N	72 22 W	62
Toluca de Lerdo: Mexico	19 17 N	99 40 W	32, 60
Tol'yatti (Stavropol'): U.S.S.R.	53 31 N	49 26 E	30, 55, 60
Tomago: Australia	32 50 S	151 44 E	32
Tomahawk: Wis., U.S.A.	45 27 N	89 42 W	25D
Tomakomai: Japan	42 38 N	141 36 E	25, 59
Tomaszów Mazowiecka: Poland	51 33 N	20 00 E	29C, 32C
Tōmatsu: Japan	43 15 N	141 55 E	60
Tommot: U.S.S.R.	58 58 N	126 19 E	48
Tom Price, *Mount*: Australia	22 49 S	117 51 E	43
Tomsk: U.S.S.R.	56 30 N	84 58 E	61, 67
Tonawanda: N.Y., U.S.A.	43 01 N	78 54 W	58B, 58F, 60B
Tongariro: *dam*, New Zealand	39 20 S	175 25 E	39
Tongnae: South Korea	35 12 N	129 05 E	40
Tønsberg: Norway	59 17 N	10 25 E	52
Tooele *Co.*: Utah, U.S.A.	40 30 N	113 25 W	49B
Topeka: Kans., U.S.A.	39 02 N	95 41 W	54, 87B
Topia: Mexico	25 13 N	106 34 W	49A
Topola: Yugoslavia	43 53 N	21 11 E	17
Toquepala: Peru	17 24 S	70 25 W	45, 50
Toral de los Vados: Spain	42 33 N	6 47 W	57C
Torari: New Hebrides	17 39 S	168 32 E	50
Torino (Turin): Italy	45 03 N	7 40 E	31B, 37B, 43B, 53B, 54B, 55A, 63A, 63B, 87D
Toronto: Canada	43 42 N	79 25 W	25D, 29, 34, 55A, 56, 58B, 62, 63, 67A, 87B
Tororo: Uganda	0 42 N	34 11 E	59
Torrance: Calif., U.S.A.	33 50 N	118 19 W	30A, 43, 53, 58, 60
Torredonjimeno: Spain	37 46 N	3 57 W	57
Torrelavega: Spain	43 21 N	4 03 W	32C, 59D, 60D
Torreón: Mexico	25 33 N	103 26 W	34, 59, 67
Torres Vedras: Portugal	39 06 N	9 16 W	17
Tórshavn: Faeroe Is.	62 01 N	6 46 W	27, 84
Tortiya: Ivory Coast	8 46 N	5 41 W	48
Toruń: Poland	53 01 N	18 35 E	32C
Torviscosa: Italy	45 45 N	13 15 E	59D
Tosa-shimizu: Japan	32 47 N	132 58 E	27D
Totoro-kō: Japan	32 31 N	131 42 E	27D
T'ou-fen: Taiwan	23 04 N	120 29 E	32, 58
Touissite: Morocco	34 29 N	1 46 W	46
Toulouse: France	43 36 N	1 26 E	53B, 53C, 58H, 61D, 61H
Tourcoing: France	50 43 N	3 09 E	29B, 31B
Tournai: Belgium	50 36 N	3 23 E	29B
Tours: France	47 23 N	0 41 E	17
Townsville: Australia	19 15 S	146 48 E	45, 84, 87
Toyama: Japan	36 41 N	137 13 E	32A, 43D, 59C, 59G, 61C, 61G, 67C, 84D
Toyoha: Japan	43 00 N	141 00 E	46
Toyohashi: Japan	34 46 N	137 23 E	32A, 43D
Toyotsu: Japan	33 40 N	130 58 E	59G
Trafford Park: England	53 30 N	2 15 W	37F
Trail: Canada	49 04 N	117 39 W	46, 59, 61
Trangslet: *dam*, Sweden	61 20 N	13 44 E	39
Transcona: Canada	49 55 N	97 00 W	59
Transvaal: *admin.*, S. Africa	24 00 S	29 00 E	16, 38, 49, 50
Träslövsläge: Sweden	57 04 N	12 16 E	27C
Travancore: *admin.*, India	9 00 N	77 00 E	47, 50
Traverse City: Mich., U.S.A.	44 46 N	85 38 W	87B
Trawsfynydd: Wales	52 54 N	3 55 W	40B
Trecate: Italy	45 26 N	8 44 E	60H
Tredyffin: Pa., U.S.A.	40 03 N	75 14 W	62
Trengganu: *admin.*, Malaysia	5 00 N	103 00 E	45C
Trento: Italy	46 04 N	11 03 E	58D, 58H
Trenton: Canada	45 37 N	62 38 W	54
Trenton: Mich., U.S.A.	42 05 N	83 06 W	37J
Trenton: N.J., U.S.A.	40 15 N	74 43 W	30, 32B
Trepča: Yugoslavia	42 56 N	20 55 E	46B, 56
Tres Cruces: Argentina	22 55 S	65 35 W	49
Três Marias: *dam*, Brazil	18 15 S	45 15 W	39
Treviso: Italy	45 40 N	12 15 E	17
Tri-City *Airport*: Tenn., U.S.A.	36 33 N	82 34 W	87C
Trident: Mont., U.S.A.	45 58 N	111 25 W	57
Trier: Germany F.R.	49 45 N	6 38 E	17
Trieste: Italy	45 40 N	13 46 E	37H, 57C, 58D, 84A
Trimmelkam: Austria	48 02 N	12 52 E	38B
Třinec: Czechoslovakia	49 41 N	18 39 E	43B
Trino: Italy	45 12 N	8 18 E	40B
Tripoli *see* Ţarābulus: Lebanon	34 27 N	35 50 E	37C, 37G,
Tripoli *see* Ţarābulus: Libya	32 54 N	13 11 E	61, 67, 84, 87
Tripura: *admin.*, India	24 00 N	92 00 E	27
Trivandrum: India	8 41 N	76 57 E	67
Troisdorf: Germany F.R.	50 49 N	7 10 E	60D
Trois Rivières: Canada	46 21 N	72 34 W	25D, 31, 84
Troitsk: U.S.S.R.	57 25 N	94 50 E	40
Trollhättan: Sweden	58 16 N	12 18 E	53, 54, 55
Trombay: India	19 01 N	72 58 E	40, 58, 59, 61
Tromsø: Norway	69 40 N	18 58 E	27, 87
Trona: Calif., U.S.A.	35 46 N	117 24 W	59
Trondheim: Norway	63 25 N	10 25 E	56, 67, 84, 87
Trondheimsfjorden: *fjord*, Norway	63 39 N	10 49 E	43, 46
Tronville-en-Barrois: France	48 43 N	5 17 E	32C
Troödos: Cyprus	34 55 N	32 53 E	50, 50B
Troutdale: Oreg., U.S.A.	45 32 N	122 22 W	47
Troy: Ind., U.S.A.	38 00 N	86 50 W	37J
Trujillo: Peru	8 06 S	79 00 W	67
Tsao-chuang: China P.R.	34 53 N	117 34 E	38C
Tselinograd: U.S.S.R.	51 10 N	71 28 E	67
Tsentr: *region*, U.S.S.R.	56 00 N	38 30 E	56
Tshikapa: Congo D.R.	6 25 S	20 48 E	48
Tsinan *see* Chi-nan: China P.R.	36 40 N	117 00 E	55, 61
Tsingtao *see* Ch'ing-tao: China P.R.	36 04 N	120 19 E	29, 31, 43, 54, 84
Tsinling Shan *see* Ch'in Ling: *mtn.*, China P.R.	34 00 N	108 00 E	50
Tsitsihar *see* Ch'i-ch'i-ha-erh: China P.R.	47 22 N	123 57 E	25, 54, 67
Tsu: Japan	34 43 N	136 31 E	29D, 32A
Tsukumi: Japan	33 04 N	131 52 E	57D
Tsumeb: South West Africa	19 13 S	17 42 E	45, 46, 49
Tsuruga: Japan	35 39 N	136 04 E	32A, 40, 57D, 59G, 60C, 84D
Tsurumi Ku: Japan	35 28 N	139 33 E	52B
Tsurusaki: Japan	33 14 N	131 41 E	30, 58G, 60C
Tuapse: U.S.S.R.	44 05 N	39 06 E	35, 36, 84
Tuba City: Ariz., U.S.A.	36 09 N	111 18 W	40A
Ţubruq (Tobruk): Libya	32 05 N	23 59 E	37D
Tu Chanh Nong Son: South Vietnam	15 43 N	108 01 E	38
Tucker: Texas, U.S.A.	31 45 N	95 35 W	37J
Tucson: Ariz., U.S.A.	32 15 N	110 57 W	67, 87
Tucupita: Venezuela	9 04 N	62 03 W	36
Tudela-Agüeria: Spain	43 19 N	5 48 W	57C
Tula: U.S.S.R.	54 12 N	37 37 E	32C, 43, 58, 61
Tula de Allende: Mexico	20 03 N	99 21 W	57
Tulsa: Okla., U.S.A.	36 07 N	95 58 W	37J, 53, 57A, 58B, 59F, 87C
Tulsa: Pa., U.S.A.	36 07 N	95 58 W	58B, 59F
Tulun: U.S.S.R.	54 35 N	100 33 E	38
Tumaco: Colombia	1 49 N	78 46 W	27
Tumut I: *dam*, Australia	35 57 S	148 23 E	39
Tumut II: *dam*, Australia	35 52 S	148 20 E	39
Tunçbilek: Turkey	39 37 N	29 29 E	38
Tundzha: *valley*, Bulgaria	42 30 N	25 30 E	17
T'ung-ch'uan: China P.R.	34 59 N	109 07 E	38
T'ung-hua: China P.R.	41 41 N	125 55 E	43
T'ung-jen: China P.R.	27 41 N	109 08 E	50
T'ung-ling: China P.R.	30 56 N	117 50 E	43, 45
Tunhovd: *dam*, Norway	60 25 N	8 55 E	39
Tunis: N.C., U.S.A.	36 35 N	76 55 W	61, 61A, 67, 87
Tūnis: Tunisia	36 48 N	10 11 E	67, 84A, 87
Tuolumne *Co.*: Calif., U.S.A.	38 00 N	120 00 W	40A
Turá al Ḩajjārah: U.A.R.	29 56 N	31 16 E	57
Turbo: Colombia	8 06 N	76 43 W	84
Turda: Romania	46 34 N	23 47 E	57C, 60D
Turgay: U.S.S.R.	49 38 N	63 30 E	50
Turin *see* Torino: Italy	45 03 N	7 40 E	31B, 37B, 43B, 53B, 54B, 55A, 63A, 63B, 87D
Türkali: Turkey	39 24 N	27 26 E	50B
Turkey *Point*: Fla., U.S.A.	25 26 N	80 19 W	40
Turkmenskaya S.S.R.: *admin.*, U.S.S.R.	40 00 N	60 00 E	27
Turku (Åbo): Finland	60 27 N	22 17 E	29, 52, 58, 67
Turnu Măgurele: Romania	43 45 N	24 52 E	61D, 61H
Turnu Severin: Romania	44 38 N	22 40 E	54B
Tuscaloosa: Ala., U.S.A.	33 12 N	87 33 W	37J, 59F
Tuscola: Ill., U.S.A.	39 49 N	88 18 W	58F, 59E, 60B, 61A
Tu-shan-tzu: China P.R.	44 20 N	84 51 E	36
Tuticorin: India	8 48 N	78 10 E	31C, 59, 60, 84
Tutunup: Australia	33 40 S	115 35 E	40

STATISTICAL SUPPLEMENT

Introduction

THE STATISTICAL SUPPLEMENT gives in tabular form for each country much of the economic data depicted on the maps. Countries are arranged in alphabetical order except that entries for dependent territories (or references to them) follow the entry for the suzerain nation.

Background and summary data on area, population, employment, trade, etc., are given first, in a standard format which is altered only when statistical information is not available. This section is followed by detailed figures for production, exports and imports. Statistics are given for the years 1963–5 and 1953–5 so that the trend of a national economy for this specific period may be studied. Also, the relative importance of various commodities in the economy of a country may be seen even if they are insignificant in the world context. They are arranged in eleven tables which group the statistics for related commodities. These, with references to the relevant map pages, are as follows:

Table		*Map pages*
1	Cereals	9–12
2	Fruit, etc.	16–17
3	Beverages, Forest Products, etc.	13–15, 24–25
4	Vegetable Oilseeds and Oils	18–19
5	Livestock, Animal Products, etc.	21–23, 26–27
6	Fibres, Textiles, etc.	28–32
7	Fuel and Power	33–41
8	Iron and Steel	42–43
9	Non-ferrous Minerals and Metals	44–50
10	Chemicals and Fertilizers	56, 58–61
11	Industry	51–57

The trade statistics are for either special trade or general trade. Special trade is defined as imports for domestic consumption or improvement and exports of home-produced or processed goods. General trade refers to total imports and total exports including re-exports. Most of the statistics in tables 1–6 are on a general trade basis; however, where imports or exports are known to be, or to include, re-exports, this has been indicated. Tables 7–11 are on a special trade basis unless otherwise stated.

Generally, mention has been made of any commodity known to be produced or traded by a country even where the quantity is not known. For certain commodities, such as cassava, no trade figures are available; in these cases the trade columns have been left blank, and the commodity has been listed only under producing countries. For certain countries, in particular those with centrally planned economies (the Sino-Soviet bloc), production and trade statistics are not always available. The omission of a commodity from the data for one of these countries does not necessarily indicate that the commodity is not a factor in its economy.

Common units, usually in the metric system, have been used wherever possible. The definitions of commodity categories have also been held constant from country to country as far as possible, but statistics for related items are not always available on the same basis. Thus, for example, many production figures for metalliferous ores refer to the weight of the metal content, whereas those for trade refer to the total weight of the ore. Attention is drawn to the Appendix which contains an alphabetical list of the commodities included in the supplement, together with definitions and other relevant information.

COUNTRY INDEX

AFGHANISTAN

Afghanistan is a constitutional monarchy; parliamentary democracy was established in 1965, and Islamic law abolished. Transit arrangements with Pakistan enable the bulk of trade to be transported through Karachi.

AREA: 657 500 sq. km. (250 000 sq. miles)

LAND USE: (percentage of total)	*1962*	*1948*
Arable and orchard	13.7	3.8
Permanent meadow and pasture	4.9	38.5
Forest and woodland	2.3	1.5
City areas, waste and other land	79.1	56.2

POPULATION: 15 751 000 (1967 estimate)

Largest city: KABUL, capital; population: 456 342 (1967)

		Year(s)
Population per physician	22 140	1966
Population per hospital bed	5 810*a*	1966
School enrolment: age 5–19 years (percentage)	10	1963–4 av.
age over 19 years (per 100 000 population)	22	1963–5 av.

a government hospitals only

EMPLOYMENT AND PRODUCTION

Agriculture (crops and sheep) is the main occupation. There are two cereal crops per annum. Sugar beet, fruit and cotton are grown. Silk, woollen and hair cloth, and carpets are made. Salt, silver, copper, coal, iron, lead, chrome, talc, and precious stones are mined in small quantities.

COMMUNICATIONS

		Year(s)
Motor vehicles in use ('000s): private	9.3	1963–5 av.
commercial	10.5	1963–5 av.
Telephones (per '000 urban population)	0.1*	1967
Radio receivers (per '000 population)	12	1963–5 av.
Daily newspapers (per '000 population)	4	1962–3 av.

FINANCE

Currency unit: The afghani

Exchange rates	*1965*	*1960*	*1957a*
Per $ U.S.	79.84*b*	42.49	23.35
Per £ sterling	223.55	118.97	62.3

		Year
National Income (million $ U.S.)	649	1958
G.N.P. per capita ($ U.S.)	70	1966

a official rate. The market rate was 50 to 55 afghanis per $ U.S. or 140 to 164 afghanis per £ sterling. *b* free rate.

TRADING

Total trade (in million $ U.S.)	*1965*
Exports (f.o.b.)	70
Imports (c.i.f.)	131

Main trading partners (percentage of total value)

Exports	*1965*	*Imports*	*1965*
U.S.S.R.	25	U.S.S.R.	47
U.K.	18	U.S.A.	15
U.S.A.	16	Germany F.R.	13
Pakistan	14	Japan	6
Germany F.R.	8	India	4
India	7	U.K.	4
Czechoslovakia	2	Pakistan	3

Distribution of trade (percentage of total value)

Exports	*1965*	*Imports*	*1965*
Crude materials and fuels	50	Loans and grant imports	57
(fur skins)	(23)	Manufactured goods	24
(cotton)	(16)	(fabrics and clothing)	(9)
Food	36	(machinery and transport equipment)	(6)
(edible nuts; dried, preserved fruits)	(26)	Food	5
Carpets	13	Fuels	3

PRODUCTION, EXPORTS AND IMPORTS

Years: **1963–5 average** and *1953–5 average* Units: '000 metric tons unless otherwise indicated

	Production		Exports		Imports	
1. CEREALS, etc.						
Barley	379.3	*283.0*[1]	—	—	—	—
Maize (corn)	717.7	na	—	—	—	—
Rice	359.7	na	—	—	—	—
Wheat	2 159.7	*2 124.0*	—	—	78.4*	*5.0**[1]
2. FRUIT, etc.						
Grapes	20.0[1]*	*20.0**	1.2*	—	—	—
Raisins	na	na	16.6*	*17.4**	—	—
3. BEVERAGES, FOREST PRODUCTS, etc.						
Sugar: beet	49.0	*30.7**				
raw	10.0	*5.7**	—	—	42.7*	*5.0*[1]*
Tea	—	—	—	—	5.2*	*2.4*[2]
Softwood *j*	686.7*	na	—	—	—	—
Hardwood *j*	4 654.0*	na	—	—	3.4[2]	—
Newsprint	—	—	—	—	0.3[1]	—
Other paper	—	—	—	—	0.3[2]	—

j '000 cu. metres of roundwood equivalent

	Production		Exports		Imports	
4. VEGETABLE OILSEEDS AND OILS						
Cottonseed	80.70	*35.00**	—	—	—	—
Linseed	na	na	13.00*	na	—	—
Sesame seed	na	na	1.89	na	—	—
Soya bean oil	—	—	—	—	0.30*	na
5. LIVESTOCK‡, ANIMAL PRODUCTS, etc.						
Cattle *d*	3 361.7*	*2 000*[1]*	—	—	—	—
Goats *d*	3 500.0*	*8 000*[1]*	} —	—	—	—
Sheep *d*	18 833.3*	*14 000*[1]*	}			
Horses *d*	268.3*	*195*[1]				
Meat‡ 'A'	145.7*	—	—	—	—	—
Eggs	18.1	na	—	—	—	—
Milk	336.0*	na	—	—	3.9*	—
Hides/skins	na	na	1.8[1]	—	—	—
Wool	na	*3**	2.4*	*0.5**	—	—

d number in thousands.

	Production		Exports		Imports	
6. FIBRES, TEXTILES, etc.						
Cotton lint	45.7	*17.7**	16.9*	*9.0*	—	—
Silk	na	na	—	—	—	—
Cotton, woven fabrics	5.5*	*2.1**	—	—	—	—
Wool, woven fabrics	na	*0.2*[2]*n*	—	—	—	—

n million metres.

	Production		Exports		Imports	
7. FUEL AND POWER						
Coal 'A'‡	117	*20*	—	—	—	—
Electricity *h*: total	245	*10*				
hydro	166[1]	*10*				
thermal	79	—				
Petroleum, refined	—	—	—	—	40	na

h million kWh.

	Production		Exports		Imports	
11. INDUSTRY						
Cement	122.0*	—	—*	—	17.0*	*17.0**
Electrical engineering *a*	—	—	—	—	1.8	na
Motor vehicles *a*	—	—	—	—	3.8	na

a million $ U.S.

na: data not available. — negligible or nil. [1] one year only. [2] two year average. * estimate. ‡ see appendix. † re-exports.

ALBANIA

Albania was occupied by the Italians and Germans from 1939–44. Elections in 1945 resulted in a communist-controlled assembly, and the following year a republic was declared. Albania withdrew from the Warsaw Pact in 1968, severed diplomatic relations with the U.S.S.R. and strengthened her ties with China P.R.

AREA: 28 748 sq. km. (11 101 sq. miles)

LAND USE: (percentage of total)	*1964*	*1943*
Arable and orchard	17.4	12.3
Permanent meadow and pasture	25.4	29.6
Forest and woodland	43.7	39.3
City areas, waste and other land	13.5	18.8

POPULATION: 1 965 000 (1967 estimate)

Largest city: TIRANË, capital; population: 156 950 (city proper, 1964)
Total working population: 730 762 (1960)

		Year(s)
Life expectancy at birth (years): male	63.7	1963–4 av.
female	66	1963–4 av.
Infant mortality (per '000)	86·8	1965
Crude birth rate (per '000)	35.2	1965
Crude death rate (per '000)	9	1965
Population per physician	2 070	1965
Population per hospital bed	170	1966
School enrolment: age 5–19 years (percentage)	107‡	1963–4 av.
age over 19 years (per 100 000 population)	677	1963–5 av.

EMPLOYMENT AND PRODUCTION

Albania is mainly an agricultural land although the raising of livestock, apart from poultry, has decreased since World War II. Cultivated and forest land is held mainly by the state and the third 5-year plan (1961–5) could not be fulfilled because Chinese aid had not made up for the withdrawal of Soviet assistance. The main crops are maize, sugar beet and wheat. Cotton, fruit, tobacco, oats and rice are also grown. An afforestation programme has been undertaken. Mineral wealth is considerable but only oil, lignite, chrome, iron ore, coal and copper are exploited. Large iron deposits with high nickel content have recently been located. Industries are concerned mainly with processing of agricultural products, and making of cement, textiles and paper.

COMMUNICATIONS

		Year(s)
Railway track (km.)	151	1964
Telephones (per '000 urban population)	0.3	1959*n*
Radio receivers (per '000 population)	51	1963–5 av.
Television sets (per '000 population)	0.4	1963–5 av.
Daily newspapers (per '000 population)	48.5	1963–4 av.

n latest data available

FINANCE

Currency unit: The lek

Exchange rates	*1965n*	*1960p*	*1950q*
Per $ U.S.	50	50	125
Per £ sterling	140	140	350

		Year(s)
National Income (million $ U.S.)	570	1966
G.N.P. per capita ($ U.S.)	300*	1966
Rate of increase of G.N.P. per capita	4.1	1960–4 av.

n middle rate. *p* official rate. *q* tourist rate

TRADING

Total trade (in million $ U.S.)	*1965*	*1955*
Exports (f.o.b.)	na	13
Imports (c.i.f.)	na	43

In 1963 49% of the exports and 59% of the imports were accounted for by China P.R. Eastern European countries took 42% of the exports and supplied 32% of the imports, there being no trade with the U.S.S.R.

PRODUCTION, EXPORTS AND IMPORTS

Years: **1963–5 average** and *1953–5 average* Units: '000 metric tons unless otherwise indicated

	Production		Exports		Imports	
1. CEREALS, etc.						
Barley	8.0*	na	—	—	—	—
Maize (corn)	181.3	na	—	—	21.2[2]	*0.3**
Oats	14.0*	na	—	—	—	—
Potatoes	30.3*	na	—	—	—	—
Rice	8.7*	na	—	—	—	—
Rye	6.0*	na	—	—	—	—
Wheat	95.3*	na	—	—	110.3[2]	na
2. FRUIT, etc.						
Figs	11.3*	na	na	na	—	—
Grapes	na	na	—	—	—	—
Olives	29.7*	na				
Oranges	2.0	na	—	—	—	—
Plums	8.7*	na	na	na	—	—
Wine *b*	na	na	7.8[2]	—	—	—

b '000 hectolitres

	Production		Exports		Imports	
3. BEVERAGES, FOREST PRODUCTS, etc.						
Sugar: beet	126.3*	na				
raw	14.7	*10.0**	—	—	9.8[2]	—
Tobacco: leaf	14.3*	*1.4*[2]*	6.0[2]	—	—	—
products	na	na	3.0*n*	na	—	—
Softwood *j*	520.0[2]	na	—	—	—	—
Hardwood *j*	1 020.0[2]*	na	—	—	—	—
Paper	na	na	na	na	—	—

j '000 cu. metres of roundwood equivalent. *n* cigarettes only.

	Production		Exports		Imports	
4. VEGETABLE OILSEEDS AND OILS						
Cottonseed	15.30	na	—	—	—	—
Olive oil	4.00*	na	—	—	—	—
5. LIVESTOCK‡, ANIMAL PRODUCTS, etc.						
Chickens *d*	1 691.0**n*	na				
Cattle *d*	412.0	na	—	—	—	—
dairy cows *d*	151.3	na				
Goats *d*	1 146.0	na	} —	—	—	—
Sheep *d*	1 613.0	na	}			
Horses *d*	45.0	na				
Pigs *d*	122.0	na	—	—	—	—
Meat‡: 'A'	44.0*	na	—	—	—	—
'B'	1.6*	na	—	—	—	—
Cheese	4.0*	*3.0*[1]	—	—	—	—
Eggs	3.1*	na	—	—	—	—
Fish	3.6*	*2.5*	—	—	—	—
Milk	80.0*	na	—	—	—	—
Hides/skins	na	na	—	—	—	—
Wool	na	*1.0*	0.4[2]	—	—	—

d number in thousands *n* incl. ducks, geese and turkeys

	Production		Exports		Imports	
6. FIBRES, TEXTILES, etc.						
Cotton lint	8.0*	na	—	—	—	—
Rubber, natural	—	—	—	—	0.3[2]	—
Cotton: yarn	7.6[1]	na	na	na	na	na
woven fabrics	3.4[1]	na	5.5[1]	na	—[1]	na
Rayon: fibre/yarn	na	na	na	na	na	na
woven fabrics	na	na	na	na	na	na
Wool, woven fabrics	1.0[2]*n*	na	—	—	—	—

n million metres

	Production		Exports		Imports	
7. FUEL AND POWER						
Coal 'B'‡	143	*190*	—	—	—	—
Coke	—	—	—	—	11	na
Electricity *h*: total	272	*80*[1]				
hydro	186[2]	*30*[1]				
thermal	86	*50*[1]				
Oil, crude	776	*210*[1]	293	na	—	—
Petroleum, refined	247	*90*[1]	—	—	20	na

h million kWh.

	Production		Exports		Imports	
8. IRON AND STEEL						
Iron ore	na	na	349	na	—	—
Pig iron	na	na	—	—	2	na
9. NON-FERROUS MINERALS AND METALS						
Chrome, ore	305.07*m*	*91.62m*	285.37	na	—	—
Copper: ore	2.54	—	—	—	—	—
metal	2.75	—	2.65	—	—	—
Zinc, metal	—	—	—	—	0.11	na

m metal content

	Production		Exports		Imports	
11. INDUSTRY						
Alcoholic beverages *b*			10.0[2]*n*	na	—	—
beer *b*	107.0	na				
Cement	136.0*	*43.0**	—*	—**p*	20.0[1]*	—**p*
Electrical engineering	—	—	—	—	5.9[2]*q*	na

b '000 hectolitres. *n* wine and cognac only. *p* excl. trade with other communist countries. *q* electric motors and radios, number in thousands.

na: data not available. — negligible or nil. [1] one year only. [2] two year average. * estimate. ‡ see appendix. † re-exports.

ALGERIA

NORTH AFRICA

Algeria became independent from French administration in 1962. This followed armed rebellion by the Moslem National Liberation Front (F.L.N.) in 1954, terrorism in France, and referenda in both countries. Within a few years of independence, 80% of the French population had left Algeria.

AREA: 2 466 833 sq. km. (952 198 sq. miles)

LAND USE: (percentage of total)

	1961	*1954*
Arable and orchard	3.0	3.1
Permanent meadow and pasture	16.1	18.2
Forest and woodland	1.3	1.4
City areas, waste and other land	79.6	77.3

POPULATION: 11 833 126 (1966 census)

Largest city: ALGER (Algiers), capital; population: 943 142 (1966)

Distribution of working population (1954)
Total working population: 3 511 934 [European: 354 510, non-European 3 157 424]

U.N. group no.		*Percentage* *Europeans*	*Non-Europeans*
0	Agriculture, forestry, fishing and hunting	11.1	82.1
1	Mining and quarrying	0.8	0.4
2/3	Manufacturing	17.2	2.9
4	Construction	9.7	1.7
5	Electricity, gas, water and sanitary services	1.2	—
6	Commerce	20.8	3.2
7	Transport, storage and communications	8.8	1.0
8	Services	25.1	2.2
9	Others	5.3	6.5

Agrarian reform and land redistribution were undertaken in 1967–8, and a five-year industrialization programme was begun with French aid in 1965.

		Year(s)
Life expectancy at birth (years): Algerians	35	1948
Non-Algerians	63	1954
Infant mortality (per '000): Algerians	86.3*	1965
Crude birth rate (per '000)	46.2*	1966
Crude death rate (per '000)	10.1*	1966
Population per physician	8 950	1964
Population per hospital bed	290	1963
School enrolment: age 5–19 years (percentage)	35	1963–4 av.
age over 19 years (per 100 000 population)	53	1963–5 av.

COMMUNICATIONS

		Year(s)
Motor vehicles in use ('000s): private	205.7	1963–5 av.
commercial	92.5	
Railway track (km.)	3 900	1964
Mail per capita: domestic	11	1963–5 av.
foreign received	1	
foreign sent	1	
Telephones (per '000 urban population)	1.2*	1967
Radio licences (per '000 population)	134	1963–5 av.
Television sets (per '000 population)	9.1	1963–5 av.
Daily newspapers (per '000 population)	24	1961

FINANCE

Currency unit: The Algerian dinar (at par with the French franc)

Exchange rates	*1965*	*1960*	*1955*	*1938*
Per $ U.S.	4.902	4.903	350	38.01
Per £ sterling	13.738	13.743	980	175

		Year
National Income (million $ U.S.)	2 272	1964
G.N.P. per capita ($ U.S.)	220	1966

TRADING

Total trade (in million $ U.S.)	*1964*	*1955*	*1938*
Exports (f.o.b.)	727	463	162
Imports (c.i.f.)	703	696	143

Main trading partners (percentage of total value)

Exports	*1964*	*1955*	*1938*	*Imports*	*1964*	*1955*	*1938*
France	78	74	83	France	71	76	75
Germany F.R.	6	3	2*a*	U.S.A.	4	3	2
Italy	3	2	–	U.K.	3	1	2
Netherlands	2	1	1	Ivory Coast	3	na	na
U.K.	1	8	5	Italy	2	1	–
Belg./Lux.	1	–	1	Germany F.R.	2	1	1*a*
Spain	1	–	–	Morocco	2	2	5*b*

a incl. Germany D.R. *b* former French Morocco

Distribution of trade (percentage of total value)

Exports	*1965*	*1955*	*1938**
Petroleum and products	54	—	—
Alcoholic beverages	18	40	49
Food	17	26	19
(citrus fruit)	(9)	(7)	(2)

Imports			
Food	22	19	15
Machinery and transport equipment	15	20	na
Textiles and clothing	14	13	14
Chemicals	11	5	7
Iron and steel	8	3	na
Wood and paper	5	6	6

A trade agreement was signed with the U.S.S.R. in November 1963 for the exchange of Soviet machinery for Algerian wheat and fruit.

PRODUCTION, EXPORTS AND IMPORTS

Years: **1963–5 average** and *1953–5 average* Units: '000 metric tons unless otherwise indicated

1. CEREALS, etc.

	Production		Exports		Imports	
Barley	**449.0**	*788.3*	**32.6*[2]**	*87.2*	na	*0.2*
Maize (corn)	**5.3***	*11.0[2]*	**0.7*[1]**	*2.3*	**0.7*[1]**	*0.3*
Millets/sorghum	**1.7***	*12.0*	—	*0.7*	na	*0.4*
Oats	**29.3**	*104.0*	—	*3.6*	**0.6*[2]**	—
Potatoes	**214.3**	*247.5[2]*	**31.5**	*88.0*	**81.4***	*96.0*
Rice	**5.3***	*8.0*	na	*0.9*	na	*3.1*
Rye	na	na	—	*1.7*	—	—
Sweet potatoes/yams	**7.0***	na				
Wheat	**1 358.3**	*1 249.0*	**7.6*[1]**	*26.9*	**308.4***	*43.3*

2. FRUIT, etc.

	Production		Exports		Imports	
Apples	**16.0***	na	na	*0.6*	**5.7***	*6.6*
Apricots	**14.7***	*11.5*	na	*3.5*	—	—
Bananas	—	—	—	*0.1†*	**17.2***	*8.8*
Dates	**110.0***	*92.3*	**20.6***	*22.9*	—	—
Figs	**59.0**	*93.3*	na	*11.2*	—	—
Grapes	**1 684.7***	*2 236.3**	**1.8[2]***	*5.5*	na	*0.2*
Lemons	**15.0**	*11.0**	**2.8[2]***	*4.7*	na	*0.1*
Olives	**153.7***	*193.5[2]*				
Oranges	**409.0**	*340.3**	**200.1***	*220.1*	**0.1[1]***	*1.8*
Other citrus fruit	**4.7**	*3.7**	**3.6***	*2.7[2]*	—	—
Peaches	**10.0***	*9.1*	na	na	—	—
Pears	**10.0***	na	—	*0.1*	**2.6***	*1.3*
Plums	**11.0***	*10.5*	na	*1.4*	—	—
Raisins	na	na	—	*0.3*	na	*1.4*
Tomatoes	**121.0***	na				
Wine *b*	**13 106.0**	*17 311.0*	**8 102.7***	*14 400.0*	na	*225.7*

b '000 hectolitres

3. BEVERAGES, FOREST PRODUCTS, etc.

	Production		Exports		Imports	
Cocoa	—	—	—	—	na	*0.3*
Coffee	—	—	—	—	**30.7[2]***	*21.0*
Sugar: beet	na	*15.0*				
raw	**1.6**	*3.7**	na	*0.1*	**234.2***	*186.3*
Tea	—	—	na	*0.1†*	na	*2.5*
Tobacco:	**6.4***	*23.1*	**1.4[2]***	*14.3*	na	*4.9*
cigars	—	*5.8e*	**0.2[1]*n***	*5.2[2]*	—	—
cigarettes	**5 585.0*e***	*7 906.0*e*				
tobacco/snuff	**3.1**	*2.4*				
Softwood *j*	**51.0[1]***	*124.5[2]*	—	*2.6[2]*	**315.2***	*324.1[2]*
Hardwood *j*	**153.0[1]***	*230.5[2]*	—	*0.8[2]*	**65.3***	*69.1*
Wood pulp	—[1]*	*23.5*	—[1]	—	**1.2[2]**	*0.5[2]*
Newsprint	—[2]*	—[2]	—[1]	—[2]	**22.0[1]**	*4.7[2]*
Other paper	**30.2[2]***	*26.5[2]**	**19.0[2]**	*13.8[2]*	**25.0[1]**	*20.7[2]*

e number in millions. *j* '000 cu. metres of roundwood equivalent.
n manufactured tobacco only.

4. VEGETABLE OILSEEDS AND OILS

	Production		Exports		Imports	
Castor oil	—	—	—	—	na	*0.01*
Copra	—	—	—	—	—	*0.30*
Coconut oil	—	—	—	—	—	*0.92[2]*
Cottonseed	**2.00***	*3.30**	—	—	—	—
Cottonseed oil	na	na	—	—	—	*3.39*
Groundnuts	—	—	na	*0.23†*	**11.90**	*8.07*
Groundnut oil	na	na	na	*0.01*	na	*8.32*
Linseed	—	*1.00[1]**	—	*0.67*	—	*0.40*
Linseed oil	—	na	—	*0.01*	na	*0.94*
Olive oil	**14.00***	*23.00**	**2.33**	*13.04*	na	*1.43*

continued

PRODUCTION, EXPORTS AND IMPORTS *continued*

4. VEGETABLE OILSEEDS AND OILS—*continued*

	Production		Exports		Imports	
Palm kernels	—	—	—	—	—	*0.20*
Palm oil	—	—	—	—	**0.47***	*1.47*
Rape seed	—	—	—	—	**66.34***	—
Rapeseed oil	na	—	—	—	**7.96***	*3.42*
Sesame seed	—	—	—	—	na	*0.27*
Soya beans	—	—	—	—	na	*1.30*
Soya bean oil	—	—	—	—	**4.09**	*2.14n*
Sunflower seed oil	—	—	—	—	—	*1.46[2]p*
Tung oil	—	—	—	—	na	na

n incl. maize oil and sunflower oil. *p* incl. other minor vegetable oils.

5. LIVESTOCK‡, ANIMAL PRODUCTS, etc.

	Production		Exports		Imports	
Chickens *d*	**6 500.0***	na				
Cattle *d*	**755.3***	*867.7*	—	*0.3*	**25.8**	*14.1*
Goats *d*	**2 536.0***	*3 279.0*	—	—	**29.3[2]***	na
Sheep *d*	**5 506.3***	*6 017.0*				
Horses *d*	**117.7**	*209.5[2]*				
Pigs *d*	**70.0**	*82.3*	—	*0.9*	na	*2.3*
Bacon/ham	**62.3***	*55.3*	—	—	**0.1***	*0.7*
Meat‡: 'A'			**0.4[2]***	*1.0*	**5.2***	*1.6*
'B'	**20.7**	na	na	*0.1*	**1.6***	*0.1*
Butter	—	—	—	—	**5.6***	*4.0*
Cheese	**10.0***	na	na	*0.1*	**5.0***	*10.9*
Eggs	**20.0***	na	—	*2.3*	**1.7***	—
Fish	**17.5**	*23.5*	**1.8**	*12.4**	**2.1**	*8.1**
Milk	**285.7***	na	—	—	**98.9***	*32.5*
Hides/skins	na	na	**7.6[1]**	*7.5[2]*	**1.7[1]**	*3.8[2]*
Wool	na	*4.3*	na	*1.1*	**0.2**	*0.3*

d number in thousands.

6. FIBRES, TEXTILES, etc.

	Production		Exports		Imports	
Cotton lint	**1.0***	*2.0*	na	*2.5*	**0.4**	*0.1*
Jute	—	—	—	—	**0.1***	—
Rubber, natural	—	—	—	—	—	*0.3*
Cotton: yarn	**1.0**	na	—	—	**0.7[2]**	*1.0[2]*
woven fabrics	**1.7[2]**	*0.1*	—	—	**3.6[2]**	*9.9*
Wool: yarn	**0.3**	*0.8*	—	—	na	*0.4*
woven fabrics	na	na	na	*0.1*	na	*0.8*

7. FUEL AND POWER

	Production		Exports		Imports	
Coal 'A'‡	**47**	*300**	na	*61*	**19[2]*n***	*274*
Electricity *h*: total	**1 094**	*880[1]*				
hydro	**313**	*290[1]*				
thermal	**781**	*590[1]*				
Natural gas *i*	**1 020**	—	**340**	—	—	—
Oil, crude	**25 620**	*60[1]*	**24 300**	na	—	—
Petroleum, refined	**1 500**	—[1]	**740**	—	**1 000**	*1 030[1]*

h million kWh. *i* million cu. metres. *n* incl. coke.

8. IRON AND STEEL

	Production		Exports		Imports	
Iron ore	**1 416*m***	*1 652m*	**2 627**	*3 261*	—	—
Pig iron	—	—	—	—	na	*1*
Steel ingots/castings	—	—	—	—	na	*16*
Iron/steel scrap	—	—	**56[2]**	*69*	—	—

m metal content.

9. NON-FERROUS MINERALS AND METALS

	Production		Exports		Imports	
Gold *k*, bullion/coins, etc.	—	—	—	—	na	*211.30*
Silver *k*: ore *m*	**281.70**	*55.70*	—	—	—	—
bullion	—	—	—	—	na	*244.67*
Asbestos: fibre	—	—	—	—	na	*2.88*
manufactured	—	—	—	—	na	*0.04*
Aluminium: bauxite	—	—	—	—	na	*3.53*
aluminium	**10.15[2]***	—	**0.97*n***	*0.24*	**0.83[2]***	*1.85*
Antimony: ore	**0.02*m***	*1.71m*	—	*5.85*	—	—
metal	—	—	—	—	na	*0.02*
Chrome, metal	—	—	—	—	na	*0.04*
Copper: ore	**1.05*m***	*0.14m*	**3.78**	*0.67*	—	—
metal	—	—	na	*1.74*	na	*8.57*
Lead: ore	**9.40*m***	*9.68m*	**12.00**	*11.65*	na	*0.25*
metal	na	na	na	*2.74*	na	*4.04*
Magnesium:						
dolomite	—	—	—	—	**1.33**	na
magnesite	—	—	—	—	**0.01**	na
Manganese, ore	—	—	—	—	na	*0.05*
Mercury *f*	—	—	—	—	na	*1.30*
Tin, metal	—	—	—	*0.03†*	na	*0.20*
Tungsten, ore	na	*0.01*	na	*0.02*	—	—
Zinc: ore	**36.67*m***	*26.61m*	**59.46**	*43.77*	—	—
metal	na	na	na	*0.45*	**1.88**	na

f metric tons. *k* '000 fine troy ounces. *m* metal content. *n* incl. scrap.

10. CHEMICALS *n* AND FERTILIZERS

	Production		Exports		Imports	
Chemicals	—		—		na	
Fertilizers:						
Phosphates	**169.0**	*714.6*	**127.6**	*660.3*	na	*9.6*
Potash	—	—	—	—	na	*18.2*
Pyrites	**24.0*x***	*12.6x*	**33.6**	*0.1*	na	*10.9*
Sulphur	**23.7*p***	na	—	—	na	*19.9*

n data not available for years 1953–5. *p* native. *x* sulphur content.

11. INDUSTRY

	Production		Exports		Imports	
Aircraft *a*	—	—	—	—	**0.3[1]**	na
Alcoholic beverages			**94.8[1]*an***	—*n*	—*n*	*4.5an*
beer *b*	**255.0**	*393.7*				
spirits	na	na				
Cement	**788.0**	*595.7*	**100.0***	*37.3*	**15.0***	*135.0*
Elec. engineering *a*	na	na	na	*2.3[2]q*	**17.8[1]*q***	*24.4[2]*
Railway vehicles *a*	—	—	—	—	**0.5[1]**	*2.8*
Machine tools *a*	—	—	—	—	**0.6[1]**	*2.6[2]*
Motor vehicles:			—	—	**26.2[1]*a***	*36.4[1]a*
commercial *d*	**2.1*p***	na				
private *d*	**3.6*p***	na				

a million $ U.S. *b* '000 hectolitres. *d* no. in thousands. *n* wines and spirits only. *p* assembly of imported parts. *q* data incomplete.

ANDORRA

EUROPE

Andorra is a neutral co-principality under the joint sovereignty of the French President and the Bishop of Urgel to both of whom the state pays dues.

AREA: 465 sq. km. (190 sq. miles)

POPULATION: 14 000 (1967 U.N. estimate)

Capital city: ANDORRA; population: 2 463 (1965)

EMPLOYMENT AND PRODUCTION

Tourism, encouraged by the absence of customs duties, is the main source of revenue. The main agricultural products are potatoes, cereals and tobacco. Stock breeding is also important. Extensive deforestation has decreased former timber resources. The working of rich deposits of iron, alum, lead, slate and stone is handicapped by lack of transport.

CURRENCY: The French franc and the Spanish peseta

na: data not available. — negligible or nil. [1] one year only. [2] two year average. * estimate. ‡ see appendix. † re-exports.

SAUDI ARABIA—see page 206
SOUTHERN YEMEN—see page 210

BAHRAIN

Bahrain is an Arab sheikdom which has special treaty relations with the U.K.

AREA: 598.3 sq. km. (231 sq. miles)

POPULATION: 182 203 (1965 census)

Capital city: AL MANĀMAH; population: 79 098 (1965)

Total working population: 45 479 (1959)

		Year(s)
Population per physician	2 030	1965
Population per hospital bed	240*b*	1966
School enrolment: age 5–19 years (percentage)	90*a*	1963–4 av.

a public education only. *b* government hospitals only.

COMMUNICATIONS

		Year(s)
Telephones (per '000 urban population)	4	1967
Radio receivers (per '000 population)	750	1963–5 av.
Television sets (per '000 population)	59.2	1963–5 av.
Daily newspapers (per '000 population)	58	1958

FINANCE

Currency unit: The Bahrain dinar replaced the Indian (external) rupee in 1965

Exchange rates	1965	1960*a*
Per $ U.S.	0.357	4.76
Per £ sterling	1.0	13.33

a rupees.

EMPLOYMENT AND TRADE

The standard of living is high in the merchant groups and rapidly rising in the lower social groups. The pearl fishing trade has now declined. Oil was discovered in 1932 and a refinery built, 80% of the oil for which is piped from Saudi Arabia. The free transit of goods for the mainland has encouraged the entrepôt trade, and by 1966 Bahrain was re-exporting 30% of its imports. Bahrain has also an international airport. Imports are food, manufactured goods, building materials, machinery and vehicles.

KUWAIT

Kuwait has long been independent and in 1961 recognition of her sovereignty was re-affirmed by the U.K. Iraqi claims to the territory were made, but British and Arab League forces supported Kuwait's independence. Since 1946 oil concessions have been made to several oil companies.

AREA: 24 280 sq. km. (9 375 sq. miles) (after partition of the Neutral Zone)

POPULATION: 467 339 (1965 census)

Largest city: AL KUWAYT, capital; population: 295 273 (1965)
Total working population: 95 533 (1961)

		Year(s)
Infant mortality (per '000)	39.8*	1965
Crude birth rate (per '000)	46.2*	1965
Crude death rate (per '000)	5.2*	1965
Accidental deaths (per 100 000 population)		
caused by motor vehicles	61.7*	1967
due to other causes	27.1	1967
Population per physician	810	1965
Population per hospital bed	140	1966
School enrolment: age 5–19 years (percentage)	97	1963–4 av.

EMPLOYMENT AND PRODUCTION

Kuwait formerly served as an entrepôt for goods for the interior and the export of hides and wool, and as a pearl fishing centre. Kuwait remains an important entrepôt centre but revenue from oil drilling has enabled her to start on large scale development plans. Some 20% of the oil was refined locally in 1965.

COMMUNICATIONS

		Year(s)
Motor vehicles in use ('000s): private	52.1	1963–5 av.
commercial	20.0	1963–5 av.
Mail per capita: domestic	3	1964–5 av.
foreign received	36	1964–5 av.
foreign sent	26	1964–5 av.
Telephones (per '000 urban population)	6.3	1967
Radio receivers (per '000 population)	340	1963–5 av.
Television sets (per '000 population)	115.3	1963–5 av.
Daily newspapers (per '000 population)	28	1964

FINANCE

Currency unit: The Kuwait dinar, at par with the pound sterling until 1968, replaced the Indian (external) rupee in 1961.

Exchange rates	1965	1960*a*
Per $ U.S.	0.357	4.76
Per £ sterling	1.0	13.33

		Year(s)
National Income (million $ U.S.)	1 487	1965
G.N.P. per capita ($ U.S.)	3 410	1966
Foreign trade (percentage of G.D.P.)	76	1963–5 av.

a rupees

TRADING

Total trade (in million $ U.S.)	1965	1960
Exports (f.o.b.)	1 250	957
Imports (c.i.f.)	377	242

Main trading partners (percentage of total value)

Exports	1965	*Imports*	1965
Italy	27	U.S.A.	21
Japan	23	U.K.	16
U.K.	19	Japan	10
France	12	Germany F.R.	9
Netherlands	6	Italy	5
		China P.R.	3
		Iran	3

Distribution of trade (percentage of total value)

*Exports**	1965	*Imports*	1965
Petroleum	94	Manufactured goods	68
Food	2	(machinery and transport equipment)	(32)
Cigarettes	2	(textiles and clothing)	(12)
Machinery and transport equipment	1	Food	21

NEUTRAL ZONE

This consists of two areas of desert which were administered jointly by Kuwait and Saudi Arabia until 1966 when they were partitioned between these two states.

Oil production which started in 1954 reached 19 million metric tons in 1965. Exploitation of oil and other natural resources will continue to be shared between Kuwait and Saudi Arabia.

OMAN

Oman is an independent sovereign sultanate extending inland to the great desert. The population is very mixed with many Indian merchants. A small tract on the Baluchistan coast was handed over to Pakistan in 1958. Close ties are maintained with the British government.

AREA: 212 000* sq. km. (82 000* sq. miles)

LAND USE: (percentage of total)

	1948
Arable and orchard	—
Permanent meadow and pasture	—
Forest and woodland	0.4
City areas, waste and other land	99.6

POPULATION: 565 000 (1967 U.N. estimate)
Capital city: MASQAṬ (Muscat); population: 6 208 (1960)

FINANCE

Currency unit: The riyal Saidi was introduced in 1970. Previously the Maria Theresa dollar and the Indian (external) rupee were circulated. A copper coin, the baiza, is still in use.

Exchange rates in 1958	*Maria Theresa dollar*	*Indian rupee*
Per $ U.S.	3.69	4.76
Per £ sterling	10.34	13.33

		Year
National income (million $ U.S.)	32	1958

LAND USE AND EMPLOYMENT

The only cultivatable area is the 10 mile wide coastal plain. Dates and sugar cane are grown and cattle are reared. Drilling for oil started in 1967. Trade is mainly with India, Pakistan, the U.K. and the Persian Gulf States. In 1964 chief exports were dates, fruit and fish. Imports included cereals, cement and vehicles.

na: data not available. — negligible or nil. [1] one year only. [2] two year average. * estimate. ‡ see appendix. † re-exports.

QATAR

Qatar is an independent Arab sheikhdom with special treaty relations with the U.K.

AREA: 10 360* sq. km. (4 000* sq. miles)

POPULATION: 75 000 (1967 estimate)

Largest city: AD DAWḤAH (Doha), capital; population: 45 000 (city proper, 1963)

FINANCE

Currency unit: The riyal replaced at par the Indian (external) rupee in 1966

Exchange rates	1968	1958
Per $ U.S.	4.76	4.76
Per £ sterling	11.43	13.33

EMPLOYMENT AND TRADE

The population consists mainly of semi-nomadic tribesmen and Bedouin using the poor grazing. Pearl fishing has declined. Development projects now depend on oil drilling, begun in 1949, on land and off-shore, and a cement factory and prawn freezing plant have been built. A large number of migrant labourers are employed.

TRUCIAL STATES

The Trucial States consist of seven independent Arab sheikhdoms which have treaty relations with the U.K. Aid is given by the other independent states of the Persian Gulf.

AREA: 83 660* sq. km. (32 300* sq. miles)

POPULATION: 136 000 (1967 estimate)
Capital city: DUBAYY (Dubai); population: 65 000 (1966)

FINANCE

Currency unit: The riyal replaced at par the Indian (external) rupee in 1966. The Bahrain dinar is also used.

Exchange rates	1968*a*	1958*b*
Per $ U.S.	4.76	4.76
Per £ sterling	11.43	13.33

a riyals. *b* rupees.

EMPLOYMENT AND TRADE

One-tenth of the population is estimated to be nomadic. The main crops are cereals, dates, vegetables, fruit and tobacco. There is a fishing trade and a declining pearl fishing industry. Revenue is derived from customs duties and oil concession payments from Abu Dhabi (since 1962). Dubai has an entrepôt trade and an international airport and Sharjah is an R.A.F. base. The chief exports are oil, dried fish and tobacco. The chief trading partners are the U.K., Japan and India.

YEMEN

In 1958 Yemen federated with the United Arab Republic (a union of Egypt and Syria) to form the United Arab States. Syria broke away in 1961, and later that year Yemen's union with Egypt was terminated.

AREA: 195 000* sq. km. (75 000* sq. miles)

POPULATION: 5 000 000 (1967 U.N. estimate)
Capital city: ṢAN 'Ā'; population: 60 000 (1956)

FINANCE

Currency unit: The silver riyal has replaced at par the Maria Theresa dollar

Exchange rates	1965	1960*a*	1958*a*
Per $ U.S.	1.1	1.1	3.69
Per £ sterling	3.08	3.08	10.34

		Year(s)
National Income (million $ U.S.)	180	1958
G.N.P. per capita ($ U.S.)	90	1966

a Maria Theresa dollars.

EMPLOYMENT AND TRADE

Semi-nomadic herding and settled agriculture occupy most of the population, since no crude oil has yet been found. The main products are millet, coffee, cotton, oilseeds, salt and hides. Soviet, Chinese and U.S. aid is received.

PRODUCTION, EXPORTS AND IMPORTS

Years: **1963–5 average** and *1953–5 average* Units: '000 metric tons unless otherwise indicated

These data are for the seven states listed above and do not include Saudi Arabia and Southern Yemen.

	Production		Exports		Imports	
1. CEREALS, etc.						
Barley	—	—	—	—	20.6*	na
Maize (corn)	—	—	—	—	0.5*	na
Millets/sorghum	—	—	—	—	4.4[2]	na
Oats	—	—	—	—	0.4*	na
Potatoes	15.7*	na	—	—	6.0*	na
Rice	—	—	3.1[1]*†	na	90.0*	na
Wheat	25.0*	na	—	—	18.7*	*20.2*[2]*
2. FRUIT, etc.						
Apples	—	—	—	—	2.0*	na
Bananas	—	—	—	—	6.1*	na
Dates	60.0**n*	na	12.9*	na	24.8*	na
Grapes	—	—	0.1[1]*†	na	0.9[1]*	na
Lemons	—	—	—	—	0.9*	na
Oranges	—	—	—	—	3.6*	na
Other citrus fruit	—	—	—	—	0.2*	na
Pears	—	—	—	—	0.1*	na
Raisins	—	—	—	—	na	na
Wine *b*	—	—	—	—	0.6*	na

b '000 hectolitres. *n* Yemen only.

	Production		Exports		Imports	
3. BEVERAGES, FOREST PRODUCTS, etc.						
Coffee	4.9*	*4.4**	4.1*	*4.4*[2]*	2.4*	—
Sugar, raw	—	—	9.5*†	na	101.0*	na
Tea	—	—	0.6[2]*†	—	4.3*	*6.4*[2]*
Tobacco: leaf	—	—	—	—	0.6*	na
cigarettes	—	—	2.2[1]*e*†	na	3.7[1]*e*	na
Newsprint	—	—	—	—	3.3[1]	na
Other paper	—	—	—	—	6.2[2]	na

e number in millions.

	Production		Exports		Imports	
4. VEGETABLE OILSEEDS AND OILS						
Copra	—	—	—	—	0.10*	na
Coconut oil	—	—	—	—	0.40*	na
Cottonseed	na	na	2.50*	na	—	—
Cottonseed oil	na	na	—	—	0.60*	na
Groundnuts	—	—	—	—	0.60*	na
Groundnut oil	—	—	—	—	0.20*	na
Linseed oil	—	—	—	—	na	na
Olive oil	—	—	—	—	0.40*	na
Palm oil	—	—	—	—	0.20*	na
Sesame seed	—	—	—	—	0.30	na
Soya bean oil	—	—	—	—	0.20*	na
Sunflower seed	—	—	—	—	0.20*	na

	Production		Exports		Imports	
5. LIVESTOCK‡, ANIMAL PRODUCTS, etc.						
Cattle *d*	1 250.0*	na	—	—	1.7*	na
Goats *d*	—	na	—	—	145.6*	na
Sheep *d*	11 493.3*	na				
Horses *d*	3.0*	na				
Butter	—	—	na	na	0.8*	na
Cheese	—	—	—	—	1.4*	na
Eggs	—	—	—	—	2.5*	na
Fish	123.0*	na	—	—	—	—
Milk	75.0*	na	—	—	49.5*	na
Hides/skins	na	na	1.6[1]	na	—	—
Wool	na	na	0.2*	na	—	—

d number in thousands. (Goats and sheep exports and imports are bracketed together.)

	Production		Exports		Imports	
6. FIBRES, TEXTILES, etc.						
Cotton lint	na	na	1.2*	na	—	na
7. FUEL AND POWER						
Electricity *ht*:						
Bahrain	137	*20*[1]				
Kuwait	584	*60*[1]				
Natural gas *i*:						
Kuwait	1 660	—	—	—	—	—
Oil, crude:						
Bahrain	2 520	*1 500*[1]	—	—	7 810	*1 280*[1]
Kuwait	104 320	*54 760*[1]	93 017	*54 030*[1]	—	—
Neutral Zone	18 713	*1 270*[1]	15 130	na	—	—
Qatar	10 060	*5 440*[1]	10 033	*5 350*[1]	—	—
Trucial States	8 413	—	8 410	na	—	—
Petroleum, refined:						
Bahrain	10 037	*9 440*[1]	8 777	*9 410*[1]	127	na
Kuwait	10 887	*1 530*[1]	6 040	*190*[1]	na	*270*[1]
Neutral Zone	3 823	—	2 723	—	10	na
Qatar	30	—[1]	—*	—[1]	37	na
Trucial States	—	—	—	—	23	na
Yemen	—	—	—	—	130	na

h million kWh. *i* million cu. metres. *t* thermal.

	Production		Exports		Imports	
11. INDUSTRY *n*						
Aircraft *a*	—	—	—	—	2.5[1]	na
Beer	na	na	0.3[1]*a*	na	na	na
Electrical engineering *a*	—	—	2.7†	na	42.6[1]	na
Merchant ships *g*	—	—	—	—	25.0	na
Motor vehicles *a*	—	—	2.0†	na	36.6	na

a million $ U.S. *g* '000 G.R.T. *n* Kuwait only.

na: data not available. — negligible or nil. [1] one year only. [2] two year average. * estimate. ‡ see appendix. † re-exports.

ARGENTINA

Argentina is a republic. The country suffered several years' economic instability due mainly to overemphasis on industrialization and frequent changes in leadership. Some attempt was made in 1957 towards more democratic government, but there was a reversion in 1966, and the president now rules by decree.

AREA: 2 808 602 sq. km. (1 084 120 sq. miles)

LAND USE: (percentage of total)

	1960	*1954*
Arable and orchard	7.0	10.8
Permanent meadow and pasture	42.6	40.7
Forest and woodland	25.2	32.3
City areas, waste and other land (incl. non-agricultural holdings)	25.2	16.2

POPULATION: 23 031 000 (1967 estimate)

Largest city: BUENOS AIRES, capital; population: 7 000 000* (1960)

Distribution of working population (1960)

Total working population: 7 599 071*

U.N. group no.		*Percentage*
0	Agriculture, forestry, fishing and hunting	19.2
1	Mining and quarrying	0.6
2/3	Manufacturing	25.2
4	Construction	5.6
5	Electricity, gas, water and sanitary services	1.1
6	Commerce	11.9
7	Transport, storage and communications	6.3
8	Services	20.0
9	Others	10.1

		Year(s)
Life expectancy at birth (years): male	63.7	1960–5 av.
female	69.5	
Infant mortality (per '000)	58.3*	1965
Crude birth rate (per '000)	22.5*	1960–5 av.
Crude death rate (per '000)	8.5*	1960–5 av.
Accidental deaths	na	
Population per physician	670	1962
Population per hospital bed	160	1965
School enrolment: age 5–19 years (percentage)	74	1963–4 av.
age over 19 years (per 100 000 population)	1 038	1963–5 av.

COMMUNICATIONS

		Year(s)
Motor vehicles in use ('000s): private	809.3	1963–5 av.
commercial	559	
Railway track (km.)	42 913	1948
Mail per capita: domestic	41	1963–5 av.
foreign received	5	
foreign sent	2	
Telephones (per '000 urban population)	6.7	1967
Radio receivers (per '000 population)	282	1963–5 av.
Television sets (per '000 population)	65.1	1963–5 av.
Daily newspapers (per '000 population)	155	1959

FINANCE

Currency unit: The peso

Exchange rates	*1965a*	*1960b*	*1950b*	*1938a*
Per $ U.S.	188.5	82.7	7.5	3.64
Per £ sterling	528.35	231.95	21.01	16.74

a selling rate. *b* official rate.

		Year(s)
National Income (million $ U.S.)	16 537	1965
G.N.P. per capita ($ U.S.)	780	1966
Rate of increase of G.N.P. per capita	0.3	1960–4 av.
Foreign trade (percentage of G.D.P.)	15	1963–5 av.

TRADING

Total trade (in million $ U.S.)	*1965*	*1955*	*1938*
Exports (f.o.b.)	1 493	929	438
Imports (c.f.)	1 199	1 173	443

Main trading partners (percentage of total value)

Exports	*1965*	*1955*	*1938*	*Imports*	*1965*	*1955*	*1938*
Italy	16	8	3	U.S.A.	23	13	17
Netherlands	11	4	7	Brazil	14	9	5
U.K.	10	22	33	Germany F.R.	9	6	10*d*
Brazil	7	14	7	Italy	7	6	6
Germany F.R.	7	6	12*d*	U.K.	6	6	20
U.S.A.	6	13	8	France	4	6	5
China P.R.	6	na	na	Japan	4	6	4

Distribution of trade (percentage of total value)

Exports	*1965*	*1955*	*1938**
Food	75	61*	70
(cereals)	(39)	(37)	(45)
(meat and meat preparations)	(22)	(21)	(24)
Crude materials and fuels	13	19*	24
(textile fibre and waste)	(8)	(14)	(11)
Imports			
Manufactured goods	57	54*	na
(machinery and transport equipment)	(25)	(18)	(15)
(iron and steel)	(15)	(16)	(9)
Crude materials and fuels	25	31*	na
(fuels)	(10)	(17)	(16)
Chemicals	11	8	6
Food	6	7	6

d incl. Germany D.R.

PRODUCTION, EXPORTS AND IMPORTS

Years: **1963–5 average** and *1953–5 average* Units: '000 metric tons unless otherwise indicated

	Production		Exports		Imports	
1. CEREALS, etc.						
Barley	**750.0**	*985.7*	**293.5**	*579.1*	—	—
Cassava	**243.7**	*304.5*[2]				
Maize (corn)	**4 950.0**	*3 622.0*	**2 863.2**	*1 210.4*	—	—
Millets/sorghum	**1 391.3**	*215.0*	**610.8**	*36.1*	—	—
Oats	**730.3**	*868.0*	**303.4**	*330.6*	**28.4**	*9.1*
Potatoes	**1 811.3**	*1 531.3*	**6.2**	*16.3*	—	—
Rice	**212.0**	*182.7*	**21.6**	*27.5*	—	—
Rye	**478.3**	*701.7*	**70.3**	*500.3*	—	—
Sweet potatoes/yams	**349.7**	*315.0*				
Wheat	**8 533.3**	*6 380.0*	**4 067.1**	*3 028.8*	—	—
2. FRUIT, etc.						
Apples	**463.0**	*286.3*	**210.6**	*57.5*	—	—
Apricots	**12.7**	*8.8*	na	na	—	—
Bananas	**69.0**	na	—	—	**173.6**	*153.5*
Cherries	**2.0**	na	na	na	—	—
Figs	**6.3**	*4.3*[2]*	na	na	—	—
Grapes	**2 345.3**	*2 007.7*	**6.2**	*5.5*	—	—
Lemons	**76.0**	*68.7*	**0.3**	—	**0.4**	—
Olives	**58.3**	*36.0*				
Oranges	**642.7**	*440.3*	**2.3**	—	**6.6**	*19.1*
Other citrus fruit	**62.0**	*13.3*	**0.2**	—	—	—

continued

	Production		Exports		Imports	
2. FRUIT, etc.—*continued*						
Peaches	**194.0**	*122.6*	na	*1.2*	—	—
Pears	**96.7**	*85.7*	**42.9**	*20.5*[2]	—	—
Pineapples	**2.0**	na	—	—	na	*8.2*
Plums	**42.0**	*32.5*	na	*1.6*	—	—
Raisins	**8.5***	*5.4*n*	**1.6**	*1.0*	—	—
Tomatoes	**318.0**	*344.3*				
Wine *b*	**18 902.0**	*13 863.0*	**4.8**	*0.7*	**0.3**	—

b '000 hectolitres. *n* commercial production.

	Production		Exports		Imports	
3. BEVERAGES, FOREST PRODUCTS, etc.						
Cocoa	—	—	—	—	**8.1**	*7.6*
Coffee	—	—	—	—	**30.2**	*30.6*
Sugar: cane	**12 292.3**	*9 451.0*				
raw	**1 097.4**	*690.7*	**149.8**	*13.3*	**0.4**	*13.3*
Tea	**11.2***	*3.8*[2]	**9.4**	na	—	*0.1*
Tobacco: leaf	**52.0**	*34.6*	**13.2**	*0.6*	**0.1**	*0.1*
cigarettes *e*	**25 961.0**	*20 180.0*	—	—	—	*0.2p*
Softwood *j*	**264.4**	*263.3**	—	—	**984.0**	*1 051.0**
Hardwood *j*	**10 209.3**[2]	*14 893.3**	**2.0**[2]	*2.8**	**318.2**	*456.6**
Wood pulp	**74.5**[2]	*59.7*	—[2]	—	**149.3***	*121.3*
Newsprint	**15.6**[2]	*35.0**	**0.3**[2]	—	**174.0**	*53.0*
Other paper	**372.5**[2]	*207.0**	**0.1**[2]	—	**15.9**	*17.7*

e no. in millions. *j* '000 cu. metres of roundwood equivalent. *p* value of tobacco manufactures in million $ U.S.

continued

PRODUCTION, EXPORTS AND IMPORTS *continued*

	Production		Exports		Imports	
4. VEGETABLE OILSEEDS AND OILS						
Castor seed	**5.00**	*2.74*	—	—	—	—
Castor oil	na	na	—	—	**0.10**	*0.19*
Coconut oil	—	—	—	—	**1.92**	*0.73*
Cottonseed	**240.70**	*238.30*	na	*0.13*	**0.01**	—
Cottonseed oil	na	na	**1.19**	—	na	*15.78*
Groundnuts	**252.96**	*117.60*	**0.19**	—	—	—
Groundnut oil	na	na	**32.92**	*1.83*	—	—
Linseed	**718.67**	*351.00n*	**7.09**	*7.00*	—	—
Linseed oil	na	na	**219.02**	*171.07*	—	—
Olive oil	**9.67**	*5.00*[2]*	**7.43**	*0.42*	**0.01**	—
Palm oil	—	—	—	—	**0.38**	*0.16*
Rapeseed	na	na	—	—	—	—
Sesame seed	—	—	—	—	na	na
Soya beans	**16.70**	*0.50*[2]	—	—	—	—
Sunflower seed	**559.67**	*460.67*	—	—	—	—
Sunflower seed oil	na	na	**13.35**	*7.39*	—	—
Tung oil	**13.50**	*12.43*	**15.45**	*12.00*	—	—

n flax grown for seed only.

	Production		Exports		Imports	
5. LIVESTOCK‡, ANIMAL PRODUCTS, etc.						
Chickens *d*	**35 566.7**	*44 500.0*[1]				
Cattle *d*	**42 406.0**	*44 429.5*[2]	**188.6**	*46.7*	**4.3**	*0.6*
dairy cows *d*	**15 826.0***	na				
Goats *d*	**5 025.0***	na	**26.7** (goats and sheep)	na	**2.7**	—
Sheep *d*	**46 139.3**	*50 728.0*				
Horses *d*	**3 760.3***	*5 849.0*[1]				
Pigs *d*	**3 439.0***	*3 750.0*[2]	**0.6**	*0.6*[2]	**0.3**	—
Bacon/ham	**2 595.3*** (bacon/ham and meat 'A')	*2 159.5*	—	*0.3*	—	—
Meat‡ 'A'			**466.1**	*208.7*	—	—
'B'	**107.4**	—	**94.8**	*25.2*	—	—
Butter	**48.3n**	*58.7n*	**10.4**	*13.9*	—	—
Cheese	**148.7**	*115.0*	**5.0**	*3.5*	—	—
Eggs	**149.0**	*155.4*[2]	**2.6**	*3.9*	**1.9**	*0.2*
Fish	**168.0**	*78.4*	**6.1**	na	**9.0**	na
Milk	**4 784.0**	*4 828.5*[2]	**2.0**	*11.2*	—	—
Whale/sperm oil	na	*7.1*	—	—	—	—
Hides/skins	na	na	**181.7**	*15.6e*	—	—
Wool	**105.8***	*108.0**	**72.9**	*75.9*	—	—

d no. in thousands. *e* no. in millions. *n* factory produce only.

	Production		Exports		Imports	
6. FIBRES, TEXTILES, etc.						
Agaves (sisal etc.)	—	—	—	—	**2.0**	*3.5*
Cotton lint	**123.3**	*124.3*	**17.1**	*30.3*	**11.1**	*2.3*
Flax fibre	**1.7***	—	—	—	—	—
Hemp fibre	—	—	—	—	**0.5**	*1.9*
Jute	—	—	—	—	**8.0**	*12.5*
Rubber: natural	—	—	—	—	**25.4**	*26.1*
synthetic	**1.2**	—	—	—	**27.4**	*1.5*[2]
Silk *f*	—	—	—	—	**2.0**	*2.3**
Cotton: yarn	**86.2**	*85.1*	**0.1**[1]	—	**0.2**[2]	*1.2*
woven fabrics	**54.9**[1]	*62.1*	—	—	**0.1**	*0.1*[2]
Rayon, fibre/yarn	**16.3**	*11.0*	na	na	**1.0**	na
Non-cellulosic fibre/yarn	**9.2**	*0.2*	—	na	**1.3**	na
Wool: yarn	na	na	**0.4**	—[2]	—	—[2]
woven fabrics	na	na	**0.1**	*0.1*[2]	—	—[2]

f metric tons.

	Production		Exports		Imports	
7. FUEL AND POWER						
Coal 'A'‡	**303**	*130*	—	—	**706**	*1 289*
Coke	—	—	—	—	**51**	*62*
Electricity *h*: total	**13 727**	*6 000*[1]				
hydro	**1 220**	*300*[1]				
thermal	**12 507**	*5 700*[1]				
Natural gas *i*	**3 790**	*981*[1]	—	—	**33**	—
Oil, crude	**13 930**	*4 370*[1]	**40**	—[1]	**1 970**	*4 130*[1]
Petroleum, refined	**14 336**	*7 460*[1]	**707**	—	**883**	*3 380*[1]
Uranium *f*	**26**	na	—	—	—	—

f metric tons. *h* million kWh. *i* million cu. metres.

	Production		Exports		Imports	
8. IRON AND STEEL						
Iron ore	**50m**	*37*m*	—	—	**942**	na
Pig iron	**574**	*33*	—	—	**57**	*104*
Steel ingots/castings	**1 182**	*192*	**20**	na	**584**	*375*
Iron/steel scrap	—	—	—	—	**3**	*1*
Iron/steel products *a*	na	na	**12**	—	**131**	*634*

a million $ U.S. *m* metal content.

	Production		Exports		Imports	
9. NON-FERROUS MINERALS AND METALS						
Diamonds	—	—	—	—	**0.04**[1]*a*	na
Gold *k*: ore *m*	na	*6.00*	—	—	—	—
bullion/coins etc.	na	na	na	*0.13*	—	—
Silver *k*: ore *m*	**2 190.70**	*1 316.70*	—	—	—	—
bullion	na	na	**386.67**	na	—	—
Asbestos: fibre	**0.35**	*0.18*[1]	—	—	—	—
manufactured	na	na	—	—	**12.80**	*8.70*
Mica	**0.44**	*0.20*	**0.63**	*0.10*	**0.02**	na
Aluminium: bauxite	—	—	—	—	**21.66**	*0.89*
aluminium	—	—	**1.10**	na	**28.35**	*11.76*
Antimony: ore	na	*0.01m*	—	—	**0.65**	*0.47*
metal	na	na	—	—	—	—
Beryl	**0.44**	*0.87*	**0.44**	*0.57*	—	—
Cadmium	—	—	—	—	—	*0.01*
Chrome, metal	—	—	—	—	na	*2.09*
Cobalt, metal	—	—	—	—	**0.06**	*1.80*
Copper: ore	**4.14m**	na	**1.34**	na	—	—
metal	na	na	—	—	**20.11**	*13.40*
Lead: ore	**28.21m**	*23.01m*	**0.25**	—	**0.16**	na
metal	**26.37**	*18.42*	—	—	**1.10**	*0.68*
Magnesium: dolomite	**98.63**	na	—	—	—	—
magnesite	—	—	—	—	**4.09**	na
metal/salts	—	—	—	—	**0.47**	*0.57*
Manganese: ore	**17.01**	*3.73*	—	—	—	—
metal	na	na	—	—	**0.94**	*2.39*
Mercury *f*	—	—	—	—	**42.80**	*0.06*
Nickel: metal	—	—	—	—	**0.41**	na
Tin: ore	**0.36m**	*0.11m*	**1.85n**	na	—	—
metal	na	na	—	—	**1.35**	*1.73*
Titanium minerals	—	—	—	—	**5.10**	*0.96*
Tungsten: ore	**0.12**	*0.83*	**0.36**	*0.40*	—	—
Vanadium	—	*0.01m*	—	—	—	—
Zinc: ore	**27.11m**	*19.00*m*	**26.63**	na	—	—
metal	**21.83**	*12.00*	**1.47**	*3.38*	**1.20**	—

a million $ U.S. *f* metric tons. *k* '000 fine troy oz. *m* metal content. *n* incl. tin-silver ore.

	Production		Exports		Imports	
10. CHEMICALS*n* AND FERTILIZERS						
Organic chemicals:						
Benzene	**177.0**[1]		na		na	
Butadiene	—		na		na	
Ethylene	na		—		na	
Methanol	**9.7**[1]		—		**7.6**	
Phenol	na		na		**0.9**[1]	
Phthalic anhydride	na		—		na	
Styrene monomer	na		na		na	
Urea	na		—		na	
Inorganic chemicals:						
Ammonia	**6.7**[1]		na		na	
Carbon black	**10.4**		—		**3.4**[2]	
Chlorine	**46.7**		na		na	
Nitric acid	**5.2**[1]		na		—	
Sodium carbonate	na		—		**108.9**	
Sodium hydroxide	**65.0**		—[1]		**12.8**	
Sulphuric acid	**140.7**		**0.1**[2]		—[2]	
Plastics:						
Polyamides	na		na		na	
Polyethylene	**18.7**[1]		**4.0**[1]		**1.0**[1]	
Polyvinyl chloride	**12.3**		—		**0.5**[2]	
Fertilizers:						
Phosphates	**0.4q**	na	—	—	—	na
Potash	—	—	—	—	**2.8**	*2.3*
Sulphur	**22.9p**	*17.2p*	—	—	**34.8**	*11.1*

n data not available for years 1953–5. *p* native. *q* guano.

	Production		Exports		Imports	
11. INDUSTRY						
Aircraft *a*	—	—	—	—	**3.2**	na
Alcoholic beverages			**0.3a**	—	**2.7a**	—
beer *b*	**1 818.0**	*3 634.0*				
Cement	**2 822.7**	*1 745.7*	**1.7**	*1.0*	**164.3**	*1.0*
Electrical engineering *a*	na	na	**3.0**	na	**64.4**	na
Locomotives	—	na	—	—	na	na
Railway vehicles *a*	na	na	**0.6**	na	**46.4**	*21.5*
Machine tools *a*	**25.0**[1]	na	—	—	—	—
Merchant ships *g*	**8.0**	na	—	—	**16.0**	*1.2*
Motor vehicles			**1.23a**	na	**84.9a**	*19.6a*
commercial	**43.1d**	—				
private	**113.2d**	—				

a million $ U.S. *b* '000 hectolitres. *d* no. in thousands. *g* '000 G.R.T.

na: data not available. — negligible or nil. [1] one year only. [2] two year average. * estimate. ‡ see appendix. † re-exports.

AUSTRALIA

The Commonwealth of Australia was established in 1901. In 1957 a preferential trade agreement was signed with the U.K., and subsequently reciprocal tariff agreements with various other countries.

AREA: 7 686 900 sq. km. (2 967 909 sq. miles)

LAND USE: (percentage of total)	*1964*	*1954*
Arable and orchard	4.6	2.9
Permanent meadow and pasture	58.1	47.0
Forest and woodland	4.6	5.4
City areas, waste and other land	32.7	44.7

POPULATION: 11 540 764 (1966 census)

Largest city: SYDNEY; population: 2 444 735 (1966)
Capital city: CANBERRA; population: 100 090 (1967)

Distribution of working population (1961)
Total working population: 4 255 096

U.N. group no.		*Percentage*
0	Agriculture, forestry, fishing and hunting	10.9
1	Mining and quarrying	1.3
2/3	Manufacturing	27.0
4	Construction	8.8
5	Electricity, gas, water and sanitary services	2.2
6	Commerce	19.6
7	Transport, storage and communications	8.6
8	Services	19.6
9	Others	2.0

		Year(s)
Life expectancy at birth (years): male	67.9	1960–2 av.
female	74.2	1960–2 av.
Infant mortality (per '000)	18.5*a*	1965
Crude birth rate (per '000)	19.7*a*	1965
Crude death rate (per '000)	8.8	1965
Accidental deaths (per 100 000 population)		
caused by motor vehicles	27.8	1965
due to other causes	26.0	1965
Population per physician	720	1965
Population per hospital bed	80	1966
School enrolment: age 5–19 years (percentage)	90*b*	1963–4 av.
age over 19 years (per 100 000 population)	1 109	1963–5 av.

a excl. pure aborigines. *b* incl. pre-school and special education.

COMMUNICATIONS

		Year(s)
Motor vehicles in use ('000s): private	2 699.7	1963–5 av.
commercial	859.7	1963–5 av.
Railway track (km.)	40 496	1964
Mail per capita: domestic	193	1963–5 av.
foreign received	141	1963–5 av.
foreign sent	10	1963–5 av.
Telephones (per '000 urban population)	25.8	1966
Radio licenses (per '000 population)	212	1963–5 av.
Television licenses (per '000 population)	163.1	1963–5 av.
Daily newspapers (per '000 population)	316.5	1962–3 av.

FINANCE

Currency unit: The Australian dollar replaced the Australian pound in 1966 at the rate A$1 to A£0.5.

Exchange rates, for Australian pounds	*1965*	*1960*	*1950*	*1938*
Per $ U.S.	0.45	0.45	0.45	0.26
Per £ sterling	1.25	1.25	1.25	1.25

		Year(s)
National Income (million $ U.S.)	18 400	1965
G.N.P. per capita ($ U.S.)	1 840	1966
Rate of increase of G.N.P. per capita	2.6	1960–4 av.
Foreign trade (percentage of G.D.P.)	29	1963–5 av.

TRADING

Trading figures refer to year ending 30th June of year stated

Total trade (in million $ U.S.)	*1965*	*1955*	*1938*
Exports (f.o.b.)	2 889	1 703	642
Imports (f.o.b.)	3 182	1 884	507

Main trading partners (percentage of total value)

Exports	*1965*	*1955*	*1938*	*Imports*	*1965*	*1955*	*1938*
U.K.	19	37	55	U.K.	26	45	41
Japan	17	8	4	U.S.A.	24	12	16
U.S.A.	10	7	7	Japan	9	2	5
New Zealand	6	5	5	Germany F.R.	6	4	4*d*
China P.R.	5	—	—	Canada	4	3	7
France	4	8	7	France	2	2	1
Italy	3	5	2	Indonesia	2	3	7

Distribution of trade (percentage of total value)

Exports	*1965*	*1955*	*1938**
Crude materials	40	53	43
(wool)	(30)	(46)	(33)
Food	39	35	46
(cereals)	(16)	(11)	(20)
(meat)	(10)	(8)	(9)
Manufactured goods	16	10	1
(non-ferrous metals)	(5)	(4)	(1)
Imports			
Manufactured goods	66	67	51
(machinery and transport equipment)	(37)	(29)	(22)
Crude materials and fuels	15	20	12
(petroleum and products)	(8)	(11)	(8)
Chemicals	9	5	6

d incl. Germany D.R.

PRODUCTION, EXPORTS AND IMPORTS

Years: **1963–5 average** and *1953–5 average* Units: '000 metric tons unless otherwise indicated

1. CEREALS, etc.

	Production		Exports		Imports	
Barley	**1 017.0**	*845.3*	**335.3**	*514.9*	—	—
Maize (corn)	**153.3**	*123.3*	**3.6**	*13.1*	—	—
Millets/sorghum	**225.7**	*149.5*[2]	**27.2**	*56.1*	—	—
Oats	**1 205.0**	*696.3*	**330.1**	*108.3*	—	—
Potatoes	**588.0**	*472.7*	**11.3**	*6.0*	**1.8**	—
Rice	**143.7**	*83.7*	**59.9**	*35.0*	**1.1**	—
Rye	**11.7**	*12.7*	**0.4**	—	—	—
Sweet potatoes/yams	**2.0**	*6.0*[1]				
Wheat	**8 677.0**	*5 100.0*	**5 585.3**	*1 490.6*	—	—

2. FRUIT, etc.

	Production		Exports		Imports	
Apples	**358.7**	*236.3*	**141.6**	*84.7*	—	—
Apricots	**41.3**	*32.9*	na	na	—	—
Bananas	**126.7**	*85.0*	—	—	—	—
Cherries	**8.0***	*6.1*	na	na	—	—
Coconuts	—	—	—	—	**6.1***n*	*4.3*[2]
Dates	—	—	—	—	**3.8**	*4.5*
Figs	**1.0***	*1.0*[2]	—	—	—	—
Grapes	**615.0**	*461.7*	**1.4**	*1.1*	—	—
Lemons	**18.7**	*16.0*[2]	**0.6**	*0.2*	—	—
Oranges	**212.3***	*136.0*[2]	**20.4**	*10.7*	—	—
Other citrus fruit	**9.0***	*5.5*[2]	—	*0.1*	—	—
Peaches	**93.7**	*64.4*	na	na	—	—
Pears	**126.0**	*84.0*	**28.6**	*24.1*	—	—
Pineapples	**85.3**	*61.7*	na	na	—	—
Plums	**27.3**	*23.4*	na	*0.3*	—	—
Raisins	**95.7**	*78.0*	**65.6**	*63.4*	—	—
Tomatoes	**146.0***	*82.0*[2]				
Wine *b*	**1 730.5**[2]	*1 091.0*	**78.0**	*57.7*	**5.0**	*2.0*

b '000 hectolitres. *n* dessicated.

3. BEVERAGES, FOREST PRODUCTS, etc.

	Production		Exports		Imports	
Cocoa	—	—	**0.1†***n*	*0.1†*	**11.5**	*7.9*
Coffee	—	—	**0.1†**	*0.1†*	**13.1**	*4.2*
Sugar: cane	**14 004.7**	*9 485.0*				
raw	**1 957.9**	*1 275.7*	**1 197.1**	*682.2*	—	*0.5*
Tea	—	—	**0.8†**	*0.3†*	**29.7**	*26.7*
Tobacco: leaf	**14.6**	*3.3*	**0.2**	—	**12.9**	*19.1*
cigars	—	*19.2e*	—	*0.9*[2]*a*	**6.5***a*	*5.9a*
cigarettes	**20 139.0***e*	*8 449.3e*				
tobacco/snuff	**4.6**	*10.2*				
Softwood *j*	**1 898.3**	*1 332.0*	**4.0**	*2.3*	**970.3**	*974.0*
Hardwood *j*	**14 104.0**	*17 089.0*	**76.7**	*105.3*	**521.4**	*221.3*
Woodpulp	**428.5**	*232.7*	—	—	**215.2**	*62.0*
Newsprint	**93.7**	*65.0*	**0.6**	*0.1*	**252.3**	*157.0*
Other paper	**568.7**	*219.3*	**14.9**	*6.4*	**139.3**	*96.0*

a million $ U.S. *e* no. in millions. *j* '000 cu. metres of roundwood equivalent. *n* incl. cocoa mass, paste or slab.

4. VEGETABLE OILSEEDS AND OILS

	Production		Exports		Imports	
Castor seed	—	—	—	—	**0.10***	*3.00*[2]*
Castor oil	na	na	**0.05**	*0.06*	**1.81**	*1.49*
Copra	na	na	na	*0.50*[1]	**33.09**	*29.13*
Coconut oil	na	na	**0.03**	*0.26*	**0.72**	—
Cottonseed	**20.70**	*1.00*	—	—	**0.30**	—
Cottonseed oil	na	na	—	—	**0.94**	*0.07*
Groundnuts	**8.63**	*10.22*	—	—	**2.52**	*1.50*
Groundnut oil	na	na	—	—	**9.50**	*2.98*
Linseed	**27.67**	*6.67n*	—	—	na	*1.00**
Linseed oil	na	na	**0.02**	*0.35*	**1.28**	*14.75*
Olive oil	—	—	—	—	**4.68**	*2.29*

n flax grown for seed only.

continued

PRODUCTION, EXPORTS AND IMPORTS *continued*

4. VEGETABLE OILSEEDS AND OILS—*continued*

	Production		Exports		Imports	
Palm kernel oil	—	—	—	—	**0.93**	na
Palm oil	—	—	—	—	**3.10**	na
Rapeseed	—	—	—	—	**0.40**	na
Rapeseed oil	—	—	—	—	**2.10**	na
Soya beans	—	—	—	—	**3.28**	na
Soya bean oil	na	na	—	—	**4.41**	na
Sunflower seed	**2.33**	*1.00*[2]	—	—	—	—
Tung oil	—	—	—	—	**1.16**	*1.73*

5. LIVESTOCK‡, ANIMAL PRODUCTS, etc.

	Production		Exports		Imports	
Chickens *d*	**21 103.3***	na				
Cattle *d*	**18 806.7**	*15 561.7*	**8.7**	*4.8*	—	*0.7*
dairy cows *d*	**11 068.0***n*	*8 932.0*				
Goats *d*	**79.0***	na	**293.3**	na	—	—
Sheep *d*	**164 742.7**	*126 955.3*				
Horses *d*	**534.3**	*808.0*				
Pigs *d*	**1 523.0**	*1 162.7*	**0.2**	*0.5*	—	—
Bacon/ham	**1 689.7***	*1 211.7*	**0.1**	*0.9*	—	—
Meat‡ 'A'			**383.0**	*202.9*	**2.0**	—
'B'	**177.4***	*134.1*	**33.2**	*31.9*	**0.2**	—
Butter	**206.7**	*175.3*	**90.0**	*56.7*	—	—
Cheese	**60.3**	*47.7*	**27.4**	*22.3*	**2.9**	*0.6*
Eggs	**149.7**	*115.9*	**2.5**	*12.9*	—	—
Fish	**75.7***q*	*52.7q*	**13.1**	na	**42.6**	na
Milk	**6 988.0**	*5 790.3*	**410.1**	*341.4*	—	*0.1*
Whale/sperm oil	**4.8**	*16.9*	—	—	—	—
Hides/skins	na	*59.0p*	**90.5***a*	*42.7a*	—	*1.1*[2]
Wool	**451.2**	*332.0*	**387.4**	*299.0*	**3.5**	*2.1*

a million $ U.S. *d* no. in thousands. *n* cows and heifers over one year old. *p* from sheep only. *q* recorded commercial catch only.

6. FIBRES, TEXTILES, etc.

	Production		Exports		Imports	
Abaca	—	—	—	—	**0.7**	*0.2*[2]
Agaves (sisal etc.)	—	—	—	—	**20.5**	*13.7*
Cotton lint	**10.7**	*1.0*	—	—	**23.4**	*19.2*
Flax fibre	**0.2***	*2.8*	—	—	**2.3**	*0.3*
Hemp fibre	—	—	—	—	**0.2**	*1.2*
Jute	—	—	—	—	**7.0**	*4.6*
Rubber: natural	—	—	—	—	**38.0**	*43.3*
synthetic	**19.0**	—	—	—	**16.3**	*1.0*
Silk *f*	—	—	—	—	**2.3**	*10.0*[2]
Cotton: yarn	**25.2**	*17.1n*	—	—	**2.3**	*2.6*
woven fabrics	**6.6***	*3.6*	—	—	**33.2**	*27.6*
Rayon: fibre/yarn	**7.0**[2]	*2.0*	**0.1**[2]	na	**8.3**[2]	*6.5*
woven fabrics	**3.0**	*2.5p*	—	—	**3.5***q*	*4.4*
Non-cellulosic fibre/yarn	**6.6***	na	**1.0**	na	**7.4**	na
Wool: yarn	**24.0**	*18.8*	**0.1**	—	**0.5**	*0.1*
woven fabrics	**13.2***t*	*25.2u*	—	—	—	—

f metric tons. *n* incl. tyre cord. *p* incl. mixture piece goods. *q* incl. synthetic piece goods. *t* weight of yarns consumed in weaving. *u* million square metres.

7. FUEL AND POWER

	Production		Exports		Imports	
Coal 'A'‡	**27 190**	*19 580*	**4 245***n*	*344n*	**10**[2]	*71*[2]
'B'	**6 500**	*10 270*	—	—	—	—
Coke	na	na	**74**	*23*	**40**	*6*
Electricity *h*: total	**32 494**	*13 910*				
hydro	**7 783**	*2 000*				
thermal	**24 710**	*11 910*				
Oil, crude	**177**	—[1]	—	—	**15 423**	*4 850*[1]
Petroleum, refined	**14 816**	*4 750*[1]	**1 670**	*180*[1]	**1 390**	*4 290*[1]
Rare earths *f*	**1 994***p*	*137pq*	**2 233**	*123*	—	—
Uranium *f*	**609**[2]	na	—	—	—	—

f metric tons. *h* million kWh. *n* incl. a small quantity in bunkers. *p* monazite content of high-grade concentrates. *q* in addition, 74 metric tons of low-grade concentrates.

8. IRON AND STEEL

	Production		Exports		Imports	
Iron ore	**3 898***m*	*2 273m*	**138**	na	**286**	*1*
Pig iron	**4 033**	*1 862*	**99**	*114*	**27**	*6*
Steel ingots/castings	**5 054**	*2 186*	**17**	*65*	**18**	*1*
Iron/steel scrap	na	na	**318**	*77*	—	—[1]
Iron/steel products *a*	na	na	**104**	*21*	**177**	*82*

a million $ U.S. *m* metal content.

9. NON-FERROUS MINERALS AND METALS

	Production		Exports		Imports	
Diamonds	na	—	**0.01***a*	*0.02a*	**4.48***a*	*2.38*
Gold *k*: ore *m*	**955.00**	*1 081.00*	**50.47**	*12.03*	—	—
bullion etc.	na	na	**479.09**	*993.20*	**144.71**	*197.69*
Platinum group metals *k*	—	*0.03*	**0.46**	*0.51*	**5.05**	*4.91*
Silver *k*: ore *m*	**18 450.00**	*13 595.00*	**3 184.03**	*1 725.55*	**1.88**	*2.07*[2]
bullion	na	na	**6 792.27**	*9 673.89*	**104.46**	*89.25*
Asbestos: fibre‡	**116.62**	*5.09*	**4.45**	*2.44*	**39.69**	*33.15*
manufactured	na	na	**233.84***n*	*34.84n*	**1 634.04***n*	*875.65n*
Mica	**0.62**	*0.52*	**56.34***np*	*24.25np*	**23.18***np*	*56.64np*

continued

9. NON-FERROUS MINERALS AND METALS—*continued*

	Production		Exports		Imports	
Aluminium:						
bauxite	**781.00**	*5.80*	**392.78**	*0.03*	**11.10**	*3.31*
alumina	**136.73**	na	—	—	**60.82***q*	na
aluminium	**69.90**	*1.27*[1]	**15.70**	*0.66*	**9.41**	*14.00**
Antimony: ore	**0.13***m*	*0.22m*	na	*0.10*	**0.04**	*0.77*
metal	na	na	na	*0.01*	**0.50**	*0.02*
Beryl	**0.09**	*0.16*	**0.09**	*0.17*	—	—
Cadmium	**0.51**	*0.30*	**0.38**	*0.20*	—	—
Chrome: ore	**0.08***m*	*2.60m*	—	—	**19.11**	*5.22*
metal	na	na	—	—	**3.92**	*1.52*
Cobalt: ore	**0.02***m*	*0.01m*	—	—	na	*0.07*[2]
metal	na	na	—	—	**0.09**	*0.93*
Copper: ore	**104.62***m*	*41.67m*	**15.17***m*	*2.30m*	—	*0.03*
metal	**82.13**	*37.14*	**35.00**	*8.60*	**18.98**	*21.26*
Lead: ore	**388.57***m*	*279.65m*	**93.59***m*	*41.29*	—	—
metal	**287.13**	*226.78*	**248.89***t*	*208.45t*	**1.13**	*0.02*
Magnesium:						
dolomite	**240.15**	na	—	—	na	na
magnesite	**38.80**	na	**1.23**	*0.09*	**32.37**	*1.46*
metal/salts	na	na	na	*0.05*	**1.04**	*1.03*
Manganese:						
ore	**67.43**	*36.75*	**36.22**	*6.25*	**60.03**	*1.54*
metal	na	na	—	—	**9.65**	*1.02*
Mercury *f*	—	—	—	—	**69.20**	*38.70*
Molybdenum *f*:						
ore	**6.35***m*	*0.60m*	na	*0.07*[2]	—	—
metal	na	na	—	—	**276.40**	*118.30*[2]
Nickel: ore	na	na	—	—	**0.61**	na
metal	na	na	**0.19**	na	**2.26**	*1.00*
Tin: ore	**3.49***m*	*1.91m*	**0.39***m*	*0.03m*	—	—
metal	**2.99**	*1.87*	**0.02**	*0.32*	**1.59**	*0.55*
Titanium minerals	**518.35**	*48.71u*	**456.10**	*47.71*	**4.30**	*15.56*
Tungsten: ore	**1.77**	*2.42*	**1.47**	*2.16*	—	—
metal	na	na	—	—	**0.03**	na
Zinc: ore *m*	**354.02**	*252.74*	**134.08**	na	na	*129.69*
metal	**191.12**	*100.18*	**92.30**	*40.16*	**2.04**	*1.59*
Zirconium minerals	**200.93**	*39.28*	**201.52**	*38.74*	—	—

a million $ U.S. *f* metric tons. *k* '000 fine troy oz. *m* metal content. *n* '000 $ U.S. *p* incl. a small quantity of manufactures. *q* incl. hydrate. *t* incl. lead content of base bullion. *u* sales only.

10. CHEMICALS*n* AND FERTILIZERS

	Production		Exports		Imports	
Organic chemicals:						
Benzene	na		na		na	
Butadiene	na		—		na	
Ethylene	na		na		na	
Methanol	na		—		**4.8**[2]	
Phenol	na		—		**0.3**	
Phthalic anhydride	na		—		**1.3**	
Styrene monomer	na		na		na	
Urea	na		—		**38.5**[1]*t*	
Inorganic chemicals:						
Ammonia	na		na		na	
Carbon black	na		—		**4.0**	
Chlorine	**43.5**[1]		—		na	
Nitric acid	**19.8**[1]		**0.1**[2]		—	
Sodium carbonate	na		**1.9**		**5.4**	
Sodium hydroxide	**64.3**		**1.7**		**6.8**	
Sulphuric acid	**138.3**		**0.1**		—[1]	
Plastics:						
Polyamides	na		—		na	
Polyethylene	**16.0**[1]		—		**10.9**	
Polyvinyl chloride	**14.0**[2]		na		na	
Fertilizers:						
Phosphates	**820.9***p*	*350.9p*	**815.8***p*	*345.9p*	**2 101.2**	*1 185.9*
Potash	—	—	—	—	**92.2**	*23.1*
Pyrites	**92.8***x*	*95.3x*	—	—	—	—
Sulphur	na	na	**60.0***q*	*63.9q*	**334.3**	*175.0*

n data not available for years 1953–5. *p* mainly from Christmas Is. *q* sulphur content of zinc concentrates. *t* year 1965–6. *x* sulphur content.

11. INDUSTRY

	Production		Exports		Imports	
Aircraft *a*	na	na	na	*1.2*	**68.4**	*17.9*
Alcoholic beverages			—	*3.8a*	**11.6***a*	*4.5a*
beer *b*	**11 921.0**	*9 434.3*				
spirits *b*	**91.2**[1]*n*	*66.7*[1]*p*				
Cement	**3 518.0**	*1 823.7*	**4.7**	*26.0*	**52.3**	*95.7*
Electrical engineering *a*	**558.0**[1]	na	**21.9**	*6.4*[2]	**167.2**	*76.8*[2]
Locomotives *c*	**54.0***	na	—	—	na	na
Railway vehicles *a*	na	na	na	*0.3*	na	*17.2*
Machine tools *a*	**35.0**	na	na	*0.3*[2]	**34.8**	*12.6*[2]
Merchant ships *g*	**33.0**	*19.0*	na	na	na	na
Motor vehicles			**38.0***a*	*5.4*[2]*a*	**290.4***a*	*170.9*[2]*a*
commercial *d*	**62.9***q*	*52.5q*				
private *d*	**291.8***q*	*226.3qt*				

a million $ U.S. *b* '000 hectolitres. *c* no. of units. *d* no. in thousands. *g* '000 G.R.T. *n* production for home consumption 1966/7. *p* 1960/1 figure. *q* incl. assembly of imported parts. *t* motor vehicle chassis and bodies only.

AUSTRALIA (TERRITORIES)

PAPUA AND NEW GUINEA

EAST INDIES

Papua and New Guinea were joined in an administrative union in 1949 as an international trusteeship under Australian administration.

AREA: 461 700 sq. km. (178 300 sq. miles)

LAND USE: (percentage of total)	*1953*
Arable and orchard	0.2
Forest and woodland	69.4
City areas, waste and other land	30.4

POPULATION: 2 129 036 (1966 census)
Largest city: PORT MORESBY, capital; population: 42 133 (1966)
Total working population: 80 000 (1964)

		Year
Infant mortality (per '000)	10.2*a*	1965
Crude birth rate (per '000)	29.0*a*	1965
Crude death rate (per '000)	3.6	1965

continued

		Year(s)
Population per physician	10 040*b*	1965
Population per hospital bed	120*b*	1966
School enrolment: age 5–19 years (percentage)	47	1963–4 av.
age over 19 years (per 100 000 population)	17	1963–5 av.

a non-indigenous population only. *b* Papua only.

COMMUNICATIONS

		Year(s)
Motor vehicles in use ('000s): private	56.7	1963–5 av.
commercial	5.4	1963–5 av.
Telephones (per '000 urban population)	0.6	1967

FINANCE
Currency unit: The Australian dollar

		Year
National Income (million $ U.S.)	300*	1966
G.N.P. per capita ($ U.S.)	140	1966

TRADING: PAPUA

Total trade (in million $ U.S.)	*1965*	*1955*	*1938*
Exports (f.o.b.)	10	6	1
Imports (f.o.b.)	37	17	2

Main trading partners (percentage of total value)

Exports	*1965*	*1955*	*Imports*	*1965*	*1955*
Australia	76	79	Australia	62	68
U.K.	13	19	U.S.A.	9	11
Japan	3	1	U.K.	7	8
			Japan	6	1

Distribution of trade (percentage of total value)

Exports	*1965a*	*1956a*
Copra	46	47
Rubber	42	47
Crocodile skins	6	na
Imports		
Manufactured goods	59	59
(machinery and transport equipment)	(26)	(27)
(textiles and clothing)	(6)	(6)
Food	21	21
(meat)	(6)	(6)
Chemicals	6	6
Crude materials and fuels	5	6

a % of national exports‡ which comprised 68% of general exports in 1965 and 88% in 1956.

TRADING: NEW GUINEA

Total trade (in million $ U.S.)	*1965*	*1955*	*1938*
Exports (f.o.b.)	44	20	4
Imports (c.i.f.)	61	21	7

Main trading partners (percentage of total value)

Exports	*1965*	*1955*	*Imports*	*1965*	*1955*
Australia	40	32	Australia	54	61
U.K.	35	60	Japan	10	5
Germany F.R.	7	–	U.K.	8	7
Netherlands	4	–	U.S.A.	6	10
Japan	4	1	Hong Kong	5	5
U.S.A.	3	6	Germany F.R.	4	2

Distribution of trade (percentage of total value)

Exports	*1965a*	*1956a*	*Imports*	*1965a*	*1956a*
Copra/coconut oil	45	75	Manufactured goods	58	52
Coffee	20	1	(machinery and transport equipment)	(25)	(19)
Cocoa	19	4	(textiles and clothing)	(9)	(9)
Wood	10	13	Food	23	24
			Chemicals	7	8
			Crude materials and fuels	4	6
			Beverages and tobacco	4	6

a % of national exports‡ which comprised 93% of general exports in 1965 and 94% in 1956.

PRODUCTION, EXPORTS AND IMPORTS

Years: **1963–5 average** and *1953–5 average* Units: '000 metric tons unless otherwise indicated

	Production		Exports		Imports	
1. CEREALS, etc.						
Potatoes	—	—	—	—	**0.9**	—
Rice	—	—	—	—	**25.1**	*13.1*
Sweet potatoes/yams	**12.7***	*8.0*				
Wheat	—	—	—	—	**0.1**	—
2. FRUIT, etc.						
Apples	—	—	—	—	**0.3**	—
Bananas	**1.0***	—	—	—	—	—
Coconuts	**643.3***e	—	**0.3**	*0.8*	—	—
Grapes	—	—	—	—	**0.1**	—
Oranges	—	—	—	—	**0.2**	—
Wine *b*	—	—	—	—	**1.8**	—

b '000 hectolitres. *e* no. in millions.

	Production		Exports		Imports	
3. BEVERAGES, FOREST PRODUCTS, etc.						
Cocoa	**17.4**	*1.3**	**16.9**	*0.8*	—	—
Coffee	**3.3***	—	**6.9**	—	—	—
Sugar, raw	—	—	—	—	**8.4**	*3.8*
Tea	—	—	—	—	**0.3**	*0.2*
Tobacco: leaf	—	—	—	—	**0.5**	na
products	—	—	—	—	na	—
Softwood *j*	**92.3***	*81.0*	**15.0**	*16.1*[1]	—	—
Hardwood *j*	**3 873.0***	*78.0**	**72.3**	*12.5*	**0.7**	*1.5*
Paper	—	—	—	—	—	na

j '000 cu. metres of roundwood equivalent.

	Production		Exports		Imports	
4. VEGETABLE OILSEEDS AND OILS						
Copra	**113.63**	*93.30*	**72.93**	*81.46*	—	—
Coconut oil	na	na	**23.80**	*7.60*	—	—
Groundnuts	**1.00***	na	**1.82**	na	—	—
Groundnut oil	—	—	—	—	**0.06**	na
Linseed oil	—	—	—	—	**0.04**	*0.02*
5. LIVESTOCK‡, ANIMAL PRODUCTS, etc.						
Chickens *d*	**77.4***	*29.0*[2]				
Cattle *d*	**31.0**	*7.4n*	—	—	**0.8**	*0.5*
Goats *d*	**2.0**	*4.0n*	—	—	—	—
Sheep *d*	—	*1.7*	—	—	—	—
Horses *d*	**1.0**	*1.0*				
Pigs *d*	**4.0**	*4.6n*	—	—	—	—

continued

	Production		Exports		Imports	
5. LIVESTOCK‡, ANIMAL PRODUCTS, etc.—*continued*						
Bacon/ham	—	—	—	—	**0.2**	—
Meat‡ 'A'	—	—	—	—	**1.8**	*0.7*[2]
'B'	—	—	—	—	**0.3**	—
Butter	—	—	—	—	**0.4**	*0.2*
Cheese	—	—	—	—	**0.2**	—
Eggs	**0.2***	—	—	—	—	—
Fish	na	*0.9*	—	—	**5.3**	na
Milk	**1.0**	—	—	—	**5.6**	*2.4**

d no. in thousands. *n* on farms only.

	Production		Exports		Imports	
6. FIBRES, TEXTILES, etc.						
Rubber, natural	**5.3**	na	**5.1**	*3.6*	—	—
7. FUEL AND POWER						
Electricity *h*: total	**75**	*19*				
hydro	**51**	*10*				
thermal	**24**	*9*				
Petroleum, refined	—	—	—	—	**93**	*50*[1]

h million kWh.

	Production		Exports		Imports	
9. NON-FERROUS MINERALS AND METALS						
Gold *k*: ore *m*	**38.30**	*94.00*	—	—	—	—
bullion/coins etc.	na	na	**39.65**	*105.59*	—	—
Platinum group: metals *k*	—	*0.01*	—	—	—	—
Silver *k*: ore *m*	**22.30**	*50.70*	—	—	—	—
bullion	na	na	na	*54.09*	—	—
Manganese, ore	—	*0.02*	—[2]	*0.07*	—	—

k '000 fine troy oz. *m* metal content.

	Production		Exports		Imports	
11. INDUSTRY						
Aircraft *a*	—	—	—	—	**1.5**	na
Cement	—	—	—	—	**36.3**	*11.3*
Electrical engineering *a*	—	—	—	—	**3.8**	na
Motor vehicles *a*	—	—	—	—	**4.3**	na

a million $ U.S.

continued

na: data not available. — negligible or nil. [1] one year only. [2] two year average. * estimate. ‡ see appendix. † re-exports.

COCOS ISLANDS

INDIAN OCEAN

The Cocos or Keeling Islands were originally incorporated with Singapore but from 1942–6 were temporarily placed under the control of Ceylon. In 1955 they were transferred to the Commonwealth of Australia. Their chief value is as a cable and wireless centre, a civil aviation and marine base, and as a meteorological station.

AREA: 14 sq. km. (5.5 sq. miles)
The islands are thickly covered with coconut palms.

POPULATION: 684 (1966 census)
Total working population: 282

NORFOLK ISLAND

PACIFIC OCEAN

AREA: 33 sq. km. (13 sq. miles)

LAND USE: (percentage of total)	*1965*	*1955*
Arable and orchard	5.5	5.7
Permanent meadow and pasture	41.7	40.0
Forest and woodland	13.9	11.4
City areas, waste and other land	38.9	42.9

POPULATION: 1 152 (1966 census)
Largest town: KINGSTON
Total working population: 311 (1961)

EMPLOYMENT AND TRADE
The chief products are citrus fruit, bananas and vegetables. Cattle are reared, and a programme of forestry has been undertaken. Tourism is the major industry. Trade, which includes the export of fish, is mainly with Australia.

AUSTRIA

EUROPE

Austria was overrun by the Germans in 1938 and liberated in 1945. Sovereignty and independence were not fully recovered until 1955. Austria is a member of the European Free Trade Association.

AREA: 83 849 sq. km. (32 366 sq. miles)

LAND USE: (percentage of total)	*1965*	*1955*
Arable and orchard	20.6	21.1
Permanent meadow and pasture	26.9	27.6
Forest and woodland	37.9	36.2
City areas, waste and other land	14.6	15.1

POPULATION: 7 323 000 (1967 estimate)
Largest city: WIEN (Vienna), capital; population: 1 638 100 (1966)

Distribution of working population (1961)
Total working population: 3 369 815

U.N. group no.		*Percentage*
0	Agriculture, forestry, fishing and hunting	22.8
1	Mining and quarrying	1.5
2/3	Manufacturing	28.6
4	Construction	9.9
5	Electricity, gas, water and sanitary services	1.0
6	Commerce	10.9
7	Transport, storage and communications	5.9
8	Services	18.3
9	Others	1.1

		Year(s)
Life expectancy at birth (years): male	66.57	1967
female	73.41	1967
Infant mortality (per '000)	28.3	1965
Crude birth rate (per '000)	17.9	1965
Crude death rate (per '000)	13.0	1965
Accidental deaths (per 100,000 population) caused by motor vehicles	24.6	1965
due to other causes	42.9	1965
Population per physician	550	1966
Population per hospital bed	90	1966
School enrolment: age 5–19 years (percentage)	69	1963–4 av.
age over 19 years (per 100 000 population)	677	1964–5 av.

COMMUNICATIONS

		Year(s)
Motor vehicles in use ('000s): private	706.8	1963–5 av.
commercial	280.0	1963–5 av.
Railway track (km.)	6 601	1964
Mail per capita: domestic	112	1963–5 av.
foreign received	19	1963–5 av.
foreign sent	19	1963–5 av.
Telephones (per '000 urban population)	14.88	1967
Radio licences (per '000 population)	296	1963–5 av.
Television licences (per '000 population)	81.37	1963–5 av.
Daily newspapers (per '000 population)	239	1962–4 av.

FINANCE
Currency unit: The schilling

Exchange rates	*1965*	*1960*	*1950*	*1938*
Per $ U.S.	25.89	26.04	21.49	5.41
Per £ sterling	72.57	73.01	60.20	24.89

		Year(s)
National Income (million $ U.S.)	7 035	1965
G.N.P. per capita ($ U.S.)	1 150	1966
Rate of increase of G.N.P. per capita	3.5	1960–4 av.
Foreign trade (percentage of G.D.P.)	39	1963–5 av.

TRADING

Total trade (in million $ U.S.)	*1965*	*1955*	*1937*
Exports (f.o.b.)	1 600	699	228
Imports (c.i.f.)	2 100	887	273

Main trading partners (percentage of total value)

Exports	*1965*	*1955*	*1937*	*Imports*	*1965*	*1955*	*1937*
Germany F.R.	29	25	15*d*	Germany F.R.	42	35	16*d*
Italy	11	17	14	Italy	8	8	6
Switzerland	7	5	5	Switzerland	6	4	3
U.S.A.	4	5	3	U.K.	5	4	5
U.K.	4	4	5	U.S.A.	4	11	6
Netherlands	4	4	2	France	4	5	3
U.S.S.R.	4	1	na	Netherlands	3	3	2

Distribution of trade (percentage of total value)

Exports	*1965*	*1955*	*1938**
Manufactured goods	74	51	na
(machinery and transport equipment)	(20)	(10)	(8)
(iron and steel)	(13)	(12)	(7)
(textiles)	(8)	(16)	(15)
Crude materials and fuels	16	23	na
(wood)	(8)	(16)	(14)
Food	5	1	na
Chemicals	5	3	na
Imports			
Manufactured goods	59	43	na
(machinery and transport equipment)	(30)	(22)	(4)
(textiles)	(8)	(6)	(5)
Crude materials and fuels	17	28	na
Food	12	19	na

d incl. Germany D.R.

na: data not available. — negligible or nil. [1] one year only. [2] two year average. * estimate. ‡ see appendix. † re-exports.

PRODUCTION, EXPORTS AND IMPORTS

Years: **1963–5 average** and *1953–5 average*   Units: '000 metric tons unless otherwise indicated

1. CEREALS, etc.

	Production 1963–5	Production 1953–5	Exports 1963–5	Exports 1953–5	Imports 1963–5	Imports 1953–5
Barley	581.7	*326.0*	0.2	—	220.1	*52.1*
Maize (corn)	197.7	*150.7*	1.5	*1.7*	387.6	*332.8*
Millets/sorghum	1.7	*2.3*	—	—	12.2	*5.2*
Oats	314.3	*352.7*	—	—	18.7	*4.1*
Potatoes	3 158.7	*3 030.3*	7.2	*13.4*	36.3	*30.0*
Rice	—	—	—	—	35.8	*28.4*
Rye	342.0	*402.3*	—	—	15.1	*50.7*
Wheat	700.7	*500.0*	—	—	61.9	*266.6*

2. FRUIT, etc.

	Production 1963–5	Production 1953–5	Exports 1963–5	Exports 1953–5	Imports 1963–5	Imports 1953–5
Apples	368.3	*273.0*	1.9	*1.0*	45.1	*23.0*
Apricots	22.7	*8.8*	na	na	—	*1.7*
Bananas	—	—	—	—	40.2	*6.4*
Cherries	30.3	*25.4*	na	na	—	*2.1*
Dates	—	—	—	—	0.5	*0.3*
Figs	—	—	—	—	na	*6.7*
Grapes	258.7*	*156.0**	—	—	27.2	*8.1*
Lemons	—	—	—	—	23.2	*12.4*
Oranges	—	—	—	—	74.4	*30.0*
Other citrus fruit	—	—	—	—	1.6	*0.3*[1]
Peaches	8.3	*4.4*	na	na	na	*6.1*
Pears	213.3	*158.7*	—	—	17.8	*14.2*
Plums	8.5	*63.7*	na	na	na	*7.7*
Raisins	—	—	—	—	4.8	*4.6*
Tomatoes	11.0	*5.0*				
Wine *b*	1 816.3	*1 088.7*	20.7	*16.7*	357.7	*85.7*

b '000 hectolitres.

3. BEVERAGES, FOREST PRODUCTS, etc.

	Production 1963–5	Production 1953–5	Exports 1963–5	Exports 1953–5	Imports 1963–5	Imports 1953–5
Cocoa	—	—	—	—	11.3	*7.0*
Coffee	—	—	0.1†	—	16.4	*5.0*
Sugar: beet	1 918.3	*1 280.7*				
raw	297.9	*201.7*	—	*0.3*	16.6	*42.2*
Tea	—	—	—	—	0.7	*0.4*
Tobacco: leaf	0.7	*0.7*	0.4	*0.8*	11.1	*9.2*
cigars	89.0*e*	*77.3e*				
cigarettes	10 027.0*e*	*6 910.3e*	— (cigars, cigarettes, tobacco/snuff)	—[2]	0.7	*0.1*[2]
tobacco/snuff	0.8	*1.3*				
Softwood *j*	9 133.0	*9 266.3*	4 782.0	*5 092.7*	35.3	*4.8*
Hardwood *j*	1 464.3	*1 465.3*	120.3	*105.8*	311.9	*9.4*
Wood pulp	715.8	*490.7*	154.0	*153.3*	39.5	*11.0*
Newsprint	134.0	*104.7*	60.7	*81.0*	—	*0.1*
Other paper	550.7	*335.7*	255.7	*159.3*	36.6	*5.6*

e no. in millions. *j* '000 cu. metres of roundwood equivalent.

4. VEGETABLE OILSEEDS AND OILS

	Production 1963–5	Production 1953–5	Exports 1963–5	Exports 1953–5	Imports 1963–5	Imports 1953–5
Castor oil	—	—	—	—	1.08	*0.45*
Copra	—	—	—	—	1.04	*1.35*[2]
Coconut oil	—	—	0.01	—	9.97	*2.97n*
Cottonseed	—	—	—	—	0.01	na
Cottonseed oil	—	—	—	—	2.54	*2.44*
Groundnuts	—	—	—	—	1.91	—
Groundnut oil	—	—	—	—	8.19	*2.85*
Linseed	—	—	—	—	0.40	*0.13*
Linseed oil	—	—	—	—	3.87	*4.42*
Olive oil	—	—	—	—	0.44	*0.90*
Palm kernels	—	—	—	—	0.33	—
Palm kernel oil	—	—	—	—	1.20	*1.36*
Palm oil	—	—	—	—	1.15	*0.99*
Rapeseed	10.00	*8.30*	5.05	—	1.14	*0.60*
Rapeseed oil	na	na	—	—	5.70	*0.36*
Sesame seed	na	na	—	—	—	—
Soya beans	—	—	—	—	0.18	—
Soya bean oil	—	—	—	—	11.97	*5.46*
Sunflower seed	3.00	na	0.73	na	4.82	*2.03*
Sunflower seed oil	na	na	—	—	21.60	*4.45*
Tung oil	—	—	—	—	0.22	*0.27*

n incl. refined palm kernel oil

5. LIVESTOCK‡, ANIMAL PRODUCTS, etc.

	Production 1963–5	Production 1953–5	Exports 1963–5	Exports 1953–5	Imports 1963–5	Imports 1953–5
Chickens *d*	10 348.3	*6 655.0*				
Cattle *d*	2 366.0	*2 317.0*	109.5	*21.4*	1.5	*6.5*
dairy cows *d*	1 240.7	*1 193.7*				
Goats *d*	121.0	*296.3*	5.9 (goats and sheep)	na	0.7	na
Sheep *d*	148.3	*298.0*				
Horses *d*	109.0	*237.0*				
Pigs *d*	2 969.0	*2 715.7*	11.8	*5.9*	116.4	*62.6*
Bacon/ham			—	—	—	*0.8*
Meat‡ 'A'	465.7 (bacon/ham and meat 'A')	*287.0*	3.0	*1.4*	7.7	*1.2*
'B'	46.6	*17.6*	1.9	*0.6*	15.2	*0.9*
Butter	42.3	*30.7*	4.6	*1.0*	0.7	*0.7*
Cheese	44.7	*21.7*	10.1	*2.3*	3.4	*1.5*
Eggs	85.8	*48.0*	—	—	15.0	*1.5*
Fish	4.9	*2.0*	0.4	*0.3**	58.2	*20.2**
Milk	3 128.7	*2 498.7*	149.0	—	12.4	*3.7**
Hides/skins	21.6	*17.2*	5.4	*2.3*[2]	13.3	*8.3*[2]
Wool	0.3	—	0.2	—	5.2	—

d no. in thousands.

6. FIBRES, TEXTILES, etc.

	Production 1963–5	Production 1953–5	Exports 1963–5	Exports 1953–5	Imports 1963–5	Imports 1953–5
Agaves (sisal etc.)	—	—	—	—	7.0	*2.3*
Cotton lint	—	—	0.1†	*0.4†*	24.8	*21.1*
Flax fibre	na	*0.5*	0.2	*0.2*	4.5	*1.6*
Hemp fibre	na	*0.5*	0.1	*0.6*	1.9	*3.2*
Jute	—	—	0.3†	—	5.3	*7.0*
Rubber: natural	—	—	—	—	12.0	*10.0*
synthetic	—	—	—	—	15.0	na
Silk *f*	—	—	—	*1.7†*	0.3	*22.7*
Cotton: yarn	25.1	*21.1*	1.1	*0.8*	5.3	*0.7*
woven fabrics	18.8	*13.8*	3.5	*1.4*	7.7	*1.7*
Rayon: fibre/yarn	64.2	*36.7*	43.4	*13.8*	4.9	*4.3*
woven fabrics	13.4	*10.5*	7.2	*3.9n*	2.2	*0.3n*
Non-cellulosic fibre/yarn	0.1	na	0.7	na	9.0	na
Wool: yarn	13.3	*11.1*	2.2	*1.1*	3.3	*1.2*
woven fabrics	7.4	*6.2*	1.0*p*	*0.5*	2.8*p*	*0.7*

f metric tons. *n* spun rayon cloth only. *p* excl. velvet and woven felt.

7. FUEL AND POWER

	Production 1963–5	Production 1953–5	Exports 1963–5	Exports 1953–5	Imports 1963–5	Imports 1953–5
Coal 'A'‡	87	*170*	—	—	4 435	*4 360*
'B'	2 877	*6 620*	16	*23*	108	*200*
Coke	na	na	1	—	946	*349*
Electricity *h*: total	20 348	*9 790*[1]				
hydro	13 739	*7 200*[1]				
thermal	6 609	*2 590*[1]				
Natural gas *i*	1 730	*435*	—	—	—	—
Oil, crude	2 710	*3 660*[1]	180	*1 450*[1]	810	na
Petroleum, refined	3 103	*2 060*[1]	180	*150*[1]	1 740	*330*[1]
Rare earths *f*	—	—	—	—	669*u*	*79u*

f metric tons. *h* million kWh. *i* million cu. metres. *u* incl. uranium salts.

8. IRON AND STEEL

	Production 1963–5	Production 1953–5	Exports 1963–5	Exports 1953–5	Imports 1963–5	Imports 1953–5
Iron ore	1 139*m*	*866m*	—	*93*	1 437	*847*
Pig iron	2 174	*1 394*	21	*383*	217	*18*
Steel ingots/castings	3 121	*1 587*	6	*55*	14	*8*
Iron/steel scrap	na	na	4	*6*	102	*59*
Iron/steel products *a*	na	na	204	*92*	60	*18*

a million $ U.S. *m* metal content.

9. NON-FERROUS MINERALS AND METALS

	Production 1963–5	Production 1953–5	Exports 1963–5	Exports 1953–5	Imports 1963–5	Imports 1953–5
Gold *k*, bullion/coins etc.	—	—	—	—	626.67‡	na
Platinum group metals *k*	na	na	0.56	*5.21*	2.72	*3.58*
Silver *k*: ore *m*	73.30	*5.00*	—	—	—	—
bullion	na	na	—	—	3 791.67	*491.67*
Asbestos: fibre	0.19	na	0.06	—	24.62	*8.24*
manufactured	na	na	14.01	*1.85*	7.94	*0.16*
Mica	na	na	0.02	*0.13*	0.34	*0.17*
Aluminium: bauxite	11.18[2]	*18.21*	3.08	*8.87*	18.10	*6.54*
alumina	15.00*	na	—	—	158.74*n*	*96.92p*
aluminium	77.66	*49.56*	59.14	*31.70*	7.94	*3.06*
Antimony: ore	0.47*m*	*0.43m*	0.80	*0.63*	—	—
metal	na	na	0.28	na	0.18	*0.11*
Cadmium	0.02	na	—	—	0.01	na
Chrome: ore	na	na	0.64	*2.05*	46.22	*59.07*
metal	—	—	—	—	14.34	*6.08*
Copper: ore	1.66*m*	*2.87m*	na	*0.45*	0.42	*0.01*
metal	14.63	*9.68*	11.39	*1.72*	31.88	*14.80*
Lead: ore	5.08*m*	*4.96m*	—	—	4.56	*4.91*
metal	7.54	*11.82*	3.44	*3.61*	13.16	*6.88*
Magnesium: dolomite	—	—	31.45	*1.76*	2.92	*0.83*
magnesite	1 595.00	na	226.09	*101.73*	25.89	*0.43*
kieserite	na	na	—	—	na	*6.76*
metal/salts	na	na	202.37	*224.40*	2.17	*2.68*
Manganese: ore	—	—	—	—	0.76	*16.23*
metal	—	—	—	—	13.71	*4.39*
Mercury *f*	na	*0.75*	—	—	20.20	*20.60*
Molybdenum *f*, metal	—	*2.72*	—	—	369.80	*67.50*
Nickel: ore	—	—	—	—	0.35	na
metal	—	—	—	—	3.23	*1.34*
Tin, metal	na	na	na	*0.04*	0.72	*0.47*
Titanium minerals	—	—	—	—	4.80	*1.14*
Tungsten: ore	0.17	—	0.16	na	3.18	*0.52*
metal	—	—	—	—	0.19	*0.16*
Zinc: ore	7.09*m*	*4.76m*	0.55	*8.22*	12.95	*4.86*
metal	12.60	*0.45*	6.73	*5.50*	8.44	*8.01*

f metric tons. *k* '000 fine troy oz. *m* metal content. *n* hydrate. *p* calcined.

continued

na: data not available. — negligible or nil. [1] one year only. [2] two year average. * estimate. ‡ see appendix. † re-exports.

PRODUCTION, EXPORTS AND IMPORTS *continued*

10. CHEMICALS*n* AND FERTILIZERS

	Production	Exports	Imports
Organic chemicals:			
Benzene	na	9.0	0.5
Butadiene	—	—	na
Ethylene	—	—	na
Methanol	na	3.0	2.3
Phenol	na	—	1.6
Phthalic anhydride	na	na	1.8
Styrene monomer	—	—	na
Urea	na	na	0.9
Inorganic chemicals:			
Ammonia	na	na	1.0
Carbon black	—	—	9.2
Chlorine	na	1.4	0.1
Nitric acid	na	na	—
Sodium carbonate	na	1.0	2.4
Sodium hydroxide	na	0.5	0.4
Sulphuric acid	208.7	9.1	20.6
Plastics:			
Polyamides	—	—	na
Polyethylene	—	—	14.4
Polyvinyl chloride	15.7	6.5*	6.7

10. CHEMICALS AND FERTILIZERS—*continued*

	Production 1963–5	Production 1953–5	Exports 1963–5	Exports 1953–5	Imports 1963–5	Imports 1953–5
Fertilizers:						
Phosphates	—	—	—	—	233.5	*27.7*
Potash	—	—	—	—	305.4	*117.0*
Pyrites	na	—	—	*39.1†*	27.5	*93.6*
Sulphur	—	—	—	—	96.8	*22.5*

n data not available for years 1953–5.

11. INDUSTRY

	Production 1963–5	Production 1953–5	Exports 1963–5	Exports 1953–5	Imports 1963–5	Imports 1953–5
Aircraft *a*	na	na	3.6	—[2]	8.4	na
Alcoholic beverages			na	*0.6a*	8.3*a*	*1.7a*
beer *b*	6 655.0	*4 201.0*				
spirits *b*	185.0[1]*n*	*456.9*[1]*p*				
Cement	3 724.3	*1 620.3*	25.0	*24.0*	15.7	*12.7*
Electrical engineering *a*	270.5[2]	na	88.1	*18.3*[2]	111.0	*24.8*[2]
Locomotives *c*	134.0[2]*	na	na	na	na	na
Railway vehicles *a*	na	na	8.3	*6.0*	na	*1.9*
Machine tools *a*	14.0	na	9.4	*1.7*[2]	27.8	*7.4*[2]
Motor vehicles			21.5*a*	*12.3a*	166.8*a*	*53.4*[2]*a*
commercial *d*	4.7	*5.2q*				
private *d*	5.9	*8.1q*				

a million $ U.S. *b* '000 hectolitres. *c* no. of units. *d* no. in thousands. *n* 1966 figure. *p* 1959–60 figure. *q* incl. assembly of imported parts.

BAHAMAS

WEST ATLANTIC

The Bahamas, a British colony, was granted internal self-government in 1964. in 1964.

AREA: 13 950 sq. km. (5 386 sq. miles)

LAND USE: (percentage of total)

	1965	*1947*
Arable and orchard	1.1	1.2
Permanent meadow and pasture	0.1	0.1
Forest and woodland	28.4	25.4
City areas, waste and other land	70.4	73.3

POPULATION: 144 000 (1967 estimate)

Largest city: NASSAU, capital; population: 80 907 (1963)

Distribution of working population (1963)
Total working population: 51 948

U.N. group no.		*Percentage*
0	Agriculture, forestry, fishing and hunting	15.5
1	Mining and quarrying	—
2/3	Manufacturing	7.6
4	Construction	14.6
5	Electricity, gas, water and sanitary services	1.1
6	Commerce	10.6
7	Transport, storage and communications	6.8
8	Services	39.7
9	Others	4.1

		Year
Infant mortality (per '000)	41	1965
Crude birth rate (per '000)	32.6	1965
Crude death rate (per '000)	8.1	1965
Population per physician	1 330	1964
Population per hospital bed	170*a*	1966
School enrolment: age 5–19 years (percentage)	88	1964
age over 19 years (per 100 000 population)	43	1964

a government hospitals only.

COMMUNICATIONS

		Year(s)
Motor vehicles in use ('000s): private	15.9	1963–5 av.
commercial	3.4	1963–5 av.
Telephones (per '000 urban population)	17.7	1967
Radio receivers (per '000 population)	248	1963–5 av.
Television sets (per '000 population)	28.9	1963–5 av.
Daily newspapers (per '000 population)	110.5	1963–4 av.

FINANCE

Currency unit: The Bahamian dollar replaced the Bahamas pound (at par with the pound sterling) in 1966 at the rate B$1 to £0.35

EMPLOYMENT AND TRADE

Tourism is now the economic mainstay of the islands. Exports consist of pulpwood, salt, cucumbers, crawfish and sponges, and imports are foodstuffs, cars, hardware and clothing, the chief trading partners being the U.S.A., the U.K. and Canada. Industries such as cement, rum distilling and fish processing are developing.

PRODUCTION, EXPORTS AND IMPORTS

Years: **1963–5 average** and *1953–5 average*   Units: '000 metric tons unless otherwise indicated

1. CEREALS, etc.

	Production 1963–5	Production 1953–5	Exports 1963–5	Exports 1953–5	Imports 1963–5	Imports 1953–5
Maize (corn)	—	—	—	—	0.3	na
Oats	—	—	—	—	0.1	na
Potatoes	—	—	—	—	2.9	na
Rice	—	—	—	—	4.3	*2.0*

2. FRUIT, etc.

	Production 1963–5	Production 1953–5	Exports 1963–5	Exports 1953–5	Imports 1963–5	Imports 1953–5
Apples	—	—	—	—	0.5*	na
Citrus fruit	—	—	—	—	—	*0.4*
Wine *b*	—	—	—	—	7.5*	na

b '000 hectolitres.

3. BEVERAGES, FOREST PRODUCTS, etc.

	Production 1963–5	Production 1953–5	Exports 1963–5	Exports 1953–5	Imports 1963–5	Imports 1953–5
Coffee	—	—	—	—	0.1	na
Sugar, raw	—	—	—	—	4.4	na
Tobacco, leaf	—	—	—	—	0.1	na
Wood *j*	357.7*	na	—	—	45.0[2]	na

j '000 cu. metres of roundwood equivalent.

5. LIVESTOCK‡, ANIMAL PRODUCTS, etc.

	Production 1963–5	Production 1953–5	Exports 1963–5	Exports 1953–5	Imports 1963–5	Imports 1953–5
Chickens *d*	525.0**n*	na				
Cattle *d*	3.7	*3.0*[1]	—	—	—	—
Goats *d*	14.0*	*14.0*[1]	—	—	—	—
Sheep *d*	22.7*	*22.0*[1]	—	—	—	—

continued

5. LIVESTOCK‡, ANIMAL PRODUCTS, etc.—*continued*

	Production 1963–5	Production 1953–5	Exports 1963–5	Exports 1953–5	Imports 1963–5	Imports 1953–5
Horses *d*	4.0*	na				
Pigs *d*	11.0*	*10.0*[1]	—	—	—	—
Bacon/ham	—	—	—	—	1.0	na
Meat‡ 'A'	—	—	—	—	3.0	na
'B'	—	—	—	—	0.6	na
Butter	—	—	—	—	0.5	*0.2**
Cheese	—	—	—	—	0.3	na
Eggs	0.2*	—	—	—	—	—
Fish	2.0	*1.4*	0.5	na	—	—
Milk	1.0	na	—	—	—	—

d no. in thousands. *n* incl. ducks, geese and turkeys.

7. FUEL AND POWER

	Production 1963–5	Production 1953–5	Exports 1963–5	Exports 1953–5	Imports 1963–5	Imports 1953–5
Electricity *ht*	124	*30*[1]				
Petroleum, refined	—	—	—	—	1 520	*40*[1]

h million kWh. *t* thermal.

11. INDUSTRY

	Production 1963–5	Production 1953–5	Exports 1963–5	Exports 1953–5	Imports 1963–5	Imports 1953–5
Cement	—	—	—	—	na	na
Merchant ships *g*	—	—	—	—	20.0	na

g '000 G.R.T.

na: data not available. — negligible or nil. [1] one year only. [2] two year average. * estimate. ‡ see appendix. ; re-exports.

BARBADOS

Barbados achieved full self-government in 1961, and in 1966 became an independent state within the British Commonwealth.

AREA: 430 sq. km. (166 sq. miles)

LAND USE: (percentage of total)	*1960*	*1955*
Arable and orchard	60.5	65.1
Permanent meadow and pasture	9.3	11.6
Forest and woodland	—	—
City areas, waste and other land	30.2	23.3

POPULATION: 246 000 (1967, U.N. estimate)
Largest city: BRIDGETOWN, capital; population: 11 452 (city proper, 1960)

Distribution of working population (1960)
Total working population: 92 200

U.N. group no.		*Percentage*
0	Agriculture, forestry, fishing and hunting	24.3
1	Mining and quarrying	0.5
2/3	Manufacturing	14.1
4	Construction	9.7
5	Electricity, gas, water and sanitary services	0.9
6	Commerce	15.9
7	Transport, storage and communications	4.8
8	Services	21.9
9	Others *a*	7.9

a incl. unemployed and those seeking employment for the first time.

		Year(s)
Life expectancy at birth (years): male	62.7	1959–61 av.
female	67.4	1959–61 av.
Infant mortality (per '000)	39.5	1965
Crude birth rate (per '000)	30.5*	1960–5 av.
Crude death rate (per '000)	9*	1960–5 av.
Accidental deaths (per 100 000 population)		
caused by motor vehicles	4.9	1965
due to other causes	20.5	1965
Population per physician	2 560	1964
Population per hospital bed	150	1966
School enrolment: age 5–19 years (percentage)	81*a*	1963–4 av.
age over 19 years (per 100 000 population)	145	1963–5 av.

a public education only.

COMMUNICATIONS		*Year(s)*
Motor vehicles in use ('000s): private	11.6	1963–5 av.
commercial	3.3	1963–5 av.
Mail per capita: domestic	22	1964–5 av.
foreign received	30	1964–5 av.
foreign sent	14	1964–5 av.
Telephones (per '000 urban population)	7.1	1967
Radio receivers (per '000 population)	174	1963–5 av.
Television sets (per '000 population)	8.3	1963–5 av.
Daily newspapers (per '000 population)	105.7	1962–4 av.

FINANCE

Currency unit: The East Caribbean dollar

Exchange rates	*1965*	*1960*	*1950*
Per $ U.S.	1.72	1.72	1.72
Per £ sterling	4.8	4.8	4.8

		Year
National Income (million $ U.S.)	88	1965
G.N.P. per capita ($ U.S.)	400	1966

TRADING

Total trade (in million $ U.S.)	*1965*	*1955*	*1938*
Exports (f.o.b.)	37	23	7
Imports (c.i.f.)	68	32	10

Main trading partners (percentage of total value)

Exports	*1965*	*1955*	*Imports*	*1965*	*1955*
U.K.	42	42	U.K.	30	40
U.S.A.	11	2	U.S.A.	16	8
Canada	8	40	Canada	12	16
Irish R.	6	na	Venezuela	8	na
Trin./Tob.	3	4	Trin./Tob.	6	6
St. Lucia	3	na	Netherlands	3	4
Dominica	2	na	New Zealand	3	2

Distribution of trade (percentage of total value)

Exports	*1965*	*1955*
Food	90	92
(sugar and molasses)	(78)	(87)
Rum	6	6
Imports		
Manufactured goods	46	42
(machinery and transport equipment)	(16)	(12)
(textiles)	(6)	(na)
Food	27	30
(meat and preparations)	(8)	(na)
Crude materials and fuels	13	12
(petroleum products)	(9)	(na)
Chemicals	7	8

PRODUCTION, EXPORTS AND IMPORTS

Years: **1963–5 average** and *1953–5 average* Units: '000 metric tons unless otherwise indicated

	Production		Exports		Imports	
1. CEREALS, etc.						
Barley	—	—	—	—	0.1	na
Cassava	1.0*	na				
Maize (corn)	1.0*	na	—	—	2.0	na
Oats	—	—	—	—	1.3	na
Potatoes	—	—	0.2	—	4.7	na
Rice	—	—	—	—	7.9	*9.3*[2]
Sweet potatoes/yams	20.7*	na				
Wheat	—	—	—	—	0.9	na
2. FRUIT, etc.						
Apples	—	—	—	—	0.3	na
Bananas	—	—	—	—	0.2	na
Oranges	—	—	—	—	1.7	na
Other citrus fruit	—	—	—	—	2.5	na
Wine *b*	—	—	0.1†	na	1.2	na

b '000 hectolitres.

	Production		Exports		Imports	
3. BEVERAGES, FOREST PRODUCTS, etc.						
Coffee	—	—	—	—	0.1	*0.1*
Sugar: cane	1 897.0*	na				
raw	185.7	*170.0*	165.5	*160.7*	0.7	*0.2*
Tea	—	—	—	—	0.1	—
Tobacco: leaf	—	—	—	—	0.2	*0.2*[2]
cigarettes	171.0*e*	na	—	—	—	—
Softwood *j*	—	—	—	—	34.3	*33.4*[1]
Hardwood *j*	—	—	—	—	2.6	*1.2*[1]
Newsprint	—	—	—	—	0.8	*0.3*[1]
Other paper	—	—	—	—	1.3	—

e no. in millions. *j* '000 cu. metres of roundwood equivalent.

	Production		Exports		Imports	
4. VEGETABLE OILSEEDS AND OILS						
Castor oil	—	—	—	—	0.02	na
Copra	—	—	—	—	3.51	na
Coconut oil	—	—	0.46	*0.20**	0.47	*0.30**
Cottonseed oil	—	—	—	—	0.03	na
Groundnuts	—	—	—	—	0.46[2]	na
Linseed	—	—	—	—	0.01	na
Linseed oil	—	—	—	—	0.05	na
Olive oil	—	—	—	—	0.01	na
5. LIVESTOCK‡, ANIMAL PRODUCTS, etc.						
Chickens *d*	329.0**n*	na	—	—	—	—
Cattle *d*	16.0*	*13.0*[1]	—	—	—	—
Goats *d*	17.0*	*16.0*[1]	0.1 (goats and sheep)	na	—	—
Sheep *d*	39.3*	*33.0*[1]			—	—
Horses *d*	1.0*	na	—	—	—	—
Pigs *d*	26.0*	*24.0*[1]	—	—	—	—
Bacon/ham	— (bacon/ham and meat 'A')	—	—	—	2.2	na
Meat‡ 'A'			—	—	1.3	na
'B'	—	—	—	—	0.7	na
Butter	—	—	—	—	0.6	*0.3**
Cheese	—	—	—	—	0.5	na
Eggs	1.1*	na	—	—	0.1	na
Fish	4.0	*3.1*	0.6	na	1.7	na
Milk	6.0*	na	0.4	na	18.1	na

d no. in thousands. *n* incl. ducks, geese and turkeys.

	Production		Exports		Imports	
7. FUEL AND POWER						
Electricity *ht*	60	*20*[1]				
Natural gas *i*	—	*2*[1]	—	—	—	—
Oil, crude	—	—	—	—	30	na
Petroleum, refined	30	*10*[1]	—	—	307	*30*[1]

h million kWh. *i* million cu. metres. *t* thermal.

	Production		Exports		Imports	
9. NON-FERROUS MINERALS AND METALS						
Asbestos, manufactured	—	—	—	—	0.03	*46.06p*
Aluminium	—	—	—	—	0.07	*22.40p*
Copper, metal	—	—	—	—	0.12	*27.73p*
Lead, metal	—	—	—	—	0.17[1]	—
Tin, metal	—	—	—	—	0.24	na
Zinc, metal	—	—	—	—	0.01	—

p '000 $ U.S.

	Production		Exports		Imports	
10. FERTILIZERS						
Potash	—	—	—	—	5.1	*3.6*
11. INDUSTRY						
Spirits	na	na	1.4*n*	*1.3n*	—	—
Cement	—	—	—	—	na	na
Electrical engineering *a*	—	—	—	—	1.3	na
Motor vehicles *a*	—	—	—	—	2.9	*0.5*

a million $ U.S. *n* rum only.

na: data not available. — negligible or nil. [1] one year only. [2] two year average. * estimate. ‡ see appendix. † re-exports.

BELGIUM

An economic union between Belgium and Luxembourg has been in operation since 1922, apart from the war years 1940–45. The Netherlands joined these two countries to form the Benelux Customs Union in 1948, and in 1960 this was replaced by a full economic union between the three, and membership of the European Economic Community. Trading figures refer to Belgium and Luxembourg

AREA: 30 513 sq. km. (11 778 sq. miles)

LAND USE: (percentage of total)	*1965*	*1955*
Arable and orchard	30.7	32.7
Permanent meadow and pasture	23.6	24.1
Forest and woodland	19.7	19.4
City areas, waste and other land	26.0	23.8

POPULATION: 9 581 000 (1967 estimate)
Largest city: BRUXELLES (Brussels) capital; population: 1 074 586 (1966)

Distribution of working population (1964)
Total working population: 3 725 700 (incl. armed forces)

U.N. group no.		*Percentage*
0	Agriculture, forestry, fishing and hunting	5.8
1	Mining and quarrying	2.8
2/3	Manufacturing	33.7
4	Construction	7.6
5	Electricity, gas, water and sanitary services	0.8
6	Commerce	14.8
7	Transport, storage and communications	6.7
8	Services	23.5
9	Others	4.3

		Year(s)
Life expectancy at birth (years): male	67.7	1959–63 av.
female	73.5	1959–63 av.
Infant mortality (per '000)	24.1	1965
Crude birth rate (per '000)	16.4	1965
Crude death rate (per '000)	12.1	1965
Accidental deaths (per 100 000 population):		
caused by motor vehicles	24.4	1965
due to other causes	35.8	1965
Population per physician	680	1965
Population per hospital bed	130	1966
School enrolment: age 5–19 years (percentage)	110‡	1963–4 av.
age over 19 years (per 100 000 population)	810	1963–5 av.

COMMUNICATIONS		*Year(s)*
Motor vehicles in use ('000s): private	1 180.7	1963–5 av.
commercial	222.6	1963–5 av.
Railway track (km.)	4 485	1964
Mail per capita: domestic	227	1963–5 av.
foreign received	19	1963–5 av.
foreign sent	20	1963–5 av.
Telephones (per '000 urban population)	17.4	1967
Radio licences (per '000 population)	325	1963–5 av.
Television licences (per '000 population)	140	1963–5 av.
Daily newspapers (per '000 population)	285	1961

FINANCE

Currency unit: The Belgian franc

Exchange rates	*1965a*	*1960a*	*1950a*	*1938b*
Per $ U.S.	49.64	49.70	50.12	29.68
Per £ sterling	139.15	139.35	140.40	136.53

		Year(s)
National income (million $ U.S.)	13 302	1965
G.N.P. per capita ($ U.S.)	1 630	1966
Rate of increase of G.N.P. per capita	4.6	1960–4 av.
Foreign trade (percentage of G.D.P.)	74	1963–5 av.

a spot rate. *b* selling rate.

TRADING (including Luxembourg)

Total trade (in million $ U.S.)	*1965*	*1955*	*1938*
Exports (f.o.b.)	6 382	2 776	730
Imports (c.i.f.)	6 497	2 830	767

Main trading partners (percentage of total value)

Exports	*1965*	*1955*	*1938*	*Imports*	*1965*	*1955*	*1938*
Netherlands	22	21	12	Germany F.R.	21	14	11*d*
Germany F.R.	22	12	12*d*	France	15	12	14
France	15	10	15	Netherlands	15	13	9
U.S.A.	8	9	7	U.S.A.	8	11	11
U.K.	5	6	14	U.K.	7	8	8
Italy	3	2	1	Italy	4	2	1
Switzerland	2	3	3	Congo D.R.	3	8	8

Distribution of trade (percentage of total value)

Exports	*1965*	*1955*	*1938**
Manufactured goods	75	73	na
(machinery and transport equipment)	(20)	(11)	(7)
(iron and steel)	(18)	(24)	(14)
Crude materials and fuels	9	14	na
Food	6	4	3
Chemicals	6	7	8
Imports			
Manufactured goods	54	44	na
(machinery and transport equipment)	(24)	(16)	(8)
Crude materials and fuels	25	33	na
(fuels)	(9)	(10)	(na)
Food	11	13	na
Chemicals	7	5	4

d incl. Germany D.R.

PRODUCTION, EXPORTS AND IMPORTS

Years: **1963–5 average** and *1953–5 average* Units: '000 metric tons unless otherwise indicated

Production data are for Belgium; data for Luxembourg are given where applicable. Trade figures apply to Belgium and Luxembourg combined.

	Production		Exports		Imports	
1. CEREALS, etc.						
Barley	506.0	*273.7*	28.3	*6.7*	282.3	*472.5*
Lux.	20.7	*13.3*				
Maize (corn)	2.0	*10.7*	85.7	*5.7*	756.4	*412.0*
Millets/sorghum	—	—	26.5	*2.0*	543.5	*113.3*
Oats	357.3	*465.0*	1.7	*1.6*	63.0	*107.4*
Lux.	34.0	*39.0*				
Potatoes	1 568.0	*2 245.7*	188.2	*126.4*	137.3	*120.2*
Lux.	87.3	*133.3*				
Rice	—	—	7.6	*6.8*	39.9	*38.6*
Rye	119.0	*226.0*	1.5	*5.5*	42.1	*139.5*
Lux.	7.3	*9.7*				
Wheat	848.3	*631.3*	199.2	*3.5*	511.6	*625.7*
Lux.	42.3	*40.0*				
2. FRUIT, etc.						
Apples	155.0	*250.0*	34.5	*41.4*	42.9	*7.7*
Lux.	11.3	na				
Bananas	—	—	4.1†	*0.8†*	70.9	*47.1*
Cherries	16.3	*30.5*	—	*2.7*	—	*0.6*
Lux.	1.0*	na				
Dates	—	—	0.1†	—	1.2	*1.4*
Grapes	11.3*	*12.7*	2.4	*0.5*	14.7	*0.4*
Lux.	20.0*	*14.7**				
Lemons	—	—	0.2†	*0.1†*	14.8	*10.0*
Oranges	—	—	6.1†	*0.3†*	132.7	*110.3*
Other citrus fruit	—	—	0.3†	—	8.3	*7.0*
Peaches	6.7	na	na	na	—	*3.6*
2. FRUIT, etc.—*continued*						
Pears	55.0	*210.0*	11.0	*16.4*	13.0	*4.9*
Lux.	1.0*	na				
Plums	16.7	*37.3*	—	*1.8*	—	*1.6*
Lux.	2.7	na				
Raisins	—	—	—	—	5.5	*5.5*
Tomatoes	74.7	na				
Wine *b*	—	—	64.3	*12.7*	873.6	*528.7*
Lux.	141.0	*105.0*				

b trade in '000 hectolitres.

	Production		Exports		Imports	
3. BEVERAGES, FOREST PRODUCTS, etc.						
Cocoa	—	—	—	*0.2†*	15.7	*8.7*
Coffee	—	—	0.8†	*1.9†*	63.7	*48.4*
Sugar: beet	2 595.3	*2 255.7*				
raw	449.9	*381.0*	95.4	*135.7*	34.0	*54.5*
Tea	—	—	0.2†	—	0.6	*0.4*
Tobacco: leaf	2.5	*3.7*	2.0	*0.2*	31.2	*21.5*
cigars	366.0*e*	*105.4e*	5.6 (cigars, cigarettes, tobacco/snuff)	*1.0*[2]	—	*0.6*[2]
cigarettes	15 188.0*e*	*9 386.0e*				
tobacco/snuff	7.4	*10.0*				
Softwood *j*	1 375.0	*1 251.7*	269.0	*130.4*	1 538.0	*1 034.1*
Lux.	77.3	*68.3*				
Hardwood *j*	1 156.7	*1 050.0*	137.3	*128.2*	587.8	*318.4*
Lux.	114.3	*81.7*				
Wood pulp	185.1	*97.7*	12.1	*17.0*	230.6	*168.7*
Newsprint	94.7	*54.3*	38.0	*10.0*	71.3	*47.0*
Other paper	403.0	*246.7*	124.0	*45.0*	363.0	*104.3*

e no. in millions. *j* '000 cu. metres of roundwood equivalent. *continued*

na: data not available. — negligible or nil. [1] one year only. [2] two year average. * estimate. ‡ see appendix. † re-exports.

BELGIUM *continued*

PRODUCTION, EXPORTS AND IMPORTS *continued*

4. VEGETABLE OILSEEDS AND OILS

	Production		Exports		Imports	
Castor seed	—	—	0.07	—	2.84	7.23
Castor oil	na	na	0.83	3.11	1.91	0.38
Copra	—	—	0.37†	—	32.02	27.53
Coconut oil	na	na	1.40	4.94	9.65	3.99
Cottonseed oil	—	—	—	10.60†	3.28	13.24
Groundnuts	—	—	0.82†	—	64.38	16.67
Groundnut oil	na	na	7.37	5.01	8.47	25.97
Linseed	20.33	19.67	11.21	6.23	29.04	40.30
Linseed oil	na	na	1.84	5.43	0.88	3.94
Olive oil	—	—	—	—	0.54	0.20
Palm kernels	—	—	0.13†	—	24.93	21.47
Palm kernel oil	na	na	1.49	2.39	1.70	2.82
Palm oil	—	—	5.61†	6.20†	35.70	44.66
Rapeseed	—	1.30	0.74†	0.47	4.44	1.80
Rapeseed oil	na	na	0.01	0.69	0.54	0.31
Soya beans	—	—	0.04†	—	125.70	20.77
Soya bean oil	na	na	3.98	2.83	3.30	0.65
Sunflower seed	—	—	0.19†	—	2.16	1.02
Sunflower seed oil	na	na	—	—	7.49	—
Tung oil	—	—	—	—	0.35	0.61

5. LIVESTOCK‡, ANIMAL PRODUCTS, etc.

	Production		Exports		Imports	
Chickens *d*	32 805.0	15 666.7				
Lux.	433.7	421.0[2]				
Cattle *d*	2 733.0	2 364.7	43.1	2.2[2]	49.9	13.3
Lux.	161.0	132.3				
dairy cows *d*	1 199.0	1 091.7*n*				
Lux.	67.7	54.3				
Goats *d*	25.0	52.7	} 18.8	na	81.8	na
Lux.	—	0.3				
Sheep *d*	156.7	129.3				
Lux.	2.3*	3.0				
Horses *d*	124.7	218.0*				
Lux.	2.7	11.6				
Pigs *d*	1 825.0	1 329.3	148.7	11.1	25.0	—
Lux.	100.0	93.7				
Bacon/ham }	478.3	371.7	{ 0.7	0.1	0.2	—
Meat‡ 'A' }			20.2	4.6	40.6	6.3
Lux.	25.7	18.7				
'B'	152.5	56.1	16.6	2.6	25.9	5.5
Lux.	3.8*	na				
Butter	83.0	88.3	7.2	—	8.6	10.1
Lux.	5.0	4.0				
Cheese	32.3*p*	13.7*p*	7.2	0.3	33.9	33.6
Lux.	1.0	1.0[2]				
Eggs	166.5	132.7	32.8	3.3	0.2	0.7
Lux.	3.6	2.3				
Fish	60.4*q*	75.7*q*	22.5	15.0[1]*	184.7	89.7[1]*
Lux.	0.6*t*	0.4*t*				
Milk	3 914.3	3 632.0	378.1	86.3	281.4	128.8
Lux.	194.0	180.7				
Whale/sperm oil	—	—	—	—	11.2	—
Hides/skins	24.2	24.2[2]	—	18.3[2]	36.7	18.4[2]
Lux.	1.0	0.9				
Wool	0.2	—[2]	17.5	11.6	60.6	35.6

d no. in thousands. *n* incl. draught cows. *p* excl. cheese produced from skim milk. *q* incl. fish landed in foreign ports. *t* sport fishing only.

6. FIBRES, TEXTILES, etc.

	Production		Exports		Imports	
Abaca	—	—	0.3†	0.5†	1.7	3.3
Agaves (sisal etc.)	—	—	4.6†	1.7†	36.7	16.0
Cotton lint	—	—	1.4†	0.9†	84.1	96.6
Flax fibre	39.1*	38.5	95.8*s*	84.5*s*	251.6	14.6
Hemp fibre	—	—	0.1†	0.2†	0.7	1.6
Jute	—	—	23.1†	4.7†	94.7	73.3
Rubber: natural	—	—	1.8†	0.5†	19.6	20.6
synthetic	12.0	—	11.9	—	22.5[2]	2.7
Silk *f*	—	—	34.7†	—	26.3	1.0
Cotton: yarn	95.5	92.5	17.2	22.2	14.4	2.3
woven fabrics	81.2	72.6	41.4	20.8	13.0	3.7
Rayon: fibre/yarn	37.4	30.2	11.0	19.1	14.7	4.1
woven fabrics	16.6	6.9*n*	15.3	4.0	10.4	5.5
Non-cellulosic fibre/yarn	7.3	1.2	7.8	—	18.3	—
Wool: yarn	63.8	39.3	24.8	11.6	6.5	2.7
woven fabrics	18.4	14.8	11.5	7.4	5.0	3.3

f metric tons. *n* incl. mixtures. *s* incl. re-exports.

7. FUEL AND POWER

	Production		Exports		Imports	
Coal 'A'‡	20 837	29 920	2 403	5 931	7 344	3 465
'B'	—	—	—	—	226	231
Coke	na	na	467	739	4 089	3 266
Electricity *h*: total	20 516	11 690*n*				
Lux.	2 122					
hydro	176	130*n*				
Lux.	737					
nuclear	49	—				
thermal	20 291	11 560*n*				
Lux.	1 385					
Natural gas *i*	70	20	—	—	—	—
Oil, crude	—	—	—	—	13 633	4 710[1]
Petroleum, refined	11 453	4 140[1]	3 217	1 800[1]	4 323	2 300[1]
Uranium *f*	—	—	—	—	7	—

f metric tons. *h* million kWh. *i* million cu. metres. *n* incl. Luxembourg.

8. IRON AND STEEL

	Production		Exports		Imports	
Iron ore	29*m*	35*m*	390	661	22 225	13 245
Lux.	1 849*m*	1 817*m*				
Pig iron	7 776	4 741	138	41	439	330
Lux.	3 974	2 869				
Steel ingots/castings	8 476	5 117	640	385	254	74
Lux.	4 392	2 904				
Iron/steel scrap	na	na	284	150	69	261
Iron/steel products *a*	na	na	1 026	544	187	69

a million $ U.S. *m* metal content.

9. NON-FERROUS MINERALS AND METALS

	Production		Exports		Imports	
Diamonds *a*	—	—	264.95†	89.07†	255.10	76.54
Gold *k*, bullion/coins etc.	—	—	204.00†	123.87†	1 013.33‡	413.00
Silver *k*, bullion	—	—	9 837.00†	3 433.00†	7 218.00	1 738.33
Asbestos: fibre	—	—	0.18†	0.22†	55.56	33.95
manufactured	—	—	216.09†	103.91†	9.15	2.54
Mica	—	—	0.18†	0.02†	1.10	1.06
Aluminium: bauxite	—	—	—	0.30†	5.30	1.30
alumina	—	—	—	0.01*n*†	11.24*p*	0.43
aluminium	—	—	107.33†	27.92†	127.18	31.83
Antimony, metal	—	—	1.53†	0.72*q*†	0.37	0.09
Cadmium	0.70	na	0.82*s*	0.12*s*	0.35	0.02
Chrome: ore	—	—	—	—	1.15	0.50
metal	—	—	—	0.05	6.05	3.39[2]
Cobalt, metal	na	na	1.35	32.97	—	—
Copper: ore	—	—	—	—	2.81	172.51
metal	—	153.6	352.97†*t*	168.19*s*	366.00	13.28
Lead: ore	—	—	—	0.29†	141.56	115.63
metal	97.50	77.01	77.40	58.87	33.41	22.95
Magnesium: dolomite	1 149.17*y*	na	498.88	130.75	16.24	6.33
magnesite	na	na	0.03	0.04	4.72	2.60
metal/salts	—*x*	—*x*	0.08	0.22	4.51	17.07
Manganese: ore	—	—	4.00†	—	267.88*u*	108.62*u*
metal	—	—	36.47[1]	9.97[2]	91.32	64.70[2]
Mercury *f*	—	—	11.30†	4.80†	95.80	36.00
Molybdenum, metal *f*	—	—	0.68†	—	317.70	114.80
Nickel, metal	—	—	0.68†	0.08†	2.32	0.62
Tin: ore	—	—	—	—	7.05	14.49
metal	5.67	10.45	5.65	10.62	3.38	1.86
Titanium minerals	—	—	12.17†	0.15†	9.20*v*	3.78
Tungsten: ore	—	—	—	—	0.02	0.11
metal	—	—	0.04†	—	0.05	0.05
Vanadium	—	—	0.39†*w*	—	0.65*w*	—
Zinc: ore	—	—	28.13†	52.08†	460.71	464.26
metal	222.88	206.15	184.78	156.12	26.03	5.59

a million $ U.S. *f* metric tons. *k* '000 fine troy oz. *n* incl. hydrates. *p* hydrate. *q* antimony oxide only. *s* incl. re-exports. *t* incl. matte. *u* incl. manganiferous iron ore. *v* ferro-titanium and titanium oxide only. *w* ferro-vanadium and vanadium oxide. *x* primary magnesium only. *y* incl. calcined.

10. CHEMICALS*n* AND FERTILIZERS

	Production		Exports		Imports	
Organic chemicals:						
Benzene	46.1		29.8		7.4	
Butadiene	—		na		na	
Ethylene	na		na		na	
Methanol	na		na		na	
Phenol	na		5.1*p*†		7.4*p*	
Phthalic anhydride	14.0		4.2		0.8	
Styrene monomer	—		0.1		1.2	
Urea	30.5[2]		55.2		6.0	

n data not available for years 1953–5. *p* incl. phenol salts.

continued

PRODUCTION, EXPORTS AND IMPORTS *continued*

10. CHEMICALS*n* AND FERTILIZERS—*continued*

	Production		Exports		Imports	
Inorganic chemicals:						
Ammonia	356.6		41.0		2.8	
Carbon black	7.5[2]*		3.6		14.0	
Chlorine	73.0		9.3		0.5	
Nitric acid	na		2.2		0.9	
Sodium carbonate	226.3		4.9		39.6	
Sodium hydroxide	58.7		14.4		25.1	
Sulphuric acid	1 357.3		101.6		47.5	
Plastics:						
Polyamides	—		0.1		5.0	
Polyethylene	17.7		11.3		22.1	
Polyvinyl chloride	40.7		na		12.3	
Fertilizers:						
Phosphates	19.1*	27.1*	28.6	3.4	1 158.5	385.9
Potash	—	—	994.2†	720.8†	1 345.6	1 109.7
Pyrites	—	—	0.3†	—	284.1	344.3
Sulphur	4.5*q*	0.4**q*	7.7†	3.9†	222.8	54.1

n data not available for years 1953–5. *q* recovered.

11. INDUSTRY

	Production		Exports		Imports	
Aircraft *a*	42.0**v*	—	92.3	1.6	62.0	12.2
Alcoholic beverages			—	1.5*a*	47.5*a*	20.3*a*
beer *b*	11 099.0	9 988.3				
Lux.	501.0	372.3				
spirits *b*	45.6[1]*n*	79.3[1]*q*				
Lux.	2.0[1]*p*	5.7[1]*t*				
Cement	5 487.0	4 563.0	1 452.3	1 821.0	30.7	11.3
Lux.	210.0	152.0				
Electrical engineering *a*	549.3[2]	—	226.0	74.8[2]	278.3	80.7[2]
Locomotives *c*	122.0*	na	na	na	na	na
Railway vehicles *a*	na	na	21.9	—	—	4.4
Machine tools *a*	24.0[1]	na	—	6.7[2]	29.7	—
Merchant ships *g*	93.0	88.9	31.0	60.5	8.0	7.0
Motor vehicles			317.4	40.8[2]	443.6	115.3[2]
commercial *d*	17.8*u*	14.7[2]*u*				
private *d*	364.5*u*	79.9*u*				

a million $ U.S. *b* '000 hectolitres. *c* no. of units. *d* no. in thousands. *g* '000 G.R.T. *n* 1967 figure. *p* 1966 figure. *q* 1961 figure. *t* 1960 figure. *u* assembly of imported parts. *v* 1965–7 av.

BERMUDA

WESTERN ATLANTIC

Bermuda, a British colony, was granted internal self-government in 1968.

AREA: 53.3 sq. km. (20.59 sq. miles)

LAND USE: (percentage of total)	*1964*	*1950*
Arable and orchard	4.0	13.3
Permanent meadow and pasture	4.0	15.0
Forest and woodland	60.0	53.3
City areas, waste and other land	32.0	18.4

POPULATION: 51 000 (1967 estimate)

Largest city: HAMILTON, capital; population: 3 000 (1965)

Total working population: 20 067 (1960)

		Year(s)
Life expectancy at birth (years): male	65.6	1965–6 av.
female	72.4	1965–6 av.
Infant mortality (per '000)	30.5	1965
Crude birth rate (per '000)	23.0	1965
Crude death rate (per '000)	7.4	1965
Population per physician	960	1964
Population per hospital bed	110	1964
School enrolment: age 5–19 years (percentage)	99	1963–4 av.

COMMUNICATIONS

		Year(s)
Motor vehicles in use ('000s): private	7.9	1963–5 av.
commercial	1.4	1963–5 av.
Mail per capita: domestic	99	1963–5 av.
foreign received	164	1963–5 av.
foreign sent	186	1963–5 av.
Telephones (per '000 urban population)	45.1*a*	1967
Radio receivers (per '000 population)	463	1963–5 av.
Television sets (per '000 population)	231.6	1963–5 av.
Daily newspapers (per '000 population)	340	1963

a excl. those of armed forces.

FINANCE

Currency unit: The Bermuda dollar replaced the Bermuda pound (at par with the pound sterling) in 1970 at the rate Bermuda $1 to £0.433 (U.S. $1.039)

EMPLOYMENT AND TRADE

The important vegetable trade with the U.S.A. has decreased owing to the imposition of tariffs, and the export of Bermuda cedarwood (juniper) ceased after the severe blight of 1943. Some fruit and concentrated essences are exported, but most foodstuffs have to be imported, as do clothing, fuel and building materials. The economy depends on the tourist trade and the use of the island as an air and naval base. Main trading partners are the U.S.A., the U.K., Canada and the Netherlands Antilles.

PRODUCTION, EXPORTS AND IMPORTS

Years: **1963–5 average** and *1953–5 average* Units: '000 metric tons unless otherwise indicated

1. CEREALS, etc.

	Production		Exports		Imports	
Oats	—	—	—	—	—	0.1
Potatoes	1.0*	1.0[2]	—	—	1.7[2]	1.7
Rice	—	—	—	—	0.3[2]	0.2

2. FRUIT, etc.

	Production		Exports		Imports	
Apples	—	—	—	—	—	0.4[2]
Bananas	1.0*	1.0	—	—	—	—
Oranges	—	—	—	—	0.5[2]	0.7
Raisins	—	—	—	—	—	0.1
Wine *b*	—	—	—	—	2.7[2]	1.0

b '000 hectolitres.

3. BEVERAGES, FOREST PRODUCTS, etc.

	Production		Exports		Imports	
Coffee	—	—	—	—	0.1[2]	0.1
Sugar, raw	—	—	—	—	2.1[2]	1.6
Tea	—	—	—	—	0.1	—

5. LIVESTOCK‡, ANIMAL PRODUCTS, etc.

	Production		Exports		Imports	
Chickens *d*	80.0	72.7				
Cattle *d*	1.7	1.0	—	—	—	—
Pigs *d*	2.0	2.0	—	—	—	—
Bacon/ham	—	—	—	—	0.4[2]	0.4
Meat‡: 'A'	—	—	—	—	1.9[2]	1.4
'B'	0.5*	na	—	—	0.8	0.4

continued

5. LIVESTOCK, ANIMAL PRODUCTS, etc.—*continued*

	Production		Exports		Imports	
Butter	—	—	—	—	0.4[2]	0.4
Cheese	—	—	—	—	0.2[2]	0.2
Eggs	0.2*	0.2[2]	—	—	0.1[2]	0.3
Fish	0.8**n*	0.6**n*	—	—	0.6[2]	na
Milk	4.0	3.0[2]	—	—	6.6	2.4

d no. in thousands. *n* marine fisheries only.

7. FUEL AND POWER

	Production		Exports		Imports	
Coal: 'A'‡	—	—	—	—	—	1
Electricity *ht*	134	60[1]	—	—		
Petroleum, refined	—	—	—	—	207	100[1]

h million kWh. *t* thermal.

9. NON-FERROUS MINERALS AND METALS

	Production		Exports		Imports	
Diamonds *a*	—	—	—	—	—[1]	0.70
Asbestos, manufactured *a*	—	—	—	—	0.03	0.04

a million $ U.S.

BHUTAN

CENTRAL ASIA

Bhutan is an independent, mainly Buddhist, state; some guidance in its external affairs has been given by India since the independence of the latter in 1949. In 1964 the king assumed direct rule, but in 1969 a more democratic form of government was introduced.

AREA: 41 400 sq. km. (16 000 sq. miles)

POPULATION: 770 000 (1967 U.N. estimate)

Summer capital: TASHI CHHO DZONG (Thimbu)
Winter capital: PUNAKHA

FINANCE

Currency unit: The Indian rupee (a sterling currency maintained at the value £0.075)

Exchange rates	*1965*	*1960*	*1955*	*1938*
Per $ U.S.	4.773	4.773	4.775	2.888

National Income (million $ U.S.) 32 (1958)

EMPLOYMENT AND TRADE

Land cultivation is primitive, the main crops being rice, maize, and millet; much of the land is under forest. There are small handicraft industries, such as weaving and metalwork. Large deposits of limestone and gypsum have been found. The main exports are timber and grain, trade being mainly with India.

BOLIVIA

SOUTH AMERICA

The Republic of Bolivia has suffered several years' political and economic instability, the latter aggravated by the lack of diversification, tin being the only important product. In 1962 aid for a development plan was received from the U.S.A. and elsewhere.

AREA: 1 098 580 sq. km. (424 160 sq. miles)

LAND USE: (percentage of total)

	1950
Arable and orchard	2.8
Permanent meadow and pasture	10.3
Forest and woodland	42.8
City areas, waste and other land	44.1

POPULATION: 3 801 000 (1967 estimate)

Largest city: LA PAZ, capital; population: 360 329 (city proper, 1965)

Distribution of working population (1950)
Total working population: 1 058 725 (excl. Indian tribes: 87 000*)

U.N. group no.		*Percentage*
0	Agriculture, forestry, fishing and hunting	63.4
1	Mining and quarrying	4.1
2/3	Manufacturing	10.3
4	Construction	2.4
5	Electricity, gas, water and sanitary services	3.9
6	Commerce	5.4
7	Transport, storage and communications	2.0
8	Services	6.6
9	Others	1.9

		Year(s)
Life expectancy at birth (years): male	49.7	1949–51 av.
female	49.7	1949–51 av.
Infant mortality (per '000)	76.5*	1965
Crude birth rate (per '000)	44*	1960–5 av.
Crude death rate (per '000)	21*	1960–5 av.
Population per physician	3 160	1966
Population per hospital bed	400	1966
School enrolment: age 5–19 years (percentage)	51	1963–4 av.
age over 19 years (per 100 000 population)	349	1964–5 av.

COMMUNICATIONS

		Year(s)
Motor vehicles in use ('000s): private	13.5	1963–5 av.
commercial	5.1	1963–5 av.
Railway track (km.)	3 580	1964
Telephones (per '000 urban population)	0.7	1967
Radio receivers (per '000 population)	127	1963–5 av.
Daily newspapers (per '000 population)	26	1961

FINANCE

Currency unit: The peso Boliviano was introduced in 1963 at the rate 1 peso Boliviano per 1 000 bolivianos

Exchange rates	*1965*	*1960b*	*1950b*	*1938b*
Per $ U.S.	11.88*a*	11 885	60.6	30.44
Per £ sterling	33.28	33 278	169.75	140.02

		Year(s)
National Income (million $ U.S.)	532	1965
G.N.P. per capita ($ U.S.)	160	1966
Rate of increase of G.N.P. per capita	3.4	1960–4 av.
Foreign trade (percentage of G.D.P.)	36	1963–5 av.

a selling rate. *b* bolivianos.

TRADING

Total trade (in million $ U.S.)	*1965*	*1955*	*1938*
Exports (f.o.b.)	129	100	27
Imports (c.i.f.)	126	81	19

Main trading partners (percentage of total value)

Exports	*1965*	*1955*	*Imports*	*1965*	*1955*
U.K.	45	33	U.S.A.	47	38
U.S.A.	42	60	Japan	13	1
Germany F.R.	5	1	Germany F.R.	12	10
Japan	2	–	Argentina	6	10
Netherlands	2	–	U.K.	6	7
Belg./Lux.	2	–	Netherlands	4	4

Distribution of trade (percentage of total value)

Exports	*1962*	*1955*
Non-ferrous ores	98	95
(tin ore)	(63)	(58)
Imports		
Food	20	26
Machinery and transport equipment	16	14
Fuel	2	4

PRODUCTION, EXPORTS AND IMPORTS

Years: **1963–5 average** and *1953–5 average* Units: '000 metric tons unless otherwise indicated

	Production		Exports		Imports	
1. CEREALS, etc.						
Barley	**93.3**	*44.0*[1]	—	—	—	—
Cassava	**154.0**	na				
Maize (corn)	**254.7**	*138.0*[1]	**0.1**	—	—	—
Millets/sorghum	—	—	—	—	**0.1**	—
Oats	**13.0**	*2.0*[1]	—	—	**0.2**	*0.7*
Potatoes	**685.0**	*189.0*[1]	—	—	—	—
Rice	**42.0**	*29.7**	—	—	**0.2**	*6.4*
Sweet potatoes/yams	**10.0***	—				
Wheat	**68.3**	*46.0*[1]	—	—	**14.4**	*54.9*
2. FRUIT, etc.						
Apples	—	—	—	—	**1.6*n***	—
Bananas	**50.0*[1]**	*50.0**	**0.4**	—	—	—
Grapes	**9.0***	na	—	—	—	—
Lemons	**40.0***	*42.0**	—	—	—	—
Oranges	**113.3***	*137.0*[2]*	—	—	—	—
Pineapples	**2.3***	na	—	—	—	—
Raisins	—	—	—	—	**0.1**	—
Wine *b*	—	—	—	—	**2.5**	—

b '000 hectolitres. *n* incl. pears and quince.

	Production		Exports		Imports	
3. BEVERAGES, FOREST PRODUCTS, etc.						
Cocoa	**2.2**	*3.0*[2]*	—	—	—	—
Coffee	**2.3**	*2.6*	**1.0**	*0.2*[2]	—	—
Sugar: cane	**1 098.0**	na				
raw	**87.3**	*6.0**	—	—	**3.1**	*50.9*
Tea	—	—	—	—	**0.3**	*0.2*
Tobacco: leaf	**1.1***	*1.0*[2]*	—	—	**0.2**[2]	*0.3*
cigarettes	**540.0*e***	*456.3e*	—	—	—	—
Softwood *j*	**3.2*[2]**	—	**0.1**	—[1]	—	—[1]
Hardwood *j*	**4 451.0**	*7 534.0*[1]	—[1]	*26.3*[2]	—	*14.4*
Newsprint	—[2]	—	—	—[1]	**0.2**[1]	*2.8*[1]
Other paper	**0.7**[2]	—	—	—[1]	**4.6**[1]	*2.3*[1]*

e no. in millions. *j* '000 cu. metres of roundwood equivalent.

	Production		Exports		Imports	
4. VEGETABLE OILSEEDS AND OILS						
Coconut oil	—	—	—	—	na	*0.01*
Cottonseed oil	—	—	—	—	**0.02**	na
Groundnuts	**6.53**	*0.70*[1]	—	—	**0.01**	na
Groundnut oil	na	na	—	—	**2.30**	na
Linseed oil	—	—	—	—	na	*0.05*
Palm kernels	na	na	**2.98**	na	—	—
Soya bean oil	—	—	—	—	**1.13***	na

continued

PRODUCTION, EXPORTS AND IMPORTS *continued*

	Production		Exports		Imports	
5. LIVESTOCK‡, ANIMAL PRODUCTS, etc.						
Chickens *d*	**2 174.3**	na				
Cattle *d*	**1 500.0**	*2 260.0*[1]*	**1.0**[1]	*0.6*	**12.0**	*7.8*[2]
Goats *d*	**1 483.0**	*1 229.0**	—	—	—	—
Sheep *d*	**6 180.3**	*6 464.0*[1]*	—	—	—	—
Horses *d*	**201.0***	na				
Pigs *d*	**667.0***	*509.0**	—	*0.1*	**0.1**	*0.3*
Meat‡: 'A'	**60.0***	—	**0.4**	—	**0.3**	—
'B'	**1.0***	—	—	—	—	—
Butter	—	—	—	—	—	*0.4*
Cheese	—	—	—	—	**0.3**	—
Eggs	**4.0***	na	—	—	—	—
Fish	**1.4**[1]*n*	*0.9*[1]*n*	—	—	**1.7**[2]	*0.8*[1]*
Milk	**44.3***	—	—	—	**45.5**	*27.5**
Wool	na	*3.0**	—	—	**0.2**	*0.3*

d no. in thousands. *n* excl. subsistence fishing.

	Production		Exports		Imports	
6. FIBRES, TEXTILES, etc.						
Cotton lint	—	—	—	—	**1.7**	*1.8*
Rubber, natural	na	na	**2.1**	*0.1**	—	*0.2*[2]
Silk *f*	—	—	—	—	**1.0**[2]	—
Cotton: yarn	**0.3**[2]	na	—	—	—	—
woven fabrics	**1.1**[1]	*0.9**	—	—	**0.4**[1]	na
Wool, woven fabrics	**1.0*n***	*1.4n*	—	—	—	—

f metric tons. *n* million metres.

	Production		Exports		Imports	
7. FUEL AND POWER						
Coal 'A'‡	**1**	*6*	—	—	—	—
Electricity *h*: total	**540**	*220*[1]				
hydro	**415**[2]	*210*[1]				
thermal	**125**	*10*[1]				
Natural gas *i*	**100**	*3*	**30**	—	—	—
Oil, crude	**430**	*350*[1]	**47**	na[1]	—	—
Petroleum, refined	**383**	*270*[1]	**3**	*20*[1]	**13**	*30*[1]

h million kWh. *i* million cu. metres.

	Production		Exports		Imports	
9. NON-FERROUS MINERALS AND METALS						
Gold *k*: ore *m*	**125.30**	*28.00*	**0.38**	*18.92*	—	—
bullion/coins etc.	na	na	**95.63**	*77.74*	—	—
Silver *k*, ore *m*	na	na	**4 598.15**	*5 894.13*	—	—
Asbestos	na	na	**0.01**	*0.26*	—	—
Antimony, ore *m*	**8.66**	*5.45*	**8.65**	*5.40*	—	—
Copper, ore *m*	na	*3.87*	**4.14**	*3.87*	—	—
Lead: ore *m*	**17.28**	*20.38*	**17.92**	*19.19*	—	—
metal	**0.55**	—	**0.02**	*1.42*	—	—
Mercury *f*	**2.17**	—	**2.80**[2]	na	—	—
Tin: ore *m*	**23.64**	*31.00*	**20.73**	*30.40*	—	—
metal	**3.21**	*0.16*	**2.74**	*0.16*	—	—
Tungsten, ore *m*	na	—	**1.24**	*2.73*	—	—
Zinc, ore *m*	**9.13**	*21.87*	**9.37**	*22.73*	—	—

f metric tons. *k* '000 fine troy oz. *m* metal content.

	Production		Exports		Imports	
10. CHEMICALS*n* AND FERTILIZERS						
Chemicals	—		—		na	
Fertilizers:						
Sulphur	na	na	**10.1**	*3.0*	—	—

n data not available for years 1953–5.

	Production		Exports		Imports	
11. INDUSTRY						
Beer *b*	**247.0**	*262.3*	—	—	—	—
Cement	**60.7**	*35.3*	—	—	**7.3**	*2.0*
Electrical engineering	—	—	—	—	na	na
Motor vehicles *a*	—	—	—	—	**7.8**	*1.9*

a million $ U.S. *b* '000 hectolitres.

BOTSWANA

SOUTHERN AFRICA

Botswana, formerly the British protectorate of Bechuanaland, became a republic within the Commonwealth in 1966, but is still linked to the South African customs union.

AREA: 575 000 sq. km. (222 000 sq. miles)

LAND USE: (percentage of total)

	1965	*1954*
Arable and orchard	0.3	0.2
Permanent meadow and pasture	72.2	57.2
Forest and woodland	1.7	1.4
City areas, waste and other land	25.8	41.2

POPULATION: 593 000 (1967 estimate)
Capital city: GABORONE; population: 4 200 (city proper, 1965)

Distribution of working population (1964)
Total working population: 250 678

U.N. group no.		*Percentage*
0	Agriculture, forestry, fishing and hunting	90.8
1	Mining and quarrying	0.8
2/3	Manufacturing	1.0
4	Construction	1.1
5	Electricity, gas, water and sanitary services	—
6	Commerce	1.0
7	Transport, storage and communications	0.9
8	Services	3.9
9	Others	0.5

COMMUNICATIONS

		Year(s)
Motor vehicles in use ('000s): private	1.5	1963–5 av.
commercial	1.7	1963–5 av.
Railway track (km.)	640	1964
Telephones (per '000 urban population)	0.4	1967
Radio licences (per '000 population)	8	1963–5 av.

FINANCE

Currency unit: The rand was introduced in 1961 at the rate R1 to £0.5 sterling

Exchange rates	*1965*	*1960a*	*1955a*
Per $ U.S.	0.714	0.357	0.357

		Year
National Income (million $ U.S.)	34*	1966
G.N.P. per capita ($ U.S.)	60	1966

a £ sterling.

EMPLOYMENT, PRODUCTION AND TRADE

Cattle-rearing and dairying are the main occupations; there is little arable farming on account of limited rainfall. Twenty per cent of the male population work on temporary contracts in the mines and industries of South Africa, producing invisible earnings which contribute to the balance of trade. Exports are mainly carcasses and animal products, and small quantities of gold, silver, asbestos and manganese. Large nickel reserves were located in 1969. Imports are mainly cereals, sugar, petroleum products and manufactured goods.

PRODUCTION, EXPORTS AND IMPORTS

Years: **1963–5 average** and *1953–5 average* Units: '000 metric tons unless otherwise indicated

	Production		Exports		Imports	
1. CEREALS, etc.						
Maize (corn)	**2.3***	*2.0*[2]	—	—	—	—
Millets/sorghum	**70.0*[1]**	*22.0*[2]	—	—	—	—
3. BEVERAGES, FOREST PRODUCTS, etc.						
Hardwood *j*	**878.7***	*19.0*	—	—	—	—

j '000 cu. metres of roundwood equivalent.

	Production		Exports		Imports	
5. LIVESTOCK‡, ANIMAL PRODUCTS, etc.						
Chickens *d*	**112.3*n***	*124.0*[2]				
Cattle *d*	**1 349.7**	*1 118.0*	—	—	—	—
dairy cows *d*	**699.3**	*564.0*[2]				
Goats *d*	**351.0**	*415.0*	— (Goats and sheep)	—	—	—
Sheep *d*	**125.6**	*191.0*				
Horses *d*	**8.7**	*7.0*[2]				
Pigs *d*	**3.0**	*4.7*	—	—	—	—

continued

	Production		Exports		Imports	
5. LIVESTOCK, ANIMAL PRODUCTS, etc.—*continued*						
Bacon/ham, Meat‡: 'A'	**21.0***	*20.0*[1]*	na	na	—	—
'B'	**3.0**	*0.2*[1]	na	na	—	—
Eggs	**0.2***	*0.2*[2]	—	—	—	—
Fish	na	na	—	—	—	—
Milk	**25.0***	*32.0*	—	—	—	—
Hides/skins	**3.5***	*0.6*[2]*p*	na	na	—	—

d no. in thousands. *n* incl. ducks, geese and turkeys. *p* from cattle only.

	Production		Exports		Imports	
9. NON-FERROUS MINERALS AND METALS						
Gold *k*, ore *m*	—	*1.06*	—	—	—	—
Silver, ore	na	na	na	na	—	—
Asbestos, fibre	**1.64**	*0.82*	na	na	—	—
Manganese, ore	**15.79**	—	na	—	—	—

k '000 fine troy oz. *m* metal content.

BRAZIL

Brazil is a federal republic with a presidential system similar to that of the U.S.A.

AREA: 8 511 965 sq. km. (3 286 500 sq. miles)

LAND USE: (percentage of total)

	1960	1955
Arable and orchard	3.5	2.3
Permanent meadow and pasture	12.6	12.6
Forest and woodland	60.8	60.8
City areas, waste and other land	23.1	24.3

POPULATION: 85 655 000 (1967 estimate)

Largest city: SÃO PAULO; population: 5 383 000 (city proper, 1967)

The new capital, BRASÍLIA, was inaugurated in 1960. In 1965 the population was estimated to be 200 000.

Distribution of working population (1960)

Total working population: 22 651 263* (excl. Indian jungle population)

U.N. group no.		*Percentage*
0a	Agriculture, forestry	51.6
1a	Mining and quarrying, fishing and hunting	2.5
2/3	Manufacturing	8.9
4	Construction	3.5
5b	Electricity, gas, water and sanitary services, and finance	9.9
6b	Commerce (excl. finance)	6.7
7	Transport, storage and communications	4.8
8	Services	12.1

		Year(s)
Life expectancy at birth (years): male	39.3	1940–50 av.
female	45.5	1940–50 av.
Crude birth rate (per '000)	42*	1960–5 av.
Crude death rate (per '000)	11*	1960–5 av.
Accidental deaths (per 100 000 population)		
caused by motor vehicles	27.2*	1960
due to other causes	31.1*	1960
Population per physician	2 290	1964
Population per hospital bed	290	1966
School enrolment: age 5–19 years (percentage)	60	1963–4 av.
age over 19 years (per 100 000 population)	184	1964–5 av.

a fishing and hunting are included in group 1 instead of group 0.
b finance is included in group 5 instead of group 6.

COMMUNICATIONS

		Year(s)
Motor vehicles in use ('000s): private	998	1963–5 av.
commercial	921	1963–5 av.
Railway track (km.)	35 349	1963
Mail per capita: domestic	35	1963–5 av.
foreign received	6	1963–5 av.
foreign sent	8	1963–5 av.
Telephones (per '000 urban population)	1.7	1967
Radio receivers (per '000 population)	95	1963–5 av.
Television sets (per '000 population)	26.5	1963–5 av.
Daily newspapers (per '000 population)	53.5	1962–3 av.

FINANCE

Currency unit: The new cruzeiro was introduced in 1967, equivalent to 1 000 old cruzeiros

Exchange rates	*1965a*	*1960a*	*1950a*	*1938a*
Per $ U.S.	2 220	205.10	18.72	16.5
Per £ sterling	6 216	574.28	52.44	75.9

		Year(s)
National Income (million $ U.S.)	17 809	1965
G.N.P. per capita ($ U.S.)	240	1966
Rate of increase of G.N.P. per capita	1.5	1960–3 av.
Foreign trade (percentage of G.D.P.)	13	1963–5 av.

a old cruzeiros.

TRADING

Total trade (in million $ U.S.)	*1965*	*1955*	*1938*
Exports (f.o.b.)	1 595	1 423	296
Imports (c.i.f.)	1 096	1 307	295

Main trading partners (percentage of total value)

Exports	*1965*	*1955*	*1938*	*Imports*	*1965*	*1955*	*1938*
U.S.A.	33	42	34	U.S.A.	30	24	24
Germany F.R.	9	7	19d	Argentina	12	12	12
Argentina	9	7	5	Germany F.R.	9	7	25d
Italy	5	3	2	Venezuela	7	7	—
Netherlands	5	3	4	Japan	3	3	—
U.K.	4	4	9	U.S.S.R.	3	na	na
France	4	4	6	France	3	5	3

Distribution of trade (percentage of total value)

Exports	*1965*	*1955*	*1938**
Food	62	75	na
(coffee)	(44)	(59)	(45)
Crude materials and fuels	25	20	na
(iron ore and concentrates)	(6)	(2)	(—)
(cotton)	(6)	(10)	(18)
Manufactured goods	7	1	na
Imports			
Manufactured goods	40	na	na
(machinery and transport equipment)	(22)	(11)	(30)
Crude materials and fuels	25	22	na
(fuels)	(21)	(19)	(7)
Food	18	17	15
(cereals)	(14)	(13)	(11)
Chemicals	16	5	na

d incl. Germany D.R.

PRODUCTION, EXPORTS AND IMPORTS

Years: **1963–5 average** and *1953–5 average* Units: '000 metric tons unless otherwise indicated

1. CEREALS, etc.

	Production		Exports		Imports	
Barley	25.3	30.3	—	—	34.2	2.8
Cassava	23 866.0	14 265.7				
Maize (corn)	10 646.0	6 929.7	440.4	30.6	0.4	16.5
Millets/sorghum	—	—	7.8n	—	11.4	7.0
Oats	20.0	13.3	—	—	12.1	10.7
Potatoes	1 226.0	842.7	4.9	—	6.9	22.9
Rice	6 555.0	3 637.7	83.1	1.8	—	3.2
Rye	17.0	18.3	—	—	—	—
Sweet potatoes/yams	1 621.7	965.0				
Wheat	540.0	914.7	—	—	2 220.3	1 570.2

n incl. other cereals.

2. FRUIT, etc.

	Production		Exports		Imports	
Apples	11.7	7.7	—	—	54.1	40.7
Bananas	4 332.7*	3 769.0	215.7	209.5	—	—
Coconuts	508.7e	na	0.6	0.3	—	—
Dates	—	—	—	—	0.1	—
Figs	15.0	9.5[2]	na	na	—	—
Grapes	484.3	316.7	—	—	0.9	5.9
Lemons	41.7	17.5[2]	0.3	—	—	—
Oranges	2 329.3	1 405.0	133.7	34.2	—	—
Other citrus fruit	na	na	3.4	—	—	—

continued

2. FRUIT, etc.—*continued*

	Production		Exports		Imports	
Peaches	82.3	44.7[1]	na	na	—	1.3
Pears	47.0	30.7	—	—	9.0	11.0
Pineapples	285.7	171.0	na	11.5	—	—
Raisins	—	—	—	—	1.6	1.4
Tomatoes	549.0	233.0				
Wine b	na	740.0*	—	—	5.4	27.0

b '000 hectolitres. *e* no. in millions.

3. BEVERAGES, FOREST PRODUCTS, etc.

	Production		Exports		Imports	
Cocoa	116.3	150.0*	78.5	117.2	—	—
Coffee	1 508.1	1 172.5	958.8	803.5	—	—
Sugar: cane	68 658.3	39 863.3				
raw	3 680.7	2 368.0*	512.1	330.3	—	—
Tea	2.2	0.7	1.7	0.4	—	—
Tobacco: leaf	221.8	142.3	53.3	26.7	—	0.1[2]
cigarettes e	58 798.0	na	—	—	—	—
Softwood j	2 192.5[2]	16 805.0	1 670.0	1 554.8	—	—
Hardwood j	115 975.0[2]	82 515.0[2]	126.7	95.1	4.5	1.1
Wood pulp	555.3*	182.0*	17.3	—	33.4	134.7
Newsprint	106.3	42.3*	—	—	78.7	121.7
Other paper	516.7*	288.0*	0.1	—	9.5	11.8

e no. in millions. *j* '000 cu. metres of roundwood equivalent.

continued

PRODUCTION, EXPORTS AND IMPORTS *continued*

4. VEGETABLE OILSEEDS AND OILS

	Production		Exports		Imports	
Castor seed	301.67	164.60	—	47.27	—	—
Castor oil	na	na	109.51	22.41	—	—
Coconut oil	—	—	—	—	0.17	—
Cottonseed	1 206.00	781.00	—	—	—	—
Cottonseed oil	na	na	1.45	—	7.02	—
Groundnuts	423.97	126.00	11.14	0.02	—	—
Groundnut oil	na	na	2.81	—	—	—
Linseed	38.67	26.67*n	10.22	—	0.06	3.70
Linseed oil	na	na	—	—	0.28[2]	—
Olive oil	—	—	—	—	8.22	6.89
Palm kernels	156.03	74.47p	—	—	—	—
Palm kernel oil	na	na	na	0.01q	0.88	—q
Palm oil	—	—	—	—	na	1.11
Rape seed	—	—	—	—	0.02	na
Sesame seed	4.00*	5.00[1]*	0.27	0.10	—	—
Soya beans	383.70	114.33	36.25	34.30	—	—
Soya bean oil	na	na	—	—	4.38	na
Sunflower seed	na	na	0.04	na	—	—
Tung oil	1.2	0.88	1.02	0.13	—	—

n flax grown for seed only. *p* babassu kernels. *q* babassu oil.

5. LIVESTOCK‡, ANIMAL PRODUCTS, etc.

	Production		Exports		Imports	
Chickens d	214 059.0	117 966.6	—	—	—	—
Cattle d	80 988.7	58 307.3	4.7	0.1	12.9	5.5
Goats d }	13 144.0	9 072.7	—	—	69.2	na
Sheep d }	20 876.0	16 855.7				
Horses d	8 945.3	7 303.0				
Pigs d	55 972.0	33 064.0	—	—	—	—
Meat‡: 'A'	2 046.0*	1 582.3	23.0	1.5	—	3.2
'B'	227.6*	31.8	4.1	1.1	—	0.1
Butter	24.0n	25.7	—	—	3.7	0.1
Cheese	40.0	33.3n	—	—	0.8	0.1
Eggs	422.3	250.9	0.2	—	—	—
Fish	371.8	174.3	2.0	0.2*	25.6	23.0*
Milk	6 239.3	3 443.0	—	—	201.5	30.7
Whale/sperm oil	0.8	—	—	—	—	—
Hides/skins	189.8	154.4	25.4	24.9[1]	—	—
Wool	17.6	16.3	7.0	4.7	0.6	0.2

d no. in thousands. *n* government inspected factory produce only.

6. FIBRES, TEXTILES, etc.

	Production		Exports		Imports	
Agaves (sisal etc.)	223.3	77.7[2]	138.6	52.6	0.1	—
Cotton lint	634.7	399.3	211.5	208.2	—	—
Flax fibre	—	—	0.2†	—	1.9	0.8
Hemp fibre	—	—	—	—	0.4	—
Jute	65.3	22.7	6.0	—	—	—
Rubber: natural	26.1	23.5	4.9	1.4	10.5	12.6
synthetic	32.7	—	4.5	—	11.0s	—
Silk f	96.7	180.0*	122.7	5.3	—	—
Cotton: yarn	106.8n	na	0.9[1]	na	—	—
woven fabrics	27.2*	na	2.5[2]	na	—	—
Rayon, fibre/yarn	41.9	30.6	na	na	—[2]	—
Non-cellulosic fibre/yarn	12.6	0.1	—	—	0.2	na
Wool, woven fabrics	19.0p	na	—	—[2]	0.2	na

f metric tons. *n* São Paulo only. *p* million metres. *s* incl. imports for re-export.

7. FUEL AND POWER

	Production		Exports		Imports	
Coal: 'A'‡	1 660	2 270	—	—	1 089	878
Coke	na	na	—	—	106	15
Electricity h: total	29 030	11 560				
hydro	22 894	9 810				
thermal	6 136	1 750				
Natural gas i	570	20	—	—	—	—
Oil, crude	4 500	280[1]	—	—	10 480	4 100[1]
Petroleum, refined	14 076	3 240[1]	5	—	867	5 190[1]
Rare earths f	594n	na	2 022p	827p	—	—
Uranium	—	—	—	—	na	4 107q

f metric tons. *h* million kWh. *i* million cu. metres. *n* monazite. *p* cerium chloride. *q* radium and radium products, in milligrams.

8. IRON AND STEEL

	Production		Exports		Imports	
Iron ore	10 814m	2 191m	10 243	1 930	—	—
Pig iron	2 526	1 030	131	21[1]	1	1
Steel ingots/castings	2 982	1 138	—	—	—	—
Iron/steel products a	na	na	21	—	62	62

a million $ U.S. *m* metal content.

9. NON-FERROUS MINERALS AND METALS

	Production		Exports		Imports	
Diamonds	350.00*l	200.00*l	—	—	0.36[2]a	na
Gold k: ore m	143.00	148.00*	—	—	—	—
bullion/coins etc.	—	—	—	—	0.68	30.70
Platinum group metals k	—	—	—	—	0.35	5.54s
Silver k: ore m	274.30	159.30	—	—	—	—
bullion	—	—	—	—	1 147.00	577.00
Asbestos: fibre	1.23	2.21	—	—	16.23	9.71s
manufactured	na	na	—	—	0.46	0.99s
Mica	1.45	1.72	1.76	0.90	0.02	na
Aluminium: bauxite	152.75	30.51	2.68	1.34	0.85	0.39
alumina	49.66	na	—	—	1.00p	0.26
aluminium	24.89	na	—	—	22.47	16.56s
Antimony: ore	—	—	—	—	0.14	—
metal	—	—	—	—	0.40	0.49s
Beryl	1.50	1.71	1.49	1.59	—	—
Cadmium	—	—	—	—	0.04	0.01
Chrome: ore	14.48mn	3.20mn	—	—	na	1.74s
metal	—	—	—	—	0.58	na
Cobalt, metal	—	—	—	—	0.03	0.40s
Copper: ore	2.72m	na	—	—	—	0.16
metal	2.50[2]	—	—	—	36.66	30.50
Lead: ore	18.00*m	3.00*m	na	12.93[1]	—	—
metal	12.91	3.12	—	—	8.24	20.72s
Magnesium:						
dolomite	343.80	na	—	} 1.95	—	—
magnesite	102.89	na	10.02	} 1.95	na	0.80
kieserite	na	na	—	} 1.95	2.34	0.78
Manganese: ore	1 334.05	202.14	913.80	145.68	—	—
metal	na	na	2.42	na	0.04	0.09s
Mercury f	—	—	—	—	93.00	76.00s
Nickel: ore	1.05m	0.05m	—	—	—	—
metal	na	na	—	—	0.54	0.23s
Tin: ore	1.27m	0.18m	—	—	1.71	0.74s
metal	1.88	1.22	—	—	—	0.29s
Titanium minerals	8.33	0.15[2]q	—	—	6.70	1.79s
Tungsten, ore	0.44	1.53	0.52	1.42	—	—
Zinc: ore	1.74m	—	na	0.46	—	—
metal	0.03*	—	—	—	40.85	22.45
Zirconium minerals	0.46	3.29	na	1.29t	—	—

a million $ U.S. *f* metric tons. *k* '000 fine troy oz. *l* '000 carats. *m* metal content. *n* Bahia only. *p* incl. hydrate. *q* rutile only. *s* incl. imports for re-export. *t* chiefly baddeleyite.

10. CHEMICALS*n* AND FERTILIZERS

	Production		Exports		Imports	
Organic chemicals:						
Benzene	na		—		na	
Butadiene	na		0.2[2]		19.6	
Ethylene	na		na		na	
Methanol	na		—		2.6[2]	
Phenol	na		—		0.4[1]	
Phthalic anhydride	na		—		2.3[1]	
Styrene monomer	na		na		na	
Urea	na		—		7.1	
Inorganic chemicals:						
Ammonia	na		—		—	
Carbon black	24.5[2]		—		3.7[2]	
Chlorine	na		na		na	
Nitric acid	na		na		—[1]	
Sodium carbonate	68.7		—		28.9[2]	
Sodium hydroxide	81.0		—		123.9	
Sulphuric acid	359.3		—		—	
Plastics:						
Polyamides	na		—		0.4	
Polyethylene	na		—		2.7	
Polyvinyl chloride	18.8[2]		—		1.2[1]	
Fertilizers:						
Phosphates	267.6p	67.4*	—	—	186.1	114.7
Potash	—	—	—	—	160.0	69.2
Pyrites	na	na	—	—	—	—
Sulphur, native	5.4q	—	—	—	170.1	74.1

n data not available for years 1953–5. *p* incl. apatite. *q* incl. recovered sulphur.

11. INDUSTRY

	Production		Exports		Imports	
Aircraft a	—	—	2.2	na	23.0	13.0[2]
Alcoholic beverages			—	—	—	2.1a
beer b	6 701.0	na				
Cement	5 420.0	2 400.3	2.0	—	21.0*	525.7
Electrical engineering a	na	na	2.4	—	64.6	7.0[2]
Railway vehicles a	—	—	—	—	15.2	18.7
Machine tools a	31.0[1]	na	—	—	15.9	na
Merchant ships g	49.0	na	—	—	1.0	13.4
Motor vehicles			2.0a	—	27.7a	25.1[2]a
commercial d	73.0	18.6[2]n				
private d	108.0	4.6[2]n				

a million $ U.S. *b* '000 hectolitres. *d* no. in thousands. *g* '000 G.R.T. *n* assembly of imported parts.

na: data not available. — negligible or nil. [1] one year only. [2] two year average. * estimate. ‡ see appendix. † re-exports.

BRITISH HONDURAS

CENTRAL AMERICA

British Honduras is a British colony with internal self-government, but the governor, who is appointed by the Crown, retains certain powers as long as the country receives financial aid from the U.K.

AREA: 22 963 sq. km. (8 867 sq. miles)

LAND USE: (percentage of total)	*1964*	*1953*
Arable and orchard	1.4	5.1
Permanent meadow and pasture	0.7	0.6
Forest and woodland	45.8	—
City areas, waste and other land	52.1	94.3

POPULATION: 113 000 (1967 estimate)

Largest city: BELIZE, capital; population: 45 572 (1964)

Distribution of working population (1960)
Total working population: 27 006

U.N. group no.		*Percentage*
0	Agriculture, forestry, fishing and hunting	39.0
1	Mining and quarrying	0.1
2/3	Manufacturing	14.1
4	Construction	7.0
5	Electricity, gas, water and sanitary services	0.9
6	Commerce	7.5
7	Transport, storage and communications	4.7
8	Services	19.7
9	Others	7.0

		Year(s)
Life expectancy at birth (years): male	45	1944–8 av.
female	49	1944–8 av.
Infant mortality (per '000)	48.5*	1965
Crude birth rate (per '000)	43.7*	1965
Crude death rate (per '000)	6.7*	1965
Population per physician	3 530	1965
Population per hospital bed	210	1966
School enrolment: age 5–19 years (percentage)	92	1963–4 av.
age over 19 years (per 100 000 population)	52	1963–4 av.

COMMUNICATIONS

		Year(s)
Motor vehicles in use ('000s): private	1.5	1963–5 av.
commercial	1.1	1963–5 av.
Telephones (per '000 urban population)	1.5	1967
Radio receivers (per '000 population)	283	1963–5 av.
Daily newspapers (per '000 population)	55	1962–4 av.

FINANCE

Currency unit: The British Honduras dollar

Exchange rates	*1965*	*1960*	*1950*	*1938*
Per $ U.S.	1.42	1.42	1.42	At par
Per £ sterling	4.0	4.0	4.0	2.8

		Year
National Income (million $ U.S.)	38*	1966
G.N.P. per capita ($ U.S.)	360	1966

TRADING

Total trade (in million $ U.S.)	*1965*	*1955*	*1938*
Exports (f.o.b.)	12	6	3
Imports (c.i.f.)	24	10	4

Main trading partners (percentage of total value)

Exports	*1965*	*1955*	*Imports*	*1965*	*1955*
U.K.	40	29	U.S.A.	37	34
U.S.A.	35	32	U.K.	32	35
Mexico	8	—	Jamaica	6	1
Canada	6	3	Canada	4	3
Jamaica	5	17	Netherlands	4	6
Guatemala	1	1	Japan	2	1
			Hong Kong	2	2

Distribution of trade (percentage of total value)

Exports	*1965*	*1955*	*1938**
Food	65	23	na
(sugar)	(33)	(5)	(na)
(fruit)	(26)	(12)	(4)
Crude materials	30	76	na
(wood)	(15)	(63)	(39)
Imports			
Manufactured goods	58	51	na
(machinery and transport equipment)	(25)	(19)	(13)
Food	22	27	17
Chemicals	8	6	na

PRODUCTION, EXPORTS AND IMPORTS

Years: **1963–5 average** and *1953–5 average* Units: '000 metric tons unless otherwise indicated

	Production		Exports		Imports	
1. CEREALS, etc.						
Maize (corn)	3.0*	*5.7*	—	*0.8*	0.3	—
Potatoes	—	—	—	—	0.7	*0.3*
Rice	1.7	*1.0*[2]	—	—	1.6	*1.3*
2. FRUIT, etc.						
Apples	—	—	—	—	0.1	—
Bananas	—	na	1.2	*0.4*	—	—
Coconuts	1.0[1]*e	na	0.3	*1.7*	—	—
Grapes	—	—	—	—	0.1	—
Oranges	34.7	—[2]	0.4	*0.1*	—	—
Other citrus fruit	9.7	*8.0**[1]	1.1[2]	*1.0*	—	—
Wine *b*	—	—	—	—	0.2	—

b '000 hectolitres. *e* no. in millions.

	Production		Exports		Imports	
3. BEVERAGES, FOREST PRODUCTS, etc.						
Cocoa	na	—	0.1	—	—	—
Sugar: cane	281.3*	*30.7*				
raw	32.8	*4.3*	31.0	*1.3*	0.5	*0.6*
Tobacco	—	—	—	—	0.1*n*	*0.1p*
Softwood *j*	52.7*	*54.3*	8.0	*42.4*	—	—
Hardwood *j*	78.7*	*53.0*	29.9	*32.6*	—	*0.1*
Newsprint	—	—	—	—	0.1[2]	—
Other paper	—	—	—	—	—[2]	*0.1*

j '000 cu. metres of roundwood equivalent. *n* cigarettes only. *p* raw and manufactured tobacco.

	Production		Exports		Imports	
4. VEGETABLE OILSEEDS AND OILS						
Copra	na	*0.17*	—	*0.10*	—	*0.05*[2]
Linseed oil	—	—	—	—	—	*0.01*

	Production		Exports		Imports	
5. LIVESTOCK‡, ANIMAL PRODUCTS, etc.						
Chickens *d*	164.0	*95.0*	—	—	—	—
Cattle *d*	27.7	*16.0*	0.2	—	—	*0.1*
Goats *d*	1.0*	*1.0*	} 0.1	—	—	—
Sheep *d*	2.0*	*2.0*				
Horses *d*	4.3*	*2.0*	—	—	—	—
Pigs *d*	14.0	*27.0*	1.4	—	—	—
Bacon/ham	} 1.0*	—	—	—	0.4	*0.1*
Meat‡: 'A'			—	—	—	—
'B'	—	—	—	—	0.5	—
Butter	—	—	—	—	0.1	*0.1*
Cheese	—	—	—	—	0.2	*0.1*
Eggs	0.3*	—	—	—	—	—
Fish	na	*0.5*	0.3	na	0.1	na
Milk	5.0*	na	0.7	—	8.9	*1.1*

d no. in thousands.

	Production		Exports		Imports	
7. FUEL AND POWER						
Electricity *h*	11*n*	—				
Petroleum, refined	—	—	—	—	27	*10*[1]

h million kWh. *n* thermal.

	Production		Exports		Imports	
11. INDUSTRY						
Alcoholic beverages *a*	—	—	—	—	0.6[2]*p*	—
Cement	—	—	—	—	8.3	*2.7*
Electrical engineering *a*	—	—	—	—	0.8	*0.3*
Motor vehicles *a*	—	—	—	—	0.9	*0.2*

a million $ U.S. *p* beer and spirits.

na: data not available. — negligible or nil. [1] one year only. [2] two year average. * estimate. ‡ see appendix. † re-exports.

BRUNEI

SOUTH EAST ASIA

Unlike the other Malay inhabited states, Brunei remained a British protectorate in 1963 at the formation of the Federation of Malaysia.

AREA: 5 800* sq. km. (2 240* sq. miles)

LAND USE: (percentage of total)	*1964*	*1955*
Arable and orchard	11.4	6.6
Permanent meadow and pasture	na	—
Forest and woodland	85.0	67.2
City areas, waste and other land	na	26.2

POPULATION: 107 000 (1967 U.N. estimate)

Capital city: BANDAR SERI BEGAWAN (Brunei Town); population: 9 702 (city proper, 1960)

Distribution of working population (1960)
Total working population: 24 830

U.N. group no.		*Percentage*
0	Agriculture, forestry, fishing and hunting	33.5
1	Mining and quarrying	15.1
2/3	Manufacturing	5.7
4	Construction	13.6
5	Electricity, gas, water and sanitary services	1.1
6	Commerce	7.8
7	Transport, storage and communications	4.0
8	Services	19.2

		Year(s)
Infant mortality (per '000)	41.0	1965
Crude birth rate (per '000)	41.5	1965
Crude death rate (per '000)	6.6	1965
Population per physician	4 590	1965
Population per hospital bed	260	1966
School enrolment: age 5–19 years (percentage)	78	1963–4 av.

COMMUNICATIONS

		Year(s)
Motor vehicles in use ('000s): private	4.6	1963–5 av.
commercial	1.8	1963–5 av.
Telephones (per '000 urban population)	1.9	1967
Radio receivers (per '000 population)	92	1963–5 av.

FINANCE

Currency unit: The Brunei dollar (at par with the Malayan dollar)

Exchange rates	*1965*	*1960*	*1955*	*1938*
Per $ U.S.	3.058	3.058	3.063	1.846
Per £ sterling	8.571	8.571	8.571	8.5

		Year
National Income (million $ U.S.)	106	1958
G.N.P. per capita ($ U.S.)	1 330	1966

TRADING

Total trade (in million $ U.S.)	*1965*	*1955*	*1938*
Exports (f.o.b.)	65	99	4
Imports (c.i.f.)	36	30	2

Main trading partners (percentage of total value)

Exports	*1965*	*Imports*	*1965*
Sarawak	98	U.K.	26
Singapore	1	U.S.A.	17
		Singapore	14
		Japan	9
		China P.R.	5
		Thailand	3
		Australia	3

Distribution of trade (percentage of total value)

Exports	*1965*	*1955*
Fuels	97	95
Imports		
Manufactured goods	65	68
(machinery and transport equipment)	(35)	(23)
Food	18	18
(cereals)	(5)	(3)
Chemicals	6	4

PRODUCTION, EXPORTS AND IMPORTS

Years: **1963–5 average** and *1953–5 average* Units: '000 metric tons unless otherwise indicated

	Production		Exports		Imports	
1. CEREALS, etc.						
Cassava	1.3*	na				
Maize (corn)	—	—	—	—	0.8[2]	—
Potatoes	—	—	—	—	0.2[2]	—
Rice	3.3	*3.7*	—	—	7.8*	*2.4*[2]
Sweet potatoes/yams	1.0	*1.2*[2]	—	—	—	—
2. FRUIT, etc.						
Apples	—	—	—	—	0.2[2]	—
Bananas	8.0*	*7.3*	—	—	0.3[2]	—
Coconuts	—	—	—	—	0.2[2]	—
Oranges	—	—	—	—	0.1[2]	—
Wine *b*	—	—	—	—	0.2[2]	—

b '000 hectolitres.

	Production		Exports		Imports	
3. BEVERAGES, FOREST PRODUCTS, etc.						
Coffee	—	—	—	—	0.1[2]	*0.1*
Sugar, raw	—	—	—	—	3.4*	*1.9*
Tobacco	—	—	—	—	0.2[2]*n*	*0.2p*
Softwood *j*	1.0	—	0.8	—	—	—
Hardwood *j*	51.0	*46.0*[1]	3.7	*0.5*[1]	9.4[2]	*20.0*[1]

j '000 cu. metres of roundwood equivalent. *n* tobacco products only. *p* raw and manufactured tobacco.

	Production		Exports		Imports	
4. VEGETABLE OILSEEDS AND OILS						
Coconut oil	—	—	—	—	0.31[2]	*0.05*[2]*
Groundnuts	—	—	—	—	0.13[2]	na
Groundnut oil			0.04[1]	na	0.33[2]	na
Soya beans	—	—	—	—	0.04[2]	na

	Production		Exports		Imports	
5. LIVESTOCK‡, ANIMAL PRODUCTS, etc.						
Chickens *d*	178.7	*67.7*	—	—	—	—
Cattle *d*	2.3	*1.0*	—	—	1.3[2]	—[1]
Goats *d*	4.0*	*1.0*	—	—	—	—
Pigs *d*	8.0	*6.7*	—	—	5.9[2]	—
Meat‡: 'A'	—	—	—	—	0.1[2]	—
'B'	—	—	—	—	0.1[2]	—
Butter	—	—	—	—	0.1[2]	*0.1**
Eggs	0.3*	*0.2*[2]	—	—	0.3[2]	—
Fish	3.8	*0.6*[2]	—[2]	—	0.8[2]	—
Milk	na	—	0.1	—	7.0	*1.9**

d no. in thousands.

	Production		Exports		Imports	
6. FIBRES, TEXTILES, etc.						
Rubber, natural	na	na	1.3*	*1.3*	—	—
7. FUEL AND POWER						
Electricity *h*	71*t*	—				
Natural gas *i*	190	*68**	53	*74*	—	—
Oil, crude	3 703	*5 310*[1]	3 643	na	—	—
Petroleum, refined	87	—[1]	23	*10*[1]	—	—

h million kWh. *i* million cu. metres. *t* thermal.

	Production		Exports		Imports	
9. NON-FERROUS MINERALS AND METALS						
Gold *k*, bullion/coins etc.	—	—	—	—	45.67[2]	—
Asbestos, manufactured	—	—	—	—	1.34[2]	—

k '000 fine troy oz.

	Production		Exports		Imports	
11. INDUSTRY						
Aircraft *a*	—	—	—	—	0.1[2]	*146.9*
Alcoholic beverages *a*	—	—	—	—	0.5[2]	*0.5*
Electrical engineering *a*	—	—	—	—	2.0[2]	*1.1*
Motor vehicles *a*	—	—	—	—	2.8	*2.1*

a million $ U.S.

na: data not available. — negligible or nil. [1] one year only. [2] two year average. * estimate. ‡ see appendix. † re-exports.

BULGARIA

Bulgaria is a member of Comecon. Formerly a principality, the country was declared a republic in 1946.

AREA: 110 911.5 sq. km. (42 823 sq. miles) (incl. territorial waters)

LAND USE: (percentage of total)	*1965*	*1947*
Arable and orchard	41.1	38.7
Permanent meadow and pasture	11.1	2.3
Forest and woodland	32.6	33.2
City areas, waste and other land	15.2	25.8

POPULATION: 8 226 564 (1965 census, based on 3% sample return)

Largest city: SOFIYA (Sofia), capital; population: 810 300 (1966)

Distribution of working population (1956)
Total working population: 4 150 207

U.N. group no.		*Percentage*
0	Agriculture, forestry, fishing and hunting	64.1
1/2/3	Mining, quarrying and manufacturing	} 15.9
5	Electricity, gas, water and sanitary services	
4	Construction	2.8
6	Commerce	3.4
7	Transport, storage and communications	3.2
8	Services	9.8
9	Others	0.8

		Year(s)
Life expectancy at birth (years): male	67.8	} 1960–2 av.
female	71.4	
Infant mortality (per '000)	30.8	1965
Crude birth rate (per '000)	15.3	1965
Crude death rate (per '000)	8.2	1965
Accidental deaths (per 100 000 population)		
caused by motor vehicles	7.2	1965
due to other causes	29.0	1965
Population per physician	600	1965
Population per hospital bed	140	1966
School enrolment: age 5–19 years (percentage)	90	1963–4 av.
age over 19 years (per 100 000 population)	1 240	1964–5 av.

COMMUNICATIONS		*Year(s)*
Motor vehicles in use ('000s): private	6	1950
commercial	5	1950
Railway track (km.)	5 771	1964
Telephones (per '000 urban population)	3.7	1967
Radio licences (per '000 population)	240	} 1963–5 av.
Television licences (per '000 population)	15.2	
Daily newspapers (per '000 population)	155	1962–4 av.

FINANCE

Currency unit: The lev. (A new lev equivalent to 10 old leva was introduced on 1 January 1962)

Exchange rates	*1965a*	*1960b*
Per $ U.S.	1.17	6.8
Per £ sterling	3.20	19.0

a official rate, new leva. *b* old leva.

		Year(s)
National Income (million $ U.S.)	5 000*	1966
G.N.P. per capita ($ U.S.)	620*	1966
Rate of increase of G.N.P. per capita	5.7	1960–4 av.

TRADING

Total trade (in million $ U.S.)	*1965*	*1955*	*1938*
Exports (f.o.b.)	1 176	236	68
Imports (f.o.b.)	1 178	250	60

Main trading partners (percentage of total value)

Exports	*1965*	*1955*	*Imports*	*1965*	*1955*
U.S.S.R.	52	47	U.S.S.R.	50	46
Germany D.R.	9	15	Germany D.R.	7	11
Czechoslovakia	8	11	Czechoslovakia	7	12
Germany F.R.	3	2	Germany F.R.	6	3
Poland	3	3	Poland	4	5
Italy	3	—	Italy	3	1
Yugoslavia	2	1	Austria	3	3

Distribution of trade (percentage of total value)

Exports	*1965*	*1955*
Food	36	34*
Machinery and transport equipment	25	na
Crude materials and fuels	21	na
Imports		
Machinery and transport equipment	44	40*
Crude materials and fuels	37	na
(fuels)	(27)	(6*)
Food	7	4*
Chemicals	6	6*

PRODUCTION, EXPORTS AND IMPORTS

Years: **1963–5 average** and *1953–5 average* Units: '000 metric tons unless otherwise indicated

	Production		Exports		Imports	
1. CEREALS, etc.						
Barley	752.7	na	0.5	*8.0**	130.6	*4.6**
Maize (corn)	1 675.3	na	120.6	*38.2**	80.5	*1.8**
Millets/sorghum	9.0[1]*	na	0.3	—	0.8	—
Oats	128.7	na	—	—	4.6[2]	—
Potatoes	399.0	na	44.0	—	—	—*
Rice	35.3	na	19.5	*4.8**	34.4	—
Rye	57.3	*162.0[2]*	—	*8.0**	8.4	—
Wheat	2 310.3	na	14.9	*149.6**	250.0	—*
2. FRUIT, etc.						
Apples	317.7	na	50.1	—	—	—
Apricots	32.7	*2.0[1]*	na	—	—	—
Bananas	—	—	—	—	0.5	—
Cherries	46.7	*6.1[1]*	na	—	—	—
Dates	—	—	—	—	0.1	—
Grapes	1 133.0	na	189.8	*28.1**	—	—
Lemons	—	—	—	—	3.1	*0.6**
Oranges	—	—	—	—	4.0	*0.4**
Peaches	80.3	*3.1*	na	na	—	—
Pears	81.0	na	1.1	—	—	—
Plums	203.3	*55.9*	na	na	—	—
Raisins	—	—	0.3	—	0.3	*0.3**
Tomatoes	724.3	—	na	—	—	—
Wine *b*	na	na	945.5	*46.0**	24.5	—

b '000 hectolitres.

	Production		Exports		Imports	
3. BEVERAGES, FOREST PRODUCTS, etc.						
Cocoa	—	—	—	—	5.6	—
Sugar: beet	1 538.0	*565.3**				
raw	211.3	*75.7**	3.1[1]	*0.2**	146.0*	—
Tea	—	—	—	—	0.5	—
Tobacco: leaf	125.9	*29.5[2]**	86.1	*21.1**	1.1	—
cigars	—	—	} 14.6*n*	*40.3a*	—	—[1]
cigarettes	24 498.0*e*	*8 860.0e*				
tobacco/snuff	144.6	—				
Softwood *j*	1 595.3*p*	na	83.0	*11.1*	149.7	—
Hardwood *j*	4 050.3*	na	79.7	*8.7*	—	—
Wood pulp	70.1	—	12.4	—	25.6	—
Newsprint	—	*6.0[2]**	—	—[1]	21.7	*11.0[1]*
Other paper	116.7	*28.5[2]**	—	—[1]	26.6	*5.9[1]*

a million $ U.S. *e* no. in millions. *j* '000 cu. metres of roundwood equivalent. *n* cigarettes only. *p* from state forests only.

	Production		Exports		Imports	
4. VEGETABLE OILSEEDS AND OILS						
Castor seed	—	*6.60[2]*	—	—	0.01	—
Castor oil	—	na	—	*0.53*	0.53	—
Coconut oil	—	—	—	—	0.70	*0.40**
Cottonseed	26.30	*36.00**	—	*4.00**	—	—
Cottonseed oil	na	na	0.86	—	—	—
Groundnuts	0.70	na	2.72	—	4.28	—
Linseed	—	na	—	—	—	*1.00**
Linseed oil	—	na	—	—	2.54	—
Olive oil	—	—	—	—	1.08	—*
Palm kernels	—	—	—	—	1.02	—
Palm oil	—	—	—	—	—	*0.06**
Rapeseed	1.30	na	2.25	*4.23**	—	—
Rapeseed oil	na	na	—	*1.10**	—	—
Sesame seed	0.20	na	—	—	0.03	—
Soya beans	0.30	na	—	—*	—	—
Sunflower seed	343.33	na	78.55	*8.43*	—	—
Sunflower seed oil	na	na	6.49	*0.53**	0.54	—
Tung oil	—	—	—	—	0.12	—
5. LIVESTOCK‡, ANIMAL PRODUCTS, etc.						
Chickens *dn*	21 591.3	*12 874.0*				
Cattle *d*	1 516.7	*1 855.0[1]*	43.0	—	1.2	—*
dairy cows *d*	621.3*	na				
Goats *d*	354.0	*765.0[2]**	} 435.0	na	2.1	na
Sheep *d*	10 285.0	*7 735.0[2]**				
Horses *d*	260.7	*468.6*				
Pigs *d*	2 257.0	*1 415.0[1]*	176.1	*9.5p*	0.2	—
Meat‡: 'A'	289.7	na	6.0	*12.9*	9.8	na
'B'	69.1*	na	8.9	—	0.2	—
Butter	11.3	na	2.1	—	—	—
Cheese	109.3	na	10.2	*0.1**	—	—
Eggs	72.6	na	23.2	*10.4*	—	—
Fish	13.5	*7.2*	—	—	—	—
Milk	907.7	na	0.8	—	21.4	na
Hides/skins	14.6[2]	na	—	*0.4[1]a*	—	—
Wool	13.3	*8.0**	—	—	1.8	*0.4*

a million $ U.S. *d* no. in thousands. *n* incl. ducks, geese and turkeys. *p* pigs over 6 months old.

continued

na: data not available. — negligible or nil. [1] one year only. [2] two year average. * estimate. ‡ see appendix. † re-exports.

PRODUCTION, EXPORTS AND IMPORTS *continued*

	Production		Exports		Imports	
6. FIBRES, TEXTILES, etc.						
Cotton lint	14.0	*22.0[2]**	1.0	—	41.6	*6.9**
Flax fibre	2.4	na	0.4	—	0.2	—
Hemp fibre	5.9	na	0.4	—	1.5	—
Jute	—	—	—	—	6.3	—
Rubber, natural	—	—	—	—	9.4	*0.5**
Silk *f*	180.0	*30.0**	73.3	*5.3**	4.0	—
Cotton: yarn	58.0	na	—	na	—	na
woven fabrics	32.8	*14.8**	4.9[2]	na	—	na
Rayon: fibre/yarn	—	na	—	na	—	na
woven fabrics	1.6	na	—	na	—	na
Wool: yarn	17.4	*8.8*	—	—	—	—
woven fabrics *q*	19.3	*10.4*	—	—	—	—

f metric tons. *q* million metres.

	Production		Exports		Imports	
7. FUEL AND POWER						
Coal‡ 'A'	607	*290*	12	—	1 742	—
'B'	11 420	*9 760*	—	—	—	—
Coke	na	na	—	—	312	—
Electricity *h*: total	8 709	*1 830*				
hydro	1 852	*650[1]*				
thermal	6 857	*1 180*				
Natural gas *i*	60	—[1]	—	—	—	—
Oil, crude	187	*150[1]*	40	na	1 486	na
Petroleum, refined	1 490	*20[1]*	37	—	1 420	na

h million kWh. *i* million cu. metres.

	Production		Exports		Imports	
8. IRON AND STEEL						
Iron ore	657*m*	na	12	—	—	—
Pig iron	472	*6*	147	—	149	—
Steel ingots/castings	508	*50*	9	—	—	—

m metal content.

	Production		Exports		Imports	
9. NON-FERROUS MINERALS AND METALS						
Asbestos, fibre	1.27	*1.07*	—	—	—	—
Cadmium	na	na	—	—	—	—
Chrome	na	na	—	—	—	—
Cobalt	na	na	—	—	—	—
Copper: ore	20.77*m*	na	—	—	—	—
metal	22.29	*3.18*	7.19	—	—	—
Lead: ore	93.39*m*	*10.00[1]*m*	—	—	—	—
metal	77.42	*3.04*	na	—	—	—
Manganese, ore	44.16	*39.00*	—	—	—	—
Zinc: ore	62.79*m*	na	—	—	—	—
metal	60.16	*0.45*	na	—	—	—

m metal content.

	Production	Exports	Imports
10. CHEMICALS*n* AND FERTILIZERS			
Organic chemicals:			
Benzene	na	—	na
Butadiene	—	—	na
Ethylene	na	na	na
Methanol	na	na	na
Phenol	na	na	na
Phthalic anhydride	na	na	na
Styrene monomer	na	na	na
Urea	25.2	na	na
Inorganic chemicals:			
Ammonia	255.0	na	na
Carbon black	na	na	na
Chlorine	na	na	na
Nitric acid	424.5	na	na
Sodium carbonate	223.4	90.6	—
Sodium hydroxide	28.1	12.7	—
Sulphuric acid	292.7	na	na
Plastics:			
Polyamides	—	—	na
Polyethylene	—	—	na
Polyvinyl chloride	na	na	na

	Production		Exports		Imports	
Fertilizers:						
Phosphates	—	—	—	—	441.2	—
Pyrites	60.0	—	—	—	—	—
Sulphur, recovered	6.7	*1.2[1]*	—	—	—	—

n data not available for years 1953–5.

	Production		Exports		Imports	
11. INDUSTRY						
Beer *b*	1 518.0	*518.3*	41.8*a*	—	—	—
Spirits *b*	143.0[1] *r*	na				
Cement	2 489.0	*768.7*	715.0[1]**p*	*57.0*p*	105.0**p*	—**p*
Electrical engineering *a*	na	na	na	na	40.8	*0.6[1]*
Machine tools *a*	—	—	—	—	—	*0.8[1]*
Merchant ships *g*	—	—	—	—	23.0	—
Motor vehicles *a*	—	—	—	—	8.6	—

a million $ U.S. *b* '000 hectolitres; trade refers to all alcoholic beverages, in million $ U.S. *g* '000 G.R.T. *p* excl. trade with other Comecon countries. *r* production for home consumption in 1967.

BURMA

Burma left the British Commonwealth to become an independent republic in 1948.

AREA: 678 000 sq. km. (261 800 sq. miles)

LAND USE: (percentage of total)	*1965*	*1954*
Arable and orchard	23.4	12.6
Permanent meadow and pasture	0.5	—
Forest and woodland	66.8	57.7
City areas, waste and other land	9.3	29.7

POPULATION: 25 811 000 (1967 estimate)

Largest city: RANGOON, capital; population: 821 800 (city proper, 1957)

		Year
Life expectancy at birth (years): male	40.8	} 1954
female	43.8	
Infant mortality (per '000)	109.3*	1965
Crude birth rate (per '000)	47.0*	1965
Crude death rate (per '000)	18.2*	1965
Accidental deaths (per 100 000 population)		
caused by motor vehicles	6.7*	1962
due to other causes	47.0*	1962
Population per physician	11 900	1965
Population per hospital bed	1 030 *b*	1966
School enrolment: age 5–19 years (percentage)	51	1964
age over 19 years (per 100 000 population)	85	1964

b government hospitals only

COMMUNICATIONS		*Year(s)*
Motor vehicles in use ('000s): private	25.6	} 1963–5 av.
commercial	22.3	
Railway track (km.)	2 990	1959
Mail per capita: domestic	2	} 1963–5 av.
foreign	0.2	
Telephones (per '000 urban population)	0.1	1967
Radio licences (per '000 population)	10	1963–5 av.
Daily newspapers (per '000 population)	9	1962

FINANCE

Currency unit: The kyat replaced the rupee in 1952

Exchange rates	*1965*	*1960*	*1958a*
Per $ U.S.	4.782	4.778	4.775
Per £ sterling	13.390	13.378	13.333

		Year(s)
National Income (million $ U.S.)	1 362	1964
G.N.P. per capita ($ U.S.)	60	1966
Rate of increase of G.N.P. per capita	1.9	1960–3 av.
Foreign trade (percentage of G.D.P.)	31	1963–4 av.

a selling rate

EMPLOYMENT AND PRODUCTION

Three-quarters of the population are employed in agriculture or forestry, rice and teak being the main products for export. Mineral deposits and oil reserves are considerable. Cement, brick and steel works have been built under the government's development plan with the aid of loans from China P.R., Japan, and Germany F.R., and a sugar refinery and H.E.P. plant are also in production.

continued

na: data not available. — negligible or nil. [1] one year only. [2] two year average. * estimate. ‡ see appendix. † re-exports.

BURMA *continued*

TRADING

Total trade (in million $ U.S.)	1965	1955 a	1938 ab
Exports (f.o.b.)	225	227	178
Imports (c.i.f.)	247	181	78

Main trading partners (percentage of total value)

Exports	1965	1955 a	1938 ab	*Imports*	1965	1955 a	1938 ab
Philippines	14	na	—	Japan	29	21	7
Ceylon	11	7	6	China P.R.	11	1	—
India	10	18	54	U.K.	9	25	18
Japan	10	18	2	U.S.A.	7	3	3
China P.R.	8	8	1	Pakistan	5	—	na
U.S.S.R.	6	7	na	India	5	18	55
U.K.	6	8	14	Netherlands	4	4	3

Distribution of trade (percentage of total value)

Exports	1965	1955 a	1938* ab
Food	75	83	na
(rice)	(62)	(75)	(44)
Crude materials and fuels	23	14	49
(raw cotton)	(4)	(4)	(2)
Imports			
Manufactured goods	68	66	na
(machinery and transport equipment)	(18)	(18)	(10)
Food	12	11	21 c
Chemicals	8	8	5
Crude materials and fuels	8	6	na

a excludes land-borne trade. *b* year beginning 1 April. *c* includes beverages and tobacco.

PRODUCTION, EXPORTS AND IMPORTS

Years: **1963–5 average** and *1953–5 average* Units: '000 metric tons unless otherwise indicated

	Production		Exports		Imports	
1. CEREALS, etc.						
Maize (corn)	58.3	32.0[2]	19.5	24.1	—	—
Millets/sorghum	43.7	na	—	—	—	—
Potatoes	53.0	na	3.5[2]	3.3	—	—
Rice	8 115.3	5 762.7	1 475.6	1 356.9	—	—
Wheat	53.0	4.5[2]	—	—	15.3[2]	3.2

	Production		Exports		Imports	
2. FRUIT, etc.						
Coconuts	50.0[1] e	na	—	—	7.2	7.6
Dates	—	—	—	—	na	1.9*
Raisins	—	—	—	—	0.1	—
Wine b	—	—	—	—	0.2	—

b '000 hectolitres. *e* no. in millions.

	Production		Exports		Imports	
3. BEVERAGES, FOREST PRODUCTS, etc.						
Sugar: cane	1 215.3	1 147.3*				
raw	68.3 n	22.0 n	—	—	39.4	21.0
Tea	—	—	—	0.1†	0.4	0.4
Tobacco: leaf	44.9	48.6*	—	0.2	—	0.4
cigarettes	970.0 e	240.3 e	—	—	—	0.2[2] p
Hardwood j	3 488.0[1]	2 077.0[2]	262.0[2]	98.4[2]	—	5.6[2]
Newsprint	—	—	—	—	15.0[1]	5.8[2]
Other paper	—	—	—	—	14.0[1]	12.6[2]

e no. in millions. *j* '000 cu. metres of roundwood equivalent. *n* in addition, non-centrifugal sugar 148* (1963–5 av.) and 113 (1953–5 av.). *p* incl. other tobacco products.

	Production		Exports		Imports	
4. VEGETABLE OILSEEDS AND OILS						
Castor oil	—	—	—	—	0.04	0.04
Copra	—	—	—	—	1.59	na
Coconut oil	na	na	—	—	6.37	14.47
Cottonseed	37.00	39.30*	—	—	0.01	na
Groundnuts	226.30	130.20	—	—	17.22	na
Groundnut oil	na	na	—	—	26.47	14.49
Linseed oil	—	—	—	—	0.29	0.24
Palm oil	—	—	—	—	na	0.22
Rapeseed	na	1.00[1] q	0.29	0.17	—	—
Sesame seed	72.13	41.67	—	—	—	—
Soya bean oil	—	—	—	—	10.16	na
Tung oil	—	—	—	—	0.01	na

q incl. mustard seed.

	Production		Exports		Imports	
5. LIVESTOCK‡, ANIMAL PRODUCTS, etc.						
Cattle d	6 053.3	4 706.7	—	—	—	—
dairy cows d	1 573.3*	na				
Goats d	523.0	217.3	—	—	—	—
Sheep d	139.0	33.0	—	—	—	—
Horses d	25.7	14.0				
Pigs d	804.0	482.3	—	—	—	—
Meat‡ 'A'	31.3	9.7	—	—	—	—
Butter	—	—	—	—	0.2	0.1
Cheese	5.0*	na	—	—	0.2	—
Eggs	8.0*	na	—	—	—	—
Fish	360.0 r	na	—	—	5.4	na
Milk	260.0	213.0[2]	—	—	119.5	66.5*
Hides/skins	na	na	na	193.5[2]	—	—

d no. in thousands. *r* incl. fish landed in foreign ports, and fish landed in Burma by foreign vessels.

	Production		Exports		Imports	
6. FIBRES, TEXTILES, etc.						
Cotton lint	18.7	20.7*	13.2	18.5	—	0.1[1]
Jute	13.3	—	1.7	—	12.9[2]	—
Rubber, natural	8.2	na	8.2	11.2	0.1	—
Silk f	—	—	2.0†	—	112.3	186.3
Cotton: yarn	5.0[2]	1.4	—	—	na	6.9
woven fabrics	1.0*	—	—	—	11.0[2]	13.5

f metric tons.

	Production		Exports		Imports	
7. FUEL AND POWER						
Coal 'A'‡	7	—	—	—	180	233
Coke	—	—	—	2†	2	8
Electricity h: total	554	180[1]				
hydro	258[2]	—[1]				
thermal	296	180[1]				
Natural gas i	na	10	—	—	—	—
Oil, crude	580	210[1]	—	—	106	na
Petroleum, refined	627	170[1]	—	—	40	150[1]

h million kWh. *i* million cu. metres.

	Production		Exports		Imports	
8. IRON AND STEEL						
Iron ore	2 540[2] m	—	—	—	—	—

m metal content.

	Production		Exports		Imports	
9. NON-FERROUS MINERALS AND METALS						
Silver k, ore	1 860.00 m	1 162.70 m	1 219.87 u	na	—	—
Asbestos: fibre	—	—	—	—	1.21	—
manufactured	—	—	—	—	0.20	—
Aluminium	—	—	—	—	3.38	—
Antimony, ore	0.15* m	0.08* m	0.01	—	—	—
Copper: ore	0.15[2] m	na	0.37	—	—	—
metal	—	—	—	—	0.26	—
Lead: ore	19.41 m	11.98 m	0.37	2.08	—	—
metal	17.25	11.47	13.95	10.68	—	—
Manganese, ore	0.10[2]	4.27	—	2.47[2]	—	—
Nickel, metal	0.07 n	0.06 n	0.45	—	—	—
Tin: ore m	0.88	1.18	0.84	0.86	—	—
metal	na	na	—	—	0.02	—
Tungsten, ore	0.56	1.95	0.86	2.15 t	—	—
Zinc: ore	7.83 m	5.99 m	15.48	31.73	—	—
metal	—	—	—	—	0.44	—

k '000 fine troy oz. *m* metal content. *n* nickel content of speiss. *t* incl. some tin-tungsten ore. *u* bullion.

	Production		Exports		Imports	
10. CHEMICALS n AND FERTILIZERS						
Chemicals	—		—		na	
Fertilizers:						
Phosphates	—	—	—	—	—	—
Potash	—	—	—	—	0.2	—
Sulphur	—	—	—	—	0.7	0.3

n data not available for years 1953–5.

	Production		Exports		Imports	
11. INDUSTRY						
Aircraft a	—	—	—	—	0.6[1]	0.4[2]
Alcoholic beverages a	—	—	—	—	0.4[1]	0.2
Cement	125.0	54.7	9.0*	—	70.0*	57.0
Electrical engineering a	—	—	—	—	9.1[1]	7.6[2]
Railway vehicles a	—	—	—	—	2.4[1]	—
Merchant ships g	—	na	—	—	8.0	6.4
Motor vehicles a	—	—	—	—	9.2[1]	5.6[2]

a million $ U.S. *g* '000 G.R.T.

BURUNDI

CENTRAL AFRICA

Burundi, as part of Ruanda-Urundi, was formerly under Belgian trusteeship, until proclaimed an independent constitutional monarchy in 1962. Joint economic arrangements with Rwanda ended two years later. Since a coup in 1966 the president has ruled through the National Revolutionary Council.

AREA: 27 834 sq. km. (10 747 sq. miles)

LAND USE: (percentage of total)	1965
Arable and orchard	37.3
Permanent meadow and pasture	22.6
Forest and woodland	2.5
City areas, waste and other land	37.6

POPULATION: 3 210 090 (1965 census)

Largest city: BUJUMBURA capital; population: 71 000 (1965)

		Year(s)
Life expectancy at birth (years): male	35*	1965
female	38.5*	1965
Infant mortality (per '000)	150*	1965
Crude birth rate (per '000)	46.1	1965
Crude death rate (per '000)	25.6*	1965
Population per physician	56 320	1965
Population per hospital bed	900	1966
School enrolment: age 5–19 years (percentage)	22	1964
age over 19 years (per 100 000 population)	6	1964–5 av.

FINANCE

Currency unit: The Burundi franc

Exchange rates	1965 a	1965 b*
Per $ U.S.	50	107
Per £ sterling	140	300

		Year
National Income (million $ U.S.)	106	1958
G.N.P. per capita ($ U.S.)	50	1966

a official rate; *b* free rate.

EMPLOYMENT AND TRADE

Subsistence agriculture accounts for well over half the gross national income; recently a fishing industry has developed on Lake Tanganyika. There are a few other small industries: food processing, brewing, cement and textile manufacturing. Trade is mainly with the U.S.A. and the U.K.

No independent production and trade figures are available for Burundi for the years 1963–5. 1953–5 data for Ruanda-Urundi are given under Rwanda.

CAMBODIA

SOUTH EAST ASIA

Cambodia, Laos and Vietnam were known as French Indo-China until 1949 when Cambodia became an independent state within the French Union. In 1954 the Geneva Conference arranged for the withdrawal of French forces following the establishment of sovereign independence.

AREA: 181 000* sq. km. (70 000* sq. miles)

LAND USE: (percentage of total)	1965	1954
Arable and orchard	16.2	17.1
Permanent meadow and pasture	na	2.9
Forest and woodland, including rough grazing	73.9	45.7
City areas, waste and other land	na	34.3

POPULATION: 6 415 000 (1967 estimate)

Largest city: PHNOM PENH, capital; population: 393 995 (city proper, 1962)

Distribution of working population (1962)

Total working population: 2 560 500

U.N. group no.		*Percentage*
0	Agriculture, forestry, fishing and hunting	80.9
1	Mining and quarrying	0.1
2/3	Manufacturing	2.8
4	Construction	0.7
5	Electricity, gas, water and sanitary services	0.1
6	Commerce	5.9
7	Transport, storage and communications	0.9
8	Services	7.1
9	Others	1.5

		Year(s)
Life expectancy at birth (years): male	44.2	1958–9
female	43.3	1958–9
Population per physician	18 760	1965
Population per hospital bed	1 320	1965
School enrolment: age 5–19 years (percentage)	46	1963–4 av.
age over 19 years (per 100 000 population)	79	1963–5 av.

COMMUNICATIONS

		Year(s)
Motor vehicles in use ('000s): private	16.6	1963–5 av.
commercial	9.3	1963–5 av.
Railway track (km.)	385	1964
Telephones (per '000 urban population)	0.1	1967
Radio receivers (per '000 population)	154	1963–5 av.
Television sets (per '000 population)	1.1	1963–5 av.
Daily newspapers (per '000 population)	8	1962

FINANCE

Currency unit: The riel

Exchange rates	1965	1960
Per $ U.S.	35.0	35.0
Per £ sterling	98.0	98.0

		Year(s)
National Income (million $ U.S.)	686	1965
G.N.P. per capita ($ U.S.)	120	1966
Rate of increase of G.N.P. per capita	2.3	1960–3 av.

TRADING

Total trade (in million $ U.S.)	1965	1955
Exports (f.o.b.)	105	40
Imports (c.i.f.)	103	48

Main trading partners (percentage of total value)

Exports	1965	1955	*Imports*	1965	1955
France a	29	26	France	20	26 a
Singapore	15	na	Japan	17	10
Hong Kong	8	5	China P.R.	14	na
China P.R.	6	na	U.K.	5	1
Philippines	5	na	Czechoslovakia	5	na
Japan	5	1	Germany F.R.	4	1
			Singapore	4	na

Distribution of trade (percentage of total value)

Exports	1965	1955
Food	60	na
(rice)	(49)	(8)
Crude materials and fuels	39	na
(rubber)	(33)	(45)
Imports		
Manufactured goods	73	na
(machinery and transport equipment)	(26)	(16)
(textiles)	(17)	(13)
Chemicals	12	6
(medicinal and pharmaceutical products)	(6)	(3)

a incl. former French overseas territories.

continued

na: data not available. — negligible or nil. [1] one year only. [2] two year average. * estimate. ‡ see appendix. † re-exports.

PRODUCTION, EXPORTS AND IMPORTS

Years: **1963–5 average** and *1953–5 average* Units: '000 metric tons unless otherwise indicated

Note—few data are available for the years 1953 and 1954, so the majority of the figures in italics refer to the year 1955 only.

	Production 1963–5	Production 1953–5	Exports 1963–5	Exports 1953–5	Imports 1963–5	Imports 1953–5
1. CEREALS, etc.						
Cassava	19.3	na	—	—	—	—
Maize (corn)	175.3	na	115.0	66.0	—	—
Potatoes	—	—	—	0.3[1]	0.1	0.2[1]
Rice	2 627.3	1 157.7*	447.4	5.9[1]	—	5.2[1]
Sweet potatoes/yams	28.0*	39.0[1]	—	—	—	—
Wheat	na	—	0.9	—	—	—
2. FRUIT, etc.						
Apples	—	—	—	—	—	0.1[1]
Bananas	156.7*	na	—	—	—	—
Coconuts	28.3*e	na	—	—	—	0.6[1]
Grapes	—	—	—	—	—	0.1[1]
Oranges	52.3	12.0[2]	—	0.3[1]	—	0.1[1]
Other citrus fruit	8.7*	6.5[2]	0.1	—	—	—
Pineapples	23.0	na	—	—	—	—
Raisins	—	—	—	—	0.1	—
Wine b	—	—	—	—	3.0	4.0[1]

b '000 hectolitres. *e* no. in millions.

	Production 1963–5	Production 1953–5	Exports 1963–5	Exports 1953–5	Imports 1963–5	Imports 1953–5
3. BEVERAGES, FOREST PRODUCTS, etc.						
Coffee	—	—	—	—	0.2	0.1[1]
Sugar, raw	—	—	na	4.3[1]	5.5	5.4[1]
Tea	—	—	—	—	0.2	0.3[1]
Tobacco: leaf	9.3	5.5[2]	0.3	0.7[1]	0.2	0.6[1]
cigarettes	—	—	—	—	—	0.2[1]
Hardwood j	518.7*	416.7	85.0	90.8	—	—
Wood pulp	—	—	—	—	0.7[2]	—
Newsprint	1.0	—	—	—	5.4[1]	0.1
Other paper	0.7	—	—	—	1.1[1]	0.3

j '000 cu. metres of roundwood equivalent.

	Production 1963–5	Production 1953–5	Exports 1963–5	Exports 1953–5	Imports 1963–5	Imports 1953–5
4. VEGETABLE OILSEEDS AND OILS						
Castor seed	2.33	—[2]	1.65	0.10[1]	—	—
Copra	5.20	na	—	—[2]	0.12	—[1]
Coconut oil	na	na	—	—[1]	1.15	0.62[1]
Cottonseed	4.00	na	2.28	0.30[1]	—	—[2]
Groundnuts	11.66	2.80	0.19	na	—	—
Groundnut oil	na	na	na	0.02[1]	0.01	0.04[1]
Linseed oil	—	—	—	—	0.08	0.02[1]
Sesame seed	10.10	2.00[2]	5.30	0.70[1]	—	—
Soya beans	8.00	8.00	6.41	3.40[1]	—	—[1]
Soya bean oil	na	na	0.11	0.47[1]	—	0.03[1]
Tung oil	—	—	0.06	—[1]	—	—

	Production 1963–5	Production 1953–5	Exports 1963–5	Exports 1953–5	Imports 1963–5	Imports 1953–5
5. LIVESTOCK‡, ANIMAL PRODUCTS, etc.						
Chickens d	2 925.0	4 000.0				
Cattle d	1 417.7	853.3	25.2*	0.1[2]	—	—[2]
dairy cows d	445.7	179.7				
Goats d	3.0*	na	—	—	—	—
Horses d	4.7	3.0				
Pigs d	822.0	384.7	4.2*	2.1[1]	—	—[1]
Meat‡ 'A'	32.0	17.7n	—	—	—	—
'B'	8.0*	7.9[2]	—	—	—	—
Butter	—	—	—	—	0.1	—
Eggs	2.4*	6.3[2]	—	0.2	—	—
Fish	162.6	150.0[2]	1.5	na	0.2	na
Milk	85.0*	na	—	—	12.0	11.5[1]
Hides/skins	0.8[2]	1.8[2]	—	—	—	—

d no. in thousands. *n* government inspected meat only.

	Production 1963–5	Production 1953–5	Exports 1963–5	Exports 1953–5	Imports 1963–5	Imports 1953–5
6. FIBRES, TEXTILES, etc.						
Cotton lint	2.3	—[2]	0.6	na	—	—[1]
Jute	2.0	—	—	—	—	—
Rubber, natural	46.8	24.9	45.1	26.2	—	—[1]
Silk f	na	20.0*	2.0	—	53.7	16.0[1]
Cotton, woven fabrics	—	—	—	—	na	na

f metric tons.

	Production 1963–5	Production 1953–5	Exports 1963–5	Exports 1953–5	Imports 1963–5	Imports 1953–5
7. FUEL AND POWER						
Electricity hn	83	30[1]				
Petroleum, refined	—	—	—	—	183	na

h million kWh. *n* thermal.

	Production 1963–5	Production 1953–5	Exports 1963–5	Exports 1953–5	Imports 1963–5	Imports 1953–5
9. NON-FERROUS MINERALS AND METALS						
Gold k: ore m	6.00	—	—	—	—	—

k '000 fine troy oz. *m* metal content.

	Production 1963–5	Production 1953–5	Exports 1963–5	Exports 1953–5	Imports 1963–5	Imports 1953–5
11. INDUSTRY						
Aircraft a	—	—	—	—	0.8	—
Alcoholic beverages a	—	—	—	—	1.2	1.7
Cement	na	na	na	na	na	na
Electrical engineering a	—	—	—	—	6.9[2]	1.9[1]
Railway vehicles a	—	—	—	—	0.3	—
Machine tools a	—	—	—	—	0.5	—
Motor vehicles a	—	—	—	—	6.5	2.9[1]

a million $ U.S.

CAMEROUN

WEST AFRICA

The Cameroun Federal Republic was formed in 1961 of the French (East) Cameroun and the southern part of the British (West) Cameroons, the northern part electing to join Nigeria. There are separate Assemblies for the East and West zones under a joint National Assembly. Cameroun joined the Equatorial Customs Union in 1966.
All pre-1961 data for West Cameroons refer to the whole of the former British Cameroons.

AREA: 474 000* sq. km. (183 012* sq. miles)

LAND USE: (percentage of total)	*1958a*	*1954b*
Arable and orchard	30.2	16.2
Permanent meadow and pasture	6.9	18.5
Forest and woodland	27.7	52.9
City areas, waste and other land	35.2	12.4

a British Cameroons. *b* French Cameroun.

POPULATION: 5 740 000 (1967 estimate)

Largest city: DOUALA; population: 200 000* (1965)

Capital city: YAOUNDÉ; population: 101 000 (city proper, 1965)

		Year(s)
Life expectancy at birth (years): male	34.3a	1964–5 av.
female	37.2a	1964–5 av.
Infant mortality (per '000)	137.2*a	1964–5 av.
Crude birth rate (per '000)	49.9*ac	1964–5 av.
Crude death rate (per '000)	25·7*a	1964–5 av.
Population per physician	33 950	1965
Population per hospital bed	480	1966
School enrolment: age 5–19 years (percentage)	69d	1964–5 av.
age over 19 years (per 100 000 population)	24	1964–5 av.

a West Cameroun only. *c* African population only. *d* incl. pre-school education.

COMMUNICATIONS

		Year(s)
Motor vehicles in use ('000s): private	15.0	1963–5 av.
commercial	20.7	1963–5 av.
Railway track (km.)	520	1963
Telephones (per '000 urban population)	0.1*	1967
Daily newspapers (per '000 population)	3	1962–4 av.

FINANCE

Currency unit: The franc CFA

Exchange rates	*1965*	*1960*	*1958b*
Per $ U.S.	246.85	246.85	210
Per £ sterling	691.18	691.18	590

		Year(s)
National Income (million $ U.S.)	520	1963
G.N.P. per capita ($ U.S.)	110	1966
Foreign trade (percentage of G.D.P.)	36	1963–4 av.

b applies to French Cameroun only.

EMPLOYMENT AND PRODUCTION

The bulk of the population is employed in agriculture, coffee and cacao being the principal products of East Cameroun; recently 'modernization centres' have been set up.
Bauxite is mined and, with the development of H.E.P., is refined locally; there are also resources of gold and tin.

continued

TRADING

Total trade (in million $ U.S.)	*1965*	*1965b*	*1955b*	*1938b*
Exports (f.o.b.)	139	118	96	7
Imports (c.i.f.)	153	137	104	6

Main trading partners (percentage of total value)

Exports	*1965b*	*1955b*	*Imports*	*1965b*	*1955b*
France	48	48	France	58	63
Netherlands	16	19	Germany F.R.	7	4
U.S.A.	10	11	U.S.A.	6	7
Germany F.R.	8	5	Guinea	5	—
Italy	3	3	Belg./Lux.	4	1
Belg./Lux.	2	—	Italy	3	1
Spain	2	—	Japan	3	na

Distribution of trade (percentage of total value)

Exports	*1965b*	*1955*b*
Food	55	na
(cocoa)	(27)	(49)
(coffee)	(23)	(14)
Manufactured goods	22	na
(aluminium alloys)	(17)	(na)
Imports		
Manufactured goods	67	na
(machinery and transport equipment)	(28)	(20)
(textiles)	(12)	(12)
Chemicals	13	1
Food	9	10

b French Cameroun only

PRODUCTION, EXPORTS AND IMPORTS

Years: **1963–5 average** and *1953–5 average* Units: '000 metric tons unless otherwise indicated

Note—data for 1953–5 refer to East (former French) Cameroun only.

	Production 1963–5	Production 1953–5	Exports 1963–5	Exports 1953–5	Imports 1963–5	Imports 1953–5
1. CEREALS, etc.						
Cassava	663.4*	601.0	—	—	—	—
Maize (corn)	193.7	98.0	—	—	—	—
Millets/sorghum	399.0	347.0	—	—	3.1	—
Potatoes	26.7*	1.7	—	—	0.7	1.8[2]
Rice	12.3*	6.0	—	0.2	5.7	3.8
Sweet potatoes/yams	226.3*	148.3	—	—	—	—
2. FRUIT, etc.						
Apples	—	—	—	—	0.2n	—
Bananas	140.6*	127.0[2]p	118.7	74.1	—	—
Coconuts e	3.0[1]*	na	—	—	—	—
Pineapples	3.0*	na	—	—	—	—
Wine b	—	—	0.2	—	133.2	225.3

b '000 hectolitres. *e* no. in millions. *n* incl. pears and quince. *p* in addition, British Cameroons: 86.5[2].

	Production 1963–5	Production 1953–5	Exports 1963–5	Exports 1953–5	Imports 1963–5	Imports 1953–5
3. BEVERAGES, FOREST PRODUCTS, etc.						
Cocoa	84.3	56.7*	72.1	55.4	—	—
Coffee	48.3	10.4	47.5	11.6	—	—
Sugar, raw	—	—	—	—	9.2	2.3
Tea	0.3*	—	0.4	—	—	—
Tobacco,	3.8*	1.5[2]	1.1	0.9	1.0	0.9
cigarettes	744.0e	—	—	—	0.1q	0.3[2]q
Softwood j	—	—	—	—[2]	—	0.1[2]
Hardwood j	5 765.3*	2 262.0[2]	227.3	105.7[2]	—	1.3[2]
Paper	—	—	—	—[2]	1.1	—[1]

e no. in millions. *j* '000 cu. metres of roundwood equivalent. *q* incl. other tobacco products.

	Production 1963–5	Production 1953–5	Exports 1963–5	Exports 1953–5	Imports 1963–5	Imports 1953–5
4. VEGETABLE OILSEEDS AND OILS						
Castor oil	—	—	—	—[2]	0.01	0.15[2]
Copra	na	na	0.06	na	—	—
Coconut oil	na	na	—	0.50	—	—
Cottonseed	17.30	12.30*	3.37	na	—	—
Groundnuts	105.93*	55.30	15.46	6.43	0.27	—
Groundnut oil	na	na	—	0.25	0.18	0.01
Linseed oil	—	—	—	—	0.01	—
Olive oil	—	—	—	—	0.02	—
Palm kernels	23.33*	21.07r	16.63	18.23	—	—
Palm kernel oil	na	na	1.02	0.89	—	—
Palm oil	42.96*	na	9.45	1.19	0.50	0.37
Sesame seed	2.40	2.10	0.32	0.17	—	—

r commercial production only.

	Production 1963–5	Production 1953–5	Exports 1963–5	Exports 1953–5	Imports 1963–5	Imports 1953–5
5. LIVESTOCK‡, ANIMAL PRODUCTS, etc.						
Chickens d	4 436.7*	2 500.0[2]				
Cattle d	2 436.7*	1 250.0	1.1	1.9	—	0.1
Goats d	1 997.0*	880.0	— (Goats and Sheep)	— (Goats and Sheep)	0.1	—
Sheep d	1 032.9*	466.7				
Horses d	46.3*	17.0[2]				
Pigs d	273.0*	250.0	—	0.1	—	—

continued

	Production 1963–5	Production 1953–5	Exports 1963–5	Exports 1953–5	Imports 1963–5	Imports 1953–5
5. LIVESTOCK‡, ANIMAL PRODUCTS, etc.—*continued*						
Meat‡ 'A'	60.0*	14.0[1]n	—	0.3	0.3	0.2
'B'	3.0*	na	—	—	0.1	—
Butter	—	—	—	—	0.2	0.1
Cheese	—	—	—	—	0.2	0.2
Eggs	4.4*	na	—	—	—	—
Fish	57.4	36.5	2.4	na	2.8	na
Milk	77.3	na	—	0.5*	3.9	3.1*
Hides/skins	na	1.3[1]	1.1	0.9[2]	—	—

d no. in thousands. *n* government inspected meat only.

	Production 1963–5	Production 1953–5	Exports 1963–5	Exports 1953–5	Imports 1963–5	Imports 1953–5
6. FIBRES, TEXTILES, etc.						
Cotton lint	17.3	6.0*	16.1	2.5	—	—
Rubber, natural	na	na	6.2	3.2	—	—
Cotton, woven fabrics	—	—	—	—	3.4	3.1
7. FUEL AND POWER						
Coal/coke	—	—	—	—	—	3
Electricity h: total	1 094	20[1]				
hydro	1 051	10[1]				
thermal	43	10[1]				
Petroleum, refined	—	—	—	—	140	90[1]

h million kWh.

	Production 1963–5	Production 1953–5	Exports 1963–5	Exports 1953–5	Imports 1963–5	Imports 1953–5
9. NON-FERROUS MINERALS AND METALS						
Gold k: ore m	1.30	1.00	—	—	—	—
bullion, coins etc.	na	na	1.03‡	1.03	—	—
Aluminium:						
alumina	—	—	—	—	101.34	—
aluminium	51.64	na	49.04	—	—	—
Tin, ore	0.04m	0.09m	0.07	0.12	—	—
Titanium minerals	—	0.08[2]	—[2]	0.11	—	—

k '000 fine troy oz. *m* metal content.

	Production 1963–5	Production 1953–5	Exports 1963–5	Exports 1953–5	Imports 1963–5	Imports 1953–5
10. CHEMICALS*n* AND FERTILIZERS						
Chemicals	—		—		na	
Fertilizers:						
Phosphates	—	—	—	—	—	—
Potash	—	—	—	—	4.0	—

n data not available for years 1953–5.

	Production 1963–5	Production 1953–5	Exports 1963–5	Exports 1953–5	Imports 1963–5	Imports 1953–5
11. INDUSTRY (see pages 102–117)						
Aircraft a	—	—	—	—	0.4	—
Alcoholic beverages			0.3[2]a	—	3.9a	4.8a
beer b	415.0	na				
Cement	—	1.7	—	—	91.3	77.3
Electrical engineering a	—	—	—	—	4.9[2]	28.3[2]
Railway vehicles a	—	—	—	—	1.5	0.8
Merchant ships g	—	—	—	—	0.3	—
Motor vehicles a	—	—	0.9†	—	12.0	4.3

a million $ U.S. *b* '000 hectolitres. *g* '000 G.R.T.

CANADA

The provinces of Canada were united as a British colony in 1867 and the country was granted complete autonomy as a member of the Commonwealth in 1931. The influence of the French settlers remains, however, particularly in Québec province, where both French and English are official languages.

AREA: 9 976 169 sq. km. (3 851 809 sq. miles)

LAND USE: (percentage of total)

	1961	1951
Arable and orchard	4.2	3.9
Permanent meadow and pasture	2.1	2.2
Forest and woodland	44.4	34.3
City areas, waste and other land	49.3	59.6

POPULATION: 20 014 880 (1966 census)

Largest city: MONTRÉAL; population: 2 436 817 (1966)
Capital city: OTTAWA; population: 494 535 (1966)

Distribution of working population (1966)
Total working population: 7 177 000

U.N. group no.		*Percentage*
0	Agriculture, forestry, fishing and hunting	7.9
1	Mining and quarrying	1.6
2/3	Manufacturing	23.5
4	Construction	6.2
5	Electricity, gas, water and sanitary services	1.0
6	Commerce	20.3
7	Transport, storage and communications	7.1
8	Services	27.8
9	Others	4.6

		Year(s)
Life expectancy at birth (years): male	68.4	1960–2 av.
female	74.2	1960–2 av.
Infant mortality (per '000)	23.6	1965
Crude birth rate (per '000)	21.4	1965
Crude death rate (per '000)	7.6	1965
Accidental deaths (per 100 000 population)		
caused by motor vehicles	25.8	1965
due to other causes	30.2	1965
Population per physician	820	1966
Population per hospital bed	90	1966
School enrolment: age 5–19 years (percentage)	82	1963–4 av.
age over 19 years (per 100 000 population)	1 386	1963–5 av.

COMMUNICATIONS

		Year(s)
Motor vehicles in use ('000s): private	5 035.4	1963–5 av.
commercial	1 297	1963–5 av.
Railway track (km.)	93 713	1964
Mail per capita	210	1963–5 av.
Telephones (per '000 urban population)	38.9	1967
Radio receivers (per '000 population)	507	1963–5 av.
Television sets (per '000 population)	258.1	1963–5 av.
Daily newspapers (per '000 population)	223	1962–3 av.

FINANCE

Currency unit: The Canadian dollar

Exchange rates	1965	1960	1950 a	1938 b
Per $ U.S.	1.075	0.9962	1.060	1.01
Per £ sterling	3.0131	2.7929	2.969	4.646

		Year(s)
National Income (million $ U.S.)	35 785	1965
G.N.P. per capita ($ U.S.)	2 240	1966
Rate of increase of G.N.P. per capita	3.2	1960–4 av.
Foreign trade (percentage of G.D.P.)	34	1963–5 av.

a mean rate. *b* spot and selling rate.

TRADING

Total trade (in million $ U.S.)	1965	1955	1938
Exports (f.o.b.)	8 109	4 384	844
Imports (c.i.f.)	7 985	4 526	674

Main trading partners (percentage of total value)

Exports	1965	1955	1938	*Imports*	1965	1955	1938
U.S.A.	58	60	33	U.S.A.	70	73	63
U.K.	14	18	41	U.K.	7	8	18
Japan	4	2	2	Venezuela	3	4	–
U.S.S.R.	2	–	na	Japan	3	1	1
Germany F.R.	2	2	2 *d*	Germany F.R.	2	1	1 *d*
Australia	2	1	4	France	1	1	1
Netherlands	1	1	1	Italy	1	–	–

Distribution of trade (percentage of total value)

Exports	1965	1955	1938*
Manufactured goods	43	41	na
(machinery and transport equipment)	(15)	(6)	(5)
(wood and paper)	(12)	(18)	(14)
Crude materials and fuels	33	32	na
(wood and paper pulp)	(12)	(17)	(11)
Food	18	18	na
(cereals)	(11)	(12)	(16)
Imports			
Manufactured goods	67	60	na
(machinery and transport equipment)	(40)	(33)	(15)
Crude materials and fuels	15	19	na
(fuels)	(7)	(10)	(14)
Food	8	9	10
Chemicals	6	6	na

d incl. Germany D.R.

PRODUCTION, EXPORTS AND IMPORTS

Years: **1963–5 average** and *1953–5 average* Units: '000 metric tons unless otherwise indicated

1. CEREALS, etc.

	Production 1963–5	Production 1953–5	Exports 1963–5	Exports 1953–5	Imports 1963–5	Imports 1953–5
Barley	4 369.0	5 008.7	689.7	1 816.5	—	—
Maize (corn)	1 259.7	632.3	5.2	22.1[2]	526.8	126.0
Millets/sorghum	na	na	8.8	10.2	3.6	—
Oats	6 298.3	5 765.3	308.5	684.5	0.1	0.3
Potatoes	2 127.0	1 716.7	187.3	120.5	73.1	92.9
Rice	—	—	—	0.3†	41.3	31.1
Rye	353.3	488.7	126.4	294.3	—	—
Wheat	17 897.0	12 855.0	12 076.1	6 244.3	—	5.7

2. FRUIT, etc.

	Production 1963–5	Production 1953–5	Exports 1963–5	Exports 1953–5	Imports 1963–5	Imports 1953–5
Apples	444.7	308.7	63.5	43.8	24.5	14.8
Apricots	3.7	3.7	—	—	na	3.0
Bananas	—	—	—	—	158.4	134.7
Cherries	19.7	13.6	na	0.5	na	1.5
Dates	—	—	—	—	7.0	10.6
Grapes	53.0	40.0	9.6	9.2	100.8	44.5
Lemons	—	—	—	—	14.8	15.0
Oranges	—	—	—	—	166.8	199.6
Other citrus fruit	—	—	—	—	57.8	59.4
Peaches	51.7	60.3	—	—	na	8.5
Pears	35.7	32.0	3.3	1.5	10.6	9.1
Plums	14.3	18.6	—	—	na	5.9
Raisins	—	—	—	—	23.6	23.9
Tomatoes	358.0	287.3	na	na	na	na
Wine *b*	na	225.0	0.1	—	139.7	59.7

b '000 hectolitres

3. BEVERAGES, FOREST PRODUCTS, etc.

	Production 1963–5	Production 1953–5	Exports 1963–5	Exports 1953–5	Imports 1963–5	Imports 1953–5
Cocoa	—	—	—	—	18.7	13.8
Coffee	—	—	0.1	0.1	76.9	46.4
Sugar: beet	1 126.3	872.7				
raw	148.2	121.7	27.5	1.2	777.2	592.4
Tea	—	—	1.1	0.2†	21.2	20.2
Tobacco: leaf	79.0	69.4	20.2	16.5	1.6	0.7
cigars	455.0 *e*	245.3 *e*				
cigarettes	41 502.0 *e*	22 820.3 *e*	—	0.5[2] *a*	—	0.6[2]
tobacco/snuff	9.5	12.4				
Softwood *j*	89 491.0[1]	81 216.7	25 791.0	16 296.2	1 820.3	874.5
Hardwood *j*	7 703.0[1]*	8 786.0	751.6	645.2	739.5[2]	332.3
Wood pulp	12 213.3*	8 458.7	3 274.5	1 955.3	73.4	46.7
Newsprint	6 555.0*	5 414.0	6 113.7	5 037.7	—	—
Other paper	2 289.3	1 462.0	319.0	99.0	134.3	80.9

a million $ U.S. *e* no. in millions. *j* '000 cu. metres of roundwood equivalent.

4. VEGETABLE OILSEEDS AND OILS

	Production 1963–5	Production 1953–5	Exports 1963–5	Exports 1953–5	Imports 1963–5	Imports 1953–5
Castor oil	—	—	—	—	2.75	2.26
Copra	—	—	—	—	—	13.37
Coconut oil	na	na	—	—	17.72	12.68
Cottonseed oil	—	—	—	—	18.69	19.94
Groundnuts	—	—	—	—	42.89	29.27
Groundnut oil	na	na	—	—	5.67	3.16
Linseed	598.33	346.30	356.97	151.83	0.61	0.73
Linseed oil	na	na	7.49	6.38	0.02	0.09
Olive oil	—	—	—	—	1.26	1.03
Palm kernel oil	—	—	—	—	3.82	—
Palm oil	—	—	—	—	8.70	25.86
Rapeseed	335.70	20.00	181.14	11.20	—	—
Rapeseed oil	na	na	0.08	1.92*	—	0.01
Soya beans	181.70	136.33	59.71	18.80*	438.57	176.77
Soya bean oil	na	na	15.89	—	14.22	9.76
Sunflower seed	15.00	5.00	5.85	—	—	—
Sunflower seed oil	na	na	—	—	—	0.14
Tung oil	—	—	—	—	1.09	1.96

continued

PRODUCTION, EXPORTS AND IMPORTS *continued*

5. LIVESTOCK‡, ANIMAL PRODUCTS, etc.

	Production 1963–5	Production 1953–5	Exports 1963–5	Exports 1953–5	Imports 1963–5	Imports 1953–5
Chickens *d*	67 531.7	65 779.7				
Cattle *d*	11 560.7	9 258.0	371.6	52.9	15.1	1.4
cows *d*	5 612.3	4 734.0 *n*				
Goats *d*	17.0*	na	13.8	na	29.3	na
Sheep *d*	878.0*	1 168.0 *n*				
Horses *d*	426.3	895.0				
Pigs *d*	5 307.0	5 129.7 *n*	5.5	18.5	0.1	—
Bacon/ham	1 295.3	1 009.0	4.0	7.8	4.7	0.1
Meat‡ 'A'			38.0	26.3	46.7	5.4
'B'	421.3*	na	22.1	9.1	5.3	7.6
Butter	161.7	151.0	8.7	1.2	0.2	—
Cheese	101.7	45.7	13.5	5.3	7.3	3.6
Eggs	292.3	252.4	1.0	4.2	3.3	0.4
Fish	1 223.6 *p*	972.2 *p*	334.8	na	30.6	na
Milk	8 363.3	7 663.0	415.9	144.1	23.0	3.3
Whale/sperm oil	2.9	—	—	—	—	—
Hides/skins *a*	na	na	15.8[2]	9.7[2]	27.8	6.5[2]
Wool	1.6	2.0	0.9	0.7 *s*	6.9	7.7

a million $ U.S. *d* no. in thousands. *n* on farms only. *p* incl. fish, except tuna, landed in foreign ports. *s* incl. re-exports.

6. FIBRES, TEXTILES, etc.

	Production 1963–5	Production 1953–5	Exports 1963–5	Exports 1953–5	Imports 1963–5	Imports 1953–5
Abaca	—	—	—	—	1.6	2.8
Agaves (sisal etc.)	—	—	—	—	40.5	25.5
Cotton lint	—	—	0.1	0.8 *s*	95.8	100.7
Flax fibre	—	0.3	—	0.5	0.2	—
Hemp fibre	—	—	—	—	0.4	0.1
Jute	—	—	0.6	—	2.4	1.8
Rubber: natural	—	—	1.2†	0.4†	43.3	45.4
synthetic	196.2	91.9	129.5	65.0[2]	27.6 *s*	5.1
Silk *f*	—	—	—	—	23.7	26.7
Cotton: yarn	78.8	66.8	—	—	6.0	3.3
woven fabrics	36.9*	30.2	4.5	—	30.6	19.0
Rayon: fibre/yarn	48.3	32.3	6.2	1.5 *q*	6.0	7.0 *q*
woven fabrics	17.5	9.5	—	—	7.0 *r*	3.9
Non-cellulosic fibre/yarn	31.2	5.8	2.5	—	7.5	—
Wool: yarn	16.5[2]	20.5	0.1	—	2.1	1.0
woven fabrics	10.5[2] *t*	11.9 *t*	—	na	4.8	5.4

f metric tons. *q* incl. spun yarn. *r* incl. synthetic piece goods. *s* incl. re-exports, or imports for re-export. *t* excl. blankets.

7. FUEL AND POWER

	Production 1963–5	Production 1953–5	Exports 1963–5	Exports 1953–5	Imports 1963–5	Imports 1953–5
Coal‡ 'A'	8 330	11 360	1 085	366	13 596	18 736
'B'	593	2 080	—	12	—	2
Coke	na	na	93	116	339	294
Electricity *h*: total	133 862	75 030				
hydro	111 413	70 610				
nuclear	116	—				
thermal	22 286	4 420				
Natural gas *i*	36 610	3 518	10 860	322	287	316
Oil, crude	39 960	17 590	13 520	2 010	20 350	12 400
Petroleum, refined	41 807	23 410	857	120[1]	5 700	4 670[1]
Rare earths *pu*	na	—	—	—	7	27
Uranium‡	5 149 *f*	1 762[1] *fq*	82 252 *u*	—	327 *ru*	529 *tu*

f metric tons. *h* million kWh. *i* million cu. metres. *p* thorium and cerium salts only. *q* 1956 figure. *r* radium and compounds. *t* radium only. *u* '000 $ U.S.

8. IRON AND STEEL

	Production 1963–5	Production 1953–5	Exports 1963–5	Exports 1953–5	Imports 1963–5	Imports 1953–5
Iron ore	18 034 *m*	5 015 *m*	28 831	7 716	5 189	3 551
Pig iron	6 059	2 683	546	317	64	25
Steel ingots/castings	8 283	3 580	340	121	12	11
Iron/steel scrap	na	na	413	499	765	182
Iron/steel products *a*	na	na	199	60	290	195

a million $ U.S. *m* metal content.

9. NON-FERROUS MINERALS AND METALS

	Production 1963–5	Production 1953–5	Exports 1963–5	Exports 1953–5	Imports 1963–5	Imports 1953–5
Diamonds *a*	—	—	—	—	14.25	9.86
Gold *k*: ore *m*	3 814.70	4 321.00	—	—	—	—
bullion/coins etc.	na	na	2 634.06‡	na	557.14‡	na
Platinum group metals *k*	399.01	344.01	503.15 *z*	0.13 / 27.23 *a*	227.58[2]	21.65 *a*
Silver *k*: ore *m*	30 553.30	29 133.70	10 003.65	6 744.24	—	—
bullion	na	na	11 827.69	15 232.84	8 853.68 *t*	144.93
Asbestos: fibre	1 234.91 *x*	876.67	1 167.04	837.06	7.30[2]	—
manufactured	na	na	1.70 *a*	1.63 *a*	0.31 / 4.96 *ap*	0.13 / 3.35 *a*
Mica	0.44	0.85	—	0.47	2.51 / 0.57 *ap*	0.06 / 0.53 *a*
Aluminium: bauxite	—	—	—	—	1 722.92[2]	2 583.65 *n*
alumina	na	na	4.67	—	757.93[2]	62.53 *q*
aluminium	723.48	519.52	652.54	462.35	70.29[2]	19.78 / 0.56 *a*
Antimony: ore	0.68 *m*	0.73 *m*	na	—	—	—
metal	—	—	—	0.40	0.77[1]	0.88

continued

9. NON-FERROUS MINERALS AND METALS—*continued*

	Production 1963–5	Production 1953–5	Exports 1963–5	Exports 1953–5	Imports 1963–5	Imports 1953–5
Cadmium	1.06	0.62	0.75	0.50	—	—
Chrome: ore	—	—	—	—	45.05[1]	62.74
metal	na	na	0.99	18.59	11.71[2]	2.56
Cobalt: ore	1.49 *m*	1.08 *m*	—	—	—	13.11
metal	na	na	0.88	20.96	0.01	0.13
Copper: ore	440.49 *m*	266.70 *m*	86.03 *m*	42.38	—	—
metal	369.56	181.43	257.56	156.33 / 1.57 *a*	14.36[1]	9.21
Lead: ore *m*	214.19	185.96	72.90	54.31	—	—
metal	149.04	145.91	102.98	94.99	2.86[1]	1.23
Magnesium:						
dolomite	na	na	—	—	20.30[2]	—
magnesite	—	—	—	—	25.84	8.00
metal/salts	8.58‡	6.32‡	3.74 *a*	2.95[1] / 4.98 *a*	14.49 / 1.13 *au*	12.11 / 0.79 *a*
Manganese: ore	—	—	—	—	96.97[1]	87.98
metal	—	—	2.17	10.37	25.38	4.18
Mercury *f*	1.07	—	—	2.6	274.00	145.50
Molybdenum *f*: ore	1 756.00 *m*	215.00 *m*	na	670.81	—	—
metal	na	na	—	—	228.30	217.70
Nickel: ore *m*	215.55	145.12	—	59.17	72.72	—
metal	na	na	141.43 *y*	85.28	12.55[2]	2.05
Tin: ore *m*	0.26	0.22	0.46	0.21	—	—
metal	—	—	—	—	4.68[2]	4.03
Titanium minerals	444.51 *v*	133.03	na	94.87	11.30[2]	30.18
Tungsten: ore	1.41	1.65	—	1.68[1]	0.29[1]	0.05
metal	na	na	—	—	0.17	0.04
Vanadium	—	—	—	—	0.27[2] *w*	—
Zinc: ore	646.52 *m*	366.38 *m*	333.72 *m*	170.37 *m*	10.17[2]	—
metal	296.42	230.08	219.22	180.41	3.99	5.03
Zirconium minerals *a*	—	—	—	—	0.35[1] *r*	0.15

a million $ U.S. *f* metric tons. *k* '000 fine troy oz. *m* metal content. *n* incl. alumina and cryolite for refining. *p* manufactures. *q* incl. bauxite not for refining. *r* excl. alloys. *t* incl. anodes. *u* bricks and alloys only. *v* excl. titanium dioxide slag (70% TiO_2). *w* ferro-vanadium. *x* sales. *y* nickel oxide. *z* excl. scrap.

10. CHEMICALS *n* AND FERTILIZERS

	Production 1963–5	Production 1953–5	Exports 1963–5	Exports 1953–5	Imports 1963–5	Imports 1953–5
Organic chemicals:						
Benzene	138.5		na		—	
Butadiene	na		na		14.4[2]	
Ethylene	225.7		na		na	
Methanol	27.8		na		3.3	
Phenol	33.5[2]		6.8		0.4	
Phthalic anhydride	9.3[2]		na		6.3	
Styrene monomer	na		na		na	
Urea	168.0		124.5[2]*		3.0[2]	
Inorganic chemicals						
Ammonia	686.0		na		21.2	
Carbon black	57.5		na		11.4	
Chlorine	489.7		28.1		37.3	
Nitric acid	573.5[2]		na		—	
Sodium carbonate	na		na		91.0	
Sodium hydroxide	588.4		na		113.8	
Sulphuric acid	2 009.2		54.2		4.1	
Plastics:						
Polyamides	na		na		na	
Polyethylene	82.0		21.2		12.8	
Polyvinyl chloride	24.1		2.4		18.6	
Fertilizers:						
Phosphates	—	—	—	—	1 336.1	547.2
Potash	900.1 *y*	—	—	—	85.7	130.1
Pyrites *x*	179.5	272.7	0.9 *a*	144.3[2]	—	—
Sulphur	1 544.2 *q*	26.4* *pq*	1 092.7	3.2	139.8	315.3

a million $ U.S. *n* data not available for years 1953–5. *p* shipments. *q* recovered sulphur. *x* sulphur content. *y* K_2O content.

11. INDUSTRY

	Production 1963–5	Production 1953–5	Exports 1963–5	Exports 1953–5	Imports 1963–5	Imports 1953–5
Aircraft *a*	456.0[1]* *q*	—	148.7	30.9 *r*	106.5	119.1
Alcoholic beverages			99.7 *a*	64.9 *a*	28.8 *a*	20.2 *a*
beer *b*	13 268.0	9 799.0				
spirits *b*	1 682.0 *n*	1 545.0 *p*				
Cement	7 026.0	3 715.0	273.7	58.3	35.7	409.3
Electrical engineering *a*	1 656.1[2]	na	143.8	32.9[2]	367.8	244.5[2]
Locomotives *c*	139.0	na				
Railway vehicles *a*	na	na	na	11.1	—	34.1
Machine tools *a*	25.0[1]	na	—	—	77.7	38.4
Merchant ships *g*	130.0	54.0	—	—	0.9	na
Motor vehicles			176.8 *a*	41.9[2] *a*	743.4 *a*	322.4 *v*
commercial *d*	118.1	89.7				
private *d*	601.7	340.9				

a million $ U.S. *b* '000 hectolitres. *c* no. of units. *d* no. in thousands. *g* '000 G.R.T. *n* 1965/66 figure. *p* 1958/59 figure. *q* 1965–7 av. *r* excl. parts.

CENTRAL AFRICAN REPUBLIC

The Central African Republic, formerly Oubangi-shari, a territory of French Equatorial Africa, and from 1958 a member state of the French Community, became independent in 1960. The country has been a member of the Equatorial Customs Union since its foundation in 1959.

AREA: 617 000 sq. km. (238 000 sq. miles)

LAND USE: (percentage of total)	*1964*
Arable and orchard	9.4
Permanent meadow and pasture	0.2
Forest and woodland	11.9
City areas, waste and other land including rough grazing	78.5

POPULATION: 1 459 000 excl. 28 000 refugees from Sudan (1967 estimate)

Largest city: BANGUI, capital; population: 150 000 (1966)
Total working population: 480 000 (1961)

		Year(s)
Life expectancy at birth (years): male	33	1959–60 av.
female	36	1959–60 av.
Population per physician	33 000	1961
Population per hospital bed	640*a*	1966
School enrolment: age 5–19 years (percentage)	30	1963–4 av.

a government hospitals only.

COMMUNICATIONS

		Year(s)
Motor vehicles in use ('000s): private	3.1	1963–5 av.
commercial	4.7	1963–5 av.
Telephones (per '000 urban population)	0.2*	1967
Radio receivers (per '000 population)	19	1963–5 av.
Daily newspapers (per '000 population)	0.3	1962–4 av.

FINANCE

Currency unit: The franc CFA

Exchange rates	*1965*	*1960*
Per $ U.S.	246.85	246.85
Per £ sterling	691.18	691.18

		Year(s)
National Income (million $ U.S.)	166	1965
G.N.P. per capita ($ U.S.)	110	1966
Foreign trade (percentage of G.D.P.)	35	1963–4 av.

TRADING

Total trade (in million $ U.S.)	*1965*	*1955*
Exports (f.o.b.)	26	16
Imports (c.i.f.)	27	18

Main trading partners (percentage of total value)

Exports	*1965*	*Imports*	*1965*
France	38	France	60
Israel	22	U.S.A.	6
U.S.A.	13	Germany F.R.	6
U.K.	7	U.K.	4
Netherlands	6	Netherlands	3
Italy	4	Belg./Lux.	3
Yugoslavia	2		

Distribution of trade (percentage of total value)

Exports	*1965*	*Imports*	*1965*
Crude materials and fuels	83	Manufactured goods	72
(diamonds)	(54)	(machinery and transport equipment)	(30)
(raw cotton)	(19)	(textiles)	(14)
Food	16	Food	11
(coffee)	(15)		

PRODUCTION, EXPORTS AND IMPORTS

Years: **1963–5 average** Units: '000 metric tons unless otherwise indicated

Note—no data are available for the years 1953–5

	Production	Exports	Imports
1. CEREALS, etc.			
Cassava	1 000.0*	—	—
Maize (corn)	29.3	—	—
Potatoes	—	—	0.1
Rice	4.3*	—	0.1
Sweet potatoes/yams	40.0*	—	—
2. FRUIT, etc.			
Apples	—	—	0.1*n*
Bananas	170.0*	—	—
Lemons	1.0*	—	—
Oranges	11.0*	—	—
Other citrus fruit	5.0*	—	—
Wine*b*	—	—	38.6

b '000 hectolitres. *n* incl. pears and quince.

	Production	Exports	Imports
3. BEVERAGES, FOREST PRODUCTS, etc.			
Coffee	10.0*	8.6	—
Tea	—	—	0.1
Tobacco, leaf	0.5*	0.4	—
Hardwood*j*	1 883.7*	20.5	—

j '000 cu. metres of roundwood equivalent.

	Production	Exports	Imports
4. VEGETABLE OILSEEDS AND OILS			
Cottonseed	19.00*	0.03	—
Groundnuts	45.97	1.47	—
Groundnut oil	na	—	0.02
Palm kernels	1.23	1.24	—
Palm oil	1.30*	—	0.20
Seasame seed	8.53	2.05	—
5. LIVESTOCK‡, ANIMAL PRODUCTS, etc.			
Chickens*d*	866.7*		
Cattle*d*	400.0*	—	0.3
dairy cows*d*	316.7*		
Goats*d*	47.0*	—	—
Sheep*d*	108.0*	—	—
Horses*d*	1.0*		
Pigs*d*	10.0	—	—
Bacon/ham } Meat‡ 'A'	8.3	—	—

continued

	Production	Exports	Imports
5. LIVESTOCK, ANIMAL PRODUCTS, etc.—*continued*			
Butter	—	—	0.1
Cheese	—	—	0.1
Eggs	5.3*	—	—
Fish	na	—	0.4
Milk	15.0*	—	2.1
Hides/skins	0.3[2]	0.8	—

d no. in thousands.

	Production	Exports	Imports
6. FIBRES, TEXTILES, etc.			
Agaves (sisal etc.)	0.2*	0.1	—
Cotton lint	10.0*	9.6	—
Rubber, natural	na	1.0	—
Cotton, woven fabrics	4.7*n*	—	—

n million metres.

	Production	Exports	Imports
7. FUEL AND POWER			
Electricity*h*: total	20		
hydro	19		
thermal	1		
Petroleum, refined	—	—	23

h million kWh.

	Production	Exports	Imports
9. NON-FERROUS MINERALS AND METALS			
Diamonds	443.67*l*	12.51*a*	—

a million $ U.S. *l* '000 carats.

	Production	Exports	Imports
10. CHEMICALS AND FERTILIZERS			
Chemicals	—	—	na
Fertilizers:			
Phosphates	—	—	0.3[2]
11. INDUSTRY			
Alcoholic beverages		—	1.0*a*
beer*b*	81.0		
Cement	—	—	17.0
Electrical engineering*a*	—	—	1.5
Motor vehicles*a*	—	—	3.3

a million $ U.S. *b* '000 hectolitres.

na: data not available. — negligible or nil. [1] one year only. [2] two year average. * estimate. ‡ see appendix. † re-exports.

CEYLON

Ceylon became an independent republic within the British Commonwealth in 1948.

AREA: 65 610 sq. km. (25 332 sq. miles)

LAND USE: (percentage of total)	*1965*	*1954*
Arable and orchard	28.6	23.1
Cultivated pasture	0.2	—
Forest and woodland	50.7	53.8
City areas, waste and other land	20.5	23.1

POPULATION: 11 741 000 (1967 estimate)

Largest city: COLOMBO, capital; population: 510 947 (city proper, 1963)
Total working population: 2 983 109

Distribution of working population (1953)

U.N. group no.		*Percentage*
0	Agriculture, forestry, fishing and hunting	53.1
1	Mining and quarrying	0.4
2/3	Manufacturing	10.2
4	Construction	1.9
5	Electricity, gas, water and sanitary services	0.2
6	Commerce	8.2
7	Transport, storage and communications	3.5
8	Services	16.2
9	Others	6.3

		Year(s)
Life expectancy at birth (years): male	61.9	1962
female	61.4	1962
Infant mortality (per '000)	53.2	1965
Crude birth rate (per '000)	33.1	1965
Crude death rate (per '000)	8.2	1965
Accidental deaths (per 100 000 population)		
caused by motor vehicles	1.4	1965
due to other causes	27.5	1965
Population per physician	5 820	1965
Population per hospital bed	320*a*	1966
School enrolment: age 5–19 years (percentage)	81*b*	1963–4 av.
age over 19 years (per 100 000 population)	120*c*	1963–5 av.

a government hospitals only. *b* includes correspondence courses. *c* excludes teacher-training and technical colleges.

COMMUNICATIONS

		Year(s)
Motor vehicles in use ('000s): private	82.6	1963–5 av.
commercial	35.5	1963–5 av.
Railway track (km.)	1 484	1964
Mail per capita: domestic	34	1963–5 av.
foreign received	1	1963–5 av.
foreign sent	1	1963–5 av.
Telephones (per '000 urban population)	0.4	1967
Radio licences (per '000 population)	38	1963–5 av.
Daily newspapers (per '000 population)	35	1964

FINANCE

Currency unit: The rupee

Exchange rates	*1965a*	*1960*	*1950*	*1938*
Per $ U.S.	4.788	4.762	4.775	2.888
Per £ sterling	13.33	13.33	13.33	13.33

		Year(s)
National Income (million $ U.S.)	1 458	1965
G.N.P. per capita ($ U.S.)	150	1966
Rate of increase of G.N.P. per capita	0.4	1960–4 av.
Foreign trade (percentage of G.D.P.)	46	1963–5 av.

a selling rate

TRADING

Total trade (in million $ U.S.)	*1965*	*1955*	*1938*
Exports (f.o.b.)	409	407	104
Imports (c.i.f.)	310	307	86

Main trading partners (percentage of total value)

Exports	*1965*	*1955*	*1938*	*Imports*	*1965*	*1955*	*1938*
U.K.	26	27	54	U.K.	18	21	21
China P.R.	9	6	na	India	9	17	22
U.S.A.	8	9	13	China P.R.	8	5	—
Australia	5	8	4	Japan	8	7	7
Iraq	5	na	na	U.S.S.R.	7	na	na
U.S.S.R.	5	na	na	Australia	6	6	3
South Africa	5	4	3	Burma	5	8	15

Distribution of trade (percentage of total value)

Exports	*1965*	*1955*	*1938**
Food	70	69	70
(tea)	(63)	(64)	(65)
Crude materials	22	24	24
(rubber)	(16)	(19)	(18)
Coconut oil	7	6	5
Imports			
Food	41	41	35
(cereals)	(17)	(21)	(21)
Manufactured goods	37	38	40
(machinery and transport equipment)	(12)	(11)	(6)
(textiles and clothing)	(11)	(12)	(9)
Crude materials and fuel	11	11	15

PRODUCTION, EXPORTS AND IMPORTS

Years: **1963–5 average** and *1953–5 average* Units: '000 metric tons unless otherwise indicated

	Production **1963–5**	Production *1953–5*	Exports **1963–5**	Exports *1953–5*	Imports **1963–5**	Imports *1953–5*
1. CEREALS, etc.						
Barley	—	—	—	—	—	*0.3*
Cassava	354.3	*234.3*	—	—	—	—
Maize (corn)	10.0	*9.0*	—	—	2.9	—
Millets/sorghum	20.0*	*22.0*	—	*0.4*	—	—
Oats	—	—	—	—	0.2	*0.7*
Potatoes	4.7*	*1.0*	—	—	66.3	*39.3*
Rice	945.7	*654.7*	0.1	*3.5*	530.3*	*399.1*
Sweet potatoes/yams	60.7	*46.7*	—	—	—	—
Wheat	—	—	—	—	0.1*n*	*0.1n*

n in addition, milled wheat 224 (1963–5 av.) and 238 (1953–5 av.).

	Production **1963–5**	Production *1953–5*	Exports **1963–5**	Exports *1953–5*	Imports **1963–5**	Imports *1953–5*
2. FRUIT, etc.						
Apples	—	—	—	—	—	*1.1*
Coconuts	2 486.7*e*	na	59.0	*65.6*	—	—
Dates	—	—	—	—	11.0	*3.3*
Pineapples	31.0	na	—	—	—	—
Raisins	—	—	—	—	0.4	*0.4*
Wine*b*	—	—	—	—	0.5	*0.3*

b '000 hectolitres. *e* no. in millions.

	Production **1963–5**	Production *1953–5*	Exports **1963–5**	Exports *1953–5*	Imports **1963–5**	Imports *1953–5*
3. BEVERAGES, FOREST PRODUCTS, etc.						
Cocoa	2.3	*2.7**	2.0	*2.8*	—	—
Coffee	—	—	—	—	—	*0.5*
Sugar: cane	83.7*	na				
raw	6.7	na	0.4	*4.7*	192.1	*149.1*
Tea	222.2	*164.8*	212.5	*160.2*	—	—

continued

	Production **1963–5**	Production *1953–5*	Exports **1963–5**	Exports *1953–5*	Imports **1963–5**	Imports *1953–5*
3. BEVERAGES, FOREST PRODUCTS, etc.—*continued*						
Tobacco: leaf	4.1*	*3.4**	—	*0.5*	0.8	*0.7*
cigars	—	—	} —	} —	—	{ *1.1*
cigarettes	1 838.0*e*	*1 492.0e*	}	}		{ na
tobacco/snuff	—	*4.1*	}	}		{ na
Softwood*j*	—	—	—	—	2.8	*1.6*
Hardwood*j*	250.3	*300.0*	0.2	*1.5*	4.8	*9.9*
Wood pulp	—	—	—	—	3.2	—
Newsprint	—	—	—	—	12.0	*10.2*
Other paper	6.3	—	—	—	12.4	*10.1*

e no. in millions. *j* '000 cu. metres of roundwood equivalent..

	Production **1963–5**	Production *1953–5*	Exports **1963–5**	Exports *1953–5*	Imports **1963–5**	Imports *1953–5*
4. VEGETABLE OILSEEDS AND OILS						
Castor oil	—	—	—	—	0.17	*0.10*
Copra	275.47	*249.93*	48.13	*46.00*	na	*0.03*
Coconut oil	na	na	96.70	*85.29*	—	—
Cottonseed	0.67	na	—	—	—	—
Groundnuts	2.80	na	—	—	0.01	*0.37*
Groundnut oil			—	—	0.04	*0.14*
Linseed oil	—	—	—	—	0.14	*0.46*
Olive oil	—	—	—	—	0.02	*0.06*
Palm kernel oil	—	—	—	—	0.27	na
Palm oil	—	—	—	—	0.26	na
Rapeseed	—	—	—	—	0.48	*0.40*[1]
Seasame seed	8.13*	*6.5*[2]	na	*1.03*	—	*0.10*

continued

na: data not available. — negligible or nil. [1] one year only. [2] two year average. * estimate. ‡ see appendix. † re-exports.

PRODUCTION, EXPORTS AND IMPORTS *continued*

	Production		Exports		Imports	
5. LIVESTOCK‡, ANIMAL PRODUCTS, etc.						
Chickens *d*	**6 166.0**	*1 673.7*				
Cattle *d*	**1 781.3**	*1 313.0*	—	—	—	*0.2*
dairy cows *d*	**1 073.3**	na				
Goats *d* }	**568.0**	*518.0*	—	—	19.8	—
Sheep *d* }	**35.0**	*96.0*				
Horses *d*	**3.0***	*3.0**				
Pigs *d*	**117.0**	*66.7*	—	—	—	—
Bacon/ham }	**18.3**	*20.0[1]n*	—	—	0.1	*0.1*
Meat‡ 'A' }			—	—	0.2	*0.3*
'B'	**2.7***	na	—	—	0.4	—
Butter	—	—	—	—	1.5	*1.0*
Cheese	—	—	—	—	0.2	*0.2*
Eggs	**20.7**	*12.2[2]*	—	—	—	*1.6*
Fish	**96.2**	*28.8*	0.2	—	37.8	*38.9[1]**
Milk	**136.7**	*103.5[2]*	0.1	—	90.9	*39.5[2]*

d no. in thousands. *n* government inspected meat only.

	Production		Exports		Imports	
6. FIBRES, TEXTILES, etc.						
Cotton lint	**0.3**	na	—	—	2.3	*0.7*
Rubber, natural	**111.6**	*97.0*	103.3	*95.8*	—	—
Cotton: yarn	**1.9[2]**	*0.8*	—	—	2.2	*0.3*
woven fabrics	**0.8***	*0.8*	—	—	11.2	*7.3*
Rayon, woven fabrics	—	—	—	—	1.3*p*	*3.3*

p incl. synthetic piece goods.

	Production		Exports		Imports	
7. FUEL AND POWER						
Coal 'A'‡	—	—	—	—	153	*288*
Electricity *h*: total	**419**	*180[1]*				
hydro	**333[2]**	*130[1]*				
thermal	**86**	*50[1]*				
Petroleum, refined	—	—	—	—	907	*960[1]*
Rare earths *fq*	**507**	*537*	144	*31[1]*	—	—

f metric tons. *h* million kWh. *q* monazite.

	Production		Exports		Imports	
8. IRON AND STEEL						
Pig iron	—	—	—	—	1	*1*
Steel ingots/castings	—	—	—	—	2	*1[1]*

	Production		Exports		Imports	
9. NON-FERROUS MINERALS AND METALS						
Diamonds *a*	—	—	—	—	—	*0.27*
Gold *k*, bullion/coins etc.	—	—	—	—	11.98‡	*6.84*
Silver *k*: ore *m*	**18.00[1]**	—	—	—	—	—
bullion	na	—	—	—	9.27	*18.73*
Asbestos: fibre	—	—	—	—	0.39	—[1]
manufactured	—	—	—	—	3.09	*11.46*
Aluminium	—	—	—	—	3.27	*0.67*
Copper, metal	—	—	—	—	0.65	—
Lead, metal	—	—	—	—	0.47	*0.07*
Magnesium, dolomite	**5.08[1]**	na	—	—	—	—
Tin, metal	—	—	—	—	3.58	*0.06*
Titanium minerals	**38.15**	—	—	—	—	—
Zinc, metal	—	—	—	—	0.22	*0.04*

a million $ U.S. *k* '000 fine troy oz. *m* metal content.

	Production		Exports		Imports	
10. CHEMICALS*n* AND FERTILIZERS						
Chemicals	—		—		na	
Fertilizers:						
Phosphates	—	—	—	—	59.9	*35.0*
Potash	—	—	—	—	57.2	*27.5*
Sulphur	—	—	—	—	2.9	*3.2*

n data not available for years 1953–5.

	Production		Exports		Imports	
11. INDUSTRY						
Aircraft *a*	—	—	—	—	1.6[1]	*0.5*
Beer *b*	**60.0**	*30.9*	—	—	—	—
Cement	**78.7**	*79.3*	—	—	196.0	*119.3*
Electrical engineering *a*	—	—	—	—	6.3[2]	*6.9[1]*
Railway vehicles *a*	—	—	—	—	2.4[1]	*18.0*
Merchant ships *g*	—	—	—	—	0.3	—
Motor vehicles *a*	—	—	—	—	11.3[1]	*11.1[1]*

a million $ U.S. *b* '000 hectolitres. *g* '000 G.R.T.

CHAD

CENTRAL AFRICA

Formerly a territory of French Equatorial Africa, and from 1958 a member state of the French Community, Chad became an independent state in 1960. Chad has been a member of the Equatorial Customs Union since its foundation in 1959.

AREA: 1 284 000 sq. km. (496 000 sq. miles)

LAND USE: (percentage of total)	*1962*
Arable and orchard	5.5
Permanent meadow and pasture	35.0
Forest and woodland	12.5
City areas, waste and other land	47.0

POPULATION: 3 410 000 (1967 estimate)

Largest city: FORT-LAMY, capital; population: 99 000 (1964)

Distribution of working population (1961)
Total working population: 1 380 000

U.N. group no.		*Percentage*
0	Agriculture, forestry, fishing and hunting	82.6
1	Mining and quarrying	0.1
2/3	Manufacturing	0.3
4	Construction	0.5
5	Electricity, gas, water and sanitary services	—
6	Commerce	0.4
7	Transport, storage and communications	0.2
8	Services	1.5
9	Others	14.4

		Year(s)
Life expectancy at birth (years): male	29	1963–4 av.
female	35	1963–4 av.
Infant mortality (per '000)	160**a*	1964
Crude birth rate (per '000)	45*a*	1964
Crude death rate (per '000)	31*	1964
Population per physician	73 330	1964
Population per hospital bed	900	1966
School enrolment: age 5–19 years (percentage)	16	1963–4 av.

a African population.

COMMUNICATIONS

		Year(s)
Motor vehicles in use ('000s): private	2.4	1963–5 av.
commercial	4.2	1963–5 av.
Telephones (per '000 urban population)	0.1	1967
Radio receivers (per '000 population)	7	1963–5 av.
Daily newspapers (per '000 population)	0.3	1962

FINANCE

Currency unit: The franc CFA

Exchange rates	*1965*	*1960*
Per $ U.S.	246.85	246.85
Per £ sterling	691.18	691.18

		Year
National Income (million $ U.S.)	192	1963
G.N.P. per capita ($ U.S.)	70	1966
Foreign trade (percentage of G.D.P.)	24	1963

TRADING

Total trade (in million $ U.S.)	*1965*	*1955*
Exports (f.o.b.)	27	20
Imports (c.i.f.)	31	24

Main trading partners (percentage of total value)

Exports	*1965*	*Imports*	*1965*
France	45	France	46
Yugoslavia	12	Neths. Antilles	13
Nigeria	11	U.S.A.	9
U.K.	8	Germany F.R.	4
Belg./Lux.	6	Cameroun	3
		Belg./Lux	3
		Japan	3

Distribution of trade (percentage of total value)

Exports	*1965*	*Imports*	*1965*
Crude materials and fuels	85	Manufactured goods	55
(raw cotton)	(77)	(machinery and transport equipment)	(21)
Food	11	(textiles)	(11)
(live animals)	(8)	Petroleum products	20
		Food	9
		Chemicals	6

continued

PRODUCTION, EXPORTS AND IMPORTS

Years: **1963–5 average** Units: '000 metric tons unless otherwise indicated

Note—no data are available for the years 1953–5

	Production	Exports	Imports
1. CEREALS, etc.			
Cassava	46.7*	—	—
Maize (corn)	12.0	—	—
Millets/sorghum	835.0*	—	0.2
Potatoes	—	—	0.4
Rice	32.3	—	0.1
Sweet potatoes/yams	50.0*	—	—
Wheat	3.3	—	0.7
2. FRUIT, etc.			
Apples	—	—	0.1*p*
Bananas	—	—	0.3
Dates	18.7*	0.3	—
Oranges	—	—	0.1
Wine *b*	—	—	19.7

b '000 hectolitres. *p* incl. pears and quince.

	Production	Exports	Imports
3. BEVERAGES, FOREST PRODUCTS, etc.			
Tea	—	—	0.8
Hardwood *j*	2 601.7*	—	12.2[2]
Newsprint	—	—	na
Other paper	—	—	na

j '000 cu. metres of roundwood equivalent.

	Production	Exports	Imports
4. VEGETABLE OILSEEDS AND OILS			
Cottonseed	62.70	—	—
Groundnuts	100.30	1.55	0.01
Groundnut oil	na	—	0.13
Olive oil	—	—	0.01
Sesame seed	5.00*	0.02	—

	Production	Exports	Imports
5. LIVESTOCK‡, ANIMAL PRODUCTS, etc.			
Cattle *d*	4 000.0*	72.0	—
Goats *d* }	2 750.0*	24.0	1.2
Sheep *d* }	1 250.0*		
Horses *d*	150.0*		
Bacon/ham }	248.0*	—	—
Meat‡ 'A' }		0.6	—
Butter	na	0.1	—
Cheese	—	—	0.1
Eggs	1.6	—	—
Fish	90.0[2]	0.3	0.1
Milk	65.0*	—	1.9
Hides/skins	0.4	0.6	—

d no. in thousands.

	Production	Exports	Imports
6. FIBRES, TEXTILES, etc.			
Agaves (sisal)	35.0	35.7	—
7. FUEL AND POWER			
Electricity *ht*:	16		
Petroleum, refined	—	—	33

h million kWh. *t* thermal.

	Production	Exports	Imports
11. INDUSTRY			
Alcoholic beverages *a*	—	—	1.3
Cement	—	—	9.0
Electrical engineering *a*	—	—	1.6
Motor vehicles *a*	—	—	2.5

a million $ U.S.

CHILE

SOUTH AMERICA

Chile is one of the more stable South American republics. The balance of the economy depends to a great extent upon the production of copper, but recently some attempt has been made towards diversification, industrialization, and social reform.

AREA: 741 767 sq. km. (286 397 sq. miles)

LAND USE: (percentage of total)	*1965*	*1955*
Arable and orchard	6.1	7.4
Permanent meadow and pasture	13.6	0.6
Forest and woodland	27.9*	22.1*
City areas, waste and other land	52.4*	69.9*

POPULATION: 8 935 000 (1967 U.N. estimate)

Largest city: SANTIAGO, capital; population: 2 313 720 (1966)

Distribution of working population (1960)
Total working population: 2 388 667

U.N. group no.		*Percentage*
0	Agriculture, forestry, fishing and hunting	27.7
1	Mining and quarrying	3.8
2/3	Manufacturing	18.0
4	Construction	5.7
5	Electricity, gas, water and sanitary services	0.8
6	Commerce	10.1
7	Transport, storage and communications	4.9
8	Services	22.8
9	Others	6.2

		Year(s)
Life expectancy at birth (years): male	49.8	1952
female	53.9	1952
Infant mortality (per '000)	101.7	1965
Crude birth rate (per '000)	35	1960–5 av.
Crude death rate (per '000)	11.5	1960–5 av.
Accidental deaths (per 100 000 population)		
caused by motor vehicles	5.8	1964
due to other causes	69.1	1964
Population per physician	2 100	1965
Population per hospital bed	260*a*	1966
School enrolment: age 5–19 years (percentage)	79	1963–4 av.
age over 19 years (per 100 000 population)	444	1963–5 av.

a government hospitals only.

COMMUNICATIONS

		Year(s)
Motor vehicles in use ('000s): private	90.1	1963–5 av.
commercial	100.3	1963–5 av.
Railway track (km.)	8 408	1964
Mail per capita: domestic	14	1961–3 av.
foreign received	na	1961–3 av.
foreign sent	1	1961–3 av.
Telephones (per '000 urban population)	3.19	1967
Radio receivers (per '000 population)	187	1963–5 av.
Television sets (per '000 population)	5.11	1963–5 av.
Daily newspapers (per '000 population)	118.5	1962–4 av.

FINANCE

Currency unit: The Chilean escudo was introduced in 1960, equivalent to 1 000 pesos

Exchange rates	*1965a*	*1960*	*1956b*	*1938b*
Per $ U.S.	3.47	1.053	31.1	31.47
Per £ sterling	9.71	2.984	87.12	144.76

		Year(s)
National Income (million $ U.S.)	4 427	1965
G.N.P. per capita ($ U.S.)	510	1966
Rate of increase of G.N.P. per capita	1	1960–4 av.
Foreign trade (percentage of G.D.P.)	23	1963–5 av.

a trade rate. *b* official rate, for pesos.

TRADING

Total trade (in million $ U.S.)	*1965*	*1955*	*1938*
Exports (f.o.b.)	688	475	139
Imports (c.i.f.)	604	376	103

Main trading partners (percentage of total value)

Exports	*1965*	*1955*	*1938*	*Imports*	*1965*	*1955*	*1938*
U.S.A.	31	42	16	U.S.A.	39	43	28
Germany F.R.	13	10	10*d*	Germany F.R.	11	11	26*d*
U.K.	11	17	22	Argentina	8	11	4
Japan	11	—	—	U.K.	6	5	10
Netherlands	11	5	—	Peru	4	8	6

Distribution of trade (percentage of total value)

	1965	*1955*	*1938**
Exports			
Minerals	90	na	na
(copper)	(68)	(70)	(49)
Imports			
Machinery and transport equipment	34	29	na
Food	13	22	na
Chemicals	10	4	na

d includes Germany D.R.

continued

PRODUCTION, EXPORTS AND IMPORTS

Years: **1963–5 average** and *1953–5 average* Units: '000 metric tons unless otherwise indicated

1. CEREALS, etc.

	Production 1963–5	Production 1953–5	Exports 1963–5	Exports 1953–5	Imports 1963–5	Imports 1953–5
Barley	131.3	82.0	1.2	9.8	—	—
Maize (corn)	193.0	103.0	—	—	4.0	—
Oats	128.0	104.0	1.9	3.9	—	—
Potatoes	768.7	611.7	3.4	—	0.1	0.7[2]
Rice	86.3	78.0	—	1.6	15.0*	2.0
Rye	14.3	6.7	—	—	—	—
Wheat	1 290.3	1 027.0	—	—	269.0	166.8

2. FRUIT, etc.

	Production 1963–5	Production 1953–5	Exports 1963–5	Exports 1953–5	Imports 1963–5	Imports 1953–5
Apples	55.0	31.3*	15.0	8.4	—	—
Apricots	4.0*	na	—	—	—	—
Bananas	—	—	—	—	30.2*	19.8
Cherries	3.3	na	—	—	—	—
Grapes	670.0*	532.0[2]	8.7	2.7	—	—
Lemons	44.7	26.0*	4.1	2.5	0.1	—
Oranges	41.0	28.3	—	—	0.2	—
Olives	20.0*	3.0[1]	—	—	—	—
Peaches	40.3*	30.1	na	0.9	—	—
Pears	11.3*	3.7*	2.9	0.8	—	—
Plums	22.7*	na	na	0.7	—	—
Raisins	0.8*	0.2*n	0.1	0.1	—	—
Tomatoes	61.3*	na				
Wine b	4 243.0[2]	3 587.0	82.6	68.3	0.1	—

b '000 hectolitres. *n* commercial production only.

3. BEVERAGES, FOREST PRODUCTS, etc.

	Production 1963–5	Production 1953–5	Exports 1963–5	Exports 1953–5	Imports 1963–5	Imports 1953–5
Cocoa	—	—	—	—	1.3	1.0
Coffee	—	—	—	—	8.8	5.8
Sugar: beet	686.7	27.3*				
raw	107.1	8.7*	—	—	179.1	230.0
Tea	—	—	—	—	6.4	3.4
Tobacco: leaf	6.2	5.0	—	0.1	1.1	0.3
cigars e	2.0	2.0	—	—	—	—
cigarettes e	6 470.0	7 688.0	—	—	—	—
Softwood j	2 506.3	764.0	90.0	145.3	1.4	6.6
Hardwood j	4 341.7	4 738.0[1]	35.7	153.1	0.6	—
Wood pulp	168.2	20.3	16.9[2]	—	6.0[2]	36.3
Newsprint	78.3	10.8	46.0[2]	—	6.2[1]	12.7
Other paper	89.0*	48.0	—[2]	—	4.2[1]	1.5

e no. in millions. *j* '000 cu. metres of roundwood equivalent.

4. VEGETABLE OILSEEDS AND OILS

	Production 1963–5	Production 1953–5	Exports 1963–5	Exports 1953–5	Imports 1963–5	Imports 1953–5
Castor seed	—	—	—	—	0.34	0.17
Copra	—	—	—	—	—	0.03
Coconut oil	—	—	—	—	0.80	—
Cottonseed oil	—	—	—	—	0.39	—
Groundnuts	—	—	—	—	0.09	0.05
Linseed	4.00*	4.67	—	—	—	0.37
Linseed oil			—	—	0.02	0.02
Olive oil	2.00*	0.50[2]	0.01	—	0.21	0.08
Palm oil	—	—	—	—	1.20	na
Rapeseed	60.00	na	0.70[2]	—[1]	—	—[1]
Sesame seed	—	—	—	—	0.01	na
Soya bean oil	—	—	—	—	12.26	0.05
Sunflower seed	43.67	69.00	—	—	—	—
Sunflower seed oil	na	na	—	—	0.16	9.00[1]n
Tung oil	—	—	—	—	0.05	na

n incl. other minor vegetable oils.

5. LIVESTOCK‡, ANIMAL PRODUCTS, etc.

	Production 1963–5	Production 1953–5	Exports 1963–5	Exports 1953–5	Imports 1963–5	Imports 1953–5
Chickens d	na	963.0[2]				
Cattle d	3 065.3	2 494.7	—	—	111.2	35.1
dairy cows d	1 023.0	na				
Goats d }	1 442.0*	800.0[1]	0.1	—	37.6	na
Sheep d }	6 483.7*	6 034.3*				
Horses d	541.7*	466.0				
Pigs d	1 010.0	855.0*	—	—	—	0.2
Meat‡ 'A'	221.3*	168.5[2]	0.9	1.0	8.8	4.4
'B'	22.2*	9.1[2]	0.2	—	—	—
Butter	5.0	7.0[1]	—	—	4.0	1.1
Cheese	9.3	11.0[2]	—	—	0.1	—
Eggs	24.0	32.5[1]*	—	—	—	—
Fish	877.1p	155.0p	120.9	0.9[1]*	0.2	0.4[1]*
Milk	837.3	771.0[1]	—	—	140.0	0.5*
Whale/sperm oil	5.7	5.4	—	—	—	—
Hides/skins	na	na	1.2q	0.3[1]	2.4a	—
Wool	11.2*	9.3*	3.2	2.3	0.6	0.6

a million $ U.S. *d* no. in thousands. *p* incl. fish landed by foreign vessels. *q* undressed skins only.

6. FIBRES, TEXTILES, etc.

	Production 1963–5	Production 1953–5	Exports 1963–5	Exports 1953–5	Imports 1963–5	Imports 1953–5
Agaves (sisal etc.)	—	—	—	—	0.3[2]	0.3[1]
Cotton lint	—	—	—	—	28.9	19.7
Flax fibre	1.0*	0.7	0.1	0.1	—	—
Hemp fibre	3.8*	3.7	0.2	1.0	—	—
Jute	—	—	—	—	0.7	3.5
Rubber, natural	—	—	—	—	7.4	3.6
Silk f	—	—	—	—	292.7	na
Cotton: yarn	27.5[1]	na	—	—	—	—
woven fabrics	11.5*	5.8*n	—	—	—	—
Rayon, fibre/yarn	4.7	3.8	—	—	1.4	na
Non-cellulosic fibre/yarn	1.1	—	—	—	1.2	na
Wool, woven fabrics	7.0[2]p	7.4[1]p	na	na	na	0.1

f metric tons. *n* incl. piece goods predominantly of cotton. *p* million metres.

7. FUEL AND POWER

	Production 1963–5	Production 1953–5	Exports 1963–5	Exports 1953–5	Imports 1963–5	Imports 1953–5
Coal‡ 'A'	1 550	2 060	1	28	191	197
'B'	30	240	—	—	—	—
Coke	na	na	—	4	—	1
Electricity h: total	5 895	3 630				
hydro	3 694	2 150				
thermal	2 201	1 480				
Natural gas i	1 810	44	—	—	—	—
Oil, crude	1 776	350[1]	—	—	520	na
Petroleum, refined	2 296	620[1]	43	—	820	1 770[1]

h million kWh. *i* million cu. metres.

8. IRON AND STEEL

	Production 1963–5	Production 1953–5	Exports 1963–5	Exports 1953–5	Imports 1963–5	Imports 1953–5
Iron ore	6 554m	1 391m	8 977	1 799	—	—
Pig iron	402	282	6	10	—	1
Steel ingots/castings	527	308	—	—	—	—
Iron/steel products a	na	na	3[1]	—	34	11

a million $ U.S. *m* metal content.

9. NON-FERROUS MINERALS AND METALS

	Production 1963–5	Production 1953–5	Exports 1963–5	Exports 1953–5	Imports 1963–5	Imports 1953–5
Gold k, ore m	67.00	133.00	59.39	70.81	—	—
Silver k, ore m	3 045.70	1 616.30	2 405.08	1 317.23	—	—
Asbestos, manufactured	—	na	—	—	7.64	4.10
Mica	—	—	—	—	0.02	0.05
Aluminium	—	—	—	—	3.16	1.13
Antimony, metal	—	—	—	—	0.05	0.05
Chrome, metal	—	—	—	—	0.28	0.46
Copper: ore	602.78m	386.76m	34.45	29.57	—	—
metal	573.06	360.41	557.70	361.09	—	—
Lead: ore	0.99m	3.00*m	1.64	2.90	—	—
metal	0.07	0.18	—	—	1.89	1.75
Magnesium: dolomite	—	—	—	—	27.39	16.78
magnesite	—	—	—	—	7.15	1.93
metal/salts	—	—	—	—	—	0.33
Manganese: ore	27.64	53.81	—	25.66	7.01	—
metal	na	na	7.03	5.93	0.01	0.04
Mercury f	15.03	9.99	6.00	—	0.40	1.50
Molybdenum f, ore	3 437.66m	1 286.85m	6 427.20	2 585.60	—	—
Nickel, metal	—	—	—	—	0.06[2]	0.07
Tin: ore	—	—	—	—	—	0.10
metal	—	—	—	—	0.75	0.41
Titanium minerals	—	—	—	—	2.10	0.46
Zinc: ore	0.97m	2.53m	3.71[1]	0.54	—	—
metal	na	na	—	—	6.83	4.23

f metric tons. *k* '000 fine troy oz. *m* metal content.

10. CHEMICALS*n* AND FERTILIZERS

	Production 1963–5	Production 1953–5	Exports 1963–5	Exports 1953–5	Imports 1963–5	Imports 1953–5
Organic chemicals:						
Benzene	na		na		na	
Butadiene	—		—		na	
Ethylene	na		—		na	
Methanol	na		—		na	
Phenol	—		—		na	
Phthalic anhydride	na		na		na	
Styrene monomer	—		—		na	
Urea	na		na		na	
Inorganic chemicals:						
Ammonia	na		—		0.1[2]	
Carbon black	—		—		3.9	
Chlorine	na		na		—[1]	
Nitric acid	0.2		—		na	
Sodium carbonate	3.8[1]		—		10.0[1]	
Sodium hydroxide	7.0[1]		na		na	
Sulphuric acid	169.0		—[1]		—[1]	
Plastics:						
Polyamides	na		na		na	
Polyethylene	—		—		na	
Polyvinyl chloride	—		—		na	
Fertilizers:						
Phosphates	32.1p	81.6*p	—	—	—	—
Potash	15.4*r	3.6r	97.8	58.0	14.5	6.6
Sulphur	40.8q	44.6q	0.1	28.1	12.2	na

n data not available for years 1953–5. *p* apatite and guano. *q* native. *r* k_2o content

11. INDUSTRY

	Production 1963–5	Production 1953–5	Exports 1963–5	Exports 1953–5	Imports 1963–5	Imports 1953–5
Alcoholic beverages			na	1.7aq	2.4[1]a	na
beer b	1 332.0	1 258.3				
Cement	1 165.3	789.7	—	8.3	10.0	1.7
Electrical engineering a	—	—	—	—	36.9	9.6[2]
Railway vehicles a	—	—	—	—	12.5	9.4
Merchant ships g	2.0	na	—	—	17.0	11.2[2]
Motor vehicles a	—	—	—	—	32.4[1]	10.1

a million $ U.S. *b* '000 hectolitres. *g* '000 G.R.T. *q* non-sparkling wines only.

continued

CHINA, PEOPLE'S REPUBLIC OF

China was proclaimed a 'People's Republic' in 1949, the communists having gained complete control of the mainland after the second world war; Mao Tse-tung was elected Chairman of the Republic, and introduced a completely reformed constitution. Taiwan (Formosa), alone, remained in Nationalist hands under Chiang Kai-shek, and, for the present at least, is effectively a separate nation.

AREA: 9 700 000* sq. km. (3 745 000* sq. miles)

LAND USE: (percentage of total)

	1954
Arable and orchard	11.2
Permanent meadow and pasture	18.2
Forest and woodland	7.9
City areas, waste and other land	62.7

In recent years great emphasis has been placed on afforestation to combat soil erosion and the reclamation of waste land. New techniques of irrigation and flood control have improved the reliability of large areas of fertile land.

POPULATION: 720 000 000 (1967 estimate)

In addition, apart from 13 million in Taiwan, about 16 million Chinese live outside China, the majority in South East Asian countries.

Largest city: SHANG-HAI; population 6 900 000 (city proper, 1957)

Capital city: PEI-P'ING (Peking); population: 4 010 000 (city proper, 1957)

		Year(s)
Infant mortality (per '000)	34*	1957
Crude birth rate (per '000)	34.1*	1957
Crude death rate (per '000)	11*	1957
School enrolment: age 5–19 years (percentage)	58*	1958
age over 19 years (per 100 000 population)	128	1960–2 av.

The death and infant mortality rates have fallen substantially due to the emphasis on public hygiene. The birth rate remains fairly constant since contraception is not popular and the emphasis of birth control propaganda is on late marriage and maternal and infant health rather than prevention of births. Much education is practical and at secondary level is combined with periods of work on the land.

EMPLOYMENT

About 80% of the population is rural and engaged principally in agriculture during the tending season and in local workshop industry during slack times. A feature of employment is the massive numbers engaged in major construction works and local projects built and financed by individual communes.

COMMUNICATIONS

		Year(s)
Railway track (km.)	31 193	1958
Telephones (per '000 urban population)	0.1a	1947
Radio licences (per '000 population)	12	1963–5 av.
Television sets (per '000 population)	0.1	1963–5 av.
Daily newspapers (per '000 population)	19a	1955

a latest available figure.

The attempt to create an industrial state has led to an expansion of communications particularly by rail and, in the south, water. A civil air service has been built up since 1949 and China now has three international-standard airports. The radio is much used as a means of propaganda and its ownership is therefore encouraged.

FINANCE

Currency unit: The yuan

Exchange rates a	1965	1960	1955
Per $ U.S.	2.34	2.34	2.34
Per £ sterling	6.859	6.859	6.859

a official rates. (1955 figure as quoted by the Bank of China.)

In the first year of communist control the galloping inflation, which had helped to contribute to the downfall of the Nationalist government, was controlled and the financial balance has since remained stable.

TRADING

Total trade (in million $ U.S.)	1965	1960
Exports (f.o.b.)	1 647	1 736
Imports (c.i.f.)	1 491	1 642

Main trading partners (percentage of total value)

Exports	1965	1960	*Imports*	1965	1960
Hong Kong	25	12	Japan	16	—
U.S.S.R.	14	49	U.S.S.R.	13	50
Japan	14	1	Australia	11	1
Cuba	8	—	Canada	7	—
U.K.	5	4	Cuba	7	2
Germany F. R.	4	4	Argentina	6	—
France	3	1	Germany F. R.	5	—
Italy	2	1	U.K.	5	5

The value of foreign trade is only about 4% of China's G.N.P. The majority of China's exports are agricultural raw materials, but the proportion of made-up textiles and light industrial goods is increasing. China has an unfavourable balance of trade only with the major grain exporting countries. A sterling balance is earned through a high level of exports to Hong Kong whence imports are virtually non-existent. Since 1960 trade with all the Comecon countries has declined.

PRODUCTION, EXPORTS AND IMPORTS

Years: **1963–5 average** and *1953–5 average* Units: '000 metric tons unless otherwise indicated

1. CEREALS, etc.

	Production 1963–5	Production 1953–5	Exports 1963–5	Exports 1953–5	Imports 1963–5	Imports 1953–5
Barley	na	12 924*n	—	2*	205*	—
Maize (corn)	na	18 812*n	175*	11*	195[2]*	—
Millets/sorghum	na	1[2]*	7*	1*	15[2]*	—
Oats	na	1 557*n	—	—	68*	—
Potatoes	na	18 150*n	25*	11*	—	—
Rice	85 000*	65 000*	724*	289*	92*	54*
Sweet potatoes/yams	na	na	—	—	—	—
Wheat	23 630*	22 635	110[2]*	—	5 063*	7*

n 1952–1956 av.

2. FRUIT, etc.

	Production 1963–5	Production 1953–5	Exports 1963–5	Exports 1953–5	Imports 1963–5	Imports 1953–5
Apples	318*	na	79*	1*	—	—
Bananas	160*	na	15*	10*	—	—
Dates	—	—	—	—	56*	—
Grapes	123*	na	2*	3*	—	—
Lemons	—	—			—	—
Oranges	na	na	37*	17*	—	—
Other citrus fruit	na	na	4*	—	—	—
Pears	831*	na	15*	—	—	—
Raisins	na	—	1*	—	—	—

Rice is the most extensive food crop in China but maize, sorghum, wheat, barley, and yams also are grown. Citrus and tropical fruits can be grown in some areas and apples are proving an important crop in Ssu-ch'uan and around Lan-chou.

3. BEVERAGES, FOREST PRODUCTS, etc.

	Production 1963–5	Production 1953–5	Exports 1963–5	Exports 1953–5	Imports 1963–5	Imports 1953–5
Cocoa	—	—	1*		6*	
Coffee	—	—	1*	—	—	—
Sugar: beet	3 693*	990[1]*				
cane	21 670*	8 350[2]*				
raw (beet) }	443*p	190[2]*p	305*	8*	438*	50*
(cane) }	1 567*	613*				
Tea	159*	12[1]*	30*	15*	2*	—
Tobacco, leaf	443*	374*	9[2]*	2*	4[2]*	—

continued

3. BEVERAGES, FOREST PRODUCTS, etc.—*continued*

	Production 1963–5	Production 1953–5	Exports 1963–5	Exports 1953–5	Imports 1963–5	Imports 1953–5
Softwood j	61 260*	na	13	na	na	na
Hardwood j	72 830*	na	2[2]	na	62	na
Wood pulp	825[2]*	na	na	na	82	na
Newsprint	350*	na	23	na	1	na
Other paper	2 567*	na	na	na	na	na

j '000 cu. metres of roundwood equivalent. *p* in addition, non-centrifugal sugar, 560* (1963–5 av.) and 315* (1953–5 av.).

Though China's tea exports have never recovered from the development of tea growing in India and Ceylon, there is sufficient demand from the home market to make tea an important crop. Tobacco also is grown for local use and coffee growing has started on a very small scale. A new timber industry is developing as a result of the afforestation programme. A great variety of trees is grown in different regions, for the production of wood-oil as well as for timber. Teak is commercially the most important wood.

4 VEGETABLE OILSEEDS AND OILS

	Production 1963–5	Production 1953–5	Exports 1963–5	Exports 1953–5	Imports 1963–5	Imports 1953–5
Castor seed	na	na	10*	23*	—	—
Copra	—	—	—*	—	2[1]*	6*
Coconut oil	—	—	—	—	13*	16*
Cottonseed	2 313*	1 550[2]*	na	3*	—	—
Cottonseed oil	na	na	na	11*	—	—
Groundnuts	1 515*	1 993*	31*	47*	—	—
Groundnut oil	na	na	5*	16*	—	—
Linseed	—	na	—*	13*	—	—
Linseed oil	na	na	—*	1*	7*	—
Rapeseed	1 092*	2 850[1]*	2*	16*	—	—
Rapeseed oil	na	na	1*	4*	—	—
Sesame seed	360*	650[1]*	3*	32*	2*	—
Soya beans	10 923*	9 100[2]*	464*	249*	—	3*
Soya bean oil	na	na	2*	8*	—	—
Sunflower seed	66*	na	3*	7*	—	—
Tung oil	75*	76*	16*	36*	—	—

Rape and sesame are both grown for oil whereas soya beans are grown principally for food, though some oil is extracted.

continued

na: data not available. — negligible or nil. [1] one year only. [2] two year average. * estimate. ‡ see appendix. † re-exports.

CHINA, PEOPLE'S REPUBLIC OF *continued*

PRODUCTION, EXPORTS AND IMPORTS *continued*

5. LIVESTOCK‡, ANIMAL PRODUCTS, etc.

	Production		Exports		Imports	
Chickens *d*	**457 850*** *n*	na				
Cattle *d*	**62 000***	*43 000**	**55***	*32**	—	—
Goats *d*	**54 000***	*39 590**	**7***	na	—	—
Sheep *d*	**65 800***	*39 590**				
Horses *d*	**7 600***	*7 220**				
Pigs *d*	**198 300***	*95 250**	**1 634***	*493**	—	—
Bacon/ham	**11 780***	na	—	—	—	—
Meat‡ 'A'			—	—	—	—
Eggs	na	na	**39***	*26**	—	—
Fish	na	*2 237**	—	—	—	—
Milk	**2 790***	na	**1***	—	**3***	—*
Wool	**46***	*28**	**14***	*10**	**10***	*1**

d no. in thousands. *n* incl. ducks, geese and turkeys.

The keeping of pigs is encouraged, principally for the production of fertilizer, and other animals are kept for draught purposes. Some sheep are bred for wool. Land which can be cultivated is rarely used for grazing which gives a lower output of calories per acre.
Fishing is growing in importance. Sea fishing is becoming mechanized and extending its range, and fresh-water fish ponds are receiving more attention.

6. FIBRES, TEXTILES, etc.

	Production		Exports		Imports	
Agaves (sisal etc.)	—	—	—	—	**7***	—
Cotton lint	**1 157***	*695[2]**	—	*4**	**136***	*51**
Flax fibre	na	na	**3***	—	—	—
Hemp fibre	na	na	—	*1**	—	—
Jute	**390***	na	—*	*1**	**47***	*8**
Rubber: natural	—	—	**3[2]***	—	**136***	*53**
synthetic	—	—	—	—	**1***	—
Silk *f*	**7 500[1]***	*4 200**	**2 110***	*1 133**	—	—
Cotton: yarn	na	na	na	na	na	na
woven fabrics	na	*488**	**67[2]***	na	—	—
Rayon, fibre/yarn	na	na	na	na	na	na
Wool, yarn	na	na	—	—	—	—

f metric tons.

Silk is the most long-standing of China's textile industries and sericulture is still practised though it is in decline. Cotton growing is increasing.

7. FUEL AND POWER

	Production		Exports		Imports	
Coal	**270 000** *p*	*190 000q*	na	na	na	na
Electricity *h t*	na	*10 100*				
Oil, crude *n*	**8 687**	*970*	—	—	**186**	na
Petroleum, refined *n*	**7 730**	*1 270*	—	—	na	na
Uranium *f*	na	na	—	—	—	—

f metric tons. *h* million kWh. *n* incl. North Vietnam, North Korea, and Mongolia. *p* 1967 figure. *q* 1958 figure. *t* thermal and hydro.

China has large resources of coal much of which is easily mined. Oil is also present in considerable quantities though it has only recently been exploited to any extent. Despite great hydro-electric potential most of the electricity is generated thermally because the development costs are less.

8. IRON AND STEEL

	Production		Exports		Imports	
Iron ore	na	*5 080** *m*	na	na	na	na
Pig iron	**17 962***	*3 235**	na	na	na	na
Steel ingots/castings	**13 638***	*2 284**	na	na	na	na

m metal content.

9. NON-FERROUS MINERALS AND METALS

	Production		Exports		Imports	
Gold *k*, ore *m*	**60**	*100[1]**	na	na	na	na
Silver *k*, ore *m*	**800**	*320**	na	na	na	na
Asbestos, fibre	**115***	—	na	na	na	na
Aluminium: bauxite	**406***	na	na	na	na	na
alumina	**200***	na	na	na	na	na
aluminium	**100**	*2** *p*	na	na	na	na
Antimony, ore *m*	**15***	*11**	na	na	na	na
Cobalt	na	na	na	na	na	na
Copper: ore *m*	**90***	*8**	na	na	na	na
metal	**100***	*8**	na	na	na	na
Lead: ore *m*	**100***	*9**	na	na	na	na
metal	**96***	*14**	na	na	na	na
Magnesium, metal/salts	**1*** *q*	na	na	na	na	na
Manganese, ore	**1 000***	na	na	na	na	na
Mercury *f*	**896***	*172[1]**	na	na	na	na
Molybdenum *f*, ore	**1 500*** *m*	na	na	na	na	na
Tin: ore *m*	**26***	*11**	na	na	na	na
metal	**26***	*10**	**9***	*5**	na	na
Tungsten, ore	**20***	*18**	na	na	na	na
Zinc: ore *m*	**100***	na	na	na	na	na
metal	**91***	*9**	na	na	na	na

f metric tons. *k* '000 fine troy oz. *m* metal content. *p* Manchuria only. *q* primary magnesium only.

China has considerable reserves of iron and is beginning to develop a highly sophisticated steel industry. She is also particularly rich in the non-ferrous minerals. Her deposits of antimony, molybdenum, tin, and tungsten may well be the richest in the world, and many other minerals, including mercury are to be found in considerable amounts.

10. CHEMICALS AND FERTILIZERS

	Production		Exports		Imports	
Chemicals	na	na	na	na	na	na
Fertilizers:						
Phosphates	**816***	*203**	na	na	na	na
Potash	na	na	na	na	na	na
Pyrites	**599*** *x*	na	na	na	na	na
Sulphur: native	**122***	—	na	na	na	na
recovered	**132***	—	na	na	na	na

x sulphur content.

The production of chemical fertilizers has developed dramatically in the past thirty years in the service of agriculture, but, despite this and the increasing degree of sophistication achieved, China was still the world's largest importer of chemical fertilizers in 1965. The manufacture of plastics began in 1958 and has developed very rapidly to include a wide range of polythene and cellulose products for farming and industrial use.

11. INDUSTRY

	Production		Exports		Imports	
Beer *b*	**640[2]***	na	—	—	—	—
Cement	**10 500***	*4 530p*	**950[1]***	*7*pq*	—	*2pq*
Machine tools *a*	**80[1]**	na	—	—	—	—

a million $ U.S. *b* '000 hectolitres. *p* incl. North Korea. *q* excl. trade with other Communist countries.

Both heavy and light industry are growing in importance. Recently the emphasis has been on industry in the service of agriculture. Tractor production is important, as is cement for construction work, and locomotives for transport. Soviet military aircraft are assembled and some manufactured under contract. Chinese ingenuity has led to a very high level of sophistication in electrical engineering.

na: data not available. — negligible or nil. [1] one year only. [2] two year average. * estimate. ‡ see appendix. † re-exports.

COLOMBIA

SOUTH AMERICA

Colombia is one of the more democratically stable republics of South America. Progress has recently been made towards industrialization and diversification to alleviate the problems of a one-product economy.

AREA: 1 138 914 sq. km. (439 735 sq. miles)

LAND USE: (percentage of total)	*1960*	*1949*
Arable and orchard	4.4	2.2
Permanent meadow and pasture	12.8	32.4
Forest and woodland	61.0	60.6
City areas, waste and other land	21.8	4.8

POPULATION: 19 191 000 (1967 estimate)

Largest city: BOGOTÁ, capital; population: 2 066 131 (city proper, 1967)

Distribution of working population (1951)
Total working population: 3 755 609

U.N. group no.		*Percentage*
0	Agriculture, forestry, fishing and hunting	53.9
1	Mining and quarrying	1.6
2/3	Manufacturing	12.3
4	Construction	3.5
5	Electricity, gas, water and sanitary services	0.3
6	Commerce	5.4
7	Transport, storage and communications	3.5
8	Services	15.9
9	Others	3.6

		Year(s)
Life expectancy at birth (years): male	44.2	1950–2 av.
female	46	
Infant mortality (per '000)	82.4*	1965
Crude birth rate (per '000)	42.5*	1960–5 av.
Crude death rate (per '000)	13*	1960–5 av.
Accidental deaths (per 100 000 population)		
caused by motor vehicles	11.4*	1965
due to other causes	32.4*	1965
Population per physician	2 470	1965
Population per hospital bed	400	1966
School enrolment: age 5–19 years (percentage)	61	1963–4 av.
age over 19 years (per 100 000 population)	207	1963–4 av.

COMMUNICATIONS		*Year(s)*
Motor vehicles in use ('000s): private	119.1	1963–5 av.
commercial	104.6	
Railway track (km.)	3 435	1964
Mail per capita: domestic	3	1959–60 av.
foreign received	1	
foreign sent	0.2	
Telephones (per '000 urban population)	2.5	1967
Radio receivers (per '000 population)	183	1963–5 av.
Television sets (per '000 population)	16.4	1963–5 av.
Daily newspapers (per '000 population)	54	1962–3 av.

FINANCE

Currency unit: The Colombian peso

Exchange rates	*1965a*	*1960*	*1950a*	*1938b*
Per $ U.S.	13.51	6.7	2.038	1.755
Per £ sterling	37.728	18.76	5.709	8.073

		Year(s)
National Income (million $ U.S.)	4 279	1965
G.N.P. per capita ($ U.S.)	280	1966
Rate of increase of G.N.P. per capita	2.1	1960–3 av.
Foreign trade (percentage of G.D.P.)	18	1963–5 av.

a principal selling rate. *b* selling rate.

TRADING

Total trade (in million $ U.S.)	*1965*	*1955*	*1938*
Exports (f.o.b.)	539	580	81
Imports (c.i.f.)	454	669	89

Main trading partners (percentage of total value)

Exports	*1965*	*1955*	*Imports*	*1965*	*1955*
U.S.A.	47	74	U.S.A.	47	63
Germany F.R.	12	8	Germany F.R.	11	10
Netherlands	5	2	U.K.	5	4
Trin./Tob.	5	1	Canada	4	3
Spain	5	1	Japan	4	1
U.K.	4	1	Sweden	3	2
Sweden	4	2	Spain	2	—

Distribution of trade (percentage of total value)

Exports	*1965*	*1955*	*1938**
Coffee	64	83	65
Crude materials and fuels	21	12	23
Imports			
Manufactured goods	64	70	na
(road motor vehicles)	(9)	(10)	
Chemicals	16	12	
Crude materials and fuels	10	10	
Food	5	7	

PRODUCTION, EXPORTS AND IMPORTS

Years: **1963–5 average** and *1953–5 average* Units: '000 metric tons unless otherwise indicated

1. CEREALS, etc.

	Production		Exports		Imports	
Barley	**85.7***	*50.0[2]*	—	—	—	*1.9*
Cassava	**1 882.0**	*734.0*	—	—	—	—
Maize (corn)	**1 047.0***	*894.3*	**0.8**	*1.1*	**6.8**	*0.1*
Millets/sorghum	—	—	—	—	**2.8**	*0.1[2]*
Oats	—	—	—	—	**6.1**	*2.1*
Potatoes	**827.0***	*600.3*	**1.2**	*0.6*	—	*0.7*
Rice	**590.0**	*297.0*	**1.1**	*6.3*	**0.3**	*11.2*
Sweet potatoes/ yams	**110.0***	na	—	—	—	—
Wheat	**107.3***	*150.7**	—	—	**141.5**	*43.1*

2. FRUIT, etc.

	Production		Exports		Imports	
Apples	—	—	—	—	—[2]	*0.8*
Bananas	**811.0***	na	**209.2**	*200.5*	—	—
Coconuts *e*	**15.0[1]***	na	—	—	—	—
Grapes	—	—	—	—	**0.1[2]**	—
Raisins	—	—	—	—	**0.3**	*0.4*
Tomatoes	**42.3***	na	na	na	—	—
Wine *b*	—	—	—	—	**6.6**	*9.7*

b '000 hectolitres. *e* no. in millions.

3. BEVERAGES, FOREST PRODUCTS, etc.

	Production		Exports		Imports	
Cocoa	**16.7**	*13.7**	—	—	**9.9**	*8.8*
Coffee	**474.2**	*404.9**	**363.6**	*365.0*	—	—
Sugar: cane	**13 945.0***	na				
raw	**427.0** *p*	*260.7*p*	**58.3**	*10.0*	—	*6.4*
Tobacco: leaf	**50.0**	*25.0**	**12.8**	*4.9*	—[2]	—
cigars	**476.0** *e*	*531.3e*	—	—	—	*0.4*
cigarettes	**17 645.0** *e*	*12 767.3e*				
tobacco/snuff	—	—				
Softwood *j*	**20.0*[1]**	*56.0[2]*	—[2]	—	—[2]	*0.7*
Hardwood *j*	**25 310.0*[1]**	*7 612.0*	**187.0[2]**	*41.1*	**1.3**	*0.7*
Wood pulp	**13.5*[2]**	*5.3**	—[1]	—	**52.2[1]**	*14.5*
Newsprint	—*[2]	—	na[1]	—	**40.0[1]**	*19.3*
Other paper	**110.0*[2]**	*15.3**	**0.2[1]**	—	**15.9[1]**	*30.0*

e no. in millions. *j* '000 cu. metres of roundwood equivalent. *p* in addition, panella, 637 (1963–5 av.) and 567 (1953–5 av.).

4. VEGETABLE OILSEEDS AND OILS

	Production		Exports		Imports	
Castor oil	—	—	—	—	—	*0.03*
Copra	**0.50***	*3.00[1]*	—	—	**11.81**	*41.03*
Coconut oil	na	na	—	—	**0.04**	*1.71q*
Cottonseed	**129.30**	*48.00**	—	—	—	*0.83*
Cottonseed oil	na	na	—	—	**0.12**	*0.45*
Linseed oil	—	—	—	—	**0.55**	*0.73*
Olive oil	—	—	—	—	**0.07**	*0.21*
Palm oil	—	—	—	—	**0.45**	*8.54*
Rapeseed	—	—	—	—	**0.01**	na
Rapeseed oil	—	—	—	—	**0.01**	—
Sesame seed	**47.20**	*10.00[1]*	—	—	—	—
Soya beans	**40.70**	na	—	—	—	—
Soya bean oil	—	—	—	—	**6.21**	*0.92*
Tung oil	—	—	—	—	**0.03[2]**	na

q incl. palm kernel oil.

5. LIVESTOCK‡, ANIMAL PRODUCTS, etc.

	Production		Exports		Imports	
Chickens *d*	**24 166.7*** *n*	*14 690.5[2]*				
Cattle *d*	**15 191.7***	*11 994.0[1]*	**20.4**	*2.4*	**0.2[2]**	*7.9*
dairy cows *d*	**5 681.0***	na				
Goats *d*	**368.0***	*294.0[1]*	—	—	**1.5**	—
Sheep *d*	**1 141.0**	*1 227.5[2]*				
Horses *d*	**1 011.0***	*1 222.0[2]*				
Pigs *d*	**2 475.0***	*1 824.0[1]*	—	—	—	*0.2*
Meat‡ 'A'	**443.3***	na	—	—	—	—
'B'	**22.1**	*32.1**	—	—	—	—
Eggs	**59.4***	*55.1**	—	—	—	
Fish	**49.7** *p*	*16.7p*	**0.8**	*0.4[1]**	**14.1**	*3.4[1]**
Milk	**1 942.0**	*1 892.0*	—	—	**1.2**	*9.9**
Hides/skins	—	na	—	*1.1*	—	—
Wool	na	*1.0[1]*	—	—	**3.3***	*0.9*

d no. in thousands. *n* incl. ducks, geese and turkeys. *p* excl. subsistence and game fishing.

continued

na: data not available. — negligible or nil. [1] one year only. [2] two year average. * estimate. ‡ see appendix. † re-exports.

COLOMBIA *continued*

PRODUCTION, EXPORTS AND IMPORTS *continued*

6. FIBRES, TEXTILES, etc.	Production		Exports		Imports	
Cotton lint	72.0	*25.0**	14.9	—	4.6	*7.8*
Flax fibre	—	—	—	—	0.1	—
Rubber, natural	—	*1.0[1]*	0.1†	—	7.0	*6.2*
Cotton: yarn	5.5[2]	na	1.0[1]	na	—	—
woven fabrics	36.9*	*21.6[2]*	0.8[1]	na	na	*1.7[2]*
Rayon, fibre/yarn	10.2	*6.2*	3.0	na	1.0	na
Non-cellulosic fibre/yarn	1.6	na	0.2	na	1.3	na
Wool: yarn	2.5[2]	na	—	—	—	*1.9*
woven fabrics	5.7r	*2.7r*	—[1]	—[2]	—[1]	*0.1*

r million metres.

7. FUEL AND POWER	Production		Exports		Imports	
Coal 'A'‡	3 090	*1 800[1]*	—	—	—	—
Electricity *h*: total	5 669	*1 640[1]*				
hydro	3 470[2]	*1 050[1]*				
thermal	2 199[2]	*590[1]*				
Natural gas *i*	790	*523[1]*	—	—	—	—
Oil, crude	9 050	*5 490[1]*	4 740	*3 590[1]*	—	—
Petroleum, refined	3 760	*1 760[1]*	603	*150[1]*	30	*480[1]*

h million kWh. *i* million cu. metres.

8. IRON AND STEEL	Production		Exports		Imports	
Iron ore	na	*—[1]*	—	—	—	—
Pig iron	204	*93[2]*	—	—	4	*1*
Steel ingots/castings	232	*77[1]*	—	—	21	*1*

9. NON-FERROUS MINERALS AND METALS	Production		Exports		Imports	
Gold *k*: ore *m*	336.30	*398.00*	—	—	—	—
bullion/coins etc.	na	na	na	*320.41*	—	—
Platinum group metals *k*	na	*28.40*	18.26	*28.40*	0.09	*0.41*
Silver *k*: ore *m*	117.30	*114.00*	—	—	—	—
bullion	na	na	na	*4.67*	57.33	*571.33*
Asbestos: fibre	—	—	—	—	9.97	*6.80*
manufactured	na	na	2.92	*1.64*	1.03	*0.41*
Mica	na	na	—	—	0.12	—
Aluminium: bauxite	—	—	—	—	6.95	na
alumina	—	—	—	—	0.12*n*	na
aluminium	—	—	—	—	6.04	*8.01*
Antimony, metal	—	—	—	—	0.03	—
Chrome: ore *m*	0.26	—	—	—	—	—
metal	—	—	—	—	—	*0.14*
Copper, metal	—	—	—	—	5.31	*5.73*
Lead: ore	0.42*m*	—	0.32	*0.71*	—	—
metal	—	—	—	—	2.05	*0.86*
Magnesium: dolomite	6.67	na	—	—	3.80	na
magnesite	0.22	na	—	—	0.05	*1.32*
metal/salts	—‡	—‡	—	—	0.61	*0.43*
Mercury *f*	0.60	*0.41*	—	—	5.60	*3.20*
Nickel, metal	—	—	—	—	0.39	*0.08*
Tin, metal	—	—	—	—	0.18	*0.04*
Titanium minerals	—	—	—	—	1.80	*0.71*
Zinc: ore	0.08*m*	—	na	*0.14*	—	—
metal	—	—	—	—	5.42	*1.63*

f metric tons. *k* '000 fine troy oz. *m* metal content. *n* incl. hydrates.

10. CHEMICALS *n* AND FERTILIZERS	Production		Exports		Imports	
Organic chemicals:						
Benzene	na		na		na	
Butadiene	—		—		na	
Ethylene	na		—		na	
Methanol	na		—		2.3[1]	
Phenol	—		—		na	
Phthalic anhydride	na		—		na	
Styrene monomer	—		—		na	
Urea	na		—		0.3[1]	
Inorganic chemicals:						
Ammonia	na		—		0.1[1]	
Carbon black	na		—		5.3[2]	
Chlorine	na		na		na	
Nitric acid	na		—		0.1[1]	
Sodium carbonate	21.7		—		7.8[1]	
Sodium hydroxide	24.7		—		2.3[1]	
Sulphuric acid	121.0		na		—	
Plastics:						
Polyamides	na		na		na	
Polyethylene	—		—		na	
Polyvinyl chloride	na		—		2.3[2]	
Fertilizers:						
Phosphates	—	—	—	—	16.8	*1.2*
Potash	—	—	—	—	40.3	*15.4*
Sulphur	14.5	*4.5*	—	—	2.7	*0.5*

n data not available for years 1953–5.

11. INDUSTRY	Production		Exports		Imports	
Aircraft *a*	—	—	—	—	7.5[2]	*6.2*
Alcoholic beverages			—	—	1.3[2]*a*	*2.9a*
beer *b*	6 672.0	*4 530.7*				
Cement	1 929.7	*961.7*	165.7	*22.0*	—	*9.7*
Electrical engineering *a*	96.7[2]	na	0.4	—	43.0	*44.7*
Railway vehicles *a*	—	—	—	—	6.4[2]	*2.8*
Machine tools *a*	—	—	—	—	8.6	—
Merchant ships *g*	—	na	—	—	27.0	*7.2*
Motor vehicles			—	—	48.8[2]*a*	*67.1a*
commercial *d*	1.1*p*	—				
private *d*	0.7*p*	—				

a million $ U.S. *b* '000 hectolitres. *d* no. in thousands. *g* '000 G.R.T. *p* assembly of imported parts.

continued

CONGO, DEMOCRATIC REPUBLIC OF THE — CENTRAL AFRICA

The former Belgian Congo was granted independence in 1960, but the departure of the Belgian administrators and technicians left a vacuum which the Congolese were not ready to fill. Tribal and regional rivalries led to the collapse of the administration and the breakaway of the province of Katanga, on which the economy of the country largely depended. U.N. intervention restored order and the country was reunited, and a 'people's republic' was declared in 1964. In 1971 the name of the country was officially changed to Zaïre.

AREA: 2 345 409 sq. km. (895 348 sq. miles)

LAND USE: (percentage of total)	*1959*	*1955*
Arable and orchard	20.9	20.7
Permanent meadow and pasture	10.0	1.0
Forest and woodland	42.7	42.3
City areas, waste and other land	35.4	26.0

POPULATION: 16 353 000 (African population only) (1967 estimate)
Largest city: KINSHASA, formerly Léopoldville, capital; population: 507 868 (city proper, 1966)

Distribution of working population (1955–7 av.)
Total working population: 6 309 941

U.N. group no.		*Percentage*
0	Agriculture, forestry, fishing and hunting	86.4
1	Mining and quarrying	1.2
2/3	Manufacturing	3.1
4	Construction	2.5
5	Electricity, gas, water and sanitary services	—
6	Commerce	1.3
7	Transport, storage and communications	1.6
8	Services	3.1
9	Others	0.8

		Year(s)
Life expectancy at birth (years): male	37.6	1950–2 av.
female	40.0	1950–2 av.
Population per physician	31 250	1966
Population per hospital bed	280	1964
School enrolment: age 5–19 years (percentage)	44	1963–4 av.
age over 19 years (per 100 000 population)	18	1963–5 av.

COMMUNICATIONS

		Year(s)
Motor vehicles in use ('000s): private	42.3	1963–4 av.
commercial	32.4	1963–4 av.
Railway track (km.)	5 174	1958
Mail per capita: domestic	2.2*a*	
foreign received	0.9*a*	1958
foreign sent	0.4*a*	1958
Telephones (per '000 urban population)	0.1*	1967
Radio receivers (per '000 population)	13	1963–5 av.
Daily newspapers (per '000 population)	1	1962

a incl. Rwanda and Burundi.

FINANCE

Currency unit: The Congolese franc

Exchange rates	*1965b*	*1960*	*1950*	*1938*
Per $ U.S.	180	65	50.12	29.68
Per £ sterling	504	182	140.4	136.53

		Year
National Income (million $ U.S.)	1 014	1964
G.N.P. per capita ($ U.S.)	60	1966

b devaluation from 65 to 180 francs per $ U.S. took place in 1963.

TRADING

Total trade (in million $ U.S.)	*1965*	*1955c*	*1938c*
Exports (f.o.b.)	336	456	52
Imports (c.i.f.)	321	379	37

Main trading partners (percentage of total value)

Exports	*1965*	*1955c*	*Imports*	*1965*	*1955c*	*1938c*
Belg./Lux.	54	52	Belg./Lux.	33	37	47
Italy	11	3	U.S.A.	24	19	8
U.K.	8	8	Germany F.R.	6	7	5*d*
France	7	7	France	5	4	2
Germany F.R.	4	3	U.K.	4	7	6
U.S.A.	4	17	Italy	3	2	1
Netherlands	3	3	South Africa	3	4	2

Distribution of trade (percentage of total value)

Exports	*1965*	*Imports*	*1965*	
Copper	52	Manufactured goods	62	
Other metals	12	(machinery and transport equipment)		(33)
Vegetable oils	8	(textiles and clothing)		(12)
Diamonds	7	Food	17	
Non-ferrous ores and concentrates	7	(cereals)		(6)
Coffee	4	Chemicals	8	
		Crude materials and fuels	5	

c 1938 and 1955 figures incl. Ruanda-Urundi (Rwanda and Burundi). *d* incl. Germany D.R.

PRODUCTION, EXPORTS AND IMPORTS

Years: **1963–5 average** and *1953–5 average* Units: '000 metric tons unless otherwise indicated

1. CEREALS, etc.	Production		Exports		Imports	
Barley	—	—	—	—	0.2	—
Cassava	6 171.3*	*7 018.7*	—	—	—	—
Maize (corn)	235.3*	*324.7*	—	*11.2*	55.4	*0.1*
Millets/sorghum	43.7*	*38.5[2]*	—	*0.5n*	—	—
Potatoes	18.0[1]*	*14.3*	—	*0.3*	3.6	*9.3*
Rice	57.0*	*184.7*	—	*0.7[2]*	26.9	*0.1*
Sweet potatoes/yams	293.3*	*336.7*	—	—	—	—
Wheat	2.7*	*4.0*	—	—	0.2	*0.2*

n may include some oilseeds.

2. FRUIT, etc.	Production		Exports		Imports	
Apples	—	—	—	—	0.4	*1.1*
Bananas	49.7*	*34.3*	13.7	*24.2*	—	—
Grapes	—	—	—	—	0.1	*0.4*
Oranges	—	—	—	—	—	*0.8*
Wine *b*	—	—	—	—	9.3	*72.0*

b '000 hectolitres.

3. BEVERAGES, FOREST PRODUCTS, etc.	Production		Exports		Imports	
Cocoa	5.6	*2.9*	5.0	*3.0*	—	—
Coffee	61.0*	*26.8*	35.9	*37.5*	—	—
Sugar: cane	333.3*	*168.3p*				
raw	35.9	*17.3*	—	—	2.0*[2]	*4.3*
Tea	4.9*	*0.7*	4.4	*0.5*	—	—
Tobacco,	3.0*	*0.2*	—	*0.1*	2.8	*3.8*
cigarettes *e*	2 808.0	*2 686.0*	—	—	na	*768.4q*
Hardwood *j*	10 939.5	*5 128.3*	149.0[2]	*203.5*	6.6[2]	*5.5*
Wood pulp	—	—	—	—	0.1[2]	*0.8*
Newsprint	—*	—	—	—	1.1[1]	*0.8*
Other paper	0.7*	—	—	—	6.0[1]	*14.7*

e no. in millions. *j* '000 cu. metres of roundwood equivalent. *p* from estates only. *q* incl. Rwanda and Burundi.

4. VEGETABLE OILSEEDS AND OILS	Production		Exports		Imports	
Castor seed	—	*1.52*	—	*1.27*	—	—
Castor oil	—	na	—	—	0.11	*0.03*
Cottonseed	16.70	*94.67*	0.08[2]	—	—	—
Cottonseed oil	na	na	0.72	*0.34*	—	—
Groundnuts	80.71	*126.70*	0.02	*1.20*	0.38	—
Groundnut oil	na	na	2.86[1]	*6.21*	0.01	—
Linseed oil	—	—	—	—	0.06	*0.27*
Olive oil	—	—	—	—	0.01	*0.10*
Palm kernels	103.27*	*118.83r*	1.38	*73.90*	—	—
Palm kernel oil	na	na	35.85	*24.80*	—	—
Palm oil	196.77	*190.67*	111.06	*139.64*	—	—
Sesame seed	6.10*	*5.23t*	—	*0.43*	—	—
Soya beans	2.00*	na	—	—	—	—

r figure possibly incomplete. *t* from villages only.

5. LIVESTOCK‡, ANIMAL PRODUCTS, etc.	Production		Exports		Imports	
Chickens *d*	na	na				
Cattle *d*	1 147.7*	*806.7*	na	*0.2*	0.3	*3.4*
Goats *d*	2 316.0*	*1 507.0*	—	—	—	—
Sheep *d*	680.7*	*537.3*	—	—	—	—
Horses *d*	1.0*	*1.0[2]*				
Pigs *d*	383.0*	*304.3*	—	*0.2*	0.3[2]	*0.3*
Bacon/ham	—	—	—	—	—	*0.1*
Meat‡ 'A'			—	—	10.5	*7.1*
'B'	—	—	—	—	2.2	*0.5*
Butter	1.0*	*0.3*	—	—	0.8	*1.5*
Cheese	—	—	—	—	0.3	*1.2*
Eggs	16.0*	na			0.1	*0.1*
Fish	75.2	*78.4*	—	—	28.3	na
Milk	27.7*	*15.0*	—	—	19.0	*21.3*
Hides/skins	na	*0.7*	1.3[2]*q*	—	—	—

d no. in thousands. *q* incl. Rwanda and Burundi.

6. FIBRES, TEXTILES, etc.	Production		Exports		Imports	
Agaves (sisal etc.)	0.2*	*0.2*	0.1	*0.2*	—	—
Cotton lint	8.3	*47.3*	6.1[2]	*42.6*	0.2	—
Jute	6.7*	*9.0*	1.9[1]	*4.5*	—	*0.1*
Rubber, natural	na	na	31.0	*22.2*	—	—
Silk *f*	na	*72.0**	—	—	—	—
Cotton, woven fabrics	9.4*	*5.5[2]*	—	—	na	*6.7*
Rayon, woven fabrics	—	—	—	—	na	*2.5*

f metric tons.

7. FUEL AND POWER	Production		Exports		Imports	
Coal 'A'‡	100	*480*	—	—	—	*158*
Electricity *h*: total	2 509	*1 260*				
hydro	na	*1 160*				
thermal	na	*100*				
Petroleum, refined	—	—	—	—	400	*400[1]*
Rare earths *f*	7*t*	*361n*	—	na	—	—
Uranium	na	na	18 200*p*	na	—	—

f metric tons. *h* million kWh. *n* monazite and bastnaesite. *p* radium content in milligrams. *t* monazite only.

8. IRON AND STEEL	Production		Exports		Imports	
Pig iron	—	—	—	—	—	*2*

9. NON-FERROUS MINERALS AND METALS	Production		Exports		Imports	
Diamonds	14 006.67*l*	*12 747.04l*	19.65*a*	*19.46a*	—	—
Gold *k*: ore *m*	164.70	*369.00*	—	—	—	—
bullion/coins etc.	na	na	na	*371.00*	—	—
Platinum group metals *k*	—	*0.18[1]*	—	—	—	—
Silver *k*: ore *m*	1 371.70	*4 529.30*	—	—	—	—
bullion	na	na	—	*37.00*	—	—
Asbestos, fibre	—	—	—	—	—	*2.23*

a million $ U.S. *k* '000 fine troy oz. *l* '000 carats. *m* metal content.

continued

na: data not available. — negligible or nil. [1] one year only. [2] two year average. * estimate. ‡ see appendix. † re-exports.

na: data not available. — negligible or nil. [1] one year only. [2] two year average. * estimate. ‡ see appendix. † re-exports.

CONGO, DEMOCRATIC REPUBLIC OF THE *continued*

PRODUCTION, EXPORTS AND IMPORTS *continued*

9. NON-FERROUS MINERALS AND METALS—*continued*

	Production		Exports		Imports	
Aluminium: bauxite	—	—	—	—	—	*0.02*
alumina	—	—	—	—	—	*0.07*
aluminium	—	—	—	—	—	*2.84*[1]
Beryl	**0.12**	*0.13q*	**0.64*n***	na	—	—
Cadmium	**0.14**	*0.09*	**0.46***	*0.07*	—	—
Cobalt: ore	**7.81*m***	*8.49m*	—	—	—	—
metal	na	na	**8.13[1]*p***	*260.35p*	—	—
Copper‡: ore	**278.83*m***	*223.36m*	—	—	—	—
metal	**278.83**	*223.36*	**284.00***	*229.84*	—	—
Lead: ore	**1.26*m***	na	—	na	—[2]	—
metal	—	—	—	—	—	*1.18*
Magnesium, metal/salts	—	—	—	—	—	*1.75*
Manganese, ore	**319.10**	*354.44*	**364.09***	*236.06*	—	—
Mercury*f*	—	—	—	—	**1.40**	*1.90*
Tin: ore	**6.20*m***	*15.38mq*	**8.13*q**	*17.65*	—	—
metal	**1.61**	*2.78*	**1.37*q**	*2.64*	—	—
Titanium minerals	—	—	—	—	—	*0.04*
Tungsten, ore	**0.22*r***	*1.46q*	**0.31***	*1.24*	—	—
Zinc: ore	**109.41*m***	*92.95m*	**82.98*m***	*116.36*	—	—
metal	**55.10**	*24.59*	**42.34***	*23.01*	—	*0.36*

f metric tons. *m* metal content. *n* exports to U.S.A. only. *p* incl. cobalt-copper ingots. *q* incl. Rwanda and Burundi. *r* incl. tungsten oxide content of tin-tungsten concentrates.

10. CHEMICALS*n* AND FERTILIZERS

	Production		Exports		Imports	
Chemicals	—		—		na	
Fertilizers:						
Potash	—	—	—	—	**1.6**[2]	—
Sulphur	—	—	—	—	—	*0.2*

n data not available for years 1953–5.

11. INDUSTRY

	Production		Exports		Imports	
Aircraft*a*	—	—	—	—	**0.9**	*4.0q*
Alcoholic beverages			—	—	**1.3*a***	—
beer*b*	**1 991.0**	*886.0*				
Cement*q*	**248.0***	*336.3*	**27.0***	*4.7*	**4.7***	*224.7*
Electrical engineering*a*	—	—	—	—	**13.5**	*10.3*[2]*q*
Railway vehicles*a*	—	—	—	—	**3.6**	*10.9*
Motor vehicles*a*	—	—	—	—	**29.5**	*20.8*[2]

a million $ U.S. *b* '000 hectolitres. *q* incl. Rwanda and Burundi.

CONGO, REPUBLIC OF THE

CENTRAL AFRICA

The Republic of the Congo, formerly known as Middle Congo, a territory of French Equatorial Africa, and from 1958 a member state of the French Community, became fully independent in 1960. The Congo has been a member of the Equatorial Customs Union since its foundation in 1959.

AREA: 342 000 sq. km. (132 046 sq. miles)

LAND USE: (percentage of total)

	1963
Arable and orchard	1.8
Permanent meadow and pasture	na
Forest and woodland	47.5
City areas, waste and other land	na

POPULATION: 860 000 (1967 U.N. estimate)

Largest city: BRAZZAVILLE, capital; population: 136 200 (1961/2 census)

		Year(s)
Life expectancy at birth (years): male / female	37	1960–1 av.
Population per physician	11 640	1966
Population per hospital bed	190	1966
School enrolment: age 5–19 years (percentage)	67	1963–4 av.
age over 19 years (per 100 000 population)	116	1964–5 av.

COMMUNICATIONS

		Year(s)
Railway track (km.)	516	1966
Telephones (per '000 urban population)	1*	1967
Television sets (per '000 population)	0.4*	1963–5 av.
Daily newspapers (per '000 population)	0.5	1963

FINANCE

Currency unit: The franc CFA

Exchange rates	*1965*	*1960*
Per $ U.S.	246.85	246.85
Per £ sterling	691.18	691.18

		Year
National Income (million $ U.S.)	106	1958
G.N.P. per capita ($ U.S.)	120	1966

TRADING

Total trade (in million $ U.S.)	*1965*	*1955*
Exports (f.o.b.)	47	10
Imports (c.i.f.)	65	43

Main trading partners (percentage of total value)

Exports	*1965*	*Imports*	*1965*
Netherlands	25	France	61
U.K.	23	U.S.A.	6
Germany F.R.	21	Germany F.R.	6
France	9	Belg./Lux.	4
Israel	5	Netherlands	3
Belg./Lux.	3	U.K.	3
South Africa	3	Italy	2

Distribution of trade (percentage of total value)

Exports	*1965*	*Imports*	*1965*
Manufactured goods	51	Manufactured goods	71
(diamonds)	(43)	(machinery and transport equipment)	(35)
Crude materials and fuels	45	Food	11
(hardwood saw and veneer logs)	(38)	Chemicals	6
		Petroleum products	6

PRODUCTION, EXPORTS AND IMPORTS

Years: **1963–5 average** Units: '000 metric tons unless otherwise indicated

Note—no data are available for the years 1953–5

1. CEREALS, etc.

	Production	Exports	Imports
Cassava	783.3*	—	—
Maize (corn)	2.0*	—	—
Potatoes	—	—	1.1
Rice	4.0*	—	1.2
Sweet potatoes/yams	60.0*	—	—
Wheat	—	—	9.6

2. FRUIT, etc.

	Production	Exports	Imports
Apples	—	—	0.3*n*
Bananas	5.0*	0.1	—
Grapes	—	—	0.1
Oranges	2.0*	—	0.1
Wine*b*	—	0.1	115.9

b '000 hectolitres. *n* incl. pears and quince.

3. BEVERAGES, FOREST PRODUCTS, etc.

	Production	Exports	Imports
Cocoa	0.8	0.8	—
Coffee	0.8*	0.7	—
Sugar: cane	323.3*		
raw	28.8	—	0.1
Tobacco: leaf	0.6*	0.3	0.6
cigarettes*e*	911.0	—	—
tobacco/snuff	0.6	—	—
Hardwood*j*	1 849.0*	505.3	—
Paper	—	—	3.3

e no. in millions. *j* '000 cu. metres of roundwood equivalent.

continued

na: data not available. — negligible or nil. [1] one year only. [2] two year average. * estimate. ‡ see appendix. † re-exports.

PRODUCTION, EXPORTS AND IMPORTS *continued*

4. VEGETABLE OILSEEDS AND OILS

	Production	Exports	Imports
Castor seed	na	0.04	—
Copra	—	—	0.01
Groundnuts	7.70*	0.47	—
Groundnut oil	na	0.11	0.10
Olive oil	—	—	0.02
Palm kernels	7.37	7.22	—
Palm kernel oil	na	0.03	0.08
Palm oil	7.10*	2.64	0.05

5. LIVESTOCK‡, ANIMAL PRODUCTS, etc.

	Production	Exports	Imports
Cattle*d*	22.3*	—	—
cows*d*	11.0*	—	—
Goats*d*	72.0*	—	—
Sheep*d*	52.0*	—	—
Pigs*d*	36.0*	—	—
Meat‡ 'B'	—	—	0.1
Butter	—	—	0.2
Cheese	—	—	0.2
Eggs	1.9	—	—
Fish	12.7	0.1	5.6
Milk	2.0*	—	3.8

d no. in thousands.

6. FIBRES, TEXTILES, etc.

	Production	Exports	Imports
Rubber, natural	0.2*	0.1	—

7. FUEL AND POWER

	Production	Exports	Imports
Electricity*h*: total	42		
hydro	27		
thermal	15		
Oil, crude	87	83	—
Petroleum, refined	—	—	90[1]

h million kWh.

9. NON-FERROUS MINERALS AND METALS

	Production	Exports	Imports
Diamonds*l*	5 416.30*	na	—
Gold*km*	3.70	na	—
Copper, ore*m*	0.29	na	—
Lead, ore*m*	1.77	na	—
Tin, ore	0.05*m*	0.06	—
Zinc, ore	4.22*m*	16.50[1]	—

k '000 fine troy oz. *l* '000 carats. *m* metal content.

10. CHEMICALS AND FERTILIZERS

Potash—A deposit, thought to be the world's largest, came into production in 1969, and is expected to yield some 500 000 tons per annum when in full production.

11. INDUSTRY

	Production	Exports	Imports
Aircraft*a*	—	—	0.4
Alcoholic beverages*a*		—	2.9
beer*b*	34.0		
Cement	—	—	50.0
Electrical engineering*a*	—	—	3.6
Railway vehicles*a*	—	—	1.8
Motor vehicles*a*	—	0.3	5.7

a million $ U.S. *b* '000 hectolitres.

COSTA RICA

CENTRAL AMERICA

Costa Rica has been an independent republic since 1821. The population, unlike that of neighbouring countries, is basically of European stock; the land is fertile, and the country economically and politically stable and advanced in the provision of social services.

AREA: 50 900* sq. km. (19 653* sq. miles)

LAND USE: (percentage of total)

	1963	*1950*
Arable and orchard	12.3	7.0
Permanent meadow and pasture	18.2	12.3
Forest and woodland	58.8	78.2
City areas, waste and other land	10.7	2.5

POPULATION: 1 594 000 (1967 provisional estimate)

Largest city: SAN JOSÉ, capital; population: 349 484 (1966)

Distribution of working population (1963)

Total working population: 395 273

U.N. group no.		*Percentage*
0	Agriculture, forestry, fishing and hunting	49.1
1	Mining and quarrying	0.3
2/3	Manufacturing	11.5
4	Construction	5.9
5	Electricity, gas, water and sanitary services	1.1
6	Commerce	9.8
7	Transport, storage and communications	3.7
8	Services	17.2
9	Others	1.4

		Year(s)
Life expectancy at birth (years): male	61.9	1962–4 av.
female	64.8	1962–4 av.
Infant mortality (per '000)	75.0	1965
Crude birth rate (per '000)	45*	1960–5 av.
Crude death rate (per '000)	8.5*	1960–5 av.
Accidental deaths (per 100 000 population)		
caused by motor vehicles	11.6	1965
due to other causes	31.8	1965
Population per physician	1 200	1967
Population per hospital bed	250	1966
School enrolment: age 5–19 years (percentage)	84*a*	1963–4 av.
age over 19 years (per 100 000 population)	471	1963–5 av.

a excl. private vocational schools; incl. evening courses.

COMMUNICATIONS

		Year(s)
Motor vehicles in use ('000s): private	20.5	1963–5 av.
commercial	10.8	1963–5 av.
Railway track (km.)	805	1966–7 av.
Telephones (per '000 urban population)	1.6	1967
Radio receivers (per '000 population)	82	1963–5 av.
Television sets (per '000 population)	22.9	1963–5 av.
Daily newspapers (per '000 population)	77	1964

FINANCE

Currency unit: The colon

Exchange rates	*1965a*	*1960*	*1950b*	*1938*
Per $ U.S.	6.62	5.6	6.24	5.62
Per £ sterling	18.54	15.68	17.48	25.85

		Year(s)
National Income (million $ U.S.)	506	1965
G.N.P. per capita ($ U.S.)	400	1966
Foreign trade (percentage of G.D.P.)	45	1963–5 av.

a export rate. *b* principal import rate.

TRADING

Total trade (in million $ U.S.)	*1965*	*1955*	*1938*
Exports (f.o.b.)	112	81	9
Imports (c.i.f.)	178	87	13

Main trading partners (percentage of total value)

Exports	*1965*	*1955*	*Imports*	*1965*	*1955*
U.S.A.	50	55	U.S.A.	40	60
Germany F.R.	12	26	Germany F.R.	10	9
Netherlands	6	3	Japan	10	2
Nicaragua	5	—	U.K.	4	7
El Salvador	4	na	France	4	1
Guatemala	4	na	Neths. Antilles	3	3
Belg./Lux.	3	2	Guatemala	3	na

Distribution of trade (percentage of total value)

Exports	*1965*	*1955*
Coffee	42	46
Fruit and vegetables (mainly bananas)	26	41
Cattle and beef	5	1
Sugar and preparations	4	1
Fertilizers	3	—
Imports		
Manufactured goods	67	63
(machinery and transport equipment)	(29)	(27)
Chemicals	18	15
Food	8	13
Mineral fuels	5	6

continued

na: data not available. — negligible or nil. [1] one year only. [2] two year average. * estimate. ‡ see appendix. † re-exports.

COSTA RICA *continued*

PRODUCTION, EXPORTS AND IMPORTS

Years: **1963–5 average** and *1953–5 average*   Units: '000 metric tons unless otherwise indicated

	Production		Exports		Imports	
1. CEREALS, etc.						
Barley	—	—	—	—	—	*0.1*
Cassava	6.0*	na	—	—	—	—
Maize (corn)	66.7*	*69.5*[2]	—	—	7.3	—
Millets/sorghum	—	—	—	—	0.1[2]	—
Potatoes	17.0*	na	0.2	—	0.1	—
Rice	71.0	*35.7**	0.1	*0.5*	1.8	*2.1*
Wheat	—	—	—	—	0.4	*5.5*
2. FRUIT, etc.						
Bananas	506.3	na	29.1	*346.9*	—	—
Coconuts e	5.0[1]*	na	—	—	—	—
Grapes	—	—	—	—	—	*0.2*
Oranges	1.0*	na	—	—	0.5[2]	—
Wine b	—	—	—	—	2.8	*4.3*

b '000 hectolitres.   *e* no. in millions.

	Production		Exports		Imports	
3. BEVERAGES, FOREST PRODUCTS, etc.						
Cocoa	10.8	*9.0**	8.5	*8.6*	—	—
Coffee	57.2	*30.1**	51.3	*26.6*	—	—
Sugar: cane	1 192.7*	na				
raw	99.4n	*31.0*n*	37.7	*6.8*	—	—
Tobacco: leaf	1.3*	*3.7**	—	—	0.1	—
cigarettes e	—	*1 022.0*	—	—	na	—
Softwood j	2.0[1]	*63.0*[1]	—	—[1]	—[2]	*0.5*[1]
Hardwood j	1 996.0*[1]	*881.0*[1]	6.6[2]	*12.7*[1]	—[2]	*0.4*[1]
Newsprint	—*[2]	—	—	—	4.6[1]	*1.7*[2]
Other paper	2.7*[2]	—	—	—[1]	18.9[1]	*3.5*[1]

e no. in millions.   *j* '000 cu. metres of roundwood equivalent.   *n* in addition, non-centrifugal sugar 35 (1963–5 av.) and 30 (1953–5 av.).

	Production		Exports		Imports	
4. VEGETABLE OILSEEDS AND OILS						
Castor oil	—	—	—	—	0.01	*0.02*
Coconut oil	—	—	—	—	0.08	*0.03*
Cottonseed	—	—	0.03	—	1.42	*0.27*
Cottonseed oil			0.02	—	1.50	*0.09*
Groundnuts	—	—	—	—	0.04	—
Linseed	—	—	—	—	0.02	—
Linseed oil			—	—	0.02	*0.07*
Olive oil	—	—	—	—	0.06	*0.05*
Palm kernels	20.00*	*7.70*[1]	—	—	—	—
Palm oil	8.20*	*1.45*[2]*	0.26	*0.21*	1.08	—
Soya bean oil	—	—	—	—	0.20	*0.11*
5. LIVESTOCK‡, ANIMAL PRODUCTS, etc.						
Chickens d	1 886.7*	*1 389.0*[1]				
Cattle d	1 083.7	*670.0*	11.0	*2.6*	0.3	*0.2*
dairy cows d	385.7	na				
Goats d	2.0*	na	—	—	—	—
Sheep d	1.0*	na	—	—	—	—
Horses d	101.0*	*85.0*[2]				
Pigs d	144.0*	*109.0*[2]	—	—	0.1	—
Meat‡ 'A'	30.3*	—	6.8	*0.5*[1]	—	—
Butter	2.3*p	*1.0*[2]*p*	0.1	—	—	—
Cheese	na	*3.0*[2]	—	—	0.1	*0.1*
Eggs	37.0*	na	—	—	—	—
Fish	3.0	*1.0*	1.1	*1.6*[1]*	1.4	*1.0*[1]*
Milk	80.0*	*146.3p*	—	—	5.8	*14.4*

d no. in thousands.   *p* factory produce only.

	Production		Exports		Imports	
6. FIBRES, TEXTILES, etc.						
Abaca	—	*3.1**	—	*3.0*	—	—
Cotton lint	na	—	1.1	—	—	—
Rubber, natural	0.1	—	0.1	—	0.1	—
Cotton, woven fabrics	—	—	—	—	1.7[1]	—
Rayon, woven fabrics	—	—	—	—	0.5[2]	—
7. FUEL AND POWER						
Electricity h: total	570	*270*[1]				
hydro	492	*240*[1]				
thermal	78	*30*[1]				
Petroleum, refined	—	—	—	—	227	*110*[1]

h million kWh.

	Production		Exports		Imports	
9. NON-FERROUS MINERALS AND METALS						
Gold k, ore m	2.30	*4.20**	na	na	—	—
Asbestos, manufactured	—	—	—	—	0.07	*0.43s*
Aluminium: alumina	—	—	—	—	—	*0.09*
aluminium	—	—	—	—	0.66	*0.09s*
Copper, metal	—	—	—	—	0.27	*12.13n*
Lead, metal	—	—	—	—	0.10	—
Manganese, ore	—	—	—	—	0.20	—
Mercury f	—	—	—	—	1.80[1]	—
Titanium minerals	—	—	—	—	0.14[1]	—

f metric tons.   *k* '000 fine troy oz.   *m* metal content.   *n* mainly copper sulphate
s incl. imports for re-export.

	Production		Exports		Imports	
10. CHEMICALS n AND FERTILIZERS						
Chemicals	—		—		na	
Fertilizers:						
Potash	—	—	—	—	4.9	—
Sulphur	—	—	—	—	0.1[2]	*0.1*

n data not available for years 1953–5.

	Production		Exports		Imports	
11. INDUSTRY						
Aircraft a	—	—	—	—	0.6	*0.8*
Alcoholic beverages			—	—	1.0a	*0.5a*
beer b	89.0	*45.9*[2]				
Cement	49.3	—	1.3	—	63.3	*52.3*
Electrical engineering a	—	—	—	—	10.7	*5.0*[2]
Railway vehicles a	—	—	—	—	0.3	*0.7*
Machine tools a	—	—	—	—	—	*0.5*[2]
Motor vehicles a	—	—	—	—	9.8	*5.6*[2]

a million $ U.S.   *b* '000 hectolitres.

CUBA

CARIBBEAN SEA

In 1959 the revolutionary movement led by Dr. Castro overthrew the former dictatorship. Close ties were formed between Cuba and the U.S.S.R., and links with the U.S.A. were severed. Trade with many western countries diminished.

AREA: 114 524 sq. km. (44 206 sq. miles)

LAND USE: (percentage of total)	*1946*
Arable and orchard	17.2
Permanent meadow and pasture	34.0
Forest and woodland	26.1
City areas, waste and other land	22.7

POPULATION: 8 033 000 (1967 estimate)
Largest city: LA HABANA (Havana) capital; population: 1 543 900 (1965)

Distribution of working population (1953)
Total working population: 1 972 266

U.N. group no.		*Percentage*
0	Agriculture, forestry, fishing and hunting	41.5
1	Mining and quarrying	0.5
2/3	Manufacturing	16.6
4	Construction	3.3
5	Electricity, gas, water and sanitary services	0.4
6	Commerce	11.8
7	Transport, storage and communications	5.3
8	Services	20.1
9	Others	0.5

Infant mortality (per '000)	38.4*	1965
Crude birth rate (per '000)	35*	1960–5 av.
Crude death rate (per '000)	8.5*	1960–5 av.
Accidental deaths (per 100 000 population)		
caused by motor vehicles	10.1*	1965
due to other causes	21.1*	1965
Population per physician	1 180	1963
Population per hospital bed	180a	1966
School enrolment: age 5–19 years (percentage)	73	1963–4 av.
age over 19 years (per 100 000 population)	340	1963–5 av.

a government hospitals only.

COMMUNICATIONS		*Year(s)*
Motor vehicles in use ('000s): private	162*	1965
commercial	103.7*	1965
Railway track (km.)	5 976a	1965
Telephones (per '000 urban population)	3*	1967
Radio receivers (per '000 population)	181	1963–5 av.
Television sets (per '000 population)	73.4	1963–5 av.
Daily newspapers (per '000 population)	88	1961

a in addition the large sugar estates operate 12 135 km. of track connecting them with the main lines.

continued

na: data not available.   — negligible or nil.   [1] one year only.   [2] two year average.   * estimate.   ‡ see appendix.   † re-exports.

FINANCE

Currency unit: The Cuban peso

Exchange rates	*1965*	*1960*	*1950*	*1938*
Per $ U.S.	1.0	1.02	1.0	1.02
Per £ sterling	2.8	2.86	2.801	4.692

		Year
National Income (million $ U.S.)	2 500*	1966
G.N.P. per capita ($ U.S.)	320*	1966

TRADING

Total trade (in million $ U.S.)	*1965*	*1955*	*1938*
Exports (f.o.b.)	686	594	143
Imports (c.i.f.)	866	575	106

Main trading partners (percentage of total value)

Exports	*1965*	*1955*	*1938*	*Imports*	*1965*	*1955*	*1938*
U.S.S.R.	47	6	na	U.S.S.R.	49	—	na
China P.R.	15	na	na	China P.R.	14	na	na
Czechoslovakia	7	—	—	U.K.	6	2	4
Spain	5	2	1	Spain	5	2	1
Germany D.R.	4	na	2f	Czechoslovakia	4	—	1
Bulgaria	3	na	na	Germany D.R.	3	na	4f
Japan	3	4	—	France	2	1	3

f incl. Germany F.R.

Distribution of trade (percentage of total value)

Exports	*1964*	*1955*	*1938**
Sugar	88	80	70
Tobacco	4	7	9
Imports			
Manufactured goods	52	na	na
(machinery and transport equipment)	(31)	(13*)	(12)
Food	22	na	na
Crude materials and fuels	14	na	na
(petroleum and products)	(8)	(8*)	(4)
Chemicals	9	na	na

PRODUCTION, EXPORTS AND IMPORTS

Years: **1963–5 average** and *1953–5 average*   Units: '000 metric tons unless otherwise indicated

	Production		Exports		Imports	
1. CEREALS, etc.						
Barley	—	—	—	—	48.6*	—[2]
Cassava	203.3*	na	—	—	—	—
Maize (corn)	194.3*	*204.7**	—	*11.2*	153.7*	*0.1*
Millets/sorghum	26.3*	na	—	—	0.1[2]	*0.7*
Oats	—	—	—	—	20.3*	*1.3*
Potatoes	87.3*	na	—	*3.1*[2]	41.5*	*34.6*[2]
Rice	192.7	*171.7**	—	*0.3*	251.8*	*186.7*
Sweet potatoes/yams	276.7*	*312.5*[2]	—	—	—	—
Wheat	—	—	—	—	422.1*	*50.1*
2. FRUIT, etc.						
Apples	—	—	—	—	2.0*	*4.4*
Bananas	63.3	na	—	*4.8*	—	—
Coconuts	10.0[1]*e	na	—	*0.3*	—	—
Grapes	—	—	—	—	0.7*[1]	*2.1**
Lemons	7.7	—	—	—	—	—
Oranges	84.7	*57.3**	—	—	—	—
Other citrus fruit	10.0	*7.7**	—	*3.1*[2]	—	—
Pineapples	100.0*	*87.7**	na	*31.0*	—	—
Tomatoes	108.0*	na	na	na	—	—
Wine b	—	—	—	—	7.0*	*13.0**

b '000 hectolitres.   *e* no. in millions.

	Production		Exports		Imports	
3. BEVERAGES, FOREST PRODUCTS, etc.						
Cocoa	1.9	*2.7**	—	*0.6*	—	—
Coffee	30.5	*42.9*	0.6*[1]	*1.4*	2.5*[2]	—
Sugar: cane	41 518.0	*43 950.0*[1]				
raw	4 830.9	*4 719.3**	4 337.4*	*4 756.1*	—	—
Tobacco: leaf	50.1	*47.6**	12.5*	*19.1*	—	—
cigars	—	*342.7e*	} 1.8	} *7.6*[2]*a*		
cigarettes	15 941.0e	*9 146.0e*			—	—
tobacco/snuff	—	—				
Softwood j	15.0[1]	*23.3**	—	—	} 229.0[2]	*367.4*[1]
Hardwood j	2 179.0*[1]	*809.0**	—	—		—[1]
Wood pulp	—[1]	*6.0**	—	—[2]	41.9[1]	*25.5*[2]*
Newsprint	6.0*[2]	—	—	na	17.0[1]	na
Other paper	74.0*[2]	—	—	—	13.2[1]	*37.6*[1]

a million $ U.S.   *e* no. in millions.   *j* '000 cu. metres of roundwood equivalent.

	Production		Exports		Imports	
4. VEGETABLE OILSEEDS AND OILS						
Castor oil	—	—	—	—	na	*0.04*[2]
Coconut oil	—	—	—	—	2.18[1]*	*2.08**
Cottonseed	8.00*	na	—	—	—	—
Cottonseed oil	na	na	—	—	—	*0.28*[2]
Groundnuts	10.03	*3.97**	—	—	13.61[2]	—
Groundnut oil	na	na	—	—	0.50*	—
Linseed oil	—	—	—	—	2.43*	*1.15*[2]
Olive oil	—	—	—	—	4.07[1]*	*6.96**
Palm kernel oil	—	—	—	—	—	*0.06*[2]
Palm oil	—	—	—	—	—	*0.01*[2]
Soya beans	—	—	—	—	25.50[1]	—
Soya bean oil	na	na	—	—	0.51[1]*	*2.25**
Sunflower seed oil	—	—	—	—	35.10*	—
5. LIVESTOCK‡, ANIMAL PRODUCTS, etc.						
Chickens d	7 467.0*n	na				
Cattle d	6 058.7*	*4 150.0*[1]		—[2]	4.8*	*0.4*
Goats d	187.0*	na	} —	} —	} 1.0*	} —
Sheep d	—	na				
Horses d	496.7*	na				
Pigs d	1 767.0*	*1 352.5*[2]	—	—	na	*0.1*
Bacon/ham	} 235.7*	} na	—	—	0.3[1]*	*5.5*
Meat‡: 'A'			—	—	—	*0.1*
'B'	4.8*	—	—	—	na	*0.1*[2]
Butter	4.0*p	*2.0*p*	—	—	4.2*	*0.3*
Cheese	3.7*	*2.3*p*	—	—	1.2*	*0.9*
Eggs	13.5*	na	—	—	—	*4.2*
Fish	37.4	*11.5*	0.8	*1.6*[1]*	34.0	*19.3*[1]*
Milk	1 190.7*	*701.3**	—	—	163.3*	*73.4*
Hides/skins	—	—	—	—	—	*2.1*

d no. in thousands.   *n* incl. ducks, geese and turkeys.   *p* factory produce only.

	Production		Exports		Imports	
6. FIBRES, TEXTILES, etc.						
Agaves (henequen)	10.0*	*11.7**	na	*7.0*	—	—
Cotton lint	4.0*	—	—	—	13.9*	*6.5**
Jute	2.7*	—	—	—	—	—
Rubber, natural	—	—	—	—	2.8*	*1.9*
Cotton: yarn	na	na	na	na	1.8[2]	na
woven fabrics	13.9[2]*	na	—	—	1.0[2]	*5.3*[2]
Rayon, fibre/yarn	1.4	*9.3*	0.5[2]	na	3.8[1]	na
Non-cellulosic fibre/yarn	—	—	—	—	0.3	—
7. FUEL AND POWER						
Coal 'A'‡	—	—	—	—	55	*37*
Coke	—	—	—	—	24	*23*
Electricity h: total	3 336	*2 000*[1]				
hydro	na	*20*[1]				
thermal	na	*1 980*[1]				
Oil, crude	40	*50*[1]	—	—	3 553	*460*[1]
Petroleum, refined	3 566	*440*[1]	10	—	1 150	*1 720*[1]

h million kWh.

	Production		Exports		Imports	
8. IRON AND STEEL						
Iron ore	na	na	—	*137*	—	—
Pig iron	—	—	—	—	26	—
Iron/steel scrap	—	—	25	—	—	—
9. NON-FERROUS MINERALS AND METALS						
Gold k, ore m	—	*1.00*	—	—	—	—
Platinum group metals k	—	—	—	—	—	*0.47s*
Silver k: ore m	na	*197.00*	—	—	—	—
bullion	na	na	na	*238.02q*	—	—
Asbestos, manufactured	—	—	—	—	9.33[2]	—
Aluminium	—	—	—	—	6.39[2]	*3.20s*
Antimony, metal	—	—	—	—	0.14[2]	—
Chrome, ore	39.61m	*73.22m*	16.40	*39.99*	—	—
Cobalt, ore	0.66m	—	—	—	—	—
Copper: ore	5.99*	*16.96m*	15.49	*81.00*	0.01	—
metal	na	na	na	*0.64*	3.12[2]	*1.75*
Lead: ore	—	*0.03m*	—	—	2.77[2]	—
metal	—	—	—	—	0.18[2]	*0.32s*
Magnesium, metal/salts	—	—	—	—	—	*0.64*
Manganese, ore	75.54	*312.33*	0.21	*288.52*	—	—
Mercury f	—	—	—	—	—	*9.30s*
Nickel, ore m	23.16	*13.16*	—	*17.62*	—	—
Tin, metal	—	—	—	—	—	*0.07s*
Zinc: ore m	—	*0.34*	—	—	—	—
metal	—	na	—	—	—	*0.29*

f metric tons.   *k* '000 fine troy oz.   *m* metal content.   *q* exports to U.S.A. only.
s incl. imports for re-export.

	Production		Exports		Imports	
10. CHEMICALS n AND FERTILIZERS						
Chemicals	—		—		na	
Fertilizers:						
Potash	—	—	—	—	39.4	*21.9*
Pyrites x	13.9*	*48.6**	—	—	—	—
Sulphur	—	—	—	—	48.5[2]	*11.8*

n data not available for years 1953–5.   *x* sulphur content.

	Production		Exports		Imports	
11. INDUSTRY						
Aircraft a	—	—	—	—	9.5[1]	—
Alcoholic beverages			4.0a	—	1.6[1]a	—
beer b	973.0	*1 189.7*				
Cement	804.0*	*417.3*	—	—	33.3*	*178.3*
Electrical engineering a	—	—	—	—	23.2[1]	*9.5*[2]
Merchant ships g	—	—	—	—	28.0	—
Motor vehicles a	—	—	—	—	57.7[1]	*35.5*

a million $ U.S.   *b* '000 hectolitres.   *g* '000 G.R.T.

na: data not available.   — negligible or nil.   [1] one year only.   [2] two year average.   * estimate.   ‡ see appendix.   † re-exports.

CYPRUS

MEDITERRANEAN SEA

Cyprus, formerly a British colony, became an independent republic in 1960 after pressure by the Greek Cypriots. There followed several years of conflict between the Greek and Turkish factions of the population. The U.N. supplied peace-keeping forces, and in 1968 the two parties met to try to find a more peaceful method of solving their problems. Cyprus remains within the Commonwealth and Britain retains rights to certain service bases.

AREA: 9 251 sq. km. (3 572 sq. miles)

LAND USE: (percentage of total)	*1965*	*1955*
Arable and orchard	46.7	46.9
Permanent meadow and pasture	10.0	10.1
Forest and woodland	18.5	18.5
City areas, waste and other land	24.8	24.5

POPULATION: 614 000 (1967 estimate)

Largest city: NICOSIA, capital; population: 106 000 (1966)

Distribution of working population (1960)

Total working population: 235 358

U.N. group no.		*Percentage*
0	Agriculture, forestry, fishing and hunting	40.3
1	Mining and quarrying	2.3
2/3	Manufacturing	13.7
4	Construction	8.7
5/8	Services, incl. electricity, gas, water and sanitary services	14.7
6	Commerce	6.9
7	Transport, storage and communications	4.1
9	Others	9.3

		Year(s)
Life expectancy at birth (years): male	63.6	1948–50 av.
female	68.8	
Infant mortality (per '000)	27.6*	1965
Crude birth rate (per '000)	24.4*	1965
Crude death rate (per '000)	6.1*	1965
Population per physician	1 320	1965
Population per hospital bed	190	1966
School enrolment: age 5–19 years (percentage)	55*a*	1963–4 av.
age over 19 years (per 100 000 population)	82	1963–5 av.

a public education only, and excluding Turkish schools.

COMMUNICATIONS		*Year(s)*
Motor vehicles in use ('000s): private	31.0	1963–5 av.
commercial	11.5	
Mail per capita: domestic	22	1964–5 av.
foreign received	25	
foreign sent	18	
Telephones (per '000 urban population)	5.0	1967
Radio licences (per '000 population)	208	1963–5 av.
Television licences (per '000 population)	17.1	1963–5 av.
Daily newspapers (per '000 population)	180.5	1963–4 av.

FINANCE

Currency unit: The Cyprus pound, at par with the pound sterling

Exchange rates	*1965*	*1960*	*1950*	*1938*
Per $ U.S.	0.357	0.357	0.357	0.215

		Year(s)
National Income (million $ U.S.)	370	1965
G.N.P. per capita ($ U.S.)	690	1966
Rate of increase of G.N.P. per capita	2	1960–4 av.
Foreign trade (percentage of G.D.P.)	55	1963–5 av.

TRADING

Total trade (in million $ U.S.)	*1965*	*1955*	*1938*
Exports (f.o.b.)	71	52	12
Imports (c.i.f.)	148	85	11

Main trading partners (percentage of total value)

Exports	*1965*	*1955*	*Imports*	*1965*	*1955*
U.K.	31	27	U.K.	33	50
Germany F.R.	20	35	Italy	10	5
Spain	9	na	Germany F.R.	8	6
Netherlands	6	6	France	6	4
U.S.S.R.	5	na	Netherlands	3	3
Italy	4	9	Greece	3	2
Israel	3	1	U.S.A.	3	4

Distribution of trade (percentage of total value)

Exports	*1965*	*1955a*
Food	48	30
(fruit and vegetables)	(37)	(16)
Copper ore and concentrates	24	31
Beverages and tobacco	8	4
Imports		
Manufactured goods	59	64
(machinery and transport equipment)	(24)	(26)
(textiles and clothing)	(11)	(11)
Food	16	13
Chemicals	9	6
Petroleum products	6	8

a These are percentages of national exports‡ which comprised 94% of general exports in 1955.

PRODUCTION, EXPORTS AND IMPORTS

Years: **1963–5 average** and *1953–5 average* Units: '000 metric tons unless otherwise indicated

	Production		Exports		Imports	
1. CEREALS, etc.						
Barley	**97.3**	*63.3*	**43.6**	*13.9*	—	*0.6*
Maize (corn)	—	—	—	—	**17.7**	—
Millets/sorghum	—	*1.0*[2]	—	—	**0.8**	—
Oats	**1.7**	*2.7*	—	—	—	—
Potatoes	**126.0**	*67.0*	**87.0**	*41.1*	**9.8**	*3.6*
Rice	—	—	—	—	**3.3**	*2.3*
Wheat	**67.0**	*66.7*	—	*11.0*	**22.4**	*38.4*
2. FRUIT, etc.						
Apples	**4.0**	*1.0*	—	—	—	—
Bananas	—	—	—	—	**1.1**	*0.4*
Figs	—	na	—	*0.2*	—	—
Grapes	**95.3**	*102.0*	**5.9**	*2.9*	—	—
Lemons	**14.7***	*5.0*	**8.3**	*2.4*	—	—
Oranges	**60.0***	*33.3*	**51.9**	*18.4*	—	—
Other citrus fruit	**22.0***	*8.7*	**18.3**	*5.3*	—	—
Olives	**14.3**	*10.0*				
Raisins	**5.8**	*6.8*	**5.8**	*5.8*	—	—
Tomatoes	**12.0**	*5.7*				
Wine*b*	**226.7**	*151.3*	**156.0**	*94.7*	**0.1**	—

b '000 hectolitres.

	Production		Exports		Imports	
3. BEVERAGES, FOREST PRODUCTS, etc.						
Coffee	—	—	—	—	**1.0**	*0.4*
Sugar, raw	—	—	—	—	**14.3**	*6.4*
Tea	—	—	—	—	**0.1**	—
Tobacco: leaf	**1.5**	*0.7*	**0.7**	*0.7*	**0.7**	*0.5*
cigars	—	—	na	*0.7*[2]	**0.2**	*0.1*[2]
cigarettes	**618.0***e*	—				
tobacco/snuff	—	—				
Softwood*j*	**45.0**	*41.3*	**0.2**	—	**52.9**	*64.6*
Hardwood*j*	**5.2**	*7.1*	—	—	**1.9**	*0.5*
Newsprint	—	—	—	—	**1.4**	*0.4*
Other paper	—	—	—	—	**4.9**[2]	*2.8**

e no. in millions. *j* '000 cu. metres of roundwood equivalent.

	Production		Exports		Imports	
4. VEGETABLE OILSEEDS AND OILS						
Coconut oil	—	—	—	—	**0.02**	*0.27*
Cottonseed	—	*1.00*	—	—	—	*1.03*
Cottonseed oil			—	—	na	*2.08*
Groundnuts	—	—	—	—	**0.53**	*0.27*
Groundnut oil			—	—	**3.18**	*0.62*
Linseed	—	*0.67*	**0.10**	*0.53*	—	—
Linseed oil			—	—	**0.06**	*0.08*
Olive oil	**2.33**	*1.30*	**0.44**	*0.32*	**0.01**	*0.04*
Palm kernel oil	—	—	—	—	**0.02**	na
Palm oil	—	—	—	—	—	*0.03*
Rapeseed oil	—	—	—	—	**1.44**	*0.03*
Sesame seed	**0.10**	*0.17*	**0.02**	—	**0.51**	*0.40*
Soya beans	—	—	—	—	**0.81**	*0.09*[2]
Sunflower seed oil	—	—	—	—	**1.17**	na
5. LIVESTOCK‡, ANIMAL PRODUCTS, etc.						
Chickens*d*	**1 972.7**	*962.3*				
Cattle*d*	**32.7**	*35.0*[1]	—	—	**0.1**	*0.2*
Goats*d*	**206.0**	*180.0*	—	—	—	—
Sheep*d*	**391.0**	*341.0*				
Horses*d*	**2.0***	*4.0*[1]				
Pigs*d*	**39.0**	*34.0*	—	—	—	—
Bacon/ham	**9.7**	*7.0*	—	—	**0.1**	—
Meat‡: 'A'			—	—	**2.7**	*0.1*
'B'	**5.6***	na	—	—	**0.1**	—
Butter	—	—	—	—	**0.4**	*0.2*
Cheese	**3.0**	*2.7*	**0.2**	*0.4*	**0.8**	*0.3*
Eggs	**3.4***	*1.1*[2]	**0.1**	—	—	—
Fish	**0.7**	*0.5*	—	—	**2.2**	na
Milk	**12.3**	*4.0*	—	—	**15.7**	*5.3*
Hides/skins	—	na	**0.8**	*0.3*[2]	—	*0.3*[2]
Wool	**0.3**	na	**0.3**	*0.3*	—	—

d no. in thousands.

continued

na: data not available. — negligible or nil. [1] one year only. [2] two year average. * estimate. ‡ see appendix. † re-exports.

PRODUCTION, EXPORTS AND IMPORTS *continued*

	Production		Exports		Imports	
6. FIBRES, TEXTILES, etc.						
Cotton lint	—	*0.7*	—	*0.3*	—	—
Hemp fibre	—	*0.1*	—	—	—	—
Rubber, natural	—	—	—	—	**0.2**	—
Cotton: yarn	—	—	—	—	**0.4**[1]	na
woven fabrics	—	—	—	—	**0.9**	*0.9*
Rayon, woven fabrics	—	—	—	—	**0.5***n*	*0.3*
Wool, yarn	—	—	—	—[1]	**0.2**	—

n incl. synthetic piece goods.

	Production		Exports		Imports	
7. FUEL AND POWER						
Coal/coke	—	—	—	—	—	*3*
Electricity*h t*	**320**	*50*				
Petroleum, refined	—	—	—	—	**350**	*160*[1]

h million kWh. *t* thermal.

	Production		Exports		Imports	
8. IRON AND STEEL						
Steel ingots/castings	—	—	—	—	**1**	na
9. NON-FERROUS MINERALS AND METALS						
Gold*k*, ore*m*	—	—	—	—	**10.28**	*0.21*
Silver*k*, bullion	—	—	—	—	**60.67**	*4.07*
Asbestos: fibre	**15.53**	*14.06*	**14.24**	*13.62*	—	—
manufactured	na	na	—	—	**3.84** / **0.15***a*	*2.57* / *0.02a*
Aluminium	—	—	—	—	**0.27**	—
Chrome, ore	**4.30***m*	na	**3.24**	*8.71*	—	—
Cobalt, ore	na	na	—	—	—	—

continued

	Production		Exports		Imports	
9. NON-FERROUS MINERALS AND METALS—*continued*						
Copper: ore	**20.87***m*	*24.24m*	**204.14**	*24.24m*	—	—
metal	na	—	**4.03**	—	**0.05**	*0.08*
Lead, metal	—	—	—	—	**0.07**	*0.03*
Magnesium, magnesite	—	—	—	—	—	*0.01*
Manganese, ore	—	—	**0.04**	—	—	—
Tin, metal	—	—	—	—	**0.01**	*0.01*
Zinc, metal	—	—	—	—	**0.06**	—

a million $ U.S. *k* '000 fine troy oz. *m* metal content.

	Production		Exports		Imports	
10. CHEMICALS*n* AND FERTILIZERS						
Chemicals	—		—		na	
Fertilizers:						
Potash	—	—	—	—	**0.4**	—
Pyrites	**413.5***x*	*555.2*x*	**859.4**	*813.3*	—	—
Sulphur	—	—	—	—	**1.7**	*1.0*

n data not available for years 1953–5. *x* sulphur content.

	Production		Exports		Imports	
11. INDUSTRY						
Aircraft*a*	—	—	—	—	**0.7**	—
Alcoholic beverages			**3.4***a*	*1.4a*	—	—
beer*b*	**54.0**	—				
spirits*b*	**9.3**[1] *p*	—				
Cement	**88.7**	—	—	—	**70.3**	*85.3*
Electrical engineering*a*	—	—	—	—	**7.1**	*5.1*[2]
Motor vehicles*a*	—	—	—	—	**8.5**	*5.4*[2]

a million $ U.S. *b* '000 hectolitres. *p* production for home consumption only, 1967.

CZECHOSLOVAKIA

EUROPE

The Czechoslovak state was broken up for the benefit of Germany, Poland, and Hungary in 1938 and re-established after the war. In 1948 a communist government was formed. A programme of liberalization in 1968 led to Soviet occupation which caused the abandonment of most of the changes planned. Czechoslovakia is a member of Comecon.

AREA: 127 870 sq. km. (49 370 sq. miles)

LAND USE: (percentage of total)	*1965*	*1948*
Arable and orchard	42.1	43.1
Permanent meadow and pasture	13.9	15.9
Forest and woodland	34.8	31.8
City areas, waste and other land	9.2	9.2

POPULATION: 14 305 000 (1967 estimate)

Largest city: PRAHA (Prague) capital; population: 1 022 621 (1965)

Distribution of working population (1950)

Total working population: 5 811 724

U.N. group no.		*Percentage*
0	Agriculture, forestry, fishing and hunting	38.0
1	Mining and quarrying	2.7
2/3	Manufacturing	28.3
4	Construction	5.1
5	Electricity, gas, water and sanitary services	0.7
6	Commerce	8.1
7	Transport, storage and communications	5.8
8	Services	10.7
9	Others	0.6

		Year(s)
Life expectancy at birth (years): male	67.3	1966
female	73.6	
Infant mortality (per '000)	25.5	1965
Crude birth rate (per '000)	16.4	1965
Crude death rate (per '000)	10.0	1965
Accidental deaths (per 100 000 population)		
caused by motor vehicles	15.4	1965
due to other causes	35.8	1965
Population per physician	540	1965
Population per hospital bed	100	1966
School enrolment: age 5–19 years (percentage)	87	1963–4 av.
age over 19 years (per 100 000 population)	1 005	1964–5 av.

COMMUNICATIONS		*Year(s)*
Motor vehicles in use ('000s): private	na	1963–5 av.
commercial	134.8	
Railway track (km.)	13 197	1965
Telephones (per '000 urban population)	11.1	1967
Radio licences (per '000 population)	263	1963–5 av.
Television licences (per '000 population)	133.8	1963–5 av.
Daily newspapers (per '000 population)	276.7*	1962–4 av.

FINANCE

Currency unit: The koruna (or crown), which is pegged to the rouble at 1.8 korunas per rouble.

Exchange rates	*1965a*	*1960*	*1950*	*1938*
Per $ U.S.	7.22	7.22	7.17	na
Per £ sterling	20.22	20.22	20.16	na

		Year(s)
National Income (million $ U.S.)	14 000*	1966
G.N.P. per capita ($ U.S.)	1 010*	1966
Rate of increase of G.N.P. per capita	0.9	1960–4 av.

a buying rate (selling rate: 20.1 per £1). There is also a tourist rate, introduced in 1964, of 44.2 korunas per £1.

TRADING

Total trade (in million $ U.S.)	*1965*	*1956*	*1937*
Exports (f.o.b.)	2 688	1 387	418
Imports (f.o.b.)	2 673	1 186	383

Main trading partners (percentage of total value)

Exports	*1965*	*1956*	*1937*	*Imports*	*1965*	*1956*	*1937*
U.S.S.R.	38	31	1	U.S.S.R.	36	33	1
Germany D.R.	10	10	15*f*	Germany D.R.	11	10	17*f*
Poland	9	7	3	Poland	8	6	3
Hungary	5	4	2	Hungary	6	5	1
Germany F.R.	3	4	*d*	Romania	4	2	5
Yugoslavia	3	1	5	Bulgaria	3	3	1
Romania	3	3	5	Germany F.R.	3	3	*d*

Distribution of trade (percentage of total value)

Exports	*1965*	*1956**
Machinery and transport equipment	43	43
Crude materials	25	39
Food	5	6
Imports		
Crude materials	40	54
Machinery and transport equipment	30	13
Food	16	29

d see Germany D.R. *f* incl. Germany F.R.

na: data not available. — negligible or nil. [1] one year only. [2] two year average. * estimate. ‡ see appendix. † re-exports.

CZECHOSLOVAKIA *continued*

PRODUCTION, EXPORTS AND IMPORTS

Years: **1963–5 average** and *1953–5 average* Units: '000 metric tons unless otherwise indicated

	Production **1963–5**	Production *1953–5*	Exports **1963–5**	Exports *1953–5*	Imports **1963–5**	Imports *1953–5*
1. CEREALS, etc.						
Barley	1 482.7	na	29.2	*15.0**	397.7	*25.6**
Maize (corn)	478.7	*395.5**[2]	6.8	—	292.4	*68.9**
Millets/sorghum	3.7	*5.5*[2]	—	—*	0.2	*0.1**
Oats	698.7	na	—	—	—	—
Potatoes	5 946.7	na	11.9	*25.5**	350.3	*6.1**
Rice	—	—	4.3	—	83.4	*18.7**
Rye	857.3	*885.5*[2]	15.0	*6.0**	44.8	*5.0**
Wheat	1 862.3	na	—	*8.1**	1 262.8	*41.0**
2. FRUIT, etc.						
Apples	128.3	na	0.5	—	56.0	*12.6**
Apricots	17.3	*17.3*	—	—	—	—
Bananas	—	—	—	—	8.7	*0.3**
Cherries	52.3	*82.3*	—	—	—	—
Dates	—	—	0.1[2]†	—	0.8	*0.1**
Grapes	68.3	*63.0**	—	—	39.8	*6.6**
Lemons	—	—	1.1[2]†	—	24.9	*14.1**
Oranges	—	—	3.4[2]†	—	26.2	*12.8*
Other citrus fruit	—	—	1.4†	—	3.6	—
Pears	40.7	na	2.5	*1.0**	1.3	—
Plums	82.3	*184.6*	—	—	—	—
Raisins	na	—	2.5	—	4.7	*0.8**
Tomatoes	122.0	na	na	na	—	—
Wine *b*	—	*380.0**	0.1	—	443.3	*74.0**

b '000 hectolitres.

	Production **1963–5**	Production *1953–5*	Exports **1963–5**	Exports *1953–5*	Imports **1963–5**	Imports *1953–5*
3. BEVERAGES, FOREST PRODUCTS, etc.						
Cocoa	—	—	—	—	13.3	*2.5**
Coffee	—	—	—	—	10.9	*3.5**
Sugar: beet	7 051.3	*5 400.0**				
raw	888.8	*775.7**	501.6	*106.2**	136.5*	*30.5**
Tea	—	—	—	—	1.6	—
Tobacco: leaf	7.3	*9.1*[2]*	2.2	—*	15.8	*5.0**
cigars *e*	79.0	*56.6*	—	—	—	—
cigarettes *e*	18 543.0	*15 425.7*	—	—	—	—
tobacco/snuff	2.7	*3.4*	—	—	—	—
Softwood *j*	10 016.0	na	1 471.0	*681.3*	312.3	*55.3*
Hardwood *j*	2 706.0	na	8.1	*7.3*	101.1	*33.4*
Wood pulp	600.0*	na	42.9	—	43.3	—
Newsprint	59.7	*63.3**	23.0	*6.0*	1.4	—
Other paper	620.7	*367.0**[2]	50.0	*41.0*[1]	13.7	*2.0*[1]

e no. in millions. *j* '000 cu. metres of roundwood equivalent.

	Production **1963–5**	Production *1953–5*	Exports **1963–5**	Exports *1953–5*	Imports **1963–5**	Imports *1953–5*
4. VEGETABLE OILSEEDS AND OILS						
Castor seed	—	—	—	—	0.06	—
Castor oil	na	na	—	*0.20**	4.39	—*
Copra	—	—	—	—	4.88*	*2.30**
Coconut oil	na	na	0.47	—	2.93*	*0.15**
Cottonseed	—	—	—	—	23.00	—
Groundnuts	—	—	0.21	—	44.98	*0.10**
Groundnut oil	na	na	1.02	*0.29**	0.41	—
Linseed	15.33	na	2.53	*0.10**	24.63	*1.83**
Linseed oil	na	na	1.00[2]	—	4.42	—
Olive oil	—	—	1.94	—	2.11	—*
Palm kernels	—	—	—	—	3.73	*0.37**
Palm kernel oil	na	na	—	—	—	*0.08**
Palm oil	—	—	—	—	0.51	*1.15**
Rapeseed	53.70	na	—	*0.87**	22.63	—
Rapeseed oil	na	na	—	*0.08**	2.16	—
Sesame seed	—	—	—	—	2.83	—
Soya beans	—	na	—	—	24.05	*0.83**
Soya bean oil	na	na	—	—	7.61	*0.96**
Sunflower seed	3.33	na	—	—	27.57	*30.18*
Sunflower seed oil	na	na	0.24	—	27.97	*3.00**
Tung oil	—	—	—	—	1.02	—

	Production **1963–5**	Production *1953–5*	Exports **1963–5**	Exports *1953–5*	Imports **1963–5**	Imports *1953–5*
5. LIVESTOCK‡, ANIMAL PRODUCTS, etc.						
Chickens *d*	27 581.0	*20 629.0*				
Cattle *d*	4 474.3	*4 061.5*[2]	—	—	4.2	*9.1**
dairy cows *d*	2 291.3	na				
Goats *d*	576.0	na	} 0.2	—	—	—
Sheep *d*	539.7	*1 017.0*[2]				
Horses *d*	228.3	*562.0*				
Pigs *d*	5 960.0	*4 472.5*[2]	56.2	—	18.6*	*17.2*n*
Bacon/ham	} 665.0*	na	1.4	—*	0.1	*0.1**
Meat‡: 'A'			8.4	*0.1*	67.3	*17.2**
'B'	66.0	na	3.0	*0.1**	10.4	*1.0**
Butter	79.7*p*	*40.0*[2]*p*	0.1	*0.3**	14.2	*4.9**
Cheese	80.0	na	3.4	*0.2**	1.4	*1.7**
Eggs	137.0	*87.2*[2]	4.4	*0.3**	2.4	*1.6**
Fish	10.4*q*	*6.5*	1.0	na	137.4	na
Milk	3 740.7	*3 392.5*[2]*	17.9	*0.2**	—	—
Hides/skins	—	—	—	na	40.3*r*	na
Wool	1.1	*1.0**	—	*0.2*[2]*	21.3*	*4.8*[2]*

d no. in thousands. *n* pigs over 6 months old. *p* factory production only. *q* excl. catches in rivers by state fish farm organizations. *r* from cattle only.

	Production **1963–5**	Production *1953–5*	Exports **1963–5**	Exports *1953–5*	Imports **1963–5**	Imports *1953–5*
6. FIBRES, TEXTILES, etc.						
Agaves (sisal etc.)	—	—	—	—	—	*0.7*
Cotton lint	—	—	—	*0.5*†*	103.7	*21.1**
Flax fibre	22.7	na	—	—	—	*3.7**
Hemp fibre	5.1	na	—	—	—	*0.8**
Jute	—	—	—	—	16.0*	*3.6**
Rubber: natural	—	—	—	—	48.3*	*16.9**
synthetic	16.7*	—	—	—	—	*12.7*[2]
Silk	na *r*	—	—	—	—	—
Cotton: yarn	106.8	na	na	na	na	na
woven fabrics	59.0	*42.5**	15.4[2]	na	na	na
Rayon: fibre/yarn	na	na	na	na	—	—
woven fabrics	7.9*t*	na	1.8	na	—	—
Wool: yarn	40.9	*30.7*[2]	na	na	—	—
woven fabrics *u*	44.3	*37.3*[2]	na	na	—	—

continued

r see Rayon: fabrics. *t* incl. natural silk fabrics. *u* million metres.

	Production **1963–5**	Production *1953–5*	Exports **1963–5**	Exports *1953–5*	Imports **1963–5**	Imports *1953–5*
7. FUEL AND POWER						
Coal‡: 'A'	28 000	*22 140*	2 433	na	4 642	na
'B'	44 423	*40 750*	1 462	na	—	—
Coke	na	na	1 827	*1 197*	—	—
Electricity *h*: total	32 011	*13 980*				
hydro	3 157	*1 350*				
thermal	28 854	*12 630*				
Natural gas *i*	1 000	*170*[1]	—	—	—	—
Oil, crude	187	*110*[1]	—	—	5 163	na
Petroleum, refined	3 817	*830*[1]	613	—	523	na

h million kWh. *i* million cu. metres.

	Production **1963–5**	Production *1953–5*	Exports **1963–5**	Exports *1953–5*	Imports **1963–5**	Imports *1953–5*
8. IRON AND STEEL						
Iron ore	870*m*	*542m*	—	—	9 398	*3 554*
Pig iron	5 647	*2 851*	—	—	142	—
Steel ingots/castings	8 191	*4 370*	—	—	—	—

m metal content.

	Production **1963–5**	Production *1953–5*	Exports **1963–5**	Exports *1953–5*	Imports **1963–5**	Imports *1953–5*
9. NON-FERROUS MINERALS AND METALS						
Silver *k*, ore *m*	2 400.00*	*1 608.00**	—	—	—	—
Asbestos, fibre	na	na	—	—	24.91	—
Aluminium	59.87*	*14.18**	—	—	—	—
Antimony, ore *m*	2.00*	*1.63**	—	—	—	—
Lead: ore *m*	13.67*	*3.16**	—	—	—	—
metal	14.15*	*8.80**	—	—	—	—
Magnesium, magnesite	—	—	—	—	146.65	—
Manganese, ore	100.00**n*	na	—	—	296.35	—
Mercury *f*	25.05*	*24.99**	—	—	—	—
Tin, ore *m*	0.21	*0.20**	—	—	—	—
Zinc	na	na	—	—	—	—

f metric tons. *k* '000 fine troy oz. *m* metal content. *n* low grade ore.

	Production **1963–5**	Production *1953–5*	Exports **1963–5**	Exports *1953–5*	Imports **1963–5**	Imports *1953–5*
10. CHEMICALS*n* AND FERTILIZERS						
Organic chemicals:						
Benzene	na		na		na	
Butadiene	—		—		na	
Ethylene	na		na		na	
Methanol	67.0[2]		na		na	
Phenol	—		—		na	
Phthalic anhydride	na		na		na	
Styrene monomer	na		na		na	
Urea	na		—		na	
Inorganic chemicals:						
Ammonia	na		na		na	
Carbon black	na		na		na	
Chlorine	na		na		na	
Nitric acid	na		na		na	
Sodium carbonate	60.8		na		na	
Sodium hydroxide	145.0		na		na	
Sulphuric acid	850.3		na		10.0[2]	
Plastics:						
Polyamides	na		na		na	
Polyethylene	—		—		na	
Polyvinyl chloride	26.2		na		na	
Fertilizers:						
Potash	—	—	—	—	320.1*	—
Pyrites *x*	140.2	na	—	—	120.2	—
Sulphur	—	—	—	—	196.1	—

n data not available for years 1953–5. *x* sulphur content.

	Production **1963–5**	Production *1953–5*	Exports **1963–5**	Exports *1953–5*	Imports **1963–5**	Imports *1953–5*
11. INDUSTRY						
Alcoholic beverages			na	na	—	—
beer *b*	17 736.0	*10 557.3*	0.4			
spirits *b*	202.0[1]*q*	*360.0*[1]*r*				
Cement	5 438.0	*2 587.7*	403.0[1]	*155.0*t*	250.0[1]*	—**t*
Electrical engineering	na	na	na	na	—	na
Locomotives	523.0*c*	*92.0*[2]*c*	67.4*a*	na	—	—
Railway vehicles	na	na	na	na	—	—
Machine tools *a*	207.0[1]	na	—	—	—	—
Merchant ships *g*	—	—	—	—	6.0	—
Motor vehicles			43.6*a*	na	17.1*a*	na
commercial *d*	47.2	*12.6*				
private *d*	58.8	*8.4*				

a million $ U.S. *b* '000 hectolitres. *c* no. of units. *d* no. in thousands. *q* 1967 figure. *r* 1957 figure. *t* excl. trade with other communist countries.

na: data not available. — negligible or nil. [1] one year only. [2] two year average. * estimate. ‡ see appendix. † re-exports.

DAHOMEY

WEST AFRICA

Dahomey, formerly a member state of French West Africa, became an independent republic in 1960. Close economic ties have been formed with Togo.

AREA: 115 762 sq. km. (44 696 sq. miles)

LAND USE: (percentage of total)

	1963
Arable and orchard	13.7
Permanent meadow and pasture	3.9
Forest and woodland	19.2
City areas, waste and other land	63.2

POPULATION: 2 505 000 (1967 U.N. estimate)

Largest city: COTONOU; population: 109 328 (city proper, 1964)
Capital city: PORTO-NOVO; population: 69 500 (city proper, 1964)
Total working population: 1 110 000* (1960)

		Year(s)
Life expectancy at birth (years)	37.3*	1961
Population per physician	20 090	1962
Population per hospital bed	930*a*	1962
School enrolment: age 5–19 years (percentage)	20	1963–4 av.
age over 19 years (per 100 000 population)	2	1964–5 av.

a government hospitals only.

EMPLOYMENT AND PRODUCTION

The population is mainly employed in agriculture, growing maize, millet and groundnuts. The forests contain oil palms which are profitably utilized. Cotton has been introduced in the north of the country and coffee in the south.

COMMUNICATIONS

		Year(s)
Motor vehicles in use ('000s): private	6.0 }	1963–5 av.
commercial	4.1 }	
Railway track (km.)	579	1965
Telephones (per '000 urban population)	0.2	1967
Radio receivers (per '000 population)	15	1963–5 av.
Daily newspapers (per '000 population)	1[2]	1962–4 av.

FINANCE

Currency unit: The franc CFA

Exchange rates	*1965*	*1960*
Per $ U.S.	246.85	246.85
Per £ sterling	691.18	691.18

		Year
National Income (million $ U.S.)	106	1958
G.N.P. per capita ($ U.S.)	80	1966

TRADING

Total trade (in million $ U.S.)	*1965*	*1955*
Exports (f.o.b.)	14	16
Imports (c.i.f.)	34	24

Main trading partners (percentage of total value)

Exports	*1965*	*Imports*	*1965*
France	55	France	55
Netherlands	11	Netherlands	5
Germany F.R.	9	Senegal	4
Italy	5	U.K.	3
U.S.A.	3	Belg./Lux.	3
		Germany F.R.	3
		Nigeria	2

Distribution of trade (percentage of total value)

Exports	*1965*	*Imports*	*1965*
Vegetable oilseeds and oils	78	Manufactured goods	62
Food	8	(textiles)	(21)
		(machinery and transport equipment)	(17)
		Food	14

PRODUCTION, EXPORTS AND IMPORTS

Years: **1963–5 average** Units: '000 metric tons unless otherwise indicated

Note—1953–5 data are not available

	Production	Exports	Imports
1. CEREALS, etc.			
Cassava	1 171.0*		
Maize (corn)	225.3	0.3[2]	—
Millets/sorghum	69.3	—[1]	—
Potatoes	—	—	0.4[2]
Rice	1.0*	—	5.5*
Sweet potatoes/yams	558.7*		
2. FRUIT, etc.			
Bananas	10.0*	—	—
Coconuts	40.0[1]**e*	0.8[2]	—
Pineapples	3.0*	—	—
Tomatoes	4.3*	—	—
Wine *b*	—	—	24.0[2]

b '000 hectolitres. *e* no. in millions.

	Production	Exports	Imports
3. BEVERAGES, FOREST PRODUCTS, etc.			
Coffee	1.3*	1.0[2]	—
Sugar, raw	—	—	6.7*
Tobacco: leaf	0.6*	0.3[2]	0.6[2]
products	—	—	0.7
Hardwood *j*	1 671.7*	0.3[2]	6.3*n*
Other paper	—	—	0.1[2]

j '000 cu. metres of roundwood equivalent. *n* incl. softwood.

	Production	Exports	Imports
4. VEGETABLE OILSEEDS AND OILS			
Castor seed	na	0.49*	—
Copra	na	1.06[2]	—
Coconut oil	na	0.05[2]	—
Cottonseed	2.70*	1.23*	—
Groundnuts	18.43	4.28	—
Linseed oil	—	—	0.01
Palm kernels	53.67	41.15	—
Palm oil	41.33	11.65	—
Soya bean oil	—	—	0.01[2]

	Production	Exports	Imports
5. LIVESTOCK‡, ANIMAL PRODUCTS, etc.			
Chickens *d*	4 000.0		
Cattle *d*	369.7	—	—
Goats *d*	497.0	—	—
Sheep *d*	387.0	—	—
Horses *d*	3.0		
Pigs *d*	302.0	—	—
Meat‡, 'A'	3.0		
Cheese	—	—	0.1[2]
Eggs	14.5	—	—
Fish	23.7	0.2	1.3
Milk	22.3*	—	1.4

d no. in thousands.

	Production	Exports	Imports
6. FIBRES, TEXTILES, etc.			
Cotton: lint	1.0*	1.1[2]	—
yarn	—	—	0.1
woven fabrics	—	—	1.7
7. FUEL AND POWER			
Electricity *h t*	16		
Petroleum, refined	—	—	47

h million kWh. *t* thermal.

	Production	Exports	Imports
11. INDUSTRY			
Alcoholic beverages *a*	na	0.1	1.1
Cement	—	—	60.0
Electrical engineering *a*	—	—	1.2
Railway vehicles *a*	—	—	0.1
Motor vehicles *a*	—	0.1	2.3

a million $ U.S.

na: data not available. — negligible or nil. [1] one year only. [2] two year average. * estimate. ‡ see appendix. † re-exports.

DENMARK

Denmark is a kingdom; the legislative power lies jointly with the king and the ' Folketing ' (parliament) in which the Faeroe Islands and Greenland are both represented. Denmark is a member of the European Free Trade Association.

AREA: 43 031 sq. km. (16 611 sq. miles)

LAND USE: (percentage of total)	*1965*	*1955*
Arable and orchard	62.9	63.5
Permanent meadow and pasture	7.5	9.1
Forest and woodland	9.3	10.2
City areas, waste and other land	20.3	17.2

POPULATION: 4 767 597 (1965 census)

Largest city: KØBENHAVN (Copenhagen), capital; population: 1 377 605 (1965)

Distribution of working population (1960)

Total working population: 2 093 631

U.N. group no.		*Percentage*
0	Agriculture, forestry, fishing and hunting	17.5
1	Mining and quarrying	0.2
2/3	Manufacturing	28.5
4	Construction	7.2
5	Electricity, gas, water and sanitary services	0.6
6	Commerce	15.0
7	Transport, storage and communications	7.2
8	Services	22.1
9	Others	1.7

		Year(s)
Life expectancy at birth (years): male	70.1	1965–6 av.
female	74.7	
Infant mortality (per '000)	18.7	1965
Crude birth rate (per '000)	18.0	1965
Crude death rate (per '000)	10.1	1965
Accidental deaths (per 100 000 population)		
caused by motor vehicles	21.9	1965
due to other causes	30.3	1965
Population per physician	750	1964
Population per hospital bed	110	1966
School enrolment: age 5–19 years (percentage)	85	1963–4 av.
age over 19 years (per 100 000 population)	911	1963–5 av.

COMMUNICATIONS		*Year(s)*
Motor vehicles in use ('000s): private	674.5	1963–5 av.
commercial	227.8	
Railway track (km.)	4 020	1964
Mail per capita: domestic	12	1963–5 av.
foreign received	10	
foreign sent	9	
Telephones (per '000 urban population)	29.1	1967
Radio licences (per '000 population)	342	1963–5 av.
Television licences (per '000 population)	214	1963–5 av.
Daily newspapers (per '000 population)	344	1962–4 av.

FINANCE

Currency unit: The krone

Exchange rates	*1965*	*1960*	*1950*	*1938*
Per $ U.S.	6.89	6.906	6.91	4.83
Per £ sterling	19.3	19.345	19.37	22.22

		Year(s)
National Income (million $ U.S.)	7 861	1965
G.N.P. per capita ($ U.S.)	1 830	1966
Rate of increase of G.N.P. per capita	4.1	1960–4 av.
Foreign trade (percentage of G.D.P.)	51	1963–5 av.

TRADING

Total trade (in million $ U.S.)	*1965*	*1955*	*1938*
Exports (f.o.b.)	2 320	1 072	335
Imports (c.i.f.)	2 822	1 179	354

Main trading partners (percentage of total value)

Exports	*1965*	*1955*	*1938*	*Imports*	*1965*	*1955*	*1938*
U.K.	22	33	56	Germany F.R.	21	19	25 *d*
Germany F.R.	17	17	20 *d*	U.K.	13	26	35
Sweden	12	7	5	Sweden	13	9	7
U.S.A.	7	7	1	U.S.A.	9	8	8
Norway	6	4	3	Netherlands	5	6	4
Italy	4	4	—	Norway	4	3	3
France	3	2	1	France	4	5	1

Distribution of trade (percentage of total value)

Exports	*1965*	*1955*	*1938**
Food	46	66	69
(pigs, bacon, etc.)	(13)	(19)	(25)
(dairy produce and eggs)	(10)	(25)	(36)
(cattle and beef)	(6)	(7)	(4)
Manufactured goods	38	24	na
(machinery and transport equipment)	(22)	(15)	(13)
Crude materials and fuels	8	5	na
Imports			
Manufactured goods	58	44	na
(machinery and transport equipment)	(25)	(15)	(10)
Crude materials and fuels	20	30	na
(mineral fuels, etc.)	(11)	(19)	(14)
Food	11	16	11
Chemicals	9	7	7

d incl. Germany D.R.

PRODUCTION, EXPORTS AND IMPORTS

Years: **1963–5 average** and *1953–5 average* Units: '000 metric tons unless otherwise indicated

1. CEREALS, etc.

	Production		Exports		Imports	
Barley	3 808.0	*2 141.7*	186.0	*169.7*	345.2	*210.5*
Maize (corn)	—	—	0.9	—	148.2	*22.5*
Millets/sorghum	—	—	0.3	*5.7*	124.4	*43.7*
Oats	757.3	*828.7*	20.6	*23.2*	76.7	*60.4*
Potatoes	1 161.3	*1 755.0*	54.2	*102.7*	8.3	*0.9*
Rice	—	—	—	*0.5*	6.5	*6.7*
Rye	292.0	*266.0*	27.8	*5.7*	9.4	*110.5*
Wheat	533.0	*276.3*	57.9	*26.9*	18.1	*226.2*

2. FRUIT, etc.

	Production		Exports		Imports	
Apples	188.7	*185.0*	11.1	*22.7*	9.3	—
Bananas	—	—	0.1	—	32.1	*28.3*
Cherries	10.0*	*6.8*	—	—	—	—
Dates	—	—	—	—	0.8	*1.0*
Grapes	—	—	0.2	—	9.2	*2.5*
Lemons	—	—	0.1	—	6.8	*4.5*
Oranges	—	—	0.5	—	42.1	*30.9*
Other citrus fruit	—	—	0.1	—[2]	3.2	*0.8*
Pears	20.7*	*18.3*	—	*0.1*	2.3	—
Plums	14.3*	*13.6*	—	—	—	—
Raisins	—	—	0.1	—	3.6	*4.0*
Tomatoes	18.7	*16.3n*				
Wine *b*	—	—	3.8	—	167.1	*96.3*

b '000 hectolitres. *n* commercial production.

3. BEVERAGES, FOREST PRODUCTS, etc.

	Production		Exports		Imports	
Cocoa	—	—	—	—	4.4	*2.8*
Coffee	—	—	0.3†	—	50.4	*26.0*
Sugar: beet	2 545.0	*2 067.7*				
raw	341.4	*303.3**	107.5	*30.1*	29.4	*0.5*
Tea	—	—	—	—	1.5	*1.2*

continued

3. BEVERAGES, FOREST PRODUCTS, etc.—*continued*

	Production		Exports		Imports	
Tobacco: leaf	—	na	0.4†	—	14.6	*10.0*
cigars	314.0*e*	*214.0e*				
cigarettes	6 941.0*e*	*4 532.7e*	na	—[2]	1.1	*0.5*[2]
tobacco/snuff	3.3	*3.5*				
Softwood *j*	920.7	*930.5*[2]	33.6	*2.8*	1 731.0	*1 176.8*
Hardwood *j*	894.3	*990.5*[2]	134.0	*34.4*	269.7	*61.9*
Wood pulp	35.7	*6.0**	23.0	*0.5*	111.3	*82.0*
Newsprint	0.1	*0.2*[1]	—	—	113.0	*62.7*
Other paper	197.7*	*118.0**	17.6	*2.5*	209.3	*84.6*

e no. in millions. *j* '000 cu. metres of roundwood equivalent.

4. VEGETABLE OILSEEDS AND OILS

	Production		Exports		Imports	
Castor oil	—	—	—	—	0.48	*0.34*
Copra	—	—	—	—	34.72	*52.17*
Coconut oil	na	na	0.43	*1.16*	0.80	*0.23*
Cottonseed	—	—	—	—	—	*6.80*[2]
Cottonseed oil	—	na	—	—	0.44	*0.35*
Groundnuts	—	—	0.04†	—	3.38	*0.43*
Groundnut oil	na	na	0.04	*0.03*	0.15	*0.46*
Linseed	—	*1.00p*	0.06†	*0.83†*	7.00	*3.23*
Linseed oil	na	na	0.02	*0.01*	5.54	*6.50*
Olive oil	—	—	—	—	0.11	*0.09*
Palm kernels	—	—	—	—	16.70	*17.80*
Palm kernel oil	na	na	1.36	*0.06*	0.30	*0.02*
Palm oil	—	—	0.12†	*0.01†*	2.50	*4.12*
Rapeseed	42.70	*11.3*	50.96	*3.10*	0.37	*1.00*
Rapeseed oil	na	na	0.36	*0.32*	0.76	*0.48*
Sesame seed	—	—	—	—	1.22	*4.60*
Soya beans	—	—	—	—	382.40	*65.07*
Soya bean oil	na	na	42.73	*1.26*	0.17	*0.11*
Sunflower seed	—	—	—	—	0.18	—
Sunflower seed oil	na	—	—	—	1.05	—
Tung oil	—	—	0.02†	—	0.39	*0.61*

p flax grown for seed only.

continued

PRODUCTION, EXPORTS AND IMPORTS *continued*

5. LIVESTOCK‡, ANIMAL PRODUCTS, etc.

	Production		Exports		Imports	
Chickens *d*	23 509.0	*24 234.3*				
Cattle *d*	3 321.7	*3 133.0*	294.3	*351.9*	0.1	*0.3*
dairy cows *d*	1 376.0	*2 189.5*[2]				
Goats *d*	5.0*	*5.0*[2]	—	—	0.3	—
Sheep *d*	75.0	*36.3*				
Horses *d*	66.0	*355.3*				
Pigs *d*	7 979.0	*4 586.7*	148.8	*134.8*	—	—
Bacon/ham	958.3	*686.7*	301.2	*225.8*	—	—
Meat‡: 'A'			151.1	*80.3*	0.6	*0.2*
'B'	130.1	*75.7*	87.8	*29.0*	0.5	—
Butter	157.0	*172.7*	107.3	*135.8*	—	—
Cheese	119.3	*85.0*	78.5	*57.0*	0.5	*0.5*
Eggs	98.9	*140.1*	29.1	*102.4*	0.5	—
Fish	853.3*q*	*375.8q*	350.6	*171.6**	213.6	*59.4**
Milk	5 228.7	*5 298.7*	490.7	*217.3*	198.4	—
Whale/sperm oil	0.1	*1.0*	—	—	—	*13.2*
Hides/skins	na	na	17.2	*10.7*	8.5	*5.1*[2]
Wool	0.1	—	0.7	*0.1*	2.8	*1.6*

d no. in thousands. *q* incl. fish landed by Danish vessels in foreign ports.

6. FIBRES, TEXTILES, etc.

	Production		Exports		Imports	
Abaca	—	—	—	—	2.6	*2.4*
Agaves (sisal etc.)	—	—	0.1†	*0.1†*	17.1	*16.6*
Cotton lint	—	—	—	—	8.6	*9.2*
Flax fibre	1.3	*4.0*[1]*	0.8	*2.0*	0.9	*0.5*
Hemp fibre	—	—	—	—	0.4	*0.3*
Jute	—	—	0.4†	—	2.4	*2.4*
Rubber: natural	—	—	—	—	6.3	*6.7*
synthetic	—	—	—	—	4.3	—
Cotton: yarn	8.1	*8.2*	0.6	—	5.5	*2.9*
woven fabrics	6.4	*6.3*	0.5	—	9.7	*7.6*
Rayon: fibre/yarn	—	—	0.3[1]†	—	5.4	*2.9*
woven fabrics	—	*1.4*[2]	0.3[2]	—	3.4	*2.6*
Non-cellulosic fibre/yarn	0.9	—	1.0	—	5.6	—
Wool: yarn	4.8[2]	*7.4*	0.4	*0.2*	4.6	*2.1*
woven fabrics	2.8	*3.7*	0.7	*0.2*	3.5	*2.7*

7. FUEL AND POWER

	Production		Exports		Imports	
Coal: 'A'‡	—	—	1†	—	3 732	*4 584*
'B'	750	*800*	35	*6*	168	*181*
Coke	na	na	50	—	1 159	*2 124*
Electricity *h*: total	7 459	*3 270*[1]				
hydro	—	*30*[1]				
thermal	7 459	*3 240*[1]				
Oil, crude	—	—	—	—	2 903	na
Petroleum, refined	2 833	*10*[1]	533	—	6 727	*3 150*[1]

h million kWh.

8. IRON AND STEEL

	Production		Exports		Imports	
Iron ore	—	—	143	*183*	4	*5*
Pig iron	72	*44*	—	—	110	*58*
Steel ingots/castings	389	*205*	3	—	39	—
Iron/steel scrap	na	na	43	*22*	1	*3*
Iron/steel products *a*	na	na	18	*4*	163	*71*

a million $ U.S.

9. NON-FERROUS MINERALS AND METALS

	Production		Exports		Imports	
Platinum group metals *k*	—	—	0.16†	*0.64†*	3.55*s*	*1.14s*
Silver *k*, bullion	—	—	40.67†	*40.70†*	3 829.70*s*	*2 221.70s*
Asbestos: fibre	—	—	0.09†	*0.04†*	21.15*s*	*9.96s*
manufactured	na	na	9.01†	*1.75†*	9.26*s*	*0.99s*
Mica	—	—	—	—	0.30	*2.10*
Aluminim: bauxite	—	—	—	*20.41†n*	43.70	*34.91s*
aluminium	na	na	3.54†	*0.66†*	27.38*s*	*9.23s*

continued

9. NON-FERROUS MINERALS AND METALS—*continued*

	Production		Exports		Imports	
Antimony, metal	—	—	—	—	0.18	*0.14*
Cadmium	—	—	—	—	0.22	—
Chrome, metal	—	—	—	—	0.36	*0.68*
Cobalt, metal	—	—	—	—	0.02	—
Copper, metal	na	na	6.28†	*3.44†*	32.65*s*	*17.01s*
Lead, metal	na	na	4.85†	*8.12†*	21.19*s*	*20.48s*
Magnesium:						
dolomite	—	—	—	—	16.89	*7.82*
magnesite	—	—	—	—	3.97	*1.29*
metal/salts	na	na	—	—	4.19	*1.76*
Manganese: ore	—	—	—	—	7.13	*2.74*
metal	na	na	—	—	2.91	*2.93*
Mercury *f*	—	—	—	—	27.30	*7.30*
Molybdenum *f*, metal	—	—	—	—	26.40	—
Nickel, metal	—	—	0.20	*0.17*	0.71	*0.10*
Tin, metal	—	—	0.87	*4.60*	1.25	*5.93*
Titanium minerals	—	—	—	—	5.50	*2.30*[2]
Zinc, metal	—	—	3.10	*1.24*	20.63	*14.39*

f metric tons. *k* '000 fine troy oz. *n* cryolite. *s* incl. imports for re-export.

10. CHEMICALS*n* AND FERTILIZERS

	Production		Exports		Imports	
Organic chemicals:						
Benzene	na		—		0.3	
Butadiene	—		—		na	
Ethylene	na		na		na	
Methanol	—		0.1		2.7	
Phenol	na		0.3		1.1	
Phthalic anhydride	na		—		4 493.5[2]	
Styrene monomer	—		—		1.1	
Urea	—		0.1		10.3	
Inorganic chemicals:						
Ammonia	—		3.2		31.8	
Carbon black	—		0.1		1.8	
Chlorine	na		0.3		0.5	
Nitric acid	na		—		4.5	
Sodium carbonate	3.8		—[2]		31.7	
Sodium hydroxide	na		—		24.6	
Sulphuric acid	18.0		7.1		2.2	
Plastics:						
Polyamides	—		—		na	
Polyethylene	16.5[2]		9.8		15.5	
Polyvinyl chloride	—		0.6		20.9	
Fertilizers:						
Phosphates	—	—	—	—	313.1	*254.1*
Potash	—	—	—	—	287.4	*303.8*
Pyrites	—	—	—	—	136.6	*128.4*
Sulphur	—	—	—	—	12.4	*0.9*

n data not available for years 1953–5.

11. INDUSTRY

	Production		Exports		Imports	
Aircraft *a*	—	—	—	*0.6*	11.3	*2.8*
Alcoholic beverages:			23.1*a*	*8.3a*	15.9*a*	*4.1a*
beer *b*	4 920.0	*2 876.0*				
spirits *b*	48.0[1]**p*	*78.0*[1]**q*				
Cement	1 812.3	*1 185.7*	129.3	*325.0*	32.3	*26.3*
Electrical engineering *a*	287.2[2]	na	87.6	*28.0*[2]	121.5	*22.5*[2]
Locomotives *c*	22.0	—	na	na	na	na
Railway vehicles *a*	na	na	0.3	—	1.1	—
Machine tools *a*	10.0[1]	na	—	—	13.7	—
Merchant ships *g*	275.0	*142.0*	141.0	*35.2*	139.0	*37.1*
Motor vehicles:			10.8*a*	*3.7*[2]*a*	160.3*a*	*63.5*[2]*a*
commercial *dr*	7.2	*4.4*				
private *dr*	24.7	*6.6*				

a million $ U.S. *b* '000 hectolitres. *c* no. of units. *d* no. in thousands. *g* '000 G.R.T. *p* 1967 figure. *q* production for home consumption in 1961. *r* assembly of imported parts.

na: data not available. — negligible or nil. [1] one year only. [2] two year average. * estimate. ‡ see appendix. † re-exports.

DENMARK (TERRITORIES)

FAEROE ISLANDS

NORTH ATLANTIC

These 21 volcanic islands have had a certain measure of home rule since 1948; they are represented by two members in the Danish Folketing.

AREA: 1 399 sq. km. (540 sq. miles)

LAND USE: (percentage of total)

	1949
Arable and orchard	2.1
City areas, waste and other land, including rough grazing	97.9

POPULATION: 38 000 (1967 estimate)
Capital city: TÓRSHAVN (Thorshavn); population 7 447 (1960)
Distribution of working population (1960)
Total working population: 14 135

U.N. group no.		*Percentage*
0	Agriculture, forestry, fishing and hunting	34.5
1	Mining and quarrying	0.8
2/3	Manufacturing	18.5
4	Construction	5.4
5	Electricity, gas, water and sanitary services	0.3
6	Commerce	10.2
7	Transport, storage and communications	10.3
8	Services	17.9
9	Others	2.1

		Year(s)
Infant mortality (per '000)	16.9*	1965
Crude birth rate (per '000)	24.0*	1965
Crude death rate (per '000)	7.1*	1965
Population per physician	1 160	1964
Population per hospital bed	150	1966
School enrolment: age 5–19 years (percentage)	104‡	1963–4 av.
age over 19 years (per 100 000 population)	16	1965

FINANCE

Currency unit: The Danish krone

EMPLOYMENT AND TRADE

The main occupations are fishing and sheep-rearing. Exports balanced imports at U.S. $ 26 million in 1965, the exports consisting primarily of fish preparations and some wool products. Denmark and the U.K. were the main trading partners.

PRODUCTION, EXPORTS AND IMPORTS

Years: **1963–5 average** and *1953–5 average* Units: '000 metric tons unless otherwise indicated

	Production		Exports		Imports	
1. CEREALS, etc.						
Barley	—	—	—	—	0.2	*0.5*
Maize (corn)	—	—	—	—	0.2	*0.1*
Potatoes	—	—	—	—	2.4	*1.6*
2. FRUIT, etc.						
Apples	—	—	—	—	0.4	*0.2*
Bananas	—	—	—	—	0.1	—
Dates	—	—	—	—	0.1	—
Oranges	—	—	—	—	0.2	*0.2*
Raisins	—	—	—	—	0.1	—
Wine *b*	—	—	—	—	0.3	—
b '000 hectolitres.						
3. BEVERAGES, FOREST PRODUCTS, etc.						
Sugar, raw	—	—	—	—	1.4	*1.3*
4. VEGETABLE OILSEEDS AND OILS						
Coconut oil	—	—	—	—	0.30	*0.28*
Cottonseed oil	—	—	—	—	—	*0.01*
Palm oil	—	—	—	—	—	*0.01*
Soya bean oil	—	—	—	—	0.14	*0.04*

	Production		Exports		Imports	
5. LIVESTOCK‡, ANIMAL PRODUCTS, etc.						
Sheep *d*	72.0*	na	—	—	—	—
Meat‡: 'A'	—	—	—	—	0.7	*0.1*
'B'	—	—	—	—	0.1	—
Butter	—	—	—	—	0.1	—
Cheese	—	—	—	—	0.2	*0.1*
Eggs	0.1*	na	—	—	0.2	*0.1*
Fish	140.3*n*	*94.6n*	67.1	*39.5**	1.2	na
Milk	—	—	—	—	1.6	*0.8*
Wool	na	na	na	na		
d no. in thousands. *n* incl. fish landed by Faeroes' vessels in foreign ports.						
7. FUEL AND POWER						
Coal, 'A'‡	—	—	—	—	3	*7*
Electricity *h*: total	45	*3*				
hydro	41	*3*				
thermal	4	—				
Petroleum, refined	—	—	—	—	40	*30*[1]
h million kWh.						
11. INDUSTRY						
Merchant ships *g*	0.8	—	—	—	0.9	—
g '000 G.R.T.						

GREENLAND

NORTH ATLANTIC

In 1953 Greenland became an integral part of the Danish realm, and is represented by two members in the Danish Folketing. Defence agreements have been signed with the U.S.A., and air force bases and weather stations have been established.

AREA: 2 175 600 sq. km. (840 000 sq. miles) of which 341 600 sq. km. (131 900 sq. miles) is ice-free land.

POPULATION: 43 000 (1967 estimate)
Capital city: GODTHAAB; population: 3 179 (1960)

Distribution of working population (1960)
Total working population: 11 800

U.N. group no.		*Percentage*
0	Agriculture, forestry, fishing and hunting	34.4
1	Mining and quarrying	2.9
2/3	Manufacturing	7.1
4	Construction	8.2
5	Electricity, gas, water and sanitary services	1.1
6	Commerce	10.3
7	Transport, storage and communications	7.9
8	Services	27.6
9	Others	0.5

		Year(s)
Life expectancy at birth (years): male	51.4*	1952–9 av.
female	53.6*	1952–9 av.
Infant mortality (per '000)	70.1*	1965
Crude birth rate (per '000)	43.5	1965
Crude death rate (per '000)	8.4	1965
Population per physician	710	1963
Population per hospital bed	60	1965
School enrolment: age 5–19 years (percentage)	110‡	1963–4 av.

FINANCE

Currency unit: The Danish krone

EMPLOYMENT AND TRADE

In recent years fishing has largely replaced fur-trapping, whaling and sealing as the main occupation. Sheep and some cattle are pastured. There are large resources of coal, but it is of low calorific value and it is planned to discontinue coal mining in 1972. Cryolite is mined, but deposits of lead and zinc also proved uneconomic to recover, and production of these ceased in 1962. Denmark has a virtual monopoly of trade although commerce with the U.K. showed a marked increase in 1965.

continued

na: data not available. — negligible or nil. [1] one year only. [2] two year average. * estimate. ‡ see appendix. † re-exports.

PRODUCTION, EXPORTS AND IMPORTS

Years: **1963–5 average** and *1953–5 average* Units: '000 metric tons unless otherwise indicated

	Production		Exports		Imports	
1. CEREALS, etc.						
Barley	—	—	—	—	na	*0.5**
Maize (corn)	—	—	—	—	na	*0.1**
Potatoes	—	—	—	—	1.9	*1.0*
Wheat	—	—	—	—	na	*0.3**
2. FRUIT, etc.						
Apples	—	—	—	—	0.5	*0.2**
Oranges	—	—	—	—	0.3	*0.1**
Raisins	—	—	—	—	0.1	—
Wine *b*	—	—	—	—	1.5	—
b '000 hectolitres.						
3. BEVERAGES, FOREST PRODUCTS, etc.						
Coffee	—	—	—	—	0.2	—
Sugar, raw	—	—	—	—	1.8	*1.4*
Softwood *j*	—	—	—	—	—	*4.5*[1]
Hardwood *j*	0.5[2]*	*0.5*	—	—	—	*0.2*[1]
j '000 cu. metres of roundwood equivalent.						
4. VEGETABLE OILSEEDS AND OILS						
Soya bean oil	—	—	—	—	0.02	—

	Production		Exports		Imports	
5. LIVESTOCK‡, ANIMAL PRODUCTS, etc.						
Chickens *d*	—	*2.0*				
Sheep *d*	33.7	*18.7*	—	—	—	—
Meat‡: 'A'	—	—	0.1	—	0.4	—
'B'	—	—	—	—	0.1	—
Butter	—	—	—	—	0.1	—
Cheese	—	—	—	—	0.2	—
Eggs	—	—	—	—	0.2	—
Fish	37.4*	*25.2**	14.5	na	0.2	na
Milk	—	—	—	—	3.5	*0.7**
d no. in thousands.						
7. FUEL AND POWER						
Coal, 'A'‡	26	*20*	—	—	12	*14*[2]
Electricity *h t*	38	*10*[1]				
Petroleum, refined	—	—	—	—	73	*40*[1]
h million kWh. *t* thermal.						
9. NON-FERROUS MINERALS AND METALS						
Aluminium, cryolite	na	na	59.31	*46.82*	—	—

DOMINICAN REPUBLIC

CARIBBEAN SEA

The Dominican Republic was established in 1844. The population, unlike that of neighbouring Haiti, is primarily of European origin. After 30 years' dictatorship ended in 1961, the country suffered considerable political unrest, culminating in civil war four years later. Peace was restored after intervention by U.S. troops, and free elections followed in 1966.

AREA: 48 442 sq. km. (18 700 sq. miles)

LAND USE: (percentage of total)

	1960	*1946*
Arable and orchard	21.9	14.0
Permanent meadow and pasture	17.8	11.9
Forest and woodland	45.7	70.6
City areas, waste and other land	14.6	3.5

POPULATION: 3 889 000 (1967 estimate)
Largest city: SANTO DOMINGO, capital; population: 577 371 (city proper, 1967)

Distribution of working population (1960)
Total working population: 820 710* (based on a 10% sample of census returns)

U.N. group no.		*Percentage*
0	Agriculture, forestry, fishing and hunting	61.4
1	Mining and quarrying	0.3
2/3	Manufacturing	8.2
4	Construction	2.5
5	Electricity, gas, water and sanitary services	0.4
6	Commerce	6.7
7	Transport, storage and communications	2.6
8	Services	11.1
9	Others	6.8

		Year(s)
Life expectancy at birth (years): male	57.2	1959–61 av.
female	58.6	1959–61 av.
Infant mortality (per '000)	72.7*	1965
Crude birth rate (per '000)	46.5*	1960–5 av.
Crude death rate (per '000)	15*	1960–5 av.
Accidental deaths (per 100,000 population)		
caused by motor vehicles	3.5*	1960
due to other causes	13.1*	1960
Population per physician	1 680	1965
Population per hospital bed	350	1966
School enrolment: age 5–19 years (percentage)	65	1962
age over 19 years (per 100 000 population)	166	1964–5 av.

COMMUNICATIONS

		Year(s)
Motor vehicles in use ('000s): private	26.5	1963–5 av.
commercial	9.7	1963–5 av.
Railway track (km.)	1 444 *a*	1963
Telephones (per '000 urban population)	0.8	1967
Radio receivers (per '000 population)	41	1963–5 av.
Television sets (per '000 population)	10	1963–5 av.
Daily newspapers (per '000 population)	27	1962

a mainly on sugar estates; no passenger services.

FINANCE

Currency unit: The peso oro, at par with the $ U.S. which, prior to 1947, was the only legal tender.

Exchange rates	*1965*	*1960*	*1950*
Per £ sterling	2.8	2.8	2.8

		Year(s)
National Income (million $ U.S.)	769	1965
G.N.P. per capita ($ U.S.)	250	1966
Rate of increase of G.N.P. per capita	3.2	1960–4 av.
Foreign trade (percentage of G.D.P.)	31	1963–5 av.

TRADING

Total trade (in million $ U.S.)	*1965*	*1955*	*1938*
Exports (f.o.b.)	126	115	15
Imports (c.i.f.)	87	98	11

Main trading partners (percentage of total value)

Exports	*1965*	*1955*	*Imports*	*1965*	*1955*
U.S.A.	80	55	U.S.A.	54	66
Netherlands	3	5	Germany F.R.	6	4
Spain	2	1	Neths. Antilles	6	6
Germany F.R.	2	1	Canada	5	4
Belg./Lux.	2	3	Japan	5	2
Italy	2	1	Netherlands	3	1
New Zealand	1	—	Italy	3	1

Distribution of trade (percentage of total value)

Exports	*1965**	*1955*	*1938**
Sugar and molasses	50	39	60
Coffee	17	25	10
Bauxite/aluminium concentrates	9	—	—

Imports	*1965*	*1955*
Machinery and transport equipment	24	27
Food	14	7
Fuels	10	8
Chemicals	10	8
Iron and steel	8	13
Edible oils	6	na
Textiles	3	12

continued

na: data not available. — negligible or nil. [1] one year only. [2] two year average. * estimate. ‡ see appendix. † re-exports.

DOMINICAN REPUBLIC *continued*

PRODUCTION, EXPORTS AND IMPORTS

Years: **1963–5 average** and *1953–5 average* Units: '000 metric tons unless otherwise indicated

1. CEREALS, etc.

	Production 1963–5	Production 1953–5	Exports 1963–5	Exports 1953–5	Imports 1963–5	Imports 1953–5
Cassava	150.0*	144.0[1]				
Maize (corn)	96.7*	87.0[2]	2.0	22.0	1.3	—
Millets/sorghum	—	—	—	—	0.2[2]	—
Oats	—	—	—	—	0.5	—
Potatoes	2.0*	2.0	—	—	1.9	1.5
Rice	146.0*	93.0*	—	0.5	25.4*	0.1
Sweet potatoes/yams	80.0*	84.0[1]				
Wheat	—	—	—	—	50.3	0.9

2. FRUIT, etc.

	Production 1963–5	Production 1953–5	Exports 1963–5	Exports 1953–5	Imports 1963–5	Imports 1953–5
Apples	—	—	—	—	0.7	0.3
Bananas	352.3	335.0	79.0	41.8	—	—
Coconuts	45.0*e	na	4.6	0.4[2]	—	—
Grapes	—	—	—	—	0.3	0.2
Lemons	3.0*	na	—	—	—	—
Oranges	25.0*	15.0*[2]	0.6	0.8	—	—
Other citrus fruit	2.0*	na	0.1	0.1	—	—
Pineapples	5.0*	na	—	—	—	—
Raisins	—	—	—	—	0.2	—
Wine *b*	—	—	—	—	3.1	1.3

b '000 hectolitres. *e* no. in millions.

3. BEVERAGES, FOREST PRODUCTS, etc.

	Production 1963–5	Production 1953–5	Exports 1963–5	Exports 1953–5	Imports 1963–5	Imports 1953–5
Cocoa	38.8	31.1	24.1	22.6	—	—
Coffee	39.6	32.1*	28.8	22.7	—	—
Sugar: cane	6 466.7*	5 429.0				
raw	738.0	647.0*	607.9	548.1	—	—
Tobacco: leaf	21.8*	17.7*	19.0	11.6	0.6	0.1
cigars	28.0e	33.7e	}			
cigarettes	1 761.0e	896.7e	—	—	na	0.4[2]a
tobacco/snuff	—	—	}			
Softwood *j*	307.5*[2]	257.0	—	1.4[2]	na	—[2]
Hardwood *j*	1 692.5*[2]	27.7p	2.4	3.3[2]	na	2.1[2]
Wood pulp	—[1]	—	—	—	na	—
Newsprint	—*	—	—	—[2]	4.6[1]	1.5[2]
Other paper	2.0*	—	—	—[2]	6.0[1]	5.3[2]

a million $ U.S. *e* no. in millions. *j* '000 cu. metres of roundwood equivalent
p production for industries only.

4. VEGETABLE OILSEEDS AND OILS

	Production 1963–5	Production 1953–5	Exports 1963–5	Exports 1953–5	Imports 1963–5	Imports 1953–5
Castor oil	—	—	—	—	0.01	—
Copra	6.50*	na	6.57	2.23	—	—
Coconut oil	na	na	0.52[2]	—	0.01[2]	—
Cottonseed	3.00*	na	—	—	—	—
Cottonseed oil	na	na	—	0.02	0.23	—
Groundnuts	35.91	21.91*	—	—	—	—
Linseed oil	—	—	—	—	0.01	—
Olive oil	—	—	—	—	0.28	0.17
Sesame seed	0.20*	na	—	—	—	—

5. LIVESTOCK‡, ANIMAL PRODUCTS, etc.

	Production 1963–5	Production 1953–5	Exports 1963–5	Exports 1953–5	Imports 1963–5	Imports 1953–5
Chickens *d*	5 250.0*	1 196.5[2]				
Cattle *d*	1 015.0*	895.0	—	1.1	0.2	0.7
Goats *d* }	928.0*	262.0[1]	—	—	—	—
Sheep *d* }	76.3*	27.0[2]				
Horses *d*	255.0*	246.0[2]				
Pigs *d*	1 082.0*	917.5[2]	—	0.6	—	1.8
Bacon/ham }	27.3*	19.0[2]	—	—	0.1[2]	—
Meat‡: 'A' }			—	1.7	—	—
'B'	—	—	—	—	0.8	—
Butter	—	—	—	—	0.4	—
Cheese	1.0*	1.0[2]	—	—	0.4	0.1
Eggs	2.5*	na	—	—	—	—
Fish	3.8*	0.7[1]	—	—	11.3	6.2*
Milk	48.0*	na	—	—	50.7*	5.4*
Hides/skins	—	2.1[1]	—	0.1[2]	0.6	1.1[2]a

a million $ U.S. *d* no. in thousands.

6. FIBRES, TEXTILES, etc.

	Production 1963–5	Production 1953–5	Exports 1963–5	Exports 1953–5	Imports 1963–5	Imports 1953–5
Agaves (sisal etc.)	0.7*	na	0.1	—	—	—
Cotton lint	2.0*	na	0.6	—	—	0.5
Rubber, natural	—	—	—	—	0.1[2]	—
Silk *f*	—	—	—	—	257.0[1]	27.7
Cotton: yarn	—	—	—	—	0.6[1]	—
woven fabrics	1.0[1]	0.3[2]	—	—	5.4[2]	2.1

f metric tons.

7. FUEL AND POWER

	Production 1963–5	Production 1953–5	Exports 1963–5	Exports 1953–5	Imports 1963–5	Imports 1953–5
Electricity *h*: total	485	190[1]				
hydro	51	—				
thermal	434	190[1]				
Petroleum, refined	—	—	—	—	437	300[1]

h million kWh.

8. IRON AND STEEL

	Production 1963–5	Production 1953–5	Exports 1963–5	Exports 1953–5	Imports 1963–5	Imports 1953–5
Iron ore	—	68m	2	96	—	—

m metal content.

9. NON-FERROUS MINERALS AND METALS

	Production 1963–5	Production 1953–5	Exports 1963–5	Exports 1953–5	Imports 1963–5	Imports 1953–5
Gold	na	na	na	na	—	—
Aluminium, bauxite	825.03	—	1 003.31	—	—	—
Copper	—	—	—	—	—	na

11. INDUSTRY

	Production 1963–5	Production 1953–5	Exports 1963–5	Exports 1953–5	Imports 1963–5	Imports 1953–5
Alcoholic beverages			—	—	2.3[2]a	0.9a
beer *b*	263.0	77.1				
Cement	244.7	177.0	13.3	36.0	2.0	1.7
Electrical engineering *a*	—	—	—	—	9.9	6.2[2]
Motor vehicles *a*	—	—	—	—	11.6	4.7[2]

a million $ U.S. *b* '000 hectolitres.

ECUADOR

SOUTH AMERICA

The Republic of Ecuador has always enjoyed democratic civilian government apart from a military junta which took over from 1963–6. The chief economic problems of the country arise from a lack of mineral resources and slow industrial development, and from the dependence for revenue on tropical crops liable to price fluctuations. Data for the Archipiélago de Colón (Galapagos Islands) are included with Ecuador.

AREA: 455 454* sq. km. (175 851* sq. miles)

LAND USE: (percentage of total)

	1961	*1953*
Arable and orchard	10.7	5.9
Permanent meadow and pasture	8.1	8.1
Forest and woodland	54.9	61.0
City areas, waste and other land	26.3	25.0

POPULATION: 5 508 000 (1967 estimate)

Largest city: GUAYAQUIL; population: 651 542 (city proper, 1965)
Capital city: QUITO; population: 401 811 (city proper, 1965)

Distribution of working population (1962)
Total working population: 1 442 590 (excl. Indian jungle population)

U.N. group no.		*Percentage*
0	Agriculture, forestry, fishing and hunting	55.6
1	Mining and quarrying	0.3
2/3	Manufacturing	14.6
4	Construction	3.3
5	Electricity, gas, water and sanitary services	0.3
6	Commerce	6.7
7	Transport, storage and communications	3.0
8	Services	13.2
9	Others	3.0

		Year(s)
Infant mortality (per '000)	93*	1965
Crude birth rate (per '000)	48.5*	1960–5 av.
Crude death rate (per '000)	14*	1960–5 av.
Accidental deaths (per 100 000 population)		
caused by motor vehicles	8.8*	1965
due to other causes	40.2*	1965
Population per physician	5 290	1964
Population per hospital bed	420	1966
School enrolment: age 5–19 years (percentage)	59	1963–4 av.
age over 19 years (per 100 000 population)	168	1963–5 av.

COMMUNICATIONS

		Year(s)
Motor vehicles in use ('000s): private	14.9 }	1963–5 av.
commercial	20.0 }	
Railway track (km.)	1 340	1964
Telephones (per '000 urban population)	0.8*	1967
Radio receivers (per '000 population)	104	1963–5 av.
Television sets (per '000 population)	6	1963–5 av.
Daily newspapers (per '000 population)	52	1962

FINANCE

Currency unit: The sucre

Exchange rates	*1965*	*1960*	*1950*	*1938*
Per $ U.S.	18.18	15.15	15.15	14.4
Per £ sterling	50.9	42.49	42.44	66.24

		Year(s)
National Income (million $ U.S.)	945	1965
G.N.P. per capita ($ U.S.)	190	1966
Rate of increase of G.N.P. per capita	0.8	1960–4 av.
Foreign trade (percentage of G.D.P.)	27	1963–4 av.

continued

TRADING

Total trade (in million $ U.S.)	*1965*	*1955*	*1938*
Exports (f.o.b.)	178a	114	9
Imports (c.i.f.)	152a	95	11

Main trading partners (percentage of total value)

Exports	*1965*	*1955*	*Imports*	*1965*	*1955*
U.S.A.	59	61	U.S.A.	41	52
Germany F.R.	14	9	Germany F.R.	12	11
Belg./Lux.	4	4	Venezuela	7	—
Colombia	4	7	Japan	6	1
Netherlands	4	1	U.K.	5	6
Italy	3	3	Sweden	3	2
France	2	2	Colombia	3	1

Distribution of trade (percentage of total value)

	1965	*1955**	*1930**
Exports			
Bananas	62	41	4
Coffee	14	26	17
Cocoa	10	21	34
Sugar	4	na	na
Imports			
Manufactured goods	63	67	na
(machinery and transport equipment)	(32)	(32)	na
Chemicals	14	10	na
Crude materials and fuels	8	7	na
Food	8	12	na

a based on export and import permits granted.

PRODUCTION, EXPORTS AND IMPORTS

Years: **1963–5 average** and *1953–5 average* Units: '000 metric tons unless otherwise indicated

1. CEREALS, etc.

	Production 1963–5	Production 1953–5	Exports 1963–5	Exports 1953–5	Imports 1963–5	Imports 1953–5
Barley	101.3	86.3	—	—[2]	—	1.5[1]
Cassava	217.3	na				
Maize (corn)	170.7	123.0	0.6	0.1[2]	—	—
Oats	2.0*	3.0	—	—	3.4	1.9[1]
Potatoes	311.7	na	—	—	—	0.1[2]
Rice	171.2	113.0*[1]	14.8	24.3	1.8	—
Rye	1.7	3.3	—	—	—	—
Sweet potatoes/yams	13.7	76.0[2]				
Wheat	65.7	32.7	—	—	45.2	48.9*

2. FRUIT, etc.

	Production 1963–5	Production 1953–5	Exports 1963–5	Exports 1953–5	Imports 1963–5	Imports 1953–5
Apples	2.7	na	—	—	0.6[2]n	—
Bananas	2 899.3	na	1 286.7*	504.3	—	—
Coconuts *e*	15.7	na	—	—	—	—
Grapes	—	—	—	—	0.2	0.1[1]
Lemons	21.3	na	—	—	—	—
Oranges	162.0	39.0*	1.9	2.8[2]	—	—
Other citrus fruit	3.5[2]	na	—	—	—	—
Peaches	4.7	na	—	—	—	—
Pineapples	57.3	na	—	—	—	—
Raisins	—	—	—	—	0.2	0.2*
Tomatoes	67.7	na				
Wine	—	—	—	—	2.8	2.5[2]

b '000 hectolitres. *e* no. in millions. *n* incl. pears and quince.

3. BEVERAGES, FOREST PRODUCTS, etc.

	Production 1963–5	Production 1953–5	Exports 1963–5	Exports 1953–5	Imports 1963–5	Imports 1953–5
Cocoa	43.2	26.4*	34.5	25.6	—	—
Coffee	53.0	27.3*	33.9	20.8	—	—
Sugar: cane	7 416.3	1 808.5[2]				
raw	168.1p	62.3p	61.7	4.6*	—	9.2*
Tobacco: leaf	1.7	1.9[2]	—	—	0.4	—
cigars	1.0e	8.5e	—	—	na	na
cigarettes	752.0e	730.0e	—	—	0.9[2]	0.4[1]
Softwood *j*	2.7	—	—[2]	—	—[2]	—[2]
Hardwood *j*	2 489.0	1 191.0[2]	14.0[2]	18.0[2]	—[2]	—[2]
Newsprint	—*	—	—	—	9.9[2]	3.4[1]
Other paper	3.3*	—	—	—	12.2[2]	1.7[1]

e no. in millions. *j* '000 cu. metres of roundwood equivalent. *p* in addition, panella **36*** (1963–5) and *26** (1953–5)

4. VEGETABLE OILSEEDS AND OILS

	Production 1963–5	Production 1953–5	Exports 1963–5	Exports 1953–5	Imports 1963–5	Imports 1953–5
Castor seed	21.06	16.26	21.43	8.30	—	—
Castor oil	na	na	—	—	—	na
Copra	3.67*	3.70[1]	—	—	—	—
Coconut oil	na	na	—	—	0.37	0.04[2]
Cottonseed	9.00	4.70*	—	—	—	—
Cottonseed oil	na	na	—	—	0.72[2]*	0.18[1]
Groundnuts	7.93	4.55[2]	0.04	—	—	—
Linseed oil	—	—	—	—	0.04	0.05[1]
Olive oil	—	—	—	—	0.28	0.07[2]
Palm kernels	7.00*	6.90[1]	—	—	—	—
Palm oil	1.30*	na	—	—	1.16	—[2]
Sesame seed	1.10	na	—	—	—	—
Soya bean oil	—	—	—	—	6.83	0.01*
Tung oil	—	—	—	—	0.01	na

5. LIVESTOCK‡, ANIMAL PRODUCTS, etc.

	Production 1963–5	Production 1953–5	Exports 1963–5	Exports 1953–5	Imports 1963–5	Imports 1953–5
Chickens *d*	5 037.0	950.0*				
Cattle *d*	1 900.0*	na	1.9	—	0.1[2]	—
Goats *d* }	164.0	na	—	—	2.2	na
Sheep *d* }	1 681.0	na				
Horses *d*	226.0	na				
Pigs *d*	1 182.0	na	—	—	—	—
Meat‡: 'A'	72.7*	33.0[1]	—	—	—	—
'B'	4.1*	na	—	—	—	—
Eggs	18.1*	na	—	—	—	—
Fish	50.0	12.2	8.6	na	0.3	1.4[1]*
Milk	395.3	na	—	—	13.6	6.3[2]
Hides/skins	na	na	—	—	—	—
Wool	0.6[2]	na	—	—	0.1	—

d no. in thousands.

6. FIBRES, TEXTILES, etc.

	Production 1963–5	Production 1953–5	Exports 1963–5	Exports 1953–5	Imports 1963–5	Imports 1953–5
Cotton lint	5.0	2.7*	—	—	1.4	1.0[2]
Rubber, natural	—	—	—	—	0.9	—
Cotton: yarn	0.8[1]	0.4[2]*	—	—	0.1[1]	na
woven fabrics	3.3	2.2	—	—	1.4	na
Wool, yarn	0.2[1]	na	—	—	—	—

7. FUEL AND POWER

	Production 1963–5	Production 1953–5	Exports 1963–5	Exports 1953–5	Imports 1963–5	Imports 1953–5
Electricity *h*: total	539	180[1]				
hydro	245	120[1]				
thermal	294	60[1]				
Natural gas	na	na	—	—	—	—
Oil, crude	370	480[1]	50	179*	337	—
Petroleum, refined	640	270[1]	—	—	23	10[1]

h million kWh.

9. NON-FERROUS MINERALS AND METALS

	Production 1963–5	Production 1953–5	Exports 1963–5	Exports 1953–5	Imports 1963–5	Imports 1953–5
Gold *k*, ore *m*	17.00	21.00	na	18.70	—	—
Silver *k*, ore *m*	103.00	56.70	47.67	na	—	—
Asbestos: fibre	—	—	—	—	0.68	0.04
manufactured	—	—	—	—	0.43	0.07
Aluminium	—	—	—	—	1.50	0.50
Copper, ore *m*	0.21	0.01	—	—	—	—
Lead: ore	0.15m	0.36m	1.41	0.17	—	—
metal	—	—	—	—	0.31	0.15
Zinc, ore	0.33	—	—	—	—	—

k '000 fine troy oz. *m* metal content.

10. CHEMICALS *n* AND FERTILIZERS

	Production 1963–5	Production 1953–5	Exports 1963–5	Exports 1953–5	Imports 1963–5	Imports 1953–5
Chemicals	—		—		na	
Fertilizers:						
Sulphur	0.2p	0.6p	—	1.6p	0.1	0.1

n data not available for years 1953–5. *p* native sulphur.

11. INDUSTRY

	Production 1963–5	Production 1953–5	Exports 1963–5	Exports 1953–5	Imports 1963–5	Imports 1953–5
Beer *b*	382.0	528.7	—	—	—	—
Cement	290.3	111.3	—	—	2.0	6.3
Electrical engineering *a*	—	—	—	—	7.5[2]	5.0[1]
Motor vehicles *a*	—	—	—	—	5.8[2]	5.3[1]

a million $ U.S. *b* '000 hectolitres.

na: data not available. — negligible or nil. [1] one year only. [2] two year average. * estimate. ‡ see appendix. † re-exports.

EL SALVADOR

CENTRAL AMERICA

The Republic of El Salvador suffered for several years frequent changes of leadership, but following elections in 1962 a more stable government was formed. Some progress has recently been made towards industrialization.

AREA: 21 393 sq. km. (8 236 sq. miles)

LAND USE: (percentage of total)	*1961*	*1950*
Arable and orchard	30.3	25.4
Permanent meadow and pasture	28.2	32.9
Forest and woodland	23.7	33.7
City areas, waste and other land	17.8	8.0

POPULATION: 3 151 000 (1967 estimate)

Largest city: SAN SALVADOR, capital; population: 315 570 (city proper, 1966)

Distribution of working population (1961)
Total working population: 807 092

U.N. group no.		*Percentage*
0	Agriculture, forestry, fishing and hunting	60.3
1	Mining and quarrying	0.1
2/3	Manufacturing	12.8
4	Construction	4.1
5	Electricity, gas, water and sanitary services	0.2
6	Commerce	6.4
7	Transport, storage and communications	2.2
8	Services	13.0
9	Others	0.9

		Year(s)
Life expectancy at birth (years): male	56.6	1960–1 av.
female	60.4	1960–1 av.
Infant mortality (per '000)	62	1966
Crude birth rate (per '000)	48*	1960–5 av.
Crude death rate (per '000)	15*	1960–5 av.
Population per physician	4 320	1964
Population per hospital bed	460	1966
School enrolment: age 5–19 years (percentage)	55	1963–4 av.
age over 19 years (per 100 000 population)	127	1963–5 av.

COMMUNICATIONS		*Year(s)*
Motor vehicles in use ('000s): private	24.1	1963–5 av.
commercial	10.8	1963–5 av.
Railway track (km.)	755	1965
Mail per capita: domestic	2	1963–5 av.
foreign received	2	1963–5 av.
foreign sent	1	1963–5 av.
Telephones (per '000 urban population)	1	1967
Radio receivers (per '000 population)	137	1963–5 av.
Television sets (per '000 population)	11.3	1963–5 av.
Daily newspapers (per '000 population)	49*	1961

FINANCE

Currency unit: The colon

Exchange rates	*1965*	*1960*	*1950a*	*1938a*
Per $ U.S.	2.5	2.5	2.503	2.502
Per £ sterling	7.0	7.0	7.008	11.509

		Year(s)
National Income (million $ U.S.)	692	1965
G.N.P. per capita ($ U.S.)	270	1966
Foreign trade (percentage of G.D.P.)	48	1963–5 av.

a selling rate.

TRADING

Total trade (in million $ U.S.)	*1965*	*1955*	*1938*
Exports (f.o.b.)	189	107	10
Imports (c.i.f.)	210	92	9

Main trading partners (percentage of total value)

Exports	*1965*	*1955*	*Imports*	*1965*	*1955*
U.S.A.	25	64	U.S.A.	31	57
Germany F.R.	23	17	Guatemala	9	2
Japan	16	4	Japan	9	3
Guatemala	11	1	Germany F.R.	8	8
Honduras	7	2	Honduras	8	4
Nicaragua	3	1	Netherlands	4	5
Netherlands	3	3	U.K.	4	3

Distribution of trade (percentage of total value)

Exports	*1965*	*1955*
Coffee	51	86
Cotton and textiles	25	9
Imports		
Manufactured goods	60	61
(machinery and transport equipment)	(27)	(22)
Chemicals	17	13
Food	14	15

PRODUCTION, EXPORTS AND IMPORTS

Years: **1963–5 average** and *1953–5 average* Units: '000 metric tons unless otherwise indicated

	Production 1963–5	Production 1953–5	Exports 1963–5	Exports 1953–5	Imports 1963–5	Imports 1953–5
1. CEREALS, etc.						
Cassava	8.0*	na				
Maize (corn)	197.3	171.3	1.2	0.2	39.6	13.7
Millets/sorghum	112.3	117.0	1.1[2]	—	1.5[2]	—
Potatoes	4.0*	3.0[1]*	1.2	0.1	2.2	0.7
Rice	31.7	17.7	2.8	1.1	1.7	4.3
Wheat	—	—	0.3	—	43.6	3.3
2. FRUIT, etc. *n*						
Apples	na	na	0.1	—	—	—
Bananas	na	na	0.6	—	—	—
Coconuts	na	na	0.6[2]	—	—	—
Oranges	na	na	0.7[2]	—	—	—
Wine *b*	na	na	0.2	—	1.2	4.7

b '000 hectolitres. *n* no production figures are available, but quantities are known to be small.

	Production 1963–5	Production 1953–5	Exports 1963–5	Exports 1953–5	Imports 1963–5	Imports 1953–5
3. BEVERAGES, FOREST PRODUCTS, etc.						
Cocoa	—	—	—	—	0.4	0.2
Coffee	117.8*	69.5*	103.4	66.6	—	—
Sugar: cane	966.0	268.3*p*				
raw	78.7	34.7**q*	17.7	1.4	—	—
Tobacco: leaf	1.2*	0.8*	—	0.1	1.5	1.7
cigarettes	1 130.0*e*	762.7*e*	—	—	0.3*t*	0.6[2]*t*
Softwood *j*	90.0[1]*	21.0[1]	—	—	96.1[2]	53.7
Hardwood *j*	2 870.0[1]*	1 053.5[2]	—[2]	—	—[2]	—
Newsprint	—[2]*	—	—	—	5.9[1]	3.3
Other paper	0.4[2]*	—	—	—	13.7[1]	6.0

e no. in millions. *j* '000 cu. metres of roundwood equivalent. *p* for centrifugal sugar only. *q* in addition, non-centrifugal sugar **22** (1963–5) and *17** (1953–5) *t* incl. other tobacco products.

	Production 1963–5	Production 1953–5	Exports 1963–5	Exports 1953–5	Imports 1963–5	Imports 1953–5
4. VEGETABLE OILSEEDS AND OILS						
Castor seed	na	—	0.02	—	—	—
Castor oil	—	—	—	0.01	0.01	0.04
Coconut oil	na	—	0.55	—	—	0.04
Cottonseed	142.70*	34.30	11.04	—	0.07	—
Cottonseed oil	na	na	3.30	0.94	0.96	0.04
Groundnuts	na	—	0.09	—	0.01	—
Linseed	—	—	—	—	0.01	—
Linseed oil	—	—	—	—	0.07	0.05
Olive oil	—	—	—	—	0.04	0.03
Sesame seed	0.83*	3.15[2]	0.97	2.13	—	0.23
Soya bean oil	—	—	—	—	0.02	—
5. LIVESTOCK‡, ANIMAL PRODUCTS, etc.						
Chickens *d*	1 933.3*	1 972.0				
Cattle *d*	919.0	803.3	16.8	28.3	9.3	24.2
dairy cows *d*	342.7*	na				
Goats *d*	15.0*	15.0	—	—	—	—
Sheep *d*	3.0*	5.3				
Horses *d*	74.0*	90.0				
Pigs *d*	323.0*	288.3	3.5*	—	41.2	41.2
Meat‡ 'A'	44.0*	9.5[2] *r*	—	—	—	—
Butter	—	—	—	—	—	0.1
Cheese	—	—	—	—	0.6	0.2
Eggs	3.6*	na	—	0.3	0.2	—
Fish	7.2	na	3.8	na	1.5	0.8*
Milk	220.3*	180.5[2]	—[2]	—	44.0	7.2*
Hides/skins	na	2.0[1]	—	—	0.3[2]	—

d no. in thousands. *r* incl. meat equivalent of live imports.

continued

na: data not available. — negligible or nil. [1] one year only. [2] two year average. * estimate. ‡ see appendix. † re-exports.

PRODUCTION, EXPORTS AND IMPORTS *continued*

	Production 1963–5	Production 1953–5	Exports 1963–5	Exports 1953–5	Imports 1963–5	Imports 1953–5
6. FIBRES, TEXTILES, etc.						
Agaves (letona)	2.9*	1.4*	0.4[2]	0.1	—	—
Cotton lint	78.3*	21.3	67.5	9.8	0.2	0.8
Rubber, natural	—	—	—	—	0.4	0.3
Cotton: yarn	3.7	0.6	1.3[2]	—	0.2[1]	—
woven fabrics	4.4	1.5	1.0[1]	—	1.8	—
Rayon, woven fabrics	—	—	—	—	0.7	—
7. FUEL AND POWER						
Coal, 'A'‡	—	—	—	—	—	1
Electricity *h*: total	379	140[1]				
hydro	340	130[1]				
thermal	39	10[1]				
Oil, crude	—	—	—	—	423	na
Petroleum, refined	423	—	193	—	60	150[1]

h million kWh.

	Production 1963–5	Production 1953–5	Exports 1963–5	Exports 1953–5	Imports 1963–5	Imports 1953–5
8. IRON AND STEEL						
Steel ingots/castings	—	—	—	—	2	1
9. NON-FERROUS MINERALS AND METALS						
Gold *k*, ore	na	10.00*m*	na	9.00*n*	—	—
Silver *k*, ore *m*	—	278.40*	4.80*n*	259.33*n*	—	—
Asbestos: fibre	—	—	—	—	0.82	0.45
manufactured	—	—	—	—	0.11	0.07
Aluminium	—	—	—	—	0.28	—
Copper, metal	—	—	—	—	0.53	—
Lead, metal	—	—	—	—	0.22	—

k '000 fine troy oz. *m* metal content. *n* bullion.

	Production 1963–5	Production 1953–5	Exports 1963–5	Exports 1953–5	Imports 1963–5	Imports 1953–5
10. CHEMICALS *n* **AND FERTILIZERS**						
Chemicals	—		—		na	
Fertilizers:						
Potash	—	—	—	—	1.8	—
Sulphur	—	—	—	—	1.2	0.1

n data not available for years 1953–5.

	Production 1963–5	Production 1953–5	Exports 1963–5	Exports 1953–5	Imports 1963–5	Imports 1953–5
11. INDUSTRY						
Aircraft *a*	—	—	—	—	0.7	—
Alcoholic beverages			—	—	0.5*a*	0.7*a*
beer *b*	133.0	—				
Cement	83.0	46.0	3.7	2.0	59.3	32.3
Electrical engineering *a*	—	—	0.7	0.1[2]	9.9	4.0[2]
Railway vehicles *a*	—	—	—	—	0.1	—
Motor vehicles *a*	—	—	—	—	13.6	7.4[2]

a million $ U.S. *b* '000 hectolitres.

EQUATORIAL GUINEA

WEST AFRICA

Equatorial Guinea, formerly Spanish Guinea, consists of the mainland territory Rio Muni and the island of Fernando Póo together with some smaller islands. A referendum in 1963 resulted in internal self-government, and complete independence from Spain followed in 1968.

AREA: Rio Muni: 26 017 sq. km. (10 045 sq. miles)
Fernando Póo: 2 034 sq. km. (785 sq. miles)

LAND USE: (percentage of total)	*1963*
Arable and orchard	7.9
Permanent meadow and pasture	3.7
Forest and woodland	81.6
City areas, waste and other land	6.8

POPULATION: Rio Muni: 201 000; Fernando Póo: 76 000 (1967 provisional estimates)

Largest city: SANTA ISABEL, capital; population: 37 237 (city proper, 1960)

		Year(s)
Infant mortality (per '000)	28.1	1965
Crude birth rate (per '000)	22.8	1965
Crude death rate (per '000)	6.3	1965
Accidental deaths (per 100 000 population)	32.5	1965
Population per physician	5 900	1961
Population per hospital bed	160	1965
School enrolment: age 5–19 years (percentage)	44	1963–4 av.

EMPLOYMENT AND TRADE

In Rio Muni, a mountainous jungle area, cocoa and coffee are grown; timber, for veneer, is the only industry. Fernando Póo is also mountainous, with forests of oil palms, ebony, mahogany and oak, and cultivated areas producing cocoa and some coffee, sugar, tobacco and vanilla. Exports are almost entirely to Spain, and in 1965 included (in percentages of total value) cacao 32, coffee 15 and wood 13; chief imports were rice 29 and oil products 26.

Total trade (in million $ U.S.)	*1964*
Exports (f.o.b.)	33
Imports (c.i.f.)	15

PRODUCTION, EXPORTS AND IMPORTS

Years: **1963–5 average** and *1953–5 average* Units: '000 metric tons unless otherwise indicated

	Production 1963–5	Production 1953–5	Exports 1963–5	Exports 1953–5	Imports 1963–5	Imports 1953–5
1. CEREALS, etc.						
Cassava	39.3	na				
Rice	—	—	—	—	—	4.8[2]
Sweet potatoes/yams	25.0*	na				
2. FRUIT, etc.						
Bananas	12.0*	na	na	2.4[2]	—	—
Coconuts *e*	6.0[1]*	na	—	—	—	—
Wine *b*	—	—	—	—	na	69.7

b '000 hectolitres. *e* no. in millions.

	Production 1963–5	Production 1953–5	Exports 1963–5	Exports 1953–5	Imports 1963–5	Imports 1953–5
3. BEVERAGES, FOREST PRODUCTS, etc.						
Cocoa *n*	32.3	21.6*	32.0*	17.1	—	—
Coffee	6.6	5.1	6.7*	5.3	—	—
Hardwood *j*	760.7*	140.5[2]	—	9.4[1]	—	—

j '000 cu. metres of roundwood equivalent. *n* mainly from Fernando Póo.

	Production 1963–5	Production 1953–5	Exports 1963–5	Exports 1953–5	Imports 1963–5	Imports 1953–5
4. VEGETABLE OILSEEDS AND OILS						
Copra	na	na	na	na	—	—
Olive oil	—	—	—	—	0.43[1]	0.25
Palm kernels	2.73*	na	na	3.37	—	—
Palm oil	3.37	na	3.04	2.58	na	0.22
5. LIVESTOCK‡, ANIMAL PRODUCTS, etc.						
Cattle *d*	2.3	na	—	—	—	—
Goats *d*	5.0*	na	—	—	—	—
Sheep *d*	25.7*	na	—	—	—	—
Pigs *d*	4.0*	na	—	—	—	—
Eggs	0.4*	na	—	—	—	—
Fish	0.9*	—[1]	—[2]	—	1.2[2]	na

d no. in thousands.

	Production 1963–5	Production 1953–5	Exports 1963–5	Exports 1953–5	Imports 1963–5	Imports 1953–5
6. FIBRES, TEXTILES, etc.						
Abaca	0.5	na	0.2[1]	na	—	—
7. FUEL AND POWER						
Petroleum, refined	—	—	—	—	25[2]	na

na: data not available. — negligible or nil. [1] one year only. [2] two year average. * estimate. ‡ see appendix. † re-exports.

ETHIOPIA

EAST AFRICA

Ethiopia, the ancient empire of Abyssinia, was conquered by the Italians in 1936 but liberated five years later. The adjacent Italian colony of Eritrea was federated to Ethiopia in 1952, and in 1962 was incorporated as a province. Data for Eritrea are included in the following.

AREA: 1 023 000 sq. km. (395 000 sq. miles)

LAND USE: (percentage of total)	*1965*	*1954*
Arable and orchard	10.3	9.7
Permanent meadow and pasture	56.4	49.6
Forest and woodland	7.3	3.5
City areas, waste and other land	26.0	37.2

POPULATION: 23 457 000 (1967 estimate)

Largest city: ADDIS ABABA, capital; population: 560 000 (city proper, 1965)

		Year(s)
Population per physician	68 520	1964
Population per hospital bed	2 470	1966
School enrolment: age 5–19 years (percentage)	6	1963–4 av.
age over 19 years (per 100 000 population)	8	1963–5 av.

EMPLOYMENT AND PRODUCTION

Ethiopia is a mountainous country; the majority of the population avoids the valleys, because of their excessive heat; however some cane sugar and cotton are grown in these lower regions. On the higher land coffee and grain are produced, and livestock are reared by the nomadic population. The forests provide potential wealth in hardwood, and exploitation of them is increasing. Mineral wealth is as yet unproven, but some salt, potash and gold are mined. With financial assistance from the World Bank, hydro-electric power is being developed, but industry is still small.

COMMUNICATIONS

		Year(s)
Motor vehicles in use ('000s): private	19.8 }	1963–5 av.
commercial	7 }	
Railway track (km.)	1 015	1965
Telephones (per '000 urban population)	0.1	1967
Radio receivers (per '000 population)	11	1963–5 av.
Television sets (per '000 population)	0.1	1963–5 av.
Daily newspapers (per '000 population)	1.5	1963–4 av.

FINANCE

Currency unit: The Ethiopian dollar

Exchange rates	*1965*	*1960*	*1950*
Per $ U.S.	2.5	2.48	2.48
Per £ sterling	7.0	6.96	6.96

		Year(s)
National Income (million $ U.S.)	942	1965
G.N.P. per capita ($ U.S.)	60	1966
Foreign trade (percentage of G.D.P.)	19	1963–5 av.

TRADING

Total trade (in million $ U.S.)	*1965*	*1955*
Exports (f.o.b.)	117	62
Imports (c.i.f.)	151	65

Main trading partners (percentage of total value)

Exports	*1965*	*1955*	*Imports*	*1965*	*1955*
U.S.A.	55	24	Italy	18	16
Italy	7	17	Japan	15	8
Saudi Arabia	5	na	U.S.A.	12	14
Germany F.R.	4	1	Germany F.R.	11	8
U.K.	4	4	U.K.	9	10
France	3	1	France	5	8
Afars/Issas	3	14	Iran	4	—

Distribution of trade (percentage of total value)

Exports	*1965*	*1955**
Coffee	67	56
Hides and skins	8	10
Oilseeds	8	10
Fruit and vegetables	7	na
Imports		
Manufactured goods	74	na
(machinery and transport equipment)	(37)	(20)
(textiles)	(12)	(28)
Crude materials and fuels	11	9
Chemicals	7	2
Food	5	3

PRODUCTION, EXPORTS AND IMPORTS

Years: **1963–5 average** and *1953–5 average* Units: '000 metric tons unless otherwise indicated

	Production		Exports		Imports	
1. CEREALS, etc.						
Barley	**785.0**	*633.0**	**0.1**	*1.0*	—	—
Maize (corn)	**713.0**	*170.0**	**1.3**	*6.5*	—	—
Millets/sorghum	**3 011.3**	*1 876.0**	**1.5**	*8.8*	**0.1**	*0.1*
Oats	**5.0^{1}***	na	—	—	—	—
Potatoes	**138.0**	*4.0**	**2.0^{2}**	*0.1*	—	—
Rice	—	—	—	—	**2.1**	*0.9*
Sweet potatoes/ yams	**68.0***	*25.0^{2}**				
Wheat	**279.0**	*188.0**	—	*3.4*	**2.2**	—
2. FRUIT, etc.						
Bananas	**35.0***	*21.5**	**12.7**	—	—	—
Dates	—	—	—	—	**1.4***	*1.0*
Lemons	**2.0***	*1.0*	—	—	—	—
Oranges	**63.0**	*10.0**	**0.4**	—	**0.1**	—
Raisins	—	—	—	—	**0.4^{1}**	*0.4*
Tomatoes	**9.0***	—				
Wine *b*	—	—	—	—	**1.5^{2}**	*1.7*

b '000 hectolitres.

	Production		Exports		Imports	
3. BEVERAGES, FOREST PRODUCTS, etc.						
Coffee	**136.0**	*46.8**	**73.0**	*40.7*	—	—
Sugar: cane	**750.0**	na				
raw	**69.2**	*11.7*	**7.5**	—	**0.8^{2}**	*18.4*
Tea	—	—	—	—	**0.6**	*0.4*
Tobacco: leaf	**1.4**	*1.5**	**0.3^{2}**	—	—	*0.1*
cigarettes	**404.0*e***	*111.5e*	—	—	**0.2*n***	—
Softwood *j*	**1 083.7***	na	—	*0.3*	**0.5**	*1.7^{1}*
Hardwood *j*	**22 545.7***	na	—	$—^{1}$	**0.1^{2}**	$—^{1}$
Wood pulp	—	—	—	—	**0.3**	—
Newsprint	**—***	—	—	$—^{1}$	**4.9*** }	*0.2^{1}*
Other paper	**0.4***	—	—	$—^{1}$	}	na

e no. in millions. *j* '000 cu. metres of roundwood equivalent. *n* incl. other tobacco products.

	Production		Exports		Imports	
4. VEGETABLE OILSEEDS AND OILS						
Castor seed	**10.67**	*11.89*	**6.16**	*4.40*	—	—
Cottonseed	**10.70**	*7.50*	**4.63***	na	—	—
Cottonseed oil	na	na	—	—	**0.13**	—
Groundnuts	**12.60**	*15.05*	**4.43^{2}**	*2.20*	—	—
Linseed	**54.00**	*52.00q*	**29.16**	*17.93*	—	—

continued

	Production		Exports		Imports	
4. VEGETABLE OILSEEDS AND OILS—*continued*						
Olive oil	—	—	—	—	**0.04**	na
Rapeseed	**5.00***	*20.00**	**1.83^{2}**	*5.27*	—	—
Sesame seed	**31.67**	*38.40*	**11.63***	*13.07*	—	—
Soya beans	**6.00***	*5.00**	—	—	—	—
Sunflower seed	**29.00***	*10.00**	**0.69**	—	—	—
Tung oil	—	—	—	—	**0.02**	—

q flax grown for seed only.

	Production		Exports		Imports	
5. LIVESTOCK‡, ANIMAL PRODUCTS, etc.						
Chickens *d*	**41 700.0*n**	na				
Cattle *d*	**25 290.3**	*21 250.0**	**8.0^{2}**	*5.0*	—	—
dairy cows *d*	**7 734.3***	na				
Goats *d*	**18 006.0**	*14 205.0** }	**14.2**	na	—	—
Sheep *d*	**24 611.0**	*18 900.0** }				
Horses *d*	**1 331.0**	*1 002.0**				
Pigs *d*	**12.0***	*12.0**	**0.3***	*0.5*	—	—
Meat‡: 'A'	**310.7** }	*411.0**	{ **3.0**	—	—	—
'B'	**53.4** }		{ —	—	—	—
Butter	**35.7***	*$2.0^{2}p$*	**0.1^{2}**	*0.2*	**1.2**	*0.1*
Cheese	—	—	—	—	**$0.1^{2}q$**	—
Eggs	**73.5**	*$50.0^{2}q$*	**0.4^{2}**	*0.1q*	—	—
Fish	**$8.9^{1}r$**	*$5.6^{2}r$*	**2.1^{2}**	na	**0.2^{2}**	na
Milk	**1 517.3***	*1 601.0*	—	—	**10.2**	*0.7**
Hides/skins	**$9.7^{1}q$**	*$1.6^{2}p$*	**9.3*a***	*11.8^{2}*	—	—
Wool	**0.2**	na	—	—	—	—

a million $U.S. *d* no. in thousands. *n* incl. ducks, geese and turkeys. *p* Eritrea only. *q* excl. Eritrea. *r* incl. fish landed by foreign vessels.

	Production		Exports		Imports	
6. FIBRES, TEXTILES, etc.						
Agaves (sisal)	**1.0***	*0.2q*	—	—	—	—
Cotton lint	**5.0**	*2.5^{2}*	—	*0.6*	**5.1**	*2.5*
Jute	—	—	—	—	**0.6**	—
Cotton: yarn	**8.3**	na	—	—	**0.8^{1}**	—
woven fabrics	**6.1**	*0.8*	—	—	**2.6^{1}**	—

q excl. Eritrea.

	Production		Exports		Imports	
7. FUEL AND POWER						
Coal 'A'‡	—	—	—	—	**5^{2}**	*10*
Electricity *h*: total	**208**	*50*				
hydro	**153**	*20^{1}*				
thermal	**55**	*30*				
Petroleum, refined	—	—	—	—	**167**	*70^{1}*

h million kWh.

continued

PRODUCTION, EXPORTS AND IMPORTS *continued*

	Production		Exports		Imports	
9. NON-FERROUS MINERALS AND METALS						
Gold *k*, ore *m*	**26.00**	*28.00*	na	na	na	na
Asbestos	na	na	—	—	—	—
Platinum group metals *k*	**0.24***	*0.38**	—	na	—	—
Manganese, ore	na	—	—	—	—	—

k '000 fine troy oz. *m* metal content.

	Production		Exports		Imports	
10. CHEMICALS*n* AND FERTILIZERS						
Chemicals	—		—		na	
Fertilizers:						
Potash	na	na	—	—	—	—

n data not available for years 1953–5.

	Production		Exports		Imports	
11. INDUSTRY						
Aircraft *a*	—	—	—	—	**3.8**	*1.2p*
Alcoholic beverages			—	—	**0.7*a***	*0.4a*
beer *b*	**137.0**	*13.0*				
Cement	**64.0**	*12.3*	—	*0.3*	**30.7***	*9.0*
Electrical engineering *a*	—	—	—	—	**7.7**	*1.4^{2}*
Railway vehicles *a*	—	—	—	—	**0.8**	—
Merchant ships *g*	—	—	—	—	**3.0**	—
Motor vehicles *a*	—	—	—	—	**13.8**	*5.8^{2}*

a million $ U.S. *b* '000 hectolitres. *g* '000 G.R.T. *p* Eritrea only.

FIJI

PACIFIC OCEAN

The Fiji Islands, previously a British colony, became an independent member of the British Commonwealth in 1970. Nadi Airport provides an important link on the trans-Pacific air route.

AREA: 18 233 sq. km. (7 036 sq. miles)

LAND USE: (percentage of total)	*1960*	*1955*
Arable and orchard	16.4	8.0
Permanent meadow and pasture	44.0	51.9
Forest and woodland	38.5	40.0
City areas, waste and other land	1.1	0.1

POPULATION: 476 727 (1966 census)

Capital city: SUVA; population: 54 900 (city proper, 1966)

Distribution of working population (1956)
Total working population: 93 257

U.N. group no.		*Percentage*
0	Agriculture, forestry, fishing and hunting	57.1
1	Mining and quarrying	2.1
2/3	Manufacturing	6.8
4	Construction	6.9
5	Electricity, gas, water and sanitary services	0.8
6	Commerce	6.7
7	Transport, storage and communications	4.3
8	Services	12.3
9	Others	3.0

		Year
Infant mortality (per '000)	24.4*	1965
Crude birth rate (per '000)	35.9	1965
Crude death rate (per '000)	5.1*	1965
Population per physician	2 370	1965
Population per hospital bed	280	1966
School enrolment: age 5–19 years (percentage)	76	1963

COMMUNICATIONS

		Year(s)
Motor vehicles in use ('000s): private	6.2 }	1963–5 av.
commercial	3.4 }	
Railway track (km.)	708*a*	1965
Mail per capita: domestic	17 }	1963–5 av.
foreign received	14 }	
foreign sent	5 }	
Telephones (per '000 urban population)	2.5	1967
Radio licences (per '000 population)	71	1963–5 av.
Daily newspapers (per '000 population)	16	1962–4 av.

a private railway, owned by the Colonial Sugar Refining Company.

FINANCE

Currency unit: The Fiji dollar replaced the Fiji pound in 1969 at the rate $F1 to £F0.5

Exchange rates	*1965a*	*1960a*
Per $ U.S.	0.396	0.396
Per £ sterling	1.11	1.11

		Year
National Income (million $ U.S.)	67	1958
G.N.P. per capita ($ U.S.)	280	1966

a Fiji pounds.

TRADING

Total trade (in million $ U.S.)	*1965*	*1955*	*1938*
Exports (f.o.b.)	50	30	8
Imports (c.i.f.)	73	36	7

Main trading partners (percentage of total value)

Exports	*1965*	*1955*	*Imports*	*1965*	*1955*
U.K.	45	41	Australia	29	24
U.S.A.	13	2	U.K.	22	37
Canada	10	19	Japan	12	1
New Zealand	7	21	New Zealand	8	8
Japan	3	—	Iran	5	na
Australia	3	2	U.S.A.	4	5
Tonga	2	2	India	3	6

Distribution of trade (percentage of total value)

Exports	*1965a*	*1955a*
Sugar	77	62
Copra and coconut oil	14	28
Imports		
Manufactured goods	43	54
(machinery and transport equipment)	(22)	(18)
(textiles)	(6)	(na)
Food	21	20
Crude materials and fuels	12	13
Chemicals	8	6

a % of national exports‡ which comprised 82% of general exports in 1965 and 87% in 1955.

continued

na: data not available. — negligible or nil. [1] one year only. [2] two year average. * estimate. ‡ see appendix. † re-exports.

PRODUCTION, EXPORTS AND IMPORTS

Years: **1963–5 average** and *1953–5 average* Units: '000 metric tons unless otherwise indicated

	Production		Exports		Imports	
1. CEREALS, etc.						
Cassava	**80.0***	*51.0*				
Potatoes	—	—	—	—	**4.9**	*2.5*
Rice	**20.3**	*24.5*[2]	—	*0.1*	**6.2**	*0.6*
Sweet potatoes/ yams	**12.3***	*16.0*				
Wheat	—	—	—	—	**0.1**	—
2. FRUIT, etc.						
Apples	—	—	—	—	**0.3**	—
Bananas	na	na	**4.2**	*11.8*	—	—
Coconuts	**228.7***e	na	**0.1**	—	—	—
Oranges	—	—	—	—	**0.1**	—
Wine *b*	—	—	—	—	**0.6**	—

b '000 hectolitres. *e* no. in millions.

	Production		Exports		Imports	
3. BEVERAGES, FOREST PRODUCTS, etc.						
Sugar: cane	**2 312.0**	*1 288.0*				
raw	**311.1**	*165.2*	**300.7**	*159.4*	**0.1**	*0.2*
Tea	—	—	—	—	**0.4**	*0.3*
Tobacco: leaf	—	—	—	—	**0.3**	—
cigarettes	**294.0***e*	—	—	—	—	*2.0n*
Softwood *j*	—	—	**8.0**	*0.8*[2]	—	*30.3*[2]
Hardwood *j*	**103.7**	*76.0*[2]	**4.3**	—[2]	**1.4**	—[2]
Newsprint	—	—	—	—[2]	**0.1**[2]	—[2]
Other paper	—	—	—	—[2]	**0.5**[2]*	—[2]

e no. in millions. *j* '000 cu. metres of roundwood equivalent. *n* incl. other tobacco products.

	Production		Exports		Imports	
4. VEGETABLE OILSEEDS AND OILS						
Castor oil	—	—	—	—	**0.04**	—
Copra	**38.43**	*37.53*	**6.53**	*6.40*	**0.07**	—
Coconut oil	na	na	**19.50**	*17.57*	—	—
Groundnuts	—	—	—	*0.03*	**0.02**	—
Groundnut oil	—	—	—	—	**1.06**	*0.16*
Linseed oil	—	—	—	—	**0.03**	*0.04*
Rapeseed oil	—	—	—	—	**0.15**	*0.23*
Soya bean oil	—	—	—	—	**0.01**	na
5. LIVESTOCK‡, ANIMAL PRODUCTS, etc.						
Chickens *d*	**142.0***	na				
Cattle *d*	**113.7**	*81.0*[1]	—	—	—	—
Goats *d*	**24.0***	*24.0*[1]	—	—	**0.1**	na
Horses *d*	**16.3***	na				
Pigs *d*	**21.0**	*9.0*[1]	—	—	—	—

continued

	Production		Exports		Imports	
5. LIVESTOCK, ANIMAL PRODUCTS etc.—*continued*						
Bacon/ham } Meat‡: 'A'	**2.0**	*2.0*[1]	{ —	—	**0.1**	*0.1*
			—	—	**1.3**	*0.5*
'B'	**0.1***	na	—	—	**0.2**	*0.1*
Butter	—	—	—	—	**0.4**	*0.3*
Cheese	—	—	—	—	**0.1**	—
Eggs	**1.0**	*0.4*	—	—	—	—
Fish	na	na	**1.5**	na	**4.3**	na
Milk	**10.0***	*25.0**	—	—	**9.7**	*5.3*
Hides/skins	—	na	—	—	—	—

d no. in thousands.

	Production		Exports		Imports	
6. FIBRES, TEXTILES, etc.						
Cotton, woven fabrics	—	—	—	—	**0.8**	*0.6*
Rayon, woven fabrics	—	—	—	—	**0.5***p*	*0.3*

p incl. synthetic piece goods.

	Production		Exports		Imports	
7. FUEL AND POWER						
Coal, 'A'‡	—	—	—	—	**5**	*19*
Electricity *h t*	**91**	*10*[1]				
Petroleum, refined	—	—	**10†**	na†	**173**	*60*[1]

h million kWh. *t* thermal.

	Production		Exports		Imports	
9. NON-FERROUS MINERALS AND METALS						
Gold *k*, ore	**105.30***m*	*73.00m*	**104.98**[2]*q*	*74.29q*	**0.27‡***q*	*0.04q*
Silver *k*, ore	**56.00***m*	*19.00m*	**60.45**[2]*q*	*14.92q*	—	*0.14q*
Copper, ore	na	na	**0.01**	—	**0.07***r*	—
Lead, metal	—	—	—	—	**0.08**	*0.01*
Manganese, ore	**3.22**	*9.99*	**5.34**	*5.81*	—	—
Tin, metal	—	—	—	—	**0.28**	—

k '000 fine troy oz. *m* metal content. *q* bullion. *r* metal.

	Production		Exports		Imports	
11. INDUSTRY						
Alcoholic beverages			—	—	**0.9***au*	*0.9au*
beer *b*	**25.0**	—				
Cement *v*	**31.0**	—	—	—	**15.3***	*17.0**
Railway vehicles *a*	—	—	—	—	**0.4**	—
Motor vehicles *a*	—	—	—	—	**3.9**	*1.2*[1]

a million $ U.S. *b* '000 hectolitres. *u* beer and spirits only. *v* incl. data for Gilbert and Ellice Islands and British Solomon Islands.

FINLAND

NORTHERN EUROPE

Finland became a republic in 1919. Territorial concessions had to be made to the U.S.S.R. in 1940 and 1944, but the two countries are now linked by a treaty of non-aggression and mutual assistance.

AREA: 337 032 sq. km. (130 129 sq. miles) incl. inland water, 31 557 sq. km.

LAND USE: (percentage of total)	*1965*	*1955*
Arable and orchard	8.1	7.7
Permanent meadow and pasture	0.4	0.8
Forest and woodland	64.6	64.3
City areas, waste and other land	26.9	27.2

POPULATION: 4 664 000 (1967 estimate)

Largest city: HELSINKI capital; population: 651 988 (1965)

Distribution of working population (1960)
Total working population: 2 033 268

U.N. group no.		*Percentage*
0	Agriculture, forestry, fishing and hunting	35.5
1	Mining and quarrying	0.3
2/3	Manufacturing	21.6
4	Construction	8.7
5	Electricity, gas, water and sanitary services	0.9
6	Commerce	11.6
7	Transport, storage and communications	6.3
8	Services	14.8
9	Others	0.3

		Year(s)
Life expectancy at birth (years): male	65.4	1961–5 av.
female	72.6	1961–5 av.
Infant mortality (per '000)	17.6	1965
Crude birth rate (per '000)	16.9	1965
Crude death rate (per '000)	9.6	1965
Accidental deaths (per 100 000 population)		
caused by motor vehicles	23.3	1965
due to other causes	34.2	1965
Population per physician	1 300	1965
Population per hospital bed	90	1966
School enrolment: age 5–19 years (percentage)	81	1963–4 av.
age over 19 years (per 100 000 population)	813	1964–5 av.

COMMUNICATIONS		*Year(s)*
Motor vehicles in use ('000s): private	387.5	1963–5 av.
commercial	86.3	1963–5 av.
Railway track (km.)	5 363	1964
Mail per capita: domestic	79	1963–5 av.
foreign received	9	1963–5 av.
foreign sent	5	1963–5 av.
Telephones (per '000 urban population)	19.2	1967
Radio licences (per '000 population)	320	1963–5 av.
Television licences (per '000 population)	136.5	1963–5 av.
Daily newspapers (per '000 population)	359	1960

continued

FINANCE

Currency unit: The new markka, or Finnmark, equivalent to 100 old markkas, was introduced in 1963

Exchange rates	*1965*	*1960*	*1955*	*1938*
Per $ U.S.	3.22	320.5	230.0	48.95
Per £ sterling	9.016	898.81	644.3	225.17

		Year(s)
National Income (million $ U.S.)	6 454	1965
G.N.P. per capita ($ U.S.)	1 600	1966
Rate of increase of G.N.P. per capita	4.4	1960–4 av.
Foreign trade (percentage of G.D.P.)	38	1964–5 av.

TRADING

Total trade (in million $ U.S.)	*1965*	*1955*	*1938*
Exports (f.o.b.)*	1 428	787	181
Imports (c.i.f.)*	1 648	769	183

Main trading partners (percentage of total value)

Exports	*1965*	*1955*	*1938*	*Imports*	*1965*	*1955*	*1938*
U.K.	20	23	43	Germany F.R.	18	9	18*d*
U.S.S.R.	16	17	2	U.S.S.R.	14	11	3
Germany F.R.	11	9	15*d*	U.K.	13	17	18
Sweden	7	2	3	Sweden	13	5	11
U.S.A.	6	6	9	U.S.A.	6	6	10
Netherlands	6	4	4	France	4	5	2
France	4	5	3	Netherlands	4	4	3

Distribution of trade (percentage of total value)

Exports	*1965*	*1955*	*1938**
Wood products and paper	69	80	80
Machinery and transport equipment	12	12	na
Dairy produce and eggs	3	1	6
Textiles and clothing	3	1	1
Imports			
Manufactured goods	60	50	na
(machinery and transport equipment)	(35)	(23)	(na)
Crude materials and fuels	19	22	na
(mineral fuels)	(10)	(12)	(10)
Chemicals	10	8	4
Food	9	19	13

d incl. Germany D.R.

PRODUCTION, EXPORTS AND IMPORTS

Years: **1963–5 average** and *1953–5 average* Units: '000 metric tons unless otherwise indicated

	Production		Exports		Imports	
1. CEREALS, etc.						
Barley	**454.7**	*279.3*	—	*5.3*	**22.6**	*1.1*[2]
Maize (corn)	—	—	—	*1.8†*	**50.4**	*37.5*
Millets/sorghum	—	—	—	*1.5†*	—	—
Oats	**860.7**	*774.0*	—	*9.4*	**23.6**	*12.0*
Potatoes	**1 109.3**	*1 178.7*	—	—	—	*3.8*
Rice	—	—	—	—	**13.4**	*7.5*
Rye	**159.0**	*127.0*	**2.7**	*3.5*	**43.7***	*96.5*
Wheat	**453.7**	*214.3*	—	*8.4*	**174.9***	*240.4*
2. FRUIT, etc.						
Apples	**26.0**	*38.3*	—	—	**37.5**	*13.7*
Bananas	—	—	—	—	**14.4**	*5.1*
Dates	—	—	—	—	**0.3**	*0.3*
Grapes	—	—	—	—	**9.4**	*0.9*
Lemons	—	—	—	—	**2.8**	*1.3*
Oranges	—	—	—	—	**35.8**	*19.7*
Other citrus fruit	—	—	—	—	**1.9**	*0.7*
Pears	—	—	—	—	**5.6**	*1.4*
Raisins	—	—	—	—	**3.7**	*5.6*
Wine *b*	—	—	—	—	**56.1**	*30.7*

b '000 hectolitres.

	Production		Exports		Imports	
3. BEVERAGES, FOREST PRODUCTS, etc.						
Cocoa	—	—	—	—	**1.3**	*0.7*
Coffee	—	—	—	—	**43.2**	*26.9*
Sugar: beet	**431.3**	*289.7*				
raw	**54.1**	*31.7*	—	—	**140.4**	*129.3*
Tea	—	—	—	—	**0.5**	*0.4*
Tobacco: leaf	—	—	—	—	**6.3**	*5.0*
cigars	**29.0**	*12.3*	—	—	—	—
cigarettes *e*	**6 415.0**	*5 476.3*	—	—	—	—
tobacco/snuff	**0.8**	*0.5*	—	—	—	—
Softwood *j*	**32 556.0**	*26 166.7*	**7 458.0**	*5 896.2*	**542.7**	*13.3*
Hardwood *j*	**12 074.7**	*6 900.0**	**121.3**	*91.8*	**25.9**	*12.9*
Wood pulp	**5 243.0**	*2 362.0*	**2 056.7**	*1 150.3*	**3.7**	*0.3*
Newsprint	**1 089.7**	*479.7*	**990.7**	*421.3*	—	—
Other paper	**1 887.7**	*631.7*	**1 500.7**	*451.7*	**8.3**	*1.5*

e no. in millions. *j* '000 cu. metres of roundwood equivalent.

	Production		Exports		Imports	
4. VEGETABLE OILSEEDS AND OILS						
Castor oil	—	—	—	—	**0.09**	*0.16*
Copra	—	—	—	—	**8.71**	—
Coconut oil	na	—	**0.03**	—	**0.35**	*8.74*
Groundnuts	—	—	—	—	**1.23**	*0.43*
Groundnut oil	na	na	—	—	**0.16**	*0.17*
Linseed	—	*1.00*[2]*	—	—	**12.38**	*1.07*
Linseed oil	na	na	**0.03**	—	**0.36**	*5.62*
Olive oil	—	—	—	—	**0.04**	*0.10*
Palm kernels	—	—	—	—	**0.34**	—
Palm kernel oil	na	—	**0.15**	—	**0.01**	*0.17*
Palm oil	—	—	—	—	**0.04**	*1.18*
Rapeseed	**7.70**	*17.30*	—	*0.23*	**2.57**	*0.07*
Rapeseed oil	na	na	**0.01**	*0.30**	**0.05**	*0.02*
Soya beans	—	—	—	—[2]	**49.99**	*19.85*[2]
Soya bean oil	na	na	**6.46**	—	**0.01**	*0.13*
Sunflower seed oil	—	—	—	—	**0.55**	—
Tung oil	—	—	—	—	**0.15**	*0.41*

	Production		Exports		Imports	
5. LIVESTOCK‡, ANIMAL PRODUCTS, etc.						
Chickens *d*	**6 859.3**	*5 930.7*				
Cattle *d*	**2 116.3**	*1 865.3*	**1.2**	*0.1*	—	—
dairy cows *d*	**1 173.0**	*1 156.3*				
Goats *d*	**2.0***	*4.7*	—	—	—	—
Sheep *d*	**219.7**	*885.0*	—	—	—	—
Horses *d*	**203.7**	*326.0*				
Pigs *d*	**597.0**	*482.3*	—	—	—	—
Meat‡: 'A'	**163.3**	*128.7*	**2.6**	*2.3*	**1.3**	*0.8*
'B'	**24.3**	*15.9*	**0.3**	*0.6*	**0.2**	—
Butter	**102.7**	*62.3*	**19.7**	*1.1*	—	*3.0*
Cheese	**35.7**	*22.3*	**19.5**	*11.2*	—	—
Eggs	**50.2**	*32.6*	**9.1**	*0.6*	—	—
Fish	**73.3**	*62.7*	—	*0.1**	**32.2**	*13.4**
Milk	**3 782.7**	*2 914.0*	**17.1**	—	—	*1.5**
Hides/skins	**9.0**[2]	*9.3*	**7.8**	*2.1*[2]	**7.7**	*8.4*[2]
Wool	**0.1**	*1.0*	—	—	**1.4**	*1.0*

d no. in thousands.

	Production		Exports		Imports	
6. FIBRES, TEXTILES, etc.						
Abaca	—	—	—	—	**0.1**	—
Agaves (sisal etc.)	—	—	—	—	**1.8**	—
Cotton lint	—	—	—	—	**14.6**	*14.7*
Flax fibre	— }	*0.2**	{ —	—	**2.7**	*1.0*
Hemp fibre	—		—	—	**0.3**	*0.1*
Jute	—	—	—	—	**0.8**	*0.7*
Rubber: natural	—	—	—	—	**7.6**	*3.8*
synthetic	—	—	—	—	**3.4***	—
Cotton: yarn	**17.6**	*13.6*	**2.3**	—	**3.6**	*2.2p*
woven fabrics	**12.7**	*9.8*	**2.8**	—	**3.4**	*2.7p*
Rayon: fibre/yarn	**25.0**	*14.8*	**18.2**	*9.2*	**2.5**	*1.5*[2]*q*
woven fabrics	**0.1**	—	**0.3**	—	**2.4***r*	*0.2r*
Non-cellulosic fibre/yarn	—	—	**0.2**	—	**4.3**	na
Wool: yarn	**6.0**[2]	*7.8*	**0.1**	—	**1.5**	*1.9*
woven fabrics	**4.4**[1]	*5.6**	**0.1***t*	—	**1.4***t*	*0.7*

p incl. spun rayon. *q* incl. nylon and waste. *r* cloth of continuous filament yarn only. *t* excl. blankets.

	Production		Exports		Imports	
7. FUEL AND POWER						
Coal	—	—	—	—	**2 377**	*1 943*
Coke	—	—	—	—	**690**	*371*
Electricity *h*: total	**13 360**	*5 970*[1]				
hydro	**8 788**	*5 350*[1]				
thermal	**4 572**	*620*[1]				
Oil, crude	—	—	—	—	**2 500**	na
Petroleum, refined	**2 193**	—[1]	—	—	**2 397**	*1 110*[1]
Uranium	na	—	—	—	—	—

h million kWh.

	Production		Exports		Imports	
8. IRON AND STEEL						
Iron ore	**331***m*	*74m*	**224**	*240*	**622**	*90*
Pig iron	**666**	*89*	**510**	*7*	**17**	*25*
Steel ingots/castings	**347**	*170*	**6**[1]	—	**52**	*33*
Iron/steel scrap	na	na	**3**	*2*	**121**	*50*
Iron/steel products *a*	na	na	**26**	*2*	**102**	*63*

a million $ U.S. *m* metal content.

continued

FINLAND *continued*

PRODUCTION, EXPORTS AND IMPORTS *continued*

9. NON-FERROUS MINERALS AND METALS

	Production		Exports		Imports	
Gold*k*, ore*m*	20.00	*18.00*	—	—	0.80[1]*n*	*47.90n*
Platinum group metals*k*	—	—	—	—	4.33[2]	*0.48*
Silver*k*, ore*m*	590.00	*233.30*	—	—	534.33*n*	*256.03n*
Asbestos: fibre	10.62	*11.66*	7.40	*3.83*	6.77	*1.19*
manufactured	na	na	0.84	*0.69*	1.10	*0.43*
Mica	—	—	0.05†	—	0.47	—
Aluminium:						
alumina	—	—	—	—	11.34*p*	*0.06*
aluminium	—	—	1.51	—	28.94	*21.73*
Chrome, metal	—	—	—	—	0.95	*0.98*
Cobalt, ore	1.72*m*	na	—	—	0.02	—
Copper: ore*m*	31.99	*20.52*	—	—	—	—
metal	33.83*q*	*21.15*	12.47	*3.65*	10.52	*2.74*
Lead: ore*m*	3.11	—	—	—	—	—
metal	na	—	0.02	—	13.44	*10.35*
Magnesium:						
magnesite	—	—	—	—	1.84	*1.13*
metal/salts	—‡	—‡	—	—	5.14	*4.31*
Manganese, metal	—	—	—	—	2.00	*1.54*
Mercury*f*	—	—	—	—	31.40	*41.60r*
Molybdenum*f*, metal	—	—	—	—	68.40	*44.30*
Nickel: ore	3.17*m*	*0.16m*	—	*0.14*	—	—
metal			2.70	*0.04*	0.22	*0.28*
Tin, metal	—	—	—	—	0.37	*0.43*
Titanium minerals	113.81	*46.24*	77.90[2]	*28.21*	1.40	*3.12*
Tungsten, ore	—	*0.09*	—	—	—	—
Vanadium	0.88*m*	—	1.27*t*	—	—	—
Zinc: ore	66.12*m*	*9.62m*	145.94	*15.39*	—	—
metal	na	na	0.08	—	8.37	*8.55*

f metric tons. *k* '000 fine troy oz. *m* metal content. *n* bullion/coins, etc. *p* hydrate. *q* incl. scrap. *r* incl. amalgam. *t* vanadium oxide.

10. CHEMICALS*n* AND FERTILIZERS

	Production	Exports	Imports
Organic chemicals:			
Benzene	0.3	—	—
Butadiene	—	—	—
Ethylene	—	—	na
Methanol	na	—	4.9
Phenol	—	—	3.0
Phthalic anhydride	—	—	0.4
Styrene monomer	—	—	—
Urea	—	—	1.9

continued

10. CHEMICALS*n* AND FERTILIZERS—*continued*

	Production		Exports		Imports	
Inorganic chemicals:						
Ammonia	66.8		0.2		0.9	
Carbon black	—		0.2		2.2	
Chlorine	95.2		—		—	
Nitric acid	4.2		—		0.2	
Sodium carbonate	0.8[2]		—		70.2	
Sodium hydroxide	107.0		1.6		3.7	
Sulphuric acid	357.3		—		22.5	
Plastics:						
Polyamides	—		—		na	
Polyethylene	—		0.1		8.2	
Polyvinyl chloride	—		—		10.5	
Fertilizers:						
Phosphates	—	—	—	—	308.5	*163.3*
Potash	—	—	—	*0.5*	170.8	*100.6*
Pyrites	257.4*x*	*115.3x*	65.3	*53.0*	—	—
Sulphur	60.0*p*	na	—	—	66.4	*39.1*

n data not available for years 1953–5. *p* recovered sulphur. *x* sulphur content.

11. INDUSTRY

	Production		Exports		Imports	
Aircraft*a*	na	—	—	—	14.3	*0.7*[2]
Alcoholic beverages			—	*0.2a*	6.6*a*	*3.2a*
beer*b*	1 083.0	*905.7*				
spirits*b*	65.0**n*	*104.6p*				
Cement	1 577.3	*1 026.3*	42.0	*54.0*	10.3	*3.7*
Electrical engineering*a*	159.7[2]	na	18.9	*3.3*[2]	98.4	*27.6*[2]
Locomotives*c*	49.0	na	na	na	na	na
Railway vehicles*a*	na	na	na	na	na	*0.6*
Machine tools*a*	—	—	—	—	19.5	—
Merchant ships*g*	136.0	*44.0*	97.0	*44.2*	7.0	*6.8*
Motor vehicles			—	*0.2*[2]*a*	132.8*a*	*36.5*[2]*a*
commercial*d*	1.1	*1.4*q*				
private	—	—				

a million $ U.S. *b* '000 hectolitres. *c* no. of units. *g* '000 G.R.T. *n* 1967 figure. *p* 1960 figure. *q* incl. assembly of imported parts.

FRANCE

EUROPE

The Fifth Republic was created in 1958 after France had recovered from German occupation during the second world war. This new constitution emphasizes the role of the president. France is a member of the European Economic Community.

AREA: 551 601 sq. km. (212 919 sq. miles)

LAND USE: (percentage of total)	*1964*	*1953*
Arable and orchard	38.1	38.6
Permanent meadow and pasture	24.3	22.3
Forest and woodland	21.8	20.7
City areas, waste and other land	15.8	18.4

POPULATION: 49 890 000 (1967 estimate)

Largest city: PARIS, capital; population: 7 369 387 (1962)

Distribution of working population (1962)
Total working population: 19 711 500

U.N. group no.		*Percentage*
0	Agriculture, forestry, fishing and hunting	19.8
1	Mining and quarrying	1.6
2/3	Manufacturing	26.9
4	Construction	8.2
5	Electricity, gas, water and sanitary services	0.9
6	Commerce	13.2
7	Transport, storage and communications	5.4
8	Services	20.1
9	Others	3.9

		Year(s)
Life expectancy at birth (years): male	68.2	1966
female	75.4	1966
Infant mortality (per '000)	21.9	1965
Crude birth rate (per '000)	17.8	1965
Crude death rate (per '000)	11.2	1965
Accidental deaths (per 100 000 population)		
caused by motor vehicles	25.2	1965
due to other causes	44.2	1965
Population per physician	900	1965
Population per hospital bed	120*a*	1965
School enrolment: age 5–19 years (percentage)	93	1963–4 av.
age over 19 years (per 100 000 population)	934	1963–5 av.

a government hospitals only.

COMMUNICATIONS

		Year(s)
Motor vehicles in use ('000s): private	8 784.3	1963–5 av.
commercial	2 062.1	1963–5 av.
Railway track (km.)	38 180	1965
Mail per capita: domestic	165	1963–5 av.
foreign received	na	1963–5 av.
foreign sent	9	1963–5 av.
Telephones (per '000 urban population)	13.2	1967
Radio licences (per '000 population)	309	1963–5 av.
Television licences (per '000 population)	112.3	1963–5 av.
Daily newspapers (per '000 population)	245	1963

FINANCE

Currency unit: The franc. The new franc, equivalent to 100 old francs, was introduced in 1960

Exchange rates	*1965*	*1960*	*1950b*	*1938b*
Per $ U.S.	4.902	4.903	350	38.01
Per £ sterling	13.738	13.743	980	175.00

		Year(s)
National Income (million $ U.S.)	70 240	1965
G.N.P. per capita ($ U.S.)	1 730	1966
Rate of increase of G.N.P. per capita	3.8	1960–4 av.
Foreign trade (percentage of G.D.P.)	21	1963–5 av.

b old francs

TRADING

Total trade (in million $ U.S.)	*1965*	*1955*	*1938*
Exports (f.o.b.)	10 051	4 911	879
Imports (c.i.f.)	10 338	4 739	1 329

Main trading partners (percentage of total value)

Exports	*1965*	*1955*	*1938*	*Imports*	*1965*	*1955*	*1938*
Germany F.R.	19	10	6*d*	Germany F.R.	18	9	7*d*
Belg./Lux.	10	7	14	U.S.A.	11	10	11
Italy	7	4	2	Belg./Lux.	8	5	7
U.S.A.	6	4	6	Italy	7	2	1
Switzerland	6	5	6	Algeria	6	8	11
Algeria	5	12	12	U.K.	5	5	7
Netherlands	5	3	4	Netherlands	5	3	3

d incl. Germany D.R.

continued

FRANCE *continued*

TRADING *continued*

Distribution of trade (percentage of total value)

Exports	*1965*	*1955*	*1938**
Manufactured goods	63	57	na
(machinery and transport equipment)	(26)	(16)	(8)
(textiles and clothing)	(9)	(11)	(12)
Food	13	12	11
Crude materials and fuels	10	17	na
Chemicals	10	8	7
Alcoholic beverages	3	3	5

Imports	*1965*	*1955*	*1938**
Manufactured goods	44	25	na
(machinery and transport equipment)	(20)	(10)	(5)
Crude materials and fuels	31	46	na
(mineral fuels)	(15)	(18)	(19)
Food	15	17	16
Chemicals	7	4	4
Alcoholic beverages	2	5	8

PRODUCTION, EXPORTS AND IMPORTS

Years: **1963–5 average** and *1953–5 average* Units: '000 metric tons unless otherwise indicated

1. CEREALS, etc.

	Production		Exports		Imports	
Barley	7 184.3	*2 478.3*	1 993.7	*32.7*	0.9	*101.0*
Maize (corn)	3 151.3	*949.7*	579.6	*0.2*	550.1	*342.9*
Millets/sorghum	75.3	*5.5*[2]	10.2	*1.2*	54.4	*35.8*
Oats	2 565.0	*3 625.7*	41.4	*16.0*	11.2	*1.9*
Potatoes	12 921.0	*15 671.0*	404.6	*223.6*	209.1	*260.7*
Rice	112.3	*67.3*	6.4	*1.7*	65.4	*58.2*
Rye	377.7	*473.7*	19.3	*0.5*	0.6	*6.5*
Wheat	12 949.0	*9 970.7*	3 214.3	*1 245.9*	684.6	*241.4*

2. FRUIT, etc.

	Production		Exports		Imports	
Apples	3 496.7	*4 134.0*	97.6	*74.3*	104.7	*30.3*
Apricots	103.7	*42.3*	na	*1.6*	na	*5.1*
Bananas	—	—	2.4	*0.7*	371.4	*266.2*
Cherries	119.7	*83.3*	na	*0.3*	na	*4.9*
Dates	—	—	9.7	*8.1*	19.3	*19.6*
Figs	4.3	—	na	—	na	*11.9*
Grapes	9 628.0*	*9 239.3*	30.5	*36.7*	7.1	*8.6*
Lemons	—	—	0.3	*0.2*	82.1	*48.2*
Oranges	2.7	*1.3*	18.8	*0.5*	733.9	*595.4*
Other citrus fruit	—	—	1.1	—	37.4	*12.2*
Olives	7.3	*30.0*				
Peaches	452.0	*160.2*	na	*0.9*	na	*1.5*
Pears	418.0*	*347.3*	24.6	*4.0n*	28.2	*4.6n*
Plums	130.3	*134.5*	na	*4.3*	na	*1.3*
Raisins	—	—	0.5	*0.7*	9.9	*7.4*
Tomatoes	510.3	*246.3*				
Wine*b*	62 204.0	*60 341.0*	4 030.4	*2 948.0p*	10 530.8	*15 255.0q*

b '000 hectolitres. *n* excl. pears for perry. *p* of which fortified wine 1 232.0. *q* excl. fortified wine.

3. BEVERAGES, FOREST PRODUCTS, etc.

	Production		Exports		Imports	
Cocoa	—	—	—	—	62.9	*47.5*
Coffee	—	—	0.6†	—	222.4	*172.2*
Sugar: beet	15 717.7	*10 259.3*[1]				
raw	2 234.8	*1 651.2*	842.1	*551.7*	427.7	*351.5*
Tea	—	—	—	—	2.2	*1.4*
Tobacco: leaf	44.3	*55.0*	1.7	*1.0*	48.6	*37.2*
cigars	311.0*e*	*97.2e*	—	*1.1*[2]	—	*1.3*[2]
cigarettes	52 256.0*e*	*38 240.7e*				
tobacco/snuff	17.9	*19.2*				
Softwood*j*	13 870.5	*12 442.7*	893.0	*1 105.1*	2 343.2	*719.1*
Hardwood*j*	30 159.5	*22 874.7*	1 084.0	*997.5*	1 485.5	*341.5*
Wood pulp	1 359.3	*1 157.3*	96.4	*10.7*	910.3	*483.0*
Newsprint	450.3	*380.0*	3.4	*13.6*	88.7	*57.0*
Other paper	2 648.3	*1 237.0*	163.3	*82.7*	393.7	*38.3*

e no. in millions. *j* '000 cu. metres of roundwood equivalent.

4. VEGETABLE OILSEEDS AND OILS

	Production		Exports		Imports	
Castor seed	—	—	0.01†	—	23.75	*18.90*
Castor oil	na	na	0.82	*0.60*	25.62	*1.20*
Copra	—	—	—	—	95.33	*87.37*
Coconut oil	na	na	1.92	*3.07*	3.87	*4.64n*
Cottonseed	—	—	—	—	—	*1.13*
Cottonseed oil	na	na	—	—	1.01	*0.31*
Groundnuts	—	—	3.63†	*0.77†*	49.17	*309.97*
Groundnut oil	na	na	16.72*	*0.24*	143.07	*84.09*
Linseed	43.67	*17.50*[2]	0.09	*0.07*	73.32	*116.07*
Linseed oil	na	na	0.92	*1.66*	13.60	*13.80*
Olive oil	1.00	*7.00**	3.03*s*	*7.70s*	18.48	*30.36**
Palm kernels	—	—	—	—	78.36	*139.23*
Palm kernel oil	na	na	0.31	na	3.81	na
Palm oil	—	—	0.87†	*0.06†*	37.64	*25.54*
Rapeseed	239.00	*96.67*	105.63	*2.83*	7.76	*13.70*
Rapeseed oil	na	na	17.01	*4.59p*	2.43	—
Sesame seed	—	—	0.36†	*0.07†*	1.24	*3.13*
Soya beans	—	—	1.63†	—	148.08	*51.03*
Soya bean oil	na	na	3.58	*0.31*	1.27	*0.20*
Sunflower seed	28.00	*3.67*	5.38	—	1.95	—
Sunflower seed oil	na	na	0.04	*0.07p*	1.73	—[2]
Tung oil	—	—	0.03†	—	2.11	*2.64*

n incl. palm kernel oil *p* incl. other minor vegetable oils. *s* incl. re-exports.

5. LIVESTOCK‡, ANIMAL PRODUCTS, etc.

	Production		Exports		Imports	
Chickens*d*	80 000*	*75 000*[1]				
Cattle*d*	20 226	*16 831*	185.8	*63.9*	20.3	*3.0*
dairy cows*d*	10 980*	*9 077*[2]				
Goats*d*	1 078	*1 273*	16.8	na	140.8	na
Sheep*d*	8 797	*7 838*				
Horses*d*	1 370	*2 275*				
Pigs*d*	9 030	*7 359*	62.2	*4.4*	333.7	*70.1*
Bacon/ham	2 943	na	1.0	*1.1*	1.2	*0.1*
Meat‡: 'A'			84.7	*37.4*	146.4	*24.0*
'B'	1 030	*805*	26.8	*5.3*	57.8	*7.8*
Butter	430	*301**	35.3	*5.5*	8.9	*9.3*
Cheese	529*	*323*	56.1	*18.5*	22.0	*8.8*
Eggs	536*	*425*[2]	4.4	*1.5*	6.3	*15.0*
Fish	763*n*	*582n*	37.3	*40.7*[2]*	318.2	*113.2**
Milk	25 801	*18 167*	925.1	*60.3*	128.5	*33.2*
Whale/sperm oil	—[1]	—	—	—	19.0	—
Hides/skins	—	—	66.3	*30.1*[2]	133.3	*84.4*[2]
Wool	10[2]	*10*	18.3	*14.7s*	90.6	*97.9*

d no. in thousands. *n* incl. fish landed by French vessels in foreign ports. *s* incl. re-exports.

6. FIBRES, TEXTILES, etc.

	Production		Exports		Imports	
Abaca	—	—	—	—	4.0	*4.9*
Agaves (sisal etc.)	—	—	0.1†	*0.1†*	60.7	*37.1*
Cotton lint	—	—	0.9†	*0.1†*	265.7	*288.1*
Flax fibre	72.5	*36.2*	121.7*s*	*6.4s*	22.4	*11.5*
Hemp fibre	2.5	*2.6*	0.6	*0.6*	2.6	*6.0*
Jute	—	—	3.0†	*0.3†*	98.5	*94.2*
Rubber: natural	—	—	0.7†	*0.8†*	132.7	*128.2*
synthetic	125.5	—	58.3	—	77.7	*18.0*
Silk*f*	5.0	*38.3*	143.7*s*	*123.0s*	765.7	*648.7*
Cotton: yarn	288.0	*231.2*	11.5	*7.4*	1.4	*1.1*
woven fabrics	216.4	*194.9n*	40.0	*48.4*	12.3	*2.8*
Rayon: fibre/yarn	138.6	*104.4*	45.7	*24.3*	12.0	*2.2*
woven fabrics	47.1	*31.0p*	12.9	*13.8*	8.9	*0.8*
Non-cellulosic fibre/yarn	87.0	*8.5*	20.4	na	15.5	na
Wool: yarn	145.1	*125.7*	25.2	*17.8*	1.8	*0.3*
woven fabrics	71.3	*64.0*	6.5	*4.8*	6.5	*1.7**

f metric tons. *n* incl. mixtures and other fabrics, except rayon and synthetic. *p* total output of broad woven fabrics by the French silk industry plus the production of rayon and synthetic fibre piece goods by the French cotton industry. *s* incl. re-exports.

7. FUEL AND POWER

	Production		Exports		Imports	
Coal: 'A'‡	50 710	*55 330*	948	*9 086*	14 675	*8 141*
'B'	1 477	*2 050*	28	*6*	478	*521*
Coke	na	na	48	*316*	4 977	*3 812*
Electricity*h*: total	94 489	*45 550*[1]				
hydro	41 510	*23 610*[1]				
nuclear	632	—[1]				
thermal	52 347	*21 940*[1]				
Natural gas*i*	5 000	*258*[1]	—	—	63	—
Oil, crude	3 063	*900*[1]	—	—	50 360	*24 900*[1]
Petroleum, refined	45 060	*21 220*[1]	8 123	*5 280*[1]	3 757	*730*[1]
Rare earths*fq*	—	—	280†	*189†*	59*r*	*631t*
Uranium*f*	1 054*m*	na	—	—	2 030*v*	*—v*

f metric tons. *h* million kWh. *i* million cu. metres. *m* metal content. *q* salts of rare earth minerals. *r* in addition, rare earth minerals 1 316. *t* in addition, monazite 84. *v* ore.

8. IRON AND STEEL

	Production		Exports		Imports	
Iron ore	17 978*m*	*14 006m*	21 640	*12 006*	3 711	*618*
Pig iron	15 304	*9 599*	364	*357*	218	*110*
Steel ingots/castings	18 759	*11 010*	489	*428*	628	*160*
Iron/steel scrap	na	na	1 510	*535*	552	*158*
Iron/steel products*a*	na	na	877	*546*	541	*71*

a million $ U.S. *m* metal content.

continued

PRODUCTION, EXPORTS AND IMPORTS *continued*

9. NON-FERROUS MINERALS AND METALS

	Production		Exports		Imports	
Diamonds a	—	—	5.50	*5.20*	22.48	*9.75*
Gold k: ore m	55.00	*37.00*	—	—	—	—
bullion, etc.	na	na	780.00[1]	*5 533.70*	10 032.00[1]	*4 396.30*
Platinum group	—	—				
metals k	—	—	59.75	*65.47*	163.59	*121.78*
Silver k: ore m	1 033.00p	*620.00p*	—	—	na	na
bullion	na	na	4 347.33	*2 334.32*	25 838.67	*9 143.17*
Asbestos: fibre	17.51	*11.12*	6.70	*3.57*	96.91	*40.86*
manufactured	na	na	42.12	*0.42*	32.58	*0.20*
Mica	0.22	—	0.77[2]s	*0.16†*	4.77	*1.65*
Aluminium: bauxite	2 374.51	*1 312.34*	202.70	*315.29*	136.40	*10.61*
alumina	802.14	na	157.41	*72.33*	71.19	—
aluminium	318.29	*120.72*	209.44	*52.67*	85.23	*2.31*
Antimony: ore	0.11m	*0.13m*	0.05	—	1.74	*6.00*
metal	na	na	0.13	*0.50*	2.40	*0.03*
Beryl	—	na	—	—	0.25[2]	na
Cadmium	0.41	*0.15*	0.08	—	0.61	*0.21*
Chrome: ore	—	—	—	—	190.45	*76.42*
metal	na	na	18.80	*8.95*	1.95	*3.28*
Cobalt: ore	—	—	—	—	10.86	*82.00*
metal	na	na	0.58	*0.75*	0.37	*0.76*
Copper: ore	0.30*m	*0.35m*	1.12	*0.01*	—	*0.02*
metal	—	—	89.99†	*13.59†*	273.74	*142.66*
Lead: ore	12.88m	*11.27m*	2.79	*0.90*	135.58	*87.90*
metal	88.59	*62.21*	25.30	*16.86*	57.03	*56.81*
Magnesium:						
dolomite	1 123.55	na	24.50	*9.66*	182.43	*170.03*
magnesite	—	—	0.47	*0.08*	34.87	*21.44*
kieserite	na	na	—	—	—	—
metal/salts	1.82w	*1.22w*	4.13†	*4.45†*	38.68	*2.26*
Manganese: ore q	—	—	1.73	*2.20*	786.07	*509.44*
metal	na	na	199.59	*68.42*	12.61	*15.22*
Mercury f	—	—	6.70†	*5.50†*	438.70	*345.70*
Molybdenum f: ore	—	—	—	—	4 550.90	na
metal	na	na	613.00	*3.50*	87.00	*6.70*
Nickel: ore	—	—	0.65†	*0.07†*	13.59	*16.16*
metal	na	na	7.61	*1.68*	35.72	*2.04*
Tin: ore	0.41m	*0.50m*	0.56	*0.46*	—	—
metal	na	na	0.26	*0.52*	11.03	*8.60*
Titanium minerals	—	—	33.70†	*0.59†*	122.40	*2.89r*
Tungsten: ore	—	*1.14*	0.06	na	1.98	na
metal	na	na	0.37	—	0.06	—
Vanadium	—	—	1.00t	—	0.41u	*0.18*
Zinc: ore	18.65m	*12.76m*	0.57	*1.41*	327.15	*236.22*
metal	183.79v	*101.33*	24.36	*5.71*	65.82	*35.21*
Zirconium minerals	—	—	—	—	24.19	na

a million $ U.S. *f* metric tons. *k* '000 fine troy oz. *m* metal content. *p* incl. silver refined from imported ore. *q* incl. manganiferous iron ore. *r* titanium oxide only. *s* incl. re-exports. *t* ferro-vanadium. *u* vanadium oxide. *v* incl. dust. *w* primary magnesium only.

10. CHEMICALS n AND FERTILIZERS

	Production		Exports		Imports	
Organic chemicals:						
Benzene	178.5		6.8		89.0	
Butadiene	22.1[2]		3.6		57.9	
Ethylene	184.3		—		—	
Methanol	112.4		20.6		10.8	
Phenol	91.9		2.6p		5.1p	
Phthalic anhydride	47.6		10.7		3.8	
Styrene monomer	58.3		4.5		44.1	
Urea	88.0		104.9		15.5	
Inorganic chemicals:						
Ammonia	1 128.6		17.1		36.9	
Carbon black	87.3		33.9		39.3	
Chlorine	532.6		4.3		1.1	
Nitric acid	2 094.3		3.7		0.3	
Sodium carbonate	1 011.0		223.1		—	
Sodium hydroxide	682.6		119.8		29.4	
Sulphuric acid	2 660.5		59.2		20.6	
Plastics:						
Polyamides	na		9.0		2.7	
Polyethylene	85.1		22.0		45.9	
Polyvinyl chloride	197.7		46.8		15.5	
Fertilizers:						
Phosphates	42.9	*103.0*	6.5	*0.9*	2 545.9	*1 295.9*
Potash	1 805.2y	*1 058.3y*	1 239.9	*1 049.5*	63.8	*6.2*
Pyrites	82.0x	*135.8x*	—	*0.7*	371.9	*482.4*
Sulphur: native	—	*3.6*	} 996.5	*12.3*	198.0	*185.5*
recovered	1 480.1r	*2.9*				

n data not available for years 1953–5. *p* incl. phenol salts. *r* from natural gas. *x* sulphur content. *y* K_2O content.

11. INDUSTRY

	Production		Exports		Imports	
Aircraft a	1 118.0*n	na	129.0	*7.8*	58.9	*34.1*
Alcoholic beverages			274.1a	*146.9a*	220.1a	*228.6a*
beer b	19 299.0	*9 915.0*p*				
spirits b	2 678.0q	*1 260.0*r*				
Cement	20 538.3	*9 665.3*	878.0	*896.3*	83.0	*10.3*
Electrical engineering a	3 546.8[2]	na	458.7	*139.3[2]*	378.8	*61.7[2]*
Locomotives c	511.0	*180.0[2]*	na	na	na	na
Railway vehicles a	na	na	33.0	*42.6*	—	*1.5*
Machine tools a	220.0[1]	na	60.1	*12.9[2]*	94.4	*34.5[2]*
Merchant ships g	479.0	*276.0*	248.0	*73.2*	25.0	*35.9*
Motor vehicles			684.6a	*228.4[2]a*	294.3a	*29.2a*
commercial d	253.6	*154.7*				
private d	1 402.4	*452.9*				

a million $ U.S. *b* '000 hectolitres. *c* no. of units. *d* no. in thousands. *g* '000 G.R.T. *n* 1965–7 av. *p* data incomplete. *q* 1967 figure. *r* 1959/60 figure.

FRANCE (OVERSEAS DEPARTMENTS)

French Guiana, Martinique, Guadeloupe, and Réunion were each given the status of a French Overseas Department in 1946.

FRENCH GUIANA

SOUTH AMERICA

AREA: 90 000* sq. km. (35 000* sq. miles)

LAND USE: (percentage of total)

	1963	*1954*
Permanent meadow and pasture (savannah)	0.6	0.6
Forest and woodland	95.0	94.9
City areas, waste and other land	4.4	4.5

POPULATION: 38 000 (1967 U.N. estimate)

Capital city: CAYENNE; population: 18 235 (1961)
Total working population: 10 415 (1961)

		Year(s)
Infant mortality (per '000)	39.6*	1965
Crude birth rate (per '000)	33.6*	1965
Crude death rate (per '000)	11.4*	1965
Population per physician	1 240	1965
Population per hospital bed	70	1965
School enrolment: age 5–19 years (percentage)	95	1963–4 av.

COMMUNICATIONS

		Year(s)
Motor vehicles in use ('000s): private	1.2	} 1963–5 av.
commercial	1.0	
Telephones (per '000 urban population)	5.2	1967
Radio licences (per '000 population)	132	1963–5 av.
Daily newspapers (per '000 population)	86	1963

FINANCE

Currency unit: The French metropolitan franc
Exchange rates—see France

		Year
National Income (million $ U.S.)	18*	1966
G.N.P. per capita ($ U.S.)	500	1966

EMPLOYMENT AND TRADE

French Guiana has about 80 000 sq. km. of tropical forest. Only a small area is cultivated, the main crops being sugar, manioc, cocoa and bananas. Shrimp fishing and gold mining are recent developments. The European Launching Development Organization has a space research station at Kourou. Exports are gold, hardwood and rum. The chief trading partners are France, the U.S.A. and the West Indies Associated States.

continued

PRODUCTION, EXPORTS AND IMPORTS

Years: **1963–5 average** and *1953–5 average* Units: '000 metric tons unless otherwise indicated

1. CEREALS, etc.

	Production		Exports		Imports	
Cassava	5.7	*11.5[2]*				
Maize (corn)	—	—	—	—	0.3	—
Potatoes	—	—	—	—	0.6	*0.5*
Rice	—	—	—	—	0.8	*0.6*
Sweet potatoes/yams	9.0*	*4.0[2]*				

2. FRUIT, etc.

	Production		Exports		Imports	
Apples	—	—	—	—	0.1	—
Bananas	3.7	na	—	—	—	—
Oranges	—	—	—	—	0.1	—
Wine b	—	—	—	—	12.0	*8.7*

b '000 hectolitres.

3. BEVERAGES, FOREST PRODUCTS, etc.

	Production		Exports		Imports	
Coffee	—	—	—	—	—	*0.1*
Sugar, raw	—	—	—	—	0.7	*0.7*
Hardwood j	51.0	*32.7*	20.4	*1.6*	0.2	*0.2*
Newsprint	—	—	—	—	—	*0.1*
Other paper	—	—	—	—	0.2	—

j '000 cu. metres of roundwood equivalent.

4. VEGETABLE OILSEEDS AND OILS

	Production		Exports		Imports	
Castor oil	—	—	—	—	—	*0.02[1]*
Coconut oil	—	—	—	—	0.01	—
Cottonseed oil	—	—	—	—	—	na
Groundnuts	—	—	—	—	0.02	—
Groundnut oil	—	—	—	—	0.08	*0.15[1]**

continued

4. VEGETABLE OILSEEDS AND OILS—*continued*

	Production		Exports		Imports	
Linseed oil	—	—	—	—	0.01	na
Palm kernel oil	—	—	—	—	0.02	—
Palm oil	—	—	—	—	—	na
Rapeseed oil	—	—	—	—	0.06	—
Soya bean oil	—	—	—	—	0.17	—

5. LIVESTOCK‡, ANIMAL PRODUCTS, etc.

	Production		Exports		Imports	
Chickens d	37.0*	*6.0[2]*				
Cattle d	3.0	*3.0[2]*	—	—	1.6	*1.6*
Goats/sheep d	—	—	—	—	0.2	—
Pigs d	6.0	*5.0[2]*	—	—	0.6	—
Meat‡: 'A'	—	—	—	—	0.2	—
'B'	—	—	—	—	0.2	—
Butter	—	—	—	—	0.1	—
Cheese	—	—	—	—	0.1	*0.1*
Fish	1.5[1]	*2.0*	0.4	na	0.4	na
Milk	—	—	—	—	1.4	*0.9*

d no. in thousands.

7. FUEL AND POWER

	Production		Exports		Imports	
Electricity h t	9	—				
Petroleum, refined	—	—	—	—	10	*10[1]*

h million kWh. *t* thermal.

9. NON-FERROUS MINERALS AND METALS

	Production		Exports		Imports	
Gold k, ore m	6.0[2]	*5.0*	na	*4.4n*	—	—

k '000 fine troy oz. *m* metal content. *n* bullion/coins etc.

11. INDUSTRY

	Production		Exports		Imports	
Cement	—	—	—	—	10.7	*4.0*

GUADELOUPE

CARIBBEAN SEA

AREA: 1 702 sq. km. (657 sq. miles)

LAND USE: (percentage of total)

	1965	*1953*
Arable and orchard	29.2	27.5
Permanent meadow and pasture	9.0	6.2
Forest and woodland	32.6	38.2
City areas, waste and other land	29.2	28.1

POPULATION: 320 000 (1967 estimate)

Capital city: POINTE-À-PITRE; population: 26 160 (1954)
Total working population: 114 267 (1961)

		Year(s)
Life expectancy at birth (years): male	62.5	} 1959–63 av.
female	66.5	
Infant mortality (per '000)	42.1*	1965
Crude birth rate (per '000)	33.7	1965
Crude death rate (per '000)	8.1	1965
Population per physician	2 110	1965
Population per hospital bed	110	1966
School enrolment: age 5–19 years (percentage)	98	1963–4 av.
age over 19 years (per 100 000 population)	79	1963–4 av.

COMMUNICATIONS

		Year(s)
Motor vehicles in use ('000s): private	13.7	} 1963–5 av.
commercial	8.6	
Telephones (per '000 urban population)	2.4	1967
Radio receivers (per '000 population)	27	1963–5 av.
Television licences (per '000 population)	1.1	1963–5 av.
Daily newspapers (per '000 population)	10	1963–4 av.

FINANCE

Currency unit: The French metropolitan franc
Exchange rates—see France

		Year
National Income (million $ U.S.)	140*	1966
G.N.P. per capita ($ U.S.)	440	1966

TRADING

Total trade (in million $ U.S.)	*1965*	*1955*	*1938*
Exports (f.o.b.)	38	34	9
Imports (c.i.f.)	85	37	7

Main trading partners (percentage of total value)

Exports	*1965*	*1955*	*Imports*	*1965*	*1955*
France	79	80	France	73	78
U.S.A.	16	1	U.S.A.	8	3
Surinam	1	na	Germany F.R.	3	na
Italy	1	—	Neths. Antilles	2	na
Morocco	1	na	Trin./Tob.	2	3
			Netherlands	2	na
			U.K.	1	1

Distribution of trade (percentage of total value)

Exports	*1965*	*1955*
Sugar	58	49
Bananas	30	40
Rum	6	6
Imports		
Manufactured goods	58	} na
(machinery and transport equipment)	(22)	
Food	21	
Chemicals	9	

continued

na: data not available. — negligible or nil. [1] one year only. [2] two year average. * estimate. ‡ see appendix. † re-exports.

FRANCE (OVERSEAS DEPARTMENTS) *continued*

GUADELOUPE *continued*

PRODUCTION, EXPORTS AND IMPORTS

Years: **1963–5 average** and *1953–5 average* Units: '000 metric tons unless otherwise indicated

	Production		Exports		Imports	
1. CEREALS, etc.						
Cassava	**5.0**	*12.0*[1]				
Maize (corn)	**1.0**	—	—	—	**1.3**	*0.3*[1]
Potatoes	—	—	—	—	**3.3**	*2.2*[2]
Rice	—	—	—	—	**7.8**	*7.5*
Sweet potatoes/ yams	**46.3***	*30.0*[1]				
2. FRUIT, etc.						
Apples	—	—	—	—	**0.4***	—
Bananas	**131.0**	*108.0*[1]	**79.7**	*70.9*	—	—
Coconuts *e*	**1.0***[1]	na	—	—	—	—
Grapes	—	—	—	—	**0.1**[2]	—
Oranges	**10.3**	na	—	—	—	—
Tomatoes	**3.0**	—				
Wine *b*	—	—	—	—	**73.4**	*59.3*

b '000 hectolitres. *e* no. in millions.

	Production		Exports		Imports	
3. BEVERAGES, FOREST PRODUCTS, etc.						
Cocoa	**0.1**	na	**0.1**	*0.2*	—	—
Coffee	**0.3**	na	**0.1**	*0.2*	**0.2**	—
Sugar: cane	**1 815.0***	na				
raw	**184.6**	*119.7**	**165.1**	*104.1*	—	—
Tobacco products	—	—	—	—	**0.2**	—
Softwood *j*	—	—	—	—	**37.0**	*28.4*
Hardwood *j*	**37.3**	*12.0*	—	—	**2.1**	*0.3*
Paper	—	—	—	—	**4.6**	*1.7*[1]

j '000 cu. metres of roundwood equivalent.

	Production		Exports		Imports	
4. VEGETABLE OILSEEDS AND OILS						
Castor oil	—	—	—	—	—	na
Groundnuts	—	—	—	—	**0.04**	—
Groundnut oil	na	—	—	—	**0.48**	na
Soya bean oil	—	—	—	—	**1.91***	—

	Production		Exports		Imports	
5. LIVESTOCK‡, ANIMAL PRODUCTS, etc.						
Chickens *d*	**423.3**	*275.0*[2]				
Cattle *d*	**70.0**	*66.3*	—	—	**0.9**	*0.3*[2]
Goats *d*	**27.0**	*28.3*	—	—	—	—
Sheep *d*	**6.3**	*10.3*				
Horses *d*	**2.0**	*4.0*[2]				
Pigs *d*	**31.0**	*36.0*	—	—	—	—
Bacon/ham	**1.0**	*1.0*[1]	—	—	**0.8***	—
Meat‡: 'A'			—	—	**1.1**[2]	—
'B'	—	na	—	—	**0.6***	—
Butter	—	—	—	—	**0.3**	*0.1**
Cheese	—	—	—	—	**0.4**	*0.2*[2]
Eggs	**0.1***	*0.1*[1]	—	—	**0.1**	—
Fish	**3.2**[1]	*1.8*	—	—	**2.2**	na
Milk	**8.3**	*6.0*[1]	—	—	**6.3**	*2.0**

d no. in thousands.

	Production		Exports		Imports	
7. FUEL AND POWER						
Electricity *h*: total	**40**	*8*				
hydro	**1**	—				
thermal	**39**	*8*				
Petroleum, refined	—	—	—	—	**70**	*30*[1]

h million kWh.

	Production		Exports		Imports	
10. CHEMICALS *n* AND FERTILIZERS						
Chemicals	—		—		na	
Fertilizers:						
Potash	—	—	—	—	**2.3**	—

n data not available for years 1953–5.

	Production		Exports		Imports	
11. INDUSTRY						
Alcoholic beverages	na	na	**2.7** *ap*	na	**2.3** *a*	na
beer *b*	na	*186.0*				
Cement	—	—	—	—	**70.7**	*30.7*
Electrical engineering *a*	—	—	—	—	**3.0**	—
Motor vehicles *a*	—	—	—	—	**6.0**	*1.6*

a million $ U.S. *b* '000 hectolitres. *p* rum only.

MARTINIQUE

CARIBBEAN SEA

AREA: 1 090 sq. km. (420 sq. miles)

LAND USE: (percentage of total)	*1964*	*1951*
Arable and orchard	29.1	26.4
Permanent meadow and pasture	18.2	19.1
Forest and woodland	24.5	24.5
City areas, waste and other land	28.2	30.0

POPULATION: 330 000 (1967 estimate)

Capital city: FORT-DE-FRANCE; population: 60 648 (1954)

Distribution of working population (1961)
Total working population: 92 344

U.N. group no.		*Percentage*
0	Agriculture, forestry, fishing and hunting	38.7
1	Mining and quarrying	0.1
2/3	Manufacturing	12.1
4	Construction	9.0
5/8	Services, including electricity, gas, water and sanitary services	24.4
6	Commerce	9.2
7	Transport, storage and communications	4.3
9	Others	2.2

		Year(s)
Life expectancy at birth (years): male	62.5	1959–63 av.
female	66.5	1959–63 av.
Infant mortality (per '000)	39.5	1965
Crude birth rate (per '000)	33.3	1965
Crude death rate (per '000)	7.4	1965
Population per physician	2 400	1961
Population per hospital bed	100 *a*	1966
School enrolment: age 5–19 years (percentage)	108‡	1963–4 av.
age over 19 years (per 100 000 population)	181	1963–5 av.

a government hospitals only.

COMMUNICATIONS

		Year(s)
Motor vehicles in use ('000s): private	14.9	1963–5 av.
commercial	8.1	1963–5 av.
Telephones (per '000 urban population)	3.7	1967
Radio receivers (per '000 population)	165	1963–5 av.
Television licences (per '000 population)	4.7	1963–5 av.
Daily newspapers (per '000 population)	13.5*	1962–4 av.

FINANCE

Currency unit: The French metropolitan franc
Exchange rates—see France

		Year
National Income (million $ U.S.)	160*	1966
G.N.P. per capita ($ U.S.)	520	1966

TRADING

Total trade (in million $ U.S.)	*1965*	*1955*	*1938*
Exports (f.o.b.)	38	26	9
Imports (c.i.f.)	91	39	7

Main trading partners (percentage of total value)

Exports	*1965*	*Imports*	*1965*
France	88	France	71
Italy	4	U.S.A.	7
Germany F.R.	2	Trin./Tob.	3
U.S.A.	2	Neths. Antilles	2
Guadeloupe	1	Netherlands	2
		Germany F.R.	2
		Italy	2

Distribution of trade (percentage of total value)

Exports	*1965*	*Imports*	*1965*
Bananas and plantains	47	Manufactured goods	57
Sugar (refined)	27	(machinery and transport equipment)	(19)
Rum	10	(Textiles and clothing)	(8)
Pineapples	8	Food	21
		Chemicals	11
		Crude materials and fuels	7

continued

MARTINIQUE *continued*

PRODUCTION, EXPORTS AND IMPORTS

Years: **1963–5 average** and *1953–5 average* Units: '000 metric tons unless otherwise indicated

	Production		Exports		Imports	
1. CEREALS, etc.						
Cassava	**3.0***	na				
Maize (corn)	—	—	—	—	**5.7**	*1.0*[1]
Oats	—	—	—	—	—	*0.9*
Potatoes	—	—	—	—	—	*2.5*[1]
Rice	—	—	—	—	**3.3**	*2.5*[2]
Sweet potatoes/ yams	**35.0***	*59.0*[1]				
2. FRUIT, etc.						
Bananas	**156.7**	na	**126.3**	*50.4*	—	—
Coconuts	na	na	—	*0.1*	—	—
Oranges	**1.0***	*1.0*[1] *n*	—	—	—	—
Pineapples	**19.7**	*6.0*[1]	na	na	—	—
Wine *b*	—	—	—	—	**54.5**	*41.7*

b '000 hectolitres. *n* incl. other citrus fruit.

	Production		Exports		Imports	
3. BEVERAGES, FOREST PRODUCTS, etc.						
Cocoa	**0.1**	*0.1*[1]	**0.1***	*0.1**	—	—
Coffee	—	*0.2*[1]	—	—	**0.4**	*0.3*[1]
Sugar: cane	**757.0**	*917.0*[1]				
raw	**71.3**	*79.7**	**65.8**	*64.3*	—	—
Softwood *j*	—	—	—	—	**32.0**	*15.3*
Hardwood *j*	**17.7**	*15.9*	—	—	**4.4**	*3.6*
Newsprint	—	—	—[2]	—	**0.4**[1]	*0.1*
Other paper	—	—	**0.5**[1]†	—	**7.6**	*0.8*

j '000 cu. metres of roundwood equivalent.

	Production		Exports		Imports	
4. VEGETABLE OILSEEDS AND OILS						
Copra	**0.30***	na	—	—	—	—
Groundnut oil	—	—	—	—	**0.12**	na
Linseed oil	—	—	—	—	—	*0.09*[1]
Soya bean oil	—	—	—	—	—	*0.08*[2]*

	Production		Exports		Imports	
5. LIVESTOCK‡, ANIMAL PRODUCTS, etc.						
Chickens *d*	**370.0**	*200.0*[1]				
Cattle *d*	**37.0**	*53.3*	—	—	**7.1**	*4.0*[1]
dairy cows *d*	**17.0**	na				
Goats *d*	**12.0**	*15.0*	—	—	—	—
Sheep *d*	**23.3**	*25.3*	—	—	—	—
Horses *d*	**6.0***	*5.0*[2]				
Pigs *d*	**35.0**	*40.0*	—	—	—	*0.1*[1]
Meat‡: 'A'	**5.0***	*3.0*[1]	—	—	**0.8**[1]	—
'B'	**1.9***	na	—	—	—	—
Butter	—	—	—	—	**0.3**	*0.1**
Cheese	—	—	—	—	**0.5**	*0.2**
Eggs	**0.4***	*0.2*[1]	—	—	—	—
Fish	**2.5**[1]	*2.8*	—	—	**3.4**	na
Milk	**10.0**	*6.0*	—	—	**6.1**	*2.2**

d no. in thousands.

	Production		Exports		Imports	
7. FUEL AND POWER						
Coal	—	—	—	—	—	*1*
Electricity *ht*	**38**	*20*				
Petroleum, refined	—	—	—	—	**77**	*40*

h million kWh. *t* thermal.

	Production		Exports		Imports	
10. CHEMICALS *n* AND FERTILIZERS						
Chemicals	—		—		na	
Fertilizers:						
Potash	—	—	—	—	**4.2**	—

n data not available for years 1953–5.

	Production		Exports		Imports	
11. INDUSTRY						
Alcoholic beverages *a*	na	na	**4.6** *p*	na	**1.7**	na
Cement	—	—	—	—	**63.0**	*21.3*
Electrical engineering *a*	—	—	—	—	**3.0**	—
Motor vehicles *a*	—	—	—	—	**6.1**	—

a million $ U.S. *p* rum only.

RÉUNION

INDIAN OCEAN

AREA: 2 508 sq. km. (968.5 sq. miles)

LAND USE: (percentage of total)	*1965*	*1954*
Arable and orchard	24.7	31.7
Permanent meadow and pasture	8.0	7.9
Forest and woodland	38.2	19.8
City areas, waste and other land	29.1	40.6

POPULATION: 418 000 (1967 estimate)

Capital city: SAINT-DENIS; population: 65 614 (1961)

Total working population: 95 869 (excluding those in compulsory military service) (1954)

		Year(s)
Life expectancy at birth (years): male	54.1	1959–63 av.
female	60.6	1959–63 av.
Infant mortality (per '000)	75.3*	1965
Crude birth rate (per '000)	42.7	1965
Crude death rate (per '000)	9.7	1965
Accidental deaths (per 100 000 population)		
caused by motor vehicles	15.2	1965
due to other causes	31.8	1965
Population per physician	3 020	1965
Population per hospital bed	150	1966
School enrolment: age 5–19 years (percentage)	90	1963–4 av.
age over 19 years (per 100 000 population)	92	1963–5 av.

COMMUNICATIONS

		Year(s)
Motor vehicles in use ('000s): private	14.4	1963–5 av.
commercial	6.9	1963–5 av.
Telephones (per '000 urban population)	2.6	1967
Radio receivers (per '000 population)	109	1963–5 av.
Television sets (per '000 population)	6.7	1963–5 av.
Daily newspapers (per '000 population)	63	1964

FINANCE

Currency unit: The franc CFA

Exchange rates	*1965*	*1960*	*1957*
Per $ U.S.	246.85	246.85	210
Per £ sterling	691.18	691.18	590

TRADING

Total trade (in million $ U.S.)	*1965*	*1955*	*1938*
Exports (f.o.b.)	34	33	6
Imports (c.i.f.)	97	41	8

Main trading partners (percentage of total value)

Exports	*1965*	*1955*	*Imports*	*1965*	*1955*
France	88	76	France	68	66
U.S.A.	3	1	Malagasy R.	6	14
Italy	2	na	Cambodia	5	6 *a*
Morocco	2	17	Italy	3	na
New Zealand	1	na	Germany F.R.	2	na

Distribution of trade (percentage of total value)

Exports	*1965*	*1955*
Sugar	78	84
Essential oils	11	4
Rum	5	4
Imports		
Manufactured goods	54	na
(machinery and transport equipment)	(20)	(14*)
(textiles and clothing)	(10)	(9*)
Food	25	28*
(cereals)	(9)	(16*)
Crude materials and fuels	5	na
Beverages and tobacco	4	2*

a incl. Laos and Vietnam.

continued

na: data not available. — negligible or nil. [1] one year only. [2] two year average. * estimate. ‡ see appendix. † re-exports.

na: data not available. — negligible or nil. [1] one year only. [2] two year average. * estimate. ‡ see appendix. † re-exports.

RÉUNION *continued*

PRODUCTION, EXPORTS AND IMPORTS

Years: **1963–5 average** and *1953–5 average* Units: '000 metric tons unless otherwise indicated

	Production		Exports		Imports	
1. CEREALS, etc.						
Cassava	**5.0**	*8.0*¹				
Maize (corn)	**15.0**	*5.0*²	—	—	**16.1**	*12.3*
Millets/sorghum	—	—	—	—	**0.1**	—
Potatoes	**3.0**	—	**0.1**	—	—	—
Rice	—	—	—	—	**42.0**	*25.7*
Sweet potatoes/ yams	**3.0**	*2.0*¹				
2. FRUIT, etc.						
Apples	—	—	—	—	**0.5**	—
Bananas	**7.3***	na	—	—	**0.1**	—
Oranges	—	—	—	—	**1.0**	—
Pineapples	**1.0**	—	—	—	—	—
Wine *b*	—	—	—	—	**72.2**	*47.0*

b '000 hectolitres.

	Production		Exports		Imports	
3. BEVERAGES, FOREST PRODUCTS, etc.						
Coffee	—	—	—	—	**1.1**	*0.8*
Sugar: cane	**1 977.7**	*1 591.7*				
raw	**234.0**	*174.7*	**204.0**	*161.0*	**0.7**	—
Tobacco: leaf	—	*0.2*²	—	—	—	—
products	—	—	—	—	**0.4**	—
Softwood *j*	—	—	—	—	**22.0**	*11.3*
Hardwood *j*	**100.7**	*93.3*	—	—	**32.3**	*4.5*
Newsprint	—	—	—	—	**0.4**	*0.3*
Other paper	—	—	—	—	**0.5**	*0.4*

j '000 cu. metres of roundwood equivalent.

	Production		Exports		Imports	
4. VEGETABLE OILSEEDS AND OILS						
Castor oil	—	—	—	—	**0.01**	*0.02*²
Coconut oil	—	—	—	—	**0.01**	*0.01*
Groundnuts	—	—	—	—	**0.08**	*0.07*
Groundnut oil	—	—	—	—	**1.71**	*0.28*
Linseed oil	—	—	—	—	**0.01**	*0.01*²
Olive oil	—	—	—	—	**0.02**	*0.40*²
Soya bean oil	—	—	—	—	**0.68**	—

	Production		Exports		Imports	
5. LIVESTOCK‡, ANIMAL PRODUCTS, etc.						
Chickens *d*	**1 700***n*	*250*				
Cattle *d*	**32**	*40*¹	—	—	**5.4**	*0.4*
Goats *d*	**10**	*25*¹	—	—	**1.1**	na
Sheep *d*	**2**	*5*¹				
Horses *d*	—	*2*¹*				
Pigs *d*	**40***	*70*¹	—	—	**6.7**	—
Bacon/ham	**5***	na	—	—	**0.3**	—
Meat‡: 'A'			—	—	**0.8**	*0.1*
'B'	—	—	—	—	**0.1**	—
Butter	—	—	—	—	**0.3**	*0.1*
Cheese	—	—	—	—	**0.3**	*0.1*²
Eggs	**2***	na	—	—	—	—
Fish	**2**²	*1*	—	—	**2.7**	na
Milk	**3***	na	—	—	**15.2**	*2.7**

d no. in thousands. *n* incl. ducks, geese and turkeys.

	Production		Exports		Imports	
6. FIBRES, TEXTILES, etc.						
Agaves (sisal etc.)	—	—	—	—	**0.1**	na
7. FUEL AND POWER						
Coal 'A'‡	—	—	—	—	na	*2*
Electricity *h*: total	**31**	*5*				
hydro	**21**	—				
thermal	**10**	*5*				
Petroleum, refined	—	—	—	—	**43**	*10*¹

h million kWh.

	Production		Exports		Imports	
10. CHEMICALS*n* AND FERTILIZERS						
Chemicals	—		—		na	
Fertilizers:						
Potash	—	—	—	—	**1.7**	na

n data not available for years 1953–5.

	Production		Exports		Imports	
11. INDUSTRY						
Alcoholic beverages *a*	na	na	**1.6***p*	*1.6p*	**2.5**	na
Cement	—	—	—	—	**103.0**	*21.3*
Electrical engineering *a*	—	—	—	—	**2.9**	*0.9*²
Motor vehicles *a*	—	—	—	—	**6.5**	*1.5*

a million $ U.S. *p* rum only.

FRANCE (OVERSEAS TERRITORIES)

NEW HEBRIDES—(Anglo-French condominium)—see page 190

COMORO ARCHIPELAGO

INDIAN OCEAN

Previously a French colony attached to Madagascar, the Comoro Islands were granted administrative autonomy in 1946, and in 1958 elected, unlike Madagascar, to remain a French Territory.

AREA: 2 170* sq. km. (838* sq. miles)

LAND USE: (percentage of total)	1955
Arable and orchard	36.9
Permanent meadow and pasture	13.8
Forest and woodland	16.1
City areas, waste and other land	33.2

POPULATION: 250 000 (1967 U.N. estimate)
Capital city: MORONI; population: 11 515 (1966)

		Year(s)
Crude birth rate (per '000)	20.6*	1964
Population per physician	16 900	1965
Population per hospital bed	470	1965
School enrolment: age 5–19 years (percentage)	19	1963–4 av.

FINANCE
Currency unit: The franc CFA

Exchange rates	*1965*	*1960*	*1957a*
Per $ U.S.	246.85	246.85	210
Per £ sterling	691.18	691.18	590

a official rate.

		Year
National Income (million $ U.S.)	13	1958
G.N.P. per capita ($ U.S.)	110	1966

EMPLOYMENT, PRODUCTION AND TRADE
The islands are self-sufficient in basic foodstuffs. The chief export crop was originally sugar cane, but now vanilla, copra, sisal, coffee, cloves, ylang and citronella are the main products, many of which are exported. Timber, for building and railway sleepers, is also exported. The majority of the trade is with France.

continued

COMORO ARCHIPELAGO *continued*

PRODUCTION, EXPORTS AND IMPORTS

Years: **1963–5 average** and *1953–5 average* Units: '000 metric tons unless otherwise indicated

	Production		Exports		Imports	
1. CEREALS, etc.						
Cassava	**31.0***	na				
Rice	—	—	—	—	**10.0**	—
Sweet potatoes/ yams	**1.0***	na				
2. FRUIT, etc.						
Coconuts *e*	**57.3***	na	—	—	—	—
Wine *b*	—	—	—	—	**1.5**	—

b '000 hectolitres. *e* no. in millions.

	Production		Exports		Imports	
3. BEVERAGES, FOREST PRODUCTS, etc.						
Coffee	—	—	**0.1**	—	—	—
Sugar: cane	na	na				
raw	na	na	—	—	**0.9**	—
4. VEGETABLE OILSEEDS AND OILS						
Copra	**3.08**	*15.00*²	**3.08**	na	—	—
5. LIVESTOCK‡, ANIMAL PRODUCTS, etc.						
Cattle *d*	**24.7***	*17.0*²	—	—	—	—
Goats *d*	**97.0***	*87.5*²	—	—	—	—
Sheep *d*	**4.0***	*4.0*²	—	—	—	—
Fish	**1.6**	na	—	—	—	—
Milk	**2.0**	na	—	—	**0.5**	—

d no. in thousands.

	Production		Exports		Imports	
6. FIBRES, TEXTILES, etc.						
Agaves (sisal etc.)	na	na	**1.0**	na	—	—
11. INDUSTRY						
Cement	—	—	—	—	**8.7**	na*p*

p see Malagasy Republic.

FRENCH POLYNESIA

PACIFIC OCEAN

French Polynesia consists of a series of island groups scattered over a wide area in the Eastern Pacific. They include the Society Islands (of which Tahiti is the most important), the Tuamotu and Gambier groups, the Austral Islands and the Marquezas Islands. These opted in 1958 to become an Overseas Territory within the French Community.

AREA: 4 000 sq. km. (1 545 sq. miles)

LAND USE: (percentage of total)	*1964*	*1950*
Arable and orchard	16.0	1.3
Permanent meadow and pasture	5.0	10.0
Forest and woodland	28.8	28.7
City areas, waste and other land	50.2	60.0

POPULATION: 98 400 (1967 census)
Capital city: PAPEETE; population: 37 485 (1967)
Total working population: 26 500 (1962)

		Year(s)
Infant mortality (per '000)	100.3*	1961
Crude birth rate (per '000)	36.1*	1964
Population per physician	1 720	1965
Population per hospital bed	120*a*	1966
School enrolment: age 5–19 years (percentage)	101‡*b*	1963–4 av.

a government hospitals only. *b* incl. pre-school education.

COMMUNICATIONS

		Year(s)
Motor vehicles in use ('000s): private	4.3	1963–5 av.
commercial	1.8	
Telephones (per '000 urban population)	4.9	1967
Radio receivers (per '000 population)	284	1963–5 av.
Daily newspapers (per '000 population)	13	1961

FINANCE
Currency unit: The franc CFP

Exchange rates	*1965*	*1960*	*1957*
Per $ U.S.	89.76	90	76
Per £ sterling	253.33	251	212

		Year(s)
National Income (million $ U.S.)	85*	1966
G.N.P. per capita ($ U.S.)	950	1966

PRODUCTION AND TRADE
The coastal plains and most of the low lying islands are covered with coconut palms. Tropical fruits such as bananas, pineapples and oranges are grown for local consumption. Copra is one of the major products for export; others include coffee, vanilla, and mother-of-pearl. Phosphate deposits were exhausted in 1966. Tourism earns almost half as much as visible exports. Main imports are metal manufactures, textiles, petroleum, sugar and flour.

PRODUCTION, EXPORTS AND IMPORTS

Years: **1963–5 average** and *1953–5 average* Units: '000 metric tons unless otherwise indicated

	Production		Exports		Imports	
1. CEREALS, etc.						
Cassava	**5.0***	*3.0*¹				
Millets/sorghum	—	—	—	—	**0.1**²	—
Potatoes	—	—	—	—	**1.1**¹	*0.7*
Rice	—	—	—	—	**2.0**	*1.1*
Sweet potatoes/ yams	**1.0***	na				
Wheat	—	—	—	—	**0.5**²	*0.2*
2. FRUIT, etc.						
Apples	—	—	—	—	**0.2**¹	—
Bananas	na	na	—	—	—	—
Coconuts	**189.7***e*	—	**0.4**¹*n*	—	—	—
Grapes	—	—	—	—	**0.1**¹	—
Wine *b*	—	—	—	—	**26.8**	*9.7*

b '000 hectolitres. *e* no. in millions. *n* desiccated.

	Production		Exports		Imports	
3. BEVERAGES, FOREST PRODUCTS, etc.						
Coffee	**0.4***	*0.1*¹	**0.1**²	—	—²	—
Sugar, raw	—	—	—	—	**4.5**	*1.5*
Hardwood *j*	**0.3**¹	—	—	—	—	—
Paper	—	—	—	—	**0.2**¹	—

j '000 cu. metres of roundwood equivalent.

	Production		Exports		Imports	
4. VEGETABLE OILSEEDS AND OILS						
Copra	**24.47**	*28.70*²	**23.06**	*20.20*	—	—
Coconut oil	na	na	**0.08**	*0.68*	—	*0.02*
Groundnut oil	—	—	—	—	**0.66**	—
Linseed oil	—	—	—	—	—	*0.02*
Olive oil	—	—	—	—	—	*0.10**²

continued

na: data not available. — negligible or nil. ¹ one year only. ² two year average. * estimate. ‡ see appendix. † re-exports.

FRENCH POLYNESIA *continued*

PRODUCTION, EXPORTS AND IMPORTS *continued*

5. LIVESTOCK‡, ANIMAL PRODUCTS, etc.

	Production		Exports		Imports	
Chickens *d*	**133.7***	*110.0*[1]				
Cattle *d*	**13.7***	*15.5*[2]	—	—	—	—
Goats *d*	**8.0***	*6.5*[2]				
Sheep *d*	**5.0**	*4.0*[2]	—	—	—	—
Horses *d*	**3.0***	*5.0*[2]				
Pigs *d*	**17.0***	*17.0*[2]	—	—	—	—
Meat‡ 'B'	—	—	—	—	**1.0**[1]	—
Butter	—	—	—	—	**0.5**	*0.2*
Cheese	—	—	—	—	**0.2**	—
Eggs	**0.3***	*0.2*[1]	—	—	—	—
Fish	**4.5**	*2.0*	—	—	**0.7**	na
Milk	—	—	—	—	**3.4**	*2.2**

d no. in thousands.

7. FUEL AND POWER

	Production		Exports		Imports	
Coal 'A'‡	—	—	—	—	—	*3*
Electricity *h*, hydro.	**16**	—				
Petroleum, refined	—	—	—	—	**47**	*10*[1]

h million kWh.

10. CHEMICALS *n* AND FERTILIZERS

	Production		Exports		Imports	
Chemicals	—		—		na	
Fertilizers:						
Phosphates *p*	**344.0**	na	**341.9**	*233.3*	—	—

n data not available for years 1953–5. *p* produced only in Makatea Is.

11. INDUSTRY

	Production		Exports		Imports	
Cement	—	—	—	—	**77.7**	*19.3*

FRENCH TERRITORY OF THE AFARS AND THE ISSAS — EAST AFRICA

Formerly French Somaliland, the French Territory of the Afars and the Issas is so named to emphasize its two main ethnic groups. The importance of the region depends largely upon the transit trade from Addis Ababa (Ethiopia) via the railway.

AREA: 23 000 sq. km. (8 900 sq. miles)

LAND USE: (percentage of total)	*1958*	*1952*
Arable and orchard	—	—
Permanent meadow and pasture	11.1	10.6
Forest and woodland	0.4	0.3
City areas, waste and other land	88.5	89.1

POPULATION: 108 000 (1966 estimate)

Capital city: DJIBOUTI; population: 43 200 (1963)

		Year(s)
Population per physician	5 300	1962
Population per hospital bed	150	1966
School enrolment: age 5–19 years (percentage)	22	1963–4 av.

COMMUNICATIONS

		Year
Motor vehicles in use ('000s): private	4.2	1965
commercial	0.8	1965
Railway track (km.)	75	1965

FINANCE

Currency unit: The Djibouti franc

Exchange rates	*1965*	*1960*	*1957*
Per $ U.S.	214	214	214
Per £ sterling	602	602	602

		Year
National Income (million $ U.S.)	48*	1966
G.N.P. per capita ($ U.S.)	570	1966

EMPLOYMENT, PRODUCTION AND TRADE

The raising of goats and other stock is very important, but crop production is small. Minerals thought to exist are gypsum, mica, amethyst and sulphur, but reserves of these are as yet unproven.

The chief items in transit from Ethiopia are hides and coffee. Major imports are fuel, sugar, cement and cotton goods. Trade is mainly with France but a few imports come from neighbouring countries.

Total trade (in million $ U.S.)	*1965*	*1955*
Exports (f.o.b.)	3.2	1.2
Imports (c.i.f.)	81.5	34.0

PRODUCTION, EXPORTS AND IMPORTS

Years: **1963–5 average** and *1953–5 average* Units: '000 metric tons unless otherwise indicated

1. CEREALS, etc.

	Production		Exports		Imports	
Millets/sorghum	—	—	—	—	**5.0**	—
Rice	—	—	—	—	**3.8**	*1.7*
Wheat	—	—	—	—	—	*1.0*

2. FRUIT, etc.

	Production		Exports		Imports	
Dates	—	—	—	—	—	na
Wine *b*	—	—	—	—	**11.2**[2]	*6.3*

b '000 hectolitres.

3. BEVERAGES, FOREST PRODUCTS, etc.

	Production		Exports		Imports	
Sugar, raw	—	—	—	—	**3.3**	*2.6*
Softwood *j*	—	—	—	—	**3.5**[2]	*4.2*[1]
Hardwood *j*	**23.0**[1]*	*4.5*[2]	—	—[2]	—	—
Newsprint	—	—	—	—[2]	**0.4**[2]	—[2]
Other paper	—	—	—	—[2]	**0.2**[2]	*0.1*[2]

j '000 cu. metres of roundwood equivalent.

5. LIVESTOCK,‡ ANIMAL PRODUCTS, etc.

	Production		Exports		Imports	
Cattle *d*	**13.3***	*10.0*	—	—	—	*3.8*[2]
Goats *d*	**499.0***	*370.0*				
Sheep *d*	**85.0***	*85.3*	—	—	—	—
Horses *d*	—	*3.0*[2]				
Meat‡: 'A'	**2.7**	*2.0*[1]*p*	—	—	—	—
'B'	**0.2**	na	—	—	—	—
Fish	**0.7**[2]	*0.7*	—	—	—	—
Milk	**1.0***	*2.0*[1]	—	—	—	—
Hides/skins	—	na	—	—	—	—

d no. in thousands. *p* government inspected meat only.

7. FUEL AND POWER

	Production		Exports		Imports	
Coal 'A'‡	—	—	—	—	—	*4*
Electricity *h*, thermal	**19***	—				
Petroleum, refined	—	—	—	—	**1 540**	*10*[1]

h million kWh.

11. INDUSTRY

	Production		Exports		Imports	
Cement	—	—	—	—	**12.3**	*8.0*

continued

NEW CALEDONIA — SOUTH WEST PACIFIC

New Caledonia and its dependencies were annexed by France in 1854. The importance of the region has risen greatly with the exploitation of its nickel reserves.

AREA: 19 103 sq. km. (7 374 sq. miles)

LAND USE: (percentage of total)	*1961*	*1955*
Arable and orchard	4.3	1.0
Permanent meadow and pasture	21.4	26.8
Forest and woodland	14.5	13.4
City areas, waste and other land	59.8	58.8

POPULATION: 86 519 (including 33 600 Europeans) (1963 census)

Capital city: NOUMÉA; population: 34 990 (city proper, 1963)

Distribution of working population (1963)
Total working population: 30 471

U.N. group no.		*Percentage*
0	Agriculture, forestry, fishing and hunting	38.0
1	Mining and quarrying	3.9
2/3	Manufacturing	12.2
4	Construction	9.3
5	Electricity, gas, water and sanitary services	0.7
6	Commerce	9.8
7	Transport, storage and communications	5.1
8	Services	19.9
9	Others	1.1

		Year(s)
Infant mortality (per '000)	32.8*	1965
Crude birth rate (per '000)	29.3*	1965
Crude death rate (per '000)	7.3*	1965
Population per physician	1 750	1965
Population per hospital bed	70	1966
School enrolment: age 5–19 years (percentage)	110‡	1963–4 av.
age over 19 years (per 100 000 population)	42	1963–4 av.

COMMUNICATIONS

		Year(s)
Motor vehicles in use ('000s): private	10.5	1963–5 av.
commercial	5.1	1963–5 av.
Mail per capita: domestic	33	1963–5 av.
foreign received	21	1963–5 av.
foreign sent	10	1963–5 av.
Telephones (per '000 urban population)	5.5	1967
Radio receivers (per '000 population)	149	1963–5 av.
Daily newspapers (per '000 population)	47	1962–4 av.

FINANCE

Currency unit: The franc CFP

Exchange rates	*1965*	*1960*	*1950*
Per $ U.S.	90	90	76
Per £ sterling	251	251	212

		Year
National Income (million $ U.S.)	140*	1966
G.N.P. per capita ($ U.S.)	1 480	1966

EMPLOYMENT, PRODUCTION AND TRADE

Agricultural products are coffee, copra, maize, vegetables, and livestock. Great mineral resources exist, especially nickel, chrome, iron and manganese. Small industries are developing. The chief exports in 1963 were chrome, iron, nickel and copra, 66% of the total going to France and the franc zone. The chief imports were coal, coke and petroleum products, 56% of the total coming from France and the franc zone.

PRODUCTION, EXPORTS AND IMPORTS

Years: **1963–5 average** and *1953–5 average* Units: '000 metric tons unless otherwise indicated

1. CEREALS. etc.

	Production		Exports		Imports	
Cassava	**4.0***	*16.0*[1]				
Maize (corn)	**2.0***	*1.0*[2]	—	—	—	—
Millets/sorghum	—	—	—	—	**0.8**	—
Potatoes	**1.0***	*1.0*[1]	—	—	**1.5**[1]	*0.8*
Rice	—	—[1]	—	—	**2.9**	*2.3*
Sweet potatoes/yams	**4.0***	*5.0*[1]	—	—	—	—

2. FRUIT, etc.

	Production		Exports		Imports	
Coconuts *e*	**12.7***	na	—	—	—	—
Wine *b*	—	—	—	—	**41.6**	*30.0*

b '000 hectolitres. *e* no. in millions.

3. BEVERAGES, FOREST PRODUCTS, etc.

	Production		Exports		Imports	
Coffee	**2.3***	*1.8**[2]	**1.5**	*1.6*	—	—
Sugar, raw	—	—	—	—	**3.5**	*2.2*
Tea	—	—	—	—	**0.1**	*0.1*
Softwood *j*	**1.9**[2]	na	—	—	—	—
Hardwood *j*	**8.9**[2]	na	—	—	—[1]	—
Paper	—	—	—	—	**1.2**[2]	—

j '000 cu. metres of roundwood equivalent.

4. VEGETABLE OILSEEDS AND OILS

	Production		Exports		Imports	
Copra	**1.73**	*3.40*[2]	**1.32**	*2.77*	—	—
Groundnut oil	—	—	—	—	**0.57**	*0.08*
Olive oil	—	—	—	—	na	*0.12*

5. LIVESTOCK‡, ANIMAL PRODUCTS, etc.

	Production		Exports		Imports	
Chickens *d*	**144.7****n*	na				
Cattle *d*	**99.0**	*102.0*[2]	—	—	—	—
Goats *d*	**19.0**	*20.0*[2]	—	—	—	—
Sheep *d*	**3.7**	*3.0*[2]	—	—	—	—
Horses *d*	**9.3**	na				
Pigs *d*	**19.0**	*14.0*[2]	—	—	—	—
Meat‡ 'B'	**0.1***	na	—	—	—	—
Butter	—	—	—	—	**0.3**	*0.1*
Cheese	—	—	—	—	**0.3**	*0.1*
Eggs	**0.5***	na	—	—	—	—
Fish	na	na	**1.0**	*0.7*	—	—
Milk	**6.0***	na	—	—	**3.7**	*2.4**

d no. in thousands. *n* incl. ducks, geese and turkeys.

7. FUEL AND POWER

	Production		Exports		Imports	
Coal 'A'‡	—	—	—	—	**172**	*156*
Coke	—	—	—	—	**83**	—
Electricity *h*: total	**337**	*60*				
hydro	**334**	*50*				
thermal	**3**	*10*				
Petroleum, refined	—	—	—	—	**12**	*30*[1]

h million kWh.

8. IRON AND STEEL

	Production		Exports		Imports	
Iron ore	**164***m*	—	**294**	—	—	—

m metal content.

9. NON-FERROUS MINERALS AND METALS

	Production		Exports		Imports	
Chrome, ore	na	*84.21m*	**7.98**	*86.92*	—	—
Magnesium, magnesite	**0.59**	na	—	—	—	—
Manganese, ore	na	*1.86*	na	*2.70*	—	—
Nickel: ore	**44.62*** *m*	*13.31*m*	**882.59**	*238.20*	—	—
metal	na	na	**44.08**	*11.00n*	—	—

m metal content. *n* ferro-nickel of which the nickel content is 32–35%.

continued

na: data not available. — negligible or nil. [1] one year only. [2] two year average. * estimate. ‡ see appendix. † re-exports.

FRANCE (OVERSEAS TERRITORIES) *continued*

ST. PIERRE AND MIQUELON

NORTH WEST ATLANTIC

St. Pierre and Miquelon are two small groups of islands off the coast of Newfoundland.

AREA: 242 sq. km. (93.5 sq. miles)

LAND USE: (percentage of total)	*1946*
Arable and orchard	12.5
Permanent meadow and pasture	—
Forest and woodland	4.2
City areas, waste and other land	83.3

POPULATION: 5 000 (1967 estimate)
Chief town: ST. PIERRE
Total working population: 1 773 (1962)

		Year
Crude birth rate (per '000)	25.5	1964
Crude death rate (per '000)	8.8	1964

FINANCE
Currency unit: The franc CFA

Exchange rates	*1965*	*1960*	*1957*
Per $ U.S.	246.85	246.85	210
Per £ sterling	691.18	691.18	590

EMPLOYMENT AND TRADE

The islands consist mainly of barren rock, and are unsuitable for agriculture. Fishing is the chief occupation and provides the main exports. Imports are textiles, wine, foodstuffs and fuels.

PRODUCTION, EXPORTS AND IMPORTS
Years: **1963–5 average** and *1953–5 average* Units: '000 metric tons unless otherwise indicated

	Production		Exports		Imports	
1. CEREALS, etc.						
Potatoes	—	—	—	—	—	*0.4**
2. FRUIT, etc.						
Wine *b*	—	—	—	—	2.8	*1.7*
b '000 hectolitres.						
3. BEVERAGES, FOREST PRODUCTS, etc.						
Sugar, raw	—	—	—	—	0.2	*0.2*
5. LIVESTOCK‡, ANIMAL PRODUCTS, etc.						
Cattle *d*	—	—	—	—	0.4*	*1.4²**
Goats/sheep *d*	—	—	—	—	0.8	na
Pigs *d*	—	—	—	—	0.4	*0.3²**
Meat‡ 'A'	—	—	—	—	—	*0.1²**
Butter	—	—	—	—	0.1	*0.1*
Fish	8.9	*6.5*	3.0	na	0.3	na
Milk	—	—	—	—	0.3	—
d no. in thousands.						
7. FUEL AND POWER						
Coal 'A'‡	—	—	—	—	9	*10*
Electricity *h*	na	—				
Petroleum, refined	—	—	—	—	17	*10¹*
h million kWh.						
11. INDUSTRY						
Cement	—	—	—	—	1.0	*1.0*

WALLIS AND FUTUNA

PACIFIC OCEAN

Previously a French Protectorate, the islands became a French Overseas Territory in 1961.

AREA: Wallis: 275 sq. km. (106 sq. miles)
Futuna: 150 sq. km. (58 sq. miles)

POPULATION: Wallis: 5 380; Futuna: 3 000* (1965 estimate)

GABON

CENTRAL AFRICA

Formerly a territory of French Equatorial Africa, and from 1958 a member state of the French Community, Gabon became an independent republic in 1960. It has been a member of the Equatorial Customs Union since its foundation in 1959.

AREA: 267 000 sq. km. (103 089 sq. miles)

LAND USE: (percentage of total)	*1962*
Arable and orchard	0.5
Permanent meadow and pasture	na
Forest and woodland (including rough grazing)	74.7
City areas, waste and other land	na

POPULATION: 473 000 (1967 estimate)
Capital city: LIBREVILLE; population: 57 000 (1967)

Distribution of working population (1963)
Total working population: 220 000

U.N. group no.		*Percentage*
0	Agriculture, forestry, fishing and hunting	84.1
1	Mining and quarrying	3.4
2/3	Manufacturing	1.9
4	Construction	1.7
5	Electricity, gas, water and sanitary services	0.1
6	Commerce	3.7
7	Transport, storage and communications	1.3
8	Services	3.2
9	Others	0.6

		Year(s)
Life expectancy at birth (years): male	25*	1960–1 av.
female	45*	
Population per physician	5 860	1964
Population per hospital bed	110	1966
School enrolment: age 5–19 years (percentage)	50	1963–4 av.
age over 19 years (per 100 000 population)	17	1964–5 av.

COMMUNICATIONS

		Year(s)
Motor vehicles in use ('000s): private	3.2	1963–5 av.
commercial	5.6	
Telephones (per '000 urban population)	0.8*	1967
Radio receivers (per '000 population)	74	1963–5 av.
Television sets (per '000 population)	2.4	1963–5 av.

FINANCE
Currency unit: The franc CFA

Exchange rates	*1965*	*1960*
Per $ U.S.	246.85	246.85
Per £ sterling	691.18	691.18

		Year(s)
National Income (million $ U.S.)	152	1963
G.N.P. per capita ($ U.S.)	400	1966
Foreign trade (percentage of G.D.P.)	76	1963–5 av.

TRADING

Total trade (in million $ U.S.)	*1965*	*1955*
Exports (f.o.b.)	96	28
Imports (c.i.f.)	62	20

Main trading partners (percentage of total value)

Exports	*1965*	*Imports*	*1965*
France	48	France	58
U.S.A.	18	U.S.A.	12
Germany F.R.	11	Germany F.R.	7
U.K.	4	Cameroun	3
Israel	3	U.K.	3

Distribution of trade (percentage of total value)

Exports	*1965*	*Imports*	*1965*
Wood	44	Manufactured goods	72
Manganese	28	(machinery and transport equipment)	(38)
Petroleum	15	Food	9
Uranium	9	Alcoholic beverages	6

continued

na: data not available. — negligible or nil. ¹ one year only. ² two year average. * estimate. ‡ see appendix. † re-exports.

PRODUCTION, EXPORTS AND IMPORTS
Years: **1963–5 average** Units: '000 metric tons unless otherwise indicated
Note—no data are available for the years 1953–5

	Production	Exports	Imports
1. CEREALS, etc.			
Cassava	126.7		
Maize (corn)	1.7*	—	0.1
Potatoes	—	—	0.7
Rice	1.0	—	1.4
Sweet potatoes/yams	2.0*		
2. FRUIT, etc.			
Apples	—	—	0.2*n*
Bananas	10.0*	—	—
Oranges	—	—	0.1
Wine *b*	—	—	89.7
b '000 hectolitres. *n* incl. pears and quince.			
3. BEVERAGES, FOREST PRODUCTS, etc.			
Cocoa	3.6	3.3	—
Coffee	2.5*	0.8	—
Sugar, raw	—	—	1.2
Tobacco: leaf	—	—	0.1
products	—	—	na
Hardwood *j*	2 771.0*¹	1 245.0	—
j '000 cu. metres of roundwood equivalent.			
4. VEGETABLE OILSEEDS AND OILS			
Groundnuts	0.70¹*	0.32	0.04
Groundnut oil	na	—	0.11
Olive oil	—	—	0.01
Palm kernels	na	0.20	—
Palm kernel oil	—	—	0.01
Palm oil	na	0.52	—
5. LIVESTOCK‡, ANIMAL PRODUCTS, etc.			
Cattle *d*	4.0*	—	0.8
Goats *d*	59.0*	—	—
Sheep *d*	47.0*	—	—
Pigs *d*	6.0*	—	—
Meat‡: 'A'	—	—	0.4
'B'	—	—	0.1
5. LIVESTOCK, ANIMAL PRODUCTS—*continued*			
Butter	—	—	0.1
Cheese	—	—	0.1
Eggs	1.6*	—	—
Fish	1.3²*p*	—	2.1
Milk	—	—	2.3
Hides/skins	na	0.1	—
d no. in thousands. *p* industrial fishing only.			
7. FUEL AND POWER			
Electricity *h t*	37		
Natural gas *i*	10	—	—
Oil, crude	1 070	1 097	—
Petroleum, refined	—	—	60
Uranium *f*	445*	1 387*u*	—
f metric tons. *h* million kWh. *i* million cu. metres. *t* thermal. *u* concentrates.			

Recent explorations have shown considerable resources of oil, natural gas and uranium, exploitation of which is increasing rapidly.

	Production	Exports	Imports
9. NON-FERROUS MINERALS AND METALS			
Gold *k*, ore *m*	38.70	32.67*n*	—
Manganese, ore	958.83	878.30	—
k '000 fine troy oz. *m* metal content. *n* bullion (may incl. a small quantity from Congo R.).			
11. INDUSTRY			
Aircraft *a*	—	—	0.7
Alcoholic beverages *a*	—	—	3.3
Cement	—	—	34.0
Electrical engineering *a*	—	—	3.0
Railway vehicles *a*	—	—	0.2
Motor vehicles *a*	—	—	6.1
a million $ U.S.			

continued

GAMBIA

WEST AFRICA

The Gambia was a British colony; however, in 1963 full internal self-government was achieved, and it became an independent member of the Commonwealth in 1965. Special arrangements regarding external affairs have been made with Senegal.

AREA: 9 301 sq. km. (3 977 sq. miles)

LAND USE: (percentage of total)	*1965*	*1955*
Arable and orchard	17.7	21.5
Permanent meadow and pasture, forest and woodland	38.4	29.4
City areas, waste and other land	43.9	49.1

POPULATION: 343 000 (1967 estimate) (excluding seasonal immigrants working on farms)
Capital city: BATHURST; population: 42 800 (1965)

		Year(s)
Life expectancy at birth (years)	43*	1962–3 av.
Infant mortality (per '000)	72.1 *a*	1965
Crude birth rate (per '000)	48.5 *a*	1965
Crude death rate (per '000)	14.1 *a*	1965
Population per physician	22 000	1965
Population per hospital bed	690 *b*	1966
School enrolment: age 5–19 years (percentage)	16	1963–4 av.

a in Bathurst only. *b* government hospitals only.

EMPLOYMENT AND PRODUCTION

Most of the population is engaged in agriculture, in particular the cultivation of groundnuts. Fishing and livestock production are considerable. No minerals are at present being exploited and groundnut processing is the only industry.

COMMUNICATIONS

		Year(s)
Motor vehicles in use ('000s): private	1.3	1963–5 av.
commercial	1.0	
Telephones (per '000 urban population)	0.4	1967
Radio receivers (per '000 population)	111	1963–5 av.
Daily newspapers (per '000 population)	5	1959

FINANCE
Currency unit: The West African pound, at par with the £ sterling

Exchange rates	*1965*	*1960*
Per $ U.S.	0.357	0.357

		Year
National Income (million $ U.S.)	20	1958
G.N.P. per capita ($ U.S.)	90	1966

TRADING

Total trade (in million $ U.S.)	*1965*	*1955*	*1938*
Exports (f.o.b.)	14	7	2
Imports (c.i.f.)	16	10	2

Main trading partners (percentage of total value)

Exports	*1965*	*1955*	*Imports*	*1965*	*1955*
U.K.	50	62	U.K.	41	48
Italy	21	—	Japan	16	7
Portugal	10	na	Burma	6	na
Netherlands	10	3	China P.R.	4	na
Switzerland	4	na	France	3	2

Distribution of trade (percentage of total value)

Exports	*1966*	*Imports*	*1966*
Groundnuts	38	Manufactured goods	64
Groundnut oil	37	(textiles and clothing)	(31)
Fodder (derived from groundnuts)	22	(machinery and transport equipment)	(19)
		Food	15
		Alcoholic beverages	7

continued

na: data not available. — negligible or nil. ¹ one year only. ² two year average. * estimate. ‡ see appendix. † re-exports.

GAMBIA *continued*

PRODUCTION, EXPORTS AND IMPORTS

Years: **1963–5 average** and *1953–5 average* Units: '000 metric tons unless otherwise indicated

1. CEREALS, etc.

	Production		Exports		mports	
Cassava	6.0*	na				
Maize (corn)	0.7*	na	—	—	—	—
Millets/sorghum	44.0*	na	—	—	—	—
Potatoes	—	—	—	—	0.1	0.2
Rice	35.0	na	—	—	8.0	3.0

2. FRUIT, etc.

	Production		Exports		mports	
Wine *b*	—	—	—	—	2.3	1.0

b '000 hectolitres.

3. BEVERAGES, FOREST PRODUCTS, etc.

	Production		Exports		mports	
Coffee	—	—	—	—	0.1	—
Sugar, raw	—	—	—	—	3.2	2.0
Tobacco: leaf	—	—	—	—	0.1	—
cigarettes	—	—	—	—	0.1	—
Softwood *j*	—	—	—	—	na	—
Hardwood *j*	146.7*	na	—	—	na	—
Other paper	—	—	—	—	0.1	—

j '000 cu. metres of roundwood equivalent.

4. VEGETABLE OILSEEDS AND OILS

	Production		Exports		mports	
Groundnuts	81.90*	42.00*	35.15	37.90	—	—
Groundnut oil	na	na	8.72	0.01	0.01[2]	0.18
Palm kernels	1.57	na	1.53	1.80	—	—
Palm oil	1.60*	2.10[1]	—	—	—	0.04

5. LIVESTOCK‡, ANIMAL PRODUCTS, etc.

	Production		Exports		Imports	
Chickens *d*	174.7**n*	300.0*n*				
Cattle *d*	184.0	145.0[2]	—	—	—	—
Goats *d*	95.0	81.0[2]	} 0.2	na	—	—
Sheep *d*	55.3	62.5[2]				
Horses *d*	na	4.0				
Pigs *d*	2.0	3.0[1]	—	—	—	—
Meat‡, 'A'	3.0*	na	—	—	—	—
Eggs	1.1*	na	—	—	—	—
Fish	na	na	0.7	na	0.1	na
Milk	—	—	—	—	1.2	1.0*

d no. in thousands. *n* incl. ducks, geese and turkeys.

6. FIBRES, TEXTILES, etc.

	Production		Exports		Imports	
Cotton, woven fabrics	—	—	—	—	1.0[2]	—
Rayon, woven fabrics	—	—	—	—	0.1[1]*p*	—

p incl. synthetic piece goods.

7. FUEL AND POWER

	Production		Exports		Imports	
Electricity *h t*	8	1	—	—	—	—
Petroleum, refined	—	—	—	—	10	10[1]

h million kWh. *t* thermal.

9. NON-FERROUS MINERALS AND METALS

	Production		Exports		Imports	
Asbestos, manufactured	—	—	—	—	0.57	—
Titanium minerals	—	na	—	0.37	—	—

11. INDUSTRY

	Production		Exports		Imports	
Alcoholic beverages			—	—	0.3*a*	—
beer *b*	215.0	43.5				
Cement	—	—	—	—	8.3	4.0
Electrical engineering *a*	—	—	—	—	0.6	0.2[2]
Motor vehicles *a*	—	—	—	—	0.6[2]	0.3

a million $ U.S. *b* '000 hectolitres.

GERMANY: DEMOCRATIC REPUBLIC

EUROPE

On the termination of World War II in 1945 the Eastern Sector of Germany came under the control of the U.S.S.R. and Poland. Separation from the Western Sector was established, and the Eastern Sector, referred to as East Germany, was declared the German Democratic Republic in 1949; this was not, however, recognized by many countries and there remains some move towards the reunification of Germany.

Germany D.R. is a member of Comecon.

Pre-war statistics refer to both sectors of Germany.

AREA: 108 174 sq. km. (41 766 sq. miles)

LAND USE: (percentage of total)

	1965	1949
Arable and orchard	46.2	47.3
Permanent meadow and pasture	13.3	12.0
Forest and woodland	27.2	27.0
City areas, waste and other land	13.3	13.7

POPULATION: 17 011 931 (1964 census) [19 102 000 in 1947]

Largest city: OST-BERLIN (East Berlin), capital; population: 1 073 647 (city proper, 1965)

Total working population: 7 229 140 (1960)

		Year(s)
Life expectancy at birth (years): male	68.5	1963–6 av.
female	73.5	1963–6 av.
Infant mortality (per '000)	24.8	1965
Crude birth rate (per '000)	16.5	1965
Crude death rate (per '000)	13.3	1965
Population per physician	750	1966
Population per hospital bed	80	1966
School enrolment: age 5–19 years (percentage)	79	1963–4 av.
age over 19 years (per 100 000 population)	476	1963–5 av.

COMMUNICATIONS

		Year(s)
Motor vehicles in use ('000s): private	583.2	1963–5 av.
commercial	282.3	1963–5 av.
Railway track (km.)	16 108	1964
Mail per capita: domestic	74	1963–5 av.
foreign received	2	1963–5 av.
foreign sent	5	1963–5 av.
Telephones (per '000 urban population)	10.1	1967
Radio licences (per '000 population)	337	1963–5 av.
Television licences (per '000 population)	164.1	1963–5 av.
Daily newspapers (per '000 population)	456	1959

FINANCE

Currency unit: The mark (M.D.N.)

Exchange rates a	1965	1960
Per $ U.S.	2.22	2.22
Per £ sterling	6.22	6.22

		Year(s)
National Income (million $ U.S.)	20 000*	1966
G.N.P. per capita ($ U.S.)	1 220	1966
Rate of increase of G.N.P. per capita	2.4	1960–4 av.

a These rates are based on a value fixed on gold, but are not recognized by the International Monetary Fund.

PRODUCTION

The Democratic Republic is economically a less diversified area than the Federal Republic; although almost self-sufficient in food, the country lacks industrial raw materials. Agriculture had been collectivized by April 1960, and industry is centrally planned. The main mineral deposits are lignite and copper, and crude steel plants have been erected as steel from the Rhur ceased to be available when Germany was divided. Industry produced about 65% of the national income in 1964.

TRADING

Total trade (in million $ U.S.)	1965	1955	1936*f*
Exports (f.o.b.)	3 070	1 278	1 925
Imports (f.o.b.)	2 810	1 173	1 709

Main trading partners (percentage of total value)

Exports	1965	1955	1936*f*	*Imports*	1965	1955	1936*f*
U.S.S.R.	43	40	4	U.S.S.R.	43	36	4
Germany F.R.	10	11		Germany F.R.	9	11	
Czechoslovakia	10	7	3	Czechoslovakia	9	6	3
Poland	9	10	1	Poland	5	10	1
Hungary	4	4	2	Hungary	4	5	2
Bulgaria	3	2	1	Bulgaria	3	3	1
Romania	2	2	2	Yugoslavia	3	—	2

f incl. Germany F.R.

DISTRIBUTION OF TRADE

In 1965, machinery and transport equipment accounted for 46% of the country's exports.

continued

na: data not available. — negligible or nil. [1] one year only. [2] two year average. * estimate. ‡ see appendix. † re-exports.

PRODUCTION, EXPORTS AND IMPORTS

Years: **1963–5 average** and *1953–5 average* Units: '000 metric tons unless otherwise indicated

1. CEREALS, etc.

	Production		Exports		Imports	
Barley	1 448.0	891.5[2]	—	2.7*	199.0	17.7*
Maize (corn)	2.3*	7.5[2]	—	—[2]	259.7	8.0*
Millets/sorghum	—	—	—	—	7.0*	—
Oats	780.0	1 356.2[2]	—	—*	—	—*
Potatoes	12 871.7	14 294.0	7.8*	1.5	207.5	1.6*
Rice	—	—	—	—	32.5	17.7*
Rye	1 825.0	2 365.5[2]	9.4*	2.4*	128.0	na
Wheat	1 476.7	1 206.5[2]	2.1	9.0*	1 183.7	41.4*

2. FRUIT, etc.

	Production		Exports		Imports	
Apples	201.3	na	—	—	73.8*	33.3*
Cherries	72.0	72.1	—	—	—	—
Dates	—	—	—	—	11.8*	—
Grapes	—	—	—	—	38.0*	7.3*
Lemons	—	—	—	—	20.0*	7.1*
Oranges	—	—	—	—	25.3*	6.2*
Pears	95.3	na	—	—	0.6[2]*	0.5*
Plums	76.7	120.9	—	—	—	—
Raisins	—	—	—	—	10.6*	1.6*
Tomatoes	23.0	na				
Wine *b*	—	—	—	0.3*	634.8	60.7*

b '000 hectolitres.

3. BEVERAGES, FOREST PRODUCTS, etc.

	Production		Exports		Imports	
Cocoa	—	—	—	—	14.6	—
Coffee	—	—	—	—	35.6	5.4[2]*
Sugar: beet	5 994.3	6 283.0*				
raw	721.7	778.0*	168.9	29.4*	165.2*	0.2*
Tea	—	—	—	—	1.6	—
Tobacco: leaf	6.8	na	—	—*	28.1	6.0*
cigars *e*	1 844.0	—	—	—	na	—
cigarettes *e*	17 915.0	17 366.0	—	—	800.8	—
tobacco/snuff	1.9	3.1	—	—	na	—
Softwood *j*	5 209.3*	8 198.0[2]	137.0[2]	16.7	2 139.0	89.0
Hardwood *j*	1 241.3	1 543.5[2]	—[2]	1.7	185.5	11.6
Wood pulp	644.1	534.0[2]	na	—[2]	116.5	13.5[2]
Newsprint	90.3	90.0*	14.7	6.9	na	0.1
Other paper	818.3	561.0*	35.0	32.3[1]	61.0	19.2[1]

e no. in millions. *j* '000 cu. metres of roundwood equivalent.

4. VEGETABLE OILSEEDS AND OILS

	Production		Exports		Imports	
Castor oil	—	—	—	—	0.62	—
Coconut oil	—	—	—	—	5.91	0.09*
Cottonseed	—	—	—	—	—	0.20*
Groundnuts	—	—	—	—	10.60[2]	—
Groundnut oil	na	na	—	—	0.24*	0.19*
Linseed	5.67	22.50[2]	—	0.13*	3.13*	0.25[2]
Linseed oil	na	na	—	—[2]	8.25*	5.51*
Olive oil	—	—	—	—[2]	0.32*	—[2]
Palm kernels	—	—	—	—	0.33*	—
Palm oil	—	—	—	—	—	0.02*
Rapeseed	172.70	167.00[2]	—	—	0.90*	—
Soya beans	—	—	—	—	6.33*	—[2]
Soya bean oil	na	—	0.49[2]*	—	0.97*	—
Sunflower seed	na	—	—	—	70.57	3.76*
Sunflower seed oil	na	na	0.99*	—	65.48*	—[2]

5. LIVESTOCK‡, ANIMAL PRODUCTS, etc.

	Production		Exports		Imports	
Chickens *d*	37 805.7*n*	23 486.3*				
Cattle *d*	4 601.3	3 821.7	4.0*	—	8.9*	13.3*
dairy cows *d*	2 393.7	na				
Goats *d*	379.0	1 142.0	} 31.7*	na	—	—
Sheep *d*	1 887.7	1 563.7				
Horses *d*	340.0	724.0				
Pigs *d*	8 698.0	8 558.3	2.5*	—	7.3*	3.6*
Bacon/ham	} 834.7*	na	{ —	—	—	0.4*
Meat‡: 'A'			—	—	—	13.7*
'B'	—	na	—	—	—	3.2*
Butter	179.3	na	—	—*	34.7	12.8*
Cheese	46.0	13.0[1]*p*	—	0.1*	15.7	9.7*
Eggs	214.5	110.6	—	—	5.5	2.7*
Fish	215.1	64.6	na	na	140.4	na
Milk	5 897.0	4 998.3	—	—	—	—
Wool	3.1[2]	2.0*	—	—	23.4	0.1*

d no. in thousands. *n* incl. ducks, geese, and turkeys. *p* factory produce only.

6. FIBRES, TEXTILES, etc.

	Production		Exports		Imports	
Agaves (sisal etc.)	—	—	—	—	0.7*	—
Cotton lint	—	—	0.1*	—	96.4	2.6*
Flax fibre	5.4	9.8[2]	0.4*	—	1.3*	0.9*
Hemp fibre	1.6	4.5[2]	—	—	1.7*	0.1*
Jute	—	—	—	—	4.4	0.1*
Rubber: natural	—	—	—	—	27.7	—
synthetic	92.7	na	na	38.1[2]	—	—
Silk	na	na	—	—	—	—
Cotton: yarn	79.2	na	na	na	7.3[1]	na
woven fabrics	33.5*	26.8*	2.8[1]	na	3.6[1]	na
Rayon	na	na	na	na	na	na
Wool: yarn	31.7	22.2	—	—	—	—
woven fabrics	38.3*q*	na	—	—	—	—

q million sq. metres.

7. FUEL AND POWER

	Production		Exports		Imports	
Coal: 'A' ‡	2 410[2]	2 680	—	60	9 575	6 308
'B'	76 200	200 610	6 581	4 088	5 485	4 246
Coke	na	na	120	30	3 248	2 426
Electricity *h*: total	50 698	26 300[1]				
hydro	623	500[1]				
thermal	50 075	25 800[1]				
Natural gas *i*	110	—[1]	—	—	—	—
Oil, crude	56	30[1]	—	—	4 183	na
Petroleum, refined	3 823	600[1]	1 143	460[1]	540	na

h million kWh. *i* million cu. metres.

8. IRON AND STEEL

	Production		Exports		Imports	
Iron ore	492*m*	427**m*	—	—	1 397*m*	890
Pig iron	2 249	1 304	—	—	740	248
Steel ingots/castings	4 256	2 334	—	—	—	—
Iron/steel products	na	na	na	na	na	na

m metal content.

9. NON-FERROUS MINERALS AND METALS

	Production		Exports		Imports	
Silver *k*, ore *m*	4 800*	4 500*	na	na	na	na
Aluminium: bauxite	—	—	—	—	301.51	na
alumina	62*	na	—	—	35.56	5.32*r*
aluminium	47*	19	—	—	na	na
Chrome: ore *m*	—	—	—	—	25.62	na
Cobalt	na	—	—	—	—	—
Copper: ore *m*	25*	20*	na	na	na	na
metal	20*	26*	na	na	na	na
Lead: ore *m*	10*	5*	na	na	na	na
metal	25*	27*	na	na	na	na
Magnesium, metal/salts	na	na	22.40	17.64	—	—
Manganese, ore *m*	—	—	—	—	81.32	na
Nickel	na	na	na	na	na	na
Tin: ore *m*	1	1	na	na	na	na
metal	1	1	na	na	na	na
Zinc: ore	10*	na	na	na	na	na
metal	10*	na	na	na	na	na

k '000 fine troy oz. *m* metal content. *r* calcined alumina.

10. CHEMICALS *n* AND FERTILIZERS

	Production		Exports		Imports	
Organic chemicals:						
Benzene	1 460.6		na		45.3	
Butadiene	na		na		na	
Ethylene	na		na		na	
Methanol	109.4		na		na	
Phenol	na		na		na	
Phthalic anhydride	na		na		na	
Styrene monomer	na		na		na	
Urea	na		na		na	
Inorganic chemicals:						
Ammonia	514.0		0.8		—	
Carbon black	14.1[1]		na		na	
Chlorine	77.9		na		na	
Nitric acid	402.3*		na		na	
Sodium carbonate	668.8		209.0		—	
Sodium hydroxide	356.4		18.7		—	
Sulphuric acid	833.4		16.0		—	
Plastics:						
Polyamides	na		na		na	
Polyethylene	3.0*		na		na	
Polyvinyl chloride	98.3		31.2		—	
Fertilizers:						
Phosphates	—	—	—	—	298.6*p*	—
Potash	1 876.0*w*	1 377.7**w*	17.4	924.3*q*	—	—
Pyrites	42.3**x*	46.0**x*	—	—	114.1*x*	199.1
Sulphur	123.2*r*	95.5[1]*r*	12.9	22.0	—	—

n data not available for years 1953–5. *p* P_2O_5 content. *q* in addition, carbonic caustic potash 14.3. *r* recovered sulphur. *w* K_2O content. *x* sulphur content.

11. INDUSTRY

	Production		Exports		Imports	
Alcoholic beverages *b*			na	na	na	278
beer	13 528	10 260				
spirits	775[1]*n*	579[1]*p*				
Cement	5 770	2 668	380[1]	275**q*	na	—**q*
Electrical engineering *a*	na	na	115*dr*	126[1]	66*dr*	na
Locomotives *c*	587	na	na	na	na	na
Railway vehicles *a*	na	na	135	na	na	na
Machine tools *a*	165[1]	na	na	na	na	na
Merchant ships *g*	172*t*	na	na	na	4[1]	na
Motor vehicles			36*a*	14*a*	16*a*	na
commercial *d*	12	20				
private *d*	93	18				

a million $ U.S. *b* '000 hectolitres. *c* no. of units. *d* no. in thousands. *g* '000 G.R.T. *n* 1965 figure. *p* 1960 figure. *q* excl. trade with other Comecon countries. *r* electrical motors, transformers and radio receivers. *t* tonnage completed for the use of the Democratic Republic only.

na: data not available. — negligible or nil. [1] one year only. [2] two year average. * estimate. ‡ see appendix. † re-exports.

GERMANY: FEDERAL REPUBLIC

The Federal Republic of, or West Germany, became a sovereign state in 1955 by the fusion of the three western zones of occupation. West-Berlin remains under tri-partite government, but is also a ' Land ' (as yet unincorporated) of the Federal Republic.

Germany F.R. is a member of the European Economic Community.

Saarland, incorporated in the French economic union in 1947, was returned to Germany in 1957. For comparative purposes, data for the Saar for 1953–5 have been included in the following tables when available.

Pre-war figures refer to both sectors of Germany.

AREA: 248 542 sq. km. (95 962 sq. miles) including West-Berlin

LAND USE: (percentage of total)

	1965	*1955*
Arable and orchard	33.4	35.4
Permanent meadow and pasture	23.5	22.9
Forest and woodland	29.0	28.6
City areas, waste and other land	14.1	13.1

POPULATION: 59 872 000 (1967 estimate)

Largest cities: WEST-BERLIN; population: 2 190 577 (city proper, 1966)
HAMBURG; population: 1 851 327 (city proper, 1966)

Capital city: BONN; population: 140 482 (city proper, 1966)

Distribution of working population (1965)
Total working population: 27 157 000

U.N. group no.		*Percentage*
0	Agriculture, forestry, fishing and hunting	10.9
1	Mining and quarrying	2.0
2/3	Manufacturing	37.5
4	Construction	8.1
5	Electricity, gas, water and sanitary services	0.8
6	Commerce	14.1
7	Transport, storage and communications	5.8
8	Services	20.5
9	Others	0.3

		Year(s)
Life expectancy at birth (years): male	67.6	1964–6 av.
female	73.5	1964–6 av.
Infant mortality (per '000)	23.8	1965
Crude birth rate (per '000)	17.9	1965
Crude death rate (per '000)	11.2	1965
Accidental deaths (per 100 000 population) caused by motor vehicles	26.4	1965
due to other causes	33.0	1965
Population per physician	650	1965
Population per hospital bed	90	1966
School enrolment: age 5–19 years (percentage)	88	1963–4 av.
age over 19 years (per 100 000 population)	566*a*	1963–5 av.

a excl. engineering schools and post-graduate teacher training.

COMMUNICATIONS

		Year(s)
Motor vehicles in use ('000s): private	8 012.4	1963–5 av.
commercial	898.6	1963–5 av.
Railway track (km.)	35 511	1964
Mail per capita: domestic	144	1963–5 av.
foreign received	6	1963–5 av.
foreign sent	10	1963–5 av.
Telephones (per '000 urban population)	15.9	1967
Radio receivers (per '000 population)	392	1963–5 av.
Television licences (per '000 population)	171.2	1963–5 av.
Daily newspapers (per '000 population)	314.7	1962–4 av.

FINANCE

Currency unit: The Deutsche mark

Exchange rates	*1965*	*1960*	*1950*	*1938*
Per $ U.S.	4.006	4.171	4.200	2.494
Per £ sterling	11.227	11.699	11.765	11.577

		Year(s)
National Income (million $ U.S.)	85 452	1965
G.N.P. per capita ($ U.S.)	1 700	1966
Rate of increase of G.N.P. per capita	3.5	1960–4 av.
Foreign trade (percentage of G.D.P.)	30	1963–5 av.

TRADING

Total trade (in million $ U.S.)	*1965*	*1955*	*1936 d*
Exports (f.o.b.)	17 892	6 135	1 925
Imports (c.i.f.)	17 472	5 793	1 709

Main trading partners (percentage of total value)

Exports	*1965*	*1955*	*1936 d*	*Imports*	*1965*	*1955*	*1936 d*
France	11	7	5	U.S.A.	13	13	6
Netherlands	10	9	8	France	11	9	2
U.S.A.	8	6	4	Netherlands	10	7	4
Belg./Lux.	8	7	4	Italy	9	4	5
Switzerland	6	6	5	Belg./Lux.	8	6	3
Italy	6	6	5*a*	U.K.	4	4	6
Austria	5	5	2	Sweden	4	5	5

Distribution of trade (percentage of total value)

Exports	*1965*	*1955*
Manufactured goods	77	74
(machinery and transport equipment)	(46)	(40)
(iron and steel)	(8)	(7)
Chemicals	12	11
Imports		
Manufactured goods	43	27
(machinery and transport equipment)	(13)	(5)
Crude materials and fuels	24	40
(mineral fuels)	(8)	(9)
Food	19	25

a incl. former Italian Somaliland. *d* incl. Germany D.R.

PRODUCTION, EXPORTS AND IMPORTS

Years: **1963–5 average** and *1953–5 average* Units: '000 metric tons unless otherwise indicated

1. CEREALS, etc.

	Production		Exports		Imports	
Barley	3 613.7	2 030.0	30.5	11.7	1 147.8	844.0
Maize (corn)	69.0	19.7	227.4	2.8	1 905.1	531.2
Millets/sorghum	—	—	19.6†	7.8†	276.4	138.4
Oats	2 227.0	2 526.6	40.2	0.5	407.9	92.1
Potatoes	21 510.3	24 983.0	36.8	55.7	518.9	167.6
Rice	—	—	16.2†	2.0†	157.4	84.6
Rye	3 224.3	3 645.7	5.0	69.9	85.6	151.0
Wheat	4 802.3	3 171.0	108.0	6.6	1 684.8	2 548.5

2. FRUIT, etc.

	Production		Exports		Imports	
Apples	1 462.7	1 228.0	5.8	0.3	528.1	262.1
Bananas	—	—	3.5†	4.7†	515.8	174.4
Cherries	233.3	174.8	na	0.7	na	10.8
Dates	—	—	—	0.1†	8.6	4.9
Grapes	779.0*	340.0*	0.3	—	228.0	100.1
Lemons	—	—	0.2†	—	129.5	81.5
Oranges	—	—	0.2†	0.2†	778.0	440.5
Other citrus fruit	—	—	0.1†	0.1†	42.2	4.4
Peaches/apricots	28.3*n*	35.6	—	—	na	68.7
Pears	397.3	402.3	0.2	—	163.3	72.7
Plums	458.3	405.1	na	0.9	na	12.3
Raisins	—	—	0.2†	—	45.3	48.4
Tomatoes	40.7	25.7				
Wine *b*	5 597.7	2 441.0	181.4	66.7	4 289.8	2 016.0

b '000 hectolitres. *n* of which apricots, 3.0.

3. BEVERAGES, FOREST PRODUCTS, etc.

	Production		Exports		Imports	
Cocoa	—	—	0.1†	0.3†	148.1	73.7
Coffee	—	—	0.9†	1.1†	256.7	100.4
Sugar: beet	12 236.0	8 997.8				
raw	1 915.2	1 340.3	6.7	6.2	205.1	192.1
Tea	—	—	0.2†	—	8.1	4.7
Tobacco: leaf	10.1	24.3	1.7	0.4	127.4	61.5
cigars	3 970.0*e*	4 692.4*e*				
cigarettes	95 400.0*e*	42 826.0*e*	—	0.1[2]	—	0.1[2]
tobacco/snuff	8.5	16.7				
Softwood *j*	16 756.3	16 082.0	348.0	95.0	6 881.0	4 226.8
Hardwood *j*	8 719.0	7 403.7	219.0	138.2	2 245.0	797.9
Wood pulp	1 379.6*	1 214.3	73.9	61.0	1 054.6	463.3
Newsprint	207.7	225.0	3.9	—	473.3	105.0
Other paper	3 792.3	2 036.7	163.7	60.8	1 214.7	225.7*

e no. in thousands. *j* '000 cu. metres of roundwood equivalent.

4. VEGETABLE OILSEEDS AND OILS

	Production		Exports		Imports	
Castor seed	—	—	—	—	29.63	17.17
Castor oil	na	na	2.86	3.27	4.58	1.42
Copra	—	—	0.29†	—	254.19	205.70
Coconut oil	na	na	1.64	0.71	48.25	55.88
Cottonseed	—	—	—	—	12.21	48.90
Cottonseed oil	na	na	0.29	0.21	72.10	36.66
Groundnuts	—	—	0.99†	0.10†	43.11	34.57

continued

PRODUCTION, EXPORTS AND IMPORTS *continued*

4. VEGETABLE OILSEEDS AND OILS—*continued*

	Production		Exports		Imports	
Groundnut oil	na	na	2.27	0.21	46.17	28.54
Linseed	—	2.67	0.48†	1.00	35.07	3.97
Linseed oil	na	na	5.15	2.47	72.07	81.85
Olive oil	—	—	0.01†	0.01†	2.82	1.75
Palm kernels	—	—	—	—	128.82	129.43
Palm kernel oil	na	na	4.53	1.31	14.82	13.54
Palm oil	—	—	3.49†	4.35†	102.04	85.16
Rapeseed	104.00	22.67	2.91	0.17	65.76*	35.30
Rapeseed oil	na	na	17.53	0.11	5.24	12.51
Sesame seed	—	—	—	—	—	16.00[2]
Soya beans	—	—	1.03	0.17	1 260.90	302.87
Soya bean oil	na	na	12.22	1.67	14.31	27.00
Sunflower seed	—	—	0.40†	—	30.94	28.14
Sunflower seed oil	na	na	4.45	1.51	59.16	6.15
Tung oil	—	—	0.03†	—	3.14	4.34

5. LIVESTOCK‡, ANIMAL PRODUCTS, etc.

	Production		Exports		Imports	
Chickens *d*	72 246.7	55 314.3				
Cattle *d*	13 141.3	11 672.0	94.3	0.7	404.8	244.5
dairy cows *d*	6 510.3	6 464.0*n*				
Goats *d*	192.0	1 041.0				
Sheep *d*	907.7	1 384.7	28.5	na	3.6	na
Horses *d*	490.0	1 278.6				
Pigs *d*	17 219.0	13 389.0	3.5	64.1	247.6	249.6
Bacon/ham	2 877.0	1 988.2	0.4	—	1.5	0.1
Meat‡: 'A'			16.4	5.2	149.8	25.6
'B'	390.0	200.0	4.5	0.3	237.0	69.5
Butter	492.7	331.0	4.9	—	18.1	18.4
Cheese	353.7	248.7	22.2	5.5	127.9	58.7
Eggs	629.3	329.5	0.2	—	137.3	143.8
Fish	634.7	761.2	83.0	30.0	740.2	363.6*
Milk	20 915.7	17 012.0	117.3	12.2	301.7	59.3
Whale oil	—	—	—	—	58.4[2]*p*	110.4
Hides/skins	115.4	106.6	—	7.8[2]	142.0	116.7[2]
Wool	1.6	2.7	3.8	1.9	71.1	62.7

d no. in thousands. *n* incl. draught cows. *p* incl. sperm oil.

6. FIBRES, TEXTILES, etc.

	Production		Exports		Imports	
Abaca	—	—	0.1†	—	2.7	4.3
Agaves (sisal etc.)	—	—	0.5†	0.1†	54.2	36.8
Cotton lint	—	—	15.3†	0.8†	284.5	263.1
Flax fibre	—	1.8	0.9†	0.2[2]†	16.1	22.1
Hemp fibre	—	1.2	0.6†	0.6†	7.1	14.9
Jute	—	—	2.3†	0.6†	55.5	89.1
Rubber: natural	—	—	0.8†	0.3†	178.1	137.7
synthetic	136.8	8.2	46.1	1.0[2]	87.6*s*	12.5
Silk *f*	—	—	275.7†	6.3†	675.3	227.0
Cotton: yarn	380.3	290.2*p*	3.0	2.6*p*	27.8	4.6*p*
woven fabrics	245.8*	233.6*	25.4	23.7*p*	30.0	9.2*p*
Rayon: fibre/yarn	285.5	192.1	104.6	41.9	33.0	16.9
woven fabrics	114.2	60.0*	21.4	14.1*q*	20.4	3.5*q*
Non-cellulosic fibre/yarn	142.6	8.1	45.5	na	20.7	na
Wool: yarn	117.3	108.5	3.5	2.1	34.0	13.2
woven fabrics	54.7	68.6*r*	4.2	1.9	26.6	11.1

f metric tons. *p* incl. mixtures predominantly of cotton. *q* rayon staple fibre cloth only. *r* yarn input to weaving mills. *s* incl. imports for re-export.

7. FUEL AND POWER

	Production		Exports		Imports	
Coal: 'A' ‡	140 317	149 140*n*	14 836	14 583	7 773	11 282
'B'	33 167	92 260	1 580	1 635	1 259	769
Coke	na	na	10 909	10 018	444	407
Electricity *h*: total	159 185	70 740*p*				
hydro	13 301	10 750*q*				
nuclear	88	—				
thermal	145 796	59 990*r*				
Natural gas *i*	2 530	284[1]*t*	—	—	17	—
Oil, crude	7 653	3 150[1]	7	na[1]	50 143	7 100[1]
Petroleum, refined	49 500	8 250[1]	4 857	790[1]	14 350	2 730[1]
Rare earths *f*	—	—	—	—	695*u*	585*u*
Uranium *f*	na	—	—	—	10	—

f metric tons. *h* million kWh. *i* million cu. metres. *n* of which 17 330 from Saar. *p* of which 2 040 from Saar. *q* of which 20 from Saar. *r* of which 2 020 from Saar. *t* of which 119 from Saar. *u* incl. salts of rare earth minerals.

8. IRON AND STEEL

	Production		Exports		Imports	
Iron ore	2 824*m*	3 889*m*	303	274	34 416	12 686
Pig iron	25 693	16 135	717	330	553	193
Steel ingots/castings	35 252	20 948	1 039	279	365	113
Iron/steel scrap	na	na	1 522	584	1 164	633
Iron/steel products *a*	na	na	1 266	376	751	244

a million $ U.S. *m* metal content.

9. NON-FERROUS MINERALS AND METALS

	Production		Exports		Imports	
Gold *k*: ore *m*	105.30	5.00	—	—	—	—
bullion/coins etc.	na	na	253.93	195.00[2]	2 986.00‡	834.50[2]
Platinum group metals *k*	—	—	209.15†	16.09†	397.04	92.71
Silver *k*: ore *m*	2 050.70	2 297.30	—	—	—	—
bullion	na	na	18 563.33	7 984.00	47 179.33	13 921.00

continued

9. NON-FERROUS MINERALS AND METALS—*continued*

	Production		Exports		Imports	
Asbestos: fibre	—	—	0.28†	0.26†	153.24	43.78
manufactured	na	na	53.08	1.88	109.07	0.52
Mica	0.01	—	0.62†	0.13†	6.06	2.46
Aluminium: bauxite	4.06	5.31	0.98*n*	0.13*p*	1 592.10	1 020.21
alumina	605.33	na	109.50*q*	77.73	54.90*q*	0.75
aluminium	221.04	124.41	69.31	72.82	231.61	53.87
Antimony: ore	—	—	—	—	2.54	1.63
metal	na	na	0.77[2]	0.27	4.69	1.59
Cadmium	0.29	0.24	0.06[2]	0.06	1.02[2]	0.29
Chrome: ore	—	—	1.58	0.31	238.92	181.46
metal	na	na	0.05	0.61	0.07	—
Cobalt: ore	—	—	—	—	—	2.78
metal	na	na	0.94	—	0.89	—
Copper: ore	1.60*m*	1.87*m*	1.33	4.27	148.53*r*	154.54[2]*r*
metal	332.17	235.23	187.90	77.03	586.99	248.00
Lead: ore	50.47*m*	65.78*m*	6.06	0.08	119.25	70.83
metal	107.26	108.53	41.92	47.23	117.12	55.25
Magnesium: dolomite	208.21[2]	na	73.99	86.12	119.31	15.39
magnesite	—	—	5.94	0.81	171.22	165.70
kieserite	na	na	193.39	48.67	—	—
metal/salts	0.50*u*	0.09*u*	113.33	47.45	153.44	9.47
Manganese: ore	—	—	7.68	2.95	742.04	309.47
metal	na	na	76.28	—	98.87	—
Mercury *f*	—	—	44.60†	4.50†	731.20	586.70
Molybdenum *f*: ore	—	—	100.10	—	8 792.20	3 088.60
metal	na	na	67.10	—	275.30	—
Nickel: ore	—	—	—	—	3.47	0.32
metal	na	na	5.68	1.12	26.71	13.12
Tin: ore	—	—	0.08	—	8.03	0.95
metal	1.24	0.49[2]	1.73	2.08	13.43	7.47
Titanium minerals	—	—	65.80†	—	357.80	98.18
Tungsten: ore‡	—	—	—	—	5.00	2.46
metal	na	na	0.26	—	0.29	—
Vanadium	—	—	—	—	—	0.39
Zinc: ore	109.52*m*	92.53*m*	41.20	10.03	130.41	68.99
metal	106.65	164.88	77.17	85.04	187.83	57.50
Zirconium minerals	—	—	1.18†	—	26.73	—

f metric tons. *k* '000 fine troy oz. *m* metal content. *p* incl. cryolite. *q* hydrate. *r* excl. burnt cupreous pyrites. *u* primary magnesium only.

10. CHEMICALS *n* AND FERTILIZERS

	Production		Exports		Imports	
Organic chemicals:						
Benzene	274.7		31.1		105.7	
Butadiene	260.2[1]		na		na	
Ethylene	694.3[1]		na		na	
Methanol	572.6		65.5		72.1	
Phenol	144.5*p*		49.3		21.2	
Phthalic anhydride	93.6		16.1		9.2	
Styrene monomer	na		na		na	
Urea	na		123.2[1]		3.0[1]	
Inorganic chemicals:						
Ammonia	1 535.1		67.1		1.5	
Carbon black	116.0		28.3		36.9	
Chlorine	1 006.0		0.1		41.4	
Nitric acid	2 431.5*		1.5		0.8	
Sodium carbonate	1 109.8[2]		43.6		64.3	
Sodium hydroxide	1 115.7		92.0		26.2	
Sulphuric acid	2 903.0		54.5		142.8	
Plastics:						
Polyamides	na		20.3[1]		5.7[1]	
Polyethylene	224.2		85.7		31.4	
Polyvinyl chloride	329.9		73.4		61.5	
Fertilizers:						
Phosphates	—	—	38.0	—	2 151.1	806.0
Potash	2 177.9*w*	1 546.3*w*	1 736.4	1 326.4	59.6	0.7
Pyrites	181.5*x*	196.4*x*	—	20.3	1 549.9	1 022.7
Sulphur	80.3*r*	72.0[1]*r*	26.1	18.2	394.4	36.2

n data not available for years 1953–5. *p* coal tar and synthetic phenol. *r* recovered sulphur. *w* K_2O content. *x* sulphur content.

11. INDUSTRY

	Production		Exports		Imports	
Aircraft *a*	118**n*	na	57.6	0.1	119.1	2.8
Alcoholic beverages			37.4*a*	17.5*a*	102.9*a*	30.6*a*
beer *b*	64 372	34 926				
spirits *b*	2 782*p*	1 694*q*				
Cement	31 511	17 095	1 068.7	1 684.3	386.3	60.3
Electrical engineering *a*	6 998[2]	na	1 320.0	408.0[2]	398.9	36.4[2]
Locomotives *c*	1 058	709[2]	na	22.0	—	—
Railway vehicles *a*	na	na	92.1	61.8	—	2.1
Machine tools *a*	725[1]	na	353.5	117.4[1]	68.9	na
Merchant ships *g*	961	903	629.0	429.3	7.0	—
Motor vehicles			2 175.0*a*	482.5[2]*a*	299.6*a*	18.5*a*
commercial *d*	246	162				
private *d*	2 599	531				

a million $ U.S. *b* '000 hectolitres. *c* no. of units. *d* no. in thousands. *g* '000 G.R.T. *n* 1965–7 av. *p* 1967 figure. *q* 1958/9 figure.

na: data not available. — negligible or nil. [1] one year only. [2] two year average. * estimate. ‡ see appendix. † re-exports.

GHANA

WEST AFRICA

In 1957, the British colony of the Gold Coast united with the British Trusteeship area of Togoland to become Ghana. The country was declared a republic within the Commonwealth in 1960.

AREA: 238 537 sq. km. (92 100 sq. miles)

LAND USE: (percentage of total)

	1961	*1954*
Arable and orchard	22.3	22.3
Permanent meadow and pasture, forest and woodland	55.1	63.9
City areas, waste and other land	22.6	13.8

POPULATION: 8 143 000 (1967 estimate)
Largest city: ACCRA, capital; population: 600 200 (1966)

Distribution of working population (1960)
Total working population: 2 725 000*

U.N. group no.		*Percentage*
0	Agriculture, forestry, fishing and hunting	58.0
1	Mining and quarrying	1.8
2/3	Manufacturing	8.6
4	Construction	3.3
5	Electricity, gas, water and sanitary services	0.5
6	Commerce	13.6
7	Transport, storage and communications	2.5
8	Services	5.7
9	Others	6.0

		Year(s)
Life expectancy at birth (years): male	37.1*	1960
female	na	
Infant mortality (per '000)	82.3*a	1963
Population per physician	12 000	1963
Population per hospital bed	770	1966
School enrolment: age 5–19 years (percentage)	57	1963–4 av.
age over 19 years (per 100 000 population)	53	1964–5 av.

a registration area only.

COMMUNICATIONS

		Year(s)
Motor vehicles in use ('000s): private	27.0	1963–5 av.
commercial	16.6	
Railway track (km.)	948	1960
Mail per capita: domestic	16	1964–5 av.
foreign received	5	
foreign sent	4	
Telephones (per '000 urban population)	0.5	1967
Radio receivers (per '000 population)	71	1963–5 av.
Television sets (per '000 population)	0.1	1963–5 av.
Daily newspapers (per '000 population)	30	1962–4 av.

FINANCE

Currency unit: The new cedi, equivalent to 1.2 cedis, was introduced in 1967. The old cedi replaced the Ghana pound in 1965 at the rate ₵1 to £G 0.305.

Exchange rates	*1965b*	*1960c*
Per $ U.S.	0.85	0.357
Per £ sterling	3.28	1.0

		Year(s)
National Income (million $ U.S.)	1 893	1965
G.N.P. per capita ($ U.S.)	230	1966
Foreign trade (percentage of G.D.P.)	35	1963–5 av.

b old cedis. *c* Ghana pounds.

PRODUCTION

Attempts to decrease reliance on cocoa as the main crop have led to diversification of agriculture by the cultivation of rubber, coffee and tobacco. Re-afforestation has been undertaken, and the fishing industry has been modernized. Recent explorations (1969) have revealed large deposits of bauxite.

TRADING

Total trade (in million $ U.S.)	*1965*	*1955*	*1938*
Exports (f.o.b.)	291	243	32
Imports (c.i.f.)	445	246	38

Main trading partners (percentage of total value)

Exports	*1965*	*1955*	*Imports*	*1965*	*1955*
U.S.A.	17	20	U.K.	26	47
U.K.	13	35	Germany F.R.	9	5
Netherlands	11	12	U.S.A.	9	4
Germany F.R.	11	13	U.S.S.R.	7	—
U.S.S.R.	11	5	Netherlands	5	8
Italy	4	2	Poland	4	na
Yugoslavia	4	na	Japan	4	10

Distribution of trade (percentage of total value)

Exports	*1965*	*1955*	*1938**
Cocoa	66	76	72
Wood	13	9	2
Diamonds	7	6	8
Manganese	5	6	14
Imports			
Manufactured goods	74	65	na
(machinery and transport equipment)	(33)	(17)	(20)
(textiles and clothing)	(15)	(38)	(12)
Food	11	15	na
Chemicals	6	6	na
Crude materials and fuels	5	7	na

PRODUCTION, EXPORTS AND IMPORTS

Years: **1963–5 average** and *1953–5 average* Units: '000 metric tons unless otherwise indicated

1. CEREALS, etc.

	Production		Exports		Imports	
Cassava	1 224.3*	*512.0²*	—	—	—	—
Maize (corn)	178.7*	*169.0*	0.2	—	1.8	*0.7*
Millets/sorghum	184.0*	*178.0*	—	—	0.1	*0.1*
Potatoes	—	—	—	—²	0.8	*1.4*
Rice	39.0*	*23.0¹*	—	—	31.9	*2.8*
Sweet potatoes/yams	1 150.3*	*481.5²*	—	—	—	—
Wheat	—	—	—	—	0.5	—

2. FRUIT, etc.

	Production		Exports		Imports	
Apples	—	—	—	—	0.3	—
Bananas	na	na	2.7	*0.4*	—	—
Coconuts	68.7*e	na	—	*1.0*	—	—
Lemons	13.0*	na	0.3n	*0.2*	—	—
Pineapples	233.0*	na	na	na	—	—
Tomatoes	15.7*	na	—	—	—	—
Wine b	—	—	—	—	12.6	*7.7*

b '000 hectolitres. *e* no. in millions. *n* incl. oranges.

3. BEVERAGES, FOREST PRODUCTS, etc.

	Production		Exports		Imports	
Cocoa	479.0	*226.1*	433.5	*222.4*	—	—
Coffee	3.0*	*1.3¹*	3.7	*0.6*	0.1	—
Sugar, raw	—	—	—	—	49.3	*26.0*
Tea	—	—	—	—	0.1	*0.1*
Tobacco: leaf	0.9*	—	—	—	1.2	*0.6*
cigarettes	1 747.0e	—	—	—	na	*1.0²p*
Softwood j	—	—	0.1	—	0.2	—
Hardwood j	9 778.0	*7 186.5²*	1 040.0	*631.7*	—	—
Newsprint	—²	—	—	—	12.1	*1.2*
Other paper	0.8*	—	—	—	9.4	*1.4²*

e no. in millions. *j* '000 cu. metres of roundwood equivalent. *p* incl. other tobacco manufactures.

4. VEGETABLE OILSEEDS AND OILS

	Production		Exports		Imports	
Castor oil	—	—	—	—	0.15	—
Copra	na	na	0.20	*2.93q*	—	—
Coconut oil	na	na	0.24	na	0.23	—
Cottonseed oil	—	—	—	—	0.08	—
Groundnuts	31.71*	*30.80*	—	—	0.29	—
Groundnut oil	na	na	—	—	0.32	—
Linseed oil	—	—	—	—	0.02	—
Olive oil	—	—	—	—	0.16*	—
Palm kernels	12.00*	na	0.66	*8.63*	—	—
Palm kernel oil	na	na	—	—	0.56	—
Palm oil	43.00*	na	—	*0.49²*	1.40	—
Soya bean oil	—	—	—	—	0.28	na

q incl. coconut oil in copra equivalent.

5. LIVESTOCK‡, ANIMAL PRODUCTS, etc.

	Production		Exports		Imports	
Chickens d	5 883.0n	na				
Cattle d	507.7	*395.0¹*	—	—	72.5	*62.9*
dairy cows d	251.7	na				
Goats d	667.0*	*428.0¹*	—	—	106.5	na
Sheep d	688.0	*464.0¹*				
Horses d	3.3*	na				
Pigs d	240.0*	*58.0¹*	—	—	0.1	—
Bacon/ham	23.3*	na	—	—	0.5	*7.2*
Meat‡: 'A'			—	—	2.3	*0.6*
'B'	na	na	—	—	1.2	—
Butter	—	—	—	—	0.4*	*0.2*
Cheese	—	—	—	—	0.2*	*0.2*
Eggs	34.7*	na	—	—	—	—
Fish	71.5*p	*24.8²*	6.4	na	35.8	*11.9**
Milk	31.0*	na	0.1	*0.8**	50.9	*12.0*

d no. in thousands. *n* incl. ducks, geese and turkeys. *p* incl. freshwater fish and molluscs.

continued

PRODUCTION, EXPORTS AND IMPORTS *continued*

6. FIBRES, TEXTILES, etc.

	Production		Exports		Imports	
Jute	—	—	—	—	2.3	—
Rubber, natural	na	na	0.3	*0.2*	—	—
Cotton: yarn	—	—	—	—	1.5¹	na
woven fabrics	12.5²q	na	—	—	9.3	na
Rayon, woven fabrics	—	—	—	—	1.4r	na

q million metres. *r* incl. synthetic.

7. FUEL AND POWER

	Production		Exports		Imports	
Coal, 'A'	—	—	—	—	38	*99¹*
Electricity h: total	494	*240n*				
hydro	36	—				
thermal	458	*240n*				
Oil, crude	—	—	—	—¹	563	na
Petroleum, refined	540	—¹	170	—¹	143	*320¹*

a million kWh. *n* incl. Togo (former French Togoland).

8. IRON AND STEEL

	Production		Exports		Imports	
Steel ingots/castings	—	—	—	—	2	—

9. NON-FERROUS MINERALS AND METALS

	Production		Exports		Imports	
Diamonds	2 541.0l	*2 197.5l*	15.13a	*12.81a*	—	—
Gold k, ore	847.0m	*735.0m*	841.30p	*784.14p*	22.61p	*0.08p*
Silver k, bullion	na	na	2.41²	*44.15*	2.32	*108.34*
Asbestos, manufactured	—	—	—	—	20.61	*20.17*

continued

9. NON-FERROUS MINERALS AND METALS—*continued*

	Production		Exports		Imports	
Aluminium: bauxite	294.32	na	255.63	*137.96*	—	—
aluminium	na	—	—	—	5.01	*0.90²*
Copper, metal	—	—	—	—	0.75	*0.37²*
Lead, metal	—	—	—	—	0.31	*0.36*
Manganese, ore	491.17	*591.27*	491.31	*587.06*	—	—
Tin, metal	—	—	—	—	0.13	*0.04²*
Zinc, metal	—	—	—	—	0.40	*0.06²*

a million $ U.S. *k* '000 fine troy oz. *l* '000 carats. *m* metal content. *p* bullion.

10. CHEMICALS*n* AND FERTILIZERS

	Production		Exports		Imports	
Chemicals	—		—		na	
Fertilizers:						
Potash	—	—	—	—	0.9	*0.1²*

n data not available for years 1953–5.

11. INDUSTRY

	Production		Exports		Imports	
Aircraft a	—	—	—	—	4.6	—²
Alcoholic beverages			—	—	0.9a	*6.4a*
beer b	215.0	*43.5*				
Cement	50.0*	—	—	—	559.7	*261.3*
Electrical engineering a	—	—	—	—	26.1	*5.4²*
Railway vehicles a	—	—	—	—	1.8	*36.0*
Merchant ships g	—	—	—	—	9.0¹	—
Motor vehicles			—	—	24.3a	*14.4a*
commercial	1.0p	—				

a million $ U.S. *b* '000 hectolitres. *g* '000 G.R.T. *p* assembly of imported parts.

GIBRALTAR

WESTERN MEDITERRANEAN

Gibraltar has been a British colony for more than two centuries, but since 1964 has had a large measure of internal self-government. In 1967 a referendum showed that an overwhelming majority of the inhabitants preferred to retain links with Britain rather than pass under Spanish sovereignty.

AREA: 6.5 sq. km. (2.5 sq. miles)

LAND USE: (percentage of total)

	1965	*1955*
City areas, waste and other land	100	100

POPULATION: 25 000* (1967 U.N. estimate)
Total working population: 9 008 (1961)

		Year(s)
Infant mortality (per '000)	20.6	1965
Crude birth rate (per '000)	27.3	1965
Crude death rate (per '000)	9.8	1965
Population per physician	1 000	1963
Population per hospital bed	110	1966
School enrolment: age 5–19 years (percentage)	70a	1963–4 av.

a public education only.

COMMUNICATIONS

		Year(s)
Motor vehicles in use ('000s): private	5.7	1963–5 av.
commercial	0.5	
Telephones (per '000 urban population)	19.3b	1967
Radio licences (per '000 population)	184	1963–5 av.
Television licences (per '000 population)	174.2	1963–5 av.
Daily newspapers (per '000 population)	300.3	1962–4 av.

b excl. telephone systems of the armed forces.

FINANCE

Currency unit: The pound sterling *c*

Exchange rates	*1965*	*1960*
Per $ U.S.	0.357	0.357

c local notes and U.K. coins in use.

EMPLOYMENT AND TRADE

Gibraltar is a free port and naval base; revenue is received from transit trade and from port dues and refuelling facilities. Small firms are engaged in food processing and clothing manufacture for local needs and export. Tourism is becoming increasingly important.

PRODUCTION, EXPORTS AND IMPORTS

Years: **1963–5 average** and *1953–5 average* Units: '000 metric tons unless otherwise indicated

2. FRUIT, etc.

	Production		Exports		Imports	
Wine b	—	—	na	*0.3†*	na	*1.0*

b '000 hectolitres.

3. BEVERAGES, FOREST PRODUCTS, etc.

	Production		Exports		Imports	
Coffee	—	—	—	—	na	*3.3¹*
Sugar, raw	—	—	—	—¹	na	*1.8¹*

5. LIVESTOCK, ANIMAL PRODUCTS, etc.

	Production		Exports		Imports	
Meat‡: 'A'	—	—	—	—	na	*0.9¹*
'B'	—	—	—	—	na	*0.1²*
Cheese	—	—	—	—	na	*0.2¹*
Fish	na	na	—	—	—	—

7. FUEL AND POWER

	Production		Exports		Imports	
Coal, 'A'‡	—	—	—	—	2	*34*
Electricity h t	39	*20¹*				
Petroleum, refined	—	—	—	—	197	*10¹*

h million kWh. *t* thermal.

11. INDUSTRY

	Production		Exports		Imports	
Cement	—	—	—	—	12.0	*4.7*

GREECE

Following a revolution in 1967 the king went into exile and a nationalist government took over all constitutional and legislative powers.

AREA: 131 944 sq. km. (50 942 sq. miles)
Land area: 129 310 sq. km. (49 927 sq. miles)

LAND USE: (percentage of total)	*1964*	*1954*
Arable and orchard	29.2	26.5
Permanent meadow and pasture	39.0	39.1
Forest and woodland	19.7	14.8
City areas, waste and other land	12.1	19.6

POPULATION: 8 716 000 (1967 estimate)

Largest city: ATHÍNAI (Athens) capital; population: 1 852 700* (1961)

Distribution of working population (1961)
Total working population: 3 638 600

U.N. group no.		*Percentage*
0	Agriculture, forestry, fishing and hunting	53.9
1	Mining and quarrying	0.6
2/3	Manufacturing	13.4
4	Construction	4.6
5	Electricity, gas, water and sanitary services	0.5
6	Commerce	7.3
7	Transport, storage and communications	4.2
8	Services	12.1
9	Others	3.4

		Year(s)
Life expectancy at birth (years): male	67.5	1960–2 av.
female	70.7	1960–2 av.
Infant mortality (per '000)	34.3	1965
Crude birth rate (per '000)	17.7	1965
Crude death rate (per '000)	7.9	1965
Accidental deaths (per 100 000 population)		
caused by motor vehicles	10.6	1965
due to other causes	26.3	1965
Population per physician	680	1965
Population per hospital bed	170	1966
School enrolment: age 5–19 years (percentage)	73*a*	1963–4 av.
age over 19 years (per 100 000 population)	569	1964–5 av.

a incl. pre-school education

COMMUNICATIONS		*Year(s)*
Motor vehicles in use ('000s): private	84.5	1963–5 av.
commercial	65.4	1963–5 av.
Railway track (km.)	2 583	1963
Mail per capita: domestic	25	1963–5 av.
foreign received	na	1963–5 av.
foreign sent	5	1963–5 av.
Telephones (per '000 urban population)	6.69	1967
Radio licences (per '000 population)	99	1963–5 av.
Daily newspapers (per '000 population)	121	1959

FINANCE

Currency unit: The drachma

Exchange rates	*1965*	*1960*	*1955*	*1938*
Per $ U.S.	30	30	30	118
Per £ sterling	84	84	84	543

		Year(s)
National Income (million $ U.S.)	4 842	1965
G.N.P. per capita ($ U.S.)	660	1966
Rate of increase of G.N.P. per capita	7.9	1960–4 av.
Foreign trade (percentage of G.D.P.)	24	1963–5 av.

TRADING

Total trade (in million $ U.S.)	*1965*	*1955*	*1938*
Exports (f.o.b.)	328	183	90
Imports (c.i.f.)	1 134	382	132

Main trading partners (percentage of total value)

Exports	*1965*	*1955*	*Imports*	*1965*	*1955*
Germany F.R.	23	25	Germany F.R.	17	17
U.S.A.	10	13	U.S.A.	10	18
U.S.S.R.	8	1	U.K.	9	11
U.K.	8	10	Italy	9	11
Italy	6	15	France	8	6
France	5	9	Belg./Lux.	4	4
Yugoslavia	4	3	Japan	3	—

Distribution of trade (percentage of total value)

Exports	*1965*	*1955*	*1938**
Tobacco	34	42	na
Food	29	22	30
(fruit)	(23)	(21)	(na)
Textiles and clothing	10	13	na
Imports			
Manufactured goods	57	45	14
(machinery and transport equipment)	(35)	(21)	(11)
Crude materials and fuels	18	26	na
Food	14	21	28
Chemicals	9	8	6

PRODUCTION, EXPORTS AND IMPORTS

Years: **1963–5 average** and *1953–5 average* Units: '000 metric tons unless otherwise indicated

1. CEREALS, etc.

	Production		Exports		Imports	
Barley	299.0	*238.3*	—	—	31.8	—
Maize (corn)	280.0	*282.7*	—	*0.1*	138.5	*5.7*
Millets/sorghum	3.3	*4.0*	—	*0.3*	5.4	*2.8*
Oats	153.0	*158.0*	—	—	—	—
Potatoes	562.3	*430.3*	11.4	—	20.3	*6.6*
Rice	98.3	*71.0*	2.3	*7.8*	3.2	*2.6*
Rye	19.7	*57.3*	—	—	—	—
Wheat	1 855.0	*1 318.3*	—	—	26.9	*222.6*

2. FRUIT, etc.

	Production		Exports		Imports	
Apples	165.7	*48.7*	13.2	—	—	—
Apricots	21.7	*8.5*	—	—	—	—
Bananas	—	—	—	—	6.9	*0.2*[2]
Cherries	19.3	*7.5*	—	—	—	—
Dates	—	—	—	—	0.2	—
Figs	121.7	*119.7*	na	*15.9*	—	—
Grapes	1 196.3	*1 055.3*	18.1	*12.2*	—	—
Lemons	110.0	*42.7*	34.9	*2.2*	—	—
Oranges	312.7	*146.7*	57.8	*9.1*	—	—
Olives	976.3	*608.3*				
Peaches	91.3	*13.2*	—	—	—	—
Pears	64.0	*36.0*	—	—	—	—
Plums	24.3*	na	—	—	—	—
Raisins	153.4	*114.7*	125.8	*109.3*	—	—
Tomatoes	499.7	*361.0*				
Wine*b*	3 249.3	*3 888.0*	358.0	*273.3*	0.7	*0.3*

b '000 hectolitres.

3. BEVERAGES, FOREST PRODUCTS, etc.

	Production		Exports		Imports	
Cocoa	—	—	—	—	3.7	*1.0*
Coffee	—	—	—	—	9.7	*5.2*
Sugar: beet	509	na				
raw	69	na	—	—	69.4	*83.3*
Tea	—	—	—	—	0.2	*0.1*
Tobacco: leaf	126	*75*	68.3	*52.1*	—	—
cigarettes	13 927*e*	*8 946e*	—	*0.1*[2]*n*	—	—[2]
Softwood*j*	271[1]*	*651*[2]	—	—	581.7	*267.3*
Hardwood*j*	2 462[1]*	*3 335*[2]	0.2	—	61.5	*3.6*
Wood pulp	—	*2**	—	—	74.8	*30.0*[2]
Newsprint	2*	—	—	—	38.3	*11.3*
Other paper	123*	*37**	3.0	—	17.4	*7.6*

e no. in millions. *j* '000 cu. metres of roundwood equivalent. *n* incl. other tobacco manufactures.

4. VEGETABLE OILSEEDS AND OILS

	Production		Exports		Imports	
Castor oil	—	—	—	—	0.03	*0.02*
Copra	—	—	—	—	—	*0.17*
Coconut oil	—	—	—	—	0.01	—
Cottonseed	140.70	*92.00*	—	—	16.85	*22.90*
Cottonseed oil	na	na	—	—	0.40	—
Groundnuts	3.97	*3.90*	—	*0.17*	0.13	—
Linseed	—	*1.00*	—	—	9.14	*3.63*
Linseed oil	na	na	—	—	0.12	*0.12*[2]
Olive oil	194.33	*138.67p*	2.06	*11.44*	—	—
Palm kernels	—	—	—	—	1.71	—
Palm oil	—	—	—	—	—	*0.01*
Rapeseed	—	—	—	—	0.07	—
Sesame seed	7.60	*12.90*	0.10	*0.23*	0.78	*0.07*
Soya bean oil	—	—	—	—	21.48*	*1.28*
Sunflower seed	3.00	*2.30*	0.57	*0.71*	0.02	—

p incl. oil extracted by solvents.

continued

PRODUCTION, EXPORTS AND IMPORTS *continued*

5. LIVESTOCK‡, ANIMAL PRODUCTS, etc.

	Production		Exports		Imports	
Chickens*d*	17 849	*10 615*[1]				
Cattle*d*	1 100	*898*	—	—	14.6	*24.7*
dairy cows*d*	688	na				
Goats*d*	4 534	*4 431*	0.1	na	518.4	na
Sheep*d*	9 231	*8 259*				
Horses*d*	320	*312*				
Pigs*d*	616	*598*	—	—	1.9	*0.1*
Meat‡: 'A'	142*	*81**	0.2	—	50.7	*4.8*
'B'	60	*23*	—	—	8.7	*0.1*
Butter	9*q*	*8r*	—	—	1.8	*1.5*
Cheese	113	*64**	0.9	—	6.2	*4.4*
Eggs	85	*31*	—	—	0.2	*0.8*
Fish	119	*53*	2.7	*0.2**	41.8	*25.5**
Milk	422	*239**	—	—	127.9	*52.0*
Hides/skins	23	*10*	6.9	*3.0*[2]	9.6	*6.6*[2]
Wool	6[1]	6	—	—	2.1	*3.4*

d no. in thousands. *q* incl. butter made from sheep's milk. *r* butter from cows' and buffaloes' milk.

6. FIBRES, TEXTILES, etc.

	Production		Exports		Imports	
Abaca	—	—	—	—	0.1	—
Agaves (sisal etc.)	—	—	—	—	2.9	*2.5*
Cotton lint	79.7	*44.3*	44.7	*14.6p*	5.8	*1.2q*
Flax fibre	0.2	*0.6*	—	—	0.7	—
Hemp fibre	—	*0.4*	—	—	0.5	*0.8*
Jute	—	—	—	—	4.5	*3.5*
Rubber, natural	—	—	—	—	3.1	*2.0*
Silk*f*	na	*40.0**	92.3	*40.7*	0.3	—
Cotton: yarn	32.1	*22.8*[2]	3.6	—	0.1	*0.3*
woven fabrics	21.4*r*	*12.5*[2]	0.5	—	3.5	*2.2*
Rayon: fibre/yarn	2.5	*1.7*	—	—	8.6	—
woven fabrics	—	—	—	—	1.3*t*	*2.4*[2]
Non-cellulosic fibre/yarn	0.3	—	0.1	—	2.4	—
Wool: yarn	10.6	*4.3*	—	*0.1*	1.4	*0.7*
woven fabrics	6.0[2]	*3.9*	0.1*u*	—	0.6*u*	*0.2*

f metric tons. *p* incl. artificial cotton. *q* incl. linters. *r* pure cotton cloth only. *t* incl. synthetic piece goods. *u* excl. blankets.

7. FUEL AND POWER

	Production		Exports		Imports	
Coal: 'A'‡	—	—	—	—	168	*271*
'B'	1 373	*786*	—	—	—	—
Coke	na	na	—	—	162	*16*
Electricity*h*: total	3 769	*1 390*[1]				
hydro	768	*330*[1]				
thermal	3 001	*1 060*[1]				
Oil, crude	—	—	—	—	1 850	na
Petroleum, refined	1 757	—[1]	23	—[1]	1 747	*1 510*[1]

h million kWh.

8. IRON AND STEEL

	Production		Exports		Imports	
Iron ore	na	*61m*	62[2]	*127*	272	—
Pig iron	—	—	—	—	25	*22*
Steel ingots/castings	209	*54**	—	—	62	*47*[2]
Iron/steel scrap	na	na	—	*9*	1	*2*[2]
Iron/steel products*a*	na	na	na	—	55	*20*

a million $ U.S. *m* metal content.

9. NON-FERROUS MINERALS AND METALS

	Production		Exports		Imports	
Gold*k*, ore*m*	—	*6.00*	—	—	—	—
Silver*k*, ore*m*	138.70	*78.70*	—	—	—	—
Asbestos: fibre	0.07	—	—	—	4.08	*0.09*
manufactured	na	na	0.46	—	4.23	
Mica	—	—	—	—	0.03	—

continued

9. NON-FERROUS MINERALS AND METALS—*continued*

	Production		Exports		Imports	
Aluminium: bauxite	1 197.58	*393.98*	1 110.29	*378.72*	—	—
alumina	73.00[1]*n*	na	na	—	1.27*p*	—
aluminium	na	—	0.79	—	9.37	*1.70**
Antimony: ore*m*	—	*0.22*	—	na	—	—
metal	—	na	—	—	0.04	
Chrome, ore	53.95*m*	*29.61m*	22.45	*28.05*	—	—
Cobalt	na	—	—	—	—	—
Copper: ore	—	na	—	*0.05*[2]	—	—
metal	—	—	0.61	—	10.19	*45.20*[2]
Lead: ore	8.87*m*	*6.56m*	8.98	*2.77*	5.05	—
metal	4.72	*2.55*	—	*0.53*	1.35	—
Magnesium: dolomite	—	—	—	—	0.12	—
magnesite	314.21	na	121.41	*42.61*	0.39	—
metal/salts	na	na	—	—	0.42	—
Manganese, ore	39.79	*18.57*	15.81	*17.30*	3.16	—
Mercury*f*	—	—	—	—	2.00	*0.10*[2]
Nickel, metal	na	na	0.24*q*	—	—	—
Tin, metal	—	—	—	—	0.25	*0.20*
Titanium minerals	—	—	—	—	1.60	—
Tungsten, metal	—	—	—	—	0.08	—
Zinc: ore	11.13*m*	*8.98m*	21.82	*12.19*	—	—
metal	—	—	—	—	9.88	*19.05*

f metric tons. *k* '000 fine troy oz. *m* metal content. *n* 1966 figure. *p* hydrate. *q* unwrought.

10. CHEMICALS*n* AND FERTILIZERS

	Production		Exports		Imports	
Organic chemicals:						
Benzene	na		—		0.1[2]	
Butadiene	—		—		na	
Ethylene	—		—		na	
Methanol	na		—		0.3	
Phthalic anhydride	—		—		na	
Styrene monomer	—		—		3.1	
Urea	—		—		0.6	
Inorganic chemicals:						
Ammonia	na		—		6.7	
Carbon black	na		—		0.7	
Chlorine	na		—		0.3	
Nitric acid	17.2[1]		—		0.4	
Sodium carbonate	—		—		16.5	
Sodium hydroxide	na		—		11.7	
Sulphuric acid	129.0[2]		0.2		29.0	
Plastics:						
Polyamides	na		—		na	
Polyethylene	—		—		na	
Polyvinyl chloride	—		—		na	
Fertilizers:						
Phosphates	—	—	—	—	129.2	*148.1*[2]
Potash	—	—	—	—	27.7	*0.9*[2]
Pyrites	64.4**x*	*99.0*x*	36.5	*142.1*	—	—
Sulphur	—	*2.5r*	8.4	—	38.4	*11.1*

n data not available for years 1953–5. *r* content of ore. *x* sulphur content.

11. INDUSTRY

	Production		Exports		Imports	
Aircraft*a*	—	—	—	—	—	*0.3*
Alcoholic beverages			5.0*a*	*3.7a*	0.7*a*	*0.1a*
beer*b*	431.0	*240.4*				
spirits*b*	73.8[1]*p*	na				
Cement	2 726.3	*896.0*	86.3	*157.7*	1.3	*2.3*
Electrical engineering*a*	na	na	—	*0.1*[2]	57.2	*13.5*[2]
Railway vehicles*a*	—	—	—	—	—	*3.3*
Merchant ships*g*	3.0	—	—	—	254.0	*56.4*
Motor vehicles*a*	—	—	1.2	*0.1*[2]	5.7	*17.1*

a million $ U.S. *b* '000 hectolitres. *g* '000 G.R.T. *p* 1961 figure.

na: data not available. — negligible or nil. [1] one year only. [2] two year average. * estimate. ‡ see appendix. † re-exports.

GUATEMALA

CENTRAL AMERICA

Guatemala is a republic of which the present constitution was promulgated in 1966 on the restoration of civilian government after three years of military rule.

AREA: 108 889 sq. km. (42 042 sq. miles)

LAND USE: (percentage of total)

	1958
Arable and orchard	13.5
Permanenet meadow and pasture	5.3
Forest and woodland	44.4
City areas, waste and other land	36.8

POPULATION: 4 717 000* (1967 estimate)

Largest city: CIUDAD DE GUATEMALA (Guatemala City), capital; population: 577 120 (city proper, 1964)

Distribution of working population (1964)

Total working population: 1 292 220* (based on a 5% sample of census returns)

U.N. group no.		*Percentage*
0	Agriculture, forestry, fishing and hunting	64.7
1	Mining and quarrying	0.2
2/3	Manufacturing	11.5
4	Construction	2.7
5	Electricity, gas, water and sanitary services	0.1
6	Commerce	6.4
7	Transport, storage and communications	2.2
8	Services	11.5
9	Others	0.7

		Year(s)
Life expectancy at birth (years): male	48.3	1963–5 av.
female	49.7	1963–5 av.
Infant mortality (per '000)	92.6	1965
Crude birth rate (per '000)	48*	1960–5 av.
Crude death rate (per '000)	19*	1960–5 av.
Accidental deaths (per 100 000 population)		
caused by motor vehicles	7.3	1965
due to other causes	28.5	1965
Population per physician	3 690	1965
Population per hospital bed	410	1966
School enrolment: age 5–19 years (percentage)	39a	1963–4 av.
age over 19 years (per 100 000 population)	161	1963–5 av.

a incl. evening courses.

COMMUNICATIONS

		Year(s)
Motor vehicles in use ('000s): private	33.5	1963–5 av.
commercial	14.6	1963–5 av.
Railway track (km.)	1 159	1962
Telephones (per '000 urban population)	0.7	1967
Television sets (per '000 population)	12.0	1963–5 av.
Daily newspapers (per '000 population)	31	1962

FINANCE

Currency unit: The quetzal

Exchange rates	*1965*	*1960*	*1950*	*1938*
Per $ U.S.	1.0	1.0	1.08	1.01
Per £ sterling	2.8	2.8	2.82	4.65

		Year(s)
National Income (million $ U.S.)	1 247	1965
G.N.P. per capita ($ U.S.)	320	1966
Rate of increase of G.N.P. per capita	2.8	1960–4 av.
Foreign trade (percentage of G.D.P.)	28	1963–5 av.

TRADING

Total trade (in million $ U.S.)	*1965*	*1955*	*1938*
Exports (f.o.b.)	187	107	18
Imports (c.i.f.)	229	107	21

Main trading partners (percentage of total value)

Exports	*1965*	*1955*	*Imports*	*1965*	*1955*
U.S.A.	37	74	U.S.A.	42	65
Germany F.R.	13	3	El Salvador	10	1
Japan	11	1	Germany F.R.	10	7
El Salvador	11	2	Japan	7	1
Honduras	4	—	U.K.	5	4
Netherlands	3	7	Venezuela	3	1
Nicaragua	3	na	Belg./Lux.	3	1

Distribution of trade (percentage of total value)

Exports	*1965*	*1955*	*1938**
Coffee	49	76	63
Textiles and clothing	23	na	na
Fruit and vegetables	4	10*	30
Sugar	3	na	na
Essential oils	3	1	na
Imports			
Manufactured goods	64	na	na
(machinery and transport equipment)	(29)	na	(6)
(textiles and clothing)	(11)	na	(14)
Chemicals	17	na	na
Food	9	na	5

PRODUCTION, EXPORTS AND IMPORTS

Years: **1963–5 average** and *1953–5 average* Units: '000 metric tons unless otherwise indicated

	Production **1963–5**	Production *1953–5*	Exports **1963–5**	Exports *1953–5*	Imports **1963–5**	Imports *1953–5*
1. CEREALS, etc.						
Cassava	**3.0***	na				
Maize (corn)	**614.7***	*389.3*	—	*1.1*	**11.2**	*19.9*
Millets/sorghum	**12.0***	*12.3*	**0.5**	—	**0.2**	—
Potatoes	**18.0***	*9.3*	**8.2**[2]	—	—[2]	—
Rice	**16.0***	*10.0*	**1.1**	*0.4*	**0.3**	*0.7*
Wheat	**35.0***	*17.7*	—	—	**65.1**	*5.6*
2. FRUIT, etc.						
Bananas	**122.7***	na	**94.4**	*153.7*	—	—
Grapes	—	—	—	—	—	*0.4*
Oranges	**30.0***	na	—	—	—	—
Wine *b*	—	—	—	—	**3.1**[2]	*1.3*

b '000 hectolitres.

	Production **1963–5**	Production *1953–5*	Exports **1963–5**	Exports *1953–5*	Imports **1963–5**	Imports *1953–5*
3. BEVERAGES, FOREST PRODUCTS, etc.						
Cocoa	**0.5**	na	**0.4**	*0.3*	—	—
Coffee	**108.2***	*71.4**	**93.5**	*55.7*	—	—
Sugar: cane	**1 633.3***	*567.7**				
raw	**143.7***n*	*44.7*n*	**44.4**	—	—	—
Tobacco: leaf	**1.9***	*1.4**	**0.1**[2]	—	**0.2**[2]	*0.3*[2]
cigars *e*	**69.0**	—	—	—	—	—
cigarettes *e*	**2 132.0**	*1 609.7*	—	—	—	—
Softwood *j*	—	*645.0*	**8.0**	*8.1*[2]	**0.3**[2]	*0.8*[1]
Hardwood *j*	**4 250.0**[1]	*564.0*[1]	**11.6**[2]	*18.5*[2]	—[2]	—[1]
Wood pulp	—[1]	—[2]	—	—[2]	**2.0**[1]	—[1]
Newsprint	—[2]*	—	—	—[2]	**4.6**[1]	*2.0*[2]
Other paper	**5.3**[2]*	—	—	—[2]	**2.5**[1]	*3.4*[1]

e no. in millions. *j* '000 cu. metres of roundwood equivalent. *n* in addition, panela 31* (1963–5 av.) and 50* (1953–5 av.).

	Production **1963–5**	Production *1953–5*	Exports **1963–5**	Exports *1953–5*	Imports **1963–5**	Imports *1953–5*
4. VEGETABLE OILSEEDS AND OILS						
Coconut oil	—	—	**0.01**[2]	—	**0.28**[2]	—
Cottonseed	**120.30***	*12.67*	**15.28**	*4.47*	**1.07**[2]	*0.20*
Cottonseed oil	na	na	**1.68**	—	**0.39**[2]	*0.08*[2]
Groundnuts	—	—	**0.01**[2]	—	—	—
Groundnut oil	—	—	—	—	—	*0.25p*
Linseed oil	—	—	—	—	**0.05**[2]	*0.54*
Olive oil	—	—	—	—	**0.14**[2]	*0.04*
Rapeseed oil	—	—	—	—	**0.01**	—
Sesame seed	**0.50***	*0.50*	**1.18**	*0.63*	—	—
Soya bean oil	—	—	—	—	**0.10**	—
Tung oil	—	—	—	—	**0.01**	—

p incl. some other vegetable oils.

	Production **1963–5**	Production *1953–5*	Exports **1963–5**	Exports *1953–5*	Imports **1963–5**	Imports *1953–5*
5. LIVESTOCK‡, ANIMAL PRODUCTS, etc.						
Chickens *d*	**5 617.0***	*4 211.3*				
Cattle *d*	**1 179.3***	*1 160.3*	**0.6**[2]	*0.1*	**36.4**[2]	*35.6*
dairy cows *d*	**637.0***	na				
Goats *d*	**89.0***	*103.7*	—	—	—	—
Sheep *d*	**694.0***	*805.7*	—	—	—	—
Horses *d*	**158.3***	*176.0*				
Pigs *d*	**417.0***	*429.0*	**2.6**[2]	*7.8*	**7.7**[2]	—
Meat‡: 'A'	**52.0***	*40.0*[2]*q*	**5.32**[2]	—	—	—
'B'	**3.1***	—	—	—	—	—
Butter	—	—	—	—	**0.1**[2]	—
Cheese	**2.0***	na	**0.2**[2]	—	**0.2**[2]	*0.1*
Eggs	**9.0***	na	**0.1**	—	**0.2**[2]	*0.4*
Fish	**3.2**	*0.7*	**1.0**	na	**1.7**[2]	na
Milk	**160.0***	*175.0*[1]	—	—	**38.3**[2]	*19.6*
Hides/skins	na	*2.5r*	—	*0.1*[2]	—	*0.6a*

a million $ U.S. *d* no. in thousands. *q* incl. meat equivalent of live animals. *r* excl. sheepskins.

continued

na: data not available. — negligible or nil. [1] one year only. [2] two year average. * estimate. ‡ see appendix. † re-exports.

PRODUCTION, EXPORTS AND IMPORTS *continued*

	Production **1963–5**	Production *1953–5*	Exports **1963–5**	Exports *1953–5*	Imports **1963–5**	Imports *1953–5*
6. FIBRES, TEXTILES, etc.						
Abaca	na	*3.2*	—	*2.4*	—	—
Agaves (letona)	**0.6***	na	—	—	—	—
Cotton lint	**75.0***	*8.0*	**57.7***	—	—	—
Jute	—	—	—	—	**1.7**[2]	—
Rubber, natural	—	—	—	—	**1.4**[2]	*0.1*
Cotton: yarn	—	—	—	—	**9.1**	—
woven fabrics	—	—	—	—	**1.7**	—
7. FUEL AND POWER						
Electricity *h*: total	**426**	*220*[1]				
hydro	**117**[1]	*130*[1]				
thermal	**309**	*90*[1]				
Oil, crude	—	—	—	—	**240**	*151**
Petroleum, refined	**206**	—[1]	—	—	**353**	*140*[1]

h million kWh.

	Production **1963–5**	Production *1953–5*	Exports **1963–5**	Exports *1953–5*	Imports **1963–5**	Imports *1953–5*
9. NON-FERROUS MINERALS AND METALS						
Silver *k*, ore *m*	**30.70**	*361.70*	na	na	**8.00p**	*18.00p*
Asbestos: fibre	—	—	—	—	**0.58**	*0.25*
manufactured	—	—	—	—	**0.14**	*0.23s*
Aluminium	—	—	—	—	—	*0.51s*
Antimony, ore	na	—	**0.01***n*	—	—	—
Chrome, ore *m*	—	*0.27*	—	—	—	—
9. NON-FERROUS MINERALS AND METALS—*continued*						
Copper, metal	—	—	—	—	**0.18**	*6.51*
Lead: ore	**0.58***m*	*4.68*m*	**0.79**	*4.66*	—	—
metal	**0.08**	*0.25**	—	—	—	—
Mercury *f*	—	—	—	—	—	*0.10s*
Zinc, ore	**0.67***m*	*6.50m*	**1.56**	*12.67*	—	—

f metric tons. *k* '000 fine troy oz. *m* metal content. *n* exports to the U.S.A. only. *p* bullion. *s* incl. imports for re-export.

	Production **1963–5**	Production *1953–5*	Exports **1963–5**	Exports *1953–5*	Imports **1963–5**	Imports *1953–5*
10. CHEMICALS *n* AND FERTILIZERS						
Chemicals	—		—		na	
Fertilizers:						
Potash	—	—	—	—	**9.1**	—
Sulphur	—	—	—	—	—	*0.1*

n data not available for years 1953–5.

	Production **1963–5**	Production *1953–5*	Exports **1963–5**	Exports *1953–5*	Imports **1963–5**	Imports *1953–5*
11. INDUSTRY						
Aircraft *a*	—	—	—	—	**1.4**	—
Alcoholic beverages			**0.4a**	—	**1.3**[2]**a**	*0.5a*
beer *b*	**203.0**	*112.0*				
Cement	**192.3**	*70.3*	**25.3***	*1.0*	**1.0**	*4.0*
Electrical engineering *a*	—	—	—	—	**10.5**	—
Railway vehicles *a*	—	—	—	—	**0.3**	—
Motor vehicles *a*	—	—	—	—	**16.5**	*5.8*

a million $ U.S. *b* '000 hectolitres.

continued

GUINEA

WEST AFRICA

Guinea, formerly the colony of French Guinea, elected to leave the French West African Community in 1958 and become an independent republic. Links with France, her main trading partner, were severed, and French financial and technical aid were replaced by assistance from the U.S.A., Germany F.R., the U.S.S.R., and China P.R.

AREA: 245 857 sq. km. (95 000 sq. miles)

POPULATION: 3 702 000 (1967 estimate)

Largest city: CONAKRY, capital; population: 197 267 (1967)

Total working population: 1 348 000 (1959)

		Year(s)
Life expectancy at birth (years): male	26*b	1955
female	28*b	1955
Population per physician	19 000	1962
Population per hospital bed	530a	1966
School enrolment: age 5–19 years (percentage)	22	1963–4 av.
age over 19 years (per 100 000 population)	16	1963–5 av.

a government hospitals only. *b* African population only.

COMMUNICATIONS

		Year(s)
Motor vehicles in use ('000s): private	8.4	1963–5 av.
commercial	12.8	1963–5 av.
Railway track (km.)	662	1965
Telephones (per '000 urban population)	0.2*	1967
Radio receivers (per '000 population)	16	1963–5 av.
Daily newspapers (per '000 population)	0.2	1959

FINANCE

Currency unit: The Guinea franc was introduced in 1960 at par with the franc CFA

Exchange rates	*1965*	*1960*
Per $ U.S.	246.85	246.85
Per £ sterling	691.18	691.18

		Year
National Income (million $ U.S.)	241	1958
G.N.P. per capita ($ U.S.)	80	1966

TRADING

Total trade (in million $ U.S.)	*1963*
Exports	46
Imports	56

PRODUCTION, EXPORTS AND IMPORTS

Years: **1963–5 average** Units: '000 metric tons unless otherwise indicated

Note—no data are available for 1953–5

	Production	Exports	Imports
1. CEREALS, etc.			
Cassava	**440.0***		
Maize (corn)	**67.3***	—	—
Millets/sorghum	**142.0***	—	—
Rice	**316.7***	—	na
Sweet potatoes/ yams	**83.3***		
2. FRUIT, etc.			
Bananas	**86.0***	**33.3***	—
Oranges	**80.7***	—	—
Pineapples	**13.0***	—	—
3. BEVERAGES, FOREST PRODUCTS, etc			
Coffee	**11.7***	na	—
Sugar, raw	—	—	**10.8**[2]*
Tobacco, leaf	**1.3**	na	—
Softwood *j*	—	—	**0.3**[2]
Hardwood *j*	**2 125.0***[1]	—	**3.3**[2]
Newsprint	—	—	**0.1**[1]
Other paper	—	—	**2.1**[1]

j '000 cu. metres of roundwood equivalent.

	Production	Exports	Imports
4. VEGETABLE OILSEEDS AND OILS			
Groundnuts	**12.37**	na	—
Palm kernels	**19.50**	**16.50***	—
Palm oil	**11.67***	na	—

continued

na: data not available. — negligible or nil. [1] one year only. [2] two year average. * estimate. ‡ see appendix. † re-exports.

PRODUCTION, EXPORTS AND IMPORTS *continued*

5. LIVESTOCK‡, ANIMAL PRODUCTS, etc.

	Production	Exports	Imports
Cattle *d*	1 716.7*	—	—
Goats *d*	410.0*	—	—
Sheep *d*	360.3*	—	—
Horses *d*	1.0*		
Pigs *d*	15.0*	—	—
Eggs	2.7*	—	—
Fish	na	—	—
Milk	137.3*	—	—

d no. in thousands.

6. FIBRES, TEXTILES, etc.

	Production	Exports	Imports
Agaves (sisal)	0.1*	—	—

7. FUEL AND POWER

	Production	Exports	Imports
Electricity *hn*	166		
Petroleum, refined	—	—	230

h million kWh. *n* hydro and thermal.

8. IRON AND STEEL

	Production	Exports	Imports
Iron ore	389*m*	560	—

m metal content.

9. NON-FERROUS MINERALS AND METALS

	Production	Exports	Imports
Diamonds *l*	66.00*	na	—
Aluminium: bauxite	1 737.45	205.35	—
alumina	495.51	486.69[1]	—

l '000 carats

11. INDUSTRY

	Production	Exports	Imports
Cement	—	—	87*
Merchant ships *g*	—	—	4*

g '000 G.R.T.

GUYANA

SOUTH AMERICA

Guyana, formerly British Guiana, became an independent member of the British Commonwealth in 1966, attaining republican status in 1970.

AREA: 215 000 sq. km. (83 000 sq. miles)

LAND USE: (percentage of total)	*1962*	*1954*
Arable and orchard	0.9	0.6
Permanent meadow and pasture	11.8	5.1
Forest and woodland	84.3	77.0
City areas, waste and other land	3.0	17.3

POPULATION: 680 000 (1967 U.N. estimate)

Largest city: GEORGETOWN (formerly Demarara), capital; population: 148 391 (1960)

Distribution of working population (1960)
Total working population: 174 730

U.N. group no.		*Percentage*
0	Agriculture, forestry, fishing and hunting	34.2
1	Mining and quarrying	3.5
2/3	Manufacturing	15.1
4	Construction	7.4
5	Electricity, gas, water and sanitary services	0.5
6	Commerce	10.4
7	Transport, storage and communications	4.4
8	Services	16.7
9	Others	7.8

		Year(s)
Life expectancy at birth (years): male	59	1959–61 av.
female	63	1959–61 av.
Infant mortality (per '000)	42.3	1965
Crude birth rate (per '000)	39.7	1965
Crude death rate (per '000)	9.5*	1960–5 av.
Accidental deaths (per 100 000 population)		
caused by motor vehicles	2.7	1962
due to other causes	41.1	1962
Population per physician	2 600	1963
Population per hospital bed	170	1966
School enrolment: age 5–19 years (percentage)	83 *a*	1963–4 av.
age over 19 years (per 100 000 population)	53 *b*	1963–5 av.

a public education only. *b* universities only.

COMMUNICATIONS

		Year(s)
Motor vehicles in use ('000s): private	9.1	1963–5 av.
commercial	2.9	1963–5 av.
Railway track (km.)	151 *a*	1964
Mail per capita: domestic	59	1963–5 av.
foreign received	na	1963–5 av.
foreign sent	37	1963–5 av.
Telephones (per '000 urban population)	1.7	1967
Radio receivers (per '000 population)	114	1963–5 av.
Daily newspapers (per '000 population)	76	1962–4 av.

a excluding about 130 km. of privately owned railway used for the transport of manganese and bauxite.

FINANCE

Currency unit: The Guyana dollar replaced, at par, the British West Indies dollar in 1966.

Exchange rates	*1965*	*1960*	*1958*
Per $ U.S.	1.71	1.71	1.71
Per £ sterling	4.8	4.8	4.8

		Year(s)
National Income (million $ U.S.)	160	1965
G.N.P. per capita ($ U.S.)	300	1966
Foreign trade (percentage of G.D.P.)	92	1963–5 av.

TRADING

Total trade (in million $ U.S.)	*1965*	*1955*	*1938*
Exports (f.o.b.)	97	53	12
Imports (c.i.f.)	104	55	11

Main trading partners (percentage of total value)

Exports	*1965*	*1955*	*Imports*	*1965*	*1955*
U.K.	25	36	U.K.	31	48
Canada	23	36	U.S.A.	24	13
U.S.A.	19	9	Trin./Tob.	11	na
Trin./Tob.	9	na	Canada	8	6
Norway	5	na	Netherlands	4	6
Jamaica	2	na	Germany F.R.	3	2
Netherlands	2	1	Japan	3	2

Distribution of trade (percentage of total value)

Exports	*1965*	*1955*	*1938**
Crude materials	46	32	
(bauxite and concentrates)	(41)	(28)	(17)
Food	46	60	na
(sugar)	(27)	(45)	(63)
(rice)	(14)	(14)	(5)
(shrimps)	(3)	(na)	(na)
Diamonds	3	2	3
Rum	3	3	na
Imports			
Manufactured goods	60	60	
(machinery and transport equipment)	(27)	(22)	(19)
(textiles and clothing)	(11)	(11)	(17)
Food	17	21	21
Chemicals	10	8	2
Petroleum products	9	8	4

continued

PRODUCTION, EXPORTS AND IMPORTS

Years: **1963–5 average** and *1953–5 average* Units: '000 metric tons unless otherwise indicated

1. CEREALS, etc.

	Production 1963–5	Production 1953–5	Exports 1963–5	Exports 1953–5	Imports 1963–5	Imports 1953–5
Cassava	10.0*	na				
Maize (corn)	1.0*	1.0[1]	—	—	1.3*	—
Oats	—	—	—	—	0.4	0.8
Potatoes	—	—	—	—	8.0[2]	8.1
Rice	239.0	151.7*	86.4	43.9	—	—
Sweet potatoes/yams	5.0*	na				

2. FRUIT, etc.

	Production 1963–5	Production 1953–5	Exports 1963–5	Exports 1953–5	Imports 1963–5	Imports 1953–5
Apples	—	—	—	—	0.4[1]	0.1
Bananas	5.0*	na	0.6[1]	—	na	—
Coconuts *e*	42.3	na	—	—	—	—
Grapes	—	—	—	—	0.1[1]	—
Lemons	2.0*	na	—	—	—	—
Oranges	10.3	na	—	—	0.2[1]	0.7
Pineapples	1.7	na	—	—	—	—
Raisins	—	—	—	—	—	0.1
Wine *b*	na	—	1.5[2]	—	0.6[1]	—

b '000 hectolitres. *e* no. in millions.

3. BEVERAGES, FOREST PRODUCTS, etc.

	Production 1963–5	Production 1953–5	Exports 1963–5	Exports 1953–5	Imports 1963–5	Imports 1953–5
Coffee	1.0	0.4[2]	0.1[1]	0.1	—	—
Sugar: cane	3 246.0	2 771.0[2]	—	—	—	—
raw	299.7	256.0	280.3	236.5	0.1[1]	—
Tea	—	—	—	—	0.1[1]	0.1
Tobacco: leaf	—	—	—	—	0.3[2]	0.3
cigarettes *e*	371.0	—	—	—	—	—
Softwood *j*	—	—	—	—	3.0[2]	6.2
Hardwood *j*	243.7	350.3	28.3[2]	53.2	145.0[2]	8.5
Newsprint	—	—	—	—	3.0[2]	0.8
Other paper	—	—	—	—	2.4[2]	8.5

e no. in millions. *j* '000 cu. metres of roundwood equivalent.

4. VEGETABLE OILSEEDS AND OILS

	Production 1963–5	Production 1953–5	Exports 1963–5	Exports 1953–5	Imports 1963–5	Imports 1953–5
Castor oil	—	—	—	—	0.01	—
Copra	5.53	4.53	—	0.03	0.43[1]	0.10[2]
Coconut oil	na	na	—	—	0.44[1]	0.42
Groundnuts	—	—	—	—	—	0.17
Linseed oil	—	—	—	—	na	0.15
Olive oil	—	—	—	—	0.01[1]	0.01
Soya bean oil	—	—	—	—	1.45[1]	—

5. LIVESTOCK‡, ANIMAL PRODUCTS, etc.

	Production 1963–5	Production 1953–5	Exports 1963–5	Exports 1953–5	Imports 1963–5	Imports 1953–5
Chickens *d*	1 783.3*	486.0[1]				
Cattle *d*	284.0	169.7*n*	0.4	—	na	—
Goats *d*	23.0*	11.7*n*	—	—	—	—
Sheep *d*	64.7*	38.7	—	—	—	—
Horses *d*	2.7*	3.5[2]				
Pigs *d*	na	27.0*n*	—	—	—	—
Bacon/ham	4.3* (Bacon/ham and Meat 'A')	2.3 (Bacon/ham and Meat 'A')	—	—	0.6[1]	0.5
Meat‡: 'A'			0.4[1]	—	0.1	0.1
'B'	0.7*	0.2[1]	—	—	—	—

continued

5. LIVESTOCK‡, ANIMAL PRODUCTS, etc.—*continued*

	Production 1963–5	Production 1953–5	Exports 1963–5	Exports 1953–5	Imports 1963–5	Imports 1953–5
Butter	—	—	—	—	0.3	0.3
Cheese	—	—	—	—	0.5[1]	0.3
Eggs	0.6*	0.5[1]	—	—	—	—
Fish	10.5	3.1	3.2	na	2.8	na
Milk	19.0	11.3	—	—	29.2	12.1
Hides/skins	—	0.2[1]	—	—	—	—

d no. in thousands. *n* excl. animals pastured on sugar plantations.

6. FIBRES, TEXTILES, etc.

	Production 1963–5	Production 1953–5	Exports 1963–5	Exports 1953–5	Imports 1963–5	Imports 1953–5
Rubber, natural	na	—	0.3[1]	—	—	—

7. FUEL AND POWER

	Production 1963–5	Production 1953–5	Exports 1963–5	Exports 1953–5	Imports 1963–5	Imports 1953–5
Coal, 'A'‡	—	—	—	—	—[1]	2
Electricity *h*: total	177	50				
hydro	na	—				
thermal	na	50				
Petroleum, refined	—	—	—	—	253	170[1]

h million kWh.

8. IRON AND STEEL

	Production 1963–5	Production 1953–5	Exports 1963–5	Exports 1953–5	Imports 1963–5	Imports 1953–5
Pig iron	—	—	—	—	1*n*	—

n incl. steel ingots.

9. NON-FERROUS MINERALS AND METALS

	Production 1963–5	Production 1953–5	Exports 1963–5	Exports 1953–5	Imports 1963–5	Imports 1953–5
Diamonds	107.67*l*	328.92*l*	3.00[2]*a*	0.76*a*	—	—
Gold *k*, ore *m*	2.30	24.00	na	13.59*q*	—	—
Silver *k*, bullion	—	—	—	—	4.46[2]	0.27
Asbestos, manufactured	—	—	—	—	1.56[2]	0.89[2]
Aluminium: bauxite	2 602.10	2 377.50	1 493.50*	2 169.89*p*	—	—
alumina	266.99	251.44*	na	na	—	—
aluminium	—	—	—	—	0.52[2]	0.42
Copper, metal	—	—	—	—	0.05[2]	—
Lead, metal	—	—	—	—	0.03[2]	—
Manganese, ore	143.45	—	164.47	—	—	—
Tin, metal	—	—	—	—	0.02[2]	—

a million $ U.S. *k* '000 fine troy oz. *l* '000 carats. *m* metal content. *p* dried and calcined. *q* bullion.

10. CHEMICALS*n* AND FERTILIZERS

	Production 1963–5	Production 1953–5	Exports 1963–5	Exports 1953–5	Imports 1963–5	Imports 1953–5
Chemicals	—		—		na	
Fertilizers:						
Potash	—	—	—	—	1.7	0.7[1]

n data not available for years 1953–5.

11. INDUSTRY

	Production 1963–5	Production 1953–5	Exports 1963–5	Exports 1953–5	Imports 1963–5	Imports 1953–5
Alcoholic beverages	na	na	2.1*aq*	1.5*aq*	0.5*a*	0.8*a*
beer *b*	40.0*	na				
Cement	—	—	—	—	30.0*	16.7
Electrical engineering *a*	—	—	—	—	na	1.6
Motor vehicles *a*	—	—	—	—	3.1	1.6

a million $ U.S. *b* '000 hectolitres. *q* rum only.

HAITI

CARIBBEAN SEA

Haiti, once a prosperous French colony, has a population primarily of African origin. The country has a long history of political upheavals, and came under U.S. control from 1915 to 1934, with the U.S. control of revenue continuing until 1947. Further unrest led to a period without a government in 1956; and since 1957 the president has ruled with 'absolute power'.

AREA: 27 750 sq. km. (10 700 sq. miles)

LAND USE: (percentage of total)	*1950*
Arable and orchard	13.4
Permanent meadow and pasture	18.0
Forest and woodland	25.2
City areas, waste and other land	43.4

POPULATION: 4 581 000 (1967 estimate)

Largest city: PORT-AU-PRINCE, capital; population: 240 000 (city proper, 1960)

Distribution of working population (1950)
Total working population: 1 747 187

U.N. group no.		*Percentage*
0	Agriculture, forestry, fishing and hunting	83.2
1	Mining and quarrying	—
2/3	Manufacturing	4.9
4	Construction	0.6
5	Electricity, gas, water and sanitary services	0.1
6	Commerce	3.5
7	Transport, storage and communications	0.4
8	Services	4.6
9	Others	2.7

Since 1950 the pattern of employment has been affected by the introduction of copper and bauxite mining and a considerable increase in the number employed in the maintenance of law and order.

continued

HAITI *continued*

POPULATION *continued*

		(Years)
Crude birth rate (per '000)	47.5*	1960–5 av.
Crude death rate (per '000)	22*	1960–5 av.
Population per physician	14 000	1965
Population per hospital bed	1 990*a*	1966
School enrolment: age 5–19 years (percentage)	26	1963–4 av.
age over 19 years (per 100 000 population)	39	1964–5 av.

a government hospitals only.

COMMUNICATIONS

		Year(s)
Motor vehicles in use ('000s): private	5.4	1963–5 av.
commercial	1.5	
Railway track (km.)	354*a*	1965
Telephones (per '000 urban population)	0.1*b*	1967
Radio receivers (per '000 population)	14	1963–5 av.
Television sets (per '000 population)	0.9	1963–5 av.
Daily newspapers (per '000 population)	6	1963

a this track (from Port-au-Prince to Verrettes) is closed to public transport but part of it is still used for transporting sugar cane. *b* much of the internal telephone system is permanently out of order, but external services are normal.

FINANCE

Currency unit: The gourde, which is fixed at the rate 5 to the U.S. dollar. U.S. coins are also in circulation.

Exchange rates	*1965*	*1960*	*1955*	*1938*
Per $ U.S.	5	5	5	5
Per £ sterling	14	14	14	23

continued

		Year(s)
National Income (million $ U.S.)	353	1965
G.N.P. per capita ($ U.S.)	70	1966
Rate of increase of G.N.P. per capita	0.4	1960–2 av.

TRADING

Total trade (in million $ U.S.)	*1965*	*1955*	*1938*
Exports (f.o.b.)	36	35	7
Imports (c.i.f.)	36	39	8

Main trading partners (percentage of total value)

Exports	*1955*	*Imports*	*1955*
U.S.A.	49	U.S.A.	66
Belg./Lux.	14	Canada	6
France	14	Germany F.R.	4
Italy	10	U.K.	4
Netherlands	3	Neths. Antilles	4
U.K.	3	France	3
S. Korea	1	Netherlands	2

Distribution of trade

Coffee accounts for two-thirds of the exports. Sisal, bananas, and sugar are also exported but in decreasing quantities. Exports of bauxite began in 1957 and of copper in 1960. The chief imports are foodstuffs, machinery, cars and chemicals. The tourist trade has decreased, because of the political unrest.

PRODUCTION, EXPORTS AND IMPORTS

Years: **1963–5 average** and *1953–5 average* Units: '000 metric tons unless otherwise indicated

	Production		Exports		Imports	
1. CEREALS, etc.						
Cassava	**118.3***	na				
Maize (corn)	**242.7***	na	—	*0.1*[1]	—	—
Millets/sorghum	**180.0***	na	—	—	—	—
Potatoes	—	—	—	—	—	*0.3*[2]
Rice	**38.7***	na	—	*0.1*[2]	**0.7***	*0.1*[1]
Sweet potatoes/ yams	**100.0***	*120.0*[1]				
Wheat	—	—	—	—	**49.1***	—
2. FRUIT, etc.						
Bananas	**225.0***	*13.0*[1]	**1.5***	*10.5*[2]	—	—
Coconuts*e*	**28.0[1]***	na	—	—	—	—
Lemons	**14.0***	na	—	—	—	—
Oranges	**6.0***	na	—	—	—	—
Wine*b*	—	—	—	—	—	*1.3*

b '000 hectolitres. *e* no. in millions.

	Production		Exports		Imports	
3. BEVERAGES, FOREST PRODUCTS, etc.						
Cocoa	**2.4**	*1.7**	—	*1.8*	—	—
Coffee	**33.4***	*33.1**	**22.9***	*23.1*	—	—
Sugar: cane	**500.0[1]***	*465.0*[2]*n*				
raw	**66.0**	*56.7*	**27.7***	*20.1*	—	*0.2*
Tobacco: leaf	**1.1***	—	—	—	—	*0.2*
cigarettes	**353.0*e***	*301.0e*	—	—	—	*0.6*[2]*ap*
Softwood*j*	**495.0[1]***	*20.0*	—	—	**2.5[2]**	*16.5*
Hardwood*j*	**7 730.0[1]***	*8 880.0*	—	*2.4*	**—[2]**	*0.4*
Newsprint	—	—	—	—	**0.3[1]**	*0.3*
Other paper	—	—	—	—	**1.2[1]**	*1.6*

a million $ U.S. *e* no. in millions. *j* '000 cu. metres of roundwood equivalent. *n* cane consumption at crushing mills. *p* incl. other tobacco products.

	Production		Exports		Imports	
4. VEGETABLE OILSEEDS AND OILS						
Castor seed	**2.0***	na	—	*5.7*[2]	—	—
Cottonseed	**2.0***	*3.0**	na	na	—	—
Groundnuts	**2.1***	na	—	—	—	—
Soya bean oil	—	—	—	—	**5.0**	*0.5*

	Production		Exports		Imports	
5. LIVESTOCK‡, ANIMAL PRODUCTS, etc.						
Chickens*d*	**5 470****q***	na				
Cattle*d*	**682***	na	—	—	—	—
Goats*d*	**882**	na	—	—	—	—
Sheep*d*	**54**	na	—	—	—	—
Horses*d*	**255**	na				
Pigs*d*	**1 143**	na	—	—	—	—
Meat‡ 'A'	**18***	na	—	—	—	—
Butter	—	—	—	—	**—***	*0.1*[2]
Cheese	—	—	—	—	**0.1***	*0.1*[2]
Fish	na	na	—	—	na	*7.3*[1]*
Milk	**17***	na	—	—	**14.9**	*3.3*[2]*
Whale/sperm oil	**9***	na	—	—	—	—
Hides/skins	na	na	—	*0.3*[2]	—	—

d no. in thousands. *q* incl. ducks, geese and turkeys.

	Production		Exports		Imports	
6. FIBRES, TEXTILES, etc.						
Agaves (sisal)	**18.6**	*25.7**	**16.6***	*25.9*	—	—
Cotton lint	**1.0***	*1.3**	na	*1.1*	—	—
Silk*f*	—	—	—	—	—	*9.0*[2]*
Cotton, woven fabrics	**0.5***	*0.3*	—	—	—	*3.5*

f metric tons.

	Production		Exports		Imports	
7. FUEL AND POWER						
Electricity*ht*	**74**	*60*[1]				
Petroleum, refined	—	—	—	—	**97**	*30*[1]

h million kWh. *t* thermal.

	Production		Exports		Imports	
9. NON-FERROUS MINERALS AND METALS						
Gold*k*, ore*m*	**7.3**	na	—	—	—	—
Silver*k*, ore*m*	**92.0**	na	—	—	—	—
Aluminium, bauxite	**401.3**	na	**413.2*p***	—	—	—
Copper, ore	**5.0*m***	na	**12.6**	—	—	—

k '000 fine troy oz. *m* metal content. *p* exports to the U.S.A. only.

	Production		Exports		Imports	
11. INDUSTRY						
Alcoholic beverages*a*	—	—	—	—	na	*0.4*
Cement	**50.3**	*20.0**	—	—	**0.7***	*23.3*
Electrical engineering*a*	—	—	—	—	—	*0.4*[2]
Motor vehicles*a*	—	—	—	—	na	*2.4*[2]

a million $ U.S.

HONDURAS

CENTRAL AMERICA

Honduras became an independent sovereign state in 1838 and adopted a republican constitution. In 1963 the government was overthrown by the armed forces, and military rule continued until 1965 when elections were held for a new civilian government.

AREA: 112 088 sq. km. (43 227 sq. miles)

LAND USE: (percentage of total)	*1963*	*1954*
Arable and orchard	7.3	7.4
Permanent meadow and pasture	30.5	17.8
Forest and woodland	26.9	43.5
City areas, waste and other land	35.3	31.3

POPULATION: 2 445 000 (1967 estimate)

Largest city: TEGUCIGALPA, capital; population: 170 535 (city proper, 1965)

Distribution of working population (1961)

Total working population: 567 988

U.N. group no.		*Percentage*
0	Agriculture, forestry, fishing and hunting	66.8
1	Mining and quarrying	0.3
2/3	Manufacturing	7.8
4	Construction	2.0
5	Electricity, gas, water and sanitary services	0.1
6	Commerce	4.8
7	Transport, storage and communications	1.4
8	Services	12.2
9	Others	4.6

		Year(s)
Infant mortality (per '000)	41.2*	1965
Crude birth rate (per '000)	48.5*	1960–5 av.
Crude death rate (per '000)	16*	1960–5 av.
Population per physician	5 400	1965
Population per hospital bed	630	1966
School enrolment: age 5–19 years (percentage)	50	1963–4 av.
age over 19 years (per 100 000 population)	107	1964–5 av.

COMMUNICATIONS

		Year(s)
Motor vehicles in use ('000s): private	8.9	1963–5 av.
commercial	7.3	
Railway track (km.)	1 152	1963
Telephones (per '000 urban population)	0.4	1967
Radio receivers (per '000 population)	59	1963–5 av.
Television sets (per '000 population)	3.3	1963–5 av.
Daily newspapers (per '000 population)	19.5	1963–4 av.

FINANCE

Currency unit: The lempira

Exchange rates	*1965*	*1960*	*1955*	*1938*
Per $ U.S.	2.0	2.0	2.02	2.04
Per £ sterling	5.6	5.6	5.7	9.4

		Year(s)
National Income (million $ U.S.)	442	1965
G.N.P. per capita ($ U.S.)	220	1956
Rate of increase of G.N.P. per capita	0.7	1960–3 av.
Foreign trade (percentage of G.D.P.)	43	1963–5 av.

TRADING

Total trade (in million $ U.S.)	*1965*	*1955*	*1937*
Exports (f.o.b.)	127	49	24
Imports	122 (c.i.f.)	54 (f.o.b.)	10 (f.o.b.)

Main trading partners (percentage of total value)

Exports	*1965*	*1955*	*Imports*	*1965*	*1955*
U.S.A.	59	68	U.S.A.	47	66
Germany F.R.	11	5	El Salvador	10	3
El Salvador	10	8	Guatemala	7	—
Guatemala	4	2	Germany F.R.	6	6
Japan	4	—	Japan	5	5
Netherlands	3	4	Neths. Antilles	4	5
Jamaica	2	—	U.K.	3	3

Distribution of trade (percentage of total value)

Exports	*1965*		*1955*		*1937**	
Food	74		78		na	
(bananas)		(42)		(50*)		(85)
(coffee)		(18)		(18)		(1)
(maize)		(4)		(—)		(na)
Crude materials	20		19		na	
(wood)		(8)		(11)		(na)
(silver, lead and zinc)		(6)		(4)		(9)
(cotton)		(5)		—		(na)
Imports						
Manufactured goods	68		62		na	
(machinery and transport equipment)		(25)		(20)		
(textiles and clothing)		(14)		(17)		
Chemicals	13		15			
Food	10		14			
Petroleum products	5		6			

PRODUCTION, EXPORTS AND IMPORTS

Years: **1963–5 average** and *1953–5 average* Units: '000 metric tons unless otherwise indicated

	Production		Exports		Imports	
1. CEREALS, etc.						
Cassava	**16.0***	*12.5*[2]				
Maize (corn)	**356.0***	*183.5*[2]	**46.8**	*6.5*	**1.2**	*1.6*
Millets/sorghum	**60.3**	*50.3*	**1.3[2]**	—	**0.2[2]**	—
Potatoes	**2.0***	*2.5*[2]	**0.2**	*0.1*	**2.7**	*0.2*
Rice	**23.7***	*14.3**	**0.8**	*0.5*	**1.8**	*1.2*
Sweet potatoes/ yams	**3.3***	*2.0*[1]				
Wheat	**1.0***	*1.0*[2]	—	—	**21.7**	*4.4*
2. FRUIT, etc.						
Bananas	**827.3***	*697.3*	**421.4**	*282.3*	—	—
Coconuts	**13.3****e*	na	**4.5**	*4.2*[2]	**0.7**	—
Oranges	**17.3*n***	*44.5*[2]*n*	**3.8**	*0.2*	—	*0.2*
Other citrus fruit	**2.7***	*15.0*[2]	**1.3**	*0.8*	—	—
Pineapples	**3.0***	*2.0*	—	—	—	—
Tomatoes	**2.0***	*3.0*[2]				
Wine*b*	—	—	—	—	**1.7**	*4.3*

b '000 hectolitres. *e* no. in millions. *n* incl. lemons.

	Production		Exports		Imports	
3. BEVERAGES, FOREST PRODUCTS, etc.						
Cocoa	**0.2**	*0.1*[2]	—	—	—	—
Coffee	**28.5***	*17.2**	**21.2**	*10.4*	—	—
Sugar: cane	**659.0**	na				
raw	**30.0*p***	*10.0*p*	**1.0**	—	**3.6**	*8.0*
Tobacco: leaf	**4.4**	*4.1*[2]	**1.8**	*1.6*	—	*0.1*
cigars	na	—	**0.2**	—	—	—
cigarettes	**1 189.0*e***	*826.0e*	na	*0.5*[2]	na	—
Softwood*j*	**2 200.0[1]**	*1 813.0**	**434.0[2]**	*265.5*[2]	**0.2[2]**	—[1]
Hardwood*j*	**1 060.0[1]**	*1 061.5*[2]	**8.1[2]**	*4.3*[2]	**—[2]**	—[1]
Newsprint	—	—	—	—[2]	**1.4[1]**	*0.5*[1]
Other paper	—	—	—	—	**13.7[1]**	*2.3*[1]

e no. in millions. *j* '000 cu. metres of roundwood equivalent. *p* in addition, non-centrifugal sugar 19* (1963–5 av.) and 21* (1953–5 av.).

	Production		Exports		Imports	
4. VEGETABLE OILSEEDS AND OILS						
Castor oil	—	—	—	—	**0.03**	*0.01*
Copra	**1.50***	na	**0.05**	*0.67*	—	—
Coconut oil	na	na	**0.24[2]**	*0.01*	**0.03[2]**	—
Cottonseed	**13.30**	*2.00*	**13.23**	—	**1.46**	—
Cottonseed oil	—	—	—	—	**0.78**	*0.12*
Groundnuts	—	—	—	—	**0.07**	—
Linseed oil	—	—	—	—	**0.01**	*0.03*
Olive oil	—	—	—	—	**0.03**	*0.04*
Palm kernels	**0.60**	*0.20*[1]	**0.10**	—	—	—
Palm kernel oil	na	na	—	*0.02*	—	*0.01*
Palm oil	**1.40***	*1.40*[1]*	**0.27[2]**	—	**0.31[2]**	—
Seasame seed	**0.50***	*0.60*[2]	**0.17**	*0.20*[1]	—	—
Soya bean oil	—	—	—	—	**0.02**	—

	Production		Exports		Imports	
5. LIVESTOCK‡, ANIMAL PRODUCTS, etc.						
Chickens*d*	**4 950.0***	*5 953.7*				
Cattle*dn*	**1 640.7**	*1 180.0*	**33.8**	*34.8*	**0.2[1]**	—
dairy cows*d*	**563.0***	na				
Goats*d*	**47.0**	*55.5*[2]	**0.4** (Goats and Sheep)	—	—	—
Sheep*d*	**8.0**	*14.0*[2]				
Horses*d*	**273.7***	na				
Pigs*d*	**754.0**	*530.0*[1]	**31.5**	*39.9*	—	—
Meat‡: 'A'	**23.7***	*23.0*[1]	—	—	—	—
'B'	**8.9***	*4.5*[1]	—	—	**0.1**	—
Butter	**4.0**	*3.3*	—	—	—	—
Cheese	**12.0**	*9.0*	**0.2**	*0.2*	—	*0.2*
Eggs	**9.0***	*7.6*[2]	—	—	**0.2**	—
Fish	na	*2.6*	**0.5**	—	**0.6**	*0.3*[1]*
Milk	**138.7**	*114.5*[2]	—	—	**20.3**	*8.3*
Hides/skins	na	*0.8*[2]	**0.8**	—	—	—

d no. in thousands. *n* cattle rearing is becoming increasingly important, and large numbers are exported to neighbouring countries.

continued

HONDURAS *continued*

PRODUCTION, EXPORTS AND IMPORTS *continued*

	Production		Exports		Imports	
6. FIBRES, TEXTILES, etc.						
Abaca	—	2.0	—	2.0	—	—
Agaves (letona)	0.1*	0.1	—	—	—	—
Cotton lint	7.7	1.0*	7.5	1.5	—	—
Rubber, natural	na	—	0.1	—	—	—
Silk *f*	—	—	—	—	7.0	—
Cotton, woven fabrics	0.4*	—	—	—	—	—

f metric tons.

	Production		Exports		Imports	
7. FUEL AND POWER						
Electricity *h*, total	133	70[1]				
hydro	na	10[1]				
thermal	na	60[1]				
Petroleum, refined	—	—	—	—	223	120[1]

h million kWh.

	Production		Exports		Imports	
8. IRON AND STEEL						
Steel ingots/castings	—	—	—	—	2	—
9. NON-FERROUS MINERALS AND METALS						
Gold *k*, ore *m*	na	23.30	1.75‡*p*	22.93*q*	—	—
Silver *k*, ore *m*	3 351.70	3 623.00	3 624.58*p*	3 649.57*q*	—	—
Asbestos, manufactured	—	—	—	—	0.06	—
Aluminium	—	—	—	—	0.20	—

continued

	Production		Exports		Imports	
9. NON-FERROUS MINERALS AND METALS—*continued*						
Copper, metal	—	—	—	—	0.04	9.53
Lead, ore	9.01*m*	1.24*m*	12.00	1.24	—	—
Zinc, ore	9.05*m*	0.86*m*	13.75	0.12	—	—

k '000 fine troy oz. *m* metal content. *p* ore and base bullion. *q* bullion.

Mineral resources are thought to be considerable and exploitation is expected to increase as transport facilities improve.

	Production		Exports		Imports	
10. CHEMICALS*n* AND FERTILIZERS						
Chemicals	—		—		na	
Fertilizers: Potash	—	—	—	—	4.7	—

n data not available for years 1953–5.

	Production		Exports		Imports	
11. INDUSTRY						
Aircraft *a*	—	—	—	—	0.4	0.3
Alcoholic beverages			—	—	0.5*a*	0.5*a*
beer *b*	170.0	108.7				
Cement	75.0	—	25.7	—	5.0	28.3
Electrical engineering *a*	—	—	—	—	5.5[2]	1.9[2]
Railway vehicles *a*	—	—	—	—	0.8	0.5
Merchant ships *g*	—	—	—	—	0.2	—
Motor vehicles *a*	—	—	—	—	8.5	3.8[2]

a million $ U.S. *b* '000 hectolitres. *g* '000 G.R.T.

HONG KONG

CHINA SEA

Hong Kong has been under British administration since 1842 apart from a period under Japanese occupation from 1941 to 1945. The recent rapid industrial development has decreased the island's long-established importance as an entrepôt, but Hong Kong remains the primary link for trade between China P.R. and the Sterling Area.

AREA: 1 013 sq. km. (391 sq. miles)

LAND USE: (percentage of total)

	1965	*1954*
Arable and orchard	12.6	12.8
Forest and woodland	9.7	33.5
City areas, waste and other land, incl. scrub and grassland	77.7	53.7

POPULATION: 3 834 000 (1967 estimate)

Largest city: VICTORIA, capital; population: 674 962 (1961)

Distribution of working population (1961)

Total working population: 1 211 999

U.N. group no.		*Percentage*
0	Agriculture, forestry, fishing and hunting	7.2
1	Mining and quarrying	0.7
2/3	Manufacturing	39.2
4	Construction	8.3
5	Electricity, gas, water and sanitary services	1.6
6	Commerce	10.8
7	Transport, storage and communications	7.2
8	Services	21.9
9	Others	3.1

		Year(s)
Life expectancy at birth (years): male	66.7	1968
female	73.3	1968
Infant mortality (per '000)	22.8	1965
Crude birth rate (per '000)	28.8	1965
Crude death rate (per '000)	4.9	1965
Accidental deaths (per 100 000 population) caused by motor vehicles	6.8	1965
due to other causes	17.1	1965
Population per physician	2 310	1965
Population per hospital bed	280	1966
School enrolment: age 5–19 years (percentage)	85	1963–4 av.
age over 19 years (per 100 000 population)	277	1963–5 av.

COMMUNICATIONS

		Year(s)
Motor vehicles in use ('000s): private	52.1	1963–5 av.
commercial	17.7	1963–5 av.
Railway track (km.)	35	1964
Mail per capita: domestic	14	1963–5 av.
foreign received	17	1963–5 av.
foreign sent	20	1963–5 av.
Telephones (per '000 urban population)	8	1967
Radio receivers (per '000 population)	143	1963–5 av.
Television licences (per '000 population)	10.3	1963–5 av.
Daily newspapers (per '000 population)	232.5	1962–4 av.

FINANCE

Currency unit: The Hong Kong dollar

Exchange rates	*1965*	*1960*	*1955*	*1937*
Per $ U.S.	5.714	5.714	5.714	3.268
Per £ sterling	16.0	16.0	16.0	15.03

		Year
National Income (million $ U.S.)	1 045	1963
G.N.P. per capita ($ U.S.)	560	1966

TRADING

Total trade (in million $ U.S.)	*1965*	*1955*	*1938*
Exports (f.o.b.)	1 143	445	185
Imports (c.i.f.)	1 569	651	188

The adverse balance of trade is offset by 'invisible' exports including insurance, investments, and income from tourists, and by remittances from nationals living abroad. In 1965 re-exports accounted for 25% of the exports.

Main trading partners (percentage of total value)

Exports	*1965*	*1955*	*Imports*	*1965*	*1955*
U.S.A.	28	3	China P.R.	26	24
U.K.	14	10	Japan	17	14
Germany F.R.	6	1	U.S.A.	11	9
Japan	6	6	U.K.	11	12
Singapore	5	na	Germany F.R.	3	3
Indonesia	3	8	Thailand	3	5
Australia	3	2	Singapore	3	na

Distribution of trade (percentage of total value)

Exports	*1965*	*1955*	*1938**
Manufactured goods	83	65	na
(textiles and clothing)	(44)	(37)	(8)
(toys)	(6)	(1)	(—)
(artificial flowers)	(4)	(na)	(—)
Food	6	12	17
Imports			
Textiles and clothing	23	25	13
Food	23	26	26
Machinery and transport equipment	13	6	6
Chemicals	7	9	6

continued

PRODUCTION, EXPORTS AND IMPORTS

Years: **1963–5 average** and *1953–5 average* Units: '000 metric tons unless otherwise indicated

	Production		Exports		Imports	
1. CEREALS, etc.						
Barley	—	—	0.1†	—	1.3	2.5
Maize (corn)	—	—	19.7†	13.7†	95.8	17.8
Millets/sorghum	—	—	0.1†	—	1.7	—
Oats	—	—	—	—	0.6	0.5
Potatoes	—	—	5.7†	10.5†	21.2	23.4
Rice	16.0	34.5[2]	35.2†	4.8†	397.8	227.5
Sweet potatoes/yams	22.7	14.0[2]				
Wheat	—	—	7.8†	—	82.5	17.6[2]
2. FRUIT, etc.						
Apples	—	—	6.8†	1.1†	27.6	7.7
Bananas	—	—	1.0†	0.1†	15.6	13.8
Grapes	—	—	0.1†	0.2†	4.5	1.8
Oranges	—	—	2.9†	7.3†	52.5	29.0
Other citrus fruit	—	—	0.2†		6.2	
Pears	—	—	2.0†	—	14.9	na
Raisins	—	—	0.2†	na†	0.9	na
Wine *b*	—	—	1.0†	0.3†	5.9	1.7

b '000 hectolitres.

	Production		Exports		Imports	
3. BEVERAGES, FOREST PRODUCTS, etc.						
Cocoa	—	—	—	—	0.1	—
Coffee	—	—	12.6†	0.2†	13.0	0.2
Sugar, raw	—	—	110.2†	85.2†	192.8	126.1
Tea	—	—	1.3†	4.0†	5.7	6.7
Tobacco: leaf			0.3†	1.2†	8.3	3.5
cigars	2*e*	na	4.9[2]*n*	0.6[2]*n*	3.7[2]*n*	1.9[2]*n*
cigarettes	8 343*e*	na				
Softwood *j*	—	—	0.7†	0.8†	15.8	42.1
Hardwood *j*	—	—	46.3†	18.6†	545.0	222.4
Wood pulp	—	—	—	—	—	6.0
Newsprint	—	—	0.8†	9.2†	33.3	24.7
Other paper	—	—	7.4†	18.6†	123.3	43.4

e no. in millions. *j* '000 cu. metres of roundwood equivalent. *n* incl. other tobacco manufactures.

	Production		Exports		Imports	
4. VEGETABLE OILSEEDS AND OILS						
Castor seed	—	—	1.23†	0.87†	0.45	0.93
Castor oil	—	—	0.01†	0.06†	0.11	0.08
Copra	—	—	1.02†	—	0.86	—
Coconut oil	—	—	0.06†	0.41†	0.64	1.32
Cottonseed	—	—	1.45†	0.13†	1.43	0.03
Cottonseed oil	—	—	0.01†	2.15†	0.22	4.53
Groundnuts	—	—	3.57†	3.33†	11.63	9.87
Groundnut oil	na	na	4.65†	2.70†	11.59	14.47
Linseed	—	—	—	2.30†	0.01	2.10
Linseed oil	—	—	0.01†	0.51†	0.59	0.72
Olive oil	—	—	—	0.02†	0.01	0.02
Palm kernels	—	—	0.44†	—	0.66	—
Palm oil	—	—	—	0.13†	—	0.20
Rapeseed oil	—	—	—	1.58†	1.45	2.26
Sesame seed	—	—	6.17†	14.27†	6.42	15.57
Soya beans	—	—	4.47†	18.80†	11.49	25.60
Soya bean oil	na	na	1.34†	2.31†	18.73	3.22
Tung oil	—	—	1.32†	7.14†	2.18	8.33
5. LIVESTOCK‡, ANIMAL PRODUCTS, etc.						
Chickens *d*	2 347.0	480.0[1]				
Cattle *d*	13.7	10.3	3.4	0.4	141.3	13.7
dairy cows *d*	3.0	3.0[2]				
Goats/sheep *d*	—	—	—	—	6.7	—
Horses *d*	1.0*	na				
Pigs *d*	290.0	46.7	1.4	0.5	1 641.7	504.0
Bacon/ham	9.0	na	0.2	0.1	3.5	0.6
Meat‡: 'A'			—	0.1	10.7	3.5
'B'	1.7	na	0.2	—	15.8	0.5
Butter	—	—	0.1†	0.1†	1.9	0.7
Cheese	—	—	—	—	0.4	0.2
Eggs	0.3*	na	1.0†	4.3†	37.6	21.7
Fish	77.7*p*	51.4*p*	13.8	9.3	62.9	31.8
Milk	5.7	4.0[2]	7.5†	10.5†	90.2	42.8
Hides/skins	—	—	1.7†*a*	2.3[2]†	—	3.1[2]
Wool	—	—	—	—	0.6	—

a million $ U.S. *d* no. in thousands. *p* refers only to fish sold through the Fish Marketing Organization.

	Production		Exports		Imports	
6. FIBRES, TEXTILES, etc.						
Abaca	—	—	0.2†	0.1†	0.4	0.6
Cotton lint	—	—	1.3†	2.5†	129.8	44.3
Hemp fibre	—	—	—	—	0.1	—
Jute	—	—	3.3†	0.1†	3.6	—
Rubber, natural	—	—	4.0†	—	8.4	5.1
Silk *f*	—	—	98.7†	230.7†	177.3	287.7
Cotton: yarn	119.5	38.2	12.3	14.4	12.1	5.6
woven fabrics	66.6*q*	na	46.5*s*	17.4*s*	38.9	12.8
Rayon: fibre/yarn	—	1.5*	—	1.5	—	—
woven fabrics	0.1*q*	—	3.2*s*	1.6*s*	6.4	6.3
Wool, yarn	6.2	—	0.2*s*	1.0†	4.5	1.4

f metric tons. *q* registered mill production only. *s* incl. re-exports.

	Production		Exports		Imports	
7. FUEL AND POWER						
Coal, 'A'‡	—	—	—	5†	177	233
Coke	—	—	—	—	5	3
Electricity *h*: total	2 393	640[1]				
hydro	na	640[1]				
thermal	na	—				
Petroleum, refined	—	—	30†	—	1 903	810[1]

h million kWh.

	Production		Exports		Imports	
8. IRON AND STEEL						
Iron ore	68	58	133	110	8	—
Pig iron	—	—	—	—	9	1
Steel ingots/castings	—	—	—	—	4	1
Iron/steel scrap	na	na	142	50*s*	80	20

s incl. re-exports.

	Production		Exports		Imports	
9. NON-FERROUS MINERALS AND METALS						
Diamonds *a*	—	—	—	1.59[2]†	24.84	7.26
Gold *k*, bullion/coins etc.	—	—	1 134.93†	1 117.00†	1 142.74	1 165.70
Platinum group metals			—	0.28†*a*	17.53*k*	0.34*as*
Silver *k*, bullion	—	—	2 218.26†	966.00†	157.23	193.33
Asbestos: fibre	—	—	—	—	0.12[2]	—
manufactured	—	—	0.04†	0.11†*a*	35.42	0.18*as*
Mica	—	—	—	0.02†	0.01	0.02*s*
Aluminium: bauxite	—	—	—	—	0.46	0.11[2]
aluminium	—	—	3.39†	0.24†	12.35	2.56
Cobalt, metal	—	—	—	—	0.04	0.71
Copper, metal	—	—	6.14†	0.81†	10.48	0.74
Lead: ore	—	na	—	0.44	—	—
metal	—	na	0.04†	0.33**s*	0.62[2]	0.29
Magnesium: magnesite	—	—	—	—	0.19	—
metal/salts	—	—	—	—	0.42	—
Manganese: ore	—	—	—	—	0.19	0.04*s*
metal	—	—	—	0.08†	—	1.55*s*
Mercury *f*	—	—	—	0.70*s*	13.80	3.30*s*
Molybdenum, ore *f*	—	0.30	—	—	—	—
Nickel, metal	—	—	0.05†	—	1.25	0.06*s*
Tin, metal	—	—	0.02†	0.03†	0.08	0.15*s*
Titanium minerals	—	—	—	0.25†	2.20	0.87*s*
Tungsten, ore	0.01	0.07	0.03	0.70*s*	—	—
Zinc, metal	—	—	0.04†	2.07*s*	5.96	4.56

a million $ U.S. *f* metric tons. *k* '000 fine troy oz. *s* incl. re-exports or imports for re-export.

	Production		Exports		Imports	
10. CHEMICALS*n* AND FERTILIZERS						
Chemicals	—		—		na	
Fertilizers: Potash	—	—	—	0.4†	0.6	0.6
Sulphur	—	—	—	—	0.8	0.9

n data not available for years 1953–5.

	Production		Exports		Imports	
11. INDUSTRY						
Aircraft *a*	—	—	—	0.2†	—	1.1
Alcoholic beverages			—	1.6*a*	11.5*a*	4.1*a*
beer *b*	189.0	46.1				
Cement	224.0	94.0	20.0	49.3	989.0	150.7
Electrical engineering *a*	na	na	45.6[2]	4.6[2]	80.0[2]	9.2[2]
Railway vehicles *a*	—	—	—	—	—	0.4
Merchant ships *g*	8.0	—	—	—	40.0	—
Motor vehicles *a*	—	—	2.8[2]	1.1[2]	30.1	7.1[2]

a million $ U.S. *b* '000 hectolitres. *g* '000 G.R.T.

na: data not available. — negligible or nil. [1] one year only. [2] two year average. * estimate. ‡ see appendix. † re-exports.

HUNGARY

EUROPE

The Hungarian republic was proclaimed in 1946 and supreme power vested in Parliament three years later. In 1956 an anti-Stalinist revolution was suppressed by Soviet troops. A Soviet-Hungarian treaty of friendship was renewed for a further twenty years in 1967. Hungary is a member of Comecon.

AREA: 93 030 sq. km. (35 900 sq. miles)

LAND USE: (percentage of total)	*1965*	*1947*
Arable and orchard	60.7	62.1
Permanent meadow and pasture	14.0	17.1
Forest and woodland	15.3	13.5
City areas, waste and other land	10.0	7.3

POPULATION: 10 212 000 (1967 estimate)

Largest city: BUDAPEST, capital; population: 1 960 000 (city proper, 1966)

Distribution of working population (1963)

Total working population: 4 790 050

U.N. group no.		*Percentage*
0	Agriculture, forestry, fishing and hunting	32.7
1	Mining and quarrying	3.5
2/3	Manufacturing	26.6
4	Construction	6.7
5	Electricity, gas, water and sanitary services	1.4
6	Commerce	7.3
7	Transport, storage and communications	6.6
8	Services	11.8
9	Others	3.4

		Year(s)
Life expectancy at birth (years): male	67.0	1964
female	71.8	
Infant mortality (per '000)	38.8	1965
Crude birth rate (per '000)	13.1	1965
Crude death rate (per '000)	10.7	1965
Accidental deaths (per 100 000 population)		
caused by motor vehicles	8.8	1965
due to other causes	31.5	1965
Population per physician	630	1965
Population per hospital bed	130	1966
School enrolment: age 5–19 years (percentage)	81	1963–4 av.
age over 19 years (per 100 000 population)	493	1964–5 av.

COMMUNICATIONS

		Year(s)
Motor vehicles in use ('000s): private	87.8	1963–5 av.
commercial	na	
Railway track (km.)	8 258	1964
Mail per capita	52	1963–5 av.
Telephones (per '000 urban population)	5.86	1967
Radio licences (per '000 population)	244	1963–5 av.
Television licences (per '000 population)	65.1	1963–5 av.
Daily newspapers (per '000 population)	166.3	1962–4 av.

FINANCE

Currency unit: The forint

Exchange rates	*1965*	*1962*	*1958*
Per $ U.S.	11.7	11.4	11.7
Per £ sterling	32.9	31.9	32.9

		Year(s)
National Income (million $ U.S.)	8 000*	1966
G.N.P. per capita ($ U.S.)	800*	1966
Rate of increase of G.N.P. per capita	4.9	1960–4 av.

TRADING

Total trade (in million $ U.S.)	*1965*	*1955*	*1938*
Exports (f.o.b.)	1 510	601	155
Imports (c.i.f.)	1 521	555	123

Main trading partners (percentage of total value)

Exports	*1965*	*1955*	*Imports*	*1965*	*1955*
U.S.S.R.	35	25	U.S.S.R.	36	19
Czechoslovakia	12	13	Czechoslovakia	9	11
Germany D.R.	9	11	Germany D.R.	9	9
Poland	7	5	Poland	6	5
Germany F.R.	5	5	Germany F.R.	5	7
Italy	4	2	Austria	3	5
Switzerland	3	2	U.K.	3	3

Distribution of trade (percentage of total value)

Exports	*1965*	*Imports*	*1965*
Manufactured goods	64	Manufactured goods	50
(machinery and transport equipment)	(32)	(machinery and transport equipment)	(27)
Food	20	Crude materials and fuels	30
(fruit and vegetables)	(6)	(mineral fuels)	(11)
Chemicals	7	Food	10
Crude materials and fuels	6		

PRODUCTION, EXPORTS AND IMPORTS

Years: **1963–5 average** and *1953–5 average* Units: '000 metric tons unless otherwise indicated

	Production		**Exports**		**Imports**	
1. CEREALS, etc.						
Barley	904.0	*690.0[2]*	—	*3.6*	200.1	*63.5**
Maize (corn)	3 580.7	*2 730.0*	60.7	*88.4**	124.3	*26.5*
Millets/sorghum	12.0	*7.0[1]*	1.8	*2.1**	1.0	*0.1**
Oats	85.3	*165.0[2]*	—	*0.2**	1.0	*0.7**
Potatoes	2 003.0	*2 230.0[2]*	37.1	*0.1**	90.2	*6.6**
Rice	34.7	*54.0[2]*	0.8	*11.5**	17.1	*7.0*
Rye	267.3	*512.0[2]*	0.3	*29.3*	10.8	*48.5**
Wheat	2 063.3	*1 895.0[2]*	50.6	*162.6**	291.7	*205.6*
2. FRUIT, etc.						
Apples	438.0	*188.0**	128.7	*15.0*	0.2	—
Apricots	90.3	*30.5[1]*	na	*4.2*	—	—
Bananas	—	—	—	—	0.7	—
Cherries	65.7	*19.3[1]*	—	—	—	—
Dates	—	—	—	—	1.1*	*0.1**
Grapes	696.7	*561.0**	21.3	*8.4**	—	—
Lemons	—	—	—	—	18.5	*3.2**
Oranges	—	—	—	—	14.1	*0.4**
Other citrus fruit	—	—	—	—	0.1	—
Peaches	38.7	*20.3[1]*	na	*1.8*	—	—
Pears	51.7	na	1.4	—	—	—
Plums	225.7	*80.3[1]*	na	*2.5*	—	—
Raisins	—	—	—	—	2.7	*0.2**
Tomatoes	327.7	na				
Wine *b*	4 071.0	*3 700.0**	555.2	*152.0*	52.8	*134.7**

b '000 hectolitres.

	Production		**Exports**		**Imports**	
3. BEVERAGES, FOREST PRODUCTS, etc.						
Cocoa	—	—	—	—	8.9	*1.3**
Coffee	—	—	—	*0.7*	10.2	*1.1*
Sugar: beet	3 480.0	*2 583.3**	—	—	—	—
raw	459.4	*325.0**	178.8	*71.0**	51.0	*53.1**
Tea	—	—	—	*0.2†*	1.2	*0.3*
Tobacco: leaf	24.6	*19.4**	9.6[2]	*2.9**	4.8	*5.9**
cigars *e*	47.0	*53.7*				
cigarettes *e*	16 894.0	*12 481.0*	na	—	na	—
tobacco/snuff	0.9	*2.3*				
Softwood *j*	252.0	*2 200.0**	20.0	*0.3*	1 665.0	*355.9*
Hardwood *j*	3 938.3		16.9	*1.9*	90.8	*2.6*
Wood pulp	61.4	na	7.1	na	49.5	na
Newsprint	—	*21.0**	—	*—[1]*	33.0	*2.1[1]*
Other paper	169.3	*125.7**	6.5	*—[1]*	68.5	*2.7[1]*

e no. in millions. *j* '000 cu. metres of roundwood equivalent.

	Production		**Exports**		**Imports**	
4. VEGETABLE OILSEEDS AND OILS						
Castor seed	0.33	*1.02[2]*	—	—	0.04	—
Castor oil	na	na	0.26	*0.05**	1.59	*0.05**
Copra	—	—	—	—	—	*3.25[2]**
Coconut oil	—	na	—	—	1.50	*0.35**
Cottonseed	na	*4.67**	—	—	0.65	—
Cottonseed oil	na	na	—	*0.95**	1.01	—
Groundnuts	—	—	—	—	6.39	—
Groundnut oil	na	—	0.47	—	0.20	—
Linseed	6.00	*2.00[2]**	0.07	—	0.12	—
Linseed oil	na	na	0.59	*0.10*	4.32	*2.58[2]*
Olive oil	—	—	—	—	0.89	—
Palm kernels	—	—	—	—	3.16	—
Palm kernel oil	na	—	0.20	—	0.49	*0.69**
Palm oil	—	—	—	—	0.97	*4.60**
Rapeseed	7.00	*2.00[2]**	0.91	*0.10**	1.16	—
Rapeseed oil	na	na	0.67	*0.23**	—	—
Sesame seed	—	—	—	—	0.09	—
Soya beans	1.30	na	—	*4.85[2]*	20.78	*33.00[2]*
Soya bean oil	na	na	—	*0.27**	1.61	—
Sunflower seed	108.33	*186.00[2]p*	13.84	*35.56*	0.01	*4.78*
Sunflower seed oil	na	na	20.99	*17.49**	4.28	—
Tung oil	—	—	—	—	0.29	—

p excl. sunflower grown with other crops.

	Production		**Exports**		**Imports**	
5. LIVESTOCK‡, ANIMAL PRODUCTS, etc.						
Chickens *d*	42 266.7	*20 725.0[2]*				
Cattle *d*	1 917.3	*2 146.3*	133.2	*17.3**	0.2	*0.5**
dairy cows *d*	836.0	na				
Goats *d*	80.0*	*160.0[2]**				
Sheep *d*	3 249.3	*1 787.7*	319.4	—	0.1	—
Horses *d*	327.7	*692.0*				
Pigs *d*	6 250.0	*5 083.0*	155.0	*126.4**	4.8	*12.6*
Bacon/ham	451.3	na	5.1	—	0.1*	—
Meat‡: 'A'			35.7	*14.0*	38.2	*3.2*
'B'	192.7	na	35.6	*11.7*	0.6	*0.1**
Butter	18.3*q*	*9.0*q*	5.3	*2.1**	3.2	*0.1**
Cheese	28.3	na	7.8	*1.5**	—[2]	—
Eggs	120.4	na	11.7	*5.4**	1.0[1]	*—**
Fish	22.8	*7.2*	3.3[2]	na	41.3[2]	na
Milk	1 806.0	*1 494.0[2]*	0.1	—	6.3	*1.3**
Hides/skins	21.2	na	1.4[2]*a*	—	16.0[2]*a*	*14.7*
Wool	4.8	*2.0**	0.5	—	4.1	*1.5*

a million $ U.S. *d* no in thousands. *q* excl. butter produced on farms.

continued

na: data not available. — negligible or nil. [1] one year only. [2] two year average. * estimate. ‡ see appendix. † re-exports.

PRODUCTION, EXPORTS AND IMPORTS *continued*

	Production		**Exports**		**Imports**	
6. FIBRES, TEXTILES, etc.						
Agaves (sisal etc.)	—	—	—	—	1.8	—
Cotton lint	—	—	—	*0.9†*	68.0	*37.0*
Flax fibre	5.7	*1.2[2]**	3.4	—	3.2	*1.5**
Hemp fibre	22.3	*18.9[2]**	4.4	*0.3*	0.5	*2.0*
Jute	—	—	0.6	—	8.6	*5.4**
Rubber: natural	—	—	—	*0.9*	15.6	*13.0**
synthetic	—	—	—	—	—	*4.6[2]*
Silk *f*	25.7	*30.0**	—	*3.3**	—	—
Cotton: yarn	67.1	*44.9*t*	na	na	0.2	na
woven fabrics	46.0*	*31.7**	21.6	na	1.1	na
Rayon: fibre/yarn	na	*0.6*	—	na	—	na
woven fabrics	2.6	na	1.2	na	—	na
Wool: yarn	16.8	*11.2*	—[1]	—	—	—
woven fabrics	29.3*r*	*21.0r*	—	—	—	—

f metric tons. *r* million sq. metres. *t* incl. mixtures.

	Production		**Exports**		**Imports**	
7. FUEL AND POWER						
Coal: 'A'‡	4 067	*2 690*	117	*551*	2 833	*836*
'B'	13 543	*19 620*	—	—	—	—
Coke	na	na	—	—	1 456	*1 059*
Electricity *h*: total	10 474	*4 940*				
hydro	77	*50[1]*				
thermal	10 397	*4 890[1]*				
Natural gas *i*	830	*540[1]*	—	—	207	—
Oil, crude	1 787	*1 600[1]*	—	—	2 036	*291**
Petroleum, refined	3 010	*1 300[1]*	500	*110[1]*	497	*110[1]*

h million kWh. *i* million cu. metres.

	Production		**Exports**		**Imports**	
8. IRON AND STEEL						
Iron ore	184*m*	*118m*	—	—	2 498	*1 213*
Pig iron	1 496	*793*	53	—	110	*151*
Steel ingots/castings	2 420	*1 555*	—	—	375	—
Iron/steel products *a*	na	na	99	na	111	na

a million $ U.S. *m* metal content.

	Production		**Exports**		**Imports**	
9. NON-FERROUS MINERALS AND METALS						
Asbestos, fibre	—	—	—	—	13.41	—
Aluminium: bauxite	1 439.40	*1 298.17*	663.98	*702.80*	—	—
alumina	250.64	na	161.70	*71.54*	—	—
aluminium	56.82	*32.49*	19.37	—	3.37	—
Antimony, ore	—	na	—	—	—	—
Chrome: ore	—	—	—	—	32.81[2]	—
metal	—	—	—	—	4.88	—
Copper, metal	—	—	—	—	24.29[2]	*17.30*
Lead: ore *m*	1.20	—	—	—	—	—
metal	0.27	—	—	—	11.78[2]	*6.40*
Magnesium:						
dolomite	491.26	na	—	—	—	—
magnesite	—	—	—	—	62.50	*41.74*
Manganese, ore	178.85	*43.24*	—	—	11.73	—
Molybdenum *f*, ore	—	—	—	—	92.80	—
Tin, metal	—	—	—	—	1.32	*0.76*

continued

	Production		**Exports**		**Imports**	
9. NON-FERROUS MINERALS AND METALS—*continued*						
Titanium minerals	—	—	—	—	0.09[2]	—
Vanadium	—	—	—	—	0.12*u*	—
Zinc: ore	2.90*m*	—	—	—	—	—
metal	1.48	—	—	—	12.05	—

f metric tons. *m* metal content. *u* ferro-vanadium.

	Production		**Exports**		**Imports**	
10. CHEMICALS *n* AND FERTILIZERS						
Organic chemicals:						
Benzene	6.3		na		na	
Butadiene	—		—		na	
Ethylene	—		—		na	
Methanol	na		na		na	
Phenol	0.3		na		na	
Phthalic anhydride	1.5		na		na	
Styrene monomer	—		—		na	
Urea	na		na		na	
Inorganic chemicals:						
Ammonia	151.9		na		na	
Carbon black	—		—		na	
Chlorine	18.0		na		na	
Nitric acid	225.4		na		na	
Sodium carbonate	—		—		na	
Sodium hydroxide	45.1		—		119.7	
Sulphuric acid	322.7		3.9		33.5	
Plastics:						
Polyamides	na		na		na	
Polyethylene	—		—		4.0	
Polyvinyl chloride	18.7[2]		na		7.0[1]	
Fertilizers:						
Phosphates	—	—	—	—	405.9	*88.6*
Potash	—	—	—	—	206.8	*27.9*
Pyrites	—	—	—	—	159.0	*92.4*
Sulphur	3.2*w*	—	—	—	150.3	—

n data not available for years 1953–5. *w* recovered sulphur.

	Production		**Exports**		**Imports**	
11. INDUSTRY						
Alcoholic beverages			—	*19.2*	—	—
beer *b*	4 249	*2 010*				
spirits *b*	189[1]*q*	*249[1]r*				
Cement	2 146	*1 394*	402.0[1]	*65.7t*	na	*—*t*
Electrical engineering *a*	na	na	101.9[2]	*69.3*	43.0[2]	na
Locomotives *c*	176	na	na	—	—	—
Railway vehicles *a*	na	na	na	—	—	—
Machine tools *a*	30[1]	na	19.5	*10.6*	15.2	—
Merchant ships *g*	11	—	—	—	—[1]	—
Motor vehicles *d*			4.5	*3.8*	12.2	—
commercial	7	*6*				

a million $ U.S. *b* '000 hectolitres. *c* no. of units. *d* no. in thousands. *g* '000 G.R.T. *q* production for home consumption in 1967. *r* production for home consumption in 1959. *t* excl. trade with other Comecon countries.

ICELAND

NORTH ATLANTIC

Formerly a Danish territory, Iceland was proclaimed an independent republic in 1944.

AREA: 103 000 sq. km. (39 770 sq. miles)

LAND USE: (percentage of total)	*1965*	*1955*
Arable and orchard	—	—
Permanent meadow and pasture	22.1	19.8
Forest and woodland	—	1.0
City areas, waste and other land	77.9	79.2

POPULATION: 200 000 (1967 U.N. estimate)

Capital city: REYKJAVÍK; population: 90 792 (1966)

Distribution of working population (1950)

Total working population: 63 595

U.N. group no.		*Percentage*
O	Agriculture, forestry, fishing and hunting	37.0
1/2/3	Mining, quarrying and manufacturing	21.3
4	Construction	9.3
5	Electricity, gas, water and sanitary services	1.2
6	Commerce	9.1
7	Transport, storage and communications	7.9
8	Services	14.2

		Year(s)
Life expectancy at birth (years): male	70.8	1961–5 av.
female	76.2	
Infant mortality (per '000)	15.0	1965
Crude birth rate (per '000)	24.5	1965
Crude death rate (per '000)	6.7	1965
Accidental deaths (per 100 000 population)		
caused by motor vehicles	13.5	1965
due to other causes	42.6	1965
Population per physician	760	1964
Population per hospital bed	90	1965
School enrolment: age 5–19 years (percentage)	105‡	1963–4 av.
age over 19 years (per 100 000 population)	549	1963–5 av.

COMMUNICATIONS

		Year(s)
Motor vehicles in use ('000s): private	25.3	1963–5 av.
commercial	6.7	
Mail per capita: domestic	38	1963–5 av.
foreign received	14	
foreign sent	8	
Telephones (per '000 urban population)	29.3	1967
Radio licences (per '000 population)	283	1963–5 av.
Daily newspapers (per '000 population)	438.7	1962–4 av.

continued

na: data not available. — negligible or nil. [1] one year only. [2] two year average. * estimate. ‡ see appendix. † re-exports.

FINANCE

Currency unit: The kronur

Exchange rates	*1965*	*1960*	*1950*	*1938*
Per $ U.S.	43.06	38.1	16.32	4.76
Per £ sterling	120.57	106.8	45.7	21.91

		Year(s)
National Income (million $ U.S.)	359	1965
G.N.P. per capita ($ U.S.)	1 740	1966
Rate of increase of G.N.P. per capita	3.7	1960–4 av.
Foreign trade (percentage of G.D.P.)	59	1963–5 av.

TRADING

Total trade (in million $ U.S.)	*1965*	*1955*	*1938*
Exports (f.o.b.)	129	52	13
Imports (c.i.f.)	137	74	11

Main trading partners (percentage of total value)

Exports	*1965*	*1955*	*Imports*	*1965*	*1955*
U.K.	20	8	U.K.	14	11
U.S.A.	16	12	U.S.A.	13	22
Germany F.R.	8	5	Germany F.R.	12	10
Denmark	7	2	Denmark	9	6
Sweden	7	5	U.S.S.R.	9	14
Italy	6	8	Norway	6	2
U.S.S.R.	5	18	Sweden	5	4

Distribution of trade (percentage of total value)

Exports	*1965*	*1955*
Fish	94	76
(meal, bait and waste)	(21)	(na)
(oil)	(14)	(4)
Imports		
Manufactured goods	67	64
(machinery and transport equipment)	(32)	(26)
(textiles and clothing)	(11)	(12)
Crude materials and fuels	13	21
(petroleum products)	(9)	(15)
Food	10	11
Chemicals	7	4

PRODUCTION, EXPORTS AND IMPORTS

Years: **1963–5 average** and *1953–5 average* Units: '000 metric tons unless otherwise indicated

	Production		Exports		Imports	
1. CEREALS, etc.						
Barley	—	—	—	—	0.4	*0.1*
Maize (corn)	—	—	—	—	0.2	*0.1*
Oats	—	—	—	—	0.1	*0.4*
Potatoes	10.3	*8.0*[2]	—	—	3.3	*3.0*[2]
Rice	—	—	—	—	0.3	*0.4*
Rye	—	—	—	—	—	*0.2*
Wheat	—	—	—	—	0.7	*0.4*
2. FRUIT, etc.						
Apples	—	—	—	—	1.7	*1.0*
Bananas	—	—	—	—	0.9	—
Dates	—	—	—	—	0.1	—
Grapes	—	—	—	—	0.2	*0.4*
Lemons	—	—	—	—	0.2	*0.1*
Oranges	—	—	—	—	1.8	*2.4*
Raisins	—	—	—	—	0.3	*0.4*
Wine *b*	—	—	—	—	4.6	*2.3*

b '000 hectolitres.

	Production		Exports		Imports	
3. BEVERAGES, FOREST PRODUCTS, etc.						
Coffee	—	—	—	—	1.9	*1.1*
Sugar, raw	—	—	—	—	10.7	*7.7*
Tobacco products	—	—	—	—	0.4	*0.3*[2]
Softwood *j*	—	—	—	—	90.1	*71.8*
Hardwood *j*	0.2[2]*	—	—	—	6.3	*4.9*
Newsprint	—	—	—	—	2.2	*1.0*
Other paper	—	—	—	—	8.3	*4.6*

j '000 cu. metres of roundwood equivalent.

	Production		Exports		Imports	
4. VEGETABLE OILSEEDS AND OILS						
Coconut oil	—	—	—	—	0.51	*1.09*
Cottonseed oil	—	—	—	—	—	*0.09*
Groundnuts	—	—	—	—	0.01	—
Groundnut oil	—	—	—	—	0.02	*0.01*
Linseed oil	—	—	—	—	0.05	*0.15*
Palm kernel oil	—	—	—	—	0.01	*0.01*
Palm oil	—	—	—	—	0.02	—
Soya bean oil	—	—	—	—	0.42	*0.36*
5. LIVESTOCK‡, ANIMAL PRODUCTS, etc.						
Chickens *d*	103.7	*83.3*				
Cattle *d*	57.7	*45.0*	—	—	—	—
dairy cows *d*	40.7	*32.0*				
Sheep *d*	758.3	*540.7*	—	—	—	—
Horses *d*	30.3	*37.6*				
Pigs *d*	2.0	*0.7*	—	—	—	—
Meat‡: 'A'	13.7	*8.7*	2.2	—	—	—
'B'	3.3	*3.2*	2.7	—	—	—
Butter	2.0	*1.0*	0.2	—	—	—
Cheese	—	—	0.5	—	—	—
Eggs	0.7*	*0.6*	—	—	—	—
Fish	985.4*n*	*453.5n*	413.8	*164.5*[1]*	0.3	—
Milk	123.7	*83.3*	5.6	—	—	—
Whale/sperm oil	3.2	*2.0*	—	—	—	—
Hides/skins	2.8	*1.7*	2.3	*2.8*[2]	—	*0.2*[2]
Wool	1.3	*1.0*	0.3	*0.2*	—	—

d no in thousands. *n* incl. fish landed in foreign ports.

	Production		Exports		Imports	
6. FIBRES, TEXTILES, etc.						
Abaca	—	—	—	—	0.2	*0.2*
Agaves (sisal etc.)	—	—	0.1†	—	0.4	—
Rubber, natural	—	—	—	—	0.2	—
Cotton: yarn	—	—	—	—	0.1[1]	—
woven fabrics	—	—	—	—	0.5[1]	—
Rayon, woven fabrics	—	—	—	—	0.2[1]*p*	—
Wool: yarn	0.5[2]	—	—[1]	—	0.1	—
woven fabrics	—	—	—	—[2]	0.2	*0.1*

p incl. synthetic piece goods.

	Production		Exports		Imports	
7. FUEL AND POWER						
Coal, 'A'‡	—	—	—	—	10	*51*
Coke	—	—	—	—	1	*1*
Electricity *h*: total	682	*410*[1]				
hydro	641	*380*[1]				
thermal	41	*30*[1]				
Petroleum, refined	—	—	—	—	433	*270*[1]

h million kWh.

	Production		Exports		Imports	
8. IRON AND STEEL						
Iron/steel scrap	na	na	2[2]	—	—	—
9. NON-FERROUS MINERALS AND METALS						
Asbestos: fibre	—	—	—	—	0.01	*0.03*
manufactured	—	—	—	—	0.15	*0.05*
Aluminium	—	—	—	—	0.33	—
Copper, metal	—	—	—	—	0.21	*0.30*
Lead, metal	—	—	—	—	0.34	*0.11*
Tin, metal	—	—	—	—	0.01	—
Titanium minerals	—	—	—	—	0.18	*0.21*
Zinc, metal	—	—	—	—	0.11	*0.03*
10. CHEMICALS*n* AND FERTILIZERS						
Chemicals	—		—		na	
Fertilizers:						
Potash	—	—	—	—	8.2	*2.9*

n data not available for years 1953–5.

	Production		Exports		Imports	
11. INDUSTRY						
Aircraft *a*	—	—	—	—	6.3	*0.5*
Alcoholic beverages			—	—	0.9*a*	*0.3a*
beer *b*	19.0	—				
Cement	112.3	—	4.0	—	—	*65.0*
Electrical engineering *a*	—	—	—	—	7.8	*3.6*[2]
Merchant ships *g*	0.1	na	—	—	8.0	*2.2*
Motor vehicles *a*	—	—	—	—	6.3	*5.2*

a million $ U.S. *b* '000 hectolitres. *g* '000 G.R.T.

INDIA

India, a union of predominantly Hindu states, became a sovereign democratic republic within the British Commonwealth in 1950, three years after its partition from Pakistan. The question of the sovereignty of Jammu and Kashmir still remains in dispute between the two countries, but data for this area are included. The Portuguese territories of Goa, Daman and Diu joined India in 1961; data for these have been added to those of India for the years 1953–5.
Data for 1938 include Pakistan.

AREA: 3 268 081 sq. km. (1 261 807 sq. miles)

LAND USE: (percentage of total)	*1964*	*1955*
Arable and orchard	49.6	45.7
Permanent meadow and pasture	4.3	2.6
Forest and woodland	17.1	14.2
City areas, waste and other land	29.0	37.5

POPULATION: 511 115 000*a* (1967 estimate)
Largest city: CALCUTTA; population: 4 764 979 (1967)
Capital city: NEW DELHI; population: 324 283*b* (city proper, 1967)

Distribution of working population (1961)
Total working population: 188 675 500*ac*

U.N. group no.		*Percentage*
0	Agriculture, forestry, fishing and hunting	72.9
1	Mining and quarrying	0.5
2/3	Manufacturing	9.5
4	Construction	1.1
5	Electricity, gas, water and sanitary services	0.3
6	Commerce	4.1
7	Transport, storage and communications	1.6
8	Services	8.8
9	Others	1.2

		Year(s)
Life expectancy at birth (years): male	41.9	1951–60 av.
female	40.6	
Accidental deaths (per 100 000 population)		
caused by motor vehicles	1.1*	1961
due to other causes	56.5*	1961
Population per physician	5 800	1962
Population per hospital bed	1 670	1965
School enrolment: age 5–19 years (percentage)	41	1963
age over 19 years (per 100 000 population)	288	1963–5 av.

a excl. the population of the area of Jammu and Kashmir under Pakistani occupation. *b* New Delhi is part of the urban agglomeration of Delhi, population 2 874 454 (1967). *c* excl. the unemployed and persons seeking employment for the first time.

COMMUNICATIONS		*Year(s)*
Motor vehicles in use ('000s): private	397.3	1963–5 av.
commercial	352.8	
Railway track (km.)	93 946	1964
Mail per capita: domestic	12	1963–5 av.
foreign received	0.2	
foreign sent	0.2	
Telephones (per '000 urban population)	0.2	1967
Radio licences (per '000 population)	9	1963–5 av.
Daily newspapers (per '000 population)	6.15	1962–4 av.

FINANCE

Currency unit: The rupee

Exchange rates	*1965*	*1960*	*1950*	*1938*
Per $ U.S.*a*	4.78	4.77	4.76	2.89
Per £ sterling	13.33	13.33	13.33	13.33

		Year(s)
National Income (million $ U.S.)	42 020	1965
G.N.P. per capita ($ U.S.)	90	1966
Rate of increase of G.N.P. per capita	0.7	1960–3 av.

a selling rates.

TRADING

Total trade (in million $ U.S.)	*1965*	*1957b*	*1955b*	*1938ab*
Exports (f.o.b.)	1 692	1 350	1 280	614
Imports (c.i.f.)	2 958	2 154	1 484	576

Main trading partners (percentage of total value)

Exports	*1965*	*1955b*	*1938ab*	*Imports*	*1965*	*1955b*	*1938ab*
U.S.A.	18	15	9	U.S.A.	38	13	6
U.K.	18	28	34	U.K.	11	25	31
U.S.S.R.	12	1	—	Germany F.R.	10	9	8*d*
Japan	7	5	9	U.S.S.R.	6	1	—
U.A.R.	3	2	1	Japan	6	5	10
Canada	3	2	1	Iran	2	2	2
Nepal	2	na	na	Canada	2	1	1

Distribution of trade (percentage of total value)

Exports	*1965*	*1957b*	*1938*ab*
Manufactured goods	47	44	na
(textiles)	(34)	(32)	(20)
Food	30	28	17
(tea)	(14)	(19)	(14)
Crude materials and fuels	18	21	na
(metalliferous ores)	(7)	(8)	(na)
Imports			
Manufactured goods	52	60	na
(machinery and transport equipment)	(35)	(30)	(13)
Food	25	9	na
(cereals)	(23)	(5)	(9)
Crude materials	14	21	na
(textile fibres)	(5)	(7)	(6)
(petroleum and petroleum products)	(5)	(10)	(9)

a incl. Pakistan. *b* year beginning 1 April. *d* incl. Germany D.R.

PRODUCTION, EXPORTS AND IMPORTS

Years: **1963–5 average** and *1953–5 average* Units: '000 metric tons unless otherwise indicated

	Production		Exports		Imports	
1. CEREALS, etc.						
Barley	2 327.7	*2 932.0*	—	—	—	*0.1*
Cassava	2 546.0	*698.7*				
Maize (corn)	4 614.3	*2 852.0*	—	*0.9*	118.2	*0.7*
Millets/sorghum	16 299.0	*15 909.0*	—	—	16.7	*148.3*[1]
Oats	—	—	—	—	0.8	*3.0*[1]*
Potatoes	3 186.0	*1 876.7*	6.7		1.8	*1.5*
Rice	53 268.3	*39 442.0*	3.1	*36.7n*	644.8	*371.9*
Sweet potatoes/yams	948.3	*1 282.7*				
Wheat	10 993.3	*8 145.3*	0.5	—	5 379.3	*764.0*

n excl. trade overland with Pakistan.

	Production		Exports		Imports	
2. FRUIT, etc.						
Bananas	2 657.0	*1 873.5*[2]	9.6	—	—	—
Coconuts	4 843.7**e*	na	0.2*	*1.7**	—	*2.1**
Dates	—	—	—	—	45.8	*80.1*
Figs	2.0*	na	—	—	—	—
Grapes	—	—	—	—	1.2	—
Lemons	450.0*	*172.3*	—	—	—	—
Oranges	763.0*	*392.0*[2]	2.2	—	—	—
Other citrus fruit	20.0*	*5.3*	—	—	0.1	—
Pears	—	—	0.1†	—	3.3	—
Raisins	—	—	—	—	9.1	*21.6*
Wine *b*	—	—	—	—	0.7	*5.7*

b '000 hectolitres. *e* no. in millions.

	Production		Exports		Imports	
3. BEVERAGES, FOREST PRODUCTS, etc.						
Cocoa	—	—	—	—	0.8	—
Coffee	62.8	*29.6*	26.7	*5.2*	—	—
Sugar: cane	114 057.3	*53 694.7*				
raw	2 942.8*r*	*1 437.0t*	350.9	*5.8*	—	*519.4*
Tea	361.2	*290.5*	211.1	*199.7*	—	*0.3**
Tobacco: leaf	364.6	*264.0*	67.3	*32.6*	0.6	*1.3*[2]
cigarettes	46 764.0*e*	*20 360.0e*	3.1*aq*	*1.7*[2]*q*	—	*1.7*[2]*q*
Softwood *j*	1 368.0[1]	*1 177.0*[1]	6.0	*4.1*	1.7	*6.3*
Hardwood *j*	14 189.0[1]	*14 657.0*[1]	17.6	*5.7*	71.6	*47.9*
Wood pulp	25.0[2]*	*77.3*	—	*5.3*	90.0	*12.0*
Newsprint	29.5[2]	*0.8*	—	—	94.3	*77.3*
Other paper	530.5[2]	*161.7*	1.6	*13.0*	24.8	*49.2*

a million $ U.S. *e* no. in millions. *j* '000 cu. metres of roundwood equivalent. *q* incl. other tobacco products. *r* in addition, gur and khandsari 6 800*. *t* in addition, gur 2 524*.

	Production		Exports		Imports	
4. VEGETABLE OILSEEDS AND OILS						
Castor seed	103.7	*117.9*	—	—	—	—
Castor oil	na	na	25.38	*31.72*	—	—
Copra	264.3*n*	*180.0*[2]*	—	—	69.73	*55.30*
Coconut oil	na	na	0.07	*0.05*	0.95	*23.20*
Cottonseed	2 135.0	*1 444.7*	—	—	0.02	*0.33*
Cottonseed oil	na	na	—	—	1.64	—
Groundnuts	3 529.1	*2 727.4*	20.28	*16.70*	—	—

n excl. Goa.

continued

INDIA *continued*

PRODUCTION, EXPORTS AND IMPORTS *continued*

4. VEGETABLE OILSEEDS AND OILS—*continued*

	Production		Exports		Imports	
Groundnut oil	na	na	45.10	72.26	0.53	—
Linseed	438.3	383.3p	0.01	—	0.62	0.50[2]*
Linseed oil	na	na	0.60	27.81	—	0.02
Olive oil	—	—	—	—	0.01	0.05
Palm oil	—	—	—	—	26.67	—
Rapeseed	1 221.0	906.3	0.19	0.17	4.07	—[1]
Rapeseed oil	na	na	0.31	0.51	0.20	—
Sesame seed	446.2	541.3	0.63	1.00	—	—
Soya beans	—	—	—	—	4.14	—
Soya bean oil	na	—	—	—	13.68	—
Sunflower seed	na	—	0.38	—	—	—
Tung oil	—	—	—	—	0.24	na

p flax grown for seed only.

5. LIVESTOCK‡, ANIMAL PRODUCTS, etc.

	Production		Exports		Imports	
Chickens *d*	121 232*n	97 372np				
Cattle *d*	185 709*	159 000p	—	0.3	—	2.8
dairy cows *d*	56 043*q	20 400p				
Goats *d*	64 628*	56 628p	} 20.1	—	1.4	—
Sheep *d*	42 693*	38 700p				
Horses *d*	1 293*	1 503p				
Pigs *d*	5 350*	4 700p	—	—	—	—
Bacon/ham }	533*	— {	—	—	—	0.1
Meat‡: 'A' }			0.1	—	—	—
'B'	161	na	0.5	—	—	—
Butter	472	549p	—	—	3.7	0.8
Cheese	—	—	—	—	0.2	0.5
Eggs	88*	na	—	—	0.3	6.2
Fish	1 233	828	17.6	31.0*	18.0	4.1*
Milk	10 235*	7 756p	—	—	422.9	269.4
Hides/skins	na	na	19.5a	10.3[2]	5.7[2]a	—
Wool	na	18*	7.3	9.3	4.8	1.5

a million $ U.S. *d* no. in thousands. *n* incl. ducks, geese and turkeys. *p* data (estimated) for the year 1955/6. *q* cows over three years old.

6. FIBRES, TEXTILES, etc.

	Production		Exports		Imports	
Abaca	—	—	—	—	2.0	0.7*
Agaves (sisal etc.)	3.0[1]*	na	0.1	—	3.8	1.3[2]*
Cotton lint	1 067.3	722.8	52.7	51.5	126.4	115.0
Flax fibre	—	—	—	—	0.8	0.1
Hemp fibre	67.1	120.4	11.2	16.9[2]	0.1	na
Jute	1 282.7	620.0n	27.1	—	65.7	236.8
Rubber: natural	43.6	22.0	—	—	22.2	3.3
synthetic	11.5	—	—	—	5.7	na
Silk *f*	1 337.5[2]	985.3*	529.0	137.0	94.7	158.3
Cotton: yarn	932.2	710.1	12.9	6.4r	na	1.0r
woven fabrics	920.9*	525.9p	68.1	85.6r	0.1[1]	0.6r
Rayon: fibre/yarn	76.2	8.5	0.1[2]	—	6.1	24.1
woven fabrics	86.8	19.3q	6.7	0.3	—r	0.5r
Non-cellulosic fibre/yarn	1.6	—	0.1	—	8.7	—
Wool: yarn	20.6	9.1[2]	0.2	—	—	1.1
woven fabrics	13.3t	7.1t	—	na	—	1.5

f metric tons. *n* in addition, mesta 174.0. *p* mill production only. *q* continuous filament piece goods only. *r* sea-borne trade only. *t* million metres.

7. FUEL AND POWER

	Production		Exports		Imports	
Coal: 'A'‡	65 187	38 840	1 160	2 013	2	—
'B'	527	—	—	—	—	—
Coke	na	na	—	28	—	1
Electricity *h*: total	33 623	9 780[1]				
hydro	14 927	3 300[1]				
thermal	18 696	6 480[1]				
Natural gas *i*	60	—	—	—	—	—
Oil, crude	2 307	350[1]	—	—	6 640	3 300[1]
Petroleum, refined	7 820	2 450[1]	360	150[1]	1 997	2 210[1]
Rare earths *fu*	2 346	na	739	—	—	—
Uranium *f*	na	—	—	—	—	—

f metric tons. *h* million kWh. *i* million cu. metres. *u* monazite.

8. IRON AND STEEL

	Production		Exports		Imports	
Iron ore	12 883m	3 629m	10 904	2 382	—	1
Pig iron	6 863	1 908	55	23	64	3
Steel ingots/castings	6 128	1 658	1	—	49	21
Iron/steel scrap	na	na	427	225	2	1[1]
Iron/steel products *a*	na	na	18	—	205	85

a million $ U.S. *m* metal content.

9. NON-FERROUS MINERALS AND METALS

	Production		Exports		Imports	
Diamonds	2.33l	—	7.28a	—	0.60a	0.14a
Gold, ore *k*	139.30m	224.00m	na	0.34n	na	2.21n
Platinum group metals *k*	—	—	—	—	2.56	—

9. NON-FERROUS MINERALS AND METALS—*continued*

	Production		Exports		Imports	
Silver, ore *k*	149.30m	110.00m	—	na	15.87n	67.16n
Asbestos: fibre	3.55	0.85	0.01	0.23	36.85	8.09
manufactured	na	na	0.09	0.87q	2.87	1.28r
Mica	32.10	16.93	34.93	17.20	—	0.09
Aluminium: bauxite	620.81	76.80	97.48	4.95	—	—
alumina	—	—	—	—	2.15	—
aluminium	59.69	5.34	11.58	—	20.78	4.20
Antimony: ore	—	—	—	—	1.59	—
metal	—	—	—	—	0.11	—
Beryl	na	na	0.46p	0.43p	—	—
Cadmium	—	—	—	—	0.11	—
Chrome: ore	53.23m	67.61m	22.68	49.53[1]	—	—
metal	—	—	—	—	0.89	0.31
Cobalt, metal	—	—	—	—	0.03	—
Copper: ore	10.20m	6.74m	—	0.33	—	18.10
metal	9.47	6.56	0.86	—	65.23	—
Lead: ore	4.27m	2.32m	—	—	0.01	0.14
metal	3.36	2.04	—	—	35.51	9.70
Magnesium: dolomite	858.29	na	—	—	—	—
magnesite	227.07	na	41.47	31.34	0.12	—
metal/salts	—‡	—‡	0.04	0.85	0.82[2]	0.65
Manganese: ore	1 438.13	1 790.24	1 292.24t	1 587.23t	6.15	—
metal	na	na	55.50	—	0.57	2.46
Mercury *f*	—	—	—	—	195.00	41.90
Nickel, metal	—	—	—	—	2.44	—
Tin, metal	—	—	0.05†	0.46†	4.92	3.51
Titanium minerals	24.37	239.41	39.40	200.70	3.30	—
Tungsten, ore	0.01	0.01	—	—	0.12	—
Zinc: ore	5.70m	2.54m	6.70	4.12	—	—
metal	—	—	2.20	—	79.59	34.28

a million $ U.S. *f* metric tons. *k* '000 fine troy oz. *l* '000 carats. *m* metal content. *n* bullion. *p* exports to U.S.A. only. *q* in addition, U.S.$144 800. *r* in addition, U.S. $1 095 900 *t* ferroginous ore.

10. CHEMICALS*n* AND FERTILIZERS

	Production		Exports		Imports	
Organic chemicals:						
Benzene	na		0.6		—	
Butadiene	na		na		na	
Ethylene	na		—		na	
Methanol	na		—		7.8	
Phenol	na		—		na	
Phthalic anhydride	—		—		3.6	
Styrene monomer	na		na		—	
Urea	19.7		—		201.9	
Inorganic chemicals:						
Ammonia	na		—		—	
Carbon black	12.0		—		12.6	
Chlorine	51.0		na		na	
Nitric acid	11.8		—		—[2]	
Sodium carbonate	290.0		—		32.3[2]	
Sodium hydroxide	187.0		—		71.3	
Sulphuric acid	645.0		—		—	
Plastics:						
Polyamides	na		—		na	
Polyethylene	10.2		—		1.9	
Polyvinyl chloride	8.1		—		1.8	
Fertilizers:						
Phosphates	8.1p	4.1p	—	—	442.9	53.3
Potash	—	—	—	0.1	102.6	24.0
Pyrites	—	0.1*x	—	—	—	—
Sulphur	—	—	—	—	261.8	68.1

n data not available for years 1953–5. *p* apatite. *x* sulphur content.

11. INDUSTRY

	Production		Exports		Imports	
Aircraft *a*					16.7[2]	11.9
Alcoholic beverages			—	—	—	2.9a
beer *b*	147.0	—				
Cement	9 876.7	4 276.0	43.7	83.7	3.0	23.7
Electrical engineering *a*	na	—	5.9	—	187.3[2]	27.5[2]
Locomotives *c*	117.0	—	—	—	na	na
Railway vehicles *a*					50.6[2]	15.7
Machine tools *a*	38.0[1]	na	—	—	—	na
Merchant ships *g*	21.0	—	—	—	151.0	—
Motor vehicles			2.4[2]a		73.4[2]a	24.9a
commercial *d*	33.1	9.3q				
private *d*	30.9	7.9q				

a million $ U.S. *b* '000 hectolitres. *c* no. of units. *d* no. in thousands. *g* '000 G.R.T. *q* assembly of imported parts.

continued

SIKKIM

CENTRAL ASIA

Sikkim was under British protection until the transfer of power in India in 1947. By a treaty of 1950 Sikkim became a protectorate of the government of India, which is responsible for communications, defence and external affairs. India is also assisting with a plan for economic development.

AREA: 7 298 sq. km. (2 818 sq. miles)

POPULATION: 183 000 (1967 estimate)
Capital city: GANGTOK; population: 6 848 (city proper, 1961)

EMPLOYMENT AND TRADE
Rice, corn, millet and fruit are produced, with potatoes as the main cash crop. The forests, which cover about one-third of the country, are as yet unexploited.

na: data not available. — negligible or nil. [1] one year only. [2] two year average. * estimate. ‡ see appendix. † re-exports.

INDONESIA

SOUTH EAST ASIA

The republic of Indonesia was formed in 1949 by the union of the states of the Netherlands East Indies with the exception of the western part of New Guinea. This latter, renamed West Irian, joined Indonesia in 1963.

Data for West Irian have been added to those for Indonesia for the years 1953–5.

AREA: 1 900 000 sq. km. (733 600 sq. miles)

LAND USE: (percentage of total)

	1954
Arable, orchard, permanent meadow and pasture	9.3
Forest and woodland	63.8
City areas, waste and other land	26.9

POPULATION: 110 920 000 (1967 estimate)
Largest city: DJAKARTA, capital; population: 2 906 533 (city proper, 1961)

Distribution of working population (1961)
Total working population: 34 578 234 (based on a 1% sample of census returns)

U.N. group no.		*Percentage*
0	Agriculture, forestry, fishing and hunting	68.0
1	Mining and quarrying	0.3
2/3	Manufacturing	5.4
4	Construction	1.7
5	Electricity, gas, water and sanitary services	0.1
6	Commerce	6.3
7	Transport, storage and communications	2.0
8	Services	9.0
9	Others	7.2

		Year
Life expectancy at birth (years): male	47.5	} 1960
female	47.5	
Infant mortality (per '000)	87.2	1964
Crude birth rate (per '000)	30.6*	1964
Crude death rate (per '000)	9.2*	1964
Population per physician	34 820a	1964
Population per hospital bed	1 450	1965
School enrolment: age 5–19 years (percentage)	44b	1961
age over 19 years (per 100 000 population)	95c	1963

a West Irian: 8 500 (1962). *b* excl. West Irian. *c* universities only.

COMMUNICATIONS

		Year(s)
Motor vehicles in use ('000s): private	146.8	} 1963–5 av.
commercial	104.3	
Railway track (km.)	6 640	1961
Mail per capita: domestic	2	
foreign received	0.1	} 1963–5 av.
foreign sent	0.1	
Telephones (per '000 urban population)	0.2	1967
Television sets (per '000 population)	0.3	1963–5 av.
Daily newspapers (per '000 population)	11a	1959

a West Irian: 2 (1961).

FINANCE

Currency unit: The rupiah

Exchange rates a*	*1964d*	*1960b*	*1955b*	*1938cd*
Per $ U.S.	402	45	3.81	1.84
Per £ sterling	1 126	126.2	10.67	8.46

Since 1949 there has been severe devaluation of the rupiah; in 1959 the value was reduced to a tenth of the nominal value, and in 1965 a new rupiah equivalent to 1 000 old rupiahs was introduced.

		Year
National Income (million $ U.S.)	8 909	1965
G.N.P. per capita ($ U.S.)	100	1966

a all rates taken at the end of the year. *b* principal import rate. *c* Dutch guilders, replaced by the rupiah in 1941. *d* basic selling rate.

TRADING (pre-1963 data exclude West Irian)

Total trade (in million $ U.S.)	*1965*	*1955*	*1938*
Exports (f.o.b.)	708	946	379
Imports (c.i.f.)	718	631	248

Main trading partners (percentage of total value)

Exports	*1965*	*1955*	*1938*	*Imports*	*1965*	*1955*	*1938*
U.S.A.	22	18	15	Japan	na	14	15
Japan	16	8	3	U.S.A.		15	9
Netherlands	13	16	21	Germany F.R.		10	10a
Australia	8	2	4	U.K.		6	8
Germany F.R.	8	4	4a	China P.R.		2	2
China P.R.	6	1	2	Burma		2	2
				Thailand		1	1

Distribution of trade (percentage of total value)

Exports	*1963*	*1955*	*1937**
Crude materials and fuels	82	82	na
(rubber)	(35)	(45)	(31)
(petroleum and petroleum products)	(39)	(22)	(17)
Food	12	10	na

Imports	*1962*	*1955*	*1937**
Manufactured goods	67	67	na
(textiles)	(20)	(27)	(na)
(machinery and transport equipment)	(29)	(16)	(12)
Food	12	9	na
Chemicals	12	9	na
Crude materials and fuel	8	8	na

a includes Germany D.R. and Austria.

PRODUCTION, EXPORTS AND IMPORTS

Years: **1963–5 average** and *1953–5 average* Units: '000 metric tons unless otherwise indicated

1. CEREALS, etc.

	Production		Exports		Imports	
Cassava	11 357.0	9 300.7				
Maize (corn)	2 803.3	2 139.3	—	9.1	—	—
Potatoes	420.0[1]*	na	na	0.3	na	0.6
Rice	12 591.0	11 278.0	—	—	758.7	247.9
Sweet potatoes/yams	3 223.0	2 051.4				

2. FRUIT, etc.

	Production		Exports		Imports	
Apples	—	—	—	0.1†	na	0.8
Bananas	—	—	—	—	—	0.2
Coconuts *e*	5 393.7	na	na	na	—	—
Dates	—	—	—	—	2.8*	6.9
Grapes	—	—	—	—	na	0.2
Oranges	—	—	—	0.1[2]	na	0.3[2]
Pineapples	—	na	na	4.4	—	—
Wine *b*	na	—	—	—	na	1.7

b '000 hectolitres. *e* no. in thousands.

3. BEVERAGES, FOREST PRODUCTS, etc.

	Production		Exports		Imports	
Cocoa	1.0	1.2	0.1[1]*	0.4	—	—
Coffee	112.0	62.3[1]	79.0*	31.2	—	—
Sugar: cane	8 921.0*	6 460.3n				
raw	680.7p	731.3p	138.5*	167.3	—	0.7
Tea	84.0*	42.5	26.4[2]	25.0	na	—
Tobacco: leaf	135.7*	9.2[2]n	12.0[1]	15.2	na	7.3
cigars	27.0e	46.3e	} —	0.3[2]	—	0.1[2]q
cigarettes	25 399.0e	16 351.0e				
Softwood *j*	76.0[2]	—	7.0[2]	—	na	3.0
Hardwood *j*	84 795.0[1]	3 893.9[2]	92.2[2]	197.3	na	3.5
Wood pulp	1.4*	6.0*	—	—	0.7[1]	1.1
Newsprint	—	—	—	—	7.9[1]	9.5
Other paper	13.7*	—	—	—	41.0[1]	69.7

e no. in millions. *j* '000 cu. metres of roundwood equivalent. *n* from estates only. *p* in addition, non-centrifugal sugar 146* (1963–5 av.) and 250* (1953–5 av.). *q* incl. other tobacco manufactures.

4. VEGETABLE OILSEEDS AND OILS

	Production		Exports		Imports	
Castor seed	2.00*	5.79	na	1.53	—	—
Copra	437.50*	760.90[2]*	156.80*	290.60	—	—
Coconut oil	na	na	—	0.65	—	—
Cottonseed	6.00*	2.30*	—	0.03	—	—
Groundnuts	299.83	262.70	3.05[1]*	9.73	—	—
Groundnut oil	na	na	—	1.76	—	—
Linseed oil	—	—	—	—	na	0.45
Palm kernels	34.23*	42.53n	30.56*	40.93	—	—
Palm oil	157.27	165.00n	122.93*	129.51	—	—
Sesame seed	2.00[1]*	na	2.00[2]*	1.53	—	—
Soya beans	367.00	350.00	—	3.55[2]	—	—

n from estates only.

5. LIVESTOCK‡, ANIMAL PRODUCTS, etc.

	Production		Exports		Imports	
Chickens *d*	101 295.0*	na				
Cattle *d*	6 357.0*	4 825.5	na	9.5	—	0.1
Goats *d*	5 112.0*	6 077.0[2]	—	—	—	—
Sheep *d*	2 380.0*	2 634.0[2]	—	—	—	—
Horses *d*	720.0*	612.0				
Pigs *d*	2 752.0*	1 379.0[1]	na	21.4	—	—
Bacon/ham }	388.7*	228.7 {	—	—	na	—
Meat‡: 'A' }			—	—	na	0.1
'B'	20.0	na	—	—	na	—
Butter	—	—	—	—	na	0.1
Cheese	—	—	—	—	na	0.2
Eggs	124.3*	na	—	—[2]	—	0.1[2]
Fish	945.8[2]	641.9	0.6[1]u	na	1.7[1]u	na
Milk	35.0*	15.0[1]	—	—	na	78.3
Hides/skins	na	na	—	1.1[2]	—	—

d no. in thousands. *u* 1962 figure.

continued

na: data not available. — negligible or nil. [1] one year only. [2] two year average. * estimate. ‡ see appendix. † re-exports.

INDONESIA *continued*

PRODUCTION, EXPORTS AND IMPORTS *continued*

6. FIBRES, TEXTILES, etc.	Production		Exports		Imports	
Abaca	0.3*	2.0	—	1.5	—	—
Agaves *q*	3.5*	29.1	na	26.5	—	—
Cotton lint	3.0	1.0[1]	—	—	na	8.3
Jute	4.7*	na	—	1.0[1]	—	—
Rubber, natural	649.3	733.9	665.8*	707.0	—	—
Silk *f*	—	—	—	—	—	38.0
Cotton: yarn	—	4.9*	—	—	13.6	13.9
woven fabrics	—	—	—	—	39.2[2]	58.6
Rayon: fibre/yarn	—	0.6	—	—	—	0.6
woven fabrics	—	na	—	—	—	5.8

f metric tons. *q* sisal and cantala.

7. FUEL AND POWER	Production		Exports		Imports	
Coal, 'A'‡	437	810	na	90	na	41
Coke	—	—	—	—	na	2
Electricity *h*: total	1 489	1 500[1]				
hydro	na	570[1]				
thermal	na	930[1]				
Natural gas *i*	2 900	1 619[1]	—	—	—	—
Oil, crude	23 244	11 830[1]	13 930	3 030[1] *t*	420	2 700[1]*
Petroleum, refined	8 640	10 210[1]	3 693	5 910[1]	143	170[1] *t*
Rare earths *f*	106 *r*	—	—	—	—	—

f metric tons. *h* million kWh. *i* million cu. metres. *r* monazite. *t* excl. data for West Irian.

8. IRON AND STEEL	Production		Exports		Imports	
Iron/steel scrap	na	na	2	75	—	—

9. NON-FERROUS MINERALS AND METALS	Production		Exports		Imports	
Diamonds *l*	2.00[1]	—	—	—	—	—
Gold, ore *km*	6.00	na	—	—	—	—
Silver, ore *km*	277.30	—	—	—	—	—
Asbestos: fibre	0.02	—	—	—	—	0.12
manufactured	na	—	—	—	—	11.85
Aluminium: bauxite	609.63	195.49	656.93	224.01	—	—
aluminium	—	—	—	—	na	6.70
Antimony, metal	—	—	—	—	—	0.09
Copper, metal	—	—	—	—	na	3.80
Lead, metal	—	—	—	—	—	1.09
Manganese, ore	4.58	24.13	na	27.70	—	—
Mercury *f*	—	—	—	—	—	16.50
Nickel, ore	2.03 *m*	—	—	—	—	—
Tin: ore	14.90 *m*	34.90 *m*	21.40[1]	46.54	—	—
metal	1.90	1.21	—	0.48	—	—
Zinc, metal	—	—	—	—	na	2.37

continued

9. NON-FERROUS MINERALS AND METALS—*continued*

f metric tons. *k* '000 fine troy oz. *l* '000 carats. *m* metal content.

10. CHEMICALS *n* AND FERTILIZERS	Production		Exports		Imports	
Chemicals	—		—		na	
Fertilizers:						
Phosphates	30.5*	4.4*	—	—	—	—
Sulphur	1.4	—	—	—	na	7.6

n data not available for years 1953–5.

11. INDUSTRY	Production		Exports		Imports	
Aircraft *a*	—	—	—	na	—	1.5
Alcoholic beverages				0.1 *a*		1.5 *a*
beer *b*	200.0	26.7[2]				
Cement	471.7*	147.3	—	—	293.3*	294.7
Electrical engineering *a*	—	—	—	na	na	20.1[2]
Railway vehicles *a*	—	—	—	—	15.1	8.2
Merchant ships *g*	0.4	—	—	—	25.0	—
Motor vehicles			—	—	28.6 *a*	19.3 *a*
commercial *dp*	na	2.7				
private *dp*	na	1.8				

a million $ U.S. *b* '000 hectolitres. *d* no. in thousands. *g* '000 G.R.T. *p* assembly of imported parts.

IRAN

MIDDLE EAST

Iran, formerly Persia, is a constitutional monarchy. A member of Cento, Iran has also signed agreements for economic development with Turkey, Pakistan and, more recently, the U.S.S.R.

AREA: 1 621 860* sq. km. (626 200* sq. miles)

LAND USE: (percentage of total)	*1960*	*1950*
Arable and orchard	7.0	10.3
Permanent meadow and pasture	4.1	6.1
Forest and woodland (including unstocked land)	7.3	11.7
City areas, waste and other land	81.6	71.9

POPULATION: 25 781 090 (1966 provisional census)

Largest city: TEHRĀN (Teheran), capital; population: 2 695 283 (city proper, 1966)

Distribution of working population (1956)

Total working population: 6 066 643

U.N. group no.		*Percentage*
0	Agriculture, forestry, fishing and hunting	54.8
1	Mining and quarrying	0.4
2/3	Manufacturing	13.5
4	Construction	5.5
5	Electricity, gas, water and sanitary services	0.2
6	Commerce	5.9
7	Transport, storage and communications	3.4
8	Services	10.8
9	Others	5.5

		Year(s)
Crude birth rate (per '000)	42.3*	1965
Crude death rate (per '000)	6.1*	1965
Population per physician	3 880	1965
Population per hospital bed	890	1966
School enrolment: age 5–19 years (percentage)	40	1964
age over 19 years (per 100 000 population)	107	1964–5 av.

COMMUNICATIONS		*Year(s)*
Motor vehicles in use ('000s): private	121.6	1963–5 av.
commercial	46.1	1963–5 av.
Railway track (km.)	3 480	1964
Telephones (per '000 urban population)	0.8	1967
Radio licences (per '000 population)	69	1963–5 av.
Television sets (per '000 population)	4.4	1963–5 av.
Daily newspapers (per '000 population)	15	1961

FINANCE

Currency unit: The rial

Exchange rates	*1965*	*1960*	*1950*	*1938*
Per $ U.S.	75.75	75.75	32.5	17.5
Per £ sterling	212.1	212.1	91.04	80.96

		Year(s)
National Income (million $ U.S.)	5 221	1965
G.N.P. per capita ($ U.S.)	250	1966
Rate of increase of G.N.P. per capita	0.2	1960–3 av.
Foreign trade (percentage of G.D.P.)	31	1963–5 av.

TRADING

Total trade (in million $ U.S.)	*1965*	*1955*	*1937*
Exports (f.o.b.)	1 303	396	159
Imports (c.i.f.)	860	312	85

Main trading partners (percentage of total value)

Exports	*1965*	*1955*	*Imports*	*1965*	*1955*
Japan	16	6	Germany F.R.	20	17
U.K.	13	11	U.S.A.	18	19
Netherlands	8	5	U.K.	13	10
France	6	7	Japan	8	8
U.S.A.	5	7	France	6	3
India	5	12	Italy	4	3
Southern Yemen	4	2	Netherlands	3	2

Distribution of trade (percentage of total value)

Exports	*1965*	*1955 a*	*1938**
Petroleum and petroleum products	87	74*	74
Carpets	4	4	4
Cotton	3	5	2
Imports			
Manufactured goods	68	69	na
(machinery and transport equipment)	(36)	(17)	na
Food	13	21	na
Chemicals	10	5	na
Crude materials	5	5	na

a the 1955 figures are percentages of total imports, excluding concessions, which amounted to 65% of the general imports‡ for that year.

continued

na: data not available. — negligible or nil. [1] one year only. [2] two year average. * estimate. ‡ see appendix. † re-exports.

PRODUCTION, EXPORTS AND IMPORTS

Years: **1963–5 average** and *1953–5 average* Units: '000 metric tons unless otherwise indicated

1. CEREALS, etc.	Production		Exports		Imports	
Barley	966.7*	840.0*	0.9[2]	4.2	1.7	—
Maize (corn)	14.0*	na	—	0.5	1.8[2]	—
Millets/sorghum	28.0*	na	—	0.2	—	—
Potatoes	107.0*	na	6.7[2]	6.5	—	—
Rice	860.0*	449.3*	5.9*	46.2	4.9*	—
Wheat	2 866.7*	2 217.7*	—	0.3[2]	99.7[2]	3.4

2. FRUIT, etc.	Production		Exports		Imports	
Apples	—	—	—	0.4	—	—
Apricots	31.7*	57.2*	—	—	—	—
Bananas	—	—	—	—	0.3[2]	—
Dates	299.3*	122.0*	24.1*	29.3	—	0.1
Figs	5.0*	na	—	—	—	—
Grapes	253.3*	na	na	1.0	—	—
Lemons	50.0*	na	—	0.1 (lemons and oranges)	0.4[2]	0.1 (lemons and oranges)
Oranges	40.0*	39.3	—		na	
Olives	15.0*	10.0[1]*				
Raisins	48.0*	52.9	31.3	32.6	—	—

3. BEVERAGES, FOREST PRODUCTS, etc.	Production		Exports		Imports	
Coffee	—	—	—	—	0.2[2]	0.1
Sugar: beet	1 283.3*	507.3*				
cane	200.0*	—				
raw (beet)	168.5	76.7*	—	—	393.9* (beet and cane)	228.4 (beet and cane)
(cane)	25.9	—	—	—		
Tea	12.4	na	—	2.0	5.2[2]	6.0
Tobacco: leaf	18.7*	14.0*	0.1	0.6	—	—
cigarettes	9 214.0 *e*	6 422.0 *e*	—	—	—	—
tobacco/snuff	4.4	5.1	—	—	—	—
Softwood *j*	—	—	0.1[2]	0.1	84.6	12.0[1]
Hardwood *j*	1 603.0	8 227.0[2]	5.4[2]	10.1	5.0[2]	—
Newsprint	—[2]	—	—	—	8.4[2]	—[1]
Other paper	5.5[2]*	—	—	—	52.5[2]	—[1]

e no. in millions. *j* '000 cu. metres of roundwood equivalent.

4. VEGETABLE OILSEEDS AND OILS	Production		Exports		Imports	
Castor seed	10.0*	8.4	—	2.40	—	—
Castor oil	na	na	—	0.10	—	—
Cottonseed	275.7	113.3*	—	6.77	—	—
Cottonseed oil	na	na	—	—	15.13	—[2]
Groundnuts	—	—	—	—	0.42[2]	na
Groundnut oil	na	na	—	—	—	0.05
Linseed	4.0[1]*	3.3*	—	5.07	—	—
Linseed oil	na	na	—	—	1.21	0.01
Olive oil	1.0*	na	na	0.02	0.49[2]	0.08
Palm oil	—	—	—	—	—	2.95 *p*
Sesame seed	6.1*	10.0*	—	2.80	—	—
Soya bean oil	—	—	—	—	31.31	—

p incl. coconut oil.

5. LIVESTOCK‡, ANIMAL PRODUCTS, etc.	Production		Exports		Imports	
Chickens *d*	26 700*	na				
Cattle *d*	4 805*	5 000[2]*	—	—	—	—
Goats *d*	12 940*	na	—	—	—	—
Sheep *d*	31 843*	17 375[2]	—	—	—	—
Horses *d*	470*	370[1]*				
Pigs *d*	7*	na	—	—	—	—
Meat‡: 'A'	239*	na	—	—	0.1[2]	—
'B'	19*	na	—	—	0.1[2]	—
Butter	—	na	—	—	2.3[2]	—
Cheese	28*	na	—	—	0.1[1]	0.1
Eggs	29*	na	—	0.6	—	—
Fish	8[2]*	25	3.8[2]	4.3[1]*	0.2[1] *q*	0.2[1]*
Milk	1 360*	na	—	—	39.8[2]	1.0*
Hides/skins	na	na	12.2	6.3	3.7	1.2
Wool	na	10*	2.0[2]	6.4	1.4[2]	0.1

d no. in thousands. *q* 1962 figure.

6. FIBRES, TEXTILES, etc.	Production		Exports		Imports	
Cotton lint	125.3*	56.7*	61.4[2]	33.3	—	—
Jute	2.7*	4.0[1]*	—	—	1.2[2]	0.1
Rubber, natural	—	—	—	—	5.8[2]	—
Silk *f*	na	109.0*	—	83.7	—	41.3
Cotton: yarn	na	na	—	—	na	0.4
woven fabrics	na	na	—	—	0.8[2]	10.4
Rayon, woven fabrics	—	—	—	—	na	3.5
Wool, woven fabrics	4.0[2] *r*	na	—	—	—	—

f metric tons. *r* million metres.

7. FUEL AND POWER	Production		Exports		Imports	
Coal, 'A'‡	250	230	—	—	—	—
Electricity *h*: total	2 200[2]	570[1]				
hydro	na	—[1]				
thermal	na	570[1]				
Natural gas *i*	1 190	—	—	—	—	—
Oil, crude	84 100	16 360[1]	63 450	8 330[1]	—	—
Petroleum, refined	18 676	7 270[1]	11 127	370[1]	—	6[2]

h million kWh. *i* million cu. metres.

8. IRON AND STEEL	Production		Exports		Imports	
Iron ore	16 934 *m*	—	2	—	—	—
Pig iron	—	—	—	—	14	—
Iron/steel scrap	na	na	—	—	6	1 *t*

m metal content. *t* incl. steel ingots.

9. NON-FERROUS MINERALS AND METALS	Production		Exports		Imports	
Asbestos: fibre	—	0.03	—	—	2.29	—
manufactured	—	—	—	—	1.38	—
Mica	—	—	—	—	0.40	—
Aluminium	—	—	—	—	4.60	0.63[2]
Antimony, ore	na	na	0.04	0.07	—	—
Chrome, ore	123.08* *m*	25.88 *m*	125.19	—	—	—
Copper, metal	—	—	—	—	4.70	1.73[2]
Lead: ore	13.97 *m*	12.70 *m*	41.45	—	—	—
metal	0.42	0.87	—	—	1.17	—
Magnesium, metal/salts	—	—	—	—	0.35	—
Manganese, ore	27.00	5.65	24.67	—	—	—
Mercury *f*	—	—	—	—	1.20	0.20
Nickel, metal	—	—	—	—	0.21	—
Tin, metal	—	—	—	—	0.25	0.16[2]
Titanium minerals	—	—	—	—	0.30	—
Zinc: ore	13.61* *m*	5.53* *m*	65.71	—	—	—
metal	na	na	—	—	2.09	0.65

f metric tons. *m* metal content.

10. CHEMICALS *n* AND FERTILIZERS	Production		Exports		Imports	
Organic chemicals:						
Benzene	—		—		na	
Butadiene	—		—		na	
Ethylene	—		—		na	
Methanol	—		—		0.2[2]	
Phenol	—		—		na	
Phthalic anhydride	—		—		na	
Styrene monomer	—		—		na	
Urea	na		na		na	
Inorganic chemicals:						
Ammonia	na		—		0.1[2]	
Carbon black	—		—		na	
Chlorine	na		—		na	
Nitric acid	na		—		0.1	
Sodium carbonate	—		—		6.4	
Sodium hydroxide	na		—		na	
Sulphuric acid	na		—[2]		0.5[2]	
Plastics:						
Polyamides	—		—		na	
Polyethylene	—		—		na	
Polyvinyl chloride	—		—		na	
Fertilizers:						
Potash	—	—	—	—	0.7	—
Sulphur	20.3* *p*	18.3[1] *p*	—	0.2[2]	2.4	—

n data not available for years 1953–5. *p* recovered sulphur.

11. INDUSTRY	Production		Exports		Imports	
Aircraft *a*	—	—	—	—	2.1	—
Beer *b*	74.0	—	—	—	—	—
Cement	801.3*	87.3	76.7*	—	10.7*	51.7
Electrical engineering *a*	—	—	—	—	41.0	6.0
Railway vehicles *a*	—	—	—	—	0.8	—
Merchant ships *g*	—	—	—	—	0.3	—
Motor vehicles *a*	—	—	—	—	50.0	5.5

a million $ U.S. *b* '000 hectolitres. *g* '000 G.R.T.

na: data not available. — negligible or nil. [1] one year only. [2] two year average. * estimate. ‡ see appendix. † re-exports.

IRAQ

MIDDLE EAST

Iraq was a monarchy until 1958 when the king was assassinated and the country declared a republic. Further coups d'état introduced a succession of republican governments during the next ten years. There has also been some internal unrest since a revolt by the Kurdish people in 1961. A customs union was formed with the U.A.R. in 1967.

AREA: 438 446 sq. km. (169 280 sq. miles)

LAND USE: (percentage of total)	*1964*	*1954*
Arable and orchard	16.7	12.3
Permanent meadow and pasture (mainly rough grazing)	9.5	2.0
Forest and woodland (incl. some rough grazing)	4.3	4.0
City areas, waste and other land	69.5	81.7

POPULATION: 8 261 527 (1965 census)

Largest city: BAGHDĀD, capital; population: 1 745 328 (city proper, 1965)

Distribution of working population (1957)
Total working population: 1 795 277 *a*

U.N. group no.		*Percentage*
0	Agriculture, forestry, fishing and hunting	47.9
1	Mining and quarrying	0.2
2/3	Manufacturing	9.5
4	Construction	4.5
5	Electricity, gas, water and sanitary services	0.6
6	Commerce	5.1
7	Transport, storage and communications	5.0
8	Services	14.2
9	Others	13.0

		Year(s)
Infant mortality (per '000)	23.7*	1965
Crude birth rate (per '000)	15.2*	1965
Crude death rate (per '000)	4.1*	1965
Population per physician	4 760	1964
Population per hospital bed	530	1966
School enrolment: age 5–19 years (percentage)	56	1963–4 av.
age over 19 years (per 100 000 population)	316	1963–5 av.

a incl. 41 000* nationals working abroad.

COMMUNICATIONS

		Year(s)
Motor vehicles in use ('000s): private	51.9	1963–5 av.
commercial	27.6	
Railway track (km.)	2 019	1961
Telephones (per '000 urban population)	0.9*	1967
Radio receivers (per '000 population)	158	1963–5 av.
Television sets (per '000 population)	16.3	1963–5 av.
Daily newspapers (per '000 population)	12	1963

FINANCE

Currency unit: The Iraqi dinar, at par with the pound sterling until 1968

Exchange rates	*1965*	*1960*	*1955*	*1938*
Per $ U.S.	0.357	0.357	0.357	0.215

		Year(s)
National Income (million $ U.S.)	1 529	1964
G.N.P. per capita ($ U.S.)	270	1966
Rate of increase of G.N.P. per capita	2.9	1960–3 av.
Foreign trade (percentage of G.D.P.)	54	1963–5 av.

TRADING

Total trade (in million $ U.S.)	*1965*	*1955*	*1938*
Exports (f.o.b.)	882	519	18
Imports (c.i.f.)	451	272	46

Main trading partners (percentage of total value)

Exports	*1965*	*1955 a*	*Imports*	*1965*	*1955 a*
U.K.	16	14	U.S.A.	12	15
France	16	—	U.K.	11	28
Italy	13	5	Germany F.R.	9	8
Netherlands	8	9	U.S.S.R.	7	na
Germany F.R.	7	13	Japan	6	8
Japan	7	1	Czechoslovakia	6	1
Spain	3	—	Poland	4	na

Distribution of trade (percentage of total value)

Exports	*1965*	*1955*	*1938**
Petroleum (crude)	94	91	74
Imports			
Machinery and transport equipment	20	28	17
Food	15	17	na
Textiles and clothing	11	13	20
Vegetable oils	4	—	na

a excl. trade in petroleum.

PRODUCTION, EXPORTS AND IMPORTS

Years: **1963–5 average** and *1953–5 average* Units: '000 metric tons unless otherwise indicated

	Production		Exports		Imports	
1. CEREALS, etc.						
Barley	**740.0**	*1 035.7*	**65.2**	*422.7*	**0.1**	*0.2*
Maize (corn)	**3.0***	*6.3*	—	*0.1*	—	—
Millets/sorghum	**11.3***	*18.0*	—	*15.5*	—	—
Potatoes	**10.0***[1]	na	—	—	**20.8**	*7.0*
Rice	**175.0**	*142.0*	—	*2.8*	**36.6**	*3.1*
Wheat	**766.7**	*793.3*	**1.1**	*34.0*	**120.0**	*11.1*
2. FRUIT, etc.						
Apples	—	—	—	—	**22.0**	—
Bananas	—	—	—	—	**6.3**	*2.9*
Coconuts	—	—	—	—	**1.2**	*0.1*
Dates	**320.0***	*357.0**	**298.9**	*240.0*	—	—
Grapes	**45.0***[1]	—	—	—	—	—
Lemons	—	—	—	—	**0.1** *n*	—
Raisins	—	—	—	—	**1.3**	*0.7*
Tomatoes	**174.0**	na				
Wine *b*	—	—	—	—	**0.3**	—

b '000 hectolitres. *n* mainly dried limes.

	Production		Exports		Imports	
3. BEVERAGES, FOREST PRODUCTS, etc.						
Coffee	—	—	—	—	**0.8**	*0.7*
Sugar: beet	**83.3***	—				
raw	**2.9**	—	—	—	**266.1***	*120.5*
Tea	—	—	—	—	**19.3**	*12.7*
Tobacco: leaf	**12.8***	*8.4*[2]*	—	—	—	—
cigarettes *e*	**4 761.0**	na	—	—	—	—
Softwood *j*	—	—	—	—	**113.6**	*119.7*
Hardwood *j*	**36.0***	*27.0*[2]	—	—	**48.5**[2]	*55.7*
Newsprint	—	—	—	—	**0.9**[2]	*0.7*
Other paper	—	—	—	—	**22.7**[2]	*6.8*

e no. in millions. *j* '000 cu. metres of roundwood equivalent.

	Production		Exports		Imports	
4. VEGETABLE OILSEEDS AND OILS						
Castor oil	—	—	—	—	**0.01**	*0.02*
Copra	—	—	—	—	**1.21**	*2.30*
Coconut oil	—	—	—	—	**0.21**	*0.94** *q*
Cottonseed	**20.00**	*10.67**	**0.03**	*0.63*	—	—
Groundnuts	—	—	—	—	**18.72**	*0.33*
Groundnut oil	na	na	—	—	**0.27**	na *r*
Linseed	**8.33**	*1.50*[2]* *p*	**5.47**	*2.03*	—	—
Linseed oil	na	na	—	—	**0.01**	*0.02*[1]
Olive oil	—	—	—	—	**0.04**	*0.10*
Palm oil	—	—	—	—	**35.64**	na *r*
Sesame seed	**7.80**	*14.70*	**0.68**	*5.53*	—	—

p flax grown for seed only. *q* incl. groundnut oil and palm oil. *r* see coconut oil.

	Production		Exports		Imports	
5. LIVESTOCK‡, ANIMAL PRODUCTS, etc.						
Chickens *d*	**4 398.0***	na				
Cattle *d*	**1 518.3**	*721.0**	**0.2**	*4.1*	—	—
Goats *d*	**2 348.0**	*1 689.0*[1]*	**0.2** (Goats and Sheep)	—	—	—
Sheep *d*	**9 980.0**	na				
Horses *d*	**168.7**	na				
Meat‡: 'A'	**86.7**	na	—	—	—	—
'B'	**5.9**	na	—	—	—	—
Butter	na	na	—	—	**0.3**	—
Cheese	**18.7***	na	—[2]	—	**0.8**	*0.2*
Eggs	**8.3***	na	—	—	—	—
Fish	**14.3** *t*	*5.4 t*	—	—	**0.3**	—
Milk	**190.0***	na	—	—	**27.6***	*4.0**
Hides/skins	**6.6**[1]	na	**4.6**	*5.3*[2]	—	—
Wool	**7.0***	*8.0**	**2.6**	*3.6*	**0.1**	—

d no. in thousands. *t* incomplete figure.

continued

PRODUCTION, EXPORTS AND IMPORTS *continued*

	Production		Exports		Imports	
6. FIBRES, TEXTILES, etc.						
Cotton lint	**10.0***	*5.3*	**2.7**	*1.9*	**1.4**	*0.1*
Jute	—	—	—	—	**3.5**	—
Rubber, natural	—	—	—	—	**0.5**	—
Silk *f*	—	—	—	—	**1.3**	*18.0*
Cotton: yarn	—	—	—	—	**0.9**	*0.3*
woven fabrics	**2.9***	na	—	—	**6.8**	*5.0*[2]
Rayon, woven fabrics	—	—	—	—	**6.9** *u*	*5.2*[2]
Wool: yarn	**0.3**[2]	na	—	—	—	—
woven fabrics	**1.0**[2] *v*	na	—	—	—	—

f metric tons. *u* incl. synthetic piece goods. *v* million metres.

	Production		Exports		Imports	
7. FUEL AND POWER						
Coal, 'A'‡	—	—	—	—	—	*1*
Coke	—	—	—	—	**1**	*1*
Electricity *h t*	**1 145**	*490*[1]				
Natural gas *i*	**750**	—	—	—	—	—
Oil, crude	**60 923**	*33 740*[1]	**58 310**	*32 150*[1]	—	—
Petroleum, refined	**2 450**	*1 100*[1]	**47**	—	—	*20*[1]

h million kWh. *i* million cu. metres. *t* thermal.

	Production		Exports		Imports	
9. NON-FERROUS MINERALS AND METALS						
Platinum group metals *k*	—	—	—	—	—	*0.92*[2]
Asbestos: fibre	—	—	—	—	**1.81**[2]	*0.04*
manufactured	—	—	—	—	**0.21**[2]	—
Aluminium	—	—	—	—	**6.45**	*2.07*
Copper, metal	—	—	—	—	**1.14**	*0.31*
Lead, metal	—	—	—	—	**0.03**[2]	—
Tin, metal	—	—	—	—	**0.13**[2]	*0.06*
Zinc, metal	—	—	—	—	**0.02**	*0.02*

k '000 fine troy oz.

	Production		Exports		Imports	
10. CHEMICALS *n* AND FERTILIZERS						
Chemicals	—		—		na	
Fertilizers:					**2.3**	—
Potash	—	—	—	—	**0.3**	—
Sulphur	—	—	—	—	**1.9**	—

n data not available for years 1953–5.

	Production		Exports		Imports	
11. INDUSTRY						
Aircraft *a*	—	—	—	—	—	*1.5*
Beer *b*	**41.0**	*17.9*	—	—	—	—
Cement	**1 077.7**	*238.0*	**383.0**	*3.7*	**10.7**	*32.7*
Electrical engineering *a*	—	—	—	—	**17.9**	*11.7*[2]
Railway vehicles *a*	—	—	—	—	—	*1.5*
Merchant ships *g*	—	na	—	—	**0.6**	*1.4*
Motor vehicles *a*	—	—	—	—	**20.3**	*22.5*

a million $ U.S. *b* '000 hectolitres. *g* '000 G.R.T.

IRISH REPUBLIC

EUROPE

After years of campaigning for home rule, Southern Ireland (or Eire) accepted dominion status in 1921 and left the British Commonwealth in 1949 to become an independent republic. The Irish Republic is a member of the European Free Trade Association and has applied (1971) to join the European Economic Community.

AREA: 68 893 sq. km. (26 600 sq. miles)

LAND USE: (percentage of total)	*1965*	*1955*
Arable and orchard	18.0	17.5
Permanent meadow and pasture	49.0	49.4
Forest and woodland	2.8	2.0
City areas, waste and other land (incl. rough grazing)	30.2	31.1

POPULATION: 2 884 002 (1966 census)
Largest city: DUBLIN, capital; population: 650 153 (1966)

Distribution of working population (1961)
Total working population: 1 108 108

U.N. group no.		*Percentage*
0	Agriculture, forestry, fishing and hunting	35.2
1	Mining and quarrying	0.9
2/3	Manufacturing	17.0
4	Construction	6.6
5	Electricity, gas, water and sanitary services	1.0
6	Commerce	14.8
7	Transport, storage and communications	5.2
8	Services	18.8
9	Others	0.5

		Year(s)
Life expectancy at birth (years): male	68.1	1960–2 av.
female	71.9	
Infant mortality (per '000)	25.2	1965
Crude birth rate (per '000)	22.1	1965
Crude death rate (per '000)	11.5	1965
Accidental deaths (per 100 000 population)		
caused by motor vehicles	10.7	1965
due to other causes	25.2	1965
Population per physician	950	1961
Population per hospital bed	70	1966
School enrolment: age 5–19 years (percentage)	91	1963–4 av.
age over 19 years (per 100 000 population)	724	1963–5 av.

COMMUNICATIONS

		Year(s)
Motor vehicles in use ('000s): private	258.5	1963–5 av.
commercial	49.5	
Railway track (km.)	2 346	1964
Mail per capita: domestic	93	1963–5 av.
foreign received	30	
foreign sent	23	
Telephones (per '000 urban population)	7.8	1967
Radio receivers (per '000 population)	212	1963–5 av.
Television sets (per '000 population)	92.4	1963–5 av.
Daily newspapers (per '000 population)	242	1963–4 av.

FINANCE

Currency unit: The Irish pound, at par with the £ sterling

Exchange rates	*1965*	*1960*	*1955*	*1938*
Per $ U.S. (selling rate)	0.357	0.357	0.357	0.215

		Year(s)
National Income (million $ U.S.)	2 249	1965
G.N.P. per capita ($ U.S.)	850	1966
Rate of increase of G.N.P. per capita	4	1960–4 av.
Foreign trade (percentage of G.D.P.)	62	1963–5 av.

TRADING

Total trade (in million $ U.S.)	*1965*	*1955*	*1938*
Exports (f.o.b.)	620	310	119
Imports (c.i.f.)	1 042	582	203

Main trading partners (percentage of total value)

Exports	*1965*	*1955*	*1938*	*Imports*	*1965*	*1955*	*1938*
U.K.	72	89	93	U.K.	51	53	50
Germany F.R.	5	1	4 *a*	U.S.A.	8	9	11
U.S.A.	4	3	—	Germany F.R.	6	5	4 *a*
Netherlands	3	1	—	France	3	1	1
France	3	1	—	Netherlands	3	3	1
Canada	1	—	—	Canada	3	3	4
Italy	1	—	—	Iran	2	na	1

Distribution of trade (percentage of total value)

Exports	*1965*	*1955*	*1938**
Food	55	62	72
(livestock and meat)	(41)	(51)	(57)
(dairy products and eggs)	(6)	(3)	(14)
Manufactured goods	24	12	na
(textiles and clothing)	(7)	(4)	(1)
Crude materials and fuels	7	8	2
Beer	3	5	9
Imports			
Manufactured goods	51	43	33
(machinery and transport equipment)	(25)	(19)	(12)
Food	16	18	25
Crude materials and fuels	15	23	na
Chemicals	9	6	na

a incl. Germany D.R. and Austria.

continued

PRODUCTION, EXPORTS AND IMPORTS

Years: **1963–5 average** and *1953–5 average* Units: '000 metric tons unless otherwise indicated

1. CEREALS, etc.

	Production		Exports		Imports	
Barley	585.3	219.3	24.2	—	28.4	23.3
Maize (corn)	—	—	—	—	103.9	199.1
Millets/sorghum	—	—	—	—	81.3	0.2
Oats	335.0	538.3	0.6	—	19.1	1.6
Potatoes	1 714.3	2 397.3	57.8	35.2	0.5	0.2
Rice	—	—	—	—	2.4	2.5
Rye	1.0	3.0	—	—	—	—
Wheat	268.7	440.0	19.1	—	244.5	161.6

2. FRUIT, etc.

	Production		Exports		Imports	
Apples	26.7	na	—	0.1	15.2	4.8
Bananas	—	—	—	—	14.2	6.8
Dates	—	—	—	—	0.2[1]	—
Grapes	—	—	—	—	1.4	0.9
Lemons	—	—	—	—	0.8[1]	0.6
Oranges	—	—	—	—	19.1	14.9
Other citrus fruit	—	—	—	—	1.3[1]	1.0
Pears	—	—	—	—	3.5	2.7
Plums	—	—	—	—	—	0.6
Raisins	—	—	—	—	7.3	9.6
Tomatoes	11.3	2.0[2]				
Wine *b*	—	—	—	0.3†	39.9	22.7

b '000 hectolitres.

3. BEVERAGES, FOREST PRODUCTS, etc.

	Production		Exports		Imports	
Cocoa	—	—	—	—	8.2	5.6
Coffee	—	—	—	—	0.4	0.4
Sugar: beet	868.0	704.7				
raw	134.7	109.7	19.1	—	45.9	69.8
Tea	—	—	—	—	11.3	10.3
Tobacco: leaf	—	—	0.1*	0.3	6.0	6.9
cigars	—	—				
cigarettes	5 377.0*e*	6 169.3*e*	—	0.5[2]	—	0.2[2]
tobacco/snuff	0.8	1.1				
Softwood *j*	278.7	112.0	11.0	1.3	473.0	352.4
Hardwood *j*	48.7	123.0	3.0	2.1	60.0	34.8
Wood pulp	31.6[2]	10.0*	0.9	0.1	36.1	28.3
Newsprint	8.0*	—[2]	—	—	36.3	26.7
Other paper	80.0*	43.8	14.3	32.7*	48.5	36.5*

e no. in millions. *j* '000 cu. metres of roundwood equivalent.

4. VEGETABLE OILSEEDS AND OILS

	Production		Exports		Imports	
Castor oil	—	—	—	—	0.15	0.10
Copra	—	—	—	—	3.68	6.37
Coconut oil	na	na	—	—	1.03	1.17
Cottonseed	—	—	—	—	1.59	na
Cottonseed oil	na	—	—	—	1.82	3.26
Groundnuts	—	—	—	—	2.16	na
Groundnut oil	na	—	0.32	—	1.30	0.83
Linseed	na	na	—	—	1.56	1.00
Linseed oil	na	na	0.27	—	1.18	1.77
Olive oil	—	—	—	—	0.07	0.06[1]
Palm kernels	—	—	—	—	2.68	1.17
Palm kernel oil	na	na	0.14	—	0.45	1.74
Palm oil	—	—	—	—	3.62	2.24
Soya beans	—	—	—	—	0.39	—
Soya bean oil	na	—	—	—	0.95	—
Sunflower seed oil	—	—	—	—	0.93	—

5. LIVESTOCK‡, ANIMAL PRODUCTS, etc.

	Production		Exports		Imports	
Chickens *d*	10 366.0	13 500.0				
Cattle *d*	5 060.3	4 461.3	684.5	463.6	129.7	0.6
dairy cows *d*	1 423.3	1 282.0				
Goats *d*	41.0*	46.0[1]	292.1	na	259.8	na
Sheep *d*	4 885.0	3 104.0				
Horses *d*	180.7	313.0				
Pigs *d*	1 159.0	879.7	4.2	0.4	19.7	—
Bacon/ham	465.0	341.7	27.3	7.2	—	—
Meat‡: 'A'			85.1	46.9	—	—
'B'	61.8	42.3	12.4	15.5	—	—
Butter	62.7	57.0	19.5	1.7	—	1.8
Cheese	15.0	2.0*n*	8.9	0.3	0.2	0.5
Eggs	44.2	54.3	0.3	8.8	—	—
Fish	31.8*p*	21.4*p*	10.5	3.7[1]*	15.7	4.4[1]*
Milk	3 011.3	2 433.7	157.1	20.8	0.8	16.8
Hides/skins	19.8	13.0	10.3	5.4[2]	—	4.3[2]
Wool	8.0	5.0	7.1	4.9	4.4	3.0

d no. in thousands. *n* factory produce only. *p* incl. fish landed by Irish vessels in foreign ports.

6. FIBRES, TEXTILES, etc.

	Production		Exports		Imports	
Agaves (sisal etc.)	—	—	—	—	6.3	1.1[2]
Cotton lint	—	—	—	—	5.7	2.7
Flax fibre	—	1.2	—	1.2	—	—
Hemp fibre	—	—	—	—	0.7	3.2[2]
Jute	—	—	—	—	9.4	6.9
Rubber, natural	—	—	—	—	3.9	4.1
Silk *f*	—	—	—	—	4.0	—
Cotton: yarn	5.7	na	1.0[2]	—	2.2	1.9
woven fabrics	3.6*	1.6	—	—	4.0	2.0

continued

6. FIBRES, TEXTILES, etc.—*continued*

	Production		Exports		Imports	
Rayon: fibre/yarn	—	—	—	—	—	0.8*t*
woven fabrics	0.8	0.4	—	—	1.0	1.6
Wool: yarn	7.3	5.1	0.8	0.3	2.0	0.9
woven fabrics	7.7*r*	6.7*r*	na	na	0.9[2]*q*	0.5*q*

f metric tons. *q* excl. blankets. *r* million sq. metres. *t* incl. spun yarn.

7. FUEL AND POWER

	Production		Exports		Imports	
Coal: 'A'‡	213	200	10	9	1 369*p*	1 745
'B'	2 110	—	—	—	—	—
Electricity *h*: total	3 221	1 600[1]				
hydro	793	490[1]				
thermal	2 428	1 110[1]				
Oil, crude	—	—[1]	—	—[1]	1 800	—[1]
Petroleum, refined	1 713	—[1]	220	—[1]	590	1 020[1]

h million kWh. *p* incl. imports for bunkering.

8. IRON AND STEEL

	Production		Exports		Imports	
Iron ore	—	—	3	20	1	1
Pig iron	—	—	—	—	20	6
Steel ingots/ castings	20	27	—	—	25	3
Iron/steel scrap	na	na	36	18	—	—

9. NON-FERROUS MINERALS AND METALS

	Production		Exports		Imports	
Gold *k*, bullion/coins etc.	—	—	1.41‡	1.20‡	12.93‡	—
Silver *k*, bullion	—	—	136.73	—	75.14[1]	0.70
Asbestos: fibre	—	—	—	—	3.84	1.95
manufactured	—	—	—	—	2.03	3.99
Aluminium	—	—	—	—	14.18	5.65
Copper: ore	—	—	0.04	—	—	—
metal	—	—	3.11*p*	1.60*p*	7.49	3.68
Lead: ore	1.26*m*	1.65*m*	—	2.37	—	—
metal	na	na	0.50	2.23	0.57	1.41[1]
Magnesium, metal	—	—	—	—	na	0.54
Nickel, metal	—	—	—	—	0.13	0.02
Tin, metal	—	—	—	—	0.06	—
Titanium minerals	—	—	—	—	1.97	—
Zinc: ore	0.48*m*	1.91*m*	—	3.59	—	—
metal	—	—	—	—	3.45	1.66

k '000 fine troy oz. *m* metal content. *p* scrap.

10. CHEMICALS *n* AND FERTILIZERS

	Production		Exports		Imports	
Organic chemicals:						
Benzene	na		—		na	
Butadiene	—		—		na	
Ethylene	—		—		na	
Methanol	—		—		na	
Phenol	—		—		0.1	
Phthalic anhydride	—		—		na	
Styrene monomer	—		—		na	
Urea	—		—		0.4[1]	
Inorganic chemicals:						
Ammonia	—		—[2]		5.1	
Carbon black	—		—		2.3	
Chlorine	—		—		0.3	
Nitric acid	—		—		0.4	
Sodium carbonate	—		—		13.9	
Sodium hydroxide	—		—		3.0	
Sulphuric acid	189.0[1]		—		2.7	
Plastics:						
Polyamides	—		—		na	
Polyethylene	—		—		3.7[2]	
Polyvinyl chloride	—		—		13.7[2]	
Fertilizers:						
Phosphates	—	na	—	—	237.9	117.7
Potash	—	—	—	—	162.9	73.8
Pyrites	—	—	—	—	2.2	42.5
Sulphur	—	—	—	—	51.9	0.2

n data not available for years 1953–5.

11. INDUSTRY

	Production		Exports		Imports	
Aircraft *a*	—	—	1.1	0.3	12.2	1.3
Alcoholic beverages			21.1*a*	14.8*a*	9.2*a*	3.9*a*
beer *b*	3 440.0	3 124.7				
spirits *b*	47.2[1]*p*	54.6[1]*q*				
Cement	1 077.7	594.7	259.3	29.3	32.3	45.0
Electrical engineering *a*	59.3[2]	na	11.2	1.2[2]	48.6	17.4[2]
Railway vehicles *a*	—	—	—	—	1.5	3.7
Merchant ships *g*	20.0[1]	—	—	—	0.6	—
Motor vehicles			0.3*a*	4.7*a*	56.4*a*	31.1*a*
commercial *dr*	4.8	4.8				
private *dr*	41.6	21.1				

a million $U.S. *b* '000 hectolitres. *d* no. in thousands. *g* '000 G.R.T. *p* 1966 figure. *q* 1960 figure. *r* assembly of imported parts.

na: data not available. — negligible or nil. [1] one year only. [2] two year average. * estimate. ‡ see appendix. † re-exports.

ISRAEL

Israel was established in 1948 as an independent sovereign state open to immigration by Jews from all countries of the world. The question of border demarcation with neighbouring Arab states led to persistant hostilities around Israel's borders, until in 1967, she was provoked into launching attacks on Jordan, the U.A.R. and Syria. This 'Six Days' War' terminated with a cease-fire negotiated by the U.N., and the territory under Israeli control increased to four times its former size. Sporadic fighting has continued and the area remains under the threat of another war.

AREA: 20 700 sq. km. (7 992 sq. miles) (1967—i.e. area within the boundaries defined by the 1948 armistice)

LAND USE: (percentage of total)

	1964	*1955*
Arable and orchard	19.9	17.6
Permanent meadow and pasture	33.9	9.7
Forest and woodland	4.6	3.0
City areas, waste and other land	41.6	69.7

POPULATION: 2 669 000 (1967 estimate)

During the period 1948–1967, 1 300 000 Jewish immigrants entered the country, thus doubling the population and creating an acute refugee problem.

Largest city: TEL AVIV-YAFO (Tel Aviv-Jaffa); population: 389 700 (1965)

Capital city: YERUSHALAYIM (Jerusalem); population: 195 700 (1966)

Distribution of working population:

Total working population: 912 400

U.N. group no.		*Percentage*
0	Agriculture, forestry, fishing and hunting	12.5
1/2/3	Mining, quarrying and manufacturing	24.5
4	Construction	10.1
5	Electricity, gas, water and sanitary services	1.7
6	Commerce	12.1
7	Transport, storage and communications	6.6
8	Services	28.7
9	Others	3.8

		Year(s)
Life expectancy at birth (years): male	70.4*a*	1967
female	73.6*a*	1967
Infant mortality (per '000)	27.4	1965
Crude birth rate (per '000)	25.8	1965
Crude death rate (per '000)	6.3	1965
Accidental deaths (per 100 000 population) caused by motor vehicles	12.3*	1965
due to other causes	22.5**b*	1965
Population per physician	410	1965
Population per hospital bed	130	1966
School enrolment: age 5–19 years (percentage)	83	1963–4 av.
age over 19 years (per 100 000 population)	933*c*	1963–5 av.

a Jewish population only. *b* includes homicide and acts of war. *c* at universities and degree-granting institutions only.

COMMUNICATIONS

		Year(s)
Motor vehicles in use ('000s): private	62.7	1963–5 av.
commercial	35.2	1963–5 av.
Railway track (km.)	692	1964
Mail per capita: domestic	67	1963–5 av.
foreign received	14	1963–5 av.
foreign sent	12	1963–5 av.
Telephones (per '000 urban population)	11.3	1967
Radio receivers (per '000 population)	271	1963–5 av.
Television licences (per '000 population)	2.7	1963–5 av.
Daily newspapers (per '000 population)	145.5	1962–3 av

FINANCE

Currency unit: The Israeli pound

Exchange rates	*1965*	*1960*	*1954*	*1953*
Per $ U.S.	3.0	1.8	1.8	1.0
Per £ sterling	8.4	5.01	5.01	2.8

		Year(s)
National Income (million $ U.S.)	2 736	1965
G.N.P. per capita ($ U.S.)	1 160	1966
Rate of increase of G.N.P. per capita	6.5	1960–4 av.
Foreign trade (percentage of G.D.P.)	37	1963–5 av.

TRADING

Total trade (in million $ U.S.)	*1965*	*1955*
Exports (f.o.b.)	406	89
Imports (c.i.f.)	811	334

Main trading partners (percentage of total value)

Exports	*1965*	*1955*	*Imports*	*1965*	*1955*
U.S.A.	14	19	U.S.A.	25	29
U.K.	12	21	U.K.	20	10
Germany F.R.	9	2	Germany F.R.	9	18
Netherlands	9	4	France	4	2
Switzerland	6	2	Italy	4	2
Belg./Lux.	5	4	Netherlands	4	3
Hong Kong	4	na	Belg./Lux.	3	1

Distribution of trade (percentage of total value)

Exports	*1965*	*1955*
Manufactured goods	60	54
(cut diamonds)	(36)	(23)
(textiles and clothing)	(9)	(5)
Food	25	41
Chemicals	6	2
Imports		
Manufactured goods	62	42
(machinery and transport equipment)	(28)	(13)
Crude materials and fuels	19	31
Food	11	22
Chemicals	5	4

PRODUCTION, EXPORTS AND IMPORTS

Years: **1963–5 average** and *1953–5 average* Units: '000 metric tons unless otherwise indicated

1. CEREALS, etc.

	Production		Exports		Imports	
Barley	73.3	65.3	—	—	64.4	26.9
Maize (corn)	5.0	20.0	—	—	176.0	7.9
Millets/sorghum	623.0	15.0	—	—	175.7	45.1
Oats	1.0	1.3	—	—	0.5	—
Potatoes	108.3	73.0	7.7	—	4.9*	15.0
Rice	—	—	—	—	14.9	3.8
Rye	—	—	—	—	2.2	9.5
Wheat	110.7	33.3	1.7[2]	—	224.8	323.5

2. FRUIT, etc.

	Production		Exports		Imports	
Apples	53.7	2.7*	0.1*p*	—	—	0.3
Bananas	48.3	13.0	16.1	—	—	—
Dates/figs	3.0	5.3*q*	—	—	0.5	0.2
Grapes	74.0	25.7	0.5	—	—	—
Lemons	33.0	16.0	12.2	4.7	—	—
Oranges	625.3	362.7	410.1	213.8	—	—
Other citrus fruit	132.3	59.7	81.2	40.1	—	—
Olives	17.3*	13.0				
Peaches/apricots	13.7	na	—	—	—	—
Pears	9.7	na	—	—	—	—

continued

2. FRUIT, etc.—*continued*

	Production		Exports		Imports	
Plums	11.7	na	—	—	—	—
Raisins	0.4	na	—	—	0.4[2]	1.0
Tomatoes	102.3	60.3				
Wine *b*	321.0	na	15.8	3.3	0.4[2]	—

b '000 hectolitres. *p* incl. pears and quince. *q* incl. avocado pears.

3. BEVERAGES, FOREST PRODUCTS, etc.

	Production		Exports		Imports	
Cocoa	—	—	—	—	1.1	1.0
Coffee	—	—	—	—	5.8	1.1
Sugar: beet	267.0	17.0*				
raw	36.5	na	—	—	83.4	61.5
Tea	—	—	—	—	1.2	0.5
Tobacco: leaf	0.9	2.8	—	—	2.2	0.7
cigars	4.0*e*	1.4*e*				
cigarettes	2 947.0*e*	2 003.3*e*	—	—	0.2[1]	—
tobacco/snuff	0.1	0.1				
Softwood *j*	8.8	0.9	—	—	468.9	288.6
Hardwood *j*	36.3	10.8	—	—	151.6	21.1
Wood pulp	—	—	—	—	22.6	9.3
Newsprint	7.9	0.3*	—	—	7.8	2.1
Other paper	38.0	6.8*	3.1	—	39.2	13.8

e no. in millions. *j* '000 cu. metres of roundwood equivalent.

continued

na: data not available. — negligible or nil. [1] one year only. [2] two year average. * estimate. ‡ see appendix. † re-exports.

PRODUCTION, EXPORTS AND IMPORTS *continued*

4. VEGETABLE OILSEEDS AND OILS

	Production		Exports		Imports	
Castor seed	—	—	—	—	0.28	—
Castor oil	na	—	—	—	0.02	0.05
Copra	—	—	—	—	4.88	8.57
Coconut oil	na	na	—	—	0.19	0.38
Cottonseed	27.30	2.70*	1.01	—	na	3.65[2]
Cottonseed oil	na	na	2.18	—	1.05	1.00
Groundnuts	8.63	9.80	3.04	—	0.21	4.53
Groundnut oil	na	na	—	—	—	0.08
Linseed	—	—	—	—	3.08	1.27
Linseed oil	na	na	—	—	0.09	0.48
Olive oil	2.00*	2.00	0.16	0.11	0.02	0.01
Palm oil	—	—	—	—	0.27	—
Rapeseed	—	—	—	—	0.02[2]	—
Sesame seed	1.30	0.50	—	—	1.70[2]	0.60
Soya beans	—	—	—	—	220.70	20.50*
Soya bean oil	na	na	23.37	—	16.98	0.61
Sunflower seed	2.67	1.00	—	—	1.19*	8.84
Sunflower seed oil	na	na	—	—	0.01	—

5. LIVESTOCK‡, ANIMAL PRODUCTS, etc.

	Production		Exports		Imports	
Chickens *d*	7 216.7	4 475.0				
Cattle *d*	225.3	94.7	0.3	—	2.2	4.9
dairy cows *d*	119.3	61.0				
Goats *d*	158.0	116.7	—	—	0.3	—
Sheep *d*	192.7	83.3				
Horses *d*	19.7	12.0*				
Meat‡: 'A'	23.3	3.0*r*	—	—	19.5	—
'B'	74.9	7.8[1]	0.4	—	0.3	6.1
Butter	3.0*t*	1.0	—	1.7	1.1	5.5
Cheese	21.0	na	—	0.8	0.3	2.4
Eggs	69.0	23.8	9.7	0.2	—	—
Fish	18.6*u*	9.2*u*	—	—	19.2	25.0[1]*
Milk	335.7	150.0	—	—	81.6	129.7
Hides/skins	—	na	—	—	9.1	4.2
Wool	0.2	—	—	0.2†	1.0	0.2

d no. in thousands. *r* government inspected meat only. *t* factory produce only. *u* incl. fish landed by Israeli vessels in foreign ports and by foreign vessels in Israeli ports.

6. FIBRES, TEXTILES, etc.

	Production		Exports		Imports	
Abaca	—	—	—	—	0.3	—
Agaves (sisal etc.)	0.6	—	0.1	—[1]	1.0	1.0[1]
Cotton lint	17.0	—	2.5	—	10.3	4.9
Flax fibre	—	0.1	—	—	0.2[2]	—
Jute	—	—	0.1	—	1.2	—
Rubber, natural	—	—	0.1	—	7.1	3.5
Cotton: yarn	21.0	na	7.5	na	—	—
woven fabrics	9.8	na	—	—	—	—
Rayon, fibre/yarn	—	—	0.1†	—	5.4	na
Non-cellulosic fibre/yarn	1.4	0.1	0.4	na	3.6	na
Wool: yarn	4.2	na	0.5	0.2	0.4	0.4
woven fabrics	1.5[1]	na	—	0.1	—	—

7. FUEL AND POWER

	Production		Exports		Imports	
Coal 'A'‡	—	—	—	—	12	25
Coke	—	—	—	—	8	3
Electricity *h t*	3 643	1 260[1]				
Natural gas *i*	40	—[1]	—	—[1]	—	—[1]
Oil, crude	183	—[1]	—	—[1]	2 960	—[1]
Petroleum, refined	3 120	960[1]	460	—[1]	360	1 220[1]*n*

h million kWh. *i* million cu. metres. *n* excl. aviation spirit. *t* thermal.

8. IRON AND STEEL

	Production		Exports		Imports	
Pig iron	—	—	—	—	28	4[2]
Iron/steel scrap	na	na	1	—	—	—

9. NON-FERROUS MINERALS AND METALS

	Production		Exports		Imports	
Diamonds *a*	—	—	135.85†*p*	16.23†	114.18*q*	14.06
Asbestos, fibre	—	—	—	—	8.44	—
Aluminium	—	—	—	0.80	7.22	1.23
Antimony, metal	—	—	—	—	—	0.02
Copper, ore	7.93*m*	na	—	—	—	—
Lead, metal	—	—	—	—	2.11	0.99
Magnesium, magnesite	—	—	—	—	1.58	—
Tin, metal	—	—	—	—	0.13	0.11
Zinc, metal	—	—	—	—	3.72	1.98

a million $ U.S. *m* metal content. *p* excl. industrial diamonds and dust. *q* excl. dust.

10. CHEMICALS*n* AND FERTILIZERS

	Production		Exports		Imports	
Organic chemicals:						
Benzene	—		—		na	
Butadiene	—		—		na	
Ethylene	4.0		—		na	
Methanol	0.4		—		3.2	
Phenol	—		—		2.7	
Phthalic anhydride	—		—		na	
Styrene monomer	—		—		0.5	
Urea	—		—		5.4[2]	
Inorganic chemicals:						
Ammonia	29.5		0.1		na	
Carbon black	3.0		1.4		2.7	
Chlorine	8.7[2]		0.1		—	
Nitric acid	12.9		—		0.1	
Sodium carbonate	—		—		17.1	
Sodium hydroxide	8.6		0.8		0.5	
Sulphuric acid	154.7		—		2.4	
Plastics:						
Polyamides	—		—		0.1	
Polyethylene	2.6		0.9		3.0	
Polyvinyl chloride	1.9		—		1.4	
Fertilizers:						
Phosphates	309.7	54.5	212.2	—	—	—
Potash	226.2**w*	8.3**w*	6.7	7.6	—	—
Sulphur	—	—	—	—	56.4	3.8[2]

n data not available for years 1953–5. *w* K_2O content.

11. INDUSTRY

	Production		Exports		Imports	
Aircraft *a*	—	—	1.4	—	6.1*t*	1.7
Alcoholic beverages:			—	0.1*a*	—	—
beer *b*	264.0	143.0				
spirits *b*	30.0[1]*q*	38.8[1]*r*				
Cement	1 127.3	564.0	125.3	120.0	12.3	9.7
Electrical engineering *a*	—	—	1.5	—	42.7	35.3
Railway vehicles *a*	—	—	—	—	1.3	—
Machine tools *a*	—	—	—	—	5.0	na
Merchant ships *g*	1.0	—	—	—	54.0	na
Motor vehicles			1.0*a*	9.3*a*	44.6*a*	1.3*a*
commercial *dp*	4.3	2.3				
private *dp*	2.8	0.6				

a million $ U.S. *b* '000 hectolitres. *d* no. in thousands. *g* '000 G.R.T. *p* assembly of imported parts. *q* 1967 data. *r* 1960 data. *t* incomplete figure.

na: data not available. — negligible or nil. [1] one year only. [2] two year average. * estimate. ‡ see appendix. † re-exports.

ITALY

Italy was declared a republic in 1946 as the result of a national referendum; this terminated a long-established monarchy in which the power of the monarch had already been relinquished. Italy is a member of the European Economic Community.

AREA: 301 224 sq. km. (116 303 sq. miles) including Vatican City

LAND USE: (percentage of total)

	1965	*1955*
Arable and orchard	50.8	52.3
Permanent meadow and pasture	17.1	17.1
Forest and woodland	20.2	19.1
City areas, waste and other land	11.9	11.5

POPULATION: 52 334 000 (1967 estimate)

Largest city: ROMA (Rome), capital; population: 2 484 737 (1965)

Distribution of working population (1965)
Total working population: 19 920 000

U.N. group no.		*Percentage*
0	Agriculture, forestry, fishing and hunting	25.1
1	Mining and quarrying	0.7
2/3	Manufacturing	28.3
4	Construction	10.6
5	Electricity, gas, water and sanitary services	0.8
6	Commerce	13.9
7	Transport, storage and communications	5.2
8	Services	14.1
9	Others	1.3

		Year(s)
Life expectancy at birth (years): male	67.2	1960–2 av.
female	72.3	
Infant mortality (per '000)	36	1965
Crude birth rate (per '000)	19.2	1965
Crude death rate (per '000)	10.	1965
Accidental deaths (per 100 000 population)		
caused by motor vehicles	20.8	1965
due to other causes	22.4	1965
Population per physician	570	1967
Population per hospital bed	100	1966
School enrolment: age 5–19 years (percentage)	63	1963–4 av.
age over 19 years (per 100 000 population)	524	1963–5 av.

COMMUNICATIONS

		Year(s)
Motor vehicles in use ('000s): private	4 685.4	1963–5 av.
commercial	634.5	
Railway track (km.)	21 043	1964
Mail per capita: domestic	101	1963–5 av.
foreign received	7	
foreign sent	7	
Telephones (per '000 urban population)	12.4	1967
Radio licences (per '000 population)	199	1963–5 av.
Television licences (per '000 population)	101	1963–5 av.
Daily newspapers (per '000 population)	101	1961

FINANCE

Currency unit: The lira

Exchange rates	*1965*	*1960*	*1950*	*1938*
Per $ U.S.	624.7	620.6	625	19.0
Per £ sterling	1 750.5	1 740.0	1 750	87.4

		Year(s)
National Income (million $ U.S.)	45 549	1965
G.N.P. per capita ($ U.S.)	1 030	1966
Rate of increase of G.N.P. per capita	5	1960–4 av.
Foreign trade (percentage of G.D.P.)	26	1963–5 av.

TRADING

Total trade (in million $ U.S.)	*1965*	*1955*	*1938*
Exports (f.o.b.)	7 200	1 857	553
Imports (c.i.f.)	7 378	2 711	593

Main trading partners (percentage of total value)

Exports	*1965*	*1955*	*1938*	*Imports*	*1965*	*1955*	*1938*
Germany F.R.	21	13	19*d*	Germany F.R.	15	13	27*d*
France	10	6	3	U.S.A.	13	15	12
U.S.A.	9	9	7	France	10	7	2
Switzerland	5	7	5	Kuwait	5	na	na
Netherlands	5	2	1	U.K.	5	5	6
U.K.	5	7	6	Netherlands	4	2	1
Belg./Lux.	4	3	1	Argentina	4	3	2

Distribution of trade (percentage of total value)

Exports	*1965*	*1955*	*1938**
Manufactured goods	70	55	na
(machinery and transport equipment)	(30)	(20)	(11)
(textile and clothing)	(15)	(15)	(14)
(shoes)	(3)	(1)	(na)
Food	11	20	23
(fruit and vegetables)	(8)	(16)	(17)
Crude materials and fuels	9	16	na
Chemicals	8	7	na
Imports			
Crude materials and fuels	37	48	na
(mineral fuels)	(16)	(20)	(22)
(textile fibres)	(6)	(21)	(12)
Manufactured goods	33	27	na
(machinery and transport equipment)	(15)	(11)	(na)
Food	21	16	9
Chemicals	7	5	na

d incl. Germany D.R.

PRODUCTION, EXPORTS AND IMPORTS

Years: **1963–5 average** and *1953–5 average* Units: '000 metric tons unless otherwise indicated

1. CEREALS, etc.

	Production		Exports		Imports	
Barley	242.3	294.3	1.3	—	732.2	77.4
Maize (corn)	3 655.3	3 123.3	333.3	41.7	4 097.4	168.7
Millets/sorghum	23.3	—	2.9	1.4	16.8	3.8
Oats	513.7	558.7	0.3	—	164.9	42.2
Potatoes	3 919.0	3 244.7	204.3	175.8	265.5	118.0
Rice	565.7	887.3	106.0	203.3	2.6	—
Rye	82.0	122.7	—	—	3.1	111.6
Sweet potatoes/yams	34.7	na				
Wheat	8 829.7	8 614.7	33.4	0.5	593.4	713.0

2. FRUIT, etc.

	Production		Exports		Imports	
Apples	2 300.7	976.0	447.8	231.5	0.4	0.1
Apricots	65.3	34.6	na	13.8	—	—
Bananas	—	—	—	—	213.8	38.9
Cherries	215.3	125.7	na	18.6	—	—
Dates	1.0*	—	0.4	0.1	5.9	6.7
Figs	269.0	327.0	na	4.4	—	—
Grapes	9 910.3	8 563.7	197.3	61.4	1.2	1.9
Lemons	591.7	342.3	293.0	180.0	—	—
Oranges	1 141.3	689.7	199.5	176.9	0.2	—
Other citrus fruit	—	—	0.5	—[1]	0.9	0.2[1]
Olives	2 323.2	1 631.0				
Peaches	1 302.0	448.1	na	107.2	—	—
Pears	1 001.7	401.3	146.1	59.8	0.4	—
Plums	128.0	95.5	na	18.5	—	—
Raisins	1.7	2.1	0.4	—	9.6	11.9
Tomatoes	3 002.3	1 510.7				
Wine *b*	63 126.0	53 809.0	2 274.4	1 190.7	77.5	51.0

b '000 hectolitres.

3. BEVERAGES, FOREST PRODUCTS, etc.

	Production		Exports		Imports	
Cocoa	—	—	1.0	—	39.6	18.2
Coffee	—	—	0.3	—	119.0	69.5
Sugar: beet	8 309	7 163				
raw	1 080	948*	3.6	—	426.2	23.0
Tea	—	—	—	—	2.2	0.9
Tobacco: leaf	73	69	6.7	12.4	20.5	8.4
cigars	241*e*	2 210*e*				
cigarettes	57 783*e*	36 603*e*	—	0.3[2]	na	0.7
tobacco/snuff	4	6				
Softwood *j*	1 438	2 145	12.0	1.6	5 301.0	2 862.9
Hardwood *j*	15 079	9 893	17.7	31.5	1 895.7	366.8
Wood pulp	639	345	4.9	10.6	876.6	277.7
Newsprint	363	129	24.1	—	9.8	21.7
Other paper	1 697	611	40.0	13.3	263.3	35.3

e no. in millions. *j* '000 cu. metres of roundwood equivalent.

4. VEGETABLE OILSEEDS AND OILS

	Production		Exports		Imports	
Castor seed	—	—	—	—	9.65	7.07
Castor oil	na	na	0.03	0.07	0.16	0.05
Copra	—	—	—	—	24.88	7.23
Coconut oil	na	na	—	—	15.72	25.65*p*
Cottonseed	8.00	16.30	—	0.63	0.68	2.07
Cottonseed oil	na	na	—	0.01[2]	0.03	0.78
Groundnuts	7.00	6.50	0.05	1.30	124.63	18.17
Groundnut oil	na	na	0.06	0.04	0.70	3.94
Linseed	4.33	11.00	0.17	0.10	4.52	23.37
Linseed oil	na	na	—	0.01	16.51	23.84[2]

p incl. palm kernel oil.

continued

na: data not available. — negligible or nil. [1] one year only. [2] two year average. * estimate. ‡ see appendix. † re-exports.

PRODUCTION, EXPORTS AND IMPORTS *continued*

4. VEGETABLE OILSEEDS AND OILS—*continued*

	Production		Exports		Imports	
Olive oil	457.67	271.00n	11.26	10.35	75.31	20.71
Palm kernels	—	—	—	—	1.06	0.10
Palm kernel oil	na	na	0.04	—	8.16	na r
Palm oil	—	—	0.01	0.07	29.54	18.81
Rapeseed	8.30	9.30	1.31	1.80	95.05	2.60
Rapeseed oil	na	na	—	0.02	0.59	3.36
Sesame seed	1.13	0.67	—	—	30.20	11.43
Soya beans	—	0.67	—	—	369.73	na
Soya bean oil	na	na	—	0.22	3.80	9.31
Sunflower seed	3.33	4.67	0.01	—	64.00	2.74
Sunflower seed oil	na	na	0.03	0.04q	2.07	1.18q
Tung oil	—	—	—	—	0.97	0.58

n oil extracted by machine only. *q* incl. other minor vegetable oils. *r* see coconut oil.

5. LIVESTOCK‡, ANIMAL PRODUCTS, etc.

	Production		Exports		Imports	
Chickens *d*	105 000*t*	75 500*				
Cattle *d*	8 981	9 014[2]	—	—	670.5	92.0
dairy cows *d*	4 751	4 291[2]				
Goats *d* }	1 247	1 890[2]	0.3	—	181.2	na
Sheep *d* }	7 828	9 819[2]				
Horses *d*	352	664[2]				
Pigs *d*	5 041	4 057[2]	7.7	—	60.1	57.0
Bacon/ham }	849	600[2]	1.3	0.2	1.0	—
Meat‡: 'A' }			0.2	0.2	298.5	36.0
'B'	500	212	0.8	0.3	10.8	11.9
Butter	59	63	—	—	33.9	7.3
Cheese	373	317	23.6	17.9	61.8	22.9
Eggs	447	314[2]	0.5	0.1	37.7	23.8
Fish	298	254	3.2	1.1[1]*	267.0	112.3[1]
Milk	8 982	5 907[2]u	1.3*	0.7*	268.1*	8.2*
Whale/sperm oil	—	—	—	—	4.4	na
Hides/skins	na	na	na	16.6[2]	165.8	52.3[2]
Wool	6	8	2.6	1.1	77.9	45.2

d no. in thousands. *t* incl. ducks, geese and turkeys. *u* excl. milk fed to livestock.

6. FIBRES, TEXTILES, etc.

	Production		Exports		Imports	
Abaca	—	—	—	—	0.8	1.3
Agaves (sisal etc.)	—	—	—	—	24.9	6.4
Cotton lint	4.7	10.7	—	4.5	212.8	152.3
Flax fibre	0.2	3.0	1.0	0.1	17.8	2.8
Hemp fibre	11.2	50.2	4.4	25.0	7.9	0.9
Jute	—	—	0.9†	0.3†	38.2	53.1
Rubber: natural	—	—	0.1†	—	91.2	54.2
synthetic	109.3	—	55.9	—[2]	49.0s	11.9
Silk *f*	588.5[2]	1 311.3	1 121.7	345.3	3 546.0	309.3
Cotton: yarn	197.5	158.6	21.9	12.7	0.7	0.4
woven fabrics	120.3	108.0	7.3	12.0	16.2	2.2
Rayon: fibre/yarn	200.1	120.8	76.7	53.1	7.1	1.2
woven fabrics	25.3	20.9	22.7	14.0	3.8	0.3
Non-cellulosic fibre/yarn	95.2	6.7	41.9	na	6.9	na
Wool: yarn	165.3	na	11.0	2.0	1.0	0.3
woven fabrics	77.1	74.0	56.6	27.7	2.7	1.0

f metric tons. *s* incl. imports for re-export.

7. FUEL AND POWER

	Production		Exports		Imports	
Coal: 'A'‡	483	1 130	10	4	10 732	9 524
'B'	593	420	—	—	40	56
Coke	na	na	123	76	437	48
Electricity *h*: total	75 770	35 380[1]				
hydro	42 675	30 510[1]				
nuclear	2 078	—				
thermal *t*	31 017	4 870[1]				
Natural gas *i*	7 580	2 964[1]	—	—	—	—
Oil, crude	2 273	260[1]	—	—	56 330	17 000[1]
Petroleum, refined	53 896	15 470[1]	11 793	4 990[1]	2 317	590[1]
Uranium	na	—	—	—	—	—

h million kWh. *i* million cu. metres. *t* incl. geothermal.

8. IRON AND STEEL

	Production		Exports		Imports	
Iron ore	458m	599m	670	402	6 093	734
Pig iron	4 375	1 491	12	9	800	231
Steel ingots/castings	10 877	4 367	100	15	992	135
Iron/steel scrap	na	na	3	1	3 864	1 597
Iron/steel products *a*	na	na	259	43	419	104

a million $ U.S. *m* metal content.

9. NON-FERROUS MINERALS AND METALS

	Production		Exports		Imports	
Gold *k*, ore	—	8.60m	—	—	1 763.30‡p	9.70r
Platinum group metals *k*	—	—	22.11†	0.29†	69.05	4.87
Silver *k*, ore	1 061.00m	861.70m	—	0.33r	na	6 429.30r
Asbestos: fibre	65.86	24.71	13.71	3.12	40.87	12.00
manufactured	na	na	44.85	14.84	16.95	0.82

continued

9. NON-FERROUS MINERALS AND METALS—*continued*

	Production		Exports		Imports	
Mica	—	—	0.11†	0.01†	2.07	4.04
Aluminium: bauxite	255.03	297.55	1.55	—	402.78	100.57
alumina	259.83q	na	14.40u	31.86	5.63u	0.05
aluminium	110.33	58.16	37.34	13.08	95.01	16.96
Antimony: ore	0.35m	0.35m	—	—	0.02[1]	0.02
metal	na	na	—	—	0.73	0.64
Cadmium	0.28	0.20	0.01	0.16	0.08[1]	0.01
Chrome: ore	—	—	1.19†	—	75.13	21.93
metal	—	—	4.43[1]	0.37†	15.66	4.25
Cobalt, metal	—	—	—	—	0.57	2.82
Copper: ore	2.18m	0.26m	1.89	—	—	—
metal	na	0.40	37.15†	6.02†	246.75	108.10
Lead: ore	33.89m	44.78m	4.84	8.97	21.03	3.35
metal	41.76	39.04	1.63	0.83	65.54	20.78
Magnesium: dolomite	920.00	na	10.29	4.36	0.87	—
magnesite	5.55	na	0.09	0.31	44.67	4.40
metal/salts	5.96x	1.99x	8.74	2.12	9.10	17.80
Manganese: ore	46.96	48.84	0.82t	0.01t	126.83t	71.35t
metal	na	na	5.58	0.91	78.28	3.82
Mercury *f*	1 950.82	1 831.34	2 417.10	1 666.50	20.50	—
Molybdenum *f*: ore	—	—	—	—	1 317.10	244.80
metal	na	na	7.10[2]	—	624.90[2]	215.00
Nickel: ore	—	—	—	0.01†	0.90	—
metal	na	—	0.96†	0.23†	9.11	2.64
Tin, metal	—	—	0.15†	0.02†	5.68	2.66
Titanium minerals	—	—	15.40†	2.07†	114.50	22.16
Tungsten: ore	—	0.03	—	—	0.05	0.09
metal	na	na	—	—	0.15	0.08
Vanadium: ore	—	—	—	—	—	0.05
metal *v*	—	na	0.03	0.04	0.44	0.04
Zinc: ore	111.42m	114.52m	39.45	63.34	3.38	1.44
metal	75.83	66.00	4.58	27.49	50.88	7.44
Zirconium minerals	—	—	—	—	12.06	0.12

f metric tons. *k* '000 fine troy oz. *m* metal content. *p* bullion and scrap. *q* aluminium oxide content. *r* bullion. *t* incl. manganiferous iron ore. *u* hydrate. *v* incl. vanadium oxide and ferro-vanadium. *x* primary magnesium only.

10. CHEMICALS*n* AND FERTILIZERS

	Production		Exports		Imports	
Organic chemicals:						
Benzene	89.7		7.1		102.0	
Butadiene	na		1.1		8.1	
Ethylene	352.1[1]		na		na	
Methanol	107.0		19.1		9.8	
Phenol	87.9		19.8		1.6	
Phthalic anhydride	63.7		20.8		0.2	
Styrene monomer	73.3		4.1		23.8	
Urea	123.6		167.9		9.3	
Inorganic chemicals:						
Ammonia	948.0*		12.9		—	
Carbon black	61.6		23.1		24.7	
Chlorine	484.7		13.2		2.4	
Nitric acid	926.6		1.1		—	
Sodium carbonate	604.7		5.8		8.7	
Sodium hydroxide	625.8		109.0		1.5	
Sulphuric acid	2 872.4		91.7		0.8	
Plastics:						
Polyamides	24.4		0.6		2.2	
Polyethylene	159.4*		56.4		7.6	
Polyvinyl chloride	285.7		126.3		3.6	
Fertilizers:						
Phosphates	—	na	—	—	1 616.8	1 257.2
Potash	198.7w	na	95.8	—	207.0	113.6
Pyrites	631.6x	576.5x	67.3	92.1	850.6	154.6
Sulphur: native }	109.4	203.2				
recovered }	1.3	5.1[1]*	5.1	24.2	45.1	—

n data not available for years 1953–5. *w* K_2O content. *x* sulphur content.

11. INDUSTRY

	Production		Exports		Imports	
Aircraft *a*	125.0*p	na	76.3	6.5	53.3	9.3
Alcoholic beverages			66.5a	27.4a	—	2.9a
beer *b*	4 168.0	1 588.7				
spirits *b*	950.0[1]r	982.0[1]t				
Cement	22 009.7	9 292.0	291.7	15.0	109.0	216.3
Electrical engineering *a*	1 341.3[2]	na	344.5	42.0[2]	286.3	57.7[2]
Locomotives *c*	na	9.0	na	na	na	na
Railway vehicles *a*	na	na	33.8	8.8	—	1.4
Machine tools *a*	126.0[1]	na	69.8	15.1	71.1	28.3
Merchant ships *g*	434.0	197.0	117.0	20.2[2]	0.1	25.1
Motor vehicles			447.3a	94.4a	204.4a	9.1a
commercial *dq*	69.5	35.5				
private *dq*	1 079.4	184.9				

a million $ U.S. *b* '000 hectolitres. *c* no. of units. *d* no. in thousands. *g* '000 G.R.T. *p* 1965–7 av. *q* excl. military vehicles. *r* 1967 data. *t* 1959 data.

na: data not available. — negligible or nil. [1] one year only. [2] two year average. * estimate. ‡ see appendix. † re-exports.

IVORY COAST

The Ivory Coast, formerly a territory of French West Africa, became an independent republic in 1960.

AREA: 322 463 sq. km. (124 300 sq. miles)

LAND USE: (percentage of total)

	1965
Arable and orchard	6.4
Permanent meadow and pasture	na
Forest and woodland, including rough grazing	74.4
City areas, waste and other land	na

POPULATION: 4 010 000 (1967 U.N. estimate)

Largest city: ABIDJAN, capital; population: 250 800 (1963)

Distribution of working population (1964)
Total working population: 1 850 000

U.N. group no.		*Percentage*
0	Agriculture, forestry, fishing and hunting	86.4
1	Mining and quarrying	0.2
2/3	Manufacturing	0.8
4	Construction	0.9
5	Electricity, gas, water and sanitary services	0.4
6	Commerce	6.8
7	Transport, storage and communications	2.3
8	Services	2.2

		Year(s)
Life expectancy at birth (years)	35	1957–8 av.
Population per physician	19 080	1965
Population per hospital bed	510*a*	1966
School enrolment: age 5–19 years (percentage)	33	1963–4 av.
age over 19 years (per 100 000 population)	37	1963–4 av.

a government hospitals only.

COMMUNICATIONS

		Year(s)
Motor vehicles in use ('000s): private	28.0	1963–5 av.
commercial	20.7	1963–5 av.
Railway track (km.)	652	1965
Telephones (per '000 urban population)	0.5	1967
Radio receivers (per '000 population)	16	1963–5 av.
Television sets (per '000 population)	0.8	1963–5 av.
Daily newspapers (per '000 population)	3.5	1962–4 av.

FINANCE

Currency unit: The franc CFA

Exchange rates	*1965*	*1960*
Per $ U.S.	246.85	246.85
Per £ sterling	691.18	691.18

		Year
National Income (million $ U.S.)	706	1964
G.N.P. per capita ($ U.S.)	220	1966

TRADING

Total trade (in million $ U.S.)	*1965*	*1955*
Exports (f.o.b.)	277	146
Imports (c.i.f.)	236	109

Main trading partners (percentage of total value)

Exports	*1965*	*Imports*	*1965*
France	38	France	62
U.S.A.	16	Germany F.R.	6
Italy	9	U.S.A.	5
Netherlands	7	Italy	3
Germany F.R.	7	Belg./Lux.	2
U.K.	3	Morocco	2
Algeria	3	Netherlands	2

Distribution of trade (percentage of total value)

Exports	*1965*	*Imports*	*1965*
Food	63	Manufactured goods	68
(coffee)	(38)	(machinery and transport equipment)	(28)
(cocoa)	(18)	(textiles and clothing)	(16)
Crude materials	31	Food	14
(hardwood)	(27)	Crude materials and fuels	7
		(petroleum products)	(5)
		Alcoholic beverages	3

PRODUCTION, EXPORTS AND IMPORTS

Years: **1963–5 average** Units: '000 metric tons unless otherwise indicated
Note—1953–5 data are not available

1. CEREALS, etc.

	Production	Exports	Imports
Cassava	1 120.0		
Maize (corn)	172.7	—	—
Millets/sorghum	82.3	—	—
Potatoes	—	0.2[2]†	na
Rice	236.3	0.2	53.9
Sweet potatoes/yams	1 887.3		
Wheat	—	—	45.6

2. FRUIT, etc.

	Production	Exports	Imports
Apples	—	—	na
Bananas	147.0	129.2	—
Coconuts *e*	10.0[1]*	na	—
Grapes	—	—	na
Oranges	—	—	na
Pineapples	45.3*	—	—
Wine *b*	—	—	325.0

b '000 hectolitres. *e* no. in millions.

3. BEVERAGES, FOREST PRODUCTS, etc.

	Production	Exports	Imports
Cocoa	115.4	116.8	—
Coffee	244.7	190.7	—
Sugar, raw	—	—	29.0
Tobacco: leaf	2.7	0.1	0.9
products	—	—	0.4
Hardwood *j*	7 731.3*	1 909.0	0.4
Newsprint	—	—	0.7[2]
Other paper	—	—	3.1[2]

j '000 cu. metres of roundwood equivalent.

4. VEGETABLE OILSEEDS AND OILS

	Production	Exports	Imports
Copra	na	0.12	—
Coconut oil	na	0.07	—
Cottonseed	6.00	5.08	—
Groundnuts	24.97	1.97	—
Groundnut oil	na	0.02	—
Palm kernels	12.73	12.71	—
Palm oil	26.83	0.84	1.74
Sesame seed	na	1.13[2]	—

5. LIVESTOCK‡, ANIMAL PRODUCTS, etc.

	Production	Exports	Imports
Cattle *d*	316.7	—	—
Goats *d*	650.0	—	—
Sheep *d*	527.3	—	—
Horses *d*	1.0*		
Pigs *d*	100.0*	—	—
Meat‡: 'A'	7.0	—	na
'B'	—	—	na
Butter	—	—	0.6
Cheese	—	—	0.4
Eggs	2.2*	—	—
Fish	51.7	1.4	2.4
Milk	14.7	—	na

d no. in thousands.

6. FIBRES, TEXTILES, etc.

	Production	Exports	Imports
Cotton lint	3.0	1.3	—
Rubber, natural	2.0	1.6	—
Cotton: yarn	—	—	0.3
woven fabrics	—	—	6.2

7. FUEL AND POWER

	Production	Exports	Imports
Electricity *h*: total	186		
hydro	115		
thermal	71		
Oil, crude	—	—	67
Petroleum, refined	57	7	237

h million kWh.

9. NON-FERROUS MINERALS AND METALS

	Production	Exports	Imports
Diamonds	192.67l	1.77a	—
Manganese, ore	151.75	130.42	—

a million $ U.S. *l* '000 carats.

11. INDUSTRY

	Production	Exports	Imports
Aircraft *a*	—	—	2.7
Alcoholic beverages *a*	—	—	5.7
Cement	5.0*	—	226.7
Electrical engineering *a*	—	—	12.5
Railway vehicles *a*	—	—	1.6
Merchant ships *g*	—	—	0.1
Motor vehicles *a*	—	0.8	18.0

a million $ U.S. *g* '000 G.R.T.

na: data not available. — negligible or nil. [1] one year only. [2] two year average. * estimate. ‡ see appendix. † re-exports.

JAMAICA

CARIBBEAN SEA

Jamaica, as one of the British West Indies, was granted self-government in 1944, and became a fully independent member of the Commonwealth in 1962.

AREA: 11 525 sq. km. (4 411 sq. miles)

LAND USE: (percentage of total)	*1964*	*1955*
Arable and orchard	21.1	15.2
Permanent meadow and pasture	23.4	20.9
Forest and woodland	19.2	17.7
City areas, waste and other land	36.3	46.2

POPULATION: 1 876 000 (1967 estimate)
Largest city: KINGSTON, capital; population: 376 520 (1960)

Distribution of working population (1960)
Total working population: 654 582

U.N. group no.		*Percentage*
0	Agriculture, forestry, fishing and hunting	36.1
1	Mining and quarrying	0.7
2/3	Manufacturing	13.7
4	Construction	7.6
5	Electricity, gas, water and sanitary services	0.5
6	Commerce	9.2
7	Transport. storage and communications	3.0
8	Services	20.3
9	Others	8.9

		Year(s)
Life expectancy at birth (years): male	62.6	1959–61 av.
female	66.6	1959–61 av.
Infant mortality (per '000)	37.4*	1965
Crude birth rate (per '000)	39.5*	1960–5 av.
Crude death rate (per '000)	8.5*	1960–5 av.
Population per physician	2 020	1964
Population per hospital bed	260 *a*	1966
School enrolment: age 5–19 years (percentage)	81	1963–4 av.
age over 19 years (per 100 000 population)	95 *b*	1963–5 av.

a government hospitals only. *b* universities only.

COMMUNICATIONS

		Year(s)
Motor vehicles in use ('000s): private	49.5	1963–5 av.
commercial	18.7	1963–5 av.
Railway track (km.)	421 *a*	1964
Mail per capita: domestic	27	1963–5 av.
foreign received	21	1963–5 av.
foreign sent	16	1963–5 av.
Telephones (per '000 urban population)	2.8	1967
Radio receivers (per '000 population)	154	1963–5 av.
Television sets (per '000 population)	10.7	1963–5 av.
Daily newspapers (per '000 population)	71	1962

a The Jamaica Railway Corporation also works 31 km. of track on behalf of one of the bauxite companies.

FINANCE
Currency unit: The Jamaican dollar replaced the Jamaican pound in 1969 at the rate J$1 to J£0.5

Exchange rates	1965 *a*	1960 *a*
Per $ U.S.	0.357	0.357
Per £ sterling	1.0	1.0

		Year(s)
National Income (million $ U.S.)	728	1965
G.N.P. per capita ($ U.S.)	460	1966
Rate of increase of G.N.P. per capita	2.3	1960–4 av.
Foreign trade (percentage of G.D.P.)	56	1963–5 av.

a rate for Jamaican pounds.

TRADING

Total trade (in million $ U.S.)	*1965*	*1955*	*1938*
Exports (f.o.b.)	220	96	25
Imports (c.i.f.)	289	128	32

Main trading partners (percentage of total value)

Exports	*1965 a*	*1955 a*	*Imports*	*1965*	*1955*
U.S.A.	38	16	U.S.A.	31	21
U.K.	27	51	U.K.	25	40
Canada	16	20	Canada	11	12
Norway	7	6	Venezuela	6	na
Sweden	2	1	Japan	3	1
Bahamas	2	—	Germany F.R.	3	2
Germany F.R.	1	1	France	2	1

Distribution of trade (percentage of total value)

Exports	*1965*	*1955*
Bauxite and alumina	47	27
Sugar and sugar preparations	22	35
Fruit and vegetables	13	20
Petroleum products	4	—
Rum	2	3
Imports		
Manufactured goods	57	57
(machinery and transport equipment)	(22)	(20)
(textiles and clothing)	(8)	(10)
Food	20	20
(cereals)	(7)	(9)
Crude materials and fuels	12	13
(mineral fuels)	(9)	(9)

a These are percentages of national exports‡ which comprised 95% of general exports in 1955 and 1965.

PRODUCTION, EXPORTS AND IMPORTS

Years: **1963–5 average** and *1953–5 average* Units: '000 metric tons unless otherwise indicated

1. CEREALS, etc.

	Production		Exports		Imports	
Cassava	**9.0**	*17.0*				
Maize (corn)	**4.3***	*12.0*	—	—	**21.6***	na
Oats	—	—	—	—	**1.0***	—
Potatoes	**11.0**	*2.7*	—	—	**3.2**	na
Rice	**3.7**	*14.3*	—	—	**27.9**	*15.0*
Sweet potatoes/yams	**214.0***	*64.0*				
Wheat	—	—	—	—	**1.0***	*0.8*

2. FRUIT, etc.

	Production		Exports		Imports	
Apples	—	—	—	—	**0.6**[2]	na
Bananas	**299.3**	*249.3*	**180.8**	*163.1*	—	—
Coconuts	**114.7** *e*	na	**0.2**	—	—	—
Grapes	—	—	—	—	**0.2**[2]	na
Lemons	**10.7**	*8.7*	—	—	—	—
Oranges	**64.0**	*67.0*	**4.1**	*2.7*	—	—
Other citrus fruit	**32.0**	*24.0*	**6.7**	*1.4*	—	—
Raisins	—	—	—	—	**0.5**[2]	na
Tomatoes	**3.0**	*4.3*				
Wine *b*	—	—	—	—	**3.2**[2]	na

b '000 hectolitres. *e* no. in millions.

3. BEVERAGES, FOREST PRODUCTS, etc.

	Production		Exports		Imports	
Cocoa	**1.7**	*2.7*	**1.7**	*1.6*	—	—
Coffee	**1.8**	*3.7*	**0.9**	*1.7*	—	—
Sugar: cane	**4 833.7***	*3 689.7*				
raw	**490.2**	*380.0*	**418.6**	*298.3*	—	*0.3*
Tea	—	—	—	—	**0.2**[2]	na
Tobacco: leaf	**2.7***	*0.5**	**0.3**	—	**1.0**	*0.6*
cigars	**21.0** *e*	*18.5e*	**7.0** *e*	*9.9e*	—	*1.2*[2] *a* (cigars and cigarettes)
cigarettes	**931.0** *e*	*585.3e*	na	na	**0.1**	
Softwood *j*	—	—	**0.2**	—	**106.4**	*54.6*[2]
Hardwood *j*	**4.7***	*4.8*	**0.2**	*0.3*	**16.4**	*6.1*
Newsprint	—	—	—	—	**5.9**[2]	*0.8*
Other paper	—	—	—	—	**18.7**[2]	—[2]

a million $ U.S. *e* no. in millions *j* '000 cu. metres of roundwood equivalent.

4. VEGETABLE OILSEEDS AND OILS

	Production		Exports		Imports	
Castor oil	—	—	—	—	**0.02**[2]	—
Copra	**15.80**	*8.30*	**0.10**	—	—	—
Coconut oil	na	na	**0.02**	—	**0.21**[2]	*0.08*
Groundnuts	—	—	—	—	**0.06**	—
Linseed	—	—	—	—	**0.01**[2]	—
Linseed oil	na	—	—	—	**0.25**[2]	—
Olive oil	—	—	—	—	**0.04**[2]	—
Palm oil	—	—	—	—	—	*0.01*[2]
Soya beans	—	—	—	—	**0.09**[2]	—
Soya bean oil	na	—	—	—	**0.04**[2]	—

5. LIVESTOCK‡, ANIMAL PRODUCTS, etc.

	Production		Exports		Imports	
Chickens *d*	**2 076.7***	*1 900.2*[2]				
Cattle *d*	**240.0**	*248.0*	**0.1**	—	—	—
dairy cows *d*	**30.3***	na				
Goats *d*	**269.0***	*350.0*	—	—	—	—
Sheep *d*	**10.0**	*17.0*	—	—	—	—
Horses *d*	**5.0**	*13.0*				
Pigs *d*	**128.0**	*145.3*	—	—	—	—
Bacon/ham	**17.0*** (bacon/ham and meat 'A')	*16.3*	—	—	**2.5**[2]	na
Meat‡: 'A'			—	—	**2.9**[2]	na
'B'	**8.0***	*4.1*	—	—	**3.6**[2]	na
Butter	—	—	—	—[2]	**3.3**	*0.8*
Cheese	—	—	—	—[2]	**1.5**	*0.6*
Eggs	**5.0***	na	—	—	**0.3**[2]	na
Fish	**15.5**	*6.0*[2]	—	—	**17.3**	na
Milk	**32.3**	*40.0*[2]	**0.2**	*0.7**	**59.0**[2]	*12.7**
Hides/skins	**1.3**[2]	*1.6*	—	—	—	—

d no. in thousands.

continued

PRODUCTION, EXPORTS AND IMPORTS *continued*

6. FIBRES, TEXTILES, etc.

	Production		Exports		Imports	
Abaca	—	—	—	—	**0.1**[2]	—
Agaves (sisal etc.)	**0.4**	*0.2*	—	—	**0.3**[2]	*0.1*
Cotton lint	—	—	—	—	**1.2**[2]	—
Jute	—	—	**2.3**[2]†	—	**3.4**[2]	—
Rubber, natural	—	—	—	—	**0.2**[2]	—
Cotton, woven fabrics	**0.8***	—	—	—	—	—
Rayon, woven fabrics	—	—	—	—	**1.3**	—

7. FUEL AND POWER

	Production		Exports		Imports	
Coal, 'A'‡	—	—	—	—	**1**	*14*
Coke	—	—	—	—	**1**	*1*
Electricity *h*: total	**723**	*130*[1]				
hydro	**142**	*80*[1]				
thermal	**581**	*50*[1]				
Oil, crude	—	—	—	—	**1 110**	na
Petroleum, refined	**986**	—[1]	**130**	*150*[1]†	**533**	*350*[1]

h million kWh.

8. IRON AND STEEL

	Production		Exports		Imports	
Iron/steel scrap	na	na	**3**	—	—	—

9. NON-FERROUS MINERALS AND METALS

	Production		Exports		Imports	
Gold *k*, bullion/coins, etc	—	—	—	—	**0.20**[1]‡	*0.10*[2]
Silver *k*, bullion	—	—	—	—	**1.00**	*1.13*
Asbestos: fibre	—	—	—	—	**0.21**	*0.03*[2]
manufactured	—	—	—	—	**1.92**	*1.39*[2]
Mica	—	—	—	—	**0.09**	—
Aluminium: bauxite	**7 866.94**	*1 979.03*	**6 067.00** *p*	*1 940.90*	—	—
alumina	**750.07**	na	**749.95**	*180.06*	—	—
aluminium	—	—	—	—	**1.76**	—
Copper, metal	—	—	—	—	**0.16**[2]	*2.76*[2]
Lead, metal	—	—	—	—	**0.22**	*0.17*
Tin, metal	—	—	—	—	**0.17**	—
Zinc, metal	—	—	—	—	**0.06**	—

k '000 fine troy oz. *p* estimated dry equivalent of actual exports which contain 8–14% free moisture.

10. CHEMICALS *n* AND FERTILIZERS

	Production		Exports		Imports	
Organic chemicals:						
Benzene	—		—		na	
Butadiene	—		—		na	
Ethylene	—		—		na	
Methanol	—		—		na	
Phenol	—		—		na	
Phthalic anhydride	—		—		na	
Styrene monomer	—		—		na	
Urea	—		—		**2.0**[1]	
Inorganic chemicals:						
Ammonia	—		—		—	
Carbon black	—		—		na	
Chlorine	—		—		**0.1**	
Nitric acid	—		—		—	
Sodium carbonate	—		—		**2.1**	
Sodium hydroxide	—		—		**63.0**	
Sulphuric acid	na		—		**0.2**	
Plastics:						
Polyamides	—		—		na	
Polyethylene	—		—		na	
Polyvinyl chloride	—		—		na	
Fertilizers:						
Potash	—	—	—	—	**7.9**	*2.0*
Sulphur	—	—	—	—	**1.1**	—

n data not available for years 1953–5.

11. INDUSTRY

	Production		Exports		Imports	
Alcoholic beverages			**3.8** *ar*	*2.6ar*	—	—
beer *b*	**218.0**	*81.4*				
spirits *b*	na	na				
Cement	**266.3**	*102.0*	**42.3**	*7.7*	**1.7**	*1.7*
Electrical engineering *a*	—	—	—	—	**9.2**	*4.1*[2]
Railway vehicles *a*	—	—	—	—	**0.4**	—
Motor vehicles *a*	—	—	—	—	**13.1**	*4.3*

a million $ U.S. *b* '000 hectolitres. *r* rum only.

JAPAN

EASTERN ASIA

Japan replaced her ancient imperialist regime by a new constitution in 1947. The Emperor remains a symbol of unity but has no powers related to government. After World War II Japan was occupied by the Allies until 1952 when her independence was regained. The Bonin Islands were returned by the U.S.A. to Japan in 1968, and the Ryuku Islands are scheduled for return in 1972.

AREA: 369 662 sq. km. (142 726 sq. miles)

LAND USE: (percentage of total)	*1960*	*1951*
Arable and orchard	16.2	13.8
Permanent meadow and pasture	2.6	3.7
Forest and woodland	68.7	61.0
City areas, waste and other land	12.5	21.5

POPULATION: 98 274 961 (1965 census)
Largest city: TŌKYŌ, capital; population: 11 005 000 (1966)
Distribution of working population (1965)
Total working population: 48 980 000*

U.N. group no.		*Percentage*
0	Agriculture, forestry, fishing and hunting	26.9
1	Mining and quarrying	0.8
2/3	Manufacturing	23.6
4	Construction	6.2
5	Electricity, gas, water and sanitary services	19.6 (5 and 7)
7	Transport, storage and communications	
6	Commerce	6.2
8	Services	15.9
9	Others	0.8

		Year(s)
Life expectancy at birth (years): male	68.4	1966
female	73.6	1966
Infant mortality (per '000)	18.5	1965
Crude birth rate (per '000)	18.6	1965
Crude death rate (per '000)	7.2	1965
Accidental deaths (per 100 000 population) caused by motor vehicles	16.5	1965
due to other causes	24.4	1965
Population per physician	900	1965
Population per hospital bed	90	1966
School enrolment: age 5–19 years (percentage)	86	1963–4 av.
age over 19 years (per 100 000 population)	1 038	1963–5 av.

COMMUNICATIONS

		Year(s)
Motor vehicles in use ('000s): private	1 696.3	1963–5 av.
commercial	3 561	1963–5 av.
Railway track (km.)	27 985	1963
Mail per capita: domestic	92	1963–5 av.
foreign received	1	1963–5 av.
foreign sent	1	1963–5 av.

continued

COMMUNICATIONS—*continued*

Telephones (per '000 urban population)	16.1	1967
Radio licences (per '000 population)	204	1963–5 av.
Television licences (per '000 population)	171.4	1963–5 av.
Daily newspapers (per '000 population)	429.5	1962–4 av.

FINANCE
Currency unit: The yen

Exchange rates	*1965*	*1960*	*1950*	*1938*
Per $ U.S.	360.9	358.3	360.8	3.7
Per £ sterling	1 010.5	1 003.2	1 010.7	17.02

		Year(s)
National Income (million $ U.S.)	68 189	1965
G.N.P. per capita ($ U.S.)	860	1966
Rate of increase of G.N.P. per capita	9.7	1960–4 av.
Foreign trade (percentage of G.D.P.)	19	1963–5 av.

TRADING

Total trade (in million $ U.S.)	*1965*	*1955*	*1938**
Exports (f.o.b.)	8 452	2 011	1 109
Imports (c.i.f.)	8 170	2 471	1 070

Main trading partners (percentage of total value)

Exports	*1965*	*1955*	*1938**	*Imports*	*1965*	*1955*	*1938**
U.S.A.	30	23	16	U.S.A.	29	31	34
Liberia *a*	4	3	na	Australia	7	7	3
Australia	4	3	3	Canada	4	4	3
Hong Kong	3	4	1	Kuwait	4	1	na
China P.R.	3	1	43	Philippines	3	4	1
Philippines	3	3	1	Iran	3	1	na
Thailand	3	3	1	U.S.S.R.	3	—	—

Distribution of trade (percentage of total value)

Exports	*1965*	*1955*	*1938**
Manufactured goods	86	82	na
(machinery and transport equipment)	(31)	(12)	(16)
(textiles and clothing)	(17)	(29)	(41)
(iron and steel)	(15)	(13)	(6)
Imports			
Crude materials and fuels	59	61	na
(petroleum and petroleum products)	(16)	(9)	(12)
Manufactured goods	17	9	na
(machinery and transport equipment)	(9)	(5)	(10)
Food	17	25	na
(cereals)	(9)	(18)	(1)
Chemicals	5	3	2

a mainly ships.

continued

PRODUCTION, EXPORTS AND IMPORTS

Years: **1963–5 average** and *1953–5 average*   Units: '000 metric tons unless otherwise indicated

1. CEREALS, etc.

	Production		Exports		Imports	
Barley	**1 065.3**	*2 360.7*	—	*5.4*	**426.2**	*682.0*
Maize (corn)	**87.7**	*74.0*	—	—	**3 102.7**	*241.4*
Millets/sorghum	**44.0***	*112.6*	—	*0.8*	**1 110.3**	*40.2*
Oats	**135.3**	*158.3*	**0.1**	—	**9.7**	*0.6*
Potatoes	**3 793.0**	*2 688.7*	**17.5**	*28.6*	—	—
Rice	**16 366.0**	*12 169.3*	**0.2**	*1.9*	**534.8**	*1 252.6*
Rye	**1.7**	*2.0*	—	—	**19.5**	*0.1*
Sweet potatoes/yams	**5 831.0**	*5 932.3*				
Wheat	**1 082.3**	*1 452.7*	—	*0.6*	**3 471.8**	*2 053.7*

2. FRUIT, etc.

	Production		Exports		Imports	
Apples	**1 125.7**	*438.3*	**16.7**	*10.1*	—	—
Bananas	—	—	—	—	**321.7**	*25.4*
Cherries	na	na	—	—	—	—
Grapes	**203.0**	*58.0*	—	—	—	—
Lemons/grapefruit	**64.3**	*22.0*	**0.2**	*0.1*[2]	**13.2**	*1.0*[2]
Oranges	**1 368.0**	*540.0*	**14.4**	*3.7*	**0.8**	*2.4*
Peaches	**211.7**	*61.3*	—	—	—	—
Pears	**346.7**	*108.7*	**5.3**	*5.0*[2]	—	—
Plums	na	*47.1*	—	—	—	—
Raisins	—	—	—	—	**16.6**	*1.3*
Tomatoes	**500.7**	*146.0*				
Wine *b*	**99.7**	na	**1.3**	—	**5.3**	*3.3*

b '000 hectolitres.

3. BEVERAGES, FOREST PRODUCTS, etc.

	Production		Exports		Imports	
Cocoa	—	—	—	—	**29.2**	*3.6*
Coffee	—	—	**0.2**	—	**19.3**	*3.0*
Sugar: beet	**1 405**	*313*				
cane	**648**	*65*				
raw (beet) }	**190**	*47*	**6.5**	*22.4*	**1 559.2**	*1 059.8*
(cane) }	**251** *n*	—*n*				
Tea	**81**	*66*	**4.0**	*15.0*	**2.9**	*0.7*
Tobacco: leaf	**188**	*122*	**7.1**	*0.6*	**23.3**	*8.2*
cigars }	**2** *e*	—				
cigarettes }	**164 289** *e*	*95 718e*	—	*0.3*[2]	**6.2** *a*	—[2]
tobacco/snuff }	**2**	*7*				
Softwood *j*	**34 673**	*29 337*	**187.0**	*146.1*	**6 703.0**	*319.3*
Hardwood *j*	**25 504**	*24 638*	**420.2**	*375.0*	**8 781.0**	*1 557.0*
Wood pulp	**4 918**	*1 682*	**3.6**	*1.3*	**501.1**	*105.7*
Newsprint	**1 131***	*437*	**6.2**	*9.1*	**29.7**	*5.0*
Other paper	**5 901**	*1 525*	**217.3**	*42.5*	**138.0**	*1.3*

a million $ U.S.   *e* no. in millions.   *j* '000 cu. metres of roundwood equivalent.
n in addition, non-centrifugal sugar 17* (1963–5 av.) and 23* (1953–5 av.).

4. VEGETABLE OILSEEDS AND OILS

	Production		Exports		Imports	
Castor seed	—	—	—	—	**37.28**	*21.87*
Castor oil	na	na	**2.31**	*0.21*	—	—
Copra	—	—	—	*0.03*†	**96.01**	*40.37*
Coconut oil	na	na	**0.53**	*0.07*	—	*0.01*
Cottonseed	—	*0.30*	—	—	**196.93**	*45.63*
Cottonseed oil	na	na	**0.02**	*0.10*[2]	**7.27**	*1.32*
Groundnuts	**96.13**	*27.00p*	—	—	**17.89**	*7.73*
Groundnut oil	na	na	**0.43**	*0.02*	—	—
Linseed	**2.33**	*3.30*	**0.14**	*0.07*	**98.69**	*50.87*
Linseed oil	na	na	**0.82**	*0.01*	**0.29**	*0.03*
Olive oil	—	—	**0.01**	—	**0.36**	*0.32*
Palm kernels	—	—	—	—[2]	**24.39**	*13.20*
Palm kernel oil	na	na	**2.00**	—	**0.28**	—
Palm oil	—	—	**0.27**†	—	**17.10**	*15.53*
Rapeseed	**123.30**	*259.67*	—	*0.50*	**94.98**	*11.10*
Rapeseed oil	na	na	**2.85**	*0.35*	—	—
Sesame seed	**4.33**	*5.53*	**0.02**	—	**33.27**	*12.53*
Soya beans	**262.70**	*437.33*	**0.17**	*0.63*	**1 666.33**	*588.13*
Soya bean oil	na	na	**4.31**	*6.87*	**0.78**	*0.10*
Sunflower seed	—	—	—	—	**5.65**	na
Tung oil	—	—	—	—	**3.94**	*3.25*

p dried.

5. LIVESTOCK‡, ANIMAL PRODUCTS, etc.

	Production		Exports		Imports	
Chickens *d*	**108 794**	*44 287*				
Cattle *d*	**3 368**	*2 880q*	**1.6**	*2.6*	**1.2**	*1.6*
dairy cows *d*	**1 937**	—				
Goats *d* }	**397**	*506q*	**0.1**	—	**0.1**	—
Sheep *d* }	**290**	*735q*				
Horses *d*	**396**	*945*				
Pigs *d*	**3 578**	*857q*	**0.8**	*0.9*	**2.3**	—
Meat‡: 'A'	**522**	*181*	**0.1**	*0.1*	**65.5**	*0.7*
'B'	**184***	na	**28.2**	—	**44.6**	*0.1*
Butter	**22** *r*	*6r*	—	—	**0.3**	*1.3*
Cheese	**13**	*1*	—	—	**8.2**	*1.0*
Eggs	**924**	*324*	**0.9**	*1.3*	**0.1**	—
Fish	**6 652**	*4 683*	**547.5**	*150.0*[1]*	**182.6**	*14.9*[1]*
Milk	**3 003**	*873*	**23.3**	*2.1*	**742.5**	*105.6*
Whale oil	**152**	*66*	—	—	—	—
Hides/skins	**44**	*18*[2]	—	*0.3*[2]	**154.0**[1]	*54.3*[2]
Wool	**1**	*2*	**0.1**	—	**140.0**	*49.7*

d no. in thousands.   *q* on farms only.   *r* factory produce only.

6. FIBRES, TEXTILES, etc.

	Production		Exports		Imports	
Abaca	—	—	—	—	**29.7**	*30.2*
Agaves (sisal etc.)	—	—	—	—	**13.3**	*7.6*
Cotton lint	—	—	**1.2**	—	**700.5**	*471.5*
Flax fibre	**4.2**	*5.3*	—	—	**9.9**	*3.2*
Hemp fibre	**0.7***	*2.6*	—	—	**0.2**	*0.1*
Jute	**0.7**	*1.3*	**1.7**	*0.3*	**86.2**	*30.3*
Rubber: natural	—	—	**1.8**	*0.2**	**206.0**	*90.9*
synthetic	**124.8**	—	**18.4**	—	**53.8** *s*	*2.7*
Silk *f*	**18 881.0**	*15 964.0*	**3 037.7**	*4 571.0*	**1 529.0**	*90.0*
Cotton: yarn	**511.1**	*395.8*	**14.3**	*11.1*	—	—
woven fabrics	**394.8**	*317.4*	**139.2**	*110.0*	—	—
Rayon: fibre/yarn	**474.1**	*284.6*	**100.1**	*9.3*	**0.9**[2]	—
woven fabrics	**164.1** *n*	*162.2*	**68.9**	*64.4*	—	—
Non-cellulosic fibre/yarn	**320.2**	*10.8*	**38.5**	—	**0.8**	—
Wool: yarn	**152.1**	*81.7*	**8.6**	*3.5*	**0.3**	*0.4*
woven fabrics	**128.8**	*141.3p*	**10.5** *q*	*3.4*	**1.4** *q*	*0.6*

f metric tons.   *n* excl. acetate fabrics.   *p* million square metres.   *q* incl. wool/silk mixture fabrics.   *s* incl. imports for re-export.

7. FUEL AND POWER

	Production		Exports		Imports	
Coal: 'A'‡	**50 837**	*42 420*	**76**	*527 r*	**13 819**	} *3 824*
'B'	**240**	*1 370*	—	—	—	
Coke	na	na	**18**	*13*	**16**	—
Electricity *h*: total	**177 314**	*59 620*				
hydro	**71 411**	*45 070*				
nuclear	**3**	—				
thermal	**105 900**	*14 550*[1]				
Natural gas *i*	**1 970**	*137*[1]	—	—	—	—
Oil, crude	**717**	*310*[1]	**3**	na	**61 746**	*6 750*[1]
Petroleum, refined	**54 570**	*6 790*[1]	**613**	—	**12 447**	*3 380*[1]

h million kWh.   *i* million cu. metres.   *r* incl. bunkers.

8. IRON AND STEEL

	Production		Exports		Imports	
Iron ore	**1 406** *m*	*890m*	—	—	**32 174**	*4 918*
Pig iron	**24 348**	*4 943*	**29**	*71*	**2 523**	*10*
Steel ingots/castings	**37 487**	*8 273*	**192**	*199*	**5**	*1*
Iron/steel scrap	na	na	**3**	*2*	**4 365**	*1 135*
Iron/steel products	na	na	**967**	*189*	**136**	*12*

a million $ U.S.   *m* metal content.

9. NON-FERROUS MINERALS AND METALS

	Production		Exports		Imports	
Diamonds *a*	—	—	**1.01**†	—	**27.44** *t*	*0.91*
Gold *k*, ore *m*	**470.70** *u*	*237.00u*	—	—	na	na
Platinum group metals *k*	**4.18**	*1.17*	—	—	**387.14**	*21.50*
Silver *k*: ore *m*	**8 838.70** *u*	*6 046.70u*	—	—	na	na
bullion	na	na	**1 054.00**	*3 777.33*	**6 117.67**	—
Asbestos: fibre	**15.92**	*5.55*	**0.31**	*0.04*	**130.99**	*19.86*
manufactured	na	na	**32.80**	*1.62*	**1.35**	*0.58*
Mica	—	—	**0.06**†	—	**5.03**	*1.24*
Aluminium: bauxite	—	—	**0.60**†	*0.15n*†	**1 579.69**	*295.80*
alumina	**575.00**	na	**105.96** *p*	—	**51.23** *p*	—
aluminium	**261.20**	*52.04*	**56.22**	*19.39*	**52.35**	*3.44*
Antimony: ore	**0.29** *m*	*0.30m*	—	—	**5.75**	*2.31*
metal	na	na	—	*0.01*	**0.55**	*0.01*
Cadmium	**1.24**	*0.28*	**0.75**	na	**0.02**	—
Chrome: ore	**43.17** *m*	*32.30m*	**1.54**	—	**327.75**	*45.83*
metal	na	na	**11.85**	*2.55*	**2.74**	*0.22*
Cobalt: ore	—	—	—	—	—	*0.10*[2]
metal	—	—	**0.01**†	—	**1.55**	*5.65*
Copper: ore	**106.64** *m*	*66.05m*	—	—	**613.06**	*38.06*
metal	**334.19**	*71.17*	**33.73**	*22.75*	**189.44**	*21.95*
Lead: ore	**53.91** *m*	*22.56m*	—	—	**62.53**	*15.39*
metal	**99.18**	*24.30*	**5.66**	*0.29*	**45.60**	*11.24*
Magnesium: dolomite	**1 753.28**	na	**2.15**	—	**12.74**	—
magnesite	—	—	—	—	**24.54**	*57.92*
metal/salts	**3.05** *x*	*0.05x*	**3.31**	—	**0.67**	*1.07*
Manganese: ore	**288.12**	*186.51*	**0.30**	*0.27*	**792.34** *q*	*133.37*
metal	na	na	**14.49**	*26.87*	—	—
Mercury *f*	**161.06**	*248.90*	**39.60**	*1.20*	**1 194.20**	*127.10*
Molybdenum *f*: ore	**296.65** *m*	*194.44m*	—	—	**3 921.60**	*389.70*
metal	na	na	—	—	**60.30**	—
Nickel: ore	—	—	—	—	**934.40**	*218.72*
metal	—	—	**0.27**	*1.50*	**10.26**[2]	*0.08*
Tin: ore	**0.83** *m*	*0.80m*	—	—	**1.72**	—
metal	**1.88**	*0.90*	**0.51**	—	**15.24**	*5.32*
Titanium minerals	**1.91** *r*	*3.31r*	**34.70**	*4.41*	**180.10**	*34.56*
Tungsten: ore	**0.79**	*0.80*	—	*0.16*	**2.23**	*0.15*
metal	na	na	**0.06**	*0.11*	—	—
Vanadium: ore	—	—	—	—	**0.03**	*0.05*[2]
metal	na	na	—	—	—	*0.03v*
Zinc: ore	**211.81**	*104.89*	—	*5.71*	**272.10**	—
metal	**322.05**	*97.86*	**57.02**[1]	*2.61*	**28.25**	*6.97*
Zirconium minerals	**0.79**	—	—	—	**25.98**[1]	—

a million $ U.S.   *f* metric tons.   *k* '000 fine troy oz.   *m* metal content.   *n* cryolite.   *p* hydrate.   *q* incl. manganiferous iron ore.   *r* titanium slag.   *t* incl. synthetic dust.   *u* incl. metal refined from imported ore.   *v* ferro-vanadium.   *x* primary magnesium only.

continued

na: data not available.   — negligible or nil.   [1] one year only.   [2] two year average.   * estimate.   ‡ see appendix.   † re-exports.

PRODUCTION, EXPORTS AND IMPORTS *continued*

10. CHEMICALS *n* AND FERTILIZERS

	Production	Exports	Imports
Organic chemicals:			
Benzene	**320.7**	**0.2**	**118.0**
Butadiene	**83.6**	—	—
Ethylene	**542.5**	—	—
Methanol	**404.2**	**43.5**	—
Phenol	**86.1**	**0.1**	—
Phthalic anhydride	**92.9**	**3.8**	**2.3**
Styrene monomer	**135.7**	**0.5**	**5.0**
Urea	**1 126.0**	**655.9**	—
Inorganic chemicals:			
Ammonia	**1 927.0**	**57.8**	—
Carbon black	**104.9**	**8.0**	**2.9**
Chlorine	**219.3**	**0.2**[1]	—
Nitric acid	na	**3.0**	**0.1**
Sodium carbonate	**714.0**	**28.3**	**4.6**
Sodium hydroxide	**1 245.0**	**42.7**	—
Sulphuric acid	**5 339.7**	**1.3**	—
Plastics:			
Polyamides	na	na	na
Polyethylene	**303.0**	**41.6**	**3.1**
Polyvinyl chloride	**435.2**	**56.6**	**2.3**

continued

10. CHEMICALS AND FERTILIZERS—*continued*

	Production		Exports		Imports	
Fertilizers:						
Phosphates	—	—	**4.1**	—	**2 265.7**	*1 363.2*
Potash	—	*0.4 y*	**12.7**	—	**1 077.7**	*628.9*
Pyrites	**1 755.4** *x*	*1 084.2x*	—	—	**29.4**[1]	*0.2*
Sulphur: native }	**225.7**	*193.4*				
recovered }	**22.3**	—	**0.2**	*11.9*	**30.8**	—

n data not available for years 1953–5.   *x* sulphur content.   *y* K_2O content.

11. INDUSTRY

	Production		Exports		Imports	
Aircraft *a*	**148.0*** *n*	—	—	*0.1*	**65.0**	*9.3*
Alcoholic beverages			—	*1.9a*	—	*0.8a*
beer *b*	**19 037.0**	*4 016.7*				
Cement	**31 555.0**	*9 966.7*	**1 736.7**	*974.0*	—	—
Electrical engineering *a*	**4 768.6**[2]	na	**644.0**	*27.0*[2]	**110.0**	*15.3*[2]
Locomotives *c*	**363.0**	na	na	na	na	na
Railway vehicles *a*	na	na	**38.9**	*13.0*	—	*0.9*
Machine tools *a*	**305.0**[1]	na	—	—	**71.5**	—
Merchant ships *g*	**3 939.0**	*600.0*	**2 350.0**	*309.0*	—	na
Motor vehicles			**313.6** *a*	*8.4a*	**31.6** *a*	*21.1a*
commercial *d*	**1 139.8**	*46.1*				
private *d*	**561.2**	*9.6*				

a million $ U.S.   *b* '000 hectolitres.   *c* no. of units.   *d* no. in thousands.   *g* '000 G.R.T.   *n* 1965–7 av.

JORDAN

MIDDLE EAST

Jordan is a constitutional monarchy, recognized in 1946 as a sovereign independent state. Since the Arab–Israeli war of 1967 a portion of Jordanian territory has been occupied by Israel. There has been considerable guerilla extremist activity within the country.

AREA: 97 740 sq. km. (37 730 sq. miles) (pre-1967)

LAND USE: (percentage of total)

	1965	*1954*
Arable and orchard	11.6	9.2
Permanent meadow and pasture	2.2	7.7
Forest and woodland, incl. unstocked land	0.7	5.4
City areas, waste and other land	85.5	77.7

POPULATION: 2 145 000 (1967 U.N. estimate)

Largest city: 'AMMĀN, capital; population: 330 396 (city proper, 1967)

Distribution of working population (1961)
Total working population: 389 978

U.N. group no.		*Percentage*
0	Agriculture, forestry, fishing and hunting	35.3
1	Mining and quarrying	2.4
2/3	Manufacturing	8.4
4	Construction	10.3
5	Electricity, gas, water and sanitary services	0.4
6	Commerce	8.0
7	Transport, storage and communications	3.1
8	Services	13.7
9	Others	18.4

		Year(s)
Life expectancy at birth (years): male	52.6*	} 1959–63 av.
female	52.0*	
Infant mortality (per '000)	42.0*	1965
Crude birth rate (per '000)	48.1	1965
Crude death rate (per '000)	5.6*	1965
Accidental deaths (per 100 000 population) caused by motor vehicles	na	
due to other causes	24.2	1965
Population per physician	4 040	1966
Population per hospital bed	580	1966
School enrolment: age 5–19 years (percentage)	71	1963–4 av.
age over 19 years (per 100 000 population)	111	1963–5 av.

COMMUNICATIONS

		Year(s)
Motor vehicles in use ('000s): private	9.7	} 1963–5 av.
commercial	5.9	
Railway track (km.)	402	1969
Mail per capita: domestic	4	} 1962–4 av.
foreign received	2	
foreign sent	3	
Telephones (per '000 urban population)	1.5	1967
Radio licences (per '000 population)	91	1963–5 av.
Daily newspapers (per '000 population)	19*	1962

FINANCE

Currency unit: The Jordan dinar, at par with the pound sterling until 1968

Exchange rates	*1965*	*1960*	*1958*
Per $ U.S.	0.357	0.357	0.215

		Year(s)
National Income (million $ U.S.)	339	1964
G.N.P. per capita ($ U.S.)	220	1966
Foreign trade (percentage of G.D.P.)	42	1963–5 av.

TRADING

Total trade (in million $ U.S.)	*1965*	*1955*	*1938*
Exports (f.o.b.)	28	8	3
Imports (c.i.f.)	157	76	6

Main trading partners (percentage of total value)

Exports	*1965*	*1955*	*Imports*	*1965*	*1955*
Lebanon	26	27	U.S.A.	15	10
Kuwait	13	2	U.K.	12	19
Saudi Arabia	12	2	Germany F.R.	9	9
Syria	11	27	Lebanon	7	11
Yugoslavia	9	—	Syria	5	7
India	8	3	Japan	5	3
Iraq	7	17	Italy	4	2

Distribution of trade (percentage of total value)

Exports	*1965*	*1955*
Food	50	46
(fruit and vegetables)	(43)	(38*)
Natural phosphates	31	na
Imports		
Manufactured goods	51	54
(machinery and transport equipment)	(18)	(15*)
(textiles and clothing)	(13)	(12*)
Food	26	33
(cereals)	(7)	(13*)
(fruit and vegetables)	(6)	(2*)
Crude materials and fuels	10	11
Chemicals	6	2

continued

na: data not available.   — negligible or nil.   [1] one year only.   [2] two year average.   * estimate.   ‡ see appendix.   † re-exports.

JORDAN *continued*

PRODUCTION, EXPORTS AND IMPORTS

Years: **1963–5 average** and *1953–5 average* Units: '000 metric tons unless otherwise indicated

	Production		Exports		Imports	
1. CEREALS, etc.						
Barley	72.0	57.3	2.0	5.9	14.1	2.6
Maize (corn)	—	—	—	0.1[2]	7.2	0.5
Millets/sorghum	8.7	17.0[2]	—	0.9	8.3	0.5
Potatoes	13.7	na	2.1	2.2	15.9	5.1
Rice	—	—	—	—	23.2	10.3
Wheat	216.3	137.3	0.6	1.6[2]	35.2	22.4
2. FRUIT, etc.						
Apples	5.0	4.0[2]	0.1	—	15.0	—
Bananas	11.0	10.0	3.0	3.6	1.7	0.2
Dates	1.0	—	—	—	7.2	10.2
Figs	19.7	29.0	—	—	—	—
Grapes	72.0	46.5[2]	0.7	0.1	2.6	0.3
Lemons	8.7	na	1.3	—	2.5	—
Oranges	30.7	na	1.4	10.2[2]	5.2	0.2[2]
Other citrus fruit	—	—	0.3	—	0.2	—
Olives	58.0	55.0[2]				
Pears	—	—	—	0.3[2]	0.5	0.2[2]
Raisins	1.2	0.9[2]*	—	—	—	0.1
Tomatoes	230.7	46.0[2]				
Wine *b*	—	—	—	—	0.1	—

b '000 hectolitres.

	Production		Exports		Imports	
3. BEVERAGES, FOREST PRODUCTS, etc.						
Cocoa	—	—	—	—	0.1	—
Coffee	—	—	—	—	1.7	0.7
Sugar, raw	—	—	—	—	54.7	25.8
Tea	—	—	—	—	1.7	0.8
Tobacco: leaf	1.6*	0.8[2]	—	0.1[2]	0.6	0.4
cigarettes	1 224.0*e*	446.0*e*	0.4[2]	—[2]	0.1*an*	—
Softwood *j*	—	1.1	—	—	} 79.6[2]	{ 31.1[2]
Hardwood *j*	17.7	72.7	—	—		—
Newsprint	—	—	—	—	0.8	0.2[2]
Other paper	—	—	—	—	5.1	2.5

a million $ U.S. *e* no. in millions. *j* '000 cu. metres of roundwood equivalent. *n* incl. other tobacco products.

	Production		Exports		Imports	
4. VEGETABLE OILSEEDS AND OILS						
Castor oil	—	—	—	—	0.03	0.02
Coconut oil	—	—	—	—[2]	na	1.26[2]
Cottonseed oil	—	—	—	—	0.76	0.54
Groundnuts	—	—	0.01	—	0.80	—
Linseed oil	—	—	—	—	0.01	0.08
Olive oil	14.33*	10.67*	0.65	3.73	0.76	—
Sesame seed	1.60	3.90[2]	0.36	1.00	3.95	0.10
Soya bean oil	—	—	—	—[1]	6.14*	—[2]
5. LIVESTOCK‡, ANIMAL PRODUCTS, etc.						
Chickens *d*	1 773.0*	na				
Cattle *d*	62.0	42.0[2]	—	—	6.8	0.2[1]
Goats *d*	622.0	446.5	} —	—	194.8	na
Sheep *d*	782.3	293.5[2]				
Horses *d*	10.0*	na				
Meat‡: 'A'	10.3*	na	—	—	—	—
'B'	3.5*	na	—	—	—	—
5. LIVESTOCK, ANIMAL PRODUCTS, etc.—*continued*						
Butter	—	—	—[2]	—	0.2	—
Cheese	—	—	0.2†	0.1†	1.2	0.3
Eggs	4.1*	na	—	—	1.1	—
Fish	0.2	0.1	—	—	1.9	na
Milk	16.3	2.5[2]*	—	—	15.8	14.2*
Hides/skins	—	—	0.8[2]	—	0.7[2]	—
Wool	0.9	—	0.1	0.1	—	—

d no. in thousands.

	Production		Exports		Imports	
6. FIBRES, TEXTILES, etc.						
Agaves (sisal etc.)	—	—	—	—	0.1	—
Cotton lint	—	—	—	—	—	0.1
Rubber, natural	—	—	—	—	0.2	—
Cotton: yarn	—	—	—	—	0.3[1]	na
woven fabrics	—	—	—	—	3.2	na
Rayon, woven fabrics	—	—	—	—	2.1	na
Wool: yarn	—	—	—	—	0.2	na
woven fabrics	—	—	—	—	1.0	na
7. FUEL AND POWER						
Coal, 'A'‡	—	—	—	—	1	—
Electricity *h*: total	135	10[1]				
hydro	na	—				
thermal	na	10[1]				
Oil, crude	—	—	—	—	370	—
Petroleum, refined	310	—[1]	—	—	33	100[1]

h million kWh.

	Production		Exports		Imports	
8. IRON AND STEEL						
Steel ingots/castings	—	—	—	—	45	—
9. NON-FERROUS MINERALS AND METALS						
Asbestos, manufactured	—	—	—	—	na	—
Aluminium	—	—	—	—	0.32	—
Copper, metal	—	—	—	—	0.17	—
Lead, metal	—	—	—	—	0.34[1]	—
Tin, metal	—	—	—	—	0.02	—
10. CHEMICALS*n* AND FERTILIZERS						
Chemicals	—		—		na	
Fertilizers:						
Phosphates	669.0	92.8	529.6	77.7	—	—
Potash	—	—	—	—	4.0	—
Sulphur	—	—	—	—	2.1	—

n data not available for years 1953–5.

	Production		Exports		Imports	
11. INDUSTRY						
Aircraft *a*			—	—	1.3[2]	—
Alcoholic beverages			—	—	0.2[2]*a*	—
beer *b*	8.0	—				
Cement	302.7	48.3*	10.3	0.3	5.3	21.7
Electrical engineering *a*	—	—	—	0.2	6.5[2]	1.0
Motor vehicles *a*	—	—	—	—	10.9	1.7

a million $ U.S. *b* '000 hectolitres.

continued

KENYA

EAST AFRICA

Kenya, formerly a British East African protectorate, became an independent member of the Commonwealth in 1963 and achieved republican status the following year. Grants for development have been received from the U.K. and China P.R. Kenya is a member of the East African Community.

AREA: 582 600 sq. km. (224 960 sq. miles)

LAND USE: (percentage of total)	1961	1953
Arable and orchard	2.9	2.7
Permanent meadow and pasture	6.7	20.6
Forest and woodland	2.9	2.2
City areas, waste and other land	87.5	74.5

Sixty per cent of the land is unproductive due to lack of water, but revenue is gained from tourist and safari attractions in this area.

POPULATION: 9 948 000 (1967 estimate)

Largest city: NAIROBI, capital; population: 314 760 (1962)

Distribution of working population (1965)
Total working population: 5 940 000

U.N. group no.		*Percentage*
0	Agriculture, forestry, fishing and hunting	35.3
1	Mining and quarrying	0.4
2/3	Manufacturing	12.0
4	Construction	3.6
5	Electricity, gas, water and sanitary services	0.4
6	Commerce	9.2
7	Transport, storage and communications	6.1
8	Services	32.8
9	Others	0.2

		Year(s)
Life expectancy at birth (years)	42.5*	1962
Infant mortality (per '000)	34.2**a*	1965
Crude birth rate (per '000)	50**b*	1965
Crude death rate (per '000)	30**b*	1965
Population per physician	12 820	1964
Population per hospital bed	780	1966
School enrolment: age 5–19 years (percentage)	48	1963–4 av.
age over 19 years (per 100 000 population)	22	1963–5 av.

a non-Africans. *b* Africans.

continued

COMMUNICATIONS

		Year(s)
Motor vehicles in use ('000s): private	70.8	} 1963–5 av.
commercial	10.7	
Railway track (km.)	926	1969
Telephones (per '000 urban population)	0.6	1967
Radio receivers (per '000 population)	31	1963–5 av.
Television sets (per '000 population)	1	1963–5 av.
Daily newspapers (per '000 population)	9	1963–4 av.

FINANCE

Currency unity: The East African shilling

Exchange rates	*1965*	*1960*	*1950a*	*1938a*
Per $ U.S.	7.143	7.143	0.357	0.215
Per £ sterling	20.0	20.0	1.0	1.0

		Year
National Income (million $ U.S.)	725	1965
G.N.P. per capita ($ U.S.)	90	1966

a East African pounds of 20 shillings.

TRADING

Note—trade with Uganda and Tanganyika is excluded.

Total trade (in million $ U.S.)	*1965*	*1955*	*1955a*
Exports (f.o.b.)	145	78	299
Imports (c.i.f.)	249	200	417

Main trading partners (percentage of total value)

Exports	*1965*	*1955a*	*Imports*	*1965*	*1955a*
U.K.	21	28	U.K.	28	44
Germany F.R.	16	10	Japan	10	4
U.S.A.	6	12	U.S.A.	10	3
Netherlands	4	4	Germany F.R.	7	6
Canada	4	2	Iran	5	2
Japan	4	2	Kuwait	3	—
Sweden	3	—	France	3	3

Distribution of trade (percentage of total value)

Exports	*1965*	*Imports*	*1965*
Food	55	Manufactured goods	59
(coffee)	(30)	(machinery and transport equipment)	(26)
(tea)	(13)	Crude materials and fuels	13
Crude materials and fuel	33	(petroleum products)	(11)
(petroleum products)	(10)	Food	11
(sisal)	(8)	Chemicals	9
(pyrethrum)	(5)		

a refers to total trade for Kenya, Uganda and Tanganyika.

PRODUCTION, EXPORTS AND IMPORTS

Years: **1963–5 average** and *1953–5 average* Units: '000 metric tons unless otherwise indicated

	Production		Exports		Imports	
1. CEREALS, etc.						
Barley	14.0	15.0	—	—	—	—
Cassava	600.0*	na				
Maize (corn)	1 125.3**n*	119.7*n*	29.5	53.3	27.3	1.6[2]
Millets/sorghum	320.0*	na	0.5	0.8	3.4	0.6
Oats	1.3	10.7	—	—	—	—
Potatoes	192.5*[2]	na	1.6	0.9	—	—
Rice	17.0	na	0.1	0.2*s*	2.5	6.5
Sweet potatoes/yams	450.0*	na				
Wheat	126.0*	128.0[2]	—	—	4.8	10.9

n from farms and estates only. *s* incl. re-exports.

	Production		Exports		Imports	
2. FRUIT, etc.						
Apples	—	—	—	—	0.8	0.5
Coconuts	65.0[1]*e*	na	1.8[1]	0.1	—	—
Dates	—	—	—	0.1	0.3	0.9*
Grapes	—	—	—	—	0.1	0.1
Citrus fruit	—	—	—	0.5[2]	—	0.2[2]
Pineapples	25.3*	na	—	—	—	—
Raisins	—	—	—	—	0.2	0.1[2]
Wine *b*	—	—	0.1	—	7.3	5.3

b '000 hectolitres. *e* no. in millions.

	Production		Exports		Imports	
3. BEVERAGES, FOREST PRODUCTS, etc.						
Coffee	45.2*	18.4[2]	39.4	16.0	—	—
Sugar: cane	408.7*	na				
raw	33.9	16.3	0.3	—	43.9	31.5
Tea	19.6	7.5	21.6*s*	4.8	6.5	na
Tobacco: leaf	0.4	0.2*	—	—	0.1	0.4
cigarettes *e*	1 900.0*	106.7*p*	} —	—	na	—
tobacco/snuff	0.1	—				
Softwood *j*	208.0[2]*	228.3	23.0	10.4	0.7	0.1[2]
Hardwood *j*	7 553.0[2]*	130.7	6.2	2.9	5.8	—[2]
Newsprint	—[2]*	—	—	—	2.9	1.3[2]
Other paper	2.5[2]*	—	—	—	26.6	4.3[2]

j '000 cu. metres of roundwood equivalent. *p* incl. small quantity of cigars. *s* incl. re-exports.

	Production		Exports		Imports	
4. VEGETABLE OILSEEDS AND OILS						
Castor seed	3.33*	na	5.88	5.37	—	—
Castor oil	na	na	—	—	0.06	0.02
Copra	1.00*	1.20[2]*q*	—	0.83	0.45	0.27
Coconut oil	na	na	0.11	0.02	0.81	1.22
Cottonseed	10.70*	5.00*	0.33	—	—	—
Cottonseed oil	na	na	0.02	0.01	—	—
Groundnuts	2.80	na	2.07	—	—	—
Groundnut oil	na	na	0.01	—	0.01	—
Linseed	—	—[1]	—	—	0.05	—
Linseed oil	na	—	—	—	0.19	0.01
Olive oil	—	—	—	—	0.03	0.02
Palm kernels	—	—	—	—	0.01	—
Palm kernel oil	—	—	—	—	0.05	—
Palm oil	—	—	—	—	3.43	—
Sesame seed	1.00	—	0.88	na	—	—
Soya bean oil	—	—	—	—	0.05	—
Sunflower seed	3.00*n*	3.00[2]*n*	1.25	2.34*v*	—	—

n from farms and estates only. *q* exports of coconut oil and copra in copra equivalent. *v* incl. data for Uganda.

	Production		Exports		Imports	
5. LIVESTOCK‡, ANIMAL PRODUCTS, etc.						
Chickens *d*	219.3*np*	198.0*np*				
Cattle *d*	7 251.7*	6 675.0*	1.7	0.2	—	0.1
dairy cows *d*	326.3*n*	na				
Goats *d*	6 367.0*	3 875.3* }	—	—	0.1	—
Sheep *d*	4 984.0	2 692.7*				
Horses *d*	2.3	5.3				
Pigs *d*	36.0*n*	42.3*n*	—	—	—	—
Bacon/ham	} 32.0**n*	16.0*n*	{ 0.4	0.7	0.1	—
Meat‡: 'A'			3.2	0.7	0.1	—
'B'	na	—	0.2	—	—	—
Butter	4.7*n*	4.7**n*	2.1	1.2	0.1	—
Cheese	1.0	—	0.1	—	—	—
Eggs	1.3*	0.9	0.1	0.1	—	—
5. LIVESTOCK, ANIMAL PRODUCTS, etc.—*continued*						
Fish	21.4	33.5	0.1	na	1.9	na
Milk	238.7*nq*	179.3*nq*	4.6	0.1	9.6	4.5*
Hides/skins	—	5.0	6.5[2]	na	—	—
Wool	0.6[2]	—	0.7	0.5	—	—

n on farms and estates only. *p* incl. ducks, geese and turkeys. *q* excl. milk fed to livestock.

	Production		Exports		Imports	
6. FIBRES, TEXTILES, etc.						
Agaves (sisal etc.)	67.8	37.7	60.2	35.6	—	—
Cotton lint	5.0*	2.3*	2.8	2.5	—	—
Flax fibre	—	na	—	0.1	—	—
Jute	—	—	—	—	2.6	—
Rubber, natural	—	—	—	—	0.7	—
Cotton, woven fabrics	—	—	—	—	7.5	na
Rayon, woven fabrics	—	—	—	—	5.2*tv*	na
Wool, yarn	—	—	—	—	0.1	—

t incl. synthetic piece goods. *v* incl. data for Uganda.

	Production		Exports		Imports	
7. FUEL AND POWER						
Coal, 'A'‡	—	—	—	—	42	19
Coke	—	—	—	—	1	2
Electricity *h*: total	305	na				
hydro	191	na				
thermal	114	na				
Oil, crude	—	—	—	—	1 186	na
Petroleum, refined	1 120	na	573	—	317	740[1]

h million kWh.

	Production		Exports		Imports	
8. IRON AND STEEL						
Iron ore	—	—	—	—	3	—
Pig iron	—	—	—	—	1	—
Steel ingots/castings	—	—	—	—	1	1
Iron/steel scrap	na	na	12	—	—	—
9. NON-FERROUS MINERALS AND METALS						
Gold *k*, ore	11.00*m*	9.00*m*	11.61*t*	9.10*t*	4.26*t*	1.63*t*
Silver *k*, ore	40.30*m*	8.30*m*	40.23*t*	—	—	—
Asbestos: fibre	0.13	0.16	—	0.05	—	—
manufactured	na	na	—	—	1.35	3.24
Mica	—	0.01	—	—	0.02	—
Aluminium	—	—	—	—	1.61	1.84
Copper, ore	2.10	—	3.09[1]	—	—	—
metal	na	—	3.41*w*	—	0.32	0.64
Lead, metal	—	—	—	—	0.14	0.03
Magnesium, magnesite	0.17	na	—	—	—	—
Tin, metal	—	—	—	—	0.11	0.12
Zinc, metal	—	—	—	—	1.37	0.08

k '000 fine troy oz. *m* metal content. *t* bullion. *w* unwrought.

	Production		Exports		Imports	
10. CHEMICALS*n* AND FERTILIZERS						
Chemicals	—		—		na	
Fertilizers:						
Potash	—	—	—	—	0.3	0.2
Sulphur	—	—	—	—	1.1	0.1

n data not available for years 1953–5.

	Production		Exports		Imports	
11. INDUSTRY						
Aircraft *a*	—	—	—	—	4.1	na
Alcoholic beverages			—	—	1.5[2]*a*	na
beer *b*	473.0	184.0				
Cement	415.3	67.3	314.3	7.0	0.7	127.0
Electrical engineering *a*	—	—	—	—	8.9	na
Railway vehicles *a*	—	—	—	—	4.7[2]	16.3*v*
Machine tools *a*	—	—	—	—	1.0	—
Motor vehicles *a*	—	—	—	—	21.4	na

a million $ U.S. *b* '000 hectolitres. *v* incl. data for Uganda.

KOREA, NORTH

The northern sector of Korea was occupied by Russian troops in 1945 at the end of World War II. In 1948 the People's Republic was established. An attempt to reunite with the southern sector in 1950 resulted in the Korean war and caused great economic hardship to the country; the boundary between North and South Korea returned to the 38th parallel in 1953.

AREA: 121 248 sq. km. (46 814 sq. miles)

LAND USE: (percentage of total)

	1960
Arable and orchard	15.7
Permanent meadow and pasture	na
Forest and woodland, including rough grazing	74.4
City areas, waste and other land	na

POPULATION: 12 700 000 (1967 U.N. estimate)
Largest city: P'YŎNGYANG, capital; population: 653 100 (city proper, 1960)

FINANCE

Currency unit: The won

Exchange rates	*1965*
Per $ U.S.	2.57
Per £ sterling	7.2

PRODUCTION AND TRADE

After the Korean war, central planning of the economy began, the more recent plans giving priority to heavy industry over agriculture; collectivization had been completed by 1958. Rice accounted for 58% of the agricultural output in 1963. Various minerals are found, the most important being coal, lead and graphite; oil drilling started in 1957. Industries, especially H.E.P., textile, metallurgical and cement production have been intensively developed by the big Japanese concerns.

Trade is mainly with China P.R. The other trading partners are almost exclusively Comecon countries.

PRODUCTION, EXPORTS AND IMPORTS

Years: **1963–5 average** and *1953–5 average* Units: '000 metric tons unless otherwise indicated

	Production		Exports		Imports	
1. CEREALS, etc.						
Barley	250.0[1]*	na	—	—	—	—
Maize (corn)	1 613.3*	na	30.3[2]*	na	33.5*	na
Millets/sorghum	402.1[1]*	na	—	—	—	—
Oats	56.0[1]*	na	—	—	—	—
Potatoes	948.3*	na	—	—	—	—
Rice	2 633.3*	na	14.5*	na	—	—
Rye	7.0[1]*	na	—	—	—	—
Sweet potatoes/ yams	273.3*	na				
Wheat	85.0[2]*	na	—	—	80.3*	na
2. FRUIT, etc.						
Apples	na	na	26.7*	na	—	—
3. BEVERAGES, FOREST PRODUCTS, etc.						
Sugar, raw	—	—	—	—	22.3	na
Tobacco, leaf	39.3*	na	6.5*	na	0.1*	—
Wood	na	na				
Newsprint	na	—	—	—	—	—
Other paper	60.0[2]*	—	—	—	—	—
4. VEGETABLE OILSEEDS AND OILS						
Coconut oil	—	—	—	—	0.17*	na
Cottonseed	na	na	—	—	—	—
Groundnuts	na	na	—	—	—	—
Linseed oil	—	—	—	—	0.44*	na
Sesame seed	na	na	—	—	—	—
Soya beans	215*	na	—	—	—	—
5. LIVESTOCK‡, ANIMAL PRODUCTS, etc.						
Cattle *d*	677	na	—	—	—	—
Goats *d*	148*	na	—	—	—	—
Sheep *d*	140*	na	—	—	—	—
Horses *d*	25*	na				
Pigs *d*	1 258	na	—	—	—	—
Meat‡, 'A'	20*	na				
Butter	—	—	—	—	0.1*	—
Eggs	4*	na	—	—	—	—
Fish	500[1]	*223*	—	—	—	—
Milk	54*	—	—	—	—	—

d no. in thousands.

	Production		Exports		Imports	
6. FIBRES, TEXTILES, etc.						
Cotton lint	na	na	—	—	9.7*	—
Hemp fibre	na	na	—	—	—	—
Rubber, natural	—	—	—	—	0.1*	—
Silk *f*	na	na	386.3	na	—	—
Cotton: yarn	na	na	na	na	na	na
woven fabrics	na	na	na	na	na	na
Rayon, yarn/fabrics	na	na	na	na	na	na

f metric tons. *p* 1957 data.

	Production		Exports		Imports	
7. FUEL AND POWER						
Coal	11 700**n*	*710[1]**	na	na	na	na
Electricity *h*	12 486	*1 010[1]**				

n 1961 data. *h* million kWh.

	Production		Exports		Imports	
8. IRON AND STEEL						
Iron ore	3 500**n*	*1 100***p*	na	na	na	na
Pig iron	1 317	*113**	na	na	na	na
Steel ingots/castings	1 128	*67*	na	na	na	na

n 1961 data. *p* 1957 data.

	Production		Exports		Imports	
9. NON-FERROUS MINERALS AND METALS						
Gold *k*, ore *m*	160.00*	na	na	na	na	na
Silver *k*, ore *m*	650.00	na	na	na	na	na
Copper: ore	8.78*	na	na	na	na	na
metal	10.59**q*	na	na	na	na	na
Lead: ore	54.43*m*	na	na	na	na	na
metal	45.36	*2.00**	na	na	na	na
Manganese, metal	na	na	na	na	na	na
Tungsten, ore	4.14*	*1.50**	na	na	na	na
Zinc: ore	101.30**m*	na	na	na	na	na
metal	68.04*	na	na	na	na	na

k '000 fine troy oz. *m* metal content. *q* electrolytic.

	Production		Exports		Imports	
10. CHEMICALS*n* AND FERTILIZERS						
Chemicals	na		na		na	
Fertilizers:						
Phosphates	200.0**p*	na	na	na	na	na
Potash	na	na	na	na	na	na
Pyrites	169.7	na	na	na	na	na

n data not available for years 1953–5. *p* apatite.

	Production		Exports		Imports	
11. INDUSTRY						
Cement	2 520.0	*265.0[1]*	na	na	na	na

Apart from cement, no information on North Korea's industrial production is available.

na: data not available. — negligible or nil. [1] one year only. [2] two year average. * estimate. ‡ see appendix. † re-exports.

KOREA, SOUTH

The Republic of Korea was established in 1948 after three years' occupation by American troops after World War II. The Korean war of 1950–3 was the result of an attempt by North Korea to reunite the two sectors of Korea; the armistice re-established the 38th parallel as the boundary between the two countries.

AREA: 98 431 sq. km. (38 004 sq. miles)

LAND USE: (percentage of total)

	1964	*1954*
Arable and orchard	22.9	20.6
Permanent meadow and pasture	0.2	—
Forest and woodland, incl. rough grazing	67.1	65.4
City areas, waste and other land	9.8	14.0

POPULATION: 29 207 856 (1966 census)
Largest city: SŎUL (Seoul), capital; population: 3 794 959 (city proper, 1966)

Distribution of working population (1965)
Total working population: 9 199 000

U.N. group no.		*Percentage*
0	Agriculture, forestry, fishing and hunting	54.4
1	Mining and quarrying	0.9
2/3	Manufacturing	8.6
4	Construction	2.7
5	Electricity, gas, water and sanitary services	0.2
6	Commerce	10.6
7	Transport, storage and communications	2.2
8	Services	13.0
9	Others	7.4

		Year(s)
Life expectancy at birth (years): male	51.1	1955–60 av.
female	53.7	1955–60 av.
Infant mortality (per '000)	5.0*	1964
Crude birth rate (per '000)	17.7*	1965
Crude death rate (per '000)	5.0*	1965
Population per physician	2 710	1965
Population per hospital bed	2 200	1966
School enrolment: age 5–19 years (percentage)	77	1963–4 av.
age over 19 years (per 100 000 population)	508	1964–5 av.

COMMUNICATIONS

		Year(s)
Motor vehicles in use ('000s): private	14.5	1963–5 av.
commercial	23.3	1963–5 av.
Railway track (km.)	4 695	1962
Mail per capita: domestic	13	1963–5 av.
foreign received	1	1963–5 av.
foreign sent	0.4	1963–5 av.
Telephones (per '000 urban population)	1.1	1967
Radio receivers (per '000 population)	65	1963–5 av.
Television licences (per '000 population)	1.3	1963–5 av.
Daily newspapers (per '000 population)	56	1962–3 av.

FINANCE

Currency unit: The won replaced the hwan in 1962 at the rate 1 won to 10 hwan

Exchange rates	*1965*	*1960 a*	*1950 a*
Per $ U.S.	271	650	500*
Per £ sterling	759	1 820	1 400*

a hwan.

		Year(s)
National Income (million $ U.S.)	2 497	1965
G.N.P. per capita ($ U.S.)	150	1966
Rate of increase of G.N.P. per capita	3.2	1960–4 av.
Foreign trade (percentage of G.D.P.)	17	1963–5 av.

TRADING

Total trade (in million $ U.S.)	*1965*	*1955*	*1938 a*
Exports (f.o.b.)	175	18	249
Imports (c.i.f.)	463	108 *b*	300

Main trading partners (percentage of total value)

Exports	*1965*	*1955*	*Imports*	*1965*	*1955*
U.S.A.	35	42	U.S.A.	39	35
Japan	25	39	Japan	36	15
S. Vietnam	9	na	Germany F.R.	3	4
Hong Kong	6	11	France	3	2
Sweden	3	na	Philippines	2	1
Thailand	2	na	Taiwan	2	5
Netherlands	2	na	Hong Kong	2	14

Distribution of trade (percentage of total value)

Exports	*1965*	*1955*
Manufactured goods	61	10
(textiles and clothing)	(27)	(na)
(plywood)	(10)	(na)
Crude materials and fuels	22	78
(metalliferous ores and metal scrap)	(10)	(32*)
Food	16	6
(fish)	(10)	(3*)

Imports	*1965*	*1955 c*
Manufactured goods	33	60
(machinery and transport equipment)	(16)	(8)
Crude materials	30	4
(textile fibres)	(13)	(na)
Chemicals	22	17
(fertilizers)	(14)	(7*)
Food	14	11
(cereals)	(12)	(na)

a incl. North Korea. *b* in addition, imports to the value U.S. $233 million financed with foreign aid. *c* these are percentages of total imports, including those financed with foreign aid.

PRODUCTION, EXPORTS AND IMPORTS

Years: **1963–5 average** and *1953–5 average* Units: '000 metric tons unless otherwise indicated

	Production		Exports		Imports	
1. CEREALS, etc.						
Barley	768.3	*844.3*	—	—	169.2	*146.5**
Maize (corn)	31.7	*12.7*	—	—[1]	9.2	*0.2[1]*
Millets/sorghum	78.0	*95.7*	0.1	—	2.1	*28.3**
Potatoes	391.7	*310.0[2]*	—	—	0.1	*0.3*
Rice	5 051.3	*3 186.3*	12.5	—	39.1	*104.4*
Rye	19.3	*22.7*	—	—	—	—
Sweet potatoes/ yams	1 317.0	*387.3*				
Wheat	136.0	*109.7*	—	—	583.0	*60.9*
2. FRUIT, etc.						
Apples	134.0	*47.3*	—	—	—	—
Bananas	—	—	—	—	0.3	—
Grapes	12.0	*2.7*	—	—	—	—
Oranges	1.0	—	—	—	—	—
Peaches	36.0	*15.2[1]*	—	—	—	—
Pears	30.7	*29.3*	—	—	—	—
Tomatoes	19.0	*7.0*				
Wine *b*	—	—	0.1	—	—	—

b '000 hectolitres.

	Production		Exports		Imports	
3. BEVERAGES, FOREST PRODUCTS, etc.						
Sugar, raw	—	—	7.1†	—	34.2	*34.8*
Tobacco: leaf	37.9	*23.5*	0.7	—	—	—
cigarettes *e*	22 470.0	*11 828.0*	—	—	—	—
tobacco/snuff	9.1	*4.6*	—	—	—	—
Softwood *j*	1 634.0*	*507.3*	—	—	144.0	*170.3*
Hardwood *j*	186.3*	*364.0*	—	—	387.0[1]	*81.4*
Wood pulp	21.7	*4.1*	—	—	65.7	*4.2*
Newsprint	43.3	*5.8*	—	—	5.0	*16.3*
Other paper	65.3	*17.6*	—	—	3.1	*22.0*

e no. in millions. *j* '000 cu. metres of roundwood equivalent.

	Production		Exports		Imports	
4. VEGETABLE OILSEEDS AND OILS						
Castor seed	2.67	na	—	—	—	—
Castor oil	na	na	—	—	0.12	—
Copra	—	—	—	—	1.49	—
Cottonseed	8.00	*20.67*	—	—	—	—
Cottonseed oil	na	na	—	—	0.01	*0.28*
Groundnuts	1.63	*0.70*	0.01	—	—	—
Linseed	—	—	—	—	0.55	—
Linseed oil	na	—	—	—	0.13	*0.14*
Sesame seed	3.67	*1.50*	—	—	—	*0.37*
Soya beans	164.36	*150.30*	—	—	5.51	*9.17**
Soya bean oil	na	na	—	—	0.09	*0.05[2]*
5. LIVESTOCK‡, ANIMAL PRODUCTS, etc.						
Chickens *d*	11 745.3	*5 544.7*				
Cattle *d*	1 324.3	*697.3*	—	—	0.5*	—
dairy cows *d*	595.7*	*509.3*				
Goats *d*	275.0	*23.3*	—	—	—	—
Sheep *d*	1.3	*1.0*	—	—	—	—
Horses *d*	26.3	*16.6*				
Pigs *d*	1 479.0	*644.3*	66.2*	—	—	—
Meat‡: 'A'	97.0*	*35.5*	0.1	—	—	—
'B'	21.1*	na	0.3	—	—	—
Butter	—	—	—	—	0.1	—
Eggs	43.0*	*4.5[2]*	—	—	—	—
Fish	589.8	*262.5*	36.6	na	0.2[2]	—
Milk	106.0*	*0.3*	—	—	82.9	*75.3*
Hides/skins	4.5[1]	*2.5[1]*	—	—	—	—
Wool	—	—	—	—	1.1	—

d no. in thousands.

continued

na: data not available. — negligible or nil. [1] one year only. [2] two year average. * estimate. ‡ see appendix. † re-exports.

KOREA, SOUTH *continued*

PRODUCTION, EXPORTS AND IMPORTS *continued*

	Production		Exports		Imports	
6. FIBRES, TEXTILES, etc.						
Abaca	—	—	—	—	3.7	—
Cotton lint	4.0	17.7*	0.1	—	66.5	14.4
Flax fibre	0.1	—	—	—	0.4	—
Hemp fibre	5.2	6.3	—	—[2]	—	—
Jute	—	—	0.3	—	—	—
Rubber, natural	—	—	—	—	11.7	2.1
Silk *f*	757.3	544.0	727.7	189.7	14.7	3.3
Cotton: yarn	64.6	20.2	—	—	—	—
woven fabrics	27.9	10.8*	14.3	—	—	—
Rayon: fibre/yarn	—	—	—	—	8.7	—
woven fabrics	5.8	6.8[2]*	—	—	—	—
Non-cellulosic fibre/yarn	1.3	—	—	—	8.6	—
Wool: yarn	3.5	0.2	—	—	—	—
woven fabrics	9.7*n*	3.2*p*	—	—	—	—

f metric tons. *n* million square metres. *p* million metres.

	Production		Exports		Imports	
7. FUEL AND POWER						
Coal: 'A'‡	9 570	1 310	240	29	130	882
'B'	7	—	—	—	—	—
Coke	—	—	—	—	8	—
Electricity *h*: total	3 005	840[1]				
hydro	729	460[1]				
thermal	2 276	380[1]				
Oil, crude	—	—[1]	—	—	767	na
Petroleum, refined	700	—[1]	—	—	647	na
Rare earths *f*	—	497[1]*q*	—	—	—	—

f metric tons. *h* million kWh. *q* monazite.

	Production		Exports		Imports	
8. IRON AND STEEL						
Iron ore	326*m*	15*m*	615	na	—	—
Pig iron	14*r*	—*r*	—	—	13	—
Steel ingots/castings	173	4	—	—	28	—
Iron/steel scrap	na	na	—	10	61	—

m metal content. *r* excl. ferro-alloys.

	Production		Exports		Imports	
9. NON-FERROUS MINERALS AND METALS						
Gold *k*, ore *m*	76.30	38.00	—	—	—	—
Silver *k*, ore *m*	427.30	51.20[2]	—	—	—	—
Asbestos, fibre	1.59	0.09	—	—	4.01	—
Aluminium	—	—	—	—	6.11	—
Cobalt	na	na	—	—	—	—
Copper: ore	0.88*m*	1.16*m*	—	—	—	—
metal	2.63	0.26	1.67	—	33.00	—
Lead: ore	3.23*m*	0.31*m*	7.69	—	—	—
metal	0.28	0.03	—	—	1.91	—
Magnesium: dolomite	na	na	12.10	—	—	—
magnesite	na	na	—	—	1.78	—
Manganese, ore	5.05	2.71	1.40	—	—	—

continued

	Production		Exports		Imports	
9. NON-FERROUS MINERALS AND METALS—*continued*						
Mercury *f*	—	—	—	—	22.00	—
Molybdenum *f*, ore	131.09*m*	9.98*m*	401.00	—	—	—
Nickel, ore	0.02*m*	—	0.18	—	—	—
Tin, metal	—	—	—	—	0.20	—
Titanium minerals	—	—	—	—	1.40	—
Tungsten, ore	5.15	5.22	4.89	3.87*t*	—	—
Zinc, ore	3.60*m*	0.01*m*	7.68	—	9.70	—

f metric tons. *k* '000 fine troy oz. *m* metal content. *t* exports to the U.S.A. only.

	Production		Exports		Imports	
10. CHEMICALS *n* AND FERTILIZERS						
Organic chemicals:						
Benzene	—		—		0.6	
Butadiene	—		—		na	
Ethylene	—		—		na	
Methanol	—		—		7.1	
Phenol	na		—		0.2	
Phthalic anhydride	—		—		na	
Styrene monomer	—		—		na	
Urea	na		—		126.3	
Inorganic chemicals:						
Ammonia	na		na		na	
Carbon black	na		—		2.7	
Chlorine	na		—		na	
Nitric acid	—		—		1.5	
Sodium carbonate	—		—		38.0	
Sodium hydroxide	6.3		—		12.0	
Sulphuric acid	13.7		—		na	
Plastics:						
Polyamides	na		—		na	
Polyethylene	—		—		na	
Polyvinyl chloride	—		—		na	
Fertilizers:						
Potash	na	na	—	—	83.1	—
Pyrites	—[2]	0.1**x*	—	—	—	—
Sulphur	—	—	—	—	2.7	—

n data not available for years 1953–5. *x* sulphur content.

	Production		Exports		Imports	
11. INDUSTRY						
Aircraft *a*	—	—	—	—	1.0	—
Alcoholic beverages			—	—	—	2.5*a*
beer *b*	266.0	na				
Cement	1 212.0	52.7	25.7	—*	102.7	291.7*
Electrical engineering *a*	—	—	1.2†	—	18.2	1.5[2]
Railway vehicles *a*	—	—	—	—	7.4	—
Merchant ships *g*	3.0	—	—	—	6.0	—
Motor vehicles			—	—	5.2*a*	0.6*a*
commercial *dp*	1.6	—				
private *dp*	0.6	—				

a million $ U.S. *b* '000 hectolitres. *d* no. in thousands. *g* '000 G.R.T. *p* assembly of imported parts.

LAOS

SOUTH EAST ASIA

Laos, Cambodia and Vietnam, previously states of French Indo-China, became independent states within the French Union in 1949. A rebel invasion of Laos was quashed in 1954 when the Geneva conference called for the withdrawal of foreign forces from Laos, but internal unrest continued and resulted in several changes of government. Rebel movements within the country continue to cause instability, and the proximity to Vietnam has led to some involvement in the Vietnamese war.

AREA: 236 800 sq. km. (91 430 sq. miles)

LAND USE: (percentage of total)	*1964*	*1955*
Arable and orchard	3.4	4.3
Permanent meadow and pasture	3.4	4.0
Forest and woodland	59.3	60.0
City areas, waste and other land	33.9	31.7

POPULATION: 2 770 000 (1967 estimate)

Largest city: VIENTIANE, capital; population: 162 297 (1962)

		Year(s)
Crude birth rate (per '000)	47*	1965
Crude death rate (per '000)	23*	1965
Population per physician	20 000	1965
Population per hospital bed	1 650	1966
School enrolment: age 5–19 years (percentage)	24	1963–4 av.
age over 19 years (per 100 000 population)	7	1964–5 av.

COMMUNICATIONS

		Year(s)
Motor vehicles in use ('000s): private	5.4	1963–5 av.
commercial	1.8	
Radio receivers (per '000 population)	19	1963–5 av.
Daily newspapers (per '000 population)	11	1962–4 av.

FINANCE

Currency unit: The kip

Exchange rates	*1965*	*1960*	*1958*
Per $ U.S.	240	80	35
Per £ sterling	672	224	98

		Year
National Income (million $ U.S.)	130	1958
G.N.P. per capita ($ U.S.)	70	1966

EMPLOYMENT AND TRADE

The chief products are rice, maize, and tobacco; much of the land is forested, and the output of teak is considerable; opium also is a source of revenue. Various minerals are found in small quantities, but only tin is mined at present. Industry is limited mainly to weaving and crafts, although there are some saw and rice mills. Exports in 1964 included tin, green coffee and timber; imports consisted of foodstuffs, manufactured goods and machinery, many of which came from the U.S.A. and the U.K. under aid agreements. The chief trading partners were Thailand, the U.S.A., France and the U.K.

continued

na: data not available. — negligible or nil. [1] one year only. [2] two year average. * estimate. ‡ see appendix. † re-exports.

PRODUCTION, EXPORTS AND IMPORTS

Years: **1963–5 average** and *1953–5 average* Units: '000 metric tons unless otherwise indicated

	Production		Exports		Imports	
1. CEREALS, etc.						
Cassava	10.0	na				
Maize (corn)	19.0*	11.0[2]*	—	—	—	—
Potatoes	14.3*	na	—	—	—	—
Rice	665.0	436.7	—	—	39.8*	23.1[1]
Sweet potatoes/yams	11.7*	na				
2. FRUIT, etc.						
Wine *b*	—	—	—	—	1.5[1]	2.0[1]

b '000 hectolitres.

	Production		Exports		Imports	
3. BEVERAGES, FOREST PRODUCTS, etc.						
Coffee	3.0	na	0.2[2]	—	—	—
Sugar, raw	—	—	—	—	2.6[2]	—
Tobacco, leaf	2.6*	0.7	—	—	0.9[2]	—
Softwood *j*	—	0.5[2]	—	—	—	—
Hardwood *j*	204.3	107.3	3.0	2.6	—	1.8
Newsprint	—	—	—	—	0.2	—
Other paper	—	—	—	—	0.5	0.1

j '000 cu. metres of roundwood equivalent.

	Production		Exports		Imports	
4. VEGETABLE OILSEEDS AND OILS						
Cottonseed	3.0*	0.3	—	—	—	—
Groundnuts	0.7	0.7[1]	—	—	—	—
Soya beans	na	na	—	0.1[1]	—	—

	Production		Exports		Imports	
5. LIVESTOCK‡, ANIMAL PRODUCTS, etc.						
Chickens *d*	7 358.0	na				
Cattle *d*	322.3	246.0[1]	—	—	—	—
Goats *d*	31.0*	na	—	—	—	—
Sheep *d*	1.0*	na	—	—	—	—
Horses *d*	16.7	na				
Pigs *d*	744.0*	177.0[1]	—	—	—	—
Meat‡, 'A'	8.3*	5.0[2]*n*	—	—	—	—
Eggs	43.3	na	—	—	—	—
Fish	na	na	—[2]	—	0.5[2]	—
Milk	25.7*	na	—	—	—	—
Hides/skins	na	0.8[2]	—	—	—	—

d no. in thousands. *n* government inspected meat only.

	Production		Exports		Imports	
6. FIBRES, TEXTILES, etc.						
Cotton: lint	2.0*	—	—	—	—	—
woven fabrics	—	—	—	—	na	na
7. FUEL AND POWER						
Electricity *ht*	12	3[1]				
Petroleum, refined	—	—	—	—	57	10[1]

h million kWh. *t* thermal.

	Production		Exports		Imports	
9. NON-FERROUS MINERALS AND METALS						
Tin: ore *m*	0.32	0.21	0.43	0.09	—	—

m metal content.

	Production		Exports		Imports	
11. INDUSTRY						
Cement	na	na	na	na	na	na

LEBANON

MIDDLE EAST

Lebanon became an independent republic in 1941 after twenty years of French mandatory rule. In 1958 a serious insurrection broke out and rebels captured several towns. The authority of the government was restored only with the help of a considerable force of U.S. troops.

AREA: 8 800* sq. km. (3 400* sq. miles)

LAND USE: (percentage of total)	*1965*	*1954*
Arable and orchard	28.5	26.5
Permanent meadow and pasture	1.0	—
Forest and woodland	9.1	7.9
City areas, waste and other land	61.4	65.6

POPULATION: 2 520 000 (1967 U.N. estimate)

Largest city: BEIRUT, capital; population: 700 000 (city proper, 1964)

		Year(s)
Crude birth rate (per '000)	32.3*	1965
Crude death rate (per '000)	3.9*	1965
Population per physician	1 390	1965
Population per hospital bed	240	1966
School enrolment: age 5–19 years (percentage)	78	1963–4 av.
age over 19 years (per 100 000 population)	768	1963–5 av.

EMPLOYMENT AND PRODUCTION

Lebanon is essentially an agricultural country. Ancient cedar forests have suffered from over exploitation, which, with unrestricted grazing of goats, has limited tree growth and led to soil erosion. Iron ore exists, but is difficult to work. Manufacturing is limited, but has doubled in the last ten years. There is a transit trade in gold, and a refinery for oil imported from Iraq and Saudi Arabia.

COMMUNICATIONS

		Year(s)
Motor vehicles in use ('000s): private	86.4	1963–5 av.
commercial	12.7	
Railway track (km.)	368	1968
Mail per capita: domestic	7	1962–4 av.
foreign received	15	
foreign sent	10	
Telephones (per '000 urban population)	4.8	1967
Radio receivers (per '000 population)	113	1963–5 av.
Television sets (per '000 population)	50.3	1963–5 av.
Daily newspapers (per '000 population)	97	1959

FINANCE

Currency unit: The Lebanese pound

Exchange rates	*1965*	*1960*	*1950 a*	*1938 a*
Per $ U.S.	3.07	3.15	2.21	1.90
Per £ sterling	8.62	8.82	6.16	8.74

		Year
National Income (million $ U.S.)	408	1958
G.N.P. per capita ($ U.S.)	480	1966

a selling rate.

TRADING

Total trade (in million $ U.S.)	*1965*	*1955*
Exports (f.o.b.)	85 (105*a*)	34 (37*a*)
Imports (c.i.f.)	182 (582*a*)	218 (241*a*)

Main trading partners (percentage of total value) *a*

Exports	*1965*	*1955*	*Imports*	*1965*	*1955*
Saudi Arabia	26	10	France	14	10
Jordan	8	5	U.K.	14	16
Iraq	7	6	Syria	11	16
Syria	7	11	U.S.A.	10	13
Kuwait	6	na	Germany F.R.	8	6
U.K.	5	5	Italy	6	4
U.S.A.	4	10			

Distribution of trade (percentage of total value)

Exports	*1965*	*1955*
Food	33	44
Manufactured goods	24	36
Crude materials and fuels	11	19
Imports		
Manufactured goods	27	49
Food	23	27
Crude materials and fuels	12	20
Chemicals	4	4

a value including gold, specie, and banknotes.

continued

na: data not available. — negligible or nil. [1] one year only. [2] two year average. * estimate. ‡ see appendix. † re-exports.

LEBANON *continued*

PRODUCTION, EXPORTS AND IMPORTS

Years: **1963–5 average** and *1953–5 average* Units: '000 metric tons unless otherwise indicated

1. CEREALS, etc.

	Production		Exports		Imports	
Barley	**12.7**	*26.3*	**4.0**	*13.2*	**57.9**	*22.2*
Maize (corn)	**10.7**	*13.5[2]*	**0.5**	*2.8*	**33.5**	*2.3*
Millets/sorghum	**9.7**	*10.0*	**0.2**	*13.7*	**3.7**	*13.8*
Oats	**2.0***	*2.0*	—	—	—	*0.1*
Potatoes	**68.0**	*33.3*	**28.8**	*13.0*	**2.3**	*5.3*
Rice	—	*0.7*	**0.3**	—	**17.6**	*10.8*
Sweet potatoes/ yams	**1.0***	na				
Wheat	**58.3**	*56.7*	**0.6**	*1.6*	**205.6**	*96.5*

2. FRUIT, etc.

	Production		Exports		Imports	
Apples	**105.0**	*30.0[2]*	**62.4**	*10.4*	**0.5**	*0.8*
Apricots	**9.7**	na	na	*0.1*	—	—
Bananas	**25.0**	*17.3*	**11.9**	*7.1*	—	—
Dates	na	na	**0.4**	*0.9*	**3.5**	*3.9*
Figs	**23.7**	*20.0*	na	*0.5*	—	—
Grapes	**91.3**	*75.0[2]*	**1.8**	*0.1*	**3.6**	*5.0*
Lemons	**66.7**	*29.0*	**28.8**	*8.9*	—	—
Oranges	**153.3**	*76.7*	**75.5**	*31.5*	—	—
Other citrus fruit	**3.0**	—	**1.2**	—	—	—
Olives	**46.3**	*25.0[2]*				
Peaches	**9.7**	*2.0[1]*	na	*0.4*	—	—
Pears	**7.7**	*11.0[2]*	**2.2**	*0.6[2]*	**0.1**	*0.2[2]*
Plums	na	na	na	*2.1*	—	—
Raisins	**0.3***	*0.2[1]*	—	—	**0.2**	*0.3*
Tomatoes	**40.3**	*23.5[2]*				
Wine *b*	—	—	**0.5**	—	**2.7**	*1.3*

b '000 hectolitres.

3. BEVERAGES, FOREST PRODUCTS, etc.

	Production		Exports		Imports	
Cocoa	—	—	—	—	**0.5**	*0.4*
Coffee	—	—	—	—	**3.2**	*1.4*
Sugar: beet	**62.3**	na				
cane	**1.7**	*1.0[1]*				
raw (beet)	**1.4**	—	**0.1**	—	**53.7**	*26.0*
Tea	—	—	—	—	**0.7**	*0.2*
Tobacco: leaf	**5.3**	*2.2*	**2.1**	*0.4*	**0.2**	*0.3*
cigarettes *e*	**1 425.0**	*970.0*	—	—	—	—
tobacco/snuff	**2.4*n***	*0.3*	—	—	—	—
Softwood *j*	**14.7***	*13.0*	**3.0[2]**	—	**171.5[1]**	*76.3*
Hardwood *j*	**21.0***	*31.0[2]*	**7.5[1]**	—	**38.0[2]*p***	*15.7*
Newsprint	**—***	—	**—[1]**	—	**2.2[1]**	*4.3*
Other paper	**8.3***	—	**0.7[1]**	—	**27.0[1]**	*7.0*

e no. in millions. *j* '000 cu. metres of roundwood equivalent. *n* sales.
p sawn logs only.

4. VEGETABLE OILSEEDS AND OILS

	Production		Exports		Imports	
Castor oil	—	—	—	—	**0.01**	—
Copra	—	—	—	—	—	*1.07**
Coconut oil	na	na	**0.05**	—	**0.64**	*0.49*
Cottonseed	—	*0.67*	**0.35†**	*0.30q*	**45.44**	*35.27q*
Cottonseed oil	na	na	—	*1.46*	—	—
Groundnuts	**3.50**	*1.40[2]*	—	—	—	—
Groundnut oil	na	na	—	—	—	*0.01*
Linseed	—	—	—	—	—	na
Linseed oil	—	na	—	*0.01*	**0.01**	*0.09*
Olive oil	**9.00***	*8.00**	**0.54**	*0.97*	—	*0.76*
Palm oil	—	—	—	—	**0.14**	*0.05*
Sesame seed	**0.23**	*1.43*	**0.31**	*0.47*	**4.73**	*2.37*

q incl. hempseed.

5. LIVESTOCK‡, ANIMAL PRODUCTS, etc.

	Production		Exports		Imports	
Chickens *d*	**11 922.7*r****	*1 640.0r*				
Cattle *d*	**102.0**	*30.0*	**0.2***	—	**123.4***	*41.0*
Goats *d*	**454.0*t***	*500.0t*	} **1.7***	na	**730.6***	na
Sheep *d*	**84.3**	*60.0*				
Horses *d*	**4.0**	*6.6*				
Pigs *d*	**9.0**	*2.7*	—	—	**0.1**	*0.8*
Meat‡: 'A'	**57.7***	*17.0*	—	—	—	—
'B'	—	—	**0.1**	—	**0.1**	—
Butter	—	—	**0.1**	—	**2.3**	*1.5*
Cheese	**7.0***	*4.5[2]*	**0.2**	*0.1*	**5.4**	*2.2*
Eggs	**9.3***	*1.5[2]*	**3.3**	*0.4*	**0.2**	*1.8*
Fish	**2.2**	na	—	—	**3.8**	na
Milk	**9.0***	na	—	—	**49.4**	*1.4**
Hides/skins	—	—	**4.0†**	*1.4†*	**9.1**	*3.3*
Wool	—	—	**2.3†**	*1.0†*	**1.7**	*0.7*

continued

5. LIVESTOCK, ANIMAL PRODUCTS, etc.—*continued*

d no. in thousands. *r* incl. ducks, geese and turkeys. *t* goats registered for taxation only.

6. FIBRES, TEXTILES, etc.

	Production		Exports		Imports	
Cotton lint	—	—	**2.5†**	*1.3†*	**5.9**	*3.6*
Hemp fibre	na	na	—	—	—	—
Jute	—	—	—	—	**0.9**	—
Rubber, natural	—	—	—	—	**0.2**	—
Silk *f*	na	*27.0*	**4.0**	*17.7*	**6.0**	—
Cotton: yarn	**3.5[1]**	na	**0.1[2]**	na	**0.4[2]**	na
woven fabrics	na	*3.5[2]*	**0.1[2]**	na	**2.1[2]**	*2.1[2]**
Rayon, woven fabrics	na	*2.9n*	na	na	na	*0.7[2]**
Wool: yarn	—	—	**—[1]**	*—[1]*	**0.3**	*0.4*
woven fabrics	na	*0.3n*	**0.2[2]*p***	—	**1.1[2]**	*0.8*

f metric tons. *n* million metres. *p* excl. blankets.

7. FUEL AND POWER

	Production		Exports		Imports	
Coal 'A'‡	—	—	**2†**	*4†*	**3**	*5*
Coke	—	—	**1†**	*1†*	**10**	*2*
Electricity *h*: total	**694**	*190[1]*				
hydro	**410[1]**	*110[1]*				
thermal	**284**	*80[1]*				
Oil, crude	—	*—[1]*	—	*—[1]*	**1 270**	*890[1]*
Petroleum, refined	**1 226**	*860[1]*	**143**	*—[1]*	**67**	*410[1]*

h million kWh.

8. IRON AND STEEL

	Production		Exports		Imports	
Iron ore	—	*21m*	—	*35*	—	—
Pig iron	—	—	—	—	**9**	*3*
Steel ingots/castings	—	—	—	—	**35**	—
Iron/steel scrap	na	na	**1**	*5*	**7**	*1*

m metal content.

9. NON-FERROUS MINERALS AND METALS

	Production		Exports		Imports	
Gold *k*, bullion/coins etc.	—	—	na	*88.50[2]†*	**2 100.00‡**	*681.30*
Platinum group metals *k*	—	—	—	—	**3.60**	*1.81*
Silver *k*, bullion	—	—	—	—	**56.37**	—
Asbestos: fibre	—	—	—	—	**3.50**	*0.36*
manufactured	na	na	**19.18**	*1.91[1]*	**0.54**	*1.46[1]*
Mica	—	—	—	—	**0.02**	—
Aluminium	—	—	—	—	**2.54**	*0.57*
Copper, metal	—	—	—	—	**0.58**	—
Lead, metal	—	—	—	—	**0.53**	*0.37*
Tin, metal	—	—	—	—	**0.01**	*0.01*
Zinc, metal	—	—	—	—	**0.87**	*0.15*

k '000 fine troy oz.

10. CHEMICALS*n* AND FERTILIZERS

	Production		Exports		Imports	
Chemicals	—		—		na	
Fertilizers:						
Potash	—	—	—	—	**3.5**	—
Sulphur	—	—	—	—	**12.7**	*0.8*

n data not available for years 1953–5.

11. INDUSTRY

	Production		Exports		Imports	
Aircraft *a*	—	—	**2.8**	—	**1.5**	*2.5*
Beer *b*	—	*23.0*	—	—	—	—
Cement	**849.3**	*366.0*	**83.3***	*38.3*	**71.7***	*6.7*
Electrical engineering *a*	—	—	—	—	**16.0**	*1.7*
Machine tools *a*	—	—	—	—	**2.1**	—
Merchant ships *g*	—	—	—	—	**0.2**	—
Motor vehicles *a*	—	—	—	—	**22.9**	*6.8*

a million $ U.S. *b* '000 hectolitres. *g* '000 G.R.T.

na: data not available. — negligible or nil. [1] one year only. [2] two year average. * estimate. ‡ see appendix. † re-exports.

LESOTHO

SOUTHERN AFRICA

Lesotho, formerly the British protectorate of Basutoland, became a republic within the Commonwealth in 1966. The country is surrounded by South African territory and is linked to the South African customs union.

AREA: 30 350 sq. km. (11 720 sq. miles)

LAND USE: (percentage of total)

	1962	*1954*
Arable and orchard	11.7	12.4
Permanent meadow and pasture	82.2	87.3
Forest and woodland	—	0 3
City areas, waste and other land	6.1	—

POPULATION: 852 459*a* (1966 census)

Capital city: MASERU; population: 18 000 (1966)

a excl. absentees working in South Africa (about 12% of the total population).

FINANCE

Currency unit: The rand was introduced in 1961 at the rate R1 to £0.5 sterling.

Exchange rates	*1965*	*1960a*	*1955a*	*1938a*
Per $ U.S.	0.714	0.357	0.357	0.218

		Year
National Income (million $ U.S.)	52*	1966
G.N.P. per capita ($ U.S.)	60	1966

a pounds.

EMPLOYMENT, PRODUCTION AND TRADE

The economy is almost exclusively agricultural, the main crops being wheat, maize, sorghum, barley, oats, and vegetables. Terracing and rotational grazing has improved the pasture for sheep and other livestock.

The main exports are wool and mohair. Remittances from many of the emigrant labourers working in South African mines and industries contribute to the country's income. Trade is mainly with South Africa.

PRODUCTION, EXPORTS AND IMPORTS

Years: **1963–5 average** and *1953–5 average* Units: '000 metric tons unless otherwise indicated

1. CEREALS, etc.

	Production		Exports		Imports	
Barley	**4.0***	—	—	—	—	—
Maize (corn)	**115.0***	na	—	—	—	—
Millets/sorghum	**55.0[1]***	na	—	—	—	—
Wheat	**41.7***	na	—	—	—	—

5. LIVESTOCK‡, ANIMAL PRODUCTS, etc.

	Production		Exports		Imports	
Cattle *d*	**352.0***	*407.0[2]*	—	—	—	—
Goats *d*	**824.0***	*599.5[2]*	—	—	—	—
Sheep *d*	**1 450.7**	*1 311.0[2]*	—	—	—	—
Horses *d*	**87.3***	*102.0[1]*				
Pigs *d*	**60.0***	na	—	—	—	—
Meat‡ 'A'	**22.0***	na	—	—	—	—
Fish	na	na	—	—	—	—
Milk	**24.7**	na	—	—	—	—
Hides/skins	na	na	—	—	—	—
Wool	**2.1***	*2.0*	na	na	—	—

d no. in thousands.

LIBERIA

WEST AFRICA

Liberia is an independent republic with a constitution modelled on that of the U.S.A. In 1950 a development programme was initiated and in 1963 the U.S.A. and Germany F.R. granted loans for construction of hydro-electric power units and road systems.

AREA: 111 000 sq. km. (43 000 sq. miles)

LAND USE: (percentage of total)

	1964	*1948*
Arable and orchard	34.5	16.3
Permanent meadow and pasture	2.2	2.3
Forest and woodland	32.5	34.9
City areas, waste and other land	30.8	46.5

POPULATION: 1 110 000 (1967 U.N. estimate)

Capital city: MONROVIA; population: 80 992 (city proper, 1962)

Distribution of working population (1962)

Total working population: 411 794

U.N. group no.		*Percentage*
0	Agriculture, forestry, fishing and hunting	80.9
1	Mining and quarrying	3.5
2/3	Manufacturing	2.1
4	Construction	2.9
5	Electricity, gas, water and sanitary services	0.1
6	Commerce	2.8
7	Transport, storage and communications	0.9
8	Services	6.0
9	Others	0.8

		Year(s)
Life expectancy at birth (years): male	36.1*	} 1962
female	38.6*	
Population per physician	11 570	1965
Population per hospital bed	600	1964
School enrolment: age 5–19 years (percentage)	22	1963–4 av.
age over 19 years (per 100 000 population)	61	1964–5 av.

COMMUNICATIONS

		Year(s)
Railway track (km.)	338	1963
Telephones (per '000 urban population)	0.3	1967
Radio receivers (per '000 population)	113	1963–5 av.
Television sets (per '000 population)	1.5	1963–5 av.
Daily newspapers (per '000 population)	2.8	1962–4 av.

FINANCE

Currency unit: the Liberian dollar, at par with the $ U.S. which is also in circulation.

Exchange rates	*1965*	*1960*	*1950*	*1938*
Per £ sterling	2.8	2.8	2.8	4.6

		Year
National Income (million $ U.S.)	154	1964
G.N.P. per capita ($ U.S.)	210	1966

TRADING

Total trade (in million $ U.S.)	*1965*	*1955*	*1938*
Exports (f.o.b.)	135	43	2
Imports (c.i.f.)	105	26	2

Main trading partners (percentage of total value)

Exports	*1965*	*1955*	*Imports*	*1965*	*1955*
U.S.A.	37	87	U.S.A.	48	62
Germany F.R.	27	4	Germany F.R.	12	11
Italy	9	—	U.K.	10	11
U.K.	7	2	Japan	5	1
Belg./Lux.	6	1	Sweden	4	na
Netherlands	5	5	Netherlands	4	7
France	4	—	Italy	3	1

Distribution of trade (percentage of total value)

Exports	*1965*	*1955*
Iron ore and concentrates	73	16
Natural rubber and rubber-like gums	22	77
Palm nuts and kernels	2	2
Imports		
Manufactured goods	67	63
(machinery and transport equipment)	(24)	(25)
Food	14	17
Crude materials and fuels	9	6
Chemicals	6	8
Beverages and tobacco	3	6

Shipping: The Liberian merchant navy had in 1963 a gross registered tonnage of 10.6 million. The Liberian government requires only a modest registration fee and a nominal annual charge, and maintains no control over the operation of ships flying the Liberian flag.

continued

na: data not available. — negligible or nil. [1] one year only. [2] two year average. * estimate. ‡ see appendix. † re-exports.

LIBERIA *continued*

PRODUCTION, EXPORTS AND IMPORTS

Years: **1963–5 average** and *1953–5 average*   Units: '000 metric tons unless otherwise indicated

	Production		Exports		Imports	
1. CEREALS, etc.						
Cassava	423.3	na	—	—		
Maize (corn)	na	na	—	—	0.1[2]	—
Potatoes	—	—	—	—	0.8[1]	*0.2*
Rice	181.3*	na	—	—	31.1*n	*7.3*

n figure derived from U.S. export statistics.

	Production		Exports		Imports	
2. FRUIT, etc.						
Apples	—	—	—	—	0.1[1]	—
Oranges	5.0*	na	—	—	—	—
Wine *b*	—	—	—	—	11.0[1]	*1.5*[2]

b '000 hectolitres.

	Production		Exports		Imports	
3. BEVERAGES, FOREST PRODUCTS, etc.						
Cocoa	1.0	*0.7*[1]	1.0[1]	*0.4*	—	—
Coffee	3.5*	*0.8*[1]	3.7[1]	*0.3*	0.1[1]	—
Sugar: cane	—	na				
raw	—	na	—	—	3.1*	*0.6*
Tobacco: leaf	—	na	—	—	0.5[1]	*0.2*
products *a*	—	—	—	—	1.3	*0.5*
Softwood *j*	—	—	—	—	—	*1.1*
Hardwood *j*	1 706.0[1]*	*8 700.0*[2]	—	—	—	*2.6*[1]
Other paper	—	—	—	—	—	*0.2*

a million $ U.S. *j* '000 cu. metres of roundwood equivalent.

	Production		Exports		Imports	
4. VEGETABLE OILSEEDS AND OILS						
Castor oil	—	—	—	—	0.01[1]	—
Groundnuts	1.40*	na	—	—	0.01	—
Groundnut oil	na	na	—	—	0.04	—
Olive oil	—	—	—	—	0.14[1]	—
Palm kernels	7.63*	na	8.16*	*12.07*	—	—
Palm oil	41.20*	na	na	*0.11*	0.05	—

	Production		Exports		Imports	
5. LIVESTOCK‡, ANIMAL PRODUCTS, etc.						
Cattle *d*	27.0*	na	—	—	5.1[1]	—
Goats *d*	54.0*	na	}			
Sheep *d*	11.3*	na	} —	—	4.5[1]	na
Pigs *d*	4.0*	na	—	—	—	—
Bacon/ham }	3.0*	na {	—	—	0.1[1]	—
Meat‡ 'A' }			—	—	0.1[1]	—
'B'	—	—	—	—	0.6[1]	—
Butter	—	—	—	—	0.2[1]	*0.1*
Cheese	—	—	—	—	0.1[1]	—
Eggs	0.1*	na	—	—	—	—
Fish	7.8*p*	*0.6p*	—	—	1.4	na
Milk	2.0*	na	—	—	6.0	*0.8*

d no. in thousands. *p* incl. fish landed by foreign vessels.

	Production		Exports		Imports	
6. FIBRES, TEXTILES, etc.						
Rubber, natural	na	na	44.4*	*34.4*	—	—

	Production		Exports		Imports	
7. FUEL AND POWER						
Electricity *h*: total	224	*30*[1]				
hydro	17	*10*[1]				
thermal	207	*20*[1]				
Petroleum, refined	—	—	—	—	177	*20*[1]

h million kWh.

	Production		Exports		Imports	
8. IRON AND STEEL						
Iron ore	7 709*m*	*959m*	11 336	*1 467*	—	—

m metal content.

	Production		Exports		Imports	
9. NON-FERROUS MINERALS AND METALS						
Diamonds *a*	na	na	3.90	*0.38*	—	—
Gold *k*, ore	2.00*m	*1.00*m*	—	*0.89q*	—	—

a million $ U.S. *k* '000 fine troy oz. *m* metal content. *q* bullion.

	Production		Exports		Imports	
11. INDUSTRY						
Alcoholic beverages			—	—	2.3[1]*a*	—
beer *b*	2.0	—				
Cement	—	—	—	—	96.7	*18.0**
Electrical engineering *a*	—	—	—	—	6.8[1]	*0.8*
Railway vehicles *a*	—	—	—	—	2.4[1]	na
Merchant ships *g p*	—	—	—	—	1 531.0	na
Motor vehicles *a*	—	—	—	*0.1*	9.5	*2.1*

a million $ U.S. *b* '000 hectolitres. *g* '000 G.R.T. *p* see note on shipping in Trading section above.

continued

LIBYA

NORTH AFRICA

In 1939 Libya, formerly a Turkish and, later, an Italian province, was incorporated into the national territory of Italy. After World War II Tripolitania and Cyrenaica were placed under British, and Fezzan under French Administration until 1949 when Libya became the first independent state to be created by the United Nations. The U.S.A. and the U.K. were granted military facilities, later extended also to the U.S.S.R., in return for economic aid.

The monarchy was overthrown in 1969 and a republic declared.

AREA: 1 759 540 sq. km. (679 358 sq. miles). Cyrenaica 49%; Tripolitania 20%; Fezzan 31%.

LAND USE: (percentage of total)

	Cyrenaica 1959	*Tripolitania 1962*	*Fezzan 1962*
Arable and orchard	0.9	4.9	0.1
Permanent meadow and pasture	0.6	23.4	—
Forest and woodland	0.5	0.1	—
City areas, waste and other land	98.0	71.6	99.9

POPULATION: 1 738 000 (1967 estimate)

Largest city: ṬARĀBULUS (Tripoli), capital; population: 213 506 (city proper, 1964)

Distribution of working population (1964)
Total working population: 405 258

U.N. group no.		*Percentage*
0	Agriculture, forestry, fishing and hunting	35.7
1	Mining and quarrying	3.5
2/3	Manufacturing	7.2
4	Construction	7.8
5	Electricity, gas, water and sanitary services	1.5
6	Commerce	6.6
7	Transport, storage and communications	5.6
8	Services	20.4
9	Others	11.7

Note—The discovery of oil in 1959 altered completely the pattern of the country's economy, and whereas 80% of the population had previously been engaged in subsistence farming, this figure had been halved by 1964, as the production of crude oil developed into a major industry.

		Year(s)
Crude birth rate (per '000)	37.2*	1966
Crude death rate (per '000)	6.7*	1966
Population per physician	3 160	1966
Population per hospital bed	310	1966
School enrolment: age 5–19 years (percentage)	53	1963–4 av.
age over 19 years (per 100 000 population)	114	1964–5 av.

COMMUNICATIONS

		Year(s)
Motor vehicles in use ('000s): private	35.3	1963–5 av.
commercial	18.1	
Mail per capita: domestic	3	1963–5 av.
foreign received	8	
foreign sent	7	
Telephones (per '000 urban population)	1.1	1967
Radio licences (per '000 population)	29	1963–5 av.
Daily newspapers (per '000 population)	5	1962–4 av.

FINANCE
Currency unit: The Libyan pound

Exchange rates	*1965*	*1960*
Per $ U.S.	0.357	0.357
Per £ sterling	1.0	1.0

		Year
National Income (million $ U.S.)	1 028	1965
G.N.P. per capita ($ U.S.)	640	1966

TRADING

Total trade (in million $ U.S.)	*1965*	*1955*	*1938*
Exports (f.o.b.)	797	13	6
Imports (c.i.f.)	320	40	46

Main trading partners (percentage of total value)

Exports	*1965*	*1955*	*Imports*	*1965*	*1955*
Germany F.R.	38	9	Italy	25	27
U.K.	21	21	U.S.A.	17	2
Italy	10	39	U.K.	15	25
France	9	—	Germany F.R.	10	3
Netherlands	8	2	France	5	6
Spain	3	na	Japan	4	1
U.S.A.	3	—	Netherlands	3	5

Distribution of trade (percentage of total value)

	1965	*1955*
Exports		
Crude oil	99	—
Imports		
Manufactured goods	74	49
(machinery and transport equipment)	(36)	(15)
(textiles and clothing)	(10)	(10)
Food	13	30
Crude materials and fuels	6	13
(petroleum products)	(4)	(5)
Chemicals	6	5

continued

na: data not available. — negligible or nil. [1] one year only. [2] two year average. * estimate. ‡ see appendix. † re-exports.

PRODUCTION, EXPORTS AND IMPORTS

Years: **1963–5 average** and *1953–5 average*   Units: '000 metric tons unless otherwise indicated

	Production		Exports		Imports	
1. CEREALS, etc.						
Barley	112.0	*35.0*[1]*p*	—	—	9.8	*3.4*
Maize (corn)	2.7*p	*1.0*[2]	—	—	—	—
Millets/sorghum	1.3	*1.5p*	—	—	0.5	—
Potatoes	11.0	*20.0*[2]*p*	—	*0.1*	1.7	*4.7*
Rice	—	—	—	—	9.9	*3.3*
Wheat	51.0*	*19.5**	—	—	10.7	*19.8*

p Tripolitania only.

	Production		Exports		Imports	
2. FRUIT, etc.						
Apples	—	—	—	—	4.4	*0.4*
Apricots	1.0*	na	—	—	—	—
Bananas	—	—	—	—	2.8	—
Cherries	6.3	na	—	—	—	—
Dates	39.3	*27.5*[2]	—	—	—	*0.4*[1]
Figs	3.7*	na	—	—	—	—
Grapes	8.0*	*3.0*[2]	—	—*p*	—	—*p*
Lemons	1.3	*0.7p*	0.2	—	—	—
Oranges	14.7*	*5.0*[2]**p*	3.1	*2.6*[2]*	—	—[2]
Olives	100.7*p*	*22.0p*				
Pears	—	—	—	—	0.4	—
Plums	6.7	na	—	—	—	—
Raisins	—	—	—	—	0.1	na
Tomatoes	114.3	na				
Wine *b*	na	na	0.6	—	1.2	*1.0*[1]

b '000 hectolitres. *p* Tripolitania only.

	Production		Exports		Imports	
3. BEVERAGES, FOREST PRODUCTS, etc.						
Coffee	—	—	—	—	0.6	*0.2*
Sugar, raw	—	—	—	—	24.5	*10.2*
Tea	—	—	—	—	4.5	*2.3*
Tobacco: leaf	1.0*	*1.6*[2]*	0.1	—	0.3	*0.3*[2]
cigars	1.3	— }				
cigarettes	843.0*e*	— }	—	—	0.4	—
tobacco/snuff	0.2	— }				
Softwood *j*	26.5[2]	*1.4*[1]	—	—	} 86.8	{ *35.0*[1]
Hardwood *j*	290.0[2]*	*27.0*[2]	—	—		{ *5.0*[1]
Newsprint	—*	—	—	—	0.3[2]	*0.2*[2]
Other paper	2.8[2]*	—	—	—	2.2	*0.8*[2]

e no. in millions. *j* '000 cu. metres of roundwood equivalent.

	Production		Exports		Imports	
4. VEGETABLE OILSEEDS AND OILS						
Castor seed	3.67*p	*3.05*	3.62	*1.85*[2]	—	—
Castor oil	na	na	—	*0.37*[2]	—	—
Coconut oil	—	—	—	—	0.24	—
Cottonseed oil	—	—	—	—	0.03	na
Groundnuts	7.00	*5.60*[1]*p*	4.31	*5.13*	0.01	*0.07*
Groundnut oil	na	na	—	—	1.06	—[1]
Linseed oil	—	—	—	—	0.12	—
Olive oil	9.67*p*	*4.33*	—	*2.20*[2]	1.79	—[2]
Palm kernel oil	—	—	—	—	0.02	—
Palm oil	—	—	—	—	0.03	—
Soya bean oil	—	—	—	—	2.11	—

p Tripolitania only.

	Production		Exports		Imports	
5. LIVESTOCK‡, ANIMAL PRODUCTS, etc.						
Chickens *d*	915.0*	*283.3u*				
Cattle *d*	121.7*	*120.5r*	—	*4.2*	2.8	—
Goats *d*	2 053.0	*1 022.5*[2]*r* }	—	—	69.9	na
Sheep *d*	1 860.0	*1 290.3r* }				
Horses *d*	37.0	*16.7*				
Pigs *d*	4.0*p*	*1.5*[2]*p*	—	*0.2*[1]	—	—
Meat‡: 'A'	10.7*	na	—	—	0.3	*0.1*
'B'	2.5*	na	—	—	0.4	—
Butter	—	—	—	—	0.3	—
Cheese	—	—	—	—	1.1	—
Eggs	2.7*	na	—	*0.2*	0.1[2]	—
Fish	0.3[2]	*2.2*	0.1	na	0.3	na
Milk	12.3*	na	—	—	17.3	*2.2**
Hides/skins	na	na	2.1	*1.1*[2]	—	—
Wool	na	*1.0*	0.7	—	—	—

d no. in thousands. *p* Tripolitania only. *r* no. registered for taxation. *u* Cyrenaica only.

	Production		Exports		Imports	
6. FIBRES, TEXTILES, etc.						
Cotton, woven fabrics	—	—	—	—	1.5[1]*	na
Wool, yarn	na	na	na	na	0.1[2]	na

	Production		Exports		Imports	
7. FUEL AND POWER						
Coal/coke	—	—	—	—	6	—
Electricity *h t*	153	*60*[1]				
Oil, crude	40 750	—[1]	40 660	na	—	—
Petroleum, refined	—	—	—	—	340	na

h million kWh. *t* thermal.

	Production		Exports		Imports	
8. IRON AND STEEL						
Iron/steel scrap	na	na	4[2]	na	—	—

	Production		Exports		Imports	
9. NON-FERROUS MINERALS AND METALS						
Silver *kq*, metal	—	—	108.58	na	—	—
Asbestos, manufactured	—	—	—	—	0.10	—

k '000 fine troy oz. *q* incl. platinum.

	Production		Exports		Imports	
11. INDUSTRY						
Aircraft *a*	—	—	—	—	0.5	*0.1*
Beer *b*	28.0	—	—	—	—	—
Cement	—	—	—	—	363.3	*41.3**
Electrical engineering *a*	—	—	—	—	22.2	*1.3*[2]
Motor vehicles *a*	—	—	—	—	43.4	*1.7*

a million $ U.S. *b* '000 hectolitres.

LIECHTENSTEIN

EUROPE

Liechtenstein has been a principality for over 500 years. Since 1924 close economic and diplomatic ties have existed with Switzerland.

AREA: 160 sq. km. (61.8 sq. miles)

LAND USE: (percentage of total)

	1953
Arable and orchard	12.5
Permanent meadow and pasture	43.7
Forest and woodland	25.0
City areas, waste and other land	18.8

POPULATION: 20 000 (1967 estimate)

Capital city: VADUZ; population: 3 514 (city proper, 1961)
Total working population: 7 575

		Year(s)
Infant mortality (per '000)	15.2*	1965
Crude birth rate (per '000)	20.6*	1965
Crude death rate (per '000)	3.1*	1965
School enrolment: age 5–19 years (percentage)	103‡	1963–4 av.

FINANCE
Currency unit: The Swiss franc

Exchange rates	*1965*	*1962*	*1957*
Per $ U.S.	4.318	4.30	4.37
Per £ sterling	12.103	12.05	12.24

EMPLOYMENT, PRODUCTION, AND TRADE

Liechtenstein has changed during the past thirty years from a predominantly agricultural to a highly industrialized country. The farming population has decreased from 70% in 1930 to 8.7% in 1965. Poultry (40 000), cattle (6 000), pigs (6 000) and sheep (1 000) are the principal livestock reared; crops include potatoes (8 000 tons annually) and maize; timber is also of importance. The rapid changeover to light industries such as textiles, ceramics, precision instruments, canned foods and heating appliances has led to a large-scale immigration of foreign workers.

Exports are sent mainly to Switzerland, Germany F.R., the U.K., France, Austria and the U.S.A. Tourism has recently been developed.

There is a customs union with Switzerland, and general trade data for Liechtenstein are included in the Swiss statistics.

na: data not available. — negligible or nil. [1] one year only. [2] two year average. * estimate. ‡ see appendix. † re-exports.

LUXEMBOURG

In 1921 a fifty-year economic union was formed between Belgium and the Grand Duchy of Luxembourg. Luxembourg became a member of Benelux in 1944, and in 1958 a member of the European Economic Community.

AREA: 2 586 sq. km. (999 sq. miles)

LAND USE: (percentage of total)

	1965	1954
Arable and orchard	26.7	30.1
Permanent meadow and pasture	24.7	23.6
Forest and woodland	33.2	33.2
City areas, waste and other land	15.4	13.1

POPULATION: 335 000 (1967 estimate)
Capital city: LUXEMBOURG; population: 78 721 (1965)

Distribution of working population (1960)
Total working population: 129 760 (excl. those in compulsory military service)

U.N. group no.		*Percentage*
0	Agriculture, forestry, fishing and hunting	14.9
1	Mining and quarrying	2.5
2/3	Manufacturing	32.3
4	Construction	8.3
5	Electricity, gas, water and sanitary services	0.6
6	Commerce	12.1
7	Transport, storage and communications	6.6
8	Services	21.7
9	Others	1.0

		Year(s)
Life expectancy at birth (years): male	61.7	1946–8 av.
female	65.8	
Infant mortality (per '000)	24	1965
Crude birth rate (per '000)	16	1965
Crude death rate (per '000)	12.3	1965
Accidental deaths (per 100 000 population)		
caused by motor vehicles	26	1967
due to other causes	22.4	1967
Population per physician	1 030	1963
Population per hospital bed	90	1966
School enrolment: age 5–19 years (percentage)	65	1963–4 av.
age over 19 years (per 100 000 population)	154	1963–5 av.

COMMUNICATIONS

		Year(s)
Motor vehicles in use ('000s): private	55.7	1963–5 av.
commercial	10.4	
Railway track (km.)	338	1964
Mail per capita: domestic	149	1963–5 av.
foreign received	69	
foreign sent	36	
Telephones (per '000 urban population)	25.8	1967
Radio licences (per '000 population)	347	1963–5 av.
Television sets (per '000 population)	74.3	1963–5 av.
Daily newspapers (per '000 population)	425	1964

FINANCE

Currency unit: The Luxembourg franc, at par with the Belgian franc

Exchange rates	*1965*	*1960*	*1950*	*1938*
Per $ U.S.	49.64	49.70	50.12	23.74
Per £ sterling	139.15	139.35	140.40	109.20

		Year
National Income (million $ U.S.)	496	1965
G.N.P. per capita ($ U.S.)	1 920	1966

PRODUCTION AND TRADE

In 1965 about 20 000 people were employed in agriculture, the principal crops being oats, potatoes and wheat; cattle and pig rearing are widespread.

The mining and metallurgical industries are the most important. Luxembourg has the highest steel production per capita in the world. Engineering is well developed and the production of beer is also of importance.

Trade statistics are included with those for Belgium.

PRODUCTION

Years: **1963–5 average** and *1953–5 average* Units: '000 metric tons unless otherwise indicated
Note—trade figures are included with those for Belgium

	Production		Exports		Imports	
1. CEREALS, etc.						
Barley	**20.7**	*13.3*				
Oats	**34.0**	*39.0*				
Potatoes	**87.3**	*133.3*				
Rye	**7.3**	*9.7*				
Wheat	**42.3**	*40.0*				
2. FRUIT, etc.						
Apples	**11.3**	na				
Cherries	**1.0***	na				
Grapes	**20.0***	*14.7**				
Pears	**1.0***	na				
Plums	**2.7***	na				
Wine *b*	**141.0**	*105.0*				

b '000 hectolitres.

	Production		Exports		Imports	
3. BEVERAGES, FOREST PRODUCTS, etc.						
Softwood *j*	**77.3**	*68.3*				
Hardwood *j*	**114.3**	*81.7*				

j '000 cu. metres of roundwood equivalent.

	Production		Exports		Imports	
5. LIVESTOCK‡, ANIMAL PRODUCTS, etc.						
Chickens *d*	**433.7**	*421.0*[2]				
Cattle *d*	**161.0**	*132.3*				
dairy cows *d*	**67.7**	*54.3*				
Goats *d*	—	*0.3*				
Sheep *d*	**2.3***	*3.0*				
Horses *d*	**2.7**	*11.6*				
Pigs *d*	**100.0**	*93.7*				

continued

	Production		Exports		Imports	
5. LIVESTOCK‡, ANIMAL PRODUCTS, etc.—*continued*						
Meat‡ 'A'	**25.7**	*18.7*				
'B'	**3.8***	na				
Butter	**5.0**	*4.0*				
Cheese	**1.0**	*1.0*[2]				
Eggs	**3.6**	*2.3*				
Fish	**0.6**[1] *t*	*0.4t*				
Milk	**194.0**	*180.7*				
Hides/skins	**1.0**	*0.9*				

d no. in thousands. *t* sport fishing only.

	Production		Exports		Imports	
7. FUEL AND POWER						
Electricity *h*: total	**2 122**	na				
hydro	**737**	na				
thermal	**1 385**	na				

h million kWh.

	Production		Exports		Imports	
8. IRON AND STEEL						
Iron ore	**1 849***m*	*1 817m*				
Pig iron	**3 974**	*2 869*				
Steel ingots/castings	**4 392**	*2 904*				

m metal content.

	Production		Exports		Imports	
9. NON-FERROUS MINERALS AND METALS						
Magnesium, dolomite	**239.5**[2]	na				
11. INDUSTRY						
Beer *b*	**501.0**	*372.3*				
Spirits *b*	**2.0**[1] *p*	*5.7*[1] *t*				
Cement	**210.0**	*152.0*				

b '000 hectolitres. *p* 1966 figure. *t* 1960 figure.

MALAGASY REPUBLIC

Malagasy, formerly the French colony of Madagascar, became an independent state within the French Community in 1960. Foreign aid has financed improvements in transport, agriculture, industry and social projects.

AREA: 594 180 sq. km. (229 233 sq. miles)

LAND USE: (percentage of total)

	1964	1954
Arable and orchard	4.9	2.2
Permanent meadow and pasture	52.0	62.7
Forest and woodland	21.7	20.3
City areas, waste and other land	21.4	14.8

POPULATION: 6 200 000 (1966 estimate)
Largest city: TANANARIVE (Antananarivo), capital; population: 335 149 (city proper, 1966)
Total working population: 3 200 000 (1964)

		Year(s)
Life expectancy at birth (years): male	37.5*	1966
female	38.3*	
Infant mortality (per '000)	65.5*	1965
Crude birth rate (per '000)	32.3*	1965
Crude death rate (per '000)	10.4*	1965
Population per physician	10 540	1965
Population per hospital bed	350	1966
School enrolment: age 5–19 years (percentage)	39	1963–4 av.
age over 19 years (per 100 000 population)	40	1963–5 av.

EMPLOYMENT AND PRODUCTION

The majority of the people are engaged in agriculture. Forest resources are abundant. Mineral products include graphite, chrome, mica, and various rarer ores. Industry includes cotton and silk weaving, metal work, food processing, cement, and the manufacture of soap.

COMMUNICATIONS

		Year(s)
Motor vehicles in use ('000s): private	29.5	1963–5 av.
commercial	25.7	
Railway track (km.)	864	1965
Mail per capita: domestic	5	1963–5 av.
foreign received	4.7	
foreign sent	2.1	
Telephones (per '000 urban population)	0.3	1967
Radio receivers (per '000 population)	49	1963–5 av.
Daily newspapers (per '000 population)	9	1962

FINANCE

Currency unit: The Malagasy franc, at par with the franc CFA

Exchange rates	*1965*	*1960*	*1958a*
Per $ U.S.	246.85	246.85	210
Per £ sterling	691.18	691.18	590

		Year
National Income (million $ U.S.)	424	1958
G.N.P. per capita ($ U.S.)	90	1966

a francs CFA.

TRADING

Total trade (in million $ U.S.)	*1965*	*1955*	*1938c*
Exports (f.o.b.)	92	82	24
Imports (c.i.f.)	138	122	17

Main trading partners (percentage of total value)

Exports	*1965*	*1955*	*Imports*	*1965*	*1955*
France	45	65	France	63	73
U.S.A.	27	15	Thailand	6	na
Réunion	6	7	U.S.A.	4	4
Germany F.R.	5	1	Germany F.R.	4	2
U.K.	3	2	Iran	2	na
Italy	1	1	Netherlands	2	1
Comoro Arch.	1	na	Senegal	2	na

Distribution of trade (percentage of total value)

Exports	*1965*	*1954**
Food	72	na
(coffee)	(32)	(43)
(vanilla)	(11)	(5)
(sugar and honey)	(5)	(na)
Crude materials and fuels	17	na
(sisal)	(6)	(2)
Tobacco	5	7
Imports		
Manufactured goods	64	na
(machinery and transport equipment)	(25)	(20)
(textiles and clothing)	(13)	(19)
Food	15	na
(rice)	(7)	(na)
Chemicals	9	2
Petroleum products	5	4
Alcoholic beverages	3	6

c includes the Comoro Archipelago.

PRODUCTION, EXPORTS AND IMPORTS

Years: **1963–5 average** and *1953–5 average* Units: '000 metric tons unless otherwise indicated

	Production		Exports		Imports	
1. CEREALS, etc.						
Cassava	**850.0**	*796.0*[1]				
Maize (corn)	**99.7***	*64.5*[2]	**1.3**	*7.5*	**0.2**	—
Millets/sorghum	**60.0**[1]*	na	—	—	—	—
Potatoes	**73.3***	*65.0*[2]	**0.3**	*0.2*	**0.3**	*0.5*
Rice	**1 237.3**	*1 013.7*	**22.0**	*32.3*	**28.4**	*2.7*
Sweet potatoes/yams	**280.0**	*303.0*[1]				
Wheat	—	—	—	—	**0.4**	—
2. FRUIT, etc.						
Apples	**10.0**	na	**0.1***n*	—	**0.1***n*	—
Bananas	**150.0**	na	**14.5**	—	—	—
Coconuts *e*	**15.3**	na	—	—	—	—
Grapes	**2.0**	na	—	—	—	—
Lemons	**2.0***	na	—	—	—	—
Oranges	**14.0***	na	—	—	—	—
Other citrus fruit	**1.0**	na	—	—	—	—
Peaches	**5.0**	na	—	—	—	—
Pineapples	**7.0***	na	—	—	—	—
Plums	**2.3**	na	—	—	—	—
Tomatoes	**8.0***	na				
Wine *b*	—	—	—	—	**119.4**	*293.3*

b '000 hectolitres. *e* no. in millions. *n* incl. pears and quince.

	Production		Exports		Imports	
3. BEVERAGES, FOREST PRODUCTS, etc.						
Cocoa	**0.4**	*0.4*[1]	**0.4**	*0.3*	—	*0.1*
Coffee	**51.7**	*46.7**	**44.1**	*41.7*	—	—
Sugar: cane	**1 116.7**	*446.0*[1]				
raw	**99.8**	*25.7*	**57.4**	*5.7*	**0.2**	*5.3*
Tea	—	—	—	—	**0.1**	—
Tobacco: leaf	**5.8***	*4.6**	**4.2**	*4.2*	**0.6**	*0.3*
cigars	—	—	}			
cigarettes	**671.0***e*	—	} **4.8**[2]	—	**0.3**	*1.0*[2]*
tobacco/snuff	**1.3**	—	}			

continued

	Production		Exports		Imports	
3. BEVERAGES, FOREST PRODUCTS, etc.—*continued*						
Softwood *j*	—	—	—[2]	*—*[2]	} **1.5**[2]	*12.5*[1]
Hardwood *j*	**3 410.0**[1]*	*2 380.0*[1]	**3.6**[2]	*0.1*[2]	}	*—*[1]
Newsprint	—	—	—	*—*[2]	} **2.3**[1]	*0.5*[2]
Other paper	—	—	—	*—*[2]	}	*1.0*[2]

e no. in millions. *j* '000 cu. metres of roundwood equivalent.

	Production		Exports		Imports	
4. VEGETABLE OILSEEDS AND OILS						
Castor seed	**1.00**	na	**0.99**	*0.77*	—	*0.37*
Castor oil	na	na	—	*0.27*	**0.01**	—
Copra	**0.27***	*1.00*[2]	—	*1.47*	**1.75**	*1.30*
Coconut oil	na	na	—	—	**0.12**	*0.41*[2]
Cottonseed	**3.00**	na	**1.09**	—	—	—
Cottonseed oil	na	na	—	—	**0.09**	—
Groundnuts	**25.20**	*16.45*	**5.32**	*7.53*	—	—
Groundnut oil	na	na	na	*0.04*	**0.17**	*0.68*
Linseed oil	—	—	—	—	**0.03**	*0.05*
Olive oil	—	—	—	—	**0.05**	*0.06*
Palm oil	—	—	—	—	—	*0.06*
Rapeseed oil	—	—	—	—	**0.15**	—
Tung oil	**1.00***	*0.51*	**0.93**	*0.41*	—	—
5. LIVESTOCK‡, ANIMAL PRODUCTS, etc.						
Chickens *d*	**13 428.3***	*13 000.0*[2]*				
Cattle *d*	**8 416.7**	*5 974.0*	**11.4**	*5.6*	—	*0.2*
dairy cows *d*	**2 180.0***	na				
Goats *d*	**300.0***	*471.0*	—	—	—	—
Sheep *d*	**300.0**	*378.3*	—	—	—	—
Horses *d*	**2.0***	*2.5*[2]				
Pigs *d*	**450.0**	*223.7*	**6.9**	—	—	—
Meat‡: 'A'	**85.7***	*54.0**	**3.2**	*1.0*	—	—
'B'	**2.1***	na	**0.2**	*0.1*	—	—
Butter	—	—	—	—	**0.5**	*0.3*
Cheese	—	—	—	—	**0.4**	*0.3*
Eggs	**14.1***	*12.5*[1]	—	—	—	—
Fish	**41.6**	*2.6**	**0.3**	na	**1.0**	*1.0*[1]*
Milk	**379.0***	na	—	—	**21.2**	*8.7**
Hides/skins	**2.4**[1]	*3.1*[2]	**2.4**	*2.8*[2]	—	—

d no. in thousands.

continued

MALAGASY REPUBLIC *continued*

PRODUCTION, EXPORTS AND IMPORTS *continued*

6. FIBRES, TEXTILES, etc.

	Production		Exports		Imports	
Agaves (sisal)	26.1	*12.1**	26.5	*8.1*	—	—
Cotton lint	2.0	na	0.2	—	—	—
Jute	2.0	*1.5*[2]	—	—	1.9	*0.7*
Silk *f*	—	—	—	—	2.7	—
Cotton: yarn	2.4[1]	na	—	—	1.2	*0.7*[2]
woven fabrics	2.4	na	—	—	4.2	*5.4*

f metric tons.

7. FUEL AND POWER

	Production		Exports		Imports	
Coal 'A' ‡	—	—	—[2]	—	14	*15*
Coke	—	—	—	—	—	*1*
Electricity *h*: total	140	*120*[1]				
hydro	80	*50*[1]				
thermal	60	*70*[1]				
Petroleum, refined	—	—	—	—	150	*100*[1]
Rare earths *f*:						
monazite	888	*22*	863	*17*	—	—
bastnaesite	—	*8*	—	*9*	—	—
uranothorianite	518*p*	—	507	—	—	—

f metric tons. *h* million kWh. *p* containing approx. 60% thorium and 20% uranium.

9. NON-FERROUS MINERALS AND METALS

	Production		Exports		Imports	
Gold *k*, ore	—	*1.00m*	—	*0.04q*	—	—
Asbestos, manufactured	—	—	—	—	0.69	—
Mica	0.76	*0.54*	0.92	*0.59*	—	—
Aluminium	—	—	—	—	0.30*r*	—
Beryl	0.21	*0.45*	0.18	*0.24*	—	—
Chrome, ore	8.45*m*	—	9.27	—	—	—
Copper, metal	—	—	—	—	0.15	—
Lead, metal	—	—	—	—	0.19	—
Tin, metal	—	—	—	—	0.01	*0.03*
Titanium minerals	4.92	—	na	—	—	—
Zinc, metal	—	—	—	—	0.09	—
Zirconium minerals	0.51	—	—	—	—[2]	—

k '000 fine troy oz. *m* metal content. *q* bullion. *r* aluminium sulphate only.
Graphite production averaged 16 480 metric tons in 1963–5.

10. CHEMICALS*n* AND FERTILIZERS

	Production		Exports		Imports	
Chemicals	—		—		na	
Fertilizers:						
Potash	—	—	—	—	1.2	—

n data not available for years 1953–5.

11. INDUSTRY

	Production		Exports		Imports	
Aircraft *a*	—	—	—	—	0.9	—
Alcoholic beverages			0.3*aq*	—	4.6*a*	*7.4a*
beer *b*	32.0	—				
spirits *b*	na	na				
Cement	41.7	—*	—	—*	78.3	*121.3p*
Electrical engineering *a*	—	—	—	—	7.8	*4.9*[2]
Locomotives *c*	1.0	—	—	—	na	na
Railway vehicles *a*	na	na	—	—	0.9	—
Merchant ships *g*	0.1	—	—	—	—	—
Motor vehicles *a*	—	—	—	—	11.9	*6.6*

a million $ U.S. *b* '000 hectolitres. *c* no. of units. *g* '000 G.R.T. *p* incl. Comoro Archipelago. *q* rum only.

continued

MALAWI

EAST AFRICA

Malawi, formerly Nyasaland, and from 1954 part of the Federation of Rhodesia and Nyasaland, became an independent member of the Commonwealth in 1963 and adopted republican status in 1966.

No independent production and trade statistics are available for the duration of the Federation 1954–1963 inclusive.

AREA: 126 338 sq. km. (48 779 sq. miles)
Land area: 95 450 sq. km. (36 853 sq. miles)

LAND USE: (percentage of total)

	1963	*1955*
Arable and orchard	10.7	23.0
Permanent meadow and pasture	3.4	4.7
Forest and woodland	8.8	14.2
City areas, waste and other land	77.1	58.1

POPULATION: 4 042 412*a* (1966 census)
Largest city: BLANTYRE; population: 109 795 (city proper, 1966)
Capital city: ZOMBA; population: 19 000 (city proper, 1966)

		Year
Population per physician	49 250	1965
Population per hospital bed	800	1965
School enrolment: age 5–19 years (percentage)	40	1964
age over 19 years (per 100 000 population)	2	1965

a excl. about one third of the adult male African labour force, working abroad in the mines, industries, and farms of Zambia and South Africa.

EMPLOYMENT AND PRODUCTION

Agriculture is the foundation of the economy, and has seen several important developments since 1967. These include a land reorganization scheme and two cotton development projects, which aim to further the transition from a subsistence agricultural economy to one of commercial crop production.

COMMUNICATIONS

		Year(s)
Motor vehicles in use ('000s): private	7.8	1963–5 av.
commercial	7.0	1963–5 av.
Railway track (km.)	450	1969
Mail per capita: domestic	3	1964–5 av.
foreign received	2	1964–5 av.
foreign sent	2	1964–5 av.
Telephones (per '000 urban population)	0.2	1967
Radio licences (per '000 population)	3	1963–5 av.

FINANCE

Currency unit: The Malawi kwacha replaced the Rhodesian pound in 1971, at the rate 1 KM to R£0.5

Exchange rates (for Rhodesian pounds)	*1965*	*1960*	*1950*	*1938*
Per $ U.S.	0.357	0.357	0.357	0.215
Per £ sterling	1.0	1.0	1.0	1.0

		Year(s)
National Income (million $ U.S.)	151	1965
G.N.P. per capita ($ U.S.)	50	1966
Rate of increase of G.N.P. per capita	1.1	1960–3 av.
Foreign trade (percentage of G.D.P.)	54	1964–5 av.

TRADING

Total trade (in million $ U.S.)	*1965*	*1955*	*1938*
Exports (f.o.b.)	40	20*e*	5
Imports (f.o.b.)	57	na	4

Main trading partners (percentage of total value)

Exports	*1965*	*Imports*	*1965*
U.K.	47	Rhodesia	36
Rhodesia	10	U.K.	25
Netherlands	4	Japan	7
South Africa	4	South Africa	5
Irish R.	3	Germany F.R.	3
France	3	U.S.A.	3
U.S.A.	3	Australia	3

Distribution of trade (percentage of total value)

Exports	*1965*	*Imports*	*1965*
Tobacco	38	Manufactured goods	70
Tea	28	(textiles and clothing)	(27)
Groundnuts	12	(machinery and transport equipment)	(21)
Cotton	8	Food	11
Vegetables	7	Chemicals	7
		Crude materials	6

e excl. trade with Rhodesia and Zambia.

continued

na: data not available. — negligible or nil. [1] one year only. [2] two year average. * estimate. ‡ see appendix. † re-exports.

PRODUCTION, EXPORTS AND IMPORTS

Years: **1964–5 average** and *1953* Units: '000 metric tons unless otherwise indicated

1. CEREALS, etc.

	Production		Exports		Imports	
Cassava	137.3*	na				
Maize (corn)	846.0*	*49.0*	13.7[1]	*35.0*	—	—
Millets/sorghum	40.0[1]*	na	0.3[1]	—	—	—
Potatoes	3.0*	—	—	—	—	—
Rice	5.0*	*4.7*	1.3[1]	*1.4*	0.5[1]	—
Sweet potatoes/yams	42.3*	na				
Wheat	—	na	—	—	—	—

2. FRUIT, etc.

	Production		Exports		Imports	
Apples	—	—	—	—	0.1[1]	—
Bananas	5.0*	na	—	—	—	—
Wine *b*	—	—	—	—	0.7[1]	—

b '000 hectolitres.

3. BEVERAGES, FOREST PRODUCTS, etc.

	Production		Exports		Imports	
Coffee	—	—	0.2[1]	—	—[1]	—
Sugar, raw	—	—	—	—	14.1*	*5.6*
Tea	12.4	*7.2*	12.5	*6.0*	0.1[1]	—
Tobacco, leaf	19.2	*14.0*	13.3[1]	*11.9*	1.9[1]	—
Softwood *j*	11.5*	*7.6*	—	—	7.0[1]	—
Hardwood *j*	3 348.0*	*5 844.7*	5.0[1]	—	5.3[1]	—
Newsprint	—	—	—	—	0.1[1]	—
Other paper	—	—	—	—	0.4[1]	—

j '000 cu. metres of roundwood equivalent.

4. VEGETABLE OILSEEDS AND OILS

	Production		Exports		Imports	
Castor seed	na	na	0.03[1]	na	—	—
Coconut oil	—	—	—	—	0.10	na
Cottonseed	7.70	*6.00**	na	*4.50*	—	—
Cottonseed oil	na	na	0.40[1]	na	—	—
Groundnuts	32.00**n*	*5.95*	17.43	*5.40*	0.44	—
Groundnut oil	na	na	—	—	0.19[1]	na
Soya beans	—	na	—	*0.60*	—	—
Sunflower seed	na	—	0.03[1]	—	—	—
Tung oil	1.47	*0.71*	1.65	*0.88*	—	—

n sales only.

5. LIVESTOCK‡, ANIMAL PRODUCTS, etc.

	Production		Exports		Imports	
Chickens *d*	2 572.0*p**	*2 502.0p*				
Cattle *d*	401.3	*290.7*	—	—	0.5[1]	—
dairy cows *d*	289.7	*184.7*				
Goats *d*	451.0*	*314.3*	—	—	—	—
Sheep *d*	81.3*	*62.0*	—	—	—	—
Pigs *d*	119.0	*84.0*	—	—	—	—
Meat‡ 'A'	6.0*	na	—[1]	—	0.2[1]	—
'B'	2.8	na	—	—	—	—
Butter	—	—	—	—	0.1[1]	—
Cheese	—	—	—	—	0.1[1]	—
Eggs	0.9*	na	—	—	—	—
Fish	15.3	na	0.1	na	0.1	na
Milk	29.3*	na	—	—	3.0	*1.0**
Hides/skins	0.4	*0.2*	na	na	—	—

d no. in thousands. *p* incl. ducks, geese and turkeys.

6. FIBRES, TEXTILES, etc.

	Production		Exports		Imports	
Agaves (sisal)	0.3*	*0.3*	0.4[1]	—	—	—
Cotton lint	3.3*	*2.0*	4.1*	*7.4*	—[1]	—
Rubber, natural	na	na	0.1[1]	—	—	—
Wool, yarn	—	—	na	na	na	na

7. FUEL AND POWER

	Production		Exports		Imports	
Coal 'A' ‡	—	na	—	—	65	*37*
Electricity *h*: total	45	na				
hydro	5	na				
thermal	40	na				
Petroleum, refined	—	—	7†	—	57	*20*

h million kWh.

9. NON-FERROUS MINERALS AND METALS

	Production		Exports		Imports	
Asbestos	—	na*r*	—	—	—	*0.67*[1]*q*
Mica	—	—	—	—	na	—
Aluminium	—	—	—	—	0.13	—
Tin, metal	—	—	—	—	0.04[1]	—

q manufactured. *r* fibre.

11. INDUSTRY

	Production		Exports		Imports	
Alcoholic beverages *a*	—	—	—	—	1.2[1]	na
Cement	31.0	na	1.0	na	0.5	na
Electrical engineering *a*	—	—	—	—	2.1	na
Motor vehicles *a*	—	—	—	—	3.5	na

a million $ U.S.

continued

MALAYSIA

SOUTH EAST ASIA

Malaysia, a member of the British Commonwealth, was created in 1963 out of the federation of Malaya (West Malaysia), Sarawak, North Borneo (Sabah) and Singapore. In 1965 Singapore seceded from this Federation of states. The constitution provides for one of the nine rulers of the Malay States to be elected as supreme head of the federation for five years. The aim is to ensure strong federal government with some autonomy for state government.

AREA: 329 600 sq. km. (127 260 sq. miles)

POPULATION: 10 071 000 (1967 estimate)
Capital city: KUALA LUMPUR; population: 316 230 (city proper, 1957)

FINANCE

Currency unit: The Malaysian dollar

Exchange rates	*1965*	*1960*	*1950*	*1938*
Per $ U.S.	3.06	3.06	3.06	1.86
Per £ sterling	8.57	8.57	8.57	8.57

		Year(s)
National Income (million $ U.S.)	2 349	1965
G.N.P. per capita ($ U.S.)	280	1966
Rate of increase of G.N.P. per capita	2.8	1963–5 av.
Foreign trade (percentage of G.D.P.)	84	1963–5 av.

SABAH

AREA: 76 115 sq. km. (29 388 sq. miles)

LAND USE: (percentage of total)

	1965	*1954*
Arable and orchard	2.7	2.7
Permanent meadow and pasture	—	2.1
Forest and woodland	96.2	80.5
City areas, waste and other land	1.1	14.7

POPULATION: 588 000 (1967 estimate)
Capital city: KOTA KINABALU (Jesselton); population: 21 719 (city proper, 1960)

Distribution of working population (1960)
Total working population: 176 626

U.N. group no.		*Percentage*
0	Agriculture, forestry, fishing and hunting	80.5
1	Mining and quarrying	0.3
2/3	Manufacturing	3.8
4	Construction	2.5
5	Electricity, gas, water and sanitary services	0.2
6	Commerce	4.4
7	Transport, storage and communications	2.6
8	Services	5.7

		Year(s)
Infant mortality (per '000)	36.5*	1965
Crude birth rate (per '000)	35.7*	1965
Crude death rate (per '000)	5.5*	1965
Accidental deaths (per 100 000 population)		
caused by motor vehicles	1.9*	1967
due to other causes	20.3*	1967
Population per physician	9 740	1965
Population per hospital bed	360	1964
School enrolment: age 5–19 years (percentage)	57	1963–4 av

COMMUNICATIONS

		Year(s)
Motor vehicles in use ('000s): private	13.5*a*	1963–5 av
commercial	4.4*a*	1963–5 av
Railway track (km.)	154	1968
Mail per capita: domestic	7	1963–5 av
foreign received	1	1963–5 av
foreign sent	3	1963–5 av
Telephones (per '000 urban population)	1.4	1967
Radio licences (per '000 population)	54*a*	1963–5 av.
Television licences (per '000 population)	3*b*	1963–5 av
Daily newspapers (per '000 population)	37	1961

a incl. Sarawak. *b* incl Sarawak and West Malaysia.

FINANCE

		Year
National Income (million $ U.S.)	119	1965

continued

na: data not available. — negligible or nil. [1] one year only. [2] two year average. * estimate. ‡ see appendix. † re-exports.

SABAH *continued*

TRADING

Total trade (in million $ U.S.)	1965	1955	1938
Exports (f.o.b.)	100	34	6
Imports (c.i.f.)	109	29	4

Main trading partners (percentage of total value)

Exports	1965	1955	*Imports*	1965	1955
Japan	50	8	U.K.	19	26
West Mal./Sing.	15	20	Hong Kong	15	8
Philippines	14	5	Singapore	13 }	11
S. Korea	4	na	West Malaysia	5 }	
Taiwan	3	—	U.S.A.	12	5
Australia	3	4*a*	Japan	7	9
Hong Kong	2	10	China P.R.	5	3

Distribution of trade (percentage of total value)

Exports	1965	1955	1938*
Crude materials and fuels	78	84	na
(wood)	(61)	(1)	(25)
(rubber)	(11)	(40)	(50)
(oilseeds)	(4)	(14)	(na)
Cigarettes	13	2	5
Imports			
Manufactured goods	48	40	na
(machinery and transport equipment)	(26)	(11)	(—)
(textiles and clothing)	(5)	(9)	(10)
Food	17	26	37
(cereals)	(6)	(10)	(na)
Cigarettes	13	na	7
Crude materials and fuels	12	18	na
Chemicals	4	4	na

a incl. New Zealand.

PRODUCTION, EXPORTS AND IMPORTS

Years: **1963–5 average** and *1953–5 average*   Units: '000 metric tons unless otherwise indicated

	Production 1963–5	Production 1953–5	Exports 1963–5	Exports 1953–5	Imports 1963–5	Imports 1953–5
1. CEREALS, etc.						
Cassava	14.0*	na				
Maize (corn)	2.7	1.0[2]	—	—	5.2[1]	—
Potatoes	—	—	—	—	0.8[1]	—
Rice	76.3	51.5[2]	—	—	32.0[2]	15.2[1]
Sweet potatoes/yams	3.3*	14.0[1]				
2. FRUIT, etc.						
Apples	—	—	—	—	0.3[1]	—
Bananas	9.0*	na	0.2	—	—	—
Coconuts	182.0*e*	na	1.4[1]	1.0[2]	0.1[1]	—
Oranges	1.0*	na	—	—	0.7[1]	—
Wine *b*	—	—	—	—	0.4[1]	—

b '000 hectolitres. *e* no. in millions.

	Production 1963–5	Production 1953–5	Exports 1963–5	Exports 1953–5	Imports 1963–5	Imports 1953–5
3. BEVERAGES, FOREST PRODUCTS, etc.						
Cocoa	—	—	0.4[2]†	—	na	—
Coffee	0.2	—	—	0.1†	0.3[2]	0.2
Sugar, raw	—	—	4.0[2]†	—	15.6*	6.6
Tea	—	—	—	—	0.1[1]	0.1
Tobacco: leaf	0.1	0.3[2]	—	0.1	—	—
cigarettes	—	—	4.8[2]†	0.2†	5.1[2]*p*	0.3*p*
Hardwood *j*	3 778.0	584.7	3 412.0*n*	380.2	58.2	2.2
Newsprint	—	—	—	—	0.4	—
Other paper	—	—	—	—	0.6	—

j '000 cu. metres of roundwood equivalent. *n* sawn wood only. *p* incl. other tobacco products.

	Production 1963–5	Production 1953–5	Exports 1963–5	Exports 1953–5	Imports 1963–5	Imports 1953–5
4. VEGETABLE OILSEEDS AND OILS						
Copra	33.00*	25.15[2]	33.00*	21.57	16.45	7.73
Coconut oil	na	na	0.28[2]	0.01[2]	0.09[2]	0.10*
Groundnuts	na *r*	—	—	—	0.22[1]	—
Groundnut oil	—	—	0.01[2]†	—	1.95[2]	0.63[2]
Palm oil	na	na *r*	0.02	—	—	—
Soya beans	—	—	—	—	0.09[1]	—
Tung oil	—	—	—	—	0.01[1]	—

r see West Malaysia.

	Production 1963–5	Production 1953–5	Exports 1963–5	Exports 1953–5	Imports 1963–5	Imports 1953–5
5. LIVESTOCK‡, ANIMAL PRODUCTS, etc.						
Chickens *d*	1 123.3	2 500.0				
Cattle *d*	15.0	15.3	1.3[1]	0.9	—	0.6
Goats *d*	18.0	14.7	0.1	na	—	—
Horses *d*	5.0	3.0				
Pigs *d*	83.0	65.3	14.7	2.3	1.2*	—
Meat‡: 'A'	4.0*	2.0[1]	—	—	0.2[1]	0.1
'B'	—	—	—	—	0.1[1]	—
Butter	—	—	—	—	0.1[1]	0.2[2]
Eggs	2.5[1]	2.5[1]	—	—	0.4[1]	—
Fish	na *r*	na *r*	1.2[1]	na	1.9	na
Milk	—	—	0.2[1]†	—	11.6[1]	4.2*
Hides/skins	na	0.1[1]	—	—	—	—

d no. in thousands. *r* see West Malaysia.

	Production 1963–5	Production 1953–5	Exports 1963–5	Exports 1953–5	Imports 1963–5	Imports 1953–5
6. FIBRES, TEXTILES, etc.						
Abaca	3.4	2.4[2]*	3.9[2]	2.0	—	0.1
Rubber, natural	na	na	23.0*	18.3	0.2[1]	0.1
7. FUEL AND POWER						
Electricity *h t*	41	10[1]				
Petroleum, refined	—	—	7†	na	107	10[1]

h million kWh. *t* thermal.

	Production 1963–5	Production 1953–5	Exports 1963–5	Exports 1953–5	Imports 1963–5	Imports 1953–5
8. IRON AND STEEL						
Steel ingots/castings	—	—	—	—	1	—
9. NON-FERROUS MINERALS AND METALS						
Gold *k*, bullion/coins etc.	—	—	—	—	10.07[2]	—
Asbestos, manufactured	—	—	—	—	3.75	1.36[1]
Aluminium	—	—	—	—	0.14	—
Copper, metal	—	—	—	—	0.10	—
Lead, metal	—	—	—	—	0.06	na *r*
Tin, metal	—	—	—	na *r*	0.11	—

k '000 fine troy oz. *r* see West Malaysia.

	Production 1963–5	Production 1953–5	Exports 1963–5	Exports 1953–5	Imports 1963–5	Imports 1953–5
10. CHEMICALS*n* AND FERTILIZERS						
Chemicals	—		—		na	
Fertilizers:						
Phosphates	—	—	—	—	0.8	0.1[2]
Potash	—	—	—	—	0.4	na

n data not available for years 1953–5.

	Production 1963–5	Production 1953–5	Exports 1963–5	Exports 1953–5	Imports 1963–5	Imports 1953–5
11. INDUSTRY						
Aircraft *a*	—	—	—	—	0.2[2]	—
Alcoholic beverages *a*	—	—	—	—	2.0[2]	0.9
Cement	na *r*	—	na *r*	—	na *r*	12.0
Electrical engineering *a*	—	—	0.1[2]†	—	4.3	0.6[2]
Railway vehicles *a*	—	—	—	—	0.3[2]	0.1
Motor vehicles *a*	—	—	0.3[2]†	—	6.9[2]	0.6[2]

a million $ U.S. *r* see West Malaysia.

na: data not available. — negligible or nil. [1] one year only. [2] two year average. * estimate. ‡ see appendix. † re-exports.

SARAWAK

AREA: 121 900 sq. km. (47 060 sq. miles)

LAND USE: (percentage of total)	1962	1952
Arable and orchard	5.6	27.6
Permanent meadow and pasture	0.1	—
Forest and woodland	73.3	71.0
City areas, waste and other land	21.0	1.4

POPULATION: 903 000 (1967 estimate)

Capital city: KUCHING; population: 50 579 (city proper, 1960)

Distribution of working population (1960)

Total working population: 294 285

U.N. group no.		*Percentage*
0	Agriculture, forestry, fishing and hunting	81.4
1	Mining and quarrying	0.8
2/3	Manufacturing	3.9
4	Construction	1.6
5	Electricity, gas, water and sanitary services	0.2
6	Commerce	4.7
7	Transport, storage and communications	1.9
8	Services	5.5

		Year(s)
Infant mortality (per '000)	42.6*	1965
Crude birth rate (per '000)	28.0	1965
Crude death rate (per '000)	5.0*	1965
Population per physician	1 290	1965
Population per hospital bed	380	1966
School enrolment: age 5–19 years (percentage)	57	1963–4 av.
age over 19 years (per 100 000 population)	18	1963–5 av.

COMMUNICATIONS		*Year(s)*
Motor vehicles in use ('000s): private	13.5*a*	1963–5 av.
commercial	4.4*a*	
Mail per capita: domestic	7	1963–5 av.
foreign received	3	
foreign sent	2	
Telephones (per '000 urban population)	1	1967
Radio licences (per '000 population)	54*a*	1963–5 av.
Television licences (per '000 population)	3*b*	1963–5 av.
Daily newspapers (per '000 population)	25	1961

a incl. Sabah. *b* incl. Sabah and West Malaysia.

FINANCE

		Year
National Income (million $ U.S.)	162	1965

TRADING

Total trade (in million $ U.S.)	1965	1955	1938
Exports (f.o.b.)	124	156	14
Imports (c.i.f.)	158	144	13

Main trading partners (percentage of total value)

Exports	1965	1955	*Imports*	1965	1955
Singapore	49 }	42	Brunei	39	66
West Malaysia	5 }		West Mal./Sing.	14	5
Japan	10	10	U.K.	13	9
Australia	8	14	China P.R.	8	2
Philippines	7	—	Japan	4	2
U.K.	5	10	U.S.A.	4	2
New Zealand	2	—	Thailand	4	4

Distribution of trade (percentage of total value) *a*

Exports	1965	1955	1938*
Petroleum products (re-exports)	36	44	45
Wood	25	5	na
Rubber	18	17	32
Pepper and pimentos	13	7	3
Imports			
Petroleum and petroleum products	44	68	30
Manufactured goods	27	12	na
(machinery and transport equipment)	(14)	(4)	(na)
Food	18	12	18
(cereals)	(6)	(na)	(na)
Chemicals	4	2	na

a these are percentages of national exports‡ (but incl. ships' bunkers), which comprised 85% of general exports in 1965; 96% in 1955.

PRODUCTION, EXPORTS AND IMPORTS

Years: **1963–5 average** and *1953–5 average*   Units: '000 metric tons unless otherwise indicated

	Production 1963–5	Production 1953–5	Exports 1963–5	Exports 1953–5	Imports 1963–5	Imports 1953–5
1. CEREALS, etc.						
Maize (corn)	—	—	0.1†	—	6.8[2]	—
Potatoes	—	—	—	—	1.0[1]	0.5
Rice	104.3	na	—	0.1[2]	53.1*	26.9[2]*
Wheat	—	—	—	—	0.4[1]	—
2. FRUIT, etc.						
Apples	—	—	—	—	0.3[1]	0.3[2]
Bananas	—	—	0.1†	—	na	—
Coconuts	46.0[1]**e*	na	0.1	—	—	—
Grapes	—	—	—	—	0.1[1]	0.1[2]
Oranges	—	—	—	—	0.3[1]	—
Raisins	—	—	—	—	0.2[1]	0.8
Wine *b*	—	—	—	—	0.4[1]	1.0

b '000 hectolitres. *e* no. in millions.

	Production 1963–5	Production 1953–5	Exports 1963–5	Exports 1953–5	Imports 1963–5	Imports 1953–5
3. BEVERAGES, FOREST PRODUCTS, etc.						
Coffee	—	—	—	0.2†	0.7[2]	0.4
Sugar, raw	—	—	—	—	19.3*	9.8
Tea	—	—	—	—	0.2[1]	0.2[2]
Tobacco: leaf	—	—	—	—	—	0.1[1]
products	—	—	—	—	0.6[2]	2.4[2]*a*
Softwood *j*	7.0	—	5.0	3.1	0.1	—
Hardwood *j*	2 018.0	579.0	1 394.0	397.3	7.2	0.9[2]
Newsprint	—	—	—	—	0.3	0.1[2]
Other paper	—	—	—	—	1.9*	—

a million $ U.S. *j* '000 cu. metres of roundwood equivalent.

	Production 1963–5	Production 1953–5	Exports 1963–5	Exports 1953–5	Imports 1963–5	Imports 1953–5
4. VEGETABLE OILSEEDS AND OILS						
Copra	10.40	2.80	—	2.43*	0.06	—
Coconut oil	na	na	2.09	0.61	0.07	0.10*
Groundnuts	na *r*	—	0.01†	—	1.19[1]	0.90
Groundnut oil	na	na	0.02[2]†	0.09[2]†	0.40[2]*	0.76
Linseed oil	—	—	—	—	—	0.03
Sesame seed	—	—	—	—	0.03[1]	—
Soya beans	—	—	—	—	0.61[1]	0.60*
5. LIVESTOCK‡, ANIMAL PRODUCTS, etc.						
Chickens *d*	33.0*	30.0[1]				
Cattle *d*	8.3	2.0[1]	0.3[1]	0.1	1.1[1]	0.7
Goats *d*	9.0	6.0[1]	—	—	—	—
Pigs *d*	284.0	20.0[1]	0.8[1]	2.2	11.0[1]	14.5
Bacon/ham }	—	—	{ —	—	0.1[1]	—
Meat‡: 'A' }			{ —	—	0.3[1]	0.1
'B'	—	—	—	—	0.1[1]	—
Butter	—	—	—	—	0.2	0.1[2]
Eggs	0.1*	—	0.1[1]	—	1.4[2]	0.9
Fish	na *r*	na *r*	0.4[1]†	na	5.1[1]	na
Milk	—	—	0.1[1]†	—	13.8[2]	1.0[2]

d no. in thousands. *r* see West Malaysia.

	Production 1963–5	Production 1953–5	Exports 1963–5	Exports 1953–5	Imports 1963–5	Imports 1953–5
6. FIBRES, TEXTILES, etc.						
Rubber, natural	na	na	43.5	28.8	1.3	0.7
7. FUEL AND POWER						
Electricity *h*, thermal	58	20[1]				
Natural gas *i*	—	—	—	—	50	79[1]
Oil, crude	50	70[1]	1 310*s*	3 230[1]*s*	3 626	5 260[1]
Petroleum, refined *p*	2 463	2 390[1]	2 273	1 840[1]	80	20[1]

h million kWh. *i* million cu. metres. *p* excl. bunkers. *s* incl. re-exports.

	Production 1963–5	Production 1953–5	Exports 1963–5	Exports 1953–5	Imports 1963–5	Imports 1953–5
9. NON-FERROUS MINERALS AND METALS						
Gold *k*, ore	3.00*m*	0.51**m*	—	0.51*q*	25.67*q*	1.94*q*
Platinum group metals *k*	—	—	—	—	0.89[2]	—
Silver *k*, bullion	—	—	—	—	0.39	6.48
Asbestos, manufactured	—	—	—	—	3.96	0.45
Aluminium: bauxite	151.73	na	170.25	na *r*	—	—
aluminium	—	—	—	—	0.57	0.28
Antimony, ore	0.04*m*	—	0.04	—	—	—
Copper, metal	—	—	—	0.10†	0.14	0.04
Mercury *f*	—	—	—	—	—	0.10[2]
Tin, metal	—	—	—	na *r*	0.03	—
Zinc, metal	—	—	—	na *r*	0.17	na *r*

f metric tons. *k* '000 fine troy oz. *m* metal content. *q* bullion. *r* see West Malaysia.

	Production 1963–5	Production 1953–5	Exports 1963–5	Exports 1953–5	Imports 1963–5	Imports 1953–5
10. CHEMICALS*n* AND FERTILIZERS						
Chemicals	—		—		na	
Fertilizers:						
Phosphates	na *p*	0.7*p*	—	—	4.4	0.1[2]
Potash	—	—	—	—	0.9	na

n data not available for years 1953–5. *p* guano.

	Production 1963–5	Production 1953–5	Exports 1963–5	Exports 1953–5	Imports 1963–5	Imports 1953–5
11. INDUSTRY						
Aircraft *a*	—	—	—	—	0.1[2]	—
Alcoholic beverages *a*	—	—	—	—	1.7[2]	1.0
Cement	na *r*	—	na *r*	—	na *r*	11.7
Electrical engineering *a*	—	—	—	—	3.9	—
Motor vehicles *a*	—	—	—	—	4.2[2]	0.3[2]

a million $ U.S. *r* see West Malaysia.

na: data not available. — negligible or nil. [1] one year only. [2] two year average. * estimate. ‡ see appendix. † re-exports.

WEST MALAYSIA

AREA: 131 587 sq. km. (50 806 sq. miles)

LAND USE: (percentage of total)

	1964	1950
Arable and orchard	18.9	16.9
Permanent meadow and pasture	na	—
Forest and woodland	65.7	73.9
City areas, waste and other land	na	9.2

POPULATION: 8 580 000 (1967 estimate)

Largest city: KUALA LUMPUR, capital; population: 316 230 (city proper, 1957)

Distribution of working population (1957)
Total working population: 2 164 861

U.N. group no.		Percentage
0	Agriculture, forestry, fishing and hunting	57.5
1	Mining and quarrying	2.7
2/3	Manufacturing	6.3
4	Construction	3.1
5	Electricity, gas, water and sanitary services	0.5
6	Commerce	9.0
7	Transport, storage and communications	3.5
8	Services	14.8
9	Others	2.6

		Year(s)
Life expectancy at birth (years): male	62.4	1965
female	64.0	1965
Infant mortality (per '000)	50	1965
Crude birth rate (per '000)	36.7	1965
Crude death rate (per '000)	7.9	1965
Population per physician	5 890	1965
Population per hospital bed	250	1966
School enrolment: age 5–19 years (percentage)	58	1963–4 av.
age over 19 years (per 100 000 population)	127	1963–5 av.

COMMUNICATIONS

		Year(s)
Motor vehicles in use ('000s): private	144.5	1963–5 av.
commercial	42.2	1963–5 av.
Railway track (km.)	1 667	1968
Mail per capita: domestic	21	1963–5 av.
foreign received	6	1963–5 av.
foreign sent	4	1963–5 av.
Telephones (per '000 urban population)	1.4	1967
Radio licences (per '000 population)	44	1963–5 av.
Television licences (per '000 population)	3*a*	1963–5 av.
Daily newspapers (per '000 population)	67	1960

a incl. Sabah and Sarawak.

FINANCE

		Year
National Income (million $ U.S.)	2 068	1965

TRADING

Note—These trading figures, representing general trade, include the considerable value of the goods from other countries in transit through West Malaysia and, prior to 1965, Singapore.

Total trade (in million $ U.S.)	1965*a*	1955*a*	1955*b*	1938*b*
Exports (f.o.b.)	1 014	755	1 358	334
Imports (c.i.f.)	852	504	1 249	315

Main trading partners (percentage of total value)

Exports	1965	1955*b*	1938*b*	*Imports*	1965	1955*b*	1938*b*
Singapore	21			U.K.	20	18	19
U.S.A.	18	17	30	Japan	12	6	5*c*
Japan	13	7	9*c*	Thailand	11	7	16
U.K.	8	18	14	Singapore	11		
U.S.S.R.	7	—	—	China P.R.	7	3	4
Germany F.R.	3	6	3*d*	Australia	6	4	2
Italy	3	4	3	U.S.A.	5	4	3

Distribution of trade (percentage of total value)

Exports	1965	1955*b*	1938* *b*
Rubber	44	58	48
Tin and alloys	28	11	17
Metalliferous ores	6	1	1
Food	5	6	10
Palm oil	3	1	1
Imports			
Manufactured goods	48	29	na
(machinery and transport equipment)	(22)	(8)	(7)
(textiles and clothing)	(7)	(7)	(6)
Food	24	22	na
(cereals)	(8)	(7)	(13)
Crude materials and fuels	15	40	na
(petroleum products)	(7)	(18)	(na)
Chemicals	8	4	na

a West Malaysia. *b* incl. Singapore. *c* incl. Taiwan and Korea. *d* incl. Germany D.R.

PRODUCTION, EXPORTS AND IMPORTS

Years: **1963–5 average** and *1953–5 average* Units: '000 metric tons unless otherwise indicated

Note—production data are for West Malaysia; data for Singapore are given where applicable. Trade figures apply to West Malaysia and Singapore combined.

1. CEREALS, etc.

	Production		Exports		Imports	
Cassava	303.3*	na				
Sing.	3.0	4.0[1]				
Maize (corn)	7.0*	na	6.6	9.8	97.1	39.0
Millets/sorghum	—	—	—	—	6.6	—
Oats				—	1.0	1.0*
Potatoes	—	—	2.0†	1.8†	39.5	31.7
Rice	851.7	664.0	78.8	49.7	618.6	471.8
Sweet potatoes/yams	98.3*	na				
Sing.	5.0	7.0[2]				
Wheat	—	—	2.2†	0.4†	103.6	14.0

2. FRUIT, etc.

	Production		Exports		Imports	
Apples	—	—	0.8†	1.3†	13.4	8.3
Bananas	332.0*	288.0[2]*	0.1	—	—	—
Sing.	—	3.0[1]				
Coconuts	732.7*e*	na	9.5	8.5	—	—
Sing.	11.3	na				
Dates	—	—	—	—	1.2*	5.3[1]*
Grapes	—	—	0.2†	0.6†	2.9	3.0
Lemons	—	—	—	0.1[1]	—	—
Oranges	—	—	1.4†	1.4†	27.0	18.6
Other citrus fruit	—	—	—	—	1.2	—
Pears	—	—	0.3†	0.5†	6.0	4.3
Pineapples	321.3*	69.0*	—	—	—	4.2[1]
Wine *b*	—	—	1.1†	1.0†	7.8	6.3

b '000 hectolitres. *e* no. in millions.

3. BEVERAGES, FOREST PRODUCTS, etc.

	Production		Exports		Imports	
Cocoa	0.6	—	0.2	—	0.1	—
Coffee	2.0*	na	30.7*s*	10.3*s*	23.1	12.9
Sugar, raw	—	—	25.2†	16.9†	283.2	182.2
Tea	3.0	2.1	3.2*s*	7.3*s*	3.7	8.4
Tobacco, leaf	2.4*	1.5*	0.1	0.2	7.9	0.6
Sing.	0.4	—				

continued

3. BEVERAGES, FOREST PRODUCTS, etc.—*continued*

	Production		Exports		Imports	
Tobacco: cigars	0.7	—				
Sing.	0.1	—				
cigarettes	5 973.0*e*	na	1.7*s*	2.5[2]*s*	3.3	10.0[2]
Sing.	2 496.0*e*	—				
tobacco/snuff	1.0	—				
Softwood *j*	—	—	7.0[2]	0.1	0.4[2]	0.1
Hardwood *j*	3 403.5[2]	1 936.0	2 089.5	276.9	1 274.9*n*	114.8
Wood pulp	—[1]	—	—[2]	—	0.5	—
Newsprint	—*	—	1.1*	0.1	31.0	9.8
Other paper	0.2*	—	8.6[2]	0.8[2]	89.0	20.7[2]

e no. in millions. *j* '000 cu. metres of roundwood equivalent. *n* sawn wood only. *s* incl. re-exports.

4. VEGETABLE OILSEEDS AND OILS

	Production		Exports		Imports	
Castor oil	—	—	—	—	0.04	0.45
Copra	127.00	155.70	22.39*s*	59.30*s*	37.22	110.97
Coconut oil	na	na	28.70	78.73	2.25	0.68
Cottonseed oil	—	—	—	—	0.38	—
Groundnuts	3.00**p*	na	0.84	1.37	14.74	11.83
Groundnut oil	na	na	1.34	1.13	3.88	2.10
Linseed oil	—	—	—	0.06†	0.38	0.45
Olive oil	—	—	0.01†	—	0.03	—
Palm kernels	32.03	14.23*pq*	14.09	13.20	2.50	0.03
Palm kernel oil	na	na	0.16	0.43	—	0.02
Palm oil	132.10	53.37*pq*	127.51	51.60	2.68	1.16
Rapeseed oil	—	—	—	—	0.05	—
Sesame seed	—	—	0.58†	0.30†	3.15	3.43
Soya beans	—	—	0.84†	0.97†	28.40	18.83
Soya bean oil	na	na	0.01	—	0.07	—
Tung oil	—	—	0.01†	—	0.15	0.07

p incl. Sabah and Sarawak. *q* estate production only. *s* incl. re-exports.

continued

PRODUCTION, EXPORTS AND IMPORTS *continued*

5. LIVESTOCK‡, ANIMAL PRODUCTS, etc.

	Production		Exports		Imports	
Chickens *d*	21 000.0*r**	10 000.0**r*				
Sing.	10 212.0*r*	4 250.0[2]*r*				
Cattle *d*	306.7	274.0	1.1	1.9	15.2	11.6
Sing.	7.0	5.0				
dairy cows *d*	145.0*	48.0[1]				
Sing.	5.0*	5.0				
Goats *d*	316.0*	277.3				
Sing.	2.0	1.0	—	—	131.8	na
Sheep *d*	41.7*	26.0				
Horses *d*	—	1.0				
Pigs *d*	476.0	332.0	—	15.3	—	23.7
Sing.	402.0	244.0				
Bacon/ham	65.3*	25.3*	0.1	—	0.6	0.6
Meat‡: 'A'			0.6	0.1	10.0	5.9
Sing.	15.7	15.5[2]				
'B'	19.8*	na	0.4	0.1	4.8	1.3
Sing.	3.2*	2.4*				
Butter	—	—	0.2†	0.4†	5.4	2.0
Cheese	—	—	0.1†	—	0.8	0.4
Eggs	11.5*	9.0[1]	1.6	0.5	4.0	8.9
Sing.	9.9	8.4[2]				
Fish	241.7*p*	141.2*p*	72.0	44.1[1]*	124.3	61.4[1]*
Sing.	11.2	6.1				
Milk	21.3*	na	8.7	13.9	331.5	226.9
Sing.	1.0	2.0[2]				
Hides/skins	na	na	—	0.9[2]	—	—

d no. in thousands. *p* incl. Sabah and Sarawak. *r* incl. ducks, geese and turkeys.

6. FIBRES, TEXTILES, etc.

	Production		Exports		Imports	
Abaca	na	—	0.3	—	—	0.1
Cotton lint	—	—	0.2†	—	1.3	—
Jute	na	—	0.5	—	0.1	—
Rubber, natural	840.3	608.9	1 059.9*s*	934.4*s*	175.9	335.2
Sing.	1.5	na				
Cotton: yarn	—	—	—	—	2.0	0.5
woven fabrics	—	—	—	—	22.4	17.8
Rayon: fibre/yarn	na	na	na	1.2*t*	—	—
woven fabrics	—	—	—	—	9.0*n*	8.3

s incl. re-exports. *t* incl. spun yarn. *n* incl. synthetic piece goods.

7. FUEL AND POWER

	Production		Exports		Imports	
Coal, 'A'‡	—	—	6[1]†*p*	na	21[1]*	74
Coke	—	—	1	—	4	4
Electricity *h*: total	1 886	1 190[1]				
hydro	483	250[1]				
thermal	1 403	940[1]				
Sing.	928*t*	na				
Oil, crude	—	—	187†	na	4 132	na
Petroleum, refined	1 360	—[1]	5 006	3 230[1]†	6 663	6 690[1]
Sing.	2 337	na				
Rare earths (monazite) *f*	na	na	638	265	—	—

f metric tons. *h* million kWh. *p* incl. Sabah and Sarawak. *t* thermal.

8. IRON AND STEEL

	Production		Exports		Imports	
Iron ore	3 908*m*	710*m*	6 615	1 243	—	—
Pig iron	—	—	1†	—	14[1]*	2*s*
Steel ingots/castings	—	—	—	—	10	1*s*
Iron/steel scrap	na	na	56*	67	19*	8

m metal content. *s* incl. imports for re-export.

9. NON-FERROUS MINERALS AND METALS

	Production		Exports		Imports	
Diamonds *a*	—	—	0.06[1]†	0.07†	3.57[1]	0.07*ps*
Gold *k*, ore *m*	6.70	21.00	—	16.19*q*	—	0.56*q*
Platinum group metals *k*	—	—	—	na	3.06	0.17*s*
Silver *k*, bullion	na	na	636.00*s*	1 084.57*s*	8.67[1]	0.57
Asbestos: fibre	—	—	—	—	14.52	1.92
manufactured	—	—	36.05†	0.03†	26.12	0.31*s*
Mica	—	—	—	—	0.01[1]	—
Aluminium: bauxite	593.03	182.87	565.36	190.64*p*	0.04	—
alumina	—	—	—	—	0.89	—
aluminium	—	—	4.71†	1.09†	10.83	3.96*s*
Copper: ore	na	—	1.78[1]	—	—	—
metal	na	—	0.65	na†	3.98	1.34*s*
Lead, metal	—	—	0.19†	0.87†	1.19	0.28*p*
Magnesium: dolomite	—	—	1.88[1]†	—	1.92	—
magnesite	—	—	0.59†	—	0.39	—
Manganese, ore	2.86	—	3.57	na†	4.06	1.44*s*
Mercury *f*	—	—	—	0.40†	12.50[1]	1.90*s*
Tin: ore	62.19*m*	60.35*m*	0.81*p*	0.09*p*	10.87[1]*p*	12.52*ps*
metal	77.16	69.16	74.65	68.82*p*	0.22[1]	0.14*s*
Titanium minerals	na	na	134.70	42.40	0.60[1]	na
Tungsten, ore	0.01	0.13	0.01[1]	0.13*s*	na	0.01*s*
Zinc: ore	—	—	—	—	1.25	na
metal	na	na	0.71	0.22*ps*	3.16	2.08*p*
Zirconium minerals	na	na	0.34*t*	0.03*t*	—	—

a million $ U.S. *f* metric tons. *k* '000 fine troy oz. *m* metal content. *p* incl. Sabah and Sarawak. *q* bullion. *s* incl. re-exports and imports for re-export. *t* zircon.

10. CHEMICALS*n* AND FERTILIZERS

	Production		Exports		Imports	
Chemicals	—		—		na	
Fertilizers:						
Phosphates	—	—	0.1†	—	88.7[1]	—
Potash	—	—	—	—	33.2	5.1
Sulphur	—	—	0.2†	—	6.1	0.2

n data not available for years 1953–5.

11. INDUSTRY

	Production		Exports		Imports	
Aircraft *a*	—	—	—	—	—	0.1
Alcoholic beverages			6.1*a*	1.8*a*	17.4*a*	9.2*a*
beer *b*	369.0[2]	—				
Sing.	302.0	na				
Cement	708.7*p*	74.0	18.3*p*	12.7	468.0*p*	327.0
Electrical engineering *a*	—	—	19.7†	4.8[2]†	90.2	26.0[2]
Railway vehicles *a*	—	—	—	—	2.5	1.7
Merchant ships *g*	2.1[2]	na	—	—	0.4[1]*p*	na
Motor vehicles *a*	—	—	55.7†	6.1†	124.2	22.5

a million $ U.S. *b* '000 hectolitres. *g* '000 G.R.T. *p* incl. Sabah and Sarawak.

MALDIVE ISLANDS

INDIAN OCEAN

The Maldive Islands were under British protection until they were granted independence in 1965; they became a republic three years later. The U.K. retains an air staging post on Gan Island.

AREA: 298 sq. km. (115 sq. miles)

POPULATION: 100 883 (1966 census)
Capital city: MALE; population: 11 202 (city proper, 1965)

		Year
Crude birth rate (per '000)	50.1*	1965
Crude death rate (per '000)	22.9*	1965
Population per hospital bed	5 050	1966

EMPLOYMENT AND TRADE

These low lying coral islands are covered with coconut palms, and some millets and fruit are grown. Fishing is the major occupation and bonito accounts for 95% of the island's exports. Fish catches amounted to some 12 000 metric tons in 1965.

MALI

WEST AFRICA

Mali, formerly French Sudan, a member state of French West Africa, became an independent republic in 1960. In 1968 the regime of the president was overthrown and a National Liberation Committee assumed control.

AREA: 1 204 021 sq. km. (464 875 sq. miles)

LAND USE

About 95% of the land is barren desert, but agriculture is increasing with collectivization and planned irrigation.

POPULATION: 4 745 000* (1967 provisional estimate)

Largest city: BAMAKO, capital; population: 165 000 (1965)

		Year(s)
Life expectancy at birth (years)	35*	1960
Population per physician	40 000	1964
Population per hospital bed	1 340*a*	1965
School enrolment: age 5–19 years (percentage)	11	1963–4 av.
age over 19 years (per 100 000 population)	4	1963–5 av.

a government hospitals only.

COMMUNICATIONS

		Year(s)
Motor vehicles in use ('000s): private	3.4	1963–5 av.
commercial	4.6	1963–5 av.
Railway track (km.)	645	1969
Telephones (per '000 urban population)	0.1	1967
Radio receivers (per '000 population)	4	1963–5 av.
Daily newspapers (per '000 population)	0.5	1962

FINANCE

Currency unit: The Mali franc replaced, at par, the franc CFA in 1962

Exchange rates	*1965*	*1960a*
Per $ U.S.	246.85	246.85
Per £ sterling	691.18	691.18

a francs CFA.

		Year
National Income (million $ U.S.)	224	1958
G.N.P. per capita ($ U.S.)	60	1966

TRADING

Total trade (in million $ U.S.)	*1965*
Exports (f.o.b.)	16
Imports (c.i.f.)	43

Main trading partners (percentage of total value)

Exports	*1965*	*Imports*	*1965*
Ivory Coast	30	France	24
Ghana	24	China P.R.	23
Senegal	17	U.S.S.R.	19
Upper Volta	12	U.A.R.	6
France	6	U.S.A.	3
U.S.S.R.	4	Ivory Coast	3
Algeria	1	Yugoslavia	3

Distribution of trade (percentage of total value)

Exports	*1965*	*Imports*	*1965*
Cattle	29	Manufactured goods	65
Fish	20	(machinery and transport equipment)	(23)
Cotton	17	(textiles and clothing)	(22)
Oilseeds	16	Food	18
		(sugar and honey)	(11)
		Crude materials and fuels	9
		Chemicals	5

PRODUCTION, EXPORTS AND IMPORTS

Years: **1963–5 average** Units: '000 metric tons unless otherwise indicated

Note—no data are available for the years 1953–5

	Production	Exports	Imports
1. CEREALS, etc			
Cassava	**153.3***		
Maize (corn)	**93.0***	—	—
Millets/sorghum	**710.3***	**0.7**	**1.0**
Potatoes	na	**0.2**	**0.4**
Rice	**148.3**	**0.1**	—
Sweet potatoes/yams	**70.0***		
Wheat	**4.0***	—	—
2. FRUIT, etc.			
Bananas	—	—	**0.3**
Dates	—	**0.2**[2]†	**0.7**
Oranges	—	—	**0.1**
Wine *b*	—	—	**3.8**

b '000 hectolitres.

	Production	Exports	Imports
3. BEVERAGES, FOREST PRODUCTS, etc.			
Coffee	—	—	**0.2**
Sugar, raw	—	**0.2**†	**21.5**
Tea	—	—	**0.4**
Tobacco: leaf	**2.4***	**0.2**	—
products	—	—	**0.3**
Hardwood *j*	**2 275.0**[1]*	—	**2.5**[2]

j '000 cu. metres of roundwood equivalent.

	Production	Exports	Imports
4. VEGETABLE OILSEEDS AND OILS			
Cottonseed	**32.30***	**3.91**	—
Groundnuts	**100.30***	**33.07**	**0.21**
Olive oil	—	—	**0.01**[1]
Palm oil	—	—	**0.27**

	Production	Exports	Imports
5. LIVESTOCK‡, ANIMAL PRODUCTS, etc.			
Cattle *d*	**4 281.7**	**65.0**	—
dairy cows *d*	**2 176.7***		
Goats *d*	**8 338.0***n*	**52.5** (goats and sheep)	—
Sheep *d*	**4 722.3***		
Horses *d*	**146.3***		
Pigs *d*	**18.0***	—	—
Meat‡, 'A'	**17.0***	—	—
Eggs	**4.6**	—	—
Fish	**90.0**[1]	**5.3**	—
Milk	**642.3***	—	**2.3***
Hides/skins	**1.4**[1]	**0.5**	—
Wool	**0.2**[1]	**0.1**	—

d no. in thousands. *n* incl. some sheep.

	Production	Exports	Imports
6. FIBRES, TEXTILES, etc.			
Agaves (sisal)	**0.2***	—	—
Cotton: lint	**16.0***	**6.7**	—
yarn	—	—	**0.6**
woven fabrics	—	—	**2.8**
7. FUEL AND POWER			
Electricity *hp*	**25**		
Petroleum, refined	—	—	**57**

h million kWh. *p* hydro and thermal.

	Production	Exports	Imports
11. INDUSTRY			
Alcoholic beverages *a*	—	—	**0.3**
Cement *q*	**192.0**	**0.7**	**34.3***
Electrical engineering *a*	—	—	**1.6**
Motor vehicles *a*	—	—	**3.5**

a million $ U.S. *q* incl. data for Mauritania and Senegal.

na: data not available. — negligible or nil. [1] one year only. [2] two year average. * estimate. ‡ see appendix. † re-exports.

MALTA

MEDITERRANEAN

Formerly a British protectorate, Malta was granted partial self-government in 1947, and independence within the Commonwealth in 1964. The agreement to British forces remaining until 1974 in return for capital aid to the extent of £51 million over the ten-year period was challenged by Malta in 1971, and was still under negotiation at the end of the year.

AREA: 316 sq. km. (122 sq. miles)

LAND USE: (percentage of total)	*1965*	*1954*
Arable and orchard	50.0	59.4
City areas, waste and other land	50.0	40.6

POPULATION: 315 765*a* (1967 estimate)

Capital city: VALLETTA; population: 17 679 (1965)

Distribution of working population (1957)

Total working population: 94 589*a*

U.N. group no.		*Percentage*
0	Agriculture, forestry, fishing and hunting	10.3
1	Mining and quarrying	0.4
2/3	Manufacturing	22.3
4	Construction	11.0
5	Electricity, gas, water and sanitary services	3.0
6	Commerce	14.2
7	Transport, storage and communications	5.9
8	Services	29.4
9	Others	3.5

		Year(s)
Life expectancy at birth (years): male	67.5	1965–7 av.
female	71.6	1965–7 av.
Infant mortality (per '000)	34.8	1965
Crude birth rate (per '000)	17.6	1965
Crude death rate (per '000)	9.4	1965
Accidental deaths (per 100 000 population)		
caused by motor vehicles	4.4	1965
due to other causes	12.8	1965
Population per physician	780	1961
Population per hospital bed	100	1965
School enrolment: age 5–19 years (percentage)	96	1963–4 av.
age over 19 years (per 100 000 population)	337	1963–5 av.

a excl. non-Maltese armed forces.

COMMUNICATIONS

		Year(s)
Motor vehicles in use ('000s): private	20.7	1963–5 av.
commercial	6.8	1963–5 av.
Mail per capita: domestic	44	1963–5 av.
foreign received	22	1963–5 av.
foreign sent	29	1963–5 av.
Telephones (per '000 urban population)	8.1	1967
Radio licences (per '000 population)	229	1963–5 av.
Television licences (per '000 population)	73.1	1963–5 av.
Daily newspapers (per '000 population)	124	1956

FINANCE

Currency unit: The pound sterling *a*

Exchange rates	*1965*	*1960*	*1955*
Per $ U.S.	0.357	0.357	0.357

		Year
National Income (million $ U.S.)	137	1965
G.N.P. per capita ($ U.S.)	510	1966

a Maltese bank notes are issued, but U.K. coins are used.

TRADING

Total trade (in million $ U.S.)	*1965*	*1955*	*1938*
Exports (f.o.b.)	24	7	3
Imports (c.i.f.)	98	59	19

Main trading partners (percentage of total value)

Exports	*1965*	*1955*	*Imports*	*1965*	*1955*
U.K.	30	21	U.K.	38	40
Italy	9	12	Italy	12	11
Libya	6	6	Netherlands	6	6
U.S.A.	5	—	France	4	5
Spain	5	na	Australia	4	3
Netherlands	4	2	Germany F.R.	4	3
Switzerland	3	—	U.S.A.	2	2

Distribution of trade (percentage of total value)

Exports	*1965*	*1955*
Manufactured goods	64	na
(textiles and clothing)	(50)	(na)
Crude materials and fuels	12	32*
Beverages and tobacco	9	11
Food	8	38
(potatoes)	(6)	(22)
Imports		
Manufactured goods	45	40
(machinery and transport equipment)	(16)	(10)
(textiles and clothing)	(10)	(6*)
Food	29	43
(cereals, fruit, vegetables)	(12)	(na)
(meat and dairy produce)	(8)	(na)
Crude materials and fuels	12	7
Chemicals	7	5

Note—the large deficit on the balance of trade was offset by receipts from ships' dues, repairs and bunkering, tourism and British government grants.

PRODUCTION, EXPORTS AND IMPORTS

Years: **1963–5 average** and *1953–5 average* Units: '000 metric tons unless otherwise indicated

	Production **1963–5**	Production *1953–5*	Exports **1963–5**	Exports *1953–5*	Imports **1963–5**	Imports *1953–5*
1. CEREALS, etc.						
Barley	**2.0**	*3.3*	—	—	**6.5**	*1.0*
Maize (corn)	—	—	—	—	**15.1**	*0.4*
Millets/sorghum	—	—	—	—	**5.7**	*9.0*
Potatoes	**20.0**	*26.3*	**9.5**	*7.4*	**4.2**	*4.9*
Rice	—	—	—	—	**0.9**	*0.9*
Wheat	**2.7**	*3.5*[2]	—	—	**58.6**	*57.3*
2. FRUIT, etc.						
Apples	—	—	—	—	**2.9**	*1.6*
Bananas	—	—	—	—	**1.1**	*0.5*
Figs	**2.0***	*2.0*	—	—	—	—
Grapes	**3.7**	*5.0*	—	—	—	—
Lemons	—	—	—	—	**0.1**	*0.1*[2]
Oranges	—	—	—	—	**3.6**	*4.9*
Pears	—	—	—	—	**0.4**	*0.2*
Raisins	—	—	—	—	**0.3**	*0.2*
Tomatoes	**6.7**	*7.0*[2]				
Wine *b*	na	na	**107.9**	*0.3*	**2.6**	*8.0*

b '000 hectolitres.

	Production **1963–5**	Production *1953–5*	Exports **1963–5**	Exports *1953–5*	Imports **1963–5**	Imports *1953–5*
3. BEVERAGES, FOREST PRODUCTS, etc.						
Coffee	—	—	—	—	**0.4**	*0.2*
Sugar, raw	—	—	—	—	**14.3**	*11.1*
Tea	—	—	—	—	**0.5**	*0.4*
Tobacco: leaf	—	—	—	—	**0.4**	*0.4*[2]
cigarettes	*e* **396.0***e*	—	**0.1**[1]	—	**0.4**[1]*n*	—
Softwood *j*	—	—	—	—	**17.4**	*16.6*
Hardwood *j*	—	—	—	—	**6.9**	*3.7*[2]
Newsprint	—	—	—	—	**0.5**[2]	*0.4*
Other paper	—	—	—	—	**0.6**[1]	*0.4*[2]*p*

e no. in millions. *j* '000 cu. metres of roundwood equivalent. *n* incl. other tobacco manufactures. *p* printing and writing paper only.

	Production **1963–5**	Production *1953–5*	Exports **1963–5**	Exports *1953–5*	Imports **1963–5**	Imports *1953–5*
4. VEGETABLE OILSEEDS AND OILS						
Cottonseed	—	—	—	—	—	*0.70*
Cottonseed oil	—	—	—	—	**0.05**	*1.67*
Groundnuts	—	—	—	—	**0.38**	*0.10*
Groundnut oil	—	—	—	—	—	*0.60*[2]
Linseed oil	—	—	—	—	—	*1.00*[2]
Olive oil	—	—	—	—	**0.03**	*0.02*
Soya bean oil	—	—	**1.95**†	—	**4.42**	*0.50*
5. LIVESTOCK‡, ANIMAL PRODUCTS, etc.						
Chickens *d*	**1 293.3**	na				
Cattle *d*	**7.7**	*5.5*[2]	—	—	**7.5**	*9.4*
Goats *d*	**28.0**	*42.0*[2]	**0.9** (goats and sheep)	na (goats and sheep)	— (goats and sheep)	— (goats and sheep)
Sheep *d*	**10.7**	*19.5*[2]				
Horses *d*	**2.0**	*2.0*[2]				
Pigs *d*	**15.0**	*23.5*[2]	—	—	—	—
Bacon/ham	**5.3*** (bacon/ham and meat 'A')	*3.7q* (bacon/ham and meat 'A')	—	—	**0.2**	*0.3**
Meat‡: 'A'			—	—	**1.6**	*1.1*
'B'	**1.2***	*0.9*	—	—	**0.5**	*0.2*
Butter	—	—	—	—	**0.5**	*0.4*
Cheese	—	—	—	—	**1.3**	*1.1*
Eggs	**3.2**	*2.2*	—	—	**0.5**	*0.8*
Fish	**1.4**	*0.9*	—	—	na	—
Milk	**15.0**	*7.0*	**0.1**	—	**21.7**	*20.3*
Hides/skins	na	*0.4*	**0.4**[1]	*0.3*[2]	—	—

d no. in thousands. *q* government inspected meat only.

	Production **1963–5**	Production *1953–5*	Exports **1963–5**	Exports *1953–5*	Imports **1963–5**	Imports *1953–5*
6. FIBRES, TEXTILES, etc.						
Cotton: lint	—	—	—	—	**1.0**	—
woven fabrics	—	—	—	—	**0.5**	*0.3*
Rayon: fibre/yarn	—[1]	—	—[1]	—	na	na
woven fabrics	—	—	—	—	**0.2***r*	*0.3*
Non-cellulosic fibre/yarn	**0.7**[1]	—	**0.6**	—	**1.3**[1]	—

r incl. synthetic piece goods.

continued

na: data not available. — negligible or nil. [1] one year only. [2] two year average. * estimate. ‡ see appendix. † re-exports.

MALTA *continued*

PRODUCTION, EXPORTS AND IMPORTS *continued*

	Production		Exports		Imports	
7. FUEL AND POWER						
Coal, 'A'‡	—	—	—	—	2*v*	*18*
Electricity *h t*	126	*40*[1]	—	—		
Petroleum, refined	—	—	—	—	217	*130*[1]

h million kWh. *t* thermal. *v* incl. imports for bunkering.

	Production		Exports		Imports	
8. IRON AND STEEL						
Steel ingots/castings	—	—	—	—	1	—
Iron/steel scrap	na	na	8	*10*[2]	—	—

	Production		Exports		Imports	
9. NON-FERROUS MINERALS AND METALS						
Diamonds *a*	—	—	—	—	0.09	*0.02*[1]
Gold *k*, bullion/coins, etc.	—	—	—	—	9.07‡	*6.70*
Silver *k*, bullion	—	—	—	*0.23*†	8.53	*4.53*
Asbestos, manufactured *a*	—	—	—	—	0.03	*0.01*

continued

	Production		Exports		Imports	
9. NON-FERROUS MINERALS AND METALS—*continued*						
Aluminium *a*	—	—	—	—	0.21	—
Copper, metal *a*	—	—	—	—	0.11	—
Zinc, ore *a*	—	—	—	—	0.03	—

a million $ U.S. *k* '000 fine troy oz.

	Production		Exports		Imports	
10. CHEMICALS*n* AND FERTILIZERS						
Chemicals	—		—		na	
Fertilizers:						
Sulphur	—	—	—	—	0.3[1]	*0.1*[2]*v*

n data not available for years 1953–5. *v* in addition, flowers of sulphur U.S. $17 900.

	Production		Exports		Imports	
11. INDUSTRY						
Alcoholic beverages *a*	na	na	0.9[1]*p*	*0.2q*	1.4[1]*p*	*0.1q*
Cement	—	—	—	—	63.0	*29.7*
Electrical engineering *a*	—	—	—	—	5.3[1]	—
Merchant ships *g*	—	—	—	—	0.1[1]	—
Motor vehicles *a*	—	—	0.2[1]†	—	3.1	*1.2*

a million $ U.S. *g* '000 G.R.T. *p* wine and beer. *q* beer only.

MAURITANIA

WEST AFRICA

Mauritania, formerly a member state of French West Africa, became an independent republic in 1960. Morocco has laid claim to the territory.

AREA: 1 085 805 sq. km. (419 232 sq. miles)

LAND USE: (percentage of total)

	1964
Arable and orchard	0.2
Permanent meadow and pasture	36.2
Forest and woodland	13.9
City areas, waste and other land	49.7

POPULATION: 1 050 000 (1964 census)

Capital city: NOUAKCHOTT; population: 15 000 (city proper, 1965)

		Year(s)
Life expectancy at birth (years)	40*	1961–2 av
Infant mortality (per '000)	187*	1964–5 av.
Crude birth rate (per '000)	45.1*	1964–5 av.
Crude death rate (per '000)	28*	1964–5 av.
Population per physician	30 000	1965
Population per hospital bed	3 720*a*	1965
School enrolment: age 5–19 years (percentage)	8	1963–4 av.

a government hospitals only.

COMMUNICATIONS

		Year(s)
Motor vehicles in use ('000s): private	1.3	1963–5 av.
commercial	2.5	1963–5 av.
Railway track (km.)	675	1969
Telephones (per '000 urban population)	0.1*	1967
Radio receivers (per '000 population)	30	1963–5 av.

FINANCE

Currency unit: The franc CFA

Exchange rates	*1965*	*1960*
Per $ U.S.	246.85	246.85
Per £ sterling	691.18	691.18

		Year
National Income (million $ U.S.)	111	1965
G.N.P. per capita ($ U.S.)	130	1966

PRODUCTION

The country's wealth lies mainly in its deposits of iron ore; output increased greatly during the decade 1960–70, the development being supported by large investments from France and the other E.E.C..countries. Copper deposits are also being exploited. Other products include cattle, gum, salt, beans and fish.

TRADING

Total trade (in mllion $ U.S.)	*1965*
Exports (f.o.b.)	58
Imports (c.i.f.)	24

Main trading partners (percentage of total value)

Exports	*1965*	*Imports*	*1965*
U.K.	25	France	47
France	20	U.S.A.	23
Germany F.R.	19	Germany F.R.	14
Italy	16	China P.R.	3
Belg./Lux.	8	U.K.	3
Netherlands	5	Canada	2
Congo R.	2		

Distribution of trade (percentage of total value)

Exports	*1965*	*Imports*	*1965*
Iron ore	94	Manufactured goods	81
Fish	4	(machinery and transport equipment)	(58)
		Food	8
		Crude materials and fuels	5

continued

PRODUCTION, EXPORTS AND IMPORTS

Years: **1963–5 average** Units: '000 metric tons unless otherwise indicated

Note—no data are available for the years 1953–5

	Production	Exports	Imports
1. CEREALS, etc.			
Maize (corn)	4.0*	—	—
Millets/sorghum	65.0[1]	—	—
Potatoes	—	—	0.1
Rice	—	—	0.1[2]
Sweet potatoes/yams	2.0*		

	Production	Exports	Imports
2. FRUIT, etc.			
Dates	6.7*	—	—
Wine *b*	—	—	1.2[2]

b '000 hectolitres.

	Production	Exports	Imports
3. BEVERAGES, FOREST PRODUCTS, etc.			
Hardwood *j*	126.0[1]	—	6.3[2]

j '000 cu. metres of roundwood equivalent.

	Production	Exports	Imports
5. LIVESTOCK‡, ANIMAL PRODUCTS, etc.			
Cattle *d*	1 733.3*	45.2[2]	
dairy cows *d*	1 023.3*		
Goats *d*	1 998.0*	267.0[2] (Goats, Sheep, Horses)	—
Sheep *d*	2 453.3*		
Horses *d*	10.0*		
Meat‡: 'A'	2.0*	—	—
Butter	—	—	0.1[2]

continued

	Production	Exports	Imports
5. LIVESTOCK‡, ANIMAL PRODUCTS, etc.—*continued*			
Eggs	2.2*	—	—
Fish	1.3[2]*n*	5.9[2]	6.3[1]
Milk	104.0*	—	0.8

d no. in thousands. *n* from marine fisheries only.

	Production	Exports	Imports
6. FIBRES, TEXTILES, etc.			
Cotton, woven fabrics	—	—	1.2
Rayon, woven fabrics	—	—	0.3*p*

p incl. synthetic piece goods.

	Production	Exports	Imports
7. FUEL AND POWER			
Petroleum, refined	—	—	33

	Production	Exports	Imports
8. IRON AND STEEL			
Iron ore	2 853*m*	3 691	—

m metal content.

	Production	Exports	Imports
11. INDUSTRY			
Aircraft *a*	—	—	0.1
Alcoholic beverages *a*	—	—	0.2[2]
Cement *q*	192.0	0.7	34.3*
Electrical engineering *a*	na	0.1	1.6
Railway vehicles *a*	—	—	4.3
Motor vehicles *a*	—	0.2†	3.0

a million $ U.S. *q* incl. data for Senegal and Mali.

MAURITIUS

INDIAN OCEAN

Mauritius became an independent state within the British Commonwealth in 1968; previously the island constituted a Crown Colony. The French language is spoken—a legacy of French possession during the eighteenth century.
Data include those for Rodrigues and the lesser dependencies.

AREA: 1 865 sq. km. (720 sq. miles)

LAND USE: (percentage of total)

	1965	*1955*
Arable and orchard	50.6	45.7
Permanent meadow and pasture	16.1	23.7
Forest and woodland	21.5	19.3
City areas, waste and other land	11.8	11.3

POPULATION: 774 000 (1967 U.N. estimate)

Largest city: PORT LOUIS, capital; population: 132 700 (1966)

Distribution of working population (1962)

Total working population: 187 400

U.N. group no.		*Percentage*
0	Agriculture, forestry, fishing and hunting	37.9
1	Mining and quarrying	0.1
2/3	Manufacturing	14.6
4	Construction	10.6
5	Electricity, gas, water and sanitary services	1.2
6	Commerce	10.0
7	Transport, storage and communications	6.3
8	Services	18.7
9	Others	0.6

		Year(s)
Life expectancy at birth (years): male	58.7	1961–3 av.
female	61.9	1961–3 av.
Infant mortality (per '000)	64.1	1965
Crude birth rate (per '000)	35.4	1965
Crude death rate (per '000)	8.6	1965
Accidental deaths (per 100 000 population)		
caused by motor vehicles	10.1	1965
due to other causes	17.9	1965
Population per physician	3 860	1965
Population per hospital bed	240	1965
School enrolment: age 5–19 years (percentage)	86	1963–4 av.
age over 19 years (per 100 000 population)	13	1965

COMMUNICATIONS

		Year(s)
Motor vehicles in use ('000s): private	12.3	1963–5 av.
commercial	5.0	1963–5 av.
Railway track (km.)	145*a*	1969
Mail per capita: domestic	11	1963–5 av.
foreign received	4	1963–5 av.
foreign sent	3	1963–5 av.
Telephones (per '000 urban population)	1.9	1967
Radio receivers (per '000 population)	139	1963–5 av.
Television sets (per '000 population)	2.4	1963–5 av.
Daily newspapers (per '000 population)	94	1962–3 av.

a mainly sugar estate lines.

FINANCE

Currency unit: The Mauritius rupee

Exchange rates	*1965*	*1960*
Per $ U.S.	4.76	4.76
Per £ sterling	13.33	13.33

		Year
National Income (million $ U.S.)	159	1965
G.N.P. per capita ($ U.S.)	210	1966

TRADING

Total trade (in million $ U.S.)	*1965*	*1955*	*1938*
Exports (f.o.b.)	66	53	14
Imports (c.i.f.)	77	53	12

Main trading partners (percentage of total value)

Exports	*1965*	*1955*	*Imports*	*1965*	*1955*
U.K.	78	82	U.K.	27	40
Canada	9	17	South Africa	10	4
U.S.A.	5	—	Australia	7	7
South Africa	4	—	Burma	6	11
Mal./Sing.	2	—	France	6	4
Hong Kong	1	—	Thailand	5	1
Réunion	1	—	Germany F.R.	4	3

Distribution of trade (percentage of total value) *a*

Exports	*1965*	*1955*	*1938**
Sugar	96	99	98
Imports			
Manufactured goods	45	45	na
(machinery and transport equipment)	(15)	(16)	na
Food	29	31	na
Chemicals	13	11	na
Crude materials and fuels	7	7	na

a percentages are of national exports‡ which comprised 95% of the general exports in 1965, and 96% in 1955.

continued

na: data not available. — negligible or nil. [1] one year only. [2] two year average. * estimate. ‡ see appendix. † re-exports.

PRODUCTION, EXPORTS AND IMPORTS

Years: **1963–5 average** and *1953–5 average* Units: '000 metric tons unless otherwise indicated

	Production		Exports		Imports	
1. CEREALS, etc.						
Cassava	0.3	*2.7*				
Maize (corn)	—	*2.7*	—	—	5.1	—
Millets/sorghum	—	—	—	—	0.1	—
Oats	—	—	—	—	0.4	*0.2*
Potatoes	5.0	*5.0*	—	—	3.7	*3.0*
Rice	—	—	—	—	68.3	*51.6*
Sweet potatoes/yams	0.7*	*1.7*				
2. FRUIT, etc.						
Apples	—	—	—	—	0.4	*0.2*
Bananas	6.7	na	—	—	—	—
Grapes	—	—	—	—	0.1	—
Coconuts	18.0*e	na	—	—	0.6	—
Oranges	—	—	—	*0.1*†	1.2	*0.5*
Other citrus fruit	—	—	—	—	0.1	—
Tomatoes	5.3	na				
Raisins	—	—	—	—	0.1	*0.1*
Wine b	—	—	0.1†	—	4.5	*3.7*

b '000 hectolitres. e no. in millions.

	Production		Exports		Imports	
3. BEVERAGES, FOREST PRODUCTS, etc.						
Sugar: cane	5 368.7	*4 383.7*				
raw	623.0	*514.7*	573.1	*486.6*	—	—
Tea	1.5	*0.5*	1.0	*0.1*	—	—
Tobacco: leaf	0.4	*0.5*	—	—	0.1	*0.1*
cigarettes	590.0e	*545.0e*	—	—	na	*0.1n*
Softwood j	13.0	*3.2*	—	—	0.1	—
Hardwood j	104.5[2]	*72.3*	—	—	18.9	*28.4*
Newsprint	—	—	—	—	0.6	*0.2*
Other paper	—	—	—	—	1.4	*0.6*

e no. in millions. j '000 cu. metres of roundwood equivalent. n incl. other tobacco products.

	Production		Exports		Imports	
4. VEGETABLE OILSEEDS AND OILS						
Castor oil	—	—	—	—	0.10	*0.06*
Copra	2.00*	*1.53*	0.98	—	—	—
Coconut oil	na	na	—	—	0.41	*0.17*
Cottonseed oil	—	—	—	—	0.45	*3.50*
Groundnuts	0.47	*0.70*	—	—	0.23	na
Groundnut oil	na	na	—	—	0.17	*0.52*
Linseed	—	—	—	—	0.01	—
Linseed oil	—	—	—	—	0.06	*0.14*
Olive oil	—	—	—	—	0.02	*0.03*
Rapeseed oil	—	—	—	—	0.04	*0.02*[2]
Soya bean oil	—	—	—	—	5.74	*0.04*
5. LIVESTOCK‡, ANIMAL PRODUCTS, etc.						
Chickens d	391.7	na				
Cattle d	44.7	*40.0**	—	—	6.7	*4.9*
dairy cows d	23.7	na				
Goats d	58.0	*54.0**				
Sheep d	2.0*	*2.0**	} —	—	2.9	na
Pigs d	4.0	*4.0**	—	—	—	—

continued

	Production		Exports		Imports	
5. LIVESTOCK‡, ANIMAL PRODUCTS, etc.—*continued*						
Bacon/ham }	1.0	*1.3* {	—	—	0.1	—
Meat‡: 'A' }			—	—	1.1	*0.3*
'B'	0.1*	*0.1*	—	—	0.4	*0.1*
Butter	—	—	—	—	0.3	*0.2*
Cheese	—	—	—	—	0.2	*0.1*
Fish	1.6*	*1.4**	—	—	3.0	na
Milk	22.7	*23.0*	—	—	25.0	*6.7**
Hides/skins	na	na	—	—	—	—

d no. in thousands.

	Production		Exports		Imports	
6. FIBRES, TEXTILES, etc.						
Agaves (sisal etc.)	na	na	na	*0.2*[2]	—	—
Jute	—	—	—	—	0.4	—
Cotton, woven fabrics	—	—	—	—	na	*1.0*
Rayon, woven fabrics	—	—	—	—	na	*0.3*
7. FUEL AND POWER						
Coal, 'A'‡	—	—	—	—	2	*21*
Electricity h: total	94	*80*[1]				
hydro	59	*30*[1]				
thermal	35	*50*[1]				
Petroleum, refined	—	—	—	—	90	*40*[1]

h million kWh.

	Production		Exports		Imports	
9. NON-FERROUS MINERALS AND METALS						
Asbestos: fibre	—	—	—	—	—	*0.22*[2]
manufactured	—	—	—	—	0.84	—
Aluminium	—	—	—	—	0.32	*0.07*
Copper, metal	—	—	—	—	0.09	*0.06*
Lead, metal	—	—	—	—	0.04	*0.04*
Tin, metal	—	—	—	—	0.01	*0.03*[1]
10. CHEMICALS n AND FERTILIZERS						
Chemicals	—		—		na	
Fertilizers:						
Phosphates	—	—	—	—	9.4p	*3.4p*
Potash	—	—	—	—	11.6	*4.9*
Sulphur	—	—	—	—	0.1	—

n data not available for years 1953–5. p phosphatic guano.

	Production		Exports		Imports	
11. INDUSTRY						
Alcoholic beverages			—	—	1.2a	*0.6a*
beer b	28.0	—				
Cement	—	—	—	—	92.7	*37.3*
Electrical engineering a	—	—	—	—	4.0	*1.1*
Railway vehicles a	—	—	—	—	—	*0.3*
Motor vehicles a	—	—	—	—	3.3	*2.0*

a million $ U.S. b '000 hectolitres.

MEXICO

CENTRAL AMERICA

Mexico is a federal republic of 29 states. The land holds considerable resources of potential mineral wealth. Recent social and industrial development has been rapid, and agricultural output is also increasing.

AREA: 1 967 183 sq. km. (761 530 sq. miles) (excl. inland waters and uninhabited islands)

LAND USE: (percentage of total)	*1960*	*1950*
Arable and orchard	12.1	9.5
Permanent meadow and pasture	40.1	34.2
Forest and woodland	22.1	19.7
City areas, waste and other land	25.7	36.6

POPULATION: 45 671 000 (1967 estimate)

Largest city: CIUDAD DE MEXICO (Mexico City), capital; population: 3 353 033 (city proper, 1967)

Distribution of working population (1960)
Total working population: 11 332 016 a

U.N. group no.		*Percentage*
0	Agriculture, forestry, fishing and hunting	54.2
1	Mining and quarrying	1.2
2/3	Manufacturing	13.7
4	Construction	3.6
5	Electricity, gas, water and sanitary services	0.4
6	Commerce	9.5
7	Transport, storage and communications	3.2
8	Services	13.5
9	Others	0.7

		Year(s)
Life expectancy at birth (years): male	57.6	} 1959–61 av.
female	60.3	}
Infant mortality (per '000)	60.7	1965
Crude birth rate (per '000)	44.5*	1960–5 av.
Crude death rate (per '000)	10.5*	1960–5 av.
Accidental deaths (per 100 000 population)		
caused by motor vehicles	6.4	1965
due to other causes	41.8	1965
Population per physician	1 810	1966
Population per hospital bed	510	1966
School enrolment: age 5–19 years (percentage)	70	1963–4 av.
age over 19 years (per 100 000 population)	303	1964–5 av.

a incl. children over 8 years of age in employment.

COMMUNICATIONS

		Year(s)
Motor vehicles in use ('000s): private	686.4	1963–5 av.
commercial	376.2	1963–5 av.
Railway track (km.)	23 672	1965
Mail per capita: domestic	19	}
foreign received	5	} 1963–5 av.
foreign sent	4	}
Telephones (per '000 urban population)	2.1	1967
Radio receivers (per '000 population)	181	1963–5 av.
Television sets (per '000 population)	33.4	1963–5 av.
Daily newspapers (per '000 population)	114*	1962–4 av.

na: data not available. — negligible or nil. [1] one year only. [2] two year average. * estimate. ‡ see appendix. † re-exports.

FINANCE

Currency unit: The Mexican peso

Exchange rates	*1965*	*1960*	*1950 b*	*1938 b*
Per $ U.S.	12.49	12.49	8.65	4.92
Per £ sterling	35.0	35.0	24.23	22.63

		Year(s)
National Income (million $ U.S.)	17 600	1965
G.N.P. per capita ($ U.S.)	470	1966
Rate of increase of G.N.P. per capita	3	1960–4 av.
Foreign trade (percentage of G.D.P.)	14	1963–5 av.

b selling rate.

TRADING

Total trade (in million $ U.S.)	*1965*	*1955*	*1938*
Exports (f.o.b.)	1 146	804	159
Imports (c.i.f.)	1 560	883	110

Main trading partners (percentage of total value)

Exports	*1965*	*1955*	*Imports*	*1965*	*1955*
U.S.A.	56	74	U.S.A.	66	77
Japan	7	6	Germany F.R.	8	4
Poland	5	na	U.K.	3	3
Germany F.R.	3	4	France	3	1
Switzerland	2	—	Italy	3	2
U.A.R.	2	na	Japan	3	1
France	1	—	Canada	2	4

Distribution of trade (percentage of total value)

Exports	*1965*		*1955*	
Food	42		24	
(cereals, fruit and vegetables)		(18)		(3*)
(sugar)		(7)		(2)
(coffee)		(7)		(13)
(cattle and beef)		(5)		(2)
(fish)		(4)		(3)
Crude materials and fuels	36		45	
(textile fibres)		(19)		(30)
Manufactured goods	16		28	
Imports				
Manufactured goods	67		63	
(machinery and transport equipment)		(50)		(44)
Chemicals	16		14	
Crude materials and fuels	12		18	
Food	4		3	

PRODUCTION, EXPORTS AND IMPORTS

Years: **1963–5 average** and *1953–5 average* Units: '000 metric tons unless otherwise indicated

	Production		Exports		Imports	
1. CEREALS, etc.						
Barley	176.7	*160.7**	—	*2.8*	48.0	*8.0*
Maize (corn)	8 063.0	*4 104.0*[2]	543.1*	*19.5*	170.9	*172.7*
Millets/sorghum	530.3	na	0.2	—	64.6	*1.3*
Oats	80.0	*54.0**	1.0	*3.4*	3.5	*2.8*
Potatoes	423.7	*155.3*	—	—	0.2	*0.9*
Rice	301.0	*177.7**	0.1	—	6.2	*0.1*
Rye	—	—	—	—	—	*2.0*
Sweet potatoes/yams	130.7	*75.3*				
Wheat	1 978.3	*796.7*	444.4	—	3.8	*104.6*
2. FRUIT, etc.						
Apples	122.3	*56.0**	0.1	—	—	*1.1*
Apricots	7.0	na	—	—	—	—
Bananas	420.0	*205.0*	14.4	*44.0*	—	—
Coconuts	823.3e	na	0.4	—	—	—
Dates	6.7	*5.5*[2]	—	—	0.1	—
Figs	7.0	*7.7*	—	—	—	—
Grapes	86.3	*43.0*[2]	0.4	—	—	*0.5*
Lemons	168.3	*80.3**	1.7	*3.2*	—	—
Oranges	860.3	*571.7**	68.4	*9.1*	—	—
Other citrus fruit	10.3	—	0.8	—	—	—
Olives	4.7	na				
Peaches	74.0	*50.8*	—	—	—	—
Pears	33.0	*17.0**	—	—	—	*0.2*[2]
Pineapples	197.3	*129.7*	—	*20.2*	—	—
Plums	56.3	*44.7*[1]	—	—	—	—
Raisins	na	na	0.3	—	—	*1.2**
Tomatoes	452.3	*371.3*				
Wine b	na	na	0.4	*1.0*	8.2	*10.7*

b '000 hectolitres. e no. in millions.

	Production		Exports		Imports	
3. BEVERAGES, FOREST PRODUCTS, etc.						
Cocoa	23.3	*11.6*	10.3	*2.9*	—	—
Coffee	154.9	*86.7**	84.0	*75.3*	—	—
Sugar: cane	23 051.0	*13 224.5*[2]				
raw	1 924.7n	*868.0*n*	483.6	*75.0*	—	—
Tobacco: leaf	68.4	*37.4**	8.9	*0.3*	3.5	*1.9*
cigars	na	*30.3e*				
cigarettes	32 811.0e	*28 465.0e*	} —	—[2]	—	*0.9*[2]
tobacco/snuff	na	*0.2*				
Softwood j	4 175.0*	*2 254.3*	25.0[2]	*159.8*	58.1[2]	*168.8*[2]
Hardwood j	1 429.0	*1 506.3*	15.6[2]	*46.8*	28.2[2]	*15.0*[2]
Wood pulp	235.1	*95.3**	—[2]	*2.7*	58.8[2]	*50.3**
Newsprint	20.3	—	—[2]	—	93.0[2]	*66.0*[2]
Other paper	531.0	*184.7**	0.4[2]	—	20.1[2]	*66.1*[1]

e no. in millions. j '000 cu. metres of roundwood equivalent. n in addition, piloncillo 120 (1963–5 av.) and 130* (1953–5 av.).

	Production		Exports		Imports	
4. VEGETABLE OILSEEDS AND OILS						
Castor seed	8.67	*3.05*	—	—	—	—
Castor oil	na	na	—	*0.01*	0.05	—
Copra	180.33	*70.10*	10.04	—	—	—
Cottonseed	964.70	*640.00**	0.07	—	1.16	*8.00*
Cottonseed oil	na	na	—	—	6.80	*3.27*
Groundnuts	66.27	*53.90**	8.67	*19.87*	—	—
Linseed	12.67p	*27.67p*	—	*4.97*	0.13	—
Linseed oil	na	na	—	—	0.73	*0.17*
Olive oil	na	na	—	—	0.65	*1.02*
Palm kernels	27.13	*13.73**	—	—	—	—
Palm oil	14.33*	na	—	—	0.06	*2.13*
Rapeseed	7.00*	*6.00**	—	—	0.13	—
Sesame seed	173.53	*82.13**	8.26	—	—	—
Soya beans	60.00	na	—	—	1.90	—
Soya bean oil	na	na	—	—	0.44*	*0.25*
Tung oil	—	—	—	—	0.16	*0.07*

p flax grown for seed only.

	Production		Exports		Imports	
5. LIVESTOCK‡, ANIMAL PRODUCTS, etc.						
Chickens d	76 153*q	*61 366*[2]*q*				
Cattle d	30 956*	*15 500*[1]*	489.4	*66.5*	19.9	*4.2*
Goats d	12 054*	*9 000*[1]*				
Sheep d	6 475*	*5 000*[1]*	} —	—	37.7	na
Horses d	4 200*	*3 950*[1]*				
Pigs d	13 724*	*7 483**	—	—[2]	1.1	*0.2*[2]
Bacon/ham }	584*	na {	—	—	—	*0.1*
Meat‡: 'A' }			26.4	*6.3**	—	—
'B'	67*	na	4.1	*0.4*	1.9	*0.3*
Butter	—	—	—	—	0.6	*0.1*
Cheese	12*	na	—	—	0.2	*0.7*
Eggs	186	*115**	—	—	—	*9.7*
Fish	250	*88*	41.4	*79.0**	34.1	*1.7*[1]*
Milk	2 305	*1 795**	0.2	—	224.8	*46.9*
Hides/skins	117[2]	na	—	—	24.1	*10.6*[2]
Wool	4	*1**	—	—	6.6	*2.8*

d no. in thousands. q incl. ducks, geese and turkeys.

	Production		Exports		Imports	
6. FIBRES, TEXTILES, etc.						
Abaca	—	—	0.3	—	—	—
Agaves (henequen)	173.4	*106.3*	41.8	*31.3*	—	—
Cotton lint	549.0	*376.7*	367.0	*273.1*	0.4	*0.1*
Flax fibre	—	—	—	—	0.1	—
Jute	—	—	—	—	0.4	*0.3*
Rubber: natural	na	na	0.9	*0.1*	14.1	*18.9*
synthetic	—	—	—	—	29.2	na
Silk f	—	—	—	—	5.7	*0.3*
Cotton: yarn	111.2	*51.0*[2]	1.1[2]	—	—	—
woven fabrics	47.3[1]	*36.5*[2]	1.7	*1.9*	—	—
Rayon: fibre/yarn	27.4	*19.2*	0.6[2]	—	0.2	—
woven fabrics	7.1	*6.2*[2]	—	—	—	—
Non-cellulosic fibre/yarn	5.6	—	—	—	3.4	—
Wool: yarn	—	*0.2*	—[1]	—	—	—
woven fabrics	3.7[1]	*2.8*	—r	—[1]	—r	—[1]

f metric tons. r excl. blankets.

continued

na: data not available. — negligible or nil. [1] one year only. [2] two year average. * estimate. ‡ see appendix. † re-exports.

MEXICO *continued*

PRODUCTION, EXPORTS AND IMPORTS *continued*

	Production		Exports		Imports	
7. FUEL AND POWER						
Coal, 'A'‡	1 147	1 340	—	—	50	43
Coke	—	—	—	—	35	11
Electricity h: total	15 522	6 330[1]				
hydro	7 236	2 940[1]				
thermal	8 286	3 390[1]				
Natural gas i	11 070	1 700[1]	1 450	—	260[1]	558[1]
Oil, crude	18 140	13 020[1]	1 050	na	30[1]	na
Petroleum, refined	17 036	10 740[1]	1 577	3 120[1]	810	1 460[1]

h million kWh. *i* million cu. metres.

	Production		Exports		Imports	
8. IRON AND STEEL						
Iron ore	1 461m	358m	11	191	—	—
Pig iron	1 134	279	—	—	32[1]	4
Steel ingots/castings	2 293	636	—	—	10	3
Iron/steel scrap	na	na	—	—	548	193
Iron/steel products a	na	na	21	—	44	7

a million $ U.S. *m* metal content.

	Production		Exports		Imports	
9. NON-FERROUS MINERALS AND METALS						
Diamonds a	—	—	—	—	0.41[2]	0.03
Gold k, ore	221.30m	417.80m	19.30n	1 363.00n	na	507.00n
Platinum group metals k	—	—	—	—	4.27	0.65s
Silver k, ore m	41 602.7	45 242.70	—	—	—	—
bullion	na	na	36 679.0	34 372.30	—	—
Asbestos: fibre	—	—	—	—	21.85	5.69
manufactured	—	—	—	—	0.72	0.88s
Mica	0.37	—	—	0.01†	0.15	0.04s
Aluminium: bauxite	—	—	—	—	8.60	—
alumina	—	—	—	—	36.86p	1.59q
aluminium	14.10	—	—	—	12.56	7.88s
Antimony: ore	4.69m	3.90m	11.77	7.46	—	—
metal	na	na	0.30	0.89	0.02	0.01s
Cadmium	na	na	1.01	0.92	—	—
Chrome, metal	—	—	—	—	0.64	1.25s
Cobalt, metal	—	—	—	—	0.04	—
Copper: ore	59.17m	56.54m	5.38	39.99	—	—
metal	52.64	47.14	19.47	46.19	0.83	0.92
Lead: ore	178.30m	216.33m	3.06[2]	7.46	—	—
metal	172.39	209.26	152.13[2]	209.70	0.01	0.04s
Magnesium:						
magnesite	na	na	—	0.02	0.04	0.23[2]
metal/salts	—	—	—	—	1.63	0.72
Manganese: ore	130.00	195.10	106.08	196.68	—	—
metal	na	na	—	—	0.43	0.35s
Mercury f	552.04	646.71	592.50	634.10	—	—
Molybdenum f, ore m	47.62	32.35	89.10	37.50	—	—
Nickel, metal	—	—	—	—	0.63	0.10s
Tin: ore	0.87m	0.48m	—	0.07	—	—
metal	0.94	0.27	—	—	0.48	0.34s
Titanium minerals	0.05	—	—	—	0.10	2.08s
Tungsten, ore	0.08	0.60	0.10	1.25	—	—
9. NON-FERROUS MINERALS AND METALS—*continued*						
Vanadium	—	na	—	0.07r	—	—
Zinc: ore	233.43m	239.83m	314.75	328.85	—	—
metal	59.64	54.68	32.28	46.91	0.08	0.09

a million $ U.S. *f* metric tons. *k* '000 fine troy oz. *m* metal content. *n* bullion, etc. *p* hydrates. *q* incl. hydrates. *r* vanadium concentrates. *s* incl. imports for re-export.

	Production		Exports		Imports	
10. CHEMICALS n AND FERTILIZERS						
Organic chemicals:						
Benzene	14.6		4.5[1]		7.2	
Butadiene	—		—		0.4[1]	
Ethylene	7.0		na		na	
Methanol	na		—		6.5	
Phenol	na		—		2.1	
Phthalic anhydride	0.5		—		3.7[1]	
Styrene monomer	na		—		9.6[1]	
Urea	74.2		na		1.2	
Inorganic chemicals:						
Ammonia	140.0		na		103.8[1]	
Carbon black	na		—		1.3[1]	
Chlorine	44.0		na		—	
Nitric acid	117.7[2]		na		—	
Sodium carbonate	107.6		—		105.6	
Sodium hydroxide	96.0		—		19.4	
Sulphuric acid	442.9[2]		—		68.7	
Plastics:						
Polyamides	na		na		na	
Polyethylene	—		—		36.2	
Polyvinyl chloride	15.0[1]		—		0.6	
Fertilizers:						
Phosphates	32.7	—	27.7	—	210.4	na
Potash	—	—	—	—	29.7	3.0
Sulphur: native	1 579.1	180.8	1 629.1 (native and recovered)	61.6 (native and recovered)	0.3 (native and recovered)	7.3 (native and recovered)
recovered	42.5	26.1[1]				

n data not available for years 1953–5.

	Production		Exports		Imports	
11. INDUSTRY						
Aircraft a	—	—	0.3	0.2	14.4	4.0
Alcoholic beverages			1.7a	0.3a	3.0a	2.0a
beer b	9 487.0	6 268.3				
Cement	4 212.0	1 831.3	—	17.3	—	30.0*
Electrical engineering a	—	—	2.1†	0.4[2]†	99.0	35.5[2]
Railway vehicles a	—	—	1.2†	—	32.0	10.6
Machine tools a	—	—	—	—	28.0	—
Merchant ships g	0.3	—	—	—	5.0	0.2[1]
Motor vehicles			0.9a	0.2a	218.8a	80.9[2]a
commercial dq	29.0	22.2				
private dq	61.1	13.5				

a million $ U.S. *b* '000 hectolitres. *d* no. in thousands. *g* '000 G.R.T. *q* assembly of imported parts.

continued

MONACO

EUROPE

Monaco, a small principality, has been under French protection since 1861. In 1962 a new constitution was promulgated maintaining the hereditary monarchy but renouncing the principle of divine right of the monarch. New neighbourhood treaties with France were signed in 1963.

AREA: 1.5 sq. km. (0.6 sq. miles)

LAND USE

All available ground is built upon. The only cultivation is in private or public gardens.

POPULATION: 24 000 (1967 U.N. estimate)

		Year
Infant mortality (per '000)	2.1*	1965
Crude birth rate (per '000)	20.5*	1965
Crude death rate (per '000)	16.0*	1965
Population per hospital bed	80a	1966
School enrolment: age 5–19 years (percentage)	53b	1964

a government hospitals only. *b* public education only.

COMMUNICATIONS

		Year(s)
Telephones (per '000 urban population)	53.9	1967
Radio receivers (per '000 population)	276	1963–5 av.
Television sets (per '000 population)	558	1963–5 av.

FINANCE

Currency unit: The French franc

TRADE

Monaco's prime source of income is tourism; there are, on average, 650 000 visitors a year. Foodstuffs and manufactured goods are imported.

na: data not available. — negligible or nil. [1] one year only. [2] two year average. * estimate. ‡ see appendix. † re-exports.

MONGOLIA

ASIA

Outer Mongolian independence from China, first proclaimed in 1921, was not recognized by China until 1946, and it was finally guaranteed in 1950 by both China P.R. and the U.S.S.R. Relations with the latter were backed by a 20-year treaty of friendship and economic assistance (1966) and with China P.R. by treaties of economic and cultural co-operation and a border agreement (1962). Since the estrangement between China P.R. and the U.S.S.R., Sino-Mongolian relations have deteriorated. The Mongolian People's Republic is a member of Comecon.

AREA: 1 565 000 sq. km. (604 250 sq. miles)

LAND USE: (percentage of total)

	1970
Permanent meadow and pasture	84.0
Forest and woodland	10.5
Other land	5.5

POPULATION: 1 170 000 (1967 estimate)

Largest city: ULAANBAATAR (Ulan Bator), capital; population: 195 300 (city proper, 1962)

		Year
Crude birth rate (per '000)	40.0*	1965
Crude death rate (per '000)	9.7*	1965
Population per physician	730	1965
Population per hospital bed	110	1966
School enrolment: age 5–19 years (percentage)	57	1961
age over 19 years (per 100 000 population)	756	1963

COMMUNICATIONS

		Year
Railway track (km.)	1 427	1965
Telephones (per '000 urban population)	1.2	1967
Daily newspapers (per '000 population)	88	1963

FINANCE

Currency unit: The tugrik replaced, at par, the rouble in 1961

Exchange rates	1965a	1960b	1958b
Per $ U.S.	4.0	4.0	4.0
Per £ sterling	11.2	11.2	11.2

a in 1965 there was a tourist exchange premium of 50% on hard-currency notes. *b* roubles.

PRODUCTION AND TRADE

The Mongols are traditionally herdsmen, and the sheep population numbers approximately 15 million; goats, cattle, horses and camels are also of importance. Some grain and vegetables are grown, wheat production in 1965 being 300 000 and potatoes 25 000 metric tons. Collectivization of agriculture was completed in 1960. The annual yield of hardwood amounts to some 700 000 cubic metres. Minerals include coal, gold, oil and wolfram. Industry is small, but is increasing with technical aid from the U.S.S.R.; and electricity production (thermal and hydro) in 1965 was in the region of 200 million kWh.

The principal exports are livestock, animal products, and gold; imports consist mainly of manufactured goods, textiles and cement.

Trade is primarily with the U.S.S.R., Switzerland being the only significant trading partner apart from the Comecon countries and China P.R.

MOROCCO

NORTH WEST AFRICA

In 1956 Morocco was formed from the union of the French and the Spanish (northern) protectorates and the international zone of Tangier. The Spanish province of Ifni was incorporated into Morocco in 1969. Ceuta and Melilla and three groups of islands off the north coast remain under Spanish sovereignty.

Note: 1953–5 statistics include data for those areas remaining under Spanish sovereignty, and are therefore not strictly comparable with later figures.

AREA: 500 000* sq. km. (193 000* sq. miles)

LAND USE: (percentage of total)

	1963	1953
Arable and orchard	17.7	20.0
Permanent meadow and pasture	17.2	23.8
Forest and woodland	12.0	10.7
City areas, waste and other land	53.1	45.5

POPULATION: 14 193 000 (1967 estimate)

Largest city: CASABLANCA; population: 1 120 000 (city proper, 1966)
Capital city: RABAT; population: 370 000 (city proper, 1966)

Distribution of working population (1960)
Total working population: 3 254 379

U.N. group no.		*Percentage*
0	Agriculture, forestry, fishing and hunting	56.3
1	Mining and quarrying	1.2
2/3	Manufacturing	8.2
4	Construction	1.7
5	Electricity, gas, water and sanitary services	0.3
6	Commerce	7.3
7	Transport, storage and communications	2.5
8	Services	9.9
9	Others (including unemployed)	12.6

		Year(s)
Life expectancy at birth (years)	47*	1962
Population per physician	12 120	1965
Population per hospital bed	660a	1965
School enrolment: age 5–19 years (percentage)	37	1963–4 av.
age over 19 years (per 100 000 population)	72	1963–5 av.

a government hospitals only.

COMMUNICATIONS

		Year(s)
Motor vehicles in use ('000s): private	157.2	1963–5 av.
commercial	60.9	1963–5 av.
Railway track (km.)	1 756	1964
Mail per capita: domestic	5	1963–4 av.
foreign received	3	1963–4 av.
foreign sent	2	1963–4 av.
Telephones (per '000 urban population)	1.1	1967
Radio licences (per '000 population)	50	1963–5 av.
Television sets (per '000 population)	1.8	1963–5 av.
Daily newspapers (per '000 population)	17	1963

FINANCE

Currency unit: The dirham replaced the Moroccan franc in 1959 at the rate DH 1 to MF 100

Exchange rates	1965	1960	1950a	1938a
Per $ U.S.	5.06	5.06	350	38.01
Per £ sterling	14.17	14.17	980	175.0

		Year(s)
National Income (million $ U.S.)	2 324	1965
G.N.P. per capita ($ U.S.)	170	1966
Rate of increase of G.N.P. per capita	0.6	1960–4 av.
Foreign trade (percentage of G.D.P.)	35	1963–5 av.

a Moroccan francs.

TRADING *e*

Total trade (in million $ U.S.)	1965	1955e	1938e
Exports (f.o.b.)	430	328	43
Imports (c.i.f.)	445	497	63

Main trading partners (percentage of total value)

Exports	1965	1955e	*Imports*	1965	1955e
France	44	45	France	38	49
Germany F.R.	8	8	U.S.A.	12	9
Spain	6	2	Cuba	8	4
U.K.	5	5	Germany F.R.	6	5
Belg./Lux.	4	3	Taiwan	4	4 (Taiwan and China P.R.)
Netherlands	3	2	China P.R.	3	
U.S.S.R.	3	na	Italy	3	3

Distribution of trade (percentage of total value)

Exports	1965	1955e*
Crude materials and fuels	45	na
(natural phosphates)	(25)	(19)
(metalliferous ores)	(12)	(10)
Food	44	na
(fruit and vegetables)	(35)	(na)
Manufactured goods	5	na
Wine	4	4
Imports		
Manufactured goods	41	na
(machinery and transport equipment)	(19)	(16)
Food	29	na
(sugar)	(17)	(9)
(cereals)	(5)	(na)
Crude materials and fuels	14	na
Chemicals	9	3

e 1938 and 1955 figures are for French Morocco only, and exclude trade with Spanish Morocco and Tangier.

continued

na: data not available. — negligible or nil. [1] one year only. [2] two year average. * estimate. ‡ see appendix. † re-exports.

PRODUCTION, EXPORTS AND IMPORTS

Years: **1963–5 average** and *1953–5 average* Units: '000 metric tons unless otherwise indicated

Note—The trade figures given for 1953–5 are the sum of the trade figures for the French Zone, the Spanish Zone, and Tangier; thus they include trade between these three states. They are therefore not comparable with the trade figures for 1963–5.

1. CEREALS, etc.

	Production		Exports		Imports	
Barley	**1 305.7**	*1 807.0**	**76.2**	*405.3*	**1.1**	*2.9**
Maize (corn)	**353.0**	*285.8*	**73.9**	*72.6*	**3.7***	*0.1*
Millets/sorghum	**81.3***	*69.3*	**40.3**	*29.4*	—	—
Oats	**17.0***	*60.0[2]*	**4.7**	*33.9*	—	—
Potatoes	**228.7**	*70.5[1]*	**91.0**	*16.5*	**39.5**	*40.6*
Rice	**19.0**	*30.5[2]*	**3.3**	*12.2*	—	*0.9*
Rye	**2.7**	*4.3[2]*	—	—	—	—
Wheat	**1 235.3**	*1 162.3**	**5.1**	*145.8*	**175.0**	*29.9*

2. FRUIT, etc.

	Production		Exports		Imports	
Apples	**6.7***	—	—	—	**2.6**	*6.5*
Apricots	**19.0**	*12.2*	—	—	—	—
Bananas	—	—	—	—	**8.3**	*7.1**
Coconuts	—	—	—	—	**0.1**	—
Dates	**83.3**	*72.3*	—	—	**1.5**	*3.4*
Figs	**66.7***	*53.5[2]*	na	na	—	—
Grapes	**441.7**	*245.0*	**0.2**	*0.9*	—	*0.7**
Lemons	**8.7**	*5.7*	**3.0**	*2.9*	—	*0.1[1]**
Oranges	**530.0**	*198.0n*	**409.1**	*140.7*	—	*2.0**
Other citrus fruit	**11.3**	*4.7n*	**5.1**	*3.3*	—	—
Olives	**186.0**	*85.0[1]*				
Peaches	**9.7**	na	—	—	—	—
Pears	**2.0***	—	—	—	—	*0.9*
Plums	**5.3***	na	—	—	—	—
Raisins	**1.5***	*0.1**	—	—	**0.9**	*0.8*
Tomatoes	**222.0***	*129.0[1]*				
Wine *b*	**2 830.0**	*1 662.0**	**1 742.1**	*800.0*	**4.3**	*98.7**

b '000 hectolitres. *n* French Morocco only.

3. BEVERAGES, FOREST PRODUCTS, etc.

	Production		Exports		Imports	
Cocoa	—	—	—	—	**0.3**	*0.2*
Coffee	—	—	—	—	**9.6**	*5.0q*
Sugar: beet	**242.7**	na				
raw	**17.9**	na	**10.6**	*27.3*	**377.0***	*315.1q*
Tea	—	—	—	*0.8*†*	**10.3**	*15.5*
Tobacco: leaf	**1.8***	*2.1**	**0.1**	*0.5*	**4.1**	*2.3*
cigarettes	**4 043.0*ep***	*2 940.0[1]e*	} —	—	**0.3[1]**	—
tobacco/snuff	**1.6**	*0.8[2]*				
Softwood *j*	**319.0[1]**	*210.2*	—[2]	*2.7[2]*	**339.4**	*264.3*
Hardwood *j*	**280.5[2]**	*787.3*	—[1]	*2.8**	**74.6**	*35.7*
Wood pulp	**28.6[2]**	—	**28.6[2]**	—	**12.7**	*7.7*
Newsprint	—	—	—[2]	—	**2.9[2]**	*3.0*
Other paper	**40.9[2]**	—	**12.5[2]**	*12.3[2]*	**25.9[2]**	*8.3*

e no. in millions. *j* '000 cu. metres of roundwood equivalent. *p* incl. cigarillos. *q* excl. Tangier.

4. VEGETABLE OILSEEDS AND OILS

	Production		Exports		Imports	
Castor seed	na	na	**0.15**	*0.60*	—	—
Castor oil	—	—	—	—	**0.04**	*0.03*
Copra	—	—	—	—	—	*0.27*
Coconut oil	—	—	—	—	**2.68**	—
Cottonseed	**12.00**	*3.30*	**1.14**	—[2]	—	—[2]
Cottonseed oil	na	na	—	—	**14.69**	*6.44*
Groundnuts	—	—	—	—	**9.52**	*5.83*
Groundnut oil	na	na	**0.02**	—	**0.69**	*3.94**
Linseed	**10.67*r***	*24.00r*	**2.37**	*12.50*	**1.24**	—
Linseed oil	na	na	na	*1.50*	—	*0.01**
Olive oil	**29.67***	*17.00**	**4.25**	*3.19*	—	*10.23*
Palm kernels	—	—	—	—	**0.65**	*2.10*
Palm kernel oil	na	na	—	—	**0.95**	*1.89*
Palm oil	—	—	—	—	**0.13**	*0.81*
Rapeseed	—	—	—	*0.07†*	**0.01**	*0.27*
Rapeseed oil	—	na	—	—	—	*0.90*
Sesame seed	—	—	**0.01†**	—	**0.02**	—
Soya beans	—	—	—	—	**7.98**	—
Soya bean oil	na	—	**0.03**	*1.00*†*	**31.01**	*3.80**
Sunflower seed	**8.33**	*2.67*	—	—	**0.03**	—
Sunflower seed oil	na	na	—	—	**6.45**	*1.80*

r flax grown for seed only.

5. LIVESTOCK‡, ANIMAL PRODUCTS, etc.

	Production		Exports		Imports	
Chickens *d*	**10 333.3***	*694.0[1]t*				
Cattle *d*	**2 922.3***	*2 744.2**	—	*4.1t*	**0.6**	*1.7**
Goats *d*	**7 449.0*u**	*10 574.2u*	} **0.8**	na	**0.1**	na
Sheep *d*	**15 093.0***	*15 112.5**				
Horses *d*	**307.7***	*241.0**				
Pigs *d*	**48.0***	*71.0**	**1.2**	*5.2*	—	*0.3*
Bacon/ham }	**133.7***	*119.5**	{ —	*0.2*	—	—
Meat‡: 'A'			—	*0.2*	—	*0.8*
'B'	**30.0***	*53.4[1]*	—	—	—	*0.1*
Butter	—	—	—	—	**4.5**	*3.3*
Cheese	—	—	—	—	**2.5**	*4.2*
Eggs	**40.0***	*50.1**	**0.4**	*4.5*	—	—
Fish	**199.5**	*112.2*	**75.2**	*76.1**	**0.2**	*3.0**
Milk	**321.7**	*458.5*	—	—	**52.8**	*26.7**
Hides/skins	**28.7[1]**	*26.6**	na	*0.9*	—	—
Wool	**5.9[2]**	*6.5**	**0.7[2]**	*2.1*	**0.2[2]**	*0.1*

d no. in thousands. *t* Spanish Morocco only. *u* number registered for taxation.

6. FIBRES, TEXTILES, etc.

	Production		Exports		Imports	
Agaves (sisal etc.)	**0.3**	*0.1[1]*	—	—	**3.1[2]**	*0.8*
Cotton lint	**6.0**	*1.7**	**5.7**	*1.6*	**4.5**	*3.5*
Hemp fibre	—	*0.3[2]*	—	—	—	—
Jute	—	—	—	*0.1†*	**3.2**	*1.4*
Rubber, natural	—	—	—	—	**1.0**	*0.5*
Silk *f*	—	—	—	—	**1.0**	—[2]
Cotton: yarn	**4.5**	*2.5*	—	—	**1.9**	*0.7[2]*
woven fabrics	**5.9[2]**	*2.0*	—	—	**9.0[2]**	*9.9*
Wool: yarn	**1.9**	*1.3[2]*	—	—	—	—
woven fabrics	**0.5**	*0.6[1]*	**0.1[2]**	*0.1*	**0.9**	*0.7*

f metric tons.

7. FUEL AND POWER

	Production		Exports		Imports	
Coal, 'A'‡	**407**	*470*	**138**	*228p*	**78**	*121*
Coke	—	—	—	—	**11**	*9*
Electricity *h*: total	**1 232**	*880[1]*				
hydro	**1 124**	*770[1]*				
thermal	**108**	*110[1]*				
Natural gas *i*	**10**	*7*	—	—	—	—
Oil, crude	**123**	*100[1]*	—	—	**806**	na
Petroleum, refined	**1 030**	*80[1]*	—	—	**137**	*770[1]*

h million kWh. *i* million cu. metres. *p* incl. small quantity of Coal 'B'.

8. IRON AND STEEL

	Production		Exports		Imports	
Iron ore	**567*m***	*765m*	**1 030**	*1 297*	**9**	na
Pig iron	—	—	—	—	**1**	*1*
Iron/steel scrap	na	na	**30**	*36*	—	*18*

m metal content.

9. NON-FERROUS MINERALS AND METALS

	Production		Exports		Imports	
Gold *k*, ore *m*	na	*4.00*	—	—	—	—
Silver *k*, ore	**658.7*m**	*2 094.70m*	**35.83*p***	*604.00p*	—	—
Asbestos: fibre	na	*0.55*	—	*0.04*	**2.34**	*0.85*
manufactured	na	na	**11.69**	—	**0.23**	*0.11*
Mica	—	*0.01*	—	*0.01*	—	*0.16*
Aluminium: bauxite	—	—	—	—	**1.99**	*1.03*
alumina	—	—	—	—	**0.12[2]q**	—
aluminium	—	—	**0.40†**	—	**3.18**	*1.66*
Antimony: ore	**1.48*m***	*0.58m*	**2.08**	*1.41*	—	—
metal	na	na	—	—	**0.01**	*0.02*
Beryl	—	*0.02*	—	*0.02*	—	—
Chrome, ore	na	na	—	*142.85*	—	*0.26r*
Cobalt, ore	**1.63*m***	*0.70m*	**14.15**	—	—	—
Copper: ore	**1.80*m***	*0.90m*	**5.66**	*3.53*	—	—
metal	na	na	**0.82**	*0.25*	**2.60**	*1.06*
Lead: ore	**74.12*m***	*84.52m*	**125.53**	*82.44*	—	—
metal	**18.28**	*26.94*	**15.12**	*27.02*	**0.19**	*0.43*
Magnesium: dolomite	na	na	—	—	**0.43[2]**	na
magnesite	na	na	—	—	**0.03[2]**	na
metal/salts	—	—	—	—	**0.54**	*0.21[1]*
Manganese, ore	**350.63**	*413.64*	**318.74**	*373.65*	—	—
Mercury *f*	—	—	—	—	**1.40**	*1.00*
Nickel, ore	**0.32*m***	*0.14m*	—	—	—	—
Tin: ore	**0.01*m***	*0.01m*	—	—	—	—
metal	**0.01**	*0.01[2]*	—	—	**0.25**	*0.24*
Titanium minerals	—	—	—	—	**0.50[2]**	—
Tungsten, ore	—	*0.01*	—	*0.02*	—	—
Zinc, ore	**42.20*m***	*37.64m*	**76.25**	*71.73*	**2.52*r***	*2.14r*

f metric tons. *k* '000 fine troy oz. *m* metal content. *p* bullion. *q* incl. hydrate. *r* metal.

10. CHEMICALS*n* AND FERTILIZERS

	Production		Exports		Imports	
Chemicals	—		—		na	
Fertilizers:						
Phosphates	**9 490.2**	*4 834.7*	**9 381.9**	*4 769.7*	—	—
Potash	—	—	—	—	**12.8**	*10.4*
Pyrites	**6.1*x***	*0.7x*	**5.0[2]**	—	—	*12.2*
Sulphur	**6.0**	—	—	—	**10.0**	*9.8*

n data not available for years 1953–5. *x* sulphur content.

11. INDUSTRY

	Production		Exports		Imports	
Aircraft *a*	—	—	—	—	**2.5[2]**	na
Alcoholic beverages			**23.6*a***	*6.6a*	**1.8[1]*a***	—
beer *b*	**269.0**	*300.0[2]*				
Cement	**826.0**	*695.6*	**27.3**	*9.7*	**14.7**	*189.3*
Electrical engineering *a*	—	—	**0.1[1]†**	—	**17.8[2]**	*13.2*
Railway vehicles *a*	—	—	—	—	—	*2.2*
Machine tools *a*	—	—	—	—	**1.8**	*1.9*
Merchant ships *g*	**0.1**	—	—	—	—	—
Motor vehicles			**1.2*a***	na	**18.9[2]*a***	*34.4a*
commercial *dp*	**1.9**	na				
private *dp*	**5.3**	na				

a million $ U.S. *b* '000 hectolitres. *d* no. in thousands. *g* '000 G.R.T. *p* assembly of imported parts.

na: data not available. — negligible or nil. [1] one year only. [2] two year average. * estimate. ‡ see appendix. † re-exports.

NAURU

PACIFIC OCEAN

From 1947 until 1968 Nauru was administered, chiefly by Australia, as a U.N. Trusteeship. Nauru then became an independent republic with a limited form of membership of the British Commonwealth.

AREA: 20 sq. km. (8 sq. miles)

LAND USE: (percentage of total)	*1963*
Arable and orchard	15
City areas, waste and other land	85

POPULATION: 6 056 (of whom 3 101 were indigenous Nauruans) (1966 census)

Total working population: 2 164 (1961), of whom approx. 1 350 are employed in phosphate mining.

PRODUCTION AND TRADE

The chief product is phosphate rock, of which some 1 600 000 metric tons were exported annually during the years 1963–5, compared with an average of 1 250 000 metric tons for the years 1953–5.

There are some 2 000 cattle and 3 000 chickens on the island, but very little land is cultivated. Annual electricity production averaged 12 million kWh. during 1963–5.

Exports, almost entirely phosphates, go to Australia, New Zealand, and the U.K.

Imports consist of foodstuffs, building materials, and machinery.

Trade for the year 1963/4 amounted to (in million $ U.S.):

Exports 9.8 Imports 12.5

NEPAL

CENTRAL ASIA

Before 1950 Nepal was ruled by a series of hereditary prime ministers. A revolutionary movement in 1950/1 restored the monarchy which, after ten unsettled years, gained executive power; and a new constitution was introduced in 1962, with a council of ministers and an indirectly elected parliament.

AREA: 141 400* sq. km. (54 600* sq. miles)

LAND USE: (percentage of total)	*1965*	*1947*
Arable and orchard	13.0	22.2
Permanent meadow and pasture	14.2	—
Forest and woodland (incl. unstocked land)	32.2	32.1
City areas, waste and other land	40.6	45.7

POPULATION: 10 500 000 (1967 estimate)

Largest city: KATMANDU, capital; population: 121 019 (city proper, 1961)

Distribution of working population (1952–4 av.)

Total working population: 4 153 455

U.N. group no.		*Percentage*
0	Agriculture, forestry, fishing and hunting	93.5
1	Mining and quarrying	—
2/3	Manufacturing	1.9
4	Construction	0.2
5	Electricity, gas, water and sanitary services	—
6	Commerce	1.4
7	Transport, storage and communications	0.5
8	Services	2.3
9	Others	0.2

		Year(s)
Population per physician	45 090	1965
Population per hospital bed	6 950	1966
School enrolment: age 5–19 years (percentage)	18	1964
age over 19 years (per 100 000 population)	73	1964–5 av.

COMMUNICATIONS

		Year(s)
Railway track (km.)	101	1969
Telephones (per '000 urban population)	0.04	1967
Daily newspapers (per '000 population)	0.8	1962–4 av.

FINANCE

Currency unit: The Nepalese rupee

Exchange rates	*1965*	*1960*	*1958*
Per $ U.S.	7.619	7.619	3.66
Per £ sterling	20.333	20.333	10.26

		Year
National Income (million $ U.S.)	665	1965
G.N.P. per capita ($ U.S.)	70	1966

TRADING

The principal exports are cereals, jute, timber, oilseeds, medicinal herbs and cattle products. The main imports are textiles, salt, fuels, sugar, machinery, paper, cereals, iron and steel. India is the main trading partner. Foreign aid and external loans contribute to the balance of trade.

The value of imports for the year 1967/8 was about U.S. $ 60 million.

PRODUCTION, EXPORTS AND IMPORTS

Years: **1963–5 average** Units: '000 metric tons unless otherwise indicated

Note—no data are available for the years 1953–5

1. CEREALS, etc.

	Production	Exports	Imports
Maize (corn)	**853.0**	—	—
Millets/sorghum	**75.3**	**0.6***	**0.1***
Potatoes	na	**0.8***	**0.1***
Rice	**2 172.0**	**32.5***	**0.1***
Wheat	**143.0**	—	**0.5***

3. BEVERAGES, FOREST PRODUCTS, etc.

	Production	Exports	Imports
Sugar: cane	**185.7**		
raw	**1.3**	—	**3.6***
Tea	na	**0.1**	**0.3***
Tobacco, leaf	na	**0.2***	**0.8***
Softwood *j*	**146.0**	**16.0**	—
Hardwood *j*	**6 826.7***	**146.3**	—
Paper	—	—	na

j '000 cu. metres of roundwood equivalent.

4. VEGETABLE OILSEEDS AND OILS

	Production	Exports	Imports
Castor seed	na	**0.82***	**0.04***
Linseed	na	**0.62***	**0.01***
Rapeseed	na	**2.99[1]**	—

5. LIVESTOCK‡, ANIMAL PRODUCTS, etc.

	Production	Exports	Imports
Cattle *d*	**2 629.3***	—	—
Goats *d*	**2 050.0***	—	—
Sheep *d*	**2 052.0***	—	—
Pigs *d*	**162.0***	—	—
Butter	na	**0.8**	—
Wool	**1.0***	—	—

d no. in thousands.

6. FIBRES, TEXTILES, etc.

	Production	Exports	Imports
Jute	**38.0**	**5.3***	**9.5[2]***
Cotton, woven fabrics	—	—	na

7. FUEL AND POWER

	Production	Exports	Imports
Electricity *h*: total	**17[2]**		
hydro	**10[2]**		
thermal	**7[2]**		
Petroleum, refined	—	—	**40**

h million kWh.

8. IRON AND STEEL

	Production	Exports	Imports
Iron/steel products	—	—	na

na: data not available. — negligible or nil. [1] one year only. [2] two year average. * estimate. ‡ see appendix. † re-exports.

NETHERLANDS

The Netherlands is a constitutional and hereditary monarchy. The central executive power rests with the Crown while the central legislative power is vested in the Crown and parliament. The country became a member of Benelux (with Belgium and Luxembourg) in 1944, and in 1961 the three became members of the European Economic Community.

AREA: 40 893 sq. km. (15 789 sq. miles) (excl. inland water)

LAND USE: (percentage of total)	*1965*	*1955*
Arable and orchard	28.8	29.7
Permanent meadow and pasture	38.3	35.9
Forest and woodland	8.6	7.1
City areas, waste and other land	24.3	27.3

POPULATION: 12 597 000 (1967 estimate)

Largest city: ROTTERDAM; population: 1 048 487 (1966)
Seat of Government: 'S GRAVENHAGE *or* DEN HAAG (The Hague); population: 743 208 (1966)

Distribution of working population (1960)
Total working population: 4 168 626

U.N. group no.		*Percentage*
0	Agriculture, forestry, fishing and hunting	10.7
1	Mining and quarrying	1.5
2/3	Manufacturing	29.9
4	Construction	9.7
5	Electricity, gas, water and sanitary services	1.1
6	Commerce	16.2
7	Transport, storage and communications	6.9
8	Services	23.5
9	Others	0.5

		Year(s)
Life expectancy at birth (years): male	71.1	1966
female	76.1	1966
Infant mortality (per '000)	14.4	1965
Crude birth rate (per '000)	19.9	1965
Crude death rate (per '000)	8.0	1965
Accidental deaths (per 100 000 population)		
caused by motor vehicles	19.7	1965
due to other causes	24.1	1965
Population per physician	860	1965
Population per hospital bed	200	1965
School enrolment: age 5–19 years (percentage)	89	1963–4 av.
age over 19 years (per 100 000 population)	1 169	1963–5 av.

COMMUNICATIONS

		Year(s)
Motor vehicles in use ('000s): private	1 707.4	1963–5 av.
commercial	217.4	1963–5 av.
Railway track (km.)	3 238	1964
Mail per capita: domestic	193	1963–5 av.
foreign received	11	1963–5 av.
foreign sent	18	1963–5 av.
Telephones (per '000 urban population)	20.1	1967
Radio licences (per '000 population)	256	1963–5 av.
Television licences (per '000 population)	151.8	1963–5 av.
Daily newspapers (per '000 population)	258.5	1962–4 av.

FINANCE

Currency unit: The guilder, or florin

Exchange rates	*1965*	*1960*	*1950*	*1938*
Per $ U.S.	3.611	3.770	3.805	1.839
Per £ sterling	10.120	10.568	10.659	8.459

		Year(s)
National Income (million $ U.S.)	15 544	1966
G.N.P. per capita ($ U.S.)	1 420	1966
Rate of increase of G.N.P. per capita	3.1	1960–4 av.
Foreign trade (percentage of G.D.P.)	75	1963–5 av.

TRADING

Total trade (in million $ U.S.)	*1965*	*1955*	*1938*
Exports (f.o.b.)	6 393	2 687	593
Imports (c.i.f.)	7 461	3 208	803

Main trading partners (percentage of total value)

Exports	*1965*	*1955*	*1938*	*Imports*	*1965*	*1955*	*1938*
Germany F.R.	28	17	15 *d*	Germany F.R.	24	18	21 *d*
Belg./Lux.	15	14	10	Belg./Lux.	20	18	11
U.K.	9	12	23	U.S.A.	10	14	11
France	8	5	6	U.K.	7	9	8
Italy	5	2	1	France	6	4	5
U.S.A.	4	6	4	Italy	4	1	1
Sweden	3	5	3	Sweden	3	3	2

Distribution of trade (percentage of total value)

Exports	*1965*	*1955*	*1938*
Manufactured goods	47	41	na
(machinery and transport equipment)	(21)	(15)	(na)
(textiles and clothing)	(9)	(9)	(6)
Food	23	30	31*
(meat)	(6)	(5)	(na)
(dairy produce and eggs)	(5)	(11)	(15)
(fruit and vegetables)	(5)	(5)	(5*)
Crude materials and fuels	17	18	na
(petroleum products)	(7)	(9)	(na)
Imports			
Manufactured goods	56	46	na
(machinery and transport equipment)	(25)	(18)	(na)
(textiles and clothing)	(9)	(6)	(4*)
Crude materials and fuels	21	31	na
(petroleum products)	(8)	(10)	(3)
Food	12	14	11*
Chemicals	7	5	na

d incl. Germany D.R.

PRODUCTION, EXPORTS AND IMPORTS

Years: **1963–5 average** and *1953–5 average*   Units: '000 metric tons unless otherwise indicated

1. CEREALS, etc.

	Production 1963–5	Production 1953–5	Exports 1963–5	Exports 1953–5	Imports 1963–5	Imports 1953–5
Barley	378.7	250.0	164.5	45.0	242.8	524.1
Maize (corn)	—	30.3	80.5†	2.0	1 870.3	533.8
Millets/sorghum	—	—	28.5†	3.0†	710.1	119.5
Oats	402.3	510.3	83.9	25.8	155.2	203.2
Potatoes	3 739.0	4 024.3	630.1	504.3	28.4	9.9
Rice	—	—	18.0†	26.1†	58.3	79.1
Rye	306.3	469.3	17.6	32.4	182.9	135.7
Wheat	644.3	332.0	173.6	11.1	702.9	768.9

2. FRUIT, etc.

	Production 1963–5	Production 1953–5	Exports 1963–5	Exports 1953–5	Imports 1963–5	Imports 1953–5
Apples	382.3*n*	328.0*n*	78.0	94.0	29.3	4.9
Bananas	—	—	0.2†	0.2†	73.9	28.5
Cherries	7.0	15.9	—	0.4	—	2.3
Coconuts	—	—	—	—	3.4	1.7
Dates	—	—	0.1†	—	0.5	1.0
Figs	—	—	—	—	—	0.7
Grapes	6.3	12.3	1.4	4.5	7.7	—
Lemons	—	—	0.1†	0.1†	9.4	5.3
Oranges	—	—	4.6†	0.7†	213.7	108.8
Other citrus fruit	—	—	0.7†	—	10.9	3.2
Peaches	1.0*	—	—	—	—	—
Pears	111.0	131.3	36.1	38.7	4.8	0.7
Plums	11.7	21.7	—	0.3	—	1.4
Raisins	—	—	—	—	21.3	16.4
Tomatoes	290.0	111.0				
Wine *b*	—	—	6.4†	3.7†	356.7	99.0

b '000 hectolitres. *n* commercial production only.

3. BEVERAGES, FOREST PRODUCTS, etc.

	Production 1963–5	Production 1953–5	Exports 1963–5	Exports 1953–5	Imports 1963–5	Imports 1953–5
Cocoa	—	—	0.6†	0.1†	108.9	59.1
Coffee	—	—	4.1†	0.2†	80.9	29.1
Sugar: beet	3 380.0	3 002.0				
raw	552.3	423.7	9.8	124.7	212.2	231.3
Tea	—	—	0.8†	0.4†	9.9	8.2
Tobacco: leaf	—	—	4.1†	5.1†	44.2	33.9
cigars	1 883.0*e*	1 112.7*e*				
cigarettes	16 170.0*e*	10 687.3*e*	na	1.9[2]	—	0.8[2]
tobacco/snuff	13.7	10.4				
Softwood *j*	485.3	332.0	34.0	11.1	4 372.6	2 982.1
Hardwood *j*	240.0	321.3	38.6	21.5	648.3	403.6
Wood pulp	149.0	421.7*	2.2	1.8	488.7	207.3
Newsprint	156.3	102.3	41.7	26.7	97.0	24.7
Other paper	1 063.0	664.7	408.0	284.7	359.3	133.7

e no. in millions. *j* '000 cu. metres of roundwood equivalent.

4. VEGETABLE OILSEEDS AND OILS

	Production 1963–5	Production 1953–5	Exports 1963–5	Exports 1953–5	Imports 1963–5	Imports 1953–5
Castor seed	—	—	0.03†	—	2.09	3.13
Castor oil	na	na	0.27	0.36	2.27	0.51
Copra	—	—	1.85†	0.53†	131.33	141.80
Coconut oil	na	na	36.16	34.86	2.14	0.72
Cottonseed oil	—	—	0.09†	5.31†	3.90	26.02
Groundnuts	—	—	9.61†	1.56†	41.34	24.53
Groundnut oil	na	na	6.16	4.29	9.23	5.23
Linseed	25.67	23.67	12.94	12.40	69.17	62.47
Linseed oil	na	na	3.74	6.41	13.88	12.88

continued

PRODUCTION, EXPORTS AND IMPORTS *continued*

4. VEGETABLE OILSEEDS AND OILS—*continued*

	Production 1963–5	Production 1953–5	Exports 1963–5	Exports 1953–5	Imports 1963–5	Imports 1953–5
Olive oil	—	—	—	—	0.17	0.05
Palm kernels	—	—	0.28†	—	124.87	86.60
Palm kernel oil	na	na	19.70	11.63	0.77	1.08
Palm oil	—	—	5.83†	9.86†	68.93	74.52
Rapeseed	10.70	15.30	13.88	5.37	11.93	9.47
Rapeseed oil	na	na	0.97	1.79	7.07	0.28
Sesame seed	—	—	—	—	0.02	10.60[2]
Soya beans	—	—	0.23†	0.30†	387.12	119.20
Soya bean oil	na	na	21.14	10.72	23.02	4.86
Sunflower seed	—	—	0.33†	—	1.29	2.03
Sunflower seed oil	na	na	0.37	0.51	7.67	4.55
Tung oil	—	—	0.02†	—	1.04	0.99

5. LIVESTOCK‡, ANIMAL PRODUCTS, etc.

	Production 1963–5	Production 1953–5	Exports 1963–5	Exports 1953–5	Imports 1963–5	Imports 1953–5
Chickens *d*	44 142.3	32 516.7				
Cattle *d*	3 671.0	2 984.7	65.5	29.9	76.4	13.0
dairy cows *d*	1 719.3*p*	1 514.0				
Goats *d*	93.0*	na	4.5	na	69.7	na
Sheep *d*	465.0	404.0				
Horses *d*	136.3	237.0				
Pigs *d*	3 314.0	2 097.0	188.2	39.4	0.1	1.4
Bacon/ham	727.0	438.3	10.4	35.3	0.3	—
Meat‡: 'A'			148.1	25.7	31.0	16.3
'B'	160.1*	73.3	100.6	18.8	23.9	1.0
Butter	95.7	79.7	33.7	49.7	2.3	—
Cheese	214.7	165.0	114.4	89.0	5.8	0.4
Eggs	288.6	195.7	105.9	113.1	0.1	—
Fish	375.3	334.0	198.7	163.6[1]*	302.9	80.3[1]*
Milk	7 036.3	5 840.3	1 587.0	968.5	1 015.5	35.6
Whale/sperm oil	8.2	14.9	—	—	25.4	50.1*r*
Hides/skins	32.6	21.7*q*	51.9	20.0[2]	65.4	40.7[2]
Wool	0.9	1.0	4.3	1.2	11.0	9.4

d no. in thousands. *p* excl. animals kept on agricultural holdings of less than one hectare. *q* cattle hides only. *r* incl. small amounts of other marine oils.

6. FIBRES, TEXTILES, etc.

	Production 1963–5	Production 1953–5	Exports 1963–5	Exports 1953–5	Imports 1963–5	Imports 1953–5
Abaca	—	—	—	—	3.1	4.2
Agaves (sisal etc.)	—	—	12.4†	5.2†	37.6	23.6
Cotton lint	—	—	2.7†	0.3†	80.0	71.9
Flax fibre	33.3	35.8	146.6*t*	22.2	7.0	3.0
Hemp fibre	—	—	0.9†	—	0.2	0.8
Jute	—	—	4.6†	0.1†	15.9	13.4
Rubber: natural	—	—	0.5†	0.1†	23.8	20.0
synthetic	91.7	—	81.2	—	14.1	2.0[2]
Silk *f*	—	—	2.0†	—	8.3	—
Cotton: yarn	72.7	67.8	12.7	6.0	16.9	13.2
woven fabrics	62.4*n*	65.3**p*	29.9	23.3	23.9	10.7
Rayon: fibre/yarn	55.1	40.5*q*	28.5	22.3	7.2	2.5
woven fabrics	11.2*n*	5.1*nr*	8.7	3.8	15.4	4.3
Non-cellulosic fibre/yarn	34.0	1.6	25.3	na	9.3	na
Wool: yarn	23.1	27.3	6.5	2.1	12.6	8.8
woven fabrics	27.7*n*	25.0*n*	6.1	5.1	9.4	3.8

f metric tons. *n* yarn consumption in licensed mills. *p* incl. spun rayon piece goods. *q* incl. tyre cord yarn. *r* continuous filament piece goods only. *t* incl. straw.

7. FUEL AND POWER

	Production 1963–5	Production 1953–5	Exports 1963–5	Exports 1953–5	Imports 1963–5	Imports 1953–5
Coal: 'A'‡	11 480	11 890	3 067	858	8 901	7 122
'B'	—	250	33	52	371	308
Coke	na	na	2 283	1 584	371	368
Electricity *h t*	22 990	10 460[1]				
Natural gas *i*	1 080	419[1]	20	—	—	—
Oil, crude	2 290	1 020[1]	7	na	23 570	11 700[1]
Petroleum, refined	22 780	12 040[1]	9 267	7 310[1]	7 340	2 620[1]

h million kWh. *i* million cu. metres. *t* thermal.

8. IRON AND STEEL

	Production 1963–5	Production 1953–5	Exports 1963–5	Exports 1953–5	Imports 1963–5	Imports 1953–5
Iron ore	—	—	217†	322†	3 059	1 149
Pig iron	2 007	624	109	224	78	20
Steel ingots/castings	2 714	927	105	1	207	128
Iron/steel scrap	na	na	384	165	77	35
Iron/steel products *a*	na	na	356	72	354	199

a million $ U.S.

9. NON-FERROUS MINERALS AND METALS

	Production 1963–5	Production 1953–5	Exports 1963–5	Exports 1953–5	Imports 1963–5	Imports 1953–5
Diamonds *a*	—	—	29.79†	20.22†	29.20	18.13
Gold *k*, bullion/coins etc.	—	—	36.37†	1 598.26†	192.70‡	1 547.30
Platinum group metals	—	—	41.66†	118.87†	75.16	139.37
Silver *k*, bullion	—	—	1 412.33†	9 957.30†	5 691.00	1 681.33

9. NON-FERROUS MINERALS AND METALS—*continued*

	Production 1963–5	Production 1953–5	Exports 1963–5	Exports 1953–5	Imports 1963–5	Imports 1953–5
Asbestos: fibre	—	—	0.08†	0.03†	19.62	10.22
manufactured	—	—	9.52†	5.18†	56.11	43.82
Mica	—	—	0.15†	0.08†	0.83	0.48
Aluminium: bauxite	—	—	0.33†	—	12.38	0.49
alumina	—	—	—	—	9.15*n*	3.33*p*
aluminium	na	na	23.20	4.07	60.78	25.95
Antimony, metal	—	—	0.14†	0.04†	0.89	0.85
Cadmium	0.04	0.01*	0.25†	—	0.27	—
Chrome: ore	—	—	1.25†	—	3.34	0.27
metal	—	—	—	0.07†	1.17	1.99
Cobalt, metal	—	—	—	—	0.18	—
Copper, metal	—	—	45.11†	22.27†	101.05	42.30
Lead: ore	—	—	—	—	0.24	2.58
metal	na	1.54	18.80†	9.79†	59.82	43.81
Magnesium:						
dolomite	—	—	—	—	333.16	35.92
magnesite	—	—	1.04†	15.61†	45.37	18.66
kieserite	na	na	—	—	—	10.63
metal/salts‡	—	—	36.42	0.79	13.61	18.91
Manganese: ore	—	—	8.14*q*†	3.50*q*†	15.44*q*	40.57*q*
metal	—	—	—	—	17.49	6.49[2]
Mercury *f*	—	—	10.60†	—	110.40	35.13
Molybdenum *f*, ore	—	—	82.30†	—	290.60	28.40
Nickel, ore	—	—	1.54†	0.06†	3.49	0.50
Tin: ore	—	—	—	—	20.53	36.51
metal	13.46	27.76	12.67	28.36	2.24	3.17
Titanium minerals	—	—	5.90†	—	17.50	6.69
Tungsten: ore	—	—	0.21†	—	0.11	0.04
metal	—	—	—	—	0.01	—
Vanadium, metal	—	—	—	—	0.01*r*	—
Zinc: ore	—	—	5.95†	—	89.17	64.81
metal	38.10	26.56	55.64*s*	23.08*s*	28.62	18.44

a million $ U.S. *f* metric tons. *k* '000 fine troy oz. *n* hydrate. *p* incl. hydrate. *q* incl. manganiferous iron ore. *r* ferro-vanadium. *s* incl. re-exports.

10. CHEMICALS*n* AND FERTILIZERS

	Production 1963–5	Production 1953–5	Exports 1963–5	Exports 1953–5	Imports 1963–5	Imports 1953–5
Organic chemicals:						
Benzene	47.0[2]		34.8		1.4	
Butadiene	na		na		na	
Ethylene	na		na		na	
Methanol	—		2.3		14.1	
Phenol	18.8		2.2		48.5	
Phthalic anhydride	11.8		1.8		7.4	
Styrene monomer	na		11.7		14.4	
Urea	404.0[1]		177.1		0.4	
Inorganic chemicals:						
Ammonia	557.0		3.2		20.2	
Carbon black	55.3[2]*		45.1		9.5	
Chlorine	137.5[2]		3.1		0.3	
Nitric acid	na		0.2		1.3	
Sodium carbonate	145.5[2]		2.0		9.7	
Sodium hydroxide	na		na		34.4	
Sulphuric acid	973.3		47.1		50.4	
Plastics:						
Polyamides	na		6.0		0.9	
Polyethylene	43.7		28.9		18.7	
Polyvinyl chloride	18.0		na		43.3	
Fertilizers:						
Phosphates	—	—	1.9	—	756.4	512.1
Potash	—	—	2.4†	1.7†	516.1	502.8
Pyrites	—	—	—	—	236.1	436.1
Sulphur	30.3*p*	7.0[1]	4.8†	7.6†	174.1	1.3

n data not available for years 1953–5. *p* recovered from sulphide ores.

11. INDUSTRY

	Production 1963–5	Production 1953–5	Exports 1963–5	Exports 1953–5	Imports 1963–5	Imports 1953–5
Aircraft *a*	84.0[1]**w*	na	151.4	10.2	77.3	16.4
Alcoholic beverages			27.6*a*	18.0*a*	—	4.7*a*
beer *b*	4 927.0	2 043.0				
spirits *b*	223.0[1]*r*	320.0[1]*t*				
Cement	2 642.7	978.0	10.0	22.3	1 758.3	1 343.0
Electrical engineering *a*	1 055.0[2]	na	553.8	169.9[2]	558.4	123.4[2]
Railway vehicles *a*	na	na	—	22.2	—	11.5
Machine tools *a*	12.0[1]	na	—	—	28.1	—
Merchant ships *g*	279.0	383.0	141.0	152.4	66.0	26.0
Motor vehicles			69.6*a*	14.5*a*	371.6*a*	109.7[2]*a*
commercial *d*	12.9*v*	5.9*v*				
private *d*	54.3*v*	14.7*u*				

a million $ U.S. *b* '000 hectolitres. *d* no. in thousands. *g* '000 G.R.T. *r* 1967 data. *t* 1961 data. *u* assembly of imported parts. *v* incl. assembly of imported parts. *w* 1966 data.

na: data not available. — negligible or nil. [1] one year only. [2] two year average. * estimate. ‡ see appendix. † re-exports.

NETHERLANDS (TERRITORIES)

NETHERLANDS ANTILLES

CARIBBEAN SEA

The Netherlands Antilles consists of the Leeward Islands (Curacao, Aruba and Bonaire) and the smaller Windward Islands. Since 1954 it has been fully autonomous in domestic affairs although it remains an integral part of the Netherlands realm.

AREA: 1 019 sq. km. (394 sq. miles)

LAND USE: (percentage of total)	*1951*
Arable and orchard	5.2
Permanent meadow and pasture	—
Forest and woodland	—
City areas, waste and other land	94.8

POPULATION: 212 000 (1967 estimate)

Capital city: WILLEMSTAD; population: 94 133 (1960)

Distribution of working population (1960)
Total working population: 60 199

U.N. group no.		*Percentage*
0	Agriculture, forestry, fishing and hunting	1.7
1	Mining and quarrying	1.1
2/3	Manufacturing	25.8
4	Construction	6.8
5	Electricity, gas, water and sanitary services	2.0
6	Commerce	13.7
7	Transport, storage and communications	6.2
8	Services	23.8
9	Others	18.9

		Year(s)
Infant mortality (per '000)	17.6*	1965
Crude birth rate (per '000)	27.3*	1965
Crude death rate (per '000)	5.0*	1965
Population per physician	1 450	1964
Population per hospital bed	110	1964
School enrolment: age 5–19 years (percentage)	112‡	1963–4 av.

COMMUNICATIONS		*Year(s)*
Motor vehicles in use ('000s): private	22.2	1963–5 av.
commercial	4.4	1963–5 av.
Mail per capita: domestic	20	1963–5 av.
foreign received	24	1963–5 av.
foreign sent	16	1963–5 av.
Telephones (per '000 urban population)	11.1	1967
Radio receivers (per '000 population)	506	1963–5 av.
Television sets (per '000 population)	4.6	1963–5 av.
Daily newspapers (per '000 population)	135	1963–4 av.

FINANCE

Currency unit: The Netherlands Antilles guilder.

Exchange rates	*1965*
Per $ U.S.	1.886
Per £ sterling	5.281

		Year
National Income (million $ U.S.)	200	1965
G.N.P. per capita ($ U.S.)	1 090	1966

TRADING

Total trade (in million $ U.S.)	*1965*	*1955*	*1938*
Exports (f.o.b.)	603	803	188
Imports (f.o.b.)	617	831	214

Main trading partners (percentage of total value)

Exports	*1965*	*1955*	*Imports*	*1965*	*1955*
U.S.A.	43	26	Venezuela	77	78
U.K.	8	14	U.S.A.	11	8
Canada	7	4	Netherlands	3	4
Netherlands	4	4	U.K.	2	4
Japan	3	na	Trin./Tob.	2	1
Germany F.R.	2	3	Colombia	1	4
Brazil	2	8	Japan	1	—

Distribution of trade (percentage of total value)

Exports	*1966*	*1955*
Petroleum and petroleum products	95	95
Imports		
Crude materials and fuels	80	88
(petroleum and petroleum products)	(79)	(88)
Manufactured goods	12	6
(machinery and transport equipment)	(4)	(2)
(textiles and clothing)	(3)	(1)
Food	4	2

PRODUCTION, EXPORTS AND IMPORTS

Years: **1963–5 average** and *1953–5 average* Units: '000 metric tons unless otherwise indicated

	Production		Exports		Imports	
1. CEREALS, etc.						
Maize (corn)	—	—	—	—	0.7	1.4
Millets/sorghum	5.0[1]*	na	—	—	0.1	—
Potatoes	—	—	—	—	6.9	6.8
Rice	—	—	—	—	5.0	2.9
2. FRUIT, etc.						
Apples	—	—	—	—	1.1	0.7
Bananas	—	—	—	—	4.3	3.2
Coconuts	—	—	—	—	0.2	0.2
Grapes	—	—	—	—	0.2	0.2
Lemons	—	—	—	—	0.1	0.2
Oranges	—	—	—	—	2.5	1.9
Other citrus fruit	—	—	—	—	0.2	0.1
Pears	—	—	—	—	0.1	—
Wine *b*	—	—	—	—	2.9	2.0

b '000 hectolitres.

	Production		Exports		Imports	
3. BEVERAGES, FOREST PRODUCTS, etc.						
Coffee	—	—	—	—	0.3	0.1
Sugar, raw	—	—	—	—	7.0	5.7
Tea	—	—	—	—	0.1	0.1
Tobacco, leaf	—	—	—	—	1.1*a*	0.4[2]
Softwood *j*	—	—	—	—	11.0	—
Hardwood *j*	—	—	—	—	4.1[2]	—
Newsprint	—	—	—	—	0.4[2]	—
Other paper	—	—	—	—	1.5[2]	—

a million $ U.S. *j* '000 cu. metres of roundwood equivalent.

	Production		Exports		Imports	
4. VEGETABLE OILSEEDS AND OILS						
Coconut oil	—	—	—	—	—	0.04*n*
Groundnuts	—	—	—	—	—	0.05
Groundnut oil	—	—	—	—	—	0.76[2]*
Linseed oil	—	—	—	—	—	0.07[2]
Soya bean oil	—	—	—	—	2.21	1.01*

n incl. some palm oil.

	Production		Exports		Imports	
5. LIVESTOCK‡, ANIMAL PRODUCTS, etc.						
Chickens *d*	57.7**p*	na				
Cattle *d*	6.0*	na	—	—	6.3	5.7
Goats *d*	85.0*	na	—	—	0.1	na
Sheep *d*	22.0*	na				
Pigs *d*	4.0*	na	—	—	—	0.4
Bacon/ham	3.0*	—	—	—	0.8	0.7
Meat‡: 'A'			—	—	2.9	1.9
'B'	—	—	—	—	1.8	0.5
Butter	—	—	—	—	0.5	0.8
Cheese	—	—	—	—	0.8	0.6
Eggs	0.5*	na	—	—	0.3	0.4
Fish	na	0.6	—	—	1.5	na
Milk	2.0*	na	—	—	24.6	17.7

d no. in thousands. *p* incl. ducks, geese and turkeys.

	Production		Exports		Imports	
7. FUEL AND POWER						
Electricity *h t*	989	220[1]				
Oil, crude	—	—	603†	2 950[1]†	40 470	42 200[1]
Petroleum, refined	36 960	40 890	35 050	36 810[1]	3 463	4 050[1]

h million kWh. *t* thermal.

	Production		Exports		Imports	
9. NON-FERROUS MINERALS AND METALS						
Asbestos, manufactured	—	—	—	—	2.76	2.95
10. CHEMICALS*n* AND FERTILIZERS						
Chemicals	—		—		na	
Fertilizers:						
Phosphates	na	na	120.9	103.7	—	—
Sulphur	31.5**p*	30.0[1]*p*	—	—	1.8	7.5

n data not available for years 1953–5. *p* recovered sulphur.

	Production		Exports		Imports	
11. INDUSTRY						
Aircraft *a*	—	—	—	0.2	—	0.4[2]
Alcoholic beverages *a*	—	—	—	—	1.4	1.9
Cement	—	—	—	—	35.0	29.3
Electrical engineering *a*	—	—	—	0.3[2]†	5.4	3.3[2]
Motor vehicles *a*	—	—	0.5	0.2	4.9	3.7[2]

a million $ U.S.

na: data not available. — negligible or nil. [1] one year only. [2] two year average. * estimate. ‡ see appendix. † re-exports.

SURINAM

SOUTH AMERICA

Since 1954 Surinam has been fully autonomous in domestic affairs, although remaining an integral part of the Netherlands realm.

AREA: 163 800 sq. km. (63 243 sq. miles)

LAND USE: (percentage of total)	*1965*	*1954*
Arable and orchard	0.3	0.2
Permanent meadow and pasture	—	—
Forest and woodland	91.2	74.6
City areas, waste and other land	8.5	25.2

POPULATION: 363 000 (1967 estimate)

Largest city: PARAMARIBO, capital; population: 110 867 (city proper, 1964)

Distribution of working population (1964)

Total working population: 80 199 (excl. tribal Indians, negroes and the armed forces)

U.N. group no.		*Percentage*
0	Agriculture, forestry, fishing and hunting	24.8
1	Mining and quarrying	7.0
2/3	Manufacturing	8.9
4	Construction	2.8
5	Electricity, gas, water and sanitary services	1.0
6	Commerce	11.1
7	Transport, storage and communications	2.4
8	Services	29.7
9	Others	12.3

		Year(s)
Life expectancy at birth (years): male	62.5	1963
female	66.7	1963
Crude death rate (per '000)	7.8	1965
Population per physician	2 410	1965
Population per hospital bed	190	1966
School enrolment: age 5–19 years (percentage)	86	1963–4 av.
age over 19 years (per 100 000 population)	229*a*	1963–4 av.

a at universities, degree-granting institutions, and teacher-training colleges only.

COMMUNICATIONS		*Year(s)*
Motor vehicles in use ('000s): private	6.8	1963–5 av.
commercial	1.9	1963–5 av.
Railway track (km.)	81	1964
Telephones (per '000 urban population)	2.6	1967
Radio receivers (per '000 population)	148	1963–5 av.
Television sets (per '000 population)	6.1	1963–5 av.
Daily newspapers (per '000 population)	33	1959

FINANCE

Currency unit: The Surinam guilder.

Exchange rates	*1965*
Per $ U.S.	1.87
Per £ sterling	5.33

		Year
National Income (million $ U.S.)	96	1964
G.N.P. per capita ($ U.S.)	360	1966

TRADING

Total trade (in million $ U.S.)	*1965*	*1955*	*1938*
Exports (f.o.b.)	58.3	26.8	3.2
Imports (c.i.f.)	95.1	27.3	3.7

Main trading partners (percentage of total value)

Exports	*1965*	*1954*	*Imports*	*1965*	*1954*
U.S.A.	73	81	U.S.A.	47	39
Canada	9	3	Netherlands	20	29
Netherlands	7	6	U.K.	6	7
Germany F.R.	3	2	Trin./Tob.	6	8
Japan	1	—	Germany F.R.	6	4
Neths. Antilles	1	—	Japan	4	3
Guyana	1	—	China P.R.	2	—

Distribution of trade (percentage of total value)

Exports	*1965*	*1955*
Bauxite and alumina	80	80
Food	11	8
Wood and wood products	7	9
Imports		
Manufactured goods	71	56
(machinery and transport equipment)	(32)	(24)
Crude materials	9	12
Food	9	16
Chemicals	9	8

PRODUCTION, EXPORTS AND IMPORTS

Years: **1963–5 average** and *1953–5 average* Units: '000 metric tons unless otherwise indicated

	Production		Exports		Imports	
1. CEREALS, etc.						
Cassava	2.0	2.3				
Maize (corn)	1.0	1.0[2]	—	—	—	—
Potatoes	—	—	—	—	2.3	1.6
Rice	84.3	63.3	18.8	8.6	—	0.1
2. FRUIT, etc.						
Bananas	8.0	2.3	4.7	—	—	—
Coconuts	6.3*e*	na	—	3.2[2]	—	—
Lemons	0.3	1.0	—	0.2	—	—
Oranges	8.7	7.7	1.9	1.3	—	—
Other citrus fruit	5.3	2.3	2.9	1.2	—	—
Tomatoes	1.0	—				
Wine *b*	—	—	—	—	0.9	0.7

b '000 hectolitres. *e* no. in millions.

	Production		Exports		Imports	
3. BEVERAGES, FOREST PRODUCTS, etc.						
Cocoa	0.2	0.1	0.2	—	—	—
Coffee	0.4	0.4	0.2	0.3	—	—
Sugar: cane	193.7	na				
raw	14.5	6.7	3.8	0.2	—	—
Tea	—	—	—	—	0.1	0.1
Tobacco: leaf	—	—	—	—	0.1	0.1
cigars	—	1.0*e*				
cigarettes	98.0*e*	66.4*e*	—	—	na	0.5[2]*a*
Hardwood *j*	263.0[2]	315.7	17.4[2]	20.5	9.8[2]	0.5[2]
Newsprint	—	—	—	—	0.4[2]	0.3[2]
Other paper	—	—	—	—	1.3[2]	0.2[2]*n*

a million $ U.S. *e* no. in millions. *j* '000 cu. metres of roundwood equivalent.
n excl. printing and writing paper.

	Production		Exports		Imports	
4. VEGETABLE OILSEEDS AND OILS						
Castor oil	—	—	—	—	0.02	—
Copra	—	—	—	—	2.77	—
Coconut oil	—	—	—	—	0.16	1.33
Cottonseed oil	—	—	—	—	na	0.04
Groundnuts	0.70	na	—	0.03	0.04	—
Linseed oil	—	—	—	—	0.10	0.16
Olive oil	—	—	—	—	—	—
Palm kernels	1.00*	0.85	—	0.10	0.02	—
Palm kernel oil	na	na	—	—	0.01	—
Soya bean oil	—	—	—	—	0.29	0.22

	Production		Exports		Imports	
5. LIVESTOCK‡, ANIMAL PRODUCTS, etc.						
Chickens *d*	320.3	262.0[1]				
Cattle *d*	38.3	33.0[1]	—	—	0.4	—
Goats *d*	11.0	5.0[1]	—	—	—	—
Sheep *d*	5.0	2.0[1]	—	—	—	—
Horses *d*	—	1.0[1]				
Pigs *d*	8.0	7.0[1]	—	—	0.1	—
Bacon/ham	1.0*	—	—	—	—	0.1
Meat‡: 'A'			—	—	—	—
'B'	0.3*	na	—	—	0.4	—
Butter	—	—	—	—	0.2	0.3
Cheese	—	—	—	—	0.4	0.3
Eggs	0.9	na	—	—	—	—
Fish	3.9	2.0*p*	0.8	na	1.7	na
Milk	8.7	na	—	—	5.7	2.7

d no. in thousands. *p* incl. shrimps landed by foreign vessels.

	Production		Exports		Imports	
6. FIBRES, TEXTILES, etc.						
Rubber, natural	na	—	0.2	—	—	—
7. FUEL AND POWER						
Coal, 'A'‡	—	—	—	—	na	2
Electricity *h*	164*r*	20*t*				
Petroleum, refined	—	—	—	—	203	100[1]

h million kWh. *r* hydro and thermal. *t* thermal.

	Production		Exports		Imports	
9. NON-FERROUS MINERALS AND METALS						
Gold *k*, ore *m*	6.00	7.00	—	—	—	—
Silver *k*, ore *m*	—	na	—	4.57	—	—
Asbestos: fibre	—	—	—	—	—	0.01
manufactured	—	—	—	—	0.94[2]	0.57
Aluminium: bauxite	3 919.24	3 253.13	3 945.11	3 254.35	—	—
alumina	71.89[1]	—	19.79	—	—	—
aluminium	1.25[1]	—	0.42	—	—	—

k '000 fine troy oz. *m* metal content.

	Production		Exports		Imports	
11. INDUSTRY						
Beer	45.0*b*	0.1*b*	—	—	0.2*a*	0.6*a*
Cement	—	—	—	—	47.0	16.3
Electrical engineering *a*	—	—	—	—	5.6	0.9[2]
Motor vehicles *a*	—	—	—	—	2.9	1.1[2]

a million $ U.S. *b* '000 hectolitres.

na: data not available. — negligible or nil. [1] one year only. [2] two year average. * estimate. ‡ see appendix. † re-exports.

NEW HEBRIDES

The New Hebrides is administered as a unique Anglo-French Condominium. An economic development plan has been set up for the expansion of agriculture and for improving communications and social services.

AREA: 14 760 sq. km. (5 700 sq. miles)

LAND USE: (percentage of total)

	1955
Arable and orchard	4.8
Permanent meadow and pasture	1.7
Forest and woodland	0.5
City areas, waste and other land	93.0

POPULATION: 77 983 (1967 census)

Capital: VILA; population: 800 (city proper, 1948)

		Year(s)
Crude birth rate (per '000)	45*	1966
Population per physician	3 780	1965
Population per hospital bed	220	1966
School enrolment: age 5–19 years (percentage)	82	1963–4 av.

FINANCE

Currency unit: The New Hebrides franc, with the value 100 per Australian dollar (which is also in circulation) replaced, at par, the franc CFP in 1970

Exchange rates a	1965	1950
Per $ U.S.	89.76	76
Per £ sterling	251.33	212

a for francs CFP.

TRADING

Total trade (in million $ U.S.)	1965	1955
Exports (f.o.b.)	9	4
Imports (c.i.f.)	7	4

Main trading partners (percentage of total value)

Exports	1965	*Imports*	1965
France	53	Australia	46
Japan	20	France	17
U.S.A.	10	Japan	6
Australia	6	U.K.	5
		Hong Kong	5
		Fiji	4

Distribution of trade (percentage of total value)

Exports	1965	*Imports*	1965
Copra	58	Manufactured goods	42
Manganese	26	Food	20
Fish	12	Crude materials and fuels	10
		Beverages and tobacco	7
		Chemicals	5

PRODUCTION, EXPORTS AND IMPORTS

Years: **1963–5 average** and *1953–5 average* Units: '000 metric tons unless otherwise indicated

	Production		Exports		Imports	
1. CEREALS, etc.						
Potatoes	—	—	—	—	—	*0.1*[2]
Rice	—	—	—	—	**2.6**	*1.5*[2]
2. FRUIT, etc.						
Coconuts *e*	**184.7**	na	—	—	—	—
Wine *b*	—	—	—	—	**7.3**	*3.7*

b '000 hectolitres. *e* no. in millions.

	Production		Exports		Imports	
3. BEVERAGES, FOREST PRODUCTS, etc.						
Cocoa	**0.6**	*0.8**	**0.6**	*0.8*	—	—
Coffee	**0.2***	*0.3*	**0.2**	*0.3*	—	—
Sugar, raw	—	—	—	—	**0.8**	*0.6*
Tobacco, cigarettes	—	—	—	—	**0.1***	—
Hardwood *j*	—	—	—	—	**6.2**[1]	—

j '000 cu. metres of roundwood equivalent.

	Production		Exports		Imports	
4. VEGETABLE OILSEEDS AND OILS						
Copra	**34.00**	*23.43*	**34.00**	*23.40*	—	—
Groundnut oil	—	—	—	—	**0.01**	—

	Production		Exports		Imports	
5. LIVESTOCK‡, ANIMAL PRODUCTS, etc.						
Cattle *d*	**60.7***	*45.0*[2]	—	—	—	—
Goats *d*	**6.0***	*5.0*[2]	—	—	—	—
Sheep *d*	**5.7**	*5.0*[2]	—	—	—	—
Horses *d*	**1.0***	*3.0*[2]				
Pigs *d*	**53.0***	*50.0*[2]	—	—	—	—
Fish	**3.1**	na	na	na	**0.5**	na
Milk	—	—	—	—	**0.5**	*0.8*

d no. in thousands.

	Production		Exports		Imports	
7. FUEL AND POWER						
Petroleum, refined	—	—	—	—	**1**	—
9. NON-FERROUS MINERALS AND METALS						
Manganese, ore	**50.80***p*	—	**57.66**	—	—	—

p sintered ore.

	Production		Exports		Imports	
11. INDUSTRY						
Alcoholic beverages *a*	—	—	—	—	**0.3**	—
Electrical engineering *a*	—	—	—	—	**0.3**[2]	—
Motor vehicles *a*	—	—	—	—	**0.3**	—

a million $ U.S.

NEW ZEALAND

New Zealand consists of two main and a number of smaller islands. Dominion status was formally adopted in 1947, with a Governor-General appointed by the British Crown. New Zealand also has responsibility for a large tract of land in the Antarctic.

AREA: 268 680 sq. km. (103 736 sq. miles)

LAND USE: (percentage of total)

	1965	1955
Arable and orchard	3.0	1.9
Permanent meadow and pasture	47.8	46.9
Forest and woodland	23.2	32.3
City areas, waste and other land	26.0	18.9

POPULATION: 2 676 919 (1966 census)

Largest city: AUCKLAND; population: 548 239 (1966)
Capital city: WELLINGTON; population: 167 859 (1966)

Distribution of working population (1961)
Total working population: 895 363

U.N. group no.		*Percentage*
0	Agriculture, forestry, fishing and hunting	14.4
1	Mining and quarrying	0.8
2/3	Manufacturing	25.0
4	Construction	9.6
5	Electricity, gas, water and sanitary services	1.3
6	Commerce	18.2
7	Transport, storage and communications	10.0
8	Services	20.3
9	Others	0.4

		Year(s)
Life expectancy at birth (years): male	68.4	1960–2 av.
female	73.8	1960–2 av.
Infant mortality (per '000)	19.5	1965
Crude birth rate (per '000)	22.9	1965
Crude death rate (per '000)	8.7	1965
Accidental deaths (per 100 000 population)		
caused by motor vehicles	20.9	1965
due to other causes	30.5	1965
Population per physician	670	1964
Population per hospital bed	100	1966
School enrolment: age 5–19 years (percentage)	90	1963–4 av.
age over 19 years (per 100 000 population)	1 884	1963–5 av.

COMMUNICATIONS

		Year(s)
Motor vehicles in use ('000s): private	658.8	1963–5 av.
commercial	149.8	1963–5 av.
Railway track (km.)	3 617	1965
Mail per capita: domestic	197	1963–5 av.
foreign received	na	1963–5 av.
foreign sent	14	1963–5 av.
Telephones (per '000 urban population)	39.9	1967
Radio licences (per '000 population)	245	1963–5 av.
Television licences (per '000 population)	108.6	1963–5 av.
Daily newspapers (per '000 population)	400	1962–4 av.

continued

FINANCE

Currency unit: The New Zealand dollar was introduced in 1967 at the rate N.Z.$1 to N.Z.£0.5

Exchange rates a	1965	1960	1950
Per $ U.S.	0.357	0.357	0.357
Per £ sterling	1.0	1.0	1.0

		Year(s)
National Income (million $ U.S.)	4 503	1965
G.N.P. per capita ($ U.S.)	1 930	1966
Rate of increase of G.N.P. per capita	1.8	1960–3 av.
Foreign trade (percentage of G.D.P.)	40	1963–5 av.

a for New Zealand pounds.

TRADING

Total trade (in million $ U.S.)	1965	1955	1938
Exports (f.o.b.)	1 006	725	225
Imports (c.i.f.)	1 052	804	217

Main trading partners (percentage of total value)

Exports	1965	1955	1938	*Imports*	1965	1955	1938
U.K.	47	65	84	U.K.	35	55	48
U.S.A.	12	6	3	Australia	17	12	13
Japan	5	1	1	U.S.A.	12	8	12
France	5	6	2	Japan	6	1	2
Australia	4	3	4	Canada	4	3	9
Germany F.R.	4	5	2 *d*	Germany F.R.	3	3	2 *d*
Belg./Lux.	3	2	1	Kuwait	2	na	na

Distribution of trade (percentage of total value)

Exports	1965	1955*	1938*
Food	55	55	70
(meat)	(28)	(27)	(28)
(dairy products and eggs)	(25)	(27)	(40)
Crude materials and fuels	38	42	28
(wool)	(29)	(36)	(21)
Chemicals	3	1	1
Manufactured goods	3	—	—
Imports			
Manufactured goods	69	72	67
(machinery and transport equipment)	(33)	(30)	(22)
(textiles and clothing)	(11)	(15)	(15)
Crude materials and fuels	13	11	na
(petroleum products)	(7)	(na)	(5)
Chemicals	10	6	6
Food	6	8	6

d incl. Germany D.R.

PRODUCTION, EXPORTS AND IMPORTS

Years: **1963–5 average** and *1953–5 average* Units: '000 metric tons unless otherwise indicated

	Production		Exports		Imports	
1. CEREALS, etc.						
Barley	**110.7**	*54.7*	—	*2.0*	—	—
Maize (corn)	**19.3**	*7.0**[2]	—	—	**0.6**	—
Millets/sorghum	—	—	—	—	**1.6***	—
Oats	**30.7**	*25.7*	—	—	—	*3.4*
Potatoes	**263.0**	*162.0*[2]	**6.7**	*2.3*	—	*2.4*
Rice	—	—	—	—	**3.4**	*2.5*
Sweet potatoes/yams	**3.7**	na				
Wheat	**257.7**	*107.0*	—	—	**174.6**	*213.4*
2. FRUIT, etc.						
Apples	**88.0**	*61.3**	**36.7**	*20.6*	—	—
Apricots	**5.3**	*3.1*	—	—	—	—
Bananas	—	—	—	—	**29.1**	*22.3*
Coconuts	—	—	—	—	**1.3***n*	*0.9*
Dates	—	—	—	—	**1.5**	*1.8*
Grapes	**7.3**	na	—	—	**0.2**	—
Lemons	**2.0**	*2.0*	—	—	—	*0.1*
Oranges	**1.0**	—	—	—	**14.8**	*13.8*
Other citrus fruit	**3.0**	*2.3*	—	—	**0.3**	*0.5*
Peaches	**18.0**	*9.1*	—	—	—	—
Pears	**15.7**	*11.5*[2]	**3.1**	*0.2*	—	—
Pineapples	—	—	—	—	na	*0.2*
Plums	**3.7**	*2.7*	—	—	—	—
Raisins	—	—	—	—	**6.6**	*5.2*
Tomatoes	**49.0***	na				
Wine *b*	**78.5**[2]	na	—	—	**11.1**	*8.3*

b '000 hectolitres. *n* mainly desiccated.

	Production		Exports		Imports	
3. BEVERAGES, FOREST PRODUCTS, etc.						
Cocoa	—	—	—	—	**3.0**	*2.6*
Coffee	—	—	—	—	**3.2**	*0.6*
Sugar, raw	—	—	**0.2†**	*0.3†*	**123.7**	*101.7*
Tea	—	—	—	—	**7.5**	*6.5*
Tobacco: leaf	**4.3**	*2.0*	—	na	**2.4**	*3.0*
cigarettes	**3 845.0***e*	*1 953.0e*	—	*0.3*[2]*r*	—	*6.7*[2]*r*
tobacco/snuff	**1.9**	*2.5*				
Softwood *j*	**5 849.0**	*3 537.7*	**499.0**	*116.9*	**79.7**	*59.0*
Hardwood *j*	**234.3**	*344.7*	**0.5**	*0.5*	**56.7**	*57.0*
Wood pulp	**398.5**	*70.0*	**62.1**	*17.1*	**18.1**	*6.8*
Newsprint	**185.7**	*3.0*	**111.0**	*0.1*	**5.8**	*39.0*
Other paper	**138.3**	*39.7*	**1.2**	*0.1*	**32.3**	*28.6*

e no. in millions. *j* '000 cu. metres of roundwood equivalent. *r* includes leaf tobacco, in million $ U.S.

	Production		Exports		Imports	
4. VEGETABLE OILSEEDS AND OILS						
Castor oil	—	—	—	—	**0.25**	*0.15*[2]
Copra	—	—	—	—	**3.51**	*2.23*
Coconut oil	na	na	—	—	—	*0.01*
Cottonseed oil	—	—	—	—	**0.11**	—
Groundnuts	—	—	—	—	**2.54**	*1.27*
Groundnut oil	na	na	—	—	**0.77**[2]	*0.18*
Linseed	**9.33***p*	*2.50*[2]*p*	**0.89**	*2.80*	—	—
Linseed oil	na	na	—	—	—	*1.59*
Olive oil	—	—	—	—	**0.11**[2]	*0.10*
Palm oil	—	—	—	—	**0.01**[2]	—

continued

	Production		Exports		Imports	
4. VEGETABLE OILSEEDS AND OILS—*continued*						
Rapeseed oil	—	—	—	—	**0.02**	—
Soya beans	—	—	—	—	**0.01**	—
Soya bean oil	—	—	—	—	**1.14**	*0.13*
Sunflower seed oil	—	—	—	—	**0.03**	—
Tung oil	—	—	—	—	**0.17**	*0.27*

p flax grown for seed only.

	Production		Exports		Imports	
5. LIVESTOCK‡, ANIMAL PRODUCTS, etc.						
Chickens *d*	**4 440***	*4 351*[1]				
Cattle *d*	**6 729**	*5 730*	**0.4**	*1.1*	—	*0.2*
dairy cows *d*	**3 466***q*	*3 766r*				
Goats *d*	**33***	na	**1.0**	na	**0.2**	—
Sheep *d*	**51 743**	*37 774*				
Horses *d*	**99**	*166*[2]				
Pigs *d*	**751**	*660*	**0.1**	—	—	—
Bacon/ham	**809**	*585*	**0.5**	*0.4*	—	—
Meat‡: 'A'			**488.8**	*346.4*	—	—
'B'	**48***	*31*	**25.7**	*19.9*	—	—
Butter	**235**	*196*	**181.1**	*151.6*	—	—
Cheese	**101**	*106*	**91.9**	*94.0*	—	—
Eggs	**45**	*31*	—	—	—	—
Fish	**45**	*38*	**4.9**	*4.4*[1]*	**2.7**	na
Milk	**5 718**	*5 136*	**741.9**	*485.0*	—	—
Whale/sperm oil	**1**	—	—	—	—	—
Hides/skins	**56**[2]	na	**43.4***a*	*28.5a*	—	*0.2*[2]*a*
Wool	**212**	*136*	**189.0**	*136.6*	**0.3**	*0.1*

a million $ U.S. *d* no. in thousands. *q* excl. cows in urban areas. *r* incl. some beef cows.

	Production		Exports		Imports	
6. FIBRES, TEXTILES, etc.						
Abaca	—	—	—	—	**0.4**[2]	*0.1*[2]
Agaves (sisal etc.)	—	—	—	—	**5.1**	*1.0*
Cotton lint	—	—	—	—	—	*0.3*
Flax fibre	**0.2**	*0.3*[1]	—	*0.1*	**0.2**	—
Hemp fibre	—	—	—	—	—	*0.4*[2]
Jute	—	—	—	—	**1.8**	*0.5*[2]
Rubber, natural	—	—	—	—	**9.3**	*8.0*
Silk *f*	—	—	—	—	**1.5**[2]	na
Cotton: yarn	—	—	—	—	**2.1**	*0.9*
woven fabrics	—	—	—	—	**8.1**	*4.9*
Rayon, woven fabrics	—	—	—	—	**2.9**	*1.8*
Wool: yarn	**6.3**	*3.3*	**0.1**	—	**0.3**	*0.7*
woven fabrics	**3.0***t*	*2.4t*	—	—	—	—

f metric tons. *t* million metres.

	Production		Exports		Imports	
7. FUEL AND POWER						
Coal: 'A'‡	**677**	*800*	—	—	**1**	*2*
'B'	**1 183**	*1 800*	—	—	—	—
Electricity *h*: total	**9 753**	*4 900*[1]				
hydro	**7 731**	*4 600*[1]				
thermal	**2 022***u*	*300*[1]				
Oil, crude	—	—	—	—	**1 140**	—[1]
Petroleum, refined	**1 063**	—[1]	**227**	—	**1 397**	*1 420*[1]

h million kWh. *u* incl. geothermal.

continued

PRODUCTION, EXPORTS AND IMPORTS *continued*

	Production		Exports		Imports	
8. IRON AND STEEL						
Iron ore	na	na	—	—	—	—
Pig iron	—	—	—	—	8	*8*
Steel ingots/castings	—	—	—	—	1	*3*
Iron/steel scrap	na	na	—	*27*	—	—
9. NON-FERROUS MINERALS AND METALS						
Diamonds *a*	—	—	—	—	0.57	*0.53*
Gold *k*: ore *m*	11.70	*35.60*	—	*0.74*	—	*0.05*
bullion/coins etc.	na	na	11.00‡	*32.70*	10.82	*0.81*
Platinum group metals *k*	—	—	—	—	2.14	*1.22*
Silver *k*: ore *m*	0.16*	*45.70*	—	*11.25*	—	—
bullion	na	na	—	*18.00*	98.38[1]	*39.18*
Asbestos: fibre	0.13	*0.05*	—	—	6.33	*3.17*
manufactured	na	na	na	*0.01a*	1.01*a*	*0.44ap*
Mica	—	—	—	—	0.13*a*	*0.05a*
Aluminium	—	—	—	—	9.74	*3.01*
Antimony, metal	—	—	—	—	—	*0.19*
Chrome, metal	—	—	—	—	—	*0.08*[2]
Cobalt, metal	—	—	—	—	0.07	*3.30*
Copper, metal	—	—	2.50†	*0.47†*	13.19	*5.32*
Lead, metal	—	—	—	*0.90†*	6.55	*6.89*
Magnesium: dolomite	7.15	na	—	—	—	—
magnesite	0.75	na	—	—	0.17	*0.06*
metal/salts	—	—	—	—	0.68	*0.71*
Manganese: ore	—	*0.23*	—	—	—	—
metal	—	na	—	—	0.56	na
Mercury *f*	—	—	—	—	5.20	*1.70*
Nickel, metal	—	—	—	—	0.21	*0.02*
Tin, metal	—	—	5.08*q*	na	0.41	*0.41*
Titanium minerals	—	—	—	—	4.40	*2.18*
Tungsten, ore	—	*0.03*	—	*0.04*	—	—
Zinc, metal	—	—	—	—	4.27	*2.09*

a million $ U.S. *f* metric tons. *k* '000 fine troy oz. *m* metal content. *p* in addition, 48 324 sq. metres of asbestos cement sheets. *q* scrap.

	Production		Exports		Imports	
10. CHEMICALS *n* AND FERTILIZERS						
Organic chemicals	—		—		na	
Inorganic chemicals:						
Ammonia	0.3[1]		—		0.1[2]	
Carbon black	—		—		na	
Chlorine	na		—		0.3[1]	
Nitric acid	na		—		na	
Sodium carbonate	—		—		16.9	
Sodium hydroxide	na		—		4.8	
Sulphuric acid	na		—		na	
Plastics	—		—		na	
Fertilizers:						
Phosphates	—	—	—	—	764.4	*522.9*
Potash	—	—	—	—	130.3	*33.4*[2]
Sulphur	—	—	—	—	178.2	*118.1*

n data not available for years 1953–5.

	Production		Exports		Imports	
11. INDUSTRY						
Aircraft *a*	—	—	—	—	8.2[2]	na
Alcoholic beverages			—	—	7.3[2]*a*	na
beer *b*	2 712.0	*1 845.0*				
spirits *b*	30.0**p*	na				
Cement	778.0	*337.0*	—	*0.7*	2.7	*172.0*
Electrical engineering *a*	104.1[2]	na	na	*0.5*	68.5	*36.3*
Railway vehicles *a*	—	—	—	—	7.0[2]	na
Machine tools *a*	—	—	—	—	6.0	na
Merchant ships *g*	—	—	—	—	6.0	na
Motor vehicles			—	—	106.1*a*	*50.8*[2]*a*
commercial *dq*	9.4	*6.9*				
private *dq*	54.8	*26.6*				

a million $ U.S. *b* '000 hectolitres. *d* no. in thousands. *g* '000 G.R.T. *p* 1967 production for home consumption only. *q* assembly of imported parts.

NEW ZEALAND (TERRITORIES)

COOK ISLANDS

PACIFIC OCEAN

The Cook Islands have had complete internal self-government since 1965, but certain links of common citizenship, etc., have been maintained with New Zealand. The High Commissioner represents both the British Crown and the New Zealand government.

AREA: 241 sq. km. (93 sq. miles)

LAND USE: (percentage of total)	*1965*	*1953*
Arable and orchard	43.5	52.2
Permanent meadow and pasture	—	—
Forest and woodland	26.1	17.4
City areas, waste and other land	30.4	30.4

POPULATION: 19 251 (1966 census)
Total working population: 5 135 (1965)

FINANCE
Currency unit: The New Zealand dollar

TRADING

Total trade (in million $ U.S.)	*1965*	*1955*
Exports (f.o.b.)	2.8	1.2
Imports (c.i.f.)	4.3	1.6

Main trading partners (percentage of total value)

Exports	*1965*	*1955*	*Imports*	*1965*	*1955*
New Zealand	99	78	New Zealand	69	74
			Japan	7	na
			Australia	6	1
			U.K.	4	10
			Hong Kong	4	na
			U.S.A.	3	4
			Fiji	2	na
			Canada	2	5

Distribution of trade (percentage of total value)

Exports	*1965*	*1955*
Fruit and vegetables	57	41
Clothing	24	14
Oilseeds (mainly copra)	13	17
Imports		
Manufactured goods	60	44
(machinery and transport equipment)	(15)	(9)
(textiles)	(13)	(14)
Food	23	32
Crude materials and fuels	7	12
Chemicals	7	7

continued

NIUE ISLAND

PACIFIC OCEAN

Niue Island, although geographically one of the Cook Islands, has been under separate administration since 1903. External affairs and defence are administered by the New Zealand government.

AREA: 259 sq. km. (100 sq. miles)

LAND USE: (percentage of total)	*1965*	*1953*
Arable and orchard	77.0	38.5
Permanent meadow and pasture	—	—
Forest and woodland	11.5	38.5
City areas, waste and other land	11.5	23.0

POPULATION: 5 194 (1966 census)
Capital: ALOFI; population: 956 (1965)

		Year(s)
Infant mortality (per '000)	10.2*	1965
Crude birth rate (per '000)	38.1*	1965
Crude death rate (per '000)	8.9*	1965
Population per physician	830	1965
Population per hospital bed	170*a*	1965
School enrolment: age 5–19 years (percentage)	104‡	1963–4 av.

a government hospitals only.

FINANCE
Currency unit: The New Zealand dollar

TRADING

Total trade (in million $ U.S.)	*1965*	*1955*
Exports (f.o.b.)	0.2	0.2
Imports (c.i.f.)	0.7	0.4

Main trading partners (percentage of total value)

Exports	*1965*	*1955*	*Imports*	*1965*	*1955*
New Zealand	86	94	New Zealand	73	78
Fiji	14	—	Australia	6	2
			U.K.	5	9
			Iran	4	na
			U.S.A.	3	1
			Japan	2	na
			Fiji	2	4

Distribution of trade (percentage of total value)

Exports	*1965a*	*1955*
Oilseeds (mainly copra)	51	80
Fruit and vegetables	32	7
Imports		
Manufactured goods	53	54
(machinery and transport equipment)	(20)	(15)
Food	28	27
Mineral fuels	7	2
Chemicals	7	9
Beverages and tobacco	5	6

a percentage of national exports‡ in 1965 which comprised 70% of general exports.

COOK AND NIUE ISLANDS

PRODUCTION, EXPORTS AND IMPORTS

Years: **1963–5 average** and *1953–5 average* Units: '000 metric tons unless otherwise indicated

	Production		Exports		Imports	
1. CEREALS, etc.						
Rice	—	—	—	—	0.1	*0.1*
2. FRUIT, etc.						
Bananas	na	na	0.3	*0.2*	—	—
Coconuts *e*	16.0[1]*	na	na	na	—	—
Oranges	na	na	1.7	*0.9*	—	—
Other citrus fruit	na	na	0.1	*0.1*	—	—
Wine *b*	—	—	—	—	0.1	—

b '000 hectolitres. *e* no. in millions.

	Production		Exports		Imports	
3. BEVERAGES, FOREST PRODUCTS, etc.						
Sugar, raw	—	—	—	—	0.9	*0.4*
Tobacco	—	—	—	—	na	*0.1*[1]*a*
Softwood *j*	—	—	—	—	—	*1.1*[2]
Hardwood *j*	49.8*	—	—	—	3.9[2]	*0.2*[1]

a million $ U.S. *j* '000 cu. metres of roundwood equivalent.

	Production		Exports		Imports	
4. VEGETABLE OILSEEDS AND OILS						
Copra: Cook Is.	1.23*	na	} 1.51	{ *1.93*	—	—
Niue Is.	na	*0.60*[2]		*na*	—	—
5. LIVESTOCK‡, ANIMAL PRODUCTS, etc.						
Chickens *d*	55.0*	*64.0*[1]				
Cattle *d*	—	*0.7*	—	—	—	—
Goats *d*	2.0*	*2.7*	—	—	—	—
Horses *d*	2.0*	*2.0*[2]				
Pigs *d*	12.0*	*9.7*	—	—	—	—
Butter	—	—	—	—	0.1*	—
Fish	na	*0.8*	—	—	—	—
Milk	—	—	—	—	0.2	—

d no. in thousands.

	Production		Exports		Imports	
11. INDUSTRY						
Electrical engineering *a*	—	—	—	—	0.1[2]	—

a million $ U.S.

TOKELAU ISLANDS

PACIFIC OCEAN

The Tokelau Islands, geographically part of the Gilbert and Ellice Is. group, became a New Zealand territory in 1949. They consist of three small atolls.

AREA: 10 sq. km. (4 sq. miles)

POPULATION: 1 900 (1966 census)
Total working population: 429 (1961)

NICARAGUA

CENTRAL AMERICA

Nicaragua has a long history of internal political conflict. A period of dictatorship was terminated in 1956 by the introduction of a more democratic form of government.

The U.S.A. has a permanent option on a canal route through the country and a 99-year option on a naval base on the Pacific coast and on Corn Island in the Caribbean Sea.

AREA: 148 000* sq. km. (57 143* sq. miles)

LAND USE: (percentage of total)	*1963*	*1950*
Arable and orchard	6.2	5.8
Permanent meadow and pasture	6.6	4.3
Forest and woodland	46.2	42.3
City areas, waste and other land	41.0	47.6

POPULATION: 1 783 000 (1967 estimate)

Largest city: MANAGUA, capital; population: 262 047 (city proper, 1965)

Distribution of working population (1963)
Total working population: 474 960

U.N. group no.		*Percentage*
0	Agriculture, forestry, fishing and hunting	59.7
1	Mining and quarrying	0.8
2/3	Manufacturing	11.7
4	Construction	3.3
5	Electricity, gas, water and sanitary services	0.3
6	Commerce	7.3
7	Transport, storage and communications	2.5
8	Services	14.2
9	Others	0.2

		Year(s)
Infant mortality (per '000)	51.6*	1965
Crude birth rate (per '000)	48.5*	1960–5 av.
Crude death rate (per '000)	15*	1960–5 av.
Accidental deaths (per 100 000 population)		
caused by motor vehicles	17.2*	1965
due to other causes	7.6*	1965
Population per physician	2 560	1965
Population per hospital bed	430	1965
School enrolment: age 5–19 years (percentage)	50*a*	1963–4 av.
age over 19 years (per 100 000 population)	188	1964–5 av.

a incl. evening courses.

COMMUNICATIONS		*Year(s)*
Motor vehicles in use ('000s): private	12.2	1963–5 av.
commercial	5	1963–5 av.
Railway track (km.)	403	1961
Telephones (per '000 urban population)	0.7	1967
Radio receivers (per '000 population)	65	1963–5 av.
Television sets (per '000 population)	8.1	1963–5 av.
Daily newspapers (per '000 population)	49	1964

FINANCE

Currency unit: The córdoba

Exchange rates	*1965a*	*1960*	*1950*	*1938*
Per $ U.S.	7.05	7.05	7.05	5.04
Per £ sterling	19.76	19.76	19.76	23.18

		Year(s)
National Income (million $ U.S.)	494	1965
G.N.P. per capita ($ U.S.)	330	1966
Rate of increase of G.N.P. per capita	4.8	1960–4 av.
Foreign trade (percentage of G.D.P.)	49	1963–5 av.

a selling rate.

TRADING

Total trade (in million $ U.S.)	*1965*	*1955*	*1938*
Exports (f.o.b.)	144	72	4
Imports (c.i.f.)	160	70	5

Main trading partners (percentage of total value)

Exports	*1965*	*1955*	*Imports*	*1965*	*1955*
Japan	34	15	U.S.A.	48	65
U.S.A.	24	35	Japan	7	2
Germany F.R.	15	18	Germany F.R.	6	6
Portugal	3	na	Costa Rica	4	—
Costa Rica	3	—	El Salvador	4	2
El Salvador	3	1	Guatemala	4	—
Netherlands	2	14	U.K.	4	3

Distribution of trade (percentage of total value)

Exports	*1965*	*1955*	*1938**
Crude materials	60	56	na
(cotton)	(46)	(43)	(6)
(oilseeds)	(8)	(7)	(na)
Food	34	43	na
(coffee)	(18)	(39)	(47)
(meat)	(5)	(—)	(na)
(sugar)	(4)	(1)	(na)
Imports			
Manufactured goods	64	64	na
(machinery and transport equipment)	(30)	(28)	na
(textiles and clothing)	(10)	(12)	na
Chemicals	19	16	na
Food	9	9	na
Crude materials and fuels	5	9	na

PRODUCTION, EXPORTS AND IMPORTS

Years: **1963–5 average** and *1953–5 average* Units: '000 metric tons unless otherwise indicated

	Production		Exports		Imports	
1. CEREALS, etc.						
Cassava	**12.3***	*6.0*[1]				
Maize (corn)	**131.7***	*117.5*	**1.0**	*4.4*	**7.2**	*0.5*
Millets/sorghum	**46.3**	*55.5*[2]	**1.1**	—	**0.6**	—
Oats	—	—	—	—	**1.3**	—
Potatoes	**2.0***	*1.5*[2]	—	*0.2*	**1.0**	—
Rice	**31.3***	*36.3**	**0.7**	*14.3*[2]	**7.5**	*0.4*
Wheat	na	na	—	*0.8*	**17.5**	—
2. FRUIT, etc.						
Apples	—	—	—	—	—	*0.1*
Bananas	na	na	**18.9**	*10.0*	—	—
Coconuts	na	na	**0.4**	*0.1*	—	—
Oranges	na	na	**0.1**	—	—	—
Other citrus fruit	na	na	**0.2**	—	—	—
Wine*b*	—	—	—	—	**2.0**	—

b '000 hectolitres.

	Production		Exports		Imports	
3. BEVERAGES, FOREST PRODUCTS, etc.						
Cocoa	**0.4**	na	**0.3**	*0.1*	**0.1**	—
Coffee	**30.3***	*20.2**	**25.2**	*19.6*	**0.2**	—
Sugar: cane	**1 038.0***	*720.0*[2]				
raw	**105.8***n*	*36.7*n*	**48.7**	*10.1*	**0.4**	—
Tobacco: leaf	**0.6***	*1.3**	—	—	**0.3**	*0.4*[2]
cigarettes*e*	**953.0**	*718.7*	—	—	—	—
Softwood*j*	**370.0***[1]	*327.0*	**38.6**[2]	*128.2*[2]	—[1]	—[1]
Hardwood*j*	**1 905.0***[1]	*774.0*[2]	**38.4**[2]	*33.8*[2]	—[1]	—[1]
Newsprint	—	—	—	*0.4*[2]	**2.3**[1]	*1.0*[2]
Other paper	—	—	—	*0.8*[2]	**1.1**[1]	*1.5*[1]

e no. in millions. *j* '000 cu. metres of roundwood equivalent. *n* in addition, non-centrifugal sugar 20* (1963–5 av.) and 23* (1953–5 av.).

	Production		Exports		Imports	
4. VEGETABLE OILSEEDS AND OILS						
Castor seed	—	na	—	*0.07*	—	—
Castor oil	—	na	—	*0.01*	**0.02**	—
Copra	na	na	**0.71**	—	—	—
Coconut oil	—	—	—	—	—	*0.07*
Cottonseed	**185.00***	*68.00**	**114.13**	*38.77*	**0.44**	*0.07*
Cottonseed oil	na	na	**0.54**	*0.03*	**0.91**	*0.03*
Groundnuts	na	—	**0.07**	—	**0.01**	—
Linseed	na	—	**0.03**	—	—	—
Linseed oil	—	—	—	—	**0.01**	*0.02*
Olive oil	—	—	—	—	**0.05**	*0.05*
Palm kernels	—	na	—	—	—	—
Palm oil	na	*0.50*[1]*	**0.20**	—	**0.15**	—
Sesame seed	**5.27**	*10.10*	**5.79**	*7.97*	—	—
Soya bean oil	—	—	—	—	**0.05**	—
5. LIVESTOCK‡, ANIMAL PRODUCTS, etc.						
Chickens*d*	**2 235***	*960**				
Cattle*d*	**1 281***	*1 000**	**3.9**	*19.7*	**1.5**	*0.1*
Goats*d*	**7***	na	—	—	—	—
Sheep*d*	**1***	na	—	—	—	—
Horses*d*	**175***	*150**				
Pigs*d*	**423***	*500**	**11.8**	*4.5*	**0.1**	—
Meat‡, 'A'	**22***	na	na	—	—	—
Butter	na	na	—	*0.1*[2]	**0.3**	—
Cheese	na	na	**0.1**	—	**0.1**	—
Eggs	**4**	na	—	—	**0.1**	—
Fish	**3***p*	na	**1.7**	na	**0.6**	na
Milk	**190**	na	—	—	**16.9**	*1.4**

d no. in thousands. *p* excl. turtles.

continued

PRODUCTION, EXPORTS AND IMPORTS *continued*

	Production		Exports		Imports	
6. FIBRES, TEXTILES, etc.						
Cotton: lint	**110.0**	*33.7**	**97.2**	*26.7*	—	—
yarn	**0.9**	na	—	—	**0.6**	—
woven fabrics	**1.4**	*0.6*[2]	—	—	**1.8**[1]	*1.5*[2]
Rayon, woven fabrics	—	—	—	—	**0.1**	—
7. FUEL AND POWER						
Electricity*h*: total	**281**	*110*[1]				
hydro	**98**	*10*[1]				
thermal	**183**	*100*[1]				
Oil, crude	—	—	—	—	**210**	na
Petroleum, refined	**203**	—[1]	—	—	**60**	*130*[1]

h million kWh.

	Production		Exports		Imports	
9. NON-FERROUS MINERALS AND METALS						
Gold*k*, ore	**209.70***m*	*244.00m*	**186.01**‡*q*	*240.28q*	—	—
Silver*k*, ore	**372.30***m*	*246.30m*	**179.34***q*	*224.00q*	—	—
Asbestos, manufactured	—	—	—	—	**0.08**	*0.41s*
Aluminium	—	—	—	—	**0.40**	—
Copper, ore	**8.90***m*	na	—	—	**0.12***r*	—
Lead, metal	—	—	—	—	**0.09**	—
Mercury*f*	—	—	—	—	—	*0.10s*
Zinc, metal	—	—	—	—	**0.28**	—

f metric tons. *k* '000 fine troy oz. *m* metal content. *q* bullion. *r* metal. *s* incl. imports for re-export.

	Production		Exports		Imports	
10. CHEMICALS*n* AND FERTILIZERS						
Chemicals	—		—		na	
Fertilizers:						
Potash	—	—	—	—	**1.9**	—
Sulphur	—	—	—	—	**2.4**	*0.1*

n data not available for years 1953–5.

	Production		Exports		Imports	
11. INDUSTRY						
Aircraft*a*	—	—	—	—	**1.0**	*0.7*[1]
Beer*b*	**98.0**	*35.8*	—	—	—	—
Cement	**60.3**	*25.3*	**0.3**	—	**8.7**	*15.3*
Electrical engineering*a*	—	—	—	—	**7.4**	*2.7*[1]
Motor vehicles*a*	—	—	—	—	**8.2**	*4.2*[1]

a million $ U.S. *b* '000 hectolitres.

NIGER

WEST AFRICA

Niger, formerly a state of French West Africa, became fully independent in 1960. The country is still, however, closely associated with France in the fields of defence and industrial expansion.

AREA: 1 188 794 sq. km. (458 996 sq. miles)

LAND USE: (percentage of total)	*1963*
Arable and orchard	11.8
Permanent meadow and pasture	2.3
Forest and woodland	12.3
City areas, waste and other land	73.6

The distribution of rainfall divides the country into a southern zone (arable), a central zone (pasture) and a northern zone (desert). In 1965 a ten-year economic plan was initiated, concentrating on the development of water resources.

POPULATION: 3 546 000 (1967 estimate)

Capital city: NIAMEY; population: 60 000 (city proper, 1967)

Distribution of working population (1960)

Total working population: 767 990*a*

	Percentage
Agriculture, forestry, fishing and hunting	96.9
Manufacturing and construction (incl. handicrafts)	0.6
Trade	0.8
Transport, storage and communications	0.2
Services	0.9
Others	0.6

		Year(s)
Life expectancy at birth (years)	37	1959–60 av.
Population per physician	65 000	1964
Population per hospital bed	1 340	1966
School enrolment: age 5–19 years (percentage)	6	1963–4 av.

a from a sample survey which excluded the inhabitants of Niamey (30 000 in 1960), some 234 000 nomads, and foreigners.

COMMUNICATIONS		*Year(s)*
Motor vehicles in use ('000s): private	2.2	1963–5 av.
commercial	4.0	1963–5 av.
Mail per capita: domestic	1	1964–5 av.
foreign received	0.6	1964–5 av.
foreign sent	0.3	1964–5 av.
Telephones (per '000 urban population)	0.1	1967
Radio receivers (per '000 population)	11	1963–5 av.
Daily newspapers (per '000 population)	0.3	1962–3 av.

FINANCE

Currency unit: The franc CFA

Exchange rates	*1965*	*1960*
Per $ U.S.	246.85	246.85
Per £ sterling	691.18	691.18

		Year
National Income (million $ U.S.)	259	1965
G.N.P. per capita ($ U.S.)	80	1966

TRADING

Total trade (in million $ U.S.)	*1965*	*1955*
Exports (f.o.b.)	25	16
Imports (c.i.f.)	38	8

Main trading partners (percentage of total value)

Exports	*1965*	*Imports*	*1965*
France	56	France	53
Nigeria	25	China P.R.	5
Algeria	3	Netherlands	5
Yugoslavia	2	Ivory Coast	5
Netherlands	2	U.S.A.	3
Dahomey	2	Germany F.R.	3
Ivory Coast	2	Senegal	3

Distribution of trade (percentage of total value)

Exports	*1965*	*Imports*	*1965*
Oilseeds and oil	64	Manufactured goods	69
Cattle and sheep	16	(textiles and clothing)	(32)
Vegetables	6	(machinery and transport equipment)	(21)
Cotton	4	Crude materials and fuels	10
		(petroleum products)	(6)
		Food	9
		Chemicals	5

continued

PRODUCTION, EXPORTS AND IMPORTS

Years: **1963–5 average** Units: '000 metric tons unless otherwise indicated
Note—no data are available for the years 1953–5

1. CEREALS, etc.

	Production	Exports	Imports
Cassava	145.0		
Maize (corn)	3.3*	—	—
Millets/sorghum	1 257.0*	1.7[2]	0.5[2]
Potatoes	—	—	0.1[2]
Rice	11.0*	—	1.8
Sweet potatoes/ yams	24.3*		
Wheat	1.0	—	—

2. FRUIT, etc.

	Production	Exports	Imports
Bananas	—	—	0.1[2]
Dates	5.0*	0.1[2]	0.7
Wine *b*	—	—	10.7

b '000 hectolitres.

3. BEVERAGES, FOREST PRODUCTS, etc.

	Production	Exports	Imports
Sugar, raw	—	—	6.9
Tea	—	—	0.2
Tobacco: leaf	0.3*	—	—
products	—	—	0.2
Hardwood *j*	1 925.0*[1]	—	1.1[2]
Paper	—	—	0.7[2]*n*

j '000 cu. metres of roundwood equivalent. *n* excl. newsprint.

4. VEGETABLE OILSEEDS AND OILS

	Production	Exports	Imports
Cottonseed	4.00*	3.03[2]	—
Groundnuts	153.53*	89.87	0.52
Groundnut oil	na	4.48	0.15
Palm oil	na	0.03	0.01

5. LIVESTOCK‡, ANIMAL PRODUCTS, etc.

	Production	Exports	Imports
Cattle *d*	3 666.7	61.8	—
Goats *d*	5 233.0	} 110.0	—
Sheep *d*	2 033.3		
Horses *d*	136.7		
Pigs *d*	2.0*	—	—
Bacon/ham	} 30.3*	0.2	—
Meat‡, 'A'		0.4	—
Eggs	1.6	—	—
Fish	7.7[2]	0.7	—
Milk	165.0*	—	0.6
Hides/skins	na	0.5	—

d no. in thousands.

6. FIBRES, TEXTILES, etc.

	Production	Exports	Imports
Cotton: lint	2.0*	1.6	—
yarn	—	—	0.2
woven fabrics	—	—	4.0

7. FUEL AND POWER

	Production	Exports	Imports
Electricity *h t*	15		
Petroleum, refined	—	—	30

h million kWh. *t* thermal.

9. NON-FERROUS MINERALS AND METALS

	Production	Exports	Imports
Tin, ore	0.05*m*	0.04	—

m metal content.

11. INDUSTRY

	Production	Exports	Imports
Alcoholic beverages *a*	—	—	0.9
Cement	—	—	11.7
Electrical engineering *a*	—	—	1.5
Motor vehicles *a*	—	0.1*	2.9[2]

a million $ U.S.

NIGERIA

Nigeria, a federation of four regions which were formerly British colonies, became sovereign and independent in 1960, and a republic in 1963. The northern part of the British (West) Cameroons joined Nigeria in 1961. The Eastern Region, Biafra, attempted to secede from the federation in 1967; fighting ensued until 1970 when the rebellion collapsed.

AREA: 923 773* sq. km. (356 669* sq. miles)

LAND USE: (percentage of total)

	1961	*1950*
Arable and orchard	23.6 }	23.1
Permanent meadow and pasture	na }	
Forest and woodland	34.2	32.0
City areas, waste and other land	na	44.9

POPULATION: 61 450 000 (1967 estimate)

Largest city: LAGOS, capital; population: 665 246 (city proper, 1963)
Total working population: 14 913 000 (1952–3 av.)

Agriculture is the main occupation, but an increasing number of people are employed in the expanding industrial sector.

		Year(s)
Accidental deaths (per 100 000 population)		
caused by motor vehicles	24.6*	1963
due to other causes	10.2*	1963
Population per physician	44 230	1965
Population per hospital bed	2 190	1966
School enrolment: age 5–19 years (percentage)	27	1963–4 av.
age over 19 years (per 100 000 population)	14	1963–5 av.

COMMUNICATIONS

		Year(s)
Motor vehicles in use ('000s): private	50.9 }	1963–5 av.
commercial	23.8 }	
Railway track (km.)	3 009	1967
Mail per capita: domestic	2 }	1963–5 av.
foreign received	0.4 }	
foreign sent	0.2 }	
Telephones (per '000 urban population)	0.1*	1967
Radio receivers (per '000 population)	9	1963–5 av.
Television sets (per '000 population)	0.3*	1963–5 av.
Daily newspapers (per '000 population)	10	1963

FINANCE

Currency unit: The Nigerian pound replaced, at par, the West African pound in 1959.

Exchange rates	*1965*	*1960*	*1950a*	*1938a*
Per $ U.S.	0.357	0.357	0.357	0.215
Per £ sterling	1.0	1.0	1.0	1.0

		Year(s)
National Income (million $ U.S.)	3 650	1965
G.N.P. per capita ($ U.S.)	80	1966
Rate of increase of G.N.P. per capita	2.5	1960–2 av.

a West African pounds.

TRADING

Total trade (in million $ U.S.)	*1965*	*1955*	*1938*
Exports (f.o.b.)	751	371	46
Imports (c.i.f.)	770	381	42

Main trading partners (percentage of total value)

Exports	*1965*	*1955*	*Imports*	*1965*	*1955*
U.K.	38	70	U.K.	31	47
Netherlands	12	8	U.S.A.	12	4
Germany F.R.	11	3	Germany F.R.	11	7
U.S.A.	10	9	Japan	9	12
France	7	2	Italy	5	3
Italy	4	2	France	4	1
Belg./Lux.	2	1	Netherlands	4	3

Distribution of trade (percentage of total value)

Exports	*1965*	*1955*	*1938**
Crude materials and fuels	64	62	na
(oilseeds)	(26)	(32)	(38)
(petroleum)	(26)	(—)	(—)
(rubber)	(4)	(4)	(1)
(cotton)	(2)	(9)	(na)
Food	19	24	na
(cocoa)	(16)	(20)	(17)
Animal and vegetable oils	9	13	na
Tin and alloys	6	—	15

Imports	*1965*	*1955*	*1938**
Manufactured goods	74	74	na
(machinery and transport equipment)	(34)	(20)	(13)
(textiles and clothing)	(17)	(27)	(23)
Crude materials and fuels	9	6	na
(petroleum products)	(6)	(5)	(4)
Food	8	10	na
Chemicals	7	5	2

continued

PRODUCTION, EXPORTS AND IMPORTS

Years: **1963–5 average** and *1953–5 average* Units: '000 metric tons unless otherwise indicated

1. CEREALS, etc.

	Production 1963–5	Production *1953–5*	Exports 1963–5	Exports *1953–5*	Imports 1963–5	Imports *1953–5*
Barley	—	—	—	—	0.3	—
Cassava	7 296.0*	na				
Maize (corn)	1 123.3*	na	0.1	0.2[2]	0.1	—
Millets/sorghum	6 483.3*	na	—	—	—	0.6[2]
Potatoes	—	—	—	—	1.7	0.6
Rice	360.0*	na	0.1	0.1	1.2	0.3
Sweet potatoes/ yams	13 338.0*	na				
Wheat	—	—	5.4†	—	46.2	—

2. FRUIT, etc.

	Production 1963–5	Production *1953–5*	Exports 1963–5	Exports *1953–5*	Imports 1963–5	Imports *1953–5*
Bananas	—	na	—[2]	80.8	—	—
Coconuts	65.0**e*	na	—	0.2	—	—
Oranges	na	na	0.2	—	—	—
Other citrus fruit	na	na	0.3	—	—	—
Wine *b*	—	—	—	—	7.1	3.0

b '000 hectolitres. *e* no. in millions.

3. BEVERAGES, FOREST PRODUCTS, etc.

	Production 1963–5	Production *1953–5*	Exports 1963–5	Exports *1953–5*	Imports 1963–5	Imports *1953–5*
Cocoa	232.4	102.8	227.7	98.7	—	—
Coffee	na	na	2.1	0.6	0.3	—
Sugar, raw	—	—	—	—	68.7	37.5
Tea	—	—	—	—	0.6	0.2
Tobacco: leaf	11.6*	10.7*	0.1	—	1.9	2.9
cigarettes	4 470.0*e*	2 294.0*e*	—	—	—	—
Softwood *j*	—	—	—	—	30.9[2]	—
Hardwood *j*	31 292.3*	898.0[1]	911.0	407.1	1.2[2]	—
Newsprint	—	—	—	—	5.1	2.1[2]
Other paper	—	—	—	—	18.3	4.7[2]

e no. in millions. *j* '000 cu. metres of roundwood equivalent.

4. VEGETABLE OILSEEDS AND OILS

	Production 1963–5	Production *1953–5*	Exports 1963–5	Exports *1953–5*	Imports 1963–5	Imports *1953–5*
Castor seed	na	na	0.22	0.57	—	—
Castor oil	na	na	1.34	na	—	—
Copra	5.90	6.57	5.80	6.57	—	—
Cottonseed	92.00	68.00*	67.13	38.13	—	—
Groundnuts	973.97*	620.67*	565.80	390.00*	—	—
Groundnut oil	na	na	81.23	28.08	0.10	—
Linseed	na	na	0.27	na	—	—
Palm kernels	414.70*	446.00*	409.13	439.47	—	—
Palm kernel oil	na	na	1.68	na	—	—
Palm oil	518.33	413.30*	138.83	200.26	—	—
Rapeseed oil	na	na	1.98	na	0.22*	na
Sesame seed	22.50	15.00[2]*	18.08	9.20	—	—
Soya beans	16.70*	9.00[2]	17.00	9.35[2]	—	—

5. LIVESTOCK‡, ANIMAL PRODUCTS, etc.

	Production 1963–5	Production *1953–5*	Exports 1963–5	Exports *1953–5*	Imports 1963–5	Imports *1953–5*
Cattle *d*	7 401.0*	na	3.5	1.7	92.6*	79.9
Goats *d*	20 278.0	na	—	—	—	—
Sheep *d*	7 221.7	na	—	—	—	—
Horses *d*	289.0	na				
Pigs *d*	663.0	na	0.3	—	—	—
Meat‡, 'A'	165.3*	na	—	—	—	—
Butter	na	—	0.3	—	0.5	0.1
Cheese	—	—	—	—	0.5	0.1
Eggs	43.9*	na	—	—	—	—
Fish	59.0[2]	42.0[1]	0.1	na	40.2	17.7
Milk	608.3*	14.0[1]	—	—	77.7	12.4
Hides/skins	na	na	8.4	8.6[2]	—	—

d no. in thousands.

6. FIBRES, TEXTILES, etc.

	Production 1963–5	Production *1953–5*	Exports 1963–5	Exports *1953–5*	Imports 1963–5	Imports *1953–5*
Cotton lint	45.7	29.0	26.7	26.0*n*	—	—
Flax fibre	na	na	1.3[2]	na	—	—
Rubber, natural	na	25.1*	64.8	24.3	0.3	—
Silk *f*	—	—	—	—	2.7	na
Cotton: yarn	na	na	—	—	2.8[2]	na
woven fabrics	12.3*	na	—	—	23.2	na
Rayon, woven fabrics	—	—	—	—	2.8*p*	na

f metric tons. *n* incl. some linters. *p* incl. synthetic piece goods.

7. FUEL AND POWER

	Production 1963–5	Production *1953–5*	Exports 1963–5	Exports *1953–5*	Imports 1963–5	Imports *1953–5*
Coal, 'A'‡	673	760	5	44	} 3	26[1]
Coke	na	na	34	—		1[1]
Electricity *h*: total	1 031	210[1]				
hydro	125	70[1]				
thermal	906	140[1]				
Natural gas *i*	60	—	—	—	—	—
Oil, crude	7 753	—[1]	7 620	na	—	—
Petroleum, refined	57	—[1]	117	10*	1 090	310[1]
Rare earths *f*	50*r*	na	na	na	—	—

f metric tons. *h* million kWh. *i* million cu. metres. *r* monazite.

8. IRON AND STEEL

	Production 1963–5	Production *1953–5*	Exports 1963–5	Exports *1953–5*	Imports 1963–5	Imports *1953–5*
Iron/steel scrap	na	na	7	2	—	—

9. NON-FERROUS MINERALS AND METALS

	Production 1963–5	Production *1953–5*	Exports 1963–5	Exports *1953–5*	Imports 1963–5	Imports *1953–5*
Gold *k*, ore	—	0.70*m*	—	0.21*t*	—	0.08*t*
Platinum group metals *k*	—	—	—	—	6.68	na
Silver *k*, bullion	—	—	—	—	20.78	9.13
Asbestos: fibre	—	—	—	—	2.13	—
manufactured	—	—	—	—	8.21	17.32[2]
Aluminium	—	—	—	—	4.95	1.45[2]
Copper, metal	—	—	—	—	1.91	0.43
Lead: ore	0.23*m*	0.02*m*	0.92	0.12	—	—
metal	na	na	—	—	0.70	0.18
Tin: ore	9.14*m*	8.23*m*	0.07	11.46	—	—
metal	9.19	—	10.43	—	0.13	0.27[2]
Tungsten, ore	—	0.01	—	0.01	—	—
Zinc: ore	—	0.22*m*	0.70	0.06	—	—
metal	—	na	—	—	0.99	0.06[2]
Zirconium minerals	0.46	—	0.30	—	—	—

k '000 fine troy oz. *m* metal content. *t* bullion/coins, etc.

10. CHEMICALS*n* AND FERTILIZERS

	Production 1963–5	Production *1953–5*	Exports 1963–5	Exports *1953–5*	Imports 1963–5	Imports *1953–5*
Chemicals	—		—		na	
Fertilizers:						
Phosphates	—	—	—	—	10.8*p*	0.8[2]
Potash	—	—	—	—	1.6	0.9[2]
Sulphur	—	—	—	—	0.1	—

n data not available for years 1953–5. *p* incl. superphosphates.

11. INDUSTRY

	Production 1963–5	Production *1953–5*	Exports 1963–5	Exports *1953–5*	Imports 1963–5	Imports *1953–5*
Aircraft *a*	—	—	—	—	2.8	1.4[2]
Alcoholic beverages			—	—	3.4*a*	—
beer *b*	522.0	74.3				
Cement	781.0	—	—	—	277.3	369.3
Electrical engineering *a*	—	—	—	—	38.5	10.8[2]
Railway vehicles *a*	—	—	—	—	5.8	6.5
Merchant ships *g*	—	—	—	—	0.2[1]	—
Motor vehicles			—	—	55.0*a*	21.8*a*
commercial *d*	3.7*p*	—				

a million $ U.S. *b* '000 hectolitres. *d* no. in thousands. *g* '000 G.R.T.
p assembly of imported parts.

na: data not available. — negligible or nil. [1] one year only. [2] two year average. * estimate. ‡ see appendix. † re-exports.

NORWAY

Norway is a constitutional and hereditary monarchy, but legislative power is vested in the 'Storting' (parliament). A member of the European Free Trade Association, Norway has applied to join the European Economic Community. Statistics include those for Svalbard (Spitsbergen) and Jan Mayen Islands.

AREA: 323 885 sq. km. (125 051 sq. miles)

LAND USE: (percentage of total)	*1965*	*1955*
Arable and orchard	2.6	2.6
Permanent meadow and pasture	0.5	0.6
Forest and woodland	21.7	23.2
City areas, waste and other land	75.2	73.6

POPULATION: 3 784 000 (1967 estimate)

Largest city: OSLO, capital; population: 484 479 (1966)

Distribution of working population (1960)
Total working population: 1 406 358

U.N. group no.		*Percentage*
0	Agriculture, forestry, fishing and hunting	19.5
1	Mining and quarrying	0.6
2/3	Manufacturing	25.5
4	Construction	9.5
5	Electricity, gas, water and sanitary services	0.9
6	Commerce	13.3
7	Transport, storage and communications	11.9
8	Services	18.4
9	Others	0.4

		Year(s)
Life expectancy at birth (years): male	71	1961–5 av.
female	75.5	1961–5 av.
Infant mortality (per '000)	16.8	1965
Crude birth rate (per '000)	17.8	1965
Crude death rate (per '000)	9.5	1965
Accidental deaths (per 100 000 population)		
caused by motor vehicles	12.2	1965
due to other causes	35.9	1965
Population per physician	810	1964
Population per hospital bed	110	1966
School enrolment: age 5–19 years (percentage)	86	1963–4 av.
age over 19 years (per 100 000 population)	494	1964–5 av.

COMMUNICATIONS		*Year(s)*
Motor vehicles in use ('000s): private	415.1	1963–5 av.
commercial	128.7	1963–5 av.
Railway track (km.)	4 360	1964
Mail per capita: domestic	113	1963–5 av.
foreign received	11	1963–5 av.
foreign sent	9	1963–5 av.
Telephones (per '000 urban population)	25.1	1967
Radio licences (per '000 population)	291	1963–5 av.
Television licences (per '000 population)	107	1963–5 av.
Daily newspapers (per '000 population)	384.3	1962–4 av.

FINANCE

Currency unit: The krone

Exchange rates	*1965*	*1960*	*1950*	*1938*
Per $ U.S.	7.15	7.15	7.15	4.30
Per £ sterling	20.02	20.02	20.02	19.76

		Year(s)
National Income (million $ U.S.)	5 409	1965
G.N.P. per capita ($ U.S.)	1 710	1966
Rate of increase of G.N.P. per capita	4.6	1960–4 av.
Foreign trade (percentage of G.D.P.)	51	1963–5 av.

TRADING

Total trade (in million $ U.S.)	*1965*	*1955*	*1938*
Exports (f.o.b.)	1 443	633	193
Imports (c.i.f.)	2 210	1 090	293

Main trading partners (percentage of total value)

Exports	*1965*	*1955*	*1938*	*Imports*	*1965*	*1955*	*1938*
U.K.	18	22	25	Sweden	21	16	11
Sweden	16	9	9	Germany F.R.	16	14	18*d*
Germany F.R.	14	11	15*d*	U.K.	12	20	16
U.S.A.	9	9	8	U.S.A.	7	9	10
Denmark	7	5	4	Denmark	5	4	3
Netherlands	3	3	7	Netherlands	5	5	3
France	3	4	7	France	4	3	3

Distribution of trade (percentage of total value)

Exports	*1965*	*1955*	*1938*
Manufactured goods	57	42	na
(machinery and transport equipment)	(17)	(7)	(5)
(paper and other wood products)	(9)	(11)	(10)
Crude materials and fuels	15	22	na
(wood and paper pulp)	(7)	(13)	(13)
Food	15	21	na
(fish)	(10)	(15)	(15)
Chemicals	9	9	9
Imports			
Manufactured goods	64	63	na
(machinery and transport equipment)	(38)	(34)	(28)
(textiles and clothing)	(7)	(7)	(9)
Crude materials and fuels	18	19	na
(petroleum products)	(6)	(8)	(na)
Food	9	12	10
Chemicals	8	4	5

d incl. Germany D.R.

PRODUCTION, EXPORTS AND IMPORTS

Years: **1963–5 average** and *1953–5 average*   Units: '000 metric tons unless otherwise indicated

1. CEREALS, etc.

	Production		Exports		Imports	
Barley	**476.0**	*213.3*	—	—	**42.9**	*55.8*
Maize (corn)	—	—	—	—	**95.4**	*81.6*
Millets/sorghum	—	—	—	—	**40.3**	*38.8*
Oats	**117.3**	*151.3*	**0.2**	*0.7*	**8.3**	*0.8*
Potatoes	**1 052.0**	*1 120.0*	**0.8**	—	**5.2**	*0.8*
Rice	—	—	—	—	**5.9**	*4.8*
Rye	**2.3**	*1.3*	—	—	**44.3**	*60.3*
Wheat	**16.7**	*37.3*	—	—	**343.4**	*300.6*

2. FRUIT, etc.

	Production		Exports		Imports	
Apples	**49.3**	*48.3*	—	—	**19.9**	*1.1*
Bananas	—	—	—	—	**28.4**	*6.6*
Cherries	**3.7**	*3.7*	—	—	—	—
Dates	—	—	—	—	**0.3**	*0.2*
Figs	—	—	—	—	na	*1.4*
Grapes	—	—	—	—	**12.8**	*1.2*
Lemons	—	—	—	—	**2.4**	*3.7*[2]*n*
Oranges	—	—	**0.2†**	—	**54.6**	*46.2*
Other citrus fruit	—	—	—	—	**1.6**	na*n*
Pears	**7.0**	*6.7*	—	—	**5.6**	*0.3*
Plums	**14.3**	*11.2*	—	—	—	—
Raisins	—	—	—	—	**3.1**	*4.2*
Tomatoes	**8.3**	*8.0*				
Wine*b*	—	—	—	—	**49.7**	*39.7*

b '000 hectolitres. *n* grapefruit incl. with lemons.

3. BEVERAGES, FOREST PRODUCTS, etc.

	Production		Exports		Imports	
Cocoa	—	—	—	—	**4.5**	*3.7*
Coffee	—	—	—	—	**32.0**	*19.0*
Sugar, raw	—	—	**0.5†**	*1.1†*	**159.0**	*133.1*
Tea	—	—	—	—	**0.5**	*0.4*

continued

3. BEVERAGES, FOREST PRODUCTS, etc.—*continued*

	Production		Exports		Imports	
Tobacco: leaf	—	—	**0.1†**	—	**5.1**	*4.3*
cigars	**17.0***e*	*12.8e*				
cigarettes	**1 217.0***e*	*1 363.3e*	—	—	**2.7***a*	*0.1*[2]
tobacco/snuff	**4.6**	*3.4*				
Softwood*j*	**7 197.7**	*8 522.3*	**273.0**	*213.7*	**347.3**	*133.9*
Hardwood*j*	**527.7**	*1 098.3*	**0.2**	*1.9*	**105.6**	*68.7*
Wood pulp	**1 743.7**	*1 192.3*	**840.4**	*657.3*	**46.5**	*24.3*
Newsprint	**290.0**	*165.0*	**234.7**	*132.7*	—	—
Other paper	**665.0**	*386.0*	**395.7**	*203.0*	**23.2**	*8.1*

a million $ U.S. *e* no. in millions. *j* '000 cu. metres of roundwood equivalent.

4. VEGETABLE OILSEEDS AND OILS

	Production		Exports		Imports	
Castor oil	—	—	—	*0.05*[2]*†*	**0.21**	*0.20*[2]
Copra	—	—	—	—	**23.40**	*39.30*
Coconut oil	na	na	**0.02**	*0.02*	**0.18**	—
Cottonseed oil	—	—	—	—	—	*0.01*
Groundnuts	—	—	—	—	**5.81**	*15.30*
Groundnut oil	na	na	—	—	**0.23**	*0.01*
Linseed	—	—	—	—	**9.75**	*20.80*
Linseed oil	na	na	—	—[2]	**0.43**	—
Olive oil	na	na	**1.14**	—	**1.44**	*1.32*
Palm kernels	—	—	—	—	—	*0.50*
Palm kernel oil	—	na	—	—	**0.01**	—
Palm oil	—	—	—	—	**0.44**	*0.04*
Rapeseed	—	—	—	—	**3.20**	—
Rapeseed oil	na	—	—	—	**0.09**	*0.04p*
Soya beans	—	—	—	—	**107.84**	*23.73*
Soya bean oil	na	na	**0.03**	*0.06*	**1.30**	*0.01*
Sunflower seed oil	—	—	—	—	**0.03**	—
Tung oil	—	—	—	—	**0.20**	*0.99*

p incl. other minor vegetable oils.

continued

na: data not available. — negligible or nil. [1] one year only. [2] two year average. * estimate. ‡ see appendix. † re-exports.

PRODUCTION, EXPORTS AND IMPORTS *continued*

5. LIVESTOCK‡, ANIMAL PRODUCTS, etc.

	Production		Exports		Imports	
Chickens*d*	**4 607.7**	*5 653.0*				
Cattle*d*	**1 095.3***n*	*1 167.3n*	**0.1**	*0.4*	—	—
dairy cows*d*	**547.3**	*825.5*[2]				
Goats*d*	**107.0***n*	*119.3n*	**0.1**	na	—	—
Sheep*d*	**1 936.7***n*	*1 953.0n*				
Horses*d*	**76.7**	*159.0*				
Pigs*d*	**539.0***n*	*416.3n*	—	*0.1*	—	—
Bacon/ham	**128.0**	*109.7*	—	—	**0.1**	*0.3*
Meat‡: 'A'			**1.6**	*1.5*	**4.0**	*0.4*
'B'	**15.9**	na	**17.2**	*0.1*	**0.5**	*0.2*
Butter	**20.0**	*16.7*	**4.7**	*2.8*	—	—
Cheese	**43.3***p*	*28.7p*	**12.2**	*2.1*	**0.3**	*0.3*
Eggs	**32.1**	*26.3*	**0.3**	*1.5*	**1.2**	—
Fish	**1 767.8***q*	*1 812.9q*	**488.4**	*511.8*[1]*	**79.9**	*33.0*[1]*
Milk	**1 671.0**	*1 591.7*	**4.7**	*1.4*[2]	**0.7**	—
Whale/sperm oil	**41.2**	*155.4*	—	—	**4.7**	*8.5*
Hides/skins	—	—	**8.0**	*6.0*[2]	**5.4**	*4.1*[2]
Wool	**3.4**	*2.7*	**1.1**	*0.6*	**1.6**	*0.7*

d no. in thousands. *n* on farms only. *p* excl. cheese made from skim milk. *q* excl. subsistence catches and fish farm production; incl. fish landed by Norwegian vessels in foreign ports.

6. FIBRES, TEXTILES, etc.

	Production		Exports		Imports	
Abaca	—	—	**0.1†**	—	**1.7**	*2.0*
Agaves (sisal etc.)	—	—	—	—	**1.5**	*1.4*
Cotton lint	—	—	—	—	**4.5**	*4.9*
Flax fibre	—	—	—	—	**0.1**	—
Hemp fibre	—	—	—	—	—	*1.0**
Jute	—	—	—	—	**0.5**	*1.1*
Rubber: natural	—	—	—	—	**5.2**	*5.0*
synthetic	—	—	—	—	**3.8**	—
Cotton: yarn	**4.7**	*3.2n*	**0.2**	—	**2.8**	*3.9*
woven fabrics	**4.2***p*	*5.2q*	**0.1**	—	**6.0**	*6.4*
Rayon: fibre/yarn	**22.9**	*15.6*	**15.9**	*11.8*	**1.5**	*1.2t*
woven fabrics	**1.9***u*	*0.6u*	**0.2***u*	—	**3.5**	*3.2u*
Non-cellulosic fibre/yarn	**0.3**	—	**0.1**	—	**5.4**	na*t*
Wool: yarn	**7.6**	*6.7*	**1.0**	—	**1.2**	*1.7*
woven fabrics	**3.3**	*4.8*	**0.3***w*	*0.1*	**1.5***w*	*1.5*

n incl. mixed yarns predominantly of cotton. *p* excl. narrow fabrics. *q* incl. spun rayon piece goods. *t* non-cellulosic fibre/yarns incl. with rayon. *u* incl. synthetic. *w* excl. blankets.

7. FUEL AND POWER

	Production		Exports		Imports	
Coal, 'A'‡	**417**	*320*	**785***r*	*574r*	**289**	*702*
Coke	na	na	**37**	—	**758**	*357*
Electricity*h*: total	**44 117**	*21 350*[1]				
hydro	**43 966**	*21 190*[1]				
thermal	**151**	*160*[1]				
Oil, crude	—	—	—	—	**2 760**	*81**
Petroleum, refined	**2 630**	*40*[1]	**1 290**	*10*[1]	**3 117**	*2 750*[1]

h million kWh. *r* incl. bunkers.

8. IRON AND STEEL

	Production		Exports		Imports	
Iron ore	**1 418***m*	*740m*	**1 453**	*1 075*	**16**	*5*
Pig iron	**911**	*293*	**571**	*204*	**11**	*19*
Steel ingots/castings	**611**	*132*	**100**	*3*	**80**	*6*
Iron/steel scrap	na	na	**8**	*1*	**41**	*10*
Iron/steel products*a*	na	na	**98**	*36*	**112**	*72*

a million $ U.S. *m* metal content.

9. NON-FERROUS MINERALS AND METALS

	Production		Exports		Imports	
Diamonds*a*	—	—	—	—	**0.01**	*0.01*
Gold*k*, bullion/coins etc.	—	—	—	—	**27.40‡**	*1.25*[2]
Platinum group metals*k*	na	na	**15.72**	*10.65*	**2.48**	*2.19*
Silver*k*, ore	na	*106.30m*	—	—	**2 452.67***n*	*1 905.00n*
Asbestos: fibre	—	—	—	—	**4.84**	*3.17*
manufactured	—	—	—	—	**15.15**	*2.50*
Mica	**3.33***	*1.40*	**3.92**	*1.11*	**4.58**	*1.53*

continued

9. NON-FERROUS MINERALS AND METALS—*continued*

	Production		Exports		Imports	
Aluminium: bauxite	—	—	—	—	**31.47**	*32.02*
alumina	**14.33***	na	—	*0.01*	**502.94**	*113.63*
aluminium	**253.99**	*62.08*	**243.40**	*54.56*	**25.27**	*11.07*
Antimony, metal	—	—	—	—	**0.10**	*0.10*
Cadmium	**0.10**	*0.10*	**0.09**	*0.06**	—	—
Chrome: ore	—	—	—	—	**72.75**	*52.40*
metal	na	na	**36.57**	*17.07*	—	—
Cobalt, metal	**0.72**	na	**0.70**	—	—	—
Copper: ore	**14.72***m*	*13.54m*	**12.07**	*29.28*	**55.99**	*34.30*
metal	**18.50**	*12.90*	**22.45**	*14.87*	**26.18**	*14.17*
Lead: ore	**3.36***m*	*0.65m*	**5.60**	*0.98*	—	—
metal	na	na	**3.60**	*1.62*	**12.36**	*10.80*
Magnesium: dolomite	**339.59**	na	**73.81**	na	**11.71**	*0.44*
magnesite	—	—	—	—	**6.35**	*0.57*
metal/salts	**23.02**	*4.98*	**22.44**	*0.05*	**49.45**	*0.93*
Manganese: ore	—	—	**5.13†**	—	**367.85**	*158.32*
metal	na	na	**182.16***r*	*81.92r*	—	—
Mercury*f*	—	—	—	—	**27.70**	*26.50*
Molybdenum*f*, ore	**219.23***m*	*155.89m*	**417.90**	*288.50*	**43.70**[1]	—
Nickel: ore	—	—	—	—	**55.99***p*	*34.39q*
metal	na	na	**30.26**	*15.98*	**1.72**	*0.04*
Tin, metal	—	—	**0.26†**	*0.19†*	**0.83**	*0.40*
Titanium minerals	**265.48**	*145.05*	**284.80**	*145.99*	**5.60**	—
Vanadium	—	na	—	—	—	—
Zinc: ore	**12.83***m*	*5.74m*	**16.22**	*3.14*	**88.91**	*78.56*
metal	**48.98**	*42.93*	**39.65**	*34.70*	**7.30**	*2.97*

a million $ U.S. *f* metric tons. *k* '000 fine troy oz. *m* metal content. *n* bullion. *p* copper-nickel matte. *q* mainly copper-nickel matte. *r* ferro-alloys.

10. CHEMICALS*n* AND FERTILIZERS

	Production		Exports		Imports	
Organic chemicals:						
Benzene	na		**0.2**		—	
Butadiene	—		—		na	
Ethylene	—		—		na	
Methanol	na		**0.3**[1]		**21.5**	
Phenol	—		—		**1.4**	
Phthalic anhydride	—		—		**3.5**	
Styrene monomer	—		—		**1.0**	
Urea	**90.0**[1]		**13.8**		—[2]	
Inorganic chemicals:						
Ammonia	**390.6**		**18.7**		**22.5**	
Carbon black	—		—		**2.3**	
Chlorine	**33.4**		**3.5**		**0.5**	
Nitric acid	**24.6**		**10.4**		—	
Sodium carbonate	**24.7**		**1.2**		**17.1**	
Sodium hydroxide	**63.4**		**11.8**		**9.3**	
Sulphuric acid	**110.5**		**12.0**		**2.0**	
Plastics:						
Polyamides	na		na		na	
Polyethylene	—		**0.1**		**15.5**	
Polyvinyl chloride	**21.7**		**14.4**		**3.3**	
Fertilizers:						
Phosphates	—	—	—	—	**174.3**	*84.6*
Potash	—	—	—	*101.7*	**122.0**	—
Pyrites	**329.2***x*	*351.4x*	**621.9**	—	—	*407.5*
Sulphur	—	*100.5y*	**2.6**	*0.2*	**46.8**	*81.4*

n data not available for years 1953–5. *x* sulphur content. *y* recovered sulphur.

11. INDUSTRY

	Production		Exports		Imports	
Aircraft*a*	—	—	—	*0.1†*	**5.7**	*2.7*
Alcoholic beverages			—	*0.2a*	—	*3.2a*
beer*b*	**1 071.0**	*734.7*				
spirits*b*	**22.1**[1]*n*	*51.9*[1]*p*				
Cement	**1 483.7**	*792.0*	**298.7**	—	**22.7**	*143.3*
Electrical engineering*a*	**201.9**[2]	na	**25.8**	*3.5*[2]	**110.8**	*40.9*[2]
Railway vehicles*a*	—	—	—	*0.1†*	—	*2.1*
Machine tools*a*	—	—	—	—	**8.6**	na
Merchant ships*g*	**386.0**	*132.0*	**56.0**	*2.5*	**1 343.0**	*574.0*
Motor vehicles*a*	—	—	**6.2†**	*0.1†*	**100.0**	*39.4*[2]

a million $ U.S. *b* '000 hectolitres. *g* '000 G.R.T. *n* 1967 figure. *p* production for home consumption in 1960.

na: data not available. — negligible or nil. [1] one year only. [2] two year average. * estimate. ‡ see appendix. † re-exports.

PAKISTAN

ASIA

When India was partitioned in 1947, Pakistan, with a population 88% Muslim, became an independent Islamic dominion of the British Commonwealth; it became a republic nine years later. The country consists (1971) of two regions, West Pakistan, containing the seat of government, and East Pakistan, which are separated by 1 000 miles of Indian territory. Pakistan is a member of Cento.

AREA: 946 720 sq. km. (365 529 sq. miles)

LAND USE: (percentage of total)	*1964*	*1955*
Arable and orchard	27.5	25.8
Permanent meadow and pasture	na	—
Forest and woodland	3.8	2.7
City areas, waste and other land	na	71.5

POPULATION: 107 258 000 (1967 estimate)

Largest city: KARÂCHI; population: 2 721 200 (1967)

Capital city: ISLÂMÂBÂD; this proposed new capital is still (1971) under construction; the temporary seat of government is Râwalpindi, the adjoining city, to which it moved from Karâchi when the new capital was first planned in 1959.

Distribution of working population (1961)

Total working population: 33 706 000* (excl. armed forces and foreigners)

U.N. group no.		*Percentage*
0	Agriculture, forestry, fishing and hunting	75.0
1	Mining and quarrying	0.1
2/3	Manufacturing	8.1
4	Construction	1.2
5	Electricity, gas, water and sanitary services	0.1
6	Commerce	4.9
7	Transport, storage and communications	1.7
8	Services	8.1
9	Others	0.8

		Year(s)
Life expectancy at birth (years): male	53.7*	1962
female	48.8*	1962
Infant mortality (per '000)	142	1964–5 av.
Crude birth rate (per '000)	49	1965
Crude death rate (per '000)	18*	1965
Population per physician	6 200	1965
Population per hospital bed	2 820	1966
School enrolment: age 5–19 years (percentage)	31	1963–4 av.
age over 19 years (per 100 000 population)	238	1963–5 av.

COMMUNICATIONS		*Year(s)*
Motor vehicles in use ('000s): private	108.4	1963–5 av.
commercial	51.2	1963–5 av.
Railway track (km.)	11 337	1964
Mail per capita: domestic	6	1962–4 av.
foreign received	1	1962–4 av.
foreign sent	1	1962–4 av.
Telephones (per '000 urban population)	0.1	1967
Radio licences (per '000 population)	5	1963–5 av.
Daily newspapers (per '000 population)	5	1962

FINANCE

Currency unit: The Pakistani rupee

Exchange rates	*1965*	*1960*	*1950*	*1938*
Per $ U.S.	4.78	4.78	3.32	2.89
Per £ sterling	13.33	13.33	11.86	13.33

		Year(s)
National Income (million $ U.S.)	8 943	1964
G.N.P. per capita ($ U.S.)	90	1966
Rate of increase of G.N.P. per capita	3.1	1960–4 av.
Foreign trade (percentage of G.D.P.)	16	963–5 av.

TRADING

Note—1938 data include India

Total trade (in million $ U.S.)	*1965*	*1955a*	*1938b*
Exports (f.o.b.)	528	401	614
Imports (c.i.f.)	1 043	290	576

Main trading partners (percentage of total value)

Exports	*1965*	*1955a*	*1938b*	*Imports*	*1965*	*1955a*	*1938b*
U.K.	13	15	34	U.S.A.	35	14	6
U.S.A.	9	8	9	U.K.	15	28	31
China P.R.	8	7	2	Germany F.R.	14	10	8*d*
India	5	13		Japan	10	15	10
Japan	5	11	9	Italy	3	1	2
Belg./Lux.	4	6	—	Canada	2	1	1
Hong Kong	4	2	—	India	2	4	

Distribution of trade (percentage of total value)

Exports	*1965*	*1955a*
Textiles	78	83*
Food	9	9*
(rice)	(5)	(4)
Imports		
Manufactured goods	64	67*
(machinery and transport equipment)	(38)	(18*)
Food	15	2*
(cereals)	(12)	(na)
Chemicals	9	8*
Crude materials and fuels	7	18*
Animal and vegetable oils	5	na

a excl. trade on government account. *b* incl. India. *d* incl. Germany D.R.

PRODUCTION, EXPORTS AND IMPORTS

Years: **1963–5 average** and *1953–5 average* Units: '000 metric tons unless otherwise indicated

1. CEREALS, etc.

	Production		Exports		Imports	
Barley	**133.0**	*137.3*	—	—	—	—
Maize (corn)	**534.7**	*444.3*	**0.2**	—	**4.1**	—
Millets/sorghum	**661.0**	*641.0*	—	*0.1*	**0.1**	—[2]
Oats	—	—	—	—	**0.1**	—
Potatoes	**504.3**	na	**0.4**	—[2]	**5.5**	na
Rice	**17 766.3**	*12 581.0*	**133.7**	*150.7*	**125.9**	—
Sweet potatoes/yams	**440.0[1]***	na	—	—	—	—
Wheat	**4 345.3**	*3 130.7*	**0.7**	*0.3*	**1 565.5**	*442.1*

2. FRUIT, etc.

	Production		Exports		Imports	
Apples	—	—	**0.1†**	—	**1.7**	—
Bananas	**1 187.3***	na	—	—	**2.3**	—
Coconuts	**80.0[1]**e***	na	—	—	**0.7**n**	—
Dates	**61.0***	na	—	—	**4.2***	*9.5*
Grapes	**19.7***	na	—	—	**15.7[2]**	—
Lemons	**31.0***	na	—	—	—	—
Oranges	**378.3***	na	**1.6**	—	**0.7**	—
Other citrus fruit	**0.7***	—	na	—	—	—
Pears	—	—	—	—	**0.2[2]**	—
Raisins	—	—	—	—	**3.0[2]**	—
Wine *b*	—	—	—	—	**0.8***	—

b '000 hectolitres. *e* no. in millions. *n* mainly desiccated.

3. BEVERAGES, FOREST PRODUCTS, etc.

	Production		Exports		Imports	
Coffee	—	—	—	—	**0.1**	—
Sugar: beet	**65.3***	—				
cane	**25 634.3**	*12 512.3*				
raw: beet	**5.8**	—	**0.3**	—	**83.1**	*75.4*
cane	**290.0**p**	*97.7p*				

continued

3. BEVERAGES, FOREST PRODUCTS, etc.—*continued*

	Production		Exports		Imports	
Tea	**26.9**	*24.3*	**1.1**	*9.6*	**0.3**	*0.2*
Tobacco: leaf	**105.0***	*95.5*	**0.6**	—	**0.6**	*0.1[2]*
cigars	na	*1.2e*	—	—	—	—
cigarettes	**18 914.0**e**	*4 472.3e*	—	—	—	—
Softwood *j*	**22.0[1]**	*149.0[1]*	—	—[1]	**4.9**	*15.4[1]*
Hardwood *j*	**3 700.0[1]**	*1 374.0*	—	—	**30.3**	—[1]
Wood pulp	**35.5*[2]**	—[1]	—	—[1]	**21.4**	—[1]
Newsprint	**33.0***	—	**8.6**	—[1]	—	*2.3[1]*
Other paper	**61.3***	—	**0.1**	—[1]	**18.0**	*23.9[1]*

e no. in millions. *j* '000 cu. metres of roundwood equivalent. *p* in addition, gur 1 505* (1963–5 av.) and 1 120* (1953–5 av.).

4. VEGETABLE OILSEEDS AND OILS

	Production		Exports		Imports	
Castor seed	**8.00***	*0.51[2]*	**1.11[2]**	*0.55[2]*	—	—
Castor oil	na	na	**0.01**	—	**0.03**	*0.05[2]**
Copra	—	—	—	—	**2.70***	*4.97*
Coconut oil	na	na	—	—	**13.91**	*4.55*
Cottonseed	**813.30**	*566.00*	**0.30**	*1.07**	**1.59**	—
Cottonseed oil	na	na	—	—[2]	**11.78***	—
Groundnuts	**20.77***	—	**0.39**	—	**2.13**	*0.10[2]*
Linseed	**13.33**r**	*13.00*r*	—	—	—	—
Linseed oil	na	na	**0.05**	—	**1.80**	*0.44*
Olive oil	—	—	—	—	**0.08**	na
Rapeseed	**324.00**	*310.30*	**0.18**	*1.05[2]*	**2.21**	—[2]
Sesame seed	**32.17**	*37.30*	—	—	—	—
Soya bean oil	—	—	—	—	**73.72**	—
Tung oil	—	—	—	—	**0.01**	—

r flax grown for seed only.

continued

na: data not available. — negligible or nil. [1] one year only. [2] two year average. * estimate. ‡ see appendix. † re-exports.

PRODUCTION, EXPORTS AND IMPORTS *continued*

5. LIVESTOCK‡, ANIMAL PRODUCTS, etc.

	Production		Exports		Imports	
Chickens *d*	na	*11 345[1]*				
Cattle *d*	**34 853***	*30 678[2]*	—	*0.1[2]*	—[2]	—
dairy cows *d*	**14 505***t**	*6 017[2]*				
Goats *d*	**11 983**	*10 067[1]*	—	—	—	—
Sheep *d*	**10 670***	*6 145[1]*	—	—	—	—
Horses *d*	**497**	*470[1]*				
Pigs *d*	**94**	*104[1]*	—	—	—	—
Bacon/ham	**351**	*264[2]*	—	—	**0.1**	—
Meat‡ 'A'			—	—	**0.1**	—
'B'	**32**	*22[2]*	—	—	—	—
Butter	**112**	na	—	—	**0.5**	—
Cheese	na	na	—	—	**0.1**	—
Eggs	**20**	*17*	**0.3**	—	—	—
Fish	**362**	*260*	**41.0**	*28.5**	**0.6**	na
Milk	**2 743***	*3 538[1]*	—	—	**106.4**	*9.5*
Hides/skins	na	na	**8.6**a**	*9.8e*	—	—
Wool	**12**	*8*	**6.7**	*8.1*	**0.2**	*0.6*

a million $ U.S. *d* no. in thousands. *e* no. in millions. *t* figures based on 1960 census.

6. FIBRES, TEXTILES, etc.

	Production		Exports		Imports	
Cotton lint	**406.7**	*283.0*	**143.8**	*196.4*	**1.8**	*2.0*
Hemp fibre	**10.0***	na	**1.5**	—	—	—
Jute	**1 068.3**	*838.7*	**762.8**	*955.2*	**0.1**	—
Rubber, natural	—	—	—	—	**6.7**	*1.6**
Silk *f*	—	—	—	—	**1.0**	*3.5[2]*
Cotton: yarn	**224.7**	*88.4*	**22.4**	*0.6[2]**	na	*7.2*
woven fabrics	**85.1***	*38.9*	**18.9**	—	na	*3.2*
Rayon: fibre/yarn	—[1]	—	—	—	**9.7[1]**	*3.9[1]**
woven fabrics	**2.8**	*1.2*	—	—	—	—
Non-cellulosic fibre/yarn	**0.1[1]**	na	na	na	**2.5**	na
Wool: yarn	**2.6[2]**	na	na	na	na	*0.1*
woven fabrics	—	—	—	—[1]	na	*0.2*

f metric tons.

7. FUEL AND POWER

	Production		Exports		Imports	
Coal 'A'‡	**917**	*380*	—	—	**986[2]**	*1 137n*
Electricity *h*: total	**3 472**	*1 000[1]*				
hydro	**1 679**	*400[1]*				
thermal	**1 793**	*600[1]*				
Natural gas *i*	**1 420**	*42[2]*	—	—	—	—
Oil, crude	**500**	*236[1]**	—	—	**2 050**	na
Petroleum, refined	**2 363**	*220[1]*	**87**	—	**943**	*870[1]*

h million kWh. *i* million cu. metres. *n* incl. coke.

8. IRON AND STEEL

	Production		Exports		Imports	
Pig iron	—	—	—	—	**59[2]**	*17*
Steel ingots/castings	—	—	—	—	**288**	*51*
Iron/steel scrap	na	na	—	—	**1[2]**	—

9. NON-FERROUS MINERALS AND METALS

	Production		Exports		Imports	
Asbestos, manufactured	—	—	—	—	**0.33[2]**	*4.20*
Aluminium: bauxite	—	*1.04[1]*	—	—	—	—
aluminium	—	na	—	—	**17.10[2]**	*4.02*

continued

9. NON-FERROUS MINERALS AND METALS—*continued*

	Production		Exports		Imports	
Antimony, ore *m*	**0.05**	—	—	—	—	—
Chrome, ore	**14.18**m**	*24.96m*	**13.36[2]**	*18.68*	—	*0.03n*
Copper, metal	—	—	—	—	**8.15[1]**	*0.28*
Lead: ore	—	—	—	—	**0.30[2]**	*0.19*
metal	—	—	—	—	**3.82[2]**	*0.37p*
Magnesium: dolomite	na	na	—	—	—	—
magnesite	**0.67**	na	—	—	—	—
metal/salts	—	—	—	—	**0.19[1]**	*0.54*
Manganese, ore	**1.13**	—	—	—	—	—
Mercury *f*	—	—	—	—	**18.60[2]**	*0.10*
Tin, metal	—	—	—	—	**0.54[2]**	*0.12*
Zinc, metal	—	—	—	—	**5.62[2]**	*1.80*

f metric tons. *m* metal content. *n* metal. *p* excl. bars, sheets, pipes and tubes.

10. CHEMICALS*n* AND FERTILIZERS

	Production		Exports		Imports	
Organic chemicals:						
Benzene	—		—		na	
Butadiene	—		—		na	
Ethylene	—		—		na	
Methanol	na		na		na	
Phenol	—		—		na	
Phthalic anhydride	—		—		na	
Styrene monomer	—		—		na	
Urea	**127.2**		na		na	
Inorganic chemicals:						
Ammonia	na		—		na	
Carbon black	—		—		na	
Chlorine	**3.1**		na		na	
Nitric acid	na		—		na	
Sodium carbonate	**31.4**		—		na	
Sodium hydroxide	**8.2**		—		na	
Sulphuric acid	**19.7**		—		na	
Plastics:						
Polyamides	—		—		na	
Polyethylene	—		—		na	
Polyvinyl chloride	—		—		na	
Fertilizers:						
Potash	—	—	—	—	**0.8**	*1.0*
Sulphur	—	—	—	—	**11.0[2]**	*0.9*

n data not available for years 1953–5.

11. INDUSTRY

	Production		Exports		Imports	
Aircraft *a*	—	—	**0.6†**	—	**6.4**	*1.3*
Alcoholic beverages			—	—	**1.1**a**	—
beer *b*	**17.0**	*13.6*				
Cement	**1 578.3**	*634.0*	**26.0***	*8.3*	**803.7***	*15.3*
Electrical engineering *a*	—	—	**0.9†**	—	**61.1**	*9.9*
Railway vehicles *a*	—	—	—	—	**32.9**	*1.1*
Machine tools *a*	—	—	—	—	**4.7**	na
Merchant ships *g*	**1.0[2]**	—	—	—	**9.0**	na
Motor vehicles *a*	—	—	**0.5†**	—	**47.2**	*6.3*

a million $ U.S. *b* '000 hectolitres. *g* '000 G.R.T.

PANAMA

CENTRAL AMERICA

The economy of Panama depends largely on the Canal Zone (*see* U.S.A. page 229), although recent attempts have been made to develop and diversify agriculture.

AREA: 75 650 sq. km. (29 201 sq. miles)

LAND USE: (percentage of total)	*1961*	*1950*
Arable and orchard	7.5	6.0
Permanent meadow and pasture	11.0	7.4
Forest and woodland	80.5	70.8
City areas, waste and other land	1.0	15.8

POPULATION: 1 329 000 (1967 estimate)

Largest city: PANAMÁ, capital; population: 358 200 (city proper, 1967)

Distribution of working population (1960)

Total working population: 336 969 (excl. tribal Indians)

U.N. group no.		*Percentage*
0	Agriculture, forestry, fishing and hunting	46.2
1	Mining and quarrying	0.1
2/3	Manufacturing	7.6
4	Construction	4.3
5	Electricity, gas, water and sanitary services	0.5
6	Commerce	9.1
7	Transport, storage and communications	3.0
8	Services	20.1
9	Others	9.1

		Year(s)
Life expectancy at birth (years): male	57.6	1960–1 av.
female	60.9	1960–1 av.
Infant mortality (per '000)	44.7*	1965
Crude birth rate (per '000)	41.5*	1960–5 av.
Crude death rate (per '000)	10.5*	1960–5 av.
Accidental deaths (per 100 000 population)		
caused by motor vehicles	10.9*	1965
due to other causes	28.6*	1965
Population per physician	2 260	1964
Population per hospital bed	330	1966
School enrolment: age 5–19 years (percentage)	71	1963–4 av.
age over 19 years (per 100 000 population)	529	1963–5 av.

COMMUNICATIONS		*Year(s)*
Motor vehicles in use ('000s): private	27.4	1963–5 av.
commercial	9.5	1963–5 av.
Railway track (km.)	111	1964
Telephones (per '000 urban population)	3.7	1967
Radio receivers (per '000 population)	341	1963–5 av.
Television sets (per '000 population)	50.6	1963–5 av.
Daily newspapers (per '000 population)	75.5	1963–4 av.

continued

na: data not available. — negligible or nil. [1] one year only. [2] two year average. * estimate. ‡ see appendix. † re-exports.

FINANCE

Currency unit: The balboa, at par with the U.S. dollar *a*

Exchange rates	*1965*	*1960*
Per £ sterling	2.81	2.81

		Year(s)
National Income (million $ U.S.)	530	1965
G.N.P. per capita ($ U.S.)	500	1966
Rate of increase of G.N.P. per capita	4.9	1960–4 av.
Foreign trade (percentage of G.D.P.)	41	1963–5 av.

a The issue of local currency is restricted to subsidiary coinage; the bulk of the money in circulation is U.S. notes and coins.

TRADING

Total trade (in million $ U.S.)	*1965*	*1955*	*1937*
Exports (f.o.b.)	79	36	8
Imports (c.i.f.)	190	76	18

Main trading partners (percentage of total value)

Exports	*1965*	*1955*	*Imports*	*1965*	*1955*
U.S.A.	65	95	U.S.A.	42	60
Canada	10	—	Venezuela	19	na
Panama C.Z.	8	na	Japan	5	1
Germany F.R.	4	1	Germany F.R.	4	4
U.K.	4	—	U.K.	3	4
Japan	3	—	Netherlands	2	1

Distribution of trade (percentage of total value)

Exports	*1965*	*1955*
Food	67	89
(bananas)	(51)	(64)
(fish)	(10)	(14)
Petroleum products	30	—
Imports		
Manufactured goods	58	59
(machinery and transport equipment)	(21)	(17)
(textiles and clothing)	(11)	(13)
Crude materials and fuels	22	11
(petroleum and products)	(21)	(10)
Chemicals	10	11
Food	9	15

PRODUCTION, EXPORTS AND IMPORTS

Years: **1963–5 average** and *1953–5 average* Units: '000 metric tons unless otherwise indicated

	Production 1963–5	Production 1953–5	Exports 1963–5	Exports 1953–5	Imports 1963–5	Imports 1953–5
1. CEREALS, etc.						
Barley	—	—	—	—	0.1	—
Cassava	45.0*	19.0[1]				
Maize (corn)	82.0	78.0	—	—	5.2	—
Oats	—	—	—	—	1.2	—
Potatoes	2.7*	1.5[2]	—	—	1.4	1.6
Rice	131.7	102.7	—	—	2.7	—
Sweet potatoes/yams	26.0*	6.0[1]				
Wheat	—	—	—	—	23.7	—
2. FRUIT, etc.						
Apples	—	—	—	—	1.4	0.7
Bananas	463.3*	340.0[2]*	300.0	216.9*	—	—
Coconuts	50.0*[1] e	na	—	2.8	—	—
Grapes	—	—	—	—	0.5	0.3
Oranges	25.0*	23.5[2]	0.1	—	—	—
Pears	—	—	—	—	0.1	0.2
Raisins	—	—	—	—	0.2	0.1
Tomatoes	5.0	4.0[2]				
Wine b	—	—	—	—	2.1	2.0

b '000 hectolitres. *e* no. in millions.

	Production 1963–5	Production 1953–5	Exports 1963–5	Exports 1953–5	Imports 1963–5	Imports 1953–5
3. BEVERAGES, FOREST PRODUCTS, etc.						
Cocoa	1.0	1.7*	0.8	2.0	—	—
Coffee	4.4	2.6	0.9	0.2	—	—
Sugar: cane	1 054.7*	310.0				
raw	45.8 n	16.7* n	14.5	5.5	—	—
Tobacco: leaf	1.1	0.3	—	—	0.2	0.2
cigarettes	788.0 e	na	—	—	0.2 p	0.4 p
Softwood j	—	—	0.1†	1.4†	11.3 (softwood and hardwood)	11.1 (softwood and hardwood)
Hardwood j	1 834.0*[1]	1 744.0[1]	2.3	12.0		
Wood pulp	—	—[2]	—	—[2]	0.4	—[2]
Newsprint	—*[2]	—	—	—	3.3	1.9
Other paper	1.0*[2]	—	0.5	—	41.1	3.6

e no. in millions. *j* '000 cu. metres of roundwood equivalent. *n* in addition, non-centrifugal sugar 4.7* (1963–5 av.) and 9.3* (1953–5 av.). *p* incl. other tobacco manufactures.

	Production 1963–5	Production 1953–5	Exports 1963–5	Exports 1953–5	Imports 1963–5	Imports 1953–5
4. VEGETABLE OILSEEDS AND OILS						
Castor oil	—	—	—	—	0.01	—
Copra	—	—	—	—	6.56	0.10
Coconut oil	na	na	—	—	0.08	0.03
Cottonseed oil	—	—	—	—	0.13	0.19
Groundnuts	—	—	—	—	0.15	0.10
Linseed oil	—	—	—	—	0.05	0.04
Olive oil	—	—	—	—	0.09	0.05
Palm kernels	—	—	—	—	—	0.10[1]
Palm oil	—	—	—	—	0.05	—
Soya bean oil	—	—	—	—	0.48	0.50
5. LIVESTOCK‡, ANIMAL PRODUCTS, etc.						
Chickens d	2 362.0	1 924.0				
Cattle d	900.7	575.0	5.7	—	—	0.1
dairy cows d	486.7	na				
Goats d	4.0*	na	—	—	—	—
Horses d	160.0*	171.0[1]				
Pigs d	188.0	227.3	—	—	—	0.1
Bacon/ham	30.7 (Bacon/ham and Meat‡ 'A')	19.0 (Bacon/ham and Meat‡ 'A')	—	—	0.2	0.5
Meat‡ 'A'			—	—	—	—
'B'	1.5*	—	—	—	—	—
Butter	—	—	—	—	1.0	0.4
Cheese	—	—	—	—	0.8	0.2
Eggs	4.7	2.8*	—	—	—	0.1
Fish	26.1	1.9	7.8	na	2.5	na
Milk	50.0*	33.0[1]	0.3	—	10.3*	7.5
Whale oil	—	21.7	—	—	—	—

d no. in thousands.

	Production 1963–5	Production 1953–5	Exports 1963–5	Exports 1953–5	Imports 1963–5	Imports 1953–5
6. FIBRES, TEXTILES, etc.						
Abaca	—	2.0*	—	2.0	—	—
Cotton lint	—	—	—	—	—	0.1
7. FUEL AND POWER						
Electricity h	358 r	140[1] t				
Oil, crude	—	—	—	—	2 163	na
Petroleum, refined	2 163	—[1]	1 240	—	83	240[1]

h million kWh. *r* thermal and hydro. *t* thermal.

	Production 1963–5	Production 1953–5	Exports 1963–5	Exports 1953–5	Imports 1963–5	Imports 1953–5
9. NON-FERROUS MINERALS AND METALS						
Asbestos, manufactured	—	—	—	—	0.30	0.76
10. CHEMICALS n AND FERTILIZERS						
Chemicals	—		—		na	
Fertilizers: Potash	—	—	—	—	0.7	—

n data not available for years 1953–5.

	Production 1963–5	Production 1953–5	Exports 1963–5	Exports 1953–5	Imports 1963–5	Imports 1953–5
11. INDUSTRY						
Alcoholic beverages			—	—	0.7 a	1.3 a
beer b	280.0	155.7				
Cement	144.0	76.7*	1.7	9.7	3.7	1.0
Electrical engineering a	—	—	—	—	8.4	2.3[2]
Merchant ships g	—	—	—	—	157.0	na
Motor vehicles a	—	—	—	—	11.5	4.5

a million $ U.S. *b* '000 hectolitres. *g* '000 G.R.T.

PARAGUAY

Paraguay has a long history of dictatorships and conflicts with neighbouring countries which has resulted in one of the poorest economies in South America. In the last thirty years there has been a tendency towards a more democratic type of government.

AREA: 406 752 sq. km. (157 042 sq. miles)

LAND USE: (percentage of total)	*1964*	*1954*
Arable and orchard	2.2	1.3
Permanent meadow and pasture (mainly rough grazing)	24.3	1.7
Forest and woodland	51.0	49.2
City areas, waste and other land	22.5	47.8

POPULATION: 2 161 000 (1967 estimate)

Largest city: ASUNCIÓN, capital; population: 305 160 (city proper, 1962)

Distribution of working population (1962)

Total working population: 616 640* (excl. Indian jungle population)

U.N. group no.		*Percentage*
0	Agriculture, forestry, fishing and hunting	52.2
1	Mining and quarrying	0.1
2/3	Manufacturing	15.2
4	Construction	3.0
5	Electricity, gas, water and sanitary services	0.2
6	Commerce	6.8
7	Transport, storage and communications	2.4
8	Services	16.7
9	Others	3.4

		Year(s)
Infant mortality (per '000)	41.5*	1965
Crude birth rate (per '000)	43.5*	1960–5 av.
Crude death rate (per '000)	13*	1960–5 av.
Population per physician	1 850	1965
Population per hospital bed	500	1966
School enrolment: age 5–19 years (percentage)	65	1963–4 av.
age over 19 years (per 100 000 population)	192	1964

COMMUNICATIONS		*Year(s)*
Motor vehicles in use ('000s): private	4.8	1963–5 av.
commercial	5.0	1963–5 av.
Railway track (km.)	1 147	1964
Mail per capita: domestic	2	1964
foreign received	3	1964
foreign sent	1	1964
Telephones (per '000 urban population)	0.8	1967
Radio receivers (per '000 population)	86	1963–5 av.
Daily newspapers (per '000 population)	37	1959

FINANCE

Currency unit: The guarani

Exchange rates	*1965*	*1960*	*1950 a*	*1938*
Per $ U.S.	126	126	3.12	2.79
Per £ sterling	352.8	352.8	8.74	12.83

		Year(s)
National Income (million $ U.S.)	378	1965
G.N.P. per capita ($ U.S.)	200	1966
Rate of increase of G.N.P. per capita	1	1960–3 av.
Foreign trade (percentage of G.D.P.)	23	1963–5 av.

a principal import rate.

TRADING

Total trade (in million $ U.S.)	*1965*	*1955*	*1938*
Exports (f.o.b.)	57	35	7
Imports (c.i.f.)	47	29	8

Main trading partners (percentage of total value)

Exports	*1965*	*1955*	*Imports*	*1965*	*1955*
Argentina	26	46	U.S.A.	21	14
U.S.A.	25	18	Argentina	21	43
U.K.	11	9	Germany F.R.	19	4
Spain	5	1	U.K.	6	7
Netherlands	5	4	Japan	6	na
Uruguay	4	3	Neths. Antilles	6	6

Distribution of trade (percentage of total value)

Exports	*1965*	*1955*
Food	43	12
(meat)	(33)	(6)
(coffee)	(6)	(—)
Wood	17	37
Cotton	8	16
Vegetable oils	8	5*
Tobacco	7	3
Quebracho extract	na	16
Imports		
Manufactured goods	64	na
(machinery and transport equipment)	(38)	(na)
Food	14	15
Mineral fuels	10	2
Chemicals	5	20

PRODUCTION, EXPORTS AND IMPORTS

Years: **1963–5 average** and *1953–5 average* Units: '000 metric tons unless otherwise indicated

	Production 1963–5	Production 1953–5	Exports 1963–5	Exports 1953–5	Imports 1963–5	Imports 1953–5
1. CEREALS, etc.						
Cassava	1 320.3	940.0[1]				
Maize (corn)	160.0	110.0	7.2	—[1]	—	—
Millets/sorghum	3.7	na	—	0.7[2]	—	—[2]
Oats	—	—	—	—	0.1	—
Potatoes	7.3*	5.0	—	—	2.1	na
Rice	19.3	19.0*	—	na	—	na
Sweet potatoes/yams	86.7	75.0[1]				
Wheat	8.3	2.0	—	—	73.0	55.5*
2. FRUIT, etc.						
Apples	—	—	—	—	0.8[2] n	—
Bananas	197.0*	na	2.7	—	—	—
Lemons	2.7*	na	0.1	na	—	—
Oranges	159.0	200.0*	0.1	0.1[2]	—	—
Other citrus fruit	24.3	12.0*	3.3	na	—	—
Pineapples	10.0*	na	—	—	—	—
Wine b	—	—	—	—	3.3	na

b '000 hectolitres. *n* incl. pears and quince.

	Production 1963–5	Production 1953–5	Exports 1963–5	Exports 1953–5	Imports 1963–5	Imports 1953–5
3. BEVERAGES, FOREST PRODUCTS, etc.						
Coffee	6.8	0.1	5.5	—	—	na
Sugar: cane	885.3	321.7				
raw	42.9	15.3	3.2	—	—	—
Tobacco: leaf	17.1	7.7	12.5	2.9	—	—
cigars	na	6.4 e	—	—	—	—
cigarettes	10.0 e	513.7 e	—	—	—	—
Hardwood j q	1 720.0*[1]	2 905.0[2]	266.0	190.6	—	—
Newsprint	—[2]*	—	—	—	1.1[1]	0.8
Other paper	0.7[2]*	—	—	—	1.4[1]	0.8[1]

e no. in millions. *j* '000 cu. metres of roundwood equivalent. *q* Quebracho trees are also grown for their medicinal bark.

	Production 1963–5	Production 1953–5	Exports 1963–5	Exports 1953–5	Imports 1963–5	Imports 1953–5
4. VEGETABLE OILSEEDS AND OILS						
Castor seed	13.00	1.02[2]	12.19	—	—	—
Castor oil	na	na	0.08	0.48*	—	—
Coconut oil	na	—	3.29	—	—	—
Cottonseed	24.00	23.67	—	—	—	—
Cottonseed oil	na	na	—	—	na	na
Groundnuts	8.87	7.00[2]	—	—	—	—

continued

	Production 1963–5	Production 1953–5	Exports 1963–5	Exports 1953–5	Imports 1963–5	Imports 1953–5
4. VEGETABLE OILSEEDS AND OILS—*continued*						
Olive oil	—	—	—	—	0.18[1]	na
Palm kernels	9.00*	na	—	—	—	—
Palm kernel oil	na	na	3.13	1.36[2]	—	—
Palm oil	5.43	2.40[1]	na	na	—	—
Soya beans	11.70	na	0.54	na	—	—
Tung oil	5.17	2.51	4.96	2.37	—	—
5. LIVESTOCK‡, ANIMAL PRODUCTS, etc.						
Chickens d	5 641.0*	3 790.0[1]				
Cattle d	5 725.3	4 167.7	—	—	0.1[2]	na
Goats d	53.0*	68.0[1]	—	—	—	—
Sheep d	401.3	220.0[2]	—	—	—	—
Horses d	612.0	345.5[2]				
Pigs d	693.0*	na	—	—	—	—
Meat‡ 'A'	133.7*	91.0[1]	na	na	—	—
'B'	na	na	na	na	—	—
Butter	—	—	—	—	0.1	—
Cheese	—	—	—	—	0.1	na
Eggs	10.7*	9.2[1]*	—	—	—	—
Fish	0.7[1]	0.4[2]	—	—	—	—
Milk	81.7	126.0[2]	—	—	11.8	—
Hides/skins	na	13.6[2]	7.9 p	0.4 e	—	—

d no. in thousands. *e* no. in millions. *p* skins of cattle and wild animals only.

	Production 1963–5	Production 1953–5	Exports 1963–5	Exports 1953–5	Imports 1963–5	Imports 1953–5
6. FIBRES, TEXTILES, etc.						
Cotton: lint	13.0	12.7*	9.2	11.6	—	—
yarn	1.2[2]	na	—	—	—	—
woven fabrics	1.9	na	—	—	—	—
Wool, woven fabrics	0.1	na	—	—	—	—
7. FUEL AND POWER						
Electricity h t	130	60[1]				
Petroleum, refined	—	—	—	—	147	na

h million kWh. *t* thermal.

	Production 1963–5	Production 1953–5	Exports 1963–5	Exports 1953–5	Imports 1963–5	Imports 1953–5
11. INDUSTRY						
Beer b	74.0	53.4	—	—	—	—
Cement	23.7	7.3	—	—*	1.0	4.0
Merchant ships g	—	—	—	—	0.2	—
Motor vehicles a	—	—	—	—	2.9	na

a million $ U.S. *b* '000 hectolitres. *g* '000 G.R.T.

PERU

SOUTH AMERICA

Peru is a republic. The constitution has been frequently amended, and a military junta seized power in 1968. There have been a number of frontier disputes with Ecuador and Bolivia, and guerillas are active.

AREA: 1 285 215 sq. km. (495 733 sq. miles)

LAND USE: (percentage of total)	*1964*	*1955*
Arable and orchard	2.0	1.4
Permanent meadow and pasture (mainly rough grazing)	21.7	9.6
Forest and woodland (includes unstocked land)	67.7	56.0
City areas, waste and other land	8.6	33.0

POPULATION: 12 385 000*a* (1967 estimate)

Largest city: LIMA, capital; population: 1 833 700 (1966)

Distribution of working population (1961)
Total working population: 3 124 579*a*

U.N. group no.		*Percentage*
0	Agriculture, forestry, fishing and hunting	49.7
1	Mining and quarrying	2.1
2/3	Manufacturing	13.2
4	Construction	3.4
5	Electricity, gas, water and sanitary services	0.3
6	Commerce	9.0
7	Transport, storage and communications	3.0
8	Services	15.3
9	Others	4.0

		Year(s)
Life expectancy at birth (years): male	52.6	1960–5 av.
female	55.5	
Infant mortality (per '000)	95.2**a*	1965
Crude birth rate (per '000)	44.5**a*	1960–5 av.
Crude death rate (per '000)	13**a*	1960–5 av.
Accidental deaths (per 100 000 population)		
caused by motor vehicles	3.5	1964
due to other causes	24.3	1964
Population per physician	1 560	1965
Population per hospital bed	410	1965
School enrolment: age 5–19 years (percentage)	68	1964
age over 19 years (per 100 000 population)	423	1963

a excl. Indian jungle population.

COMMUNICATIONS		*Year(s)*
Motor vehicles in use ('000s): private	130	1963–5 av.
commercial	92.6	
Railway track (km.)	2 654	1960
Telephones (per '000 urban population)	1.2	1967
Radio receivers (per '000 population)	184	1963–5 av.
Television sets (per '000 population)	15.8	1963–5 av.
Daily newspapers (per '000 population)	47	1959

FINANCE

Currency unit: The sol

Exchange rates	*1965*	*1960*	*1950*	*1938*
Per $ U.S.	26.82	26.76	14.95	4.7*a*
Per £ sterling	75.1	74.93	41.88	23.05

a official selling rate.

		Year(s)
National Income (million $ U.S.)	2 536	1965
G.N.P. per capita ($ U.S.)	320	1966
Rate of increase of G.N.P. per capita	3.4	1960–4 av.
Foreign trade (percentage of G.D.P.)	34	1963–5 av.

TRADING

Total trade (in million $ U.S.)	*1965*	*1955*	*1938*
Exports (f.o.b.)	666	268	76
Imports (c.i.f.)	719	300	59

Main trading partners (percentage of total value)

Exports	*1965*	*1955*	*Imports*	*1965*	*1955*
U.S.A.	34	36	U.S.A.	40	50
Germany F.R.	13	7	Germany F.R.	12	9
Japan	9	4	Japan	7	2
Netherlands	9	4	Argentina	7	5
U.K.	6	10	U.K.	5	9
Belg./Lux.	5	6	Canada	4	2
Italy	3	1	Italy	3	2

Distribution of trade (percentage of total value)

Exports	*1965*	*1955**	*1938**
Non-ferrous ores and metals	36	28	28
Textiles	19	25	7
Sugar	12	14	5
Petroleum and products	2	8	18
Imports			
Machinery and transport equipment	43	34	na
Food	15	13	9
Chemicals	10	10	7
Textiles	7	4	13

PRODUCTION, EXPORTS AND IMPORTS

Years: **1963–5 average** and *1953–5 average* Units: '000 metric tons unless otherwise indicated

	Production		Exports		Imports	
1. CEREALS, etc.						
Barley	**183.0***	*220.0*	—	—	**16.0**	—
Cassava	**478.3**	*214.7*				
Maize (corn)	**504.0***	*306.7*	**0.8**	*0.5*	**9.3**	*0.8*
Millets/sorghum	—	—	—	—	**0.5**	—
Oats	**2.3***	na	—	—	**3.9**	*0.1*
Potatoes	**1 486.0***	*1 409.0*	—	—	—	*0.1*[2]
Rice	**301.7***	*253.0**	—	*18.1*	**46.9**	—
Sweet potatoes/yams	**165.0***	*82.7*				
Wheat	**148.0**	*161.3*	—	—	**397.5**	*264.4*
2. FRUIT, etc.						
Apples	—	—	—	—	**10.1**	*1.4*
Bananas	na	na	**0.4**	*0.3*	**7.0**	na
Coconuts	na	na	**0.1**	—	**0.2***n*	—
Figs	**5.0***	na	—	—	—	—
Grapes	**56.3***	*46.5*[2]	—	—	**0.1**	—
Lemons	na	na	**0.1**	—	—	—
Oranges	**202.0***	na	**0.1**	—	**2.7**	*3.2*
Olives	**10.3***	*6.0*[1]	—	—	—	—
Pears	—	—	—	—	**1.2**	—
Raisins	—	—	—	—	**0.8**	*0.4*
Tomatoes	**35.3**	na				
Wine*b*	na	*101.7*	**0.1**	—	**2.2**	*1.0*

b '000 hectolitres. *n* desiccated.

	Production		Exports		Imports	
3. BEVERAGES, FOREST PRODUCTS, etc.						
Cocoa	**2.7**	*4.1*	**0.1**	*0.1*	**0.7**	—
Coffee	**51.5***	*10.4**	**39.0**	*5.4*	**0.5**	*0.2*
Sugar: cane	**7 799.7***	*5 955.5*[2]				
raw	**779.7***p*	*650.7*p*	**427.6**	*442.1*	—	—

continued

	Production		Exports		Imports	
3. BEVERAGES, FOREST PRODUCTS, etc.—*continued*						
Tea	**1.2***	*0.7*	**0.1**	—	**0.1**	*0.1*
Tobacco: leaf	**3.0**	*3.5*	—	—	—	*0.3*
cigars	—	*1.3e*	—	—	na	—
cigarettes	**1 971.0***e*	*2 436.3e*	—	—	na	—
tobacco/snuff	**0.5**	*0.7*	—	—	na	—
Softwood*j*	**11.0**[2]	na	**0.1**[2]	*0.2*	**143.4**	*126.2*
Hardwood*j*	**2 972.0***[2]	*1 651.7*	**10.4**[2]	*12.8*	**1.2**[2]	*4.5*
Wood pulp	—[2]	*12.0*[2]	—[2]	—	**17.5**[2]	*8.8*
Newsprint	—[2]	—	—[2]	—	**34.0**[2]	*9.5*
Other paper	**64.9**[2]	*24.0**	**0.1**[2]	*0.5*	**7.8**[2]	*8.2*

e no. in millions. *j* '000 cu. metres of roundwood equivalent. *p* in addition, chancaca 20* (1963–5 av.) and 27* (1953–5 av.).

	Production		Exports		Imports	
4. VEGETABLE OILSEEDS AND OILS						
Castor seed	**7.33***	*1.02*[2]	**0.45**	na	—	—
Castor oil	na	na	—	*0.04*	—	—
Coconut oil	—	—	—	—	**1.27**	*0.30*
Cottonseed	**237.70**	*168.30*	na	*0.13*	—	—
Cottonseed oil	na	na	—	—	**0.40**	*0.27*
Groundnuts	**1.40**	*0.70*	—	—	**0.12**	—
Groundnut oil	na	na	—	—	**0.01**	*0.02*
Linseed	—	—	—	—	**0.01**[2]	—
Linseed oil	—	—	—	—	**0.17**	*0.29*
Olive oil	—	—	—	—	**0.19**	*0.24*
Palm kernels	—	—	—	—	**0.15**	—
Palm oil	—	—	—	—	**0.01**	—
Sesame seed	**0.20***	na	—	—	—	—
Soya bean oil	—	—	—	—	**7.36**	*0.01*
Sunflower seed oil	—	—	—	—	**2.05**	—
Tung oil	—	—	—	—	**0.01**	—

continued

na: data not available. — negligible or nil. [1] one year only. [2] two year average. * estimate. ‡ see appendix. † re-exports.

PRODUCTION, EXPORTS AND IMPORTS *continued*

	Production		Exports		Imports	
5. LIVESTOCK‡, ANIMAL PRODUCTS, etc.						
Chickens*d*	**21 825.3***q*	*11 135.0q*				
Cattle*d*	**3 784.7**	*3 359.0*	—	—	**82.5**	*19.3*
Goats*d*	**4 033.0**	*2 257.7*	—	—	**6.7**	na
Sheep*d*	**15 589.0**	*16 305.0*				
Horses*d*	**1 173.7**	*532.0*				
Pigs*d*	**1 727.0**	*1 321.7*	—	—	—	—
Meat‡: 'A'	**161.0***	*105.7*	—	—	**6.8**	*5.4*
'B'	**20.3***	na	—	—	**4.8**	*0.2*
Butter	**3.0***	*2.0*[2]	—	—	**5.6**	*1.5*
Cheese	**8.7***	*9.0*[2]	—	—	**1.2**	*0.6*
Eggs	**20.0**	*5.6*	—	—	—	—
Fish	**7 885.8**	*198.7*	**1 455.5**	*31.5**	**0.8**	*0.5*[1]*
Milk	**491.0**	*388.0*[2]	**0.1**	—	**96.1**	*40.4*
Whale oil	**7.6**	na	—	—	—	—
Hides/skins	na	na	**1.2**[1]*a*	*1.7*[2]	**0.5**[1]*a*	—
Wool	**6.1***	*4.7*	**2.2**	*0.8*	—	—

a million $ U.S. *d* no. in thousands. *q* incl. ducks, geese and turkeys.

	Production		Exports		Imports	
6. FIBRES, TEXTILES, etc.						
Agaves (sisal etc.)	—	—	—	—	**0.8**	—
Cotton lint	**142.7**	*106.7*	**116.4***	*57.4*	—	—
Jute	**3.3***	—	—	—	**0.3**[2]	—
Rubber, natural	**2.9***r*	*3.1r*	—	*0.4*	**2.0**	—
Cotton: yarn	**17.6**	na	—	—	—	—
woven fabrics	**10.9**[2]*	na	—	—	—	—
Rayon, fibre/yarn	**1.5**	*0.9*	—	—	**4.1**	—
Non-cellulosic fibre/yarn	**0.5**	—	—	—	**2.6**	na
Wool: yarn	**4.4**	na	—[2]	—	—[2]	—
woven fabrics	**6.0***t*	na	—[2]	—	**0.1**[2]	*0.2*

r from plantations only. *t* million metres.

	Production		Exports		Imports	
7. FUEL AND POWER						
Coal 'A'‡	**137**	*140*	**11**	*18*	**1**	—
Coke	—	—	—	—	**6**	*1*
Electricity*h*: total	**3 649**	*1 480*[1]				
hydro	**2 411**	*850*[1]				
thermal	**1 238**	*630*[1]				
Natural gas*i*	**600**	*17*	—	—	—	—
Oil, crude	**3 153**	*2 410*[1]	**370**	*31*[1]	**93**	na
Petroleum, refined	**2 893**	*1 910*[1]	**107**	*570*[1]	**630**	*70*[1]

h million kWh. *i* million cu. metres.

	Production		Exports		Imports	
8. IRON AND STEEL						
Iron ore	**5 424***m*	*1 064m*	**5 776**	*1 505*	—	—
Pig iron	**25***t*	*—t*	—	—	**1**	*1*
Steel ingots/castings	**84**	—	—	—	—	—

m metal content. *t* excl. ferro-alloys.

	Production		Exports		Imports	
9. NON-FERROUS MINERALS AND METALS						
Gold*k*: ore*m*	**99.7**	*153.0*	**5.02**	*23.34*	—	—
bullion/coins etc.	na	na	**37.59**	*61.05*	—	—
Silver*k*: ore*m*	**35 364.0**	*21 001.7*	**14 184.95**	*8 662.24*	—	—
bullion	na	na	**19 898.47**	*9 736.58*	—	—
Asbestos: fibre	—	—	—	—	**3.35**	*1.30*
manufactured	na	na	**0.01**	*0.02*	**0.61**	*0.29*
Mica	—	—	—	—	**0.12**	*0.01*
Aluminium	—	—	—	—	**4.51**	*3.30*
Antimony, ore*m*	**0.65**	*0.89*	**0.85**	*1.03*	—	—

continued

	Production		Exports		Imports	
9. NON-FERROUS MINERALS AND METALS—*continued*						
Cadmium	**0.20**	*0.03*	**0.20**	*0.01*	—	—
Chrome, metal	—	—	—	—	—	*0.11*
Copper: ore*m*	**177.08**	*39.08*	**22.54**	*10.25*	—	—
metal	**156.06**	*27.17*	**152.40**	*26.63*	**2.09**	*1.03*
Lead: ore*m*	**151.40**	*114.47*	**65.24**	*47.17*	—	—
metal	**85.89**	*59.04*	**80.86**	*59.06*	**0.09**	*0.20*
Magnesium:	**1.42**	na	—	—	—	—
magnesite	—	—	—	—	**1.06**	*1.44*
metal/salts	na	na	na	*0.66*	**0.38**	*0.19*
Manganese, ore	**0.63**	*2.37*	**0.67**	*4.74*	—	—
Mercury*f*	**108.98**	*2.59*	**93.00**	*2.40*	**0.90**	*0.60*
Molybdenum*f*, ore*m*	**535.40**	*2.27*	**547.30**	*1.50*	—	—
Tin: ore*m*	**0.03**	—	—	—	**0.02**	—
metal	na	—	**0.03**	*0.01†*	**0.16**	*0.05*
Titanium minerals	—	—	—	—	**0.60**	*0.29*
Tungsten, ore	**0.65**	*0.83*	**0.41***m*	*0.54m*	—	—
Vanadium*m*	—	*0.20*	—	*0.19*	—	—
Zinc: ore*m*	**228.68**	*154.58*	**187.63**	*104.34*	—	—
metal	**59.90**	*13.78*	**55.57**	*14.60*	**0.66**	*0.49*

f metric tons. *k* '000 fine troy oz. *m* metal content.

	Production		Exports		Imports	
10. CHEMICALS*n* AND FERTILIZERS						
Organic chemicals:						
Benzene	na		na		na	
Butadiene	—		—		na	
Ethylene	—		—		na	
Methanol	na		—		na	
Phenol	—		—		na	
Phthalic anhydride	—		—		na	
Styrene monomer	—		—		na	
Urea	—		—		**0.7**	
Inorganic chemicals:						
Ammonia	na		—		—	
Carbon black	—		—		**1.9**[2]	
Chlorine	na		**0.2**[1]		na	
Nitric acid	**32.8**		—		**0.1**	
Sodium carbonate	—		—		**15.1**	
Sodium hydroxide	**8.0**		—		**10.5**	
Plastics:						
Polyamides	na		na		na	
Polyethylene	—		—		na	
Polyvinyl chloride	—		—		na	
Fertilizers:						
Phosphates	**187.2***p*	*281.4p*	—	—	**9.6**	*1.0*
Potash	—	—	—	—	**4.9**	*0.6*
Sulphur	—	*1.7*	—	*0.6*	**13.7**	*4.1*

n data not available for years 1953–5. *p* guano.

	Production		Exports		Imports	
11. INDUSTRY						
Beer*b*	**1 670.0**	*898.7*	—	—	—	—
Spirits*b*	**180.0**[1]**q*	na	—	—	—	—
Cement	**864.3**	*492.3*	—	*0.7*	**30.3**	*46.7*
Electrical engineering*a*	—	—	—[1]	—	**50.4**	*18.6*
Merchant ships*g*	**4.0**	na	—	—	**0.1**	—
Motor vehicles			—	—	**35.9**[1]*a*	*32.1a*
commercial*dr*	**1.0**	—				
private*dr*	**0.6**	—				

a million $ U.S. *b* '000 hectolitres. *d* no. in thousands. *g* '000 G.R.T. *q* production for home consumption in 1967. *r* assembly of imported parts.

PHILIPPINES

SOUTH EAST ASIA

The Philippines gained U.S. 'Commonwealth' status in 1934 followed by independence as a republic in 1946. An agreement with the U.S.A. guarantees certain military base facilities until 1974.

AREA: 299 400* sq. km. (115 600* sq. miles)

LAND USE: (percentage of total)	*1963*	*1953*
Arable and orchard	26.4	19.9
Permanent meadow and pasture	11.0	3.9
Forest and woodland	41.2	53.0
City areas, waste and other land	21.4	23.2

POPULATION: 34 656 000 (1967 estimate)

Largest city: MANILA; population: 1 402 000 (city proper, 1966)
Manila is the present (1971) capital, but QUEZON CITY, population 501 800 (city proper, 1966), a suburb of Manila, has been designated as the future capital.

Distribution of working population (1965)

Total working population: 10 543 000 (excl. armed forces)

U.N. group no.		*Percentage*
0	Agriculture, forestry, fishing and hunting	57.4
1	Mining and quarrying	0.3
2/3	Manufacturing	11.6
4	Construction	2.8
5	Electricity, gas, water and sanitary services	0.2
6	Commerce	10.6
7	Transport, storage and communications	3.5
8	Services	13.5
9	Others	0.1

continued

na: data not available. — negligible or nil. [1] one year only. [2] two year average. * estimate. ‡ see appendix. † re-exports.

PHILIPPINES *continued*

POPULATION—*continued*

		Year(s)
Life expectancy at birth (years): male	48.8*	1946–9 av.
female	53.4*	
Infant mortality (per '000)	72.9*	1965
Crude birth rate (per '000)	24.6*	1965
Crude death rate (per '000)	7.3*	1965
Accidental deaths (per 100 000 population)		
caused by motor vehicles	2.7*	1965
due to other causes	8.5*	1965
Population per physician	1 330	1966
Population per hospital bed	730	1966
School enrolment: age 5–19 years (percentage)	81*	1963–4 av.
age over 19 years (per 100 000 population)	1 315*	1963–4 av.

COMMUNICATIONS

		Year(s)
Motor vehicles in use ('000s): private	130.2	1963–5 av.
commercial	97.9	
Railway track (km.)	1 136	1963
Telephones (per '000 urban population)	0.6	1967
Radio receivers (per '000 population)	40	1963–5 av.
Television sets (per '000 population)	2.8	1963–5 av.
Daily newspapers (per '000 population)	17.5	1962–3 av.

FINANCE

Currency unit: The Philippine peso

Exchange rates	*1965 a*	*1960*	*1950 b*	*1938 b*
Per $ U.S.	3.92	2.015	2.015	2.006
Per £ sterling	10.98	5.644	5.644	9.228

		Year(s)
National Income (million $ U.S.)	7 091	1965
G.N.P. per capita ($ U.S.)	160	1966
Rate of increase of G.N.P. per capita	0.8	1960–4 av.
Foreign trade (percentage of G.D.P.)	30	1963–5 av.

a import rate. *b* selling rate with tax.

TRADING

Total trade (in million $ U.S.)	*1965*	*1955*	*1938*
Exports (f.o.b.)	794	413	116
Imports (f.o.b.)	835	534	132

Main trading partners (percentage of total value)

Exports	*1965*	*1955*	*1938*	*Imports*	*1965*	*1955*	*1938*
U.S.A.	48	60	78	U.S.A.	35	65	68
Japan	26	15	6	Japan	24	8	10
Netherlands	10	7	2	Germany F.R.	4	2	3 *d*
Germany F.R.	4	2	1 *d*	U.K.	4	2	2
Taiwan	2	—	—	Burma	4	na	na
Sweden	1	1	—	Canada	3	3	1
South Korea	1	1	—	Netherlands	2	2	2

Distribution of trade (percentage of total value)

Exports	*1965*	*1955*	*1938**
Crude materials and fuels	55	na	na
(copra)	(21)	(30)	(13)
(wood)	(19)	(10)	(2)
(metalliferous ores)	(10)	(7)	(na)
Food	26	na	44
(sugar)	(19)	(27)	(39)
(fruit and vegetables)	(4)	(5)	(na)
Coconut oil	8	4	9
Imports			
Manufactured goods	57	59	na
(machinery and transport equipment)	(31)	(19)	(15)
(textiles and clothing)	(6)	(17)	(20)
Food	20	19	14
(cereals)	(12)	(7)	(4)
Crude materials and fuels	13	11	na
(petroleum products)	(9)	(na)	(na)
Chemicals	9	8	na

d incl. Germany D.R.

PRODUCTION, EXPORTS AND IMPORTS

Years: **1963–5 average** and *1953–5 average* Units: '000 metric tons unless otherwise indicated

1. CEREALS, etc.

	Production		Exports		Imports	
Cassava	**618.7**	*284.0*[2]				
Maize (corn)	**1 328.7**	*810.7*	—	*0.1*	**0.8**	—
Millets/sorghum	—	—	—	—	**3.6**	—
Oats	—	—	—	—	**1.4**	—
Potatoes	**17.0**	*7.3*	—	—	**0.2**	*2.0*
Rice	**3 969.3**	*3 219.0*	**0.1**	*0.5*	**371.5**	*35.7*
Sweet potatoes/ yams	**736.7**	*768.3*				
Wheat	—	—	—	—	**396.2**	*273.2n*

n incl. wheat flour.

2. FRUIT, etc.

	Production		Exports		Imports	
Apples	—	—	—	—	**8.8**	*3.1*
Bananas	**713.0***	*239.3*	—	—	—	—
Coconuts	**7 124.7e**	na	**69.5p**	*47.9*	—	—
Grapes	—	—	—	—	**2.3**	*2.0*
Lemons	**9.0**	na	—	—	—	—
Oranges	**34.0**	*12.7*	—	—	**2.2**	*3.1*
Other citrus fruit	**21.7**	*16.3*	—	—	**0.1**	*0.1*
Pears	—	—	—	—	**0.3**	*0.5*
Pineapples	**160.7***	*100.7*	—	—	—	—
Raisins	—	—	—	—	**0.9**	*0.5*[2]
Tomatoes	**57.7**	*37.7*				
Wine *b*	—	—	—	—	**1.3**	*1.0*

b '000 hectolitres. *e* no. in millions. *p* desiccated.

3. BEVERAGES, FOREST PRODUCTS, etc.

	Production		Exports		Imports	
Cocoa	**3.7**	*1.7*	—	—	**5.3**	*0.9*
Coffee	**39.1**	*7.4*[2]	—	—	**0.4**	*1.5*
Sugar: cane	**12 776.7***	*12 726.3*				
raw	**1 630.8q**	*1 217.0q*	**1 110.6**	*877.5*	—	—
Tea	—	—	—	—	**0.3**	*0.1*
Tobacco: leaf	**59.5**	*32.0*	**27.6**	*9.5*	**1.2**	*9.8*
cigars	**85.0e**	*92.0e*	} —	—		
cigarettes	**23 001.0e**	*14 494.3e*	} —	—	—	*1.7*
tobacco/snuff	**0.9**	*0.4*	} —	—		
Softwood *j*	—	*121.7*	—	—	**0.4**	*0.1*
Hardwood *j*	**8 591.3***	*3 714.0*	**6 608.0**	*2 462.9*	—[2]	—
Wood pulp	—*	*5.0**	—	—	**21.1**[2]	—
Newsprint	—[2]	—	—	—	**43.5**[2]	*23.0*
Other paper	**127.3***	*10.0**	—	—	**53.4**[2]	*13.7*[1]

e no. in millions. *j* '000 cu. metres of roundwood equivalent. *q* in addition, muscovado and panocha 52* (1963–5 av.) and 77* (1953–5 av.).

4. VEGETABLE OILSEEDS AND OILS

	Production		Exports		Imports	
Castor seed	—	—	**0.07†**	—	na	*0.10**
Castor oil	—	—	—	—	**0.06**	*0.04*
Copra	**1 462.03**	*967.13*	**936.36**	*762.27*	—	—
Coconut oil	na	na	**223.00**	*66.12*	—	—
Cottonseed oil	—	—	—	—	**0.83**	*0.32*

continued

4. VEGETABLE OILSEEDS AND OILS—*continued*

	Production		Exports		Imports	
Groundnuts	**9.80***	*12.60*	**0.12**	*0.03*	—	—
Linseed oil	—	—	—	—	**1.74**	*0.54*
Olive oil	—	—	—	—	**0.06**	*0.04*
Palm kernel oil	—	—	—	—	**0.30**	—
Palm oil	—	—	—	—	**5.69**	*2.41*[2]
Sesame seed	—	—	—	—	—	*0.13*
Soya beans	**1.30***	—	—	—	**9.51**	*3.30*
Soya bean oil	na	na	**0.88**	—	**0.55***	—
Tung oil	—	—	—	—	**0.10**	—

5. LIVESTOCK‡, ANIMAL PRODUCTS, etc.

	Production		Exports		Imports	
Chickens *d*	**52 400.3**	*44 893.0*				
Cattle *d*	**1 380.0**	*793.0*	—	—	**2.9**	*3.7*
Goats *d*	**4 544.0**	*407.0*	—	—	—	—
Sheep *d*	**14.0***	*21.7*	—	—	—	—
Horses *d*	**242.3**	*206.0*				
Pigs *d*	**6 596.0**	*5 238.0*	—	—	**0.3**	*0.1*[2]
Bacon/ham	} **199.7***	*58.0r*	—	—	—	*0.1*
Meat‡ 'A'	}		—	—	**2.1**	*1.8*
'B'	**33.0**	*39.7*[1]	—	—	**0.2**	*0.1*
Butter	—	—	—	—	**2.6**	*0.8*
Cheese	—	—	—	—	**2.1**	*1.3*
Eggs	**64.8**	*49.2**	—	—	—	—
Fish	**624.9**	*353.9*	**0.3**	*0.8*[1]*	**50.5**	*31.2*[1]*
Milk	**41.7***	na	—	—	**420.6**	*229.9*

d no. in thousands. *r* government inspected meat only.

6. FIBRES, TEXTILES, etc.

	Production		Exports		Imports	
Abaca	**112.5**	*116.0**	**106.2**	*106.4*	—	—
Agaves (cantala)	**2.5***	*0.8*[2]	—	—	—	—
Cotton lint	—	—	—	—	**31.0**	*2.5*
Jute	—	—	—	—	**5.6**	—
Rubber, natural	**5.7**	*1.3*	—	*0.2*	**6.2**	—
Silk *f*	—	—	—	—	**1.3**	*9.3*
Cotton: yarn	**10.2**	*0.6*	—	—	—	—
woven fabrics	**17.3***	*1.6*	—	—	**10.0**[2]*	na

f metric tons.

7. FUEL AND POWER

	Production		Exports		Imports	
Coal 'A'‡	**120**	*130*	—	—	—	—
Coke	—	—	—	—	**16**	*5*
Electricity *h*: total	**4 596**	*1 190*				
hydro	**1 500**	*380*				
thermal	**3 096**	*810*				
Oil, crude	—	—	—	—	**4 123**	na
Petroleum, refined	**4 147**	*600*[1]	**133**	—	**120**	*1 570*[1]

h million kWh.

8. IRON AND STEEL

	Production		Exports		Imports	
Iron ore	**809m**	*788m*	**1 407**	*1 309*	—	—
Pig iron	—	—	—	—	**17**	*1*[2]
Steel ingots/castings	—	—	—	—	**67**	—
Iron/steel scrap	na	na	—[2]	*12*	—	—

m metal content.

continued

PRODUCTION, EXPORTS AND IMPORTS *continued*

9. NON-FERROUS MINERALS AND METALS

	Production		Exports		Imports	
Gold *k*: ore *m*	**413.00**	*438.60*	**54.80t**	*22.90*	—	—
bullion/coins etc.	na	na	**310.41**	*56.48*	—	*139.22*[2]
Silver *k*: ore *m*	**893.30**	*533.70*	**370.47**	*39.53*	—	—
bullion	na	na	—	*0.93*	—	—
Asbestos: fibre	—	—	—	—	**1.51**	*0.63*
manufactured	**0.31**	—	—	—	**0.28**	*1.29*
Mica	—	—	—	—	**0.06**	—
Aluminium	—	—	—	—	**9.99**	*2.55*[2]
Antimony, metal	—	—	—	—	—	*0.01*
Chrome, ore	**493.91m**	*517.75m*	**538.79**	*486.36*	—	—
Copper: ore	**62.49m**	*14.84m*	**269.23**[2]	*74.79*	—	—
metal	na	na	**1.05**[2]	*0.13*	**4.41**	—
Lead, ore	**0.09m**	*2.19m*	—	*2.25*	**3.06u**	*0.93*[2]*u*
Magnesium:						
dolomite	**5.15**	na	—	—	**2.94**	—
magnesite	—	—	—	—	**0.48**	—
metal/salts	—	—	—	—	**0.33**	—
Manganese, ore	**22.47**	*14.27*	**9.89**	*18.02*	—	—
Mercury	**86.54**	*7.30*	**64.20**	—	**0.40**	*0.80*[2]
Molybdenum *f*, ore	**96.31m**	—	**199.10**	—	—	—
Nickel, ore	—	—	**0.02**[2]†	—	**0.04**	—
Tin, metal	—	—	—	—	**1.94**	*0.12*
Titanium minerals	—	—	—	—	**3.20**	—
Zinc, ore	**2.70m**	*0.25m*	**6.92**	*0.48*	**12.33u**	*1.02u*

f metric tons. *k* '000 fine troy oz. *m* metal content. *t* exports to the U.S.A. only. *u* metal.

10. CHEMICALS*n* AND FERTILIZERS

	Production		Exports		Imports	
Organic chemicals:						
Benzene	—		—		na	
Butadiene	—		—		na	
Ethylene	—		—		na	
Methanol	na		—		na	
Phenol	—		—		na	
Phthalic anhydride	—		—		na	
Styrene monomer	—		—		na	
Urea	—		—		na	

continued

10. CHEMICALS*n* AND FERTILIZERS—*continued*

	Production		Exports		Imports	
Inorganic chemicals:						
Ammonia	na		—		**30.3**	
Carbon black	na		—		**4.6**	
Chlorine	na		—		—	
Nitric acid	—		—		**0.2**	
Sodium carbonate	na		na		na	
Sodium hydroxide	**12.0**		—		**18.9**[2]	
Sulphuric acid	**38.0**		—		**0.1**	
Plastics:						
Polyamides	—		—		na	
Polyethylene	—		—		**3.7**	
Polyvinyl chloride	—		—		**3.1**	
Fertilizers:						
Phosphates	**3.6p**	*1.0p*	—	—	**29.6**	—
Potash	—	—	—	—	**35.2**	*1.2*
Pyrites	**32.5x**	*5.5x*	—	—	—	—
Sulphur	**0.1**	*1.9**	—	—	**9.6**	*5.8*

n data not available for years 1953–5. *p* incl. guano. *x* sulphur content.

11. INDUSTRY

	Production		Exports		Imports	
Beer *b*	**1 236.0**[2]	*517.0*	—	—	—	—
Cement	**1 243.0***	*350.7*	—*	—	**166.0***	*49.3*
Electrical engineering *a*	—	—	—	—	**41.4**	*17.6*
Railway vehicles *a*	—	—	—	—	**2.5**	na
Merchant ships *g*	—	na	—	—	**10.0**	*5.6*[1]
Motor vehicles			—	—	**58.7a**	*15.9a*
commercial *dq*	**6.2**	*3.1*				
private *dq*	**7.0**	*1.0*				

a million $ U.S. *b* '000 hectolitres. *d* no. in thousands. *g* '000 G.R.T. *q* assembly of imported parts.

POLAND

EUROPE

Poland was overrun by Germany from the west and the U.S.S.R. from the east in 1939, and liberated, with certain adjustments to territory, in 1945. In 1947 a communist government was established. An uprising in 1956 was quashed, and further unrest in 1968 led to government purges. Poland is a member of Comecon.

AREA: 311 730 sq. km. (120 359 sq. miles)

LAND USE: (percentage of total)	*1965*	*1955*
Arable and orchard	50.3	52.0
Permanent meadow and pasture	13.7	13.4
Forest and woodland	25.8	23.8
City areas, waste and other land	10.2	10.8

POPULATION: 31 944 000 (1967 estimate)

Largest city: WARSZAWA (Warsaw), capital; population: 1 261 300 (1966)

Distribution of working population (1960)

Total working population: 13 967 442	*Percentage*
Agriculture, forestry, fresh-water fishing and hunting	47.7
Mining and quarrying, sea fishing, manufacturing, gas and electricity services	23.3
Construction	5.7
Commerce	5.8
Transport, storage and communications	4.8
Services, water and sanitary services, and others	12.7

		Year(s)
Life expectancy at birth (years): male	67.5	1963–5 av.
female	72.9	
Infant mortality (per '000)	41.7	1965
Crude birth rate (per '000)	17.3	1965
Crude death rate (per '000)	7.4	1965
Accidental deaths (per 100 000 population)		
caused by motor vehicles	8.0	1965
due to other causes	30.8	1965
Population per physician	800	1965
Population per hospital bed	130	1966
School enrolment: age 5–19 years (percentage)	90	1963–4 av.
age over 19 years (per 100 000 population)	771	1964–5 av.

COMMUNICATIONS

		Year(s)
Motor vehicles in use ('000s): private	215.0	1963–5 av.
commercial	173.5	
Railway track (km.)	26 886	1964
Mail per capita: domestic	30	1960
foreign received	1	
foreign sent	1	
Telephones (per '000 urban population)	4.4	1967
Radio licences (per '000 population)	184	1963–5 av.
Television licences (per '000 population)	54.3	1963–5 av.
Daily newspapers (per '000 population)	148	1962–4 av.

FINANCE

Currency unit: The zloty

Exchange rates a	*1965*	*1960*	*1958*
Per $ U.S.	4.0	4.0	4.0
Per £ sterling	11.2	11.2	11.2

		Year(s)
National Income (million $ U.S.)	20 000*	1966
G.N.P. per capita ($ U.S.)	730*	1966
Rate of increase of G.N.P. per capita	4.8	1960–4 av.

a official rates; the tourist rate in 1970 was 24 zloty per $ U.S. (57.4 per £ sterling).

TRADING

Total trade (in million $ U.S.)	*1965*	*1955*	*1938*
Exports (f.o.b.)	2 228	920	225
Imports (f.o.b.)	2 340	932	248

Main trading partners (percentage of total value)

Exports	*1965*	*1955*	*1938*	*Imports*	*1965*	*1955*	*1938*
U.S.S.R.	35	31	—	U.S.S.R.	31	34	1
Czechoslovakia	9	8	4	Germany D.R.	12	13	23 *a*
Germany D.R.	7	14	24 *a*	Czechoslovakia	10	9	3
U.K.	6	9	18	Hungary	5	3	1
Germany F.R.	5	3	*b*	U.K.	4	5	11
Hungary	4	3	1	Germany F.R.	4	3	*b*
U.S.A.	3	na	5	Mexico	3	—	—

Distribution of trade (percentage of total value)

Exports	*1965*	*1955**	*1938**
Manufactured goods	48	19	na
(machinery and transport equipment)	(34)	(12)	(na)
Crude materials, fuels, minerals and metals	30	59	na
Foods	18	16	35
Chemicals and rubber	4	3	2
Imports			
Manufactured goods	40	35	na
(machinery and transport equipment)	(33)	(31)	(20)
Crude materials and fuels	39	49	na
Foods	13	13	11
Chemicals and rubber	8	3	na

a incl. Germany F.R. and Austria. *b* see Germany D.R.

continued

PRODUCTION, EXPORTS AND IMPORTS

Years: **1963–5 average** and *1953–5 average*   Units: '000 metric tons unless otherwise indicated

	Production		Exports		Imports	
1. CEREALS, etc.						
Barley	1 402.7	1 162.0[2]	58.9	27.3	401.7	1.1*
Maize (corn)	15.7	na	—	—	366.6	4.3
Millets/sorghum	29.0	na	0.3	1.0*	160.0	—
Oats	2 529.7	2 180.0[2]	—	12.5*	17.7	0.1*
Potatoes	45 330.3	31 341.5[2]	632.3	7.0*	0.5	1.0*
Rice	—	—	—	—*	73.8	13.4*
Rye	7 459.0	6 423.5[2]	—	—	136.4	397.3
Wheat	3 177.0 n	2 068.0	—	38.1*	1 754.4	389.0

n in addition, buckwheat 39.3.

	Production		Exports		Imports	
2. FRUIT, etc.						
Apples	472.3	123.0*[2]	17.8	—	4.6	0.4*
Bananas	—	—	—	—	0.9	—
Cherries	71.3	64.0	na	na	—	—
Dates	—	—	—	—	0.9	—
Grapes	—	—	—	—[2]	28.4	1.1*
Lemons	—	—	—	—	30.4	2.6*
Oranges	—	—	—	—	13.1	2.6*
Other citrus fruit	—	—	—	—	0.7	—
Pears	75.0	25.0[2]*	0.2	—	—	—
Plums	85.0	41.7	na	na	—	—
Raisins	—	—	—	—	1.8	0.4*
Tomatoes	284.0	na				
Wine b	—	—	0.4†	—	173.8	6.7*

b '000 hectolitres.

	Production		Exports		Imports	
3. BEVERAGES, FOREST PRODUCTS, etc.						
Cocoa	—	—	—	—	14.5 p	2.0*
Coffee	—	—	—	—	11.7	0.9*
Sugar: beet	11 849.7	7 039.0*				
raw	1 517.1	1 147.0*	422.9	365.0*	45.0	1.7*
Tea	—	—	—	—	5.1	1.2
Tobacco: leaf	73.3	27.8[2]*	2.8	—	17.2	6.4*
cigars e	65.0	28.0[1]	—	—	—	—
cigarettes e	55 606.0	34 154.3	—	—	—	—
tobacco/snuff	0.3	0.4[1]	—	—	—	—
Softwood j	14 228.7	15 656.0[2]	1451.0	573.9	198.0	—
Hardwood j	2 710.3	1 618.0[2]	22.3	17.3	30.4	3.4
Wood pulp	496.2	356.0[2]	—	2.0[2]	136.0	55.0[2]
Newsprint	77.0	70.0*	20.7	10.0[1]	0.3	—
Other paper	713.7	357.7*	18.0	7.0[1]	19.3	14.0[1]

e no. in millions. *j* '000 cu. metres of roundwood equivalent. *p* incl. cocoa paste.

	Production		Exports		Imports	
4. VEGETABLE OILSEEDS AND OILS						
Castor seed	—	—	—	—	0.20	—
Castor oil	—	—	—	0.02*†	2.00	—
Copra	—	—	—	—	0.68	3.50*
Coconut oil	—	—	—	—	6.97	1.39*
Cottonseed	—	—	—	—	0.17	—
Cottonseed oil	—	—	—	—	5.49	—
Groundnuts	—	—	—	—	26.82	—
Groundnut oil	na	—	—	0.01*†	0.06	0.15*
Linseed	64.33	na	0.03	0.03*	2.82	1.37*
Linseed oil	na	na	—	0.01*	14.98	0.32*
Olive oil	—	—	—	—	1.53	0.01*
Palm kernels	—	—	—	—	17.21	—
Palm oil	—	—	—	—	1.86	2.10*
Rapeseed	332.70	126.00*	22.06	0.13*	8.54	—
Rapeseed oil	na	na	1.43	—	2.61	—
Sesame seed	—	—	—	—	3.65	—[2]
Soya beans	—	—	—	—	29.98	—
Soya bean oil	na	—	—	—	20.39	—
Sunflower seed	—	—	—	—	2.33	—
Sunflower seed oil	na	—	—	—	6.74	—
Tung oil	—	—	—	—	2.62	2.18

	Production		Exports		Imports	
5. LIVESTOCK‡, ANIMAL PRODUCTS, etc.						
Chickens d	124 849	na				
Cattle d	9 909	7 661	68.7*	—	0.6	—
dairy cows d	6 249	na				
Goats d }	222	na }	14.1*	na	0.2	—
Sheep d }	3 046	3 914 }				
Horses d	2 589	2 644				
Pigs d	12 783	10 135	89.2*	36.7*	8.4*	—*
Bacon/ham }	1 646	na	{ 51.7	54.8*	—	—
Meat‡ 'A' }			{ 37.2	0.7*	38.4	0.2*
'B'	223	na	27.3	2.1*	—	—
Butter	163	61[2]	19 0	2.7*	5.2	2.5*
Cheese	169	11[2] q	1.4	—	0.4	—
Eggs	338	206[2]	40.2	18.3	—	—
Fish	263	117	16.7	na	67.9	na
Milk	12 855	9 761[2]	20.1	—	—	2.0*
Hides/skins	70	na	—	—	32.7	na
Wool	4	4*	—	—	16.0	7.5

d no. in thousands. *q* factory produce only.

	Production		Exports		Imports	
6. FIBRES, TEXTILES, etc.						
Abaca	—	—	—	—	0.4	—
Agaves (sisal etc.)	—	—	—	—	9.9	1.0
Cotton lint	—	—	—	—	139.2	65.3*
Flax fibre	51.8	52.8[2]	8.0	0.2*	6.6	3.1*
Hemp fibre	16.0	9.8[1]*	1.1	0.1*	—	—
Jute	—	—	—	—	22.3	15.1*
Rubber: natural	—	—	—	—	36.2	17.8*
synthetic	38.4	—	—	—	—	7.1[2]
Silk f	na	13.0*	—	—	—	—
Cotton: yarn	175.6	109.3*	—	na	—	na
woven fabrics	91.8	64.8*	16.9	na	1.4	na
Rayon: fibre/yarn	na	44.6	na	na	na	na
woven fabrics	14.8 r	na	23.6 s	na	na	na
Wool: yarn	63.0	50.8	na	na	na	na
woven fabrics	88.3 t	72.7 t	na	na	na	na

f metric tons. *r* incl. natural silk products. *s* incl. re-exports. *t* million metres.

	Production		Exports		Imports	
7. FUEL AND POWER						
Coal‡ 'A'	116 443	94 480	19 068	24 205	1 276	—
'B'	5 823	6 040	5 439	4 096[1]*	596	—
Coke	na	na	2 309	1 996	—	—
Electricity h: total	40 449	15 630[1]				
hydro	769	710[1]				
thermal	39 680	14 920[1]				
Natural gas i	1 200	390[1]	—	—	330	—
Oil, crude	297	200[1]	—	—	2 116	473*
Petroleum, refined	1 820	510[1]	680	—	2 463	712*

h million kWh. *i* million cu. metres.

	Production		Exports		Imports	
8. IRON AND STEEL						
Iron ore	925 m	511 m	—	—	9 055	3 869
Pig iron	5 599	2 711	30	—	392	—
Steel ingots/castings	8 555	3 993	na	na	na	na
Iron/steel scrap	na	na	—	—	2	—

m metal content.

	Production		Exports		Imports	
9. NON-FERROUS MINERALS AND METALS						
Silver k, ore m	129.00	97.00	—	—	—	—
Asbestos, fibre	—	—	—	—	25.19	—
Mica	—	—	—	—	0.89	—
Aluminium: bauxite	—	—	—	—	89.09	—
alumina	—	—	—	—	89.41	—
aluminium	47.22	11.48[2]*	—	—	—	—
Cadmium	0.42	0.23*	0.33	—	—	—
Chrome, ore	—	—	—	—	119.32	—
Cobalt	na	—	—	—	—	—
Copper: ore	14.27 m	4.87 m	—	—	15.96	—
metal	34.60	9.03	—	—	32.29	—
Lead: ore	39.40 m	38.50* m	8.14	—	—	—
metal	40.60	21.65	—	—	17.97	—
Magnesium:						
magnesite	35.53	na	—	—	135.95 u	—
kieserite	na	na	2.44	—	—	—
metal/salts	—‡	—‡	—	—	7.15	—
Manganese, ore	—	—	—	—	344.07	—
Mercury f	—	—	—	—	211.80	—
Molybdenum f, ore	—	—	—	—	226.20	—
Nickel, ore m	1.14	—	—	—	—	—
Tin, metal	—	—	—	—	2.53	—
Titanium minerals	—	—	—	—	3.50	—
Tungsten, ore	—	—	—	—	2.47	—
Zinc: ore	149.96 m	120.35* m	—	—	153.97	73.63
metal	186.15	145.57*	115.71[1]	98.79	—	—

f metric tons. *k* '000 fine troy oz. *m* metal content. *u* calcined and caustic.

	Production	Exports	Imports
10. CHEMICALS n AND FERTILIZERS			
Organic chemicals:			
Benzene	83.8[2]	33.3[2]	—
Butadiene	—	—	20.0
Ethylene	na	na	na
Methanol	61.4[2]	12.5[2]	—
Phenol	41.2[2]	3.7	—
Phthalic anhydride	13.0[1]	1.8[2]	—
Styrene monomer	na	—	1.3[1]
Urea	170.0[1]	3.0[2]	—
Inorganic chemicals:			
Ammonia	523.3	na	6.9[2]
Carbon black	16.8[2]*	3.5	2.6
Chlorine	88.4	1.8	—
Nitric acid	765.7	na	na
Sodium carbonate	605.1[2]	210.7[2]	16.2
Sodium hydroxide	223.7[1]	14.4[1]	—
Sulphuric acid	983.7	—	18.6[1]

n data not available for years 1953–5.

continued

na: data not available. — negligible or nil. [1] one year only. [2] two year average. * estimate. ‡ see appendix. † re-exports.

PRODUCTION, EXPORTS AND IMPORTS *continued*

	Production		Exports		Imports	
10. CHEMICALS n AND FERTILIZERS—*continued*						
Plastics:						
Polyamides	na		na		na	
Polyethylene	—		—		1.7[2]	
Polyvinyl chloride	22.8		2.5		9.5	
Fertilizers:						
Phosphates	82.3	na	—	—	997.7 p	—
Potash	—	—	1.8†	—	1 011.3	—
Pyrites	88.7*	56.8*	20.1[2]	—	24.3[1]	—
Sulphur	320.3	—	172.0	—	17.9	—

n data not available for years 1953–5. *p* incl. apatite.

	Production		Exports		Imports	
11. INDUSTRY						
Alcoholic beverages			na	na	—	—
beer b	7 523.0	5 131.3				
spirits b	945.0[1] p	1 474.0[1] q				
Cement	8 668.7	3 503.3	685.0[1]	366.7* r	321.0[1]	—[1] r
Electrical engineering	na	na	—	—	5.8	39.1[1]
Locomotives c	328.0 t	na	na	248.0[2]	na	na
Railway vehicles	na	na	73.0 au	2 938.0[2] c	—	—
Machine tools a	54.0[1]	na	na	5.4[1]	—	—
Merchant ships g	260.0	103.8[1] v	271.0[1]	na	14.0	na
Motor vehicles			7.1 a	na	21.7 a	na
commercial d	34.2	12.2				
private d	21.8	2.4				

a million $ U.S. *b* '000 hectolitres. *c* no. of units. *d* no. in thousands. *g* '000 G.R.T. *p* production for home consumption in 1967. *q* 1960 figure. *r* excl. trade with Eastern Europe, the U.S.S.R. and China P.R. *t* excl. narrow gauge. *u* freight and passenger cars only. *v* 1956 figure.

PORTUGAL

Portugal is a republic and a member of the European Free Trade Association. Data for Madeira and the Azores, which are considered integral parts of Portugal for administrative purposes, are included with statistics for Portugal.

AREA: 91 641 sq. km. (35 383 sq. miles)

LAND USE: (percentage of total)	*1963*	*1939*
Arable and orchard	49.2	38.0
Permanent meadow and pasture	6.0	16.7
Forest and woodland	28.1	27.7
City areas, waste and other land	16.7	17.6

POPULATION: 9 440 000 (1967 U.N. estimate)

Largest city: LISBOA (Lisbon), capital; population: 825 800 (city proper, 1966)

Distribution of working population (1960)

Total working population: 3 423 551

U.N. group no.		*Percentage*
0	Agriculture, forestry, fishing and hunting	42.3
1	Mining and quarrying	0.8
2/3	Manufacturing	20.3
4	Construction	6.7
5	Electricity, gas, water and sanitary services	0.4
6	Commerce	8.0
7	Transport, storage and communications	3.6
8	Services	14.6
9	Others incl. compulsory military service	3.3

		Year(s)
Life expectancy at birth (years): male	60.7	1959–62 av.
female	66.4	1959–62 av.
Infant mortality (per '000)	64.9	1966
Crude birth rate (per '000)	22.9	1965
Crude death rate (per '000)	10.3	1965
Accidental deaths (per 100 000 population)		
caused by motor vehicles	13.8	1965
due to other causes	27.7	1965
Population per physician	1 180	1965
Population per hospital bed	170	1966
School enrolment: age 5–19 years (percentage)	66	1963–4 av.
age over 19 years (per 100 000 population)	344	1963–4 av.

COMMUNICATIONS		*Year(s)*
Motor vehicles in use ('000s): private	193.5*	1963–4 av.
commercial	61.8*	1963–4 av.
Railway track (km.)	3 597	1964
Mail per capita: domestic	40	1963–5 av.
foreign received	8	1963–5 av.
foreign sent	9	1963–5 av.
Telephones (per '000 urban population)	6.3	1967
Radio licences (per '000 population)	123	1963–5 av.
Television licences (per '000 population)	16.4	1963–5 av.
Daily newspapers (per '000 population)	657*	1962–4 av.

FINANCE

Currency unit: The Portuguese escudo

Exchange rates	*1965*	*1960*	*1950*	*1938*
Per $ U.S.	28.83	28.83	28.95	23.67
Per £ sterling	80.82	80.82	81.10	108.9

		Year(s)
National Income (million $ U.S.)	3 233	1965
G.N.P. per capita ($ U.S.)	380	1966
Rate of increase of G.N.P. per capita	5.3	1960–3 av.
Foreign trade (percentage of G.D.P.)	38	1963–5 av.

TRADING

Total trade (in million $ U.S.)	*1965*	*1955*	*1938*
Exports (f.o.b.)	576	285	50
Imports (f.o.b.)	923	398	101

Main trading partners (percentage of total value)

Exports	*1965*	*1955*	*1938*	*Imports*	*1965*	*1955*	*1938*
U.K.	18	15	21	Germany F.R.	16	15	17 d
Angola	14	13	5	U.K.	13	14	17
U.S.A.	11	10	5	U.S.A.	8	10	12
Mozambique	8	7	5	Angola	8	5	5
Germany F.R.	8	8	13 d	France	8	8	6
France	5	5	8	Italy	5	3	2
Sweden	3	2	2	Mozambique	5	6	3

Distribution of trade (percentage of total value)

Exports	*1965*	*1955*	*1938**
Manufactured goods	54	37	na
(textiles and clothing)	(24)	(13)	(7)
(diamonds)	(6)	(—)	(—)
Food	17	20	na
(fish)	(9)	(12)	(16)
Crude materials and fuels	12	26	30
Wine	7	8	20
Chemicals	7	5	na
Imports			
Manufactured goods	51	49	na
(machinery and transport equipment)	(27)	(25)	(16)
(iron and steel)	(6)	(9)	(1)
Crude materials and fuels	26	31	53
(textile fibres)	(11)	(11)	(5)
(petroleum products)	(7)	(10)	(na)
Food	11	10	17

d incl. Germany D.R.

continued

na: data not available. — negligible or nil. [1] one year only. [2] two year average. * estimate. ‡ see appendix. † re-exports.

PORTUGAL *continued*

PRODUCTION, EXPORTS AND IMPORTS

Years: **1963–5 average** and *1953–5 average* Units: '000 metric tons unless otherwise indicated

1. CEREALS, etc.

	Production 1963–5	Production 1953–5	Exports 1963–5	Exports 1953–5	Imports 1963–5	Imports 1953–5
Barley	59.7	92.7	—	0.1	5.2	0.1
Maize (corn)	526.3	375.3	0.1	21.6	109.7	45.1
Millets/sorghum	—	—	0.1†	—	1.5	0.1
Oats	88.7	122.0	—	—	—	—
Potatoes	1 011.7	1 099.3	13.5	8.1	47.7	33.6
Rice	162.0	159.0	1.2	3.9	18.3	0.7
Rye	197.3	177.7	—	—	1.7	na
Sweet potatoes/yams	37.0[1]	na				
Wheat	558.7	659.7	—	8.7	257.0	99.0

2. FRUIT, etc.

	Production 1963–5	Production 1953–5	Exports 1963–5	Exports 1953–5	Imports 1963–5	Imports 1953–5
Apples	90.7	42.0*[2]	0.3	0.1	—	—
Apricots	7.3*	6.1	—	—	—	—
Bananas	—	—	—	2.4	6.0	0.1
Cherries	32.0	36.6	—	—	—	—
Figs	351.3*	na	—	3.5	—	—
Grapes	1 912.3	1 729.3*n	0.5	0.6	—	—
Lemons	10.3*	na	—	—	—	—
Oranges	101.0*	na	0.1	—	0.5	—
Other citrus fruit	2.0*	—	—	—	0.2	—
Olives	502.3	na	—	—	—	—
Peaches	43.7	23.7	—	—	—	—
Pears	56.0*	26.0[2]*	0.2	—	—	—
Pineapples	na	na	na	1.8p	—	—
Plums	36.7	18.0	—	—	—	—
Raisins	0.1*	0.1	—	—	—	—
Wine b	13 766.0	11 752.0	2 159.8	1 329.7	1.0	1.0

b '000 hectolitres. *n* excl. Madeira and the Azores. *p* from the Azores.

3. BEVERAGES, FOREST PRODUCTS, etc.

	Production 1963–5	Production 1953–5	Exports 1963–5	Exports 1953–5	Imports 1963–5	Imports 1953–5
Cocoa	—	—	—	—	2.0	0.8
Coffee	—	—	0.1†	—	12.5	9.4
Sugar: beet	105.3*	na				
cane	48.3*	na				
raw (beet)	9.2	9.7	—	—	171.2	116.0
(cane)	5.7					
Tea	0.1*	na	—	—	0.2	0.1
Tobacco: leaf	—	—	—	—	6.2	5.0
cigars	na	8.7e	—	—	—	—
cigarettes	6 378.0e	4 402.3e	—	—	—	—
tobacco/snuff	0.6	1.2	—	—	—	—
Softwood j	4 000.0	2 753.3	627.0	46.3	53.3	15.4
Hardwood j	1 933.3	2 256.0	4.7	0.2	70.5	32.9
Wood pulp	148.4	29.7	100.1	30.5	33.6	22.3
Newsprint	15.3	3.3	1.0	—	13.1	13.0
Other paper	117.7*	45.0	6.4	4.3	7.1	4.1

e no. in millions. *j* '000 cu. metres of roundwood equivalent.

4. VEGETABLE OILSEEDS AND OILS

	Production 1963–5	Production 1953–5	Exports 1963–5	Exports 1953–5	Imports 1963–5	Imports 1953–5
Castor seed	—	—	—	0.07†	0.78	2.30
Castor oil	—	—	—	—	0.05	—
Copra	—	—	—	—	12.03	7.17
Coconut oil	na	na	0.13	—	0.02	—
Cottonseed	—	—	0.04†	—	8.26	1.10
Cottonseed oil	na	na	—	—	0.11	—
Groundnuts	—	—	0.03†	0.03†	72.53	23.23
Groundnut oil	na	na	0.75	0.36	4.65	0.96
Linseed	—	—	—	—	3.61	0.53
Linseed oil	na	na	0.03	0.02	0.81	1.28
Olive oil	74.67	79.67	7.92	9.13	8.40	—*
Palm kernels	—	—	—	—	17.92	18.93
Palm kernel oil	na	na	0.44	na	0.63	na
Palm oil	—	—	0.01†	—	14.53	8.99
Rapeseed	—	—	—	—	0.02	—
Sesame seed	—	—	—	—	4.26	1.65[2]
Soya bean oil	—	—	—	—	0.25	—
Tung oil	—	—	—	—	0.15	—

5. LIVESTOCK‡, ANIMAL PRODUCTS, etc.

	Production 1963–5	Production 1953–5	Exports 1963–5	Exports 1953–5	Imports 1963–5	Imports 1953–5
Chickens d	8 160.0*	na				
Cattle d	1 087.0*	na	0.2	—	0.2	0.5[2]
Goats d	631.6*	na	33.6	na	0.2	—
Sheep d	5 097.3*	na				
Horses d	79.0*	na				
Pigs d	1 694.0*	na	—	1.3[2]	—	—
Bacon/ham	161.7	99.7q	0.2	0.5	0.1	—
Meat‡ 'A'			—	0.3	13.2	0.3
'B'	32.8*	31.4	—	—	—	—
Butter	2.0p	5.7p	0.3	0.5	0.5	—
Cheese	20.7	10.0p	1.4	0.5	0.3	—
Eggs	32.7	23.1	—	—	0.1	—
Fish	565.7	435.0	109.3	54.9[1]*	29.8	25.5[1]*
Milk	356.3	192.7	16.4	1.7*	1.3	—
Whale/sperm oil	2.8	3.0	—	—	—	—
Hides/skins	10.0[2]	7.1	—	0.2[2]	10.5	5.1[2]
Wool	5.0*	5.0	0.5	1.0	3.6	1.3

d no. in thousands. *p* factory produce only. *q* incl. meat equivalent of live imports.

6. FIBRES, TEXTILES, etc.

	Production 1963–5	Production 1953–5	Exports 1963–5	Exports 1953–5	Imports 1963–5	Imports 1953–5
Abaca	—	—	—	—	0.3	0.1
Agaves (sisal etc.)	—	—	0.1†	—	39.8	5.4
Cotton lint	—	—	—	0.2†	79.4	45.0
Flax fibre	0.2*	—	—	—	0.2	0.1
Hemp fibre	—	—	—	—	0.2	—
Jute	—	—	0.4†	—	24.0	6.8
Rubber: natural	—	—	—	—	5.9	3.7
synthetic	—	—	—	—	5.7	—
Silk f	—	—	—	—	0.7	—
Cotton: yarn	73.3	39.2	13.9n	1.5n	—	—
woven fabrics	41.3	30.6	28.1	13.8	0.7	0.3
Rayon: fibre/yarn	4.0	1.4	0.3[2]	—	9.4	5.9
woven fabrics	6.4p	1.8p	1.5p	0.1	0.1[1]	—
Non-cellulosic fibre/yarn	0.5	na	0.1	na	6.6	na
Wool: yarn	13.8[2]	4.7	0.4	—	0.1	—
woven fabrics	6.8	5.2	0.5	0.2	0.1	—

f metric tons. *n* incl. sewing and embroidery thread. *p* incl. synthetic fabrics.

7. FUEL AND POWER

	Production 1963–5	Production 1953–5	Exports 1963–5	Exports 1953–5	Imports 1963–5	Imports 1953–5
Coal‡ 'A'	430	400	—	3	431	499
'B'	53	90	—	—	—	
Coke	na	na	—	—	224	21
Electricity h: total	4 566	1 640				
hydro	4 068	1 390				
thermal	498	250				
Oil, crude	—	—	—	—	1 580	na
Petroleum, refined	1 530	870	190	210[1]	1 070	540[1]
Uranium	19f	na	—	—	494q	na

f metric tons. *h* million kWh. *q* radium salts, in milligrams.

8. IRON AND STEEL

	Production 1963–5	Production 1953–5	Exports 1963–5	Exports 1953–5	Imports 1963–5	Imports 1953–5
Iron ore	114m	75m	52	190	—	—
Pig iron	262	—	17	—	—	—
Steel ingots/castings	242	—	—	—	—	12
Iron/steel scrap	na	na	36	19	3	3
Iron/steel products a	na	na	6	1	49	32

a million $ U.S. *m* metal content.

9. NON-FERROUS MINERALS AND METALS

	Production 1963–5	Production 1953–5	Exports 1963–5	Exports 1953–5	Imports 1963–5	Imports 1953–5
Diamonds a	—	—	na	—	28.16u	12.11u
Gold k, ore m	21.70	21.00	—	—	—	—
Platinum group metals	—	—	—	—	1.58	0.16
Silver k: ore m	53.30	57.30	—	—	—	—
bullion	—	—	—	—	931.67	1 525.00
Asbestos: fibre	0.03	0.06	0.03	0.02	2.75	2.16
manufactured	na	na	0.56	—	0.39	0.06
Mica	—	—	—	—	0.13	0.03
Aluminium: bauxite	—	—	—	—	0.39	0.02
alumina	—	—	—	—	102.88n	—
aluminium	—	—	—	—	10.83	3.23
Antimony, ore	0.01m	—	—	0.01	—	0.03p
Beryl	0.02	0.34	0.05	0.31	—	—
Chrome, ore	na	0.01m	—	—	—	0.06p
Cobalt, metal	—	—	—	—	—	0.05
Copper: ore	4.00m	0.57m	0.79	—	0.01	0.02
metal	na	na	1.26	0.16	15.01	9.00
Lead: ore	0.19m	1.65m	—	—	—	—
metal	1.26	1.29	0.15	0.02	8.12	2.50
Magnesium: dolomite	4.09	na	—	—	—	—
magnesite	—	—	—	—	0.52	0.21
metal/salts	—	—	—	—	1.98	1.63
Manganese, ore	7.77	8.75	5.83	7.84	—	—
Mercury f	—	—	—	1.20†	14.20	8.11
Nickel, metal	—	—	—	—	0.15	0.04
Tin: ore	0.66m	1.38m	0.09	0.73	—	—
metal	0.63	0.73	0.27	0.06	0.03	—
Titanium minerals	0.06	0.66	—	0.81	2.40[2]	0.33
Tungsten: ore	1.68	4.77	1.22	4.06	—	—
metal	na	na	0.25	0.25	—	—
Zinc: ore	1.36	na	3.19	na	—	—
metal	na	na	0.08	0.07	8.61	3.72

a million $ U.S. *f* metric tons. *k* '000 fine troy oz. *m* metal content. *n* excl. hydrate. *p* metal. *u* imports from Angola only.

10. CHEMICALS*n* AND FERTILIZERS

	Production 1963–5	Production 1953–5	Exports 1963–5	Exports 1953–5	Imports 1963–5	Imports 1953–5
Organic chemicals:						
Benzene	—		—		na	
Butadiene	—		—		na	
Ethylene	—		—		na	
Methanol	na		—[2]		0.1	
Phenol	—		—		0.2	
Phthalic anhydride	—		—		0.5	
Styrene monomer	—		—		na	
Urea	15.0[2]		na		1.1	

n data not available for years 1953–5.

continued

PRODUCTION, EXPORTS AND IMPORTS *continued*

10. CHEMICALS*n* AND FERTILIZERS—*continued*

	Production 1963–5	Production 1953–5	Exports 1963–5	Exports 1953–5	Imports 1963–5	Imports 1953–5
Inorganic chemicals:						
Ammonia	na		—		5.1	
Carbon black	—		—		4.0[1]*	
Chlorine	na		—		na	
Nitric acid	111.2		—		—	
Sodium carbonate	0.3[1]		0.1		—	
Sodium hydroxide	na		0.2		0.1	
Sulphuric acid	412.7		6.3		0.1	
Plastics:						
Polyamides	na		na		na	
Polyethylene	—		—		na	
Polyvinyl chloride	4.5[1]		0.9*		0.3*	
Fertilizers:						
Phosphates	—	—	—	—	268.2	239.7
Potash	—	—	0.8†	—	28.1	10.4
Pyrites	279.8x	285.9x	296.4	380.1	—	—
Sulphur	10.5p	15.7[1]p	0.3	0.6	41.7	2.5

n data not available for years 1953–5. *p* recovered sulphur. *x* sulphur content.

11. INDUSTRY

	Production 1963–5	Production 1953–5	Exports 1963–5	Exports 1953–5	Imports 1963–5	Imports 1953–5
Aircraft a	—	—	—	0.1	3.0	1.9
Alcoholic beverages			38.1a	23.8a	na	0.3a
beer b	469.0	168.3				
spirits b	112.3[1]n	80.0[1]p				
Cement	1 638.7	772.3	267.7	152.0	1.0	0.3
Electrical engineering a	29.7[2]	na	5.8	0.7[2]	43.2	14.5[2]
Locomotives c	10.0	—				
Railway vehicles a	—	—	—	0.2†	1.4	2.2
Machine tools a	4.0[1]	na	—	—	—	—
Merchant ships g	3.0	6.0	na	17.3s	9.0	15.8
Motor vehicles			1.2a	0.3a	49.3a	24.8a
commercial dq	4.6	na				
private dq	16.9	na				

a million $ U.S. *b* '000 hectolitres. *c* no. of units. *d* no. in thousands. *g* '000 G.R.T. *n* 1967 figure. *p* 1960 figure. *q* assembly of imported parts. *s* incl. re-exports.

PORTUGAL (TERRITORIES)

In 1951 the former Portuguese colonies of Angola, Cape Verde Islands, Macao, Mozambique, Portuguese Guinea, Portuguese Timor, and São Tome and Principe were given the status of 'overseas territories' with financial and administrative autonomy. Customs duties with Portugal were abolished in 1964. The former Portuguese territories in India were incorporated into the Indian Union in 1961.

ANGOLA

CENTRAL AFRICA

AREA: 1 246 700 sq. km. (481 351 sq. miles)

LAND USE: (percentage of total)

	1953	1937
Arable and orchard	0.7	0.7
Permanent meadow and pasture	23.3	23.3
Forest and woodland	34.6	50.7
City areas, waste and other land	41.4	25.3

POPULATION: 5 203 000 (1967 estimate)

Largest city: LUANDA; population: 224 540 (1960)

Luanda is the present (1971) capital, but NOVA LISBOA has been designated as the new capital.

		Year(s)
Life expectancy at birth (years)	35a	1940
Infant mortality (per '000)	15.6*	1965
Crude birth rate (per '000)	22.2	1965
Crude death rate (per '000)	1.7*	1965
Accidental deaths (per 100 000 population)		
caused by motor vehicles	2.2*	1965
due to other causes	12.4*	1965
Population per physician	13 140	1964
Population per hospital bed	410	1966
School enrolment: age 5–19 years (percentage)	na	
age over 19 years (per 100 000 population)	10	1963–5 av.

a latest available figure.

EMPLOYMENT

The majority of the working population is engaged in subsistence farming and the processing of agricultural produce. Mining provides alternative employment and a small number are engaged in oil and copper refining.

COMMUNICATIONS

		Year(s)
Motor vehicles in use ('000s): private	39.0	1963–5 av.
commercial	16.2	
Railway track (km.)	3 256	1964
Mail per capita: domestic	4	1963–5 av.
foreign received	0.3	
foreign sent	0.2	
Telephones (per '000 urban population)	0.3	1967
Radio licences (per '000 population)	15	1963–5 av.
Daily newspapers (per '000 population)	8	1962–3 av.

FINANCE

Currency unit: The Portuguese escudo

		Year
National Income (million $ U.S.)	261	1958
G.N.P. per capita ($ U.S.)	170	1966

TRADING

Total trade (in million $ U.S.)	1965	1955	1938
Exports (f.o.b.)	200	98	15
Imports (c.i.f.)	195	93	10

Main trading partners (percentage of total value)

Exports	1965	1955	*Imports*	1965	1955
Portugal	35	23	Portugal	48	47
U.S.A.	23	23	U.K.	11	12
Netherlands	12	9	Germany F.R.	8	10
Germany F.R.	5	8	U.S.A.	8	14
France	4	3	France	4	2
Congo D.R.	3	2	Belg./Lux.	3	4
Belg./Lux.	2	3	Sweden	2	1

Distribution of trade (percentage of total value)

Exports	1965	1955
Food	61	64
(coffee)	(47)	(45)
Diamonds	16	12
Sisal	5	7
Oilseeds and vegetable oils	3	4
Imports		
Manufactured goods	37	32
(machinery and transport equipment)	(13)	(14)
(cotton piece goods)	(7)	(9)
Wine	8	9
Food	6	5

continued

ANGOLA *continued*

PRODUCTION, EXPORTS AND IMPORTS

Years: **1963–5 average** and *1953–5 average* Units: '000 metric tons unless otherwise indicated

1. CEREALS, etc.

	Production 1963–5	Production 1953–5	Exports 1963–5	Exports 1953–5	Imports 1963–5	Imports 1953–5
Cassava	1 340.0*	na				
Maize (corn)	385.3*	na	119.6	76.3	—	—
Millets/sorghum	na	—	1.9[2]	—	0.1[2]	—
Potatoes	—	—	0.3[2]†	0.4†	5.3	0.3
Rice	27.7*	na	1.8	1.1	1.5[2]	—
Wheat	13.0[2]	na	—	—	31.8	2.3

2. FRUIT, etc.

	Production 1963–5	Production 1953–5	Exports 1963–5	Exports 1953–5	Imports 1963–5	Imports 1953–5
Bananas	na	na	2.8[2]	—	—	—
Oranges	na	na	0.1[2]	0.1[2]	—	—
Wine *b*	—	—	0.8[2]†	—	732.7	417.0

b '000 hectolitres.

3. BEVERAGES, FOREST PRODUCTS, etc.

	Production 1963–5	Production 1953–5	Exports 1963–5	Exports 1953–5	Imports 1963–5	Imports 1953–5
Cocoa	0.3	—[1]	0.3	0.3	—	—
Coffee	174.0*	65.0*	145.3	58.7	—	—
Sugar: cane	733.3*	367.5[2]				
raw	65.7	44.0*	27.3	29.4	—	—
Tobacco: leaf	3.6*	na	1.8	0.5	0.4	0.1
cigarettes	1 540.0*e*	645.0*e*	0.1	—	—	—
tobacco/snuff	—	0.1				
Hardwood *j*	5 902.5[2]*	na	131.5[2]	60.0[1]	—	—
Wood pulp	21.8[2]	na	18.9[2]	—[2]	—[2]	—[1]
Paper	2.9[2]	—	—[2]	—[1]	2.5[2]	na

e no. in millions. *j* '000 cu. metres of roundwood equivalent.

4. VEGETABLE OILSEEDS AND OILS

	Production 1963–5	Production 1953–5	Exports 1963–5	Exports 1953–5	Imports 1963–5	Imports 1953–5
Castor seed	5.00*	4.06	1.29	2.73	—	—
Castor oil	na	na	0.17	1.01	—	0.01
Cottonseed	10.30*	12.50[2]*	1.13	10.00*	—	—
Cottonseed oil	na	na	0.11	—	0.01[2]	—
Groundnuts	22.63*	na	2.95	2.90	—	—
Groundnut oil	na	na	0.12[2]	—	0.04[2]	0.15
Linseed oil	—	—	—	—	0.10[2]	0.07
Olive oil	—	—	—	—	3.52	2.27
Palm kernels	16.34*	na	16.34	10.37	—	—
Palm kernel oil	na	na	1.68	—	—	—
Palm oil	18.33*	na	16.38	9.20	0.06	0.02
Sesame seed	1.00[1]*	na	1.53	0.33	—	—

5. LIVESTOCK‡, ANIMAL PRODUCTS, etc.

	Production 1963–5	Production 1953–5	Exports 1963–5	Exports 1953–5	Imports 1963–5	Imports 1953–5
Cattle *d*	1 383.3*	1 187.3	0.1	0.4	0.8[2]	0.1
Goats *d*	475.0*	448.3	—	—	—	—
Sheep *d*	129.7*	130.0	—	—	—	—
Horses *d*	1.0*	1.0[2]				
Pigs *d*	302.0*	257.3	—	0.1	—	—
Bacon/ham }	53.7*	6.0	—	—	0.1	—
Meat‡ 'A' }			2.1	0.4	—	—
Butter	—	—	—	—	0.2	0.2
Cheese	—	—	—	—	0.6	0.2
Eggs	1.6*	na	—	—	—	—
Fish	284.1	257.3	69.4	73.2[1]*	3.8	1.5[1]*
Milk	131.7*	na	—	0.2	—	3.5*
Hides/skins	na	na	1.0	1.5[2]	—	—

d no. in thousands.

6. FIBRES, TEXTILES, etc.

	Production 1963–5	Production 1953–5	Exports 1963–5	Exports 1953–5	Imports 1963–5	Imports 1953–5
Agaves (sisal etc.)	na	na	56.5	34·7	—	—
Cotton lint	5.3*	5.7*	4.1	3.8	—	—
Jute	2.0*	—	—	—	4.5	—
Rubber, natural	—	0.1[2]	—	—	0.2[2]	—
Cotton, woven fabrics	0.9	0.3	—	—	5.2	3.3

7. FUEL AND POWER

	Production 1963–5	Production 1953–5	Exports 1963–5	Exports 1953–5	Imports 1963–5	Imports 1953–5
Coal 'A'‡	—	—	—	—	15	26
Coke	—	—	—	—	5	—
Electricity *h*: total	na	49				
hydro	na	9				
thermal	264	40				
Oil, crude	783	—[1]	260	na	—	—
Petroleum, refined	493	—[1]	80	—	33	100[1]

h million kWh.

8. IRON AND STEEL

	Production 1963–5	Production 1953–5	Exports 1963–5	Exports 1953–5	Imports 1963–5	Imports 1953–5
Iron ore	511*m*	—[2]	825	—	—	—

m metal content.

9. NON-FERROUS MINERALS AND METALS

	Production 1963–5	Production 1953–5	Exports 1963–5	Exports 1953–5	Imports 1963–5	Imports 1953–5
Diamonds	1 129.33*l*	731.44*l*	28.16*a*	12.11*a*	—	—
Platinum group metals	na	na	na	na	—	—
Asbestos: fibre	—	—	—	—	0.99	0.63
manufactured	—	—	—	—	0.19	0.02
Mica	—	0.19	—	0.05	—	—
Aluminium	—	—	—	—	1.54	0.24
Copper: ore	na	2.15*m*	—	0.02	—	—
metal	0.10[1]	1.23	0.08	1.44	0.48	0.17
Lead, metal	—	—	—	—	0.15	0.04
Magnesium metal/salts	—	—	—	—	0.37	—
Manganese, ore	na	43.04	4.47	40.68	—	—
Mercury *f*	—	—	—	—	4.00	0.03
Vanadium	—	0.01*m*	—	—	—	—
Zinc, ore	—	0.03*m*	—	—	0.14*r*	0.13*r*

a million $ U.S. *f* metric tons. *l* '000 carats. *m* metal content. *r* metal.

10. CHEMICALS*n* AND FERTILIZERS

	Production 1963–5	Production 1953–5	Exports 1963–5	Exports 1953–5	Imports 1963–5	Imports 1953–5
Chemicals	—		—		na	
Fertilizers:						
Potash	—	—	—	—	1.1	—
Sulphur	—	—	—	—	0.4	0.1

n data not available for years 1953–5.

11. INDUSTRY

	Production 1963–5	Production 1953–5	Exports 1963–5	Exports 1953–5	Imports 1963–5	Imports 1953–5
Aircraft *a*	—	—	—	—	0.5[1]	0.1
Alcoholic beverages			—	—	13.7*ap*	10.2*a*
beer *b*	305.0	31.7				
Cement	217.7	47.0	55.7	—	2.3*	80.7
Electrical engineering *a*	—	—	—	—	2.1*q*	1.2[2]
Railway vehicles *a*	—	—	—	—	—[1]	1.3
Merchant ships *g*	0.4	—	—	—	—	—
Motor vehicles *a*	—	—	—	—	11.5	7.6[2]

a million $ U.S. *b* '000 hectolitres. *g* '000 G.R.T. *p* wine only. *q* incomplete figure.

CAPE VERDE ISLANDS

ATLANTIC OCEAN

AREA: 4 033 sq. km. (1 557 sq. miles)

LAND USE

The islands are mountainous and the climate poor, with very high temperatures and low seasonal rainfall. Agriculture is limited to small areas. Occasional earthquakes have been recorded and there is one active volcano.

POPULATION: 232 000 (1967 estimate)

Capital city: PRAIA; population: 13 142* (1960)

Distribution of working population (1960)

Total working population: 105 570*

U.N. group no.		*Percentage*
0	Agriculture, forestry, fishing and hunting	40.2
1	Mining and quarrying	0.2
2/3	Manufacturing	1.0
4	Construction	4.0
6	Commerce	1.3
7	Transport, storage and communications	1.2
8	Services	51.9
9	Others	0.2

		Year(s)
Infant mortality (per '000)	76.7	1965
Crude birth rate (per '000)	43.0	1965
Crude death rate (per '000)	10.6	1965
Accidental deaths (per 100 000 population)		
caused by motor vehicles	1.3	1965
due to other causes	20	1965
Population per physician	8 800	1964
Population per hospital bed	490	1966
School enrolment: age 5–19 years (percentage)	30	1963–4 av.

COMMUNICATIONS

		Year(s)
Telephones (per '000 urban population)	0.3	1967
Radio licences (per '000 population)	15	1963–5 av.

EMPLOYMENT, PRODUCTION AND TRADE

Agriculture and fishing are the main occupations of the people, the chief products being bananas, coffee, nuts, tuna and pozzolana. Trade is mainly with Portugal. Mindelo is an important bunkering station on the South Atlantic route from Europe to South America, and there is an air base on Sal.

continued

PRODUCTION, EXPORTS AND IMPORTS

Years: **1963–5 average** and *1953–5 average* Units: '000 metric tons unless otherwise indicated

1. CEREALS, etc.

	Production 1963–5	Production 1953–5	Exports 1963–5	Exports 1953–5	Imports 1963–5	Imports 1953–5
Barley	—	—	—	—	0.1	—
Maize (corn)	15.0*[1]	na	—	—	6.9	1.0
Potatoes	—	—	0.1[2]	0.1	0.4[2]	—
Rice	—	—	—	—	1.4	0.5
Wheat	—	—	—	—	—	0.2

2. FRUIT, etc.

	Production 1963–5	Production 1953–5	Exports 1963–5	Exports 1953–5	Imports 1963–5	Imports 1953–5
Bananas	na	na	3.0	na	—	—
Wine *b*	—	—	—	—	10.2	5.0

b '000 hectolitres.

3. BEVERAGES, FOREST PRODUCTS, etc.

	Production 1963–5	Production 1953–5	Exports 1963–5	Exports 1953–5	Imports 1963–5	Imports 1953–5
Coffee	na	0.2[2]	na	0.1	—	—
Sugar, raw	—	—	—	—	3.2	1.4
Wood *j*	—	—	—	—	3.0[2]	—

j '000 cu. metres of roundwood equivalent.

4. VEGETABLE OILSEEDS AND OILS

	Production 1963–5	Production 1953–5	Exports 1963–5	Exports 1953–5	Imports 1963–5	Imports 1953–5
Castor seed	na	na	0.04	1.40	—	—
Cottonseed oil	—	—	—	—	0.03	—
Groundnuts	na	na	0.32	na	—	—
Groundnut oil	na	na	—	—	0.07	na
Linseed oil	—	—	—	—	—	0.01[1]
Olive oil	—	—	—	—	0.14	0.04*

5. LIVESTOCK‡, ANIMAL PRODUCTS, etc.

	Production 1963–5	Production 1953–5	Exports 1963–5	Exports 1953–5	Imports 1963–5	Imports 1953–5
Cattle *d*	20.0*	9.5[2]	—	0.2	—	—
Goats *d*	na	38.0[2]	—	—	—	—
Sheep *d*	3.0*	2.5[2]	—	—	—	—
Horses *d*	1.0*	1.0[2]				
Pigs *d*	15.0*	11.0[2]	—	—	—	—
Fish	2.5[2]*n*	1.6*n*	1.5	na	—	—
Milk	—	—	—	—	0.2	—

d no. in thousands. *n* incomplete figure.

7. FUEL AND POWER

	Production 1963–5	Production 1953–5	Exports 1963–5	Exports 1953–5	Imports 1963–5	Imports 1953–5
Coal 'A'‡*n*	—	—	—	—	na	6
Electricity *ht*	na	—				
Petroleum, refined *n*	—	—	—	—	420	480[1]

h million kWh. *n* for bunkers. *t* thermal.

11. INDUSTRY

	Production 1963–5	Production 1953–5	Exports 1963–5	Exports 1953–5	Imports 1963–5	Imports 1953–5
Cement	8.3	—	—	—	—	—

MACAO

SOUTH EAST ASIA

AREA: 16 sq. km. (6 sq. miles)

POPULATION: 169 299 (1960 census)

Largest city: MACAU, capital; population: 161 252 (city proper, 1960)

Distribution of working population (1960)

Total working population: 41 533

U.N. group no.		*Percentage*
0	Agriculture, forestry, fishing and hunting	5.3
1/2/3	Mining, quarrying and manufacturing	30.1
4	Construction	3.5
5	Electricity, gas, water and sanitary services	1.2
6	Commerce	26.6
7	Transport, storage and communications	8.0
8	Services	23.5
9	Others	1.8

		Year
Crude birth rate (per '000)	14.6*	1965
Population per physician	3 720	1963
Population per hospital bed	160	1966
School enrolment: age 5–19 years (percentage)	93*a*	1963

a incl. pre-school education.

COMMUNICATIONS

		Year(s)
Telephones (per '000 urban population)	1.1	1967
Radio receivers (per '000 population)	21	1963–5 av.
Daily newspapers (per '000 population)	119	1962–3 av.

FINANCE

Currency unit: The Portuguese escudo; also the pataca for which the exchange rate in 1960 was about 5 per $ U.S. (14 per £ sterling)

TRADE

Trade is mainly transit trade by Portuguese, British and Dutch ships, and is handled by Chinese merchants. In 1963, 4 322 vessels, totalling 2 753 700 G.R.T., entered the port.

PRODUCTION, EXPORTS AND IMPORTS

Years: **1963–5 average** and *1953–5 average* Units: '000 metric tons unless otherwise indicated

1. CEREALS, etc.

	Production 1963–5	Production 1953–5	Exports 1963–5	Exports 1953–5	Imports 1963–5	Imports 1953–5
Maize (corn)	—	—	—	—	1.2	—
Millets/sorghum	—	—	—	—	0.5	—
Potatoes	—	—	—	0.1[2]†	1.1	1.9[2]
Rice	—	—	—	4.4†	21.0	28.4
Wheat	—	—	—	—	0.7	—

2. FRUIT, etc.

	Production 1963–5	Production 1953–5	Exports 1963–5	Exports 1953–5	Imports 1963–5	Imports 1953–5
Wine *b*	—	—	—	—	3.2	7.0[1]

b '000 hectolitres.

3. BEVERAGES, FOREST PRODUCTS, etc.

	Production 1963–5	Production 1953–5	Exports 1963–5	Exports 1953–5	Imports 1963–5	Imports 1953–5
Coffee	—	—	0.2†	—	0.4	0.1[1]
Sugar, raw	—	—	—	—	3.2	1.8
Tea	—	—	—	—	0.2	0.2[1]
Tobacco, leaf	—	—	—	—	0.4	—
Hardwood *j*	—	—	—	—	30.1[2]	—
Paper	—	—	—	—	4.3[2]	—

j '000 cu. metres of roundwood equivalent.

4. VEGETABLE OILSEEDS AND OILS

	Production 1963–5	Production 1953–5	Exports 1963–5	Exports 1953–5	Imports 1963–5	Imports 1953–5
Coconut oil	—	—	—	—	0.01	0.02[1]
Groundnuts	—	—	—	—	1.13	0.10[2]
Groundnut oil	na	na	0.16	0.15[2]	0.95	0.45*

continued

4. VEGETABLE OILSEEDS AND OILS—*continued*

	Production 1963–5	Production 1953–5	Exports 1963–5	Exports 1953–5	Imports 1963–5	Imports 1953–5
Linseed oil	—	—	—	—	0.01	—
Olive oil	—	—	—	—	0.02	0.02*
Sesame seed	—	—	—	—	0.13	0.03
Soya bean oil	—	—	na	na	na	na
Tung oil	—	—	—	—	0.07	—

5. LIVESTOCK‡, ANIMAL PRODUCTS, etc.

	Production 1963–5	Production 1953–5	Exports 1963–5	Exports 1953–5	Imports 1963–5	Imports 1953–5
Cattle *d*	na	na	—	—	1.5	—
Goats *d*	1.0*	na	—	—	—	—
Pigs *d*	84.0*	na	—	—	15.1	—
Meat‡ 'A'	—	—	—	—	0.1	—
'B'	—	—	—	—	0.6	—
Butter	—	—	—	—	0.2	—
Eggs	—	—	—	0.1[2]†	1.7	0.2[2]
Fish	8.9	4.8	6.9	na	2.5[2]	na
Milk	—	—	—	—	2.6	0.5[2]*

d no. in thousands.

6. FIBRES, TEXTILES, etc.

	Production 1963–5	Production 1953–5	Exports 1963–5	Exports 1953–5	Imports 1963–5	Imports 1953–5
Cotton lint	—	—	—	—	0.1	0.1
Rubber, natural	—	—	—	—	0.1	—

7. FUEL AND POWER

	Production 1963–5	Production 1953–5	Exports 1963–5	Exports 1953–5	Imports 1963–5	Imports 1953–5
Electricity *ht*	26	3				
Petroleum, refined	—	—	—	—	37	na

h million kWh. *t* thermal.

MOZAMBIQUE

EAST AFRICA

AREA: 784 961 sq. km. (303 074 sq. miles)

LAND USE: (percentage of total)	*1961*	*1948*
Arable and orchard	3.4	2.6
Permanent meadow and pasture	56.2	57.1
Forest and woodland	24.8	25.1
City areas, waste and other land	15.6	15.2

POPULATION: 7 124 000 (1967 estimate)

Largest city: LOURENÇO MARQUES, capital; population: 177 929 (1960)

Distribution of working population (1950)
Total working population: 1 672 829

U.N. group no.		*Percentage*
0	Agriculture, forestry, fishing and hunting	75.3
1	Mining and quarrying	0.1
2/3	Manufacturing	4.7
4/5	Construction and electricity, gas, water and sanitary services	1.2
6	Commerce	1.4
7	Transport, storage and communications	1.0
8	Services	6.9
9	Others	9.4

		Year(s)
Life expectancy at birth (years)	45a	1940
Infant mortality (per '000)	100.9*	1965
Crude birth rate (per '000)	2.4*	1965
Crude death rate (per '000)	1.1*	1965
Accidental deaths (per 100 000 population)		
caused by motor vehicles	2.8*	1965
due to other causes	6.5*	1965
Population per physician	17 990	1964
Population per hospital bed	650	1964
School enrolment: age 5–19 years (percentage)	26	1963–4 av.
age over 19 years (per 100 000 population)	6	1963–4 av.

a latest available figure.

COMMUNICATIONS

		Year(s)
Motor vehicles in use ('000s): private	46.1	1963–5 av.
commercial	8.6	1963–5 av.
Railway track (km.)	3 621	1963
Mail per capita: domestic	2	1963–5 av.
foreign received	2	1963–5 av.
foreign sent	2	1963–5 av.
Telephones (per '000 urban population)	0.3	1967
Radio licences (per '000 population)	15	1963–5 av.
Daily newspapers (per '000 population)	6	1963

FINANCE

Currency unit: The Portuguese escudo

		Year
National Income (million $ U.S.)	253	1958
G.N.P. per capita ($ U.S.)	100	1966

TRADING

Total trade (in million $ U.S.)	*1965*	*1955*	*1938*
Exports (f.o.b.)	108	53	8
Imports (c.i.f.)	173	90	22

Main trading partners (percentage of total value)

Exports	*1965*	*1955*	*Imports*	*1965*	*1955*
Portugal	37	44	Portugal	35	29
India	15	8	U.K.	11	15
South Africa	12	6	South Africa	11	8
U.S.A.	5	6	Germany F.R.	8	14
U.K.	5	8	Iraq	5	na
Angola	4	—	U.S.A.	4	8
Germany F.R.	4	4	Japan	4	1

Distribution of trade (percentage of total value)

Exports	*1965*	*1955*
Crude materials and fuels	46	na
(cotton)	(18)	(28)
Food	37	na
(cashew nuts)	(19)	(8)
(sugar)	(9)	(14)
(tea)	(7)	(10)
Imports		
Manufactured goods	56	na
(machinery and transport equipment)	(28)	(23)
(textiles and clothing)	(11)	(16)
Crude materials and fuels	9	na
Food	8	na
Beverages	6	na

PRODUCTION, EXPORTS AND IMPORTS

Years: **1963–5 average** and *1953–5 average* Units: '000 metric tons unless otherwise indicated

	Production		Exports		Imports	
1. CEREALS, etc.						
Barley	—	—	—	—	na	na
Cassava	39.7*	na				
Maize (corn)	145.0*n	na	—	2.2	36.4	4.7
Millets/sorghum	25.7*[1]	na	—	0.3	na	0.4
Potatoes	11.3*n	8.0[1]*n	0.3	0.2	5.2[2]	3.0
Rice	137.7*n	na	1.9	4.4	—	—
Wheat	9.7*n	na	—	—	44.6	19.5

n from farms and villages only.

	Production		Exports		Imports	
2. FRUIT, etc.						
Bananas	24.7*	16.0*	18.3	15.9	—	—
Coconuts	423.3*e	na	—	—	—	—
Lemons	1.0*	—	0.1[1]	—	—	—
Oranges	8.3*	na	4.0[1]	1.2	—	—
Other citrus fruit	4.0*	na	2.1[1]	0.7	—	—
Tomatoes	1.0*	—				
Wine b	—	—	0.1†	—	413.7	215.7

b '000 hectolitres. *e* no. in millions.
Cashew nuts are also grown and exported.

	Production		Exports		Imports	
3. BEVERAGES, FOREST PRODUCTS, etc.						
Coffee	—	—	—	—	0.2[1]	0.1[2]
Sugar: cane	1 533.3*	na				
raw	165.8	102.7*	101.0	68.6	—	—
Tea	9.8	4.5*[2]	9.2	4.7	—	—
Tobacco: leaf	2.5*	1.0*	0.7[2]	0.1	0.5[2]	0.2
cigarettes	1 517.0e	758.3e	0.1p	—	—	—
Hardwood j	7 470.0*[1]	na	150.1[2]	129.0[1]	11.5[2]	12.0*
Newsprint	—	—	—	—[1]	2.5[2] (Newsprint and Other paper)	0.8[1]
Other paper	—	—	—	—[1]		0.1[1]

e no. in millions. *j* '000 cu. metres of roundwood equivalent. *p* incl. other tobacco manufactures.

	Production		Exports		Imports	
4. VEGETABLE OILSEEDS AND OILS						
Castor seed	1.00*	na	1.28	2.23	—	—
Castor oil	na	na	0.01	0.06	—	—
Copra	52.47	49.00*	39.60	36.67	—	—
Coconut oil	na	na	8.18	5.89	—	—
Cottonseed	64.30*	58.00[2]*	9.85	17.07	—	—
Cottonseed oil	na	na	1.07	2.45	—	—
Groundnuts	17.03*	na	—	2.87	0.01	—
Groundnut oil	na	na	6.09	1.73	—	—
Linseed oil	—	—	—	—	—	0.08
Olive oil	—	—	—	—	1.34	0.71
Sesame seed	1.60*	1.70[1]	1.59	1.83	—	—
Sunflower seed	1.00*	na	—	—	—	—

	Production		Exports		Imports	
5. LIVESTOCK‡, ANIMAL PRODUCTS, etc.						
Chickens d	190.0*	128.0[1]				
Cattle d	1 131.3	801.7	—	0.4	0.8[1]	0.3
dairy cows d	280.3	na				
Goats d	423.0*	371.7	—	—	—	—
Sheep d	102.0*	76.0	—	—	—	—
Horses d	na	8.0				
Pigs d	93.0	77.7	—	—	—	—
Bacon/ham	11.7* (Bacon/ham and Meat‡ 'A')	5.0[2]	—	—	—	0.1
Meat‡ 'A'			—	0.2	—	—
Butter	na	na	—[2]	—	0.5[2]	0.3
Cheese	na	—	0.1	—	0.7	0.3
Eggs	0.3*	0.3	—	—	—	—
Fish	6.1[2]	4.9	0.7	0.3[1]*	9.4	3.2[2]*
Milk	51.0*	6.5[2]	—	—	17.2	10.4*
Hides/skins	na	na	0.9	0.6[2]	—	—

d no. in thousands.

	Production		Exports		Imports	
6. FIBRES, TEXTILES, etc.						
Agaves (sisal)	31.5*	24.7*	30.9	23.7	—	—
Cotton lint	32.3	30.0*	31.8	25.5	—	—
Jute	2.3*	na	—	—	5.9	0.1
Rubber, natural	—	—	—	—	0.3	—
Cotton: yarn	1.8	na	—	—	—	—
woven fabrics	1.4[1]	na	0.5[1]	na	5.1[1]	na

continued

na: data not available. — negligible or nil. [1] one year only. [2] two year average. * estimate. ‡ see appendix. † re-exports.

PRODUCTION, EXPORTS AND IMPORTS *continued*

	Production		Exports		Imports	
7. FUEL AND POWER						
Coal‡ 'A'	253	170	63q	45q	319	226
Coke	na	na	—	—	1	1
Electricity h: total	228[2]n	50				
hydro	na	—				
thermal	na	50				
Oil, crude	—	—	—	—	483	—
Petroleum, refined	473	—[1]	280	—	77	90[1]
Uranium minerals f	na	na	na	13	—	—

f metric tons. *h* million kWh. *n* consumption. *q* incl. bunkers.

	Production		Exports		Imports	
8. IRON AND STEEL						
Iron/steel scrap	na	na	7	2	—	—

	Production		Exports		Imports	
9. NON-FERROUS MINERALS AND METALS						
Gold k, bullion/coins etc.	na	1.50[2]*	360.33‡	0.80	71.40‡	106.00
Silver k, ore m	na	1.00[2]*	na	na	na	na
Asbestos: fibre	na	0.15	0.05	0.12	0.61	0.58
manufactured	—	—	—	—	0.04	0.01
Mica	0.01[1]	0.01	—	—	—	—
Aluminium: bauxite	6.10	2.73	6.40	2.03	—	—
aluminium	—	—	—	—	0.31	0.04

continued

	Production		Exports		Imports	
9. NON-FERROUS MINERALS AND METALS—*continued*						
Beryl	0.38	0.68	0.45	0.61	—	—
Copper, metal	—	—	—	—	0.54	0.14
Lead, metal	—	—	—	—	0.16	0.05
Mercury f	—	—	—	—	0.04	0.06
Tin, metal	—	—	—	—	0.05	0.01
Zinc, metal	—	—	—	—	0.10	0.03

f metric tons. *k* '000 fine troy oz. *m* metal content.

	Production		Exports		Imports	
10. CHEMICALS n AND FERTILIZERS						
Chemicals	—		—		na	
Fertilizers:						
Sulphur	—	—	—	—	0.5	0.6

n data not available for years 1953–5.

	Production		Exports		Imports	
11. INDUSTRY						
Aircraft a	—	—	—	—	0.1[1]	—
Alcoholic beverages			—	—	na	4.7a
beer b	126.0	45.8				
Cement	190.3	98.0	—	0.7	1.0*	28.7
Electrical engineering a	—	—	—	—	6.4	0.6[2]
Railway vehicles a	—	—	—	—	2.6	4.4
Motor vehicles a	—	—	—	—	9.0	5.0[2]

a million $ U.S. *b* '000 hectolitres.

PORTUGUESE GUINEA

WEST AFRICA

AREA: 36 125 sq. km. (13 948 sq. miles)

LAND USE

The clearance of the mangrove swamps in the low deltaic region of the coast has enabled this area to be developed as paddy fields. Savannah vegetation, with coconut and oil palms, is found on the higher ground inland. On the interior plateau millet and groundnuts are grown, and cattle are reared.

POPULATION: 528 000 (1967 estimate)

Capital city: BISSAU; population: 18 309 (1950)
Total working population: 312 031 (1950)

		Year(s)
Infant mortality (per '000)	80.2*	1966
Crude birth rate (per '000)	7.3*	1965
Crude death rate (per '000)	4.3*	1965
Population per physician	15 410	1963
Population per hospital bed	620a	1966
School enrolment: age 5–19 years (percentage)	11	1963–4 av.

a government hospitals only.

COMMUNICATIONS

		Year
Telephones (per '000 urban population)	0.2	1967
Daily newspapers (per '000 population)	2	1964

TRADE

In 1965 exports amounted to about U.S. $4 million and imports to $15 million, the adverse balance being aggravated by expenditure on the maintenance of law and order. Trade is mainly with Portugal; most foodstuffs and virtually all manufactured goods are imported; exports consist of groundnuts and palm kernels, and a little natural rubber.

PRODUCTION, EXPORTS AND IMPORTS

Years: **1963–5 average** and *1953–5 average* Units: '000 metric tons unless otherwise indicated

	Production		Exports		Imports	
1. CEREALS, etc.						
Cassava	35.7*	na				
Potatoes	—	—	—	—	1.8[2]	—[1]
Rice	130.0*[1]	na	—	0.4[2]	5.7[2]	—
2. FRUIT, etc.						
Wine b	—	—	—	—	36.2[2]	14.5[2]

b '000 hectolitres.

	Production		Exports		Imports	
3. BEVERAGES, FOREST PRODUCTS, etc.						
Coffee	—	—	—	—	0.1[1]	—
Sugar, raw	—	—	—	—	1.4*	na
Tobacco, leaf	—	—	—	—	0.5[2]	—
Hardwood j	460.0*[1]	na	16.6[2]	na	—	—

j '000 cu. metres of roundwood equivalent.

	Production		Exports		Imports	
4. VEGETABLE OILSEEDS AND OILS						
Groundnuts	45.27*	na	24.53	24.63	—	—
Groundnut oil	na	na	0.06[2]	—	—	—
Olive oil	—	—	—	—	0.15[2]	0.05[2]*

continued

	Production		Exports		Imports	
4. VEGETABLE OILSEEDS AND OILS—*continued*						
Palm kernels	12.03	na	9.48	8.00[1]*	—	—
Palm oil	8.00*	na	0.08[1]	0.60[2]*	—	—
Sesame seed	na	na	0.14[1]	—	—	—
5. LIVESTOCK‡, ANIMAL PRODUCTS, etc.						
Cattle d	230.0*	na	—	—	0.4[1]	—
Goats d	152.0*	na	—	—	—	—
Sheep d	57.3*	na	—	—	—	—
Pigs d	100.0*	na	—	—	—	—
Meat‡, 'A'	1.0*	na	—	—	—	—
Fish	0.8	0.5	—[1]	—	na	—
Milk	—	—	—	—	1.1[2]	—

d no. in thousands.

	Production		Exports		Imports	
6. FIBRES, TEXTILES, etc.						
Rubber, natural	na	na	na	0.1	—	—
7. FUEL AND POWER						
Petroleum, refined	—	—	—	—	20	na
11. INDUSTRY						
Cement	—	—	—	—	18.0*	13.7*

continued

na: data not available. — negligible or nil. [1] one year only. [2] two year average. * estimate. ‡ see appendix. † re-exports.

PORTUGUESE TIMOR

SOUTH EAST ASIA

AREA: 14 925 sq. km. (5 763 sq. miles)

LAND USE

About 60% of the country is under forest; the remainder of the land is not readily cultivable, but subsistence crops of grain and vegetables are grown, and coffee is produced for export.

POPULATION: 570 000 (1967 estimate)

Capital city: DÍLI; population: 52 158 (city proper, 1960)

		Year
Crude birth rate (per '000)	19*	1965
Crude death rate (per '000)	9.9*	1965
Population per physician	27 150	1964
Population per hospital bed	780	1966
School enrolment: age 5–19 years (percentage)	8	1961

COMMUNICATIONS

		Year(s)
Telephones (per '000 urban population)	0.1	1967
Radio licences (per '000 population)	2	1963–5 av.

FINANCE

Currency unit: The Portuguese escudo

TRADE

Trade is mainly with Portugal, exports being coffee, copra, natural rubber, and wax. All manufactured goods and most foodstuffs are imported.

PRODUCTION, EXPORTS AND IMPORTS

Years: **1963–5 average** and *1953–5 average* Units: '000 metric tons unless otherwise indicated

	Production		Exports		Imports	
1. CEREALS, etc.						
Cassava	**15.0***	*14.0*[1]				
Maize (corn)	**21.0***	*22.5*[2]	—	—	—	—
Rice	**15.7***	*7.0*[1]	**0.2**	—	—	—
Sweet potatoes/yams	**10.0***	*3.0*[1]				
2. FRUIT, etc.						
Coconuts *e*	**12.0[1]***	na	—	—	—	—
Wine *b*	—	—	—	—	**3.6**[1]	*2.0**
b '000 hectolitres. *e* no. in millions.						
3. BEVERAGES, FOREST PRODUCTS, etc.						
Coffee	**1.3***	na	**2.4**	*1.2*[2]	—	—
Sugar, raw	—	—	—	—	**0.4***	*3.2*
Tobacco, leaf	—	*0.3*[2]*	—	—	—	—
4. VEGETABLE OILSEEDS AND OILS						
Copra	**1.00***	*1.00*[2]	**1.58**	*1.27*	—	—
Groundnuts	na	*0.70*[1]	—	—	—	—
Olive oil	—	—	—	—	na	*0.02*
5. LIVESTOCK‡, ANIMAL PRODUCTS, etc.						
Cattle *d*	**36.0***	*9.0*	—	—	—	—
Goats *d*	**228.0***	*173.0*	—	—	—	—
Sheep *d*	**50.0***	*40.7*	—	—	—	—
Horses *d*	**94.0***	*64.0*				
Pigs *d*	**225.0***	*168.3*	—	—	—	—
Fish	**0.1**	na	—	—	—	—
d no. in thousands.						
6. FIBRES, TEXTILES, etc.						
Rubber, natural	**0.3***	*0.2*	na	*0.2*	—	—

SÃO TOMÉ AND PRINCIPE

ATLANTIC OCEAN

AREA: 964 sq. km. (372 sq. miles)

POPULATION: 60 000* *a* (1967 estimate)

Capital city: SÃO TOMÉ; population: 5 714 (city proper, 1960)

		Year(s)
Infant mortality (per '000)	76.6	1965
Crude birth rate (per '000)	53.3	1965
Crude death rate (per '000)	15.9	1965
Accidental deaths (per 100 000 population)	na	
Population per physician	3 050	1964
Population per hospital bed	30	1966
School enrolment: age 5–19 years (percentage)	31	1963–4 av.

a incl. 17 000 immigrant labourers under 4-year contracts.

COMMUNICATIONS

		Year(s)
Motor vehicles in use ('000s): private	0.8	1963–5 av.
commercial	0.3	
Telephones (per '000 urban population)	0.9	1967
Radio licences (per '000 population)	25	1963–5 av.

FINANCE

Currency unit: The Portuguese escudo

PRODUCTION AND TRADE

The chief commercial products are cacao, copra, coffee, palm oil and cinchona, cacao providing 80% of the exports in 1964. Manufactured goods and most foodstuffs are imported.

PRODUCTION, EXPORTS AND IMPORTS

Years: **1963–5 average** and *1953–5 average* Units: '000 metric tons unless otherwise indicated

	Production		Exports		Imports	
1. CEREALS, etc.						
Cassava	**2.0***	na				
Maize (corn)	—	—	—	—	**1.6**	*3.3*
Potatoes	—	—	—	—	**0.6**	*0.4*
Rice	—	—	—	—	**1.3**	*1.8*
2. FRUIT, etc.						
Bananas	**4.3***	na	—	—	—	—
Coconuts *e*	**46.0***	na	—	—	—	—
Wine *b*	—	—	—	—	**23.2**	*20.3*
b '000 hectolitres. *e* no. in millions.						
3. BEVERAGES, FOREST PRODUCTS, etc.						
Cocoa	**8.9**	*7.6**	**8.9**	*8.0*	—	—
Coffee	**0.2**	na	**0.2**	*0.3*	—	—
Sugar, raw	—	—	—	—	**0.9**[2]	*0.4*
4. VEGETABLE OILSEEDS AND OILS						
Copra	**5.63***	na	**5.71**	*4.73*	—	—
Groundnuts	—	—	—	—	**0.02**	—
Linseed oil	—	—	—	—	—	*0.01*[1]
Olive oil	—	—	—	—	**0.10**	*0.06*
Palm kernels	**3.03***	na	**3.54**	*5.23*	—	—
Palm oil	**1.47***	na	**0.82**	*2.08*	—	—
5. LIVESTOCK‡, ANIMAL PRODUCTS, etc.						
Cattle *d*	**3.7***	*4.7*	—	—	—	*0.1*
Goats *d*	**1.0***	*2.0**	—	—	—	—
Sheep *d*	**2.7**	*4.0**	—	—	—	—
Pigs *d*	**4.0**	*7.0*	—	—	—	—
Fish	**0.7**	*0.4*	—	—	**0.8**[2]	na
d no. in thousands.						
7. FUEL AND POWER						
Electricity *h t*	**6**	—				

Cinchona is also grown, and the bark exported.

h million kWh. *t* thermal.

na: data not available. — negligible or nil. [1] one year only. [2] two year average. * estimate. ‡ see appendix. † re-exports.

RHODESIA

CENTRAL AFRICA

Rhodesia, formerly Southern Rhodesia and a member of the Federation of Rhodesia and Nyasaland from 1954–1963, attained the status of a self-governing British Protectorate upon the dissolution of the Federation. The government made a unilateral declaration of independence in 1965, whereupon the U.N. called on all nations to impose economic sanctions on Rhodesia.

No independent data for Rhodesia are available for the years of the Federation, 1954–1963.

AREA: 390 622 sq. km. (150 820 sq. miles)

LAND USE: (percentage of total)	*1965*	*1955*
Arable and orchard	4.7	4.7
Permanent meadow and pasture	12.5	12.2
Forest and woodland	60.0	64.0
City areas, waste and other land	22.8	19.1

POPULATION: 4 530 000 (1967 estimate)

Largest city: SALISBURY, capital; population: 330 000 (1966)

			Year(s)
Life expectancy at birth (years):	Africans	50	1962
	Europeans: male	66.9	1961–3 av.
	female	74.0	
Infant mortality (per '000)	Asians	34.5	1965
	Africans	34.3*	
	Europeans	23.0	
Crude birth rate (per '000)	Asians	32.6	1965
	Africans	32.1*	
	Europeans	18.3	
Crude death rate (per '000)	Asians	5.1	1965
	Africans	4.5*	
	Europeans	6.3	
Accidental deaths (per 100 000 population) caused by motor vehicles		39.7 *b*	1965
due to other causes		21.9 *b*	
Population per physician		7 570	1964
Population per hospital bed		280	1966
School enrolment: age 5–19 years (percentage)		72 *a*	1963–4 av.
age over 19 years (per 100 000 population)		16	1963–5 av.

a Africans only, but excl. those at mission schools. *b* Europeans only.

EMPLOYMENT AND PRODUCTION

Approximately half the land in Rhodesia is reserved for ownership by the Africans, who constitute 95% of the population. Cereal crops, particularly maize, form the basis of the subsistence agriculture. Tobacco is the principal commercial crop. Industry is becoming increasingly important. In 1967 the largest sources of employment for African labour were (in descending order) agriculture, manufacturing, construction, mining, and domestic service.

COMMUNICATIONS

		Year(s)
Motor vehicles in use ('000s): private	106.8	1963–4 av.
commercial	31.8	
Railway track (km.)	3 350	1966
Mail per capita: domestic	15	1964–5 av.
foreign received	5	
foreign sent	4	
Telephones (per '000 urban population)	2.4	1967
Radio licences (per '000 population)	53*	1965
Daily newspapers (per '000 population)	30	1959

FINANCE

Currency unit: The Rhodesian dollar replaced the Rhodesian pound in 1970 at the rate R$1 to R£0.5.

Exchange rates (for Rhodesian pounds)	*1965*	*1950*	*1938*
Per $ U.S.	0.357	0.357	0.215
Per £ sterling	1.0	1.0	1.0

		Year
National Income (million $ U.S.)	877	1965
G.N.P. per capita ($ U.S.)	210	1966

TRADING

Total trade (in million $ U.S.)	*1965*	*1950*	*1938*
Exports (f.o.b.)	442	117	30
Imports (f.o.b.)	335	165	47

Main trading partners (percentage of total value)

Exports	*1965*	*1950*	*1938*	*Imports*	*1965*	*1950*	*1938*
Zambia	25	8	7	U.K.	30	47	50
U.K.	22	54	73	South Africa	23	27	15
South Africa	11	11	4	U.S.A.	7	5	9
Germany F.R.	9	1	2 *a*	Japan	6	na	na
Malawi	6	1	—	Germany F.R.	4	1	3 *a*
Japan	5	na	na	Zambia	3	2	1
Netherlands	3	1	—	Iran	3	3	1

Distribution of trade (percentage of total value) *b*

Exports	*1965*	*1950**	*1938**
Tobacco	34	50	26
Manufactured goods	31	na	na
(footwear and clothing)	(5)	(6)	(3)
(machinery and transport equipment)	(6)	(—)	(—)
Food	10	2	6
Asbestos	8	15	26
Coal and electric energy	5	1	5
Metalliferous ores	4	5	10
Imports			
Manufactured goods	67	na	na
(machinery and transport equipment)	(32)	(17)	(19)
(textiles and clothing)	(14)	(15)	(13)
Chemicals	11	3	4
Crude materials and fuels	9	na	na
Food	8	5	3
Beverages and tobacco	3	1	—

a incl. Germany D.R. and Austria. *b* % of national exports‡ which comprised 90% of general exports in 1965, 82% in 1950 and 80% in 1938.

PRODUCTION, EXPORTS AND IMPORTS

Years: **1964–5 average** and *1953* Units: '000 metric tons unless otherwise indicated

	Production		Exports		Imports	
1. CEREALS, etc.						
Barley	**1.3***	—	—	—	**0.8**	—
Maize (corn)	**752.7*** *p*	*484.0 p*	**10.1**	*0.5*	**37.2**	*9.1*
Millets/sorghum	**254.0***	*147.0*	**0.2**	*0.5*	**8.6**	—
Oats	—	—	—	—	**1.0**	*0.3*
Potatoes	**22.3**	*10.3*	**2.4**	*0.4*	**0.3**	*2.0*
Rice	**3.0***	na	**0.2**	—	**3.6**	*0.9*
Sweet potatoes/yams	—	*1.0*				
Wheat	**3.3**	*1.0*	**5.9** *s*	—	**89.6**	*50.0*
p from farms and estates only. *s* incl. re-exports.						
2. FRUIT, etc.						
Apples	—	—	**0.1†**	—	**2.1**	—
Bananas	—	—	**0.1†**	—	**5.7**	—
Coconuts	—	—	—	—	**0.1**	*0.1*
Dates	—	—	—	—	—	*0.1*
Grapes	—	—	**0.1†**	—	**0.8**	—
Lemons	**1.0***	—	**0.5**	—	**0.1**	—
Oranges	**17.0***	*9.0*	**1.4**	*0.1*	**0.4**	*0.5*
Other citrus fruit	**4.0***	na	—	—	—	—
Raisins	—	—	—	—	**0.2**	*0.2*
Wine *b*	—	—	**2.4†**	*2.0†*	**9.0**	*6.0*
b '000 hectolitres.						
3. BEVERAGES, FOREST PRODUCTS, etc.						
Coffee	—	—	**0.1†**	—	**0.4**	*0.1*
Sugar: cane	**1 214.7**	*27.5*[2]				
raw	**167.9**	*2.3*	**172.3**	*8.0*	**0.1**	*33.5*
Tea	**1.4**	*0.5*	**0.5**	*0.1†*	**1.0**	*0.5*
Tobacco: leaf	**115.3**	*55.3*[2]	**112.4**	*39.2 s*	**10.9**	*4.5*
products	na	na	**2.6**	—	—	—
Softwood *j*	**80.0**	*88.3*	**3.0**	—	**48.1**	—
Hardwood *j*	**3 741.0**[1]	*2 386.0*	**33.5**	—	**41.2**	—
Wood pulp	**4.1**	—	—[1]	—	**4.2**	—
Newsprint	**4.4**	—	**1.3**	—	**1.4**	—
Other paper	**5.9**	—	**3.8**	—	**25.4**	—
j '000 cu. metres of roundwood equivalent. *s* incl. re-exports.						
4. VEGETABLE OILSEEDS AND OILS						
Castor seed	na	na	**0.04**	na	—	—
Castor oil	na	na	—	—	**0.04**	*0.03*
Coconut oil	—	—	—	—	**1.37**	*0.06*
Cottonseed	**6.00**	*0.30*	**0.45**	—	**0.27**	—
Cottonseed oil	na	na	—	—	**1.23**	*0.18*
Groundnuts	**78.87***	*52.50*	**2.25**	—	**0.26**	—
Groundnut oil	na	na	**1.77**	*1.80*	**0.22**	*0.02*

continued

na: data not available. — negligible or nil. [1] one year only. [2] two year average. * estimate. ‡ see appendix. † re-exports.

PRODUCTION, EXPORTS AND IMPORTS *continued*

4. VEGETABLE OILSEEDS AND OILS—*continued*

	Production		Exports		Imports	
Linseed oil	—	—	—	*0.01†*	0.11	*0.09*
Olive oil	—	—	—	—	0.02	*0.01*
Palm kernel oil	—	—	—	—	0.05	*1.58*
Palm oil	—	—	—	—	0.49	*0.76*
Soya beans	na	na	0.10	—	—	—
Soya bean oil	—	—	—	—	0.31[1]	—
Sunflower seed	2.00*p	*1.00*p*	0.27	—	0.22	—
Sunflower seed oil	na	na	0.02	—	0.14	—
Tung oil	—	—	—	—	0.01	—

p from farms and estates only.

5. LIVESTOCK‡, ANIMAL PRODUCTS, etc.

	Production		Exports		Imports	
Chickens *d*	778.0*	*562.0*				
Cattle *d*	3 587.7	*3 031.0*	1.2	*3.1*	4.6	*1.7*
dairy cows *d*	841.3*p*	*630.3np*				
Goats *d*	557.0*	*482.0*	0.2 (Goats and Sheep)	—	7.1	na
Sheep *d*	391.7	*294.3*				
Horses *d*	6.7*	*6.0*				
Pigs *d*	133.0	*121.3*	—	*0.1*	0.2	*0.2*
Bacon/ham	77.3 (Bacon/ham and Meat 'A')	*55.3q*	0.7	*0.9*	—	—
Meat‡: 'A'			15.8	*1.6*	1.3	—
'B'	9.7*	*6.3*	1.5	—	—	—
Butter	1.0	*0.3*	0.2	—	—	*1.1*
Cheese	na	—	0.2	—	0.1	*0.3*
Eggs	1.5*	*1.1*	0.2	—	—	—
Fish	1.6	na	0.2	—	12.8	na
Milk	104.7*	*55.3*	9.7	*1.3*	22.6	*8.6*
Hides/skins	na	*4.5*	8.6	na	—	—

d no. in thousands. *n* incl. some beef cows. *p* on farms and estates only. *q* government inspected meat only.

6. FIBRES, TEXTILES, etc.

	Production		Exports		Imports	
Cotton lint	3.0	—	1.9	*0.1*	2.5	*1.0*
Jute	—	—	—	—	0.1	*2.4*
Rubber, natural	—	—	0.2†	—	5.1	*0.2*
Cotton: yarn	na	*2.8*	na	na	na	na
woven fabrics	na	na	0.5	—	3.2	na
Rayon, woven fabrics	—	—	—	—	na	na
Wool, yarn	na	na	—	—	—	*0.1*

7. FUEL AND POWER

	Production		Exports		Imports	
Coal, 'A'‡	3 097	na	1 488	*886*	11 (Coal and Coke)	*8*
Coke	na	na	126	*80*		*1*
Electricity *h*: total	3 764	na				
hydro	3 526	na				
thermal	238	na				
Oil, crude	—	—	—	—	170	—
Petroleum, refined	143	—	40	—	297	*180*
Uranium *f*	na	na	—	—	—	—

f metric tons. *h* million kWh.

8. IRON AND STEEL

	Production		Exports		Imports	
Iron ore	na	41*m*	304	na	—	—
Pig iron	268	na	236	*6*[2] (Pig iron and Steel)	2 (Pig iron and Steel)	*3*
Steel ingots/castings	114	na	29	na		—

m metal content.

9. NON-FERROUS MINERALS AND METALS

	Production		Exports		Imports	
Gold *k*: ore *m*	561.70	*521.00*	1.00[1]‡	*4.90*	2.20[1]‡	*0.13*
bullion/coins etc.	na	na	565.10	*505.56*	—	—
Silver *k*, ore	89.40*m*	*81.30m*	89.78*n*	*81.69n*	—	—
Asbestos: fibre	142.69	na	164.36[2]	*64.98*	—	—
manufactured	na	na	1.58*a*	*0.72a*	—	*4.96p*
Mica	0.12	*0.16*	0.35[1]	*0.17*	—	—
Aluminium: bauxite	2.03	—	—	—	—	—
aluminium	na	—	—	*0.04†*	1.03	*0.04*
Antimony, ore	0.10*m*	*0.10m*	0.20	*0.24*	—	*0.01q*
Beryl	0.16	*1.15*	0.12	*1.49*	—	—
Chrome: ore	462.73*m*	na	545.38	*369.17*	—	—
metal	na	na	na	*3.10*	21.98	na
Copper: ore	17.12*m*	*0.51m*	7.06	*0.50*	—	—
metal	15.69	na	18.70	na	5.31	*0.40*
Lead: ore	na	na	na	*0.02*	—	—
metal	—	—	—	—	0.80	*0.18*
Magnesium:						
dolomite	na	na	0.12[1]	na	—	—
magnesite	28.35	na	28.94	*8.62*	—	—
Manganese, ore	—	*0.40*	—	*2.26*	—	—
Mercury *f*	—	—	—	—	na	*3.70*
Nickel: ore	na	na	0.71[1]	*0.07*	—	—
metal	0.33	na	—	—	0.03	na
Tin: ore	0.51*m*	*0.19m*	0.06	*0.02*	—	—
metal	0.51	*0.02*	0.44	—	0.08	*0.06*
Tungsten, ore	0.01	*0.29*	0.03[1]	*0.28*	—	—
Zinc, metal	—	—	—	—	0.94	*0.12*

a million $ U.S. *f* metric tons. *k* '000 fine troy oz. *m* metal content. *n* bullion. *p* in addition, asbestos valued at U.S. $ 154 000. *q* metal.

10. CHEMICALS *n* AND FERTILIZERS

	Production		Exports		Imports	
Chemicals	—		—		na	
Fertilizers:						
Phosphates	2.8	—	—	—	84.8[1]*y*	—
Potash	—	—	—	—	33.3	—
Pyrites	28.5**x*	*13.5x*	na	*21.7*	—	—
Sulphur	—	—	—	—	na	—

n data not available for 1953. *x* sulphur content. *y* 1963 data; incl. Nyasaland and Northern Rhodesia.

11. INDUSTRY

	Production		Exports		Imports	
Aircraft *a*	—	—	—	—	2.8	na
Alcoholic beverages *a*	na	na	2.4	na	2.1	na
Cement	212.0	na	6.0	na	3.0	na
Electrical engineering *a*	na	na	8.4	na	15.4	na
Railway vehicles *a*	—	—	—	—	5.5	na
Motor vehicles			7.6*a*	na	29.1*a*	na
commercial *dr*	1.3	—				
private *dr*	5.0	—				

a million $ U.S. *d* no. in thousands. *r* assembly of imported parts.

ROMANIA

EUROPE

In 1947 the king abdicated under political pressure, and the 'People's Republic' (later known as the 'Socialist Republic') was proclaimed. Romania is a member of Comecon.

AREA: 237 500 sq. km. (91 699 sq. miles)

LAND USE: (percentage of total)	*1965*	*1955*
Arable and orchard	44.1	39.2
Permanent meadow and pasture	18.2	14.3
Forest and woodland	26.8	26.6
City areas, waste and other land	10.9	19.9

POPULATION: 19 105 056 (1966 census)

Largest city: BUCUREȘTI (Bucharest), capital; population: 1 518 725 (1966)

Distribution of working population (1956)

Total working population: 10 466 258

U.N. group no.		*Percentage*
0/1/2/3	Agriculture and hunting *a*	69.6
	Mining, quarrying, forestry, fishing and manufacturing	14.2
4	Construction	2.5
5/8	Services, incl. electricity, gas, water and sanitary services	6.8
6	Commerce	3.3
7	Transport, storage and communications	2.8
9	Others	0.8

		Year(s)
Life expectancy at birth (years): male	63.4	1963
female	70.3	1963
Infant mortality (per '000)	44.1	1965
Crude birth rate (per '000)	14.6	1965
Crude death rate (per '000)	8.6	1965
Population per physician	760	1965
Population per hospital bed	130	1966
School enrolment: age 5–19 years (percentage)	85	1963–4 av.
age over 19 years (per 100 000 population)	669	1964–5 av.

a incl. unpaid family workers.

COMMUNICATIONS		*Year(s)*
Motor vehicles in use ('000s): private	na	1963–5 av.
commercial	30.8	1963–5 av.
Railway track (km.)	956	1964
Mail per capita	75	1963–5 av.
Telephones (per '000 urban population)	2.7*	1967
Radio licences (per '000 population)	141	1963–5 av.
Television licences (per '000 population)	19.4	1963–5 av.
Daily newspapers (per '000 population)	170	1962–4 av.

continued

na: data not available. — negligible or nil. ¹ one year only. ² two year average. * estimate. ‡ see appendix. † re-exports.

FINANCE

Currency unit: The lei

Exchange rates a	*1965*	*1960*	*1957*
Per $ U.S.	6.0	6.0	6.0
Per £ sterling	16.8	16.8	16.8

a since 1957 there has been a special tourist rate of 18 per $ U.S. (50.4 per £ sterling).

		Year(s)
National Income (million $ U.S.)	12 000*	1966
G.N.P. per capita ($ U.S.)	650	1966
Rate of increase of G.N.P. per capita	8.2	1960–4 av.

TRADING

Total trade (in million $ U.S.)	*1965*	*1956*	*1938*
Exports (f.o.b.)	1 102	397	157
Imports (f.o.b.)	1 077	352	137

Main trading partners (percentage of total value)

Exports	*1965*	*Imports*	*1965*
U.S.S.R.	40	U.S.S.R.	38
Czechoslovakia	9	Germany F.R.	10
Germany D.R.	7	Czechoslovakia	6
Italy	6	Germany D.R.	6
Germany F.R.	6	Italy	5
Poland	4	France	5
Hungary	3	U.K.	4

Distribution of trade (percentage of total value)

Exports	*1965*	*1956**
Crude materials, fuels, metals	39	63
Manufactured goods	33	na
(machinery and transport equipment)	(19)	(10)
Food	21	24
Chemicals and rubber	7	na
Imports		
Manufactured goods	47	na
(machinery and transport equipment)	(39)	(20)
Crude materials, fuels, minerals, metals	43	68
Chemicals and rubber	6	na
Food	3	7

PRODUCTION, EXPORTS AND IMPORTS

Years: **1963–5 average** and *1953–5 average* Units: '000 metric tons unless otherwise indicated

1. CEREALS, etc.

	Production		Exports		Imports	
Barley	394.7	*415.0*[2]*	—	*0.4*	—	—[2]
Maize (corn)	6 197.3	*5 415.0*[2]*	857.2*	*112.1**	—	*6.5**
Millets/sorghum	na	*20.5*[2]	2.1*	*1.1**	—	—
Oats	109.0	*365.0*[2]*	—	—	—	—
Potatoes	2 508.7	*2 502.0*[2]*	19.2	—	3.3*	—
Rice	50.3	*42.0*[2]*	—	*0.5**	36.3	*2.1**
Rye	98.3	*192.0*[2]	16.1	*5.3**	—	—
Wheat	4 520.0	*2 573.0*[2]*	195.8*	*77.5**	208.2*[2]	*45.7**

2. FRUIT, etc.

	Production		Exports		Imports	
Apples	180.7	*26.0*[1]*	9.2*	—	—	—
Apricots	30.3	*8.1*[1]	—	—	—	—
Cherries	45.3	*39.6*[1]	—	—	—	—
Dates	—	—	—	—	0.1*[2]	—
Grapes	918.7	*942.0*[2]*	51.0	—	—	—
Lemons	—	—	—	—	10.4*	*2.9**
Oranges	—	—	—	—	6.7*	*2.0**
Other citrus fruit	—	—	—	—	0.5*	—
Peaches	7.3	na	—	—	—	—
Pears	45.0	*40.0*[1]*	—	—	—	—
Plums	558.7	*473.5*	—	—	—	—
Raisins	—	—	—	—	0.4*[2]	—
Tomatoes	503.7	na				
Wine *b*	na	*4 655.0*	375.0	—	17.0*	*5.7**

b '000 hectolitres.

3. BEVERAGES, FOREST PRODUCTS, etc.

	Production		Exports		Imports	
Cocoa	—	—	—	—	4.4	—
Coffee	—	—	—	—	1.5*	*0.2**
Sugar: beet	3 080.0	*1 541.7**				
raw	376.5	*184.3**	59.1	—[2]	16.3	*26.3**
Tea	—	—	—	—	0.1*	—
Tobacco: leaf	38.7	*18.5*[2]*	5.9*	—	1.6[2]	—
cigarettes *en*	22 148.0	na	—	—	—	—
Softwood *j*	6 215.5[2]	na	2 322.0	*781.0*	0.2	—
Hardwood *j*	15 226.0[2]	na	1 055.0	*54.5*	1.1	—
Wood pulp	217.0[2]	na	37.8	—	14.2	—
Newsprint	50.0[2]	*46.0**	4.3	*1.8*	0.5	na
Other paper	212.0[2]	*30.3*[1]*	6.5	na	11.2	na

e no. in millions. *j* '000 cu. metres of roundwood equivalent. *n* incl. cigars.

4. VEGETABLE OILSEEDS AND OILS

	Production		Exports		Imports	
Castor seed	12.3	*3.1*[2]	—	—	—	—
Castor oil	na	na	2.77	—*	—	—
Coconut oil	—	—	—	—	0.95*	*0.02**
Cottonseed	na	*15.3**	na	*14.50*[2]*	—	—
Cottonseed oil	na	na	—	—	1.79	—
Groundnuts	—	—	—	—	0.57*	—
Linseed	25.7	*10.0*[2]*	0.07*	—	—	*1.07**
Linseed oil	na	na	—	—	1.79*	*0.37**
Palm kernel oil	—	—	—	—	0.01[2]*	—
Palm oil	—	—	—	—	—	*0.01**
Rapeseed	na	*8.0*[2]*	1.33*	*0.33**	—	—
Soya beans	2.0	*13.0*[2]*	—	—	0.03*	—
Sunflower seed	529.3	*280.0*[2]*	4.00	—	—	—
Sunflower seed oil	na	na	35.62	—	0.37	*0.51**
Tung oil	—	—	—	—	0.06*	—

5. LIVESTOCK‡, ANIMAL PRODUCTS, etc.

	Production		Exports		Imports	
Chickens *d*	37 473*n*	*31 250*[2]*n*				
Cattle *d*	4 653	*4 715*[2]*	11.6*	*0.1**	0.2[2]*	—
dairy cows *d*	1 962*p*	na				
Goats *d*	638	*345*[1]*	32.0* (Goats and Sheep)	na	—	—
Sheep *d*	12 434	*11 135*[1]				
Horses *d*	726	*1 097*[2]				
Pigs *d*	5 070	*4 660*[2]*	40.0	*1.6**	0.1*	—
Meat‡, 'A'	537*	na	—	—	—	—
Butter	19*q*	na	5.6*	—	—	*0.2**
Cheese	50	na	1.4*	—	—	—
Eggs	111	na	8.8	*0.2**	1.2*	*0.7**
Fish	35[2]	na	—	—	—	—
Milk	2 727*	*1 985**	—	—	1.7*	—
Hides/skins	—	—	—	—	11.0	—
Wool	15	*10**	1.0*	—[2]	0.8*	*0.7**

d no. in thousands. *n* incl. ducks, geese and turkeys. *p* incl. buffalo cows. *q* factory produced butter only.

6. FIBRES, TEXTILES, etc.

	Production		Exports		Imports	
Agaves (sisal etc.)	—	—	—	—	1.3*	—
Cotton lint	—	*8.0*[2]*	—	—	66.3	*3.8**
Flax fibre	8.9*	*6.4*[2]*	0.3*	—	—	—
Hemp fibre	13.1*	*25.4*[2]*	0.6[2]	—	—	*0.2**
Jute	—	—	—	—	3.8*	*0.1**
Rubber, natural	—	—	—	—	20.2	*0.1**
Silk *f*	na	*10.0**	71.7*	—	—	—
Cotton: yarn	74.2	*45.6*[2]*	—	na	1.5[2]	na
woven fabrics	41.4	*31.0**	5.3[2]	na	—	na
Rayon: fibre/yarn	na	*1.4*[1]*	na	na	na	na
woven fabrics	3.2	na	na	na	na	na
Wool: yarn	23.8	*17.7*[1]	na	na	na	na
woven fabrics	40.0[1]*r*	*31.3*[1]*r*	na	na	na	na

f metric tons. *r* million sq. metres.

7. FUEL AND POWER

	Production		Exports		Imports	
Coal: 'A'‡	4 943	*3 350*	—	—	707	—
'B'	1 660	*2 750*	—	—	—	—
Coke	—	—	—	—	931	—
Electricity *h*: total	14 249	*3 810*[1]				
hydro	709	*320*[1]				
thermal	13 540	*3 490*[1]				
Natural gas *i*	14 180	*5 660*[1]	203	—	—	—
Oil, crude	12 760	*10 760*[1]	—	—	—	—
Petroleum, refined	11 176	*9 660*[1]	5 533	na	—	—

h million kWh. *i* million cu. metres.

8. IRON AND STEEL

	Production		Exports		Imports	
Iron ore	1 003*m*	*301m*	—	—	2 388	—
Pig iron	1 883	*487**	—	—	43	—
Steel ingots/castings	3 057	*705*	—	—	—	—

m metal content.

continued

na: data not available, — negligible or nil. ¹ one year only. ² two year average. * estimate. ‡ see appendix. † re-exports.

PRODUCTION, EXPORTS AND IMPORTS *continued*

9. NON-FERROUS MINERALS AND METALS

	Production		Exports		Imports	
Silver *k*, ore *m*	643.00*	643.00*	na	na	na	na
Aluminium: bauxite	32.85*	15.20*	2.67	na	na	na
alumina	na	na	na	na	na	na
aluminium	22.80[1]	5.62[1]*	na	na	na	na
Chrome, ore	na	—	na	—	na	na
Lead: ore *m*	na	11.10[1]*	—	—	—	—
metal	13.55*	10.53*	na	na	—	—
Manganese, ore	161.93	281.83	75.26	na	—	—
Mercury *f*	6.65	na	na	na	na	na
Zinc	na	na	na	na	na	na

f metric tons. *k* '000 fine troy oz. *m* metal content.

10. CHEMICALS*n* AND FERTILIZERS

	Production	Exports	Imports
Organic chemicals:			
Benzene	44.0	na	na
Butadiene	na	na	na
Ethylene	na	na	na
Methanol	na	na	na
Phenol	16.6[1]	13.1[1]	na
Phthalic anhydride	na	na	na
Styrene monomer	na	na	na
Urea	na	na	na
Inorganic chemicals:			
Ammonia	154.9[2]	na	na
Carbon black	35.1	17.9	—
Chlorine	203.0[1]	na	na
Nitric acid	225.5[2]*	na	na
Sodium carbonate	337.8	186.6	—
Sodium hydroxide	198.4	102.9	—
Sulphuric acid	434.7	na	na

continued

10. CHEMICALS*n* AND FERTILIZERS—*continued*

	Production		Exports		Imports	
Plastics:						
Polyamides	na		na		na	
Polyethylene	na		na		na	
Polyvinyl chloride	6.4[2]		na		na	
Fertilizers:						
Phosphates	—	—	—	—	139.7*p*	—
Potash	—	—	—	—	9.3*	—
Pyrites	152.7*x*	na	—	—	—	—

n data not available for years 1953–5. *p* P_2O_5 content. *x* sulphur content.

11. INDUSTRY

	Production		Exports		Imports	
Alcoholic beverages			45.3	na	—	—
beer *b*	2 435.0	1 308.0[1]				
spirits *b*	330.0[1]*q*	500.0*r*				
Cement	4 842.7	1 829.0	1 538.0[1]	233.3*t*	na	—*t*
Electrical engineering *a*	na	na	43.2*u*	na	31.1*u*	na
Railway vehicles *c*	185.0*w*	na	na	na		
Machine tools *a*	39.0[1]	na	na	na	na	na
Merchant ships *g*	—	—	—	—	8.0	na
Motor vehicles			—	—	8.1*a*	—
commercial *d*	15.7	3.1[1]*v*				

a million $ U.S. *b* '000 hectolitres. *c* no. of units. *d* no. in thousands. *g* '000 G.R.T. *q* production for home consumption in 1966. *r* 1961 figure. *t* excl. trade with Eastern Europe, the U.S.S.R., and China P.R. *u* electric machine apparatus. *v* trucks only. *w* locomotives only.

RWANDA

CENTRAL AFRICA

Rwanda and Burundi which together formed the Belgian territory of Ruanda-Urundi, separated in 1959 after a period of inter-tribal friction. Internal self-government was granted to Rwanda in 1962, but the country is still supported by Belgian aid. The customs union with Burundi was broken off in 1964. Pre-1960 data are for the former Ruanda-Urundi.

AREA: 26 330 sq. km. (10 166 sq. miles)

LAND USE: (percentage of total)

	1963
Arable and orchard	37.8
Permanent meadow and pasture	33.0
Forest and woodland	5.9
City areas, waste and other land	23.3

POPULATION: 3 306 000*a* (1967 estimate)

Capital city: KIGALI; population: 4 273 (1959)

		Year(s)
Crude birth rate (per '000)	21.3*	1965
Crude death rate (per '000)	4.8*	1965
Population per physician	97 350	1964
Population per hospital bed	750	1966
School enrolment: age 5–19 years (percentage)	44	1963–4 av.
age over 19 years (per 100 000 population)	3	1963–5 av.

a African population only.

FINANCE

Currency unit: The Rwanda franc, at par with the Belgian franc until April 1966, thereafter at par with the $ U.S.

Exchange rates	1965*a*	1960
Per $ U.S.	50	50
Per £ sterling	140	140

		Year
National Income (million $ U.S.)	95	1958
G.N.P. per capita ($ U.S.)	40	1966

a official rate; the free rate was about 118 per $ U.S. (330 per £ Sterling).

TRADING

Total trade (in million $ U.S.)	1965*a*
Exports (f.o.b.)	14
Imports (c.i.f.)	18

Main trading partners (percentage of total value)

Exports	1965*a*	*Imports*	1965*a*
U.S.A.	49	Belg./Lux.	26
Belg./Lux.	38	Uganda	17
Germany F.R.	3	Germany F.R.	11
Congo D.R.	2	Burundi	6
U.K.	2	U.S.A.	4
		Japan	4
		U.K.	4

Distribution of trade (percentage of total value)

Exports	1965	*Imports*	1965
Coffee	54	Manufactured goods	71
Tin	37	(machinery and transport equipment)	(28)
Pyrethrum	2	(textiles and clothing)	(16)
Tea	2	Crude materials and fuels	10
		Food	8
		Chemicals	7

a for earlier trade figures, see Congo D.R.

continued

na: data not available. — negligible or nil. [1] one year only. [2] two year average. * estimate. ‡ see appendix. † re-exports.

PRODUCTION, EXPORTS AND IMPORTS

Years: **1963–5 average** and *1953–5 average* Units: '000 metric tons unless otherwise indicated

Note—1953–5 data are for the former Ruanda-Urundi, i.e. include Burundi.

1. CEREALS, etc.

	Production		Exports		Imports	
Barley	—	1.7	—	—	—	—
Cassava	1 033.0*	1 977.0				
Maize (corn)	143.3*	136.0	—	—	—	—
Millets/sorghum	218.3	211.3	—	—	—	—
Potatoes	100.0*	130.7	—	—	—	—
Rice	2.7*	1.0	—	—	—	—
Sweet potatoes/yams	966.7*	1 713.0				
Wheat	5.0*	9.3	—	—	—	—

3. BEVERAGES, FOREST PRODUCTS, etc.

	Production		Exports		Imports	
Coffee	9.1	16.8	na	na	—	—
Tea	0.3	0.2[2]*	na	na	—	—
Tobacco	1.5*n*	1.6*n*	—	—	na	na

n leaf tobacco.

4. VEGETABLE OILSEEDS AND OILS

	Production		Exports		Imports	
Castor seed	na	na	na	na	—	—
Copra	na	na	na	na	—	—
Cottonseed	4.30*	4.67	na	na	—	—
Groundnuts	4.90*	4.20	na	na	—	—
Palm kernels	0.20*	na	na	na	—	—
Palm oil	1.00*	na	na	na	—	—
Soya beans	na	4.00	na	na	—	—

5. LIVESTOCK‡, ANIMAL PRODUCTS, etc.

	Production		Exports		Imports	
Cattle *d*	1 216.7*	928.7	—	—	—	—
Goats *d*	1 890.0*	1 303.7	—	—	—	—
Sheep *d*	680.0*	401.7	—	—	—	—
Pigs *d*	56.0*	49.0	—	—	—	—
Meat‡: 'A'	10.0*	na	—	—	—	—
'B'	3.0*	na	—	—	—	—

continued

5. LIVESTOCK‡, ANIMAL PRODUCTS, etc.—*continued*

	Production		Exports		Imports	
Eggs	1.9*	na	—	—	—	—
Fish	na	5.1	—	—	—	—
Milk	55.0*	5.3	—	—	—	—
Hides/skins	0.1[1]	1.3	—	—	—	—

d no. in thousands.

6. FIBRES, TEXTILES, etc.

	Production		Exports		Imports	
Agaves (sisal)	—	0.1	—	—	—	—
Cotton lint	2.3*	2.0	na	na	—	—

7. FUEL AND POWER

	Production		Exports		Imports	
Electricity *h*: total	11	—				
hydro	10	—				
thermal	1	—				
Petroleum, refined	—	—	—	—	17	na

h million kWh.

9. NON-FERROUS MINERALS AND METALS

	Production		Exports		Imports	
Gold *k*, ore *m*	na	na	na	na	—	—
Beryl	0.24	na	na	na	—	—
Tin, ore	1.37*m*	na*p*	na*p*	na	—	—
Tungsten, ore	0.15	na*p*	na	na	—	—

k '000 fine troy oz. *m* metal content. *p* see Congo D.R.

11. INDUSTRY

	Production		Exports		Imports	
Beer *b*	265.0[2]	na	0.1*a*	—	—	—
Cement *p*	na	na	na	na	na	na
Electrical engineering *a*	—	—	—	—	0.7	na
Motor vehicles *a*	—	—	—	—	11.6	na

a million $ U.S. *b* '000 hectolitres. *p* see Congo D.R.

RYUKYU ISLANDS

CHINA SEA

The administration of the Ryukyu Islands of which the largest and most important is Okinawa, was assigned to the U.S.A. after the surrender of Japan in 1945. It has been agreed that the islands should revert to Japanese control in 1972.

AREA: 2 196 sq. km. (848 sq. miles)

LAND USE: (percentage of total)

	1964	1955
Arable and orchard	25.5	19.5
Permanent meadow and pasture	0.9	7.3
Forest and woodland	54.5	52.7
City areas, waste and other land	19.1	20.5

POPULATION: 934 176 (1965 census)

Largest city: NAHA, capital; population: 257 177 (city proper, 1965)

Distribution of working population (1965)
Total working population: 417 000

U.N. group no.		*Percentage*
0	Agriculture, forestry, fishing and hunting	35.7
2/3	Manufacturing	8.9
4	Construction	7.0
5	Electricity, gas, water and sanitary services }	4.6
7	Transport, storage and communications }	
6	Commerce	18.0
8	Services	22.5*a*
9	Others	3.3

		Year(s)
Life expectancy at birth (years): male	68.0	1960
female	74.6	1960
Infant mortality (per '000)	9.8	1965
Crude birth rate (per '000)	22.3	1965
Crude death rate (per '000)	5.3	1965
Accidental deaths (per 100 000 population)		
caused by motor vehicles	8.9	1965
due to other causes	16.4	1965
Population per physician	1 940	1964
Population per hospital bed	290*b*	1965
School enrolment: age 5–19 years (percentage)	130‡	1963–4 av.
age over 19 years (per 100 000 population)	511	1964–5 av.

a 13% of the labour force was employed by U.S. military and naval establishments. *b* government hospitals only.

COMMUNICATIONS

		Year(s)
Motor vehicles in use ('000s): private	10.9	1963
commercial	11.0	1963
Telephones (per '000 urban population)	4.3*c*	1967
Television sets (per '000 population)	108.3*	1963–5 av.
Daily newspapers (per '000 population)	255*	1964

c excl. telephones of the U.S. armed forces.

FINANCE

Currency unit: The U.S. dollar

		Year
National Income (million $ U.S.)	144	1958
G.N.P. per capita ($ U.S.)	450	1966

continued

na: data not available. — negligible or nil. [1] one year only. [2] two year average. * estimate. ‡ see appendix. † re-exports.

RYUKYU ISLANDS *continued*

PRODUCTION, EXPORTS AND IMPORTS

Years: **1963–5 average** and *1953–5 average* Units: '000 metric tons unless otherwise indicated

	Production		Exports		Imports	
1. CEREALS, etc.						
Barley	—	na	—	—	1.3	—
Maize (corn)	—	—	—	—	8.1*	—
Potatoes	6.0*	3.0	—	—	5.9	—
Rice	12.0	18.0[2]	—	—	93.4	40.0
Sweet potatoes/yams	67.0*	261.7				
Wheat	na	1.0	—	—	24.1	—
2. FRUIT, etc.						
Apples	—	—	—	—	2.2	—
Bananas	1.7*	1.0	0.1	—	1.5	—
Grapes	—	—	—	—	0.1	—
Oranges	—	—	—	—	4.7	—
Other citrus fruit	—	—	—	—	0.1	—
Pineapples	47.3	na	—	—	—	—
Tomatoes	1.3*	1.3				
3. BEVERAGES, FOREST PRODUCTS, etc.						
Sugar: cane	1 823.3	283.0				
raw	na n	7.0 n	186.9*	17.5	21.1	4.4
Tea	0.1*	0.1	—	—	0.7	—
Tobacco, leaf	0.5	—	—	—	1.6*	na
Softwood *j*	} 69.0	na	—	—	278.0*	na
Hardwood *j*		na	—	—	30.3[1] *q*	na
Newsprint	—	—	—	—	3.8[1]	na
Other paper	—	—	—	—	9.7[1]	na

j '000 cu. metres of roundwood equivalent. *n* in addition, black sugar 18.0 (1963–5 av.) and 19.3 (1953–5 av.). *q* sawn wood only.

	Production		Exports		Imports	
4. VEGETABLE OILSEEDS AND OILS						
Cottonseed oil	—	—	—	—	0.05	na
Groundnuts	—	—	0.06[2]†	—	0.23	—
Rapeseed oil	—	—	—	—	1.71	na
Soya beans	na	4.00	na	0.33	11.46	—
Soya bean oil	na	na	0.08	—	2.44	0.21[2]
5. LIVESTOCK‡, ANIMAL PRODUCTS, etc.						
Chickens *d*	971.7	261.0				
Cattle *d*	18.3	16.3	1.0	0.1	3.4	0.9
Goats *d*	57.0	92.7	—	—	—	—
Horses *d*	15.7	19.0				
Pigs *d*	121.0	143.0[1]	0.1	—	0.5	—
Meat‡, 'A'	9.7	4.0[2]	—	—	—	—
Eggs	8.8	na	—	—	0.6	—
Fish	21.0	12.5	5.1	na	12.0	na
Milk	1.0*	na	—	—	30.2*	0.3

d no in thousands.

	Production		Exports		Imports	
6. FIBRES, TEXTILES, etc.						
Cotton lint	—	—	—	—	0.4	—
Silk *f*	na	1.0[1]	—	1.5[2]	—	—

f metric tons.

	Production		Exports		Imports	
7. FUEL AND POWER						
Electricity *ht*	652	na				
Petroleum, refined	—	—	—	—	300	na

h million kWh. *t* thermal.

	Production		Exports		Imports	
11. INDUSTRY						
Cement	33.3*	—	—	—	273.7*	143.3*

SAN MARINO

EUROPE

San Marino is a small ancient republic surrounded by Italian territory. A long-established treaty of friendship and a customs union with Italy have been preserved.

AREA: 61.2 sq. km. (23.6 sq. miles)

POPULATION: 18 000 (1967 estimate)

Capital city: SAN MARINO; population: 3 817 (1964)

		Year(s)
Infant mortality (per '000)	14.0*	1965
Crude birth rate (per '000)	16.4*	1965
Crude death rate (per '000)	8.5*	1965
School enrolment: age 5–19 years (percentage)	43	1963–4 av.

COMMUNICATIONS

		Year(s)
Telephones (per '000 urban population)	9.5	1967
Radio receivers (per '000 population)	169	1963–5 av.
Television licences (per '000 population)	76.5	1963–5 av.

FINANCE

Currency unit: The lira *a*

Exchange rates	1965	1960	1955	1938
Per $ U.S.	624.7	620.6	625	19
Per £ sterling	1 750.5	1 740	1 750	87.4

a Italian and Vatican City notes are in use, but local coins and postage stamps are issued.

EMPLOYMENT, PRODUCTION AND TRADE

The principal farm products are cereals, wine and cattle. Industries include quarrying and dressing building stone, ceramics, textiles and paint manufacture. The tourist trade is considerable; 2 400 000 tourists visited the republic in 1964.

SAUDI ARABIA

MIDDLE EAST

The Saudi Arabian Kingdom was so named in 1932, and executive power remained with the king until a cabinet system of government became effective in 1962. Agreements for trade and co-operation were signed with Kuwait in 1942 and Jordan in 1962. Revenue from oil has been used to finance a recent programme of agricultural, social and industrial development.

AREA: 2 100 000* sq. km. (810 000* sq. miles)

LAND USE: (percentage of total)

	1965	1952
Arable and orchard	0.2	0.1
Permanent meadow and pasture (mainly rough grazing)	37.7	58.0
Forest and woodland	0.8	0.3
City areas, waste and other land	61.3	41.6

POPULATION: 6 990 000 (1967 U.N. estimate)

Largest city: AR RIYĀḌ (Riyadh), capital; population: 225 000 (city proper, 1965)

Employment: Camels and sheep are reared by the nomadic population of the Nejd plateau. Some cereal crops and fruit are grown around most of the oases. Oil is the most important industry; others include thermal electricity and cement.

		Year(s)
Population per physician	13 000	1964
Population per hospital bed	1 150	1966
School enrolment: age 5–19 years (percentage)	12	1963–4 av.
age over 19 years (per 100 000 population)	24	1963–5 av.

COMMUNICATIONS

		Year(s)
Motor vehicles in use ('000s): private	44.8	} 1963–5 av.
commercial	36	
Telephones (per '000 urban population)	0.4*	1967
Television sets (per '000 population)	3.8	1963–5 av.
Daily newspapers (per '000 population)	2.5	1962–3 av.

FINANCE

Currency unit: The riyal

Exchange rates	1965	1960	1958
Per $ U.S.	4.5	4.5	3.69
Per £ sterling	12.6	12.6	10.34

		Year
National Income (million $ U.S.)	850	1958
G.N.P. per capita ($ U.S.)	240	1966

continued

TRADING

Note—data are for the Islamic lunar year of 354 days

Total trade (in million $ U.S.)	1965	1965 *a*	1955 *a*
Exports (f.o.b.)	1 326	1 385	561
Imports (c.i.f.)	350	376	186

Main trading partners (percentage of total value)

Exports	1965	*Imports*	1965
Japan	19	U.S.A.	20
Italy	12	U.K.	9
U.S.A.	7	Japan	7
Bahrain	7	Lebanon	7
Germany F.R.	5	Germany F.R.	6
France	4	Italy	6
Australia	4	Syria	5

Distribution of trade (percentage of total value)

Exports	1965	*Imports*	1965
Crude petroleum	84	Manufactured goods	54
Petroleum products	16	(machinery and transport equipment)	(28)
		Food	28
		(cereals)	(10)
		Wood	3

a trade including the value of gold, specie and banknotes.

PRODUCTION, EXPORTS AND IMPORTS

Years: **1963–5 average** and *1953–5 average* Units: '000 metric tons unless otherwise indicated

	Production		Exports		Imports	
1. CEREALS, etc.						
Barley	3.0	na	—	—	34.0*	5.3[1]
Maize (corn)	—	na	—	—	22.9*[2]	7.1[1]
Millets/sorghum	65.0*	75.5[2]	0.2*	—[1]	32.5*	8.3[1]
Potatoes	—	—	—	—	6.6*	na
Rice	2.7	na	—	—	149.4*	20.6
Wheat	136.0	na	—	—	55.9*	27.3[1]
2. FRUIT, etc.						
Apples	—	—	—	—	9.5*	na
Bananas	—	—	—	—	8.9*[2]	na
Dates	299.3*	na	3.7*	na	1.4*	10.3*[2]
Grapes	—	—	—	—	1.0*	na
Lemons	—	—	—	—	1.5*	na
Oranges	—	—	—	—	15.3	na
Other citrus fruit	—	—	—	—	0.1*	na
Pears	—	—	—	—	0.4*	na
Tomatoes	59.3*	na				
3. BEVERAGES, FOREST PRODUCTS, etc.						
Coffee	0.1	—	0.1*	—	4.1*[2]	na
Sugar, raw	—	—	—	—	55.0*	22.5[1]
Tea	—	—	—	—	3.4	na
Tobacco: leaf	—	—	—	—	0.4[1]	—
cigarettes	—	—	—	—	0.3[2]	—
Wood	—	—	—	—	na	na
4. VEGETABLE OILSEEDS AND OILS						
Castor oil	—	—	—	—	0.01*	—
Coconut oil	—	—	—	—	0.23	na
Cottonseed	—	—	—	—	0.04[2]	na
Cottonseed oil	—	—	—	—	1.40	na
Groundnuts	—	—	—	—	0.48	na
Linseed oil	—	—	—	—	0.02[2]	na
Olive oil	—	—	—	—	0.34	na
Rapeseed oil	—	—	—	—	0.09*	na
Sesame seed	0.37*	na	0.16	na	1.80[2]*	na
Soya bean oil	—	—	—	—	0.19*	na

	Production		Exports		Imports	
5. LIVESTOCK‡, ANIMAL PRODUCTS, etc.						
Cattle *d*	67.0*	na	—	—[1]	6.9*	na
Goats *d*	2 306.0*	na	} 8.1	na	308.4*	na
Sheep *d*	2 750.0*	na				
Horses *d*	na	na				
Butter	—	—	—	—	0.7*	na
Cheese	—	—	—	—	1.5*	na
Eggs	9.9	na	—	—	0.8	na
Fish	20.5	na	—	—	—	—
Milk	4.0*	na	—	—	38.3*	na
Wool	na	na	0.1*	—	—	—

d no. in thousands.

	Production		Exports		Imports	
6. FIBRES, TEXTILES, etc.						
Agaves (sisal etc.)	—	—	—	—	0.1*	—
7. FUEL AND POWER						
Electricity *ht*	149 *n*	50[1]				
Natural gas *i*	490	—	—	—	—	—
Oil, crude	89 293	47 540[1]	75 020	37 470[1]	—	—
Petroleum, refined	13 900	9 740	10 367	na	67	—

h million kWh. *i* million cu. metres. *n* incomplete figure, referring to the production in three cities only. *t* thermal.

	Production		Exports		Imports	
9. NON-FERROUS MINERALS AND METALS						
Gold *k*, ore *m*	na	39.00	na	na	na	na
Silver *k*, ore *m*	na	71.70	na	na	na	na

k '000 fine troy oz. *m* metal content.

	Production		Exports		Imports	
11. INDUSTRY						
Aircraft *a*	—	—	—	—	1.8	na
Cement *p*	214.7*	—	—*	—	1 123.3*	700.0*
Electrical engineering *a*	—	—	—	—	13.0	na
Motor vehicles *a*	—	—	—	—	81.5[2]	na

a million $ U.S. *p* incl. data for other Arabian Peninsular States.

SENEGAL

WEST AFRICA

Senegal, formerly a state of French West Africa, and from 1959–60 a partner in the Federation of Mali, became an independent republic in 1960.

AREA: 197 161 sq. km. (76 124 sq. miles)

LAND USE: (percentage of total)

	1963
Arable and orchard	28.0
Forest and woodland	27.1
Permanent meadow and pasture } City areas, waste and other land	44.9

POPULATION: 3 670 000 (1967 U.N. estimate)

Largest city: DAKAR, capital; population: 374 700 (1961)

Total working population: 1 317 580 (1960/1)

		Year(s)
Life expectancy at birth (years)	37*	1957
Infant mortality (per '000)	90.2 *a*	1965
Population per physician	18 760	1965
Population per hospital bed	660 *b*	1966
School enrolment: age 5–19 years (percentage)	26	1963–4 av.
age over 19 years (per 100 000 population)	77	1964–5 av.

a in Dakar only. *b* government hospitals only.

COMMUNICATIONS

		Year(s)
Motor vehicles in use ('000s): private	26.6	} 1963–5 av.
commercial	17.6	
Railway track (km.)	390	1964
Telephones (per '000 urban population)	0.7	1967
Radio licences (per '000 population)	53*	1963–5 av.
Daily newspapers (per '000 population)	6	1963

FINANCE

Currency unit: The franc CFA

Exchange rates	1965	1960
Per $ U.S.	246.85	246.85
Per £ sterling	691.18	691.18

		Year
National Income (million $ U.S.)	519	1965
G.N.P. per capita ($ U.S.)	210	1966

continued

SENEGAL *continued*

TRADING

Total trade (in million $ U.S.)	*1965*	*1955a*
Exports (f.o.b.)	128	92
Imports (c.i.f.)	160	197

Main trading partners (percentage of total value)

Exports	*1965*	*Imports*	*1965*
France	81	France	54
Germany F.R.	3	Cambodia	6
Malagasy R.	2	Germany F.R.	5
Japan	2	U.S.A.	4
Italy	1	Thailand	4
U.K. and Irish R.	1	Ivory Coast	4
South Africa	1	Italy	3

Distribution of trade (percentage of total value)

Exports	*1965*	*Imports*	*1965*
Groundnuts (incl. oil and cake)	79	Manufactured goods	48
Natural phosphates	8	(textiles and clothing)	(16)
		(machinery and transport equipment)	(15)
		Food	35
		(cereals)	(17)
		Crude materials and fuels	8
		Chemicals	6

a incl. data for Mali and Mauritania.

PRODUCTION, EXPORTS AND IMPORTS

Years: **1963–5 average** Units: '000 metric tons unless otherwise indicated

Note—no data are available for 1953–5

	Production	Exports	Imports
1. CEREALS, etc.			
Barley	—	—	0.3
Cassava	159.3		
Maize (corn)	45.7	—	16.0
Millets/sorghum	536.7	—	22.3
Potatoes	5.3*	0.2	11.6
Rice	108.7	—	154.7
Sweet potatoes/yams	9.7		
Wheat	—	0.1†	63.6
2. FRUIT, etc.			
Apples	—	—	3.2*n*
Bananas	4.0*	—	1.4
Coconuts	10.0*[1]*e*	—	—
Dates	—	—	1.4
Grapes	—	—	0.3
Lemons	—	—	0.1
Oranges	3.0*	—	5.2
Other citrus fruit	—	—	0.1
Wine *b*	—	0.2†	114.4

b '000 hectolitres. *e* no. in millions. *n* incl. pears and quince.

	Production	Exports	Imports
3. BEVERAGES, FOREST PRODUCTS, etc.			
Coffee	—	—	0.4
Sugar, raw	—	0.5†	71.8
Tea	—	—	1.3
Tobacco: leaf	—	—	0.7
cigarettes	1 550.0*e*	0.1*p*	na
Softwood *j*	—	—	6.8
Hardwood *j*	2 110.0	—	20.2
Wood pulp	—	—	0.3[2]
Paper	—	—	13.0[2]

e no. in millions. *j* '000 cu. metres of roundwood equivalent. *p* incl. other tobacco products.

	Production	Exports	Imports
4. VEGETABLE OILSEEDS AND OILS			
Castor seed	na	0.10	—
Castor oil	na	—	0.01
Groundnuts	721.70	211.70	0.05
Groundnut oil	na	125.23	—
Linseed oil	—	—	0.10
Olive oil	—	—	0.02
Palm kernels	3.83	4.02	—
Palm oil	—	—	0.20

	Production	Exports	Imports
5. LIVESTOCK‡, ANIMAL PRODUCTS, etc.			
Chickens *d*	2 881.0*		
Cattle *d*	1 884.7	0.6	0.2
dairy cows *d*	949.0*		
Goats *d*	590.0*	} —	0.1
Sheep *d*	500.0*		
Horses *d*	111.0*		
Pigs *d*	42.0	—	—
Meat‡: 'A'	31.3*	—	—
'B'	—	—	0.1
Butter	—	—	0.5
Cheese	—	—	2.1
Eggs	9.2*	—	0.2
Fish	124.5	7.1	10.8
Milk	150.7*	—	25.6
Hides/skins	0.3[1]*	1.2	—

d no. in thousands.

	Production	Exports	Imports
6. FIBRES, TEXTILES, etc.			
Agaves (sisal etc.)	—	—	2.0
Rubber, natural	—	—	0.3
Cotton: yarn	0.5	—	0.2
woven fabrics	1.4	—	6.7
7. FUEL AND POWER			
Coal, 'A'‡	—	—	1
Electricity *h t*	192		
Oil, crude	—	—	253
Petroleum, refined	237	—	1 010

h million kWh. *t* thermal.

	Production	Exports	Imports
9. NON-FERROUS MINERALS AND METALS			
Titanium minerals	4.76	5.34	—
Zirconium minerals	1.21	1.10*q*	—

q zircon.

	Production	Exports	Imports
10. CHEMICALS AND FERTILIZERS			
Chemicals	—	—	na
Fertilizers:			
Phosphates	798.6	582.2	—
11. INDUSTRY			
Alcoholic beverages		—	2.2*a*
beer *b*	102.0		
Cement *r*	192.0	0.7	34.3*
Electrical engineering *a*	na	0.4†	6.2
Railway vehicles *a*	na	0.2	1.0
Merchant ships *g*	—	—	0.1
Motor vehicles *a*	—	0.7†	7.6

a million $ U.S. *b* '000 hectolitres. *g* '000 G.R.T. *r* incl. data for Mali and Mauritania.

na: data not available. — negligible or nil. [1] one year only. [2] two year average. * estimate. ‡ see appendix. † re-exports.

SIERRA LEONE

Sierra Leone, previously a British protectorate, became a sovereign and independent member of the Commonwealth in 1961.

AREA: 73 326 sq. km. (27 925 sq. miles)

LAND USE: (percentage of total)	*1965*	*1955*
Arable and orchard	51.1	50.6
Permanent meadow and pasture	30.7	30.4
Forest and woodland	4.2	4.2
City areas, waste and other land	14.0	14.8

POPULATION: 2 439 000 (1967 estimate)

Largest city: FREETOWN, capital; population: 148 000 (city proper, 1966)

Distribution of working population (1963)
Total working population: 937 737

U.N. group no.		*Percentage*
0	Agriculture, forestry, fishing and hunting	74.8
1	Mining and quarrying	5.1
2/3	Manufacturing	4.4
4	Construction	1.7
5	Electricity, gas, water and sanitary services	0.2
6	Commerce	5.7
7	Transport, storage and communications	1.7
8	Services	3.1
9	Others	3.3

		Year(s)
Infant mortality (per '000)	117.6*	1965
Crude birth rate (per '000)	43.6*	1965
Crude death rate (per '000)	18.6*	1965
Population per physician	16 440	1965
Population per hospital bed	1 210	1963
School enrolment: age 5–19 years (percentage)	16	1963–4 av.
age over 19 years (per 100 000 population)	36	1964–5 av.

COMMUNICATIONS		*Year(s)*
Motor vehicles in use ('000s): private	9.2	} 1963–4 av.
commercial	4.3	
Railway track (km.)	500	1964
Mail per capita: domestic	3	
foreign received	2	} 1963–5 av.
foreign sent	2	
Telephones (per '000 urban population)	0.2	1967
Radio receivers (per '000 population)	44	1963–5 av.
Television sets (per '000 population)	0.3	1963–5 av.
Daily newspapers (per '000 population)	7.5	1962–4 av.

FINANCE

Currency unit: The leone replaced the West African pound in 1964 at the rate Le1 to WA£0.5

Exchange rates	*1965*	*1960a*	*1954a*	*1938a*
Per $ U.S.	0.714	0.357	0.357	0.215
Per £ sterling	2.0	1.0	1.0	1.0

		Year(s)
National Income (million $ U.S.)	290	1965
G.N.P. per capita ($ U.S.)	150	1966
Foreign trade (percentage of G.D.P.)	55	1963–5 av.

a West African pounds.

TRADING

Total trade (in million $ U.S.)	*1965*	*1955*	*1938*
Exports (f.o.b.)	83	29	11
Imports (c.i.f.)	108	48	7

Main trading partners (percentage of total value)

Exports	*1965*	*1955*	*Imports*	*1965*	*1955*
U.K.	75	71	U.K.	33	60
Netherlands	11	6	U.S.A.	14	2
Germany F.R.	7	12	Japan	8	2
Italy	3	—	Netherlands	6	3
France	1	—	France	6	1
U.S.A.	1	6	Germany F.R.	4	2
			Italy	4	2

Distribution of trade (percentage of total value) *a*

Exports	*1965*	*1955*
Diamonds	64	14
Iron ore and concentrates	19	37
Palm kernels	10	25
Coffee and cocoa	4	12
Imports		
Manufactured goods	64	59
(machinery and transport equipment)	(29)	(15)
(textiles and clothing)	(16)	(22)
Food	14	18
Crude materials and fuels	10	7
(petroleum products)	(9)	(4)
Chemicals	5	4

a % of national exports‡ which comprised 91% of general exports in 1965 and 97% in 1955.

PRODUCTION, EXPORTS AND IMPORTS

Years: **1963–5 average** and *1953–5 average* Units: '000 metric tons unless otherwise indicated

	Production		Exports		Imports	
1. CEREALS, etc.						
Cassava	60.7*	*37.7*				
Maize (corn)	9.3*	na	—	—	—	—
Millets/sorghum	23.3*	*27.3*	—	—	—	—
Potatoes	—	—	—	—	1.0	*0.5*
Rice	324.0*	*221.7*	—	*0.3*	13.6	*8.7*
Sweet potatoes/yams	9.0*	*10.0*				
2. FRUIT, etc.						
Bananas	na	na	—	*0.5*	—	
Coconuts	na	na	—	*0.1*	—	—
Oranges	91.0*	na	—	—	—	—
Wine *b*	—	—	—	—	3.6	*21.7*

b '000 hectolitres.

	Production		Exports		Imports	
3. BEVERAGES, FOREST PRODUCTS, etc.						
Cocoa	3.6	*2.0**	3.2	*1.9*	—	—
Coffee	5.4	na	4.6	*1.9*	—	—
Sugar, raw	—	—	—	—	17.5	*5.3*
Tobacco: leaf	—	—	—	—	1.1	*0.8*
cigarettes	419.0*e*	na	—	—	0.1[2]*p*	*0.2*[2]
Hardwood *j*	2 688.0[1]	*2 647.3*[1]	—	—	13.0[2]*n*	*4.0*[1]
Newsprint	—	—	—	—	1.8[2]	*0.1*[2]
Other paper	—	—	—	—	0.2[2]*	*0.3*[2]

e no. in millions. *j* '000 cu. metres of roundwood equivalent. *n* incl. softwood. *p* incl. other tobacco products.

	Production		Exports		Imports	
4. VEGETABLE OILSEEDS AND OILS						
Groundnuts	5.83*	*3.97*	na	*0.90*	—	—
Groundnut oil	na	na	na	na	0.55	na
Palm kernels	52.23	na	52.23	*65.93*	—	—
Palm oil	37.67*	na	na	*0.44*	0.20	na
Sesame seed	na	na	na	*0.27*	—	—
Soya bean oil	—	—	—	—	0.97	na
5. LIVESTOCK‡, ANIMAL PRODUCTS, etc.						
Chickens *d*	2 000.0*	*966.7*				
Cattle *d*	183.3	*100.0*	—	—	—	—
Goats *d*	33.0*	*21.7*	}			
Sheep *d*	27.3	*11.7*	—	—	0.2	—
Pigs *d*	7.0*	*5.0*	—	—	—	—
Bacon/ham }	11.7*	na	{ —	—	0.2	—
Meat‡ 'A'			—	—	—	*0.1*
Butter	—	—	—	—	0.2	*0.1*
Cheese	—	—	—	—	0.1	—
Fish	30.2	na	0.1	na	5.5	na
Milk	—	—	—	—	13.3	*2.0**

d no. in thousands.

	Production		Exports		Imports	
6. FIBRES, TEXTILES, etc.						
Silk *f*	—	—	—	—	46.3	na
Cotton: yarn	—	—	—	—	0.1[1]	—
woven fabrics	—	—	—	—	3.5	na
Rayon, woven fabrics	—	—	—	—	0.3*n*	na

f metric tons. *n* incl. synthetic piece goods.

	Production		Exports		Imports	
7. FUEL AND POWER						
Coal, 'A'‡	—	—	—	—	3*n*	*27*
Electricity *h t*	87	*30*[1]				
Petroleum, refined	—	—	—	—	307	*30*[1]

h million kWh. *n* incl. coke. *t* thermal.

	Production		Exports		Imports	
8. IRON AND STEEL						
Iron ore	1 358*m*	*716m*	2 110	*1 155*	—	—

m metal content.

	Production		Exports		Imports	
9. NON-FERROUS MINERALS AND METALS						
Diamonds	1 437.67*l*	*6 005.27l*	50.92*a*	*4.01a*	—	—
Gold *k*, ore	—	*1.00m*	—	*1.77p*	—	—
Platinum group metals *k*	—	na	—	na	0.48[2]	—
Silver *k*, bullion	—	—	—	—	4.13[2]	*2.72*
Asbestos, manufactured	na	na	0.39	na	na	*1.04*[2]
Aluminium: bauxite	130.39*	—	108.26	—	—	—
aluminium	—	—	—	—	0.07	*0.04*[2]
Chrome, ore	0.93*m*	*21.63m*	2.95	*19.97*	—	—
Copper, metal	—	—	—	—	0.06	—
Lead, metal	—	—	—	—	0.04	*0.01*
Titanium minerals	na	—	0.30	—	—	—

a million $ U.S. *k* '000 fine troy oz. *l* '000 carats. *m* metal content. *p* bullion.

	Production		Exports		Imports	
10. CHEMICALS*n* AND FERTILIZERS						
Chemicals	—		—		na	
Fertilizers:						
Potash	—	—	—	—	0.1	na

n data not available for years 1953–5.

	Production		Exports		Imports	
11. INDUSTRY						
Alcoholic beverages *a*	—	—	—	—	1.7[1]	*2.4p*
Cement	15.0	—	—	—	68.3	*26.0*
Electrical engineering *a*	—	—	—	—	6.1[2]	*0.4*[2]
Railway vehicles *a*	—	—	—	—	1.2[2]	*1.1*
Motor vehicles *a*	—	—	—	—	7.7[2]	*1.1*[2]

a million $ U.S. *p* beer and wine only.

na: data not available. — negligible or nil. [1] one year only. [2] two year average. * estimate. ‡ see appendix. † re-exports.

SINGAPORE

Singapore, an independent state since 1959, became a state within Malaysia in 1963 but seceded two years later, regaining its sovereignty, to become an independent member of the British Commonwealth. Agreements for external defence and mutual assistance have been signed with Malaysia. Singapore's economy relies chiefly on the importance of the port as an entrepôt.

AREA: 581* sq. km. (224* sq. miles) (incl. adjacent islets)

LAND USE: (percentage of total)

	1965	1954
Arable and orchard	22.4	21.3
Permanent meadow and pasture	—	—
Forest and woodland	20.7	26.7
City areas, waste and other land	56.9	52.0

POPULATION: 1 956 000 (1967 estimate)

Capital city: SINGAPORE

Distribution of working population (1957)

Total working population: 480 267

U.N. group no.		*Percentage*
0	Agriculture, forestry, fishing and hunting	8.4
1	Mining and quarrying	0.3
2/3	Manufacturing	13.9
4	Construction	5.1
5	Electricity, gas, water and sanitary services	1.2
6	Commerce	25.3
7	Transport, storage and communications	10.5
8	Services	33.2
9	Others	2.1

		Year(s)
Infant mortality (per '000)	26.3	1965
Crude birth rate (per '000)	31.1	1965
Crude death rate (per '000)	5.6	1965
Accidental deaths (per 100 000 population)		
caused by motor vehicles	13.6	1966
due to other causes	15.2	1966
Population per physician	2 020	1964
Population per hospital bed	290*a*	1966
School enrolment: age 5–19 years (percentage)	82	1963–4 av.
age over 19 years (per 100 000 population)	708*	1963–5 av.

a government hospitals only.

COMMUNICATIONS

		Year(s)
Motor vehicles in use ('000s): private	98.9	1963–5 av.
commercial	20.5	1963–5 av.
Railway track (km.)	26	1965
Mail per capita: domestic	22	1965
foreign received	20	1965
foreign sent	15	1965
Telephones (per '000 urban population)	4.9	1967
Radio licences (per '000 population)	231	1963–5 av.
Television licences (per '000 population)	27.3	1963–5 av.
Daily newspapers (per '000 population)	272.3	1962–4 av.

FINANCE

Currency unit: The Singapore dollar, at par with the Malaysian dollar

Exchange rates	*1965*	*1960*	*1955*	*1938*
Per $ U.S.	3.06	3.06	3.06	1.86
Per £ sterling	8.57	8.57	8.57	8.57

		Year
National Income (million $ U.S.)	948	1965
G.N.P. per capita ($ U.S.)	570	1966

TRADING

Total trade (in million $ U.S.)	*1965*	*1955a*	*1938a*
Exports (f.o.b.)	981	583	334
Imports (c.i.f.)	1 244	745	315

Main trading partners (percentage of total value)

Exports	*1965*	*1955a*	*1938a*	*Imports*	*1965*	*1955a*	*1938a*
West Malaysia	31			West Malaysia	23		
U.K.	6	18	14	Japan	11	6	2*b*
Sarawak	5	2	2	U.K.	11	18	19
Hong Kong	4	1	1	China P.R.	6	3	4
Sabah	4	1	—	U.S.A.	5	4	3
U.S.S.R.	4	—	—	Sarawak	5	5	4
U.S.A.	4	17	30	Australia	4	4	2

Distribution of trade (percentage of total value)

Exports	*1965*	*Imports*	*1965*
Crude materials and fuels	42	Manufactured goods	38
(rubber)	(23)	(machinery and transport equipment)	(14)
(petroleum products)	(14)	(textiles and clothing)	(9)
Manufactured goods	27	Crude materials and fuels	32
(machinery and transport equipment)	(10)	(rubber)	(15)
Food	15	(petroleum products)	(13)
Chemicals	4	Food	20

a incl. West Malaysia. *b* incl. Taiwan and North and South Korea.

PRODUCTION

Years: **1963–5 average** and *1953–5 average* Units: '000 metric tons unless otherwise indicated

Note—Trade figures for Singapore are included with Malaysia

	Production		Exports		Imports	
1. CEREALS, etc.						
Cassava	**3.0**	*4.0*[1]				
Sweet potatoes/yams	**5.0**	*7.0*[2]				
2. FRUIT, etc.						
Bananas	—	*3.0*[1]				
Coconuts*e*	**11.3**	na				

e no. in millions.

	Production		Exports		Imports	
3. BEVERAGES, FOREST PRODUCTS, etc.						
Tobacco: leaf	**0.4**	—				
cigars	**0.1**	—				
cigarettes*e*	**2 496.0**	—				

e no. in millions.

	Production		Exports		Imports	
5. LIVESTOCK‡, ANIMAL PRODUCTS, etc.						
Chickens*d*	**10 212.0***r*	*4 250.0*[2]*r*				
Cattle*d*	**7.0**	*5.0*				
dairy cows*d*	**5.0***	*5.0*				
Goats*d*	**2.0**	*1.0*				
Pigs*d*	**402.0**	*244.0*				

continued

	Production		Exports		Imports	
5. LIVESTOCK‡, ANIMAL PRODUCTS, etc.—*continued*						
Meat‡ 'A'	**15.7**	*15.5*[2]				
'B'	**3.2***	*2.4**				
Eggs	**9.9**	*8.4*[2]				
Fish	**11.2**	*6.1*				
Milk	**1.0**	*2.0*[2]				

d no. in thousands. *r* incl. ducks, geese and turkeys.

	Production		Exports		Imports	
6. FIBRES, TEXTILES, etc.						
Rubber, natural	**1.53**	na				
7. FUEL AND POWER						
Electricity*ht*	**928**	—				
Petroleum, refined	**2 337**	na				

h million kWh. *t* thermal.

	Production		Exports		Imports	
11. INDUSTRY						
Beer*b*	**302.0**	na				

b '000 hectolitres.

na: data not available. — negligible or nil. [1] one year only. [2] two year average. * estimate. ‡ see appendix. † re-exports.

SOMALI REPUBLIC

Somalia, formerly Italian Somaliland, was united with British Somaliland to form the Somali Republic in 1960.

AREA: 637 660 sq. km. (246 135 sq. miles)

LAND USE: (percentage of total)

	1960*	1955
Arable and orchard	1.5	1.5
Permanent meadow and pasture	32.3	32.3
Forest and woodland	22.6	22.6
City areas, waste and other land	43.6	43.6

POPULATION: 2 660 000 (1967 estimate)

Largest city: MOGADISCIO (Mogadishu), capital; population: 170 000 (city proper, 1966)

Employment: Livestock rearing is the chief occupation, 75% of the population being nomadic. The remainder of the population is engaged mainly in the production of subsistence crops.

		Year(s)
Population per physician	30 000	1960
Population per hospital bed	560	1964
School enrolment: age 5–19 years (percentage)	5	1963–4 av.
age over 19 years (per 100 000 population)	3	1963–5 av.

COMMUNICATIONS

		Year(s)
Motor vehicles in use ('000s): private	4.3	1963–5 av.
commercial	6.1	1963–5 av.
Telephones (per '000 urban population)	0.2	1967
Radio receivers (per '000 population)	12	1963–5 av.
Daily newspapers (per '000 population)	2	1964

FINANCE

Currency unit: The Somali shilling was introduced in 1960 to replace, at par, the Italian somalo and the British East African shilling

Exchange rates	*1965*	*1960*	*1958a*
Per $ U.S.	7.14	7.14	7.2
Per £ sterling	20.2	20.2	20.2

		Year
National Income (million $ U.S.)	96	1958
G.N.P. per capita ($ U.S.)	50	1966

a somalos.

TRADING

Total trade (in million $ U.S.)	*1965*	*1955a*
Exports (f.o.b.)	33	10
Imports (c.i.f.)	50	14

Main trading partners (percentage of total value)

Exports	*1965*	*1955a*	*Imports*	*1965*	*1955a*
Italy	49	78	Italy	29	57
Arab. Pen. States	39	10	U.S.S.R.	8	na
U.A.R.	4	na	Kenya*b*	7	16
Kenya*b*	3	2	U.K.	6	1
U.S.A.	2	3	France	5	na
Afars/Issas	1	—	Japan	5	na
			U.S.A.	5	3

Distribution of trade (percentage of total value)

Exports	*1965*	*1955a*
Bananas and plantains	46	67
Livestock	29	3
Hides and skins	6	10
Wood charcoal	5	1

Imports	*1965*	*1955a*
Manufactured goods	52	56
(machinery and transport equipment)	(24)	(21)
(textiles and clothing)	(9)	(16)
Food	26	21
(rice)	(8)	(4)
Crude materials and fuels	10	12
Chemicals	5	6
Vegetable oils	4	1

a former Italian Somaliland only. *b* incl. Tanzania and Uganda.

PRODUCTION, EXPORTS AND IMPORTS

Years: **1963–5 average** and *1953–5 average* Units: '000 metric tons unless otherwise indicated

Note—the trade figures given for 1953–5 are the sum of the trade figures for the former Italian and British Somalilands; thus they include trade between these two regions, and are not, therefore, comparable with the trade figures for 1963–5.

	Production		Exports		Imports	
1. CEREALS, etc.						
Cassava	**18.3***	na				
Maize (corn)	**38.0***	*36.3*	—	—	**4.9**[2]	*1.4*
Millets/sorghum	**54.3***	*67.0*	—	*0.3*[2]	**2.0**[2]	*3.8*[2]
Oats	—	—	—	—	—	*0.5*
Potatoes	—	—	—	—	**0.6**[1]	*0.8*
Rice	—	—	—	—	**29.8**[2]	*6.3*
Sweet potatoes/yams	**2.0***	—				
Wheat	—	—	—	—	**0.2**[2]	—
2. FRUIT, etc.						
Bananas	**141.0**	*66.0*	**102.4***	*40.5*	—	—
Coconuts*e*	**1.0***[1]	na	—	—	—	—
Citrus fruit	**4.0***	*3.0*	**0.3**[2]	—	—	—
Dates	—	—	—	—	**9.1***	*7.0*[2]
Wine*b*	—	—	—	—	**1.0**[2]	*5.0*

b '000 hectolitres. *e* no. in millions.

	Production		Exports		Imports	
3. BEVERAGES, FOREST PRODUCTS, etc.						
Coffee	—	—	—	—	**1.5**[2]	*0.9*
Sugar: cane	**173.7**	*85.5*[2]				
raw	**13.7**	*8.3*	—	*0.1*	**13.8***	*7.5*
Tea	—	—	—	—	**1.6**[2]	*0.4*
Tobacco: leaf	**0.1***	—	—	—	—	—
products	—	—	—	—	**0.3**	*0.1*[2]*n*
Softwood*j*	—	—	—	—[2]	**8.0**[1]	*3.0*[1]
Hardwood*j*	**560.3**[2]	*41.5*[2]	—	—[2]	na	—[1]
Newsprint	—	—	—	—[2]	**0.1**[1]	*0.4*[2]
Other paper	—	—	—	—[2]	**0.3**[1]	*0.2*[2]

j '000 cu. metres of roundwood equivalent. *n* in addition cigarettes (in millions) 47.4.

	Production		Exports		Imports	
4. VEGETABLE OILSEEDS AND OILS						
Coconut oil	—	—	—	—	**1.27**[1]	*0.19*
Cottonseed	**2.00***	*1.30*	—	—	—	*0.03*
Cottonseed oil	na	na	—	—	**1.58***	—
Groundnuts	**1.40***	*0.70*	—	*0.17*	—	—
Groundnut oil	na	na	—	*0.01*	**0.62**[1]	—
Olive oil	—	—	**0.02†**	*0.01†*	**0.34**[2]	*0.12*
Sesame seed	**5.17***	*3.47*	—	*0.17*	—	*0.05*

	Production		Exports		Imports	
5. LIVESTOCK‡, ANIMAL PRODUCTS, etc.						
Chickens*d*	**4 000****p*	*3 000**				
Cattle*d*	**1 351***	*1 122**	**50.8***	*8.5*	—	—
Goats*d*	**4 563***	*4 314*[2]*	**858.3**[2] (goats and sheep)	na	—	—
Sheep*d*	**3 823***	na				
Horses*d*	na	na				
Pigs*d*	**4***	*2**	—	—	—	—
Meat‡, 'A'	**22***	na	—	—	—	—
Butter	na	na	**0.1**[2]	—	**0.2**[1]	—
Eggs	**13***	na	—	—	—	—
Fish	**5**[2]*	na	—	—	—	—
Milk	**77***	na	—	—	—	—
Hides/skins	na	*2*[2]*	**3.8**[2]	*1.8*[2]	—	—

d no. in thousands. *p* incl. ducks, geese and turkeys.

	Production		Exports		Imports	
6. FIBRES, TEXTILES, etc.						
Cotton: lint	**1.0***	*0.3*	**0.4**[2]	*0.7*	—	—
woven fabrics	—	—	—	—	na	*0.7*
7. FUEL AND POWER						
Electricity*ht*	**11**	*3*				
Petroleum, refined	—	—	—	—	**37**	*10*[1]

h million kWh. *t* thermal.

	Production		Exports		Imports	
9. NON-FERROUS MINERALS AND METALS						
Beryl	—	*0.01*	—	*0.01*	—	—
10. CHEMICALS*n* AND FERTILIZERS						
Chemicals	—		—		na	
Fertilizers:						
Phosphates	na	na	na	*0.2p*	—	—

n data not available for years 1953–5. *p* guano.

	Production		Exports		Imports	
11. INDUSTRY						
Aircraft*a*	—	—	—	—	**0.1**	—
Alcoholic beverages*a*	—	—	—	—	**0.4**	*0.2r*
Cement	—	—	—	—	**38.3**	*7.4*
Electrical engineering*a*	—	—	—	—	**1.5**	*0.4*
Motor vehicles*a*	—	—	**0.1†**	—	**4.5**	*0.9*

a million $ U.S. *r* beer and wine only.

na: data not available, — negligible or nil. [1] one year only. [2] two year average. * estimate. ‡ see appendix. † re-exports.

SOUTH AFRICA

The Union of South Africa withdrew from the British Commonwealth in 1961 to become the Republic of South Africa. In 1966 the U.N. General Assembly terminated South Africa's trusteeship of South West Africa, but South Africa continues to administer the territory.

AREA: 1 221 042 sq. km. (471 445 sq. miles) (excl. Walvis Bay *a*)
a see South West Africa.

LAND USE: (percentage of total)	*1960*	*1954*
Arable and orchard	9.9	7.5
Permanent meadow and pasture	74.0	75.7
Forest and woodland	1.3	0.9
City areas, waste and other land	14.8	15.9

POPULATION: 18 733 000 (1967 estimate)
Largest city: JOHANNESBURG; population: 1 152 525 (1960)
Administrative capital: PRETORIA; population: 422 590 (1960)
Legislative capital: CAPE TOWN; population: 807 221 (1960)

Distribution of working population (1960)
Total working population: Africans *c* and Asians 4 551 361
Europeans 1 140 469

U.N. group no.		*Percentage* Africans *c* and Asians	*Europeans*
0	Agriculture, forestry, fishing and hunting	34.9	10.3
1	Mining and quarrying	11.9	5.5
2/3	Manufacturing	9.9	20.1
4	Construction	4.5	6.3
5	Electricity, gas, water and sanitary services	0.6	0.9
6	Commerce	4.9	20.5
7	Transport, storage and communications	2.0	10.7
8	Services	21.4	22.1
9	Others	9.9	3.6

	Africans c	*Asians*	*Europeans*	*Year*
Life expectancy at birth (years): male	49.6*	57.7*	64.7*	1960
female	54.3*	59.6*	71.7*	1960
Infant mortality (per '000)	134.0	55.9	24.5	1965
Crude birth rate (per '000)	44.2	32.3	24.0	1965
Crude death rate (per '000)	15.2	7.7	9.0	1965
Accidental deaths (per 100 000 population) caused by motor vehicles	43.8	26.9	38.6	1966
due to other causes	42.5	19.6	28.0	1966
Population per physician			1 900 *b*	1963
Population per hospital bed			190 *b*	1962
School enrolment: age 5–19 years (percentage)			69 *b*	1963
age over 19 years (per 100 000 population)			329 *ab*	1965

a at universities only. *b* data for total population. *c* incl. coloured population.

COMMUNICATIONS		*Year(s)*
Motor vehicles in use ('000s): private	1 016	1963–5 av.
commercial	262	1963–5 av.
Railway track (km.)	21 203	1962
Mail per capita: domestic	53	1964–5 av.
foreign received	6	1964–5 av.
foreign sent	4	1964–5 av.
Telephones (per '000 urban population)	6.9	1967
Radio receivers (per '000 population)	126	1963–5 av.
Daily newspapers (per '000 population)	57	1961

FINANCE

Currency unit: The rand replaced the South African pound in 1961 at the rate R1 to SA £0.5

Exchange rates	*1965*	*1960 a*	*1950 a*	*1938 a*
Per $ U.S.	0.714	0.357	0.357	0.215
Per £ sterling	2.0	1.0	1.0	1.0

		Year(s)
National Income (million $ U.S.)	8 900 *b**	1965
G.N.P. per capita ($ U.S.)	550 *b*	1966
Rate of increase of G.N.P. per capita	3.5 *bc*	1960–4 av.
Foreign trade (percentage of G.D.P.)	36	1963–5 av.

a South African pounds. *b* incl. South West Africa. *c* incl. Botswana, Lesotho and Swaziland.

TRADING

Total trade (in million $ U.S.)	*1965*	*1955*	*1938*
Exports excluding gold (f.o.b.)	1 485	1 033	157
Exports of gold (f.o.b.)	1 074	497	355
Imports (c.i.f.)	2 459	1 350	463

Main trading partners (percentage of total value excl. gold)

Exports	*1965*	*1955*	*1938*	*Imports*	*1965*	*1955*	*1938*
U.K.	34	31	77	U.K.	28	35	39
U.S.A.	9	8	1	U.S.A.	19	21	17
Japan	7	2	1	Germany F.R.	11	6	5 *d*
Germany F.R.	5	5	7 *d*	Japan	6	2	3
Belg./Lux.	4	5	2	Italy	4	2	1
Italy	4	5	1	Canada	3	4	3
France	3	4	3	France	3	1	1

Distribution of trade (percentage of total value excl. gold)

Exports	*1965*	*1955*	*1938* b*
Crude materials and fuels	34	na	na
(textile fibres)	(13)	(18*)	(34)
(metalliferous ores)	(10)	(5*)	(na)
Manufactured goods	34	na	na
(diamonds)	(13)	(10)	(9)
Food	23	20	27
(fruit and vegetables)	(11)	(7*)	(12)
Imports			
Manufactured goods	73	na	na
(machinery and transport equipment)	(42)	(19*)	(16)
(textiles and clothing)	(9)	(13*)	(21)
Crude materials and fuels	13	na	na
Chemicals	7	5	4
Food	4	5	6

b 1938 figures are percentages of the value excl. government stores and trade with South West Africa and Zambia. *d* incl. Germany D.R.

PRODUCTION, EXPORTS AND IMPORTS

Years: **1963–5 average** and *1953–5 average* Units: '000 metric tons unless otherwise indicated

1. CEREALS, etc.	Production		Exports		Imports	
Barley	35.7	55.0[2]*	2.8	13.9	1.0[2]	—
Maize (corn)	4 956.7n	3 409.7	1 410.3	406.2	0.5	47.0
Millets/sorghum	337.3*	163.3	103.6	42.0	1.2	0.3
Oats	120.0	na	—	8.8	13.5	7.6
Potatoes	417.3*	184.0[1]	15.0	16.7	8.0	5.3
Rice	2.0*	8.0[1]	0.3	0.3s	60.2	18.0
Rye	13.3	na	—	—	1.2	—
Sweet potatoes/yams	61.0*	na				
Wheat	875.3	657.0	—	0.6	155.0	234.7

n from farms and villages only. *s* incl. re-exports.

2. FRUIT, etc.	Production		Exports		Imports	
Apples	139.7*	56.0[1]*	79.8	18.4	0.2[2]	—
Apricots	30.3	21.7*	na	0.6	—	—
Bananas	57.7	na	—	0.4	9.7	12.8
Coconuts	—	—	—	—	2.2q	1.4
Dates	—	—	—	—	1.3	1.5
Figs	1.0*	1.0[1]	—	—	—	—
Grapes	721.3*	502.3*	28.7	18.7	—	—
Lemons	22.0*	4.0	9.7	2.6	—	—
Oranges	452.7*	258.0	262.4	173.9	0.4	—
Other citrus fruit	51.7*	14.3	27.7*	10.9	0.1	—

continued

2. FRUIT, etc.—*continued*	Production		Exports		Imports	
Peaches	122.7*	49.8*	na	1.9	—	—
Pears	60.7*	26.0[2]p	30.3	19.6	—	—
Pineapples	111.0*	74.3*	na	3.5	—	—
Plums	12.0*	14.2*	na	2.4	—	—
Raisins	8.2*	8.6	3.3	3.2	0.1	—
Tomatoes	140.0*	na				
Wine b	4 008.5[2]	2 886.0*	187.1	128.3	23.9	2.3

b '000 hectolitres. *p* total handled by the Deciduous Fruit Board. *q* incl. desiccated coconut.

3. BEVERAGES, FOREST PRODUCTS, etc.	Production		Exports		Imports	
Cocoa	—	—	—	—	4.1	3.3
Coffee	—	—	0.4†	0.1†	13.0	10.8
Sugar: cane	9 668.7	6 532.3	—	—	—	—
raw	1 259.7	754.0	513.4	190.2	18.7	0.2
Tea	—	—	0.3†	3.0†	16.5	11.7
Tobacco: leaf	26.5	17.1	7.7	1.2	2.4	2.0
cigarettes e	11 535.0	10 038.0	na	—	na	—
tobacco/snuff	10.7	9.8[2]				
Softwood j	2 468.0[2]	1 150.0[2]*	1.0	na	318.8	463.7*
Hardwood j	4 215.0[2]	na	9.4	na	464.0	na
Wood pulp	204.0[1]	43.7*	134.6	na	23.9	10.0*
Newsprint	99.5[2]	na	—	na	52.7	46.3
Other paper	330.5[2]	85.0*	11.2	na	153.3	113.0[1]*

e no. in millions. *j* '000 cu. metres of roundwood equivalent. *continued*

PRODUCTION, EXPORTS AND IMPORTS *continued*

4. VEGETABLE OILSEEDS AND OILS	Production		Exports		Imports	
Castor seed	12.67	5.79	1.37	—	—	0.23
Castor oil	na	na	—	0.14	0.13	0.11
Copra	—	—	—	—	—	0.17
Coconut oil	—	—	—	—	7.70	6.87
Cottonseed	26.00*	11.00	—	0.47	0.05	—
Cottonseed oil	na	na	—	—	0.22	—
Groundnuts	157.73	142.80	55.51	27.60	0.04[2]	—
Groundnut oil	na	na	9.50	16.63	0.03[2]	0.04
Linseed	—	—	—	—	0.03[2]	0.03
Linseed oil	na	na	0.17s	0.05s	5.45	6.11
Olive oil	—	—	—	—	0.11	0.13
Palm kernel oil	—	—	—	—	1.91	2.59
Palm oil	—	—	—	—	—	1.16
Soya beans	2.70*	na	—	—	0.05	—
Soya bean oil	na	na	—	—	0.76	0.24n
Sunflower seed	84.00	55.67	3.41	3.76	—	—
Sunflower seed oil	na	na	0.73	0.24	—	0.02
Tung oil	—	—	—	—	0.35[2]	—

n incl. maize oil. *s* incl. re-exports.

5. LIVESTOCK‡, ANIMAL PRODUCTS, etc.	Production		Exports		Imports	
Chickens d	11 168.7*	15 840.0*				
Cattle d	12 366.7*	11 629.5[2]	11.6	26.5	0.6	103.2
dairy cows d	3 805.0*	2 908.0[1]n				
Goats d	5 288.0*	5 482.0[2]	6.3	na	—	—
Sheep d	38 233.3*	36 567.0[2]				
Horses d	460.0*	na				
Pigs d	1 440.0*	514.0[2]	0.1	3.9	—	—
Bacon/ham	563.0*	390.5[2]q	0.6	2.1p	0.3	—
Meat‡: 'A'			15.6	5.4	0.3	2.5
'B'	130.8*	98.5[2]q	3.9	1.4	—	—
Butter	42.7	37.3	1.2	1.3	6.7	2.2
Cheese	14.0*	11.7	0.2	0.8	1.5	0.2
Eggs	70.4*	40.1[2]	7.3	4.1	—	—
Fish	621.3	363.8	357.8	75.4*	5.1	15.2[2]*
Milk	2 526.7*	2 058.5	0.9	5.1	31.2	1.5
Whale oil	16.5	30.5	—	—	—	—
Hides/skins	na	na	24.6a	31.5	1.2a	—
Wool	67.2*	64.7	62.8	57.6	3.5	4.3

a million $ U.S. *d* no. in thousands. *n* on farms and estates only. *p* incl. canned bacon. *q* government inspected meat only.

6. FIBRES, TEXTILES, etc.	Production		Exports		Imports	
Abaca	—	—	—	—	0.6	1.4[2]*
Agaves (sisal etc.)	1.8*	na	—	—	5.1	5.3
Cotton lint	13.0*	5.7	0.6	0.2	23.9	2.5
Flax fibre	—	—	—	—	—	1.4
Hemp fibre	—	—	—	—	0.6[2]	na
Jute	2.7*	na	—	—	—	16.2*
Rubber: natural	—	—	0.1†	—	26.3	27.3
synthetic	7.3	—	0.3	—	19.6[2]	4.1
Cotton: yarn	38.2	7.7[2]*	0.1[1]	—	2.2	4.2
woven fabrics	11.0	1.1*	—	—	15.6	24.1
Rayon: fibre/yarn	—[2]	—	0.2[2]†	—	31.1[2]	5.8
woven fabrics	na	na	—	—	8.7	16.3
Non-cellulosic fibre/yarn	2.7[2]	na	0.1	na	9.0	na
Wool: yarn	9.8	11.4[1]	0.1[2]	—	1.3	1.3
woven fabrics	4.0r	15.0[1]*	—	—	na	11.9

r million metres.

7. FUEL AND POWER	Production		Exports		Imports	
Coal, 'A'‡	45 287	32 150	1 375	1 059p	57	15[2]
Coke	na	na	2	6	11	na
Electricity h: total	29 900*	14 778[1]				
hydro	40	8[1]				
thermal	29 860*	14 770[1]				
Oil, crude	—	—	—	—	3 903	940[1]
Petroleum, refined	3 803	850[1]	353	80[1]	1 813	2 280p
Rare earths (monazite) f	696	na	—	—	—	—
Uranium f	3 062	3 353u	3 755[1]v	45a	—	—

a million $ U.S. *f* metric tons. *h* million kWh. *p* incl. bunkers. *u* 1956 data. *v* U_3O_8 content of concentrates.

8. IRON AND STEEL	Production		Exports		Imports	
Iron ore	3 482m	1 223m	1 022	3	—	—
Pig iron	2 973	1 240	555	35	1	—[2]
Steel ingots/castings	3 090	1 417	2	—		1[2]
Iron/steel products a	na	na	62	—	77	41

a million $ U.S. *m* metal content.

9. NON-FERROUS MINERALS AND METALS	Production		Exports		Imports	
Diamonds	4 590.33l	2 714.32l	142.63a	105.37as	0.42an	28.72a
Gold k: ore m	29 032.70	13 259.70	—	6.13	—	—
bullion/coins etc.	na	na	29 889.67	12 909.70	—	—
Platinum group metals k	554.37	346.44	13.68[1]a	301.67	2.45	0.29
Silver k, ore	2 928.70m	1 296.30m	2 050.69p	0.24p	47.75[2]p	169.73p
Asbestos: fibre	200.21[1]	97.87	212.94	110.56q	6.58[2]	—
manufactured	na	na	0.87a	1.21a	2.41a	0.72[2]a
Mica	2.51	2.46	2.12	3.09	0.63	0.04
Aluminium: bauxite	—	—	—	—	8.27	—
alumina	—	—	—	—	0.52	—
aluminium	na	—	1.17[2]†	0.85†	25.03r	5.60*
Antimony, ore	12.25m	8.52m	20.29	14.40	0.32[1]v	0.18v
Beryl	0.19	0.26	0.15	0.26	—	—
Chrome, ore	861.26m	635.88m	648.02	483.73	63.87[2]	—
Copper: ore	58.36m	41.04m	2.75m	1.11m	5.57[2]	—
metal	54.50	39.68	84.32[2]	37.59	36.26	13.94[2]
Lead: ore	0.02m	0.39m	—	0.07	na	na
metal	na	na	47.97	0.12	11.89	10.96[2]
Magnesium: magnesite	89.98	na	3.36	—	31.17[2]	—
metal/salts	—	—	—	—	11.09[1]	9.63
Manganese: ore	1 398.43	705.97	943.65	523.07[2]	0.57[2]	—
metal	na	na	124.33	—	—	0.72
Mercury f	—	—	—	—	25.90	34.90[2]
Nickel: ore m	2.63	2.00	na	1.62	—	—
metal	na	na	0.92[2]	—	—	—
Tin: ore	1.60m	1.34m	1.30	1.21	—	—
metal	1.00	0.80	na	0.51t	0.61	0.34
Titanium minerals	9.80	0.87[2]	10.40	0.57	—	—
Tungsten, ore	0.01	0.30w	0.01	0.40w	—	—
Vanadium	1.27m	—	2.08u	—	—	—
Zinc, metal	—	—	0.18†	0.08†	40.09	20.95[1]
Zirconium minerals	0.80	—	0.87	—	—	—

a million $ U.S. *f* metric tons. *k* '000 fine troy oz. *l* '000 carats. *m* metal content. *n* cut and polished diamonds only. *p* bullion. *q* incl. data for Swaziland and Bechuanaland. *r* excl. aluminium sulphates. *s* incl. re-exports. *t* middlings. *u* vanadium-oxide. *v* metal. *w* waste.

10. CHEMICALS *n* AND FERTILIZERS	Production		Exports		Imports	
Organic chemicals:						
Benzene	na		—		na	
Butadiene	—		—		na	
Ethylene	na		—		na	
Methanol	na		0.2[1]		0.3[1]	
Phenol	—		—		na	
Phthalic anhydride	na		—		na	
Styrene monomer	na		—		1.8[2]	
Urea	na		0.2[1]		24.5[1]	
Inorganic chemicals:						
Ammonia	na		—		—	
Carbon black	na		—		7.6[2]	
Chlorine	na		0.4[1]		—	
Nitric acid	na		0.1[1]		—[1]	
Sodium carbonate	na		—		88.7[2]	
Sodium hydroxide	35.0[1]*		—		10.6	
Sulphuric acid	na		7.6[1]		—[1]	
Plastics:						
Polyamides	na		na		na	
Polyethylene	na		0.1[2]		20.8	
Polyvinyl chloride	5.0[1]		0.6[1]		8.1[2]	
Fertilizers:						
Phosphates	547.6	103.6	12.0	—	265.6	323.5z
Potash	—	—	—	—	108.3	24.8
Pyrites	172.7x	88.4x	3.8[2]	—	—	—
Sulphur	5.0y	na	0.2	0.1	154.2	69.9[2]

n data not available for years 1953–5. *x* sulphur content. *y* recovered sulphur only. *z* incl. South West Africa.

11. INDUSTRY	Production		Exports		Imports	
Aircraft a	—	—	—	—	18.0	na
Alcoholic beverages			7.2a	8.0a	7.3a	4.4a
beer b	1 422.0	959.0[2]				
spirits b	177.0n	285.0p				
Cement	3 405.7	2 207.3	41.0	35.0	33.7q	26.7q
Electrical engineering a	253.1[2]	na	6.4	na	133.1	42.3[2]
Locomotives c	158.0*	na	na	—	na	na
Railway vehicles a	na	na	1.7	—	17.3	na
Machine tools a	na	na	0.1	—	27.3	6.5
Merchant ships g	0.6	—	—	—	20.0	na
Motor vehicles			5.8	13.1[2]	275.8	7.2[2]
commercial dr	43.5	na				
private dr	130.0	na				

a million $ U.S. *b* '000 hectolitres. *c* no. of units. *d* no. in thousands. *g* '000 G.R.T. *n* 1965 data. *p* 1962 data. *q* incl. data for South West Africa. *r* assembly of imported parts.

SOUTH WEST AFRICA

Since 1920 South West Africa has been administered by South Africa in whose parliament it is represented. In 1968 the U.N. General Assembly proclaimed that South West Africa would, in future, be known as Namibia; and it urged the immediate termination of the South African administration of the territory, but this has not yet (1971) been effected.

Walvis Bay (980 sq. km.), the main trading port, is an integral part of South Africa, but is administered by South West Africa.

AREA: 824 295 sq. km. (318 261 sq. miles) (excl. Walvis Bay)

LAND USE: (percentage of total)	*1960*	*1954*
Arable and orchard	0.8	0.1
Permanent meadow and pasture	64.2	62.0
Forest and woodland	6.4	6.1
City areas, waste and other land	28.6	31.8

POPULATION: 594 000 (1967 U.N. estimate)

Capital city: WINDHOEK; population: 36 051 (1960)

Distribution of working population (1960)

Total working population: 203 323

U.N. group no.		*Percentage*
0	Agriculture, forestry, fishing and hunting	58.5
1	Mining and quarrying	5.9
2/3	Manufacturing	4.3
4	Construction	6.1
5	Electricity, gas, water and sanitary services	0.4
6	Commerce	4.3
7	Transport, storage and communications	3.2
8	Services	11.9
9	Others	5.4

	Africans	*Europeans*	*Year*
Infant mortality (per '000)	111.1*	39.1*	1964
Crude birth rate (per '000)	57.3*	23.0	1964
Crude death rate (per '000)	15.2	6.9	1964
School enrolment: age 5–19 years (percentage)	36*a*		1963

a Africans and Europeans.

COMMUNICATIONS		*Year*
Motor vehicles in use ('000s)	41.5	1966
Railway track (km.)	2 338	1964
Telephones (per '000 urban population)	4.4	1967
Daily newspapers (per '000 population)	12	1964

FINANCE

Currency unit: The South African rand

TRADE

90% of the trade is with South Africa.

PRODUCTION, EXPORTS AND IMPORTS

Years: **1963–5 average** and *1953–5 average* Units: '000 metric tons unless otherwise indicated

	Production		Exports		Imports	
1. CEREALS, etc.						
Maize (corn)	**9.3***	*23.0*[1]	—	—	na	*0.8*[1]
Millets/sorghum	**15.0***	*17.3*	—	—	na	*0.1*
Oats	—	—	—	—	na	*0.1*[2]
Potatoes	—	—	na	*0.2*[2]†	na	*1.5*[2]
Rice	—	—	—	—	na	*0.3*
Wheat	**1.0***	*1.0*[2]	—	—[2]	na	*12.3n*

n wheat flour.

	Production		Exports		Imports	
2. FRUIT, etc.						
Apples	—	—	—	—	na	*0.1*[1]
Bananas	—	—	—	—	na	*0.3*
Grapes	—	—	—	—	na	*0.2*[2]
Oranges	—	—	—	—	na	*0.4*
Raisins	—	—	—	—	na	*0.1*
Wine *b*	—	—	—	—	na	*4.7*

b '000 hectolitres.

	Production		Exports		Imports	
3. BEVERAGES, FOREST PRODUCTS, etc.						
Coffee	—	—	—	—	na	*0.1*
Sugar, raw	—	—	—	—	na	*5.5*
Tea	—	—	—	—	na	*0.1*
Softwood *j*	—	—	—	—	na	*24.3*[2]
Hardwood *j*	na	*168.0*[2]	—	—	na	*0.3*[2]
Newsprint	—	—	—	—	na	*0.1*
Other paper	—	—	—	—	na	*0.2*[2]

j '000 cu. metres of roundwood equivalent.

	Production		Exports		Imports	
4. VEGETABLE OILSEEDS AND OILS						
Groundnut oil	—	—	—	—	na	*0.04*
Linseed oil	—	—	—	—	na	*0.02*

	Production		Exports		Imports	
5. LIVESTOCK‡, ANIMAL PRODUCTS, etc.						
Chickens *d*	**314.0***n*	*180.0*				
Cattle *d*	**2 291.3**	*1 550.0*	—	*109.0*	—	*0.4*
Goats *d*	**1 533.0***	*533.3*	—	—	—	—
Sheep *d*	**3 621.0**	*3 266.7*	—	—	—	—
Horses *d*	**31.0***	*36.0*				
Pigs *d*	**19.0***	*23.3*	—	—	—	*3.3*
Meat‡, 'A'	**64.0***	*36.0*[2]	—	*3.3*	—	—
Butter	**3.3**	*4.3*	—	*1.7*	—	—
Cheese	—	na	—	*0.1*	—	—
Eggs	**0.1***	*0.1*[1]	—	—	—	*0.1*
Fish	**634.8***p*	*259.8p*	na	*76.3**	—	*0.1*[1]*
Milk	**60.0***	*115.5*[2]	—	—	—	*1.1*
Wool	na	*4.0*[2]	—	*2.2*	—	—

d no. in thousands. *n* incl. ducks, geese and turkeys. *p* incl. fish landed in Walvis Bay.

	Production		Exports		Imports	
7. FUEL AND POWER						
Coal, 'A'‡	—	—	—	—	na	*68*[2]
Electricity *h t*	**188**	—				
Petroleum, refined	—	—	na	na	na	na

h million kWh. *t* thermal.

	Production		Exports		Imports	
8. IRON AND STEEL						
Iron ore	na	—[2]*m*	—	—	—	—

m metal content.

	Production		Exports		Imports	
9. NON-FERROUS MINERALS AND METALS						
Diamonds	**1 464.00***l*	*699.38l*	**1 328.67***l*	*35.91a*	—	—
Silver *k*, ore *m*	**1 373.30**	*951.70*	**474.84**	*1 279.21*[1]	—	—
Asbestos, manufactured	—	—	—	—	—	*0.23*[2]*a*
Mica	**0.35**	na	**0.31**	—	—	—
Aluminium	—	—	—	—	—	*0.01*[2]
Beryl	**0.04**	*0.49*	**0.02**	*0.43*	—	—
Cadmium	**0.01**	*0.64*	**0.36**	*0.47*	—	—
Copper: ore *m*	**35.66**	*15.91*	**8.87**	*15.45*	—	—
metal	**26.33**	na	—	—	na	*0.19*[2]
Lead: ore *m*	**85.89**	*73.53*	**57.22**	*66.56*	—	—
metal	**38.55**	—	**37.74**	—	—	*0.02*[2]
Manganese, ore	**1.27**	*35.26*	**0.43**[1]	*29.35*[2]	—	—
Mercury *f*	—	—	—	—	—	*0.10*[2]
Tin, ore	**0.45***m*	*0.33m*	**0.36**	*0.45*	—	—
Tungsten, ore	**0.19**	*0.13*	**0.66**	*0.14*	—	—
Vanadium *m*	**1.06**	*0.56*	**0.88***	*0.54*	—	—
Zinc, ore	**31.74***m*	*17.81m*	**35.13***m*	*18.42*	—	—

a million $ U.S. *f* metric tons. *k* '000 fine troy oz. *l* '000 carats. *m* metal content.

	Production		Exports		Imports	
10. CHEMICALS*n* AND FERTILIZERS						
Chemicals	—		—		na	
Fertilizers:						
Phosphates	**1.07***p*	*1.7p*	**0.5**	*1.2*	na	na*y*

n data not available for years 1953–5. *p* guano. *y* see South Africa.

	Production		Exports		Imports	
11. INDUSTRY						
Beer *b*	**60.0**	na	—	—	—	—
Cement	—	—	—	—	na*y*	na*y*

b '000 hectolitres. *y* see South Africa.

na: data not available. — negligible or nil. [1] one year only. [2] two year average. * estimate. ‡ see appendix. † re-exports.

SOUTHERN YEMEN

The Federation of South Arabia was overrun by the forces of the National Liberation Front in 1967 and was declared the Southern Yemen People's Republic. The last of the British troops and civilians left Aden (formerly a British colony) the same year. The name was amended in 1970 to 'The People's Democratic Republic of Yemen'.

AREA: 160 300 sq. km. (61 890 sq. miles)

LAND USE: (percentage of total)	*1965*	*1945*
Arable and orchard	0.9	0.4
Permanent meadow and pasture (rough grazing)	31.3	62.0
Forest and woodland (mainly scrub)	8.9	—
City areas, waste and other land	58.9	37.6

POPULATION: 1 170 000 (1967 estimate)

Largest city: ADEN; population: 225 000 (1964)

Capital city: MADĪNET AL SHAAB (formerly Al Ittiḥād)

		Year(s)
Infant mortality (per '000)	75.8*a*	1965
Crude birth rate (per '000)	38.4*a*	1965
Crude death rate (per '000)	8.2*a*	1965
Population per physician	2 140*a*	1966
Population per hospital bed	780*a*	1964
School enrolment: age 5–19 years (percentage)	46*a*	1963–4 av.

a Aden State only.

COMMUNICATIONS		*Year(s)*
Motor vehicles in use ('000s): private	11.8	1963–5 av.
commercial	2.8	(1963–5 av.)
Telephones (per '000 urban population)	0.7	1967
Radio receivers (per '000 population)	217	1963–5 av.

FINANCE

Currency unit: The South Arabian dinar, at par with the pound sterling, was introduced in 1965.

Exchange rates	*1965*	*1960a*	*1956a*
Per $ U.S.	0.357	7.14	7.2
Per £ sterling	1.0	20.0	20.0

a East African shillings, used in Aden.

EMPLOYMENT, PRODUCTION AND TRADE

Extensive irrigation in recent years now enables cash crops of fruit and vegetables to be grown, and in particular the Abyan long-staple cotton, which has (1970) become the country's major export. Subsistence grain-crops are also grown in the higher areas. In the drier parts, nomadic communities live by herding livestock.

The importance of Aden as a bunkering station was greatly reduced by the closure of the Suez Canal.

TRADING

Total trade (in million $ U.S.)	*1965*	*1955a*	*1938*
Exports (f.o.b.)	190	177	16
Imports (c.i.f.)	301	198	30

Main trading partners (percentage of total value)

Exports	*1965*	*1955a*	*Imports*	*1965*	*1955a*
U.K.	21	7	Iran	17	3
Yemen	7	7	Japan	11	5
Japan	5	1	U.K.	11	9
South Africa	4	1	Kuwait	11	31
Afars/Issas	3	3	India	4	7
Australia	3	3	Trucial States	4	na
			Qatar	3	na

Distribution of trade (percentage of total value)

	1965	*1955a*
Exports		
Crude materials and fuels *b*	84	na
(petroleum products)	(78)	(68)
Food	9	10*
Manufactured goods	4	7*
Imports		
Crude materials and fuels	43	na
(petroleum and products)	(39)	(44)
Manufactured goods	33	na
(textiles and clothing)	(12)	(8)
Food	18	na

a Aden State (former Aden Colony) only. *b* incl. ships' bunkers.

PRODUCTION, EXPORTS AND IMPORTS

Years: **1963–5 average** and *1953–5 average* Units: '000 metric tons unless otherwise indicated

	Production		Exports		Imports	
1. CEREALS, etc.						
Barley	—	—	—	—	**0.1**	—
Maize (corn)	—	—	—	*0.4*†	—	*0.5*
Millets/sorghum	**25.0**	*33.7*	**6.6**	*9.7*	**12.7**	*12.9*
Potatoes	—	—	**0.2**†	—	**7.3**	*2.7*
Rice	—	—	**18.5**†	*12.0*†	**29.4**	*16.2*
Wheat	**8.3**	*4.7*	**14.3**	*0.5*	**37.8**	*3.0*
2. FRUIT, etc.						
Apples	—	—	**0.1**†	—	**1.8**	—
Coconuts	—	—	—	—	—	*0.1*
Dates	**8.0**	*13.7*	—	—	**10.9***	*10.5**[2]
Grapes	—	—	—	—	**0.4**	—
Oranges	—	—	**0.1**†	—	**1.5**	*0.6*
Other citrus fruit	—	—	—	—	**0.3**	—
Pears	—	—	—	—	**0.2**	—
Wine *b*	—	—	**0.1**†	—	**0.7**	—

b '000 hectolitres.

	Production		Exports		Imports	
3. BEVERAGES, FOREST PRODUCTS, etc.						
Coffee	na	na	**4.6**	*8.0*	**4.4**	*9.3*
Sugar, raw	—	—	**17.6**†	*16.9*†	**53.2**	*26.8*
Tea	—	—	**0.3**†	*0.5*†	**2.0**	*1.0*
Tobacco: leaf	—	—	**1.5**†	*1.6*[2]†	**4.4**	*3.7*
products	na	na	**0.2**[2]	*0.2*[2]	**1.2**[2]	*1.1*[2]
Hardwood *j*	—	—	**20.0**[1]†	—	**123.6**	—
Other paper	—	—	—	—	**0.8**[1]	—

j '000 cu. metres of roundwood equivalent.

	Production		Exports		Imports	
4. VEGETABLE OILSEEDS AND OILS						
Coconut oil	—	—	**0.07**†	*0.04*†	**0.28**	*1.01*
Cottonseed	**11.70**	*7.00*	**9.44**	*3.75*[2]	**0.15**	*3.75*[2]
Cottonseed oil	na	na	**0.03**	na	**0.49**	*0.26*[1]
Groundnuts	—	—	**0.03**†	na	**0.16**	na
Groundnut oil	—	—	**0.01**†	*0.09*†	**0.68**	*0.31*
Linseed oil	—	—	—	—	**0.04**	*0.08*
Olive oil	—	—	—	—	**0.11**	*0.02*
Sesame seed	**0.90**	*1.20*	—[2]	—	—	*0.40*[2]
Soya bean oil	—	—	—	—	**0.12**	na

	Production		Exports		Imports	
5. LIVESTOCK‡, ANIMAL PRODUCTS, etc.						
Cattle *d*	**71.7***	*68.0*	—	*0.2*[2]	—	*21.7*
Goats *d*	**802.0***	*855.0*	**0.9** (Goats, Sheep)	—	**333.9**	na
Sheep *d*	**202.3***	*200.0*				
Horses *d*	na	*7.0*				

continued

	Production		Exports		Imports	
5. LIVESTOCK‡, ANIMAL PRODUCTS, etc.—*continued*						
Bacon/ham	—	—	—	—	**0.2**	—
Meat‡: 'A'	—	—	—	—	**0.2**	—
'B'	—	—	—	—	**0.5**	*0.2*
Butter	—	—	**1.6**†	*0.3*[1]†	**7.8**	*1.9*
Cheese	—	—	—	—	**0.3**	*0.1*
Eggs	—	—	—	—	**0.9**	—[2]
Fish	**53.1**	*54.2*	**4.7**	*7.1*[1]*	**2.4**	*4.5*[1]*
Milk	—	—	**1.5**†	*0.8*†	**33.4**	*4.6*
Hides/skins	na	na	**3.7**[2]*a*	*6.4*[2]*e*	**2.4***a*	*8.0*[2]*e*

a million $ U.S. *d* no. in thousands. *e* no. in millions.

	Production		Exports		Imports	
6. FIBRES, TEXTILES, etc.						
Cotton: lint	**6.0**	*2.7*	**5.2**	*8.0*[2]	**0.1**	*5.0*[2]
woven fabrics	—	—	—	—	**5.8**	*9.4*
Rayon, woven fabrics	—	—	—	—	**3.7**[1]*n*	*1.7*

n incl. synthetic piece goods.

	Production		Exports		Imports	
7. FUEL AND POWER						
Coal, 'A'‡	—	—	—	—	**1**[1]	*31*
Coke	—	—	—	—	—	*1*
Electricity *h t*	**194**[2]	*100*[1]				
Natural gas *i*	**10**	na	—	—	—	—
Oil, crude	—	—	—	—	**6 760**	na
Petroleum, refined	**6 640**	*4 050*[1]	**4 107**	*1 930*[1]	**1 487**	*980*[1]

h million kWh. *i* million cu. metres. *t* thermal.

	Production		Exports		Imports	
8. IRON AND STEEL						
Iron/steel scrap	na	na	**1**	—	—	—

	Production		Exports		Imports	
9. NON-FERROUS MINERALS AND METALS						
Asbestos, manufactured	—	—	—	—	na	*0.21*
Aluminium	—	—	—	—	**0.23**	na
Tin, metal	—	—	—	—	**1.24**	*0.19*

	Production		Exports		Imports	
11. INDUSTRY						
Alcoholic beverages *a*	—	—	—	—	**1.2**[1]	na
Cement	—	—	**5.0***†	—	**109.0***	*40.7*
Electrical engineering *a*	—	—	**1.4**[2]†	na	**11.8**	na
Motor vehicles *a*	—	—	**1.6**†	na	**8.3**[2]	*2.2*[2]

a million $ U.S.

na: data not available. — negligible or nil. [1] one year only. [2] two year average. * estimate. ‡ see appendix. † re-exports.

SPAIN

The current regime in Spain was established at the conclusion of the Spanish Civil War, in 1939, with General Franco as 'Head of the Spanish State'. Included in metropolitan Spain are the Islas Baleares (Balearic Islands), the Islas Canarias (Canary Islands), three small groups of islands off the coast of Morocco, and the North African towns Ceuta and Melilla.

AREA: 504 748 sq. km. (194 883 sq. miles)

LAND USE: (percentage of total)	*1965*	*1955*
Arable and orchard	40.8	39.7
Permanent meadow and pasture	28.1	19.0
Forest and woodland (incl. some rough grazing)	23.0	27.4
City areas, waste and other land	8.1	13.9

POPULATION: 32 140 000 (1967 estimate)

Largest city: MADRID, capital; population: 2 599 330 (1965)

Distribution of working population (1965)

Total working population: 12 183 600*a*

U.N. group no.		*Percentage*
0	Agriculture, forestry, fishing and hunting	34.5
1	Mining and quarrying	1.4
2/3	Manufacturing	24.3
4	Construction	7.9
5	Electricity, gas, water and sanitary services	0.8
6	Commerce	11.6
7	Transport, storage and communications	4.8
8	Services	14.3
9	Others	0.4

		Year(s)
Life expectancy at birth (years): male	67.3	1960
female	71.9	1960
Infant mortality (per '000)	37.8	1965
Crude birth rate (per '000)	21.3	1965
Crude death rate (per '000)	8.6	1965
Accidental deaths (per 100 000 population)		
caused by motor vehicles	9.8	1965
due to other causes	19.9	1965
Population per physician	800	1965
Population per hospital bed	320	1966
School enrolment: age 5–19 years (percentage)	70	1963–4 av.
age over 19 years (per 100 000 population)	386	1964–5 av.

a based on a labour force sample survey.

COMMUNICATIONS		*Year(s)*
Motor vehicles in use ('000s): private	644.2	1963–5 av.
commercial	304.6	1963–5 av.
Railway track (km.)	18 942	1966
Mail per capita: domestic	68	1963–5 av.
foreign received	8	1963–5 av.
foreign sent	7	1963–5 av.
Telephones (per '000 urban population)	9.6	1967
Radio receivers (per '000 population)	133	1963–5 av.
Television sets (per '000 population)	39.4	1963–5 av.
Daily newspapers (per '000 population)	131.5	1962–3 av.

FINANCE

Currency unit: The peseta

Exchange rates	*1965*	*1960*	*1950*	*1938*
Per $ U.S.	59.99	60.15	11.22	9.10
Per £ sterling	167.97	168.42	31.42	41.86

		Year(s)
National Income (million $ U.S.)	18 765	1965
G.N.P. per capita ($ U.S.)	640	1966
Foreign trade (percentage of G.D.P.)	18	1963–5 av.

TRADING

Total trade (in million $ U.S.)	*1965*	*1955*	*1935*
Exports (f.o.b.)	967	446	191
Imports (c.i.f.)	3 004	617	286

Main trading partners (percentage of total value)

Exports	*1965*	*1955*	*1935*	*Imports*	*1965*	*1955*	*1935*
Germany F.R.	14	15	13*d*	U.S.A.	18	19	17
U.K.	13	16	22	Germany F.R.	14	10	14*d*
U.S.A.	12	10	10	France	11	11	6
France	11	8	12	U.K.	9	10	11
Netherlands	5	5	5	Italy	6	2	3
Cuba	4	2	3	Netherlands	4	3	4
Italy	4	2	3	Saudi Arabia	3	na	na

Distribution of trade (percentage of total value)

Exports	*1965*	*1955*	*1935**
Food	40	45	53
(fruit and vegetables)	(33)	(39)	(38)
Manufactured goods	33	18	na
(machinery and transport equipment)	(10)	(2)	(1)
Crude materials and fuels	11	25	na
Chemicals	8	3	6
Wine	5	5	7
Imports			
Manufactured goods	49	38	26
(machinery and transport equipment)	(27)	(25)	(16)
(iron and steel)	(9)	(5)	(1)
Crude materials and fuels	23	40	na
(petroleum and products)	(9)	(15)	(5)
Food	14	7	12
(cereals)	(5)	(1*)	(—)
Chemicals	9	9	13

d incl. Germany D.R.

PRODUCTION, EXPORTS AND IMPORTS

Years: **1963–5 average** and *1953–5 average* Units: '000 metric tons unless otherwise indicated

1. CEREALS, etc.

	Production		Exports		Imports	
Barley	**1 963.0**	*1 800.0*	—	—	**558.8**	*41.8*
Maize (corn)	**1 172.0**	*691.3*	**0.1**	—	**1 223.5**	*27.1*[2]
Millets/sorghum	**41.0**	*1.0*[2]	**0.3**	*0.4*	**39.5**	*0.9*
Oats	**408.7**	*488.7*	—	—	**0.3**	—
Potatoes	**4 473.0**	*3 912.3*	**124.2**	*72.2*	**213.9**	*56.6*
Rice	**382.3**	*394.3*	**64.7**	*55.3*	—	—
Rye	**373.0**	*475.0*	—	*0.5*	**0.8**	—
Sweet potatoes/ yams	**75.0**	*135.3*				
Wheat	**4 521.7**	*3 947.3*	—	*0.2*	**140.1**	*424.3*

2. FRUIT, etc.

	Production		Exports		Imports	
Apples	**417.7**	*246.3*	**0.1**	*0.2*	**0.2**	—
Apricots	**140.3**	*60.3*	na	*12.1*	—	—
Bananas	**359.0***n*	*223.0n*	**106.8***n*	*172.5n*	—	*57.7*
Cherries	**54.7**	*34.9*	—	—	—	—
Coconuts	—	—	—	—	**2.9**	na
Dates	**14.7**	*7.0*	**0.1**	—	**1.1**	—
Figs	**145.0**	*170.0*	na	*1.1*	—	—
Grapes	**4 646.0**	*3 116.0*	**92.1**	*42.4*	—	—
Lemons	**111.3**	*44.7*	**34.7**	*35.9*	—	*0.1*[1]
Oranges	**1 891.3**	*1 159.0*	**1 054.0**	*937.6*	**0.5**	—
Other citrus fruit	**4.0**	*2.0*	**2.8**	*0.6*	—	—
Olives	**1 771.3**	*1 545.3*				
Peaches	**151.3**	*105.0*	na	—	—	—
Pears	**162.0**	*77.0*	**14.9**	—	—	—
Plums	**75.3**	*51.8*	na	*0.8*	—	—
Raisins	**11.3***	*9.5*	**4.9**	*5.0*	—	—
Tomatoes	**1 342.0**	*816.0*				
Wine *b*	**28 864.7**	*19 270.0*	**2 007.6**	*1 256.7*	**2.0**	*0.7*

b '000 hectolitres. *n* produced mainly in the Canary Islands.

3. BEVERAGES, FOREST PRODUCTS, etc.

	Production		Exports		Imports	
Cocoa	—	—	—	—	**27.3***	*14.1*
Coffee	—	—	—	—	**38.1**	*6.0*
Sugar: beet	**3 250.3**	*2 205.0**				
cane	**375.0**	*360.0*				
raw (beet)	**467.1**	*302.0*	—	*60.5*	**232.2**	*20.5*
(cane)	**34.0**	*31.0*				
Tea	—	—	—	—	**0.5**	*0.2p*
Tobacco: leaf	**29.8**	*33.1n*	**0.1**	—	**35.4**	*21.0*
cigars	**350.0***e*	*591.7e*				
cigarettes	**37 543.0***e*	*14 310.0e*	—	—	**2.9**	*0.6*
tobacco/snuff	**4.3**	*13.8*				
Softwood *j*	**5 461.7**	*3 198.7*	**39.5**	*4.8*[1]	**982.6**	*53.4*[1]
Hardwood *j*	**9 731.0**	*4 812.3*	**0.4**	*0.7*[1]	**179.3**	*0.2*[1]
Wood pulp	**256.9**	*186.0*	**8.4**	—[2]	**179.7**	*95.0*[2]
Newsprint	**66.0**	*27.0*	—	—[2]	**41.0**	*8.9*[2]
Other paper	**505.7**	*187.0*	**2.0**	*0.4*[2]	**44.9**	*5.1*[2]

e no. in millions. *j* '000 cu. metres of roundwood equivalent. *n* excl. the Canary Is. *p* incl. substitutes.

4. VEGETABLE OILSEEDS AND OILS

	Production		Exports		Imports	
Castor seed	—	—	—	—	**0.38**	*0.60*[2]
Castor oil	—	—	—	—	**1.88**	—
Copra	—	—	—	—	**10.79**	*7.00*
Coconut oil	—	—	—	—	**1.87**	*0.40*
Cottonseed	**169.30**	*52.67*	**0.01**	—	**1.45**	—
Cottonseed oil	na	na	—	—	**0.39**	—
Groundnuts	**5.37**	*8.40*	**0.23**	—	**21.75**	—
Groundnut oil	na	na	**0.20**	—	**48.41**	—
Linseed	**2.67***	*4.50*[2]	—	—[2]	**15.57**	*0.57*
Linseed oil	na	na	—	*0.20*[2]*p*	**4.17**	*0.37*[2]

p incl. other vegetable oils.

continued

na: data not available. — negligible or nil. [1] one year only. [2] two year average. * estimate. ‡ see appendix. † re-exports.

PRODUCTION, EXPORTS AND IMPORTS *continued*

4. VEGETABLE OILSEEDS AND OILS—*continued*

	Production		Exports		Imports	
Olive oil	**374.67**	*303.33*	**65.31**	*26.52*	—	—
Palm kernels	—	—	—	—	**0.42**	*0.93*
Palm kernel oil	—	—	—	—	**0.17**	—
Palm oil	—	—	—	—	**0.30**	*2.42*
Rapeseed oil	—	—	—	—	**0.11**	—
Sesame seed	—	—	**0.10†**	—	**0.53**	—
Soya beans	—	—	—	—	**137.27**	*7.30**
Soya bean oil	—	—	**0.13†**	—	**86.85***	*1.11**
Sunflower seed	**7.30**	*1.00*[2]	—	—	—	—
Sunflower seed oil	—	—	—	—	**26.54**	—
Tung oil	—	—	—	—	**0.44**	—

5. LIVESTOCK‡, ANIMAL PRODUCTS, etc.

	Production		Exports		Imports	
Chickens *d*	**39 830.3**	*28 676.5*[2]				
Cattle *d*	**3 692.0**	*3 097.5*[2]	**1.1**	*2.2*	**3.0**	*0.7*
Goats *d*	**2 408.0**	*3 591.0*[2]				
Sheep *d*	**19 194.7**	*16 772.5*[2]	**96.7**	na	**12.2**	na
Horses *d*	**394.0**	*606.5*[2]				
Pigs *d*	**5 733.0**	*5 156.0*	**3.8**	*1.5*	**21.0**	*0.1*
Bacon/ham	**615.0**	*410.7*	—	—	**0.2**	—[2]
Meat‡: 'A'			**0.6**	—	**68.5**	*1.8*
'B'	**252.3***	*99.3*	**0.3**	—	**4.0**	—
Butter	**3.3**	*7.3**	—	—	**1.0**	*0.1*
Cheese	**47.6**	*40.7**	—	—	**7.4**	*0.6*
Eggs	**294.3**	*141.7*	**0.2**	—	**2.8**	*4.1*
Fish	**1 223.4***q*	*690.3*	**67.0**	*20.8*[1]*	**104.1**	*26.6*[1]*
Milk	**2 387.3**	*2 463.3p*	**0.1**	*0.9*	**319.6**	*1.1*
Whale oil	**1.0**	—	—	—	—	—
Hides/skins	na	*16.2r*	**5.5**	*0.7*	**42.0**	*10.7*
Wool	**12.8**	*22.7**	**2.3**	—	**5.6**	*1.6*

d no. in thousands. *p* excl. milk fed to livestock. *q* incl. fish landed by Spanish vessels in foreign ports. *r* cattle hides only.

6. FIBRES, TEXTILES, etc.

	Production		Exports		Imports	
Abaca	—	—	—	—	**0.3**	*0.4*
Agaves (sisal etc.)	—	—	—	—	**10.9**	*3.0*[2]
Cotton lint	**83.7**	*26.3*	**8.4**	—	**17.3**	*66.5*
Flax fibre	**4.8***	*8.0*	—	—	**2.4**	*0.3*
Hemp fibre	**5.2**	*10.1*	**0.5**	*0.2*	—	—
Jute	**0.3**	—	—	—	**26.9**	*17.5*
Rubber: natural	—	—	—	*0.1†*	**38.1**	*13.7*
synthetic	—	—	—	—	**26.8**	—
Silk *f*	**56.7**	*46.7*	**49.0**	—	**33.3**	*4.0*
Cotton: yarn	**126.1**	*55.3*	**6.5**	*0.2*	—	—
woven fabrics	**99.9**	*47.7*	**6.9**	*3.7*	—	*0.3*
Rayon: fibre/yarn	**60.0**	*39.5*	**10.9**	*0.3*[2]	**0.9**	*0.8*[2]*p*
woven fabrics	**16.1***q*	na	**1.6**	na	**0.6***r*	na
Non-cellulosic fibre/yarn	**12.7**	*0.1*	**0.5**	—	**11.4**	na
Wool: yarn	**29.7**	*15.3*	**0.1**	na	**0.2**	na
woven fabrics	**22.0***t*	na	**0.5**	*0.3*	**0.2**	—

f metric tons. *p* incl. waste. *q* incl. natural silk fabrics. *r* incl. synthetic fabrics. *t* incl. carpets; excl. felt.

7. FUEL AND POWER

	Production		Exports		Imports	
Coal: 'A'‡	**12 683**	*12 430*	**4**	*84*	**1 783**	*811*
'B'	**1 330**	*1 830*	**26**	*9*	**99**	—
Coke	—	—	**1**	*2*	—	*152*
Electricity *h*: total	**29 396**	*10 490*[1]				
hydro	**20 792**	*8 110*[1]				
thermal	**8 604**	*2 380*[1]				
Oil, crude	**63**	*30*[1]	**27**	na	**12 180**	*3 630*[1]
Petroleum, refined	**10 503**	*1 970*[1]	**1 123**	*540*[1]	**2 353**	*1 730*[1]
Uranium *f*	**88**[2]	na	—	—	—	—

f metric tons. *h* million kWh.

8. IRON AND STEEL

	Production		Exports		Imports	
Iron ore	**2 617***m*	*1 456m*	**2 090**	*1 597*	**180**	*299*
Pig iron	**2 120**	*910*	**152**	*30*	**13**	*6*
Steel ingots/castings	**3 053**	*1 145*	**50**[2]	—	**456**	*3*
Iron/steel scrap	na	na	—	—	**296**	*50*
Iron/steel products *a*	na	na	**16**	*2*	**167**	*26*

a million $ U.S. *m* metal content.

9. NON-FERROUS MINERALS AND METALS

	Production		Exports		Imports	
Gold *k*, ore *m*	**21.70**	*9.00*	—	—	—	—
Platinum group metals *k*	—	—	—	—	**0.59**[2]	*0.07*
Silver *k*, ore *m*	**3 077.00**	*1 328.00*	—	—	na	—
Asbestos: fibre	na	*0.05*	—	—	**46.89**	*6.08*
manufactured	na	na	**0.98**	*0.07*	**2.28**	*0.15*

continued

9. NON-FERROUS MINERALS AND METALS—*continued*

	Production		Exports		Imports	
Mica	na	*0.11*	**0.01**	—	**0.69**	—
Aluminium: bauxite	**7.79**	*5.77*	—	—	**68.47**	*9.18*
alumina	—	—	—	—	**102.88**	*13.01*
aluminium	**49.01**	*3.88*	**9.53**	—	**18.70**	*3.55*
Antimony: ore	**0.07***m*	*0.18m*	—	—	**0.58**	—
metal	na	na	—	—	**0.41**	—
Cadmium	**0.06**	*0.01*	—	—	**0.01**	—
Chrome: ore	—	—	—	—	**21.00**	—
metal	—	—	—	—	**2.00**	*0.02*
Cobalt	na	—	—	—	—	—
Copper: ore	**7.55***m*	*7.28m*	—	—	**20.21**	—
metal	**25.31**	*9.95*	**7.19**	*0.17*	**60.44**	*13.30*
Lead: ore	**59.07***m*	*57.38m*	**0.01**	—	**0.07**	—
metal	**57.96**	*57.22*	**4.65**	*25.89*	**8.76**	*0.10*
Magnesium:						
dolomite	na	—	**2.39**	—	**1.64**	—
magnesite	**92.88**	—	**25.93**	—	**5.60**	—
metal/salts	—‡	—‡	—	—	**0.23**	—
Manganese: ore	**16.19**	*37.48*	—	—	**112.89**	*14.37*
metal	—	—	—	—	**1.58**	*3.57*
Mercury *f*	**2 505.46**	*1 412.33*	**2 121.90**	*1 372.70*	—	—
Nickel: ore	—	—	—	—	**0.36**	—
metal	—	—	—	—	**1.85**	*0.55*
Tin: ore	**0.12***m*	*1.04m*	—	—	**2.83**	—
metal	**1.64**	*0.71*	**0.26**	*0.27*	**0.04**	*0.07*
Titanium minerals	**42.22**	*3.14*	**23.80**	—	**5.20**	—
Tungsten, ore	**0.09**	*2.28*	**0.04**	*2.43*	—	—
Zinc: ore	**73.15***m*	*88.06m*	**21.20**	—	—	*100.76*
metal	**60.89**	*23.42*	**18.12**	—	**0.93**	*0.66*

f metric tons. *k* '000 fine troy oz. *m* metal content.

10. CHEMICALS *n* AND FERTILIZERS

	Production		Exports		Imports	
Organic chemicals:						
Benzene	**7.2**		—		**0.8**	
Butadiene	—		—		na	
Ethylene	na		na		na	
Methanol	**7.5**		—		**9.8**	
Phenol	**2.3**		—		**2.3**	
Phthalic anhydride	**6.0**		**0.3**		**0.5**	
Styrene monomer	—		—		**14.8**	
Urea	**30.7**		**2.4**		**9.8**	
Inorganic chemicals:						
Ammonia	**205.2**[2]		**0.6**		**3.2**	
Carbon black	**1.2**[1]		—		**17.3**	
Chlorine	**60.5**		—		**0.5**	
Nitric acid	**153.1**		—		**1.8**	
Sodium carbonate	**198.9**		—		**11.8**	
Sodium hydroxide	**160.5**		**2.3**		**2.3**	
Sulphuric acid	**1 449.7**		**1.6**		**40.3**	
Plastics:						
Polyamides	na		—		**1.1**	
Polyethylene	—		—		**39.5**	
Polyvinyl chloride	**29.7***		**0.1***		**4.1***	
Fertilizers:						
Phosphates	—	*22.7*	—	—	**1 063.3**	*716.4*
Potash	**358.6***w*	*208.2w*	**332.6**	*245.7*	**0.4**	—
Pyrites	**1 072.9***x*	*973.2*x*	**1 139.1**	*1 460.8*	—	—
Sulphur: native	**8.0***	*5.8*	**0.4**	—	**31.9**	*4.4*
recovered	**63.2**	*35.1*				

n data not available for years 1953–5. *w* K_2O content. *x* sulphur content.

11. INDUSTRY

	Production		Exports		Imports	
Aircraft *a*	**13.0****n*	na	—	—	**10.9**	*2.7*
Alcoholic beverages			**43.5***a*	*24.6a*	—	*0.3a*
beer *b*	**6 697.0**	*1 452.3*				
spirits *b*	**1 200.0****p*	*782.8q*				
Cement	**8 355.7**	*3 280.0*	**11.7***	*4.0*	**1 805.3**	*24.3*
Electrical engineering *a*	**578.5**[2]	na	**7.6**	*1.6*	**123.2**	*26.2*
Locomotives *c*	**71.0**	*45.0*[2]	na	na	na	na
Railway vehicles *a*	na	na	**2.1**	na	**13.2**	*17.3*
Machine tools *a*	**50.0**[1]	na	**8.4**	na	**37.8**	*10.9*
Merchant ships *g*	**229.0**	*56.0*	**98.0**	*1.0*	—	*8.2*
Motor vehicles			**12.7***a*	*0.2a*	**52.6***a*	*26.8a*
commercial *d*	**64.2**	*0.8r*				
private *d*	**121.0**	*8.8r*				

a million $ U.S. *b* '000 hectolitres. *c* no. of units. *d* no. in thousands. *g* '000 G.R.T. *n* 1965–67 av. *p* 1967 figure. *q* 1962 figure. *r* incl. assembly of imported parts.

SPANISH SAHARA

Spanish Sahara is the only African state remaining (1971) as a Spanish Overseas Province. Claims to the territory have been made by both Morocco and Mauritania; 7 000 sq. km. of the land was ceded by Spain to Morocco in 1958.

AREA: 266 000 sq. km. (102 680 sq. miles)

POPULATION: 48 000 (1967 U.N. estimate)

Capital city: EL AAIÚN; population: 5 500 (city proper, 1961)

		Year(s)
Crude birth rate (per '000)	3.8*	1964
Crude death rate (per '000)	3.9*	1967
Population per physician	2 530	1964
Population per hospital bed	250	1965
School enrolment: age 5–19 years (percentage)	21	1963–4 av.

Employment and production: The inhabitants are largely nomadic, but there is also some fishing, and a little maize and barley is grown. Rich deposits of phosphates were discovered in 1963.

na: data not available. — negligible or nil. [1] one year only. [2] two year average. * estimate. ‡ see appendix. † re-exports.

SUDAN

NORTH EAST AFRICA

The Sudan was administered jointly by the U.K. and the U.A.R. (then Egypt) until 1956 when it became a sovereign independent republic. There followed several changes of government with a period (1958–64) under military rule. A 10-year development plan (1961–1971) has led to improvements in industry, irrigation, transport and education.

AREA: 2 505 813 sq. km. (967 500 sq. miles)

LAND USE: (percentage of total)

	1954
Arable and orchard	2.8
Permanent meadow and pasture	9.6
Forest and woodland	36.5
City areas, waste and other land	51.1

POPULATION: 14 355 000 (1967 estimate)

Largest city: UMM DURMĀN (Omdurman); population: 198 000 (city proper, 1966)
Capital city: AL KHURṬŪM (Khartoum); population: 185 000 (city proper, 1966)

Distribution of working population (1956)
Total working population: 4 844 000*

U.N. group no.		*Percentage*
0	Agriculture, forestry, fishing and hunting	85.8
2/3	Manufacturing	5.0
4	Construction	0.6
6	Commerce	2.1
7	Transport, storage and communications	0.6
8	Services	4.6
9*a*	Others	1.3

		Year(s)
Life expectancy at birth (years)	40*	1950
Population per physician	30 720	1964
Population per hospital bed	1 010	1965
School enrolment: age 5–19 years (percentage)	15	1963–4 av.
age over 19 years (per 100 000 population)	51	1964–5 av.

a incl. groups 1 and 5.

COMMUNICATIONS

		Year(s)
Motor vehicles in use ('000s): private	21.1	1963–5 av.
commercial	18.4	
Railway track (km.)	5 403	1965
Telephones (per '000 urban population)	0.3	1967
Radio receivers (per '000 population)	17	1963–5 av.
Television sets (per '000 population)	0.8	1963–5 av.

FINANCE

Currency unit: The Sudanese pound

Exchange rates	*1965*	*1960*	*1950*	*1938*
Per $ U.S.	0.348	0.348	0.348	0.210
Per £ sterling	0.975	0.975	0.975	1.007

		Year(s)
National Income (million $ U.S.)	1 221	1965
G.N.P. per capita ($ U.S.)	100	1966
Rate of increase of G.N.P. per capita	3.8	1960–2 av.
Foreign trade (percentage of G.D.P.)	34	1963–5 av.

TRADING

Total trade (in million $ U.S.)	*1965*	*1955*	*1938*
Exports (f.o.b.)	196	145	30
Imports (c.i.f.)	208	140	32

Main trading partners (percentage of total value)

Exports	*1965*	*1955*	*Imports*	*1965*	*1955*
Germany F.R.	11	8	U.K.	23	30
Italy	10	9	Japan	9	3
U.K.	10	28	India	9	11
China P.R.	8	1	U.S.A.	7	2
Netherlands	7	2	Germany F.R.	5	4
U.S.S.R.	6	—	U.A.R.	4	11
India	6	14	U.S.S.R.	4	—

Distribution of trade (percentage of total value)

Exports	*1965*	*1955*
Crude materials	84	92*
(cotton)	(47)	(62)
(oilseeds)	(23)	(17*)
(gum arabic)	(11)	(10)
Food	14	8
(fodder)	(6)	(na)
Imports		
Manufactured goods	58	58
(machinery and transport equipment)	(21)	(11*)
(textiles and clothing)	(20)	(18*)
Food	22	24
(sugar)	(7)	(7*)
(cereals)	(5)	(4*)
Chemicals	10	5*
Crude materials and fuels	7	10

PRODUCTION, EXPORTS AND IMPORTS

Years: **1963–5 average** and *1953–5 average* Units: '000 metric tons unless otherwise indicated

	Production		Exports		Imports	
1. CEREALS, etc.						
Barley	**0.3**	—[2]	—	—	—	—
Cassava	**121.3***	na				
Maize (corn)	**21.0**	*22.0*[1]	—	*5.4*	—	—
Millets/sorghum	**1 525.0**	*1 201.0*[2]	**88.2**	*46.5*	—	—
Potatoes	**25.0***	*2.0**	—	—	**1.5**	*2.3*
Rice	—	—	—	—	**4.9**	*3.4*
Sweet potatoes/ yams	**11.0***	na				
Wheat	**41.3**	*15.0*[2]	—	—	**51.2**	—
2. FRUIT, etc.						
Apples	—	—	—	—	**2.1**	*0.2*
Bananas	**10.0***	na	**0.7**	—	—	—
Dates	**42.3**	*24.0*[1]	**0.5**	*6.2*	**3.9***	*6.8*
Grapes	—	—	—	—	**0.1**	—
Lemons	—	na	—	—	—	—
Oranges	**1.0***	na	—	—	**0.9**	*2.1*
Raisins	—	—	—	—	**0.4**	*0.1*
Wine *b*	—	—	—	—	**2.9**	*39.3*

b '000 hectolitres.

	Production		Exports		Imports	
3. BEVERAGES, FOREST PRODUCTS, etc.						
Coffee	—	—	—	—	**10.9**	*5.3*
Sugar: cane	**196.7***	—				
raw	**19.3**	—	—	—	**152.3**	*97.8*
Tea	—	—	**0.6**†	—	**9.9**	*6.9*
Tobacco products	—	—	—	—	**0.7**	*0.5*[2]
Softwood *j*	**2.3**	—	—	—[2]	**124.9**	*67.7*[2]
Hardwood *j*	**21 180.0**	*13 588.0*	—	—[2]	**0.7**	—[2]
Wood pulp	—[2]	—	—	—	—	*0.2*
Newsprint	—*	—	—	—[2]	**1.3**	*0.4*
Other paper	**17.3***	—	—	—[2]	**4.5**	*0.4*

j '000 cu. metres of roundwood equivalent.

Acacia trees are grown and the gum arabic is an important export.

	Production		Exports		Imports	
4. VEGETABLE OILSEEDS AND OILS						
Castor seed	**7.67**	—[2]	**4.73**	—	—	—
Castor oil	na	—	—	—	**0.01**	—
Coconut oil	—	—	—	—	**0.54**	*0.20*
Cottonseed	**272.70**	*172.30*	**88.26**	*108.30*	—	—
Cottonseed oil	na	na	**9.01**	*4.55*	—	*0.01*
Groundnuts	**203.90**	*23.10*[1]*	**142.31**	*26.03*	—	—
Groundnut oil	na	na	**0.72**	*0.04*[2]	**0.01**	—
Linseed oil	—	—	—	—	**0.20**	*0.04*[2]
Olive oil	—	—	—	—	**0.03**	*0.03*
Palm kernels	—	—	—	—	**0.04**	na
Palm oil	—	—	—	—	**0.11**	*0.38*
Sesame seed	**172.53**	*122.00*[1]*	**74.37**	*23.17*	—	—
5. LIVESTOCK‡, ANIMAL PRODUCTS, etc.						
Cattle *d*	**7 030***	*2 227**	**14.7**	*36.9*	**0.4**	*1.5*
Goats *d*	**6 762***	*5 000*[1]*	**126.8**	na	—	—
Sheep *d*	**8 525***	*6 000*[1]*				
Horses *d*	**21***	*21*[2]*				
Pigs *d*	**5***	na	—	—	—	—
Bacon/ham	**141***	na	—	—	—	*0.1*[1]
Meat‡, 'A'			**0.1**	—	—	—
Butter	—	—	—	—	—	*0.2*
Cheese	—	—	—	—	—	*0.1*
Eggs	**15***	na	—	—	—	—
Fish	na	*13*	**0.5**	*2.7*[1]*	**0.3**	*0.2*[1]*
Milk	**958***	na	—	—	**15.4**	*1.6*
Hides/skins	na	na	**5.0**	*3.9*[2]	—	—

d no. in thousands.

	Production		Exports		Imports	
6. FIBRES, TEXTILES, etc.						
Cotton lint	**138.3**	*91.0*	**132.6**	*81.8*	—	—
Jute	—	—	—	—	na	na
Rubber, natural	—	—	—	—	**0.4**	na
Cotton: yarn	**4.5**[2]	na	—	—	**1.4**[2]	na
woven fabrics	**4.4**[2]	na	—	—	**11.9**	*10.2*
Rayon, woven fabrics	—	—	—	—	**3.4***n*	*2.7*

n incl. synthetic piece goods.

continued

PRODUCTION, EXPORTS AND IMPORTS *continued*

	Production		Exports		Imports	
7. FUEL AND POWER						
Coal, 'A'‡	—	—	—	—	**8**	*48*
Coke	—	—	—	—	**1**	*2*[2]
Electricity *h*: total	**170**	*10*				
hydro	na	—				
thermal	na	*10*				
Oil, crude	—	—	—	—	**243**	na
Petroleum, refined	**217**	—[1]	—	—	**420**	*270*[1]

h million kWh.

	Production		Exports		Imports	
8. IRON AND STEEL						
Iron ore	na	na	**12**	na	—	—
Pig iron	—	—	—	—	—	*10*
Iron/steel scrap	na	na	**2**	na	—	—
9. NON-FERROUS MINERALS AND METALS						
Gold *k*, ore	na	*1.90m*	**0.10**[2]*p*	*0.23p*	**0.03**[2]*p*	*0.30*p*
Silver *k*, bullion	—	—	—	—	—	*2.20*
Asbestos, manufactured	—	—	—	—	na	*7.91*
Mica	—	—	—	—	**0.02**	—
Aluminium	—	—	—	—	**1.70**	—
Chrome, ore	**21.29***m*	—	**3.83**	—	—	—
Copper, metal	—	—	—	—	**0.43**	*0.24*
Lead, metal	—	—	—	—	**0.19**	na

continued

	Production		Exports		Imports	
9. NON-FERROUS MINERALS AND METALS—*continued*						
Manganese, ore	**3.27**	—	—	—	—	—
Mercury *f*	—	—	—	—	—	*0.10*
Tin, metal	—	—	—	—	**0.16**	*0.02*
Zinc, metal	—	—	—	—	**0.15**	na

f metric tons. *k* '000 fine troy oz. *m* metal content. *p* bullion.

	Production		Exports		Imports	
10. CHEMICALS *n* AND FERTILIZERS						
Chemicals	—		—		na	
Fertilizers:						
Potash	—	—	—	—	**0.1**	—

n data not available for years 1953–5.

	Production		Exports		Imports	
11. INDUSTRY						
Aircraft *a*	—	—	—	—	**1.6**	*0.5*
Alcoholic beverages			—	—	**0.6***a*	*1.5a*
beer *b*	**71.0**	—				
Cement	**79.7**	*40.0**	—	*1.7*	**233.0**	*29.0*
Electrical engineering *a*	—	—	—	—	**11.5**	*1.0*[2]
Railway vehicles *a*	—	—	—	—	**7.6**	na
Merchant ships *g*	—	—	—	—	**3.0**	na
Motor vehicles *a*	—	—	—	—	**16.7**	*2.9*[2]

a million $ U.S. *b* '000 hectolitres. *g* '000 G.R.T.

SWAZILAND

SOUTHERN AFRICA

Swaziland, formerly a British protectorate, became an independent member of the Commonwealth in 1968, but remains part of the South African customs union.

AREA: 17 400 sq. km. (6 705 sq. miles)

LAND USE: (percentage of total)

	1964	*1954*
Arable and orchard	14.5	5.5
Permanent meadow and pasture	73.4	89.6
Forest and woodland	7.4	2.8
City areas, waste and other land	4.7	2.1

POPULATION: 374 697 (1966 estimate)

Capital city: MBABANE; population: 8 390 (1962)
Total working population: 54 144 (1956)

		Year(s)
Life expectancy at birth (years)	44*a*	1966
Population per physician	7 500	1965
Population per hospital bed	420	1966
School enrolment: age 5–19 years (percentage)	66	1963–4 av.

a African population only.

COMMUNICATIONS

		Year(s)
Railway track (km.)	220	1964
Telephones (per '000 urban population)	0.9	1967
Radio licences (per '000 population)	17	1963–5 av.

FINANCE

Currency unit: The South African rand was introduced in 1961.

Exchange rates	*1965*	*1960a*	*1950a*	*1938a*
Per $ U.S.	0.714	0.357	0.357	0.215
Per £ sterling	2.0	1.0	1.0	1.0

a South African pounds.

		Year
National Income (million $ U.S.)	100*	1966
G.N.P. per capita ($ U.S.)	290	1966

EMPLOYMENT, PRODUCTION AND TRADE

Forty-five per cent of the land is in European ownership for the exploitation of minerals, but the agricultural and grazing rights of the natives are safeguarded and delimited. The chief crops are maize, cotton, tobacco, sugar, fruit, rice and vegetables. Re-afforestation has been undertaken. The largest mineral products are iron ore and asbestos, and the output of coal is increasing. The chief exports are iron, asbestos, sugar and wood. Trade is mainly with South Africa.

PRODUCTION, EXPORTS AND IMPORTS

Years: **1963–5 average** and *1953–5 average* Units: '000 metric tons unless otherwise indicated

	Production		Exports		Imports	
1. CEREALS, etc.						
Maize (corn)	**33.3***	*45.0*[1]	—	—	na	na
Millets/sorghum	**20.0***[1]	*18.0*[1]	—	—	—	—
Potatoes	**1.0***	na	—	—	—	—
Rice	**6.7***	*2.0*[1]	—	—	—	—
Sweet potatoes/ yams	**8.0***	na				
2. FRUIT, etc.						
Bananas	**1.0***	na	—	—	—	—
Oranges	**4.7**	na	—	—	—	—
Other citrus fruit	**2.7**	na	—	—	—	—
Pineapples	**3.7***	na	—	—	—	—
Tomatoes	**3.0***	na				
3. BEVERAGES, FOREST PRODUCTS, etc.						
Sugar: cane	**866.7***	na				
raw	**119.5**[1]	na	na	na	—	—
Tobacco, leaf	**0.2***	*0.2*	—	—	—	—
Softwood *j*	**424.5***[2]	na	**37.0**	na	—	—
Hardwood *j*	**115.5***[2]	*108.3*	—	*4.3*	—	—
Wood pulp	**52.7***	na	**2.1**[1]	—	—	—

j '000 cu. metres of roundwood equivalent.

	Production		Exports		Imports	
4. VEGETABLE OILSEEDS AND OILS						
Cottonseed	**3.7**	na	—	—	—	—
Tung oil	—	*0.3*	—	—	—	—
5. LIVESTOCK‡, ANIMAL PRODUCTS, etc.						
Chickens *d*	**311.3**	*247.3*				
Cattle *d*	**529.0**	*424.7*	—	—	—	—
dairy cows *d*	**228.7**	*137.5*[2]				
Goats *d*	**230.0**	*145.7*	—	—	—	—
Sheep *d*	**40.0**	*31.3*	—	—	—	—
Horses *d*	**2.3**	*2.0*[2]				
Pigs *d*	**9.0**	*9.3*	—	—	—	—
Meat‡: 'A'	**12.7***	*20.5*[2]	—	—	—	—
'B'	**14.3***	*2.3*[2]	—	—	—	—
Eggs	**2.6***	na	—	—	—	—
Milk	**32.0***	*21.0*[2]	—	—	—	—
Hides/skins	na	*0.4*[1]	—	—	—	—

d no. in thousands.

	Production		Exports		Imports	
6. FIBRES, TEXTILES, etc.						
Cotton lint	**2.0**	na	—	—	—	—
7. FUEL AND POWER						
Coal	**11**	—	na	—	—	—
8. IRON AND STEEL						
Iron ore	**227***m*	na	na	na	—	—

m metal content.

	Production		Exports		Imports	
9. NON-FERROUS MINERALS AND METALS						
Gold *k*, ore *m*	**2.00**	na	na	na	—	—
Asbestos, fibre	**34.50**	*28.08*	na	na	—	—
Tin, ore	na	*0.03m*	—	—	—	—

k '000 fine troy oz. *m* metal content.

SWEDEN

Sweden is an hereditary monarchy. Parliamentary government was established in 1917, but executive power remains with the king. Sweden is a member of the European Free Trade Association.

AREA: 449 793 sq. km. (173 665 sq. miles)

Land area: 411 260 sq. km. (158 787 sq. miles)

LAND USE: (percentage of total)	*1965*	*1955*
Arable and orchard	7.1	8.4
Permanent meadow and pasture	1.2	1.6
Forest and woodland	50.0	50.0
City areas, waste and other land	41.7	40.0

POPULATION: 7 765 981 (1965 census)

Largest city: STOCKHOLM, capital; population: 1 262 402 (1966)

Distribution of working population (1960)

Total working population: 3 244 084

U.N. group no.		*Percentage*
0	Agriculture, forestry, fishing and hunting	13.8
1	Mining and quarrying	0.7
2/3	Manufacturing	34.2
4	Construction	9.1
5	Electricity, gas, water and sanitary services	1.1
6	Commerce	13.5
7	Transport, storage and communications	7.5
8	Services	19.8
9	Others	0.3

		Year(s)
Life expectancy at birth (years): male	71.6	1961–5 av.
female	75.7	1961–5 av.
Infant mortality (per '000)	13.3	1965
Crude birth rate (per '000)	15.9	1965
Crude death rate (per '000)	10.1	1965
Accidental deaths (per 100 000 population) caused by motor vehicles	17.9	1965
due to other causes	26.1	1965
Population per physician	910	1965
Population per hospital bed	70	1966
School enrolment: age 5–19 years (percentage)	76	1963–4 av.
age over 19 years (per 100 000 population)	794	1963–5 av.

COMMUNICATIONS		*Year(s)*
Motor vehicles in use ('000s): private	1 671.5	1963–5 av.
commercial	137.9	1963–5 av.
Railway track (km.)	13 722	1964
Mail per capita: domestic	169	1963–5 av.
foreign received	11	1963–5 av.
foreign sent	8	1963–5 av.
Telephones (per '000 urban population)	47.9	1967
Radio licences (per '000 population)	385	1963–5 av.
Television licences (per '000 population)	255.2	1963–5 av.
Daily newspapers (per '000 population)	398	1962–4 av.

FINANCE

Currency unit: The krona

Exchange rates	*1965*	*1960*	*1950*	*1938*
Per $ U.S.	5.18	5.18	5.18	4.19
Per £ sterling	14.52	14.54	14.51	19.25

		Year(s)
National Income (million $ U.S.)	17 000*	1966
G.N.P. per capita ($ U.S.)	2 270*	1966
Rate of increase of G.N.P. per capita	4.7	1960–4 av.
Foreign trade (percentage of G.D.P.)	42	1963–5 av.

TRADING

Total trade (in million $ U.S.)	*1965*	*1955*	*1938*
Exports (f.o.b.)	3 969	1 726	464
Imports (c.i.f.)	4 375	1 997	525

Main trading partners (percentage of total value)

Exports	*1965*	*1955*	*1938*	*Imports*	*1965*	*1955*	*1938*
Germany F.R.	14	13	18*d*	Germany F.R.	22	22	22*d*
U.K.	13	20	23	U.K.	15	14	12
Norway	12	10	7	U.S.A.	9	10	16
Denmark	9	6	5	Denmark	6	4	3
U.S.A.	6	5	9	Norway	5	3	4
Netherlands	5	6	3	Netherlands	5	7	4
Finland	5	2	5	France	4	5	3

Distribution of trade (percentage of total value)

Exports	*1965*	*1955*	*1938**
Manufactured goods	66	50	43
(machinery and transport equipment)	(35)	(22)	(14)
(wood and paper)	(10)	(12)	(10)
Crude materials and fuels	27	44	41
(wood and paper pulp)	(18)	(32)	(27)
Imports			
Manufactured goods	63	51	43
(machinery and transport equipment)	(30)	(20)	(16)
(textiles and clothing)	(9)	(9)	(11)
Crude materials and fuels	18	26	24
(petroleum and products)	(9)	(12)	(6)
Food	10	13	9
Chemicals	8	6	9

d incl. Germany D.R.

PRODUCTION, EXPORTS AND IMPORTS

Years: **1963–5 average** and *1953–5 average* Units: '000 metric tons unless otherwise indicated

1. CEREALS, etc.

	Production		Exports		Imports	
Barley	1 322.3	412.3	101.4	22.7	15.0	42.7
Maize (corn)	—	—	—	—	39.2	43.4
Millets/sorghum	—	—	—	0.5	6.2	33.9
Oats	1 314.7	801.7	84.3	11.0	2.1	24.0
Potatoes	1 642.3	1 480.3	0.2	1.5	28.3	48.9
Rice	—	—	—	—	10.7	8.3
Rye	123.7	256.0	11.0	47.3	83.2	13.7
Wheat	933.0	908.3	264.5	268.4	138.4	30.6

2. FRUIT, etc.

	Production		Exports		Imports	
Apples	237.0	172.0	0.8	0.3	47.3	33.6
Bananas	—	—	—	—	47.5	44.3
Cherries	9.3	7.8	—	—	na	1.5
Coconuts	—	—	—	—	2.0	—
Dates	—	—	—	—	0.4	0.3
Figs	—	—	—	—	na	1.7
Grapes	—	—	0.5†	—	23.4	11.4
Lemons	—	—	0.1†	—	5.5	4.5
Oranges	—	—	1.0†	0.1†	105.6	92.8
Other citrus fruit	—	—	0.1†	—	4.2	1.9
Peaches	—	—	—	—	na	2.8

continued

2. FRUIT, etc.—*continued*

	Production		Exports		Imports	
Pears	54.3	31.0	0.2	—	17.2	19.5
Plums	23.0	17.6	—	—	na	1.5
Raisins	—	—	—	—	3.9	4.2
Wine *b*	—	—	0.1†	—	328.1	92.7

b '000 hectolitres.

3. BEVERAGES, FOREST PRODUCTS, etc.

	Production		Exports		Imports	
Cocoa	—	—	—	—	7.7	6.6
Coffee	—	—	0.3	—	90.1	50.8
Sugar: beet	1 548.3	1 826.0				
raw	242.2	286.0	4.1	7.7	83.6	66.7
Tea	—	—	0.1	—	1.4	1.1
Tobacco: leaf	0.1	0.3	0.1	—	10.1	8.8
cigars	12.5[2]*e*	17.8*e*	—	—[2]	1.6	0.9[2]
cigarettes	7 646.0*e*	4 741.3*e*				
tobacco/snuff	3.9	4.3				
Softwood *j*	41 300.0	35 300.0	8 984.0	7 641.5	292.7	368.7
Hardwood *j*	6 333.3	3 900.0	33.3	28.4	194.6	113.0
Wood pulp	6 297.3	3 578.0	3 348.3	2 232.7	4.4	0.8
Newsprint	646.0	346.7	438.7	196.3	—	0.1
Other paper	2 270.3*	1 031.3*	1 378.7	574.7	38.8	12.3*

e no. in millions. *j* '000 cu. metres of roundwood equivalent.

continued

na: data not available. — negligible or nil. [1] one year only. [2] two year average. * estimate. ‡ see appendix. † re-exports.

PRODUCTION, EXPORTS AND IMPORTS *continued*

4. VEGETABLE OILSEEDS AND OILS

	Production		Exports		Imports	
Castor oil	—	—	0.06†	0.01†	1.31	0.83
Copra	—	—	—	—	62.60	49.20
Coconut oil	na	na	0.58	3.73	4.04	4.87
Cottonseed	—	—	—	—	0.02	—
Cottonseed oil	—	—	0.25†	—	6.11	0.01
Groundnuts	—	—	0.02†	—	0.59	0.23
Groundnut oil	na	na	0.03	0.15	1.49	0.30
Linseed	na	3.67*n*	—	0.70	0.46	5.50
Linseed oil	na	na	0.03	0.01	10.53	10.10
Olive oil	—	—	—	—	0.13	0.09
Palm kernel oil	—	—	0.02†	—	0.80	0.13
Palm oil	—	—	0.17†	0.03†	2.04	0.92
Rapeseed	164.70	124.30*p*	50.97	39.13	0.72	3.90
Rapeseed oil	na	na	14.71	14.37	0.03	0.10*q*
Soya beans	—	—	—	—	1.78	8.06
Soya bean oil	na	na	1.18*s*	0.85*s*	10.05	0.68
Sunflower seed oil	—	—	—	—	0.05	—
Tung oil	—	—	—	—	0.87	1.12

n flax grown for seed only. *p* seed delivered to oil factories. *q* incl. other minor vegetable oils. *s* incl. re-exports.

5. LIVESTOCK‡, ANIMAL PRODUCTS, etc.

	Production		Exports		Imports	
Chickens *d*	9 667.7	11 735.0*r*				
Cattle *d*	2 344.0	2 552.3	13.1	0.4	0.9	0.3
dairy cows *d*	1 529.7	2 039.3				
Goats *d*	15.0*	na	—	—	0.2	—
Sheep *d*	212.3	196.7				
Horses *d*	132.0	336.0				
Pigs *d*	1 855.0	1 534.7	1.4	24.8	—	—
Bacon/ham	374.3	321.0	10.0	3.1	1.3	—
Meat‡: 'A'			28.0	4.4	13.2	17.3
'B'	48.8	43.3	1.8	0.5	6.9	2.1
Butter	81.7	93.3	8.9	10.1	0.3	—
Cheese	57.3	54.3	5.2	4.2	8.6	4.2
Eggs	96.7	83.3	7.1	8.1	1.6	—
Fish	359.0*u*	206.8*u*	227.4	57.1[1]*	149.6	na
Milk	3 688.7	4 328.0	46.4	30.0	1.3	—
Whale/sperm oil	—	—	—	—	2.0	—
Hides/skins	—	na	18.0	9.1[2]	25.2	19.1[2]
Wool	0.2	—	0.6	0.4	4.8	4.2

d no. in thousands. *r* incl. ducks, geese and turkeys. *u* excl. freshwater fish; incl. fish landed by Swedish vessels in foreign ports.

6. FIBRES, TEXTILES, etc.

	Production		Exports		Imports	
Abaca	—	—	—	—	0.7	0.3
Agaves (sisal, etc.)	—	—	—	0.1†	5.6	5.9
Cotton lint	—	—	0.1†	—	20.1	29.0
Flax fibre	1.8	2.7	1.0	1.4	3.1	2.7
Hemp fibre	0.6	0.8	0.3	—	0.1	0.4
Jute	—	—	0.3†	0.2†	5.1	5.3
Rubber: natural	—	—	2.6†	—	26.5	22.2
synthetic	—	—	—	—	27.1	—
Cotton: yarn	19.7	25.1*v*	0.1	0.1	9.0	3.5
woven fabrics	19.5	22.4	2.5	0.8	12.2	8.1
Rayon: fibre/yarn	34.8	16.0	22.0	7.7	5.7	3.5
woven fabrics	11.7	7.6	2.9*w*	0.4	10.5*w*	3.6
Non-cellulosic fibre/yarn	0.2	—	0.2	—	10.6	—
Wool: yarn	11.7	14.4	0.3	0.1	3.9	2.1
woven fabrics	8.0	11.0	0.9	0.6	4.0	5.5

v incl. mixed yarns. *w* incl. synthetic fibres.

7. FUEL AND POWER

	Production		Exports		Imports	
Coal, 'A'‡	57	190	11	2	1 833	3 456*q*
Coke	na	na	10	38	1 554	2 178
Electricity *h*: total	45 053	23 620[1]				
hydro	42 480	21 740[1]				
thermal	2 573	1 880[1]				
Oil, crude	73	110[1]	—	—	3 340	1 700[1]
Petroleum, refined	3 060	1 770[1]	243	7[1]	14 227	6 190[1]
Uranium	na	—	—	—	—	—

h million kWh. *q* incl. lignite and brown coal.

8. IRON AND STEEL

	Production		Exports		Imports	
Iron ore	16 258*m*	9 971*m*	23 359	14 907	98	—
Pig iron	2 276	1 102	120	105	300	90
Steel ingots/castings	4 357	1 908	109	7	12	—
Iron/steel scrap	na	na	17	9	204	51
Iron/steel products *a*	na	na	284	82	206	109

a million $ U.S. *m* metal content.

9. NON-FERROUS MINERALS AND METALS

	Production		Exports		Imports	
Diamonds *a*	—	—	0.18	0.08	1.05	1.00
Gold *k*, ore *m*	116.30	99.00	55.70‡*p*	50.70*p*	201.30‡*p*	34.47*p*
Platinum group metals *k*	—	—	—	4.97†	—	0.61
Silver *k*, ore *m*	3 273.00	2 061.70	698.00*p*	540.00*p*	470.00*p*	2 642.30*p*
Asbestos: fibre	—	—	0.07	—	18.25	12.72
manufactured	na	na	20.38	0.03	18.85	1.86
Mica	0.02[2]	0.17[2]	0.01	0.02	1.19	0.84
Aluminium: bauxite	—	—	—	—	23.67	22.60
alumina	—	—	—	—	59.45	19.48
aluminium	26.42	10.12	21.29	11.34	54.66	22.82
Antimony, metal	—	—	0.03	0.06	0.38	0.36
Beryl	0.02	—	—	—	—	—
Cadmium	—	—	—	—	0.15	0.10
Chrome: ore	—	—	—[2]	0.01	136.23	59.56
metal	na	na	20.84	8.66	11.98	2.03
Cobalt, metal	na	na	0.01	0.02	0.19	1.69
Copper: ore	1.90*m*	14.14*m*	—	—	83.09	41.49
metal	47.12	17.18	56.19	37.74	95.05	52.31
Lead: ore	69.15*m*	29.13*m*	44.19	10.48	—	—
metal	40.45	19.16	12.42	6.01	12.12	18.06
Magnesium: dolomite	73.13*t*	na	4.02	—	26.65	—
magnesite	—	—	0.19	0.03	8.06	1.39
metal/salts	—‡	—‡	0.16†	na	40.73	16.66
Manganese: ore	12.00**n*	14.51*n*	8.93	0.87	76.77	32.20
metal	na	na	3.94	0.88	22.51	2.81
Mercury *f*	na	na	9.30	1.30	92.10	52.00
Molybdenum *f*: ore	—	na	—	—	2 952.30	1 079.00
metal	na	na	338.30	91.00	585.20	59.70
Nickel: ore	—	—	—	—	0.44	na
metal	na	na	0.96	0.01	12.56	3.43
Tin, metal	—	—	0.14	0.05	1.02	0.79
Titanium minerals	—	—	0.10†	0.35†	16.90	7.84
Tungsten: ore	0.09	0.45	0.09	0.10	1.50	0.41
metal	na	na	0.17	0.13	0.56	0.02
Vanadium *r*	—	—	0.15†	0.03†	0.10	0.03
Zinc: ore	80.36*m*	54.10*m*	148.54	97.78	—	—
metal	na	na	2.23	1.15	39.93	38.10

a million $ U.S. *f* metric tons. *k* '000 fine troy oz. *m* metal content. *n* low-grade ore. *p* bullion. *r* ferro-vanadium. *t* excl. calcined.

10. CHEMICALS *n* AND FERTILIZERS

	Production		Exports		Imports	
Organic chemicals:						
Benzene	0.5[1]		na		na	
Butadiene	na		na		na	
Ethylene	na		na		na	
Methanol	0.8		—		36.6	
Phenol	2.0*r*		1.1		7.9	
Phthalic anhydride	3.7		0.2		5.6	
Styrene monomer	—		0.1[1]		6.9	
Urea	na		—		14.3	
Inorganic chemicals:						
Ammonia	99.4		0.1		15.6	
Carbon black	—		—		20.1	
Chlorine	199.1		3.2		2.6	
Nitric acid	179.1		—		6.1	
Sodium carbonate	1.5		—		103.2	
Sodium hydroxide	230.1		4.1		28.6	
Sulphuric acid	522.2		17.0		8.9	
Plastics:						
Polyamides	na		—		1.0	
Polyethylene	16.5[2]		9.0		30.1	
Polyvinyl chloride	26.9		7.5		13.5	
Fertilizers:						
Phosphates	—	—	0.2	—	433.4	327.1
Potash	—	—	2.7†	1.8†	179.7	187.8
Pyrites	212.0*x*	194.3*x*	16.2	12.7	58.9	89.9
Sulphur	25.1*q*	28.9[1]*q*	0.2	3.4	124.6	49.5

n data not available for years 1953–5. *q* recovered sulphur. *r* incl. phenol alcohols. *x* sulphur content.

11. INDUSTRY

	Production		Exports		Imports	
Aircraft *a*	76.0**t*	na	—	1.5	19.8	10.8
Alcoholic beverages			—	0.4*a*	26.7*a*	12.9*a*
beer *b*	3 002.0	2 082.7				
spirits *b*	211.0**u*	344.8*v*				
Cement	3 550.0	2 414.0	90.7	325.7	8.0	7.0
Electrical engineering *a*	806.0[2]	na	202.6	62.0[2]	255.8	70.4[2]
Locomotives *c*	69.0	71.0[2]	na	na	na	na
Railway vehicles *a*	na	na	10.3	1.6	na	4.5
Machine tools *a*	46.0[1]	na	22.1	14.0	35.1	10.6[2]
Merchant ships *g*	1 026.0	518.0	815.0	372.2	167.0	14.3
Motor vehicles			205.3*a*	30.4[2]*a*	310.9*a*	139.2[2]*a*
commercial *d*	22.9	16.1*w*				
private *d*	163.3	41.5*w*				

a million $ U.S. *b* '000 hectolitres. *c* no. of units. *d* no. in thousands. *g* '000 G.R.T. *t* 1965–7 av. *u* production for home consumption in 1967. *v* production for home consumption in 1960. *w* incl. assembly of imported parts.

na: data not available. — negligible or nil. [1] one year only. [2] two year average. * estimate. ‡ see appendix. † re-exports.

SWITZERLAND

A long-established democracy, Switzerland has been a republic since 1798, and maintains a policy of political neutrality. Banking, insurance and tourism are all important factors in the economy. Switzerland is a member of the European Free Trade Association.

AREA: 41 288 sq. km. (15 941 sq. miles)

LAND USE: (percentage of total)	*1964*	*1955*
Arable and orchard	10.2	10.8
Permanent meadow and pasture	42.2	41.8
Forest and woodland	23.8	23.8
City areas, waste and other land	23.8	23.6

POPULATION: 6 050 000 (1967 U.N. estimate)

Largest city: ZÛRICH; population: 657 400 (1967)
Capital city: BERN; population: 250 600 (1967)

Distribution of working population (1960)

Total working population: 2 512 411

U.N. group no.		*Percentage*
0	Agriculture, forestry, fishing and hunting	11.2
1	Mining and quarrying	0.3
2/3	Manufacturing	39.7
4	Construction	9.5
5	Electricity, gas, water and sanitary services	0.9
6	Commerce	13.8
7	Transport, storage and communications	5.4
8	Services	19.0
9	Others	0.2

		Year(s)
Life expectancy at birth (years): male	68.7	1958–63 av.
female	74.1	
Infant mortality (per '000)	17.8	1965
Crude birth rate (per '000)	18.8	1965
Crude death rate (per '000)	9.3	1965
Accidental deaths (per 100 000 population)		
caused by motor vehicles	21.2	1965
due to other causes	37.2	1965
Population per physician	760	1965
Population per hospital bed	80	1965
School enrolment: age 5–19 years (percentage)	62*p*	1963–4 av.
age over 19 years (per 100 000 population)	519*p*	1963–5 av.

p public education only.

COMMUNICATIONS

		Year(s)
Motor vehicles in use ('000s): private	835.5	1963–5 av.
commercial	87.3	
Railway track (km.)	5 112	1963
Mail per capita: domestic	252	
foreign received	28	1963–5 av.
foreign sent	34	
Telephones (per '000 urban population)	39.3	1967
Radio licences (per '000 population)	276	1963–5 av.
Television licences (per '000 population)	84.1	1963–5 av.
Daily newspapers (per '000 population)	369.3	1962–4 av.

FINANCE

Currency unit: The Swiss franc

Exchange rates	*1965*	*1960*	*1950*	*1938*
Per $ U.S.	4.318	4.305	4.294	4.438
Per £ sterling	12.103	12.068	12.028	20.415

		Year(s)
National Income (million $ U.S.)	11 460	1965
G.N.P. per capita ($ U.S.)	2 250	1966
Rate of increase of G.N.P. per capita	3.1	1960–4 av.
Foreign trade (percentage of G.D.P.)	49	1963–5 av.

TRADING

Total trade (in million $ U.S.)	*1965*	*1955*	*1938*
Exports (f.o.b.)	2 959	1 307	302
Imports (c.i.f.)	3 697	1 489	366

Main trading partners (percentage of total value)

Exports	*1965*	*1955*	*1938*	*Imports*	*1965*	*1955*	*1938*
Germany F.R.	17	13	16*d*	Germany F.R.	30	24	23*d*
U.S.A.	10	12	7	France	15	12	14
France	8	7	9	Italy	10	10	7
Italy	8	8	7	U.S.A.	8	13	8
U.K.	7	5	11	U.K.	7	5	6
Austria	4	3	2	Belg./Lux.	4	4	4
Netherlands	4	4	5	Netherlands	4	5	3

Distribution of trade (percentage of total value)

Exports	*1965*	*1955**	*1938**
Manufactured goods	72	na	na
(machinery and transport equipment)	(30)	(23)	(18)
(watches)	(14)	(19)	(18)
(textiles and clothing)	(10)	(13)	(16)
Chemicals	20	16	15
Food	4	2	5
Imports			
Manufactured goods	60	na	na
(machinery and transport equipment)	(24)	(15)	(8)
Food	14	16	23
Crude materials and fuels	13	na	na
Chemicals	9	8	7

d incl. Germany D.R.

PRODUCTION, EXPORTS AND IMPORTS

Years: **1963–5 average** and *1953–5 average* Units: '000 metric tons unless otherwise indicated

1. CEREALS, etc.

	Production 1963–5	Production 1953–5	Exports 1963–5	Exports 1953–5	Imports 1963–5	Imports 1953–5
Barley	98.7	62.7	—	—	272.2	179.8
Maize (corn)	17.0	4.0	0.3	—	161.5	79.3
Millets/sorghum	—	—	—	—	18.8	11.9
Oats	34.0	67.3	—	—	140.3	115.6
Potatoes	1 152.3	1 160.3	37.0	11.1	15.8	73.1
Rice	—	—	0.4†	—	19.3	20.6
Rye	57.0	41.0	—	—	0.8	3.2
Wheat	347.3	304.0	—	—	372.0	348.5

2. FRUIT, etc.

	Production 1963–5	Production 1953–5	Exports 1963–5	Exports 1953–5	Imports 1963–5	Imports 1953–5
Apples	335.0	413.0	5.2	43.8	23.6	16.8
Apricots	8.0	3.7	—	—	na	8.4
Bananas	—	—	0.1†	—	54.7	18.4
Cherries	42.3	54.9	na	—	na	3.1
Dates	—	—	—	—	1.1	1.1
Figs	—	—	—	—	na	1.6
Grapes	126.3	95.3	—	—	31.7	15.8
Lemons	—	—	—	0.1[1]†	17.2	13.6
Oranges	—	—	0.1†	0.1†	90.6	59.9
Other citrus fruit	—	—	—	—	7.7	5.4
Peaches	—	—	—	—	na	13.2
Pears	138.7	266.7	8.2	1.0	8.8	3.4
Pineapples	—	—	—	—	na	0.4
Plums	39.3	39.0	—	—	na	2.8
Raisins	—	—	—	—	2.9	2.6
Tomatoes	20.7	9.7				
Wine *b*	812.3	658.7	9.3	28.3	1 552.1	1 022.3

b '000 hectolitres.

3. BEVERAGES, FOREST PRODUCTS, etc.

	Production 1963–5	Production 1953–5	Exports 1963–5	Exports 1953–5	Imports 1963–5	Imports 1953–5
Cocoa	—	—	—	0.3†	14.8	10.8
Coffee	—	—	5.5†	—	38.3	18.7
Sugar: beet	319.0	214.0				
raw	48.6	34.0	3.1	2.7	230.1	172.8
Tea	—	—	0.1†	0.1†	1.4	0.8
Tobacco: leaf	1.7	2.1	—	—	18.6	11.8
cigars	652.0*e*	499.3*e*		na		
cigarettes	16 680.0*e*	8 026.3*e*	5.7	2.8[2]*e*	—	—
tobacco/snuff	1.6	2.2		na		
Softwood *j*	2 780.0	2 986.7	87.0	29.9	672.0	205.0
Hardwood *j*	1 146.7	845.0	58.7	8.1	370.8	216.4
Wood pulp	255.7	169.0	10.3	8.5	145.0	67.0
Newsprint	107.7	60.0	—	2.1	6.9	—
Other paper	470.7	248.3*	11.7	5.7	85.7	13.3

e no. in millions. *j* '000 cu. metres of roundwood equivalent.

4. VEGETABLE OILSEEDS AND OILS

	Production 1963–5	Production 1953–5	Exports 1963–5	Exports 1953–5	Imports 1963–5	Imports 1953–5
Castor seed	—	—	—	—	—	0.05[2]
Castor oil	—	—	—	0.03†	1.46	0.74
Copra	—	—	—	—	16.91	26.80
Coconut oil	na	na	0.41	—	3.17	4.63
Cottonseed oil	—	—	—	—	—	na
Groundnuts	—	—	0.03†	—	70.82	36.73
Groundnut oil	na	na	0.39	—	4.49	5.40
Linseed	—	—	—	—	8.72	8.53
Linseed oil	na	na	0.40*	2.20*p*	3.85	7.72*p*

p incl. other inedible oils.

continued

PRODUCTION, EXPORTS AND IMPORTS *continued*

4. VEGETABLE OILSEEDS AND OILS—*continued*

	Production 1963–5	Production 1953–5	Exports 1963–5	Exports 1953–5	Imports 1963–5	Imports 1953–5
Olive oil	—	—	—	—	4.63	1.55
Palm kernels	—	—	—	—	4.98	0.30
Palm kernel oil	na	—	0.39	—	0.56	—[1]
Palm oil	—	—	—	—	2.37	0.62
Rapeseed	13.00	5.30	—	—	0.90	0.50
Rapeseed oil	na	na	—	—	1.52	0.11*
Sesame seed	—	—	—	—	0.71	1.83
Soya beans	—	—	—	—	0.33	0.07
Soya bean oil	na	—	—	—	3.59	0.46
Sunflower seed oil	—	—	0.21†	—	12.28	—
Tung oil	—	—	—	—	0.28*	—

5. LIVESTOCK‡, ANIMAL PRODUCTS, etc.

	Production 1963–5	Production 1953–5	Exports 1963–5	Exports 1953–5	Imports 1963–5	Imports 1953–5
Chickens *d*	5 960.3	6 300.7				
Cattle *d*	1 729.0	1 603.7	12.0	11.6	27.5	9.2
dairy cows *d*	1 052.3	886.7				
Goats *d*	82.0*	135.7	0.3	na	0.2	na
Sheep *d*	239.7	191.7				
Horses *d*	77.0	124.0				
Pigs *d*	1 471.0	1 001.7	0.1	—	6.0	14.2*
Bacon/ham	255.7	195.0	—	—	0.3	—
Meat‡: 'A'			0.1	0.1	39.6	0.3
'B'	47.0*	31.1	—	—	24.8	8.4
Butter	32.7	26.3	—	—	6.6	4.6
Cheese	74.7	58.7	34.6	20.3	11.6	3.0
Eggs	30.6	29.5*p*	0.1	—	23.5	13.4
Fish	2.9	2.0	0.7	0.3[1]*	61.9	na
Milk	3 115.7	2 757.0	59.6	25.2	137.2	9.1
Hides/skins	15.6	13.1	7.9*a*	—	—	9.7[2]
Wool	0.3	—	0.4	—	4.9	4.7

a million $ U.S. *d* no. in thousands. *p* excl. eggs for hatching.

6. FIBRES, TEXTILES, etc.

	Production 1963–5	Production 1953–5	Exports 1963–5	Exports 1953–5	Imports 1963–5	Imports 1953–5
Agaves (sisal, etc.)	—	—	—	—	2.9	0.9[2]
Cotton lint	—	—	0.2†	2.9†	41.8	36.7
Flax fibre	—	—	0.1†	—	2.1	0.4
Hemp fibre	—	—	—	—	1.2	2.0[2]
Jute	—	—	0.2†	—	2.4	1.0
Rubber: natural	—	—	—	—	7.8	7.2
synthetic	—	—	—	—	10.1	—
Silk *f*	—	—	154.0†	46.0†	678.7	430.3
Cotton: yarn	37.3	29.8	4.3	3.6	0.9	1.2
woven fabrics	21.4*q*	19.4	5.0	5.2	4.6	2.2
Rayon: fibre/yarn	22.7	21.2	14.0	16.9	5.5	0.7*r*
woven fabrics	na	na	4.0	2.5	4.1	0.7
Non-cellulosic fibre/yarn	18.6	1.7	15.8	na	6.8	na
Wool: yarn	1.7	na	2.2	1.3	2.2	1.5
woven fabrics	7.2	4.5[1]	1.5	1.0	2.5	2.3

f metric tons. *q* yarn consumption in weaving mills. *r* incl. some nylon.

7. FUEL AND POWER

	Production 1963–5	Production 1953–5	Exports 1963–5	Exports 1953–5	Imports 1963–5	Imports 1953–5
Coal, 'A'‡	—	—	1†	9†	1 722	2 011
Coke	—	—	—	5†	553	632
Electricity *h*: total	23 112	14 030[1]				
hydro	22 785	13 920[1]				
thermal	327	110[1]				
Oil, crude	—	—	—	—	803	na[1]
Petroleum, refined	707	—[1]	70	—	6 193	1 790[1]

h million kWh.

8. IRON AND STEEL

	Production 1963–5	Production 1953–5	Exports 1963–5	Exports 1953–5	Imports 1963–5	Imports 1953–5
Iron ore	41**m*	56**m*	83	115	3	66
Pig iron	34	44	14	4	74	120
Steel ingots/castings	337	158	—	—	237	—
Iron/steel scrap	na	na	26	3	7	17
Iron/steel products *a*	na	na	18	3	223	97

a million $ U.S. *m* metal content.

9. NON-FERROUS MINERALS AND METALS

	Production 1963–5	Production 1953–5	Exports 1963–5	Exports 1953–5	Imports 1963–5	Imports 1953–5
Gold *k*, bullion/coins etc.	—	—	525.33‡	34.20	157.30	55.17
Platinum group metals *k*	—	—	27.59	2.08	40.00	11.18
Silver *k*, bullion	—	—	596.00	297.73	8 543.67	4 712.67
Asbestos: fibre	—	—	0.08	0.01*n*	12.86	5.02*n*
manufactured	na	na	4.32	0.46	6.74	2.59
Mica	—	—	0.18	na*n*	0.94	na*n*
Aluminium:						
bauxite	—	—	—	—	2.73	—
alumina	—	—	0.10	0.01	127.28	60.26
aluminium	63.83	28.50	39.00	13.94	19.59	7.90
Antimony: metal	—	—	—	—	0.29	0.18
Copper: ore	—	—	—	1.30	—	1.28
metal	—	—	22.11	10.82	61.09	31.04
Lead: ore	—	—	—	0.88	—	—
metal	—	—	7.56	1.22	22.92	15.53
Magnesium:						
dolomite	—	—	—	—	9.59	—
magnesite	—	—	—	—	3.95	—
metal/salts	—*x*	0.08*x*	—	—	7.00	—
Mercury *f*	—	—	5.50	22.30	43.70	44.20
Nickel, ore	—	—	1.52	0.93	2.08	1.08
Tin, metal	—	—	0.21	0.16	1.00	0.06
Titanium minerals	—	—	—	—	6.50	—
Zinc, metal	—	—	1.21	5.21	27.40	24.76

f metric tons. *k* '000 fine troy oz. *n* mica incl. with asbestos. *x* primary magnesium only.

10. CHEMICALS*n* AND FERTILIZERS

	Production	Exports	Imports
Organic chemicals:			
Benzene	na	na	na
Butadiene	—	—	na
Ethylene	na	na	na
Methanol	na	0.1	17.0
Phenol	na	na	na
Phthalic anhydride	na	0.7[2]	2.9[2]
Styrene monomer	—	—	na
Urea	na	3.3	0.4
Inorganic chemicals:			
Ammonia	na	—	20.9
Carbon black	na	0.4	6.7
Chlorine	na	11.1	—
Nitric acid	na	0.1	0.3
Sodium carbonate	na	2.2	3.6
Sodium hydroxide	na	2.1	5.5
Sulphuric acid	167.0	19.0	0.4
Plastics:			
Polyamides	na	na	na
Polyethylene	—	—	na
Polyvinyl chloride	10.5[2]	3.4[2]	7.8[2]

Fertilizers:	Production 1963–5	Production 1953–5	Exports 1963–5	Exports 1953–5	Imports 1963–5	Imports 1953–5
Phosphates	—	—	—	—	36.2	24.7*
Potash	—	—	—	2.3†	116.9	78.3
Pyrites	—	—	—	—	39.1	—
Sulphur	—	—	—	—	66.5	56.1

n data not available for years 1953–5.

11. INDUSTRY

	Production 1963–5	Production 1953–5	Exports 1963–5	Exports 1953–5	Imports 1963–5	Imports 1953–5
Aircraft *a*	50.0[1]	na	—	—	32.5	6.0
Alcoholic beverages			—	—	43.2*a*	17.3*an*
beer *b*	4 371.0	2 426.3*p*				
spirits *b*	84.0*q*	145.0*r*				
Cement	4 066.7	1 829.7	84.3	7.3	84.7	74.3
Electrical engineering *a*	na	na	187.5	6.8[2]	190.4	12.9[2]
Locomotives *c*	72.0*	na	na	na	—	—
Machine tools *a*	121.0[1]	na	113.2	54.3	36.8	19.4[2]
Merchant ships *g*	—	—	—	—	0.6	5.0
Motor vehicles			—	5.0[2]*a*	241.1*a*	69.9*a*
private *dt*	17.7	6.5[2]				

a million $ U.S. *b* '000 hectolitres. *c* no. of units. *d* no. in thousands. *g* '000 G.R.T. *n* wine only. *p* sales by breweries. *q* 1966/7 figure. *r* 1956–60 av. *t* assembly of imported parts.

na: data not available. — negligible or nil. [1] one year only. [2] two year average. * estimate. ‡ see appendix. † re-exports.

SYRIA

MIDDLE EAST

Syria, mandated to France after World War I, became an independent republic during World War II. A brief union with Egypt in 1958, forming the United Arab Republic, was broken when Syria seceded three years later.

AREA: 185 680 sq. km. (71 700 sq. miles)

LAND USE: (percentage of total)	*1964*	*1955*
Arable and orchard	35.9	22.2
Permanent meadow and pasture	33.0	34.1
Forest and woodland	2.4	2.4
City areas, waste and other land	28.7	41.3

POPULATION: 5 600 000 (1967 estimate)

Largest city: DIMASHQ (Damascus), capital; population: 618 457 (city proper, 1966)

Distribution of working population (1965)

Total working population: 1 424 267

U.N. group no.		*Percentage*
0	Agriculture, forestry, fishing and hunting	55.5
1	Mining and quarrying	0.8
2/3	Manufacturing	11.6
4	Construction	5.5
5	Electricity, gas, water and sanitary services	0.7
6	Commerce	9.9
7	Transport, storage and communications	2.9
8	Services	11.9
9	Others	1.2

		Year(s)
Infant mortality (per '000)	22.3*	1965
Crude birth rate (per '000)	33.4*	1965
Crude death rate (per '000)	4.6*	1965
Population per physician	5 110	1963
Population per hospital bed	900	1966
School enrolment: age 5–19 years (percentage)	50	1963–4 av.
age over 19 years (per 100 000 population)	630	1964–5 av.

COMMUNICATIONS		*Year(s)*
Motor vehicles in use ('000s): private	25.0	1963–5 av.
commercial	13.8	
Railway track (km.)	961	1964
Telephones (per '000 urban population)	1.6	1967
Radio receivers (per '000 population)	297	1963–5 av.
Television sets (per '000 population)	9.2	1963–5 av.
Daily newspapers (per '000 population)	15	1962–4 av.

FINANCE

Currency unit: The Syrian pound

Exchange rates	*1965*	*1960*	*1938*
Per $ U.S.	3.82	3.58	1.9
Per £ sterling	10.71	10.05	8.75

		Year(s)
National Income (million $ U.S.)	781	1963
G.N.P. per capita ($ U.S.)	180	1966
Rate of increase of G.N.P. per capita	8.2	1960–4 av.

TRADING

Total trade (in million $ U.S.)	*1965*	*1955*	*1955a*
Exports (f.o.b.)	168	128	132
Imports (c.i.f.)	212	179	196

Main trading partners (percentage of total value)

Exports	*1965*	*1955a*	*Imports*	*1965*	*1955a*
Lebanon	22	21	Germany F.R.	12	10
U.S.S.R.	10	—	U.K.	8	13
China P.R.	10	—	Iraq	8	6
Italy	6	10	U.S.A.	7	11
Romania	6	—	France	6	10
France	5	21	Italy	6	5
Saudi Arabia	5	2	Lebanon	5	6

Distribution of trade (percentage of total value)

Exports	*1965*	*1955*
Textiles and clothing	56	63*
Food	34	23
(cereals, fruit and vegetables)	(17)	(9*)
Imports		
Manufactured goods	49	60*
(machinery and transport equipment)	(16)	(15*)
(textiles and clothing)	(13)	(13*)
Food	20	16
(cereals, fruit and vegetables)	(10)	(6*)
Crude materials and fuels	18	19
Chemicals	12	4*

a incl. gold and specie.

PRODUCTION, EXPORTS AND IMPORTS

Years: **1963–5 average** and *1953–5 average* Units: '000 metric tons unless otherwise indicated

	Production		Exports		Imports	
1. CEREALS, etc.						
Barley	**703.7**	*414.7*	**284.9**	*204.5*	—	*0.2*
Maize (corn)	**6.7**	*21.3*	**1.7**	*2.7*	**2.9**	*0.1*
Millets/sorghum	**59.3**	*103.3*	**8.5**	*26.4*	—	—
Oats	**2.3**	*4.7*	—	*0.1*	**0.5**	—
Potatoes	**43.0***	*29.7*	**0.9**	*0.9*	**15.8**	*8.6*
Rice	**1.3**	*15.3*	—	*1.0*	**28.1**	*11.3*
Rye	na	—	**0.2**	—	—	—
Wheat	**1 111.3**	*757.2*	**133.9**	*148.7*	**7.7**	*10.4*
2. FRUIT, etc.						
Apples	**24.7**	*8.7*	**1.2**	*1.1*	**12.8**	*2.2*
Apricots	**22.0**	*20.3*	na	na	—	—
Bananas	—	—	—	*0.3†*	**8.0**	*5.5*
Cherries	**1.0**	na	—	—	—	—
Dates	—	—	—	*0.1†*	**22.1**	*26.1*
Figs	**55.0**	*53.0*	na	na	—	—
Grapes	**198.3**	*235.7*	**6.1**	*4.7*	**0.4**	—
Lemons	**2.0**	*1.7*	—	*0.1*	**12.5**	*2.7*
Oranges	**4.7**	*3.3*	—	*0.8*	**57.4**	*21.8*
Other citrus fruit	—	—	—	—	**0.7**	—
Olives	**85.7**	*38.0*				
Peaches	**3.0**	na	—	—	—	—
Pears	**6.0**	*2.0*	**0.2**	—	**0.5**	—
Plums	**2.7***	na	—	—	—	—
Raisins	**10.0***	*17.0*	**0.1**	*0.4*	—	—
Tomatoes	**134.7**	*67.7*				
Wine *b*	—	—	—	—	**0.7**	*1.0*

b '000 hectolitres.

	Production		Exports		Imports	
3. BEVERAGES, FOREST PRODUCTS, etc.						
Cocoa	—	—	—	—	**0.1**	—
Coffee	—	—	**0.8†**	—	**3.3**	*1.1*
Sugar: beet	**143.3**	*44.3**				
cane	**2.7**	—				
raw	**17.4**	*5.7**	—	—	**73.7**	*31.5*
Tea	—	—	—	—	**3.0**	*1.0*

continued

	Production		Exports		Imports	
3. BEVERAGES, FOREST PRODUCTS, etc.—*continued*						
Tobacco: leaf	**8.0**	*5.2*	**0.5**	*0.7*	**0.4**	*0.7*
cigarettes	**2 763.0e**	*1 756.7e*	—	—	**0.2[2]**	—
tobacco/snuff	**1.5**	*1.1*				
Softwood *j*	**2.0**	*350.0*	—[1]	—	**168.0[2]**	*43.6*
Hardwood *j*	**78.0*[1]**	*350.0[1]*	**1.8[1]**	—	**27.8[2]**	*49.2*
Newsprint	—*	—	—	—	**0.7[2]**	*0.6*
Other paper	**3.2***	—	—	—[2]	**19.4[2]**	*5.7*

e no. in millions. *j* '000 cu. metres of roundwood equivalent.

	Production		Exports		Imports	
4. VEGETABLE OILSEEDS AND OILS						
Castor seed	—	—	—	—	**0.03**	na
Castor oil	—	—	—	—	na	*0.01*
Copra	—	—	—	*0.20†*	**1.22**	*3.37*
Coconut oil	—	—	—	—	**0.21**	*0.01*
Cottonseed	**279.00**	*123.00*	**38.06**	*45.47*	**0.23**	*0.80*
Cottonseed oil	na	na	**7.44**	*1.30*	**0.02**	*0.03*
Groundnuts	**4.20***	*2.10*	**3.89**	*1.07**	—	*0.07*
Linseed	—	—	—	—	**1.14**	na
Linseed oil	—	—	—	—	na	*0.15*
Olive oil	**16.00***	*8.67*	**2.75**	*0.83*	**0.21**	*1.78*
Palm kernels	—	—	—	—	**0.21**	—
Palm oil	—	—	—	*0.01*	**2.06**	*3.28*
Sesame seed	**5.53**	*12.67*	**0.07**	*0.97*	**2.99**	*0.87*
Sunflower seed	—	—	—	—	—	*0.02*
5. LIVESTOCK‡, ANIMAL PRODUCTS, etc.						
Chickens *d*	**4 092.7**	*2 986.3*				
Cattle *d*	**454.0**	*516.0*	**32.6**	*47.8*	**13.9**	*1.6*
dairy cows *d*	**330.7**	*268.5[2]*				
Goats *d*	**1 352.0***	*1 612.7*	**420.0**	na	**376.6**	na
Sheep *d*	**4 632.0**	*3 753.7*				
Horses *d*	**67.7***	*100.6*				
Pigs *d*	na	na	—	*0.4**	—	—

d no. in thousands.

continued

na: data not available. — negligible or nil. [1] one year only. [2] two year average. * estimate. ‡ see appendix. † re-exports.

PRODUCTION, EXPORTS AND IMPORTS *continued*

	Production		Exports		Imports	
5. LIVESTOCK‡, ANIMAL PRODUCTS, etc.—*continued*						
Meat‡: 'A'	**59.3***	*29.7n*	—	—	—	—
'B'	**4.6***	*1.6[2]n*	—	—	—	—
Butter	**2.3p**	*12.5[2]p*	**0.6**	*0.8*	**1.0**	*0.1*
Cheese	**28.3**	*15.5[2]*	**0.4**	*1.3*	**1.1**	*0.2*
Eggs	**14.3**	*9.2*	**0.6**	*1.8*	—	—
Fish	na	na	**0.9**	*0.4**	**3.5**	*0.7**
Milk	**56.7***	*152.5[2]**	**3.2**	—	**18.5**	*1.8[2]**
Hides/skins	na	*4.2[2]*	**1.9[2]**	*1.0*	**4.1[2]**	*3.1*
Wool	**5.2[2]**	*4.3*	**4.7**	*2.9*	**0.1**	*0.5*

n government inspected meat only. *p* factory produce only.

	Production		Exports		Imports	
6. FIBRES, TEXTILES, etc.						
Cotton lint	**169.0**	*70.3*	**138.8**	*61.7*	—	—
Hemp fibre	**0.5**	*2.0*	—	—	—	—
Rubber: natural	—	—	—	—	**0.2**	—
Silk *f*	na	*11.0*	**11.7**	*10.7*	**0.7**	*6.7*
Cotton: yarn	**17.2**	*7.2[2]**	**0.5**	na	**0.9**	na
woven fabrics	**15.7**	na	**2.6**	na	**0.8**	na
Wool: yarn	**0.3**	na	—	—	**0.6**	*0.5*
woven fabrics	**0.7r**	na	—	—	**1.7**	*0.9*

f metric tons. *r* million metres.

	Production		Exports		Imports	
7. FUEL AND POWER						
Coal, 'A'‡	—	—	—	—	**2**	*4*
Coke	—	—	—	—	**2**	*1*
Electricity *h*: total	**572**	*270[1]*				
hydro	na	*10[1]*				
thermal	na	*260[1]*				
Oil, crude	—	—	—	—	**970**	na
Petroleum, refined	**920**	—[1]	**30**	*10[1]*	**293**	*510[1]*

h million kWh.

	Production		Exports		Imports	
8. IRON AND STEEL						
Pig iron	—	—	—	—	**1**	*1*
Iron/steel scrap	—	—	—	—	**2**	*1*
9. NON-FERROUS MINERALS AND METALS						
Gold *k*, bullion/coins etc.	—	—	—	—	**11.80[1]t**	*264.30*
Asbestos, manufactured	—	—	—	—	**4.63**	*0.79[2]*
Aluminium	—	—	—	—	**0.38**	*0.32[2]*
Lead, metal	—	—	—	—	**0.43**	*0.22[2]*
Magnesium: magnesite	—	—	—	—	—	*0.03[2]*
metal/salts	—‡	—‡	—	—	**0.04[1]**	*0.15[2]*
Tin, metal	—	—	—	—	**0.08**	*0.09*
Zinc, metal	—	—	—	—	**0.66**	*0.43*

k '000 fine troy oz. *t* gross weight of bullion and scrap.

	Production		Exports		Imports	
10. CHEMICALS *n* AND FERTILIZERS						
Chemicals	—		—		na	
Fertilizers:						
Sulphur	—	—	—	—	**0.7**	*0.6*

n data not available for years 1953–5.

	Production		Exports		Imports	
11. INDUSTRY						
Aircraft *a*	—	—	—	—	**0.5[2]**	—
Alcoholic beverages			—	—	**0.3[2]a**	—
beer *b*	**25.0**	*0.9*				
Cement	**665.0**	*246.0*	—	—	**13.3**	*39.7*
Electrical engineering *a*	—	—	**0.1†**	—	**13.6[2]**	*3.0*
Motor vehicles *a*	—	—	**0.3[2]p**	—	**5.4**	*9.9*

a million $ U.S. *b* '000 hectolitres. *p* used.

TAIWAN

CHINA SEA

Taiwan (the Republic of China), also called Formosa, is controlled by the remnant of the Nationalist government of China. The U.S.A. has pledged protection of Taiwan and its off-shore islands. The Chinese seat at the U.N. was occupied by Taiwan until 1971 when the People's Republic of China took its place.

AREA: 35 961 sq. km. (13 885 sq. miles)

LAND USE: (percentage of total)	*1965*	*1955*
Arable and orchard	24.7	24.3
Permanent meadow and pasture	na	1.7
Forest and woodland	70.9	49.1
City areas, waste and other land	na	24.9

POPULATION: 13 383 357* (1966 census)

Largest city: T'AI-PEI, capital; population: 1 155 191 (city proper, 1965)

Distribution of working population (1956)

Total working population: 2 993 029

U.N. group no.		*Percentage*
0	Agriculture, forestry, fishing and hunting	50.1
1	Mining and quarrying	1.5
2/3	Manufacturing	10.9
4	Construction	2.1
5	Electricity, gas, water and sanitary services	0.5
6	Commerce	6.7
7	Transport, storage and communications	3.6
8	Services	14.2
9	Others	10.4

		Year(s)
Life expectancy at birth (years): male	65.8	1965
female	70.4	1965
Infant mortality (per '000)	22.2*a*	1965
Crude birth rate (per '000)	32.7*a*	1965
Crude death rate (per '000)	5.5	1965
Accidental deaths (per 100 000 population)		
caused by motor vehicles	7.7	1965
due to other causes	29.5	1965
Population per physician	2 470	1965
Population per hospital bed	1 030	1966
School enrolment: age 5–19 years (percentage)	80	1963–4 av.
age over 19 years (per 100 000 population)	553	1963–5 av.

a Chinese population only.

COMMUNICATIONS		*Year(s)*
Motor vehicles in use ('000s): private	12.8	1963–5 av.
commercial	15.2	
Railway track (km.)	4 500	1964
Mail per capita: domestic	31	1963–5 av.
foreign received	1	
foreign sent	1	
Telephones (per '000 urban population)	1.5	1967
Radio licences (per '000 population)	99	1963–5 av.
Television licences (per '000 population)	3.1	1963–5 av.
Daily newspapers (per '000 population)	64	1963

FINANCE

Currency unit: The Taiwan dollar

Exchange rates	*1965a*	*1960*
Per $ U.S.	40.1	39.85
Per £ sterling	112.28	111.56

		Year(s)
National Income (million $ U.S.)	2 297	1965
G.N.P. per capita ($ U.S.)	230	1966
Rate of increase of G.N.P. per capita	3.6	1960–3 av.
Foreign trade (percentage of G.D.P.)	34	1963–5 av.

a selling rate.

TRADING

Total trade (in million $ U.S.)	*1965*	*1955*
Exports (f.o.b.)	450	123
Imports (c.i.f.)	557	104*a*

Main trading partners (percentage of total value)

Exports	*1965*	*1955*	*Imports*	*1965*	*1955*
Japan	31	59	Japan	40	30
U.S.A.	22	4	U.S.A.	32	48
S. Vietnam	10	na	Iraq	4	na
Germany F.R.	7	1	Germany F.R.	3	2
Hong Kong	6	5	Philippines	2	1
Thailand	4	4	Australia	2	—
Morocco	2	—			

Distribution of trade (percentage of total value)

Exports	*1965*	*1955**
Food	51	85
(fruit and vegetables)	(25)	(8)
(sugar and honey)	(13)	(49)
Textiles and clothing	15	na
Wood and paper	10	na
Imports		
Manufactured goods	46	na
(machinery and transport equipment)	(29)	(9)
Crude materials and fuels	31	na
(textile fibres and waste)	(10)	(12)
Chemicals	13	16
Food	8	16
(cereals)	(6)	(7)

a excl. U.S. $82 million 'aid imports' from the U.S.A.

continued

na: data not available. — negligible or nil. [1] one year only. [2] two year average. * estimate. ‡ see appendix. † re-exports.

PRODUCTION, EXPORTS AND IMPORTS

Years: **1963–5 average** and *1953–5 average* Units: '000 metric tons unless otherwise indicated

1. CEREALS, etc.

	Production 1963–5	Production 1953–5	Exports 1963–5	Exports 1953–5	Imports 1963–5	Imports 1953–5
Barley	0.7	—	—	—	7.8	—
Cassava	241.3	126.7				
Maize (corn)	39.3	9.3	—	—	23.6	—
Millets/sorghum	9.0	6.0	—	—	4.3	—
Oats	—	—	—	—	0.1	—
Potatoes	15.0	2.0	6.3		0.3	—
Rice	2 779.0	2 053.0	168.2	88.4	13.4	1.7
Sweet potatoes/ yams	2 876.0	2 429.7				
Wheat	20.7	16.0	—	—	349.4	176.1

2. FRUIT, etc.

	Production 1963–5	Production 1953–5	Exports 1963–5	Exports 1953–5	Imports 1963–5	Imports 1953–5
Apples	—	—	—	—	2.7	—
Bananas	284.0	93.0	187.1	26.4	—	—
Grapes	3.0	na	—	—	—	—
Lemons	4.7	2.0	—	—	—	—
Oranges	84.7	22.0	6.9	1.1	—	—
Other citrus fruit	8.7	7.0	—	—	—	—
Olives	2.3	na				
Peaches	3.0	na	—	—	—	—
Pears	2.0	na	—	—	0.3	—
Pineapples	207.0	68.3	na	na	—	—
Plums	17.3	na	—	—	—	—
Raisins	—	—	—	—	0.4	—
Tomatoes	27.7	10.3				

3. BEVERAGES, FOREST PRODUCTS, etc.

	Production 1963–5	Production 1953–5	Exports 1963–5	Exports 1953–5	Imports 1963–5	Imports 1953–5
Cocoa	—	—	—	—	0.1	—
Sugar: cane	8 465.7*	5 643.0[2]				
raw	891.5n	740.7*n	771.6	673.7	—	—
Tea	20.0	13.2	16.3	11.1	—	—
Tobacco: leaf	17.7	12.1*	2.0	0.1	1.8	0.7
cigarettes e	12 983.0	9 447.7	—	—	—	—
tobacco/snuff	0.3	0.1	—	—	—	—
Softwood j	726.3	455.0[1]	123.0	na	1.2	—
Hardwood j	484.0	463.0[1]	71.4	na	545.1	—
Wood pulp	22.7	21.3	6.9	na	29.4	na
Newsprint	14.7	10.0*	2.2	na	—	—
Other paper	171.0*	33.0*	15.0	na	4.2	—

e no. in millions. *j* '000 cu. metres of roundwood equivalent. *n* in addition, non-centrifugal sugar 24 (1963–5 av.) and 16 (1953–5 av.).

4. VEGETABLE OILSEEDS AND OILS

	Production 1963–5	Production 1953–5	Exports 1963–5	Exports 1953–5	Imports 1963–5	Imports 1953–5
Castor oil	—	—	—	—	0.04	0.02
Copra	—	—	—	—	2.90	—
Coconut oil	na	—	—	—	—	1.38
Cottonseed	2.00	3.00[2]	—	—	—	—
Groundnuts	77.70	45.01	0.21	—	3.20	—
Groundnut oil	na	na	0.02	—	1.06	—
Linseed oil	—	—	—	—	0.25	0.19
Rapeseed	21.00	1.00	0.01	—	1.87	—
Sesame seed	2.57	2.00	0.09	—	1.46	—
Soya beans	59.00	20.30	—	—	175.23	100.50[2]
Soya bean oil	na	na	0.38	—	3.17	0.64

5. LIVESTOCK‡, ANIMAL PRODUCTS, etc.

	Production 1963–5	Production 1953–5	Exports 1963–5	Exports 1953–5	Imports 1963–5	Imports 1953–5
Chickens d	8 262.3	6 368.0				
Cattle d	101.3	75.7	—	—	0.2	—
Goats d	143.0	161.7	—	—	—	—
Pigs d	2 772.0	2 767.3	10.3	—	0.2	—
Meat‡: 'A'	235.7	81.3*	—	—	—	—
'B'	26.9*	na	—	—	—	—
Butter	—	—	—	—	0.2	—
Eggs	5.0*	3.5	0.3	—	—	—
Fish	369.7p	154.3p	1.6	0.2[1]*	3.3	19.8[1]*
Milk	11.3	2.0	—	—	48.0	12.6
Hides/skins	1.5	0.6	—	—	—	—
Wool	—	—	—	—	1.7	—

d no. in thousands. *p* incl. fish landed by Taiwanese vessels in foreign ports.

6. FIBRES, TEXTILES, etc.

	Production 1963–5	Production 1953–5	Exports 1963–5	Exports 1953–5	Imports 1963–5	Imports 1953–5
Abaca	—	—	—	—	0.2	—
Agaves (sisal)	10.9	0.9	1.5	—	—	—
Cotton lint	1.0	1.5[2]	—	—	61.8	—
Flax fibre	2.2	0.2	1.9	—	—	—
Hemp fibre	4.0	na	—	—	—	—
Jute	12.0	12.3	0.3	—	2.6	—
Rubber, natural	—	—	—	—	6.1	1.9*
Silk f	31.5[2]	106.0[1]	3.0	—	—	—
Cotton: yarn	51.2	22.6	7.2	na	0.2[1]	—
woven fabrics	28.0	18.5	13.1	na	—	—
Rayon, fibre/yarn	4.6	na	0.3	na	9.9	na
Non-cellulosic fibre/yarn	0.7	na	1.2	na	5.4	na
Wool: yarn	3.2	0.8	1.1	na	—	na
woven fabrics	4.3q	1.4q	0.1	na	0.2	na

f metric tons. *q* million metres.

7. FUEL AND POWER

	Production 1963–5	Production 1953–5	Exports 1963–5	Exports 1953–5	Imports 1963–5	Imports 1953–5
Coal, 'A'‡	4 963	2 360	63	120	—	—
Coke	na	na	—	—	10	7
Electricity h: total	5 952	1 970[1]				
hydro	2 258	1 530[1]				
thermal	3 694	440[1]				
Natural gas i	180	30[1]	—	—	—	—
Oil, crude	13	—[1]	—	—	1 520	na
Petroleum, refined	1 420	600[1]	57	—	40	780[1]

h million kWh. *i* million cu. metres.

8. IRON AND STEEL

	Production 1963–5	Production 1953–5	Exports 1963–5	Exports 1953–5	Imports 1963–5	Imports 1953–5
Iron ore	—	—	—	—	51	11
Pig iron	63	8	7	—	—	—
Steel ingots/castings	338	28	—	—	3	7
Iron/steel scrap	na	na	—	—	288	4

9. NON-FERROUS MINERALS AND METALS

	Production 1963–5	Production 1953–5	Exports 1963–5	Exports 1953–5	Imports 1963–5	Imports 1953–5
Gold k, ore m	27.30	27.00	—	—	77.67r	—
Silver k, ore m	69.70	48.00	—	—	—	—
Asbestos: fibre	0.61	0.17	0.06	—	1.19	0.37
manufactured	na	na	0.36	—	0.37	0.47
Mica	—	0.02	—	—	—	—
Aluminium: bauxite	—	7.55[1]	—	—	82.54	26.86
alumina	37.00*	na	—	—	—	—
aluminium	16.74	6.35	9.00[1]	2.49	0.02	—
Chrome, ore	—	—	—	—	0.21[2]	—
Copper: ore	1.68m	0.59m	12.24	5.23	—	—
metal	1.85	0.90	0.09	—	4.54	0.55
Lead, metal	—	—	—	—	2.87	1.73
Magnesium: dolomite	38.06	na	—	—	—	—
metal/salts	na	—‡	0.57	—	—	—
Mercury f	—	1.17	—	—	40.70	2.20
Nickel, metal	—	—	—	—	0.13	—
Tin, metal	—	—	—	—	0.17	0.17
Titanium minerals	—	—	—	—	1.20	—
Zinc, metal	—	—	—	—	6.25	3.28

f metric tons. *k* '000 fine troy oz. *m* metal content. *r* bullion.

10. CHEMICALS*n* AND FERTILIZERS

	Production 1963–5	Production 1953–5	Exports 1963–5	Exports 1953–5	Imports 1963–5	Imports 1953–5
Organic chemicals:						
Benzene	na		0.2		0.1	
Butadiene	—		—		na	
Ethylene	—		—		na	
Methanol	na		—		0.4[1]	
Phenol	na		—		0.5	
Phthalic anhydride	—		—		na	
Styrene monomer	—		—		na	
Urea	132.8		na		na	
Inorganic chemicals:						
Ammonia	131.5[2]		0.3[1]		—	
Carbon black	na		0.1		1.3	
Chlorine	9.0		—		—	
Nitric acid	38.4		—		—	
Sodium carbonate	14.7		—		0.5	
Sodium hydroxide	53.5		3.9		0.1	
Sulphuric acid	138.3		0.1		—[1]	
Plastics:						
Polyamides	na		—		0.2[2]	
Polyethylene	—		—		12.5[2]	
Polyvinyl chloride	2.4[2]		3.4[2]		1.8[2]	
Fertilizers:						
Phosphates	—	—	—	—	—	42.6y
Potash	—	—	—	—	77.4	17.1
Pyrites	16.9x	9.9x				
Sulphur: native	6.1	4.8	—	—	82.3	na
recovered	2.5	—				

n data not available for years 1953–5. *x* sulphur content. *y* apatite.

11. INDUSTRY

	Production 1963–5	Production 1953–5	Exports 1963–5	Exports 1953–5	Imports 1963–5	Imports 1953–5
Beer b	169.0	66.6	—	—	—	—
Cement	2 347.3	548.7	830.3	25.0	—	38.0
Electrical engineering a	na	na	6.5	—	21.9	2.2
Railway vehicles a	—	—	—	—	1.4	na
Machine tools a	na	na	—	—	—	0.2
Merchant ships g	5.0	na	—	—	8.0	na
Motor vehicles			—	—	12.8a	0.5a
commercial du	0.6	—				
private du	1.5	—				

a million $ U.S. *b* '000 hectolitres. *d* no. in thousands. *g* '000 G.R.T. *u* assembly of imported parts.

TANZANIA

Tanzania, an independent member of the British Commonwealth, was formed in 1964 of the union of the Trust Territory of Tanganyika and the Protectorate of Zanzibar. Tanzania is a member of the East African Community.

Where data are given separately, T refers to Tanganyika and Z to Zanzibar, including Pemba.

AREA: T 937 060 sq. km. (361 800 sq. miles)
Z 2 640 „ (1 020 „)

LAND USE: (percentage of total)

	1963	1954
Arable and orchard	12.7	11.6
Permanent meadow and pasture	36.9	16.0
Forest and woodland	37.6	38.2
City areas, waste and other land	12.8	34.2

POPULATION: T 11 876 982, Z 354 360 (1967 census)

Largest city: DAR ES SALAAM, capital; population: 272 515* (city proper, 1967)

Employment: Agriculture and forestry are the principal occupations in Tanganyika. Cash crops of cotton and coffee are grown on plantations, some of which are now owned by Africans. There is some mining, and industry is being developed. In Zanzibar, particularly on the island of Pemba, clove growing is the major occupation; coconuts are also grown, and fishing is important.

continued

			Year(s)
Life expectancy at birth (years)	T	37.5*	1957
	Z	42.8*	1958
Infant mortality (per '000)	Z	19.9*	1965
Crude birth rate (per '000)	Z	26*	1965
Crude death rate (per '000)	Z	3.7*	1965
Population per physician	.	18 240	1965
Population per hospital bed	T	560	1966
	Z	410a	1966
School enrolment: age 5–19 years (percentage)		21	1963–4 av.
age over 19 years (per 100 000 population)	.	3	1963–5 av.

a government hospitals only.

COMMUNICATIONS

			Year(s)
Motor vehicles in use ('000s): private	T	31.4	1963–5 av.
	Z	1.6	1963–5 av.
commercial	T	9.4	1963–5 av.
	Z	0.6	1963–5 av.
Railway track (km.)	T	3 782	1969
Telephones (per '000 urban population)	.	0.2	1967
Radio receivers (per '000 population)	.	10*	1963–5 av.
Daily newspapers (per '000 population)	T	3*	1962
	Z	5*	1962

FINANCE

Currency unit: The Tanzanian shilling replaced, at par, the East African shilling in 1966. Prior to 1960, East African pounds of 20 shillings were used

Exchange rates	*1965a*	*1960a*	*1955b*	*1938b*
Per $ U.S.	7.143	7.143	0.357	0.215
Per £ sterling	20.0	20.0	1.0	1.0

			Year(s)
National Income (million $ U.S.)	T	625	1965
	Z	31	1965
G.N.P. per capita ($ U.S.)	.	80	1966
Rate of increase of G.N.P. per capita	T	1.3	1960–4 av.
Foreign trade (percentage of G.D.P.)	.	46	1963–5 av.

a East African shillings. *b* East African pounds.

TRADING: TANGANYIKA

Note—trade with Kenya and Uganda is excluded

Total trade (in million $ U.S.)	*1965*	*1955*	*1955a*	*1938*
Exports (f.o.b.)	176	102	299	15
Imports (c.i.f.)	140	122	417	14

Main trading partners (percentage of total value)

Exports	*1965*	*1955a*	*Imports*	*1965*	*1955a*
U.K.	30	28	U.K.	32	44
Hong Kong	8	2	Japan	9	4
Germany F.R.	8	10	Germany F.R.	8	6
India	8	15	Italy	8	3
China P.R.	7	—	India	7	6
U.S.A.	6	12	U.S.A.	6	3
Netherlands	5	4	Netherlands	4	3

Distribution of trade (percentage of total value)

Exports	*1965*	*Imports*	*1965*
Sisal and other agaves	23	Manufactured goods	78
Cotton	20	(machinery and transport equipment)	(32)
Coffee	14	(textiles and clothing)	(19)
Diamonds	12	Chemicals	8
Fruit and vegetables	8	Food	7

a refers to the total trade for Kenya, Uganda and Tanganyika.

TRADING: ZANZIBAR

Total trade (in million $ U.S.)	*1965*	*1955*	*1938*
Exports (f.o.b.)	11	16	4
Imports (c.i.f.)	12	16	5

Main trading partners (percentage of total value)

Exports	*1965*	*1955*	*Imports*	*1965*	*1955*
Indonesia	22	40	U.K.	14	33
India	14	21	Tanganyika	12	na
China P.R.	11	na	Japan	9	5
Tanganyika	9	14a	China P.R.	7	na
U.S.S.R.	7	na	Iran	7	na
Pakistan	6	1	India	5	14
U.K.	4	4	U.S.A.	5	—

Distribution of trade (percentage of total value *b*)

Exports	*1965*	*1955*
Cloves and clove oil	69	82
Copra and coconut oil	23	13
Imports		
Food	40	43
Manufactured goods	36	34
Crude materials and fuels	12	13
Chemicals	5	2

a incl. Kenya and Uganda. *b* % of national exports‡ which comprised 83% of general exports in 1965 and 86% in 1955.

PRODUCTION, EXPORTS AND IMPORTS

Years: **1963–5 average** and *1953–5 average* Units: '000 metric tons unless otherwise indicated

Note—data for Tanganyika and Zanzibar are given separately where available; but, where they are combined, the trade figures include internal trade between the two states.

1. CEREALS, etc.

		Production 1963–5	Production 1953–5	Exports 1963–5	Exports 1953–5	Imports 1963–5	Imports 1953–5
Cassava	T	1 033.0*	1 861.0[1]				
	Z	80.0*	87.3				
Maize (corn)	.	623.3*	na	10.7r	14.0	6.3r	17.6[2]
Millets/sorghum	.	1 084.3*	915.5[2]	0.5	5.7	0.7r	0.5
Potatoes	.	9.3	3.0[1]	0.1	0.5	—r	0.8
Rice	T	105.7	52.0[2]	—	0.5	1.6*	0.5
	Z	9.7	9.0[2]	na	4.0	10.2[1]	17.8
Sweet potatoes/ yams	T	250.0*	na				
	Z	9.0*	9.0*				
Wheat	.	23.7	14.0[1]	—	—	3.3r	1.2

r data for Zanzibar na.

2. FRUIT, etc.

		Production 1963–5	Production 1953–5	Exports 1963–5	Exports 1953–5	Imports 1963–5	Imports 1953–5
Apples	.	—	—	—	—	0.2r	—
Bananas	Z	12.0*	14.0	—	—	—	—
Coconuts e	T	110.0*	na	—	—	—	—
	Z	150.0*	na	na	0.9[1]	—	—
Dates	.	—	—	—	—	0.9	1.0[2]
Oranges/lemons	.	5.3n	3.5[2]	na	—	—	—
Raisins	.	—	—	—	—	0.1r	—
Wine b	.	—	—	—	—	3.2r	2.0

b '000 hectolitres. *e* no. in millions. *n* total sales. *r* data for Zanzibar na.

continued

TANZANIA *continued*

PRODUCTION, EXPORTS AND IMPORTS *continued*

3. BEVERAGES, FOREST PRODUCTS, etc.

		Production		Exports		Imports	
Coffee		37.7	18.3	29.5r	18.8	—r	0.1
Sugar: cane	T	800.0*	na				
raw		59.6	12.0	0.6r	0.1	9.4*	31.1
Tea		5.2	1.6	4.3r	1.5	—r	0.2
Tobacco: leaf	T	3.9	2.3	0.7	0.4	—	0.3
cigarettes		1 516.0e	—	—	—	0.1rt	0.2rt
Softwood j		30.3	46.0	7.0	4.1	5.4	3.6
Hardwood j		11 414.3	18 924.5[2]	25.5	21.7	4.1	3.1
Newsprint		—	—	—	—	0.7	0.2[2]
Other paper		—	—	—	—	2.9	0.1u

e no. in millions. j '000 cu. metres of roundwood equivalent. r Zanzibar data na. t incl. other tobacco manufactures. u Tanganyika data na.

4. VEGETABLE OILSEEDS AND OILS

		Production		Exports		Imports	
Castor seed	T	15.67*	na	16.93	9.90	—	—
Copra	T	13.47	12.43	4.37	2.83	0.77	0.17
	Z	13.33*	12.80	11.20*	5.77	—	—
Coconut oil	T	na	na	0.12	0.49	0.03	0.23
	Z	na	na	3.40*	4.21	—	0.01
Cottonseed	T	97.00*	32.67	0.47	1.57	—	—
Cottonseed oil		na	na	1.08	0.29	0.19	0.03
Groundnuts		12.13n	19.25	9.91r	4.67	—r	0.13
Groundnut oil		na	na	0.01	—	—r	0.03
Linseed oil	T	na	na	—	—	0.07	0.16
Olive oil	T	—	—	—	—	0.02	0.02
Palm kernels	T	1.03	—	1.84	0.57	0.52	0.03
Palm oil		0.50	na	0.10	—	0.05	0.07
Sesame seed		9.30	6.70[2]r	8.78	2.50	—r	0.05[2]
Soya beans	T	3.50[2]	1.00[1]*	1.82	0.60	—	—
Soya bean oil		na	na	—	—	0.32	—
Sunflower seed	T	8.00	na	8.13	9.86	—	—
Tung oil	T	—	—	0.01	—	0.01	—

n total sales. r Zanzibar data na.

Zanzibar is important for the production of cloves and clove oil, the greater part of the world's supply being produced here, mainly on the island of Pemba.

5. LIVESTOCK‡, ANIMAL PRODUCTS, etc.

		Production		Exports		Imports	
Chickens d	Z	166.7*	na				
Cattle d		8 429.0	6 616.0r	2.0	4.4	—r	4.8
dairy cows dq	T	3 925.7*r	na				
Goats d		4 408.0	3 986.0r	5.0 (Goats and Sheep)	na	—r	—
Sheep d	T	2 765.0	2 842.7				
Pigs d	T	21.0	15.0	—	—	—	—
Meat‡: 'A'		89.0*	117.0[1]	—	0.2	0.1	—
'B'	T	—	—	—	—	0.1	—
Butter		1.0*	1.0[1]	—r	0.1	—r	0.4
Eggs		1.9*	0.3[1]u	—	—	na	na
Fish	T	83.5[2]	50.8	2.0 (T and Z)	na	1.6	na
	Z	10.1	8.8				
Milk	T	189.0	135.0[1]	0.1	—	30.8	11.4*
	Z	3.0	5.0[2]	na	0.3*	na	3.4*
Hides/skins		7.1[1]	4.7[1]p	6.4[2]	na	—	—

d no. in thousands. p of cattle only. q all cows over 3 years old. r Zanzibar data na. u Tanganyika data na.

6. FIBRES, TEXTILES, etc.

		Production		Exports		Imports	
Agaves (sisal)	T	222.9	165.7	214.6	180.2	—	—
Cotton: lint	T	56.0	16.7	50.0	25.3	—	—
yarn		—	—	—	—	5.1[2]	na
woven fabrics		—	—	—	—	5.7	na
Rayon, woven fabrics		—	—	—	—	1.3q	na

q incl. synthetic piece goods.

7. FUEL AND POWER

		Production		Exports		Imports	
Coal		—	—	—	—	—	41
Coke	T	—	—	—	—	—	1
Electricity h: total		197	na				
hydro		135	na				
thermal		62	na				
Petroleum, refined		—	—	40†	—	387	200[1]

h million kWh.

8. IRON AND STEEL

	Production		Exports		Imports	
Pig iron	—	—	—	—	1	—
Iron/steel scrap	na	na	4	—	—	—

9. NON-FERROUS MINERALS AND METALS

	Production		Exports		Imports	
Diamonds	693.67l	2 746.13l	17.79a	7.53a	—	—
Gold k: ore m	95.70	70.00	na	4.37	—	—
bullion/coins etc.	na	na	95.46	70.04	1.80	1.07
Silver k: ore m	23.70	42.00	na	231.25	—	—
bullion	—	—	23.57	42.23	—	—
Asbestos, manufactured	—	—	—	—	0.70	1.65
Mica	0.26	0.19	0.21	0.19	—	—
Aluminium	—	—	—	—	1.90	0.45
Copper, ore	na	0.50m	na	0.49	0.09q	0.27q
Lead, ore	na	3.11m	na	2.87	0.05q	0.02q
Magnesite	1.14	na	0.54	0.14	—	—
Tin, ore	0.26m	0.04m	0.36	0.06	0.04q	0.06q
Tungsten, ore	—	0.01	—	0.02	—	—
Zinc, metal	—	—	—	—	1.28	0.01

a million $ U.S. k '000 fine troy oz. l '000 carats. m metal content. q metal.

10. FERTILIZERS

	Production		Exports		Imports	
Phosphates	na	0.1v	—	—	—	—
Potash	—	—	—	—	1.3	0.3
Sulphur	—	—	—	—	0.3	0.1

v bat guano.

11. INDUSTRY

		Production		Exports		Imports	
Alcoholic beverages				—	—	1.0a	0.2au
beer b		103.0	24.6				
Cement		—	—	—	0.3	152.3	141.3
Electrical engineering a		na	na	—	—	7.7	0.3[2]u
Railway vehicles a	T	na	na	—	—	0.4[2]	4.2
Motor vehicles a		—	—	—	—	15.1	0.4u

a million $ U.S. b '000 hectolitres. u Tanganyika data na.

THAILAND

Thailand, formerly known as Siam, is an independent sovereign state. The king no longer exercises absolute power, but since 1958 has ruled through the national assembly. Substantial technical and military aid is received from the U.S.A.

AREA: 514 000 sq. km. (198 400 sq. miles)

LAND USE: (percentage of total)

	1964	1954
Arable and orchard	21.9	15.2 (arable and pasture)
Permanent meadow and pasture	—	
Forest and woodland	52.8	62.8
City areas, waste and other land	25.3	22.0

POPULATION: 32 680 000 (1967 estimate)

Largest city: KRUNG THEP (Bangkok), capital; population: 1 608 305 (1963)

Distribution of working population (1960)

Total working population: 13 836 984

U.N. group no.		Percentage
0	Agriculture, forestry, fishing and hunting	82.0
1	Mining and quarrying	0.2
2/3	Manufacturing	3.4
4	Construction	0.5
5	Electricity, gas, water and sanitary services	0.1
6	Commerce	5.6
7	Transport, storage and communications	1.2
8	Services	4.7
9	Others	2.3

		Year(s)
Life expectancy at birth (years): male	53.6*	1960
female	58.7*	
Infant mortality (per '000)	31.2*	1965
Crude birth rate (per '000)	36.4*	1965
Crude death rate (per '000)	7.1*	1965
Population per physician	8 820	1965
Population per hospital bed	1 090	1966
School enrolment: age 5–19 years (percentage)	56	1963–4 av.
age over 19 years (per 100 000 population)	180	1963–5 av.

COMMUNICATIONS

		Year(s)
Motor vehicles in use ('000s): private	63.1	1963–5 av.
commercial	80.0	
Railway track (km.)	3 519	1964
Mail per capita: domestic	2	1963–5 av.
foreign received	0.4	
foreign sent	0.2	
Telephones (per '000 urban population)	0.3	1967
Radio receivers (per '000 population)	54	1963–5 av.
Television sets (per '000 population)	5.8	1963–5 av.
Daily newspapers (per '000 population)	12	1962–4 av.

FINANCE

Currency unit: The baht

Exchange rates	1965	1960	1950	1938
Per $ U.S.	20.83	21.14	21.14	2.34
Per £ sterling	58.32	59.19	59.19	10.76

		Year(s)
National Income (million $ U.S.)	3 204	1965
G.N.P. per capita ($ U.S.)	130	1966
Rate of increase of G.N.P. per capita	2.4	1960–3 av.
Foreign trade (percentage of G.D.P.)	34	1963–5 av.

continued

na: data not available. — negligible or nil. [1] one year only. [2] two year average. * estimate. ‡ see appendix. † re-exports.

TRADING

Total trade (in million $ U.S.)	1965	1955	1938
Exports (f.o.b.)	622	337	89
Imports (c.i.f.)	771	342	57

Main trading partners (percentage of total value)

Exports	1965	1955	*Imports*	1965	1955
Japan	18	18	Japan	32	18
West Malaysia	14	24 (West Malaysia and Singapore)	U.S.A.	19	19
Singapore	6		Germany F.R.	10	6
India	7	—	U.K.	9	11
Hong Kong	7	9	Netherlands	3	8
U.S.A.	6	30	Hong Kong	3	10
Germany F.R.	5	1	Taiwan	2	2

Distribution of trade (percentage of total value)

Exports	1965	1955	1938*
Food	54	52	na
(rice)	(34)	(45)	(45)
Rubber	16	26	14
Tin	9	6*	23
Jute and kenaf	9	—	na
Imports			
Manufactured goods	68	69	na
(machinery and transport equipment)	(31)	(19)	(6)
(textiles and clothing)	(11)	(21)	(20)
Crude materials and fuels	11	11	na
Chemicals	10	8	na
Food	6	9	13

PRODUCTION, EXPORTS AND IMPORTS

Years: **1963–5 average** and *1953–5 average* Units: '000 metric tons unless otherwise indicated

1. CEREALS, etc.

	Production		Exports		Imports	
Barley	—	na	—	0.4[2]	—	—
Cassava	2 003.0	259.0[1]				
Maize (corn)	931.0	60.0	904.6	42.7*	—	—
Millets/sorghum	na	na	23.3	—	—	—
Potatoes	2.0*	—	—	—	0.2	0.5[2]
Rice	9 793.3	7 220.0	1 753.7*	1 193.3		
Sweet potatoes/yams	189.3	na				
Wheat	—	—	—	—	7.6*	27.4[1]*n

n milled wheat.

2. FRUIT, etc.

	Production		Exports		Imports	
Bananas	763.0*	na	5.2	—	—	—
Coconuts	911.3e	na	—	—	1.9[2]	—
Lemons	na	na	0.2	—	—	—
Oranges	na	na	0.3	0.6[2]	—	—
Other citrus fruit	na	na	0.3	1.1[2]	—	—
Pineapples	287.7*	na	—	—	—	—
Tomatoes	12.7*	na				
Wine b	—	—	—	—	1.3*	—[2]

b '000 hectolitres. e no. in millions.

3. BEVERAGES, FOREST PRODUCTS, etc.

	Production		Exports		Imports	
Coffee	—	—	—	—	4.1	2.2[2]
Sugar: cane	4 435.7	2 318.7				
raw	238.1p	43.0*p	65.3*	—	0.1	35.5[2]
Tea	—	—	—	—	1.6	1.2[2]
Tobacco: leaf	53.1	52.8	5.1	0.2	4.8	2.9[2]
cigars	3.0e	0.8e	— (cigars and cigarettes)	0.3[2]	—	0.2[2]
cigarettes	10 242.0e	7 190.7e				
Hardwood j	3 802.7	3 305.7	181.0	169.2	4.1[1]	—
Wood pulp	—	1.8	—[2]	—	6.2	—
Newsprint	—	—	—[2]	—	26.0[2]	10.4
Other paper	3.6	2.0	0.3[2]	—	24.6[2]	17.4

e no. in millions. j '000 cu. metres of roundwood equivalent. p in addition, crude brown sugar 140* (1963–5 av.) and 26* (1953–5 av.).

4. VEGETABLE OILSEEDS AND OILS

	Production		Exports		Imports	
Castor seed	41.33	17.58	34.81	19.30*	—	—
Castor oil	na	na	0.04*	0.05[2]	0.02	0.01[2]
Copra	20.93*	na	0.14	1.43	0.33*	na
Coconut oil	na	na	—	0.66[2]	0.74	0.16*
Cottonseed	32.70	16.30	11.63	1.65[2]	—	—
Groundnuts	82.60	61.60	14.32	16.47*	0.02[2]	—[2]
Groundnut oil	na	na	0.55	0.33[2]*	—	—
Linseed oil	—	—	—	—[2]	0.17*	0.23[2]
Olive oil	—	—	—	—	0.02*	—
Palm oil	—	—	—	—	0.04*	—
Sesame seed	15.53	9.90	3.15*	3.20[2]	—	—
Soya beans	32.30	21.00	3.44	2.60*	—	—
Soya bean oil	na	na	—	0.59[2]	0.05*	—[2]
Tung oil	na	na	0.05*	—	0.01*	—

5. LIVESTOCK‡, ANIMAL PRODUCTS, etc.

	Production		Exports		Imports	
Chickens d	30 300.0*	na				
Cattle d	5 341.3	5 509.0	56.3	12.6[2]	0.1	—
Goats d	28.0*	28.0[1]	—	—	—	—
Sheep d	14.0*	na	—	—	—	—
Horses d	181.7*	156.0[2]				
Pigs d	4 488.0*	3 133.3	20.4	13.6[2]	—	—[2]
Meat‡: 'A'	217.7*	na	—	—	—	—
'B'	33.1*	na	—	—	—	—
Butter	—	—	—	—	0.4	0.1[2]
Cheese	—	—	—	—	0.1	—
Eggs	82.0*	na	4.6	2.5[2]	—	—
Fish	536.9	215.9	12.4	18.4[1]*	9.0	3.1[1]*
Milk	374.0*	na	0.2	—	180.6	100.8
Hides/skins	na	na	6.9	5.9[2]	—	—

d no. in thousands.

6. FIBRES, TEXTILES, etc.

	Production		Exports		Imports	
Cotton lint	16.3	8.3	0.1	—	14.8	1.6[2]
Jute	7.0*q	1.0[2]	0.4*	—	—	—
Rubber, natural	208.4*	117.0	208.2	121.2	—	—
Silk f	na	na	19.7	18.0[1]	0.3	17.0[1]
Cotton: yarn	16.5	na	—	—	5.4	na
woven fabrics	21.8*	na	0.1[2]	—	12.5	na
Rayon, woven fabrics	—	—	—	—	5.7	na

f metric tons. q in addition, kenaf 295.0*; no other data for kenaf are available.

7. FUEL AND POWER

	Production		Exports		Imports	
Coal: 'A'‡	—	—	—	—	—	54
'B'	40	—	—	—	—	—
Coke	—	—	—	—	3	2
Electricity h: total	1 135[2]	320[1]				
hydro	565[2]	—[1]				
thermal	570[2]	320[1]				
Oil, crude	7	—[1]	—	—	643	—
Petroleum, refined	683[1]	—[1]	67	—	1 547	440[1]

h million kWh.

8. IRON AND STEEL

	Production		Exports		Imports	
Iron ore	200m	3m	—	—	—	—
Pig iron	—	3	—	—	1	—
Steel ingots/castings	—	2	—	—	—	—
Iron/steel scrap	na	na	3	—	—	—

m metal content.

9. NON-FERROUS MINERALS AND METALS

	Production		Exports		Imports	
Asbestos: fibre	—	—	—	—	8.08	—
manufactured	na	—	3.52	—	5.45	3.08s
Mica	—	—	—	—	0.01	—
Aluminium	—	—	—	—	5.64	2.98[1]s
Antimony, ore	1.05m	0.05m	1.44	0.11	—	—
Copper, metal	—	—	—	—	3.20	—
Lead, ore	3.83m	4.69m	7.58	6.63[1]	0.98r	—
Magnesium, salts	—‡	—‡	—	—	0.55	—
Manganese, ore	17.03	—	9.37	—	—	—
Mercury f	—	—	—	—	2.00	—
Tin: ore m	17.01	10.47	14.18	10.41	—	—
metal	5.61[1]	—	—	—	—	—
Titanium minerals	na	na	—	—	—	—
Tungsten, ore	0.40	1.40	0.18	1.52	—	—
Zinc, ore	1.45m	2.48m	—	—	12.42r	—

f metric tons. m metal content. r metal. s incl. imports for re-export.

10. CHEMICALS n AND FERTILIZERS

	Production		Exports		Imports	
Organic chemicals:						
Urea	—		—		2.2[1]	
Other organic chemicals	—		—		na	
Inorganic chemicals:						
Ammonia	na		—		0.3[1]	
Carbon black	—		—		2.1[1]	
Chlorine	na		—		0.1[1]	
Nitric acid	—		—		0.4[1]	
Sodium carbonate	—		—		12.2[1]	
Sodium hydroxide	na		—		9.0[1]	
Sulphuric acid	na		—		—[1]	
Fertilizers:						
Potash	—	—	—	—	2.8	—
Sulphur	—	—	—	—	7.1	0.4

n data not available for years 1953–5.

11. INDUSTRY

	Production		Exports		Imports	
Aircraft a	—	—	—	—	3.5	1.2[1]
Alcoholic beverages a	—	—	—	—	—	1.2
Cement	1 103.0	353.7	112.7	2.0	22.7	48.3
Electrical engineering a	—	—	—	—	42.1	15.8[2]
Railway vehicles a	—	—	—	—	7.0	—
Merchant ships g	—	—	—	—	5.0	—
Motor vehicles a	—	—	—	—	64.7	17.0[2]

a million $ U.S. g '000 G.R.T.

na: data not available. — negligible or nil. [1] one year only. [2] two year average. * estimate. ‡ see appendix. † re-exports.

TOGO

WEST AFRICA

Togo, formerly the French trusteeship territory of Togoland, became an independent republic within the French Union in 1960; (the British trusteeship territory elected to be incorporated into Ghana). Togo has close economic co-operation with Dahomey, has defence and financial agreements with France, and is an associate member of the European Economic Community.

AREA: 56 000 sq. km. (21 600 sq. miles)

LAND USE: (percentage of total)	*1965*	*1955*
Arable and orchard	38.2	37.3
Permanent meadow and pasture	3.5	3.5
Forest and woodland	9.4	8.8
City areas, waste and other land	48.9	50.4

POPULATION: 1 724 000 (1967 estimate)
Largest city: LOMÉ, capital; population: 128 900 (1966)
Total working population: 648 550 (1958–60 av.)

Employment: The majority of the population is employed in agriculture, both in the production of subsistence crops and in the commercial production of coffee, cocoa, groundnuts, and palm kernels. Since the discovery of large phosphate deposits in 1953, the mining of phosphate rock has provided alternative employment.

		Year(s)
Life expectancy at birth (years): male	31.6	1961
female	38.5	1961
Infant mortality (per '000)	127*	1961
Crude birth rate (per '000)	34.2* *a*	1965
Crude death rate (per '000)	7.6* *a*	1965
Population per physician	36 400	1965
Population per hospital bed	740 *b*	1966
School enrolment: age 5–19 years (percentage)	31	1963–4 av.
age over 19 years (per 100 000 population)	4	1965

a African population. *b* government hospitals only.

COMMUNICATIONS		*Year(s)*
Motor vehicles in use ('000s): private	0.4	1963–5 av.
commercial	0.3	1963–5 av.
Railway track (km.)	443	1964
Mail per capita: domestic	1	1963–5 av.
foreign received	1	1963–5 av.
foreign sent	1	1963–5 av.
Telephones (per '000 urban population)	0.2*	1967
Radio receivers (per '000 population)	18	1963–5 av.
Daily newspapers (per '000 population)	7.5	1963–4 av.

FINANCE

Currency unit: The franc CFA

Exchange rates	*1965*	*1960*	*1955*
Per $ U.S.	246.85	246.85	210
Per £ sterling	691.18	691.18	590

		Year
Gross National Income (million $ U.S.)	135	1965
G.N.P. per capita ($ U.S.)	100	1966

TRADING

Total trade (in million $ U.S.)	*1965*	*1955*	*1938*
Exports (f.o.b.)	27	22	2
Imports (c.i.f.)	45	18	2

Main trading partners (percentage of total value)

Exports	*1965*	*Imports*	*1965*
France	43	France	31
Netherlands	12	Germany F.R.	19
Germany F.R.	9	Japan	14
Italy	9	U.K.	6
Belg./Lux.	6	U.S.A.	3
Japan	4	Netherlands	3
Australia	4	Ghana	2

Distribution of trade (percentage of total value)

Exports	*1965*	*Imports*	*1965*
Coffee and cocoa	46	Manufactured goods	72
Natural phosphates	33	(machinery and transport equipment)	(32)
Oilseeds	12	(textiles and clothing)	(19)
Cotton	4	Food	10
		Beverages and tobacco	7
		Crude materials and fuels	5
		Chemicals	5

PRODUCTION, EXPORTS AND IMPORTS

Years: **1963–5 average** and *1953–5 average* Units: '000 metric tons unless otherwise indicated

	Production		Exports		Imports	
1. CEREALS, etc.						
Cassava	**963.3**	*368.3*				
Maize (corn)	**91.3**	*51.3*	—	*0.4*	—	—
Millets/sorghum	**122.7**	*115.7*	—	—	—	—
Potatoes	—	—	—	—	**0.3**	*0.1*
Rice	**22.7**	*12.0*	**0.1**	*0.1*	**2.8**	*1.3*
Sweet potatoes/yams	**1 002.0***	*387.0*				
2. FRUIT, etc.						
Coconuts *e*	**32.3***	na	—	—	—	—
Wine *b*	—	—	—	—	**20.3**	*25.0*

b '000 hectolitres. *e* no. in millions.

	Production		Exports		Imports	
3. BEVERAGES, FOREST PRODUCTS, etc.						
Cocoa	**14.2**	*5.5*	**13.6**	*11.5*	—	—
Coffee	**13.1**	*3.8*	**11.0**	*3.4*	—	—
Sugar, raw	—	—	—	—	**4.0**	*1.7*
Tobacco: leaf	—	—	—	—	**0.1**	—
products	—	—	—	—	**0.5**	—
Softwood *j*	—	—	—	—[2]	**3.3**	—[1]
Hardwood *j*	**948.7***	*49.0*[1]	—	—[2]	**11.2**[2]	*1.9*[1]
Newsprint	—	—	—	—[2]	**0.1**	—[1]
Other paper	—	—	—	—[2]	**0.1**[2]	—[1]

j '000 cu. metres of roundwood equivalent.

	Production		Exports		Imports	
4. VEGETABLE OILSEEDS AND OILS						
Castor seed	**0.33**	na	**0.48**	*0.30*	—	—
Copra	**2.60**	*5.07*	**2.58**	*5.90*	—	—
Coconut oil	na	na	—	*0.04*	—	—
Cottonseed	**4.70**	*2.67*	**2.45**	*1.53*	—	—
Groundnuts	**12.83**	*9.10*	**2.51**	*0.50*	—	—
Groundnut oil	na	na	—	—	**0.28**	*0.04*
Palm kernels	**14.23**	*9.80*	**14.18**	*9.63*	—	—
Palm oil	**1.67**	na	**0.10**	*0.43*	**0.12**	*0.34*
Soya bean oil	—	—	—	—	**0.01**[2]	na

	Production		Exports		Imports	
5. LIVESTOCK‡, ANIMAL PRODUCTS, etc.						
Chickens *d*	**1 260.7**	*746.0p*				
Cattle *d*	**155.0**	*109.0*	**0.3***	*1.4*	**2.6**	—
dairy cows *d*	**84.0***	na				
Goats *d*	**426.0**	*208.3*	**0.9** (goats and sheep)	na	**2.1**[2]	na
Sheep *d*	**505.3**	*260.0*				
Horses *d*	**0.7**	*1.0*				
Pigs *d*	**200.0**	*189.3*	—	*1.5*	—	—
Meat	na	na	—	—	—	—
Eggs	**0.7***	*0.1*	—	—	—	—
Fish	**4.7**	*3.3*	—	—	**4.6**	—
Milk	**8.3***	*27.7*	—	—	**123.2**	*0.6**
Hides/skins	—	*0.1*	—	—	—	—

d no. in thousands. *p* incl. ducks, geese and turkeys.

	Production		Exports		Imports	
6. FIBRES, TEXTILES, etc.						
Cotton: lint	**2.7**	*1.7*	**2.1**	*0.8*	—	—
yarn	—	—	—	—	**0.1**	na
woven fabrics	—	—	—	—	**2.6**	*1.0*
7. FUEL AND POWER						
Electricity *h*: total	**28**	—				
hydro	**2**	—				
thermal	**26**	—				
Petroleum, refined	—	—	—	—	**40**	*20*[1]

h million kWh.

	Production		Exports		Imports	
10. CHEMICALS *n* AND FERTILIZERS						
Chemicals	—		—		na	
Fertilizers:						
Phosphates	**753.0**	—	**685.5**	—	—	—

n data not available for years 1953–5.

	Production		Exports		Imports	
11. INDUSTRY						
Alcoholic beverages *a*	—	—	—	—	**1.7**	na
Cement	—	—	—	—	**37.7**	*16.7*
Electrical engineering *a*	—	—	—	—	**1.7**	na
Railway vehicles *a*	—	—	—	—	**0.7**	na
Motor vehicles *a*	—	—	**0.1** *p*	—	**2.3**	na

a million $ U.S. *p* used.

TONGA

PACIFIC OCEAN

The kingdom of Tonga, or the 'Friendly Islands', previously a British protected state, became an independent member of the Commonwealth in 1970. The group consists of some 150 islands.

AREA: 700 sq. km. (270 sq. miles)

LAND USE: (percentage of total)	*1965*	*1955*
Arable and orchard	78.5	68.6
Permanent meadow and pasture	2.9	1.4
Forest and woodland	15.7	15.7
City areas, waste and other land	2.9	14.3

POPULATION: 77 429 (1966 census)
Capital city: NUKUALOFA; population: 15 545 (city proper, 1966)

		Year(s)
Infant mortality (per '000)	8.7*	1965
Crude birth rate (per '000)	33.6*	1965
Crude death rate (per '000)	3.5*	1965
Population per physician	3 040	1965
Population per hospital bed	370 *a*	1966
School enrolment: age 5–19 years (percentage)	101‡	1963–4 av.

a government hospitals only.

COMMUNICATIONS		*Year(s)*
Telephones (per '000 urban population)	1.1	1967
Radio receivers (per '000 population)	46	1963–5 av.

FINANCE

Currency unit: The pa'anga, or Tongan dollar, at par with the Australian dollar, replaced the Australian pound in 1967 at the rate T$1 to A£0.5

Exchange rates (for Australian pounds)	*1965*	*1960*	*1950*	*1938*
Per $ U.S.	0.45	0.45	0.45	0.26
Per £ sterling	1.25	1.25	1.25	1.25

TRADING

Total trade (in million $ U.S.)	*1964*
Exports (f.o.b.)	2.6
Imports (c.i.f.)	4.3

Exports consist mainly of copra and bananas.

PRODUCTION, EXPORTS AND IMPORTS

Years: **1963–5 average** and *1953–5 average* Units: '000 metric tons unless otherwise indicated

	Production		Exports		Imports	
1. CEREALS, etc.						
Cassava	**19.0***	*7.0*[2]				
Sweet potatoes/yams	**70.0***	*27.7*				
2. FRUIT, etc.						
Bananas	na	*21.0**	**6.7**	*4.4*	—	—
Coconuts	**59.7*** *e*	na	**0.8** *n*	—	—	—
Lemons	**2.0***	na	—	—	—	—
Oranges	**1.7***	na	—	—	—	—

e no. in millions. *n* incl. desiccated.

	Production		Exports		Imports	
3. BEVERAGES, FOREST PRODUCTS, etc.						
Sugar, raw	—	—	—	—	**0.7**[1]	*0.3*
4. VEGETABLE OILSEEDS AND OILS						
Copra	**10.17**	*18.83*	**9.37**	*16.37*	—	—
5. LIVESTOCK‡, ANIMAL PRODUCTS, etc.						
Chickens *d*	na	na				
Cattle *d*	**2.7**	*2.0*	—	—	—	—
Goats *d*	**3.0**	*1.7*	—	—	—	—
Sheep *d*	**27.0**	na	—	—	—	—
Horses *d*	**7.0**	*6.6*				
Pigs *d*	**27.0**	*30.0*	—	—	—	—
Eggs	**0.1***	na	—	—	—	—

d no. in thousands.

TRINIDAD AND TOBAGO

CARIBBEAN SEA

The islands of Trinidad and Tobago, formerly a British colony and a member of the West Indies Federation, became an independent member of the Commonwealth in 1962.

AREA: 5 128 sq. km. (1 980 sq. miles)

LAND USE: (percentage of total)	*1961*	*1953*
Arable and orchard	34.1	33.5
Permanent meadow and pasture	1.0	1.2
Forest and woodland	45.0	45.6
City areas, waste and other land	19.9	19.7

POPULATION: 1 030 000 (1967 U.N. estimate)
Capital city: PORT-OF-SPAIN; population: 93 954 (city proper, 1960)

Distribution of working population (1960)
Total working population: 278 147

U.N. group no.		*Percentage*
0	Agriculture, forestry, fishing and hunting	19.9
1	Mining and quarrying	4.6
2/3	Manufacturing	14.7
4	Construction	10.8
5	Electricity, gas, water and sanitary services	1.9
6	Commerce	12.6
7	Transport, storage and communications	5.8
8	Services	24.0
9	Others	5.7

		Year(s)
Life expectancy at birth (years): male	62.2	1959–61 av.
female	66.3	1959–61 av.
Infant mortality (per '000)	38.1	1965
Crude birth rate (per '000)	38*	1960–5 av.
Crude death rate (per '000)	8*	1960–5 av.
Accidental deaths (per 100 000 population)		
caused by motor vehicles	14.4	1966
due to other causes	16.0	1966
Population per physician	3 820	1965
Population per hospital bed	230 *a*	1965
School enrolment: age 5–19 years (percentage)	87 *b*	1963
age over 19 years (per 100 000 population)	77	1963–5 av.

a government hospitals only. *b* public education only.

COMMUNICATIONS		*Year(s)*
Motor vehicles in use ('000s): private	51.7	1963–5 av.
commercial	15.4	1963–5 av.
Railway track (km.)	175	1964
Telephones (per '000 urban population)	4.2	1967
Radio receivers (per '000 population)	168	1963–5 av.
Television licences (per '000 population)	27.6	1963–5 av.
Daily newspapers (per '000 population)	84	1963

continued

TRINIDAD AND TOBAGO *continued*

FINANCE

Currency unit: The Trinidad and Tobago dollar replaced, at par, the British West Indies dollar in 1962

Exchange rates	*1965*	*1960a*	*1958a*
Per $ U.S.	1.71	1.71	1.71
Per £ sterling	4.8	4.8	4.8

		Year(s)
National Income (million $ U.S.)	488	1965
G.N.P. per capita ($ U.S.)	630	1966
Rate of increase of G.N.P. per capita	7.3	1960–1 av.
Foreign trade (percentage of G.D.P.)	121	1963–4 av.

a B.W.I. dollars.

TRADING

Total trade (in million $ U.S.)	*1965*	*1955*	*1938*
Exports (f.o.b.)	403	166	35
Imports (c.i.f.)	477	172	35

Main trading partners (percentage of total value)

Exports	*1965*	*1955*	*Imports*	*1965*	*1955*
U.S.A.	34	3	Venezuela	26	26
U.K.	16	39	U.S.A.	17	9
Sweden	6	3	U.K.	17	38
Netherlands	5	5	Saudi Arabia	16	na
Canada	4	6	Colombia	6	1
France	3	3	Canada	5	9
Guyana	2	2	Guyana	1	2

Distribution of trade (percentage of total value)

Exports	*1965*	*1955*
Petroleum and petroleum products	83	76
Sugar	6	11
Chemicals	5	1
Imports		
Petroleum and petroleum products	49	28
Manufactured goods	33	45
(machinery and transport equipment)	(16)	(17)
Food	11	17
Chemicals	4	5

PRODUCTION, EXPORTS AND IMPORTS

Years: **1963–5 average** and *1953–5 average* Units: '000 metric tons unless otherwise indicated

	Production		Exports		Imports	
1. CEREALS, etc.						
Cassava	5.0*	na				
Maize (corn)	3.0*	na	—	—	16.3[2]	na
Millets/sorghum	—	—	—	—	0.6[2]	na
Oats	—	—	—	—	1.3[2]	na
Potatoes	—	—	0.4[2]†	—	12.5[2]	na
Rice	10.3*	na	—	0.1	28.8	17.8
Sweet potatoes/yams	15.0*	na				
Wheat	—	—	—	—	0.2[2]	—
2. FRUIT, etc.						
Apples	—	—	—	—	1.1[2]	na
Bananas	25.7*	na	0.2	2.0	1.0[2]	—
Coconuts	117.7*e	na	—	—	—	—
Grapes	—	—	—	—	0.2	—
Lemons	2.0*	na	—	—	—	—
Oranges	15.0*	4.0	2.5	2.0	—	—
Other citrus fruit	29.0*	16.7	4.7	5.1	—	—
Tomatoes	3.0*	—	—	—	—	—
Wine *b*	—	—	—	—	3.2[2]	na

b '000 hectolitres. *e* no. in millions.

	Production		Exports		Imports	
3. BEVERAGES, FOREST PRODUCTS, etc.						
Cocoa	5.4	8.5	5.3	8.5	—	—
Coffee	4.1*	na	3.6	1.4	—	—
Sugar: cane	2 348.3*	1 800.3				
raw	238.8	178.7	202.6	152.1	0.2[2]	—
Tea	—	—	—	—	0.2[2]	na
Tobacco: leaf	—	—	—	—	0.7	0.7
cigarettes *e*	765.0	688.3	—	—	—	—
Softwood *j*	—	—	0.3†	0.2†	77.5[2]	56.2
Hardwood *j*	131.0[1]	169.7	0.9	0.7	3.3[2]	1.4
Newsprint	—	—	—	—	3.4[1]	2.1[2]
Other paper	—	—	—	—	17.1[1]	14.0

e no. in millions. *j* '000 cu. metres of roundwood equivalent.

	Production		Exports		Imports	
4. VEGETABLE OILSEEDS AND OILS						
Castor oil	—	—	—	—	0.01[2]	—
Copra	13.47*	15.50[2]	—	—	1.96	—
Coconut oil	na	na	0.26	0.90	0.35[2]	—
Groundnuts	—	—	—	—	1.29[2]	0.03
Groundnut oil	na	—	—	—	0.03[2]	na
Linseed oil	—	—	—	—	0.17[2]	na
Olive oil	—	—	—[2]	—	0.15[2]	na
Palm oil	—	—	—	—	—	0.24
Rapeseed oil	—	—	—	—	0.02[2]	na
Soya bean oil	—	—	—	—	0.11	na
Tung oil	—	—	—	—	0.21[2]	na
5. LIVESTOCK‡, ANIMAL PRODUCTS, etc.						
Chickens *d*	933.3*n	na				
Cattle *d*	52.7*	38.0[1]	—	—	—	0.1
Goats *d*	30.0*	32.1[1]	} —	—	5.3[2]	na
Sheep *d*	5.0*	4.0				
Horses *d*	1.0*	na				
Pigs *d*	40.0*	34.0[1]	—	—	—	—
Bacon/ham }	2.0*	1.7p	{ —	—	2.5[2]	—
Meat‡: 'A'			0.2	—	4.6[2]	—
'B'	0.7*	na	—[2]	—	3.0[2]	0.6
Butter	—	—	—	—	1.8	1.0
Cheese	—	—	—	—	1.3	0.8
Eggs	3.0*	na	—	—	0.3	—
Fish	9.6	4.0	0.1	na	4.8	na
Milk	5.0*	na	0.6	0.5*	70.8	42.4*

d no. in thousands. *n* incl. ducks, geese and turkeys. *p* government inspected meat only.

	Production		Exports		Imports	
6. FIBRES, TEXTILES, etc.						
Agaves (sisal, etc.)	—	—	—	—	0.1[2]	na
Cotton: lint	—	—	—	—	0.2[2]	na
woven fabrics	na	na	0.1	na	—	—
Rayon, woven fabrics	—	—	—	—	1.0	na
7. FUEL AND POWER						
Coal, 'A'‡	—	—	—	—	1	6
Electricity *h t*	784	280[1]				
Natural gas *i*	1 030	505[1]	—	—	—	—
Oil, crude	6 970	3 600[1]	1 370	390[1]*	11 540	2 590[1]
Petroleum, refined	17 360	5 280[1]	14 630	3 820[1]	20	120[1]

h million kWh. *i* million cu. metres. *t* thermal.

	Production		Exports		Imports	
8. IRON AND STEEL						
Iron/steel scrap	na	na	3	11	—	—
9. NON-FERROUS MINERALS AND METALS						
Gold *k*, bullion/coins etc.	—	—	—	—	8.72[1]	1.01
Silver *k*, bullion	—	—	—	—	18.32	0.57
Asbestos, manufactured	—	—	—	—	1.18	1.47
Mica	—	—	—	—	0.01	—
Aluminium	—	—	—	—	2.19[2]	0.16
Copper, metal	—	—	—	—	0.24	0.04
Lead, metal	—	—	—	—	0.11	0.10
Magnesium, magnesite	—	—	—	—	0.07	—
Tin, metal	—	—	—	—	2.56	na
Zinc, metal	—	—	—	—	0.03	na

k '000 fine troy oz.

	Production		Exports		Imports	
10. CHEMICALS*n* AND FERTILIZERS						
Organic chemicals:						
Benzene	na		na		na	
Butadiene	—		—		na	
Ethylene	—		—		na	
Methanol	—		—		na	
Phenol	—		—		na	
Phthalic anhydride	—		—		na	
Styrene monomer	—		—		na	
Urea	na		na		na	
Inorganic chemicals:						
Ammonia	na		na		na	
Carbon black	—		—		na	
Chlorine	—		—		na	
Sodium carbonate	—		—[2]		1.9[2]	
Sodium hydroxide	—		—		2.3	
Sulphuric acid	na		0.4		—	
Plastics	—		—		na	
Fertilizers:						
Potash	—	—	—	—	3.0	1.8
Sulphur	5.3r	5.1[1]*r	—	1.4	15.1	—

n data not available for years 1953–5. *r* recovered sulphur.

	Production		Exports		Imports	
11. INDUSTRY						
Aircraft *a*	—	—	—	—	5.4	1.1
Alcoholic beverages			1.8a	1.2a	2.0a	2.4a
beer *b*	90.0	26.6				
Cement	176.0	48.7	50.7*	22.0	11.3*	36.7
Electrical engineering *a*	—	—	—	—	12.8	4.8[2]
Railway vehicles *a*	—	—	—	—	—	0.2
Motor vehicles *a*	—	—	—	—	10.6	6.8

a million $ U.S. *b* '000 hectolitres.

na: data not available. — negligible or nil. [1] one year only. [2] two year average. * estimate. ‡ see appendix. † re-exports.

TUNISIA

Tunisia, formerly a French protectorate, became an independent sovereign state in 1956. The following year the monarchy was abolished and the country was declared a republic. A customs union with France has been maintained.

AREA: 164 150 sq. km. (63 362 sq. miles)

LAND USE: (percentage of total)	*1964*
Arable and orchard	34.6
Rough grazing land	45.2
Forest and woodland	6.7
City areas, waste and other land	13.5

POPULATION: 4 457 862 (1966 census)

Largest city: TÚNIS, capital; population: 662 000 (1964)

Distribution of working population (1956)

Total working population: 1 327 520* (excl. foreigners)

U.N. group no.		*Percentage*
0	Agriculture, forestry, fishing and hunting	68.1
1	Mining and quarrying	1.1
2/3	Manufacturing	6.2
4	Construction	2.1
5	Electricity, gas, water and sanitary services	0.2
6	Commerce	4.7
7	Transport, storage and communications	2.0
8	Services	6.4
9	Others	9.2

		Year(s)
Infant mortality (per '000)	74.3*	1960
Crude birth rate (per '000)	44.3	1965
Crude death rate (per '000)	11.8*	1965
Population per physician	8 990	1964
Population per hospital bed	390a	1966
School enrolment: age 5–19 years (percentage)	61	1963–4 av.
age over 19 years (per 100 000 population)	107	1963–5 av.

a government hospitals only.

COMMUNICATIONS		*Year(s)*
Motor vehicles in use ('000s): private	48.7 }	1963–5 av.
commercial	28.1 }	
Railway track (km.)	2 016	
Telephones (per '000 urban population)	0.8*	1967
Radio licences (per '000 population)	72	1963–5 av.
Television sets (per '000 population)	0.8	1963–5 av.
Daily newspapers (per '000 population)	28	1962

FINANCE

Currency unit: The Tunisian dinar, equivalent to 1 000 Tunisian francs, was introduced in 1958

Exchange rates	*1965*	*1960*	*1950a*	*1938a*
Per $ U.S.	0.52	0.42	350	38
Per £ sterling	1.456	1.176	980	175

		Year(s)
National Income (million $ U.S.)	789	1965
G.N.P. per capita ($ U.S.)	200	1966
Rate of increase of G.N.P. per capita	3.3	1960–4 av.
Foreign trade (percentage of G.D.P.)	38	1963–5 av.

a Tunisian francs.

TRADING

Total trade (in million $ U.S.)	*1965*	*1955*	*1938*
Exports (f.o.b.)	120	106	39
Imports (c.i.f.)	245	181	45

Main trading partners (percentage of total value)

Exports	*1965*	*1955*	*Imports*	*1965*	*1955*
France	31	55	France	39	75
Italy	12	8	U.S.A.	16	2
U.K.	5	11	Italy	7	4
Yugoslavia	4	na	Germany F.R.	5	1
Greece	4	1	U.K.	4	1
Algeria	4	5	U.S.S.R.	2	na
India	4	na	Brazil	2	1

Distribution of trade (percentage of total value)

Exports	*1965*	*1955*
Phosphates and phosphatic fertilizers	34	20
Olive oil	21	9
Food	18	21*
(fruit and vegetables)	(10)	(3*)
Metalliferous ores and scrap	6	na
Imports		
Manufactured goods	66	na
(machinery and transport equipment)	(31)	(10*)
(textiles and clothing)	(11)	(14*)
(iron and steel)	(9)	(na)
Food	14	15*
(cereals)	(7)	(na)
Crude materials and fuels	11	na
(petroleum and products)	(5)	(7*)
Chemicals	6	5*

PRODUCTION, EXPORTS AND IMPORTS

Years: **1963–5 average** and *1953–5 average* Units: '000 metric tons unless otherwise indicated

	Production		Exports		Imports	
1. CEREALS, etc.						
Barley	222.7	143.7	11.6	25.2	20.8	11.6
Maize (corn)	— }	2.0[2]	{ —	0.5	5.7	—
Millets/sorghum	5.0* }		0.1	1.7	0.1	0.2
Oats	10.0*	7.3	1.7	3.7	0.6	—
Potatoes	48.0*	19.0	2.0	0.4	6.2	24.7
Rice	—	—	—	—[2]	1.0	1.2
Wheat	628.7	533.0	72.7	168.5	137.5	9.5
2. FRUIT, etc.						
Apples	8.3	2.5[2]	—	0.1	1.1	2.2
Apricots	14.7	6.1[1]	—	—	—	—
Bananas	—	—	—	—	2.2	2.4
Dates	42.0	37.0	2.8	2.7	0.2	0.4
Figs	18.3	13.0[2]	—	—	—	—
Grapes	261.3	134.0*	—	—	—	0.2
Lemons	14.7	10.0*	5.0	4.5	—	—
Oranges	73.3	41.7*	34.8	15.1	—	0.4
Other citrus fruit	1.0*	—	0.4	—	—	—
Olives	392.3	na				
Peaches	10.7	na	—	—	—	—
Pears	4.7	1.0[1]	—	—	0.2	—
Plums	5.3	na	—	—	—	—
Raisins	0.1*	0.1*[2]	—	—	0.1	0.3
Tomatoes	102.7	25.7				
Wine *b*	1 830.0	944.0*	1 293.0	449.0	1.8	3.7

b '000 hectolitres.

	Production		Exports		Imports	
3. BEVERAGES, FOREST PRODUCTS, etc.						
Cocoa	—	—	—	—	0.3	0.1
Coffee	—	—	—	—	2.3	1.3
Sugar: beet	44.0	—				
raw	5.5	—	0.5	—	75.7	62.6
Tea	—	—	—	—	4.8	2.3
Tobacco: leaf	1.4	1.7*[2]	0.1	0.2	2.6	2.3
cigars	—	3.0e	}			
cigarettes	2 581.0e	1 898.3e	} —	—	0.1	—
tobacco/snuff	0.9	0.7	}			
Softwood *j*	54.0*[2]	16.1	—	—	na	67.3
Hardwood *j*	1 219.5*[2]	100.0	—	—	na	35.8
Newsprint	—*	—[2]	—[1]	—	} 17.0[2]	{ 2.5[1]
Other paper	4.5*[2]	3.8[2]	0.1[1]	—	}	{ 4.2

e no. in millions. *j* '000 cu. metres of roundwood equivalent.

	Production		Exports		Imports	
4. VEGETABLE OILSEEDS AND OILS						
Castor oil	—	—	—	—	0.01	—
Coconut oil	—	—	—	—	—	0.04
Cottonseed	na	na	0.31	—	—	—
Cottonseed oil	na	na	—	0.05	—	0.03
Groundnuts	—	—	—	0.13†	0.61	1.27
Groundnut oil	na	na	—	0.03	—[2]	0.38
Linseed	1.00*	1.00[2]	0.46	0.63	—	0.07
Linseed oil	na	na	—	—	0.23	0.35
Olive oil	90.67	58.67	42.24	23.72	—	0.43
Rapeseed oil	—	—	—	—	—	0.01
Sesame seed	—	—	0.01†	—	0.94	0.83
Sunflower seed	—	—	—	—	0.12	—

continued

na: data not available. — negligible or nil. [1] one year only. [2] two year average. * estimate. ‡ see appendix. † re-exports.

TUNISIA *continued*

PRODUCTION, EXPORTS AND IMPORTS *continued*

5. LIVESTOCK‡, ANIMAL PRODUCTS, etc.

	Production		Exports		Imports	
Chickens *dr*	5 406.3*	5 500.0[2]				
Cattle *d*	654.0*	489.0	0.1	—	2.7	1.1
dairy cows *d*	222.3*	na				
Goats *d*	477.0	1 665.3	0.7	na	14.3	na
Sheep *d*	3 689.0*	3 089.7				
Horses *d*	83.0	79.5[2]				
Pigs *d*	4.0	15.0	—	1.9	—	—
Bacon/ham	41.7*	35.0[1]	—	0.1	—	—
Meat‡: 'A'			0.1	0.3	0.3	—
'B'	8.4*	na	—	—	—	—
Butter	—	—	—	—	1.0	0.9
Cheese	1.3*	1.0[1]	0.2	0.1	0.8	1.6
Eggs	11.3*	15.0[2]	—	—	—	0.3
Fish	23.3	12.0	3.0	na	0.4	na
Milk	124.0*	59.5[2]	—	—	24.7	13.9*
Hides/skins	na	0.7[2]	1.0	2.4[2]	—	0.2[2]
Wool	1.5[2]	1.0[2]	—	0.7	—	—

d no. in thousands. *r* incl. ducks, geese and turkeys.

6. FIBRES, TEXTILES, etc.

	Production		Exports		Imports	
Cotton lint	na	na	0.2	—	1.5	—
Jute	—	—	—	—	1.8	—
Rubber, natural	—	—	—	—	0.1	0.1
Silk *f*	—	—	—	—	—	0.7
Cotton: yarn	—	—	—	—	2.4	0.7[2]
woven fabrics	—	—	—	—	2.7	4.5
Wool: yarn	—	—	—	—[2]	1.2[2]	0.2[2]
woven fabrics	—	—	—[2]	0.1[2]	0.4[2]	0.5[2]

f metric tons.

7. FUEL AND POWER

	Production		Exports		Imports	
Coal, 'A'‡	—	—	—	—	31	57
Coke	—	—	—	—	12	11
Electricity *h*: total	436	220[1]				
hydro	37	—				
thermal	399	220[1]				
Natural gas *i*	10	—	—	—	—	—
Oil, crude	—	—[1]	—	—	463	—
Petroleum, refined	450	—	3	—	227	430[1]

h million kWh. *i* million cu. metres.

8. IRON AND STEEL

	Production		Exports		Imports	
Iron ore	525*m*	572*m*	836	1 016	—	—
Iron/steel scrap	na	na	9	35	na	2

m metal content.

9. NON-FERROUS MINERALS AND METALS

	Production		Exports		Imports	
Silver *k*: ore *m*	19.00	79.00	—	—	—	—
Asbestos: fibre	—	—	—	—	0.23	—
manufactured	—	—	—	—	9.29	—
Mica	—	—	—	—	0.05	0.03
Aluminium	na	na	0.23	na	0.44	0.18
Copper, metal	—	—	0.76*q*	—	0.74	0.83
Lead: ore	14.25*m*	25.64*m*	na	0.57	0.01[2]	1.44
metal	12.96	27.27	12.80	25.17	—	0.03
Mercury *f*	2.00	1.91	—	—	7.50	0.20
Tin, metal	—	—	—	—	0.05	0.04
Titanium minerals	—	—	—	—	0.20	—
Zinc, ore	4.15*m*	4.85*m*	6.08	9.82	0.32*p*	0.39*p*

f metric tons. *k* '000 fine troy oz. *m* metal content. *p* metal. *q* mainly scrap.

10. CHEMICALS*n* AND FERTILIZERS

	Production		Exports		Imports	
Chemicals	—		—		na	
Fertilizers:						
Phosphates	2 720.3	1 880.7	2 147.0	1 782.7	—	—
Potash	—	—	—	—	6.8	1.7
Pyrites	—	—	—	—	11.3	11.1
Sulphur	—	—	—	—	35.9	18.1

n data not available for years 1953–5.

11. INDUSTRY

	Production		Exports		Imports	
Aircraft *a*	—	—	—	—	1.7[2]	na
Alcoholic beverages			—	—	0.3*a*	6.5*a*
beer *b*	184.0	98.3				
Cement	423.3	298.0	82.3	104.7	8.3	7.3
Electrical engineering *a*	—	—	—	—	13.4	2.6[1]
Railway vehicles *a*	—	—	—	—	2.2	na
Machine tools *a*	—	—	—	—	1.6	0.5
Merchant ships *g*	—	—	—	—	0.7	na
Motor vehicles *a*	—	—	—	—	12.4	7.7[2]

a million $ U.S. *b* '000 hectolitres. *g* '000 G.R.T.

TURKEY

EASTERN MEDITERRANEAN

Turkey was declared a republic in 1923, and there followed a long process of reform and 'Westernization'.

Turkey is a member of Cento and an associate member of the European Economic Community; agreements for co-operation and development have been signed with Iran and Pakistan.

AREA: 780 576 sq. km. (301 380 sq. miles)

LAND USE: (percentage of total)

	1965	*1955*
Arable and orchard	33.5	29.0
Permanent meadow and pasture	36.2	40.3
Forest and woodland	13.5	13.4
City areas, waste and other land	16.8	17.3

POPULATION: 31 391 421 (1965 census)

Largest city: İSTANBUL; population: 2 052 368 (1965)
Capital city: ANKARA; population: 971 069 (1965)

Distribution of working population (1960)

Total working population: 12 993 245

U.N. group no.		*Percentage*
0	Agriculture, forestry, fishing and hunting	75.0
1	Mining and quarrying	0.6
2/3	Manufacturing	6.8
4	Construction	2.2
5	Electricity, gas, water and sanitary services	0.1
6	Commerce	3.1
7	Transport, storage and communications	1.9
8	Services	5.2
9	Others	5.1

		Year(s)
Life expectancy at birth (years)	53.7 *	1966
Infant mortality (per '000)	155*	1966
Crude birth rate (per '000)	43*	1966
Crude death rate (per '000)	16*	1966
Accidental deaths (per 100 000 population)		
caused by motor vehicles	3.9*a**	1965
due to other causes	8.6*a**	1965
Population per physician	2 860	1965
Population per hospital bed	550	1966
School enrolment: age 5–19 years (percentage)	55	1964
age over 19 years (per 100 000 population)	283	1963–5 av.

a in provincial capitals and district centres only.

COMMUNICATIONS

		Year(s)
Motor vehicles in use ('000s): private	79.7	1963–5 av.
commercial	99.0	
Railway track (km.)	7 929	1964
Mail per capita: domestic	10	1963–5 av.
foreign received	1	
foreign sent	1	
Telephones (per '000 urban population)	1.2	1967
Radio licences (per '000 population)	68	1963–5 av.
Television sets (per '000 population)	0.1	1963–5 av.
Daily newspapers (per '000 population)	45	1961

FINANCE

Currency unit: The lira, or Turkish pound

Exchange rates	*1965 a*	*1960 a*	*1955 b*	*1938 b*
Per $ U.S.	9.0	9.0	2.83	1.26
Per £ sterling	25.2	25.2	7.91	5.81

		Year(s)
National Income (million $ U.S.)	7 593	1965
G.N.P. per capita ($ U.S.)	280	1966
Rate of increase of G.N.P. per capita	1.6	1960–4 av.
Foreign trade (percentage of G.D.P.)	12	1963–5 av.

a export rate. *b* basic selling rate.

continued

na: data not available. — negligible or nil. [1] one year only. [2] two year average. * estimate. ‡ see appendix. † re-exports.

TRADING

Total trade (in million $ U.S.)	*1965*	*1955*	*1938*
Exports (f.o.b.)	464	313	115
Imports (c.i.f.)	577	498	119

Main trading partners (percentage of total value)

Exports	*1965*	*1955*	*1938*	*Imports*	*1965*	*1955*	*1938*
U.S.A.	18	16	12	U.S.A.	28	22	10
Germany F.R.	16	16	43*d*	Germany F.R.	15	18	47*d*
U.K.	9	7	3	U.K.	10	8	11
Italy	7	8	10	Italy	6	4	5
Belg./Lux.	5	2	2	France	4	6	1
Lebanon	5	—	na	Saudi Arabia	3	3	—
France	4	7	3	U.S.S.R.	3	2	4

Distribution of trade (percentage of total value)

Exports	*1965*	*1955*	*1938**
Food	37	34	42
(fruit and vegetables)	(24)	(20)	(26)
Crude materials and fuels	35	33	na
(cotton)	(22)	(15)	(7)
Tobacco	20	28	27
Imports			
Manufactured goods	61	69	na
(machinery and transport equipment)	(37)	(35)	(23)
Crude materials and fuels	18	15	na
Chemicals	16	17	6

d incl. Germany D.R.

PRODUCTION, EXPORTS AND IMPORTS

Years: **1963–5 average** and *1953–5 average* Units: '000 metric tons unless otherwise indicated

1. CEREALS, etc.

	Production		Exports		Imports	
Barley	3 596.0	3 008.3	46.8[2]	101.0	3.7	40.3
Maize (corn)	996.7	842.7	—	10.2[2]	11.7	—
Millets/sorghum	57.7	94.3	10.4	8.5	—	—
Oats	530.0	365.7	—	—	—	13.9
Potatoes	1 660.0	1 038.7	1.2	—	0.1	1.0
Rice	200.3	153.0	1.1*	8.2	0.1	0.5[2]
Rye	803.3	606.7	40.5	46.9	—	—
Wheat	9 069.0	6 718.7	—	571.3	405.4	74.2

2. FRUIT, etc.

	Production		Exports		Imports	
Apples	342.0	136.3	—	0.3	—	—
Apricots	88.7	68.6	—	—	—	—
Cherries	68.7	41.7	—	—	—	—
Figs	208.0	104.0	—	12.6	—	—
Grapes	2 944.3	2 047.7	6.0	0.1	—	—
Lemons	62.0	22.7	7.9	5.4	—	—
Oranges	324.3	145.7	14.9	2.8	—	—
Other citrus fruit	2.7	—	1.1	—	—	—
Olives	569.0	325.3				
Peaches	80.0	20.3	—	—	—	—
Pears	143.0	108.7	—	—	—	—
Plums	95.0	60.6	—	—	—	—
Raisins	270.0*	130.8	61.4	39.7	—	—
Wine *b*	332.0	209.0*	19.1	20.0	—	—

b '000 hectolitres.

3. BEVERAGES, FOREST PRODUCTS, etc.

	Production		Exports		Imports	
Cocoa	—	—	—	—	1.1	0.7
Coffee	—	—	—	—	1.1	6.4
Sugar: beet	3 802.7	1 357.0	—	—	—	—
raw	624.8	224.7	88.8	3.6	—	2.0
Tea	11.0	0.7[1]	1.4	—	0.7	2.4
Tobacco: leaf	150.0	113.3	56.7	65.4	—	—
cigarettes	33 952.0*e*	22 095.0*e*	—	—	—	—
tobacco/snuff	0.2	2.8	—	—	—	—
Softwood *j*	5 531.0	2 096.7	2.0	1.5	—	452.9
Hardwood *j*	4 526.5[2]	3 619.7	16.2	15.5	1.6	7.2
Wood pulp	73.6	31.0	—	—	7.6	—
Newsprint	20.7	5.6	—	—	17.0	10.1
Other paper	76.3	31.4	—	—	24.4	20.3

e no. in millions. *j* '000 cu. metres of roundwood equivalent.

4. VEGETABLE OILSEEDS AND OILS

	Production		Exports		Imports	
Castor oil	—	—	—	—	0.21	0.04
Copra	—	—	—	—	0.35	0.10
Coconut oil	na	na	—	—	0.01	—
Cottonseed	491.30	266.30	11.28	13.10[2]	0.31	—
Cottonseed oil	na	na	—	—	15.55	4.15
Groundnuts	17.71	10.01	0.94	0.87	—	—
Linseed	16.67	19.00	0.74	1.13	—	—
Linseed oil	na	na	—	—	—	0.06
Olive oil	94.67	54.67*	14.13	0.38	—	—
Rapeseed	6.70	2.30	—	—	—	—
Sesame seed	36.00	49.50	0.40	—	—	—
Soya beans	5.30	3.67	1.29	2.00	—	—
Soya bean oil	na	na	—	—	36.26	—
Sunflower seed	137.33	124.00	0.39	2.50[2]	0.01	—

5. LIVESTOCK‡, ANIMAL PRODUCTS, etc.

	Production		Exports		Imports	
Chickens *d*	27 812.3	22 970.3				
Cattle *d*	12 859.0	10 774.0	107.8	19.3[2]	0.4	—
dairy cows *d*	4 437.7*	na				
Goats *d*	21 581.0	21 029.0	714.3	na	—	—
Sheep *d*	32 182.3	26 876.3				
Horses *d*	1 206.7	1 211.0				
Pigs *d*	12.0	4.0[2]	—	—	—	—

continued

5. LIVESTOCK‡, ANIMAL PRODUCTS, etc.—*continued*

	Production		Exports		Imports	
Meat‡: 'A'	199.0	113.5[2]*r*	—	—	—	—
'B'	24.5	na	—	—	—	—
Butter	na	—	0.1	—	—	—
Cheese	na	—	0.1	—	—	—
Eggs	69.1	55.4	—	3.0	—	—
Fish	129.4	111.1	10.8	4.8[1]*	0.3	0.2[1]*
Milk	2 411.3	1 444.3	—	—	0.8	1.0[1]
Hides/skins	na	na	7.0	2.3[2]	7.6	2.3[2]
Wool	23.7	20.0	2.4	0.4	5.7	3.4

d no. in thousands. *r* government inspected meat only.

6. FIBRES, TEXTILES, etc.

	Production		Exports		Imports	
Agaves (sisal, etc.)	—	—	—	—	1.0	0.2
Cotton lint	299.0	146.0	153.5	71.0	—	—
Flax fibre	4.8	4.2	—	—	—	—
Hemp fibre	9.5	11.4	—	—	—	—
Jute	—	—	—	—	0.4	—
Rubber: natural	—	—	—	—	10.9	4.8
synthetic	—	—	—	—	4.5	—
Silk *f*	na	253.3*	124.0	9.0	—	—
Cotton: yarn	100.5	22.8	—	—	na	1.2
woven fabrics	21.8*t*	16.0*t*	2.4	—	na	9.5
Rayon, fibre/yarn	1.6	0.8	—	—	7.6	1.7*p*
Non-cellulosic fibre/yarn	0.5	na	—	na	4.1	na
Wool: yarn	20.7	9.2	—	—[2]	—	0.1
woven fabrics	24.0*q*	4.3*qt*	—	—	—	0.2

f metric tons. *p* incl. spun yarn. *q* million metres. *t* production by state-owned mills only.

7. FUEL AND POWER

	Production		Exports		Imports	
Coal: 'A'‡	4 330	3 500	11	2	—[2]	—
'B'	953	1 480	—	—	—	—
Coke	—	—	—	—	4	—
Electricity *h*: total	4 453	1 380				
hydro	1 973	80				
thermal	2 480	1 300				
Oil, crude	1 063	180[1]	—	—	3 190	na
Petroleum, refined	3 783	60[1]	670	—	23	960[1]

h million kWh.

8. IRON AND STEEL

	Production		Exports		Imports	
Iron ore	606*m*	392*m*	4	208	—	—
Pig iron	432	205	6[2]	—	27	—
Steel ingots/castings	513	176	—	7	89	2
Iron/steel scrap	na	na	—	6	22	—

m metal content.

9. NON-FERROUS MINERALS AND METALS

	Production		Exports		Imports	
Platinum group metals *k*	—	—	—	—	1.19	0.02
Silver *k*, bullion	—	—	—	—	5.33	40.33
Asbestos: fibre	0.93	0.09	—	—	2.12	0.02
manufactured	na	na	—	0.04	4.43	2.39
Mica	—	—	—	—	0.09	—
Aluminium: bauxite	7.11[2]	—	—	—	—	—
alumina	—	—	—	—	0.04	—
aluminium	—	—	—	—	9.15	4.12
Antimony: ore	1.74*m*	1.17*m*	3.38	1.39	—	—
metal	—	—	0.11	0.05	—	—
Chrome: ore	418.14*m*	707.93*m*	327.01	531.54	—	—
metal	na	na	4.39	—	0.03	0.14
Cobalt, metal	—	—	—	—	—	0.02

k '000 fine troy oz. *m* metal content.

continued

na: data not available, — negligible or nil. [1] one year only. [2] two year average. * estimate. ‡ see appendix. † re-exports.

TURKEY *continued*

PRODUCTION, EXPORTS AND IMPORTS *continued*

9. NON-FERROUS MINERALS AND METALS—*continued*	Production		Exports		Imports	
Copper: ore	32.10m	na	5.51	*4.20*	—	—
metal	25.69	*23.94*	14.46	*13.82*	3.00	*1.55*
Lead: ore	1.95m	*2.03m*	3.04	*1.11*	—	—
metal	1.59	—	—	*0.07*	1.67	*2.59*
Magnesium:						
dolomite	370.00*p	na	—	—	—	—
magnesite	44.19	na	—	—	0.04	—
metal/salts	—‡	—‡	31.93[2]	—	0.65	*0.67*[2]
Manganese, ore	13.60	*63.26*	15.04	*46.26*	4.31r	—
Mercury f	96.66	*12.66*	95.30	*12.10*	—	*0.10*
Nickel, metal	—	—	—	—	0.09	*0.01*
Tin, metal	—	—	—	—	0.77	*0.78*
Titanium minerals	—	—	—	—	1.80v	—
Zinc, ore	5.84m	*3.41m*	3.54	*0.29*	8.24r	*6.26r*
Zirconium minerals	—	—	—	—	na	—

f metric tons. *m* metal content. *p* 1966 figure. *r* metal. *v* titanium-oxide only.

10. CHEMICALS*n* AND FERTILIZERS	Production	Exports	Imports
Organic chemicals:			
Benzene	na	na	na
Butadiene	—	—	na
Ethylene	—	—	na
Methanol	na	na	na
Phthalic anhydride	—	—	na
Styrene monomer	—	na	0.1[2]
Urea	—	—	na

continued

10. CHEMICALS*n* AND FERTILIZERS—*continued*	Production		Exports		Imports	
Inorganic chemicals:						
Ammonia	na		—		—	
Carbon black	—		—		6.1[2]	
Chlorine	na		na		na	
Nitric acid	na		—		0.1	
Sodium carbonate	na		—		32.1	
Sodium hydroxide	na		—		21.4[2]	
Sulphuric acid	22.3		—		26.5[1]y	
Plastics:						
Polyamides	na		—		na	
Polyethylene	—		—		na	
Polyvinyl chloride	na		—		na	
Fertilizers:						
Phosphates	—	—	—	—	103.1	*21.7*
Potash	—	—	—	—	4.2	*1.1*
Pyrites	52.5x	*12.3x**	101.4	—	—	—
Sulphur, native	21.3	*10.4*	na	*0.3*	0.2	*0.5*

n data not available for years 1953–5. *x* sulphur content. *y* incl. oleum.

11. INDUSTRY	Production		Exports		Imports	
Aircraft a	—	—	—	—	0.4	*0.3*
Alcoholic beverages			na	na	na	na
beer b	287.0	*275.7*				
spirits b	206.0t	*119.0w*				
Cement	2 952.7	*678.7*	0.7	—	77.0	*660.0*
Electrical engineering a	—	—	—	—	40.6	*27.9*[2]
Railway vehicles a	—	—	—	—	7.3	*8.1*
Machine tools a	—	—	—	—	6.1	*2.5*
Merchant ships g	3.0	—	—	—	—	—
Motor vehicles a	—	—	—	—	43.7	*27.2*

a million $ U.S. *b* '000 hectolitres. *g* '000 G.R.T. *t* production for home consumption in 1967. *w* 1957 figure.

UGANDA

EAST AFRICA

Uganda, formerly a British East African protectorate, became a fully independent member of the Commonwealth in 1962. In 1966 the prime minister suspended the constitution and assumed full powers of government until the following year when the country became a republic and a new constitution was formed. Uganda is a member of the East African Community.

AREA: 243 410 sq. km. (93 981 sq. miles)

LAND USE: (percentage of total)	*1964*	*1952*
Arable and orchard	16.0	11.7
Permanent meadow and pasture	na	—
Forest and woodland	7.0	7.1
City areas, waste and other land	na	81.2

POPULATION: 7 934 000 (1967 estimate)

Largest city: KAMPALA, capital; population: 123 332 (1959)

		Year(s)
Infant mortality (per '000)	160*	1959
Crude birth rate (per '000)	42*a	1959
Crude death rate (per '000)	20*a	1959
Population per physician	11 600	1965
Population per hospital bed	890	1966
School enrolment: age 5–19 years (percentage)	30	1963–4 av.
age over 19 years (per 100 000 population)	15	1963–5 av.

a African population.

Employment: The majority of the population is employed in agriculture. The cash crops produced include cotton, coffee, oilseeds, tea, sugar, and tobacco. Copper is mined and smelted.

COMMUNICATIONS		*Year(s)*
Motor vehicles in use ('000s): private	28.4	1963–5 av.
commercial	5.6	1963–5 av.
Railway track (km.)	1 160	1969
Telephones (per '000 urban population)	0.3	1967
Radio receivers (per '000 population)	18	1963–5 av.
Television sets (per '000 population)	0.5	1963–5 av.
Daily newspapers (per '000 population)	5	1964

FINANCE

Currency unit: The Uganda shilling replaced, at par, the East African shilling in 1966. Prior to 1960 East African pounds of 20 shillings were used.

Exchange rates	*1965 a*	*1960 a*	*1950 b*	*1938 b*
Per $ U.S.	7.143	7.143	0.357	0.215
Per £ sterling	20.0	20.0	1.0	1.0

		Year(s)
National Income (million $ U.S.)	585	1965
G.N.P. per capita ($ U.S.)	100	1966
Rate of increase of G.N.P. per capita	0.5	1960–4 av.

a East African shillings. *b* East African pounds.

TRADING

Note—trade with Kenya and Tanganyika is excluded

Total trade (in million $ U.S.)	*1965*	*1955*	*1955 a*
Exports (f.o.b.)	179	118	299
Imports (c.i.f.)	114	95	417

Main trading partners (percentage of total value)

Exports	*1965*	*1955 a*	*Imports*	*1965*	*1955 a*
U.S.A.	22	12	U.K.	38	44
U.K.	17	28	Japan	10	4
Belg./Lux.	11	3	Germany F.R.	9	6
China P.R.	10	—	India	5	6
India	6	15	U.S.A.	5	3
Canada	3	10	Italy	4	3
Germany F.R.	3	10	France	4	3

Distribution of trade (percentage of total value)

Exports	*1965*	*Imports*	*1965*
Coffee	49	Manufactured goods	78
Cotton	27	(machinery and transport equipment)	(36)
Copper	13	(textiles and clothing)	(19)
		Chemicals	8
		Food	5

a refers to the total trade for Kenya, Uganda and Tanganyika.

na: data not available. — negligible or nil. [1] one year only. [2] two year average. * estimate. ‡ see appendix. † re-exports.

PRODUCTION, EXPORTS AND IMPORTS

Years: **1963–5 average** and *1953–5 average* Units: '000 metric tons unless otherwise indicated

1. CEREALS, etc.	Production		Exports		Imports	
Cassava	1 447.0*	na				
Maize (corn)	212.0*	na	2.3	*15.0*[2]	0.1	—[2]
Millets/sorghum	672.3	na	0.4	—	—	—
Potatoes	19.0*	na	—	—	—	—
Rice	1.7*	na	0.1	—	5.4	*6.2*
Sweet potatoes/yams	1 330.0*	na				
Wheat	—	na	—	—	1.0	—

2. FRUIT, etc.	Production		Exports		Imports	
Apples	—	—	—	—	0.1	—
Dates	—	—	—	—	0.1	—
Raisins	—	—	—	—	0.1	—
Wine b	—	—	0.1†	—	2.1	*1.3*

b '000 hectolitres.

3. BEVERAGES, FOREST PRODUCTS, etc.	Production		Exports		Imports	
Coffee	190.9	*50.1*[2]	148.3	*52.1*	—	—
Sugar: cane	1 533.3*	*499.3*				
raw	122.4	*60.7*	2.9	—	0.3	*6.1*
Tea	7.4	*2.7*	6.1	*2.0*	—	—
Tobacco: leaf	3.6	*1.8**	0.1	—	—	—
cigarettes	1 205.0e	*2 961.7e*	—	—	—	—
tobacco/snuff	—	*0.3*	—	—	—	—
Softwood j	5.4	*2.5*[2]	0.2	—	6.7	*2.6*
Hardwood j	10 747.7*	*12 117.3*	9.7	*0.7*	1.1	*0.5*
Newsprint	—	—	—	—	0.7	*0.2*[2]
Other paper	—	—	—	—	2.0	*0.8*[1]

e no. in millions. *j* '000 cu. metres of roundwood equivalent.

4. VEGETABLE OILSEEDS AND OILS	Production		Exports		Imports	
Castor seed	2.33*	—	2.06	*8.77*	—	—
Coconut oil	—	—	—	—	0.65	*0.60*
Cottonseed	156.00	*130.67*	—	*16.50*[2]	—	—
Cottonseed oil	na	na	1.11	*1.94*	—	—
Groundnuts	114.10*	*119.00*[1]	2.58	*6.00*	—	—
Groundnut oil	na	na	na	*0.10*	—	—
Linseed	—	na	—	*0.03*	—	—
Linseed oil	—	—	—	—	0.01	*0.01*
Olive oil	—	—	—	—	0.01	—
Palm oil	—	—	0.10†	—	0.69	—
Sesame seed	30.50*	*32.00*[2]*	0.89	na	—	—
Soya beans	1.30*	*1.00*[1]	0.15	*1.47*	—	—
Sunflower seed	—	—	0.10	*2.34v*	—	—

v incl. data for Kenya.

5. LIVESTOCK‡, ANIMAL PRODUCTS, etc.	Production		Exports		Imports	
Cattle d	3 529.7	*2 898.0*	—	—	—	—
Goats d	2 001.0	*2 577.7*	—	—	—	—
Sheep d	804.0	*1 100.0*	—	—	—	—
Pigs d	19.0*	*13.5*[2]	—	—	—	—
Meat‡, 'A'	121.7	*53.0*[1]*	0.6	—	—	—
Eggs	34.4*	na	—	—	—	—
Fish	72.2	*28.0*	0.1	na	0.1	na
Milk	328.0*	*234.0*[2]	—	—	8.2	*3.0**
Hides/skins	3.0[2]	*1.8n*	4.2[2]	na	—	—

d no. in thousands. *n* cattle hides only.

6. FIBRES, TEXTILES, etc.	Production		Exports		Imports	
Agaves (sisal)	0.3	*1.0*	0.3	*0.7*	—	—
Cotton lint	71.0	*64.0*	64.4	*64.8*	—	—
Rubber, natural	—	—	—	—	0.1	—
Cotton, woven fabrics	3.2*	na	—	—	na	na
Rayon, woven fabrics	—	—	—	—	5.2v	na

v incl. data for Kenya.

7. FUEL AND POWER	Production		Exports		Imports	
Electricity, hydro h	530	na				
Petroleum, refined	—	—	33†	—	190	*120*[1]

h million kWh.

9. NON-FERROUS MINERALS AND METALS	Production		Exports		Imports	
Gold k, bullion/coins etc.	—	—	0.03‡	*0.41*	1.64	*0.90*
Silver k, bullion	—	—	—	*0.07*	na	—
Asbestos: fibre	—	—	—	—	0.67	*0.10*[2]
manufactured	—	—	—	—	0.59	*2.03*
Mica	—	na	—	*0.03*	—	—
Aluminium	—	—	—	—	0.23	*1.12*
Beryl	0.32	*0.07*	0.37	*0.07*	—	—
Cobalt	na	na	—	—	—	—
Copper: ore	na	na	—	—	—	—
metal	17.21‡	na	17.21	na	0.09	*0.06*
Lead, ore	—	na	—	*0.05*	0.05q	*0.01q*
Tin, ore	0.19m	*0.08m*	0.29	*0.12*	0.03q	*0.02q*
Tungsten, ore	0.02	*0.18*	0.03	*0.15*	—	—
Zinc, metal	—	—	—	—	0.09	na

k '000 fine troy oz. *m* metal content. *q* metal.

10. CHEMICALS*n* AND FERTILIZERS	Production		Exports		Imports	
Chemicals	—		—		na	
Fertilizers:						
Phosphates	11.2p	*3.7p*	0.4	*3.8*	—	—
Potash	—	—	—	—	1.4	*0.1*
Sulphur	—	—	—	—	3.1	*0.4*

n data not available for years 1953–5. *p* apatite.

11. INDUSTRY	Production		Exports		Imports	
Aircraft a	—	—	—	—	0.4[2]	na
Alcoholic beverages			—	—	0.6a	na
beer b	150.0	*23.3*				
Cement	86.3	*36.3*	—	*1.3*	13.0	*67.3*
Electrical engineering a	—	—	—	—	7.2	na
Railway vehicles a	—	—	—	—	na	*16.3v*
Motor vehicles a	—	—	—	—	14.1	na

a million $ U.S. *b* '000 hectolitres. *v* incl. data for Kenya.

UNION OF SOVIET SOCIALIST REPUBLICS

The revolution of 1917 terminated the rule of the Russian Empire by the Tsars, and introduced the socialist system of government, with central planning of the economy. The Union consists of fifteen Soviet Socialist Republics, and local and central power is vested in the Working Peoples' Deputies. The U.S.S.R. is the nucleus of Comecon.

AREA: 22 400 000 sq. km. (8 650 000 sq. miles)

LAND USE: (percentage of total)	*1964*	*1954*
Arable and orchard	10.3	9.8
Permanent meadow and pasture	16.6	11.9
Forest and woodland	40.6	33.2
City areas, waste and other land	32.5	45.1

POPULATION: 235 543 000 (1967 estimate)

Largest city: MOSKVA (Moscow), capital; population: 6 507 000 (1967)

Distribution of working population (1959)
Total working population: 108 995 013

U.N. group no.		*Percentage*
0	Agriculture, forestry, fishing and hunting	35.2
1	Mining and quarrying	33.6
2/3	Manufacturing	
4	Construction	
5	Electricity, gas, water and sanitary services	
7	Transport, storage and communications	
6	Commerce	4.7
8	Services	13.3
9	Others (incl. armed forces)	13.2

		Year(s)
Life expectancy at birth (years)	70	1966–7 av.
Infant mortality (per '000)	27.6	1965
Crude birth rate (per '000)	18.4	1965
Crude death rate (per '000)	7.3	1965
Population per physician	480	1965
Population per hospital bed	100	1966
School enrolment: age 5–19 years (percentage)	99	1963–4 av.
age over 19 years (per 100 000 population)	1 570	1963–5 av.

COMMUNICATIONS		*Year(s)*
Railway track (km.)	129 300	1965
Mail per capita	22	1963–5 av.
Telephones (per '000 urban population)	3.6*	1967
Radio licences (per '000 population)	315	1963–5 av.
Television licences (per '000 population)	57.1	1963–5 av.
Daily newspapers (per '000 population)	229	1964

FINANCE

Currency unit: The rouble

Exchange rates	*1965 a*	*1960*	*1958*
Per $ U.S.	0.9	0.9	4.0
Per £ sterling	2.5	2.5	11.2

		Year(s)
National Income (million $ U.S.)	200 000*	1966
G.N.P. per capita ($ U.S.)	890*	1966
Rate of increase of G.N.P. per capita	4.8*	1960–4 av.

a middle rate.

continued

na: data not available. — negligible or nil. [1] one year only. [2] two year average. * estimate. ‡ see appendix. † re-exports.

UNION OF SOVIET SOCIALIST REPUBLICS *continued*

TRADING

Total trade (in million $ U.S.)	*1965*	*1955*	*1938*
Exports (f.o.b.)	8 174	3 427	256
Imports (f.o.b.)	8 058	3 061	272

Main trading partners (percentage of total value)

Exports	*1965*	*1955*	*1938*	*Imports*	*1965*	*1955*	*1938*
Germany D.R.	17	14	7*f*	Germany D.R.	16	17	5*f*
Czechoslovakia	11	10	1	Czechoslovakia	13	13	1
Poland	9	12	1	Poland	10	9	—
Bulgaria	7	4	na	Bulgaria	8	4	na
Hungary	7	3	—	Hungary	6	5	na
Romania	5	8	—	Romania	5	7	—
Cuba	5	na	na	Cuba	4	1	na

Distribution of trade (percentage of total value)

Exports	*1965*	*1955*
Manufactured goods	44	37*
(machinery and transport equipment)	(21)	(17*)
Raw materials and fuels	35	30*
(petroleum)	(12)	(5*)
(wood)	(5)	(4*)
Food	7	11*
Imports		
Manufactured goods	61	49
(machinery and transport equipment)	(34)	(30)
Food, beverages and tobacco	21	14
Raw materials and fuels	15	32

f incl. Germany F.R.

PRODUCTION, EXPORTS AND IMPORTS

Years: **1963–5 average** and *1953–5 average* Units: '000 metric tons unless otherwise indicated

1. CEREALS, etc.

	Production		Exports		Imports	
Barley	22 867.0	na	1 109.3	91.6*	—	9.0*
Maize (corn)	10 930.7	na	637.6	36.9*	—	—
Millets/sorghum	2 546.7*	na	—	—	—	—
Oats	5 194.7	na	20.7	26.7*	—	—
Potatoes	84 484.0	na	—	—	—	—
Rice	472.7	na	6.5	1.2*	264.9	71.9*
Rye	13 865.7	na	334.1	433.4*	—	—
Wheat	61 229.0*n*	na	2 599.6	650.5*	5 569.7	6.7*

n in addition, buckwheat 724.7.

2. FRUIT, etc.

	Production		Exports		Imports	
Apples	na	na	—	0.8*	140.5	—
Bananas	—	—	—	—	20.3	0.2*
Dates	—	—	—	—	16.7	1.9*
Grapes	2 974.3	na	na	0.2*	100.5	5.5*
Lemons	na	na	—	—	38.9	15.8*
Oranges	na	na	na	0.1*	128.3	28.0*
Pineapples	—	—	—	—	na	0.6[1]
Raisins	na	na	na	0.5*	44.3	9.4*
Wine *b*	12 650.3	4 473.0	na	na	1 080.0	—

b '000 hectolitres

Apricots, cherries, peaches, pears, and plums are also grown, but no figures are available.

3. BEVERAGES, FOREST PRODUCTS, etc.

	Production		Exports		Imports	
Cocoa	—	—	—	—	69.7	17.5*
Coffee	—	—	—	—[2]	30.3	—
Sugar: beet	65 589	24 533				
raw	7 774	3 505	635.7	157.1*	1 779.7	404.9*
Tea	45*	na	9.1	—	30.2	—
Tobacco: leaf	194*	na	2.4	1.5*	108.9	22.1*
cigars	—	2*e*	—	—	} 51.0*a*	—
cigarettes	280 800*e*	196 270*e*	715.3*e*	1 044.5*e*		
tobacco/snuff	na	na	—	—		
Softwood *j*	305 900[2]*	238 600*	15 780.0	2 566.1	157.0[2]	494.1
Hardwood *j*	51 735[2]*	62 750*	68.0	12.7	421.9	172.0[2]
Wood pulp	3 907[1]	1 870[2]	254.9[2]	59.0	84.0[1]	32.3
Newsprint	598[2]	427*	122.0[2]	12.9	57.0[2]	12.0[2]
Other paper	3 389[2]*	1 878*	70.5[2]	0.5[2]	129.5[2]	75.0[1]

a million $ U.S. *e* no. in millions. *j* '000 cu. metres of roundwood equivalent.

4. VEGETABLE OILSEEDS AND OILS

	Production		Exports		Imports	
Castor seed	46.7	17.3[2]	—	—	1.4	—
Castor oil	na	na	—	—	16.6	0.2*
Copra	—	—	—	—	10.2	—
Coconut oil	—	—	—	—	11.2	0.5[2]*
Cottonseed	3 530.0*	2 535.0*	—	—	—	—
Cottonseed oil	na	na	—	—	—	1.9*
Groundnuts	—	—	—	—	25.3	—
Groundnut oil	na	—	—	—	—	0.7*
Linseed	430.0*	—	—	—	12.4	1.4*
Linseed oil	na	na	—	2.1*	28.6	39.4
Olive oil	—	—	—	—	5.2	0.2*
Palm kernels	—	—	—	—	3.6	—
Palm oil	—	—	—	—	2.4	—
Rapeseed	25.3*	na	—	—	—	—
Sesame seed	0.5*	na	—	—	10.1	—
Soya beans	380.0*	na	—	9.6*	31.1	—[2]
Sunflower seed	5 252.7	na	97.0	53.9[1]	—	6.1[1]
Sunflower seed oil	na	na	209.2	—	2.0	1.5*
Tung oil	0.3*	0.7	—	—	1.8	12.2[1]

5. LIVESTOCK‡, ANIMAL PRODUCTS, etc.

	Production		Exports		Imports	
Chickens *d*	485 100*p*	na				
Cattle *d*	86 536	61 534	—	—	97.0	3.0*
dairy cows *d*	38 365	30 000*				
Goats *d*	5 930	18 650	} —	—	1 264.0	na
Sheep *d*	132 952	108 888				
Horses *d*	8 500	15 270				
Pigs *d*	54 555	42 406	—	—	69.2	29.4*

continued

	Production		Exports		Imports	
5. LIVESTOCK‡, ANIMAL PRODUCTS, etc.—*continued*						
Meat‡: 'A'	6 827	na	—	—	—	61.1
'B'	1 075	na	0.1	—	12.8	—
Butter	1 007	na	44.4	—	4.3	18.3*
Cheese	467*	na	4.4	—	4.4	2.5*
Eggs	1 574	na	—	—	24.3	3.6*
Fish	4 518	2 245	206.9	—	94.1	—
Milk	64 503	na	60.2	—	163.0	—
Whale oil	118	43	—	—	—	—
Hides/skins	—	—	—	—	49.6*e*	—
Wool	214	na	26.1	0.1*	47.2	13.6*

d no. in thousands. *e* no. in millions. *p* incl. ducks, geese and turkeys.

6. FIBRES, TEXTILES, etc.

	Production		Exports		Imports	
Agaves (sisal, etc.)	—	—	—	—	5.1	—
Cotton lint	1 821.3	na	390.9	108.1*	184.5	15.9*
Flax fibre	389.7	na	28.9	1.4*	—	—
Hemp fibre	105.0*	na	2.5	—	0.4	1.7*
Jute	60.0*	na	—	—	29.1*	9.1*
Rubber: natural	—	—	23.3†	—	251.9	14.5*
synthetic	na	na	—	23.4[1]*s*	23.9	25.4[1]
Silk *f*	2 782.5[2]	na	1 500.0*	20.0*	—	—
Cotton: yarn	1 262.0	na	5.7	na	13.7*	na
woven fabrics	813.3*	682.1*	—	na	10.0	na
Rayon: fibre/yarn	na	na	na	na	na	na
woven fabrics	109.4	na	na	na	na	na
Wool: yarn	239.0	154.7	—	—	1.0	—
woven fabrics	369.0*q*	234.7*q*	—	—	—	—

f metric tons. *q* million metres. *s* incl. re-exports.

7. FUEL AND POWER

	Production		Exports		Imports	
Coal: 'A'‡	207 740*	276 640	22 164	1 437[1]	5 656	8 664[1]
'B'	213 957*	114 620	—	2 875[1]*r*	—	—
Coke	na	na	3 849	1 617[1]	659	450[1]
Electricity *h*: total	459 343	151 110				
hydro	} 78 217	20 320				
nuclear		—				
thermal	381 126	130 790				
Natural gas *i*	108 700	8 980	327	—	—	—
Oil, crude	224 187	70 790[1]	36 790	2 920[1]	180	1 580[1]
Petroleum, refined	16 718	61 000[1]	20 270	5 040[1]	1 840	na[1]
Uranium	na	na	—	—	—	—

h million kWh. *i* million cu. metres. *r* may incl. re-exports.

8. IRON AND STEEL

	Production		Exports		Imports	
Iron ore	87 448*m*	38 102*m*	23 573	8 817	—	—
Pig iron	62 417	30 239	3 287	1 200	198	588
Steel ingots/castings	85 428	41 600	820	186	55	—
Iron/steel scrap	na	na	436	52[1]	—	—
Iron/steel products *a*	na	na	691	na	293	na

a million $ U.S. *m* metal content.

9. NON-FERROUS MINERALS AND METALS

	Production		Exports		Imports	
Diamonds	4 000*l*	—	—	—	—	—
Gold *k*, ore *m*	4 683	9 000*	—	—	—	—
Platinum group metals *k*	1 300*	108*	800.0*p*	126.5*p*	—	—
Silver *k*, ore *m*	29 300*	25 000*	—	—	—	—
Asbestos, fibre	735	340	213.6	67.1[1]**s*	—	—
Mica	—	—	—	0.2[1]	0.3	—
Aluminium: bauxite	4 403*	965*	—	1.9*	457.2*q*	—
aluminium	808*	355*	209.4	41.6[1]**s*	6.4	7.0[1]**s*
Antimony: ore	6**m*	na	—	—	—	—
metal	na	na	3.4	1.6**s*	—	7.0[1]**s*
Beryl	1**r*	na	—	—	—	—
Cadmium	2	—	0.9	0.2[1]*	0.2	—

k '000 fine troy oz. *l* '000 carats. *m* metal content. *p* total for available countries. *q* imports from Greece only. *r* cobbed; only 10–12% BeO. *s* incl. re-exports or imports for re-export.

continued

PRODUCTION, EXPORTS AND IMPORTS *continued*

9. NON-FERROUS MINERALS AND METALS—*continued*

	Production		Exports		Imports	
Chrome: ore	1 317**m*	544**m*	659.3	15.8[1]*	—	—
metal	na	na	14.5	—	—	—
Cobalt, metal	1	na	0.2	2.5[1]	—	na
Copper: ore	717*m*	na	—	—	—	—
metal	649	324	101.2	44.8[1]*	36.7	—
Lead: ore	na	na				
metal	332*	207*	103.0	26.2[1]	45.5	17.6[1]
Magnesium:						
magnesite	—	—	—	—	105.2	40.1[1]
metal/salts	32**x*	47**x*	2.8	1.7[1]	—	—
Manganese: ore	7 112*	4 658*	1 007.6[1]	866.6[1]	—	—
metal	na	na	61.3	—	—	—
Mercury *f*	1 264	424	207.9	191.0[1]	—	—
Molybdenum *f*: ore	5 967*m**	na	—	—	—	—
metal	na	na	4 369.0	—	—	—
Nickel, ore	83*m*	na	—	—	—	—
Tin: ore	na	na	—	—	—	—
metal	22*	10*	0.2	2.1[1]*s*	6.4	16.9[1]**s*
Tungsten, ore	11	8	—	—	8.0*t*	—
Zinc: ore	432**m*	na	—	37.0[1]	—	—
metal	497[1]	242*	122.0	35.5[1]	70.1	47.4[1]
Zirconium minerals	na	na	—	—	—	—

f metric tons. *m* metal content. *s* incl. re-exports or imports for re-export. *t* imports from China P.R. only. *x* primary magnesium only.

10. CHEMICALS*n* AND FERTILIZERS

	Production		Exports		Imports	
Organic chemicals:						
Benzene	637		120.2		—	
Butadiene	na		na		na	
Ethylene	na		na		na	
Methanol	848[2]		36.9		—	
Phenol	455		14.3		—	
Phthalic anhydride	85[1]		2.2		0.5	
Styrene monomer	na		na		na	
Urea	220[1]		19.5		—	

continued

10. CHEMICALS*n* AND FERTILIZERS—*continued*

	Production		Exports		Imports	
Inorganic chemicals:						
Ammonia	na		na		na	
Carbon black	442[2]		13.4		16.5	
Chlorine	1 458[2]*		na		na	
Nitric acid	na		na		na	
Sodium carbonate	2 719		74.5		190.1	
Sodium hydroxide	1 168		29.7		191.0	
Sulphuric acid	7 677		79.1		—	
Plastics:						
Polyamides	na		na		na	
Polyethylene	na		—		4.7	
Polyvinyl chloride	106[1]		—		28.3	
Fertilizers:						
Phosphates	11 167**p*	4 493**p*	2 977.5*y*	988.5[1]*y*	—	—
Potash	2 200**w*	588**w*	857.3	46.0[1]	7.9	
Pyrites	1 714*x*	na	1 063.5	—	—	—
Sulphur: native	982*	na	} 135.0	29.7[1]	85.4	12.5[1]
recovered	417*	163[1]*				

n data not available for years 1953–5. *p* incl. apatite. *w* K_2O content. *x* sulphur content. *y* apatite.

11. INDUSTRY

	Production		Exports		Imports	
Aircraft *a*	na	na	na	na	—	—
Alcoholic beverages			na	na	na	na
beer *b*	29 353	18 573				
spirits	na	na				
Cement	66 116	19 146	2 016.0[1]	140.0*n*	67.0[1]	—*n*
Electrical engineering *a*	na	na	—	—	83.6	93.3[1]
Locomotives *c*	2 137	924	—	—	—	169.0
Railway vehicles *a*	na	na	—	—	153.5	—
Machine tools *a*	790[1]	na	34.4	—	91.9	107.9[1]
Merchant ships *g*	428*p*	na	na	na	666.0[1]	—
Motor vehicles			123.5*a*	328.6*a*	—	—
commercial *d*	602	300				
private *d*	186	93				

a million $ U.S. *b* '000 hectolitres. *c* no. of units. *d* no. in thousands *g* '000 G.R.T. *n* excl. trade with other Comecon countries, China P.R., North Vietnam and North Korea. *p* production for home registration only.

UNITED ARAB REPUBLIC

NORTH AFRICA

The United Arab Republic was the title given to the short-lived union between Egypt and Syria in 1958; when Syria withdrew from the union, the name was retained by Egypt.

The Egyptian monarchy terminated in 1953, and the country was declared a republic. Colonel Nasser assumed the presidency in 1956, and, with foreign aid, effected flood-control of the Nile thus providing great advances in agricultural efficiency and the development of hydro-electric power. The Six-Days' War in 1967 led to a destructive interruption in the country's progress, the closure of the Suez Canal, and Israeli occupation of the Gaza Strip and the Sinai Peninsula.

AREA: 1 000 000 sq. km. (386 200 sq. miles)

LAND USE: (percentage of total)	*1965*	*1954*
Arable and orchard	2.7	2.6
Permanent meadow and pasture	—	—
Forest and woodland	—	—
City areas, waste and other land	97.3	97.4

POPULATION: 30 083 419 (1966 census)

Largest city: AL QĀHIRAH (Cairo), capital; population: 4 219 853 (city proper, 1966)

Distribution of working population (1960)

Total working population: 7 769 067 *a*

U.N. group no.		*Percentage*
0	Agriculture, forestry, fishing and hunting	56.7
1	Mining and quarrying	0.3
2/3	Manufacturing	9.1
4	Construction	2.0
5	Electricity, gas, water and sanitary services	0.5
6	Commerce	8.1
7	Transport, storage and communications	3.3
8	Services	17.3
9	Others (incl. unemployed)	2.7

		Year(s)
Life expectancy at birth (years): male	51.6	} 1960
female	53.8	
Infant mortality (per '000)	113.2*	1965
Crude birth rate (per '000)	41.4*	1965
Crude death rate (per '000)	14.0*	1965
Accidental deaths (per 100 000 population)		
caused by motor vehicles	0.1*	1965
due to other causes	39.0*	1965
Population per physician	2 380	1964
Population per hospital bed	560 *b*	1966
School enrolment: age 5–19 years (percentage)	50	1963–4 av.
age over 19 years (per 100 000 population)	540	1963–5 av.

a excl. nomads and foreigners. *b* government hospitals only.

COMMUNICATIONS		*Year(s)*
Motor vehicles in use ('000s): private	91.9	} 1963–5 av.
commercial	23.4	
Railway track (km.)	4 231	1964
Mail per capita: domestic	9	} 1963–5 av.
foreign received	2	
foreign sent	2	
Telephones (per '000 urban population)	1.1*	1967
Radio receivers (per '000 population)	59	1963–5 av.
Television sets (per '000 population)	9.2	1963–5 av.
Daily newspapers (per '000 population)	15*	1964

FINANCE

Currency unit: The Egyptian pound

Exchange rates	*1965*	*1960*	*1950 a*	*1938 a*
Per $ U.S.	0.35	0.35	0.35	0.21
Per £ sterling	0.98	0.98	0.98	1.01

		Year(s)
National Income (million $ U.S.)	2 370	1958
G.N.P. per capita ($ U.S.)	160	1966
Foreign trade (percentage of G.D.P.)	32	1963–4 av.

a selling rate.

continued

UNITED ARAB REPUBLIC *continued*

TRADING

Total trade (in million $ U.S.)	*1965*	*1955*	*1938*
Exports (f.o.b.)	604	419	147
Imports (c.i.f.)	933	525	184

Main trading partners (percentage of total value)

Exports	*1965*	*1955*	*1938*	*Imports*	*1965*	*1955*	*1938*
U.S.S.R.	22	5	1	U.S.A.	20	12	7
Czechoslovakia	10	6	3	Germany F.R.	9	10	10 d
China P.R.	8	6	na	U.S.S.R.	9	1	1
Germany F.R.	6	6	} 11	India	6	4	2
Germany D.R.	4	1		Italy	6	8	8
Italy	5	5	6	France	5	9	5
India	4	9	5	U.K.	5	13	23

Distribution of trade (percentage of total value)

Exports	*1965*	*1955*	*1938**
Crude materials and fuels	65	83	na
(textile fibres and waste)	(57)	(79)	(75)
Manufactured goods	20	6	na
(textile yarn and clothing)	(17)	(4)	(na)
Food	14	10	6
Imports			
Manufactured goods	41	53	na
(machinery and transport equipment)	(23)	(25)	(15)
Food	24	11	10
(cereals and preparations)	(16)	(—)	(—)
Crude materials and fuel	18	18	na
Chemicals	13	12	11

d incl. Germany D.R.

PRODUCTION, EXPORTS AND IMPORTS

Years: **1963–5 average** and *1953–5 average* Units: '000 metric tons unless otherwise indicated

1. CEREALS, etc.

	Production		Exports		Imports	
Barley	**135.0**	*115.3*	**1.2**	*0.3*	**1.7**	*5.2*
Maize (corn)	**1 967.3***	*1 711.7*	**1.0**	*0.4*	**247.1**	*3.2*
Millets/sorghum	**736.3***	*556.0*	**0.4**	*1.1*	**11.9**	*2.2*
Potatoes	**412.3**	*198.0*	**62.9**	*25.5*	**14.1**	*21.1*
Rice	**2 039.0***	*1 026.7*	**412.5**	*77.3*	—	—
Sweet potatoes/yams	**85.3**	*42.3*				
Wheat	**1 531.0**	*1 575.7*	**1.0**	*0.2*	**1 004.1**	*159.0*

2. FRUIT, etc.

	Production		Exports		Imports	
Apples	**6.0**	*3.7*	—	—	**2.4**[2]	*8.1*
Apricots	**7.0**	*4.1*[1]	—	—	—	—
Bananas	**56.7**	*37.5*[2]	**1.0**	*0.4*	—	—
Coconuts	—	—	—	—	—	*0.7*
Dates	**384.3**	*332.3*	—	—	**5.8***	*22.4*
Figs	**4.0**	*9.7*	—	—	na	*2.0*
Grapes	**95.3**	*90.7*	**0.1**	*0.5*[2]	—	*0.1*
Lemons	**73.7**	*37.0*	**0.4***n*	—	—	—
Oranges	**389.7**	*315.3*	**7.5**	*0.5*	—	*5.6*
Olives	**9.3**	*3.7*				
Peaches	**5.3**	—	—	—	—	—
Pears	**12.7**	*4.0*	—	—	—	*0.2*
Plums	**1.7**	—	—	—	—	—
Raisins	—	—	—	—	**1.1**	*2.0*
Tomatoes	**1 163.7**	*509.0*				
Wine *b*	na	—	**13.1**	—	**0.4**	*4.3*

b '000 hectolitres. *n* incl. grapefruit.

3. BEVERAGES, FOREST PRODUCTS, etc.

	Production		Exports		Imports	
Cocoa	—	—	—	—	**1.0**	*0.4*
Coffee	—	—	—	—	**3.5**	*4.3*
Sugar: cane	**4 744.0**	*3 722.7*				
raw	**408.9**	*301.7*	**18.6**	*2.9*	**49.2**	*26.4*
Tea	—	—	—	—	**26.1**	*17.9*
Tobacco: leaf	—	—	—	—	**13.5**	*11.0*
cigars	**1.3***e*	na	}			
cigarettes	**12 535.0***e*	na	} **0.3**	*0.1*[2]	—	*0.2*[2]
tobacco/snuff	**3.8**	na	}			
Softwood *j*	na	*7.8*	—	— }	**753.0**	{ *346.2*
Hardwood *j*	**147.0***[1]	*11.0*	—	— }		{ *255.3*
Wood pulp	—	*2.9**	—	—	**49.1**	*7.8*
Newsprint	—*	*10.0*[2]	—	—	**42.0**	*20.3*
Other paper	**101.7***	*20.2*[1]	—	—	**37.3**	*48.7*

e no. in millions. *j* '000 cu. metres of roundwood equivalent.

4. VEGETABLE OILSEEDS AND OILS

	Production		Exports		Imports	
Castor seed	—	—	—	—	**0.01**	*0.05*[2]
Castor oil	—	—	—	—	**0.08**	*0.28*
Coconut oil	—	—	—	—	**1.92**	*3.51*
Cottonseed	**923.0**	*641.0*	—	—	**5.41**	*12.37*
Cottonseed oil	na	na	**0.44**	*8.31*	**40.82**	*1.59*
Groundnuts	**32.9**	*17.7*	**4.76**	*3.93*	**0.08**	*0.80*
Groundnut oil	na	na	—	*0.06*	—	*0.25*
Linseed	**11.7**	*4.3*	—	—	**0.20**	—
Linseed oil	na	na	—	*0.03*[2]	**5.30**	*0.77*
Olive oil	na	*1.0*[1]*	—	—	**0.53**	*1.36*
Palm kernel oil	—	—	—	—	—	*0.02*
Palm oil	—	—	—	—	**0.20**	*0.51*
Sesame seed	**23.9**	*13.0**	**3.62**	*0.30*	**7.15**	*2.27*
Soya bean oil	—	—	**0.01**†	—	**13.87***	—

5. LIVESTOCK‡, ANIMAL PRODUCTS, etc.

	Production		Exports		Imports	
Chickens *d*	**22 676.3**	*61 406.0*[2]				
Cattle *d*	**1 587.0**	*1 353.0*	**0.1**	—	**48.0**	*35.3*
Goats *d*	**784.0**	*739.5*[2]	} **4.6**	na	**23.6**	na
Sheep *d*	**1 772.0**	*1 226.5*[2]	}			
Horses *d*	**54.3**	*41.0*[2]	—	—	—	—
Pigs *d*	**12.0**	*19.0*[2]	—	—	—	—

continued

5. LIVESTOCK‡, ANIMAL PRODUCTS, etc.—*continued*

	Production		Exports		Imports	
Meat‡: 'A'	**245.0**	*196.0*[2]	—	—	**6.3**	*3.5*
'B'	**76.7**	*44.0*	—	—	**2.1**	—
Butter	**11.0**	na	—	—	**0.6**	*2.3*
Cheese	**254.7**	na	**0.2**	*0.2*	**2.7**	*7.4*
Eggs	**42.3**	*30.6*	**0.1**	—	—	—
Fish	**112.3**	*57.4*	**2.1**	*0.4*[1]*	**6.8**	*12.0*[1]*
Milk	**379.0***	*296.3*	—	—	**74.4***	*10.2*
Hides/skins	na	na	—	*0.4*[2]	**4.1**	*0.6*[2]
Wool	**1.8**	*2.0**	—	*0.1*	**1.4**	*0.6*

d no. in thousands.

6. FIBRES, TEXTILES, etc.

	Production		Exports		Imports	
Agaves (sisal, etc.)	—	—	—	—	**0.2**	*0.2*
Cotton lint	**488.7***	*333.3*	**303.5**	*303.9*	—	—
Flax fibre	**9.3**	*3.3*	**7.9**	*3.0*	—	—
Jute	—	—	**0.3**[2]†	—	**18.5**	*1.6*
Rubber, natural	—	—	—	—	**4.2**	*0.7*
Silk *f*	**12.3**	*2.0*[2]	—	—	**48.0**	*52.0*
Cotton: yarn	**130.6**	*65.6*	**32.5**	*9.0*	—	*0.1*
woven fabrics	**85.7**	*45.4**	**14.1**	*0.9*	—	*0.9*
Rayon: fibre/yarn	**12.2**	*6.3*	**2.7**	—	—	*2.7*[2]
woven fabrics	**8.9**[2]	—	**0.6**[2]	—	—	*0.2*
Non-cellulosic fibre/yarn	**0.5**	—	—	—	**0.1**	—
Wool: yarn	**9.5**	*2.6*	—	—	—	*0.4*
woven fabrics	**5.7**[2]	*2.9*	—	—	**0.1***p*	*0.7*

f metric tons. *p* excl. blankets.

7. FUEL AND POWER

	Production		Exports		Imports	
Coal, 'A'‡	**10**[2]	—	—	—	**246**	*100*
Coke	—	—	—	—	**172**	*9*
Electricity *h*: total	**5 013**	*1 410*[1]				
hydro	**1 575**	*20*[1]				
thermal	**3 438**	*1 390*[1]				
Oil, crude	**6 153**	*1 830*[1]	**2 700**	na	**4 350**	*970*[1]
Petroleum, refined	**7 020**	*2 460*[1]	**1 430**	*10*[1]	**773**	*1 210*[1]
Rare earths *f*	na	*5q*	—	—	—	—

f metric tons. *h* million kWh. *q* monazite.

8. IRON AND STEEL

	Production		Exports		Imports	
Iron ore	**481**	*1*	—	—	—	—
Pig iron	**190**	—	—	—	**82**	*4*
Steel ingots/castings	**184**	*59*	—	—	**74**	*3*
Iron/steel scrap	na	na	—	*5*	**42**	*2*
Iron/steel products *a*	na	na	**1**	—[2]	**49**	*26*

a million $ U.S.

9. NON-FERROUS MINERALS AND METALS

	Production		Exports		Imports	
Gold *k*, ore	—	*12.70m*	—	—	na	*6.77u*
Platinum group metals *k*	—	—	—	—	—	*0.30*
Silver *k*, bullion	—	—	—	—	—	*9.70*
Asbestos: fibre	**1.56**	*0.07*	—	*0.08*[2]	**5.29**	*1.98*
manufactured	na	na	—	—	**0.55**	*0.32*
Mica	—	—	—	—	na	—
Aluminium	—	—	—	—	**5.75***n*	*8.57*[1]
Chrome, ore	—	*0.53m*	—	*0.28*[2]	—	*0.04u*
Copper, metal	—	—	—	*0.08*†	**5.69**[1]	*2.84*
Lead, ore	**0.17***m*	*0.17m*	—	—	**4.70**[2]*pu*	*0.75u*
Magnesium: dolomite	—	—	—	—	**2.96***q*	*3.24q*
metal/salts	—‡	—‡	—	—	na	*0.41*
Manganese, ore	**225.42***	*225.00**	**156.10**	*213.73*	—	—
Mercury *f*	—	—	—	—	na	*1.00*
Nickel, metal	—	—	—	—	na	*0.03*
Tin, metal	—	—	—	—	**0.91**	*0.24*
Titanium minerals	**0.19**	*2.53*	—	—	—	—
Tungsten, ore	—	*0.01*	—	*0.01*[2]	—	—
Zinc, ore	na	na	na	*1.24*[2]	**1.65***t*	*3.74*
Zirconium minerals	**0.03**	*0.15*	—	—	—	—

f metric tons. *k* '000 fine troy oz. *m* metal content. *n* excl. aluminium sulphates. *p* excl. semi-manufactures. *q* incl. magnesite. *t* unwrought metal only. *u* metal.

continued

na: data not available. — negligible or nil. [1] one year only. [2] two year average. * estimate. ‡ see appendix. † re-exports.

PRODUCTION, EXPORTS AND IMPORTS *continued*

10. CHEMICALS *n* AND FERTILIZERS

	Production		Exports		Imports	
Organic chemicals:						
Benzene	na		—		na	
Phenol	na		—		na	
Other organic chemicals	—		—		na	
Inorganic chemicals:						
Carbon black	—		—		na	
Sodium carbonate	—		—		na	
Sodium hydroxide	**17.6**[2]		—		**45.0**[2]*	
Other inorganic chemicals	na		—		na	
Plastics	na		na		na	
Fertilizers:						
Phosphates	**606.3**	*555.1*	**373.8**	*398.4*	—	—
Potash	—	—	—	—	na	*0.7*
Pyrites	na	na	**88.8**	na	—	—
Sulphur: native	**0.2***	na	} —	—		
recovered	**2.9**	*3.8*[1]	}		**9.8**	*5.8*

n data not available for years 1953–5.

11. INDUSTRY

	Production		Exports		Imports	
Aircraft *a*	—	—	—	—	**5.5**	*2.0*
Alcoholic beverages			—	—	—	*0.9a*
beer *b*	**206.1**	*97.7*				
spirits *b*	na	*16.0*[1]*				
Cement	**2 487.7**	*1 235.0*	**229.0**	*102.3*	**120.3**	*7.3*
Electrical engineering *a*	**96.6**[2]	na	—	—	**60.6**	*25.2*[2]
Railway vehicles *a*	—	—	—	—	**12.6**	*6.0*
Machine tools *a*	na	na	—	—	na	*5.5*[2]
Merchant ships *g*	**6.0**	na	—	—	**1.0**	*6.6*
Motor vehicles			—	—	**52.3***a*	*19.5a*
commercial *d*	**1.9***p*	—				
private *d*	**4.5***p*	—				

a million $ U.S. *b* '000 hectolitres. *d* no. in thousands. *g* '000 G.R.T. *p* assembly of imported parts.

UNITED KINGDOM

EUROPE

The United Kingdom, comprising England, Scotland, Wales and Northern Ireland, is a constitutional monarchy, but executive and legislative power are vested in the parliament. The U.K. is a member of the European Free Trade Association and has applied (1971) to join the European Economic Community.

AREA: 229 827 sq. km. (88 736 sq. miles)

LAND USE: (percentage of total)	*1965*	*1955*
Arable and orchard	30.7	29.1
Permanent meadow and pasture	49.7	50.4
Forest and woodland	7.4	6.6
City areas, waste and other land	12.2	13.9

POPULATION: 55 068 000 (1967 estimate)

Largest city: LONDON, capital; population: 7 913 600 (1966)

Distribution of working population (1951)

Total working population: 24 856 500 (1966)

U.N. group no.		*Percentage*
0	Agriculture, forestry, fishing and hunting	3.1
1	Mining and quarrying	2.3
2/3	Manufacturing	34.8
4	Construction	7.8
5	Electricity, gas, water and sanitary services	1.7
6	Commerce	16.0
7	Transport, storage and communications	6.6
8	Services	27.0
9	Others	0.7

E/W: England and Wales; S: Scotland; NI: Northern Ireland

			Year(s)
Life expectancy at birth (years): male		68.1	} 1963–5 av.
female		74.2	}
Infant mortality (per '000)		19.6	1965
Crude birth rate (per '000)		18.3	1965
Crude death rate (per '000)		11.5	1965
Accidental deaths (per 100 000 population) caused by motor vehicles	E/W	15.7	} 1965
	S	15.2	
	NI	14.0	
due to other causes	E/W	23.6	
	S	32.4	
	NI	21.5	
Population per physician		830	1964
Population per hospital bed *a*	E/W	100	} 1966
	S	90	
	NI	90	
School enrolment: age 5–19 years (percentage)	E/W	93	} 1963–4 av.
	S	89	
	NI	99	
age over 19 years (per 100 000 population)	E/W	434	} 1963–5 av.
	S	564	
	NI	507	

a government hospitals only.

COMMUNICATIONS

		Year(s)
Motor vehicles in use ('000s): private	8 483.0	} 1963–5 av.
commercial	1 757.9	}
Railway track (km.)	24 006	1965
Mail per capita: domestic	197	} 1963–5 av.
foreign received	8	
foreign sent	10	
Telephones (per '000 urban population)	20.7	1967
Radio licences (per '000 population)	297	1963–5 av.
Television licences (per '000 population)	243.3	1963–5 av.
Daily newspapers (per '000 population)	506.5	1962–4 av.

FINANCE

Currency unit: The pound sterling

Exchange rates	*1965*	*1960*	*1950*	*1938*
Per $ U.S.	0.357	0.357	0.357	0.213

The pound is an important currency in international monetary transactions. Its devaluation in 1967 affected particularly the countries of the Sterling Area, many of which also devalued so that their currencies should remain pegged to the pound.

		Year(s)
National Income (million $ U.S.)	79 213	1965
G.N.P. per capita ($ U.S.)	1 620	1966
Rate of increase of G.N.P. per capita	2.6	1960–4 av.
Foreign trade (percentage of G.D.P.)	31	1963–5 av.

TRADING

Total trade (in million $ U.S.)	*1965*	*1955*	*1938*
Exports (f.o.b.)	13 723	8 613	2 741
Imports (c.i.f.)	16 103	10 029	4 582

Main trading partners (percentage of total value)

Exports	*1965*	*1955*	*1938*	*Imports*	*1965*	*1955*	*1938*
U.S.A.	11	6	4	U.S.A.	12	11	13
Australia	6	10	8	Canada	8	9	9
South Africa	6	6	8	Netherlands	5	3	3
Germany F.R.	5	3	4 d	Germany F.R.	5	2	3 d
Sweden	5	3	2	Australia	4	7	8
Canada	4	5	5	Sweden	4	4	3
Netherlands	4	4	3	South Africa	4	2	2

d incl. Germany D.R.

Distribution of trade (percentage of total value)

Exports a	*1965*	*1955*	*1938**
Manufactured goods	75	74	73
(machinery)	(27)	(22)	(9)
(transport equipment)	(15)	(15)	(8)
(textiles and clothing)	(7)	(12)	(18)
Chemicals	9	8	5
Food	3	3	3
Imports			
Manufactured goods	34	20	na
(machinery and transport equipment)	(11)	(4)	(1)
(non-ferrous metals)	(6)	(6)	(4)
Crude materials and fuels	29	38	na
(petroleum and products)	(11)	(9)	(5)
Food	27	34	41
(fruit and vegetables)	(5)	(6)	(5)
Chemicals	5	3	na

a these are percentages of national‡ exports which comprised 97% of the general exports in 1965, 94% in 1955, and 84% in 1938. *d* incl. Germany D.R.

continued

na: data not available. — negligible or nil. [1] one year only. [2] two year average. * estimate. ‡ see appendix. † re-exports.

UNITED KINGDOM *continued*

PRODUCTION, EXPORTS AND IMPORTS

Years: **1963–5 average** and *1953–5 average* Units: '000 metric tons unless otherwise indicated

1. CEREALS, etc.

	Production 1963–5	Production 1953–5	Exports 1963–5	Exports 1953–5	Imports 1963–5	Imports 1953–5
Barley	7 473.0	2 608.0	141.4	64.6	328.0	1 115.2
Maize (corn)	—	—	4.6†	0.2†	3 400.5	1 416.2
Millets/sorghum	—	—	1.1†	0.4†	388.4	210.5
Oats	1 346.3	2 699.0	7.9s	0.2	26.8	62.1
Potatoes	7 108.0	7 404.7	87.0s	83.9s	322.9	244.8
Rice	—	—	0.8†	0.5†	111.9	77.3
Rye	22.7	42.0	—	—	5.9	1.2[2]
Wheat	3 638.0	2 725.3	51.8s	1.7†	4 086.9	4 055.5

s incl. re-exports.

2. FRUIT, etc.

	Production 1963–5	Production 1953–5	Exports 1963–5	Exports 1953–5	Imports 1963–5	Imports 1953–5
Apples	645.7	555.0	3.3†	2.8†	231.7	149.0
Bananas	—	—	0.8†	0.6†	365.3	290.3
Cherries	16.0	19.6	—	—	na	1.8
Coconuts	—	—	0.2†	0.4†	20.6	27.1
Dates	—	—	0.8†	3.3†	13.6	13.5
Figs	—	—	—	—	na	3.2
Grapes	—	—	0.8†	1.5†	57.7	35.6
Lemons	—	—	0.6[2]†	0.2†	34.2	30.6
Oranges	—	—	4.8†	13.4†	401.3	397.0
Other citrus fruit	—	—	3.1[2]†	0.9†	67.9	51.4
Peaches	—	—	—	—	na	13.2
Pears	73.0	45.3	1.8†	2.4†	59.5	59.6
Pineapples	—	—	—	—	na	4.3
Plums	69.0	89.8	—	—	na	6.6
Raisins	—	—	0.3†	4.6†	117.7	139.2
Tomatoes	78.7	112.0				
Wine *b*	—	—	53.6†	41.0†	1 301.4	546.0

b '000 hectolitres.

3. BEVERAGES, FOREST PRODUCTS, etc.

	Production 1963–5	Production 1953–5	Exports 1963–5	Exports 1953–5	Imports 1963–5	Imports 1953–5
Cocoa	—	—	2.9†	7.3†	92.2	133.0
Coffee	—	—	2.8†	4.4†	71.0	32.8
Sugar: beet	6 156.3	4 860.7				
raw	882.3	700.3	425.4s	748.9s	2 346.8	2 606.1
Tea	—	—	17.7†	15.2†	250.7	232.0
Tobacco: leaf	—	—	1.9†	2.7†	139.7	146.9
cigars	461.0e	119.0[1]e	13.0 (cigars, cigarettes, tobacco/snuff)	19.7[2]	—	0.3[2]
cigarettes	114 437.0e	112 378.0[1]e				
tobacco/snuff	15.9	16.5[1]				
Softwood *j*	1 476.7	1 735.0	—	3.8	14 709.0	11 824.4
Hardwood *j*	1 864.3	1 541.0	5.0	11.3	1 972.3	1 703.0
Wood pulp	278.3*	133.7	—	—	2 889.1	1 953.3
Newsprint	741.7	621.3	14.1	132.7	644.7	326.7
Other paper	3 621.0	2 398.7	171.3	110.7	1 106.3	549.2

e no. in millions. *j* '000 cu. metres of roundwood equivalent. *s* incl. re-exports.

4. VEGETABLE OILSEEDS AND OILS

	Production 1963–5	Production 1953–5	Exports 1963–5	Exports 1953–5	Imports 1963–5	Imports 1953–5
Castor seed	—	—	—	—	20.25	19.13
Castor oil	na	na	1.00	1.20	17.63	11.96
Copra	—	—	0.02†	0.20[2]†	63.91	91.10
Coconut oil	na	na	1.26†	3.40†	44.34	34.97
Cottonseed	—	—	—	—	132.46	160.40
Cottonseed oil	na	na	2.07	2.05	17.05	19.61
Groundnuts	—	—	2.32†	5.53†	146.09	360.27
Groundnut oil	na	na	7.17	13.09	55.74	36.33
Linseed	—	2.30	0.17†	—	117.78	28.37
Linseed oil	na	na	2.72	10.07	43.76	97.48
Olive oil	na	na	0.08†	0.93†	2.69	2.99
Palm kernels	—	—	0.06†	0.53†	203.99	373.10
Palm kernel oil	na	na	7.12	19.19	0.33	0.19
Palm oil	—	—	0.65†	2.08†	115.68	201.42
Rapeseed	—	—	—	—	17.46	8.13
Rapeseed oil	na	na	0.05	0.04	1.40	0.75
Sesame seed	—	—	—	1.23†	—	10.30
Soya beans	—	—	—	—	283.37	64.60
Soya bean oil	na	na	1.01	4.35	21.33	0.13
Sunflower seed oil	—	—	—	—	3.63	0.92n
Tung oil	—	—	0.26†	—	5.26	10.29

n incl. other minor vegetable oils.

5. LIVESTOCK‡, ANIMAL PRODUCTS, etc.

	Production 1963–5	Production 1953–5	Exports 1963–5	Exports 1953–5	Imports 1963–5	Imports 1953–5
Chickens *d*	110 629	83 843				
Cattle *d*	11 762q	10 617q	265.0	2.3	619.0	551.2
dairy cows *d*	4 963	4 520q				
Goats *d*	21*q	39[2]*q	407.7 (Goats and Sheep)	na	272.6	na
Sheep *d*	29 637q	22 759q				
Horses *d*	160*	325*				
Pigs *d*	7 406q	5 753q	31.9	1.2	1.2	0.8
Bacon/ham	2 028 (Bacon/ham and Meat 'A')	1 502	1.6s	0.9s	397.5	311.7
Meat‡: 'A'			18.8s	3.8†	698.0	703.0
'B'	534	237	5.2s	2.3	155.8	88.0
Butter	39	25	2.1s	2.3s	447.7	294.8
Cheese	111	79	2.7s	2.2s	148.1	137.8
Eggs	822	543	2.7s	0.8s	15.5	79.2
Fish	994	1 098	58.6	65.1[1]*	731.7	386.4[1]*
Milk	12 620	10 849	271.4s	90.7	882.5	592.4
Whale/sperm oil	5	85	—	—	34.9	112.1p
Hides/skins	na	82	—	12.4[2]	81.8	109.2[2]
Wool	38	32	32.7s	36.2s	177.5	223.3

d no. in thousands. *p* produced mainly on factory ships and land stations of British registration. *q* on farms only. *s* incl. re-exports.

6. FIBRES, TEXTILES, etc.

	Production 1963–5	Production 1953–5	Exports 1963–5	Exports 1953–5	Imports 1963–5	Imports 1953–5
Abaca	—	—	—	—	17.4	16.1
Agaves (sisal, etc.)	—	—	1.2†	0.5†	70.5	68.5
Cotton lint	—	—	7.0†	3.9†	226.5	339.3
Flax fibre	na	6.8	1.7	1.1	44.2	42.3
Hemp fibre	—	—	—	—	4.1	11.6
Jute	—	—	2.7†	1.1†	124.1	145.3
Rubber: natural	—	—	22.7†	32.6†	201.9	277.2
synthetic	152.5	—	43.2	—	56.0s	14.9
Silk *f*	—	—	43.3†	0.3†	422.3	266.3
Cotton: yarn	224.0	360.0q	6.0	17.8	16.2	4.2s
woven fabrics	149.5*	208.8	29.2	70.4	98.2	24.7s
Rayon: fibre/yarn	230.8	190.1[1]	50.6	23.0[2]	12.8	2.8[2]
woven fabrics	90.5	73.2r	16.3	16.3	14.2	6.0s
Non-cellulosic fibre/yarn	126.7	15.2	34.6	na	22.3	na
Wool: yarn	251.2	243.7	14.5	12.2	2.1	1.4
woven fabrics	106.7*	na	22.9	28.8	9.1	4.0

f metric tons. *q* incl. yarn of cotton waste. *r* incl. mixtures. *s* incl. imports for re-export.

7. FUEL AND POWER

	Production 1963–5	Production 1953–5	Exports 1963–5	Exports 1953–5	Imports 1963–5	Imports 1953–5
Coal, 'A'‡	195 387	225 170	5 941	13 520	12	5 019
Coke	na	na	1 591	1 632	—	—
Electricity *h*: total	184 155	78 720				
hydro	4 103	1 900				
nuclear	10 217	—				
thermal	169 835	76 820				
Natural gas *i*	180	—	—	—	250	—
Oil, crude	113	150[1]	680v	na	59 236	27 300[1]
Petroleum, refined	52 700	25 770[1]	9 410	6 090[1]	18 560	8 390[1]
Rare earths *f*	—	—	—	—	na	40t
Uranium	—	—	—	14u	—	11u

f metric tons. *h* million kWh. *i* million cu. metres. *t* compounds only *u* radium compounds in grams. *v* incl. partly refined.

8. IRON AND STEEL

	Production 1963–5	Production 1953–5	Exports 1963–5	Exports 1953–5	Imports 1963–5	Imports 1953–5
Iron ore	4 266m	4 447m	—	1	17 537	12 007
Pig iron	16 705	12 032	105	40	557	671
Steel ingots/castings	25 659	18 939	69	3	250	379
Iron/steel scrap	na	na	835	20	46	1 182
Iron/steel products *a*	na	na	611	400	242	176

a million $ U.S. *m* metal content.

9. NON-FERROUS MINERALS AND METALS

	Production 1963–5	Production 1953–5	Exports 1963–5	Exports 1953–5	Imports 1963–5	Imports 1953–5
Diamonds *a*	—	—	433.47[2]†	—	457.14[2]	116.09v
Gold *k*: ore *m*	—	—	—	—	2.86‡	146.70
bullion/coins etc.	—	—	39 490.30†	6 335.50†	38 648.1	14 758.58
Platinium group metals *k*	—	—	849.72†	488.73†	104.64t	79.83
Silver *k*: ore *m*	—	—	—	—	75.0[2]	3 847.33
bullion	na	28.40*	17 018.02s	12 119.02s	33 557.1	28 765.40
Asbestos: fibre	—	—	6.71†	4.63†	175.02	127.87
manufactured	na	na	75.28s	149.16s	23.74	6.30
Mica	—	—	3.46†	1.10†	10.00	6.24
Aluminium: bauxite	—	—	—	—	426.13	330.77
alumina	—	—	19.48†	15.76†	7.82	0.02
aluminium	33.16	29.45	99.89	86.46	348.64	213.86
Antimony: ore	—	—	—	—	13.20[2]	13.10
metal	na	na	1.28	1.38	—	—
Beryl	—	—	—	—	na	0.18v
Cadmium	0.18	0.16	—	0.04	1.46	0.65
Chrome: ore	—	—	—	—	197.18	151.41
metal	na	na	0.56	3.15	52.64	20.82
Cobalt, metal	na	na	0.52*	11.69	2.63[2]	47.59
Copper: ore	—	—	—	—	0.78	—
metal	na	—	170.07†	98.93†	544.19	379.36
Lead: ore *m*	0.17	8.17	—	—	25.57	—
metal	0.18	6.64	49.88	12.31	185.41	201.68
Magnesium: dolomite	3 556.19	na	—	—	12.15	—
magnesite	—	—	—	—	78.19	29.78
metal/salts	5.03x	5.31x	2.38	17.06	9.36	20.16[1]
Manganese: ore	—	—	—	—	448.34	473.74
metal	na	na	8.22*	4.25	101.72	16.53
Mercury *f*	—	—	—	23.00†	703.00	597.20
Molybdenum *f*: ore	—	—	—	—	6 774.00	5 256.00
metal	na	na	192.00	335.30	82.30	3.70
Nickel: ore	—	—	—	—	61.25	33.78
metal	na	na	36.91	19.84	22.32	12.47
Tin: ore	1.28m	1.04m	—	—	45.05	61.55
metal	17.19	28.31	10.71	12.42	8.66	1.04
Titanium minerals	—	—	1.10†	0.33†	269.20[2]	159.50
Tungsten: ore	—	0.08	0.02	0.03	5.08	4.26
metal	na	na	1.12	0.45	0.23	0.01
Vanadium	—	na	0.04	0.05	0.13	0.27w
Zinc: ore	—	3.10m	0.86	2.21	252.29	189.11
metal	106.16	79.69	20.77	12.38	193.80[2]	151.80
Zirconium minerals	—	—	—	—	41.95	6.55

a million $ U.S. *f* metric tons. *k* '000 fine troy oz. *m* metal content. *s* incl. re-exports. *t* in addition, U.S.$ 48.5 million of ore. *v* incomplete figure. *w* ore. *x* primary magnesium only.

continued

PRODUCTION, EXPORTS AND IMPORTS *continued*

10. CHEMICALS*n* AND FERTILIZERS

	Production	Exports	Imports
Organic chemicals:			
Benzene	162.5[2]	na	na
Butadiene	109.0[1]	na	na
Ethylene	492.3	na	na
Methanol	200.0[1]	9.0	4.1
Phenol	64.9	17.1	5.9[2]
Phthalic anhydride	55.8	na	8.0[2]
Styrene monomer	76.4[1]	na	13.6
Urea	na	na	na
Inorganic chemicals:			
Ammonia	na	4.5	na
Carbon black	148.8	38.6	14.1
Chlorine	na	na	na
Nitric acid	na	na	na
Sodium carbonate	na	188.8	na
Sodium hydroxide	na	170.6	na
Sulphuric acid	3 107.3	24.9	1.1[1]
Plastics:			
Polyamides	na	na	na
Polyethylene	205.5	85.9	19.5
Polyvinyl chloride	172.5	2.5	46.9

continued

10. CHEMICALS AND FERTILIZERS—*continued*

	Production 1963–5	Production 1953–5	Exports 1963–5	Exports 1953–5	Imports 1963–5	Imports 1953–5
Fertilizers:						
Phosphates	—	—	—	—	1 546.5	1 125.3
Potash	—	—	0.1	3.9	770.7	559.2
Pyrites	10.2*x	3.1x	—	—	240.1	502.6
Sulphur	50.2y	46.6[1]y	2.1	1.8	698.0	315.0

n data not available for years 1953–5. *x* sulphur content. *y* recovered sulphur.

11. INDUSTRY

	Production 1963–5	Production 1953–5	Exports 1963–5	Exports 1953–5	Imports 1963–5	Imports 1953–5
Aircraft *a*	1 140.0[1]*	na	158.9	105.7r	49.0	66.0
Alcoholic beverages			na	133.3a	150.6a	71.6a
beer *b*	47 733.0	39 948.3				
spirits	3 435.0bp	837.5bq	287.3a			
Cement	16 022.0	12 087.0	302.0	1 966.7	596.7	257.7
Electrical engineering *a*	6 144.6[2]	na	899.8	506.8[2]	314.4	55.2[2]
Locomotives *c*	705.0	1 191.0[2]	na	36.0	—	—
Railway vehicles *a*	na	na	53.7	119.0	—	3.3
Machine tools *a*	340.0[1]	na	132.1	84.6	92.0	46.2
Merchant ships *g*	1 014.0	1 400.0	190.0	461.9	322.0	46.8
Motor vehicles			1 494.6	720.0	139.1	28.8[2]
commercial *d*	441.2	282.6				
private *d*	1 743.6	753.9				

a million $ U.S. *b* '000 hectolitres. *c* no. of units. *d* no. in thousands. *g* '000 G.R.T. *p* production in England only for 1966/7. *q* production for home consumption in England only in 1961. *r* excl. parts.

UNITED KINGDOM (TERRITORIES)

BAHAMAS—see page 125
BERMUDA—see page 127
BRITISH HONDURAS—see page 130
BRUNEI—see page 130
GIBRALTAR—see page 158
HONG KONG—see page 163
NEW HEBRIDES—see page 190
WEST INDIES ASSOCIATED STATES—see page 233

BRITISH SOLOMON ISLANDS

PACIFIC OCEAN

The British Solomon Islands Protectorate comes under the jurisdiction of the Western Pacific High Commission, the headquarters of which are at Honiara, on the islands.

AREA: 29 785 sq. km. (11 500 sq. miles)

LAND USE: (percentage of total)

	1965	1952
Arable and orchard	4.9	4.9
Permanent meadow and pasture	1.3	1.3
Forest and woodland	89.4	89.4
City areas, waste and other land	4.4	4.4

POPULATION: 144 000 (1967 unofficial estimate)

Capital city: HONIARA; population: 4 300 (city proper, 1964)

FINANCE

Currency unit: The Australian dollar replaced the Australian pound in 1966 at the rate A$1 to A£0.5

Exchange rates (for Australian pounds)	1965	1960	1950	1938
Per $ U.S.	0.45	0.45	0.45	0.26
Per £ sterling	1.25	1.25	1.25	1.25

PRODUCTION AND TRADE

Most of the land is covered with coconut palms and copra accounted for 94% of the exports in 1965. The cultivation of rice is important, and is developing rapidly. Timber, cocoa, sorghum and trochus shell are also exported, and some income is derived from tourism. Imports include foodstuffs, machinery and building materials.

Exports in 1965 amounted to U.S.$ 538 000; imports, to U.S.$ 735 000.

PRODUCTION, EXPORTS AND IMPORTS

Years: **1963–5 average** and *1953–5 average* Units: '000 metric tons unless otherwise indicated

1. CEREALS, etc.

	Production 1963–5	Production 1953–5	Exports 1963–5	Exports 1953–5	Imports 1963–5	Imports 1953–5
Millets/sorghum	na	na	na	na	0.1	—
Rice	na	na	—	—	3.0	1.7
Sweet potatoes/yams	50.0*	na				

2. FRUIT, etc.

	Production 1963–5	Production 1953–5	Exports 1963–5	Exports 1953–5	Imports 1963–5	Imports 1953–5
Coconuts *e*	158.7*	na	na	na	—	—
Wine *b*	—	—	—	—	0.2	—

b '000 hectolitres. *e* no. in millions.

3. BEVERAGES, FOREST PRODUCTS, etc.

	Production 1963–5	Production 1953–5	Exports 1963–5	Exports 1953–5	Imports 1963–5	Imports 1953–5
Cocoa	na	—	0.1	—	—	—
Sugar, raw	—	—	—	—	0.7	0.4
Softwood *j*	3.0	na	2.0	—	—	—
Hardwood *j*	165.7*	na	4.3[1]	—	0.7	—

j '000 cu. metres of roundwood equivalent.

4. VEGETABLE OILSEEDS AND OILS

	Production 1963–5	Production 1953–5	Exports 1963–5	Exports 1953–5	Imports 1963–5	Imports 1953–5
Copra	25.43	na	24.07	18.80	—	—
Linseed oil	—	—	—	—	na	na

5. LIVESTOCK‡, ANIMAL PRODUCTS, etc.

	Production 1963–5	Production 1953–5	Exports 1963–5	Exports 1953–5	Imports 1963–5	Imports 1953–5
Cattle *d*	4.3*	3.0[1]	—	—	—	—
Pigs *d*	5.0*	na	—	—	—	—
Fish	na	na	—	—	0.2	—
Milk	—	—	—	—	1.5	—

d no. in thousands.

7. FUEL AND POWER

	Production 1963–5	Production 1953–5	Exports 1963–5	Exports 1953–5	Imports 1963–5	Imports 1953–5
Petroleum, refined	—	—	—	—	7	—

9. NON-FERROUS MINERALS AND METALS

	Production 1963–5	Production 1953–5	Exports 1963–5	Exports 1953–5	Imports 1963–5	Imports 1953–5
Gold *k*, ore	0.16m	—	0.22p	—	—	—

k '000 fine troy oz. *m* metal content. *p* bullion.

11. INDUSTRY

For cement data see Fiji.

continued

na: data not available. — negligible or nil. [1] one year only. [2] two year average. * estimate. ‡ see appendix. † re-exports.

CAYMAN ISLANDS — CARIBBEAN SEA

The Cayman Islands, which had been administered by the Governor of Jamaica were placed under the jurisdiction of the British Colonial Office when Jamaica became independent in 1962.

AREA: 260 sq. km. (100 sq. miles)

LAND USE: (percentage of total)

	1965
Arable and orchard	1.9
Permanent meadow and pasture	8.9
Forest and woodland	25.0
City areas, waste and other land	64.2

POPULATION: 9 000 (1967 U.N. estimate)

Capital city: GEORGETOWN; population: 2 573 (1960)
Total working population: 3 159 (1960)

		Year
Infant mortality (per '000)	39.7*	1961
Crude birth rate (per '000)	26.9*	1965
Crude death rate (per '000)	7.0*	1965
School enrolment: age 5–19 years (percentage)	74	1964

EMPLOYMENT AND TRADE

The principal occupations are shipping, fishing, and rope-making. Tourism has developed recently. Imports consist of foodstuffs, textiles and building materials, exports are rope, shark skin and turtle.

CHANNEL ISLANDS — EUROPE

The Channel Islands are a group of islands off the north coast of France, which have belonged to the British Crown since the eleventh century. They consist of Jersey, Guernsey, Alderney, Sark, and several smaller islands. They each have their own legislature; remnants of feudal government survive on Sark.

AREA: 194 sq. km. (75 sq. miles)

(Jersey 115 sq. km.; Guernsey 63 sq. km.; Alderney 8 sq. km.; Sark 4 sq. km.)

POPULATION: 116 000 (1967 U.N. estimate)

(1961 distribution: Jersey 63 345; Guernsey 47 198; Alderney 1 449; Sark 560)

PRODUCTION AND TRADE

The chief commercial crops are early potatoes, flowers, tomatoes and fern; and dairy cattle are reared. Granite is also exported. The tourist trade flourishes, and provides a reliable source of income. Imports consist mainly of fuel, building materials and foodstuffs, trade being primarily with the U.K.

PRODUCTION, EXPORTS AND IMPORTS

Years: **1963–5 average** and *1953–5 average* Units: '000 metric tons unless otherwise indicated

Note—since 1960 trade with the U.K. has been regarded as 'internal', and, as the greater part of the islands' trade is with the U.K., few trade figures for 1963–5 are available. Those figures shown for this period exclude trade with the U.K.

	Production		Exports		Imports	
1. CEREALS, etc.						
Millets/sorghum	—	—	—	—	na	*0.5*
Oats	—	*1.0*	—	—	na	*0.3*
Potatoes	**57.0**	na	na	*44.2*	na	*5.0*
Wheat	—	*0.3*	—	—	na	*2.2*
2. FRUIT, etc.						
Bananas	—	—	—	—	na	*0.5*
Grapes	—	—	na	*0.2*	na	*0.4*
Oranges	—	—	—	—	na	*0.6*
Tomatoes	**59.4**	na				
Wine *b*	—	—	—	—	na	*5.4*
b '000 hectolitres.						
3. BEVERAGES, FOREST PRODUCTS, etc.						
Coffee	—	—	—	—	na	*0.2*
Sugar, raw	—	—	—	—	na	*3.8*
Tea	—	—	—	—	na	*0.7*
5. LIVESTOCK‡, ANIMAL PRODUCTS, etc.						
Chickens *d*	**133.7**	*70.3*				
Cattle *d*	**13.0**	*15.0²*	na	*0.5*	—	—
Horses *d*	na	*1.0²*				
Pigs *d*	**3.0**	*5.0*	na	*0.7*	na	*0.2*

continued

	Production		Exports		Imports	
5. LIVESTOCK‡, ANIMAL PRODUCTS, etc.—*continued*						
Bacon/ham	—	—	—	—	na	*0.8*
Meat‡: 'A'	—	—	—	—	na	*3.4*
'B'	—	—	—	—	na	*0.3*
Butter	—	—	—	—	na	*0.7*
Cheese	—	—	—	—	na	*0.5*
Eggs	**0.3**	*0.1*	—	—	na	*0.8*
Fish	na	na	—	—	—	—
Milk	**23.3**	*21.8*	—	—	na	*1.3*
d no. in thousands.						
7. FUEL AND POWER						
Coal, 'A'‡	—	—	—	—	**158**	*286*
Coke	na	na	**15†**	—	**6**	*17*
Electricity *h t*	na	*20*				
Petroleum, refined	—	—	—	—	na	*60¹*
h million kWh. *t* thermal.						
8. IRON AND STEEL						
Iron/steel scrap	na	na	**2**	*2*	—	—
9. NON-FERROUS MINERALS AND METALS						
Asbestos, manufactured	—	—	—	—	**2.38**	*0.84*
Lead, metal	—	—	—	—	**0.52**	—

continued

na: data not available. — negligible or nil. ¹ one year only. ² two year average. * estimate. ‡ see appendix. † re-exports.

FALKLAND ISLANDS — SOUTH ATLANTIC

The Crown colony of the Falkland Islands is administered by a governor. The population is almost exclusively of British birth or descent.

AREA: 12 000 sq. km. (4 630 sq. miles)

LAND USE: (percentage of total)

	1961
Arable and orchard	—
Permanent meadow and pasture	86.6
Forest and woodland	—
City areas, waste and other land	13.4

POPULATION: 2 500 (1967 U.N. estimate)

Capital city: STANLEY; population: 1 074 (1962)
Total working population: 1 163 (1962)

		Year(s)
Population per physician	500	1965
Population per hospital bed	60	1966
School enrolment: age 5–19 years (percentage)	93	1963–4 av.

FINANCE

Currency unit: The Falkland Islands pound, at par with the pound sterling which is also in circulation

Exchange rates—see U.K.

EMPLOYMENT AND TRADE

The islanders are principally engaged in sheep farming, wool being the chief export; whaling has now declined. Trade is mainly with the U.K.

TRADING

Total trade (in million $ U.S.)	*1965*	*1955*	*1938*
Exports (f.o.b.)	7	11	3
Imports (c.i.f.)	2	8	2

Distribution of trade (percentage of total value)

Exports	*1965*	*Imports*	*1965*
Crude materials (mainly wool)	43	Manufactured goods (machinery and transport equipment)	47 (13)
Food	22	Crude materials and fuels	19
Animal and vegetable oils	14	Food	18
		Beverages and tobacco	9

PRODUCTION, EXPORTS AND IMPORTS

Years: **1963–5 average** and *1953–5 average* Units: '000 metric tons unless otherwise indicated

	Production		Exports		Imports	
5. LIVESTOCK‡, ANIMAL PRODUCTS, etc.						
Chickens *d*	**2.3**	na				
Cattle *d*	**11.0**	*12.0²*	—	—	—	—
Sheep *d*	**630.0**	*597.0²*	—	—	—	—
Horses *d*	**3.3**	*2.5²*				
Meat‡, 'A'	**3.0***	na	—	—	—	—
Fish	na	na	—	na	**13.6**	na

continued

	Production		Exports		Imports	
5. LIVESTOCK‡, ANIMAL PRODUCTS, etc.—*continued*						
Milk	**1.0***	na	—	—	—	—
Wool	na	*1.3**	**1.5**	*1.3*	—	—
d no. in thousands.						
7. FUEL AND POWER						
Coal, 'A'‡	—	—	—	—	—	*1*
Petroleum, refined	—	—	—	—	**20**	*180¹*

GILBERT AND ELLICE ISLANDS — PACIFIC OCEAN

The Crown colony of the Gilbert and Ellice Islands comes under the jurisdiction of the Western Pacific High Commission. Included also in the group are Ocean Island, the Phoenix Islands and all but five of the Line Islands.

AREA: 955 sq. km. (369 sq. miles)

LAND USE: (percentage of total)

	1964	*1955*
Arable and orchard	47.1	39.8
Permanent meadow and pasture	—	—
Forest and woodland	2.3	2.2
City areas, waste and other land	50.6	58.0

POPULATION: 48 780 (1963 census)

Capital city: TAPIWA; population: 8 953 (city proper, 1967)

		Year(s)
Life expectancy at birth (years): male	56.9*	1958–62 av.
female	59.0*	1958–62 av.
Infant mortality (per '000)	124.3*	1965
Crude birth rate (per '000)	23.8*	1965
Crude death rate (per '000)	7.4*	1965
Population per physician	2 360	1964
Population per hospital bed	110	1966
School enrolment: age 5–19 years (percentage)	86	1964

FINANCE

Currency unit: The Australian dollar replaced the Australian pound in 1966 at the rate A$1 to A£0.5

Exchange rates (for Australian pounds)	*1965*	*1960*	*1950*	*1938*
Per $ U.S.	0.45	0.45	0.45	0.26
Per £ sterling	1.25	1.25	1.25	1.25

PRODUCTION, EXPORTS AND IMPORTS

Years: **1963–5 average** and *1953–5 average* Units: '000 metric tons unless otherwise indicated

	Production		Exports		Imports	
1. CEREALS, etc.						
Rice	—	—	—	—	na	*0.8²*
2. FRUIT, etc.						
Coconuts *e*	**46.7**	na	—	—	—	—
e no. in millions.						
3. BEVERAGES, FOREST PRODUCTS, etc.						
Sugar, raw	—	—	—	—	na	*0.3*
4. VEGETABLE OILSEEDS AND OILS						
Copra	**7.40**	*9.33*	**6.93***	*7.45²*	—	—

	Production		Exports		Imports	
5. LIVESTOCK‡, ANIMAL PRODUCTS, etc.						
Pigs *d*	**11.0**	*9.0²*	—	—	—	—
Fish	na	na	—	—	—	—
d no. in thousands.						
10. CHEMICALS *n* AND FERTILIZERS						
Chemicals	—		—		na	
Fertilizers:						
Phosphates *p*	**351.7**	na	**351.7**	*299.2*	—	—

n data not available for years 1953–5. *p* from Ocean Island.

11. INDUSTRY

For cement data see Fiji.

continued

na: data not available. — negligible or nil. ¹ one year only. ² two year average. * estimate. ‡ see appendix. † re-exports.

ISLE OF MAN — IRISH SEA

The Isle of Man is administered by its own Court of Tynwald, and is not, in general, bound by the Acts of the U.K. Parliament.

AREA: 588 sq. km. (227 sq. miles)

LAND USE: (percentage of total)	1965
Arable and orchard	40.7
Permanent meadow and pasture	11.9
Forest and woodland	3.4
City areas, waste and other land	44.0

POPULATION: 50 423 (1966 census)

Capital city: DOUGLAS; population: 19 517 (1966)

Distribution of working population (1951)
Total working population: 23 257

U.N. group no.		*Percentage*
0	Agriculture, forestry, fishing and hunting	10.9
1	Mining and quarrying	1.4
2/3	Manufacturing	12.0
4	Construction	13.2
5	Electricity, gas, water and sanitary services	2.7
6	Commerce	15.8
7	Transport, storage and communications	9.4
8	Services	26.6
9	Others	8.0

		Year
Infant mortality (per '000)	19.7	1965
Crude birth rate (per '000)	14.9	1965
Crude death rate (per '000)	17.7	1965

PRODUCTION AND TRADE

The main source of income is the tourist industry, half a million British tourists visiting the island annually. The main agricultural products are oats, barley, and root crops, small quantities of which are exported.

PRODUCTION, EXPORTS AND IMPORTS

Years: **1963–5 average** and *1953–5 average* Units: '000 metric tons unless otherwise indicated

	Production		Exports		Imports	
1. CEREALS, etc.						
Barley	**3.3**	*1.0*[2]	—	—	—	—
Oats	**9.0**	*13.5*[2]	—	—	—	—
Potatoes	**11.7**	*8.0*[2]	—	—	—	—
Wheat	**0.3**	*1.0*[2]	—	—	—	—
5. LIVESTOCK‡, ANIMAL PRODUCTS, etc.						
Chickens *d*	**99.0**	*67.3*	—	—	—	—
Cattle *d*	**29.3**	*25.7*	—	—	—	—
Sheep *d*	**115.0**	*82.7*	—	—	—	—
Horses *d*	**0.7**	*1.0*	—	—	—	—
Pigs *d*	**5.0**	*7.3*	—	—	—	—
Fish	na	na	—	—	—	—
Milk	**14.0**	*14.0*[2]	—	—	—	—
Hides/skins	na	na	—	—	—	—

d no. in thousands.

ST. HELENA — ATLANTIC OCEAN

St. Helena is a rugged, mountainous island in mid-Atlantic which was, before the building of the Suez Canal, a prosperous and important port of call on the route to India. The island is a Crown colony, administered by a governor and legislative council responsible also for the administration of Ascension Island and Tristan da Cunha (see below).

AREA: 121.7 sq. km. (47 sq. miles)

LAND USE: (percentage of total)	1962
Arable and orchard	4.8
Permanent meadow and pasture	4.8
Forest and woodland	2.3
City areas, waste and other land	88.1

POPULATION: 4 649 (1966 estimate)
Capital: JAMESTOWN; population: 1 475 (city proper, 1966)
Total working population: 1 898 (1956) (including Ascension Is.)

		Year(s)
Infant mortality (per '000)	17.7*	1965
Crude birth rate (per '000)	24.6*	1965
Crude death rate (per '000)	9.2*	1965
Population per physician	1 670	1964
Population per hospital bed	70	1966
School enrolment: age 5–19 years (percentage)	114‡	1963–4 av.

PRODUCTION AND TRADE

Flax is grown on the island, and flax fibre, tow, rope, and twine are exported. Lace-making is another industry. Rice, sugar and other foodstuffs and most consumer goods are imported.

ASCENSION ISLAND

Ascension Island is a small island 700 miles north west of St. Helena from which it is administered.

Area: 88 sq. km. (34 sq. miles)

Population: 1 217 (1968 estimate)

Capital: GEORGETOWN

TRISTAN DA CUNHA

Tristan da Cunha is a small group of volcanic islands in the South Atlantic. A volcanic eruption in 1961 led to the evacuation of the islands for two years.

Area: 116 sq. km. (45 sq. miles)

Population: 271 (1969)

Only a small portion of the islands is cultivable, the main crop being potatoes. Cattle, sheep and geese are reared, and a small amount of fruit grown. Fish are plentiful.

continued

na: data not available. — negligible or nil. [1] one year only. [2] two year average. * estimate. ‡ see appendix. † re-exports.

SEYCHELLES — INDIAN OCEAN

The Seychelles has long been a Crown colony. In 1965 several outlying islands were added as dependencies of the Seychelles under the name 'British Indian Ocean Territory'. Chronic unemployment of 14% has made the islands dependent on British aid since 1958, and has delayed self-government. There are plans to develop the tourist industry to make the islands more self-reliant.

AREA: 259 sq. km. (100 sq. miles) (including dependencies)

LAND USE: (percentage of total)	1965	1954
Arable and orchard	42.1	42.1
Permanent meadow and pasture	1.0	1.0
Forest and woodland	12.4	9.9
City areas, waste and other land	44.5	47.0

POPULATION: 48 000 (1967 estimate)
Capital city: VICTORIA; population: 10 504 (1960)

*Distribution of working population** (1960)

Total working population: 17 665	*Percentage*
Agriculture, forestry and fishing	47
Skilled work	16
Domestic service	13
Trade and commerce	3
Public works	19
Public administration	2

		Year(s)
Life expectancy at birth (years): male	60.8	1960
female	65.9	1960
Infant mortality (per '000)	58.7*	1965
Crude birth rate (per '000)	37.4*	1965
Crude death rate (per '000)	11.9*	1965
Population per physician	3 290	1964
Population per hospital bed	140*a*	1966
School enrolment: age 5–19 years (percentage)	69	1963–4 av.
age over 19 years (per 100 000 population)	76	1963–5 av.

a government hospitals only.

COMMUNICATIONS

		Year(s)
Telephones (per '000 urban population)	0.8	1967
Radio receivers (per '000 population)	61	1963–5 av.
Daily newspapers (per '000 population)	35.3	1962–4 av.

FINANCE

Currency unit: The Seychelles rupee

Exchange rates	*1965*	*1960*	*1955*
Per $ U.S.	4.76	4.78	4.78
Per £ sterling	13.32	13.33	13.33

TRADING

Total trade (in million $ U.S.)	*1965*	*1955*	*1938*
Exports (f.o.b.)	2.1	1.3	0.3
Imports (c.i.f.)	3.9	1.9	0.4*a*

Distribution of trade (percentage of total value)

Exports	1965	*Imports*	1965
Copra	62	Manufactured goods	40
Food (mainly fish and cinnamon)	25	(machinery and transport equipment)	(13)
		Food	33
		Crude materials and fuels	10
		Beverages and tobacco	9
		Chemicals	6

a (f.o.b.)

PRODUCTION, EXPORTS AND IMPORTS

Years: **1963–5 average** and *1953–5 average* Units: '000 metric tons unless otherwise indicated

	Production		Exports		Imports	
1. CEREALS, etc.						
Cassava	**1.0***	*1.0*[2]				
Maize (corn)	—	—	—	—	**0.2**	*0.8*
Potatoes	—	—	—	—	**0.2**	*0.1*
Rice	—	—	—	—	**3.4**	*2.4*
2. FRUIT, etc.						
Coconuts *e*	**49.0***	na	na	na	—	—
Wine *b*	—	—	—	—	**0.9**	*0.7*
b '000 hectolitres. *e* no. in millions.						
3. BEVERAGES, FOREST PRODUCTS, etc.						
Sugar, raw	—	—	—	—	**1.2**	*1.0*
4. VEGETABLE OILSEEDS AND OILS						
Copra	**6.07**	*6.50*	**6.04**	*6.50*	—	—
Coconut oil	na	na	na	*0.10*	**0.01**	—
Cottonseed oil	—	—	—	—	**0.01**	—
Groundnuts	—	—	—	—	**0.01**[2]	—
Groundnut oil	—	—	—	—	**0.02**	—
Linseed oil	na	na	**0.01**[2]	—	—	—
5. LIVESTOCK‡, ANIMAL PRODUCTS, etc.						
Cattle *d*	**3.0**	na	—	—	—	—
Goats *d*	**2.0***	na	—	—	—	—
Pigs *d*	**3.0**	na	—	—	—	—
Fish	**1.5**[2]*	*1.5**	na	na	—	—
Milk	—	—	—	—	**0.8**	*0.7**
d no. in thousands.						
9. NON-FERROUS MINERALS AND METALS						
Asbestos, manufactured	—	—	—	—	—	*0.03*[1]
10. CHEMICALS*n* AND FERTILIZERS						
Chemicals	—		—		na	
Fertilizers: Phosphates	na	na	**5.6*p***	*7.2p*	—	—
n data not available for years 1953–5. *p* guano.						
11. INDUSTRY						
Cement	—	—	—	—	**3.7**	*1.3*

TURKS AND CAICOS ISLANDS — WEST ATLANTIC

These islands, which had been administered by the Governor of Jamaica, were placed under the jurisdiction of the British Colonial Office when Jamaica became independent in 1962.

AREA: 430 sq. km. (166 sq. miles)

POPULATION: 6 000 (1967 U.N. estimate)
Capital city: GRAND TURK; population: 2 339 (city proper, 1960)
Total working population: 2 108 (1960)

		Year
Infant mortality (per '000)	114.1*	1965
Crude birth rate (per '000)	23.1*	1965
Crude death rate (per '000)	10.2*	1965

EMPLOYMENT AND TRADE

A U.S. air base and naval facilities, and a cable station are situated on Grand Turk. The tourist industry is developing rapidly. The chief exports are salt (decreasing), sisal, crawfish, and conches. Earnings of the considerable number of islanders working abroad in the Bahamas are another source of income.

na: data not available. — negligible or nil. [1] one year only. [2] two year average. * estimate. ‡ see appendix. † re-exports.

UNITED STATES OF AMERICA

The U.S.A. is a federation of 50 states each of which has its own constitution, judicial system, and legislature. The form of federal government laid down in the Constitution gives executive power to a directly elected president whilst legislative power rests with a two chamber Congress.
In 1959 Alaska and Hawaii became the 49th and 50th states. For the purpose of comparisons, the 1953–5 data for these two areas have been included with those for the U.S.A.

AREA: 9 191 802 sq. km. (3 548 974 sq. miles)

LAND USE: (percentage of total)

	1959	*1954*
Arable and orchard	19.8	20.1
Permanent meadow and pasture	27.4	27.4
Forest and woodland	32.2	34.9
City areas, waste and other land	20.6	17.6

POPULATION: 199 118 000 (1967 estimate)

Largest city: NEW YORK; population: 11 410 000* (1966)
Capital city: WASHINGTON, D.C.; population: 2 615 000* (1966)

Distribution of working population (1965)

Total working population: 78 357 000*

U.N. group no.		*Percentage*
0	Agriculture, forestry, fishing and hunting	6.2
1	Mining and quarrying	0.7
2/3	Manufacturing	25.6
4	Construction	6.4
5	Electricity, gas, water and sanitary services	1.4
6	Commerce	23.0
7	Transport, storage and communications	4.8
8	Services	27.6
9	Others	4.3

		Year(s)
Life expectancy at birth (years): male	67.0	1967
female	74.2	
Infant mortality (per '000)	24.7	1965
Crude birth rate (per '000)	19.4	1965
Crude death rate (per '000)	9.4	1965
Accidental deaths (per 100 000 population)		
caused by motor vehicles	25.4	1965
due to other causes	30.4	1965
Population per physician	670	1965
Population per hospital bed	120	1966
School enrolment: age 5–19 years (percentage)	103‡	1963–4 av.
age over 19 years (per 100 000 population)	2 709	1963–5 av.

COMMUNICATIONS

		Year(s)
Motor vehicles in use ('000s): private	71 743.8	1963–5 av.
commercial	13 511.7	1963–5 av.
Railway track (km.)	344 949	1964
Mail per capita: domestic and foreign, incl. packages	358	1963–5 av.
foreign received	10	
foreign sent	3	
Telephones (per '000 urban population)	49.9	1967
Radio receivers (per '000 population)	1 140	1963–5 av.
Television sets (per '000 population)	345.9	1963–5 av.
Daily newspapers (per '000 population)	315.3	1962–4 av.

FINANCE

Currency unit: The U.S. dollar

Exchange rates	*1965*	*1960*	*1950*	*1938*
Per £ sterling	2.8	2.8	2.8	4.64

The $ U.S. which since 31 January 1934 has been fixed at $35 per oz. of fine gold, is the world's leading currency. Other currencies are normally quoted in terms of the $ U.S.

		Year(s)
National Income (million $ U.S.)	562 938	1965
G.N.P. per capita ($ U.S.)	3 520	1966
Rate of increase of G.N.P. per capita	2.7	1960–4 av.
Foreign trade (percentage of G.D.P.)	7	1963–5 av.

TRADING

Total trade (in million $ U.S.)	*1965*	*1955*	*1938*
Exports (f.o.b.)	27 532	15 556	3 102
Imports (f.o.b.)	21 431	11 568	2 191

Main trading partners (percentage of total value)

Exports	*1965*	*1955*	*1938*	*Imports*	*1965*	*1955*	*1938*
Canada	21	20	15	Canada	23	23	13
Japan	8	4	8	Japan	11	4	7
Germany F.R.	6	4	3a	U.K.	7	5	6
U.K.	6	6	17	Germany F.R.	6	3	3a
Mexico	4	5	2	Venezuela	5	5	1
Netherlands	4	3	3	Mexico	3	3	2
France	4	2	4	Italy	3	2	2

Distribution of trade (percentage of total value)

Exports	*1965*	*1955*	*1938**
Manufactured goods	55	58	na
(machinery)	(25)	(20)	(11)
(transport equipment)	(12)	(15)	(14)
Food	15	11	13
(cereals and preparations)	(10)	(6)	(7)
Crude materials and fuels	14	17	na
Chemicals	9	7	3
Imports			
Manufactured goods	49	32	na
(machinery and transport equipment)	(14)	(4)	(—)
(textiles and clothing)	(6)	(4)	(6)
Crude materials and fuels	25	34	na
(petroleum and products)	(10)	(9)	(2)
(metalliferous ores and scrap)	(4)	(6)	(na)
Food	16	26	26
(coffee)	(5)	(12)	(7)

a incl. Germany D.R.; also Austria for the period 7 May–31 December.

PRODUCTION, EXPORTS AND IMPORTS

Years: **1963–5 average** and *1953–5 average* Units: '000 metric tons unless otherwise indicated

1. CEREALS, etc.

	Production		Exports		Imports	
Barley	8 500.7	7 424.3	1 379.7	804.6	177.9	591.6
Maize (corn)	98 114.3	80 268.0	12 832.5s	2 676.5	24.2	41.4
Millets/sorghum	14 799.3	4 978.3	2 943.1s	769.4	8.1*	14.7
Oats	13 280.3	19 944.0	179.8	127.6	54.3	636.5
Potatoes	12 115.3	10 207.0	96.7	155.7	89.8	66.3
Rice	3 322.0	2 611.7	1 358.9s	589.5	10.5	7.7
Rye	803.3	619.3	190.7s	54.2	33.1	205.0
Sweet potatoes/yams	754.7	861.7				
Wheat	33 981.3	28 015.7	18 586.7s	5 885.2	76.0	223.3

s incl. re-exports.

2. FRUIT, etc.

	Production		Exports		Imports	
Apples	2 910.0	2 275.0	92.9s	35.9	26.3	32.5
Apricots	197.0	206.9	na	2.6	—	—
Bananas	3.7*	3.0*	56.5†	21.5†	1 460.7	1 490.3
Cherries	245.0	208.3	na	1.3	na	0.5
Coconuts	—	—	—	—	60.7	56.4
Dates	20.3	17.3	3.5s	0.8	16.4	18.7
Figs	58.0	78.3	na	0.6	na	2.9
Grapes	3 515.0	2 571.0	97.7s	52.5	14.8	10.1
Lemons	628.7	524.7	101.6	38.9	2.5n	2.5
Oranges	4 748.3	5 273.0	194.7s	333.7	49.5	3.2
Other citrus fruit	1 493.0	1 612.0	79.0s	65.5	na	2.4
Olives	48.7	35.0				
Peaches	1 672.7	1 294.1	na	7.8	na	1.1

continued

2. FRUIT, etc.—*continued*

	Production		Exports		Imports	
Pears	519.7	644.3	25.7s	16.9	6.9	4.6
Pineapples	935.0*	725.4*	na	0.5	na	41.4
Plums	527.3	502.6	na	5.8	na	1.1
Raisins	232.3	188.8	50.3s	61.1	0.9[1]	0.1
Tomatoes	4 868.3	3 663.7				
Wine b	13 313.0	8 918.0	10.9s	6.7	572.7	315.3

b '000 hectolitres. *n* incl. grapefruit. *s* incl. re-exports.

3. BEVERAGES, FOREST PRODUCTS, etc.

	Production		Exports		Imports	
Cocoa	—	—	6.9†	15.5†	305.7	239.1
Coffee	3	4	37.7s	12.9s	1 362.1	1 154.8
Sugar: beet	20 451	11 610				
cane	21 680	15 079				
raw (beet)	2 732	1 693	3.5	26.6	3 609.9	4 457.1
(cane)	2 041	1 552				
Tea	—	—	0.3†	0.3†	59.0	49.5
Tobacco: leaf	972	982	225.9s	228.2	78.5	48.9
cigars	8 062e	5 837e	124.7a	62.9[2]a	—	3.1[2]a
cigarettes	547 009e	412 409e				
tobacco/snuff	78	93				
Softwood j	219 149	200 979	7 667.0	2 674.5	19 307.0	11 987.0
Hardwood j	88 075	91 308	783.3	490.2	1 479.8	1 417.7
Wood pulp	28 775	17 149	1 347.8	374.0	2 673.0	1 942.0
Newsprint	1 967	1 124	96.7	119.0	5 349.3	4 583.0
Other paper	33 713	22 627	1 197.0	386.0	170.3	190.3

a million $ U.S. *e* no. in millions. *j* '000 cu. metres of roundwood equivalent. *s* incl. re-exports.

continued

4. VEGETABLE OILSEEDS AND OILS

	Production		Exports		Imports	
Castor seed	27.3	12.9	—	—	0.94	47.00
Castor oil	na	na	0.40s	1.19s	48.90	42.17
Copra	—	—	0.02	0.13	254.53	301.03
Coconut oil	na	na	3.60s	4.86	177.17	63.97
Cottonseed	5 607.7	5 594.3	5.98	14.00	0.17	—
Cottonseed oil	na	na	231.11	182.31	—	—
Groundnuts	679.9	631.0	45.20	26.40	0.90	18.50
Groundnut oil	na	na	22.93	1.53	—	5.74
Linseed	769.0	1 009.0	120.91	124.90	0.01	0.20
Linseed oil	na	na	10.94	102.29	—	—
Olive oil	na	2.0*	—	—	22.08	25.19
Palm kernel oil	—	—	—	—	38.06	22.11n
Palm oil	—	—	—	—	5.50	22.09
Rapeseed	1.0*	0.5[2]	0.03	—	12.56	14.60
Rapeseed oil	na	na	—	—	1.96*	2.25
Sesame seed	0.5*	—	—	—	11.43	5.93
Soya beans	20 372.7	8 919.0	5 554.16	1 380.73	—	0.03
Soya bean oil	na	na	541.37	38.81	—	—
Sunflower seed	na	na	—	—	4.23	0.30
Sunflower seed oil	na	na	—	—	0.12*	0.03
Tung oil	7.0	13.0	0.85s	0.27	10.87	12.26

n incl. babassu oil. *s* incl. re-exports.

5. LIVESTOCK‡, ANIMAL PRODUCTS, etc.

	Production		Exports		Imports	
Chickens d	370 735n	390 965n				
Cattle d	105 888	95 672q	46.3	20.3	842.4	192.2
cows dp	49 641	48 302q				
Goats d	3 882rt	2 646r	26.5	na	11.9	na
Sheep d	28 135n	31 625				
Horses d	2 869	3 011u				
Pigs d	56 770	49 182	10.9	2.2	5.0*	16.9
Bacon/ham	14 364	11 637	13.8s	25.2	5.8	7.0
Meat‡: 'A'			48.1s	10.2	389.3	30.4
'B'	5 579	3 466	180.0s	36.9	12.7	1.6
Butter	645	727	35.4s	39.3	0.3	0.3
Cheese	1 055	810	7.7s	13.8	36.3	23.9
Eggs	3 800	3 750	9.1	31.2	0.3	2.2
Fish	2 716v	2 748	119.4	109.2[1]*	915.8	482.0[1]*
Milk	57 012	55 620	5 208.5	1 756.5	13.3	10.9
Whale/sperm oil	1	—	—	—	30.1	18.0w
Hides/skins	na	na	92.2a	1 027.8e	75.9a	56.6e
Wool	54	61	1.5s	0.3	91.9	113.3

a million $ U.S. *d* no. in thousands. *e* no. in millions. *n* excl. Hawaii and Alaska. *p* incl. beef cows. *q* on farms only. *r* Angora goats only. *s* incl. re-exports. *t* Texas only. *u* excl. Alaska. *v* incl. fish landed in foreign ports for transhipment to U.S.A. *w* incl. sperm oil‡.

6. FIBRES, TEXTILES, etc.

	Production		Exports		Imports	
Abaca	—	—	0.5†	1.3†	30.6*	40.7
Agaves (sisal, etc.)	—	—	8.8†	21.0†	90.0*	152.3
Cotton lint	3 300.0	3 247.3	1 017.6s	716.8	25.4	36.7
Flax fibre	—	na	—	—	4.0	3.5
Hemp fibre	—	na	—	—	—	0.9
Jute	—	—	1.1†	0.4†	65.2*	68.2
Rubber: natural	—	—	27.3†	9.0†	433.8	638.8
synthetic	1 756.9	826.7	300.5	63.5[2]	30.8s	13.9
Silk f	—	—	1 009.3†	28.3†	2 932.0	3 024.3
Cotton: yarn	1 842.6	1 691.6*	2.8	7.9	9.3	0.1
woven fabrics	1 321.1*	1 213.3	44.9	69.8	63.5	8.9
Rayon: fibre/yarn	651.3	535.7	18.8	12.1	48.4	46.0
woven fabrics	297.4	183.0n	11.4	18.7	8.3p	0.6
Non-cellulosic fibre/yarn	656.1	137.7	44.4	na	14.8	na
Wool: yarn	236.6	313.0	0.1	0.1	4.5	0.8
woven fabrics	107.4*q	285.7r	0.4	0.6	10.5	5.6

f metric tons. *n* in addition, rayon tyre cord and fabric 175.3. *p* incl. synthetic. *q* excl. mixtures containing less than 50% virgin wool. *r* excl. mixtures con-aining less than 25% virgin wool.

7. FUEL AND POWER

	Production		Exports		Imports	
Coal: 'A'‡	453 480	442 420	11 853	37 834	242	172
'B'	867	2 870	—	—	—	69
Coke	na	na	547	435	104	121
Electricity h: total	1 084 183	562 713				
hydro	182 030	112 547				
nuclear	3 404	—				
thermal	898 749n	450 166n				
Natural gas i	435 780	250 556	590	879	12 320	308
Oil, crude	397 297	352 120[1]	180	1 560[1]	60 200	40 600
Petroleum, refined	426 430	344 510	5 087	12 290[1]	53 000	25 330[1]
Rare earths f	na	na	421[2]p	20q	3 194r	5[2]qs
Uranium f	9 362	4 572[1]t	5u	614v	5 065w	69 493x

f metric tons. *h* million kWh. *i* million cu. metres. *n* incl. geothermal. *p* thorium and cerium. *q* cerium only. *r* monazite and thorium. *s* incl. imports for re-export. *t* 1956 figure. *u* in addition, radium products 244 milligrams. *v* radium content in milligrams. *w* in addition, radium salts 44 660[1] milligrams. *x* radium salts in milligrams.

8. IRON AND STEEL

	Production		Exports		Imports	
Iron ore	47 077m	51 818m	7 065	4 035	40 909	17 055
Pig iron	77 954	65 382	189	56	929	473
Steel ingots/castings	111 218	95 845	596	224	246	87
Iron/steel scrap	na	na	6 520	2 140	215	194
Iron/steel products a	na	na	606	560	877	173

a million $ U.S. *m* metal content.

9. NON-FERROUS MINERALS AND METALS

	Production		Exports		Imports	
Diamonds a	—	—	48.6	3.3	336.4[2]	181.8
Gold k: ore m	1 538.3	1 902.0	33.8	5.3	306.7	851.9
bullion/coins etc.	na	na	18 171.3	877.3[2]	1 478.2	935.9
Platinum group metals k	41.8	24.5	—	27.7	950.9	747.2
Silver k: ore m	37 127.3	36 597.0	1 503.7	33.7	44 212.3	47 450.6
bullion	na	na	58 677.7	2 505.7	10 936.0	38 191.5
Asbestos: fibre	86.4p	44.3	24.2	2.1	643.1	638.4
manufactured	na	na	17.3	17.3q	40.9r	7.1
Mica	104.3	75.9	3.9	2.7	8.7	11.0
Aluminium: bauxite	1 618.9	1 816.4	—	19.8	10 550.3	4 902.2
alumina	—	—	266.0†	—	203.3	—
aluminium	2 304.2	1 293.7	310.4	44.1	474.5	261.6
Antimony: ore	0.6m	0.5m	0.2[2]	—	9.3m	6.1m
metal	na	na	0.1[1]	0.3	5.8	4.3
Beryl	0.2u	0.6	0.1	—	5.9	6.0
Cadmium	4.6	4.5	0.4	0.4	0.6	1.2
Chrome: ore	—	113.5m	7.0	1.0	1 309.9	1 672.5
metal	na	na	7.5	6.7	34.2	15.2
Cobalt: ore	0.3m	0.6m	0.7m	22.0m	—	50.9
metal	na	na			6.0	143.0
Copper: ore	1 152.6m	834.7m	5.2m	4.8m	21.0m	106.9
metal	2 428.4	1 779.5	384.6	240.0	968.0	467.5
Lead: ore	254.2m	304.3m	—[2]	0.8	118.4	126.9
metal	381.8	433.4	18.4	6.5	232.3	288.0
Magnesium: dolomite	1 902.8	na	229.9[1]	—	—	—
magnesite	478.7[1]	na	70.2	8.4	69.6[2]	66.2
kieserite	na	na	—	—	35.2	41.4
metal/salts	71.6x	62.7x	11.6	4.3	26.4	
Manganese: ore	19.9	196.8	11.2	5.8	2 820.1	2 449.4
metal	na	na	5.5[2]	1.4	155.2	75.1
Mercury f	607.2	595.6	91.0	21.7	1 155.0	1 938.6
Molybdenum f: ore m	31 447.6	26 867.0	18 533.8	8 867.9	—	72.8
metal	na	na	1 045.5	199.9	140.7[2]	—
Nickel: ore	11.2m	1.6m	—[2]	—	—	1.4
metal	na	na	44.7s	14.7s	126.4[2]	118.1
Tin: ore	—	0.1	—	—	4.9	26.5
metal	3.4	25.3[2]	6.8	6.9	41.7	67.8
Titanium minerals	873.6	504.1	29.3[2]	48.9	304.2[2]	252.7
Tungsten: ore	6.9p	12.0p	—	—	2.7	21.6
metal	na	na	0.2[2]	0.2	0.4	0.4
Vanadium m	4.1p	7.2p	0.9v	0.4	—	0.7
Zinc: ore	518.7m	464.3m	—[2]	0.9	329.8	397.7
metal	859.1	811.0	35.4	39.1	144.9	181.2
Zirconium minerals	0.9t	20.7	1.9	0.8	47.1	21.9

a million $ U.S. *f* metric tons. *k* '000 fine troy oz. *m* metal content. *p* mine shipments. *q* in addition, brake and clutch linings valued at U.S.$5 530 000. *r* in addition, brake and clutch linings valued at U.S.$6 580 000. *s* incl. re-exports. *t* zirconium sponge metal only. *u* chiefly low-grade ores. *v* in addition, ferro-vanadium 0.5. *x* primary magnesium only.

10. CHEMICALS n AND FERTILIZERS

	Production		Exports		Imports	
Organic chemicals:						
Benzene	2 542.0		344.5		43.4	
Butadiene	1 120.0[1]		na		na	
Ethylene	na		na		na	
Methanol	1 156.9		na		na	
Phenol	468.8*		13.1		—	
Phthalic anhydride	246.0		10.1[2]		0.5[1]	
Styrene monomer	1 131.6		125.3		—	
Urea	799.5		31.4		237.2	
Inorganic chemicals:						
Ammonia	6 919.6		167.0[1]		na	
Carbon black	1 068.0[1]		103.4		1.2	
Chlorine	5 420.9		37.4		26.3	
Nitric acid	4 169.2		0.2[2]		na	
Sodium carbonate	4 402.0		222.6		—	
Sodium hydroxide	5 686.6		323.8		1.5	
Sulphuric acid	20 633.9		8.4		34.6	
Plastics:						
Polyamides	34.3		na		na	
Polyethylene	1 187.4		186.1		0.1[1]	
Polyvinyl chloride	734.8		31.0		2.7[2]	
Fertilizers:						
Phosphates	23 401.7	13 069.7	5 740.9	2 287.3	152.0	115.3
Potash	2 691.6w	1 792.4w	864.2	131.1	1 260.9	235.6
Pyrites	356.3x	404.6x	—	—	197.3	280.5
Sulphur: native	5 495.9	5 612.8	2 097.3	1 551.8	1 605.6	12.6
recovered	1 078.2	405.2[1]				

n data not available for years 1953–5. *w* K_2O content. *x* sulphur content.

continued

UNITED STATES OF AMERICA *continued*

PRODUCTION, EXPORTS AND IMPORTS *continued*

11. INDUSTRY	Production		Exports		Imports	
Aircraft a	10 465[2]w	na	1 003.6	741.5n	104.8	28.2
Alcoholic beverages			—	9.2a	380.9a	163.8a
beer b	120 860	106 691p				
spirits b	4 001q	10 324r				
Cement	60 993	46 863	109.3t	276.7	660.3u	343.7u
Electrical engineering a	37 863	na	1 592.0	786.5[2]	492.6	59.8[2]
Locomotives c	1 524	1 676[2]v	na	na	—	—

continued

11. INDUSTRY—*continued*	Production		Exports		Imports	
Railway vehicles a	na	na	131.1	110.1	—	2.0
Machine tools a	1 160[1]	na	234.2	145.0	—	—
Merchant ships g	280	359	0.8	113.3	0.2	18.5
Motor vehicles			1 779.5a	1 293.6a	801.8a	75.3[2]a
commercial d	1 585	1 166				
private d	8 232	6 532				

a million $ U.S. *b* '000 hectolitres. *c* no. of units. *d* no. in thousands. *g* '000 G.R.T. *n* number on order. *p* incl. Puerto Rico. *q* 1967 figure. *r* 1959 figure. *t* incl. Puerto Rico's exports. *u* excl. imports from Puerto Rico. *v* excl. parts. *w* 1965–7 av.

UNITED STATES OF AMERICA (TERRITORIES)

RYUKYU ISLANDS—see page 205

AMERICAN SAMOA

PACIFIC OCEAN

American Samoa is an unincorporated territory of the U.S.A. Its indigenous inhabitants are U.S. nationals. In 1952 civilian control replaced the naval administration.

AREA: 197 sq. km. (76 sq. miles)

LAND USE: (percentage of total)	*1964*	*1955*
Arable and orchard	40	30
Forest and woodland	20	60
City areas, waste and other land	40	10

POPULATION: 29 000 (1967 estimate)

Capital: PAGO PAGO; population: 1 251 (city proper, 1960)
Total working population: 5 889 (1960)

		Year(s)
Infant mortality (per '000)	33.6	1965
Crude birth rate (per '000)	42.9	1965
Crude death rate (per '000)	6.1	1965
Population per physician	1 100	1965
Population per hospital bed	140	1966
School enrolment: age 5–19 years (percentage)	124‡	1963–4 av.
age over 19 years (per 100 000 population)	200	1965

FINANCE

Currency unit: The U.S. dollar

		Year
National Income (million $ U.S.)	15*	1966
G.N.P. per capita ($ U.S.)	580	1966

PRODUCTION AND TRADE

Coconuts, tropical fruit, and copra are the main products of the islands; fishing is also of commercial importance, and some livestock are reared. Trade is mainly with the U.S.A., the chief exports being copra, tuna, and handicrafts.

PRODUCTION, EXPORTS AND IMPORTS

Years: **1963–5 average** and *1953–5 average* Units: '000 metric tons unless otherwise indicated

	Production		Exports		Imports	
1. CEREALS, etc.						
Rice	—	—	—	—	0.5[2]	—
2. FRUIT, etc.						
Bananas	1.0*	14.7	na	na	—	—
Coconuts e	7.3*	na	na	na	—	—
e no. in millions.						
3. BEVERAGES, FOREST PRODUCTS, etc.						
Sugar, raw	—	—	—	—	0.5[2]	0.2
Hardwood j	—	—	—	—	3.1[2]	—
j '000 cu. metres of roundwood equivalent.						
4. VEGETABLE OILSEEDS AND OILS						
Copra	0.80	1.57	0.78	0.93	—	—
5. LIVESTOCK‡, ANIMAL PRODUCTS, etc.						
Chickens d	80.0*	67.0[2]				
Cattle d	na	na	—	—	—	—
Pigs d	13.0	13.5[2]	—	—	—	—
Fish	na	3.1[2]	na	na	0.4[1]	na
d no. in thousands.						
7. FUEL AND POWER						
Electricity h t	21[1]	—				
Petroleum, refined	—	—	—	—	40	na
h million kWh. *t* thermal.						

continued

na: data not available. — negligible or nil. [1] one year only. [2] two year average. * estimate. ‡ see appendix. † re-exports.

GUAM

WEST PACIFIC

Guam, the largest and most southerly of the Mariana or Ladrone Islands, is of great strategic importance. It reverted to U.S. control in 1944 after three years' Japanese occupation. In 1950 civilian control replaced the post-war naval administration, and full U.S. citizenship was granted to the inhabitants.

AREA: 540 sq. km. (209 sq. miles)

LAND USE: (percentage of total)	*1960*	*1955*
Arable and orchard	21.8	22.2
Permanent meadow and pasture	14.5	14.8
Forest and woodland	18.2	18.5
City areas, waste and other land a	45.5	44.5

a about one third of the land is occupied by U.S. naval and air forces.

POPULATION: 94 000 (1967 estimate)

Capital city: AGANA; population: 1 642 (city proper, 1960)
Total working population: 20 315 (1964)

		Year(s)
Infant mortality (per '000)	32.5	1965
Crude birth rate (per '000)	33.0	1965
Crude death rate (per '000)	4.4	1965
Population per physician	2 500	1965
Population per hospital bed	270	1966
School enrolment: age 5–19 years (percentage)	90	1963–4 av.
age over 19 years (per 100 000 population)	1 864	1964–5 av.

COMMUNICATIONS

		Year(s)
Motor vehicles in use ('000s): private	16.4	1963–5 av.
commercial	2.2	1963–5 av.
Telephones (per '000 urban population)	23.1	1967
Radio receivers (per '000 population)	364	1963–5 av.
Television sets (per '000 population)	364	1963–5 av.
Daily newspapers (per '000 population)	182	1962–4 av.

		Year
National Income (million $ U.S.)	120*	1966
G.N.P. per capita ($ U.S.)	1 550	1966

EMPLOYMENT, PRODUCTION AND TRADE

Many of the inhabitants of the island are employed by the U.S. Navy or Air Force. There is a little agriculture, producing maize, bananas and coconuts, and some livestock are reared; but most food and all consumer goods and building materials have to be imported. The island is the only American territory to have a large measure of free trade, excise duties being levied only on tobacco, alcoholic beverages and fuel. Income is derived primarily from the U.S. government but a little copra and some tropical fruits and vegetables are exported.

PRODUCTION, EXPORTS AND IMPORTS

Years: **1963–5 average** and *1953–5 average* Units: '000 metric tons unless otherwise indicated

	Production		Exports		Imports	
1. CEREALS, etc.						
Maize (corn)	na	na	na	na	0.3*[2]	—
Potatoes	—	—	—	—	0.4	na
Rice	—	—	1.6[2]†	—	4.2[2]	na
3. BEVERAGES, FOREST PRODUCTS, etc.						
Sugar, raw	—	—	—	—	1.4[2]	na
5. LIVESTOCK‡, ANIMAL PRODUCTS, etc.						
Chickens d	148.0*n	199.7n				
Cattle d	5.3n	5.5[2]n	—	—	—	—
Goats d	3.0n	3.0[2]n				

continued

	Production		Exports		Imports	
5. LIVESTOCK‡, ANIMAL PRODUCTS, etc.—*continued*						
Pigs d	6.0n	10.5[2]n	—	—	—	—
Meat‡: 'A'	—	—	—	—	1.9	—
'B'	0.1	—	—	—	—	—
Eggs	0.5*	na	—	—	—	—
Fish	0.2	0.2	—	—	0.4[2]	na
d no. in thousands. *n* on farms only.						
7. FUEL AND POWER						
Electricity h t	355	na				
Petroleum, refined	—	—	—	—	110	na
h million kWh. *t* thermal.						

PACIFIC ISLANDS, TRUST TERRITORY OF

The territory, known also as Micronesia, includes the Caroline, Marshall and Mariana Islands (except Guam). Under a U.N. trusteeship agreement the U.S.A. administers these islands which were formerly mandated to Japan.

AREA: 1 779 sq. km. (687 sq. miles)

LAND USE: (percentage of total)	*1965*	*1955*
Arable and orchard	29.8	34.3
Permanent meadow and pasture	10.1	6.2
Forest and woodland	22.5	18.5
City areas, waste and other land	37.6	41.0

POPULATION: 91 448 (1967 census)

FINANCE

Currency unit: The U.S. dollar

		Year
National Income (million $ U.S.)	24*	1966
G.N.P. per capita ($ U.S.)	270	1966

PRODUCTION AND TRADE

Copra, cacao, black pepper and ramie are the chief products. Commercial tuna fishing has been developed. Copra is the main export, and guano is obtained from some of the smaller islands.

PRODUCTION, EXPORTS AND IMPORTS

Years: **1963–5 average** and *1953–5 average* Units: '000 metric tons unless otherwise indicated

	Production		Exports		Imports	
1. CEREALS, etc.						
Cassava	5.0*	9.7				
Rice	—	—	—	—	na	0.5[2]
Sweet potatoes/ yams	4.0*	6.0				
2. FRUIT, etc.						
Bananas	3.0*	2.7	—	—	—	—
Coconuts e	82.7*	na	—	—	—	—
Pineapples	na	0.7	—	—	—	—
e no. in millions.						
3. BEVERAGES, FOREST PRODUCTS, etc.						
Sugar, raw	—	—	—	—	na	0.3
4. VEGETABLE OILSEEDS AND OILS						
Copra	12.47	10.93	10.78	10.20[2]	—	—
5. LIVESTOCK‡, ANIMAL PRODUCTS, etc.						
Chickens d	105.0	71.3				
Cattle d	5.3	1.3	—	—	—	—
Goats d	3.0	4.0[1]	—	—	—	—
Pigs d	19.0	9.7	—	—	—	—
Meat‡, 'A'	—	—	—	—	—	0.1[2]
Eggs	na	na	—	—	—	—
Fish	na	na	—	—	—	—
Milk	—	—	—	—	na	0.2*
d no. in thousands.						
10. CHEMICALS n AND FERTILIZERS						
Chemicals	—		—		na	
Fertilizers:						
Phosphates	na	na	na	90.6p	—	—
n data not available for years 1953–5. *p* from Angaur Is.						

continued

na: data not available. — negligible or nil. [1] one year only. [2] two year average. * estimate. ‡ see appendix. † re-exports.

PANAMA CANAL ZONE

CENTRAL AMERICA

A treaty of 1903 authorized the U.S.A. to take over the French Canal Co. with sovereign rights over a ten mile wide strip of Panama territory in return for a capital payment and an annuity. In 1965 the status of the Canal Zone changed; a measure of agreement was reached by the U.S.A. and Panama, and the territory is now administered by the Panama Canal Zone Government.

AREA: 1 676 sq. km. (647 sq. miles) (including water area)

LAND USE: (percentage of total)

	1951
Arable and orchard	0.7
Permanent meadow and pasture	7.7
Forest and woodland (including brush-land)	39.2
City areas, waste and other land	52.4

POPULATION: 56 000*a* (1967 estimate)
Administrative centre: BALBOA HEIGHTS; population: 3 665 (1965) (incl. Balboa and Ancon)
a incl. armed forces.

COMMUNICATIONS

		Year(s)
Motor vehicles in use ('000s): private	15.0	1963–5 av.
commercial	0.8*	1963
Railway track (km.)	77	1964
Telephones (per '000 urban population)	22.9	1966

TRANSIT TRADE
In 1966, 11 926 ships used the canal, the majority of which were registered in the U.S.A., Norway, the U.K., Germany F.R., or Liberia. The net weight of cargo amounted to 78 918 013 tons.

PRODUCTION, EXPORTS AND IMPORTS

Years: **1963–5 average** and *1953–5 average* Units: '000 metric tons unless otherwise indicated

	Production		Exports		Imports	
1. CEREALS, etc.						
Potatoes	—	—	—	—	0.1	*3.4**
Wheat	—	—	—	—	0.5	na
2. FRUIT, etc.						
Apples	—	—	—	—	—	*0.2**
Grapes	—	—	—	—	—	*0.1**
Raisins	—	—	—	—	—	*0.1**
3. BEVERAGES, FOREST PRODUCTS, etc.						
Sugar, raw	—	—	—	—	na	*1.1*[2]

	Production		Exports		Imports	
5. LIVESTOCK‡, ANIMAL PRODUCTS, etc.						
Bacon/ham	—	—	—	—	—[2]	*0.4**
Cheese	—	—	—	—	0.1[2]	*0.2*[1]*
Eggs	—	—	—	—	na	*0.5**
Milk	—	—	—	—	3.0[2]	*9.7**
7. FUEL AND POWER						
Electricity *h*: total	410	na				
hydro	277	na				
thermal	133	na				
Petroleum, refined	—	—	180†	na	2 713	na
11. INDUSTRY						
Cement	na	—	na	—	na	*25.0**

h million kWh.

PUERTO RICO

CARIBBEAN SEA

Puerto Rico is a self-governing territory under the protection of the U.S.A. The people have U.S. citizenship, and the island has a non-voting representative in the U.S. Congress. The U.S.A. has agreed to grant complete independence when it is requested.

AREA: 8 891 sq. km. (3 435 sq. miles)

LAND USE: (percentage of total)

	1965	*1954*
Arable and orchard	30.4	40.2
Permanent meadow and pasture	35.3	35.8
Forest and woodland	13.3	12.1
City areas, waste and other land	21.0	11.9

POPULATION: 2 697 000 (1967 estimate)
Largest city: SAN JUAN, capital; population: 754 300 (1966)

Distribution of working population (1966)
Total working population: 819 500

U.N. group no.		*Percentage*
0	Agriculture, forestry, fishing and hunting	17.1
1	Mining and quarrying	1.5
2/3	Manufacturing	18.6
4	Construction	9.5
5/8	Services, including electricity, gas, water and sanitary services	28.5
6	Commerce	17.1
7	Transport, storage and communications	6.8
9	Others	0.9

		Year(s)
Life expectancy at birth (years): male	67.1	1959–61 av.
female	71.9	
Infant mortality (per '000)	42.8	1965
Crude birth rate (per '000)	30.2	1965
Crude death rate (per '000)	6.7	1965
Accidental deaths (per 100 000 population)		
caused by motor vehicles	16.1	1965
due to other causes	22.6	1965
Population per physician	980	1965
Population per hospital bed	220	1966
School enrolment: age 5–19 years (percentage)	98*c*	1963–4 av.
age over 19 years (per 100 000 population)	1 583	1964–5 av.

c incl. pre-school education.

COMMUNICATIONS

		Year(s)
Motor vehicles in use ('000s): private	226	1963–5 av.
commercial	48	
Telephones (per '000 urban population)	8.1	1967
Daily newspapers (per '000 population)	59.5	1962–4 av.

FINANCE
Currency unit: The U.S. dollar

		Year(s)
National Income (million $ U.S.)	2 525	1965
G.N.P. per capita ($ U.S.)	1 090	1966
Rate of increase of G.N.P. per capita	5.9	1960–4 av.

PRODUCTION AND TRADE
The chief crops are sugar (accounting for 60% of the exports), tobacco, coffee, fruit, maize and yams. Trade is mainly with the U.S.A.

continued

na: data not available. — negligible or nil. [1] one year only. [2] two year average. * estimate. ‡ see appendix. † re-exports.

PRODUCTION, EXPORTS AND IMPORTS

Years: **1963–5 average** and *1953–5 average* Units: '000 metric tons unless otherwise indicated
Note—Trade figures are included with those for the U.S.A., except for the items shown below

	Production		Exports		Imports	
1. CEREALS, etc.						
Cassava	6.0	*10.3*				
Maize (corn)	11.7	*16.7*				
Rice	2.0*[1]	*2.7*				
Sweet potatoes/ yams	27.0	*37.3*				
2. FRUIT, etc.						
Bananas	114.7	*138.3*				
Coconuts	15.0*e*	na				
Lemons	3.3	*2.0*[2]				
Oranges	35.7	*28.3*				
Other citrus fruit	15.3	*17.7**				
Pineapples	64.0	*24.0*				
Tomatoes	20.3	*8.3*				
3. BEVERAGES, FOREST PRODUCTS, etc.						
Coffee	15.0	*13.0*				
Sugar: cane	8 489.3	*9 392.3*				
raw	870.7	*1 064.7*	na	*969.4n*	—	—
Tobacco: leaf	15.8	*14.8*				
cigars*e*	na	*120.7*				
cigarettes*e*	na	*3.9*[2]				
Hardwood*j*	45.1	*197.0*				

e no. in millions. *j* '000 cu. metres of roundwood equivalent. *n* all exported to U.S.A.

	Production		Exports		Imports	
5. LIVESTOCK‡, ANIMAL PRODUCTS, etc.						
Chickens*d*	3 624.0	*727.0*				
Cattle*d*	502.7*p*	*399.7p*				
dairy cows*d*	302.0	na				
Goats*d*	25.0**p*	*26.0p*				
Sheep*d*	na	na				
Horses*d*	23.0*	*38.0*[2]*				
Pigs*d*	160.0*p*	*74.0p*				
Meat‡: 'A'	27.3	*15.3*				
'B'	11.5*	*5.9*				
Eggs	12.5	*5.1*				
Fish	4.6	*2.5*				
Milk	336.0	*198.7*				
7. FUEL AND POWER						
Electricity*h*: total	3 634	*1 050*[1]				
hydro	222	*210*[1]				
thermal	3 412	*840*[1]				
Oil, crude	—	—	—	—	5 340	*450*[1]
Petroleum, refined	5 380	*330*[1]	2 500[1]	na	340	na
11. INDUSTRY						
Beer*b*	855.0	na				
Cement	1 274.3	*651.0*	na	*76.0q*	90.3	—

d no. in thousands. *p* on farms only.
h million kWh.
b '000 hectolitres. *q* excl. exports to the U.S.A.

VIRGIN ISLANDS (U.S.A.)

CARIBBEAN SEA

The U.S. Virgin Islands were bought from Denmark in 1917 for strategic reasons. The inhabitants were made U.S. citizens in 1927 but the islands are constitutionally an unincorporated territory, and the U.S. Department of the Interior retains full jurisdiction.

AREA: 344.5 sq. km. (133 sq. miles)

LAND USE: (percentage of total)

	1960	*1955*
Arable and orchard	14.7	32.4
Permanent meadow and pasture	20.6	
Forest and woodland	5.9	50.0
City areas, waste and other land	58.8	17.6

POPULATION: 56 000 (1967 U.N. estimate)
Capital city: CHARLOTTE AMALIE; population: 12 880 (city proper, 1960)

Distribution of working population (1960)
Total working population: 11 334

U.N. group no.		*Percentage*
0	Agriculture, forestry, fishing and hunting	5.4
1	Mining and quarrying	0.2
2/3	Manufacturing	7.7
4	Construction	12.0
5	Electricity, gas, water and sanitary services	1.7
6	Commerce	18.4
7	Transport, storage and communications	7.0
8	Services	43.0
9	Others	4.6

		Year(s)
Infant mortality (per '000)	30.0	1965
Crude birth rate (per '000)	46.0	1965
Crude death rate (per '000)	9.6	1965
Population per physician	1 000	1963
Population per hospital bed	250	1966
School enrolment: age 5–19 years (percentage)	126‡	1963–4 av.
age over 19 years (per 100 000 population)	908	1964–5 av.

FINANCE

		Year
National Income (million $ U.S.)	25*	1966
G.N.P. per capita ($ U.S.)	2 320	1966

PRODUCTION, EXPORTS AND IMPORTS

Years: **1963–5 average** and *1953–5 average* Units: '000 metric tons unless otherwise indicated

	Production		Exports		Imports	
1. CEREALS, etc.						
Rice	—	—	—	—	2.1[2]	—
3. BEVERAGES, FOREST PRODUCTS, etc.						
Sugar: cane	162.3*	*110.7*				
raw	10.8	*9.0*	na	*9.9*	—	—
5. LIVESTOCK‡, ANIMAL PRODUCTS, etc.						
Chickens*d*	20.7	*15.5*[2]				
Cattle*d*	7.0	*15.5*[2]	0.4[1]	—	0.6[21]	—
Goats*d*	3.0	*2.0*[2]	—	—	0.8[1]	na
Sheep*d*	2.0	*2.0*[2]				
Horses*d*	0.7	*1.0*				
Pigs*d*	1.0	*1.0*[1]	—	—	0.4[2]	—

continued

	Production		Exports		Imports	
5. LIVESTOCK‡, ANIMAL PRODUCTS, etc.—*continued*						
Meat‡, 'A'	3.0*	*1.0*[2]	—	—	—	—
Cheese	—	—	—	—	0.1[2]	—
Eggs	—	—	—	—	0.1[2]	—
Fish	4.7	na	—	—	—	—
Milk	2.0	*1.7*	—	—	—	—
7. FUEL AND POWER						
Electricity*h t*	81	*10*[1]				
Petroleum, refined	—	—	—	—	87	—

d no. in thousands.
h million kWh. *t* thermal.

na: data not available. — negligible or nil. [1] one year only. [2] two year average. * estimate. ‡ see appendix. † re-exports.

UPPER VOLTA

Upper Volta was reconstituted as a separate state of French West Africa in 1947 after fifteen years' partition between the Ivory Coast, Mali, and Niger, and became an independent republic in 1960. Ties with France concerning finance and technical assistance were retained. The army assumed power in 1966 but there was a partial return to civilian government in 1970.

AREA: 274 122 sq.km. (105 839 sq. miles)

LAND USE: (percentage of total)

	1960
Arable and orchard	17.9
Permanent meadow and pasture	na
Forest and woodland	7.3
City areas, waste and other land	na

POPULATION: 5 054 000 (1967 estimate)

Capital city: OUAGADOUGOU; population: 59 126 (city proper, 1961)

		Year(s)
Life expectancy at birth (years): male	32.1*	1960–1 av.
female	31.1*	
Infant mortality (per '000)	182*	1960–1 av.
Population per physician	63 000	1964
Population per hospital bed	1 680 *a*	1966
School enrolment: age 5–19 years (percentage)	8	1963–4 av.

a government hospitals only.

COMMUNICATIONS

		Year(s)
Motor vehicles in use ('000s): private	3.5	1963–5 av.
commercial	3.6	
Telephones (per '000 urban population)	0.1*	1967
Radio receivers (per '000 population)	10	1963–5 av.
Television sets (per '000 population)	0.1	1964–5 av.
Daily newspapers (per '000 population)	0.1	1957

FINANCE

Currency unit: The franc CFA

Exchange rates	*1965*	*1960*
Per $ U.S.	246.85	246.85
Per £ sterling	691.18	691.18

		Year
National Income (million $ U.S.)	145	1958
G.N.P. per capita ($ U.S.)	50	1966

TRADING

Total trade (in million $ U.S.)	*1965*	*1955*
Exports (f.o.b.)	14	5
Imports (c.i.f.)	37	na

Main trading partners (percentage of total value)

Exports	*1965*	*Imports*	*1965*
Ivory Coast	52	France	54
Ghana	19	Ivory Coast	16
France	8	Mali	6
Mali	5	Senegal	3
Italy	3	Germany F.R.	2
		Ghana	2
		U.S.A.	2

Distribution of trade (percentage of total value)

Exports	*1965*	*Imports*	*1965*
Food	70	Manufactured goods	53
(cattle)	(42)	(machinery and transport equipment)	(19)
(sheep and goats)	(14)	(textiles and clothing)	(13)
Crude materials	23	Food	21
(oilseeds)	(11)	(sugar)	(5)
(cotton)	(7)	Crude materials and fuels	16

PRODUCTION, EXPORTS AND IMPORTS

Years: **1963–5 average** Units: '000 metric tons unless otherwise indicated

Note—no data are available for the years 1953–5

	Production	Exports	Imports
1. CEREALS, etc.			
Cassava	32.0*		
Maize (corn)	118.7*	—	0.2
Millets/sorghum	1 198.3	0.7	—
Potatoes	—	—	0.5
Rice	31.7*	—	3.3
Sweet potatoes/yams	51.0*		
2. FRUIT, etc.			
Apples	—	—	0.1 *n*
Bananas	—	—	1.2
Dates	—	—	0.1
Oranges	—	—	0.6
Wine *b*	—	—	16.1

b '000 hectolitres. *n* incl. pears and quince.

	Production	Exports	Imports
3. BEVERAGES, FOREST PRODUCTS, etc.			
Coffee	—	—	0.1
Sugar, raw	—	—	9.3
Tobacco: leaf	0.4*	—	0.1
products	—	—	0.4
Softwood *j*	—	—	na
Hardwood *j*	3 045.0*[1]	—	12.4[2]

j '000 cu. metres of roundwood equivalent.

	Production	Exports	Imports
4. VEGETABLE OILSEEDS AND OILS			
Cottonseed	8.70*	3.18	0.03
Groundnuts	93.57*	3.50	—
Groundnut oil	na	0.07	0.01
Palm oil	—	—	0.06[2]
Sesame seed	5.37	2.20	—

	Production	Exports	Imports
5. LIVESTOCK‡, ANIMAL PRODUCTS, etc.			
Chickens *d*	3 183.0*		
Cattle *d*	1 973.3*	58.9*	—
dairy cows *d*	792.0*		
Goats *d*	1 900.0	131.1 (goats and sheep)	—
Sheep *d*	1 066.7*		
Horses *d*	63.7		
Pigs *d*	110.0	—	—
Meat‡, 'A'	32.0*	—	—
Butter	—	—	0.1
Eggs	11.4	—	—
Fish	3.3	0.1	1.8
Milk	118.3*	—	3.4
Hides/skins	0.5[2]	0.5	0.1

d no. in thousands.

	Production	Exports	Imports
6. FIBRES, TEXTILES, etc.			
Cotton: lint	3.7*	1.7	—
yarn	na	—	0.6[2]
woven fabrics	—	—	1.8
7. FUEL AND POWER			
Electricity *h t*	18		
Petroleum, refined	—	—	33

h million kWh. *t* thermal.

	Production	Exports	Imports
9. NON-FERROUS MINERALS AND METALS			
Gold *k*: ore	37 *m*	39 *p*	—

k '000 fine troy oz. *m* metal content. *p* bullion.

	Production	Exports	Imports
11. INDUSTRY			
Alcoholic beverages		—[2]	0.8[2] *a*
beer *b*	35.0		
Cement	—	—	29.3
Electrical engineering *a*	—	—	1.4
Motor vehicles *a*	—	0.1	2.9

a million $ U.S. *b* '000 hectolitres.

na: data not available. — negligible or nil. [1] one year only. [2] two year average. * estimate. ‡ see appendix. † re-exports.

URUGUAY

Uruguay has been a republic since 1830. Apart from the years 1952–66, when executive power was vested in a nine-man 'Council of State', there has been a presidential system of government. The country has an advanced social welfare system.

AREA: 186 926 sq. km. (72 172 sq. miles)

LAND USE: (percentage of total)

	1961	*1954*
Arable and orchard	12.0	12.3
Permanent meadow and pasture	74.1	67.8
Forest and woodland	3.2	2.7
City areas, waste and other land	10.7	17.2

POPULATION: 2 783 000 (1967 estimate)

Largest city: MONTEVIDEO, capital; population: 1 158 632 (city proper, 1963)

Distribution of working population (1963)

Total working population: 1 015 500*

U.N. group no.		*Percentage*
0	Agriculture, forestry, fishing and hunting	17.9
1	Mining and quarrying	0.2
2/3	Manufacturing	20.8
4	Construction	4.8
5	Electricity, gas, water and sanitary services	1.7
6	Commerce	13.0
7	Transport, storage and communications	6.1
8	Services	27.4
9	Others	8.1

		Year(s)
Infant mortality (per '000)	49.8*	1965
Crude birth rate (per '000)	24.5*	1960–5 av.
Crude death rate (per '000)	9*	1960–5 av.
Accidental deaths (per 100 000 population)		
caused by motor vehicles	7.5	1966
due to other causes	29.1	1966
Population per physician	850	1963
Population per hospital bed	200 *b*	1966
School enrolment: age 5–19 years (percentage)	72	1963–4 av.
age over 19 years (per 100 000 population)	587 *a*	1963–5 av.

a universities and degree granting institutions only. *b* government hospitals only.

COMMUNICATIONS

		Year(s)
Motor vehicles in use ('000s): private	112	1963–5 av.
commercial	81.1	
Railway track (km.)	3 102	1964
Telephones (per '000 urban population)	6.9*	1967
Radio receivers (per '000 population)	342	1963–5 av.
Television sets (per '000 population)	66.4	1963–5 av.
Daily newspapers (per '000 population)	249.5	1962–3 av.

FINANCE

Currency unit: The Uruguayan peso

Exchange rates	*1965*	*1960*	*1950*	*1938*
Per $ U.S.	59.9 *a*	11.03	1.5	1.84
Per £ sterling	157.72	30.88	4.21	8.46

		Year(s)
National Income (million $ U.S.)	1 458	1965
G.N.P. per capita ($ U.S.)	570	1966
Rate of increase of G.N.P. per capita	1.3	1960–3 av.
Foreign trade (percentage of G.D.P.)	23	1963–4 av.

a official import rate.

TRADING

Total trade (in million $ U.S.)	*1965*	*1955*	*1938*
Exports (f.o.b.)	191	184	62
Imports (c.i.f.)	150	229	62

Main trading partners (percentage of total value)

Exports	*1965*	*1955*	*1938*	*Imports*	*1965*	*1955*	*1938*
U.S.A.	17	9	4	U.S.A.	13	19	12
U.K.	16	14	26	Germany F.R.	12	8	16 *d*
Netherlands	9	23	3	U.K.	10	11	20
Germany F.R.	8	4	24 *d*	Brazil	9	17	8
Spain	8	—	—	Venezuela	9	5	—
Italy	7	4	4	Argentina	6	1	5
France	6	5	7	Kuwait	4	na	na

Distribution of trade (percentage of total value)

Exports	*1965*	*1955*	*1938**
Wool	47	57	44
Animals and meat	32	5	23
Hides and skins	8	8	12
Imports			
Machinery and transport equipment	26	na	na
Fuels	17	12	20
Food	6	9	13
Chemicals	4	2	1

d includes Germany D.R.

PRODUCTION, EXPORTS AND IMPORTS

Years: **1963–5 average** and *1953–5 average* Units: '000 metric tons unless otherwise indicated

	Production 1963–5	Production *1953–5*	Exports 1963–5	Exports *1953–5*	Imports 1963–5	Imports *1953–5*
1. CEREALS, etc.						
Barley	27.7*	39.7	0.9	1.7	1.6	1.0
Cassava	—	2.5[2]				
Maize (corn)	120.0	207.3	—	1.8	20.4	0.6
Millets/sorghum	2.0*	5.0[2]	0.3	—	0.1[2]	—
Oats	77.0*	44.0	—	—	5.3	2.8[2]
Potatoes	84.0*	72.3	0.1	—	26.4*	45.1
Rice	71.3	65.3	19.3	14.3	—	—
Sweet potatoes/yams	77.3*	60.7				
Wheat	434.3*	835.0	43.3	190.9	2.5	—
2. FRUIT, etc.						
Apples	27.7	33.0[1]	—	—	—	—
Bananas	—	—	—	—	23.9	17.0
Coconuts	—	—	—	—	0.1 *n*	0.1
Grapes	122.3*	143.0[1]	—	—	—	—
Lemons	12.7*	6.3*	—	—	—	—
Oranges	46.7*	45.0	—	—	—	—
Other citrus fruit	1.0*	—	—	—	—	—
Olives	1.0*	1.0[2]				
Peaches	18.7	na	—	—	—	—
Pears	4.0*	3.0[1]	—	—	—	—
Plums	5.0*	na	—	—	—	—
Raisins	—	—	—	—	0.3[2]	0.4
Tomatoes	21.7	23.0[1]	—	—		
Wine *b*	730.0[1]	830.5[2]	—	—	0.1	1.3

b '000 hectolitres. *n* desiccated.

	Production 1963–5	Production *1953–5*	Exports 1963–5	Exports *1953–5*	Imports 1963–5	Imports *1953–5*
3. BEVERAGES, FOREST PRODUCTS, etc.						
Cocoa	—	—	—	—	0.5	0.8
Coffee	—	—	—	—	2.5	3.5
Sugar: beet	347.7*	224.0*				
cane	176.7*	74.3				
raw (beet)	40.5	21.7*	—	—	36.3	72.3
(cane)	10.4	3.7*				
Tea	—	—	—	—	0.6	0.3
Tobacco: leaf	0.2*	0.4*	—	—	3.2	4.1
cigars	—	na	—	—	—	—
cigarettes	2 560.0 *e*	na				
Softwood *j*	130.0	65.0[1]	—	—	108.5	290.6[1]
Hardwood *j*	1 135.0[2]*	635.0[1]	—	na	22.4[2]	44.0[1]
Wood pulp	3.4[2]	52.0[2]	—	—	14.0[1]	12.5*[2]
Newsprint	—[2]*	—	—	na	20.0[1]	21.5[2]
Other paper	32.0[2]*	—	—	na	1.5[1]	na

e no. in millions. *j* '000 cu. metres of roundwood equivalent.

	Production 1963–5	Production *1953–5*	Exports 1963–5	Exports *1953–5*	Imports 1963–5	Imports *1953–5*
4. VEGETABLE OILSEEDS AND OILS						
Castor oil	—	—	—	—	0.15	0.18
Copra	—	—	—	—	na	0.10
Coconut oil	—	—	—	—	0.97	0.60 *p*
Cottonseed	1.00	na	—	—	—	—
Cottonseed oil	na	na	0.04	na	—	—
Groundnuts	3.50	4.20	—	—	0.01[2]	na
Groundnut oil	na	na	0.30	—[2]	—	—
Linseed	72.33	59.30 *n*	0.55	20.13	0.02[2]	na
Linseed oil	na	na	20.02	31.32	—	—

n flax grown for seed only. *p* incl. palm oil and shea seed oil.

continued

na: data not available. — negligible or nil. [1] one year only. [2] two year average. * estimate. ‡ see appendix. † re-exports.

URUGUAY *continued*

PRODUCTION, EXPORTS AND IMPORTS *continued*

4. VEGETABLE OILSEEDS AND OILS—*continued*

	Production		Exports		Imports	
Olive oil	—	—	—	—	0.02	*0.36*
Soya beans	—	—	—	—	0.05	na
Sunflower seed	63.00	*79.30*	—	—	—	—
Sunflower seed oil	na	na	1.53[2]	*3.94q*	—	—
Tung oil	—	—	—	—	0.02	na

q incl. other minor vegetable oils.

5. LIVESTOCK‡, ANIMAL PRODUCTS, etc.

	Production		Exports		Imports	
Chickens *d*	7 266.7*	*5 672.0*[1]*				
Cattle *d*	8 717.7	*7 916.0*	5.4	—[2]	0.1	—[1]
Goats *d*	18.0*	na	} 73.7	na	0.1	—
Sheep *d*	21 869.3	*26 227.5*[2]				
Horses *d*	463.0	na				
Pigs *d*	427.0	*256.7*	—	—	—	na
Meat‡: 'A'	370.3*	*366.7*	90.6	*35.1*	—	—
'B'	21.7*	*29.4*[1]	3.3	*1.2*	—	—
Butter	7.0*	*4.0*[2]	1.3	*0.1*	—	*0.1*
Cheese	9.3*	*5.7**	—	—	—	—
Eggs	16.3*	*16.7**	1.3[2]	—	—	—
Fish	12.0	*4.1*	0.6	—	0.5	—
Milk	719.0	*576.0*[2]	—	—	—	—
Hides/skins	36.2[1]	na	31.5	*30.3*[2]	—	—
Wool	51.4*	*58.3*	25.9	*43.4*	—	—

d no. in thousands.

6. FIBRES, TEXTILES, etc.

	Production		Exports		Imports	
Agaves (sisal, etc.)	—	—	—	—	0.2	*0.2*
Cotton lint	0.7	—	—	—	6.2	*8.8*
Hemp fibre	—	—	—	—	0.1	*0.1*
Jute	—	—	—	—	0.7	*1.2*
Rubber, natural	—	—	—	—	3.4	*3.0*
Cotton, woven fabrics	—	—	—	—	na	*0.5*
Rayon, fibre/yarn	0.8	*0.9*	—	—	1.5	na
Non-cellulosic fibre/yarn	0.7	—	—	—	0.7	na
Wool: yarn	na	na	0.3	*0.1*	na	na
woven fabrics	na	na	0.2	na	—[2]	—

7. FUEL AND POWER

	Production		Exports		Imports	
Coal, 'A'‡	—	—	—	—	33[1]	*86*
Coke	—	—	—	—	2[1]	*3*
Electricity *h*: total	1 650	*930*				
hydro	992	*680*[1]				
thermal	658	*250*				
Oil, crude	—	—	—	—	1 520	*1 100*[1]
Petroleum, refined	1 453	*1 100*[1]	7	*239*[1]*	83	*190*[1]

h million kWh.

8. IRON AND STEEL

	Production		Exports		Imports	
Iron ore	1	na	—	—	—	—
Steel ingots/castings	11	—	—	—	27	*17*

9. NON-FERROUS MINERALS AND METALS

	Production		Exports		Imports	
Gold *k*, bullion/coins etc.	—	—	—	—	—	*0.21*[1]
Platinum group metals *k*	—	—	—	—	0.19[1]	*0.31*[1]
Asbestos, manufactured	—	—	—	—	1.30[1]	*1.68*[1]
Mica	na	*0.01*[1]	—	—	—	—
Aluminium	—	—	—	—	0.43[1]	*4.48*[1]
Antimony, metal	—	—	—	—	0.01	—[1]
Chrome, metal	—	—	—	—	—	*0.15*[1]
Copper, metal	—	—	—	—	1.05[1]	*0.81*[1]
Lead, metal	—	—	—	—	1.09[1]	*2.01*
Magnesium, dolomite	24.72*r*	na	9.79	na	—	—
Mercury *f*	—	—	—	—	0.06	*0.20*[1]
Tin, metal	—	—	—	—	0.05[1]	*0.07*[1]
Zinc, metal	—	—	—	—	1.04[1]	*1.13*[1]

f metric tons. *k* '000 fine troy oz. *r* dolomitic limestone.

10. CHEMICALS*n* AND FERTILIZERS

	Production	Exports	Imports
Organic chemicals:			
Benzene	na	na	na
Butadiene	—	—	na
Ethylene	—	—	na
Methanol	—	—	na
Phenol	—	—	na
Phthalic anhydride	—	—	na
Styrene monomer	—	—	na
Urea	—	—	na
Inorganic chemicals:			
Ammonia	na	—	na
Carbon black	—	—	na
Chlorine	na	na	na
Nitric acid	na	na	na
Sodium carbonate	—	—	na
Sodium hydroxide	na	—	2.5[1]
Sulphuric acid	na	na	na
Plastics:			
Polyamides	na	na	na
Polyethylene	—	—	na
Polyvinyl chloride	—	—	na

	Production		Exports		Imports	
Fertilizers:						
Phosphates	—	—	—	—	31.3	na
Potash	—	—	—	—	0.1	*1.0*[1]
Sulphur	—	—	—	—	8.6	*4.8*

n data not available for years 1953–5.

11. INDUSTRY

	Production		Exports		Imports	
Aircraft *a*	—	—	—	—	0.6[1]	na
Beer *b*	764.0	na	—	—	—	—
Cement	417.3	*294.7*	17.3*	—	—	*91.0*
Merchant ships *g*	0.1	na	—	—	0.1	*2.0*[1]
Motor vehicles *a*	—	—	—	—	0.9	*5.2*[2]

a million $ U.S. *b* '000 hectolitres. *g* '000 G.R.T.

VENEZUELA

SOUTH AMERICA

Venezuela is one of the more economically stable of the South American republics, due mainly to the considerable revenue from oil. In 1958 a democratic form of civilian government was introduced after five years' military rule.

AREA: 912 050* sq. km. (352 143* sq. miles)

LAND USE: (percentage of total)

		1961
Arable and orchard	on agricultural holdings	5.7
Permanent meadow and pasture	on agricultural holdings	18.3
Forest and woodland		52.6
City areas, waste and other land		23.4

POPULATION: 9 352 000 (1967 estimate)

Largest city: CARACAS, capital; population: 1 764 274 (1966)

Distribution of working population (1961)
Total working population: 2 406 725* *a*

U.N. group no.		*Percentage*
0	Agriculture, forestry, fishing and hunting	32.1
1	Mining and quarrying	1.9
2/3	Manufacturing	12.3
4	Construction	5.3
5	Electricity, gas, water and sanitary services	1.1
6	Commerce	12.6
7	Transport, storage and communications	4.4
8	Services	23.8
9	Others	6.5

		Year(s)
Life expectancy at birth (years)	66.4	1961
Infant mortality (per '000)	47.7* *a*	1965
Crude birth rate (per '000)	47.0* *a*	1960–5 av.
Crude death rate (per '000)	9.5* *a*	1960–5 av.
Accidental deaths (per 100 000 population) caused by motor vehicles	22.2*	1966
due to other causes	25.2*	1966
Population per physician	1 210	1965
Population per hospital bed	310	1966
School enrolment: age 5–19 years (percentage)	83	1963–4 av.
age over 19 years (per 100 000 population)	498	1963–5 av.

a excl. Indian jungle population.

COMMUNICATIONS

		Year(s)
Motor vehicles in use ('000s): private	341.3	1963–5 av.
commercial	139.9	1963–5 av.
Railway track (km.)	773	1964
Mail per capita: domestic	21	1965
foreign received	29	1965
foreign sent	10	1965
Telephones (per '000 urban population)	3.4	1967
Radio receivers (per '000 population)	190	1963–5 av.
Television sets (per '000 population)	70.9	1963–5 av.
Daily newspapers (per '000 population)	78	1963

continued

na: data not available. — negligible or nil. [1] one year only. [2] two year average. * estimate. ‡ see appendix. † re-exports.

FINANCE

Currency unit: The bolivar

Exchange rates b	*1965*	*1960*	*1955*	*1938*
Per $ U.S.	4.5	3.35	3.35	3.19
Per £ sterling	12.6	9.38	9.38	14.67

		Year(s)
National Income (million $ U.S.)	6 497	1965
G.N.P. per capita ($ U.S.)	850	1966
Rate of increase of G.N.P. per capita	1.5	1960–4 av.
Foreign trade (percentage of G.D.P.)	47	1963–5 av.

b official selling rates.

TRADING

Total trade (in million $ U.S.)	*1965*	*1955*	*1938*
Exports (f.o.b.)	2 745	1 873	181
Imports (c.i.f.)	1 297	943	96

Main trading partners (percentage of total value)

Exports	*1965*	*1955*	*1938*	*Imports*	*1965*	*1955*	*1938*
U.S.A.	37	38	na	U.S.A.	51	59	56
Neths. Antilles	24	37		Germany F.R.	9	9	12 *d*
Canada	10	2		Canada	6	4	—
U.K.	8	4		U.K.	6	8	7
Trin./Tob.	5	2		Japan	5	2	—
Brazil	3	4		Italy	5	3	2
Netherlands	2	3		France	3	4	3

Distribution of trade (percentage of total value)

	1965	*1955**	*1938**
Exports			
Petroleum	65	94	92
Petroleum products	28		
Iron ore	5	3	na
Imports			
Manufactured goods	72	na	na
(machinery and transport equipment)	(43)	(34)	(30)
(iron and steel)	(7)	(11)	(16)
Food	10	9	5
(cereals and cereal preparations)	(4)	(3)	(2)
Chemicals	10	6	4

d incl. Germany D.R.

PRODUCTION, EXPORTS AND IMPORTS

Years: **1963–5 average** and *1953–5 average* Units: '000 metric tons unless otherwise indicated

1. CEREALS, etc.

	Production		Exports		Imports	
Barley	—	—	—	—	0.2	*8.0**
Cassava	318.3	*201.3*				
Maize (corn)	475.3	*326.0*	—	—	68.2	*1.0*
Millets/sorghum	—	—	—	—	0.6[2]	—
Oats	—	—	—	—	12.2	*13.7*
Potatoes	123.7	*38.3*	—	—	10.6	*37.5*
Rice	165.7	*76.7**	—	—	1.4	*3.3*
Rye	—	—	—	—	0.1	—
Sweet potatoes/yams	99.7	*53.5*[2]				
Wheat	1.0	*4.5*[2]	—	—	502.0	—

2. FRUIT, etc.

	Production		Exports		Imports	
Apples	—	—	—	—	12.3	*4.1**
Bananas	1 296.3	*50.5*[2]	11.0	*3.1**	—	—
Coconuts	170.7*e*	na	0.3	*0.1*[2]	0.1*n*	—
Grapes	—	—	—	—	6.1	*3.9**
Oranges	40.0*	na	—	—	0.1[2]	—[1]
Pears	—	—	—	—	5.0	*1.1**
Pineapples	40.0	na	—	—	—	—
Raisins	—	—	—	—	0.9	*0.4**
Tomatoes	66.3	na				
Wine *b*	—	—	—	—	27.3	*49.3*

b '000 hectolitres. *e* no. in millions. *n* desiccated.

3. BEVERAGES, FOREST PRODUCTS, etc.

	Production		Exports		Imports	
Cocoa	21.2	*15.3**	12.3	*16.5*	—	—
Coffee	57.1	*47.0*	20.6	*36.8*	—	—
Sugar: cane	3 826.3*	*2 134.7*				
raw	317.4*p*	*143.7*p*	19.5	—	—	*24.8*
Tea	—	—	—	—	0.2[2]	—
Tobacco: leaf	8.7	*6.0**	—	—	0.2	*0.4*[2]
cigars *e*	93.0	*70.6*	—	—	—	—
cigarettes *e*	8 822.0	*3 000.0*				
Softwood *j*	—	—	—[2]	—	7.3	*145.9*
Hardwood *j*	5 139.0*	*1 349.0*	2.6	*1.6*		*9.5*
Wood pulp	—*[2]	—[2]	—	—	75.0	*5.9*
Newsprint	—	—[1]	—	—	36.0	*17.7*
Other paper	131.4	*4.4*[1]	—	—	40.0[2]	*49.3*

e no. in millions. *j* '000 cu. metres of roundwood equivalent. *p* in addition, papelón and panella 44* (1963–5 av.) and 73* (1953–5 av.).

4. VEGETABLE OILSEEDS AND OILS

	Production		Exports		Imports	
Castor oil	—	—	—	—	0.07*	*0.07*
Copra	15.90	*14.95*[2]	—	—	44.96	*48.90*
Cottonseed	24.30	*8.67*	—	—	0.04	—
Cottonseed oil	na	na	—	—	9.98	—
Groundnuts	1.17	*1.05*[2]	—	—	0.34	*0.03*
Groundnut oil	na	na	—	—	3.70[2]	—
Linseed	—	—	—	—	0.03[2]	—
Linseed oil	—	—	—	—	0.67	*0.94*
Olive oil	—	—	—	—	0.52	*0.71*
Palm kernels	na	na	—	—	—	—
Palm kernel oil	—	—	—	—	0.01	—
Palm oil	1.50*	*1.33*	—	—	—	—
Rapeseed	—	—	—	—	0.03[2]	—
Sesame seed	43.87	*9.30*	—	—	12.36	*10.20*
Soya beans	—	—	—	—	14.95	—
Soya bean oil	na	—	—	—	0.92[2]	*0.07*
Sunflower seed	—	—	—	—	0.06	—
Tung oil	—	—	—	—	0.07[2]	—

5. LIVESTOCK‡, ANIMAL PRODUCTS, etc.

	Production		Exports		Imports	
Chickens *d*	29 162.3*q*	na				
Cattle *d*	6 618.3	*6 230.0*[1]	—	*0.1*	4.8*	*0.7*
dairy cows *d*	3 240.0*	na				
Goats *d*	1 247.0	na	—	—	—	—
Sheep *d*	80.3	na	—	—	—	—
Horses *d*	398.3*	na				
Pigs *d*	1 867.0	na	—	—	0.4	—
Bacon/ham	187.7	*96.0*	—	—	0.2	*3.1*
Meat‡: 'A'			—	—	7.0	—
'B'	42.3*	na	—	—	—	—
Butter	4.3*r*	*2.7r*	—	—	—	*0.9*
Cheese	16.0	*16.0*[2]	—[2]	—	4.2	*5.2*
Eggs	30.0*	na	—	—	1.9	*13.4*
Fish	109.0	*61.6*	6.5	*1.3*[1]*	18.7	na
Milk	602.7	*308.0*[2]	—	—	438.9	*180.0**

d no. in thousands. *q* incl. ducks, geese and turkeys. *r* factory produce only.

6. FIBRES, TEXTILES, etc.

	Production		Exports		Imports	
Agaves (sisal)	11.9	*5.7**	—	*0.5*[1]	—	—
Cotton lint	14.0	*4.0*	—	—	6.0[2]	*1.2*
Hemp fibre	—	—	—	—	—	*0.3*[2]
Rubber, natural	—	—	0.3†	—	5.1[2]	*8.1*
Silk *f*	—	—	—	—	3.5[2]	—
Cotton: yarn	15.2	*0.9*	—	—	1.0[1]	na
woven fabrics	8.0	*1.8*	—	—	1.4	na
Rayon: fibre/yarn	2.7	*2.3*	0.2	na	3.8	na
woven fabrics	4.1	*2.9t*	—	—	2.7*u*	na
Non-cellulosic fibre/yarn	1.4	na	—	—	2.5	na
Wool, woven fabrics	3.3*v*	*0.6v*	na	na	0.2[2]	na

f metric tons. *t* incl. mixed yarn. *u* incl. synthetic piece goods. *v* million metres.

7. FUEL AND POWER

	Production		Exports		Imports	
Coal, 'A'‡	37	*30*		*1*	9	*1*
Coke	—	—	—	—	167	na
Electricity *h*: total	7 536	*1 600*[1]				
hydro	1 233	*250*[1]				
thermal	6 303	*1 350*[1]				
Natural gas *i*	6 080	*2 420*[1]	—	—	—	—
Oil, crude	177 180	*115 540*[1]	119 830	*87 700*[1]	—	—
Petroleum, refined	56 326	*26 080*[1]	44 927	*21 470*[1]	7	*110*[1]

h million kWh. *i* million cu. metres.

8. IRON AND STEEL

	Production		Exports		Imports	
Iron ore	9 609*m*	*3 446m*	14 740	*5 071*	—	—
Pig iron	320	—	—	—	8	*2*
Steel ingots/castings	476	—	—	—	3	—
Iron/steel scrap	—	—	—	—	6[1]	—
Iron/steel products *a*	na	na	11	—	79	*85*

a million $ U.S. *m* metal content.

9. NON-FERROUS MINERALS AND METALS

	Production		Exports		Imports	
Diamonds	91.67*l*	*107.64l*	1.90[1] *a*	*1.99a*	—	—
Gold *k*, ore	28.30*m*	*48.20m*	—	*9.00p*	—	—
Platinum group metals *k*	—	—	—	—	17.61	—[1]

a million $ U.S. *k* '000 fine troy oz. *l* '000 carats. *m* metal content. *p* bullion.

continued

na: data not available. — negligible or nil. [1] one year only. [2] two year average. * estimate. ‡ see appendix. † re-exports.

VENEZUELA *continued*

PRODUCTION, EXPORTS AND IMPORTS *continued*

9. NON-FERROUS MINERALS AND METALS—*continued*

	Production		Exports		Imports	
Asbestos: fibre	—	*0.36*	—	*0.40*	3.89	*1.98*
manufactured	—	—	—	—	10.29	*2.44s*
Mica	—	—	—	—	0.28	*0.61²s*
Aluminium:						
alumina	—	—	—	—	0.28	—
aluminium	na	—	—	—	17.12	*1.60*s*
Antimony, metal	—	—	—	—	0.02	*0.02²s*
Copper, metal	—	—	—	—	7.18	*0.27²*
Lead, metal	—	—	—	—	3.72	*0.75²s*
Magnesium:						
magnesite	na	na	—	—	1.21	*0.03²*
metal/salts	—‡	—‡	—	—	0.50	*0.12²*
Mercury *f*	—	—	—	—	6.60	*24.60²s*
Tin, metal	—	—	—	—	0.16	*0.13s*
Titanium minerals	—	—	—	—	3.10	*0.93²s*
Zinc, metal	—	—	—	—	3.79	*0.81²*

a million $ U.S. *f* metric tons. *k* '000 fine troy oz. *l* '000 carats. *m* metal content. *p* bullion. *s* incl. imports for re-export.

10. CHEMICALS*n* AND FERTILIZERS

Organic chemicals:	Production	Exports	Imports
Benzene	na	—	—²
Butadiene	—	—	na
Ethylene	—	—	na
Methanol	—	—	1.1
Phenol	—	—	0.4
Phthalic anhydride	—	—	na
Styrene monomer	—	—	na
Urea	na	—	3.5

continued

10. CHEMICALS*n* AND FERTILIZERS—*continued*

	Production		Exports		Imports	
Inorganic chemicals:						
Ammonia	na		—		0.7	
Carbon black	3.5²		na		0.9²	
Chlorine	na		na		na	
Nitric acid	na		—		0.1	
Sodium carbonate	—		—		26.4²	
Sodium hydroxide	15.0²		—		14.4	
Sulphuric acid	42.0²		—		0.2	
Plastics:						
Polyamides	na		na		na	
Polyethylene	—		—		na	
Polyvinyl chloride	—		—		na	
Fertilizers:						
Phosphates	2.1*	—	—	—	—	—
Potash	—	—	—	—	15.2	*1.1²*
Sulphur	—	—	—	—	22.4	*1.4*

n data not available for years 1953–5.

11. INDUSTRY

	Production		Exports		Imports	
Aircraft *a*	—	—	—	—	8.6	na
Alcoholic beverages			—	—	7.6*a*	*7.9a*
beer *b*	2 631.0	*1 290.7*				
Cement	1 845.7	*1 159.0*	210.7	*1.3**	0.7	*25.0*
Electrical engineering *a*	—	—	—	—	91.3	*29.7²*
Merchant ships *g*	—	—	—	—	1.0	*15.8*
Motor vehicles			—	—	120.0*a*	*90.3a*
commercial *dn*	10.8	*5.6*				
private *dn*	29.3	*8.6*				

a million $ U.S. *b* '000 hectolitres. *d* no. in thousands. *g* '000 G.R.T. *n* assembly of imported parts.

VIETNAM, NORTH

SOUTH EAST ASIA

Vietnam, Laos and Cambodia comprised the former territory of French Indo-China. In 1954 at the Geneva Conference the rift between North and South Vietnam was generally recognized, and the northern zone was established as the Democratic Republic of Vietnam. It has since been the aim of North Vietnam, which now has a centrally planned economy, to work for reunification with the South.

AREA: 164 103 sq. km. (63 360 sq. miles)

LAND USE: (percentage of total)

	1965
Arable and orchard	12.7
Permanent meadow and pasture	na
Forest and woodland, incl. rough grazing	49.8
City areas, waste and other land	na

POPULATION: 20 100 000 (1967 estimate)

Largest city: HA NOI, capital; population: 643 576 (1960)

COMMUNICATIONS

		Year
Railway track (km.)	901	1967

FINANCE

Currency unit: The dong

Exchange rates	*1965 b*	*1960 b*
Per $ U.S.	3.6	3.6
Per £ sterling	10.08	10.08

		Year(s)
Rate of increase of G.N.P. per capita	2.8	1960–3 av.

b official rate.

EMPLOYMENT, PRODUCTION AND TRADE

Two-thirds of the cultivated land is under rice, which in good years supplies the needs of the country. The majority of the people are employed in the paddy fields, or in the cultivation of other crops which include sugar cane, root crops, and cotton. Silk is also grown, and anthracite and phosphates are mined.

The chief trading partners are China P.R. and the Comecon countries.

PRODUCTION, EXPORTS AND IMPORTS

Years: **1963–5 average** Units: '000 metric tons unless otherwise indicated

Note—no data are available for 1953–5

1. CEREALS, etc.	Production	Exports	Imports
Cassava	841.3*		
Maize (corn)	252.0*	—	25.6*
Rice	4 469.3*	6.9*	16.1*
Sweet potatoes/yams	820.3*		
2. FRUIT, etc.			
Bananas	na	8.4*	—

3. BEVERAGES, FOREST PRODUCTS, etc.	Production	Exports	Imports
Coffee	1.1*	0.9*	—
Sugar: cane	760.7*		
raw	na	5.5*	32.6*
Tea	3.8*	0.9*	—
Tobacco, leaf	4.6*	0.3*	—
Wood	na	—	—

continued

na: data not available. — negligible or nil. ¹ one year only. ² two year average. * estimate. ‡ see appendix. † re-exports.

PRODUCTION, EXPORTS AND IMPORTS *continued*

4. VEGETABLE OILSEEDS AND OILS	Production	Exports	Imports
Castor seed	2.00*	0.12*	—
Castor oil	na	0.02	—
Coconut oil	—	—	1.39
Cottonseed	4.00*	—	—
Groundnuts	24.27*	2.32	—
Groundnut oil	na	0.64*	—
Sesame seed	2.77*	0.36*	—
Soya beans	8.00*	0.57*	0.50¹*
Tung oil	na	0.06*	—

5. LIVESTOCK‡, ANIMAL PRODUCTS, etc.	Production	Exports	Imports
Chickens	na		
Cattle *d*	800.7	0.6*	—
Horses *d*	30.0*		
Pigs *d*	4 226.0	11.5*	—
Eggs	na	0.2*	—
Fish	na	—	—
Milk	—	—	2.7*

d no. in thousands.

6. FIBRES, TEXTILES, etc.	Production	Exports	Imports
Cotton lint	2.0*	—	—
Jute	16.0*	3.1*	—
Rubber, natural	na	0.4*	1.8*
Silk *f*	na	11.7*	—

f metric tons.

7. FUEL AND POWER	Production	Exports	Imports
Coal, 'A'‡	na	na	—
Electricity *h*	504²		

h million kWh.

10. CHEMICALS AND FERTILIZERS	Production	Exports	Imports
Chemicals	—	—	na
Fertilizers:			
Phosphates	1 000**p*	na	—

p apatite.

11. INDUSTRY	Production	Exports	Imports
Cement	614.7*	100.0*	—

VIETNAM, SOUTH

SOUTH EAST ASIA

South Vietnam became a republic in 1954, and since that date there has been a series of military and civilian administrations. The North Vietnamese attempts to reunite the country are vigorously resisted by the South Vietnamese who fear the enforcement of communist principles. In this resistance South Vietnam has the active support of the U.S.A. and of some other Western nations.

AREA: 171 665 sq. km. (66 280 sq. miles)

LAND USE: (percentage of total)

	1965
Arable and orchard	17.2
Permanent meadow and pasture	16.8
Forest and woodland	32.8
City areas, waste and other land	33.2

POPULATION: 16 973 000 (1967 estimate)

Largest city: SAI GON, capital; population: 1 485 300 (1965)
Total working population: 4 750 000

Employment: the majority of the population is employed in agriculture; rubber and rice being the most important products; although considerable diversification has been planned, progress to this end has been slow because of the war against North Vietnam.

There has been some industrial development but this, and trends in employment distribution are distorted by the conditions of war.

		Year(s)
Infant mortality (per '000)	36.7*	1965
Crude birth rate (per '000)	27.7*	1965
Crude death rate (per '000)	6.4*	1965
Population per physician	19 960	1963
Population per hospital bed	590	1966
School enrolment: age 5–19 years (percentage)	57	1963–4 av.
age over 19 years (per 100 000 population)	152	1963–5 av.

COMMUNICATIONS

		Year(s)
Motor vehicles in use ('000s): private	32.5	1963–5 av.
commercial	30.3	1963–5 av.
Railway track (km.)	1 400	1967
Mail per capita: domestic	3	1963–5 av.
foreign received	1	1963–5 av.
foreign sent	1	1963–5 av.
Telephones (per '000 urban population)	0.2	1967
Radio receivers (per '000 population)	58	1963–5 av.
Daily newspapers (per '000 population)	32.3	1962–4 av.

FINANCE

Currency unit: The piastre

Exchange rates	*1965*	*1960*
Per $ U.S.	60*a*	35
Per £ sterling	168	98

		Year(s)
National Income (million $ U.S.)	1 828	1965
G.N.P. per capita ($ U.S.)	120	1966
Rate of increase of G.N.P. per capita	0.1	1960–3 av.
Foreign trade (percentage of G.D.P.)	19	1963–5 av.

a trade rate.

TRADING

Total trade (in million $ U.S.)	*1965*	*1955*	*1938 a*
Exports (f.o.b.)	35	69	54*
Imports (c.i.f.)	357	263	84*

Main trading partners (percentage of total value)

Exports	*1965*	*1955*	*Imports*	*1965*	*1955*
France	34	31	U.S.A.	45	12
Germany F.R.	16	1	Taiwan	13	3
U.K.	12	2	Japan	9	13
Japan	11	3	South Korea	5	na
West Mal./Sing.	7	7	Malaysia	4	—
Hong Kong	5	4	France	3	51
Italy	5	1	Germany F.R.	2	2

Distribution of trade (percentage of total value)

Exports	*1965*	*1955*
Rubber	73	58
Food	15	na *b*
(tea)	(6)	(—)
Imports		
Manufactured goods	57	na
(machinery and transport equipment)	(20)	(15*)
(iron and steel)	(13)	(4*)
(textiles)	(9)	(16*)
Chemicals	14	na
(medicinal and pharmaceutical products)	(5)	(4*)
Food	14	na
(dairy products and eggs)	(5)	(5*)
Crude materials and fuels	12	na

a incl. North Vietnam. *b* mainly rice.

continued

na: data not available. — negligible or nil. ¹ one year only. ² two year average. * estimate. ‡ see appendix. † re-exports.

PRODUCTION, EXPORTS AND IMPORTS

Years: **1963–5 average** and *1953–5 average* Units: '000 metric tons unless otherwise indicated

	Production 1963–5	Production 1953–5	Exports 1963–5	Exports 1953–5	Imports 1963–5	Imports 1953–5
1. CEREALS, etc.						
Cassava	304.7	na				
Maize (corn)	42.3	30.0[1]	—	1.4[1]	14.0	1.4[1]
Millets/sorghum	—	—	—	—	—	0.1[1]
Potatoes	6.7	—	—	—	0.3[2]	9.4[1]
Rice	5 111.3	2 669.0[2]	123.8	69.6[1]	80.6	0.3[1]
Sweet potatoes/ yams	293.0	na				
2. FRUIT, etc.						
Apples	—	—	—	—	0.4[2]	1.5[1]
Bananas	210.3	na	0.3	—	—	—
Coconuts	144.7*e*	na	—	0.5[1]	—	—
Dates	—	—	—	—	0.1	1.8[1]
Grapes	—	—	—	—	0.2	1.0[1]
Oranges	—	—	—	—[1]	—	2.1[1]
Pineapples	55.7	na	—	—	—	—
Pears	—	—	—	—	0.2[2]	—
Raisins	—	—	—	—	0.1	0.6[1]
Wine *b*	—	—	—	—	4.7	82.0[1]

b '000 hectolitres. *e* no. in millions.

	Production 1963–5	Production 1953–5	Exports 1963–5	Exports 1953–5	Imports 1963–5	Imports 1953–5
3. BEVERAGES, FOREST PRODUCTS, etc.						
Coffee	3.5	1.5[2]	0.3	0.2[1]	—	0.2[1]
Sugar: cane	1 082.7	660.0[1]				
raw	7.0*p*	2.0[2]	—	—[1]	59.2	54.9[1]
Tea	5.3	3.7[2]	2.2	0.2[1]	—	0.2[1]
Tobacco: leaf	7.2	7.2[2]	—	0.7[1]	3.3	4.9[1]
cigarettes *e*	6 202.0	na	—	—	—	6.2[2]*n*
Softwood *j*	16.0	44.3	—	—	—	0.7
Hardwood *j*	710.7	607.7	—	0.4	0.3	58.6
Wood pulp	2.0	—	—	—	11.7[2]	—
Newsprint	—	—	—	—	5.5	3.2
Other paper	15.7*	—	—	—	26.0*	18.2

e no. in millions. *j* '000 cu. metres of roundwood equivalent. *n* incl. other tobacco manufactures. *p* in addition, non-centrifugal sugar 35*.

	Production 1963–5	Production 1953–5	Exports 1963–5	Exports 1953–5	Imports 1963–5	Imports 1953–5
4. VEGETABLE OILSEEDS AND OILS						
Castor seed	—	—	—	—[1]	—	0.10[1]
Castor oil	—	—	—	—	0.07[2]	—
Copra	24.83	19.75[2]	0.03	—[2]	—	0.40[1]
Coconut oil	na	na	0.43	0.31[1]	—	—[1]
Cottonseed	—	2.00[2]	—	—[2]	—	0.30[1]
Cottonseed oil	—	—	—	—[1]	2.41	1.17[1]
Groundnuts	23.80	11.90[2]	4.32	—	—	—
Groundnut oil	na	na	0.86	—[1]	0.01	0.17[1]
Linseed oil	—	—	—	—	0.01	—
Olive oil	—	—	—	—[1]	0.01	0.01
Sesame seed	0.57	na	0.27	0.10[1]	—[1]	—
Soya beans	4.30	na	—	—[2]	0.94	0.80[1]
Soya bean oil	—	—	—	—[2]	1.70[2]	—[2]

	Production 1963–5	Production 1953–5	Exports 1963–5	Exports 1953–5	Imports 1963–5	Imports 1953–5
5. LIVESTOCK‡, ANIMAL PRODUCTS, etc.						
Cattle *d*	1 050.7	na	—	—[2]	—	0.1[2]
dairy cows *d*	39.7*	na				
Goats *d*	33.0	na	—	—	—	—
Sheep *d*	3.7	na	—	—	—	—
Horses *d*	11.0	na				
Pigs *d*	3 313.0	na	2.9*	—	—	—
Meat‡: 'A'	121.3*	na	—	—	—	—
'B'	na	na	0.3	—	—	—
Butter	—	—	—	—	0.2	0.9
Cheese	—	—	—	—	0.3	1.5[1]
Eggs	2.4*	—	1.4	1.3[2]	—	—
Fish	383.5	120.0[1]	1.1	na	0.1	na
Milk	1.0	—	—	—	71.7	32.8[2]
Hides/skins	na	1.0[2]	—	0.2[2]	—	—

d no. in thousands.

	Production 1963–5	Production 1953–5	Exports 1963–5	Exports 1953–5	Imports 1963–5	Imports 1953–5
6. FIBRES, TEXTILES, etc.						
Cotton lint	—	1.0[2]	—	na	13.8	—
Jute	3.7	—	0.2	—	3.5	1.0[1]
Rubber, natural	71.7	58.2	66.2	54.4[1]	1.2	—
Cotton: yarn	7.6	na	—	—	6.8[1]	na
woven fabrics	5.6	na	—	—	0.9[1]	8.8[1]
7. FUEL AND POWER						
Coal, 'A'‡	60	—	—	166[1]	16	26[1]
Electricity *h*, thermal	430*p*	70[1]				
Petroleum, refined	—	—	—	—	1 100	330[1]

h million kWh. *p* in addition, hydro 33.

	Production 1963–5	Production 1953–5	Exports 1963–5	Exports 1953–5	Imports 1963–5	Imports 1953–5
9. NON-FERROUS MINERALS AND METALS						
Chrome, ore	na	—	—	—	—	—
Tin, ore	2.25**m*	—*m*	—	—	—	—

m metal content.

	Production 1963–5	Production 1953–5	Exports 1963–5	Exports 1953–5	Imports 1963–5	Imports 1953–5
10. FERTILIZERS						
Potash	—	—	—	—	11.8	—
11. INDUSTRY						
Aircraft *a*	—	—	—	—	1.6[2]	—
Alcoholic beverages			na	—	—	8.1[2]*a*
beer	941.0*b*	663.3*b*	0.2*a*			
Cement	na	na	na	na	na	na
Electrical engineering *a*	—	—	—	—	13.2	8.6[2]
Railway vehicles *a*	—	—	—	—	3.8	—
Motor vehicles *a*	—	—	—	—	15.1	10.7

a million $ U.S. *b* '000 hectolitres.

WESTERN SAMOA

PACIFIC OCEAN

Western Samoa, previously administered by New Zealand under a U.N. Trusteeship Agreement, became an independent sovereign state in 1962. The island remains within the British Commonwealth, New Zealand acting as a liaison in external affairs.

AREA: 2 842 sq. km. (1 097 sq. miles)

LAND USE: (percentage of total)	1965	1955
Arable and orchard	31.7	11.3
Permanent meadow and pasture	2.1	0.7
Forest and woodland	64.8	63.1
City areas, waste and other land	1.4	24.9

POPULATION: 131 377 (1966 census)

Capital city: APIA; population: 25 480 (1966)

Distribution of working population (1961)
Total working population: 27 941

U.N. group no.		*Percentage*
0	Agriculture, forestry, fishing and hunting	68.5
1	Mining and quarrying	—
2/3/4	Manufacturing and construction	6.1
5/8	Services, including electricity, gas, water and sanitary services	13.5
6	Commerce	7.8
7	Transport, storage and communications	2.7
9	Others	1.4

		Year(s)
Infant mortality (per '000)	42.5*	1965
Crude birth rate (per '000)	30.7*	1965
Crude death rate (per '000)	5.7*	1965
Population per physician	2 240	1966
Population per hospital bed	240*a*	1966
School enrolment: age 5–19 years (percentage)	105‡	1963–4 av.
age over 19 years (per 100 000 population)	79	1964

a government hospitals only.

FINANCE

Currency unit: The tala, at par with the New Zealand dollar, replaced the Western Samoa pound in 1966 at the rate 1 tala to WS£0.5

Exchange rates (for Western Samoa pounds)	1965	1960
Per $ U.S.	0.357	0.357
Per £ sterling	1.0	1.0

TRADING

Total trade (in million $ U.S.)	1965	1955	1938
Exports (f.o.b.)	6	7	1
Imports (c.i.f.)	9	5	1

Main trading partners (percentage of total value)

Exports	1965	*Imports*	1965
New Zealand	44	New Zealand	29
Netherlands	16	Australia	19
U.K.	15	U.K.	10
Germany F.R.	12	U.S.A.	10
American Samoa	5	Japan	9

Distribution of trade (percentage of total value)

Exports	1965	*Imports*	1965
Copra	41	Manufactured goods	43
Bananas and plantains	30	(machinery and transport equipment)	(14)
Cocoa beans	22	(textiles and clothing)	(9)
		Food	31
		(meat)	(9)
		(cereals)	(7)
		Crude materials and fuels	12

continued

PRODUCTION, EXPORTS AND IMPORTS

Years: **1963–5 average** and *1953–5 average* Units: '000 metric tons unless otherwise indicated

	Production 1963–5	Production 1953–5	Exports 1963–5	Exports 1953–5	Imports 1963–5	Imports 1953–5
1. CEREALS, etc.						
Potatoes	—	—	—	—	—	0.1
Rice	—	—	—	—	1.0	0.4
2. FRUIT, etc.						
Bananas	na	11.4	19.8	11.4	—	—
Coconuts *e*	108.0*	na	—	—	—	—

e no. in millions.

	Production 1963–5	Production 1953–5	Exports 1963–5	Exports 1953–5	Imports 1963–5	Imports 1953–5
3. BEVERAGES, FOREST PRODUCTS, etc.						
Cocoa	4.0	3.5*	3.9	3.1	—	—
Sugar, raw	—	—	—	—	3.0	2.0
Tobacco: leaf	—	—	—	—	0.1	—
products	—	—	—	—	0.3*a*	
Softwood *j*	—	—	—	—	} 9.6	3.3
Hardwood *j*	56.0*[1]	na	—	—		—

a million $ U.S. *j* '000 cu. metres of roundwood equivalent.

	Production 1963–5	Production 1953–5	Exports 1963–5	Exports 1953–5	Imports 1963–5	Imports 1953–5
4. VEGETABLE OILSEEDS AND OILS						
Copra	14.87*	na	14.52	14.27	—	—
5. LIVESTOCK‡, ANIMAL PRODUCTS, etc.						
Cattle *d*	18.3	11.0[2]	—	—	—	—
Horses *d*	2.7	na				
Pigs *d*	36.0*	na	—	—	—	—
Butter	—	—	—	—	0.1	0.1
Fish	na	na	—	—	—	—
Milk	—	—	—	—	—	0.1

d no. in thousands.

	Production 1963–5	Production 1953–5	Exports 1963–5	Exports 1953–5	Imports 1963–5	Imports 1953–5
7. FUEL AND POWER						
Electricity *h*: total	7	—				
hydro	5	—				
thermal	2	—				
Petroleum, refined	—	—	—	—	10	—[1]

h million kWh.

	Production 1963–5	Production 1953–5	Exports 1963–5	Exports 1953–5	Imports 1963–5	Imports 1953–5
11. INDUSTRY						
Alcoholic beverages *a*	—	—	—	—	0.2	—
Electrical engineering *a*	—	—	—	—	0.4[2]	—
Motor vehicles *a*	—	—	—	—	0.6	—

a million $ U.S.

WEST INDIES ASSOCIATED STATES

The West Indies Federation, which was established in 1958, was dissolved in 1962 after Jamaica and Trinidad had seceded. In 1967 the West Indies Associated States was established, consisting of the former British colonies of: Antigua, Dominica, Grenada, Montserrat, St. Kitts with Nevis and Anguilla, St. Lucia, St. Vincent and the Virgin Islands (U.K.). These were given self-government in association with Britain who retains powers and responsibilities for the defence and external affairs of these Caribbean islands.

FINANCE

Currency unit: The East Caribbean dollar replaced, at par, the British West Indies dollar in 1965

Exchange rates	1965	1960	1955
Per $ U.S.	1.71	1.71	1.71
Per £ sterling	4.8	4.8	4.8

ANTIGUA

AREA: 442 sq. km. (171 sq. miles)

LAND USE: (percentage of total)	1964	1955
Arable and orchard	54.6	36.4
Permanent meadow and pasture	4.5	9.1
Forest and woodland	13.6	9.1
City areas, waste and other land	27.3	45.4

POPULATION: 61 000 (1967 estimate)

Capital city: SAINT JOHNS; population: 21 595 (1960)
Total working population: 18 212 (1960)

		Year(s)
Life expectancy at birth (years): male	60.5	1959–61 av.
female	64.3	1959–61 av.
Infant mortality (per '000)	45.4	1965
Crude birth rate (per '000)	30.4	1965
Crude death rate (per '000)	8.4	1965
Population per physician	3 750	1964
Population per hospital bed	140	1964
School enrolment: age 5–19 years (percentage)	109‡	1963–4 av.
age over 19 years (per 100 000 population)	82	1963

COMMUNICATIONS		*Year(s)*
Telephones (per '000 urban population)	2.1	1967
Radio receivers (per '000 population)	58	1963–5 av.
Television sets (per '000 population)	8.4	1963–5 av.
Daily newspapers (per '000 population)	17	1962–4 av.

FINANCE		*Year*
National Income (million $ U.S.)	18*	1966
G.N.P. per capita ($ U.S.)	300	1956

Antigua is less hilly and wooded than the other Leeward Is. and sugar cane and cotton are cultivated and exported. Tourism is developing. Parts of the island are leased to the U.S.A. for military and naval bases.

TRADING

Total trade (in million $ U.S.)	1965
Exports (f.o.b.)	4
Imports (c.i.f.)	19

DOMINICA

AREA: 728 sq. km. (289.5 sq. miles)

LAND USE: (percentage of total)	1963	1955
Arable and orchard	7.3	25.3
Permanent meadow and pasture	0.9	1.3
Forest and woodland	46.3	32.9
City areas, waste and other land	45.5	40.5

POPULATION: 70 000 (1967 estimate)

Capital city: ROSEAU; population: 10 417 (1960)

Distribution of working population (1960)
Total working population: 23 409

U.N. group no.		*Percentage*
0	Agriculture, forestry, fishing and hunting	50.0
1	Mining and quarrying	0.1
2/3	Manufacturing	10.8
4	Construction	10.2
5	Electricity, gas, water and sanitary services	0.7
6	Commerce	8.3
7	Transport, storage and communications	2.3
8	Services	13.6
9	Others	4.0

		Year(s)
Life expectancy at birth (years): male	57.0	1958–62 av.
female	59.2	1958–62 av.
Infant mortality (per '000)	53.6	1965
Crude birth rate (per '000)	42.7	1965
Crude death rate (per '000)	8.9	1965
Population per physician	5 600	1963
Population per hospital bed	200	1963
School enrolment: age 5–19 years (percentage)	79	1963–4 av.

FINANCE		*Year*
National Income (million $ U.S.)	15*	1966
G.N.P. per capita ($ U.S.)	230	1966

TRADING

Total trade (in million $ U.S.)	1963	1955
Exports (f.o.b.)	5	3
Imports (c.i.f.)	7	4

The chief trading partner in 1963 was the U.K.

Distribution of trade (percentage of total value)

Exports	1954	*Imports*	1954
Food	81	Manufactured goods	43
(bananas)	(55)	Food	36
Chemicals	9	Chemicals	8
Crude materials (excl. fuels)	8	Crude materials and fuels	7

continued

GRENADA

AREA: 344 sq. km. (133 sq. miles)

LAND USE: (percentage of total)	*1965*	*1953*
Arable and orchard	47.1	55.9
Permanent meadow and pasture	2.9	8.8
Forest and woodland	11.8	14.7
City areas, waste and other land	38.2	20.6

POPULATION: 99 000 (1967 estimate)

Capital city: SAINT GEORGES; population: 7 303 (1960)

Distribution of working population (1960)

Total working population: 27 314

U.N. group no.		*Percentage*
0	Agriculture, forestry, fishing and hunting	39.9
1	Mining and quarrying	0.2
2/3	Manufacturing	9.5
4	Construction	10.6
5	Electricity, gas, water and sanitary services	0.7
6	Commerce	10.8
7	Transport, storage and communications	3.2
8	Services	17.1
9	Others	8.0

		Year(s)
Life expectancy at birth (years): male	60.1	1959–61 av.
female	65.6	
Infant mortality (per '000)	42.5	1965
Crude birth rate (per '000)	30.5	1965
Crude death rate (per '000)	8.5	1965
Accidental deaths (per 100 000 population)		
caused by motor vehicles	3.3	1961
due to other causes	22.2	1961
Population per physician	4 550	1962
Population per hospital bed	160	1964
School enrolment: age 5–19 years (percentage)	95	1963–4 av.

COMMUNICATIONS		*Year(s)*
Motor vehicles in use ('000s): private	2.1	1963–5 av.
commercial	0.6	
Telephones (per '000 urban population)	2.1	1967
Radio receivers (per '000 population)	104	1963–5 av.
Daily newspapers (per '000 population)	16.3	1962–4 av.

FINANCE		*Year*
National Income (million $ U.S.)	22*	1966
G.N.P. per capita ($ U.S.)	230	1966

TRADING

Total trade (in million $ U.S.)	*1964*
Exports (f.o.b.)	5
Imports (c.i.f.)	11

In 1964 the main exports were cocoa, bananas and nutmegs, while imports consisted of flour, dried fish and hardware. The chief trading partners were the U.K., Canada and the U.S.A.

MONTSERRAT

AREA: 101 sq. km. (39 sq. miles)

LAND USE: (percentage of total)	*1963*
Arable and orchard	50.0
Permanenet meadow and pasture	12.5
Forest and woodland	25.0
City areas, waste and other land	12.5

POPULATION: 14 000 (1967 U.N. estimate)

Capital city: PLYMOUTH; population: 1 911 (1960)

Total working population: 4 332 (1960)

		Year(s)
Life expectancy at birth (years): male	49.5	1946
female	54.8	
Infant mortality (per '000)	54.8	1965
Crude birth rate (per '000)	27.4	1965
Crude death rate (per '000)	10.5	1965
Population per physician	3 500	1964
Population per hospital bed	200	1966
School enrolment: age 5–19 years (percentage)	75	1963–4 av.

TRADING

Total trade (in million $ U.S.)	*1964*
Exports (f.o.b.)	0.3
Imports (c.i.f.)	4

The chief exports are bananas, vegetables and Sea Island cotton.

ST. KITTS, NEVIS AND ANGUILLA

AREA: 400 sq. km. (155 sq. miles)

LAND USE: (percentage of total)	*1962*	*1955*
Arable and orchard	40.0	37.5
Permanent meadow and pasture	10.0	5.0
Forest and woodland	17.5	17.5
City areas, waste and other land	32.5	40.0

POPULATION: 60 000 (1967 unofficial estimate)

Capital city: BASSETERRE; population: 15 726 (city proper, 1960)

Distribution of working population (1960)

Total working population: 19 616

U.N. group no.		*Percentage*
0	Agriculture, forestry, fishing and hunting	46.0
1	Mining and quarrying	0.1
2/3	Manufacturing	10.6
4	Construction	8.1
5	Electricity, gas, water and sanitary services	0.8
6	Commerce	8.8
7	Transport, storage and communications	4.2
8	Services	18.1
9	Others	3.3

		Year(s)
Life expectancy at birth (years): male	58.0	1959–61 av.
female	61.9	
Infant mortality (per '000)	59.1	1965
Crude birth rate (per '000)	32.7	1965
Crude death rate (per '000)	9.8	1965
Population per physician	4 290	1965
Population per hospital bed	270	1966
School enrolment: age 5–19 years (percentage)	104‡	1963–4 av.

FINANCE		*Year*
National Income (million $ U.S.)	15*	1966
G.N.P. per capita ($ U.S.)	260	1966

TRADING

Total trade (in million $ U.S.)	*1965*	*1955*
Exports (f.o.b.)	5	5
Imports (c.i.f.)	9	5

Distribution of trade (percentage of total value)

Exports	*1965*	*1954a*
Food	91	94
(sugar)	(89)	(92)
Imports		
Manufactured goods	46	46
(machinery and transport equipment)	(15)	(22)
Food	31	27
Chemicals	9	7
Crude materials and fuels	8	9
Beverages and tobacco	5	5

a St. Kitts and Nevis only.

The chief products of St. Kitts are sugar and cotton; of Nevis, cotton and coconuts sent mainly to Barbados; cattle-rearing and vegetable growing are other activities. The chief product of Anguilla is salt.

continued

na: data not available. — negligible or nil. ¹ one year only. ² two year average. * estimate. ‡ see appendix. † re-exports.

ST. LUCIA

AREA: 616 sq. km. (238 sq. miles)

LAND USE: (percentage of total)	*1965*	*1953*
Arable and orchard	33.9	30.6
Permanent meadow and pasture	4.8	6.5
Forest and woodland	21.0	35.5
City areas, waste and other land	40.3	27.4

POPULATION: 105 000 (1967 U.N. estimate)

Capital city: CASTRIES; population: 4 353 (city proper, 1960)

Distribution of working population (1960)

Total working population: 31 372

U.N. group no.		*Percentage*
0	Agriculture, forestry, fishing and hunting	48.3
1	Mining and quarrying	—
2/3	Manufacturing	11.0
4	Construction	8.3
5	Electricity, gas, water and sanitary services	0.7
6	Commerce	7.9
7	Transport, storage and communications	2.0
8	Services	12.7
9	Others	9.1

		Year(s)
Life expectancy at birth (years): male	55.1	1959–61 av.
female	58.5	
Infant mortality (per '000)	41.9	1965
Crude birth rate (per '000)	46.4	1965
Crude death rate (per '000)	8.7	1965
Accidental deaths (per 100 000 population)		
caused by motor vehicles	3.1	1963
due to other causes	20.4	1963
Population per physician	6 800	1963
Population per hospital bed	200	1966
School enrolment: age 5–19 years (percentage)	78*a*	1964

a includes pre-school education.

FINANCE		*Year*
National Income (million $ U.S.)	20*	1966
G.N.P. per capita ($ U.S.)	190	1966

TRADING

Total trade (in million $ U.S.)	*1964*
Exports (f.o.b.)	6
Imports (c.i.f.)	11

The chief exports are bananas, copra and cocoa, and the imports flour, machinery and textiles. Trade is mainly with the U.K.

ST. VINCENT

AREA: 389 sq. km. (150 sq. miles)

LAND USE: (percentage of total)	*1964*	*1955*
Arable and orchard	50.0	50.0
Permanent meadow and pasture	2.9	—
Forest and woodland	44.2	50.0
City areas, waste and other land	2.9	—

POPULATION: 91 000 (1967 unofficial estimate)

Capital city: KINGSTOWN; population: 4 308 (city proper, 1960)

Distribution of working population (1960)

Total working population: 24 856

U.N. group no.		*Percentage*
0	Agriculture, forestry, fishing and hunting	40.1
1	Mining and quarrying	0.5
2/3	Manufacturing	11.0
4	Construction	11.4
5	Electricity, gas, water and sanitary services	0.9
6	Commerce	11.0
7	Transport, storage and communications	3.9
8	Services	14.9
9	Others	6.3

		Year(s)
Life expectancy at birth (years): male	58.5	1959–61 av.
female	59.7	
Infant mortality (per '000)	69.5	1965
Crude birth rate (per '000)	43.0	1965
Crude death rate (per '000)	9.5	1965
Accidental deaths (per 100 000 population)		
caused by motor vehicles	2.4	1961
due to other causes	11.0	1961
Population per physician	10 000	1962
Population per hospital bed	210*a*	1962
School enrolment: age 5–19 years (percentage)	96	1963–4 av.

a government hospitals only.

FINANCE		*Year*
National Income (million $ U.S.)	20*	1966
G.N.P. per capita ($ U.S.)	230	1966

TRADING

Total trade (in million $ U.S.)	*1965*	*1955*	*1938*
Exports (f.o.b.)	4	2	1
Imports (c.i.f.)	9	4	1

The main trading partner in 1964 was the U.K.

Distribution of trade (percentage of total value)

Exports	*1965*	*Imports*	*1965*
Food	82	Manufactured goods	42
Crude materials	16	(machinery and transport equipment)	(13)
		Food	30
		Chemicals	12
		Crude materials and fuels	7
		Beverages and tobacco	4

VIRGIN ISLANDS (U.K.)

Eleven of the forty-two British islands are inhabited, Tortola being the largest of the group.

AREA: 130* sq. km. (59 sq. miles)

LAND USE: (percentage of total)	*1955*
Arable and orchard	13.3
Permanent meadow and pasture	26.7
Forest and woodland	6.7
City areas, waste and other land	53.3

POPULATION: 9 000 (1968 U.N. estimate)

Capital city: ROAD TOWN; population: 891 (city proper, 1960)

Total working population: 2 164 (1960)

		Year(s)
Infant mortality (per '000)	66.7	1964
Crude birth rate (per '000)	26.5	1964
Crude death rate (per '000)	8.8	1964
Population per physician	4 000	1961
Population per hospital bed	230	1966
School enrolment: age 5–19 years (percentage)	92	1963–4 av.

TRADING

Total trade (in million $ U.S.)	*1964*
Exports (f.o.b.)	0.1
Imports (c.i.f.)	2.4

The principal exports are livestock, fish, charcoal, vegetables and fruit.

continued

na: data not available. — negligible or nil. ¹ one year only. ² two year average. * estimate. ‡ see appendix. † re-exports.

WEST INDIES ASSOCIATED STATES *continued*

PRODUCTION, EXPORTS AND IMPORTS

Years: **1963–5 average** Units: '000 metric tons unless otherwise indicated

Note—the trade figures given are the sum of the trade figures for the separate members of the Associated States, and therefore include inter-trade (if any) amongst them. The 1953–5 data for the West Indies Federation are not comparable due to the inclusion of Jamaica and Trinidad, and have therefore been omitted from the tables.

	Production	Exports	Imports
1. CEREALS, etc.			
Maize (corn)	—	—	0.9
Oats	—	—	0.2
Potatoes	—	—	0.9
Rice	—	—	5.6
Sweet potatoes/yams	7.0*	—	—
2. FRUIT, etc.			
Bananas	152.7*	148.6*	—
Coconuts	58.0**e*	0.5	—
Citrus fruit	12.4*	1.1[1]	—
Wine *b*	—	0.3	1.2

b '000 hectolitres. *e* no. in millions.

	Production	Exports	Imports
3. BEVERAGES, FOREST PRODUCTS, etc.			
Cocoa	3.1	3.0	—
Sugar: cane	534.3		
raw	62.7	59.1	5.9
Hardwood *j*	41.5[1]	—	—

j '000 cu. metres of roundwood equivalent.

	Production	Exports	Imports
4. VEGETABLE OILSEEDS AND OILS			
Copra	9.90*	5.78*	—
Coconut oil	na	0.95[2]	0.02[1]
Cottonseed	na	0.09[1]	—
Groundnuts	na	0.08[1]	0.06
Olive oil	—	—	0.02

	Production	Exports	Imports
5. LIVESTOCK‡, ANIMAL PRODUCTS, etc.			
Chickens *d*	113.3*n*	0.7	—
Cattle *d*	47.0	0.7[1]	—
dairy cows *d*	7.0		
Goats *d*	56.0	} 0.9[1]	—
Sheep *d*	48.7		
Horses *d*	5.3		
Pigs *d*	60.0	0.4[1]	—
Bacon/ham	} —	{ —	0.3
Meat‡: 'A'		—	0.1
'B'	—	—	0.4
Butter	—	—	0.2
Cheese	—	—	0.2
Eggs	0.3*	—	—
Fish	3.2*	—	2.1
Milk	5.0	—	9.2

d no. in thousands. *n* incl. ducks, geese and turkeys.

	Production	Exports	Imports
6. FIBRES, TEXTILES, etc.			
Cotton: lint	na	0.2	—
woven fabrics	—	—	4.8
Rayon, woven fabrics	—	—	0.6*
7. FUEL AND POWER			
Electricity *h t*	9		
Petroleum, refined	—	—	66

h million kWh. *t* thermal.

	Production	Exports	Imports
10. FERTILIZERS			
Potash	—	—	2.1

YUGOSLAVIA

EUROPE

In 1945 Yugoslavia was proclaimed a republic and two years later the members of the royal family were deprived of their nationality and property. A new constitution in 1953 made the working people the sole authority at all levels of government and in 1963 the name of the country became the Socialist Federal Republic of Yugoslavia.

AREA: 255 804 sq. km. (98 766 sq. miles)

LAND USE: (percentage of total)	*1965*	*1955*
Arable and orchard	32.5	32.0
Permanent meadow and pasture	25.2	25.6
Forest and woodland	34.4	30.9
City areas, waste and other land	7.9	11.5

POPULATION: 19 958 000 (1967 estimate)

Largest city: BEOGRAD (Belgrade), capital; population: 585 234 (1961)

Distribution of working population (1961)

Total working population: 8 340 400

U.N. group no.		*Percentage*
0	Agriculture, forestry, fishing and hunting	57.0
1	Mining and quarrying	1.7
2/3/5	Manufacturing, electricity, gas, water and sanitary services	12.0
4	Construction	3.8
6	Commerce	3.2
7	Transport, storage and communications	3.0
8	Services	8.7
9	Others	10.6

		Year(s)
Life expectancy at birth (years): male	62.4	} 1961–2 av.
female	65.6	
Infant mortality (per '000)	71.8	1965
Crude birth rate (per '000)	20.9	1965
Crude death rate (per '000)	8.7	1965
Population per physician	1 200	1965
Population per hospital bed	170	1966
School enrolment: age 5–19 years (percentage)	85	1963–4 av.
age over 19 years (per 100 000 population)	916	1964–5 av.

COMMUNICATIONS		*Year(s)*
Motor vehicles in use ('000s): private	147.4	} 1963–5 av.
commercial	57.4	
Railway track (km.)	11 847	1964
Mail per capita: domestic	52	} 1963–5 av.
foreign received	3	
foreign sent	3	
Telephones (per '000 urban population)	2.3	1967
Radio receivers (per '000 population)	134	1963–5 av.
Television licences (per '000 population)	30.8	1963–5 av.
Daily newspapers (per '000 population)	82.5	1962–4 av.

FINANCE

Currency unit: The Yugoslav dinar; the new dinar equivalent to 100 old dinars was introduced in 1966

Exchange rates (for old dinars)	*1965a*	*1960a*	*1950*	*1938*
Per $ U.S.	1 250	300	50	41.4
Per £ sterling	3 500	840	140	190.6

		Year(s)
National Income (million $ U.S.)	10 000*	1966
G.N.P. per capita ($ U.S.)	510	1966
Rate of increase of G.N.P. per capita	7.7	1960–4 av.

a official rates.

TRADING

Total trade (in million $ U.S.)	*1965*	*1955*	*1938*
Exports (f.o.b.)	1 092	257	117
Imports (c.i.f.)	1 288	441	114

Main trading partners (percentage of total value)

Exports	*1965*	*1955*	*Imports*	*1965*	*1955*
U.S.S.R.	17	7	U.S.A.	15	33
Italy	13	15	Italy	11	10
Germany F.R.	9	13	Germany F.R.	9	13
Germany D.R.	7	1	U.S.S.R.	8	3
Czechoslovakia	7	3	Czechoslovakia	5	2
Poland	6	2	Germany D.R.	5	1
U.S.A.	6	11	U.K.	5	5

Distribution of trade (percentage of total value)

Exports	*1965*		*1955*	
Manufactured goods	58		32	
(machinery and transport equipment)		(24)		(2)
(textiles and clothing)		(8)		(3)
Food	21		24	
(animals and meat)		(15)		(10)
Crude materials and fuel	11		30	
(wood)		(5)		(17)
Chemicals	5		5	
Imports				
Manufactured goods	53		38	
(machinery and transport equipment)		(28)		(25)
(iron and steel)		(10)		(4)
(textiles and clothing)		(4)		(2)
Crude materials and fuels	22		26	
(textile fibre and waste)		(9)		(13)
Food	15		27	
(cereals and preparations)		(8)		(18)
Chemicals	9		7	

continued

na: data not available. — negligible or nil. [1] one year only. [2] two year average. * estimate. ‡ see appendix. † re-exports.

PRODUCTION, EXPORTS AND IMPORTS

Years: **1963–5 average** and *1953–5 average* Units: '000 metric tons unless otherwise indicated

	Production		Exports		Imports	
1. CEREALS, etc.						
Barley	580.0	*367.0*	16.9	—	45.1	*5.0*
Maize (corn)	6 086.7	*3 581.3*	57.8	*61.1*	49.8	*54.1*
Millets/sorghum	31.0	*18.3*	3.1	*1.9*	—	—
Oats	325.3	*287.7*	—	—	—	*17.0*
Potatoes	2 743.3	*2 077.3*	0.4	*1.0*	11.5	*1.9*
Rice	24.3	*22.7*	—	*1.1*	34.1	*9.2*
Rye	162.3	*254.0*	—	—	—	—
Wheat	3 769.3	*2 112.7*	0.1	—	1 080.7	*855.0*
2. FRUIT, etc.						
Apples	191.3	*175.3*	0.1	*5.6*	2.0	—
Apricots	23.6	*16.9*	—	*1.2*	—	—
Bananas	—	—	—	—	9.6	*0.1*
Cherries	82.0	*66.0*	—	*1.3*	—	—
Dates	—	—	—	—	0.6	—
Figs	22.3	*19.3*	—	—	—	—
Grapes	1 236.7	*861.0*	14.7	*6.1*	—	—
Lemons	—	—	—	—	22.1	*2.5*
Oranges	—	—	—	—	32.0	*3.7*
Other citrus fruit	—	—	—	—	2.0	—
Olives	33.3	*26.7*				
Peaches	34.0	*16.9*	—	*0.5*	—	—
Pears	72.0	*67.3*	0.1	*0.3*	—	—
Plums	645.0	*778.3*	—	*8.1*	—	—
Raisins	—	—	—	*0.5*	2.1	*1.2*
Tomatoes	292.7	*135.3*				
Wine *b*	5 633.3	*3 992.0*	446.0	*171.7*	0.6	—

b '000 hectolitres.

	Production		Exports		Imports	
3. BEVERAGES, FOREST PRODUCTS, etc.						
Cocoa	—	—	—	—	10.1	*1.4*
Coffee	—	—	—	—	17.0	*1.7*
Sugar: beet	2 706.7	*1 381.0*	—	—	—	—
raw	353.0	*155.7*	13.5	—	92.4	*29.6*
Tea	—	—	—	—	0.5	—
Tobacco: leaf	56.2	*33.4*	21.0	*9.2*	4.5	*0.5*
cigars	—	*0.2e*	—	—	—	—
cigarettes	24 369.0*e*	*15 006.7e*	—	—	—	—
tobacco/snuff	0.1	*26.7*	—	—	—	—
Softwood *j*	4 370.7	*5 084.0*	600.0	*839.0*	35.9	—
Hardwood *j*	13 676.0	*13 963.3*	743.8	*469.2*	9.8	—
Wood pulp	326.8	*66.7*	46.1	*12.0*	39.4	*3.2*
Newsprint	41.3	*3.4*	1.1	—	14.7	*13.0*
Other paper	335.7	*68.7*	42.3	*3.1*	23.9	*7.9*

e no. in millions. *j* '000 cu. metres of roundwood equivalent.

	Production		Exports		Imports	
4. VEGETABLE OILSEEDS AND OILS						
Castor seed	3.3	*2.0*	—	—	—	*1.30[2]*
Castor oil	na	na	0.51	*0.13*	0.02	*0.31*
Copra	—	—	—	—	4.20	*0.83*
Coconut oil	—	—	—	—	11.76	*1.77*
Cottonseed	5.0	*4.0**	—	—	0.02	—
Cottonseed oil	na	na	—	—	0.85	*0.53*
Groundnuts	0.7	*0.2*	0.01	—	1.34	—
Groundnut oil	—	—	—	—	—	*0.06*
Linseed	—	*0.3*	—	—	24.43	—
Linseed oil	—	—	—	—	0.35	*3.36*
Olive oil	6.0	*3.7*	—	—	0.30	*0.60*
Palm kernels	—	—	—	—[2]	0.62	—
Palm kernel oil	—	—	—	—	0.24	*0.14*
Palm oil	—	—	—	—	2.05	—
Rapeseed	3.0	*7.7*	0.01	*0.03*	—	*1.80*
Rapeseed oil	na	na	—	—	0.27	*1.70*
Sesame seed	0.6	*0.4*	—	—	0.13	—
Soya beans	9.0	*2.0*	—	—	—	*3.00*
Soya bean oil	na	na	—	—	32.35	*0.50*
Sunflower seed	252.0	*113.3*	5.46	—[2]	0.03	*4.78*
Sunflower seed oil	na	na	—	—	0.51	—
Tung oil	—	—	—	—	0.17	—

	Production		Exports		Imports	
5. LIVESTOCK‡, ANIMAL PRODUCTS, etc.						
Chickens *d*	28 163.3	*21 971.0[2]*				
Cattle *d*	5 216.0	*5 133.7*	55.4	*65.1*	1.2	*0.6*
dairy cows *d*	2 617.0	*2 406.3*				
Goats *d*	200.0*	*420.5[2]*	} 116.1	na	—	—
Sheep *d*	9 731.7	*11 830.0*				
Horses *d*	1 141.3	*1 187.0*				
Pigs *d*	6 003.0	*4 541.7*	7.6	*58.7*	131.2	*1.2*
Bacon/ham	} 567.3	*336.7*	{ 3.3	—	—	—
Meat‡: 'A'			108.5	*11.4*	0.8	—
'B'	180.3*	*68.3*	5.8	*2.9*	0.1	—
Butter	15.0	na	—	—	1.8	*2.4*
Cheese	91.7	na	1.0	*1.4*	—	*0.2*
Eggs	82.0	*50.6*	0.9	*10.3*	3.9	—
Fish	38.2	*23.8*	21.9	*5.4[1]**	44.9	*1.5[1]**
Milk	2 237.0	*1 583.7*	—	na	188.9	—
Hides/skins	50.4[2]	na	—	*2.0[2]*	34.3	*12.0[2]*
Wool	7.5	*9.7*	0.2	*0.8*	8.3	*2.0*

d no. in thousands.

	Production		Exports		Imports	
6. FIBRES, TEXTILES, etc.						
Abaca	—	—	—	—	0.7	—
Agaves (sisal etc.)	—	—	—	—	4.9	*0.1*
Cotton lint	2.3	*2.0*	—	*0.2*	80.3	*32.1*
Flax fibre	2.4	*3.6*	—	—	0.6	*0.2*
Hemp fibre	44.7	*43.1*	10.9	*9.6*	—	—
Jute	—	—	—	*0.1†*	13.6	*3.4*
Rubber: natural	—	—	—	—	18.1	*4.6*
synthetic	—	—	—	—	11.2	—
Silk *f*	55.0[2]	*49.3**	64.3	*34.3*	—	—
Cotton: yarn	80.9	*33.3n*	3.6	—	1.0	—
woven fabrics	49.5	*20.7*	14.5	*4.3*	2.6	—
Rayon: fibre/yarn	na	na	—	—	na	na
woven fabrics	2.8*p*	*1.2[2]**	1.0	*1.2r*	5.2	na
Wool: yarn	29.6	*4.0*	—	—	0.5	*0.6*
woven fabrics	51.7*q*	*21.0q*	0.6	*0.1*	0.4	—

f metric tons. *n* incl. yarn predominantly of cotton. *p* continuous filament piece goods only. *q* million sq. metres. *r* incl. mixtures.

	Production		Exports		Imports	
7. FUEL AND POWER						
Coal 'A'‡	1 240	*1 130*	94	*74**	1 891	} *689*
'B'	13 860	*14 070*	54	*78*	—	
Coke	—	—	—	—	178	*192*
Electricity *h*: total	14 416	*3 590*				
hydro	8 196	*1 970*				
thermal	6 220	*1 620*				
Natural gas *i*	260	*64*	—	—	—	—
Oil, crude	1 837	*260[1]*	300	*na[1]*	883	*na[1]*
Petroleum, refined	2 063	*650[1]*	143	*40[1]*	207	*40[1]*

h million kWh. *i* million cu. metres.

	Production		Exports		Imports	
8. IRON AND STEEL						
Iron ore	1 050*m*	*494m*	153	*7*	392	*2*
Pig iron	1 103	*393*	28	*6*	167	*14*
Steel ingots/castings	1 678	*658*	9	—	17	*2*
Iron/steel scrap	na	na	1	*1*	89	*34*
Iron/steel products *a*	na	na	33	*4*	112	*22*

a million $ U.S. *m* metal content.

	Production		Exports		Imports	
9. NON-FERROUS MINERALS AND METALS						
Diamonds *a*	—	—	—	—	0.07	—
Gold *k*, ore *m*	98.30	*41.00*	—	—	—	—
Platinum group metals *k*	—	—	4.89[1]	—	15.27	*0.51*
Silver *k*: ore	3 992.30*m*	*2 953.70m*	2 688.70*t*	*2 092.00[2]t*	—	—
Asbestos: fibre	8.75	*3.64*	4.75	*0.74*	12.21	*2.44*
manufactured	na	na	3.63	—	0.82	*0.29*
Mica	0.04	—	—	*0.01[2]*	0.05	—
Aluminium: bauxite	1 384.20	*651.76*	1 008.20	*561.99*	4.20	*0.94*
alumina	88.46	na	12.93	*9.09*	1.11	—
aluminium	37.33	*5.93*	21.32	*1.92*	15.25	*0.70*
Antimony, ore	2.72*m*	*1.52m*	2.20*m*	*1.25m*	0.13[1]	—
Cadmium	0.04	—	0.03[2]	—	0.01	—
Chrome: ore	87.33*m*	*125.88m*	20.35	*36.19*	57.89	*0.35*
metal	na	na	8.14	*2.44*	—	—
Cobalt, metal	—	—	—	—	0.04	*0.04*
Copper: ore	62.61*m*	*29.91m*	1.15[2]	—	—	—
metal	53.14	*29.91*	25.23	*14.37*	15.31	—
Lead: ore	111.08*m*	*86.45m*	na	na	na	—
metal	102.25	*71.05*	62.82	*61.25*	3.19[2]	—
Magnesium:						
dolomite	—	—	—	—	0.96[2]	—
magnesite	478.44	na	112.79	*38.64*	—	*0.21*
metal/salts	—‡	—‡	28.62	*0.14*	1.37	*3.98*
Manganese: ore	8.00	*4.57*	—	—	40.28	*8.10*
metal	na	na	8.22	*3.26*	0.45	—
Mercury *f*	569.67*	*497.67**	404.30	*435.10*	70.00*	—
Molybdenum *f*, ore	na	*500.00**	—	—	—	—
Nickel, metal	—	—	—	—	0.67	*0.04*
Tin, metal	—	—	—	—	1.63	*0.49*
Titanium minerals	—	—	—	*0.10[1]*	3.40	*0.27[2]*
Tungsten: ore	0.09	—	—	—	0.09	—
metal	—	—	—	—	0.04	—
Zinc: ore	90.63*m*	*58.95m*	25.89	*38.53*	—	—
metal	44.27	*13.99*	16.94	*6.43*	3.88	—

a million $ U.S. *f* metric tons. *k* '000 fine troy oz. *m* metal content. *t* bullion.

	Production	Exports	Imports
10. CHEMICALS*n* AND FERTILIZERS			
Organic chemicals:			
Benzene	na	2.2[1]	—[1]
Butadiene	—	—	na
Ethylene	na	na	na
Methanol	7.3[2]	1.9	2.0
Phenol	2.8[2]	1.5	1.0
Phthalic anhydride	1.3[1]	—	0.6
Styrene monomer	6.0[1]	—	0.1
Urea	—	—	31.3[2]

n data not available for years 1953–5.

continued

na: data not available. — negligible or nil. [1] one year only. [2] two year average. * estimate. ‡ see appendix. † re-exports.

PRODUCTION, EXPORTS AND IMPORTS *continued*

10. CHEMICALS*n* AND FERTILIZERS—*continued*	Production		Exports		Imports	
Inorganic chemicals:						
Ammonia	119.0		—		0.1	
Carbon black	7.7[1]*		0.7		1.9	
Chlorine	31.8		3.9		—	
Nitric acid	213.3		0.6[2]		0.2	
Sodium carbonate	108.7		18.0		14.2	
Sodium hydroxide	77.2		26.3		14.9	
Sulphuric acid	432.8		1.8		18.0	
Plastics:						
Polyamides	na		—		na	
Polyethylene	5.6		na		na	
Polyvinyl chloride	8.7		3.1[1]		10.2[1]	
Fertilizers:						
Phosphates	—	—	—	—	552.5	*60.7*
Potash	—	—	—	—	297.2	*38.1*
Pyrites	158.5*x	*89.7*x*	184.0	*138.9*	—	—
Sulphur	—	—	—	—	15.6	*5.9*[2]

n data not available for years 1953–5. *x* sulphur content.

11. INDUSTRY	Production		Exports		Imports	
Aircraft*a*	—	—	—	—	5.1	*1.1*
Alcoholic beverages			10.3*a*	*2.6a*	0.3*a*	—
beer*b*	2 635.0	*724.3*				
spirits*b*	506.0**u*	—				
Cement	2 971.7	*1 411.0*	245.3	*256.0*	355.3	*40.0*
Electrical engineering*a*	na	na	46.3	*1.9*[2]	63.0	*19.5*[2]
Locomotives*c*	130.0[1]	na	na	na	na	na
Railway vehicles*a*	na	na	19.8	*2.7*	7.6	*5.2*
Machine tools*a*	8.0[1]	na	4.1	na	22.2	na
Merchant ships*g*	232.0	na	195.0	na	24.0	na
Motor vehicles			9.7*a*	*0.1a*	39.1*a*	*7.1a*
commercial*d*	12.8	*2.5p*				
private*d*	26.1	*0.7q*				

a million $ U.S. *b* '000 hectolitres. *c* no. of units. *d* no. in thousands. *g* '000 G.R.T. *p* incl. assembly of imported parts. *q* assembly of imported parts only. *u* production for home consumption in 1966.

ZAMBIA

CENTRAL AFRICA

Zambia, formerly Northern Rhodesia, became an independent republic within the British Commonwealth in 1964 following the dissolution of the Federation of Rhodesia and Nyasaland. Due to the lack of transport facilities and of fuel resources, the economy of the country has been seriously affected by the economic sanctions imposed upon Rhodesia.

No separate production or trade figures are available for Zambia for the duration of the Federation, 1954–63.

AREA: 752 262 sq. km. (290 586 sq. miles)

LAND USE: (percentage of total)	*1963*	*1955*
Arable and orchard	2.6	40.6 (Arable and orchard; Permanent meadow and pasture)
Permanent meadow and pasture	43.8	
Forest and woodland	50.0	49.7
City areas, waste and other land	3.6	9.7

POPULATION: 3 947 000 (1967 estimate)

Largest city: LUSAKA, capital; population: 152 000 (1966)

Employment: The mines and associated industries of Zambia, Rhodesia and South Africa provide employment for much of the indigenous population of Zambia. Only about half the adult male population (as well as the women) is engaged in agriculture. The soil is relatively infertile and the savannahs infested with tsetse fly, limiting agricultural activities. In 1967 about a third of the country's agricultural production came from farms run by the few (less than 1 500) Europeans farming in Zambia.

		Year(s)
Life expectancy at birth (years)	40	1963
Infant mortality (per '000)	259*	1950
Crude birth rate (per '000)	51.4**a*	1963
Crude death rate (per '000)	19.6**a*	1963
Population per physician	21 820	1964
Population per hospital bed	380	1966
School enrolment: age 5–19 years (percentage)	43*a*	1963–4 av.

a Africans only.

COMMUNICATIONS		*Year(s)*
Motor vehicles in use ('000s): private	41.6	1963–5 av.
commercial	11.2	1963–5 av.
Railway track (km.)	1 005*	1969
Mail per capita: domestic	7	1964–5 av.
foreign received	5	1964–5 av.
foreign sent	3	1964–5 av.
Telephones (per '000 urban population)	1	1967
Radio licences (per '000 population)	2	1963–5 av.
Daily newspapers (per '000 population)	6	1964

FINANCE

Currency unit: The kwacha replaced the Rhodesian pound in 1968 at the rate K1 to R£ 0.5

Exchange rates (for Rhodesian pounds)	*1965*	*1960*	*1950*	*1938*
Per $ U.S.	0.357	0.357	0.357	0.215
Per £ sterling	1.0	1.0	1.0	1.0

		Year(s)
National Income (million $ U.S.)	647	1965
G.N.P. per capita ($ U.S.)	180	1966
Rate of increase of G.N.P. per capita	0.5	1960–4 av.

TRADING

Total trade (in million $ U.S.)	*1965*	*1955e*	*1950*	*1938*
Exports (f.o.b.)	532	328	140	50
Imports (f.o.b.)	295	na	75	25

Main trading partners (percentage of total value)

Exports	*1965*	*1950*	*1938*	*Imports*	*1965*	*1950*	*1938*
U.K.	38	48	40	Rhodesia	34	13	15
Germany F.R.	13	5	32	U.K.	20	40	43
Japan	12	—	na	South Africa	20	28	16
Italy	8	—	10	U.S.A.	6	7	10
France	7	—	na	Japan	4	—	2
South Africa	7	9	3	Germany F.R.	3	—	na
Rhodesia	3	2	1	Italy	2	1	na

Distribution of trade (percentage of total value)

Exports	*1965*	*1950*	*1938**
Copper	92	87	88
Zinc, lead, and cobalt	4	9	na
Tobacco	1	2	1
Imports			
Manufactured goods	69	na	na
(machinery and transport equipment)	(33)	(30)	(37)
(textiles and clothing)	(12)	(12)	(10)
Crude materials and fuels	12	na	na
Chemicals	10	3	na
Food	8	3	na

e excl. trade with Rhodesia and Malawi.

continued

PRODUCTION, EXPORTS AND IMPORTS

Years: **1964–5 average** and *1953* Units: '000 metric tons unless otherwise indicated

1. CEREALS, etc.	Production		Exports		Imports	
Cassava	152.0*	na				
Maize (corn)	207.3*	*69.7n*	24.7	—	10.7	*36.3*
Millets/sorghum	256.0*	na	0.5	—	9.5	*1.1*
Oats	—	—	—	—	0.3	—
Potatoes	2.7	*2.3*	0.2	—	2.4	*2.2*
Rice	—	na	—	—	1.9	—
Sweet potatoes/yams	12.0*	na				
Wheat	1.0*	na	—	—	22.4	*9.1*

n produce of farms only.

2. FRUIT, etc.	Production		Exports		Imports	
Apples	—	—	—	—	1.0	—
Bananas	—	—	—	—	1.2	—
Grapes	—	—	—	—	0.2	—
Oranges	1.0*	na	0.1	—	—	—
Other citrus fruit	—	—	—	—	0.1	—
Raisins	—	—	—	—	—	*0.1*
Wine*b*	—	—	—	—	3.3	*4.0*

b '000 hectolitres.

3. BEVERAGES, FOREST PRODUCTS, etc.	Production		Exports		Imports	
Coffee	—	—	—	—	0.2	—
Sugar, raw	—	—	1.5†	—	22.7	*8.2*
Tea	—	—	—	—	0.4	*0.2*
Tobacco, leaf	10.3	*3.9*[2]	11.0	*4.8*	—	—
Softwood*j*	—	—	—	—	42.1[1]	—
Hardwood*j*	3 824.0*	*1 409.9*	23.0[1]	—	6.7[1]	—
Newsprint	—	—	—	—	1.0[1]	—
Other paper	—	—	—	—	4.5[1]	—

j '000 cu. metres of roundwood equivalent.

4. VEGETABLE OILSEEDS AND OILS	Production		Exports		Imports	
Castor seed	na	na	—	—	—	—
Castor oil	—	—	—	—	0.01	—
Coconut oil	—	—	—	—	0.08	—
Cottonseed	na	na	0.27	na	—	—
Cottonseed oil	na	na	—	—	0.16	—
Groundnuts	25.43**p*	na	1.67	*0.90*	2.53	*0.80*
Groundnut oil	na	na	na	*0.36*	1.33	*0.55*
Linseed oil	—	—	—	—	0.02	*0.01*
Olive oil	—	—	—	—	0.01	—
Palm kernel oil	—	—	—	—	0.49	*0.15*
Palm oil	—	—	—	—	—	*0.33*
Sunflower seed	na	*0.30n*	0.11[2]	na	—	—
Sunflower seed oil	na	na	—	—	0.02	—

n produce of farms and estates only. *p* sales only.

5. LIVESTOCK‡, ANIMAL PRODUCTS, etc.	Production		Exports		Imports	
Cattle*d*	1 269.0	*969.0*	0.5	—	7.6	*29.2*
dairy cows*d*	534.0*	*480.3**				
Goats*d*	157.0*	*97.3*	— (Goats and Sheep)	—	0.1	—
Sheep*d*	36.3	*9.7*				
Pigs*d*	64.0	*43.0*	0.1	—	0.1	*0.1*
Bacon/ham	15.7* (Bacon/ham and Meat 'A')	na	—	—	—	*0.4*
Meat‡: 'A'			0.5	*2.5*	2.9	—
'B'	1.3*	na	—	—	1.0	—
Butter	—	—	—	—	0.4	*0.5*
Cheese	—	—	—	—	0.2	*0.1*
Eggs	0.7*	na	—	—	0.1	—
Fish	40.8	*16.1q*	4.2	na	6.4	na
Milk	91.0*	*5.0*[2]	—	—	10.9	*6.5*
Hides/skins	na	na	0.5[2]*a*	na	—	—

a million $ U.S. *d* no. in thousands. *q* incomplete figure.

6. FIBRES, TEXTILES, etc.	Production		Exports		Imports	
Cotton lint	na	na	0.3	na	—	—
Rubber, natural	—	—	—	—	0.1	—

7. FUEL AND POWER	Production		Exports		Imports	
Coal 'A'‡	—	na	—	—	1 069	*808*
Coke	—	—	—	—	63	*15*
Electricity*h*: total	709	na				
hydro	297	na				
thermal	412	na				
Petroleum, refined	—	—	—	—	160	*70*

h million kWh.

8. IRON AND STEEL	Production		Exports		Imports	
Iron ore	na	982*m*	—	—	—	—
Pig iron	na	na	—	—	6	*6*

m metal content.

9. NON-FERROUS MINERALS AND METALS	Production		Exports		Imports	
Diamonds*a*	—	—	—	—	0.34	—
Gold*k*, ore*m*	5.00	—	—	—	—	—
Silver*k*, ore	1 047.00*m*	*436.30m*	21.27*r*	na	2.54[1]*r*	na
Asbestos: fibre	na	na	—	—	1.06	—
manufactured	na	na	—	—	1.20*a*	*1.11a*
Mica	—[1]	—	—	—	0.01	—
Aluminium	—	—	—	—	0.27	*0.38*
Antimony, metal	—	—	—	—	0.06	—
Cadmium	0.02	na	0.01	—	—	—
Chrome, ore	—	—	—	—	0.34	—
Cobalt, ore	1.23*m*	*0.87m*	1.02*t*	*28.10t*	—	—
Copper: ore	638.71*m*	*376.42m*	1.46	—	—	—
metal	634.85	*367.25*	682.61*n*	*378.02*	0.65	—
Lead: ore	na	na	—	—	—	—
metal	18.04	*14.41*	14.52	*12.78*	—	*0.08*
Magnesium:						
magnesite	—	—	—	—	0.26[1]	—
metal/salts	—‡	—‡	—	—	0.08[1]	—
Manganese, ore	34.03	*14.01*	29.80	na	—	—
Tin, ore	0.01*m*	—[2]*m*	0.08	na	0.05*t*	na
Zinc: ore	44.24*m*	*36.71m*	—	—	—	—
metal	47.87	*27.02*	45.52	na	—	—

a million $ U.S. *k* '000 fine troy oz. *m* metal content. *n* excl. semi-manufactures. *r* bullion. *t* metal.

10. CHEMICALS*n* AND FERTILIZERS	Production		Exports		Imports	
Chemicals	—		—		na	
Fertilizers:						
Potash	—	—	—	—	—	*0.1*
Pyrites	—	—	—	—	—	*5.4*
Sulphur	—	—	—	—	5.1[1]	na

n data not available for 1953.

11. INDUSTRY	Production		Exports		Imports	
Aircraft*a*	—	—	—	—	1.2	na
Alcoholic beverages*a*	—	—	—	—	1.6	na
Cement	203.0	na	3.0*	na	5.5*	—
Electrical engineering*a*	—	—	—	—	16.6	na
Railway vehicles*a*	—	—	—	—	0.9	na
Motor vehicles*a*	—	—	—	—	23.0	na

a million $ U.S.

APPENDIX

Background and summary data

Area

The area given includes that of inland waters. Where this is significantly different from the land area both figures have been given.

Population

The population of a city refers to that of the urban agglomeration unless otherwise stated.

The terms Africans, Europeans, etc. are used where separate statistics are available for countries with ethnically-mixed populations.

The school enrolment percentages, published by UNESCO, are intended to give a rough indication of the development of education in each country and should not be used for direct comparisons between countries. Figures over 100 are due to the actual age range of pupils not corresponding exactly to the age-standardized population.

Communications

Data for mail per capita give the number of letters per annum.

Data for daily newspapers refer to the number printed per day. The figures should be taken as only an approximate indication of the circulation, as they are, in many cases, based on incomplete data.

The number of radio and television receivers is given where possible, but where only the number of licences issued is available, this figure has been given.

Items have been omitted from the standard format of this table where information was not available or the figure was negligible or nil.

Finance

The observation that a currency is tied to the pound sterling does not necessarily apply after the sterling devaluation of 1967.

The currencies of the ' franc zone ' include the franc CFA and the franc CFP which are used by the French Union states of the African and Pacific Financial Communities respectively.

Foreign trade (given as a percentage of the Gross Domestic Product) is defined as the sum of exports and imports.

Trading

Trading figures given are for general trade except where footnoted ' national exports '; these are defined as the exports of domestic (or home-produced) merchandise only.

Trade in gold, specie and banknotes is excluded; but where gold is significant in a country's economy, and where the trade distribution percentages are available only for a total figure which includes trade in gold, then the trade data for gold have also been shown.

Commodities

Notes marked P *apply to production only;* T *to trade only*

Commodity (Table no.)	Standardized units and definitions
Abaca (6)	'000 metric tons
Agaves (6)	'000 metric tons sisal, henequen, letona and cantala
Aircraft (11)	million $ U.S. P data for 1965–7 only
Alcoholic beverages (11)	T million $ U.S. beer, spirits and wine
beer	P '000 hectolitres
spirits	P '000 hectolitres available only for year stated
Aluminium (9)	'000 metric tons
bauxite	T incl. cryolite
alumina	P 1953–5 data not available
aluminium	T incl. semi-manufactures, alloys, salts and scrap
Ammonia (10)	'000 metric tons 1953–5 data not available
Anthracite *see* Coal 'A'	
Antimony (9)	'000 metric tons
ore	P metal content of ore and concentrates T incl. concentrates
metal	P not available T incl. regulus, alloys, salts, and scrap
Apples (2)	'000 metric tons
Apricots (2)	'000 metric tons
Asbestos (9)	'000 metric tons
fibre	incl. crude and waste
manufactured	P not available T incl. asbestos cement products
Automobiles *see* Motor vehicles	
Bacon/ham (5)	'000 metric tons P not available separately, but included in Meat 'A'
Baddeleyite *see* Zirconium minerals	
Bananas (2)	'000 metric tons P excl. plantains
Barley (1)	'000 metric tons
Bastnaesite *see* Rare earths	
Bauxite *see* Aluminium	
Beef *see* Meat 'A'	
Beer *see* Alcoholic beverages	
Benzene (10)	'000 metric tons 1953–5 data not available
Beryl (9)	'000 metric tons data incomplete
Bituminous coal *see* Coal 'A'	
Brown coal *see* Coal 'B'	
Butadiene (10)	'000 metric tons 1953–5 data not available
Butter (5)	'000 metric tons
Cadmium (9)	'000 metric tons P smelter production T incl. flue-dust, alloys, salts, and scrap
Cantala *see* Agaves	
Carbon black (10)	'000 metric tons 1953–5 data not available
Cassava (1)	'000 metric tons T not available
Castor oil (4)	'000 metric tons P not available (average commercial extraction rate 45%)
Castor seed (4)	'000 metric tons
Cattle (5)	'000 head P population
dairy cows	P population of cows and heifers over two years, and heifers (under two years) in calf T not available
Cement (11)	'000 metric tons
Cerium *see* Rare earths	
Cheese (5)	'000 metric tons
Cherries (2)	'000 metric tons T 1963–5 not available
Chickens (5)	P population in '000 head T not available
Chlorine (10)	'000 metric tons 1953–5 data not available
Chrome (9)	'000 metric tons
ore	P chromite T incl. concentrates
metal	P not available T incl. salts and alloys
Cigars and cigarettes *see* Tobacco	
Citrus fruit (2)	'000 metric tons
lemons	incl. limes
oranges	incl. clementines and tangerines
other citrus fruit	mainly grapefruit
Clementines *see* Citrus fruit	
Coal (7)	'000 metric tons T excl. coal for bunkering
'A'	anthracite and bituminous coal
'B'	lignite or brown coal P weight of hard coal equivalent
Cobalt (9)	'000 metric tons
ore	P metal content of ore, concentrates, matte and salts
metal	P not available T incl. alloys, salts, and scrap
Cocoa (cacao) (3)	'000 metric tons
Coconuts (2)	P millions (approx. equivalent to '000 metric tons) 1953–5 data not available T '000 metric tons weight in shell unless otherwise stated
Coconut oil (4)	'000 metric tons P not available (average commercial extraction rate from copra 64%)
Coffee (3)	'000 metric tons
Coke (7)	'000 metric tons P not available
Copper (9)	'000 metric tons
ore	P metal content of ore T incl. concentrates and matte
metal	P smelter production T incl. unwrought copper, alloys, salts, scrap, and copper content of copper-gold and copper-lead ores
Copra (4)	'000 metric tons *see also* Coconut oil
Corn *see* Maize	
Cotton (6) lint yarn woven fabrics	'000 metric tons
Cottonseed (4)	'000 metric tons
Cottonseed oil (4)	'000 metric tons P not available (average commercial extraction rate 18%)
Cows *see* Cattle	
Cryolite *see* Aluminium	
Currants *see* Raisins	
Dairy cows *see* Cattle	
Dates (2)	'000 metric tons
Diamonds (9)	P '000 carats T million $ U.S. incl. rough, cut and polished, industrial and gem diamonds, bort and dust
Dolomite *see* Magnesium	
Eggs (5)	'000 metric tons hens' eggs in the shell only
Electrical engineering (11)	million $ U.S. equipment powered by electricity P 1964 data only
Electricity (7)	million kilowatt hours T not available
hydro	
nuclear	
thermal	incl. geothermal where stated

Commodities *continued*

Commodity (Table no.)	Standardized units and definitions
Ethylene (10)	'000 metric tons 1953–5 data not available
Figs (2)	'000 metric tons
Fish (5)	'000 metric tons fish and other aquatic animals landed in domestic ports, but excluding landings by foreign vessels
Flax fibre (6)	'000 metric tons incl. straw, tow, and waste
Flaxseed *see* Linseed	
Gas *see* Natural gas	
Gasoline *see* Petroleum	
Geothermal electricity *see* Electricity	
Goats (5)	'000 head P population T incl. sheep 1953–5 data not available
Gold (9)	'000 fine troy ounces T where reference to the Appendix (‡) is made the trade in gold was recorded by value only, and the weight obtained by dividing this by the official annual average price of gold per fine troy ounce, but no account was taken of the premium
ore	metal content of ore and concentrates
bullion/coins, etc.	
Grapefruit *see* Citrus fruit	
Grapes (2)	'000 metric tons
Groundnuts (4)	'000 metric tons shelled equivalent (approx. 70% of weight in shell)
Groundnut oil (4)	'000 metric tons P not available (average commercial extraction rate from shelled nuts 46%)
Ham *see* Bacon/ham	
Hardwood (3)	'000 cubic metres of roundwood equivalent
Hemp fibre (6)	'000 metric tons
Henequen *see* Agaves	
Hides/skins (5)	'000 metric tons
Horses (5)	P population in '000 head T not available *see also* Meat 'B'
Hydro-electricity *see* Electricity	
Ilmenite *see* Titanium minerals	
Iridium *see* Platinum group metals	
Iron ore (8)	'000 metric tons P metal content of ore T incl. burnt iron pyrites

Commodity (Table no.)	Standardized units and definitions
Iron/steel (8)	P not available
scrap	'000 metric tons
products	million $ U.S.
Jute (6)	'000 metric tons
Kieserite *see* Magnesium	
Lamb *see* Meat 'A'	
Lead (9)	'000 metric tons
ore	P metal content of ores and concentrates
metal	P smelter production T incl. alloys, salts, scrap and lead content of base bullion
Lemons *see* Citrus fruit	
Letona *see* Agaves	
Lignite *see* Coal 'B'	
Limes *see* Citrus fruit	
Linseed (flaxseed) (4)	'000 metric tons
Linseed oil (4)	'000 metric tons P not available (average commercial extraction rate 34%)
Livestock (5)	'000 head P population
Locomotives (11)	P number T incl. with railway vehicles, in million $ U.S.
Machine tools (11)	million $ U.S. P 1953–5 data not available
Magnesium (9)	'000 metric tons
dolomite	P 1953–5 data not available
magnesite	P 1953–5 data not available
kieserite	P not available
metal/salts	P primary magnesium only
Maize (corn) (1)	'000 metric tons
Manganese (9)	'000 metric tons
ore	
metal	P not available T incl. spiegeleisen and ferro-manganese
Meat (5)	'000 metric tons
'A'	beef, veal, pork, mutton, and lamb P incl. bacon and ham
'B'	edible offals, poultry, horsemeat, etc.
Merchant ships (11)	'000 gross registered tons T the importing country refers to the country of registration
Mercury (9)	metric tons excl. compounds
Methanol (10)	'000 metric tons
Mica (9)	'000 metric tons incl. micanite and phlogopite

Commodity (Table no.)	Standardized units and definitions
Milk (5)	'000 metric tons T evaporated, condensed, and powdered milk in approximate weight of fresh milk equivalent
Millets/sorghum (1)	'000 metric tons
Molybdenum (9)	metric tons
ore	P metal content of ores and concentrates T incl. concentrates
metal	P not available T incl. alloys, salts, and scrap
Monazite *see* Rare earths	
Motor vehicles (11)	T million $ U.S. commercial and private vehicles, incl. motor cycles
commercial	P number in thousands
private	P number in thousands, excl. motor cycles
Mustard seed *see* Rapeseed	
Mutton *see* Meat 'A'	
Natural gas (7)	million cubic metres
Newsprint (3)	'000 metric tons
Nickel (9)	'000 metric tons
ore	P metal content of ore, concentrates, and matte T incl. concentrates and matte
metal	P not available T incl. alloys, salts, and scrap
Nitric acid (10)	'000 metric tons
Non-cellulosic (synthetic) fibre/yarn (6)	'000 metric tons T 1953–5 data not available
Nuclear energy *see* Electricity	
Oats (1)	'000 metric tons
Oil, crude (7)	'000 metric tons
Olives (2)	'000 metric tons T not available
Olive oil (4)	'000 metric tons
Oranges *see* Citrus fruit	
Osmiridium and osmium *see* Platinum group metals	
Palladium *see* Platinum group metals	
Palm kernels (4)	'000 metric tons
Palm kernel oil (4)	'000 metric tons P not available (average commercial extraction rate 48%)
Palm oil (4)	'000 metric tons
Paper, other (3)	'000 metric tons incl. paperboard and all paper other than newsprint
Peaches (2)	'000 metric tons T 1963–5 not available
Peanuts *see* Groundnuts	
Pears (2)	'000 metric tons

Commodity (Table no.)	Standardized units and definitions
Petroleum, refined (7)	'000 metric tons T excl. ships' bunkers except where specified
Phenol (10)	'000 metric tons 1953–5 data not available
Phosphates (10)	'000 metric tons incl. apatite and guano where indicated; excl. manufactured and semi-manufactured phosphates P phosphate rock, chalk and dust T incl. compounds
Phthalic anhydride (10)	'000 metric tons 1953–5 data not available
Pig iron (8)	'000 metric tons incl. ferro-alloys
Pigs (5)	'000 head P population
Pineapples (2)	'000 metric tons T 1963–5 data not available
Platinum group metals (9)	'000 fine troy ounces incl. alloys, iridium, osmiridium, osmium, palladium, rhodium, ruthenium and concentrates; excl. platinum sent by post
Plums (2)	'000 metric tons T 1963–5 data not available
Polyamides (10)	'000 metric tons 1953–5 data not available
Polyethylene (10)	'000 metric tons 1953–5 data not available
Polyvinyl chloride (10)	'000 metric tons 1953–5 data not available
Pork *see* Meat 'A'	
Potash (10)	'000 metric tons P K_2O content or equivalent T incl. salts and compounds
Potatoes (1)	'000 metric tons
Poultry *see* Chickens and Meat 'B'	
Pyrites (10)	'000 metric tons P sulphur content T iron and cupreous pyrites *see also* Iron ore
Radium *see* Uranium	
Railway vehicles (11)	million $ U.S. P not available *see also* locomotives
Raisins (2)	'000 metric tons incl. currants and sultanas
Rapeseed (4)	'000 metric tons incl. mustard seed
Rapeseed oil (4)	'000 metric tons P not available (average commercial extraction rate 38%)

Commodities *continued*

Commodity (Table no.)	Standardized units and definitions
Rare earths (7)	metric tons incl. monazite, thorite, bastnaesite, and cerium
Rayon (cellulosic) (6) fibre/yarn woven fabrics	'000 metric tons
Rhodium *see* Platinum group metals	
Rice (1)	'000 metric tons T milled equivalent
Rubber (6) natural synthetic	'000 metric tons
Ruthenium *see* Platinum group metals	
Rutile *see* Titanium minerals	
Rye (1)	'000 metric tons
Scheelite *see* Tungsten	
Sesame seed (4)	'000 metric tons
Sesame seed oil (4)	'000 metric tons P not available (average commercial extraction rate 48%)
Sheep (5)	'000 head P population T incl. goats 1953–5 data not available
Ships *see* Merchant ships	
Silk (6)	metric tons
Silver (9) ore	'000 fine troy ounces metal content of ore and concentrates
bullion	T incl. scrap
Sisal *see* Agaves	
Skins *see* Hides/skins	
Snuff *see* Tobacco	

Commodity (Table no.)	Standardized units and definitions
Sodium carbonate (10)	'000 metric tons 1953–5 data not available
Sodium hydroxide (10)	'000 metric tons 1953–5 data not available
Softwood (3)	'000 cubic metres of roundwood equivalent
Sorghum *see* Millets/sorghum	
Soya beans (4)	'000 metric tons
Soya bean oil (4)	T '000 metric tons P not available (average commercial extraction rate 18%)
Sperm oil *see* Whale/sperm oil	
Spiegeleisen *see* Manganese	
Spirits *see* Alcoholic beverages	
Steel ingots/castings (8)	'000 metric tons
Steel products and scrap *see* Iron/steel	
Styrene monomer (10)	'000 metric tons 1953–5 data not available
Sugar (3)	'000 metric tons
beet	T not available
cane	T not available
raw	raw equivalent of beet or cane, incl. refined
Sulphur (10)	'000 metric tons
Sulphuric acid (10)	'000 metric tons 1953–5 data not available
Sultanas *see* Raisins	
Sunflower seed (4)	'000 metric tons
Sunflower seed oil (4)	T '000 metric tons P not available (average commercial extraction rate 35%)
Sweet potatoes/yams (1)	'000 metric tons T not available

Commodity (Table no.)	Standardized units and definitions
Tangerines *see* Citrus fruit	
Tea (3)	'000 metric tons
Thermal electricity *see* Electricity	
Thorite *see* Rare earths	
Tin (9)	'000 metric tons
ore	P metal content of ore and concentrates T incl. concentrates
metal	T incl. alloys
Titanium minerals (9)	'000 metric tons incl. ilmenite, rutile, alloys, and salts
Tobacco (3)	
leaf	'000 metric tons
cigars	P number in millions T '000 metric tons
cigarettes	P number in millions T '000 metric tons
tobacco/snuff	'000 metric tons
Tomatoes (2)	'000 metric tons T not available
Tung oil (4)	'000 metric tons
Tungsten (9)	'000 metric tons
ore	P WO_3 content (estimated as 60% of ore) T incl. wolfram and scheelite ores and concentrates
metal	P not available T incl. alloys and scrap
Uranium (7)	metric tons P metal content of uranium minerals T ores and concentrates, or radium products, etc. where specified
Urea (10)	'000 metric tons 1953–5 data not available

Commodity (Table no.)	Standardized units and definitions
Vanadium (9)	'000 metric tons P content of ores and concentrates T content of ores and concentrates, or ferro-vanadium, where specified
Veal *see* Meat 'A'	
Whale/sperm oil (5)	'000 metric tons T whale oil only
Wheat (1)	'000 metric tons incl. spelt T incl. meslin; excl. flour
Wine (2)	'000 hectolitres T *see also* Alcoholic beverages
Wolfram *see* Tungsten	
Wood *see* Softwood and Hardwood	
Wood pulp (3)	'000 metric tons
Wool	'000 metric tons
raw (5)	clean wool equivalent
yarn (6)	incl. mixtures predominantly of wool
woven fabrics (6)	incl. mixtures predominantly of wool
Yams *see* Sweet potatoes/yams	
Zinc (9)	'000 metric tons
ore	P metal content of ore
metal	P smelter production T incl. lithopone, salts and scrap
Zirconium minerals (9)	'000 metric tons incl. concentrates, zircon, baddeleyite, etc. as individually specified